level G P

CURRENT LAW YEAR BOOK 1986

AUSTRALIA AND NEW ZEALAND
The Law Book Company Ltd.
Sydney : Melbourne : Perth

CANADA AND U.S.A.
The Carswell Company Ltd.
Agincourt, Ontario

INDIA
N. M. Tripathi Private Ltd.
Bombay
and
Eastern Law House Private Ltd.
Calcutta and Delhi
M.P.P. House
Bangalore

ISRAEL
Steimatzky's Agency Ltd.
Jerusalem : Tel Aviv : Haifa

MALAYSIA : SINGAPORE : BRUNEI
Malayan Law Journal (Pte.) Ltd.
Singapore

PAKISTAN
Pakistan Law House
Karachi

CURRENT LAW YEAR BOOK 1986

Being a Comprehensive Statement of
the Law of 1986

Editor in Chief
PETER ALLSOP, C.B.E., M.A.
Barrister

General Editor
KEVAN NORRIS, LL.B.
Solicitor

Assistant General Editor
JULIE HARRIS, LL.B.

Administration
GILLIAN BRONZE, LL.B.

Editors

English Cases:

NICHOLAS BAATZ, M.A., B.C.L., *Barrister*
STEPHEN BRANDON, B.A., LL.M., *Barrister*
REX BRETTEN, Q.C., M.A., LL.B., *Barrister*
CHRISTOPHER BUTLER, LL.B., *Barrister*
JOHN ELVIDGE, M.A., LL.B., *Barrister*
SHAUN FERRIS, B.A., *Barrister*
IAN GOLDSWORTHY, *Barrister*
DAVID GRANT, M.A., LL.B., *Barrister*
CHARLES JOSEPH, B.A., *Barrister*
SIMON LEVENE, M.A., *Barrister*
STEPHEN LEVINSON, LL.B., *Solicitor*
ANN McALLISTER, B.A., LL.M., *Barrister*
STEPHEN MORGAN, LL.B., M.A., *Barrister*
LIONEL PERSEY, LL.B., *Barrister*
ANTHONY PITTS, *Barrister*
JOHN PUGH-SMITH, M.A., *Barrister*
CLARE RENTON, *Barrister*
CHARLES SCOTT, LL.B., *Barrister*
JOHN STEPHENS, *Barrister*
PATRICK STEWART, *Barrister*
STEPHEN SUTTLE, M.A., *Barrister*
HELEN TATE, LL.B., *Barrister*
AVTAR VIRDI, *Solicitor*
ROBERT WEBB, LL.B., *Barrister*

European Communities:

ALISON GREEN, LL.M., *Barrister*

Delegated Legislation:

JOHN TATE, LL.B., *Barrister*

Northern Ireland:

FRED MARTIN, LL.B., *Barrister*

Damages Awards:

DAVID KEMP, B.A., *Barrister*
DERRICK TURRIFF, *Barrister*

Commonwealth Cases and Articles:

ANDREW BURR, M.A., *Barrister*

LONDON
SWEET & MAXWELL LTD.   STEVENS & SONS LTD.
1987

The Mode of Citation

of the CURRENT LAW YEAR BOOK

is *e.g.*:

[1986] C.L.Y. 1282

ISBN: This volume only: 0 421 38400 X
with Citators : 0 421 38390 9

Published in 1987 by
Sweet & Maxwell Limited of
11 New Fetter Lane, London,
and printed in Great Britain
by The Eastern Press Limited
of London and Reading

PREFACE

THIS volume completes forty years of Current Law publishing. It supersedes the monthly issues of *Current Law* for 1986 and covers the law from January 1 to December 31 of that year.

Citators

The Case Citator and the Statute Citator are contained in separate volumes, issued with this volume.

The *Current Law Citators* cover cases during the years 1977–86 and statutes during the period 1972–86. There are permanent bound volumes covering cases during the period 1947–76 and statutes during 1947–71.

The present volume contains a table of cases digested and reported in 1986 and the usual tables covering 1986 Statutory Instruments and their effect on the orders of earlier years and a table of Northern Ireland Statutory Rules and Orders.

Books and Articles

Indices of the books and articles published in 1986 are included at the back of this volume. The full title, reference and the name of the author is given in each case and both indices are arranged under Current Law headings.

Index

The Subject-matter Index in this volume has been compiled by Helen Tate, LL.B., *Barrister*. Owing to the ever-increasing size of the index in 1977 it was decided to include references from 1972 onwards only. This provides an overlap of five years in the index which covers in great detail the whole of the law decided, enacted, issued or published during the years 1972–86. In addition this index includes all statutes enacted since 1947. The full thirty-year Index from 1947–76 may be found in the 1976 *Year Book*.

Statutes and Orders

Sixty-eight Acts received the Royal Assent during the year. A complete list of Statutes appears under the title STATUTES AND ORDERS.

Alphabetical and numerical lists of the Statutory Instruments of 1986 are contained in this volume, together with a table showing the affect of the 1986 Instruments on previous delegated legislation.

Cases

The number of cases digested exceeds 2,500. This figure does not include the short reports showing what damages have been awarded in cases of injury or death. These decisions have been collected and edited by Mr. David Kemp and Mr. Derrick Turriff. The Quantum of Damages Table at the front of this volume provides a guide to the personal injury decisions reported in 1986.

The *Year Book* again includes a selection of cases of persuasive force from the Scottish courts and the courts of the Commonwealth and from the English county courts. It also includes a section on the law of the European Communities.

Court of Appeal

As a service to the profession *Current Law* continues the publication of brief notes of decisions of the Court of Appeal (Civil Division) which have not hitherto been reported but whose transcripts are available in the Supreme Court Library at the Royal Courts of Justice. *Current Law* is indebted to Mr. Avtar S. Virdi, *Solicitor*, who has prepared the notes of the details of the cases. Transcripts of these cases were previously available in the Bar Library.

Northern Ireland

All Northern Irish Acts and Orders and the cases reported from the courts of Northern Ireland have been digested together with a selection of the cases reported from the courts of the Republic of Ireland. This work has been carried out by our editor in Northern Ireland, Mr. S. F. R. Martin.

Cases "ex relatione"

We welcome short reports of cases submitted by members of both branches of the legal profession. They are noted as "*ex rel.* A.B., Barrister" or "*ex rel.* C.D., Solicitors," as the case may be. These reports, we believe, are of considerable value to the profession since the contributor can properly be regarded as having first hand knowledge of the facts. Unfortunately, occasional instances have recently been brought to our notice in which reports of this kind have been misleading or even incorrect. We are grateful to those who bring such matters to our attention and we seek to correct the report in a later issue or in the "*Current Law Year Book.*" We must stress, however, that we are entirely dependent on the contributor for the accuracy of his or her report. It is impracticable for us independently to check the facts stated to us.

The General Editor thanks those who have pointed out errors and have sent in notes of interesting cases.

May 1987.   P. A.

CONTENTS

THE LAW OF 1986 DIGESTED UNDER TITLES:

Administrative Law, § 1
Agency, § 31
Agriculture, § 38
Aliens, § 76
Animals, § 77
Arbitration, § 90
Armed Forces, § 120
Atomic Energy, § 133
Auctioneers and Valuers, § 136
Aviation, § 137

Bailments, § 151
Banking, § 152
Bankruptcy, § 172
Bastardy and Legitimation, § 183
Bills of Exchange, § 185
British Commonwealth, § 186
Building and Engineering, Architects and Surveyors, § 197
Building Societies, § 235
Burial and Cremation, § 251

Canals, § 253
Capital Taxation, § 254
Carriers, § 267
Charities, § 274
Civil Defence, § 279
Commons, § 280
Company Law, § 285
Compulsory Purchase, § 347
Conflict of Laws, § 361
Constitutional Law, § 368
Consumer Credit, § 370
Contract, § 377
Copyright, § 427
Coroners, § 443/4

Corporation Tax, § 449
County Court Practice, § 455
Criminal Law, § 470
Crown Practice, § 950
Customs and Excise, § 955

Damages, § 970
Death Duties, § 1072
Divorce and Matrimonial Causes, § 1073

Easements and Prescriptions, § 1113
Ecclesiastical Law, § 1117
Education, § 1125
Election Law, § 1154
Electricity, § 1161
Emergency Laws, § 1163
Employment, § 1164
Equity, § 1296
Estoppel, § 1301
European Communities, § 1303
Evidence, § 1499
Executors and Administrators, § 1520
Extradition, § 1521

Factories, § 1536
Family Allowances, § 1542
Firearms, § 1543
Fish and Fisheries, § 1547
Food and Drugs, § 1557
Forestry, § 1571
Fraud, Misrepresentation and Undue Influence, § 1572
Friendly Societies, § 1576

CONTENTS

TABLE OF CASES

9

TABLE OF CASES

10

TABLE OF CASES

TABLE OF CASES

13

TABLE OF CASES

TABLE OF CASES

16

TABLE OF CASES

TABLE OF CASES

TABLE OF CASES

TABLE OF CASES

23

TABLE OF CASES

24

25

TABLE OF CASES

26

TABLE OF CASES

TABLE OF CASES

TABLE OF CASES

TABLE OF CASES

TABLE OF CASES

TABLE OF CASES

33

TABLE OF CASES

TABLE OF CASES

35

TABLE OF CASES

TABLE OF CASES

TABLE OF CASES

COURT OF APPEAL

SUPREME COURT LIBRARY TRANSCRIPTS

TABLE OF UNREPORTED CASES

Decisions of the Court of Appeal (Civil Division) of which transcripts have been lodged in the Supreme Court Library.

The following cases will be found in the Unreported Cases Court of Appeal (Civil Division) section.

Realistics *v.* LP Marsh (Properties) (1986 No. 291), § 65

Rosalie Co. S.A. *v.* Khalid (1985 No. 295), § 55

Rowark *v.* National Coal Board (1986 No. 45), § 42

Sargent *v.* Walsall Metropolitan Borough Council (1985 No. 335), § 45

Second WRVS Housing Society *v.* Blair, § 24

Short *v.* Short (1985 No. 877), § 48

Skibs A/S Avanti, Skins A/S Glarona; Skibs A/S Navahs (t/a Parrederiet Sibotre) *v.* Okeanis Shipping Corp., § 2

Smith *v.* British Railways Board (1985 No. 577), § 20

Stanton *v.* Smith (1985 No. 345), § 64

Supercoral *v.* Taube (Michael) (1986 No. 88), § 66

Sutton *v.* Jones (1985 No. 624), § 43

TDI *v.* Stride Micro (A Nevada Corporation) (1986 No. 119), § 52

Taylor *v.* National Coal Board (1986 No. 202), § 36

Trustees of the Eyre Estate *v.* Hall (1986 No. 230), § 3

Tucker *v.* Hampshire County Council (1986 No. 99), § 18

Wiltshire London *v.* Mayor and Burgesses of Lambeth London Borough (1985 No. 258), § 54

ERRATUM

QUANTUM OF DAMAGES
PERSONAL INJURIES OR DEATH

The fourth column (headed "Reference".) of the Quantum of Damages Table on pages 43 to 45 incorrectly lists the paragraph references to the 1986 *Current Law Monthly Digests*. This column should therefore be ignored. The cases referred to in the Table can all be found at paragraph 988 *et seq.*

QUANTUM OF DAMAGES
PERSONAL INJURIES OR DEATH

The table below is a cumulative guide to quantum of damages cases reported in Current Law in 1986

Injury	Case	Award General	Total	Reference
		£	£	
Maximum Severity	*Brightman* v. *Johnson*	413,500	580,547	1 C.L. 106
	Francis v. *Bostock*	225,000	413,945	1 C.L. 106
	Thirtle v. *Suckling*	280,555	342,263	6 C.L. 88
	Jenkinson v. *Lumbis*	284,600	296,600	10 C.L. 97
	Rotchford		122,000	9 C.L. 87
Multiple Injuries	*Doyle* v. *Edmunds*	46,000	49,893	10 C.L. 97
	Podmore v. *Higgins*	8,500		5 C.L. 103
	Bush v. *Philip (1)*	2,700	3,600.55	5 C.L. 103
Skin	*Butler* v. *Marconi Electronic Devices*	3,000	3,040	9 C.L. 87
Burns and Scars	*Laker* v. *Townsend*	20,000	20,582	3 C.L. 86
	Keith v. *Tennens*	3,500		1 C.L. 106
	Russell v. *Staveley Chemicals*	2,500		2 C.L. 98
	Sargent v. *Walsall M.B.C.*	750		10 C.L. 97
Face	*Thorne*	6,500	6,560	3 C.L. 86
	Vujanic	2,500	2,553	5 C.L. 103
	Singh	1,250		7 C.L. 91
Sight	*White*	20,000		6 C.L. 88
	Angol	15,000	15,050	6 C.L. 88
Neck	*Peters* v. *Ministry of Defence*	16,631	30,019	2 C.L. 98
	Holton v. *Roberts*	6000		8 C.L. 67
	Marsh v. *M.I. Electrical Installations*	2,500		7 C.L. 91
	Bowen v. *O'Neill (1)*	1,800		1 C.L. 106
Shoulder	*Cooper*	5,000		8 C.L. 67
Spine below neck	*Beaman*	35,000	38,572	5 C.L. 103
Spine	*Davies* v. *Massey Ferguson Perkins*	1,250		7 C.L. 91
Respiratory Organs	*Needham* v. *Charles Portway and Son*	74,000	94,000	9 C.L. 87
	Clarke v. *Murex*	68,580	71,185	1 C.L. 106
	Grodentz v. *Tate and Lyle Refineries*	35,000	49,162	9 C.L. 87
	Jones v. *Willbrow Manufacturing*	12,000		9 C.L. 87
	Fanning	1,250	1,521	6 C.L. 88

Personal Injuries or Death—*continued*

Injury	Case	Award General	Total	Reference
		£	£	
Internal Organs— Kidney	Baker v. Turtle	15,000	15,184	3 C.L. 86
Liver	Baker v. East Yorkshire Health Authority	8,000	8,229.17	3 C.L. 86
Rectum	Harkness v. Oxfordshire Health Authority	4,000		5 C.L. 103
Reproductive Organs	Miller v. Peterborough Health Authority	5,000	5,060	8 C.L. 67
Arm	Hinds v. Latter (A) and Co.		76,700	11 C.L. 85
	Edkins v. B.L. Cars	61,070	68,740	7 C.L. 91
	Jamieson v. Thomas	42,500	45,069	3 C.L. 86
	Boore v. Harland Tyres	8,500	31,244	5 C.L. 103
	Hutley v. Prudential Assurance	4,250	12,727.74	5 C.L. 103
	Hawkins v. Esso Petroleum	5,000		5 C.L. 103
	Bastable v. Bush	4,500		5 C.L. 103
Elbow	Kent v. Scholey	1,500		10 C.L. 97
Wrist	Steele v. Britannia (Cheltenham)	2,250	3,090	6 C.L. 88
	Kerr v. Langdon	2,950		10 C.L. 97
Pelvis and Hip	Smith v. Naylor	8,000		10 C.L. 97
Pelvis	Gilbert v. Romano	4,000		2 C.L. 98
Hip	Gifford v. Keeling	11,900		3 C.L. 86
Leg	Hughes v. Odeco Drilling	74,100	98,025	5 C.L. 103
	Bennett v. National Coal Board	46,415	64,557.93	10 C.L. 97
	Hawker v. Golding		16,000	11 C.L. 85
	Wakeham v. Bournemouth District Council	10,000	11,444·73	6 C.L. 88
	Bailey	4000		11 C.L. 85
	Bowen v. O'Neill (2)	2,000		1 C.L. 106
Fingers and Thumb	Madeley v. Baxters Butchers	15,000	19,374	8 C.L. 67
	Jones v. William George (Wath)	8,500	8,788.99	1 C.L. 106
	Lambert v. Raffatac	4,500	7,279.75	8 C.L. 67

Personal Injuries or Death—*continued*

Injury	Case	Award General	Total	Reference
		£	£	
Knee	*Steer* v. *Royal Borough of Kensington and Chelsea*	4,300	6,118·18	7 C.L. 91
Ankle	*Johnson* v. *British Railways Board*	8,000	8,764	3 C.L. 86
	Corsi v. *Linfood Holdings*	5,000		5 C.L. 103
Foot	*Weiss-Stoll* v. *Baldwin*	87,500	105,975·53	7 C.L. 91
Neurosis	*Ackers* v. *Wigan Area Health Authority*	13,700	13,775	3 C.L. 86
	S. v. *Meah*	12,500	12,610	9 C.L. 87
Miscellaneous Conditions				
Neuroma	*Daly* v. *Wolverhampton Health Authority*	6,000	6,050	10 C.L. 97
Pharyngitis	*Lee*	7,500	7,679	2 C.L. 98
Minor Injuries	*Fairless* v. *Kingston-upon-Hull City Council*	2,000	2,123	8 C.L. 67
	Hanby v. *Mawdsley*	1,750		2 C.L. 98
	Payne v. *Donley*	1,750	1,815	7 C.L. 91
	Roberts v. *National Coal Board*	1,750		9 C.L. 87
	Dulieu v. *Silcock and Colling*	1,000		2 C.L. 98
	Chapman v. *Bowater U.K. Paper Co.*	800	854.93	9 C.L. 87
	Khania	750		7 C.L. 91
	Herrington v. *Leece*	600	850	9 C.L. 87
	Brook v. *Hampshire County Council*	600	630·95	6 C.L. 88
	Parsons v. *(Unknown)*	650		10 C.L. 97
	Stevenson v. *North Derbyshire Health Authority*	600		9 C.L. 87
	Murray v. *Murray (A.W.)*	500	671.71	3 C.L. 86
	Bush v. *Philip (2)*	425		5 C.L. 103

1

ALPHABETICAL TABLE OF

STATUTORY INSTRUMENTS

1986

ALPHABETICAL TABLE OF S.I. 1986

ALPHABETICAL TABLE OF S.I. 1986

ALPHABETICAL TABLE OF S.I. 1986

ALPHABETICAL TABLE OF S.I. 1986

ALPHABETICAL TABLE OF S.I. 1986

55

ALPHABETICAL TABLE OF S.I. 1986

ALPHABETICAL TABLE OF S.I. 1986

ALPHABETICAL TABLE OF S.I. 1986

59

ALPHABETICAL TABLE OF S.I. 1986

ALPHABETICAL TABLE OF S.I. 1986

ALPHABETICAL TABLE OF S.I. 1986

ALPHABETICAL TABLE OF S.I. 1986

ALPHABETICAL TABLE OF S.I. 1986

81

ALPHABETICAL TABLE OF S.I. 1986

ALPHABETICAL TABLE OF S.I. 1986

85

NUMERICAL TABLE OF
STATUTORY INSTRUMENTS

Note: References to paragraph numbers exceeding 3553 are to the Scottish edition of the Current Law Year Book 1986

1986		C.L.Y.	1986		C.L.Y.
1		2046	74		2340
2		3534	75		2340
3		2200	76		25546
4		2016	77		3462
5		81	78	(C. 2)	3593
6		176	79		959
7	(S. 1)	4139	80	(C. 3)	3461
8		3253	81		3449
9		2126	82		960
10		2126	83		1567
12		254	84		1610
13		3534	89		3029
21		4544	90		3029
23		2130	91		3029
24		2520	92		3029
25		3124	93		3029
26		3019	96		2046
27		3028	100		162
28		3029	101		4622
29		3029	102	(C. 4)	1578
30		3029	103		1580
31		3029	104		1158
32		3029	105		2338
33		3029	106		3028
34		3029	107		3028
35		3029	108		3028
36		3028	109		3028
37		3028	110		1555
38		3028	111		2519
39		3028	114		2484
40		3028	117		3029
41		3028	118		3029
42		3028	120		4091
43		3028	121		4402
44		3028	124		3082
45		3028	125	(C. 5)	32
46		3028	126		33
47		3028	127		32
48		3028	128	(C. 6)	3392
49		3029	129		2007
50		3029	130		3028
51		3029	131		3028
56		2929	132		3028
57		61	133		3029
58		3526	134		3029
59		4077	136		3534
60		4077	137		3082
67		1247	139		4015a
68		1557	140		4526
69		1608	143		84
70		1608	144		3089
71		3467	148		2046

1986		C.L.Y.	1986		C.L.Y.
149		2114	231		2099
150	(S. 11)	4528	236		3028
151		2046	237		2021
152		1608	245		3534
153		1608	246		3534
154		2065	247		3534
155		145	249		3534
156		2062	250		1555
157		3028	251		1555
160		192	252		4131
162		2747	253		4468
163		3028	254		4468
164		3029	255		4055
165		3029	256		2037
166		3029	257		1608
174		2756, 4521	258		1608
175		1568	259		2965
176		1143	260		966
177		56	262		2962
178		2910	264		2962
179		2989	265		2028
180		2989	266		4067
181		2962	267		4646
183		2975	271		1163
184		2975	272		1972
185	(C. 7)	176	273		1970
189		1608	274		1970
190		1608	275		1965
192		2046	276		1978
193		3019	277		2756
194		72	278		1609
195		72	280		2021
196		72	281		2014
197		72	282		2036
198		3124	283		1551
199		2246	286		186
200		3028	294		1193
201		3028	296		3092
202		3028	297		2035
203		3028	298		2058
204		3029	299		2050
205		3029	300		2046
206		3029	301		3082
207		2744	302		3430
208		2029	303		4318
209	(S. 12)	4241	304		3670
210		4241	305		3497
211		2026	306		2903
212		2034	307		674
213		4074	309		2124
214		4391	310		3105
215		3029	311		137
216		1789	312		137
217		1790	313		2958
218		1508	314		1137
219		1791	315		2988
220		1530	316		2988
222		2407	317		2525
223		3223	318		1247
224		1734	319	(C. 8)	188
225		2962	320		4512
226		2003	321		2014
227		2057	328		1753
228		2131	329		2808
230		2034	330		2067

NUMERICAL TABLE OF S.I. 1986

1986		C.L.Y.	1986		C.L.Y.
331		2240	407		4249
333		2021	408		4572
334		3084	409		4391
335		3498	410		4005
336		3494	411		4529
337	(C. 9)	3484	412		4395
338		74	413		2046
339		71	414	(C. 13)	3461
341		4428	416		639
342		4527	417		1163
343		2756	420		3291
344		2808	424		1806
345		2053	425		2046
346		957	426		2046
347		957	427		2992
348		957	428		58
349		1608	429		1569
350		1608	430		1610
351		1597	431		2005
353		3028	432		2234
354		3028	433		3028
355		3028	434		3028
356		3028	435		2046
357		3028	436		2046
358		3028	437		2046
359		3029	439		2046
360		3029	440		2244
361		3029	441		1562
362		3029	442		2046
363		3029	443		2046
364	(C. 10)	2560	444		1970
365	(C. 11)	3484	445		1965
366		2508	446		1778
367	(C. 1)	2078	447		1809
368		2864	448		4313
369		2958	449		4059
370		2968	450		4054
371		2987	451		4066
372		2987	452		2046
373		4394	453		3024
374		4303	454		1555
378		76	455		2546
379		2046	456		2123
380		2520	457		2113
381		2240	458		2245
382		1549	459		2234
383		1158	460		3028
384	(C. 12)	3217	461		3029
385		2832	462		3029
386		1745	463	(C. 14)	303
387		266	464		680
388		4149	465		2522
389		4149	466	(C. 15)	3530
390		4401	467		3529
391		2518	468		3529
392		1193	469		4076
397		1608	470		52
399		2046	471		2046
400		956	472		2953
401		3534	473		4076
402		3094	474		4076
403		148	475		3394
404		2330	476		72
405		543	477		1247
406		235	478		1247

1986		C.L.Y.	1986		C.L.Y.
482		1726	583		2495
484		3119	584		2494
485		3124	585		2531
486		3119	586		2128
495		955	587		4317
496		1547	588		4258
497		1547	589		2905
498		73	590		3515
501		2046	592		2509
502		3311	593	(N.I. 2)	2451
507		1608	594	(N.I. 3)	2336
509		4129	595	(N.I. 4)	2393
510		4005	597		1155
511		1608	598		697
512		1608	599		138
513		4666	600		2006
514		4428	601		3039
515		4428	605		3028
516		4313	606		3029
517		3598	607		2973
518		3634	608		1770
521		1608	609		240
523		2046	610		1603
524		2240	611		295
525		1797	612		295
526		2021	613		1810
527		254	614		3403
528		263	615		1810
529		1765	616		1810
530		3516	617		1810
531		3495	618		1810
532		3494	619		334
533		2021	620		1576
535		2021	621		1769
537	(C. 16)	3215	622		1769
538		1548	623		3321
539		1727	624		2046
540		960	625		2141a
541		1887	626		3665
542		1134	628		2530
543		4429	629		3212
544		138	630		2129
545		4304	631		2141a
546		3028	632	(L. 2)	2609
548		3029	633		461
549		3029	634		1106
550		3029	635	(C. 17)	1105
522		3029	636	(L. 3)	466
553		2046	637		2634
555		4622	638		2753a
556		2021	639	(C. 18)	1160
557		1608	641		4525
559		1143	642		4128
560		2748	643		1965
561		3320	645		2021
562		3160	647		1555
563		2046	648		1555
564		2046	660		2129
565		1608	666		2931
566		3450	667		1608
567		3450	669		1193
568		3094	672		4741
573		2046	673		4058
576		4403	674		3799
582		2046	675		1608

1986		C.L.Y.	1986		C.L.Y.
676		1608	814		2512
678		4149	815		3029
679		1608	816		3029
680		1550	817		57
681	(S. 66)	4058	818		3028
682		1608	819		3028
688		3283	820		3028
690		2756	821		3028
691		3409	822		3028
692	(S. 69)	4647	824		3028
693	(S. 67)	4760	825		3028
694	(S. 68)	4428	826		3028
696	(L. 4)	1081	827		3028
697		27536	828		3028
701	(S. 70)	4392	829		3028
702		1729	830		3028
703		1729	831		3535
704		3488	832	(C. 21)	1583
705		1520	833		1581
706		2454	834		1581
707	(C. 19)	59	836		4078
711		2033	837		3080
714		3082	840	(C. 22)	303
716		3488	841		3024
720		1567	842		543
721		1567	843		4138
722		1567	848		146
723		1567	852		1610
724		2012	853		3529
726		1608	854		2020
731		1597	857		2066
739		2992	861		3121
740		3534	862		88
748		2935	864		1825
751		2525	865		3029
752		2935	866		1825
753		3451	867		2046
754		460	868		2935
758		3001	869		3451
760	(C. 20)	3390b	870		253
765		2099	882		2920
766		1534	887		2112
767	(N.I. 5)	228	889		3028
768		1577	890		1193
769		163	892		4514
770		2846	896		3489
771		1732	897		1608
772		160	900		3216
774		3532	901		3394
775		3532	902		2752
778		1607	903		3123
779		1555	904		2987
784		2554a	909		3499
786		2120	910		958
787		967	915		3028
788		4084	916		2240
789		4080	918		2060
790		4084	923	(L. 5)	2081
791		4084	924		4313
797		1614	925		4318
799		4428	926		1555
803		2044	934		3482
809		3125	938		958
812		3354	939		3498
813		957	940		2527

1986		C.L.Y.	1986		C.L.Y.
941		3028	1036		2292
942		3028	1038	(S. 89)	4686
943		3028	1039		3222
944		4315	1040		3089
945		2100	1043		3537
946		2519	1044		2745
947		1353	1045		2745
948		76	1046		2525
949		108	1047		2406
950		2240	1048	(C. 26)	2177
951		177	1049	(C. 27)	1105
952		177	1050		4312
963		2239	1051		3095
964		2239	1052	(C. 28)	3091
965		4322	1057		2099
966		4322	1059		1560
967		4054	1063		2021
968	(C. 23)	3483	1064		1608
969		3483	1065		1608
970		3483	1066		3089
971		1796	1067		3089
972		3451	1068		3089
974	(C. 24)	2236	1069		3089
975		2243	1070		3089
976		2243	1071		3089
977		4379	1072		3089
978		4066	1073		3089
980		1590	1074		3089
981		140	1075		3089
982		2131	1078		2908
986		1543	1079	(L. 6)	2092
987		1565	1080	(C. 29)	1160
988		1556	1081		1158
989		1137	1082		3543
990		1125	1088	(C. 30)	3461
991		1125	1089		2992
994		3451	1090		2931
995		3393	1091		2338
996	(S. 87)	4072	1092		3028
1000		2756	1095		2530
1002		135	1096		1096
1007		3028	1101		3029
1008		3028	1102		967
1009		1610	1103		4005
1010		3185	1104		4005
1011		3159	1105		372
1012		3028	1106		1608
1013		3394	1107		1608
1014		2247	1110		61
1015		2247	1111		4015a
1016		374	1113		3219
1017		1608	1114		74
1018		1608	1115		1552
1019		966	1116		2518
1020		3097	1117		3119
1021		2533	1118		3119
1027		1560	1119		3143
1028		2036	1120		3132
1029	(C. 25)	682	1121		1560
1030		3451	1125	(C. 31)	945
1031		1137	1128		4056
1032	(N.I. 6)	2302	1129		4068
1033	(N.I. 7)	2300	1130		3029
1034	(N.I. 8)	2303	1131		3028
1035	(N.I. 9)	2301	1132		3028

1986		C.L.Y.	1986		C.L.Y.
1133		2031	1219		3025
1135		72	1220	(C. 34)	3025
1136		2243	1221	(C. 35)	3026
1137		1163	1222		3025
1138		51	1223	(C. 36)	3025
1141	(L. 7)	2073	1224		2909
1142	(L. 8)	2640	1225		2962
1143		1117	1226	(C. 37)	3978
1144		1120	1227		4005
1145		3283	1228	(C. 38)	143
1146		2408	1229		141
1147	(C. 32)	2979	1230		4666
1148		1123	1231		4428
1149		1608	1232		1560
1150		1608	1233		51
1151		1608	1234		1585
1154		4468	1236		2809
1156		1610	1237	(C. 39)	3977
1157		196	1238		4273
1158		196	1239		4274
1159		2175	1240		1730
1161		189	1241		126
1162		148	1243		4513
1163		3089	1244		1608
1164		1122	1245		3445
1165	(N.I. 10)	2452	1247		1560
1166	(N.I. 11)	2418	1248		3098
1167	(N.I. 12)	2419	1249		693
1168		25	1250		949
1169		2486a	1253		3455
1170		3283	1256		46
1172		1542	1259		3160
1173		3160	1260		3538
1174		3553a	1266		1808
1175		2980	1271		2009
1176		3310	1272		1555
1177		2973	1273	(C. 40)	3428
1178		2454	1274	(C. 41)	3423
1179		1560	1275		3218
1180		2131	1277		3527
1181		1745	1278		3619
1182	(C. 33)	3929	1280		680
1185		1560	1281		3028
1186		1976	1282		3028
1187	(L. 9)	2695	1283		3028
1188		2066	1284		3028
1189	(L. 10)	466	1287		4755
1190		2013	1288		4082
1191		3847	1290		81
1192		4322	1291		1202
1193		3028	1292		3160
1194		3028	1293		3160
1195		3028	1294		1560
1196		3028	1295		61
1197		3028	1296		2745
1198		3028	1297	(C. 42)	3004
1199		3028	1298		192
1200		3029	1299		428
1201		1555	1300		1530
1202		148	1301	(N.I. 13)	2363
1208		1825	1302	(N.I. 14)	2471
1209		1825	1303		3405
1210		3537	1304		139
1217		3023	1305		3083
1218		138	1306		1126

1986		C.L.Y.	1986		C.L.Y.
1315	(C. 43)	1588	1412		1560
1316	(C. 44)	1589	1413		1560
1317		1589	1414		2121
1318		1589	1415		1608
1319		3426	1416		1608
1322		2823	1419		53
1323		3001	1422		1560
1324		1151	1427		2473
1325		1150	1428		2927
1326	(C. 45)	3460	1429		1597
1327		3446	1431		1560
1328		2991	1432		1560
1329		2929	1433		4238
1330		3446	1434		1607
1331		1560	1435		1560
1332	(L. 11)	2092	1436		3311
1333	(L. 12)	2079	1437		1555
1334	(C. 46)	682	1438		1555
1335		525	1439		1555
1336	(C. 47)	2977	1440		1747
1338		2920	1441		3097
1342		72	1442		2842
1343	(C. 48)	1659	1444		2842
1344		1560	1445		2842
1345		2122	1446		960
1346		1126	1447		3409
1347		137	1448		1586
1348		137	1449		4391
1352		957	1450	(C. 49)	3461
1353		4010	1451		1608
1357		1502	1452		1608
1358		4468	1453		1608
1359		4468	1454		1608
1360		1560	1455		1608
1361		2666	1456		2918
1364		2016	1458		2918
1365		2762	1459		2918
1367		3410	1460		1158
1368		2108	1461		2484
1372		3393	1462		3028
1373		1557	1463		3028
1379		2526	1464		3028
1380		2526	1465		3028
1381		2529	1466		3029
1382		3311	1467		2926
1384		1560	1469		1608
1386		3457	1475	2918,	4086
1387		3457	1477		3394
1389		1608	1479		1560
1390		2114	1480		2747
1391		2931	1483		1560
1392		3028	1484	(C. 50)	48/49
1393		3028	1485	(C. 51)	3575
1394		3028	1486		2240
1395		3028	1487	(C. 52)	143
1396		3029	1489		1618
1397		1126	1488	(C. 53)	547
1398		2046	1490		1618
1399		1813	1491		1560
1400		1608	1492		2918
1407		1608	1493		2918
1408		1608	1494		1616
1409		1608	1498	(L.13)	1082
1410		1560	1499		2235
1411		1560	1500		1193

1986		C.L.Y.	1986		C.L.Y.
1501		2992	1615		1560
1502		141	1616		1560
1503	(C. 54)	2560	1617	(C. 59)	4473
1504		3452	1618		3534
1505	(L. 14)	462	1619		2014
1507		4318	1620		1555
1508		1560	1621		1560
1509		3311	1622		4544
1510		70	1623		2752
1511		1618	1626		3082
1512		1608	1627		1162
1513		1608	1628		3451
1514		1608	1629		3451
1515		1970	1642		2240
1516		1608	1643		961
1528		87	1644		2860
1530		66	1645		2860
1531		3532	1646		1607
1532		3534	1647		1608
1534		1819	1648		3454
1535		1560	1649		3454
1536		1816	1650		3454
1537		1819	1651		3454
1540		1560	1652		3454
1541		3145	1653		3454
1542		2918	1657		4323
1543		148	1662		1560
1544		148	1663		2517
1546	(C. 55)	3752	1664		1560
1545		3149	1665		3028
1547		3463	1666		3028
1552		1560	1667		3029
1557		3274	1668		3451
1558		1607	1669		2918
1559		1965	1670		3532
1560	(C. 56)	237	1671		3451
1561		3138	1672		3453
1571		4316	1673		3453
1572		3283	1674		3453
1574		1560	1675		3453
1575		3532	1676		3453
1576		1560	1677		3453
1577		3028	1681		1560
1578		3028	1682		3537
1579		3028	1683		3545
1580		3028	1684		3536
1581		3028	1685		3542
1582		3028	1686		3858
1583		3028	1687		3792
1584		3028	1688		1560
1585		3028	1689		1560
1586		3029	1690		3532
1587		1794	1691		3451
1590		4076	1695		1643
1591		2206	1696		2556
1592		1560	1700		4290
1595		1560	1702		3459
1596	(C. 57)	48/49	1703		3459
1597		2908	1704		2126
1609	(C. 58)	3157	1707		1560
1610		3394	1709		1193
1611		65	1710		3206
1612		66	1711		3206
1613		4085	1712		163
1614		4085	1713		2100

NUMERICAL TABLE OF S.I. 1986

1986		C.L.Y.	1986		C.L.Y.
1715		249	1836		4191
1716		2515	1837		1560
1717		2525	1838		3029
1718		2525	1839		3028
1719	(C. 60)	3157	1840		3028
1720		1560	1841		3028
1729		1825	1842		3028
1733		3534	1843		3028
1734		87	1844		3028
1735		82	1845		3028
1736		1607	1846		2549
1737		1608	1849		1560
1738		1608	1856		1606
1739		3532	1858		1606
1740		3028	1859		2990
1741		3028	1860	(C. 66)	2511
1742		3028	1865		319
1743		3028	1874	(C. 67)	4757
1744		3028	1875		4622
1745		3028	1876		2116
1746		3028	1877		243
1747		3029	1878		238
1755		81	1880		4755
1756		1560	1881		1676
1757		3411	1882		2905
1758		3411	1883	(N.I. 15)	2316
1759	(C. 61)	3099	1884		538
1760		1597	1885		1161
1761		2115	1886	(N.I. 16)	2346
1763		244	1887	(N.I. 17)	2458
1764		307	1888	(N.I. 18)	2464
1765		1560	1889		25
1772		3123	1890		3426
1774		2046	1891		2755
1775		1560	1892		3072
1776		3534	1893		3072
1777		3106	1894		75
1778		147	1896		1556
1779		3457	1897		2242
1780		3459	1899		1648
1781	(C. 62)	2585	1900		1560
1782		251	1901		1556
1791		1608	1902		1597
1792		1608	1909		2014
1794	(C. 63)	3461	1911		86
1795		2751	1912		2021
1800		1608	1913	(C. 68)	3593
1801		141	1914		3596
1803	(C. 64)	3797	1915		3666
1807		1608	1916		3665
1808		3587	1917		3663
1809	(C. 65)	1588	1918		3667
1810		1591	1919		1808
1811		2338	1922		1193
1812		2908	1924		303
1813		2908	1925		308
1814		1608	1929		2046
1818		543	1932		3104
1819		963	1933		3151
1820		968	1934		960
1823		3579	1935		3089
1824		1608	1936		1555
1832		1745	1937		4428
1833		3206	1940	(C. 69)	2851
1835		1970	1941		4428

96

1986		C.L.Y.	1986		C.L.Y.
1942		1072	2024	(N.I. 21)	2447
1943		2332	2025		131
1944		263	2026		131
1945	(C. 70)	4221	2027		2636
1946		4666	2030		306
1947		4654	2031	(C. 76)	2851
1948		1755	2032		2551
1951		2905	2033		2540
1952		3532	2034	(S. 155)	4257
1953		148	2035		4093
1954		4544	2038		3089
1955		4428	2041	(C. 77)	687
1956		4742	2042		1630
1957		3455	2044	(C. 78)	2586
1958	(C. 72)	3157	2046		2852
1959	(C. 73)	3157	2048		3283
1960		1205	2049		3539
1961		3185	2050		3029
1962	(L. 15)	2093	2051		3028
1963		2021	2052		3028
1964		2021	2053		3028
1965		4526	2055		3028
1966		4666	2056		3028
1967		1608	2057		3028
1980		2119	2058		3028
1981		1584	2059		3028
1982		1555	2060		1552
1983	(C. 74)	4374	2061		79
1984	(S. 154)	4544	2062		85
1985		2537	2063		2046
1986		3532	2066	(C. 79)	3090
1987		1607	2067		297
1988		1607	2068		2031
1989		3514	2069		962
1992		2752	2070		2525
1993		1560, 4079	2071	(C. 80)	122
1994		308	2072		132
1995		307	2073		132
1996		308	2074		132
1997		2131	2075		1552
1998	(C. 75)	1294	2076		2972
1999		178	2077		2016
2000		331	2088	(C. 81)	78
2001		181	2089		86
2002		312	2090		1555
2003		278	2092		2046
2004		2239	2093		2046
2005		2239	2097		300
2006		2239	2098		247
2007		2239	2099		248
2008		2016	2100		2927
2009		2016	2101		2973
2011		1526	2102		2454
2012		1527	2103		2002
2013		1528	2105		965
2014		1529	2106		2031
2015		1531	2107		4405
2016		1532	2109		3537
2017		1792	2113		2099
2018		134	2114		2099
2019		1163	2115	(L. 16)	2640
2020		1533	2116		1819
2021	(N.I. 19)	2453	2117	(C. 82)	1815
2022		1525	2118		1819
2023	(N.I. 20)	2401	2119		2532

NUMERICAL TABLE OF S.I. 1986

1986		C.L.Y.	1986		C.L.Y.
2120		148	2208		1560
2121		148	2209		1368
2122		1557	2210		3534
2123		305	2212		1758
2124	(C. 83)	122	2213	(S. 163)	4015
2125		120	2214		1154
2126		123	2215		1154
2128		2972	2216		245
2129		138	2217		3148
2130		3082, 4678	2218		3115
2134		309	2219		2486
2135		1977	2220		3089
2136		3534	2221		1788
2137	(C. 84)	4141	2222		1791
2138		4145	2223		3092
2139		4142	2224		3089
2140		4148	2225		3092
2141		964	2226		696
2142		311	2229		2401a
2143		461	2230		648
2144		2634	2231		1155
2145	(C. 85)	547	2233		4419
2146		1163	2234		4704
2147		1757	2235		438
2148		964	2236		3426
2149		1608	2237		3221
2150		2756	2238		138
2151	(L. 17)	542	2239		2001
2152		242	2240		1825
2153		148	2241		2551
2154		3160	2242		1560
2155		239	2243		3082
2156		1608	2244		3082
2157		1608	2245		310
2158		1608	2246	(C. 88)	2851
2159		1608	2247		307
2160		1608	2248		1560, 4079
2161		167a	2250		2338
2168		250	2255	(S. 164)	4543
2169		246	2256		4543
2170		148	2258		3102
2171		2525	2259	(C. 89)	2560
2172		3144	2260	(C. 90)	2560a
2173		3144	2261		2688
2174		967	2262	(C. 92)	1631
2175		76	2264		1597
2176		76	2265		81
2177		2109	2266	(C. 93)	3752
2179		957	2268		693
2180		1825	2271		3029
2181		1825	2272		3028
2183		1610	2273		3028
2184	(S. 162)	3805	2274		3028
2185		2685	2278		2014
2186		372	2279		2014
2187		2754	2281		1250
2191		1747	2282		1295
2192		2099	2283		1187
2193		1643	2284		1250
2194		1643	2285		3053
2195		1643	2286		3283
2202	(C. 86)	3530	2287		204
2203	(C. 87)	1132	2288		3515
2204		3403	2289		2695
2207		468	2290		3515

NUMERICAL TABLE OF S.I. 1986

1986		C.L.Y.	1986		C.L.Y.
2291	(S. 167)	3634	2313		1245
2292		957	2316		680
2293		2046	2317		680
2294		2242	2318		680
2295		81	2319		1608
2296		4647	2320		1608
2297		4648	2321		1607
2298		4428	2328		1794
2299		1567	2329		1555
2300		2752	2330		639
2301		48/49	2331		639
2302		53	2332		639
2310	(S. 171)	4318	2355		1608
2312		1541	2356		3082

TABLE OF S.R. & O. and S.I.

AFFECTED BY

STATUTORY INSTRUMENTS OF 1986

This Table describes the effect on existing Statutory Rules and Orders and Statutory Instruments of Statutory Instruments of 1986. The first entry, for example, shows that Statutory Instrument No. 105 of 1890 was amended by Statutory Instrument 648 of 1986, and that the 1986 Instrument is digested at paragraph 1555. For the effect on post 1946 Statutory Instruments of all subsequent Statutory Instruments see the Table of Statutory Instruments Affected in the *Current Law Legislation Citator*.

Note: References to paragraph Numbers exceeding §3553 are to the Scottish edition of the Current Law Year Book.

1890
   105 amended No. 648 § 1555
   296 revoked No. 647 § 1555

1900
   292 revoked No. 1201 § 1555

1904
  1476 revoked No. 647 § 1555

1906
   644 revoked No. 1201 § 1555

1921
  1536 amended No. 76

1925
  1093 amended No. 1534 § 1819
   795 amended No. 2001 § 181
  1093 amended No. 1536 § 1816
  1093 amended No. 1537 § 1819
  1093 amended No. 2001 § 181
  1093 amended No. 2116 § 1819
  1093 amended No. 2118 § 1819

1930
  1125 revoked No. 468 § 3529
  1126 revoked No. 467 § 3529

1933
   295 revoked No. 1201 § 1555
   789 amended No. 83 § 1567

1934
  1346 amended No. 857 § 2066

1935
   488 amended No. 1129 § 4068

1936
  1297 revoked No. 1755 § 81
  1367 amended No. 2312 § 1541

1938
   607 amended No. 2312 § 1541
   640 amended No. 2312 § 1541
   661 amended No. 691 § 3409
   661 revoked No. 1319 § 3426

1938—*cont.*
   727 revoked No. 2312 § 1541
   728 revoked No. 2312 § 1541
   729 revoked No. 2312 § 1541
  1163 revoked No. 2312 § 1541
  1228 amended No. 2312 § 1541
  1245 revoked No. 2312 § 1541
  1509 revoked No. 24 § 2520
  1528 revoked No. 2312 § 1541
  1612 revoked No. 2312 § 1541

1939
   56 revoked No. 24 § 2520
   509 revoked No. 2312 § 1541
   510 amended No. 2312 § 1541
   621 amended No. 2312 § 1541
   642 amended No. 2312 § 1541
   857 revoked No. 2312 § 1541
  1490 revoked No. 2312 § 1541
  1888 amended No. 2312 § 1541

1940
   109 amended No. 2312 § 1541
   729 revoked No. 2312 § 1541
  1419 amended No. 2001 § 181

1944
  1129 amended No. 2001 § 181

1947
   184 amended No. 2312 § 1541
   871 revoked No. 1755 § 81
  1176 revoked No. 1755 § 81
  1443 revoked No. 1951 § 2905
  1659 amended No. 390 § 4401
  2600 amended No. 2312 § 1541

1948
   631 revoked No. 214 § 4391
  1131 revoked No. 214 § 4391
  1949 revoked No. 214 § 4391
  1250 revoked No. 214 § 4391
  1256 revoked No. 214 § 4391
  1954 revoked No. 214 § 4391

1949
    35 amended No. 2312 § 1541
   330 amended No. 619 § 334
  1097 revoked No. 431 § 2005

1950
  1837 revoked No. 2312 § 1541

1952
   114 revoked No. 401 § 3534
  1869 amended No. 1444 § 2842
  2231 revoked No. 1820 § 968

1954
  1212 revoked No. 24 § 2520
  1227 revoked No. 24 § 2520
  1382 revoked No. 401 § 3534

1955
   990 revoked No. 1078 § 2908
  1911 amended No. 693 § 4760

1956
   782 revoked No. 13 § 3534

1957
   191 revoked No. 1951 § 2905
   439 revoked No. 1078 § 2908
   972 revoked No. 1078 § 2908
  1154 amended No. 13 § 3534
  2027 revoked No. 401 § 3534
  2233 amended No. 136 § 3534
  2242 revoked No. 401 § 3534

1958
   165 amended No. 58 § 3526
   257 revoked No. 1951 § 2905
   313 revoked No. 1951 § 2905
   962 revoked No. 1951 § 2905
  1208 amended No. 770 § 2846
  1819 revoked No. 2312 § 1541

1959
     3 amended No. 1962 § 2093
   861 revoked No. 1299 § 428
  2053 revoked No. 1078 § 2908
  2115 revoked No. 401 § 3534
  2282 amended No. 1733 § 3534

1960
  1410 amended No. 1776 § 3534
  1552 amended No. 136 § 3534
  2195 amended No. 1358 § 4468
  2332 revoked No. 103 § 1580

1961
   257 revoked No. 120 § 4091
  1214 amended No. 1414 § 2121
  2100 amended No. 58 § 3526
  2213 revoked No. 647 § 1555

1962
   737 revoked No. 1532 § 3534
   767 amended No. 1738 § 1608
  1404 revoked No. 401 § 3534
  1765 amended No. 660 § 2129
  1978 amended No. 2210 § 3534
  2045 amended No. 609 § 240
  2527 revoked No. 1951 § 2905
  2576 amended No. 995 § 3393

1962—*cont.*
  2641 revoked No. 1002 § 135
  2767 revoked No. 1002 § 135

1963
   629 revoked No. 1755 § 81
  1710 amended No. 1682 § 3537
  1834 revoked No. 1002 § 135
  1880 revoked No. 1002 § 135
  1881 revoked No. 1002 § 135

1964
   227 amended No. 691 § 3049
   227 revoked No. 1319 § 3426
  1107 revoked No. 923 § 2081
  1346 revoked No. 401 § 3534
  1529 amended No. 399 § 2046

1965
   321 amended No. 514 § 4428
   321 amended No. 694 § 4428
   321 amended No. 799 § 4428
   321 amended No. 1128 § 4056
   321 amended No. 1231 § 4428
   540 amended No. 452 § 2046
   753 revoked No. 399 § 2046
  1301 revoked No. 401 § 3534
  1681 amended No. 249 § 3534
  1776 amended No. 632 § 2609
  1776 amended No. 1187 § 2695
  1776 amended No. 2001 § 181
  1776 amended No. 2289 § 2695
  1839 amended No. 21 § 4544
  1995 amended No. 621 § 1769

1966
   233 amended No. 455 § 2546
   897 revoked No. 399 § 2046
  1044 amended No. 1532 § 3534
  1190 revoked No. 1951 § 2905
  1287 revoked No. 399 § 2046

1967
    29 amended No. 1353 § 4010
   954 amended No. 2001 § 181
  1310 amended No. 621 § 1769
  1345 revoked No. 399 § 2046
  1447 revoked No. 399 § 2046
  1875 revoked No. 724 § 2012

1968
    43 revoked No. 183 § 2975
   357 revoked No. 887 § 2112
   571 revoked No. 1951 § 2905
   746 revoked No. 399 § 2046
   935 revoked No. 1002 § 135
   936 revoked No. 1002 § 135
   953 revoked No. 1002 § 135
   954 revoked No. 1002 § 135
  1039 revoked No. 401 § 3534
  1231 amended No. 274 § 1970
  1314 revoked No. 1039 § 3222
  1558 amended No. 2105 § 965
  1645 revoked No. 724 § 2012
  2049 amended No. 1442 § 2842

1969
   258 revoked No. 1079 § 2092
   284 amended No. 1558 § 1607

1969—*cont.*
463 revoked No. 179 § 2989
1272 revoked No. 923 § 2081
1342 amended No. 2001 § 181
1437 revoked No. 1953 § 148
1712 revoked No. 724 § 2012
1787 amended No. 1846 § 2549

1970
147 amended No. 2100 § 1526
230 revoked No. 1079 § 2092
257 amended No. 1459 § 2918
1109 revoked No. 724 § 2012
1126 revoked No. 214 § 4391
1356 revoked No. 401 § 3534
1370 revoked No. 1683 § 3545
1437 revoked No. 1299 § 428
1621 amended No. 1532 § 3534
1710 revoked No. 1684 § 3536
1711 amended No. 1682 § 3537
1714 revoked No. 1684 § 3536
1780 revoked No. 1442 § 2842
1945 revoked No. 1951 § 2905
1958 amended No. 1328 § 2991

1971
40 revoked No. 1683 § 3545
90 revoked No. 978 § 4066
129 revoked No. 1445 § 2842
231 amended No. 422 § 2046
311 revoked No. 498 § 73
450 amended No. 607 § 2973
450 amended No. 1177 § 2973
450 amended No. 2101 § 2973
492 amended No. 518 § 3634
495 revoked No. 399 § 2046
618 revoked No. 1951 § 2905
818 amended No. 1459 § 2918
1036 revoked No. 498 § 73
1040 revoked No. 1951 § 2905
1061 revoked No. 1951 § 2905
1062 revoked No. 1951 § 2905
1197 revoked No. 1537 § 1819
1217 revoked No. 1445 § 2842
1218 revoked No. 1442 § 2842
1493 revoked No. 178 § 2910
1743 revoked No. 1882 § 2905
1848 revoked No. 1299 § 428
1861 amended No. 1357 § 1502
1930 revoked No. 129 § 2007
2102 amended No. 2012 § 1527
2103 amended No. 2016 § 1532

1972
171 amended No. 442 § 2046
172 amended No. 442 § 2046
173 amended No. 422 § 2046
316 amended No. 2126 § 123
385 revoked No. 312 § 137
419 amended No. 2125 § 120
545 amended No. 690 § 2756
641 amended No. 2001 § 181
681 revoked No. 401 § 3534
729 revoked No. 259 § 2965
764 amended No. 2001 § 181
765 amended No. 2001 § 181
941 amended No. 1434 § 1607
1268 amended No. 2001 § 181
1344 revoked No. 590 § 3515

1972—*cont.*
1375 revoked No. 498 § 73
1481 revoked No. 399 § 2046
1483 amended No. 1277 § 3527

1973
79 revoked No. 2214 § 1154
118 revoked No. 400 § 956
334 amended No. 2212 § 1758
390 amended No. 254 § 4468
390 amended No. 673 § 4058
390 amended No. 1359 § 4468
417 amended No. 422 § 2046
428 amended No. 1379 § 2526
490 amended No. 706 § 2454
498 amended No. 1776 § 3534
798 amended No. 2332 § 639
982 revoked No. 399 § 2046
1028 revoked No. 180 § 2989
1064 revoked No. 722 § 1567
1230 revoked No. 1893 § 3072
1268 amended No. 625 § 2141a
1360 amended No. 208 § 2029
1468 amended No. 1499 § 2235
1756 amended No. 2014 § 1529
1897 revoked No. 1951 § 2905
1910 revoked No. 2215 § 1154
2061 amended No. 561 § 3320
2124 amended No. 26 § 3019
2173 revoked No. 498 § 73
2199 revoked No. 1201 § 1555
2200 revoked No. 647 § 1555
2221 revoked No. 1951 § 2905

1974
84 revoked No. 2215 § 1154
160 amended No. 381 § 2240
160 amended No. 916 § 2240
160 amended No. 1486 § 2240
284 amended No. 976 § 2243
287 revoked No. 975 § 2243
419 amended No. 420 § 3291
420 amended No. 420 § 3291
447 revoked No. 724 § 2012
488 revoked No. 1002 § 135
500 revoked No. 1002 § 135
505 amended No. 1571 § 4316
506 amended No. 925 § 4318
506 amended No. 1507 § 4318
507 revoked No. 965 § 4322
518 amended No. 282 § 2036
519 amended No. 345 § 2053
520 revoked No. 24 § 2520
529 amended No. 464 § 680
529 amended No. 945 § 2100
529 amended No. 1280 § 680
529 revoked No. 1713 § 2100
539 amended No. 435 § 2046
544 revoked No. 887 § 2112
572 amended No. 1445 § 2842
668 amended No. 1962 § 2093
768 amended No. 1342 § 72
812 amended No. 1449 § 4391
1286 amended No. 2001 § 181
1356 amended No. 791 § 4084
1366 revoked No. 541 § 1887
1377 amended No. 976 § 2243
1440 amended No. 966 § 4322
1740 amended No. 391 § 2518

103

1974—*cont.*
1838 amended No. 587 § 4317
1934 revoked No. 590 § 3515
1942 amended No. 1951 § 2905
2057 amended No. 2001 § 181
2211 amended No. 2062 § 85

1975
59 revoked No. 1713 § 2100
205 amended No. 620 § 1576
229 revoked No. 1319 § 3426
267 revoked No. 178 § 2910
297 revoked No. 1713 § 2100
299 revoked No. 1322 § 2823
536 amended No. 302 § 3430
539 amended No. 267 § 4646
563 amended No. 486 § 3119
563 amended No. 1545 § 3149
563 amended No. 1561 § 3138
789 revoked No. 965 § 4322
837 amended No. 1191 § 3847
873 revoked No. 1713 § 2100
928 revoked No. 26 § 3019
1023 amended No. 1249 § 693
1023 amended No. 2268 § 693
1054 revoked No. 541 § 1887
1077 revoked No. 1713 § 2100
1180 revoked No. 1713 § 2100
1562 revoked No. 178 § 2910
1573 amended No. 1541 § 3145
1573 amended No. 2217 § 3148
1803 amended No. 1142 § 2640
1960 amended No. 1240 § 1730
1803 amended No. 2155 § 2640
1992 revoked No. 260 § 966
1994 revoked No. 1713 § 2100
2029 revoked No. 180 § 2989
2030 revoked No. 179 § 2989
2031 revoked No. 259 § 2965
2124 amended No. 1016 § 374
2233 revoked No. 411 § 4529

1976
98 amended No. 2204 § 3403
179 revoked No. 1713 § 2100
185 amended No. 1716 § 2515
248 amended No. 333 § 2021
335 revoked No. 401 § 3534
905 revoked No. 541 § 1887
963 amended No. 2217 § 3248
965 amended No. 2217 § 3148
1073 amended No. 576 § 4403
1263 amended No. 1045 § 2745
1267 amended No. 1172 § 1542
1290 amended No. 1987 § 1607
1419 amended No. 443 § 2046
1447 amended No. 1493 § 2918
1641 revoked No. 1713 § 2100
1679 revoked No. 944 § 4315
1758 amended No. 2217 § 3148
1825 revoked No. 965 § 4322
1973 revoked No. 1713 § 2100
1981 revoked No. 1683 § 3545
1987 amended No. 2001 § 181
2012 amended No. 2001 § 181
2031 revoked No. 1039 § 3222
2065 revoked No. 2214 § 1154
2066 revoked No. 2215 § 1154
2105 revoked No. 2174 § 967
2144 amended No. 2020 § 1533

1977
87 amended No. 1241 § 126
139 revoked No. 1713 § 2100
204 amended No. 1782 § 251
228 amended No. 443 § 2046
248 revoked No. 1335 § 525
288 revoked No. 697 § 2753b
289 amended No. 435 § 2046
314 revoked No. 1202 § 148
344 amended No. 634 § 1106
548 amended No. 1224 § 2909
564 amended No. 1277 § 3527
665 amended No. 435 § 2046
717 amended No. 111 § 2519
717 amended No. 946 § 2519
746 amended No. 294 § 1193
776 revoked No. 2067 § 297
827 amended No. 23 § 2130
833 revoked No. 724 § 2012
910 revoked No. 2141 § 964
928 amended No. 2299 § 1567
982 revoked No. 1892 § 3072
985 amended No. 424 § 1806
1017 revoked No. 590 § 3515
1033 revoked No. 723 § 1567
1043 revoked No. 882 § 2920
1043 amended No. 1338 § 2920
1079 revoked No. 13 § 3534
1121 revoked No. 24 § 2520
1173 revoked No. 862 § 88
1210 amended No. 1217 § 3023
1301 revoked No. 1892 § 3072
1309 amended No. 752 § 2935
1309 amended No. 868 § 2935
1317 revoked No. 262 § 2963
1341 revoked No. 24 § 2520
1379 revoked No. 2331 § 639
1413 revoked No. 2128 § 2972
1521 revoked No. 399 § 2046
1653 amended No. 465 § 2522
1653 amended No. 940 § 2527
1672 revoked No. 1713 § 2100
1721 revoked No. 2061 § 79
1760 revoked No. 590 § 3515
1845 revoked No. 24 § 2520
1884 revoked No. 1713 § 2100
1956 revoked No. 24 § 2520
1999 revoked No. 975 § 2243
2052 amended No. 406 § 235
2069 revoked No. 1335 § 525
2103 amended No. 1813 § 2908

1978
32 amended No. 5 § 81
32 amended No. 1290 § 81
216 amended No. 583 § 2495
245 revoked No. 1202 § 148
266 revoked No. 24 § 2520
415 amended No. 625 § 2141a
484 amended No. 1082 § 3543
484 revoked No. 1082 § 3543
564 amended No. 560 § 2748
652 revoked No. 1713 § 2100
707 revoked No. 259 § 2965
813 revoked No. 1713 § 2100
814 revoked No. 1713 § 2100
822 revoked No. 24 § 2520
950 amended No. 976 § 2243
1014 revoked No. 175 § 1568

S.R. & O. AND S.I. AFFECTED IN 1986

1978—*cont.*
1017 revoked No. 1078 § 2908
1106 amended No. 220 § 1530
1128 revoked No. 887 § 2112
1129 revoked No. 335 § 3498
1133 amended No. 1512 § 1608
1133 amended No. 1513 § 1608
1133 amended No. 1514 § 1608
1157 revoked No. 1458 § 2918
1163 revoked No. 923 § 2081
1233 revoked No. 1078 § 2908
1235 revoked No. 1078 § 2908
1240 revoked No. 1776 § 3534
1263 revoked No. 1078 § 2908
1317 revoked No. 1078 § 2908
1345 revoked No. 184 § 2975
1347 revoked No. 181 § 2963
1364 revoked No. 1492 § 2918
1423 amended No. 266 § 4067
1424 amended No. 255 § 4055
1738 revoked No. 24 § 2520
1739 revoked No. 24 § 2520
1823 revoked No. 401 § 3534
1878 revoked No. 1493 § 2918
1932 revoked No. 1532 § 3534
1938 revoked No. 1493 § 2918

1979
2 revoked No. 24 § 2520
138 revoked No. 1078 § 2908
142 revoked No. 887 § 2112
218 revoked No. 416 § 639
237 revoked No. 1202 § 148
305 revoked No. 1305 § 3083
427 amended No. 1951 § 2905
453 amended No. 2013 § 1528
591 amended No. 198 § 3124
591 amended No. 485 § 3124
592 revoked No. 24 § 2520
628 amended No. 1561 § 3138
628 amended No. 1772 § 3123
628 amended No. 2217 § 3148
660 revoked No. 175 § 1568
705 amended No. 966 § 4322
785 amended No. 409 § 4391
843 revoked No. 1078 § 2908
937 amended No. 622 § 1769
1062 revoked No. 1078 § 2908
1088 amended No. 369 § 2958
1122 revoked No. 724 § 2012
1146 amended No. 1820 § 968
1198 amended No. 313 § 2958
1230 amended No. 1696 § 2556
1285 revoked No. 1713 § 2100
1436 revoked No. 1684 § 3536
1470 amended No. 784 § 2554a
1470 amended No. 2032 § 2551
1470 amended No. 2241 § 2551
1534 revoked No. 24 § 2520
1613 revoked No. 2049 § 3539
1644 amended No. 1642 § 2240
1715 amended No. 2235 § 438
1727 amended No. 2033 § 2540
1737 amended No. 918 § 2060
1746 amended No. 1457 § 4086
1746 amended No. 2076 § 2972

1980
107 revoked No. 965 § 4322
108 amended No. 1962 § 2093

1980—*cont.*
139 revoked No. 1078 § 2908
140 revoked No. 1078 § 2908
160 revoked No. 416 § 639
216 revoked No. 24 § 2520
224 revoked No. 1713 § 2100
233 revoked No. 24 § 2520
234 revoked No. 24 § 2520
287 revoked No. 1078 § 2908
320 amended No. 442 § 2046
330 amended No. 338 § 74
335 amended No. 1437 § 1555
347 amended No. 100 § 162
420 amended No. 195 § 72
443 revoked No. 443 § 2046
449 amended No. 196 § 72
450 amended No. 197 § 72
499 amended No. 194 § 72
529 amended No. 1075 § 3089
538 amended No. 1072 § 3089
542 revoked No. 1071 § 3089
574 revoked No. 986 § 1543
604 revoked No. 996 § 4072
610 revoked No. 1078 § 2908
623 revoked No. 1372 § 3393
638 revoked No. 902 § 2752
811 revoked No. 647 § 1555
819 amended No. 696 § 1081
821 amended No. 637 § 2634
821 amended No. 2144 § 2634
822 revoked No. 1201 § 1555
861 revoked No. 1390 § 2114
880 revoked No. 1078 § 2908
1009 revoked No. 939 § 3498
1012 revoked No. 938 § 958
1020 revoked No. 1713 § 2100
1064 revoked No. 2049 § 3539
1070 amended No. 1082 § 3543
1070 revoked No. 1082 § 3543
1072 amended No. 57 § 61
1100 revoked No. 1951 § 2905
1120 amended No. 366 § 2508
1162 revoked No. 1713 § 2100
1166 revoked No. 1078 § 2908
1233 revoked No. 392 § 1193
1254 amended No. 412 § 4395
1261 revoked No. 1713 § 2100
1279 amended No. 472 § 2953
1342 revoked No. 2193 § 1643
1354 revoked No. 1691 § 3451
1437 amended No. 2217 § 3148
1449 revoked No. 1713 § 2100
1503 amended No. 432 § 2234
1580 revoked No. 2217 § 3148
1582 amended No. 1498 § 1082
1630 amended No. 276 § 1978
1633 revoked No. 401 § 3534
1641 amended No. 1259 § 3160
1656 revoked No. 1713 § 2100
1641 amended No. 2173 § 3144
1674 amended No. 448 § 4313
1742 amended No. 1082 § 3543
1742 revoked No. 1082 § 3543
1789 revoked No. 1078 § 2908
1793 revoked No. 253 § 4468
1828 revoked No. 1713 § 2100
1850 revoked No. 1039 § 3222
1866 amended No. 788 § 4084
1894 amended No. 272 § 1972

105

1980—*cont.*

1894 amended No. 1186 § 1976
1894 amended No. 2001 § 181
1894 amended No. 2135 § 1977
1898 amended No. 275 § 1965
1931 revoked No. 1319 § 3426
1941 revoked No. 2187 § 2754
2001 revoked No. 1372 § 3393
2025 revoked No. 1935 § 3089

1981

91 revoked No. 561 § 3320
101 amended No. 458 § 2245
121 revoked No. 193 § 3019
152 revoked No. 416 § 639
180 revoked No. 724 § 2012
193 revoked No. 568 § 3094
257 amended No. 370 § 2968
257 amended No. 1812 § 2908
258 amended No. 994 § 3451
258 revoked No. 1668 § 3451
259 revoked No. 1628 § 3451
261 revoked No. 1078 § 2908
264 revoked No. 1691 § 3451
289 amended No. 442 § 2046
305 revoked No. 975 § 2243
307 amended No. 976 § 2243
316 revoked No. 724 § 2012
327 amended No. 1236 § 2809
354 amended No. 334 § 3084
359 amended No. 966 § 4322
360 revoked No. 965 § 4322
362 revoked No. 403 § 148
390 revoked No. 1713 § 2100
500 amended No. 373 § 4394
536 amended No. 442 § 2046
552 amended No. 1332 § 2092
553 amended No. 1333 § 2079
560 amended No. 435 § 2046
622 revoked No. 848 § 146
644 amended No. 442 § 2046
697 revoked No. 1078 § 2908
747 revoked No. 862 § 88
803 revoked No. 1202 § 148
804 amended No. 443 § 2046
804 amended No. 623 § 3321
815 amended No. 2217 § 3148
859 amended No. 1859 § 2990
861 amended No. 705 § 1520
861 amended No. 2185 § 2685
915 revoked No. 1078 § 2908
931 amended No. 2100 § 2927
952 amended No. 748 § 2935
1017 amended No. 1353 § 4010
1059 amended No. 1951 § 2905
1080 revoked No. 335 § 3498
1081 amended No. 435 § 2046
1082 amended No. 435 § 2046
1086 amended No. 542 § 1134
1135 revoked No. 1536 § 1816
1189 revoked No. 1078 § 2908
1239 revoked No. 1755 § 81
1250 revoked No. 24 § 2520
1260 amended No. 1819 § 963
1311 amended No. 1733 § 3534
1341 revoked No. 1713 § 2100
1432 revoked No. 1039 § 3222
1449 revoked No. 1713 § 2100
1455 amended No. 2295 § 81

1981—*cont.*

1509 revoked No. 24 § 2520
1514 amended No. 2210 § 3534
1525 amended No. 562 § 3160
1525 amended No. 2154 § 3160
1526 amended No. 1010 § 3185
1527 amended No. 1292 § 3160
1527 amended No. 1293 § 3160
1528 amended No. 1259 § 3160
1528 amended No. 1961 § 3185
1528 amended No. 2173 § 3144
1529 amended No. 1259 § 3160
1529 amended No. 2173 § 3144
1580 revoked No. 1078 § 2908
1596 amended No. 1278 § 3619
1631 amended No. 302 § 3430
1663 revoked No. 1078 § 2908
1687 amended No. 636 § 466
1687 amended No. 1189 § 466
1687 amended No. 2001 § 181
1688 revoked No. 1078 § 2908
1694 amended No. 372 § 2987
1694 amended No. 904 § 2987
1707 amended No. 1295 § 61
1743 amended No. 420 § 3291
1747 amended No. 1069 § 3089
1825 amended No. 831 § 3535
1847 revoked No. 331 § 2240

1982

7 amended No. 1501 § 2992
125 revoked No. 724 § 2012
137 revoked No. 56 § 2929
137 revoked No. 101 § 4622
144 revoked No. 2049 § 3539
217 amended No. 9 § 2126
218 amended No. 10 § 2126
218 amended No. 1704 § 2126
219 revoked No. 416 § 639
275 revoked No. 724 § 2012
284 amended No. 976 § 2243
291 revoked No. 179 § 2989
292 revoked No. 180 § 2989
293 revoked No. 259 § 2965
301 amended No. 442 § 2046
333 amended No. 966 § 4322
356 revoked No. 403 § 148
467 revoked No. 967 § 4054
555 amended No. 443 § 2046
586 amended No. 1505 § 462
586 amended No. 2001 § 181
612 amended No. 79 § 959
626 amended No. 1980 § 2119
717 amended No. 583 § 2495
718 revoked No. 1319 § 3426
719 amended No. 2001 § 181
719 amended No. 2103 § 2002
811 amended No. 1043 § 3537
834 amended No. 2074 § 132
863 amended No. 459 § 2234
863 amended No. 950 § 2240
894 amended No. 477 § 1247
898 amended No. 516 § 4313
898 amended No. 924 § 4313
908 revoked No. 24 § 2520
938 revoked No. 1148 § 1123
949 revoked No. 1104 § 4005
992 revoked No. 561 § 3320
1000 amended No. 1021 § 2533

1982—*cont.*

1009 amended No. 151 § 2046
1057 revoked No. 1078 § 2908
1093 revoked No. 403 § 148
1109 amended No. 2151 § 542
1132 revoked No. 1078 § 2908
1135 amended No. 1811 § 2338
1143 revoked No. 177 § 56
1197 amended No. 273 § 1970
1197 amended No. 444 § 1970
1197 amended No. 1515 § 1970
1197 amended No. 1835 § 1970
1223 revoked No. 1078 § 2908
1229 amended No. 1208 § 1825
1241 amended No. 2217 § 3148
1271 amended No. 427 § 2992
1272 revoked No. 1078 § 2908
1400 revoked No. 2218 § 3115
1408 amended No. 1118 § 3119
1408 amended No. 1561 § 3138
1408 amended No. 2217 § 3148
1422 revoked No. 1078 § 2908
1457 amended No. 476 § 72
1478 amended No. 371 § 2987
1480 revoked No. 1078 § 2908
1496 amended No. 890 § 1193
1506 amended No. 641 § 4525
1513 amended No. 1985 § 2537
1514 revoked No. 24 § 2520
1554 revoked No. 1492 § 2918
1576 revoked No. 1078 § 2908
1579 amended No. 1277 § 3527
1623 revoked No. 1501 § 2992
1706 amended No. 633 § 461
1706 amended No. 2143 § 461
1784 amended No. 2153 § 148
1812 revoked No. 1713 § 2100

1983

70 revoked No. 392 § 1193
104 revoked No. 2217
111 revoked No. 724 § 2012
112 revoked No. 1078 § 2908
132 revoked No. 2181 § 1825
196 revoked No. 416 § 639
210 revoked No. 862 § 88
250 amended No. 442 § 2046
253 amended No. 382 § 1549
256 amended No. 251 § 1555
256 revoked No. 2090 § 1555
302 amended No. 459 § 2234
309 amended No. 976 § 2243
312 amended No. 440 § 2244
315 amended No. 2001 § 181
349 revoked No. 403 § 148
362 amended No. 516 § 4313
382 amended No. 614 § 3403
415 revoked No. 2223 § 3092
416 revoked No. 2225 § 3092
417 amended No. 597 § 1155
425 revoked No. 428 § 58
483 amended No. 610 § 1603
435 amended No. 104 § 1158
436 amended No. 105 § 2338
471 revoked No. 1078 § 2908
481 amended No. 1346 § 1126
708 amended No. 1163 § 3089
506 amended No. 625 § 2141a

1983—*cont.*

548 amended No. 139 § 4015a
548 revoked No. 1111 § 4015a
560 revoked No. 401 § 3534
573 revoked No. 334 § 3084
587 amended No. 2001 § 181
667 amended No. 2294 § 2242
670 revoked No. 1039 § 3222
686 amended No. 628 § 2530
713 amended No. 2001 § 181
713 amended No. 754 § 460
713 amended No. 1361 § 2666
713 amended No. 2207 § 468
843 revoked No. 1713 § 2100
873 amended No. 786 § 2120
873 amended No. 1345 § 2122
873 amended No. 1897 § 2242
883 amended No. 592 § 2509
932 revoked No. 1078 § 2908
938 revoked No. 791 § 4084
939 revoked No. 788 § 4084
941 amended No. 1755 § 81
947 amended No. 910 § 958
969 revoked No. 1202 § 148
971 revoked No. 967 § 4054
1000 amended No. 2217 § 3148
1029 revoked No. 1238 § 4273
1030 revoked No. 1104 § 4005
1080 revoked No. 334 § 3084
1087 revoked No. 1856 § 1606
1150 revoked No. 1103 § 4005
1153 revoked No. 2215 § 1154
1154 revoked No. 2214 § 1154
1182 amended No. 1623 § 2752
1185 amended No. 1325 § 1150
1190 amended No. 443 § 2046
1204 amended No. 1439 § 1555
1206 amended No. 1438 § 1555
1209 amended No. 1244 § 1608
1212 amended No. 586 § 2128
1269 revoked No. 24 § 2520
1270 revoked No. 24 § 2520
1271 amended No. 24 § 2520
1351 amended No. 1015 § 2247
1352 amended No. 1014 § 2247
1375 amended No. 864 § 1825
1383 revoked No. 998 § 1556
1390 amended No. 1210 § 3537
1399 amended No. 1173 § 3160
1399 amended No. 1292 § 3160
1399 amended No. 1293 § 3160
1439 revoked No. 428 § 58
1450 amended No. 392 § 1193
1508 amended No. 720 § 1567
1509 amended No. 721 § 1567
1514 amended No. 790 § 4084
1515 amended No. 789 § 4080
1518 amended No. 1881 § 1676
1598 amended No. 484 § 3119
1598 amended No. 1011 § 3159
1598 amended No. 1118 § 3119
1649 amended No. 392 § 1193
1653 revoked No. 1685 § 3542
1669 revoked No. 1713 § 2100
1740 revoked No. 1981 § 1584
1761 amended No. 1271 § 2009
1770 revoked No. 400 § 956
1808 amended No. 1591 § 2206
1818 revoked No. 2090 § 1555

1983—*cont.*
1830 revoked No. 453 § 3024
1838 revoked No. 2069 § 962
1845 revoked No. 1713 § 2100
1865 amended No. 769 § 163
1865 revoked No. 1712 § 162
1908 amended No. 3 § 2200
1914 revoked No. 1713 § 2100
1915 revoked No. 1713 § 2100

1984
62 revoked No. 149 § 2144
91 revoked No. 193 § 2019
137 revoked No. 2209 § 1368
165 revoked No. 416 § 639
174 amended No. 678 § 4149
176 amended No. 666 § 2931
176 amended No. 1391 § 2931
195 amended No. 1078 § 2908
210 revoked No. 24 § 2520
230 amended No. 378 § 76
252 amended No. 449 § 4057
256 amended No. 450 § 4054
261 revoked No. 400 § 956
266 amended No. 21 § 4544
284 amended No. 314 § 1137
293 amended No. 966 § 4322
295 amended No. 516 § 4313
295 amended No. 924 § 4313
297 amended No. 2001 § 181
299 amended No. 976 § 2243
300 amended No. 459 § 2234
300 revoked No. 950 § 2240
310 amended No. 392 § 1193
331 revoked No. 1078 § 2908
368 revoked No. 1304 § 139
380 amended No. 317 § 2525
380 amended No. 1716 § 2515
386 revoked No. 1078 § 2908
396 revoked No. 1712 § 163
421 amended No. 433 § 2046
426 revoked No. 1713 § 2100
451 amended No. 1259 § 3160
451 amended No. 1541 § 3145
451 amended No. 2217 § 3148
451 amended No. 2218 § 3115
455 amended No. 538 § 1548
457 amended No. 625 § 2141a
458 amended No. 2217 § 3148
460 revoked No. 1442 § 2842
461 revoked No. 1445 § 2842
519 amended No. 681 § 4058
520 amended No. 674 § 3799
549 amended No. 2235 § 438
561 revoked No. 1755 § 81
577 revoked No. 1713 § 2100
613 revoked No. 2218 § 3115
614 amended No. 1716 § 2525
614 amended No. 2171 § 2525
641 revoked No. 403 § 148
679 revoked No. 1078 § 2908
698 revoked No. 724 § 2012
770 revoked No. 862 § 88
779 amended No. 2001 § 181
813 revoked No. 1078 § 2908
817 revoked No. 1078 § 2908
840 revoked No. 1104 § 4005
841 revoked No. 1103 § 4005
880 amended No. 2030 § 306
887 amended No. 2001 § 181

1984—*cont.*
938 amended No. 2217 § 3148
981 amended No. 739 § 2292
1042 revoked No. 1148 § 1123
1045 revoked No. 815 § 3029
1047 revoked No. 740 § 3534
1048 revoked No. 740 § 3534
1075 amended No. 2001 § 181
1098 amended No. 1031 § 1137
1132 revoked No. 967 § 4054
1144 revoked No. 2331 § 639
1150 revoked No. 2221 § 1788
1175 revoked No. 2194 § 1643
1204 revoked No. 1713 § 2100
1206 amended No. 1643 § 961
1216 amended No. 1074 § 3089
1217 amended No. 1067 § 3089
1218 amended No. 1070 § 3089
1244 amended No. 1922 § 1193
1244 amended No. 1951 § 2905
1268 revoked No. 550 § 3029
1303 amended No. 1933 § 3151
1303 amended No. 2218 § 3115
1316 amended No. 1260 § 3538
1317 revoked No. 2049 § 3539
1345 amended No. 457 § 2113
1383 revoked No. 1646 § 1607
1519 amended No. 836 § 4078
1523 amended No. 988 § 1556
1538 revoked No. 740 § 3534
1543 revoked No. 1078 § 2908
1551 revoked No. 404 § 2330
1566 revoked No. 987 § 1565
1578 amended No. 456 § 2123
1628 revoked No. 1713 § 2100
1640 revoked No. 26 § 3019
1705 revoked No. 1494 § 1616
1714 amended No. 1288 § 4082
1787 revoked No. 740 § 3534
1809 revoked No. 1078 § 2908
1811 revoked No. 1078 § 2908
1814 amended No. 600 § 2006
1823 amended No. 222 § 2407
1874 amended No. 853 § 3529
1890 amended No. 392 § 1193
1902 amended No. 294 § 1193
1920 amended No. 2120 § 148
1927 revoked No. 1501 § 2992
1956 revoked No. 2090 § 1555
1960 amended No. 2217 § 3148
1970 amended No. 701 § 4392
1989 amended No. 584 § 2494
1991 revoked No. 2218 § 3115
2005 amended No. 1894 § 75
2020 revoked No. 2284 § 1250
2037 revoked No. 67 § 1247

1985
24 revoked No. 5 § 81
91 revoked No. 1078 § 2908
94 amended No. 140 § 4526
95 amended No. 2002 § 312
100 revoked No. 479 § 1547
108 revoked No. 816 § 3029
138 revoked No. 416 § 639
159 amended No. 2218 § 3115
175 amended No. 853 § 3529
185 revoked No. 678 § 4149
186 amended No. 466 § 3530
213 amended No. 2001 § 181

1985—*cont.*

214 amended No. 753 § 3451
214 amended No. 869 § 3451
214 amended No. 972 § 3451
221 revoked No. 424 § 1806
246 amended No. 407 § 4249
251 revoked No. 402 § 3094
279 revoked No. 392 § 1193
298 revoked No. 975 § 2243
300 revoked No. 302 § 3430
338 revoked No. 608 § 1770
343 revoked No. 620 § 1576
344 revoked No. 621 § 1769
345 revoked No. 622 § 1769
349 revoked No. 403 § 148
255 revoked No. 965 § 4322
357 amended No. 339 § 71
359 revoked No. 1399 § 1813
371 amended No. 459 § 2234
394 revoked No. 134 § 3029
426 revoked No. 724 § 2012
440 amended No. 430 § 1610
464 revoked No. 1225 § 2963
487 amended No. 926 § 1555
489 revoked No. 24 § 2520
506 revoked No. 510 § 4005
508 revoked No. 459 § 2234
509 revoked No. 740 § 3534
510 revoked No. 1202 § 148
555 (except para. 3) revoked No. 967
556 amended No. 140 § 4526
564 revoked No. 1712 § 163
572 revoked No. 1712 § 163
573 revoked No. 2049 § 3539
677 amended No. 84 § 1610
677 amended No. 852 § 1610
677 amended No. 1009 § 1610
677 amended No. 1156 § 1610
677 amended No. 2183 § 1610
684 amended No. 989 § 1137
685 amended No. 991 § 1125
691 revoked No. 816 § 3029
692 revoked No. 816 § 3029
699 revoked No. 1020 § 3097
730 revoked No. 1078 § 2908
751 amended No. 2015 § 1531
757 amended No. 2186 § 372
764 revoked No. 815 § 3029
777 amended No. 1082 § 3543
777 revoked No. 1082 § 3543
784 revoked No. 584 § 2494
785 amended No. 583 § 2495
790 revoked No. 815 § 3029
793 revoked No. 117 § 3029
827 amended No. 451 § 4066
829 revoked No. 2067 § 297
830 amended No. 990 § 1125
849 amended No. 82 § 960
849 amended N 540 § 960
849 amended No. 1446 § 960
849 amended No. 1934 § 960
854 amended No. 2097 § 300
863 revoked No. 344 § 2808
866 amended No. 71 § 3467
886 amended No. 305 § 3497
886 amended No. 335 § 3498
899 revoked No. 816 § 3029
921 amended No. 691 § 3049
921 revoked No. 1319 § 3426
928 revoked No. 92 § 3029

1985—*cont.*

937 revoked No. 1511 § 1618
946 revoked No. 29 § 3029
967 amended No. 1561 § 3138
969 amended No. 816 § 3029
970 revoked No. 816 § 3029
993 revoked No. 442 § 2046
996 amended No. 2001 § 181
997 revoked No. 1256 § 48
1012 amended No. 8 § 3253
1050 amended No. 1144 § 1120
1062 revoked No. 34 § 3029
1072 revoked No. 1501 § 2992
1076 revoked No. 1104 § 4005
1084 revoked No. 1713 § 2100
1086 amended No. 853 § 3529
1120 revoked No. 1227 § 4005
1126 revoked No. 1306 § 1126
1156 revoked No. 1713 § 2100
1166 amended No. 583 § 2495
1174 revoked No. 5 § 81
1183 revoked No. 1103 § 4005
1226 revoked No. 33 § 3029
1317 revoked No. 861 § 3121
1323 amended No. 317 § 2525
1323 amended No. 1716 § 2515
1325 amended No. 576 § 4403
1333 amended No. 392 § 1193
1363 revoked No. 1078 § 2908
1377 revoked No. 938 § 958
1384 revoked No. 939 § 3498
1411 amended No. 318 § 1247
1416 amended No. 1357 § 1502
1428 revoked No. 1778 § 147
1430 revoked No. 1777 § 3106
1431 revoked No. 133 § 3029
1433 revoked No. 118 § 3029
1435 revoked No. 31 § 3029
1437 revoked No. 215 § 3029
1464 revoked No. 815 § 3029
1492 amended No. 199 § 2246
1496 revoked No. 49 § 3029
1497 revoked No. 90 § 3029
1510 revoked No. 361 § 3029
1511 revoked No. 165 § 3029
1512 revoked No. 31 § 3029
1515 revoked No. 24 § 2520
1523 revoked No. 606 § 3029
1524 revoked No. 1200 § 3029
1530 revoked No. 1050 § 4312
1571 revoked No. 1118 § 3119
1576 amended No. 2287 § 204
1581 revoked No. 2103 § 2002
1607 amended No. 837 § 3080
1630 amended No. 348 § 957
1630 amended No. 813 § 957
1630 amended No. 1352 § 957
1630 amended No. 2179 § 957
1643 amended No. 2238 § 138
1646 revoked No. 1989 § 3514
1648 revoked No. 28 § 3029
1649 revoked No. 30 § 3029
1665 amended No. 296 § 3092
1691 revoked No. 814 § 2512
1692 revoked No. 109 § 3028
1693 revoked No. 816 § 3029
1705 amended No. 140 § 4526
1714 amended No. 544 § 138
1714 amended No. 2121 § 148
1720 revoked No. 89 § 3029

1985—*cont.*

1737 amended No. 306 § 2903
1752 revoked No. 816 § 3029
1759 revoked No. 1713 § 2100
1768 revoked No. 51 § 3029
1769 revoked No. 35 § 3029
1770 revoked No. 91 § 3029
1771 revoked No. 815 § 3029
1801 amended No. 2076 § 2972
1802 revoked No. 2128 § 2972
1807 amended No. 2001 § 181
1810 revoked No. 815 § 3029
1811 revoked No. 865 § 3029
1819 revoked No. 2072 § 132
1820 revoked No. 2073 § 132
1823 amended No. 982 § 2131
1823 amended No. 1997 § 2131
1824 revoked No. 50 § 3029
1845 revoked No. 1712 § 163
1848 revoked No. 2214 § 1154
1850 revoked No. 887 § 2112
1867 revoked No. 816 § 3029
1868 revoked No. 93 § 3029
1870 revoked No. 1713 § 2100
1875 revoked No. 2161 § 167a
1880 amended No. 445 § 1965
1880 amended No. 1559 § 1965
1881 revoked No. 307 § 674
1884 amended No. 564 § 2046
1894 revoked No. 164 § 3029
1895 revoked No. 166 § 3029
1905 revoked No. 1668 § 3451
1906 revoked No. 1628 § 3451
1907 revoked No. 1691 § 3451
1920 revoked No. 24 § 2520
1929 amended No. 2171 § 2525
1930 amended No. 751 § 2525
1931 amended No. 751 § 2525
1931 amended No. 1046 § 2525
1931 amended No. 2171 § 2525
1939 amended No. 2129 § 138
1948 revoked No. 865 § 3029
1949 revoked No. 362 § 3029
1950 revoked No. 206 § 3029
1964 revoked No. 1713 § 2100
1965 revoked No. 1713 § 2100
1972 revoked No. 815 § 3029
1973 revoked No. 815 § 3029
1982 revoked No. 8 § 3253
2004 revoked No. 1713 § 2100
2011 amended No. 2300 § 2752
2031 revoked No. 1713 § 2100
2032 revoked No. 2283 § 1187
2033 revoked No. 2281 § 1250
2039 revoked No. 1078 § 2908
2041 amended No. 787 § 967
2051 revoked No. 1078 § 2908
2066 amended No. 2330 § 639

1986

36 revoked No. 462 § 3029
38 revoked No. 815 § 3029
39 revoked No. 815 § 3029
40 revoked No. 205 § 3029
41 revoked No. 360 § 3029
42 revoked No. 204 § 3029
43 revoked No. 815 § 3029
44 revoked No. 548 § 3029
45 revoked No. 815 § 3029
46 revoked No. 1130 § 3029

1986—*cont.*

47 revoked No. 363 § 3029
48 revoked No. 815 § 3029
68 amended No. 1737 § 1557
107 revoked No. 815 § 3029
108 revoked No. 815 § 3029
111 revoked No. 946 § 2519
130 revoked No. 815 § 3029
131 revoked No. 359 § 3029
132 revoked No. 2050 § 3029
139 revoked No. 1111 § 4015a
148 amended No. 413 § 2046
148 amended No. 564 § 2046
148 amended No. 2293 § 2046
157 revoked No. 461 § 3029
163 revoked No. 815 § 3029
177 revoked No. 1735 § 82
192 amended No. 426 § 2046
192 amended No. 582 § 2046
200 revoked No. 865 § 3029
201 revoked No. 552 § 3029
202 revoked No. 815 § 3029
203 revoked No. 1200 § 3029
251 revoked No. 2090 § 1555
260 amended No. 1019 § 966
236 revoked No. 815 § 3029
300 revoked No. 379 § 2046
331 revoked No. 524 § 2240
353 revoked No. 915 § 3028
354 revoked No. 915 § 3028
355 revoked No. 1130 § 3029
356 revoked No. 549 § 3029
357 revoked No. 815 § 3029
358 revoked No. 815 § 3029
403 amended No. 2170 § 148
405 amended No. 842 § 543
405 amended No. 1250 § 949
405 amended No. 1818 § 543
413 amended No. 573 § 2046
426 amended No. 582 § 2046
433 revoked No. 815 § 3029
460 revoked No. 815 § 3029
464 revoked No. 1713 § 2100
465 revoked No. 940 § 2527
446 revoked No. 815 § 3029
553 amended No. 1398 § 2046
590 amended No. 2290 § 3515
611 revoked No. 2134 § 309
691 revoked No. 1447 § 3409
769 revoked No. 1712 § 163
818 revoked No. 915 § 3028
822 revoked No. 1396 § 3029
823 revoked No. 915 § 3028
824 revoked No. 1101 § 3029
825 revoked No. 1101 § 3029
826 revoked No. 1101 § 3029
827 revoked No. 1667 § 3029
828 revoked No. 1130 § 3029
869 amended No. 972 § 3451
941 revoked No. 1101 § 3029
942 revoked No. 1130 § 3029
943 revoked No. 1130 § 3029
945 revoked No. 1713 § 2100
951 revoked No. 1995 § 307
966 amended No. 1192 § 4322
944 revoked No. 1668 § 3451
1007 revoked No. 1130 § 3029
1027 revoked No. 1121 § 1560
1046 amended No. 1717 § 2525
1059 revoked No. 1179 § 1560

ALPHABETICAL TABLE OF
NORTHERN IRELAND
STATUTORY RULES AND ORDERS 1986

ALPHABETICAL TABLE OF N. IRELAND S.R. & O. 1986

NORTHERN IRELAND

NUMERICAL TABLE OF STATUTORY RULES AND ORDERS 1986

1985	C.L.Y.	1986		C.L.Y.
359	2411	65		2400
362	2411	66		2287
364	2476	67		2289
365	2334	68		2400
366	2467	69		2400
367	2353	71		2463
368	2411	72		2463
		75		2310
1986	C.L.Y.	76		2380
1	2462	77		2380
2	2290	78		2430
3	2454	79		2290
4	2454	80		2380
5	2454	81		2334
7	2429	82		2463
10	2293	83		2341
11	2293	88		2310
12	2293	89		2388
16	2463	96		2393
17	2450	101		2380
18	2391	102		2454
19	2361	103		2388
21	2355	107	(C. 1)	2393
22	2353	110		2353
23	2463	111		2353
24	2289	112		2353
25	2289	113		2289
26	2289	114		2463
27	2289	115		2429
28	2351	116		2290
33	2454	117		2454
34	2334	118		2411
35	2345	119		2355
36	2345	120		2472
37	2459	123		2454
38	2334	124	(C. 3)	2358
39	2380	125		2358
40	2355	126		2358
45	2463	127		2358
46	2412	128		2412
47	2412	129		2364
48	2290	130		2364
51	2462	131		2355
52	2391	132		2299
53	2391	133		2388
54	2341	137		2364
55	2473	138		2364
56	2371	139		2463
57	2463	140		2388
61	2293	141		2472
62	2454	142		2472
64	2463	143		2353
		144		2353

1986	C.L.Y.	1986	C.L.Y.
145	2353	230	2454
148	2454	231	2454
150	2353	232	2412
151	2410	233	2333
152	2395	235	2361
154	2380	236	2463
155	2410	237	2380
156	2361	238	2454
157	2463	239	2361
158	2361	240	2463
159	2361	241	2412
160	2463	243	2454
161	2454	244	2450
162	2454	246	2289
163	2400	247	2341
164	2400	253	2290
165	2334	254	2289
166	2391	261	2289
167	2391	262	2463
168	2479	264	2299
169 (C. 4)	2463	265	2472
170	2400	266	2463
171	2454	267	2454
173	2454	268	2352
174	2393	270	2463
175	2388	271	2454
176	2450	273	2361
177	2454	275	2463
179	2463	276	2463
184	2412	278	2410
185	2428	279	2410
188	2344	280	2334
191	2472	281	2334
192	2472	282	2454
193	2393	283	2454
194	2338	284	2411
195	2310	286	2450
197	2454	287	2299
200	2410	288	2290
202	2463	289	2400
203	2412	290	2472
204	2537	291	2287
205	2334	292	2454
206	2341	293	2454
207	2463	294	2410
208	2463	295	2289
209	2364	296	2467
210	2412	298	2454
211	2463	299	2289
212	2463	300	2289
213	2410	301	2349
214	2356	302	2341
215	2454	303	2463
216	2454	304	2299
218	2310	305	2299
219	2388	306	2299
221	2463	307	2476
222	2479	308	2476
223	2463	309	2400
224	2472	311	2476
225	2463	313	2428
226	2476	314	2411
227	2355	315	2411
228	2454	320	2463
229	2454	330 (C. 5)	2393

1986	C.L.Y.	1986	C.L.Y.
331	2296	354	2351
332	2450	355	2351
334	2289	357	2400
345	2463	358	2448
346	2412	359	2388
347	2310	360	2412
348	2310	361	2412
349	2364	363 (C. 8)	2463
350	2351	364 (C.9)	2290
351	2351	365	2463
352	2351	368	2454
353 (C. 71)	2351	369	2412
		706	2454

TABLE OF ABBREVIATIONS

A.B.L.R. = Australian Business Law Review.
A.C. = Appeal Cases (Law Reports).
A.J.I.L. = American Journal of International Law.
A.L.J. = Australian Law Journal.
A.L.J.R. = Australian Law Journal Reports.
A.L.M.D. = Australian Legal Monthly Digest.
A.L.R. = Australian Law Reports.
A.R. = Alberta Reports 1977–
ATLA L.Rep. = Association of Trial Lawyers of America Reporter.
A.T.R. = Australian Tax Review.
Acct. = Accountant.
Acct.Rec. = Accountants Record.
Accty. = Accountancy.
Admin. = Administrator.
All E.R. = All England Law Reports.
Anglo-Am. = Anglo-American Law Review.
Art. = Article.
Aus. = Australia.

B.C.L.R. = British Columbia Law Reports.
B.L.R. = Business Law Review.
B.T.R. = British Tax Review.
Brit.J.Criminol. = British Journal of Criminology.
Build.L.R. = Building Law Reports.
Bull.E.C. = Bulletin of the European Communities.
Bull.J.S.B. = Bulletin of Judicial Studies Board.
Bus.Ed. = Business Education.

c. = Chapter (of Act of Parliament).
C.A. = Court of Appeal.
C.A.T. = Court of Appeal Transcript.
C. & S.L.J. = Company and Securities Law Journal.
C.C.A. = Court of Criminal Appeal.
C.C.L.T. = Canadian cases on the Law of Torts 1976–
C.I.L.J.S.A. = Comparative and International Law Journal of Southern Africa.
C.I.L.L. = Construction Industry Law Letter.
C.I.P.A. = The Journal of the Chartered Institute of Patent Agents.
C.J.Q. = Civil Justice Quarterly.
C.L. = Current Law.
C.L.B. = Commonwealth Law Bulletin.
C.L.C. = Current Law Consolidation.
C.L.J. = Cambridge Law Journal.
C.L.L.R. = City of London Law Review.
C.L.P. = Current Legal Problems.
C.L.R. = Commonwealth Law Reports.
C.L.Y. = Current Law Year Book.
C.M.L.R. = Common Market Law Reports.
C.M.L.Rev. = Common Market Law Review.
C.Q.S. = Chartered Quantity Surveyor.
C.S.W. = Chartered Surveyor Weekly.
Can. = Canada.
Can. Bar J. = Canadian Bar Journal.
Can.B.R. or Canadian B.R. = Canadian Bar Review.
Can.C.L. = Canadian Current Law.

Ch. = Chancery (Law Reports).
Co.Law. = Company Lawyer.
Co. Law Dig. = Company Law Digest.
Com.Cas. = Commercial Cases.
Commercial Acct. = Commercial Accountant.
Comp.L.P. = Computer Law & Practice.
ConLR = Construction Law Reports.
Const.L.J. = Construction Law Journal.
Conv.(N.S.) (or Conv. or Conveyancer) = Conveyancer and Property Lawyer (New Series).
Cox C.C. = Cox's Criminal Cases.
Cr.App.R. = Criminal Appeal Reports.
Cr.App.R.(S.) = Criminal Appeal Reports (Sentencing).
Crim.L.R. = Criminal Law Review.
Crim.R. = Criminal Reports.
Ct. = Court.
Cts.-Martial App.Ct. = Courts-Martial Appeal Court.

D.C. = Divisional Court.
D.L.R. = Dominion Law Reports.

E. = England.
E.A.T. = Employment Appeal Tribunal.
E.C.C. = European Commercial Cases.
E.C.L.R. = European Competition Law Review.
E.C.R. = European Court Reports.
E.C.S.C. = European Coal and Steel Community.
E.E.C. = European Economic Community.
E.G. = Estates Gazette.
E.I.P.R. = European Intellectual Property Review.
E.H.R.R. = European Human Rights Reports.
E.L.Rev. = European Law Review.
E.O.R. = Equal Opportunities Review.
E.P.L. Leaflet = Excess Profits Levy Leaflet.
E.P.T. Leaflet = Excess Profits Tax Leaflet.

F.L.R. = Federal Law Reports.
F.L.R. = Family Law Reports.
FLR = Financial Law Reports.
F.S.R. = Fleet Street Reports.
Fam. = Family Division (Law Reports).
Fam.Law = Family Law.

G.W.D. = Green's Weekly Digest.

H.L. = House of Lords.
H.L.R. = Housing Law Reports.
Harv.L.R. or Harvard L.R. = Harvard Law Review.

I.B.L. = International Business Lawyer.
I.C.L.Q. = International and Comparative Law Quarterly.
I.C.L.R. = International Construction Law Review.
I.C.R. = Industrial Cases Reports.

125

I.L.J. = Industrial Law Journal.
I.L.P. = International Legal Practitioner.
I.L.R.M. = Irish Law Reports Monthly.
I.L.T. *or* Ir.L.T. = Irish Law Times.
I.L.T.R. = Irish Law Times Reports.
Imm.A.R. = Immigration Appeals Reports.
Imm. and Nat.L. & P. = Immigration and Nationality Law and Practice.
Ins.L.P. = Insolvency Law & Practice.
I.R. *or* Ir.R. = Irish Reports (Eire).
I.R.L.R. = Industrial Relations Law Reports.
Ir.Jur. = Irish Jurist.
Ir.Jur.(N.S.) = Irish Jurist (New Series).
Ir.Jur.Rep. = Irish Jurist Reports.
I.T.R. = Industrial Tribunal Reports.

J. *and* JJ. = Justice, Justices.
J.A.L. = Journal of African Law.
J.B.L. = Journal of Business Law.
J.C. = Justiciary Cases.
J.C.L. = Journal of Criminal Law.
J.C.L. & Crim. = Journal of Criminal Law and Criminology.
J.Crim.L., C. & P.S. = Journal of Criminal Law, Criminology and Police Science.
J.E.R.L. = Journal of Energy and Natural Resources Law.
J.I.B. = Journal of the Institute of Bankers.
J.L.A. = Jewish Law Annual.
J.L.H. = Journal of Legal History.
J.L.S. = Journal of the Law Society of Scotland.
J.P. = Justice of the Peace Reports.
J.P.L. = Journal of Planning and Environment Law.
J.P.N. = Justice of the Peace Journal.
J.R. = Juridical Review.
J.S.W.L. = Journal of Social Welfare Law.
Jam. = Jamaica.

K.B. = King's Bench (Law Reports).
K.I.R. = Knight's Industrial Reports.

L.C. = Lord Chancellor.
L.C.J. *or* C.J. = Lord Chief Justice.
L.Exec. = Legal Executive.
L.G.C. = Local Government Chronicle.
L.G.R. = Local Government Reports.
L.G.Rev. = Local Government Review.
L.J. = Law Journal Newspaper.
L.J. *and* L.JJ. = Lord Justice, Lords Justices.
L.J.A.C.R. = Law Journal Annual Charities Review.
L.J.N.C.C.R. = Law Journal Newspaper County Court Reports.
L.J.R. = Law Journal Reports.
L.M.C.L.Q. = Lloyd's Maritime and Commercial Law Quarterly.
L.P. = Reference to denote Lands Tribunal decisions (transcripts available from the Lands Tribunal).
L.Q.R. = Law Quarterly Review.
L.R. = Law Reports.
L.R.R.P. = Reports of Restrictive Practices Cases.
L.S. = Legal Studies.
L.S.Gaz. = Law Society's Gazette.
L.T. = Law Times.

L.Teach. = Law Teacher.
L.T.J. = Law Times Journal.
L.V.App.Ct. = Lands Valuation Appeal Court (Scotland).
L.V.C. = Reference to denote Lands Tribunal decisions (transcripts available from the Lands Tribunal).
L. & J. = Law and Justice.
Ll.L.Rep. = Lloyd's List Reports (before 1951).
Ll.P.C. = Lloyd's Prize Cases.
Lit. = Litigation.
Liverpool L.R. = Liverpool Law Review.
Lloyd's Rep. = Lloyd's List Reports (1951 onwards).

M.L.J. = Malayan Law Journal.
M.L.R. = Modern Law Review.
M.R. = Master of the Rolls.
McGill L.J. = McGill Law Journal.
Mag.Ct. = Magistrates' Court.
Mal. = Malaya.
Mal.L.R. = Malaya Law Review.
Man.Law = Managerial Law.
Med.Sci. & Law = Medicine, Science and the Law.
Melbourne Univ.L.R. = Melbourne University Law Review.
Mel.L.J. = Melanesian Law Journal.

NATO R. = NATO Review.
N.I. = Northern Ireland; Northern Ireland Reports.
N.I.J.B. = Northern Ireland Judgment Bulletin.
N.I.L.Q. = Northern Ireland Legal Quarterly.
N.I.L.R. = Northern Ireland Law Reports.
N.Z.L.R. = New Zealand Law Reports.
N.Z.U.L.R. = New Zealand Universities Law Review.
New L.J. = New Law Journal.
New L.R. = New Law Reports, Ceylon.
Nig.L.J. = Nigerian Law Journal.

O.H. = Outer House of Court of Session.
O.J. = Official Journal of the European Communities.
O.J.L.S. = Oxford Journal of Legal Studies.
Oklahoma L.R. = Oklahoma Law Review.
Ord. = Order.
Osgoode Hall L.J. = Osgoode Hall Law Journal.

P. = Probate, Divorce and Admiralty (Law Reports).
P. & C.R. = Property and Compensation Reports.
P.C. = Privy Council.
PCC = Palmer's Company Cases.
P.L. = Public Law.
P.N. = Professional Negligence.
P.S. = Petty Sessions.
P.T. = Profits Tax Leaflet.
Pr.A.S.I.L. = Proceedings of the American Society of International Law.

TABLE OF ABBREVIATIONS

Q.B. = Queen's Bench (Law Reports).
Q.J.P.R. = Queensland Justice of the Peace Reports.
Q.L.R. = Queensland Law Reporter.
Q.S. = Quarter Sessions.
Q.S.R. = Queensland State Reports.

r. = Rule.
R.A. = Rating Appeals.
R. & I.T. = Rating and Income Tax.
R. & V. = Rating and Valuation.
R.C.N. = Rating Case Notes.
R.F.L. = Reports of Family Law (Canadian).
R.I.C.S. = Royal Institution of Chartered Surveyors, Scottish Lands Valuation Appeal Reports.
R.P.C. = Reports of Patent, Design and Trade Mark Cases.
R.P.Ct. = Restrictive Practices Court.
R.P.R. = Real Property Reports (Canada).
R.R.C. = Ryde's Rating Cases.
R.T.R. = Road Traffic Reports.
R.V.R. = Rating and Valuation Reporter.
reg. = Regulation.
Reg.Acct. = Registered Accountant.
Rep. of Ir. = Republic of Ireland.

s. = Section (of Act of Parliament).
S. or Scot. = Scotland.
S.A. = South Africa.
S.A.L.J. = South African Law Journal.
S.A.L.R. = South African Law Reports.
S.A.S.R. = South Australian State Reports.
S.C. = Session Cases.
S.C.C.R. = Scottish Criminal Case Reports.
S.C.(H.L.) = Session Cases (House of Lords).
S.C.(J.) = Session Cases (High Court of Justiciary).
SCOLAG = Journal of the Scottish Legal Action Group.
S.I. = Statutory Instrument.
S.J. = Solicitors' Journal.
S.J.Suppl. = Supplement to the Solicitors' Journal.
S.L.C.R. = Scottish Land Court Reports.
S.L.C.R.App. = Scottish Land Court Reports (appendix).
S.L.G. = Scottish Law Gazette.
S.L.R. = Scottish Law Reporter (Reports 1865–1925).
S.L.R. = Scottish Law Review (Articles 1912–63).
S.L.R. = Scottish Law Review (Sheriff Court Reports 1885–1963).
S.L.R. (and date) = Statute Law Reform Act (Statute Citator only).
S.L.R. = Statute Law Revision.
S.L.T. = Scots Law Times.

S.L.T.(Land Ct.) = Scots Law Times Land Court Reports.
S.L.T.(Lands Tr.) = Scots Law Times Lands Tribunal Reports.
S.L.T.(Lyon Ct.) = Scots Law Times Lyon Court Reports.
S.L.T.(News) = Scots Law Times, News section.
S.L.T.(Notes) = Scots Law Times Notes of Recent Decisions (1946–1981).
S.L.T.(Sh.Ct.) = Scots Law Times Sheriff Court Reports.
S.N. = Session Notes.
S.P.L.P. = Scottish Planning Law and Practice.
S.R. & O. = Statutory Rules and Orders.
S.T.C. = Simon's Tax Cases.
Sc.Jur. = Scottish Jurist.
Sh.Ct.Rep. = Sheriff Court Reports (Scottish Law Review) (1885–1963).
Sol. = Solicitor.
Stat.L.R. = Statute Law Review.
Sydney L.R. = Sydney Law Review.

T.C. or Tax Cas. = Tax Cases.
T.C. Leaflet = Tax Case Leaflet.
T.L.R. = Times Law Reports.
T.P.G. = Town Planning and Local Government Guide.
T.U.L.B. = Trade Union Law Bulletin.
Tas.S.R. = Tasmanian State Reports.
Tax. = Taxation.
Tr.L. = Trading Law.
Traff.Cas. = Railway, Canal and Road Traffic Cases.
Trial = Trial.
Trib. = Tribunal.
Trust L. & P. = Trust Law and Practice.
Tulane L.R. = Tulane Law Review.

U.G.L.J. = University of Ghana Law Journal.
U.S. = United States Reports.
U.T.L.J. = University of Toronto Law Journal.

V.A.T.T.R. = Value Added Tax Tribunal Reports.
V.L.R. = Victorian Law Reports.

W.A.L.R. = West Australian Law Reports.
W.I.A.S. = West Indies Associated States.
W.I.R. = West Indian Reports.
W.L.R. = Weekly Law Reports.
W.N. = Weekly Notes (Law Reports).
W.W.R. = Western Weekly Reports.
Washington L.Q. = Washington Law Quarterly.

Yale L.J. = Yale Law Journal.

UNREPORTED CASES

COURT OF APPEAL (CIVIL DIVISION)

This section contains brief notes of decisions of the Court of Appeal (Civil Division) which have not appeared in any other recognised series of law reports. The transcripts of these decisions are available in the Supreme Court Library at the Royal Courts of Justice.

1. Administrative Law—judicial review—premature application

In 1961 the applicant broke his neck when he dived into the Thames and was severely paralysed as a result but he could get about, stand up, walk, feed himself and so on. Since then he had lived with a friend in his (the friend's) house and the friend had looked after him. Until 1980 the local council were providing home help to the household at the rate of ten hours per week. From 1980 the council began reducing the amount of the home help. The applicant applied for judicial review of the council's decision to provide him with five hours of home help per week which he considered was inadequate for his requirements. *Held,* that this was essentially a case where, before judicial review was moved for, the route via the Secretary of State ought to be taken pursuant to s.85 of the National Health Service Act 1977. It was accordingly premature to apply for judicial review and the application would be refused (*R. v. Ealing London Borough Council, ex p. Leaman.* (Unreported, February 1984, Mann J. considered.) November 18, 1985. (C.A.T. No. 731.) R. *v.* EALING LONDON BOROUGH COUNCIL, *ex p.* GOSSINGTON.

2. Arbitration—agreement—variation of agreement—whether arbitration clause in agreement applicable to issue between parties

The parties were respectively buyers and sellers of a ship under a contract (negotiated through brokers) which incorporated the standard terms of the Norwegian Sale Form as amended by their special bargain. The contract included the following arbitration clause: "If any dispute should arise in connection with the interpretation and fulfilment of this contract, same shall be decided by arbitration in the City of London, English Law to apply." The terms of the contract were originally agreed in December 1984 but the sellers alleged that there was a variation in the terms in January 1985. The parties were agreed that (i) there was a contract in existence between them for the sale of the ship and (ii) the contract had been repudiated. The dispute was whether the contract was repudiated by the sellers or whether it was repudiated by the buyers and in order to determine this the issue of whether there was a variation in the terms of the contract alleged by the sellers would have to be decided. The sellers contended that "this contract" on their view was a different contract from "this contract" on the buyers' view, and therefore there was no single arbitration clause which governed the issue of whether anybody had failed to fulfil the contract, and accordingly there was no arbitral tribunal which could resolve the issue between the parties. *Held,* that the sole issue of who failed to fulfil the contract fell within the scope of the arbitration clause; the issue was one of fulfilment of only the one contract, namely "this contract" and there was no reason why the parties had not agreed that that issue would be determined by arbitration rather than by litigation. Appeal from Hobhouse J. November 20, 1985. (C.A.T. No. 741.) SKIBS A/S AVANTI, SKIBS A/S GLARONA, SKIBS A/S NAVAHS (T/A PARREDERIET SIBOTRE) *v.* OKEANIS SHIPPING CORP.

3. Bankruptcy—bankruptcy of contractual tenant—disclaimer of lease by trustee—objection to disclaimer—possession against tenant

In September 1978 P granted to D a lease of a dwelling-house for a term of seven and a quarter years from June 24, 1978. The rateable value of the premises was within the limits of the Rent Acts and accordingly if the lease expired while D were the tenants under it, they would thereafter hold over as statutory tenants. The lease included covenants whereby (1) there was an absolute prohibition against assignment or sub-letting of the premises or any part thereof, (2) the use of the property was restricted to a dwelling house, (3) full repairing obligations were imposed on D who were to deliver up the premises in good repair at the end of the term, and (4) D were required in the last three months of the last year of the term to paint the interior and exterior of the premises. In August 1984 a receiving order was made against D and they were in due course adjudicated bankrupt. In January 1985 a trustee in bankruptcy was appointed and the unexpired term of the lease vested in the trustee. In February 1985 the trustee gave notice of his intention to disclaim and in August 1985 he disclaimed the lease under s.54 of the Bankruptcy Act 1914 and rule 278 of the Bankruptcy Rules 1952 on the ground that the land was burdened with onerous covenants. In October 1985 P issued proceedings against D for possession, the particulars of claim reciting, *inter alia*, the terms of the lease, the appointment of the trustee and the notice of disclaimer. The judge dismissed the claim holding that there was no evidence before him to suggest that the property was burdened with onerous covenants and that accordingly the disclaimer by the trustee was null and void. *Held*, allowing P's appeal and granting an order for possession, that (1) this was a lease which was on its face onerous and which the trustee was entitled to disclaim, as he might otherwise have been held liable for breach of the covenants as to repairs and painting. The evidence could not be read as indicating that all the covenants had been complied with to the extent that the covenant for delivery up in good repair had also been complied with and the covenant for painting in the last three months. Furthermore, it was unsatisfactory that there should be a ruling on the validity of a disclaimer by a trustee in bankruptcy in proceedings to which the trustee was not a party in circumstances where whether or not there had been a disclaimer was said to depend on matters of fact. Where it was a question of saying whether covenants in a lease burdening land were in truth onerous on the facts of the particular case, then the appropriate tribunal to decide that was the bankruptcy court in proceedings by way of appeal by the bankrupt who was wanting to set up that there had been no disclaimer, under s.80 of the Bankruptcy Act 1914 against the trustee's decision to disclaim. (*Re Mercer and Moore* (1869) 14 Ch. D. 287 and *Metropolis Estates* v. *Wilde* [1940] 2 K.B. 536 considered); (2) D had no right to remain in the property and there was no answer to P's claim for possession. This was so whether the disclaimer was valid or invalid as the lease became vested in the trustee in bankruptcy on D's bankruptcy and remained vested in him until he validly disclaimed it or if the disclaimer was invalid, until the term expired by effluxion of time; immediately before then the protected tenant was the trustee and not D. (*Smalley* v. *Quarrier* [1975] C.L.Y. 1907 applied). March 6, 1986. (C.A.T. No. 230). TRUSTEES OF THE EYRE ESTATE v. HALL.

4. Bankruptcy—costs—petitioning creditors costs—enforcement of order—leave of the court

As the bankrupt was legally aided, the Court of Appeal, in dismissing the bankrupt's appeal against the adjudication order, ordered that the petitioning creditor's costs of appeal when taxed should not be enforced without further order of that court. The costs were taxed in the sum of £1,391·06 and the petitioning creditor applied for leave to enforce the order for costs. An affidavit from the trustee in bankruptcy exhibited an interim account that showed that all the claims of the preferential creditors, amounting to some £3,554, had been paid and a first dividend of 20 pence in the pound had been paid to the unsecured creditors. That left some £2,454 for further distribution to the unsecured creditors. *Held*, that similar principles as had been stated in the case of *Esal (Commodities), Re* [1985] C.L.Y. 325 *i.e.* that "a winding-up petition was not a normal suit between parties in which one side beat the other, but a case in which the remedy sought was a class remedy, the petitioner representing all the unsecured creditors of the company," were, by analogy, applicable to the present bankruptcy case. It was no fault of the petitioning creditor that the costs of the proceedings had been substantially increased by unsuccessful appeals by the bankrupt. Justice to all concerned would best be served by allowing this application. Though the effect of the order would enable the petitioner creditor to receive its taxed cost in full, it would still only receive payment of the same proportion of the debt on which its petition was founded as the other unsecured creditors would receive in respect of their debts. October 2, 1985. (C.A.T. 536.) DEBTOR A, *Re* (No. 5 of 1978).

5. Bankruptcy—petition—adjournment of hearing—disputed debt

The petitioning creditor obtained summary judgment in the sum of £52,731 against the debtor, his former business partner, in respect of certain transactions, and commenced bankruptcy proceedings against him on that judgment debt. At the hearing of the bankruptcy petition the debtor contended that the petition should be adjourned pending the taking of the partnership accounts in accordance with the partnership deed submitting that until that was done it was impossible to be sure that there was a valid debt. The registrar refused an adjournment on the ground that the parties could not possibly resolve the debtor's claim for an account within the foreseeable future even if in the end it might be found that the debtor was owed something by the petitioning creditor. The debtor appealed. *Held,* dismissing the appeal, that the registrar was fully entitled, on the very full information which he had, to come to the conclusion that that was a matter of such complexity that it would be a long time before it was resolved and that in the exercise of his discretion he would refuse an adjournment and make the receiving order (*A Debtor (No. 452 of 1948) Re* (1949) C.L.C. 686 and *L. F. H. Wools, Re* [1969] C.L.Y. 408 considered). Appeal from Mr. Registrar Dewhurst. November 29, 1985. (C.A.T. No. 787.) DEBTOR, A, *Re*; DEBTOR *v.* BROWN.

6. Building and Engineering, Architects and Surveyors—standard form contract incorporating J.C.T. conditions—retention monies—setting aside separate trust fund

By an agreement made in July 1981 P contractor contracted with D employer to build the Holiday Inn, Croydon, for a sum of just over £7,000,000. The agreement was in standard form incorporating the J.C.T. conditions (July 1977 Revision). The Holiday Inn opened on March 12, 1984. However, disputes had arisen between the parties under the agreement and had been referred to arbitration. In the arbitration proceedings, which were due to be heard in April 1986, P was claiming £4,000,000 and D resisted the claim and counterclaimed that there was in fact a balance owing to it. A sum of £355,179, representing the accumulated "retention percentage" of the total value of the work done by P and material and goods as certified by Interim Certificates issued by the architect, had been properly retained by D pursuant to Cl. 30(3) of the conditions. Furthermore the extended date for completion, March 29, 1983, had not been met by P and the architect had issued certificates under Cl. 22 of the conditions which, in relation to the period up to February 1984, entitled D to liquidated and ascertained damages in excess of the retention monies of £355,179. Pending the determination of the issues in the arbitration P sought interlocutory relief by way of a mandatory injunction ordering D forthwith to pay the sum of £355,179 into a separate bank account to be applied in accordance with the trust specified in Cl. 30(4)(*a*) of the conditions. D contended that the effect of the architect's certificates was to discharge it from any obligation under cl. 30(4)(*a*) to appropriate and set aside a separate trust fund. The judge held that the relationship between D and P was at the most that of debtor and creditor and that he could not order security to be given for the payment of the disputed debt and accordingly dismissed P's application. *Held,* dismissing P's appeal, that the question depended upon the true construction and effect of cll. 22 and 30(4)(*a*) of the conditions. Upon their true construction there was no obligation imposed on the employer by cl. 30(4)(*a*) of the conditions to appropriate and set aside retentions as a separate trust fund enforceable by the contractor in a case where damages for non-completion in excess of the amount of retentions were payable by the contractor under cl. 22 pursuant to architect's certificates whose validity was disputed. There was no subsisting obligation on D to appropriate and set aside a separate trust fund under cl. 30(4)(*a*) or, in other words, D could not at present be joined with P in the relationship of trustee and beneficiary and at the most their relationship was that of debtor and creditor. It followed that no injunction could be granted, it being the invariable practice of the Court not to order security of payment of a disputed debt (*Rayack Construction* v. *Lampeter Meat Co.* [1980] C.L.Y. 206). Appeal from David Thomas J. September 5, 1985. (C.A.T. No. 521.) Boot (Henry) Building v. Croydon Hotel and Leisure Co.

7. Consumer Credit—extortionate credit bargain—excessive interest rate—no general upper limit

P finance company contended that it had been established by decisions of the courts that a credit bargain could not be extortionate within the Consumer Credit Act 1974, if the rate of interest payable did not exceed 48 per cent. per annum. *Held,* that the courts had not laid down that a rate of interest not exceeding 48 per cent. per annum could not be grossly exorbitant. Interest charged not exceeding 48 per cent. per annum could be held excessive under s.10(1) of the Money Lenders Act 1927 and it still could. Particular factors which may point to such interest being excessive were that the principal of the loan was amply secured and that the loan was for a short term only and so could be called in if there was any default in payment of proper interest. Further, while the court was directed by s.138(2) of the 1974 Act to have regard to such evidence as was adduced concerning interest rates prevailing at the time the bargain was made, the court must also be entitled to have regard to its own general knowledge of normal interest rates (*Catley (A.)* v. *Scott* [1981] I.C.R. 241 explained; *Woodstead Finance* v. *Petrou,* unreported, January 22, 1986, (C.A.T. No. 38), considered). March 25, 1986. (C.A.T. No. 284). Castle Phillips Finance Co. v. Williams.

8. Contract—implied terms—fixed term employment contract—renewal after expiry of fixed term—duration of renewed employment

When a contract for a fixed term terminated and the parties continued the one to be employed and the other to pay, what must be inferred depended on the circumstances of each individual case. If there was nothing to point to an intention on the part of both parties to create a renewal of the same duration as the original fixed term, then the implication was that the employment was for an indefinite period and subject to termination by reasonable notice (*Richardson* v. *Koefod* [1969] C.L.Y. 1235 considered, *Messer* v. *Barrett Co.* [1927] 1 D.L.R. 284 (Ontario Supreme Court) applied). October 15, 1985. Appeal from Taylor J. (C.A.T. No. 583.) Rawle v. James Cubitt and Partners (A Firm).

9. County Court Practice—injunction—non-molestation injunction—limitation in scope and time

P, who lived together with D from 1980 to 1984, complained of a series of molestations and assaults directed by D against her at various times from July 27, 1985 to late in September 1985, consisting of assaults upon her person, unwelcome visits to and damage at her dwelling house, telephone threats and harrassment by means of "heavy breathing" telephone calls at "unsocial hours". The judge granted P an injunction restraining D from assaulting, molesting or otherwise interfering with P or from entering her property "until further order". D appealed contending, *inter alia,* that molestation and interference were not in the circumstances of the case, in

132

which no question of matrimonial nexus arose and where there were no children to protect, actionable wrongs and therefore it was not just to grant an injunction to restrain them. *Held,* that was correct, unless there was evidence that P's health was being impaired by molestation or interference calculated to create such impairment, in which case relief would be granted by way of an injunction to the extent that it would be necessary to avoid that impairment of health. Although there was evidence that the telephone threats caused an impairment of P's health, beyond that impairment of health was not supported by any evidence. Accordingly the generalised prohibition against molestation and interference went too wide. It was therefore proper for the court under R.S.C., Ord. 59, r.10(3), while disallowing the wider prohibition generally of molestation and interference, to substitute a prohibition against the narrower form of wrong which was attested by the evidence as being one which involved an impairment of P's health. Further, as was proper in the case of interlocutory relief, the order below should be altered as by being delimited as regard time by reference to "judgment in the action of further order". Subject to those matters, D's appeal would be dismissed (*Egan* v. *Egan* [1975] C.L.Y. 2637 explained; *Beddow* v. *Beddow* (1878) 9 Ch. 89 and *Janvier* v. *Sweeney* [1919] 2 K.B. 316 followed). March 6, 1986. (C.A.T. No. 227). BURNETT *v.* GEORGE.

10. County Court Practice—judgment—setting aside judgment in absence of party

P deliberately chose to remain absent from the hearing of the case and judgment was given in D's favour. P appealed against the refusal of the judge to set aside the judgment and order a re-hearing contending that once his contumacious conduct had been dealt with, apologised for, punished and so purged, that conduct was to be disregarded when it came to an application for a re-hearing and the main question which the court hearing such an application had to consider in those circumstances was the doing of justice between the parties. *Held,* dismissing the appeal, that it was not only the interests of the parties which had to be considered; the public interest had to be considered also, the interest that litigation should not be prolonged and that a decision which had been given, and which on the face of it appeared to be a final decision, should not be set aside where the reason for the decision having been given in absence of one of the parties was wholly because of the failure of that party to attend the trial and his misbehaviour in relation to the trial. In considering justice between the parties, the conduct of the person applying for an order for a re-hearing had to be taken into consideration as well as the matters arising in the litigation itself. Where a party had been clearly notified of a day for trial and deliberately chose to absent himself, it was a most real consideration to be taken into account in assessing where the interests of justice lay. February 19, 1986. (C.A.T. No. 159). CRADDOCK *v.* BARBER.

11. County Court Practice—solicitors—solicitor ceasing to act for party—notice by party to act in person

On November 9 H gave notice under C.C.R. 1981, Ord. 50, r.5(3) by letters written to the county court, his solicitors and W's solicitors that he would henceforth be acting in person and would be representing himself at the hearing fixed for November 20 and stating his address for service. Prior to that, H's solicitors had made an application under Ord. 50, r.5(4) to remove their name from the court record. On November 20 the judge granted their application with costs to be paid by H. H appealed. *Held,* allowing the appeal and discharging the order made by the judge, that the solicitors were not entitled to make an application to the court under Ord. 50, r.5(4) because it was a matter which had already been disposed of under Ord. 50, r.5(3). There was no occasion for the making of an order removing the solicitors from the record because the client had already given notice, and equally, there was no reason why the client should have borne the costs of that application. June 24 1985. (C.A.T. No. 327.) HOLMES *v.* HOLMES.

12. County Court Practice—summons—successive summonses—extension of time for issue

On November 16, 1979, P issued proceedings in the county court claiming damages in respect of injuries she suffered in a motor car accident. Her solicitors were unsuccessful in effecting service of the proceedings as they were unable to ascertain D's whereabouts at the time. On December 15, 1981, P's solicitors filed an application to serve the proceedings out of time supported by an affidavit setting out at length the history of the attempts to trace D for service. On February 5, 1982, the registrar granted the application and pursuant to that order on February 22, 1982, the summons was served on D. On June 6, 1984, on D's application to set aside the re-issue of the summons, it was held that P's solicitors had adopted the wrong procedure and that they should have made application for successive summonses under C.C.R. (1936), Ord. 8, r.32(4). The order of February 5, 1982, was therefore null and void because the original summons had expired on November 16, 1980, 12 months after the date of issue and no application having been made to serve a successive summons under r.32, there was no summons in existence. *Held*, allowing P's appeal, that (1) there was power to extend the time under C.C.R., Ord. 8, r.32(4) at the time, on February 2, 1982, when the irregular order was made; (2) the irregularity in the form of the order could be cured under C.C.R., Ord. 37, r.4; (3) in the exceptional circumstances of the case the discretion both to extend the time and cure the irregularities should be exercised in P's favour (*Lewis* v. *Wolkin Properties* [1977] C.L.Y. 448 followed; *Bernstein* v. *Jackson* [1982] C.L.Y. 2593 explained). March 7, 1986. (C.A.T. No. 238) GABBIDANE v. ALLI.

13. Damages—negligence—wrongful imprisonment—quantum

Owing to an order of the court not being properly drawn up, P, who suffered from arthritis and was disabled in that he had to have a prosthesis (a false foot) was arrested and kept in a police cell for 53 hours including two nights provided with only two blankets. The jury awarded P £200 damages. P appealed. *Held*, that the damages would be increased to £500. Any substantial loss of liability was a serious matter and must be properly compensated in damages. Appeal from Hodgson J. February 12, 1986. (C.A.T. No. 134) BECKETT v. WALKER.

14. Divorce and Matrimonial Causes—decree absolute—appeal to Court of Appeal—leave to appeal

At the hearing of the divorce suit H failed to produce in evidence a document the genuineness of which was disputed by W. The judge granted W a decree nisi. H applied for a rehearing under M.C.R. 1977, r.54 making his representations in writing and exhibiting a photocopy of the document and on March 15, 1983 the application was refused. On March 21, 1983 the decree nisi was made absolute on application by W. In July 1984 in ancillary proceedings the judge found on a balance of probabilities that the document was genuine. H applied contending that he was not precluded by s.18(1)(d) of the Supreme Court Act 1981 from appealing the decree absolute. *Held*, dismissing the application, that the provisions of s.18(1)(d) were objective and absolute. They were based on the obvious necessity of public policy to bring a state of finality in questions of matrimonial status so that everybody, including children and others and the parties themselves may be sure of the position. A person who had failed to avail himself of the opportunity to appeal from the decree nisi within the ordinary time provided was under a heavy burden to bring himself within s.18(1)(d). There was no room here for H to avail himself of a right of appeal against the decree nisi in this case. October 14, 1985. (C.A.T. No. 575). CROSBY v. CROSBY.

UNREPORTED CASES

15. Divorce and Matrimonial Causes—legal aid—charge on property recovered or preserved—disadvantage in contesting trivial issues—duty of solicitors to warn litigants

The divorce proceedings in which both parties (with three children now aged thirteen, nine and six years) were legally aided had been protracted, acrimonious and costly. There had been many applications to and orders of the court. The combined costs of both sides to date, which the Law Society were entitled, subject to certain exceptions, to recover out of the property recovered or preserved in the proceedings already amounted to some £8,000. The family's only substantial asset was the matrimonial home in which the equity was some £18,000 to £19,000. In the result, nearly half of this family asset, which was initially available to provide for the parties and their children, had already been eaten up in costs. It seemed highly likely that more yet would be so consumed. The court expressed the opinion that that was a sad but all too familiar situation and that it could not be stressed too strongly that it was incumbent on solicitors to explain and constantly reiterate to legally aided clients that legal aid did not mean that they conducted litigation free of charge forever. Often, particularly where relations between parties to a broken marriage were bitter, comparatively trivial issues were contested, the contesting of which issues could only result in a loss even if the contest was successful. That situation was likely to prevail in the present case if the parties were unable to agree with regard to the contents of the matrimonial home, a matter which remained at the moment in potential contest. Legal aid could in such circumstances be a disadvantage rather than a benefit, and the question which should always be to the forefront in everyone's mind was whether the contest of an issue was likely to produce or preserve more that the costs involved in success. If it was not so likely, contesting the issue was not only a useless exercise but a disadvantageous one. August 30, 1985. (C.A.T. 518.) ANTHONY *v.* ANTHONY.

16. Equity—ownership of property—non-owner making mortgage repayments—whether inequitable for true owner to benefit

In 1980 P, then aged 70, formed a relationship with D (2), who at that time was living with her son D (1) (aged 27). P wished to buy a house costing £16,000 for himself and D (2) to live in. He had £6,000 in cash available but was unable to raise finance for the balance because of his age. Accordingly an agreement was made in February 1981 whereby the house was purchased in D (1)'s name on a mortgage taken out by D (1) but on the understanding that P would be making the mortgage repayments. The judge found that, by contract, for his own convenience, P had agreed that the property should be bought in D (1)'s name and that, after the purchase, P should have no interest in it whatsoever. P and D (2) started living in the house but their relationship broke down and in the middle of 1982 D (2) left. P thereafter stayed on in the house making the mortgage repayments. In April 1983 P issued proceedings claiming that the house was his beneficially. P contended, *inter alia,* that after D (2) left, P, to the knowledge of D (1) went on paying the mortgage repayments in the belief induced by D (1) that, as long as he did so, he would go on staying in the property and, once the mortgage had been paid off, he could stay there for the rest of his life. The question arose as to whether it was inequitable for D (1) at the very least, to repay to P all the payments which P had made after D (2) left. *Held,* that in February 1981, P knew he had no claim to the property. For his own reasons in March 1982 he decided to claim the property. He was making a false claim at that stage and he made the payments in that knowledge and went on doing so after he knew at the beginning of the proceedings that his case was being challenged by D (1) and D (2). In those circumstances there was nothing inequitable about D (1) getting the benefit of those payments. P had been unwise enough to make them for his own reasons and when his own reasons were not accepted by the court, he must take the consequences of them. Appeal from Whitford J. February 25, 1986. (C.A.T. No. 193). BIRD *v.* PHILLIPS.

17. Evidence—fresh evidence—leave to adduce—deliberate decision by counsel not to adduce such evidence in court below

A deliberate decision was made by leading counsel not to raise a certain issue and refer to the evidence in support of it on the hearing of the application for judicial review. The question was, where counsel had taken a deliberate decision to conduct a case on one basis and had made a concession which went to the root of the matter, should counsel in the Court of Appeal be allowed to reopen the matter on an entirely different basis seeking to adduce fresh evidence in support. *Held,* on principle, that to allow counsel to do that would be a wrong exercise of discretion by the Court of Appeal. The court did, however, have to look at all the circumstances of the case. There might be a case involving the liberty of the subject where it would be right to allow the case to be reopened on a different basis having regard to the fact that counsel in the court below had made a decision which the Court of Appeal did not think was right (*R.* v. *Secretary of State for the Home Department, ex p. Mumin Ali* [1984] C.L.Y. 1737 applied). Appeal from Glidewell J. October 31, 1985. R. *v.* SECRETARY OF STATE FOR THE HOME DEPARTMENT, *ex p.* YATES.

18. Factories—building—building operations—ladders

A fire in a school hall had caused the deposit of soot and oily substances on the walls. P, the school caretaker, was injured when a step ladder he was using to clean the walls overbalanced and he fell to the ground. P claimed, *inter alia,* under the Factories Acts, contending that the cleaning, being attributable to the soot and oily substance deposited by the fire, was maintenance of a special nature and came within the words "building operation" as defined in s.176 of the Factories Act 1961. *Held,* dismissing P's appeal, that the fact that Parliament had found it specifically necessary to include external cleaning of a structure in the definition of maintenance indicated clearly that they were not directing their minds to internal cleaning of a structure, which was something of a scale and nature quite different from the elaborate scaffolding and water washing inherent in external cleaning of a structure. February 3, 1986. (C.A.T. No. 99.) TUCKER *v.* HAMPSHIRE COUNTY COUNCIL.

19. Factories—passageway—duty to keep free from obstruction—loose materials

P stepped upon a substantial bolt lying in passageway about one metre wide at D's (his employer's) premises and fell on his back damaging his knee. P alleged a breach of the Construction (General Provisions) Regulations 1961 (S.I. 1961 No. 1580), reg. 48(2). The judge held that assuming that the bolt constituted a loose material within reg. 48(2), nevertheless it did not restrict unduly the passage of persons in this case and accordingly there was no breach of reg. 48(2). P appealed. *Held*, dismissing the appeal, that on a true and proper construction of reg. 48(2), looking at the words as a whole, what was intended was that if loose materials were left which restricted unduly the passage of persons, then such loose materials had to be removed so as to leave an unobstructed passage. The obligation on the employer was to leave a passage which did not restrict unduly the passage of persons. It was not possible to fasten upon the word "obstructed" in reg. 48(2) and read it in such a way as to require everything to be removed from a walkway or area ignoring the opening words of the regulations. Appeal from Boreham J. December 16, 1985. (C.A.T. No. 848). READER *v.* BRITISH STEEL CORP.

20. Factories—safe means of access to place of work—access to storage area—provision of ladder

No particular ladder was made available by employers D for employees to reach a storage area 10 feet above ground level at D's factory. The frequency of use of a ladder to reach the storage area was of the order of 20 times a week. P, employee, fell breaking his arm and leg when a long ladder that he was using (which extended some four feet above the storage area into the roof space above it) slipped, being unfastened and unfooted. *Held,* that in order to comply with the duty imposed by s.29 of the Factories Act 1961, to provide and maintain, so far as was reasonably practicable, a safe means of access to every place to which any person had at any time to work, some means of easily fastening the ladder was called for. More probably, a permanently fastened ladder was needed to give access to the storage area. A system whereby workmen could help themselves to any available ladder from the ladder store was not good enough. It was plainly foreseeable that, with that frequency of use, men would use the ladder without having it footed. Appeal from Hodgson J. October 14, 1985. (C.A.T. No. 577.) SMITH *v.* BRITISH RAILWAYS BOARD.

21. Hire Purchase—car leasing agreement—breach—damages

P purchased a Ford Granada car from HPJ Co. for some £8,500 and in March 1980 leased it to D for three years. In November 1980 D handed the car over HPJ and took delivery of a smaller car which he leased through arrangements made by HPJ with a different hire purchase company. P found out what had happened and entered into an arrangement with HPJ whereby HPJ agreed to pay P a sum of money required to settle D's lease. HPJ accordingly sent a cheque but it was not met. D contended that the fact that the offer was accepted by HPJ, albeit that the cheque was not met, ratified the agreement to sell the car to HPJ entered into by him. *Held,* dismissing D's appeal, that P were not setting aside the lease with D, nor were they ratifying D's action. They were merely seeing whether they could help D in that they were assuming, until the cheque was not met, that HPJ could pay what D owed (*Verschures Creameries* v. *Hull & Netherlands Shipping Co.* [1921] 2 K.B. 608, *United Australian* v. *Barclays Bank* [1941] A.C. 1, *Brewer* v. *Sparrow* 108 E.R. 739 explained). Further, P's action in requesting a garage owner, who then had possession of the car, to repossess the car on their behalf was not a *novus actus interveniens* preventing further damages from accruing but a step reasonably taken by P to mitigate the damage which D had caused by selling the car. January 16, 1986. (C.A.T. No. 14.) LOMBARD NORTH CENTRAL *v.* WALKER.

22. Housing—local authority—small holdings—long term retention

Before the coming into force of the Housing and Building Control Act 1984, which, *inter alia,* conferred on public sector tenants security of tenure and certain other rights, D council considered a report of its County Farms Panel which recommended that in order to safeguard operational requirements in relation to statutory smallholdings, notices to quit be served in respect of those properties which in the opinion of the county land agent and valuer it was desirable to retain on estate management grounds or to meet an operational need, whether in the long term or short, and decided that notices to quit be served on certain tenants prior to the coming into force of the 1984 Act. The reason which motivated the committee to reach its decision was that, as a smallholdings authority, the council needed, and would need indefinitely, resources of accommodation for tenants and others, including students. Although it was apparent that there was no immediate need of the properties for smallholdings purposes, the committee was conscious that it might in the long term regret the loss of houses not needed in the short term. The applicant, one of the tenants served with a notice to quit, applied for judicial review of the council's decision to serve notices to quit contending, *inter alia,* that it was not established that the council had a genuine need to retain the properties and that the benefit to be derived by the council in retaining them was purely speculative. *Held,* dismissing the applicant's appeal, that although, having regard to the past history of the properties and their present use, it seemed improbable that they would be needed for smallholdings purposes in the foreseeable future, nevertheless, there was no reason why the council should not take the view that they might require the properties in the long term and it was therefore prudent to retain them. February 6, 1986. (C.A.T. No. 118.) R. *v.* DURHAM COUNCIL *ex p.* EGAN.

UNREPORTED CASES

23. Housing—mobile home—protected site—meaning

On a true and proper construction the meaning of a protected site in s.1(2) of the Caravan Sites Act 1968 was a site in respect of which planning permission had been granted for the stationing of one or more caravans. If planning permission had not been granted then the site was not a protected site within the meaning of that Act, or, it followed, by virtue of s.5 of the Mobile Homes Act 1983, within the meaning of the 1983 Act (*Brice* v. *National By-Products* [1984] C.L.Y. 1914 explained). July 19, 1985. (C.A.T. No. 396). GUTTELIN v. MULLANE.

24. Housing—secure tenancy—possession—reasonableness of order

In considering whether it was reasonable under s.34(3) of the Housing Act 1980 to make an order for possession on the ground of non-payment of rent against D, who held a secured tenancy under s.34 of the 1980 Act and was in receipt of housing benefit from the Department of Health and Social Security but spent the rent money on food instead, the judge failed to take into account the suggestion by the Law Centre representing D that they would make sure that necessary steps were taken to see that the rent was paid direct to the landlord by the D.H.S.S. *Held,* allowing D's appeal, that that was a very important factor which should have been taken into account. It was well known that arrangement could be made with the D.H.S.S. when housing benefit was payable to see that the rent was paid direct to the landlord. The case would accordingly be remitted to the county court for reconsideration. March 6, 1986. (C.A.T. No. 228). SECOND W.R.V.S. HOUSING SOCIETY v. BLAIR.

25. Husband and Wife—contempt of court—breach of undertaking—immediate custodial sentence

In April 1984 H gave an undertaking to the court not to assault, molest or otherwise interfere with W. In February 1985 H wrote a letter in "extremely abusive terms" to W and she issued a notice of committal against him. The judge adjourned W's application generally with liberty to either party to restore it, thereby warning H that that was how the situation would stand unless and until there was some further breach. On April 6, 1985, when W was picking up the children from a visit to H, H yelled and screamed at her and used obscene language. Then on April 28, 1985 H again used obscene and abusive language in the presence of the children, when W came to collect the children accompanied by a lady with whom W appeared to be living in a lesbian relationship. The judge held H to be in contempt and sentenced him to four weeks imprisonment. H appealed. *Held,* dismissing the appeal, that H's actions amounted to serious molestations which were in breach of his undertaking and accordingly H was in contempt of court. The effect of the adjournment of the application for committal was very similar to the deferment of the imposition of a sentence in criminal proceedings and when the matter came to be considered again H was inevitably at risk of an immediate custodial sentence. There was no error in the judge's approach. (*Ansah* v. *Ansah* [1977] C.L.Y. 1567 explained). Appeal from Arnold P. August 13, 1985. (C.A.T. No. 510) GEORGE v. GEORGE.

26. Husband and Wife—financial provision—lump sum award—benefit to persons other than wife

The judge ordered H to pay his former wife, W, who was cohabiting with a man B, a lump sum payment of £600,000. H appealed contending, *inter alia,* that the judge wrongly exercised his discretion because in reaching his decision he failed to take into account or give sufficient weight to the fact that W was cohabiting with a man who would benefit from the capital which H had been ordered to pay. *Held,* dismissing the appeal, that the judge was wholly justified in failing to take that fact into account since it was irrelevant. He had to consider what were the reasonable needs of W under the circumstances, and it was accepted that the sum to meet those reasonable needs, after she had had the house transferred to her, was the annual disposable sum, the net figure of £28,000. How she spent her money was her affair. The fact that she might spend some part of it upon B, who as a result would benefit from it, would merely reduce the satisfying of her reasonable needs which required *ex hypothesi* the sum of £28,000 per annum. It was just as irrelevant that she should be spending part of her money upon B as if she decided to have living with her an impecunious friend or an elderly relative, who, again, would be an expense which she herself would defray out of the income which had been assessed as being appropriate solely for her needs. Appeal from Reeve J. (C.A.T. No. 756.) November 25, 1985. DUXBURY *v.* DUXBURY.

27. Husband and Wife—financial provision—order for indemnity for costs incurred overseas—jurisdiction

On appeal from an order of the Registrar relating to financial provision between the parties after divorce, the judge ordered, *inter alia,* that H should indemnify W in respect of costs incurred in undefended proceedings by her in the Isle of Man whereby she obtained an *ex parte* injunction to protect sums of money which she thought were in two bank accounts held by H there. *Held,* that there was no jurisdiction to order one party to indemnify another party for costs, however meritoriously incurred, in another jurisdiction as a direct order, as it were, from an unliquidated liability. Ss.23 and 24 of the Matrimonial Causes Act 1973, which were applicable here, did not provide a jurisdiction to order an indemnity for costs incurred overseas. January 29, 1986. (C.A.T. No. 85) BOWIE *v.* BOWIE.

28. Husband and Wife—matrimonial home—exclusion of spouse—common law right to live in matrimonial home

The judge refused W's application under s.1 of the Matrimonial Homes Act 1983 for an order, *inter alia,* that H permit her to return to the matrimonial home which was owned jointly in the names of H and his father. W appealed, contending that quite apart from the 1983 Act she had an independent right to live in the matrimonial home at common law, and that the judge had no discretion to keep her out on the basis of the decision in *Gurasz* v. *Gurasz* [1969] C.L.Y. 1645. *Held,* dismissing the appeal, that the decision in *Gurasz* did not apply in the present case and was limited to cases where the matrimonial home was a dwelling which was owned, using the word in the widest sense, whether it be freehold, leasehold as a tenant or however, by one or other spouse or the spouses jointly; as soon as one found that there was a third person who was the owner occupier along with a spouse, then a common law right could not exist against the person who was not a spouse (*Gurasz* v. *Gurasz* [1969] C.L.Y. 1645 and *Hoggett* v. *Hoggett* [1980] C.L.Y. 1621 explained). December 17, 1985. (C.A.T. No. 853.) CHAUDHRY *v.* CHAUDHRY.

29. Husband and Wife—matrimonial home—meaning—objective test

In deciding whether a dwelling house, had ever become a matrimonial home of H and W, the judge asked the question whether the house was the place where H and W had really set up home together, and, having looked at all the circumstances, the judge declared that the property was at no time a matrimonial home and that, pursuant to s.1(1) of the Matrimonial Homes Act 1983, the provisions of that Act did not apply thereto and accordingly W had no right to occupation of the property. *Held,* dismissing W's appeal, that the test of what was a matrimonial home in the context of the 1983 Act was an objective test. Parliament had used the language in that Act in its ordinary sense and had not attempted to give a special or artificial meaning in the interpretation section of the statute. In order to answer the question the judge had to look at all the circumstances of the case. The judge had directed himself correctly as a matter of law. The court would not seek to cloud the problem of construction by formulating any other indicia or test. March 18, 1986. (C.A.T. No. 262). MACKINTOSH *v.* MACKINTOSH.

30. Husband and Wife—property adjustment order—appeal—leave to appeal out of time

On December 21, 1984, the judge made an order on an appeal from an order of the registrar relating to property adjustment between the parties who were now divorced. On January 11, 1985, W died. On June 10, 1985, H applied for leave to appeal out of time against the judge's order. *Held,* granting leave to appeal out of time, that if the registrar, when he made his order on October 29, 1984, or the judge, when he was dealing with the appeal on December 21, 1984, had known that on January 11, 1985 W was going to die, he would have made an order less favourable to her by way of transfer of part of the equitable interest of H to her, because her need would have been quite different from that which was contemplated by the Court making the order. H was thus entitled to leave to appeal out of time (*Wells* v. *Wells,* unreported, June 18, 1980, C.A.T. No. 526 followed). March 10, 1986. (C.A.T. No. 240.) PASSMORE *v.* GILL.

31. Immigration—appeal—appeal to Immigration Appeal Tribunal—Tribunal to consider case de novo

On an appeal from a decision of the Immigration Appeal Tribunal the judge concluded that the Tribunal had erred in law in holding that the adjudicator had overlooked para. 117 of H.C. 394 and held that he must accordingly quash the order of the Tribunal. *Held,* that it was clear that under s.20(1) of the Immigration Act 1971 it was the duty of the Tribunal to consider the case *de novo.* On an application for judicial review of a decision of the Tribunal, the question to be asked was whether the decision of the Tribunal itself was open to challenge on the *Wednesbury* principle. Accordingly, if the Tribunal did erroneously conclude that the adjudicator had overlooked para. 117 of the Immigration Rules, that was of itself no ground for quashing their decision. The true approach by the judge should have been, not simply to reconsider the decision of the Tribunal, but rather to consider whether the decision which the Tribunal made was open to challenge on the ordinary *Wednesbury* principle. Appeal from Webster J. October 23, 1985. (C.A.T. No. 584.) PROPOSED APPLICATION FOR JUDICIAL REVIEW BY OSEI, *Re.*

32. Immigration—detention—refusal of leave to enter—temporary admission subject to restrictions

On its true construction, para. 126 of HC 169, which dealt with a man admitted to U.K. "in a temporary capacity" who married a woman settled here, did not apply to persons who were "temporarily admitted" to the U.K. under para. 21 of Sched. 2 to the Immigration Act 1971. Para. 126 dealt with a situation where people had had leave to enter or remain and were seeking variations of that leave (*R.* v. *Immigration Appeal Tribunal, ex p. Alexander* [1982] 1 C.L.Y. 1553 applied). Appeal from Hodgson J. July 2, 1985. (C.A.T. No. 348). R. *v.* SECRETARY OF STATE FOR THE HOME DEPARTMENT, *ex p.* KHAN (TAJ MOHAMMED).

33. Immigration—illegal entrant—entry by fraud in 1969—leave to enter or remain

R, a Commonwealth citizen who was subject to control under the Commonwealth Immigrants Act 1962 and 1968, entered the U.K. in 1969 by the use of a forged passport. In October 1985 he was detained as an illegal entrant. R contended that he had a right to remain here indefinitely by virtue of s.34(2) and (3) of the Immigration Act 1971 and that the powers conferred by para. 9 of Sched. 2 of the 1971 Act were not exercisable in his case even though he was an illegal entrant. R argued as follows: (1) He was a person who was given leave to enter the U.K. by virtue of the 1962 and 1968 Acts and in view of the decision in *Khawaja* [1983] C.L.Y. 1908 that leave could not be treated as a nullity even though it was obtained by fraud. (2) By virtue of s.34(2) of the 1971 Act he had therefore to be "treated as having been given leave to enter under the 1971 Act." (3) Furthermore, by virtue of s.34(3) of the 1971 Act he had to be treated as having indefinite leave to remain in the U.K. (4) Accordingly, as from January 1, 1983, he had a statutory right to be treated as a person who had been given leave to enter and an indefinite leave to remain in the U.K. (5) In view of this statutory right, he, albeit an illegal entrant, had been "given leave to enter or remain" in the U.K. within para. 9 of Sched. 2 to the 1971 Act. *Held,* dismissing R's appeal, that on the true construction of para. 9 of Sched. 2, an illegal entrant such as R who had entered the country in breach of the immigration laws, could bring himself outside the ambit of para. 9 only if, *subsequent* to his illegal entry, he had been given leave to enter or remain in the U.K. Para. 9 did not contemplate that a person may simultaneously both become an illegal entrant and be given leave to enter and remain in the U.K. indefinitely. Further, s.34(2) and (3) did not give R any statutory right to remain indefinitely in the U.K. They were expressed to operate without prejudice to the generality of s.34(1) which itself operated to render R an illegal entrant. The force of the words of s.34(2) is simply that a person other than an illegal entrant who had been given leave to enter under the 1962 and 1968 Acts was spared the necessity of making a new application for leave to enter under the 1971 Act after that Act came into force. They did not absolve an illegal entrant from the need to make such application (*Khawaja* [1983] C.L.Y. 1908 and *Azam* [1973] C.L.Y. 4 considered). Appeal from Kennedy J. March 25, 1986. (C.A.T. No. 307). R. *v.* SECRETARY OF STATE FOR THE HOME DEPARTMENT, *ex p.* RAZAK.

34. Landlord and Tenant—business premises—occupied for business purposes—occupation by tenant's company

L applied to strike out T's application for a new tenancy under the Landlord and Tenant Act 1954 on the ground that T had not been in occupation of the premises for the purposes of a business within s.23 of the 1954 Act. A company of which T owned all the shares had been conducting business at the premises. T contended that the reality of the position was that the business was in fact the business of T who were using a vehicle in the form of a company to carry on their business and that by virtue of s.30 of the 1954 Act (as added to by s.6 of the Law of Property Act 1969). *Held,* dismissing T's appeal, that the company was a legal entity entirely separate from T. T was accordingly not in occupation of the premises within s.23 of the 1954 Act (*Tunstall* v. *Steigman* [1962] C.L.Y. 1718 applied, *Pegler* v. *Craven* [1952] C.L.Y. 1961 explained). May 16, 1985. (C.A.T. No. 305.) CRISTINA *v.* SEEAR.

35. Landlord and Tenant—rent restriction—possession—landlord's work needs—acquisition of other house suitable to work needs

On its true construction para (*f*) of Part V of the Rent Act 1977 (as added by the Housing Act 1980) required a connection between the landlord's aquisition of a dwelling-house as his residence and use of the proceeds of the sale of the existing house for that purpose. It required a connection within a reasonable time. It would not be sufficient for a landlord merely to say that sometime in future he might want to use the money. Further, the application of the provision was not limited to the acquiring of an existing dwelling-house but was wide enough to cover the building of a new house for that purpose. June 18, 1985. (C.A.T. No. 286.) BISSESSAR *v.* GHOSA.

36. Mining Law—equipment of mine—good construction—breach of duty

D's employee, an experienced miner, hit his head against a gangway in D's mine and suffered injuries from which he died shortly afterwards. P contended, *inter alia,* that there was a breach of s.81(1) of the Mines and Quarries Act 1954 in that the gangway confined the work space of the deceased and was not high enough and that created a danger and accordingly the apparatus including the gangway was not of good construction. *Held,* that there was no breach of s.81. There was nothing in s.81 which required that some appliance in a mine should be so constructed or positioned that when it was in use for its purpose, it was out of reach of a man going about his work upright. In a mine that was an untenable submission. It mattered not whether the apparatus was of good construction because it had no causative element as far as the deceased's injury was concerned. The place was well lit. Further, reg. 2 of the Coal and Other Mines (Managers and Officials) Regulations 1956 required some foresight by the manager or under manager, as the case may be. It was a providing regulation and not an enforcing regulation. What had to be provided was suitable materials and appliances. But what the manager could not do was to foresee everything which may happen in a mine, which, in the end resulted in injury. What he had to do was to make available the materials necessary to ensure the safety of persons employed in the mine. Safety and danger were opposite sides of the same coin, particularly where they were used as words and expressions under the Factories Acts and coal mines Legislation. The point about the present case was that nobody thought it was reasonably foreseeable, indeed foreseeable at all, that the deceased, in a well lit part of the mine with his lamp on, should walk straight into something which he had been working with for several weeks and knew perfectly well was there. (*Smith* v. *A. Davies & Co. (Shopfitters)*) [1969] C.L.Y. 319 considered). Appeal from Otton J. February 27, 1986. (C.A.T. No. 202) TAYLOR *v.* NATIONAL COAL BOARD.

37. Minors—access—access to grandparents—no right

The judge declined to order access to either the child's father or to the paternal grandparents. The grandparents who sought access to the child, now aged four years, appealed contending that it was universally or at least usually in the interests of a child to have continuing access to members of the child's family, both on the maternal and the paternal side, including the grandparents, and that the judge flew in the face of that principle unless it could be demonstrated that there were reasons for such a departure from that general principle. *Held,* dismissing the appeal, that there was no such principle. There was certainly a principle to be derived from the decided cases, that it was normal that both parents of the child should have access to that child and that if any other solution was reached there had to be material upon which that departure could be based. But in the case of relations other than the parents, the matter was quite different and there had to be performed in every case a balancing exercise, in the one scale being placed those items of evidence which suggested that there would be a benefit to the child from the access which was sought and in the other such factors as there may be to demonstrate either that there would be no such benefit or that there were other reasons for refusing access. There was in this case no material whatsoever to suggest that access to the grandparents would be advantageous to the child. March 19, 1986. (C.A.T. No. 269). HOLT *v.* HOLT.

38. Minors—wardship—confidentiality of wardship proceedings—ex parte applications

F issued summonses in the magistrates' court alleging perjury on various occasions against M who had been given care and control of the child of their marriage in wardship proceedings in which there had been several applications. F applied *ex parte* for copies of the affidavits used in the wardship proceedings to be sent to the magistrates. The judge granted the application making an order containing directions designed to preserve the confidentiality of the wardship proceedings and protect the interests of the ward by restricting the disclosure of the affidavits for certain purposes and to certain persons only. M appealed. *Held,* allowing M's appeal and quashing the judge's order, that the order should never have been made *ex parte* because M and the ward were very much concerned with it. The result of the order would be, if there was a committal for trial, that there would be a public trial which would defeat the whole purpose of the confidentiality of wardship proceedings. The provisions of confidentiality which the judge rightly sought to impose would not prevent this, because it would be at the trial, if there was a trial, that trouble would arise. Furthermore, it should be a guiding rule that *ex parte* applications should only be allowed in wardship cases where there was an urgent necessity for them. In all wardship cases it was essential that the Official Solicitor should know what was going on and should have an opportunity of appearing if he thought it right or necessary to do so. Quite apart from representations, in such a case as this the court should be sure that there was a case. The judge mentioned consultation with the Director of Public Prosecutions, but this should be done at an earlier stage. If there was to be any application which, if granted, would interfere with the confidentiality of the wardship proceedings, it would be preferable for it to be made by the Director of Public Prosecutions. If the Director had been consulted, a decision would have been made as to whether there was a case of perjury. Appeal from His Honour Judge Head. June 14, 1985. (C.A.T. No. 311). H. (A MINOR), *Re.*

39. Minors—wardship—jurisdiction—supervision of local authority

M a boy born in December 1984 to an unmarried mother, was taken into voluntary care under s.2 of the Child Care Act 1980. The mother wished to place him for adoption and M was placed with Mr. and Mrs. R on a short-term fostering basis. In June 1985 Mr. and Mrs. R requested the local council to consider them as prospective adopters of M. The adoption panel of the council decided that Mr. and Mrs. R were not suitable either as adoptive parents in general or as adoptive parents of M in particular. Mr. and Mrs. R were dissatisfied with that decision and issued an originating summons making M a ward of court and seeking, *inter alia,* his care and control. The judge on the application of the council ordered that M should no longer remain a ward of the court. Mr. and Mrs. R appealed, contending that the only way in which relief could be achieved by them was to keep the wardship proceedings open, not to use the wardship proceedings as a convenient alternative to an application for judicial review of the council's decision under R.S.C., Ord. 53, but to use them having achieved jurisdiction by establishing a situation applicable with Ord. 53 in order to exercise normal wardship jurisdiction over the functions of the council under the statutory code. *Held,* dismissing the appeal, that the process under s.31 of the Supreme Court Act 1981 and R.S.C., Ord. 53 was specifically designed so that the courts supervise the proper execution of their statutory duties by bodies upon whom those duties rested. That process was protected in a number of ways, such as the necessity to apply for leave to move for the relief, and in doing so, it was incumbent upon the applicant to state specifically the statutory duty the breach of which was alleged, and the manner in which the breach was alleged to have taken place. Then the whole matter was considered by the court on its merits. Those safeguards could not be put to one side where children were concerned. The local authority in exercising its powers should not be subjected to supervision or possible interference by applications in wardship proceedings, unless it could be shown that they behaved in such a way as to bring upon themselves the supervision of the court under the provisions of s.31 and Ord. 53 (*A.* v. *Liverpool City Council* [1981] C.L.Y. 1796 considered). Appeal from Booth J. December 18, 1985. (C.A.T. No. 858.) M (A MINOR), *Re.*

40. Minors—welfare report—order that mother reside in matrimonial home with children pending preparation—jurisdiction

W appealed against an order of the judge that she reside in the matrimonial home with the two children of the marriage, then both aged two and a half, pending the preparation of a welfare report. *Held,* allowing the appeal, that it was unnecessary to consider whether there was any jurisdiction to make the order. On the facts of the case there were no grounds whatever for the judge to make such an order. Not surprisingly H had consented to the appeal against that order being allowed. He had not appeared and had given his consent, very properly, in order to save costs. February 3, 1986. (C.A.T. No. 100) RATCLIFF *v.* RATCLIFF.

41. Negligence—occupier's liability—child trespasser—foreseeability of risk

A school had round it a chain link fence six feet high with spikes at the top. Inside the fence were two oak trees with their branches overhanging the pavement. P, an infant, was playing in the road outside the fence. She saw two boys throwing sticks up into the trees from the road in order to try and get down some acorns. She went to help, found some sticks and threw them up. A stick became wedged between two branches and P decided to dislodge it by climbing the fence. Whilst on the fence P's body jerked, her foot fell out of the holes in the fence and her arm became impaled on the spikes at the top from where she dangled until rescued by a friend. The judge found against D who accepted that there was a possibility that a child might climb the fence and be injured trying to get at the acorns liable in negligence to P. *Held,* allowing D's appeal, that the possibility of some injury might have been foreseeable but this accident was of a special kind. It was not somebody attempting to climb over the fence in order to get inside but somebody climbing a fence in order to get a piece of wood that had been thrown into the trees. That was not something that could have been reasonably foreseen. D, having considered the matter, were entitled to regard the risk as being so remote as not to call upon them to take any special measure to avoid it (*British Railways Board* v. *Herrington* [1972] C.L.Y. 2344 and *Pannett* v. *McGuiness* [1972] C.L.Y. 2343 applied). January 24, 1986. (C.A.T. No. 59.) HULSE *v.* MANCHESTER CITY COUNCIL.

42. Negligence—remoteness of damage—foreseeable harm—whether precise nature of injury to be foreseen

P, an employee, claimed damages against D, his employers, for personal injuries in the form of tenosynovitis of the left wrist, caused due to work performed by him in the course of his duties at Markham Main Colliery in South Yorkshire. P appealed against the decision of the judge, on the ground, *inter alia,* that having found upon the evidence that a strain, or sprain, or twist to some part of the body, including the wrist, was foreseeable, the judge was not justified in holding that tenosynovitis was an injury of a different kind and thus not a foreseeable consequence of the work performed, or any breach of duty relating thereto. *Held,* allowing the appeal, that having found that an injury such as a sprain or strain was foreseeable, including injuries of that nature to the wrist, the judge should not have excluded an injury such as tenosynovitis as being not foreseeable. That could consist of no more than a specific variant of the foreseeable injury, and was within the ambit of injuries found to be foreseeable. The precise nature of the injury did not need to be foreseen if its general nature could, and the fact that tenosynovitis was an inflammation of the tendon or its sheath was not sufficient to categorise it as a kind which was not foreseeable, whereas strains or sprains and the like were (*Bradford* v. *Robinson Rentals* [1967] C.L.Y. 1197 and *Tremain* v. *Pike* [1969] C.L.Y. 2412 considered). January 23, 1986. (C.A.T. No. 45) ROWARK *v.* NATIONAL COAL BOARD.

43. Negligence—res ipsa loquitur—driving motor vehicle in foggy conditions—only one rear light working

To drive a motor vehicle on a road in foggy conditions when only one of two rear lights was lit raised a presumption of negligence on the part of the driver. That presumption could be discharged by the defendant either providing an explanation of how that rear light came to be off which did not connote negligence on his part or by showing that he had in fact taken reasonable steps and that notwithstanding that, the rear light had gone out. October 25, 1985. (C.A.T. No. 624.) SUTTON *v.* JONES.

44. Negligence—res ipsa loquitur—pot of boiling water falling on plaintiff—vicarious liability

D2, a nurse, was employed by D1, a health authority. D2 went to the kitchen in the geriatric ward where he was on duty, to get a pot of boiling water, some cups and coffee. He came back into the ward and as he put the tray down on the table, the pot of boiling water fell off into P's, a fellow nurse's, lap and burnt her. *Held*, that (1) this was a case of *res ipsa loquitor* and no explanations having been given by D2, negligence was established against him; (2) D1 was vicariously liable for the negligence of D2 as D2 was acting in the course of his employment. D2 was acting within the terms of his written employment functions, *inter alia*, "to satisfy the human needs of patients and staff with particular regard to their well being, dignity and comfort." December 4, 1985. (C.A.T. No. 810.) McPHERSON *v.* DEVON AREA HEALTH AUTHORITY.

45. Negligence—vicarious liability—child in care boarded out—injury by negligence of foster parents—whether council vicariously liable

P child was taken into care by D1 local authority and boarded out to D2 and D3 foster parents. By an unexplained accident P suffered severe burns to her feet whilst she was with the foster parents. Proceeding on the principle of *res ipsa loquitur* the judge found D3 negligent and therefore responsible for P's injuries. It was contended, *inter alia*, that there was a relationship of principal and agent or of a sufficient proximity between the foster parents and D1 to make D1 liable for the acts of the foster parents. *Held*, that the relationship between P and D1 and between P and D2 and D3 was one which was regulated simply and solely by the provisions of the statutory scheme under the Children Act 1948 and the regulations relating to it. That was inconsistent with the notion that the foster parents were in any way the agents of D1 in carrying out the duties. It was the duty of D1 to provide accommodation for the child, and the duty was satisfied by the provision of accommodation by boarding out. The foster parents were not in any way fulfilling D1's duty to provide accommodation. They were the means by which D1 carried out its own duty. It was inconsistent with the statutory scheme that they should be treated as agents of D1. June 6, 1985. (C.A.T. No. 335.) SARGENT *v.* WALSALL METROPOLITAN BOROUGH COUNCIL.

46. Practice—action—striking out—want of prosecution—duty of counsel in "two-judge appeals"

D applied to strike out the action by P for want of prosecution. The judge found that shortly before D had issued their summons to strike out they had acted in such a way as to give rise to the fair inference that they intended to proceed with the litigation despite the delay and that P's solicitors acted upon this implied representation in continuing to take steps on the action and to spend money in doing so. The judge held that in these circumstances, despite the delay and consequent prejudice, he retained no discretion whether or not to strike out the action but was bound to refuse D's application, although had he still retained the relevant discretion, he would have exercised it in D's favour. D appealed. The appeal was listed for hearing before a two-judge court. It came on for hearing before Kerr and May L.JJ. *Held*, dismissing the appeal and granting leave to appeal to the House of Lords; *Per* Kerr L.J.: the court was not precluded from granting the application upon appropriate terms as to costs in such circumstances. *Per* May L.J.: the court was so precluded (*Allen* v. *McAlpine* [968] C.L.Y. 3104 considered). Further, due to the pressure of work in the Court of Appeal, appeals which could be heard by a two-judge court were prima facie listed to be dealt with in this way. But many interlocutory appeals and appeals from the county court presented problems of considerable difficulty which may well give rise to differences of opinion in the Court of Appeal. Such cases may be difficult to identify by the Registry of Civil Appeals when they were listed, and by the time the court saw the papers, shortly before the hearing of the appeal, it was often administratively difficult or impossible to rearrange the hearing before a court of three. On the other hand these cases should be identifiable by the counsel instructed on the appeal. They should therefore bear this in mind and inform the Registry in good time whenever it appeared to them that an appeal which may be heard by a court of two should more appropriately be heard by a court of three, so that their views in this regard could be considered before the case was listed. Appeal from Staughton J. July 31, 1985. (C.A.T. No. 497.) BANLADESH BIMAN v. PAN AYER S.A.

47. Practice—Anton Piller order—retrospective discharge of executed order—general jurisdiction

A fully executed Anton Piller order could be discharged if it was established that it should never have been made. This was so whenever a defendant raised this contention and sought to enforce the plaintiff's cross-undertaking in damages on the basis of which the order against him was made.

If the sole reason for seeking a retrospective discharge of the order was to enforce the cross-undertaking as to damages, then there was no ground for any immediate application. Any issues as to the validity of the order or as to the consequences of its invalidity should generally be left to be dealt with at the trial of the action. If the action was settled, then any disputes concerning the order were likely to be settled as well. But exceptional cases could arise if a defendant was in some way affected in his reputation or otherwise by the fact that the order remained apparently valid in the interim.

It was important that the profession should be reminded of certain of the main requirements of the Anton Piller jurisdiction.

The Anton Piller order was at the extremity of the court's powers. It was an exceptional remedy only to be granted where "if the defendant were forewarned, there is a grave danger that vital evidence will be destroyed, that papers will be burnt or lost or hidden, or taken beyond the jurisdiction, and so the ends of justice be defeated . . . that there is real possibility that (the defendants) may destroy such material before any application inter partes can be made."

The phrase "a real possibility" was to be contrasted with the extravagant fears which seemed to afflict all plaintiffs who had complaints of breach of confidence, breach of copyright or passing off. Where the production and delivery up of documents was in question, the courts had always proceeded, justifiably on the basis that the overwhelming majority of people in this country would comply with the court's orders, and that defendants would therefore comply with orders to, for example, produce and deliver up documents without it being necessary to empower the plaintiff's solicitors to search the defendant's premises.

It followed that the making of an Anton Piller order against a trading company may well be regarded as a serious stigma on that company's commercial reputation. It followed that there was a responsibility in each case on the plaintiff's advisers to consider seriously whether it was justifiable to seek an Anton Piller order against the particular defendant, or whether it would be enough to obtain negative injunctions with, if appropriate, an order to deliver up documents or material, for example, where the documents sought were the property of the plaintiff.

Since the Anton Piller orders were always made on *ex parte* application, the plaintiffs' advisers had a duty to put candidly before the court all relevant material. If, even inadvertently, there had been a failure to put material information before the court, the court had a discretion to set aside the order, or refuse to continue it, without even going into the merits of the plaintiffs' claim for relief. Again, because the Anton Piller order was exceptional and because the application for it was made *ex parte,* it was the duty of counsel for the plaintiff to ensure (usually by putting a draft minute of order before the judge) that the order he was asking for contained all proper safeguards for the absent defendant.

These safeguards should normally include (and the list was not exhaustive) the following: (1) an undertaking by the plaintiffs that the order would be served on the defendant by a solicitor and that the solicitor who served the order would at the same time supply the defendants served with copies of all affidavits and other documents which were put before the judge on the *ex parte* application, or in so far as there were no such affidavits, with affidavits, or at the least written statements setting out the substance of the matters of fact which were explained to the judge by counsel for the plaintiff on that application; (2) an undertaking by the plaintiffs that the solicitor who served the order would explain its terms to the defendant served and would advise him to seek immediate advice; (3) express liberty to each defendant to apply to the court on short notice to vary or discharge the order; (4) a cross undertaking in damages; and (5) an undertaking by the plaintiffs to issue a writ if the *ex parte* application for the Anton Piller order was made before there had been time to issue the writ.

It was unjust to the defendant if the evidence on which the order had been obtained was not produced to him when the order was served, because if he was not told what the case against him was he was gravely hampered in endeavouring to have the order set aside or varied by the court. Moreover, the service of an Anton Piller order, involving as it did the arrival of a number of strangers to search the defendant's premises, was a delicate matter requiring tactful handling by the solicitor concerned, whether the defendant was innocent or guilty of what was alleged against him. Justice required that he must be shown the case against him at the earliest moment. To avoid lax practice developing, these safeguards ought to be embodied in the undertakings to the court in the *ex parte* order.

There was no doubt that a defendant could apply to set aside the Anton Piller order on the ground that it ought never to have been made.

Ordinarily, an application to set aside an Anton Piller order which had already been fully executed, though important to the defendant, was not a matter of overwhelming urgency. Ordinarily, therefore, in a case where, as was normal practice in the Chancery Division, the negative injunctions granted with an Anton Piller order were granted for a period of a few days only in the expectation that by the end of that period the plaintiff would be applying *inter partes* for a continuation of those injunctions, the defendant ought to make his application for setting aside of the Anton Piller order returnable not earlier than the return date for the plaintiffs' *inter partes* application for the continuation of the negative injunctions. The two applications could then be taken together.

Again, ordinarily in a case where, as was usual in the Queen's Bench Division, the *ex parte* injunctions had been granted until further order, and not over a fixed date, albeit with liberty to apply, it was undesirable that application for the retrospective discharge of an already executed order should be made with excessive haste. Excessive haste could readily lead to disorder in the parties' preparations for the hearing of the application. It would ordinarily be far better if a few days were allowed to elapse before the application was made, so as to give both parties a better opportunity to put their tackle in order before the application was heard.

It was the responsibility of counsel not to waste the time of the court, and it would seldom if ever be necessary to hear cross-examination of witnesses on an application in advance of the trial to set aside an Anton Piller order which had been fully executed. Such an application was not to be taken by counsel for any party as an opportunity to interrogate, or elicit admissions for use at the trial or to probe the strength of the substantive cases which the other party may seek to make at the trial.

An application to set aside an Anton Piller order which had not yet been executed had of course to be decided with expedition in order to establish whether or not the order will be executed. It was otherwise where the order had already been fully executed, and in such a case the judge to whom an application to set aside such an order was made would be entitled in his discretion, if he thought fit in a particular case, to direct that the application to set aside the order, with any ancillary matters of costs or of directing an inquiry as to damages on the cross-undertaking, be adjourned to the judge at trial of the action. Appeal from Park J. April 3, 1985. (C.A.T. No. 137) BOOKER MCCONNELL *v.* PLASCOW.

48. Practice—appeal—appeal out of time—leave to appeal

H and W, Australian by birth, had lived in this country for several years. They were still married but W had commenced divorce proceedings in Australia. W applied pursuant to s.30 of the Law of Property Act 1925 for an order for the sale of the matrimonial home and for division of the proceeds of sale. The matter was heard by the Registrar on September 25, 1985, but was not concluded and the hearing was adjourned to October 23. W had given evidence and had been cross-examined by H but H had not himself presented his case by giving evidence on his own behalf. On October 4 H wrote to the Registrar indicating that he would in fact have to visit Australia on October 23 and asking that the hearing date be vacated. The Registrar replied to H's address in England that such an informal request could not be accepted and that there would have to be an application on notice to vacate the date. H said that he never received that letter. On October 21 H telephoned the clerk to the Registrar from Australia and was told that he would have to appear before the Registrar if he wished to vacate date of hearing. On October 23 the hearing was resumed in H's absence, W completed her case and the Registrar gave judgment in W's favour to the effect that the matrimonial home should be sold at a price advised by a reputable estate agent. On October 26, H wrote a letter to the Clerk of the Rules indicating that he wanted a stay of the Registrar's decision with the intention of appealing. The letter was not accepted as a proper notice of appeal and H then instructed solicitors to act for him and they issued a Notice of Appeal in a proper form on November 7. By virtue of R.S.C., Ord. 58, r.3(2) the time for appealing the order of the Registrar had expired on October 30 and accordingly H applied for leave to appeal. The judge concluded that H's failure to attend the hearing before the Registrar on October 23 was his own fault and that he could have attended if he had wished to and considered that there was no merit in H's appeal and accordingly refused the application. H applied to the Court of Appeal for leave to appeal from the judge's decision contending that the period of delay in appealing was short, being only eight days, and he should not be deprived of his right of appeal which he would have had if the notice had been given in time. *Held,* refusing leave to appeal that the application was without merit and there was no error made by the judge in coming to his decision (*Palata Investments* v. *Burt* [1985] C.L.Y. 2590 explained). Appeal from Swinton-Thomas J. December 20, 1985. (C.A.T. No. 877.) SHORT *v.* SHORT.

49. Practice—contempt of court—block sentence for a number of contempts—wrong finding of one contempt

The judge found D guilty of a number of contempts and imposed a general sentence for all the contempts. One of the contempts was said to be that by an order of the court D had been restrained, *inter alia,* from causing or inciting dogs to stray on any part of a certain golf course. *Held,* that (1) permitting a dog to stray did not amount to a breach of the order and was not contempt. Accordingly the judge's order was on the face of it invalid; (2) assuming that the judge made a finding of fact which would have justified a correction of the order under the Slip Rule, and that the matter could have been corrected before the order was drawn, one could not now, in a case affecting the liberty of the subject, amend the order at this stage, after the contemnor had been committed to prison in pursuance of it; it was not permissible now to correct it in order to eradicate an invalidity upon the face of it; (3) the defect could not be severed from the rest of the contempts which were not disputed. It may be that the judge's decision would have been the same even without this particular item but on a matter affecting the liberty of the subject one could not properly assume that to be the case. There was no discretion in the matter and the whole of the order of the judge must be set aside (*Hastings, Re* [1985] C.L.Y. 795 considered and *Cinderby* v. *Cinderby*, unreported, April 26, 1978 C.A.T. No. 272 followed). Appeal from Walton J. December 3, 1985. (C.A.T. No. 804.) Cullen v. Rose.

50. Practice—contempt of court—leave to apply to commit for alleged contempt—late application

In May 1985 the applicant applied under R.S.C., Ord. 59, r.14(3) for leave to apply to commit a detective chief inspector of the City of London Police for alleged contempts which took place in the early part of 1984. *Held, inter alia,* that the application was far too late and would be refused, January 20, 1986. (C.A.T. No. 24.) Kemper's Application, *Re.*

51. Practice—costs—security for costs—appropriate order on appeal

The court decided to make an order that the appellant provide £80,000 security for costs within three weeks and stated that in the trial division it was usual for such an order to be on terms that the action be stayed if the money was not provided within that period. In the context of an appellate court, that was not the appropriate order as otherwise the court should merely have an endless series of appeals sitting stayed waiting until such time as the appellants saw fit to provide the money. The appropriate order in an appellate context when the respondent had had his case investigated and had succeeded in front of the trial judge was that unless the security was provided within the stated period, the appeal stood dismissed. Appeal from Hirst J. January 17, 1986. (C.A.T. No. 23.) Black King Shipping Corp. v. Massie.

52. Practice—costs—security for costs—jurisdiction to order

Instead of finding that there was reason to believe that P company would be unable to pay D's costs of successfully defending the case, the judge made a specific finding that there was a risk that P company would be unable to pay D's costs if successful in their defence and ordered P to give security for D's costs under s.726 of the Companies Act 1985. *Held,* allowing P's appeal, that a mere risk that P would be unable to pay the costs was not enough to render s.726 applicable. Accordingly, the judge had no jurisdiction to proceed with the matter of discretion of whether security should be given. February 6, 1986. (C.A.T. No. 119). TDI v. Stride Micro (A Nevada Corporation).

53. Practice—Court of Appeal—appeal—leave to appeal—appeal against refusal of leave to appeal out of time

P applied for leave to appeal to the Court of Appeal from a decision of the judge refusing leave to appeal out of time from a decision of the master. *Held,* that the judge's decision on the point was final. The judge had a discretionary power to extend the time for leave to appeal to him. The discretion was his and he exercised it adversely to the applicant. He made no order on the appeal. There was no order from which the Court of Appeal could hear an application for leave to appeal (*Lane* v. *Esdaile* [1891] A.C. 210 and *In the Matter of the Housing of the Working Classes Act 1890 ex p. Stevenson* [1892] 1 Q.B. 609 followed). Appeal from Tudor Price J. July 17, 1985. (C.A.T. No. 388.) Nicholson v. National Westminster Bank.

54. Practice—Court of Appeal—appeal—leave to appeal—Order 14 proceedings

In R.S.C., Ord. 14 proceedings the judge refused leave to defend and gave P judgment for the sum claimed by them. D appealed. P contended that the appeal required the leave of the Court under s.18(1)(*h*) of the Supreme Court Act 1981 arguing that s.18(2)(*a*) of the Act only applied in cases where the court below had given conditional leave to defend and that it did not apply where P had given judgment. *Held,* allowing D's appeal and granting unconditional leave to defend,

149

that s.18(2)(*a*) was not limited to cases where conditional leave had been given in Ord. 14 proceedings; it covered all orders under Ord. 14 where unconditional leave had been refused and an order giving judgment for the plaintiff for the whole sum was necessarily an order refusing unconditional leave to defend. No leave to appeal was necessary in that case. Appeal from Official Referee. June 5, 1985. (C.A.T. No. 258.) WILTSHIRE LONDON *v.* MAYOR AND BURGESSES OF LAMBETH LONDON BOROUGH.

55. Practice—Court of Appeal—appeal—setting down—extension of time

D served a notice of appeal on P but owing to his solicitor's mistake the appeal was not set down and after five months' delay which had been fully and frankly explained D applied for an extension of time to set down the appeal. *Held,* dismissing D's appeal from the refusal of the registrar to grant an extension of time, that although there was a discretion in suitable cases to extend the time limits, it would not be appropriate in a case where delay of this length had taken place. Appeal from Mr. Registrar Adams. June 20, 1985. (C.A.T. No. 295.) ROSALIE COMPANY S.A. *v.* KHALID.

56. Practice—Court of Appeal—order on appeal—ordering retrial

By virtue of R.S.C., Ord. 59, r.11(1)(2), whilst the court had a discretion to order a retrial "if it thinks fit," it was only obliged to order a retrial if it was satisfied there had been a wrong or miscarriage of justice. The word "wrong" in R.S.C., Ord. 59, r.11(2) could extend to a situation in which a party had not been afforded the right of full audience before the court even though there had not been a miscarriage of justice, *e.g.* where evidence on which, *inter alia,* the judge below had based his conclusion had been only partly deployed because of an attitude by the judge at an early stage of the hearing which was in direct conflict with his attitude at the end. June 25, 1985. (C.A.T. No. 298.) ALJOE *v.* NYARKO.

57. Practice—immigration—renewed application for judicial review—abuse of process—administrative arrangements for listing application

In dismissing a renewed application for judicial review by the applicant who had sought leave to visit the U.K. for three months but had been refused entry by the immigration officer on March 12, 1985 but admitted under the temporary admission procedure, Sir John Donaldson M.R. considered the application an abuse of the process of the court and stated, *inter alia,* as follows: I have been very troubled about the case because the notice of intention to renew the application for judicial review was given in October 1985. It is now January 1986. I have therefore made administrative arrangements with the Civil Appeals Office that in cases of this class, if there is a renewed application, they should be considered at once to see whether it is merely an attempt to buy time or whether there are reasonable grounds for thinking that the application might succeed. If there are no such grounds, administrative measures will be taken to list it at the earliest possible opportunity. I desire to make this clear in order that those who think they can simply buy time by an abuse of the process of the court will realise that in future they will be unsuccessful. Appeal from McNeill J. (C.A.T. No. 62.) January 27, 1986. R. *v.* SECRETARY OF STATE FOR THE HOME DEPARTMENT *ex p.* KARIM.

58. Practice—injunction—interlocutory injunction—interests of innocent third parties

P were granted an *ex parte* injunction restraining D1 and D2 former employees (investment consultants) of P, from acting in breach of a "non-solicitation" clause in their terms of employment with P. At the hearing *inter partes* the judge discharged that head of the injunction on the ground that to maintain it could have a very serious effect on the customers, innocent parties, who had already been solicited. P appealed contending that if the rights of third parties were likely to be seriously affected then their proper course was to apply to intervene in the proceedings under the provisions of R.S.C., Ord. 15, r.6 and under that rule a third party may only intervene in certain limited circumstances which did not obtain here. *Held*, dismissing the appeal, that applications for and the granting of interlocutory injunctions had to be kept as flexible as possible. It would be quite wrong to say that it was improper for the judge to take third party rights into consideration merely because they had not applied to join the proceedings under R.S.C., Ord. 15, r.6. Appeal from McCullough J. December 5, 1985. (C.A.T. No. 814.) MERRIL LYNCH PIERCE FENNER & SMITH INC. *v.* BESMANP.

59. Practice—interim payment—affidavit—time limit for service of affidavits

P claimed damages for personal injuries suffered at his place of employment with D. He applied for interim payment under R.S.C., Ord. 29, r.10 and served an affidavit in support of his application. The master dismissed the application and P appealed. The appeal was set down for hearing on March 19. While the appeal was pending two affidavits were sworn on behalf of D and served on P on March 1 and 7 respectively. P decided to put in a further affidavit in reply to D's affidavits. He had this affidavit sworn and served on D on March 15. The judge admitted P's further evidence. D contended, *inter alia,* that the judge should not have admitted the further affidavit of P without allowing D an adjournment. *Held,* that it was clear that the wording in Ord. 29, r.10(4) referring to the affidavit in support and documents exhibited thereto being served not less than 10 clear days before the return date, referred to the essential affidavit in support of an application and not to subsequent affidavits, be they affidavits in reply or affidavits supplementing the original affidavit. There was therefore no mandatory time limit of 10 clear days binding the judge to grant an adjournment. It was a matter for his discretion to decide whether there should have been an adjournment granted to enable D to deal with P's second affidavit. Appeal from Sir Neil Lawson. June 11, 1985. (C.A.T. No. 272.) BARSTOW *v.* ROBERTS (A.) & CO. (BUILDING).

60. Practice—judgment—stay of execution—stay pending hearing of "counterclaim"

P obtained judgment against D in default of defence for £19,644 being the arrears said to be owed by D under a licence agreement. D's application to set aside the judgment was refused. D then applied to file an amended defence, set off and counterclaim and for execution of the judgment to be stayed pending the trial of the counterclaim but that application was also refused although a stay of execution of the judgment was granted pending an appeal. D later commenced a separate action against P claiming damages for breaches of collateral warranties in relation to the agreement and applied for a stay of execution of the judgment against him pending the determination of his action. *Held,* allowing D's appeal and granting the stay, that D's claim went to the very matters out of which P's judgment arose. If the matter had been properly dealt with at the outset, there would have been no question of P being able to obtain a summary judgment. It was a situation where there would have been leave to defend if there had been an application under R.S.C., Ord. 14. The matter was one which undoubtedly would have had to go to trial. D had certain personal difficulties both in regard to his health and in regard to obtaining proper assistance from his previous legal advisors. Looking at the situation as a whole, this was a case where justice would be only served if D was granted a stay of execution so as to be able to proceed with the proceedings which he had now launched. The power to grant a stay was contained in R.S.C., Ord. 47, r.1 and that power was irrespective of the judgment being set aside. Furthermore the application for a stay could be made under the rule either at the time of the judgment or subsequent thereto, although of course in practice, if there was delay that could well affect the outcome (*C.S.I. International Co.* v. *Archway Personnel (Middle East)* [1980] C.L.Y. 2125 considered). Appeal from McCowan, J. January 27, 1986. (C.A.T. No. 65.) ESSO PETROLEUM *v.* NORTHCOTT.

UNREPORTED CASES

61. Practice—Mareva injunction—ex parte application—duty of disclosure

An oversight or error of judgment was no answer to the failure to disclose the full facts of the case as they were known and documents which were available to the applicant for a Mareva injunction. There was a heavy duty of disclosure upon any applicant for a Mareva injunction. The test was whether the facts to be disclosed were in fact relevant and not whether the party, who should have disclosed them, thought they were relevant or even was aware of their significance (*The King* v. *The General Commissioners for the Purposes of the Income Tax Acts for the District of Kensington* [1917] 1 K.B. 486 and *Dalglish* v. *Jarvie* 2 Mac. & G. 231 applied). Appeal from Skinner J. June 12, 1985. (C.A.T. No. 276.) MARTIGNY INVESTMENTS S.A. v. ELMBRANCH.

62. Practice—matrimonial proceedings—Anton Pillar and Mareva Orders—jurisdiction

The court could in appropriate circumstances in matrimonial proceedings grant both an Anton Pillar Order and a Mareva Injunction. So far as the Anton Pillar Order was concerned, the court should not grant such an order save on strong evidence. February 26, 1986. (C.A.T. No. 197). FRANCIS v. FRANCIS.

63. Practice—originating notice of motion—form—lack of Royal Arms replica—irregularity

P issued out of the District Registry a notice of motion, which they apparently intended to be an originating notice of motion, seeking an injunction against D their former partner. The notice of motion was given a case number, stamped by the Registry, and the fee appropriate to an originating process was paid by P. However it did not bear at the top, as required by R.S.C., Ord. 8 either stamped or embossed, a replica of the Royal Arms. *Held,* that that defect did not invalidate the whole proceedings because under R.S.C., Ord. 2 that defect was an irregularity only and could and should have been cured upon terms, and in particular such terms as to costs as the court might direct. It was an irregularity which in fact caused no embarrassment to D and which was not misleading in any way. The proceeding was obviously intended to be originating and the relief which it was seeking was set out perfectly clearly so that D was not misled. Appeal from his Honour Judge Fitzhugh Q.C. February 24, 1986. (C.A.T. No. 191) PAGET v. BRITTON.

64. Practice—payment into court—dismissal of action for want of prosecution—payment out to plaintiff upon dismissal

D admitted liability for a road traffic accident in July 1978 which resulted in injuries to P and in August 1982 paid into court a sum of £4,000 in settlement of P's claim for damages which amounted to nearly £11,000 at the time of issue of the writ in July 1981. In February 1985 the judge, on appeal from the registrar, upheld the order of the registrar dismissing P's action for want of prosecution but allowed P to accept the £4,000 which was still in court. *Held,* allowing D's appeal, that under the rules, the judge had power to grant P's application to take out the money out of time; the judge was entitled to do so at any time during the subsistence of the action. The order to strike out the action, although he had concluded that it should be struck out, had not yet been formally made, let alone drawn up. The possibility of making an order of this kind appeared in the Annual Practices in note 25.1.8 (p.423) dealing with applications to strike out for want of prosecution. No authority was cited for the last sentence there but it would be right to follow the course of giving the plaintiff a last chance to accept the money in court in cases in which the justice to both parties really required that to be done. It would not be desirable to suggest what such cases might be. However, given the existence of the power, it had to be exercised with great caution. Once the court had concluded that the action ought to be struck out for want of prosecution, then prima facie that is what the court should do, with the consequence that any money in court went back to the defendants.

Another matter to be taken into account was that it would be unfortunate if the fact that money had been paid into court in an action were somehow to influence the diligence and speed with which it was pursued. It would be unfortunate if those acting for the plaintiff took the view that the fact that there was money in court might provide a salvation against inordinate, inexcusable and prejudicial delay, because there would or might always be a chance to ask for the money to be paid out at a late stage. To that extent the presence of money in court, and if it were to become a practice to do what the judge did in the present case, would involve the danger of creating a charter for delay on the part of plaintiffs. Appeal from Mars-Jones J. July 2, 1985. (C.A.T. No. 345.) STANTON *v.* SMITH.

65. Practice—striking out claim—failure to comply with final order—approach to exercise of jurisdiction

The judge made an order under R.S.C., Ord. 24, r.16 striking out P's counterclaim against D on the ground, *inter alia,* that they had failed to serve a list of documents within 21 days as required by an Order of the court which was stated to be final, the judge taking the view that D had had enough time, although D stated that the papers were before counsel and the list would be provided within a few days. *Held,* on the question of how the jurisdiction to strike out should be exercised, allowing P's appeal and granting a further extension of time to provide the list, that the approach which was approved by the House of Lords in *Birkett* v. *James* [1977] C.L.Y. 2410 which was a case involving striking out through want of execution, was of general application and would apply where the court was concerned to discover whether or not it would be right in the exercise of the court's discretion to strike out an action for failure to comply either with some rule of court laying down a time limit or with some order of the court specifying a time limit within which some particular action was to be taken. As a general rule in all cases of this kind the court should exercise the power to strike out in accordance with the guidelines approved by the House of Lords in *Birkett* v. *James.* Thus, the court should seek to see first whether the party in default had failed to comply with a peremptory order or otherwise had acted in a contumelious manner or had been guilty of some abuse of the process of the court, and secondly, whether the party involved had been guilty of inordinate or inexcusable delay and whether that delay had caused some prejudice to the other party. In the second class of case it was always relevant to discover whether the limitation period had expired which might prevent the party involved from initiating fresh proceedings. The words "contumelious" and "abuse of the process of the court" had no precise meaning and they involved the following question which the court had to ask itself: Was there to be found in the conduct of the party concerned some clear and unmistakable defiance of an order of the court? In other words, had the party gone ahead and continued with a certain course of conduct or failed to comply with an order despite a warning and despite the fact that he knew the consequences? It was in that sense that the word "peremptory" order was used, where the court gave a clear warning to a party that if he failed to take some action within a stipulated time, then certain precise consequences were going to follow. There was no such order in the present case and it was not a case of contumelious behaviour. There was no clear evidence of any prejudice to D. Further, where a court on application to exercise this power was told by a responsible person that within a few days the order was going to be complied with, that was a factor to which great weight must in the ordinary way be attached. There will always be cases where in the circumstances, though assurances of that kind were given, the court was entitled to give little weight to them, but in the ordinary way such assurances should be weighed in the balance very carefully (*Greek City Co.* v. *Demetriou* [1983] C.L.Y. 3068 and *Husband's of Marchwood* v. *Drummond Walker Developments* [1975] C.L.Y. 2609 considered and applied). Appeal from the Official Referee. March 6, 1986 (C.A.T. No. 291). REALISTICS *v.* LP MARSH (PROPERTIES).

153

66. Practice—summary judgment—conditional leave to defend—whether condition can attach to counterclaim

P claimed a sum of money for the price of goods sold and delivered. D served a defence and counterclaim that the money was not due for a number of reasons. On P's application for summary judgment the Master gave unconditional leave to defend. On appeal, the judge thought that it would be wholly wrong to give judgment for P but that there were indications that part of D's evidence was tenuous if not shadowy. He accordingly ordered that D have leave to defend on condition that D pay into Court a sum of £15,000 within 28 days and if the said sum was not so paid the counterclaim stand dismissed. *Held,* that that order was not competent for the judge to make because in effect he was giving unconditional leave to defend by way of set off but ordering that D, in order to pursue their counterclaim, should bring money into court. There was no power to make such an order under R.S.C., Ord. 14, r.3. Accordingly the appeal would be allowed, the judge's order set aside and the Master's order restored. January 29, 1986. (C.A.T. No. 88) SUPERCORAL v. MICHAEL TAUBE.

67. Practice—writ—renewal—extension of validity—discharging order extending validity

On June 29, 1982, P issued an endorsed writ against D and on June 7, 1983 on an *ex parte* application by P, the register renewed the validity of the writ for six months (until December 29, 1983). On December 20, 1983 the writ was served on D. On January 3, 1984, D lodged an acknowledgement of service and agreed to extend time for service of the statement of claim until January 31, which was served on January 10. On January 18, 1984, P agreed to extend the time for service of the defence until February 29, 1984. On February 7, 1984 D wrote to the registrar asking for a copy of the affidavit filed by P in support the *ex parte* application to renew the validity and a copy was supplied on February 10. It was then agreed between the parties that the action would be transferred to the Official Referee and P granted a general extension of time for service of a defence on the basis that D undertook to issue a time summons within seven days of the transfer. The action was transferred to the Official Referee on March 6, 1984, and P applied (as agreed) for directions by the Official Referee and D for further time for serving a defence. The applications were heard on April 25, 1984, when D indicated to P for the first time that they wished for time to consider whether an application to strike out the writ should be made. D were granted time to apply to discharge the registrar's order extending the validity of the writ and D made an application to that effect on May 30. *Held,* that D in February 1984 and thereafter, so conducted themselves as to lead P to believe that they intended to utilise the extension of time for the preparation of a defence and for no other purpose; they thus elected to follow that course and may not follow any other. On February 7, 1984 D's solicitors may not have known that an application to set aside the order extending validity of the writ would succeed, but they must have appreciated that they were entitled to make such an application, and that they might decide to do so. This was sufficient to constitute an election in the circumstance of this case. D, having made the representation and P having acted upon it to their potential detriment, were not entitled to apply to discharge the order renewing the validity of the writ within the time extended for service of the defence. The rule of law which prevented D from making such an application was not "estoppel" but more accurately categorised as "quasi-estoppel" or "election." D's appeal would accordingly be dismissed (*Kammins Ballrooms Co.* v. *Zenith Investments (Torquay)* [1970] C.L.Y. 1525 applied). January 23, 1986. (C.A.T. No. 51.) DEVON AND CORNWALL HOUSING ASSOCIATION v. DONALD BUTLER ASSOCIATES (A FIRM).

68. Practice—writ—renewal—good and sufficient cause—removal of legal aid limitation

P was granted a legal aid certificate limited to carrying out certain expert investigation and to the issuing but not the service of the writ. D knew of the legal aid granted to P. P issued a writ but in August 1980 had been unable to satisfy the legal aid authority that they should lift the limitation restricting service of it on D. The writ was renewed *ex parte* (under R.S.C., Ord. 6, r.8) on four separate occasions, namely in July 1981, May 1982, July 1983 and June 1984 pending the lifting of the legal aid limitation. *Held,* allowing D's appeal, that the question of legal aid was to be ignored in considering whether to renew the writ and it mattered not whether or not D knew that P was legally aided (*Baker* v. *Bowketts Cakes* [1966] C.L.Y. 9987 and *Stevens* v. *Services Window and General Cleaning Co.* [1967] C.L.Y. 3258 applied). Appeal from Sir Neil Lawson. June 18, 1985. (C.A.T. No. 317.) MADRON v. ARUN DISTRICT COUNCIL.

69. Rating and Valuation—recovery or rates—distress warrant—no power in justices to delay execution

In issuing a distress warrant for the recovery of rates, justices had no power to order that there shall be any delay in the execution of the warrant. The justices' function in issuing a distress warrant was ministerial and not judicial. *The Queen on the Prosecution of Astin* v. *Handsley* (1881) 7 Q.B.D. 398 followed. Further the words "to show cause why" in s.97(1) of the General Rate Act 1967 meant to show cause why, *as a matter of law,* the rates had not been paid and did not apply to a situation in which a person was saying that he was not financially in a position to pay the rates. July 31, 1985. (C.A.T. No. 505.) DICHINSON v. STOCKPORT COUNTY COUNCIL.

70. Real Property and Conveyancing—rescission of contract—vendor unable to satisfy requisition—notice to purchaser withdraw requisition

V and his two sisters were the beneficiaries of the estate of their mother who died intestate in September 1973. In February 1976 V obtained a grant of letters of administration to her estate. By a deed of assignment dated March 3, 1976, and made between the three children, the two sisters assigned their beneficial interests in a freehold property included in their mother's estate to V in consideration of the payment by him of the sum of £1,000 to each of them. By an assent made on the same day V assented to the vesting in himself of the freehold property. In April 1976 V sold the property at auction to P at a price of £17,500. The sale was expressed to be subject to the Law Society's General Conditions of Sale (1980 Edition). Shortly afterwards V's solicitors delivered an epitome of title to P's solicitors which unnecessarily disclosed the assignment dated March 3, 1976. The disclosure resulted in P's solicitors raising a requisition that they must be satisfied that there was no possibility of the transaction being set aside in view of V's fiduciary relationship. V was unable to satisfy the requisition and eventually gave notice to P under General Condition 16(1) requiring him to withdraw the requisition. P refused to withdraw the requisition and V gave notice to rescind the agreement under General Condition 16. P thereupon brought an action seeking, *inter alia,* a declaration that V's notice of rescission was ineffective. The question arose as to whether V's conduct in unnecessarily disclosing in the epitome of title the assignment of March 3, 1976 amounted to "recklessness" thereby disentitling him from relying on General Condition 16. *Held,* that the act of disclosing what appeared to be a perfectly proper deed which in normal circumstances would strenghthen the title could not in itself be said to be reckless (*Selkirk* v. *Romar Investments* [1964] C.L.Y. 3750 applied). November 21, 1985. (C.A.T. No. 789.) OWEN v. WILLIAMS.

71. Solicitors—resolution by Law Society to intervene in solicitor's practice—application to withdraw notice of resolution

Pursuant to para. 6 of Sched. 1 to the Solicitors Act 1974 the Law Society informed solicitor B that they had resolved that they suspected him of dishonesty and vested in themselves money connected with his practice. In October 1982 B's practising certificate expired and applications for its renewal were refused. In November 1982 B applied to the court under para. 6(4) for an order that the society withdraw its notice and for certain consequential relief. There then followed a series of interlocutory applications in those proceedings. In July 1984 B was adjudicated bankrupt and prior to the adjudication there had been unspecified money judgments against him. The judge took the view that this was not a case for a substantive hearing or for dealing with the question whether there was any foundation for the society's suspicions of dishonesty on B's part. In view of the various events and in the light of the bankruptcy, which by virtue of para. 1(1)(d) entitled the society to exercise the same powers, the judge could not make an effective order that the society should withdraw the notice and consequently revert monies in B and he accordingly dismissed B's application. B appealed contending that he had a right to have the question of honesty or dishonesty adjudicated upon. *Held,* dismissing the appeal, that he had no such right; what the statute gave him was a right to apply to the court to have the notice withdrawn. Whether or not the society had proper grounds for suspicion in the first place, the decision had to be made at the time of the hearing. At the time of the hearing before the judge (as indeed now) there was no effective way in which the notice could be withdrawn because apart from the supervening events, there was no practice left to be re-established and there was virtually no money left in the client account. But in any event B was not in a position, because of supervening events, to resume his practice, and therefore no court could order the withdrawal of the notice with the consequence that monies should be re-vested in B (*Buckley* v. *The Law Society* (No. 2) [1984] C.L.Y. 2621 approved). Appeal from Peter Gibson J. October 9, 1985. (C.A.T. No. 561.) BUCKLEY v. LAW SOCIETY.

72. Tort—false imprisonment—damages—exemplary damages

P who was wrongfully arrested by a police officer and kept in a holding cell at a police station for about 20 minutes brought an action for damages for imprisonment. The only method of arrest was that the police officer held P's arm in a perfectly proper manner and no complaint was made about the officer's conduct other than that the arrest was not lawful. The judge ruled that in the circumstances of the case it was not open to the jury to consider exemplary damages and so that matter was not left to the jury. With regard to compensatory damages the judge directed the jury that the case involving the policeman in making a mistake did not call for "ample compensation." The jury awarded P £5 damages. P appealed. *Held,* allowing the appeal and ordering a retrial, that (1) exemplary damages having already been excluded, it was difficult to see what could be meant and what could be understood by the jury from the phrase "ample compensation" other than that it meant full or ample compensation or "quite enough." Whatever it may truly have been intended to mean there was a danger of indicating to the jury that in some way they should reduce the compensation which they otherwise would have awarded, because the arrest arose out of a mistake on the part of the police. That was a confusing and misleading direction. It would not be safe to allow the verdict to stand because it may well be that in coming to the admittedly low figure of £5 the jury may well have been influenced by the direction of the judge that they did not have to give full compensation because the policeman made a mistake; (2) the question whether or not to award exemplary damages should have been left to the jury with appropriate directions as to what special features of the case they might in their discretion take into account in deciding whether or not to award such damages, and if so, how much. The judge applied the wrong test when he said in the examples that he gave that either there must be evidence of oppressive behaviour, malicious arrest, cruelty in the mode of arrest, insolence or prolonged imprisonment for there to be exemplary damages (*Rookes* v. *Barnard* [1964] C.L.Y. 3703 considered). November 28, 1985. (C.A.T. No. 790.) HOLDEN v. CHIEF CONSTABLE OF LANCASHIRE.

73. Trade Unions—professional association—constitution and activities—whether a trade union

The constitution of P Association stated, *inter alia*, that it "shall be concerned with the professional interests of its members". *Held,* that when dealing with persons who were of professional standing the words "professional interests of the members" were not to be taken as confining attention simply to the status of the profession to which the members belonged but dealt in a wider context with the interests of the individual members in their profession. In the context of the constitution the phrase "professional interests" was apt to cover the interests of individual members in their profession including their interests *vis-à-vis* their employers. Further the activities that the association engaged in were such that it could be said that one of its principal purposes included the regulation of relations between its members and their employers associations. Accordingly P Association fell within the definition of a trade union within s.28 of the Trade Union and Labour Relations Act 1974 and was capable of suing or being sued in its own name. Appeal from Sir Neil Lawson Q.C. March 3, 1986. (C.A.T. No. 217). BRITISH ASSOCIATION OF ADVISERS & LECTURERS IN PHYSICAL EDUCATION *v.* NATIONAL UNION OF TEACHERS.

DATES OF COMMENCEMENT

Statutes

(in alphabetical order)

This section contains all statutory dates of commencement during 1986. Where an Act or part of an Act is brought into force by a Statutory Instrument the Instrument's number and *Current Law* paragraph reference is given. Otherwise the commencement provisions are contained in the Act itself and the *Current Law* reference refers to the brief digest of the Act. References to paragraph numbers exceeding 3553 are to the Scottish edition of the Current Law Year Book 1986.

For a complete guide to the commencement, amendment, judicial consideration, repeal, etc. of Statutes since 1947 see the *Current Law Statute Citators*.

ADMINISTRATION OF JUSTICE ACT 1985
    Ss.2, 4, 5, 7, 8, 12, 46, 67(2), Scheds. 1, 3, 8, Pt. III (in part): March 12, 1986 (S.I. 1986 No. 364: [1986] C.L.Y. 2560a.)
    Ss.13, 22, 23, 38, 47, 51, 55, 67(1) (in part), 67(2) in part: October 1, 1986 (S.I. 1986 No. 1503: [1986] C.L.Y. 2560a.)
    S.50: April 28, 1986 (S.I. 1986 No. 364: [1986] C.L.Y. 2560a.)
AGRICULTURAL HOLDINGS ACT 1984
    Ss.8, 10(2), Sched. 4 (in part): January 1, 1986 (S.I. 1985 No. 1644: [1986] C.L.Y. 44.)
AGRICULTURAL HOLDINGS ACT 1986
    All provisions: June 18, 1986 ([1986] C.L.Y. 45.)
AGRICULTURE ACT 1970
    S.113(3), Sched. 5, Pt. II (repeals): May 1, 1986 (S.I. 1986 No. 707: [1986] C.L.Y. 59).
    Sched. 5, Pt. II: May 1, 1986 (S.I. 1986 No. 707: [1986] C.L.Y. 59.)
AGRICULTURE ACT 1986
    Ss.1–7, 9, 11, 17, 18(pt.) 19–23: September 25, 1986 ([1986] C.L.Y. 47.)
    S.8(2): September 8, 1986 (S.I. 1986 No. 1596: [1986] C.L.Y. 48/9)
    S.10: December 31, 1986 (S.I. 1986 No. 2301: [1986] C.L.Y. 48/9.)
    Ss.12, 18(3): July 25, 1986 ([1986] C.L.Y. 47.)
    Ss.13, 15: September 25, 1986 (S.I. 1986 No. 1484: [1986] C.L.Y. 48/9.)
    Ss.14 and 16 (Scotland): September 25, 1986 (S.I. 1986 No. 1485 [1986] C.L.Y. 3575.)
AIRPORTS ACT 1986
    Ss.1, 3, 75, 76(1) to (4), 77(5)(6), 79 to 82, 85: July 8, 1986 ([1986] C.L.Y. 142.)
    Ss.12 to 28, 29 to 35, 68, 70 to 72, 78, 84 (*Ibid.*)
    Ss.57 to 62 (incl. Sched. 2), s.83(1), (Pt.), Sched. 4, paras. 1 and 2: July 31, 1986 (S.I. 1986 No. 1228: [1986] C.L.Y. 143.)
    Ss.63 to 66, 83(1)(pt.), 83(5)(pt.), Sched. 3, Sched. 4, para. 10, Sched. 6, pt. II: August 1, 1986: (S.I. 1986 No. 1228: [1986] C.L.Y. 143.)
    Pt. IV (including Sched. 1), ss.67, 69, 73, 74, 83(1)(3)(5), Sched. 4, paras. 3–8, 6, Pt. II: October 1, 1986 (S.I. 1986 No. 1487: [1986] C.L.Y. 143.)
APPROPRIATION ACT 1986
    All provisions: July 25, 1986 ([1986] C.L.Y. 2845.)
ARMED FORCES ACT 1986
    Ss.1, 15, 17: June 26, 1986 ([1986] C.L.Y. 121.)
    Ss.14, 16(2) (in part): December 30, 1986 (S.I. 1986 No. 2071: [1986] C.L.Y. 122.)
    Repeal of s.1 of Armed Forces Act 1985: September 1, 1986 ([1986] C.L.Y. 121.)

159

DATES OF COMMENCEMENT

ATOMIC ENERGY AUTHORITY ACT 1986
All provisions: April 1, 1986: ([1986] C.L.Y. 133.)

AUSTRALIA ACT 1986
All provisions: March 3, 1986 (S.I. 1986 No. 319: [1986] C.L.Y. 188.)

BANKRUPTCY (SCOTLAND) ACT 1985
Ss.1(1)(b), (2) and (6), 2(2)–(4), 72, 73 (except for the definition of "preferred debt") and 76: February 1, 1986 (S.I. 1985 No. 1924 (C.47): [1986] C.L.Y. 3694.)
All provisions not yet in force save for s.51(2), the definition of "preferred debt" in s.73(1), Sched. 3, Sched. 7, paras. 13 and 14(3), and certain repeals in Sched. 8: April 1, 1986 (S.I. 1985 No. 1924 (C.47) as amended by S.I. 1986 No. 78 (C.2): [1986] C.L.Y. 3593.)
All remaining provisions. December 29, 1986. (S.I. 1986 No. 1913: [1986] C.L.Y. 3593.)

BETTING, GAMING AND LOTTERIES (AMENDMENT) ACT 1984
S.2: March 10, 1986 (S.I. 1986 No. 102: [1986] C.L.Y. 1578.)

BRITISH COUNCIL AND COMMONWEALTH INSTITUTE SUPERANNUATION ACT 1986
All provisions (British Council only): November 10, 1986 (S.I. 1986 No. 1860: [1986] C.L.Y. 2511.)

BRITISH SHIPBUILDERS (BORROWING POWERS) ACT 1986
All provisions: June 26, 1986 ([1986] C.L.Y. 3391.)

BUILDING SOCIETIES ACT 1986
Ss.1–4 and Sched. 1: September 25, 1986 ([1986] C.L.Y. 236.)
Ss.7 (in part), 18 (in part), 38–40 (in part), 109 (in part), 112(1)(3)(4), 113 (in part), 115, 116, 118, 119, 120(4) (in part), 122, 123, Sched. 20, paras. 1, 2, 8–11, 17: September 25, 1986 (S.I. 1986 No. 1560: [1986] C.L.Y. 237.)
Ss.120(4)(pt.), 121, 125, Sched. 20, para. 7: July 25, 1986 ([1986] C.L.Y. 236.)

CABLE AND BROADCASTING ACT 1984
Ss.37–41, 57(1) (in part), Sched. 5 (in part): April 1, 1986 (S.I. 1986 No. 537: [1986] C.L.Y. 3215.)

CHARITIES ACT 1985
All provisions: January 1, 1986 (S.I. 1985 No. 1583: [1985] C.L.Y. 265.)

CHILD ABDUCTION AND CUSTODY ACT 1985
All provisions: August 1, 1986 (S.I. 1986 No. 1048: [1986] C.L.Y. 2177.)

CHILDREN ACT 1975
Ss.47, 48(1)(2), 49–55: April 1, 1986 (Scotland only). (S.I. 1985 No. 1557: [1985] C.L.Y. 3725.)

CIVIL AVIATION (EUROCONTROL) ACT 1983
Ss.1, 2, 3(1): January 1, 1986 (S.I. 1985 No. 1915: [1986] C.L.Y. 142.)

CIVIL JURISDICTION AND JUDGMENTS ACT 1982
S.35(1): November 14, 1986 (S.I. 1986 No. 1781 [1986] C.L.Y. 2585.)

CIVIL PROTECTION IN PEACETIME ACT 1986
All provisions: August 26, 1986 ([1986] C.L.Y. 279.)

COMMONWEALTH DEVELOPMENT CORPORATION ACT 1986
All provisions: June 26, 1986 ([1986] C.L.Y. 190.)

COMPANY DIRECTORS DISQUALIFICATION ACT 1986
All provisions: December 29, 1986 ([1986] C.L.Y. 290 and S.I. 1986 No. 1924: [1986] C.L.Y. 303.)

CONSOLIDATED FUND ACT 1986
All provisions: March 18, 1986 ([1986] C.L.Y. 2848.)

CONSUMER SAFETY ACT 1978
S.10(1), Sched. 3: August 8, 1986 (S.I. 1986 No. 1297: [1986] C.L.Y. 3004.)

CONSUMER SAFETY (AMENDMENT) ACT 1986
All provisions: August 8, 1986 ([1986] C.L.Y. 3003.)

CORNEAL TISSUE ACT 1986
All provisions: August 26, 1986 ([1986] C.L.Y. 2110.)

DATES OF COMMENCEMENT

CROWN AGENTS (AMENDMENT) ACT 1986
All provisions: July 25, 1986 ([1986] C.L.Y. 31.)

DOCKYARD SERVICES ACT 1986
All provisions: September 25, 1986 ([1986] C.L.Y. 1184.)

DRUG TRAFFICKING OFFENCES ACT 1986
Ss.1(3), 2(1), 24, 34, 38, 40: September 30, 1986 (S.I. 1986 No. 1488: [1986] C.L.Y. 547.)
Ss.24(3)(a), 34 and (so far as extending to Scotland) 38 and 40: September 30, 1986 (S.I. 1986 No. 1546 [1986] C.L.Y. 3752.)
S.35: July 8, 1986 ([1986] C.L.Y. 546.)
Ss.27–29, 31, 33: December 30, 1986 (S.I. 1986 No. 2145: [1986] C.L.Y. 547.)

EDUCATION ACT 1986
Ss.2 to 6: July 18, 1986 ([1986] C.L.Y. 1129.)
S.1: September 18, 1986 ([1986] C.L.Y. 1129.)

EDUCATION (AMENDMENT) ACT 1986
All provisions: February 17, 1986 ([1986] C.L.Y. 1130.)

ENDURING POWERS OF ATTORNEY ACT 1985
All provisions: March 10, 1986 (S.I. 1986 No. 125: [1986] C.L.Y. 33.)

FAMILY LAW (SCOTLAND) ACT 1985
All provisions (save s.25): September 1, 1986 (S.I. 1986 No. 1237; [1986] C.L.Y. 3977.)

FINANCE ACT 1985
Royal Assent: July 25, 1986. Certain provisions are deemed to come into force prior to the Royal Assent. Dates of commencement are contained in the text of the Act.
S.19, October 1, 1986 (S.I. 1986 No. 968 (C.23): [1986] C.L.Y. 3483.)
S.20, October 1, 1986 (S.I. 1986 No. 970: [1986] C.L.Y. 3483.)
S.27(3), appointed day: July 1, 1986 (S.I. 1986 No. 934: [1986] C.L.Y. 3482.)
S.30, Sched. 8: April 1, 1986 (S.I. 1986 No. 365: [1986] C.L.Y. 3484.)
S.32(1): April 1, 1986 (S.I. 1986 No. 337: [1986] C.L.Y. 3484.)

FINANCIAL SERVICES ACT 1986
Ss.177, 178(1)(2)(a)(6), 179 (in part) 180 (in part), 198(2)(a), 199(1)(a)(3)–(6)(8)(9) (in part), 200(1)(b) (in part), 201(1), 202, 203, 205, 207, 209, 210 Sched. 13, paras. 3, 4, 6, 7, 9–11, 13, 14 (in part): November 15, 1986 (S.I. 1986 No. 1940: [1986] C.L.Y. 2851).
Ss.182, 211(3) (part), 212(1), (3), Sched. 13 (part) and Sched. 17 (part): November 27, 1986 (S.I. 1986 No. 2031: [1986] C.L.Y. 2851)

FOOD AND ENVIRONMENT PROTECTION ACT 1985
All remaining provisions: January 1, 1986 (S.I. 1985 No. 1698: [1985] C.L.Y. 1551.)

FORESTRY ACT 1986
All provisions: September 8, 1986 ([1986] C.L.Y. 1571.)

GAMING (BINGO) ACT 1985
All provisions: June 9, 1986 (S.I. 1986 No. 832 (c.21): [1986] C.L.Y. 1583.)

GAS ACT 1986
Ss.1, 65, 68, Sched. 1: August 18, 1986 (S.I. 1986 No. 1315: [1986] C.L.Y. 1588.)
Ss.2, 63, 64, Sched. 2: August 23, 1986 (S.I. 1986 No. 1315: [1986] C.L.Y. 1588.)
S.62: November 14, 1986 (S.I. 1986 No. 1809: [1986] C.L.Y. 1588.)
Remaining provisions of Pt. I, ss.66; 67(1), (2), (3), (4); Scheds. 7, 8 (Pt. I), 9 (Pt. I): August 23, 1986 (S.I. 1986 No. 1316: [1986] C.L.Y. 1589.)

HEALTH AND SOCIAL SECURITY ACT 1984
Ss.1(3), (5)(a), (6) (7), 24 (in pt.), Pts. I and II of Sched. 1, repeals in Sched. 8 (in pt.): July 1, 1986 (S.I. 1986 No. 974 (C.24): [1986] C.L.Y. 2236)

HEALTH SERVICE JOINT CONSULTATIVE COMMITTEES (ACCESS TO INFORMATION) ACT 1986
All provisions: August 26, 1986 ([1986] C.L.Y. 2237.)

DATES OF COMMENCEMENT

HIGHWAYS (AMENDMENT) ACT 1986
All provisions: July 2, 1986 ([1986] C.L.Y. 1601.)

HORTICULTURAL PRODUCE ACT 1986
All provisions: August 26, 1986 ([1986] C.L.Y. 60.)

HOUSING ACT 1985
All provisions: April 1, 1986 ([1985] C.L.Y. 1641.)

HOUSING ASSOCIATIONS ACT 1985
All provisions: April 1, 1986 ([1985] C.L.Y. 1641.)

HOUSING (CONSEQUENTIAL PROVISIONS) ACT 1985
All provisions: April 1, 1986 ([1985] C.L.Y. 1641.)

INCEST AND RELATED OFFENCES (SCOTLAND) ACT 1986
All provisions: November 1, 1986. (S.I. 1986 No. 1803 [1986] C.L.Y. 3797.)

INDUSTRIAL DEVELOPMENT ACT 1985
S.3: April 1, 1986 ([1985] C.L.Y. 3488.)

INDUSTRIAL TRAINING ACT 1986
All provisions: July 20, 1986 ([1986] C.L.Y. 3395.)

INSOLVENCY ACT 1985
Ss.3(1)(3)–(5), 4(1)(*a*)(*b*) (2)–(6), 5(1)(2)(*a*) (4) (5), 6–9, Sched. 1, paras. 1–3, 4(1)–(3)(5), 5, 6: July 1, 1986 (S.I. 1986 No. 840: [1986] C.L.Y. 303).

Ss.3(2), 4(1)(*c*), 5(2)(*b*) (3), Sched. 1, para. 4(4): June 1, 1986 (S.I. 1986 No. 840 (c.22): [1986] C.L.Y. 303)

Ss.10, 11, 106(pt.)(1), 108(3), 213(2), (7), (8), (9), 226(pt.), 232, 236(1)–(4), Sched. 5(pt.): February 1, 1986 (S.I. 1986 No. 6: [1986] C.L.Y. 303.)

Ss.12–16, 18, 108 (in part), 216, Scheds. 2, 6, paras. 1–7, 15(1)(2), Sched. 9, paras. 2–4, Sched. 10 (in part): April 28, 1986 (S.I. 1986 No. 463: [1986] C.L.Y. 303.)

Ss.45, 108(1), (3), 109(3), 235(2), Sched. 9, paras. 7, 8: March 1, 1986 (S.I. 1986 No. 6: [1986] C.L.Y. 303.)

Ss.106(pt.), 108(1), (3), 109(1), (2)(pt.), 226(pt.), 235(1), (3), Sched. 5(pt.), Sched. 6(pt.), Sched. 8(pt.), Sched. 10(pt.): March 1, 1986 (S.I. 1986 No. 185: [1986] C.L.Y. 303.)

Ss.213(1), (3)–(6), 234, Sched. 8, para. 36, Sched. 10(pt.): April 1, 1986 (S.I. 1986 No. 185: [1986] C.L.Y. 303.)

S.214 (in part), Sched. 8, para. 27 (in part), Sched. 10 (in part): April 1, 1986 (S.I. 1986 No. 463: [1986] C.L.Y. 303.)

All remaining provisions: December 29, 1986 (S.I. 1986 No. 1924: [1986] C.L.Y. 303).

INSOLVENCY ACT 1986
All provisions: December 29, 1986 ([1986] C.L.Y. 304 and S.I. 1986 No. 1924: [1986] C.L.Y. 303.)

INTERCEPTION OF COMMUNICATIONS ACT 1985
All provisions: April 10, 1986 (S.I. 1986 No. 384: [1986] C.L.Y. 3217.)

LANDLORD AND TENANT ACT 1985
All provisions: April 1, 1986 ([1985] C.L.Y. 1641.)

LATENT DAMAGE ACT 1986
All provisions: September 18, 1986 ([1986] C.L.Y. 2273.)

LAW REFORM (MISCELLANEOUS PROVISIONS) (SCOTLAND) ACT 1985
Ss.14, 15, and 19, Sched. 2, paras. 8, 12, 13 and 24 (and s.59(1) so far as it relates to these paragraphs). December 8, 1986. (S.I. 1986 No. 1945: [1986] C.L.Y. 4221.)

S.35: January 1, 1986 (S.I. 1985 No. 1908: [1986] C.L.Y. 4323.)

S.36: January 1, 1986 (S.I. 1985 No. 2055: [1986] C.L.Y. 4323.)

S.50: February 1, 1986 (S.I. 1985 No. 1908: [1986] C.L.Y. 4323.)

LAW REFORM (PARENT AND CHILD) (SCOTLAND) ACT 1986
All provisions: December 8, 1986 (S.I. 1986 No. 1983: [1986] C.L.Y. 4374.)

DATES OF COMMENCEMENT

LEGAL AID (SCOTLAND) ACT 1986
Ss.1(1) and (3)—(6), 2(2) and (3), 3(1), (2) and (4)—(6), 40(1)(b) and (2)(b), 41, 45(1) (in part) and Scheds. 1 and 3, paras. 3 and 4: October 1, 1986 (S.I. 1986 No. 1617 [1986] C.L.Y. 4473.)

LOCAL GOVERNMENT ACT 1985
Abolition date: April 1, 1986 ([1985] C.L.Y. 2046.)

LOCAL GOVERNMENT ACT 1986
Ss.1, 7, 9–12: March 26, 1986 ([1986] C.L.Y. 2030.)
Ss.2–4, 6, 8: April 1, 1986 ([1986] C.L.Y. 2030.)

LOCAL GOVERNMENT (ACCESS TO INFORMATION) ACT 1985
All provisions: April 1, 1986 ([1985] C.L.Y. 2045.)

MARRIAGE (PROHIBITED DEGREES OF RELATIONSHIP) ACT 1986
All provisions: November 1, 1986 (S.I. 1986 No. 1343: [1986] C.L.Y. 1659.)

MARRIAGE (WALES) ACT 1986
All provisions: March 18, 1986 ([1986] C.L.Y. 1660.)

MATRIMONIAL AND FAMILY PROCEEDINGS ACT 1984
S.10, Sched. 1. paras. 21, 23–26: October 1, 1986 (S.I. 1986 No. 1049: [1986] C.L.Y. 1105.)
Ss.32–40, 42, 43, Sched. 1, paras. 3, 16–18, 19(b), 20(b), 29–31, Sched. 3 (in part): April 28, 1986 (S.I. 1986 No. 635: [1986] C.L.Y. 1105).)
Pt. V (apart from ss.40, 41, 44), Scheds. 1, paras. 3, 16, 18, 19(b), 20(b), 29–31; Sched. 3 (in part): April 28, 1986 (S.I. 1986 No. 635: [1986] C.L.Y. 1105).
All provisions extending to Scotland: September 1, 1986 (S.I. 1986 No. 1226: [1986] C.L.Y. 3978.)

MERCHANT SHIPPING ACT 1979
Ss.17, 18, 19(1)(4), 50(4) (in part), Scheds. 4, 5, 7, Pt. I: December 1, 1986 (S.I. 1986 No. 1052: [1986] C.L.Y. 3091.)

MUSEUM OF LONDON ACT 1986
All provisions: April 1, 1986 ([1986] C.L.Y. 2004.)

NATIONAL HERITAGE (SCOTLAND) ACT 1985
Ss.11, 12, 13, 14, 15, 17 (in part), 18(6), 24 (in part being all remaining provisions): April 1, 1986 (S.I. 1985) No. 851: [1985] C.L.Y. 4327.)

PATENTS, DESIGNS AND MARKS ACT 1986
Ss.1(pt), 3(1)(pt), Sched. 1, paras. 1, 2 and 3, Pt. I(pt): October 1, 1986: (S.I. 1986 No. 1274: [1986] C.L.Y. 3423.)
Ss.2, 3(pt.) and Sched. 2: October 1, 1986 ([1986] C.L.Y. 3422.)

POLICE AND CRIMINAL EVIDENCE ACT 1984
Ss.1 (in part), 2–6, 7(1)(2)(a), 8–22, 24–36, 37(1)(10)(15), 38–58, 60(1)(a), 61–65, 68–82, 107, 113(1)(2), 114, 116, 117, 119, Scheds. 1, 2, 3, 6 (in part), 7 (in part): January 1, 1986 (S.I. 1985 No. 1934: [1985] C.L.Y. 663.)

PORTS (FINANCE) ACT 1985
Ss.3, 4, 5: January 1, 1986 (1985 S.I. No. 1153: [1985] C.L.Y. 3221.)

POWERS OF ATTORNEY ACT 1985
All provisions: March 10, 1986 (S.I. 1986 No. 125 [1986] C.L.Y. 33.)

PREVENTION OF OIL POLLUTION ACT 1986
All provisions: May 18, 1986 ([1986] C.L.Y. 3096.)

PROSECUTION OF OFFENCES ACT 1985
Ss.1, 2, 3(pt.) 4–8, 10, 14, 23, 25, 26, 27; Sched. 1, paras. 1–3, Sched. 2(pt.) (these provisions only come into force in the following areas: Durham, Greater Manchester, Merseyside, Northumberland, South Yorkshire, Tyne and Wear, West Midlands, West Yorkshire): April 1, 1986 (S.I. 1985 No. 1849: [1985] C.L.Y. 675.)
Ss.1–8, 10, 14, 15 (in part), 23, 25, 26, 27, Sched. 1, paras. 1–3, Sched. 2 (in part): October 1, 1986 (S.I. 1986 No. 1029: [1986] C.L.Y. 682.)

DATES OF COMMENCEMENT

Pt. I, Ss.23, 25, 26, 27, Sched. 1, paras. 1, 2, 3, Sched. 2 (in part) (specified counties): April 1, 1986 (S.I. 1985 No. 1849: [1985] C.L.Y. 675.)

Ss.24, 28, 31(5)(6), Sched. 1, para. 4, 5, Sched. 2(pt): April 1, 1986 (S.I. 1985 No. 1849: [1985] C.L.Y. 675.)

Pt. II, Scheds. 1, paras. 6–10; 2 (in part): October 1, 1986 (S.I. 1986 No. 1334: [1986] C.L.Y. 682.)

PROTECTION OF CHILDREN (TOBACCO) ACT 1986
All provisions: October 8, 1986 ([1986] C.L.Y. 2205.)

PROTECTION OF MILITARY REMAINS ACT 1986
All provisions: September 8, 1986 ([1986] C.L.Y. 130.)

REGISTERED HOMES ACT 1984
S.1 (in part): January 1, 1986 (S.I. 1984 No. 1348 [1984] C.L.Y. 2163.)

REPRESENTATION OF THE PEOPLE ACT 1985
Sched. 4, para. 69: April 21, 1986 (S.I. 1986 No. 639: [1986] C.L.Y. 1160.)

RESERVOIRS ACT 1975
Ss.2, 3, 11, 15(4), 16, 17 (in part), 18, 21(5)(6), 22, 24 (Greater London and the metropolitan counties): April 1, 1986 (S.I. 1986 No. 466: [1986] C.L.Y. 3530.)

Ss.6–10 12–14, 15(1)–(5), 19, 20, 21(1)–(6), 22, 23, 25–28, Sched. 2 (areas other than Greater London and the metropolitan counties): April 1. 1986 (S.I. 1986 No. 466: [1986] C.L.Y. 3530.)

ROAD TRAFFIC (DRIVING INSTRUCTION) ACT 1984
S.1.: September 30, 1986 (S.I. 1986 No. 1336: [1986] C.L.Y. 2977.)

ROAD TRAFFIC REGULATION ACT 1984
S.90: July 31, 1986: (S.I. 1986 No. 1147: [1986] C.L.Y. 2979.)

ROAD TRAFFIC REGULATION (PARKING) ACT 1986
All provisions: September 8, 1986 ([1986] C.L.Y. 2978.)

ROADS (SCOTLAND) ACT 1984
S.126 and Sched. 7 and s.156(3) and Sched. 11 in so far as they relate to Sched. 10 to the Road Traffic Regulation Act 1984 (c.27): January 1, 1986 (S.I. 1985 No. 1953 [1985] C.L.Y. 4240.)

SAFETY AT SEA ACT 1986
Ss.10, 11, 14(pt.), 15: October 30, 1986 (S.I. 1986 No. 1759: [1986] C.L.Y. 3099.)

SOCIAL SECURITY ACT 1985
Ss.1, 2, 3, 4 (in part), 5, 6(1)–(4), 29(1)(2) (in part), Scheds. 1, 2 (in part), 3, Pt. II, 5, paras. 1–4, 18–21, 23, 24, 27, 28, 30–32, Sched. 6 (in part): January 1, 1986 (S.I. 1985 No. 1364: [1985] C.L.Y. 3288.)

Ss.18, 20: April 6, 1986. ([1985] C.L.Y. 3287.)

Ss.21 (in part), 29(1) (in part), Sched. 5, para. 37; 6 (in part): April 6, 1986 (1985 S.I. No. 1125: [1985] C.L.Y. 3288.)

S.29(1) (in part), Sched. 5, paras. 25, 38: April 6, 1986 (S.I. 1985 No. 1364: [1985] C.L.Y. 3288.)

SOCIAL SECURITY ACT 1986
Ss.8, 16, 86(pt.), Scheds. 10(pt.), 11(pt.): November 1, 1986 (S.I. 1986 No.1719: [1986] C.L.Y. 3157.)

Ss.30(pt.), 37, 38(pt), 45, 61, 63, 64, 70, 71(pt), 72, 74, 76, 81, 83, 84, 85, 86(pt.), 87, 88, 89, 90; July 25, 1986 ([1986] C.L.Y. 3156.)

Ss.39 (in part), 51(1) *(b)(c)(d)(e)*, 62, 67(1), 71(1)–(3), 86(1)(2)(in part), Sched. 3, paras. 1, 2, 3, 5(1) (in part), (2), 13, 14, 15, 17, Sched. 10, paras. 68, 83, 84, 88–93, 95, 97, 100, 104, 105, Sched. 11 (in part): October 1, 1986 (S.I. 1986 No. 1609: [1986] C.L.Y. 3157.)

Ss.42, 43, 44: October 5, 1986 (save effect of s.42 in certain cases which comes into force on October 4, 1987) (S.I. 1986 No. 1609: [1986] C.L.Y. 3157.)

Ss.62, 67(1), 71(1)–(3), Sched. 3 (in part): October 1, 1986 (S.I. 1986 No. 1609: [1986] C.L.Y. 3157.)

DATES OF COMMENCEMENT

STATUTE LAW (REPEALS) ACT 1986

All provisions: May 2, 1986, ([1986] C.L.Y. 3210.)

TOWN AND COUNTRY PLANNING (MINERALS) ACT 1981

Pt. I so far as not already in force, s.34 so far as it applies to provisions of Sched. 1: May 19, 1986 (S.I. 1986 No. 760 (c.20): [1986] C.L.Y. 3390b.)

TRADE MARKS (AMENDMENT) ACT 1984

All provisions: October 1, 1986 (S.I. 1986 No. 1273: [1986] C.L.Y. 3428.)

TRANSPORT ACT 1982

Ss.27–51 (except s.39), 73, 75, 76, Scheds. 1 and 3: October 1, 1986 (S.I. 1986 No. 1326 [1986] C.L.Y. 3460.)

Ss.27(2) and (4), 29(1), (6)(a) and (b) and (7), 31, 32, 33(3), (5) and (6), 36, 37, 38, 45, 46, 47(6) and (7), 49(2)–(13), 51, Sched. 3. December 1, 1986. (S.I. 1986 No. 1874: [1986] C.L.Y. 4757.)

TRANSPORT ACT 1985

Ss.1(pt) 2, 3, 4(pt.) 5, 12, 13(pt.), 16, 29, 30, 32(pt), 34, 47–56, 57(pt.), 59–84, 87, 88–92, 106, 110, 112, 113, 118–124, 125, 127(pt.), 128, 129–138, 139(pt.), Sched. 1, paras. 1, 2, 3(pt.) 4-6, 12–14, 15(pt.) 16, Sched. 2, Sched. 3 (save for paras. 8 and 26), Sched. 5, Sched. 6, paras. 1–11, 13, 15, 19–21, 26, Sched. 7, paras. 1, 4, 6, 10–14, 18, 20, 21(pt.), 23, Sched. 8(pt.): January 6, 1986 (S.I. 1985 No. 1887: [1986] C.L.Y. 3546.)

Ss.1 (remaining pt.), 4 (remaining pt.), 6, 24–28, 32 (remaining pt.), 35–46, 111, 126 (pt.), 127(4) (remaining pt.), 139(1) (remaining pt.), 139(2)–(3) (pt.), Scheds. 1, 6, 7 (remaining pts.), 8 (remaining pt. except as specified): October 26, 1986 (S.I. 1986 No. 1794: [1986] C.L.Y. 3461.)

Ss.7–9, 126(3): July 14, 1986 (S.I. 1986 No. 1088: [1986] C.L.Y. 3461.)

Ss.10, 11, 13, 17, 18, 22, 23, 33, 126(1)(2), 127(1)(2)(4), 139(2), Sched. 7, paras. 2, 21(2): August 1, 1986 (S.I. 1986 No. 1088: [1986] C.L.Y. 3461.)

Ss.31, 104, 117, 139(1)–(3) in relation to Scheds. 6, 7, 8 in force under this order, Sched. 4, Sched. 6, paras 24, 25, Sched. 7, paras. 7, 8, 15, 21(3), (11), Sched. 8 in relation to repeals under this Order: September 15, 1986 (S.I. 1986 No. 1450: [1986] C.L.Y. 3461.)

Ss.57(6), 93(8)(b), 102, 108, 109, 116(1), 139(1)(2)(3), Scheds. 3, paras. 8, 24, 26, Sched. 6, paras. 22, 23, Sched. 7, paras. 3, 9, 17, 19, 22, 24, Sched. 8: April 1, 1986 (S.I. 1986 No. 414: [1986] C.L.Y. 3461.)

S.58 (save subs. (5)): April 1, 1986. ([1985] C.L.Y. 3086.)

Ss.93–101 (save for s.93(8)(b)), 103, 105, Sched. 6, paras. 22, 23, Sched. 7, para. 19(pt.): February 14, 1986 (S.I. 1986 No. 80: [1986] C.L.Y. 3461.)

S.107: April 1, 1986 (S.I. 1985 No. 1887: [1985] C.L.Y. 3546.)

Ss.114, 115, 116(2)(3), 139(3), Sched. 8: July 26, 1986 (S.I. 1986 No. 1088: [1986] C.L.Y. 3461.)

TRUSTEE SAVINGS BANK ACT 1976

Sched. 5, para. 19 and 20: July 20, 1986 (S.I. 1986 No. 1221: [1986] C.L.Y. 3025.)

TRUSTEE SAVINGS BANK ACT 1985

Appointed day for certain repeals under the Act: July 20 and 21, 1986 (S.I. 1986 No. 1220) and (S.I. 1986 No. 1223: [1986] C.L.Y. 3026.)

Vesting day: July 21, 1986 (S.I. 1986 No. 1222: [1986] C.L.Y. 3026.)

VALUE ADDED TAX ACT 1983

S.39(8) (appointed day): October 1, 1986 (S.I. 1986 No. 969: [1986] C.L.Y. 3483.)

VIDEO RECORDINGS ACT 1984

Ss.9 and 10 (for certain purposes): September 1, 1986 (S.I. 1986 No. 1125: [1986] C.L.Y. 945.)

Ss.9, 10 (in part) (Scotland): September 1, 1986 (S.I. 1986 No. 1182: [1986] C.L.Y. 3929.)

DATES OF COMMENCEMENT

WAGES ACT 1986

S.24, 25(1)–(3), 27, 28, 29, 31, 32(pt.), Sched. 4(pt.), Sched. 5 (Pt. I): July 25, 1986 ([1986] C.L.Y. 1293.)

Ss.12–23, 25(pt.), 30(pt.), 32(pt.), Scheds. 2, 3, 4 (paras. 4–7), 5 (Pt. II): September 25, 1986 ([1986] C.L.Y. 1293.)

WEIGHTS AND MEASURES ACT 1985

All provisions (save s.43): January 30, 1986. ([1985] C.L.Y. 3638.)

CURRENT LAW YEAR BOOK

1986

ADMINISTRATIVE LAW

1. Broadcasting—powers—judicial review

[Broadcasting Act 1981 (c.68), s.20(5).] The Court could not judicially review the IBA decision not to give permission to Rank Organisation to exercise voting rights over shares exceeding five per cent. of the issued voting shares of Granada Group as they were not exercising any function under the Act. R. *v*. INDEPENDENT BROADCASTING AUTHORITY, *ex p*. RANK ORGANISATION, *The Times*, March 14, 1986, Mann J.

2. Chief constables—duty of care—victim of murderer

A chief constable owes no duty of care to the victim of a murderer even though he had killed many people. Even if such a duty existed it would be excluded because of the impossibility of defining the class of persons at risk and in any event the harm committed was too remote to constitute a breach of duty: HILL *v*. CHIEF CONSTABLE FOR WEST YORKSHIRE (1986) 136 New L.J. 238, Lawson J.

3. Council on Tribunals

The Annual Report of the Council on Tribunals for 1985/86 has been published. Copies of the report are available from H.M.S.O. (H.C. 42) [£8·30.]

4. Foreign proceedings—obtaining evidence—procedure

[Extradition Act 1873 (c.60); Evidence (Proceedings in Other Jurisdictions) Act 1975 (c.34).] The Home Secretary is at liberty to decide which of these routes he will select in responding to a request from a foreign government for an order to obtain evidence for use in foreign criminal proceedings. Nor was he himself under any duty to consider the questions of law raised by the request: R. *v*. SECRETARY OF STATE FOR THE HOME DEPARTMENT, *ex p*. SPERMACET WHALING AND SHIPPING CO. S.A., *The Times*, November 14, 1986, D.C.

5. Judicial review—availability of remedy—alternative remedy—appeal against tax assessments—costs

Taxpayers were granted leave to apply for judicial review against the decision of a tax inspector on the ground that it was an abuse of his powers even though they could have appealed to the Special Commissioners, since they would not be able to recover their costs in such an appeal.

A Jersey company purchased land in the U.K. for £325,000 in 1981. Later that year it sold the land to a wholly-owned subsidiary, a U.K. company of which the applicants were directors, for £1,125,000. The U.K. company then sold the land to an independent purchaser for £1,150,000. The applicants were assessed to tax under s.488(8) of the Income and Corporation Taxes Act 1970 on the basis that they had directly or indirectly provided an opportunity for another person, the Jersey company, to realise a gain. There was no evidence that the applicants were or ever had been beneficially entitled to the Jersey company's gain or to the land. They applied for judicial review to quash the assessments on the grounds that they were *ultra vires* the inspector. Leave was refused and they renewed their application, contending that there was no evidence on which the inspector could have judged that tax was due from them, and that he acted improperly in that the assessments had been made with an intention other than that of recovering tax genuinely believed to be due and in order to make inquiries about other individuals of a kind not authorised by the statutory powers of inquiry. *Held*, that it was arguable that the inspector's decision was irrational and might be an abuse of his powers. Although the points could equally well be taken on an appeal by the applicants to the Special Commissioners, the applicants, if successful, would be prejudiced in that they would not be able to recover their costs in such an appeal. Leave to apply for judicial review was therefore granted. (*R* v. *Commissioner for the Special Purposes of the Income Tax Acts, ex p. Stipplechoice* [1985] C.L.Y. 2688 applied).

R. v. INSPECTOR OF TAXES, *ex p.* KISSANE [1986] 2 All E.R. 37, Nolan J.

6. Judicial review—certiorari—to quash conviction—new evidence

Following R's unsuccessful appeal against conviction of assaulting a police officer in the execution of his duty at a trial at which R and the officer, X, were the only witnesses, it came to light that X had told a sergeant, shortly after the relevant incident, that he did not know what had happened and that there must have been a clash of heads. *Held,* granting judicial review and quashing the conviction, that the ambit of certiorari, was wide enough to cover the present situation: R. v. LIVERPOOL CROWN COURT, *ex p.* ROBERTS [1986] Crim.L.R. 622, D.C.

7. Judicial review—challenged authority—disclosure of information. See R. v. LANCASHIRE COUNTY COUNCIL, *ex p.* HUDDLESTON, § 1141.

8. Judicial review—commissioners—refusal to grant adjournment. See R. v. BRENTFORD GENERAL COMMISSIONERS, *ex p.* CHAN, § 2854.

9. Judicial review—decision of Commonwealth Games Federation

The court would refuse to exercise its jurisdiction to grant a declaration to a potential competitor in the Commonwealth Games since there was no claim of right and no contractual relationship between her and the Federation, and as a person adversely affected her case had been properly put before the relevant body. Moreover the Federation had in any event properly construed "domicile" in their constitution by using its normal everyday meaning. Furthermore, even if given its legal meaning, the necessary requirements could not have been made out. (*Prenn* v. *Simmonds* [1971] C.L.Y. 1711, *McInnes* v. *Onslow-Fane* [1978] C.L.Y. 21 considered): COWLEY v. HEATLEY, *The Times,* July 24, 1986, Browne-Wilkinson V.C.

10. Judicial review—declaration—whether power to grant

[Supreme Court Act 1981 (c.54), s.31(2); R.S.C., Ord. 53, r.1(2).] The Divisional Court has power under s.31(2) of the Supreme Court Act 1981 and Ord. 53, r.1(2) to grant a declaration on an application for judicial review, even if it is not possible to make a prerogative order. For a declaration to be granted, however, it must be more than merely a comment on past events: it must be of practical use for the future: R. v. SECRETARY OF STATE FOR THE ENVIRONMENT *ex p.* NOTTINGHAMSHIRE COUNTY COUNCIL, *The Times,* November 10, 1986, D.C.

11. Judicial review—delay in application for leave to apply—whether good reason for extending time. See R. v. STRATFORD-ON-AVON DISTRICT COUNCIL, § 2662.

12. Judicial review—immigration cases

All applications for judicial review of immigration decisions will be screened to see whether they are bona fide applications, or merely devices to buy time. If there appears to be no merit in an application, it will be listed at the earliest possible opportunity: KARIM, *ex p. The Times,* February 4, 1986, D.C.

13. Judicial review—leave to apply—discovery

On an interlocutory appeal against a decision to order discovery it was not open to D to challenge the original grant of leave to pursue an application for judicial review. The court may conduct or permit the conduct of fact-finding in judicial review proceedings (*R.* v. *Deputy Governor of Camp Hill Prison ex p. King* [1985] C.L.Y. 2752, *R.* v. *Board of Visitors of Hull Prison, ex p. St. Germain* [1979] C.L.Y. 2195 considered): R. v. GOVERNOR OF PENTONVILLE PRISON, *ex p.* HERBAGE (NO. 2), *The Times,* November 7, 1986, C.A.

14. Judical review—mental health proceedings—civil proceedings. See WALDRON, *ex p.,* § 2134.

15. Judicial review—non-payment of rates—committal—delay. See R. v. LAMBETH BOROUGH COUNCIL, *ex p.* STERLING (AHIJAH), § 2805.

16. Judicial review—refusal of bail

Judicial review is an inappropriate relief to seek when a person has been refused bail by justices and subsequently a judge in chambers. The appropriate course is to reapply to the Judge. *Re* HERBAGE, *The Times,* October 25, 1985, D.C.

17. Judicial review—renewed application

[Supreme Court Act 1981 (c.54), s.18(1)(*a*).] The section deprives the Court of Appeal of jurisdiction to hear appeals in "any criminal cause or matter" and therefore it cannot consider a renewed application for leave to apply for judicial review of a justices refusal to issue a summons for breach of the peace: R. *v.* BOLTON JUSTICES, *ex p.* GRAEME, *The Times,* March 14, 1986, C.A.

18. Judicial review—Revenue documents—discovery

The applicants in judicial review proceedings sought discovery of documents relating to the practice of the Inland Revenue in applying F.A. 1973, Sched. 19, para. 10, in relation to share exchanges. *Held,* that the Revenue's practice in operating the relevant provisions of the 1973 Act was likely to illuminate the issues of fact, and discovery should be ordered, but should be confined to internal documents of the Revenue of a general character, excluding documents indicating how particular individual cases had been dealt with: R. *v.* I.R.C., *ex p.* ROTHSCHILD (J.) HOLDINGS [1986] S.T.C. 410, Simon Brown J.

19. Judicial review—when available

[Supreme Court Act 1981 (c.54) s.31(2)] The court could grant declaratory relief in respect of public law issues whenever it was just and convenient to do so, but it was neither just nor convenient if there was an alternative remedy, and the jurisdiction would not be exercised unless there was a point of general public importance which needed to be resolved in the public interest (*Gillick* v. *West Norfolk Area Health Authority* [1985] C.L.Y. 2230 a considered): R. *v.* SECRETARY OF STATE FOR THE ENVIRONMENT, *ex p.* G.L.C., *The Times,* December 30, 1985, Woolf J.

20. Judicial review—whether available—police disciplinary procedure. See R. *v.* CHIEF CONSTABLE OF MERSEYSIDE POLICE, *ex p.* CALVELEY, § 2542.

21. Library authorities—abuse of power—newspaper ban

[Public Libraries and Museums Act 1964 (c.75).] P published a newspaper which was involved in a labour dispute. D was a local authority which supported P's workers against P, and accordingly refused to provide P's newspapers at any of its libraries. *Held,* that the ban was imposed for ulterior political reasons that had nothing to do with D's duty to service public libraries under the Public Libraries and Museums Act 1964. D was abusing its powers by applying improper considerations, and its ban was therefore unlawful: R. *v.* EALING, HAMMERSMITH AND FULHAM, AND CAMDEN LONDON BOROUGH COUNCILS, *ex p.* TIMES NEWSPAPERS, *The Times,* November 6, 1986, D.C.

22. Minister's duty to consult—whether mandatory—whether sufficient consultation. See R. *v.* SECRETARY OF STATE FOR SOCIAL SERVICES, *ex p.* ASSOCIATION OF METROPOLITAN AUTHORITIES, § 1635.

23. Natural justice—board of visitors—disciplinary proceedings. See R. *v.* BOARD OF VISITORS OF FRANKLAND PRISON, *ex p.* LEWIS, § 2735

24. National Coal Board—executive decision—whether subject to judicial review

[Coal Industry Nationalisation Act 1946 (c.59), s.46.] S.46 of the Coal Industry Nationalisation Act 1946 imposes a duty on the National Coal Board to establish machinery for the settlement of terms and conditions of employment and other matters. It does not extend beyond that to the realms of consultation as a matter of statutory duty. The decision to close a colliery is part of executive or business or management duties of the NCB; it is not part of its activities as a public body, and it is therefore not subject to judicial review: R. *v.* NATIONAL COAL BOARD, *ex p.* NATIONAL UNION OF MINEWORKERS, *The Times,* March 8, 1986, D.C.

25. Parliamentary commissioner

PARLIAMENTARY COMMISSIONER ORDER 1986 (No. 1168) [45p], made under the Parliamentary Commissioner Act 1967 (c.13), s.5(4); operative on August 8, 1986; amends Sched. 3 to the 1967 Act.

PARLIAMENTARY COMMISSIONER (NO. 2) ORDER 1986 (NO. 1889) [45p], made under the Parliamentary Commissioner Act 1967 (c.13), s.4(2); operative on December 8,

1986; adds the Ordnance Survey to the departments subject to investigation by the Parliamentary Commissioner for Administration.

26. **Public inquiry—effect of government policy—inspector ignoring objections because of policy.** See R. v SECRETARY OF STATE FOR TRANSPORT, *ex p.* GWENT COUNTY COUNCIL, § 3447.

27. **Statutory powers of ministers—guidance to local authorities over expenditure—whether lawful**

[Local Government, Planning and Land Act 1980 (c.65), (as amended by Local Government Finance Act 1982 (c.32), s.8), s.59(6)(*cc*)(11A).]

Whilst the Secretary of State must adhere to one set of principles in giving guidance to local authorities over spending, the principles themselves may lawfully reflect the differences between local authorities, for example as to their past spending patterns. Where the Secretary of State exercises his powers in such circumstances the court should not interfere merely on the ground of "unreasonableness."

The Secretary of State gave guidance to local authorities over their spending which the respondent authorities felt unfairly discriminated against them as being over-spending councils. They contended that the differentiation between high-spending and low-spending authorities was unlawful. *Held,* that the guidance given by the Secretary of State was lawful and proper. The Secretary of State was obliged to adhere to consistent principles, but those principles themselves could properly contain matters differentiating between high-spending and low-spending authorities. Only if there was an allegation of bad faith, or something akin thereto, could the court properly intervene on a ground of "unreasonableness," particularly where the matter was one for the political judgment of the Secretary of State.

NOTTINGHAMSHIRE COUNTY COUNCIL *v.* SECRETARY OF STATE FOR THE ENVIRONMENT; CITY OF BRADFORD METROPOLITAN COUNCIL *v.* SECRETARY OF STATE FOR THE ENVIRONMENT [1986] 2 W.L.R. 1, H.L.

28. **Tribunal—health authority—procedure**

A disciplinary tribunal of a health authority which had reached its conclusion on the balance of probabilities was in breach of its own rules and its decision was therefore quashed: R. *v.* SOUTH GLAMORGAN HEALTH AUTHORITY, *ex p.* PHILLIPS, *The Times,* November 21, 1986, Russell J.

29. **Tribunals—right to counsel**

Whether or not persons appearing before domestic tribunals have a right to legal representation, there is a discretion to allow it to them and a probable duty to do so where they are charged with infamous conduct: MANCHANDA *v.* MEDICAL EYE CENTRE ASSOCIATION, (1986) 83 L.S.Gaz. 3673, C.A.

30. **Union rules—validity of decision.**

The Court held that a decision by equity, consequent on a referendum of its members, to instruct members not to work in South Africa was invalid as outside the union rules: GORING *v.* BRITISH ACTORS EQUITY ASSOCIATION, *The Times,* August 5, 1986, Sir Nicholas Browne-Wilkinson, V.-C.

AGENCY

31. **Crown Agents (Amendment) Act 1986 (c.43)**

This amends s.17 of the Crown Agents Act 1979 (interest on Crown Agents' commencing capital debit payable during initial period only if Secretary of State so determines).

The Act received the Royal Assent on July 25, 1986.

32. **Enduring powers of attorney**

COURT OF PROTECTION (ENDURING POWERS OF ATTORNEY) RULES 1986 (No. 127) [£2·80], made under the Enduring Powers of Attorney Act 1985 (c.29), s.10(1)(*d*) and the Mental Health Act 1983 (c.20), ss.106, 107, 108; operative on March 10, 1986; supplement S.I. 1984 No. 2035 in relation to enduring powers of attorney.

ENDURING POWERS OF ATTORNEY (PRESCRIBED FORM) REGULATIONS 1986 (No. 126) [£1·35], made under the Enduring Powers of Attorney Act 1985 (c.29), s.2(2); operative on March 10, 1986; prescribes the form of an enduring power of attorney.

33. Enduring Power of Attorney Act 1985—commencement
ENDURING POWERS OF ATTORNEY ACT 1985 (COMMENCEMENT) ORDER 1986 (No. 125 (C.5)) [40p]; made under the Enduring Powers of Attorney Act 1985 (c.29), s.14(2); brings the 1985 Act into force on March 10, 1986.

34. Estate agent—commission—whether lost through "unprofessional" conduct
D engaged P, a firm of estate agents, to act for them in finding a property for the provision of shelter and nursing services, and undertook to pay a commission if they succeeded in purchasing a property to which P had introduced them. D subsequently did purchase the property, but refused to pay commission on the grounds that P had committed a breach going to the root of the contract of agency of terms to be implied both by common law and pursuant to the rules of the Incorporated Society of Valuers and Auctioneers, by simultaneously acting for two rival prospective purchasers with the result that the price which D had had to pay had been substantially increased. The judge found that, although there had been preliminary negotiations about the property with the prospective rivals, in neither case had these progressed to the point where P could be said to be acting for the prospective rivals within the meaning of the terms contended for by D. Furthermore D were aware of the interest of these rivals, and had expected to attend a joint view of the premises with them. *Held,* giving judgment for P, that (1) a term was to be implied into the contract of agency that P would act in accordance with the rules: these provided that no member should act for two parties in the same transaction without the full knowledge and consent of both parties; (2) the duty not so to act arose as soon as a client demonstrated a real intent to buy; (3) in this case P had not acted in breach of that duty once it had so arisen; (4) any duty to be implied by common law was co-extensive with the duty under the rules, and that P were not therefore in breach of it; (5) even if P had been in breach of duty, they would not in the circumstances have been disentitled to their commission (*Andrews* v. *Ramsay & Co.* [1903] 2 K.B. 635 distinguished): STANSFIELD (ERIC V.) (A FIRM) v. SOUTH EAST NURSING HOME SERVICES (1985) 277 E.G. 311, Mr. Charles Whitby Q.C.

35. Estate agent—commission contract—construction—whether requirement of "effective cause"
D, a property company who were seeking a tenant for new office premises, circularised estate agents in the following terms: "We . . . offer a full-scale letting fee to your company should you introduce a tenant by whom you are unable tᴏ be retained, and with whom we have not been in previous communication, and who subsequently completes a lease." A subsequent circular letter offered double commission on otherwise similar terms. In April 1982 P introduced M, who were seeking new premises, and subsequently "chased" them, but M decided later that year that they would not move for the time being. In 1983 M's interest in a move revived and R, another agent, purported to reintroduce M to D. R were ineligible for commission from D, since they were retained by M and since M had been in previous communication with D. When M eventually completed a lease, P claimed that they had satisfied all D's requirements and were accordingly entitled to double commission. D objected, claiming that P had not been the effective cause of the letting: they conceded that the requirements of the commission clause had in other respects been satisfied. *Held,* giving judgment for P, that (1) the effective cause of the letting was not P but R; (2) a requirement that an introduction by an estate agent should be the effective cause of an eventual letting was not to be implied if the terms of the contract were otherwise clear (*Luxor (Eastbourne)* v. *Cooper* [1941] A.C. 108 applied); (3) the wording of the commission clause was clear in its intention that the party entitled to commission was to be the one who first introduced the eventual lessee, thus avoiding arguments about who was the effective cause of the letting; (4) P had accordingly fulfilled all the requirements of the commission clause: COOPER (BRIAN) & CO. v. FAIRVIEW ESTATES (INVESTMENTS) (1986) 278 E.G. 1094, H.H. Judge Tibber.

36. Estate agent—professional charges—quantum meruit
D employed P, a firm of estate agents, to "provide valuations orally of the premises and business, to prepare an inventory of fixtures and fittings, to take details of trading figures and generally to assist . . . at negotiations . . . with the vendors", in connection with the purchase by D of a night-club. P submitted an invoice for professional charges based on scale 17(b) of the scale of charges of the RICS and,

when D denied that such a basis for payment had been agreed, served a statement of claim "for the sum of £5,980 being the cost of work done on behalf of the defendant and to his order." The judge held that there was no term of the agreement entitling P to payment on scale 17(b), but that P was entitled to a substantial sum by way of quantum meruit. On appeal D contended that the judge had not been entitled to make such an award, because P's claim had not contained an alternative quantification by way of quantum meruit. *Held*, dismissing D's appeal, that whilst P had not contended for remuneration on a quantum meruit basis, D's own case had recognised that P was entitled to some remuneration on such a basis, and the judge had therefore been entitled to adopt that basis in making his assessment of D's liability to P: WITHEY ROBINSON (A FIRM) *v.* EDWARDS, (1985) 277 E.G. 748, C.A.

37. **Ostensible authority—agent having no authority to agree terms—whether principal bound**

   A principal is not liable on a charterparty negotiated without authority or consent by an employee in the absence of any representation by them as to his authority.

   The plaintiffs were formed to purchase a ship from the defendants on the basis that the ship was to be chartered back. M, the defendants' chartering manager, told the plaintiffs that he had authority to agree to the sale of the ship with a three year charter back to the defendants. Documents purporting to be a 12 month and three year charterparty came into existence, but the defendants knowing only of the 12 month charterparty redelivered the vessel. The plaintiffs sued for breach of the three year agreement, M admitted he had signed the charterparty without the knowledge or authority of the defendants. The judge found the defendants liable. The Court of Appeal reversed the decision. *Held,* on appeal, dismissing the appeal, that M could not, in the absence of a representation by the defendants as to his authority, reasonably be believed to have authority to complete the agreement (*Russo-Chinese Bank* v. *Li Yau Sam* [1910] A.C. 174 applied).
   ARMAGAS *v.* MUNDOGAS [1986] 2 W.L.R. 1063, H.L.

AGRICULTURE

38. **Agricultural holdings—arrears of rent—whether discharged by unpresented cheque—whether payment into court appropriated to arrears—whether notice to remedy valid**

   [Agriculture (Forms of Notices to Remedy) Regulations 1978 (S.I. 1978 No. 258).] Under a tenancy agreement for an agricultural holding, T covenanted to pay an annual rent totalling £3,800 in equal twice-yearly payments, and was also required to make twice-yearly payments in respect of interest on the cost of improvements carried out by L. In August 1980 L served a notice to quit under s.2(3) Case E of the Agricultural Holdings (Notices to Quit) Act 1977 alleging that part of the farm had been unlawfully sub-let and, for fear of prejudicing their claim pending the arbitrator's decision, made no demand for the rent falling due in September 1980 and March 1981. T nonetheless sent cheques in respect of the rent (but not the interest on improvements), but these remained unrepresented and their validity subsequently expired. In due course the arbitrator found for L (although this finding was subsequently set aside on appeal) and L then demanded the rent for September 1980 and March 1981. Eventually L obtained a distress warrant, which was ordered to be set aside on payment into court by T of "the sum of £3,800 on account of any moneys due from (T) to (L)." T subsequently made no payment of the rent and interest due in September 1981, which meant that he was effectively one half-year in arrears on the rent, and three half-years in arrears on the interest. In January 1982 L served a notice to pay in respect of the September 1981 rent, and a notice to remedy pursuant to the Agriculture (Forms of Notices to Remedy) Regulations 1978 in respect of the interest arrears, and subsequently served another notice to quit pursuant to s.2(3) Cases D(a) and (b) respectively of the 1977 Act, on the grounds of T's failure to comply with these notices. The arbitrator having stated a case for the court, the judge held that T had failed to comply with the notice to pay rent, but that the notice to remedy was not in proper form. Both parties appealed, and T argued that he had discharged his obligation to pay all rent due up to and including September 1981, either because the unpresented cheque was a valid discharge of the obligation to pay the September 1980 rent, whilst the payment into court had discharged the March and September 1981 rent; or because the payment into court was appropriated to the March and September 1981 rent, whilst the notice to pay had not referred to the September 1980 rent. *Held,* dismissing T's appeal and allowing L's cross-appeal, that (1) the mere receipt by L of the unpresented cheques had not discharged T's liability for the September 1980 or March 1981 rent (*Beevers v. Mason* [1979] C.L.Y. 50 distinguished); (2) at the time of the payment into court of the £3,800 there had been no appropriation by T of that money to the March or September 1981 rent, neither did the order for payment into court suffice so to appropriate the money (*Leeson v. Leeson* [1936] 2 K.B. 156 applied); (3) thereafter the rights of appropriation had devolved upon L (*Cory Brothers & Co. v. Owners of the Turkish Steamship "Mecca"* [1897] A.C. 286 applied); (4) accordingly T was in default as to the September 1981 rent; (5) the notice to remedy, despite some inaccuracy and terseness, had sufficiently indicated the source of the obligation sought to be enforced, and was accordingly valid: OFFICIAL SOLICITOR *v.* THOMAS (1986) 279 E.G. 407, C.A.

39. **Agricultural holdings—covenant against assigning or underletting part of the premises without permission—whether permission necessary to underletting of the whole.** See FIELD *v.* BARKWORTH, § 1823.

40. **Agricultural holdings—disposal of produce—duty of Minister**
     The Minister of Agriculture, Fisheries and Food is obliged to make arrangements for the disposal of the marketable produce of smallholdings let on his behalf by the Land Settlement Association Ltd. He is not, however, obliged to provide any specific services unless at any particular time he considers it expedient in the common interests of his tenants—a question he must keep constantly under review: WILLIAMS *v.* MINISTER OF AGRICULTURE, FISHERIES AND FOOD, *The Times,* October 17, 1986, H.L.

41. **Agricultural holdings—joint tenancy—termination—counternotice**
     [Agricultural Holdings (Notices to Quit) Act 1977 (c.12), s.2(1)(*b*).]
     Where an agricultural tenancy is granted to three joint tenants, including a company wholly owned by the landlord, who farm the land as a partnership, a clause in the partnership agreement purporting to prevent the joint tenants serving a counternotice under s.2(1)(*b*) of the Agricultural Holdings (Notices to Quit) Act 1977 without the consent of the company is void and unenforceable.
     S and L were joint tenants of land to which the Agricultural Holdings (Notices to Quit) Act 1977 applied. L was a company wholly owned by the landlords, F. S and L farmed the land pursuant to a partnership agreement. The agreement contained a clause providing that no counternotice under s.24 of the Agricultural Holdings Act 1948 (the predecessor to the 1977 Act) could be served by any partner on F without the consent of L. On September 26, 1983 F served notices to quit the land on S and L. Two days later L served notice to dissolution of the partnership in accordance with the agreement on S. S served counternotices on F pursuant to s.2(1)(*b*) of the Agricultural Holdings (Notices to Quit) Act 1977 on October 14, 1983. S purported to serve the counternotices on behalt of the partnership which was described as the tenant. The counternotices were served without the consent, and contrary to the wishes of L. F sought a declaration that the counternotices were invalid; S counterclaimed for a declaration that they were valid. The trial judge held that for the purposes of s.2(1)(*b*) of the Act where "the tenant" was a joint tenant "the tenant" might mean all the joint tenants acting together or only some depending upon the circumstances of the case. He also held that the particular circumstances of the present case did not require all the joint tenants to join in serving the counternotices and that the counternotices were valid. *Held,* that on F's appeal, the meaning of "the tenant" in s.2(1)(*b*) of the Act could not fluctuate in the manner indicated by the trial judge. Where there was a joint tenancy "the tenant" meant all the joint tenants. Where one of the joint tenants was the landlord it was open to argument that "the tenant" meant all the joint tenants with the exception of the landlord. As that argument did not arise on the facts of the present case the court did not express a concluded view upon it. The clause in the partnership agreement preventing S from serving the counternotices without L's consent was void and unenforceable. It was conceded that F and L fell to be regarded as one and the same by public policy which required that F should not by such a clause deprive S of the security of tenure granted by the 1977 Act. In the circumstances the counternotices must be treated as having been served with the authority of L. Appeal dismissed (*Leak and Moorlands Building Society v. Clark* [1952] C.L.Y. 1947, *Johnson v.*

Moreton [1970] C.L.Y. 42) *Greenwich London Borough Council* v. *McGrady* [1983] C.L.Y. 2099 applied, *Howson* v. *Buxton* [1928] All E.R. Rep. 434, *Fairclough (T. M.) and Sons* v. *Berliner* [1931] 1 Ch. 60, *Lloyd* v. *Sadler* [1978] C.L.Y. 1806 considered).

FEATHERSTONE *v.* STAPLES [1986] 2 All E.R. 461, C.A.

42. Agricultural holdings—rent arbitration notice—whether capable of being withdrawn without consent

[Agricultural Holdings Acts 1948 (c.63), s.8(1) and 1986 (c.5), s.12(1).]

By a notice given in September 1982 pursuant to s.8(1) of the Agricultural Holdings Act 1948 (now s.12(1) of the 1986 Act) L demanded an arbitration as to the amount of rent payable for an agricultural holding, but later purported to withdraw the notice. T nonetheless applied in due time for the appointment of an arbitrator, and an arbitrator was duly appointed. *Held,* that the notice was a trigger setting in motion the statutory machinery, and that it could not therefore be withdrawn unilaterally without the consent of the other party: BUCKINGHAMSHIRE COUNTY COUNCIL *v.* GORDON (1986) 279 E.G. 853, H.H. Judge Barr.

43. Agricultural holdings—succession—whether T's "only or principal source of income"

[Agriculture (Miscellaneous Provisions) Act 1976 (c.55), s.18(2).] B farmed land in Yorkshire in partnership with his father from 1961 until his father's retirement in 1971, and thereafter worked the farm on his own along with another very small holding. Between 1978 and his death in 1983 the father was an invalid, and during this period B worked solely on the farm, from which he derived his only income, drawn from a farm account held jointly with his father. This account was in profit until the end of 1981, but thereafter until the end of 1982 was in overdraft. B duly applied to succeed to the tenancy under the Agriculture (Miscellaneous Provisions) Act 1976, arguing that, between 1977 and 1981, the farm had been his only or principal source of income within the meaning of s.18(2) of the Act. The tribunal rejected this submission, basing its decision not on the five-year period relied on by T, but on the full seven years between 1977 and 1983; and it further found that the farm had not in any case been B's sole or principal source of livelihood in 1981, because the father had in that year paid into the joint farm account his pension, attendance allowance and sums from his deposit account. *Held,* allowing B's appeal by way of case stated under s.6(1) of the Agriculture (Miscellaneous Provisions) Act 1954, and remitting the case to the tribunal, (1) that the tribunal had erred in considering the full seven years as opposed to the five years relied on by B; (2) that the tribunal had been misled by the existence of the joint farm account, and that the fact that part of the capital employed in the business in 1981 came from B's father was irrelevant to the question of whether the farm had been B's sole or principal source of livelihood: BAILEY *v.* SITWELL (1986) 279 E.G. 1092, Hodgson J.

44. Agricultural holdings—tenancy agreement lost—estoppel by convention

A tenancy of an agricultural holding created by a written agreement made in 1923 was vested jointly in T, his brother and his father. The agreement, which contained a covenant against assignment or under-letting without L's consent, had by 1970 been lost and forgotten. In 1970 and 1974 rent arbitrations were conducted in relation to the holding under s.8 as amended of the Agricultural Holdings Act 1948, in each case upon the assumption by L, T and the arbitrator that there was no written tenancy agreement. In 1980 T, by now the sole surviving joint tenant, assigned the holding to his son. When L, who had by now discovered the agreement of 1923, sought to forfeit the tenancy for irremediable breach of covenant, T. denied that the breach was incapable of remedy, and contended that L was in any event estopped from relying upon the 1923 covenant. The judge, on a case stated by the arbitrator, found that the breach was incapable of remedy and that L were not so estopped. *Held*, allowing T's appeal, that (1) the breach was incapable of remedy (*Scala House and District Property Co.* v. *Forbes* [1973] C.L.Y. 1896 applied); (2) L were however estopped by convention from relying upon the 1923 covenant with respect to the 1980 assignment, since both parties had in 1970 and 1975 conducted their affairs upon the common basis that there was no written agreement (*Amalgamated Investment & Property Co.* v. *Texas Commerce International Bank* [1981] C.L.Y. 1273 applied); (3) the effect of the estoppel was however spent as regards any future assignment: TROOP *v.* GIBSON (1986) 277 E.G. 1134, C.A.

45. Agricultural Holdings Act 1986 (c.5)
This Act consolidates certain enactments relating to agricultural holdings, and gives effect to recommendations of the Law Commission.
The Act received the Royal Assent on March 18, 1986.

46. Agricultural holdings—units of production
AGRICULTURAL HOLDINGS (UNITS OF PRODUCTION) ORDER 1986 (No. 1256) [£1·40], made under the Agricultural Holdings Act 1986 (c.5), Sched. 6, para. 4; operative on September 12, 1986; prescribes units of production for various enterprises relating to agricultural land.

47. Agriculture Act 1986 (c.49)
This Act makes further provision relating to agriculture and agricultural and other food products, horticulture and the countryside.
The Act received the Royal Assent on July 25, 1986.

48/49. Agriculture Act 1986—commencement
AGRICULTURE ACT 1986 (COMMENCEMENT) (No. 1) ORDER 1986 (No. 1484 (c.50)) [45p], made under the Agriculture Act 1986 (c.49), s.24; brings into force on September 25, 1986 sections 13 and 15 of the 1986 Act.
AGRICULTURE ACT 1986 (COMMENCEMENT No. 3) ORDER 1986 (No. 1596 (C.57)) [45p], made under the Agriculture Act 1986 (c.49), s.24(2); brings into force on September 8, 1986 section 8(2) of the 1986 Act.
AGRICULTURE ACT 1986 (COMMENCEMENT No. 4) ORDER 1986 (No. 2301) [45p], made under the Agriculture Act 1986 (c.49), s.24(2); brings into force on December 31, 1986 s.10 of the 1986 Act which provides for the abolition of the Egg Authority.

50. Butter. See FOOD AND DRUGS.

51. Cereals
CEREALS CO-RESPONSIBILITY LEVY REGULATIONS 1986 (No. 1233) [£1·40], made under the European Communities Act 1972 (c.68), s.2(2); operative on August 5, 1986; provide for the administration, collection and enforcement of co-responsibility levy imposed in respect of specified cereals.
HOME-GROWN CEREALS AUTHORITY (RATE OF LEVY) ORDER 1986 (No. 1138) [80p], made under the Cereals Marketing Act 1965 (c.14), s.13; operative on August 1, 1986; specifies in respect of home-grown wheat, barley and oats the rate of levy to be raised to meet the amounts apportioned to finance the said Authority.

52. Dairy produce
DAIRY PRODUCE QUOTAS REGULATIONS 1986 (No. 470) [£4·40], made under the European Communities Act 1972 (c.68), s.24(2); operative on March 31, 1986; make provision with respect to dairy produce quotas.

53. Eggs
EGGS AUTHORITY (ABOLITION) ORDER 1986 (No. 2302) [45p], made under the Agriculture Act 1986 (c.49), s.9(2); abolishes the Egg Authority with effect from December 31, 1986.
EGGS AUTHORITY (TRANSFER OF ASSETS) (APPOINTED DATE) ORDER 1986 (No. 1419) [45p], made under the Agriculture Act 1986 (c.49), s.9(5); provides that the appointed date, on which the property, rights and liabilities of the Eggs Authority shall vest in the Ministers, shall be October 1, 1986.

54. Eggs—levies. See FOOD AND DRUGS, § 1562.

55. Environmentally sensitive areas
Orders made under the Agricultural Act 1986 (c.49). s.18(1)(4):
S.I. 1986 Nos. 2249 (South Downs) [£1·40]; 2251, (Wert Fenwith) [£1·40] ; 2252 (Somerset Levels and Moors) [£1·40]; 2253 (Pennine Dales) [£1·40]; 2254 (The Broads) [£1·40]; 2257 (Cambrian Mountains) [£1·40].

56. Feeding stuffs
FEEDING STUFFS REGULATIONS 1986 (No. 177) [£5·40], made under the Agriculture Act 1970 (c.40), ss.66(1), 68(1)(1A)(3), 69(1)(3), 70(1), 73(3), 74(1), 74A, 84; operative on March 10, 1986; replace S.I. 1982 No. 1143 and implement specified Council Directives.

57. Grants
AGRICULTURAL AND HORTICULTURAL CO-OPERATION GRANTS (EXTENSION OF PERIOD) ORDER 1986 (No. 817) [45p], made under the Agriculture Act 1967 (c.22) ss.61(6)

and 62; operative on May 15, 1986, further extends the period within which applications for grant aid purposes connected with co-operation activities in agriculture may be submitted to the organisation "Food from Britain."

58. Heather and grass burning

HEATHER AND GRASS etc. (BURNING) REGULATIONS 1986 (No. 428) [£1·35], made under the Hill Farming Act 1946 (c.73), s.20(1); operative on April 1, 1986; regulate the burning of heather, rough grass, bracken, gorse and vaccinium throughout England and Wales.

59. Hill farming

HILL FARMING (APPOINTED DAY FOR REPEAL) ORDER 1986 (No. 707 (c.19)) [45p], made under the Agriculture Act 1970 (c.40), s.113(3), Sched. 5, Pt. II; appoints May 1, 1986 as the day for the repeal of the provisions relating to hill farming which are set out in Sched. 5, Pt. II to the 1970 Act.

60. Horticultural Produce Act 1986 (c.20)

This Act confers on authorised officers (within the meaning of Pt. III of the Agriculture and Horticulture Act 1964) powers in relation to the movement of horticultural produce and connected purposes.

The Act received the Royal Assent on June 26, 1986 and comes into force on August 26, 1986. It does not extend to Northern Ireland.

61. Horticulture

AGRICULTURE AND HORTICULTURE GRANT (VARIATION) SCHEME 1986 (No. 57) [40p], made under the Agriculture Act 1970 (c.45), ss.28 and 29; operative on January 25, 1986; varies S.I. 1980 No. 1072 and extends to Northern Ireland only.

FARMS AND HORTICULTURE DEVELOPMENT (AMENDMENT) REGULATIONS 1986 (No. 1295) [£1·90], made under the European Communities Act 1972 (c.68), s.2(2); operative on July 26, 1986; amend S.I. 1981 No. 1707.

HORTICULTURAL DEVELOPMENT COUNCIL ORDER 1986 (No. 1110) [£1·90], made under the Industrial Organisation and Development Act 1947 (c.40), ss.1-6, 14; operative on July 1, 1986; establishes a development council for the horticulture industry.

62/3. Levies. See CUSTOMS AND EXCISE, § 955.

64. Milk marketing. See FOOD AND DRUGS, § 1567.

65. Milk production—compensation

MILK (COMMUNITY OUTGOERS SCHEME) (ENGLAND AND WALES) REGULATIONS 1986 (No. 1611) [£2·90], made under the European Communities Act 1972 (c.68), s.2(2); operative on September 19, 1986; implement Council Regulation (EEC) No. 1336/86, which fixes compensation for discontinuation of milk production, and Commission Regulation (EEC) No. 2321/86.

66. Milk quotas

MILK (PARTIAL CESSATION OF PRODUCTION) (ENGLAND AND WALES) SCHEME 1986 (No. 1612) [£2·90], made under the Milk (Cessation of Production) Act 1985 (c.4), s.1; operative on September 19, 1986; provides for the payment of compensation to certain holders of milk quotas who undertake to surrender between 50 per cent. and 95 per cent. of their quota.

MILK QUOTA (CALCULATION OF STANDARD QUOTA) ORDER 1986 (No. 1530) [80p], made under the Agriculture Act 1986 (c.49), Sched. 1, para. 6; operative on September 25, 1986; prescribes the quota per hectare and the average yield per hectare to be taken into account in determining the "standard quota" for the purposes of Sched. 1 to the 1986 Act.

67. Milk quotas—area of production—meaning

[Dairy Produce Quotas Regulations 1984 (S.I. 1984 No. 1047) Sched. 2, para. 6(3)(e).]

On the true construction of para. 6(3)(e) of Sched. 2 to the Dairy Produce Quotas Regulations 1984, an "area used for milk production" is not restricted to current milk production, but includes land used for support of the herd and to provide for future production.

The holding consisted of two farms, A, and B. There was a dairy unit on each farm. B was transferred to transferees. The transferees objected to the minister's division of the quota of milk sales, and to an arbitrator's finding in the matter, on the basis that an area was "used for milk production" if it was used for the current production of milk, under para. 6(3) of Sched. 2 to the Dairy Produce Quotas Regulations 1984. _Held,_ that an "area used for milk production" was not restricted to current milk production, but included used in support of the herd and to provide for future production, such as land used for dry cows and heifers, for buildings and yards of a dairy unit, and land used for dairy or dual-purpose bulls bred for the herd.

PUNCKNOWLE FARMS _v._ KANE [1985] 3 All E.R. 790, P. J. Crawford sitting as a Deputy High Court Judge.

68. Milk quotas—reserve quota—"exceptional hardship" provisions

[Dairy Produce Quotas Regulations 1984 (S.I. 1984 No. 1047) Sched. 2, Pt. II paras. 16, 17] A and his brother, each of whom were partners with their father in an active dairy farm which received a primary milk quota, each completed the purchase of a farm of their own during 1984, and applied before the prescribed date for a share in their region's regional wholesale reserve of quota under the "exceptional hardship" provisions set out in paras. 16 and 17 of Pt. II of Sched. 2 to the Dairy Produce Quotas Regulations 1984. The Dairy Produce Quotas Tribunal rejected the applications because neither applicant would be producing, selling or delivering milk from his respective farm before the end of the first quota year on March 31, 1985. _Held,_ allowing an application to quash the decision, and remitting the matter to a differently constituted tribunal, that (1) it was arguable that A and his brother were "producers" within the regulations, by virtue of their partnership with their father, and could thereby be persons "intending to go into business" within the meaning of para. 17(3)(_b_) of the Schedule; (2) the tribunal had not carried out a "balancing exercise" or paid sufficient attention to the considerations of "exceptional hardship"; (3) the tribunal's decision appeared to impose a "cut-off" date which was not expressly imposed by the regulations: R. _v._ DAIRY PRODUCE QUOTA TRIBUNAL FOR ENGLAND AND WALES, _ex p._ ATKINSON (1985) 276 E.G. 1159, Macpherson J.

69. Overseas development. See INTERNATIONAL LAW.

70. Pesticides

CONTROL OF PESTICIDES REGULATIONS 1986 (No. 1510) [£1·90], made under the Food and Environment Protection Act 1985 (c.48), ss.16(2), 24(3); operative on October 6, 1986 save for reg. 3(3) which is operative on July 1, 1987, reg. 4(1) which is operative on January 1, 1987 and reg. 4(5)(_b_)(i) which is operative on January 1, 1988; make provision for the control of the use of pesticides in Great Britain.

71. Plant breeders

PLANT BREEDERS' RIGHTS (FEES) (AMENDMENT) REGULATIONS 1986 (No. 339) [£1·35], made under the Plant Varieties and Seeds Act 1964 (c.14), ss.9(1), 36; operative on April 1, 1986; amends S.I. 1985 No. 357 by substituting a new schedule of increased fees.

72. Plant health

IMPORT AND EXPORT (PLANT HEALTH) (GREAT BRITAIN) (AMENDMENT) ORDER 1986 (No. 195) [40p], made under the Plant Health Act 1967 (c.8), ss.2, 3(1)(2); operative on March 10, 1986; amends S.I. 1980 No. 420 by omitting references to non-indigenous plant pests and certain other pests.

IMPORT AND EXPORT (PLANT HEALTH) (GREAT BRITAIN) (AMENDMENT) (NO. 2) ORDER 1986 (No. 1135) [45p], made under the Plant Health Act 1967 (c.8), ss.2 and 3(1) and (2); operative on August 1, 1986; prohibits the landing in Great Britain of pea seeds for use as breeder's seed, pre-basic seed or basic seed within the meaning of S.I. 1985 No. 975.

IMPORT AND EXPORT OF TREES, WOOD AND BARK (HEALTH) (GREAT BRITAIN) (AMENDMENT) ORDER 1986 (No. 196) [40p], made under the Plant Health Act 1967, ss.2, 3(1)(2); operative on March 10, 1986; amends S.I. 1980 No. 449 by omitting references to non-indigenous tree pests and certain other pests.

PLANT PESTS (GREAT BRITAIN) (AMENDMENT) ORDER 1986 (No. 194) [40p], made under the Plant Health Act 1967, s.3(1)(2); operative on March 10, 1986; amends S.I. 1980 No. 449 so as to prohibit the keeping without a licence of any plant pest referred to in either Sched. 1 or 2 to S.I. 1980 No. 420 and redefines "non-indigenous plant pest."

RESTRICTION ON MOVEMENT OF SPRUCE WOOD (AMENDMENT) ORDER 1986 (No. 476) [80p], made under the Plant Health Act 1967 (c.8), s.3(1), (2) and (4); operative on

April 8, 1986; adds to the list of areas in respect of which the movement of spruce wood is restricted.

TREE PESTS (GREAT BRITAIN) (AMENDMENT) ORDER 1986 (No. 197) [40p], made under the Plant Health Act 1967, s.3(1)(2); operative on March 10, 1986; amends S.I. 1980 No. 450 so as to prohibit the keeping without a licence of any tree pest referred to in Scheds. 1 or 2 to S.I. 1980 No. 449.

WATERMARK DISEASE (LOCAL AUTHORITIES) (AMENDMENT) ORDER 1986 (No. 1342) [45p], made under the Plant Health Act (c.8), ss.3(1)(2)(4), 5(1) as read with the Agriculture (Miscellaneous Provisions) Act 1972 (c.62), s.20; operative on August 27, 1986; amends S.I. 1974 No. 768 in order to prevent the spread of the said disease.

73. Poultry

LIVE POULTRY RESTRICTIONS (REVOCATION) ORDER 1986 (No. 498) [45p] made under the Animal Health Act 1981 (c.22), ss.1, 8(1), 25, 87(5); operative on March 14, 1986; revokes S.I. 1971 No. 311 as amended.

74. Seeds

SEEDS (FEES) (AMENDMENT) REGULATIONS 1986 (No. 1114) [£1·90], made under the Plant Varieties and Seeds Act 1964 (c.14), s.16(1)(1A)(e)(5)(a)(8); operative on August 1, 1986; amend S.I. 1985 No. 981 by prescribing revised fees.

SEEDS (NATIONAL LISTS OF VARIETIES) (FEES) (AMENDMENT) REGULATIONS 1986 (No. 338) [£1·35], made under the Plant Varieties and Seeds Act 1964 (c.14), s. 16(1)(1A)(e)(8); operative on April 1, 1986; amend S.I. 1980 No. 330 by inserting a new schedule which increases fees.

75. Sheep

SHEEP ANNUAL PREMIUM (AMENDMENT) REGULATIONS 1986 (No. 1894) [45p], made under the European Communities Act 1972 (c.68), s.2(2); operative on November 28, 1986; amend S.I. 1984 No. 2005 in relation applications for the premium.

ALIENS

76. British nationality

BRITISH NATIONALITY (FEES) (AMENDMENT) REGULATIONS 1986 (No. 378) [40p], made under the British Nationality Act 1981 (c.61), s.41(2)(3); operative on April 1, 1986; amends S.I. 1984 No. 230 so as to increase fees payable thereunder.

BRITISH NATIONALITY (HONG KONG) REGULATIONS 1986 (No. 2175) [£1·40], made under the British Nationality Act 1981 (c.61), s.41(1) and (3); operative on July 1, 1987; contains general provisions for carrying into effect the purposes of S.I. 1986 No. 948.

HONG KONG BRITISH NATIONALITY ORDER 1986 (No. 948) [1·40], made under the Hong Kong Act 1985 (c.15), Sched. 1, para. 2; operative on July 1, 1986; makes provisions with regard to the British nationality status persons who are British Dependent Territories citizens by virtue of a connection with Hong Kong.

STATUS OF BRITISH NATIONAL (OVERSEAS) (DEPRIVATION) RULES 1986 (No. 2176) [80p], made under the British Nationality Act 1981 (c.61), s.40(8) as applied by S.I. 1986 No. 948; operative on July 1 1987; make provisions for the practice and procedure of inquiries set up under s.40 of the 1981 Act as upheld by the 1986 Order.

ANIMALS

77. Animals (Scientific Procedures) Act 1986 (c.14)

This Act makes new provisions for the protection of animals used for experimental or other scientific purposes.

The Act received the Royal Assent on May 20, 1986, and comes into force on dates to be appointed.

78. Animals (Scientific Procedures) Act 1986—commencement

ANIMALS (SCIENTIFIC PROCEDURES) ACT (COMMENCEMENT) ORDER 1986 (No. 2088 (c.81)) [45p], made under the Animals (Scientific Procedures) Act 1986 (c.14), s.30(3); brings the Act into force on January 1, 1987.

79. Badgers

BADGERS (CONTROL AREAS) (REVOCATION) ORDER 1986 (No. 2061) [45p], made under the Animal Health Act 1981 (c.22), ss.1, 21(2)(4)(5); operative on December 29, 1986; revokes S.I. 1977 No. 1721.

80. Captive animal—maiming wild animal—whether protection
[Protection of Animals Act 1911 (c.27, s.15(c).] S.15 of the Protection of Animals Act 1911 defines "animal" as "any domestic or captive animal": beating a wild animal so as to maim it and bring it under the domination of the beater does not make it a captive animal. In s.15(c), the word "maimed" should read together with the words ". . . for the purpose of hindering or preventing its escape" (*Rowley* v. *Murphy* [1964] C.L.Y. 84 applied): HUDNOTT v. CAMPBELL, *The Times*, June 27, 1986, D.C.

81. Diseases
BRUCELLOSIS (ENGLAND AND WALES) (AMENDMENT) ORDER 1986 (No. 2295) [45p], made under the Annual Health Act 1981 (c.22), ss.1, 6, 7(1), 28 34(7), 35(3), 87(2); operative on January 1, 1987; amends S.I. 1981 No. 1455 so as to prohibit the keeping of pregnant bovine animals for resale within 30 days of their calving on premises which have not been approved.

DISEASES OF ANIMALS (APPROVED DISINFECTANTS) (AMENDMENT) (NO. 2) ORDER 1986 (No. 1290) [80p], made under the Animal Health Act 1981 (c.22), ss.1, 7(1)(*a*)–(*c*), (2) and 23(*f*) and (*g*); operative on July 31, 1986; amends S.I. 1978 No. 32.

DISEASES OF ANIMALS (APPROVED DISINFECTANTS) (AMENDMENT) ORDER 1986 (No. 5) [£1·85], made under the Animal Health Act 1981 (c.22), ss.1, 7(1)(*a*)–(*c*), (2) and 23 (*f*) and (*g*); operative on January 31, 1986; amends S.I. 1978 No. 32.

IMPORTATION OF SALMONID VISCERA ORDER 1986 (No. 2265) [80p], made under the Animal Health Act 1981 (c.22), ss.1, 10(1)(2); operative on February 1, 1987; prohibits the importation of any viscera of fish of the family *Salmonidae* except without a licence.

INFECTIOUS DISEASES OF POULTRY ORDER 1986 (No. 1755) [£2·40], made under the Animal Health Act 1981 (c.22), ss.1, 7, 8(1), 15(4)(5), 17, 23, 25, 72, 87(5)(*a*), 88(4)(*a*); operative on October 22, 1986; consolidates with amendments S.R. & O. 1936 No. 1297, as amended, and makes provision for the control of diseases of poultry.

82. Feeding stuffs
FEEDING STUFFS (NO. 2) REGULATIONS 1986 (No. 1735) [£6·00], made under the Agriculture Act 1970 (c.40), ss.66(1), 68(1)(1A)(3), 69(1)(3), 70(1), 73(3), 74(1), 74A, 84 and the European Communities Act 1972 (c.68), s.2(2); operative on December 3, 1986; implement various Council and Commission Directives and make provision for the composition, storage, handling, use and supply of specified animal feeding stuffs.

83. Hormone growth promoters. See MEDICINE, § 2116.

84. Marine nature reserves
WILDLIFE AND COUNTRYSIDE (BYELAWS FOR MARINE NATURE RESERVES) REGULATIONS 1986 (No. 143) [80p] made under the Wildlife and Countryside Act 1981 (c.69), s.37(5); operative on March 5, 1986; modifying byelaws made under the Local Government Act 1972 in relation to their application to Marine Nature Reserves.

85. Rabies
RABIES (IMPORTATION OF DOGS, CATS AND OTHER MAMMALS) (AMENDMENT) ORDER 1986 (No. 2062) [45p], made under the Animal Health Act 1981 (c.22), ss.1, 10(1)–(5), 95(1); operative on January 1, 1987; amends S.I. 1974 No. 2211.

86. Scientific procedures
ANIMALS (SCIENTIFIC PROCEDURES) ACT (FEES) ORDER 1986 (No. 2089) [45p], made under the Animals (Scientific Procedures) Act 1986 (c.14), ss.8, 28; operative on January 1, 1987; prescribes fees payable under s.6 of the 1986 Act.

ANIMALS (SCIENTIFIC PROCEDURES) (PROCEDURE FOR REPRESENTATIONS) RULES 1986 (No. 1911) [80p], made under the Animals (Scientific Procedures) Act 1986, s.12(7); operative on December 10, 1986; prescribe the procedure to be followed in the making and consideration of representations made under s.12 of the 1986 Act.

87. Sheep—export
EXPORT OF SHEEP (PROHIBITION) ORDER 1986 (No. 1528) [45p], made under the Animal Health Act 1981 (c.22), s.11; operative on September 4, 1986; prohibits the export of sheep from the United Kingdom which come from designated areas so long as they remain as such.

EXPORT OF SHEEP (PROHIBITION) (NO. 2) ORDER 1986 (No. 1734) [45p], made under the Animal Health Act 1981, s.11; operative on October 8, 1986; prohibits the export of sheep to a Member State of the EEC from designated areas.

88. Sheep scab
SHEEP SCAB ORDER 1986 (No. 862) [£4·90], made under the Animal Health Act 1981 (c.22), ss.1, 7(1), 8(1), 14(1), 15(4), 17(1), 23 and 25; operative on June 3, 1986; consolidates S.I. 1977 No. 1173 and amending instruments.

89. Slaughter—pre-stunning of poultry before slaughter—exemptions
[Slaughter of Poultry Act 1967 (c.24), s.2(*b*); Animal Health and Welfare Act 1984 (c.40).] On appeal against conviction, the appellants (the owner of a poultry slaughterhouse and his Muslim slaughterman) were unable to show that all the three elements required to plead the exemption to pre-stunning of poultry before slaughter were present. These are that without causing unnecessary suffering (1) the slaughter was by the Muslim method, (2) by a Muslim and (3) for the food of Muslims. Although (1) and (2) were not in dispute, the purchaser of a live chicken (an R.S.P.C.A. Chief Inspector wearing a crucifix) was not asked which type of slaughter he required to be carried out on the bird. It was slaughtered by the Muslim method. Evidence showed that he had no intention of using the bird "for the food of Muslims" and would have said so if he had been asked. The proprietor had issued no instructions to his staff to enquire about this. "Local knowledge" of the premises being used only for "Halal" (Muslim slaughter) was not enough since the premises were in the Petticoat Lane market area renowned for tourist interest and milling with people with no local knowledge. *Held*, that unless it could be shown that all three elements existed as a matter of fact, the exemption would not apply and the bird should have been pre-stunned: MALINS *v.* COLE & ATTARD, Knightsbridge Crown Court. (*Ex rel. K. B. Muriel, Solicitor*).

ARBITRATION

90. Abandonment—abandonment by silence and/or inactivity
An arbitration can be abandoned by silence and/or inactivity where the claimant's conduct could reasonably lead the respondent to assume that an offer to abandon had been made; *a fortiori* where the lapse of time was so great that the respondent could reasonably have ceased to give any consideration to the proceedings at all (*The Bremer Vulkan* [1981] C.L.Y. 119, *The Hannah Blumenthal* [1982] C.L.Y. 139, *The Leonidas D* [1985] C.L.Y. 110 considered): GOLDEN BEAR, THE, *Financial Times*, November 14, 1986, Staughton J.

91. Appeal—leave to appeal—finality of judge's decision
[Arbitration Act 1979 (c.42), s.1(3)(*b*) (6A) (as amended by Supreme Court Act 1981 (c.54), s.148(2).]
A judge's decisions to refuse leave to appeal to the High Court from the decision of arbitrators and to refuse leave to appeal to the Court of Appeal were unappealable.
A dispute between the owners and the charterers of a vessel was referred to arbitration before three arbitrators who by a majority decided in favour of the owners. The charterers applied under s.1(3)(*b*) of the Arbitration Act 1979 for leave to appeal to the High Court but this was refused by the judge, as was a later application under s.1(6A) for leave to appeal from his decision to the Court of Appeal. The Court of Appeal declined to hear appeals by the charterers from the judge's decision under either subs. (3)(*b*) or (6A). *Held*, that the discretion of a judge under subs. (3)(*b*) was absolute, and was unappealable by the express terms of subs. (6A). Even if it could be shown that the judge had not exercised his discretion under subs. (3)(*b*) judicially or at all, a refusal of leave to appeal to the Court of Appeal under subs. (6A) was itself final and unappealable. But there was no evidence that the judge in refusing leave under either subsection had failed to exercise his discretion either judicially or at all, and accordingly the Court of Appeal had neither the jurisdiction nor the justification to interfere with the judge's orders. (*Lane v. Esdaile* [1891] A.C. 210, H.L. and in *Racal Communications, Re* [1980] C.L.Y. 273 applied; *Pioneer Shipping v. B.T.P. Tioxide (The Nema)* [1981] C.L.Y. 76 and *Antaios Compania Naviera S.A. v. Salen Rederierna A.B. (The Antaios)* [1984] C.L.Y. 96 considered; *Scherer v. Counting Instruments (Note)* [1986] C.L.Y. 2572, distinguished). *Per* Sir John Donaldson M.R.: It was unfortunate that the recommendation for the establishment of an Arbitration Rules Committee was

rejected. A power in the Arbitration Act 1979 to amend the Act by subordinate legislation might have obviated the need for a great deal of judicial effort, regarded by some as more legislative than adjudicative and the idea of a specialist body with legislative powers seems worth reviving.
ADEN REFINERY CO. *v.* UGLAND MANAGEMENT CO. [1986] 3 W.L.R. 949, C.A.

92. Arbitration clause—summary judgment—arguable point of law—stay. See S.I. SETHIA LINERS *v.* STATE TRADING CORP. OF INDIA, § 2711.

93. Arbitration proceedings—inactivity—mutual abandonment
P and D had arbitration proceedings wherein pleadings were started in mid-1981. Thereafter nothing was done until late 1984 when D's solicitors served a list of documents. D contended that the arbitration had been mutually abandoned. *Held* on the facts and the evidence that there had been a mutual abandonment by implied agreement: GEBR. VAN WEELDE SCHEEPVAARTKANTOR BV *v.* COMPANIA NAVIERA SEA ORIENT S.A. THE AGRABELE [1985] 2 Lloyd's Rep. 496, Evans J.

94. Arbitrator—powers—GAFTA rules
An arbitrator appointed under the GAFTA rules has no power to override the statutory limitation periods: COMPAGNIE EUROPEENE DE CEREALS *v.* TRADAX EXPORT, *The Financial Times,* April 15, 1986, Hobhouse J.

95. Arbitrator—revocation of authority—considerations
[Arbitration Act 1950 (c.27), s.1.] P engaged D to execute extension works to their hotel; the contract was in the RIBA JCT standard form. Shortly afterwards they also engaged D under a separate contract to execute works to the hotel entrance; the second contract did not incorporate JCT conditions. Disputes arose under both contracts and respectively arbitration and High Court proceedings were commenced. At the first meeting before the arbitrator P challenged his jurisdiction but the challenge was rejected by the arbitrator. P then issued an originating summons seeking a stay of the arbitration proceedings and the revocation of the arbitrator's authority pursuant to s.1 of the Arbitration Act 1950. The grounds argued in support of the application were that the existence of both the arbitration and the High Court proceedings in connection with the two closely linked contracts would create unnecessary expense and that P would be unable to join into the arbitration the suppliers of allegedly defective windows. *Held,* that s.1 of the 1950 Act was passed in Order to make the revocation of an arbitrators' authority more difficult and revocation pursuant to the section should only be granted in very exceptional circumstances. The application was based upon considerations of convenience rather than justice and would be refused: PROPERTY INVESTMENTS (DEVELOPMENT) *v.* BYFIELD BUILDING SERVICES (1985) 31 Build.L.R. 47, Steyn J.

96. Arbitrator—whether validly appointed–estoppel
Disputes arose under FOSFA sale contracts. S claimed arbitration, and on the date upon which the time for nomination of an arbitrator expired, B indicated that they had appointed X. X had not, it appeared, in fact been notified of the appointment by B. However, when X was approached by S's arbitrator, he assumed that he had been appointed and asked B for directions. None were forthcoming. X and the other arbitrator proceeded to an award. B contended that the award was not enforceable as X had not been authorised to act as arbitrator. *Held,* dismissing B's appeal, that (1) B had failed to take up an opportunity of repudiating the appointment of X when the latter had sought directions; (2) B was estopped from assailing the authority of X: LEGUMBRES S.A.C.I.F.I.A. *v.* CENTRAL SUL [1986] 1 Lloyd's Rep. 401, C.A.

97. Award—arbitrators stating grounds—whether reasoned award—application for further reasons
[Arbitration Act 1979 (c.42), s.1(5)(6).]
Where an arbitrator's award did not constitute a "reasoned award" within s.1(5) of the Arbitration Act 1979, the court cannot order the arbitrator to state further reasons.
A dispute between buyers and sellers of a vessel was referred to arbitration. The arbitrator published an interim final award, and at a later date sent the parties privileged reasons for the decision. The sellers applied for an order under s.1(5) directing the arbitrators to state further reasons for the award. The judge declined to make the order. *Held,* dismissing the appeal, that the arbitrators' decision did not constitute a "reasoned award" within the meaning of s.1(5), and that s.1(6) therefore

deprived the court of jurisdiction to order the arbitrators to state reasons for the award (dicta in *Warde* v. *Feedex International Inc.* [1984] C.L.Y. 111 referred to). TRAVE SCHIFFAHRTSGESELLSCHAFT mbh v. NINEMIA MARITIME CORP. [1986] 2 W.L.R. 773, C.A.

98. **Award—no reasons asked for—misunderstanding—reasons sought—whether "special reason" for making order—whether appealable point of law**
[Arbitration Act 1979 (c.42), s.1(5), (6).]
Both parties to an arbitration indicated to commercial arbitrators that they did not want a reasoned award. In fact O's solicitors were under standing instructions to ask for reasons and had failed to instruct counsel accordingly. O lost, and wanted to appeal. They therefore made an application under s.1(5)(6) of the Arbitration Act 1979, the burden being on them to demonstrate a "special reason" why reasons should be ordered. *Held*, that (1) an internal misunderstanding was right at the threshold of providing a special reason; (2) it was right that the Court should look to see if there was a realistic prospect of the case containing an appealable point of law. The case, however, turned on a question of fact and there was no basis for exercising discretion in favour of O: GEBR. VAN WEELDE SCH. B.V. v. SOCIÉTÉ INDUSTRIELLE D'ACIDE PHOSPHORIQUE ET DÉNGRAIS; DYNASHINKY, THE [1986] 1 Lloyd's Rep. 435, Hobhouse J.

99. **Award—remission—procedural mishap—fresh evidence**
[Arbitration Act 1950 (c.27), s.22.] A charterparty dispute between O and C was referred to arbitration. Both parties made submissions in 1984. On March 25, 1985, the arbitrator sent a telex to both parties stating that there was no proof of payments allegedly made by C to O, but requesting C to adduce such proof in the meantime. On April 1, 1985, the arbitrator announced that he would publish his award on April 4, 1985. On April 3, 1985, C informed their solicitors that the relevant documentary proof was contained in a letter sent to the solicitors dated March 10, 1985. C's solicitors requested copies, but neglected to apply for an adjournment. On April 4, 1985, the arbitrator published his award. On April 23, 1985, C's solicitors received copies of March 10, 1985 letter. C applied for an order for remission of the award under the Arbitration Act 1950, s.22 on the grounds of procedural mishap and fresh evidence. *Held*, that (1) the arbitrator was not acting under a misunderstanding. It was irrelevant that the arbitrator may erroneously have supposed that he had the totality of the evidence which the parties wished to put before him. The jurisdiction to remit on this basis will not be exercised where the misunderstanding arises from the failure by the party who seeks remission to use the information that was in his possession; (2) for a remission to be justified on the basis of fresh evidence, the evidence must be such as would have been likely to have had a substantial effect on the decision of the arbitrator and must have been unavailable to the party, at the hearing. The first criterion was not satisfied on the facts, and the second condition also failed, as the relevant evidence was in C's possession at the time submissions in the arbitration were made: COMPAGNIE NATIONALE ALGERIENNE DE NAVIGATION v. HECATE SHIPPING Co. [1985] 2 Lloyd's Rep. 588, Leggatt J.

100. **Award—retrospective effect**
[Arbitration Act 1950 (c.27), s.19A as introduced by Administration of Justice Act 1982 (c.53), s.15 and Sched. 1.] The section acts retrospectively: FOOD CORPORATION OF INDIA v. MARASTRO CIA NAVIERA SA, (1986) 136 New L.J. 607, C.A.

101. **Award—sale of goods—construction—whether certificate of weight and quality conclusive—FOFSA time limt**
By a sale contract dated July 5, 1982, S, the original sellers, sold to T, the intermediate sellers, a quantity of Malaysian palm fatty acid distillate in sound second-hand drums. The contract provided "confirmed shipped quality/shipped weight final". The next day T sold the goods to the buyers P, under a contract providing "shipped weight and quality to be final as per certificate of independent surveyor." Both contracts provided under the heading "quality" "TSM 9.5%; M & I max. 3 %, FFA min 70%" and incorporated FOFSA 53 and the FOFSA arbitration rules. Superintendents at the local port subsequently issued a "certificate of weight and quality" which showed that the samples of the product analysed complied with the sale contract. The goods were shipped, but on arrival at destination it was found that the contents of some drums contained palm acid oil and a solid black substance, and that some drums were empty. P rejected the goods and the disputes were referred to

arbitration. *Held,* allowing the appeals, that (1) the superintendent's certificate certified the results of their chemical analysis and not the nature of the commodity itself. The certificates were only final and conclusive on matters covered by the quality clause *viz.* the percentage items of constituent , and not the commodity itself; (2) this was a claim other than on "quality and/or condition" wither FOFSA Rule 2, as it was a claim for non-compliance with description. The FOFSA time bar was therefore inapplicable: DAUDRUY (CH) VAN CAUWENBERGHE *v.* TROPICAL PRODUCTS SALES S.A. [1986] 1 Lloyd's Rep 535, Hirst J.

102. Award—setting aside—procedural mishap—failure of arbitrators to permit full argument or damages

A dispute under a voyage charterparty was submitted to arbitrators for resolution. At a first hearing the arbitrators were to deal with liability only. They found against O, but also made certain findings on quantum. When they proceeded to an interim hearing on quantum they relied on those earlier findings. O applied to have both interim awards set aside. *Held,* allowing O's appeal on the award on quantum, that the tribunal had wrongfully precluded O from making all his arguments on mitigation and the award would be set aside: FIFTH KAMBOS SHIPPING CORPORATION OF MONROVIA *v.* EURICO S.p.A: THE DONA MARGARITA [1986] 2 Lloyd's Rep. 135, Gatehouse J.

103. Commencement of arbitration out of time—extension of time

P entered into certain contracts of sale with D. Each contract contained a London arbitration clause and contained a 28 day period in which claims had to be brought. There were substantial shortfalls in the shipments. P dishonoured bills of exchange and D commenced an action under those bills. P then sought an extension of time under s.27 of the Arbitration Act 1950. D obtained summary judgment and P's application was dismissed. *Held,* allowing P's appeal, that this was a case where undue hardship would be caused if an extension of time was not given. The sum at stake was large and no prejudice had been caused to D in the presentation of this case: GRAHAM H. DAVIES (U.K.) *v.* RICH (MARC) & Co. [1985] 2 Lloyd's Rep. 423, C.A.

104. County court—procedure—cross examination. See CHILTON *v.* SAGA HOLIDAYS § 455.

105. Delay in prosecution of reference—abandonment—estoppel

By two contracts subject to the arbitration rules of GAFTA 125, P agreed to sell to D quantities of tapioca chips c.i.f. Dunkirk, shipment to be in January and February 1979. P failed to appropriate the requisite goods to their contracts with D, and declared themselves in default. The dispute between D and P was referred to arbitration, the respective arbitrators being appointed on March 15 and March 19, 1979. In support of their claim, D submitted three invoices to P on July 31, 1979, which were rejected by P on August 9, 1979. Four years of inactivity ensued. On August 19, 1983, D informed P that their arbitrator was no longer able to act. On August 22, 1983, P replied that there was no arbitration in existence. Between August and October 1983, there were various communications between P and D concerning the claims, but no reference was made to abandonment of the arbitration. On May 25, 1984, D informed P that they would apply to GAFTA for the appointment of an arbitrator. On June 18, 1984, P replied that there was no claim for arbitration: *Held,* that (1) to rely on abandonment, P must show D's conduct amounted to an offer to abandon, and that P, by their conduct, accepted D's offer; (2) such an offer to abandon was not supported on the evidence; silence and inactivity between August 1979 and August 1983 did not clearly suggest an intention to abandon on the part of D, and was not reasonably so to be understood. Such conduct was most consistent with dilatoriness on the part of D; (3) P's conduct did not amount to an unequivocal acceptance of an offer to abandon, as their conduct in "lying low" was equally consistent with a belief that the references were still alive; (4) consequently there was no consensual abandonment. Neither was there an estoppel in the absence of a clear and unequivocal representation by conduct by D and in the absence of reliance by P: CIE FRANCAISE D'IMPORTATION ET DE DISTRIBUTION S.A *v.* DEUTSCHE CONTI; [1985] 2 Lloyd's Rep. 592, Bingham J.

106. Extension of time—arbitrators' jurisdiction to decide—Court's discretion

[Arbitration Act 1950 (c.27), s.27.]

The GAFTA 125 rules contain a provision whereby, if a claim is brought out of time, it shall be waived and absolutely barred unless the arbitrators in their absolute discretion, or the Board of Appeal, in their absolute discretion determine otherwise. S commenced their claim out of time and both arbitral tribunals held that the time bar was applicable. S then sought an extension of time pursuant to s.27 of the Arbitration Act 1950. B contended that s.27 could not apply where the arbitrators had jurisdiction to determine the issue of time bar. *Held,* that the existence of a jurisdiction in the arbitrators did not preclude the Court from exercising a discretion pursuant to s.27. In the present case, however, that jurisdiction would not be exercised in favour of S: EUROPEAN GRAIN & SHIPPING *v.* DANSK LANDBRUGS GROVVARESLSKAB [1985] 1 Lloyd's Rep. 163, Leggatt J.

107. Fees—of arbitrators—fees of legal advisors to arbitrators
[Arbitration Act 1950 (c.27), ss.18, 19.] P and D had a dispute which was arbitrated by the Board of Appeal of the Cocoa Association. The board members were very senior traders. The fees of the board were disputed. They consisted of the board members own fees at an hourly rate of £75, and the fee of their legal advisor at an hourly rate of £100, and a secretarial charge of £875. The total was £15,500, of which £8,750 was attributable to the legal advisor. *Held,* that the board members' fees had not been shown to be unreasonable, but they had not properly considered the legal advisor's fee, nor the secretarial charge since they were not aware of the charge of £200 per hour for Sunday work, nor of the charge of £150 for evening work, nor of the secretarial charge at the time that they considered the fees. In view of the size of the total bill the board should have made closer inquiries to ensure that the fees were fair and reasonable. The second part of the bill would be set aside (*Government of Ceylon v. Chandris* [1963] C.L.Y. 136 approved): KURKJIAN (SN) (COMMODITY BROKERS) *v.* MARKETING EXCHANGE FOR AFRICA, *Financial Times,* June 11, 1986, Staughton J.

108. Foreign awards
ARBITRATION (FOREIGN AWARDS) ORDER 1986 (No. 949) [45p], made under the Arbitration Act 1975 (c.3), s.7(2); operative on June 26, 1986; specifies Malaysia as a State which is a party to the New York Convention on the Recognition and Enforcement of Foreign Arbitral Awards (Cmnd. 6419).

109. Injunction—delay in prosecution—whether mutual abandonment of reference
In 1975 arbitrators were appointed in respect of demurrage claims brought by O against C. Nothing was done by O to prosecute the claims and in 1978 the arbitrators closed their files. There were no further communications between the parties until 1983. When O sought to prosecute the claims in 1983 C claimed a declaration that the arbitration had been abandoned by mutual consent. *Held,* on the facts and on the evidence that there was no implied agreement to abandon the reference and C had failed to show any prejudice arising out of the delay: FOOD CORP. OF INDIA *v.* ANTCLIZO SHIPPING CORP. [1986] 1 Lloyd's Rep. 181, Evans J.

110. Interest on award—enforcement of interest on award as judgment—debt
Arbitration Act 1950 (c.27), ss.20, 26; Supreme Court Act 1981 (c.54), s.35A.]
Arbitrators awarded P a sum inclusive of interest. D did not pay, and the award thereby incurred interest at the judgment rate pursuant to s.20 of the Arbitration Act 1950. P sought to enforce the award in Germany. D paid the principal sum but not the interest thereon. P could not recover the interest in Germany, and therefore sought a judgment for the interest under s.26 of the Arbitration Act 1950, together with interest thereon to date. D contended that such interest would be compound interest. *Held,* that there was no substance in the defence. D's liability was for a debt together with interest thereon and fell within s.35A of the Supreme Court Act 1981: COASTAL STATES TRADING (U.K.) *v.* MEBRO MINERALOEL GmbH [1986] 1 Lloyd's Rep. 465, Hobhouse J.

111. Jurisdiction—agreement not to arbitrate. See PARTINGTON & SON (BUILDERS) *v.* TAMESIDE METROPOLITAN BOROUGH COUNCIL, § 225.

112. London Bar Arbitration Scheme. See PRACTICE, § 2668.

113. Remission to arbitrators—scope of remission—arbitrator's jurisdiction
An award was remitted by the Court of Appeal to arbitrators so that they could investigate a further issue in a safe port arbitration, namely whether there was a sufficient turning circle for the vessel in that port. O, at whose instance the remission had been granted, amended their pleadings not only to include the "turning circle point" but also to raise other contentions as to the unsafety of the port. C contended

that those other contentions were outwith the jurisdiction of the arbitrators. *Held,* that C was correct. The jurisdiction of the arbitrators had been revived for one limited purpose only: INTERBULK *v.* AIDEN SHIPPING CO.: THE VIMEIRA (No. 3) [1986] 2 Lloyd's Rep. 75, Steyn J.

114. Rent review—application for leave to appeal. See LUCAS INDUSTRIES *v.* WELSH DEVELOPMENT AGENCY, § 1907.

115. Rent review—extension of time. See PITTALIS *v.* SHEREFETTIN, § 1906.

116. Sealed open offer—whether offer lapsed

O let their vessel to C. There was a collision and C made certain deductions of hire. Disputes were referred to arbitration, and C made an open offer to settle the dispute for 100,000 DM. During the course of the hearing it became apparent that not all issues could be resolved. The arbitrator made an interim declaratory award in favour of C. O then purported to accept the open offer. C contended that it was no longer open: *Held,* that the offer lapsed when the major part of the claim had been determined by decision and the making of such an award signalled the end of a reasonable time for acceptance of the award: KRUPP HANDEL GmbH *v.* INTERMARE TRANSPORT GmbH: THE ELBE ORE [1986] 1 Lloyd's Rep. 176, Bingham J.

117. Sole arbitrator—whether validly appointed

[Arbitration Act 1950 (c.27), s.7.]

A dispute arose between O and C over the charter of a vessel. O appointed their arbitrator and gave C seven days notice in which to appoint their arbitrator. C did not reply and the arbitrator proceeded to make a default award against C. O claimed payment, and C applied for a declaration that the arbitrator had no jurisdiction and that the award was not binding: *Held,* that the declaration would be granted as O had never appointed the arbitrator as sole arbitrator in accordance with s.7(*b*) of the Arbitration Act 1950: MINISTRY OF FOOD, GOVERNMENT OF BANGLADESH *v.* BENGAL LINER; THE BENGAL PRIDE [1986] 1 Lloyd's Rep. 167, Leggatt J.

118. Stay of proceedings—whether dispute at date of writ

[H.K.] D engaged P as a main contractor to construct some industrial buildings. On July 7, 1984 the architect issued a certificate for H.K. $7.2 million which under the terms of the contract was payable within 14 days. No payment was made when on September 10, 1984 P issued a writ for the amount of the certificate. The architect then issued a revised certificate on September 19, 1984 reducing the sum due from HK $7.2 million to HK $4.9 million. The reduction was in respect of plumbing and drainage works allegedly overvalued and an instruction issued in relation to a cement/sand screed for which there was no written instruction until September 19, 1984. P applied for summary judgment and D issued a summons to stay the action under s.6 of the Arbitration Ordinance of Hong Kong. *Held,* that at the time of the issue of the writ there was no dispute because the evidence showed that the issues raised by D in relation to the plumbing and drainage or cement/sand screed had not by then been raised with P. Accordingly the court had no jurisdiction to stay the proceedings. On Ord. 14 application D had shown a triable issue only in relation to the plumbing and drainage issue and judgment would be given in the amount of the original certificate less the amount of the alleged overvalue of the plumbing and drainage works: LEUNG (PETER) CONSTRUCTION CO. *v.* TAI POON (1985) 4 Constr.L.J. 299, H.K. C.A.

119. Written arbitration clause—partially oral contract—whether binding

[Arbitration Act 1975 (c.3), s.7.] A contract was made partly orally and partly in writing. The written part contained an arbitration clause. *Held,* that this was "an agreement in writing . . . to submit to arbitration" within the meaning of s.7 of the Arbitration Act 1975. It was not necessary by some writing that a party has assented for the arbitration clause to be binding. If a document with a written arbitration clause forms part of a contract, a party's oral assent to arbitration is sufficient (*The Saint Raphael* [1985] C.L.Y. 120 applied): ZAMBIA STEEL & BUILDINGS SUPPLIES *v.* JAMES CLARK & EATON, *The Financial Times,* August 15, 1986, C.A.

ARMED FORCES

120. Air force—rules of procedure

RULES OF PROCEDURE (AIR FORCE) (AMENDMENT) RULES 1986 (No. 2125) [£1·40], made under the Air Force Act 1955 (c.19), ss.103, 106 and 209; operative on January 1, 1987; amend S.I. 1972 No. 419.

121. Armed Forces Act 1986 (c.21)

This Act continues the Army Act 1955, the Air Force Act 1955 and the Naval Discipline Act 1957 and amends those Acts and the Armed Forces Acts of 1976 and 1981. The amendments deal with certain offences, sentences, applications of the Acts to civilians and reserve liability of women.

The Act received the Royal Assent on June 26, 1986.

122. Armed Forces Act 1986—commencement

ARMED FORCES ACT 1986 (COMMENCEMENT NO. 1) ORDER 1986 (No. 2071 (c.80)) [45p], made under the Armed Forces Act 1986 (c.21), s.17; brings into force on December 30, 1986 sections 14 and 16(2) (in part) of the 1986 Act.

ARMED FORCES ACT 1986 (COMMENCEMENT No. 2) ORDER (No. 2124 (c.83)) [45p], made under the Armed Forces Act 1986 (c.21), s.17; brings into force on January 1, 1987 sections 2–8), 10–13, 16 (so far as it is not already in force) of the 1986 Act.

123. Army

RULES OF PROCEDURE (ARMY) (AMENDMENT) RULES 1986 (No. 2126) [£1·40], made under the Army Act 1955 (c.18), ss.103, 106 and 209; operative on January 1, 1987; amend S.I. 1972 No. 316.

124. Court-martial—jurisdiction—offence committed before transfer or discharge

[Air Force Act 1955 (c.19), ss.12(1), 13(1).]

Where an airman commits an offence in the period between being given a discharge certificate and his actual discharge, he will be liable to air force law if those responsible for his discharge have a reasonable suspicion of the commission of the offence before his actual discharge.

G, a regular airman in the R.A.F. was given a discharge certificate on June 9 and began terminal leave before his transfer to the reserve on July 12. While on leave he stole a credit card from a fellow airman, used it and then admitted the offences under interrogation by R.A.F. police on July 7. His transfer to the reserve was cancelled. At his trial before a court-martial G offered a plea to the jurisdiction in that he had ceased to be a regular airman on July 12 and was not subject to air force law. The plea was rejected and G pleaded guilty. His appeal was rejected. *Held,* dismissing the appeal, that under s.13(1) of the 1955 Act an airman had "become liable . . . to be proceeded against for an offence" if before the date of his discharge a transfer to the reserve those responsible for his discharge or transfer were aware that there was a reasonable suspicion that he had committed a relevant offence; since G had admitted the offences before July 12 he had become liable to proceedings under s.13(1) and therefore remained subject to air force law under s.12(1).

R. *v.* GARTH [1986] 2 W.L.R. 80, H.L.

125. Court-martial—retrial—convening order

[Army Act 1955 (c.18), s.134(3).] A convening order is "issued" within the meaning of s.134(3) of the Army Act 1955 if it is signed by the convening officer and directs a court to convene at a particular time and place. The convening officer has power to order a retrial. When a commanding officer refuses to confirm a finding of guilt, it is as though the court-martial has never taken place. There can therefore be a retrial without the laying of a fresh charge: R. *v.* AMOS, *The Times*, March 18, 1986, Courts-Martial Appeal Court.

126. Courts-martial

COURTS-MARTIAL AND STANDING CIVILIAN COURTS (ADDITIONAL POWERS ON TRIAL OF CIVILIANS) (AMENDMENT) REGULATIONS 1986 (No. 1241) [45p], made under the Army Act 1955 (c.18), Sched. 5A, para. 17, the Air Force Act 1955 (c.19), Sched. 5A, para. 17 and the Naval Discipline Act 1957 (c.53), Sched. 4A, para. 17; operative on January 1, 1987; increases the maximum and minimum number of hours to be worked under a Community Service Order.

127. Museums. See LITERARY AND SCIENTIFIC INSTITUTIONS.

128. Pensions. See PENSIONS AND SUPERANNUATION, § 2509.

129. Police and Criminal Evidence Act 1984. See CRIMINAL LAW, § 674.

130. Protection of Military Remains Act 1986 (c.35)

This Act protects from unauthorised interference the remains of military aircraft and vessels that have crashed, sunk or been stranded and of associated human remains.

The Act received the Royal Assent on July 8, 1986 and comes into force on September 8, 1986. It extends to Northern Ireland.

131. Reserve and auxiliary forces

RESERVE FORCES ACTS 1980 AND 1982 (ISLE OF MAN) ORDER 1986 (No. 2026) [80p], made under the Reserve Forces Act 1980 (c.9), s.158(3); operative on December 23, 1986; extends to the Isle of Man the Reserve Forces Acts 1980 and 1982.

RESERVE FORCES (SAFEGUARD OF EMPLOYMENT) ACT 1985 (ISLE OF MAN) ORDER 1986 (No. 2025) [80p], made under the Reserve Forces (Safeguard of Employment) Act 1985 (c.17), s.22 operative on December 23, 1986; extends to the Isle of Man the 1985 Act.

132. Terms of service

ARMY TERMS OF SERVICE REGULATIONS 1986 (No. 2072) [£1·90], made under the Armed Forces Act 1966 (c.45), s.2; operative on January 1, 1987; re-enacts S.I. 1985 No. 1819 with modifications which relate to women, recruits and persons entering under the Army Youth Short Service Scheme.

ROYAL AIR FORCE TERMS OF SERVICE (AMENDMENT) REGULATIONS 1986 (No. 2073) [45p], made under the Armed Forces Act 1966, s.2; operative on January 1, 1987; amend S.I. 1985 No. 1820 enabling a person to enlist under the Royal Air Force Youth Training Scheme for either 12 months or two years.

ROYAL NAVY TERMS OF SERVICE (RATINGS) (AMENDMENT) REGULATIONS 1986 (No. 2074) [45p], made under the Armed Forces Act 1966, s.2; operative on January 1, 1987; amend S.I. 1982 No. 834 by enabling a person to enter into naval service under the Royal Navy Youth Training Scheme for either 12 months or two years.

ATOMIC ENERGY

133. Atomic Energy Authority Act 1986 (c.3)

This Act puts the finances of the United Kingdom Atomic Energy Authority on a trading fund basis.

It received the Royal Assent on February 17, 1986 and comes into force on April 1, 1986.

134. Nuclear installations

NUCLEAR INSTALLATIONS (HONG KONG) (AMENDMENT) ORDER 1986 (No. 2018) [45p], made under the Nuclear Installations Act 1965 (c.57), s.28, and the Energy Act 1983 (c.25), s.33; operative on November 25, 1986; provides for the Hong Kong Secretary for Monetary Affairs to certify the Hong Kong dollar equivalent of amounts expressed in special drawing rights for the purposes of S.I. 1983 No. 1890.

135. Radioactive substances

RADIOACTIVE SUBSTANCES (SUBSTANCES OF LOW ACTIVITY) EXEMPTION ORDER 1986 (No. 1002) [80p], made under the Radioactive Substances Act 1960 (c.34), ss.2(6), 6(5), 7(4), 20(*a*); operative on July 14, 1986; provides for exemptions and exclusions under the 1960 Act in respect of certain substances of low radioactivity.

AUCTIONEERS AND VALUERS

136. Exclusion clause—construction—whether negligence

P entrusted to D in 1977 for sale by auction a valuable and uninsured diamond, and signed a form which stated, *inter alia*, ". . . whilst you take all reasonable care in handling the property . . . you are not responsible for loss or damage of any kind whether caused by negligence or otherwise . . ." Whilst on view on the day before the auction the diamond was stolen, despite the presence of security guards, whilst the attention of D's single porter was momentarily distracted by the need to serve another customer. The judge held that the exemption clause had been incorporated in the contract and served to exclude liability for negligence on D's part, and that D had not in any case been negligent. *Held*, dismissing P's appeal, that (1) D's security system for the viewing of jewellery had in 1977 not been reasonably safe, since it was inevitable that the single porter would from time to time have to divert his attention from one customer in order to deal with others; (2) however the exemption clause was clear and adequate to exclude liability for negligence by D or those for whom D was responsible: SPRIGGS *v.* SOTHEBY PARKE BERNET & Co. (1986) 278 E.G. 969, C.A.

AVIATION

137. Aerodromes

AERODROMES (DESIGNATION) (BYELAWS) ORDER 1986 (No. 311) [40p], made under the Civil Aviation Act 1982 (c.16), s.33(1); operative on April 1, 1986; designates specified aerodromes for the purposes of s.33 of the 1982 Act.

AERODROMES (DESIGNATION) (DETENTION AND SALE OF AIRCRAFT) ORDER 1986 (No. 312) [40p], made under the Civil Aviation Act 1982 (c.16), s.88(10); operative on April 1, 1986; designate specified aerodromes for the purposes of s.88 of the 1982 Act.

AERODROMES (DESIGNATION) (DETENTION AND SALE OF AIRCRAFT) (No. 2) ORDER 1986 (No. 1347) [45p], made under the Civil Aviation Act 1982 (c.16), s.88(10); operative on August 5, 1986; designates certain airports as aerodromes to which s.88 applies (the person owning or managing the said aerodrome must detain and sell aircraft where default is made in the payment of airport charges).

AERODROMES (DESIGNATION) (FACILITIES FOR CONSULTATION) ORDER 1986 (No. 1348) [45p], made under the Civil Aviation Act 1982, s.35; operative on August 5, 1986; designates certain airports for the purposes of s.35 of the 1982 Act (duty to provide adequate facilities for consultation for users of the aerodrome).

138. Air navigation

AIR NAVIGATION (AIRCRAFT AND AIRCRAFT ENGINE EMISSIONS) ORDER 1986 (No. 599) [£1·40], made under the Civil Aviation Act 1982 (c.16), ss.60, 61, 101, 102; operative on May 1, 1986; make provision in relation to engine emissions from gas turbine engines manufactured after May 1, 1986.

AIR NAVIGATION (AMENDMENT) ORDER 1986 (No. 2238) [£1·40], made under the Civil Aviation Act 1982 (c.16), s.60, 61, 102; operative on January 27, 1987; amend S.I. 1985 No. 1643.

AIR NAVIGATION (DANGEROUS GOODS) (AMENDMENT) REGULATIONS 1986 (No. 2129) [45p], made under S.I. 1985 No. 1643; operative on January 1, 1987; amend S.I. 1955 No. 1939.

AIR NAVIGATION (RESTRICTION OF FLYING) (FARNBOROUGH) REGULATIONS 1986 (No. 1218) [45p], made under S.I. 1985 No. 1643; operative on August 26, 1986; impose restrictions on flying in the specified airspace during the exhibition of flying at Farnborough Aerodrome.

RULES OF THE AIR AND AIR TRAFFIC CONTROL (AMENDMENT) REGULATIONS 1986 (No. 544) [80p], made under S.I. 1985 No. 1643; operative on April 10, 1986; amend S.I. 1985 No. 1714.

139. Aircraft engine noise

AIR NAVIGATION (NOISE CERTIFICATION) ORDER 1986 (No. 1304) [£2·90], made under the Civil Aviation Act 1982 (c.16), ss.60, 61, 101, 102; operative on August 1, 1986; replaces S.I. 1984 No. 368.

140. Airport shops

EXETER AIRPORT SHOPS ORDER 1986 (No. 981) [45p], made under the Shops (Airports) Act 1962 (c.35), s.1(2); operative on June 16, 1986; designates Exeter Airport for the purposes of the 1962 Act.

141. Airports

AIRPORTS ACT 1986 (MODIFICATIONS IN SCHEDULE 4 TO THE TRANSPORT ACT 1968) ORDER 1986 (No. 1801) [£1·90], made under the Airports Act 1986 (c.31), s.75(5); modifies Sched. 4 of the 1968 Act for the purposes of its application to transfers under s.15(7) of the 1986 Act.

AIRPORTS ACT 1986 (NOMINATED COMPANY) ORDER 1986 (No. 1229) [45p], made under the Airports Act 1986 (c.31), s.2(2); provides that the company nominated by the Secretary of State to take over the property, rights and liabilities to which the British Airports Authority was entitled is BAA plc.

ECONOMIC REGULATION OF AIRPORTS (DESIGNATION) ORDER 1986 (No. 1502) [45p], made under the Airports Act 1986 (c.31), operative on October 1, 1986; designates Gatwick, Heathrow, Manchester and Stansted airports for the purposes of s.40 of the 1986 Act.

142. Airports Act 1986 (c.31)

This Act provides for the dissolution of the British Airports Authority and the vesting of its property, rights and liabilities in a company nominated by the Secretary of State. It provides for the reorganisation of other airport undertakings in the public sector, the regulation of the use of airports and imposition of economic controls at certain airports. It makes other amendments to the law relating to airports, and provides for control of capital expenditure by local authority airport undertakings.

The Act received the Royal Assent on July 8, 1986. Ss.1, 3, 75, 76(1)–(4), 77(5) (6), 79–82, 85 came into force on July 8, 1986. Other sections of the Act came into force on various appointed days.

143. Airports Act 1986—commencement
AIRPORTS ACT 1986 (COMMENCEMENT NO. 1 AND APPOINTED DAY) ORDER 1986 (No. 1228 (C.38)) [80p], made under the Airports Act 1986 (c.31), ss.2(1), 79(5), 85(5)(6); brings into force on July 31, 1986 Pt. V, s.83(1) and Scheds. 2, 4, paras. 1 and 2, and brings into force on August 1, 1986 ss.63–66, 83(1)(5), Scheds. 3, 4, para. 10, 6, Pt. II.

AIRPORTS ACT 1986 (COMMENCEMENT NO. 2) ORDER 1986 (No. 1487 (C.52)) [80p], made under the Airports Act 1986 (c.31), s.85(5)(6); brings into force on October 1, 1986 Pt. IV (including Sched. 1), sections 67, 69, 73, 74, 83(1)(3)(5), Sched. 4, paras. 3–8, 6, Pt. II.

144. Airports—local government reorganisation. See LOCAL GOVERNMENT, § 2046.

145. Air travel reserve fund
AIR TRAVEL RESERVE FUND (WINDING UP OF FUND AND DISSOLUTION OF AGENCY) ORDER 1986 (No. 155) [40p], made under the Air Travel Reserve Fund Act 1975 (c.36), s.6; operative on February 27, 1986; provides for the winding up of the said Fund.

146. British Aerospace Act 1980
BRITISH AEROSPACE ACT 1980 (GOVERNMENT SHAREHOLDING) ORDER 1986 (No. 848) [45p], made under the British Aerospace Act 1980 (c.26), s.7(4); operative on June 13, 1986; revokes S.I. 1981 No. 622 and reduces the Government's target investment limit in British Aerospace to nil.

147. Carriage by air
CARRIAGE BY AIR (STERLING EQUIVALENTS) ORDER 1986 (No. 1778) [45p], made under the Carriage by Air Act 1961 (c.27), s.4(4); operative on November 7, 1986; specifies the sterling equivalents of amounts expressed as gold francs as the limit of an air carrier's liability under the 1929 Warsaw Convention, as amended.

148. Civil aviation
AIR NAVIGATION (INVESTIGATION OF AIR ACCIDENTS INVOLVING CIVIL AND MILITARY AIRCRAFT OR INSTALLATIONS) REGULATIONS 1986 (No. 1953) [£2·90], made under the Civil Aviation Act 1982 (c.16), s.75; operative on December 8, 1986; re-enact S.I. 1969 No. 1437 with amendments.

CIVIL AVIATION ACT 1982 (GUERNSEY) ORDER 1986 (No. 1162) [45p], made under the Civil Aviation Act 1982 (c.16), s.108(1); operative on October 1, 1986; extends to Guernsey s.97(1) of the 1982 Act, which extends to seaplanes the power contained in the Merchant Shipping Act 1894 to make regulations for the prevention of collisions at sea.

CIVIL AVIATION AUTHORITY (ECONOMIC REGULATION OF AIRPORTS) REGULATIONS 1986 (No. 1544) [£1·90], made under the Civil Aviation Act 1982 (c.16), s.7(2) and the Airports Act 1986 (c.31), ss.36(3), 38(2)–(6), 41(6), 48(7) and 51(5) and (7); operative on October 1, 1986; prescribe procedures to be followed by the Civil Aviation Authority in exercising its functions in relation to the economic regulation of airports under Pt. IV of the 1986 Act.

CIVIL AVIATION (CANADIAN NAVIGATION SERVICES) REGULATIONS 1986 (No. 1202) [£1·40], made under the Civil Aviation Act 1982, ss.73 and 74; operative on August 11, 1986; increase charges for certain air navigation services provided by or on behalf of the Government of Canada.

CIVIL AVIATION (JOINT FINANCING) (FOURTH AMENDMENT) REGULATIONS 1986 (No. 2153) [80p], made under the Civil Aviation Act 1982, ss.73, 74; operative on January 1, 1987; further amends S.I. 1952 No. 1784.

CIVIL AVIATION (NAVIGATION SERVICES CHARGES) REGULATIONS 1986 (No. 403) [£1·85], made under the Civil Aviation Act 1982 (c.16), ss.73, 74; operative on April 1, 1986; consolidate with amendments S.I. 1981 No. 362, as amended.

CIVIL AVIATION (NAVIGATION SERVICES (CHARGES) (AMENDMENT) REGULATIONS 1986 (No. 2170) [45p], made under the Civil Aviation Act 1982 (c.16), ss.73, 74; operative on January 12, 1987; amend S.I. 1986 No. 403.

CIVIL AVIATION (ROUTE CHARGES FOR NAVIGATION SERVICES) (THIRD AMENDMENT) REGULATIONS 1986 (No. 2120) [£1·40], made under the Civil Aviation Act 1982, ss.73, 74; operative on January 1, 1987; further amend S.I. 1984 No. 1920.

ECONOMIC REGULATION OF AIRPORTS (EXPENSES OF THE MONOPOLIES AND MERGERS COMMISSION) REGULATIONS 1986 (No. 1543) [80p], made under the Airports Act 1986, s.47; operative on October 1, 1986; provide for charges to be paid by airport operators in respect of the Commission's expenses.

RULES OF THE AIR AND AIR TRAFFIC CONTROL (SECOND AMENDMENT) REGULATIONS 1986 (No. 2121) [45p], made under S.I. 1985 No. 1643; operative on January 27, 1987 save for reg. 2(3) which is operative on April 9, 1987; amends S.I. 1985 No. 1714.

149. Civil aviation—detention of aircraft—payment of charges pending
[Civil Aviation Act 1982 (c.16), s.74(4).] The Civil Aviation authority is empowered by s.74(4) of the Civil Aviation Act 1982 to make regulations for the detention of aircraft in respect of which charges have been incurred, regardless of whether they are still operated by the people who incurred the charges: R. *v.* CIVIL AVIATION AUTHORITY, *ex p.* EMERY AIR FREIGHT CORP., *The Times*, November 10, 1986, C.A.

150. Seaplanes—collision at sea. See SHIPPING AND MARINE INSURANCE, § 3072.

BAILMENTS

151. Agreement to park caravan on site—loss—obligations of site owner
The agreement provided a license whereby the owner of a caravan was permitted to station it on a site. No bailment was thereby established, and no term was to be implied that the site owner would take reasonable care of the caravan. (*Halbauer* v. *Brighton Corporation* [1954] C.L.Y. 582 considered): HINKS *v.* FLEET (T/A SILVER SANDS CARAVAN PARK), *The Times*, October 7, 1986, C.A.

BANKING

152. Assignment of chose in action—priority
Where the customer of a bank gives "irrevocable permission" to someone to pay future income to the bank in consideration of the bank not proceeding against him this constitutes a contract to assign future choses in action and takes priority over subsequent judgments against the customer: WINN *v.* BURGESS, *The Times*, July 8, 1986, C.A.

153. Bank account—unauthorised debits—failure to inform bank—release of securities by bank—estoppel
L was a company acquired by B.P. RS and his son DS. L maintained an account with BCCI. DS also maintained accounts with BCCI including a deposit account in credit to the extent of £100,000. L arranged an overdraft facility of £100,000 secured in part against DS's deposit account. The mandate given by L to BCCI provided for BCCI to honour cheques, bills of exchange and promissory notes drawn, signed, accepted or made on behalf of L by either RS or DS and B or P and to act on any instructions given by the persons so authorised with regard to any accounts. On November 15, 1978 £40,000 was transferred from L's account to DS's account. There were six more transfers made between November 25, 1978 and January 17, 1979 totalling £258,000. All the transfers were executed by BCCI on oral instructions received from RS. BCCI were instructed to send statements to B but failed to do so. By November 29, 1978 B and P had seen bank statements disclosing the £40,000 transfer and wrote to BCCI querying a number of entries in the statements but not the £40,000 transfer. The letter reiterated to the bank they should only act upon instructions from DS or RS in conjunction with B or P. On February 20, 1979 L's business was transferred to the Midland Bank along with DS's. The Midland Bank discharged Ls overdraft of £105,143.63 and DS's overdraft of £15,412.83. The £100,000 in DS's deposit account was transferred to the Midland Bank and credited to L's account. In effect DS paid L about £84,000. At the end of May 1979 B eventually obtained statements for L's account from BCCI. In December 1979 B's solicitors wrote to BCCI pointing out that the transfers were unauthorised and

claiming the sum of £258,000. L sued to recover that sum. BCCI claimed that the transfers were authorised; that L was estopped from claiming the sums; that any claims against the bank were impliedly abandoned when L's account was closed; and that the bank was entitled to credit against the total claimed liabilities of L discharged by DS, in particular the £84,000 odd paid by DS to L. *Held,* that the transfers were unauthorised. The words "to act on any instructions given by the persons so authorised" did not entitle any of the authorised persons to act alone in giving valid instructions to BCCI but required either RS or DS to give instructions jointly with either B or P. No authority was given to DS or RS to instruct BCCI to make the transfers. The fact that L's letter to BBCI on November 29, 1978 was silent regarding the £40,000 transfer and the fact that RS, DS, B and P were aware of the transfer amounted to a representation that the transfer was authorised. In the light of the express instructions to BCCI concerning the authorisation of transactions contained in the letter that representation could not extend to the subsequent transactions. BCCI acted to its detriment on February 20, 1979 by releasing the securities it held. In consequence L was estopped from claiming that the £40,000 transfer was unauthorised. The remaining transfers did not come to B and Ps knowledge until after May 1979. Thereafter L could elect to pursue BCCI for the money or to treat the money as owed to it by DS. The fact that the money in question was recorded in the company's books as debits to "DS loan account" was not an unequivocal act showing that L had chosen DS rather than BCCI as its debtor. It was an act that could logically be analysed without inputing an approval of the unauthorised transfers by L. In the circumstances BCCI failed to prove that the transfers were ratified by L. It was not possible to imply any term that L had abandoned any claims against BCCI upon closing its account with the bank. Such a term was not so obvious that it did not need to be expressed nor necessary to give business efficacy to the transaction. BCCI was entitled to credit against L's claim to the extent that the proceeds of the transfers were paid to L by DS either directly or indirectly by discharging liabilities of L. £93,000 fell to be deducted from L's claim on that basis. L was entitled to recover £125,000 from BCCI. (*Bannatyne* v. *MacIver* (D. & C.) [1906] 1 K.B. 103, *Harrisons & Crossfield* v. *London & North-Western Railway Co.* [1917] 2 K.B. 755, *British America Elevator Co.* v. *Bank of British North America* [1919] A.C. 658, *Liggett (B.) (Liverpool)* v. *Barclays Bank* [1928] 1 K.B. 48, *Lloyd's Bank* v. *Chartered Bank of India, Australia & China* [1929] 1 K.B. 40, *London Intercontinental Trust* v. *Barclays Bank* [1980] C.L.Y. 157 considered): LIMPGRANGE *v.* BANK OF CREDIT AND COMMERCE INTERNATIONAL S.A. [1986] FLR 36, Staughton J.

154. Bankers' books—production—foreign customer. See MACKINNON *v.* DONALDSON, LUFKIN AND JENRETTE SECURITIES, § 1501.

155. Bond—demand bond—when challengeable. See GKN CONTRACTORS *v.* LLOYDS BANK, § 2655.

156. Borrowers—receiver—duty of bank
    When a bank exercises a power under documents of security to appoint a receiver of assets it does not owe a duty to other borrowers or guarantors and is not obliged therefore to consider "all relevant matters" such as the fact that finance was being raised to repay part of a loan due to the bank: SHAMJI *v.* JOHNSON MATTHEY BANKERS, *Financial Times*, January 17, 1986, C.A.

157. Commodity broker—security—whether deposit
    [Banking Act 1979 (c.37), s.1(1).] Brokers in commodity and financial futures who receive sums of money referable to the giving of security for the provision of property or services do not receive "deposits" so as to commit an illegal act under the Act: SCF FINANCE CO. v. MASRI, *The Times*, August 12, 1986, C.A.

158. Conversion of cheques—false indorsement—bank acting in good faith and without negligence—whether liable when cheque paid into third party account
    [Cheques Act 1957 (c.36), s.4.]
    A bank must take reasonable care to see that its customer has a proper title to a cheque presented for collection but unless there are unusual facts, or matters such as to put a reasonable banker upon enquiry as to the true ownership of the cheque a bank is entitled to assume that its customer is the true owner thereof.
    T arranged with a director of a company R, that false invoices for plant and machinery would be submitted to AJ, a dealer in the sort of machines concerned. As

part of the plot two cheques were presented to the bank for collection, one payable to T and apparently indorsed by him, and one payable to the director and indorsed by him. A comparison of the signatures would have shown that they were from the same person and it was subsequently ascertained that the director had in fact forged T's signature. T never received his part of the proceeds of the plot and sued the bank. *Held,* that (i) the circumstances here were sufficiently unusual to put the bank upon enquiry, and although there was no want of good faith on the part of the bank they should have detected the fraud. But (ii) T was himself fully aware of the fraudulent nature of the scheme whereby the cheque was obtained in the first place, and even if he was not so aware the court would not aid his recovery since the claim was to recover the very proceeds of the fraud. Action dismissed. (*Marfani & Co. v. Midland Bank* [1968] C.L.Y. 175 applied).

THACKWELL *v.* BARCLAYS BANK [1986] 1 All E.R. 676, Hutchinson J.

159. Deposit account—insolvency—priority. See SPACE INVESTMENTS *v.* CANADIAN IMPERIAL BANK OF COMMERCE TRUST CO. (BAHAMAS), § 285.

160. Deposit protection fund

DEPOSIT PROTECTION FUND (EXCLUDED INSTITUTIONS) ORDER 1986 (No. 772) [45p], made under the Banking Act 1979 (c.37), s.23(2); operative on May 21, 1986; excludes the Norddeutsche Landesbank Girozentrale from s.23(1) of the 1979 Act, thus exempting it from the requirement to contribute to the deposit protection fund established by s.21 of the Act.

161. Duty of care by underwriters—breach of good faith—liability

Insurers who underwrite a series of loans by banks owe a duty of utmost good faith and at common law to inform the banks when they discover after the first loan had been made that the broker who had arranged insurance had acted fraudulently. BANQUE KEYSER ULLMAN SA *v.* SKANDIA (U.K.) INSURANCE CO., *The Times,* October 4, 1986, Steyn J.

162. 1819 Banks

BANKING ACT 1979 (REMOVAL OF 1819 BANKS) ORDER 1986 (No. 100) [40p], made under the Trustee Savings Banks Act 1985 (c.58), s.6(4); operative on January 28, 1986; amends S.I. 1980 No. 347 so removing the 1819 Banks from Sched. 1 to the 1979 Act.

163. Exempt transactions

BANKING ACT 1979 (EXEMPT TRANSACTIONS) (AMENDMENT) REGULATIONS 1986 (No. 769) [80p], made under the Banking Act 1979 (c.37), s.2(1) and (5); operative on May 20, 1986; add a further category of exempt transaction to which the prohibition on deposit-taking imposed by s.1 of the 1979 Act does not apply.

BANKING ACT 1979 (EXEMPT TRANSACTIONS) REGULATIONS 1986 (No. 1712) [£2·90], made under the Banking Act 1979 (c.37), s.2(1)(5); operative on October 27, 1986; consolidate with amendments S.I. 1983 No. 1865, as amended.

164. Letter of credit—bills of lading—alleged internal inconsistency on face of bills—issuing bank refused to pay—UCP Article 20(b)

P2 agreed to sell goods c.i.f. to X. X instructed the bank D to open an irrevocable letter of credit ("LC") in favour of P2. The LC was made available against beneficiary's draft at sight drawn on D accompanied by, *inter alia,* a full set of clean on board ocean bills of lading. The LC incorporated the terms of the Uniform Customs and Practice for Documentary Credits (UCP). Bills of Lading were issued on "received for shipment" forms although they were indorsed "shipped on board." P2 negotiated the LC to P1, but D refused to pay, contending that the bill did not comply with UCP in that there notation on the face of the bill "shipped on board" had not been signed or initialled as required by Article 20(*b*). The Court of Appeal of New South Wales agreed with that contention. *Held,* allowing the appeal of P1 and P2, that (1) the bill was not internally inconsistent and that the notation made it clear that the goods had been shipped; (2) the bills therefore complied with the terms upon which the LC was issued and D was bound to make payment thereunder: WESTPAC BANKING CORP. *v.* SOUTH CAROLINA NATIONAL BANK [1986] 1 Lloyd's Rep. 311, P.C.

165. Letter of credit—confirming bank—rejection of documents—whether documents conformed to requirements

P agreed to sell their vessel to B. The D2 bank issued an irrevocable letter of credit in favour of P. The D1 bank confirmed the letter of credit. The letter of credit required a notice of readiness to be signed by B and certain other documents to be presented to D1 in London. B attempted to refuse to take delivery, and eventually delivery was ordered by the English courts. D1 contended that the documents presented by P did not conform to those required by the letter of credit. *Held,* that on the facts and the evidence the documents presented did not conform to the requirements of the letter of credit and P's claim failed: Astro Excito Navegacion S.A. *v.* Chase Manhattan Bank N.A.: Messianiki Tolmi, The [1986] 1 Lloyd's Rep. 455, Leggatt J.

166. Letter of credit—non-payment on sale of goods—refusal to accept drafts

[Uniform Customs and Practice for Documentary Credits (1983) (I.C.C. publication no. 400) art. 10(b) (iii).]

A marginal note to such effect means that the Uniform Customs and Practice is deemed incorporated into a documentary credit unless there is anywhere an express statement to the contrary, and in the absence of any such statement there may be no reason for implying any such exclusion.

P were beneficiaries under irrevocable letters of credit issued by a bank in Pakistan, and confirmed by a London bank; each letter bore a marginal note stating that unless expressed to the contrary the Universal Customs were deemed to be incorporated into the letters. D refused to accept the letters and P sued, proceeding under Order 14. The judge gave leave to defend, but gave leave to appeal. *Held,* that P's appeal would be allowed. It was clear from the marginal notes that the Universal Customs had to be incorporated. There was no express exclusion and no ground for an implied exclusion. The terms of the Universal Customs were quite unambiguous and D had to pay.

Forestal Mimosa *v.* Oriental Credit [1986] 1 W.L.R. 631, C.A.

167. Money held on trust—customer's right to trace if clearly identifiable

The plaintiff company sought a declaration that a sum of £123,000 was held on trust by the defendant bank, SIB. In addition the plaintiff sought a tracing enquiry to ascertain whether the missing sums could be recovered. *Held,* granting the declaration but refusing to make a tracing order, that although the plaintiffs were entitled to trace money held on trust even where mixed with that of other customers, where clearly identifiable, it was not so entitled when the funds had been repaid to other customers or dissipated in settlement of the bank's debts: Magenta Finance and Trading Co. *v.* Savings and Investment Bank 1985 [FLR] 237, Ch.D., Isle of Man High Ct.

167a. National Savings Bank

National Savings Bank (Interest on Ordinary Deposits) Order 1986 (No. 2161) [45p], made under the National Savings Bank Act 1971 (c.29), s.5(5); operative on January 1, 1987; continues the two-tier interest rate structure for ordinary deposits in the N.S.B., contained in S.I. 1985 No. 1875.

168. Performance bond—demand presented thereunder—whether guarantor entitled to investigate the facts underlying the demand—enforceability

P sold two quantities of tallow c. & f. Alexandria to B on terms, *inter alia,* that the D bank would put up performance bonds for 10 per cent. of the contract price. The actual payment for the tallow was to be made by confirmed irrevocable transferable letter of credit. P claimed that the letter of credit had not been opened in the correct way and that B was, therefore, in default. B sought to correct the letters of credit but to no avail. P then sought to enforce the performance bonds against D by presenting letters of demand. D denied that the performance bonds imposed absolute obligations to pay on demand, contended that the demands themselves were inadequate, and also that P has suffered no proven financial loss. P contended that the bond created an absolute obligation to pay on the face of the demand. *Held,* that P should succeed, in that (1) the commercial purpose of a bond was to provide security, and that security would only be obtained in circumstances where payment under the bond, upon receipt of a proper first demand, was guaranteed. The bank guarantor was not concerned with the rights and wrongs of the underlying transaction; (2) on the facts and the evidence the demands made were good demands; (3) the letters of credit issued by B did not in fact conform with the requirements of the contract; (4) P was not obliged to prove actual loss: SIPOREX TRADE S.A. *v.* BANQUE INDOSUEZ [1986] 2 Lloyd's Rep. 146, Hirst J.

169. Performance bond—liability—whether conditional—whether validity of bond extended

On May 22, 1981, R agreed to sell to E 10,000 tonnes sugar c & f free out Alexandria or Port Said. On May 21, 1981, OCL, who were R's bankers, had instructed WF through their Egyptian correspondents, BDC, to establish a bid bond and to add their confirmation. On June 1, 1981, OCL wrote to WF asking them to telex BDC a performance bond in lieu of and cancelling the bid bond. The performance bond was expressed to be "valid until 16.00 hrs. Cairo time on the 45th day after the arrival of the ship or 15 September 1981, whichever is earlier upon which date this bond shall be automatically cancelled." In its final form, the performance bond incorporated the "U.C.P." and read "We undertake to pay the said amount on your written demand in the event that the supplier fails to execute the contract in perfect performance." On September 5, 1981, E wrote to BDC requesting an extension of the validity of the bond to December 15, 1981. WF failed to pass on the inquiry to OCL. On November 29, 1981, E made a further request for extension to BDC. WF passed on the request to OCL but made no reference to the earlier request. R refused to authorise the extension, on the grounds the bond had expired on September 15, 1981. E made a further request for extension and then, on February 3 1982, E demanded the amount of the bond from OCL. E instituted proceedings and obtained judgment against BDC in Egypt on February 23, 1984, which judgment is final and binding. BDC claimed Ord. 14 judgment against WF who in turn claimed summary judgment against OCL. *Held,* dismissing an appeal by OCL and WF giving summary judgment against WF and OCL, that (1) E, when making their demands, did not assert that R had failed to perform their contract. However, BDC did not pay under and pursuant to any demands made by E, but only by virtue of the order of the Egyptian tribunal. BDC added their confirmation to the bond at the request of WF, and BDC were entitled to be indemnified by WF for all consequences flowing from this, including the Egyptian judgment; (2) BDC had no authority to extend the validity of the bond and had not done so on the facts; (3) there was no reason to suppose that R had not intended the performance bond to be confirmed by BDC; (4) no term would be implied that WF would notify OCL promptly in the event of a demand being made under the bond, and thus OCL could not raise an arguable case of breach of this term so as to give them leave to defend; (5) BDC's unauthorised incorporation of the "U.C.P." into the performance bond was not causative of the Egyptian tribunal's adverse findings of liability against BDC: ESAL (COMMODITIES) *v.* ORIENTAL CREDIT [1985] 2 Lloyd's Rep. 546, C.A.

170. Solicitors' client account—misappropriation of funds—liability of bank as constructive trustee

[Gaming Act 1845 (c.109), s.18; Bills of Exchange Act 1882 (c.61), s.29(1)(*b*); Solicitors Act 1974 (c.47), s.85.]

P was a firm of solicitors. Cass was a partner in the firm and was also a compulsive gambler. D1 was the operator of a casino at which Cass gambled. D2 was a bank that maintained a personal account for Cass and a clients' account for P. From 1979 onwards Cass took money from the clients' account to fund his gambling. In November 1980 Cass gave D1 a draft for £3,735 belonging to P to fund his gambling. D1 duly presented the draft and was paid. In early 1979 the bank first acquired knowledge of Cass's gambling. Thereafter the manager observed large numbers of cheques for cash being drawn upon Cass's account. Accounts at other banks came to light indicating that Cass had lied to D2 earlier in stating that D2 was his only bank. On July 3, 1980, Fox, D2's manager, discussed with Cass his continued gambling. Fox recorded that he told Cass that he did not accept his comment that it was a controlled outlay. Thereafter all the indicia of Cass's account being used for gambling became more apparent. Fox failed to inform his superiors that Cass was a gambler and a liar. At a meeting with P in February 1982 Fox denied all knowledge that Cass was a gambler. In October 1980 Cass's partners discovered Cass had drawn £1,810·56 and £2,105·76 as travelling expenses to which he was not entitled. Cass's partnership was terminated in early October 1980 to take effect from the end of the year. P did nothing to alter their bank mandate which authorised Cass to draw upon the clients' account on his signature alone. Cass took £323,222·14 in total from the clients' account and paid back only £100,313·16. Between October 10, 1980 and November 21, 1980 he stole £120,698·91. P sought to recover the stolen money from D1 and D2. *Held,* that a contract for the sale of gaming chips at a casino could not be described as a contract preparatory to gaming. Such a contract was a contract by way of gaming and accordingly moneys and cheques passed by Cass to D1 passed under a void contract. The moneys were not recoverable as money had and received notwithstanding that the moneys were stolen by Cass. Similarly winnings cheques were not recoverable. Section 18 of the Gaming Act 1845 applied. D1 converted the draft for £3,735. The circumstances in which it passed to D1 clearly raised doubts on the part of D1 as to whether Cass was entitled to pass it. Accordingly D1 did not take the draft in good faith without notice of any defect in Cass's title to it within the meaning of s.29(1)(*b*) of the Bills of Exchange Act 1882. Contributory negligence on the part of P did not provide D1 with any defence to P's claim for conversion. A breach of contract by D2 could render it liable to P as a constructive trustee. Section 85 of the Solicitors Act 1974 gave a banker protection in respect of potential claims by beneficial owners of moneys in a solicitor's client account. The section did not create a special category of such accounts to which constructive trusteeship could not apply. The court was entitled to take into account any contributory negligence on the part of P in considering any breach of contract by D2. D1 would be liable as constructive trustees if they received the moneys from Cass with knowledge of their source, namely P's client account. D2 would be liable as constructive trustees by assisting Cass to misappropriate funds from P's client account with knowledge of Cass's misappropriation. Knowledge for this purpose meant actual knowledge or wilfully shutting one's eyes to the obvious or wilfully and recklessly failing to make such enquiries as an honest and reasonable man would make. There must also be a want of probity on the part of the defendant. So far as D1 was concerned at no time could it be said that D1 possessed the requisite knowledge. So far as D2 was concerned Fox's conduct in suppressing information that Cass was a gambler and a liar and in lying to P about D2's knowledge that Cass was a gambler was only explicable on the basis that Fox was shutting his eyes to the obvious source of Cass's money to gamble with or was wilfully and recklessly failing to make such enquiries as an honest and reasonable man would make. D2 were liable as constructive trustees from July 3, 1980 onwards. P's actions in early October 1980, having discovered Cass's dishonesty in connection with travel expenses, in permitting Cass to remain authorised to draw upon the client account on his signature alone were totally inadequate. From that time P was responsible for the losses sustained. It was inequitable to grant relief in respect of those losses (*Barnes* v. *Addy* (1874) L.R. 9 Ch.App. 244; *Transvaal & Delagoa Bay Inv. Co.* v. *Atkinson* [1944] 1 All E.R. 579; *Nelson* v. *Larholt* (1948) C.L.C. 3887; *Selangor United Rubber Estates* v. *Cradock (No. 3)* [1968] C.L.Y. 418; *Carl Zeiss Stiftung* v. *Smith (Herbert) & Co. (No. 2)* [1968] C.L.Y. 3704; *Karak Rubber Co.* v. *Burden (No. 2)* [1972] C.L.Y. 206; *Belmont Finance Corp.* v. *Williams Furniture* [1978] C.L.Y. 242; *Baden* v. *Société Gen. du Commerce S.A.* [1983] B.C.L.C. 325 considered; *Marintrans (A.B.)* v. *Comet Shipping Co.* [1985] C.L.Y. 3170 not followed; *Montague's Settlement, Re* (Ch.D., March 29, 1985, unreported, applied; *Forsikringsaktieselskapet Vesta* v. *Butcher* [1986] 366 followed): Lipkin Gorman *v.* Karpnale and Lloyds Bank [1986] F.L.R. 271, Alliott J.

170a. Trustee savings bank—depositors—status
    [Trustee Savings Bank Act 1981 (c.65)] The depositors with the bank have no interest beyond their contractual entitlement to repayment of their deposits with interest gained thereon and the trustees' obligation is to hold their assets for that purpose subject to statutory obligations and their rules: TSB Central Board *v.* Vincent, *The Times,* April 29, 1986, Scott J.

171. Trustee savings banks—whether proprietary interest of depositors
    [Trustee Savings Banks Act 1981 (c.65), ss.1(3)(*a*), 4, 32.]
    Depositors in the T.S.B. have no proprietary rights against the bank or its assets.
    The Trustee Savings Banks Act 1985 provided a scheme for the reorganisation of the four certified T.S.B.'s. A depositor challenged the scheme seeking declarations that the banks were unincorporated associations, the members of which were the depositors. *Held,* by the House of Lords, dismissing the depositors' appeal, that the

depositors were only entitled to the return of principal and interest, and had no residual interest in the assets, accordingly they had no proprietary rights.

Ross *v.* Lord Advocate [1986] 1 W.L.R. 1077, H.L.

BANKRUPTCY

172. Application to rescind receiving order—debt below statutory minimum—jurisdiction to make receiving order

[Bankruptcy Act 1914 (c.59), ss.4(1)(*a*), 5(2)(5).]

A petitioning creditor seeking a receiving order under the Bankruptcy Act 1914 must show that the debt exceeds the statutory minimum both at the time when the petition is presented and at the date of the hearing, otherwise there is no jurisdiction to make the order.

A petitioner presented a bankruptcy petition claiming a debt due of £904·50. Prior to the hearing of the petition the debtor paid off some £250 of the debt, thus reducing it below the statutory minimum of £750. The county court registrar made the receiving order sought, and the debtor's application for rescission of the order was dismissed. *Held,* that on the true construction of s.5(2) and (5) of the 1914 Act a petitioner had to show that the debt exceeded the statutory minimum both at the time when he presented the petition, and at the date of the hearing. The original order and the order refusing rescission had been made, therefore, without jurisdiction and had to be set aside.

Patel (A Debtor), Re [1986] 1 W.L.R. 221, D.C.

173. Effect on protected tenancy—covenants in lease—whether onerous. See Eyre *v.* Hall, § 1826.

174. Execution of judgment debt—stay of part—bankruptcy notice

[Bankruptcy Act 1914 (c.59), s.1(1)(*g*).]

Where a stay of execution has been granted in respect of part only of a judgment debt, the balance of the debt can support the issue of a bankruptcy notice.

D, the debtor, was ordered to pay a certain sum to the petitioning creditor by the High Court. He was granted a stay of execution in respect of part of the debt pending trial of a counterclaim. On D's failure to pay, a bankruptcy notice was issued. An order for substituted service provided that it might be posted to D. The notice was posted on May 2. The petition stated that the notice had been served on May 3. *Held,* that (1) when a stay of execution had been granted in respect of part only of a judgment debt, the balance could support the issue of a bankruptcy notice; however, (2) service of the notice was completed on placing it in the post, *i.e.* May 2. The error was one of substance and not merely one of form, and the receiving order would be discharged. (*Bates, ex p. Lindsey, Re* (1887) 57 L.T. 417, *Child, ex p. Child, Re* [1891–4] All E.R. Rep. 899 and *Miller, ex p. Furniture and Fine Arts Depositories, Re* [1912] 3 K.B. 1 applied).

James *v.* Amsterdam-Rotterdam Bank N.V. [1986] 3 All E.R. 179, D.C.

175. Insolvency *See also* Company Law.

176. Insolvency Act 1985—commencement. *See* Company Law.

177. Insolvency practitioners

Insolvency Practitioners (Authorisation by Relevant Authority) Regulations 1986 (No. 951) [£1·40], made under the Insolvency Act 1985 (c.65), ss.4, 5, 10; operative on July 1, 1986; make provision for the granting or refusal of applications for authorisation to act as an insolvency practitioner made to the relevant authority.

Insolvency Practitioners Tribunal (Conduct of Investigations) Rules 1986 (No. 952) [£1·40], made under the Insolvency Act 1985, Sched. 1 para. 4(4) and the Tribunals and Inquiries Act 1971 (c.62), s.10; operative on July 1, 1986; sets out the procedure under which the Insolvency Practitioners Tribunal is to conduct the investigation of a case referred to it.

178. Insolvent estates of deceased persons

Administration of Insolvent Estates of Deceased Persons Order 1986 (No. 1999) [£3·40], made under the Insolvency Act 1986 (c.45), s.421; operative on December 29, 1986; specifies the provisions of the 1986 Act which apply to the administration in bankruptcy of the insolvent estates of deceased persons.

179. Notice of motion—service out of jurisdiction

[Bankruptcy Rules 1962, r.86; R.S.C., Ord. 11, r.1(1)(*a*)–(*f*).] The court has a discretionary power under r.86 of the Bankruptcy Rules 1962 to give leave to serve a notice of motion of bankruptcy out of the jurisdiction. Leave should not be given under r.86 unless the case can be brought within R.S.C., Ord. 11, r.1(1)(*a*)–(*f*); *i.e.* that one or more of the specified requirements are satisfied, and the court is satisfied that it is a proper case to be brought: re JOGIA, *Re;* TRUSTEE IN BANKRUPTCY *v.* PENNELLIER (D) & Co. (1986) 136 New L.J. 776, Browne-Wilkinson V.-C.

180. Practice Notes. see PRACTICE.

181. Subordinate legislation

INSOLVENCY (AMENDMENT OF SUBORDINATE LEGISLATION) ORDER 1986 (No. 2001) [£1·40], made under the Insolvency Act 1986 (c.45), ss.439, 441(1); operative on December 29, 1986; makes consequential amendments to U.K. bankruptcy provisions as a result of the coming into force of the 1986 Act.

182. Trustee—remuneration—creditors' failure to attend meetings—jurisdiction of court.

[Bankruptcy Act 1914 (4 & 5 Geo. 5, c.59), ss.82(1), 105(1).]

The court, exercising its bankruptcy jurisdiction, has a wide general power to do all that is necessary to achieve justice between the parties.

The applicant was appointed by creditors of a bankrupt estate as trustee. After completing his duties he submitted his papers with a note claiming suitable remuneration. The creditors failed to attend a meeting he convened to consider the matter, and then failed to attend five subsequent meetings. The applicant applied to the registrar under s.105(1) of the Act to fix his remuneration. The registrar refused the application. *Held*, allowing the appeal, that the court had a wide general power by virtue of s.105(1) to do justice between the parties where the system has broken down (*Burn (J.), Re* [1932] 1 Ch. 24 considered).

COLGATE (A BANKRUPT), *Re, ex p.* TRUSTEE OF THE PROPERTY OF THE BANKRUPT [1986] 2 W.L.R. 137, C.A.

BASTARDY AND LEGITIMATION

183. Affiliation—corroboration—blood tests—whether "other evidence" capable of corroboration

[Affiliation Proceedings Act 1957 (c.55), s.4(1) (as amended by Affiliation Proceedings Act (Amendment) Act 1972 (c.49), s.1(1).]

A report of blood tests relating to the parties was "other evidence" capable of corroborating the mother's evidence in a material particular for the purposes of affiliation proceedings.

The mother of an illegitimate girl born in April 1984 complained against the defendant alleging that he was the father and seeking an affiliation order. She gave evidence before the justices that she had had intercourse with him once in July 1983 but with no other man at any time. As corroboration she produced a serologist's report on her, the child, and the defendant which showed that the defendant was not excluded from paternity, and that 998 men out of 1,000 chosen at random could be excluded when subjected to the same tests. The justices dismissed the case on the ground that there was no case for the defendant to answer since there was not sufficient evidence of corroboration as required by s.4(1) of the Affiliation Proceedings Act 1957. *Held*, allowing the mother's appeal that the report was "other evidence" capable of corroborating the mother's evidence in a material particular within s.4(1) of the Act of 1957 (*S. v. McC. (orse S.) and M. (D. S. intervener); W. v. W.* [1970] C.L.Y. 762 considered; *Reffell* v. *Morton* (1906) 70 J.P. 347 distinguished). Since the result of the blood tests showed that there was a high statistical probability that the defendant could be the father the justices were wrong to dismiss the complaint before hearing his evidence and evaluating it with that of the mother. The case was remitted to them for further hearing.

TURNER *v.* BLUNDEN [1986] 2 W.L.R. 491, D.C.

184. Paternity—blood tests. See EVIDENCE, § 1502.

BILLS OF EXCHANGE

185. Cheque—company cheque—signature of director—personal liability

A company director is not rendered personally liable merely by signing a company cheque.

W, a director of R, signed a company cheque, in favour of B, which was dishonoured. B sued R, which had gone into liquidation, and W. W failed to put in a defence and judgment was entered against him. His application to set the judgment aside on the ground that he was not personally liable for the debt was refused, though he was given conditional leave on the question of consideration. *Held*, allowing W's appeal, that a company director who signs a cheque printed with the company's name and account number adopts all the printing and writing on the cheque, so that the cheque is deemed to be drawn on the company's account and the person signing the cheque is not rendered personally liable on it merely because he has placed his signature on it (*Chapman* v. *Smethurst* [1909] 1 K.B. 927 applied).

BONDINA *v*. ROLLAWAY SHOWER BLINDS [1986] 1 All E.R. 564 C.A.

BRITISH COMMONWEALTH

186. Asian Development Bank

ASIAN DEVELOPMENT BANK (EXTENSION OF LIMIT ON GUARANTEES) ORDER 1986 (No. 286) [40p], made under the Overseas Development and Co-operation Act 1980 (c.63), s.7; operative on February 11, 1986; increases sums payable under s.7(1)(*a*) of the 1980 Act to the Asian Development Bank to £140,000,000.

187. Australia Act 1986 (c.2)

This Act terminates the power of the Parliament of the United Kingdom to legislate for Australia, terminate appeals to Her Majesty in Council and deals with other related matters.

The Act received the Royal Assent on February 17, 1986 and comes into force on such day as the Secretary of State may appoint.

188. Australia Act 1986—commencement

AUSTRALIA ACT 1986 (COMMENCEMENT) ORDER 1986 (No. 319 (C.8)) [40p], made under the Australia Act 1986 (c.2), s.17(2); brings the 1986 Act into force on March 3, 1986.

189. Bahamas

JUDICIAL COMMITTEE (THE COMMONWEALTH OF THE BAHAMAS) ORDER 1986 (No. 1161) [45p], made under the Judicial Committee Amendment Act 1895 (c.44), s.1(1); operative on July 12, 1986; names the Supreme Court of the Bahamas as a superior court for the purposes of the 1895 Act.

190. Commonwealth Development Corporation Act 1986 (c.25)

This Act extends the powers of the Commonwealth Development Corporation. It enables the Secretary of State to make grants to the Corporation and to impose restrictions on and give guarantees in respect of borrowing by the Corporation's subsidiaries.

The Act received the Royal Assent on June 26, 1986. It extends to Northern Ireland.

191. Fugitive offenders. See EXTRADITION, § 1525.

192. Hong Kong

HONG KONG (LEGISLATIVE POWERS) ORDER 1986 (No. 1160) [45p], made under the Hong Kong Act 1985 (c.15), Sched., para. 3; operative on August 6, 1986; confers on the legislature of Hong Kong the power to repeal or amend enactments of the U.K., in so far as they are part of the law of Hong Kong, which relate to civil aviation, merchant shipping or admiralty jurisdiction.

HONG KONG (LEGISLATIVE POWERS) ORDER 1986 (No. 1298) [45p], made under the Hong Kong Act 1985 (c.15), Sched., para. 3; operative on August 26, 1986; confers on the legislature of Hong Kong the power to repeal or amend enactments of the U.K., insofar as they are part of the law of Hong Kong, which relate to civil aviation, merchant shipping or admiralty jurisdiction.

193. Hong Kong (British Nationality) Order 1986. See ALIENS, § 76.

194. Trinidad and Tobago—judicature—Chief Justice continuing in office after retirement. See SOOKOO *v*. ATT.-GEN. of TRINIDAD AND TOBAGO, § 369.

195. Trinidad and Tobago—registration of English judgment—application out of time. See QUINN *v*. PRES-T-CON, § 2690.

196. Turks and Caicos Islands

TURKS AND CAICOS ISLANDS (CONSTITUTION) (INTERIM AMENDMENT) ORDER 1986 (No. 1157) [80p], made under the West Indies Act 1962 (c.19), s.5; suspends certain provisions of the constitution of the Turks and Caicos Islands concerning the executive and legislature and makes temporary provision in place thereof.

TURKS AND CAICOS ISLANDS (LAWS) (INTERIM AMENDMENT) ORDER 1986 (No. 1158) [45p], made under the Turks and Caicos Islands (Constitution) Orders 1976–86; provides for an amendment to the laws of the Turks and Caicos Islands empowering the governor to act in his discretion in place of the Chief Minister, a Minister or Permanent Secretary.

BUILDING AND ENGINEERING, ARCHITECTS AND SURVEYORS

197. A.C.E. conditions of engagement—fees entitlement on termination

A engaged R as their consulting engineers in relation to the proposed development of a coal mine in the Vale of Belvoir. The contract was based upon the terms of the A.C.E. conditions of engagement. R rendered substantial services in connection with the project until March 25, 1982 when after a public inquiry, the Secretary of State refused planning permission for the mine. For a year after that announcement no services were requested of R nor did they render any nor was the agreement suspended by A under the provisions of the agreement. On March 31, 1983 the agreement was formally terminated. R sought payment pursuant to clause 18 of the contract and the claim was determined by an arbitrator who awarded under clause 18(1)(*a*) the whole of the profit which R would have made out of the project but for the termination. The arbitrator rejected any claim for disruption pursuant to clause 18(1)(*c*) of the contract finding as a fact that there was no impairment of profitability on R's part as a result of termination. A appealed. *Held*, that on the true construction of clause 18(1)(*a*) R were entitled to receive a proportion of their total fee represented by the proportion which they have performed of the whole of the work and not the whole of the fees which they would have earned had the project been completed: NATIONAL COAL BOARD *v.* LEONARD & PARTNERS (A FIRM) (1983) 31 Build.L.R. 117, Leggatt J.

198. Actions against local authorities—limitation—damages recoverable—whether inspectors acting infra vires

P were owners of a house constructed in 1969. D by their building inspectors had passed plans and inspected the works during their construction. In 1972 and 1973 cracking appeared in the house and P sought the advice of D's building inspector who recommended a builder for remedial work. This work consisting of underpinning appeared to have been successful but in 1977 cracking re-appeared and it was discovered that the house had been built upon the site of an old pond. P sued D for breach of statutory duty and negligence arising out of their building control functions. D contended that the action was barred by the Limitation Act 1980. *Held,* that D were in breach of their common law duty and that the cause of action arose when there was first a present or imminent threat to health and safety. This had first occurred on the facts in 1982. The fact that the ineffective remedial works of 1973 had delayed this was irrelevant. The damages recoverable by P were not limited to the cost of remedial works necessary to remove the threat to health and safety but the principle of *restitutio in integrum* applied so that the costs of redecoration were recoverable. In advising in 1973 the building inspector had been acting *intra vires* notwithstanding that there had been no relevant applications in respect of these works: BILLAM AND BILLAM *v.* CHELTENHAM BOROUGH COUNCIL (1984) 3 Con.L.R. 99, Mr. Recorder Cyril Newman Q.C.

199. Breach of regulations—failure to comply with time limits—whether continuing breach

[Public Health Act 1961 (9 & 10 Eliz. 11, c.64), s.4(6) (as amended by Health and Safety at Work Act 1974 (c.37), s.61(4) Sched. 6, para. 4); Building Regulations 1976 (S.I. 1976 No. 1676), regs. A10, A11; Magistrates Courts Act 1980 (c.43), s. 127(1).]

Offences of failing to comply with regs. A10 and A11 of the 1976 Building Regulations are not continuing offences.

On various dates before May 18, 1983 builders carried out work to which the 1976 regulations applied. The builders failed to comply with time limits set out in regulations A10 and A11. On November 18, 1983 more than six months after the relevant time periods had expired, the authority preferred informations alleging contravention of the relevant regs. The justices held that the offences were not continuing offences and they had no jurisdiction. *Held,* dismissing the appeal, that the failure to comply with the regulations was complete at the expiry of the relevant periods for compliance; failure to prefer informations within six months of those times deprived the court of jurisdiction. (*Estate Products (Frozen Foods)* v. *Doncaster Borough Council* [1980] C.L.Y. 209 overruled; dicta in *Hodgetts* v. *Chiltern District Council* [1983] C.L.Y. 3655 applied).

HERTSMERE BOROUGH COUNCIL *v.* DUNN (ALAN) BUILDING CONTRACTORS (1985) 84 L.G.R. 214, D.C.

200. Building arbitration—guarantee of builder's obligations—action against guarantors prior to determination of arbitration

[Aus.] A building contract contained an arbitration clause in the *Scott* v. *Avery* form. A dispute arose between the parties and steps were taken to refer the same to arbitration. Pending such a reference, a guarantee was given to the employers, by which the sureties guaranteed the builder's obligations under the contract, including any loss incurred by reason of the builder's inability to meet any judgment or award in favour of the employers. Before the hearing and determination of the arbitration, the employers sued the sureties under the guarantee, seeking to recover losses allegedly suffered by reason of the builder's default under the building contract. *Held,* that the obtaining of an award against the builder was a condition precedent to the liability of the sureties under the guarantee (*Queen Frederica, The* [1978] C.L.Y. 1539 referred to): ROUX *v.* LANGTREE [1985] V.R. 799, Supreme Ct. of Victoria, Beach J.

201. Building contract. See also NORTHERN IRELAND, § 2297.

202. Building contract—architect's certificate—set off

P, a building contractor, claimed from D sums due on foot of an architect's certificate under a building contract. D claimed a right to set off an unliquidated sum as damages for P's negligence and delay in executing the works. *Held,* refusing P's application to enter final judgment, that (1) an amount included in an architect's certificate does not constitute a debt of a particular character and enjoys no special immunity from a cross-claim or right of set off; (2) there is a presumption that each party to a building contract is entitled to all those remedies for its breach as would arise by operation of law; (3) parties to a building contract are entitled to incorporate in it any clause, including a clause extinguishing, curtailing or enlarging the ordinary rights of set off, and whether they have extinguished, curtailed or enlarged the right of set off depends on the construction of the contract; and (4) the terms of the contract were not inconsistent with the right of set off (*Modern Engineering (Bristol)* v. *Gilbert-Ash (Northern)* [1973] C.L.Y. 262 followed): HEGARTY & SONS *v.* ROYAL LIVER FRIENDLY SOCIETY [1985] I.R. 524, Murphy J.

203. Building contract—tender—whether acceptance by conduct. See NORTHERN CONSTRUCTION CO. *v.* GLOGE HEATING & PLUMBING, § 377.

204. Building regulations

BUILDING (AMENDMENT OF PRESCRIBED FEES) REGULATIONS 1986 (No. 2287) [£1·40], made under the Building Act 1984 (c.55), ss.1, 3, 16(10), 34, 35 50(3); Sched. 1, paras. 2, 5, 10(c); operative on February 1, 1987; increase fees payable to a local authority.

205. Causes of action—amendment to statement of claim.

[R.S.C., Ord.20, r.5(5)] P engaged Ds as architects, engineers and builders in or about the construction of a block of flats. Defects appeared. In 1966 proceedings were commenced and the statement of claim served in April 1967 alleged breaches by each of Ds of their respective duties in contract and in negligence. The statement of claim pleaded a series of defects in the building, principally faults in the brickwork. In April 1970 P first wrote complaining of defects in the roof of the building and in November 1970 they issued a summons to amend the statement of claim so as to introduce those allegations. The judge allowed the amendment. Ds appealed. *Held,* dismissing the appeal, that the amendment should be allowed notwithstanding that the original statement of claim made no complaint in relation to the roofs because the allegations sought to be introduced did not constitute a new cause of action being, as were the previous allegations, allegations of breach of duty by the respective Ds. Even if new allegations were a new cause of action the amendment should be allowed pursuant to R.S.C., Ord. 20, r.5(5) because the new allegations arose out of substantially the same facts as the facts out of which previous allegations arose: IDYLL *v.* DINERMAN DAVISON & HILLMAN (1985) 4 Constr.L.J. 294, C.A.

206. Certificate in error—obligation
Where a building contract stated that an employer should pay a contractor on the basis of an architect's certificate, the Court of Appeal held that he was bound so to do on the true construction of the agreement even though the certificate was in error and for the wrong amount: LUBENHAM FIDELITIES AND INVESTMENT CO. *v.* SOUTH PEMBROKESHIRE DISTRICT COUNCIL, *The Times,* April 8, 1986, C.A.

207/8. Certificate of proper performance—whether conclusive against action.
[H.K.] P were developers, D were mechanical and electrical sub-contractors who had entered into a side agreement with P whereunder, *inter alia*, D warranted their work to P. The sub-contract also provided that the issue of a certificate of final sub-contract completion by P's consultants in respect of D's work " will be conclusive that the sub-contractor has duly performed all his obligations in respect of the sub-contract works [with certain exceptions]." In November 1984 P issued proceedings against D's alleging bad workmanship and delay. In February 1984 P's consultants issued a certificate of final sub-contract completion in respect of D's works. D's applied to strike out the statement of claim relying upon the consultants' certificate. *Held,* that on the true construction the side agreement provided that the certificate should be conclusive as to the state of the premises and as to D's due discharge of its obligations both at the time of and before its issue. P had no greater rights against D in tort than they had in contract and therefore, the point being one purely of construction, P's action in both contract and tort should be struck out (*William Hill Organisation* v. *Bernard Sunley & Sons* [1982] C.L.Y. 252 applied]: WHARF PROPERTIES *v.* CUMINE (ERIC) ASSOCIATES (1984) 29 Build.L.R. 106, H.K. High Ct., Hunter J.

209. Cost plus informal contract—cost certified by architect—whether certificate can be opened up by court
P, a builder, was engaged on a contract known as the Valentin contract to which certain standard terms and conditions applied including an arbitration clause. The supervising officer on that contract was a Mr. Edwards. In December 1979 P and Mr. Edwards had a meeting in connection with another contract at which P was told he could do the work and that the contract would be run as the Valentin contract. Work proceeded on a cost plus basis with P being paid against Mr. Edwards' certificates. P claimed at the end of the contract for sums over and above those certified. A preliminary issue was ordered to be tried as to whether the Court had jurisdiction to open up, review or revise Mr. Edwards' certificates. *Held,* that the terms of the Valentin contract had not been incorporated by reference and therefore there was no arbitration clause in the second contract. However the Court could not go behind Mr. Edwards' certificates because those certificates were not ordinary interim certificates as commonly used in building contracts but certificates verifying records of expenditure for the purpose of a cost plus contract and that the work had been done. The parties having chosen that mechanism for payment the court could not reopen past certificates (*Northern Regional Health Authority* v. *Derek Crouch Construction Co.* [1984] C.L.Y. 117 and *Oram Builders* v. *Pemberton* [1985] C.L.Y. 207 considered and applied: REED *v.* VAN DER VORM (1985) 5 Con.L.R. 111, H.H. Judge Lewis Hawser Q.C., O.R.

210. Defective foundations—whether local authority liable—whether consequent damage a "present or imminent risk to the health and safety of occupiers"
P was the owner under a long lease and former occupier of a house built on inadequate foundations on back-filled land, and sued the local authority for negligence in the performance of its duties under the building regulations or by-laws. The plans had required that there be a concrete raft with an integral five inch concrete floor slab on top, but the floor slab was omitted in favour of suspended floor timbers, the garage had a six inch layer of hard-core beneath the garage floor, and a subsequent extension was built on strip foundations not tied in (as they should have been) to the raft foundation. A number of problems ensued, including cracking of brickwork, ceilings and internal walls; tilting of the house on its raft; differential settlement of the exterior; cracking of the garage floor slab; sticking of doors; draughts; leaking; a risk to services especially drains; and a certainty of future deterioration because under-pinning was inappropriate. The judge found that successive local authorities

had been negligent in permitting departures from the plans and in permitting the extension to be built with strip foundations only, but found that the problems did not constitute a present or imminent danger to the health or safety of the occupiers, and accordingly gave judgment for the authority on the principle of *Anns* v. *Merton London Borough Council* [1977] C.L.Y. 2030. He ordered that the authority should none the less pay two-thirds of P's costs up to the start of the trial, on the grounds that they had not pleaded this line of defence until the first day of trial. *Held,* dismissing P's appeal and allowing D's cross-appeal, that (1) there had been ample evidence to support the judge's finding that the problems did not constitute a present or imminent danger to health or safety; (2) the judge had erred in his order as to costs, since the requirement of proving such a danger had been on P throughout. The Court would substitute a direction that there be no order for costs up to the end of the trial at first instance: PERCIVAL v. WALSALL METROPOLITAN BOROUGH COUNCIL (1986) 279 E.G. 218, C.A.

211. Defective foundations—whether local authority negligent—accrual of cause of action. See JONES v. STROUD DISTRICT COUNCIL, § 1993.

212. Design—workmanship—causes of action. See CIRCLE 33 HOUSING TRUST v. FAIRVIEW ESTATES (HOUSING) § 2700

213. Duties of local authorities—scope of duties. See HAMBRO LIFE ASSURANCE v. WHITE, YOUNG AND PARTNERS, § 230.

214. Duties of local authorities—standard of care—limitation—negligence
P1 and P2 were the owners of semi-detached houses in Holland-on-Sea, Essex. The houses had been built in 1965 on a site which had probably been wooded. The foundation design had been prepared by engineers, G, and the foundations had been built by R. The plans were approved and the works inspected by the local authority T. In 1976 P1 and P2 discovered cracks in their houses and in 1980 thereof issued proceedings against G, R and T claiming damages for negligence and breach of statutory duty. It was agreed that the cracks were due to movement of the clay subsoil caused by long term recovery heave due to the absorption by the subsoil of water previously absorbed by the trees. *Held,* that (1) T did not owe to P1 and P2 an absolute statutory duty to ensure that the premises as built complied with the relevant building byelaws (dicta of Woolf J. in *Worlock* v. *SAWS* [1983] C.L.Y. 2521 followed); (2) on the facts none of G, R or T had been negligent and therefore the claims failed; (3) when limitation is pleaded the plaintiff must prove that he has suffered damage within the limitation period and if he can the burden of proving that the case is statute-barred falls upon the defendant; (4) the cause of action in negligence accrued to the benefit of the owner who was such when the damage occurred and unless the cause of action is assigned a successor in title has no right to sue; (5) a failure to commission a pre-purchase structural survey was on the facts contributorily negligent: PERRY v. TENDRING DISTRICT COUNCIL; THURBON v. SAME (1984) 30 Build.L.R. 118, H.H. Judge Newey Q.C. O.R.

215. Duty of care—whether owed to building contractor by architect—application to strike out statement of claim.
[H.K.] P were main contractors and D were architects engaged on two building projects. P brought two actions against D alleging breach of common law duties of care owed by D to P arising out of the performance by D of their functions under the respective building contracts; the breaches alleged constituted failures to act fairly and impartially and failures to exercise reasonable skill and care in or about the discharge of their functions. D applied to strike out the statement of claim in both actions. *Held,* refusing the application, that it was not possible to say that architects clearly did not owe duties of care to builders as alleged in the statement of claim. The distinction between the architect as certifier and as the owners' agent, if any, was not relevant to the existence of such duties. The duties of care were not confined to circumstance where there had been reliance as in *Hedley Byrne* v. *Heller* [1963] C.L.Y. 2416 but arose out of the proximity of the parties. P's loss was recoverable even although it was financial loss. The fact that P would have a concurrent remedy against the building owner was irrelevant because of the usual rules against double recovery. Even if P's recovery against D were simply the amount of interest which P had lost by being kept out of his money such a claim was not prohibited by the common law as to interest because until the arbitrator should have issued a certificate

no debt would have existed: SHUI ON CONSTRUCTION CO. *v.* SHUI KAY CO. (1985) 4 Const.L.J. 305 H.K. High Ct., Hunter J.

216. Employers' duty to re-nominate—contractors right to reject—effect of termination of nominated sub-contract

A engaged R to construct a leisure complex under the terms of the JCT standard form of building contract. Part of the work involved specialist work in connection with a swimming pool. A nominated G Co. for this work and R entered into a sub-contract with G Co., G. Co., abandoned their work and R lawfully terminated the sub-contract and requested A to re-nominate an alternative sub-contractor. R purported to re-nominate M Co., upon terms that M Co., would take longer than the unexpired main contract period to complete their work. The purported nomination also related only to work left uncompleted by G Co., and not to work which G Co. had executed defectively. A purported to instruct R to rectify this defective work. R objected to the nomination. *Held,* that (1) on the true construction of clause 27(a) of the main contract R were entitled to reject the nomination on the grounds that M Co., were not prepared to undertake to complete their work within the unexpired main contract period. The fact that there had been some discussion between the parties to the effect that the contract period might be extended did not affect the position (dicta of Sir D. Cairns in *Percy Bilton* v. *G.L.C.* [1982] C.L.Y. 236 followed); (2) the purported nomination was also invalid because the proposed sub-contract did not cover remedial work. R were under no obligation to do prime cost work *North West Metropolitan Regional Hospital Board* v. *T.A. Bickerton & Son* [1970] C.L.Y. 241 applied); (3) on the true construction of clause 23 (g) as amended by the parties R were only entitled to an extension of time in respect of delay by G Co., nominated sub-contractor, if G Co. had been delayed by reasons for which R could obtain an extension of time under the contracts; (4) A were entitled to be credited by R with the amount paid by A to R in respect of G Co.'s work but R were not responsible to A for the greater cost of rectifying and completing the work of G Co.: FAIRCLOUGH BUILDING *v.* RHUDDLAN BOROUGH COUNCIL (1985) 30 Build. L.R. 26, C.A.

217. FASS/NFBTE sub-contract—employers' set off of liquidated damages—whether equivalent to payment.

[H.K.] P were sub-contractors to D upon terms similar to those of the NFBTE/FASS nominated sub-contract. D in turn were engaged by M upon terms similar to those of the JCT RIBA standard form of contract 1963 edition. The architect issued interim certificates on favour of D under the main contract. He also issued a clause 22 certificate against them. M purported to set off the liquidated damages deductible pursuant to the clause 22 certificate against the sums due under the terms of the interim certificates. P issued proceedings against D for sums certified in the interim certificates in respect of their sub-contract work contending that the set off by M of the liquidated damages (arising out of delay not concerning P) was equivalent to payment within the meaning of clause 11(6) of the sub-contract. D applied to stay P's action so that the dispute could be referred to arbitration. The judge gave P judgment, holding that he was entitled to decide the point of law involved upon an application for summary judgment and that the set off by M constituted payment of the amounts certified to D since the clause 22 certificate could not be challenged by D under the terms of the main contract until after practical completion. *Held,* allowing the appeal, that given the complexity of the chain of contract between M, D and P, questions raised were not fit for determination in proceedings for summary judgment even though their resolution depended upon legal interpretation of contractual documents: SCHINDLER LIFTS (HONG KONG) *v.* SHUI ON CONSTRUCTION CO. (1984) 29 Build.L.R. 95, H.K. C.A.

218. FCEC sub-contract—proper law by implication. See JMJ CONTRACTORS *v.* MARPLES RIDGEWAY, § 361.

219. Financing charges—written application—effect of negotiations—compound interest

P undertook to construct a housing estate for D. The contract was in the JCT standard form of building contract. P were delayed on the execution of their works by, *inter alia,* variations and late instructions and made claims for loss and/or expense. In the period between practical completion and 1974 and 1979 P and D entered into negotiations in connection with the claim but these were finally inconclusive. In 1979, for the first time P wrote asking specifically for financing charges as part of its loss and expense due under the contract. Also in 1979 the architect certified a sum in respect of P's claim for loss and expense but refused to certify anything either in respect of interest in general or in respect of financing charges in particular. P issued a writ claiming financing charges for the whole period. *Held*, that (1) a written application made under clauses 11(6) and 24(1) of the contract in relation to financing charges must make some reference to the fact that the contractor has suffered loss or expense by reason of being out of his money in respect of the relevant variation or late instruction or whatever; (2) on the facts of the present case D were estopped from challenging the timeousness of the application because the parties had entered into a course of negotiations; (2) practical completion was not a cut off point in relation to financing charges which could constitute direct loss or expense raised by a variation etc., until the date of the last application made before the issue of the certificate issued in respect of the primary loss or expense incurred by reason of the relevant variation; (3) financing charges which accrued during the period of negotiations were not recoverable because the period of delay to which they referred was due to an independent cause, *i.e.* the negotiations; (4) financing charges were recoverable upon the basis of compound interest: REES & KIRBY *v*. SWANSEA CITY COUNCIL (1985) 30 Build.L.R. 1, C.A.

220. I.C.E. conditions—tendered programme

D tendered for the construction of a tunnel. The tender incorporated the I.C.E. conditions of contract, 5th edition. Cl. 107 of the specification required D to supply with his tender a programme for the execution of the works and D did this; the programme provided for the works to be executed in the upstream direction. The programme was approved at a pre-contract meeting and a contract subsequently concluded incorporating the minutes of that meeting, the tender, and the programme. In the event it was impossible for D to execute the works in any order other than downstream. D contended that this was a variation to the contract and that they were entitled to a variation order pursuant to cl. 51(1) of the I.C.E. Conditions. The dispute was referred to arbitration and the arbitrator's interim award on the point was appealed pursuant to the Arbitration Act 1979, s.1(2) and (3). *Held*, that the programme was provided not under cl. 14 of the contract but under cl. 107 of the specification; when therefore the programme could not be followed due to physical impossibility within the meaning of cl. 13(1), D were entitled, pursuant to cl. 13(3), to a variation order and to payment accordingly: YORKSHIRE WATER AUTHORITY *v*. SIR ALFRED MCALPINE & SON (NORTHERN) (1985) 32 Build.L.R. 114, Skinner J.

221. Income tax. See INCOME TAX.

222. J.C.T. conditions—loss and expense—damages—implied terms

C, a building contractor, agreed to construct an estate of 287 dwellings for M; the contract was in the J.C.T. standard form. Disputes arose between the parties, C contending, *inter alia*, that late instructions and varied works entitled them to extensions of the contract period for completion and to loss and expense pursuant to the contract or to damages for breach of the contract. The disputes were referred to arbitration. The arbitrator made an interim award upon a number of preliminary issues; the interim award was, in part, appealed pursuant to the Arbitration Act 1979. *Held*, as to each of the 11 issues appealed, (1) Issue 1. There were implied terms of the contract (a) that M would not hinder C in the execution by C of the contract work (dicta of Vaughan Williams L.J. in *Barque Quilpue* v. *Bryant* [1904] 2 K.B. 261 at p.274 applied); (b) that each party would do whatever was necessary in order to enable a contract to be carried out (dicta of Lord Blackburn in *Mackay* v. *Dick* (1881) 6 A.C 251 at p.263 applied). It was a particular application of that term that the architect should provide correct information concerning the work and M as the employer would be liable for the architect's failure so to provide correct information; (2) Issue 5. A document prepared by C which set out in diagrammatic form the planned programme for the work and indicated the dates by which information was required could be a specific application within cl. 23(*f*) and 24(1)(*a*) whenever delivered, provided that the "required by" dates satisfied the requirements of those clauses; such a document would also have to be revised to suit the actual progress of the works from time to time; (3) Issue 14. It was not a condition precedent to the architects considering whether an extension of time should be granted under cl. 23 that C had given notice, but a failure by C to give such a notice was a breach of contract on his part and if such a breach had caused a delay which would otherwise have been avoidable then C would be disentitled from recovering for the avoidable delay; (4) Issue 6. A valid notice of delay by C pursuant to cl. 23 must relate to some past event but not necessarily to some past delay. The notice must be in writing and must specify a cause of delay but need not specify which of the sub-clauses of cl. 23 are the applicable sub-clauses or provide the architect with sufficient information to make that assessment; C however was under a duty to give the architect as much information as possible as to the cause of delay so as to assist the architect in performing his duty; (5) Issues 7 and 8. C's applications for loss and expense must be framed with sufficient particularity to enable the architect to do what he is required to do and must for the same reason be made within a reasonable time. What degree of particularity would be required will depend upon the circumstances; (6) issue 9. Where it is impracticable to disentangle or disintegrate the separate items of loss and expense and to show that each item was caused by some discrete event constituting a head of claim, then it is permissible to assess the loss and expense as a global sum; provided that the difficulty was not caused by C and that the conditions which have to be satisfied before an award can be made have been so satisfied in respect of each head of claim in respect of which a global award is to be made; (7) Issue 10. C was entitled but not obliged to make applications pursuant to cl. 11(6) and cl. 24(1); if he did so the applications should be made with the particularity indicated above. Once he was satisfied that the necessary conditions had been fulfilled the architect was under a duty to ascertain the loss and expense or to instruct the quantity surveyor to ascertain it; C was then under a duty to co-operate breach of which duty could result in his not being entitled to recover the loss and expense; (8) Issue 11. C were entitled to recover damages for such breaches of contract as they could show in addition to their right to recover pursuant to cl. 24(1) and cl. 30; they could make a claim under cl. 24(1) in order to obtain prompt reimbursement and later claim damages for breach of contract in respect of the same events bringing into account sums recovered pursuant to cl. 24; (9) Issue 13. C could not recover upon a partial quantum meruit; recovery upon a total quantum meruit would only arise were it to be shown that the contract machinery for valuation had broken down. (10) Issue 15. The arbitrator had no power to waive or cure any deficiencies in any notice or written application which C was required to make: MERTON LONDON BOROUGH *v.* STANLEY HUGH LEACH, 32 Build.L.R. 51. Vinelott J.

223. JCT RIBA conditions—clause 18(2) and 20(c)—contract for liability for negligence
    P1 were freeholders and P2 lessees of office premises. P2 engaged D to execute certain building works for the provision of a computer room at the premises. During the works fire damage occurred due to D's negligence to P's building and P2's equipment on the premises. P1 and P2 sued D for the damage which they suffered in negligence and P2 also sued for breach of contract. D contended that their contract with P2 was upon the terms of the RIBA JCT standard form of building contract and that by virtue of clause 18(2) and clause 20c they were not liable to P2 and were entitled to be defended by P2 against any claim by P1. *Held*, that (1) the contract did not incorporate the RIBA JCT conditions; (2) if it had then by virtue of clause 18(2) and clause 20(c) D were not liable to P2 for the fire damage. (*Archdale Co.* v. *Comservices* [1954] C.L.Y. 581 followed); (3) The contract was governed by D's standard conditions but where relevant these did not exclude liability for negligence (*Smith* v. *South Wales Switchgear Co.* [1978] C.L.Y. 339 followed); (4) D's claiming against P2 for an indemnity against any liability to P1 could not succeed even if clause 20(c) formed part of the contract: COLEMAN STREET PROPERTIES *v.* DENCO MILLER (1982) 31 Build.L.R. 32, Lawson J.

224. JCT RIBA standard form—retention money—trust fund.
    [H.K.] P the main contractor undertook the erection of a block of flats for D under terms similar to those of the JCT RIBA standard form 1963 edition. During the course of the works interim certificates were issued from which D retained certain sums as entitled to do so by terms of the contract. After practical completion the architect issued two interim certificates which D refused to honour contending that by reason of defects in the works and delayed completion for which P were responsible, they were entitled to set off their losses against the certificates. These contentions were disputed by P and in the meantime P sought an injunction requiring D to pay all retention moneys into a separate bank account and to hold the same on trust in accordance with clause 30(4)(a) of the conditions. *Held*, that the injunction

should be granted so that D should establish such a bank account and hold the moneys as trustee to apply the same in accordance with clause 30(4) of the contract with only such right of recourse thereto as arose out of D's substantiated claims for liquidated amounts (*Rayack Construction* v. *Lampeter Meat Co.* [1980] C.L.Y. 206 followed). Such an injunction should normally be granted as a matter of course, unless there were substantiated heads of deduction. In considering whether to grant injunctions in circumstances such as these, the court was not constrained by principles generally applicable to the grant of mandatory injunctions but which did apply where there were special factors, when the court should approach the matter on the broad principle of doing what it can to avoid injustice (*Cayne* v. *Global Natural Resources* [1984] C.L.Y. 2656 approved): CONCORDE CONSTRUCTION CO. v. COLGAN (1984) 29 Build.L.R. 120 H.K. High Court. Rhind J.

225. JCT standard form—jurisdiction of arbitrator

In 1977 D engaged P to design and build an estate of houses; the contract was in the JCT standard form 1963 edition, 1976 revision. Progress was delayed beyond the contract date for completion and various disputes arose between the parties which involved a review of the architect's certificates, opinions and decisions. P's application for summary judgment on an alleged interim certificate was dismissed in 1981 but no application to stay the proceedings and refer the dispute to arbitration was made because the parties agreed that the court should have the same powers as the arbitrator to open up, review and revise any certificate of the architect. The action progressed at a leisurely pace. In 1984 certain observations of the Court of Appeal in *Northern Regional Health Authority* v. *Crouch (Derek) Construction Co.* led the parties to believe that the court might not have jurisdiction over the disputes. D therefore sought a declaration that the court did have all the powers that an arbitrator under the contract would have and in particular powers to open up, review and revise all certificates, opinions and decisions of the architect. *Held,* granting the declaration, that the powers of the arbitrator under cl.35 were no different from those which would be possessed by a judge if a court were to be seized of the dispute (*Northern Regional Health Authority* v. *Crouch (Derek) Construction Co.* [1984] C.L.Y. 117 considered): PARTINGTON & SON (BUILDERS) v. TAMESIDE METROPOLITAN BOROUGH COUNCIL (1985) 32 Build. L.R. 150, Davies Q.C., O.R.

226. JCT standard form 1980 Edition—responsibility of contractor for defaulting sub-contractor—determination

D engaged P, building contractors to erect 50 dwellings; the contract was on the RIBA JCT standard form of building contract 1980 Edition. E Co. were nominated as piling sub-contractors.

In the event E Co. failed to perform their work properly on time; their piles failed to comply with the performance specification. The architect wrote to P on July 15, 1983 to the effect that it would be imprudent to proceed further with the groundworks and that they should cease work on that element of the contract. At a meeting held between P, E Co. and the architect P determined E Co's sub-contracts. The following day, August 2, 1983, P wrote to the architects requesting a re-nomination. On September 8 not having by then received such a re-nomination P wrote determining their employment pursuant to clause 28.1.3.4. of the contract on the grounds that the whole or substantially the whole of the uncompleted works had been and were suspended for a continuous period of one month. D refused to accept that this determination was valid and purported to determine the contract for Ps non-performance pursuant to clause 27. D further contended that P were liable for damages arising out of E. Co.'s failure to perform. *Held,* that (1) on its true construction the architect's letter of July 15, 1983 had been an instruction to postpone the works for the purposes of clause 23.2; (2) P had suspended the works pursuant to that instruction; (3) the architects instruction had not been caused by the negligence or default of the contractor within clause 28 because it had been caused by E. Co.'s failure to comply with the performance specification; clause 35.21. of the main contract and clause 2 of the sub-contract NSC/2 together had the effect that the main contractor was not responsible to the employer for the sub-contractors' failure, *inter alia*, to comply with the performance specification. At the same time the failure of the piles constituted a failure by E. Co. to use adequate materials and workmanship but that was not necessarily a breach by P until final performance by them of the main contract was tendered and in any event it did not follow from the fact that E

Co.'s breach was in this respect P's breach that the postponement notice was caused by the "negligence or default of the contractor" within the meaning of clause 28.1.3.4. (*North West Metropolitan Regional Hospital Board* v. *Bickerton* [1970] C.L.Y. 241 considered); (4) P's notice had not been given unreasonably or vexatiously since the circumstances did not constitute a gross disparity between the benefit to P and the burden to D (observation of Ormrod L.J. in *J. & M. Hill & Son* v. *London Borough of Camden* [1982] C.L.Y. 245) referred to: JARVIS (JOHN) v. ROCKDALE HOUSING ASSOCIATION (1985) 5 Con.L.R. 118, Mr. Recorder Ronald Bernstein, Q.C.

227. **Limitation—accrual of cause of action—defective construction** See ALBERNI DISTRICT CREDIT UNION v. CAMBRIDGE PROPERTIES, § 1992.

228. **Limitation—date of accrual of cause of action**
P were the individual owners of dwellings in a terrace. Subsidence damage occurred to the terrace as a result of inadequate foundations having been provided. P sued the builders in negligence and for breach of statutory duty imposed by the building regulations and the local authority for negligent performance of a statutory duty or power to inspect. *Held,* that (1) both defendants had been in breach of their respective duties; (2) from the middle of 1978 serious subsidence damage had occurred to the terrace due to those breaches; (3) each individual owner had a separate cause of action because each had a separate interest in their respective dwelling; those causes of action accrued against the builder when damage first occurred and against the local authority when there was first an imminent danger to the health and safety of the occupier. The latter test denoted a danger which had already arisen or was so likely to occur in the immediate future that it would be unrealistic not to regard it as already existing for the purpose of determining the time when the cause of action arose. The issue was to be considered in the light of circumstances as they obtained at the time when the issue arose. On the facts the cause of action had arisen in the middle of 1978 by which date the building was moving at an unpredictable rate: THOMAS v. PHILLIPS (T. A.) (BUILDERS) and TAFF ELY BOROUGH COUNCIL (1985) 2 Const.L.J. 64, H. H. Judge Davies Q.C., O.R.

229. **Liquidated damages provision—penalty—sectional completion.**
S engaged B upon the terms of the JCT RIBA standard form 1963 edition to erect 123 dwellings and associated works. The appendix provided that liquidated and ascertained damages were to be at the rate of £20 per week for each uncompleted dwelling. The architect issued a clause 22 certificate and S deducted liquidated damages. B challenged S's entitlement to liquidated damages contending that since the contract contained no express provisions for sectional completion of the works, the liquidated damages provisions were rendered unenforceable by reason of the operation of clauses 12(1) and 16(e) of the conditions. The arbitrator rejected his contention and B applied for leave to appeal pursuant to s.1(4) of the Arbitration Act 1979. *Held,* granting leave to appeal and allowing the appeal, that because the contract did not provide for sectional completion S would have been entitled to deduct liquidated damages on all the dwellings and on all the associated works up to the date of practical completion of all the works irrespective of whether they had taken possession of dwellings during the course of the works (clause 16(e) could not be operated with the Appendix). In consequence the liquidated damages provisions were capable of operating as a penalty since the liquidated damages could exceed substantially the actual loss sustained, and were therefore invalid however reasonably S had in fact operated those provisions: BRAMALL & OGDEN v. SHEFFIELD CITY COUNCIL (1983) 29 Build.L.R. 73, O.R.

230/1. **Local authorities—negligence—breach of statutory duty**
P bought the freehold of a tenanted industrial estate in 1979. The estate had been completed in 1975. In 1980 significant settlement appeared caused by differential settlement of foundations to walls; the settlement increased to such an extent that each of the units on the estate constituted a present or imminent danger to the health and safety of occupants and visitors. P sued the local authority for negligence and for breach of statutory duty in or about the execution of their functions of passing plans and inspecting the works pursuant to the Building Regulations. The local authority, *inter alia,* denied that they owed a duty to the plaintiffs contending that as a non-occupying investor P did not fall within the class of those to whom the duty was owed because their health and safety were not likely to be affected by its acts and omissions. A preliminary issue was tried as to whether the local authority owed the

duty of care. *Held,* that the local authority did not owe the duty of care (*Peabody Donation Fund (Governors)* v. *Parkinson (Sir Lindsay) & Co.* [1984] C.L.Y. 2298 and *Investors in Industry Commercial Properties* v. *South Bedfordshire District Council* [1986] C.L.Y. 2259 followed): HAMBRO LIFE ASSURANCE *v.* WHITE YOUNG & PARTNERS (1986) 33 Build. L.R. 119. O.R.

232. Main contractors design liabilities—JCT standard form clause 12(1)

D engaged P to build a warehouse and office block under the terms of the JCT standard form of building contract. XP were consultant structural engineers to the project and, *inter alia,* designed the reinforced concrete floor slab of the basement area. The main contract bills imposed an obligation upon P to construct the basement slabs and maintain it so that it was impervious to water. The floor cracked and water penetration occurred. *Held,* that (1) XP had failed to exercise the requisite skill and care in their design of the slab and the water penetration was the consequence of this inadequate design; (2) on their true construction the bills did not impose a design obligation upon P and if they did then clause 12(1) prevented the modification of the contract conditions by provisions of the bills and such an obligation could not stand together with the conditions of contract which took precedence: MOWLEM (JOHN) & CO. *v.* BRITISH INSULATED CALLENDERS PENSIONS TRUST (1977) 3 Con.L.R. 64.

233. Prevention—not provided for by contract—effect on liquidated damages.

P, builders issued summonses pursuant to R.S.C., Ord. 14 and Ord. 29 against D, employers for sums certified by an architect. The contract was on the JCT RIBA standard form 1963 edition. D counterclaimed liquidated and in the alternative unliquidated damages for delay. D relied upon a clause 2 certificate issued by the architect. P contended that because D had been guilty of an act of prevention constituting a breach of contract with which the contract did not deal in its provisions for extensions of time, the liquidated damages provisions were unenforceable. The official referee gave P judgment but stayed execution of part thereof. *Held,* allowing D's appeal, that (1) the official referee's findings of fact were not so unreasonable that no reasonable tribunal could have reached them and therefore the court proceeded on the basis that there had been an act of prevention (failure to give possession of site) by D, causing appreciable delay to P; (2) the act of prevention constituted a breach of contract which not being dealt with by the provision for extension of time was fatal to the liquidated damages provision (*Peak Construction (Liverpool)* v. *McKinney Foundations* [1971] C.L.Y. 999 applied); (3) the clause 22 certificate was therefore inconclusive as determining the rights of the parties (*Northern Regional Health Authority* v. *Derek Crouch Construction Co.* [1984] C.L.Y. 117 referred to); (4) the counterclaim for unliquidated damages could not be dismissed as shadowy or having been made in bad faith and it could exceed D's claim. Therefore the judge, should have given unconditional leave to defend (*Sable Contractors* v. *Bluett Shipping* [1979] C.L.Y. 2165 applied); (5) no leave to appeal was required from the decision of the official referee since the order appealed from was not an interlocutory order: RAPID BUILDING GROUP *v.* EALING FAMILY HOUSING ASSOCIATION (1984) 29 Build.L.R. 5, C.A.

234. Standard form contract—damage by fire due to contractors' negligence—risk of fire on employers—whether contractors liable

[Standard Form of Building Contract, Local Authorities Edition with Quantities, 1963 ed. (July 1977 rev.) cll.18(2), 20[C].]

On the true construction of clauses 18(2) and 20[C] of the Standard Form of Building Contract, Local Authorities Edition with Quantities, 1963 ed. (July 1977 rev.) the entire risk of damage by fire lies on the employer, even where occurring through negligence on the part of the contractors.

W agreed on the standard form contract to modernise houses owned by S; during the course of the work one of the houses was damaged by fire. For the purpose of a special case it was assumed that the fire had been caused by the negligence of the contractors. *Held,* that on the true construction of clauses 18(2) and 20[C] the employer bore the whole risk of damage by fire, even where caused by the contractors' negligence (*Archdale (James) & Co.* v. *Comservices* [1954] C.L.Y. 581 approved).

SCOTTISH SPECIAL HOUSING ASSOCIATION *v.* WIMPEY CONSTRUCTION U.K. [1986] 1 W.L.R. 995, H.L.

BUILDING SOCIETIES

235. Authorised investments

BUILDING SOCIETIES (AUTHORISED INVESTMENTS) (AMENDMENT) ORDER 1986 (No. 406) [40p], made under the Building Societies Act 1962 (c.37), s.58; operative on April 1, 1986; amends S.I. 1977 No. 2052.

236. Building Societies Act 1986 (c.53)

This Act makes fresh provision with respect to building societies and further provision with respect to conveyancing services.

The Act received the Royal Assent on July 25, 1986.

237. Building Societies Act 1986—commencement

BUILDING SOCIETIES ACT 1986 (COMMENCEMENT NO. 1) ORDER 1986 (No. 1560 (c.56)) [£1·40], made under the Building Societies Act 1986 (c.53), s.126(3); brings into force in September 25, 1986 sections 7 (in part), 18 (in part), 38–40 (in part), 109 (in part), 112(1)(3)(4), 113 (in part), 115, 116, 118, 119, 120(4) (in part), 122, 123, Sched. 20, paras. 1, 2, 8–11, 17; brings into force on January 1, 1987 Parts II (save for s.7), III (save for s.18), IV, Section 34, Part VI (save for ss.36(5)(6)(8) (9)(11)(b)(c)(e)(f)(12), 38–40), VII, VIII, IX (except ss.83(1)–(5), 84(8)–(10)), sections 90 (in part), 93–96, 103(1) (in part) (2)–(9), 104, 105, 106, 107, 108, 109 (in part), 110, 111, 112(2), 113 (in part), 114, 117, 120 (in part), Scheds. 2 (except para. 30), 3–14, 15, paras. 58, 59, 16, 18, 19 (in part), 20, paras. 3–6, 12–16, 18; brings into force in July 1, 1986 section 83(1)–(5), 84(8)–(10); brings into force on January 1, 1988 sections 18, 36(5)(6)(8)(9)(11)(b)(c)(e)(f) (12), 86–92 (in part), 103(1) (in part), 120(2) (in part), Sched. 2, para. 30, Scheds. 15 (in part), 17, 19 (in part).

238. Capital resources

BUILDING SOCIETIES (DESIGNATED CAPITAL RESOURCES) ORDER 1986 (No. 1878) [45p], made under the Building Societies Act 1986 (c.53), s.45(5); operative on January 1, 1987; specifies that where a building society has issued shares, where there are restrictions on the payment of interest and repayment of capital, they may be treated as capital resources which may be aggregated to a limit of £75,000 with reserves for the purposes of the first criterion of prudent management.

239. Charge towards Commission

BUILDING SOCIETIES (GENERAL CHARGE AND FEES) REGULATIONS 1986 (No. 2155 [£1·40], made under the Building Societies Act 1986 (c.53), ss.2(2) and 116(2); operative on January 1, 1987; provide for building societies to pay a charge towards the expenses of the Commission established by the 1986 Act.

240. Fees

BUILDING SOCIETIES (FEES) REGULATIONS 1986 (No. 609) [80p], made under the Building Societies Act 1962 (c.37), s.123(1); operative on April 28, 1986; increase fees payable in connection with the operation of Building Societies.

241. Income tax on payments. See INCOME TAX, § 1726.

242. Mergers

BUILDING SOCIETIES (MERGERS) REGULATIONS 1986 (No. 2152) [95p], made under the Building Societies Act 1986 (c.53), s.96(5); operative on January 1, 1987; prescribe the relevant limit of bonus to be distributed among members of building societies participating in an amalgamation or transfer.

243. Mobile home loans

BUILDING SOCIETIES (MOBILE HOME LOANS) ORDER 1986 (No. 1877) [45p], made under the Building Societies Act 1986 (c.53), s.15(2); operative on January 1, 1987; prescribes different types of security which a building society may accept as security for a mobile home loan.

244. Money transmission guarantee

BUILDING SOCIETIES (MONEY TRANSMISSION GUARANTEE LIMIT) ORDER 1986 (No. 1763) [45p], made under the Building Societies Act 1986 (c.53), Sched. 8, Pt. IV, para. 1; operative on January 1, 1987; prescribes a maximum limit of £100 for any guarantee given by a building society in respect of any single operation of an account by means of which money transmission services are provided.

245. Mortgages

BUILDING SOCIETIES (SUPPLEMENTARY PROVISIONS AS TO MORTGAGES) RULES 1986 (No. 2216) [45p], made under the Building Societies Act 1986 (c.53), Sched. 4, para.

3; operative on January 1, 1987; prescribe those particulars which the notice sent by a building society to a mortgagor after the sale by the society of the mortgaged property must contain.

246. Powers

BUILDING SOCIETIES ACT 1986 (POWERS AND MISCELLANEOUS TRANSITIONAL PROVISIONS) ORDER 1986 (No. 2169) [£1·40], made under the Building Societies Act 1986 (c.53), s.121; operative on January 1, 1987; provides for the transition from the Building Societies Act 1962 and the Building Societies Act (Northern Ireland) 1967 to the 1986 Act in relation to specified matters.

247. Prescribed contracts

BUILDING SOCIETIES (PRESCRIBED CONTRACTS) ORDER 1986 (No. 2098) [80p], made under the Building Societies Act 1986 (c.53), s.23(2); operative on January 1, 1986; prescribes sterling interest rate swaps and capital and interest currency swaps as types of contracts a building society may enter into under s.23 of the 1986 Act.

248. Prescribed equitable interests

BUILDING SOCIETIES (PRESCRIBED EQUITABLE INTERESTS) ORDER 1986 (No. 2099) [80p], made under the Building Societies Act 1986 (c.53), s.10(6); operative on January 1, 1987; prescribes three types of equitable interest which building societies may accept as security for an advance of money.

249. Qualifying bodies

BUILDING SOCIETIES (DESIGNATION OF QUALIFYING BODIES) ORDER 1986 (No. 1715) [80p], made under the Building Societies Act 1986 (c.53), s.18(2)(c); operative on October 14, 1986; designates certain bodies corporate as qualifying bodies in which building societies may invest.

250. Rules

BUILDING SOCIETIES ACT 1986 (RULES AND MISCELLANEOUS TRANSITIONAL PROVISIONS) ORDER 1986 (No. 2168) [£1·90] made under the Building Societies Act 1986 (c.53), s.121; operative on January 1, 1987; provides for the transition from the Building Socities Act 1962 and the Building Societies Act (Northern Ireland) 1967 to the 1986 Act in relation to specified matters.

BURIAL AND CREMATION

251. Burial records

LOCAL AUTHORITIES' CEMETERIES (AMENDMENT) ORDER 1986 (No. 1782) [80p], made under the Local Government Act 1972 (c.70), s.214(3)(4); operative on November 7, 1986; amends S.I. 1977 No. 204 so as to permit burial records to be kept on computer.

252. Protection of Military Remains Act 1986 (c.35). See ARMED FORCES, § 130.

CANALS

253. Droitwich Canals Trust

DROITWICH CANALS TRUST (CONFERMENT OF POWERS TO MAKE BYELAWS) ORDER 1986 (No. 870) [80p], made under the Transport Act 1968 (c.73), s.113; operative on May 30, 1986; provides for the making of byelaws for the proper control and use of Droitwich Canal.

CAPITAL TAXATION

254. Capital gains tax

CAPITAL GAINS TAX (ANNUAL EXEMPT AMOUNT) ORDER 1986 (No. 527) [40p], made under the Capital Gains Tax Act 1979 (c.14), s.5(10); specifies £6,300 as the amount which, under s.5 of the 1979 Act, is the exempt amount for the year 1986–7 unless Parliament otherwise determines.

CAPITAL GAINS TAX (GILT-EDGED SECURITIES) ORDER 1986 (No. 12) [40p], made under the Capital Gains Tax Act 1979 (c.14), Sched. 2, para. 1; specifies gilt-edged securities which are exempt from tax on capital gains if held for more than 12 months or if disposed of on or after July 2, 1986.

255. Capital gains tax—asset—disposal—covenant not to compete
[Finance Act 1965 (c.25), s.22(1)(3).]
Where a company sold shares in subsidiary companies and was paid money in
return for an agreement not to compete with the buying company, that money was
not assessable to corporation tax as a chargeable gain since it did not accrue from the
disposal of any asset and did not derive from the shares in the subsidiaries retained
and controlled by them.
The taxpayer company agreed to sell shares in subsidiary companies to G.E. It
also covenanted that no company in its group would compete with G.E. for five
years. G.E. paid the taxpayer company $575,000 in respect of that covenant as well
as sums for the price of the shares in the subsidiary companies. The taxpayer
company was assessed to corporation tax on the basis that the $575,000 constituted a
chargeable gain by virtue of s.22 of the Finance Act 1965 so that it fell to be taken
into account in computing its liability for corporation tax. The taxpayer company
appealed to the special commissioners, who upheld their position that by entering the
covenant they had not disposed of an asset within the meaning of the capital gains
tax legislation. The Crown's appeal was dismissed. *Held*, that (1) the provisions of
s.22(1)(c) of the Finance Act 1965 applied only to assets that existed prior to their
disposal and not to disposals that consisted of an act of creation; the covenant given
at the time of the sale of the shares was not an asset for the purposes of the capital
gains tax legislation; (2) the capital sum was paid because of the company's ability to
control its subsidiaries and that ability was separate from its shareholding in the
subsidiary. Accordingly, the shareholding was not to be regarded as the source from
which the capital sum paid for the covenant was received, and the provisions of
s.22(3) did not apply to bring the payment into charge; (3) the taxpayer company's
freedom to carry on business through its trading subsidiaries was not an asset within
the scope of s.22 and thus it could not be the subject matter of any disposal by the
taxpayer company so as to bring the capital sum received into charge to the tax.
KIRBY (INSPECTOR OF TAXES) *v*. THORN E.M.I. [1986] 1 W.L.R. 851, Knox J.

256. Capital gains tax—enhancement expenditure—expenditure incurred
[Capital Gains Tax 1979 (c.14), s.32.] In 1973 T purchased a house occupied by his
mother-in-law (Mrs. W) as a protected tenant. In 1981 he agreed to sell the house
with vacant possession for £26,000, and in order to obtain such possession agreed to
pay Mrs. W £9,400 to give up her tenancy. Subsequently, T and Mrs. W varied their
agreement, T undertaking, in lieu of the payment of £9,400, to provide Mrs. W with
rent-free accommodation for the rest of her life, and for this purpose T constructed
an extension to his house at a cost of approximately £25,000. *Held*, allowing T's
appeal, that the value of the accommodation provided by T to Mrs. W should be
included as enhancement expenditure within C.G.T.A. 1979, s.32(1)(b), in calculating
the chargeable gain accruing to T on the disposal of the house: CHANEY *v*. WATKIS
[1986] S.T.C. 89, Nicholls J.

257. Capital gains tax—exemption—dwelling-house—caravan
[Capital Gains Tax Act 1979 (c.14), s.101] T kept a caravan in the courtyard of an
old farmhouse which was uninhabitable and in the course of renovation. The caravan
was occupied by T sporadically while work was carried out on the house. The
caravan had no electricity or water laid to it. Subsequently, T disposed of the
farmhouse and grounds and claimed exemption under C.G.T.A. 1979, s.101. *Held*,
dismissing T's appeal, that the exemption was not available, as the caravan was not
on the facts a dwelling-house within C.G.T.A. 1979, s.101: MOORE *v*. THOMPSON
[1986] S.T.C. 170, Millet J.

258. Capital gains tax—losses—tax avoidance
[Finance Act 1971 (c.68), Sched. 10, para. 10.] T Co. carried out a scheme
designed to secure that chargeable gains on the disposal of its factory premises
accrued in an accounting period in which trading losses were available for set-off.
Held, dismissing T Co.'s appeal, that the scheme was not effective to secure a
disposal under a contract made in an accounting period in which trading losses were
available and, in any event, the decisions in *Ramsay (W.T.)* v. *I.R.C.* [1981] C.L.Y.
1385, and in *Furniss* v. *Dawson* [1984] C.L.Y. 270, would have applied to frustrate
the scheme: MAGNAVOX ELECTRONICS CO. (IN LIQUIDATION) *v*. HALL [1986] S.T.C.
561, C.A.

259. Capital gains tax—option—abandonment—disposal—capital sum
[Finance Act 1965 (c.25), s.22(3), and Sched. 7, para. 14(3).] T Co. owned an option to participate in a property development. Subsequently, by way of settlement of litigation, it consented to an order whereunder in consideration of £2m. it released and abandoned the option. T Co. claimed that as, under F.A. 1965, Sched. 7, para. 14(3), the abandonment of an option was not the disposal of an asset, it was not liable for corporation tax in respect of the receipt of £2m. *Held*, allowing the Crown's appeal, that Sched. 7, para. 14(3), did not exclude a disposal, and consequent charge, under F.A. 1965, s.22(3), where a capital sum was received (*Golding* v. *Kaufman* followed): POWLSON v. WELBECK SECURITIES [1985] C.L.Y. 241; [1986] S.T.C. 423, Hoffman J.

260. Capital gains tax—residuary legatee—base cost of property
[Finance Act 1965 (c.25), Sched. 6, para. 4.] T was the residuary legatee of his mother's estate which, after deduction of debts and expenses, was worth substantially less than £6,000. Comprised in the estate was a tenanted house valued at £6,000 which T wished to acquire. Accordingly, he borrowed £2,500 which he paid over to the executor; the executor was then able to transfer the house to T. Nearly three years later, T sold the house for £9,000. T contended that, under F.A. 1965, Sched. 6, para. 4(1)(*b*) (expenses of establishing etc. title), the sum of £2,500 was deductible in computing the chargeable gain. *Held*, dismissing T's appeal, that the sum of £2,500 was not laid out in establishing, preserving or defending title, so that para. 4(1)(*b*) could not apply: PASSANT v. JACKSON [1986] S.T.C. 164, C.A.

261. Capital gains tax—share exchange—group of companies—disposal
[Finance Act 1965 (c.25), Sched. 7, paras. 4 and 6, Sched. 13, para. 2.] In 1965 the parent company of a group (P) acquired shares in three companies at a cost of £1,270,380; it subsequently transferred those to a subsidiary company (T) in exchange for shares issued by T; subsequently, T sold those shares for £601,235 (their then market value) to another subsidiary (W). In 1972 W disposed of the shares in the course of its liquidation, and claimed that the disposal gave rise to a loss of the difference between £1,270,380 (the original cost to the group) and the market value of the shares at the time of the liquidation. The Inland Revenue contended that on the share exchange T must have been taken as acquiring the shares at market value, the provisions of F.A. 1965, Sched. 7, para. 4, preventing these being a "disposal" to T for the purposes of Sched. 13, para. 2, so that subsequently W inherited T's lower base cost of £601,235. *Held*, dismissing the Crown's appeal, that F.A. 1965, Sched 7, para. 4, applied only to regulate the tax position of P, and did not apply to prevent Sched. 13, para. 2, operating in relation to T's acquisition of the shares from P: WESTCOTT v. WOOLCOMBERS [1986] S.T.C. 182, Hoffmann J.

262. Capital gains tax—tax avoidance scheme—whether single composite transaction
[Taxes Management Act 1970 (c.9), s.114.]
Where there was a share exchange designed to postpone indefinitely capital gains tax, and later a sale to a third party which had not been prearranged at the time of the exchange, so that the two were not one single composite transaction, the gain arising on the sale to the third party did not constitute a chargeable gain.
G was the managing director of and a shareholder in PGI, a company, and also trustee of a family trust holding shares in the company.
In order to postpone indefinitely capital gains tax otherwise payable on a sale of the entire share capital of PGI to C Co., an Isle of Man company, PGH, was set up to exchange its shares for those of PGI and to sell the PGI shares on to C Co. The proceeds of sale would then be lent, interest free, to the original shareholders of PGI. C Co. ended negotiations in February 1974, but the share exchange proceeded and was completed in March 1974. In January 1976 PGH sold all its shares in PGI to a third party H Co. The Revenue raised assessments for 1973–4 on all the shareholders on the ground that the share exchange constituted a chargeable disposal. In March 1982 further assessments were raised for the year 1975–6 on the sale to H Co. By a typing error the year of assessment on the trustees was given as 1974–5. By the time the Revenue noticed the error it was too late to raise any further assessment for 1975–6, and so the inspector vacated the assessment for 1974–75 but did not tell the trustees. In the meantime the assessments were appealed, and the Special Commissioners allowed the appeals. The Crown appealed, contending that the Revenue could not withdraw an

assessment unilaterally, and the wrong assessment could be corrected under s.114(1) of the Taxes Management Act 1970. *Held,* that an assessment was made when a notice of assessment was completed and entered and a certificate of entry into the assessment book was signed. It could be amended at any time before service. Thereafter it could only be altered in accordance with s.29(6) of the Act or varied under s.54. There was no statutory provision under which the assessment could be altered unilaterally by an inspector after it was made and served. But where the error was a genuine mistake, and it was clear that the assessment could only have been understood in the circumstances to refer to the right year, the court could correct the error under s.114(1). The further assessment was therefore valid for the year 1975–6 (dictum of Megarry J. in *Fleming (Inspector of Taxes)* v. *London Produce Co.* [1968] C.L.Y. 1857; [1968] 2 All E.R. at 986–987 not followed). As the sale to H had not been prearranged or preordained at the time of the share exchange the two transactions were not a single composite transaction. There were therefore no grounds for disregarding the share exchange and so the gain arising on the sale to H did not constitute a chargeable gain. The Crown's appeal would therefore be dismissed (*Craven (Inspector of Taxes)* v. *White* [1985] C.L.Y. 243 and *I.R.C.* v. *Bowater Property Developments* [1985] C.L.Y. 3407 followed: *Ramsay (W. T.)* v. *I.R.C.* [1981] C.L.Y. 1385; *I.R.C.* v. *Burmah Oil Co.* [1982] C.L.Y. 1576 and *Furniss (Inspector of Taxes)* v. *Dawson* [1984] C.L.Y. 270 considered).
BAYLIS (INSPECTOR OF TAXES) *v.* GREGORY [1986] 1 All E.R. 289, Vinelott J.

263. Capital transfer tax
CAPITAL TRANSFER TAX (INDEXATION) ORDER 1986 (No. 528) [40p], made under the Capital Transfer Tax Act 1984 (c.51), s.8(4); substitutes new tables of rate bands and rates in Sched. 1 to the 1984 Act.
INHERITANCE TAX AND CAPITAL TRANSFER TAX (INTEREST ON UNPAID TAX) ORDER 1986 (No. 1944) [45p], made under the Inheritance Tax Act 1984 (c.51), s.233; operative on December 16, 1986; reduces the annual rates of interest on unpaid inheritance tax or unpaid capital transfer tax.

264. Capital transfer tax—protective trust—advancement of property—avoidance scheme
[Finance Act 1975 (c.7), Sched. 5, paras. 4 and 18.] The trustees held property on such trusts as the sixth Marquess of Cholmondeley and the trustees should appoint and subject thereto on trust for the marquess for life in tail male. On June 11, 1979, the trustees appointed part of the settled property (three tenanted farms in Cheshire) to be held on protective trusts for the marquess for life, with power to advance capital to the remaindermen. On the following day, the trustees by deed advanced the three farms to Lord Rocksavage absolutely. The trustees contended that the charge to capital transfer tax under F.A. 1975, Sched. 5, para. 4(2), on the determination of the life interest of the marquess in the three farms was excluded by para. 18(2) of that Schedule. *Held,* dismissing the trustees' appeal, that para. 18(2) applied only to the failure or determination of the protected life interest as such and did not cover the case of removal of the property from the settlement (*Thomas* v. *I.R.C.* [1981] C.L.Y. 211, and *Egerton* v. *I.R.C.* [1983] C.L.Y. 293 applied): CHOLMONDELEY *v.* I.R.C. [1986] S.T.C. 384, Scott J.

265. Increase in share capital of subsidiary company—assumption of liabilities—EEC directive. See NATIONAL SMOKELESS FUELS *v.* I.R.C., § 000.

266. Parallel pooling
CAPITAL GAINS TAX (PARALLEL POOLING) REGULATIONS 1986 (No. 387) [£1·85], made under the Finance Act 1985 (c.54), Sched. 19, para. 21; operative on April 1, 1986; extends indexation relief for CGT to companies which had elected to have securities of the same class pooled so as to be treated as a single asset.

CARRIERS

267. Carriage by air—carrier of goods—damages limited by the Warsaw-Hague Convention—interest
[Carriage by Air Act 1961 (c.27), Sched. 1, art. 22(2)(a).]
The limits imposed by the Warsaw-Hague Convention and the Carriage by Air Act 1961, Sched. 1, art. 22(a) are comprehensive of everything except costs and may not be exceeded by an award of interest upon damages.

Plaintiffs were awarded damages against air carriers of the maximum sums recoverable under the Warsaw-Hague Convention and art. 22(a) of Sched. 1 of the Carriage by Air Act 1961. *Held*, on the question of whether the plaintiff's were entitled to interest, that if the damages had been less than the limit, interest could have been awarded up to the limit. But the limit applied to everything except costs, and once it was reached, no interest could be awarded which brought the total award above it.

SWISS BANK CORP. *v.* BRINK'S-MAT [1986] 2 All E.R. 188, Bingham J.

268. Carriage by road. See ROAD TRAFFIC, § 2905.

269. Carriage by road—C.M.R. Convention—sub-contracted carriage

[Carriage of Goods by Road Act 1965 (c.37), s.1 and Sched.; R.S.C. Ord. 11, r.(1)(1).]

The words "carriers concerned" in article 39, paragraph 2 of the C.M.R. convention do not include a carrier claiming indemnity or contribution under article 37.

Carriers who each carry separate parts of one consignment, under separate consignment notes, cannot be "successive . . . carriers" to each other under article 34.

The Rules of the Supreme Court, including those relating to service outside the jurisdiction, take effect subject to statutory provisions such as those under the 1965 Act, and the C.M.R.

A. Co. ordered 200 video machines from Taiwan and employed M. Co. to arrange carriage to Edinburgh. M. Co. employed C. Co. to carry the goods by air from Taiwan to Luxembourg. There, the goods were split into three consignments for onward carriage by road and a separate consignment note was issued for each, in accordance with the C.M.R. C. Co. employed a different carrier for each consignment. On arrival, some goods from each consignment were found to be damaged. M. Co. sued A. Co., who brought in C. Co. as third party. C. Co. attempted to bring in the three carriers, but one was served in Luxembourg and applied to have the fourth party notice set aside, despite being itself a Luxembourg company. Another of the three was a British company, and C. Co. claimed that all three were successive road carriers, within article 34, so it could bring its claim in England, being a "country in which one of the carriers concerned is ordinarily resident", under article 39. It further claimed to be able to serve proceedings in Luxembourg pursuant to Ord. 11 r.1(1)(*l*). *Held,* granting the application, that (1) "carrier concerned" in article 39 of C.M.R. did not include the carrier claiming indemnity or contribution under article 37. *Cummins Engine Co.* v. *Davis Freight Forwarding* [1981] C.L.Y. 218 applied; (2) these were not "successive carriers" within article 34 since article 34 clearly provided that successive carriers were such under a single consignment note. Thus leave to serve out of the jurisdiction could not be justified by C. Co. on the basis of article 39 and R.S.C., Ord. 11, r.1(1)(*l*); (3) the Rules of the Supreme Court took effect subject to any statutory provision such as the 1965 Act and the C.M.R. In the circumstances, C. Co. had failed to make out a case for extra-territorial jurisdiction under R.S.C., Ord. 11, r.1(1)(*l*), so the leave to serve the fourth party notice should be set aside, along with all proceedings under that notice.

ARCTIC ELECTRONICS CO. (U.K.) *v.* MCGREGOR SEA AND AIR SERVICES [1986] R.T.R. 207, Hobhouse J.

270. Carriage by road—written claim made on carrier's underwriters—whether time suspended

[C.M.R. Convention, Art. 32(2).] In this case P sought to contend that the sending of a letter of claim to the underwriters of D, a C.M.R. carrier, was sufficient to suspend this running of time under Article 32(2) of the C.M.R. Convention. D contended that the underwriters had no authority to receive the written claim on his behalf. *Held*, dismissing D's appeal, that (1) it was for D to adduce evidence of lack of authority, which he had failed to do, and (2) on the evidences the fact indicated that the underwriters were expressly or impliedly authorised to deal with the claim: POCLAIN S.A. *v.* S.C.A.C. S.A. [1986] 1 Lloyd's Rep. 404, C.A.

271. Carriage by sea—bill of lading—transhipment—whether Hague Visby rules applicable—package limitation. See ANDERS MAERSK, THE, § 3060.

272. Carriage by sea—freight forwarders—agreement to procure carriage—whether acting as principals or agents

D agreed with P to arrange for the carriage of a cargo of steel plate from Hamburg to Manchester. D entered into a charterparty with the owners of the carrying vessel in their own name. Inadequate dunnage was supplied at Hamburg, and the vessel missed her arrival dates in the U.K. She had to be switched to another port for discharge. P paid for the vessel to be discharged in the face of D's failure to co-operate. P claimed that there was a breach of contract on the part of D in failing to procure the shipment at the agreed freight rate (inclusive of discharge costs). D contended that they had acted merely as freight forwarders and as agents and were not therefore, liable. *Held,* that although D did act as freight forwarders they had not acted in purely an agency capacity and it was their obligation to procure a seaworthy vessel and provide for the carriage and discharge of the cargo: HARLOW & JONES v. P. J. WALKER SHIPPING & TRANSPORT [1986] 2 Lloyd's Rep. 141, Bingham J.

273. Damaged goods—c.i.f. contract—buyer's risk. See TRIANGLE STEEL & SUPPLY CO. v. KOREAN UNITED LINES INC., § 2251.

CHARITIES

274. Charity Commissioners' Annual Report

The Report of the Charity Commissioners for England and Wales for the year 1985 has been published. Copies may be obtained from H.M.S.O. (ISBN 0 10 239186 6) [£5·90.]

275. Charity proceedings—action brought by donor—authority of Charity Commissioners

[Charities Act 1960 (c.58), s.28(1)(2)(8).]

B, a governor of a charity established to run a private hospital, brought an action against the defendant governors and by motion sought an order restraining the sale of the hospital. In bringing the action B relied on an alleged contract between himself and the governors thereby excluding, under s.28 of the 1960 Act, the necessity of obtaining an order from the Charity Commissioners to bring charity proceedings. The preliminary points concerned whether the proceedings were "charity proceedings" within s.28, and, if so, whether it was still necessary to join the Attorney-General to the proceedings. *Held,* that (1) the Constitution did not create a contract regulating the rights and obligations of the governors *inter se*; the legal nature of such rights did not differ whether donations were made or not; since in both cases the governors acquired their rights for the benefit of the charity s.28 applied and the proceedings required an order of the Commissioners; (2) the Attorney-General needed to be made a party.

BROOKS v. RICHARDSON [1986] 1 W.L.R. 385, Warner J.

276. House to house collections—representations that proceeds to charity—whether collection for charitable purpose

[House to House Collections Act 1939 (2 & 3 Geo. 6, c.44), ss.1(2), 11(1).]

A promotion for a charitable purpose which involves an exchange of goods for money is a "collection" within the meaning of s.11 of the House to House Collection Act 1939.

The defendants were principals of St Mary's Charity Aids, a private company. They sold goods on a house to house basis representing the company as a registered charity, and stating that donations were made to a named charity. The company was not a registered charity although it did make donations. The defendants were summonsed for promoting a collection for charitable purposes without a licence, and convicted. *Held,* dismissing the appeal, that the 1939 Act was to be construed on its own; a promotion for a charitable purpose which involved an exchange of goods for money was a "collection" within the meaning of s.11 of the Act. (*Carasu* v. *Smith* [1968] C.L.Y. 1743 followed).

COOPER v. COLES [1986] 3 W.L.R. 888, D.C.

277. Trust for education and welfare—whether limited to education—whether validly a charitable purpose

A gift for "education and welfare" may, on its true construction, amount to two separate purposes with the result that the gift was not charitable, gifts for the welfare of a certain class not being capable of being charitable.

T left an estate to be held on trust for ". . . the education and welfare of Bahamian children and young people . . .". The trustee of the estate sought the determination of the court on the question whether that gift was validly charitable or not. *Held*, that the gift was not charitable. The words "education and welfare" had to be construed disjunctively, and thus the gift had two purposes, rather than the single purpose of educational welfare. A trust solely for the welfare of a certain class was not capable of being charitable, so the trusts contained in that clause were void, and the moneys concerned fell into residue (*Re Eades* [1920] 2 Ch. 353 approved).

ATT.-GEN. OF THE BAHAMAS *v.* ROYAL TRUST CO. [1986] 1 W.L.R. 1001, D.C.

278. William Lambe (London) Trust

CHARITIES (WILLIAM LAMBE (LONDON) TRUST) ORDER 1986 (No. 2003) [£1·40], made under the Charities Act 1960 (c.58), s.19(2); operative on December 8, 1986; gives effect to a scheme of the Charity Commissioners for six charities known collectively as the William Lambe (London) Trust.

CIVIL DEFENCE

279. Civil Protection in Peacetime Act 1986 (c.22)

This Act enables local authorities to use their civil defence resources in connection with emergencies and disasters unconnected with any form of hostile attack by a foreign power.

The Act received the Royal Assent on June 26, 1986 and comes into force two months from that date. It does not extend to Northern Ireland.

COMMONS

280. Issue before Commissioner—not raised in instant objection—whether raised

The matter of the registration of all the land in question, as provisionally registered, was before the Commissioner as a result of certain objections, but not as a result of the objection of the party who wished to call evidence about the land. *Held*, that as the question was whether the registration should be confirmed, it necessarily involved the question whether any part of the land was not common land. Such evidence should be considered. If there was a discretion, it would be exercised in these circumstances to admit the evidence: ARKENGARTHDALE COMMON, *Re*. (Ref. Nos. 268/D/464–476).

281. Levancy—couchancy—rights of grazing

In the course of a lengthy hearing, the Commons Commissioner *held*, (1) that section 15 of the Commons Registration Act 1965 intended to abolish levancy and couchancy; and (2) section 10 of the 1965 Act did not require the court to assume that the right owner could graze at all times and in all circumstances the number of animals mentioned in the register without regard to the circumstances in which the right came into existence: BLACK MOUNTAIN, DINEFWR, DYFED (Ref. Nos. 272/D/441–777) *Re*.

282. Non-attendance at inquiry—whether registration properly made

It was contended that the propriety of registration was established merely because nobody attended the hearing to support the relevant objection. *Held*, that such non-attendance could not constitute evidence that the registrations were properly made (*Sutton Common, Wimborne, Re* [1982] C.L.Y. 290; *Corpus Christi College v. Gloucestershire County Council* [1982] C.L.Y. 291 and *West Anstey Common, Re* [1985] C.L.Y. 276 referred to): BUCKFASTLEIGH MOOR, SOUTH HAMS DISTRICT, DEVON (Ref. 209/D/406) *Re*.

283. Registration—continued grazing by tenant—effect

Abergwesyn Hill is an area of 18,000 acres provisionally registered as a common in June 1968. The dispute concerned an area on the north west side known as Esgairadar. From at least 1884 successive tenants of a farm adjoining Esgairadar grazed sheep on Esgairadar. *Held*, that (1) the right to be presumed in such circumstances was one in favour of the owners in fee simple of the farm, based on the long user by their tenants; (2) on the facts, the claimant had not established that there was any other right of grazing, whether brought about by prescription or otherwise. (*Att. Gen. v. Tomline* (1880) 15 Ch.D. 150 distinguished): ABERGWESYN HILL, LLANFIHANGEL, *Re*, Ref. No. 276/D/800–823, Commons Commissioner.

284. Registration—whether land "of a manor"—evidence as to existence of the manor

There were no rights of common registered concerning the subject land. In considering whether the land was waste land of a manor, the Commissioner *held*, that the documentary evidence as to the existence of a relevant manor was scanty, and did not in fact clearly indicate its identity; however, the absence of evidence of manorial records, together with statements by Inclosure Applicants, were factors of considerable significance in coming to the view that there was no existing manor as at the date of registration: LIZARD DOWNS AND CLAY PITS, LANDEWEDNACK, CORNWALL, *Re* (Ref. No. 206/D/540–2), Commons Commissioner.

COMPANY LAW

285. Bank depositing trust money with itself as trustee—winding up—whether beneficiaries have priority over unsecured creditors

Where a bank lawfully deposits trust moneys with itself, the beneficiaries have no priority over unsecured creditors in the event of a winding up.

The bank acted as trustee of various settlements, and was empowered to deposit trust money with any bank including itself. The bank did this in relation to a number of accounts. In a winding-up the court held that the deposited trust money was still impressed with a trust in favour of the beneficiaries who took priority over other unsecured creditors. *Held,* allowing the appeal, that since the bank had not misappropriated trust moneys, the moneys became the property of the bank, accordingly the beneficiaries were only entitled to claim as unsecured creditors without priority.

SPACE INVESTMENTS *v.* CANADIAN IMPERIAL BANK OF COMMERCE TRUST CO. (BAHAMAS) [1986] 1 W.L.R. 1072, P.C.

286. Building company—booking deposits for apartments—no contracts executed—winding-up—whether depositors secured creditors

[Ire.] A building company received booking deposits from persons interested in purchasing proposed new apartments. No building agreement was signed or contract executed and the deposits were returnable upon notification by either party. The company created an equitable mortgage of the site of the proposed apartments by deposit of the title deeds with a bank. The company was later ordered to be wound up compulsorily. *Held,* allowing an appeal from a decision of the High Court that the depositors were secured creditors, that as no contracts were executed, the only payments made were the booking deposits and it had been accepted that the proposed purchases would be the subject of written contracts, the depositors acquired no estate or interest in the apartments and were unsecured creditors: BARRETT APARTMENTS, *Re,* [1985] J.R. 350, Supreme Ct.

287. Capital reduction—absence of special resolution—written resolution signed by all members—whether reduction be confirmed by court

[Companies Act 1948 (c.38), s.66(1).]

The court can confirm a reduction in the share capital of a company in the absence of a special resolution to that effect where all the members of the company sign a written resolution to that effect.

The company wished to effect a reduction in its share capital. All four members of the company signed what was described as a written resolution reducing the share capital of the company. No special resolution was passed at a shareholders meeting to that effect. The company sought the confirmation by the court of the proposed reduction. *Held,* confirming the reduction, that the court had the power to confirm the reduction of the company's share capital where no special resolution to that effect had been passed at a shareholders' meeting but instead all the members of the company signed a written resolution to that effect. It was most unlikely that in future the court would confirm a reduction of capital in similar circumstances (*Re Pearce Duff & Co.* [1960] C.L.Y. 425, *Cane v. Jones* [1980] C.L.Y. 269 applied).

BARRY ARTIST, *Re* [1985] 1 W.L.R. 1305, Nourse J.

288. Companies offences—committed prior to new Act—under which Act properly charged

[Companies Act 1976 (c.69), ss.12(1)(10) and (11); Companies (Consolidation) (Consequential Provisions) Act 1985 (c.9), s.31; Interpretation Act 1978 (c.30), s.16(1)(*b*)(*d*).]

D was charged with failing, as an officer of a company, prior to October 1983, to keep accounting records of the company's transactions, contrary to ss.12(1)(10) and (11) of the 1976 Act. *Held,* allowing the prosecutor's appeal, that magistrates had wrongly accepted D's submission that, as a result of s.31 of the 1985 Act, the offences should be charged under the 1985 Act's corresponding provisions.

S.16(1)(*b*)(*d*) of the 1978 Act applied and the offences were properly charged: TAYLOR *v*. MCGIRR [1986] Crim.L.R. 544, D.C.

289. Company cheque—signature of director—personal liability. See BONDINA *v*. ROLLAWAY SHOWER BLINDS, § 185.

290. Company Directors Disqualification Act 1986 (c.46)
This Act consolidates certain enactments relating to the disqualification of persons from being directors of companies and from being otherwise concerned with a company's affairs.
The Act received the Royal Assent on July 25, 1986.

291. Conduct of affairs—minority members entitlement to relief against former member
[Companies Act 1985 (c.6), s.461(1)(2).]
Relief can be granted under s. 461(1) of the Companies Act 1985 in respect of the conduct of a respondent who is no longer a member of the company.

F, his wife and four daughters held all the shares in a private family company. In 1982 they agreed that H, the husband of one of the daughters, should acquire a controlling interest in the company and a transfer was made to him though the daughters continued to hold a substantial minority interest. Three of the daughters complained that between 1982 and 1984 H had conducted the company's affairs contrary to the agreement and to their interests. In June 1985 negotiations commenced for H to buy out their share but in July they were informed that H's shares had been acquired by a Gibralterian company. the daughters sought relief under s.461 of the 1985 Act. H applied to be struck out as a respondent to the petition on the ground that he was no longer a member. *Held*, dismissing the application, that s.461(1) of the 1985 Act was wide enough to enable the court to grant relief in respect of a complaint that the company's affairs had been conducted by a respondent who was no longer a member of the company in a manner unfairly prejudicial to the interests of members.

COMPANY, A, *Re* (No. 005287 of 1985) [1986] 1 W.L.R. 281, Hoffmann J.

292. Covenanted payments—close company—apportionment—judicial review. See R. *v*. H.M. INSPECTOR OF TAXES, *ex p*. LANSING BAGNALL, § 1749.

293. Debenture—created less than twelve months before insolvency—validity
[Companies Act 1948 (c.38), s.322(1).]
Section 322(1) of the Companies Act 1948 invalidated a floating charge to which it applied only on a winding-up and therefore did not invalidate the repayment of a debt secured which had been made by a company prior to the commencement of its winding up.

On May 21, 1981 the plaintiff, a company incorporated in Scotland, granted the defendant, to whom it owed £94,500, in consideration of a further advance by him to the company, a debenture containing a floating charge over the company's assets and undertaking to secure an indebtedness up to a total of £100,000. By a letter dated October 12, 1981 the defendant formally demanded repayment, with which the plaintiff company could not and did not comply. On November 2, 1981 the defendant exercised his right under the debenture to appoint himself receiver, and on November 3, 1981 as receiver he sold the company's assets for £95,000 and applied the money towards repayment of the debt due to him. On May 20, 1982 the company went into liquidation and by a writ dated April 28, 1983 the liquidator claimed repayment of the proceeds of sale on the ground that the floating charge, having been created within 12 months of the commencement of the winding up at a time when the company was insolvent, was invalid by virtue of s.322(1) of the Companies Act 1948. It was agreed at the hearing that the company had not been solvent at the date when the debenture was granted. The judge dismissed the claim, and the liquidator's appeal was dismissed. *Held,* that s.322(1) invalidated a floating charge to which it applied only on a winding up and did not invalidate the repayment of a debt secured which had been made by the company prior to the commencement of its winding up. By virtue of s.17(1) of the Companies (Floating Charges and Receivers) (Scotland) Act 1972 when the defendant as receiver realised the assets and applied the proceeds towards repayment of his debt, he did so as agent of the company, and so repayment was neither invalidated nor required to be repaid under s.322(1) (*Re Parkes Garage (Swadlincote)* [1929] 1 Ch. 139, D.C. considered).

MACE BUILDERS (GLASGOW) *v*. LUNN [1986] 3 W.L.R. 921, C.A.

294. Debenture—debt—unspecified amount

A demand for monies due under powers contained in a debenture need not specify the amount owing. When the debenture provides for the creditor to be fully indemnified against all costs of enforcing payment of the debt, the court still has an overriding discretion on costs: BANK OF BARODA v. PANESSAR, *The Times*, July 10, 1986, Walton J.

295. Directors

INSOLVENT COMPANIES (DISQUALIFICATION OF UNFIT DIRECTORS) PROCEEDINGS RULES 1986 (No. 612) [80p], made under the Insolvency Act 1985 (c.65), s.106; operative on April 28, 1986; set out the code of procedure for an application by the Secretary of State or the official receiver for the disqualification of directors by the court under sections 12 and 13 of the 1985 Act.

INSOLVENT COMPANIES (REPORTS ON CONDUCT OF DIRECTORS) RULES 1986 (No. 611) [£2·90], made under the Insolvency Act 1985, s.106; operative on April 28, 1986; makes provision for the manner in which a voluntary liquidator or administrative receiver shall report the conduct of directors of insolvent companies where they appear to be unfit to be directors of companies.

296. Directors—personal liability—ultra vires acts

A company's articles may protect a director from personal liability even for loss incurred through acts *ultra vires* the company.

[Jersey] A Jersey company contracted to buy property in England, payment to be by instalments. After only two payments, the goods of the company were declared "en désastre" by the Royal Court of Jersey. The viscount began proceedings in the Jersey court against the director for their loss on the ground that the expenditure was *ultra vires* the company. There was no suggestion of dishonesty. Under art. 46, every director was entitled to be indemnified against all losses incurred by him "in the conduct of the company's business," and no director should be liable "for any loss which shall happen in the course of the duties of his office or in relation thereto, unless the same shall happen through his own dishonesty." *Held*, that art. 46 was to be construed as exonerating a director from personal liability and in the absence of dishonesty the directors were protected in relation to loss caused by *ultra vires* acts (*Claridge's Patent Asphalte Co., Re* [1921] 1 Ch. 543 applied; dictum in *Cullerne* v. *London and Suburban General Permanent Building Society* (1890) 25 Q.B.D. 485, 488 C.A. disapproved.)

VISCOUNT OF THE ROYAL COURT OF JERSEY v. SHELTON (BARRY) [1986] 1 W.L.R. 985, P.C.

297. Disqualification orders

COMPANIES (DISQUALIFICATION ORDERS) REGULATIONS 1986 (No. 2067) [£1·40], made under the Company Directors Disqualification Act 1986 (c.46), s.18 and the Companies Act 1985 (c.6), s.301; operative on December 29, 1986; replace S.I. 1985 No. 829 so as to take account of the additional grounds for disqualification introduced by the Insolvency Act 1985 and the 1986 Act.

298. Dissolution of company—accrual of debt after dissolution

[Companies Act 1948 (c.38), s.353.]

The name of the company will not be restored to the register if the party making the application was not a member or creditor at the date of dissolution, but only became such a person after dissolution (*Timbiqui Gold Mines, Re* [1961] Ch. 319 considered): AGA ESTATE AGENCIES Re, *The Times*, June 4, 1986, Harman J.

299. Financial services—disclosure of information. See REVENUE AND FINANCE, § 2852.

300. Forms

COMPANIES (FORMS) (AMENDMENT) REGULATIONS 1986 (No. 2097) [45p], made under the Companies Act 1985 (c.6), ss.469(1), 470(3), 481(1)(*b*) and (2), 482(1), 485, 486, 495(2)(*a*), (*b*), 496(1)(*e*), 497(2), 498(3) and 744; operative on December 29, 1986; revoke certain provisions in S.I. 1985 No. 854 relating to receivers or to receivers and managers.

301. Fraudulent trading—liability of parent company—whether knowingly party to fraudulent trading

[Companies Act 1948 (c.38), s.332(1); now Companies Act 1985 (c.6), s.630.]

Augustus Barnett & Son was a subsidiary of Rumasa, a Spanish company with substantial interests in the production and marketing of wines and sherries. Augustus Barnett had a substantial deficiency of current assets so that its auditors refused to certify its accounts in the absence of a letter from Rumasa confirming it would continue to support the company. In their last such letter in June 1982 Rumasa undertook to provide capital to maintain the company's trading position for the next 12 months and to provide such long term finance as was necessary. In February 1983 Rumasa was nationalised. In March 1983 the directors of Augustus Barnett sought assurances of financial support from Rumasa. Rumasa provided further financial support in the form of a loan to the company from another of its subsidiaries. Further assurances of support were given by Rumasa. In June the company sought additional financial support from Rumasa which was not forthcoming and in September entered into a creditors' voluntary liquidation. The liquidation sought a declaration that Rumasa was knowingly party to the carrying on of the business of the company with intent to defraud creditors under s.332 of the Companies Act 1948. The liquidator alleged in his points of claim that Rumasa induced the company to continue trading and induced suppliers and creditors to continue doing business with the company by giving the letters of comfort, providing financial support and making statements of intention to continue supporting the company. The liquidator alleged that Rumasa had no intention of honouring its assurances and was knowingly party to and concurred in the carrying on of the business of the company with intent to defraud the creditors of the company. Those allegations were inferences from the facts pleaded, in essence that on several occasions Rumasa declared an intention to support the company but in the end failed to do so. It was not alleged that Rumasa itself carried on the company's business or that the company's board of directors had any intention of defrauding the company's creditors. Rumasa applied to strike out the points of claim. *Held,* allowing the application, that before the court could make an order under s.332 of the Act it must be satisfied that someone had done an act which could be described as carrying on some business of the company with an intent to defraud. The words "persons . . . party to" may extend to persons who participated in a company's fraudulent acts although that person was not involved in carrying on the company's business but they could not extend to such a person where there were no fraudulent acts on the part of the company even if that person acted with intent to defraud. In any event the inference of an intention to defraud the creditors of the company on the part of Rumasa could not be drawn from the pleaded facts: AUGUSTUS BARNETT AND SON, *Re* 1986 PCC 167, Hoffmann J.

302. Fraudulent trading—single transaction—dishonesty. See R. *v.* LOCKWOOD, § 608.

303. Insolvency Act 1985—commencement
INSOLVENCY ACT 1985 (COMMENCEMENT No. 1) ORDER 1986 (No. 6) [80p], made under the Insolvency Act 1985 (c.65), s.236(2); brings into force on February 1, 1986, and March 1, 1986, scheduled provisions of the 1985 act.
INSOLVENCY ACT 1985 (COMMENCEMENT No. 2) ORDER 1986 (No. 185 (C.7)) [£1·35], made under the Insolvency Act 1985; bring into force on March 1, 1986 sections 106 (in part), 108(1)(3), 109(1)(2) (in part), 226 (in part), 235(1)(3), Scheds. 5 (in part), 6 (in part), 8 (in part) and 10 (in part), and brings into force on April 1, 1986 sections 213(1)(3)(4)(5)(6), 234, Sched 8, para. 36, Sched. 10 (in part).
INSOLVENCY ACT 1985 (COMMENCEMENT No. 3) ORDER 1986 (No. 463 (c.14)) [£1·35], made under the Insolvency Act 1985 (c.65), s.236(2); brings into force on April 1, 1986, s. 214 (in part) and Scheds. 8, para. 27 (in part); 10 (in part) and brings into force on April 28, 1986 ss.12, 13, 14, 15, 16, 18, 108 (in part), 216, Scheds. 2; 6, paras. 1–7, 15(1)(2); 9, paras. 2–4; 10 (in part).
INSOLVENCY ACT 1985 (COMMENCEMENT No. 4) ORDER 1986 (No. 840 (c.22)) [£1·40], made under the Insolvency Act 1985 (c.65), s.236(2); bring into force on June 1, 1986 sections 3(2), 4(1)(c), 5(2)(b)(3) and Sched 1, para. 4(4) to the 1985 Act and bring into force on July 1, 1986 sections 3(1)(3)–(5), 4(1)(a)(b),(2)–(6), 5(1)(2)(a)(4)(5), 6–9, Sched. 1, paras. 1–3, 4(1)–(3)(5), 5, 6 to the 1985 Act.
INSOLVENCY ACT 1985 (COMMENCEMENT No. 5) ORDER 1986 (No. 1924 (C.71)) [80p], made under the Insolvency Act 1985 (c.65), s.236(2); brings into force on December 29, 1986 all provisions of the 1985 Act not yet in force.

304. Insolvency Act 1986 (c.45)
This Act consolidates: the enactments relating to company insolvency and winding up; enactments relating to the insolvency and bankrupcty of individuals; and other enactments dealing with related matters.
It received the Royal Assent on July 25, 1986.

305. Insolvency courts

Co-operation of Insolvency Courts (Designation of Relevant Countries and Territories) Order 1986 (No. 2123) [45p], made under the Insolvency Act 1986 (c.45), s.426(11); operative on December 29, 1986; designates relevant countries and territories for the purposes of s.426 of the 1986 Act.

306. Insolvency fees

Insolvency Fees Order 1986 (No. 2030) [£1·40], made under the Bankruptcy Act 1914 (c.59), s.133, the Insolvency Act 1986 (c.45), ss.414, 415 and the Public Offices Fees Act 1879 (c.58), s.2; operative on December 29, 1986; prescribe fees charged in company and individual insolvency proceedings in England and Wales to which the 1986 Act applies.

307. Insolvency practitioners

Insolvency Practitioners (Recognised Professional Bodies) Order 1986 (No. 1764) [45p], made under the Insolvency Act 1985 (c.65), ss.3(2), 10; operative on November 10, 1986; specifies bodies which are declared to be recognised professional bodies for the purposes of s.3 of the 1985 Act.

Insolvency Practitioners Regulations 1986 (No. 1995) [£2·40], made under the Insolvency Act 1985 (c.65), ss.4, 5, 10 and the Insolvency Act 1986 (c.45), ss.390, 392, 393, 419; operative on December 29, 1986; makes provision in relation to the authorisations of insolvency practitioners.

Insolvency Practitioners (Amendment) Regulations 1986 (No. 2247) [45p], made under the Insolvency Act 1986 (c.45), ss.390, 419; operative on December 29, 1986; amend S.I. 1986 No. 1995 to provide that the maximum amount of the specified penalty sum under any bond entered into by an insolvency practitioner shall be £5 million.

308. Insolvency proceedings

Insolvency Proceedings (Monetary Limits) Order 1986 (No. 1996) [80p], made under the Insolvency Act 1986 (c.45), ss.416, 418, Sched. 6, paras. 9, 12; operative on December 29, 1986; increases the sums specified in ss.184(3) and 206(1)(*a*)(*b*) of the 1986 Act, the monetary limits for the bankruptcy provisions of that Act and the maximum level of the preferential claim of an employee.

Insolvency Regulations 1986 (No. 1994) [£2·90], made under S.I. 1986 No. 1925 and the Insolvency Act 1986 (c.45), ss.411, 412, Scheds. 8, para. 27; 9, para. 30; operative on December 29, 1986; make provision in relation to matters which are of an administrative as opposed to a judicial nature.

Insolvency Rules 1986 (No. 1925) [£19·30], made under the Insolvency Act 1986 (c.45), ss.411 and 412; operative on December 29, 1986; set out the detailed procedure for the conduct of all company and individual insolvency proceedings in England and Wales under the 1986 Act.

309. Insolvency—directors conduct—reports

Insolvent Companies (Reports on Conduct of Directors) No. 2 Rules 1986 (No. 2134) [£3.40], made under the Insolvency Act 1985 (c.65), s.126, the Insolvency Act 1986 (c.45), s.411 and the Company Directors Disqualification Act 1986 (c.46), s.21; operative on December 29, 1986; makes provision for the order in which a voluntary liquidator, administrative receiver or an administrator of a company appointed after December 29, 1986, shall make to the Secretary of State the required report as to the conduct of persons who have been directors or shadow directors of insolvent companies which makes such directors appear to be unfit to be concerned in the management of a company.

310. Insolvency—land registration rules

Insolvency (Land Registration Rules) Order 1986 (No. 2245) [45p], made under the Insolvency Act 1986 (c.45), s.439; operative on December 28, 1986; revokes an entry in S.I. 1986 No. 2001 relating to S.R. & O. 1925 No. 1093.

311. Insolvency—partnerships order

Insolvent Partnerships Order 1986 (No. 2142) [£4·90], made under the Insolvency Act 1986 (c.45), s.420, and the Company Directors Disqualification Act 1986 (c.46), s.21(2); operative on December 29, 1986; specifies the provisions of the Insolvency Act 1986 which apply in relation to insolvent partnerships.

312. Insurance companies

INSURANCE COMPANIES (WINDING-UP) (AMENDMENT) RULES 1986 (No. 2002) [£1·40], made under the Insolvency Act 1986 (c.45), s.411 and the Insurance Companies Act 1982 (c.50), s.59; operative on December 29, 1986; amend S.I. 1985 No. 95 consequential upon the Insolvency Act 1986, S.I. 1986 Nos. 1925 and 1994.

313. Legal proceedings action to recover director's loan—directors' authority to commence action—continuation of proceedings

[Isle of Man] In 1976 P commenced an action against D claiming repayment of a director's loan and interest thereon. The action was commenced on the instructions of A and B who were validly appointed directors of P at the time. In 1977 A and B sold their shares in the company to X and Y. In consequence A and B lost their qualification to act as directors. No other directors were appointed. The Particulars of Claim and Defence were both served after that time. Discovery took place thereafter. At the trial D claimed that as P had not validly appointed directors there was no-one to give authority or instructions for the actions taken on the company's behalf prior to the hearing nor to give proper instructions at the hearing. D claimed that the action ought to be struck out. *Held,* that the action would not be struck out. At the time the action was commenced A and B were validly appointed directors and as such authorised to give instructions for the commencement of proceedings. Having regard to the fact that the action was a simple one based on a director's loan the instructions given at the outset were sufficient for the action to be continued without further instructions from P. The fact that P carried on the action without any validly appointed directors was not sufficient in the circumstances to bring about a cessation or abrogation of the authority given to P's legal advisors to carry the proceedings to a conclusion: C.H.S. (REAL ESTATE) *v.* HEWISON AND POTTS [1986] PCC 113, Deemster Luft.

314. Liquidation—duty to help liquidator

[Companies Act 1985 (c.6) s.561.] There is a general duty upon those involved in an insolvent company's affairs to assist the liquidator (*Rolls Razor (No. 2) Re* [1970] C.L.Y. 302, *Castle New Homes, Re* [1979] C.L.Y 282, *Spiraflite, Re (Note)* [1979] C.L.Y. 283 considered): RHODES (JOHN T.), *Re, The Times,* July 12, 1986, Hoffmann J.

315. Minority shareholder's action—company in liquidation—whether action should proceed in name of company

A minority shareholder cannot sue derivatively on behalf of a company in liquidation.

Fargro and Superior Group each held 50 per cent. of the shares of Bridge Produce Marketing ("the company"). The company was a deadlocked company. Fargro claimed that Superior and others diverted assets and opportunity belonging to the company for their own benefit. The company went into liquidation. Thereafter Fargro commenced an action against Superior and the others, claiming to sue derivatively on behalf of the company. The defendants conceded Fargro would be entitled to pursue its minority shareholders' action if the company were not in liquidation as it would be impossible for Fargro to have the company take action against the defendants. The defendants contended that as the company was in liquidation Fargro was not entitled to pursue a minority shareholders' action. *Held,* that once the company went into liquidation its rights became vested in the liquidator. A shareholder seeking to pursue an action on behalf of the company can ask the liquidator to bring the action in the name of the company. If the liquidator refuses to do so or imposes unreasonable terms on the shareholder the shareholder can apply to the court for an order that the liquidator bring the action in the name of the company or that the shareholder be entitled to bring an action in the name of the company. Once a company has gone into liquidation the basis upon which a minority shareholders' action can be pursued, namely the impossibility of the company bringing an action in its own name, ceases to exist. Accordingly the action would be reconstituted to permit the action to be brought in the name of the company with the liquidator's consent (*Cape Breton Co. v. Fenn* (1881) 17 Ch.D. 198 considered, *Ferguson v. Wallbridge* [1935] 3 D.L.R. 66 applied).

FARGRO *v.* GODFROY [1986] 1 W.L.R. 1134, Walton J.

316. Minority shareholders—action against company and directors—indemnity for costs—procedure

P's application for an indemnity as to costs in a minority shareholders' action against a company should normally be *inter partes,* not *ex parte.*

P brought a minority shareholders' action against a company and the directors alleging excessive remuneration. The plaintiffs applied *ex parte* for an order indemnifying them against costs until conclusion of discovery and inspection. The master granted the order sought and made a limited order on taxation. *Held,* allowing the application to set aside the order, that the plaintiffs should not be granted such an order unless it would cause injustice; normally the application should be *inter partes. (Wallersteiner* v. *Moir (No. 2)* [1973] C.L.Y. 2602 distinguished).

SMITH v. CROFT [1986] 1 W.L.R. 580, Walton J.

317. Minority shareholders—unfair prejudice—directors' advice on offer for shares

Shareholders in a private company petitioned under s.459 of the 1985 Act, alleging the directors had acted in manner unfairly prejudicial to their interests. The directors urged shareholders to accept an offer in which they the directors had a financial interest, while ignoring a much more favourable alternative offer. The directors moved to strike out the petition. *Held,* dismissing the motion, that the concept of "unfairness" conferred a wide jurisdiction on the court, and should be given its ordinary meaning; the directors' letter of advice could be construed as unfairly impairing their chances of selling their shares: COMPANY (No. 008699 of 1985) A, *Re* 1986 PCC 296, Hoffman J.

318. Minority shareholders—unfairly prejudicial conduct towards—strike out of petition

[Companies Act 1985 (c.6), s.459.] The court would refuse to strike out a petition for relief where the "unfair" conduct related to the petitioner's directorship, since it was at any rate possible that his shareholding, or the circumstances of its acquisition, might give him a legitimate expectation of remaining a director. Unfairness covered wider equitable considerations as well as strict legal rights: COMPANY A, *Re* (No. 00477 of 1986), *The Times,* April 8, 1986, Hoffman J.

319. Modified accounts

COMPANIES (MODIFIED ACCOUNTS) AMENDMENT REGULATIONS 1986 (No. 1865) [80p], made under the Companies Act 1985 (c.6), s.251(1); for the purposes of ss.249 and 250 raise the thresholds for turnover and balance sheet total for each of the three thresholds.

320. New forms—statutory return

From July 1, 1986 companies will be required to use new forms when making their statutory return to the Companies Registration Office. Supplies of the new form and lists of changed form numbers are available, free of charge, from the Stationery Section, Companies Registration Office, Crown Way, Maindy, Cardiff CF4 3UZ.

321. Person dealing with company—lack of good faith—capacity of company

[European Communities Act 1972 (c.68), s.9(1).]

Lack of good faith cannot be established against a person dealing with a company, under s.9(1) of the European Communities Act 1972 merely because having been put on inquiry, he fails to inquire into the limits of a company's capacity or its rules of management.

G executed a power of attorney but failed to seal it, although it bore the words "signed, sealed and delivered." By a document executed thereafter by the donee, G's solicitor, G gave an unlimited guarantee. TCB knew of the power of attorney and relied upon the execution of the guarantee in lending money to two companies, X and Y. A debenture in G's favour was executed by Y, signed by the attorney for G as one of the directors. The articles of association provided only for the directors to sign personally. G contended that since the power of attorney was unsealed it was invalid, and that Y had no power to delegate the power to execute the debenture. *Held,* that (1) G was estopped from denying that the power of attorney was sealed; (2) there was no lack of faith under s.9(1) simply because being put on inquiry, a person failed to inquire into the limits of a company's capacity or its rules of management. (*First National Securities* v. *Jones* [1978] C.L.Y 792 and *Stromdale & Ball* v. *Burden* (1952) C.L.C. 5559 followed.)

TCB v. GRAY [1986] 1 All E.R. 587, Browne-Wilkinson V.C.

322. Receivers. See RECEIVERS.

323. **Receivership—ability of company to pay debts—possible future assets—charge by defectively sealed document**
[Companies Act 1948 (c.38), s.223 (see now Companies Act 1985 (c.6), s.518).] In deciding whether a company could pay its debts regard could not be had to a possibility of future assets which was unenforceable. Only contracts in existence at the relevant date weighed in the balance. The defective sealing of the charge was of no practical effect, since the charge merely operated as an agreement to execute a deed, and would be enforceable by specific performance (*Re European Life Assurance Society* (1869) L.R. 9 Eq. 122 considered): BYBLOS BANK *v.* AL KHUDHAIRY, *Financial Times,* November 7, 1986, C.A.

324. **Registration of charge certificate—unsecured creditor**
[Companies Act 1948 (c.38), ss.95(1), 98(2); Tribunals and Inquiries Act 1971 (c.62), s.14(1) and Companies (Forms) Regulations 1983 (S.I. 1983 No. 1021) Form 47.]
When a company is being compulsorily wound up an unsecured creditor can apply for judicial review of the Registrar of Companies' decision to issue a certificate of registration of a charge against the company; however, the certificate is conclusive evidence that the requirements of registration have been complied with, so another court cannot hear evidence on the matter.
A bank sought to register under s.95(1) of the Companies Act 1948 a charge purportedly created on February 9, 1984. Form 47 was lodged but it did not contain all the prescribed particulars, although all the documents relied upon by the bank to substantiate the charge were included with the application. After being advised of the error the bank re-submitted a fresh form 47 on or about March 29, 1984, bearing the date February 29. Registration was recorded by the Registrar as at February 29. The company sought judicial review to quash the registration. The judge ordered that the unsecured creditor be joined as co-applicant, granted an order, holding that although the Registrar's certificate was conclusive in ordinary litigation, as a matter of public policy it was nevertheless susceptible to judicial review. He ordered the bank to pay the costs of both the company and the unsecured creditor. The bank appealed against the order on the ground that the unsecured creditor had no locus standi. *Held,* that the unsecured creditor had sufficient locus standi to apply; any person or body with a sufficient interest could apply to quash the decision of a person or body performing a public function for lack of jurisdiction or breach of natural justice. Section 98(2) of the Companies Act did not exclude the jurisdiction of the court; it merely excluded the admission of evidence. However, (2), allowing the Registrar's appeal, on that basis the court was precluded on an application to judicial review by any person other than the Attorney-General from inquiring into the facts on which the registration had been made.
R. *v.* REGISTRAR OF COMPANIES, *ex p.* CENTRAL BANK OF INDIA [1986] 1 All E.R. 105, C.A.

325. **Resolution of company—reduction of capital—trivial error**
[Companies Act 1985 (c.6), s.137.] The draughtsman of a company's resolution made a trivial error in that he miscalculated a figure of nearly 15 million shares by three. The shareholder sought a corrective special resolution to rectify. *held,* that it was an unnecessary and unwarranted expense, and the application would be struck out as disclosing no reasonable cause of action: WILLAIRE SYSTEMS, *Re, The Times,* July 17 1986, C.A.

326. **Shares—classes of shares—rights of individual shareholder—whether class rights**
[Companies Act 1985 (c.6), s.125.]
A company which issued shares to a shareholder and amended its articles to grant the shareholder particular rights to prevent a take-over could not later cancel the articles since the shareholder had rights attached to a class of shares which could not be abrogated.
P and D were both publishers of newspapers. They negotiated a transaction whereby D would acquire one of P's papers and P would acquire 10 per cent. of D's share capital. D duly issued the 10 per cent. shareholding and as part of the agreement under which the shares were issued amended its articles to grant P rights of pre-emption over other ordinary shares, rights in respect of unissued shares, and the right to appoint a director. The purpose of such rights was to enable P as a shareholder to prevent a take-over of D. After several years, the directors of D

proposed to convene an extraordinary general meeting and to pass a special resolution to cancel the articles which gave special rights to P. P sought a declaration that the rights were class rights which could not be abrogated without his consent, and an injunction restraining D from holding the meeting. *Held,* granting the declaration, that the special rights granted by the articles were rights which although not attached to any particular shares were conferred on P as a shareholder in D and were attached to the shares held for the time being by P without which it was not entitled to the rights. Accordingly P had "rights attached to a class of shares" and since s.125 of the Companies Act 1985 provided that class rights could not be varied or abrogated without the consent of the class members, the special rights enjoyed by P could not be varied or abrogated without his consent. (*Bushell* v. *Faith* [1970] C.L.Y. 285 applied.) On the facts, the adoption of articles by D conferring the special rights on P was a condition precedent to the agreement between the parties and was not a contractual obligation of D. Accordingly, it was not a term of the agreement that P would have the benefit of the special rights conferred on it by the articles, nor could such a term be implied.

CUMBRIAN NEWSPAPERS GROUP *v.*CUMBERLAND & WESTMORLAND HERALD NEWSPAPER & PRINTING CO. [1986] 3 W.L.R. 26, Scott J.

327. Shares—transfer—restrictions on transfer—registration

Phoenix Property and Investment Co. ("the company") was a private property investment company limited by shares. Its articles of association provided, *inter alia,* that "(E) . . . no share shall be transferred by a member or by any person entitled to transfer the same to any person not already a member of the company if any member for the time being of the company or the wife, husband, parent or child (not being a minor) of any member shall be willing to purchase the same" and "(F) Where any shares shall subject to the provisions of subd. (E) be offered for sale the same shall unless the parties shall be able to agree as to the sale price be so offered and may be purchased at a fair value as determined by the auditors for the time being of the company." In February 1982 P purchased 90 shares in the company from the executors of the estate of a deceased shareholder. On February 26, 1982 the executors executed a transfer of the shares to P and subsequently forwarded the same to the company secretary requesting him to register the transfer and provide a new certificate in respect of the holding for P. The company secretary declined to register the transfer and in April 1982 the board of directors resolved to notify shareholders that 90 shares in the company were being offered for sale. The company secretary issued a circular to all the shareholders inviting bids for the shares within 14 days. Three bids were received from existing shareholders. P commenced an action seeking an order that the company register P as the holder of the 90 shares in question. The trial judge held that the transfer dated February 26, 1982 was effective between P and the executors giving rise to a beneficial interest in P's favour in the shares but that P could not become the legal owner until the transfer was registered. The trial judge further held that P was entitled to have the transfer registered by the company. The company appealed against the latter part of the judgment but not the former part. *Held,* allowing the appeal, that in its terms (E) took away the right of a member to transfer his shares to an outsider to the company only if another member or a specified relative was willing to purchase the shares. The provision was not wholly void as being unworkable. The parties to the contract embodied in the articles clearly contemplated that existing shareholders and their specified relatives should be given an opportunity to purchase shares in the company before they were sold to an outsider. In order to achieve that end and give business efficacy to the articles the court was entitled to and would imply a further term into the articles that any person wishing to sell shares in the company shall first take reasonable steps to give the other members and their specified relatives a reasonable opportunity to make an offer to purchase the shares at a fair value to be determined by the company's auditors in default of agreement. The fact that there might be difficulties in notifying the specified relatives that the shares were for sale was a matter relevant to whether a vendor had taken reasonable steps on the facts of each particular case. Such difficulties as might exist did not preclude the court from implying the term into the articles. No reasonable notice of the proposed sale of the shares had been given by the executors to the other members of the company or the specified relatives. Accordingly the transfer of the shares to P was in breach of (E). In consequence the board of directors were bound by the articles to refuse to register the transfer to P: TETT v. PHOENIX PROPERTY AND INVESTMENT CO. [1986] PCC 210, C.A.

328. Shares—transfer—whether required transfer

Companies Act 1985 (c.6), s.459.] Under s.459 of the Companies Act 1985, a petition may be presented to the courts by a member of a company who feels that the conduct of its affairs are prejudicial to himself or other members. The articles of association of X provided that a shareholding member was bound to execute a transfer of his shares if he ceased to be an employee or a director (unfair dismissal was excluded). In the absence of agreement of the value of the shares, the company's auditor was to value them. Because of a breakdown in the relationship between K, a minority shareholder director, and T, a majority shareholder, K was dismissed, and required to transfer his shares. *Held*, that it could not be accepted that if there was an irretrievable breakdown in relations between members of a corporate quasi-partnership, the exclusion of K from management was *ipso facto* unfairly prejudicial conduct within s.459. Unfairness would depend on whether it was reasonable for him rather than another to be dismissed, and on the provisions of the articles of association. K could have no legitimate expectation that in the event of a breakdown between himself and T, he would not be relied on to sell his shares at a fair value (*Postgate & Denby, Financial Times,* July 1, 1986 applied): XYZ, Re, *The Financial Times,* August 12, 1986, Hoffman J.

329. Shares—valuation—procedure

Where a company's articles of association lay down a machinery for valuing a member's shares, the member should use that machinery, and will not ordinarily be entitled to complain of unfairness unless he has done so: COMPANY, A, Re (No. 004377 of 1986), *The Times,* August 27, 1986, Hoffmann J.

330. Trading in shares and land—hotel property—Malaysia. See LIM FOO YONG SDN BHD v. COMPTROLLER-GENERAL OF INLAND REVENUE, § 1768.

331. Unfair prejudice applications

COMPANIES (UNFAIR PREJUDICE APPLICATIONS) PROCEEDINGS RULES 1986 (No. 2000) [£1·40], made under the Insolvency Act 1986 (c.45), s.411; operative on December 29, 1986; sets out a new procedure in relation to petitions presented to the Court under Pt. XVII of the Companies Act 1985.

332. Valuation of shares—capitalisation of future profits—methods of allowing for risk

Where the shares of a private company making handsome profits but having little in the way of assets are to be valued, the proper valuation method is to capitalise those profits making a due allowance for risk.

B was a minority shareholder in a private company which had virtually no break-up value, but which was making very good profits. Following a consent order in the proceedings dealing with liability, he sought a valuation of the shares. *Held*, that the proper method was to capitalise the future profits making an allowance for risk, but being careful not to allow twice over for what might in reality be the same risk. Thus, either the future profits can be estimated, making there an allowance for risk, and a price/earnings ratio chosen; or the risk allowance can be incorporated into the price/earnings figure; or partly one method, and partly the other may be adopted. But always care should be taken not to take risk into account more than was strictly proper.

BUCKINGHAM v. FRANCIS [1986] 2 All E.R. 738, Staughton J.

333. VAT certificates—administrative receivers. See RECEIVERS, § 2832.

333a. Voluntary liquidation—liquidator appointed by director—majority of creditors seeking compulsory winding up

[Companies Act 1985 (c.6), s.645.]

The court, in deciding whether to wind up a company under the Companies Act 1985, s.645, can take into account the values of the creditors' debts, and the general principles of fairness and commercial morality.

Shortly after the petitioning creditor obtained judgment for £50,000 the company went into voluntary liquidation. The liquidator was in effect appointed by the sole director of the company. At a meeting from which the creditor and other independent creditors were excluded, the appointment of the liquidator was confirmed. The petitioning creditor with the support of other large value creditors presented a petition for compulsory winding up. The petition was opposed by some of the smaller creditors. *Held,* granting the petition, that the court in having regard to the wishes of creditors, was entitled to have regard to the value of their debts and their probable motives.

PALMER MARINE SURVEYS, *Re* [1986] 1 W.L.R. 573, Hoffmann J.

334. Winding up
COMPANIES (WINDING UP) (AMENDMENT) RULES 1986 (No. 619) [45p], made under the Insolvency Act 1985 (c.65), s.106; operative on April 28, 1986; amend S.I. 1949 No. 330 to take account of the 1985 Act.

335. Winding up—advertisement—practice direction. See PRACTICE DIRECTION (Ch.D.) (No. 1 of 1986) (COMPANIES COURT: ADVERTISEMENT OF WINDING UP PETITIONS), § 2721.

336. Winding up—assignment of petitioning creditor's debts—substitution
[H.K.] [Companies Ordinance (Laws of Hong Kong 1984 rev. c.32), s.179(1); Companies (Winding-up) Rules (1984 ed. c.32), r.33.]
The court had an unfettered discretion to substitute a petitioner for winding-up who has acquired the debt by assignment after the date of the petition.
A finance company assigned to a bank debts owed to it by the appellant companies. Both the company and the bank presented joint winding-up petitions, and the bank subsequently assigned the debts to the assignee. The company and bank applied for the assignee to be substituted as sole petitioner, the judge making the orders. The companies appealed on the basis that the assignee was not a creditor at the date of the petition. *Held,* dismissing the companies' appeals, that the court had an unfettered discretion to permit the substitution of a petitioner who had acquired the debt after the presentation of the petition (*Paris Skating Rink Co., Re* (1887) 5 Ch.D. 959 explained).

PERAK PIONEER *v.* PETROLIAM NASIONAL BHD [1986] 3 W.L.R. 105, P.C.

337. Winding up—attendance before registrar—jurisdiction of registrar
[Companies Act 1985 (c.6), s.520; Companies (Winding up) Rules 1949 (S.I. 1949 No. 330); rr.27, 33.] P presented a petition to wind up a company, C, which was served on C by post. The petition was not advertised., At the Rule 33 hearing, P applied for and was granted leave to withdraw the petition. On the same day C applied to strike out the petition on the forthcoming hearing. C was not told of the registrar's order. The judge dismissed the petition and ordered P to pay C's costs with liberty to P to apply to set aside the order. P applied to set aside the order. *Held,* dismissing the application, that even though the petition had not been advertised, the registrar had no jurisdiction to give leave to withdraw the petition on the application of P alone (*Insurance Co., Re*) [1875] 33 L.T. 49, *Royal Mutual Benefit Building Society, Re* (1960) C.L.Y. 442 applied; *Five Oaks Construction, Re* [1968] C.L.Y. 458 considered): COMPANY A, *Re*, May 20, 1986, H.H. Judge Cox; Exeter County Court. [*Ex rel. S. R. Davies, Barrister.*]

338. Winding-up—bankruptcy rules—mutual credit and set-off—preferential and non-preferential debts—rateable set off
[Bankruptcy Act 1914 (c.59), s.31.]
Section 31 of the Bankruptcy Act 1914 gives no right to either debtor or creditor to appropriate any credit to any particular debt or part of a debt. Accordingly the principle that equality is equity operates so that credits should be set off rateably between preferential and non-preferential parts of a debt.
A company went into liquidation with sufficient assets to meet the claims of preferential creditors but not to meet those of the ordinary creditors. A debt was owed to the D.H.S.S. which was partly preferential and partly non-preferential. At the same time, the Crown, represented by the Customs and Excise, owed the company £2,750·69 as a refund of value added tax. The Crown sought to set off this sum, pursuant to s.31 of the Bankruptcy Act 1914, against that part of the debt owed to it (through the D.H.S.S.) which was non-preferential, which would otherwise be irrecoverable. The liquidator disputed this action of the Crown claiming that the debt due to the company should be set off first against the preferential part of the debt, which would leave more funds available for distribution among the other preferential creditors or even, if there were sufficient funds, for the unsecured creditors. The D.H.S.S. applied to the court for a determination on whether the £2,570·69 should be set off first against the preferential part of the debt owed to it, or first against the

non-preferential part of that debt, or rateably against the respective parts of the debt. *Held,* that s.31 was not intended to benefit a debtor or creditor or any class of creditors at the expense of any other but to provide a means of conducting an accounting exercise and it gave no right to either debtor or creditor to appropriate any credit to any particular debt or part of a debt. Accordingly the principle that equality was equity operated so that the credit should be set off rateably between the preferential and the non-preferential part of the debt (dictum of Buckley J. in *E. J. Morel* (1934), *Re* [1961] C.L.Y. 1200; not followed).

UNIT 2 WINDOWS (IN LIQUIDATION), *Re* [1985] 1 W.L.R. 1383, Walton J.

339. Winding up—compulsory—presentation of petition by contributory—interlocutory injunction restraining presentation—availability of minority shareholder relief

[Companies Act 1985 (c.6), ss.459, 517(g), 520(2).]

C S and W were directors of Coulon Sanderson & Ward ("the company"). In 1979 C went into semi-retirement, and in 1983 S resigned as a director and disposed of his shares in the company. W was the managing director of the company with day to day control of its activities. After S resigned C had majority control of the voting rights in the company. Disputes arose between C and W which proved incapable of resolution and resulted in W giving one month's notice of resignation as a director in March 1985. The difficulties between C and W were such that it was agreed that W's resignation should take effect on an earlier date. W started in business in competition with the company and thereafter by letters dated April 30 and May 30, 1985 written by his solicitors stated his intention to petition for the company to be compulsorily wound up under s.222(f) Companies Act 1948 (now s.517(g) Companies Act 1985). W contended the company's business was in effect a partnership business from which he had been expelled by C's conduct and that C was mismanaging the company in such a manner as to jeopardise its existence and greatly diminish the value of W's shareholding. The letters set out W's contentions at great length citing details of the facts relied upon. The company sought an undertaking from W not to present a petition without first giving seven days' notice thereof. When W refused to give such an undertaking the company commenced proceedings on July 2, 1985 seeking an injunction to restrain W from presenting a winding up petition or from advertising any such petition. On the same day, the company issued a notice of motion for hearing on July 5 seeking an injunction in the same terms. It was contended on behalf of the company that the presentation of a winding-up petition as opposed to a petition for minority shareholder relief under s.75 of the Companies Act 1980 (now s.459 Companies Act 1985) would be an abuse of the process of the court. At the hearing W said he wished to answer the company's evidence. The judge was referred to the material parts of the evidence before the court including the lengthy letters written by W's solicitors and heard full argument on both sides. The judge stated that he did not propose to decide whether the proposed petition was an abuse until all the evidence was filed. The motion was adjourned for seven days and an injunction in the terms sought granted in the meantime to "do no more than hold the ring." On July 12 the motion came on before a different judge with only 15 minutes to spare in which to consider it. An order was made adjourning the motion to a date to be fixed and continuing the injunction in the meantime. *Held,* allowing W's appeal, that the court should not, on the hearing of an interlocutory motion, interfere with what would otherwise appear to be a legitimate right to present a winding-up petition unless the evidence before it is sufficient to establish prima facie that the company would succeed in establishing that the presentation of the petition would constitute an abuse of the process. That principle should be applied whether the injunction was sought *ex parte* or *inter partes* unless in exceptional circumstances time did not permit an adequate consideration of the issues. Before granting the injunction on July 5 the judge had first to satisfy himself on the evidence then available whether the company had established prima facie that the presentation of a winding-up petition by W was an abuse of process. As the judge had not come to that conclusion the injunction ought not to have been granted on July 5. Had W's complaints related solely to mismanagement on the part of C the remedies available in the form of minority shareholder relief were prima facie adequate so that a winding-up order would be unobtainable by virtue of s.520(2) of the Companies Act 1985. As W raised complaints of a quasi-partnership nature it was doubtful whether those complaints fell within the ambit of s.459 of the Companies Act 1985 so as to entitle W to minority shareholder relief. The order made on July 12, 1985 was made without reference to the evidence and on the assumption that the injunction was properly granted on July 5. Accordingly the order made on July 12 must be set aside (*Bryanston Finance* v. *De Vries (No. 2)* [1975] C.L.Y. 319 applied, *Beese* v. *Woodhouse* [1970] C.L.Y. 2287 distinguished): WARD v. COULON, SANDERSON AND WARD [1986] PCC 57, C.A.

340. Winding up—contributions—unpaid dividends—holding company as member
[Companies Act 1948 (11 and 12 Geo. 6, c.38), s.212(1)(*g*).]

H, a wholly owned subsidiary of H Holdings, declared dividends between 1974 and 1981 which were not paid over to H Holdings but retained for use in the business. In 1982 H went into a creditors' voluntary winding up and H Holdings claimed £3½ million as a loan due to it from H. The liquidator rejected the claim since it was for unpaid dividends and was not payable in competition with other creditors of H. H Holdings applied for an order reversing the liquidator's decision. *Held,* refusing the application, that the burden was on H Holdings to show that the unpaid dividends were subject to some agreement creating a loan or that it was to be treated as though the dividends had been paid and then loaned back. There was no evidence of such an agreement and no consideration to support it. Further there was no evidence that H, when it declared the dividend, did not have the cash to pay them and the striking of a balance on mutual debts required the use of real money. With the passage of time the unpaid dividends had not been recognised by H and H Holdings as being left on loan. The liquidator was correct to treat the sums due to H Holdings as being due in its character as a member and therefore H Holdings was not entitled to be paid in competition with other creditors of H under s.212(1)(*g*) of the 1948 Act.

HOLLIDAY (L.B.) & Co. *Re,* [1986] 2 All E.R. 367, Mervyn Davies J.

341. Winding up—expenses incurred "previously" to compulsory winding up—voluntary liquidator
[Companies (Winding-Up) Rules 1949 (S.I. 1949 No. 330 (L4)), r.195.] A voluntary liquidator's expenses are expenses incurred before the making of the compulsory winding up order, and are costs incurred in the winding-up *Waterloo Manufacturing Co. (Burnley) Re* (1936) 3 L.J. CCR considered): SORGE (A.V.) & Co, *Re, The Times,* July 18, 1986, Hoffmann J.

342. Winding up—hearing in chambers—whether permissible
[Cayman Is.] [Companies Law, s.94.]

Petitioning creditors applied for the hearing of winding-up petitions in respect of two companies to be held *in camera,* or in chambers. The basic reason was to avoid the risk of breach of confidentiality as regards overseas investors who had been assured of confidentiality for their investment activities. *Held,* adjourning the proceedings into chambers, that the court would exercise its discretion under s.94, not strictly because it was in the interests of justice, but as a matter of public policy and to protect investors' rights of confidentiality: S (A COMPANY, *Re;* T (A COMPANY), *Re* [1986] PCC 241, Grand Ct., Cayman Islands.

343. Winding up—insurance company failing to pay debt—petition—whether abuse of process
[Companies Act 1985 (c.6), s.158(1)(*e*).]

Where a company, even a well-known insurance company, fails to pay a specific sum it concedes it owes, it is not an abuse of process to file a petition for its winding-up.

P, a well known insurance company, paid to D most of their insurance claim. Oral agreement was reached as to the balance of £1,154. Despite frequent attempts to obtain the money, D received no reply from the company. D presented a petition to wind up the insurance company on the ground that it was unable to pay its debts. The company applied for an injunction alleging abuse of process, in that given their standing and reputation D could not swear they believed the company to be insolvent. *Held,* refusing the injunction, that where a company was under an undisputed obligation to pay a specific sum and failed so to do, it could be inferred that it was unable to do so (*Mann* v. *Goldstein* [1968] C.L.Y. 456 applied).

CORNHILL INSURANCE v. IMPROVEMENT SERVICES [1986] 1 W.L.R. 114, Harman J.

344. Winding up—persistent default by liquidator—order of disqualification
[Companies Act 1948 (11 and 12 Geo. 6, c.38), s.188(1)(*b*)(4) as amended by Companies Act 1981 (c.62), s.93(1); Companies Act 1976 (c.69), s.28.]

The court was not restricted, in respect of an application under s.93 of the Companies Act 1981, to considering defaults occurring after the coming into force of the section on June 15, 1982.

The Secretary of State applied pursuant to s.188(1)(*b*) as amended, for an order for an accountant to be disqualified as a liquidator. The ground of the application was persistent default in the sending of returns. The amendment came into force on June 15, 1982, but most of the evidence of default related to matters before that date. *Held,* that the amendment did not restrict the court to matters occurring after the relevant date, and the court was entitled to make the order notwithstanding the defendant had not been convicted in respect of any default. (*Grantham Wholesale Fruit, Vegetable and Potato Merchants, Re* [1972] C.L.Y 394 considered).

ARCTIC ENGINEERING *Re,* [1986] 1 W.L.R. 686, Hoffmann J.

345. Winding up—set off—right to retain money against future liabilities. See CHARGE CARD SERVICES, *Re,* § 390.

346. Winding up—whether fixed or floating charges

[Ire.] A company created in favour of a bank what was stated to be a first fixed charge over its book debts and other debts present and future and two days later created a debenture in favour of the bank which charged by way of a first fixed legal charge the company's present and future book debts. All moneys received in respect of the book debts were to be paid into a special bank account, the bank having an absolute discretion to allow the company to transfer moneys from this account to its working account. In certain circumstances the bank could ensure that no moneys be withdrawn from this special account. On a winding up of the company the liquidator applied to the court for a direction as to whether the charges created were fixed or floating charges. *Held,* on appeal, that (1) a fixed charge may be created in respect of book debts and other debts present and future but that the use of the words "fixed charge" was not conclusive; and (2) the requirement that the proceeds of the book debts be paid into the special account under the bank's control deprived the company of the free use of the proceeds. The charges were, accordingly fixed charges: KEENAN BROS. *Re,* [1985] I.R. 401, Supreme Ct.

COMPULSORY PURCHASE

347. Acquisition of land—delay before notice of inquiry—effect

[Mal.] [Government Proceedings Ordinance 1956 (F. M. Ordinance 58 of 1956, rev. 1965), s.29(1)(*b*); Land Acquisition Act 1960 (No. 34 of 1960, rev. 1976), ss. 3, 8(1), 10(1), 68, Sched. 1, para. 1(1).]

An acquiring authority has a duty to complete the compulsory acquisition of land within a reasonable time.

The State Authority decided to acquire land compulsorily under s.3 of the 1960 Act. The declaration of that decision was published in the Gazette in 1972, under s.8, but the Collector failed to give notice of an inquiry to assess compensation until 1979. An award was made in 1980 based on the value of the land in 1972. The landowners, who were precluded under s.68 of the 1960 Act from bringing a suit against the Collector applied for certiorari to quash the award on the grounds of delay. The judge quashed the declaration and all subsequent decisions. On appeal by the Collector the Federal Court allowed the appeal in part. The Collector appealed and the landowners cross-appealed. *Held,* dismissing the Collector's appeal, that (1) an acquiring authority had a duty to complete the compulsory acquisition of land within a reasonable time and it was implicit within s.10 of the 1960 Act that the Collector could not delay giving notice of the holding of the inquiry; the seven-year delay invalidated the inquiry and the award and the court had properly set them aside; dictum of Upjohn L.J. in *Simpson's Motor Sales (London)* v. *Hendon Corporation* [1963] C.L.Y. 455 applied; (2) dismissing the cross-appeal, the Collector was not entitled to possession of the land and must restore it; although the Federal Court had properly set aside the order for repossession of the land since under s.29(1)(*b*) of the 1956 Ordinance the court had no power to make such an order against the Collector, the landowners would be granted a declaration that they were entitled, as against the State Authority, to possession of the land.

COLLECTOR OF LAND REVENUE SOUTH WEST DISTRICT PENANG *v.* KAM GIN PAIK [1986] 1 W.L.R. 412, P.C.

348. Alternative routes—relevance

Melton Borough Council made a compulsory purchase order on land required for a rear service road to a main shopping street. Alternative routes had been considered. An inquiry was held. The Secretary of State refused to confirm the order. Melton Borough Council applied for judicial review of the minister's decision. *Held*, that (1) the local authority must establish that the acquisition was necessary; (2) the local authority must provide the minister with all relevant information; (3) the Secretary of State was entitled to find that the case for the non-viability of the alternative route had not been made out. Application dismissed: R. *v.* SECRETARY OF STATE FOR THE ENVIRONMENT, *ex p.* MELTON BOROUGH COUNCIL [1985] J.P.L. 190, Forbes J.

349. Blight notice—whether jurisdiction to strike out

[Town and Country Planning Act 1971 (c.78) s.195.]

The Lands Tribunal has no jurisdiction to strike out a blight notice.

B purported to serve a blight notice under s.193(1) of the Town and Country Planning Act 1971 in the respect of certain land of which he was the freehold owner. The land formed part of a larger plot of land owned by B. Section 193(2)(*a*) of the Act provided that B could not serve a notice under s.193 of the Act in respect of land forming part of a hereditament or agricultural unit the entirety of which he owned. The Secretary of State served a counter-notice on B objecting to the blight notice on the ground that the land did not constitute an agricultural unit nor was it a separate or part of a separate hereditament in the Valuation List. The counter-notice was referred to the Lands Tribunal. The Secretary of State applied to strike out B's notice as a preliminary point of law in reliance on the provisions of s.193(2)(*a*) of the Act. *Held*, dismissing the application, that B's notice contravened s.193(2)(*a*) of the Act. That point was not raised nor could it be raised by virtue of s.194(2) of the Act. By s.195 of the Act the Lands Tribunal only had jurisdiction to uphold the objections raised in the counter-notice, in which event the blight notice would not take effect, or to declare the blight notice valid. The Tribunal had no jurisdiction to strike out the blight notice (*Essex County Council* v. *Essex Incorporated Congregational Church Union* [1963] C.L.Y. 3432 applied).

BINNS *v.* SECRETARY OF STATE FOR TRANSPORT (1985) 50 P. & C.R. 468, Lands Tribunal.

350. Compensation—disturbance—regional development grant—deduction

[Land Compensation Act 1961 (c.33), s.5.]

It is contrary to public policy to lessen the inducement afforded by payment of a regional development grant to relocate in a development area by deducting the amount of the grant from compensation payable for disturbance.

The local authority agreed to buy P's premises at a price equivalent to the compensation which would have been payable had the acquisition been by way of compulsory purchase. Most of the price was compensation for disturbance. P acquired new premises and carried out works the cost of which were agreed to fall within the compass of disturbance and on which they received a regional development grant. The local authority sought to deduct the grant from the price they were otherwise liable to pay. The Lands Tribunal held that the compensation should be assessed without any deduction. *Held*, dismissing the appeal, that compensation for compulsory purchase was to be assessed in the same way as damages at common law; it was contrary to public policy to lessen the inducement of a regional development grant by deducting the grant from the compensation; the loss caused by disturbance was different in kind from the payment of the grant; there was no right to make the deduction (*Rickets* v. *Metropolitan Railway Co.* (1865) 34 L.J.Q.B. 257; *Horn* v. *Sunderland Corporation* [1941] 2 K.B. 26, *Parry* v. *Cleaver* [1969] C.L.Y. 906 applied; *West Suffolk County Council* v. *W. Rought* [1956] C.L.Y. 1275 distinguished).

PALATINE GRAPHIC ART CO. *v.* LIVERPOOL CITY COUNCIL [1986] 2 W.L.R. 285, C.A.

351. Compensation—meaning of "no general demand or market"

[Land Compensation Act 1961 (c.33), s.5(5).]

In considering whether no general demand or market for land for a particular use existed in ascertaining the appropriate basis for compensation on a compulsory purchase the court was concerned with the existence of an actual existing demand and not a latent demand that might arise if land for that particular use became available.

The appellants owned a livestock auction market in Carlisle which the county council agreed to acquire. The agreement provided that the purchase price should be the compensation that would be payable if the property had been compulsorily purchased. The appellants sought a price based on the compensation payable on a reinstatement basis as provided by s.5(5) of the Land Compensation Act 1961. The county council contended that the appellants could not be entitled to the cost of reinstating an equivalent property on the ground that there existed a general demand or market for land and premises for use as a livestock auction mart. The county council adduced evidence that there had been 18 transactions in livestock markets since 1957 and that although they rarely came on the market they were invariably bought when they did. The Land Tribunal held that there was a latent demand for property for livestock markets that became apparent when land devoted or intended to be devoted to the purpose of a livestock market was offered for sale. There was, therefore, a general demand or market for land for use as a livestock market so that s.5(5) of the Act could not provide the basis for ascertaining the purchase price to be paid by the county council. The Court of Appeal upheld that decision. *Held*, allowing the appeal that the relevant question for the purposes of s.5(5) of the Act was whether "there is no general demand or market for land" for the purposes of livestock marts. In that event the purchase price could be ascertained on a reinstatement basis. The word "general" referred to "demand" and not to "market". For the purposes of s.5(5) of the Act the existence of a general demand had to be determined at the time compensation fell to be assessed, *i.e.* the present time, and not with reference to some conditions or state of circumstances that may or may not exist at some future time. There was no evidence of the existence of a market in land for the purposes of livestock marts. There was no general demand for land for that purpose presently in existence. The latent demand identified by the Land Tribunal might only come into existence at a future date if a livestock mart was offered for sale and could not be described as an ever-present unsatisfied demand for land for the purposes of a livestock mart. The price to be paid by the county council could be ascertained on a reinstatement basis in accordance with s.5(5) of the Act.

HARRISON & HETHERINGTON *v.* CUMBRIA COUNTY COUNCIL (1985) 50 P. & C.R. 396, H.L.

352. Compensation—purchase after entry—whether purchaser entitled to compensation—whether purchase price relevant

A purchaser who purchases land after notice to treat and entry under a compulsory purchase order is nevertheless entitled to compensation, and the purchase price is irrelevant to the amount.

This was a reference to determine the amount of compensation payable in respect of the compulsory acquisition, in order to construct a new road, of land which formed part of the curtilage of a freehold shop and warehouse at Sevenoaks, Kent. The principal issue was as to injurious affection of the remainder of the premises which, eleven days after the date of entry, had been purchased by the claimant, subject to the benefit of the claim for compensation, for £200,000. The acquiring authority had carried out work valued at £3,000 to provide alternative vehicular access to the remainder of the premises, and it was agreed that the award of compensation should take this into account. Both parties advanced a "before and after" approach to valuation, the claimant seeking £168,000 and the authority contending that the value of the remainder of the premises was greater than that of the whole before acquisition. The authority made a preliminary submission that the claimant had suffered no loss because it had received value for money. *Held*, that the purchaser was nevertheless entitled to compensation, and the purchase price was irrelevant to the amount. Nonetheless, the claimants' figure was far too high, and they would be awarded £3,250 in injurious affection and £100 for land taken.

LANDLINK TWO AND BARCLAYS BANK *v.* SEVENOAKS DISTRICT COUNCIL (1986) 51 P. &. C.R. 100, Lands Tribunal.

353. Home loss payment—redevelopment—purpose for which land was acquired

[Land Compensation Act 1973 (c.26), s.29(1)(c).]

"Purposes for which the land was acquired" in s.29(1)(c) of the Land Compensation Act 1973 refers to broad and general purposes, rather than any specific scheme.

In 1963 a local authority compulsorily purchased land in order to clear it and erect housing. In 1967 before any clearance the defendant became a tenant of a dwelling on the land; in 1980 the authority decided not to erect its own housing but to sell it to a private developer. A little later the defendant vacated and was relocated. The question arose whether he was entitled to a home loss payment under s.29(1)(c) of the 1973 Act. The judge held that that he was not so entitled. *Held,* allowing the appeal, that "purpose for which the land was acquired" was to be given a broad purposive construction; it did not refer to the precise scheme envisaged at the time of acquisition (*Follows* v. *Peabody Trust* (1983) 10 H.L.R. 62 applied).

GREATER LONDON COUNCIL *v.* HOLMES [1986] 1 All E.R. 739, C.A.

354. Lands Tribunal decisions

ADVANCE GROUND RENTS *v.* MIDDLESBROUGH BOROUGH COUNCIL (Ref./174/1985) (1986) 280 E.G. 1015. (The local authority sought compulsorily to acquire a house in Middlesbrough as part of a clearance scheme, and served notice to treat and notice of entry in August 1977 on S, who were described in the order as "owners or reputed owners." In September 1977 D (who traded in the name of S) submitted a claim form, which revealed that the house was mortgaged to L. Possession was taken and the house demolished in July 1979, and compensation agreed with D in August 1979, but it subsequently transpired that L had died and that his interest had been disposed of to A. A's title was proved to the authority's satisfaction by August 1981, but no notice to treat was served on A until February 1985, in response to which A claimed the freehold interest and £7,000 by way of compensation. The tribunal found that service of notice to treat on A had taken place well outside the three-year time limit from the time the compulsory purchase order became operative prescribed by s.4 of the Compulsory Purchase Act 1965; and that it was also served well beyond the six-month time limit from the time that A's title had been established in law prescribed by s.22(3) of the Act. Hence the notice to treat served on A was invalid, the authority had lost the opportunity to rectify the omission, and the tribunal had no jurisdiction to determine compensation under s.1 of the Land Compensation Act 1961. In case the tribunal's findings as to jurisdiction should prove incorrect, the tribunal determined compensation at the V.O.'s figure of £59, in the absence of any other evidence.)

355. PAYNE *v.* KENT COUNTY COUNCIL (Ref./127/1984) (1986) 280 E.G. 645. (This was a reference to determine the compensation payable following the compulsory acquisition for highway purposes of the freehold interest in a petrol filling station with a small showroom, workshop and small cafe business on the outskirts of Chatham. The valuation date was December 17, 1982. The tribunal, taking into account the facts that there had been a nearby garage in a "milking" position which would, but for the new scheme, have been redeveloped and modernised; that there had been a drop in throughput in 1981–82 not entirely attributable to the scheme of acquisition; and that there had been price-cutting, the effect of which, though marginal, was properly to be taken into account, concluded that a prospective purchaser would base his valuation on an estimated annual throughput of 1,500,000 gallons. The tribunal then considered the appropriate multiplier to apply to the gallonage. On the rental approach, it applied a figure of 3·5p per gallon, capitalised at six per cent., giving a total of £871,500; whilst it arrived at a capital value of £882,353 by adopting a figure of 1·7 gallons to the pound. It then rounded off the gross compensation at £875,000, from which was to be deducted £175,000 in respect of the cost of redevelopment. The tribunal further found that there was insufficient room for a modern catering business, but added £50,000 in respect of a small catering unit, which could be operated without too much dislocation on the forecourt. Total compensation was thus assessed at £750,000.)

356. SMITH *v.* WEST MIDLANDS COUNTY COUNCIL (Ref./240/1983) (1986) 278 E.G. 419. (This was a reference to determine the compensation payable following the compulsory purchase of 1,860 sq. yards of residential backland in the centre of Birmingham. Forty-two garages and workshops on the site had been demolished prior to the valuation date of December 20, 1982, and it was not disputed that outline planning permission would have been granted for the erection of three terraced houses with access by private road. The claimant contended for a figure of £6 per sq. yard, giving a total of £11,160; whereas the authority argued that the site was not economically viable and valued the land at £1,180, on the basis that it could be used to accommodate 37 prefabricated garages. The tribunal, noting that the land was unique with no helpful comparables, accepted the claimant's valuation and assessed compensation at £11,160.)

357. Lands Tribunal for Northern Ireland decision

MAHOOD v. DEPARTMENT OF THE ENVIRONMENT FOR NORTHERN IRELAND (Ref./33/1983) (1985) 277 E.G. 654 (This was a reference to determine the proper measure of surveyors' fees payable in respect of the compulsory acquisition of land fronting a main road which was being widened. It was agreed that the correct scale was RICS Scale 5, but disputed whether the fee should be based solely on the amount of compensation for land taken (agreed at £30) or additionally upon the cost (£234) of accommodation works consisting of replacing the old fence with a new post and wire fence. The parties accepted that the correct test, one of fact and degree in every case, was whether there had been "negotiation" of the accommodation works between the Department and the surveyors acting as the claimant's agents. The tribunal found that the Department had made simple proposals for a replacement fence which were accepted without demur by the surveyors, subject to two minor amendments. There had thus been no negotiation as required by Scale 5, and the fees were to be calculated on the figure of £30 at the minimum fee of £7.50.)

358. Notices to treat and enter—service on an agent—whether good service

[Compulsory Purchase Act 1965 (c.56), s.30.]

The service of notices to treat and enter in respect of a property served on an agent for the owner of it was not proper service within the requirements of the Compulsory Purchase Act 1965, s.30.

PF owned property within the urban district of Huyton-with-Roby, now the metropolitan borough of Knowsley, which was subject to a compulsory purchase order. In 1972 PF emigrated to Australia, thereafter the property was dealt with by RF, his brother. The Council served a notice to treat and subsequently a notice of entry on RF. The matter came before the Lands Tribunal where the Council conceded that the notices had not been served in accordance with s.30 of the Compulsory Purchase Act 1965. The Lands Tribunal held that the notices had been properly served on RF as the general agent of PF with full authority to receive statutory notices. RF on behalf of PF appealed by way of case stated. *Held*, allowing the appeal, that s.30 of the Act set out a complete code for the service of the notices. The notices were not properly served in accordance with that code. It was not possible to escape from the provisions of the Act by providing for service upon the agent of the owner as the Lands Tribunal had sought to do. The notices were therefore invalid (*Shepherd* v. *Corporation of Norwich* (1855) 30 Ch.D. 553 applied, *Townsends Carriers* v. *Pfizer* [1978] C.L.Y. 1790 distinguished).

FAGAN v. KNOWSLEY METROPOLITAN BOROUGH COUNCIL (1985) 50 P. & C.R. 363, C.A.

359. S.52 reservation—whether restrictive covenant—if so, whether obsolete

[Town and Country Planning Act 1971 (c.78), s.52.] In 1976 the District Council gave outline planning permission in relation to 34.3 acres of agricultural land near Towcester for "residential development (343 units) incorporating associated open space, a site for a primary school and local shopping provision." At the same time the developer entered into an agreement under s.52 of the Town and Country Planning Act 1971 which provided that, ". . . an area of 1.3 hectares adjacent to the playing field and amenity open space shall be reserved for school purposes . . ." The designated area was not shown on the plans annexed to the agreement, but was shown on those attached to the outline planning permission. When the specified land was subsequently acquired compulsorily for a primary school, the developer argued that the s.52 reservation had not created a restrictive covenant running with the land, that such restriction as had been created was of limited duration, and that the specified area could therefore be valued for compensation purposes under rule (2) of s.5 of the Land Compensation Act 1961 without reference to the reservation for school purposes. The Lands Tribunal upheld these contentions, and further held that, if a restrictive covenant had been created, it had become obsolete and should be discharged under s.84(1) of the Law of Property Act 1925, on account of the compulsory purchase order and its consequences. *Held*, allowing the district council's appeal, that (1) the s.52 agreement had created a restrictive covenant over land, the identity of which could be and was ascertained by the developers themselves; (2) having regard to the terms of the s.52 agreement and the continuing need for a school, the covenant was of unlimited duration; (3) for the same reasons the covenant had not become obsolete and should not be discharged; (4) the land was therefore to be valued for compensation purposes subject to the reservation: ABBEY HOMESTEADS (DEVELOPMENTS) *v.* NORTHAMPTONSHIRE COUNTY COUNCIL (1986) 278 E.G. 1249, C.A.

360. Valuation—actual rents—lands tribunal decision. See MUSLIM *v.* ISLINGTON LONDON BOROUGH COUNCIL, § 2784.

CONFLICT OF LAWS

361. Contract—proper law by implication

D undertook to execute certain engineering works in Iraq for an Iraqi state organisation. The contract was in the FIDIC standard form and the proper law was expressly stated to be Iraqi law. D engaged P to execute part of the works as sub-contractors upon the terms of the FCEC "blue" form of sub-contract, conventionally used in conjunction with the ICE form of engineering contract. Disputes arose between P and D and a preliminary issue was ordered to be tried as to the proper law of the contract. *Held,* that (1) since there was no express choice of proper law, therefore the question was whether a choice of the proper law could be inferred from all relevant contemporary circumstances and in default of that what was the system of law with which the transaction had the closest and most real connection (*Amin Rasheed Corp.* v. *Kuwait Insurance Co.* [1982] C.L.Y. 2914 and *Whitworth Street Estates (Manchester)* v. *Milter (James) & Partners* [1970] C.L.Y. 326 followed); (2) on the balance of the relevant contemporary circumstances the proper law of the sub-contract was Iraqi law; an important consideration was that the sub-contract would not operate in isolation but would operate by reference to the main contract which was governed by Iraqi law; (3) further, if it were necessary to consider the second test, the transaction had its most real and closest connection with Iraqi law because the sub-contract was expressly linked to the main contract which was governed by Iraqi law: JMJ CONTRACTORS *v.* MARPLES RIDGWAY (1985) 31 Build.L.R. 100, Davies J.

362. Foreign arbitration award—recognition by English courts—conclusiveness of award—English proceedings

The English courts will normally recognise the validity of the decision of a competent foreign arbitration tribunal.

In 1980 P, an American citizen, brought proceedings against an Iranian state enterprise. The upheavals in Iran frustrated the proceedings, and relations between the two countries were broken off. Eventually an arbitration tribunal was established at the Hague to settle finally all outstanding matters. The tribunal dismissed his claim. P then brought an action in England, the causes of action all relating to the initial transactions but framed differently: P alleged, that the tribunal had arrived at a wrong decision. D applied to strike out the claim on the ground that it had already been the subject of litigation before a competent tribunal. *Held,* that the English courts would recognise the validity of decisions of a foreign arbitration tribunal whose competence derived from international law or practice; it followed that the court would recognise the Hague tribunal. P's action was an abuse of process and would be struck out (*Messina* v. *Petrococchino* (1872) L.R. 4 P.C. 144 applied).

DALLAL *v.* BANK MELLAT [1986] 1 All E.R. 239, Hobhouse J.

363. Foreign law—recognition—expropriation of company assets

[R.S.C., Ord. 18, r.19; Ord. 33, r.3.]

The courts of England will recognise foreign laws providing for the compulsory acquisition of property without consideration of their merits, and will not allow arguments that the enforcement of those laws amounts to an attempt by that other country to collect its taxes to frustrate that principle.

An application to strike out a pleading should be refused where it would necessarily involve long and complex argument, but the court may accede to such an application where it is satisfied that striking out would obviate the need for a long trial, or where it would have the effect of substantially reducing the issues between the parties.

Certain decrees were passed in Spain in 1983 as a result of which control of WH passed to the State of Spain. Actions were commenced over the ownership of certain trade marks by WH and others under the control of Spain. The defendants to the action sought to defend on the basis that the expropriation decrees were penal in nature and should not, therefore, or for some other reason, be enforced. The plaintiff moved to strike out the amendment. *Held,* that the defence had been correctly struck out. The nature of the claim was not to enforce the decrees, because they had already had the effect in Spain of perfecting the title of the State to the property in question. Thus there was nothing in the point raised in the defence. In so far as it was argued that striking out was not appropriate in the circumstances, whilst the court would ordinarily be wary of such an application where there would be needed long and serious argument, such a course could be taken where the court was satisfied that striking out would be beneficial in terms of saving time and/or reducing the burdens of the trial by reducing the issues in contention (*Drummond-Jackson* v. *British Medical Association* [1970] C.L.Y. 1575 and *McKay* v. *Essex Area Health Authority* [1982] C.L.Y. 3117 disapproved).

WILLIAMS AND HUMBERT v. W. & H. TRADE MARKS (JERSEY) [1986] 2 W.L.R. 24, H.L.

364. Foreign proceedings—restraint of foreign proceedings—U.S. anti-trust proceedings

The extra-territorial jurisdiction and pre-trial procedure of United States anti-trust suits are, by English standards, prima facie offensive.

L went into liquidation in 1982. The liquidator brought proceedings in the U.S. against a number of other airlines alleging breach of anti-trust laws by conspiracy to fix predatory air fares. M lent money to L and was involved in an attempt to rescue L but withdrew its support. M had a subsidiary in the U.S. which was not subject to direct control by M and had no dealings with L. The liquidator, believing that M was involved in the conspiracy, threatened to institute proceedings against M in the U.S. which had extra-territory application. This action would expose M to onerous discovery obligations enabling the liquidator to obtain evidence to support his claim even if he had no evidence at the outset. M sought a declaration that it was not liable in the U.S. for L's collapse and an injunction restraining the liquidator from commencing proceedings. The injunction was granted but later discharged. M appealed against the discharge. *Held,* allowing the appeal that (1) the extra-territorial jurisdiction and pre-trial procedure of U.S. anti-trust suits were, by English standards, prima facie offensive; only if the complaining party had voluntarily submitted to U.S. law would it be prevented from obtaining an injunction; M's dealings with L had taken place in England and had no connection with the U.S. or with the other airlines alleged to have conspired against L; the presence of M's subsidiary was irrelevant; M had not submitted and was entitled to the injunction (*British Airways Board* v. *Laker Airways* [1984] C.L.Y. 2641 distinguished); (2) the fact that the liquidator had no evidence of M's involvement in the alleged conspiracy did not make it unjust or unconscionable for him to proceed because in the absence of other reasons for making it unjust or unconscionable he was entitled to commence his action, but the weakness of his evidence was a factor the English court should take into account; the fact that the anti-trust jurisdiction would subject M to liability in respect of acts done in England to defend M's own legitimate interests, being acts intended to be governed by English law and not giving rise to any claim in England, was decisive; M was entitled to the injunction.

MIDLAND BANK v. LAKER AIRWAYS [1986] 1 All E.R. 526, C.A.

365. Proper law—judgment mortgage—currency in which debt to be paid

[Ire.] In 1978, before the Republic of Ireland entered the European Monetary System, P obtained a High Court declaration that certain sums were well charged on D's lands on the Republic. In 1983, after the Republic had entered the European Monetary System, the High Court declared that the balance due should be paid in the currency of the Republic. P appealed on the ground that, as the contract for the advances was made in Northern Ireland, the proper law of the contract was Northern Ireland law and, accordingly, that the balance should be paid in sterling. *Held,* dismissing the appeal, that although the proper law of the contract was Northern Ireland law money advanced and secured on immovable property in the Republic must be construed as being in the currency of the Republic: NORTHERN BANK v. EDWARDS [1985] I.R. 284, Supreme Ct.

366. Reinsurance contract—original insurance governed by Norwegian law—reinsurance contract with Lloyd's in London—insurance and reinsurance contracts in same terms

Where a contract of reinsurance entered into by Lloyd's underwriters in London is in the same terms as the original contract of insurance to which Norwegian law applies, the liability of the underwriters is governed by the liability imposed on the Norwegian insurance company by the application of Norwegian law to the original contract of insurance.

In a case where concurrent duties in tort and in contract to take reasonable care are imposed on a defendant, contributory negligence is available as a defence although the plaintiff's claim is made in contract.

P was a Norwegian insurance company. D1 was a syndicate of Lloyd's underwriters specialising in insuring fish farms and D2 were brokers of such insurance. P entered into a contract of insurance, on standard terms prepared by D1 and provided to P by D2, with A to insure A's fish farm against loss of fish from any cause whatsoever. P reinsured the risk by entering into a contract of reinsurance with D1 through D2. The contract of reinsurance was in the same terms as the original contract of insurance. Both contracts required A to keep records of stock and a 24 hour watch over the fish farm. The reinsurance contract provided that in the event of a loss no payment, offer or compromise should be made without the consent of D1 who should have control of all negotiations. A advised P that he could not comply with the requirement to keep a 24 hour watch. P contacted D2 with a view to altering that requirement. D2 failed to raise the matter with D1 and P failed to pursue the matter with D2. Some months later A made a claim against P on the policy. It was accepted that Norwegian law applied to the contract between A and P and that pursuant to that law P was obliged to meet A's claim. D1 refused to accept liability under the contract of reinsurance. P met A's claim and sued D1 on the reinsurance contract and D2 for negligence in contract and in tort in connection with the required alteration to the provision requiring A to keep a 24 hour watch. D1 denied liability under the reinsurance policy on the grounds (a) P had settled A's claim without their consent, (b) A had failed to keep proper stock records and (c) A had failed to keep a 24 hour watch on his fish farm. *Held*, that D1 was liable to P on the reinsurance contract. The clause concerning settlement of claim by P without D1's consent merely provided that any settlement entered into by P without consent was not binding on D1. It did not entitle D1 to avoid the reinsurance contract. Although A had not kept proper stock records the requirement under the contracts of insurance and reinsurance to do so was not a warranty the breach of which rendered the insurance and reinsurance null and void. D1 could not evade liability on grounds (a) or (b) whether English or Norwegian law applied. The contracts of insurance and reinsurance provided that the failure to keep a 24 hour watch on the fish farm rendered the insurance null and void. Under English law the insurance would be avoided. Norwegian law prevented P avoiding the contract of insurance with A on account of the fact that the failure to keep a 24 hour watch did not contribute to the loss suffered by A and could not have prevented it. Applying English conflict of law principles the proper law of the reinsurance contract was English law subject to the construction and effect of its terms as if they had formed part of the original contract of insurance being determined in accordance with Norwegian law. The parties must have contemplated that the original contract of insurance was governed by Norwegian law and that the liability reinsured by D1 was P's liability under that contract as Norwegian law applied to it. Accordingly D1 was liable to P. D2 owed a professional duty of care to P both in contract and in tort. D2 were negligent in failing to take up the requirement to keep a 24 hour watch with D1 and report back to P. P was also negligent in failing to note that D2 had not replied on that matter and failing to raise the matter again with D2. D2 was 25 per cent. to blame and P 75 per cent. to blame for any loss P might have suffered in consequence. Where concurrent tortious and contractual duties to take care existed, contributory negligence could be raised as a defence to a claim for breach of that duty unless the contract specifically provided otherwise (*Sayers* v. *Harlow Urban District Council* [1958] C.L.Y. 2220 applied, *Hamlyn & Co.* v. *Talisker Distillery* [1894] A.C. 202, *Wagg (Helbert) & Co., Re* [1956] C.L.Y. 1351, *Colchester Estates (Cardiff)* v. *Carlton Industries* [1984] C.L.Y. 2588, *Insurance Co. of Africa* v. *Scor (U.K.) Reinsurance Co.* [1983] C.L.Y. 2007 considered, *Basildon District Council* v. *Lesser (J. E.) (Properties)* [1984] C.L.Y. 368 distinguished, *A. B. Marintrans* v. *Comet Shipping Co., The Shinjitsu Maru (No. 5)* [1985] C.L.Y. 317 not followed).

FORSIKRINGSAKTIESELSKAPET VESTA *v.* BUTCHER [1986] 2 All E.R. 488, Hobhouse J.

367. **Sovereign immunity—diplomatic immunity—registration of local land charges against property—severed diplomatic relations**

Once there is a dispute on the registration of a charge under the Land Registration Act 1925 the appropriate process is an originating summons, which must be served on a foreign state in accordance with s.12(1) of the State Immunity Act 1978. *Per curiam*: the diplomatic immunity of a mission premises under art. 22 of the Vienna Convention only extended to premises currently so used.

The Westminster Council in the exercise of its statutory powers shored up the Iranian Embassy after the siege. Diplomatic relations were severed between Iran and the U.K. Iran refused to pay for the work. Westminster applied to have charges registered under the Land Registration Act 1925. The Iranian government's solicitors objected on the ground that the premises enjoyed diplomatic immunity. Westminster took out an originating summons. Iran's solicitors refused to accept service, and service under s.12(1) of the State Immunity Act 1978 was impossible due to the absence of diplomatic relations. *Held*, that the court had no jurisdiction to entertain the summons.

WESTMINSTER CITY COUNCIL v. GOVERNMENT OF THE ISLAMIC REPUBLIC OF IRAN [1986] 1 W.L.R. 979, Peter Gibson J.

CONSTITUTIONAL LAW

368. **Sovereign immunity—International Tin Council—contractual undertaking to waive immunity**

[International Tin Council (Immunities and Privileges) Order 1972 (S.I. 1972 No. 120) art. 6.]

A contractual undertaking on the part of the International Tin Council to submit to the jurisdiction of the High Court was a sufficient waiver of the immunity from suit and legal process granted to the Council for the purposes of art. 6(*a*) International Tin Council (Immunities and Privileges) Order 1972.

By a facility letter P agreed to lend the International Tin Council £10 million. The letter contained a term providing for it to be governed by English law and stating that "you [the Council] hereby irrevocably submit to the non-exclusive jurisdiction of the High Court of Justice in England and consent to the giving of any relief and/or the issue of any process for enforcement or otherwise against you." The Council defaulted on the repayment of the loan. P sued. The Council applied to set aside the writ on the ground that the Council was immune from suit and legal process by virtue of the International Tin Council (Immunities and Privileges) Order 1972. Art. 6 of the Order provides: "The Council shall have immunity from suit and legal process except: (a) to the extent that the Council shall have expressly waived such immunity in a particular case. . . ." *Held*, dismissing the summons, that article 23 of the Headquarters Agreement between the government and the Council did not provide an exclusive code for dealing with contractual disputes by way of arbitration. Accordingly P was not debarred from suing subject to art. 6 of the Order. The contractual undertaking by the Council to submit to the jurisdiction of the High Court was a sufficient waiver within the meaning and for the purposes of art. 6 of the Order. To be effective the waiver relied upon must relate to a specific transaction and could be given either before or after the commencement of proceedings in connection with that transaction. The Council was not a body enjoying sovereign immunity. It was a body of which sovereign states were members and its immunity and privileges were limited to those which were granted to it by the government. Accordingly it was not necessary for the Council to actually submit to the jurisdiction in the face of the court before it could be bound by the proceedings (*Exchange (Schooner)* v. *McFaddon* (1812) 7 Cranch 116 (U.S.S.C.) distinguished).

STANDARD CHARTERED BANK v. INTERNATIONAL TIN COUNCIL [1986] 3 All E.R. 257, Bingham J.

369. **Trinidad and Tobago—judicature—Chief Justice continuing in office after retirement age**

[Constitution of the Republic of Trinidad and Tobago Act 1976 (No. 4 of 1976) Sched., s.136(1)(2).]

Under the Constitution of Trinidad and Tobago the President is empowered to permit a judge to continue in office after reaching retirement age for a fixed period to complete matters already commenced, and during this period he can also do extra-judicial duties such as the witnessing of writs, and new work which would be completed within the extended tenure.

By s.136(1) of the Constitution of Trinidad and Tobago a retirement age for judges, including the Chief Justice, was set at 65. By s.136(2) the President could empower a judge to continue in office for such period "as may be necessary to enable him to deliver judgment or to do any other thing in relation to proceedings that were commenced before him before he attained that age." The Chief Justice attained 65 on July 15, 1985, and previously in June he had been empowered by the President to continue in office until December 21, 1985 to complete unfinished business. On July 16 the plaintiffs' solicitor sought to issue a writ for negligence, which had to be witnessed by the Chief Justice according to the Rules of the Supreme Court. The plaintiffs on July 16 applied by originating summons to determine whether on the proper construction of s.136(1) and (2) the President had power to extend the tenure of the Chief Justice. The judge of first instance held that he had no such power, but the Court of Appeal reversed that decision. The plaintiffs appealed to the Judicial Committee. *Held,* dismissing the appeal, that The President was empowered to permit a Chief Justice to continue in office for a fixed period under s.136(2). Although the extension granted was to enable him to deliver judgment or do any other thing in relation to proceedings commenced before him before he reached retirement age, during the period of the extension he had to perform all the functions and duties appertaining to the office of Chief Justice, including such extra-judicial duties as the witnessing of writs, but he should not undertake new work which might not be finished within his extended tenure of office. *Quaere*: Whether the Constitution permits a second extension of a judge's tenure of office.

SOOKOO v. ATT. GEN. OF TRINIDAD AND TOBAGO [1985] 3 W.L.R. 1021, P.C.

CONSUMER CREDIT

370. Brokerage—provision of display boxes and application forms—whether effecting introduction to consumer credit business

[Consumer Credit Act 1974 (c.39), ss.39, 145 and 147.] V Co. agreed with R.C.C. Co. that R.C.C. Co. should provide credit facilities, R.C.C. Co. having the appropriate licence. V Co. displayed a sign in its shop offering instant credit and provided display boxes and leaflets containing application forms prepared and printed by V. Co. and setting out R.C.C. Co.'s standard terms. V. Co. pleaded guilty to carrying on ancillary credit business (credit broking) without a licence, contrary to ss.39 and 147 of the 1974 Act. *Held,* dismissing the prosecutor's appeal against a subsequent acquittal of R.C.C. Co. on an information alleging aiding, abetting, counselling or procuring V. Co.'s alleged offences, that the provision of display boxes and application forms did not amount to the introduction of a person seeking credit to a common credit business within s.145. 2. *Obiter*: s.170(1) of the 1974 Act did not necessarily exclude liability under s.8 of the Accessories and Abettors Act 1861 and s.44 of the Magistrates' Courts Act 1980: BROOKES v. RETAIL CREDIT CARDS [1986] Crim.L.R. 327, D.C.

371. Consumer hire agreements—misrepresentations of dealer

[Consumer Credit Act 1974 (c.39), ss.9, 15 and 56] M entered into a leasing agreement with G for the hire of an ice shake dispenser. The agreement was for 36 months with no right to terminate. During prior negotiations between G and U (who sold the machine to M) U misrepresented to M (1) that at the end of the agreement she could buy the machine for £25, and (2) if it proved unprofitable she could terminate the agreement at any time and would only be liable for instalments then due and the cost of removing the machine. The machine was not profitable. G repudiated the agreement and M removed the machine, sold it and claimed £1,200 against G under the liquidated damages clause in the agreement. In answer to the claim G sought to invoke the agency provisions of s.56 saying (1) U acted as "negotiator" under s.56 and were the agents of M who were liable for those misrepresentations, and (2) that a consumer hire agreement under s.15 was also a consumer credit agreement under s.12(*a*) to which agreements s.56 applies, arguing that although there was no cash loan under s.9, there was "any other form of financial accommodation" and thus credit because M were providing G with the financial means with which to acquire possession of the machine. *Held,* that although U had made misrepresentations, M were not liable for them. The agreement in question was a consumer hire agreement and not a consumer credit agreement because it did not afford credit of any sort nor "any other form of financial accommodation." All M had done was to hire out the machine. They had not deferred any existing indebtedness which is an essential ingredient of credit. U were not the agents of the plaintiffs so as to fall within s.56 since they were not acting as negotiators: MOORGATE MERCANTILE LEASING *v.* ISOBEL GELL AND UGOLINI DISPENSERS (U.K.), October 21, 1985; H.H. Judge Rice; Grays Thurrock County Ct. (*Ex. rel. D H. P. Levy & Co., Solicitors*).

372. Exempt agreements

CONSUMER CREDIT (EXEMPT AGREEMENTS) (No. 2) (AMENDMENT) ORDER 1986 (No. 1105) [80p], made under the Consumer Credit Act 1974 (c.39), ss.16(1)(4), 182(2)(4); operative on July 23, 1986; amends S.I. 1985 No. 757.

CONSUMER CREDIT (EXEMPT AGREEMENTS) (No. 2) (AMENDMENT No. 2) ORDER 1986 (No. 2186) [80p], made under the Consumer Credit Act 1974 (c.39), ss.16(1)(4), 182(2)(4); operative on January 2, 1987 save for Art. 2(c)(d)(e) which is operative on January 7, 1987; amends S.I. 1985 No. 757 as a consequence of the coming into force of certain specified provisions of the Building Societies Act 1986 and the Housing and Planning Act 1986.

373. Extortionate credit bargain—rate of interest—whether justified

[Consumer Credit Act 1974 (c.39), s.138.]

A credit bargain was not extortionate within the meaning of s.138 of the Consumer Credit Act of 1974 where the borrower had been warned of the cost of the credit and where the risk taken by the lender justified the rate of interest charged and the rate was not out of line with that charged by other lending bodies.

On August 1, 1979 P, after consulting solicitors, entered into a deferred sale agreement with D and became entitled to enter into occupation of a house which they were contractually bound to purchase in 12 months' time, with payment of interest meanwhile on the balance of the purchase price. They fell behind in their interest payments, but on September 2, 1980 completed the purchase and executed a charge over it to pay D the principal sum lent of £17,450 plus interest at the rate of 25.785 per cent. per annum over 10 years. They missed instalments, tried and failed to sell the house, and in January 1982 D started possession proceedings. In March P found a buyer and in April the house was transferred and the mortgage redeemed. D made no charge for interest on arrears of instalments. In May 1984 P brought proceedings seeking an order that the rate of interest stipulated under the legal charge be reduced to a proper rate on the grounds that the loan and terms of repayment constituted an extortionate credit bargain within the meaning of s.138 of the Consumer Credit Act 1974, that the rate of interest was "grossly exorbitant," and that the circumstances surrounding the loan and the charge "grossly contravenes ordinary principles of fair trading." The claim failed. *Held,* that it was for the court to determine whether a credit bargain was "extortionate" and the meaning of the word was confined to the meaning given in s.138 (dictum of Browne-Wilkinson J. in *Multiservice Bookbinding* v. *Marden* [1979] Ch. 84, 110; [1978] C.L.Y. 2023 considered). On the evidence P could not rely on their lack of business experience or financial pressure as relevant factors since they had been warned by independent solicitors and D that a mortgage would be expensive, and no advantage was taken of them by D. The degree of risk, accepted by D on the security offered was a relevant factor and justified the rate of interest charged, since P had found difficulty in obtaining a building society or other institutional loan. As to the remaining factor set out in s.138, namely prevailing interest rates, regard should be had to the true rate of interest, *i.e.* the annual percentage rate of charge calculated in accordance with the Consumer Credit (Total Charge for Credit) Regulations 1980 even though they did not apply to the loan in question. A comparison of rates charged by other lending bodies showed that the payments required of P fell far short of constituting the legal charge an "extortionate credit bargain" under s.138 or one which "grossly contravened" the principles of fair dealing (dictum of Sir John Donaldson in *Wills* v. *Wood* [1984] C.L.Y. 2039 applied).

DAVIES *v.* DIRECTLOANS [1986] 1 W.L.R. 823, Edward Nugee, Q.C. sitting as a deputy High Court judge.

374. Licence

CONSUMER CREDIT (PERIOD OF STANDARD LICENCE) (AMENDMENT) REGULATIONS 1986 (No. 1016) [45p], made under the Consumer Credit Act 1974 (c.39), ss.22(1)(*a*) 147(1), 189(1); operative on August 1, 1986, vary S.I. 1975 No. 2124 by extending to 15 years the duration of a standard licence.

375. Restricted use credit agreement—second agreement—antecedent negotiations

[Consumer Credit Act 1974 (c.39), ss.11(1)(*a*) and 12(*a*).] W obtained a first vehicle on a two-year HP contract from U.D.T. Nearly a year later he took it to a garage who promised to take it in part-exchange for a second vehicle, to be financed through F.N.S. by a "restricted use credit agreement" and to pay off W's debt to U.D.T. W handed over the first vehicle to the garage, entered into the agreement with F.N.S. and took possession of the second vehicle. The garage failed to pay U.D.T. and went into liquidation. W was then left with two debts. W elected to pay off the sum due to F.N.S. so that he could keep the second vehicle as a means of getting to work. U.D.T. sued W. W consented to judgment being entered against him, not to be enforced pending his third party proceedings against F.N.S., claiming that the garage's promise was an "antecedent negotiation" to the second agreement, so that the garage was the agent of F.N.S. *Held*, that the promise by the garage to pay off W's debt was sufficiently related to the second vehicle for the promise to form part of the antecedent negotiations for which F.N.S. were liable. Leave to appeal was granted to F.N.S.: U.D.T. *v.* WHITFIELD, June 12, 1986; Judge Vos, Newcastle County Ct. [*Ex rel. Roger Thorn, Barrister.*]

376. Undue influence—unauthorised third party—agent. See COLDUNELL *v.* GALLON, § 1299.

CONTRACT

377. Acceptance by conduct—tender by contractor—contract formed upon submission

[Can.] N, a general building contractor, invited sub-contractors to tender on a construction contract. G, a mechanical sub-contractor, submitted a telephonic bid in accordance with prevailing practice in the industry. G's tender was conveyed twenty minutes before N's deadline to submit its tender to the prospective employer. G knew that N would select one of the sub-contractors' bids and rely upon the same and that N's tender to the employer would be irrevocable. N used G's tender in making its own. Thereafter, G attempted to withdraw its tender, upon discovering a miscalculation therein. The employer accepted N's offer but G refused to sign a formal sub-contract or to do the work. N was forced to engage another sub-contractor at a higher price and successfully sued G for the difference. *Held*, dismissing G's appeal, that a party inviting tenders is making an offer to others to submit tenders, which is accepted by the submission of a tender in accordance with the invitation. G was aware of the industry custom and knew that N might select its tender and rely upon it in submitting its own. G also knew that N's own tender would be irrevocable. Further, industry practice was that sub-contractors' tenders could be withdrawn up to the point of any deadline but that thereafter they remained irrevocable for the same period as the main contractor's so remained. G's contract with N was therefore concluded when it submitted its tender. Not having been withdrawn prior to N's own tender, it remained irrevocable. G was therefore liable to N (*R. in Right of Ont.* v. *Ron Engr. & Const. (Eastern)* [1981] 1 S.C.R. 111 applied): NORTHERN CONSTRUCTION CO. *v.* GLOGE HEATING AND PLUMBING [1986] 2 W.W.R. 649, Alberta Ct. of Appeal.

378. Agreement for lease—subsequent grant—whether merger

N.U. agreed to take a lease of land, and covenanted to erect a building on it, *inter alia*, in good and workmanlike manner. N.U. agreed to make a sub-lease of the building to I.P.C., and agreed to erect the building in accordance with its earlier covenant with the freeholder. I.P.C. took the sub-lease and entered into occupation. The building was defective. The sub-lease itself was silent as to the erection of the building. *Held*, that the terms of the agreement for the sub-lease did not merge into the sub-lease itself since those terms were collateral to the terms of the sub-lease, and in no way incompatible with it, and there were no express provisions providing for the terms of the agreement to cease to have effect on the granting of the sub-lease, or at any other time (*Leggatt* v. *Barratt* 15 Ch. 306, *Knight Sugar* v. *Alberta Railways* [1938] 1 All E.R. 266, *Palmer* v. *Johnson* [1884] 13 Q.B. 350, *Lawrence* v.

Cassel [1930] K.B. 83 considered): INTERNATIONAL PRESS CENTRE *v.* NORWICH UNION, *Financial Times,* May 16, 1986, Judge Esyr Lewis Q.C.

379. Auctioneer—exclusion clause—whether negligence. See SPRIGGS *v.* SOTHEBY PARKE BERNET & CO., § 136.

380. Breach—consideration

P I Co. traded in the futures market through the agency of C B Co. and in October 1981 owed C B Co. about £36,000. At a meeting between the managing director of C B Co. and D, who was the sole beneficial owner of the shares in P I Co., D agreed to pay off the amount due at the rate of £1,000 per month. Two payments were made. *Held,* dismissing a claim by C B Co., that the agreement amounted to an indemnity and not a guarantee but, as no request was made to C B Co. to forbear from bringing proceedings against P I Co., the indemnity was not given for consideration and was, accordingly, unenforceable: COMMODITY BROKING *v.* MEEHAN [1985] I.R. 12, Barron J.

381. Breach—default of antecedent obligations—assessment of damages

In a contract for the sale of goods, B, the buyer, had obligations antecedent to his obligations to pay for the goods and to provide a ship to receive them. The contract entitled S, the seller, to wait until the last day for shipment to see if B would perform the contract. B was in breach of the antecedent obligations. S could have treated the contract at an end at that point, but chose to affirm it, and left the contract open until the last day for shipment. *Held,* that S was entitled to opt for certainty and clarity if he chose, by waiting until the end of the shipment period, and the date as at which damages for breach should be assessed was the last possible date for shipment, because it was only then that B's default under the main contract became certain. *Kyprianou (Phoebus D.) Co.* v. *Pim (Wm. H.) Jnr. & Co.* [1978] C.L.Y 2642 applied) LUSOGRAIN COMMERCIO INTERNACIONAL DE CEREAS *v.* BUNGE, *The Financial Times,* July 11, 1986, Staughton J.

382. Breach—repudiation—penalty

P hired a computer to D. The leasing contract provided for the timing of the leasing payments to be of the essence, and further provided for the payment of overdue monies, payment of all monies that would have fallen due, payment of damages and the termination of the contract. *Held,* that the late payments were repudiatory breaches since the parties had made time of the essence, therefore the clause entitling P to the various payments was not a penalty, and P was entitled to recover under each head (*Steedman* v. *Drinkle* [1916] A.C. 275, *Financings* v. *Baldock* [1963] C.L.Y. 1639 considered): LOMBARD NORTH CENTRAL *v.* BUTTERWORTH (1986) 83 L.S.Gaz, 2750, C.A.

383. Breach—whether using best endeavours enough—mitigation of loss

T booked a holiday for himself, his wife and four-year-old daughter in a three-star hotel in Majorca, having chosen it from O's brochure. The hotel was described as very reliable with a reputation for good service and cuisine, a tasteful décor and a friendly atmosphere. T chose O's holiday because the brochure indicated that flights were scheduled ones, daytime and direct to the airport of destination. His daughter was shy and insecure and would be difficult if travelling at night. The plane was over-booked and he was offered a non-direct night flight with no guarantees that he would make his connection at the other end. T refused this offer and re-booked the first direct flight available. He attempted to telex the hotel, and returned home losing two days of his holiday. T flew out two days later to find the hotel over-booked. He had to spend two nights in an apartment with a defective toilet, peeling wallpaper, beds with no springs and a dirty, rusty wash-basin. O argued (1) that the contract with T was only to use his best endeavours to arrange the flight and hotel and that (2) if there was a breach due to the over-booking, T had failed to mitigate his loss by not accepting the alternative flight. *Held,* that (a) the contract with T was to provide the flight and hotel accommodation; (b) T had not failed to mitigate his loss as O had not proved that he had failed to be reasonable within the meaning of the law; (c) T was entitled to out-of-pocket expenses of £100 and a sum attributable to a national rebate in respect of four days' lost hotel accommodation (£129·29) and £300 for general damages for inconvenience, which would have been more had T not exaggerated the problems. Total award: £529·29: TUCKER *v.* O.T.A. TRAVEL, December 17, 1985; Mr. Assistant Recorder Fay, Salisbury County Ct. (*Ex rel. Mark Horton, Barrister.*)

384. C. & f. contract—title to property—whether right to sue in tort. See LEIGH AND SILLIVAN *v.* ALIAKMON SHIPPING CO., § 2252

385. C.i.f. contract—intention—whether enforceable. See HARYANTO (YANI) *v.* MAN (E.D. & F.) (SUGAR), § 2999.

386. Commodities contract—futures—whether closing out agreed

In this action P, who were commodity brokers, claimed that D owed them a large sum, being losses incurred by P on D's gold and silver account. D, however, contended that P had been given specific instructions to close all D's positions on a certain date and had they done so there would have been monies owing to D. *Held*, on the facts and the evidence, that no instructions had been given to P to close the positions, and P's claim therefore succeeded in full: DREXEL BURNHAM LAMBERT INTERNATIONAL B.V. *v.* NASR [1986] 1 Lloyd's Rep. 356, Staughton J.

387. Concluded agreement—effect of words "subject to survey"

B and L signed a document headed "Quotations/Contract" which provided for the fitting of double-glazed windows at B's house. The document was a contract save that the words "subject to survey" appeared next to L's signature. The survey was for L to ensure that the replacement windows described in the document could be fitted. No survey took place because B decided not to proceed, arguing that the words "subject to survey" meant that there was no concluded agreement. *Held*, that (1) there was a concluded agreement, and (2) the effect of the words "subject to survey" was to suspend L's contractual obligations until after the survey at which point there was an option as to whether L was to proceed. The words had no effect upon B's obligations (*Ee* v. *Kakar* [1980] C.L.Y. 2798 applied): BIRING v. LIGHTNING WINDOWS, February 4, 1986; Warwick County Ct.; Judge Francis Allen. (*Ex rel. David Worster, Barrister*).

388. Contract of affreightment—lien—bill of lading. See SCANCARRIERS A/S *v.* AOTEAROA INTERNATIONAL; BARRANDUNA, THE, § 3076.

389. Contributory negligence—whether defence to a claim in contract

[Law Reform (Contributory Negligence) Act 1945 (c.28), s.1(1).]

The Law Reform (Contributory Negligence) Act 1945 does not provide a defendant with any defence to a claim in contract where negligence on the part of the plaintiff contributes to the defendant's breach of contract.

Comet Shipping Co. (C) chartered a ship from A.B. Marintrans (M). The ship was ordered to carry a cargo of palletised milk powder. The ship was not suitable for such a task but could be made suitable if the cargo was properly loaded. After the cargo had been loaded the master of the ship asked advice of a surveyor appointed by C's agents concerning the way in which the cargo was stowed. The master was not happy with the advice but, in reliance upon it, put to sea whereupon the cargo shifted in bad weather necessitating a return to port. The surveyor's advice was negligent in that the stowage was seriously defective making the ship unseaworthy when it sailed. C claimed certain sums from M alleging a breach of the charterparty. M claimed to be entitled to rely upon the provisions of the Law Reform (Contributory Negligence) Act 1945 to reduce any award made against them. The arbitrators made a reduction in the damages recoverable by C on account of the surveyor's negligent advice. C appealed to the Commercial Court. *Held*, allowing the appeal, that contributory negligence did not provide a defence to a claim in contract before the Act came into force. The Act amended the law relating to contributory negligence by providing for an apportionment of liability whereas previously contributory negligence, where it applied, was a complete defence. The Act did not have effect so as to provide a defence of contributory negligence where that defence did not exist prior to its commencement. The wording of s.1(1) of the Act is directed towards tortious liabilities alone and is not apt to cover breaches of contractual duties of care. The apportionment provided for in s.1(1) of the Act does not apply to a claim in contract (*De Meza & Stuart* v. *Apple van Straten Shena & Stone* [1975] C.L.Y. 391, *Quinn* v. *Burch Bros. (Builders)* [1966] C.L.Y. 3452, *James (A. S.) Pty.* v. *Duncan* [1970] V.R. 705, *Rowe* v. *Turner, Hopkins & Partners* [1980] 2 N.Z.L.R. 550, *Basildon D.C.* v. *Lesser (Properties)* [1984] C.L.Y. 368 considered).

A.B. MARINTRANS *v.* COMET SHIPPING CO.; SHINJITSU MARU NO. 5, THE [1985] 3 All E.R. 442, Neill L.J.

390. Credit card purchase—whether further liability for payment

Where a purchaser pays for goods by way of a credit card he is discharged from any further liability to pay for the goods as such payment is not a conditional payment on the part of the purchaser.

A debtor of a company in liquidation is entitled to set off against moneys owed to the company any liabilities of the company to the debtor arising after the date of the winding up provided those liabilities arise under a contract entered into by the debtor and the company prior to the date of the winding up.

Charge Card Services ("C") operated a scheme involving the provision of charge cards to account holders for the purposes of purchasing petrol and diesel from participating garages. There was an agreement between C and each account holder under which C undertook to pay for fuel supplied to the account holder. C provided monthly statements to the account holders who were liable to pay the same within 14 days. There was a separate agreement between C and each participating garage. The garages undertook to honour the charge card by supplying fuel to account holders on the same terms as for cash sales. C agreed to reimburse the garages for the cost of fuel purchased by account holders less commission due to C. C also undertook to establish a guarantee for the benefit of participating garages of its obligation to reimburse them. When a charge card was presented at a garage to pay for fuel supplied, the garage completed a sales voucher with details of the transaction and imprinted it with the account holder's card. The account holder was given one copy, the garage retained one copy and a copy was submitted to C for payment. To finance the scheme C entered into an agreement to factor its receivables, *i.e.* the debts due from account holders to Commercial Credit Services. Under the agreement Commercial Credit undertook to maintain an account in C's name. The agreement provided for Commercial Credit to credit to the account sums payable to C, *e.g.* the purchase price for the receivables and debit the account with sums payable by C to Commercial Credit. Condition 3B of the agreement provided that any credit balance in the account was payable to C less any amount that Commercial Credit should in its absolute discretion decide to retain as security against any claims made against C, any risk of non-payment by account holders and any amount prospectively chargeable to C that Commercial Credit would be entitled to debit to the account. In February 1985 C went into liquidation. In consequence the garages were not paid for fuel supplied to account holders. The liquidator collected £2 million from account holders in respect of fuel supplied. The garages contended that the account holders were liable to pay the garages and so the money should be paid to them. A second completely separate issue arose between C and Commercial Credit. In the exercise of its discretion under condition 3B, Commercial Credit had retained a substantial sum of money from the balance in the account standing to C's credit. The liquidator claimed to be entitled to that money. By originating summons the liquidator sought the determination of the court on the two issues. *Held,* that (1) on the use of the fuel card three separate bilateral contracts came into existence between the three parties, one of which was a contract between the garage and the account holder for the supply of fuel. That contract imposed an obligation to pay the price of the fuel supplied on the account holder. The acceptance of the use of the card by the garage was merely a subsequent agreement between the garage and account holder as to how the consideration under the contract, *i.e.* the price, may be satisfied. Payment by use of the card was not a conditional discharge of the account holders' liability to pay the price but was an absolute discharge of that liability. The discharge of the account holders' liability under the supply contract was not conditional upon receipt by the garage of payment from C. The features normally present whenever payment is made by a credit or charge card support a presumption that payment by such means is not a conditional payment only. The liability of the account holders to pay C was not dependant upon C having first paid the garages. Accordingly the garages were not entitled to the £2 million recovered by the liquidator from the account holders; (2) the right of retention given to Commercial Credit by condition 3B of the contract between C and Commercial Credit was not a charge over C's book debts. A charge in favour of a debtor (Commercial Credit) of its own indebtedness to the chargor (the credit balance on the account payable to C) was conceptually impossible. The condition gave rise to a right of set off effective against the liquidator provided it did not go beyond what was permitted by s.31 of the Bankruptcy Act 1914. Commercial Credit was entitled to set off against the sums owing to C liabilities that were contingent at the date of the winding up order provided they arose from a transaction or agreement between the parties entered into prior to the date of the winding up order. There was no distinction between a liability, the very existence of which was contingent at the date of the winding up order, and a liability that was certain but the amount of which could not be ascertained because it was dependant on future events. A debtor of a company in liquidation was entitled to set off both liabilities against his debt to the company. Accordingly, Commercial Credit was entitled to the sums retained pursuant to condition 3B, and C was not entitled to be paid the purchase price for its receivables free from any deduction by Commercial Credit ((1) *Richardson* v. *Worrall* [1985] C.L.Y. 1777 considered; (2) *Asphaltic Wood Pavement Co., Re* (1885) 30 Ch.D. 216, *Hiley* v. *Peoples Prudential Assurance Co.* (1938) 60 C.L.R. 468 applied, *Sovereign Life Assurance Co.* v. *Dodd* [1892] 2 Q.B. 573, *Palmer* v. *Day & Sons* [1895] 2 Q.B. 618, *Daintrey, Re* [1900] 1 Q.B. 546, *Taylor, Re* [1910] 1 K.B. 562, *National Benefit Assurance Co., Re* [1924] 2 Ch. 339, *City Life Assurance Co., Re* [1926] Ch. 191, *Palmer* v. *Carey* [1926] A.C. 703, *Fenton, Re* [1931] 1 Ch. 85, *Debtor (No. 66 of 1955), A, Re* [1956] C.L.Y. 632, *Halesowen Presswork & Assemblies* v. *Westminster Bank* [1971] 1 Q.B. 1 considered, *Carreras Rothmans* v. *Freeman Mathews Treasure* [1984] C.L.Y. 332 not followed).

CHARGE CARD SERVICES, *Re* [1986] 3 W.L.R. 697, Millett J.

391. Debt—payable on demand—right to enforce security—reasonable time for compliance

[Aus.] A debtor required to pay a debt payable on demand must be allowed a reasonable opportunity to meet the demand before the creditor may enforce his security. It is not essential to the validity of a notice calling up a debt that it correctly states the amount of the debt. However, in determining whether the debtor has had such an opportunity it will be relevant to take account of the debtor's knowledge, lack of knowledge and means of knowledge of the amount due and of the information which the creditor has provided in that respect, including the response which he has made to any inquiry by the debtor (*Toms* v. *Wilson* (1862) 122 E.R. 524 applied; *Massey* v. *Sladen* (1868) L.R. 4 Ex. 13 not followed): BUNBURY FOODS PROPRIETARY *v.* NATIONAL BANK OF AUSTRALASIA [1983–84] 153 C.L.R. 491, High Ct. of Australia.

392. Estate agent—professional charges—quantum meruit. See WITHEY ROBINSON (A FIRM) *v.* EDWARDS, § 36.

393. Estoppel—agreement ultra vires one party

ENIT made an agreement in London within the bounds of its constitution, but without the consent of the Minister in Rome. J was misled into thinking that all the formalities had been completed, and relied upon them. *Held,* that Italian law rendered ENIT's side of the bargain voidable, not void, and English law (which governed the contract) provided that ENIT were estopped from denying the agreement (*Bodley Head* v. *Flegon* [1972] CLY 532 considered): JANRED PROPERTIES *v.* ENTE NATIONALE PER IL TURISMO (No. 2), *Financial Times,* December 17, 1985, Knox J.

394. Exchange control—Bretton Woods Agreements—payment by cheque—enforceability

[Bretton Woods Agreements Order in Council 1946, Sched., Pt. 1, art. viii, s.2(*b*).]

The court will not enforce a contract which constitutes in reality an exchange contract contrary to the Bretton Woods Agreement.

P, an Iranian settled in England, devised a scheme to get his money out of Iran. He arranged with D, a travel agent, to purchase airline tickets in Iran and to forward them to him in England for exchange. A cheque for £33,334 made payable to P under this arrangement was stopped. P sued on the cheque. The judge refused to enforce the cheque on the grounds that the contract was contrary to the Bretton Woods Agreements. *Held,* dismissing the appeal, that the court had a duty to refuse to enforce any monetary transaction, however concealed, which constituted an exchange contract contrary to the Bretton Woods Agreement (*United City Merchants (Investments)* v. *Royal Bank of Canada* [1982] C.L.Y. 215 applied).

MANSOURI *v.* SINGH [1986] 2 All E.R. 619, C.A.

395. Illegality—part of agreement prohibited by statute—whether whole object was to violate regulation

[Can.] The parties agreed in writing to settle litigation between themselves. The agreement provided for the plaintiffs to pay a sum in return for the defendant's release of any interest he might have in certain mineral claims. If the plaintiffs failed to pay the sum by a certain date, they would pass their interests in the mineral claims to the defendant. The documents relating to these alternative transactions were placed in escrow. The plaintiffs realized that they would be unable to pay in time and applied for and obtained an order extending time for payment and a further order restraining the escrow agent from releasing the relevant documents. The defendant successfully appealed those orders. Meanwhile, the plaintiffs sought a declaratory judgment that the settlement agreement was void for illegality, contending that the defendant was not entitled under local statute to acquire the relevant interests by transfer, not being a registered licensee. At first instance it was held that the transfer provision was illegal but was severable, leaving the remainder of the agreement valid and enforceable. *Held*, on appeal, that the agreement's purpose was to settle litigation and did not appear to contemplate the application of the relevant regulations. The parties must be taken to have expected that the routine licensing requirements would be fulfilled if and when necessary. The whole object of the contract was not to violate the regulations but to give commercial effect to the parties' agreement. The arrangement did not offend against public policy, which was why illegal contracts were not enforced. The agreement should be enforced (*St. John Shipping Corporation* v. *Rank (Joseph)* [1956] C.L.Y. 8303 applied): DODGE v. EISENMAN, 68 B.C.L.R. 327, British Columbia C.A.

396. Illegality—recovery of consideration—ignorance of illegality of pyramid scheme
[Can.] O paid Z $2,200 to participate in an illegal pyramid scheme, which required O to find eight other people to join the same. O would then receive $17,600. Z promised to pay the amount of O's original investment should the scheme "stop," assuring O that the scheme was legal. Soon after O paid Z, there was newspaper publicity into such schemes and Z suspended all further meetings with O. O recruited no participants and recovered the $2,200 at trial. *Held*, dismissing Z's appeal, that there are two exceptions to the rule that a party cannot recover under an illegal contract: first, where the parties are not in *pari delicto,* and secondly where the plaintiff "repents" before performing the contract. Here, the parties were in *pari delicto* because their common design was to participate in a scheme which was in fact unlawful. Ignorance of the law was no excuse. O, however, fell within the second exception by not carrying into effect the illegal purpose in a substantial manner prior to abandoning the scheme. Z's greater degree of turpitude was also relevant; OUSTON v. ZUROWSKI [1985] 5 W.W.R. 169, British Columbia C.A.

397. Implied terms—quantity delivered—non-payment
P delivered bread daily to D who owned a supermarket. The only evidence in writing of the contract was the daily delivery note left by P's roundsman with D, showing the amount of bread delivered, on which appeared the words "Customers are requested to check deliveries and extensions and any errors must be notified immediately." In practice D paid each week's account shortly after the end of that week. P claimed for the unpaid price of bread delivered in two particular weeks. D refused to pay on the grounds that over a previous period of 45 weeks P had delivered to D less bread than stated on the delivery notes. D counterclaimed for the monies previously paid to P for bread allegedly not delivered. In addition to relying on the above wording of the delivery notes as an express term, P alleged that there were implied terms, namely (1) that P would not accept responsibility for short delivery if the same was not notified to P within a reasonable time, (2) that in the absence of such notification, D would be deemed to have accepted the correctness of the quantity delivered, and (3) that by reason of D's payment for bread stated to have been delivered by P, D would be deemed to have accepted the correctness of the quantity. *Held*, that (1) the express words of the delivery note amounted to no more than an exhortation to customers, but that (2) each of the alleged implied terms were terms of the contract on which P could rely: SUNBLEST BAKERIES v. WHITE-SANSOM, July 2, 1986; H.H. Judge Taylor, Q.C., Sheffield County Ct. [*Ex rel. Hon. Michael McLaren, Barrister.*]

398. Licence agreement—implied term—mistake of lawyer
Where a person was allowed, by a licence, the use of an old oven for the storage and display of antiques it was not necessary to imply a term that the licensor would make and keep the oven watertight. Moreover a mistake in the presentation of a case by counsel would rarely lead to a re-trial in order to avoid unfairness to the

other side (*Doyle* v. *Olby (Ironmongers)* [1969] C.L.Y. 1528 considered): MORRIS-THOMAS *v.* PETTICOAT LANE RENTALS, *The Times,* June 18, 1986, C.A.

399. Loan—third party lender—right of subrogation. See BOODLE HATFIELD *v.* BRITISH FILMS, § 1991.

400. Management agreement—duty to insure—underinsurance—breach
The issue for determination in an arbitration was whether the managers of a vessel were under a duty to insure the vessel for more than the sum for which they had in fact insured her. The arbitrator found that they were, and awarded O damages. The Court of Appeal agreed. *Held,* dismissing M's appeal, that on a true construction of the relevant documents and the evidence, that M ought to have insured the vessel for a greater sum: GLAFKI SHIPPING CO. S.A. *v.* PINIOS SHIPPING CO. NO. 1; THE MAIRA (No. 2) [1986] 2 Lloyd's Rep. 12, H.L.

401. Merchantability—samples—evidence
The fact that a contract provides for sampling to establish whether a cargo complies with the description in the contract does not preclude a buyer adducing other evidence of unmerchantability or other non compliance: FORD (CHARLES E.) *v.* FEE (A.) INC., *Financial Times,* February 14, 1986, Bingham J.

402. Negotiations—whether binding contract concluded
This is a case which was decided purely on its own facts. The issue for determination was whether two parties had concluded a binding contract for the voyage charter of a vessel. Leggatt J. held that on all the evidence no binding contract had been reached. *Held,* dismissing an appeal, that the judge was right. The correspondence amply demonstrated that the parties were at all material times engaged in continuing negotiations that had not come to fruition: HOFFLINGHOUSE & CO. *v.* C-TRADE S.A.: THE INTRA TRANSPORTER [1986] 2 Lloyd's Rep. 132, C.A.

403. Non-payment—settlement—frustration. See NILE CO. FOR THE EXPORT OF AGRICULTURAL CROPS *v.* BENETT (H. & J.M.) (COMMODITIES), § 3015.

404. Offer—letter of intent—whether a binding acceptance
P responded by tender to an invitation by D to sell sugar. They conducted negotiations and P presented to D an offer which was to remain open until June 12, 1981. D issued a letter of intent for the supply of materials as per the terms of the offer and required P to put up a performance bond within seven days. P duly did this. D did not go ahead with the deal, and contended that there was no concluded contract between the parties. *Held,* that on the fact and the evidence the letter of intent was intended to constitute an acceptance of the offer and had contractual significance: WILSON SMITHETT & CAPE (SUGAR) *v.* BANGLADESH SUGAR AND FOOD INDUSTRIES CORP. [1986] 1 Lloyd's Rep. 378, Leggatt J.

405. Option to purchase—deposit to be paid within specified time—document exchange
Payment made by document exchange, where the document exchange box number be cleared each normal working day, will be deemed to be received on the day of the next normal collection.
D granted P an option to purchase land by October 4. The solicitors of both parties belonged to a document exchange. By the rules of the agency, each member's box had to be cleared at least once each normal working day, and delivery to the box was to be accepted as delivery to the member's office. P's solicitors gave notice of P's intention to exercise the option in September. On October 3 they paid the cheque for the deposit with an accompanying letter in D's solicitor's box at the document exchange. The next normal collection would have been October 4. D's solicitors then claimed that payment was made on October 5, and that D had elected to rescind the agreement. *Held,* that P's failure to pay the deposit by October 4 would only have been a breach entitling D to fix a date for payment in any event, and D was not entitled to rescind the agreement. Further, parties who instructed solicitors to do acts on their behalf empowered the solicitors to carry out their business in whatever manner they considered appropriate. D's solicitors were party to an agreement whereby D must be deemed to have received payment on October 4 (*Millichamp* v. *Jones* [1982] C.L.Y. 3370 applied; *Hare* v. *Nicoll* [1966] C.L.Y. 1410 and *United Scientific Holdings* v. *Burnley Borough Council* [1977] C.L.Y.1758 distinguished).
WILMOTT (JOHN) HOMES *v.* READ (1986) 51 P. & C.R. 90, Whitford J.

406. Order for specific performance—whether vendor entitled to resell land
Where a vendor of land obtains a judgment for specific performance against the purchaser he cannot thereafter elect to resell the land to a third party without first having the order for specific performance dissolved.

P entered into a contract to sell a warehouse and certain equipment to D. D paid a deposit of £12,500 and completion was to take place in October 1983. D failed to complete the purchase on the appropriate date. In June 1984 P issued a writ seeking, *inter alia*, an order for specific performance of the agreement. In July 1984 in default of defence Warner J. ordered that the agreement be specifically performed and carried into execution and that completion should take place at a time and place to be appointed by the court after the conveyance had been executed. Thereafter correspondence passed between P and D but P took no steps to enforce the order. In November 1984 P sold the property to a third party for £25,000 less than the price agreed with D. In January 1985 P issued and served a notice of motion seeking a declaration that P was entitled to treat the contract with D as at an end and resell the property notwithstanding the order of Warner J., a declaration that D's deposit be forfeited and damages. *Held,* dismissing the motion, that on obtaining an order for specific performance the contract between P and D remained in effect. If the property was to be dealt with in any other way it could only be done by agreement or by first obtaining a further order of the court. P should have applied to the court for an order dissolving the order for specific performance. Such an application was not a mere formality. In the present case, had such an application been made it would have been refused. P had no right to elect to resell the property whilst the order for specific performance remained in force (*Johnson* v. *Agnew* [1979] C.L.Y. 2733 applied; dictum of Megarry V.-C. in *Singh (Sudagar)* v. *Nazeer* [1978] C.L.Y. 3056 followed).

G.K.N. Distributors *v.* Tyne Tees Fabrication (1985) 50 P. & C.R. 403, Nourse J.

407. Parole evidence rule. See Law Reform, § 1955.

408. Performance bond—demand presented thereunder—whether guarantor entitled to investigate facts underlying demand—enforceability. See Siporex Trade S.A. *v.* Banque Indosuez, § 168.

409. Personal services—negative covenant—enforcement
P employed D, two terms of whose contract of employment were (1) that he would give 12 months' notice of termination of the contract, and (2) that for the duration of the contract he would not work for P's business rivals. D gave two months' notice, intending to work for M, P's rival. P sought an interlocutory injunction to prevent D from working for M, and offered to pay D's wages during the remainder of the 12-month notice period, and pending the outcome of the case. *Held,* that the Courts were reluctant to grant injunctions that would force a defendant either to work for his former employer, to starve, or to remain idle, but in view of P's offer, however, these disadvantages were overcome, and the balance of convenience lay in P's favour. An injunction would therefore be granted: Evening Standard *v.* Henderson, *The Times,* November 15, 1986, C.A.

410. Record—released to public—meaning
It was held that a record was "released to the public" when a recording company gave an irrevocable instruction to distributors to release it to retailers whether or not the record had actually arrived at outlets in sufficient quantities for sale over the counter: McLelland *v.* Carlin Music Corp., *The Times,* April 19, 1986, Rokison Q.C.

411. Reinsurance contract—original insurance governed by Norwegian law—reinsurance contract with Lloyd's in London—insurance and reinsurance contracts in same terms. See Forsikringsaktieselskapet Vesta *v.* Butcher, § 366.

412. Restraint of trade—use of confidential information—injunction
D gained confidential information from P, his employer. He left P, and P obtained an injunction preventing D from using the information for his, D's, business. The contract of employment provided for a period of one year from its termination during which D would not trade in competition. *Held,* that the injunction should not be continued beyond a period of one year from the date of termination of the contract (*Faccenda Chicken* v. *Fowler* [1985] C.L.Y. 1134, *Robb* v. *Green* [1895] 2

Q.B. 1, *Potters-Ballotini* v. *Weston-Baker* [1976] C.L.Y. 2157, *Harrison* v. *Project & Design (Redcar)* [1978] C.L.Y. 2235, *Fisher-Karpark Industries* v. *Nichols* [1983] C.L.Y. 2882, *Terrapin* v. *Builders Supply Co. (Hayes)* [1960] C.L.Y. 2520, *Seager* v. *Copydex* [1967] C.L.Y. 1486, *Coco* v. *A. N. Clark (Engineers)* [1968] C.L.Y. 1458 considered): BULLIVANT (ROGER) *v.* ELLIS, *The Times,* June 5, 1986, C.A.

413. Restrictive covenant—doctor—whether valid. KERR *v.* MORRIS, § 3399.

414. Retention of title—terms of contract

P sought to restrain D from disposing of equipment, or the proceeds of its sale, for which no payment had been made. P had sought to incorporate a retention of title clause in the contract, but D had made counter-proposals. No formal acceptance was ever given, but P delivered the goods to D. *Held,* that the delivery of the goods was an acceptance by P of the counter-proposals made by D. Since they contained no clause retaining title P's application for interlocutory relief failed: SAUTER AUTOMATION *v.* GOODMAN (H. C.) (MECHANICAL SERVICES), *Financial Times,* May 14, 1986, Mervyn Davies J.

415. Sale of goods. See SALE OF GOODS.

416. Sale of land—fixtures and fittings—vacant possession. See HYNES *v.* VAUGHAN, § 3523.

417. Sale of ship—commission—settlement See AUNE (CARL) AGENCIA MARITIMA AFRETA-MENTOS *v.* ENGENHARIA E. MAQUINAS S.A., § 3100.

418. Shipbuilding contracts—commission agreement—entitlement to commission

The P shipbrokers entered into 16 commission agreements for the construction of vessels for Greek shipping groups. In all but two cases the ultimate purchasers cancelled the building contracts. P claimed their commission from D. *Held,* that (1) upon a true construction of the agreements commission was only payable after relevant payment had been made under the building contracts. However (2) there was an implied term that D would not break the shipbuilding contracts so as to deprive P of commission under the agreements. This they had done and P's claim succeeded: MOUNDREAS (GEORGE) & CO. S.A. *v.* NAVIMPEX CENTRALA NAVALA [1985] 2 Lloyd's Rep. 515, Saville J.

419. Special condition—export certificate—obligation

A provision in a contract for the sale of goods that the seller will "provide for" an export certificate imposes an absolute obligation on him to obtain such a certificate: TRADAX OCEAN TRANSPORTATION *v.* PAGNAN, *The Financial Times,* July 8, 1986, Steyn J.

420. Supply of services—implied terms. See LAW REFORM, § 1945.

421. Surgery—sterilisation of patient—result contracted for—warranty

A contract for the sterilisation of a patient was not a contract for the result that the patient would never again become pregnant.

P was a woman who with her husband decided not to have any more children. P consulted D who was an experienced consultant gynaecological surgeon about a sterilisation operation. D suggested a laparoscopy and emphasised to P and her husband that the operation was irreversible. D failed to advise P that there was a chance of 2 to 6 in 1,000 that she might become pregnant again after the operation. P agreed to the operation being carried out privately and in due course signed a form consenting to the operation of a laparoscopy sterilisation the effect and nature of which had been explained to her. After the operation P became pregnant and sued D for breach of contract. In his defence D admitted that P was advised that the operation must be regarded as a permanent procedure and that P was not warned of the slight risk of failure. In cross-examination D conceded that it was reasonable for P to have left his consulting rooms with the impression that she would be sterilised and that would be an end of the matter. The trial judge dismissed P's claim. P appealed and argued that (1) there was a contract that she would be 100 per cent. sterile, (2) there was an express warranty that she would not become pregnant after the operation, and (3) there was an implied warranty to that effect. *Held,* dismissing the appeal, that (1) D did not contract to render P absolutely sterile, he contracted to carry out a laparoscopy operation; (2) the representation that the operation was irreversible did not give rise to a warranty that as a result of the operation P would be absolutely sterile; it meant no more than that the operative procedure could not be reversed; (3) the intelligent lay bystander on hearing the discussion between P and D prior to the operation could not reasonably infer that D was giving a warranty that the operation would be 100 per cent. successful. In the absence of any express warranty the court should be slow to imply against a medical man an unqualified warranty as to the results of an intended operation. The nature of the contract does not depend upon what P or D thought in their own minds but on what the court objectively considers that the words used by the parties must be reasonably taken to have meant (*The Moorcock* (1889) 14 P.D. 64 considered).

EYRE *v.* MEASDAY [1986] 1 All E.R. 488, C.A.

422. Surgery—vasectomy—nature of contract—whether contract for particular result

A doctor carrying out surgery is not to be regarded as guaranteeing or warranting that the operation will achieve a particular result, but if he fails to warn the patient that failure is a possibility he may be liable in damages for any consequences flowing from that failure to warn.

T and his wife wished to avoid having any more children and consulted M, a surgeon, with a view to T having a vasectomy. M carried out the operation, but subsequently, by a rare chance, T became fertile again and his wife conceived. Knowing of the operation T's wife believed she could not be pregnant and did not consult her doctor, who confirmed her pregnancy, until it was too late for an abortion. The judge awarded £9,677 damages for the birth and upkeep of the child. *Held,* on appeal, that (i) a surgeon could not be said to guarantee or warrant that surgery would achieve a particular result and although the contract between surgeon and patient should require the surgeon to exercise all proper skill and care, the fact that the desired result was not achieved did not, of itself, mean that the surgeon was in breach of the contract; (ii) the failure of M to warn that the operation might, rarely, fail amounted to negligence as he should have appreciated that T's wife would have delayed consulting her doctor until it was too late to do anything about her pregnancy; (iii) T and his wife were entitled to damages for the distress, pain and suffering inherent in the birth, and this was not cancelled out by the joys of having a healthy baby.

THAKE *v.* MAURICE [1986] 1 All E.R. 497, C.A.

423. Trade descriptions—"act or default of some other person"—acting in course of trade or business. See OLGEIRSSON *v.* KITCHING, § 3020.

424. Unconscionable deal—setting aside sale at undervalue—requirements

Poverty with ignorance is one of the requirements for setting aside a sale at an undervalue as an unconscionable bargain. P was old, incapacitated in judgment, and desirous of a quick sale. *Held,* that the requirement was satisfied: WATKIN *v.* WATSON-SMITH, *The Times,* July 3, 1986, Michael Wheeler Q.C.

425. Undue influence—charge over wife's property—whether manifest and unfair disadvantage to wife

Mr. P ran a hairdressing business. Mr. and Mrs. P obtained a loan of £10,000 from the Midland Bank. The loan was secured by a charge over a house belonging solely to Mrs. P. Mrs. P acquired the house in the settlement of divorce proceedings involving her first husband and occupied the house with Mr. P and her children from her first marriage. Mr. P got into difficulties with the bank and in consequence the bank took proceedings for possession of the house. On March 26, 1981 an order for possession in 28 days was made. Mr. P's accountant advised him to acquire long term finance from a building society and short term finance to meet the bank's claim. Mr. P's solicitor introduced him to another of his clients, Woodstead Finance. W agreed to lend Mr. P £25,000 over a six month period at an annual rate of interest of 42 per cent. The loan was to be secured on the house owned by Mrs. P. All the necessary documents were prepared by Mr. P's solicitor and their execution supervised by Mr. P's accountant. Mrs. P was given a letter advising her of the terms of the loan, the effect of the charge against the house and to seek independent advice from a solicitor. At the meeting at which the documents were executed the accountant fully explained the situation to Mrs. P and advised her to seek independent advice if she wished but that if she did seek independent advice it had to be done quickly. The trial judge found that Mrs. P was aware of the urgency and that no other source of finance could be found and rejected the suggestion of obtaining independent advice. Mrs. P executed a guarantee and charge over her house in respect of the loan. Mr. P failed to comply with the terms of the loan for paying interest to W and disappeared. Mrs. P received no benefit from the £25,000. W sought to recover the loan from Mrs.

P who defended the claim on the grounds that the execution of the guarantee and charge had been obtained by the exercise of undue influence over her and that the terms of the loan were extortionate. The trial judge found that the terms were not extortionate and the defence of undue influence was not established. *Held,* dismissing Mrs. P's appeal, that unless it could be demonstrated that the grant of the legal charge by Mrs. P to W constituted a manifest and unfair disadvantage to Mrs. P any defence based on undue influence could not succeed. On the evidence the terms of the loan were not manifestly disadvantageous to Mrs. P. They were the normal terms upon which people in the position of Mr. and Mrs. P could obtain short term finance. Having regard to the fact that the bank held an order for possession of the house and Mr. P's financial position there was no other realistic alternative to entering into the arrangements agreed with W. There was no disadvantage to Mrs. P sufficient to raise a prima facie likelihood of undue influence. The disadvantages that existed were due to the acute financial crisis in which Mr. and Mrs. P found themselves. On the evidence adduced at the trial it was not an extortionate credit bargain under the Consumer Credit Act 1974 (*National Westminster Bank* v. *Morgan* [1985] C.L.Y. 413 applied): PETROU v. WOODSTEAD FINANCE [1986] F.L.R. 158, C.A.

426. Undue influence—presumption—circumstances
Undue influence will be presumed in a relationship when (i) A has ceded to B such trust and confidence that B is obliged out of public policy to show that he has not abused or betrayed it; (ii) where B is in a position to influence A into effecting the transaction of which complaint is made; and (iii) Where the gift made by A is so large, or the transaction entered into is so improvident, that friendship, charity, or other usual motives cannot reasonably account for it. It is not necessary to prove either dishonesty or conscious abuse of power, and there is no limit to the relationships in which the presumption might apply (*Tufton* v. *Sperni* [1952] C.L.Y. 1485 affirmed; *Holder* v. *Holder* [1968] C.L.Y. 1572 and *National Westminster Bank* v. *Morgan* [1985] C.L.Y. 413 considered): GOLDSWORTHY v. BRICKELL, *The Times,* July 21, 1986, C.A.

COPYRIGHT

427. Computer programs—importation
[France] The Court decided for P in an action for breach of copyright, fraudulent imitation of trade mark and various ancillary claims by P whose computer and software had been copied and then imported by D: APPLE COMPUTER INC. v. SEGIMEX [1985] F.S.R. 608, Tribunal de Grande Instance, Paris.

428. Copyright Act 1956
COPYRIGHT (ISLE OF MAN) ORDER 1986 (No. 1299) [£1·40], made under the Copyright Act 1956 (c.74), ss.31(1), (2) and 47(3); operative on September 1, 1986; extends to the Isle of Man the 1956 Act as amended.

429. Dramatic and musical performers' protection—private rights of action—whether enforceable after death
[Dramatic and Musical Performers' Protection Act 1958 (c.44).] A performer's right to give or withhold his consent under the Dramatic and Musical Performers' Protection Act 1958 survives his death and vests in his personal representatives. Although the Act makes it a criminal offence to use material without the performer's consent, it also confers a civil right of action on him: RICKLESS v. UNITED ARTISTS CORP., *The Times,* December 12, 1986, C.A.

430. Elements of offence—proof of offence
[Copyright Act 1956 (c.74), s.21(4A).] The elements of an offence under s.21(4A) of the Copyright Act 1956 are: (1) that copyright in the article subsists; (2) that first authorised publication took place in a country to which the section extends; and (3) that the copies are infringing copies. These elements may be proved by people other than the makers or the owners of the copyright: MUSA v. LE MAITRE, *The Times,* December 11, 1986, D.C.

431. Infringement—home-taping—declaration—duty of care—incitement
[Copyright Act 1956 (c.74), ss.1, 18, 21.] P manufactured and sold audio equipment which could copy pre-recorded cassettes. They warned customers that the recording in some circumstances might not be permissible. They sought a declaration that their action was not unlawful, in advertising and offering for sale such equipment. The

declaration was refused at first instance. *Held,* on appeal by P, that (1) P were not infringers or joint tortfeasors; (2) P was not authorising infringement, since they had no control over the use of the machines; (3) there was no duty of care to copyright owners; (4) the advertising of the machines might amount to an incitement to infringe. Declaration refused: AMSTRAD CONSUMER ELECTRONICS *v.* BRITISH PHONOGRAPHIC INDUSTRY [1986] F.S.R. 159, C.A.

432. Infringement—indirect copying—car exhaust pipes

A car manufacturer is not entitled to interfere with a car owner's inherent right to repair his car as economically as possible by asserting its copyright in vehicle parts.

A, which did not have a licence from B.L. to copy and sell spare parts, produced replacement exhaust pipes by copying the shape and dimensions of the original. B.L. commenced proceedings alleging infringement of copyright. The judge granted B.L. an injunction. The Court of Appeal upheld the decision. *Held,* by the House of Lords that (1) for the purposes of the Copyright Act 1956 the manufacture of the exhaust pipes, although achieved by indirect copying, amounted to an infringement by A of B.L.'s copyright in the drawings (*L.B. (Plastics)* v. *Swish Products* [1979] C.L.Y. 355 followed); (2) allowing the appeal, that car owners had an inherent right to repair their cars in the most economical way possible and to have means to a free market in spare parts, and B.L. was not entitled to derogate from or interfere with that right by asserting their copyright (*Browne* v. *Flower* [1911] 1 Ch. 219 and *O'Cedar* v. *Slough Trading Co.* [1927] 2 K.B. applied).

BRITISH LEYLAND MOTOR CORP. *v.* ARMSTRONG PATENTS CO. [1986] 2 W.L.R. 400, H.L.

433. Infringement—innocent infringement—director's liability

[Copyright Act 1956 (c.74), ss.17, 18 R.S.C., Ord. 14.] P owned the copyright in drawings which led to the production of an electric alarm. D2 was asked by a German company to manufacture alarms similar to P's. D1, the company, manufactured and sold the alleged copies. D2 wrongly formed the view there was no copyright. *Held,* that (1) D1 could not rely on ss.17, and 18 since he should have been aware that there was copyright; (2) D2 was personally liable as a joint tortfeasor. Summary judgment was given for P: BESSON (A. P.) *v.* FULLEON AND AMLANI [1986] F.S.R. 319, Harman J.

434. Infringement—passing off—Kiwifruit pocket packs

[N.Z.] [Copyright Act (N.Z.) 1962, ss.5, 7, 9; Copyright Act 1956 (c.74), s.4(3) Kiwifruit Licensing Regulations (N.Z.) 1977 S.R. 281/77.] P were the first manufacturers of "pocket packs" for kiwifruit. They were the only ones approved by the New Zealand Kiwifruit Authority who specified suitable forms. D endeavoured to manufacture packs which did not infringe, working alone without reference to existing pocket packs. D's product looked similar. P alleged copyright infringement and passing off. *Held,* that (1) D had copied and infringed by using the verbal descriptions of the Kiwifruit Authority, which were substantially derived from P's product; (2) when the packs were removed from their cartons purchasers might be confused, and the goodwill of P might be damaged. Injunction granted: PLIX PRODUCTS *v.* WINSTONE (FRANK M.) [1985] F.S.R. 63, H.Ct. of N.Z.

435. Infringement—programs for microcomputers—whether source and object codes original literary works

[Aus.] [Copyright Act 1968 (Cth.), Copyright Act 1911 (c.46), s.1(2), 35.]

D imported WOMBAT microcomputers. P manufactured and sold microcomputers under the name Apple II. At first instance the judge found that neither the object code programs nor the source code programs were protected by copyright. The full court reversed this but considered that they should not infer the requisite knowledge. D appealed and P cross-appealed. *Held,* allowing D's appeal, that (1) the source code of each program was an original literary work; (2) the object code was not an original literary work; (3) a programmed Apple II or WOMBAT ROM was not a reproduction or adaptation of the written expression of the relevant program expressed in source code: COMPUTER EDGE PTY. *v.* APPLE COMPUTER INC. [1986] F.S.R. 537, High Ct. of Australia.

436. Infringement—unlawful interference with goods—photographs

[Contempt of Court Act 1981 (c.49), s.10.]

P were a film company. D published in its newspaper photographs of the film star on P's set. The photographs had been taken by P's employee on set, and then allegedly stolen. D purchased the photographs. P sought an order, *inter alia,* that D deliver up the photographs and disclose the identity of the person from whom they purchased the photographs. *Held,* that P had not established that it was necessary in the interests of justice to make the order for disclosure. Further such disclosure should not in any event be ordered at the interlocutory stage: HANDMADE FILMS (PRODUCTIONS) *v.* EXPRESS NEWSPAPERS [1986] F.S.R. 463, Browne-Wilkinson, V.-C.

437. Infringement—video cassettes—possession—whether "by way of trade"
[Copyright Act 1956 (c.74), s.21(4A).] D purchased video cassettes from a person whom he knew to be in the trade of buying and selling pirate videotapes. *Held,* allowing D's appeal against convictions of possessing by way of trade an infringing copy, contrary to s.21(4A) of the 1956 Act as amended, that "by way of trade" meant "in the course of trade." A person purchasing for his own consumption and not in the course of trade cannot be guilty under s.21(4A): REID *v.* KENNET [1986] Crim.L.R. 456, D.C.

438. International conventions
COPYRIGHT (INTERNATIONAL CONVENTIONS) (AMENDMENT) ORDER 1986 (No. 2235) [80p], made under the Copyright Act 1956 (c.74), ss.31, 32, 47; operative on January 27, 1987; corrects an error in S.I. 1984 No. 549 and extends S.I. 1979 No. 1715 to dependent countries of the Commonwealth.

439. Joint ownership—agreement by one owner—injunction
H and W jointly owned the copyright in photographs of their wedding. W fell into a coma, and was only kept alive by a life-support machine. After W lost consciousness, H granted M, a newspaper, an exclusive licence to publish the photographs. E, another newspaper, sought to publish the photographs, and, when E tried to restrain it, said that one joint owner of copyright could not grant an exclusive licence without the other's consent. *Held,* that there was a serious issue to be tried as to whether W was already dead, and on the balance of convenience an injunction would be granted to restrain E's use of the photographs: MAIL NEWSPAPERS *v.* EXPRESS NEWSPAPERS, *The Times,* October 10, 1986, Millett J.

440. Partnership asset—magazine—sale by receiver
[Aus.] [Copyright Act (Australia) 1968, ss. 36, 196] The partnership of D and P1 included copyright in a magazine. When the partnership was to be wound up a receiver agreed with D to sell "all the right title and interest . . . in the magazine. . . ." P contended that there had not been any assignment of P1's interest in the copyright and that copyright was not vested in D. *Held,* dismissing the appeal, that (1) the receiver had the right to sell the copyright in the magazine; (2) the fact that the copyright had not been expressly mentioned in the agreement did not prevent it from being an "assignment" under the Act; (3) the agreement had been signed by the receiver on behalf of the partners which was sufficient signature by the assignors, within the Act: MURRAY *v.* KING [1986] F.S.R. 116, Fed. Court of Australia.

441. Protection—intellectual work—video games. See ATARI IRELAND *v.* VALADON (ALAIN) AND TARAYRE (CLAUDE GUILLEMIN), § 000.

442. Video games—hiring out—protection
[Germany] The Court dismissed an appeal by P, a video games cassette manufacturer for alleged breach of copyright against a purchaser who then sold on and commercially hired out his cassettes on the basis that (a) it was doubtful whether copyright existed; and (b) if the games could be protected P's failure to mark his cassettes "not for hire" had the effect of extinguishing his rights at the point of sale: HIRING OF VIDEO GAMES CASSETTES, *Re* [1985] F.S.R. 606 Karlsruhe C.A.

CORONERS

443/4. Inadequate direction to jury—costs
[Coroners Act 1887 (c.71), s.6(1).] Where the Coroner fails adequately to identify the issues for the jury and the requirements of the section are satisfied, all findings are quashed and an order for costs may be made against the Coroner. The Act does not limit the jury in the opinions they may express: INQUEST INTO THE DEATH OF ADAM BITHELL (DEC'D.), *Re* (1986) 150 J.P.N. 348, D.C.

445. Inquest—death in prison—evidence not disclosed at inquest—application for fresh inquest

[Coroners Act 1887 (50 & 51 Vict., c.71), s.6 Coroners (Amendment) Act 1926 (16 & 17 Geo. 5, c.59), s.19.]

The Court may grant an application for a new inquest, notwithstanding that it cannot be shown that new evidence will probably result in a different verdict, if the interests of justice demand it.

At an inquest into the death of a prisoner, a jury returned an open verdict. The coroner subsequently read in a report, which had not been submitted at the inquest, about possible solvent sniffing prior to death. The coroner applied for a fresh inquest. *Held,* granting the application, that although it had not been shown that there would probably be a different verdict if a new inquest was held, the matters raised had not been examined, and it was in the interests of justice that a new inquest should be ordered (*R. v. Cardiff City Coroner, ex p. Thomas* [1970] C.L.Y. 389; *Davis, decd., Re* [1967] C.L.Y. 663 distinguished).

RAPIER, DECD., *Re* [1986] 3 W.L.R. 830, D.C.

446. Inquest—second post-mortem—refusal of consent—order

[Coroners Rules 1984 (S.I. 1984 No. 552), r.19.]

Although a coroner has jurisdiction over a body while in his or her possession the power to order a post-mortem is not exclusive to the coroner, and she could be directed to give consent to one.

On Saturday, August 3, 1985 the deceased was taken into police custody and about 10 p.m. found unconscious in his cell. He was taken to hospital and found to be dead on arrival. On the Monday, August 5, the widow's solicitor learnt that a post-mortem was being held that morning but, there being insufficient time to attend, she arranged with the coroner's office for a second post-mortem. On August 9 she heard that the coroner had refused permission for a second post-mortem. She applied for judicial review to quash this decision and to order the coroner to give her consent to the holding of a second post-mortem. *Held,* granting application, that although the coroner had jurisdiction over the body while it was in her possession and her consent to a second post-mortem was required, the power to order a post-mortem was not exclusively in her. There were no sufficient grounds advanced by the coroner for her refusal to order a second post-mortem, and her decision was unsustainable and would be quashed. She would be directed to give consent for a second post-mortem as soon as practicable (*R. v. Bristol Coroner, ex p. Kerr* [1974] C.L.Y. 477 considered).

R. *v.* H.M. CORONER FOR GREATER LONDON (SOUTHERN DISTRICT), *ex p.* RIDLEY [1985] 1 W.L.R. 1347, Saville J.

447. Inquest verdict—application to quash—rights of interested parties

[Coroners Act 1887 (c.71), s.6; Coroners Amendment Act 1926 (c.59), s.19.] Persons troubled or aggrieved by an inquest verdict, who cannot point to a clear error in the conduct of the inquest, should (with the Attorney General's fiat) seek to have the verdict quashed on an application under s.6 of the Coroners Act 1887 and s.19 of the Coroners Amendment Act 1926. The Courts then have the power to grant relief if in all the circumstances the verdict was unsafe and unsatisfactory—which it cannot do on an application for judicial review. A coroner has no duty to inform interested parties of their right to examine witnesses at an inquest: R. *v.* H.M. CORONER FOR THE COUNTY OF CENTRAL CLEVELAND, *ex p.* DENT, *The Times,* February 17, 1986, D.C.

448. Summonsing a jury—exercise of discretion

[Coroners (Amendment) Act 1926 (c.59), s.13(2)] A coroner has very wide discretion as to whether or not to summon a jury, and in order to obtain judicial review of a decision not to do so it is necessary to show that he took into account something that he should not, or failed to take into account something that he should, when coming to his decision (*R. v. H.M. Coroner at Hammersmith ex p. Peach* [1980] C.L.Y. 385 considered): R. *v.* H.M. CORONER OF THE EASTERN DISTRICT OF THE METROPOLITAN COUNTY OF WEST YORKSHIRE, *ex p.* NATIONAL UNION OF MINEWORKERS, YORKSHIRE AREA, (1985) 150 J.P. 58, D.C.

CORPORATION TAX

449. Capital allowances—whether allowances mandatory

[Finance Act 1965 (c.25), s.56.] B.P. Tyne and B.P. Oil incurred capital expenditure on the provision of machinery and plant for trading purposes prior to the end of 1972. F (No. 2) A. 1975, s.43, prevented them carrying forward losses incurred before the end of 1972. The companies, therefore, decided not to claim allowances in respect of the expenditure for the periods before the end of 1972, giving them increased allowances for 1973 and subsequent years. The Inland Revenue claimed that the companies were obliged to take the allowances in the periods in which the expenditure was incurred. *Held,* dismissing the Crown's appeals, that the legislation did not oblige the companies to take the allowances in the periods in which the expenditure was incurred; they were free to renounce the allowances for those periods: ELLISS v. B.P. OIL NORTHERN IRELAND REFINERY; ELLISS v. B.P. TYNE TANKER CO., *The Times,* December 16, 1986, C.A.

450. Double taxation—overseas life assurance company—investment income

[Double Taxation Relief (Taxes on Income) (Canada) Order 1967 (S.I. 1967 No. 482), Sched., art. 6; Double Taxation (Taxes on Income) (Canada) Order 1980 (S.I. 1980 No. 7091, Sched., art. 7; Income Tax Act 1952 (c.10), s.430; Income and Corporation Taxes Act 1970 (c.10), s.316.] T Co. was an overseas life assurance company; its head office was in Canada; it had a branch in the U.K. and branches in five other countries. For accounting periods from 1972 to 1977, it was assessed to corporation tax under I.C.T.A. 1970, s.316, on a proportion of its worldwide income from the investment of its life assurance fund. The proportion was calculated by the formula $\frac{A \times B}{C}$ in s.316, where "A" was the worldwide investment income, "B" was the average of U.K. policyholders' liabilities, and "C" was the average liabilites to all policy holders. Originally, under I.T.A. 1952, s.30, the proportion was based on premiums; in 1969 it was changed to liabilities to policy holders. T Co. claimed that the assessments were precluded by the Double Taxation Conventions with Canada. In particular, it was contended by T. Co. that (1) I.C.T.A. 1970, s.316, was in breach of the 1967 Convention and should be disregarded, (2) s.316 was in conflict with art. 7(2) of the 1980 Convention and should be disregarded, and (3) in any event, component "B" in the formula should have omitted proposals received through agents in the foreign countries where T Co. had offices. *Held,* dismissing T Co's appeal, that (1) the change from premium basis of apportionment to a liability basis enacted in I.C.T.A. 1970, s.316, was not in breach of the 1967 Convention; (2) s.316 satisfied the principle in Art. 7(2) of the 1980 Convention; and (3) proposals for policies effected by agents in foreign countries were effected "through" the U.K. branch and so should be included in component "B": SUN LIFE ASSURANCE CO OF CANADA v. PEARSON [1986] S.T.C. 335, C.A.

451. Double taxation relief—set off for advance corporation tax

[Income and Corporation Taxes Act 1970 (c.10), ss.497, 501, 505; Finance Act 1972 (c.41), ss. 84, 85, 100.] In the accounting period to June 1980, T Co. was entitled to relief under I.C.T.A. 1970, s.497, from double taxation by way of credit for foreign withholding tax and foreign underlying tax in respect of dividends which it had received. For the same accounting period, T Co. had available for relief under F.A. 1972, s.85, advance corporation tax attributable to dividends of £2.2m. paid by it. The Inland Revenue claimed that the relief for the advance tax must be taken before double taxation relief was given under I.C.T.A. 1970, s.497. *Held,* dismissing the Crown's appeal, that T. Co. was entitled to take credit for double taxation relief before set-off advance corporation tax: COLLARD v. MINING AND INDUSTRIAL HOLDINGS [1986] S.T.C. 230, Walton J.

452. Trade—acquisition of loans—whether a trading transaction

W, a bank, and T Co. were subsidiaries of GUS. In 1974 and 1975 W transferred certain loans secured on land to T Co., which was dormant, at face value. T Co. was put in funds by GUS to buy the loans. The loans transferred in 1975 were repaid; those transferred in 1974 were not. After considerable trouble, T Co. sold the underlying securities, incurring substantial losses. T Co. claimed that the losses were trading losses eligible for group relief. The General Commissioners accepted evidence that the loans had been transferred at a proper price and with a reasonable expectation of T Co. making profit, but that, nevertheless, T Co. was not trading. *Held,* allowing T Co.'s appeal, that, (1) having regard to the evidence accepted by the Commissioners, the transactions were entered into by T Co. by way of trade, and (2) the costs of acquiring the loans from W were proper deductions in computing T Co.'s profits or losses: TORBELL INVESTMENTS *v.* WILLIAMS [1986] S.T.C. 397, Harman J.

453. Trade—contributions to employee pension trust fund—whether capital or revenue expenditure

Payments made by a company to a trust fund it sets up to provide pension and retirement benefits for its employees are not capital expenditure but are revenue expenditure and thus deductible from the company's profits in computing corporation tax payable by the company.

With a view to providing pension and retirement benefits to their employees Ringtons set up a trust fund in accordance with the Companies Act 1948, s.54(1)(*b*). The company intended to pay into the fund approximately five per cent. of its profits in each year. The company was not bound to make payments into the fund. The trust was empowered to use its funds to purchase shares in the company and given a discretion to retain money on deposit at the bank. The trust was set up in 1978 and was to last for 79 years. There was no set target for the fund to reach in value. In 1980 at various times the company paid a total of £35,000 into the trust fund. The company was assessed to corporation tax for 1980 on the basis that the £35,000 was capital expenditure and thus not an allowable deduction in computing the company's trading profits. The company appealed to the Special Commissioners who held the payments to be revenue expenditure and thus deductible. The Crown appealed by way of case stated. *Held,* dismissing the appeal, that the payment of £35,000 was a revenue expenditure and not a capital expenditure. It was one of a series of voluntary payments to a fund that had no recognisable ceiling or target and, as such, could not be described as an instalment of some capital sum to be paid to the trust fund. The payment did not create nor acquire for the company an asset or enduring advantage of a capital nature, the intended amount and duration of the fund was uncertain and was distributable by the trustees in their own discretion. As such the trust fund might exist for a very short period of time and not the 79 years intended (*Heather (Inspector of Taxes) v. P.-E. Consulting Group* [1972] C.L.Y. 1755 followed, *British Insulated and Helsby Cables v. Atherton (Inspector of Taxes)* [1926] A.C. 205, *Tucker (Inspector of Taxes) v. Granada Motorway Services* [1979] C.L.Y. 374 considered).

JEFFS (INSPECTOR OF TAXES) *v.* RINGTONS [1986] 1 All E.R. 144, Scott J.

454. Trade—payments to employees' trust—profits—deduction of payments

[Income and Corporation Taxes Act 1970 (c.10), s.130.] T Co. traded as fishmongers; its shares were held by two elderly directors and their wives. The employees were concerned that on the deaths of the directors the company would be unable to continue in its original form. Accordingly, on advice of accountants, a trust was constituted for the benefit of T Co.'s employees with a view to acquiring the share capital of T Co. The company made an initial payment to the trustees of £2,500 and two further payments of £2,224 and £1,000. The Inspector refused to allow deduction of these payments in computing the company's Schedule D, Case I, profits. *Held,* allowing T Co.'s appeal, that the payments were made wholly and exclusively for its trade within I.C.T.A. 1970, s.130(*a*), and deduction should have been allowed: BOTT (E.) *v.* PRICE, *The Times,* December 8, 1986, Hoffmann J.

COUNTY COURT PRACTICE

455. Arbitration—procedure—cross-examination

[C.C.R., Ord. 19, r.5(2).]

When one party to a county court arbitration is legally represented that party cannot be prevented from cross-examining an unrepresented party.

C brought an action against S which was referred to arbitration before the registrar under C.C.R., Ord. 19. C appeared in person and S was represented by a solicitor. The registrar refused to allow S's solicitor to cross-examine C on the ground that it would give S an unfair advantage. He stated that all questions to C were to be put through the registrar. The judge refused S's appeal. *Held,* allowing the appeal, that although arbitrations were intended to be informal, it did not mean that the arbitrator could adopt a procedure which deprived a party of the services of a solicitor or counsel if he wished to have them. It was the duty of the arbitrator, without entering the arena to the extent that he was no longer acting judicially, to make good any deficiencies of the unrepresented party.

CHILTON *v.* SAGA HOLIDAYS [1986] 1 All E.R. 841, C.A.

456. Contempt—breach of undertaking—committal—whether penal notice required—whether service of order required

[C.C.R., Ord. 29, r.1(2)(6)(7).]

C.C.R., Ord. 29, r.1 has no direct application to cases of committal for breach of an undertaking, where the procedural requirements are less onerous and proof of service is unnecessary.

Per curiam: it is good practice that when an undertaking is given instead of an injunction granted, the undertaking should be recorded in the order of the Court, which order should be served and indorsed with a notice explaining what would happen in the event of a breach.

H gave a non-molestation undertaking during the course of divorce proceedings; the undertaking was recited in the order, but no penal notice was endorsed thereon and the order was never served. Following a breach of the undertaking the judge dispensed with service of the original order and committed H. *Held*, that the appeal would be dismissed. Strictly speaking, Ord. 29, r.1 was of no application because it was the undertaking itself which was being enforced. A person giving an undertaking is presumed to know of it so it is unnecessary to prove service, nor need a penal notice be indorsed thereon. The order for committal was perfectly proper and the appeal would be dismissed (*Nguyen* v. *Phung* [1984] C.L.Y. 470 and *Williams* v. *Fawcett* [1985] C.L.Y. 471 distinguished).

HUSSAIN *v.* HUSSAIN [1986] 1 All E.R. 961, C.A.

457. Contempt—committal—general procedure

[County Courts Act 1984 (c.28), s.14(1)(*b*).] The County Court judge should generally give a person against whom a contempt has been proved an opportunity to make representations why he should not be committed to prison: STILWELL *v.* WILLIAMSON, *The Times,* September 1, 1986, C.A.

458. Contempt—committal order—particularity

[C.C.R. (S.I. 1981 No. 1687), Ord. 13, r.3; Ord. 29, r. 167)] A mother and daughter (the plaintiffs) had brought proceedings to stop an alleged campaign of harassment by D, a man living with the mother's other daughter. D had given a non-molestation undertaking. On August 28, 1985 a notice to show cause why he should not be committed to prison was served personally on D. The notice set out what was alleged to be the breach in vague and general terms and was supported by an affidavit. On October 2, the matter was adjourned and a new notice in identical items was served personally on D giving October 11 as the date for the hearing. On that day D failed to appear and the matter was adjourned until October 18. In order to notify D the plaintiffs' solicitors served a further copy of the original notice which was posted through the letter-box of the home of D's parents on October 16. D did not appear at the hearing on October 18. The judge made an order committing D to prison for 28 days. *Held*, allowing D's appeal, that where requirements were imposed for the protection of a defendant they must be strictly complied with. The notice of the hearing on October 18 if regarded as a notice of an adjourned hearing under Ord. 13, r. 3, had not been served personally by the proper officer; and if regarded as a fresh notice of application under Ord. 13, r. 1 had not been served within the time prescribed by the rules. The Court could have dispensed with service under Ord. 29, r. 1(7) but normally that was only done in urgent cases and that fact should be stated in the committal order. As a consequence D had not had any opportunity to make representations. Furthermore the judge had relied on matters between October 2 and 11 of which D had had no notice since they were not comprised in any affidavit or in the notice of application. For these technical reasons the order could not be allowed to stand (*Williams* v. *Fawcett* [1985] C.L.Y. 471 considered): TABONE *v.* SEGUNA (1986) 16 Fam.Law 188, C.A.

459. Costs—inflated claims—payment into court—whether further costs allowed

[C.C.R., Ord. 19, rr.2(3) and 6.] In June 1985 vehicles belonging to P1 and D were involved in a road traffic accident. P2 was driving P1's vehicle. P1 claimed £186 and in the same pleading it was said that P2 was shocked and shaken, stiff and sore (did not seek medical attention however). The damages claimed by P1 and P2 were limited to £600 in each case. A "common form" defence was filed and payment into court of £308 was made. The question arose as to whether P were entitled to further costs other than those paid into court. P's solicitors applied under Ord. 11, r.3(5) for further costs to which they would normally have been entitled. The application was opposed on the basis that the way in which P1 and P2's cases had been presented was an abuse of the process of the court. D argued that P1 and 2's cases had been purposely inflated so as to prevent the operation of Ord. 19, rr.2(3) or 6. *Held,* that the court was satisfied that the claims had been purposely inflated to prevent the operation of a rule disallowing further costs. Judgment for D on basis that P entitled to no more costs than those paid into court already by D (*Hobbs* v. *Marlowe* [1977] C.L.Y. 433 followed): BARROWCLOUGH v. BRITISH GAS CORP., July 25, 1986; Mr. Registrar Haythornthwaite. [*Ex rel. Forbes & Partners, Solicitors.*]

460. County court names
CIVIL COURTS (AMENDMENT) ORDER 1986 (No. 754) [45p], made under the County Courts Act 1984 (c.28), s.2(1); operative on May 28, 1986; changes the names of specified courts and revises the schedule of county courts whose designated names differ from the place in which they are held.

461. Fees
COUNTY COURT FEES (AMENDMENT) ORDER 1986 (No. 633) [45p], made under the County Courts Act 1984 (c.28), s.128; operative on April 28, 1986; increases fees payable under S.I. 1982 No. 1706.
COUNTY COURT FEES (AMENDMENT No. 2) ORDER 1986 (No. 2143) [80p], made under the Insolvency Act 1986 (c.45), ss.414 and 415, and the County Courts Act 1984 (c.25), s.128; operative on December 29, 1986; amends S.I. 1982 No. 1706 concerning fees.

462. Forms
COUNTY COURT (FORMS) (AMENDMENT) RULES 1986 (No. 1505 (L.14)) [£1·40], rr. 1, 3, 4 operative on October 1, 1986 and Rules 2, 5, 6 operative on January 1, 1987; amend S.I. 1982 No. 586 so as to substitute certain new forms.

463. Jurisdiction—application to wrong court—application to correct court out of time
[County Courts Act 1984 (c.28), s.75(3)(a); C.C.R. 1981 (S.I. 1981 No. 1687 (L.20)), Ord. 4, r.8, Ord. 16, r.2.]
An application received by the "wrong" County Court within set time limits, but forwarded to the "correct" court out of time, is a valid application which the "correct" court has jurisdiction to hear.
The applicant was a tenant of business premises within the district of the Dartford County Court. The landlord served a s.25 notice on the tenant who replied by letter that he was unwilling to give up the premises. The time limit for an application for a new tenancy expired on September 17. On that date an application was received by the Tunbridge Wells court who forwarded it to Dartford. It arrived there on September 18. Judge Clapham held that it was out of time and declined jurisdiction. *Held,* allowing the appeal, that the county court's jurisdiction was a general one; although the applicant had chosen the wrong court as prescribed in the rules, it had jurisdiction to deal with the matter, and the application had been made in time.
SHARMA v. KNIGHT [1986] 1 W.L.R. 757, C.A.

464. Possession—squatters—warrant of possession—whether valid against subsequent squatters
[C.C.R., Ord. 24 and Ord. 26, r.17(5).] P obtained an Ord. 24 judgment in August 1985 against persons unknown and on September 3, 1985, warrant of possession issued. The premises were boarded up by P on September 26. On October 3, more squatters entered and were evicted on October 22, pursuant to the warrant of possession by bailiffs. On October 23 the premises were again boarded up. On that day D and other squatters entered. P applied for a warrant of restitution. There was a cross-application by a squatter to be joined as defendant and to set aside the warrant of possession. *Held,* that (1) the initial boarding up of the premises did not prevent the subsequent execution of the warrant of possession against squatters other than the original persons unknown; (2) the re-entry into possession of squatters albeit not those who were originally evicted come within the ambit of C.C.R., Ord. 26, r.17(5), and P was therefore entitled to its warrant of

restitution (*Wiltshire County Council* v. *Frazer, The Times,* September 27, 1985 and *McPhail* v. *Persons, Names Unknown* [1973] C.L.Y. 2800, followed): LAMBETH LONDON BOROUGH v. GUYT, December 10, 1985, H. H. Judge Holroyd-Pearce, Q.C., Lambeth County Ct. (*Ex rel. Ann McAlister, Barrister*).

465. Registry of County Court Judgements
From January 2, 1986, the operation of the Registry of County Court Judgments has been transferred from the Lord Chancellor's Department to a private company— Registy Trust Ltd. The Registry will operate from 171/173 Cleveland Street, London W1P 5PE. Tel. 01-387-8279.

466. Rules
COUNTY COURT (AMENDMENT) RULES 1986 (No. 636 (L.3)); operative on April 28, 1986; amend S.I. 1981 No. 1687.
COUNTY COURT (AMENDMENT No. 2) RULES 1986 (No. 1189 (L.10)) [80p], operative on August 1, 1986 save for Rules 2, 3 and 4 which are operative on October 1, 1986; amend S.I. 1981 No. 1687 so as to amend Rule 41, to provide for notice to be given to the person entitled to relief against forfeiture in proceedings brought by a landlord seeking forfeiture and give effect to the Child Abduction and Custody Act 1985.

467. Striking out defence—enforcement of interim orders
[County Courts Act 1984 (c.28), s.50(2); R.S.C., Ord. 45.] There is no equivalent of R.S.C., Ord. 45 in the County Court, so it cannot order that unless a defendant pays an amount outstanding under an interim order, the defence will be struck out. This would be counter to s.50(2) of the County Courts Act 1984: H. H. PROPERTY Co. v. RAHIM, *The Times,* November 8, 1986, C.A.

468. Transfer of proceedings
CIVIL COURTS (AMENDMENT No. 3) ORDER 1986 (No. 2207) [45p], made under the County Courts Act 1984 (c.28), s.2(1) and the Supreme Court Act 1981 (c.54), s.99(1); operative on January 31, 1987; closes the Hyde County Court and transfers its business to the Tameside County Court.

469. Transfer of proceedings—jurisdiction to make order
[C.C.R., 1981, Ord. 13, r.2, Ord. 16.] Only a Judge or Registrar can make an order transferring proceedings from one Court to another: RHODES (JOHN T.), *ex p.* HAYWARD, *The Times,* July 15, 1986, C.A.

CRIMINAL LAW

470. Abuse of process—acquittal of co-defendant at first trial—relevance at second trial
At the first trial D's brother was acquitted and the jury were unable to agree in relation to D on charges concerning importation of heroin. At D's second trial the prosecution maintained their case that D's brother had been D's "lookout". *Held,* dismissing D's appeal against conviction, that there had been no abuse of process. Against D's brother the prosecution had to prove that he was assisting D and that he knew what D was doing. The case was very different from the situation where a man had been acquitted and the same man was prosecuted again (*R.* v. *Humphreys* [1977] C.L.Y. 622 distinguished): R. v. IJAZ HAIDER MIRZA [1986] Crim.L.R. 45, C.A.

471. Administering noxious thing—injure—intent
[Offences against the Person Act 1861 (c.100), s.24.] In the offence under s.24 of the Offences against the Person Act 1861, of administering a poison or noxious thing with intent to injure, the word "injure" is used in the sense of "causing physical harm". An intention merely to keep awake the person to whom the drug is administered is not enough: R. v. HILL (FREDERICK), *The Times,* July 28, 1986, H.L.

472. Alternative verdict—direction in summing up—no previous consideration
[Road Traffic Act 1972 (c.20), ss.2, 3; Criminal Law Act 1977 (c.45), s.50(1).]
It is an irregularity in the course of the trial for the judge in his summing up to leave the jury to consider a charge about which neither the Crown nor the defence have had an opportunity to argue or make submissions.
At 2.15 a.m. H left a nightclub with two young women and was involved in an incident with some youths. Thereafter he drove off in his car with his companions to a roundabout when the same youths ran into the road and chased after the car. H turned his car round 360 degrees and drove off hitting one of the youths who suffered serious injury. H was charged, *inter alia,* with reckless driving. In summing

up the judge, without prior warning to counsel, directed the jury to consider the alternative of careless driving if they rejected the reckless driving charge. H was convicted of careless driving. *Held,* allowing the appeal, that inviting a jury to consider a charge about which neither the Crown nor the defence had had an opportunity to make submissions, was an irregularity in the trial, in the present circumstances the conviction must be quashed.

R. *v.* HAZELL [1985] R.T.R. 369, C.A.

473. Alternative verdict—judge's refusal to direct—whether material irregularity

Where there exists an alternative, and less serious, offence to that charged the judge must direct the jury on that lesser offence only where there is evidence to support that lesser offence on the case as presented at the trial.

F was alleged to have caused the death of another motorist by reckless driving, the essence of the prosecution case being that he had been driving far too fast having regard to the nature of the road; there was some evidence, however, that he had been driving much more slowly than the prosecution alleged. The judge refused to direct the jury that it was open to them to convict of the lesser offence of careless driving, and F was convicted. *Held,* allowing his appeal, that where, on the case as presented by the prosecution, there was evidence to support an alternative lesser offence, the jury should be directed upon it. The judge could refuse to do so only if there was no such evidence.

R. *v.* FAIRBANKS [1986] 1 W.L.R. 1202, C.A.

474. Appeal—perjured evidence of prosecution witness—whether conviction unsafe

A police officer gave perjured evidence, but his evidence overall was peripheral to the main issues involved. *Held,* that the conviction was not unsafe: R. *v.* CUMMINS; R. *v.* PERKS, *The Times,* June 23, 1986, C.A.

475. Appeal—sentence—frivolous appeals

The Court of Appeal reiterated that, notwithstanding the support of counsel, frivolous and groundless appeals against sentence can lose the appellant the benefit of time served awaiting appeal: R. *v.* GAYLE, *The Times,* May 28, 1986, C.A.

476. Appeal to Crown Court from Magistrates' Court—appellant absent—refusal of Crown Court to hear appeal—withdrawal of appeal

Where a person appealing to the Crown Court is represented at the hearing by counsel there is no obligation upon him to be present in person.

C and two others were convicted in the magistrates' court of assaulting a police officer in the execution of his duty. All three appealed to the Crown Court. C decided not to attend the hearing of the appeal for reasons connected with employment he had recently obtained. All three appellants were represented by the same counsel who made an application on behalf of C that his appeal might be heard in his absence. The application was refused, leaving C's counsel no option but to withdraw his appeal. At the conclusion of the hearing the other two appellants were acquitted. C applied for judicial review of the decision of the Crown Court that his appeal could not proceed in his absence. *Held,* allowing the application, that where a person appealing to the Crown Court against a decision of a magistrates' court is represented by counsel at the hearing of his appeal there was no obligation upon him to attend personally at the hearing. By virtue of the presence of counsel the appellant is deemed not to be absent. The manner in which the appeal was withdrawn was not an abandonment of the appeal that would prevent the Crown Court from considering the appeal afresh (*R. v. Medway* [1975] C.L.Y. 502 distinguished).

R. *v.* CROYDON CROWN COURT, *ex p.* CLAIR [1986] 1 W.L.R. 746, D.C.

477. Appeals to Crown Court—notice of abandonment—application to withdraw

D gave notice under Rule 11 of the Crown Court Rules 1982 of abandonment of his appeal against a conviction by magistrates. Three months later, a Crown Court judge allowed D's application to have his appeal re-instated. *Held,* quashing the judge's decision, that leave to withdraw an abandonment of an appeal to the Crown Court could only be given if the abandonment was given in circumstances making it a nullity (*R. v. Essex Quarter Sessions, ex p. Larkin* [1961] C.L.Y. 5257 applied; *R. v. Keating* [1982] C.L.Y. 504 considered): R. *v.* KNIGHTSBRIDGE CROWN COURT, *ex p.* COMMISSIONERS OF CUSTOMS AND EXCISE [1986] Crim.L.R. 324, D.C.

478. Arson—director setting fire to company premises—whether lawful excuse
[Criminal Damage Act 1971 (c.48), s.1(1)(3).]
A company director who fraudulently sets fire to his company building is not entitled to claim "lawful excuse."
The appellant set fire to a store belonging to a company of which he was managing director. A submission of no case on the grounds that he was owner of the premises failed; the appellant was convicted. He appealed on the grounds that the appellant must be taken to have consented to the damage. *Held,* dismissing the appeal, and distinguishing *R. v. Denton,* that the appellant could not be held to be entitled to consent to a fraudulent purpose (*R. v. Denton* [1981] C.L.Y. 358 distinguished). R. *v.* APPLEYARD (1985) 81 Cr.App.R. 319, C.A.

479. Assaulting police officer in execution of duty—whether acting in execution of duty
[Police Act 1964 (c.48), s.51(1).] D approached his girlfriend, X, who had run away from D after an argument, in order to see if she was all right and to ask the way home. A police officer, Y, approached D to check him out in case he was following X. D continued and, when Y approached again, attacked Y, punching and kicking him. Justices acquitted D of assaulting a police officer in the execution of his duty, contrary to s.51(1) of the 1964 Act, on the basis that Y had not been acting in the execution of his duty since he had no reason to believe that any offence had been, was being or would be committed. *Held,* allowing the prosecutor's appeal, that providing the officer's intention in attempting to speak to a person was in pursuit of the preservation of peace or prevention of crime, he acted in the execution of his duty. (*Donnelly v. Jackman* [1970] C.L.Y. 2218, *Collins v. Wilcock* [1984] C.L.Y. 506 and *McManus v. Whittington* April 29, 1986) considered): WEIGHT *v.* LONG [1986] Crim.L.R. 746, D.C.

480. Assisting—whether conviction prior to conviction of principal proper
[Criminal Law Act 1967 (c.58), s.4(1).] D1 and D2 were convicted of assisting X to commit a robbery contrary to s.4(1) of the 1967 Act. They were alleged to have sheltered X, knowing him to have committed robbery, with intent to impede his arrest. X had not attended for trial but the prosecution adduced evidence of his involvement in the robbery. *Held,* dismissing appeals against conviction, that the convictions were proper. R. *v.* DONALD AND DONALD [1986] Crim.L.R. 535, C.A.

481. Attempt—attempt to procure act of gross indecency—whether offence
[Sexual Offences Act 1956 (c.69), s.13; Criminal Attempts Act 1981 (c.47), s.1(4)(b).] S.13 of the Sexual Offences Act 1956 makes it an offence to procure the commission of an act of gross indecency, "procurement" being an essential element of the offence. Attempting so to procure is an offence under s.1(1) of the Criminal Attempts Act 1981, even though by s.1(4)(b) of that Act procuring of an offence is excluded: it is only excluded where it is not an essential element of the substantive offence: CHIEF CONSTABLE OF HAMPSHIRE *v.* MACE, *The Times,* June 20, 1986, C.A.

482. Attempt—impossibility—importation of prohibited drugs
[Customs and Excise Management Act 1979 (c.2), s.170(1)(b); Criminal Attempts Act 1981 (c.47), s.1.]
It is no defence for a defendant charged with a criminal attempt for him to say that it would in fact have been impossible to commit the crime (*Anderton v. Ryan* [1985] C.L.Y. 506 (H.L.) overruled).
The appellant was tried on counts of attempting to be knowingly concerned in dealing with and harbouring a controlled drug, namely heroin, contrary to s.1(1) of the Criminal Attempts Act 1981 and s.170(1)(b) of the Customs and Excise Management Act 1979. He was carrying a package containing a powdered substance and more such was found at his flat. The prosecution case was that he admitted having drugs in police interview and in a statement under caution stated that he very deeply suspected that the substance was heroin. In fact it was a vegetable material akin to snuff. In evidence he denied making any admission and denied that the statement under caution amounted to a confession. He was found guilty and appealed on the grounds that because the substance was not a drug he could not be guilty in law. His appeal was dismissed by the Court of Appeal and by the House of Lords. *Held,* that (1) in order to prove a charge under s.170(1) of the 1979 Act of being knowingly concerned in harbouring or dealing with goods the importation of which was prohibited, it was sufficient to prove that the person knew that the goods concerned were prohibited goods and no proof was required that he knew the goods

to be of a particular category, irrespective of the different penalties attaching to the importation of different categories of prohibited goods. Accordingly, it was immaterial that the appellant was unsure of the exact nature of the substance in his possession, in that in any event he believed he was dealing with controlled drugs the importation of which was prohibited (*R.* v. *Hussain* [1969] C.L.Y. 854 approved); (2) on the true construction of s.1 of the Criminal Attempts Act 1981 the *actus reus* of the statutory offence of attempt required an act which was more than merely preparatory to the commission of an offence and which the defendant did with the intention of committing an offence, notwithstanding that the commission of the actual offence was, on the true facts, impossible. The appellant had on the facts of the case been rightly convicted; (3) the distinction which the House of Lords had previously drawn in regard to s.1 between acts which were "objectively innocent" and those which were not, could not be maintained. *Anderton* v. *Ryan* [1985] C.L.Y. 506 had been wrongly decided and since it was indistinguishable from the present case would be departed from under the *Practice Statement (Judicial Precedent)* [1966] C.L.Y. 9921. *Per* Lord Hailsham, Lord Elwyn-Jones and Lord Mackay: Even if the Practice Statement had not been applied, the appeal would still have been dismissed by distinguishing the facts of the present case from those in *Anderton* v. *Ryan*, on the basis that the appellant was guilty on the clear wording of section 1(1) and (2) of the 1981 Act and that no recourse was therefore necessary to the wording of section 1(3), which would be irrelevant.

R. *v.* SHIVPURI [1986] 2 W.L.R. 988, H.L.

483. Attempt—obtaining services by deception—hire-purchase agreement
Obtaining a hire-purchase agreement amounts to obtaining services but cannot properly be described as credit facilities.

D was convicted of attempting to obtain services dishonestly, namely credit facilities to purchase a motor vehicle. D went to a garage to purchase a motor vehicle. He completed a hire-purchase agreement proposal form in the name and address of his next door neighbour. The proposal form was to enable the finance company to investigate the applicant's credit worthiness as a preliminary step before entering into any hire-purchase agreement. *Held,* allowing D's appeal, that the benefits of a hire-purchase agreement could not be described as "credit facilities" as stated in the particulars of the indictment. The indictment was therefore defective. Obtaining the benefits of a hire-purchase agreement could amount to obtaining services. The steps taken by D could only be described as preparatory to committing the offence of dishonestly obtaining services by deception and were not sufficiently proximate to the offence to be categorised as an attempt. Had the finance company responded favourably D would have had to complete a hire purchase agreement form before he could obtain any services (*R.* v. *Ilyas* [1984] C.L.Y. 511 applied, *R.* v. *Halai* [1983] C.L.Y. 729 distinguished).

R. *v.* WIDDOWSON [1986] R.T.R. 124, C.A.

484. Attempt—supplying drugs—incomplete offence
When, if the facts were as the defendant believed, the attempted offence would have been possible even though, on the true facts, the attempted offence was impossible a conviction for attempt under section 1 of the Criminal Law Act 1977 is possible.

T pleaded guilty to attempting to supply drugs. He had sold pieces of paper that he believed were impregnated with LSD. In fact the pieces of paper were not so impregnated. He later appealed because of the change in the law brought about by the House of Lords' decision in *Anderton* v. *Ryan. Held,* applying *R.* v. *Shivipuri,* that a conviction for attempting to supply drugs was possible on these facts and so the conviction would stand. *R.* v. *Shivpuri* [1985] C.L.Y. 507 and *Anderton* v. *Ryan* [1985] C.L.Y. 506 applied).

R. v. TULLOCH (W.A.) (1986) 83 Cr.App.R. 1, C.A.

485. Attempt—theft from handbag—indictment
The appellants had admitted trying to steal whatever was in X's handbag. They were charged with attempting to steal "some or all of the contents" of that handbag. X did not give evidence. *Held,* dismissing appeals against conviction, that since the Criminal Attempts Act 1981 it was irrelevant whether there were any contents in the bag. The wording of the charge in the indictment did not mean that the prosecution

were alleging that there was property in the bag: R. *v.* SMITH AND SMITH [1986] Crim.L.R. 166, C.A.

486. Attempted rape—mens rea—self-induced intoxication
[Criminal Attempts Act 1981 (c.47), s.1(1).]
D was charged with five counts including one of attempted rape contrary to s.1(1). He broke into the house of a 63-year-old woman and subjected her to a series of acts that were capable of being interpreted as an attempt to rape. Before the incident, D had consumed over a gallon of beer, a quantity of amphetamines and possibly some LSD. D gave evidence to the effect that due to this consumption, he was in such an intoxicated state as to have no recollection of the incident. His defence was that, as he had no knowledge of where he was or what he was doing at the time of the *actus reus*, he could not and did not form the necessary *mens rea* for attempted rape. *Held*, that self-induced intoxication was relevant to the offence of attempted rape and if D was so intoxicated as not to know that he was trying to have intercourse, then he would not be guilty of that offence. The judge directed the jury that they must be satisfied that at the time when the acts described were performed, that it was D who was doing them and that he both knew that he was doing them and intended to do them. D was convicted on all five counts: R. *v.* WEBSTER, February 12, 1986; Turner J. (*Ex rel. Steven Robinson, Barrister*).

487. Bail—bail pending appeal—applications to High Court judge on circuit—whether proper
[Criminal Appeal Act 1968 (c.19), ss.18(1), 31(1)(2)(*e*); Criminal Appeal Rules 1968 (S.I. 1968 No. 1262), r.2(1).]
It is not proper for counsel to make a bail application to a High Court judge on circuit until a formal application for leave to appeal has been made.
S was sentenced at the Crown Court and on the same day was granted bail by a High Court judge on circuit who purported to act under s.31 of the 1968 Act. His sentence was varied on appeal, and the question arose as to whether it was proper for a judge to grant bail before any formal application for leave to appeal had been received by the registrar. *Held,* that it was improper to ask a High Court judge to act until the proper application for leave had been made.
R. *v.* SUGGETT (1985) 81 Cr.App.R. 243, C.A.

488. Bail—bail pending appeal
The disadvantage of bail pending appeal to the Court of Appeal is that the defendant may not have spent sufficient time in custody before being granted bail to meet the justice of the case, and so has to be returned to custody: R. *v.* NEAL, *The Times*, January 29, 1986, C.A.

489. Bail—failure to surrender—conduct of trial. See SCHIAVO *v.* ANDERTON, § 2069.

490. Bail—failure to surrender—whether reasonable excuse
[Bail Act 1976 (c.63), s.6(1).] Where D failed to surrender to his bail because he mistakenly thought his court appearance was on a later date because of an administrative blunder by his solicitors, there was no reasonable excuse for the failure to surrender because the date should have been known to him in any event, although the circumstances provided mitigation on his behalf: LAIDLAW *v.* ATKINSON, *The Times,* August 2, 1986, D.C.

491. Bail—refusal—remedies
When a defendant is refused bail by justices, he must exhaust the remedies available to him in the Crown Court before applying to the Divisional Court: R. *v.* GUILDHALL JUSTICES, *ex p.* PRUSHINOWSKI, *The Times*, December 14, 1985, D.C.

492. Bail—surety—forfeiture of recognisance
[Magistrates' Courts Act 1980 (c.43), s.120.] H stood surety for a defendant. Subsequently the total amount of sureties required was reduced by the court without notification to H, and the defendant was released. He absconded, and it transpired that H did not have sufficient assets to pay the sum ordered to be forfeited. He had misled the court. He was imprisoned. *Held,* that a period of imprisonment was correct, but in the circumstances the maximum sentence (which had been imposed) was not appropriate, and would be quashed so that H would be released immediately (*i.e.* after about two months) (*R. v. Southampton Justices, ex p. Green* [1975] C.L.Y. 2038 considered): R. *v.* BOW STREET MAGISTRATES' COURT, *ex p.* HALL, *The Times,* October 27, 1986, C.A.

493. Bail—surety—forfeiture of recognisance

In deciding whether to forfeit part or the whole of a surety's recognisance the court should have regard to the conduct of the surety when D absconded, and also to the surety's knowledge or lack thereof as to any relaxation of the conditions of bail which might have been relevant to his willingness to remain a surety (*R.* v. *Southampton Justices, ex p. Green* [1975] C.L.Y. 2038, *R.* v. *Waltham Forest Justices, ex p. Parfrey* [1980] C.L.Y. 436, *R.* v. *Wells Street Magistrates' Court, ex p. Albanese* [1982] C.L.Y. 516 considered): R. *v.* INNER LONDON CROWN COURT, *ex p.* SPRINGALL, *The Times,* December 2, 1986, D.C.

494. Bankruptcy order—whether a nullity

[Powers of Criminal Courts Act 1973 (c.62), s.40.] A judge is not obliged to afford counsel the opportunity to address the judge before making a criminal bankruptcy order but it was desirable as a matter of common courtesy: R. *v.* PREFAS, *The Times,* November 12, 1986, C.A.

495. Binding over—young offender—refusal to be bound over—power of justices. See HOWLEY *v.* OXFORD, § 2072.

496. Breach of statutory duty—contempt of statute—whether offence created

[Broadcasting ACT 1981 (c.68), s.4(3).]

A modern statute is not to be construed as creating an offence unless it expressly or by necessary implication so provides.

A summons was issued against the broadcasting authority by magistrates alleging breach of statutory duty in that they had failed to satisfy themselves that a broadcast did not include "subliminal" messages and images. The authority applied for judicial review on the grounds that a breach of s.4(3) of the 1981 Act was not a crime, and the court had no jurisdiction. *Held,* granting the application, that the doctrine of "contempt of statute" was more readily applicable to ancient than modern statutes, in the absence of the express creation of a criminal offence in the 1981 Act, the proper inference was that Parliament did not intend to create an offence.

R. *v.* HORSEFERRY ROAD JUSTICES *ex p.* INDEPENDENT BROADCASTING AUTHORITY [1986] 3 W.L.R. 132, D.C.

497. Breach of the peace—constable's belief

[Public Order Act 1936 (c.6), s.5.] Whether an officer's belief that a breach of the peace is likely is reasonable or not must take into account the circumstances in which the officer makes a spur of the moment decision: G. *v.* CHIEF SUPERINTENDENT OF POLICE, STROUD, *The Times,* November 29, 1986, D.C.

498. Breach of the peace—homosexual conduct—whether insulting behaviour—defendants unaware of other people being present

[Metropolitan Police Act 1839 (c.47), s.54(13).]

Conduct may be "insulting . . . behaviour" within the meaning of the Metropolitan Police Act 1839, s.54(13), whenever there are persons present who might be insulted by the behaviour, notwithstanding that those committing the offence may not intend such insult, or indeed be aware that there is anyone else present.

Per curiam: overt heterosexual, as well as homosexual, conduct may be insulting behaviour if there is another person, such as a young woman, who feels it objectionable.

D1 and D2, both men, were kissing and cuddling on Oxford Street at about 2 a.m. Two girls walked past, one raising her hand to her mouth and running up to her boyfriend, who was walking ahead. The defendants were convicted of using insulting behaviour whereby a breach of the peace might be committed. *Held,* that the fact that the defendants might not have been aware of anyone else's presence on the street was irrelevant. The conduct was insulting, and might have caused a breach of the peace, and that was sufficient. (*Parkin* v. *Norman* [1982] C.L.Y. 632 considered). MASTERSON *v.* HOLDEN [1986] 1 W.L.R. 1017, D.C.

499. Building regulations—failure to comply with time limits—whether continuing breach. See HERTSMERE BOROUGH COUNCIL *v.* DUNN (ALAN) BUILDING CONTRACTORS, § 199.

500. Burglary—"building"—meaning

[Theft Act 1968 (c.60), s.9.] S and G were convicted of attempted burglary of two articulated lorry trailers being used as temporary storage space during building redevelopment by a supermarket. The trailers had been unhitched and left on their wheels and struts where buildings had been. An electric cable supplied power to each trailer. Steps were made and placed against each trailer. *Held,* allowing appeals against the convictions, that the trailers were not "buildings" within s.9 of the 1968 Act (*B. and S.* v. *Leathley* [1979] C.L.Y. 412 and *Estate Products (Frozen Foods)* v. *Doncaster Borough Council* [1980] C.L.Y. 209 considered): NORFOLK CONSTABULARY v. SEEKINGS AND GOULD [1986] Crim.L.R. 167, Norwich Crown Court.

501. Burglary—entering building as a trespasser with intent to steal—limited authority to enter—authority exceeded—whether trespass
[Aus.] The local equivalent of the Theft Act contained the words "enters . . . as a trespasser." *Held,* that (1) the words should have their ordinary meaning at common law; (2) a person who enters premises for a purpose alien to the terms of a licence given to him to enter them enters as a trespasser (*R.* v. *Pratt* (1855), 119 E.R. 319, *Taylor* v. *Jackson* (1898), 78 L.T. 555, *Harrison* v. *Duke of Rutland* [1893] 1 Q.B. 142 and *R.* v. *Jones and Smith* [1976] C.L.Y. 409 applied): BARKER v. THE QUEEN (1983) 153 C.L.R. 338, High Ct. of Australia.

502. Burglary with intent—no express evidence
[Theft Act 1968 (c.60), s.9(1)(*a*).] D was charged with burglary with intent to cause grievous bodily harm. There was no specific express evidence of such intent, no weapons were carried on entering the premises, and no grievous bodily harm had been caused, although the occupiers had been assaulted. *Held,* that the charge should not have been left to the jury, there being no evidence of intent to harm at the time of entry: R. v. O'NEILL, MCMULLEN AND KELLY, *The Times,* October 17, 1986, C.A.

503. Case stated—recognisance required—applicant's means
[Magistrates' Courts Act 1980 (c.43), s.114; Crown Court Rules 1982 (S.I. 1982 No. 1109), r.26(11).] Justices must have regard to a defendant's means before requiring a recognizance before stating a case: R. v. NEWCASTLE UPON TYNE JUSTICES, *ex p.* SKINNER, *The Times,* October 27, 1986, D.C.

504. Causing grievous bodily harm—intent—direction to jury
The correct direction to the jury in a trial for causing grievous bodily harm is "You must feel sure that the defendant intended to cause serious bodily harm to the victim. You can only decide what his intention was by considering all the relevant circumstances and in particular what he did and what he said about it."
P pleaded guilty to causing grievous bodily harm. He later appealed on the basis that his plea was based on the passage dealing with intent in *Archbold* but that passage had been disapproved of in *R.* v. *Moloney* [1985] C.L.Y. 642. *Held,* that the appeal was misconceived. By pleading guilty P admitted that he intended to harm his victim. The passage in *Archbold,* even before the decision in *Moloney* was only very rarely used in cases other than cases of murder and would not have been used in this case. (*R.* v. *Moloney* [1985] C.L.Y. 642 and *R.* v. *Hancock and Shankland* [1986] C.L.Y. 652 considered).
R. v. PURCELL (1986) 83 Cr.App.R. 45, C.A.

505. Causing nuisance and disturbance—glue-sniffing
[Local Government (Miscellaneous Provisions) Act 1982 (c.30), s.40.] H and M were found in a school playground, after school hours, sniffing glue. Such conduct had previously necessitated clearing up to avoid danger to schoolchildren. *Held,* allowing the prosecutor's appeal, that the justices had erred in deciding that merely inhaling solvents unobserved without others present could not of itself constitute a nuisance and in consequently dismissing a charge of being unlawfully on the premises, causing a nuisance and disturbance to the annoyance of persons who lawfully used the premises, contrary to s.40 of the 1982 Act. Undue interference with the comfortable and convenient use of land, as indicated by the schools' headmistress evidence of annoyance and distress, could be sufficient (*Schwab* v. *Costaki* [1956] 1 All E.R. 652 applied): SYKES v. HOLMES AND MAW [1985] Crim.L.R. 791, D.C.

506. Cheque card fraud—pecuniary advantage—use of card abroad
[Theft Act 1968 (c.60), s.16.] D obtained an overdraft at a London bank by presenting a cheque backed by a cheque card overseas. *Held,* that the matter was triable in England since the pecuniary advantage was obtained in England although the conduct leading to it was committed abroad (*Treacy* v. *D.P.P.* [1971] C.L.Y. 2188, *R.* v. *Baxter* [1972] C.L.Y. 745, *D.P.P.* v. *Stonehouse* [1977] C.L.Y. 1450 considered): R. v. BEVAN, *The Times,* October 24, 1986, C.A.

507. Committal—calling of witnesses

[Magistrates' Courts Rules 1981 (S.I. 1981 No. 552), rr.6(2), 7(10)] A defendant is entitled to call witnesses in his defence at a committal without giving evidence himself: R. *v.* BLYTH VALLEY JUSTICES, *ex p.* FAWCUS, *The Times,* April 30, 1986, D.C.

508. Committal for sentence—social enquiry report—power of magistrates to commit

A magistrates' court is entitled to obtain and consider a social enquiry report before deciding whether to commit an offender to the Crown Court for sentence under the Magistrates Courts Act 1980, s.38.

A defendant pleaded guilty before a magistrates' court to a number of offences of dishonesty against his employer. The court decided to deal with the case summarily but was then told that the defendant wanted 19 other offences to be taken into consideration, and that the total sum involved was over £4,000. The court adjourned the case for a social enquiry report, and then committed the defendant for sentence to the Crown Court. Before the Crown Court it was conceded that the committal was bad and that the magistrates' court had retained jurisdiction by asking for the social enquiry report. The Crown Court declined to sentence the defendant and the prosecutor sought mandamus against it to order it to do so. *Held,* that the order of mandamus should go to the Crown Court. Obtaining a social enquiry report was one means of obtaining information about the character and antecedents of a defendant and a magistrates' court which obtained an order did not thereby prevent itself from committing the case to the Crown Court.

R. *v.* SOUTHWARK CROWN COURT, *ex p.* COMMISSIONER OF POLICE FOR THE METROPOLIS (1984) 6 Cr.App.R.(S.) 304, D.C.

509. Committal for trial—no evidence offered by prosecution—whether discharge proper.

See R. *v.* HORSEFERRY ROAD MAGISTRATES' COURT, *ex p.* O'REGAN, § 2075.

510. Common law conspiracy to defraud—evidence supporting conspiracy to commit specific statutory offences—indictment

[Criminal Law Act 1977 (c.45), s.1(1), Criminal Attempts Act 1981 (c.47), s.5.]

Where an indictment necessarily involves allegations of contraventions of the Theft Act 1968 the indictment should not allege a common law conspiracy to defraud.

G and another operated a scheme to induce people to invest in chalets abroad. The scheme was fraudulent in that people were induced to invest money by inaccurate statements. G was charged with conspiracy to defraud by dishonestly making false or reckless statements, failing to disclose the absence of planning consent, fraudulently obtaining the release of investor's funds. G appealed against conviction. *Held,* that the indictment necessarily involved an allegation of conspiracy to contravene one or more of the provisions of the Theft Act 1968. Where there was conduct, some of which amounted to an offence under s.1(1) of the Criminal Law Act 1977 only a conspiracy contrary to that section could be charged. However, as the judge's summing up had covered the questions of conspiracy, dishonesty, obtaining and deception, in the light of the verdict, the misdescription had not had any effect. Accordingly there had been no miscarriage of justice and the conviction would be upheld (*R.* v. *Ayres* [1984] C.L.Y. 538, *R.* v. *Tonner* [1985] C.L.Y. 671 applied, *R.* v. *Duru and Asghar* [1973] C.L.Y. 581 considered).

R. *v.* GRANT (1986) 82 Cr.App.R. 324, C.A.

511. Compensation order—garnishee proceeding to enforce—effect of pending appeal

[Criminal Appeal Act 1968 (c.19), s.42; Powers of Criminal Courts Act 1973 (c.62), s.36; Magistrates' Courts Act 1980 (c.43), s.87(1)(3); Supreme Court Act 1981 (c.54), s.18(1)(*a*).]

A magistrate does not have power to authorise his clerk to issue garnishee proceedings in respect of a compensation order while the judgment debtor's petition for leave to appeal to the House of Lords is pending.

E was convicted on charges of theft and forgery and ordered to pay compensation of £11,700 and costs of £5,000. On his appeal the Court of Appeal reduced the compensation order but left the costs undisturbed. E petitioned the House of Lords for leave to appeal. Meanwhile a magistrate, while enforcing the compensation and costs orders, conducted an inquiry into E's means during which it emerged that he had a bank account with sufficient funds to pay the orders. The magistrate made an order under s.87(3) of the 1980 Act authorising the clerk of the court, G, to obtain a garnishee order. G obtained an order nisi and served it on the bank which mistakenly paid the money to G before the order absolute was made. E had the order nisi discharged and obtained summary judgment against the bank, which reclaimed and was repaid the money by G. G then obtained a second garnishee order nisi. E applied to discharge it on the ground that G's authority to take garnishee proceedings expired on the discharge of the first order. G appealed against the discharge. E contended that the court did not have jurisdiction to hear the appeal, that G was not authorised to obtain the second order nisi and that the original authorisation was invalid while E was petitioning the House of Lords. *Held,* allowing the appeal in part, that (1) s.18(1)(*a*) of the 1981 Act did not preclude an appeal to the Civil Division of the Court of Appeal in the present circumstances because by s.87(1) of the 1980 Act the convicted person was deemed to be a judgment debtor and the clerk a judgment creditor both having all the usual rights including the right to appeal, and the appeal was not therefore in respect of a "criminal cause or matter"; (2) the clerk was authorised for the purposes of s.87(3) of the 1980 Act to obtain the garnishee order nisi since no restriction was imposed on the magistrates' court on when or how such proceedings could be taken; (3) since by s.87(3) the enforcement procedure could only be used to recover a "sum adjudged to be paid," the magistrate had no power to authorise G to issue garnishee proceedings in respect of the compensation order while E's petition to the House of Lords was pending since s.42 of the 1968 Act had with s.36 of the 1973 Act suspended the operation of that order. But these provisions did not apply to the costs order and G's appeal would be allowed in so far as it related to the costs, and the order limited to the sum of £5,000 would be made absolute.

GOOCH *v.* EWING (ALLIED IRISH BANK, GARNISHEE) [1985] 3 All E.R. 654, C.A.

512. Consecutive sentences—whether appropriate for repeated conspiracies—criminal bankruptcy and fine—whether appropriate in combination fine and imprisonment—whether appropriate together

Ordinarily offences arising from the same incident should not be made the subject of consecutive sentences of imprisonment, but that course may be taken where the circumstances justify it.

The imposition of a fine, with a substantial term of imprisonment in default, and a term of immediate imprisonment is permissible where there are grounds for believing that the defendant has not disclosed all his assets, but provided that the total term of imprisonment would not be excessive if the defendant had to serve the entire combined period.

A criminal bankruptcy order may be made in conjunction with the imposition of a fine, but circumstances justifying such a course would be rare.

M and his co-appellants were convicted on various counts of conspiracy to evade the provisions requiring payment of value added tax on imported gold. Fines, sentences of imprisonment (including consecutive sentences of and approaching the maximum sentence) and criminal bankruptcy orders were imposed. *Held,* that (1) the judge had been entitled to impose consecutive sentences in the circumstances of the case, notwithstanding the ordinary rule that offences arising out of the incident should be dealt with by concurrent sentences. This was a massive fraud; (ii) the imposition of substantial terms of imprisonment in default of the fines being paid was not, however, correct because its effect was to increase substantially the maximum sentence. Such a course was improper even though the maximum sentence was hopelessly inadequate; (iii) a criminal bankruptcy order would not ordinarily be appropriate where fines had been imposed. The appeals would be allowed to the limited extent that all the fines would be quashed.

R. *v.* MICHEL (1984) 6 Cr.App.R.(S.) 379, C.A.

513. Conspiracy—common law and statutory conspiracy—considerations of the court

Where a defendant was charged with a statutory conspiracy to commit a specific offence and with conspiracy to defraud at common law the court must first consider whether the statutory conspiracy was made out and, if it was not, whether the common law conspiracy was made out.

J and A were involved in an enterprise to manufacture devices for reversing electricity meters. They agreed to sell their devices to W who was a middleman rather than an end user. J and A were charged with conspiracy to defraud at common law. At the conclusion of the prosecution case it was accepted that as the law then stood the prosecution was in difficulty. In consequence an alternative count of statutory conspiracy to incite others to dishonestly and without due authority abstract electricity contrary to s.13 of the Theft Act 1968 was added to the indictment. J and A were convicted on the alternative count and a not guilty verdict was returned on the conspiracy to defraud count on the direction of the trial judge. J and A appealed. *Held,* allowing the appeal, that there was no evidence that J and A conspired to incite W to use the devices personally. Similarly it was not shown on the evidence that there was a conspiracy to incite W to incite others to use the devices personally. There was no direction to the jury on what "incite" meant nor on what evidence was available that J and A intended to incite W. The convictions could not be said to be safe nor satisfactory. J and A having been acquitted on the common law conspiracy to defraud count that count could not now be revived. In dealing with cases where both a statutory and a common law conspiracy was alleged the court should first consider whether the statutory conspiracy was made out. If it was proved the common law conspiracy was as a matter of law necessarily excluded. If the court was not satisfied that the statutory conspiracy was proved it should consider whether or not the common law conspiracy was proved. The jury would need a careful direction as to what was required (*R.* v. *Hollinshead* [1985] C.L.Y. 524 considered).

R. *v.* JAMES AND ASHFORD (1986) 82 Cr.App.R. 226, C.A.

514. Conspiracy—knowingly introducing people for procuring cocaine—whether conspiracy to possess cocaine

[Criminal Law Act 1977 (c.45), s.1(1)] G knowingly introduced two people, X and Y, in order that one should procure cocaine. *Held,* dismissing G's appeal against conviction of conspiracy to unlawfully possess cocaine, contrary to s.1 of the 1977 Act, that it was sufficient if X had asked to be introduced to Y so that one of them could obtain cocaine and G knew that such was the purpose of the introduction (*R.* v. *Walker* [1962] C.L.Y. 552 distinguished): R. *v.* EL-GHAZAL [1986] Crim.L.R. 52, C.A.

515. Conspiracy to defraud

The Eighteenth Report of the Criminal Law Revisions Committee on *Conspiracy to Defraud* has been published. The report recommends that the law should be restored to its pre-1977 position. It is hoped that this will be implemented in the forthcoming Criminal Justice Bill. The report is available from H.M.S.O. (Cmnd. 9873) [£3·10.]

516. Conspiracy to defraud—acts with two specific and different objectives

A count of conspiracy is bad where it particularises acts with two specific and different objectives, the one unlawful the other lawful.

The appellants were charged with a number of counts of fraudulent trading. Counts 12 and 13 charged conspiracies, the former statutory, the latter at common law. Both counts contained identical particulars under five heads, relating to two different specific unlawful objects.

The first three particulars related to substantive offences, the latter two did not. the trial judge quashed count 12, but the appellants were convicted on count 13. They appealed on the grounds that the particulars alleged two conspiracies, one involving a substantive offence, the other no offence known to law. *Held,* allowing the appeal, that the count contained an agreement to achieve two distinct purposes, one of which involved an offence against s.15 of the Theft Act, the other acts which involved no offence; the count was bad (dictum in *R.* v. *Ayres* [1984] C.L.Y. 538 applied).

R. *v.* ZEMMEL (1985) 81 Cr.App.R. 279, C.A.

517. Conspiracy to defraud—charge at common law—defence alleging commission of statutory offence—whether conviction to be upheld

[Theft Act 1968 (c.60), ss.15(1), 25(1); Criminal Law Act 1977 (c.45), ss.1(1), 5(1) (as amended by Criminal Attempts Act 1981 (c.47), s.5).]

Common law conspiracy to defraud may properly be charged notwithstanding that the evidence discloses in addition a clear statutory conspiracy to commit a substantive offence.

C was charged with conspiracy to defraud in that as a member of the staff employed on a British Rail Buffet Car he, and others, had brought on to the train their own raw materials, failing to account to BR for the proceeds of the sales they thereby made. One of the grounds of appeal was that the charge amounted to a substantive offence, namely going equipped for cheat. *Held,* allowing an appeal by the Crown, that the conviction was proper because conspiracy to defraud could be charged at common law notwithstanding that the evidence might in addition disclose a substantive offence. (*R.* v. *Ayres* [1984] C.L.Y. 538 and *R.* v. *Tonner* [1985] C.L.Y. 671 considered).

R. *v.* Cooke [1986] 3 W.L.R. 327, H.L.

518. Contempt—Crown Court—abuse of judge

H shouted from the public gallery that a judge was biased and a racist. When she refused to apologise she was detained overnight. On the following day the judge committed her to prison for seven days. *Held,* dismissing her appeal, that where any person disturbs a Crown Court by publicly abusing the judge in a way which cannot be overlooked, it is for the judge to take steps to safeguard the court's authority; including, when appropriate, the offender's immediate arrest and detention, informing the offender distinctly what the contempt is said to have been, giving an opportunity to apologise and of being advised and represented by counsel and making any necessary legal aid order for such purpose, granting any necessary adjournment, entertaining counsel's submissions and then imposing any penalty within the limits fixed by statute which the judge is satisfied is merited: R. *v.* Hill [1986] Crim. L.R. 457, C.A.

519. Contempt—"insulting"—meaning

[Contempt of Court Act 1981 (c.49), s.12(1)(*a*)] P, a witness at a summary trial, after giving evidence threatened to "get" the defendant and his solicitor who were waiting outside court whilst the magistrates considered their decision. *Held,* allowing P's appeal against a finding by the magistrates that he was in contempt and against a fine for such contempt, that a threat was not an "insult" within s.12(1)(*a*) of the Contempt of Court Act 1981. Accordingly, the magistrates had no power to deal with P. *Obiter:* the Crown Court has no jurisdiction to hear an appeal from a finding of contempt (an appeal from the penalty imposed could be heard by the Crown Court): R. *v.* Havant Magistrates' Court and Portsmouth Crown Court, *ex p.* Palmer [1985] Crim.L.R. 658, D.C.

520. Contempt—"legal proceedings held in public"—meaning

[Contempt of Court Act 1981 (c.49), s.4.] H.T.V. Co's camera crew filmed the arrest of S for drug offences. H.T.V. Co. intended to include the film in a programme about drugs trafficking. S pleaded guilty. Justices made an order under s.4(2) of the 1981 Act that publication of the film be postponed. *Held,* quashing the order, that there was no jurisdiction to make the order, since the film was not a report of "legal proceedings held in public," which words meant proceedings in court at a hearing of charge of a person for a criminal offence. If it was thought that a report might prove embarrassing and prejudicial to a trial, the proper remedy was to seek an injunction in the High Court, which would no doubt grant an injunction if there was a danger of the "strict liability rule" being breached: R. *v.* Rhuddlan Justices, *ex p.* H.T.V. [1986] Crim.L.R. 329, D.C.

521. Control of sex establishment—meaning of "significant"—selling or displaying sex articles to a significant degree

[Local Government (Miscellaneous Provisions) Act 1982 (c.30).]

To decide whether a business consists to a significant degree of selling, displaying or demonstrating sex articles the word "significant" implied a higher standard than merely "more than insignificant." A number of factors have to be considered.

G owned a business which included the sale of magazines, newspapers, stationery and confectionery. The shop also displayed a number of magazines which, it was conceded, amounted to sex articles within the terms of the Local Government (Miscellaneous Provisions) Act 1982. The sale of these magazines represented a very small proportion of the shop's total turnover. G's appeal against conviction by the justices for using premises as a sex establishment without a licence was upheld in the Crown Court. On appeal by the local council the question was whether there had been a "significant degree" of selling or displaying of sex articles. *Held,* that the word "significant" has more than one meaning but in this context it means more than just "not insignificant." A higher standard is required. The standard cannot be prescribed. It depends upon a number of factors such as; the nature of the other business, the ratio between the sexual and other aspects, the quantity of sales, the nature of the display and the nature of the articles themselves. There was nothing in the present case to indicate that the Crown Court had not directed itself in a manner consistent with that approach and so the appeal would be dismissed.

LAMBETH LONDON BOROUGH COUNCIL *v.* GREWAL (1986) 82 Cr.App.R. 301, C.A.

522. Copyright infringement—pirate videotapes—possession—whether by way of trade. See REID *v.* KENNET, § 437.

523. Coroners. See CORONERS.

524. Corruption—local councillor—accepting money for past favour
[Public Bodies Corrupt Practices Act 1889 (c.69), s.1(1).]
It is a corrupt practice for a councillor to accept money in return for a past favour.

The appellant was chairman of a district council planning committee. After a building firm was granted planning permission in a proper way, sums of money were given to him by a representative of the building firm. He was charged with corruption contrary to s.1 of the Public Bodies Corrupt Practices Act 1889. He denied the offence stating that he had not been influenced by the money received which was merely reflecting the firm's pleasure at having been granted planning permission. The jury were directed that corruption included the receipt of money for a past favour without any prior agreement, and the offence lay not in showing favour to the application but in accepting a reward for doing so. He was convicted and appealed on the ground that this direction was wrong in law, but it was upheld on appeal (dicta of Lawton L.J. in *R.* v. *Wellburn* [1980] C.L.Y. 447; (1979) 69 Cr.App.R. 254, 264, 265 applied).

R. *v.* PARKER (1985) 82 Cr.App.R. 69, C.A.

525. Costs
COSTS IN CRIMINAL CASES (GENERAL) REGULATIONS 1986 (No. 1335) [£2·40], made under the Prosecution of Offences Act 1985 (c.23), ss.19, 20; operative on October 1, 1986; make provision in relation to the payment of costs in criminal cases.

526. Costs—excessive order
[Costs in Criminal Cases Act 1973 (c.14), s.2(2).] D was fined £400 and ordered to pay £600 in costs. He was unemployed. He was ordered to pay £10 per week. *Held,* that even if he could pay £10 per week, which was doubtful, the order was grossly excessive in that it would take two years for payment to be made. The costs order would be quashed in its entirety: R. *v.* NOTTINGHAM JUSTICES, *ex p.* FOHMANN, *The Times,* October 27, 1986, D.C.

527. Crime prevention
The Home Office has published a booklet describing some of the projects undertaken through the Community Programme initiative. The booklet is entitled; *Crime Prevention The Community Programme: A Practical Guide* and is available from the Home Office Crime Prevention Unit, Queen Anne's Gate, London SW1H 9AT.

The Home Office Crime Prevention Unit has published a paper on prepayment coin meters. *Prepayment Coin Meters: a target for burglary,* by Nigel Hill is available free of charge from the Home Office Crime Prevention Unit, 50 Queen Anne's Gate, London SW1H 9AT. (ISBN 0 86252 245 5).

528. Criminal damage—erasure of computer program—meaning of damage to property
[Criminal Damage Act 1971 (c.48), ss.1(1) and 10(1).]
Erasing a program from a printed circuit card is damage to property.

D deliberately erased the program from a printed circuit card that operated an automatic computerised saw, rendering the saw inoperable. He was convicted of criminal damage. He appealed arguing that the erasure did not amount to damage to property. *Held,* that the property referred to was the printed circuit card. The removal of the program made it necessary for time, labour and money to be expended to replace the program. D did cause damage to the card. The erasure of the program does constitute damage within the meaning of the Criminal Damage Act 1971 (*R.* v. *Henderson & Battley* [1984] Unreported and *R.* v. *Fisher* (1865) L.R. 1 C.C.R. 7 applied).

Cox *v.* RILEY (1986) 83 Cr.App.R. 54, D.C.

529. Criminal damage—intent to endanger life—bullets fired into house—whether causal link

[Criminal Damage Act 1971 (c.48), s.1(2)(*b*).]

S.1(2) of the Criminal Damage Act 1971 is directed to the possible danger to life caused by the damaged property itself, not to the dangers inherent in the method of causing the damage.

The appellant, after an argument with a business partner, went to the partner's house at night and fired bullets from a rifle at the windows and front door. He was charged with causing criminal damage with intent. The judge rejected a submission of no case. *Held*, allowing the appeal, that the section was directed towards the endangering of life caused by the damage itself. Here lives had been endangered by the discharge of bullets, not by the damage to the property.

R. *v.* STEER [1986] 1 W.L.R. 1286, C.A.

530. Criminal damage—meaning of "damage"

[Criminal Damages Act 1971 (c.48), s.1.] The appellants painted silhouettes on a pavement as part of a protest, using soluble paint which would be washed away eventually by rainwater. The local authority washed the markings away with high pressure jets. *Held*, dismissing their appeals against convictions of causing damage to the pavement, that there had been "damage" within the meaning of s.1 of the 1971 Act (*Samuels* v. *Stubbs* 4 S.A.S.R. 200 approved; *A. (A Juvenile)* v. *The Queen* [1978] C.L.Y 447 considered): HARDMAN *v.* THE CHIEF CONSTABLE OF AVON & SOMERSET CONSTABULARY [1986] Crim.L.R. 330, Bristol Crown Court.

531. Criminal damage—right to jury trial—assessing value of damage

[Magistrates' Courts Act 1980 (c.43), s.22(2), (3) and (4).] D and about 30 others drove vehicles into a field, thus ruining a crop valued at £5,800. Being unable to calculate the damage done by each individual the prosecution calculated the damage done in each case by taking the distance between the field boundary and the vehicle's stopping point. On such basis the value involved did not exceed £400 in any individual case. *Held*, refusing applications for certiorari to quash the magistrates' decision that the offences were triable only summarily under s.22(2) of the 1980 Act, that the prosecution were entitled to say that they could and would prove only the minimum damage. Only if there was other material in an individual case giving rise to a real doubt as to the applicability of the calculation would the prosecution's approach be wrong. There was no right to jury trial under s.22(3)(4) of the 1980 Act in this case: R. *v.* SALISBURY MAGISTRATES' COURT *ex p.* MASTIN [1986] Crim.L.R. 545, D.C.

532. Criminal damage—self defence—recklessness

During a dispute between D and X, X fell though a shop window. D claimed that he had acted in reasonable self defence and held on to X when X attacked him and X had then fallen through the window. *Held*, allowing D's appeal, that having acquitted D of assault occasioning X actual bodily harm, they could not properly convict him of criminal damage to the window on the basis of reckless behaviour, since it had not been proved that he had acted other than in reasonable self defence: SEARS *v.* BROOME [1986] Crim.L.R. 461, D.C.

533. Criminal damage—smearing mud on wall

D smeared mud graffiti on a police cell wall. Cleaning the wall cost £7. *Held*, that what constituted criminal damage was a matter of fact and degree for the justices to decide. They had erred, however, in finding that what D had done could not amount, as a matter of law, to criminal damage. The damage need not be permanent to be criminal damage (*Cox* v. *Riley* [1986] C.L.Y. 528 and *R.* v. *Henderson and Battley* (C.A.C.D., November 29, 1984) applied): ROE *v.* KINGERLEE [1986] Crim.L.R. 735, D.C.

534. Criminal injuries compensation

From November 7, 1986 compensation will be payable under the scheme only if the injury is one for which compensation of at least £550 will be awarded. The new limit will apply also to injuries sustained before November 7, 1986 if the application is received after January 6, 1987. There is no longer a separate limit in respect of family violence case.

535. Criminal injuries compensation—crime of violence—meaning—entitlement to compensation

[Criminal Injuries Compensation Scheme (1979 revision), para. 4.)

A crime of violence within the meaning of para. 4 of the Criminal Injuries Compensation Scheme (1979 revision) was a crime of a violent nature not a crime that, in the circumstances of the particular case, had violent consequences.

The four applicants were train drivers. Each had run over and killed a person on a railway line whilst driving a train. In three of the cases a verdict of suicide and in the other a verdict of accidental death had been returned by coroners' courts. The deceased in the suicide cases were guilty of an offence contrary to s.34 of the Offences against the Person Act 1861. In the fourth case the deceased was senile and may have lacked the necessary *mens rea* to be convicted of a similar offence. It was an offence contrary to s.34 of the 1861 Act to endanger or cause to be endangered the safety of any person being conveyed or being in or upon a railway by any unlawful act, wilful omission or neglect. Each of the applicants suffered physical and psychiatric injuries in the incidents. The Criminal Injuries Compensation Board refused to award compensation to the applicants under the Criminal Injuries Compensation Scheme on the ground that their injuries were not directly attributable to a crime of violence. The Divisional Court upheld the Board's decision. *Held,* dismissing the applicants' appeals, that a crime of violence within the meaning of para. 4 of the scheme was a crime of a violent nature not merely a crime that had, in a particular case, violent consequences. It was a matter of fact for the Board to decide in each case whether the crime in question was of a violent nature. In the fourth case had the deceased been found not guilty on account of a lack of *mens rea* due to his mental condition of senility it amounted to an immunity at law within the meaning of para. 4 of the scheme so that for the purposes of the scheme a "crime" would have been committed (*R. v. Criminal Injuries Compensation Board, ex p. Clowes* [1977] C.L.Y. 473 considered).

R. *v.* CRIMINAL INJURIES COMPENSATION BOARD, *ex p.* WARNER [1986] 2 All E.R. 478, C.A.

536. Criminal Injuries Compensation Board

The Criminal Injuries Compensation Board has published its Twenty-Second Report. Copies of the Report are available from H.M.S.O. (CM 42) [£5·00].

537. Criminal justice

The Home Office has published a working paper entitled *Criminal Justice: a working paper* which sets out the Government's five point strategy for combating crime and fear of crime. Copies are available from Room 1001, Home Office, 50 Queen Anne's Gate, London SW1H 9AT.

The Research and Planning Unit has published two papers on modelling the criminal justice system: "Modelling the Criminal Justice System," by Patricia Morgan and "The Criminal Justice System Model: the Flow Model," by Hugh Pullinger. The papers, Nos. 35 and 36 respectively, are available from the Research and Planning Unit, Home Office, 50 Queen Anne's Gate, London SW1H 9AH.

538. Criminal Justice Act 1982—Guernsey

CRIMINAL JUSTICE ACT 1982 (GUERNSEY) ORDER 1986 (No. 1884) [80p], made under the Criminal Justice Act 1982 (c.48), s.81(11); operative on December 1, 1986; extends to Guernsey, with modifications, the provisions of the Criminal Law Act 1977, the Magistrates' Courts Act 1980 and the Criminal Justice Act 1982.

539. Crown court—appeal from Magistrates' Court—amended information—re-hearing

On appeal from a magistrates' court, a Crown Court has no power to amend an information. Thus where a defendant is convicted before justices on an amended information and appeals to the Crown Court, that court is required to re-hear the case on the information in its amended and not in its original form.

F had been charged with failing to conform to the indication of Pelican Crossing Light signals. The prosecutor obtained leave in the magistrates' court to amend the information to failing to comply with automatic traffic signals. The defendant was convicted and appealed to the Crown Court which refused to hear the appeal with the information as laid originally but only as amended. They dismissed the appeal. The Divisional Court *held* that the Crown Court had to deal with the information in its amended form, and dismissed F's appeal (dictum of Lord Goddard C.J. in *Drover v. Rugman* [1951] C.L.Y. 6011 and of Lord Widgery C.J. in *Garfield v. Maddocks*

[1973] C.L.Y. 470 applied. Dictum of Lord Parker C.J. in *Wright* v. *Nicholson* [1970] C.L.Y. 1651 disapproved).

FAIRGRIEVE *v.* NEWMAN (1986) 82 Cr.App.R. 60, D.C.

540. Crown court business—justices' sittings—practice direction

The Lord Chief Justice made a practice direction on July 28, 1986 in the following terms:

With the concurrence of the Lord Chancellor and pursuant to s.75(2) of the Supreme Court Act 1981 I direct that the directions and distribution of Crown Court Business given by the Lord Chief Justice on October 14, 1971 shall be amended by inserting in para. 13 after the words "any other proceedings" the words "apart from cases listed for plea of not guilty." This amendment is to take effect from October 1, 1986.

PRACTICE DIRECTION (CRIME: CROWN COURT BUSINESS) (JUSTICES' SITTINGS IN THE CROWN COURT) July 28, 1986.

541. Crown court—jurisdiction on appeal against conviction—appeal against one of several convictions

[Supreme Court Act 1981 (c.54), s.48.]

Where a defendant appeals to the Crown Court against one of a number of convictions by a magistrates' court, the Crown Court has jurisdiction to consider all the matters that are before the magistrates' court and is not limited to considering solely the conviction appealed against.

D was convicted of a number of road traffic offences by the justices including driving without insurance. The justices disqualified D from driving for that offence. In consequence the justices were unable to order any penalty points to be endorsed on D's driving licence in respect of the other offences. D appealed to the Crown Court against his conviction for driving without insurance. The notice of appeal was limited to that offence. D's appeal was allowed. The Crown Court then proceeded to impose penalty points on D's driving licence in respect of the other offences not included in D's notice of appeal. D appealed by way of case stated. *Held,* dismissing D's appeal, that the Crown Court could only consider imposing penalty points if the "decision which is the subject of the appeal" within the meaning of the Supreme Court Act 1981, s.48 was not limited to the conviction stated in the notice of appeal. The word "decision" in s.48 was used in a wide sense. It was clear from the wording of the section that the Crown Court should have the right to confirm, reverse or vary the whole decision made by the magistrates' court at the time the conviction or sentence expressly appealed against was made. The Crown Court has jurisdiction in respect of all the matters before the magistrates' court and is not constrained to deal solely with the subject matter of the notice of appeal.

DUTTA *v.* WESTCOTT [1986] 3 W.L.R. 746, D.C.

542. Crown court rules

CROWN COURT (AMENDMENT) RULES 1986 (No. 2151 (L.17)) [45p], made under the Supreme Court Act 1981, ss.54(1) and s.6, and the Drug Trafficking Offences Act 1986 (c.32), s.27(6); operative on December 30, 1986; amend S.I. 1982 No. 1109 so as to insert two new rules concerning provisions in the 1986 Act.

543/4. Crown prosecution service

CROWN PROSECUTION SERVICE (WITNESSES' ALLOWANCES) (AMENDMENT) REGULATIONS 1986 (No. 842) [45p], made under the Prosecution of Offences Act 1985 (c.23), s.14(1)(*b*)(2); operative on June 2, 1986; increases the maximum financial loss allowance payable under S.I. 1986 No. 405.

CROWN PROSECUTION SERVICE (WITNESSES' ALLOWANCES) (AMENDMENT No. 3) REGULATIONS 1986 (No. 1818) [45p], made under the Prosecution of Offences Act 1985 (c.23), s.14(1)(*b*)(2); operative on November 17, 1986; increases the maximum overnight subsistence allowance payable to witnesses.

CROWN PROSECUTION SERVICE (WITNESSES' ALLOWANCES) REGULATIONS 1986 (No. 405) [£1·35], made under the Prosecution of Offences Act 1985 (c.23), s.14(1)(*b*)(2); operative on April 1, 1986; provide for the payment of costs and expenses to witnesses who give evidence at the instance of the Crown Prosecution Service.

545. Drug abuse—supply—duress—direction to jury

The direction on duress should be "has the prosecution made you sure that the defendant was not acting under duress in the sense that he did not commit the crime charged because of threats being made, either of death or serious injury to himself or another."

O, a Colombian citizen in London with his family, was approached by C who required a courier for a substantial drugs operation. C threatened D's wife and child. Later a suitcase containing three packets of cocaine arrived at O's flat. The police who had O under observation, arrested him and charged him with supplying and possessing cocaine. The judge directed the jury to ask themselves whether O had acted "solely" as a result of the threats. *Held,* that the direction was correct although the word "solely" was best omitted as it might raise unnecessary complications. The conviction would be upheld.

R. *v.* Ortiz (Fernando) (1986) 83 Cr.App.R. 173, C.A.

546. Drug Trafficking Offences Act 1986 (c.32)
This Act provides for the recovery of the proceeds of drug trafficking. It also prohibits the supply of articles for administering or preparing controlled drugs and increases the number of assistant commissioners of police of the metropolis.

The Act received the Royal Assent on July 8, 1986, and comes into force, with the exception of s.35, on days to be appointed. S.35 came into force on July 8, 1986.

547. Drug Trafficking Offences Act 1986—commencement
Drug Trafficking Offences Act 1986 (Commencement No. 1) Order 1986 (No. 1488 (C.53)) [45p], made under the Drug Trafficking Offences Act 1986 (c.32), s.40(2); brings into force on September 30, 1986 sections 1(3), 2(1), 24, 34, 38 and 40 of the 1986 Act.

Drug Trafficking Offences Act 1986 (Commencement No. 3) Order 1986 (No. 2145 (C.85)) [45p], made under the Drug Trafficking Offences Act 1986 (c.48), s.40(2); brings into force on December 30, 1986 sections 27–29, 31 and 33, and brings into force on January 12, 1987 all remaining provisions of the said Act not yet in force.

548. Duplicity—unlicensed tree felling
[Forestry Act 1967 (c.10), (as amended), s.17(1)] D appealed against conviction of felling trees without a licence, contrary to s.17(1) of the 1967 Act, as amended. The charge concerned 90 trees worth £1,330. *Held,* dismissing the appeal, that, although D's actions had spanned three days, it was quite possible for magistrates to decide which of the trees had been felled illegally and to impose penalties accordingly. That a number of issues may arise in the trial did not convert one activity into two or more. The information was not bad for duplicity. Duplicity is a question of fact and degree (*R.* v. *Bristol Crown Court, ex p. Purnell* (unreported 1985), *R.* v. *Wilson* [1979] C.L.Y. 592 and *Jemmison* v. *Priddle* [1972] C.L.Y. 1599 applied): Cullen *v.* Jardine [1985] Crim.L.R. 668, D.C.

549. Equivocal plea—appeal to Crown Court—evidence of equivocality—position of justices
[Supreme Court Act 1981 (c.54), s.48(2)(*b*).]
Where the Crown Court has inquired into the issue of equivocality of a plea of guilty before justices, and concluded on the evidence that the plea was equivocal, it has power to remit the case to the justices for a re-hearing.

D pleaded guilty to being in charge of a motor vehicle with excess alcohol in his blood. The justices accepted the plea and fined him. A letter from his solicitor, which was before the justices, claimed that he was not in charge because the car had broken down. On appeal the Crown Court decided that the plea must have been equivocal if that letter had indeed been before the justices, and granted D leave to appeal, adjourning the matter for affidavits from the clerk to the justices and the chairman. The clerk took the view that the plea was unequivocal and declined to provide affidavits. The Crown Court heard the matter and decided that the plea was indeed equivocal and remitted the matter to the justices. The clerk refused to arrange a rehearing. The chief constable appealed. *Held,* that the Crown Court had properly conducted an inquiry into the equivocality of the plea and reached a justifiable conclusion on sufficient evidence. In such circumstances the Crown Court had jurisdiction to order the justices to rehear the case (*R.* v. *Rochdale Justices, ex p. Allwork* [1981] C.L.Y. 505 applied; *R.* v. *Plymouth Justices, ex p. Whitton* [1981] C.L.Y. 512 not followed).

R. *v.* Plymouth Justices, *ex p.* Hart [1986] 2 W.L.R. 976, D.C.

550. Escaping from prison—meaning of "prison"—escape from magistrates' court
[Prison Act 1952 (c.52), s.39.]
The offence of aiding a prisoner to escape or to attempt to escape from a prison under s.39 of the Prison Act 1952 is limited to a prisoner in a prison, Borstal, or remand or detention centre, and does not cover other forms of imprisonment or legal custody. Aiding a prisoner to escape from these is a common law offence.

A prisoner was remanded in custody in one of H.M. Prisons. He was taken to a magistrates' court where he was remanded in custody for another week. While there the appellants helped him to escape and were charged under s.39 of the Prison Act 1952. At their trial it was submitted that their conduct did not constitute an offence contrary to s.39 since the prisoner was not in a prison at that time. They were convicted and appealed. *Held,* that s.39 plainly dealt with a prisoner held in a prison or remand or detention centre or Borstal and nothing else. In the present case the offence was not made out, since the offence was a common law offence. The court were not entitled to substitute a conviction for that offence and the convictions were quashed (*Nicoll* v. *Catron* [1986] C.L.Y. 615 applied).
R. *v.* Moss; R. *v.* HARTE (1985) 82 Cr.App.R. 116, C.A.

551. Evidence—admissibility—confession of paranoid schizophrenic—whether discretion to admit
The judge has discretion to admit a confession provided he is satisfied that it is voluntary, and he may exercise that discretion notwithstanding that the accused may have been in an irrational state of mind when he made the confession.

During the course of his being interviewed by a police officer who was aware he was a paranoid schizophrenic M made both an oral and a written confession to killing his girlfriend. Shortly afterwards, in an agitated state, he sought to retract the statements. The trial judge refused to exclude the statements, saying that the jury would be able to separate out the factual material from the delusions from which M was suffering. *Held,* that the discretion was to admit or exclude evidence of a confession depending upon whether the judge was satisfied that it was voluntary, and that discretion existed notwithstanding that the person making the statement might be suffering from delusions. The judge had weighed very carefully the exercise of his discretion, and it could not be said that he had erred in its exercise.
R. *v.* MILLER (A. R.) [1986] 1 W.L.R. 1191, C.A.

552. Evidence—admissibility—letters—hearsay—letters written by defendant's wife
Where incriminating letters had been written by a defendant's wife they should be placed before him in cross-examination and if he says that he was aware of the contents, the incriminating passages can be put to him. They should not be put before the jury earlier.

Customs officers found cannabis concealed in a TV set. The drug was removed and the set delivered to the house where the appellant and his wife lived in a flat. He signed for the set stating that he believed the owner lived in the house and took the set inside. It was found in his living room. There were also two letters written by the appellant's wife and signed in both their names written five days before the delivery and incriminating them in drug trafficking. He was charged with fraudulent evasion of the prohibition on the importation of a controlled drug. He denied this and said that he was unaware of the letters and merely took in the TV to discover to whom it belonged. His wife did not give evidence. The jury were told to disregard the letters unless satisfied that the defendant knew of their contents. He was convicted and appealed on the ground that the letters were hearsay and were an attempt to get round the rule that prevents a wife giving evidence against her husband. *Held,* on appeal, that the proper procedure was for the prosecution to prove the finding of the letters as part of the case to give notice to the defence of the use to which they might be put but not to give any indication of the contents to the jury. If the defendant gave evidence, as the appellant did, they should be placed before him and he should have been asked whether he was aware of their contents. If he said yes the passages relating to the shortage of drugs could be asked about. Nevertheless, as the judge had dealt fairly with the approach of the jury to the letters and diminished the effect of their contents, and the case against him was overwhelming, the proviso to s.2(1) of the Criminal Appeal Act 1968 would be applied (*R.* v. *Gillespie and Simpson* [1967] C.L.Y. 749 applied).
R. *v.* COOPER (1985) 82 Cr.App.R. 74, C.A.

553. Evidence—admissibility—mixed statement to police raising defence—free choice of defendant to give evidence

Where a defendant in the course of an interview with the police raises a defence or makes assertions in his favour they do amount to evidence. Where a judge rules otherwise and so forces a defendant to give evidence himself, the defendant is deprived of his free choice whether or not to give evidence and his conviction is unsafe.

The appellant was involved in an incident with a man who was punched and knocked down. The appellant was seen by the police and in oral and written statements raised the issue of self defence. He was charged with causing grievous bodily harm contrary to s.20 of the Offences against the Person Act 1861. At the close of the prosecution case it was submitted that there was no case to answer since it was for the prosecution to disprove self-defence. The judge overruled that, saying there was no evidence of self-defence at that stage although the appellant's statements were before the jury. He said he would so direct the jury unless it was raised by evidence. The appellant was thus called to give evidence and was convicted. He argued on appeal that he had been compelled to give evidence. *Held,* allowing the appeal, that where a defendant in the course of interview makes an oral or written statement which makes excuses for his conduct or assertions in his favour in a "mixed" statement, *i.e.* partly admissions partly exculpatory statements, these excuses and assertions form part of the evidence in the case, although they might not carry as much weight as the admissions. As a result of the judge's ruling, there had been a breach of the fundamental principle of an English trial in that the appellant had been deprived of a free choice whether to give evidence or not, and the conviction had to be quashed (*R.* v. *Duncan* [1981] C.L.Y. 437 applied).

R. *v.* HAMAND (1985) 82 Cr.App.R. 65, C.A.

554. Evidence—admissibility—prisoner—prison legal aid officer

Whilst they should normally remain confidential, conversations between prisoners and legal aid officers are not covered by privilege: R. *v.* UMOH, *The Times,* November 29, 1986, C.A.

555. Evidence—aiding and abetting attempted rape—corroboration

Where there is corroborative evidence to support evidence against the principal offender it would be absurd to re-apply the corroboration rule to the same evidence affecting the aider and abettor.

O was charged with aiding and abetting P who was charged with attempted rape. The judge directed the jury that the complainant's evidence against the principal offender had to be corroborated but did not give the jury the same direction in relation to the complainant's evidence against O. He appealed against conviction. *Held,* that the essence of corroboration is to confirm in the minds of the jury the creditworthiness of the witness whose evidence has been corroborated. If the jury do not accept the complainant's evidence, corroboration is valueless. In the present case, where the evidence against the principal offender was corroborated, the jury must have accepted the complainant's evidence when convicting the principal offender. In those circumstances it would be absurd to re-apply the corroboration rule in regard to an aider and abettor. To do so would be to re-establish what was already known—that she was a reliable witness (*D.P.P.* v. *Hester* [1972] C.L.Y. 631 applied).

R. *v.* OLALEYE (1986) 82 Cr.App.R. 337, C.A.

556. Evidence—alibi—whether warning necessary

There is no rule which requires that a judge should warn a jury that the mere fact that a defendant has told lies in support of an alibi does not prove his guilt.

The appellant was charged with burglary. The principal evidence was scientific which was not challenged and could not sensibly have been challenged. The defence was an alibi. The judge in summing up did not suggest that the jury should, if they concluded that the alibi was untrue, regard that as supporting or corroborating the forensic evidence, and he dealt in the most neutral terms with the discrepancies between what the appellant said to the police and his evidence. He was convicted and appealed on the ground that the judge had failed to direct the jury that, even if they found that the alibi was untrue, that did not necessarily mean that the appellant had committed the offence. *Held,* on appeal, that there was no rule requiring the judge to do so. No warning need be given whenever the veracity of the defendant or the truth of an alibi defence was challenged (*R.* v. *Turnbull* [1976] C.L.Y. 451 considered and distinguished).

R. *v.* Penman (1985) 82 Cr.App.R. 44, C.A.

557. Evidence—character—cross-examination of defendant on previous convictions—exercise of judge's discretion

Where D's defence to a charge of possessing cannabis with intent to supply was, in effect, that four police officers conspired to concoct a case against him, that evidence was planted in his house and that two officers made up contemporaneous notes of an interview the trial judge correctly exercised his discretion in allowing D to be cross-examined about previous convictions for possessing cannabis, and a large amount of cash found in D's house on an earlier occasion.

In November 1983 the police raided D's house. They found 60 small plastic bags, a pair of scales the pan of which had traces of cannabis on it, £1,300 in cash, a large bag of herbal mixture to make cannabis go further, and various quantities of cannabis totalling 47·45 grammes. D was interviewed when contemporaneous notes were made which D refused to sign. During the interview D made substantial admissions to substantial parts of the case. On a prior raid on D's house in March 1983 4·35 grammes of cannabis were found and £1,900 in cash. D was charged with possessing 4·35 grammes of cannabis (count 1), supplying cannabis to another (count 2) and possession of cannabis with intent to supply (count 4). D pleaded guilty to count 1 but denied the other counts. He stated that the police had concocted the evidence of cannabis at his house, that they deliberately contaminated the pan of his scales with cannabis, that he had not been asked the questions nor given the answers recorded in the contemporaneous notes of interview, that the herbal material was plant food and that the money represented £800 belonging to a friend, £200 being a win on the horses and the remainder savings from a job that finished 10 months beforehand. Upon the application of the prosecution the trial judge gave leave for D to be cross-examined about his guilty plea to count 1, a previous conviction for possessing cannabis and the £1,900 discovered in March 1983. D was convicted on counts 2 and 4 and appealed. *Held,* dismissing the appeal, that the imputations made against the prosecution witness were such that the trial judge had jurisdiction to permit D to be cross-examined about his previous convictions. The trial judge should exercise his discretion in accordance with the following guidelines. (1) The prejudicial effect of the questions must be weighed against the damage caused by the attack on the prosecution witnesses so as to ensure a fair trial for both sides; (2) evidence of character would not be admitted where it was unjust and gravely prejudicial to D; (3) in the ordinary and normal case the trial judge may feel it appropriate for the jury to have the necessary material to judge whether D can be believed in his attack on the prosecution witnesses; (4) the Court of Appeal will only interfere where the trial judge has erred in principle or there is no material upon which the trial judge's decision can properly be supported. In the present case there was an abundance of material to support the conclusion that it was fair to permit D to be cross-examined as to his previous convictions. D could be cross-examined about the £1,900 as it was relevant to establishing the truth of D's explanation about the sum of £1,300 found in his possession (*Selvey* v. *D.P.P.* [1968] C.L.Y. 687 applied, *R.* v. *Watts* [1983] C.L.Y. 661, *R.* v. *John and Braithwaite* (unreported), 24 November 1983 considered).

R. *v.* Burke (1986) 82 Cr.App.R. 156, C.A.

558. Evidence—character—cross-examination on previous convictions

[Criminal Evidence Act 1898 (c.36), s.1(*f*)(ii).]

Where a defendant makes a deliberate attack on the conduct of a prosecution witness calculated to discredit him wholly, thus raising a real issue for the jury to try, the judge is entitled to allow the jury to know of the previous convictions of the defendant even where they closely resembled the offences charged.

The appellant was tried on a count of knowingly living wholly or in part on the earnings of prostitution contrary to s.30 of the Sexual Offences Act 1956. The police evidence was that he was habitually in the company of prostitutes, exercised control over them, and took money from them. His defence was that the police evidence was a total fabrication and his financial position was such that he did not need to take money from prostitutes. The judge exercised his discretion under s.1(*f*)(ii) of the Criminal Evidence Act 1898 to allow cross-examination of the appellant about previous convictions he had for allowing his premises to be used for the purpose of prostitution. He was convicted and appealed. *Held,* dismissing the appeal that where a deliberate attack was made on the conduct of a prosecution witness calculated to discredit him wholly, which the jury had to determine in order to reach a verdict, the judge was entitled to allow a jury to know the previous convictions of the person making the attack. The fact that the convictions were for offences closely resembling the offences charged were matters for the judge to take into consideration when exercising his discretion but did not oblige him to disallow the proposed cross-examination. The trial judge had rightly exercised his discretion in permitting cross-examination not only because of the attack on the police witnesses but also because the appellant had put his own good character in issue. Although these were cumulative grounds, if either had stood alone, the court would not have intervened with the judge's exercise of his discretion (*R.* v. *Selvey* [1968] C.L.Y. 687 applied; *R.* v. *Watts* [1983] C.L.Y. 661 not followed).

R. *v.* POWELL [1985] 1 W.L.R. 1364, C.A.

559. Evidence—confessions—admissibility—similar acquittals

Where the main evidence against a defendant were his alleged admissions which he was challenging, it was proper to tell the jury that other defendants had been acquitted where similarly the main evidence against them had been confessions recorded by the same officer arising out of his investigation of the same group of offences: R. *v.* COOKE, *The Times,* November 11, 1986, C.A.

560. Evidence—conflicting identification evidence—corroboration—documents made by another—whether admissible against defendant

On a charge of conspiracy, documents made by one defendant were admissible in evidence against a co-defendant provided the document was prepared in furtherance of a purpose common to both defendants and there was some other evidence of the existence of that common purpose.

A direction to a jury that the corroborative evidence they must look for was evidence that tended to show the witness to be a witness of truth was not defective where the trial judge elaborated on the direction by putting forward a number of pieces of undoubtedly potentially corroborative evidence for the jury's consideration.

D and S were convicted of conspiracy to evade the prohibition on the importation of controlled drugs. The case for the prosecution was that D, S and another arranged for W to smuggle suitcases of cannabis into Britain from France via the port of Poole. W met D and the others in Cherbourg where he was given the suitcase in question and again in Poole where it was returned. W was caught and gave evidence for the prosecution. In chief he identified D having picked him out at an identity parade. In cross-examination W changed his evidence and stated D was not the person he had met in Cherbourg and Poole previously. The documentary evidence relied upon by the prosecution included a document from a Bureau de Change in Cherbourg with W's telephone number and some expenses relating to the enterprise written on the back and two documents containing profit and loss calculations for the enterprise for the three people involved. The documents were found in S's possession. In directing the jury the trial judge stated it would be very dangerous to act on the evidence of W alone without corroboration, that any corroborative evidence must come from a source independent of W and that the evidence for which they should look was evidence which tended to show W was a witness of truth. D appealed contending that the direction was inadequate and that the judge was wrong to allow the jury to consider the documents as evidence against anyone other than S. *Held,* dismissing the appeal, that the direction given to the jury was, taken alone, inadequate in that the jury were not directed to look for evidence that also tended to implicate D. However the trial judge went on to put forward for the jury's consideration a number of pieces of potentially corroborative evidence that did implicate D. In the circumstances the inadequacy of the direction was corrected by the nature of the evidence drawn to the jury's attention. The documentary evidence was admissible against D if it disclosed some common purpose upon which S and D were engaged and where there was other evidence of the existence of that common purpose. The jury were properly directed in their consideration of the first limb of the test and there was ample evidence to link D with the documents given that S stated in evidence that D was one of the people referred to in the profit and loss calculations (*R.* v. *Baskerville* [1916] 2 K.B. 658, *R.* v. *Walters* [1979] C.L.Y. 492 considered).

R. *v.* DONAT (1986) 82 Cr.App.R. 173, C.A.

561. Evidence—corroboration—criminal and mentally ill witness—duty of judge

When the prosecution evidence consists solely of the testimony of witnesses who are not within the accepted classes of suspect witnesses, but are nevertheless suspect because of their mental condition and criminality, the judge must warn the jury of the danger of acting on their uncorroborated evidence.

The appellants, nurses at Rampton secure hospital, were accused in two separate trials of ill-treating their patients. In both cases the evidence consisted wholly of witnesses who had serious criminal convictions and/or were mentally ill. In both cases the judge directed the jury to approach the evidence with great caution, but he gave no specific direction as to the danger of convicting without corroboration. The appellants were convicted, and the convictions were upheld by the Court of Appeal. *Held,* by the House of Lords allowing certain appeals on other grounds, that in such circumstances the judge was required to warn the jury that it would be dangerous to convict without corroboration; however, the judge's direction had been adequate and fair, and the appeal based on those grounds would be dismissed. (*R.* v. *Beck* [1982] C.L.Y. 563 approved; *D.P.P.* v. *Kilbourne* [1973] C.L.Y. 524 considered; *R.* v. *Bagshaw* [1984] C.L.Y. 594 overruled; *R.* v. *Sawyer* [1981] C.L.Y. 1482 applied).

R. *v.* Spencer; R. *v.* Smails [1986] 2 All E.R. 928, H.L.

562. Evidence—corroboration—rape—use and effect of corroborating evidence—lies and admissions by defendant

It was wrong to direct a jury that they could convict a defendant of rape on the basis of corroborating evidence where they considered the evidence of the complainant could not be relied upon.

D was convicted of rape. The complainant was his sister-in-law who said D had threatened her with a knife after grabbing her by the throat and thereafter committed a number of acts of rape and buggery on her. The next day she went to her sister's house in a state of great distress and related what had happened. D was arrested. Among the statements he made to the police was an admission that much against his will sexual intercourse took place with the complainant. At the trial D said he found the complainant with another man, that she tried to seduce him so that he would not tell his brother about the other man, that sexual intercourse did not take place and that the complainant's injuries were caused when he pushed her away from him. There were striking inconsistencies in the complainant's evidence. The trial judge directed the jury on the danger of convicting D unless the jury found independent evidence from a source other than the complainant that tended to show D was guilty. The judge went on to emphasise the unreliable nature of the complainant's evidence and stated "If you think looking at the whole matter that she really cannot be relied upon at all and that the other matters do not carry the case on their own, well no doubt you would acquit". The judge also directed the jury that D's interview with the police was an area where corroboration might be found but should be treated with caution without explaining why. D appealed. *Held,* allowing the appeal, that the judge ought to have expanded on his direction regarding the requirement for corroboration evidence by setting out the issues that required corroborative evidence for their resolution. The failure to do so did not mean the verdict was unsafe or unsatisfactory. The judge's direction on the reliability of the complainant's evidence left open to the jury the possibility of discarding the complainant's evidence, and convicting on the corroborating evidence alone. The jury should have been directed that if they chose to discard the complainant's evidence there was no evidence that required corroboration. So far as the police interviews were concerned, the judge should have directed the jury that if D's admission was true it was capable of corroborating the complainant's allegation that sexual intercourse took place. If D lied to the police the lies were capable of corroborating the complainant's evidence provided the jury were satisfied that (1) the statement was a lie, (2) the lie was deliberate, (3) the lie related to a material issue and (4) the motive for the lie was the realisation of guilt and fear of the truth on the part of D (*D.P.P.* v. *Kilbourne* [1973] C.L.Y. 524, *R.* v. *Lucas* [1981] C.L.Y. 400 applied, *James* v. *R.* [1971] C.L.Y. 2290 considered).

R. *v.* Rahmoun (1986) 82 Cr.App.R. 217, C.A.

563. Evidence—corroboration—refusal of defendant to give comparative samples—accomplice evidence

Refusal to provide comparative body samples can in some circumstances amount to corroboration of an accomplice's evidence.

S was charged with robbery. He did not give evidence, and the prosecution relied on the evidence of an accomplice together with the fact that S refused to give hair samples to compare with hairs found at the scene of the crime. The jury were directed that the refusal was capable of corroborating the accomplice's evidence. *Held*, dismissing the appeal, that the refusal to give comparative samples, could, and in this case did, provide corroborative evidence; each case depended on its facts (*R. v. Gilbert* [1977] C.L.Y. 559, dictum in *R. v. Chandler* [1976] C.L.Y. 459 considered). R. *v.* SMITH (R. W.) (1985) 81 Cr.App.R. 286, C.A.

564. Evidence—cross-examination—caution

A defendant may not be cross-examined on his reasons for refusing to be interviewed by police after being cautioned: W. *v.* BOOTHBY, *The Times*, July 4, 1986, D.C.

565. Evidence—cross-examination—reference to another's plea of guilty

S denied robbery and the police evidence. He claimed in cross-examination that C, to whom S had admitted selling a Barclaycard stolen in the robbery, had planted the Barclaycard on S. S was cross-examined about C's plea of guilty, in separate proceedings, to handling the card. *Held*, dismissing C's appeal against conviction, that (1) C's plea was irrelevant and there was no evidence of it; (2) provided that it is made clear that pleas or statements of co-defendants are not to be regarded as evidence against the defendant being tried, there is nothing wrong in juries learning of such pleas or statements; (3) no objection had been taken to the questioning at the time. It would not have been wrong to refuse an application for a new trial, had one been made. Counsel had made a tactical decision not to seek a re-trial. The irregularity was not material: R. *v.* SUTTON [1986] Crim.L.R. 241, C.A.

566. Evidence—destruction of evidence before trial—whether possible to commit

[Customs and Excise Management Act 1979 (c.2), s.68(2).] Where secondary evidence exists of the goods that have been destroyed justices may commit D for trial notwithstanding that there is no primary evidence of the goods in question (*R. v. Lushington, ex p. Otto* [1894] 1 Q.B. 430 considered): R. *v.* UXBRIDGE JUSTICES, *ex p.* SOFAER, *The Times*, December 4, 1986, D.C.

567. Evidence—diminished responsibility—burden of proof

[Homicide Act 1957 (c.11), s.2(2).] It was for the defence to raise the question of diminished responsibility as a defence (*R. v. Kooken* [1982] C.L.Y. 649 considered): R. *v.* CAMPBELL, *The Times*, November 4, 1986, C.A.

568. Evidence—diminished responsibility—medical opinions based on hearsay

It was for the defendant himself with the advice of counsel to decide whether or not to give evidence in the light of any guidance he himself requested from the trial judge in relation to establishing a defence of diminished responsibility to murder.

The defendant was charged with murder, and raised the issue of diminished responsibility. His counsel asked the judge for guidance as to how far the medical witnesses could be allowed to give evidence as to what he had told them and to give opinions based thereon, and whether the judge would comment adversely in the event of his not giving evidence. The judge said it was for counsel to decide how to present his case but ruled that if the truth of what he said to the doctors was in question the only course was for the defendant to give evidence, or for other evidence to be called, to prove those facts. He had completely recovered from any abnormality of mind but gave evidence that he was suffering from delusions at the time of the killing. He appealed against conviction. *Held*, dismissing the appeal, that it was for counsel to decide how to conduct the defence and to accept or reject the guidance he had sought from the judge. The defendant had to decide in the end. A doctor could not state what a patient had told him about past symptoms to prove the truth of what the patient said but could do so to explain the grounds upon which he had reached a conclusion as to the patient's condition. Thus if the doctor's evidence was not supported by evidence from the defence the judge was justified in telling the jury that his case was flimsy or non-existent. Even if the judge's guidance had been wrong, the defendant had made no more admissions in evidence than he had already made to the police and formally for the trial and there was no miscarriage of justice (*R.* v. *Bathurst* [1968] C.L.Y. 909 applied).

    R. *v.* BRADSHAW (1985) 82 Cr.App.R. 79, C.A.

569. Evidence—ex-wife a witness where ex-husband a defendant—competence and compellability

    In proceedings in which her ex-husband is a defendant an ex-wife is competent with regard to matters pre-dating the marriage, and can be cross-examined as to credit about matters occurring during it.

    The defendant A was charged with others with conspiring to pervert the course of justice. The Crown called his former wife to give evidence of matters after the divorce. She said she did not want to answer questions concerning events during her marriage. The judge was asked to rule as to the proper scope of cross-examination. *Held,* that a wife was only incompetent as to matters arising during the marriage but could give evidence of matters pre-dating it, and could be cross-examined as to credit by reference to matters which arose during the marriage (*R.* v. *Algar* [1953] C.L.Y. 771, *R.* v. *Deacon* [1973] C.L.Y. 598 applied; *Shenton* v. *Tyler* [1939] Ch. 620 distinguished).

    R. *v.* ASH (LEONARD) (1985) 81 Cr.App.R. 294, Hobhouse J.

570. Evidence—finger-prints and palm-prints of juvenile—meaning of "palm-print"

    [Magistrates' Courts Act 1980 (c.43), s.49(1).]

    M.L. aged 14 was charged with burglary and taken into custody where he gave his finger prints and palm prints by consent. Three days later he was charged with the murder of a police officer. An application was made by a chief inspector for an order under s.49 of the Magistrates' Courts Act 1980 that the finger prints and palm prints of M.L. be taken. The chief inspector was interested in the prints of the "leading edge" of the hand. The order was granted. M.L. sought an order of certiorari on the basis that the application was not for a "finger-print" or "palm-print" within s.49. *Held,* that Parliament had left it to the good sense of the justices to decide whether, in the particular circumstances of the case, what was sought was a "palm-print." There was no reason why that part of the hand from which prints were sought should not be described as the palm. The application would therefore be refused.

    R. *v.* TOTTENHAM JUSTICES, *ex p.* M.L. (1986) 82 Cr.App.R. 277, C.A.

571. Evidence—hostile witness—cross-examination on previous inconsistent statement—where witness denies making statement

    Under cross-examination as a hostile witness X, in the absence of the jury, denied making a written statement implicating B in an assault on X. He admitted making parts of the statement and that the signatures on it were his. *Held,* dismissing B's appeal against conviction of assaulting X occasioning actual bodily harm, that the judge had not erred in allowing X to be cross-examined on the statement before the jury: R. *v.* BALDWIN [1986] Crim.L.R. 681, C.A.

572. Evidence—hostile witness—re-examination

    The prosecution were allowed to treat a witness as hostile and to examine him on previous inconsistent statements. *Held,* that the prosecution, following cross-examination by the defence, should be allowed to re-examine the witness but only upon completely and genuinely new matters which had arisen from defence cross-examination and that such matters should be defined before re-examination: R. *v.* WONG [1986] Crim.L.R. 683, Southwark Crown Court.

573/4. Evidence—identification

    X, aged 13, was raped. She described the rapist, his clothing and his bicycle to police and identified C at an identification parade. In evidence her description varied somewhat from that which she had given the police. A bicycle owner at about the time of the rape had identified C as someone he suspected of the theft but could not be positive in giving evidence as to identification. *Held,* dismissing C's appeal against conviction by applying the proviso, that although the judge had erred in failing to warn the jury of the special need for caution before convicting in reliance on the identification, and the importance of such a direction should be emphasised, the prosecution case was exceptionally strong (*R.* v. *Turnbull* [1976] C.L.Y. 451 approved): R. *v.* CLIFTON [1986] Crim.L.R. 399, C.A.

575. Evidence—imputations against prosecution witnesses—cross examination of defendant on previous convictions

[Criminal Evidence Act 1898 (c.36), s.1.]

Where prosecution witnesses are cross examined in such a way as gives rise to a necessary implication that they had fabricated their evidence, then cross examination of the defendant on his previous convictions was rightly allowed.

O was charged with theft of a purse. Police officers had seen him drop the purse from inside his jacket. In interview O said that the police were lying. The officers were cross examined on the basis that they were mistaken. The prosecution applied successfully for leave to cross examine the defendant on his previous convictions. *Held,* dismissing O's appeal against conviction, that the effect and purport of the cross examination had to be judged objectively. The necessary implication in the questions was that the officers had made up their evidence. Thus there was no basis for interfering with the exercise of the judge's discretion. (*R.* v. *Britzmann* [1983] C.L.Y. 631; *R.* v. *Cook* [1959] C.L.Y. 674, *R.* v. *Powell* [1985] C.L.Y. 590 considered.)

R. v. Owen (A.C.) (1986) 83 Cr.App.R. 100, C.A.

576. Evidence—indecent assault—secret motive

[Sexual Offences Act 1956 (c.69), s.14(1).] D spanked a schoolgirl, admitting that he had a buttock fetish. He was charged with indecent assault under s.14(1) of the Sexual Offences Act 1956. *Held,* that it was open to the prosecution to call evidence of an admitted secret motive which actuated the accused to commit the offence charged, although the existence of a secret sexual motive is not necessarily always admissible as a makeweight on the issue of objective indecency. A jury should be directed that a secret motive cannot turn circumstances into indecency if they would not regard them as indecent without it: R. v. Court, *The Times,* October 20, 1986, C.A.

577. Evidence—intent to kill—record

[Offences Against the Person Act 1861 (c.100), s.16.] On a charge of making a threat to kill, evidence is admissible, at the discretion of the judge of a defendant's previous conduct as tending to show whether he intended his words to be taken seriously or not: R. v. Williams (Clarence Ivor), *The Times,* Octover 28, 1986, C.A.

578. Evidence—knowledge of child—child below 14

Before a conviction can properly ensue there must be material before the justices to rebut the presumption that a child over 10 but below 14 does not know or appreciate the difference between right and wrong. The material must go further than an appreciation of childish mischief: H. (A Minor) v. Chief Constable of South Wales, *The Times,* July 5, 1986, D.C.

579. Evidence—mental capacity of defendant—expert

M and two others were charged with rape. M may have been persuaded to act as he did by the other accused in order to silence him as a witness. M was neither insane nor psychiatrically ill. The judge refused to admit expert evidence that M had an intelligence quotient placing him on the boundaries of dull-normal and sub-normal intelligence, was extremely immature, limited in his understanding of people, likely to judge events at face value and be confused as to willingness or unwillingness and had a strong desire to please and conform to expectations of others. *Held,* dismissing M's appeal against conviction, that (1) M's capacity to understand was a relevant issue; (2) generally, evidence that a defendant had an I.Q. of 69 or less should be admitted on such an issue but where he was within (though at the lower end) of the scale of normality, expert evidence should not generally be admitted (*R.* v. *Turner* [1975] C.L.Y. 562, *D.P.P.* v. *Jordan* [1977] C.L.Y. 615 and *R.* v. *Chard* [1972] C.L.Y. 638 considered; *Kavery* v. *D.P.P.* [1974] A.C. 85 distinguished): R. v. Masih [1986] Crim.L.R. 395, C.A.

580. Evidence—murder—use of past events to establish state of mind

Evidence of the history of the relationship between the murderer and victim should not generally be admitted to prove the killer's state of mind at the time of the killing.

B was charged with the murder of his former mistress. The prosecution were allowed to call evidence of past incidents and of the relationship between the two. B was convicted and appealed. *Held,* that this was a motiveless crime. To use the evidence of past events as evidence of motive which went to intent was a fallacious approach. The evidence was remote from the act and its only effect could be to prejudice the jury. It should not have been admitted. However, as this was as clear a case of murder as there could be, the proviso of s.2(1) of the Criminal Appeal Act 1968 would be applied. (*R.* v. *Ball* (1911) 6 Cr.App.R. 31 considered.)

R. *v.* BERRY (D.R.) (1986) 83 Cr.App.R. 7, C.A.

581. Evidence—notes of deceased—scientific officer's notes on possible arson—whether admissible

The notes of a deceased scientific officer on a possible arson are admissible but not his opinions.

M was charged with arson at an hotel owned by his wife. The prosecution sought to put in evidence a report of a scientific officer, who had made working notes and given an opinion, in its entirety, although the officer had died before the trial. The judge ruled that the part of the report dealing with the facts was admissible. *Held,* dismissing the application, that the judge was right to admit the notes as evidence, but that did not apply to the officer's opinion (dictum in *Djambi (Sumatra) Rubber Estates, Re* (1913) 107 L.T. 631 applied; dicta in *Myers* v. *D.P.P.* [1964] C.L.Y. 1641 considered).

R. *v.* McGUIRE (1985) 81 Cr.App.R. 323, C.A.

582. Evidence—oath—affirmation—whether irregularity

Where a witness was improperly required by a judge to give evidence on affirmation because the witness neither understood nor believed in the divine sanction attaching to an oath, the irregularity could not be described as material.

D was convicted of rape. The complainant was a single woman aged 33 and of low mental ability; her mental age was said to be about 10 years. Before evidence was given the trial judge enquired of the complainant about the extent of her knowledge and belief in God and the extent of her understanding generally concerning telling the truth. The judge formed the view that she did not have sufficient belief in the existence of God to be competent to take a binding oath but that she sufficiently understood the requirement and necessity of telling the truth. The judge ordered that her evidence should be given on affirmation rather than oath. *Held,* dismissing D's appeal, that whilst the judge was right to enquire into the complainant's competence as a witness, he ought not to have embarked on a detailed examination of her theological awareness. Having come to the conclusion that she was a competent witness the judge ought to have allowed her to give her evidence on oath if she did not object to being sworn. The judge's enquiry ought properly to be directed to ascertaining whether the witness had a sufficient understanding of the solemnity of the occasion and the responsibility to tell the truth. It was impossible to conclude that the irregularity was a material irregularity (*R.* v. *Hayes* [1977] C.L.Y. 673, *R.* v. *Campbell* [1983] C.L.Y. 633 applied).

R. *v.* BELLAMY (1986) 82 Cr.App.R. 222, C.A.

583. Evidence—photofit picture—admissibility

Neither the hearsay rule nor the rule against the admission of previous consistent statements prevents the production of a photofit picture by a prosecution witness during examination in chief. A sketch similarly made, or a photograph of the defendant in the course of committing the offence, are also admissible (*R.* v. *Smith (Percy)* [1976] C.L.Y. 449 approved): R. *v.* COOK, *The Times,* December 10, 1986, C.A.

584. Evidence—police informant—identity—rule of exclusion

At the defendant's trial on charges of drugs offences the judge refused an application that identities of persons who had given information to the police leading to the defendant's apprehension should be disclosed to the defence. *Held,* dismissing the appeals, that evidence as to informants' identities should be excluded unless the judge decides that it is necessary to admit the evidence in order to prevent a miscarriage of justice and in order to prevent the possibility that exclusion of the evidence may deprive a defendant of the opportunity to cast doubt on the case against him; R. *v.* HALLETT [1986] Crim.L.R. 463, C.A.

585. Evidence—pre-trial review—admissions made—use in evidence at trial—the ex improviso principle

Although a pre-trial review does not have the force of law, it is undesirable and wrong that anything said or done in the course of it should be used for evidential purposes at the subsequent trial unless the party affected by it consents.

The *ex improviso* principle does not require that the prosecution take note of fanciful or unreal statements, no matter from what source they emanate, as possible warnings of evidence likely to be given at the trial.

The appellant was charged with murder, rape and aggravated burglary. It was said at a pre-trial review that identity would be in issue. Later his solicitor wrote to the D.P.P. denying the murders but admitting his client was in the house at the time. The appellant wrote a letter, passed on to the D.P.P. containing allegations against a journalist B. At the trial the appellant gave evidence that the girl in the house had consented to sexual intercourse, had told him that B was the murderer, and pointed to B who was present in court. He was convicted and appealed on the grounds (1) that the judge should not have allowed a transcript of the pre-trial review to be shown to the jury and (2) should not have allowed B to be called in rebuttal. *Held,* on (1), that it was wrong to allow the pre-trial review to be used in evidence at the trial unless the party affected consented. The action in this case allowing the pre-trial review to be used was an irregularity. However, in the light of the solicitor's letter which qualified or destroyed the appellant's alibi, it did not damage the appellant's defence and so the irregularity was not a material one. On (2) the appellant contended that his allegations against B were not made *ex improviso* since the contents of the letter to the D.P.P. were sufficient to have alerted the prosecution to the possibility that he would say in evidence that B was the murderer. This contention was without substance since the contents were such that it was unreasonable to say that the prosecution should have anticipated that anything said in it would be repeated and therefore call for an answer in anticipation as part of the prosecution case. The judge could not be faulted for disregarding as mere hearsay what the appellant said and did on that occasion, and it was right and proper to allow B to be called to give evidence in rebuttal of his case (dictum of Tindal C.J. in *R.* v. *Frost* (1839) 9 C. & P. 129, 195 applied).

R. *v.* Hutchinson (1986) 82 Cr.App.R. 51, C.A.

586. Evidence—press photographs—order to produce

[Police and Criminal Evidence Act 1984 (c.60), s.9, Sched. 1, para. 2.] A judge was entitled to conclude that press photographs of riots would contain newsworthy material of benefit to a criminal investigation that he was therefore entitled to order their production: *Ex p.* Bristol Press & Picture Agency, *The Times,* November 11, 1986, D.C.

587. Evidence—previous acquittal on similar charge based on evidence of same police officer—whether admissible evidence at later trial

Where the prosecution put D's previous convictions in evidence at a trial D was entitled to put in evidence a previous acquittal on a similar charge to that for which he was being tried where the same police officer was the principal witness for the prosecution at both trials.

D was convicted of conspiracy to supply heroin. Some six months previously D had been tried on a similar charge and acquitted. The main witness for the prosecution at both trials was the same police officer. At the second trial D's counsel sought to cross-examine the officer about the earlier acquittal with a view to showing that the officer's evidence had proved unacceptable to the jury at the earlier trial and thereby cast doubt on the reliability of the officer's evidence. The trial judge prevented D's counsel from so doing and gave leave to the prosecution to put D's previous convictions in evidence upon an unopposed application for leave to do so. After D had been cross-examined about his convictions the trial judge refused to allow D's counsel to re-examine D about the earlier acquittal. D appealed. *Held,* that it did not follow from D's acquittal at the earlier trial that the officer was lying or that his evidence was necessarily unreliable at the later trial. Accordingly the trial judge was right to prevent D's counsel from cross-examining the officer about the earlier acquittal. The trial judge was wrong to prevent D's counsel from re-examining him about the earlier acquittal where one of the previous convictions relied upon by the prosecution arose from the earlier trial. As such there was a material irregularity so that D's appeal should be allowed and the conviction quashed (*R. v. Hay* [1983] C.L.Y. 660 distinguished).

R. *v.* Doosti (1986) 82 Cr.App.R. 181, C.A.

588. Evidence—refreshing memory

It is proper for a prosecution witness to refresh his memory from his statement, and the suggestion that he might like to do so may come from the judge. It is better that the witness remain in court to refresh his memory: R. *v.* Tyagi, *The Times,* July 21, 1986, C.A.

589. Evidence—sample of body fluid taken from suspect without consent—admissibility

There is no rule of law that anything taken from a suspect could not be admitted in evidence unless the suspect consented to the taking.

A raped three girls, attempting to bugger two of them. Each of the attacks occurred after A, posing as a minicab driver, had picked up the girls. The strongest evidence against A was that each of the girls had contracted an unusual strain of gonorrhea. A, whilst in prison awaiting trial was seen by a consultant physician and allowed him to take a sample of body fluid because he had been told by the prison authorities that he had to do so. The sample showed that A had the same strain of gonorrhea as the three victims. The prosecution called evidence to that effect at the trial and A was convicted. A appealed, contending that the evidence was the physical equivalent to an oral confession and so was inadmissible. *Held,* that the basic rule is that evidence which is relevant should be admitted unless there is some rule which says it should not. There is no rule of law that says that evidence of anything taken from a suspect, whether it is body fluid, hair or an article hidden in an orifice of the body, cannot be admitted in evidence unless the suspect consented to the taking. A had not been tricked into giving the evidence and so it was not unfair for the prosecution to use it. The trial judge had been right in his discretion not to include it (*R. v. Sang* [1979] C.L.Y. 448 considered; *R. v. Payne* [1963] C.L.Y. 3051 distinguished).

R. *v.* Apicella (1986) 82 Cr.App.R. 295, C.A.

590. Evidence—similar fact

Evidence of sexual conduct by a defendant given by a consenting partner was admissible in evidence under the similar fact principle where it bore striking resemblance to the behaviour of a defendant charged with indecent assault and rape: R. *v.* Butler, *The Times,* June 24, 1986, C.A.

591. Evidence—surveillance from police observation post—whether permissible to exclude evidence of location of observation post.

Where premises are used as an observation post by the police to gather evidence against a defendant the trial judge of his own volition is empowered to prevent questions being asked to establish the exact location of the premises where the interests of justice in preserving the co-operation of the public with the police or the protection of the occupier of the premises is required, provided no miscarriage of justice is caused to the defendant.

D was convicted of unlawfully supplying a controlled drug to another person. The prosecution case was based upon the observations and identifications of two police officers positioned in an observation post. Upon the application of the prosecution the trial judge held he would not compel the officers to answer questions about the location of the observation post that might embarrass or imperil their sources of co-operation. D appealed on the ground that it was wrong in law to permit the prosecution to conceal the location of the observation post. *Held,* dismissing the appeal, that the public interest required that nothing should be done to discourage the co-operation of members of the public with the police in the prevention and detection of crime. In the same way that an officer cannot be asked about the identity of his informant so the officers could not be asked to identify the exact location of their observation post. If the need to avoid a miscarriage of justice required the provision of the information it must be provided. It was for the defendant to show good reason why the information should be provided. The trial judge was obliged to apply those rules whether or not he was invited so to do by the prosecution (*Att.-Gen. v. Briant* (1846) 15 M. & W. 169, *Marks v. Beyfus* (1890) 25 Q.B.D. 494, *R. v. Hennessey (Timothy)* [1979] C.L.Y. 472 applied, *Webb v. Catchlove* (1886) 3 T.L.R. 159 not followed).

R. *v.* Rankine [1986] 2 W.L.R. 1075, C.A.

592. Evidence—tape recording—police interviews

The Home Office has issued a draft code of practice for the tape recording of police interviews with suspects. The code is issued under the terms of s.60(1)(*a*) of the Police and Criminal Evidence Act 1984.

593. Evidence—video recording

Notwithstanding that an original video recording was not produced in court, evidence of the contents are admissible: TAYLOR *v.* CHIEF CONSTABLE OF CHESHIRE, *The Times,* October 28, 1986, D.C.

594. Evidence—video recording—admissibility

At T's trial on a charge of reckless driving during a chase of T by police: *held,* that a video recording of the alleged route of the chase, made by a technician of the Avon and Somerset Constabulary, was admissible to remove the necessity for maps and photographs and convey a picture of the roads more accurately and helpfully and to enable a police witness to tie up his notes with the visual presentation of the recording. (*Barber (J.) and Sons* v. *Lloyd's Underwriters* [1986] C.L.Y. 1507 applied). R. *v.* THOMAS (STEVEN) [1986] Crim.L.R. 682, Bristol Crown Court.

595. Evidence—witness becoming ill—discretion to allow trial to continue

The complainant in a sexual assault trial having given evidence in chief, she became ill and incapable of giving further evidence after some hours of cross-examination. *Held,* that the trial judge had a discretion to allow the trial to continue on the basis of such evidence as she had given: R. *v.* STRETTON AND McCALLION, *The Times,* November 25, 1986, C.A.

596. Evidence—witness—bigamous wife

A woman with whom a man has gone through a bigamous ceremony of marriage is a competent witness against him for the prosecution: she is in the same position evidentially as a mistress (*R.* v. *Yacoob* [1981] C.L.Y. 410 applied): R. *v.* KHAN (JUNAID), *The Times,* June 10, 1986, C.A.

597. Factual basis for sentence—determination by judge—appeal to Court of Appeal

Where there is a dispute as to the factual basis upon which an offender is to be sentenced, and that dispute is determined by the judge, an appeal against his determination will lie to the Court of Appeal, but the Court of Appeal may approach the matter as it would approach a finding of fact in a civil matter.

P pleaded guilty to one count of living on the earnings of prostitution, and one count of aiding and abetting buggery in the form of bestiality. In mitigation he alleged that the woman had consented to prostitution, and had willingly participated in the act of bestiality. The prosecution case was that he had coerced the woman, using threats and violence. The judge heard evidence and determined the matter under the principle in *R.* v. *Newton* ([1983] C.L.Y. 815). The judge rejected P's account and sentenced him to 4 years' for living on the earnings of prostitution, and 3 years' consecutive for the offence of buggery. *Held,* on appeal, when the judge's findings of fact were challenged, that the Court of Appeal had jurisdiction to entertain the appeal and review the judge's decision on the facts. The test to be applied would be that appropriate to a civil appeal, but in the circumstances it was impossible so to do. The judge had seen and heard the witnesses (*R.* v. *Newton* [1983] C.L.Y. 815 considered).

R. *v.* PARKER (1984) 6 Cr.App.R.(S.) 444, C.A.

598. Factual basis for sentence—facts used in mitigation—whether hearing required to determine their truth

Three years' imprisonment for burglary upheld: a judge is not bound to hear oral evidence from a probation officer of a change of heart by the accused.

O pleaded guilty to burglary of a jewellers' shop. He had a number of previous convictions, and this offence was committed shortly before the expiry of a parole licence after being released from sentence of 3 years' imprisonment. A probation officer felt that O had had a change of heart after his last release from prison, but the judge declined to hear oral evidence thereof. He sentenced O to 3 years' imprisonment. *Held,* that the question of whether there had, or had not, been some sort of change of heart by O was not within the principle of *Newton.* Even had there been such a change of approach by O the sentence was still proper. Appeal dismissed (*R.* v. *Newton* [1983] C.L.Y. 815 considered).

R. *v.* ODEY (1984) 6 Cr.App.R.(S.) 318, C.A.

599. False improvement—father of daughter—whether unlawful imprisonment

A parent can be held to have unlawfully imprisoned their child if the restraint goes beyond the bounds of parental discipline.

A Bangladesh father, whose daughter had been fostered out, abducted her against her will in an attempt to take her back to Bangladesh. She was rescued from a car by police. The father was charged, *inter alia*, with false imprisonment. A submission of no case was rejected and he changed his plea. *Held*, dismissing the appeal, that parental restraint was not only unlawful where a court order was in existence, but also where it was of a nature or duration to take it out of the category of parental discipline (*R. v. D.* [1984] C.L.Y. 651 considered).

R. *v.* RAHMAN (1985) 81 Cr.App.R. 349, C.A.

600. Firearms. See FIREARMS.

601. Fixed penalties. See ROAD TRAFFIC.

602. Food and drugs. See FOOD AND DRUGS.

603. Forfeiture order—conspiracy to supply controlled drug—money deemed to be proceeds of sale—whether order valid.

[Powers of Criminal Courts Act 1973 (c.62), s.43(1).]

S.43 of the Powers of Criminal Courts Act 1973 is to be construed as meaning property "that has been used for the purpose of committing an offence by him," that is the convicted person.

When the appellant's premises were searched the police found 4,500 grammes of cannabis and £1,136 in cash. A further £436 was found on his person; he made no admissions that the money came from drug dealing; he was charged with conspiracy to supply a controlled drug. The judge made a forfeiture order in respect of the £1,136. *Held,* allowing the appeal, that an order under this section could be made in respect of property which had been used for the purpose of committing the offence of which he was convicted; there was no power to make the order on a plea of conspiracy to supply (*R. v. Cuthbertson* [1980] C.L.Y. 526 considered).

R. *v.* SLATER (J. K.) [1986] 1 W.L.R. 1340, C.A.

604. Forfeiture order—order against a person not a defendant—judicial review

[Misuse of Drugs Act 1971 (c.38), s.27(1); Supreme Court Act 1981 (c.54), s.29(1)(3).]

The Divisional Court has power to hear an appeal by way of judicial review from an order of the Crown Court forfeiting property belonging to a non-defendant, since otherwise he would have no right of appeal. A forfeiture order would be quashed where such a person had no knowledge of the purpose to which his goods would be used by the defendant.

The applicant's son was charged with two offences of supplying heroin, on November 8 and 13, 1984. He used different motor cars on each occasion which belonged to his father. He pleaded guilty to the second charge and was sentenced to four years' imprisonment. The trial judge found that the applicant was unaware that his son was dealing in drugs, but ordered the forfeiture of the two cars under s.27(1) of the Misuse of Drugs Act 1971. The applicant applied to quash the forfeiture order by way of certiorari. *Held,* granting the application that the forfeiture order was not a sentence or order dealing with an offender and could not affect the conduct of the son's trial. Accordingly, the order was not one relating to trial on indictment and the court's jurisdiction to review the order was not excluded by s.29(3) of the Supreme Court Act 1981 (*Re Smalley* [1985] C.L.Y. 555 applied; *R. v. Cardiff Crown Court, ex p. Jones* [1973] C.L.Y. 2674 and *R. v. Smith (Martin)* [1974] C.L.Y. 554 doubted). Since one of the cars was not used in the transaction to which the son had pleaded guilty, that car had not been shown to relate to an offence within s.27(1) of the Misuse of Drugs Act 1971. Although a forfeiture order was proper where a lender of a motor car should have been put on notice that the car was going to be used for illegal purposes, it should not be ordered where he was unaware of his son's criminal activities.

R. *v.* MAIDSTONE CROWN COURT, *ex p.* GILL [1986] 1 W.L.R. 1405, D.C.

605. Forgery—child allowance vouchers—no intention to prejudice—whether offence

[Forgery and Counterfeiting Act 1981 (c.45), ss.3, 10.]

An offence is committed under s.3 of the Forgery Act 1981 only if there has been an intention both to induce someone to accept an instrument as genuine and an intention that the other should act to his prejudice. During a period when his wife and four children had left the U.K. and were living abroad, the appellant signed in his wife's name vouchers claiming child allowance. He was prosecuted under s.3 of the 1981 Act. He gave evidence that he genuinely believed he was entitled to the money. *Held,* allowing the appeal, that on his version he had a defence, and the judge should have directed the jury to consider whether he intended the Secretary of State to act to his prejudice.

R. *v.* TOBIERRE [1986] 1 W.L.R. 125, C.A.

606. Forgery—obtaining by deception—false name on form—whether necessary for jury to agree on means of deception

[Forgery and Counterfeiting Act 1981, (c.45), s.9(1)(*h*).]

M opened a building society account in a false name and paid into it a cheque which had been sent to a wrong address. He then presented a withdrawal form for £5,000 and obtained a cheque which was cashed by a bank on the authorisation of the building society. He was convicted of theft of the original cheque, obtaining the £5,000 cheque by deception and forgery of the withdrawal form. *Held,* dismissing his appeal, that (1) the recorder had correctly ruled that the withdrawal form was a false instrument because it "purported to have been made . . . by an existing person but he did not in fact exist", within s.9(1)(*h*) of the 1981 Act; (2) it is not necessary for each member of a jury, satisfied that a charge was proved, to reach his conclusion by precisely the same route. A direction on the lines set out in *R. v. Brown* was comparatively rarely needed and only where there was an obvious risk of disagreement between jurors as to whether a particular necessary ingredient of an offence is proved or as to the making, falsity and efficacy of at least one of the representations used to obtain by deception; (3) *R. v. Brown* should not be applied to a defence of duress. (*R. v. Brown* [1984] C.L.Y. 624 distinguished): R. *v.* MOORE [1986] Crim.L.R. 552, C.A.

607. Fraud trials. See LAW REFORM, § 1949.

608. Fraudulent trading—single transaction—dishonesty

[Companies Act 1948 (c.38), s.332(3), as amended] L was convicted of fraudulent trading, contrary to s.332(3) of the 1948 Act, as amended. *Held,* dismissing L's appeal, that (1) the judge had not erred in directing the jury as to dishonesty in accordance with *R. v. Ghosh.* Such a direction was of general application and applied in cases of commercial fraud; (2) nor had the judge erred in directing that a single dishonest transaction carried out with intent to defraud a creditor, could constitute carrying on business with intent to defraud creditors. The judge was clearly referring to a transaction in the course of business (*R. v. Ghosh* [1982] C.L.Y 659, *R. v. Grantham* [1984] C.L.Y. 627 and *R. v. Cooper (Gerald) Chemicals* [1978] Ch. 262 considered): R. *v.* LOCKWOOD [1986] Crim.L.R. 244, C.A.

609. Grievous bodily harm—defence

Defendants charged with assault occasioning grievous bodily harm claimed that the injuries arose in the course of rough and undisciplined horseplay to which their victim had consented. *Held,* that this could have afforded a defence, and should have been left to the jury to decide (*Att.-Gen.'s Reference (No. 6 of 1980)* [1981] C.L.Y. 362 considered): R. *v.* MUIR, *The Times,* March 18, 1986, C.A.

610. Handling—assisting in disposal of property

C knew that his wife was stealing cash and spending it on goods and their living expenses. He was convicted of handling £650 which she had paid to their solicitors with regard to the purchase of a flat in their joint names. C agreed that the bill was for them both. *Held,* allowing C's appeal, that the *actus reus* of the offence was assisting in the disposal of the money, rather than obtaining the benefit of it. Assisting included encouraging or helping. From the evidence the jury could have made inferences justifying a conviction. The judge's direction, however, was wrong and the jury might have inferred that C's wife made the decisions without assistance: R. *v.* COLEMAN [1986] Crim.L.R. 56, C.A.

611. Handling—dishonesty—offer to return goods

[Theft Act 1968 (c.60), s.22(1).] In response to an advertisement R, using a false name, contacted loss adjusters and offered to return some stolen paintings for reward provided that no attempt was made to arrest him. At his trial on a charge of handling stolen goods, his defence was that he was an honest businessman who found out about the paintings by chance. He gave no evidence. *Held,* dismissing R's appeal against conviction, that (1) "dishonest" in s.22(1) of the 1968 Act did not necessarily mean dishonest in relation to the loser of the goods; and (2) unless the defendant has raised the issue of whether he knew that anybody would regard what he did as dishonest, it was not necessary for the full subjective test set out in *R.* v. *Ghosh* to be referred to in the summing up (*R.* v. *Ghosh* [1982] C.L.Y. 659 considered): R. *v.* ROBERTS [1986] Crim.L.R. 122, C.A.

612. Handling—guilty knowledge—evidence of previous convictions
[Theft Act 1968 (c.60), s.27(3)(*b*).] Evidence of D's previous convictions for handling stolen goods should not be adduced as a matter of course, but only where it was demanded by the interests of justice: R. *v.* RASINI, *The Times*, March 20, 1986, C.A.

613. Handling—"knowing or believing"—meaning
[Theft Act 1968 (c.60), s.22(1).]
Guidelines on the approach to be followed on "knowing or believing" goods to be stolen.
H was convicted of handling stolen goods. He appealed his conviction on the basis of a misdirection by the judge on the *mens rea* of the offence. *Held,* dismissing the appeal, that "knowledge" is where a defendant is told by someone with first-hand knowledge (the thief), that goods are stolen; "belief" is something short of knowledge, where there could be no other reasonable conclusion in the light of all the circumstances (*R.* v. *Griffiths* [1975] C.L.Y. 595 distinguished).
R. *v.* HALL (1985) 81 Cr.App.R. 260, C.A.

614. Handling—recent possession of other stolen property
[Theft Act 1968 (c.60), s.27(3).] S was convicted of receiving a stolen music centre between November 17, 1982 and October 5, 1983 and of receiving a stolen video recorder between April 13, 1983, and October 5, 1983. *Held,* allowing S's appeal against conviction on the first count, that (1) the prosecution had relied upon the doctrine of recent possession and s.27(3) of the 1968 Act re both counts; (2) since there was no satisfactory evidence of when the music centre came into S's possession, the jury should have been told that with regard to that count there was no evidence of recent possession but there was evidence on which they could apply s.27(3) of the 1968 Act (consideration of evidence that the accused was in possession of two different stolen articles within the previous twelve months on the issue of whether he knew he was handling stolen goods): R. *v.* SIMMONS [1986] Crim.L.R. 397, C.A.

615. Harbouring escaped prisoner—escape en route to remand centre—whether escape from "prison or other institution"
[Prison Act 1952 (c.52), ss.13(2), 39, 43(3); Criminal Justice Act 1961 (c.39), s.22(2).]
The yard of a police station is not a "prison or other institution" within the meaning of s.39 of the Prison Act 1952.
A prisoner awaiting trial was remanded in custody. He was later brought to a magistrates' court and there remanded again; while in a police van in the local station yard he escaped and took refuge in the defendant's house. The defendant was charged with "harbouring a prisoner." The defence submitted that the station yard was not a "prison or other institution." *Held,* allowing the appeal, that on a strict construction of the relevant sections the wrong offence had been charged (*R.* v. *Abbott* [1956] C.L.Y. 1725 distinguished).
NICOLL *v.* CATRON (1985) 81 Cr.App.R. 339, D.C.

616. Health and safety at work—person injured not in employ of company
[Health and Safety at Work Act 1974 (c.37), s.3(1).] The Act clearly provides for the conviction of a company director who is responsible for faulty equipment, where that equipment is used by a person not in the employ of the company, but with permission: R. *v.* MARA, *The Times,* November 13, 1986, C.A.

617. Importation of drugs—knowledge of prohibition on importation of other goods
[Misuse of Drugs Act 1971 (c.38), ss.3(1), 28(3); Customs and Excise Management Act 1979 (c.2), s.170(2).] D could properly be convicted of being knowingly concerned in the fraudulent evasion of a prohibition on the importation of goods contrary to the 1979 Act even when the prohibition on the importation of the goods that D mistakenly thought he was importing was contained in the 1971 Act. (*R.* v.

Hennessey (Timothy) [1979] C.L.Y. 472 followed; *R.* v. *Hussain* [1969] C.L.Y. 854, *R.* v. *Courtie* [1984] C.L.Y. 523 considered; *R.* v. *Taaffe* [1984] C.L.Y. 581, *R.* v. *Shivpuri* [1986] C.L.Y. 482 distinguished): R. *v.* ELLIS AND STREET; R. *v.* SMITH (GLORIA MARIE), *The Times,* August 12, 1986, C.A.

618. Incest and Related Offences (Scotland) Act 1986 (c.36)
This Act makes provision for Scotland in respect of incest and related offences. It received the Royal Assent on July 18, 1986 and extends to Scotland only.

619. Incitement—inciting another to counsel and abet a third person—whether an offence
[Criminal Law Act 1977 (c.45), s.5(7).]
If A incites B to agree with C that C will wound D, A's incitement of B is not an offence under s.5(7) of the Criminal Law Act 1977.
S wished for the death or serious injury of his wife. He urged B to pay a man (who was in fact non-existent) to do so or to procure the deed. S was charged with incitement to cause grievous bodily harm. The trial judge directed the jury that if S had urged B to incite a third person to cause grievous bodily harm S would be guilty of incitement. S was convicted and appealed. *Held,* that S may have been convicted of an offence for which he was not charged—incitement to incite to cause grievous bodily harm (not incitement to cause grievous bodily harm as charged). Further he may have been convicted of a non-existent offence—inciting B to agree with someone else to cause grievous bodily harm. Accordingly the appeal would be allowed.
R. *v.* SIRAT (MOHAMMED) (1986) 83 Cr.App.R. 41, C.A.

620. Incitement to commit offence—copyright—civil liability
[Copyright Act 1956 (c.74), s.21(3)] Incitement to commit the offence might lead to civil liability, and an injunction restraining such incitement was therefore justified: CBS SONGS *v.* AMSTRAD CONSUMER ELECTRONICS, *The Times,* May 9, 1986, Whitford J.

621. Indecent or obscene articles—prohibition on importation—goods which can lawfully be made and sold within U.K. See CONEGATE *v.* H.M. CUSTOMS AND EXCISE, § 000.

622. Indictment—amendment—conspiracy—whether jurisdiction to hear amended indictment
[Trade Descriptions Act 1968 (c.29), s.19(1).]
An indictment alleging conspiracy to defraud could not be amended successfully to allege conspiracy to commit offences under the Trade Descriptions Act 1968 where the time limit imposed by s.19 of the Act for the prosecution of offences under the Act had expired.
P, J and H were involved in a plot to manufacture and market bogus Chanel scent and toilet water. They appeared before Aylesbury Crown Court on an indictment containing counts alleging, *inter alia,* conspiracy to defraud. Defence submissions that the counts were bad in the light of the decision in *R.* v. *Ayres* in that they did not allege a conspiracy to commit a specific criminal offence were upheld by the trial judge. The trial judge allowed the prosecution to amend the indictment to allege a conspiracy to commit offences under the Trade Descriptions Act 1968 without objection from the defence. J and H pleaded guilty. P was convicted by the jury. The amendment was made to the indictment outside the time limit for the prosecution of offences under the Act set out in s.19(1) of the Act. P, J and H appealed and submitted that by reason of s.19 of the Act the trial judge did not have jurisdiction to hear the amended counts alleging conspiracy to commit offences under the Act. *Held,* allowing the appeals, that although the facts upon which the counts of conspiracy to defraud were based were substantially the same facts as the counts of conspiracy to commit offences under the Act, a prosecution alleging conspiracy to defraud could not properly be described as a prosecution for offences under the Act. Accordingly the Crown Court had no jurisdiction to hear the amended counts in the indictment (*R.* v. *Newcastle upon Tyne Justices, ex p. John Bryce (Contractors)* [1975] C.L.Y. 2056 considered).
R. *v.* PAIN, JORY AND HAWKINS (1986) 82 Cr.App.R. 141, C.A.

623. Indictment—joinder of counts—application of proviso
[Indictment Rules 1971 (S.I. 1971 No. 1253), r.9.]
The appellant gave evidence at the trial of his brother for wounding with intent that he, and not his brother, had been responsible for the act. The brother was acquitted and the appellant was then charged with wounding with intent and perjury. The two charges were tried together and B was found guilty of perjury. He appealed

against conviction arguing that the two counts should not have been tried together because the offences were not founded on the same or similar facts. *Held,* that regardless of the merits of trying the two counts together the Court had no hesitation in saying that no miscarriage of justice had occurred and so the proviso of the Criminal Appeal Act 1968, s.2(1) would be applied. (*R. v. Barrell and Wilson* (1969) 69 Cr.App.R. 250 considered.)

R. *v.* BARNES (T) (1986) 83 Cr.App.R. 38, C.A.

624. Joinder of counts—legal or factual similarities—series of offences

On the question of joinder of counts the court should seek to ascertain whether or not the counts had similar or dissimilar legal characteristics, whether or not they had similar or dissimilar factual characteristics such as enabled the offences properly to be described as a series of offences.

M was charged with five offences on one indictment and pleaded guilty to one of them. The first count was one of reckless driving, the second was of intentional or reckless causing of damage, the third was of assault, the fourth and fifth counts, of criminal damage and reckless driving, arose out of the same set of facts. M applied to sever the third count on the indictment and that application was rejected. *Held,* that there was no legal similarity between count one and count three. The factual similarities did not amount to a series of offences of similar character. The convictions would be quashed. (*Ludlow* v. *Metropolitan Police Commissioner* [1970] C.L.Y. 458; *R.* v. *Harward* [1981] C.L.Y. 470 considered).

R. *v.* MARSH (STEPHEN LESLIE) (1986) 83 Cr.App.R. 165, C.A.

625. Judicial review—Crown Court—counts to be on file—whether subject to review

[Supreme Court Act 1981 (c.54), s.29(3).]

The High Court has no jurisdiction to entertain an application for judicial review in respect of a judge's order that counts of an indictment lie on the file.

The applicant was convicted of theft on a count that had been severed from an indictment containing 14 other counts. After sentence, the defendant was arraigned on the other matters, pleaded not guilty, and the common serjeant ordered that those counts lie on the file; he made a similar order in respect of another indictment. *Held,* dismissing the application for judicial review, that the order was an order affecting the conduct of a trial, and therefore came within the exception of s.29(3) of the 1981 Act. The court had no jurisdiction to entertain the application (*Smalley, Re* [1985] C.L.Y. 555 applied).

R. *v.* CENTRAL CRIMINAL COURT, *ex p.* RAYMOND [1986] 1 W.L.R. 710, C.A.

626. Juries. See JURIES.

627. Justices—costs—acquittal of defendant—prosecution ordered to pay defence costs. See R. *v.* HORSEFERRY ROAD JUSTICES, *ex p.* UNDERWOODS (CASH CHEMISTS), § 2077.

628. Juvenile attaining 17—committal—jurisdiction of juvenile court

[Magistrates Courts Act 1970 (c.43), s.24.]

Where a defendant under 17 appeared before a juvenile court on an indictable offence other than homicide, the material date for determining whether he was to be tried there or committed to the Crown Court was whether he had attained 17 when he first appeared before them, *i.e.* when the charge was put to him and the proceedings were ready to commence.

B, then aged 16, was charged with robbery, and bailed. On March 22, 1984 he appeared to answer his bail before a juvenile court but the case was adjourned since his solicitor was ill and the charge was not put or a plea entered. Before the adjourned hearing on May 3, 1984 B attained 17 and the justices took the view that s.24 of the Magistrates Court Act 1980 only permitted them to decide whether or not to commit him for trial but not to try him. The applicant applied to the Divisional Court to quash the justices' decision on the ground that the justices should have dealt with him as he first appeared before the court when aged under 17. The application for certiorari was refused. The material date for determining the mode of trial was held to be the date when he appeared when the charge was put to him and the proceedings were ready to be commenced. In the present case this was on May 3, 1984 by which date he had attained 17 (dicta of Lord Diplock in *R.* v. *Islington North Juvenile Court, ex p. Daley* [1982] C.L.Y. 742 applied).

R. *v.* VALE OF GLAMORGAN JUVENILE JUSTICES, *ex p.* BEATTIE (1985) 82 Cr.App.R. 1, D.C.

629. Law reform. *See* LAW REFORM.

630. Legal aid—"date fixed for trial"—review
[Legal Aid in Criminal Proceedings (General) Regulations 1968 (S.I. 1968 No. 1231), reg. 6E(2)(*c*) (as inserted by Legal Aid in Criminal Proceedings (General) (Amendment) Regulations 1983 (S.I. 1983 No. 1863), reg. 9).]
Since the court alone and not the police have the power to fix the date for a trial, a defendant's first appearance at court cannot be the "date fixed for the trial" within the meaning of reg. 6E(2)(*c*) of the Legal Aid in Criminal Proceedings (General) Regulations 1968.
The applicant, aged 17, was charged on May 6, 1986 with obtaining property by deception contrary to s.15(1) of the Theft Act 1968, an offence triable either way, and released on bail to appear before justices on June 3. His solicitor's application for legal aid was refused on May 14 on the ground, pursuant to reg. 6C(1)(*a*) of the Regulations, that it did not appear to the court or the proper officer of the court desirable in the interests of justice to grant the application. He was sent a notice of refusal by the court which informed him that he was not entitled to apply for a review of that decision to a criminal legal aid committee. By reg. 6E(2) an application for review would lie where the offence was triable either way and "(*c*) the application for a legal aid order was made no later than 21 days before the date fixed for the trial of an information or the inquiry into an offence as examining justices where such date had been fixed at the time that the application was made." The applicant applied for judicial review of the decision not to grant a review and requiring the justices to discharge their duty under the Regulations. *Held,* allowing the application, that since the court alone could fix the date for the trial or an inquiry, a defendant's first appearance at court could not be the "date fixed for the trial". Since it had not been fixed the justices were wrong to tell the applicant that he was not entitled to apply to a criminal legal aid committee for a review of the refusal of legal aid. If the court did decide to proceed on the first appearance, it would be the decision of the justices to proceed to hear the case or to act as examining justices which would make it the "date fixed for the trial . . . or the inquiry" and not the fact that the date was fixed by the police or the prosecution service.
R. *v.* BURY JUSTICES, *ex p.* N. [1986] 3 W.L.R. 965, D.C.

631. Licensed hackney carriage—attempt to retain ownership
[Town Police Clauses Act 1847 (c.89), s.40; Local Government (Miscellaneous Provisions) Act 1976 (c.57), s.55.] The licence plate issued by the local authority remained their property, and when the vehicle to which it was attached was sold the former owner of the vehicle lost all the benefits from the licence plate: CHALLONER *v.* EVANS, *The Times,* November 22, 1986, D.C.

632. Licensing—purchasing intoxicating liquor—person under 18
[Licensing Act 1964 (c.26), s.169(2).] X, an adult, purchased drink for B and O (both under 18) using their money whilst they waited outside. *Held,* dismissing the prosecutor's appeal against acquittals of B and O on charges of purchasing lager contrary to s.169(2) of the 1964 Act, that although B and O were the real purchasers, they had not committed an offence under s.169(2) since they were not on the premises when the drink was sold. There is no offence under the section unless the defendant bought or attempted to buy intoxicating liquor for consumption in a bar in licenced premises: WOBY *v.* B. AND O. [1986] Crim.L.R. 183, D.C.

633. Loitering—self-incrimination—duty to answer
[H.K.] (Crimes Ordinance (Laws of Hong Kong, 1984 rev., c.200), s.160(1).]
A person who was suspected of loitering in suspicious circumstances had a duty under the Crimes Ordinance of Hong Kong to answer questions about his conduct. Those answers could not be used to incriminate him in other proceedings.
Per curiam: If the answer given would amount to the admission of an offence under other than s.160(1) the answer, if given under the direct threat of arrest on a charge of loitering would be inadmissible upon a charge of that other offence as not having been given voluntarily. If no answer is given, that does no more than help to indicate that the loiterer has no satisfactory explanation for his presence.
Police officers in Hong Kong saw the defendant at 5 a.m. looking at entrances to buildings and pulling and pushing at grilles preventing access to flats. He went up the stairs in one building. He was asked to explain this but gave no reply. He was charged with loitering contrary to s.160(1) of the Crimes Ordinance. At the end of

the prosecution case the magistrate ruled that there was no case for the defence to answer because, since he was entitled not to answer questions that might incriminate him of an offence other than loitering; he had therefore not been given a proper opportunity to give an account of himself and an explanation. The Court of Appeal dismissed the Attorney-General's appeal. The Attorney-General's further appeal to the Judicial Committee was allowed. *Held,* that the offence created by s.160(1) was a lingering in suspicious circumstances and a failure to give a satisfactory explanation. Accordingly the police officer had to ask the defendant to explain himself, and the submission did not protect him from answering the officers. It placed him in the position in the absence of a satisfactory answer, of either having to admit to an offence under the section or to another offence. Since he had been asked for an explanation the magistrates had erred in law in holding that he had no case to answer (*R.* v. *Ma Kui* [1985] H.K.L.R. 414, [1985] H.K.C.L. 635 overruled).

ATT.-GEN. OF HONG KONG *v.* SHAM CHUEN [1986] 3 W.L.R. 245, P.C.

634. Malicious wounding—recklessness—direction to jury
[Offences against the Person Act 1861 (c.100), s.20.] Where a jury were not given a proper direction on the issue of recklessness where recklessness was a material part of the case that was a material irregularity leading to the quashing of the conviction: R. *v.* DUME (CONSTANTINE), *The Times*, October 16, 1986, C.A.

635. Manslaughter—causing death by reckless conduct—unlawful and dangerous act—direction to jury
In a case of manslaughter by an unlawful and dangerous act the correct direction for the jury was that where the defendant did an unlawful act of such a kind as all sober and reasonable people would inevitably recognise a risk of some harm resulting therefrom, and death was caused thereby, the defendant was guilty of manslaughter. It was not necessary for the unlawful act to be directed at the victim so long as there was no intervening cause before death. In an *R.* v. *Lawrence* type of case the jury ought to be directed that they should be satisfied that the defendant was acting in such a manner as to create an obvious risk of danger and physical injury to some person and, having recognised that there was some risk, the defendant had nevertheless gone ahead.

G wished to be rehoused but, because he was in arrears with his rent, he would not be rehoused. He planned to burn down his house, rescue the occupants and obtain another house from the local council. He doused the living room with petrol and threw a petrol bomb through the window. Because of the rapid spread of the flames it was not possible to rescue all of the occupants and three of them died. G was convicted of manslaughter. *Held,* dismissing the appeal, that the case was capable of being either an unlawful act or the *Lawrence* type of manslaughter. The judge's direction, based upon the *Lawrence* type of case, was therefore not open to criticism. (*Kong Cheuk Kwan* v. *The Queen* [1986] C.L.Y. 636, *D.P.P.* v. *Newbury and Jones* [1976] C.L.Y. 496, *R.* v. *Church* [1965] C.L.Y. 848 applied; *R.* v. *Dalby* [1982] C.L.Y. 639 explained.)

R. *v.* GOODFELLOW (1986) 83 Cr.App.R. 23, C.A.

636. Manslaughter—collision at sea—direction to jury
Where there was a collision at sea causing death the jury should have been directed in accordance with the model direction suggested by the House of Lords in R. v. *Lawrence* [1981] C.L.Y. 2382.

In perfect weather one morning in July 1982 a collision occurred between two hydrofoils travelling at a combined speed of 64 m.p.h. between Hong Kong and Macau. Two people were killed. The appellant was the captain of one of the vessels and his first mate and the captain and deck officer of the other vessel were all charged with manslaughter. None of them gave evidence at the trial in Hong Kong. There was much anecdotal evidence but little direct oral evidence of the positions of the two vessels and their movements before the collision. Only the appellant was convicted. He appealed on the ground that the judge had misdirected the jury in his direction that the relevant risk they had to consider was the risk of causing some injury albeit not necessarily serious but not so slight that an ordinarily prudent individual would feel justified in treating it as negligible (adopting a passage in Archbold 41st ed. para. 20–49, 2nd Supp.). The Court of Appeal of Hong Kong dismissed the appeal. *Held,* by the Privy Council, quashing the conviction on the grounds of a fundamental misdirection, that the model direction suggested in

Lawrence [1981] C.L.Y. 2382 applied in this case. The jury should have been directed to consider whether the appellant's act of navigation created an obvious and serious risk of causing physical damage to some other ship and thus to other persons who might have been in the area of the collision at the relevant time. Where such a risk was created, the jury should have considered whether the appellant had navigated without giving any thought to the possibility of that risk or whether he had recognised that risk existed, but had nevertheless gone on to take it. The case was not one for the operation of the proviso to s.2(1) of the Criminal Appeal Act 1968. *R.* v. *Lawrence* as explained by Lord Diplock in *R.* v. *Caldwell* [1981] C.L.Y. 385; and dictum of Watkins L.J. in *R.* v. *Seymour* [1984] C.L.Y. 525 applied.

KONG CHEUK KWAN *v.* THE QUEEN (1985) 82 Cr.App.R. 18, P.C.

637. Manslaughter—of child—parents jointly indicted—no evidence implicating one rather than the other

[Children and Young Persons Act 1933 (c.12), s.1(1).]

Where parents responsible for the care of their child are jointly charged with manslaughter, but there is no evidence which of them was in charge of the child when she died or whether the other was then present, a submission of no case to answer must succeed.

Per curiam: Some consideration might be given to increasing the maximum penalty which may be imposed in cases which fall within s.1 of the Children and Young Persons Act 1933.

The appellants were mother and stepfather of a small child. She sustained serious injuries and died. She died from a fractured skull sustained at some time between noon and 8.30 p.m. during which period both parents had been absent from the home at times, and also present at times. They both denied responsibility. The prosecution invited the jury to draw the inference that they were both responsible, and the trial judge rejected a submission of no case to answer by both defendants on the basis that there was sufficient prima facie evidence of this. Neither gave evidence and they were convicted. The judge directed the jury that they could draw the inference that they were jointly responsible. *Held*, allowing their appeals, that the evidence against each appellant, taken separately did not establish his or her presence when the child was injured or any participation. Both had told lies but lies did not lead to the inference of their presence. The judge ought to have acceded to the submission of no case to answer (dictum of Lord Goddard C.J. in *R.* v. *Abbott* [1955] C.L.Y. 559 applied, *R.* v. *Gibson and Gibson* [1985] C.L.Y. 584 considered). Evidence of general custody and care did not establish presence but was only a step towards proof. The jury were invited to draw inferences which the evidence did not allow.

R. *v.* LANE AND LANE (1985) 82 Cr.App.R. 5, C.A.

638. Metropolitan police—detention—requirement to explain reasons

[Metropolitan Police Act 1839 (c.47), s.66.] When H was stopped by police who suspected that the car he was driving was stolen, he gave a false name and claimed to be driving with the consent of the car's owner. After questioning, he began to walk away. When the officers brought him back and told him not to walk away as they had further questions, H pushed one officer and all three fell to the ground in the ensuing struggle. *Held*, dismissing H's appeal against conviction of assault occasioning bodily harm, that an officer lawfully detaining a person under s.66 of the 1839 Act must make it clear to that person that he is no longer free and why he is being detained, unless he makes it impossible for the officer to do so or the reason for detention is obvious. There was evidence from which the jury could properly conclude that H had had these things made clear to him (*Pedro* v. *Diss* [1981] C.L.Y. 2090 and *Christie* v. *Leachinsky* [1947] A.C. 543 applied).

R. *v.* HAMILTON [1986] Crim.L.R. 187, C.A.

639. Misuse of drugs

MISUSE OF DRUGS (AMENDMENT) REGULATIONS 1986 (No. 2330) [80p], made under the Misuse of Drugs Act 1971 (c.38), ss.7, 10, 31; operative on April 1,1987; amend S.I. 1985 No. 2066.

MISUSE OF DRUGS (DESIGNATION) ORDER 1986 (No. 2331) [80p], made under the Misuse of Drugs Act 1971 (c.38), s.7(4)(5); operative on April 1, 1987; replaces S.I. 1977 No. 1379 and designated specifies certain drugs to which s.7(3) of the 1971 Act will not apply.

MISUSE OF DRUGS (LICENCE FEES) REGULATIONS 1986 (No. 416) [80p], made under the Misuse of Drugs Act 1971 (c.38), ss.30, 31; operative on April 1, 1986; prescribe the fee payable in relation to a licence to produce, supply, offer to supply or possess controlled drugs.

MISUSE OF DRUGS (SAFE CUSTODY) (AMENDMENT) REGULATIONS 1986 (No. 2332) [45p], made under the Misuse of Drugs Act 1971 (c.38), ss.10(2)(*a*), 31; operative on April 1, 1987; amend S.I. 1973 No. 798 by substituting a new Schedule 1.

640. Misuse of drugs—"concerned in supplying"—meaning
[Misuse of Drugs Act 1971 (c.38), s.4(1), (3)(*b*)(*c*).]
A judge in his summing-up must give specific directions on the meaning of "being concerned in" the supply of drugs.
The appellant was charged with being concerned in the supply of a controlled drug (Ritalin tablets). The judge in his summing up read s.4(3) to the jury, but despite promptings by counsel, gave the jury no assistance on the meaning of "concerned in" *Held*, allowing the appeal, that the judge had failed to give assistance with regard to the meaning of "concerned in"; it was impossible to apply the proviso (*R*. v. *Blake and O'Connor* [1979] C.L.Y. 500 considered).
R. *v*. HUGHES (1985) 81 Cr.App.R. 344, C.A.

641. Misuse of drugs—possession—dried out psilocybin mushrooms—whether an ester of psilocin
[Misuse of Drugs Act 1971 (c.38), Sched. 2, Part 1, para. 5.] C picked and dried out about 100 psilocybin mushrooms, which he used in tea. Psilocybin was a derivative of psilocin and the latter was a Class A drug listed in Sched. 2, Part 1, para. 1 of the 1971 Act. *Held*, dismissing C's appeal against conviction of possession of a Class A controlled drug, that the dried mushrooms were a "preparation" containing a substance or product specified in para. 1, within para. 5 of Part 1 of Schedule 2. For the mushrooms to have been prepared they had to cease being in their natural growing state and in some way altered by the hand of man to put them in a condition in which they could be used (*R*. v. *Stevens* [1981] C.L.Y. 483 applied): R. *v*. CUNCLIFFE [1986] Crim.L.R. 547, C.A.

642. Misuse of drugs—possession—preparation containing less than 0.2 per cent. morphine
[Misuse of Drugs Act 1971 (c.38); Misuse of Drugs Regulations (S.I. 1973 No. 797), reg. 4.] Regulation 4 of the Misuse of Drugs Regulations provides, *inter alia*, that the Misuse of Drugs Act 1971 shall not apply to a preparation of morphine that contains less than 0.2 per cent. of morphine. This regulation defines an essential ingredient of the offence of possessing unlawful drugs, and the onus is therefore on the prosecution to prove the percentage of morphine in the drugs the subject of the charge: R. *v*. HUNT (RICHARD), *The Times*, December 13, 1986, H.L.

643. Misuse of drugs—possession—whether dependent on memory
[Misuse of Drugs Act 1971 (c.38), s.5(1)(2).]
Whether someone is in "possession" of a drug does not depend on his memory and recollection of its existence.
D had a small quantity of cannabis resin in a wallet found in his pocket. He sought a ruling as to whether he had a defence on the the assumption that he had been given the drug two years earlier and had forgotten all about it. The judge ruled that these facts did not afford him a defence. He pleaded guilty. *Held*, dismissing the appeal, that "possession" did not depend on the powers of memory of the possessor; if he had known at one time of its existence, he remained in possession (*R*. v. *Buswell* [1972] C.L.Y. 609 followed; *R*. v. *Russell* (1984) 81 Cr.App.R. 315 not followed).
R. *v*. MARTINDALE [1986] 1 W.L.R. 1042, C.A.

644. Misuse of drugs—strategy document
A new edition of the Government's strategy document, *Tackling Drug Misuse*, was published on March 26, 1986. Copies are available from the Home Office, E5 Division (Drugs Branch), Room 236, 50 Queen Anne's Gate, London SW1H 9AT.

645. Misuse of drugs—supply—issuing of NHS prescription in bad faith
[Misuse of Drugs Act 1971 (c.38), s.4.] T, a general practitioner, prescribed on various occasions a controlled drug and issued NHS prescriptions for it. *Held*, that there was no case for T to answer on charges of supplying the drug contrary to s.4 of the 1971 Act, even assuming that T had issued the prescriptions unlawfully and in

bad faith. Supplying involved the physical passage of the drug from supplier to supplied: R. v. TAYLOR [1986] Crim.L.R. 680, St. Alban's Crown Court.

646. Misuse of drugs—supply—meaning
[Misuse of Drugs Act 1971 (c.38), ss.4(3) and 5.]
Handing over quantities of a controlled drug to someone else for them to hold temporarily does not amount to "supplying" the drug. To "supply" is to do something which is designed to benefit the recipient.
D1 was a registered drug addict and had obtained a quantity of Physeptone from a doctor lawfully. He gave some of the drug to D2 to prevent himself from overdosing. D1 was charged with supplying a controlled drug to D2 contrary to s.4(3) of the Misuse of Drugs Act 1971. D2 was charged with possession of a controlled drug. The trial judge, at the end of the prosecution case, ruled that neither of them had a defence. Both then changed their pleas to guilty. On appeal. Held, that the word supply required an act designed for the benefit of the recipient. It did not include the depositing of an object for safekeeping. D2 did not come within any of the defences to the charge of possessing a controlled drug. Accordingly D1's appeal would be allowed and his conviction quashed. D2's appeal would be dismissed.
R. v. DEMPSEY AND DEMPSEY (1986) 82 Cr.App.R. 291, C.A.

647. Misuse of drugs—supply—return to owner
[Misuse of Drugs Act 1971 (c.38), s.5(3).]
Where the owner of drugs resumes actual possession of the articles placed by him in the custody of another, there is not a sufficient return of the article to constitute a "supply" by the bailee.
M pleaded guilty to possession of cannabis but not guilty to "intent to supply." His evidence was that a package, under the seat of his car, had been left there by a friend who was expected to come round and pick it up. The judge ruled that on his own evidence the appellant was guilty of the s.5(3) offence. Held, allowing the appeal, that there must be a transfer of physical control to the benefit of the recipient of the article; the facts here were not sufficient to constitute the return of the article an act of supply (R. v. Dempsey and Dempsey [1986] C.L.Y. 646 followed; R. v. Delgado [1984] C.L.Y. 663 not followed).
R. v. MAGINNIS [1986] 2 W.L.R. 767, C.A.

648. Misuse of Drugs Act 1971
MISUSE OF DRUGS ACT 1971 (MODIFICATION) ORDER 1986 (No. 2230) [80p], made under the Misuse of Drugs Act 1971 (c.38), s.2(2); operative on April 1, 1987; adds certain drugs to Pt. I of Sched. 2 to the 1971 Act (which specifies the class A drugs which are subjecy to control under the Act).

649. Murder—duress—whether defence
Duress provides no defence to a charge of murder.
H and B aided and abetted the killing of E, took part in the killing of P and conspired to kill R. They were tried on counts of murdering E and P and conspiring to murder R. Their defence was duress. The judge left duress as an issue on the counts of murdering E and conspiring to murder R, but did not do so on the count of murdering P. They were convicted on the three counts.
B and C were tried on a charge of murder of a man shot by B. C denied any involvement. B's defence was that he agreed to shoot the man because he feared that C would kill him, but in fact the gun went off accidentally so he did not have the necessary mens rea. The judge left B's defence of duress to the jury in respect of manslaughter only. B and C were convicted of murder. The appeals were heard together and were dismissed. Held, that (1) duress by threats of the immediate infliction of death or grievous bodily harm is no defence to a charge of murder, though it is a defence to a person charged with aiding and abetting a murder; R. v. Dudley and Stephens (1884) 14 Q.B.D. 273 and D.P.P v. Lynch [1975] C.L.Y. 622 applied; Abbott v. The Queen [1976] C.L.Y. 513 considered; (2) the test in duress was whether the threat was of such gravity that it might well have caused a reasonable man in the same situation to act in the same way and whether a sober man of reasonable firmness sharing the defendant's characteristics would have responded to the threat by taking part in the killing; R. v. Graham (Paul) [1982] C.L.Y. 556 applied; (3) the trial judge had correctly directed the jury that if B was guilty only of manslaughter, then C could at most only be found guilty of manslaughter; R. v. Richards [1974] C.L.Y. 510 doubted.
R. v. HOWE; R. v. BANNISTER; R. v. BURKE; R. v. CLARKSON [1986] 2 W.L.R. 294, C.A.

650. Murder—incitement to solicit—incitement to conspire
[Criminal Law Act 1977, (c.45), s.5(7).] E was charged with unlawfully inciting B to solicit, encourage, persuade, endeavour to persuade and propose to a person or persons unknown, to murder X. E offered B £1,000 to see someone who could "put a contract out" on X, saying she wanted X dead. B informed the police. E met police who were pretending to be "hit-men" and gave them details, saying that they could make it appear an accident. *Held,* dismissed E's convictions of incitement to solicit to murder and of soliciting to murder, that incitement to solicit murder was not necessarily the same as incitement to conspire with someone to murder. S.5(7) of the 1977 Act had abolished only incitement to conspire. The facts of E's incitement of B were not actually to enter into an agreement with anyone for commission of a crime, but to procure an assassin (although a conspiracy might have resulted). (*R. v. Sirat* [1986] C.L.Y. 619 considered): *R. v.* Evans [1986] Crim.L.R. 470, C.A.

651. Murder—mental element—direction equating foresight with intention
To equate foresight with intention in a direction on the *mens rea* of murder is clearly wrong as explained in recent authorities.
N was tried for murder. The Crown's case was that he poured paraffin through a house letter box and set it alight; a child died. N admitted the arson but added he did not want anyone to die. The judge's direction equated foresight with intention. *Held,* allowing the appeal and substituting a conviction for manslaughter, that in the light of subsequent authorities the direction was clearly wrong (*R. v. Moloney* [1985] C.L.Y. 642, *R. v. Hancock and Shankland* [1986] C.L.Y. 652 applied).
R. v. Nedrick [1986] 1 W.L.R. 1025, C.A.

652. Murder—mental element—foresight of consequences
The House of Lords disapproved its own recent guidelines for directions to a jury in a murder trial involving foresight of consequences.
H and S were striking miners who pushed a block of concrete off a bridge onto a motorway underneath, killing the driver of a taxi which was carrying a miner to work. They were convicted of murder after the judge had directed the jury following the guidelines laid down in *R. v. Moloney.* The Court of Appeal substituted convictions for manslaughter. *Held,* dismissing the Crown's appeal, that when it was necessary to direct a jury on the issue of intent by reference to foresight of consequences, the words "natural consequences" were not by themselves sufficient to imply probability; the judge should refer to probability and explain to the jury that the greater the probability of the consequence the more likely it was that the consequence was foreseen, and that if it was foreseen the more likely it was that it was intended; since the judge's direction was liable to have misled the jury into concentrating exclusively on the causal link between the act and its consequences, the murder convictions had been rightly quashed (dictum of Lord Bridge of Harwich in *R. v. Moloney* [1985] C.L.Y. 642 disapproved).
R. v. Hancock and Shankland [1986] 2 W.L.R. 357, H.L.

653. Murder—provocation
[Homicide Act 1957 (c.11), s.3.] D eventually admitted that he had covered his baby son with cushions and knelt on him to stop him crying. He said he had been extremely tired, trying to look after his wife and son and had been annoyed by the crying. *Held,* substituting for D's conviction of murder one of manslaughter, that the judge had erred in ruling that D was not able on such evidence to raise a defence of provocation under s.3 of the 1957 Act: *R. v.* Doughty [1986] Crim.L.R. 625, C.A.

654. Murder—verdict—jury unable to agree—conviction of manslaughter—whether proper
[Criminal Law Act 1967 (c.58), s.6(2).]
On a proper construction of s.6 of the Criminal Law Act 1967, a jury can return a verdict of guilty of manslaughter in an indictment containing only a count of murder.
S was tried on a count of murder; the prosecution had indicated they would accept a plea to manslaughter but none was forthcoming. At the end of the trial the jury were unable to agree on the murder count, and the judge directed them that a verdict of manslaughter would be acceptable. The jury returned a unanimous verdict and S was sentenced to life imprisonment. The appeal was on the point of whether, having failed to agree on the murder count before them, the jury were entitled to

return a verdict of guilty of manslaughter on that count. *Held* dismissing the appeal, that the verdict was valid.

R. *v.* SAUNDERS [1986] 1 W.L.R. 1163, C.A.

655. Natural justice—bias of judge—reasonable suspicion—justice to be seen to be done

[Scot.] At a social function a sheriff remarked in the presence of a solicitor that he would not grant legal aid to a miner. He subsequently dismissed applications by that solicitor for the sheriff to disqualify himself from hearing cases in which miners were charged with breach of the peace at picket lines. *Held,* allowing the miners' appeals against conviction that since a reasonable person on hearing of the sheriff's remark would be likely to conclude that he was biased, so far as cases involving miners were concerned, he was disqualified whether or not bias in fact existed (*Law* v. *Chartered Institute of Patent Agents* (1919) 2 Ch 276, 289 applied): BRADFORD *v.* McLEOD (1986) Crim.L.R. 690, High Court of Justiciary in Scotland.

656. Not guilty plea—plea of guilty to lesser charge included in the offence charged—effect

L's plea of guilty to unlawful wounding contrary to s.20 of the Offences Against the Person Act 1861 was not accepted and he was tried on a charge of wounding with intent, contrary to s.18. In summing up, the judge told the jury that L had pleaded guilty to s.20 and that they must in any event convict him of that. *Held,* allowing L's appeal against conviction of the s.20 offence, that such a plea not accepted by the Crown had to be withdrawn and was a nullity. L had not admitted the s.20 offence during the trial. The verdict was a nullity. (*R.* v. *Hazeltine* [1967] C.L.Y. 855 applied): R. *v.* LEE [1985] Crim.L.R. 798, C.A.

657. Obstructing a police officer—actus reus

[Police Act 1964 (c.48), s.51.] During a police raid upon a restaurant D, a customer, told X (a policewoman in plain clothes) that she would be all right if she said she had a meal and had not bought a drink after midnight. *Held,* quashing D's conviction of obstructing a police officer contrary to s.51 of the 1964 Act, that an intention to make the task of the police more difficult did not amount to obstruction in itself. It had to be shown that that task had been made more difficult by D's act (*Bastable* v. *Little* [1907] 1 K.B. 59 considered): BENNETT *v.* BALE [1986] Crim.L.R. 404, D.C.

658. Obstructing a police officer—aiding and abetting

[Police Act 1964 (c.48), s.51(3).] Police officers halted a convoy of vehicles intending to go to Stonehenge and told those in the leading vehicle they could not proceed further, whereupon the leading vehicle was driven into an adjoining field followed by the other vehicles. The respondent was in a van which, when police entered the field, was driven into and about another field causing considerable damage. After police tried unsuccessfully to stop the van, it became embedded in soft ground. The respondent and the driver shouted abuse at the officer, who had to smash a window to gain entry to arrest them. *Held,* allowing the prosecutor's appeal against an acquittal of obstructing a police officer in the execution of his duty, that the court could not see how the magistrate could properly have avoided convicting the respondent: SMITH *v.* HANCOCK [1986] Crim.L.R. 560, D.C.

659. Obstructing a police officer—aiding and abetting

[Police Act 1964 (c.48), s.51(3).] Police officers halted a convoy of vehicles intending to go to Stonehenge and told those in the leading vehicle they could not proceed further, whereupon the driver drove into an adjoining field, followed by the other vehicles. When told by loud hailers that they would be arrested if they did not leave, none left. Missiles were thrown at the police and police attempting to enter the field were attacked. The respondents were passengers in a vehicle driven at one of the police officers. *Held,* allowing the prosecutor's appeal against a finding of no case to answer on charges of wilfully obstructing a police officer in the execution of his duty, that the magistrate had erred in confining himself to considering the situation from the time when the van was driven at the officer. The convoy were resolved to confront the police and resist arrest and intended to proceed to Stonehenge knowing that thereby they would be likely to obstruct the police in the execution of their duty. The respondents being of the same mind gave encouragement to the driver, by remaining in the van, to adopt any available means to avoid their arrest (*Lewis* v. *Cox* [1984] C.L.Y. 676, *Parrish* v. *Garfitt* [1984] C.L.Y. 706, *Allen* v. *Ireland* [1984] C.L.Y. 707 and *R.* v. *Allan* [1963] C.L.Y. 621 considered): SMITH *v.* REYNOLDS [1986] Crim.L.R. 559, D.C.

660. Obstructing a police officer—wilful obstruction
[Police Act 1964 (c.48), s.51(3).] Police officers halted a convoy of vehicles intending to go to Stonehenge. D was in a coach driven by X, whom D did not know. When a sergeant told them that they would be arrested if they proceeded further, X said "my mind is made up. We will go." The passengers all got back into the coach, D thinking that X intended to drive past Stonehenge and leave the area. X drove off the road, round a police car blocking the road and towards Stonehenge. *Held*, allowing the prosecutor's appeal against a finding of no case to answer on a charge of wilfully obstructing a police officer in the execution of his duty, that the inference from D returning to the coach was that he intended to be a party to obstructing the officer in carrying out his duty: SMITH *v.* LOWE [1986] Crim.L.R. 561, D.C.

661. Obstructing highway—matters to be taken into account
[Highways Act 1980 (c.66), s.137.]
It is a matter of fact and degree whether the use made of the highway by a member of the public was so unreasonable as to amount to a wilful obstruction of free passage along the highway contrary to s.137 of the Highways Act 1980.

D was convicted of wilfully obstructing the free passage along the highway contrary to s.137 of the Highways Act 1980 by the justices. D worked as a tout for a club in Soho. On four occasions within the space of 13 minutes he was seen to approach small groups of pedestrians and engage them in conversation for a minute or so, causing the footway to become blocked and other pedestrians to pass by walking in the roadway. D's appeal to the Crown Court was unsuccessful. D appealed by way of case stated. *Held*, that a member of the public has a right to pass and re-pass along a highway and to do everything that is reasonable thereto, *e.g.* talk to a passing friend. An offence under s.137 of the Highways Act 1980 is committed where as a matter of fact and degree the use of the highway is so unreasonable as to amount to an obstruction. All the circumstances were to be considered including the length of time the obstruction continues, the place were it occurs, the purpose for which it is done and whether other persons are in fact obstructed. If the defendant was merely exercising his ordinary right of passing and re-passing any obstruction caused would not be unlawful. In the present case the finding of the justices and the Crown Court was fully justified on the evidence (*Pitcher* v. *Lockett* [1967] C.L.Y. 1796, *Nagy* v. *Weston* [1965] C.L.Y. 1778 considered).

COOPER *v.* METROPOLITAN POLICE COMMISSIONER (1986) 82 Cr.App.R. 238, D.C.

662. Obstruction of police—removal of motor vehicle—drunken driver. See LIEPENS *v.* SPEARMAN, § 2974.

663. Obtaining pecuniary advantage—tenancy of public house—whether an "office"—whether an opportunity to apply for office
[Theft Act 1968 (c.60), s.16] M made false statements in order to obtain the provisional tenancy of a public house, which took effect upon M becoming the registered holder of a justices' licence. *Held*, allowing M's appeal against conviction of obtaining a pecuniary advantage by deception contrary to s.16 of the 1968 Act, that (1) the tenant of a public house did not hold an "office" within s.16; (2) assuming that the holder of a justices' licence does hold an "office", an opportunity to apply for an office in which remuneration will be earned does not amount itself to an opportunity to earn remuneration; (3) *Obiter:* if the Crown had relied upon what M had said to the justices, that would probably have provided foundation for offences: R. *v.* McNIFF [1986] Crim.L.R. 57, C.A.

664. Offensive weapon—defence of forgetfulness—direction to jury
The trial judge must direct the jury in an offensive weapon case where the issue is forgetfulness, that the prosecution must prove the defendant had the object with him "knowingly."

Police stopped the appellant's car, and found a knife concealed under the dashboard and a cosh under the driver's seat. He was acquitted of the charge of possessing offensive weapons in a public place on the count of the knife but convicted on the cosh. His defence to the cosh had been "I put it there, but then forgot all about it." The judge failed to direct the jury that it was for the prosecution to prove that he had it with him "knowingly." *Held*, allowing the appeal, that however unlikely the defence was to succeed, the defence was properly raised and it should have been left to the jury in terms (dicta in *Sweet* v. *Parsley* [1969] C.L.Y. 2210 applied; *R.* v. *Cugullere* [1961] C.L.Y. 1646 explained).

R. *v.* RUSSELL (R.) (1985) 81 Cr.App.R. 315, C.A.

665. Offensive weapon—glass door broken in domestic dispute—assault with glass

[Vagrancy Act 1824 (5 Geo. 4, c.83), as amended by Theft Act 1968 (c.60), s.33(3), Sched. 3).]

The offence of carrying an offensive weapon contrary to s.4 of the Vagrancy Act 1824 is not the actual use of the weapon, but the premeditated carrying of the article for use.

Two police officers went to the defendant's home to deal with a domestic dispute; the door was slammed breaking the glass panel. He then lunged at the officers with the broken glass. He was convicted, *inter alia,* of having an offensive weapon with intent to commit an arrestable offence. *Held,* allowing the appeal, that the offence was not the use of the weapon but the premeditated carrying of it (*Ford* v. *Falcone* [1971] C.L.Y. 11861; *Ohlson* v. *Hylton* [1975] C.L.Y. 644 applied).

WOOD *v.* COMMISSIONER OF POLICE OF THE METROPOLIS [1986] 1 W.L.R. 796, C.A.

666. Offensive weapon—police truncheon—whether reasonable excuse

[Prevention of Crime Act 1953 (c.14), s.1(1), (3), (4); Criminal Law Act 1967 (c.58), s.2(1).] A policeman's truncheon is an offensive weapon *per se,* but carrying one as part of a fancy dress outfit, namely a policeman's uniform, is a reasonable excuse for being in possession of one. Since the potential offence was not an arrestable offence, and since H had not even been asked for his name and address, still less refused to give it, his arrest and imprisonment was unlawful (*Tims* v. *John Lewis & Co.* [1952] C.L.Y. 2157, *Wershof* v. *Commissioner of Police of the Metropolis* [1979] C.L.Y. 2093 considered): HOUGHTON *v.* CHIEF CONSTABLE OF GREATER MANCHESTER, *The Times,* July 24, 1986, C.A.

667. Offensive weapon—possession—requirements of offence

[Prevention of Crime Act 1953 (c.14), ss.1 and 4.]

An indictment of possessing an offensive weapon need not have two counts (one in respect of the weapon being offensive *per se* and the other referring to the intent of the accused).

F was found in possession of a knife in a public place and was charged with contravening s.1(1) of the Prevention of Crime Act 1953. The jury were directed to approach the case in two stages, first whether or not the weapon was offensive *per se* and, if not, whether the accused intended to cause injury to the person by use of the weapon. On appeal on the basis of a failure properly to direct the jury that it must be unanimous in concluding either that the weapon was offensive or that the accused had the necessary intent. *Held,* that no reasonable jury could have been left with the impression that some of them could base their verdict on the nature of the article, whilst others could base their verdict on the appellant's intention. They must have reached their conclusion on one basis or the other. It is unnecessary to have two counts on the indictment for such an offence (*R.* v. *Brown (K.)* [1984] C.L.Y. 624 and *R.* v. *Agbim* [1979] C.L.Y. 475 considered.)

R. *v.* FLYNN (JAMES) (1986) 82 Cr.App.R. 319, C.A.

668. Official secrets—meaning of "employed under"

[Official Secrets Act 1911 (c.28), s.2(1).] D was convicted of offences contrary to s.7 of the Official Secrets Act 1920 and s.2(1) of the 1911 Act. He had been employed under a contract with a county council but worked solely for the police as a computer operator at a police station under the supervision of a police officer and was expected by the Council to take his instructions from a police officer. The issue was whether D was a "person who was employed under" a person who held an office under Her Majesty (*i.e.* the policeman). *Held,* dismissing D's appeals, that "employed under" in s.2(1) did not mean "employed by." D had been employed under the police officer (*R.* v. *Reason* (1853) 17 J.P.R. 743 considered): LOAT *v.* JAMES [1986] Crim.L.R. 744, D.C.

669. Parole—further conviction—effect

[Criminal Justice Act 1967 (c.80), ss.60 and 62.] Where a person is sentenced to imprisonment during the currency of a parole licence in respect of a previous sentence and the court elects to revoke that licence, the defendant cannot become entitled within one year from the revocation to be considered for parole in respect of any sentence: R. _v._ McKinnon (William Harold), _The Times,_ November 26, 1986, C.A.

670. Perjury—corroboration of evidence—direction to jury
[Perjury Act 1911 (c.6), ss.1 and 13.]
Where, at the trial of a person charged with perjury, the prosecution set out to prove the falsity of statements made by the accused and did not invite a conviction on any other basis, the judge should always bring s.13 of the Perjury Act 1911 to the attention of the jury unless the accused admitted that the statement was untrue.

R obtained a divorce by forging her husband's signature on the relevant court documents. She swore an affidavit in the usual form that her husband had signed the documents. When prosecuted for perjury the only evidence of the falsity of that statement came from her husband. R appealed against conviction on the basis that the judge had failed to direct the jury's attention to s.13 of the Perjury Act 1911. _Held,_ that there had been a material irregularity but the proviso of s.2(1) of the Criminal Appeal Act 1968 would be applied.

R. _v._ Rider (Theresa Ann) (1986) 83 Cr.App.R. 207, C.A.

671. Personation of electors—parliamentary election—whether imprisonment correct
[Representation of the People Act 1983 (c.2) s.60(1).]
Two months' imprisonment on a woman of good character who had impersonated two electors at a parliamentary election upheld.

Per curiam: ordinarily a sentence of more than 2 months' imprisonment is going to be proper for the offence of personation committed during a parliamentary election.

P, a woman of impeccable character, fraudulently signed and returned a postal ballot form in the name of a man of 80, and also returned a ballot paper sent by mistake to a neighbour who had died some while earlier. She was sentenced to 2 months' imprisonment, ordered to pay £1,500 towards the costs of the prosecution, and disqualified from voting or holding public office for 5 years. _Held,_ that the offences were very grave and fully merited the immediate custodial sentence imposed. Normally a sentence of greater than 2 months' imprisonment would be proper for such an offence.

R. _v._ Phillips (C. K.) (1984) 6 Cr.App.R.(S.) 293, C.A.

672. Perverting the course of justice—police officer—discretion to abort proceedings
In trivial cases a police officer has a discretion to abort proceedings. What is a trivial case for these purposes is a question of fact for the jury.

C was a police sergeant in charge of a police station when a motorist who had provided a positive roadside breath test, was brought in for breath analysis. C recognised the motorist as the son of a police inspector who had a serious heart condition such that stress or worry might precipitate further illness. C released the motorist and was charged with conduct tending and intending to pervert the course of justice. After expert evidence had been given of a discretion to abort proceedings, the judge ruled that the existence of such a discretion depended on the seriousness of the case and it was for the jury to decide on which side of the line a case fell. C appealed. _Held,_ that the judge's approach was the right one, and the conviction was not unsafe or unsatisfactory.

R. _v._ Coxhead [1986] R.T.R. 411, C.A.

673. Plea of guilty under influence of drugs—conviction—jurisdiction to quash
S changed his plea to guilty of attempted robbery during his trial. His co-accused was acquitted. _Held,_ quashing S's conviction, that, on the evidence, there was a very real risk that S had been affected by delusion caused by L.S.D. at the time of changing his plea and for a short time thereafter. The conviction was unsafe and unsatisfactory. R. _v._ Swain [1986] Crim.L.R. 480, C.A.

674. Police and Criminal Evidence Act 1984
Police and Criminal Evidence Act 1984 Codes of Practice (Armed Forces) Order 1986 (No. 307) [40p], made under the Police and Criminal Evidence Act 1984 (c.60), s.113(5); operative on March 1, 1986; appoints March 1, 1986 as the date on which codes of practice made under s.113(3) will come into operation.

675. Police powers of entry—purpose of entry unrelated to Act empowering entry—whether entry valid
Once a police officer is lawfully on premises by virtue of the provisions of any one of the Acts giving him power to enter those premises he is lawfully there for all purposes.

Police officers entered an unlicensed night café. A power of entry was provided by s.14 of the Gaming Act 1845 for the sole purpose of detecting offences under the Misuse of Drugs Act 1971. After entry the officers saw what appeared to be prohibited drugs being discarded. They had no warrant under the Misuse of Drugs Act 1971 to search suspects. The defendant was charged with obstructing a constable in the execution of his duty. The magistrate dismissed the information on the ground that the purpose of the police entry was to search for drugs. Anything following, in the absence of a warrant was in excess of the officer's duty. *Held,* that once lawful entry had been effected, the officer was lawfully there for all purposes. In searching the defendant they were acting in the execution of their duty, notwithstanding the absence of a search warrant.

FOSTER v. ATTARD (1986) 83 Cr.App.R. 214, D.C.

676. Possession of wild bird—strict liability

[Wildlife and Countryside Act 1981 (c.69), s.1(2).] Possession under the 1981 Act is an offence of strict liability: KIRKLAND v. ROBINSON, *The Times,* December 4, 1986, D.C.

677. Power of arrest—constable—reasonable suspicion

[Criminal Law Act 1967 (c.58), s.2(4).] A constable who has formed reasonable grounds to suspect an offence has been committed is not obliged to discount all possible defences or seek complete proof before carrying out an arrest: WARD v. CHIEF CONSTABLE OF AVON AND SOMERSET CONSTABULARY, *The Times,* June 26, 1986, C.A.

678. Precedent—Divisional Court decision

H sought to argue, contrary to a previous Divisional Court decision, that evidence directed to alleged unreliability of the Lion Intoximeter generally was admissible. *Held,* dismissing H's appeal, that the Divisional Court will only depart from what was said in a previous decision when it was convinced that what was previously said was wrong (*R.* v. *Greater Manchester Coroner, ex p. Tal* [1984] C.L.Y. 447 considered): HORNIGOLD v. CHIEF CONSTABLE OF LANCASHIRE [1985] Crim.L.R. 792, D.C.

679. Prevention of shop theft

The Home Office Crime Prevention Unit has published a paper on the subject of shop theft. The report, one of a series of occasional papers, is entitled *The Prevention of Shop Theft: an approach through crime analysis.* It's author is Paul Ekblom. Copies are available free of charge from the Home Office Crime Prevention Unit, 50 Queen Anne's Gate, London SW1H 9AT. (ISBN 0 86252 237 4).

680. Probation

COMBINED PROBATION AREAS (AMENDMENT) ORDER 1986 (No. 464) [40p], made under the Powers of Criminal Courts Act 1973 (c.62), s.54(4) and Sched. 3, para. 1; operative on April 1, 1986; amends S.I. 1974 No. 529 to take account of the Local Government Act 1985.

COMBINED PROBATION AREAS (CORNWALL) ORDER 1986 (No. 2316) [45p], made under the Powers of Criminal Courts Act 1973, s.54(4) and Sched. 3, para. 1; operative on January 1, 1987; amends S.I. 1986 No. 1713 to take account of the combination of the petty sessional divisions of East Middle, East South and Liskerrett.

COMBINED PROBATION AREAS (NORTHUMBRIAN) ORDER 1986 (No. 1280) [45p], made under the Powers of Criminal Courts Act 1973 (c.62), s.54(4) and Sched. 3, para. 1; operative on September 1, 1986; amends S.I. 1974 No. 529.

COMBINED PROBATION AREAS (NORTHUMBRIA) ORDER 1986 (No. 1318) [45p], made under the Powers of Criminal Courts Act 1973, s.54(4) and Sched. 3, para. 1; operative on January 1, 1987; amends S.I. 1986 No. 1713 to take account of the combination of the petty sessional divisions of Banburgh and East Coquetdale and West Coquetdale Ward.

COMBINED PROBATION AREAS (OXFORDSHIRE) ORDER 1986 (No. 2317) [45p], made under the Powers of Criminal Courts Act 1973, s.54(4) and Sched. 3, para. 1; operative on January 1, 1987; amends S.I. 1986 No. 1713 to take account of the combination of the petty sessional divisions of Bampton East and Bampton West.

681. Probation statistics

The probation statistics for England and Wales for 1984 have been published. Copies are available from the Home Office Statistical Department, Room 844/5, 50 Queen Anne's Gate, London SW1H 9AT, or by personal application to the Publications Officer, Home Office Library. [£4·00.]

682. Prosecution of Offences Act 1985—commencement

PROSECUTION OF OFFENCES ACT 1985 (COMMENCEMENT No. 2) ORDER 1986 (No. 1029 (c.25)) [80p], made under the Prosecution of Offences Act 1985 (c.23), s.31(2)(3); brings into force on October 1, 1986, for all areas where they are not already in force sections 1–8, 10, 14, 15 (in part), 23, 25, 26, 27, Sched. 1, paras. 1–3, Sched. 2 (in part).

PROSECUTION OF OFFENCES ACT 1985 (COMMENCEMENT No. 3) ORDER 1986 (No. 1334 (c.46)) [80p], made under the Prosecution of Offences Act 1985 (c.23), s.31(2)(3); brings into force on October 1, 1986, Pt. II, and Sched. 1, paras. 6–10 and Sched. 2 (in part).

683. Prostitution—off-street offences—report. See LAW REFORM, § 1957.

684. Protection from eviction. See LANDLORD AND TENANT

685. Psychopathic offenders. See LAW REFORM, § 1958.

686. Public Order Act 1986 (c.64)

Part I of the Act creates a comprehensive and graduated range of public order offences. Three newly-defined offences of riot, violent disorder and affray replace the old common law offences. In addition, the offence of threatening behaviour, at present in s.5 of the Public Order Act, is revised and extended to private as well as public places. Finally, a new offence of disorderly conduct is created.

Part II establishes a new framework for the holding of processions, demonstrations and assemblies.

Part III of the Act introduces measures to protect individuals from those who incite racial hatred.

Part IV introduces a new exclusion order scheme which aims to tackle soccer hooliganism.

Part V of the Act contains miscellaneous provisions. New offences are created connected with the contamination of or interference with goods with the intention of causing public alarm or injury or economic loss to any person as a result of that action. The final part of the Act also creates a new police power to deal with certain acts of aggravated trespass.

Lastly, a number of amendments to the Sporting Events (Control of Alcohol, etc.) Act 1985 are made. A new offence of possessing fireworks and smoke bombs at football grounds is introduced.

The Act comes into force on a day to be appointed. The legislation in general applies to England and Wales, although some parts, most notably the incitement to racial hatred provisions, apply to Scotland. The provisions on contamination of consumer products apply to Northern Ireland.

687. Public Order Act 1986—commencement

PUBLIC ORDER ACT 1986 (COMMENCEMENT No. 1) ORDER 1986 (No. 2041 (c.77)) [80p], made under the Public Order Act 1986 (c.64), s.41; brings into force on January 1, 1987, the provisions of the 1986 Act specified in the schedule.

688. Public order—using insulting words or behaviour whereby breach of peace may be occasioned—statutory offence

[Metropolitan Police Act 1839 (c.47), s.54(13)] T asked a group of youths including G, in a shopping centre, to stop swearing. G continued, despite a warning that he might be arrested, and the others surrounded T (a police officer). Other people were in the area and a couple walked away hurriedly. T arrested G for using insulting words and behaviour, G punched T and a fight ensued. T claimed he arrested G because of the couple's reaction to G's language. *Held,* dismissing G's appeal against conviction of an offence contrary to s.54(13) of the 1839 Act as amended, that under s.54(13) the power to arrest was wider than the common law power to arrest for breach of the peace. It was not necessary to establish a reasonable belief that a breach would be committed. It was also open to the justices to convict on the basis that G used threatening, etc. words as behaviour with intent to provoke a breach of the peace (*R.* v. *Howell* [1982] C.L.Y. 151, *Read* v. *Jones* [1984] C.L.Y. 522 and

Simcock v. *Rhodes* [1978] C.L.Y. 586 considered): GRANT v. TAYLOR [1986] Crim.L.R. 252, D.C.

689. Rape—by victim's husband—separation deed—non-molestation injunction—expiry of injunction—whether implied consent revived

In June 1984 R was restrained by injunction from molesting his wife or going near to her for two months and was ordered to leave the matrimonial home. A formal deed of separation was entered into on the same day but it contained no non-cohabitation or non-molestation clause. *Held,* dismissing R's appeal against conviction of rape of his wife, that her implicit consent to intercourse with R did not revive when the injunction expired (*R.* v. *Steele* [1978] C.L.Y. 589 applied): R. v. ROBERTS [1986] Crim.L.R. 188, C.A.

690. Rape—consent—corroboration of complainant's evidence—direction to jury

Where consent is in issue on a charge of rape the jury must be directed about the necessity of corroboration of the complainant's evidence.

B, P and T were convicted of rape. The complainant, S, was a 15 year old girl who was educationally sub-normal with a mental age of about 11. S attended a party where she drank a considerable amount of alcohol and became unwell. She was placed on a bed and left lying there fully clothed. B, P and T found S there. All had sexual intercourse with her. Their defence to the charge of rape was that S had consented. The prosecution case was that S was insensible and incapable of giving any consent. S was called as a witness and gave evidence that she was aware of what was going on but did not consent. B, P and T appealed on the ground that the jury had not been directed on the necessity for corroboration of S's evidence that she had not consented. *Held,* allowing the appeals, that the issue between the prosecution and defence being whether or not S had consented it was vital that the jury should have been directed about the necessity for corroboration of S's evidence. It could not be said that no corroboration was required on account of the evidence of other witnesses at the trial, nor that the prosecution had placed minimal or no reliance upon S's evidence. Given there was a clear issue on consent it was not a proper case in which to apply the proviso to s.2 of the Criminal Appeal Act 1968 (*R.* v. *Trigg* [1963] C.L.Y. 707 applied).

R. v. BIRCHALL, POLLOCK AND TATTON (1986) 82 Cr.App.R. 208, C.A.

691. Rape—cross-examination—other sexual activity of complainant

[Sexual Offences (Amendment) Act 1976 (c.82), s.2.] The complainant should be allowed to be questioned about other similar events if it would be unfair to the defendant to prevent such a line of cross-examination (*R.* v. *Viola* [1982] C.L.Y. 596 considered): R. v. COX (DAVID), *The Times,* June 18, 1986, C.A.

692. Reckless driving—high speed chase through city—whether imprisonment appropriate

Immediate imprisonment may be appropriate for reckless driving involving a high speed chase through the streets of a city but the sentence of 9 months would be cut to 4.

M drove powerful car at high speed through the streets of London at 5 a.m., going through a number of traffic lights and being pursued all the while by a police car. He skidded often, and drove on the pavement. *Held,* that immediate imprisonment was correct for this was a serious case of bad driving, but 9 months was too long as M had no record of bad driving. A sentence of 4 months would be imposed.

R. v. MODESTE (1984) 6 Cr.App.R.(S.) 221, C.A.

693. Rehabilitation of offenders

REHABILITATION OF OFFENDERS ACT 1974 (EXCEPTIONS) (AMENDMENT) ORDER 1986 (No. 1249) [80p], made under the Rehabilitation of Offenders Act 1974 (c.53), s. 4(4); operative on July 18, 1986; amends S.I. 1975 No. 1023 so that neither section 4(2) nor section 4(3)(*b*) of the 1974 Act apply to offices or employments which involve access to persons under 18 years of age.

REHABILITATION OF OFFENDERS ACT 1974 (EXCEPTIONS) (Amendment No. 2) ORDER 1986 (No. 2268) [80p], made under Rehabilitation of Offenders Act 1974 (c.53), ss.4(4), 7(4), 10(1); in part operative on January 1, 1987 otherwise on same date as Financial Services Act 1986, s.189, Sched. 14 comes into force; amends S.I. 1975 No. 1023 in relation to the Building Societies Commission.

694. Remands in custody
The Home Office has published a consultation document on remands in custody. The document proposes changes to the procedure for assessing the length of the remand period. Copies of the document are available from the Home Office, C2 Division, Room 416, 50 Queen Anne's Gate, London SW1H 9AT. Tel: 01-213-3205. Comments should be sent to that address by January 31, 1987.

695. Reparation—consultative document. See LAW REFORM, § 1959.

696. Repatriation of prisoners
REPATRIATION OF PRISONERS (OVERSEAS TERRITORIES) ORDER 1986 (No. 2226) [£1·90], made under the Repatriation of Prisoner Act 1984 (c.47), s.9(4); operative on February 1, 1987; extends the provisions of the 1984 Act to specified territories.

697. Repatriation of Prisoners Act 1984
REPATRIATION OF PRISONERS ACT 1984 (ISLE OF MAN) ORDER 1986 (No. 598) [80p], made under the Repatriation of Prisoners Act 1984 (c.47), s.9(4); operative on April 26, 1986; extends to the Isle of Man the provisions of the 1984 Act.

698. Research and Planning Unit programme
The Home Office has published the 1986–87 research programme of its Research and Planning Unit. Copies of the programme are available free of charge from the Research and Planning Unit, Room 278, 50 Queen Anne's Gate, London SW1H 9AT.

699. Research studies
A collection of research studies has been published by the Home Office Research and Planning Unit. Research Bulletin No. 20 contains 13 articles on various aspects of the criminal justice system. Copies of the Bulletin are available from Research and Planning Unit, Home Office, 50 Queen Anne's Gate, London SW1H 9AT.
The Home Office Research and Planning Unit has published a collection of research studies which examine the various aspects of the criminal justice system. *Research Bulletin 21* is available from Research and Planning Unit, Home Office, 50, Queen Anne's Gate, London SW1H 9AT.
The Home Office Research and Planning Unit has published a collection of research studies in Research Bulletin 22. The Bulletin contains 10 articles which reflect the range of the Unit's work. Copies are available from the Home Office Research and Planning Unit, 50 Queen Anne's Gate, London SW1H 9AT.

700. Robbery—street mugging—defendant under 21—whether custodial sentence
Street mugging of two elderly women: 5 years' youth custody upheld.
O'B was the driver of a car used by two other robbers to make their escape after two separate robberies of elderly women, one aged 90, and the other aged 83. As a result of injuries sustained in the course of the robbery it was likely that the 83 year old lady would be bed-ridden for the remainder of her life. *Held,* that 5 years' youth custody was entirely appropriate for such a crime, whether the appellant was a "mere" driver of the escape car, or one of the active participants.
R. *v.* O'BRIEN (1984) 6 Cr.App.R.(S.) 274, C.A.

701. Sale of prescription only medicine—whether offence of strict liablity
[Medicines Act 1968 (c.67), s.58(2)(*a*).]
S.58(2(*a*) of the Medicines Act 1968 creates an offence of strict liability.
The stipendiary magistrate dismissed certain informations against the defendant Pharmaceutical Society, alleging sale of medicine contrary to s.58(2) and 67(2) of the Medicines Act 1968. The magistrate was of the view that the offences required proof of *mens rea. Held,* allowing the prosecution's appeal, that s.58(2)(*a*) of the Medicines Act 1968 creates an offence of strict liability.
PHARMACEUTICAL SOCIETY OF GREAT BRITAIN *v.* STORKWAIN [1986] 2 All E.R. 635, H.L.

702. Self defence—honest belief—whether reasonableness of belief relevant
A was alleged to have run at X with his arms raised and, when X raised her arms to protect herself, to have pushed her, causing her to fall to the ground. A alleged that X had leapt at him and that he grabbed her wrists, thinking that X intended to scratch him, as a result of which X fell. *Held,* dismissing A's appeal against conviction of assault occasioning actual bodily harm, that (1) as the simple question was whether the prosecution had proved that X had not come at A with her arms

raised, no question of A's belief or of mistake arose; (2) had it been necessary to decide the question, the court would have been minded to say that Lane, C.J.'s judgment in *Gladstone Williams* correctly set out the test where, in relation to self defence, an issue arises as to the defendant's belief in the existence of a state of affairs (*i.e.* once the belief is found to have been genuinely held, reasonableness of the belief is irrelevant) (*R.* v. *Williams (Gladstone)* [1984] C.L.Y 502 approved; *R.* v. *Abraham* [1973] C.L.Y. 481, *R.* v. *Chisam* [1963] C.L.Y. 784, *R.* v. *Fennell* [1970] C.L.Y. 418 and *D.P.P.* v. *Morgan* [1975] C.L.Y. 682 considered): R. v. ASBURY [1986] Crim.L.R. 258, C.A.

703. Sentence—adjournment to obtain social enquiry report—indication of probability of custodial sentence
Where a sentencer adjourns for a social enquiry report and community service assessment, but makes it clear that a custodial sentence is the likely course, no expectation of a non-custodial sentence is created and there is no injustice in the sentencer imposing a custodial report when the social enquiry report recommends community service. The appellants were convicted of robbery. After conviction the judge adjourned for a social enquiry report but said that "an immediate custodial sentence is likely to be the conclusion that it will come to" and indicated later that he felt that a custodial sentence was likely. The reports described the appellants as suitable for community service but both were sentenced to detention centre orders of three months: *Held,* that the judge made it quite plain that a custodial sentence was the likely outcome. No expectation of a non-custodial sentence can have been created and so the principles set out in the cases of *R.* v. *Gillam* (1980) 2 Cr.App.R.(S.) 267 and *R.* v. *Millwood* [1983] C.L.Y. 761 have no application to the present case. The judge acted properly in imposing custodial sentences and the sentences were not too long for this type of offence: (*R.* v. *Gillam* (1980) 2 Cr.App.R.(S) 267 and *R.* v. *Millwood* [1983] C.L.Y. 761 distinguished).
R. v. HORTON AND ALEXANDER (1985) 7 Cr.App.R.(S.) 299, C.A.

704. Sentence—affray—guidelines
The leaders and organisers of serious affrays can expect sentences of seven years imprisonment and upwards. Sentences on others more marginally involved should reflect their individual circumstances: R. v. KEYS, *The Times,* November 22, 1986, C.A.

705. Sentence—affray—spontaneous affray
In dealing with affrays a distinction must be drawn between deliberate, premeditated affrays and spontaneous affrays.
The appellants pleaded guilty or were convicted of affray. They had been drinking heavily in a number of public houses on a "stag night" when a fight broke out between the appellants and another party. Several people were injured. Those convicted were sentenced to three years' imprisonment or youth custody. Those who pleaded guilty received two years' imprisonment. *Held,* that this was not a premeditated affray. No weapons were taken along. It was a case of a party getting out of hand. Although a deterrent sentence was necessary, the sentences imposed failed to take into account the distinction between premeditated and spontaneous affrays. Accordingly the sentences would be reduced to two years' and 18 months' imprisonment.
R. v. ANDERSON (1985) 7 Cr.App.R.(S.) 210, C.A.

706. Sentence—appeal from justices—power of Crown Court
[Magistrates' Courts Act 1980 (c.43), s.10(3); Supreme Court Act 1981 (c.54), s.48.] The court cannot adjourn after conviction solely to allow D to reach the age of 21 before sentence: ARTHUR v. STRINGER, *The Times,* October 11, 1986, D.C.

707. Sentence—appeal—police informer
D's sentence of nine years imprisonment for robbery was reduced to six years in consideration of his having given information to the police: R. v. McEVILLY, *The Times,* November 4, 1986, C.A.

708. Sentence—appeals
Adjournment for reports
R. v. RENNES [1986] Crim.L.R. 193 (Magistrates adjourned R's case to obtain a social enquiry report and a community service assessment; despite favourable assessment, committed to Crown Court for sentence—12 months' imprisonment

altered to conditional discharge since R's legitimate expectation that a community service order would be made if the reports were favourable ought not to have been defeated and R had already served 5 months—sentence otherwise proper and appeal would have been dismissed if R had not been led to expect community service if reports favourable: no warning given by the magistrates when case adjourned).

709. *Arson*
R. *v.* BROWNSWORD [1986] Crim.L.R. 638 (pleaded guilty to arson and criminal damage—sentencer referred to fact that house next door was occupied—since no charge of arson involving recklessness, improper to refer to family next door when sentencing but sentences upheld as correct in any event).

710. *Breach of trust*
R. *v.* MOSSOP [1986] Crim.L.R. 72 (Dentist made false remission claims re patients allegedly exempt from charges, false claims of emergency treatment and a claim re a fictitious patient; £6,826 to £10,000 obtained over at least 9 months—9 months' imprisonment upheld).

711. R. *v.* POULTER [1986] Crim.L.R. 73 (Aged 27—postman opened letters likely to contain small amounts of cash, including letters to children and on one occasion stole a parcel containing a bathroom cabinet; total amount stolen: £100—18 months' imprisonment reduced to 12 to reflect plea of guilty and evident remorse).

712. *Causing death by reckless driving*
R. *v.* DANIELS [1986] Crim.L.R. 484 (After drinking four pints of beer drove with drinking friends and tried to overtake shortly before corner; passengers killed in ensuing crash—74 microgrammes of alcohol per 100 millilitres of breath—18 months' imprisonment reduced to 12; five-year disqualification reduced to three).

713. *Community service*
R. *v.* WHITTINGHAM [1986] Crim.L.R. 572 (180 hours' community service; failed to attend regularly after performing 68½ hours—order revoked and two months' imprisonment substituted with no credit being given for satisfactory completion of 68½ hours—sentence varied to allow immediate release, 2½ weeks having been served, as credit should be given for the 68½ hours completed).

714. R. *v.* WILLIAMS [1986] Crim.L.R. 754 (helped burglar to move stolen property to different address—180 hours' community service—after completing 149 hours remanded in custody several months re matters in which prosecution ultimately offered no evidence; failed to resume community service even after brought before magistrates for breach—eventually, at Crown Court, sentenced to 12 months' imprisonment for original offence—suspended for two years—reduced to three months suspended, to give credit for community service performed).

715. *Compensation—counsel's duties*
R. *v.* BOND [1986] Crim.L.R. 413 (aged 64; stole employers' property worth £8,192 over two-year period—no previous convictions—six month's imprisonment suspended and £3,200 compensation order—mitigation on basis B may be able to pay substantial compensation and that employers had retained £3,000 owing to B in wages during suspension since commencement of investigation—in fact employers owed only £604 wages and paid this to B, who used £400 to pay mortgage arrears and balance to pay debts; B was on supplementary benefit and had no capital—compensation order quashed: counsel should be wary of instructions of this kind given orally on day of hearing and court should be careful to ensure there was proper financial basis for compensation order).

716. *Compensation order*
R. *v.* BUTT [1986] Crim.L.R. 755 (obtained supplementary benefit for two years by deception—18 months' imprisonment with £6,540·56 compensation order, on basis that B had house which could be sold—compensation order quashed: even if there was a house, compensation order inappropriate where only asset from which order could be satisfied was matrimonial home still occupied by members of defendant's family).

717. R. *v.* HILLS [1986] Crim.L.R. 756 (book-keeper stole £6,058 in sophisticated way— 100 hours' community service and £5,000 compensation order to be paid at £200 per month—compensation order reduced to £1,440 payable at £120 per month: H could afford only £120 per month and usual maximum period for compensation should be 12 months).

718.   R. v. HUISH [1985] Crim.L.R. 800 (Before sentence H's counsel told the judge H had sufficient assets to pay £22,900 compensation in full—on appeal out of time it was shown that H could not do so; he claimed he had been too afraid to say so in case he was sent to prison—compensation order quashed—before compensation orders made, evidence should be given orally or on affidavit; most careful examination required).

719. *Conspiracy to manufacture amphetamine*
     R. v. MORGAN [1986] Crim.L.R. 485 (M pleaded guilty; B and A were convicted—concerned with others in producing amphetamine sulphate and planned to produce two kilos per week (street value £20,000 per kilo); conspiracy lasted about three months; about 2½ kilos sold—seven years' imprisonment for A, eight for B and six for M upheld).

720.   R. v. SHAW [1986] Crim.L.R. 485 (Arranged to purchase substantial amount of B.M.K. and took delivery of 112 litres, for which paid £7,700 cash—arrested on returning to flat with next part of consignment—other chemicals necessary for production of amphetamine sulphate found in flat—profits might have been £2 million to £7 million—10 years' imprisonment upheld: manufacture was analogous to importing).

721. *Corruption*
     R. v. OZDEMIR [1986] Crim.L.R. 263 (Age: 38; convicted of corruption; offered police officer £50 or free meal at O's restaurant not to report O's son for driving without a licence—no previous convictions—12 months' imprisonment with six to serve and remainder suspended—three months' immediate imprisonment substituted).

722. *Custody for life*
     R. v. TURTON [1986] Crim.L.R. 642 (Age: 17—broke into school and caused extensive damage; threatened youth in street at midnight with breadknife, demanding money and when youth ran away caused wounds to face and hand—five offences taken into consideration including assault by striking another on head with pint glass—several previous appearances including burglary, assault, criminal damage and threatening behaviour—not mentally ill—custody for life for the attempted robbery and wounding with intent; 12 months' youth custody for burglary—varied to eight years' youth custody: sentencer had not had in mind criteria in *R. v. Pither* (1979) 1 Cr.App.R.(S.) 209).

723. *Defendant's misconduct in court—relevance to sentence*
     R. v. POWELL [1985] Crim.L.R. 802 (Original sentence: 3 months' detention; following swearing and shouting from the dock, sentence altered to 6 months' youth custody—original sentence restored: contempt should be dealt with separately under clear procedure laid down, not by review of original sentence).

724/5. *Detention of juvenile—youth custody—credit for time in care in secure accommodation pending trial*
     R. v. MURPHY AND DUKE [1986] Crim.L.R. 571 (M: 16, D: 17; broke into house, stole items including shotgun cartridges; later returned and stole shotgun; agreed with X to rob shop; shortened barrel; failed to carry out robbery as too many people around but subsequently committed robbery at garage stealing £136 and cigarettes, D carrying gun—M: four years' detention; D: four years' youth custody—reduced on appeal by six months in each case to take into account period spent in secure accommodation in assessment centre pending trial).

726. *Disqualification*
     R. v. LANE [1986] Crim.L.R. 574 (Age: 18 or 19; used car in course of burglary—sentences: detention centre orders for some; community service for others—all disqualified from driving under Powers of Criminal Courts Act 1973, s.44—though not wrong in principle, disqualifications quashed as before ordering such disqualification the court should indicate to counsel it had in mind such order and should give counsel opportunity to draw attention of court to any relevant considerations).

727. *Extended sentence*
     R. v. PARKER [1985] Crim.L.R. 804 (Burglaries of dwelling-houses—5 years' imprisonment, certified as an extended sentence—4 years' ordinary imprisonment

substituted as P had kept out of trouble for 13 months following his last release from prison: extended sentence only appropriate where defendant had made no attempt to rehabilitate himself and had commenced committing offences almost immediately after last release from prison).

728. *Factual basis for sentence*
R. *v.* BENT [1986] Crim.L.R. 415 (aged 20; stole scotch eggs from supermarket; prosecution alleged B punched security officer and hit him with stick; B claimed he pushed the officer and threatened with stick—unfavourable social enquiry report—nine months' youth custody, judge referring to B having hit security officer with stick—upheld: trial of issue not necessary where no substantial conflict and difference was only in emphasis, as in degree; gravamen of charge was resisting arrest).

729. R. *v.* HAWKINS [1986] Crim.L.R. 194 (Pleaded guilty to burglary—dropped brother and another off and drove back to collect them 1 hour later after burglary committed—claimed did not know of plan to commit burglary and pleaded guilty on basis only realised when returned to collect others but became party to the theft at that stage—sentenced on basis H's account rejected without evidence on the issue being heard—appeal dismissed: since H's claim manifestly false and incredible, judge entitled to reject it without hearing evidence).

730. R. *v.* MACKENZIE [1986] Crim.L.R. 346 (M was alleged to have hidden in a cubicle of a ladies' lavatory and to have attacked a lady, hitting her several times and trying to put a bicycle tyre around her arms, causing cuts and bruising to the lady, who escaped with her handbag and shopping—pleaded guilty to assault occasioning actual bodily harm but denied using tyre and any motive of theft and claimed he had gone to lavatory because drunk—sentencer accepted prosecution version without evidence being called—*Held,* though defence version absurd, judge should not have sentenced without more: might have heard M's evidence and then only heard victim's evidence if M's was in the slightest degree credible; might also have reminded M's counsel that discount for plea might be largely nullified if victim caused to give evidence—three years' imprisonment reduced to two as M now had to be sentenced on his own version).

731. R. *v.* SMITH [1986] Crim.L.R. 640 (using firearm with intent to resist arrest—issue as to whether air-pistol discharged towards police officer accidentally or intending to shoot him—three years' imprisonment reduced to two because sentencer had sentenced on basis of intention to shoot: although defence counsel had declined judge's offer to try the issue, indicating that he preferred to rely upon S's statement to the police, it was for the court to decide whether to try the issue of fact if relevant to sentence and it should do so if not prepared to sentence on basis of defendant's version).

732. *Indecent assault by woman*
R. *v.* HANCOCK [1986] Crim.L.R. 697 (Age: under 21—whilst in charge of neighbour's three-year-old son, masturbated him, bit his penis, inserted finger in anal passage and invited him to fondle her indecently; other occasions invited boys aged 11 and 12 to fondle her indecently—12 months' youth custody for indecent assault upheld: in most cases women offenders to be treated on same basis as men—court disapproved of practice of imposing no separate penalty on certain counts in indictment).

733. *Indecent assault—persistent offender*
R. *v.* HOUGHTON [1986] Crim.L.R. 566 (Aged 27—pleaded guilty to two indecent assaults on nine-year-old son of woman in whose home H was staying and eight-year-old son of a friend of that woman; touched boy's penis in each case but desisted when boy objected—five previous appearances for similar offences and one buggery: sentences up to 30 months' imprisonment—had severe personality disorder but not violent or aggressive—likely to repeat such offences—six years' imprisonment with six months consecutive for earlier offence for which on probation—reduced to four years with six months consecutive since statutory procedure for extended sentence had not been used).

734. *Importing cocaine*
R. *v.* RYAN [1986] Crim.L.R. 757 (imported 881 grammes cocaine worth £140,000—pleaded not guilty—nine years' imprisonment upheld).

734a. R. v. VAN HUBBARD [1986] Crim.L.R. 758 (went through green customs channel with 177 grammes cocaine in jacket sleeve with street value £26,000—seven previous convictions including one for importing cannabis—pleaded guilty—six years' imprisonment upheld: experienced traveller warned by previous conviction rather than courier).

734b. *Juvenile—detention*

R. v. SMITH [1986] Crim.L.R. 343 (Age: under 17—six months' youth custody for one assault occasioning actual bodily harm, 12 months for another and 18 months' detention under s.53(2) of the Children and Young Persons Act 1933 for blackmail— 18 months' detention reduced to 12 months' youth custody, although longer sentence might well have been passed, since court had to begin on assumption 18 months was correct and it had been held that where 18 months was suitable, there was insufficient differential between that and maximum youth custody (12 months) to make youth custody unsuitable).

735. *Juvenile—detention—affray*

R. v. RHOOMS [1986] Crim.L.R. 567 (Aged 16—with others attacked two men; R struck one with knife, causing wound to hip, and threatened other with knife; minor injuries to both victims—co-defendant sentenced to 18 months' youth custody for affray—psychiatric report described R as having character disorder with poor impulse control but no formal psychiatric disorder—six years' detention reduced to four).

736. *Juvenile—detention—arson*

R. v. CUMMINS [1986] Crim.L.R. 483 (Age: 16—broke into youth club, drank, tried to steal from machine and set fire to premises by lighting chairs after stacking them—cost of replacing building £235,000—five other offences taken into consideration including entering schools and causing damage—five years' detention upheld).

737. *Juvenile—detention—burglary*

R. v. HORROCKS [1986] Crim.L.R. 412 (aged 16; with another broke into house and stole property worth several £100's and caused extensive damage; on occasion attempted to burgle another house; twice handled property stolen in other burglaries— several previous findings of guilt for theft, disorderly behaviour and criminal damage—sentence: 18 months' detention under Children and Young Persons Act 1933, s.53(2) for burglary with 12 months' youth custody for attempt and six for handling, all concurrent—12 months' youth custody substituted for the 18 months sentence as sentences had inappropriately used s.53(2) to get round restrictions on length of youth custody sentences: generally s.53(2) used for substantial terms of three years or more).

738. *Juvenile—detention—lack of powers where no conviction on indictment*

R. v. CORCORAN [1986] Crim.L.R. 568 (Aged 17; very serious robberies, burglaries, etc.—committed to Crown Court for sentence under Magistrates' Courts Act 1980, s.37—three years' detention under Children and Young Persons Act 1933, s.53(2) quashed, though entirely deserved, since no power to order s.53(2) detention in absence of conviction on indictment; 12 months' youth custody substituted: justices should not accept jurisdiction in cases of such gravity).

739. *Juvenile detention—robbery*

R. v. DAVIS [1986] Crim.L.R. 486 (Ages: all 15 or 16—agreed to rob garage by holding up attendant with a pistol loaded with darts—went to garage and abandoned plan because little in till—next week F and P and robbed girl cashier of £100 at another garage, threatening with pistol—F and P: 30 months' detention with concurrent sentences for the offences; D: 21 months' detention—F's and P's sentences upheld, though normally s.53(2) detention only appropriate for at least three years: extremely serious offence for which three years could have been imposed; other concurrent sentences reduced to 12 months' youth custody—D's sentence reduced to 12 months' youth custody since s.53(2) detention inappropriate where sentence only nine months longer than maximum youth custody).

740. R. v. METCALFE [1986] Crim.L.R. 569 (Aged 16; committed to Crown Court for sentence for two burglaries under Magistrates' Courts Act 1980, s.37—pleaded guilty to indictment alleging attempted robbery: broke into home of 69-year-old man carrying axe and wearing hood and ran away when man blew whistle—four years' detention under Children and Young Persons Act 1933, s.53(2) for attempted robbery and two years' concurrent for burglaries—four year sentence reduced to three years in view of frankness, admissions and plea and since sentencer had wrongly said appropriate sentence might have been seven years if M were adult).

741. *Kidnapping*

R. *v.* MOIED [1986] Crim.L.R. 488 (M employed W and X, private detectives, to bring back to the family home A's 20-year-old daughter, who had moved away to go to college, for a fee of £3,000—W and X persuaded her to go with them by pretending to be police and that her sister was seriously ill; blindfolded her during seven-hour journey—held at house of nephew (AM) until A confessed during police interview—A: 18 months' imprisonment; M: two years; AM: six months (for false imprisonment); W: three years—upheld).

742. R. *v.* RAPHAEL [1985] Crim.L.R. 803 (After X left R, taking their child, R visited house where X staying, forced entry into room, struck X with hammer on thigh, dragged her to car and drove her to flat where they had been living—18 months' imprisonment upheld).

743. *Living on earnings of prostitution*

R. *v.* EL-GAZZAR [1986] Crim.L.R. 698 (operated escort agency for prostitutes visiting clients in hotels and other premises; prostitutes collected £3 agency fee and charged own fee in addition—no inducements, threats or force—12 months' imprisonment and £2,000 fine with 90 days' imprisonment in default upheld: *R. v. Farrugia* [1979] C.L.Y. 540 approved; *R. v. Colton* [1981] C.L.Y. 525 disapproved).

744. *Long-term detention of juvenile for series of petty offences*

R. *v.* CRAIG [1986] Crim.L.R. 640 (Age: 16—burgled old people's homes pretending to be police officer and stealing small sums—many previous appearances: detention centre twice; supervision orders—five years' detention under Children and Young Persons Act 1933, s.53(2) upheld).

745. *Manslaughter*

R. *v.* HARWOOD [1986] Crim.L.R. 264 (Drug addict whose prescribed dose was being reduced attacked 96-year-old grandmother when she refused to discuss problems—repeated blows about head with brick wrapped in shirt—then ransacked house seeking money or drugs—convicted of manslaughter on indictment for murder—many previous convictions none since 1972—10 years' imprisonment upheld).

746. R. *v.* PHILLIPS [1985] Crim.L.R. 802 (During argument with X, struck X about face causing X to fall and strike head, suffering fatal injuries—about 12 months' imprisonment (or even sometimes no imprisonment) usually appropriate in cases of manslaughter by punch causing victim to fall and strike head on pavement; in this case P had propensity to behave violently; accordingly, 7 years' imprisonment reduced to 2).

747. R. *v.* TOMINEY [1986] Crim.L.R. 639 (whilst appellants were attempting to rob a van, a sawn-off shotgun accidentally went off causing fatal injuries to a security guard—Sentences: 22, 18 and 17 years' imprisonment respectively for manslaughter; for attempted robbery: 15 years for one who pleaded guilty and 12 for the others—submitted that where manslaughter was in course of a criminal act, sentence should not greatly exceed that for the substantive offence—22 years' sentence reduced to 18, 18 year sentence to 14 and 17 years sentence to 13 since the manslaughter sentences were higher than necessary).

748. *Parole—irrelevance in sentencing*

R. *v.* KENWAY AND CUNNINGHAM [1986] Crim.L.R. 345 (Judge commented when passing extended sentence on C that if he passed sentence reflecting gravity of offence alone (about two years' imprisonment) C would be released on licence after about eight months, which would not sufficiently protect the public against C—C's total sentences reduced from five years extended to three, not extended: improper to take parole into account when sentencing and extended sentence should not be passed when, as here, offender had endeavoured to lead an honest life for a period after his most recent release from custody; K's sentence reduced from 21 months' to 15 months' imprisonment).

749. *Possessing stolen travellers' cheques with intent*

R. *v.* LIMA [1986] Crim.L.R. 129 (Aged 53; pleaded guilty—found at airport with 9 different passports, 2 identity cards and stolen travellers' cheques with face value £22,000—3 previous convictions, one being in England in 1974; escaped from sentence imposed in 1974—5 years' imprisonment reduced to 3½ years in view of guilty plea and fact sentence to be served consecutively to 1974 sentence).

750. *Probation*

R. *v.* BARNETT [1986] Crim.L.R. 758 (theft of tape recorder from shop—committed further theft day before sentenced—consented to probation order if alternative was imprisonment but B said he considered it an onerous sentence—order upheld: defendant should have full appreciation of the realistic alternatives when considering whether or not to consent to probation; here, a short custodial sentence was probably the only alternative—B's consent was therefore valid).

751. *Probation order—court's power to deal with breach of suspended sentence*

R. *v.* BARNES [1986] Crim.L.R. 573 (Arson—two years' probation and suspended sentence of nine months' imprisonment for previous driving offences dealt with by extending operational period for two years from date of probation order—held: technically court had power to deal with suspended sentence because did so on same occasion as making probation order but not desirable to have probation order running with suspended sentence; accordingly, probation order quashed but supervision order added to suspended sentence).

752. *Relevance of defence allegations against police*

R. *v.* EVANS [1986] Crim.L.R. 757 (sentencer commented that normally would impose fine for offence such as E's but took into account E's attitude to society and in particular the police, as evidenced by allegations made by E against one officer—three months' imprisonment suspended for one year varied to £25 fine: fact that offender attacked police in course of defence should not add to sentence).

753. *Relevance of sentence causing likely separation of woman and young child*

R. *v.* OULESS AND OULESS [1986] Crim.L.R. 702 (Mr. O pleaded guilty to series of offences concerning robberies of banks, post offices and shop in most of which sawn-off shotgun carried and in some of which warning shots fired; £61,000 total stolen—Mrs. O pleaded guilty to five robberies or attempted robberies: had helped plan them and had waited for Mr. O in car whilst robberies taking place—she was pregnant; gave birth some time after sentenced—15 years' imprisonment for Mr. O upheld; five years' youth custody for Mrs. O upheld: submission that sentence should be reduced to term which, after allowing for remission, would allow mother and child not to be separated under normal Home Office practice rejected: sentencers should ignore remission and treatment of the child was matter for Home Office).

754. *Robbery*

R. *v.* O'DRISCOLL [1986] Crim.L.R. 701 (With another went into home of man aged 80, hit him over head, shoulders and legs with hammer, found wallet, held lighted poker to his face and tied him up with wire and gagged him—15 years' imprisonment upheld).

755. *Social security fraud*

R. *v.* MITCHELL [1986] Crim.L.R. 265 (Age: 28—obtained unemployment benefit totalling £5,000, to which not entitled, by deception—offences began shortly after put on probation for deception and theft—drew some benefit using false name—18 months' imprisonment reduced to nine).

756. *Supplementary benefits fraud*

R. *v.* FORD [1986] Crim.L.R. 483 (Obtained supplementary benefit over six-year period; he and wife employed during first three years; wife employed part-time during last three years; £7,265 overpayment—12 months' imprisonment upheld: longer sentences should be passed for such offences than had been passed for several years).

757. *Suspended sentence—activation*

R. *v.* JAGODZINSKI [1986] Crim.L.R. 700 (12 months' imprisonment suspended for two years with supervision order for stabbing wife following matrimonial problems—subsequently fined £75 for possessing small amount of cannabis during operational period of suspended sentence—Crown Court order activating suspended sentence with term reduced to eight months quashed).

758. *Suspended sentence—activation—after community service order imposed*

R. *v.* CRESSWELL [1986] Crim.L.R. 565 (Aged 22—six months' imprisonment suspended for two years for shoplifting—three months later magistrates imposed 240 hours' community service order for offence committed in breach of the suspended sentence—order in Crown Court, activating suspended sentence and quashing the community service order, quashed: though court had sympathy with sentencer, Crown Court had lost opportunity as result of magistrates' court order, since C had ensured that the magistrates were aware of the suspended sentence).

759. Theft—by accountant
R. v. MILLER [1986] Crim.L.R. 127 (Pleaded guilty—assistant chief cashier with considerable control over company's accounts stole over £500,000 over 9 years; some repaid; final deficiency exceeded £300,000—4 years' imprisonment reduced to 3).

760. Theft—by conveyancer
R. v. GRANT [1986] Crim.L.R. 127 (Pleaded guilty—cut price conveyancer competing with solicitors lost £22,000 of clients' money by gambling; used whole of bankers' draft, received from another couple for purchase of house, in further gambling—previously in prison for robbery and blackmail committed in order to obtain money for gambling—psychiatric report indicated G a psychopathic gambler—4 years' imprisonment upheld as appropriate even after giving discount for plea).

761. Theft—by employee
R. v. KELLY [1986] Crim.L.R. 641 (Shop assistant stole from till £50, £9·98 and £17·56 respectively on separate occasions—pleaded not guilty—six months' imprisonment upheld).

762. Theft—by solicitor
R. v. OFFORD [1986] Crim.L.R. 192 (Solicitor pleaded guilty to defrauding clients of £242,000 total over 18 month period—5 years' imprisonment reduced to 2).

763. Threatening to kill
R. v. BOWDEN [1986] Crim.L.R. 699 (Woman with whom B had lived for three years with her children rejected him after period in hospital when B treated for alcoholism; B knocked on her door late at night and threatened her brandishing sword from his collection; barricaded himself with her in bedroom for two hours until police forced way in—five years' imprisonment upheld).

764. Young offender
R. v. McKENNA [1986] Crim.L.R. 195 (Aged 16—convicted of rape and indecent assault—sentences: 2 years' detention under Children and Young Persons Act 1933, s.53(2) for rape and 12 months consecutive for robbery for which magistrates had committed M for sentence under Magistrates' Courts Act 1980, s.37—varied to 3 years' detention for rape with no separate sentence for robbery, since no power existed to impose detention under s.53(2) on a committal for sentence; undesirable to vary the 12 months' detention to 12 months' youth custody in view of difference in methods of release on licence from the 2 types of sentence).

765. Youth custody
R. v. BASSETT (Girl aged 20—went on shoplifting expedition—arrested and bailed—went on second expedition within week—in breach of prior conditional discharge, of bail condition and failing to surrender—served nine days on remand prior to sentence—judge said she had failed to co-operate, committed an offence on bail, and unless a custodial sentence was imposed she would continue to commit offences—sentenced to two months' youth custody on each count to run consecutively (four months in total)—on appeal, judge said four months was too stringent a reaction—appeal allowed in part to substitute a term of youth custody to effect her immediate release), November 28, 1985, C.A. (Ex rel. G. J. Reeds, Barrister).

766. R. v. McAUSLANE [1986] Crim.L.R. 126 (Pleaded guilty—attempted to snatch young woman's handbag and stabbed her in back when she resisted, causing severe injuries which were successfully repaired by surgery—no previous convictions—6 years' youth custody in all upheld).

767. R. v. REYNOLDS [1986] Crim.L.R. 125 (Pleaded guilty to robbery and attempted robbery—attack on old lady, pushing her to ground and stealing handbag containing £38; subsequently went into shop with accomplice, concealing faces and with pistol—but fleeing when threatened with knitting needle—no previous convictions—12 months' youth custody upheld despite guilty plea as lesser sentence would be inadequate).

768. R. v. RICHARDS [1986] Crim.L.R. 414 (aged 17; planned mugging of 53-year-old man, knocking him unconscious and kicking his shoulder, stealing wallet with £620; two burglaries of shops; 18 similar offences taken into consideration ("sneak thefts" from shops)—three previous convictions for dishonesty—three years' youth custody for robbery with six months consecutive for burglaries upheld: without guilty plea, proper total sentence would have been 4½ years' youth custody).

769. Sentence—armed robbery of sub post offices—length of sentence

Sentences of 14 years' imprisonment are appropriate penalties for offences of robbery and attempted robbery at two sub post offices.

F and another pleaded guilty to robbery and attempted robbery of sub post offices. Both offences involved the use of armed weapons and were well planned. Violence was used against staff or customers. Both men had poor criminal records and a history of drug addiction. They were sentenced to 14 years' imprisonment. *Held,* that sub post offices are by nature more in need of protection than High Street banks as they are relatively defenceless and so need all the protection that the court can afford them. The fact that one of the appellants was the getaway driver does not reduce the role he played in the robbery and so does not avail him and he is equally deserving of a substantial sentence. The usual bracket for such offences is 15 to 18 years' imprisonment and, allowing for the single mitigating factor, that the appellants both pleaded guilty the sentence is entirely appropriate (*R. v. Turner* [1975] C.L.Y. 559 applied).

R. v. FENLON AND JARPUR (1985) 7 Cr.App.R.(S.) 175, C.A.

770. Sentence—arson causing £500,000 worth of damage—committed while affected by drink

Four years' imprisonment is appropriate for an offender who, whilst intoxicated, set fire to his employers premises causing £500,000 worth of damage and who had a long history of such behaviour.

F pleaded guilty to arson. He had broken into his employers warehouse and set fire to a box. The fire caused substantial damage. He was intoxicated at the time. From 1971 F had a record of offences involving assault, criminal damage and threatening behaviour. On each of the occasions that he was committed he had been drinking to excess. *Held,* that the impression given by F's conduct is that he is a menace when under the influence of drink. It was almost inevitable that he would eventually wreak substantial damage. It is not inevitable that the scale of the damage of an unlawful act should substantially affect the length of sentence but here the court cannot be criticised for taking it into account. The sentence passed was an appropriate one.

R. v. FAIRMINER (1985) 7 Cr.App.R.(S.) 3, C.A.

771. Sentence—arson—juvenile setting fire to school

When sentencing a juvenile for the arson of his school it is necessary for a deterrent sentence to be imposed. That sentence should not be so long that, for a person of the offender's age, the end of the sentence would appear to be out of sight.

G aged 16 was convicted of arson. He had set fire to foam mattresses to create a diversion while he and another stole the school dinner money. The fire caused £1 million worth of damage, though C did not intend to cause that much damage. Sentenced to five years' detention. *Held,* that a deterrent sentence was necessary. The amount of damage caused was not a critical factor in determining sentence— more important is the offender's intention in starting the fire. Whilst this sentence would have been entirely appropriate for an older offender, for one of C's age the end would seem out of sight. He would not have a target against which to measure his conduct whilst in detention. The sentence should be reduced to three years' detention. (*R. v. Storey* [1985] C.L.Y. 810 discussed and applied).

R. v. CONWAY (1985) 7 Cr.App.R.(S.) 303, C.A.

772. Sentence—arson at school—whether non custodial sentence cannot be justified

An offence of arson at a school is not necessarily so serious that a non-custodial sentence cannot be justified for the purposes of the Criminal Justice Act 1982, s.1(4).

D, aged 17 and of good character, pleaded guilty to one count of arson. He had set fire to a door at his school, causing £200 worth of damage. Sentenced to 12 months' youth custody. *Held,* that this offence came within the lower range of cases of arson. D played a minor part in the offence, he was of good character and had immediately admitted his guilt. This was not so serious an offence that a non custodial sentence could not be justified. The youth custody sentence would be quashed and a community service order for 50 hours would be substituted. (*R.* v. *Storey* [1985] C.L.Y. 810 applied).

R. *v.* DEWBERRY AND STONE (1985) 7 Cr.App.R.(S.) 202, C.A.

773. Sentence—arson—nurse setting fire to hospital
Sentence of 30 months' imprisonment substituted for 4 years' imprisonment for a nurse who started four fires in a hospital whilst under great domestic stress.

Z was an agency nurse employed at the Royal Free Hospital. The standard of her work and qualifications was such that her services were specifically requested by the hospital. In November 1983 whilst on night duty she set fire on four successive nights to four different unoccupied rooms at the hospital. No real danger was occasioned to patients except that a patient in strict isolation had to be moved causing a serious health hazard. Approximately £10,000 damage was done and some very important medical records were destroyed. In consequence Z faced 8 counts of arson to which she pleaded guilty. Z was 30 years old and married. The social inquiry report disclosed that Z was under a great deal of stress at the time in consequence of domestic and family problems. Her actions were considered to be a "cry for help". Z was not suffering from any identifiable psychiatric illness. She was of previous good character and remorseful. Z was sentenced to 4 years' imprisonment. *Held,* allowing Z's appeal, that the gravity of the offences called for a sentence of immediate imprisonment particularly in the light of the fact that there was no psychiatric illness or abnormality present. Z's personal circumstances were such that the sentence imposed could properly be reduced from what was otherwise an appropriate sentence to one of 30 months' imprisonment.

R. *v.* ZYWINA (1984) 6 Cr.App.R.(S.) 434, C.A.

774. Sentence—assault—assault on process server
Sentence of 18 months' imprisonment for assault occasioning actual bodily harm to a person serving a court summons reduced to 8 months.

W was convicted on two counts of assault occasioning actual bodily harm. The victim was a process server who was attempting to serve a summons for a variation of maintenance issued by his wife upon him. The process server was punched on the nose once and then pushed around by W. W was aged 40, separated from his wife and had previous convictions although none of great significance in recent years. The judge observed that the machinery of justice was based upon the service of documents, and that it was essential that persons serving such documents should be able to do so unmolested. W was sentenced to 18 months' imprisonment. *Held,* allowing W's appeal, that the court agreed with the observations made by the judge. Whilst the offences were serious they were not so grave as to warrant a sentence of 18 months' imprisonment. The sentence would be reduced to 8 months' imprisonment.

R. *v.* WATKIN (1984) 6 Cr.App.R.(S.) 416, C.A.

775. Sentence—assault by 20 year old causing bruising and puncture wound—youth custody
Five months' youth custody was not excessive for a 20 year old who committed assault occasioning actual bodily harm.

E and others were eating a take away meal from another restaurant in the forecourt of an Indian restaurant. When the proprietor complained they attacked him. E went off and came back with a jack handle shouting racial abuse. He struck the proprietor on the arm causing bruising and a small puncture wound. E was sentenced to 5 months' youth custody. *Held,* that although E had no record of violence in the past this was a disgraceful and violent incident with racial overtones. Those who commit offences of this kind should know that substantial sentences of youth custody will follow. The sentence was appropriate and would be upheld.

R. *v.* ENGLISH (1985) 7 Cr.App.R.(S.) 65, C.A.

776. Sentence—assault by youths occasioning actual bodily harm—whether offence so serious that non-custodial sentence could not be justified
[Criminal Justice Act 1982, (c.48), s.1(4).]

An assault by a gang of youths on a boy who was unknown to them was so serious that a non-custodial sentence could not be justified.

J pleaded guilty to assault occasioning actual bodily harm. He and five other youths had attacked a boy who was unknown to them after an incident at a dance. They punched and kicked the boy, inflicting injuries to the eye, stomach and chest, from which he recovered quickly. J was sentenced to three months' detention. *Held,* that the sentencer had to bear in mind s.1(4) of the Criminal Justice Act 1982. The only consideration here was whether a non-custodial sentence could be justified. Notwithstanding all that could be said in favour of the appellants, this was a cowardly attack and a serious offence. The sentence was entirely appropriate.

R. *v.* JEOFFROY (1985) 7 Cr.App.R.(S.) 135, C.A.

777. Sentence—assault occasioning actual bodily harm—custodial sentence

A custodial sentence is inevitable for assault occasioning actual bodily harm to a police officer by driving a car with the officer on the bonnet but the Court must also consider mitigating factors.

A pleaded guilty to assault occasioning actual bodily harm and reckless driving. He had been signalled to stop by a police officer but drove at the officer, carrying him on the bonnet for about 100 yards before stopping and handing over his keys. He was sentenced to 6 months' imprisonment and disqualified from driving for 12 months. *Held,* that a custodial sentence was inevitable for conduct of this kind and, for this class of offence 6 months was generally the minimum. The Court should also consider A's repentance, free admission of guilt, excellent background and good working record. The sentence of 6 months would be upheld but half of it would be suspended.

R. *v.* AGUILAR (1985) 7 Cr.App.R. (S.) 178, C.A.

778. Sentence—assault—whether mitigation

It is no mitigation of the gravity of an assault that it occurred in a domestic setting: R. *v.* CUTTS, *The Times,* December 3, 1986, C.A.

779. Sentence—assisting police by giving information—whether ground for reduction of sentence

Where an offender has given assistance to the police and has been beaten up as a result it is appropriate to reduce his sentence.

T pleaded guilty to theft. He had siphoned petrol from parked cars on a number of occasions. He gave valuable information to the police but was beaten up by other men as a result and had to spend four days in hospital. He was sentenced to one month's imprisonment and a nine months' suspended sentence activated with the term reduced to six months.

Held, that the case of *R. v. Sinfield* had drawn the courts' attention to the value of encouraging people to give information to the police so that more serious offences may be resolved. Bearing in mind the assistance given by T and his subsequent injuries he did deserve some reduction of sentence. The suspended sentence would be reduced to three months' imprisonment (*R. v. Sinfield* (1981) 3 Cr.App.R.(S.) 258 applied).

R. *v.* THOMAS (K. G.) (1985) 7 Cr.App.R.(S.) 95, C.A.

780. Sentence—blackmail—posing as police officer and demanding sums of money

B pleaded guilty to counts of blackmail and theft. He posed as a police officer and purported to arrest people visiting a public lavatory. He then offered to release them for sums of money which the victims paid over. Sentenced to eight years imprisonment. *Held,* that there were only two points of mitigation; the small sums involved (£100 and £30) and the fact that B had pleaded guilty. The case of *R. v. Scanlon* [1986] C.L.Y. 781, where a blackmailer was sentenced to 10 years' imprisonment, could be distinguished because that offender was on probation at the time of the offences. The present sentence was a little too high and would be reduced to six years' imprisonment. (*R. v. Scanlon* [1986] C.L.Y. 781 distinguished).

R. *v.* BURCHE (1985) 7 Cr.App.R.(S.) 379, C.A.

781. Sentence—blackmail—threat to disclose homosexual behaviour

Ten years' imprisonment was reduced to seven in the case of a man who persistently blackmailed men whom he met in public lavatories.

S pleaded guilty to two counts of blackmail among other offences. On two occasions he met men in public lavatories, and pretended to engage in homosexual activity; stole money and a document from each man, and threatened to inform their wives. He was on probation at the time for similar offences. He was sentenced to ten years' imprisonment. *Held,* on appeal, that a severe sentence had to be passed because of the nature of the offences, their persistence, and because he was in breach of probation for similar offences. However the overall sentence was too long and would be reduced to seven years.

R. *v.* SCANLON (1984) 6 Cr.App.R.(S.) 199, C.A.

782. Sentence—breach of community service order made by magistrates' court—power to commit to Crown Court for sentence

[Powers of Criminal Courts Act 1973 (c.62), s.16(3).]

Where there is a breach of a community service order made by a magistrates' court the magistrates' court dealing with the offender has no power to commit him to the Crown Court for sentence.

The offender was ordered by the magistrates' court to perform 100 hours' community service. He later appeared before the magistrates' court having failed to comply with the order. He was committed to the Crown Court for sentence. The Crown Court declined to sentence him. *Held*, that there was no power to enable the magistrates' court to commit the offender to the Crown Court in these circumstances. The duty of the magistrates' court in these circumstances is to pass sentence on the offender there and then.

R. *v.* WORCESTER CROWN COURT, *ex p.* LAMB (1985) 7 Cr.App.R.(S.) 44, D.C.

783. Sentence—buggery of adolescent boy

Three years' imprisonment was upheld on a man who buggered a boy of 13 whom he had met through a scout troop.

Q pleaded guilty to one count of gross indecency and two of buggery. He met a boy, then aged 12, through a scout troop of which he was an instructor. After the boy left the scouts, the association continued, and eventually acts of masturbation and buggery took place. Q gave the boy money after acts of buggery. Q had no previous conviction for a sexual offence. *Held*, upholding the sentence of 3 years' imprisonment, that having considered *R.* v. *Tanner* [1983] C.L.Y. 764, *R.* v. *Armston* [1982] C.L.Y. 684; and *R.* v. *Thornton* [1984] C.L.Y. 824 the sentence did not appear in any way out of line. The boy was only 13 when the first offence was committed, Q admitted at least 10 occasions, and there was an element of corruption. The sentencer rightly took into account public feeling, the deterioration in the boy's behaviour resulting in his being placed in voluntary care, and the plea of guilty. He had weighed all the factors correctly.

R. *v.* QUEEN (1984) 6 Cr.App.R.(S.) 178, C.A.

784. Sentence—buggery of boy aged 15.

Thirty months' imprisonment is an appropriate sentence for an offender who committed buggery with a 15-year-old boy.

D pleaded guilty to the buggery of two youths, one of them aged 15. The appellant had taken the boy in after the boy had left home following a row with his parents. A few days later the boy went to bed with the appellant and another youth. There were acts of indecency between the youth and the boy. The next morning the appellant buggered the boy. Medical examination revealed that the boy had not practised buggery before. *Held*, that where young boys of 15 are involved the court must make it clear that such youths need and are entitled to the protection of the courts. Others should be deterred from taking advantage of young boys who fall out with their parents and seek refuge with homosexuals. There is therefore no reason to interfere with the sentence passed (*R.* v. *Armston* [1982] C.L.Y. 684 applied).

R. *v.* DRIVER (1985) 7 Cr.App.R.(S.) 55, C.A.

785. Sentence—buggery of boy aged 16 years

Thirteen months' imprisonment is an appropriate sentence for a man who buggered a boy of 16.

W pleaded guilty to buggery of a boy of 16. W had several previous convictions including one for indecent assault on a 16 year old. W met his victim in a public house. The boy did not want to go back to his home so he went to W's home where the offence was committed. Both W and the victim were of limited intelligence. W was sentenced to 13 months' imprisonment. *Held*, bearing in the mind the principle that the effect of the sentence on others as well as the offender must be considered, it was not possible to say that the sentence was wrong. W was not of previous good character and the victim had a mental age of about 8. To pass a lesser sentence would be to fail in the duty to protect others (*R.* v. *Thornton* [1984] C.L.Y. 824 and *R.* v. *Armston* [1982] C.L.Y. 684 considered).

R. *v.* WHARMBY (1985) 7 Cr.App.R.(S.) 25, C.A.

786. Sentence—buggery of 17 year old male prostitute

Thirty months' imprisonment is too severe a sentence for offences of buggery and gross indecency with a 17 year old male prostitute.

W, aged 43, pleaded guilty to offences of gross indecency and buggery. W and another picked up a male prostitute and indulged in acts of gross indecency with him. W had a suspended sentence for attempted buggery of a 14 year old and had a history of such offences. He was sentenced to a total of 30 months' imprisonment.

Held, that the court had to consider a deterrent element when sentencing offenders of this sort. However, in this case there was no question of corrupting the male prostitute. The totality of the sentence was too great and would be reduced to 18 months' imprisonment (*R. v. Armston* [1982] C.L.Y. 684 and *R. v. Dighton* [1984] C.L.Y. 825 applied).

R. *v.* WINDLE (1985) 7 Cr.App.R.(S.) 31, C.A.

787. Sentence—buggery of young boys—untreatable personality disorder

The relevant question was how to balance the need to keep the offender out of circulation for an appropriate length of time against what was just for him.

L pleaded guilty to charges of indecent assault, attempting to procure the commission of acts of gross indecency and buggery involving boys aged 11, 13 and 14. L had previously been convicted of attempted buggery, sexual intercourse and indecent assault on two 12 year old girls. He was sentenced to 10 years' imprisonment. *Held*, that L was of inadequate personality, had been in and out of mental homes since he was 12 years old and was not susceptible to treatment. The only problem is to keep him out of circulation for a proper length of time having regard to his own interests and those of young people who may be subject to his attention. The sentence was not inappropriate or excessive in length.

R. *v.* LIDDLE (1985) 7 Cr.App.R.(S.) 59, C.A.

788. Sentence—burglary by juvenile—whether detention justified.

D, aged 16, pleaded guilty to counts of burglary, with four other burglaries taken into consideration. He entered the homes of middle aged or elderly ladies while they were in the garden and stole jewellery or cash to a value of £3,500 (£964 worth was recovered). He was sentenced to 30 months' detention under the Children and Young Persons Act 1933, s.53(2). *Held*, that the prime reasons for the section were the protection of the public and the punishment of the offender. Those reasons justified the sentence passed. The present offences were persistent and artful, they could not adequately be dealt with by a sentence of 12 months' youth custody. The sentence would be upheld.

R. *v.* DOHERTY (1985) 7 Cr.App.R.(S.) 277, C.A.

789. Sentence—burglary of homes of elderly people—quoting previous cases on sentencing appeals

Six years' imprisonment was varied to five in the case of a man with a substantial record who burgled the homes of elderly persons. It was not appropriate in appeals on sentence to quote to the Court of Appeal earlier reported decisions on length of sentence.

S pleaded guilty to two counts of burglary and one of theft. He gained entry to the flat of a lady of 66 by posing as a council workman and stole a purse containing £40. A few days later he broke into the flat of a man of 82 and stole his Post Office savings book. He then called on the man, claimed to have found the book, and demanded money for its return. The owner was persuaded to go the the Post Office and draw out £100 of which the appellant kept £90. He had a substantial record including offences of this kind. He was sentenced to six years, which was varied to five on appeal, since six was to some extent too long. *Held*, following *R. v. Large* [1981] C.L.Y. 525 that it was not appropriate on sentence appeals to draw the Court's attention to earlier cases on sentence. Sentencing was extremely difficult, and the particular sentence depended wholly on the facts and circumstances of the individual case in front of the sentencing judge, facts which may not appear in any report made of the comments of the Court of Appeal in allowing or dismissing an appeal. The Court was fully aware from its general experience of the general range of sentences for a particular offence. The task of the sentencing judge and the Court of Appeal was to determine at what particular point on the range the sentence should be pitched. Where no point of principle arose, the Court should not be referred to earlier sentencing reports.

R. *v.* SAWYER (1984) 6 Cr.App.R.(S.) 459, C.A.

790. Sentence—burglary of laboratory as part of demonstration

A short sentence of imprisonment, suspended, is the right sentence where a burglar is not motivated by the desire for personal gain but by reasons of moral justification.

S was one of 17 animal welfare campaigners who entered the office of a member of a university department and ransacked it. He was found by the police to have three slides on him, which illustrated methods of injecting rodents. He claimed that he intended to return the slides having made them available to the press. He pleaded guilty to burglary. He was sentenced to 28 days immediate imprisonment and was bound over in the sum of £100 for two years. On appeal, as he had been in custody for seven days, the sentence was varied to one of 7 days immediate imprisonment. The Court held that it was clear that the appellant was not motivated by any desire for personal gain, and considered he was morally justified in what he did. The law was not to be taken into the hands of campaigners and those who invaded property must inevitably expect a custodial sentence. But in circumstances such as the present, it should be wholly suspended. The right sentence would have been 28 days, suspended for two years.

R. *v.* STOCK (1984) 6 Cr.App.R.(S.), 234, C.A.

791. Sentence—calculated fraud on D.H.S.S.

Two years' youth custody was an appropriate sentence for a calculated fraud on the D.H.S.S.

A pleaded guilty to seven counts of obtaining by deception with 40 similar offences to be taken into consideration. He had claimed supplementary benefit in the names of other people by obtaining birth certificates of children who had died. He had obtained £7,000 worth of benefit to which he was not entitled. Sentenced to two years' youth custody. *Held,* that this case was much worse than cases of non disclosure or "signing on" twice and drawing two lots of benefits. Such offences usually attracted sentences of six months' or 15 months' imprisonment. This was a deliberate and ingenious fraud which made it one of the most serious of its kind. Accordingly the sentence would be upheld. (*R. v. Boyle* [1981] C.L.Y. 525, *R. v. Sequeira* [1983] C.L.Y. 803, *R. v. Burns* [1984] C.L.Y. 894, *R. v. Stafford* [1985] C.L.Y. 735 distinguished.)

R. *v.* ADAMS (1985) 7 Cr.App.R.(S.) 411, C.A.

792. Sentence—causing death by reckless driving—custodial sentence

Nothing must be done to suggest that a person who knocks down a pedestrian on a controlled crossing and does not stop can expect other than substantial punishment.

B pleaded guilty to causing death by reckless driving. He drove across a pelican crossing against the lights and collided with an old lady who died later. B drove on and passed another red light. He was sentenced to 6 months' immediate imprisonment and disqualified from driving for 2 years. *Held,* that although there were mitigating factors such as B's good character, his plea of guilty and the time he had to wait for his case to be dealt with, there were also aggravating factors. These were that the pedestrian was on a controlled crossing and, more seriously, B drove off without stopping. There was no doubt that a custodial sentence was the only possible disposal of the case and the sentence was well within the bracket open to the trial judge (*R. v. Boswell* [1984] C.L.Y. 831 applied).

R. *v.* BROWN (V.) (1985) 7 Cr.App.R.(S.) 97, C.A.

793. Sentence—causing death by reckless driving—custodial sentence.

Applying the guidelines set out in *R. v. Boswell* [1984] C.L.Y. 831 a sentence of 12 months' youth custody is not too severe for causing death by reckless driving.

L was convicted of causing death by reckless driving. He had been driving along a country lane at speed. He had to go over a number of humpback bridges. His passenger had warned him about his speed. At one humpback the car "took off" and landed on top of a car coming in the opposite direction, killing the two people in it. L was badly injured and had not been drinking. He was sentenced to 12 months' youth custody and disqualified from driving for seven years. *Held,* that although L had no previous driving convictions, was of good character, had not been drinking and had not been chasing through town at great speed, this was not an isolated piece of inadvertence. L's passenger had already warned him about his speed. It was a terrifying piece of driving. It is essential to maintain consistency in cases of this nature. The sentence of youth custody was appropriate but seven years' disqualification was too long a period to keep L off the road and that part of the sentence would be reduced to three years (*R.* v. *Boswell* [1984] C.L.Y. 831 applied).

R. *v.* LAWSON (1985) 7 Cr.App.R.(S.) 165, C.A.

794. Sentence—causing death by reckless driving—15-year-old in car taken without consent

Six months' youth custody is an appropriate sentence for a youth who caused death by reckless driving in a car taken without consent whilst showing off to friends.

E aged 15 pleaded guilty to causing death by reckless driving. E and a friend were in a car that had been taken without consent. E, showing off to friends, reversed into a kerb and overturned the car, killing the passenger. He was sentenced to 6 months' youth custody and disqualified from driving for 5 years. *Held,* that the mitigating factors of the guilty plea, remorse, and previous good record were outweighed by the fact that E knew that the car was not his to drive from the outset and that E was showing off to friends. This wicked piece of conduct required marking as such and which E should expiate by way of a custodial sentence. Therefore the sentence was an appropriate one.

R. *v.* EASTWOOD (MARK) (1985) 7 Cr.App.R.(S.) 77, C.A.

795. Sentence—causing death by reckless driving—guidelines for custodial sentence

Three years and six months' imprisonment with 10 years' disqualification from driving was too severe for causing two deaths by reckless driving.

J, with no previous conviction for road traffic offences, pleaded guilty to two counts of causing death by reckless driving. He had been at a party until 5 a.m. where he had consumed alcohol. He left with four passengers in his father's car which was found to be in poor condition and had sub-standard tyres. J drove at high speed swerving to and fro despite repeated protests from his passengers. The car collided with a lamp post, killing two passengers. J was a learner driver and had no insurance. He was sentenced to 3½ years' imprisonment and disqualified from driving for 10 years. *Held,* having considered the aggravating and mitigating factors set out in *R.* v. *Boswell* [1984] C.L.Y. 831 and applying those to this case the proper sentence is two years' imprisonment with five years' disqualification from driving (*R.* v. *Boswell* [1984] C.L.Y. 831 applied).

R. *v.* JANES (1985) 7 Cr.App.R.(S.) 170, C.A.

796. Sentence—causing death by reckless driving—ignoring warning from passengers—drink

A sentence of 18 months was appropriate for causing death by reckless driving where the offender, although of previous good record, had been drinking and ignored warnings from his passengers.

H pleaded guilty to causing death by reckless driving. He had spent four hours drinking with others. They set off in a car with H driving. Having overtaken two cars in a dangerous fashion, H lost control of the car, hit the verge and somersaulted off the road. Two of the passengers were thrown out of the car and one of them later died. H was sentenced to 18 months' imprisonment and disqualified from driving for six years. *Held,* that although three of the mitigating factors referred to in the case of *Boswell* [1984] C.L.Y. 831 were present, namely good character, good driving record and remorse and shock, three of the aggravating features were also present—driving after consuming alcohol, ignoring warnings from passengers and competitive driving to show off. The court was obliged to follow the guidelines imposed recently and had to consider such aggravating features. The sentence was not an excessive one (*R.* v. *Boswell* [1984] C.L.Y. 831 applied).

R. *v.* HEPPINSTALL (1985) 7 Cr.App.R.(S.) 20, C.A.

797. Sentence—causing death by reckless driving—no aggravating factors

A custodial sentence is not appropriate for an offender who causes death by reckless driving where none of the aggravating factors listed in *R.* v. *Boswell* are present.

W aged 17 pleaded guilty to causing death by reckless driving. He had only just passed his driving test when, whilst driving at 45 mph around an "S" bend, he lost control of the car, mounted the kerb and killed two pedestrians. There was no suggestion of alcohol. He was sentenced to 12 months' youth custody and disqualified for three years.

Held, that applying *R.* v. *Guilfoyle* [1973] C.L.Y. 2987, this was not an act of selfish disregard for others but of momentary misjudgment by an inexperienced driver. The only possible aggravating factor was speed but W's speed was not of the order of 70 or 80 mph. W was young, of good character and sober. None of the aggravating factors listed in *R. v. Boswell* [1984] C.L.Y. 831 were present. In those circumstances there was an alternative to a custodial sentence. The sentence would be varied to 100 hours' community service and the period of disqualification would be reduced to 18 months (*R. v. Guilfoyle* [1973] C.L.Y. 2987 and *R. v. Boswell* [1984] C.L.Y. 831 considered).

R. *v.* WHITMORE (1985) 7 Cr.App.R.(S.) 193, C.A.

798. Sentence—causing grievous bodily harm with intent—setting fire to victim

Five years' imprisonment is at the very bottom of the scale for offences of this sort and in most cases a sentence of life imprisonment may be appropriate.

T was convicted of causing grievous bodily harm with intent. After a row with her lesbian lover T poured petrol over the woman and set fire to her. T immediately tried to put the flames out but the victim still suffered intensive and severe burns requiring long term medical treatment. T was sentenced to five years' imprisonment. *Held*, that it was becoming common for robbers to tie up victims, douse them with petrol and threaten to ignite them. If the victim dies it would be murder. If the victim does not die the offence would, in all probability, merit a sentence of life imprisonment. This was not such a case as there were strong mitigating circumstances— T's remorse, the fact that she had acted on the spur of the moment and would not be likely to repeat the act, and her immediate attempts to put the flames out. However, T did set her victim on fire—she must have known the consequences. In all the circumstances the sentence was an appropriate one. It was at the very bottom of the scale for this kind of case and, unless the circumstances are most extraordinary, nobody who commits this sort of offence is likely to receive a lesser sentence.

R. *v.* THOMAS (P. A.) (1985) 7 Cr.App.R.(S.) 87, C.A.

799. Sentence—"clocking" used cars—custodial sentence

[Trades Descriptions Act 1968 (c.29).]

Second hand car dealers who dishonestly "clock" motor cars and fail to disclose that they are selling cars in the course of a business deserve an immediate custodial sentence and a substantial fine.

G pleaded guilty to one count of obtaining by deception, one of applying a false trade description to goods, two of obtaining services by deception and two of failing to disclose that goods were being sold in the course of a business. 35 other offences were considered. G advertised cars in newspapers without disclosing that he was a dealer. He sold one car that had done 77,000 miles as having a mileage of 44,000 miles. He was sentenced to 12 months' imprisonment. *Held*, that second-hand car dealers who "clock" motor cars in this way deserve a sentence of immediate custody and a substantial fine. It was important that profits from this kind of behaviour should be taken from the dishonest dealer. Having regard to G's previous good character and his plea of guilty his sentence would be varied to a partly suspended sentence with six months' to serve and the balance held in suspense.

R. *v.* GUPTA (KULDIP) (1985) 7 Cr.App.R.(S.) 172, C.A.

800. Sentence—cocaine—possession of small quantity for personal use

Eight months' imprisonment with two to serve and the balance held in suspense, together with a £4,000 fine was not too severe for a man aged 34 of previous good character.

D, of previous good character, was convicted of possessing 13·6 grammes of powder containing 25 per cent. cocaine. *Held*, that the use of drugs of this sort for social purposes must be stamped out. D was an educated man, not unaware of the risks he was taking in possessing the drug and he runs his own company successfully. He cannot claim to be driven to drugs by unemployment. The custodial sentence and the fine passed were both entirely appropriate.

R. *v.* DIAMOND (PATRICK) (1985) 7 Cr.App.R.(S.) 152, C.A.

801. Sentence—combined sentence of imprisonment, fine, and criminal bankruptcy order

It is possible to combine a sentence of a maximum sentence of imprisonment with a fine and sentence of imprisonment in lieu thereof where it is apparent that there are funds available to pay the fine, and in very rare cases also to impose a criminal bankruptcy order but only where it is completely clear that there are ample funds to pay the creditors, after the fine is paid.

Per curiam: a criminal bankruptcy order, of itself, has no practical effect. All it does is provide conclusive proof of an act of bankruptcy upon which the official petitioner can petition for a receiving order. It will only be in very rare cases that a fine should be imposed as well as a criminal bankruptcy order. In cases where the Crown is not the creditor, the effect of a fine, if it is paid before a petition is presented, will be to reduce the funds available to compensate the victims named as creditors in the order. Where the Crown is the creditor it will almost always be better to omit making a criminal bankruptcy order if a fine is imposed, leaving it to the commissioners to petition in bankruptcy for the tax avoided if they wish to do so.

The appellant G. operating through a company, J Co., was aided by the appellant B, to defraud the Customs and Excise of almost £2 million in value added tax. He also operated a similar scheme through L Co. with the aid of the appellant H but the sum involved of £127,000 was later repaid by G and H *inter alia*. G and B were convicted of conspiring to contravene s.38 of the Finance Act 1972 in respect of J Co. and G and H in respect of L Co. G and B were sentenced to the maximum term of two years imprisonment on the first count, G was fined £100,000 and B £25,000 and criminal bankruptcy orders were made in the sum of £1,939,923·59. On the second count G was sentenced to 2 years' imprisonment consecutive and fined £50,000, H to 15 months imprisonment and fined £20,000 which he later paid. Receiving orders were made against G and B. *Held*, allowing the appeals against sentence, that a distinction should have been drawn between the first count where the maximum term was right, and the second lesser fraud: G's sentence on the second count would be reduced to 1 year, and H having served 6 months would be released. Provided the fine did not exceed the amount that a defendant could pay it could be imposed as a punishment or a means of forcing a defendant to hand over the profits of his crime. There was nothing wrong in principle in imposing a maximum sentence and a fine. But since the Customs and Excise Commissioners had applied for receiving orders the appellants could no longer lawfully pay the fines; and therefore they would be quashed and it would be left to the Commissioners to obtain from them their profits which had been transferred abroad.

R. *v.* GARNER; R. *v.* BULLEN; R. *v.* HOWARD [1986] 1 W.L.R. 73, C.A.

802. Sentence—combined sentence of imprisonment and disqualification
[Powers of Criminal Courts Act 1973 (c.62), s.44.]
There is no absolute rule that a period of disqualification should not last longer than a sentence of imprisonment imposed at the same time.

A pleaded guilty to 2 counts of handling stolen goods with 5 other offences taken into consideration. As a part-time taxi driver he was involved in driving for men whom he knew to be burglars and allowed his taxi to be used to dispose of stolen property. He was sentenced to 3 months' imprisonment and disqualified from driving under Powers of Criminal Courts Act 1973 section 44 for 12 months. *Held*, that there is no rule that a period of disqualification imposed under section 44 must always and automatically be such as to come to an end on the offender's release from prison. The nature of the offence, the antecedents and the extent to which the offender would be handicapped by not being able to drive upon his release were all relevant considerations. As A would not be able to return to his main employment as a British Telecom engineer on his release the period of disqualification would be reduced to 6 months. It was right that there should be some employment disadvantage as additional punishment by way of disqualification (*R. v. Wright* [1979] C.L.Y. 2299, *R. v. Hansel* [1983] C.L.Y. 817 considered).

R. *v.* ARIF (MOHAMMED), (1985) 7 Cr.App.R. (S.) 92, C.A.

803. Sentence—commercial fraud by director of a company
In times of economic stress the court should mark offences of commercial fraud with severe penalties to deter others.

K, the sole director of a company was convicted of one offence of attempting to evade liability by deception, three of obtaining by deception, one of theft and of fraudulent trading. When the company was known to be in serious financial difficulty K continued to order stock without paying for it. When pressed for payment he issued a cheque which he then stopped before being cleared. A sum of £11,500 was transferred from the company to a partnership in which K had an interest. The company eventually went into liquidation with deficiencies of £100,000. K was sentenced to four years' imprisonment with a criminal bankruptcy order for £52,000 and was disqualified from being a company director for five years. *Held*, that when temptations to indulge in dishonesty were strong because of economic stress it was important to mark offences of this sort with severe penalties to deter others. The sentence was appropriate (*R.* v. *Pal* (1981) 3 Cr.App.R.(S.) 343 considered).

R. *v.* KAZMI (1985) 7 Cr.App.R.(S.) 115, C.A.

804. Sentence—community service order—breach—custodial sentence—relevance of time spent on remand

[Criminal Justice Act 1967 (c.80), s.67.]

Where an offender spends time in custody on remand before the imposition of a community service order, if he subsequently receives a custodial sentence for being in breach of that order it may be appropriate to make some reduction of the sentence to take into account the period in custody on remand which does not count towards the sentence.

M pleaded guilty to charges of taking a motor vehicle, driving whilst disqualified and making a false statement. He was sentenced to 200 hours' community service but failed to comply with the order and so, upon being brought back to court, was sentenced to 15 months' youth custody. *Held,* that section 67 of the Criminal Justice Act 1967 makes it clear that a period in custody on remand before a community service order will not be deducted from the time to be served on a sentence of imprisonment for breach of that order. The time spent in custody on remand is therefore a relevant factor when deciding what sentence to impose for a breach of a community service order. As M had spent four months in custody on remand his sentence would be reduced to a total of 12 months' youth custody.

R. *v.* MCINTYRE (1985) 7 Cr.App.R.(S.) 196, C.A.

805. Sentence—community service order—when effective

[Powers of Criminal Courts Act 1973 (c.62), s.14(6).]

A community service order comes into force and becomes effective at the time when the order is orally pronounced in court.

G consented to the making of a community service order against him. The justices pronounced the order orally in open court. No copy of the order was served on G as required by s.14(6) of the Powers of Criminal Courts Act 1973. G failed to keep appointments with the probation officer dealing with the implementation of the order. Upon being summonsed for breach of the order G claimed the order was not effective by virtue of the fact that it had not been served on him. The justices upheld that contention and sought the opinion of the court on the question of whether the community service order need be served on a defendant before it became effective. *Held,* that a community service order came into force on, and was effective from the time it was orally pronounced in open court. S.14(6) of the Act was an administrative provision directing service of the written order on the defendant and did not provide a prerequisite to the coming into force of the order (*R.* v. *Dugdale* [1981] C.L.Y. 375 disapproved, *Cooper* v. *Chief Constable of Lancashire* [1984] C.L.Y. 531 approved, *Cohen* v. *Cohen* (1947) C.L.C. 2923 considered).

THORPE *v.* GRIGGS (1984) 6 Cr.App.R.(S.) 286, D.C.

806. Sentence—compensation order—guidelines

The court should not make a compensation order unless (1) careful enquiry has been made into the defendant's capacity to pay; (2) if there be some capacity to pay, the time given for the defendant to pay should not be excessive; and (3) the order should be in precise terms.

S pleaded guilty to counts of obtaining by deception. He was sentenced to 18 months' imprisonment suspended for two years and ordered to pay £7,024·95 in compensation at the rate of £4 per week for the first £1,000 and the balance as quickly as possible. *Held,* that the judge erred in principle. The order was imprecise in its terms, the time for repayment was interminable and it was not sure how the balance of the order could be paid after the first £1,000 was paid. The order would be quashed.

R. *v.* SCOTT (formerly LUTTA) (1986) 83 Cr.App.R. 221, C.A.

807. Sentence—compensation order—length of time over which order should be payable

A compensation order should not be made in an amount greater than the offender can pay within one year.

H pleaded guilty to counts of burglary, theft and attempted theft. He and a number of youths had been involved in a number of burglaries of schools. H was sentenced to three months' detention and ordered to pay £598·14 as compensation. Following conviction H had lost his job and was unable to find another. The compensation order would take six years to pay off at the rate prescribed. *Held,* that the court should be slow to order offenders to pay substantial compensation except where the money is readily available to the offender. H's financial circumstances after this case were worse than before it. A compensation order which, because of the offender's lack of means takes more than a year to pay off is wrong in principle. Although many of the observations relate to fines they are equally apt for compensation orders. A compensation order of £100 would therefore be substituted.

R. *v.* HOLDEN (1985) 7 Cr.App.R.(S.) 7, C.A.

808. Sentence—conviction by jury—factual basis for sentencing
The trial judge, having heard the evidence in the case was entitled to reach his own conclusions on the facts of the case for the purposes of sentencing the defendant W was charged with causing grevious bodily harm contrary to s.20 of the Offences Against the Person Act 1861. The victim was an 11 month old child. There were four areas of injury, bruising to the back, bruising to the right eye and cheek, bruises on both legs, and a fractured clavicle. After retiring the jury asked whether the injuries to the face in isolation constituted grevious bodily harm. After a further direction the jury returned a unanimous verdict of guilty. Upon further enquiry the foreman of the jury stated that they had not reached a unanimous verdict on whether W was guilty in respect of the broken clavicle. W's counsel objected to any further enquiry of the matter. The trial judge formed the view that W was responsible for that injury and sentenced W to 15 months' imprisonment. *Held,* dismissing W's appeal, that the trial judge having heard all the evidence was entitled to form his own view of the facts of the case for the purposes of sentencing W. The fact that the foreman of the jury had indicated there was no unanimous agreement in respect of the fractured clavicle could not prevent the trial judge forming the view that W was responsible for it. The sentence could not be said to be excessive (*R. v. Solomon* [1984] C.L.Y. 764 applied).

R. *v.* WILCOX (1984) 6 Cr.App.R.(S.) 276, C.A.

809. Sentence—counterfeiting—custodial sentence
The passing of forged bank notes is a serious offence which in a normal way demands a sentence of imprisonment. Those who distribute forged bank notes are just as much part of the chain of dishonesty as those who produce them.

H was convicted of passing counterfeit currency, tendering a counterfeit note and possessing counterfeit notes with intent to pass them off. H had gone shopping with another whose identity she did not disclose. She passed three counterfeit £50 notes but was detected at her fourth attempt. She was found to be in possession of seven other counterfeit notes. She was sentenced to nine months' immediate imprisonment. *Held,* that whilst the appellant was only a distributor she was just as dishonest as those who produced counterfeit currency. The courts had often emphasised the gravity of the offence of passing forged bank notes. The offender should normally face immediate imprisonment. The sentence in this case was correct in principle and right in length. (*R. v. Bibi* [1980] C.L.Y. 575; *R. v. Carter* [1984] C.L.Y. 846 and *R. v. Lewis* [1984] C.L.Y. 772, considered).

R. *v.* HORRIGAN (1985) 7 Cr.App.R.(S.) 112, C.A.

810. Sentence—criminal bankruptcy order—no victim of offence in indictment—jurisdiction
[Powers of Criminal Courts Act 1973 (c.62), s.39.]
Provided that it is satisfied that a loss of the required level has been suffered, a court may make a criminal bankruptcy order even though the loss concerned was not an integral part of the offence in respect of which the offender was convicted.

After seven days of trial M pleaded guilty to two counts of forgery. The allegation had been that he had entered into a bogus agreement with an Iranian businessman to supply 1,500 tonnes of metal to him, in the course of which he had forged a bill of lading and a document purporting to show that the metal had been delivered to Iran. Payment was to be by letter of credit opened at a London bank; in due course M drew the whole amount from the bank, which was reimbursed by the businessman. M's defence was that the entire transaction had been bogus and designed to enable the businessman to evade Iranian exchange control regulations. The plea of guilty was tendered on the basis that the bank had suffered no loss. M was sentenced to 12 months' imprisonment and a criminal bankruptcy order was made on the basis of the loss suffered by the businessman. *Held,* provided that a loss had been suffered which was of the prescribed amount, the court had jurisdiction to invoke the provisions of s.39 of the 1973 Act. There was no requirement that the loss be an ingredient of the offence concerned. Prior to the plea being tendered, the judge had indicated that a criminal bankruptcy order was in his mind, on the basis of the businessman's loss, and there was no reason to interfere with his decision.

R. v. MAYER (1984) 6 Cr.App.R.(S.) 193, C.A.

811. Sentence—custodial sentence—offence committed during currency of community service order—substantial part of community service order performed

When sentencing an offender for an offence in respect of which a community service order was originally made the sentencer may make allowance for the fact that a substantial part of the community service order had been performed.

C pleaded guilty to handling stolen goods. He had previously been convicted of handling stolen goods and ordered to perform 80 hours' community service. He had already performed 61 of the 80 hours at the time of sentence. Sentenced to two years' imprisonment for the latest offence and six months' consecutive for the offence for which the Community Service Order was made. *Held,* that to give some allowance for the substantial performance of the Community Service Order would be appropriate. The six months' imprisonment would be made to run concurrently with the sentence of two years. (*R. v. Anderson* [1983] C.L.Y. 789 discussed).

R. v. COOK (1985) 7 Cr.App.R.(S.) 249, C.A.

812. Sentence—dealing in heroin on small scale—guidelines

A pleaded guilty to counts of possessing heroin with intent to supply and of supplying heroin. 35 grammes of heroin were found in his motor car and four ounces of heroin were found at his home. He admitted supplying small quantities to three other people but he had not imported the drug from abroad. Sentenced to seven years' imprisonment. *Held,* that although the time may be near when the sentences suggested in *Aramah* [1983] C.L.Y. 764 may require revision they would be applied in this case. The amount of heroin involved did not place the offence at the higher end of the scale. The age and good character of the offender were irrelevant as he was precisely the sort of person those distributing the drug sought to employ. It would be wrong not to reduce the appellant's sentence but no criticism should be implied against the sentencer who was right in seeing a need to impose a deterrent sentence. In the light of authority the sentences were too harsh and would be reduced to five years' imprisonment. (*R. v. Aramah* [1983] C.L.Y. 764, *R. v. Hyam* [1984] C.L.Y. 868 and *R. v. Mansour* [1984] C.L.Y. 864 applied).

R. v. ANSARI (1985) 7 Cr.App.R.(S.) 312, C.A.

813. Sentence—deprivation of property order—property used in commission of offence

Where an order depriving an offender of his rights in property used in the commission of the offence is combined with a fine, the overall penalty should be commensurate with the offence.

S pleaded guilty to burglary. He had driven to the scene in his Rover motor car and had used it to carry away the stolen goods. S was a driller for oil and received £500 per week. He was sentenced to nine months' imprisonment, suspended, fined £5,000 and deprived of his rights in the car valued at £10,000.

Held, that S was in receipt of a substantial income and the £5,000 fine was appropriate but having regard to the overall penalty the confiscation of S's car was too heavy a punishment in the circumstances of the case. The order would be quashed.

R. v. SCULLY (1985) 7 Cr.App.R.(S.) 119, C.A.

814. Sentence—detention centre order—single offence by youth of previous good character

[Criminal Justice Act 1982 (c.48), s.1(4).]

The burglary of a dwelling-house is not necessarily "so serious that a non-custodial sentence cannot be justified" for the purposes of the Criminal Justice Act 1982, s.1(4).

B, aged under 21 with no previous convictions pleaded guilty to burglary of a dwelling-house with several other youths. He was sentenced to one month's detention centre order. *Held,* that there was no reason why it was necessary to pass a custodial sentence. Although burglary was a serious offence, in this case the appropriate sentence would have been a community service order. As B had already served some time in a detention centre the sentence would be varied to a conditional discharge.

R. v. BATES (JOHN) (1985) 7 Cr.App.R. (S.) 105, C.A.

815. Sentence—discount for plea of guilty—changing plea after tactical plea of not guilty

Defendants who put up tactical pleas of not guilty and then change them to guilty pleas cannot expect to get the same discount they would have done had they pleaded guilty at the outset.

H and E were arraigned on a number of offences involving burglary, robbery and conspiracy to rob. At the pre-trial review they pleaded not guilty. On re-arraignment they pleaded guilty to all charges against them and were sentenced to 14 years imprisonment. *Held,* dismissing the appeals, that discounts on sentence depend upon the circumstances of the case. Where a suspect, when arrested, immediately tells the police that he is guilty and co-operates with them thereafter he can expect a substantial discount. Where an accused is in a position where he cannot hope to put forward a plea of not guilty he cannot expect much by way of discount if he does so and changes his plea later. Here there was nothing wrong with the sentences imposed.

R. v. HOLLINGTON AND EMMENS (1986) 82 Cr.App.R. 281, C.A.

816. Sentence—disparity of sentence—offenders dealt with by different judges

B pleaded guilty to two counts of burglary. On the first count he had been assisted by an accomplice. Both offences involved burglary of residential dwellings. The accomplice, sentenced by a different judge, was ordered to perform 200 hours' community service. B was sentenced to 12 months' youth custody. *Held,* that the sentencer of the accomplice stated that she had considered a custodial sentence but had decided that it was an exceptional occasion where the personal circumstances of that offender justified the court in the view that the normally inevitable custodial sentence that should be imposed for the domestic burglary would not be appropriate. To obtain justice in the round B's sentence would be reduced to six months' youth custody. (*R.* v. *Stanburg* [1981] C.L.Y. 525 referred to).

R. *v.* BERRY (R.C.) (1985) 7 Cr.App.R.(S.) 392, C.A.

817. Sentence—disparity—test

When an appeal against sentence is based on the disparity between the appellant's sentence and that of his co-accused, the appellant's sense of grievance is irrelevant. The test is whether right-thinking members of the public, knowing all the facts, would say "Something has gone wrong here with the administration of justice, which has resulted in one or more convicted persons being treated unfairly": R. *v.* TOWLE, R. *v.* WINTLE, *The Times,* January 23, 1986, C.A.

818. Sentence—disparity—whether different sex of offenders justifies disparity—position where unduly lenient sentence

A difference in sex is no good reason for drawing a distinction between two offenders who are equally to blame for a crime.

The two appellants were each sentenced to 5 years' imprisonment for possessing heroin with intent to supply. A woman, who was equally involved in the criminal enterprise, was sentenced to 2 years, solely on the ground that she was a woman. The appellants appealed on the ground of disparity. *Held,* that the fact of the matter was that the sentence on the woman was wholly wrong in principle and was far too lenient. That was no ground for interfering. No distinction on the ground of sex should be made between men and women when sentencing offenders who were equally culpable. On the facts, however, the judge had failed properly to distinguish between the roles played by the two appellants, and had failed to make a proper allowance for the fact the one of them had simply been an intermediary: his sentence would be reduced to 4 years (*R.* v. *Williams* [1953] C.L.Y. 811 followed).

R. *v.* OKUYA (1984) 6 Cr.App.R.(S.) 253, C.A.

819. Sentence—disqualification from driving—vehicle used for other offence—whether court to invite submissions before disqualifying

[Powers of Criminal Courts Act 1973 (c.62), s.44.]

If a sentencer has in mind to disqualify from driving an offender who has used a motor vehicle in the course of committing another offence he should inform counsel of the possibility and invite submissions thereon.

P was concerned in a "smash and grab" at a jeweller's and in addition to other penalties he was disqualified from driving for 4 years. The first time it had become apparent that this was in the judge's mind was when the judge passed sentence: counsel had no opportunity to make submissions on the point. *Held,* that the judge had been mistaken in not intimating to counsel that he had in mind the imposition of a period of disqualification and that part of the sentence would therefore be quashed.

R. *v.* POWELL (M. B.) (1984) 6 Cr.App.R.(S.) 354, C.A.

820. Sentence—disqualification from driving—vehicle used in commission of crime

[Powers of Criminal Courts Act 1973 (c.62), s.44.]

A disqualification from driving under the Powers of Criminal Courts Act 1973 may be imposed only where there is evidence that the vehicle was used in the crime for which the offender is convicted.

P pleaded guilty to handling stolen electronic scales that had been stolen from a butcher's shop. P's car had been seen outside a shop while he was arranging to sell the scales to the owner of that shop. P was sentenced to four months' imprisonment and disqualified from driving for 12 months. *Held,* that there was no evidence to show that the vehicle had been used in connection with the offence of handling stolen goods (although it may have been used in connection with the disposal of the goods on behalf of another). The disqualification was not within the requirements of the statute and would be quashed.

R. *v.* PARRINGTON (1985) 7 Cr.App.R.(S.) 18, C.A.

821. Sentence—disqualification from driving until test passed—circumstances where apppropriate

Only where there is some reason to doubt the competence of an offender to drive should he be disqualified until he has passed a test: to do otherwise is wrong in principle.

P pleaded guilty to causing grievous bodily harm and to reckless driving. Whilst driving a van P shot out from a side turning obstructing a cyclist who was on the main road. When the cyclist protested at this conduct P got out of his van and seriously assaulted the cyclist, causing him grievous bodily harm. P was sentenced to 15 months' imprisonment for the assault, and was disqualified from driving for 3 years, and thereafter until he had passed a driving test. *Held,* that the period of imprisonment was perfectly justifiable, if not lenient. In so far as the period of disqualification was concerned, however, that was too long. P had never been disqualified in respect of any similar offence before, and the length of the period was such as to provoke him into the commission of fresh offences. Further the disqualification of P until he had passed a new driving test was wrong in principle: there was no evidence to show that P, who was an experienced driver, was incapable of proper driving, and nothing to show any general incompetence, whatever may have been the faults of the particular incident of reckless driving for which he was being sentenced.

R. *v.* PEAT (1984) 6 Cr.App.R.(S.) 311, C.A.

822. Sentence—disqualification where driving essential to employment—vehicle used in commission of offence

Where an offender's livelihood depends upon him being able to drive then, if the offence discloses nothing adverse as to his driving capability any period of disqualification may be tempered so as not to inhibit the offender from working after serving his sentence of imprisonment.

D pleaded guilty to counts of taking a vehicle without authority and theft from vehicles of £450 worth of goods. He was sentenced to nine months' youth custody and disqualified for 2 years. D was a vehicle mechanic and needed to be able to drive as part of his job. *Held,* that where an offender depends upon being able to drive for his job and where his offence involved using the vehicle in the commission of the crime rather than disclosing anything adverse on his driving ability then the court may, if it sees fit, temper any period of disqualification accordingly. The circumstances of this case indicated that it would be appropriate to do so. The period of disqualification would be reduced to 12 months, to enable D to drive immediately (*R. v. Kent and Tanser* [1983] C.L.Y. 760 considered).

R. *v.* DAVEGUN (1985) 7 Cr.App.R.(S.) 110, C.A.

823. Sentence—drugs offences

Seven years imprisonment for possession of cannabis with intent to supply was justified on the facts, and sentencing for serious drug offences could be heavier than the guidelines (*R. v. Aramah* [1983] C.L.Y. 764 considered: R. *v.* GILMORE, *The Times,* May 21, 1986, C.A.

824. Sentence—exportation of prohibited material—custodial sentence

[Export of Goods (Control) Order 1981 (S.I. 1981 No. 1641).]

Immediate custodial sentences are necessary for offences involving exportation of prohibited goods but, for this offender, two years' imprisonment was too harsh.

L, of previous good character, pleaded guilty to 13 counts of exporting prohibited goods to Bulgaria. The computers that were exported were believed to be of no military use. L was sentenced to the maximum sentence for this offence—two years' imprisonment. *Held,* that the offence is not one that could be punished by a financial penalty—an immediate custodial sentence is necessary. Had the offender known or believed that the computers were for military use that would have aggravated the offence. Bearing in mind L's impeccable character up to now, the fact that he pleaded guilty and the frankness he exhibited to the police, he should not have been given the maximum sentence. The sentence would be reduced to 12 months' imprisonment (*R.* v. *Carrigan* (Unreported) considered).

R. *v.* LUDLAM (1985) 7 Cr.App.R.(S.) 154, C.A.

825. Sentence—extended sentence—taking parole into account

It is improper to take account of parole when sentencing an offender. An intended sentence should not be passed on an offender who had attempted to lead an honest life after his most recent release from custody.

C pleaded guilty to counts of burglary, attempted burglary and taking without the owner's consent. The sentencer referred to the probability of C's parole reducing the usual sentence for offences of this gravity and remarked that the public would not be afforded sufficient protection from him should such a sentence be passed. So C was sentenced to five years' imprisonment extended. *Held,* that C had endeavoured to lead an honest life for a period following his last release from custody. It was inappropriate that he should now be made the subject of an extended sentence. It was also improper to take the possibility of parole into account when passing sentence. The sentence would be reduced to three years' imprisonment, not extended. (*R.* v. *Gisbourne* [1977] C.L.Y. 643 and *R.* v. *Kenworthy* [1969] C.L.Y. 718 applied).

R. *v.* CUNNINGHAM (1985) 7 Cr.App.R.(S.) 457, C.A.

826. Sentence—failure to comply with enforcement notice—permission subsequently granted

There was nothing wrong with a £100 fine and £300 costs as a penalty for failure to comply with an enforcement notice under the Town and Country Planning Act 1971 even though planning permission was granted after the sentence was imposed.

F carried out extensive building works to his bungalow without planning permission. After a number of appeals against the refusal of planning permission, enforcement notices and the refusal of later applications for planning permission, F was prosecuted for failing to comply with the enforcement notice. After a number of deferments of sentence, one of them to give F an opportunity to comply with the notice, he was sentenced to a £100 fine with £300 costs. *Held,* that the penalty would be upheld. It would not be expunged by virtue of the fact that F later obtained planning permission. The court is bound to accept the validity of the notice and not to attempt to second guess the result of subsequent appeals to the Secretary of State. The appellant had obtained an advantage by his long failure to comply with the law by securing his ultimate objective. He should not be given an additional advantage by being allowed to avoid any penalty for that failure to comply with the law. To allow that would bring the law into disrespect.

R. *v.* FEHILY (1985) 7 Cr.App.R.(S.) 82, C.A.

827. Sentence—fine—related to gravity of offence

A court determining the amount of a fine should first decide what is appropriate for the offence and then consider the offender's financial resources and whether the offender is capable of paying such a fine.

C, who was of previous good character, pleaded guilty to handling stolen goods. She had been found in possession of stolen jewellery and £1,000 in cash. She was sentenced to a fine of £1,000. *Held,* that judged by the gravity of the crime itself the fine was excessive for a person of good character. It was wrong to assume that the £1,000 was available to pay the fine. The correct approach was to decide the appropriate sentence for the offence and the offender and then to consider the offender's resources. In this case the appropriate fine was £150.

R. *v.* CLEMINSON (1985) 7 Cr.App.R. (S) 128, C.A.

828. Sentence—football hooligan
Life imprisonment for a persistent football hooligan is wrong in principle: R. *v.* WHITTON, *The Times,* May 20, 1986, C.A.

829. Sentence—forfeiture—profits from trafficking in prohibited drugs
[Misuse of Drugs Act 1971 (c.38), s.27.]
A defendant, having invited the trial judge to forfeit assets gained through drug trafficking and impose a reduced sentence of imprisonment, could not on appeal successfully argue that the assets did not relate to the specimen charge to which he pleaded guilty within the meaning of s.27 of the Misuse of Drugs Act 1971.
M and J pleaded guilty to conspiracy to contravene s.20 of the Misuse of Drugs Act 1971 and assisting in the unlawful supply of cannabis resin in a place outside the U.K. between certain dates (count 2 on the indictment). A voluntary bill of indictment had been preferred by order of a High Court judge after discussions between counsel for M, J and the prosecution. Count 2 was chosen as a specimen count with the knowledge and agreement of the leaders appearing for M and J and expressly included to allow the trial judge to make a forfeiture order pursuant to s.27 of the Misuse of Drugs Act 1971. M and J had been involved in drug trafficking in Holland. When arrested, large amounts of cash in sterling and guilders was discovered in their possession. Further amounts of cash were found in bank safety deposit boxes and building society accounts. The defendants were also in possession of other goods and property purchased with the proceeds of their enterprise. The trial judge was invited by counsel for M and J to strip them of the proceeds and assets acquired and then impose a reduced sentence of imprisonment. The trial judge made forfeiture orders in the sum of £117,000 and £170,000 against M and J respectively and imposed a reduced sentence of imprisonment. M and J then appealed against the forfeiture orders contending, *inter alia,* that as there was only one specimen charge between certain dates all the money subjected to the forfeiture orders could not relate to that charge within the meaning of s.27 of the Act. *Held,* dismissing the appeal, that M and J having conceded through their counsel that the money was related to the charge and invited the judge to make the forfeiture order could not argue that the money forfeited did not relate to the charge. The order against M would be varied in so far as it included assets purchased with the proceeds of the enterprise and moneys held in bank and building society accounts as the former did not relate directly to the charge and the latter were choses in action which could not be made the subject of a forfeiture order. The fact that the cash seized was paid into a bank account and thus became a chose in action did not prevent a forfeiture order being made. The time to consider the nature of the assets seized was the time at which they were seized (*R. v. Cuthbertson* [1980] C.L.Y. 526 considered).
R. *v.* MARLAND AND JONES (1986) 82 Cr.App.R. 134, C.A.

830. Sentence—fraudulently obtaining unemployment benefit
Thirty months' imprisonment is too severe a sentence for a man who obtained £5,300 in unemployment benefit to which he was not entitled.
S pleaded guilty to three counts of obtaining by deception and asked for 28 other offences to be taken into consideration. He had been collecting unemployment benefit whilst at the same time receiving money from the D.H.S.S. for taking in lodgers at two houses that he owned. He collected £5,300 worth of benefit to which he was not entitled. He was sentenced to 30 months' imprisonment.
Held, that S has a long history of previous offences of dishonesty. Even so the sentence was too harsh in the light of his plea of guilty and his admission to the police. A sentence of 15 months' imprisonment should be substituted for the original sentence (*R. v. Byrne* (1983) 5 Cr.App.R.(S.) 370, *R. v. Boyle* [1981] C.L.Y. 525, *R. v. Bateman* [1981] C.L.Y. 525, *R. v. Baker* [1982] C.L.Y. 684, *R. v. Morton* [1983] C.L.Y. 886, *R. v. Sequeira* [1983] C.L.Y. 803 and *R. v. Hassan* (1981) 3 Cr.App.R.(S.) 306 applied).
R. *v.* STAFFORD (1985) 7 Cr.App.R.(S.) 62, C.A.

831. Sentence—handling—substantial quantities of stolen goods—length of sentence
Four years' imprisonment, and an order to pay prosecution costs of £6,000, upheld for man convicted of handling stolen cigarettes worth £160,000, being part of a consignment worth £1,000,000.
P was convicted of handling stolen cigarettes worth £160,000. Those cigarettes were part of a large quantity worth £1,000,000 which had been stolen from a depot owned by

the manufacturer. He had previously been sentenced to 6 years for importing drugs. *Held,* that this was a case justifying a sentence towards the top of the scale. In some cases the existence of the handler was of great advantage to the thief and those cases, of which this was one, demanded severe sentences. Appeal dismissed.

R. *v.* PATEL (1984) 6 Cr.App.R.(S.) 191, C.A.

832. Sentence—handling—statutory power to make criminal bankruptcy order
[Powers of Criminal Courts Act 1973 (c.62), s.39.]
Burglars stole property worth £2·75m from a bank strongroom. C and J were convicted of conspiracy to commit burglary and handling stolen goods. Both were sentenced to terms of imprisonment and criminal bankruptcy orders were made against both of them. They appealed on the grounds as to whether it had been shown that the gold that persons listed in the schedule to the criminal bankruptcy order had lost had ever been handled by C or J. *Held,* that although no gold was found on their premises or on C or J the court must look at the matter from a common sense point of view. There was evidence that gold had been melted at J's premises and the necessary equipment was found during a police search. It was therefore shown that the loss of the gold listed in the schedule did result from offences committed by C and J. Accordingly the court was within its jurisdiction under the Powers of Criminal Courts Act 1973 in imposing the criminal bankruptcy orders (*R. v. Cain* [1984] C.L.Y. 557; *R. v. Howell* [1978] C.L.Y. 595; *R. v. Reilly* [1983] C.L.Y. 910 considered).

R. *v.* CANNON (1986) 82 Cr.App.R. 286, C.A.

833. Sentence—importing and dealing in cocaine
No distinction is to be drawn between the various categories of Class A drugs for sentencing purposes: 4 years' imprisonment upheld for importing cocaine.
M was a citizen of Colombia who had lived in the U.K. since 1974. He was convicted of importing cocaine with a street value of about £3,000 by receiving a letter addressed to him containing the drug. He was of previous good character and was sentenced to 4 years' imprisonment. *Held,* that the sentence was entirely proper. No distinction in principle should be drawn betwen the different categories of Class A drugs. Those who imported cocaine or L.S.D. could expect to be dealt with in the same way as those who imported heroin (*R. v. Aramah* [1983] C.L.Y. 764 explained).

R. *v.* MARTINEZ (1984) 6 Cr.App.R.(S.) 364, C.A.

834. Sentence—importation of large quantity of cannabis—guidelines
It is not necessary to draw the line between large scale importation and medium scale importation of cannabis precisely. Medium quantities would justify sentences of three to six years' imprisonment whilst large scale importation required sentences of up to 10 years' imprisonment.
P pleaded guilty to importing between 60 and 80 kilogrammes of cannabis from Morocco. He was sentenced to seven years' imprisonment. *Held,* that in the light of the appellant's previous convictions for drug offences and the fact that this could be described as an offence towards the bottom of the large scale importation of cannabis the sentence would have been appropriate had the appellant been convicted of the offence. However, the sentencer failed to give sufficient credit for his guilty plea and so the sentence would be reduced to 5½ years' imprisonment (*R. v. Aramah* [1983] C.L.Y 764 applied, *R. v. Forsythe* [1980] C.L.Y. 571, *R. v. Chisti* [1981] 3 Cr.App.R.(S.) 99 considered).

R. *v.* PRICE (1985) 7 Cr.App.R.(S.) 190, C.A.

835. Sentence—indecent assault—assault on girl aged 12—not of most serious nature
Nine months' imprisonment for an indecent assault, not of the most serious nature, on a 12 year old girl is too severe.
C, aged 45, pleaded guilty to indecently assaulting a 12-year-old girl but he disputed her version of the incident. The trial judge, rather than call the girl to give evidence accepted C's version. This was that he visited a neightbour's house, found the girl there and, after some sexual conversation with her, pulled down her knickers and put his face on her stomach. He released her when she protested. C was sentenced to 9 months' imprisonment. *Held,* that the judge had correctly acted on C's account of events. The conduct was at the bottom of the scale of offences involving interference with young girls. It was an isolated lapse by a man of previous good character. The sentence would be reduced to 3 months' imprisonment.

R. *v.* CANK (1985) 7 Cr.App.R. (S.) 99, C.A.

836. Sentence—isolated incident of attempted incest with 13 year old daughter—custodial sentence.

A sentence of 18 months' imprisonment for an isolated attempted incest was appropriate.

J pleaded guilty to attempted incest with his 13 year old daughter. Penetration did not occur because of last minute remorse by J. No physical or mental injury was suffered by the child although it was uncertain what could emerge in the long term. J was of previous good character and was deeply remorseful for what had happened. He was unlikely to re-offend. J was sentenced to 18 months' imprisonment. *Held,* that one of the matters to be considered is the importance of re-establishing stability in the fostering situation in which the daughter had been placed. There was, therefore, no urgency about restoring contact between father and daughter. Of course that should in no way go to lengthen the sentence or to inhibit a remission of the sentence if other things dictated it. In the circumstances of the case the sentence was entirely appropriate.

R. *v.* JAMES (1985) 7 Cr.App.R.(S.) 147, C.A.

837. Sentence—kidnapping

A and another pleaded guilty to kidnapping. They had seized a man in an attempt to make him tell them the whereabouts of a former girlfriend of A. The man was held captive for half an hour and was threatened with violence. A sentence of 2½ years' imprisonment was imposed on both men. *Held,* that it is entirely appropriate that this sort of conduct should attract a prison sentence but 2½ years was rather on the long side. Accordingly the sentence would be reduced to 18 months' imprisonment.

R. *v.* AHMAD AND WOOLLEY (1985) 7 Cr.App.R.(S.) 433, C.A.

838. Sentence—kidnapping—detaining with violence for a short time

Life imprisonment was varied to nine years where a defendant kidnapped a young woman driver and held her captive under threats of violence for an hour and a half, and stole a small sum of money from her.

The second appellant pleaded guilty to kidnapping and robbery: a count for indecent assault was not proceeded with. The first appellant pleaded guilty to the same two counts, and also to a charge of indecent assault in an unrelated incident. They had got into a van in which a girl was waiting for her companion to return from shopping. The second appellant threatened her with a knife and later with scissors, while the first appellant drove the van. She was forced to hand over £5 from her purse. She was released after an hour and a half. The second appellant was sentenced to life imprisonment and the first to five years, with two years consecutive for the unrelated indecent assault. *Held,* on appeal, that a sentence of life imprisonment was not really necessary and nine years would suffice. The sentence on the first appellant was correct (*R. v. Hodgson* [1968] C.L.Y. 848; *R. v. Hercules* [1980] C.L.Y. 571 considered).

R. *v.* SINGLETON; R. *v.* BUTLER (1984) 6 Cr.App.R.(S.) 430, C.A.

839. Sentence—kidnapping—deterrent sentence

The courts must do all that lies in their power to prevent the new and comparatively rare crime of kidnapping.

B was convicted of conspiracy to kidnap, kidnapping, false imprisonment and blackmail. He had been involved in the kidnapping of a youth of 18 years who was driven to an hotel and detained for some 30 hours. Demands were made to the youth's father for a payment of £200,000 for the youth's release. The youth was released after the father had delivered some money which remained uncollected. *Held,* that the express inclusion of an element of deterrence in the sentence of 14 years' imprisonment was justified. The crime of kidnapping is a new one and is comparatively rare. The courts must do all they can to prevent it. The sentence was fully justified and not inappropriate to the gravity and circumstances of the crime.

R. *v.* BELMONT (1985) Cr.App.R. (S.) 139, C.A.

840. Sentence—kidnapping—extortion

Eighteen years' imprisonment upheld for kidnapping and blackmail.

P was convicted of kidnapping, false imprisonment and blackmail. He had broken into a young couple's house and held them for several days, making demands for substantial sums of money from the father of the husband. Eventually the couple were released. He was sentenced to 10 years for the kidnapping, and 8 years consecutive for blackmailing the husband's father. *Held,* that the totality of the sentence was entirely proper. The offence of blackmail was properly made consecutive as it involved a different victim (the husband's father) and the totality of the period of imprisonment was proper (*R.* v. *Parker* [1981] C.L.Y. 525 and *R.* v. *Karunaratne* [1983] C.L.Y. 764 considered).

R. *v.* PANAE (1984) 6 Cr.App.R.(S.) 410, C.A.

841. Sentence—kidnapping—political refugee

B and others pleaded guilty to counts of kidnapping and administering stupefying drugs. The plan was to seize a man who had been part of the Nigerian Government but was now a refugee in this country and take him back to Nigeria where he was accused of corruption. To this end the man was seized in the street, drugged and put into a crate to be flown to Nigeria. The appellants were sentenced to between 10 and 14 years' imprisonment. *Held,* that the large number of political refugees in this country must be free from threat or fear of forcible abduction. The method of abduction used here was an affront to the rule of law. It was a carefully planned operation, the victim was seized on a public street and rendered unconscious by drugs, he was put into a crate which was nailed shut. There is a need for deterrence in cases of this sort. Accordingly the sentences imposed were appropriate.

R. *v.* BARAK (1985) 7 Cr.App.R.(S.) 404, C.A.

842. Sentence—kidnapping—unpremeditated and involving violence

Five years' imprisonment is not too long a sentence for kidnapping a young woman and detaining her for 20 minutes.

B, whilst on bail for charges of burglary and whilst under the influence of drugs, got into a parked car with the intention of using it to go home. The owner came to the car and tried to open the door. B grabbed her, held a pen knife to her throat and forced her into the car. Eventually the woman escaped after a struggle but sustained minor injuries. B pleaded guilty to kidnapping, false imprisonment, burglary, assault occasioning actual bodily harm and taking a vehicle without consent. He was sentenced to a total of 5 years' imprisonment, including concurrent sentences of 5 years' on the counts of kidnapping and false imprisonment. *Held,* that this was not a case of a family dispute or lover's tiff. Violence had been used and, although it arose without premeditation, it was a serious case. In the circumstances 5 years' for the kidnapping was not too long (*R.* v. *Spence and Thomas* [1984] C.L.Y. 876 distinguished).

R. *v.* BROWN (DAVID RITCHIE) (1985) 7 Cr.App.R. (S.) 15, C.A.

843. Sentence—kidnapping—unpremeditated without motive of ransom

D and H, both aged 19, pleaded guilty to kidnapping and having a firearm in a public place. They wished to regain a necklace they had lost at a party to N. They went to the house of N's girlfriend with a loaded shotgun and a flick knife. They forced the girl to go with them to find N but were intercepted by the police. It was accepted that there was no intention to hold the girl to secure a money ransom. Both offenders were sentenced to 10 years' youth custody. *Held,* that H was the prime mover and D had played a lesser role. Both sentences were too long. H, who carried the gun, would be sentenced to six years' youth custody and D to five years' youth custody.

R. *v.* DWYER AND HARVEY (1985) 7 Cr.App.R.(S.) 332, C.A.

844. Sentence—kidnapping a diplomat

R was convicted of murder and pleaded guilty to false imprisonment. B pleaded guilty to kidnapping. Both had been involved in the kidnapping of an Indian diplomat who was held hostage while certain demands were made. The victim, after two days' captivity, was shot and killed. R was sentenced to 18 year's imprisonment for false imprisonment (as well as a life sentence for murder). B was sentenced to 20 years' imprisonment. A third offender was sentenced to 12 years' imprisonment for false imprisonment and did not appeal against sentence. *Held,* that this case involved kidnap, false imprisonment and violence against the victim. The victim of this terrorist offence was selected because he was an easy target. He was a diplomat whose safety was guaranteed by this county. The deterrent effect for offences of this sort was important. However the sentence of 20 years on B did not allow enough room for an appropriate sentence on the ringleaders of this plot (who had escaped) should they be brought to justice. Further, the discrepancy between the sentences imposed on R and the third offender for the offence of false imprisonment was too great. Accordingly, B's sentence would be reduced to 18 years' imprisonment and R's to 15 years' imprisonment.

R. *v.* RAJA AND BHATTI (1985) 7 Cr.App.R.(S.) 425, C.A.

845. Sentence—LSD possession with intent to supply

Those who supply drugs, particularly Class A drugs, can expect to lose their liberty for a long time.

B-P pleaded guilty to possessing 92 doses of LSD, a Class A drug, with intent to supply. He had a number of convictions for drug offences. He was sentenced to four years' imprisonment. *Held,* that it was clear that B-P had not learnt his lesson and was still using and supplying LSD. The sentence of four years' imprisonment was correct (*R. v. Aramah* [1983] C.L.Y. 764; *R. v. Virgin* [1984] C.L.Y. 853 considered).

R. *v.* BOWMAN-POWELL (1985) 7 Cr.App.R. (S.) 85, C.A.

846. Sentence—life imprisonment—false imprisonment—criteria

Life imprisonment should be upheld for a grave case of false imprisonment where the defendant is a danger to the public.

The appellant, aged 43, lured a 13 year old boy to his flat. There he tied and gagged him and proceeded to various acts of indecency and attempted buggery. During the course of these activities a knife was used to threaten the boy. The appellant pleaded guilty to counts of false imprisonment, attempted buggery and gross indecency. Medical reports showed he was a homosexual pederast with deviant sadomasochistic tendencies. He was sentenced to life imprisonment on the false imprisonment count, no separate penalties on the others. *Held,* dismissing the appeal, that life was a proper sentence as the appellant was plainly abnormal and a danger to the public.

R. *v.* PATE (1980) 80 Cr.App.R. 349, C.A.

847. Sentence—long term detention of juvenile

[Children and Young Persons Act 1933 (c.12), s.53(2).]

Where a court imposes on a juvenile a sentence of detention under the Children and Young Persons Act 1933. s.53(2), the term of detention should not be longer than would be passed on an offender aged over 17 or on an adult for the same offences.

B, aged 16, pleaded guilty to counts of robbery, attempted robbery and possessing a firearm with intent to commit an indictable offence. He and an accomplice had gone to 3 garages and held up the assistant, stealing a total of £2,750. B had 7 previous findings of guilt including robbery. He was sentenced to 5 years' detention on each count of robbery or attempted robbery, all concurrent and 2 years on each count of possessing a firearm, all concurrent but consecutive to the terms of 5 years. The trial judge passed the sentences "in the knowledge that the Secretary of State has the power and discretion" to release B. *Held,* that the view that the maximum term of youth custody was inadequate to mark the gravity of the offences was correct. It was therefore appropriate to deal with B under the Children and Young Persons Act 1933, s.53(2). However it seemed that the judge had passed a longer sentence than he would have if sentencing an older offender. The sentencer should not allow the provisions for early release by the Home Secretary to affect the determination of the length of the period of detention. The sentence of 7 years was longer than was absolutely necessary and terms of 4 years for the robberies and 6 months for the firearms offences would be substituted (*R. v. Butler* [1985] C.L.Y. 815 considered).

R. *v.* BURROWES (1985) 7 Cr.App.R. (S.) 106, C.A.

848. Sentence—making a false statement as to services provided—immediate custodial sentence

[Trade Descriptions Act 1968 (c.29), s.20(1).]

It is important to discourage offences where it is impossible for the customer to tell whether repairs had been done to machinery as claimed or not.

B pleaded guilty to 4 offences under the Trade Descriptions Act 1968, s.20(1), of making false statements as to the nature of services provided. He was the director of a small company which repaired washing machines. On a number of occasions invoices were submitted for repairs that had not been carried out, involving a total of about £200. B was sentenced to 9 months' imprisonment, with 3 to serve and the balance held in suspense. *Held,* that although B was an elderly man facing a criminal charge for the first time and was not in good health it was important that dishonest tradesmen should be discouraged from taking advantage of the public who could not determine whether repairs had been carried out or not. The sentence, if anything was on the light side (*R.* v. *Lester* [1976] C.L.Y. 586 and *R.* v. *Edelson* [1978] C.L.Y. 595 distinguished).

R. *v.* BURRIDGE (1985) 7 Cr.App.R. (S.) 125, C.A.

849. Sentence—manslaughter—death during fight—length of sentence

Where two men caused the death of a third unintentionally while giving him a beating 7 years' imprisonment was reduced to 4.

The deceased was living with the daughter of one appellant and sister of the other. They went to his home and fought with him, in the course of which he died. Both appellants were charged with murder, but acquitted thereof and convicted of manslaughter. *Held,* that by their verdict the jury had indicated that they were not satisfied that the appellants had intended to kill their victim. The court would ordinarily in such a case endeavour to disregard the fact that the victim had died: on such a basis, had the deceased not in fact, accidentally, been killed the appellants would have been convicted of malicious wounding with a maximum sentence of 5 years. On that basis 7 years' imprisonment was too severe and the sentences would be reduced to 4 years.

R. *v.* MCNAMARA (1984) 6 Cr.App.R.(S.) 356, C.A.

850. Sentence—manslaughter—provocation

Five years' imprisonment reduced to four for a man convicted of manslaughter by reason of provocation.

M was convicted of manslaughter. While he was serving a prison sentence his wife formed an association with another man. After his release he returned to his wife who boasted of that association as well as mocking M's sexual prowess. He strangled her with a sash cord. He was sentenced to five years' imprisonment. *Held,* that in view of the mitigating factors, in particular the gross provocation and the remorse felt afterwards by the appellant—as shown by his attempt to commit suicide—the sentence was too severe. The sentence would be reduced to four years' imprisonment.

R. *v.* MELLENTIN (1985) 7 Cr.App.R.(S.) 9, C.A.

851. Sentence—manslaughter—young child killed by father—single incident by man of good character—length of sentence

Four years' imprisonment is the suitable sentence for a man of previous good character who violently beat his daughter on one occasion causing her death.

W pleaded guilty to manslaughter. In the course of chastising his 3 year old daughter he hit her on the buttocks with a stick. In consequence of the beating she sustained the daughter died. There was no evidence of any previous maltreatment of the child and W was a man of good character. W was sentenced to 7 years' imprisonment. *Held,* substituting a sentence of 4 years imprisonment, that it was an isolated incident in which W lost his temper and hit his daughter too hard with the result that she died. Having regard to the circumstances in which the offence was committed and W's character 7 years' imprisonment was excessive.

R. *v.* WILLIAMS (DANIEL LEROY) (1984) 6 Cr.App.R.(S.) 298, C.A.

852. Sentence—mental illness supervening after prison sentence—judicial and executive powers

[Mental Health Act 1983 (c.20), ss.37, 47, 49.]

Where mental illness supervenes after the imposition of a prison sentence the court will seldom interfere as the executive has sufficient powers to make the necessary orders.

C pleaded guilty to importing cocaine and was sentenced to five years' imprisonment. At the time of his trial there was no suggestion of mental illness, but subsequently he became ill and was transferred to hospital where a restriction order was made; because of a shortage of beds he was transferred back to prison while still mentally ill. *Held,* dismissing the appeal, that the public was entitled to be protected, the sentence would stand, and if any further action needed to be taken it could be by the executive order s.37 or by a deportation order.

R. *v.* CASTRO (1985) 81 Cr.App.R. 212, C.A.

853. Sentence—mitigation—consistency

Magistrates should consider whether they should exercise their discretion to permit a change of plea where mitigation is advanced which is inconsistent with a guilty plea: R. *v.* SOUTH SEFTON JUSTICES, *ex p.* RABACA, *The Times,* February 20, 1985, Div. Ct.

854. Sentence—obscene exhibitions—sentence of immediate imprisonment and fine in addition appropriate

Twelve months' imprisonment was appropriate where a man was convicted of being involved in the management of a cinema showing obscene films.

C was part owner of a cinema club where a film showing scenes of buggery was found. He had a previous conviction for an offence involving obscene publications. Within 10 months of his release from that sentence he had become involved in the cinema club. He was convicted and sentenced to 12 months' immediate imprisonment and a fine of £10,000. *Held,* that the sentence of 12 months could not be considered wrong in principle having regard to the fact that this was C's second conviction. The fine was not merely punitive, it was also intended to deprive C of at least part of the proceeds of the commercial exploitation of pornography. Having regard to the comparatively short period of C's involvement with the cinema the fine would be reduced to £5,000 (*R. v. Rolt* [1985] C.L.Y. 802, *R. v. Zampa* (1984) 6 Cr.App.R. (S.) 110, *R. v. Holloway* [1982] C.L.Y. 700 considered).

R. *v.* CALLEJA (1985) 7 Cr.App.R. (S.) 13, C.A.

855. Sentence—obscene publications—selling obscene video tapes to sex shops

Sentence of 18 months' imprisonment reduced to nine months' for supplying obscene video tapes to sex shops.

V was convicted on two separate indictments of possessing obscene articles for publication for gain. On two occasions V delivered video tapes to sex shops. On the first occasion V was carrying 14 cassettes in a plastic bag and when stopped admitted that the cassettes were his and that he sold them for £15 each. On the second occasion in similar circumstances V had one obscene video tape in his possession. V was aged 47, lived with a lady who had 2 children aged 4 and 7 by him, had sporadic previous convictions and had worked variously in the sex business in the Soho area. V was sentenced to 18 months' imprisonment in respect of the second offence, where his not guilty plea resulted in a jury being shown a film that caused them great distress and anger, and six months' imprisonment concurrent for the first offence. *Held,* allowing V's appeal, that V was little more than a delivery man and not making a lot of money for himself from those activities. He was not a man behind a pornographic enterprise. The sentence of 18 months' imprisonment was out of proportion and would be reduced to 9 months' in total consisting of 3 months for the first offence and 6 months' for the second (*R. v. Holloway* [1982] C.L.Y. 700 considered).

R. *v.* VELLA (1984) 6 Cr.App.R.(S.) 373, C.A.

855a. Sentence—obtaining small sums of money by deception—offender with long record of similar offences

A sentence of 3½ years' imprisonment is too harsh for an offender who was more of a pest and nuisance than a vicious and wicked criminal.

C pleaded guilty to 5 offences of obtaining by deception with 42 other offences to be taken into consideration. The sums involved were about £5. C had been sentenced to imprisonment on 10 previous occasions. The trial judge sentenced him to 3½ years' imprisonment. *Held,* that the sentence passed is one that one would expect to be passed where a man is a really vicious and persistent criminal. This was not that type of case. However in view of C's past record of persistent offending a prison sentence was inevitable. The sentence of 3½ years' imprisonment was quashed and a sentence of 12 months imprisonment was substituted.

R. *v.* COCKERILL (1985) 7 Cr.App.R.(S) 27, C.A.

856. Sentence—partly suspended sentence—appropriate sentence

The court could properly impose a sentence of immediate youth custody equal to the length of imprisonment a defendant would have served under a partly suspended sentence where such a sentence could not be imposed by reason of the defendant's age.

T pleaded guilty to an offence of wounding contrary to s.20 of the Offences against the Person Act. T stabbed a man in the course of a fight in the car park of a public house after a heated discussion on politics in the public house. The victim spent 10 days in hospital having undergone surgery for a wound that could have been a great deal more serious. T was of previous good character, had a good education and was supported by a good social inquiry report. T made no attempt to escape after the incident, co-operated fully with the police and was instrumental in obtaining help for his victim. T was sentenced to two years' youth custody. *Held,* allowing T's appeal, that two years' imprisonment was the correct sentence for the offence. Having regard to T's character it was appropriate to suspend part of that sentence. A partly suspended sentence could not be imposed on T by virtue of his age. In the circumstances it was proper to impose a sentence of imprisonment equivalent in length to the period of imprisonment that would have been served under a partly suspended sentence. A sentence of 15 months' youth custody was substituted for the sentence of two years' youth custody (*R. v. Dobbs and Hitchings* [1984] C.L.Y. 939 applied).

R. *v.* Trew (1984) 6 Cr.App.R.(S.) 345, C.A.

857. Sentence—partly suspended sentence—offender already subject to sentence of imprisonment

It is not good sentencing practice to impose a partly suspended sentence upon an offender who is already serving a term of imprisonment.

Y pleaded guilty to the theft of a car. At the time of sentence he was already serving an immediate sentence of 15 months' imprisonment. He was sentenced to 18 months' imprisonment with nine months to serve and the balance held in suspense.

Held, that although not quite the same as passing a fully suspended sentence upon someone already serving a custodial sentence, a partly suspended sentence was still bad practice although it could not be said to be unlawful. As the sentence was not excessive, however, there was no reason to alter it.

R. *v.* Young (1985) 7 Cr.App.R.(S.) 72, C.A.

858. Sentence—partly suspended sentence—offence committed whilst defendant serving period of imprisonment—activation of suspended part of sentence

[Criminal Law Act 1977 (c.45), s.47.]

A sentence of imprisonment suspended on a partly suspended sentence could be activated where the defendant committed a further offence during the period of imprisonment served initially.

T was sentenced to 18 months' imprisonment for burglary. T was ordered to serve twelve months' of that sentence and the remaining six months' was suspended. In the course of serving the initial twelve months imprisonment T absconded from prison and commited a number of thefts by taking food, clothing and maps from shops. For the shop-lifting offences T was sentenced to one months' imprisonment for each offence to run concurrently. The judge activated the suspended part of the partly suspended sentence. T appealed. *Held,* dismissing T's appeal, that T had been convicted of offences punishable with imprisonment and committed during the whole period of the original sentence within the meaning of s.47(3) of the Criminal Law Act 1977. "The whole period" included the initial period of imprisonment and the period which was suspended.

R. *v.* Taylor (J. S.) (1984) 6 Cr.App.R.(S.) 448, C.A.

859. Sentence—passing counterfeit notes

The passing of counterfeit notes requires a custodial sentence to punish the wrongdoer and to act as a deterrent to him and others.

H, of previous good character, pleaded guilty to having custody of counterfeit currency and of tendering a counterfeit note. By the quantity of notes in his possession it was obvious that he was close to the source of the counterfeit notes. He was sentenced to two years' imprisonment. *Held,* that the issue of counterfeit notes undermines the economy and causes great loss to innocent people. This type of offence, in nearly every case will require a custodial sentence to punish the offender, to deter him from committing the same sort of offence again and to deter others from so doing. Therefore the sentence was entirely appropriate.

R. *v.* Howard (1986) 82 Cr.App.R. 262, C.A.

860. Sentence—passing counterfeit notes

Three years' imprisonment is an appropriate sentence for an offender who, over a period of time, persistently passes counterfeit £50 notes.

H pleaded guilty to three counts of passing counterfeit notes and 32 similar offences were taken into consideration. He was arrested when he attempted to purchase a pair of sunglasses with a counterfeit £50 note. He was sentenced to three years' imprisonment. *Held,* that H was only a distributor but he was operating in a skilled way and had passed off counterfeit notes for a period of about two and a half weeks making a profit of £900. He was persistent in what he was doing. He had a record of drug addition and of dishonesty. The offence he committed was a serious one and so the sentence was an appropriate one.

R. *v*. HUNTINGDON (1985) 7 Cr.App.R.(S.) 168, C.A.

861. Sentence—police informer—guidelines on sentencing reduction

A large-scale police informer can expect a reduction in his proper sentence from about one-half to two-thirds according to the circumstances of the case, but no hard and fast rule can be laid down.

The appellant pleaded guilty to one count of robbery and six of burglary, which entailed theft of high value goods from commercial premises, and valued at £150,000 in all. He was the organiser of 31 professionally executed burglaries and three robberies, snatches rather than violent robberies. He had previous convictions but not since between 1976 and 1983 and had not served a previous term of imprisonment. He was sentenced to 6 years' imprisonment having given information after apprehension that led to the conviction of 17 others and to the detection of others. The Court of Appeal said that no hard and fast rule could be laid down as to the amount of reduction of sentence for a large scale informer. The court should first assess the gravity and number of the offences of the informer to reach a starting figure. Where robberies involve firearms, disguises, detailed plans, or attacks on security guards, the guidelines in *R. v. Turner* (1975) 61 Cr.App.R. 132 will be applied to reach a figure in the region of 18 years or more. In the case of multiple burglaries where no violence has been used the starting figure will usually be less, depending on the number of cases and whether the property was houses or commercial premises. The amount of the reduction will depend on a number of variables, such as the quality and quantity of the information, its accuracy, the informer's willingness to confront other criminals or give evidence against them, and the degree of risk of reprisal to himself and his family. He could then expect a substantial mitigation to produce the information, varying from about one-half to two-thirds reduction, according to the circumstances, in what would otherwise be the proper sentence. Applying these principles the starting point in the appellant's case was 10 years. As the assistance given to the police was great, the proper net figure was 4½ years imprisonment, and the sentence was reduced accordingly (*R. v. Sinfield* (1981) 3 Cr.App.R.(S) 258 considered).

R. *v*. KING (1986) 82 Cr.App.R. 120, C.A.

862. Sentence—possessing firearm with intent to commit indictable offence—length of sentence

It is not wrong in principle to impose a longer term of imprisonment for the offence of possessing a firearm with intent to commit an indictable offence than could have been imposed had that offence been committed.

S was convicted of possessing an imitation pistol with the intention of committing an assault. S had planned to use the pistol to threaten another man to give him certain information. He was sentenced to two years' imprisonment. S argued that this was wrong in principle because the maximum sentence for the intended offence— common assault—was limited to 12 months.

Held, that the use of a real or imitation firearm took the matter into a more serious area. The maximum sentence for the offence of possessing a firearm with intent to commit an indictable offence was 14 years' imprisonment. There is no restriction on the sentence to that applicable to the offence intended. The indictable offence contemplated does not restrict the sentence. The sentence imposed was correct.

R. *v*. SHELDRAKE (1985) 7 Cr.App.R.(S.) 49, C.A.

863. Sentence—possibility of psychiatric treatment—referred to by judge

A sentencer imposing a sentence of imprisonment should not express the hope that the offender will be sent to a particular prison for treatment.

W pleaded guilty to two counts of obtaining by deception with 71 other offences taken into consideration. All of the offences involved the dishonest use of cheque books and cheque cards. W had a long history of such behaviour. He was sentenced to a total of two years' imprisonment (which included two activated suspended sentences). The sentencer expressed the hope that W might go to Grendon Underwood prison for psychiatric treatment.

Held, that a sentencing judge should not make reference to the possibility of treatment at Grendon Underwood. Where an offender goes to prison is not a matter for the court—the reference to a particular prison would create an expectation that may not be fulfilled. The sentence would be reduced to a total of 15 months' imprisonment (*R.* v. *Thompson* [1984] C.L.Y. 929; *R.* v. *Hook* (1980) 2 Cr.App.R.(S.) 353 and *R.* v. *Tate* [1983] C.L.Y. 828 considered).

R. *v.* WATSON (J. G.) (1985) 7 Cr.App.R.(S.) 79, C.A.

864. Sentence—power of Crown Court to alter sentence—interval of several days
[Supreme Court Act 1981 (c.54), s.47(2).]
N was convicted of conspiracy to defraud and of three counts of false imprisonment. He was sentenced to 10 years' imprisonment on each count concurrently. Fourteen days later the sentencer, after hearing counsel, varied the sentences to run consecutively. N was then subject to a total of 20 years' imprisonment. *Held,* that this is not a case where the judge has altered sentence because of an earlier lapse of memory. The sentence was altered because after 14 days the judge felt that the sentences he had passed did not reflect the full culpability of the offender. The case should be approached on the basis that it may not appear that justice has been done. This does not mean that under no circumstances can sentences be increased but in this case the original sentence will be restored (*R.* v. *Grice* [1978] C.L.Y 625, *R.* v. *Sodhi* [1978] C.L.Y. 632, *R.* v. *Newsome and Browne* [1970] C.L.Y 513 considered).

R. *v.* NODJOUMI (1985) 7 Cr.App.R.(S.) 183, C.A.

865. Sentence—power to disqualify from acting as director of company
The power to disqualify an offender from acting as a director of a company under s.188(1) of the Companies Act 1948 (Now s.295 of the Companies Act 1985) is not limited to cases of offences related to the internal management of the company.
A pleaded guilty to nine charges relating to fraudulent hire purchase transactions. He had been the director of companies set up to raise money by fraudulent hire purchase transactions and obtained about £300,000. He was sentenced to three years' imprisonment, ordered to pay compensation of £83,000 and disqualified from being a director of a company for 10 years. He appealed, arguing that the power to disqualify was limited to offences that related to the internal management of the company. *Held,* applying *R.* v. *Corbin* [1985] C.L.Y. 790 that the power to disqualify applied to offences "committed in connection with the management of the company" and that applied to both internal and external affairs. The period of disqualification was appropriate. (*R.* v. *Corbin* [1985] C.L.Y. 790 applied).

R. *v.* AUSTEN (1985) 7 Cr.App.R.(S.) 214, C.A.

866. Sentence—qualification for parole—activated partially suspended sentence
[Criminal Law Act 1977 (c.45), s.47; Eligibility for Release on Licence Order (S.I. 1983 No. 1958).]
Activation of the suspended portion of a partially suspended sentence under s.47 of the Criminal Law Act 1977 is not wrong even where, by reason of the anomalous position produced by the Eligibility for Release on Licence Order 1983 the offender is thus worse off than he might have been had the whole term been imposed immediately.
D committed an offence and was sentenced to 18 months imprisonment of which 12 were suspended. He served 4 and was then released having earned 2 months remission for good conduct. During the suspension he committed another offence and was sentenced to one month's imprisonment and the 12 months was activated consecutively. He was entitled to parole after serving 6 months or one-third of his sentence whichever was the longer. He appealed, claiming that even if he got parole he would have to serve a minimum of 6 months the second time whereas if the whole of the 18 months had been imposed immediately, he might only have to serve 6 months on qualifying for parole instead of a minimum of 10. *Held,* that even though an anomaly had arisen out of the Eligibility for Release on Licence Order 1983 the sentence was correct and it was not one of the considerations a court should take into account in deciding whether or not to activate a partially suspended sentence under s.47(4) of the Criminal Law Act 1977.

R. *v.* HANNELL (1985) 82 Cr.App.R. 41, C.A.

867. Sentence—rape by burglar
B pleaded guilty to counts of burglary and one count of rape. He had entered a dwelling house in the early hours of the morning and raped the 19 year old occupant.

Sentenced to 10 years' imprisonment for the rape. *Held,* that B was not armed, there was no conversation between him and the victim, the rape was not pre-meditated and B now showed remorse. In the light of these factors the sentence is out of line with the reported offences of this nature. The sentence of 10 years' imprisonment will be quashed and a sentence of 7 years' imprisonment substituted therefor. (*R.* v. *Roberts* [1982] C.L.Y. 703 discussed).

R. *v.* BLACK (1985) 7 Cr.App.R.(S.) 325, C.A.

868. Sentence—rape—guidelines

The Court of Appeal has laid down guidelines for sentences for rape, attempted rape, and associated offences.

The Court of Appeal when considering sentences in 17 cases of rape and other associated offences said that statistics revealed that sentences were too low, and gave guidelines.

Rape was a serious crime calling for custodial sentence other than in wholly exceptional cases, as in *R.* v. *Taylor* [1984] C.L.Y. 911. Where there was no aggravating or mitigating feature, rape by an adult should merit a starting point of five years in a contested case. Where there were two or more men acting together, or where it was committed after a man broke into where the victim was, or where it was by a person in a position of responsibility to the victim or by a person who abducts the victim and holds her captive, the starting point should be eight years. Where there was a campaign of rape of a number of victims, 15 years or more might be appropriate. Where the behaviour was perverted or showed psychopathic tendencies or gross personality disorder, and the defendant was likely to remain a danger for an indefinite time if left at large, a life sentence is not inappropriate. The crime is aggravated if there is additional violence, or a weapon is used to frighten or wound, or if the rape is repeated, or is carefully planned, or if the defendant has previous convictions for rape or other serious offences of a violent or sexual kind, or if the victim is subjected to further sexual indignities or perversions, or the victim is very old or young, or if the effect is specially serious. Where the offence is aggravated the starting point should be substantially higher. A plea of guilty which would obviate a victim giving evidence should normally result in a reduction of sentence depending on all the circumstances, including the likelihood of a verdict of not guilty had the matter been contested. The fact that a victim acted imprudently, *e.g.* by accepting a lift from a stranger is not a mitigating factor, and her previous sexual experience is irrelevant. There should be some mitigation if the defendant was led to believe that she would consent to sexual intercourse. Previous good character is only of minor significance. The starting point for attempted rape should be less especially if desisted from early on but aggravating features might make it more serious than rape itself. Youths under 21 should receive youth custody but reduced to reflect their age. A juvenile court should never accept jurisdiction to deal with a rape case.

R. *v.* BILLAM [1986] 1 W.L.R. 349, C.A.

869. Sentence—rape of former wife—former wife living with offender

C pleaded guilty to rape. The victim was his former wife who, after the divorce, returned to live with C until alternative accommodation could be found. They shared the same bed and had sexual intercourse from time to time. One night C had been drinking heavily, came home and had intercourse with his former wife against her will. She reported the matter to the police. Sentenced to four years' imprisonment. *Held,* that C was not entitled to act in the way he did. It was a rape with aggravating features. However, it was an exceptional case and the sentence could be reduced to three years' imprisonment.

R. *v.* Cox (1985) 7 Cr.App.R.(S.) 422, C.A.

870. Sentence—rape—young adult offender—whether custody right—length of sentence

Four years' youth custody upheld for man of 20 who raped girl of 11.

P, aged, 20, had raped an educationally retarded girl of 11 who had come to his home to play with his daughter. He was for practical purposes of previous good character. *Held,* that 4 years' imprisonment was appropriate on the facts of the case, and could not be said to be excessive. He had admitted the offence without argument and expressed considerable and genuine remorse; he had a good work record. But the fact was that this was an appalling offence and the judge had fully considered the many mitigating factors present in passing a sentence of 4 years' imprisonment. It was quite impossible to say that that sentence was manifestly excessive, and the appeal would be dismissed.

R. *v.* PEARTON (1984) 6 Cr.App.R.(S.) 314, C.A.

871. Sentence—reasons for imprisonment—drug addiction

Curing an offender of drug addiction is an improper reason for passing a long sentence of imprisonment.

B pleaded guilty to various counts of burglary, obtaining by deception and possessing a controlled drug. He had committed the offences to obtain money to buy heroin to which he was addicted. He was sentenced to 5 years imprisonment, the judge observing that a considerable period in custody was the only hope for B. *Held*, that that was an improper reason for passing a long sentence of imprisonment. The sentence would be reduced to a total of 3 years' imprisonment.

R. *v.* BASSETT (1985) 7 Cr.App.R. (S.) 75, C.A.

872. Sentence—reckless driving—causing injuries—repeatedly overtaking and slowing down

Eighteen months' imprisonment is too harsh for a driver who persistently overtakes motor cyclists and then slows down causing a collision and injuries.

C pleaded guilty to reckless driving. He was driving his car and was overtaken by 2 motor cyclists. He overtook them and then slowed down. This happened several times until a collision occurred. C was subsequently found to have excess alcohol in his blood and was dealt with for the offence by a magistrate's court. He was sentenced to 18 months' immediate imprisonment and disqualified from driving for 7 years. *Held*, that having regard to the facts that this was not the most serious instance of reckless driving (although it is a very serious case), the collision had not been caused deliberately and C had pleaded guilty, the sentence of 18 months' was too long and would be reduced to 12 months' imprisonment. The period of disqualification was also unnecessarily long and would be reduced to 3 years.

R. *v.* CARRIER (1985) 7 Cr.App.R. (S.) 57 C.A.

873. Sentence—reckless driving—custodial sentence

A sentence of 6 months' imprisonment is correct for reckless driving resulting in serious injury.

B pleaded guilty to reckless driving. He had been drinking at 5 public houses and consumed 14 pints of beer. He was found to have 3 times the permitted level of alcohol in his body. He was driving a car knowing that the brakes were defective. He drove at high speed to beat another car to a particular point when, on a bend, the car turned on one side. One of B's passengers was paralysed from the waist down. B had no previous convictions for bad driving, and he was sentenced to 6 months' imprisonment and disqualified from driving for 3 years. *Held*, that if death had resulted the appropriate sentence would have been in the region of 18 months. As the only mitigating factors were that B had pleaded guilty and had no previous convictions for bad driving and these had been taken into account by the judge, the sentence was right in principle and not excessive.

R. *v.* BILTON (1985) 7 Cr.App.R. (S.) 103, C.A.

874. Sentence—reckless driving—offender aged 20 of good character

Community service rather than youth custody is appropriate for a young offender of previous good character for reckless driving.

E aged 20 and of previous good character stole a parked motor cycle. He was seen by the police and a chase ensued during which E drove through 2 red traffic lights, exceeded the speed limit, went the wrong way round a bollard, caused traffic to stop and finally mounted a pavement. He was immediately arrested and admitted what had happened. He pleaded guilty to charges of taking a conveyance without authority and reckless driving and was sentenced to 1 month and 6 months' youth custody consecutive. *Held*, allowing the appeal, that the taking of the motorcycle was premeditated and the reckless driving bad and persistent, but for a young man of good character the appropriate sentence would be 150 hours' community service and since E had served 46 days' youth custody, the sentence would be varied so that he serve 100 hours community service.

R. *v.* EMERY [1985] R.T.R. 415, C.A.

875. Sentence—restitution order

A restitution order should only be made where it is clear that the money or goods involved fall within the provisions of s.28 of the Theft Act 1968. No order should be made if there be any doubt.

C pleaded guilty to handling stolen property. She had received sums from V who had been stealing the money from her employer. Some of the money was used to buy household items. C was sentenced to 12 months' imprisonment suspended, and a restitution order was made relating to the whole sum stolen and certain items of property. *Held*, that C disputed that certain items of property had been bought with stolen funds. Although the judge had ample evidence on which the order relating to the specified items could have been justified, C had not given evidence. The order should not have been made as the trial judge had not fully investigated the matter. The order relating to specific items would therefore be quashed.

R. *v.* CALCUTT AND VARTY (1985) 7 Cr.App.R.(S.) 385, C.A.

876. Sentence—robbery—'mugging' an old lady—youth custody

Where two youths had "mugged" a partially blind 78-year-old lady substantial periods of imprisonment or youth custody were required. Anything other than a substantial sentence would be an affront to the public.

J and S pleaded guilty to robbery. They had been drinking and behaving in a loutish manner at a bus stop. A 78-year-old lady got off a bus and they "rushed" her and grabbed a music case. She was not physically hurt but suffered shock the next day. Both offenders had previous convictions for dishonesty. They were sentenced to four years' youth custody. *Held*, that although it is important not to allow emotion to carry away a sentencer, this was a serious offence where substantial terms of imprisonment or youth custody had to be imposed or else the public would be affronted. In the circumstances the sentences were perfectly proper and were not excessive.

R. *v.* JACQUES AND SHAW (1985) 7 Cr.App.R.(S.) 61, C.A.

877. Sentence—robbery—possession of firearm with intent—consecutive sentences

It is an established exception to the principle that where two or more offences are committed in the course of one transaction the sentences should be concurrent but that where a firearm is used in the course of a robbery the offender should receive consecutive sentences for the robbery and for possession of a firearm.

B pleaded guilty to robbery and possession of a firearm with intent to commit an indictable offence. B and another robbed a bingo club of £4,000. B carried a sawn-off shotgun and his accomplice a knife. B was sentenced to seven years' imprisonment for the robbery and one years' imprisonment for possession of a firearm, both sentences to run consecutively. The co-defendant was sentenced to four years' youth custody. B appealed. *Held*, that B was the older man, he had planned the robbery and had a bad record, the disparity between the sentences of the two defendants was therefore appropriate. The total sentence was not excessive. The public interest demanded that sentences imposed for the offences of robbery and of possession of a firearm with intent should run consecutively not concurrently. This was stated in the case of *R. v. Faulkner* [1972] C.L.Y. 1550 and confirmed in *R. v. French* [1983] C.L.Y. 757. The case of *R. v. Rouse* [1985] C.L.Y. 741 did not limit the principle laid down in *Faulkner*. An offender who commits a robbery while carrying a firearm must normally expect a substantial consecutive sentence for the offence of carrying a firearm. (*R. v. Faulkner* [1972] C.L.Y. 1550, *R. v. French* [1983] C.L.Y. 757 applied, *R. v. Rouse* [1985] C.L.Y. 741 distinguished).

R. *v.* BOTTOMLEY (1985) 7 Cr.App.R.(S.) 355, C.A.

878. Sentence—robbery—shorter sentence on driver than on perpetrators

No distinction is to be drawn between the various participants in a robbery—each has his role to play in the commission of the offence.

C pleaded guilty to robbery. C and two others had robbed Post Office employees of £104,000. C took part in the actual robbery whilst P was the driver of the escape car. P also pleaded guilty and was sentenced to 10 years' imprisonment. C was sentenced to 12 years' imprisonment. *Held*, applying the general principles set out in *R. v. Britt* (unreported) that no distinction was to be drawn between the participants in a robbery to avoid objectionable disparity in sentences where no real difference in culpability existed. Accordingly C's sentence would be reduced to 10 years' imprisonment. (*R. v. Britt* (unreported) discussed).

R. *v.* CHURCH (1985) 7 Cr.App.R.(S.) 370, C.A.

879. Sentence—robbery—youths wearing masks and carrying imitation firearms

C pleaded guilty to robbery. With three other youths, all masked and carrying imitation firearms, he robbed a residential establishment, struck three people and stole £350. Sentenced to six years' youth custody. *Held,* that given the aggravating features of this case (the masks, the imitation firearms, the violence initiated by C) the sentence was entirely correct.

R. *v.* CHRISTOPHER (1985) 7 Cr.App.R.(S.) 308, C.A.

880. Sentence—soliciting to murder

The offence of soliciting to murder required a substantial element of deterrence. A sentence of 10 years' imprisonment was fully justified.

P pleaded guilty to two counts of soliciting to murder. P was in financial difficulties, approached a man and promised him £5,000 to murder P's wife and daughter. P then took out an insurance policy on his wife's life. P was sentenced to 10 years' imprisonment. *Held,* that P had insisted on the murder of his wife and of his daughter and had paid considerable sums of money to that end. It was a grave case and a substantial element of deterrence was necessary in such cases. The sentence was an appropriate one (*R. v. Raw* [1984] C.L.Y 917 distinguished; *R. v. Walker and Cook* (1981) 3 Cr.App.R.(S.) 235 considered).

R. *v.* PEATFIELD (1985) 7 Cr.App.R.(S.) 132, C.A.

881. Sentence—statutory limitation on length—disparity—whether ground for reducing sentence

Where disparity in the sentences of two defendants was caused by a statutory limitation on the length of imprisonment to be imposed on one, that disparity could not be a ground for reducing the term of imprisonment imposed upon the other.

T was convicted of possessing an offensive weapon and wounding with intent to do grievous bodily harm contrary to s.18 of the Offences against the Person Act 1861. W was convicted of possessing an offensive weapon and unlawful wounding contrary to s.20 of the Offences against the Person Act 1861. T and W had armed themselves with wooden clubs studded with nails. In addition T had a 6 inch long kitchen knife. For no reason at all T and W attacked their victim and in the course of the fight T stabbed the victim in the back and punctured his lung. The victim spent 4 days in an intensive care unit and thereafter recovered. The trial judge formed the view that T and W had armed themselves with dreadful weapons to hunt down innocent people and cause them injury. At the time of the offences T was 16 and W 15. At trial both were one year older. T was sentenced to six years' youth custody and W to 12 months' youth custody. By virtue of the provisions of s.7(8) of the Criminal Justice Act 1982 12 months youth custody was the maximum term that could be imposed on W. *Held,* allowing T's appeal, that the disparity between the sentences imposed on T and W resulted from the application of statutory provisions. It was not a disparity in the accepted sense of the word that might justify a reduction in the sentence imposed on T. The length of sentence imposed on T was right for the offence but having regard to his young age and the support he would receive from his family it was proper to reduce the sentence imposed upon him to four and a half years' youth custody.

R. *v.* TYRE (1984) 6 Cr.App.R.(S.) 247, C.A.

882. Sentence—suspended sentence—new offence—magistrates deciding to impose fresh suspended sentence—position of Crown Court

On an offender committing a fresh offence during the period of deferment of a sentence of imprisonment suspended by the Crown Court and being sentenced by a magistrates' court to a new suspended sentence the Crown Court may still activate the original suspended sentence.

In July 1983 H had been sentenced to 4 months' imprisonment suspended for 2 years for an offence of theft. During the period of suspension he was sentenced to further periods of imprisonment, again suspended, for offences of criminal damage and being on enclosed premises. When the new offences were reported to the Crown Court that court activated the first sentence in full. He appealed. *Held,* that the fact that the magistrates had decided to deal with the new offences themselves was no reason for the Crown Court to feel itself bound not to activate the original suspended sentence. The Crown Court retained full discretion in the matter, and it was impossible on the facts of the case to say that the Crown Court had erred (*R. v. Ipswich Crown Court, ex p. Williamson* [1983] C.L.Y. 891 considered).

R. *v.* HAMILTON (1984) 6 Cr.App.R.(S.) 451, C.A.

883. Sentence—suspended sentence—where appropriate

It is inappropriate to pass a suspended sentence of imprisonment where a sentence of imprisonment is not appropriate.

J was convicted of stealing an electric fire worth £10·99 from his landlady. He was fined £100, ordered to pay £100 prosecution costs and sentenced to 28 days' imprisonment suspended for two years. *Held,* that the sentence was wrong in principle. Although the offence merited a fine it did not merit a sentence of imprisonment. It followed that it was inappropriate to pass a suspended sentence. The court should first consider whether a sentence of imprisonment was appropriate and then go on to consider suspending that sentence in whole or part. The sentence of imprisonment would be quashed.

R. *v.* JEFFREY (1985) 7 Cr.App.R.(S.) 11, C.A.

884. Sentence—theft—breach of trust

C was convicted of theft. He had stolen £350 in cash whilst he was the honorary booking secretary of a community centre. Sentenced to 4½ months' immediate imprisonment. *Held,* that the sentence was not inappropriate or incorrect. Applying the guidelines set out in *R. v. Barrick* [1985] C.L.Y. 765, an immediate custodial sentence was inevitable in cases of breach of trust by theft unless there were exceptional circumstances or the amounts involved were small. Here there were no exceptional circumstances—it was a straightforward breach of trust and, the sum involved was not insignificant. The sentence should therefore be sufficiently severe to mark publicly the gravity of the offence (*R. v. Barrick* [1985] C.L.Y. 765 applied).

R. *v.* CHATFIELD (1985) 7 Cr.App.R.(S.) 262, C.A.

885. Sentence—theft—breach of trust

C pleaded guilty to counts of obtaining by deception, attempting to obtain by deception and false accounting with five other offences to be considered. C was employed as a clerk with authority to certify invoices for payment. He obtained false invoices, certified them for payment and shared the proceeds with an accomplice. His employers were defrauded of £1,000. Sentenced to six months' imprisonment. *Held,* applying *R. v. Barrick* [1985] C.L.Y. 765, that the circumstances of this case were not so exceptional, nor was the amount involved so small as to fall within the category of cases where an immediate custodial sentence was not necessary. The sentence would be upheld. (*R. v. Barrick* [1985] C.L.Y. 765 applied).

R. *v.* COLLEY (1985) 7 Cr.App.R.(S.) 264, C.A.

886. Sentence—theft by baggage handlers

Three years immediate imprisonment was the starting point for persistent, systematic and extensive pilfering. On a plea of guilty some reduction would be made, but such a plea was watered down in the circumstances, where D was recorded on film committing the offences, and would not otherwise have been caught: R. *v.* DHUNAY, *The Times*, April 2, 1986. C.A.

887. Sentence—theft from employer

Two months' immediate imprisonment for a shop assistant who stole £1,700 from her employer is not wrong in principle or extent.

B pleaded guilty to 2 counts of theft and 2 of false accounting, with 30 similar offences taken into consideration. She had been employed in a supermarket and, over a period of several months stole sums of £100 by falsely recording till purchases. The judge took into account her good character, her frankness to the police, her willingness to pay back £500 and her plea of guilty but the breach of trust placed in her by her employer weighed against this as well as the fact that the offences were committed over a long period of time. *Held,* that there was nothing wrong either in principle or extent of the sentence imposed (*R. v. Weston* (1980) 2 Cr.App.R. (S.) 391 considered).

R. *v.* BAGNALL (1985) 7 Cr.App.R. (S.) 40, C.A.

888. Sentence—theft—large sums of money by insurance broker

Sentence of 5 years' imprisonment upheld for theft by defendant of over £80,000 entrusted to him in his capacity as an insurance broker.

T was a partner in a firm called Equity brokers. In 1982 the firm was in financial difficulties and T obtained employment as a branch manager with a company called Property Growth Assurance Co. He stole £36,000 from the company by diverting premiums from life assurance policies to Equity Brokers. He stole £600 from a fund set up by the Assurance Co. to assist employees in financial difficulties. He also stole

£46,000 from sums paid by individuals to Equity Brokers to be invested. T co-operated fully with the police once the offences came to light making their investigation one of the easiest they had undertaken. T pleaded guilty. He was 49, had no previous convictions, was married with 3 children, was an articulate and intelligent man and at the time of the offences earning £50,000 per year. The stolen money was not recovered and T was bankrupted with liabilities in excess of £150,000. The individual customers of Equity Brokers were unlikely to receive their money back but no loss to the customers of Assurance Co. was occasioned. T was sentenced to 5 years' imprisonment. *Held*, dismissing T's appeal, that there were no grounds for criticising the sentence imposed.

R. *v*. Taylor (M. J.) (1984) 6 Cr.App.R.(S.) 394, C.A.

889. Sentence—theft of large sum by employee

Four years' imprisonment is too long a sentence where the offender pleads guilty to the theft of large sums from his employer.

A pleaded guilty to nine counts of theft with five other offences taken into consideration. He had paid cheques in respect of VAT refunds into his own account rather than that of his employer. He had stolen some £185,000 which he gambled away. Sentenced to four years' imprisonment. *Held*, that had the trial judge had the advantage of having the case of *R*. v. *Barrick* [1985] C.L.Y. 765 before him he would have been impelled to impose a lesser sentence. Applying the guidelines laid down in that case a sentence of four years' imprisonment where the offender had pleaded guilty was too harsh. A sentence of three years' imprisonment would be substituted for the original sentence. (*R*. v. *Barrick* [1985] C.L.Y. 765 applied).

R. *v*. Ali (1985) 7 Cr.App.R.(S.) 337, C.A.

890. Sentence—unlawful wounding—striking victim in face with unbroken glass

The offence of unlawful wounding was not as serious as wounding with intent and so a long period of imprisonment is not appropriate.

M pleaded guilty to unlawful wounding. He had some previous convictions for assault. He had struck the victim in the face with an unbroken glass, inflicting cuts which needed stitches and left some minor scarring. He was sentenced to three years' imprisonment. *Held*, that the offence was not so serious as wounding with intent. A custodial sentence was appropriate but it should be reduced to two years' imprisonment.

R. *v*. McLoughlin (1985) 7 Cr.App.R.(S.) 67, C.A.

891. Sentence—unlawful wounding by youth of 19—youth custody sentence

[Offences against the Person Act 1861 (c.100), s.20.]

Three years' youth custody is an appropriate sentence for a 19-year-old who stabbed a man.

K pleaded guilty to unlawful wounding contrary to section 20 of the Offences against the Person Act 1861. After an argument in a public house he stabbed a man three times. One of the wounds was within three-quarters of an inch of the victim's heart. He also slashed the victim's nose. He was sentenced to three years' youth custody. *Held*, that although K has behaved well in prison, has a girlfriend who was pregnant and accepted responsibility for his acts and expressed remorse the offence was a serious one. He came very close to killing his victim and had gone to the public house equipped with the knife. This was a vicious and cruel attack and the sentence was an appropriate one.

R. *v*. Knight (D.) (1985) 7 Cr.App.R.(S.) 5, C.A.

892. Sentence—unlicensed fishing for salmon and trout on a commercial basis—imprisonment

A sentencer is entitled to conclude that the offenders were engaged in fishing on a commercial basis and to use his general knowledge of the incidence of unlicensed fishing in the area to determine the sentence.

J and G were convicted of unlicensed fishing. They were seen fishing with a drift net and were caught with three salmon and other fish. They were sentenced to three months' imprisonment. *Held*, that the sentences passed by the trial judge in the particular experience he had, were entirely proper in the circumstances of the offence.

R. *v*. Jacobs and Gillespie (1985) 7 Cr.App.R.(S.) 43, C.A.

893. Sentence—violence to young children

Six years' imprisonment upheld for a man who used violence on his two children on two occasions.

S was convicted of inflicting grievous bodily harm and of assault occasioning actual bodily harm. He had punched his two year old son on the head causing a fracture and had poured boiling water over his eight month old daughter. He was sentenced to six years' imprisonment.

Held, that the sentence must express public abhorrence for this sort of behaviour. It should also contain an element of punishment for the offender. In the circumstances the sentences were fully justified.

R. *v.* SIMS-REES (1985) 7 Cr.App.R.(S.) 120.

894. Sentence—whether probation order a "conviction"—suspended sentence

[Powers of Criminal Courts Act 1973 (c.62), ss.13(1), 22(1), 23(1)(*c*) and 26(10)(*b*).]

For the purposes of section 23(1)(*c*) of the Powers of Criminal Courts Act 1973 a probation order made in the Crown Court was a "conviction". It was not desirable to have a probation order and a suspended sentence running at the same time.

B was convicted of driving offences at the Crown Court and sentenced to nine months' imprisonment suspended for two years. Ten months later he was convicted of arson. The judge made a probation order for two years and further extended the period of suspension to run from the date of the second conviction. B appealed on the question as whether a probation order was a conviction and as to whether it was appropriate to vary the suspended sentence. *Held,* that the probation order had been made in the Crown Court, not the Magistrates' Court and was therefore a conviction. The Crown Court was therefore entitled to use its powers to vary the original suspended sentence. However, because it is undesirable to have a suspended sentence and a probation order running at the same time, the sentence, though technically lawful, would be amended by allowing the amended suspended sentence to stand and substitute for the probation order a sentence of one day's imprisonment (*R. v. Tarry* [1970] C.L.Y. 512 considered).

R. *v.* BARNES (W. T.) (1986) 83 Cr.App.R. 58, C.A.

894a. Sentence—wounding with intent—revenge attack

Twelve years' imprisonment was upheld on a man convicted of wounding with intent who attacked with an axe the wife of a man who had killed his son.

S was convicted of wounding with intent and unlawful wounding. S's son had been killed in a fight with L. L had been tried for murder but was acquitted on the basis of self-defence. Two years later when L was shopping with his wife and two small children, S came towards him with an axe. When L left the shop, S attacked L's wife with the axe causing facial injuries and fracturing her jaw. He then picked up her two-year-old son and threw him onto the shop counter. He was sentenced to twelve years for wounding with intent and five years concurrent for unlawfully wounding the child. *Held,* that the sentence was not too long. One of the reasons for the existence of the criminal law was to prevent people taking the law into their own hands, in particular in revenge feuds and vendettas. It was necessary for the judge to make clear that this kind of violence would be punished severely.

R. *v.* SAKHI (1984) 6 Cr.App.R.(S.) 309, C.A.

895. Sentence—youth custody—arson

Two years' youth custody is an inappropriate sentence for a youth of 17 who sets fire to a cafe.

S pleaded guilty to arson. After problems arose in relation to an association he had formed with a young girl he set fire to a cafe by pouring petrol over a pile of leaves next to the cafe wall and igniting it. The fire spread causing £60,000 worth of damage. S was sentenced to two years' youth custody.

Held, that as this was S's first custodial sentence and he had never been associated with an offence of this sort before, the sentence was too severe. A sentence of 12 months' youth custody would be substituted for the original sentence.

R. *v.* SWALLOW (1985) 7 Cr.App.R.(S.) 22, C.A.

896. Sentence—youth custody—criminal damage

Six months' youth custody is not an appropriate sentence for youths who damage a large number of car tyres.

T and others aged between 15 and 17 were convicted of criminal damage. After a party they had slashed a number of car tyres, causing damage to the value of £1,000. They were sentenced to six months' youth custody.

Held, that although an immediate custodial sentence was necessary here, regardless of the fact that the offenders were of previous good character and that the sentence may affect their education, a sentence of youth custody was not appropriate. A detention centre order for three months would be appropriate.

R. v. TRAVIS (1985) 7 Cr.App.R.(S.) 149, C.A.

897. Sentence—youth custody—criteria for imposition

[Criminal Justice Act 1982 (c.48), s.1(4).]

The theft of £2 by a sales assistant from her employer was not "so serious that a non custodial sentence cannot be justified".

B, aged 20 and of previous good character, pleaded guilty to theft of £2 from her employer. She was sentenced to 3 months' youth custody. *Held*, that on the facts of this case there was no basis for saying that B would not be able to respond to a non-custodial sentence or that a custodial sentence was necessary for the protection of the public. The theft of £2 was not "so serious that a non custodial sentence could not be justified". This would only apply to the kind of offence which, when committed by a young person would make right-thinking members of the public, knowing all the facts, feel that justice had not been done by the passing of any sentence other than a custodial one. The sentence was quashed and a conditional discharge for 12 months substituted for it.

R. v. BRADBOURN (1985) 7 Cr.App.R. (S.) 180, C.A.

898. Sentence—youth custody—grievous bodily harm with intent—robbery

Twelve years' youth custody is an appropriate sentence for a 19 year old youth who has stabbed two people in the course of two robberies.

S, aged 19, pleaded guilty to causing grievous bodily harm with intent and robbery. He had demanded money from an 81 year old lady and, when she refused to hand over her savings, he stabbed her in the right eye. A few days later S stabbed the manageress of a bookshop in the neck and stole £300 from the till. S was sentenced to 12 years' youth custody.

Held, that although the judge was under a duty to pass as short a sentence as possible on a young man, there was also a duty to protect the public. S had shown himself to be merciless and unrepentant and had a history of behaviour of this sort. In the circumstances the sentence was entirely correct.

R. v. STEWART (1985) 7 Cr.App.R.(S.) 33, C.A.

899. Sentence—youth custody—manslaughter by reason of provocation

A sentence of six years' youth custody was entirely proper for a 17-year-old convicted of manslaughter by reason of provocation.

H aged 17 was convicted of manslaughter on an arraignment for murder. He had met the deceased at a club and had been invited back to play the piano. On arrival at the deceased's flat H found that he had been tricked and that there was no piano. The deceased made homosexual advances to him by grabbing at his testicles saying "I want you." H bitterly resented this and reacted violently to it. Using a hammer that he had been given to demolish a caravan he hit the deceased over the head several times. H was sentenced to six years' youth custody. *Held*, that although there were mitigating factors, such as H's good character and previously non-violent personality, this was a serious case of manslaughter and a substantial period of custodial sentence was bound to follow. The sentence passed was entirely correct.

R. v. HOWARD (DAVID EDWARD) (1985) 7 Cr.App.R.(S.) 130, C.A.

900. Sentence—youth custody—manslaughter—stabbing in course of a chase.

Six years' youth custody was too severe a sentence for a 16 year old who had stabbed another boy who had been chasing him.

L pleaded guilty to manslaughter. He had gone out drinking with a gang of youths and had consumed some two litres of lager. They were recognised by a rival gang and L was chased by a boy who was bigger than he was. L eventually stopped and stabbed his pursuer with a sheath knife that L was carrying with him. The blow was fatal. L telephoned the police and waited there for them. He had no previous convictions, had a job and had just recently lost his father. The trial judge sentenced him to six years' youth custody. *Held*, that although this was obviously a case for a custodial sentence, the factors of provocation and the extreme youth of the offender indicate that the sentence was too harsh and would be reduced to four years.

R. v. LOUGHTON (1985) 7 Cr.App.R.(S.) 91, C.A.

901. Sentence—youth custody—robbery

A sentence of youth custody is appropriate for an 18 year old who attacks a man in the street and steals a small sum of money.

S, aged 18, pleaded guilty to robbery. He chased and kicked a man in the street and stole £3 from him. S was drunk at the time. He was sentenced to four years' youth custody.

Held, that it was necessary to look at the matter not only from the appellant's point of view but also from the point of view of the public who should be protected from this sort of offence. However in view of the appellant's youth, his guilty plea and the fact that this was his first period of youth custody, the sentence could be reduced to three years' youth custody.

R. *v.* SPENCER (1985) 7 Cr.App.R.(S.) 1, C.A.

902. Sentence—youth custody—sentence on juvenile—guilty plea

Twelve months' youth custody, being the maximum possible sentence for a juvenile, is not appropriate after a plea of guilty.

P, aged 16 pleaded guilty to four offences of burglary with 11 others taken into consideration. He had had six previous appearances before the courts. The sentencer, having indicated that he had taken the plea of guilty into account, sentenced P to 12 months' youth custody. *Held,* that the sentence passed was the maximum possible in this case. The sentencer must have overlooked the limitations on his powers. Although P richly deserved the sentence passed it would be reduced to nine months' youth custody.

R. *v.* PILFORD (1985) 7 Cr.App.R.(S.) 23, C.A.

902a. Sentence—youth custody—setting fire to school

The length of sentence should not be affected by the amount of damage that had been done, although the offenders should not be treated differently by reason of their education and further prospects.

Two youths, aged 17 had broken into a school where they were and had been pupils. They caused substantial damage to various rooms and furniture. They then broke into another school and started a fire which spread and caused damage to the extent of £90,000. Both youths had been drinking. They were sentenced to two years' youth custody having pleaded guilty to charges of criminal damage, burglary and reckless arson. *Held,* that it would be wrong to treat the appellants differently because they were educated and had a bright future. It was necessary for them to understand that they had committed serious offences and would be punished accordingly. However there should not be any relationship between the penalty and the extent of the damage they had caused. Bearing that and the fact that both offenders would be unlikely to offend again the sentences should be reduced to 12 months' youth custody.

R. *v.* INNIS AND HOPKINS (1985) 7 Cr.App.R.(S.) 52, C.A.

903. Sentence—youth custody sentence—statutory criteria

[Criminal Justice Act 1982 (c.48), s.1(4).]

A youth custody sentence should not be imposed unless the statutory criteria are satisfied.

G pleaded guilty to two offences of burglary. He had no previous convictions. He had broken into a school and stolen some electronic equipment and had broken into a house that was unoccupied and stolen some bathroom furniture. Most of the property was recovered. He was sentenced to six months' youth custody even though a social inquiry report recommended community service. *Held,* that the statutory criteria under s.1(4) of the Criminal Justice Act 1982 had to be satisfied before a sentence of youth custody could be imposed. Although these offences were serious they were not at the upper end of the scale as far as criminality was concerned. Presented with this offender and this offence the court should have in mind the following criteria—whether there was any other method of dealing with him that was appropriate, whether G was able or willing to comply with non-custodial measures and whether a custodial sentence was necessary for the protection of the public. In this case G was a suitable candidate for community service, a custodial sentence was not necessary for the protection of the public and the offence was not sufficiently serious to deserve a custodial sentence. A community service order would have been appropriate but as G had been in custody for eight weeks the sentence would be varied to such a term of detention as would result in his immediate release.

R. *v.* GRIMES (1985) 7 Cr.App.R.(S.) 137, C.A.

904. Sentence—youth custody—whether to run consecutively to detention
[Children and Young Persons Act 1933 (c.12), s.53(2).]
A youth custody sentence should not be imposed to run consecutively to an order for detention under the Children and Young Persons Act 1933, s.53(2).

G, aged 16 pleaded guilty to robbery. He and two other youths forced entry into the home of an 88-year-old man, held a penknife to his throat and demanded his life savings. He was arrested for this offence and, whilst on bail, was involved in a burglary in which £4,000 worth of metal ingots were stolen. He was also involved in other offences arising out of the theft of a transit van. He had been before the magistrate's court on four previous occasions and had been conditionally discharged three times. He was sentenced to two years' detention under the Children and Young Persons Act 1933 for the robbery and nine months' youth custody for the burglary. *Held,* that for a robbery of this kind a sentence of 12 months' youth custody would have been inadequate. The imposition of two years' detention was correct. However, it was not appropriate to impose a sentence of youth custody to run consecutively for the burglary because of the difference in the provisions for early release, licence and supervision after release. The sentence of youth custody would be varied to a sentence of nine months' detention consecutive to the two years' for the robbery.
R. *v.* GASKIN (1985) 7 Cr.App.R.(S.) 28, C.A.

905. Sentence—wounding with intent—stabbing wife
Five years' imprisonment was, if anything, a moderate sentence for an unprovoked and savage attack by a husband on his ex-wife.

G, who had previous convictions for dishonesty and violence, was convicted of wounding with intent. He had asked his ex-wife if he could spend the night at her house. She agreed but slept in a separate room with her children. During the night G, who had been drinking, entered the room and stabbed his ex-wife five times. *Held,* that this was a savage and unprovoked attack in the presence of two children. The sentence cannot be regarded as too severe.
R. *v.* GHUMAN (1985) 7 Cr.App.R.(S.) 114, C.A.

906. Sentencing—guidelines
Cases in which sentencing guidelines are laid down are for assistance only, and are not to be used as rules never to be departed from: R. *v.* NICHOLAS, *The Times,* April 23, 1986, C.A.

907. Sentencing—young offenders—guidelines
[Children and Young Persons Act 1933 (c.12), s.53(2); Criminal Appeal Act 1968 (c.19), s.4(2); Criminal Justice Act 1982 (c.48), s.7(8).] The Court of Appeal laid down guidelines for sentencing young offenders to detention and youth custody. (1) the use of detention under s.53(2) of the Children and Young Persons Act 1933 is not limited to cases of exceptional gravity such as attempted murder, armed robbery, etc.; (2) however, s.53(2) should not be used simply because a 12 months' youth custody seems to be on the low side in a particular case; (3) where a sentence of 12 months' youth custody seems too light, and a sentence of two years or more youth custody would be appropriate if the offender were over 17, s.52(2) is appropriate. If the offence calls for more than 12 but less than 24 months' detention and the offender is aged 17 or over, the sentence should normally be one of youth custody, not s.53(2) detention; (4) where several offences are involved, only one of which deserves detention, it is appropriate to give detention for it, and either consecutive or concurrent sentences of detention for the others; (5) where a 15- or 16- year-old commits two offences, one of which (A) carries a minimum sentence of 14 years, and the other (B) a lower maximum, it is not usually proper to sentence under s.53(2) for A (which would not otherwise deserve it) in order to compensate for the inadequacy of a maximum sentence of 12 months for B. Where, however, the same course of conduct gives rise to both A and B, such a sentence may properly be passed; (6) it is undesirable for a sentence of s.53(2) custody to run consecutively or concurrently with a sentence of youth custody. Where there is no alternative, however, the solution may be to impose no separate penalty for the offence for which s.53(2) custody is not available. If there is then a successful appeal against the conviction for the s.53(2) offence, the court is entitled under s.4(2) of the Criminal Appeal Act 1968 to sentence for offences for which no separate sentences have been passed; (7) although time spent in custody awaiting sentence is allowed off sentences of youth custody or detention centre, it does not count towards s.53(2) sentences. In imposing

a s.53(2) sentence, this should be borne in mind (*R.* v. *Oakes* [1984] C.L.Y. 875, *R.* v. *Butler* [1985] C.L.Y. 815 considered): R. *v.* FAIRHURST, *The Times,* August 2, 1986, C.A.

908. Sentencing powers—handbook
The fourth edition of *The Sentence of the Court* has been published. This Home Office booklet is a handbook for courts on the treatment of offenders. (ISBN 0 11 340807 2) It is available from H.M.S.O. [£3·50].

909. Sex establishment—licence—knowledge
[Local Government (Miscellaneous Provisions) Act 1982 (c.30), Sched. 3, paras. 6(1), 20(1)(*a*).]
In order to prove a charge of knowingly using premises as a sex establishment, it must be shown that the defendant had actual knowledge that they were being so used.
By Sched. 3 to the Local Government (Miscellaneous Provisions) Act 1982, para. 6, it was provided that premises should not be used as sex establishments except in accordance with the terms of a licence. By para. 20(1)(*a*) of the Schedule a person who "knowingly uses, or knowingly causes or permits the use of, any premises . . . contrary to paragraph 6 above . . . shall be guilty of an offence."
The appellant council resolved that Sched. 3 should apply to their area, pursuant to s.48 of the Act. It came into force in the area on February 1, 1983. The defendant company were the owners of premises that were used, with their permission, by a sub-tenant as a sex establishment from before the first advertisement of the council's resolution until after February 24, 1983. No licence had been applied for. Informations were preferred against the company and a director of the company for breach of para. 6. The defendants contended that they believed that application for a licence had been made by the sub-tenant and had not been determined. The magistrate dismissed the informations, holding that it had not been proved beyond reasonable doubt that they had known that no application had been made. The informations alleged offences on February 8 and 24. The council's appeals to the Divisional Court of the Queen's Bench Division and the House of Lords were dismissed. *Held,* that knowledge that the use of premises as a sex establishment was in contravention of the prohibition imposed by para. 6(1) was a necessary ingredient of the offence. Since this had not been proved, the defendants were entitled to be acquitted.
WESTMINSTER CITY COUNCIL *v.* CROYALGRANGE [1986] 1 W.L.R. 674, H.L.

910. Sexual offences—gross indecency—attempt to procure
[Criminal Attempts Act 1981 (c.47), s.1.] D passed a note of invitation to an act of gross indecency through a hole between public toilet cubicles to a man who was a police officer. *Held,* allowing the prosecutor's appeal against dismissal of a charge of attempting to procure the commission by a man of an act of gross indecency in a public place, contrary to s.1(1) of the 1981 Act, that s.13 of the Sexual Offences Act 1956 creates an alternative substantive offence of procuring the commission by a man of an act of gross indecency with another. A charge of attempting to commit that offence was not precluded by s.1(4)(*b*) of the 1981 Act: HAMPSHIRE *v.* MACE [1986] Crim.L.R. 752, D.C.

911. Sexual offences—indecent assault on children under 16—ingredients of offence
[Sexual Offences Act 1956 (4 & 5 Eliz. 2, c.69), ss.14(1)(2), 15(1)(2), 46.]
Where a defendant is charged with indecent assault on a child under 16, the acts complained of must amount to more than an assault and be accompanied by circumstances of indecency.
T was caretaker at a middle school for girls. He was charged with indecent assaults on two of them, one aged 11, the other 12. Neither girl gave sworn evidence; nobody else witnessed the incident. The 12-year-old stated he had touched the bottom of her skirt, rubbed it, and when pushed had walked away. T was convicted on both counts. *Held,* allowing the appeal on both counts, that there was no corroborative evidence of the 11-year-old's story; the circumstances of the other offence might be an assault but did not have the necessary ingredient of indecency (dictum in *Faulkner* v. *Talbot* [1981] C.L.Y. 463 applied).
R. *v.* THOMAS (E.) (1985) 81 Cr.App.R. 331, C.A.

912. **Special procedure material—application for discovery—whether notice must contain details of documents sought**

[Police and Criminal Evidence Act 1984 (c.60), s.9, Sched. 1.]

When making an application under the Police and Criminal Evidence Act 1984 for discovery of "special procedure material" the police are obliged to set out in the notice a description of all material they seek to be produced.

Applications were made to the court for the discovery of "special procedure" material under s.9 and Sched. 1 of the 1984 Act. The hearing was *inter partes* and the notice to the recipients contained no detail at all of the relevant documents or material the subject of the application. The judge granted the applications. *Held,* allowing the appeal and quashing the orders, that the police are obliged to set out in the relevant notice a description of all material which is sought to be discovered, despite the risk that the evidence might be destroyed.

R. *v.* CENTRAL CRIMINAL COURT, *ex p.* ADEGBESAN [1986] 3 All E.R. 113, D.C.

913. **Statistics—annual volume**

The annual volume, *Criminal Statistics, England and Wales, 1985* has been published. Copies are available from H.M.S.O. (Cm. 10) [£14·20].

914. **Statistics—cautions, court proceedings and sentencing**

The Home Office has published summary statistics for 1985 on offenders dealt with by formal police cautions or criminal court proceedings in England and Wales. The statistics are contained in statistical bulletin issue 23/86 which is available from the Statistical Department, Home Office, Lunar House, Croydon, Surrey, CRO 9YD. Tel. 01-760–2850. [£1·50.]

914a. **Statistics—misuse of drugs**

The Home Office has published its annual bulletin showing statistics on the misuse of controlled drugs in the U.K. during 1985. Copies of the bulletin are available from the Statistical Department, Home Office, Lunar House, Croydon, Surrey CR0 9YD. Tel: 01-760-2850. (Issue 28/86) [£2·50].

915. **Statistics—notifiable offences**

The Home Office has published statistics of notifiable offences recorded by the police in England and Wales during the first quarter of 1986. Statistical bulletin issue 16/86 is available from the Statistical Department, Home Office, Tolworth Tower, Surbiton, Surrey, KT6 7DS. Tel: 01-399-5191, ext. 298. [£1·50.]

The Home Office has published a statistical bulletin which sets out details of notifiable offences recorded by the police in England and Wales during the second quarter of 1986. The bulletin, Issue 25/86, is available from the Statistical Department, Home Office, Lunar House, Croydon, Surrey, CRO 9YD. Tel. 01-760–2850. [£1·50.]

The Home Office has published statistics of notifiable offences recorded by the police in England and Wales during 1985. The statistics show an increase in rape offences of 29 per cent. over the year. Statistical bulletin issue 4/86 is available from Statistical Department, Home Office, Tolworth Tower, Surbiton, Surrey, KT6 7DS. Tel. 01-399-5191, ext. 298 [£1·50].

916. **Statistics—notification of arrest**

The Home Office has published *Statistics on the Operation of section 62 of the Criminal Law Act 1977 England and Wales 1985.* The Statistical Bulletin (Issue 9/86) is available from Statistical Department, Home Office, Tolworth Tower, Surbiton, Surrey KT6 7DS. Tel: 01-399-5191, ext. 298. [£1·50.]

917. **Statistics—Police and Criminal Evidence Act 1984**

The Home Office has published statistics on the operation of certain police powers under the Police and Criminal Evidence Act 1984 during the first quarter of 1986. The statistics are published in Statistical Bulletin Issue 24/86 which is available from the Statistical Department, Home Office, Lunar House, Croydon, Surrey CRO 9YD. Tel. 01-760–2850. [£2·20.]

918. **Statistics—police powers**

Statistics on the operation of certain police powers under the Police and Criminal Evidence Act 1984 for the third quarter of 1986 have been published. Statistical Bulletin 41/86 is available from the Statistical Department, Home Office, Lunar House, Croydon, Surrey CR0 9YD. Tel: 01-760-2850.

The Home Office has published a statistical bulletin giving details of the operation of certain police powers under the Police and Criminal Evidence Act 1984 during the second quarter of 1986. The bulletin (Issue 32/86) is available from the Statistical Department, Home Office, Lunar House, Croydon, Surrey CR9 9YD. Tel: 01-760-2850. [£2·50.]

919. Statistics—prevention of terrorism
Statistics on the operation of the Prevention of Terrorism (Temporary Provisions) Acts 1974, 1976 and 1984 during the last quarter of 1985 have been published. Copies of the statistics (Issue 1/86) are available from Statistical Department, Home Office, Tolworth Tower, Surbiton, Surrey, KT6 7DS. Tel: 01-399-5191, ext. 298. [£2·50.]
The Home Office has published a statisticial bulletin giving details of the operation of the prevention of terrorism legislation during the second quarter of 1986. Copies of the bulletin (Issue 20/86) are available from Statistical Department, Home Office, Lunar House, Croydon, Surrey CR0 9YD. Tel: 01-760 2850 [£2·50].
The Home Office has published statistics on the operation of the prevention of terrorism legislation during the third quarter of 1986. Copies of the bulletin (Issue 33/86) are available from the Statistical Department, Home Office, Lunar House, Croydon, Surrey CR0 9YD. Tel: 01-760-2850. [£2·50.]

920. Statistics—prison population
The Home Office has published a statistical bulletin detailing the ethnic origins of prisoners. The bulletin (Issue No. 17/85) is entitled *The Ethnic Origins of Prisoners: The Prison Population on 30 June 1985 and Persons Received, July 1984–March 1985.* Copies are available from: Statistical Department, Home Office, Tolworth Tower, Surbiton, Surrey, KT6 7DS. Tel.: 01-399-5191, ext. 298 [£2·50].

921. Statistics—probation
The Home office has published the probation statistics for England and Wales for 1985. Copies are available from the Home Office Statistical Department, Room 844/5, 50 Queen Anne's Gate, London SW1H 9AT. [£4·50.]

922. Statistics—public disorder
The Home Office has published a statistical bulletin (Issue 10/86) detailing statistics of those arrested in connection with the serious incidents of public disorder during September and October 1985. The bulletin, which is an interim report, is available from Statistical Department, Home Office, Tolworth Tower, Surbiton, Surrey, KT6 7DS. Tel: 01-399-5191, ext. 298. [£1·50.]

923. Statistics—reconvictions
The Home Office has published a statistical bulletin giving the results of a study of the reconvictions in England and Wales of those given probation orders. Copies of the bulletin (Issue 34/86) are available from the Statistical Department, Home Office, Lunar House, Croydon, Surrey CR0 9YD. Tel: 01-760-2850. [£2·50.]

924. Statistics—reconvictions and recalls of life licensees
The Home Office has published a statistical bulletin giving details of the reconviction and/or recall of those released on life licence up to the end of 1984. Copies of the bulletin (Issue 22/86) are available from the Statistical Deparment, Home Office, Lunar House, Croydon, Surrey CRO 9YD. Tel. 01-760–2850. [£2.50.]

925. Statistics—sentence—young offenders
The Home Office has published a statistical bulletin dealing with the sentencing of young offenders under the Criminal Justice Act 1982 during the years from July 1983 to June 1985. The bulletin, Issue 14/86, is available from the Statistical Department, Home Office, Tolworth Tower, Surbiton, Surrey, KT6 7DS. Tel: 01-399–5191, ext 298. [£2·50.]

926. Summing up—observation to jury—whether proper
Defence submissions at the close of the prosecution case that there is no case for the defendant to answer should be made in the absence of the jury, and, if the trial proceeds thereafter, should not be referred to by the judge in his summing-up or elsewhere; R. *v.* SMITH (WILLIAM) AND DOE, *The Times,* December 3, 1986, C.A.

927. Suppression of terrorism. See EMERGENCY LAWS, § 1163.

928. Tachograph records—falsification—whether imprisonment right
[Transport Act 1968 (c.73), s.99(5).]
Twenty-eight days' immediate imprisonment reduced to 7 days for long distance lorry drivers who had falsified tachograph records on their lorries.

H and other long distance lorry drivers pleaded guilty to a number of offences of falsifying the tachograph records in their vehicles. Each was sentenced to 3 months' imprisonment, of which 28 days was immediate, the balance being suspended. The drivers claimed that the offences had been committed following pressure from the employer, who had had the gain therefrom. *Held,* that on the facts of these cases custodial sentences would not have been considered appropriate had the court been sitting at first instance. Immediate imprisonment would be right, however, in cases of blatant or repeated breaches of the Act as it was designed to prevent accidents caused by drivers becoming overtired.

R. *v.* PARKINSON (1984) 6 Cr.App.R.(S.) 423, C.A.

929. Theft—appropriation—payment by cheque and card—account in fictitious name—whether appropriation of bank's money
[Theft Act 1968 (c.60), s.3(1).]
The use of a cheque backed by a guarantee card drawn on an account in a fictitious name, in which there are no funds, is not an "appropriation" within the meaning of s.3(1) of the Theft Act, 1968 and is therefore not theft.

The appellant used false names to open various accounts. Subsequently he drew 12 cheques at casinos for gaming chips, when there was no money in the accounts. Each cheque was accompanied by a bankers card. He was charged with theft; the judge directed the jury that there was an appropriation on these facts. *Held,* allowing the appeal, that use of a cheque and card in these circumstances was not an appropriation within s.3(1).

R. *v.* NAVVABI [1986] 3 All E.R. 102, C.A.

930. Theft—attempted theft—distracting dogs on race track
[Criminal Attempts Act 1981 (c.47), s.1(1), (4).] D backed a greyhound to win a race. Once the race had started, it became clear that the greyhound would not win; D therefore ran on to the track to distract the dogs, in the hope that the stewards would declare "no race," and the bookmakers would then have to return all stakes. He was charged with attempting under s.1(1), (4) of the Criminal Attempts Act 1981 to steal his stake. *Held,* that it could not be said of D that in jumping on to the track he was in the process of committing theft. There was no evidence that in so doing he had got beyond the stage of mere preparation (*R.* v. *Ilyas (Mohammed)* [1984] C.L.Y. 511 considered; *D.P.P.* v. *Stonehouse* [1977] C.L.Y. 1450 not followed), R. *v.* GULLEFER, *The Times,* November 25, 1986, C.A.

931. Theft—company cheque—use for unauthorised purpose
[Theft Act 1968 (c.60), s.6(1)] As a company director, S drew company cheques to pay his debts and obligations including an Access account used by S and his wife. *Held,* dismissing S's appeal against conviction, *inter alia,* of theft of a company cheque used to discharge an Access account liability, that (1) if a person uses a company cheque in part for an unauthorised purpose, unless such user is *de minimis,* he demonstrates an intent to treat the cheque as his own to dispose of regardless of the company's rights within s.6(1) of the 1968 Act; (2) The high proportion which the unauthorised subject matter bears of the overall cheque may make it clear that the transaction was prima facie dishonest: R. *v.* SOBEL [1986] Crim.L.R. 261, C.A.

932. Theft—handling distinguished—guidelines
The Court of Appeal gave the following guide to cases where theft and handling might be charged as alternatives: (1) both offences should be charged when there was more than a merely fanciful possibility that the evidence at trial might support one rather than the other; (2) there is a danger that juries might be confused by references to second or later appropriations; (3) juries should be told that a person can be both a thief and a handler, but that he cannot be convicted of both; (4) handling is the more serious offence; (5) if the jury cannot agree on which of the two offences has been proved, they should be discharged; and (5) judges and advocates should, when addressing juries, keep it short and simple: R. *v.* SHELTON, *The Times,* June 3, 1986, C.A.

933. Theft—secret profit—sale on employer's premises—whether constructive trust arises—whether "property belonging to another"
[Theft Act 1968 (c.60), s.5(1)(3).]
An employee who makes a secret profit by selling his own goods on his employer's premises is not guilty of theft of that money.

A pub manager employed by brewers, contracted only to sell the brewer's beer on the premises. In fact he was "buying out" from a wholesaler and making a secret profit which he retained. He and a barman who was helping him were acquitted of theft and going equipped for cheat. The case was referred on a reference on the questions of whether the manager held the moneys on account for the brewery, whether he was a constructive trustee, and whether therefore the moneys came within s.5(3) of the 1968 Act. *Held,* that (1) the money was not held on account of the brewers but on his own account; (ii) the person in a fiduciary position who made a secret profit was not a trustee within the meaning of s.5; (iii) the brewers had no proprietary interest in the money, and it could not be said to "belong to another."

ATT.-GEN.'S REF. (No. 1 of 1985) [1986] 2 W.L.R. 733, C.A.

934. Theft—taking a conveyance—evidence—case to answer
[Theft Act 1968 (c.60), s.12(1): Road Traffic Act 1972 (c.20), s.143(1).]
Evidence of a denial of ever having been in the type of car concerned, plus evidence of a thumb-print in the particular vehicle, does not constitute a case to answer on charges of taking a conveyance without consent and driving whilst uninsured.

J was interviewed in connection with the taking of a car, and said that he had never been in such a type of car. His thumb-print was found on the rear-view mirror of the vehicle in question. The justices dismissed the charge of taking the vehicle without consent and driving whilst not insured on the grounds that there was no evidence of possession or control. *Held,* that the prosecutor had to prove not just that J had been in the vehicle, but also that he had taken it for his own use, and used it. This was not proved by the evidence before them, so the justices were right in dismissing the charges.

CHIEF CONSTABLE OF AVON AND SOMERSET CONSTABULARY v. JEST [1986] R.T.R. 372, D.C.

935. Trial—decision to offer no evidence—whether matter for trial judge or prosecuting counsel
It is part of the personal responsibility of prosecuting counsel to decide whether to offer evidence against a defendant, although he should be ready to explain that decision to the trial judge.

J was convicted of criminal damage. Before his trial had started prosecuting counsel informed the trial judge that the prosecution proposed to offer no evidence. The trial judge disapproved and the trial continued. *Held,* that the proper approach for judges in this position is set out in "Guidance to Prosecution Counsel" issued by the Bar Committee of the Senate. The decision is one for prosecution counsel alone. The conviction would be quashed.

R. v. JENKINS (MALCOLM) (1986) 83 Cr.App.R. 152, C.A.

936. Trial—direction to jury—duty to allow counsel to address judge
L was convicted of assault occasioning actual bodily harm. The Crown case was that L had deliberately and intentionally driven at a crowd. In summing up the judge directed the jury that it was open to them to convict on the basis of recklessness. *Held,* allowing L's appeal, that the judge should have given both counsel an opportunity to address him on that point and if necessary call further evidence if he thought it necessary so to direct the jury: R. v. LUNN [1985] Crim.L.R. 797, C.A.

937. Trial—in absence of defendant—judge's discretion
On the third day of O's trial on charges of conspiracy to steal and theft, he failed to appear. The judge issued a warrant. On the following day the judge ruled that the case should continue in O's absence and O's counsel and solicitor withdrew from the case. *Held,* dismissing O's appeal against conviction, that the Court of Appeal would not lightly interfere with the exercise of a judge's discretion unless it was wrong or unreasonable. The judge had been entitled to take into account as important that the prosecution might not be able, on a re-trial, to call two foreign witnesses who were businessmen resident outside the jurisdiction (*R. v. Jones, (No. 2)* [1972] C.L.Y. 759 considered): R. v. O'NIONE [1986] Crim.L.R. 342, C.A.

938. Trial—joint trial—whether sufficient nexus
Three defendants were charged with carrying offensive weapons. Two of them were arrested within 15 minutes and a quarter of a mile of the third, who had been arrested at the scene of the fight. *Held,* that there was sufficient nexus in the

circumstances of the apprehension and arrest to warrant a prima facie conclusion that all three had before the arrest been associated with a scene of violence. A joint trial would therefore be of no prejudice: R. *v.* LIVERPOOL JUVENILE COURT, *ex p.* B., D., and M., *The Times*, May 13, 1986, D.C.

939. Trial—summing up

When a judge intends to direct the jury on a matter that has not been canvassed during the trial, he should tell counsel before they start their speeches, so that they can have the opportunity of addressing the jury on it: R. *v.* CRISTINI (LUIGI), *The Times*, November 8, 1986, C.A.

940. Trial—summing up—evidence—police—judge's comments

H claimed that police officers had put undue pressure upon him and denied in any event their evidence that he had made admissions. The trial judge posed the question to the jury: "Do you take the view that these Detective Constables would have put their careers on the line?" *Held*, dismissing H's appeal against conviction, that whilst it was undesirable for comments to be made in a summing up which placed police witnesses in any special category, or which suggested that adverse consequences would follow to such witnesses in the event of an acquittal, taking the summing up as a whole, no material irregularity had occurred (*R. v. Fisher* [1983] C.L.Y. 938; *R. v. Culbertson* [1970] C.L.Y. 544 and *R. v. Wellwood-Kerr* [1978] C.L.Y. 655 considered): R. *v.* HARRIS [1986] Crim.L.R. 123, C.A.

941. Unlawful export of goods—involvement in enterprise

[H.K.] [Import and Export Ordinance, ss.2, 18(1)(*b*); Import and Export (General) Regulations, reg. 4.] D agreed to transport unlicensed and unmanifested goods to a destination within Hong Kong territorial waters, where they would be transported to another ship for unlawful export by others, those others not being controlled by D, nor acting with his authority. *Held*, that D could not be convicted of attempting to export prohibited articles since he had not attempted to export them: ATT.-GEN. OF HONG KONG *v.* TSE HUNG-LIT, (1986) 83 L.S.Gaz. 1995, P.C.

942. VAT offences—duplicity—admissibility of evidence of previous conduct

[Finance Act 1972 (c.41), s.38.]

Section 38(3) of the Finance Act 1972 is intended to create one offence covering numerous offences which can be individually charged under s.38(1) and (2). The proper time for applying to quash an indictment for duplicity is before a plea is taken.

The appellant was tried on one count only of the commission of VAT offences under s.38(1) and (2) of the Finance Act 1972 contrary to s.38(3) of the Act. The Crown alleged the issue of invoices for zero-rated goods in relation to standard-rated goods and failure to issue invoices relating to sales. The prosecution called evidence of transactions prior to the period covered by the indictment to set the overall system of trading from which inferences could be drawn. The appellant submitted at the close of the prosecution's case that the indictment was bad for duplicity and the judge overruled that submission. He was convicted. *Held*, on appeal, that the offence charged under s.38(3) related to a "person's conduct during a specified period" and created one offence embracing the commission of numerous offences which themselves could have been charged under s.38(1) and (2). The indictment was not bad for duplicity. The judge was right in the exercise of his discretion to admit the earlier conduct of the business, although the judge ought to have specifically told them the relevance of the evidence. The proper time to apply to quash an indictment was before the plea was taken except in exceptional circumstances (*R. v. Maywhort* [1955] C.L.Y. 599; *R. v. Heane* (1864) 4 B. & S. 947; *R. v. James* (1871) 12 Cox C.C. 127 and *R. v. Wilmott* (1933) 23 Cr.App.R. 63 considered).

R. *v.* ASIF (1985) 82 Cr.App.R. 123, C.A.

943. Verdict—alteration after discharge of defendant—discretion of trial judge

Where a jury seeks to alter a verdict pronounced by the foreman the judge has a discretion whether to allow the alteration.

D was charged with cruelty to a child contrary to s.1(1) of the Children and Young Persons Act 1933 jointly with his wife. At the end of the summing up the judge advised the jury that if either defendant were found guilty on account of wilful neglect as opposed to assault or ill treatment the verdict returned should be guilty of wilful neglect. After their deliberations the jury returned their verdict. In answer to the clerk's questions the foreman gave a verdict of not guilty in respect of D and guilty in respect of his wife. D was discharged and the court proceeded to deal with the wife's antecedents and mitigation. Ten minutes after the verdicts were taken the trial judge received a note from the jury stating "we thought we found D guilty of wilful neglect. What happens now." D was brought back into the dock and a verdict of guilty of wilful neglect was returned by the jury. D appealed. *Held,* dismissing the appeal, that the trial judge has a discretion whether to allow an alteration to be made to a verdict returned by the jury. All the circumstances of the case must be taken into account in the exercise of that discretion. Important considerations are the length of time between the initial verdict and the jury's wish to alter it, the probable reason for the initial mistake, and the necessity to ensure justice for both the defendant and the prosecution. The fact that a defendant had been discharged did not preclude the alteration of the jury's verdict. If there were any question that the desire of the jury to alter the verdict resulted from anything heard after their initial verdict the alteration could not be permitted. In the present case the foreman was most likely waiting for the clerk to ask whether D was guilty of wilful neglect. The judge exercised his discretion correctly (*R.* v. *Parkin* (1824) 1 Mood. C.C. 45, *R.* v. *Vodden* (1853) Dears. C.C. 229 followed).

    R. *v.* ANDREWS (1986) 82 Cr.App.R. 148, C.A.

944. Verdict—necessity for jury to give verdict—change of plea

It is necessary to secure the verdict of the jury before sentencing a defendant, even if he has changed his plea to guilty during the course of the trial.

W was charged with reckless driving. He originally pleaded not guilty but when the trial judge ruled that the defence of necessity was not open to him he changed his plea to guilty. The judge immediately proceeded to sentence him. After sentence had been passed, the judge was reminded of the need for the jury to return a verdict. The judge invited the foreman to return a guilty verdict without giving him an opportunity to consult other jury members. *Held,* allowing the appeal, that once a defendant is put in the charge of a jury he could only come out by the jury returning a verdict, even where he had changed his plea. The judge could not pass sentence until a guilty verdict was returned by the jury. The conviction was therefore unsafe and must be set aside.

    R. *v.* WILLER (MARK EDWARD) (1986) 83 Cr.App.R. 225, C.A.

945. Video Recordings Act 1984—commencement

VIDEO RECORDINGS ACT 1984 (COMMENCEMENT No. 3) ORDER 1986 (No. 1125 (c.31)) [80p], made under the Video Recordings Act 1984 (c.39), s.23(2); brings into force on September 1, 1986 ss.9 and 10 of the 1984 Act.

946. View of alleged scene of crimes—whether justices should be accompanied by parties or representatives

At her trial on an information alleging driving without due care and attention D gave no evidence. After her solicitor had addressed the magistrates, they indicated that they intended to view the scene over the luncheon adjournment. They did so and later dismissed the information. *Held,* dismissing the prosecutor's appeal, that it was undesirable for justices to have a view unaccompanied by the parties or their representatives and a view should take place at or before the evidence had been concluded. The justices had, however, impliedly invited the parties or their representatives to attend and the magistrates had only visited the scene to supplement information they had from oral evidence and photographs (*Salsbury* v. *Woodland* [1969] C.L.Y. 2432 applied): PARRY *v.* BOYLE [1986] Crim.L.R. 551, D.C.

947. Voluntary bill of indictment—powers of Crown Prosecutor

[Prosecution of Offences Act 1985 (c.23), s.1(6); Supreme Court Act 1981 (c.54), s.29(3); Indictments (Procedure) Rules 1971 (S.I. 1971 No. 2084), r.8.] A Crown Prosecutor does not need to file an affidavit in an application to a High Court judge for a voluntary bill of indictment deposing to the truth of the statements in the application: BRAY, *Ex p., The Times,* October 7, 1986, D.C.

948. Witness summons—judicial review

Judicial review is not available in a matter relating to trial on indictment. The issuing of witness summons to attend and give evidence at a trial on indictment is such a matter: REES, *ex p. The Times,* May 7, 1986, D.C.

949. Witnesses

CROWN PROSECUTION SERVICE (WITNESSES' ALLOWANCES) (AMENDMENT NO. 2) REGULATIONS 1986 (No. 1250) [45p], made under the Prosecution of Offences Act 1985 (c.23), s.14(1)(*b*) and (2); operative on August 11, 1986; increase the maximum locum and compensatory allowances payable to a professional witness who attends court to give evidence at the instance of the Crown Prosecution Service and thereby incurs expenditure or suffers loss.

CROWN PRACTICE

950. Certificate of Secretary of State—judicial review—whether available

[Crown Proceedings Act 1947 (c.44), s.40(3)(*a*); State Immunity Act 1978 (c.33), s.21; Tribunals and Inquiries Act 1971 (c.62), s.14.] The Secretary of State issued a number of certificates containing matters of fact and law. T sought judicial review of the issue of the certificates on the basis that they were plainly wrong. *Held*, that since statute provided for the certificates to be conclusive they were not reviewable if the basis of the application required extrinsic evidence to be called in respect of the matters certified. Moreover the matters certified were "matters of state" and so not reviewable in any event (*Anisminic* v. *Foreign Compensation Commission* [1969] C.L.Y. 1866, *R.* v. *Registrar of Companies, ex p. Central Bank of India* [1985] C.L.Y. 331 *Council of Civil Service Unions* v. *Minister for the Civil Service* [1985] C.L.Y. 12 considered): R. *v.* SECRETARY OF STATE FOR FOREIGN AND COMMONWEALTH AFFAIRS, *ex p.* TRAWNIK, *The Times,* February 21, 1986, C.A.

951. Crown as landlord—whether bound by statute

See DEPARTMENT OF TRANSPORT *v.* EGOROFF, § 1934.

952. Crown proceedings—exemption from liability in tort—soldier referred to civilian hospital

[Crown Proceedings Act 1947 (c.44), s.10(1)(*a*)(*b*).]

The immunity of the Secretary of State from suit is restricted to injury suffered by a serviceman while on duty or while on Crown land.

The deceased B, a soldier stationed in West Germany, sustained head injuries during horseplay in barrack's. He was transferred from the army medical reception centre to a local civilian hospital, but the army doctor failed to give the hospital accurate notes of B's injuries resulting in a significant delay in making an accurate diagnosis. B died. B's father, suing as administrator of his estate brought an action for damages against the Secretary of State alleging negligence by the army doctor. The Secretary of State claimed immunity from suit pursuant to s.10(1) of the 1947 Act, and issued a certificate under s.10(1)(*b*) attributing B's death to his military service. The question whether the Secretary of State was entitled to rely on the immunity was tried as a preliminary issue. The judge upheld the Secretary of State's claim. *Held*, allowing the appeal, that (1) by s.10(1)(*b*) the Secretary of State was entitled to issue such a certificate of entitlement to an award even though when it was issued it was clear that there was no one entitled to receive such an award and the only effect was to enable the Secretary of State to claim immunity from suit since the certificate was merely declaratory of the fact that death was attributable to military service and it did not follow that an award would be made; *Adams* v. *War Office* [1955] C.L.Y. 2110 approved; (2) the injury suffered by B, *i.e.* the failure by the army doctor to give the civilian hospital accurate information about B had occurred at the civilian hospital and not on Crown land, and therefore the Secretary of State was not entitled to claim immunity because under s.10(1)(*a*) such immunity was restricted to an injury suffered by a serviceman while on duty or while on Crown land.

BELL *v.* SECRETARY OF STATE FOR DEFENCE [1985] 3 All E.R. 661, C.A.

953. Judicial review—prisoner—injunction sought—jurisdiction

[Crown Proceedings Act 1947 (10, 11, 12 Geo. 6, c.44), ss.21(1)(2), 38(2); Supreme Court Act 1981 (c.54), s.31(1)(2), R.S.C., Ord. 53, r.3(10).]

The Queen's Bench Division on the Crown side has jurisdiction to grant prerogative orders against officers of the Crown.

The applicant was remanded in custody pending extradition. He complained of being detained under inhumane conditions and applied for judicial review and an injunction against the Secretary of State and the prison governor to ensure he was contained more humanely. He applied for an interim injunction. *Held* dismissing the application, that (1) the Queen's Bench Division did have jurisdiction to grant prerogative orders against an officer of the Crown; but (2) the court could not exercise control over a prison governor in the exercise of his responsibilities (*R.* v. *Secretary of State for the Home Department, ex p. Kirkwood* [1984] C.L.Y. 1538 distinguished).

R. v. GOVERNOR OF PENTONVILLE PRISON *ex p.* HERBAGE [1986] 3 W.L.R. 504, Hodgson J.

954. Prerogative—treaty-making power—Anglo-Irish Agreement—whether invalid or justiciable

[Union with Ireland Act 1800 (c.67), art. 6; Ireland Act 1949 (c.41), s.2.]

The Anglo-Irish Agreement of November 15, 1985 is not invalid, and it is not the function of the court to inquire into the exercise of the Crown prerogative in either entering into or implementing the agreement.

By an agreement of November 15, 1985 the Governments of the U.K. and Ireland agreed to establish an Intergovernmental Conference concerned with Northern Ireland and relations between the two parts of Ireland to deal with political and legal matters, security, and the promotion of cross-border co-operation. It was accepted that the Irish Government could put its views on certain matters in Northern Ireland but it was stated that there was no derogation from the sovereignty of either government which retained responsibility for its own decisions and administration. The applicants were members of the Ulster Unionist Council opposed to the agreement who claimed that the agreement was invalid as fettering the statutory duties and powers of the Secretary of State for Northern Ireland, in diminishing the rights of subjects of Northern Ireland contrary to the Union with Ireland Act 1800, and that the establishment of a new standing body was unlawful. Leave to apply for judicial review was refused on a renewed application.

Held, that section 2 of the Ireland Act 1949 expressly stated that the Republic of Ireland was not to be regarded as a foreign power and the agreement did not deprive the people of Northern Ireland of any privileges or place them on a different footing from others in the U.K., and so the agreement did not conflict with art. 6 of the Union with Ireland Act 1800. As the Intergovernmental Conference had no legislative or executive power its establishment did not contravene any statute or rule of common law or constitutional convention, nor fetter the discretion of the Secretary of State. It was of an international nature, and as the agreement concerned relations with another sovereign state it was akin to a treaty, and accordingly it was not the function of the court to inquire into the exercise of the prerogative in either entering into or implementing the agreement.

Ex p. MOLYNEAUX [1986] 1 W.L.R. 331, Taylor J.

CUSTOMS AND EXCISE

955. Agricultural levies

AGRICULTURAL LEVY RELIEFS (FROZEN BEEF AND VEAL) ORDER 1986 (No. 495) [£1·35], made under the Customs and Excise Duties (General Reliefs) Act 1979 (c. 3), s.4; operative on April 4, 1986; requires the Minister of Agriculture to allocate the U.K.'s share of a quota for the levy-free import of frozen beef and veal under the provisions of E.E.C. Reg. No. 193/86.

956. Betting duty

GENERAL BETTING DUTY REGULATIONS 1986 (No. 400) [£2·80], made under the Betting and Gaming Duties Act 1981 (c.63), s.12(2) and Sched. 1, para. 2; operative on March 30, 1986; introduce new arrangements for the administration of general betting duty.

957. Customs duties

CUSTOMS DUTIES (ECSC) (No. 2) (AMENDMENT No. 2) ORDER 1986 (No. 348) [40p], made under the European Communities Act 1972 (c.68), s.5(1)(3), Sched. 2, para. 4; operative on March 1, 1986; amends S.I. 1985 No. 1630 as a consequence of S.I. 1986 No. 346.

CUSTOMS DUTIES (ECSC) (No. 2) (AMENDMENT No. 3) ORDER 1986 No. 813) [45p], made under the European Communities Act 1972 (c.68), s.5(1) and (3), Sched. 2, para. 4; operative on May 9, 1986; amends S.I. 1985 No. 1630.

CUSTOMS DUTIES (ECSC) (No. 2) (AMENDMENT No. 4) Order 1986 (No. 1352)

[45p], made under the European Communities Act 1972 (c. 68), s.5(1)(3), Sched. 2, para. 4; operative on August 4, 1986; amends S.I. 1985 No. 1630.

CUSTOMS DUTIES (ECSC) (No. 2) (AMENDMENT No. 5) ORDER 1986 (No. 2179) [45p], made under the European Commission Act 1972 (c.68), s.5(1) and (3) and Sched. 2, para. 4; operative on January 1, 1987; amends S.I. 1985 No. 1630.

CUSTOMS DUTIES (ECSC) (QUOTA AND OTHER RELIEFS) ORDER 1986 (No. 2292) [£1·40], made under the Customs and Excise Duties (General Reliefs) Act 1979 (c.3), ss.1,4; operative on January 1, 1987; provides for relief from customs duties on certain iron and steel products originating in specified developing countries.

CUSTOMS DUTIES (PORTUGAL) ORDER 1986 (No. 347) [£3·30], made under the European Communities Act 1972 (c.68), s.5(2) and (3); operative on March 1, 1986; implements obligations of the U.K. concerning Portugal.

CUSTOMS DUTIES (SPAIN) ORDER 1986 (No. 346) [£8·80], made under the European Communities Act 1972 (c.68), s.5(2) and (3); operative on March 1, 1986; implements obligations of the UK concerning Spain under the treaty of accession of Spain and Portugal to the EEC from March 1, 1986.

958. Excise duties

EXCISE DUTIES (DEFERRED PAYMENT) (AMENDMENT) REGULATIONS 1986 (No. 910) [45p], made under the Customs and Excise Management Act 1979 (c.2), ss.93, 127A; operative on July 1, 1986; amend S.I. 1983 No. 947.

EXCISE DUTIES (SMALL NON-COMMERCIAL CONSIGNMENTS) RELIEF REGULATIONS 1986 (No. 938) [80p], made under the European Communities Act 1972 (c.68), s.2(2); operative on July 1, 1986; provide for relief from excise duty on small consignments sent from abroad from a private individual to another private individual for his use.

959. Excise warehousing

EXCISE WAREHOUSING (ETC.) (AMENDMENT) REGULATIONS 1986 (No. 79) [40p], made under the Customs and Excise Management Act 1979 (c.2), s.93 and the Alcoholic Liquor Duties Act 1979 (c.4), s.15; operative on February 17, 1986; modify the requirements for occupiers of excise warehouses and the proprietors of goods in those warehouses to keep and produce records relating to warehoused goods and to their businesses.

960. Export and import controls

EXPORT OF GOODS (CONTROL) (AMENDMENT No. 4) ORDER 1986 (No. 82) [40p], made under the Import, Export and Customs Powers (Defence) Act 1939 (c.69), s.1; operative on January 22, 1986; amends S.I. 1985 No. 849.

EXPORT OF GOODS (CONTROL) (AMENDMENT No. 5) ORDER 1986 (No. 540) [£1·85], made under the Import, Export and Customs Powers (Defence) Act 1939 (c.69), s.1; operative on March 24, 1986; amends S.I. 1985 No. 849.

EXPORT OF GOODS (CONTROL) (AMENDMENT No. 6) ORDER 1986 (No. 1446) [80p], made under the Import, Export and Customs Powers (Defence) Act 1939 (c.69), s.1; operative on September 1, 1986; further amends S.I. 1985 No. 849.

EXPORT OF GOODS (CONTROL) (AMENDMENT No. 7) ORDER 1986 (No. 1934) [45p], made under the Import, Export and Customs Powers (Defence) Act 1939 (c.69), s.1; operative on November 17, 1986; futher amends S.I. 1985 No. 849 by introducing export controls on carbon-bonded thermal insulating materials.

961. Free zones

FREE ZONE (BELFAST AIRPORT) DESIGNATION (VARIATION) ORDER 1986 (No. 1643) [45p], made under the Customs and Excise Management Act 1979 (c.2), s.100A(4)(a)(ii); operative on September 24, 1986; varies the area of the free zone at Belfast Airport.

962. Gaming machine licence duty

GAMING MACHINE LICENCE DUTY (VARIATION OF MONETARY LIMITS AND EXEMPTIONS) ORDER 1986 (No. 2069) [45p], made under the Betting and Gaming Duties Act 1981 (c.63), s.22(3), Sched. 4, para. 3; operative on January 1, 1987; increases the small prize machine limit and the maximum amounts which may be paid as a prize in respect of gaming by machine at a pleasure fair.

963. Import and export by sea

SHIP'S REPORT, IMPORTATION AND EXPORTATION BY SEA (AMENDMENT) REGULATIONS 1986 (No. 1819) [45p], made under the Customs and Excise Management Act 1979 (c.2), ss.35(4), 42(1); operative on December 1, 1986; amends the method of ship's report as contained in S.I. 1981 No. 1260.

964. Inward processing relief

INWARD PROCESSING RELIEF ARRANGEMENTS (CUSTOMS DUTIES AND AGRICULTURAL LEVIES) REGULATIONS 1986 (No. 2148) [45p], made under the European Communities Act 1972 (c.65), s.2(2); operative on January 1, 1987; provide for the payment of customs duties and agricultural levies in respect of goods which on their importation were previously relieved of duties and levies under inward processing relief arrangements.

INWARD PROCESSING RELIEF (REVOCATION) REGULATIONS 1986 (No. 2141) [45p], made under the Customs and Excise Duties (General Reliefs) Act 1979 (c.3), s.2(1); operative on January 1, 1987; revoke S.I. 1977 No. 910.

965. Personal relief

CUSTOMS DUTY (PERSONAL RELIEFS) (NO. 1) ORDER 1968 (AMENDMENT) ORDER 1986 (No. 2105) [45p], made under the Customs and Excise Duties (General Reliefs) Act 1979 (c.3), s.13; operative on January 1, 1987; increases the "other goods" allowance to £250 in respect of goods obtained duty and tax paid within the Community and increases to £32 the allowance for goods obtained elsewhere or duty and tax free within the Community.

966. Postal packets

POSTAL PACKETS (CUSTOMS AND EXCISE) (AMENDMENT) REGULATIONS 1986 (No. 1019) [45p], made under the Post Office Act 1953 (c.36), s.16(2); operative on July 1, 1986; modify s.43(2)(c) of the Customs and Excise Management Act 1979 in its application to postal packets.

POSTAL PACKETS (CUSTOMS AND EXCISE) REGULATIONS 1986 (No. 260) [£1·35], made under the Post Office Act 1953 (c.36), s.16(2); operative on March 1, 1986; set out customs requirements relating to incoming and outgoing postal packets and the goods contained in them.

967. Quota reliefs

CUSTOMS DUTIES (ECSC) (QUOTA AND OTHER RELIEFS) (AMENDMENT) ORDER 1986 (No. 787) [45p], made under the Customs and Excise Duties (General Reliefs) Act 1979 (c.3), s.1; operative on May 2, 1986; amends S.I. 1985 No. 2041.

CUSTOMS DUTIES (QUOTA RELIEF) ORDER 1986 (No. 1102) [45p], made under the Customs and Excise Duties (General Reliefs) Act 1979 (c.3), s.4; operative on July 1, 1986; provides for the administration of the U.K.'s share of the tariff quota opened for the period July 1, 1986–June 30, 1987, by the EEC, providing exemption from customs duty on import into the U.K. for home use of rum, arrack and tafia originating in various African, Caribbean and Pacific states.

CUSTOMS DUTIES QUOTA RELIEF (ADMINISTRATION) ORDER 1986 (No. 2174) [45p], made under the Customs and Excise Duties (General Reliefs) Act 1979 (c.3), s.4; operative on January 1, 1987; provides for the implementation and administration of reliefs within a tariff quota from customs duty as provided for under s.1 of the 1979 Act.

968. Stills

STILLS (REVOCATION) REGULATIONS 1986 (No. 1820) [45p], made under the Alcoholic Liquor Duties Act 1979 (c.4), s.82(1); operative on November 30, 1986; revokes S.I. 1952 No. 2231 and amends S.I. 1979 No. 1146 which regulated the manufacture, keeping and using of stills by persons other than distillers and rectifiers.

969. Warehousing regulations—keeping of records—whether requirements ultra vires

Customs and Excise Management Act 1979 (c.2), s.93(2)(g) (as amended); Excise Warehousing (Etc.) Regulations 1982 (S.I. 1982 No. 612), reg. 8.]

Regulation 8 of the Excise Warehousing (Etc.) Regulations 1982 is, *ultra vires* s.93(2) of the Customs and Excise Management Act 1979, and does not empower the Customs and Excise to inspect records relating to the non-excisable aspects of a warehouse's business.

P, wine and spirit merchants, used their warehouses for various types of storage, but only partially for the storage of excisable goods. The different activities were all carried on together as a whole. The Commissioners of Customs and Excise claimed that reg. 8(1) and (3) of the Excise Warehousing (Etc.) Regulations 1982 which empowered them to inspect "all records relating to the business" meant that they could inspect all P's records, not merely those relating to excisable goods. *Held,* that reg. 8 was *ultra vires* the creating statute, s.93(2) of the Customs and Excise Management Act 1979, and there was no power to inspect the records relating to the non-excisable aspects of P's business. (Dictum of Viscount Dilhorne in *Daymond* v. *South West Water Authority* [1975] C.L.Y. 2788 applies).

R. *v.* CUSTOMS AND EXCISE COMMISSIONERS, *ex p.* HEDGES & BUTLER [1986] 2 All E.R. 164, D.C.

DAMAGES

970. Assault—excessive force by police. See LEON *v.* COMMISSIONER OF POLICE FOR THE METROPOLIS, § 2538.

971. Assessment of damages—currency

P's vessel, which was Panamanian registered, collided with D's vessel. D's vessel was entirely to blame and liability was agreed. The Admiralty Registrar awarded P damages in United States dollars. D applied to vary the order, contending that P traded in drachmas. *Held,* varying the Registrar's assessment, that P traded in Greek drachmas and this was the currency in which they felt their loss: THE LASH ATLANTICO [1985] 2 Lloyd's Rep. 464, Sheen J.

972. Breach of confidence—confidential information—basis of assessment

Where the tort of breach of confidence has been committed the damages payable by the defendant should be such as to put the plaintiff in the position he would have been in had the tort not been committed.

P was the owner of certain confidential information consisting of the names and addresses of the suppliers of various component parts for a new type of landing leg for articulated lorry trailers developed by P. D obtained the information and used it to enter into competition with P. By a consent order D admitted the information was confidential and an inquiry was ordered into the damage suffered by P in consequence of D's use of the information. D issued a summons in which they sought the determination of the court of the proper basis for the assessment of damages. The court determined the proper basis to be the profits lost by P in consequence of the wrongful disclosure and use of the information. D appealed contending that as the information in question was obtainable elsewhere P's damages ought properly to be assessed with reference to the value of the information itself. *Held,* dismissing the appeal, that the damages payable by D should be such as to put P in the position they would have been in had the tort not been committed. Had it been the case that P would have licensed others to use the information the measure of damages would be the price that P could have commanded for the information and the question of loss of profits would not arise. Where, as in the present case, a manufacturer intended to use the information in his business rather than make the information available to his competitors the measure of damages should be ascertained by reference to the profits lost by the manufacturer (*General Tire and Rubber Co.* v. *Firestone Tyre and Rubber Co.* [1975] C.L.Y. 2503 applied, *Saltman Engineering Co.* v. *Campbell Engineering Co.* (1948) C.L.C. 7033 considered, *Seager* v. *Copydex (No. 2)* [1969] C.L.Y. 1303 distinguished).

DOWSON & MASON *v.* POTTER [1986] 2 All E.R. 418, C.A.

973. Breach of statutory duty—injury caused by attempt to remove obstruction—liability

[Construction (Working Places) Regulations 1966 (S.I. 1966 No. 94), reg. 30(2).]

When there is a breach of statutory duty, employers may be liable despite a human intervention between breach and injury which is a natural and probable consequence of the breach.

P tried to unblock a walkway at D Co.'s plant under which ladles containing molten metal were moved. In the process he suffered a whiplash injury. He claimed damages for breach of statutory duty for failure to keep the walkway free from obstruction contary to reg. 30(2) of the Construction (Working Places) Regulations 1966. The judge found in favour of P. *Held,* dismissing D Co.'s appeal, that it was necessary to examine whether the human intervention between breach of duty and injury was a natural and probable consequence of the breach and if so whether the intervention was sufficient to break the chain of causation. In the circumstances it was very likely that a person finding the obstruction would attempt to remove it; P's injury was caused by the breach, and the precise manner in which the injury was suffered was immaterial (*Gorris* v. *Scott* (1874) L.R. 9 Ex. 124 and *Grant* v. *National*

Gas Board [1956] C.L.Y. 5537 applied; *Stapley* v. *Gypsum Mines* [1953] C.L.Y. 2287 and *Millard* v. *Serck Tubes* [1969] C.L.Y. 1465 considered).
McGovern v. British Steel Corp. [1986] I.C.R. 608, C.A.

974. False imprisonment—counterclaim
[Law Reform (Miscellaneous Provisions) Act 1970 (c.33), s.3(2)]. In September 1983, S and P became engaged. In October S gave P an engagement ring. In January 1984 P terminated the engagement due to S's behaviour. She agreed to meet S in his car and S was very aggressive. P tried to leave but S locked the door and held her by the wrists. P was very distressed. She screamed for help and after five minutes was allowed to leave. S brought an action to recover the ring. P counterclaimed for, *inter alia*, damages for false imprisonment. *Held*, that the claim should be dismissed under s.3(2) and the counterclaim should succeed. Damages for false imprisonment assessed at £250: Simmons v. Polak, March 26, 1986; H.H. Judge Lowe; Willesden County Ct. (*Ex rel. David Nelson, Barrister*).

975. Holiday—cancellation—inconvenience and disappointment
In January 1985 P purchased a holiday for himself, his wife, mother and son at a five star hotel in Israel from D for £2,455. The holiday was for seven days in April 1985. P wished to spend the Jewish festival of Passover at the hotel but did not tell D this. The day before departure, D told P that he could not stay at the five-star hotel contracted for, and offered him an inferior hotel at the same resort. P refused the offer, the holiday was cancelled and D returned the price to P. P claimed damages for inconvenience and disappointment, including that suffered because the family had to spend Passover at home. *Held*, that P was entitled to general damages for disappointment, etc. P was not obliged to accept an alternative holiday. The court took into account that P and his family had another holiday in Israel in May 1985 and frequently took foreign holidays. P was not entitled to extra damages because it was Passover since that was too remote, P not having told D that he was a religious Jew to whom Passover was important. Special damages (for loss of earnings and telephone calls) assessed at £210. General damages: £250: Jacobs v. Thomson Travel, April 11, 1986; H.H. Judge Honig, Bloomsbury County Ct. (*Ex rel. Anthony Radersky, Barrister*).

976. Holiday—loss of enjoyment—quantum
C paid £859 for a two-week holiday for herself, her husband and three children in a self-contained exclusive villa in Majorca. It was discovered on arrival that the villa had been built very recently and a plumber was still carrying out repairs in the bathroom. The inside of the villa was damp and cold—the plasterwork had not been dried out prior to C's arrival. The family's clothing and bedding became damp and they slept in sweatshirts and socks. The swimming pool could not be used. C felt unable to allow the children to play around the villa because a vicious dog on a long chain from a nearby farm was able to encroach upon the property. The villa was burgled on the tenth day, upon which C's family moved to a hotel. *Held*, that the facilities at the villa fell below what a reasonable person could anticipate. For diminution in value of the holiday, special damages of £359 were awarded. For mental distress, inconvenience and disappointment, general damages of £1,000 were awarded: Carter v. Thomson Travel, February 7, 1986; Oldham County Ct. (*Ex rel. Nicholas Braslavsky, Barrister*).

977. Holiday—mitigation of loss—best endeavours of tour operator. See Tucker v. O.T.A. Travel, § 383.

978. Injuries resulting in divorce—divorce costs—whether recoverable
D injured P. As a result of P's injuries, his marriage broke down, and in the subsequent proceedings he was ordered to pay maintenance and the cost of the proceedings to his wife. He sued D for damages, including the costs incurred in his divorce. *Held*, that although the maintenance ordered was not recoverable from D, the Court had a discretion to order D to pay the taxed costs of P's divorce (*Jones* v. *Jones* [1984] C.L.Y. 1096 distinguished, *Aiden Shipping Co.* v. *Interbulk* [1986] C.L.Y. 2606 applied): Pritchard v. J. H. Cobden, *The Times*, December 3, 1986, C.A.

979. Judicial review—appropriateness
L, an education authority, had a statutory duty to pay its employees. However, it owed C, one of its lecturers, £600. C sought an order of mandamus to order L to pay

the money it owed him, as well as damages for distress and inconvenience. *Held*, that judicial review was a wholly inappropriate way to claim such damages, although under s.31(4) of the Supreme Court Act 1981 and R.S.C., Ord. 53, r.7 the arrears themselves could be claimed by such proceedings (*Archer* v. *Brown* [1984] C.L.Y. 1580 distinguished): R. *v.* LIVERPOOL CITY COUNCIL, *ex p.* COADE, *The Times*, October 10, 1986, Simon Brown J.

980. Late payment—knowledge of loss—whether recoverable

A payee under a contract cannot recover damages by way of interest merely because payment is late. Such damages can be recovered, however, when the contracting parties know that, because of special circumstances, loss will result from late payment. The essential question is whether the loss was reasonably within the contemplation of the parties at the time of making the contract (*Hadley* v. *Baxendale* [1854] 9 Exch. 341 and *London Chatham & Dover Railway* v. *South Eastern Railway* [1893] A.C. 429 applied): LIPS MARITIME CORP. *v.* PRESIDENT OF INDIA, *The Financial Times*, November 4, 1986, C.A.

981. Loss of earnings—pension rights—entitlement to contributions towards pension

A plaintiff who has suffered no loss of pension rights is not entitled to a sum representing earnings that would have been compulsorily deducted as contributions towards that pension, as the contributions would not have been at his disposal.

P was injured at work and D were liable. P was required by his contract of employment to belong to a pension scheme under which he had to contribute a percentage of his earnings as a contribution towards the pension. He was off work for 31 weeks, during the latter part of which he received no pay, and accordingly no deductions could be made from his earnings for his pension. He suffered no loss of pension rights. The judge allowed P's claim for damages for his lost contribution, but this decision was reversed on appeal. *Held,* that pension contributions were different in kind from wages received, and his real loss did not include the contributions he would have made to the pension scheme. The sole question was what he had lost, and since he would never have received the amount of his pension contribution, and it would never have been at his disposition, he was not entitled to recover that as damages (*British Transport Commission* v. *Gourley* [1955] C.L.Y. 724 and *Parry* v. *Cleaver* [1969] C.L.Y. 906 considered).

DEWS *v.* NATIONAL COAL BOARD [1986] 3 W.L.R. 227, C.A.

982. Over-dumping of spoil—measure of damage

In 1976 the parties agreed that D should have the right to dump spoil on P's land during construction of the A34. In breach of contract, D over-dumped and dumped where they were not entitled. D contended that the measure of damage was the diminution in value of the land (about £800), whilst P contended that they were entitled to the cost of removing the spoil (some £78,000), arguing that this was required in order for planning permission to be obtained. The judge found that P had a substantial chance of obtaining such permission despite earlier failures, and held that the measure of damage was the cost of removing the spoil. *Held*, dismissing D's appeal, that (1) damages should put the plaintiff in the same position as if the breach of contract or tort had not occurred, but should be reasonable as between the plaintiff and defendant (*Taylor (CR) (Wholesale)* v. *Hepworths* [1977] C.L.Y. 2020 and *Ward* v. *Cannock Chase District Council* [1985] C.L.Y. 2313 followed); (2) the judge had had ample evidence from which to infer that P had a substantial chance of obtaining planning permission; (3) it was accordingly fair and reasonable for him to order reinstatement; (4) the cost of removal should not be reduced pro rata to reflect the possibility that planning permission might not be obtained): MINSCOMBE PROPERTIES *v.* SIR ALFRED MCALPINE & SON (1986) 279 E.G. 759, C.A.

983. Personal injuries—ankle—quantum

Twisted ankle, causing little disability but resulting in permanent and worsening pain in the ankle. General damages: £1,750: WILKINSON *v.* MINISTRY OF DEFENCE *The Times*, July 12, 1986 C.A.

984. Personal injuries—future loss of earnings—increased taxation

In awarding damages for future loss of earnings, a judge decided that the appropriate multiplier was 14, but he increased it to 15 to take account of the higher rate of taxation that the award would attract. *Held*, that this was a relevant and reasonable consideration: THOMAS *v.* WIGNALL, *The Times*, December 11, 1986, C.A.

985. Personal injuries—limitation—several injuries

[Limitation Act 1980 (c.58), s.14(1).] When P suffers a series of injuries in a single accident and settles an action which he has started in respect of one of them he cannot commence another action in respect of another injury which he becomes aware of later (allegedly arising from the same accident) if the date when he becomes aware lies outside the limitation period which would have been applicable to the original action: BRISTOW v. GROUT, *The Times*, November 3, 1986, Jupp J.

986. Personal injuries—loss of earning capacity or handicap on open market—assessment

There is no conventional sum nor any formula for the assessment of damages for loss of earning capacity or handicap on the open labour market, and each case is to be treated on its own: PAGE v. ENFIELD AND HARINGEY AREA HEALTH AUTHORITY, *The Times*, November 7, 1986, C.A.

987. Personal injuries or death—quantum

Details have been received of the following cases in which damages for personal injuries or death were awarded. The classification and sequence of the classified awards follows that adopted in Kemp and Kemp, *The Quantum of Damages*, Vol. 2. Unless there is some statement to the contrary the age of the applicant is his age at the time of the court hearing. The damages are stated on the basis of full liability, *i.e.* ignoring any deduction made for contributory negligence. The sum is the total amount of the damages awarded unless otherwise stated. Interest is excluded in all cases.

Injuries of Maximum Severity

988. BRIGHTMAN v. JOHNSON (*The Times*, December 17, 1985; Tudor Price J.). single woman, aged 18 at date of accident and 22 at date of hearing. Former clerical assistant. Popular, athletic girl, who was described as having "the bloom and self-confidence of a young adult at peace with life." Very severe injuries to neck and throat resulting in complete tetraplegia from below neck, loss of larynx and power of speech and permanent tracheostomy. Life shattered. Had suffered severe bouts of depression and one stage often said she wished she had been killed. But had faced up to her disabilities with remarkable courage. At Stoke Manderville had won gold medal presented to bravest patient of the year and described by judge as "a shining example of the capacity of the human spirit to fight and triumph against almost overwhelming physical odds." Would require constant care and attendance for rest of life. Parents had provided devoted care for some time. Now lived in specially converted flat near them with resident housekeeper and two nurses working shifts. General damages for pain and suffering and loss of amenities assessed at £95,000 and cost of future care at £318,500. *Total award*: £580,547.

989. HOUSECROFT v. BURNETT [1986] 1 All E.R. 332, C.A. Where nursing care is provided for a severely disabled plaintiff by a relative the appropriate sum to be awarded as damages is not that arrived at by calculating the cost of the care provided at commercial rates. P was injured in a road traffic accident caused by D's negligence. In consequence P suffered tetraplegia. P was a 16 year old girl at the time of the accident and 19 at the date damages were assessed. P's intellectual and mental faculties were unimpaired but she was in need of constant attention being unable to do anything for herself. Although she was relatively free from pain and discomfort she was completely aware of the damage caused to herself and the loss of a future of great potential. Her life expectancy was between 25 and 32 years. P was awarded damages of £323,050 including £80,000 for pain, suffering and loss of amenity; £108,550 for her future care; and, £56,000 for loss of future earnings. Future care was calculated by applying a multiplier of 13 to a multiplicand of £8,350. The multiplicand consisted of £5,350 being the commercial cost of providing additional care and assistance to supplement that to be provided by the plaintiff's mother and £3,000 for the care provided by the mother. Future loss of earnings was calculated by applying a multiplier of 10 to a multiplicand of £5,600. No separate award for "last years" was made. P appealed against the award. *Held*, dismissing the appeal, that as a future guideline the proper figure to award for pain, suffering and loss of amenity for an average case of tetraplegia in April 1985 is £75,000. The time had come to start afresh and discard references to cases of the last 10 to 15 years. More should be awarded if there was continuing pain and/or any diminution in the powers of speech, sight or hearing. Less should be awarded where the plaintiff was unaware of the condition or had a reduced expectation of life. In the average case the plaintiff was not in physical pain, fully aware of the disability, had an expectation of life in excess of 25 years and full powers of speech, sight and hearing. The award of £80,000 could not be described at too low. The judge erred in failing to make provision in the cost of future care for the need to employ extra assistance at commercial rates for one month each year to give the plaintiff's mother a holiday. The judge did not err in failing to calculate the cost of future care on the basis that the plaintiff's mother would play no part in providing that care. The multiplicand of £3,000 being the value put on the care to be provided by the mother was not to be interfered with. It was not correct to value the care provided by the mother at commercial rates nor was it correct to award nothing in respect of that care. The plaintiff should be awarded sufficient to provide for her future care and needs including the need to make some monetary acknowledgement to her mother for the care rendered by her. £39,000 was sufficient for the latter pupose in the present case. The assessment would vary according to the facts of each case. A multiplier of 10 in calculating the loss of future earnings was sufficient to take into account the "last years" having regard to the difficulties of predicting what the plaintiff's future earnings would be. The lack of provision for the mother's holidays in the damages for future care was accounted for by the generosity of the award for pain, suffering and loss of amenity (*Donnelly* v. *Joyce* [1973] C.L.Y. 727, *Harris* v. *Harris* [1973] C.L.Y. 741, *Walker* v. *McClean (John) & Sons* [1979] C.L.Y. 664, *Wright* v. *British Railways Board* [1983] C.L.Y. 1063, *Hughes* v. *McKeown* [1985] C.L.Y. 955 considered).

990. FRANCIS *v.* BOSTOCK (*The Times*, November 9, 1985; Russell J.; Manchester). Single woman, aged 21. Student. As result of accident in September 1982 suffered spinal injury resulting in paraplegia from below waist and severe disability in both arms. In hospital about six months. then cared for at home by mother for 18 months. Now studying law and computing at Polytechnic. General damages for pain and suffering and loss of amenities assessed at £77,000, for future nursing expenses at £140,000 and for physiotherapy at £8,000. Further sums were awarded for future loss of earnings and value of mother's services. *Total award:* £413,945.

991. [Scot.] ROTCHFORD (May 26, 1986; Criminal Injuries Compensation Board; Edinburgh). Male, aged 16 at date of offence and 24 at date of hearing. Former furniture manufacturer's apprentice with school leaving certificate only. Had worked for only a few weeks when run over by motor vehicle whilst being chased by thugs. Major head injury involving diffuse brain damage and resulting in dense right hemiparesis; major fracture of pelvis; bruised kidneys and multiple abrasions. In hospital a year. Loss of most of vision; unable to speak and could only make garbled noises indicative of discomfort or pleasure; doubly incontinent; right leg shortened; some spontaneous movement of left arm and left leg only; no capacity to perform even elementary tasks; somewhat stimulated by music and television. Required special wheelchair and constant attendance to dress, sit, be fed and care for his incontinence and constant care throughout the night for turning him. Any mobilisation very restricted, for short periods and then only with 2 attendants. Aware of his condition and surroundings. Surrounded by numerous and loving family. Home had been altered and specially equipped. Damages for solatium assessed at £70,000; for cost of past care at £10,000 (based on multiplier of 5 and multiplicand of £2,000); for cost of future care at £42,000. Loss of earnings were agreed and were based on multiplier of 16. *Total award* exceeded £122,000. (*Ex rel. J. D. Campbell of the Scottish Bar*).

992. JENKINSON *v.* LUMBIS (June 8, 1986; Kennedy J.; Leeds). Female, aged 19 at date of accident and 22 at date of hearing. Before accident had high average IQ of 115; had been normal, happy, sociable teenager, who was good at sports; had done well at school (attaining 4 passes in CSE and 5 GCE 'O' levels) and had left with glowing report; had obtained a Diploma in hotel catering after 2 years at Technical College, where she was in top 25 per cent. of her year and among best in practical tasks; had begun working in parents' hotel and intended to go into catering industry. Devastating injuries, including very severe closed head injury with fracture of base of skull; gross multiple facial lacerations resulting in severe cosmetic disability; partial loss of sight in left eye; ruptured spleen and torn liver. In hospital 3 months, deeply unconscious 1 month and had 6 months' retrograde amnesia. Underwent tracheotomy and operation for repair of liver. Left with severe intellectual, physical and emotional disabilities. Now had mentality of an 11 year old, overall IQ of 85, loss of short-term memory, serious difficulty with speaking and inability to enunciate words, suffered from emotional liability, alternating between bouts of weeping and giggling, and profound personality change. She was childish, irresponsible and lacking in motivation and carried soft toys and children's books around with her. Visual acuity in left eye was reduced to a half and had to wear tinted lens permanently. Had difficulty in swallowing and drinking and had to wear denture. Persistent weakness in left arm and hand, had difficulty in lifting things, running and walking, was unsteady on her feet and tended to trip. Acutely conscious of her facial disfigurement and had moments of insight into her condition. Unable to manage her affairs or handle money and needed constant supervision. Condition permanent. Life expectancy normal viz. about 54 years. Parents had shown great devotion and would continue to care for her for foreseeable future. Did not require psychiatrically trained nurse, but needed companion to keep an eye on her, cope with her emotional outbursts and deal with any emergencies. Parents' claim for recovery of losses sustained due to run-down of hotel business caused by care devoted to plaintiff was rejected. Damages were assessed or agreed as follows: (1) for pain and suffering and loss of amenities: £54,000; (2) agreed pre-trial loss of earnings of plaintiff: £10,000; (3) for plaintiff's loss of future earnings: £88,000 (based on multiplier of 16 and multiplicand of £5,500; (4) for value of parents' services to trial: £13,000; (5) for cost of future care: £104,400 consisting of (a) £27,000 for value of parents' services (based on multiplier of 9 and multiplicand of £3,000) and (b) £77,400 for institutional care (based on same multiplier and multiplicand of £8,800); (6) for future cost of contact lenses: £2,700 (based on multiplier of 18 and multiplicand of £150); (7) for future costs of administration by Court of Protection: £12,500; (8) other agreed pre-trial special damages (including cost of holiday in Australia for plaintiff and parents, cost of conversion of part of family home into a flat and expenses incurred in visiting plaintiff in hospital): £12,000. *Total Damages:* £296,600 (*Ex rel. Paul Worsley, Barrister*).

993. THIRTLE *v.* SUCKLING (October 25, 1986; Michael Davies J.; Leeds). Male, aged 33 at date of accident and 39 at date of trial. Single and of barely average intelligence. Apparently right-handed. Former scrap metal burner. Described by employer as conscientious and valued employee, but previous work record to some degree inconsistent. Fracture of skull with cerebral contusion resulting in permanent brain damage; major fractures of right arm, and lower right leg. Underwent operations for insertion and removal of plates in arm and leg. His intellectual level was reduced, his memory was poor, he lacked concentration, his sense of balance was impaired resulting in falls and difficulty with stairs, he suffered from headaches, dizziness and insomnia and was intolerant of noise, he was subject to depression and abnormal variations in mood, he had tendency to sit in chair for long periods and smoke very heavily and occasionally indulged in anti-social behaviour when taken out. There was continuing limitation of pronation and supination of right arm and discomfort in arm and leg and he had intermittent backache due to falls and lack of activity. Lived with parents in isolated bungalow. Able to wash, shave, attend to own toilet, dress and feed himself, but inadvisable for him to venture out alone. Enjoyed outings but not holidays. Clung to desire to return to work, though now incapable of work of any kind. Life expectancy reduced by 5 years. Parents, who were in their mid-60s and did not enjoy best of health, were expected to be able to continue to care for him for further 5 years. Thereafter employment of housekeeper and part-time handyman would be necessary and sister would give occasional support. Special damages were assessed as follows: (1) for past loss of earnings: £24,359 (after deducting 15 per cent. to reflect past work record); (2) for past care by parents: £28,300; (3) for miscellaneous pre-trial expenses: £9,049. General damages were assessed as follows: (1) for pain and suffering and loss of amenities: £50,000; (2) for future loss of earnings: £76,135; (3) for cost of future care by parents: £28,250 (based on multiplier of 5 and multiplicand of £5,650); (4) for cost of future care by others: £79,970 (based on multiplier of 10); (5) for accommodation: £14,700; (6) for future cost of vehicles: £17,500; (7) for Court of Protection fees: £12,500; for loss of expectation of life: £1,500. *Total Special Damages*: £61,708. *Total General Damages*: £280,555. (*Ex rel. A. R. Dent, Barrister*).

Multiple Injuries

994. Doyle *v.* Edmunds (May 15, 1986; Caulfield J.). Male, aged 19 at date of accident and 24 at date of trial. Former despatch clerk. Right-handed. Single. Had been keen football, tennis and snooker player. Injury to right brachial plexus resulting in total paralysis and partial loss of sensation in right arm; severe comminuted fractures of right femur, tibia, fibula and lateral malleolus; total lesion of right lateral popliteal nerve resulting in "foot drop" condition; later consequential fall causing fracture of humerus. In hospital 4 months. Had 6 operations including bone grafting. Due to remarkable efforts within 16 months obtained secure employment with R.A.F. Right arm wasted and useless; right leg shortened by 1¾″ necessitating "leg equalisation" operation; crepitus in right knee; extensive scarring to right hip and lower leg. Unable to use stick when walking, to run or pursue any active recreations save horse riding and swimming. Probability of osteo-arthritis in right knee within 10 to 15 years. No future loss of earnings or loss of earning capacity, but locked into present job for life. *Special Damages:* £3,893 (including pre-trial loss of earnings and costs of adapting car to enable plaintiff to drive). *General Damages:* £46,000. (*Ex rel. James Gibbons, Barrister*).

995. Podmore *v.* Higgins (October 18, 1985; Saville J.; Birmingham). Housewife, aged 56. Right-handed. Enjoyed darts and played to high standard. Multiple injuries, including severe comminuted fracture of right wrist, fractures of left humerus and one rib on right side, lacerations of both shins, two black eyes and and other bruises. Had suffered some depression. Left with (1) considerable stiffness and restriction of movement of right wrist: there was no movement of backward extension and rotation was restricted; (2) stiffness of left shoulder and likely permanent restriction of abduction of left arm to about 135°; (3) unsightly scars on right shin, which caused her to wear trousers instead of skirts. Now unable to play darts and had difficulty with housework, in lifting a kettle or saucepan and bathing herself: *General Damages*: £8,500. (*Ex rel. Rutherfords, Solicitors*).

Face

996. Laker *v.* Townsend (July 25, 1985; Deputy Judge Inskip; Q.B.D.; Winchester). Female, aged 20 at date of accident and 27 at date of hearing. Unmarried. Junior scientific officer Grade 2 in hospital bio-chemistry department. Intelligent, attractive, shy and sensitive girl, who was lacking in self confidence, less mature than average, prone to slight acne, and was just establishing herself in adult life at time of accident. Led active life regularly attending dances, parties and the like. Had just begun science course at college. Front seat passenger in car involved in head-on collision and head went through windscreen. Severe multiple facial lacerations and fractures of 2 incisors. In hospital 4 days initially. Underwent 2 operations under general anaesthetic, first for suturing wounds and second for exploration of wounds and removal of glass fragments. Attended hospital for out-patient treatment for some time. Severe and extensive facial scarring, resulting in appearance graphically described in one medical report as a "mincemeat face", included: (1) horizontal linear scar 2 cm. above right eyebrow; (2) 24 mm. semi-lunar shaped gouged scar above same eyebrow; (3) 26 mm. linear scar running from outer part of right temple downwards into eyebrow; (4) 77 mm. long by average 6 mm. wide scar on right cheek running forward and horizontally to border of lower jaw and ending in right side of lower lip; (5) 11 mm. long livid hypertrophic scar; (6) two 7mm. long gouged scars; (7) 21 mm. linear scar; (8) 8 mm. long by 5 mm. wide gouged, depressed scar. For better part of 3 years suffered very unsightly eruption of acne due to use of lanolin cream to massage scars, which was additional blow to her morale and left her with pock marks. After about 3 years underwent plastic surgery to scar on right cheek involving "Z plasty" operation. As result of accident life between ages of 20 and 27 had been a "disaster". Facial disfigurement had severely affected her. She became extremely self-conscious and embarrassed by her appearance, felt she was ugly and developed a phobia of meeting people and hence depression. Unconsciously she always tried to hide her face from passers by. She shunned strangers. Her social life almost ceased. She had no close friends and rarely went out. She suffered great distress whenever the accident and the extent of her injuries were mentioned. Viewed objectively there had been some improvement in her facial appearance and she was still attractive and had a pleasing personality. But she was left with permanent scarring which would always be obvious and would attract attention. She had agreed to see a clinical psychologist who it was hoped would help her to overcome at least some of the psychological effects of her disfigurement. But she would always be embarassed when meeting strangers and would suffer some social disadvantage. Following accident she had passed her college examinations with a grade 2:2, had become a junior scientific officer and after an oral examination had been promoted to her present position. In 1985 she had sat her fellowship examinations, but had not yet learnt the results. There was shortly to be a vacancy for a senior scientific officer. But there was no evidence as to her abilities or prospects at her present hospital or elsewhere. No award was made for loss of future earnings or loss of earning capacity. *Agreed Special Damages*: £582. *General Damages*: £20,000. (*Ex rel. Townsends, Solicitors*).

997. THORNE (September 25, 1985; Criminal Injuries Compensation Board; London). Male, aged 18 at date of injury and 24 at date of hearing. Stabbed by broken bottle in right jaw and neck below ear. Severance of the facial nerve causing complete right-sided facial paralysis. Nerve transplant operation performed resulting after 18 months in almost complete recovery from paralysis, but leaving long hypertrpohic scar. After about 4 years underwent plastic surgery, but this had resulted in more disfiguring 3″×2″ W-shaped scar on jaw line and neck, which was visibly hypertrophic, most unsightly and was painful in cold weather or if touched. *Special Damages:* £60. *General Damages:* £6,500. (*Ex rel. John S. Church, Barrister*).

998. SINGH (February 5, 1986; Criminal Injuries Compensation Board; Birmingham). Male, aged 33. Laceration of right eyebrow. No bony injury. Wound sutured by application of steri-strips. Left with permanent L-shaped scare 1¾″ long, which itched in warmer weather. *General damages:* £1,250. (*Ex rel. Haynes Duffell, Kentish and Co., Solicitors.*)

Jaw

999. VUJANIC (November 19, 1985; Criminal Injuries Compensation Board; Leeds). Male, aged 41 at date of offence and 43 at date of hearing. Punched and kicked by two men. Bilateral compound fractures of lower jaw with damage to nerves of jaw, bruising to body and abrasions to both shins. In hospital a week. Fractures reduced and fixed with wire and sound molar tooth removed. Wiring in place for about a month, during which time he could take only liquid nourishment. Permanent loss of sensation around lower lip and chin causing difficulty in shaving and initially in eating. Necks of teeth where jaw wired now sensitive to hot and cold food and liquids. Permanent unsightly abrasions on both shins. *Agreed Special Damages*: £53. *General Damages*: £2,500. (*Ex rel. Michael Slater, Barrister*).

Skin

1000. BUTLER *v.* MARCONI ELECTRONIC DEVICES (June 6, 1986; Deputy Judge A. W. Hamilton Q.C.; Q.B.D.; Lincoln). Female, aged 59. Due to work with expoxy resins contracted dermatitis in February 1982. Thereafter suffered intermittently on her fingers for 3 years. In February 1985 developed severe eczema on neck, which lasted about 1 month. No further attacks thereafter. In May 1986 retired early due to anxiety. Left with 2 small scars on back resulting from patch tests. Permanent propensity to dermatitis from contact with domestic adhesives and the like. Wished to obtain work as shop assistant, but feared that mention of condition would hinder prospects. *Special Damages*: £40. *General Damages*: £3,000 (including small sum for loss of earning capacity). (*Ex rel. Andrew & Co., Solicitors*).

Burns and Scars

1001. KEITH *v.* TENNENS (August 16, 1985; Mr. Registrar Simons; Southend County Court). Female, aged 16 at date of accident and 19 at date of hearing. Trapped in car which burst into flames after accident. Large burn to left shoulder, singed hair and ears and cut to brow above hair line. In hospital nine days. Good recovery. Left with unsightly 25 cm. × 15 cm. scar on shoulder. No continuing pain. Upset by adverse comments when wearing low-backed clothing. No special damages. *General Damages*: £3,500 (including £500 for trauma of accident). (*Ex rel. Stephen Weddle, Barrister.*)

1002. SARGENT *v.* WALSALL METROPOLITAN BOROUGH COUNCIL (June 27, 1985; Court of Appeal). Girl, aged 2 at date of accident and 12 at date of trial. Full thickness burns to whole of right sole and outer aspect of left sole. Admitted to hospital after 10 to 14 days, during which period would have suffered considerable pain. In hospital 8 weeks, of which about 4 weeks were attributable to accident. No surgery required. Full recovery. Burns had healed leaving scar tissue which was not adherent to underlying tissues. Slight risk of contraction of scarring, but this would be amenable to treatment. Claim dismissed. Court of Appeal dismissed plaintiff's appeal on liability and quantum. *General Damages* assessed at £750. (*Ex rel. J. E. Fletcher, Barrister*

1003. RUSSELL v. STAVELEY CHEMICALS (July 12, 1985; Mr. Assistant Recorder M. J. G. Harris; Chesterfield County Court). Male, aged in about the mid-30s. Fitter. Apparently right-handed. Acid burn to back of left hand. Attended regularly for changes of dressing initially. Resumed pre-accident work after 3 weeks. Initially suffered some abnormal sensation on palmar surface of fingers and some embarrassment, pain and discomfort from scarring, which for 18 months was quite conspicuous and resembled a spider or tattoo. Good recovery. Left with permanent, large, irregular scar, which was not adherent to underlying structures, had faded considerably and was now only slightly noticeable. *General Damages:* £2,500. (*Ex rel. Evill and Coleman, Solicitors*).

Sight

1004. WHITE (February 11, 1986; Criminal Injuries Compensation Board; Bristol). Boy, aged 14 at date of injury and 15 at date of hearing. Hit in right eye by air-gun pellet. Permanent loss of vision and eye shrunken. Cosmetic prosthesis fitted with no ill-effect. Vision in left eye improved since injury. Before injury had displayed artistic talents—might have become a graphic designer. Poor prospects now of non-manual full-time employment due to backwardness at school. *General Damages:* £20,000. (*Ex rel. Declan O'Mahony, Barrister*).

1005. ANGOL (December 11, 1985; Criminal Injuries Compensation Board; London). Male, aged 45 at date of injury and 47 at date of hearing. Previously unemployed and receiving long term invalidity benefit. Acid thrown in face. Permanent loss of vision in right eye; permanent impairment of vision in left eye; acute pain and suffering; scarring. Condition had stabilised and scarring and pain had lessened with time, but no prospect of impairment in condition of either eye. Now wore dark glasses to hide ugly appearance of right eye, which embarrassed him. No award for loss of earnings. General damages for loss of right eye assessed at £12,000 and for other injuries at £3,000. *Special Damages:* £50. *Total General Damages:* £15,000. (*Ex rel. Angela Glenn, Barrister*).

Neck

1006. PETERS v. MINISTRY OF DEFENCE (May 17, 1985; Bristow J.; Winchester). Male, aged 44 at date of accident and 54 at date of trial. Former long-distance lorry driver. Multiple injuries, including non-specific injury to neck causing chronic dysrhythmia and degenerative changes at level of cervical vertebrae 5/6 and 6/7; injury to both acromio-clavicular joints; sprain of right wrist; and multiple bruising. Wrist in plaster 2 weeks. Resumed pre-accident work after 6 weeks. Thereafter continued to suffer from pain in shoulder and elbow and aching, weakness and restriction of movement in neck, which were not severe initially but persistent. Underwent two manipulations of spine and one of shoulder under general anaesthetic; two injections of shoulder and one of elbow with hydro-cortisone; two hemi-excisions of clavicles under general anaesthetic; occasionally used soft collar; and finally in April 1983 underwent spinal fusion at C5/6 and C6/7 levels, which had resulted in major improvement in condition of neck. Treatment had necessitated periodic absences from work, chronic neck discomfort had caused him difficulty in loading and roping heavy lorries and hence transfer to driving container lorries and he was made redundant in March 1983. At date of trial was still unemployed. General damages for pain and suffering and loss of amenities assessed at £11,000; for 1 year's future loss of earnings at £4,631; and for loss of earning capacity at £1,000. *Special Damages:* £13,388. *Total General Damages:* £16,631. (*Ex rel. Richard Tyson, Barrister*).

1007. HOLTON v. ROBERTS (March 25, 1986; Mr. Registrar Bird; Yeovil County Court). Married woman, aged 61 at date of hearing. Retired cook. Whiplash injury to neck.

Severe pain from neck radiating across shoulders and down her arms. Had physiotherapy and pain-killers but pain persisted. Would continue to suffer right-sided neck and upper shoulder aching lasting throughout the day. Aching aggravated by daily heavy lifting which was unavoidable as she cared for her paraplegic husband. Prognosis was that neck disability was permanent. *General damages* (for pain, suffering and loss of amenity): £6,000. (*Ex rel. Declan O'Mahony, Barrister*).

1008. MARSH *v.* M. I. ELECTRICAL INSTALLATIONS (February 21, 1986; Judge McGregor; Peterborough County Court). Female, aged 21 at date of accident and 23 at date of trial. Police constable. Whiplash injury to neck resulting in pain extending into left shoulder and back pain. For 6 weeks wore collar for decreasing periods and off work. Resumed sports with discomfort after 3 months. Thereafter suffered discomfort only after long periods of driving or sports. Expected to be symptom-free within 3 years of accident. *General damages:* £2,500. (*Ex rel. Russell Jones and Walker, Plaintiff's Solicitors.*)

1009. BOWEN *v.* O'NEILL (1) (March 5, 1985; Drake J.; Manchester). Male, aged about 25 at date of accident and 27 at date of trial. Tractor driver. Whiplash injury to neck causing some pain and stiffness on rotation. In soft collar six weeks and off work 14 weeks. Left with very mild discomfort which would gradually lessen, but not disappear entirely, amounting to inconvenience rather than disability. *General Damages*: £1,800. (*Ex rel. James Chapman & Co., Solicitors.*)

Spine Below Neck

1010. BEAMAN (December 17, 1985; Criminal Injuries Compensation Board (Michael Ogden Q.C., Chairman); Nottingham). Married woman, aged 31 at date of offence and 40 at date of hearing. Former nursing assistant. Lesion of lumbar intervertebral disc at L5/S.I. level and fracture of proximal segment of coccyx. Put into plaster jacket, then underwent traction and heat treatment. Unfit to resume pre-accident work and eventually dismissed on grounds of ill health. Fracture of coccyx had united with some backward displacement of distal fragments. Post-traumatic degenerative changes affecting disc had developed and were likely to become progressively worse. Continuing pain and discomfort in back; agility impaired; unable to lift or carry heavy weights, bend, kneel or work in cramped spaces; unable to do heavy housework or go dancing; sexual relations impaired. Suffered from bouts of depression. Had put on 4 stone in weight due to inactivity. Change of personality. Now more irritable and had resorted to drinking heavily with risk of becoming dependent on alcohol. Had difficulty in undertaking even sedentary occupation due to inability of sit or stand for long periods and was virtually unemployable. General damages for pain and suffering and loss of amenities assessed at £15,000 and for loss of future earnings at £20,000 (based on multiplier of 10). *Agreed Special Damages*: £3,572. *Total General Damages*: £35,000. (*Ex rel. Keith Hornby, Barrister*).

1011. DAVIES *v.* MASSEY FERGUSON PERKINS (January 30, 1986; Evans J.). Male, aged 50 at date of accident. Pre-existing degenerative condition of spine which had already caused symptoms. Missed step when descending stairs. Minor twisting injury to lumbar spine, which did not exacerbate previous condition, and caused symptoms for at most 6 months. For several weeks suffered increasing pain and stiffness. After about 2 months underwent traction, which assisted. After about 3 to 4 months had further physiotherapy. In quite severe pain for some time, which gradually resolved. When pain severe unable to do gardening, suffered pain on any minor jarring of back, such as stepping off kerb into road, had difficulty dressing himself and managing ordinary household activities and needed wife's help. Off work only on days when attended hospital for treatment. Any residual symptoms after 6 months attributable to pre-existing condition. *General damages:* £1,250. (*Ex rel. Robert P. Glancy, Barrister.*)

Respiratory Organs

1012. NEEDHAM *v.* CHARLES PORTWAY AND SON (May 15, 1986; Deputy Judge Piers Ashworth Q.C.; Q.B.D.). Male, aged 54. Former chargehand fitter. As result of exposure to asbestos between 1956 and 1968 developed pleural disease involving cuirass-type pleural thickening, which restricted his breathing capacity. First symptoms of disease exhibited in 1976. Between then and 1980 he suffered minor dyspnoea. In

1981 he was made redundant and, although capable of light work, had since been unable to find alternative employment. By date of trial pleural disease was extensive and progressive, he had developed underlying mild asbestosis, he suffered from chest pains, anxiety and depression and was substantially disabled. Able to walk only 200 yards on the flat at his own face. 50 per cent. risk of lung cancer and small risk of mesothelioma. Expectation of life reduced. No realistic prospect of obtaining work. In last year of life would require extra assistance from his wife. General damages for pain and suffering and loss of amenities assessed at £30,000, for loss of future earnings and at £42,500 (based on agreed multiplier of 7) and for wife's future services at £1,500. *Special Damages*: £20,000. *Total General Damages*: £74,000. (*Ex rel. Field Fisher & Martineau, Solicitors*).

1013.   CLARKE *v.* MUREX (February 29, 1984; Latey J.; Birmingham). Male, aged 50. Former clerical worker in motor industry. As result of exposure to berylium in course of employment as process worker between 1952 and 1960 developed form of pneumonconiosis known as berylliosis. Condition diagnosed in 1985 when X-rays revealed changes in lung tissue. In 1968 disability assessed at 5 per cent. From between 1972 and 1977 became increasingly short of breath. By 1982 had throaty cough, but no history of chest pain, able to manage half-mile walk to work on the flat only slowly, became breathless on attempting hills or hurrying, at end of working day felt exhausted and went to bed early. In October 1982 volunteered for redundancy because of condition. In November 1982 disability assessed at 20 per cent. and year later at 40 per cent. Since retirement had led sedentary life, doing light gardening and odd jobs around house. Able to manage only short walk on the flat, became breathless if he attempted one flight of stairs, painting upset chest and had to give up fishing. Sexual relations limited to three or four occasions a year and on last occasion became so breathless that wife wanted to call doctor. Lung function would deteriorate gradually but progressively. Life expectancy 10 to 15 years. Wife had given up part-time work, not because plaintiff required nursing, but to enable her to enjoy his remaining years with him and do work around house which he could not do. Award included wife's loss of earnings. In assessing plaintiff's loss of earnings no deduction made in respect of *ex gratia* payment made by former employers under voluntary redundancy scheme, but statutory payment deducted on ground that there had been no redundancy in department in which he had worked and special case made for him because of ill-health. General damages for pain and suffering and loss of amenities assessed at £27,000 and for loss of future earnings at £41,580 based on multiplier of six. *Special Damages*: £2,605. *Total General Damages*: £71,185. (*Ex rel. Robin Thompson and Partners, Solicitors*.)

1014.   GRODENTZ *v.* TATE AND LYLE REFINERIES (March 21, 1986; Deputy Judge Richard Rougier Q.C.; Q.B.D.). Male, aged 56. Former taxi driver. Pre-existing ankylosing spondylitis. As result of past work with asbestos, in 1979 to 1980 developed pleural disease with plaques and extensive pleural thickening causing breathlessness, chest pains and anxiety. In April 1985 had to give up taxi driving. Underwent thoracostomy to prevent mesothelioma. In 1986 overall disability assessed at 60 per cent. Continuing breathlessness and chest pain, latter partly due to spondylitis. Some risk of lung cancer and mesothelioma. General damages for pain and suffering and loss of amenities assessed at £22,500 and for future loss of earnings at £12,500. *Special Damages*: £14,162. *Total General Damages*: £35,000. (*Ex rel. Field Fisher & Martineau, Solicitors*).

1015.   JONES *v.* WILLBROW MANUFACTURING (April 15, 1986; Michael Davies J.; Cardiff). Male, aged 59. Former planer in welding shop. As result of long exposure to welding fumes, particularly from 1965 to 1971, developed late onset asthma causing loss of fitness and enjoyment of life over number of years. Made redundant in 1981, but it was agreed that this was not attributable to condition. General health good, but able to walk only about 100 yards, unable to dig his garden and always had to carry inhaler. Disability partly attributable to his smoking in earlier years. Did not have good change of obtaining alternative employment in 1981, but impossible to say that he had no such chance. General damages for pain and suffering and loss of amenities assessed at £10,000 and for loss of chance of employment at £2,000. *Total General Damages*: £12,000. (*Ex rel. Robin Thompson and Partners, Solicitors*).

1016.   FANNING (November 29, Criminal Injuries Compensation Board; Liverpool). Male, aged 38. A Fire Officer. Inhaled large quantity of smoke and suffered scorched bronchi. Within hour became breathless and had sharp pains in chest on breathing. For about 5 weeks chest pain prevented him from walking more than short distances. Then improved and returned to work after 6/7 weeks. Complete recovery after about 6 months apart from feeling that now more affected by smoke inhalation than before. *Special Damages*: £271. *General Damages*: £1,250. (*Ex rel. Richard Barnett and Co., Solicitors*).

Reproductive Organs

1017. MILLER v. PETERBOROUGH HEALTH AUTHORITY (March 13, 1986; Judge McGregor; Peterborough County Court). Male, aged 19 at date of operation and 25 at date of trial. Self-employed wood merchant. Married shortly before trial. In hospital, suffering from left inguinal hernia. During operation, left testicular artery severed or constricted cutting off blood supply to left testicle. Subsequently left testicle swollen and painful, eventually atrophied. Complete loss of testicle's reproductive and hormonal functions—complaints of premature ejaculation and inability to maintain an erection due to psychological rather than physiological reasons. Young man of particular sensitivity, bordering on hypochondria. Fertility not affected. Cosmetic effect negligible. *Special damages*: £60. *General damages* for pain and suffering: £5,000. (*Ex rel. Micheal Yelton, Barrister*).

Internal Organs—Liver

1018. BAKER v. EAST YORKSHIRE HEALTH AUTHORITY (October 15, 1985; Jupp J.; Leeds). Male, aged 59. Maintenance fitter. Teetotaller. In course of employment by defendants exposed to fumes of perchloroethylene, a dry-cleaning solvent, resulting in liver damage. In December 1978 began to suffer symptoms including anorexia, lassitude, permanent unpleasant taste in mouth and lost about 1½ stone in weight. Liver biopsy revealed inflammation of some portal tracts suggestive of local hepatitis. After about a month symptoms subsided. In 1980, late 1982 and 1983 suffered further exacerbations, each episode lasting between 4 and 11 weeks, juxtaposed with periods of relative good health. Later biopsies revealed severe portal tract fibrosis with evidence of bridging consistent with hepatic necrosis. In 1983 prescribed Prednisolone, a cortico-steroid, which he had taken ever since. This had stabilised liver condition and there had been no further incidents of hepatitis. Previous hobbies of gardening, swimming and badminton now inhibited through lassitude. Work unaffected. Remote possibility of peptic ulceration, diabetes and osteoporosis as result of steroid treatment. *Agreed Special Damages*: £229·17. *General Damages*: £8,000. (*Ex rel. Julina N. Goose, Barrister*).

Internal Organs—Kidney

1019. BAKER v. TURTLE (October 19, 1985; Deputy Judge Roger Titheridge Q.C.; Q.B.D.). Female, aged 13 at date of accident and 17 at date of trial. Struck by motor vehicle. Kidney ruptured and divided into three pieces; suffered serious psychological effects; minor abrasions of skin and ankle. In hospital 16 days. Nephrectomy performed. Was depressed for some time and used to lie awake at night crying. Suffered frequent nightmares about accident and complete loss of self-confidence. Was very apprehensive when crossing roads, to such extent that she was embarassed when with friends. Very good recovery from kidney injury. Remaining kidney had adapted naturally to maintain normal renal function. Remote possibility of adhesions developing. If remaining kidney was damaged, she would be in hazardous position, though this would to some degree be alleviated by modern dialysis and transplant techniques. Prospect of such damage impossible to predict. Left with 8″ x ⅜″ post-operative abdominal scar, which was pale and soundly healed; 2 circular drain scars, each 1″ in diameter, with subsequent appendicectomy scar leading from lower scar; 1″ diameter scar on shin and 1¼″ by 1½″ scar on inner side of ankle. Of these only the abdominal scar gave rise to any significant degree of disfigurement. Plaintiff was very concerned about its appearance, would not wear a bikini, was embarassed at school and when swimming and worried about its effect on boyfriends. She still suffered nightmares about once a month, was still nervous of crossing roads and was only slowly regaining her self-confidence. These remaining psychological symptoms were expected to improve greatly once litigation was concluded. *Agreed Special Damages*: £184·60. *General Damages*: £15,000. *Per Curiam*.

The analogy drawn by Cantley J. in *Hughes* v. *Armitage Brothers* [1974] C.L.Y. 927 between loss of a kidney and loss of an eye could not be taken too far. The one differs from the other since, in the normal course, a plantiff will not be troubled by a lost kidney. Furthermore, it would be wrong to up-date the award in *Hughes* for loss of a kidney *simpliciter* for two reasons: (1) (Though this did not appear from the reports of the case in *Kemp and Kemp* at para. 7–812 and *Current Law*) the award there made included a sum for aggravation of a pre-existing back injury); (2) The prospects of a plaintiff who suffers damage to a remaining kidney are almost certainly better today than in 1974 due to improvements in transplant and dialysis techniques. The appropriate bracket for the loss of a kidney *simpliciter* is £8,000 to £9,000. (*Ex rel. Jonathan S. Fisher, Barrister*).

Internal Organs—Rectum

1020. HARKNESS *v*. OXFORDSHIRE HEALTH AUTHORITY (January 17, 1986; Court of Appeal (Sir John Donaldson M.R., Stephen Brown L.J. and Sir Edward Eveleigh)). Male, aged 29 at date of accident. Surgeon. Central spike of operating theatre stool entered rectum. Potentially devastating injury, but suffered only tears to perianal skin and anal sphincter. No damage to urethra, bladder, bowels or rectum. Developed haematoma the size of an orange. In hospital total of 16 days. Underwent 2 operations under general anaesthetic to make and close a colostomy, which was maintained for 8 weeks. Full recovery after 3 months apart from 11 cm. colostomy scar, which caused comment in surgeons' locker room, flatus on exertion and uncomfortable sensation after drinking fizzy liquids. Court allowed plaintif's to appeal against Master Grant's award of £3,000 general damages for pain and suffering. *General Damages*: £4,500. (*Ex rel. Kieran Coonan, Barrister*).

Hip

1021. GIFFORD *v*. KEELING (November 15, 1985; Deputy Judge Partick Bennett Q.C.; Q.B.D.). Male, aged 44 at date of accident and 47 at date of trial. Lorry driver. Posterior dislocation of right hip with small fracture at rear margin of joint; contusion to right thigh and knee; shock. In hospital for 3 to 4 months. Dislocation reduced by manipulation under general anaesthetic. Right leg in traction for 3 months. Steel pin inserted in upper tibia for this purpose had to be removed owing to infection and thereafter skin traction applied, causing blistering. After 3 months began to mobilise on crutches. Returned to work after 4½ months doing normal duties but at much slower pace. For some time sleep disturbed by back ache, but problem largely resolved by use of orthopaedic bed. Left with ugly scars on skin. Continuing deep aching pain in right hip, low back ache and pain in rear left hip, which was intermittent but frequent. Had difficulty getting into and out of lorry cab and in lifting and carrying. Able to drive lorry all day, but unable comfortably to drive car for more than about an hour. Recreations of swimming and taking long walks now restricted. Would be some late degenerative changes in right hip and at about retiring age might need hip replacement operation at agreed cost of £3,500 at current prices. If operation not performed before that time, it was unlikely to be required due to his reduced activity. General damages for pain and suffering and loss of amenities assessed at £9,000, for loss of earning capacity at £2,000 and for chance of future surgery at £900. *Total General Damages*: £11,900. (*Ex rel. Robert P. Glancy, Barrister*).

1022. SMITH *v*. NAYLOR (January 29, 1986; MacPherson J.; Liverpool). Female, aged 19 at date of accident and 21 at date of trial. Now married. Since leaving school at 16 had wanted to join W.R.N.S. and had been accepted shortly before accident. Thrown from vehicle in "frightening and very unpleasant accident." Multiple fractures to pelvis and numerous superficial lacerations and bruises. In hospital 7 weeks. Required catheterisation and leg in traction 6 weeks. Resumed pre-accident work after 4 months. Good recovery. Left with small scar above right eye and lump on side of thigh, which constituted permanent cosmetic blemish and embarassed her when wearing swimming costumes. Now unable to pursue proposed career in W.R.N.S., which caused her real disappointment. General damages for pain and suffering and loss of amenities assessed at £6,000 and for loss of career opportunity at £2,000. *Total General Damages:* £8,000. (*Ex rel. J. Benson, Barrister*).

Pelvis

1023. GILBERT *v.* ROMANO (July 16, 1985; Hodgson J.; Sheffield). Female, aged 46 at date of accident and 50 at date of trial. Struck by car while crossing road. Fractures of right superior and inferior pubic rami and chip fracture of symphysis pubis. In hospital 9 weeks. Thereafter needed walking stick for about 2 months. Full function of right hip regained within 4 months. Now unable to move bulky objects such as furniture and left with general aching of right pelvic region, especially in cold and damp weather, which would be permanent, but was controlled by painkillers; but these did not constitute "significant disability". No degenerative changes expected. *General Damages*: £4,000. (*Ex rel. Mark Grenyer, Barrister*).

Shoulder

1024. COOPER (April 17, 1986; Criminal Injuries Compensation Board, Manchester). Male, aged 47. Police sergeant. Right-handed. Sustained blows to head and body, rendering him unconscious. Nine stitches in cut at back of head. Headaches and dizziness for two months after the incident. Fractured cheek—required no treatment. Soft tissue injury to left shoulder. Physiotherapy manipulation, cortisone injections and heat treatment failed to eradicate the stiffness. Could not bear weight on left arm. If shoulder remained in one position for long, became stiff and painful. Pain woke him at least once each night. No bony injury so no further disability expected to develop, but symptoms unlikely to improve. Hobbies of decorating, gardening and golf affected. Off work four months. Worked in administrative capacity and had been able to avoid active work. When he retired in three years time, would have to seek a clerical occupation. *General damages*: £5,000. (*Ex rel. Michael Booth, Barrister*).

Arm

1025. HINDS *v.* LATTER (A.) AND CO. (December 9, 1985; Deputy Judge Sir Douglas Frank; Q.B.D.). Male, aged 47 at date of accident and 48 at date of trial. Former machiner operator. Right-handed. Keen do-it-yourself man, who had redecorated home to good standard and serviced own car. Right arm caught between rollers of printer/slotter machine resulting in traumatic amputation of arm below elbow. In hospital 3½ weeks. Required surgical re-amputation 2″ to 3″ above elbow to make stump suitable for fitting of prosthesis. Had difficulty in fitting satisfactory prosthesis. Unfit for work for about 15 months. Ultimately obtained work as decorator on community project under job creation scheme, but with substantial earnings loss. Prosthesis supplied had minimal functional and cosmetic value and he preferred not to wear it due to rubbing on stump. Continuing tingling and "phantom limb" sensations in stump. Able to paint interiors and exteriors, but unable to work on ladders and considered himself to be carried by workmates. Unable to do former D.I.Y. work and could only drive car with automatic gearbox. Developing median nerve neuroma and might require operation to remove it within year or two. Present job would end within year and future prospects uncertain. General damages for pain and suffering and loss of amenities assessed at £33,000; for future loss of earnings at £37,400 (based on multiplier of 11 and agreed multiplicand of £3,400); for future costs of employing others to do decorating and car maintenance work and additional cost of automatic gearbox cars at £6,300 (based on multiplier of 12 and multiplicand of £525). *Agreed Special Damages:* £3,500. *Total General Damages:* £76,700 (*Ex re. Clifford and Co., Solicitors*).

1026. JAMIESON *v.* THOMAS (October 10, 1985; Eastham J.; Swansea). Male, aged 18 at date of accident and 22 at date of hearing. Right-handed. Temporarily employed as warehouse and delivery boy, but intended to become theatre lighting technician. Thrown from motor cycle onto roadway. Damage to left brachial plexus causing complete paralysis of left shoulder and upper limb; undisplaced fracture of right wrist, mild concussion, small left pneumothorax and lacerations to left knee, from which made uneventful recovery. After about a month nerve graft operation performed in attempt to restore some function and feeling to arm, which met with only limited success. After 2 years there was a partial return of power to the biceps brachii and a flicker of activity in the flexors of the fingers, but very poor recovery of skin sensibility in the hand and all digits. He was able to flex his elbow, which enabled him to carry objects with his left forearm against his chest. Apart from this limited function his overall disability was equivalent to that resulting from an amputation of the left upper limb. Possibility of arthrodeses of shoulder and wrist to provide some improvement in control of position of arm. Unable to pursue previous hobbies of rock climbing and motorcycling and hampered in sailing and hill walking. Scar on left knee which was tender on kneeling. Unemployed since accident. Prospects of obtaining employment in his chosen field substantially reduced. General damages for pain and suffering and loss of amenities assessed at £27,500 and for loss of earning capacity at £15,000. *Agreed Special Damages*: £2,569. *Total General Damages*: £42,500. *Per curiam*. In one way this was a more serious injury than an amputation since it was impossible to fit an artificial limb to provide some function. But to counterbalance this the plaintiff still had his arm. (*Ex rel. Christopher McKay, Barrister*).

1027. EDKINS *v*. B.L. CARS (January 29, 1986; Otton J., Birmingham). Male, aged about 38 at date of accident and 42 at date of trial. Car worker. Fracture of head of left radius with chip fracture of lateral humeral epicondyle and damage to surface of coronoid process of ulna. In hospital 2 weeks. Radial head excised. Resumed pre-accident work after 4 months, but found job too strenuous and had to be "carried" by workmates. After about 14 months underwent operation to excise part of ulna and equalise lengths of ulna and radius, which ended previous discomfort, but resulted in psendarthrosis between severed bone ends. After about 22 months underwent further operation for excision of part of ulna. Proximal end of ulna still flicked across when arm was twisted causing pain, elbow ached on use and plaintiff wore leather support on wrist. Loss of about 50 per cent. active pronation and supination of forearm, flexion limited to 120 degrees and loss of grip. Pain in forearm likely to worsen from time to time and increased in cold weather. Defendants had treated him well and found him lighter job, but there was continuing loss of earnings of £720 p.a., present job might be phased out and some risk of his becoming redundant. Now required car with automatic gearbox at agreed cost of £250 p.a. Ability to do D.I.Y. jobs restricted and loss in this respect agreed at £520. General damages for (1) pain and suffering and loss of amenities assessed at £13,500; (2) for future loss of earnings at £9120 (based on multiplier of (2); (3) for loss of earning capacity or handicap on labour market at £20,000; (4) for additional car expenses at £3,500 (based on multiplier of 14); and for additional costs of former D.I.Y. work at £7,280 (based on multiplier of 14). *Agreed Special Damages:* £7,670. *Total General Damages:* £61,070. (*Ex rel. Nicholas J. Worsley, Barrister.*)

1028. BOORE *v*. HARLAND TYRES (November 25, 1985; Gatehouse J.) Male, aged 24 at date of accident and 32 at date of trial. Pressure builder machinist. Right-handed. Compound fracture of right radius and ulna; severe bruising to right groin, which resolved after 8 weeks. Fracture reduced and arm put in plaster. After about a month underwent operation for plating of radius and ulna. Thereafter wore elbow cast for 4 months, then Colles-type plaster for 3 months. Radius united satisfactorily, but ulna failed to unite. After about 26 months plate in ulna removed and bone graft performed, then in plaster for 6 months. After 3¾ years resumed light work. After just under 5 years ulna still not united. Underwent further plating operation, followed by 3 months in plaster, which resulted in satisfactory union. After 7 years right arm almost asymptomatic and ulnar plate removed. Good recovery. Left with minor scarring, odd aches and pains on unusual activity and about 5% limitation of pronation and supination of forearm. Some difficulty in lifting heavy weights and now unable to enjoy swimming or do arduous do-it-yourself work. Off work total of 214 weeks. General damages for pain and suffering and loss of amenities assessed at £7,500 and for handicap on labour market at £1,000. *Agreed Special Damages*: £22,744. *Total General Damages*: £8,500. (*Ex rel. John Cooper, Barrister*).

1029. HAWKINS *v*. ESSO PETROLEUM (October 17, 1985; Farquharson J.). Male, aged 40 at date of accident and 43 at date of trial. Former truck fitter. Apparently right-handed. Fell from ladder. Fracture dislocation of right elbow and simple fracture of head of left radius. In hospital one day. Dislocation reduced and fragments of radial head removed under general anaesthetic. Sutures removed after 16 days. Right arm in plaster for 1 month and left arm rested but not immobilised. Physiotherapy for 3 months. Would have been fit to return to pre-accident work after 9 months, but had retired due to supervening medical condition unrelated to accident. At date of trial there was 15° loss of extension and 10° loss of supination in right elbow, and slight loss of grip in right hand and he had occasional aching in both wrists in wet weather.

No significant risk of osteoarthritis. No special damages. *General Damages*: £5,000. (*Ex rel. Mark Pelling, Barrister*).

1030. BASTABLE *v.* BUSH (October 3, 1985; Tudor Price J.; Cardiff). Male, aged 33 at date of accident and 38 at date of trial. Street lighting attendant. Right handed. Keen cricketer and darts player. Fracture of head of right radius. In hospital 10 days. Underwent operation to excise radial head. 3 months physiotherapy. Resumed pre-accident work after 4½ months. Continuing weakness and lack of rotation in forearm and some discomfort. Further improvement expected, but there would be some permanent loss of strength. Had learned to compensate for disability by increased use of left arm. Had given up darts and now seldom played cricket. Risk of osteoarthritis developing when he was nearing retirement age. No handicap on labour market. *General Damages*: £4,500. (*Ex rel. Keith Bush, Barrister*).

1031. HUNTLEY *v.* PRUDENTIAL ASSURANCE (October 2, 1985; Mr. Deputy Recorder Langan Q.C.; Guildford County Court). Widower, aged 82 at date of accident and 84 at date of hearing. Fit and active woman, who lived alone in a flat, was able to do own shopping and housework and enjoyed many recreational and social activities. Displaced comminuted fracture of left olecranon. In hospital 4 days. Underwent open reduction of fracture and fixation with tension band wiring. Left with 30% loss of extension and continuing pain in elbow and permanent surgical scar with tenderness over tips of wires. Unable to carry heavy weights or lift heavy objects. In constant fear of people accidentally knocking into arm. Now able to walk outdoors a little more confidently with aid of walking stick. Manner of life now markedly changed. Unable to cope in flat without assistance. Had required services of qualified night nurse for 9 weeks and daily home help until March 1985. Would require some continuing assistance in future. *Special Damages*: £8,474·74 (including cost of past and future care). *General Damages*: £4,250. (*Ex rel. S. J. Widdup, Barrister*).

Elbow

1032. KENT *v.* SCHOLEY (April 28, 1986; Judge Astill; Scunthorpe County Court). Male, aged 34 at date of injury. Assaulted. Fracture of left olecranon and laceration to forehead. Fracture fixed internally with wire. Full recovery of movement in elbow within 6 weeks. After about 14 months underwent out-patient operation to remove fixing wire. Left with permanent 11 cm. scar behind elbow and 1.5 cm. scar on forehead. Remote possibility developing in elbow sooner than usual. *General Damages:* £1,500. (*Ex rel. Mark Grenier, Barrister*).

Wrist

1033. KERR *v.* LANGDON (June 26, 1985; Jupp J.; Nottingham). Female, aged 55 at date of accident and 57 at date of trial. Right-handed. Pre-existing degenerative changes in neck. Undisplaced fracture of radial styloid process of right wrist and pain in neck. Not admitted to hospital. Wrist in plaster about 6 weeks. Resumed pre-accident work after about 2½ months. Fracture united without deformity. Diminishing pain in wrist for about 16 months. Grip slightly reduced. Intermittent pain and stiffness and restriction of movement in neck, but not attributable to accident. *General Damages:* £2,950. (*Ex rel. J. E. Fletcher, Barrister*).

1034. STEELE *v.* BRITANNIA (CHELTENHAM) (February 25, 1986; French J.; Bristol). Male aged 29. Roofing sub-contractor. Fell 10 feet through skylight. Fracture of right scaphoid bone without amalgamation. Wrist in plaster 12 weeks. Unfit for work for about 20 weeks. Virtually complete recovery. Wrist now had normal appearance and full range of movements. Some aching after strenuous use of right hand, which his job required. No risk of osteo-arthritis. *Agreed Special aDamages*: £840. *General Damages*: £2,250. (*Ex rel. Edward Hess, Barrister*).

Fingers and Thumb

1035. MADELEY *v.* BAXTERS BUTCHERS (November 5, 1985; Wood J.; Birmingham). Married woman with two children. Aged 45 at date of accident. Right handed. Injured right hand in unguarded machinery. Laceration to tip of right thumb and fracture; severe fracture to index finger which was amputated at the knuckle joint the following day; fracture of two of the phalanges of the middle finger and damage to tendons and nerves of middle finger. Underwent 6 operations including skin graft from ring finger and thigh. Major part of useful function of hand gone. Pain and aching in hand aggravated by use and by cold. Middle finger grossly deformed—thinner and fixed at 45 degrees at second joint. Operation 16 months after accident improved range of movement of middle finger though still fixed at 40 degrees. Virtually full movement in thumb, ring and little finger. Scar on ring finger. Self conscious of deformity. Ability to do housework and hobbies of knitting and gardening affected. Off work 90 weeks. Returned to work with same employers but to different work done with left hand. *Agreed special damages* £1,374, *"Smith* v. *Manchester"* award £3,000, *General damages* for pain and suffering and loss of amenities £15,000. (*Ex rel. Rawleys & Blewitts, Solicitors*).

1036. JONES *v.* WILLIAM GEORGE (WATH) (December 13, 1984; Deputy Judge Saville; Q.B.D.; Sheffield). Male, aged 32 at date of accident and 34 at date of trial. Apparently right-handed. Amputation through terminal phalanges of right index and middle fingers and injury to right ring finger. Left with some scarring and sensory loss to tip of ring finger, marked limitation on movement of proximal interphalangeal joints of middle and index fingers (though there was satisfactory movement of both metacarpo-phalangeal joints), severe impairment of power grip and impairment of fine function of hand, especially handling of small objects. Well-motivated man who had adapted well to his disablilities. General damages for pain and suffering and loss of amenities assessed at £7,000 and for loss of earning capacity at £1,500. *Special Damages*: £288·99. *Total General Damages*: £8,500. (*Ex rel. Irwin Mitchell, Solicitors*.)

1037. LAMBERT *v.* RAFFATAC (April 15, 1986; Alliott J.; Leeds). Male, aged 29 at date of accident and 30 at date of trial. Right handed. Machine operator. Left hand trapped in machine roller. Crush injury to left thumb; x-rays showed a comminuted fracture of terminal phalanx, severe dorsal laceration and loss of skin and soft tissue; minor crush injury to left index finger, loss of nail on middle finger which was also fractured and suffered loss of sensation which was unlikely to improve. Off work 20½ weeks. Left with some loss of movement in thumb, index and middle fingers. Painful symptoms in hand especially in cold weather unlikely to improve. *Agreed Special Damages* £279.75, *"Smith* v. *Manchester" damages* £2,500, *General damages* for pain and suffering and loss of amenities £4,500. (*Ex rel. Simon Hickey, Barrister*.)

Leg

1038. BENNETT *v.* NATIONAL COAL BOARD (May 30, 1986; Deputy Judge Cotton; Q.B.D.; Sheffield). Male, aged 34 at date of accident and 40 at date of trial. Former coal face development worker. As result of fall of coal suffered severe laceration to left foot. Underwent unsuccessful skin graft operations. After 2 years of continuous severe pain underwent below-knee amputation. Thereafter suffered "phantom limb" sensations at night. Due to difficulty and discomfort with temporary prosthesis about 3 years after accident underwent further operation in which stump re-fashioned. 2 months later painful neuroma was removed and after further 2 months temporary prosthesis was fitted. Due to need to keep removing prosthesis and get around on crutches, he developed pain and limitation of movement in left shoulder necessitating cortisone injections and physiotherapy. After about 3¾ years fitted with satisfactory prosthesis and returned to work as horizontal strata bunker operator, a job at which he could remain seated. There was a real risk that he would lose this job before the end of his normal working life and he was likely to accept redundancy or early retirement some time after he was 50. His chances of obtaining alternative employment would be minimal. General damages for pain and suffering and loss of amenities were assessed at £30,000; for future loss of earnings at about £11,415 consisting of about £6,865 in respect of continuing loss of earnings in his present job (based on a multiplier of 12) and £4,550 in respect of further continuing loss of earnings resulting from a re-grading (based on a multiplier of 10); and for loss of earning capacity or handicap on the labour market at £5,000. *Special Damages:* £18,142.93. *Approximate total General Damages:* £46,415. (*Ex rel. Brian Thompson and Partners, Solicitors*).

1039. HUGHES *v.* ODECO DRILLING (November 7, 1985; Hutchinson J.). Male, aged 30 at date of accident and 37 at date of trial. Former oil rig labourer. Severe open comminuted fractures of left tibia and fibula resulting in below knee amputation after 3½ years. In hospital initially for almost 6 months. Over long period underwent 7 operations in unsuccessful attempt to unite fracture and required plastic surgery for replacement of necrotic skin. Now able to walk about a $\frac{1}{2}$ mile and suffered occasional discomfort in stump. Had worked only few months since accident and unemployed at trial. Likely future net earnings £3,400 p.a. Agreed general damages for pain and suffering and loss of amenities of £30,000; future loss of earnings assessed at £37,300 (based on multiplier of 14) and for handicap on labour market at £6,800 (based on multiplier of 2). *Special Damages*: £23,925. *Total General Damages*: £74,100. (*Ex rel. Robin F. Rowland, Barrister*).

1040. HAWKER *v.* GOLDING (May 9, 1986; Tucker J.). Married woman, aged 42 at date of accident and 45 at date of trial. Before accident took active part in management of pub, of which husband licensee, and in charitable fund raising through Ladies Auxiliary and enjoyed badminton and dancing. Knocked down by motor vehicle. Compound fractures of upper third of both tibiae; fractures of both fibulae; laceration over occipital region of scalp. Underwent immediate operation under general anaesthetic to fix tibial fractures and both legs immobilised in full-length plaster casts. After 9 months underwent bone graft to right leg and cast on left leg removed. After a year underwent further operation to remove fixing plate and screws and cast on right leg removed. Then had 6 weeks' physiotherapy. On crutches 18 months. Unable to help in bar of pub for 2 years. Left with 5° bowing and $\frac{3}{4}$″ shortening of left leg, 7″ vertical pale scar on front of right shin and 3″ pale scar on right knee. Unable to kneel or squat, as able to approximate right foot only to within 7″ of buttocks and left foot to within 10″. Walked with slight limp and unable to go more than about $\frac{3}{4}$ mile without rest. Aching in left knee would continue indefinitely and osteo-arthritis likely to develop in about 5 years. Needed help with shopping and household tasks requiring some strength or agility, unable to pursue pre-accident activities and amount of work now able to do in pub substantially reduced. Employed domestic helper at cost of £11 a week and daughter helped with shopping and housework. Would always need some help with domestic tasks. General damages for pain and suffering and loss of amenities assessed at £14,000, for cost of future domestic assistance at £1,000 and for loss of earning capacity at £1,000. *Agreed Special Damages:* £5,000. *Total General Damages:* £16,000 (*Ex rel. Martin Reynolds, Barrister*).

1041. WAKEHAM *v.* BOURNEMOUTH DISTRICT COUNCIL (February 14, 1986; H.H. Judge Lauriston Q.C., sitting as High Court Judge; Winchester). Male, aged 38 at date of accident and 42 at date of trial HGV lorry-driver. Slipped on ice and hit head. Brief period of unconsciousness. Right fibula and medial malleolus broken. Fibula fixed with a plate and 6 screws; malleolus with a single screw. Leg in plaster 2 months. Left with a 13 cm. scar on right leg and reduction of movement in ankle. Ankle ached in cold or wet weather. Unable to run at all. Walking on rough ground painful. Had difficulty in kneeling or squatting. Off work 3 months initially. Unable to continue in job as ankle become stiff if he drove far. Limited in jobs he could apply for—semi-sedentary work preferable obtained employment at lesser rate of pay which he gave up after 5 months for personal reasons. *General Damages* for pain and suffering assessed at £7,500 and for loss of earning capacity at £2,500. *Agreed Special Damages*: £1441·73. *Total General Damages*: £10,000. (*Ex rel. Christopher Naish, Barrister*).

1042. BOWEN *v.* O'NEILL (2) (March 5, 1985; Drake J.; Manchester). Married woman aged about 25 at date of accident and 27 at date of trial. Accounts clerk. Knee injury; trivial injury to right middle finger which was painful for 12 months. Left with minor scar on knee and discomfort on vigorous use of knee. Would continue to suffer minor, but not trivial, symptoms in knee. *General Damages*: £2,000. (*Ex rel. James Chapman & Co., Solicitors.*)

Knee

1043. STEER *v.* ROYAL BOROUGH OF KENSINGTON AND CHELSEA (March 13, 1986; Deputy Judge Tibber; Q.B.D.). Female, aged 43 at date of accident and 46 at date of trial. As result of fall on pavement sustained undisplaced transverse fracture of left patella and cut lip. Knee aspirated under local anaesthetic and plaster cylinder applied. Physiotherapy for over a year. By date of trial had developed osteo-arthritis in knee, which was stiff on waking in mornings until she "got going." 50 per cent. possibility of requiring patellar excision. *Agreed Special Damages:* £1,818·18. *General Damages:*

£4,300 (consisting of £4,250 for injury to knee and £50 for injury to lip). (*Ex rel. Alastair McFarlane, Barrister.*)

1044. BAILEY (June 13, 1986; Criminal Injuries Compensation Board). Male, aged 31 at date of injury and about 34 at date of award. Displaced spiral fracture of left tibia and fracture of upper left fibula. In hospital 12 days. Following operation to fix tibia with screws pre-existing diabetes out of control for a week. In plaster 2½ months; weight bearing after 3 months; resumed work after 5 months, but needed extra rest periods and ankle ached for further 3 months. Returned to hospital for 2 days for removal of screw and off work for 3 weeks. Left with "nuisance value" aching of ankle on fast running or walking, slight swelling of ankle and 5½" scar on lower shin, but otherwise complete recovery. *General Damages:* £4,000 (*Ex rel. Vivienne Gay, Barrister*).

Ankle

1045. JOHNSON *v.* BRITISH RAILWAYS Board (November 27, 1985; Rose J.; Leeds). Married woman, aged 44 at date of accident and 46 at date of trial. Very active person. Slipped and fell heavily resulting in injury to left ankle. This caused ankle to "give way" 4 months later resulting in extensive, if not complete and irremediable tear of lateral ligament of ankle and possible minor damage to hyaline cartilage. In plaster 7 weeks, then had physiotherapy. Left with chronically unstable ankle, which gave way about once a week with increasing pain. Her way of life was severely affected. She was now able to walk for only 2 miles in comfort; she could not do heavy shopping; her ability to do housework, gardening, decorating and similar tasks was severely restricted; her ability to drive and cycle was limited; she could no longer go fell-walking, and dancing was painful. There was a real risk of osteo-arthritis in about 10 years time. She was unlikely to require arthrodesis of ankle before she was 60. *Agreed Special Damages*: £764. *General Damages*: £8,000. (*Ex rel. P.J.M. Heppel, Barrister*).

1046. CORSI *v.* LINFOOD HOLDINGS (October 14, 1985; Mr. Assistant Recorder Morton; Caerphilly County Court). Female, aged 33 at date of accident and 37 at date of trial. Security officer. Right ankle trapped between tailgate and body of van resulting in severe bruising, swelling and pain. Lower leg in plaster 1 week, then required physiotherapy. Unable to bear weight on leg for 5 weeks. Off work 5 months. After 3 years still suffered slight discomfort, particularly in cold weather. Full recovery by date of trial. *General Damages*: £1,500. (*Ex rel. Keith Bush, Barrister*).

Foot

1047. WEISS-STOLL *v.* BALDWIN (January 30, 1986; Deputy Judge Patrick Bennett Q.C.; Q.B.D.). Female, aged 32 at date of accident and 37 at date of hearing. Unmarried. Former self-employed caterer earning £55 p.w. net, whose ambition was to become a catering manager. No academic qualifications. Keep-fit enthusiast, who enjoyed running, swimming, tennis, aerobics and dancing and was training for London marathon. Unusually severe comminuted fracture—dislocation of mid-tarsal region of left foot with dorsal subluxation of part of navicular bone and fracture of cuboid bone; other superficial injuries. In hospital 11 days. Operation to reduce and fix with wires fracture-dislocation. In plaster up to knee for 6 weeks. Further operation to remove wires. Physiotherapy for 7 months. After a year obtained employment as catering manager at sports club ultimately earning £176 p.w. net, which would have risen to £204 p.w. net by date of hearing. Greatly valued by employers, but after 15 months forced to give up job because of pain caused by being constantly on her feet. Later worked for 2 months as restaurant supervisor earning £132 p.w. net. At date of hearing earning £58 p.w. net from sedentary clerical job. Had developed severe degenerative osteo-arthritis in foot, but arthrodesis not recommended; movement of sub-talar joint reduced by ⅓ and suffered some stiffness, tenderness and swelling. Now walked on outer side of foot, restricted by pain to ¼ hour walks, had difficulty on uneven ground, unable to tiptoe or squat and sleep disturbed. Footwear permanently restricted to training shoes and slippers and had to wear bandage and valgus insole. Unable to resume pre-accident activities. Had acquired management skills and experience and ought to be able to find work at current net pay of £100 p.w. General damages for pain and suffering and loss of amenities assessed at £12,500 and for future partial loss of earnings at £75,000 (based on multiplier of 13, which took account of fact that she would have continued work until at least 60, and multiplicand of £5,769, which took account of fact that difference between current earning capacity and earnings as catering manager might widen in future). *Special Damages:* £18,475·53. *Total General Damages:* £87,500. (*Ex rel. Janet Waddicor, Barrister.*)

Neurosis

1048. ACKERS *v.* WIGAN HEALTH AUTHORITY (June 6, 1985; Russell J.; Liverpool). Married woman, aged 26 at date of accident and 31 at date of hearing. Planned to have 3 children. Required caesarian section operation for delivery of first child. Due to negligence was not anaesthetised, but was paralysed by pre-operation muscle relaxant drugs. Surgeon and theatre staff unaware of plight. During 1¼ hour operation was fully conscious, felt every sensation and was additionally terrified and distressed by artificial ventilation of lungs. Developed severe reactive depression. For first 3 months after birth had negative feelings towards child and thus denied some of pleasures of new motherhood. Subsequently became pregnant again in belief normal delivery possible. Owing to position of foetus further caesarian section delivery became necessary and for 10 weeks she suffered exceptional terror and misery in anticipation of operation. Continuing depression which manifested itself in mood changes irritability, phobia of general anaesthetics and hospitals, severe proximal insomnia and in fear of further pregnancy, which severely impaired her sexual relationship with her husband. Also suffering from painful and embarassing varicose veins and bladder cyst, but unable to face required surgery. Course of abreactive therapy planned, which would involve reliving her experiences and would be very unpleasant. Prognosis guardedly optimistic. General damages for pain and suffering and loss of amenities assessed at £12,000 and for cost of future psychiatric treatment at £1,700. *Agreed Special Damages:* £75. *Total General Damages:* £13,700. (*Ex rel. Jane Tracy Forster, Barrister*).

1049. S. *v.* MEAH (July 14, 1986; Master Topley). Female, aged 30 at date of assault and about 34 at date of hearing. "Bonny, placid" person with 2 daughters, aged 11 and 7. Subjected to vicious sexual assault by friend of husband lasting some 2 hours, in course of which compelled at knife point to participate in oral sex and, whilst defending herself, was struck or stabbed several times resulting in 2 superficial wounds each requiring 4 stitches. Daughters drawn into room by her screams. Developed depression, anxiety state and personality change and suffered exacerbation of pre-existing asthma. Speedy recovery from physical injuries. Obtained divorce in 1982, though breakdown in marriage not attributable to assault. Attempted suicide in 1983. Could no longer live normal life. Continuing nightmares, unable to live alone and had to have female relative with her every night, panicked if she had to be alone with a man, as in a lift, was prone to depression and had continuing asthma. Prognosis poor. Unlikely to be capable of forming normal relationship with a man. *W.* v. *Meah;* and *D.* v. *Meah* [1986] 6 C.L. 90 considered. General damages for pain and suffering and loss of amenities assessed at £10,000 and aggravated damages at £2,500. *Special Damages:* £110. *Total General Damages:* £12,500. *Per Master Topley.* The present case was more analogous to *D.* v. *Meah.* But if he had decided those cases, he would have awarded higher general damages. (*Ex rel. Vivienne Gay, Barrister*).

Miscellaneous Conditions—Neuroma

1050. DALY *v.* WOLVERHAMPTON HEALTH AUTHORITY (June 10, 1986; Deputy Judge Patrick Bennett Q.C.; Q.B.D.). Female, aged 23 at date of accident and 27 at date of hearing. Unmarried. Developed permanent neuroma on thigh due to damage to nerve and/or blood vessel caused by injection. Suffered bruising and blistering initially and required daily dressings for over 6 weeks due to discharge from wound. Left with permanent round scare on thigh, which was "visible, unsightly and nasty," embarassed her and inhibited her from swimming or sunbathing, and aching and burning sensation in thigh after walking for more than half an hour or standing for any length of time, which was likely to resolve eventually. *Agreed Special Damages:* £50. *General Damages:* £6,000. (*Ex rel. Pamela D. Macdougall, Barrister*).

Miscellaneous Conditions—Pharyngitis

1051. LEE (June 25, 1985; Criminal Injuries Compensation Board Appeal Committee; Newcastle-upon-Tyne). Male, aged 19 at date of offence and 21 at date of hearing. Severe blow to left jaw. Fracture of mandible involving lower left wisdom tooth and leading to serious and unusual complications and sequelae. Developed severe infection of mandible necessitating emergency operation involving tracheostomy. In intensive care 3 days. Since operation had suffered from chronic, secondary pharyngitis, which caused him to suffer from a "sore throat" virtually every day, would necessitate a tonsillectomy and was likely to be permanent. Left with three post-operative scars whose appearance could be improved by plastic surgery, but would always constitute a gross cosmetic disability: (1) "lumpy" scar over angle of left jaw measuring 3 cm. by ½ cm.; at broadest point; (2) further "lumpy" scar beneath chin measuring 2 cm. by ½ cm.; (3) particularly unsightly tracheostomy scar over front of neck measuring 5½ cm. by 2 cm. at broadest point. Embarrassed by scarring, tended to avoid wearing open-necked shirts and had difficulty shaving. *Special Damages*: £179. *General Damages*: £7,500. (*Ex rel. Meikle, Skene and Company, Solicitors*).

Minor Injuries

1052. BUSH v. PHILIP (1) (December 8, 1985; Deputy Judge Fife; Bromley County Court). Male, aged 42 at date of accident and about 44 at date of hearing. Involved in road traffic accident at start of cycling holiday with son. Injury to right thumb; lacerations to head requiring sutures; bruises and abrasions; concussion; shock. Taken to hospital but not detained. Lost enjoyment of first week of holiday. Some permanent limitation of flexion and extension of thumb, some loss of manual dexterity and continuing aching in thumb in cold and damp weather. No likelihood of degenerative changes. Unobtrusive but permanent scarring of temple. No longer enjoyed cycling. General damages for pain and suffering and loss of amenity assessed at £2,500 and for loss of holiday at £200. *Total Special Damages*: £990·55. *Total General Damages*: £2,700. (*Ex. rel. Anthony Snelson, Barrister*).

1053. PAYNE v. DONLEY (March 20, 1986; Mr. Registrar Taylor; Hereford County Court). Female, aged 23. W.R.A.F. clerk. Assaulted. Minimially displaced fracture through distal end of left radius, which was manipulated under general anaesthetic. In plaster 7 weeks. After 9 weeks had 25 degree loss of extension in left wrist, but able to resume typing. Therafter no further treatment, but had continuing dull ache in wrist during cold weather. At date of hearing residual symptoms "minimal". Post-traumatic osteoarthritis highly unlikely. *Special Damages:* £65. *General Damages:* £1,750. (*Ex rel. Jonathan Furness, Barrister.*)

1054. ROBERTS v. NATIONAL COAL BOARD (August 13, 1986; Judge Gibbon Q.C., Pontypridd County Court). Male, aged 18 at date of accident and 23 at date of trial. Coal-miner. Fractures of 4th and 5th metacarpels of right hand. Plastercast for 6 weeks. Relatively satisfactory bony union but with slight angulation/shortening. Full recovery save for continuing minor discomfort in hand due to soft tissue scarring. Off work 8 weeks. *General damages*: £1,750. [*Ex rel. Patrick Griffiths, Barrister.*]

1055. FAIRLESS v. KINGSTON UPON HULL CITY COUNCIL (April 18, 1986; Judge Hunt; Kingston-upon-Hull County Court). Widow, aged about 68 at date of accident and 71 at date of trial. Thrown violently about 'bus. Struck head. Swelling to back of head; bruising and lacerations to face. Suffered shock. Bruising to body. For several months after accident experienced dizziness and headaches. Left with 2 inch vertical scar on forehead and indentation of forehead at site of scar. Left with phobia of 'bus travel which had been pre-accident hobby. *Agreed special damages*: £123. *General damages*: £2,000. (*Ex rel. P. J. M. Heppel, Barrister*).

1056. HANBY v. MAWDSLEY (July 23, 1985; Court of Appeal). Female, aged 42 at date of trial. Kitchen worker. Apparently right-handed. Severe blow to left shoulder causing "frozen shoulder". No fracture. Resumed work after 2 weeks, but continued to suffer from minor pain and restriction of movement in shoulder, which caused her difficulty in pegging out washing, carrying shopping and heavy work. After 2 years still had 10° restriction of movement and general ache in shoulder region. But anticipated that, if she received treatment, these symptoms would resolve within 3 to 6 months; and that, if she did not, would resolve spontaneously within 12 months. Court dismissed defendant's appeal against award of Mr. Assistant Recorder V. Hall, Newark County

Court. *General Damages*: £1,750. *Per curiam*. Award was perhaps on the generous side. But pain and suffering is a very subjective matter and the trial judge, who sees the injured party, is in the best position to assess the effect it has upon the claimant. (*Ex rel. Mark Grenyer, Barrister*).

1057.   DULIEU *v.* SILCOCK AND COLLING (May 13, 1985; Mr. Registrar Lipton; Ilford County Court). Male, aged 44. Car transporter driver. Right-handed. Fell from top of transporter. Sprain to left wrist, minor fracture to hand. Metatarsal of left foot and shock. Not detained in hospital. Wrist strapped. No other medical treatment. Resumed pre-accident work after 2 weeks. Wrist quite painful initially, but after about 4 months it was free from discomfort. For about 3 or 4 weeks left foot was painful on weight bearing, after about 6 weeks pain had eased considerably and within 2 months or so had almost completely resolved. On medical examination some 7 months after accident there was minor residual muscle wasting in left calf and he had occasional slight ache in foot during cold weather. Complete recovery within about a year. *General Damages*: £1,000. (*Ex rel. Robin Thompson and Partners, Solicitors*).

1058.   CHAPMAN *v.* BOWATER U.K. PAPER CO. (June 24, 1986; Judge Batterbury; Medway County Court). Male, aged 52. Factory worker. Both eyes injured by escape of paper dust. Temporarily blinded and in pain until all dust removed. Treated initially at place of work, then twice attended hospital as out-patient. Off work a week during which eyes watered and he had difficulty reading. Thereafter eyes were bloodshot and watered for 9 months. Full recovery. *Special Damages*: £54.93. *General Damages*: £800. (*Ex rel. Simon Wheatley, Barrister*).

1059.   KHANIA (February 26, 1986; Criminal Injuries Compensation Board; London). Male, aged 40. Right-handed. Struck on back of left hand with chair leg. Deep bruising to 4th and 5th metacarpals. No bony injury. Off work 10 days. Severe pain for 2 weeks. Unable to lift heavy objects with left hand or drive car for a month. Complete functional recovery after 18 months. Slight swelling on dorsum expected to resolve within a year. *General Damages: £750. (ex rel. Simon Molyneux, Barrister.)*

1060.   PARSONS *v.* (UNKNOWN) (May 20, 1986; Mr. Deputy Registrar Masters; Exeter County Court). Boy, aged about 5. Struck by car and thrown into air. Concussion, laceration to scalp necessitating stitches and grazing to both legs. Unconscious for some minutes. Detained in hospital for 4 days during which time he suffered from nausea and vomitting and was rather lethargic. Full recovery. Some scarring of scalp which was likely to fade in time. *Agreed General Damages* of £650 approved by court. (*Ex rel. Christopher Naish, Barrister*).

1061.   STEVENSON *v.* NORTH DERBYSHIRE HEALTH AUTHORITY (June 27, 1986; Judge Wilcox; Chesterfield County Court). Female, aged 21 at date of accident and 23 at date of trial. Catering assistant. Laceration of right calf. Left with 4 cm. oblique scar, noticeable but not vivid, becoming purple in cold weather. Cramp in leg for ½ hour after swimming. *General damages* (for pain, suffering and loss of amenity): £600. [*Ex rel. Stephen Killalea, Barrister*].

1062.   BROOK *v.* HAMPSHIRE COUNTY COUNCIL (December 3, 1985; Judge Stock Q.C.; Southampton County Court). Female, aged 16 at date of accident and 19 at date of trial. Right-handed. Youth scheme employee. Air pistol pellet traversed palm for about 3 cm. and lodged at base of left index finger. In hospital 48 hours. Pellet extracted under general anaesthetic and 10 stitches inserted, which were removed after 10 days. Returned to work after 3 weeks. Pain and discomfort continued for further 3 weeks. Thereafter full recovery, apart from minimal discomfort and limitation of movement in finger in cold weather and small scars to finger and palm, which did not constitute a real cosmetic disability. *Special Damages*: £30·95. *General Damages*: £600. (*Ex rel. Philip Glen, Barrister*).

1063.   HERRINGTON *v.* LEECE (July 1, 1986; Judge Edmonson; Barrow in Furness and Ulverston County Court). Male, aged 41 at date of accident and 43 at date of trial. Thrown off motor cycle. Injury to left knee, probably involving patellar cartilage, and cut to mouth. Off work 1 day and knee painful and swollen for 4 or 5 days. Left with occasional pain and stiffness under knee with occasional clicking beneath patella. No chance of osteo-arthritis. *Agreed Special Damages*: £250. *General Damages*: £600. (*Ex rel. Townsends, Solicitors*).

1064. MURRAY *v.* A. W. MURRAY (November 25, 1985; Judge Barr; Brentford County Court). Male, aged 19 at date of accident. Deep abrasion of elbow and small wound and superficial abrasion of knee. Wounds cleaned and sutured in hospital, but not detained. Developed infection of elbow. Out-patient for 2 weeks then returned to work and resumed driving. Within 3 weeks resumed swimming and squash. "Nervous" driver for nearly a year. Left with ¾″ square scar on elbow. *Agreed Special damages*: £171·71. *General Damages*: £500. (*Ex rel. Andrew W. Lewis, Barrister*).

1065. BUSH *v.* PHILIP (2) (December 8, 1985; Deputy Judge Fife; Bromley County Court). Male, aged 15 at date of accident and about 17 at date of hearing. Involved in road traffic accident at start of cycling holiday with father. Bruises, abrasions and shock. Taken to hospital but not detained. Lost enjoyment of first week of holiday. No longer enjoyed cycling. Agreed general damages for pain and suffering and loss of amenity of £225. General damages for loss of enjoyment of holiday assessed at £200. *Total General Damages*: £425. (*Ex rel. Anthony Snelson, Barrister*).

1066. Personal injuries litigation. See LAW REFORM, § 1956.

1067. Personal injury—loss of earning capacity—deduction of benefits
[Law Reform (Personal Injuries) Act 1948 (c.41) s.2(1).]
   It is appropriate to deduct sickness, invalidity, injury or disablement benefits which have accrued to a plaintiff from an award of damages for loss of earning capacity.
   F, a council employee brought an action for damages for personal injuries and was awarded £12,500 for pain, suffering and loss of amenity and £35,000 for loss of earning capacity from which was deducted pursuant to s.2(1) of the 1948 Act, the sum of £1,250 representing one half of benefits accrued to F. F appealed against the deduction. *Held*, dismissing the appeal, that since an award of damages for loss of earning capacity or for handicap in the labour market will not be made unless it is probable that there will be some prospective loss of earnings, an award for loss of earning capacity is to be treated as a loss of earnings within s.2(1) and half the value of any relevant benefit for the five years beginning with the time when the cause of action accrued is deductible.
   FOSTER *v.* TYNE AND WEAR COUNTY COUNCIL [1986] 1 All E.R. 567 C.A.

1068. Personal injury—medical negligence—whether aggravated damages appropriate—whether damages for grief—whether damages for future pregnancy
   Although the concept of aggravated damages has no place in the area of medical negligence, the compensatory damages may include damages for distress where the distress has made it more difficult for the plaintiff to recover, damages for grief where that has led to "nervous shock" and where the grief has made it more difficult for her to recover from the original injury and damages representing the financial loss in having another pregnancy to replace a child lost as a result of the medical negligence.
   During attempted delivery of twins in hospital the obstetrician put his arm inside P to attempt manual manipulation of the head of one of the babies. Shortly after birth the child died as a result of that treatment which was described as horrific and wholly unacceptable. P had had one child already, and she and her husband had planned to have three, so she claimed, in addition to the usual damages, damages for the future financial cost of replacing the dead child. Only quantum was in issue. *Held,* that (i) aggravated damages *per se* are not appropriate in cases of medical negligence, but where particular distress has been caused to the patient (as in the circumstances of this case) and that distress makes it more difficult for the patient to recover that fact can be taken into account in assessing the compensatory damages; (ii) similarly, grief itself is not compensatable unless it leads to nervous shock and if it does, and that causes the plaintiff to take longer to recover, that factor may lead to an increase in damages; (iii) the financial cost of a future pregnancy to replace a child whose death is caused by medical negligence is not too remote.
   KRALJ *v.* McGRATH [1986] 1 All E.R. 54, Woolf J.

1069. Remoteness—personality change after accident—criminal offences
   Damages are not recoverable from a person who caused an accident to compensate the victims of the plaintiffs' resultant personality change.
   D caused an accident in which P suffered severe head injuries. The injuries resulted in a personality change whereby P developed a propensity to attack women. One, who was raped, recovered some £10,000 from him; another, who was indecently

assaulted, recovered some £7,000. P sought to recover those sums from D. *Held,* dismissing the action, that P was seeking to recover damages paid as compensation to persons who could not have claimed against D themselves due to remoteness and lack of duty of care, and P should not be allowed compensation for the consequences of his crimes, on the grounds of public policy (dicta of Lane J. in *Malcolm* v. *Broadhurst* [1970] C.L.Y. 744 and of Watkins L.J. in *Lamb* v. *Camden London Borough* [1981] C.L.Y. 1855 and *Gray* v. *Barr (Prudential Assurance Co., third party)* [1971] C.L.Y. 6012 applied; *Jones* v. *Jones* [1984] C.L.Y. 1096 distinguished; *Overseas Tankship (U.K.)* v. *Morts Dock and Engineering Co., The Wagon Mound (No. 1)* [1961] C.L.Y. 2343 and *McLoughlin* v. *O'Brian* [1982] C.L.Y. 2153 considered).

MEAH v. MCCREAMER (NO. 2) [1986] 1 All E.R. 943, Woolf J.

1070. Still-born child—assessment of damages
Due to a hospital's negligence, P gave birth to a still-born child. She subsequently suffered severe depression, which threatened her marriage, and there was a 50 per cent. risk of mortality in any future pregnancy. As a result, she decided not to attempt to have further children, and this decision was accepted as reasonable. *Held,* on assessment of damages, that the recoverable heads of damage were (1) Loss of happiness and satisfaction in bringing her pregnancy to a successful conclusion; (2) although not entitled to damages for the loss of the society of her still-born child, she was entitled to be compensated for the loss associated with its physical loss; (3) the considerable physical illness brought on by her misfortune. Without breaking the figures down, a total of £18,000 would be awarded (*Udale* v. *Bloomsbury Area Health Authority* [1984] C.L.Y. 1005 distinguished): BAGLEY v. NORTH HERTS HEALTH AUTHORITY (1986) 136 New L.J. 1014, Simon Brown J.

1071. Trespass to the person—rape and indecent assault—relationship to personal injuries awards
The primary purpose of damages will be to compensate the victims, and the award for aggravated damages will be moderate.
D suffered severe head injuries in an accident, which resulted in a personality change whereby D developed a propensity to attack women. After a series of offences, he was sentenced to life imprisonment. One woman whom he had raped and another whom he had indecently assaulted claimed damages. Liability was admitted. Both women remained affected by their experience. *Held,* that the primary purpose of damages must be to compensate the plaintiffs, and so far as aggravated damages were concerned, the award must be moderate. In the circumstances damages would be assessed at £6,750 in the one case, and £10,250 in the other.
W. v. MEAH; D. v. MEAH [1986] 1 All E.R. 935, Woolf J.

DEATH DUTIES

1072. Estate duty
ESTATE DUTY (INTEREST ON UNPAID DUTY) ORDER 1986 (No. 1942) [45p], made under the Finance Act 1970 (c.24), s.30; operative on December 16, 1986; provides that interest on unpaid estate duty will run at eight per cent. under the various provisions which impose a fixed rate of interest.

DIVORCE AND MATRIMONIAL CAUSES

1073. Ancillary relief—future likely inheritance—whether property
[Matrimonial Causes Act 1973 (c.18), s.25(2)(*a*).] A person's expectation of inheriting property under a will can in certain cases be property which that person "is likely to have in the foreseeable future" under s.25(2)(*a*) of the Matrimonial Causes Act 1973, but such cases will be rare. In most cases, uncertainties both as to fact of inheritance and to the time when it will occur will make it impossible to consider such property under the section: MICHAEL v. MICHAEL, *The Times,* May 28, 1986, C.A.

1074. Breach of undertaking—committal—whether penal notice required—whether service of order required. See HUSSAIN v. HUSSAIN, § 456.

1075. Consent orders—practice direction. See PRACTICE DIRECTION (FAM.D.) (MATRIMONIAL CAUSES RULES 1977: RULE 76A: CONSENT ORDERS), § 2670.

1076. Decree nisi—notice to respondent
[Matrimonial Causes Rules (S.I. 1977 No. 344), r.48(2).] In divorce proceedings neither W, who was residing in Canada, nor her English solicitors with whom H's solicitors were otherwise content, had been given notice of the hearing of the decree nisi, as required by r.48(2). *Held,* allowing W's appeal and setting aside the decree, that there was no possible justification for a court to grant a decree nisi without notice being given to the respondent since, quite apart from a breach of the rules, it would be an affront to the rules of natural justice: WALKER *v.* WALKER, *The Times,* June 2, 1986, C.A.

1077. Decree nisi—rescission—adultery—naming the co-respondent
[Matrimonial Causes Act 1973 (c.18), s.49: Matrimonial Causes Rules (S.I. 1977 No. 344, r.13.] The parties marriage had broken down in 1980 when W had left to live with another man. W agreed to sign a draft confession statement only on condition that the co-respondent would not be named in the proceedings. H was advised by an inexperienced clerk to file petition based on the allegation that W had committed adultery with a man whose identity was unknown to H. H's supporting affidavit stated that the contents of the petition were true although, in fact, H was aware of the identity of the co-respondent. *Held,* upon the summons of the Queen's Proctor to rescind the decree nisi, that there had been a clear breach of s.49 and r.13. His Lordship was disturbed by a sentence in *Rayden on Divorce (14th edition)* at para. 5 on p.198 which stated that "in practice this rule was circumvented." The decree nisi would be rescinded: BRADLEY *v.* BRADLEY (QUEEN'S PROCTOR INTERVENING) (1986) 16 Fam.Law 25, Eastham J.

1078. Divorce—appeal—limitations
[Supreme Court Act 1981 (c.54), s.18(1)(*d*).] In June 1984 W had been granted a decree nisi. Form no. D1298 was sent to H stating that the marriage would be dissolved unless sufficient cause be shown to the court within 6 weeks from the making of the decree why such decree should not be made absolute. H said that he had understood that to mean 6 weeks in which to appeal by way of communicating with the trial court. In August 1984 the error was pointed out to him. H did nothing and the decree was made absolute in September 1984. In February 1985 H communicated by letter to the civil appeals officer that he wished to appeal. *Held,* dismissing H's appeal, that H had had ample time and opportunity to launch his appeal and had failed to act promptly once he had been informed of his error. In those circumstances he could not bring himself within a situation which would exempt him from the provisions of s.18(1)(*a*): MCCARNEY *v.* MCCARNEY (1986) 1 F.L.R. 312, C.A.

1079. Divorce—application for leave to appeal out of time—marriage irretrievably broken down—costs
The county court had dismissed H's application to set aside a decree nisi, mistakenly believing he had no jurisdiction to entertain it. *Held,* dismissing H's appeal for leave to appeal out of time, that whether or not H had grounds for contending that the marriage had not broken down it was now clear that the marriage had undoubtedly broken down irretrievably and that W had left the matrimonial home with the children. No useful purpose would be served in a sterile argument which would eventually have to be financed out of the matrimonial home: ORSBORNE *v.* ORSBORNE (1986) 16 Fam.Law 99, Griffiths L.J.

1080. Domicile of choice—considerations
A settled intention to live indefinitely in England so as to acquire a domicile of choice could not be established merely by a foreigner having a desire, that was reciprocated, to marry, as soon as it became possible to do so, a resident Englishman and thereafter to live in England. It was for the court to make an objective assessment of the situation: CRAMER *v.* CRAMER, *The Times,* May 15, 1986, C.A.

1081. Fees
MATRIMONIAL CAUSES FEES (AMENDMENT) ORDER 1986 (No. 696 (L.4)) [45p], made under the Matrimonial Causes Act 1973 (c.18), s.51; operative on May 5, 1986; increase the fees on an application for ancillary relief and introduces new fees for applications concerning children, appeals from a registrar to a judge, applications

fixing a date for a defended cause, applications for financial relief after an overseas divorce and other interlocutory applications.

1082. Financial provision

MAGISTRATES' COURTS (MATRIMONIAL PROCEEDINGS) (AMENDMENT) RULES 1986 (No. 1498 (L.13)) [£1·40], made under the Magistrates' Courts Act 1980 (c.43), ss.144, 145; operative on October 1, 1986; amend S.I. 1980 No. 1582 so as to make provision for applications made in relation to financial provision to be given in a new form.

1083. Financial provision—consent order—appeal out of time—fresh evidence

On April 17, 1984 the court had made a consent order whereby H transferred to W his interest in the tenancy of their council house and a bond of £2,000, H's only capital asset. W's claims for maintenance for herself and other financial relief were dismissed. Maintenance of £13·10 per week was ordered for the youngest child of the family. The order expressly recorded that H had no present intention of accepting voluntary redundancy from the company for whom he had worked for the last 20 years. On June 26, 1984 H applied for voluntary redundancy and received a severance payment of £25,000 under a scheme which had come into existence after the order, the terms of which being an improvement upon an earlier scheme. He contended that a disability resulting from a recent car accident had affected his work prospects and prompted his application. He did not inform W of the payment but applied for a downward variation of the maintenance order. On September 19, 1984, having found out about the redundancy payment, W applied for leave to appeal out of time and for the consent order to be set aside on the basis of fresh evidence, mistake, fraudulent misrepresentation and non-disclosure. *Held,* allowing W's appeal, that the time for appealing the consent order would be extended, fresh evidence would be admitted and the order would be set aside as it had been made on a fundamentally false basis. The court had jurisdiction to grant such relief notwithstanding that the fresh evidence did not disprove specific facts found to be proved at the original hearing. It was sufficient that events subsequent to the making of the order had falsified the basic assumptions on which the order had been made or had brought about a radical change in the circumstances in which it had been contemplated that the order would operate. The order could equally be set aside on the grounds of mistake and fraudulent misrepresentations. Having considered the parties' circumstances *de novo* a fresh order would be made by which H should pay a lump sum of £10,000 in addition to the transfer of the bond (*Minton* v. *Minton* [1979] C.L.Y. 766 and *Toleman* v. *Toleman* [1985] C.L.Y. 1672 distinguished; *Murphy* v. *Stone Wallwork (Charlton)* [1969] C.L.Y. 901; *Mulholland* v. *Mitchell* [1971] C.L.Y. 3232; *Skone* v. *Skone* [1971] C.L.Y. 3489; *Daubney* v. *Daubney* [1976] C.L.Y. 791; *Wales* v. *Wadham* [1977] C.L.Y. 839; *Thwaite* v. *Thwaite* [1981] C.L.Y. 701; *Allsop* v. *Allsop* [1981] C.L.Y. 702; *Brusselen* v. *Brusselen* (1981) 131 New L.J. 1310; *Tommey* v. *Tommey* [1982] C.L.Y. 907; *Robinson* v. *Robinson* [1982] C.L.Y. 1485; *Wells* v. *Wells* [1982] C.L.Y. unreported cases 183; *O'Dougherty* v. *O'Dougherty* [1983] C.L.Y. 1841; *Warren* v. *Warren* [1983] C.L.Y. 1855 and *Livesey* v. *Jenkins* [1985] C.L.Y. 1049 considered): REDMOND *v.* REDMOND (1986) 16 Fam. Law 260; (1986) 2 F.L.R. 173, H.H. Judge Stannard.

1084. Financial provision—consent order—implementation of term—death of husband

[Law Reform (Miscellaneous Provisions) Act 1934 (c.41), s.1(1).] In 1977 a consent order had been made whereby it was to transfer to W a lump sum and some investments and she was to transfer to him her reversionary interest in a family settlement and her estate and interest in a property in Jersey. In addition she was to execute a power of attorney in favour of a person nominated by H to enable the transfer of property to be carried out. The power of attorney was executed and the stipulated transfers effected except for the transfer of W's interest in the property which had not been completed by H at the time of his death in an accident in 1983. W promptly cancelled the power of attorney and went to live in the property. The executors of H's estate instituted proceedings in Jersey and in the Family Division of the High Court, *inter alia,* for a declaration that the 1977 Order in so far as it remained unperformed was valid and enforceable against W, notwithstanding H's death. *Held,* that as H, prior to his death, could have applied to the court for an order compelling W to comply with the terms of the 1977 Order there was vested in him, at the date of his death, a "cause of action" within the meaning of s.1(1) which survived for the benefit of his estate. W had not attempted to argue to the contrary on this point but asserted that the granting of the declaration was a discretionary matter and that, in the circumstances, such a discretion should not be exercised in favour of the executors. As they had a real, and not a theoretical, interest in raising the matter and there were no merits in W's actions the declaration would be granted (*Russian Commercial and Industrial Bank* v. *British Bank for Foreign Trade* [1921] A.C. 438 and *Vine* v. *National Dock Harbour Board* [1957] C.L.Y. 1264 considered): LANE (DECEASED) *Re*, LANE *v.* LANE (1986) 16 Fam. Law 74 C.A.

1085. Financial provision—disabled husband—whether claim against wife
[Matrimonial Causes Act 1973 (c.18), s.25A(3).] H and W divorced. W was a schoolteacher. H was so severely incapacitated by a stroke that he could barely speak, and could not possibly look after himself. His parents looked after him. On H's application for maintenance, the judge dismissed the claim under s.25A(3) of the Matrimonial Causes Act 1973. He held that because of the dramatic nature of his disabilities there was no financial help W could give him that would enhance his life, because his limited opportunities for pleasure were reasonably satisfied. *Held*, on appeal, that this was a suitable case for disentitling H under s.25A(3) from making any future claim against W. The judge was right to hold that it would be unjust to make W support H out of an income which, after paying her outgoings, enabled her to do no more than lead a reasonable life as a professional teacher. No order made against W could benefit H: SEATON *v.* SEATON, *The Times,* February 24, 1986, C.A.

1086. Financial provision—family business—capital reflection—considerations
H and W had married in 1964 and had two children. In 1971 H had started a small engineering company which, with W's active help and support, had been built up into a sound business by the time the parties had separated in 1976. In ancillary relief proceedings W contended that the orders sought, besides representing a proper proportion of the present capital and financial resources of the parties, should also reflect the likelihood of substantial capital being acquired by H in the future in the event of a flotation of the family company or a takeover or sale of shares. The use of a trust scheme to cover such a disposal was proposed. *Held*, that whilst W had assisted in the build up of the business this had only been for four years out of a 12 year marriage. She was at present, and would be in future, entitled to participate in the income derived from it. By reason of the recession the company would require a sustained and substantial product build up over a good number of years before the capital contingency and benefits envisaged could arise. Accordingly, there was no ascertainable contingency, in the forseeable future which was likely to create a capital prospect (*Calder* v. *Calder* [1976] C.L.Y. 776 and *Priest* v. *Priest* [1980] C.L.Y. 782 distinguished; *Trippas* v. *Trippas* [1973] C.L.Y. 925a and *SD* v. *SD* [1975] C.L.Y. 983 considered); BURGESS *v.* BURGESS (1986) 16 Fam. Law 155, H. H. Judge Callman.

1087. Financial provision—lump sum—anticipation of Army gratuity—whether order to be made
[Army Act 1955 (c.18), s.203(1)(2); Matrimonial Causes Act 1973 (c.18), ss.23(1)(c), 25(1)(a).]
An order which purports to require a husband to make a lump sum payment out of a gratuity due from the Army in the future amounts to a charge thereon and is void. Nor should the court adjourn such an application for more than four or five years so as to enable a wife to make such a claim after the gratuity had in fact been paid. Following a divorce W applied for an order that H, a serving soldier, should pay a lump sum to her out of the gratuity he would be receiving on discharge from the Army. Decree nisi was in 1981 and the gratuity would not become payable before 1988. The registrar made an order that W receive one-quarter of the gratuity when paid; subsequent to the hearing before the registrar W re-married and H was promoted as a result of which he would probably be remaining in the Army until 2003. *Held*, that (1) the order amounted to a charge on the lump sum and was void by virtue of s.203 of the 1955 Act, although once H had received the gratuity the situation might be different; (2) a lump sum was in any event inappropriate as there was no capital out of which it could have been paid, and the family assets had already been divided; (3) it would be wrong to adjourn such an application for longer than four or five years and so W's application would be dismissed. (*Walker* v.

Walker [1983] C.L.Y. 1695 and *Milne* v. *Milne* [1981] C.L.Y. 716 applied): ROBERTS
v. ROBERTS [1986] 1 W.L.R. 437, Wood J.

1088. Financial provision—lump sum—application of one-third rule—valuation
   The judge, having found that W had no source of income, made an order for H to
pay her a lump sum of £100,000. H was a director and minority shareholder in a
largely family firm. On expert evidence the judge valued his interest in the company
by computing a proportion of the company's assets in terms of the fraction of the
shareholding which belonged to H. The judge awarded one-third of the total figure
by way of a lump sum. *Held*, dismissing H's appeal, that in the circumstances of the
case where there was a reason and a not unconvincing presentation by an experienced
valuer in favour of the method adopted by the judge he could not be blamed for the
line he had taken. Equally, the adoption of one-third proportion did not render his
judgment one which should be overturned; for the cases since *O'D* v. *O'D* did not
constitute a direction to the court to reject the application of the one-third rule (*O'D*
v. *O'D* [1975] C.L.Y. 983; *P.* v. *P.* [1978] C.L.Y. 813; *Potter* v. *Potter* [1982] C.L.Y.
935 and *Smith* v. *Smith* [1983] C.L.Y. 1099 considered. BULLOCK *v.* BULLOCK (1986)
16 Fam.Law 129, C.A.

**1089. Financial provision—lump sum—application on variation of periodical payments—no
jurisdiction—drafting of consent orders**
   [Matrimonial Causes Act 1973 (c.18), s.31(7); Matrimonial and Family Proceedings
Act 1984 (c.42), ss.5, 6, Pt. II.] In 1975 a consent order had been made transferring
the former matrimonial home, its contents, a car and a caravan to W absolutely. In
1976 a periodical payments order was also made by consent for the benefit of W and
the children. In 1983 W applied for a variation. H was dilatory and unco-operative.
In early 1984 he moved to Spain with his third wife. The Registrar gave leave *ex
parte* to W to amend her application to include a lump sum and award £50,000 in full
and final settlement of her claims. H appealed successfully to Ewbank J. contending
that the Registrar had had no jurisdiction under s.31 as amended by the 1984 Act, to
grant such leave. The judge discharged the Registrar's order and defined a fixed
period for periodical payments to be made to W. *Held*, dismissing W's appeal, that
the judge had been right in his findings that there had been an overall capital
settlement in the 1975 consent order although no formal dismissal had been included
of W's claim to a lump sum care should be taken to ensure that consent orders truly
embodied beyond equivocation what the parties agreed upon and should include any
provisions which were consequential upon that agreement (*Minton* v. *Minton* [1979]
C.L.Y. 766 and *Pearce* v. *Pearce* [1981] C.L.Y. 712 considered): SANDFORD *v.*
SANDFORD (1986) 16 Fam.Law 104, C.A.

1090. Financial provision—lump sum—appropriateness—legally aided parties—heavy charge
   The marriage had broken down in 1982. However, due to bitter and protracted
litigation, cross-applications for ancillary relief were not heard until June 1985. W
was now living with the two children of the marriage in a council house which she
was entitled to buy at an advantageous rate. H was living in the former matrimonial
home with another woman and her three children. She worked with H in his business
which had begun to prosper and which was likely to continue so to do. The judge
decided that W was entitled to half the matrimonial assets and, with additional
compensation for the dismissal of her entitlement for periodical payments. H was
ordered to pay a lump sum representing 62½ per cent. of such assets. H appealed
contending that the judge had failed to appreciate that the lump sum ordered would
force the sale of the matrimonial home, which he needed both as a home and as a
base for his business and that W should receive a deferred charge. Both parties were
legally aided. At the time of the first instance hearing the costs amounted to £16,000
and the costs of appeal to a further £5,000. *Held,* allowing the appeal to the extent of
delaying the sale by six months, that the judge had been fully entitled to reach his
conclusion and had been correct in holding that H's intractability had prevented a
satisfactory settlement on the basis of a sale before crippling legal costs had been
incurred. There was no evidence of need on the part of H which justified an
alternative order. Justice between the parties would be met by there being no order
as to costs *inter partes* in the Court of Appeal and the court below. It was imperative
that litigants who received legal aid should fully understand the dangers when
deciding to pursue contentious matters: MASON *v.* MASON (1986) 16 Fam. Law 217,
C.A.

1091. Financial provision—lump sum—available capital in future—power of adjournment

In ancillary relief proceedings the registrar had made a lump sum order in favour of W on the basis that H's farming partnership was failing and likely to be dissolved, thus releasing the necessary capital. On appeal the judge adjourned W's application with liberty to apply to both parties on the basis that an immediate lump sum order would force it out of business as the partnership was not doomed as W had contended. H exercised his liberty to apply but the judge adhered to his original order. *Held,* dismissing H's appeal against the adjournment (but allowing his appeal as to the quantum of periodical payments) that whilst it was settled law that lump sum applications should ordinarily be disposed of once and for all, where there was a real possibility of capital becoming available in the near future from a specific source then it was within the court's jurisdiction to order an adjournment and, in particular, where it was the only means of doing justice between the parties (*Morris* v. *Morris* [1978] C.L.Y. 1600 and *Priest* v. *Priest* [1980] C.L.Y. 782 considered): DAVIES *v.* DAVIES (1986) 16 Fam. Law 138, (1986) 1 FLR 497, C.A.

1092. Financial provision—lump sum—factors

[Matrimonial Causes Act 1973 (c.18), ss.23 and 25.] In assessing a lump sum the Court should take account only of the factors set out in s.25 of the Act: COLLINS *v.* COLLINS, *The Times,* August 12, 1986, C.A.

1093. Financial provision—periodical payments—arrears

[Magistrates Courts Act 1980 (c.43), s.95.] An order had been made in divorce proceedings requiring H to make periodical payments of £105 p.m. to the two children of the family. The order was registered in the magistrates' court. H learned that a creditor of W was in financial difficulties. He therefore paid the balance of the loan, some £500, to the creditor and wrote to W stating that he proposed to deduct £50 from his monthly payments to recover the £500. W did not reply. He made two deductions. W applied to enforce the arrears. The justices remitted £100 and indicated that they would remit eight further sums of £50 p.m. *Held,* allowing W's appeal, that whilst the justices had a very wide discretion to remit arrears under s.95 that discretion must be exercised judicially, and that involved having regard to the relevant considerations. The fact that the justices had failed to consider that the periodical payments were to the children and not to W wholly vitiated the way they had exercised their discretion. The order would be set aside: PARRY *v.* MEUGENS (1986) 1 F.L.R. 125, Reeve J.

1094. Financial provision—periodical payments—arrears—appeal. See BERRY *v.* BERRY, § 2094.

1095. Financial provision—periodical payments—arrears—remission

The maintenance order had been registered in the magistrates' court. W sought enforcement of arrears in the sum of £1,056. H sought to reduce this amount submitting, *inter alia,* that arrears which had accrued 12 months before the issue of the complaint should be remitted under the *Ross* v. *Pearson* rule. The justices remitted part of the arrears to take into account a period of unemployment by H and an uncredited payment but declined to remit any of the arrears on the *Ross* v. *Pearson* principle on the ground that the county court order was of relatively recent origin. *Held,* dismissing H's appeal, that the remission of arrears was governed by a rule of practice rather than law. This dated from the days of the Ecclesiastical Courts, the underlying philosophy being that if the complainant had waited a year before enforcing the order she did not need the money. In the instant appeal the maintenance order had been made within the 12 month period before the complaint to enforce. This was a justifiable reason for the justices to distinguish the case from the usual rule (*Kerr* v. *Kerr* [1897] 2 Q.B. 439, *Pilcher* v. *Pilcher (No. 2)* [1956] C.L.Y. 2764 and *Fowler* v. *Fowler* [1980] C.L.Y. 760 considered; *Ross* v. *Pearson* [1975] C.L.Y. 986 distinguished: RUSSELL *v.* RUSSELL (1986) 16 Fam. Law 156, (1986) 1 F.L.R. 465, C.A.

1096. Financial provision—periodical payments—clean break—termination date

[Matrimonial Causes Act 1973 (c.18), ss. 25A, 31(7).] H and W had married in 1953 and had divorced in 1977. In 1984 W, now aged 56, applied for an increase of her maintenance. H was aged 60. He was employed by the National Trust and lived at a low rent in tied accommodation but had to retire at the age of 65. The judge varied the registrar's increased order by adding to it provisions that the order should cease to have effect when H no longer had tied employment or reached the age of 65. *Held,* allowing W's appeal, that a termination date should only be made after consideration whether the recipient would be able to adjust to the "clean break" without undue hardship. This had not been considered by the judge. The effect of the order was to put into H's hands the opportunity to cease work out of perversity. It was plainly wrong and the additional phrases would be struck out: Morris *v.* Morris (1986) 16 Fam.Law 24, C.A.

1097. Financial provision—periodical payments—conduct—inappropriateness of transfer to High Court

[Matrimonial Causes Rules (S.I. 1977 No. 344), r.80.] H and W had married in 1952 and finally separated in 1979. In subsequent ancillary relief proceedings in 1983 H swore an affidavit setting out W's conduct during the marriage. Most of his complaints related to slovenly behaviour but two raised serious issues relating to her adultery in 1953 and 1959. W now appealed contending that the county court judge had erred in ruling that W's alleged conduct was of a nature likely to affect the determination of her application for ancillary relief. No account was taken of the time elapsed between such conduct and the breakdown of the marriage and there was no capital issue in dispute since W lived in a council house. *Held,* allowing W's appeal in part, that the only purpose of s.80 was to regulate which court should try a contested issue of conduct. However, the terms of the rule were absolute. Here, as the adultery was admitted, the issue was not contested. All the argument would be, if it came to a hearing, was whether or not the adultery in 1959 should or should not affect the ancillary relief issue. In practical terms there was no reason why the matter could not be left in the county court to proceed in the ordinary way, it being open to H to raise the uncontested issues if he wished. The appeal was misconceived though since W was contending that H's affidavit did not raise any issue of conduct and that the application to transfer should be dismissed, thereby shutting out any evidence of that kind: Coley *v.* Coley (1986) 16 Fam Law. 74 C.A.

1098. Financial provision—periodical payments—husband's application

Upon W's application to execute a maintenance agreement H applied on his own motion, for a periodical payments order in favour of W. The registrar struck out the application on the ground that a spouse could not claim for an order for periodical payments against himself. *Held,* allowing H's appeal, that H was not prohibited from seeking such an order by any statutory provision. There could be fiscal or family reasons for a husband to seek such an order *e.g.* a wife could be under a disability (*Peacock* v. *Peacock* [1982] C.L.Y. 1123 followed): Simister *v.* Simister (1986) 83 L.S.Gaz. 3001, Waite J.

1099. Financial provision—periodical payments—net effect—subsistence level

W received supplementary benefits of £60 per week. H earned £134 gross per week and paid £20 per week to his mother for his keep. He had purchased a house on a mortgage for £13,250 and his repayments and rates amounted to £36 per week. The recorder found that although H was justified in wanting to have a place of his own he should be prepared to make some sacrifices for acquiring it. He therefore computed that H could afford to pay maintenance of £35 per week to W and the two children of the family after taking into account his net income of £53·71. *Held,* allowing H's appeal, that the recorder had not been justified in regarding the property acquired by H as anything more than necessary accommodation to which H was entitled. It was a modest property and was costing him no more than he would have to pay as a tenant, whether in private or council accommodation. Therefore it was the wrong approach to impose on H a penalty. The recorder had also failed to consider the effect of his order on the money available to H which would only just place him above DHSS subsistence limits. In the circumstances the registrar's original order totalling £15 per week would be restored (*Bellenden* v. *Satterthwaite* (1948) C.L.C. 3046; *Peacock* v. *Peacock* [1984] C.L.Y. 1123 and *G.* v. *G. (Minors: Custody Appeal)* [1985] C.L.Y. 2594 followed: Allen *v.* Allen (1986) 16 Fam. Law 269; (1986) 2 F.L.R. 265, C.A.

1100. Financial payments—periodical payments—school fees—payments against custodial parent. See Sherdley *v.* Sherdley, § 2203.

1101. Financial provision—variation of periodical payments order—whether jurisdiction to terminate order on payment of capital sum

[Matrimonial Causes Act 1973 (c.18), s.31(7) (as substituted by Matrimonial and Family Proceedings Act 1984 (c.42), s.6).]

S.31(7) of the Matrimonial Causes Act 1973 (as substituted by s.6 of the Matrimonial and Family Proceedings Act 1984) should be construed so as to permit the court to order a termination of periodical payments on payment of a sufficient capital sum to properly compensate her, having regard to the welfare of any children of the family and the need that the wife should be able to adjust without undue hardship on the termination of the order.

Both H and W applied for orders varying a periodical payments order in favour of W. H sought to commute the order on payment of a capital sum to W. *Held*, that under s.31 of the 1973 Act, as introduced by s.6 of the 1984 Act, the court was entitled to give effect to the clean break principle, and to order that the periodical payments should terminate upon W being paid a sufficient capital sum.

S. *v.* S. [1986] 3 W.L.R. 518, Waite J.

1102. Financial provision and property adjustment—consent order—wife's suicide—whether leave to appeal out of time

Events subsequent to a consent order made in full and final settlement of divorce proceedings cannot constitute a fundamental mistake vitiating the order.

The matrimonial home was owned jointly by husband and wife. In divorce proceedings a consent order was made transferring the husband's interest in the home to her. After the time limit for appealing but before the execution of the order the wife killed the children and committed suicide. The husband applied for leave to appeal out of time against the consent order which application was opposed by the wife's mother. The judge granted the application and set aside the order. *Held*, allowing the appeal, that (1) events subsequent to the order could not constitute a fundamental mistake vitiating the consent order; and (2) events occurring after the order could not provide a ground for appealing out of time (*Thwaite* v. *Thwaite* [1981] C.L.Y. 701; *Jenkins* v. *Livesey* [1985] C.L.Y. 1049 considered).

BARDER *v.* BARDER [1986] 3 W.L.R. 145, C.A.

1103. Financial relief—foreign decrees—retrospective effect

[Matrimonial and Family Proceedings Act 1984 (c.42), s.12(1).]

The provisions of s.12 of the Matrimonial and Family Proceedings Act 1984 which give the court jurisdiction to entertain applications for financial relief based on foreign decrees are retrospective in effect.

H and W who were married in Lebanon settled in the United Kingdom. They remained here, but H was granted a decree of divorce in the Lebanon in April 1985. In September 1985, s.12 of the Matrimonial and Family Proceedings Act 1984 came into effect, giving the court power to entertain applications for financial relief based on foreign decrees. W applied for leave to apply for financial relief. *Held*, that the provisions of this section were retrospective in effect and the court had jurisdiction to entertain the application. (*Powys* v. *Powys* [1971] C.L.Y. 3594, *Williams* v. *Williams* [1971] C.L.Y. 5471 and *Chaterjee* v. *Chaterjee* [1975] C.L.Y. 969 applied; *Lewis (H)* v. *Lewis (G)* [1985] C.L.Y. 1692 considered.)

CHEBARO *v.* CHEBARO [1986] 3 W.L.R. 95, Sheldon J.

1104. Injunction—non-molestation—decree absolute—jurisdiction

H and W had been divorced, the decree absolute having been made in March 1984. In September 1985 W made an *ex parte* application for a non-molestation injunction and to prevent H from returning to the former matrimonial home. The county court judge refused the application on the ground that he had no jurisdiction but indicated that he would otherwise have made the order sought. *Held*, allowing W's appeal, that there was jurisdiction to grant the injunction sought even though the marriage had been dissolved by decree absolute. The application would be remitted back to the County Court to be heard *inter partes* and an interim injunction would be made to continue until such hearing (*Robinson* v. *Robinson* [1963] C.L.Y. 1675, *Ruddell* v. *Ruddell* [1967] C.L.Y. 1890 and *Beasley* v. *Beasley* [1969] C.L.Y 1648 followed): WEBB *v.* WEBB [1986] 1 F.L.R. 541, C.A.

1105. Matrimonial and Family Proceedings Act 1984—commencement

MATRIMONIAL AND FAMILY PROCEEDINGS ACT 1984 (COMMENCEMENT NO. 3) ORDER 1986 (No. 635 (c.17)) [80p], made under the Matrimonial and Family Proceedings

Act 1984 (c.42), s.47(1)(*c*)(*e*); brings into force on April 28, 1986 the provisions of Pt. V, other than sections 40, 41 and 44, Sched. 1, paras. 3, 16, 17, 18, 19(*b*), 20(*b*), 29–31 and Sched. 3 so far as it is not already in force.

MATRIMONIAL AND FAMILY PROCEEDINGS ACT 1984 (COMMENCEMENT NO. 4) ORDER 1986 (No. 1049 (c.27)) [45p], made under the Matrimonial and Family Proceedings Act 1984 (c.42), s.47(1)(*a*)(*c*); brings into force on October 1, 1986 section 10 and Sched. 1, paras. 21, 23–26.

1106. Matrimonial Causes Rules

MATRIMONIAL CAUSES (AMENDMENT) RULES 1986 (No. 634) [£1·40], made under the Matrimonial Causes Act 1973 (c.18), s.50; operative on April 28, 1986; make provision in relation to the distribution of, and the transfer of, matrimonial proceedings between the High Court and county courts.

MATRIMONIAL CAUSES (AMENDMENT NO. 2) RULES 1986 (No. 1096) [45p], made under the Matrimonial Causes Act 1973 (c.18), s.50; operative on August 1, 1986; amend S.I. 1977 No. 344.

1107. Non-molestation injunction—breach—whether committal

[Domestic Violence and Matrimonial Proceedings Act 1976 (c.50), s.2(1).] Although it is not wrong in principle for a judge to commit a person in breach of a non-molestation injunction *ex parte* to prison, it is preferable to arrest him and pass sentence after learning the evidence of both sides: NEWMAN *v.* BENESCH, *The Times,* September 22, 1986, C.A.

1108. Polygamous marriage—desertion—whether just cause

[Matrimonial Causes Act 1973 (c.18), s.1(2)(*c*)] H and W both Muslim and citizens of Bangladesh, had married in Karachi in 1964. There were no children of the marriage. They were both doctors and had come to live in England. In 1979 H took employment in Kuwait and, in the hope of having children, entered into a second marriage, by proxy, with a Bangladeshi woman. When he returned H and W lived together for a short while. W repeatedly asked that H divorce his second wife and when he refused, she left him. She made a complaint to the justices alleging desertion. The justices dismissed it on the ground that both parties had accepted expert opinion evidence on Muslim law that a Muslim wife had no basis for complaint in relation to a second marriage. In 1981 H petitioned for divorce under s.1(2)(*c*). The only issue before the judge was whether W had had just cause to leave H based on the second marriage. The judge dismissed the petition concluding that since both parties had been resident in England for over 10 years and were educated people the action of H in taking a second wife without the consent of W seriously risked the continuance of the marriage. H appealed contending that the judge should have accepted, without qualification, the expert opinion evidence that polygamy was not a just cause for desertion. *Held,* dismissing H's appeal, that it was the personal circumstances of the parties that was of vital importance on the facts the judge had come to the right conclusions that H had not been able to prove desertion and that W had just cause to live apart from him: QUORAISHI *v.* QUORAISHI (1985) 15 Fam. Law 308, C.A.

1109. Special procedure lists—practice direction. See PRACTICE, § 2671.

1110. Special procedure—rescission of decree nisi—proof of petition

[Matrimonial Causes Act 1973 (c.18), s.1(2).] W had filed a divorce petition based on H's unreasonable behaviour. H accepted that the marriage had broken down irretrievably but he disputed the allegations of behaviour made against him. H stated in the acknowledgment of service that he wished to defend the suit. W's solicitors took the view that it was unlikely that H would be granted legal aid to defend and entered the cause in the special procedure list. H's solicitors made an application to set aside the Registrar's certificate of satisfaction and for leave to file an answer but the application could not be served before the date fixed for the pronouncement of the decree nisi. H was wrongly informed that this hearing would take place in the afternoon, in consequence of which the decree nisi was made. *Held,* allowing H's appeal, that under s.1(2) it was not enough for a party to allege, even if it was admitted by the other side, that the marriage had broken down irretrievably. The petitioner had to go on and prove one of the relevant facts. H was therefore entitled to contest the case and had been debarred, by a mistake which was no fault of his, from so doing (*Mitchell* v. *Mitchell* [1984] C.L.Y. 1681 considered): CAHILL *v.* CAHILL (1986) 16 Fam.Law 102, C.A.

1111. Talaq divorce—talaq pronounced in British Isles—recognition

[Recognition of Divorces and Legal Separations Act 1971 (c.53), ss.2, 3(1) (as amended by Domicile and Matrimonial Proceedings Act 1973 (c.45), s.15(2)).]

Pronouncement of talaq in the U.K. amounts to the institution of proceedings for divorce in Pakistan but on the true construction of ss.2 and 3(1) of the Recognition of Divorces and Legal Separations Act 1971 only one set of proceedings in one country was contemplated.

A Pakistani pronounced talaq in the U.K. against a wife resident in Pakistan; he carried out the administrative requirements of talaq. Subsequently he acted as sponsor for a fiancee to enter the U.K., but the immigration officer refused her entry on the ground that he was not satisfied that the marriage could take place within a reasonable time, the divorce not being recognised in England. F's appeals were dismissed. *Held*, on further appeal, that the immigration officer had been correct. The 1971 Act contemplated one set of proceedings in one country and the pronouncement of talaq in the U.K. amounted to the institution of proceedings subsequently completed in Pakistan.

R. *v*. SECRETARY OF STATE FOR HOME DEPARTMENT, *ex p*. FATIMA [1986] 2 W.L.R. 693, H.L.

1112. Validity of divorce—appropriate procedure

[Matrimonial Causes Act 1973 (c.18), s.45.] The appropriate procedure for determining whether a valid marriage still subsisted or had been dissolved was by way of a petition seeking a declaration under the inherent jurisdiction of the court. It was only where the validity of the marriage at its inception was called into question that the petition for a declaration should be presented under s.45 of the 1973 Act: WILLIAMS *v*. ATT.-GEN., *The Times*, October 29, 1986, Latey J.

EASEMENTS AND PRESCRIPTION

1113. Covenant to repair—contribution to maintenance of roads—whether binding

The predecessors in title of D in 1899 covenanted to contribute to the costs of repair of two roads. The estate on which the property was situated contained many other roads. Since some time in the 1920s the total expenditure on all roads had simply been divided among the property owners according to the length of property frontage. *Held*, that the payments since the 1920s did not change the effect of the original covenant, nor was there any evidence of an easement requiring the burden of a payment for the benefit thereof. There was no evidence of an implied collateral contract at the time D purchased the property. D could only be required to make a contribution in respect of the two roads abutting his property: FOUR OAKS ESTATE *v*. HADLEY, *The Times*, July 2, 1986, C.A.

1114. Right of way—disturbance—whether actionable interference

An injunction should not be granted restraining a landlord from interfering with the tenant's quiet enjoyment when it is beyond the landlord's power to interfere in the manner complained of.

A granted a 99 year lease of land to B to construct a filling station and car-wash. The projected site for the car-wash turned out to be an obstruction of various rights of way granted by X, A's predecessors in title. The beneficiaries of the rights of way were granted injunctions against A and B to restrain the construction of the car wash. The judge granted both injunctions, but on B's claim by way of contribution notice against A, held that the claim should fail, since A was not in breach of any covenant in the lease. The judge ordered that A and B should jointly pay two-thirds of the plaintiff's costs. A appealed against the injunction. B complained that if A's appeal was successful, B would be left to pay the whole of the costs. *Held*, allowing A's appeal, that (1) since the lease was for 99 years, it was beyond A's power to interfere with the rights of the plaintiffs in the manner complained of. Accordingly, the injunction was unnecessary and should be discharged, however, (2) although the ordinary award as to costs would have been against the plaintiffs, in the present case, A had disputed and lost on all substantive matters in the action, and accordingly there should be no order as to A's costs. B could seek to recover the increased costs in the contribution proceedings against A.

CELSTEEL *v*. ALTON HOUSE HOLDINGS [1986] 1 All E.R. 608, C.A.

1115. Right of way—failure to clear ice and snow—whether obstruction

The failure of the owner of a road to clean frozen rutted ice and snow is not an obstruction of a right of way: CLUTTENHAM v. ANGLIAN WATER AUTHORITY, *The Times,* August 14, 1986, C.A.

1116. Right to light—obstructed by extension to servient tenement—whether actionable

[Prescription Act 1832 (2 & 3 Will. 4, c.71), s.3.]

A dominant owner's right under s.3 of the Prescription Act 1832 is an easement for access of light to a building not to a particular room within it.

In 1968 P purchased a property whose second floor was lighted naturally by two windows situate at the rear that had been in position for more than 20 years. In 1976 P subdivided the rooms on the second floor, the two rear rooms of which were still lighted by the relevant windows facing D's premises. D subsequently added two floors to their premises. P sought damages claiming a prescriptive right to light. *Held,* that P had established an actionable nuisance and damages were assessed at £8,000 (*Price* v. *Hilditch* [1930] 1 Ch. 500 applied).

CARR-SAUNDERS v. McNEIL (DICK) ASSOCIATES [1986] 1 W.L.R. 922, Millett J.

ECCLESIASTICAL LAW

1117. Church dignitaries

CHURCH DIGNITARIES (RETIREMENT) RULES 1986 (No. 1143) [£2·40], made under the Church Dignitaries (Retirement) Measure 1949 (No. 1), s.17; operative on October 1, 1986; provide for the retirement of church dignitaries.

1118. Clergy pensions

CLERGY PENSIONS (AMENDMENT) REGULATIONS 1985 (No. 2081) [£1·35], made under the Clergy Pensions (Amendment) Measure 1972 (No. 5), s.6(1); operative on April 1, 1986; make provision in relation to clerical pensions.

1119. Faculty—reordering of church—duty to future generations

It is the duty of the consistory court to have regard to future generations as much as the present one.

The vicar and his two churchwardens petitioned for a faculty to allow the reordering of the church by removing the holy table from its position underneath a baldachino several paces towards the west end, and by erecting a sacrament house under the baldachino for reserving. The petition was unopposed. *Held,* granting the petition; that (1) the reservation was lawful since there would be no holy table beneath the baldachino and the sacrament house would be several paces behind the holy table. (*Lapford Re,* [1954] C.L.Y. 1066, *Bishopwearmouth (Rector and Churchwardens)* v. *Adey* [1958] C.L.Y. 1109 and *St. Peter and St. Paul, Leckhampton (Rector and Churchwardens)* v. *Barnard* [1968] C.L.Y. 1322 applied); (2) the proposed changes were not necessary and were based on the fashion for the priest taking a westward facing position to celebrate services; the fashion was likely to change and it was the court's duty to have regard to the interests of future generations; but the proposals were popular and the petition would be granted.

ST. MATTHEWS, WIMBLEDON, *Re* [1985] 3 All E.R. 670, Southwark Consistory Ct.

1120. Fees

LEGAL OFFICERS' FEES ORDER 1986 (No. 1144) [£1·90], made under the Ecclesiastical Fees Measure 1962 (No. 1), s.1; operative on January 1, 1987; increases certain fees.

1121. Holy table—quality of table—material and moveability—whether required to be "a table"

[Holy Table Measure 1964, s.1; Revised Canons Ecclesiastical, Canon F2, para 1.]

A holy table is not illegal simply because it is immoveable, but it must still be a "table" within the ordinary usage of that word before it may be introduced into a church.

Per curiam: the onus is on petitioners who wish to introduce a sculpture into a church, and while the Court would always try to give effect to the wishes of parishioners, that approach might not be appropriate in cases of unusual parishes such as are found in the City.

The rector and one of his churchwardens sought a faculty permitting the introduction of an altar, sculpted in marble, into his church. The church was by Sir Christopher Wren, and a masterpiece, being the first domed church in England. The intention was that the altar should be placed under the dome, the priest moving around it to conduct services. The parochial church council were unanimous in their support of the idea, but the diocesan advisory committee were not so sure, and an appearance to the petition was entered by the archdeacon to put the rector to proof. The question, therefore, was whether the altar was a table, so that it could be introduced into the church as a holy table, or alternatively whether, if not a table, it could nonetheless be introduced as a sculpture. *Held,* that the simple fact that a table was immoveable did not prevent it from being a holy table within the meaning of the 1964 Measure, but it had still to be "a table" within the ordinary meaning and usage of that word. The sculpture was not, on any ordinary usage of the word, "a table", and the petition failed as a matter of law.

Re ST. STEPHEN WALBROOK, [1986] 2 All E.R. 705, Newsom Ch.

1122. Methodist Church Act 1976
METHODIST CHURCH ACT 1976 (JERSEY) ORDER 1986 (No. 1164) [80p], made under the Methodist Church Act 1976 (c.xxx), ss.28 and 30; operative on September 1, 1986; extends the 1976 Act to Jersey.

1123. Parochial fees
PAROCHIAL FEES ORDER 1986 (No. 1148) [£1·40], made under the Ecclesiastical Fees Measure 1962 (No. 1), s.2(1); operative on January 1, 1987; establishes a new table of fees for matters in connection with baptisms, marriages, burials, the erection of monuments and other miscellaneous matters.

1124. Religious or public benevolent institution—Scientology—whether exemption from pay-roll tax. See CHURCH OF THE NEW FAITH *v.* COMMISSIONER OF PAY-ROLL TAX, § 2862.

EDUCATION

1125. Assisted places
EDUCATION (ASSISTED PLACES) (AMENDMENT) REGULATIONS 1986 (No. 991) [80p], made under the Education Act 1980 (c.20), ss.17(6), 35(4). Pt. I and Pt. II for the purposes specified in Reg. 1(2)(*a*)(*b*) are operative on July 8, 1986 and Pt. II for all other purposes is operative on September 1, 1986; amend S.I. 1985 No. 685.

EDUCATION (ASSISTED PLACES) (INCIDENTAL EXPENSES) (AMENDMENT) REGULATIONS 1986 (No. 990) [45p], made under the Education Act 1980, ss.18, 35(4); operative on September 1, 1986 save for Reg. 1(2)(*a*)(*b*) which is operative on July 8, 1986; amend S.I. 1985 No. 830.

1126. Awards
EDUCATION (MANDATORY AWARDS) REGULATIONS 1986 (No. 1306) [£4·40], made under the Education Act 1962 (c.12), ss.1 and 4(2) and Sched. 1, paras. 3, 4; operative on September 1, 1986; supersede S.I. 1985 No. 1126.

EDUCATION (MANDATORY AWARDS) (AMENDMENT) REGULATIONS 1986 (No. 1397) [45p], made under the Education Act 1962 (c.12), ss.1 and 4(2); operative on September 1, 1986; amends S.I. 1986 No. 1306.

EDUCATION (TEACHER TRAINING AWARDS) (AMENDMENT) REGULATIONS 1986 (No. 1346) [45p], made under the Education Act 1962, ss.3(*a*) and 4; operative on September 1, 1986; increase certain training awards.

1127. Closure and amalgamation of schools—proper procedure—inadequate period of consultation—whether proposals ultra vires
[Education Act 1944 (7 & 8 Geo VI, c.31), s.6, Sched. 1, part 11, para. 7.]
Parents have a legitimate expectation tantamount to a legal right to be properly consulted by a local education authority prior to the making of proposals affecting closure and amalgamation of local schools.

In July 1983 after proper public consultation, a local education authority made proposals regarding future education in the area. In December after a political change further reports were ordered. A brief consultative document was prepared which contained little information and copies were sent to parents barely three weeks before the deadline for written representations. The authority then made new proposals materially different from the originals. An application was made to quash the decisions as being *ultra vires. Held,* granting the application, that (1) the local authority had not acted according to the proper procedural requirements; (2) the parents had a legitimate right to proper consultation which had been met with a wholly inadequate consultative document and an unreasonable time for consultation (*Associated Provincial Picture Houses, v. Wednesbury Corp* (1948) C.L.C. 8107 applied; *R.* v. *Liverpool City Council, ex p. the Professional Association of Teachers* [1984] C.L.Y. 1172 followed).

R. *v.* BRENT LONDON BOROUGH COUNCIL, *ex p.* GUNNING (1985) 84 L.G.R. 168, Hodgson. J.

1128. Disciplinary investigation—investigation by governors completed—further investigation by local education authority

[Education Act 1944 (c.31), ss.17, 24(1).] Upon a proper construction of the articles of government of the school and of the head teacher's contract of employment, the local authority was entitled to conduct an investigation into a complaint made about the head, notwithstanding that the school governors had already conducted and concluded an investigation into the same complaint (*Honeyford* v. *Bradford City Metropolitan Council* [1986] C.L.Y. 1177 considered): McGOLDRICK *v.* BRENT LONDON BOROUGH COUNCIL, *The Times,* November 20, 1986, C.A.

1129. Education Act 1986 (c.40)

This Act provides for the making of grants by the Secretary of State to the Fellowship of Engineering and the Further Education Unit and makes further provision in relation to the arrangements under the Local Government, Planning and Land Act 1980, Part VI (Rate Support Grant) for the pooling of expenditure by local authorities on education.

The Act received the Royal Assent on July 18, 1986 and extends to England and Wales only.

1130. Education (Amendment) Act 1986 (c.1)

This Act increases the limit in s.2(1) of the Education (Grants and Awards) Act 1984 (limit on expenditure approved for grant purposes) and excludes remuneration for midday supervision from the Remuneration of Teachers Act 1965

The Act received the Royal Assent on February 17, 1986 and came into force on that date.

1131. Education (No. 2) Act 1986 (c.61)

This Act amends the law relating to education. It deals with school government.

The Act received the Royal Assent on November 7, 1986.

1132. Education (No. 2) Act 1986—commencement

EDUCATION (NO. 2) ACT 1986 (COMMENCEMENT NO. 1) ORDER 1986 (No. 2203 (c.87)) [£1·40], made under the Education (No. 2) Act 1986 (c.61), s.66; brings into force on January 7, 1987 sections 17, 30, 31, 33, 44–46, 47(11), 50–53, 56, 67(4) (in part) (5) (in part) Sched. 4, paras. 5, 7 and Sched. 6 (in part), also, brings into force on April 1, 1987 sections 54, 55, 67(4) (in part), Sched. 4, para. 1.

1133. Education committee—"experience in education"—construction

[Education Act 1944 (c.31), Sched. 1, part 2, para. 5.] By para. 5 of part 2 of Sched. 1 to the Education Act 1944, members of education committees must be people "of experience in education." "Experience" is to be construed widely: it is not restricted to experience of teaching, and does not imply any technical qualification: R. *v.* CROYDON LONDON BOROUGH COUNCIL, *ex p.* LENEY, *The Times,* November 27, 1986, D.C.

1134. GCSE training

EDUCATION (SCHOOLS AND FURTHER EDUCATION) (AMENDMENT) REGULATIONS 1986 (No. 542) [40p], made under the Education Act 1980 (c.20), ss.27 and 35(4); operative on April 18, 1986; amends S.I. 1981 No. 1086 in relation to the duration of the school year and day.

1135. Grant application—reconsideration—whether duty on local authority

[Education Act 1962 (c.12).] In 1978, E, an education authority, refused P a grant because of a mistaken legal assumption. In 1983 the House of Lords ruled in another case that the assumption was incorrect, and P applied for his original application to be reconsidered. E refused, because of a policy directive from the Secretary of State to reconsider only applications for the academic years 1979/80 and after. P sought judicial review of the 1978 and 1983 decisions. *Held,* that E's duty under the Education Act 1962 was not only to bestow awards, but also to consider whether each applicant qualified for one. The duty to pay the award thereafter was quite separate. In determining in 1978 that P did not qualify for an award, E had therefore performed its duty, albeit mistakenly. E had the power, as well as a duty, to reconsider the application after the House of Lords' decision. E's adoption of the Secretary of State's directive was reasonable, but the directive itself was flawed by error, because the subject of the House of Lords case had himself been a pre-1979 student, and, having won his case, good public administration demanded that all students of the same or later years should be treated equally: R. *v.* HERTFORDSHIRE COUNTY COUNCIL, *ex p.* CHEUNG, R. *v.* SEFTON METROPOLITAN BOROUGH COUNCIL, *ex p.* PAU, *The Times,* April 4, 1986, C.A.

1136. Grant application—refusal of grant—failure to exercise discretion.
[Education Act 1962 (c.12), s.1(1); Education (Mandatory Awards) Regulations 1982 (S.I. 1982 No. 954), reg. 11(2)(*d*)] Each local authority failed to exercise its discretion to treat an application for a grant as having been made in time although it was in fact made shortly after time had expired, and after the case of *Shah.* In each case officials had told the applicants not to bother applying. *Held,* that the decisions not to make grants would be quashed (*R.* v. *Barnet London Borough Council, ex p. Shah* [1983] C.L.Y. 1157, *Howell* v. *Falmouth Boat Construction Co.* [1951] C.L.Y. 9617, *H.T.V.* v. *Price Commission* [1976] C.L.Y. 2344, *R.* v. *I.R.C. ex p. Preston* [1985] C.L.Y. 1728 *R.* v. *Haringey London Borough Council ex p. Sai Shun Lee* (unrep. July 25, 1984 considered): R. *v.* WEST GLAMORGAN COUNTY COUNCIL, *ex p.* GHEISSARY; R. *v.* EAST SUSSEX COUNTY COUNCIL *ex p.* KHATIBSHAHIDI, *The Times,* December 18, 1985, Hodgson J.

1137. Grants
BLOCK GRANT (EDUCATION ADJUSTMENTS) (WALES) REGULATIONS 1986 (No. 314) [£2·30], made under the Local Government, Planning and Land Act 1980 (c.65), Sched. 10, paras. 2, 5, 6, 7; operative on March 26, 1986; provides for the adjustment of the block grant payable to local authorities in Wales for education purposes in the year 1985/6 and subsequent years.
EDUCATION (GRANTS) (MUSIC AND BALLET SCHOOLS) (AMENDMENT) REGULATIONS 1986 (No. 989) [80p], made under the Education Act 1944 (c.31), s.100(1)(*b*)(3); Pt. I and Pt. II for the purposes specified in Reg. 1(2)(*a*)(*b*) are operative on July 8, 1986 and Pt. II for all other purposes is operative on September 1, 1986; amend S.I. 1985 No. 684.
EDUCATION SUPPORT GRANTS (AMENDMENT) REGULATIONS 1986 (No. 1031) [45p], made under the Education (Grants and Awards) Act 1984 (c.11), s.1(2); operative on September 1, 1986; further amend S.I. 1984 No. 1098.

1138. Grants—EEC nationals wishing to attend courses at U.K. colleges—whether vocational courses—discrimination.
[Education (Mandatory Awards) Regulations 1983 (S.I. 1983 No. 1135), reg. 9(2), (4), Regulation (E.E.C.) No. 1612/68, art. 7, Treaty of Rome, Arts. 7, 128.]
Nationals of E.E.C. Member States do not have to be resident in the U.K. for three years before they become entitled to an educational grant provided they intend to pursue a course of training in a vocational school. A vocational school is an establishment providing vocational training courses on a substantial and continuing basis and includes schools training students to enter a profession.
H was a national of Republic of Ireland who intended to attend an LL.B. course at Queen Mary College, London University with a view to becoming a lawyer. D was a national of France who intended to attend a postgraduate course for a Postgraduate Certificate in Education at Kings College, London University with a view to becoming a teacher. P was a national of Republic of Ireland who was accepted to attend a similar course at Edge Hill College, Knowsley with a view to becoming a religious education teacher. All three applied to their relevant local authority for education awards to enable them to undertake their respective courses. H and D's applications were refused on the grounds that they had not been ordinarily resident for three years and that their courses were not vocational courses at vocational schools. P's application was refused on the ground that Edge Hill College was not on the recognised list of establishments for European Community migrant workers. All sought judicial review of the decisions of the local authorities concerned. At the hearing it was conceded that Edge Hill College was a vocational school if teacher training fell within the definition of vocational training. *Held,* that (1) a vocational school was not simply a school offering courses in manual or technical training, a vocation included a profession such as teaching. There was nothing in art. 7(3) of E.E.C. regulation No. 1612/28 to indicate that rights of access to training are to

exclude professional training; (2) the combined effect of Art. 128 and Art. 7 of the Treaty of Rome was a general prohibition on discrimination on grounds of nationality in respect of access to vocational training in Member States. The decisions refusing awards breached that prohibition on discrimination; (3) the applicants were not deprived of the same social advantages as U.K. nationals in breach of art. 7(2) of Regulation E.C.C. No. 1612/68 because they were no longer workers, having become students. The relevant time was the time at which the social advantage was to be enjoyed; (4) if an educational establishment provides a vocational training course on a substantial or continuing basis it is a vocational school; (5) H's LL.B. course was not designed nor intended to equip H for a career or a job but was academic in nature. H was not attending a course of vocational training. D and P's courses were vocational training. D and P's applications were allowed and H's dismissed. It was not appropriate to make any reference to the European Court pursuant to Art. 177 Treaty of Rome (*MacMahon* v. *Department of Education and Science* [1982] C.L.Y. 1180 followed, *Forcheri* v. *Belgium State* [1984] C.L.Y. 1406, *Bulmer (H.P.)* v. *Bollinger (J)*. *S.A.* [1972] C.L.Y. 3434 applied).

R. *v.* INNER LONDON EDUCATION AUTHORITY, *ex p.* HINDE (1985) 83 L.G.R. 695, Taylor J.

1139. Grants—sex discrimination—equal treatment directive

[Council Directive 76/207/EEC] The principle of equal treatment for the sexes enshrined in the Council Directive 76/207/EEC is prima facie not being observed if, in a situation where there is an equal number of women and men in the population, one sees a practice working in reality in such a way that many more women than men are adversely affected by it: R. *v.* SECRETARY OF STATE FOR EDUCATION, *ex p.* SCHAEFFTER, *The Times,* August 18, 1986, Schiemann J.

1140. Headmaster—disciplinary procedure—powers of Governors and Assistant Director of Education. See HONEYFORD *v.* CITY OF BRADFORD METROPOLITAN COUNCIL, § 1177.

1141. Local authority grant—lengthy but temporary residence overseas—whether "ordinarily resident" in United Kingdom

[Education Act 1962 (c.12), s.1(1); Education (Mandatory Awards) Regulations 1983 (S.I. 1983 No. 1135), reg. 5(4).]

Lengthy but temporary residence overseas may render an applicant for a grant not ordinarily resident within a local authority's locality.

Per curiam: a local authority whose decision was challenged in proceedings for judicial review should not be partisan and should assist the court in the same manner as the judge of an inferior court.

A, the applicant, moved from Lancashire to Hong Kong at the age of five when her father became employed there. The family always intended to return to Lancashire, and they kept their home there. Thirteen years later, A sought a grant for study from the Lancashire County Council, but was refused, on the ground that she has not been ordinarily resident within the locality for three years preceding the application. A's application for judicial review was dismissed. A appealed to the Court of Appeal. *Held,* dismissing the appeal, that the council's refusal was not unreasonable, and it was entitled to find that A's residence abroad had ceased to be merely temporary.

R. *v.* LANCASHIRE COUNTY COUNCIL, *ex p.* HUDDLESTON [1986] 2 All E.R. 941, C.A.

1142. Local authority—report—relevant criteria

[Education Act 1944 (c.31), Sched. 1, para. 7.] In discharging their functions in respect of education under the Schedule an education committee must make an evaluation of all issues relevant to making a decision: R. *v.* KIRKLEES METROPOLITAN BOROUGH COUNCIL, *ex p.* MOLLOY, *The Times,* November 5, 1986, Mann J.

1143. Remuneration of teachers

REMUNERATION OF TEACHERS (FURTHER EDUCATION) (AMENDMENT) ORDER 1986 (No. 176) [£1·85], made under the Remuneration of Teachers Act 1965 (c.3), ss.2(6), 7(3); operative on February 18, 1986; provides for new remuneration scales for teachers in higher education.

REMUNERATION OF TEACHERS (PRIMARY AND SECONDARY EDUCATION) (AMENDMENT) ORDER 1986 (No. 559) [£2·30], made under the Remuneration of Teachers Act 1965 (c.3), ss.2(6) and 7(3); operative on March 25, 1986; amends a document setting out pay scales in primary and secondary schools maintained by local education authorities.

1144. School attendance—failure to comply with order—subsequent failure
[Education Act 1944 (c.31), s.37(5).] When parents have been once convicted under s.37(5) of the Education Act 1944 of failing to comply with a school attendance order, they cannot be convicted a second time of failing to comply with the same order: ENFIELD LONDON BOROUGH COUNCIL *v.* FORSYTH, *The Times,* November 19, 1986, C.A.

1145. School attendance—walking distance between school and home—route unsafe for unaccompanied child—whether "nearest available route"
[Education Act 1944 (c.31), s.39.]
The "nearest available route" for a child to walk to school is the nearest route along which the child could walk with reasonable safety accompanied if necessary.
R's daughter was of compulsory school age and on the register at a local comprehensive. The shortest route to school was 2·94 miles but involved using an isolated and partly unmade track which R regarded as unsuitable for their child to use unaccompanied. The next shortest route was over three miles. The local authority were obliged to provide free transport to school for children who would otherwise have to walk over three miles. The local authority refused to provide free transport for Rs' daughter. R refused to send her to school and were duly convicted by the justices of an offence under the Education Act 1944, s.39. R appealed contending that the nearest available route for their daughter to walk to school was more than three miles so that s.39(2)(c) relieved them of liability for their daughter's non-attendance at school. R were successful in the Divisional Court. Held, allowing the council's appeal, that before a route could be described as "available" it must be reasonably capable of being used by a child to walk to school. Availability was not to be judged by what it was reasonable for an unaccompanied child to use. For a route to be "available" within the meaning of s.39(5) of the Act, it must be a route along which a child accompanied as necessary can walk with reasonable safety to school. A route does not fail to be "available" merely because it could not safely be used by an unaccompanied child (*Farrier* v. *Ward* [1954] C.L.Y. 1096 considered).
ROGERS *v.* ESSEX COUNTY COUNCIL [1986] 3 W.L.R. 689, H.L.

1146. School governors—challenge to election—remedy
[Education Act 1944 (c.31), s.99.] P sought to challenge the election of parent governors to the governing body of a county school. *Held,* that judicial review was not the appropriate remedy. P should use s.99 of the Education Act 1944, and complain to the Secretary of State for Education and Science: R. *v.* NORTHAMPTON COUNTY COUNCIL, *ex p.* GRAY, *The Times,* June 10, 1986, D.C.

1147. School governors—exclusion from meeting
[Education (School Governing Bodies) Regulations (S.I. 1981 No. 809).] The regulations do not provide an exclusive and exhaustive set of circumstances in which a governor can be obliged to withdraw from a meeting: LOCKETT *v.* CROYDON LONDON BOROUGH COUNCIL, *The Times,* August 6, 1986, C.A.

1148. Special educational needs—statement—discretion of education authority
[Education Act 1981 (c.60), ss.5, 7.] Where an education authority decides under s.5 of the Education Act 1981 that a child has or probably has special educational needs, s.7 does not oblige it to determine the special educational provisions that should be made for the child or make a statement of the child's special educational needs, although it has a discretion to do so: R. *v.* HEREFORD AND WORCESTER COUNTY COUNCIL, *ex p.* LASHFORD, *The Times,* November 10, 1986, C.A.

1149. Speech therapy—whether non-educational provision—whether duty to provide
[Education Act 1981 (c.60), s.7(2); Education Act 1944 (c.31), s.81; Local Government Act 1972 (c.70), s.111(1); Scholarships and Other Benefits Regulations 1977 (S.I. 1977 No. 1443), reg. 4(a).] A local authority may reasonably conclude that speech therapy is "non-educational provision." There is no power to make a grant to pay for such therapy: R. *v.* OXFORDSHIRE EDUCATION AUTHORITY, *ex p.* W, *The Times,* November 22, 1986, D.C.

1150. Students' dependants allowances

EDUCATION (STUDENTS' DEPENDANTS ALLOWANCES) (AMENDMENT) REGULATIONS 1986 (No. 1325) [80p], made under the Education Act 1973 (c.16), s.3; operative on September 1, 1986; amend S.I. 1983 No. 1185.

1151. Teachers

EDUCATION (BURSARIES FOR TEACHER TRAINING) REGULATIONS 1986 (No. 1324) [80p], made under the Education Act 1962 (c.12), ss.3(*a*) and 4; operative on September 1, 1986; empower the Secretary of State to pay training bursaries to persons undergoing initial training as teachers in mathematics, physics, craft, design and technology.

1152. Teachers—refusal to take classes for absent colleagues—deductions made by employers—whether teachers contractually bound

Teachers are contractually bound to comply with the head's reasonable directions for the proper administration of the school, which includes "cover" for absent colleagues.

The plaintiffs were teachers employed in a secondary school. It was their normal practice to "cover" for absent teachers. Following union instructions they refused to do so, but remained at school occupied in their normal tasks. The employers deducted a small part of their salary for "breach of contract." The actual written contracts were silent on this point. The teachers issued writs asserting that they were not contractually bound to cover for absent colleagues. *Held,* that the deductions were properly made; teachers were professionals and it was their contractual duty to discharge all their professional obligations which included the head's reasonable directions on the proper administration of the school (*Liverpool City Council* v. *Irwin* [1976] C.L.Y. 1532; *Redbridge London Borough Council* v. *Fishman* [1978] C.L.Y. 1125 applied).

SIM *v.* ROTHERHAM METROPOLITAN BOROUGH COUNCIL [1986] 3 W.L.R. 851, Scott J.

1153. Teachers' superannuation. See PENSIONS AND SUPERANNUATION, § 2529a.

ELECTION LAW

1154. Local elections

LOCAL ELECTIONS (PARISHES AND COMMUNITIES) RULES 1986 (No. 2215) [£5·40], made under the Representation of the People Act 1983 (c.2), s.36(2); provide for the conduct of parish and community council elections.

LOCAL ELECTIONS (PRINCIPAL AREAS) RULES 1986 (No. 2214) [£4·90], made under the Representation of the People Act 1983 (c.2), s.36(2); provide for the conduct of elections of councillors of the council of a principal area i.e. a county, district or London Borough and the members of ILEA.

1155. Parliamentary constituencies

PARLIAMENTARY CONSTITUENCIES (ENGLAND) (MISCELLANEOUS CHANGES) ORDER 1986 (No. 597) [£1·40] made under the House of Commons (Redistribution of Seats) Act 1949 (c.66), s.3; operative on April 9, 1986; gives effect to the recommendations of the Boundary Commission for England dated January 23, 1986.

PARLIAMENTARY CONSTITUENCIES (WALES) (MISCELLANEOUS CHANGES) ORDER 1986 (No. 2231), [50p], made under the House of Commons (Redistribution of Seats) Act 1949 (c.66), s.3; operative on December 30, 1986; gives effect to the recommendations contained in the report of the Boundary Commission for Wales of July 2, 1986.

1156. Parliamentary Constituencies Act 1986 (c.56)

This Act consolidates the House of Commons (Redistribution of Seats) Acts 1949 to 1979.

The Act received the Royal Assent on November 7, 1986 and comes into force on February 7, 1986. It extends to Northern Ireland.

1157. Personation of electors—parliamentary election—whether imprisonment correct. See R. *v.* PHILLIPS (C.K.), § 671.

1158. Representation of the people

REPRESENTATION OF THE PEOPLE (AMENDMENT) REGULATIONS 1985 Order 1986 (No. 104) [£1·85], made under the Representation of the People Act 1983 (c.2), ss.53 and 201(1) and Sched. 2, paras. 11, 11A and 12; operative on February 3, 1986; amend S.I. 1983 No. 000.

REPRESENTATION OF THE PEOPLE REGULATIONS 1986 (No. 1081) [£6·50], made under the Representation of the People Act 1983 (c.2), ss.7(4), 10(*b*), 14(1), 15(2)(4), 16, 18(8) 36(3C), 53, 56(1)(5), 75(3), 89(1), 20(1), Scheds. 1 rules 24, 28(3), 32(3); 2; 4, para. 8(1) and the Representation of the People Act 1985 (c.50), ss.2(3), 3(5)(6)(7), 6(1)(5), 7(1)(3), 8(6)(7), 9(4)(7)(8), 15(5); operative when specified provisions of the 1985 Act come into force; make provision in relation to the representation of the people.

REPRESENTATION OF THE PEOPLE (VARIATION OF LIMITS OF CANDIDATES' ELECTION EXPENSES) ORDER 1986 (No. 383) [40p], made under the Representation of the People Act 1983 (c.2), s.76A(1), 197(3); operative on March 2, 1986; increases the maximum amount of expenses.

REPRESENTATION OF THE PEOPLE (WELSH FORMS) ORDER 1986 (No. 1460) [£1·90], made under the Welsh Language Act 1967 (c.66), s.2(1); operative on September 26, 1986; prescribes versions partly in Welsh and partly in English of the forms set out in Sched. 2 to S.I. 1986 No. 1081.

1159. Representation of the people. See also NORTHERN IRELAND, § 2338.

1160. Representation of the People Act 1985—commencement

REPRESENTATION OF THE PEOPLE ACT 1985 (COMMENCEMENT No. 2) ORDER 1986 (No. 639 (c.18)) [45p], made under the Representation of the People Act 1985 (c.50), s.29(2); brings into force on April 21, 1986 Sched. 4, para. 69 to the 1985 Act.

REPRESENTATION OF THE PEOPLE ACT 1985 (COMMENCEMENT No. 3) ORDER 1986 (No. 1080 (c.29)) [£1·40], made under the Representation of the People Act 1985 (c.50), s.29(2); bring into force on February 16, 1987 sections 5–11, 12(3), 15, 16, 19 (in part), 21, Scheds. 2, 4, paras. 7, 9, 73, 79, 80, 84–86, Sched. 5 (in part).

ELECTRICITY

1161. Fuel and Electricity (Control) Act 1973—continuation

FUEL AND ELECTRICITY (CONTROL) ACT 1973 (CONTINUATION) (JERSEY) ORDER 1986 (No. 1885) [45p], made under the Fuel and Electricity (Control) Act 1973 (c.67), s.10(3); operative on November 30, 1986; continues the 1973 Act in force in Jersey for a further year.

1162. Meters

METERS (DETERMINATION OF QUESTIONS) (EXPENSES) REGULATIONS 1986 (No. 1627) [45p], made under the Electric Lighting (Clauses) Act 1899 (c.19), s.57(5); operative on October 13, 1986; provides for the payment by the Electricity Boards of sums towards the administrative expenses of the Secretary of State incurred in connection with determining the correctness of electricity meters.

EMERGENCY LAWS

1163. Prevention of terrorism

PREVENTION OF TERRORISM (TEMPORARY PROVISIONS) ACT 1984 (CONTINUANCE) ORDER 1986 (No. 417) [40p], made under the Prevention of Terrorism (Temporary Provisions) Act 1984 (c.8), s.17(2)(*a*); provides that the provisions of the 1984 Act shall continue in force for a further 12 months from March 22, 1986.

SUPPRESSION OF TERRORISM ACT 1978 (APPLICATION OF PROVISIONS) (UNITED STATES OF AMERICA) ORDER 1986 (No. 2146) [£1·40], made under the Suppression of Terrorism Act 1978 (c.26), s.5(1)(*i*); applies certain provisions of the 1978 Act to the extradition of offenders to the USA.

SUPPRESSION OF TERRORISM ACT 1978 (DESIGNATION OF COUNTRIES) ORDER 1986 (No. 271) [40p], made under the Suppression of Terrorism Act 1978 (c.26), s.8; operative on March 13, 1986; designates Belgium, The Netherlands, Portugal and Switzerland for the purposes of the 1978 Act.

SUPPRESSION OF TERRORISM ACT 1978 (DESIGNATION OF COUNTRIES) (No. 2) ORDER 1986 (No. 1137) [45p], made under the Suppression of Terrorism Act 1978 (c.26), s.8; operative on August 26, 1986; designates Italy and Liechtenstein for the purposes of the 1978 Act.

SUPPRESSION OF TERRORISM ACT 1978 (OVERSEAS TERRITORIES) ORDER 1986 (No. 2019) [£1·40], made under the Suppression of Terrorism Act 1978 (c.26), s.7(3); operative on December 17, 1986; extends ss.1–5, 8, 9 of the 1978 Act to specified territories.

EMPLOYMENT

1164. Appeal—costs—preliminary hearing procedure

[Employment Appeal Tribunal Rules 1980 (S.I. 1980 No. 2035), r.27.] An appeal under the preliminary hearing procedure which was dismissed did not necessarily attract an award of costs unless the appeal was "unnecessary": RATTAN *v.* BRITISH AIRWAYS, *The Times,* July 18, 1986, E.A.T.

1165. Appeal to Employment Appeal Tribunal—no dispute over industrial tribunal decision—whether appeal proper

An appeal to the Employment Appeal Tribunal where there is no dispute between the parties is an abuse of process and will not be entertained by the Tribunal.

B and others worked for S Co. and believed themselves to be self-employed. S Co. agreed with this, but the Inland Revenue disagreed. B and his colleagues brought the application to test their status and subsequently appealed, after receiving a favourable decision from the industrial tribunal, in order to enhance the status of the decision. *Held,* that the appeal was an abuse of process and should not be entertained. There was no dispute between the parties to the appeal, and the one party with whom there was a genuine dispute, the Inland Revenue, was not a party.

BAKER *v.* SUPERITE TOOLS [1986] I.C.R. 189, E.A.T.

1166. Appeals—fresh evidence

[Industrial Tribunals (Rules of Procedure) Regulations 1985 (S.I. 1985 No. 16), r.10(1)(*d*)] Fresh evidence will only be admitted if its existence could not have reasonably been known or foreseen (*Bagga* v. *Heavy Electricals (India)* [1972] C.L.Y. 1223, *International Aviation Services U.K.* v. *Jones* [1979] C.L.Y. 863 doubted): BORDEN U.K. *v.* POTTER, *The Times,* May 3, 1986, E.A.T.

1167. Confidentiality—information acquired in course of business

An ex-employee may use confidential information acquired in the course of his previous employment, though not to the extent of memorising or recording such information during the course of the employment for the purpose of such use afterward.

P Co, who marketed fresh chickens employed D as its sales manager, employing a system suggested by D. D left P Co and set up a similar business in the same area employing a number of P Co's staff. There was no contractual agreement governing the activities of employees after ceasing employment. P Co.'s application for an injunction restraining D from using their confidential sales information was refused. *Held,* dismissing P Co.'s appeal, (1) an ex-employee did not owe the same duty of fidelity as an employee, and confidential information short of a trade secret was not protected, so long as the ex-employee had not abused his duty of fidelity whilst an employee by memorising or recording it then. Furthermore, such information short of a trade secret could not be protected by a restrictive covenant; (2) in considering whether information was a trade secret or the equivalent of a trade secret, the court should have regard to (a) the nature of the employment and the status of the employee, (b) the nature of the information, (c) whether the employer had stressed the confidentiality of the information to the employee and (d), whether the information could be isolated from other non-confidential information. In the circumstances, the sales information fell short of a trade secret and was not protected (*Herbert Morris* v. *Saxelby* [1916–17] All E.R. Rep. 317, *Printers and Finishers* v. *Holloway* [1964] All E.R. 736, *Worsley (E) & Co.* v. *Cooper* [1939] 1 All E.R. 290, *Robb* v. *Green* [1895–9] All E.R. Rep. 1053 and *Wessex Dairies* v. *Smith* [1935] All E.R. Rep. 75 considered).

FACCENDA CHICKEN *v.* FOWLER; FOWLER *v.* FACCENDA CHICKEN [1986] 1 All E.R. 617, C.A.

1168. Constructive dismissal—provision of safe system of work—whether reasonable precautions

[Employment Protection (Consolidation) Act 1978 (c.44), ss.55(2)(*c*); Health and Safety at Work Act 1974 (c.37), s.2(1).]

When an employee claims for constructive dismissal, having resigned due to inadequate safety precautions, the proper test is whether, objectively, the precautions on those which would have been taken by a reasonable employer.

P worked as a clerk in a building society agency. There were two armed robberies. The agency was protected by heavy glass, alarms, a steel plate and a dummy camera.

P resigned on the ground that she was too frightened to continue working there. She complained for constructive dismissal for failure to supply a safe system of work. The tribunal upheld this complaint on the ground that the precautions were inadequate. *Held,* allowing the employers' appeal, that the test was an objective one, whether the precautions were those which would have been taken by a reasonable employer, and the tribunal had erred in law.

DUTTON & CLARK *v.* DALY [1985] I.C.R. 780, E.A.T.

1169. Consultant surgeon—sole recommended applicant—whether right to employment
[National Health Service Act 1977 (c.49), Sched. 5, para. 10(1) as amended; National Health Service (Appointment of Consultants) Regulations 1982 (S.I. 1982 No. 276), reg. 8.] The statutory process provides a screening system to ensure that proper candidates are put before the authority, but the decision whether to employ any of such candidates is entirely that of the authority, ungoverned by any statutory criteria. Therefore the authority's decision in the instant case not to employ the only candidate recommended, but to re-advertise, was not susceptible to judicial review since the necessary statutory underpinning did not exist (*R.* v. *East Berkshire Health Authority, ex p. Walsh* [1984] C.L.Y. 14, *R.* v. *Secretary of State for the Home Department, ex p. Benwell* [1984] C.L.Y. 12, *R.* v. *Hertfordshire County Council, ex p. Nupe* [1985] C.L.Y. 1149 considered): R. *v.* TRENT REGIONAL HEALTH AUTHORITY, *ex p.* JONES, *The Times,* June 19, 1986, Macpherson J.

1170. Continuous employment—accumulation of short term contracts—whether global contracts—redundancy payments
A series of short term contracts for trawlermen do not give rise to a global employment contract entitling them to claim redundancy payments.

The applicants were trawlermen who had sailed exclusively for the employers for periods from 3 to 33 years, with voyages of several weeks interspersed with short periods of leave. Due to a decline in the industry the entire fleet was taken out of service. On their application for redundancy payments the tribunal found that the accumulation of short term contracts gave rise to a global contract which qualified them for redundancy. *Held,* allowing the appeal, that the tribunal had misdirected themselves, there was no evidence of a global contract of employment (*Dobie* v. *Burns International Security Services UK* [1984] C.L.Y. 1310 applied).

HELLYER BROTHERS *v.* McLEOD [1986] I.C.R. 122, E.A.T.

1171. Continuous employment—illegal agreement—effect
[Employment Protection (Consolidation) Act 1978 (c.44), s.64(1)(*a*) (as amended by Unfair Dismissal (Variation of Qualifying Period) Order 1979 (S.I. 1979 No. 959) art. 2).]

"Continuously employed" means continuously employed under a legal contract of employment.

H was employed from 1967 until dismissal on May 11, 1983. For four weeks in May and June 1982 he was paid a tax free lodging allowance to which he was not entitled and which was illegal. On H's application the Industrial Tribunal held that he had not been continuously legally employed for a period of one year ending with his dismissal and dismissed his application. *Held,* dismissing the appeal, that during the four week period when the lodging allowance was paid the contract of employment was illegal; "continuously employed" in s.64(1)(*a*) of the 1978 Act meant under a legal contract of employment so that H could not rely on that period in considering the year up to his dismissal; since the period when the illegality ended and the date of his dismissal was less than a year, the Industrial Tribunal's decision had been correct.

HYLAND *v.* BARKER (J. H.) (NORTH WEST) [1985] I.C.R. 861, E.A.T.

1172. Contract of employment—Church minister—inducted into full-time paid pastorate
A minister inducted into a full-time pastorate of the Presbyterian Church of Wales in accordance with the Book of Order and Rules of the church is not employed under a contract of employment.

D was an ordained minister of the Presbyterian Church of Wales. D was inducted pastor of the United Pastorate of Tabernacle, Whitchurch and Herman, Tongwynlais in October 1975 in accordance with the Book of Order and Rules of the Presbyterian Church in Wales. The pastorate was of indeterminate time and not subject to determination by notice. The book of rules provided for D to be paid a stipend and have a manse free of rent and rates from the Church's sustentation fund. Payments

were only made from the fund to the extent that resources permitted. D was dismissed from his pastorate after a visitation and disciplinary and other proceedings of the Church in accordance with the Rule Book. D claimed to be employed by the Church under a contract of employment and that he had been unfairly dismissed. D appealed against the decision of the Court of Appeal that there was no contract of employment. *Held*, dismissing the appeal, that it was possible for a person to carry out spiritual duties under a contract of employment but in the present case there was no contract between D and the Church. No contractual duties were imposed upon D, he devoted his whole life to his religion and had answered and accepted the call of the pastorate to attend their spiritual affairs. His duties were dictated by his conscience, not a contract. The Church was not contractually bound to pay a stipend to D and discharge the expenses of the manse. The Church was obligated to deal with its property in accordance with the trusts contained in the Book of Rules. The stipend was paid and manse made available to D in discharge of those obligations (*Methodist Conference (President of the)* v. *Parfitt* [1984] C.L.Y. 1241 followed, *Forbes* v. *Eden* (1867) L.R. 1 H.L. Sc. & Div. 508 considered).
DAVIES v. PRESBYTERIAN CHURCH OF WALES [1986] 1 W.L.R. 323, H.L.

1173. Contract of employment—collective agreement—binding in honour only—whether enforceable
Redundancy terms were contained in a collectively negotiated contract of employment, and were stated to be binding in honour only. *Held*, that it was fully legally binding (*Robertson* v. *British Gas Corp.* [1983] C.L.Y. 1213 applied): MARLEY v. FORWARD TRUST GROUP, *The Times*, July 1, 1986, C.A.

1174. Contract of employment—collective agreement—whether employee entitled to benefit of life assurance scheme
C's letter of employment with a local authority in Scotland stated that his post was subject to the Conditions of Service of the relevant National Joint Council, "and as supplemented by the Authorities' Rules and as amended from time to time." C claimed that his employers were bound in the terms of his contract of employment to provide a non-contributory life assurance scheme. One of the rules of the Authority stated that the employing Council had introduced a non-contributory life assurance scheme. *Held*, dismissing the action, that as a matter of construction the rules were to be regarded as made unilaterally by the employers notwithstanding consultations having taken place with a trade union; they were not rules which had been the subject of agreement between the employers and C and that they were not agreed rules. There was no limitation placed on the employers rights to vary, alter or cancel any of the provisions in the rule and it was within the contemplation of the parties that these rules might be altered. Accordingly the employers were entitled to alter the rules and C could not require them to provide him with the life assurance scheme: CADOUX v. CENTRAL REGIONAL COUNCIL [1986] I.R.L.R. 131, Court of Session (Lord Ross).

1175. Contract of employment—date of appointment—teacher
The date of appointment of a teacher is when he is first employed as such, not when a salary grade changes or ought to change: BRIDGEN v. LANCASHIRE COUNTY COUNCIL, *The Times*, February 8, 1986, E.A.T.

1176. Contract of employment—domestic disciplinary procedure—whether debarred by prior criminal proceedings
[Offences Against the Person Act 1861 (c. 100), s. 44, s. 45; Employment Protection (Consolidation) Act 1978 (c. 44), s. 57.] S was employed as a school keeper. In 1983 after a full hearing before a magistrate he was acquitted of a charge of an assault against a pupil. The school subsequently commenced disciplinary proceedings for misconduct against S which proceedings were not concluded. S brought this action for a declaration that the disciplinary proceedings commenced by the school or the continuation of those proceedings was unlawful and for an injunction restraining the school from continuing with the proceedings. The grounds relied upon by S were (i) that the disciplinary proceedings put him in double jeopardy; (ii) the staff code provided that where disciplinary proceedings took place after a conviction, the decision of the Court should not be questioned; (iii) the effect of a certificate under s. 44 of the Offences against the Person Act 1861 was to release S "from all further or other proceedings, civil or criminal, for the same cause" and it was submitted that the disciplinary proceedings were "other civil proceedings"; (iv) it

was submitted that it was unfair and oppressive for S to be subjected to identical proceedings after he had been exposed to the trouble and expense of a criminal trial, particularly where he might lose his job as a result. *Held,* rejecting the claim for a declaration and an injunction, that (1) the burden of proof in the disciplinary proceedings differs from that in the magistrates' court and therefore the question of double jeopardy did not apply as the disciplinary body was not a Court of competent jurisdiction; (2) whilst it is not unknown in civil litigation for a conviction to be treated as prima facie evidence, it was wrong to suggest that an acquittal cannot be challenged in disciplinary proceedings; (3) the effect of a certificate of acquittal was to release the defendant from "further or other proceedings" but this did not include matters coming before a domestic tribunal which should not be prevented from investigating such a matter; (4) whilst a court is entitled to interfere in order to protect the rights of an individual which have been infringed, the disciplinary hearing was not a trial and the school had an obligation by contract to conduct the enquiry. Their functions were quite different from the criminal proceedings. (*R. v. Hampshire County Council, ex p. Ellerton* [1985] C.L.Y. 1531; *D.P.P. v. Connolly* [1964] A.C. 1254; *D.P.P. v. Nasralla (Patrick)* [1967] C.L.Y. 706, applied; *R. v. British Broadcasting Corp., ex p. Lavelle* [1983] C.L.Y. 15, referred to): SAEED v. GREATER LONDON COUNCIL (INNER LONDON EDUCATION AUTHORITY) [1986] I.R.L.R. 23, POPPLEWELL J.

1177. Contract of employment—headmaster—disciplinary procedures—respective powers of Governors and Assistant Director of Education

[Education Act 1944 (c. 31) ss. 8, 17, 23, 24, 27.] H was employed as a headmaster. His views on the method of education to be adopted in a school with large numbers of children whose mother tongue was not English led him to a dispute with the school's Assistant Director of Education. The Assistant Director complained to the school Governors recommending H's dismissal. The Governors rejected the complaint and recommended reinstatement. The local education authority took the view that under the terms of the conditions of service for H, the Governors recommendation was not final and that the disciplinary procedure could continue. H issued a writ asking for a declaration that the disciplinary procedure had been exhausted and that his suspension should come to an end. At first instance the judge declared that H's suspension should come to an end and that he was entitled to resume his duties in that post forthwith and that the disciplinary proceedings which had been started against him had been exhausted. The local authority appealed to the Court of Appeal. *Held,* allowing the appeal; taking into account the statutory background of ss. 8 and 17 of the Education Act 1944 the proper construction of H's service contract was such that it cannot have been the intention that in all cases the recommendation of school Governors should be accepted. This was the case notwithstanding that such a construction might lead to the Assistant Director of Education becoming a Judge in his own cause. The Council were entitled to continue disciplinary proceedings against H on the allegations against him and they would have an inherent power to suspend him pending a final decision: HONEYFORD v. CITY OF BRADFORD METROPOLITAN COUNCIL [1986] I.R.L.R. 32, C.A.

1178. Contract of employment—illness of employee—dismissal—whether frustration

[Employment Protection (Consolidation) Act 1978 (c.44), s.50(1), Sched. 3, para. 3(3).]

Where it became apparent to both employer and employee that the employee would never again, through illness or incapacity, be able to perform his obligations under the contract, that was such a change in the mutual obligations of the parties that the doctrine of frustration applied and the employee was not entitled to be paid during any period of notice under the Employment Protection (Consolidation) Act 1978.

N had been employed by UE as a skilled workman since 1957 when in 1983 he suffered a heart attack. By 1984 it was clear that he would never be able to work again. The contract as such provided that he was entitled to no pay whilst absent from work through sickness. UE gave N 12 weeks' notice. N claimed sick pay under para. 3 of Sched. 3 to the 1978 Act. *Held,* that the doctrine of frustration applied when the mutual obligations of the parties had changed to such a significant degree as when N was no longer able ever again to work. The service of notice terminating N's contract of employment was otiose in that the contract had already been terminated by frustration when it became clear that N would never again be able to work. Mere service of the notice did not entitle N to payment during any period of notice and he was not entitled to sick pay (*Davis Contractors* v. *Fareham Urban District Council* [1956] C.L.Y. 874 applied; *Harman* v. *Flexible Lamps* [1980] C.L.Y. 1047 doubted).

NOTCUTT *v.* UNIVERSAL EQUIPMENT CO. (LONDON) [1986] 1 W.L.R. 641, C.A.

1179. Contract of employment—series of contracts—whether aggregation of hours worked

[Employment Protection (Consolidation) Act 1978 (c.44), Sched. 13, paras. 3, 9(1)(*b*).] P was employed as a teacher by D over a period of time under a series of different contracts, each relating to a particular college for the duration of the college term. Eventually D refused to renew P's contract. *Held*, on the question of whether P qualified by the length of her service under para. 3 of Sched. 13 to the Employment Protection (Consolidation) Act 1978, that the tribunal was entitled to aggregate the hours of work which P's various contracts of employment usually involved in any one week. The periods between terms, and therefore between periods of employment, did not break the continuity of her employment. Para. 9(1)(*b*) operated to preserve the continuity of her employment: SURREY COUNTY COUNCIL *v.* LEWIS (1986) 130 S.J. 785, C.A.

1180. Contract of employment—unilateral variation—whether the employee is entitled to damages for breach

K and W were employed by a local authority and for several years each had been entitled to receive essential car user allowances and the use of their own motor vehicles on council business. In 1984 the local authority informed both employees that the nature of their duties had been reviewed and that it was no longer considered that it was essential for them to have their own cars at their disposal whenever required. That being the case it was proposed that the essential user allowance would not be payable in the future. The alternative arrangements proposed were generally less advantageous than those previously enjoyed. Both employees issued a writ claiming an injunction restraining the local authority from implementing the proposed breach and also damages. At trial the judge concluded that the claims were well founded. He ordered the local authority to pay the two plaintiffs damages to be assessed. He further made a declaration in favour of the two employees that the withdrawal of their entitlement to essential car user allowances was in breach of their contract of employment and that they were essential car users and as such entitled to the appropriate allowances. *Held*, rejecting the appeal of the local authority, that on a proper construction of the language of the National Joint Council Conditions of Service for Administrative, Professional, Technical and Clerical Staff which were incorporated in both contracts of employment, employees either were or were not within the designated category of "essential users." If within the category of essential user the local authority did not have the right to withdraw the essential user allowance in the absence of a change in the nature of the duties of such employees. No such change was relied upon in these cases. Accordingly, the local authority were in breach of contract in purporting to withdraw the allowances in the case of both employees. The obligation to provide the allowances was capable of being discharged, but only either by agreement of the parties or because of a change in the nature of the duties: KEIR AND WILLIAMS *v.* HEREFORD AND WORCESTER COUNTY COUNCIL [1985] I.R.L.R. 505, C.A.

1181. Contributions to employees provident fund—service charge collected from hotel guests—whether employee's share "wages"

[Mal.] [Employees Provident Fund Act 1951 (Laws of Malaysia, Act 272, 1982 rev.), s.2(*a*).]

Where an employee's share of a service charge levied by hotel management is part of his contractual remuneration it may be "wages" such as to attract employee and employer contributions to a provident fund.

The Employees Provident Fund Act 1951 requires contributions to be made by both employees and employers in respect of wages paid to the employees. The hotel levied a compulsory 10 per cent. service charge which was distributed pro rata to the employees under the provisions of the contract of service negotiated by the employees' union. *Held*, on the question whether the share of service charge amounted to "wages" for the purpose of being liable to contributions, that the share of the service charge was remuneration to which the employee was entitled under his contract of service. Accordingly contributions had to be paid under the provisions of the 1951 Act.

PEREIRA *v.* HOTEL JAYAPURI BHD [1986] 1 W.L.R. 449, P.C.

1182. Covenant in restraint of trade. See TRADE AND INDUSTRY, § 3399.

1183. Defective equipment—whether "equipment" includes ship
[Employers' Liability (Defective Equipment) Act 1969 (c.37), s.1(1)(3).]
A ship is "equipment" for the purposes of an action by a crew member against his employer for damages due to defective equipment under the Employer's Liability (Defective Equipment) Act 1969.

D's ship sank with the loss of all hands. The estate of a crew member claimed damages under s.1 of the Employer's Liability (Defective Equipment) Act 1969 on the ground that the ship was unseaworthy. *Held,* on a preliminary issue whether the ship was "equipment" as opposed to a crew member's place of work, that if a train or an aircraft was "equipment", then it followed that a ship must be "equipment" as well.

COLTMAN *v.* BIBBY TANKERS; DERBYSHIRE THE [1986] 2 All E.R. 65, Sheen J.

1184. Dockyard Services Act 1986 (c.52)
This Act makes provision in connection with any arrangements that may be made by the Secretary of State for or with a view to the provision by contractors of certain dockyard services.

The Act received the Royal Assent on July 25, 1986.

1185. Effective date of termination—relevance of receipt of P45
[Employment Protection (Consolidation) Act 1978 (c.44), ss.55(2)(*a*), 55(4)(*b*)] W was dismissed from his job as a caretaker on February 9, 1983. He did not apply to an Industrial Tribunal until June 24, 1983. The Industrial Tribunal found that they had no jurisdiction to hear the claim. W appealed to the Employment Appeal Tribunal on the ground that he had not been effectively dismissed until he received his form P45 on June 27, 1983. The Employment Appeal Tribunal ordered that the case be remitted to the Industrial Tribunal for the point to be argued. The employers appealed to the Court of Appeal. *Held,* upholding the appeal, that the P45 has nothing whatever to do with the date on which the employment terminates. This is governed both by statute and case law and it is clear that the effective date of termination is the date on which W was summarily dismissed. The Employment Appeal Tribunal had been in error because of what was clearly a false point taken on the form P45: NEWHAM LONDON BOROUGH *v.* WARD [1985] I.R.L.R. 509, C.A.

1186. Employment Appeal Tribunal—costs—preliminary hearing
The Employment Appeal Tribunal is entitled to award costs in appropriate circumstances at preliminary hearings: RAVELIN *v.* BOURNEMOUTH BOROUGH COUNCIL, *The Times,* July 19, 1986, E.A.T.

1187. Employment protection
EMPLOYMENT PROTECTION (VARIATION OF LIMITS) ORDER 1986 (No. 2283) [80p], made under the Employment Protection (Consolidation) Act 1978 (c.44), ss.15(5), 122(6), 148, 154(3), 154(4), Sched. 14, paras. 8(2)–(4); operative on April 1, 1987; varies certain limits which are reviewable under s.148 of the 1978 Act.

1188. Equal opportunities—guidelines for employers operating in Northern Ireland
[U.S.A.] [Fair Employment (Northern Ireland) Act 1976 ss.(1)(1), 3(1), 12(1), 12(2), 16, 17.] NYCERS is a pension fund in New York. It sought to urge U.S. owned companies who operated in Northern Ireland to initiate or support shareholders' resolutions requiring the implementation of the MacBride Principles which were a set of equal opportunity guidelines. NYCERS sought a preliminary injunction requiring AB, a U.S. company operating a subsidiary in Northern Ireland, to circularise its members concerning their proposal before an Annual General Meeting. AB argued that the principles would entail unlawful positive discrimination against Protestants. This view was supported by an affidavit by the Industrial Development Board. *Held,* that it was probable that upon a full trial NYCERS could show that the principles could be legally implemented notwithstanding the affidavit filed by the Industrial Development Board. The Fair Employment (Northern Ireland) Act did not require an employer to ignore the religion of employees or potential employees or the religious composition of the workforce. The proposed principles did not require discrimination but development training programmes and affirmative

action similar to that already carried out by the Fair Employment Agency. Accordingly, NYCERS were granted a preliminary injunction prohibiting AB from seeking proxies from shareholders without informing them of the equal opportunity principles proposed and also requiring an additional mailing to be made to inform shareholders of the proposals made by NYCERS: NEW YORK CITY EMPLOYEES' RETIREMENT SYSTEMS *v.* AMERICAN BRAND [1986] I.R.L.R. 239, U.S. District Court.

1189. Equal pay—job evaluation study—whether required for defence
[Equal Pay Act 1970 (c.41), ss.1(2)(*c*), (3), 2A(2) as amended; Industrial Tribunals (Rules of Procedure) Regulations 1980 (S.I. 1980 No. 884), regs. 7A, 8.] It is not necessary in every case where the value of work is challenged for the employer to produce a job evaluation if either the employer produces evidence that the job does not require the same degree of skill or effort, or if the difference in pay is due to a material factor other than sex: FOREX NEPTUNE (OVERSEAS) *v.* MILLER, *The Times,* November 18, 1986, E.A.T.

1190. Equal pay—material difference—whether justified
[Equal Pay Act 1970 (c.41), s.1(3), Sex Discrimination Act 1975 (c.65), s.8(1).] H, a Health Board, wished to attract X, Y and Z, privately-employed prosthetists, to work for it, so it offered them salaries above the Whitley Council scale. They all happened to be men. G, a female prosthetist who was already working for the N.H.S., was employed by H at the Whitley Council rate. She claimed that she was being less favourably treated than X, Y and Z, within the meaning of s.1(3) of the Equal Pay Act 1970, as substituted by s.8(1) of the Sex Discrimination Act 1975. *Held,* that in the circumstances it was not unreasonable for X, Y and Z to be offered higher rates of pay, and that the circumstances of their employment amounted to a "material difference (other than the difference of sex) between [G's case and theirs]". G was therefore not entitled to claim an income equal to theirs: RAINEY *v.* GREATER GLASGOW HEALTH BOARD, *The Times,* November 28, 1986, H.L.

1191. Equal Pay—whether "equal pay" relates only to remuneration or terms and conditions of employment considered as a whole
[Equal Pay Act 1970 (c.41), ss.1(1), 1(2)(*c*), 1(3); EEC Treaty: Art. 119.] An Industrial Tribunal held that H, who was a canteen cook, was employed on work of equal value to that of her male comparators who were shipyard workers. It was accepted that H was not paid the same wage or overtime rates as the comparators but it was argued that she should not receive the same wage or overtime rates because, considered as a whole, her terms and conditions were not less favourable and it was sought to introduce evidence to that effect. The Industrial Tribunal deferred calculating an award pending an appeal on the point to the Employment Appeal Tribunal. For H it was submitted that once it was shown that she did work of equal value, she was entitled to point to specific terms in her contract of employment which were less favourable and have those terms amended accordingly and that it mattered not if, when all the other terms or conditions were considered, her position was better than the comparators. *Held,* the terms of s.1(2) of the Equal Pay Act 1970 were ambiguous and accordingly the court must apply Art. 119. Taking that course the Tribunal should look at the overall package (*Sorbie* v. *Trusthouse Forte Hotels* [1976] C.L.Y. 891, considered; *Bulmer (H. P.)* v. *Bollinger (J.) S.A.* [1974] C.L.Y. 1471, applied): HAYWARD *v.* CAMMELL LAIRD SHIPBUILDERS [1986] I.R.L.R., 287 E.A.T.

1192. Factories. See FACTORIES.

1193. Health and safety at work
BAKING AND SAUSAGE MAKING (CHRISTMAS AND NEW YEAR) REGULATIONS 1986 (No. 1709) [45p], made under the Health and Safety at Work etc. Act 1974 (c.37), s.15(1)(5)(*a*); operative on November 10, 1986; provide for a temporary exemption from statutory restrictions to enable women over 18 to be employed on specific Saturday afternoons and Sundays in December 1986 in baking and sausage making.
CLASSIFICATION, PACKAGING AND LABELLING OF DANGEROUS SUBSTANCES (AMENDMENT) REGULATIONS 1986 (No. 1922) [80p], made under the Health and Safety at Work etc. Act 1974 (c.37), ss.15(1)(4)(*a*)(6)(*b*), 82(3)(*a*); operative on December 9, 1986; amend S.I. 1984 No. 1244.
ELECTRICALLY OPERATED LIFTS (EEC REQUIREMENTS) REGULATIONS 1986 (No. 1500) [£1·90], made under the European Communities Act 1972 (c.68), s.2(2); operative on

September 30, 1986; implement Council Directive 84/528/EEC and 84/529/EEC as amended by Commission Directive 86/312/EEC in relation to electrical lifts.

HEALTH AND SAFETY (LOCAL GOVERNMENT) (CONSEQUENTIAL AMENDMENT) REGULATIONS 1986 (No. 294) [40p], amend S.I. 1977 No. 746 and S.I. 1984 No. 1902 as a consequence of the abolition of the GLC and the Metropolitan County Councils.

HEALTH AND SAFETY (MISCELLANEOUS FEES) REGULATIONS 1986 (No. 392) [£2·30], made under the Health and Safety at Work Etc. Act 1974 (c.37), ss.43(2)(4)(5)(6), 82(3)(*a*); operative on April 1, 1986; fix or determine fees payable to the Health and Safety Executive in respect of specified matters.

IONISING RADIATIONS (FEES FOR APPROVALS) REGULATIONS 1986 (No. 669) [80p], made under the Health and Safety at Work etc. Act 1974 (c.37), s.43(2)(4)(5)(6); operative on May 6, 1986; provide for the fixing and determination of fees to be paid to the Health and Safety Executive in respect of approvals of services and apparatus under S.I. 1985 No. 1333.

NOTIFICATION OF NEW SUBSTANCES (AMENDMENT) REGULATIONS 1986 (No. 890) [80p], made under the European Communities Act 1972 (c.68), s.2(2) and the Health and Safety at Work etc. Act 1974 (c.37), ss.2, 15(1)(2), Sched. 3, paras. 1(1)(*b*), (4), 15(1); operative on June 18, 1986; amend S.I. 1982 No. 1496 so as to provide a simplified notification procedure for new substances.

1194. Industrial training levy—double glazing units—whether installation "alteration" or "repair" of building

Industrial Training (Construction Board) Order (S.I. 1980 No. 1274) Sched. 1, para. 1(a)(*c*) (as amended by Industrial Training (Construction Board) Order 1964 (Amendment) Order 1982 (S.I. 1982 No. 922).]

The manufacture and installation of double glazing units is to be treated as just one activity the greater part of which amounts to the manufacture of components for the insulation of buildings rather than activities within the construction industry and thus does not amount to the alteration or repair of a building.

Each company was engaged in the manufacture and installation of double glazing units; each was assessed to industrial training levy by the CITB. Manufacture of the units was 40 per cent. of the selling price, and installation 20 per cent. thereof. *Held,* that neither company was engaged in activities of the construction industry, as neither could be said to be involved in the alteration or repair of buildings within the meaning of the 1980 Regulations. No industrial training levy was accordingly payable.

CONSTRUCTION INDUSTRY TRAINING BOARD *v.* CHILTERN INSULATIONS [1986] I.C.R. 394, Webster J.

1195. Industrial tribunal—adjournment—action in both industrial tribunal and High Court

An industrial tribunal need not adjourn a complaint of unfair dismissal when High Court proceedings are pending, but it should be extremely careful to have regard to the doctrine of *res judicata* when making findings of fact.

E was dismissed for breach of an implied term of his contract of employment to use his best endeavours to serve his employers. He claimed damages in the High Court for wrongful dismissal and complained of unfair dismissal to an industrial tribunal. The industrial tribunal refused to adjourn the hearing pending the outcome of the High Court action. *Held,* dismissing the employers' appeal, that the tribunal was entitled to reach that decision; it should, however, be extremely careful to have regard to the doctrine of *res judicata* when making findings of fact (*Green* v. *Hampshire County Council* [1980] C.L.Y. 933 considered).

AUTOMATIC SWITCHING *v.* BRUNET [1986] I.C.R. 542, E.A.T.

1196. Industrial tribunal—conflict of fact

[Industrial Tribunals (Rules of Procedure) Regulations (S.I. 1985 No. 16.] An Industrial Tribunal is placed in an impossible position if it is required to resolve a dispute of fact on the basis of written representations from both sides: TESCO STORES *v.* PATEL, *The Times,* March 15, 1986, E.A.T.

1197. Industrial tribunal—finding of fact—duty to decide

An industrial tribunal is under a duty to decide important issues of fact; it may not reach its ultimate decision on the basis of failure to reach a conclusion upon such a fact.

The industrial tribunal was unable to decide whether the employee was dismissed, as he claimed, or left of his own accord, as the employers claimed. They therefore dismissed the employee's claim, on the ground that he had failed to discharge the onus of showing that he had been dismissed. *Held,* allowing the employee's appeal, that the tribunal was under a duty to decide important issues of fact, and could not reach its ultimate decision on the basis of failure to reach a conclusion (*Bray* v. *Palmer* [1953] C.L.Y. 2472 and *Baker* v. *Market Harborough Industrial Co-operative Society* [1953] C.L.Y. 2473 applied).

Morris *v.* London Iron and Steel Co. [1986] I.C.R. 629, E.A.T.

1198. Industrial tribunal—interlocutory application review of decision—jurisdiction of chairman

[Industrial Tribunals (Rules of Procedure) Regulations 1980 (S.I. 1980 No. 884), reg. 2, Sched. I, rr.12(4), 13(2).]

A chairman of an industrial tribunal, sitting alone, has jurisdiction to make a further order for directions notwithstanding that the tribunal may already have made an order.

Prior to the hearing of N's complaint of unfair dismissal N obtained an order for directions from the tribunal; subsequently he sought a "review" from the chairman, who, sitting alone heard N's application and made a further order. He refused, however, to make an order for specific discovery as sought by N, who appealed. *Held,* that the chairman had jurisdiction to make the order sought and had reached the correct conclusion.

Nikitas *v.* Solihull Metropolitan Borough Council [1986] I.C.R. 291, E.A.T.

1199. Industrial tribunal—notice of hearing—date notice "sent" by post

[Industrial Tribunals (Rules of Procedure) Regulations 1985 (S.I. 1985 No. 16), Sched. 1, r.5.]

A notice of hearing is "sent" under r.5 of Sched. 1 to the Industrial Tribunal (Rules of Procedure) Regulations 1985 when it is received or deemed to have been received.

The industrial tribunal posted notice to the employers on March 21 of a hearing to take place on April 7. The letter was received on March 24. The employers argued that the tribunal had no jurisdiction to hear the case, there not being 14 days notice within r.5 of Sched. 1 to the Industrial Tribunal (Rules of Procedure) Regulations 1985. The tribunal held that "send" under rule 5 referred to the date of posting. *Held,* allowing the employers' appeal, that "send" under r.5 referred to the date when notice was received or deemed to have been received, and the tribunal lacked jurisdiction to hear the claim.

Derrybaa *v.* Castro-Blanco [1986] I.C.R. 546, E.A.T.

1200. Industrial tribunal—sex discrimination cases—discovery of application forms of candidates

[Sex Discrimination Act 1975 (c.65), s.7.]

Where a complainant alleges discrimination on grounds of sex in respect of an application for employment the industrial tribunal ought not to order discovery of the application forms of other candidates but should ensure the complainant is provided with the essential information contained in those forms to enable the complainant to have a fair hearing in every sense of the word.

W applied for a job at a children's home run by the respondent county council. The home was staffed exclusively by women. A short list of three men and four women was drawn up and after those applicants were interviewed a woman was appointed to the job. W claimed he had been discriminated against because of his sex and that the respondent ought to have discriminated positively in favour of appointing a man. W's claim was dismissed by the tribunal. Thereafter W made fresh applications for employment at the children's home all of which were unsuccessful. W made a number of complaints to the industrial tribunal alleging discrimination on grounds of sex. W sought further particulars of the respondent's answers which the tribunal refused to order. In reaching that decision the tribunal considered W's complaints and the respondent's answers but did not consider questionnaires completed by the respondent at W's request pursuant to s.74 of the Sex Discrimination Act 1975. W also sought an order for discovery of the application forms of the other candidates for employment by the respondent at the children's home. The tribunal ordered disclosure of photocopies of the application forms. W appealed against the decisions of the tribunal. *Held,* that s.7 of the Act provided a defence to a respondent against whom a charge of positive discrimination had been made. It did not give an applicant the right to require a respondent to discriminate positively in his favour. The dismissal of W's first claim could not be overturned. In deciding whether or not to order further particulars of the respondent's answer the tribunal ought to have regard to the questionnnaires completed by the respondent. The order refusing further particulars should be set aside and the matter remitted to the tribunal for further consideration. It was quite wrong to order the disclosure in the process of discovery of personal information given in confidence to an employer by a candidate in competition with the applicant for the job in question. The applicant was entitled to know about the qualifications, work experience, age and sex of the other candidates for the job. The industrial tribunal must maintain a balance between the maintenance of the confidence and trust between potential employees and the employer and the necessary information to be supplied to the applicant so as to ensure a fair hearing in every sense of the word. The essential information should be extracted from the application form held by the respondent and given to the applicant in a separate document that could be checked by the tribunal against the application forms if so required. The information given should not permit the identification of the candidate concerned. The order for photocopies of the application forms should be set aside.

WILLIAMS *v.* DYFED COUNTY COUNCIL [1986] I.C.R. 449, E.A.T.

1201. Industrial tribunal—striking out—lapse of time
[Industrial Tribunals (Rules of Procedure) Regulations 1980 (S.I. 1980 No. 884), Sched. 1, r.12(2)(*b*).]

Proceedings before industrial tribunals are swift, and will not tolerate the leisurely approach to litigation which obtains in the High Court.

E was dismissed on October 26, 1984 and complained to an industrial tribunal of unfair dismissal. D Co. entered an appearance on November 19. In January 1985 just before the hearing, E was granted an adjournment with a view to settlement. In April the tribunal asked for information about the current position and received no reply. On July 2 E was directed to show cause why the complaint should not be struck out for want of prosecution. On July 15 the application was struck out pursuant to r.12(2)(*b*) of Sched. 1 to the Industrial Tribunals (Rules of Procedure) Regulations 1980. *Held,* dismissing E's appeal, that proceedings before industrial tribunals were swift and would not tolerate the leisurely approach to litigation which obtained in the High Court.

O'SHEA *v.* IMMEDIATE SOUND SERVICES [1986] I.C.R. 598, E.A.T.

1202. Job Release Act 1977—continuation
JOB RELEASE ACT 1977 (CONTINUATION) ORDER 1986 (No. 1291) [45p], made under the Job Release Act 1977 (c.8), s.1(4)(*b*); operative on September 30, 1986; s.1 of the 1977 is to continue in force until September 29, 1987.

1203. Judicial review—disciplinary procedure—whether available when other avenue of appeal is open
[Police Act 1964 (c.48), s.37, Police (Discipline) Regulations 1977 (S.I. 1977 No. 580), reg. 7.] Five police officers were found guilty of disciplinary offences by their Chief Constable. They were dismissed from the force or required to retire. Their dismissal took place some three years after the incident alleged against them. The officers were not informed that an investigation was taking place into their conduct for a period of two and a half years from the date of the incident. A statutory right of appeal to the Secretary of State existed but the officers sought judicial review of the Chief Constable's decision as an alternative. The Divisional Court held that although judicial review might be the appropriate remedy after the appeal had been heard and determined by the Secretary of State, the five officers were premature in their application. An appeal was made from this decision to the Court of Appeal. *Held,* granting the appeal, that Regulation 7 of the Police (Discipline) Regulations 1977 required an investigating officer to inform the officers of the investigation "as soon as is practicable." The operation of this regulation is an essential protection for police officers facing disciplinary charges and, save in the rare case when an investigation would be prejudiced by the giving of that notice, it would be difficult to justify any appreciable delay. There had been far too much delay in this case. Whilst the general rule was that judicial review should not arise where other appeal procedures are provided by Parliament, the present case illustrated circumstances in which it would be appropriate to subject such a decision to judicial review. This had been so serious a departure from the police disciplinary procedure that the Court

should, in the exercise of its discretion, grant a review. It was emphasised that this was an exceptional case and that normally an applicant would be left to pursue the alternative remedy available to him (*R.* v. *Paddington Valuation Officer, ex p. Peachy Corporation (No. 2)* [1965] C.L.Y. 3337 considered): CALVELEY v. MERSEYSIDE POLICE [1986] I.R.L.R. 177, C.A.

1204. Lock-out—definition
[Employment Protection (Consolidation) Act 1978 (c.44), Sched. 13, para. 24.] For there to be a "lockout" within para. 24 of Sched. 13 of the Employment Protection (Consolidation) Act 1978, it is not necessary for the employer to be acting in breach of contract: EXPRESS AND STAR v. BUNDAY, *The Times,* October 20, 1986, E.A.T.

1205. Maternity pay
STATUTORY MATERNITY PAY (GENERAL) REGULATIONS 1986 (No. 1960) [£2·90], made under The Social Security Act 1986 (c.50), ss.46(4), (7) and (8), 47(1), (3), (6) and (7), 48(3), (6), 50(1), (2), (4) and (5), 51(1)(*g*), (*k*), (*n*) and (*r*), 54(1), 83(1), 84(1) and Sched. 4, paras. 6, 8 and 12(3); operative on March 15, 1987 as to regs. 1, 22 and 23, and on April 6, 1987 as to the remainder; provide for statutory maternity pay.

1206. Notice period—date of commencement
Seven days' notice of dismissal means seven days exclusive of a day on which work had been done, so an employee orally dismissed with one week's notice can count on the day after she is told to leave as the first day of her notice: WEST v. KNEELS, *The Times,* July 10, 1986, E.A.T.

1207. Pay statements—particulars to be included—obligation
[Employment Protection (Consolidation) Act 1978 (c. 44), ss. 8, 11(1)(8).]
Section 8 of the Employment Protection (Consolidation) Act 1978 creates an inherent right in an employee to an itemised pay statement, whether or not the employee asks for such a statement at the time of payment.
P had never been given, nor had she asked for, an itemised pay statement. On her dismissal she applied to an industrial tribunal under s. 11(1) of the Employment Protection (Consolidation) Act 1978 to determine what particulars should have been included to comply with s. 8. The tribunal refused on the ground her right to such a statement had not been denied her, since she never asked for one. *Held,* allowing P's appeal, that s. 8 created an inherent right, and an obligation on the employers, with which they had failed to comply.
COALES v. WOOD (JOHN) & CO.]1986] I.C.R. 71, E.A.T.

1208. Payment of salary—local authority's decision to withhold—whether reasonable
On March 7, 1985 trade unions took strike action in support of a particular cause. The applicants to the court were members of the National Union of Teachers and officers of its Liverpool division. That union, after a ballot, decided not to participate in the day of action. Many of its members reported for work but they found that their schools were closed because caretakers had participated in the day of action. Those teachers who reported for work signed a register to indicate that they had so done and that register was passed by the appropriate head teacher, to the respondent's education department. The two applicants complained about a decision of the local authority that only those who worked on March 7, 1985 should be paid for that day. The Court decided as a preliminary point that the second applicant, who was a branch secretary of the Liverpool division of the National Union of Teachers did have *locus standi* to bring the claim and also that the issue was justiciable. Correspondence before the court made it clear that those who were willing and able to work and reported as such, but who were prevented from working by the activities of other trade unionist, were not to be paid. Such a decision was wholly unreasonable and would be quashed. A date was specified by which all payments to which there was an entitlement should be paid with liberty to apply: R. v. LIVERPOOL CITY CORPORATION, *ex p.* FERGUSON AND FERGUSON [1985] I.R.L.R. 501, D.C.

1209. Racial discrimination—academic qualifications—whether detrimental
[Race Relations Act 1976 (c.74), ss.1(1)(*b*), 4(1).]
To insist on 'O' level English as a job qualification is prima facie discriminatory against foreigners; but such discrimination may be justified on the grounds of being irrespective of race, or of not amounting to a detriment.

P was a 44-year-old Asian woman who had not obtained 'O' level English Language. She had sufficient fluency and ability to obtain the qualification if she was prepared to sit the examination, but she was not. She applied for a job as a clerical officer with the D.H.S.S. 'O' level English Language is an essential qualification for a clerical officer with the Civil Service. P was rejected. She claimed that such a requirement was indirect discrimination on the grounds of race. The tribunal found (1), that Asians were not inherently less able to obtain the qualification, and the requirement was not discriminatory; (2), even if it was, it was justifiable irrespective of race within s.1(1)(*b*)(ii) and did not amount to a detriment within s.1(1)(*b*)(iii). *Held,* dismissing P's appeal, (1) that the tribunal was wrong in finding that the requirement was not discriminatory, but that (2) the tribunal was entitled to find that the requirement was justifiable irrespective of race and did not amount to a detriment.

RAVAL *v.* D.H.S.S. [1985] I.C.R. 685, E.A.T.

1210. Racial discrimination—British ship sailing outside territorial waters—recruitment of crew—whether "establishment in Great Britain"

[Race Relations Act 1976 (c.74), ss.4(1), 8(1)(2), 14(1)(4).]

The question whether a place of employment is "an establishment in Great Britain" is to be answered by examining where the parties contemplated the employment would take place.

The respondents undertook to act as a recruiting agency for crew for the SS. *Uganda,* a British ship which was requisitioned, to go to the Falklands as a hospital ship. The crew were to fly to Gibraltar to join the ship, and then to fly back from there at the end of her Falkland service. The applicants who were Somali seamen were turned down on racial grounds. The applicants complained of discrimination, and before the hearing the SS. *Uganda* did in fact sail into Southampton. The tribunal dismissed their claim holding that the ship was not "an establishment in Great Britain" in the contemplation of the parties. *Held,* dismissing the appeal, that the question had to be determined by reference to what was contemplated by the parties to be the intended place of work; since it was never contemplated that the ship would enter territorial waters, the discrimination was lawful.

DERIA *v.* GENERAL COUNCIL OF BRITISH SHIPPING [1986] I.C.R. 172, C.A.

1211. Racial discrimination—complaints to tribunals

The Commission for Racial Equality has published a research report which discusses the position of *Industrial Tribunal Applicants under the Race Relations Act 1976.* Copies of the report are available, free of charge, from the Commission for Racial Equality, Eliot House, 10/12 Allington Street, London SW1E 5EH.

1212. Racial discrimination—language—characteristics of racial group

[Race Relations Act 1976 (c.74) s.1.] An applicant for a job in Wales was turned down because she could not speak Welsh. *Held,* that she had not been unlawfully discriminated against under s.1 of the Race Relations Act 1976. It was wrong in law to use language alone to define a racial group: the Welsh-speaking Welsh were therefore not a distinct ethnic group (*Manla* v. *Dowell Lee,* [1983] C.L.Y. 1163 applied): GWYNEDD COUNTY COUNCIL *v.* JONES, *The Times,* July 28, 1986, E.A.T.

1213. Racial discrimination—racial insult—whether capable of being "detriment"

[Race Relations Act 1976 (c.74), s.4(2)(*c*).]

Where an employee is subjected to a racial insult at her place of work there is no unlawful racial discrimination unless in consequence she is disadvantaged in the circumstances in which she has to work.

S was a coloured woman employed by the respondent as a secretary/personal assistant. She overheard the manager telling K, another employee, to give some typing to "the wog". She complained that she had been subjected to unlawful discrimination. Although the incident concerning the insult was not one of the matters specifically complained of, it was put forward as evidence of racial prejudice. The tribunal considered the insult and found that someone had said "give the typing to the wog" but were unable to find whether it was the manager or K. The tribunal concluded that there was an element of racial prejudice at S's place of work. The industrial tribunal dismissed the complaint. S appealed to the Employment Appeal Tribunal where the sole question related to the racial insult. The E.A.T. held it was impossible to say that the use of the phrase "the wog," deplorable though it was, could properly be described as a detriment. *Held,* dismissing S's appeal, that s.4(2) of the Racial Discrimination Act 1976 provided by para. (*c*) that it was unlawful for a person to discriminate against an employee by "subjecting him to any other detriment". Before the employee could be said to be subjected to some "other detriment" the tribunal must find that by reason of the acts complained of a reasonable worker would or might take the view that he had been disadvantaged in the circumstances in which he had to work. To racially insult the employee was not enough by itself even though it might cause distress. By virtue of s.32 the Act the employer was liable, whether the employee who caused the disadvantage to the employee was of managerial status or not. "Detriment" was not limited to dismissal or disciplinary action by the employer or some action by the employee, such as leaving the employment or seeking a transfer to another department, but included the employee continuing to work and put up with the harassment. S could not be said to have been "treated" less favourably by the person who used the phrase "the wog" unless that person intended her to hear it or knew or ought reasonably to have known that it would be passed on to her or that she would become aware of it. There were no findings of fact to that extent nor any findings that the complainant was disadvantaged. The complaint was bound to fail (*Ministry of Defence* v. *Jeremiah* [1980] C.L.Y. 967, *Kirby* v. *Manpower Services Commission* [1980] C.L.Y. 950, *B.L. Cars* v. *Brown* [1983] C.L.Y. 1260, *Porcelli* v. *Strathclyde Regional Council* [1985] C.L.Y. 1221 considered).

DE SOUZA *v.* AUTOMOBILE ASSOCIATION [1986] I.C.R. 514, C.A.

1214. Racial discrimination—residence—membership of political party
[Race Relations Act 1976 (c.74), s.1(1)(*b*).] It is a rule of the Labour Party that only those who have been resident in Great Britain for one year are eligible for party membership. P, a resident of Northern Ireland, sought a job with the Party as a research assistant, but was refused for not fulfilling this requirement. *Held,* that the requirement was not discriminatory within s.1(1)(*b*)(i) of the Race Relations Act 1976, but that even if it were, it would be justifiable under s.1(1)(*b*)(ii) to demand that research assistants to a political party and constituency agents were party members: MCALISTER *v.* LABOUR PARTY, *The Times,* June 5, 1986, E.A.T.

1215. Racial discrimination—Sikh—protective headgear requirement—whether justifiable
[Race Relations Act 1976 (c.74), s.1(1)(*b*)(ii).]
The requirement that all personnel, including Sikhs, wear protective headgear in a repair shop is not unlawful discrimination.
The applicant, a Sikh, worked in the carriage repair shop. In 1983 for safety reasons the employers introduced a requirement that safety headgear should be worn. The applicant was unable to wear the hard hat over his turban, and was forced to take less well-paid work. On his application, the tribunal found that it was discriminatory, but justified and dismissed the complaint. *Held,* dismissing the appeal, that the tribunal were entitled to take into account all the matters they had, and their decision was not perverse.
SINGH *v.* BRITISH RAIL ENGINEERING [1986] I.C.R. 22, E.A.T.

1216. Racial discrimination—union pressure—inference of discrimination
[Race Relations Act 1976 (c.74), ss.1(1)(*a*), 4(2)(*b*), 58(5).]
A coloured road sweeper, E, employed by the council was given a temporary appointment as a refuse collector by R, a council officer. Officials of E's trade union at a meeting with R objected to the appointment ostensibly on the ground that because of E's attendance record, the appointment was in breach of a collective agreement. R revoked the appointment. The Commission interviewed R who said he thought the true reason for the union objection was E's colour; that R did not want to jeopardise the collective agreement since union action was an implicit threat if E were appointed; that R reluctantly stopped E getting the job. The Commission purporting to give notice under s.58(5)(*a*) of the 1976 Act wrote to the council warning of the discrimination and thereafter, despite the council's representations, served a non-discrimination notice under s.58. The council applied for judicial review to quash the notice. At the hearing it was conceded by the commission that it accepted what R had said and it was not disputed that R himself was in no way racially prejudiced. The judge dismissed the application. *Held,* dismissing the appeal that (1) there was material which could satisfy the commission and entitle it to infer that R had discriminated against E by bowing to industrial pressure and treating E as he would not have treated him had he been white; (2) the concession was limited to

the acceptance of R's evidence and was not directed to the reason given by R to E for the withdrawal of the appointment; the council knew that the commission did not accept that E's record was the reason for the withdrawal, and it had not therefore acted in breach of the rules of natural justice or unfairly in failing to give R separate notification of the intention to serve a notice on the council naming him.

R. *v.* COMMISSION FOR RACIAL EQUALITY, *ex p.* WESTMINSTER CITY COUNCIL [1985] I.C.R. 827, C.A.

1217. Redundancy—consultation with union—protective award
[Employment Protection Act 1975 (c.71), ss.99(1), 101(1), (4), (5).] The period of a protective award where the employer had failed to consult a trade union started at the date when the proposed dismissals took effect, not when the first actual dismissal was made. Leave to appeal was granted (*Green and Son (Castings)* v. *ASTMS* [1984] C.L.Y. 1264 approved, *G.K.N. Sankey* v. *National Society of Motor Mechanics* [1980] C.L.Y. 954 not followed): T.G.W.U. *v.* LEDBURY PRESERVES (1928), *The Times,* July 24, 1986, E.A.T.

1218. Redundancy—continuing work after receipt of pension—dismissal—entitlement to redundancy payment—notice
[Redundancy Payments Pensions Regulations 1965 (S.I. 1965 No. 1932), regs. 4(1), 5(1)(*a*).]
The Redundancy Payments Pensions Regulations 1965 are not excluded because an employee has enjoyed pension rights prior to the actual termination of his employment.
Under a superannuation scheme, employees reaching 60 who wished to continue working could take their pension immediately or at 65. The employee chose to take his pension at 60 in January 1981. In March 1984 he was dismissed and applied for a redundancy payment; the employers gave notice that his right to a payment was excluded. The tribunal found that the relevant regulations did not apply where an employee had been in receipt of pension prior to the termination of his employment. *Held,* allowing the appeal, that the tribunal had erred in deciding that the Regulations were excluded because the employee had enjoyed his pension rights before employment actually ended.
BRITISH TELECOMMUNICATIONS *v.* BURWELL [1986] I.C.R. 35, E.A.T.

1219. Redundancy—disabled employee
[Disabled Persons (Employment) Act 1944 (c.10), s.9(5).]
An employer must, before he dismisses an employee who is registered as disabled, consider the employee's personal circumstances before he decides that he has reasonable cause.
P was a registered disabled person. He was a skilled inspector with G.E.C. A redundancy situation arose. There was a screening operation after which P together with a number of employees, some of whom were more capable, some less, were dismissed for redundancy. The employers did not assess the position with particular reference to a registered disabled person. P complained for unfair dismissal. The tribunal found in favour of the employers, on the ground that they had reasonable cause to dismiss for reasons unconnected with P's disability. *Held,* allowing P's appeal, that the employers, and also the tribunal should have first considered P's personal circumstances, and the case would be remitted to a fresh tribunal (*Seymour* v. *British Airways Board* [1983] C.L.Y. 1322 applied).
HOBSON *v.* G.E.C. TELECOMMUNICATIONS [1985] I.C.R. 777, E.A.T.

1220. Redundancy—local government privatisation—property transfer order—whether compensation
[London Government Act 1963 (c.33), s.23(2)] The GLC employed P as a gardener at property which was later transferred to Wandsworth London Borough Council; P continued to do the same job. In 1983, Wandsworth decided to privatise its gardening services, and P was made redundant. He claimed that his loss of employment was attributable to the making of a property transfer order under s.23(2) of the London Government Act 1963, and that he was entitled to compensation. *Held,* that his loss of employment was entirely due to Wandsworth's need to economise, and its decision to employ private contractors: it had nothing to do with the 1963 Act: FLEMING *v.* WANDSWORTH LONDON BOROUGH COUNCIL, *The Times,* December 23, 1985, C.A.

1221. Redundancy—necessity to consult within a group of companies

[Employment Protection (Consolidation) Act 1978 (c.44), s.57(3).] S was employed by a subsidiary of a large group of companies. He was dismissed by reason of redundancy but no enquiries about alternative job opportunities for him were made within the group. The Industrial Tribunal found the dismissal unfair relying in particular on the authority of *Vokes* v. *Bear*. The employers appealed to the Employment Appeal Tribunal. *Held,* allowing the appeal, that the Industrial Tribunal had not distinguished between lack of consultation on the one hand and failure to look for job opportunities elsewhere within the group on the other hand. The argument of the Industrial Tribunal was so closely intertwined as to make it impossible to sever. Both influences contributed to the Industrial Tribunal's conclusion but the failure to enquire within the group contributed to it a good deal more powerfully than their views on the absence of consultation. It was an error of law on the Tribunal's part to treat *Vokes* v. *Bear* as virtually conclusive of unfairness. That case did not give rise to any principle that was binding upon them or force them into a conclusion upon any similar facts basis. The claim was remitted to be heard afresh by a different Industrial Tribunal (*Vokes* v. *Bear* [1984] C.L.Y. 1338, not followed, *Dobie* v. *Burns International Security Services (UK)* [1984] C.L.Y. 1310, followed): MDH *v.* SUSSEX [1986] I.R.L.R. 123, E.A.T.

1222. Redundancy—offer of alternative employment—whether in writing and whether sufficient

[Employment Protection (Consolidation) Act 1978 (c.44), ss.84(5)(*b*), 84(5)(*d*) and 84(6)(*b*).] M was made redundant on February 11, 1983 but offered alternative employment on a six-month trial basis. This was accepted. At the end of that period the employers extended the trial period by a further six months. M accepted this extension. M did not attain the standard which the employers expected of him and in the course of the extension period, they terminated his employment. He was declared redundant from his original job. M was paid the monies to which he was entitled in that respect. An Industrial Tribunal found that he had been fairly dismissed. M appealed to the Employment Appeal Tribunal. *Held,* rejecting the appeal, that the offer of alternative employment was contained in a letter dated February 11, 1983 written by the employers to M. It was countersigned by M on that date. There was no doubt that this indicated that he accepted those terms. The extension beyond the first six months was the subject of another letter from the employers to M dated August 22, 1983. M did not countersign that letter but the Industrial Tribunal found as a fact that he accepted its terms and worked in accordance with it until November 29, 1983. The requirement of s.84(5) that such an offer must be "in writing" means that a unilateral document signed only by the employer would be insufficient. The employee must do something to indicate acceptance. M had done this in the present case by countersigning the first letter. Although he had not countersigned the second letter, the two documents could be read together. The latter document specifically referred back to the former. Moreover M had accepted its terms and worked in accordance with it. This did constitute an agreement in writing as required by s.84(5)(*b*). It was not necessary for such a letter to contain all the particulars which an employer is bound to give under s.1 of the 1978 Act. The appeal was dismissed: McKINDLEY *v.* HILL (WILLIAM) (SCOTLAND) [1985] I.R.L.R. 492, E.A.T.

1223. Redundancy—re-engagement—pregnancy

[Employment Protection (Consolidation) Act 1978 (c.44), s.60(1).] S.60 of the Employment Protection (Consolidation) Act 1978 renders dismissal on the ground of pregnancy unfair. P was made redundant, and was not re-engaged because she would have been on maternity leave at the start of her contract. *Held,* that s.60 applied to dismissal, but not to re-engagement: STOCKTON-ON-TEES BOROUGH COUNCIL *v.* BROWN, *The Times,* August 18, 1986, E.A.T.

1224. Redundancy—re-engagement by associated company—whether employee dismissed

[Employment Protection (Consolidation) Act 1978 (c.44), s.84(1).]

In s.84(1) of the Employment Protection (Consolidation) Act 1978 the phrase "his employer" includes for any employee an associated employer of the company last employing him which has no employees at the time when it offers employment, and thus an offer of employment by such a company precludes redundancy.

L and his co-applicant were directors of J Co., which went into liquidation. They caused a dormant company, which was associated with J Co., to be re-activated and offered themselves and their workforce re-employment, contending that they had been dismissed by J Co., and were thus entitled to redundancy payments. *Held,* that s.84(1) of the 1978 Act had been satisfied because an associated company, which had no employees when it made an offer of employment, was within the meaning of the phrase "his employer" as used in s.84(1). Thus L was not dismissed by J Co. and was not entitled to any redundancy payment.

Lucas *v.* Henry Johnson (Packers & Shippers) [1968] I.C.R. 384, E.A.T.

1225. Redundancy—selection for redundancy

[Employment Protection (Consolidation) Act 1978 (c.44), s.57(3) (as amended by Employment Act 1980 (c.42), s.6).]

In considering whether objective criteria for selection for redundancy have been established it is necessary to consider good industrial practice.

D and others were foremen in RR's car division. Following consultations RR decided to select foremen for redundancy on the basis of an assessment of them by departmental managers under the headings experience, capability, flexibility and future career and prospects. After discussion of those criteria at meetings the managers conducted the assessment and dismissed D and others. On their complaint of unfair dismissal the Industrial Tribunal held that since the managers had not been given written guidelines about the selection, RR had failed to establish objective criteria for selection and the dismissals were unfair under s.57(3) of the 1978 Act. *Held,* allowing RR's appeal, that the Industrial Tribunal ought to have considered the selection procedure in the light of good industrial practice and then considered whether the dismissals were unfair instead of holding that the failure to establish objective criteria made the dismissals unfair. *Per curiam*: in *Williams* v. *Compair Maxam* [1982] C.L.Y. 1122, the E.A.T. did not lay down the rules for selection for redundancy which, if breached, gave rise to a claim for unfair dismissal.

Rolls Royce Motors *v.* Dewhurst [1985] I.C.R. 869, E.A.T.

1226. Redundancy—selection for redundancy—criteria for selection—failure to consult

[Employment Protection (Consolidation) Act 1978 (c.44), s.57(3).] G, an upholsterer, was dismissed for redundancy. One of the criteria relied upon by his employers was "the attitude of the persons evaluated to their work." This was a criterion which had been agreed with the recognised union. G was selected for redundancy principally because of his attitude to work and his use of bad language. The quality of his work was also taken into account. When it was decided that G should be dismissed, he was called to a meeting without any prior warning and told that he was to be made redundant. He was not given a opportunity of consultation on the issue of his redundancy. An Industrial Tribunal found the dismissal to be fair. The criterion, unusual though it was, was said to be fair having regard to the fact that it had been agreed with the union. On the second ground relating to the lack of consultation, it was conceded that this was a procedural fault but it was immaterial, because even if consultation had taken place, it would not possibly have made any difference. G appealed to the Employment Appeal Tribunal. *Held,* upholding the appeal, that the Industrial Tribunal had reached a perverse decision. Whilst the Employment Appeal Tribunal were not willing to go the length of saying that no reasonable Tribunal could have found that the criterion relating to attitude was acceptable, the decision that consultation would have made no difference was startling and unsupportable. The decision of the Industrial Tribunal was set aside and there was substituted for it a declaration that G was unfairly selected for redundancy. The claim was remitted to the Industrial Tribunal to consider the question of remedy: Graham *v.* ABF [1986] I.R.L.R. 90, E.A.T.

1227. Redundancy—selection for redundancy—effect of lack of consultation

[Employment Protection (Consolidation) Act 1978 (c.44), ss.57(3).] H was one of 33 employees dismissed by reason of redundancy without any prior notification or consultation. An Industrial Tribunal held, the Chairman dissenting, that the dismissal was fair. They found that the selection criteria were reasonable that it was not reasonably practicable for management to consult and consultation would have made no difference. H appealed to the Employment Appeal Tribunal. *Held,* that although no Court has ever gone so far as to hold that consultation is so essential that the absence of it will render any dismissal unfair automatically, in this case there were no cogent reasons for denying consultation which could have been arranged. There must have been a sporting chance that H could have pointed to her own good performance record, her experience and her age and seniority as factors in favour of her retention to persuade management to take her name off the redundancy list and the majority of the Industrial Tribunal, in allowing themselves to be influenced by a presumed need for secrecy, went beyond the bounds of permissible speculation. The Employment Appeal Tribunal substituted a finding of unfair dismissal and directed that the claim be restored to the Industrial Tribunal to assess the appropriate remedy (*Payne* v. *Spook Erection* [1984] C.L.Y. 1291 applied, *Williams* v. *Compair Maxam* [1982] C.L.Y. 1122 referred to): HOLDEN *v.* BRADVILLE [1985] I.R.L.R. 483, E.A.T.

1228. Redundancy—selection for redundancy—effect of lack of consultation

[Employment Protection (Consolidation) Act 1978 (c.44), ss.57(3).] G, a trainee quantity surveyor was dismissed by reason of redundancy. The Tribunal found that the employers selected on the basis of capability, reliability, conduct and service which criteria were applied to all employees and the reason for the dismissal was a genuine redundancy. By a majority, an Industrial Tribunal held the dismissal unfair for three reasons which were: (i) lack of notice of prior consultation, (ii) inadequate consideration of the point that G although employed within a roofing department was a general surveyor, and (iii) the employers had acted unfairly in dismissing G at a crucial stage in his career. The employers appealed to the Employment Appeal Tribunal. *Held,* sustaining the appeal, that (1) notwithstanding that there had been discrimination between G and his trade union colleagues on the question of consultation, they having been consulted whilst he was not, it would still be a proper cause open to a reasonable employer to have selected G for redundancy. The method of selection applied had been fair and the only effect of consultation would have involved a departure from that method; (2) the ground that G was employed as a general surveyor was not relied upon in the originating application and the majority were not entitled to rely upon it as a reason for holding the selection for redundancy based upon accepted criteria as being unfair; and (3) the facts did not suggest that G had been dismissed at too crucial a stage in his career; however, once it is accepted that the basis of selection was capability, reliability, conduct and service and that such a basis was a fair one and applied to the entire workforce including trainees this ground ceases to have relevance in deciding whether the appellants had acted reasonably within the meaning of s.57(3). The Employment Appeal Tribunal also upheld an appeal against the level of compensation being assessed at six months net pay and bonus on the grounds that it was arbitrary and unrelated to any estimated period of legitimate unemployment brought about by the dismissal (*Atkinson* v. *Lindsay (George) & Co.* [1980] C.L.Y. 962 referred to): LAFFERTY (F.) CONSTRUCTION *v.* DUTHIE [1985] I.R.L.R. 487, E.A.T.

1229. Redundancy—short-time working—piecework available but no agreement as to rate of pay—whether work "provided"

[Employment Protection (Consolidation) Act 1978 (c.44), s.87.]

Where work was made available to an employee on a piecework basis but the employee failed to agree a rate of pay for the work with the employer the employee was "provided" with work for the purposes of s.87 of the Employment Protection (Consolidation) Act 1978 (redundancy on account of employer's failure to provide work).

T was employed by S on a piecework basis as a metal polisher. Work was short and an associated company decided to send its polishing work to S. S and T could not agree a rate of pay at which T would do the work. In consequence T went on short-time. The work was carried out elsewhere at a lower rate of pay than T had been offered. T served a notice on S claiming that he had been laid off for four weeks and thus entitled to redundancy pay. The industrial tribunal held that T had been on short-time work and that the work he refused to do could not have been provided for him in the absence of any agreement as to the rate of pay. In consequence T was entitled to a redundancy payment pursuant to the provisions of s.87 of the Employment Protection (Consolidation) Act 1978. *Held,* allowing S's appeal, that an employee was entitled to a redundancy payment pursuant to s.87 of the Act where he was on short-time work for four consecutive weeks as a result of the failure of his employer to provide work for him. S.87 of the Act says nothing about pay for the work, it merely relates to "work of the kind which he is employed to do." T was provided with work of a kind he was employed to do but refused to do it. In consequence he was not entitled to a redundancy payment under s.87 of the Act.

SPINPRESS v. TURNER [1986] I.C.R. 433, E.A.T.

1230. Redundancy—temporary cessation of work—whether affecting period of continuous employment

[Employment Protection (Consolidation) Act 1978 (c.44), Sched. 13, para. 9(1)(b).]

Where an industrial tribunal has to consider the effect of gaps in employment of employees engaged in work where the seasonal demand varies, the proper course is not to conduct a mathematical exercise such as determining the percentages of gaps and employment over the two-year period envisaged by Sched. 13 to the Employment Protection (Consolidation) Act 1978, but rather to examine and consider the whole period of the employee's employment, looking at all the circumstances.

F and the other applicants were employed by K in a department where the workload varied with the seasons; when light they were dismissed, and when heavy they were re-employed. The length of time during which each was employed, when compared with the lay-off periods, varied. Eventually the department was closed and all the applicants were dismissed. *Held*, on their appeal from the industrial tribunal's refusal to grant redundancy payments, that the tribunal had been wrong simply to carry out the mathematical exercise of calculating the lay-off periods as compared with the periods of employment, and further to limit its consideration to the two-year period envisaged by Sched. 13 of the 1978 Act. The correct approach was to look at the entire history of the applicants' employment with K, and all the circumstances surrounding their employment (*Fitzgerald* v. *Hall Russell & Co.* [1969] C.L.Y. 1281 applied; *Ford* v. *Warwickshire County Council* [1983] C.L.Y. 1230 explained).

FLACK v. KODAK [1986] 2 All E.R. 1003, C.A.

1231. Redundancy—transfer of trade or business—dismissals and transfer on same day—liability for redundancy payments

[Transfer of Undertakings (Protection of Employment) Regulations 1981 (S.I. 1981 No. 1794), reg. 5.]

When dismissals for redundancy and the transfer of a trade or business take place on the same day, it does not matter which occurs first; the transferee will be liable for redundancy payments.

The sellers agreed to sell their hotel to the buyers on April 2, 1984, and the employees were given notice terminating their employment on that date. The sellers paid the redundancy payments and then sought rebate from the Secretary of State. The Secretary of State refused the rebate, on the grounds that by virtue of reg. 5 of the Transfer of Undertakings, (Protection of Employment) Regulations 1981, the buyers were liable for the redundancy payments. An industrial tribunal granted the sellers' application for rebate, on the ground that the dismissals were antecedent to the transfer. *Held*, allowing the appeal to the Secretary of State that, construing the regulations broadly, the effect of reg. 5 was that the transferee was liable, and the sellers were not entitled to rebate (*Apex Leisure Hire* v. *Barratt* [1984] C.L.Y. 1316 distinguished).

SECRETARY OF STATE FOR EMPLOYMENT v. ANCHOR HOTEL (KIPPFORD) [1985] I.C.R. 724, E.A.T.

1232. Redundancy—transfer of undertaking—meaning of "immediately before"

[Transfer of Undertakings (Protection of Employment) Regulations 1981 (S.I. 1981 No. 1794), regs. 3, 5(1)(3).]

Regulation 5 of the Transfer of Undertakings Regulations 1981 refers to contracts of employment actually subsisting at the moment of transfer.

In November 1983 the employers went into receivership; after a series of negotiations they dismissed the entire workforce at 11.00 a.m. on November 28, and sold the company at 2.00 p.m. that same day. On the next day the whole workforce was re-employed by the new owners. The applicants claimed they were entitled to redundancy payments as they were not employed "immediately before the transfer." The tribunal upheld their claim. *Held*, dismissing the Secretary of State's appeal, that on a proper construction of reg. 5(3), the provisions were concerned with contracts subsisting at the time of the transfer of undertakings. The applicants here were dismissed before the relevant transfer of undertakings. (*Premier Motors (Medway)* v. *Total Oil Great Britain* [1984] C.L.Y. 1266 approved; *Wendelboe* v. *L.J. Music ApS (in liquidation)* [1985] 1 C.M.L.R. 476, applied.)

SECRETARY OF STATE FOR EMPLOYMENT v. SPENCE [1986] 3 W.L.R. 380, C.A.

1233. Redundancy upon return from maternity leave—refusal of Manpower Services Commission to fund job—whether "suitable available vacancy"
[Employment Protection (Consolidation) Act 1978 (c.44), s.45(3).]
A job funded by the Manpower Services Commission under the Community Programme that is a suitable vacancy for an employee returning from maternity leave who is redundant is available within the meaning of s.45(3) of the Employment Protection (Consolidation) Act 1978 notwithstanding the fact that the Commission would not fund the job because the employee failed to fulfil the criteria of the Community Programme.
The employer was a job creation agency funded almost entirely by the Manpower Services Commission. The agency was split into divisions including a Y.T.S. division and a Community Programme division. R was an employee in the Y.T.S. division. R took maternity leave. Upon her return the employer had reorganised its staff with the result that R was redundant. There was a vacancy in the Community Programme division that was suitable for R. Because R was not a long-term unemployed adult fulfilling the criteria of the Community Programme the Commission refused to fund the job if R was employed to do it. In consequence R was not employed to do the job and her employment ended by virtue of redundancy. R complained to the industrial tribunal that she had been unfairly dismissed. The tribunal held that a suitable vacancy was available for R within the meaning of s.45(3) of the Employment Protection (Consolidation) Act 1978 and therefore her dismissal was deemed to be unfair. *Held*, dismissing the employer's appeal, that the word "available" in s.45(3) of the Act was an ordinary English word not a term of art. It could not be said that the tribunal were wrong in concluding that the vacancy in question was available. The Manpower Services Commission was not a party to the relationship existing between R and her employer. Availability for the purposes of s.45(3) of the Act was not expressed to be qualified by considerations of what was economic or reasonable. It was not right that a third party should, by imposing on the employer requirements of eligibility for jobs make unavailable for the purposes of s.45(3) of the Act a suitable vacancy otherwise available.
COMMUNITY TASK FORCE *v.* RIMMER [1986] I.C.R. 491, E.A.T.

1234. Repeated short-term contracts—trawlerman—whether continuous employment—whether dismissed
Evidence that there was a global contract of employment covering a period of many short-term contracts may justify the conclusion that an applicant has been dismissed when he is not selected for one of the contracts.
P worked for BL for 30 years as a trawler skipper, in his case on the basis that he would keep himself available for BL, and BL would choose their crews from their own pool of seamen. When not sailing he was not paid and drew unemployment benefit. With the decline in the fishing industry P sailed ever more infrequently, until BL chose an outside skipper to sail their last trawler. P claimed unfair dismissal. *Held*, that the industrial tribunal had been correct in their application of the test of mutuality and in holding that there was a global contract of employment. They had erred, however, in concluding that P had been made redundant and no reasonable tribunal could have reached that conclusion (*Hellyer Brothers* v. *McLeod* [1986] C.L.Y. 1170 distinguished).
BOYD LINE *v.* PITTS [1986] I.C.R. 244, E.A.T.

1235. Sex discrimination. See also EUROPEAN COMMUNITIES.

1236. Sex discrimination—Community Programme restrictions—whether conditions justifiable
Where the Secretary of State determined to apply as a condition of eligibility for a job through the Community Programme run by the Manpower Services Commission that the applicant be in receipt of certain benefits and that condition had a discriminatory effect on grounds of sex, the condition could not be said to be unjustifiable merely because the Secretary of State did not first consult the Equal Opportunities Commission.
In October 1982 the Secretary of State introduced the Community Programme. Its object was to provide temporary work of benefit to the community for long-term unemployed adults. So as to enable those in the greatest need to find a place on the Programme the Secretary of State made it a condition that any applicant for a job on the Programme had to be in receipt of an appropriate benefit. The partner of a

recipient of an appropriate benefit also qualified. C applied for a job on the Programme as an advice worker at a local advice centre. C was not appointed as she failed to satisfy the condition of receiving an appropriate benefit. C was a married woman with three youngish children. C complained to the industrial tribunal with the support of the Equal Opportunities Commission that she had been unlawfully discriminated against in breach of the provisions of the Sex Discrimination Act 1975. It was admitted by the Secretary of State that the condition had a discriminatory effect that was unlawful but claimed the condition was justified in that it was a simple workable condition likely to ensure that those in greatest need benefited from the Programme. The tribunal held that the discriminatory effect of the condition was not justified on the ground that the Secretary of State had enough time to devise a condition which fulfilled the policy objectives without discriminating against women. The tribunal gave the following reasons for its decision—(1) there was sufficient time for the Secretary of State to give further consideration to the discriminatory effect of the condition, (2) it was not a good answer to say that the discriminatory effect was a consequence of the decision by a woman not to pay a full National Insurance contribution when in employment, (3) the Secretary of State failed to consider whether families in receipt of benefits such as family income supplement, rent or rate rebates might also be as much in need of a job as those in receipt of appropriate benefits, (4) there was no evidence that the Secretary of State had considered whether or not the condition breached an E.E.C. Council directive, and (5) the Secretary of State failed to consult the Equal Opportunities Commission before imposing the condition. *Held*, remitting the matter to the industrial tribunal on the Secretary of State's appeal, that whether or not the discriminatory effect was justified was a question of fact. The appeal could only succeed if the tribunal applied the wrong test or in applying the right test had regard to irrelevant matters or failed to have regard to relevant matters. With the exception of (3) none of the reasons advanced by the tribunal provided valid support for the tribunal's conclusion. Reason (1) was no more than the demolition of an argument not raised before the tribunal, namely that there was no time for further consideration. Reason (2) amounted to no more than an assertion that a defence not relied upon by the Secretary of State was not a good defence. Reason (4) was conceded to be an illegitimate consideration. With regard to reason (5) the tribunal erred in thinking that the mere fact that the Secretary of State failed to consult the Equal Opportunities Commission was a factor to be relied upon in support of the view that the condition and its effect were not justifiable. Reason (3) was a potentially valid consideration to which the tribunal ought to have regard. In the circumstances the tribunal had regard to matters that were irrelevant in reaching its decision. In the light of (3) it could not be said that a tribunal would inevitably have held the condition to be justified and in consequence the matter would have to be remitted to the industrial tribunal for rehearing.

SECRETARY OF STATE FOR EMPLOYMENT *v.* CHANDLER [1986] I.C.R. 436, E.A.T.

1237. Sex discrimination—contract personally to execute work or labour—newspaper distribution contract

[Sex Discrimination Act 1975 (c.65), ss.6(1)(*c*), 82(1).]

In deciding whether employment is under a "contract personally to execute any work or labour", it is necessary to consider whether the party is under an obligation personally to execute any work or labour and whether that obligation is the dominant purpose of the contract.

G, a woman, was employed by her father in his business as a wholesale distributor of newspapers. On her father's retirement G applied to M. Group to distribute its papers but was rejected and the contract placed elsewhere. G complained to the Industrial Tribunal that M. Group had unlawfully discriminated against her. The Tribunal held that it had jurisdiction and the E.A.T. upheld that ruling. *Held*, allowing M. Group's appeal, that whether employment was under "a contract personally to execute any work or labour" within s.82(1) of the 1975 Act depended on whether there was an obligation on the party that he would personally execute any work or labour and whether that obligation was the dominant purpose of the contract. In this case the father's contract was not personally to execute any work or labour and therefore G would not be employed under such a contract. Any discrimination against G did not relate to her employment. Therefore the Tribunal did not have jurisdiction.

GUNNING *v.* MIRROR GROUP NEWSPAPERS [1986] 1 All E.R. 385, C.A.

1238. Sex discrimination—dismissal—time limit for complaint

[Sex Discrimination Act 1975 (c.65), ss.6(2)(*b*), 76(1).]

For the purpose of a complaint of sex discrimination by dismissal, the act of discrimination is the actual dismissal not the notice, and time begins to run from the later date.

Mr. and Mrs. E were stewards of a club. It was a term of their employment that they would not have children. Mrs. E became pregnant. On February 18 they were given notice of dismissal to take effect on April 7. On July 3 they presented a complaint for sex discrimination contrary to s.6(2)(*b*) of the Sex Discrimination Act 1975. The question was raised whether the complaint was outside the three month time limit. *Held,* that the act of discrimination was the actual dismissal not the notice, and therefore the industrial tribunal had jurisdiction to hear the claim (*Lupetti* v. *Wrens Old House* [1984] C.L.Y. 1254 applied).

GLOUCESTER WORKING MEN'S CLUB & INSTITUTE v. JAMES [1986] I.C.R. 603, E.A.T.

1239. Sex discrimination—dismissal for pregnancy

[Sex Discrimination Act 1975 (c.65), ss.1(1), 6(2)(*b*).]

The Sex Discrimination Act 1975 may apply to cases where a woman claims to have been the victim of unlawful discrimination connected with pregnancy.

Two applicants complained that they had been dismissed because they had become pregnant. In both cases the tribunals dismissed the complaints on the basis of *Turley* v. *Allders Department Stores* [1980] C.L.Y. 971, where it was decided that dismissal because of pregnancy could not amount to discrimination between the sexes by virtue of "less favourable treatment", because a man could not get pregnant. *Held,* allowing the appeal, that the Act could apply in such cases; the correct approach was to ask whether the pregnancy was capable of being matched by analogous circumstances, for example by comparing the circumstances of a pregnant female employee with those of a sick male employee. Accordingly, both cases would be remitted to different tribunals for reconsideration on that basis (*Turley* v. *Allders Department Stores* [1980] C.L.Y. 971 not followed.)

HAYES v. MALLEABLE WORKING MEN'S CLUB AND INSTITUTE; MAUGHAN v. NORTH EAST LONDON MAGISTRATES' COURT COMMITTEE, [1985] I.C.R. 703, E.A.T.

1240. Sex discrimination—indirect discrimination—compliance with condition

[Sex Discrimination Act 1975, (c.65), s.1(1)(*b*).]

On a complaint for unlawful discrimination, if no women employees at all can comply with a condition, then it cannot be said that a "considerably smaller proportion" can comply with it under s.1(1)(*b*) of the Sex Discrimination Act 1975.

P, a woman, worked at a working men's club whose membership was open only to men. Only male employees were eligible for membership. Only employees who were club members had the right to be heard before being disciplined. P was suspended without the right to be heard. She complained of unlawful discrimination contrary to s.1(1)(*b*) of the Sex Discrimination Act 1975. Her complaint was upheld. On appeal, the club argued that if no women at all could comply with the condition, then it could not be said that "a considerably smaller proportion" of women could comply. *Held,* dismissing the appeal, that such an argument was contrary to the spirit of the Act, and the tribunal had been entitled to reach its decision.

GREENCROFT SOCIAL CLUB AND INSTITUTE v. MULLEN [1985] I.C.R. 796, E.A.T.

1241. Sex discrimination—industrial tribunal—jurisdiction

[Sex Discrimination Act 1975 (c.65), ss.6(1)(2), 10.]

An industrial tribunal has no jurisdiction to entertain a complaint for sexual discrimination where a complainant works mainly outside the U.K. unless she works on a British registered ship, aircraft, or hovercraft operated by a person resident in, or whose principal place of business is in, Great Britain.

The applicant was employed as a cashier on a ship registered in Hamburg and owned by the employers, a company registered in England with offices at Sheerness. The ship sailed between Sheerness and Flushing. She complained to an industrial tribunal of harassment and sexual discrimination on board ship contrary to section 6 of the Sex Discrimination Act 1975. The tribunal ruled that they had no jurisdiction to hear her claim, and her appeal to the Employment Appeal Tribunal was dismissed. She further appealed to the Court of Appeal. *Held,* that section 10 of the Act was unambiguous on its true construction, and defined employment at an establishment in Great Britain in the context of ships, aircraft, and hovercraft. It excluded claims by those whose work was done wholly or mainly outside Great Britain unless it was done on a British registered ship, aircraft, or hovercraft operated by a person whose principal place of business, or whose ordinary residence, was in Great Britain, and was not done wholly outside Great Britain. Since the applicant's work was done mainly outside territorial waters on a German registered ship, the industrial tribunal had no jurisdiction to hear her claim.

HAUGHTON v. OLAU LINE (U.K.) [1986] 1 W.L.R. 504, C.A.

1242. Sex discrimination—safeguarding national security—differences in treatment between men and women police officers. See JOHNSTON v. CHIEF CONSTABLE OF THE ROYAL ULSTER CONSTABULARY, § 1462.

1243. Sex discrimination—sexual harassment—detriment to employee
[Sex Discrimination Act 1975 (c.65), ss.1, 6.]
On hearing a sex discrimination complaint the tribunal should ask itself first, whether there was sexual harassment, and secondly, was it to the detriment of the applicant.

The council employed three laboratory technicians, who were all female and included E, the applicant, at one of their schools. Two left, and were replaced by men. P alleged that they conducted a campaign of harassment, including sexual harassment, against her with a view to forcing her to leave. She was in the event transferred to another school at her own request. The tribunal found that she had been discriminated against by the two men but that they would have been as unpleasant to a male whom they disliked so that the council could not be said to have treated her less favourably than they would have treated a man. The Employment Appeal Tribunal allowed E's appeal on the ground that the tribunal should first have asked itself whether there was sexual harassment. *Held,* dismissing the council's appeal, that s.1(1)(*e*) of the Sex Discrimination Act 1975 was not concerned with the motive for particular treatment of an applicant, only with the treatment itself. Since part of the treatment of E was only meted out because she was a woman, the tribunal should have first asked itself whether there had been sexual harassment. Since there had, E had been treated less favourably than a man for the purposes of s.1(1)(*a*) and 6(2)(*b*).

PORCELLI v. STRATHCLYDE REGIONAL COUNCIL [1986] I.C.R. 564, Court of Session, First Division.

1244. Sex Discrimination Act 1986 (c.59)
This Act amends the Sex Discrimination Act 1975 and the Equal Pay Act 1970 to bring them into line with European Community law. The Act also repeals protective legislation applying to one sex only.
The Act received the Royal Assent on November 7, 1986.

1245. Sex Discrimination Act 1986—commencement
SEX DISCRIMINAL ACT (COMMENCEMENT) ORDER 1986 (No. 2313 (c.95)) [80p], made under the Sex Discrimination Act 1986 (c.59), s.10(3); brings into force on February 27, 1987 section 7, 8, Sched. 1, Pt. III.

1246. Short-time work—reduced remuneration—whether lawful
An employer who unilaterally introduces short time working is not entitled to avoid his contractual obligation to pay his employee his due remuneration: MILLER v. HAMWORTHY ENGINEERING, *The Times,* May 14, 1986, C.A.

1247. Sick pay
STATUTORY SICK PAY (ADDITIONAL COMPENSATION OF EMPLOYERS) (COMPUTATION) REGULATIONS 1986 (No. 318) [40p], made under the Social Security and Housing Benefits Act 1982 (c.24), ss.9(1A)(*a*), 26(1), 47; operative on April 6, 1986; amend S.I. 1985 No. 1411.
STATUTORY SICK PAY (GENERAL) AMENDMENT REGULATIONS 1986 (No. 477) [£1·35], made under the Social Security and Housing Benefits Act 1982 (c.24), ss.2(3A), 3(4A) and (5), 17(4), 18 and 26(1); operative on April 6, 1986; contain provisions relating to statutory sick pay.
STATUTORY SICK PAY (GENERAL) AMENDMENT (TRANSITIONAL) REGULATIONS 1986 (No. 478) [40p], made under the Social Security Act 1985 (c.53), s.32(6); operative on April 6, 1986; makes provision in connection with the coming into force of s.18 of the 1985 Act and S.I. 1986 No. 477.

STATUTORY SICK PAY UP-RATING ORDER 1986 (No. 67) [40p], made under the Housing Benefits Act 1982 (c.24), s.7(5), (6) and (10), operative on April 6, 1986; increases statutory sick pay.

1248. Termination of contract—whether dismissal—whether automatic termination

H was employed by an Education Department on terms contained in a written contract which included the following: "the appointment will last only as long as sufficient funds are provided either by the Manpower Services Commission or by other firms/sponsors to fund it." The employer subsequently wrote to H informing her that they had not received any contracts from the MSC for courses at the College and that her course would not receive funding after the present contract expired and, as a result, in accordance with the terms of her employment, it would terminate. An Industrial Tribunal found that H was employed for a specific purpose; that that specific purpose having ceased, the contract was discharged by performance; or alternatively it was terminable on the happening or non-happening of a future event and it was terminable in a sense that it automatically terminated when the non-payment occurred. H appealed to the Employment Appeal Tribunal. *Held*, dismissing the appeal, that it was not particularly easy to see that this was a contract for a particular purpose but the contract was terminable on the happening or non-happening of a future event. It came to an end automatically (*Wiltshire County Council v. National Association of Teachers in Further and Higher Education and Guy* [1980] C.L.Y. 1024, considered): BROWN *v.* KNOWSLEY BOROUGH COUNCIL [1986] I.R.L.R. 102, E.A.T.

1249. Trade unions. See TRADE UNIONS.

1250. Unfair dismissal

UNFAIR DISMISSAL (INCREASE OF COMPENSATION LIMIT) ORDER 1986 (No. 2284) [45p], made under the Employment Protection (Consolidation) Act 1978 (c.44), ss.75(2), 154(3), 154(4); operative on April 1, 1987; increase to £8,500 the amount which can be awarded by an industrial tribunal in claims for unfair dismissal as the compensatory award.

UNFAIR DISMISSAL (INCREASE OF LIMITS OF BASIC AND SPECIAL AWARDS) ORDER 1986 (No. 2281) [45p], made under the Employment Protection (Consolidation) Act 1978 (c.44), ss.73(4B), 75A(7), 154(3)(4), operative on April 1, 1987; increases the basic award to £2,300 and increases limits for the calculation of special awards to £11,500, £23,000 and £17,250.

1251. Unfair dismissal—agreement to settle claim prior to institution of proceedings—involvement of ACAS officer—economic duress—validity of agreement

[Employment Protection (Consolidation) Act (c.44), ss.134(3), 140(2)(*d*).]

Where an employee faced with being summarily dismissed or being made redundant with compensation agreed after consulting an ACAS officer to accept the latter alternative and agreed not to make any claim against his employer in consequence of the termination of his employment that agreement was binding on the employee.

On November 10, 1983 H and his employers fell out. H was told by his employer, the respondent, that he was to be summarily dismissed. He was given the alternative of being made redundant, receiving a payment of £3,800, salary to the end of the month and certain other benefits for a limited time. H was given until November 18, 1983 to consider his position. If he accepted the latter alternative he would have to sign an agreement to be prepared by ACAS. H was informed that an ACAS officer would deal with the matter. H discussed the matter with the ACAS officer and his solicitor. On November 18 H accepted the latter alternative and signed the agreement because the former alternative was penury and would leave him entirely without means. The agreement was expressed to be in full and final settlement of all claims which H could bring against the respondent before an industrial tribunal. H thereafter applied to the industrial tribunal for compensation for unfair dismissal and contended that the agreement was void under s.140 of the Act and voidable at common law as having been reached under economic duress. The tribunal rejected that contention and the Employment Appeal Tribunal dismissed H's appeal. *Held*, dismissing H's appeal, that it could not be said that at the time the agreement was signed no action had been taken in respect of which H could have presented a complaint to the tribunal within the meaning of s.134(3) of the Act. It was clear that on November 10 H was given notice that come what may his employment would be terminated on November 18, 1983. Accordingly H was entitled to make a complaint to the industrial tribunal under s.67(4) of the Act at any time after November 10. The word "claims" in s.134(3)(*a*) merely meant that a state of affairs existed giving rise to the right to make a claim, whether successful or not, vested in the complaint. It was not necessary for H to have got to the stage of considering presenting a complaint before s.134(3) could apply. It could not be said that the ACAS officer had not acted in accordance with s.134(3) of the Act as required by s.140(2)(*d*) of the Act. It was not for the industrial tribunal to investigate whether the ACAS officer correctly interpreted his duties under s.134 of the Act. It was sufficient that he intended and purported to act under that section. In the circumstances the agreement was effective to exclude the jurisdiction of the industrial tribunal pursuant to the provisions of s.140 of the Act. Although such an agreement could be avoided on grounds of economic duress it could not be said in the circumstances of the present case that H's entering into the agreement was involuntary. H had a real alternative to entering into the agreement in that he could have been summarily dismissed, claimed supplementary benefit and made a claim for unfair dismissal in the ordinary course of events. "It is entirely sensible to observe that in real life it must be very rare to encounter economic duress of an order which renders actions involuntary. It follows that if the applicant's situation was not uncommon, it is highly unlikely that he was subject to the necessary degree of economic duress." (*Pao On* v. *Lau Yiu Long* [1979] C.L.Y. 331 considered).

HENNESSY *v.* CRAIGMYLE & Co. [1986] I.C.R. 461, C.A.

1252. Unfair dismissal—alleged dismissal for trade union membership—redundancy and absence of consultation
B was employed as a charge hand together with H. Both were members of the TGWU. Both were active in supporting the union. Both were made redundant at a time when B had accrued a right to bring a claim for unfair dismissal but H had not. Both brought claims to an Industrial Tribunal claiming that they had been dismissed for an inadmissible reason. The Industrial Tribunal rejected this claim but found that B had been unfairly dismissed because he had been unfairly selected for redundancy; the basis of unfairness being the lack of consultation. The employers appealed on four grounds: (1) it was wrong for the Industrial Tribunal to have considered the issue of the fairness of selection for redundancy because arguments had only been directed at the question of union activity; (2) the Industrial Tribunal had failed to make a positive finding that the failure to consult would have made any difference; (3) the Tribunal fell into error by misstating the proper test setting out the burden of proof; (4) the findings of the Industrial Tribunal were inconsistent. *Held*, allowing the appeal, that (1) it was too late to raise the argument that the issue of unfair redundancy should not have been considered. No objection was taken at the Industrial Tribunal hearing when it had been made clear that they propose to deal with this issue; (2) it would impose an unnecessary and intolerable burden on Industrial Tribunals to say that they were bound in every case to make a positive finding on the balance of probability as to what would have happened if the omitted consultation had taken place; (3) there had been a material misdirection in relation to the burden of proof. It was for this reason that the appeal succeeded. The case was remitted to a specially constituted Industrial Tribunal in part because of the fourth ground of appeal relating to the inconsistent basis of the Industrial Tribunals decision (*British United Shoe Machinery Co.* v. *Clarke* [1978] C.L.Y. 993, *Yate Foundry* v. *Walters* [1984] C.L.Y. 1311 discussed): HOWARTH TIMBER (LEEDS) *v.* BISCOMB [1986] I.R.L.R. 52, E.A.T.

1253. Unfair dismissal—award—civil proceedings—stay. See SCHOFIELD *v.* CHURCH ARMY, § 2719.

1254. Unfair dismissal—basic award—whether new owners liable for basic award
[Transfer of Undertakings (Protection of Employment) Regulations 1981 (S.I. 1981 No. 1794), regs. 5(2), 8(1)(2).]
Where an employee has been unfairly dismissed by the transferor and then unfairly by the transferee, the transferee could be liable for the basic award arising from both dismissals.
F was employed by the owners of a hotel; on their deciding to sell the business they dismissed her. The new owners re-engaged her, but within six weeks dismissed her on grounds of redundancy. The industrial tribunal found in F's favour and ordered compensation from the new owners and from the original owners. F

appealed. *Held,* that the new owners could be liable for the basic awards arising from both dismissals. On the facts however the industrial tribunal had failed to consider the reasons for the first dismissal and so the case would be remitted for further consideration.

FENTON *v.* STABLEGOLD [1986] I.C.R. 236, E.A.T.

1255. Unfair dismissal—compensation—award limited to one year—date of assessment

The correct basis for assessment of compensation for unfair dismissal is to examine the situation at the date of the hearing with regard to what has actually occurred.

In July 1982 a county council dismissed their school meals staff and offered them new contracts at reduced pay. A number of employees successfully claimed unfair dismissal. The tribunal in assessing compensation held that since the service would have closed in any event within 12 months, the loss of earnings should be limited to one year from date of dismissal. *Held,* allowing the employee's appeal, that the tribunal had erred in basing their assessment on the future prospects of the service at the date of the dismissals, they ought to have had regard to the situation at the date of the hearing and to what had actually occurred.

GILHAM *v.* KENT COUNTY COUNCIL (No. 3) [1986] I.C.R. 52, E.A.T.

1256. Unfair dismissal—compensation—mitigation of loss

[Employment Protection (Consolidation) Act 1978 (c.44), s.74(4).]

On a complaint for unfair dismissal, an industrial tribunal has a duty under s.74(4) of the Employment Protection (Consolidation) Act 1978 to consider whether an employee has tried to mitigate his loss by seeking alternative employment (semble) the burden of proof being on the employee.

E's dismissal was held to be unfair. On the hearing to assess compensation the employers brought evidence that alternative employment had been available to E. The tribunal accepted E's evidence that she had been to a job centre, but failed to find employment. *Held,* allowing the appeal, that under s.74(4) of the Employment Protection (Consolidation) Act 1978 the tribunal had a duty to consider whether E had tried to mitigate her loss by seeking alternative employment (*semble*) the burden of proof being on E, and the tribunal's decision was one which could not have been reached by a reasonable tribunal (dicta of Roskill L.J. in *Bessenden Properties* v. *Corness (Note)* [1978] C.L.Y. 1156 and of Lord McDonald in *Lanton Leisure* v. *Zonfrillo* (unreported), September 20, 1985 considered).

SCOTTISH & NEWCASTLE BREWERIES *v.* HALLIDAY [1986] I.C.R. 577, E.A.T.

1257. Unfair dismissal—complaint—whether delivered in time

[Employment Protection (Consolidation) Act 1978 (c.44), s.67(2).] The Central Office of Industrial Tribunals made a special arrangement with the Post Office that post received for delivery on a Saturday should be kept until the Monday. *Held,* that this constitutes the Post Office the Tribunal's bailee of the mail, and so the time limit for presenting a complaint under s.67(2) of the Employment Protection (Consolidation) Act 1978 is met if the complaint comes to the Post Office's hands by the Saturday, even if time expires then (*Hodgson* v. *Armstrong* 1967 C.L.Y. 2241 applied): LANG *v.* DEVON GENERAL, *The Times,* August 19, 1986, E.A.T.

1258. Unfair dismissal—continuous employment—associated employer—equal division of shareholding

[Employment Protection (Consolidation) Act 1978 (c.44), s.153(4).]

A company in which shares are held equally by a husband and wife cannot be an associated employer of a company in which the husband has a majority shareholding in the absence of any evidence that the husband controls the voting rights attaching to the shares held by the wife.

L was an employee of SWL Co. in which Mr. S held 50 shares and his son three. L had been employed by SWL Co. for more than one year but less than two years. Throughout the time the number of persons employed by SWL Co. did not exceed 19. Mr. S was also a shareholder in a number of other companies. The shares in those companies were divided equally between Mr. S and his wife. L claimed that SWL Co. and the other companies were associated employers so that she was entitled to make a claim for unfair dismissal. The industrial tribunal held the companies to be associated employers as the companies were being run as a family business by Mr. S. The Employment Appeal Tribunal overturned that finding. *Held,* dismissing L's appeal, that Mr. and Mrs. S could not be treated as a composite person for the purpose of identifying who controlled the other companies. It was doubtful whether the Act admitted the concept of plural control. In any event the composite person of Mr. and Mrs. S could not be said to be the same person as Mr. S for the purposes of s.153(4) of the Act. The section requires that for companies to be associated employers control of the companies shall be in the hands of the same person. There was no evidence to show as a matter of fact that Mr. S was the ultimate controller of the other companies. It was not enough to show that he had day to day control of their business. There was no presumption that in a family company one shareholder had expressly or tacitly agreed to vote in accordance with the other shareholder's wishes and no presumption that a husband controlled his wife's shares and votes (*Zarb* v. *British & Brazilian Produce Co. (Sales)* [1978] C.L.Y. 1105 explained, *Floor* v. *Davis* [1979] C.L.Y. 446, *Poparm* v. *Weekes* [1985] C.L.Y. 1230 considered).

SOUTH WEST LAUNDERETTES *v.* LAIDLER [1986] I.C.R. 455, C.A.

1259. Unfair dismissal—contract of apprenticeship—sentence of borstal training—whether contract frustrated

A lengthy sentence of custody is capable of frustrating a contract of apprenticeship.

In September 1979 the applicant entered into a four year contract of apprenticeship. In June 1981 he was convicted of a serious criminal offence and sentenced to Borstal training. The employers refused to take him back. The applicant successfully applied to a tribunal for unfair dismissal. *Held,* allowing the employers' appeal, that the imposition of the custodial sentence was capable of, and did on these facts, frustrate the contract (*Hare* v. *Murphy Bros.* [1975] C.L.Y. 1097 not followed).

SHEPHERD (F. C.) & Co. *v.* JERROM [1986] 3 W.L.R. 801, C.A.

1260. Unfair dismissal—dishonesty of wife—subsequent dismissal of husband—whether breakdown of trust and confidence

[Employment Protection (Consolidation) Act 1978 (c.44), ss.57(1)(*b*), 57(3).] Mr. and Mrs. W were both employed by EE. Mrs. W was arrested and convicted for offences of dishonesty. Mr. W was subsequently dismissed and complained to an Industrial Tribunal that he had been unfairly dismissed. The Tribunal held that he had been dismissed for a substantial reason of a kind such as to justify his dismissal and that dismissal was fair. EE were a small firm operating in a small town. The Tribunal felt that the trust and confidence between employer and employee had completely broken down in this case which would have been sufficient to justify the employment terminating. A second ground was the effect on customers of the continuation of Mr W's employment. The Tribunal did not elaborate on its finding that the dismissal was in all the circumstances fair and reasonable. Mr W appealed to the Employment Appeal Tribunal. *Held,* upholding the appeal, that it had not been the act of the employee that had caused any breakdown of trust and confidence and it was impossible to accept that the behaviour of Mrs. W could lead to a breach of confidence in the trust residing in Mr. W. Further, the Industrial Tribunal had not considered the issue of fairness and the surrounding circumstances adequately. It is only exceptionally that the Employment Appeal Tribunal would interfere with the finding of an Industrial Tribunal on the ground of perverseness but this case fell to be regarded as one of those exceptional cases: WADLEY *v.* EAGER ELECTRICAL [1986] I.R.L.R. 93, E.A.T.

1261. Unfair dismissal—employer's breach of contract—contract affirmed—subsequent conduct of employer causing resignation—whether repudiation

[Employment Protection (Consolidation) Act 1978 (c.44), ss.55(2)(*c*).]

Where an employer's conduct entitles an employee to terminate his contract, the test as to whether that conduct amounted to a repudiation is an objective test.

In 1981 the employer demoted the employee and altered his pay in flagrant breach of contract. The employee affirmed the contract nevertheless. Subsequently persistent criticism and threats led to resignation and a complaint of unfair dismissal. The tribunal dismissed the claim on the grounds that the breach of contract was irrelevant once affirmed, and that subsequent conduct did not amount to a repudiation. The decision was upheld on appeal. *Held,* allowing the appeal, that the original breach could be relied on together with subsequent conduct as cumulatively amounting to a repudiatory breach of the implied obligation of trust and confidence. The test as to whether the conduct was repudiatory was objective.

LEWIS *v.* MOTORWORLD GARAGES [1986] I.C.R. 157, C.A.

1262. Unfair dismissal—less than two years' employment—more than twenty employees—relevant date

[Employment Protection (Consolidation) Act 1978 (c.44), s.64A (as inserted by Employment Act 1980 (c.42), s.8); Transfer of Undertakings (Protection of Employment) Regulations 1981 (S.I. 1981 No. 1794), reg. 5.]

On its true construction, s.64A(1)(*b*) of the Employment Protection (Consolidation) Act 1978 provides that an employee of less than two years' service may take proceedings for unfair dismissal if the employers have had more than 20 employees at any time during the period of employment.

P was employed by a company with more than 20 employees. After 9 months, the undertaking was transferred to a company which had less than 20 employees. Four months later, P was dismissed. An industrial tribunal held that P was entitled to present a claim for unfair dismissal under s.64A(1) of the Employment Protection (Consolidation) Act 1978. *Held,* dismissing the employers' appeal, that the number of employees did not fall to be assessed at the date of dismissal. Section 64A(1) comprehended any time during the period of employment.

KEABEECH *v.* MULCAHY [1985] I.C.R. 791, E.A.T.

1263. Unfair dismissal—long-term holiday agreement—consensual termination on failure to return—whether provision valid

[Employment Protection (Consolidation) Act 1978 (c.44), s.140.]

A provision for the automatic termination of an employee's contract of employment upon the failure of the employee to report for work on a specified future date has the effect of limiting the operation of ss.54 and 55 of the Employment Protection (Consolidation) Act 1978 and thus is void pursuant to s.140 of the Act.

I wished to go on holiday for a period longer than her contractual entitlement. Her employer agreed to her extended holiday absence. It was a condition of the employer's agreement that I should return to work on September 28, 1983. It was agreed that if she failed to do so her contract of employment would automatically terminate on that date. On her return from holiday I was struck down with gastric flu and was unable to return to work on September 28. Her employer wrote informing her that her contract of employment had automatically terminated. Her employer indicated she might be considered for re-employment if a medical certificate were provided. I provided a medical certificate but was not re-employed. I claimed she had been unfairly dismissed. The industrial tribunal and the Employment Appeal Tribunal held that I had not been dismissed but that there had been a consensual termination of her contract of employment. *Held,* allowing I's appeal, that it offended against common sense to say that there had been a consensual termination of I's contract of employment in the circumstances. The termination of a contract of employment by agreement does not of itself prevent an employee being dismissed for the purposes of the Employment Protection (Consolidation) Act 1978. If the employer's argument were correct up until the agreement for I's extended holiday absence I was entitled to the benefit of ss.54 and 55 of the Act. Thereafter that benefit would be subject to the condition that she reported for work on September 28, 1983. It was impossible to avoid the conclusion that the provision for automatic termination had the effect, if valid, of limiting the operation of the Act. It was therefore void by virtue of the provisions of s.140(1)(*a*) of the Act (*British Leyland U.K.* v. *Ashraf* [1978] C.L.Y. 1183 overruled).

IGBO *v.* JOHNSON MATTHEY CHEMICALS [1986] I.C.R. 505, C.A.

1264. Unfair dismissal—loss of statutory rights—compensation

The conventional sum of £20 awarded for loss of statutory rights should now be raised to £100: HEAD *v.* MUFFETT, *The Times,* July 24, 1986, E.A.T.

1265. Unfair dismissal—meaning of redundancy—reasonableness of the decision to dismiss in absence of consultation

[Employment Protection (Consolidation) Act 1978 (c.44), ss.57(2)(*c*), 57(3), 81(2)(*b*).] P was engaged for most of his time in the work of a sole layer/pre-sole fitter. Another employee, H, also carried out work as a sole layer/pre-sole fitter. He was found, as a matter of fact, to carry out this work satisfactorily and that his attendance was substantially better than P's. In 1983 there was a recession in the shoe trade. The employers decided it was necessary to reduce the workforce and selected P for redundancy having consulted the relevant trade union and followed procedures agreed with them. P was not consulted prior to the dismissal. An

Industrial Tribunal found that P's dismissal was not in breach of a customary agreement or an agreed procedure and that it had been fair because the procedures agreed with the trade union had been applied and because P had wrongfully refused to carry out an order and had a poor attendance record. He had also been responsible for damage to some equipment. P raised two grounds of appeal against the decision of the Industrial Tribunal. He first submitted that the Tribunal applied the wrong test in the definition of redundancy and secondly, submitted that the decision that the dismissal was fair was perverse. P contended that the Industrial Tribunal had been wrong to consider the question of whether there was a diminishing need for the work for which he was required to perform under his contract of employment rather than a particular kind of work which he actually carried out. *Held,* rejecting the appeal, that there is consistent and binding authority that the Industrial Tribunal was not in error when they applied as the appropriate test, the diminishing need for the kind of work which he was employed to do under his contract of employment. Further the approach of the Tribunal was amply supported by the evidence and whilst the lay members of the Employment Appeal Tribunal wish to emphasise that it is not desirable for an employer to seek to discharge his duty by referring questions of redundancy solely to a trade union instead of consulting the employee as well, all were of the view that this Industrial Tribunal was justified in concluding on the facts that the individual consultation would have made no difference (*Nelson* v. *British Broadcasting Corp.* [1977] C.L.Y. 1123, *Nelson* v. *British Broadcasting Corp.* (No. 2) [1980] C.L.Y. 1018, *Cowen* v. *Haden Carrier* [1983] C.L.Y. 1276, applied; *Williams* v. *Compair Maxam* [1982] C.L.Y. 1122 referred to): PINK *v.* WHITE; PINK *v.* WHITE & CO. (EARLS BARTON) [1985] I.R.L.R. 489, E.A.T.

1266. Unfair dismissal—misconduct

[Employment Protection (Consolidation) Act 1978 (c.44), s.57.] P was dismissed summarily for dishonesty. The industrial tribunal found that it would have been a "meaningless formality" to have put the allegations to P in the light of the circumstances. *Held,* that the tribunal had considered the necessary questions, and had made findings available to it on the evidence. The decision that the dismissal was fair could not be criticised as perverse (*British Home Stores* v. *Burchell* [1980] C.L.Y. 1004, *British Labour Pump* v. *Byrne* [1979] C.L.Y. 993, *Polkey* v. *A. E. Daunton Services, The Times,* October 23, 1986 considered): PRITCHETT *v.* J. McINTYRE, *The Times,* October 24, 1986, C.A.

1267. Unfair dismissal—misconduct—employee expressing intention to compete

The expression of an intention in the future by employees to compete with their employers expressed in a letter to suppliers is not in itself a breach of the duty of loyalty justifying dismissal.

Warehousemen employed by nuts and bolts suppliers wrote to 10 of the employers' suppliers informing them that they intended to start up in business on their own and asking for details of their products. They were dismissed for gross misconduct. The industrial tribunal found that they were in breach of their duty of loyalty, and that the dismissals were not unfair. *Held,* allowing the employees' appeal, that the employees action was not a breach of their duty of loyalty, and their dismissals were unfair (*Harris & Russell* v. *Slingsby* [1973] C.L.Y. 1131 considered). LAUGHTON *v.* BAPP INDUSTRIAL SUPPLIES [1986] I.C.R. 634, E.A.T.

1268. Unfair dismissal—money in lieu of notice—whether deduction from compensation

When an employee is unfairly dismissed, and given money in lieu of notice, this money should not be deducted from any compensation awarded by an industrial tribunal: ADDISON *v.* BABCOCK FATA, *The Times,* July 10, 1986, E.A.T.

1269. Unfair dismissal—non-compliance with reinstatement order—re-engagement on different duties—limit on compensation

[Employment Protection (Consolidation) Act 1978 (c.44), ss.69(1)(2), 71(1), 75, 75A (as substituted by Employment Act 1982 (c.46), s.5(6)).]

Reinstatement on different duties does not amount to compliance with a reinstatement order, which may be the subject of compensation under s.75A(2) of the Employment Protection (Consolidation) Act 1978 without being subject to the limitations in s.69(2).

S and others had been employed as security guards, with a few minor duties of a general nature. They were unfairly dismissed. The industrial tribunal ordered reinstatement, in purported compliance with which A re-engaged them as cleaners, with a few security duties. *Held,* that reinstatement meant that the employer had to treat the employee as though he had never been dismissed. Re-employment as cleaners did not amount to reinstatement of the employees, in respect of which a special award under s.75A(2) of the 1978 Act. The limits provided by s.69 applied only to matters ancillary to the unfair dismissal itself.

ARTISAN PRESS *v.* SRAWLEY [1986] I.C.R. 328, E.A.T.

1270. Unfair dismissal—normal retiring age—manner in which it may be varied

[Employment Protection (Consolidation) Act 1978 (c.44), s.64(1)(*b*), 153(1).] M was first employed by HIDB in March 1976 when he was aged 42 as a clerk. He was informed verbally that his normal retiring age was 65. In 1975 the HIDB decided as a matter of policy to change the normal retiring age for their existing male staff from 65 to 60. The change was promulgated in 1975 in a number of staff circulars. M was 60 on June 11, 1983. By that time he was an administrative officer and he was retained in that position until October 31, 1983. He was re-engaged on November 1, 1983 as a clerk at a reduced salary. M complained to an Industrial Tribunal that his dismissal from his post as administrative officer was unfair. The Industrial Tribunal decided that it had jurisdiction to hear his complaint and rejected an argument that it was debarred by s.64(1)(*b*). HIDB appealed to the Employment Appeal Tribunal which decided that the question to be asked was what would the group of which the Respondent was a member, reasonably regard as their normal retiring age. They further decided that the appropriate group to be considered in the case of M was those administrative officers employed by HIDB who had been taken on for 1975. HIDB appealed to the Court of Session. *Held,* allowing the appeal, that the Employment Appeal Tribunal had relied upon the decision of the English Court of Appeal in *Hughes* v. *Department of Health and Social Security.* That decision had been overruled on appeal to the House of Lords. It followed that the appropriate group to be considered were all administrative officers employed at the date of the termination of M's employment. If this was the appropriate group to be taken into account there was no dispute that the normal retiring age was 60 and not 65. The proper test is to ascertain what would be the reasonable expectation or understanding of the employees holding that position at the relevant time. Whilst the contractual retiring age will prima facie be the normal retiring age, it may be displaced by evidence that it is regularly departed from in practice (*Waite* v. *Government Communication Headquarters* [1983] C.L.Y. 1327, *Hughes* v. *Department of Health and Social Security* [1984] C.L.Y. 1295, and [1985] C.L.Y. 1246 considered): THE HIGHLANDS AND ISLANDS DEVELOPMENT BOARD *v.* MACGILLIVRAY [1986] I.R.L.R. 210, Court of Session.

1271. Unfair dismissal—normal retiring age—manner in which it may be varied

[Employment Protection (Consolidation) Act 1978 (c.44), s.64(1)(*b*).] M was a prison officer. His contractual retiring age was 55. He was dismissed at the age of 56 years and four months. In practice his employers regularly departed from the contractual retiring age and in fact prison officers retired at a variety of higher ages. M complained to an Industrial Tribunal that he had been unfairly dismissed and the Tribunal decided as a preliminary point that they had jurisdiction to entertain his complaint. The employers appealed to the Employment Appeal Tribunal. *Held,* rejecting the appeal, that the Tribunal has found that the contractual retiring age was not superseded by definite higher age but it had ceased to be the normal retiring age. There was no authority for the view that the contractual retiring age had to be given up absolutely rather than parted from sufficiently resulting in the retiral of employees at a variety of higher ages. This would be sufficient to rebut the presumption (*Waite* v. *Government Communications Headquarters* [1983] C.L.Y. 1327, *Department of Health and Social Security* v. *Hughes and Coy* [1985] C.L.Y. 1246 applied): SECRETARY OF STATE FOR SCOTLAND *v.* MEIKLE [1986] I.R.L.R. 208, E.A.T.

1272. Unfair dismissal—normal retiring age—whether sufficiently definite to constitute normal retiring age

[Employment Protection (Consolidation) Act 1978 (c.44), s.64(1)(*b*).]

An age for retirement of between 62 and 63 was not sufficiently definite to constitute a normal retiring age for the purposes of s.64(1)(*b*) of the Employment Protection (Consolidation) Act 1978.

S was a district alkali officer employed by the Health and Safety Executive. When he was first employed the Civil Service Pay and Conditions of Service Code provided a contractual age for retirement of 60. His normal retiring age was the completion of 30 years' service or 65 whichever came soonest. S would have reached 65 first. In 1982 the chief alkali inspector was under pressure to retire staff before the age of 65 and at an annual staff meeting that year announced that those with 20 years' service would have to retire at 60 but that district alkali inspectors might be allowed to stay until aged 63. S's employment was terminated in June 1983 when he was 63 years and seven months old. S claimed he was unfairly dismissed. His employer claimed his employment terminated after his normal retiring age so that any claim was excluded by s.64(1)(*b*) of the Employment Protection (Consolidation) Act 1978. The industrial tribunal held that at the time his employment commenced his normal retiring age was 65 but that it had been changed to between 62 and 63 and that change had been clearly communicated to S. In consequence, the tribunal had no jurisdiction to entertain his claim. *Held*, allowing S's appeal, that as a matter of law the employer was not prevented from altering S's normal retirement age provided the change was clearly communicated to S. The finding that it was so communicated was a finding of fact with which the appeal tribunal could not interfere. Although the tribunal found that S would normally have been retired between the age of 62 and 63 that age could not be said to be a normal retiring age. It did not constitute a definite age but encompassed a variety of ages. As it was not possible to specify the normal retiring age from the evidence the statutory alternative of 65 prevailed and the tribunal had jurisdiction to hear S's complaint (*Waite* v. *Government Communications Headquarters* [1983] C.L.Y. 1327 applied).

SWAINE *v.* HEALTH AND SAFETY EXECUTIVE [1986] I.C.R. 498, E.A.T.

1273. Unfair dismissal—offer of alternative employment—acceptance for trial period—dismissal during trial period—redundancy

[Employment Protection (Consolidation) Act 1978 (c.44), s.84(1)(6)(*b*).]

Where an employee who would otherwise have been made redundant accepts alternative employment offered by her employer, and during the currency of a trial period with regard to that new employment is dismissed, that dismissal falls to be considered in its own right rather than relating back to the original redundancy, and may therefore found a claim for unfair dismissal.

H was given notice that she would be made redundant, during the course of which her employers offered her employment with another division, subject to an eight week trial period, during which if either side found the new employment unsatisfactory it would be terminated. During that trial period WHS did terminate H's employment, and she claimed unfair dismissal. The industrial tribunal held that in consequence of s.84 of the 1978 Act H's dismissal related back to her initial redundancy, and questions of unfair dismissal did not therefore arise. *Held,* allowing the appeal, that the tribunal was wrong. S.84 was restricted to Part VI of the Act, and did not extend to Part V. The case would accordingly be remitted to another tribunal to consider the merits.

HEMPELL *v.* W. H. SMITH & SONS [1986] I.C.R. 365, E.A.T.

1274. Unfair dismissal—procedure at an Industrial Tribunal—allegations of bias of Chairman

C resigned from her employment and claimed that she had been constructively dismissed. Her application came before an Industrial Tribunal in December 1984. Before the case was completed however it was adjourned and in the period before the further hearing an application was made by the respondents for a re-hearing on the grounds of allegedly biased comments made by the Chairman. The same Chairman directed a re-hearing before a freshly constituted Tribunal. At a subsequent hearing the lay members reversed the Chairman's decision. The employers then appealed to the Employment Appeal Tribunal. *Held,* upholding the appeal, that the proper test where there is an allegation of bias is an objective one. Would the reasonable observer present at the hearing, not being a party, or associated with a party, to the proceedings but knowing the issues, reasonably gain the impression of bias. That impression may be given by the appearance of a closed mind against a party on a matter which calls for decision by the Tribunal when that party has not yet presented all his evidence relevant to the point or had the opportunity of addressing the Tribunal on that evidence.

In the present case the Chairman had, on balance, made certain comments which were injudicious and untimely. Accordingly whilst such a decision was wholly exceptional an order would be made directing that the case be heard afresh by another Tribunal. Further, the Industrial Tribunal had failed to give adequate consideration to the staleness of the evidence and submissions that had been heard given that the hearing had been commenced more than two years before its decision: SIMPER (PETER) & CO. *v.* COOKE [1986] I.R.L.R. 19, E.A.T.

1275. Unfair dismissal—reason—failure to establish
[Employment Protection (Consolidation) Act 1978 (c.44), ss.57(1), 57(2).] A was a refuse collection driver who, whilst reversing his refuse collection vehicle, knocked down and killed an old lady. A was suspended and subsequently dismissed following a disciplinary meeting. A had been offered but rejected an opportunity to accept demotion. An Industrial Tribunal found that although there was no evidence before them as to the reasons why the employers had reached their conclusions, they were satisfied that A had committed a dismissible offence by carrying out a dangerous manoeuvre and that it was unnecessary for the employer in such circumstances to explain the reason for their decision to dismiss. The dismissal was found to have been fair. A appealed to the Employment Appeal Tribunal. *Held,* allowing A's appeal, that the Tribunal had committed a fundamental error of law in failing to apply the provisions of s.57(1). It was not right for a Tribunal simply to consider whether there had been a dismissible offence without having regard to the reason or absence of reason given by the employer. A finding was substituted that the dismissal was unfair: ADAMS *v.* DERBY CITY COUNCIL [1986] I.R.L.R. 163, E.A.T.

1276. Unfair dismissal—reason for dismissal—substitution of reason—whether prejudice suffered
H was dismissed from his post as a regional sales manager and his employers contended that the dismissal was by reason of redundancy. An Industrial Tribunal found that the reason for the dismissal was a reorganisation constituting a substantial reason and not redundancy. H appealed to the Employment Appeal Tribunal arguing that he had been unfairly deprived of the opportunity of developing his case and possibly of calling evidence and certainly of arguing in ways different from those which he adopted on the basis that his employers relied on the fact that he had been dismissed by reason of redundancy. *Held,* dismissing the appeal, that H could not show that he had been prejudiced on the facts of this case. The Industrial Tribunal had considered the bona fides of and the reasons for the decision to reorganise. The Industrial Tribunal would not have considered any other factual issues had the employer relied upon some other substantial reason. Where the different grounds are really different labels and nothing more, there is no basis for saying that the late introduction, even without pleading or without argument, is a ground for interference on appeal; but where the difference goes to facts and substance, there would or might have been some substantial or significant difference in the way the case was conducted. An appeal would succeed if the Tribunal relied upon a different ground without affording an opportunity for argument (*Nelson* v. *British Broadcasting Corp.* [1977] C.L.Y. 1123, *Banerjee* v. *City & East London Area Health Authority* [1979] C.L.Y. 1030, *Murphy* v. *Epsom College* [1984] C.L.Y. 1262, and *Hotson* v. *Wisbech Conservative Club* [1985] C.L.Y. 1262, considered): HANNAN *v.* TNT-IPEC (U.K.) [1986] I.R.L.R. 165, E.A.T.

1277. Unfair dismissal—reasonableness—errors in dismissal procedure not prejudicial—contributory conduct—whether basic award to be reduced
[Employment Protection (Consolidation) Act 1978 (c.44), ss.73(7B), 74 (as amended by Employment Act 1980 (c.42), s.9(4).]
An industrial tribunal is entitled to hold that a dismissal is unfair where the employer has unreasonably delayed dismissal procedures, even where the delay has not prejudiced the employee. Where the tribunal reduces the compensatory award it is only in exceptional circumstances that the tribunal should not reduce the basic award.
The R.S.P.C.A. alleged that C was guilty of gross misconduct in the way that he carried out an investigation into complaints of cruelty against two dogs. Disciplinary proceedings (in respect of other matters) were already pending against C and the disciplinary procedure in respect of that investigation was not commenced for some six months or thereabouts. The industrial tribunal held that the R.S.P.C.A. had

acted unreasonably in delaying the investigation, albeit that C had suffered no prejudice because he would have been dismissed in any event. The tribunal decided, however, that C had contributed to his own dismissal to such an extent that it reduced the compensatory award to nil, but it left intact the basic award. *Held,* that the tribunal's decision on liability was not perverse and could be sustained, notwithstanding that C had not been prejudiced. Only exceptionally, however, could it be justified to reduce the compensatory award and not to reduce the basic award commensurately. The R.S.P.C.A.'s appeal against the basic award would be allowed, and it would be reduced to nil.

R.S.P.C.A. *v.* CRUDEN [1986] I.C.R. 205, E.A.T.

1278. Unfair dismissal—reasonableness—jurisdiction of appellate courts

The Employment Appeal Tribunal is not entitled to interfere with a finding of an industrial tribunal that a dismissal is fair where the tribunal has regard to all the relevant matters and the finding is not perverse.

N was employed as a music teacher by the respondent county council. In consequence of his conduct in the course of invigilating an "A" level examination on June 15, 1983 the respondent's Divisional Education Officer purported to summarily dismiss N, on June 16, 1983. After objections from N and his union representative he was suspended on full pay. Thereafter N's conduct was considered at a meeting of the respondent's schools sub-committee. After hearing evidence the committee resolved that N should be dismissed for gross misconduct. The voting followed the pattern of the committee's political party composition. N appealed to the respondent's appeals committee to no avail. N complained that he had been unfairly dismissed. The industrial tribunal found that N was guilty of misconduct. It criticised the respondent's disciplinary procedure. It found that no injustice resulted to N from the procedural short-comings and that the decision to dismiss N fell within the band of reasonable responses of a reasonable employer in the circumstances. An appeal against the decision that N's dismissal was fair was allowed by the Employment Appeal Tribunal which stated that the total response of the respondents to N's conduct regarded in the round displayed too much haste, stubbornness and secrecy and too little concern for the appearance of fairness as well as its substance to be seen in the eyes of any reasonable tribunal as conduct which would commend itself to a reasonable employer in their position. *Held*, allowing the respondent's appeal, that as an appellate court the Employment Appeal Tribunal was not entitled to reverse the decision of an industrial tribunal unless the tribunal had misdirected itself on the law or reached a decision that no reasonable tribunal could properly reach. In the present case the E.A.T. had wrongly substituted its own decision on whether N's dismissal was fair for the decision made by the tribunal. The tribunal considered all the relevant matters and applied the law correctly. The tribunal's decision could not be described as perverse. The tribunal had regard to matters that were not relied upon by the parties but were relevant in considering the procedures followed by the respondents. It was proper for the tribunal to consider such matters and attach such weight to them as they saw fit in the circumstances of the case as a whole. The parties ought to be given an opportunity to deal with such matters by the tribunal. In considering such matters the tribunal should pay careful and proper attention to the course of the hearing and the way in which and the extent to which a point has been made or relied upon (*Iceland Frozen Foods* v. *Jones* [1983] C.L.Y. 1325, *Dobie* v. *Burns International Security Services (U.K.)* [1984] C.L.Y. 1310, *Gilham* v. *Kent County Council (No. 2)* [1985] C.L.Y. 1259 applied).

NEALE *v.* HEREFORD AND WORCESTER COUNTY COUNCIL [1986] I.C.R. 471, C.A.

1279. Unfair dismissal—reasonableness—ill-health incapacity—employee unable to perform her duties

[Employment Protection (Consolidation) Act 1978 (c.44), s.57(2)(*a*).]

Where an employee is unable through ill-health to perform all her duties the employer is entitled to dismiss her.

S was employed by ELB as a residential social worker, which required her to lift handicapped patients. After she developed back trouble, ELB's medical advisers concluded that she was incapable of performing her duties, with which view S's own doctor concurred (although he thought she might be capable of light work). When a suitable post became available ELB offered it to S, who turned it down because she would have to move. ELB then dismissed S. The industrial tribunal rejected the complaint of unfair dismissal. *Held,* on appeal, that the simple fact was that S was incapable of performing her duties, however widely her contract was drawn. That ELB could enforce mobility itself with regard to S's employment did not mean that there was a corresponding obligation upon ELB to provide work elsewhere within its organisation (*Gunton* v. *Richmond London Borough Council* [1980] C.L.Y. 895 applied).

SHOOK v. EALING LONDON BOROUGH COUNCIL [1986] I.C.R. 314, E.A.T.

1280. Unfair dismissal—reasonableness—subsequent events

[Employment Protection (Consolidation) Act 1978 (c.44), s.57(3).]

When considering whether an employee has been unfairly dismissed it is necessary to take account of the whole process of dismissal, and events occurring during the notice period are not excluded from consideration.

In November 1983 the employers thought that a redundancy situation would arise by the following May and in February 1984, as part of a programme of phased redundancies gave the employee notice that he would be made redundant as from May 4. They then obtained a fresh contract bringing new work opportunities from April 1984 and recruited a number of new staff, but did not offer the employee a job. On his claim for unfair dismissal, an industrial tribunal held that although the employers had acted unreasonably, they were precluded in law from holding the dismissal unfair because if it was fair at the date of the dismissal notice, subsequent events during the notice period could not render it unfair, and the complaint was dismissed. *Held,* allowing the employee's appeal, that when considering whether there was unfair dismissal within section 57(3) of the Employment Protection (Consolidation) Act 1978 it was necessary to take account of the whole process of dismissal initiated by the giving of notice and completed by its expiry, rather than regarding the giving of notice as fixing the moment of dismissal and precluding consideration of events which occurred during the notice period. The employers acted unfairly in failing to offer the employee fresh employment when it became available during the period of notice, and his complaint would be upheld (*Davis (W.) & Sons* v. *Atkins* [1977] C.L.Y. 1160 distinguished; *Abernethy* v. *Mott, Hay and Anderson* [1974] C.L.Y. 1285 considered).

STACEY v. BABCOCK POWER [1986] 2 W.L.R. 207, E.A.T.

1281. Unfair dismissal—re-engagement—payment of arrears—date at which earnings to be assessed

[Employment Protection (Consolidation) Act 1978 (c.44), s.69.]

When an industrial tribunal makes an order for the re-engagement of an employee and payment of arrears of pay, the arrears should be calculated on the basis of the employee's pay at the date of dismissal.

P was employed by E as a technical writer in the computer business. She was dismissed and alleged unfair dismissal on the ground of her trade union activities. The industrial tribunal did not accept that, but found that she had been dismissed on the ground of redundancy; they concluded that dismissal was unfair for lack of proper consultation. They ordered that she should be re-engaged as a trainee programmer. Previously she had been earning about £8,000. Now she would be earning about £5,000. When the tribunal came to consider what arrears should be paid under s.69(4)(*d*) of the Employment Protection (Consolidation) Act 1978 the question arose whether their calculations should be based on the larger or the smaller figure. They chose the higher figure. *Held,* dismissing E's appeal, that arrears should be calculated by reference to the employee's pay on the date of dismissal.

ELECTRONIC DATA PROCESSING v. WRIGHT [1986] I.C.R. 76, E.A.T.

1282. Unfair dismissal—reinstatement—contributory fault

[Employment Protection (Consolidation) Act 1978 (c.44), ss.69(5), 74(6))] Where an industrial tribunal examined the question of contributory fault in deciding on a compensatory award, it was not necessary to re-open the question when deciding on reinstatement: BOOTS CO. v. LEES-COLLIER, *The Times,* January 24, 1986, E.A.T.

1283. Unfair dismissal—right of appeal—denial of right

Where a contract of employment contains a right of appeal against dismissal, and the employee is denied that right, his dismissal is unfair (*West Midlands Co-operative Society* v. *Tipton* [1986] C.L.Y. 1285 applied): NATIONAL COAL BOARD v. NASH, *The Times,* May 7, 1986, E.A.T.

1284. Unfair dismissal—short term contracts—non-renewal—whether redundancy

[Employment Protection (Consolidation) Act 1978 (c.44), s.55(2)(*b*), 57(1)(*b*).]

The non-renewal of a fixed-term contract can constitute "some other substantial reason" for dismissal within the meaning of the Employment Protection (Consolidation) Act 1978.

The employee, a teacher, was employed between 1981–1983 on a series of short-term fixed contracts. Her last contract was not renewed, and she was deemed to have been dismissed. She claimed redundancy or unfair dismissal in the alternative. The tribunal found that there was neither redundancy nor unfair dismissal. The E.A.T. held that since on the facts the need for teachers had been reduced by one, a redundancy situation existed. *Held*, allowing the appeal, that (1) the appeal tribunal had proceeded on an erroneous assumption of fact; and (2) the non-renewal of a fixed-term contract could constitute "some other substantial reason" for dismissal (*Terry* v. *East Sussex County Council* [1976] C.L.Y. 876, approved; *Nottinghamshire County Council* v. *Lee* [1980] C.L.Y. 960 distinguished).

FAY v. NORTH YORKSHIRE COUNTY COUNCIL [1986] I.C.R. 133, C.A.

1285. Unfair dismissal—summary dismissal—refusal of employer to entertain appeal—whether relevant in determining reasonableness of dismissal

[Employment Protection (Consolidation) Act 1978 (c.44), s.57(3) (as amended by Employment Act 1980 (c.42), s.6).]

On the question of whether an employer has acted reasonably in summarily dismissing an employee an Industrial Tribunal is entitled to take into account the employer's refusal to entertain the employee's contractual right of appeal, and in certain cases such a refusal by the employer may of itself justify a finding of unfair dismissal.

Per curiam: following summary dismissal, success by the employee under the domestic appeals procedure would operate as from the date of the dismissal; if the appeal fails, then the effective date is the date when notice of immediate dismissal is given.

T was warned that unless his attendance record improved he would be liable to dismissal. Subsequently he was dismissed for poor attendance, but the employer refused to allow him to exercise his right, under an agreed procedure, to appeal. The Industrial Tribunal held that the dismissal was unfair, primarily because of the employer's refusal to hear the appeal. *Held*, on the question of whether that was an admissible consideration, that the Tribunal was entitled to consider the employer's refusal to hear T's appeal. In the absence of any admitted serious misconduct such a refusal could itself be a ground for a finding of unfair dismissal. (*National Heart and Chest Hospitals Board of Governors* v. *Nambiar* [1981] C.L.Y. 973, *Greenall Whitley* v. *Carr* [1985] C.L.Y. 1251 and *Sainsbury (J.)* v. *Savage* [1981] C.L.Y. 968 approved; *Devis (W.) & Sons* v. *Atkins* [1977] C.L.Y. 1160 distinguished.

WEST MIDLANDS CO-OPERATIVE SOCIETY v. TIPTON [1986] 2 W.L.R. 306, H.L.

1286. Unfair dismissal—time limits—whether "reasonably practicable" to have presented in time

[Employment Protection (Consolidation) Act 1978 (c.44), s.67(2).]

The fact that a claimant delays putting in a claim for unfair dismissal, relying on the advice of a third party, is not normally a ground for saying it was not reasonably practicable to present a claim in time.

The two employees were dismissed by their employers, a health authority. They were advised by a member of their representative body to delay their applications to a tribunal until the internal appeal processes were exhausted. Their appeals failed and one year after dismissal they applied to a tribunal. On a preliminary point as to time limits the tribunal found they had jurisdiction. *Held*, allowing the appeal, that the quality and accuracy of the advice of a third party was not normally a ground for contending it was not reasonably practicable to present a complaint.

CROYDON HEALTH AUTHORITY v. JAUFURALLY [1986] I.C.R. 4, E.A.T.

1287. Unfair dismissal—transfer of business—effective date

[Transfer of Undertakings (Protection of Employment) Regulations (S.I. 1981 No. 1794).] An employee who is dismissed between exchange of contracts for the sale of a business and completion is entitled to bring a claim for unfair dismissal against the purchasing company: KESTONGATE v. MILLER, *The Times,* May 28, 1986, E.A.T.

1288. Unfair dismissal—transfer of business—re-engagement on new terms

[Transfer of Undertakings (Protection of Employment) Regulations 1981 (S.I. 1981 No. 1794), regs. 5(1)(2)(3), 8(1) (2).]

Where a dismissal is in consequence of a transfer of a business it is automatically unfair, and remains so where there are no changes in the workforce.

On the sale of a newsagents' business, B, who had been employed as a part-time assistant since 1978, was given notice of dismissal and made redundant on Friday June 21. The buyer, P, offered B re-engagement on the Saturday, to commence the following Monday. The incidence of B's working hours, but not their quantity were changed. A month later B left P's employ, and claimed unfair dismissal by P on the transfer of the business. *Held*, that by virtue of reg. 8(1) of the 1981 Regulations the dismissal of June 21, occurring as it did in consequence of the transfer of the business, was deemed to be unfair; it remained so notwithstanding reg. 8(2) as there were "changes in the workforce". Further, albeit that there was a two-day gap between the ending of B's employment with the vendor of the business and her re-engagement by P, she was nonetheless employed in the business immediately before the transfer and was thus deemed to have been dismissed by P (*Apex Leisure Hire* v. *Barratt*) [1984] C.L.Y. 1316 and *Fenton* v. *Stablegold* [1986] C.L.Y. 1254 applied).

BULLARD *v.* MARCHANT [1986] I.C.R. 389, E.A.T.

1289. Unfair dismissal—transfer of undertakings—construction

[Transfer of Undertakings (Protection of Employment) Regulations (S.I. 1981 No. 1794), A Quaker school enjoying charitable status was held not to be an undertaking in the nature of a commercial venture so that teachers employed immediately prior to the sale of the school were obliged to direct their claims for unfair dismissal against the original management of the school rather than the new owners: WOODCOCK *v.* COMMITTEE OF THE FRIENDS SCHOOL, *The Times*, April 29, 1986, E.A.T.

1290. Unfair dismissal—whether transfer of undertaking—whether dismissal for a reason connected with the transfer.

[Transfer of Undertakings (Protection of Employment) Regulations 1981 (S.I. 1981 No. 1794), regs.2(1), 5.] H was employed by a Student Union as a manageress of their catering facilities. Losses occurred and the Students Union entered into a 12 month agreement with outside caterers who undertook the management and supervision of the catering services. They were paid on a commission basis. H was dismissed by the Students Union and went to work for the caterers. Subsequently the Students Union terminated the agreement with the caterers but failed to re-engage H who considered that she had been automatically transferred to the employment of the Students Union by the operation of the Transfer Regulations. An Industrial Tribunal by a majority concluded that there had been no relevant transfer of an undertaking and that her application failed. *Held*, rejecting H's appeal, that whether or not a particular undertaking had been relevantly transferred is always a question of fact and degree and it was not advisable or even possible to lay down legal principles as to what did or did not amount to a relevant transfer of an undertaking. Whilst the correct interpretation of the Regulations is clearly a matter of law, the circumstances of a particular case giving rise to an inference that an undertaking has been relevantly transferred is a question of fact and degree. It was not possible to say in this case that the majority of the Tribunal had failed to take account of any material circumstances in this regard or had misdirected themselves in their approach. For this reason the Appellant's argument failed. The Employment Appeal Tribunal did hold however that the Industrial Tribunal had misdirected itself in holding, by a majority, that there had been a dismissal because an employer cannot claim to have dismissed an employee if he uses terms which are vague and unspecific as they had done in the present case. If the Employment Appeal Tribunal had had to decide this aspect of the argument they would have agreed with the dissenting member of the Industrial Tribunal (*International Computers* v. *Kennedy* [1981] C.L.Y. 827, applied): HADDEN *v.* UNIVERSITY OF DUNDEE STUDENTS' ASSOCIATION [1985] I.R.L.R. 449 E.A.T.

1291. Vicarious liability—criminal act of employee—damages

[Ire.] D provided a specialist security protection service at P's premises. One of D's employees stole goods from the premises. *Held*, allowing P's claim for damages, that (1) as D was specifically engaged to protect P's property he was under a duty to take due care to do so and as he had delegated that duty to an employee he was vicariously liable for the act of that employee notwithstanding that it was a criminal one; and (2) P was entitled to recover the replacement value of the stolen goods together with the costs incurred by him in investigating the theft: JOHNSON AND JOHNSON (IRELAND) v. C. P. SECURITY [1985] I.R. 362, Egan J.

1292. Wages—deductions in respect of losses—calculated by employer—whether "for or in respect of any fine"

[Truck Act 1896 (59-60 Vict., c.44), s.1(1).]

A petroleum company's contract with an employee permitting arbitrary deductions calculated by the employers "for or in respect of any fine," may be unfair and unreasonable and contravene the Truck Act 1896.

B worked as a forecourt attendant; he signed a form setting out the main terms of his employment including a clause permitting deductions for any loss caused by his negligence or breach of contract. The company was to calculate any deduction, but no details were given of the method. He was told he would be liable for any shortages attributable to his shift, although other staff had access to the till. He worked for three weeks, in which on one occasion a £20 deduction was made, and on another the whole of his wage was retained. The company was charged and convicted of an offence contrary to the Truck Act 1896. *Held*, dismissing the appeal, that as the deduction was entirely at the discretion of the company, and in view of the arbitrary nature of the powers reserved to them, the amount of the fine authorised by the contract could not be regarded as fair and reasonable, and the contract contravened s.1(1) (*Bristow* v. *City Petroleum* [1985] C.L.Y. 1146 considered).

SEALAND PETROLEUM CO. v. BARRATT [1986] 1 W.L.R. 700, C.A.

1293. Wages Act 1986 (c.48)

This Act makes fresh provision with respect to the protection of workers in relation to the payment of wages; makes further provision with respect to wages councils; restricts redundancy rebates to employers with less than ten employees and abolishes certain similar payments.

The Act received the Royal Assent on July 25, 1986.

1294. Wages Act 1986—commencement

WAGES ACT 1986 (COMMENCEMENT) ORDER 1986 (No. 1998 (C.75)) [45p], made under the Wages Act 1986 (c.48), s.33; brings into operation on January 1, 1987, Pt. 1 of the 1986 Act.

1295. Wages councils

WAGES COUNCILS (PRESERVATION OF ACCRUED RIGHTS UNDER WAGES ORDER) ORDER 1986 (No. 2282) [45p], made under the Wages Act 1986 (c.48), Sched. 6, para. 6; operative on January 28, 1987; continues in force rights in relation annual holidays and paid annual holiday which workers currently enjoy after wages orders cease to have effect under the 1986 Act.

EQUITY

1296. Company—loan—termination of purpose

The secondary trust established when money is lent to a company for the specific purpose of purchasing certain items is spent when those itself are purchased and does not revive if the purchase falls through and part of the money reverts to the receiver of the company: EVTR, *Re, Financial Times,* July 18, 1986, Michael Wheeler Q.C. (sitting as deputy High Court Judge).

1297. Equitable rights—cause of action—foreign state—export documents claimed to be forged

Although declaratory relief could only be granted to protect a legal or equitable right, a foreign government was entitled to claim such relief where it alleged that its export licences had been forged since it was in their interests that they have credibility.

A painting by Goya was exported from Spain and bought by D2 who arranged for D1 to sell it at auction. The Kingdom of Spain brought proceedings alleging that the picture had been illegally exported and that three documents apparently authorising the export had been forged. Ds applied to strike out the action as showing no cause of action and as an abuse of the process of the court. The application was dismissed. *Held*, that although P had no legal title to the picture and sought only a declaration, it was possible that the use of forged documents purporting to be those of a foreign state could debase the genuine export licences issued by the state. P had therefore an arguable case that it had an equitable right to bring an action in this country to protect its property from damage or pecuniary loss (*Emperor of Austria* v. *Day* (1861) 3 de G.F. & J. 217 and *R.C.A. Corp.* v. *Pollard* [1982] C.L.Y. 436 considered). The bona fides of P was not in question since the court was satisfied that the proceedings had not been brought in order to depress the value of the picture at the auction, and therefore Ds had not shown that the action should be struck out as an abuse of the court.

KINGDOM OF SPAIN v. CHRISTIE, MANSON & WOODS [1986] 1 W.L.R. 1120, Browne-Wilkinson V.-C.

1298. Proprietary estoppel—reliance on fictitious letter—whether bar to equitable relief

L brought proceedings against T for possession of a flat, on grounds that were agreed to be good at law. T however claimed a proprietary estoppel on the grounds that they had expended substantial sums on the property in reliance upon an alleged representation by L that T could live in the premises rent free for as long as they wished. In support of this claim they relied upon a letter which the assistant recorder found was known to one of them to be a forgery. He held that this behaviour disentitled T to any equitable relief. *Held*, dismissing Ts' appeal, that this conclusion was quite correct: WILLIS (J.) & SON v. WILLIS (1986) 277 E.G. 1133, C.A.

1299. Undue influence—unauthorised third party—agent

[Consumer Credit Act 1974 (c.39), s.138(1)(*b*).]

A commercial trader is not liable for the unconscionable conduct of a third party when the third party had not been constituted the lender's agent.

G and his wife who were both in their eighties offered to help their son who needed some money. The son arranged for them to borrow £20,000 from C who were licensed moneylenders on a short term loan secured by a charge on G's house. C expected the loan to be repaid by the son, and referred the matter to their solicitors for completion. The solicitors sent the parents by post or via the son a legal charge to be signed by G, a consent to the loan to be signed by his wife and a letter to each parent advising them to seek independent legal advice. The letter did not reach the parents but they signed the documents in the presence of the son's solicitor who explained the consent form to the mother but did not advise them on the nature of the transaction. The son was given the cheque on which he forged G's indorsement and kept the money. The loan was not repaid. C brought proceedings to enforce the charge and G contended that the transaction had been obtained by undue influence and that the bargain was extortionate within s.138 of the 1974 Act. The judge set the charge aside. *Held*, allowing C's appeal that (1) a commercial lender was not liable for a third party's unconscionable conduct which affected the debtor's agreement to or execution of a loan if the third party's conduct was an unauthorised intervention in the transaction; when the third party has not been appointed the lender's agent the lender's only duty is to point out the desirability of taking independent legal advice; the duty does not extend to ensuring that the debtor is independently advised or that the documents are executed in the presence of a solicitor; though the son had exercised undue influence he was not constituted C's agent or the agent of C's solicitors and his unilateral assumption of the conduct of the transaction could not constitute him their agent; *Turnbull* v. *Duval* [1902] A.C. 429. *Chaplin* v. *Brammall* [1908] 1 K.B. 233, *Avon Finance* v. *Bridger* [1979] C.L.Y. 1832, *Kings North Trust* v. *Bell* [1985] C.L.Y. 1650 distinguished; (2) there was nothing unusual about the transaction and since the rate of interest was reasonable and C had acted in the normal way, they had discharged the burden of showing that the bargain was not extortionate.

COLDUNELL v. GALLON [1986] 1 All E.R. 429, C.A.

1300. Unjust enrichment—unconscionable bargain—whether duty to advise obtaining of independent legal advice

[Can.] L, an undischarged bankrupt, and W decided to buy five lots and build homes on them. L's mother, M, gave L $20,000 to make the initial payment and agreed to purchase L's interest in the lots in her name. The plaintiff bank approved a loan to W and M, who signed a joint account agreement, a lodgement of title to the five lots and a demand note for $150,000 to the bank. The documents were signed at L's lawyer's home, where L, who was the only person able to speak to M in her native tongue, explained the general effect of the documents but assured her they had nothing to do with her home, her only major asset. M never spoke with anyone from the bank, nor did she receive any independent legal advice. The venture failed and the bank took foreclosure proceedings and obtained personal judgment on the note against W and M. *Held*, that relief is granted for an unconscionable bargain where an unfair advantage is gained by an unconscientious use of power by a stronger party against a weaker, as demonstrated by evidence of the substantial unfairness of the bargain and inequality of the parties. Here, M's only objective was to assist her son; she did not seek to gain anything personally. Everyone involved in this venture thought it would succeed and it was not a case of additional security being extracted for an additional loan. L did not act as the bank's agent in obtaining execution of the documents. It was as likely as not that, even had she obtained legal advice, she would have signed the documents. Under the circumstances, the bank owed no duty to M to get such advice. The agreement was not unfair, nor was there any evidence of an unfair advantage gained by an unconscientious use of power by a stronger party against a weaker (*Lloyds Bank* v. *Bundy* [1974] C.L.Y. 1691 distinguished): TORONTO-DOMINION BANK v. WONG AND LIM, 65 B.C.L.R. 243, British Columbia, C.A.

ESTOPPEL

1301. Equitable licence—occupation of house by unmarried mother and child—burden of proof as to detriment

A woman who had a child by her lover and moved into a house provided by him was not entitled to a transfer of the property to her based on proprietary estoppel or contractual licence, in the absence of any detriment caused to her.

Per curiam: The onus to prove an absence of detriment does not shift to the other party once a claimant proves that she has changed her position in reliance on alleged assurances. There is merely a rebuttable presumption, where, following assurances by the other party, a claimant has adopted a course of conduct prejudicial or detrimental to her, that she did so in reliance on the assurances (*Greasley* v. *Cook* [1980] C.L.Y. 1066 considered).

P and D were both married to others when they became lovers. D told P that he wished them to live together and they discussed having a child. He bought a house, and when P became pregnant by D she left her husband and moved into the house, giving up her job two months before the birth. D did not move in but visited her regularly, paid all the bills, and gave her an allowance for herself and the child. This arrangement continued when he bought another house into which P moved with the child. She redecorated and improved the house and garden. She asked him to put the house into joint names but he refused, assuring her though that he would always provide for her and provide her with a roof over her head. After ten years, the relationship ended, he offered her £10,000 to move out, but she refused. She started affiliation proceedings, in the course of which D undertook to permit P and the child to occupy the house until the child was 17. She brought an action based on proprietary estoppel and contractual licence for an order that the property be conveyed to her absolutely or alternatively, a declaration that she was entitled to occupy it for life. *Held*, that the action be dismissed. When P moved into the first house she did nothing that amounted to providing consideration for, and it was impossible to infer, a contract between the parties that D would provide her with a house for the rest of her life (*Tanner* v. *Tanner* [1976] C.L.Y. 2170 distinguished). On the evidence, P had not held a mistaken belief that she would have the right to remain indefinitely against D's wishes, since they had not discussed what was to happen if their relationship broke down, and a belief that D would always provide a roof over her head was not sufficient. Further, P had not acted to her detriment in becoming pregnant, leaving her husband, looking after the house and child or in not looking for a job. She had not therefore established the elements necessary to give rise to an equity in her favour to remain in the house once the child was 17. The action was dismissed on D's undertaking to provide accommodation at the house for P and the child until then (*Pascoe* v. *Turner* [1979] C.L.Y. 1083 distinguished; *Willmott* v. *Barber* (1880) 15 Ch.D. 96 considered).

COOMBES v. SMITH [1986] 1 W.L.R. 808, Jonathan Parker Q.C. sitting as a deputy High Court judge.

1302. Personal right of occupation—possession—unmarried couple
[Fiji; Native Land Trust Act (Fiji), s.121.]
Where a couple lived together unmarried, and one partner gave up her flat to live with the other on his representation that it would be a permanent home for her and her children, he was estopped from denying that she could remain there permanently and was not entitled to possession against her.

The Native Land Trust Board of Fiji leased native land to the Fiji Housing Authority which made it available to married couples. In 1968 P began associating with D who had two children, and a child of the parties was born in 1970. In 1973 when they were living as man and wife, P applied to the housing authority for land stating that he was married to D and undertaking to use the land solely for the erection of a house for him and his family. D supported the application having been told by P that the land would be for their family use. P financed and built a house, and D in reliance on his representation that it would be a permanent home for her and her family gave up her flat and went to live with him in the house. She used her earnings to look after the family. P left in 1980 and later took possession proceedings. The judge dismissed the action but the Court of Appeal of Fiji allowed an appeal, holding that when P left he conferred on D a licence to occupy the house which was an unlawful dealing with land under s.12 of the Native Land Trust Act, the prior consent of the Native Land Trust Board not having been obtained. *Held*, allowing D's appeal to the Judicial Committee, that as it would be inequitable for P to evict D he was estopped from denying that she had his permission to remain permanently in the house. Such a promissory or equitable estoppel, being a purely personal right not amounting to a property interest, was not a dealing with the land for the purposes of s.12 of the Native Land Trust Act and so was not defeated by that section. P was not entitled to an order for vacant possession (*Kulamma* v. *Manadan* [1968] C.L.Y. 241 followed); *Chalmers* v. *Pardoe* [1963] C.L.Y. 2981 distinguished).

Semble: When a union between an unmarried couple comes to an end, one who is sole owner in law and in equity of the property hitherto their home may in certain circumstances obtain an order for possession against the other. It was the particular combination of facts in this case which led to the estoppel
MAHARAJ (SHEILA) v. JAI CHAND [1986] 3 W.L.R. 440, P.C.

EUROPEAN COMMUNITIES

1303. Agricultural produce—export licences—whether forfeiture penalty too drastic
E.D. & F. Man (Sugar) (the plaintiff) wished to export sugar to a non-EEC State. Under the common organisation of the sugar market, surplus sugar might be exported to non-EEC States provided an export licence was obtained and a deposit was lodged in accordance with the conditions laid down in European Commission Reg. No. 1880/83. The issue of an export licence was conditional upon the lodging of a deposit which guaranteed that the export would be effected during the period of validity of the licence and which was forfeited wholly or partially if the transaction was not effected, or was only partially effected within that period. The plaintiff lodged the necessary deposit, but applied for a licence a couple of hours after the time-limit for such application had expired. The Intervention Board for Agricultural Produce declared the deposit forfeit as a result of that delay. The plaintiff brought proceedings in the English High Court for repayment of the deposit. Mr. Justice Glidewell asked the European Court under Art. 177 EEC for a preliminary ruling on the interpretation and validity of Art. 6(3) of Reg. 1880/83. *Held,* that Art. 6(3) was invalid in as much as it laid down forfeiture of the entire deposit as the penalty for failure to comply with the time-limit imposed for the submission of applications for export licences. Automatic forfeiture of the entire deposit was too drastic a penalty to be imposed in the event of an infringement less serious than the failure to fulfil the primary obligation to export.
R. v. INTERVENTION BOARD FOR AGRICULTURAL PRODUCE, *ex p.* E. D. & F. MAN (SUGAR) [1985] 3 C.M.L.R. 759. European Ct.

1304. Agriculture—directives, decisions and regulations
Corrigenda to Commission Regulation (EEC) No. 3154/85 of November 11, 1985 laying down detailed rules for the administrative application of monetary compensatory amounts (O.J. No. L310 of 21.11.1985). (O.J. 1986 L5/11.)

Corrigendum to Commission Regulation (EEC) No. 3153/85 of November 11, 1985 laying down detailed rules for the calculation of monetary compensatory amounts (O.J. No. L310 of 21.11.1985). (O.J. 1986 L5/10.)

Corrigendum to Commission Regulation (EEC) No. 3155/85 of November 11, 1985 providing for the advance fixing of monetary compensatory amounts (O.J. No. L310 of 21.11.1985). (O.J. 1986 L5/11.)

Commission Regulation (EEC) No. 992/86 of April 4, 1986 suspending advance fixing of the monetary compensatory amounts. (O.J. 1986 L90/39.)

Commission Regulation (EEC) No. 1002/86 of April 7, 1986 amending Regulation (EEC) No. 3155/85 providing for the advance fixing of monetary compensatory amounts. (O.J. 1986 L93/8.)

Commission Regulation (EEC) No. 1013/86 of April 8, 1986 amending Regulation (EEC) No. 1677/85 as regards the fixing of the correcting factor to be used to calculate the monetary compensatory amounts applicable for certain agricultural products. (O.J. 1986 L94/18.)

Commission Regulation (EEC) No. 1019/86 of April 8, 1986 repealing Regulation (EEC) No. 992/86 suspending advance fixing of the monetary compensatory amounts. (O.J. 1986 L94/30.)

Commission Regulation (EEC) No. 1022/86 of April 8, 1986 on transitional measures concerning the application of certain monetary compensatory amounts. (O.J. 1986 L94/37.)

Commission Regulation (EEC) No. 1302/86 of April 30, 1986, amending Regulation (EEC) No. 1022/86 on transitional measures concerning the applications of certain monetary compensatory amounts. (O.J. 1986 L114/82.)

Commission Regulation (EEC) No. 1303/86 of April 30, 1986, on transitional measures concerning the application of certain monetary compensatory amounts. (O.J. 1986 L114/83.)

Commission Regulation (EEC) No. 1377/86 of May 7, 1986 on transitional measures concerning the application of certain monetary compensatory amounts. (O.J. 1986 L.120/35.)

Council Regulation (EEC) No. 3642/85 of December 19, 1985 amending Regulation (EEC) No. 1035/72 on the common organisation of the market in fruit and vegetables. (O.J. 1985 L348/1.)

Council Regulation (EEC) No. 1006/86 of March 25, 1986 amending Regulation (EEC) No. 2727/75 on the common organisation of the market in cereals with regard to arrangements for production refunds. (O.J. 1986 L94/1.)

Council Regulation (EEC) No. 1007/86 of March 25, 1986 amending Regulation (EEC) No. 1418/76 on the common organisation of the market in rice in respect of the arrangements for production refunds. (O.J. 1986 L94/3.)

1305. Agriculture—intervention—adulterated milk powder

The defendant sold skimmed-milk powder to the plaintiff intervention board, having bought it originally from a producer who was later convicted of adulterating its product. A few years later the plaintiff considered that the dried milk product which the defendant had sold to it, did not constitute skimmed-milk powder and sued the defendant for damages for non-performance. The defendant disputed before the German courts that it had delivered powder which had been adulterated. The defendant was ordered to pay damages. The defendant appealed to the Bundesgerichtshof (the German Federal Supreme Court). *Held,* allowing the appeal in part, that it was not to be assumed without evidence that all or part of the powder delivered by the defendant was adulterated. The case was remitted for further inquiry.

STORAGE OF ADULTERATED MILK POWDER, *Re* [1986] 2 C.M.L.R. 123, German Federal Supreme Court.

1306. Agriculture—milk—discrimination

Mr. Bozzetti, an Italian dairy farmer, sought repayment of an amount deducted, on behalf of the Ministero del Tesoro, as the co-responsibility levy, from the sale price of the milk which he produced. He argued that the co-responsibility levy gave rise to discrimination between EEC producers because it was calculated by reference to the price of milk containing 3·7 per cent. fat, whilst milk produced in Italy had a lower fat content. He argued that Italian farmers had less responsibility for the surpluses which it was sought to end, but were still required to pay the same rate of levy as other EEC producers. Therefore, he alleged that the levy was unlawful and should not be payable. Mr. Bozzetti brought proceedings for repayment of the sums he had paid before the Pretore (Magistrate), Cremona. The latter asked the European Court under Art. 177 EEC for a preliminary ruling on the interpretation and validity of European Council Reg. 1079/77 of May 17, 1977 on a co-responsibility levy and on measures for expanding the markets in milk and milk products and European Commission Reg. 1822/77 of August 5, 1977 laying down detailed rules for the collection of the co-responsibility levy introduced in respect of milk and milk products, as amended and supplemented. *Held,* that (1) EEC law requires that the co-responsibility levy introduced by Reg. 1079/77 and regulated in detail by Reg. 1822/77 be defined by reference to its economic purpose as one of the intervention measures aimed at stabilising the market in milk products. It is for the domestic court to draw from that finding the conclusions which are necessary to resolve whether it has jurisdiction in this regard; (2) none of the arguments put forward affected the validity of Regs. 1079/77 and 1822/77. The Regs. could not be regarded as discriminatory, nor could the machinery set up under those Regs. be regarded as inconsistent, since the method by which the co-responsibility levy is calculated accorded with the common organisation of the market.

BOZZETTI *v.* INVERNIZZI SpA AND THE MINISTERO DEL TESORO (No. 179/84) [1986] 2 C.M.L.R. 246, European Ct.

1307. Agriculture—milk—non-marketing premium

European Council Regulation 1078/77 of May 17, 1977 introduced a system of premiums for the non-marketing of milk and milk products and for the conversion of dairy herds. Dr. von Menges (the "plaintiff") farmed his own land in Germany and kept a herd of dairy cows. In 1980 he obtained a premium for the non-marketing of milk and milk products. In accordance with Art. 2(2)(*a*) of Regulation 1078/77 he undertook not to market milk or milk products for five years. In 1981 the plaintiff leased his farm to a farmer who planned, *inter alia,* to use it to raise milk sheep. The plaintiff sought a declaration from the German courts that the marketing of ewe's milk and ewe's milk products was not prejudicial to the grant of the non-marketing premium. The Administrative Court of Appeal for the Land of North Rhine-Westphalia asked the European Court under Art. 177 EEC for a preliminary ruling on the interpretation of Art. 2(2)(*a*) of Reg. 1078/77. *Held,* that the words "milk and milk products" in Art. 2(2)(*a*) of Reg. 1078/77 applied to ewe's milk and ewe's milk products. If ewe's milk was regarded as not covered by the "milk" that the recipient of a non-marketing premium undertakes not to market, this would be incompatible with the objectives of the premium system, especially as such an interpretation would lead to the premium system itself encouraging replacement of dairy cows by milk sheep and would therefore tend to create new surpluses.

VON MENGES (KLAUS) *v.* LAND NORDRHEIN-WESTFALEN (No. 109/84) [1986] 2 C.M.L.R. 309, European Ct.

1308. Agriculture—milk production—compensation for discontinuation. See AGRICULTURE, § 65.

1309. Agriculture—monetary compensatory amounts—payment

The plaintiff, Continental Irish Meat (in receivership), exported beef from Ireland to the U.K. and Italy. It therefore became liable to the defendant, representing the Irish intervention agency, for monetary compensatory amounts ("m.c.a.s") upon exportation. Since Ireland, U.K. and Italy had exercised the option contained in Art. 2a of Council Reg. 974/71, the Irish intervention agency became liable to the plaintiff in respect of the m.c.a.s payable on importation of the beef into U.K. and Italy. The Irish intervention agency paid to the plaintiff's receiver the difference between the sum payable by way of m.c.a.s upon importation against the m.c.a.s owed by the plaintiff upon exportation. The plaintiff brought proceedings for the remainder of the sum on the basis that the intervention agency had been acting in one capacity when dealing with m.c.a.s on exports and in another capacity when dealing with m.c.a.s on imports, and was not entitled to set-off the sums. The Supreme Court of Ireland asked the European Court under Art. 177 EEC for a preliminary ruling on the interpretation of Art. 2a of European Council Reg. 974/71 on certain measures of short-term economic policy to be taken in agriculture following the temporary widening of the margins of fluctuation for the currencies of certain Member States, as amended by Art. 2

of Council Reg. 1112/73. *Held,* that Art. 2a of Reg. 974/71, as amended by Art. 2 of Reg. 1112/73, had to be interpreted as meaning that where an exporting EEC State has entered into an agreement with an importing EEC State for the payment of m.c.a.s which should be granted by the latter State, the first State is acting in the same capacity when it pays that amount as when it recovers the m.c.a.s payable upon exportation of the product from its country. Thus, an intervention agency is acting in the same capacity when paying to and receiving from the undertaking the relevant m.c.a.s and is entitled, if national law so allows, to set-off such amounts.

CONTINENTAL IRISH MEAT *v.* MINISTER FOR AGRICULTURE (No. 125/84) [1985] 3 C.M.L.R. 713, European Ct.

1310. Agriculture—Potato Marketing Board—levies
The Potato Marketing Board, the plaintiff, sued Mr. Drysdale, the defendant potato grower, for payment of levies due under the potato marketing scheme. The defendant argued that the potato marketing scheme was contrary to EEC law and sought to rely, *inter alia,* on the defences raised by the defendants in *Potato Marketing Board* v. *Robertsons* [1983] C.L.Y. 1639. The plaintiff obtained summary judgment under Order 14 of the Rules of the Supreme Court. The defendant appealed. *Held,* dismissing the appeal, that no prima facie case had been established by the defendant that Arts. 16, 34, 37 or 86 EEC provided a defence to the action. There was no triable issue and no need to seek a preliminary ruling from the European Court of Justice. The case of *Potato Marketing Board* v. *Robertsons (supra)* was followed. It would be inappropriate in applications under Order 14 involving questions of EEC law to hold that a defendant is estopped by any default judgment which may have been given against him previously: POTATO MARKETING BOARD *v.* DRYSDALE (JOHN M.) [1986] 3 C.M.L.R. 331, English Court of Appeal.

1311. Agriculture—reduced price butter—edible ices
P brought proceedings against decisions of the German intervention agency. By their decisions the agency forfeited the processing securities provided by P, which had purchased intervention butter at a reduced price, on the ground that the end use to which the processed product was put was in breach of EEC regulations. The Higher Administrative Court of Hesse accepted that the butter was duly processed into powder for the preparation of edible ices in accordance with Art. 6(1)(c) of Commission Regulation 1259/72. The Court asked the European Court under Art. 177 EEC for a preliminary ruling on the interpretation of Art. 6 of Reg. 1259/72 and whether the subsequent separation of the processed product and its use for purposes other than the production of edible ices justified the forfeiture of the security under Art. 18(2) of Reg. 1259/72. *Held,* that (1) Art. 6(a), which was inserted into Reg. 1259/72 by Commission Regulation 1910/73, applied to powder for the preparation of edible ices within Art. 6(1)(c) of Reg. 1259/72. Art. 6(a) allowed further processing of the products mentioned in Art. 6(1)(c) only if the resulting products were also products referred to in that Article; (2) where the security had not already been released, the national intervention agency had to declare it forfeit if it established that although powder for the preparation of edible ices was produced from the butter in accordance with Art. 6(1)(c) of Reg. 1259/72, as amended, the powder was not used for the preparation of edible ices, but was separated into products falling within headings of the Common Custom Tariff other than those referred to in Art. 6(1)(c), as amended; (3) the insertion of the additive sodium caseinate to powder for the preparation of edible ices did not adversely affect the right to release of the security where the conditions set by Art. 6(1)(c) of Reg. 1259/72 were met within the prescribed period.

FIRMA JOSEF HOCHE & ROOMBOTERFABRIEK 'DE BESTE BOTER' *v.* BUNDESANSTALT FÜR LANDWIRTSCHAFTLICHE MARKTORDNUNG (Nos. 154–155/83) [1986] 2 C.M.L.R. 632, European Ct.

1312. Agriculture—rosé wine—labelling
Mr. Ramel and others (the defendants) were prosecuted in France for producing and selling as "rosé table wines" certain wines obtained by coupage of rosé table wines from Italy and red table wines originating in various EEC States, without observing traditional French practices for the production of rosé wine. The defendants argued that the proceedings had no legal basis under EEC rules on the organisation of the common market in wine, which did not prohibit the mixtures at issue or the

marketing thereof. The Court of Appeal, Montpellier, asked the European Court under Art. 177 EEC for a preliminary ruling on the interpretation of EEC rules on the common organisation of the market in wine. *Held,* that (1) European Council Regulations 337/79 and 355/79 had to be interpreted as permitting the coupage of red table wine with a rosé table wine, where the two wines concerned originate in more than one EEC State. The Regulations allowed the marketing of the resulting mixture within the EEC under the description "rosé table wine from various countries of the European Communities" in so far as the term "rosé" is not inconsistent with an objective characteristic of the wine, which enables it to be differentiated from red wine or white wine solely by reason of its colour; (2) Art. 2(2)(*h*) of Regulation 355/79 did not permit an EEC State to prescribe that a table wine may not be described as "rosé wine" or be marketed, solely on the ground that a particular table wine was not produced in accordance with traditional local or national practices.

FEDERATION NATIONALE DES PRODUCTEURS DE VINS DE TABLE ET VINS DE PAYS *v.* RAMEL (No. 89/84) [1986] 2 C.M.L.R. 529, European Ct.

1313. Agriculture—sheep. See AGRICULTURE, § 000.

1314. Approximation of laws—directives, decisions and regulations
85/573/EEC:
Council Directive of December 19, 1985 amending Directive 77/436/EEC on the approximation of the laws of the Member States relating to coffee extracts and chicory extracts. (O.J. 1985 L372/22.)
85/581/EEC:
Council Directive of December 20, 1985 adapting, on account of the accession of Spain and Portugal, Directive 85/210/EEC on the approximation of the laws of the Member States concerning the lead content of petrol. (O.J. 1985 L372/37.)
85/647/EEC:
Commission Directive of December 23, 1985 adapting to technical progress Council Directive 71/320/EEC on the approximation of the laws of the Member States relating to the braking devices of certain categories of motor vehicles and their trailers. (O.J. 1985 L380/1.)
86/94/EEC:
Council Directive of March 10, 1986 amending for the second time Directive 73/404/EEC on the approximation of the laws of the Member States relating to detergents. (O.J. 1986 L80/51.)
86/96/EEC:
Council Directive of March 18, 1986 amending Directive 80/232/EEC on the approximation of the laws of the Member States relating to the ranges of nominal quantities and nominal capacities permitted for certain prepackaged products. (O.J. 1986 L80/55.)
86/102/EEC:
Council Directive of March 24, 1986 amending for the fourth time Directive 74/329/EEC on the approximation of the laws of the Member States relating to emulsifiers, stabilisers, thickeners and gelling agents for use in foodstuffs. (O.J. 1986 L88/40.)
86/199/EEC:
Eighth Commission Directive of March 26, 1986 adapting to technical progress Annexes II, IV and VI to Council Directive 76/768/EEC on the approximation of the laws of the Member States relating to cosmetic products. (O.J. 1986 L.149/38.)
86/217/EEC:
Council Directive of May 26, 1986 on the approximation of the laws of the Member States relating to tyre pressure gauges for motor vehicles. (O.J. 1986 L.152/48.)
86/218/EEC:
Fourth Commission Decision of May 16, 1986 relating to the application of Council Directive 72/166/EEC on the approximation of the laws of the Member States relating to insurance against civil liability in repect of the use of motor vehicles, and to the enforcement of the obligation to insure against such liability. (O.J. 1986 L.153/52.)
86/219/EEC:
Fifth Commission Decision of May 16, 1986 relating to the application of Council Directive 72/166/EEC on the approximation of the laws of the Member States

relating to insurance against civil liability in respect of the use of motor vehicles, and to the enforcement of the obligation to insure against such liability. (O.J. 1986 L.153/53.)

86/220/EEC:

Sixth Commission Decision of May 16, 1986 relating to the application of Council Directive 72/166/EEC on the approximation of the laws of the Member States relating to insurance against civil liability in respect of the use of motor vehicles, and to the enforcement of the obligation to insure against such liability. (O.J. 1986 L.153/54.)

86/247/EEC:

Twenty-first Council Directive of 16 June 1986 on the harmonisation of the laws of the Member States relating to turnover taxes—Deferment of the introduction of the common system of value-added tax in the Hellenic Republic. (O.J. 1986 L164/27.)

86/290/EEC:

Commission opinion of May 30, 1986 addressed to the French Government on their draft decree concerning the implementation of various provisions of Council Regulation (EEC) No. 543/69 as amended, on the harmonisation of certain social legislation relating to road transport. (O.J. 1986 L182/28.)

86/295/EEC:

Council Directive of May 26, 1986 on the approximation of the laws of the Member States relating to roll-over protective structures (ROPS) for certain construction plant. (O.J. 1986 L186/1.)

86/296/EEC:

Council Directive of May 26, 1986 on the approximation of the laws of the Member States relating to falling-object protective structures (FOPS) for certain construction plant. (O.J. 1986 L186/10.)

86/297/EEC:

Council Directive of May 26, 1986 on the approximation of the laws of the Member States relating to the power take-offs of wheeled agricultural and forestry tractors and their protection. (O.J. 1986 L186/19.)

86/312/EEC:

Commission Directive of June 18, 1986 adapting to technical progress Council Directive 84/529/EEC on the approximation of the laws of the Member States relating to electrically operated lifts. (O.J. 1986 L196/56.)

86/388/EEC:

Commission Directive of July 23, 1986 amending Council Directive 83/229/EEC on the approximation of the laws of the Member States relating to materials and articles made of regenerated cellulose film intended to come into contact with foodstuffs. (O.J. 1986 L.228/32.)

86/431/EEC:

Seventh Commission Directive of June 24, 1986 adapting to technical progress Council Directive 67/548/EEC on the approximation of laws, regulations and administrative provisions relating to the classification, packaging and labelling of dangerous substances. (O.J. 1986 L247/1.)

86/508/EEC:

Commission Directive of October 7, 1986 adapting to technical progress for the second time Council Directive 77/728/EEC on the approximation of the laws, regulations and administrative provisions of the Member States relating to the classification, packaging and labelling of paints, varnishes, printing inks, adhesives and similar products. (O.J. 1986 L295/31.)

86/562/EEC:

Commission Directive of November 6, 1986 adapting to technical progress Council Directive 71/127/EEC on the approximation of the laws of the Member States relating to the rear-view mirrors of motor vehicles. (O.J. 1986 L327/49.)

1315. Businessman's Guide

The Businessman's Guide to E.E.C. Legal Developments 1986 has been published by S. J. Berwin & Co. The booklet is a guide to the current year's development of the European Communities. Enquiries should be addressed to Stephen Kon, S. J. Berwin & Co., Capital House, 42 Weston Street, London S.E.1. 3QN; Tel: 01–403–3111 [£1·50.]

1316. Civil Jurisdiction and Judgments Act 1982

The United Kingdom has ratified the 1978 Accession Convention to the 1968 Convention on Jurisdiction and the Enforcement of Judgments in Civil and Commercial matters. The Convention enters into force for the U.K. on January 1, 1987 and the Civil Jurisdiction and Judgments Act 1982 will be brought into force similarly on January 1, 1987.

1317. Civil Jurisdiction and Judgments Act 1982—commencement. See PRACTICE, § 2585/2586.

1318. Coal and steel—directives decisions and regulations

85/553/ECSC:

Decision of the representatives of the Governments of the Member States of the European Coal and Steel Community, meeting within the Council of December 17, 1985 applying for 1986 the generalised tariff preferences for certain steel products originating in developing countries. (O.J. 1985 L352/235.)

85/637/ECSC:

Commission Decision of December 20, 1985 derogating from High Authority recommendation No. 1–64 on tariff protection in order to enable the generalised tariff preferences to be applied to certain iron and steel products originating in the developing countries. (O.J. 1985 L379/54.)

Commission Decision No. 3484/85/ECSC of November 27, 1985 establishing Community rules for aid to the steel industry. (O.J. 1985 L340/1.)

Commission Decision No. 3485/85/ECSC of November 27, 1985 on the extension of the system of monitoring and production quotas for certain products of undertakings in the steel industry. (O.J. 1985 L340/5.)

Commission Decision No. 3486/85/ECSC of November 27, 1985 fixing the rates of abatement for the first quarter of 1986 in accordance with Decision No. 3485/85/ECSC on the extension of the system of monitoring and production quotas for certain products of undertakings in the steel industry. (O.J. 1985 L340/41.)

Commission Decision No. 3501/85/ECSC of December 11, 1985 amending Decision No. 528/76/ECSC regarding the Community system of measures taken by the Member States to assist the coal-mining industry. (O.J. 1985 L335/8.)

Commission Decision No. 3612/85/ECSC of December 20, 1985 amending Decision 73/287/ECSC concerning coal and coke for the iron and steel industry in the Community. (O.J. 1985 L344/33.)

Commission Decision No. 3613/85/ECSC of December 20, 1985 on retrospective Community surveillance of imports and exports of certain iron and steel products covered by the Treaty establishing the European Coal and Steel Community originating in certain non-member countries. (O.J. 1985 L344/34.)

Commission Decision No. 3614/85/ECSC of December 18, 1985 fixing the rate of the levies for the 1986 financial year and amending Decision No. 3–52 on the amount of and methods for applying the levies provided for in Arts. 49 and 50 of the ECSC Treaty. (O.J. 1985 L344/37.)

Commission Decision No. 3699/85/ECSC of December 23, 1985 relating to the suspension of Decision No. 3715/83/ECSC fixing minimum prices for certain steel products (O.J. 1985 L351/53.)

Commission Decision No. 3700/85/ECSC of December 23, 1985 modifying for the second time Decision No. 3716/83/ECSC instituting a guarantee system for certain steel products. (O.J. 1985 L351/54.)

Commission Decision No. 3701/85/ECSC of December 23, 1985 amending for the second time Decision No. 3483/82/ECSC concerning the requirement for Community undertakings to declare the quantities of certain steel products delivered. (O.J. 1985 L351/55.)

Commission recommendation No. 3658/85/ECSC of December 23, 1985 on Community surveillance in respect of the importation of certain iron and steel products covered by the ECSC Treaty and originating in certain non-member countries. (O.J. 1985 L348/32.)

86/3/ECSC:

Decision of the Representatives of the Governments of the Member States of the European Coal and Steel Community, meeting within the Council, and of the Commission of the European Communities of January 7, 1986 determining the arrangements to be applied with regard to imports into Spain and Portugal, originating in Algeria, Egypt, Israel, Jordan, Lebanon, Morocco, Syria, Tunisia,

Turkey and Yugoslavia of products falling within the ECSC Treaty. (O.J. 1986 L12/27.)

86/37/EEC, ECSC:

Recommendation of the Commission of February 28, 1986 to the Member States on the extension of the period of validity of the transitional measures adopted in respect of ACP States and overseas countries and territories:—Council Regulation (EEC) No. 485/85,—Council Regulation (EEC) No. 486/85,—Council Decision 85/159/EEC.—Decision 85/160/ECSC of the representatives of the Government of the Member States of the European Coal and Steel Community, meeting within the Council of February 26, 1985. (O.J. 1986 L55/109.)

86/38/ECSC:

Decision of the representatives of the Governments of the Member States, meeting within the Council of February 28, 1986 establishing the arrangements to be applied to imports into Spain and Portugal of products covered by the ECSC Treaty originating in Austria, Finland, Norway, Sweden or Switzerland and covered by the Agreements between the Community and those countries. (O.J. 1986 L56/119.)

86/48/ECSC:

Decision of the representatives of the governments of the Member States, meeting within the Council of March 3, 1986 extending Decision 80/1187/ECSC opening tariff preferences for products within the province of the ECSC Treaty and originating in the overseas countries and territories associated with the Community. (O.J. 1986 L.63/184.)

86/49/ECSC:

Decision of the representatives of the governments of the Member States, meeting within the Council of March 3, 1986 establishing arrangements for trade between Spain and Portugal on the one hand and the African, Caribbean and Pacific States (ACP States) on the other in products falling within the ECSC Treaty. (O.J. 1986 L.63/185.)

86/50/ECSC:

Decision of the representatives of the governments of the Member States, meeting within the Council, of March 3, 1986 establishing arrangements for trade between Spain and Portugal on the one hand and the overseas countries and territories (OCT) on the other in products falling within the ECSC Treaty. (O.J. 1986 L.63/189.)

86/89/ECSC:

Decision of the representatives of the Governments of the Member States meeting within the Council of March 14, 1986 opening tariff preferences in Greece for products covered by the ECSC Treaty and originating in Austria, Finland, Norway, Sweden and Switzerland. (O.J. 1986 L78/29.)

86/97/ECSC:

Commission Decision of March 5, 1986 authorising Spain to adopt protective measures in respect of imports of certain steel products. (O.J. 1986 L80/57.)

86/98/ECSC:

Decision of the representatives of the Governments of the Member States, meeting within the Council of March 3, 1986 on the uniform application of the customs nomenclature with regard to products falling within the province of the ECSC Treaty. (O.J. 1986 L81/29.)

86/116/EEC:

Commission Decision of March 7, 1986 concerning the zones referred to in Art. 2(3) of Regulation (EEC) No. 2616/80 instituting a specific Community regional development measure contributing to overcoming constraints on the development of new economic activities in certain zones adversely affected by restructuring of the steel industry. (O.J. 1986 L99/25.)

86/133/ECSC:

Commission Decision of March 13, 1986 derogating from High Authority recommendations No. 1/64 concerning an increase in the protective duty on iron and steel products at the external frontiers of the Community (121 derogation). (O.J. 1986 L101/42.)

86/134/ECSC:

Commission Decision of March 13, 1986 derogating from High Authority recommendation No. 1/64 concerning an increase in the protective duty on iron and steel products at the external frontiers of the Community (122 derogation). (O.J. 1986 L101/43.)

86/184/ECSC:

Commission Decision of April 2, 1986 establishing the delivery levels of ECSC steel products of Spanish origin on to the rest of the common market, excluding Portugal. (O.J. 1986 L.132/37.)

86/185/ECSC:

Commission Decision of April 2, 1986 establishing the delivery levels of ECSC steel products of Portuguese origin on to the rest of the common market, excluding Spain. (O.J. 1986 L.132/38.)

86/400/ECSC

Commission Decision of July 10, 1986 authorising the Member States to institute intra-Community surveillance of the importation for home use of certain iron and steel products originating in certain third countries, covered by the Treaty establishing the European Coal and Steel Community and in free circulation in the Community. (O.J. 1986 L233/7.)

86/518/ECSC

Commission Decision of October 1, 1986 authorising Spain to adopt protective measures in respect of imports of certain steel products. (O.J. 1986 L305/46.)

86/589/EEC

Commission Decision of November 26, 1986 accepting undertakings given in connection with the anti-dumping proceeding concerning imports of potassium permanganate originating in Czechoslovakia, the German Democratic Republic and the People's Republic of China and terminating the investigation. (O.J. 1986 L339/32.)

86/596/EEC:

Commission Decision of November 26, 1986 relating to a proceeding under Article 85 of the EEC Treaty (IV/31.204—MELDOC). (O.J. 1986 L348/50.)

Commission Decision No. 978/86/ECSC of March 24, 1986 amending Decision No. 2873/82/ECSC on the monitoring by the Community of exports of certain steel products to the United States of America. (O.J. 1986 L91/49.)

Commission Decision No. 1031/86/ECSC of April 9, 1986 prohibiting alignment on offers of steel products originating from certain third countries. (O.J. 1986 L95/14.)

Commission Decision No. 1566/86/ECSC of February 24, 1986 on iron and steel statistics. (O.J. 1986 L.141/1.)

Commission Decision No. 1618/86/ECSC of May 26, 1986 fixing the rates of abatement for the third quarter of 1986 in accordance with Decision No. 3485/85/ECSC on the extension of the system of monitoring and production quotas for certain products of undertakings in the steel industry. (O.J. 1986 L.142/31.)

Commission Decision No. 2308/86/ECSC of July 22, 1986 fixing the amended rates of abatement for the third quarter of 1986 in accordance with Decision No. 3485/85/ECSC on the extension of the system of monitoring and production quotas for certain products of undertakings in the steel industry. (O.J. 1986 L201/24.)

Commission Decision No. 2365/86/ECSC of July 28, 1986 laying down the conditions and criteria for the application of Article 7 of Decision No. 3485/85/ECSC on the extension of the system of monitoring and production quotas for certain products of undertakings in the steel industry. (O.J. 1986 L205/21.)

Commission Decision No. 2827/86/ECSC of September 11, 1986 amending Decision No. 2872/82/ECSC on the restriction of exports of certain steel products to the United States of America. (O.J. 1986 L262/12.)

Commission Decision No. 2828/86/ECSC of September 11, 1986 amending Decision No. 2873/82/ECSC on the monitoring by the Community of exports of certain steel products to the United States of America. (O.J. 1986 L262/16.)

Commission Decision No. 2829/86/ECSC of September 11, 1986 concerning exports of semi-finished iron and steel products to the United States of America. (O.J. 1986 L262/19.)

Commission Decision No. 2852/86/ECSC of September 15, 1986 fixing the rates of abatement for the fourth quarter of 1986 in accordance with Decision No. 3485/85/ECSC on the extension of the system of monitoring and production quotas for certain products of undertakings in the steel industry. (O.J. 1986 L264/18.)

Commission Decision No. 3673/86/ECSC of December 1, 1986 fixing the rates of abatement for the first quarter of 1987 in accordance with Decision No.

3485/85/ECSC on the extension of the system of monitoring and production quotas for certain products of undertakings in the steel industry. (O.J. 1986 L339/20.)

Commission Decision No. 3746/86/ECSC of December 5, 1986 amending Decision No. 3485/85/ECSC on the extension of the system of monitoring and production quotas for certain products of undertakings in the steel industry. (O.J. 1986 L348/1.)

Commission Regulation (EEC) No. 977/86 of March 24, 1986 amending Regulation (EEC) No. 2874/82 on the monitoring by the Community of exports of certain steel products to the United States of America. (O.J. 1986 L91/1.)

Commission Regulation (EEC) No. 979/86 of March 24, 1986 amending Regulation (EEC) No. 61/85 on the monitoring by the Community of exports of steel tubes and pipes to the United States of America. (O.J. 1986 L91/96.)

Commission Regulation (EEC) No. 2826/86 of September 11, 1986 amending Regulation (EEC) No. 2874/82 on the monitoring by the Community of exports of certain steel products to the United States of America. (O.J. 1986 L262/9.)

Council Regulation (EEC) No. 2823/86 of September 11, 1986 amending Regulation (EEC) No. 2870/82 on the restriction of exports of certain steel products to the United States of America. (O.J. 1986 L262/1.)

Council Regulation (EEC) No. 2824/86 of September 11, 1986 concerning exports of semi-finished iron and steel products to the United States of America. (O.J. 1986 L262/6.)

1319. Companies—accounts—partnerships

The European Commission submitted a proposal for a Council Directive amending Directive 78/660 on annual accounts and Directive 83/349 on consolidated accounts so that the rules contained therein applied to partnerships, limited partnerships and unlimited companies whose unlimited members consist of either public or private limited companies.

DRAFT DIRECTIVE ON COMPANY ACCOUNTS (PARTNERSHIPS) [1986] 2 C.M.L.R. 661, E.C. COMMISSION.

1320. Competition—abuse of dominant market position—cars

British Leyland (BL) brought proceedings under Art. 173 EEC seeking annulment of the European Commission's decision that it had abused its dominant position with regard to the reimportation of left hand drive Metro cars. BL sought, in the alternative, a reduction in the 350,000 ECU fine imposed. *Held,* that BL's application was dismissed. Three ways in which BL had handled the issue of National Type Approval Certificates for left hand Metro cars had been obstructive to the reimportation of such cars into the U.K. and constituted abuse of a dominant position contrary to Art. 86 EEC: BRITISH LEYLAND *v.* EUROPEAN COMMISSION (No. 226/84), *The Times,* November 12, 1986, European Ct.

1321. Competition—air transport—fares

Ds were travel agencies who sold "soft currency" airline tickets, which they bought from travel agents or airlines situated abroad. These tickets started from abroad by air, but passed via Germany and were much cheaper than fares approved by the German Minister for Transport. P complained that Ds were acting anti-competitively and illegally. *Held,* judgment on the appeal was stayed pending a preliminary ruling from the European Court of Justice on the compatibility, *inter alia*, of the German law on tariffs on airline flights, with EEC Law.

FIRMA AHMED SAEED FLUGREISEN *v.* ZENTRALE ZUR BEKÄMPFUNG UNLAUTEREN WETTBEWERB EV [1986] 3 C.M.L.R. 158, German Federal Supreme Court.

1322. Competition—banking—negative clearance

The Irish Banks' Standing Committee applied under Council Regulation 17 to the European Commission for negative clearance on behalf of its members for a number of agreements in force between them.

The Commission issued a Notice stating that it proposed to make a favourable decision in relation to these agreements. Prior to any such decision being taken, it invited comments thereon from interested third parties.

APPLICATION OF THE IRISH BANKS' STANDING COMMITTEE, *Re* [1986] 2 C.M.L.R. 425, European Commission Notice.

1323. Competition—book prices—national law

Two French booksellers' trade associations brought summary proceedings against Argendis S.A. for a declaration that it was acting contrary to the French Book Prices

Act 1981 by undercutting book prices and for an order that it should desist, *inter alia,* from affixing two price labels to books (one label showing the statutory price and another label showing its own cheaper price) and from advertising the cheaper price. The associations also sought damages. Argendis S.A. argued that the judge had no jurisdiction to give such relief on the ground that this case involved a serious question on the compatibility of the 1981 Act with EEC Law, or alternatively Argendis S.A. argued that a reference to the European Court under Art.177 EEC should be made. The judge declared that he had no jurisdiction. The trade associations appealed. *Held,* allowing the appeal, that applications by the associations were admissible and justified. Argendis was offering discount on the retail sale of books contrary to French Law, which had not been shown to be manifestly contrary to EEC Law (in particular Arts. 3(f), 5 and 85 EEC). Thus, the judge dealing with summary matters had jurisdiction on a provisional basis and pending a judicial decision settling the main issue, to take preventive measures or to award damages.

L'UNION SYNDICALE DES LIBRAIRES DE FRANCE *v.* ARGENDIS S.A. [1986] E.C.C. 197, Court of Appeal, Versailles.

1324. Competition—commodity futures market—petroleum

The International Petroleum Exchange of London (IPE) notified its articles of association and rules and regulations to the European Commission and applied for negative clearance under Council Regulation 17.

The Commission issued a Notice stating that it proposed to take a favourable decision in relation to IPE's articles of association and rules and regulations. Prior to taking such a decision, the Commission invited interested third parties to make their comments within 28 days.

INTERNATIONAL PETROLEUM EXCHANGE OF LONDON, *Re* [1986] 2 C.M.L.R. 525, European Commission Notice.

1325. Competition—computers—collaboration agreements

International Computers and Fujitsu notified the European Commission of agreements for their collaboration in the computer field. The Commission issued a Notice that it intended either to grant exemption to these agreements under Art. 85(3) EEC or to have its Directorate-General for Competition send a provisional letter as described in the notice on procedures concerning notifications. The Commission invited interested third parties to send their comments within one month.

INTERNATIONAL COMPUTERS AND FUJITSU, *Re* [1986] 3 C.M.L.R. 154, European Commision Notice.

1326. Competition—defamation—privilege

In proceedings under Art. 85 EEC a complaint was made by a customer (Orbinson) to his retailer (Hodes) that the manufacturer, Hasselblad, would not service his appliance because it had been bought through unauthorised channels. The letter was passed to the Commission for use in proceedings. Hasselblad alleged that the letter was libellous and sued the customer in defamation, the action being struck out as against the public interest (*Hasselblad (G.B.)* v. *Orbinson* [1984] C.L.Y. 1373). Hasselblad brought libel proceedings against Hodes alleging that Hodes had concocted the letter as part of a trumped-up case. *Held,* that the action was struck out as being against the public interest, following the case of *Hasselblad (G.B.)* v. *Orbinson.*

HASSELBLAD (G.B.) *v.* HODES [1985] 3 C.M.L.R. 664, Sir Douglas Frank Q.C.

1327. Competition—directives, decisions and regulations

85/542/EEC:

Commission Decision of December 12, 1985 accepting an undertaking given in connection with the anti-dumping investigation concerning imports of roller chains for cycles originating in the USSR and terminating the investigation. (O.J. 1985 L335/63.)

85/559/EEC:

Commission Decision of November 27, 1985 relating to a proceeding under Art. 85 of the EEC Treaty (IV/30.846—Ivoclar. (O.J. 1985 L369/1.)

85/560/EEC:

Commission Decision of December 2, 1985 relating to a proceeding under Art. 85 of the EEC Treaty (IV/30.971—BP/Kellogg). (O.J. 1985 L369/6.)

85/561/EEC:

Commission Decision of December 13, 1985 relating to a proceeding under Art. 85 of the EEC Treaty (IV/30.017—Breeders' rights: roses). (O.J. 1985 L369/9.)

85/562/EEC:

Commission Decision of December 13, 1985 relating to a proceeding under Art. 85 of the EEC Treaty (IV/30.570 etc.—Sole distribution agreements for whisky and gin. (O.J. 1985 L369/19.)

85/563/EEC:

Commission Decision of December 13, 1985 relating to a proceeding under Art. 85 of the EEC Treaty (IV/27.590—London Sugar Futures Market Limited. (O.J. 1985 L369/25.)

85/564/EEC:

Commission Decision of December 13, 1985 relating to a proceeding under Art. 85 of the EEC Treaty (IV/27.591—London Cocoa Terminal Market Association Limited). (O.J. 1985 L369/28.)

85/565/EEC:

Commission Decision of December 13, 1985 relating to a proceeding under Art. 85 of the EEC Treaty (IV/27.592—Coffee Terminal Market Association of London Limited). (O.J. 1985 L369/31.)

85/566/EEC:

Commission Decision of December 13, 1985 relating to a proceeding under Art. 85 of the EEC Treaty (IV/27.593—London Rubber Terminal Market Association Limited). (O.J. 1985 L369/34.)

85/592/EEC:

Commission Decision of July 31, 1985 concerning aids granted by the French Government in the beef and veal sector. (O.J. 1985 L373/1.)

85/609/EEC:

Commission Decision of December 14, 1985 relating to a proceeding under Article 86 of the EEC Treaty (IV/30.698—ECS/AKZO). (O.J. 1985 L374/1.)

85/615/EEC:

Commission Decision of December 16, 1985 relating to a proceeding pursuant to Art. 85 of the EEC Treaty (IV/30.373—P & I clubs). (O.J. 1985 L376/2.)

85/616/EEC:

Commission Decision of December 16, 1985 relating to a proceeding pursuant to Art. 85 of the EEC Treaty (IV/30.665—Villeroy & Boch). (O.J. 1985 L376/15.)

85/617/EEC:

Commission Decision of December 16, 1985 relating to a proceeding pursuant to Art. 85 of the EEC Treaty (IV/30.839—Sperry New Holland). (O.J. 1985 L376/21.)

85/618/EEC:

Commission Decision of December 18, 1985 relating to a proceeding pursuant to Art. 85 of the EEC Treaty (IV/30.739—Siemens/Fanuc). (O.J. 1985 L376/29.)

Council Regulation (EEC) No. 3521/85 of December 12, 1985 definitively collecting the provisional anti-dumping duty imposed on imports of roller chains for cycles, originating in the USSR, and extending the provisional anti-dumping duty imposed on imports of roller chains for cycles, originating in the People's Republic of China. (O.J. 1985 L335/61.)

86/21/EEC:

Commission Decision of February 4, 1986 accepting undertakings given in connection with the anti-dumping investigation concerning imports of certain clogs originating in Sweden. (O.J. 1986 L32/28.)

86/33/EEC:

Commission Decision of February 13, 1986 accepting an undertaking given in connection with the anti-dumping investigation concerning imports of roller chains for cycles originating in the People's Republic of China and terminating that investigation. (O.J. 1986 L40/27.)

86/34/EEC:

Commission Decision of February 12, 1986 terminating the anti-dumping proceedings concerning imports of electronic typewriters manufactured by Nakajima All Precision Co. Ltd and originating in Japan. (O.J. 1986 L40/29.)

86/35/EEC:

Commission Decision of February 21, 1986 accepting undertakings given in connection with the anti-dumping proceeding concerning imports of fibre building board from Finland and Sweden and terminating the investigation. (O.J. 1986 L46/23.)

86/36/EEC:
Commission Decision of February 26, 1986 accepting undertakings entered into connection with the anti-dumping proceeding concerning imports into Greece of certain categories of glass originating in Turkey, Yugoslavia, Romania, Bulgaria, Hungary and Czechoslovakia and terminating the investigation. (O.J. 1986 L51/73.)

86/59/EEC:
Council Decision of March 6, 1986 terminating the anti-dumping proceeding concerning imports of dead-burned (sintered) natural magnesite originating in the People's Republic of China and North Korea. (O.J. 1986 L70/41.)

86/86/EEC:
Commission Decision of March 18, 1986 terminating the anti-dumping proceeding concerning imports of stainless steel household cooking ware originating in South Korea. (O.J. 1986 L74/33.)

86/99/EEC:
Commission Decision of March 24, 1986 terminating the anti-dumping proceeding concerning imports of hardboard originating in Portugal. (O.J. 1986 L81/30.)

86/207/EEC:
Commission Decision of April 10, 1986 concerning applications submitted by Beckman & Vagedes, KG, Bocholt, for refund of anti-dumping duties collected on certain imports of cotton yarn originating in Turkey. (O.J. 1986 L.151/26.)

86/208/EEC:
Commission Decision of April 10, 1986 concerning applications submitted by Industrieverband Gewebe, Frankfurt/Main, on behalf of Hecking & Co., Leo Middelhoff GmbH & Co. KG and Frottierweberei Vossen GmbH, for refund of anti-dumping duties collected on certain imports of cotton yarn originating in Turkey. (O.J. 1986 L.151/28.)

86/209/EEC:
Commission Decision of April 10, 1986 concerning applications submitted by Carl Weiske, Hof/Saale, for refund of anti-dumping duties collected on certain imports of cotton yarn originating in Turkey. (O.J. 1986 L.151/30.)

86/210/EEC:
Commission Decision of April 10, 1986 concerning applications submitted by Textilveredlungs- und handelsgesellschaft mbH & Co. KG, Neuenkirchen, for refund of anti-dumping duties collected on certain imports of cotton yarn originating in Turkey. (O.J. 1986 L.151/32.)

86/211/EEC:
Commission Decision of April 10, 1986 concerning applications submitted by Cotimex GmbH, Düsseldorf, for refund of anti-dumping duties collected on certain imports of cotton yarn originating in Turkey (O.J. 1986 L.151/34.)

86/212/EEC:
Commission Decision of April 10, 1986 concerning applications submitted by Textil—Imex GmbH, Bremen, for refund of anti-dumping duties collected on certain imports of cotton yarn originating in Turkey (O.J. 1986 L.151/36.)

86/232/EEC:
Commission Decision of June 9, 1986 accepting undertakings given in connection with the anti-dumping proceeding concerning imports of hardboard originating in Argentina, Switzerland and Yugoslavia and terminating the investigation. (O.J. 1986 L.157/61.)

86/344/EEC:
Commission decision of July 17, 1986 terminating the anti-dumping proceedings concerning imports of Portland cement originating in the German Democratic Republic, Poland and Yugoslavia. (O.J. 1986 L202/43.)

86/398/EEC
Commission Decision of April 23, 1986 relating to a proceeding under Article 85 of the EEC Treaty (IV/31.149—Polypropylene) (O.J. 1986 L230/1.)

86/497/EEC:
Commission Decision of October 7, 1986 accepting undertakings given inconnection with the anti-dumping proceeding concerning imports of silicon carbide originating in the People's Republic of China, Norway, Poland and the USSR, and terminating the investigation regarding imports of that product originating in the People's

Republic of China, Norway, Poland, Czechoslovakia, the USSR and Yugoslavia. (O.J. 1986 L287/25.)

86/589/EEC:

Commission Decision of November 26, 1986 accepting undertakings given in connection with the anti-dumping proceeding concerning imports of potassium permanganate originating in Czechoslovakia, the German Democratic Republic and the People's Republic of China and terminating the investigation. (O.J. 1986 L339/32).

86/596/EEC:

Commission Decision of November 26, 1986 relating to a proceeding under Article 85 of the EEC Treaty (IV/31.204—MELDOC). (O.J. 1986 L348/50.)

Commission Decision No. 2645/86/ECSC of July 30, 1986 implementing Decision No. 2064/86/ECSC establishing Community rules for State aid to the coal industry. (O.J. 1986 L242/1.)

Commission Decision No. 2767/86/ECSC of September 5, 1986 imposing a provisional anti-dumping duty on imports of certain sheets and plates, of iron or steel, originating in Yugoslavia. (O.J. 1986 L254/18.)

Commission Regulation (EEC) No. 2640/86 of August 21, 1986 imposing a provisional anti-dumping duty on imports of plain paper photocopiers originating in Japan. (O.J. 1986 L239/5.)

Commission Regulation (EEC) No. 2495/86 of August 1, 1986 imposing a provisional anti-dumping duty on imports of potassium permanganate originating in Czechoslovakia, the German Democratic Republic and the People's Republic of China. (O.J. 1986 L217/12.)

Council Decision No. 813/86/ECSC of March 14, 1986 on protection against imports which are the subject of dumping between the Community of Ten and the new Member States or between the new Member States during the period throughout which the transitional measures laid down by the Act of Accession of Spain and Portugal apply. (O.J. 1986 L78/1.)

Council Regulation (EEC) No. 113/86 of January 20, 1986 amending Regulation (EEC) No. 1698 imposing a definitive anti-dumping duty on imports of electronic typewriters originating in Japan. (O.J. 1986 L17/2.)

Council Regulation (EEC) No. 264/86 of February 4, 1986 imposing a definitive anti-dumping duty on imports of certain clogs originating in Sweden and definitively collecting the provisional anti-dumping duty. (O.J. 1986 L32/1.)

Council Regulation (EEC) No. 265/86 of February 4, 1986 extending the provisional anti-dumping duty on imports of certain electronic weighing scales originating in Japan. (O.J. 1986 L32/4.)

Council Regulation (EEC) No. 338/86 of February 14, 1986 imposing a definitive anti-dumping duty on imports of roller chains for cycles originating in the People's Republic of China and definitively collecting the provisional anti-dumping duty of those imports. (O.J. 1986 L40/25.)

Council Regulation (EEC) No. 677/86 of March 3, 1986 extending the provisional anti-dumping duty on imports of copper sulphate originating in Yugoslavia. (O.J. 1986 L62/1.)

Council Regulation (EEC) No. 812/86 of March 14, 1986 on protection against imports which are the subject of dumping between the Community of Ten and the new Member States or between the new Member States during the period throughout which the transitional measures laid down by the Act of Accession of Spain and Portugal apply. (O.J. 1986 L78/1.)

Council Regulation (EEC) No. 1058/86 of April 8, 1986 imposing a definitive anti-dumping duty on imports of certain electronic scales originating in Japan. (O.J. 1986 L97/1.)

Council Regulation (EEC) No. 1946/86 of June 24, 1986 amending Regulation (EEC) No. 273/83 imposing a definitive anti-dumping duty on imports of light sodium carbonate originating in Bulgaria, the German Democratic Republic, Poland, Romania and the Soviet Union. (O.J. 1986 L169/1.)

Council Regulation (EEC) No. 2127/86 of July 7, 1986 amending Regulation (EEC) No. 1698/85 imposing a definitive anti-dumping duty on imports of electronic typewriters originating in Japan. (O.J. 1986 L187/3.)

Council Regulation (EEC) No. 2336/86 of July 24, 1986 concerning the existing anti-dumping duties applicable to imports from third countries into Spain and Portugal. (O.J. 1986 L203/8.)

Council Regulation (EEC) No. 3661/86 of November 26, 1986 imposing a definitive anti-dumping duty on imports of potassium permanganate originating in the People's Republic of China and definitively collecting the provisional anti-dumping duty imposed on imports of potassium permanganate originating in Czechoslovakia, the German Democratic Republic and the People's Republic of China. (O.J. 1986 L339/1.)

1328. Competition—distribution franchise agreement—partitioning of markets

Mrs. Schillgalis (the defendant) sold bridalwear under franchising agreements with the plaintiff, Pronuptia de Paris GmbH ("Pronuptia") and its parent company. Under the agreements the defendant had the exclusive right to use the Pronuptia trade-mark in Hamburg, Oldenburg and Hanover, and the right to advertise in those areas, subject to Pronuptia's approval of the advertising. In return for the advantages of this franchise, the defendant had to pay licence fees of ten per cent. of her turnover. The plaintiff brought proceedings in Germany to recover the licence fees, the defendant argued that she was not liable to pay such fees as the agreements were void under Art. 85(1) EEC. The German Federal Court of Justice asked the European Court under Art. 177 EEC for a preliminary ruling on the interpretation of Art. 85 EEC and of Reg. 67/67. *Held*, that (1) the Court would restrict its comments to distribution franchise agreements. The compatibility of such agreements with Art. 85(1) EEC could not be assessed in the abstract, but depended on the clauses contained in the agreements and on the economic context in which they were included; (i) clauses whose purpose was to protect the franchisor's know-how, or the identity and reputation of the distribution network, which was symbolised by the brand name, did not constitute restrictions of competition within Art. 85(1) EEC; (ii) clauses which resulted in a partitioning of markets between franchisor and franchisees or among franchisees amounted to restrictions of competition within Art. 85(1) EEC; (iii) notification of recommended prices by the franchisor to franchisees did not constitute a restriction on competition provided, however, that between the franchisor and franchisees or among franchisees there was no concerted practice with a view to the effective application of those prices; (2) Reg. 67/67 was not applicable to the type of distribution franchise agreements in issue in these proceedings.

PRONUPTIA DE PARIS GmbH, FRANKFURT AM MAIN *v.* SCHILLGALIS (No. 161/84) [1986] 1 C.M.L.R. 414, European Ct.

1329. Competition—dominant position—abuse

C.I.C.C.E. sought a declaration under Art. 173(2) EEC that the European Commission's decisions of July 12 and October 28, 1983 to the effect that no further action would be taken on an application made by the C.I.C.C.E. under Art. 3 of Council Regulation 17 of February 6 are void. C.I.C.C.E. had alleged in its application that by insisting on very low licence fees for broadcasting films the three French television companies were in breach of Art. 86 EEC. C.I.C.C.E. argued that since the three French television companies had the exclusive rights to provide television in France, they held a dominant position in the EEC and alleged that their conduct was unfair. The Commission found that C.I.C.C.E.'s application failed to substantiate the alleged abuses. *Held*, that (1) a letter from a Director-General in the European Commission which affirms the Commission's intention to close the file on a complaint under Regulation 17 is a "decision" against which the complainant may appeal under Art. 173(2) EEC; (2) C.I.C.C.E. had not established that the Commission's decision to take no further action was vitiated by an error such as to justify it being declared void. Neither the documents in the case nor the proceedings before the Court shed doubt on the Commission's assessment. Accordingly, the decisions were not annulled; (3) when the European Commission investigates under Regulation 17 allegedly restrictive practices which have already been found by a national anti-trust body to be abusive of a dominant position under national law, it is in no way bound to come to the same conclusion under EEC competition law, even if the EEC and the national rules are substantially the same.

COMITÉ DES INDUSTRIES CINÉMATOGRAPHIQUES DES COMMUNAUTÉS EUROPÉENNES *v.* E.C. COMMISSION (No. 298/83) [1986] 1 C.M.L.R. 486, European Ct.

1330. Competition—dominant position—abuse

The European Commission found that AKZO Chemie BV ("AKZO") occupied a dominant position in the supply of organic peroxides in the EEC. The Commission decided (1) AKZO had abused its dominant position contrary to Art. 86 EEC by pursuing against Engineering and Chemical Supplies (Epsom and Gloucester) Ltd. (ECS) a course of conduct aimed at damaging ECS's business or at pushing ECS out of the EEC organic peroxides markets or both. Such conduct consisted, *inter alia,* of direct threats to ECS and offering product at unreasonably low prices to ECS's customers; (2) a fine of 10 million ECUs was to be imposed on AKZO; (3) AKZO was to cease the actions which were contrary to Art. 86 EEC. In so far as AKZO failed to do so, a daily penalty of 1,000 ECUs would be imposed until AKZO rectified its actions; (4) AKZO was to supply an annual compliance report to the Commission for a period of five years from January 1, 1986.

Engineering and Chemical Supplies (Epsom and Gloucester) *v.* AKZO Chemie BV (No. IV/30.698) (1986) 3 C.M.L.R. 273, European Commission.

1331. Competition—dominant position—abuse. See R. *v.* Monopolies and Mergers Commission, *ex p.* Argyll Group, § 3397.

1332. Competition—dominant position—interim measures—undertaking

The European Commission commenced proceedings to take interim measures against Hilti A.G., which it believed to be dominant in the market of powder actuated tools and their nails and cartridge magazines. The Commission objected to the marketing moves whereby Hilti allegedly tied together the supply of Hilti magazines and nails. Whilst not admitting the Commission's allegations, Hilti offered an undertaking not to tie the supply of magazines and nails. The Commission thereupon suspended proceedings and, for the first time, accepted an undertaking in lieu of a formal Decision in proceedings for interim measures.

Hilti A.G., *Re* [1985] 3 C.M.L.R. 619, European Commission Notice.

1333. Competition—dominant position—television advertising

The plaintiff, a Belgian tele-marketing company, brought proceedings in Belgium against the first defendant, which runs the R.T.L. television station, and against Information Publicité Benelux S.A. ("I.P."), which is R.T.L.'s exclusive agent for television advertising aimed at the Benelux countries. The plaintiff claimed an injunction restraining the first defendant and I.P. from refusing to sell it television time on the R.T.L. station for telephone marketing operations using a telephone number other than that of I.P., arguing that this constituted abuse of a dominant position contrary to Art. 86 EEC. The Tribunal de Commerce, Brussels, asked the European Court under Art. 177 EEC for a preliminary ruling on the interpretation of Art. 86 EEC. In its order for reference the Tribunal stated that the first defendant and I.P. dominated the market in television advertising aimed at viewers in French-speaking Belgium as there was no commercial advertising allowed on Belgian television stations and the advertising of other French-language stations which can be received in Belgium is aimed only rarely or not at all at Belgium viewers. *Held,* that (1) Art. 86 EEC applies to an undertaking with a dominant position on a particular market, even where that position is due not to the activities of the undertaking itself, but to the fact that because of national legislative provisions there can be no competition or only very limited competition on that market; (2) an abuse contrary to Art. 86 EEC occurs where, without any objective need, an undertaking with a dominant position on a particular market reserves to itself or to an undertaking belonging to the same group an ancillary activity which might be carried out by another undertaking as part of its activities on a neighbouring, but separate market, with the possibility of eliminating all competition from such undertaking; (3) it followed that subjecting the sale of broadcasting time to the condition that only the telephone number of an advertising agent belonging to the same group as the television station should be used, amounted in practice to a refusal to supply the services of that station to any other tele-marketing undertaking. If such refusal could not be justified by technical or commercial requirements relating to the nature of the television, but was intended to reserve to the agent any tele-marketing broadcast by the television station, with the possibility of eliminating all competition from another undertaking, such conduct amounted to an abuse contrary to Art. 86 EEC, provided that the other conditions of Art. 86 EEC were met.

CENTRE BELGE D'ETUDES DE MARCHÉ-TÉLÉ-MARKETING S.A. *v.* COMPAGNIE LUXEMBOURGEOISE DE TÉLÉDIFFUSION S.A. (No. 311/84) [1986] 2 C.M.L.R. 558, European Ct.

1334. Competition—exclusive distributorship agreements—guarantees

ETA, a Swiss company produced "Swatch" watches which it distributed with 12 months guarantees in Belgium through an exclusive dealer network. ETA brought proceedings against parallel importers of "Swatch" watches seeking to have them prohibited from including ETA's guarantees with the watches which they sold. The Commercial Court, Brussels, asked the European Court under Art. 177 EEC for a preliminary ruling on the compatibility of such a guarantee clause contained in an exclusive distribution agreement with Art. 85 EEC. *Held,* that a clause in an exclusive distribution agreement, by which a supplier undertook, in relation to its exclusive dealers, to grant guarantees on its products to their customers, and by virtue of which, it refused the guarantees to customers of parallel distributors, was contrary to Art. 85 EEC to the extent to which the restriction on competition which might arise, affected trade between EEC States.

ETA FABRIQUES D'EBAUCHES *v.* DK INVESTMENT (No. 31/85) [1986] 2 C.M.L.R. 674, European Ct.

1335. Competition—franchise agreements—cosmetics

The European Commission issued a Notice stating that it proposed to adopt a favourable attitude towards the standard-form distribution franchise agreements which Yves Rocher had notified. The notified agreements contained the terms of the franchise agreements which Yves Rocher concluded with its exclusive retailers for the marketing of its cosmetics. The European Commission invited interested third parties to send their comments on the case within one month.

FRANCHISE AGREEMENTS OF YVES ROCHER, *Re* [1986] 2 C.M.L.R. 95, European Commission Notice.

1336. Competition—group membership—computer software

Various large information technology companies notified agreements to the European Commission concerning the X/Open Group, which they had formed. The Group proposed to establish a "common application environment" for software to run on Unix operating systems. This was aimed at increasing the range of software that could be offered and which would be compatible with different companies' computer systems. The Commission intended to adopt a favourable decision provided it was immediately told of any changes in membership and received an annual report on any applicant refused membership of the Group. Before adopting such a decision the Commission invited interested third parties to provide their comments within a month.

THE X/OPEN GROUP, *Re* [1986] 3 C.M.L.R. 373, European Commission Notice.

1337. Competition—illicit commercial practice—U.S. exclusion order

Enkva BV, the sole producer of aramid fibres in the EEC, complained to the European Commission about an order of the U.S. International Trade Commission ("USITC"). By its order USITC excluded from the U.S.A. imports of certain forms of aramid fibre manufactured outside the U.S.A. by the Akzo group, including Enkva. Enkva alleged that such an order was made in breach of the USA's international obligations under GATT. The European Commission considered that the complaint raised an important question on the interpretation of GATT and had considerable economic implications; accordingly, in the interests of the EEC, the European Commission commenced an examination in accordance with Art. 6 of European Council Regulation 2641/84 of September 17, 1984. The European Commission invited views from interested parties and parties who could show that they were primarily concerned by the outcome of the procedure.

UNITED STATES LITIGATION BETWEEN E.I. DUPONT DE NEMOURS & CO. AND AKZO N.V., *Re* [1986] 1 C.M.L.R. 410, European Commission Notice.

1338. Competition—injunction—television and radio schedules

Radio Telefis Eireann (R.T.E.) publishes programme schedules and commentaries on the programmes. R.T.E. claims copyright in the schedules and commentaries, but provides them free of charge to newspapers and other publications who request them, but subject to a licence containing certain terms and conditions. R.T.E. claimed that the defendant had infringed its copyright by being in breach of a previously obtained licence by publishing a week's TV and radio programme schedules in advance. R.T.E. claimed, *inter alia*, an injunction to restrain that breach. The defendant claimed that R.T.E. were in breach of Arts. 85 and 86 EEC and had requested the European Commission to investigate the alleged breach of EEC competition law. *Held*, that an interlocutory injunction was granted to R.T.E. Once a plaintiff was entitled to an interlocutory injunction in Irish law the existence of an enquiry by the European Commission into a breach of EEC law did not justify the refusal of such an injunction.

RADIO TELEFIS EIRANN *v.* MAGILL TV GUIDE [1985] E.C.C. 574, Irish High Ct.

1339. Competition—interim measures—coin operated machines

The plaintiff supplied coin operated machines to some 57 Humberside tied public houses owned by Northern County Breweries ("Northern"). The machines were supplied pursuant to agreements with the tenants of the public houses. The defendant bought Northern and introduced a new "coin operated equipment policy", whereby all tenants had to operate equipment from the defendant's list of nominated suppliers. The defendants refused to place the plaintiff on that list. The plaintiff brought proceedings against the defendant alleging, *inter alia,* breaches of Art. 85 EEC and Art. 86 EEC, and sought an interim injunction. *Held,* that an interim injunction would be granted to restrain the defendant from (a) wrongfully interfering with the plaintiff's agreements with the tenants; (b) interfering with the plaintiff's equipment on the tenants' premises and (c) taking any action which would limit the freedom of the tenants to place orders for the plaintiff's equipment. An interim injunction would be granted as there was a series of serious questions to be tried in relation to Art. 85 EEC and damages would not be an adequate remedy for the plaintiff. The plaintiff's case in relation to Art. 86 EEC failed, as there was no evidence that the defendant occupied a dominant position within the EEC.

CUTSFORTH (T/A FOR AMUSEMENT ONLY (HULL)) *v.* MANSFIELD INNS [1986] 1 C.M.L.R. 1, Sir Neil Lawson.

1340. Competition—joint research and development—process plant

BP International (BP) and M. W. Kellogg Company (Kellogg) notified the European Commission of their arrangements regarding the joint development of a design for the construction of ammonia plant using BP's catalyst. BP, a company in the BP group, had developed a catalyst which could be used for the production of ammonia. BP sought Kellogg's assistance in devising a suitable process plant as Kellogg were experienced process plant designers. *Held*, that (1) certain restrictions imposed by the arrangements were contrary to Art. 85 EEC, in particular to restrict BP's supply of the catalyst to certain persons (unless Kellogg was prepared to agree to the supply to others) and various restrictions on the development or sale of other processes by Kellogg; (2) the agreement did not qualify for exemption by virtue of Commission Regulation 418/85 on the application of Art. 85(3) EEC to categories of research and development agreements, since several of its clauses went beyond the scope of that Regulation as they restricted the exploitation of products and processes which had not been jointly developed by the parties and which were not covered by Arts. 4 and 5 of that Regulation; (3) an individual exemption under Art. 85(3) EEC was granted as the successful development of the process would promote technical and economic progress, especially energy saving, which would benefit consumers, and the restrictions could be justified. Exemption was granted for seven years from June 1, 1983 (the date when the arrangements were notified).

APPLICATION OF BP INTERNATIONAL & THE M. W. KELLOGG CO., *Re* [1986] 2 C.M.L.R. 619, E.C. Commission Decision.

1341. Competition—joint venture—air filtration devices

Mitchell Cotts & Co. (Engineering) Ltd. ("Mitchell"), an English company, and Sofiltra Poelman S.A. ("Sofiltra"), a French company, notified to the European Commission certain agreements concerning their joint venture in the U.K. The joint venture was to make and sell air filtration devices under a know-how licence granted by Sofiltra. Mitchell was to lease the production premises and to supply commercial know-how. The agreements contained various restrictions, which the parties sought to justify. The Commission indicated that it proposed to adopt a favourable decision, but before doing so, it asked interested third parties to submit their comments within a month.

MITCHELL COTTS AIR FILTRATION, *Re* [1986] 3 C.M.L.R. 370, European Commission Notice.

1342. Competition—joint venture agreement—comfort letter

Dunlop ("Dunlop") and Pirelli General PLC ("Pirelli"), two U.K. companies, notified agreements concerning a joint venture relating to the supply of hydraulic and electro-hydraulic umbilicals and other ancillary equipment. Dunlop and Pirelli sought exemption from the European Commission for these agreements under Art. 85(3) EEC. The European Commission issued a Notice stating that it proposed to take no action and that the procedure might be closed by a "comfort letter". The Commission invited interested third parties to send their comments within one month.

AGREEMENTS BETWEEN DUNLOP & PIRELLI GENERAL, *Re* [1986] 2 C.M.L.R. 192, European Commission Notice.

1343. Competition—joint venture agreement—comfort letter

Vallourec, a French company, and Nyby Uddeholm A.B. ("NUAB"), a Swedish company, notified to the European Commission an agreement to set up a joint subsidiary, for which they sought negative clearance under Art. 85(1) EEC or exemption under Art. 85(3) EEC. The object of the joint venture being to produce steel powder for sale to the two parent companies which they would turn into tubes, bars and sections, as well as the joint venture subsidiary being able to produce small-dimension tubes, bars and sections. The European Commission issued a Notice stating that it proposed to either grant an exemption under Art. 85(3) EEC or send a "comfort letter". The Commission invited interested third parties to send their comments within one month.

AGREEMENT BETWEEN VALLOUREC & NYBY UDDEHOLM AB, *Re* [1986] 2 C.M.L.R. 194, European Commission Notice.

1344. Competition—metal cans—comfort letter

SOFREB applied to the European Commission for negative clearance from Art. 85(1) EEC or exemption under Art. 85(3) EEC for the agreements by which it was set up. SOFREB was a company set up by a large tin can producer and by a major steel group in order to manufacture two-piece metal drink cans. The Commission issued a Notice stating that it proposed to take no action with regard to the agreement and that the matter might be closed by the sending of a "comfort letter." The Commission invited interested parties to send their comments within one month from publication of the Notice.

SOCIÉTÉ FRANCAISE DE DEVELOPPEMENT DE LA BOITE-BOISSONS (SOFREB), *Re* [1986] 1 C.M.L.R. 226, European Commission.

1345. Competition—performing right society—royalty

SYNDIS, a French association of discotheques, challenged various practices of S.A.C.E.M., a French performing right association. SYNDIS argued that S.A.C.E.M.'s levying of a royalty fee at a flat rate of 8·82 per cent. of the total receipts of discotheques, whether the music was French or foreign, and its agreements with various discotheque owners, were contrary to Arts. 85 and 86 EEC. *Held,* that S.A.C.E.M. had not conducted itself contrary to EEC competition law. S.A.C.E.M. was awarded compensation against SYNDIS as the latter had organised an unjustified refusal by its members to pay their royalites.

CHAMBRE SYNDICALE NATIONALE DE LA DISCOTHEQUE (SYNDIS) *v.* SOCIETE DES AUTEURS, EDITEURS, ET COMPOSITEURS DE MUSIQUE (S.A.C.E.M.) [1986] E.C.C. 400, Tribunal de Grande Instance.

1346. Competition—production plant for coated glass—exemption

Boussois S.A. ("Boussois") and Interpane—Entwicklungs- und Beratungsgesellschaft mbH & Co. K.G. ("Interpane") notified an agreement between them to the European Commission for negative clearance or exemption under Art. 85(3) EEC. The agreement related to the sale by Interpane to Boussois of a production plant to be built in France, for applying insulating coatings to flat glass for double glazing units. By the agreement Interpane licensed Boussois to use a body of technology, some of which was patented. The Commission issued a Notice stating that it proposed to grant an exemption under Art. 85(3) EEC, but before doing so, it invited interested third parties to send their comments within a month.

AGREEMENT BETWEEN BOUSSOIS S.A. AND INTERPANE- ENTWICKLUNGS- UND BERATUNGSGESELLSCHAFT mbH & Co. K.G., *Re* (No. IV/31.302) [1986] 3 C.M.L.R 222, E.C. Commission Notice.

1347. Competition—selective distribution system—newspapers

S.A. Binon & Cie (plaintiff), a seller of, *inter alia,* books and stationery, in Charleroi, Belgium, brought proceedings against S.A. Agence et Messageries de la Presse (defendant). The plaintiff sought an order requiring the defendant to refrain from refusing to sell or supply the plaintiff with Belgian and foreign newspapers and journals distributed by the defendant in Belgium. The Tribunal de Commerce, Brussels, asked the European Court for a preliminary ruling under Art. 177 EEC on the interpretation of Arts. 85 and 86 EEC in relation to the selective distribution system of newspapers and journals in Belgium. *Held,* that (1) Art. 85(1) EEC is applicable to a set of agreements between an agency which specialises in the distribution of newspapers and journals in one EEC State, the majority of the publishers of newspapers and periodicals who are established in that State and various publishers established in other EEC States, if the practical effect of the agreements is that the approval of retail sales outlets is a question for that agency or a body set up by it within the framework of the said agreements: (2) a selective distribution system for newspapers and periodicals which affects trade between EEC States is contrary to Art. 85(1) EEC if (a) re-sellers are chosen on the basis of quantitative criteria. (However, the Commission may be prepared to give an exemption under Art. 85(3) EEC if it considers that such criteria can be justified by a particular applicant); or if (b) the criteria determining the choice of re-sellers are applied less strictly in relation to undertakings which are part of a particular group of undertakings than in relation to other retailers; (3) an obligation on retailers to abide by fixed prices in the framework of a selective distribution system for newspapers and periodicals which affects trade between EEC States, is contrary to Art. 85(1) EEC. (However, the Commission may be prepared to give an exemption under Art. 85(3) if it is justified in a particular case).

S.A. BINON & CIE *v.* S.A. AGENCE ET MESSAGERIES DE LA PRESSE (No. 243/83) [1985] 3 C.M.L.R. 800, European Ct.

1348. Competition—sole distribution agreements—spirits

The Distillers Company ("Distillers"), the leading producer of spirits in the EEC notified, on behalf of several subsidiaries, 21 sole distribution agreements made between those subsidiaries and various companies in EEC States. The agreements were covered by the block exemption provided by Commission Regulation 67/67, which has been superseded by Regulations 1983/83 and 1984/83. *Held,* that (1) the block exemption provided by Regulation 1983/83 would apply to Agreements 1 to 17 as the parties to the agreements were not regarded as manufacturers of equivalent goods within the meaning of Art. 3(b) of Reg. 1983/83. Block exemption under Reg. 1983/83 would apply after December 31, 1986; (2) Agreements 18 to 21 involved parties who were mutual competitors as both manufactured alcoholic beverages in the category to which the agreements related. Such agreements could not benefit from the exemption provided by Reg. 1983/83. The agreements were granted individual exemptions under Art. 85(3) EEC as the conditions of Art. 85(3) were met. Such individual exemptions were granted for 10 years commencing from January 1, 1987.

APPLICATION OF THE DISTILLERS CO., *Re* [1986] 2 C.M.L.R. 664, E.C. Commission Decision.

1349. Competition—terms for admission to exhibition—Notice

National Boat Shows ("NBS") notified to the European Commission the terms and conditions upon which exhibitors were admitted to the annual London International Boat Show. Following discussions with the Commission, NBS modified the notified conditions. The Commission issued a Notice that it proposed to take no action with regard to the modified conditions, but invited interested third parties to send their observations within one month.

LONDON INTERNATIONAL BOAT SHOW, *Re* [1985] 3 C.M.L.R. 622, European Commission Notice.

1350. Confidentiality—Commission—damages for breach of duty

EEC Treaty (Cmnd. 5179–II) Arts. 214, 215; Protocol on the Statute of the Court of Justice of the EEC (Cmnd. 5179–II) Art. 43.]

The principle of confidentiality contained in Art. 24 of the EEC Treaty extends to information supplied by an individual to the Communities if the information is by its nature confidential.

A, a senior executive of H.R. a large Swiss company, wrote to the Commissioner for Competition of the European Communities alleging that H.R. engaged in anti-competition practices, contrary to a free trade agreement between Switzerland and the EEC. He expressly asked that his name should not be revealed. A met officials from the Directorate General for Competition (D.G. IV) and gave them certain documents. No action was taken until A left H.R. and the officials knew that he had gone to Italy but he did not ask to be kept informed nor query the use to be made of the documents he had supplied. The documents were shown to H.R. in the belief that their origin could not be traced, copies were given to H.R. which admitted their authenticity. Later a lawyer for H.R. approached the officials asking for the name of the informant and suggested that H.R. would not prosecute him and would co-operate with D.G.IV A was not made aware of this. D.G.IV refused to do this and H.R. laid a complaint of economic espionage against a person unknown but indicating that A was the prime suspect having investigated the copied documents. When A crossed from Italy into Switzerland he was arrested and admitted that he was the informant. He was charged and confined but he caused a letter to be written to D.G.IV giving details of his arrest. An official at D.G.IV told H.R.'s lawyer that A was the informant and A was released on bail. Thereafter H.R. was fined by the Commission for anti-competitive practices and A was convicted in his absence at Basle and given a one year suspended prison sentence. The Commission paid A's bail and legal fees and made a substantial payment which A refused to accept in final settlement. In case 145/83 he claimed compensation under Art. 215 of the Treaty for loss suffered by breach of the Commission's duty of confidentiality, and in case 53/84 compensation for failing to refer Switzerland's economic espionage offence to a joint-committee contrary to the agreement between Switzerland and the EEC. *Held* that (1) the principle of confidentiality set out in Art. 214 included information supplied by individuals to an institution of the Communities if the information was by its nature confidential; A's letter made it clear that the Commission was bound by a duty of confidentiality which was unlimited and continuing; (2) the Commission was at fault in failing to bring to A's attention the offer by H.R.'s lawyer not to take criminal proceedings against him but was not at fault in disclosing A's identity to H.R. after A had done so to the Swiss police; (3) A's claim was not barred by the five year limitation period under Art. 43 of the Protocol since a plea under Art. 43 could not defeat a claim by a person who only belatedly became aware of his cause of action; A had only become aware of the discussion between the Commission and H.R.'s lawyer after the defence had been filed; (4) the Commission would pay A compensation in case 145/83 which would be reduced by one-half because of A's failure to indicate that he could be identified from the documents, his failure to ask to be kept informed and his return to Switzerland without checking his criminal liability then; (5) matters relating to the free trade agreement with Switzerland relating to anti-competitive practices could only be referred to the joint committee for reasons concerning the general interest of the Community, following an essentially political assessment, and was not open to challenge by any individual; A's claim in case 53/84 failed.

ADAMS *v.* E.C. COMMISSION [1986] 2 W.L.R. 367, European Ct.

1351. Confidentiality—credit institutions—depositions by witnesses
The plaintiff local authority deposited sums with a Dutch bank which became insolvent. The plaintiff obtained under Dutch law an order for the provisional examination of witnesses, including Mr. Hillenius. Mr. Hillenius was head of the accountancy division of De Nederlandsche Bank, the supervisory authority for banks in the Netherlands for the purposes of European Council Directive No. 77/780 on the co-ordination of laws, regulations and administrative provisions relating to the taking up and pursuit of the business of credit institutions. Mr Hillenius refused to answer questions on the manner in which De Nederlandsche Bank had exercised supervision of the bankrupt bank because he was covered by the obligation of banking secrecy imposed upon him by the Dutch law which implemented the Directive. The Supreme Court of the Netherlands asked the European Court under Art. 177 EEC for a preliminary ruling on the interpretation of Art. 12 of Directive No. 77/780. *Held,* that (1) Art. 12(1) of Directive No. 77/780 provided for an obligation of professional

secrecy on present and past employees of competent authorities. This meant that any confidential information which such employees might have received in the course of their duties might not be disclosed to any person or authority even by way of depositions made as a witness in civil proceedings, except by virtue of provisions laid down by national law; (2) National legislation of EEC States might provide exceptions to the requirement of maintaining professional secrecy. Where such legislation was of a general nature, it was for the national court to balance the interest in establishing the truth against the interest of maintaining the secrecy of certain information, before deciding whether a witness in possession of confidential information, might rely upon an obligation of secrecy: GEMEENTE HILLEGOM *v.* HILLENIUS (No. 110/84), *The Times,* January 2, 1986, European Ct.

1352. Confidentiality—duty of European Commission—business secrets
Engineering & Chemical Supplies (Epsom & Gloucester) ("ECS") complained to the European Commission that the AKZO Group had infringed EEC competition law. The European Commission carried out an investigation into the alleged infringements under Council Reg. 17. The Commission sent ECS a copy of its statement of objections alleging infringements of Art. 86 EEC. The copy of the statement of objections listed numerous annexes. Some of the annexes contained confidential information concerning AKZO. On December 14, 1984 the Commission decided to send some of the annexes to ECS at ECS's request. On December 18, 1984 the Commission informed AKZO that it had sent the annexes to ECS. AKZO applied to the European Court for annulment of the Commission's decision to provide ECS with certain confidential documents. *Held,* that (1) the obligation of professional secrecy set out in Art. 20(2) of Reg. 17 was qualified in respect of those to whom Art. 19(2) gave the right to be heard, such as the complainant. The commission could supply the latter with information covered by the obligation to professional secrecy to the extent that such disclosure was necessary to the smooth conduct of the investigation. However, documents containing business secrets were not to be disclosed to a complainant; (2) it was for the Commission to determine whether a document contained business secrets. After giving the undertaking concerned an opportunity to give its views, the Commission should take a properly reasoned decision and notify it to the undertaking so that the latter has the chance to challenge the decision in the European Court; (3) the Commission's decision to provide ECS with certain confidential information was annulled as the Commission had decided to do so before notifying its views to AKZO. Thus, it had denied AKZO the possibility of using Arts. 173 and 185 EEC to prevent the implementation of the decision. In the circumstances the decision was annulled without it being necessary to decide whether the documents actually contained business secrets.
AKZO CHEMIE BV & AKZO UK *v.* E.C. COMMISSION, ENGINEERING & CHEMICAL SUPPLIES (EPSOM & GLOUCESTER) intervening (No. 53/85), *The Times,* July 7, 1986 European Ct.

1353. Designation of Ministers
EUROPEAN COMMUNITIES (DESIGNATION) ORDER 1986 (No. 947) [45p], made under the European Communities Act 1972 (c.68), s.2(2); operative on July 11, 1986; designates Ministers and departments who may make regulations under s.2(2) of the 1972 Act in relation to specified matters.

1354. Directives—draft proposal—semi-conductor chips
The European Commission submitted to the European Council a proposal for a Council Directive on the legal protection of original topographies of semi-conductor products.
DRAFT SEMICONDUCTOR CHIPS DIRECTIVE [1986] 1 C.M.L.R. 682, European Council.

1355. Directives—shares—information
The European Commission submitted to the European Council a proposal for a Directive on information to be published when major holdings in the capital of a listed company are acquired or disposed of.
DRAFT DIRECTIVE ON SHARE TRANSACTIONS [1986] 2 C.M.L.R. 241, E.C. Council.

1356. Draft Directive—freedom of establishment—companies' branch information
The European Commission proposed a Council Directive based on Art. 54(3)(*g*) EEC concerning disclosure requirements in respect of branches opened in an EEC State by certain types of companies governed by the law of another State.
DRAFT COMPANY LAW (BRANCH INFORMATION) DIRECTIVE [1986] 3 C.M.L.R. 364.

1357. Draft Directive—harmonisation—television broadcasting
The European Commission proposed a Council Directive on the co-ordination of certain provisions laid down by law, regulation or administrative action in EEC States concerning the pursuit of broadcasting activities.
DRAFT DIRECTIVE ON TELEVISION BROADCASTING [1986] 3 C.M.L.R. 350.

1358. Economic affairs—directives, decisions and regulations
85/543/EEC:
Council Decision of December 9, 1985 concerning a Community loan in favour of the Hellenic Republic. (O.J. 1985 L341/17.)
Commission Regulation (EEC) No. 2573/86 of August 12, 1986 amending Regulations (EEC) No. 1871/86 and (EEC) No. 2096/86 with regard to documents covering intra-Community movement of cereals exempted from the co-responsibility levy. (O.J. 1986 L229/28.)

1359. Education—vocational training—discrimination. See R. *v.* INNER LONDON EDUCATION AUTHORITY, *ex p.* HINDE, § 1138.

1360. Employment—business transfer—employee
Mr. Mikkelsen was employed as works foreman by A/S Danmols Inventar (the defendant), which suspended payments of its debts in September 1981 and dismissed Mr. Mikkelsen with effect from December 31, 1981. In October 1981 the business was transferred to another company, in which Mr. Mikkelssen held 33 per cent. of shares, 50 per cent. of the voting rights and was chairman. Mr. Mikkelsen retained his post as works foreman, carrying out the same work and receiving the same pay. On December 2, 1981 the defendant was declared insolvent, whereupon Mr. Mikkelsen lodged a claim for compensation for premature termination of employment and holiday pay. The Vestre Landsret Denmark, asked the European Court under Art. 177 EEC for a preliminary ruling on the interpretation of Council Directive 77/187 of February 14, 1977 on the approximation of the laws of the Member States relating to the safeguarding of employees' rights in the event of transfers of undertakings, businesses or parts of businesses. *Held*, that (1) Art. 3(1) of Directive 77/187 did not cover the transfer of the rights and obligations of persons who were employed by the transferor at the date of the transfer but who, by their own accord, do not continue to work as employees of the transferees; (2) the meaning of "employee" for the purpose of Directive 77/187 covered any person who, in the EEC State concerned, is protected as an employee under national labour law. It is for the national court to decide whether a person falls within such a category.
MIKKELSEN *v.* DANMOLS INVENTAR A/S (No. 105/84) [1986] 1 C.M.L.R. 316, European Ct.

1361. Employment—business transfer—dismissal
The plaintiffs were employed by L.J. Music ApS ("Music") and were dismissed four days before "Music" was declared insolvent. The day after it was declared insolvent it was bought by a new company. The new company engaged the plaintiffs at a higher salary, but the plaintiffs lost their seniority. The plaintiffs brought proceedings for a declaration that they were entitled to compensation for unlawful dismissal and holiday pay. The Western Division of the Danish Court asked the European Court under Art. 177 EEC for a preliminary ruling on the interpretation of Council Directive 77/187 of February 14, 1977 on the approximation of the laws of EEC States relating to the safeguarding of employees' rights in the event of transfer of undertakings, businesses or parts of businesses. *Held*, that Council Directive 77/187 provides that the transferor company's rights and obligations arising from a contract of employment existing on the date of transfer shall be transferred to the transferee. It is for the national law and national courts to establish whether employees were employed at the date of transfer. The Directive does not require EEC States to pass legislation under which the transferee of an undertaking becomes liable in respect of obligations regarding holiday pay and compensation to employees who were not employed in the undertaking on the date of transfer.
KNUD WENDELBOE *v.* L.J. MUSIC ApS (No. 19/83) [1986] 1 C.M.L.R. 476, European Ct.

1362. Employment—business transfer—employee's rights

Mr. Spijkers was employed by Colaris, which operated a slaughterhouse. In December 1982 Colaris's activities ceased and the slaughterhouse, together with various other items, bought by Benedik Abbattoir CV (Benedik). All the employees of Colaris, except for Mr. Spijkers and another, were taken over by Benedik. In March 1983 Colaris were declared insolvent. Mr. Spijkers took proceedings in Holland for recovery of his wages from December 1982 onwards and sought an order that he be provided with work by Benedik. He argued that there had been a transfer of undertaking within the meaning of the Dutch legislation which was enacted to implement Council Directive 77/187 of February 14, 1977, which would automatically imply the transfer to Benedik of the rights and obligations arising from his contract of employment with Colaris. The Hoge Raad asked the European Court under Art. 177 EEC for a preliminary ruling on the interpretation of Art. 1(1) of Directive 77/187. *Held,* that the words "transfer of an undertaking, business or part of a business to another employer" in Art. 1(1) of Directive 77/187 were to be interpreted as envisaging the case in which the business in issue retained its identity. In order to determine whether or not such a transfer had occurred, it was necessary to consider whether, having regard to all the facts characterising the transaction, the business was disposed of as a going concern, as would be indicated, *inter alia,* by the fact that its operation was actually continued or resumed by the new employer with the same or similar activities. Such a determination was to be made by the national courts.

Spijkers *v.* Gebroeders Benedik Abbattoir C.V. (No. 24/85) [1986] 2 C.M.L.R. 296, European Ct.

1363. Employment—business transfer—partial transfer

The plaintiffs were employees of a company which was declared insolvent. A new company (the defendant) was formed which took over certain departments of the old company and the staff in those departments. It also engaged certain other employees of the old company, but not the plaintiffs whose departments were not taken over. The plaintiffs claimed that their dismissal was invalid and sought payments from the defendant, in the Cantonal Court, Rotterdam. The latter asked the European Court under Art. 177 EEC for a preliminary ruling on the interpretation of European Council Directive 77/187 of February 14, 1977. *Held,* that (1) Art. 1(1) of Directive 77/187 does not apply to the transfer of a business or part of a business of an insolvent transferor although EEC States can choose to apply the principles of the Directive to such a transfer if they wish. The Directive does apply where a business or part of a business is transferred to another employer in the course of a procedure such as "surséance van betaling" (judicial leave to suspend payment of debts); (2) Art. 3(1) of Directive 77/187 does not cover the transferor's rights and obligations arising from contracts of employment existing on the date of transfer and entered into with employees who were not yet employed in the transferred departments. This is so even if those employees had carried out certain duties for the benefit of the departments transferred.

Botzen *v.* Rotterdamsche Droogdok Maatschappij (No. 186/83) [1986] 2 C.M.L.R. 50, European Ct.

1364. Employment—collective redundancies—compensation

H. Nielsen & Søn Maskinfabrik A/S ("Nielsen") informed the bankruptcy court that it was suspending payment of its debts. Two trade union ("plaintiffs") asked Nielsen to provide a bank guarantee for the future payment of wages to its workers. No such guarantee was forthcoming and the workers stopped work on the plaintiffs' advice. Within a week Nielsen went bankrupt and dismissed its workers. The plaintiffs claimed monies under Danish legislation, which provided that if an employer does not give the authorities 30 days notice of proposed collective redundancies he must pay the workers an allowance equal to their salary for that period. The legislation had been passed pursuant to European Council Directive 75/129 of February 17, 1975 on the approximation of the laws of the Member States relating to collective redundancies. The Danish Højesteret asked the European Court under Art. 177 EEC for a preliminary ruling on the interpretation of Directive 75/129. *Held,* that (1) the termination by workers of their contracts of employment after an employer has said that he is suspending payment of his debts cannot be regarded as dismissal by the employer for the purposes of Directive 75/129; (2) Directive 75/129 is applicable only where an employer has actually contemplated collective redundancies or has prepared a plan for collective redundancies.

DANSK METALARBEJDERFORBUND *v.* NIELSEN (H.) & SØN MASKINFABRIK A/S (No. 284/83) [1986] 1 C.M.L.R. 91, European Ct.

1365. Employment—collective redundancies—implementation

The European Commission brought proceedings against Belgium under Art. 169 EEC for failing to adopt within the prescribed period all the measures necessary to comply with Council Directive 75/129 of February 17, 1975 on the approximation of the laws of EEC States relating to collective redundancies. *Held,* that Belgium had failed to fulfil its obligations under the EEC by failing to adopt all the measures necessary to comply fully with Directive 75/129. Belgian legislation did not properly implement the Directive as it (i) did not apply to collective redundancies arising from the closure of the enterprise in question, where such closure did not come about as the result of a judicial decision; and (ii) excluded from the benefit of the Directive ship repairers, port workers and manual workers in the building industry.

COLLECTIVE REDUNDANCIES, *Re*; E.C. COMMISSION *v.* BELGIUM (No. 215/83) [1985] 3 C.M.L.R. 624, European Ct.

1366. Establishment—nationality—discrimination

Mr. Steinhauser, a German artist, residing in Biarritz, tendered to lease exhibition premises from the municipal authorities of Biarritz. The mayor of Biarritz informed Mr. Steinhauser that his application could not be considered because one of the conditions in the tender specifications was that applicants should be French nationals. Mr. Steinhauser brought proceedings for annulment of this decision as being contrary to the right of establishment enshrined in Art. 52 EEC. The Tribunal Administratif asked the European Court under Art. 177 EEC for a preliminary ruling on the interpretation of Art. 52 EEC. *Held,* that Art. 52 EEC does not permit conditions in a tendering scheme for the allocation of municipal public property according to which acceptance of applications is conditional upon nationality.

STEINHAUSER *v.* CITY OF BIARRITZ (No. 197/84) [1986] 1 C.M.L.R. 53, European Ct.

1367. Euratom—directives, decisions and regulations

85/593/Euratom:

Commission Decision of November 20, 1985 on the reorganisation of the Joint Research Centre (JRC). (O.J. 1985 L373/6.)

86/61/EEC, Euratom, ECSC:

Commission Decision of January 8 1986 amending the provisional rules of procedure of the Commission of July 6, 1967. (O.J. 1986 L72/34.)

86/62/EEC, Euratom, ECSC:

Commission Decision of February 3, 1986 concerning the French Republic pursuant to Art. 13(2) of Regulation (EEC, Euratom, ECSC) No. 2892/77 concerning own resources accruing from value added tax. (O.J. 1986 L72/(35.)

86/88/EEC, Euratom:

Council Decision of March 10, 1986 concerning the conclusion of the Framework Agreement for scientific and technical cooperation between the European Communities and the Kingdom of Norway. (O.J. 1986 L78/26.)

1368. European Assembly—elections

EUROPEAN ASSEMBLY ELECTIONS REGULATIONS 1986 (No. 2209) [£4·90], made under the European Assembly Elections Act 1978 (c.10), Sched. 1, para. 2; provide for the conduct of the election of representatives to the European Assembly in England, Wales and Scotland.

1369. ECSC—directives, decisions and regulations

Commission Decision No. 1328/86/ECSC of May 5, 1986 fixing the amended rates of abatement for the second quarter of 1986 in accordance with Decision No. 3485/85/ECSC on the extension of the system of monitoring and production quotas for certain products of undertakings in the steel industry. (O.J. 1986 L117/19.)

1370. ECSC—exceeding quotas—fines

The European Commission imposed fines on 14 iron and steel undertakings under Art. 58 ECSC for exceeding their respective quotas

THE COMMUNITY *v.* BADISCHE STAHLWERKE A.G. [1985] 3 C.M.L.R. 756, Decision 85/C285/03.

1371. ECSC—pricing practices—fines

The European Commission imposed fines on six iron and steel undertakings for having infringed Art. 60 ECSC.

THE COMMUNITY *v.* COCKERILL-SAMBRE [1985] 3 C.M.L.R. 755, Decision 85/C261/03.

1372. European Communities (Amendment) Act 1986 (c.58)

This Act amends the European Communities Act 1972 so as to include in the definition of "the Treaties" and "the Community Treaties" certain provisions of the Single European Act signed at Luxembourg and The Hague on February 17 and 28, 1986. It extends certain provisions to courts attached to the European Court and amends references to the European Assembly.

The Act received the Royal Assent on November 7, 1986.

1373. European Development Fund—directives, decisions and regulations

86/90/EEC:

Council Decision of March 10, 1986 giving a discharge to the Commission in respect of the implementation of the operations of the European Development Fund (1963) (Second EDF) for the financial year 1984. (O.J. 1986 L80/46.)

86/91/EEC:

Council Decision of March 10, 1986 giving a discharge to the Commission in respect of the implementation of the operations of the European Development Fund (1969) (Third EDF) for the financial year 1984. (O.J. 1986 L80/48.)

86/92/EEC:

Council recommendation of March 10, 1986 concerning the discharge to be given to the Commission in respect of the implementation of the operations of the European Development Fund (1975) (Fourth EDF) for the financial year 1984. (O.J. 1986 L80/49.)

86/93/EEC:

Council recommendation of March 10, 1986 concerning the discharge to be given to the Commission in respect of the implementation of the operations of the European Development Fund (1979) (Fifth EDF) for the financial year 1984. (O.J. 1986 L80/50.)

1374. European Court procedure—interim measures—education

The European Commission asked the European Court to grant interim measures, pursuant to Art. 186 EEC and Art. 83 of the Rules of Procedure, ordering Belgium to take immediate measures to ensure, until the European Court gave judgment in the main action, that students who are nationals of other EEC States can have access to Belgian University education in the same way as students who are Belgian nationals. *Held*, pending judgment in the main action, that Belgium is required (1) to take immediately all necessary measures to safeguard access by students who are nationals of other EEC States to studies forming part of vocational training given by Belgian University institutions in the same way as Belgian students. However, such access might be made conditional on the student giving an undertaking to pay supplementary fees (a "minerval") if Belgium succeeded on the merits; (ii) to inform the European Commission and the European Court within not more than one month of the measures Belgium has taken to conform with (i).

EDUCATION FEES, *Re*, E.C. COMMISSION *v.* BELGIUM (No. 293/85 R) [1986] 1 C.M.L.R. 594, Lord Mackenzie Stuart C.J.

1375. European Court procedure—production quotas—time limit for challenging fine

The European Commission fined the applicant for exceeding steel production quotas by Decision of January 26, 1984. The Decision, although duly delivered and received on February 3, was addressed to Metalgoi SNC instead of to Metalgoi SpA, since unbeknown to the Commission it had changed its corporate status. The time limit for lodging an appeal with the European Court expired on March 14, 1984. An appeal was lodged on March 26, 1984. The Commission argued that the application was inadmissible as it had been lodged out of time. *Held,* that the application was dismissed as inadmissible. The mistake as to the correct name of the company did not vitiate the delivery of the decision; the Decision reached the applicant in proper time and the applicant realised that it was the addressee. Thus, time ran from February 3, 1984 and the application was out of time.

METALGOI SPA *v.* E.C. COMMISSION (No. 82/84) [1986] 2 C.M.L.R. 335, President of the European Ct.

1376. European Court procedure—provisional measures—suspension

Application was made to the President of the European Court for interim suspension of Arts. 1, 2 and 3 of Commission Regulation 2677/84 of September 20, 1984 relating to transitional measures for the revaluation of the "green" Deutschmark in relation to corn, sugar and potato starch. Germany had also taken proceedings for annulment of those provisions. *Held,* that the application for interim suspension was refused. Provisional measures were not appropriate as the applicant had not proved "urgency" in the sense that serious or irreparable damage would be caused to the applicant if the application was rejected. Where application is made for suspension of legislation, the measures sought must be provisional in the sense that they must not prejudice the decision on the main issue. In the circumstances a suspension would have amounted to prejudging the result of the main action.

AGRICULTURAL PRICES, *Re;* GERMANY *v.* EUROPEAN COMMISSION (No. 278/84R) [1986] 1 C.M.L.R. 64, President of the European Ct.

1377. European Court procedure—requests of Registrar—production of documents

Twenty-five applicants brought proceedings in the European court for damages under Art. 178 EEC and Art. 215(2). The Registrar of the Court requested the applicants, pursuant to Art. 387 of the Rules of procedure, to produce (a) the instruments constituting and regulating the companies in question and (b) proof that the authority granted to the applicant's lawyer was properly conferred on him by a duly authorised person. Nineteen of the applicants produced the requisite documents, but six failed to do so. *Held*, that applications by six applicants were dismissed as inadmissible because of their non-compliance with the Registrar's requests.

G.A.A.R.M. *v.* E.C. COMMISSION (No. 289/93) [1986] 1 C.M.L.R. 602, European Ct.

1378. EEC Judgments Convention—enforcement—costs

A French court had awarded the plaintiff damages in French francs for non-delivery of certain goods. The French Court had applied German Law as the proper law of the contract. The plaintiff sought to enforce the judgment in Germany. *Held*, that (1) a set-off could be considered even though it was in a different currency from that awarded in the judgment; (2) the judgment debtor could not challenge the judgment so far as costs were concerned (costs not being specifically awardable in German Law); (3) a foreign judgment which included an element of future unascertained costs could be enforced under the EEC Judgments Convention.

ENFORCEMENT OF A FOREIGN COSTS ORDER, *Re* [1986] E.C.C. 481, Frankfurt am Main Court of Appeal.

1379. EEC Judgments Convention—enforcement—protective measures

Mr. Pelkmans (plaintiff) obtained judgment in Breda, Holland, against Mr. Capelloni and Mr. Aquilini (defendants). The plaintiff obtained judgment from the Appeal Court, Brescia, authorising enforcement of the Breda judgment pursuant to the EEC Judgments Convention. The defendants appealed. Prior to the appeal being heard, the plaintiff obtained an order for protective measures pursuant to Art. 39 of the EEC Judgments Convention, authorising him to sequester the defendants' immovable property. The plaintiff sought confirmation of the sequestration from the Italian courts. The Corte Suprema di Cassazione asked the European Court for a preliminary ruling on the interpretation of Art. 39 of the Convention. *Held*, that (1) Art. 39 of the EEC Judgments Convention enables a party, who has obtained authorisation for enforcement, to proceed, within the requisite period, directly with protective measures against the property of the party against whom enforcement is sought. The party seeking protective measures does not need to obtain specific authorisation; (2) a party who has obtained authorisation for enforcement may proceed with the protective measures mentioned in Art. 39 until the expiry of the period set out in Art. 36 for lodging an appeal and, if such an appeal is filed, until a decision is given thereon; (3) a party who has proceeded with the protective measures mentioned in Art. 39 is under no obligation to obtain, in respect of those measures, any confirmatory judgment from a national court, even though national law might require that.

CAPELLONI & AQUILINI *v.* PELKMANS (No. 119/84) [1986] 1 C.M.L.R. 388, European Ct.

1380. EEC Judgments Convention—enforcement—service

Rosco B.V. ("Rosco") obtained a judgment in the Hague District Court against Fraisgel, a French company. Rosco sought to enforce the judgment in France. Fraisgel had received notice of the proceedings through diplomatic channels the day after the hearing date given, but had made no attempt thereafter to find out what had occurred or to take steps to have the judgment set aside. *Held,* That Rosco was entitled to an order for execution. It could not be said that the judgment was unenforceable as improperly served under Art. 27(2) of the EEC Judgments Convention, when there was no evidence that Fraisgel had tried to discover what had happened or had sought to set the judgment aside.

Rosco B.V. *v.* Sàrl Fraisgel [1986] E.C.C. 175, Tribunal de Grande Instance, Paris.

1381. EEC Judgments Convention—enforcement—service of documents

W. M. Brähmer applied to enforce a German judgment against two Dutch nationals. The German legal documents commencing the proceedings had been served by post in the Netherlands. The method of serving German legal documents in the Netherlands was governed by the Dutch-German Conventions on facilitating legal relations of August 30, 1962, by the Hague Convention on Services of Documents Abroad of November 16, 1965 and by Art. IV of the Protocol to the EEC Judgments Convention. On the basis of these Conventions service of those documents had to be through the Public Prosecutor's Department, through diplomatic or consular channels, or by sending the documents from a German bailiff to a Dutch bailiff. *Held,* that enforcement of the judgment would be refused because the documents commencing the proceedings had been served by post contrary to the Conventions binding Germany and the Netherlands.

Brähmer (W. M.) *v.* Louer-Van Loon (Maria) & Wigleven-Eijsermans (Cornelia) [1986] E.C.C. 178, District Court, Breda.

1382. EEC Judgments Convention—enforcement order—interested third party

Deutsche Genossenschaftsbank, a German bank, sought enforcement in the French courts of a notarial deed against its German debtor, DGV, which had assets in France. The President of the Regional Court, Strasbourg, made an order for enforcement and in doing so relied, in particular, on the EEC Judgments Convention. Brasserie du Pêcheur S.A. (Pêcheur) another of DGV's creditors, applied to have the order set aside. Pêcheur made its application under a provision in French law, which permitted any person affected by a judicial decision given *ex parte* to make an application to the Court. The President allowed Pêcheur's application and set aside the order for enforcement. The bank appealed to the Court of Appeal, Colmar which asked the European Court for a preliminary ruling on the interpretation of Art. 36 of the EEC Judgments Convention. *Held,* that (1) Art. 36 of the EEC Judgments Convention excludes procedures whereby interested third parties may challenge an enforcement order, even though such a procedure exists under the national law of the State in which the enforcement order is made; (2) the EEC Judgments Convention deals with the procedure for obtaining enforcement orders, but does not deal with their execution. Execution is governed by the national law of the court in which execution is sought, so interested third parties may contest execution in accordance with the procedures available to them under national laws.

Deutsche Genossenschaftsbank *v.* Brasserie du Pêcheur S.A. (No. 148/84) [1986] 2 C.M.L.R. 496, European Ct.

1383. EEC Judgments Convention—enforcement order—service of documents

The defendant appealed against enforcement in Germany of a Belgian judgment against him. *Held,* that enforcement was refused as the defendant had not been properly served with the documents commencing proceedings. The defendant was described on the documents by the abbreviated name of "O", which was incorrect, and no certificate of service was produced.

Enforcement of a Belgian Judgment, *Re* [1986] E.C.C. 478, Düsseldorf Court of Appeal.

1384. EEC Judgments Convention—jurisdiction—expired written agreements

In 1956 the parties made a written agreement for a year. In 1958 the parties made another written agreement for a year, which was to lapse, failing renewal in writing. No written renewal occurred, but the parties carried on business for over 20 years by applying the agreements. The parties were in dispute and the appellant argued in the

Belgian Courts that a jurisdiction clause contained in one of the two original agreements was applicable and conferred jurisdiction on the Court at Turin. The Court of Cassation, Brussels, asked the European Court for a preliminary ruling on Art. 17 of the EEC Judgments Convention. *Held,* that where a written agreement containing a jurisdiction clause had expired, but the agreement continued to form the legal basis for the parties' contractual relations, that jurisdiction clause met the formal requirements of Art. 17 if either (i) the relevant national law allowed the parties to extend the initial agreement without observing the requirements of writing; or (ii) one of the parties had confirmed the clause in writing without the other party objecting to it after receiving such confirmation: Iveco Fiat SpA *v.* Van Hool NV (No. 313/85), *The Times,* November 17, 1986, European Ct.

1385. EEC Judgments Convention—jurisdiction clause—bill of lading

The Belgian Cour de Cassation had asked the European Court of Justice for a preliminary ruling on whether a third holder of a bill of lading was to be regarded as bound by rights and duties ascribed to a shipper in a bill of lading, including the jurisdiction clause (see No. 71/83 [1985] C.L.Y. 1452). *Held,* that (1) the ruling of the European Court of Justice in No. 71/83 applied. Following that ruling, it was a matter of national law whether a third holder of a bill of lading was bound by the rights and duties of the shipper; (2) the lower court's judgment was reversed. The third holder was bound by a jurisdiction clause contained in the bill of lading.

Partenreederei M.S. Tilly Russ *v.* Haven en Vervoerbedrijf "Nova" N.V. [1986] ECC 493, Belgian Cour de Cassation.

1386. EEC Judgments Convention—jurisdiction—agreement

Berghoefer GmbH ("Berghoefer"), a German company with its registered office in München-Gladbach, sued ASA S.A., a French company with a French registered office, in respect of termination of an agency agreement. Berghoefer brought proceedings in München-Gladbach. A dispute arose as to the validity of a jurisdiction clause which was originally agreed in writing, but was subsequently amended orally. On appeal the Bundesgerichtshof asked for a preliminary ruling on the interpretation of Art. 17 of the European Convention on Jurisdiction and the Enforcement of Judgments in Civil and Commercial Matters 1968 ("EEC Judgments Convention"). *Held,* that the first paragraph of Art. 17 of the EEC Judgments Convention had to be interpreted as meaning that the formal requirements therein set out are fulfilled if it is shown that the jurisdiction was conferred by an oral agreement dealing expressly with that point, that written confirmation of that agreement by one of the parties was received by the other and that the latter raised no objection.

Berghoefer (F.) GmbH & Co. KG *v.* ASA S.A. (No. 221/84) [1986] 1 C.M.L.R. 13, European Ct.

1387. EEC Judgments Convention—jurisdiction—agreement

The plaintiff, a German firm, sued the defendant, a French customer, for the price of gut which it had supplied pursuant to the defendant's verbal order. The plaintiff sent the defendant a bill of account and then delivered the gut. The plaintiff brought proceedings in Germany and relied on a forum clause which was printed on the back of the bill as being part of the parties' agreement. *Held,* that there was no effective agreement on a jurisdiction clause within Art. 17 of the EEC Convention on Jurisdiction and the Enforcement of Judgments in Civil and Commercial Matters 1968.

Written Confirmation of an Oral Contract, *Re* [1986] E.C.C. 39, Hanseatic Court of Appeal.

1388. EEC Judgments Convention—jurisdiction—exclusive concession

Carl Freudenberg KG ("Freudenberg"), a German company, granted Mr. Van Oppens an exclusive sales concession in Belgium and Luxembourg of its floor coverings products. Mr. van Oppens brought proceedings in Belgium in respect of the unilateral termination of his concession. Freudenberg disputed the jurisdiction of the Belgian courts. *Held,* that the Court had jurisdiction under Art. 5(1) of the EEC Judgments Convention. All the claims for compensation in the case were the consequence of the breach of the obligation in question, as defined by the EEC Judgments Convention. Since the place of performance of the obligation was Belgium, Belgian courts had jurisdicition.

Freudenberg (Carl) K.G. *v.* Bureau R.C. Van Oppens Sàrl [1986] E.E.C. 366, Belgian Cour de Cassation.

1389. EEC Judgments Convention—jurisdiction—forum clause

Mr. Anterist acted as a guarantor of a firm's debts vis-à-vis the Crédit Lyonnais, a French bank. He signed a guarantee which stated that the court within whose jurisdiction (the relevant branch of the bank) is situated shall have exclusive jurisdiction to adjudicate upon all matters concerning the performance of this agreement. As a result of the firm's failure to pay its debt, the bank brought proceedings in Germany against the guarantor. Mr. Anterist challenged the jurisdiction of the German Courts arguing that under the terms of the agreement contained in the guarantee a French Court should have exclusive jurisdiction. The Bundesgerichtshof asked the European Court for a preliminary ruling on the interpretation of Art. 17 of the EEC Judgments Convention. *Held,* that (1) Art. 17 of the EEC Judgments Convention permitted the parties to select, by agreement, the court(s) which were to have jurisdiction in relation to any disputes between them. Para. 1 of Art. 17 conferred exclusive jurisdiction on the court(s) referred to in the clause, while para. 3 preserved the right of the party for whose benefit the clause had been included to bring proceedings before any other court which had jurisdiction by virtue of the Convention; (2) para. 3 of Art. 17 was to be interpreted so as to give effect to the joint intention of the parties on the conclusion of the agreement; (3) an agreement conferring jurisdiction was not to be regarded as having been concluded for the benefit of only one of the parties within the meaning of para. 3 of Art. 17, when it was established only that the parties had agreed that jurisdiction was to be conferred upon the court(s) of the contracting State in which that party was domiciled: ANTERIST v. CRÉDIT LYONNAIS (No. 22/85) *The Times,* July 4, 1986, European Ct.

1390. EEC Judgments Convention—jurisdiction—mortgage

P did tile-laying work for D's building scheme on German land. P sued D for failing to pay for the work. Under German law P had a right to a building trade worker's mortgage for the amount due, which could be attached to the land. D disputed the Court's jurisdiction. *Held,* that the Court had national and international jurisdiction sufficient to enable it to require D to consent to the mortgage on the building land. The Court had international jurisdiction pursuant to Art. 5(1) of the EEC Judgments Convention. In accordance with Art. 16(1) of the EEC Judgments Convention P's claim for consent to the registration of a mortgage was a contractual claim for a declaration of intention.

JURISDICTION IN THE MORTGAGE OF LAND FOR CONTRACTUAL DEBT, *Re* [1986] E.C.C. 363, Oberlandesgericht, Köln.

1391. EEC Judgments Convention—jurisdiction—penalty

In previous proceedings between S. C. Johnson & Sons Inc. and Mobilar Export Import GmbH. the President of the Arrondissementsrechtbank, Rotterdam, issued an order prohibiting Mobilar from exporting aerosol sprays to the Middle East and fixed the amount of the penalty for any violation. Johnson claimed that Mobilar should be ordered to pay penalties for Mobilar's violation of the order. Mobilar agued that the Court did not have jurisdiction, since neither party was domiciled or resident in Holland and since the Dutch court had not been given jurisdiction, either by Dutch national laws or by the EEC Judgments Convention. *Held,* that the Court had jurisdiction in accordance with Arts. 24 and 43 of the EEC Judgments Convention. The Court was entitled to quantify the amount of the penalties payable.

JOHNSON (S. C.) & SON INC. v. MOBILAR EXPORT IMPORT GMBH [1986] E.C.C. 360, Arrondissementsrechtbank, Rotterdam.

1392. EEC Judgments Convention—jurisdiction—security

Brennero, an Italian shoe manufacturer, obtained judgment against Wendel, a German shoe manufacturer, in an Italian Court. Brennero obtained an order from a German Court for the enforcement of that order. Wendel appealed against that order and the appellate Court, before giving judgment on the appeal, made enforcement of the Italian judgment conditional on Brennero providing security. Brennero appealed on a point of law (Rechtsbeschwerde) to the Bundesgerichtshof. The latter asked the European Court under Art. 177 EEC for a preliminary ruling on the interpretation of Arts. 37 and 38 of the EEC Judgments Convention. *Held,* that (1) Art. 38(2) of the EEC Judgments Convention allows a Court to which an appeal has been launched against an order authorising enforcement under the Convention, to make enforcement conditional on the provision of security only when it delivers judgment on the appeal; (2) Art. 37(2) of the Convention means that an appeal in cassation (in Germany, a Rechtsbeschwerde), may be lodged only against the judgment given on appeal. It followed that there was no right of appeal to the Bundesgerichtshof as no judgment had been given on the appeal. It would be for the lower appellate Court to revoke the order in so far as it required security to be provided without giving judgment on the appeal.

CALZATURIFICIO BRENNERO S.A.S. *v.* WENDEL GMBH SCHUPRODUKTION INTERNATIONAL (No. 258/83) [1986] 2 C.M.L.R. 59, European Ct.

1393. EEC Judgments Convention—service—enforcement

The respondent objected to enforcement of a French judgment on him on the basis that he had not been properly served with the documents instituting the proceedings and that none of these documents had been translated into German. *Held*, that the judgment was enforced. The documents originating the proceedings were served on the respondent properly and in enough time to enable him to prepare his defence. Service had been in accordance with French internal law, with the Hague Convention on the Service of Documents Abroad 1965 and with Art. 27(2) of the EEC Judgments Convention. It was irrelevant to the question of service whether the formal requirements of Art. 5 of the Hague Convention were observed or whether the notice to appear needed to be accompanied by a German translation.

ENFORCEMENT OF A FRENCH JUDGMENT, *Re* [1986] E.C.C. 472, Düsseldorf Court of Appeal.

1394. EEC Judgments Convention—service of document—time limit

In 1980 Mr. and Mrs. Debaecker (the plaintiffs) let business premises in Antwerp to Mr. Bouwman, a Dutchman. On September 21, 1981 Mr. Bouwman left the premises without prior notice and without leaving a forwarding address. On September 24, 1981 the plaintiffs applied for a summons (returnable on October 1, 1981 before the Cantonal Judge, Antwerp) which was "served" on him pursuant to the Belgian Judicial Code at the Antwerp police station, where he was registered as a resident of Antwerp. Mr. Bouwman terminated his tenancy by a letter, dated September 25, 1981, which was received by the plaintiffs' lawyer on September 28. Mr. Bouwman stated therein that his new address was a Post Office number in Essen. The plaintiffs' lawyer did not inform Mr. Bouwman of the hearing of October 1, 1981. At the latter hearing judgment was given in default of appearance and Mr. Bouwman was ordered to pay damages. The plaintiffs sought to enforce the order in Holland. The Hoge Raad asked the European Court for a preliminary ruling on the interpretation of service of documents in Art. 27(2) of the EEC Judgments Convention. *Held*, that (1) the obligation in Art. 27(2) of the EEC Judgments Convention that service of a document commencing proceedings should have been effected in sufficient time is applicable where service was effected within a time limit set by the court of the State in which the judgment was given or where the defendant resided within the jurisdiction of that court or in the same State as that court; (2) in deciding whether service was effected in sufficient time, the court in which enforcement is sought may consider any exceptional circumstances which occur after service was effected; (3) in deciding whether service was effected in sufficient time, the court in which enforcement is sought may take into account the fact that the plaintiffs learnt of the defendant's new address after service was effected and the fact that the defendant was responsible for failure of the document to reach him.

DEBAECKER *v.* BOUWMAN (No. 49/84) [1986] 2 C.M.L.R. 400, European Ct.

1395. European Parliament—budget—interim measures

The U.K. brought proceedings for (1) the annulment of the act whereby the President of the European Parliament declared, on December 18, 1985, the final adoption of the general budget of the European Communities; (2) the total or partial annulment of the general budget of the European Communites for 1986. The U.K. applied for an interim order pending final judgment in the main action, that EEC States should make limited payments in respect of VAT for the 1986 budget. *Held*, that the U.K. had shown that serious and irreparable damage would occur if interim measures were not granted. Accordingly, the following interim orders were made: (1) the Commission shall implement, until July 10, 1986 or until judgment is given in the case of *European Council* v. *European Parliament*, (No. 34/86) [1986] 11 C.L. 109, whichever date shall be the earlier, the budget for 1986 on the basis of the draft budget established by the Council on November 27, 1985 (subject to certain amendments made by the Parliament on December 12, 1985); (2) in the first demand which the Commission makes, following this order, on the U.K. for funds relating to the 1986 budget, it shall reduce the sums claimed, on the basis of the draft budget of November 27, 1985, by the amount of any overpayments made by the U.K. before this order on the basis of the budget declared by the President of the European Parliament on December 18, 1985.

THE EUROPEAN COMMUNITY BUDGET 1986, *Re*; U.K. *v.* EUROPEAN PARLIAMENT (No. 23/86) [1986] 3 C.M.L.R. 82, President of the European Ct.

1396. European Parliament—budget—non-compulsory expenditure

The European Council brought proceedings pursuant to Art. 173 EEC and Art. 146 Euratom against the European Parliament for (1) the partial or total annulment of the general budget of the European Communities for 1986 and for (2) the annulment of the act of December 18, 1985 whereby the President of the European Parliament declared the final adoption of that budget. The European Council (and the intervening Governments) complained that the European Parliament increased certain budgetary appropriations in breach of the Treaties, in particular in breach of Art. 203(9) EEC and equivalent provisions in the Euratom and ECSC Treaties. These increases brought a rise in the non-compulsory expenditure in the 1986 budget, as compared with the like expenditure for the financial year 1985, which exceeded the maximum rate of increase set in conformity with Art. 203(9). *Held*, that (1) the act of the President of the European Parliament of December 18, 1985, whereby he declared the adoption of the budget for 1986 had been finally adopted, was void; (2) the annulment of the said act of December 18, 1985 did not affect the validity of payments made and commitments entered into, in implementation of the budget for 1986 as published in the Official Journal, before the date of delivery of this judgment; (3) Parliament and Council were to resume the budgetary procedure as regards the joint fixing of the maximum rate of increase of non-compulsory expenditure.

1986 BUDGET, *Re:* E.C. COUNCIL (GERMANY, FRANCE AND U.K. intervening) *v.* EUROPEAN PARLIAMENT (No. 34/86) [1986] 3 C.M.L.R. 94, European Ct.

1397. European Parliament—elections—campaign costs

The general budget of the EEC included item 3708 which provided for appropriations intended as a "contribution to the costs of preparations" for the next European elections. On October 12, 1982, the Bureau of the European Parliament adopted a decision establishing the distribution of the appropriations allocated to item 3708. That decision was elaborated upon by rules adopted on September 29, 1983. The rules provided that 31 per cent. of the appropriations allocated to item 3708 were to be distributed to political groupings which took part in the 1983 elections while the remaining 69 per cent. were to be divided amoung the parties represented in the European Parliament elected in 1979. The French Ecologist Party, Les Verts, sought the annulment of the 1982 decision and the 1983 rules on the ground, *inter alia,* that in accordance with Art. 138 EEC and Art. 7(2) of the Act concerning the election of the representatives of the assembly by direct universal suffrage of September 20, 1976 that financial scheme was to be governed by the national legislation of the EEC States and that parties already represented in the 1974 Parliament were able to draw on both the 69 per cent. and the reserve fund of 31 per cent. and were thereby given a considerable advantage by comparison with political groupings which had no representatives in the assembly elected in 1979. *Held*, that (1) an action for annulment might be brought against acts of the European Parliament which were intended to have legal force with regard to third parties; (2) "Les Verts" was an association which was individually concerned by the disputed acts; (3) at the present stage of EEC law, the establishment of a system of reimbursement of election campaign costs and the determination of its detailed implementation remained within the competence of the Member States pursuant to Art. 7(2) of the Act. Thus, the European Parliament had infringed Art. 7(2) of the Act by the adoption of the decision of 12th October 1982 and the 1983 rules. Accordingly, the decision and rules were void.

LES VERTS—PARTI ECOLOGISTE *v.* EUROPEAN PARLIAMENT (No. 294/83) *The Times,* April 24, 1986, European Ct.

1398. European Parliament—location—powers
    Luxembourg brought proceedings pursuant to Arts. 31 and 38 ECSC and, in the alternative, pursuant to Art. 173 EEC and Art. 146 Euratom, seeking annulment of the resolution of the European Parliament of July 7, 1981. The resolution was on the consequences to be drawn from the European Parliament's adoption, on July 7, 1981, of the Zaga Report. The resolution required the re-organisation of the Parliament's staff so that those who mostly dealt with the functioning of its committees should be based in Brussels and those who mostly dealt with the functioning of the "part-sessions" of Parliament in Strasbourg should be based in Strasbourg. Luxembourg argued that Parliament had exceeded its powers under the Treaties; that whilst Parliament had the right to take measures to ensure the smooth working of its departments, it had to respect the EEC States' right to fix the seat of the institutions. *Held,* that the European Parliament by adopting the resolution had exceeded the limits of its powers under the Treaties. Consequently, the resolution of July 7, 1981 was void.
    LUXEMBOURG *v.* EUROPEAN PARLIAMENT (NO. 2) (No. 108/83) [1986] 2 C.M.L.R 507.

1399. European Parliament—Member of European Parliament—legal immunity
    Mr. Faure, a Member of the European Parliament (a "MEP") was summoned to appear in the Tribunal Correctionel, Paris to answer a charge of being an accessory to the public defamation of a civil servant. It was argued on Mr. Faure's behalf that he enjoyed, during the sessions of the Parliament, the immunities, including legal immunity, conferred by Art. 10 of the Protocol on the Privileges and Immunities of the European Communities ("the Protocol"). The Parliament had been in session from March 5, 1982 to March 7, 1983, although not actually sitting on the date of summons, January 27, 1983. The Cour d'Appel asked the European Court under Art. 177 EEC for a preliminary ruling on the interpretation of Art. 10 of the Protocol. *Held,* that Art. 10 of the Protocol which granted MEPs immunity "during the sessions of the Assembly", was to be interpreted as meaning that the European Parliament was to be regarded as being in session, even if it was not actually sitting, up to the time of the closure of the annual or extraordinary sessions. An interpretation of "sessions" to merely times when the Parliament was actually sitting would jeopardise the achievement of the various activities of the Parliament: WYBOT *v.* FAURE (No. 149/85) *The Times,* July 24, 1986, European Ct.

1400. European Social Fund—directives, decisions and regulations
    85/568/EEC:
        Council Decision of December 20, 1985 amending, on account of the accession of Spain and Portugal, Decision 83/516/EEC on the tasks of the European Social Fund. (O.J. 1985 L370/40.)
    85/645/EEC:
        Commission Decision of December 23, 1985 amending, with a view to the accession of Spain and Portugal, Decision 85/420/EEC on the amounts of assistance from the European Social Fund towards expenditure on recruitment and employment premiums. (O.J. 1985 L/379/65.)
    85/646/EEC:
        Commission Decision of December 23, 1985 derogating in favour of Spain and Portugal from Decision 83/673/EEC in respect of the deadline for submission to the European Social Fund of applications for assistance for specific operations. (O.J. 1985 L379/66.)
    Council Regulation (EEC) No. 3823/85 of December 20, 1985 amending, on account of the accession of Spain and Portugal, Regulation (EEC) No. 2950/83 on the implementation of Decision 83/516/EEC on the tasks of the European Social Fund. (O.J. 1985 L370/23.)
    Council Regulation (EEC) No. 3824/85 of December 20, 1985 amending, with a view to its extension to cover self-employed persons, Regulation (EEC) No. 2950/83 on the implementation of Decision 83/516/EEC on the tasks of the European Social Fund. (O.J. 1985 L370/25.)
    86/221/EEC:
        Commission Decision of April 30, 1986 on the Guidelines for the Management of the European Social Fund in the financial years 1987 to 1989. (O.J. 1986 L.153/59.)

86/413/EEC:

Commission Decision of July 30, 1986 on the rates of assistance from the European Social Fund towards expenditure on recruitment and employments premiums. (O.J. 1986 L237/35.)

1401. External affairs—directives, decisions and regulations

85/557/EEC:

Council Decision of December 17, 1985 on the conclusion of the Agreement between the European Economic Community and the Government of the Republic of Senegal amending, for the second time, the Agreement on fishing off the coast of Senegal, and the conclusion of the new Protocol thereto. (O.J. 1985 L361/86.)

85/567/EEC:

Decision of the representatives of the governments of the Member States, meeting within the Council, and the Commission of December 20, 1985 concerning the conclusion of Agreements in the form of an Exchange of Letters between the Member States and the European Coal and Steel Community, on the one hand, and the Republic of Austria, the Republic of Finland, the Republic of Iceland, the Kingdom of Norway, the Kingdom of Sweden and the Swiss Confederation respectively, on the other, on the arrangements applicable to trade between Spain and Portugal, on the one hand, and Austria, Finland, Iceland, Norway, Sweden and Switzerland respectively on the other, from January 1 to February 28, 1986. (O.J. 1985 L370/38.)

Commission Decision No. 3712/85/ECSC of December 11, 1985 on the conclusion of an Arrangement extending and amending the Arrangement of October 21, 1982 concerning trade in certain steel products. (O.J. 1985 L355/101.)

Commission Decision No. 3713/85/ECSC of December 11, 1985 amending Decision No. 2872/82/ECSC on the restriction of exports of certain steel products to the United States of America. (O.J. 1985 L355/155.)

Commission Regulation (EEC) No. 3531/85 of December 12, 1985 laying down certain technical and control measures relating to the fishing activities of vessels flying the flag of Spain in the waters of the other Member States, except Portugal. (O.J. 1985 L336/20.)

Commission Regulation (EEC) No. 3532/85 of December 12, 1985 concerning the stopping of fishing for plaice by vessels flying the flag of the United Kingdom. (O.J. 1985 L336/27.)

Commission Regulation (EEC) No. 3539/85 of December 13, 1985 concerning the stopping of fishing for mackerel by vessels flying the flag of Ireland. (O.J. 1985 L336/48.)

Commission Regulation (EEC) No. 3561/85 of December 17, 1985 concerning information about inspections of fishing activities carried out by national control authorities. (O.J. 1985 L339/29.)

Commission Regulation (EEC) No. 3587/85 of December 16, 1985 amending, by reason of the accession of Spain and Portugal, Regulation (EEC) No. 3321/82 as regards the list of fishery products and sizes qualifying for the carry-over premium. (O.J. 1985 L343/16.)

Commission Regulation (EEC) No. 3617/85 of December 20, 1985 concerning the stopping of fishing for herring by vessels flying the flag of the Netherlands. (O.J. 1985 L344/43.)

Commission Regulation (EEC) No. 3661/85 of December 23, 1985 concerning the stopping of fishing for shrimp by vessels flying the flag of France. (O.J. 1985 L348/41.)

Commission Regulation (EEC) No. 3693/85 of December 23, 1985 laying down rules for calculating withdrawal prices and fixing the withdrawal prices, for the 1986 fishing year, for the fishery products listed in Annex I (A) and (D) to Regulation (EEC) No. 3796/81 and for certain products landed in areas very distant from the main areas of consumption in the Community. (O.J. 1985 L351/35.)

Commission Regulation (EEC) No. 3694/85 of December 23, 1985 fixing the standard values to be used in calculating the financial compensation and the advance pertaining thereto in respect of fishery products withdrawn from the market during the 1986 fishing year. (O.J. 1985 L351/41.)

Commission Regulation (EEC) No. 3695/85 of December 23, 1985 fixing the amount of the carry-over premium for certain fishery products for the 1986 fishing year. (O.J. 1985 L351/43.)

Commission Regulation (EEC) No. 3696/85 of December 23, 1985 fixing the reference prices for fishery products for the 1986 fishing year. (O.J. 1985 L351/45.)

Commission Regulation (EEC) No. 3703/85 of December 23, 1985 laying down detailed rules for applying the common marketing standards for certain fresh or chilled fish. (O.J. 1985 L351/63.)

Commission Regulation (EEC) No. 3715/85 of December 27, 1985 laying down certain technical and control measures relating to the fishing activities of vessels flying the flag of Portugal in the waters of the other Member States except Spain. (O.J. 1985 L360/1.)

Commission Regulation (EEC) No. 3716/85 of December 27, 1985 laying down certain technical and control measures relating to the fishing activities in Spanish waters of vessels flying the flag of another Member State except Portugal. (O.J. 1985 L360/7.)

Commission Regulation (EEC) No. 3717/85 of December 27, 1985 laying down certain technical and control measures relating to the fishing activities in Spanish waters of vessels flying the flag of Portugal. (O.J. 1985 L360/14.)

Commission Regulation (EEC) No. 3718/85 of December 27, 1985 laying down certain technical and control measures relating to the fishing activities in Portuguese waters of vessels flying the flag of Spain. (O.J. 1985 L360/20.)

Council Regulation (EEC) No. 3551/85 of December 12, 1985 allocating the 1986 Community catch quotas in Canadian waters among Member States. (O.J. 1985 L339/1.)

Council Regulation (EEC) No. 3552/85 of December 12, 1985 opening, allocating and providing for the administration of Community tariff quotas for certain fishery products (1986). (O.J. 1985 L339/3.)

Council Regulation (EEC) No. 3602/85 of December 17, 1985 fixing the guide prices for the fishery products listed in Annex I(A) and (D) of Regulation (EEC) No. 3796/81 for the 1986 fishing year. (O.J. 1985 L344/1.)

Council Regulation (EEC) No. 3603/85 of December 17, 1985 fixing the guide prices for the fishery products listed in Annex II to Regulation (EEC) No. 3796/81 for the 1986 fishing year. (O.J. 1985 L344/3.)

Council Regulation (EEC) No. 3605/85 of December 17, 1985 fixing the Community producer price for tuna intended for the canning industry for the 1986 fishing year. (O.J. 1985 L344/11.)

Council Regulation (EEC) No. 3708/85 of December 10, 1985 on the conclusion of an Arrangement in the form of an Exchange of Letters with the United States of America extending and amending the Arrangement of October 21, 1982 relating to trade in certain steel products. (O.J. 1985 L355/1.)

Council Regulation (EEC) No. 3709/85 of December 10, 1985 amending Council Regulation (EEC) No. 2870/82 on the restriction of exports of certain steel products to the United States of America. (O.J. 1985 L355/55.)

Council Regulation (EEC) No. 3710/85 of December 10, 1985 on the conclusion of an Arrangement in the form of an Exchange of Letters with the United States of America extending the Arrangement of January 10, 1985 concerning trade in steel pipes and tubes. (O.J. 1985 L355/97.)

Council Regulation (EEC) No. 3711/85 of December 10, 1985 amending Council Regulation (EEC) No. 60/85 on the restriction of exports of steel pipes and tubes to the United States of America. (O.J. 1985 L355/100.)

Council Regulation (EEC) No. 3720/85 of December 20, 1985 amending for the fourth time Regulation (EEC) No. 1/85 fixing, for certain fish stocks and groups of fish stocks, provisional total allowable catches for 1985 and certain conditions under which they may be fished. (O.J. 1985 L361/1.)

Council Regulation (EEC) No. 3721/85 of December 20, 1985 fixing, for certain fish stocks and groups of fish stocks, total allowable catches for 1986 and certain conditions under which they may be fished. (O.J. 1985 L361/5.)

Council Regulation (EEC) No. 3723/85 of December 20, 1985 amending Regulation (EEC) No. 2057/82 establishing certain control measures for fishing activities by vessels of the Member States. (O.J. 1985 L361/42.)

Council Regulation (EEC) No. 3724/85 of December 20, 1985 fixing the flat-rate amounts of hake, horse mackerel and blue whiting allocated to Spain for 1986. (O.J. 1985 L361/45.)

Council Regulation (EEC) No. 3725/85 of December 20, 1985 allocating quotas between Member States for vessels fishing in Swedish waters. (O.J. 1985 L361/47.)

Council Regulation (EEC) No. 3726/85 of December 20, 1985 laying down for 1986 certain measures for the conservation and management of fishery resources applicable to vessels flying the flag of Sweden. (O.J. 1985 L361/49.)

Council Regulation (EEC) No. 3728/85 of December 20, 1985 amending Regulation (EEC) No. 2204/82 laying down general rules for the granting of a special carry-over premium for Mediterranean sardines and anchovies. (O.J. 1985 L361/57.)

Council Regulation (EEC) No. 3729/85 of December 20, 1985 laying down for 1986 certain measures for the conservation and management of fishery resources applicable to vessels flying the flag of certain non-member countries in the 200-nautical-mile zone off the coast of the French department of Guiana. (O.J. 1985 L361/58.)

Council Regulation (EEC) No. 3730/85 of December 20, 1985 allocating certain catch quotas between Member States for vessels fishing in the Norwegian economic zone and the fishery zone around Jan Mayen. (O.J. 1985 L361/66.)

Council Regulation (EEC) No. 3731/85 of December 20, 1985 laying down for 1986 certain measures for the conservation and management of fishery resources applicable to vessels registered in the Faroe Islands. (O.J. 1985 L361/69.)

Council Regulation (EEC) No. 3732/85 of December 20, 1985 allocating catch quotas between Member States for vessels fishing in Faroese waters. (O.J. 1985 L361/76.)

Council Regulation (EEC) No. 3733/85 of December 20, 1985 amending Regulation (EEC) No. 2908/83 on a common measure for restructuring, modernising and developing the fishing industry and for developing aquaculture. (O.J. 1985 L361/78.)

Council Regulation (EEC) No. 3734/85 of December 20, 1985 laying down for 1986 certain measures for the conservation and management of fishery resources applicable to vessels flying the flag of Norway. (O.J. 1985 L361/80.)

Council Regulation (EEC) No. 3737/85 of December 20, 1985 amending Regulation (EEC) No. 2909/83 on measures to encourage exploratory fishing and cooperation through joint ventures in the fishing sector. (O.J. 1985 L361/56.)

Council Regulation (EEC) No. 3825/85 of December 20, 1985 concerning the conclusion of Agreements in the form of an exchange of letters between the European Economic Community on the one hand and the Republic of Austria, the Republic of Finland, the Republic of Iceland, the Kingdom of Norway, the Kingdom of Sweden and the Swiss Confederation respectively, on the other, on the arrangements applicable to trade between Spain and Portugal on the one hand, and Austria, Finland, Iceland, Norway, Sweden and Switzerland respectively on the other, from January 1 to February 28, 1986. (O.J. 1985 L370/26.)

Council Regulation (EEC) No. 3829/85 of May 20, 1985 concerning the conclusion of the Agreement between the European Economic Community and the Republic of Colombia on trade in textile products. (O.J. 1986 L378/1.)

Council Regulation (EEC) No. 3836/85 of December 20, 1985 concerning the conclusion of the Agreement between the European Economic Community and the Republic of Singapore on trade in textile products. (O.J. 1985 L381/84.)

86/8/EEC:

Council Decision of January 20, 1986 on the conclusion of an Agreement in the form of exchanges of letters between the European Economic Community and the Kingdom of Norway concerning reciprocal trade in cheese. (O.J. 1986 L22/25.)

86/87/EEC, Euratom:

Council Decision of March 10, 1986 concerning the conclusion of the Framework Agreement for scientific and technical cooperation between the European Communities and the Republic of Finland. (O.J. 1986 L78/23.)

86/101/EEC:

Council Decision of February 24, 1986 concerning the conclusion of an exchange of letters between the European Economic Community and the Government of Canada concerning exports of boneless manufacturing beef from the Community to Canada. (O.J. 1986 L87/33.)

86/123/EEC:

Council Decision of April 8, 1986 concerning the conclusion of an Agreement in the form of an exchange of letters between the European Economic Community and the Government of Canada relating to the claim by the European Economic Community for compensation arising from the extension of quotas on imports into Canada of women's and girls' footwear for the period December 1, 1985 to November 30, 1988. (O.J. 1986 L100/26.)

86/124/EEC:

Council Decision of April 8, 1986 authorising extension or tacit renewal of certain trade agreements concluded between Member States and third world countries. (O.J. 1986 L100/30.)

86/182/EEC:

Council Decision of May 6, 1986 on the conclusion of an Agreement in the form of an exchange of letters concerning an extension of the Protocol annexed to the Agreement between the European Economic Community and the Government of the Republic of Guinea-Bissau on fishing off the coast of Guinea-Bissau for a period of three months from March 15, 1986. (O.J. 1986 L.131/51.)

86/236/EEC:

Commission Decision of April 16, 1986 changing the import arrangements established by Council Decision 85/648/EEC and applied in the Member States in respect of imports of various agricultural and industrial products from the People's Republic of China. (O.J. 1986 L.161/33.)

86/237/EEC:

Council Decision of June 9, 1986 authorising the extension or tacit renewal of certain trade agreements conducted between the Member States and third countries. (O.J. 1986 L.162/30.)

86/283/EEC

Council Decision of June 30, 1986 on the association of the overseas countries and territories with the European Economic Community. (O.J. 1986 L175/1.)

86/416/EEC

Council Decision of April 8, 1986 concerning the conclusion of the Agreement between the European Economic Community and the Islamic Republic of Pakistan on trade in textile products. (O.J. 1986 L245/1.)

86/417/EEC

Council Decision of April 8, 1986 concerning the conclusion of the Agreement between the European Economic Community and the Republic of the Philippines on trade in textile products. (O.J. 1986 L245/46.)

86/418/EEC

Council Decision of April 8, 1986 concerning the conclusion of the Agreement between the European Economic Community and the People's Republic of Poland on trade in textile products, and of the Agreement in the form of an Exchange of Letters. (O.J. 1986 L245/90.)

86/419/EEC

Council Decision of April 8, 1986 concerning the conclusion of the Agreement between the European Economic Community and the Socialist Republic of Romania on trade in textile products. (O.J. 1986 L245/141.)

86/420/EEC

Council Decision of April 8, 1986 concerning the conclusion of the Agreement between the European Economic Community and the Democratic Socialist Republic of Sri Lanka on trade in textile products. (O.J. 1986 L245/192.)

86/421/EEC

Council Decision of April 8, 1986 concerning the conclusion of the Agreement between the European Economic Community and the Czechoslovak Socialist Republic on trade in textile products. (O.J. 1986 L245/239.)

86/422/EEC

Council Decision of April 8, 1986 concerning the conclusion of the Agreement between the European Economic Community and the Kingdom of Thailand on trade in textile products. (O.J. 1986 L245/289.)

86/423/EEC

Council Decision of April 8, 1986 concerning the conclusion of the Supplementary Protocol to the Cooperation Agreement between the European Economic Community and the Socialist Federal Republic of Yugoslavia on trade in textile products. (O.J. 1986 L245/338.)

86/449/EEC:
Council Decision of September 8, 1986 on the conclusion of an Agreement in the form of an Exchange of Letters concerning the provisional application, as from June 16, 1986, of the Agreement amending for the second time the Agreement between the European Economic Community and the Government of the Republic of Guinea-Bissau on fishing off the coast of Guinea-Bissau. (O.J. 1986 L261/20.)

Council Regulation (EEC) No. 439/86 of February 17, 1986 on the conclusion of the Agreement in the form of an Exchange of Letters between the European Economic Community and the People's Democratic Republic of Algeria fixing the additional amount to be deducted from the levy on imports into the Community of untreated olive oil, originating in Algeria, for the period from November 1, 1985 to February 28, 1986. (O.J. 1986 L50/1.)

Council Regulation (EEC) No. 440/86 of February 17, 1986 on the conclusion of the Agreement in the form of an Exchange of Letters between the European Economic Community and the Kingdom of Morocco fixing the additional amount to be deducted from the levy on imports into the Community of untreated olive oil, originating in Morocco, for the period November 1, 1985 to February 28, 1986. (O.J. 1986 L50/3.)

Council Regulation (EEC) No. 441/86 of February 17, 1986 on the conclusion of the Agreement in the form of an Exchange of Letters between the European Economic Community, and the Republic of Tunisia fixing the additional amount to be deducted from the levy on imports into the Community of untreated olive oil, originating in Tunisia, for the period November 1, 1985 to February 28, 1986. (O.J. 1986 L50/5.)

Council Regulation (EEC) No. 780/86 of February 24, 1986 concerning the conclusion of the Agreement between the European Economic Community and the Government of the Democratic Republic of Madagascar on fishing off the coast of Madagascar. (O.J. 1986 L73/25.)

Council Regulation (EEC) No. 781/86 of March 6, 1986 concerning the conclusion of the Agreement in the form of an exchange of letters relating to Art. 9 of Protocol No. 1 to the Agreement between the European Economic Community and the State of Israel and concerning the import into the Community of preserved fruit salads originating in Israel (1986).

Council Regulation (EEC) No. 782/86 of March 6, 1986 on the conclusion of the Agreement in the form of an exchange of letters between the European Economic Community and the People's Democratic Republic of Algeria concerning the import into the Community of preserved fruit salads originating in Algeria (1986). (O.J. 1986 L74/3.)

Council Regulation (EEC) No. 783/86 of March 6, 1986 on the conclusion of the Agreement in the form of an exchange of letters between the European Economic Community and the Kingdom of Morocco concerning the import into the Community of preserved fruit salads originating in Morocco (1986). (O.J. 1986 L74/6.)

Council Regulation (EEC) No. 784/86 of March 6, 1986 on the conclusion of the Agreement in the form of an exchange of letters between the European Economic Community and the Republic of Tunisia concerning the import into the Community of preserved fruit salads originating in Tunisia (1986). (O.J. 1986 L74/9.)

Council Regulation (EEC) No. 785/86 of March 6, 1986 on the conclusion of the Agreement in the form of an exchange of letters between the European Economic Community and the People's Democratic Republic of Algeria on the importation into the Community of tomato concentrates originating in Algeria (1986). (O.J. 1986 L74/12.)

Council Regulation (EEC) No. 814/86 of March 14, 1986 on the conclusion of the Agreement in the form of an exchange of letters between the European Economic Community and the Socialist Republic of Romania amending Annex II to the Protocol annexed to the Agreement on trade in industrial products. (O.J. 1986 L78/19.)

Council Regulation (EEC) No. 1196/86 of April 22, 1986 on the conclusion of the Agreement for commercial economic and development co-operation between the European Economic Community and the Islamic Republic of Pakistan. (O.J. 1986 L108/1.)

Council Regulation (EEC) No. 1443/86 of April 28, 1986 on the application of Decision No. 1/86 of the EEC-Austria Joint Committee supplementing and amending Lists A and B annexed to Protocol No. 3 concerning the definition of the concept of "originating products" and methods of administrative cooperation. (O.J. 1986 L.134/1.)

Council Regulation (EEC) No. 1542/86 of April 8, 1986 on the application of Decision No. 2/85 of the EEC-Austria Joint Committee—Community transit—on the Spanish and Portuguese texts of the Agreement between the European Economic Community and the Republic of Austria on the application of the rules on the Community transit and amending the Appendices thereto. (O.J. 1986 L.143/1.)

Council Regulation (EEC) No. 1543/86 of April 8, 1986 on the application of Decision No. 2/85 of the EEC-Switzerland Joint Committee—Community transit— on the Spanish and Portuguese texts of the Agreement between the European Economic Community and the Swiss Confederation on the application of the rules on Community transit and amending the Appendices thereto. (O.J. 1986 L.143/187.)

Council Regulation (EEC) No. 2009/86 of June 24, 1986 concerning the conclusion of the Cooperation Agreement between the European Economic Community, of the one part, and the countries parties to the General Treaty on Central American Economic Integration (Costa Rica, El Salvador, Guatemala, Honduras and Nicaragua) and Panama, of the other part. (O.J. 1986 L172/1.)

Information on the date of entry into force of the Third ACP-EEC Convention signed at Lomé on December 8, 1984. (O.J. 1986 L86/209.)

1402. Fisheries—directives, decisions and regulations

Corrigendum to Council regulation (EEC) No. 3720/85 of December 20, 1985 amending for the fourth time Regulation (EEC) No. 1/85 fixing, for certain fish stocks and groups of fish stocks, provisional total allowable catches for 1985 and certain conditions under which they may be fished. (O.J. No. L361 of 31.12.1985). (O.J. 1986 L62/42.)

Corrigendum to Council Regulation (EEC) No. 3721/85 of December 20, 1985 fixing, for certain fish stocks and groups of fish stocks, total allowable catches for 1986 and certain conditions under which they may be fished (O.J. No. L361 of 31.12.1985). (O.J. 1986 L62/42.)

Corrigendum to Council regulation (EEC) No. 3724/85 of December 20 1985 fixing the flat-rate amounts of hake, horse mackerel and blue whiting allocated to Spain for 1986 (O.J. No. L361 of 31.12.1985). (O.J. 1986 L62/43.)

Corrigendum to Council Regulation (EEC) No. 3734/85 of December 20, 1985 laying down for 1986 certain measures for the conservation and management of fishery resources applicable to vessels flying the flag of Norway (O.J. No. L361 of 31.12.1985). (O.J. 1986 L62/43.)

Corrigendum to Council Regulation (EEC) No. 3777/85 of December 31, 1985 amending Regulation (EEC) No. 3721/85 fixing, for certain fish stocks and groups of fish stocks, the total allowable catches for 1986 and certain conditions under which they can be fished (O.J. No. L363 of 31.12.1985). (O.J. 1986 L62/44.)

Corrigendum to Council Regulation (EEC) No. 3778/85 of December 31, 1985 establishing, for 1986, certain measures for the conservation and management of fishery resources, applicable to vessels flying the flag of Member States, other than Spain and Portugal, in waters falling under the sovereignty or within the jurisdiction of Spain (O.J. No. L 363 of 31.12.1985). (O.J. 1986 L62/44.)

Corrigendum to Council Regulation (EEC) No. 3780/85 of 31 December 1985 establishing, for 1985, certain measures for the conservation and management of fishery resources applicable to vessels flying the flag of Portugal in waters falling under the sovereignty or within the jurisdiction of other Member States, apart from Spain and Portugal (O.J. No. L.363 of 31.12.1985). (O.J. 1986 L62/45.)

Corrigendum to Council Regulation (EEC) No. 3783/85 of December 31, 1985 allocating, for 1986, Community catch quotas in Greenland waters (O.J. No. L363 of 31.12.1985). (O.J. 1986 L62/45.)

86/78/EEC:

Commission Decision of February 21, 1986 approving a programme for the fishery sector submitted by the Netherlands pursuant to Council Regulation (EEC) No. 355/77. (O.J. 1986 L76/56.)

86/186/EEC:

Commission Decision of October 9, 1985 on aids granted by the French Government to producers' organisations in the fisheries sector. (O.J. 1986 L.136/55.)

86/238/EEC:

Council Decision of June 9, 1986 on the accession of the Community to the International Convention for the Conservation of Atlantic Tunas, as amended by the Protocol annexed to the Final Act of the Conference of Plenipotentiaries of the States Parties to the Convention signed in Paris on July 10, 1984. (O.J. 1986 L.162/33.)

86/351/EEC:

Commission Decision of July 4, 1986 on the guidance programme for the fishing fleet submitted by Portugal for 1986 in accordance with Council Regulation (EEC) No. 2908/83. (O.J. 1986 L205/46.)

86/352/EEC:

Commission Decision of July 10, 1986 concerning extensions in the implementation by Germany of certain measures to adjust capacity in the fisheries sector, pursuant to Council Directive 83/515/EEC. (O.J. 1986 L205/50.)

86/381/EEC

Commission Decision of July 23, 1986 relating to the specific programme concerning the processing and marketing of fish and fish products in Germany for the period of 1985 to 1989 forwarded by the Federal Republic of Germany pursuant to Council Regulation (EEC) No. 355/77. (O.J. 1986 L226/14.)

86/382/EEC

Commission Decision of July 23, 1986 relating to the specific programme concerning the processing and marketing of fish and fish products in Denmark for the period 1986 to 1990 forwarded by Denmark pursuant to Council Regulation (EEC) No. 355/77. (O.J. 1986 L226/17.)

86/383/EEC

Commission Decision of July 23, 1986 relating to the specific programmes concerning the processing and marketing of fish and fish products in France for the period 1986 to 1990 forwarded by France pursuant to Council Regulation (EEC) No. 355/77. (O.J. 1986 L226/20.)

86/384/EEC

Commission Decision of July 23, 1986 relating to the specific programme concerning the processing and marketing of fish and fish products in Ireland for the period 1985 to 1989 forwarded by Ireland pursuant to Council Regulation (EEC) No. 355/77. (O.J. 1986 L226/24.)

86/385/EEC

Commission Decision of July 23, 1986 relating to the specific programme concerning the processing and marketing of fish and fish products in Italy for the period 1986 to 1988 forwarded by Italy pursuant to Council Regulation (EEC) No. 355/77. (O.J. 1986 L226/27.)

86/386/EEC

Commission Decision of July 23, 1986 relating to the specific programmes concerning the processing and marketing of fish and fish products in the United Kingdom for the period 1985 to 1989 forwarded by the United Kingdom pursuant to Council Regulation (EEC) No. 355/77. (O.J. 1986 L226/30.)

86/401/EEC

Commission Decision of July 28, 1986 on measures to encourage exploratory fishing pursuant to Council Regulation No. 2909/83 (EXP/FR/1/85). (O.J. 1986 L233/13.)

86/471/EEC:

Commission Decision of September 5, 1986 on the guidance programme in respect of the fishing fleet submitted by Spain for 1986 pursuant to Regulation (EEC) No. 2908/83. (O.J. 1986 L279/46.)

Commission Regulation (EEC) No. 255/86 of February 4, 1986 suspending the duties applicable to fresh fishery products originating in Morocco and coming from joint fishery ventures set up between natural or legal persons from Portugal and Morocco, on the direct landing of such products in Portugal. (O.J. 1986 L31/15.)

Commission Regulation (EEC) No. 314/86 of February 11, 1986 laying down detailed rules for the grant of a storage premium for certain fishery products. (O.J. 1986 L39/8.)

Commission Regulation (EEC) No. 544/86 of February 27, 1986 opening tariff quotas for fishery products coming from joint ventures set up between natural or legal persons from Spain and from other countries. (O.J. 1986 L55/44.)

Commission Regulation (EEC) No. 546/86 of February 27, 1986 laying down detailed rules for applying the supplementary trade mechanism to fishery products. (O.J. 1986 L55/47.)

Commission Regulation (EEC) No. 654/86 of February 28, 1986 fixing, for the 1986 fishing year, the overall foreseeable level of imports for the products subject to the supplementary trade mechanism in the fisheries sector. (O.J. 1986 L66/6.)

Commission Regulation (EEC) No. 655/86 of February 28 1986. Fixing, for the 1986 fishing year, the annual import quotas for the products subject to the rules for the application by Spain and Portugal of quantitative restrictions on fishery products. (O.J. 1986 L66/9.)

Commission Regulation (EEC) No. 656/86 of February 28, 1986 concerning the fixing, for the period March 1 to December 31, 1986, of the withdrawal and selling prices for certain fishery products and amending Regulation (EEC) No. 3693/85 as regards the withdrawal prices for Atlantic sardines and anchovies. (O.J. 1986 L66/11.)

Commission Regulation (EEC) No. 657/86 of February 28, 1986 fixing the reference prices for certain fishery products for the period March 1 to December 31, 1986. (O.J. 1986 L66/16.)

Commission Regulation (EEC) No. 658/86 of February 28, 1986 fixing the reference prices for intra-Community trade in anchovies and Atlantic sardines for the 1986 fishing year. (O.J. 1986 L66/18.)

Commission Regulation (EEC) No. 659/86 of February 28, 1986 fixing the compensatory allowance for Mediterranean sardines. (O.J. 1986 L66/19.)

Commission Regulation (EEC) No. 660/86 of February 28, 1986 fixing the storage premium for certain fishery products for the period from March 1 to December 31, 1986. (O.J. 1986 L66/20.)

Commission Regulation (EEC) No. 661/86 of February 28, 1986 amending Regulation (EEC) No. 3695/85, by reason of the accession of Spain and Portugal, in respect of the list of fishery products for which a carry-over premium is granted. (O.J. 1986 L66/22.)

Commission Regulation (EEC) No. 990/86 of April 4, 1986 concerning the stopping of fishing for saithe by vessels flying the flag of Germany. (O.J. 1986 L90/35.)

Commission Regulation (EEC) No. 1051/86 of April 10, 1986 concerning the stopping of fishing for plaice, sole, cod, whiting and hake by vessels flying the flag of the Netherlands. (O.J. 1986 L96/23.)

Commission Regulation (EEC) No. 1220/86 of April 24, 1986 concerning the stopping of fishing for salmon by vessels flying the flag of Denmark. (O.J. 1986 L109/12.)

Commission Regulation (EEC) No. 1482/86 of May 15, 1986 amending Regulation (EEC) No. 3717/85 laying down certain technical and control measures relating to the fishing activities in Spanish waters of vessels flying the flag of Portugal. (O.J. 1986 L.130/21.)

Commission Regulation (EEC) No. 1483/86 of May 15, 1986 amending Regulation (EEC) No. 3718/85 laying down certain technical and control measures relating to the fishing activities in Portuguese waters of vessels flying the flag of Spain. (O.J. 1986 L.130/23.)

Commission Regulation (EEC) No. 1601/86 of May 26, 1986 concerning the stopping of fishing for redfish by vessels flying the flag of France. (O.J. 1986 L.140/22.)

Commission Regulation (EEC) No. 1602/86 of May 26, 1986 concerning the stopping of fishing for cod, whiting and sole by vessels flying the flag of the Netherlands. (O.J. 1986 L.140/23.)

Commission Regulation (EEC) No. 1771/86 of June 6, 1986 concerning the stopping of fishing for sole by vessels flying the flag of Belgium. (O.J. 1986 L.153/32.)

Commission Regulation (EEC) No. 2168/86 of July 10, 1986 amending Regulation (EEC) No. 655/86 fixing, for the 1986 fishing year, the annual import quotas for the products subject to the rules for the application by Spain and Portugal of quantitative restrictions on fishery products. (O.J. 1986 L189/11.)

Commission Regulation (EEC) No. 2189/86 of July 11, 1986 concerning the stopping of fishing for saithe by vessels flying the flag of the United Kingdom. (O.J. 1986 L190/55.)

Commission Regulation (EEC) No. 2190/86 of July 11, 1986 concerning the stopping of fishing for haddock by vessels flying the flag of the Netherlands. (O.J. 1986 L190/54.)

Commission Regulation (EEC) No. 2191/86 of July 11, 1986 concerning the stopping of fishing for sole by vessels flying the flag of Belgium. (O.J. 1986 L190/55.)

Commission Regulation (EEC) No. 2326/86 of July 24, 1986 amending Regulation (EEC) No. 3598/83 in the matter of the list of representative wholesale markets and ports for fishery products. (O.J. 1986 L202/23.)

Commission Regulation (EEC) No. 2621/86 of August 21, 1986 concerning the stopping of fishing for plaice by vessels flying the flag of the Netherlands. (O.J. 1986 L236/23.)

Commission Regulation (EEC) No. 2836/86 of September 12, 1986 concerning the stopping of fishing for anglerfish by vessels flying the flag of Spain. (O.J. 1986 L261/10.)

Commission Regulation (EEC) No. 2890/86 of September 18, 1986 concerning the stopping of fishing for cod by vessels flying the flag of Belgium. (O.J. 1986 L267/14.)

Commission Regulation (EEC) No. 2911/86 of September 19, 1986 repealing Regulation (EEC) No. 2189/86 concerning the stopping of fishing for saithe by vessels flying the flag of the United Kingdom. (O.J. 1986 L271/17.)

Commission Regulation (EEC) No. 3465/86 of November 13, 1986 concerning the stopping of fishing for cod and "other species" by vessels flying the flag of France. (O.J. 1986 L319/29.)

Commission Regulation (EEC) No. 3483/86 of November 13, 1986 concerning the stopping of fishing for cod by vessels flying the flag of France. (O.J. 1986 L320/17.)

Commission Regulation (EEC) No. 3565/86 of November 21, 1986 concerning the stopping of fishing for sole by vessels flying the flag of the United Kingdom. (O.J. 1986 L327/34.)

Commission Regulation (EEC) No. 3582/86 of November 24, 1986 concerning the stopping of fishing for herring by vessels flying the flag of Ireland. (O.J. 1986 L332/5.)

Commission Regulation (EEC) No. 3583/86 of November 24, 1986 concerning the stopping of fishing for cod by vessels flying the flag of the United Kingdom. (O.J. 1986 L332/6.)

Commission Regulation (EEC) No. 3637/86 of November 28, 1986 amending Regulation (EEC) No. 655/86 fixing, for the 1986 fishing year, the annual import quotas for the products subject to the rules for the application by Spain and Portugal of quantitative restrictions on fishery products. (O.J. 1986 L336/42.)

Commission Regulation (EEC) No. 3641/86 of November 28, 1986 amending Regulation (EEC) No. 654/86 fixing, for the 1986 fishing year, the overall foreseeable level of imports for the products subject to the supplementary trade mechanism in the fisheries sector. (O.J. 1986 L336/55.)

Commission Regulation (EEC) No. 3647/86 of November 28, 1986 concerning the stopping of fishing for sole by vessels flying the flag of the United Kingdom. (O.J. 1986 L336/63.)

Commission Regulation (EEC) No. 3672/86 of December 1, 1986 concerning the stopping of fishing for cod by vessels flying the flag of the Netherlands. (O.J. 1986 L339/19.)

Commission Regulation (EEC) No. 3683/86 of December 2, 1986 concerning the stopping of fishing for herring by vessels flying the flag of Ireland. (O.J. 1986 L340/8.)

Commission Regulation (EEC) No. 3714/86 of December 4, 1986 concerning the stopping of fishing for hake by vessels flying the flag of Ireland. (O.J. 1986 L342/20.)

Commission Regulation (EEC) No. 3715/86 of December 4, 1986 concerning the stopping of fishing for cod by vessels flying the flag of a Member State. (O.J. 1986 L342/21.)

Commission Regulation (EEC) No. 3753/86 of December 9, 1986 revoking Regulation (EEC) No. 3337/86 concerning the stopping of fishing for blue ling and ling by vessels flying the flag of France. (O.J. 1986 L348/39.)

Commission Regulation (EEC) No. 3754/86 of December 9, 1986 revoking Regulation (EEC) No. 3419/86 concerning the stopping of fishing for hake by vessels flying the flag of Germany. (O.J. 1986 L348/40.)

Council Regulation (EEC) No. 114/86 of January 20, 1986 extending until December 31, 1986 the validity of Regulations (EEC) No. 3721/85, No. 3730/85, No. 3784/85 and No. 3777/85 concerning fisheries. (O.J. 1986 L17/4.)

Council Regulation (EEC) No. 448/86 of February 24, 1986 establishing, for the period from March 3 to June 30, 1986, certain measures for the conservation and management of fishery resources applicable to vessels flying the Japanese flag in waters falling under the sovereignty or jurisdiction of Portugal. (O.J. 1986 L50/34.)

Council Regulation (EEC) No. 568/86 of February 24, 1986 concerning the application of Protocol No. 4, annexed to the Act of Accession of Spain and Portugal, with regard to the mechanism for additional responsibilities within the framework of fisheries agreements concluded by the Community with third countries. (O.J. 1986 L55/103.)

Council Regulation (EEC) No. 573/86 of February 28, 1986 laying down the arrangements applicable to trade in certain fishery products with Norway and Sweden, consequent upon the accession of Spain and Portugal. (O.J. 1986 L56/110.)

Council Regulation (EEC) No. 1418/86 of May 6, 1986 fixing the number of vessels flying the flag of Portugal authorised to fish for albacore tuna in waters under the sovereignty or jurisdiction of Spain. (O.J. 1986 L.129/1.)

Council Regulation (EEC) No. 1419/86 of May 6, 1986 fixing the number of vessels flying the flag of Spain authorised to fish for albacore tuna in waters under the sovereignty or jurisdiction of Portual. (O.J. 1986 L.129/3.)

Council Regulation (EEC) No. 1420/86 of May 6, 1986 amending Regulations (EEC) No. 3542/85, No. 3543/85 and No. 3544/85 on the opening, allocation and administration of Community tariff quotas for certain fish and fillets of fish. (O.J. 1986 L.129/5.)

Council Regulation (EEC) No. 1866/86 of June 12, 1986 laying down certain technical measures for the conservation of fishery resources in the waters of the Baltic Sea, the Belts and the Sound. (O.J. 1986 L.162/1.)

Information concerning the date of entry into force of the Agreement between the European Economic Community and the Government of the Democratic Republic of Madagascar on fishing off the coast of Madagascar. (O.J. 1986 L.137/27.)

Council Regulation (EEC) No. 2056/86 of June 25, 1986 allocating additional catch quotas among Member States for vessels fishing in Swedish waters. (O.J. 1986 L176/1.)

Council Regulation (EEC) No. 2057/86 of June 25, 1986 amending for the third time Regulation (EEC) No. 3721/85 fixing, for certain fish stocks and groups of fish stocks, the total allowable catches for 1986 and certain conditions under which they may be fished. (O.J. 1986 L176/3.)

Council Regulation (EEC) No. 2296/86 of July 21, 1986 amending Regulation (EEC) No. 2245/85 laying down certain techincal measures for the conservation of fish stocks in the Antarctic. (O.J. 1986 L201/2.)

Council Regulation (EEC) No. 2315/86 of July 21, 1986 amending Annex VI to Regulation (EEC) No. 3796/81 on the common organisation of the market in fishery products. (O.J. 1986 L202/1.)

Council Regulation (EEC) No. 2334/86 of July 21, 1986 fixing catch possibilities for certain fish stocks and groups of fish stocks in the Regulatory Area as defined in the NAFO Convention. (O.J. 1986 L203/1.)

Council Regulation (EEC) No. 2374/86 of July 24, 1986 amending for the fourth time Regulation (EEC) No. 3721/85 fixing, for certain fish stocks and groups of fish stocks, the total allowable catches for 1986 and certain conditions under which they may be fished. (O.J. 1986 L205/4.)

Council Regulation (EEC) No. 2375/86 of July 24, 1986 amending Regulation (EEC) No. 3783/85 allocating, for 1986, Community catch quotas in Greenland Waters. (O.J. 1986 L205/6.)

Council Regulation (EEC) No. 2930/86 of September 22, 1986 defining characteristics for fishing vessels. (O.J. 1986 L274/1.)

Council Regulation (EEC) No. 2972/86 of September 23, 1986 making Regulation (EEC) No. 2908/83 on a common measure for restructuring, modernising and developing the fishing industry and for developing aquaculture applicable to the Canary Islands. (O.J. 1986 L279/1.)

Council Regulation (EEC) No. 3221/86 of October 21, 1986 amending for the fifth time Regulation (EEC) No. 3721/85 fixing, for certain fish stocks and groups of fish stocks, total allowable catches for 1986 and certain conditions under which they may be fished. (O.J. 1986 L300/2.)

Council Regulation (EEC) No. 3777/85 of December 31, 1985 amending Regulation (EEC) No. 3721/85 fixing, for certain fish stocks and groups of fish stocks, the total allowable catches for 1986 and certain conditions under which they can be fished. (O.J. 1985 L363/1.)

Council Regulation (EEC) No. 3778/85 of December 31, 1985 establishing, for 1986, certain measures for the conservation and management of fishery resources, applicable to vessels flying the flag of Member States, other than Spain and Portugal, in waters falling under the sovereignty or within the jurisdiction of Spain. (O.J. 1985 L363/20.)

Council Regulation (EEC) No. 3779/85 of December 31, 1985 establishing, for 1986, certain measures for the conservation and management of fishery resources, applicable to vessels flying the flag of a Member State, other than Spain and Portugal, in waters falling under the sovereignty or within the jurisdiction of Portugal. (O.J. 1985 L363/22.)

Council Regulation (EEC) No. 3780/85 of December 31, 1985 establishing for 1986, certain measures for the conservation and management of fishery resources applicable to vessels flying the flag of Portugal in waters falling under the sovereignty or within the jurisdiction of other Member States, apart from Spain and Portugal. (O.J. 1985 L363/24.)

Council Regulation (EEC) No. 3781/85 of December 31, 1985 laying down the measures to be taken in respect of operators who do not comply with certain provisions relating to fishing contained in the Act of Accession of Spain and Portugal. (O.J. 1985 L363/26.)

Council Regulation (EEC) No. 3782/85 of December 31, 1985 amending for the sixth time Regulation (EEC) No. 171/83 in particular by the addition of technical conservation measures applicable to maritime waters falling within the sovereignty or jurisdiction of Spain and Portugal. (O.J. 1985 L363/28.)

Council Regulation (EEC) No. 3783/85 of December 31, 1985 allocating, for 1986, (O.J. 1985 L363/32.)

Corrigendum to Council Regulation (EEC) No. 2057/86 of June 25, 1986 amending for the third time Regulation (EEC) No. 3721/85 fixing, for certain fish stocks and groups of fish stocks, the total allowable catches for 1986 and certain conditions under which they may be fished (O.J. No. L176 of 1.7.1986). (O.J. 1986 L191/22.)

1403. Free movement of goods—imports—prosecutions

Mr. Abink was prosecuted in Holland for being in breach of Dutch legislation regarding the evasion of tax on the importation of certain motor vehicles. Mr. Abink was a Dutch employee of a German business. He had a residence in Holland and in Germany. He drove his employer's German registered car between Germany and Holland. The car was used on Dutch roads under a "temporary importation" arrangement under which no VAT was payable on "importation" into Holland. The District Court, Arnhem, asked the European Court for a preliminary ruling under Art. 177 EEC on the compatibility with EEC Law on the free movement of goods of Dutch legislation, whereby any resident of the Netherlands was prohibited from driving a foreign-registered car unless normal customs duties (including VAT) had been paid on it. *Held*, that the provisions of the EEC Treaty regarding free movement of goods do not prevent national legislation from imposing on persons residing in an EEC State a ban, subject to criminal penalties, on the use of motor vehicles admitted under temporary importation arrangements and thus exempt from payment of VAT, even if that legislation makes no exception for cases in which such vehicles are used without any intention of evading tax.

CRIMINAL PROCEEDINGS AGAINST JAN GERRIT ABINK (No. 134/83) [1986] 1 C.M.L.R. 579, European Ct.

1404. Free movement of goods—quantitative restrictions—prohibition of oil sales to Israel—whether policy compatible with Community law

[EEC Treaty, arts. 5, 34, 113.]

The United Kingdom policy prohibiting export of oil to certain destinations, or to countries which might re-export to those destinations, was not a policy likely to restrict or distort trade within the EEC, and was not therefore in breach of Community law.

The United Kingdom had a policy, which was not enshrined in legislation, or the subject of any legal provision, preventing the export of North Sea oil to a number of countries including Israel. Sellers agreed to sell a large quantity of such oil to buyers, but when the buyers' vessel arrived for loading the terminal refused to load the vessel because they had by then become aware of the oil's eventual destination, namely Israel. The arbitrator held that buyers were in breach of contract with the sellers, and awarded the sellers damages of $13m. *Held*, on a reference to the European Court, that the policy of the United Kingdom prohibiting such exports was not incompatible with EEC law, as it did not restrict or distort trade between Member States.

BULK OIL (ZUG) AG *v.* SUN INTERNATIONAL (No. 2) (No. 174/84) [1986] 2 All E.R. 744, European Ct.

1405. Free movement of workers—criminal proceedings—language

Mr. Mutsch, a Luxembourg national, resided in Saint Vith, a German speaking municipality in Belgium, which was within the territorial jurisdiction of the Criminal Court, Verviers. Mr. Mutsch argued that he was entitled to the benefit of s.17(3) of the Act of June 15, 1935. S.17(3) provides that where an accused of Belgian nationality resides in a German speaking municipality within the jurisdiction of the Criminal Court Verviers and so requests, the court proceedings shall be in German. The Cour d'Appel, Liège, asked the European Court for a preliminary ruling under Art. 177 EEC on the compatibility of s.17(3) of the Act of 1935 with EEC Law. *Held*, that the principle of free movement of workers as set out in Art. 48 EEC and European Council Regulation 1612/68, requires that a worker who is a national of one EEC State and habitually resides in another EEC State should be entitled to insist that criminal proceedings against him be conducted in a language other than the language usually used in proceedings before that Court, if workers who are nationals of the host EEC State have that right in the same circumstances.

MINISTÈRE PUBLIC *v.* MUTSCH (No. 137/84) [1986] 1 C.M.L.R. 648, European Ct.

1406. Free movement of workers—residence permits—non-married partners

Miss Reed, a U.K. national went to the Netherlands. She applied for a residence permit in order to be able to live there with Mr. W, a U.K. national, who was working in the Netherlands. Miss Reed and Mr. W had had a stable relationship for about five years. Miss Reed's application for a residence permit was rejected. She applied to the Dutch Courts for an order to restrain the Netherlands from taking any measure which might result in her deportation. She was granted such an order, but the State appealed. The Supreme Court of the Netherlands asked the European Court for a preliminary ruling under Art. 177 EEC. *Held*, that the right granted by an EEC State to its own nationals to enable them to obtain permission for their non-married partners, who were not nationals of that EEC State, to reside on its territory, was a social advantage within Art. 7(2) of Council Regulation 1612/68. Therefore, an EEC State which granted such an advantage to its national workers could not refuse it to workers who were nationals of other EEC States without discriminating on the ground of nationality contrary to Arts. 7 and 48 EEC.

THE NETHERLANDS *v.* REED (ANN FLORENCE) (No. 59/85) *The Times*, April 21, 1986, European Ct.

1407. Freedom of establishment and services—recognition of qualifications—harmonisation of training

The European Commission took proceedings against Italy under Art. 169 EEC for failing to adopt within the prescribed period the measures needed to comply with Council Directive 78/1026 and not fully implementing Council Directive 78/1027. Directive 78/1026 set out provisions for the mutual recognition of diplomas, certificates and other evidence of formal qualifications in veterinary medicine. Directive 78/1027 provides for the co-ordination of provisions in relation to the activities of veterinary surgeons. *Held*, that Italy had failed to fulfil its obligations under the EEC Treaty by

(1) not adopting within the prescribed period the provisions needed to comply with Directive 78/1026. Italy could not rely, as a defence, on the fact that the Bill implementing the Directive had been delayed due to the premature dissolution of the Italian Chamber of Deputies; (2) not fully implementing Directive 78/1027 and by failing to provide for compulsory instruction in the subjects known as "animal ethology and protection" and "food hygiene and technology" as part of the curriculum for veterinary surgeons.

VETERINARY TRAINING, *Re*; E.C. COMMISSION *v.* ITALY (No. 221/83) [1985] 3 C.M.L.R. 654, European Ct.

1408. Freedom of establishment—company registered office—sickness benefit
[EEC Treaty, Art. 52, 58.] Articles 52 and 58 of the EEC treaty oblige Member States to treat companies equally, wherever in the EEC those companies' registered offices may be: SEEGERS *v.* BESTUUR VAN DE BEDRIJFSVERENIGING VOOR BANK—EN VERZEKERINGSWEZEN GROOTHANDEL EN VRIJE BEROEPEN, *The Times,* August 27, 1986, European Ct.

1409. Freedom of movement for persons and services—recognition of qualifications—harmonisation of training
The European Commission submitted a proposal for a Council Directive on a general system for the recognition of higher education diplomas.

DRAFT HIGHER EDUCATION DIPLOMAS (RECOGNITION) DIRECTIVE [1985] 3 C.M.L.R. 703, E.C. Council.

1410. Freedom of movement—migrant worker—public service employment
Mrs. Lawrie-Blum, a British national, passed the first State examination for appointment as a secondary school teacher at a German University. She applied to the Oberschulamt, Stuttgart, to be accepted as a trainee secondary school teacher. Such a trainee had to comply with the requirements for the appointment of a civil servant, including the requirement of German nationality. The Oberschulamt refused her application because she was not a German national. She brought proceedings for annulment of that decision as being contrary to Art. 48 EEC. The Bundesverwaltungsgericht (the Federal Administrative Court) asked the European Court under Art. 177 EEC for a preliminary ruling on the interpretation of Art. 48 EEC. *Held*, that (1) a trainee teacher engaged in teaching practice, during which she gave lessons and for which she received payment, was to be regarded as a worker within Art. 48(1) EEC irrespective of the legal nature of the employment relationship; (2) teaching practice in preparation for the teaching profession was not to be considered as employment in the public service within the meaning of Art. 48(4) EEC, admission to which might be restricted to nationals of the EEC State involved.

LAWRIE-BLUM *v.* LAND BADEN WÜRTTEMBERG (No. 66/85) *The Times,* July 7, 1986, European Ct.

1411. Freedom of movement—migrant workers—family
Mrs. Diatta, a Senegalese national, married a French national, who lived and worked in West Berlin. From 1978 she lived apart from her husband and intended to divorce him. Mrs. Diatta applied for an extension of her residence permit, but the Berlin police authorities refused an extension on the ground that she was no longer a member of the family of an EEC national and did not live with her husband. Mrs. Diatta challenged that refusal in the German Courts. The Federal Administrative Court asked the European Court for a preliminary ruling under Art. 177 EEC upon the interpretation of Arts. 10 and 11 of Council Reg. No. 1612/68 on the freedom of movement for workers within the EEC. *Held,* that for the purposes of Art. 10 of Reg. No. 1612/68 members of the family of a migrant worker did not necessarily have to live permanently with him in order to have a right of residence in the EEC State in which he worked.

DIATTA *v.* LAND BERLIN (No. 267/83) [1986] 2 C.M.L.R. 164, European Ct.

1412. Freedom of movement—migrant workers—financial assistance from public funds
Mr. Kempf, a German, moved to Holland. He worked part-time as a music teacher and also obtained supplementary benefit under Dutch law. The Secretary of State for Justice refused his application for a Dutch residence permit on the ground that he was not "a favoured EEC citizen" within the meaning of Dutch legislation on aliens since, having sought financial support from Dutch public funds, he had shown he was unable to support himself from his own paid activity. Mr. Kempf brought

proceedings against that decision before the Judicial Division of the State Council. The latter asked the European Court under Art. 177 EEC for a preliminary ruling which would clarify the judgment in *Levin* v. *Staatssecretaris van Justitie* [1982] C.L.Y. 1235. *Held,* that an EEC national who followed an effective and genuine activity as an employed person on a part-time basis in another EEC State, could not be excluded from EEC law relating to free movement of workers by reason of his claiming financial benefit from public funds in order to augment the income which he obtained from that activity: KEMPF *v.* STAATSSECRETARIS VAN JUSTITIE (No. 139/85) *The Times,* June 6, 1986. European Court.

1413. Fuel and Power—directives, decisions and regulations
Council Regulation (EEC) No. 3640/85 of December 20, 1985 on the promotion, by financial support, of demonstration projects and industrial pilot projects in the energy field. (O.J. 1985 L350/29.)

1414. Harmonisation—credit institutions—reorganisation and winding up
The European Commission submitted to the European Council a proposal for a Council Directive on the co-ordination of laws, regulations and administrative provisions relating to the reorganisation and winding up of credit institutions. DRAFT BANK FAILURES DIRECTIVE [1986] 2 C.M.L.R. 361.

1415. Human rights—nationalisation—compensation
Sir William Lithgow and others (the plaintiffs) brought proceedings against the UK, in which they argued that the Aircraft and Ship Building Industries Act 1977 (the "Act") was incompatible with Art. 1 of the First Protocol to the European Convention on Human Rights. The plaintiffs were shareholders in companies which were nationalised pursuant to that Act. The plaintiffs criticised the way compensation for nationalisation was assessed under that Act and pointed out the disparity between the compensation and the value of their nationalised interests. *Held,* that the Act was not incompatible with Art. 1 of the First Protocol. Nationalisation was a measure of a general economic nature in regard to which the the State had to be allowed a wide discretion. In the exercise of its wide margin of appreciation, the U.K. was reasonably entitled to decide to adopt compensation provisions which did not allow (i) for alterations in the value of the assets between the dates of their valuation and the dates when the assets became vested in public ownership; (ii) for inflation or (iii) for the size of the public ownership of the shareholders' holding: LITHGOW *v.* U.K., *The Times,* July 7, 1986, European Court of Human Rights.

1416. Imports—agricultural products—levies—ACP States
H. Spitta & Co. ("Spitta"), a German importer of beef, objected to the levy fixed on a beef consignment from Madagascar. The beef had been classified under subheading 16.02 B III b 1(aa). The levy had been calculated in accordance with the provisions of Commission Regulation 932/77 of April 29, 1977 fixing the amount by which import charges on beef and veal originating in the African, Caribbean and Pacific States ("ACP") had to be reduced. Spitta brought proceedings contesting the charging of the levy in the Hessisches Finanzgericht. The latter asked the European Court under Art. 177 EEC for a preliminary ruling on whether the reduction fixed at 143·956 units of account by Reg. 932/77 for goods falling under subheading 16.02 B III b 1(aa) was valid. *Held,* that the validity of Reg. 932/77 was upheld. The method of calculation adopted by the Commission could not be criticised and was not discriminatory.
SPITTA (H.) & CO. *v.* HAUPTZOLLAMT FRANKFURT AM MAIN-OST (No. 124/84) [1986] 2 C.M.L.R. 686, European Ct.

1417. Imports—agriculture—milk—health
A prosecution was brought in Holland against C.M.C. Melkunie BV (the "defendant"), a Dutch importer, for holding in stock milk products imported from Germany, which were alleged to be unfit for human consumption contrary to a Dutch Milk Order. The Order was made under a Dutch Act which set out the conditions that pasteurised and sterilised goods must satisfy in order to be marketed in Holland. The defendant appealed to the Hoge Raad against the imposition of fines for contravening this legislation. The Hoge Raad asked the European Court for a preliminary ruling under Art. 117 EEC on the compatibility of such national legislation with Art. 30 EEC and whether it could be justified under Art. 36 EEC. *Held,* that national legislation banning the marketing of goods lawfully produced and

marketed in the exporting EEC State on the ground that they do not satisfy the microbiological conditions set by the importing EEC State amount to a measure equivalent in effect to a quantitative restriction contrary to Art. 30 EEC; (2) national legislation which (i) does not permit active coliform bacteria to be present in a pasteurised milk product, and (ii) is intended to prevent such a product from containing at the time of its consumption non-pathogenic micro-organisms to a level which may constitute a risk to the health of the most sensitive consumers and to that end sets the maximum number of such micro-organisms that may be present on the date of sale of the product on the basis of its deterioration in the time between its sale and consumption, can be justified on health grounds under Art. 36 EEC.

C.M.C MELKUNIE BV (now called MELKUNIE HOLLAND B.V.) (No. 97/83) [1986] 2 C.M.L.R. 318, European Ct.

1418. Imports—anti-dumping—potatoes

G.A.A.R.M. and other associations of French potato producers (the applicants) brought proceedings against the E.C. Commission for damages under Art. 215 EEC. They sought compensation for the damage which they said they had suffered because the Commission failed to take measures to stop the large imports of Greek new potatoes on to the German, U.K. and French markets or to oblige the Greek Government to suspend the aid granted by it for the export of new potatoes. The applicants claimed this resulted in their being unable to sell French potatoes on those markets and having to destroy them. *Held*, that (1) the applicants had *locus standi* in so far as the proceedings were based on the loss suffered by them in their capacity as dealers in new potatoes; (2) proceedings for damages were dismissed as the Commission was not under any obligation to adopt any of the measures urged by the applicants, as (i) although the prices of imported Greek potatoes undercut U.K. prices, they were not so many as to affect the general market price; (ii) there was no evidence of concerted agreements between Greek producers in contravention of Art. 85 EEC; (iii) the potatoes were exempt from EEC rules on State aids as they were not covered by a common organisation of the market under the C.A.P.; (iv) Art. 131 of the Act of Greek Accession (which allowed the Commission to take anti-dumping measures pending the expiry of transition measures) did not apply to new potatoes; (v) there were no grounds for finding that the balance of competition had been jeopardised on the U.K., French and German markets.

GROUPEMENT DES ASSOCIATIONS AGRICOLES POUR L'ORGANISATION DE LA PRODUCTION ET DE LA COMMERCIALISATION DES POMMES DE TERRE ET LÉGUMES DE LA RÉGION MALOUINE (G.A.A.R.M.) *v.* E.C. COMMISSION (No. 289/83) [1986] 3 C.M.L.R. 15, European Ct.

1419. Imports—anti-dumping—steel

In June 1982 P imported steel sheets from Eastern Germany into the Netherlands. The Dutch authorities levied anti-dumping duties based on the Commission Communication of December 29, 1981 amending the basic prices for certain iron and steel products. P objected on the ground that the basic prices fixed by the Commission should have been converted into Dutch guilders, not at the ECU rate applicable on January 1, 1982 as required by the Communication of December 29, 1981, but at the daily rate published by the Commission which was applicable at the date when the importation took place. The College van Beroep asked the European Court of Justice for a preliminary ruling. *Held*, that (1) the provisions of Council Regulation (EEC) 2779/78 of November 23, 1978 did not apply to goods which came within the scope of the ECSC Treaty; (2) the Commission gained from Art. 74 ECSC and from Recommendation 77/329/ECSC of April 15, 1977 the power to issue Recommendation 3140/78/ECSC of December 29, 1979, of which the Commission's communication of December 30, 1978 was an essential part; (3) prolonged adherence to compulsory conversion rates for calculating anti-dumping duties applicable to goods coming within the scope of the ECSC was not to be regarded as contrary to European Community law, unless it was shown that the resulting calculation conflicted with the requirements of Commission Recommendation 77/329/ECSC of April 15, 1977, and especially Art. 19(3) thereof.

GERLACH & Co. B.V. *v.* MINISTER FOR ECONOMIC AFFAIRS (No. 239/84) [1986] 3 C.M.L.R. 30, European Ct.

1420. Imports—ban on imports—public morality

U.K. Customs and Excise authorities seized consignments of various erotic items which had been imported from Germany by Conegate. Uxbridge Magistrates' Court ordered the forfeiture of these goods as being indecent or obscene articles, whose importation into the U.K. was prohibited by s.42 of the Customs Consolidation Act 1876. On Conegate's appeal, the English High Court asked the European Court under Art. 177 EEC for a preliminary ruling on the interpretation of Art. 30 EEC and Art. 36 EEC. *Held,* that (1) an EEC State might not rely upon public morality within the meaning of Art. 36 EEC in order to ban the importation of items from other EEC States on the ground that they were indecent or obscene, where such provisions, which prohibited transmission of such goods by post, or restricted their public display or licensed some premises for their sale, could not be regarded as equivalent in substance to a prohibition on manufacture and marketing; (2) Art. 234 EEC meant that an agreement made prior to the entry into force of the EEC Treaty might not be relied upon in order to justify restrictions on trade between EEC States.

CONEGATE *v.* H.M. CUSTOMS AND EXCISE, (No. 121/85), *Re* [1986] 1 C.M.L.R. 739, European Ct.

1421. Imports—common customs tariff—art work

A West German art dealer imported a three dimensional wall relief by an American artist. The wall relief was composed of cardboard and expanded polystyrene, sprayed with black paint and oil and fixed to a wooden panel by means of wire and synthetic resin. The German Customs authorities gave it the tariff classification appropriate for articles comprised of artificial resins and plastic materials. The dealer challenged this classification and argued that it should have been given the tariff classification appropriate for "original sculptures and statuary," which would have resulted in a lower rate of duty than that imposed. The Finanzgericht, Berlin, asked the European Court under Art. 177 EEC for a preliminary ruling on the interpretation of tariff heading 99.02 of the Common Customs Tariff (CCT). *Held,* that an item accepted as being a work of art by the customs authority had to be classified under "original sculptures and statuary, in any material" under heading 99.03 of the CCT.

ONNASCH *v.* HAUPTZOLLAMT BERLIN-PACKHOF (No. 155/84) [1986] 2 C.M.L.R. 456, European Ct.

1422. Imports—common customs tariff—classification of jeans

In December 1975 a German importer purchased jeans of traditional style from outside the EEC. It declared these to be jeans for women falling within the Common Customs Tariff ("CCT") heading 61.02. That meant the jeans were free of duty under that heading. The Hauptzollamt demanded customs duties on the ground that the trousers were men's trousers under CCT heading 61.01 because the front fastening was from left to right. The importer challenged that decision in the German Courts, arguing that jeans of traditional style were also worn by females, and, thus, it was not possible to classify them solely as menswear. The Bundesfinanzamt (Federal Finance Court) asked the European Court under Art. 177 EEC for a preliminary ruling on the interpretation of the CCT. *Held,* that jeans of a traditional style, with a front fastening from left to right, were to be classified as male outer garments under CCT heading 61.01: HAUPTZOLLAMT OSNABRÜCK *v.* KLEIDERWERKE HELA LAMPE GMBH & Co. K.G. (No. 255/85), *The Times,* July 24, 1986, European Ct.

1423. Imports—customs checks—delay

P, a French importer of wine from Italy, brought proceedings against the French authorities in respect of delays caused at customs whilst checks were made that the wine met certain qualifying standards. Average delays occasioned by such checks rose from 40 days in 1978 to 180 days in 1981. *Held,* that although the custom authorities had a right to analyse the wines, they could not use this procedure in order to apply restrictions to the import of wine from Italy contrary to EEC Law. Further, although the authorities were not bound by a set time limit within which to effect these customs clearance operations, such operations should be carried out within a reasonable time (21 days being a reasonable time). By grossly exceeding this period, without giving proper justification for such delay, the State was at fault and had to compensate the plaintiff.

SOCIÉTÉ TRESCH-ALSACAVES *v.* MINISTRE DE L'ECONOMIE, DES FINANCES ET DU BUDGET [1986] 2 C.M.L.R. 625, Tribunal Administratif, Strasbourg.

1424. Imports—customs classification—direct action

Casteels Pvba, a Belgian importer of windscreen-wiper motors into the EEC complained that the customs authorities of Belgium and France differed as to which tariff heading of the Common Customs Tariff (CCT) was appropriate to such products. Casteels brought an action under Art. 173(2) EEC for annulment of Commission Regulation 3529/83 on the classification of goods under subheading 85-01Bl(b) of the CCT adopted pursuant to Council Regulation 97/69 on measures to be taken for uniform application of the nomenclature of the CCT. *Held,* that (1) the application for annulment was dismissed as inadmissible as Casteels was not directly and individually concerned by Regulation 3529/83. That Regulation was of general application, since it concerned all products of the type specified and took effect, in the interests of the uniform application of the CCT, in relation to all EEC customs authorities and all importers; (2) an importer is not directly and individually concerned by the Regulation just because it is in dispute with customs authorities regarding some imported products. It may contest the authorities' classification in a national court which may ask for a preliminary ruling of the European Court under Art. 177 EEC.

CASTEELS PVBA *v.* EUROPEAN COMMISSION (No. 40/84) [1986] 2 C.M.L.R. 475, European Ct.

1425. Imports—duty-free imports—frontier residents

Mr. Paul bought 250 cigarettes in a Dutch district near the frontier some 80 kilometres from his home in Germany. The German customs authorities refused to allow him to import more than 40 cigarettes duty-free. The authorities relied on German rules for duty exemption for imports by frontier-zone residents, whereby 40 cigarettes are exempt from duty (as opposed to the general limit of 300 cigarettes) when the importation is made by residents near the frontier whose journey into the opposite foreign territory has not exceeded 15 kilometres in depth. Mr. Paul considered the opposite territory to be constituted by an area 15 kilometres in radius the centre of which is the customs post nearest to the district of residence, the authorities considered that it covered a single 15 kilometres strip running along the whole of the frontier. Mr. Paul challenged the authorities' view in the German courts. The Finanzgericht, Düsseldorf, asked the European Court under Art. 177 EEC for a preliminary ruling on the interpretation of "imported: in frontier-zone travel" in Art. 4 of Council Regulation 1544/69 of July 23, 1969. *Held,* that (1) Regulation 1544/69, as amended, applies only to travellers from a non-EEC State; (2) this case was concerned with imports of goods between EEC States, and thus, it was necessary to look at Council Directive 69/169, as amended; (3) "frontier zone" in Art. 5(5) of Directive 69/169, as amended by Directive 72/230, has to be interpreted as meaning a circular zone having a radius of 15 kilometres and its centre at the customs crossing.

PAUL *v.* HAUPTZOLLAMT EMMERICH (No. 54/84) [1986] 2 C.M.L.R. 465, European Ct.

1426. Imports—film distribution—video cassettes

French legislation prohibited the marketing of video cassettes or video discs of a film until a year had passed since a certificate had been issued authorising the film's first showing in a French cinema. Video cassettes of the films *Furyo* and *Le Marginal* were placed on the French market before the requisite time period had passed. The distributors of the cassettes argued that the time-limit set by the legislation was contrary to EEC law. The Tribunal de Grande Instance, Paris, asked the European Court under Art. 177 EEC for a preliminary ruling on the interpretation of Arts. 30, 34, 36 and 59 EEC with a view to assessing the compatibility of the French legislation with EEC law. *Held,* that Art. 30 EEC did not apply to national legislation which regulated the distribution of cinematographic works by banning their simultaneous exploitation in cinemas and in video cassette form for a limited period of time, provided that (a) the ban applied equally to home-produced and imported cassettes and (b) any barriers to intra-EEC trade created thereby did not exceed what was required for ensuring that the exploitation in cinemas of cinematographic works of all origins held priority over other means of distribution.

CINÉTHÈQUE S.A. *v.* FEDERATION NATIONALE DES CINEMAS FRANÇAIS (Nos. 60–61/84) [1986] 1 C.M.L.R. 365, European Ct.

1427. Imports—health inspections—animal feedingstuffs
Denkavit Futtermittel GmbH (Denkavit), a German importer of feedingstuffs, brought proceedings in the German courts for a declaration that it was entitled to import compound animal feedingstuffs without a licence or certificate. Denkavit argued that Council Directive 79/373 on the marketing of compound feedstuffs for animals precluded EEC States from purporting to justify health inspections by relying on Art. 36 EEC. The Higher Administrative Court for North Rhine—Westphalia asked the European Court under Art. 177 EEC for a preliminary ruling on the interpretation of Arts. 3 and 9 of Directive 79/373 and Art. 30 EEC and 36 EEC. *Held,* that Directive 79/373, in particular Arts. 3 and 9 thereof, together with Art. 30 EEC, had to be interpreted as meaning that EEC States are not prohibited from requiring, in reliance on Art. 36 EEC, that the importation of compound feedingstuffs from other EEC States had to be subject to health inspections evidenced by (i) production of a certificate issued by the veterinary authorities of the exporting State, or (ii) an import licence issued by the veterinary authorities of the importing State, provided that such a licence is issued on terms that are in reasonable proportion to the requirements set out in Art. 36 EEC.
DENKAVIT FUTTERMITTEL GmbH *v.* LAND NORDRHEIN-WESTFALEN (No. 73/84) [1986] 2 C.M.L.R. 482, European Ct.

1428. Imports—health protection tax—pigmeat
French legislation introduced a health-protection and meat-market organisation tax assessed on the carcase weight of pigs. The tax was charged on national products when slaughtering took place and on imported products when released for consumption. Pigmeat from other EEC States was already subject to health inspection and health inspection fees in the framework of the common organisation of the market in pigmeat. Thus, pigmeat from non-EEC States suffered double taxation. The Tribunal d'Instance, Lille, ordered the Customs Administration to reimburse Société Rungis Porcs in respect of the health-protection tax it had paid on imports of pigmeat from other EEC States. The Customs Administration appealed. *Held,* that the appeal would be dismissed. The health-protection tax constituted a tax having an effect equivalent to a customs duty, contrary to Arts. 9, 12 and 13 EEC.
ADMINISTRATION DES DOUANES *v.* SOCIÉTÉ RUNGIS PORCS [1986] 1 C.M.L.R. 757, Cour d'Appel, Douai.

1429. Imports—monetary compensatory amounts—refusal to pay
The plaintiff in Eire sold grain to purchasers in Northern Ireland. The intervention agency in Eire refused to pay Monetary Compensatory Amounts (MCAs) to the plaintiff as it believed that some of the grain had been clandestinely re-imported into Eire for re-exportation to the U.K. The plaintiff was not party to any such irregularity or fraud and he brought proceedings in Eire to recover the MCAs. The Supreme Court of Ireland asked the European Court under Art. 177 EEC for a preliminary ruling on the obligation to pay MCAs. *Held,* that (1) the exporting EEC State, which had the obligation to pay the MCAs, was justified in refusing to pay those MCAs where the produce had not entered the importing EEC State for home use due to the purchaser's fraud, even though the necessary formalities and forms had been completed and the exporter had acted in good faith; (2) the exporting EEC State had to justify such refusal to make payment on the basis of grave suspicions formed on objective grounds which had not been dispelled by its inquiries. In such circumstances refusal to pay MCAs was justified, unless proof was given that the produce had actually entered the importing EEC State for home use: IRISH GRAIN BOARD (TRADING) *v.* MINISTER FOR AGRICULTURE (No. 254/85), *The Times,* November 17, 1986, European Ct.

1430. Imports—patents—drugs
Hoechst held parallel patents in the Netherlands and in the U.K. relating to the manufacture of frusemide. DDSA Pharmaceuticals ("DDSA") obtained a compulsory licence under Hoechst's U.K. parallel patent for the manufacture of frusemide. The licence was valid solely for the U.K. and prohibited exportation. DDSA sold frusemide tablets to Pharmon which intended to market the tablets in the Netherlands. Pharmon sought a declaration that an interim order prohibiting it from infringing Hoechst's Netherlands' patent did not extend to frusemide which Pharmon had

bought from DDSA and that enforcement of that prohibition by Hoechst was unlawful. The Hoge Raad asked the European Court for a preliminary ruling under Art. 177 EEC. *Held,* that (1) it was not contrary to Arts. 30 and 36 EEC for a patent holder to prevent the importation and distribution in a Member State of a product protected by that patent, where that product had been lawfully manufactured in another EEC State by the holder of a compulsory licence under a parallel patent owned by the same patent holder; (2) it was irrelevant whether or not the compulsory licence contained a prohibition on export, whether or not it provided for royalties in favour of the patent holder and whether or not the latter had accepted or rejected such royalties.

PHARMON B.V. *v.* HOECHST A.G., *Re* (No. 19/84) [1985] 3 C.M.L.R. 775, European Ct.

1431. Imports—prices—books

FNAC launched an operation called "books at European prices" whereby FNAC acquired books in Belgium, which had been published in France, and then placed them on sale in France at prices 20 per cent. below those fixed by publishers in accordance with the French Book Prices Act 1981. Editions Gallimard obtained injunctions to restrain FNAC from pursuing this operation. FNAC argued, *inter alia,* that the Act was contrary to EEC law and appealed against the granting of the injunctions. *Held,* injunctions were confirmed for various reasons, including the fact that FNAC was trying, by artificially creating an international commercial circuit, to gain for itself the opportunity of offering for sale various books, without being obliged to observe the minimum prices imposed on the French market by the Act. In the particular circumstances of this case FNAC was not entitled to rely on the general principles of free trade embodied in EEC law.

S.A. FNAC *v.* S.A. EDITIONS GALLIMARD [1986] E.C.C. 59, Cour d'Appel, Paris.

1432. Imports—quantitative restrictions—confectionery

On October 20, 1978 the Italian Ministry of Health issued an order limiting the use of animal gelatin to certain limited percentages for preserved meat products, ice cream and confectionery products. The European Commission regarded that order as being a measure having an effect equivalent to a quantitative restriction on imports contrary to Art. 30 EEC since it prevented the importation of foodstuffs containing a higher percentage of animal gelatin which had been lawfully manufactured and marketed in another EEC State. The Commission brought proceedings in the European Court against Italy under Art. 169 EEC. *Held,* that by restricting the importation of confectionery products which contained more than one per cent. of animal gelatin and which are lawfully manufactured and marketed in other EEC States, Italy had failed to fulfil its obligations under Art. 30 EEC.

GELATIN IN SWEETS, *Re*; E.C. COMMISSION *v.* ITALY (No. 51/83) [1986] 2 C.M.L.R. 274, European Ct.

1433. Imports—quantitative restrictions—discrimination

French legislation gave certain tax advantages to publishers publishing newspapers or journals dealing mainly with political affairs. An amendment of that legislation in 1980 provided that publishers should not benefit from those tax advantages in respect of publications which they print abroad. The European Commission brought proceedings in the European Court against France under Art. 169 EEC arguing that the amendment was contrary to Art. 30 EEC. *Held,* that France had failed to fulfil its obligations under Art. 30 EEC by depriving publishers of certain tax advantages in respect of publications which they print in other EEC States.

AID TO FRENCH NEWSPAPERS, *Re*; E.C. COMMISSION *v.* FRANCE (No. 18/84) [1986] 1 C.M.L.R. 605, European Ct.

1434. Imports—quantitative restrictions—drugs

The Secretary of State for Health & Social Security decided to change the basis upon which reimbursement was to be made to chemists in respect of medicines purchased by them for dispensation under the National Health Service prescriptions. The change affected the prices and discounts that importers could charge chemists for imported drugs. Bomore Medical Supplies and Eurochem (importers of drugs) challenged that decision by way of judicial review as being contrary to Art. 30 EEC. *Held,* that the decision constituted a measure of equivalent effect to a quantitative restriction on imports of medicines within Art. 30 EEC and was accordingly unlawful and in breach of the statutory duty imposed by Art. 30 EEC and s.2(1) of the

European Communities Act 1972. The decision discriminated against imported drugs. Any scheme whose object, let alone effect, was to reduce the competitiveness of cheaper imported drugs in the UK was contrary to Art. 30 EEC.

R. *v*. SECRETARY OF STATE FOR SOCIAL SERVICES, *ex p*. BOMORE MEDICAL SUPPLIES & EUROCHEM [1986] 1 C.M.L.R. 228, C.A.

1435. Imports—quantitative restrictions—pharmaceutical goods

Belgian companies (plaintiffs) applied to the Luxembourg Minister for Health for authorisation to import pharmaceutical goods and to sell them wholesale directly to pharmacists in Luxembourg. The Minister refused the applications on the ground that, contrary to Luxembourg regulations, the plaintiffs did not have either a registered office or premises for the storage of medicinal preparations there. The plaintiffs appealed against such refusals to the Contentious Proceedings Division of the State Council. The latter asked the European Court under Art. 177 EEC for a preliminary ruling on the interpretation of Art. 30 EEC and of Directive 75/319 of May 20, 1975 on the approximation of provisions laid down by law, regulation or administrative action relating to proprietary medicinal products. *Held*, that EEC Law did not permit the authorities of an EEC State to require a supplier of pharmaceutical goods, whose headquarters were in another EEC State, and which wished to supply retail pharmacists in the importing EEC State directly, to keep within the latter State storage premises and technical equipment, when that supplier met the conditions set by the law of the EEC State in which its headquarters were sited: LEGIA *v*. MINISTRE DE LA SANTÉ (Nos. 87 & 88/85), *The Times,* June 6, 1986, European Ct.

1436. Imports—quantitive restrictions—payments

The European Commission brought proceedings against Greece under Art. 169 EEC for failing to comply with Art. 38 of the Act of Greek Accession. Art. 38 provides that cash payments with regard to imports from other EEC States are to be reduced in accordance with the following timetable: January 1, 1981, 25 per cent.; January 1, 1982, 25 per cent.; January 1, 1983, 25 per cent. and January 1, 1984, 25 per cent. The Greek Minister of Commerce issued a decision on January 23, 1981, whereby certain goods in respect of which as at December 31, 1980 payment in cash was required in full upon importation, could thereafter be imported without having to satisfy that condition. On the other hand, certain other goods would be subject to the requirement to pay for them fully in cash. The European Commission considered that by taking that decision Greece had failed properly to fulfil its obligations; instead of completely liberalising a certain number of goods Greece ought to have reduced by 25 per cent. the amount required to be paid in cash with regard to all the products to which Art. 38 applies. *Held*, that Greece had failed to fulfil its obligations under Art 38 of the Act of Greek Accession by continuing in 1981 to subject the importation of certain goods from other EEC States to the requirement that they should be paid for fully in cash.

IMPORT PAYMENTS *Re*; E.C. COMMISSION *v*. GREECE (No. 58/83) [1986] 1 C.M.L.R. 673, European Ct.

1437. Imports—quantitative restrictions—remedies for breach—whether damages for disrupted trade

[European Economic Community Treaty, art. 30]

The implementation by the U.K. Government of measures in breach of the ban on quantitative restrictions contained in art. 30 EEC Treaty does not of itself give a right to damages for any disruption caused to an individual's trade or business by the measures.

B was engaged in the business of importing turkeys from France into the U.K. pursuant to a general licence so to do. In 1981 the government of the U.K. introduced a policy of preventing imports of turkeys from countries where vaccination rather than slaughter was used to control disease. In consequence, the existing general licence was withdrawn and replaced by one that prevented the import of turkeys from France. The European Court held that the new general licence was a restriction imposed in breach of art. 30, EEC Treaty. Thereafter B was able to resume importing turkeys from France in November 1982. B issued a writ claiming damages for the disruption of the business of importing turkeys claiming, *inter alia,* a breach of the defendant's statutory duty imposed by art. 30, EEC Treaty banning quantitative restrictions on imports. That part of B's claim was tried as a preliminary issue and judgment entered against the defendant for damages to be assessed. The defendant appealed. *Held,* allowing the appeal, that art. 30, EEC Treaty created individual rights of a public law nature having regard to the fact that it restricted legislative and executive actions to control imports by quantitative restrictions. A breach of art. 30 gave rise to a right to judicial review, by anyone with a sufficient interest. A mere breach of the article would not give rise to a right to damages. If it could be shown that in implementing the measures there had been an abuse of power then damages could be claimed. The measures implemented by the U.K. Government were a simple excess of power and not a breach of statutory duty. If an abuse of power were shown B could claim damages for the commission of the tort of misfeasance in public office. The proof of malice upon the part of the officer concerned was not necessary but it must be proved that the officer knew that he had no power to act as he did and that he knew his act would injure the plaintiffs (*Bayerische H.N.L. Vermehrungsbetriebe GmbH & Co. K.G.* v. *E.C. Council and Commission* [1979] C.L.Y. 1201, *Koninklijke Scholten Honig N.V.* v. *E.C. Council and Commission* [1980] C.L.Y. 1146 applied, *Garden Cottage Foods* v. *Milk Marketing Board* [1983] C.L.Y. 2987, *An Bord Bainne Co-op* v. *Milk Marketing Board* [1984] C.L.Y. 1344 distinguished, *Dunlop* v. *Woollahra Municipal Council* [1981] C.L.Y. 1846 considered).

Bourgoin S.A. *v.* Ministry of Agriculture, Fisheries and Foods [1985] 3 All E.R. 585, C.A.

1438. Imports—valuation for customs purposes—freight charges
Mainfrucht Obstverwertung GmbH (M.O.) imported consignments of fruit from Bulgaria into Germany. For each consignment the suppliers drew up two invoices; the first showed a net price per tonne for the fruit carriage paid at the German border. The second showed the cost of transport from the German border to M.O.'s premises in Bavaria. A dispute arose between M.O. and Hauptzollamt as to the value of the goods for customs purposes under European Council Reg. No. 1224/80 on the valuation of the goods for customs purposes. The Federal Finance Court asked the European Court for a preliminary ruling under Art. 177 EEC. *Held,* that where a purchaser had paid a foreign seller, in addition to the price of the goods, a specific sum in respect of freight charges for transport within the EEC, on the basis of a separate invoice, the transaction value for the purposes of Art.3(1) of Reg. No. 1224/80 included only the first of those two sums. Thus, the value for customs purposes of goods imported into the EEC from non-Member States, did not include the cost of transporting the goods within the EEC: Hauptzollamt Schweinfurt *v.* Mainfrucht Obstverwertung GmbH (No. 290/84), *The Times,* January 2, 1986, European Ct.

1439. Income tax—supplements and allowances out of Community Budget—exemption from tax
[EEC Treaty, arts. 5 and 7; Act of Accession, art. 3.] T was the headmaster of the European School at Culham, Oxfordshire, established pursuant to the Statute of the European School of 1957 and the Protocol of 1962. Pursuant to regulations and a decision of the Board of Governors (composed of delegates of the Member States), he was paid (in addition to his standard salary) a "differential allowance" the cost of which fell directly on the Community budget, and which pursuant to the Board of Governors' decision was to be exempt from tax. The Inland Revenue assessed the differential allowance to income tax. T appealed to the Special Commissioners, who, considering that their decision depended upon questions of interpretation of Community Law, referred certain questions to the European Court. *Held,* that (1), the Court had jurisdiction to interpret Art. 3 of the Act of Accession to determine the scope of measures covered by it; (2) Art. 3 applied the 1957 decision of the Board of Governors; (3) Art. 5 of the Treaty imposed obligations upon Member States, but did not enable T (a subject of a Member State) to enforce directly against the U.K. the obligation not to tax the differential allowance; and (4) neither Art. 7 of the Treaty nor the general principles of Community law required a Member State to exempt salaries and allowances of its own nationals from tax: Hurd *v.* Jones [1986] S.T.C. 127, European Ct.

1440. Institutions—directives, decisions and regulations
Council Regulation (ECSC, EEC, Euratom) No. 3517/85 of December 12, 1985 introducing special and temporary measures applicable to the recruitment of

officials of the European Communities as a result of the accession of Spain and Portugal. (O.J. 1985 L335/55.)

Council Regulation (ECSC, EEC, Euratom) No. 3518/85 of December 12, 1985 introducing special measures to terminate the service of officials of the European Communities as a result of the accession of Spain and Portugal. (O.J. 1985 L335/56.)

Council Regulation (ECSC, EEC, EURATOM) No. 3520/85 of December 12, 1985 amending Regulation (Euratom, ECSC, EEC) No. 549/69 determining the categories of officials and other servants of the European Communities to whom the provisions of Art. 12, the second paragraph of Art. 13 and Art. 14 of the Protocol on the Privileges and Immunities of the Communities apply. (O.J. 1985 L335/60.)

Council Regulation (ECSC, EEC, Euratom) No. 3580/85 of December 17, 1985 adjusting the remuneration and pensions of officials and other servants of the European Communities and the weightings applied thereto. (O.J. 1985 L343/1.)

Council Regulation (ECSC, EEC, Euratom) No. 3678/85 of December 20, 1985 adapting the representation and special-duty allowances for the President and members of the Commission and the President, Judges, Advocates-General and Registrar of the Court of Justice. (O.J. 1985 L351/1.)

86/1/EEC, Euratom, ECSC:
Decision of the representatives of the governments of the Member States of the European Communities of January 1, 1986 appointing Members of the Commission of the European Communities. (O.J. 1986 L8/32.)

86/2/EEC, Euratom, ECSC:
Decision of the representatives of the governments of the Member States of the European Communities of January 1, 1986 appointing a Judge and an Advocate-General to the Court of Justice. (O.J. 1986 L8/33.)

86/4/EEC, Euratom, ECSC:
Decision of the Representatives of the Governments of the Member States of the European Communities of January 15, 1986 appointing a Judge to the Court of Justice. (O.J. 1986 L18/37.)

86/13/EEC, Euratom, ECSC:
Decision of the Representatives of the Governments of the Member States of the European Communities of January 22, 1986 appointing a Vice-President to the Commission of the European Communities. (O.J. 1986 L27/66.)

86/14/EEC, Euratom, ECSC:
Council Decision of January 27, 1986 appointing two additional members to the Court of Auditors. (O.J. 1986 L27/67.)

Corrigendum to Council Regulation (EEC, Euratom, ECSC) No. 123/86 of January 20, 1986 amending Regulation (ECSC, EEC, Euratom) 1826/69 laying down the form of the 'laissez-passer' to be issued to members and servants of the institutions (O.J. No. L 18 of 24.1.1986). (O.J. 1986 L40/31.)

86/183/EEC, Euratom, ECSC:
Council Decision of May 6, 1986 appointing a Member of the Court of Auditors. (O.J. 1986 L.131/54.)

Council Regulation (EEC, Euratom, ECSC) No. 3619/86 of November 26, 1986 correcting the weightings applicable in Denmark, Germany, Greece, France, Ireland, Italy, the Netherlands and the United Kingdom of the remuneration and pensions of Officials and Other Servants of the European Communities. (O.J. 1986 L336/1.)

1441. Interim measures—parallel imports—removal of registration restrictions

Since July 1984 the Italian Government had made it increasingly difficult to register imported cars. These administrative measures were taken in reaction to a dramatic increase in parallel imports of cars into Italy. The Commission considered that these measures caused damage to other EEC exporters, Italian importers and finally to customers. The European Commission brought proceedings against Italy under Art. 169 EEC for a declaration that by making the registration of cars imported from other EEC States as parallel imports subject to formalities not justified by EEC law, Italy had failed to fulfil its obligations under Art. 30 EEC. The European Commission applied to the European Court for interim measures to ensure the immediate registration and free movement of cars imported into Italy from other EEC States. *Held,* that the interim order would be granted to the effect that Italy must implement the necessary measures to ensure that no requirement is imposed on parallel importers which is more stringent than those in being prior to July 1984. Italy was ordered to report every fortnight to the Commission the number of registrations made and the reasons for any delay.

IMPORT OF FOREIGN MOTOR VEHICLES, *Re*; E.C. COMMISSION *v.* ITALY (No. 154/85R) [1986] 2 C.M.L.R. 159, President of the European Ct.

1442. Interim measure—remission of import duty—negligence of national authorities
The Greek Ministry of Finance asked the European Commission pursuant to Art. 13 of Council Reg. 1430/79, to allow import duties by the applicants to be remitted on the ground that, as a result of negligent advice on the part of the Greek authorities, the applicants had not applied for advance fixing of the duties. The Commission rejected the request by Decision E (84) 557 of April 25, 1984. The applicants brought an action for annulment of that Decision and applied for interim measures to suspend the operation of that Decision. *Held,* interim order granted to the effect that the Commission should inform the Greek authorities that the import levy should not be demanded before November 1, 1984 provided that the applicants lodged a bank guarantee securing the payment of the disputed amount at that date.

ORYZOMYLI KAVALLAS OEE *v.* E.C. COMMISSION (No. 160/84R) [1986] 2 C.M.L.R. 269, President of the European Ct.

1443. Interim measures—stay—bank guarantee
On October 9, 1985 the European Commission fined Finsider SpA for exceeding its steel production quotas. By letter, dated October 14, 1985, the Commission stated that if Finsider brought an action before the European Court the Commission would not take steps to recover the fine while the case was pending before the Court, provided Finsider gave a bank guarantee to cover the fine and interest. Finsider commenced proceedings in the European Court for annulment of the decision of October 9, 1985. Finsider sought interim measures by way of a stay of the decision pending the Court's judgment in the main action. Finsider argued that payment of the fine or even provision of a bank guarantee would have severe financial consequences for it. *Held,* that (1) applications for interim measures must specify the circumstances showing urgency. Such urgency must be assessed by reference to the necessity for a provisional ruling in order to prevent serious, irreparable damage to the applicant; (2) Finsider had failed to show exceptional circumstances which justified exemption from the Commission's requirement of a bank guarantee pending the Court's decision in the main action. Finsider was a large manufacturing company which would have no difficulty in obtaining a bank guarantee. Provision of such a guarantee was not likely to cause Finsider serious irreparable harm; (3) a stay would be granted with regard to the payment of the fine provided that Finsider furnished the requisite bank guarantee.

FINSIDER SPA *v.* EUROPEAN COMMISSION (No. 392/85 R) [1986] 2 C.M.L.R. 290, President of the European Ct.

1444. Interim measures—stay—steel production quotas
The liquidators of Cockerill-DRC S.A. ("Cockerill") brought proceedings under Art. 33(2) ECSC for the annulment of the Commission's Decision of January 13, 1986. By that decision the Commission ordered the transfer of Cockerill's annual steel reference production and quantities to Sacilor to which Cockerill's plant had been sold. The liquidators sought suspension of the operation of the Commission's Decision until the European Court gave its judgment in the main proceedings. *Held,* that the application to suspend the operation of the Commission's Decision was dismissed. The liquidators had failed to make out a prima facie case for the interim measures sought.

COCKERILL-DRC S.A. (CAUET J. AND JOLIOT B., LIQUIDATORS) *v.* E.C. COMMISSION (No. 48/86R) [1986] 3 C.M.L.R. 378, European Ct., Lord Mackenzie Stuart C.J.

1445. Interim measures—urgency—intervention
Silver Seiko, Silver Reed (UK) and Silver Reed International GmbH (hereafter all referred to as "Silver") applied for interim suspension, as regards Silver, of the effect of Council Regulation 1698/85 of June 19, 1985, or other interim measures, until the European Court gave judgment on Silver's main application for annulment of Reg. 1698/85 which imposed definitive anti-dumping duties on imports of electronic typewriters originating in Japan. A European trade association, CETMA, applied to intervene in the case in support of the conclusions of the European Council. *Held,*

application for interim measures dismissed. Silver had not produced adequate evidence that Silver would suffer serious and irreparable damage establishing the urgency of the interim measures sought. Leave was given to CETMA to intervene because it had an interest in the result of the case within Art. 37(2) of the Statute of the European Court and it could receive a copy of Silver's application, subject to deletion of certain confidential information which was contained therein.

SILVER SEIKO *v.* EUROPEAN COUNCIL (No. 273/85R) [1986] 1 C.M.L.R. 214, The President of the European Court.

1446. Interim measures—urgency—serious and irreparable damage

Canon Inc., Canon France SA, Canon Rechner Deutschland GmbH and Canon (UK) (hereafter all referred to as "Canon") applied for interim suspension, as regards Canon, of the effect of Council Regulation 1698/85 of June 19, 1985, or other interim measures, until the European Court gave judgment on the main application. Canon's main application was for the annulment of Reg. 1698/85 which imposed definitive anti-dumping duties on imports of electronic typewriters produced by Canon. *Held,* application for interim measures dismissed. Canon had put forward factual and legal grounds which showed a prima facie case for suspending the application of Reg. 1698/85, but had failed to produce adequate evidence that Canon would suffer serious and irreparable damage establishing the urgency of the interim measures sought.

CANON INC. *v.* EUROPEAN COUNCIL (No. 277/85R & 300/85R) [1986] 1 C.M.L.R. 220, The President of the European Court.

1447. Interim measure—urgency—serious and irreparable damage

Tokyo Electric Company TEC Belgium, TEC Electronic GmbH, TEC Europe and TEC France (hereafter all referred to as "TEC") applied (1) for interim suspension, as regards TEC, of the definitive anti-dumping duty imposed by Council Regulation 1698/85 of June 19, 1985, on imports of electronic typewriters manufactured by Tokyo Electric Company Ltd., in so far as that duty exceeded the level of provisional anti-dumping duty imposed; alternatively, (2) for suspension of the time limit of three months for applications for reimbursement of anti-dumping duties pending the outcome of TEC's application to the European Court for annulment of Arts. 1 and 2 of Reg. 1698/85. *Held,* application for interim measures dismissed because in (1) TEC had failed to put forward factual and legal grounds which showed a prima facie case for the interim measures sought; and in (2) TEC had failed to establish adequately that TEC would suffer irreparable damage.

TOKYO ELECTRIC CO. *v.* EUROPEAN COUNCIL (No. 260/85R) [1986] 1 C.M.L.R. 209, The President of The European Court.

1448. Jurisdiction—EEC Judgments Convention—set-off

The plaintiff, a German company, brought proceedings in Germany against the defendant, a French resident, for unjust enrichment. The Regional Court of Baden-Baden ruled that the German Courts had no jurisdiction. It later made an order for costs against the plaintiff. The plaintiff lodged an application to avoid enforcement proceedings and sought, in any event, to set off against the order for costs the claim regarding unjust enrichment. On appeal, the German Federal Supreme Court asked for a preliminary ruling on Art. 16(5) of the EEC Judgments Convention. *Held,* that applications to oppose enforcement, as permitted under s.767 of the German Code of Civil Proceedings, came within the jurisdiction provision set out in Art. 16(5) of the EEC Judgments Convention. However, that provision did not enable those seeking to oppose enforcement in the courts of the Contracting State in which enforcement is to occur, to plead a set-off between the right whose enforcement is being sought and a claim over which the courts of that State would have no jurisdiction if it were raised independently.

AS-AUTOTEILE SERVICE GmbH *v.* MAHLÉ (PIERRE) (No. 220/84) [1986] 3 C.M.L.R. 321, European Ct.

1449. Movement of goods—directives, decisions and regulations

Commission Regulation (EEC) No. 254/86 of February 4, 1986 laying down detailed rules for the progressive abolition of the quantitative restrictions applicable in the Member States other than Spain and Portugal for preserved sardines and tuna originating in Spain. (O.J. 1986 L31/13.)

Commission Regulation (EEC) No. 409/86 of February 20, 1986 on methods of administrative co-operation to safeguard the transitional period of the free movement of goods between the Community as constituted on December 31, 1985 on the one hand and Spain and Portugal on the other and between those two new Member States. (O.J. 1985 L46/5.)

Council Regulation (EEC) No. 241/86 of January 27, 1986 introducing quantitative restrictions on imports of certain products originating in the United States of America. (O.J. 1986 L30/1.)

1450. Quantitative Restrictions—directives, decisions and regulations.

Commission Regulation (EEC) No. 545/86 of February 27, 1986 laying down detailed rules for applying the arrangements for a security as provided for in Regulation (EEC) No. 360/86 laying down rules for the application by Spain and Portugal of quantitative restrictions on fishery products. (O.J. 1986 L55/46.)

Commission Regulation (EEC) No. 593/86 of February 28, 1986 laying down certain detailed rules for the application of the quantitative restrictions on imports into Spain and Portugal of agricultural products from third countries and the system of import and export licences. (O.J. 1986 L58/6.)

Commission Regulation (EEC) No.1636/86 of May 28, 1986 laying down the detailed rules for applying quantitative restrictions on imports into Portugal of oil-cake from third countries. (O.J. 1986 L.144/23.)

Council Regulation (EEC) No. 182/86 of January 14, 1986 making the importation into Spain and Portugal of textile products originating in certain third countries subject to quantitative limitations. (O.J. 1986 L26/1.)

Council Regulations (EEC) No. 360/86 of February 17, 1986 laying down the rules for the application by Spain and Portugal of quantitative restrictions on fishery products. (O.J. 1986 L43/8.)

Council Regulation (EEC) No. 1647/86 of May 26, 1986 amending Regulation (EEC) No. 241/86 introducing quantitative restrictions on imports of certain products originating in the United States of America. (O.J. 1986 L.145/1.)

Council Regulation (EEC) No. 2825/86 of September 11, 1986 repealing Regulation (EEC) No. 241/86 introducing quantitative restrictions on imports of certain products originating in the United States of America. (O.J. 1986 L262/8.)

1451. Regional policy—directives, decisions and regulations

85/544/EEC:

Commission Decision of July 31, 1985 amending Decision 82/740/EEC on the designation of development areas pursuant to Art. 11 of the Belgian Law of December 30, 1970. (O.J. 1985 L341/19.)

85/545/EEC:

Commission Decision of December 4, 1985 approving a supplementary outline programme presented by France pursuant to Council Regulation (EEC) No. 269/79 establishing a common measure for forestry in certain Mediterranean zones of the Community. (O.J. 1985 L341/21.)

85/546/EEC:

Commission Decision of December 9, 1985 approving a programme for the flower and ornamental plant sector in the Land North Rhine-Westphalia pursuant to Council Regulation (EEC) No. 355/77. (O.J. 1985 L341/22.)

85/596/EEC:

Commission Decision of December 11, 1985 correcting Decision 82/462/EEC on the replacement of the Annex to Council Directive 75/270/EEC concerning the Community list of less-favoured areas within the meaning of Council Directive 75/268/EEC. (O.J. 1985 L373/43.)

85/599/EEC:

Commission decision of December 12, 1985 adjusting the boundaries of less-favoured areas in France within the meaning of Council Directive 75/268/EEC. (O.J. 1985 L373/46.)

Council Regulation (EEC) No. 3634/85 of December 17, 1985 on the establishment of specific Community regional development measures in 1985 and amending Regulation (EEC) No. 1787/84. (O.J. 1985 L350/4.)

Council Regulation (EEC) No. 3635/85 of December 17, 1985 amending Regulation (EEC) No. 2617/80 instituting a specific Community regional development measure contributing to overcoming constraints on the development of new economic activities in certain zones adversely affected by restructuring of the shipbuilding industry. (O.J. 1985 L350/8.)

Council Regulation (EEC) No. 3636/85 of December 17, 1985 amending Regulation (EEC) No. 219/84 instituting a specific Community regional development measure contributing to overcome constraints on the development of new economic activities in certain zones adversely affected by restructuring of the textile and clothing industry. (O.J. 1985 L350/10.)

Council Regulation (EEC) No. 3637/85 of December 17, 1985 amending Regulation (EEC) No. 2619/80 instituting a specific Community regional development measure contributing to the improvement of the economic and social situation of the border areas of Ireland and Northern Ireland. (O.J. 1985 L350/12.)

Council Regulation (EEC) No. 3638/85 of December 17, 1985 instituting a specific Community regional development measure contributing to the development of new economic activities in certain zones affected by the implementation of the Community fisheries policy. (O.J. 1985 L350/17.)

Council Regulation (EEC) No. 3641/85 of December 20, 1985 amending Regulation (EEC) No. 1787/84 on the European Regional Development Fund. (O.J. 1985 L350/40.)

86/39/EEC:
Commission Decision of December 23, 1985, instituting in the prefecture of Grevena, Greece, a pilot action in preparation for the integrated Mediterranean programmes. (O.J. 1986 L62/25.)

86/40/EEC:
Commission Decision of December 23, 1985 instituting in the area of Lake Trasimeno, region of Umbria, Italy, a pilot action in preparation for the integrated Mediterranean programmes. (O.J. 1986 L62/30.)

86/41/EEC:
Commission Decision of December 23, 1985 amending Decision 84/77/EEC instituting a pilot action in preparation for the integrated Mediterranean programmes. (O.J. 1986 L62/34.)

86/42/EEC:
Commission Decision of December 23, 1985 amending Decision 84/73/EEC instituting a pilot action in preparation for the integrated Mediterranean programmes. (O.J. 1986 L62/36.)

86/43/EEC:
Commission Decision of December 23, 1985 amending Decision 84/70/EEC instituting a pilot action in preparation for the integrated Mediterranean programmes. (O.J. 1986 L62/38.)

86/477/EEC:
Commission Decision of August 20, 1986 approving an integrated Mediterranean programme for the island of Crete (Greece). (O.J. 1986 L282/21.)

1452. Research—directives, decisions and regulations
86/28/Euratom
Council Decision of January 20, 1986 approving the conclusion by the Commission of a Memorandum of Understanding between the European Atomic Energy Community and the Government of Canada concerning cooperation in the field of fusion research and development. (O.J. 1986 L35/9.)

1453. Right of establishment—directives, decisions and regulations
85/584/EEC:
Council Directive of December 20, 1985 amending, on account of the accession of Spain and Portugal, Directive 85/433/EEC concerning the mutual recognition of diplomas, certificates and other evidence of formal qualifications in pharmacy, including measures to facilitate the effective exercise of the right of establishment relating to certain activities in the field of pharmacy. (O.J. 1985 L372/42.)

85/614/EEC:
Council Directive of December 20, 1985 amending, on account of the accession of Spain and Portugal, Directive 85/384/EEC on the mutual recognition of diplomas, certificates and other evidence of formal qualifications in architecture, including measures to facilitate the effective exercise of the right of establishment and freedom to provide services. (O.J. 1985 L376/1.)

1454. Right of establishment—services—medical and dental professions
The French Public Health Code required that a doctor or dentist wishing to practise in a French department had to be enrolled on that department's register and

not on any other. In particular, it prohibited a doctor or dentist enrolled or registered as a doctor or dentist in a State other than France from being enrolled on any department's register. Legislation required applicants for such registration to produce either a certificate showing cancellation of any previous enrolment or registration, or evidence that there had been no previous registration or enrolment. The European Commission took proceedings against France under Art. 169 EEC for failing to meet its obligations under the EEC Treaty, in particular those relating to the freedom to provide services and the right to establishment. *Held,* that France had failed to meet its obligations under Arts. 48, 52 and 59 EEC by requiring doctors and dentists established in another EEC State to cancel their enrolment or registration in that other State in order to be able to practise their profession in France.

REGISTRATION OF FOREIGN DOCTORS, *Re*; E.C. COMMISSION *v.* FRANCE (No. 96/85) [1986] 3 C.M.L.R. 57, European Ct.

1455. Sex discrimination—access to employment—compensation

The plaintiffs, female social workers, applied for posts at a male prison in West Germany. The authorities appointed two male candidates with lesser qualifications to those posts. The Labour Court, Hamm, found that there had been discrimination and awarded the plaintiff's compensation pursuant to s.611a(2) of the German Civil Code. That section purported to implement Council Directive 76/207 on the implementation of equal treatment for men and women as regards access to employment. The Court found that that section only enabled it to award reimbursement of travelling expenses incurred by the plaintiffs in pursuing their applications for the posts. The Court asked the European Court under Art. 177 EEC for a preliminary ruling on the interpretation and direct applicability of Directive 76/207. *Held,* that (1) National Courts have to interpret Directive 76/207 in the light of its wording and its purpose; (2) Directive 76/207 does not require a sanction to be imposed on an employer who discriminates on grounds of sex with regard to access to employment, whereby that employer has to make a contract of employment with the applicant discriminated against; (3) as regards sanctions for any sexual discrimination, Directive 76/207 does not contain any unconditional and sufficiently precise obligation which, in the absence of implementing measures taken within the set time limits, may be relied on by an individual in order to obtain specific compensation under the Directive, where this is not available under domestic law; (4) Directive 76/207 lets each EEC State choose what sanction it wishes to impose for breach of the prohibition of discrimination contained in the Directive. Nevertheless, if an EEC State chooses to penalise infringements of the prohibition by the award of compensation, such compensation has to be adequate in relation to the damage sustained. Compensation has to be more than merely nominal damages, for example, more than mere reimbursement of travelling expenses incurred by a candidate.

VON COLSON AND KAMANN *v.* LAND NORDRHEIN-WESTFALEN (No. 14/83); HARZ (DORIT) *v.* DEUTSCHE TRADAX GmbH (No. 79/83), [1986] 2 C.M.L.R. 430, European Ct.

1456. Sex discrimination—dismissal from employment—retirement age

Ms Marshall was dismissed at the age of 62 years, as she had passed the normal retirement age applied by her employers to female employees. The employers had followed a policy that the normal retirement age was the age at which social security pensions became payable, *i.e.* 65 years for men and 60 years for women. She commenced proceedings in the industrial tribunal and argued that her dismissal and the reason for dismissal constituted unlawful discrimination on the ground of sex contrary to the Sex Discrimination Act 1975 and EEC Law. On appeal, the Court of Appeal of England and Wales asked the European Court under Art. 177 EEC for a preliminary ruling. *Held,* that (1) dismissal of a woman solely because she had reached or passed the qualifying age for a state pension, where that age was different under national law for men and for women, amounted to discrimination on the ground of sex contrary to Art 5(1) of Council Directive 76/207; (2) Art. 5(1) of Directive 76/207, which prohibited any discrimination on the ground of sex with regard to working conditions, including dismissal was sufficiently precise and unconditional to be capable of being relied upon by an individual before a national court as against a State authority acting in its capacity as employer, in order to avoid the application of any national provision which did not conform to Art. 5(1).

MARSHALL *v.* SOUTHAMPTON & SOUTH-WEST HAMPSHIRE AREA HEALTH AUTHORITY (No. 152/84) [1986] 1 C.M.L.R. 688.

1457. Sex discrimination—employment—exceptions
    The European Commission brought proceedings against West Germany under Art. 169 EEC for a declaration that it had failed to meet its obligations under the EEC Treaty by not fully transposing into national law Council Directive 76/207 on the implementation of the principle of equal treatment for men and women as regards access to employment, vocational training and promotion, and working conditions and Council Directive 75/117 on the approximation of the laws of the EEC States relating to the application of the principle of equal pay for men and women. *Held,* that (1) the following complaints made by the Commission against West Germany were rejected, namely the complaints of failure to apply the principle of equal treatment in the public service and in the independent professions, the complaint of failure to give legal effect to the provisions concerning offers of employment and the complaint of failure to transpose Directive 75/117 into national law with regard to remuneration in the public service; (2) West Germany failed to meet its obligations under the EEC Treaty by failing to take the measures necessary to apply Art. 9(2) of Council Directive 76/207 in relation to the occupational activities excluded from the scope of that principle by virtue of Art. 2(2) of Directive 76/207. It is primarily the responsibility of EEC States to make a list, in whatever form, of the occupations and activities excluded from the application of the principle of equal treatment and to notify the results to the Commission so that the latter can supervise the nature of the exceptions claimed.
    SEX DISCRIMINATION LAWS *Re*: E.C. COMMISSION *v.* WEST GERMANY (NO. 248/83) [1986] 2 C.M.L.R. 588, European Ct.

1458. Sex discrimination—employment—occupational pensions
    Bilka, a German store, had an occupational pension scheme for its employees. Part-time employees were only admitted to that scheme if they had worked full-time for a minimum of 15 years out of a total of 20 years. Mrs. Weber had worked for Bilka full-time from 1961 to 1972 and part-time from 1972 until the termination of her employment. Since she had not finished the minimum of 15 years of full-time work Bilka refused to grant her an occupational pension. Mrs. Weber challenged the legality of that refusal claiming, *inter alia*, that the occupational pension scheme was contrary to the principle of equal pay for men and women enshrined in Art. 119 EEC. She alleged that setting a minimum period of full-time work put female employees at a disadvantage since, in order to be able to care for their family, they would be more likely than male workers to seek part-time work. The German Federal Labour Court asked the European Court under Art. 177 EEC for a preliminary ruling on the compatibility of the store's policy with Art. 119 EEC. *Held,* that (1) the exclusion of part-time employees from an occupational scheme was contrary to Art. 119 EEC where that measure affected a much greater number of female than male employees, unless that measure was attributable to factors which were objectively justified and were not related to any discrimination based on sex; (2) a store might justify having a pay policy which excluded part-time workers from an occupational pension scheme, regardless of their sex, by arguing that it tried to employ as few part-time workers as possible, provided it was shown that the means selected to achieve that objective corresponded to the genuine requirements of the employer and were appropriate and necessary to reach that end; (3) Art. 119 EEC did not require an employer to organise the occupational pension scheme which he provided for his employees in such a manner as to take into account the particular problems encountered by workers with family responsibilities in fulfilling the conditions of entitlement to such a pension.
    BILKA-KAUFHAUS GMBH *v.* KARIN WEBER VON HARTZ (NO. 170/84) [1986] 2 C.M.L.R. 701, European Ct.

1459. Sex discrimination—employment—pension contributions
    Mr. Newstead, a 57-year-old bachelor joined the Civil Service in 1969. In 1969 he chose not to contribute to the Civil Service Widows' and Children's Pension Scheme, to which contributions were optional. In 1973 he became subject to a new national pension scheme for the Civil Service under which men became liable to suffer a compulsory deduction from their gross salary by way of contribution to a pension for their widow (repayable if they should retire or die unmarried), but female civil

servants were under no corresponding obligation. Mr. Newstead argued before the Employment Appeal Tribunal that this compulsory contribution requirement on men amounted to sexual discrimination contrary to EEC law and, in particular, contrary to Art. 119 EEC. The Employment Appeal Tribunal asked the European Court under Art. 177 EEC for a preliminary ruling on the interpretation of Art. 119 EEC and the European Council Directives 75/117 and 76/207. It also asked whether Directive 76/207 had direct effect in EEC States.

NEWSTEAD *v.* DEPARTMENT OF TRANSPORT & H.M. TREASURY [1986] 2 C.M.L.R. 196, E.A.T.

1460. Sex discrimination—equal pay—implementation of directive
The European Commission considered that the Danish Act 32 of February 4, 1976 on equal pay for men and women did not fulfil the obligations arising from European Directive 75/117 of February 10, 1975 on the approximation of the laws of the Member States relating to the application of the principle of equal pay for men and women. The Commission found that the Act was deficient in that it did not require employers to pay men and women the same salary for work to which equal value is attributed and did not provide any means of redress for workers to pursue claims for breach of the principle of equal pay for work of equal value. The Commission took proceedings against Denmark under Art. 169 EEC. *Held,* that (1) by failing to adopt within the prescribed period the measures necessary to implement Directive 75/117, the Kingdom of Denmark had failed to fulfil its obligations under the EEC Treaty; (2) While EEC States may leave implementation of the principle of equal pay in the first instance to representatives of management and labour in the Member States, they must still ensure by suitable legislative and administrative provisions, that all workers receive the protection provided for in the Directive. The Danish law did not possess the clarity and precision required to ensure the protection of workers' rights pursuant to the directive.

EQUAL PAY CONCEPTS, *Re;* EUROPEAN COMMISSION *v.* DENMARK (No. 143/83) [1986] 1 C.M.L.R. 44, European Ct.

1461. Sex discrimination—redundancy—pensions
Ms. Roberts was made redundant at 53 years of age as part of a mass redundancy on closure of a depot by Tate and Lyle Industries Ltd. ("Tate"). Ms. Roberts was a member of an occupational pension scheme, which provided for compulsory retirement at the age of 65 years for men and 60 years for women. As part of the terms of the mass redundancy Tate agreed to grant an immediate pension to both men and women who were over 55 years of age. Ms. Roberts brought proceedings against Tate that her dismissal amounted to unlawful discrimination contrary to the Sex Discrimination Act 1975 and contrary to EEC Law, in particular European Council Directive 76/207 of February 9, 1976 on the implementation of equal treatment for men and women as regards access to employment, vocational training and promotion, and working conditions. Ms. Roberts alleged that it was discriminatory that a male employee should receive an immediate pension 10 years before the normal retirement age for men whereas a female employee was not so entitled until five years before the normal retirement age for females. The Court of Appeal of England and Wales asked the European Court under Art. 177 EEC for a preliminary ruling on the interpretation of Directive 76/207. *Held,* that it was not contrary to Directive 76/207 for an employer to arrange for both men and women who are made redundant to receive a pension at 55 years of age. This did not constitute sexual discrimination contrary to Art. 5(1) of Directive 76/207, even though in the result men would receive pensions at a time which is earlier in relation to their normal pensionable age than that applicable to women.

ROBERTS (JOAN) *v.* TATE & LYLE INDUSTRIES (No. 151/84) [1986] 1 C.M.L.R. 714, European Ct.

1462. Sex discrimination—safeguarding national security—difference in treatment between men and women police officers
[Sex Discrimination (Northern Ireland) Order 1976; art. 53(1)(2); E.C. Council Directive 76/207, arts. 2(1)(2)(3), 3(1), 4, 6.]
On a complaint for sex discrimination, the government's certificate that an act of discrimination is excluded for reasons of national security or protecting public order is not conclusive and cannot exclude review by the courts.

J was employed as a member of the full-time Royal Ulster Constabulary Reserve. Although carrying out the usual duties of uniformed police officers, she was not armed in carrying out those duties. The Chief Constable considered that if women were armed, it would increase the risk, they might become targets for assassination, that armed women officers would be less effective in areas for which women were better suited such as welfare work, and that the public would regard it as a much greater departure from the ideas of an unarmed police force. In 1980 the Chief Constable decided not to offer women new contracts of full-time employment on the grounds that a substantial part of general police duties involved the use of firearms. J claimed that she had been unlawfully discriminated against. The Secretary of State for Northern Ireland issued a certificate stating that the action was for the purpose of safeguarding national security. The Industrial Tribunal sought the European Court's ruling on whether a Member State could exclude acts of sex discrmination on the grounds of national security or protecting public order, whether employment as an armed member of a police force was an activity when the sex of the worker constituted a determining factor, whether the Chief Constable's policy could be justified out of a concern to protect women within art. 2(3) of the E.C. Council Directive 76/207 and whether J could rely on the directive before the national court. *Held,* that (1) the principle of effective judicial control did not allow a certificate to be treated as conclusive evidence so as to exclude review by the courts; (2) acts of discrimination for the protection of public safety must be examined in the light of derogations from the principle of equal treatment for men and women; (3) in deciding whether in the context of the activities of a police officer sex constituted a determining factor a Member State might take into consideration requirements of public safety in order to restrict general policing duties; (4) differences in treatment allowed to protect women did not include risks and danger such as those to which any armed police officer was exposed in the performance of his duties in a given situation, that did not specifically affect women as such; (5) the application of the principle of equal treatment to the conditions governing access to jobs and to training was unconditional and sufficiently precise to be relied on by individuals against a Member State which failed to implement it correctly.

JOHNSTON *v.* CHIEF CONSTABLE OF THE ROYAL ULSTER CONSTABULARY [1986] 3 All E.R. 135, European Ct.

1463/4. Sex discrimination—voluntary extension of maternity leave—whether properly reserved to women

[Council Directive (76/207/EEC), arts. 1, 2, 5(1).]

A voluntary extension of maternity leave may properly be reserved to women to the exclusion of men under art. 2(3) of Council Directive (76/207/EEC).

P was the father of an illegitimate child born in West Germany. Under West German law the mother, after a period of eight weeks from the birth, could claim additional maternity leave until the child was aged six months. She would then be entitled to a daily allowance from the state. The mother elected not to do so, and returned to work. P left work in order to look after the child unpaid. The German courts refused him the daily allowance. P argued that that refusal was in breach of Council Directive (76/207/EEC) art. 1, which requires equality of treatment to working conditions, art. 2(1) which forbids sex discrimination by reference to marital or family status, and art. 5(1) which provides that men and women must be guaranteed the same working conditions without discrimination on the grounds of sex. The question was referred to the European Court of Justice. *Held,* that the provision fell within art. 2(3), which expressly excepted from the directive provisions concerning the protection of women, particularly as regards pregnancy and maternity, and was therefore valid.

HOFMANN *v.* BARMER ERSATZKASSE [1985] I.C.R. 731, European Court.

1465. Social affairs—directives, decisions and regulations

Council Regulation (EEC) No. 3820/85 of December 20, 1985 on the harmonisation of certain social legislation relating to road transport. (O.J. 1985 L370/1.)

Council Regulation (EEC) No. 3821/85 of December 20, 1985 on recording equipment in road transport. (O.J. 1985 L370/8.)

1466. Social security—pensions—deductions

The European Commission brought proceedings against Belgium under Art. 169 EEC for failing to fulfil its obligations under Art. 33 of Reg. 1408/71 on the application of social security schemes to employed persons and their families moving within the Community and under Art. 5 EEC. Belgian legislation required recipients of a pension from a Belgian social security fund to pay social security contributions (in the form of deduction at source from the pensions payment) in respect of contributions for sickness and maternity, not only where recipients resided in Belgium, but also where the recipients resided in other EEC States. The Commission objected to the legislation in so far as it applied to those not resident in Belgium, as being contrary to Art. 33. *Held,* that by deducting contributions from pensions in respect of EEC nationals residing in another EEC State, Belgium failed to fulfil its obligations under the EEC Treaty.

PENSION DEDUCTIONS, *Re*; E.C. COMMISSION *v.* BELGIUM (No. 275/83) [1985] 3 C.M.L.R. 749, European Ct.

1467. Social security—self-employed person—residence requirement

The plaintiff was a Dutch priest who worked from 1955 to 1980 as a missionary in Zaire. During a period of leave in 1977 he resided in Holland and registered as a voluntary insured person under a Dutch law, known as the AAW. Art. 77 of AAW authorised voluntary insurance contributions to be paid in respect of periods when the insured was pursuing an activity in a developing State, such as Zaire. The plaintiff returned to Holland in March 1981 after becoming incapacitated for work in Zaire. The defendant awarded him benefits under the AWW. However, having learnt that he had gone to reside permanently in a monastery in Belgium the defendant suspended payments on the ground that he had not been incapacitated for work in Holland for an uninterrupted period of 52 weeks within the meaning of the AAW. The plaintiff brought an action for annulment of that decision before the Social Security Court, Utrecht. The latter asked the European Court under Art. 177 EEC for a preliminary ruling. *Held,* that (1) a missionary priest could be regarded as a "self-employed person" for the purposes of Art. 1(*a*)(iv) of Reg. 1408/71 as amended by Reg. 1390/81 even if he received contributions to meet his needs from third parties who were the beneficiaries of his priestly services; (2) a national regulation on social security matters whose effects applied to people carrying out or who had carried out activities partly or fully outside the EEC was to be regarded as "legislation" within Art. 2 of Reg. 1408/71; (3) Art. 2(4) of Reg. 1390/81 applied to the refusal by a social security body to grant invalidity benefit, on the ground that the insured person had not previously resided in the EEC State concerned during a certain uninterrupted period. However, the insured person could not rely on that provision until July 1, 1982.

VAN ROOSMALEN *v.* BESTUUR VAN DE BEDRIJFSVERENIGING VOOR DE GEZONDHEID, GEESTELIJKE EN MAATSCHAPPELIJKE BELANGEN (No. 300/84), *The Times,* October 29, 1986, European Ct.

1468. Social security—sex discrimination—invalidity care allowance

[Social Security Act 1975 (c.14), s.37(3)(*a*)(i), Council Directive 79/7, arts. 1, 3(1)(*a*), 4.]

The provisions of s.37(3) of the Social Security Act 1975 regarding payment of invalidity benefit to a married woman are discriminatory and contrary to the E.C. Council Directive.

The applicant was a married woman living with her husband. She had worked for a number of years, but gave up when her disabled mother moved in to her home. She applied for a care allowance under s.37(3)(*a*)(1), but was refused, although it was accepted that the benefit was payable to a man in the same circumstances. The matter was referred to the European Court on the question of discrimination contrary to art. 4(1). *Held,* that s.37(3) placed a woman living with a man at a disadvantage in respect of entitlement to the relevant benefit, and was discriminating and contrary to art. 4(1).

DRAKE *v.* CHIEF ADJUDICATION OFFICER (No. 150/85) [1986] 3 All E.R. 65, European Ct.

1469. Social security—unemployment benefit—contribution conditions. See SOCIAL SECURITY DECISION No. R(U) 7/85, § 3186.

1470. State aids—annulment proceedings—locus standi

The Commission had been investigating, pursuant to Art. 93(2) EEC, the tariff structure for natural gas supplied to Dutch producers of ammonia and of nitrate fertilisers, which the applicants argued amounted to a State aid by the Dutch

Government. The Dutch Government abolished the tariff structure which had been objected to and introduced a new tariff "F". The Commission terminated its procedure under Art. 93(2) EEC as it regarded tariff "F" as compatible with EEC law and not a State aid. French manufacturers of nitrate fertilisers (the applicants) brought proceedings for annulment of the decision whereby the European Commission terminated the procedure initiated against the Dutch Government under Art. 93(2) EEC. The applicants had been involved in the initial complaint against the Dutch Government. The Commission argued that the decision was not of individual concern to the applicants and that the applicants had no *locus standi. Held,* the decision was of direct and individual concern to the applicants and, accordingly, the application was admissible.

COMPAGNIE FRANÇAISE DE L'AZOTE (COFAZ) S.A. *v.* E.C. COMMISSION (No. 169/84) [1986] 3 C.M.L.R. 385, European Ct.

1471. State aids—interim measures—need to show serious and irreparable damage
Germany brought proceedings for a declaration that Commission Decision 85/12 of July 23, 1984 was void in so far as it prohibited investment aids in the German labour market areas of Borken-Bocholt and Siegen. Germany applied for an order that the execution of the Commission Decision be stayed until the Court's judgment in the main action. *Held,* that the plaintiff's application was dismissed as the plaintiff had failed to show that the order was necessary for the purpose of avoiding serious, irreparable damage. In this case the regional aids were not decisive for investment decisions by firms, the Decision imposing the ban allowed a one year adjustment period and permitted the aid to be granted even after the cut-off date if application had been submitted before then. Further, Germany had not proved that the ban would prevent any important investment projects.

GERMAN LOCAL INVESTMENT AIDS, *Re*; GERMANY *v.* E.C. COMMISSION (No. 248/84R) [1985] 3 C.M.L.R. 710, European Ct., Lord Mackenzie Stuart.

1472. State aids—local authorities—locus standi
The European Commission, by Decision 83/397 addressed to Luxembourg, declared that certain aids which the Luxembourg Government proposed to grant to steel undertakings were compatible with the EEC provided that these undertakings reduced production and closed certain of their factories. Five Luxembourg municipalities brought proceedings under Art. 173 EEC and Art. 31 ECSC for declaration that the Decision was void. *Held,* that the action was dismissed as inadmissible because (i) the municipalities had no locus standi to sue under Art. 33 ECSC since they were not EEC States, nor the Council, nor undertakings, nor associations of undertakings within Art. 48 ECSC; (ii) the municipalities had no locus standi to sue under Art. 173(2) EEC since they were not "directly and individually concerned". The Decision left such a margin of discretion to the State and to the undertakings concerned when deciding where production should be reduced and factories closed, that the Decision could not be said to be of direct and individual concern to the municipalities, with which the undertakings affected, happened to be connected by virtue of the sites of their factories.

MUNICIPALITY OF DIFFERDANGE, THE *v.* E.C. COMMISSION (No. 222/83) [1985] 3 C.M.L.R. 638, European Ct.

1473. State aids—procedure to challenge grants—grants to farmers
The French Government notified to the European Commission under Art. 93(3) EEC grants payable to farmers with turnovers of less than 250,000 francs. The grants were payable out of the operating surplus accumulated by the Caisse Nationale de Credit Agricole ("the Fund"). The Commission commenced the procedure under Art. 93(2) EEC. The French Government argued that the grants were not State aids as the Fund's surplus came from private, as opposed to State, funds. It also stated that the decision to allocate money for such grants was made by the Fund's board, on which the State representatives were in a minority. On the basis of those arguments the Commission considered that the grants were not State aids and stopped its procedure under Art. 93(2) EEC. Instead the Commission brought proceedings under Art. 169 EEC for a declaration that by encouraging the Fund to make grants to the poorest farmers, France had failed to fulfil its obligations under Art. 5 EEC, having regard to the EEC Treaty's objectives regarding competition and, in particular, Art. 92 EEC. *Held,* that (1) the application was dismissed as inadmissible in as much as it was based directly on Art. 169 EEC and the Commission

had failed to comply with the preliminary stage of the procedure set out in Art. 93 EEC; (2) the procedure contained in Art. 93(2) EEC provides all parties concerned with guarantees, which are designed for the particular problems created by State aids with regard to competition in the EEC and which go much further than those provided in the preliminary procedure set out in Art. 169 EEC, in which only the Commission and the EEC State involved participate. It follows that, although the existence of that specific procedure does not prevent the compatibility of an aid scheme in relation to EEC rules other than those contained in Art. 92 EEC from being assessed under the procedure contained in Art. 169 EEC, the Commission must use the procedure set out in Art. 93(2) EEC if it wishes to prove that that scheme, as aid, is incompatible with the Common Market.

GRANTS TO POOR FARMERS, *Re*: E.C. COMMISSION *v.* FRANCE (No. 290/83) [1986] 2 C.M.L.R. 546, European Ct.

1474. State aids—restructuring—public investments

The Belgian State had, through a regional agency, granted finance in the form of loans and an injection of capital into Intermills S.A., a Belgian paper-making group. The loans were pursuant to a restructuring plan. Under that plan Intermills stopped bulk production and started manufacturing special papers with a high added value. The European Commission had approved the loans under Art. 92 EEC since they were linked to a restructuring plan, but it had prohibited by its Decision 82/670/EEC of the July 22, 1982 the capital investment on the ground that it amounted to "rescue aid" to pay the Intermills' debts. *Held*, that both forms of finance amounted to "aid", but the Commission had given no verifiable reasons to justify its findings that the capital investment was not compatible with the EEC Treaty and, in particular Art. 92 EEC. Accordingly Decision 82/670 EEC was void.

INTERMILLS S.A. *v.* E.C. COMMISSION (No. 323/82) [1986] 1 C.M.L.R. 614, European Ct.

1475. Steel—production quotas—fine

Queensborough Rolling Mill Co. ("Queensborough") brought proceedings under Art. 33(2) ECSC for the annulment of the Commission Decision imposing a fine on Queensborough for exceeding its production quotas for the third and fourth quarters of 1981. *Held*, application dismissed as Queensborough was unable to show that the Decision was unlawful.

QUEENSBOROUGH ROLLING MILL COMPANY *v.* E.C. COMMISSION (No. 64/84) [1986] 2 C.M.L.R. 211, European Ct.

1476. Taxation—capital taxes—exemption

National Smokeless Fuels (the appellant) owed £30 million to various banks. On June 29, 1983 the share capital of the appellant was increased by the creation of 30 million new ordinary shares of £1 each. Those shares were allotted to the appellant's parent company in consideration of the discharge by the parent company of the appellant's debts to the bank. The Commissioners of Inland Revenue assessed stamp duty of £300,000 on that allotment on the basis that the transaction was subject to capital duty of one per cent. under s.47 of the Finance Act 1973, applying EEC Directive 69/335. The appellant appealed against that assessment and argued that it was entitled to exemption from that duty under para. 10 of Sched. 19 to the Finance Act 1973, implementing EEC Directive 73/79. *Held*, dismissing the appeal, that consideration of the Act and the relevant Directives led to the conclusion that acquisition by a parent company of a new issue of shares in its already wholly-owned subsidiary was not covered by the exemption from capital duty.

NATIONAL SMOKELESS FUELS LTD. *v.* I.R.C. [1986] 3 C.M.L.R. 227, Warner J.

1477. Taxation—directives, decisions and regulations

86/246/EEC:

Council Directive of June 16, 1986 amending Directive 72/464/EEC on taxes other than turnover taxes which affect the consumption of manufactured tobacco. (O.J. 1986 L164/26.)

86/247/EEC:

Twenty-first Council Directive of June 16, 1986 on the harmonisation of the laws of the Member States relating to turnover taxes—Deferment of the introduction of the common system of value-added tax in the Hellenic Republic. (O.J. 1986 L164/27.)

86/560/EEC:
Thirteenth Council Directive of November 17, 1986 on the harmonisation of the laws of the Member States relating to turnover taxes—Arrangements for the refund of value added tax to taxable persons not established in Community territory. (O.J. 1986 L326/40.)
Council Regulation (ECSC, EEC, Euratom) No. 3519/85 of December 12, 1985 amending Regulation (EEC, Euratom, ECSC) No. 260/68 laying down the conditions and procedure for applying the tax for the benefit of the European Communities. (O.J. 1985 L335/59.)
Council Regulation (ECSC, EEC, Euratom) No. 3735/85 of December 20, 1985 extending the term of validity of Regulation (EEC, EURATOM, ECSC) No. 2892/77 implementing, in respect of own resources accruing from value added tax, the decision of April 21, 1970 on the replacement of financial contributions from Member States by the Communities' own resources. (O.J. 1985 L356/1.)

1478. Taxes—discrimination—cars

France imposed annually a differential tax on cars less than 16 CV and a special tax on cars more powerful than 16 CV. The special tax was fixed at a rate much higher than the highest rate of the differential tax. Mr. Humblot was charged the special tax on his 36 CV Mercedes-Benz. He brought proceedings against the tax authorities, challenging the imposition of the special tax. Mr. Humblot argued that this tax was imposed only on foreign cars since private cars more powerful than 16 hp were not manufactured in France and that this consititued discrimination contrary to Art. 95 EEC. The Tribunal de Grande Instance, Belfort, asked the European Court for a preliminary ruling under Art. 117 EEC. *Held,* that a special tax imposed upon cars which exceeded a certain fiscal rating was contrary to Art. 95 EEC when the only cars affected by the special tax were imported, in particular from other EEC States.

HUMBLOT *v.* DIRECTEUR DES SERVICES FISCAUX (No. 112/84) [1986] 2 C.M.L.R. 338, European Ct.

1479. Transport—air transport—competition

D were prosecuted for infringing the French Civil Aviation Code when selling air tickets by applying tariffs that had not been submitted to the French Minister for Civil Aviation for approval or were different from the approved tariffs. The approved tariffs were those agreed in I.A.T.A. The Tribunal de Police de Paris asked the European Court under Art. 177 for a preliminary ruling to enable it to assess the compatibility of provisions of the Code with EEC Law. *Held,* that (1) air transport is subject to the general rules of the EEC Treaty, including Arts. 85 and 86 EEC, but it is not subject to the direct enforcement procedures of the European Commission through Regs. 17 and 1017/68; (2) air transport continues to be governed by Arts. 88 and 89 EEC. Under Art. 88 EEC the authorities in EEC States rule on the compatibility of agreements and practices with Arts. 85 and 86 EEC; (3) where the national authorities have not given a ruling under Art. 88 EEC and the Commission has not made a finding under Art. 89 EEC that a breach has occurred, a national court which is not a "national authority" does not have jurisdiction to find that the conduct in issue is contrary to Art. 85(1) EEC. If, however, a ruling or finding has been made under Art. 85 EEC or Art. 89 EEC, then the national courts can apply Art. 85(2) EEC; (4) it is contrary to Art. 5, Art. 3(f)) and Art. 85 EEC for EEC States to approve air tariffs and to reinforce the effects thereof where it has been found pursuant to Art. 88 or Art. 89(2) EEC that those tariffs are the result of an agreement, a decision or concerted practice contrary to Art. 85 EEC.

MINISTÈRE PUBLIC *v.* ASJES (No. 209-213/84) [1986] 3 C.M.L.R. 173, European Ct.

1480. Transport—combined road/rail transport—transport authorisation

German transporters carrying goods from Germany to Northern Italy transported their vehicles by rail to Lugano station, Switzerland as that station was closer to the point of unloading of the goods than Italian stations equipped for unloading road vehicles. Italian customs authorities insisted on a transport authorisation on the vehicles' entry into Italy by road because they considered that the European Council Directive 75/130 of February 17, 1975 on the establishment of common rules for certain types of combined road/rail carriage of goods between Member States did not apply where the unloading station was in a non-EEC State. That Directive provides for the liberalisation of road/rail carriage between EEC States, in particular, by liberalising such carriage from quota systems and from systems of authorisation. The

European Commission brought proceedings under Art. 169 EEC against Italy for failing to fulfil its obligations under Directive 75/130. *Held*, that Italy failed to fulfil its obligations under Directive 75/130 by requiring a transport authorisation for road vehicles registered in Germany and transported by rail as far as Lugano station, when that is the closest suitable rail unloading station to the point of unloading of the goods and the transporter is able to prove the distance covered by rail in accordance with the provisions of Art. 3 of the Directive.

ROAD/RAIL TRANSPORT TO LUGANO, *Re*; E.C. COMMISSION *v.* ITALY (No. 2/84) [1986] 2 C.M.L.R. 86, European Ct.

1481. Transport—common transport policy—failure to act
The European Parliament brought proceedings under Art. 175(1) EEC for a declaration that the European Council had infringed the EEC Treaty, especially Arts. 3(e), 61, 74, 75 and 84 EEC, by failing to introduce a common policy for transport and, in particular, to lay down the framework of such a policy in a binding manner and further by failing to reach a decision on 16 specified proposals submitted by the European Commission with regard to transport. *Held*, that the European Council was in breach of the EEC Treaty by failing to ensure freedom to provide services in the sphere of international transport and to lay down the conditions under which non-resident carriers might undertake transport services in an EEC State. The absence of a common transport policy which the EEC Treaty required to be brought into existence did not in itself necessarily amount to a failure to act sufficiently specific in nature to establish a cause of action under Art. 175 EEC, whereas the EEC Treaty obligations relating to freedom to provide services were sufficiently specific for disregard of them to be the subject of a finding of failure to act pursuant to Art. 175 EEC.

EUROPEAN PARLIAMENT *v.* EUROPEAN COUNCIL (No. 13/83) [1986] 1 C.M.L.R. 138, European Ct.

1482. Transport—directives, decisions and regulations
85/636/EEC:
  Commission Decision of December 20, 1985 amending Decision 84/520/EEC granting financial assistance for special measures of Community interest relating to transport infrastructure. (O.J. 1985 L379/52.)
  Corrigendum to Commission Decision 85/516/EEC of November 18, 1985 setting up a Joint Committee on Road Transport (O.J. No. L317 of 28.11.1985). (O.J. 1986 L7/15.)
  Council Regulation (EEC) No. 3677/85 of December 20, 1985 amending Regulation (EEC) No. 3164/76 on the Community quota for the carriage of goods by road between Member States. (O.J. 1985 L354/46.)
86/242/EEC:
  Commission Recommendation of April 25, 1986 addressed to the Government of the Grand Duchy of Luxembourg on a draft law on the division of goods transported between rail and road. (O.J. 1986 L.163/41.)
86/290/EEC:
  Commission opinion of May 30, 1986 addressed to the French Government on their draft decree concerning the implementation of various provisions of Council Regulation (EEC) No. 543/69 as amended, on the harmonisation of certain social legislation relating to road transport. (O.J. 1986 L182/28.)
86/360/EEC:
  Council Directive of July 24, 1986 amending Directive 85/3/EEC on the weights, dimensions and certain other technical characteristics of certain road vehicles. (O.J. 1986 L217/19.)
86/597/EEC:
  Commission opinion of November 26, 1986 to the Portuguese Government on implementation of Council Directive 79/115/EEC, concerning pilotage of vessels by deep-sea pilots in the North Sea and English Channel. (O.J. 1986 L348/66.)
86/598/EEC:
  Commission opinion of November 26, 1986 addressed to the French Government on the draft Decree concerning the implementation of Council Directive 82/714/EEC laying down technical requirements for inland waterway vessels. (O.J. 1986 L348/67.)

1483. Transport—statistical returns—force majeure

Council Directive 78/546 of June 12, 1978 required EEC States to make annual statistical returns to the European Commission from 1979 onwards in respect of the carriage of goods by road. In 1979 and 1980 Italy informed the Commission that due to a bomb attack on the Ministry of Transport's data processing centre and the consequent destruction of the vehicle register it was not possible for Italy to comply with the time limit set out in Directive 78/546 for making the returns. By 1982 Italy had still not made complete returns and could not give any indication of the date when complete returns could be made. The Commission took proceedings against Italy under Art. 169 EEC. *Held,* that (1) Italy had failed to fulfil its obligations under Directive 78/546 by failing to make statistical returns in respect of carriage of goods by road in accordance with the rules set out in that Directive; (2) although the bomb attack, which occurred before January 18, 1979, may have amounted to *force majeure,* its effect could only last for the period of time required for an administration with a normal degree of diligence to replace the equipment destroyed and to collect and prepare the data. Italy was not entitled to rely on that event to justify the continuing failure to comply with its obligations years later.

TRANSPORT STATISTICS, *Re*; E.C. COMMISSION *v.* ITALY (No. 101/84) [1986] 2 C.M.L.R. 352, European Ct.

1484. VAT—goods—repairs

P carried out repairs to old school books. P was paying VAT in respect of such repairs at the reduced rate of four per cent charged under Dutch law on supplies of books. The Dutch customs authorities decided that those repairs did not constitute a supply of goods under Dutch law, but rather the provision of services, to which a rate of 18 per cent applied. Accordingly the authorities issued a re-assessment notice on P requiring the paying of the additional VAT P brought proceedings against the customs authorities' decision. P argued that the various things it did to repair tattered books resulted in the manufacture of a new book and that it should be regarded as supplying books. The Hoge Raad asked the European Court under Art. 177 EEC for a preliminary ruling on the interpretation of Art. 5 of Council Directive 67/228 on the harmonisation of legislation of EEC States concerning turnover taxes (the 2nd VAT Directive) and Art. 5 of Council Directive 77/388 on the harmonisation of the laws of the EEC States relating to turnover taxes (the 6th VAT Directive). *Held,* that the production of goods from customers' materials, as referred to in Art. 5 of the 2nd VAT Directive, only occurred where a contractor produced a new product from the materials supplied to him by his customer. A new product was produced when the contractor's work resulted in a product whose function was generally regarded as different from that of the materials provided. Thus, the references in Art. 5 of the 2nd VAT Directive and Art. 5 of the 6th VAT Directive to "supply of goods" by goods made from customers' own materials only applied to the making of new goods and not to the repair of old goods. It followed that the repair of old books amounted to the provision of a service.

VAN DIJK BOEKHUIS B.V. *v.* STAATSSECRETARIS VAN FINANCIEN (No. 139/84) [1986] 2 C.M.L.R. 575, European Ct.

1485. VAT—imports—privately owned goods

Ms. Bergeres-Becque, a Belgian national, living in France, imported a car which had been a gift to her, from Belgium. She appealed against the calculation of VAT on importation because the French customs authorities had charged the rate applying in France, on the value of the car assessed according to a used rating normally applied in France. The Tribunal d'Instance asked the European Court for a preliminary ruling under Art. 177 EEC on the interpretation of Art. 95 EEC. *Held,* that (1) when applying Art. 95 EEC to the levying of VAT on imports of goods by a private person, no distinction is to be made according to whether or not the transaction giving rise to the importation was effected for consideration; (2) where an EEC State levies VAT on the importation from another EEC State of goods supplied by a private person, the taxable amount does not include the amount of VAT paid in the exporting EEC State which is still contained in the value of the goods when they are imported; that value is to be assessed on the basis of the relevant data in the exporting EEC State; (3) the amount of VAT paid in the exporting EEC State which is still contained in the value of the goods when they are imported is equal: (i) in cases in which the value of the goods has diminished between the date on which VAT was last charged in the exporting EEC State and the date of importation, to the amount of VAT paid in the exporting EEC State, less a percentage representing the proportion by which the goods have depreciated; (ii) in cases in which the value of the goods has appreciated over the same period, to the full amount of VAT paid in the exporting EEC State.

BERGERES-BECQUE v. HEAD OF THE INTER-REGIONAL CUSTOMS SERVICE (No. 39/85) [1986] 2 C.M.L.R. 143, European Ct.

1486. VAT—6th VAT Directive—business activity

The appellant was registered for VAT as a consultant. He acquired and restored various ex-naval patrol boats. He claimed that certain costs in connection therewith should be treated as input tax and therefore VAT deductible. The Commissioners of Customs and Excise refused to allow such deductions as they said that he has failed to show that such costs were in respect of "any business carried on or to be carried on by him". *Held,* that (1) the 6th VAT Directive was binding on the U.K. legislature, who had now incorporated it in the Value Added Tax Act 1983. Since the provisions of the latter Act reflected the intent of the 6th VAT Directive, there was no need to rely any further on the Directive as the Statute superseded it; (2) the appellant's activity constituted a business activity carried on by him or to be carried on by him under s.14(3) of the Value Added Tax Act 1983. Therefore, the costs were deductible as VAT inputs.

HAYDON-BAILLIE (W.G.) v. H.M. CUSTOMS & EXCISE [1986] 3 C.M.L.R. 74, V.A.T Tribunal, London.

1487. VAT—6th VAT Directive—direct effect

The VAT Tribunal considered the basis for deducting input tax in the case of a charity, which ran the Whitechapel Art Gallery but made no admission charge, and which also ran ancillary activities of a profit-earning kind, the inputs in question not being clearly attributable to one rather than the other. *Held,* that the relevant parts of Art. 17 and Art. 19 of the 6th VAT, namely para. 2(a) to (c) and para. 5(a) to (e) of Art. 17 and para. 1 of Art. 19 were permissive and did not have direct effect. An apportionment would be made pursuant to s.14(4) VAT Act 1983 in relation to goods and services so that only part of the tax referring to supplies used or to be used for the purposes of a business carried on by the charity could be regarded as input tax.

WHITECHAPEL ART GALLERY v. COMMISSIONERS OF CUSTOMS AND EXCISE [1986] 1 C.M.L.R. 79, VAT Tribunal, London.

1488. VAT—6th VAT Directive—discrimination

The Eastern Division of the Danish High Court referred to the European Court for a preliminary ruling under Art. 177 EEC several questions on the interpretation of Art. 95 EEC and of the 6th Council Directive 77/388 ("the 6th VAT Directive") in order to enable it to decide whether Danish legislation on VAT was compatible with those provisions. *Held,* that (1) the 6th VAT Directive does not prevent an EEC State from applying to imports different accounting periods and payment periods from those for internal transactions; (2) differences between the national time limits allowed for the payment of VAT on imports and those allowed for the payment of VAT on domestic transactions may, in certain circumstances, infringe Art. 95 EEC. However, tax periods which serve as a basis for calculating the net tax position of each taxable person under the internal system need not be taken into consideration in the comparison of the periods for payment. Therefore, there is nothing in the national legislation described by the national court which constitutes discrimination contrary to Art. 95 EEC.

DANSK DENKAVIT ApS v. MINISTERIET FOR SKATTER og AFGIFTER (No. 42/83) [1985] 3 C.M.L.R. 729, European Ct.

1489. VAT—6th VAT Directive—exemption from double imposition of VAT

Mr. Profant, a Luxembourgeois, studied in Belgium, from 1976 to 1981. He remained registered at his mother's address in Luxembourg during this period and returned to that address regularly. Between 1976 and 1981 he purchased two cars in Luxembourg where VAT was paid and where they were registered. In 1978 he married a French national in Luxembourg. From 1978 he and his wife lived in Belgium. In 1981 they went to live in Luxembourg. In 1980 the Belgian tax authorities informed Mr. Profant that he was deemed to be normally resident in Belgium since his marriage and that he was obliged to pay VAT on the importation of his two cars. Belgian tax authorities generally granted Luxembourg students who were normally resident in Luxembourg and who studied in Belgium the benefit of the exemption from VAT for cars registered in Luxembourg. However, that benefit was not granted to married students who were deemed to have their normal residence in Belgium. Having refused to pay the VAT on the cars, criminal proceedings were brought against Profant. The Cour d'Appel, Brussels, asked the European Court under Art. 177 EEC for a preliminary ruling. *Held,* that (1) VAT levied by one EEC State on a car imported from another EEC State was not a customs duty or a charge having equivalent effect to such a duty within the meaning of Arts. 12 and 13 EEC; (2) the rules of EEC law, and, in particular, those established by the sixth VAT Directive prevented an EEC State from levying VAT on the import of a car bought in another EEC State in which VAT was paid, and where the car was registered, where that car was used by a national of the second EEC State who had a residence in that State, but who was a student in the first EEC State where, for the duration of those studies he was registered as a foreigner. In that respect it was irrelevant whether or not the person in question was married; (3) when tax authorities of an EEC State applied their national legislation relating to exemption from VAT of cars used by students from another EEC State, they were obliged to apply the concept of temporary importation in such a way as to avoid restricting, by double taxation of the cars, the freedom of EEC nationals to study in the EEC States of their choice.

MINISTÈRE PUBLIQUE AND MINISTÈRE DES FINANCES *v.* PROFANT (No. 249/84) [1986] 2 C.M.L.R. 378, European Ct.

1490. VAT—6th VAT Directive—imports—private goods

Gaston Schul Douane—Expediteur BV ("Schul") imported into Netherlands a second-hand boat on behalf of a private person resident in the Netherlands who had bought it in France from another private person. The boat had been built in Monaco and had been imported into France. VAT had been paid on its importation into France. Dutch tax authorities charged VAT on that importation at the rate of 18 per cent. on the sale price, which was the normal rate applied within the Netherlands on the sale of goods for valuable consideration. Schul challenged the VAT assessment on the basis, *inter alia*, that VAT would not have been charged on a similar transaction effected between private persons in the Netherlands. The Supreme Court of the Netherlands asked the European Court for a preliminary ruling under Art. 177 EEC on the interpretation of Art. 95 EEC and the 6th VAT Directive. *Held*, that (1) where an EEC State charges VAT on the importation, from another EEC State, of goods sold by a private person, but does not charge VAT on sales of similar goods by private persons within its own State, the VAT payable on importation must be assessed by taking into account the amount of VAT paid in the EEC State of exportation that is still contained in the value of the goods at the time of importation in such a manner that that amount is not included in the taxable amount and is in addition deducted from the VAT payable on importation; (2) the amount of VAT paid in the EEC State of exportation that is still contained in the value of the goods at the time of importation is equal: (a) in instances where the value of the goods has gone down between the date on which VAT was last charged in the EEC State of exportation and the date of importation: to the amount of VAT actually paid in the EEC State of exportation, minus a percentage representing the proportion by which the goods have depreciated; (b) in instances where the value of the goods has gone up over the same period: to the full amount of the VAT actually paid in the EEC State of exportation.

STAATSSECRETARIS VAN FINANCIËN *v.* GASTON SCHUL DOUANE-EXPEDITEUR BV (No. 47/84) [1986] 1 C.M.L.R. 559, European Ct.

1491. VAT—6th VAT Directive—imports—private goods

The European Commission issued a Notice on the Gaston Schul Cases (Nos. 15/81 and 47/84) relating to the importation by a private person of used goods purchased in another EEC State from another private person. The Commission set out its views and policy in the light of the European Court's decision in those cases.

VAT ON IMPORTS OF PRIVATE PROPERTY [1986] 1 C.M.L.R. 555, European Commission's Practice Note.

1492. VAT—6th VAT Directive—land and fishing rights

The owner of a hotel and of fishing rights in Plas Madoc Water, which were treated as business assets of the hotel, sold the hotel to one buyer and the fishing rights to another buyer, accounting for VAT on both transactions. *Held*, that the 6th VAT Directive had direct effect in the U.K. and prevailed over the Value Added Tax Act 1983, where there were any differences between them. Under Art. 13B of the 6th VAT Directive the transfer of an estate in land, including the bed of a river, to which the fishing rights were appurtenant, was exempt from VAT Thus, no VAT was chargeable.

PARKINSON *v*. CUSTOMS & EXCISE COMMISSIONER [1986] 3 C.M.L.R. 1, Value Added Tax Tribunal, London.

1493. VAT—6th VAT Directive—part-exchanged goods
The European Commission brought proceedings against the Netherlands under Art. 169 EEC for failing to bring into effect measures required for its compliance with Art. 11 of the Sixth Council Directive on VAT ("6th VAT Directive"). The European Commission brought proceedings against Ireland under Art. 169 EEC for a declaration that, by continuing to apply s.10(2) of the VAT Act 1972, Ireland had failed to fulfil its obligations under Art. 11 of the 6th VAT Directive. Dutch and Irish provisions provided that in cases of part-exchange the taxable amount for new goods was to be arrived at after deducting the value of second hand goods taken in part exchange. The Commission alleged that such provisions were contrary to Art. 11 of the 6th VAT Directive. Netherlands and Ireland argued that such provisions amounted to special systems applicable to used goods and were permissible under Art. 32 of the 6th VAT Directive. *Held*, Commission's applications dismissed. The Dutch and Irish provisions at issue were covered, both as regards their objects and effects, by Art. 32 of the 6th VAT Directive and did not infringe Art. 11 of the Directive.

VAT ON PART-EXCHANGED GOODS, *Re*; E.C. COMMISSION *v*. THE NETHERLANDS & IRELAND (Nos. 16/84 & 17/84) [1986] 1 C.M.L.R. 336, European Ct.

1494. VAT—6th VAT Directive—postal services—exemptions
German legislation exempted from VAT the transportation of mail by the German Federal Railways, the German airline Lufthansa and by certain private railway companies under contracts made with the German Post Office. The European Commission considered that these German exemptions went wider than the exemptions permissible under Art. 13 of the 6th Council Directive 77/388/EEC of May 18, 1977 (the "6th Directive"). Accordingly, the Commission brought proceedings under Art. 169 EEC against Germany. *Held*, that by exempting from VAT the services provided by transport undertakings for the German Post Office, Germany had failed to fulfil its obligations under the EEC Treaty and under the 6th Directive.

VAT ON POSTAL TRANSPORT, *Re*; E.C. COMMISSION *v*. GERMANY (No. 107/84) [1986] 2 C.M.L.R. 177, European Ct.

1495. VAT—6th VAT Directive—shipping—exemption
The plaintiff, a German firm, installed and operated gaming machines on board German ferry boats which travelled between Germany and Denmark. The plaintiff's employees would attend the ferries from time to time in order to maintain, repair and replace the machines. A dispute arose as to what proportion of the machines' turnover was liable to the imposition of VAT by the German tax authorities. The Finanzgericht, Hamburg, asked the European Court under Art. 177 EEC for a preliminary ruling on the interpretation of Art. 9(1) and Art. 15, No. 8 of the 6th Council Directive 77/388 (the 6th VAT Directive). *Held*, that (1) Art. 9(1) of the 6th VAT Directive had to be interpreted as meaning that facilities for conducting a business such as the operation of gambling machines on board a ship sailing on the high seas outside the territory of the EEC State may be viewed as a fixed establishment within the meaning of Art. 9(1) only if the establishment requires a permanent combination of human and technical resources necessary for the provision of those services in question and if it is impractical to connect the services with the place where the supplier has established his business; (2) the exemption provided for in Art. 15, No. 8 of the 6th VAT Directive does not cover the operation of gaming machines on board the sea-going ships referred to in that Article.

GUNTER BERKHOLZ *v*. FINANZAMT HAMBURG-MITTE-ALTSTADT (No. 168/84) [1985] 3 C.M.L.R. 667, European Ct.

1496. VAT—6th VAT Directive—voyage through international waters
The plaintiff, Trans Tirreno Express SpA, transports passengers and goods by sea from Livorno, Italy, to Olbia, Sardinia. The provincial VAT Office, Sassari, claimed

VAT from the plaintiff for such transport for the whole of the crossing. The plaintiff argued that it should not have to pay tax for the part of the voyage which crosses international waters. The Commissione Tributaria di Secondo Grado, Sassari, asked the European Court under Art. 177 EEC for a preliminary ruling on Art. 9(2)(*b*) of the 6th Council Directive 77/388/EEC of May 17, 1977 (the "6th Directive"). *Held,* that Art. 9(2)(*b*) of the 6th Directive does not preclude an EEC State from applying its VAT legislation to transport between two places within its national territory, even where part of the voyage occurs outside its territorial limits, provided that it does not encroach on the tax jurisdiction of other States.

TRANS TIRRENO EXPRESS SpA *v.* PROVINCIAL VAT OFFICE, SASSARI (No. 283/84) [1986] 2 C.M.L.R. 100, European Ct.

1497. VAT—sparkling wines—discrimination

The European Commission brought proceedings against Italy under Art. 169 EEC for a declaration that Italy was in breach of Art. 95 EEC by applying to sparkling wines imported from other EEC States a rate of VAT higher than that applicable to sparkling wines produced in Italy. *Held,* that the definition given by Italian legislation of the class of sparkling wines subject to the highest rate of VAT had been framed in such a way as to cover only imported wines and to protect comparable national wines by subjecting them to significantly lower rates of VAT. Hence, the classification was contrary to Art. 95 EEC and Italy had violated its obligations thereunder.

ITALIAN VAT ON SPARKLING WINES, *Re*; E.C. COMMISSION (France intervening) *v.* ITALY (No. 278/83) [1985] 3 C.M.L.R. 688, European Ct.

1498. VAT—taxable supplies—business activities

Mr. Steele carried on a precious metals business under the name "Atlas Marketing" as well as pursuing his career as a professional racing driver. Atlas Marketing appealed against an assessment of VAT *Held,* that Mr. Steele's motor racing activities were not carried on as a hobby, but amounted to a business activity whose financial transactions were subject to VAT as inputs or outputs. The Commissioners of Customs and Excise's statement of the criterion of business activity, namely whether or not receipts from sponsorships for the sport exceeded the costs and expenses incurred, was not correct in law (*Rompelman* v. *Minister van Financiën* [1985] C.L.Y. 1499 followed).

ATLAS MARKETING *v.* COMMISSIONERS OF CUSTOMS AND EXCISE [1986] 1 C.M.L.R. 71, VAT Tribunal, London.

EVIDENCE

1499. Admissibility—oppression—reasonable doubt

G, a girl of 20 and of previous good character, was arrested by the police on suspicion of her involvement in an armed robbery at a trustee savings bank. No caution was given by the arresting officer. She was kept in custody for 37 hours during which time she was interviewed eight times. In between each interview she was kept in a detention room. No caution was given before any of the first seven interviews. G was throughout in a distressed condition. She was not allowed to see her mother nor anybody independent. The eighth interview began at 8.40 p.m. and ended at 12.20 a.m. During this interview certain admissions were allegedly made by G. The police alleged that she was cautioned at the beginning of the last interview. It was submitted that the final interview should be excluded as being inadmissible on the grounds that it had not been made voluntarily by reason of oppression. *Held,* that evidence of the eighth interview was inadmissible. Before evidence could be admissible, it had to be established beyond reasonable doubt that the answers were made voluntarily, namely not under oppression. The test to be applied was to put oneself in the position of the defendant. Having regard to (1) the defendant's characteristics and (2) the fact that she was not allowed to see her mother, and to the number of interviews, the period of time and to her being shut in a detention room, then by the time of the final interview, G's free will had been sapped. It could not be said beyond reasonable doubt that there was not oppression looked at subjectively: R. v. GARDNER, May 1, 1986; Lymbery J. [*Ex rel. R. Paradysz, Barrister.*]

1500. Admissibility—truth test

As a matter of principle evidence produced by the administration of some mechanical, chemical or hypnotic truth test is not admissible in evidence: FENNELL *v.* JEROME PROPERTY MAINTENANCE, *The Times,* November 26, 1986, Tucker J.

1501. Bankers books—bank in U.S.A.—account of foreign customer—ex parte order and subpoena requiring bank to produce books—sovereignty of U.S.A.

An order under the Bankers' Books Evidence Act 1879 directed to a foreign bank requiring it to permit inspection and the taking of copies of entries in its books relating to the account of a foreign customer should not be made save in very exceptional circumstances and should not be made *ex parte* without notice being given to the bank.

P brought an action against a number of defendants including a Bahamian company alleging fraud. When P sought to serve the writ it was discovered that the company no longer existed, having been struck off the Bahamian companies register at the instigation of its directors. In consequence P could not obtain discovery from the company in connection with its bank account. The company banked with Citibank in New York. Six months later, in September 1985 and two months before the trial, P applied *ex parte* for an order under s.7 of the Bankers' Books Evidence Act 1879 requiring Citibank to permit P to inspect and take copies of entries in its books for the account of the company. Two days later P caused subpoenas to be issued to Citibank requiring it to attend the trial and produce its records relating to the company's account. The order and subpoenas were directed to Citibank's London office. Citibank applied by motion to discharge the order and set aside the subpoenas on the grounds that they exceeded the international jurisdiction of the court and infringed the sovereignty of the U.S.A. *Held*, that the order and subpoenas were directed to a bank that was not a party to the action in respect of an account, documents and transactions that took place in the U.S.A. As the order and subpoenas were to take effect in New York there was an infringement of the sovereignty of the U.S.A. notwithstanding the fact that Citibank had a London office over which the court had jurisdiction. Such an order and subpoenas should not be made save in very exceptional circumstances. There were no exceptional circumstances in the present case. P could have obtained the necessary information by applying for the issue of letters of request to the courts of New York pursuant to R.S.C., Ord. 39 or, with the leave of the court, applying directly to the courts of New York under the provisions of the legislation enforceable in those courts. Either course of action would not involve the infringement of the sovereignty of the U.S.A. It appeared there was still sufficient time for P to apply directly to the New York courts before the trial started. The fact that the information was obtainable from the company by way of discovery in the action had the company continued to exist did not assist P. Orders concerning documents outside the jurisdiction should ordinarily be made on notice to the bank concerned. The order and subpoenas were discharged. (*R.* v. *Grossman* [1981] C.L.Y. 2306 applied, *British South Africa Co.* v. *De Beers Consolidated Mines* [1910] 2 Ch. 502, *Acrow Automation* v. *Rex Chainbelt Inc.* [1971] C.L.Y. 9259, *Norwich Pharmacal Co.* v. *Customs and Excise Commissioners* [1973] C.L.Y. 2643, *Bankers Trust Co.* v. *Shapira* [1980] C.L.Y. 2136, *X A.G.* v. *A Bank* [1983] C.L.Y. 365 considered).

MacKinnon *v.* Donaldson, Lufkin and Jenrette Securities Corp. [1986] 2 W.L.R. 453, Hoffmann J.

1502. Blood tests

Blood Tests (Evidence of Paternity) (Amendment) Regulations 1986 (No. 1357) [80p], made under the Family Law Reform Act 1969 (c.46), s.22; operative on September 1, 1986; increase the charges which may be made in respect of blood tests carried out for the purpose of determining paternity in civil proceedings.

1503. Committal proceedings—contempt of court—hearsay evidence

[R.S.C., Ord. 41, s.5(2).] Committal proceedings are not interlocutory, therefore hearsay evidence is not admissible on an application for committal (*Salter Rex & Co.* v. *Ghosh* [1971] C.L.Y. 9150, *White* v. *Brunton* [1984] C.L.Y. 2614, *Gilbert* v. *Endean* (1878) 9 Ch.D. 259, *Norwich Pharmacal Co.* v. *Commissioners of Customs and Excise* [1973] C.L.Y. 2643, *New Brunswick Electrical Power Commission, Re* [1976] 73 DLR (3d) 94, *Comet Products U.K.* v. *Hawkex Plastics* [1971] C.L.Y. 9083 considered): Savings & Investment Bank *v.* Gasco Investments (Netherlands) BV, (1986) 136 New L.J. 657, Scott J.

1504. Cross-examination—spent convictions—judge's discretion

[Rehabilitation of Offenders Act 1974 (c.53).] In civil proceedings, a person may not be cross-examined on convictions that are spent under the Rehabilitation of

Offenders Act 1974, unless the judge is satisfied that it is not possible for justice to be done without such cross-examination. Where the convictions are not spent, however, the judge has no power to exclude such cross-examination if the convictions are relevant to the issue of credibility: D. *v.* YATES, *The Times,* December 3, 1986, C.A.

1505. Disclosure—medical report received in prior action—whether use in subsequent action
In a previous action, P claimed damages for a personal injury. P's solicitors obtained a medical report which they disclosed to D's solicitors. In the present action (in respect of another injury) D wished to rely on the same report. The report was a disclosable document in the first action, though privileged until P elected to produce it as part of his evidence. D received the report in the first action subject to an obligation not to use it for any purpose outside that action and specifically not for the purpose of any subsequent action. *Held,* that D cannot use, as evidence in a subsequent action, a report made to the solicitors acting for the same plaintiff in a previous action against the same defendants unless P hereafter waives the legal professional privilege which attaches to it (*Harman* v. *Home Office* [1983] 1 A.C. 280 and *Riddick* v. *Thames Board Mills* [1977] C.L.Y. 1368 applied; *Harmony Shipping Co.* v. *Davis* [1981] C.L.Y. 2487 considered): DINHAM *v.* BRITISH STEEL CORP., March 26, 1986; Evans J., Cardiff. [*Ex. rel. Dolmans, Solicitors.*]

1506. Expert evidence—disclosure—where expert is a party
The rules concerning advance disclosure of expert evidence apply equally where the expert is a party to the proceedings.
Shell sued engineers for negligence in the construction of offices. Shell disclosed their experts' report. The engineers did not, asserting that they were entitled to give evidence on their own behalf without advance disclosure. *Held,* that the rules in R.S.C., Ord. 38 referred to "expert evidence" not evidence given by independent experts, and they applied equally to "in-house" experts, and to the parties themselves (*Buckley* v. *Rice Thomas* (1554) 1 Plowd. 118 applied; *Folker* v. *Chadd* (1783) 3 Doug. K.B. 157 considered).
SHELL PENSIONS TRUST *v.* PELL FRISCHMANN & PARTNERS (A FIRM) [1986] 2 All E.R. 911, His Honour Judge Newey Q.C.

1507. Foreign tribunal—videotaped examination of witnesses—considerations
R.S.C., Ord 70; Evidence (Proceedings in Other Jurisdictions) Act 1975 (c.34).]
[Examinations in England under R.S.C, Ord. 70 for the purpose of obtaining evidence for foreign courts should follow the procedural norms for proceedings in England, but, the court will permit the admission of videotaped examinations of witnesses under certain considerations.
P started an action in a court in the United States against DS in pursuit of insurance claims. DS included underwriters in London, from whom P wished to take evidence by deposition. Some of them were unwilling to give evidence on a videotape. P obtained letters of request from the United States court addressed to the English court and applied under R.S.C., Ord. 70, r. 4 and the Evidence (Proceedings in Other Jurisdictions) Act 1975 for an order that the depositions be taken before an examiner and that the examination be videotaped. The judge in chambers granted the order sought *ex parte*, and four of DS sought to have the order discharged or varied. *Held,* that the depositions go ahead since the question whether they should do so had been fully argued in the United States court and the English court would not interfere with their request for depositions to be taken in England. Further, the order would not be varied to delete a reference to videotaping. Examinations under R.S.C., Ord. 70 should follow the procedural norms for proceedings in England. However, where the foreign court made a request as to the manner for taking depositions, the English court should, subject to the exercise of judicial discretion in any particular case, normally employ that method unless it was totally contrary to established English procedures. Since proceedings for taking evidence outside court were not limited to the permitted method of recording proceedings in court, and since video recordings were admissible in English courts it could not be said that the use of video recordings was necessarily inconsistent with English procedure. The value and convenience of such recordings was not outweighed by any stress that might be caused to DS (dictum of Cockburn C.J. in *Desilla* v. *Fells & Co.* (1879) 40 L.T. at 424 applied).
BARBER (J.) & SONS (A FIRM) *v.* LLOYD'S UNDERWRITERS [1986] 2 All E.R. 845, Evans J.

1508. Foreign proceedings
     EVIDENCE (PROCEEDINGS IN OTHER JURISDICTIONS) (ANGUILLA) ORDER 1986 (No.
218) [£1·35], made under the Evidence (Proceedings in Other Jurisdictions) Act 1975
(c.34), s.10(3); operative on April 1, 1986; extends the provisions of the 1975 Act to
Anguilla.

1509. Interview notes—inadmissibility
     [Civil Evidence Act 1968 (c.64), ss.2(1), 4(1).] In wardship proceedings between F,
the paternal grandparents and the maternal grandparents concerning the care and
control of a girl aged three years, the maternal grandparents applied for the notes of
an interview between a solicitor and M, who was later killed in a road accident
concerning contemplated divorce proceedings, to be admitted either under s.2(1)
(admissibility of out-of-court statements) or s.4 (admissibility of certain records) of
the 1968 Act. *Held,* refusing the application, that the notes could not be put in under
s.2(1) as a statement since they were the subjective notes of the solicitor and had not
been agreed or approved by the relevant person, namely, M. Equally, they were not
a record under s.4 since they constituted an *aide memoire,* being selective and
necessarily subjective, so fell short of being a total and complete record (*J.* v. *C.*
[1969] C.L.Y. 1082; *R.* v. *Tirado* [1974] C.L.Y. 662; *H.* v. *Schering (Chemicals)*
[1983] C.L.Y. 1671 and *Savings and Investment Bank* v. *Gasco Investments
(Netherlands) BV* [1984] C.L.Y. 1531 considered): D (A MINOR) (WARDSHIP:
EVIDENCE), *Re,* (1986) 16 Fam. Law 263; (1986) 2 F.L.R. 189, Wood J.

1510. Journalists sources—disclosure
     [Contempt of Court Act 1981 (c.49), s.10.] A journalist will only be required to
disclose his source if it was necessary in the technical sense in the administration of
justice (*Secretary of State for Defence* v. *Guardian Newspapers* [1984] C.L.Y. 2596
followed): MAXWELL *v.* PRESSDRAM, *The Times,* November 12, 1986, C.A.

1511. Letters of request—disputed tax assessment
     Evidence (Proceedings in other Jurisdictions) Act 1975 (c.34).) J, a wealthy
Norwegian shipowner, died in 1982. In September 1983, the Norwegian tax authorities
levied an additional assessment on J's estate in respect, *inter alia,* of J's beneficial
interest in a trust consisting of shares in a Panamanian company, C.T.C. In
proceedings by the estate in Norway to have the assessment set aside, an application
was made under the 1975 Act requesting the examination of K and H, being persons
resident in England, and who had knowledge of C.T.C. matters, and for discovery of
documents in their possession. K and H both owed a duty of confidentiality to J.
Held, that (1) the proceedings in Norway were "civil proceedings" within the
meaning of the 1975 Act; (2) compliance with the letter of request would not be
contrary to public policy, even though it concerned a foreign resident's tax liability;
(3) the request was not prejudicial to U.K. sovereignty; (4) the Court had a
discretion to comply with the request once it was shown that its primary purpose was
bona fide for use in civil proceedings; (5) the Court would not allow the 1975 Act to
be used as a vehicle for a "fishing expedition" and the terms of the request were
too wide; (6) the balance was against K and H being ordered to break their duty of
confidentiality Appeal allowed in part: JAHRE (ANDERS), *Re* [1986] 1 Lloyd's Rep.
496, C.A.

**1512. Letters rogatory—whether "civil or commercial matter"—terms of letter—whether
"fishing expedition"**
     [Evidence (Proceedings in Other Jurisdictions) Act 1975 (c.34), ss.1, 2, 9(1).]
     The question of whether proceedings in a foreign court are proceedings in a civil
or commercial matter for the purposes of s.9(1) of the Evidence (Proceedings in
Other Jurisdictions) Act 1975 is to be determined having regard to the classification
of the proceedings in the law of the country in question and the classification of the
proceedings in English law.
     In September 1983 the Vestfold County Tax Committee in Norway raised a
retrospective supplementary tax assessment for the years 1972 to 1982 against the
estate of Anders Jahre, a wealthy Norwegian shipowner who died in 1982, in the
sum of 338 million kroner. The assessment was made because the Tax Committee
formed the view that Jahre had evaded tax by concealing a large part of his assets

behind the cloak of a Panamanian company called Continental Trust Co. Inc. (CTC). The ownership of that company passed to a trust or foundation. The Tax Committee believed Jahre to be the person controlling the foundation directly or indirectly and thus liable to tax. The estate commenced proceedings in the Sandefjord City Court to set aside the assessment. Later the estate also appealed to the National Tax Committee against the assessment. In the course of the proceedings, at the request of the State and the estate, the Sandefjord court sent a letter rogatory to "the competent court in Britain" requesting that H and K be ordered to appear before the English court to be orally examined on oath as witnesses in the Norwegian proceedings. H was a senior employee of Lazard Brothers & Co. ("Lazards") and was appointed assistant secretary to CTC and treasurer in 1978. He retired from CTC in 1984. K was a director of Lazards and acted as an adviser to the foundation that owned CTC. Lazards were the foundation's bankers. The questions sought to be put to H and K were directed to ascertain the identities of those who owned or controlled CTC and the foundation, whether Anders Jahre had any dealings with either of them, the extent and nature of assets held by CTC and the foundation, and the nature and location of the accounts and other records kept in relation to their activities. H and K objected to having to appear and give evidence on the following grounds: (1) the proceedings in Norway were not proceedings in a civil or commercial matter within the meaning of s.9(1) of the Evidence (Proceedings in Other Jurisdictions) Act 1975; (2) compliance with the letter rogatory meant assisting a foreign State in gathering tax from one of its own subjects contrary to public policy as applied by English law; (3) the terms of the letter rogatory were so wide as to amount to a fishing expedition and did not constitute a proper or acceptable request for evidence under the Act; (4) to answer any questions would amount to a breach of the duty of confidence owed by H and K to the foundation and CTC. Notwithstanding their objections the Master made an order for H and K to appear for examination as witnesses. Their appeal to the judge in chambers succeeded to the extent that the ambit of the questions to be put was limited. _Held_, allowing H and K's appeal, that (1) in deciding whether proceedings were proceedings in a civil or commercial matter within the meaning of s.9(1) of the Act the court should have regard to the classification of the proceedings under the law applicable in both the requesting court and the addressed court. The court would satisfy itself that the proceedings concerned a civil or commercial matter under the law of the requesting court but would only accept such a categorisation provided it did not conflict with established principles applied in the court addressed. That test was satisfied in the present case, given that the letter rogatory described the Norwegian proceedings as a civil case and the evidence that the proceedings were civil for the purposes of the administration of justice in Norway. The proceedings were clearly "civil" proceedings within the English classification of proceedings; (2) it was doubtful whether the court was debarred from considering the request for evidence as a matter of public policy on the ground that it was a proceeding for the enforcement of the revenue law of a foreign State. As a matter of policy the court would not be disposed to comply with the letter rogatory if the estate, as the taxpayer, objected. As jurisdiction to deal with the request was established under the Act it could not be contrary to public policy to accede to a request for evidence being made jointly by the State and the tax payer; (3) a request for evidence which was in effect a roving inquiry designed to obtain information that might lead to obtaining evidence in general support of a party's case as opposed to evidence proving properly particularised allegations of fact amounted to a fishing expedition. The terms of the request made by the Norwegian court were so wide as to amount to a fishing expedition. Whilst the court was obliged to strive to give effect to the letter of request, if necessary by substantial amendment, it was not obliged to redraft the request in different terms. It was not possible to amend the request in such a way as to make it acceptable to the court; (4) the court was required to carry out a balancing exercise between the desirable policy of assisting foreign courts in their proceedings and the desirability of upholding the duty of confidence in relationships in which it is clearly entitled to recognition and respect. In balancing those conflicting demands all the circumstances of the case were relevant. In the present case the balance was against compelling a breach of H and K's duty of confidence, having regard to the width of the letter of request, the international importance attached to banks maintaining their clients' confidence and the fact that the case was essentially a tax dispute. In addition if such an order were made it was unlikely to meet with any international reciprocity whatsoever (*Tournier v. National Provincial and Union Bank of England* [1924] 1 K.B. 461; *Government of India* v. *Taylor* [1955] C.L.Y. 377; *Radio Corp. of America* v. *Rauland Corp.* [1956] C.L.Y. 6731; *Westinghouse Electric Corp. Uranium Contract Litigation M.D.L. Docket No. 325 (No. 2), Re* [1978] C.L.Y. 1422; *Bankers Trust Co.* v. *Shapira* [1980] C.L.Y. 2136; *British Steel Corp.* v. *Granada Television* [1980] C.L.Y. 2132; *State of the Netherlands* v. *Rüffer* [1981] C.L.Y. 1037; *Williams and Humbert* v. *W. & H. Trade Marks (Jersey)* [1986] C.L.Y. 363; *Gemeente Hillegom* v. *Hillenius* [1986] C.L.Y. 1351 considered).

STATE OF NORWAY'S APPLICATION, *Re* [1986] 3 W.L.R. 452, C.A.

1513. Parol evidence rule—counsel's opinion—whether admissible in construing a deed

A written opinion prepared by counsel is not admissible as evidence for the purposes of construing a deed of settlement drafted by counsel where the wording of the deed is not in dispute.

Gerson Berger Association was an association founded by Gerson Berger and his son Sighismond for the advancement of Jewish education. Sighismond and Gerson Berger's other children wished to assist the funding of the Association. The children each entered into a charitable trust deed on April 1, 1968 declaring that certain income and property to which they were entitled as beneficiaries under a trust should be held upon such public charitable trusts as might be appointed within three months and subject thereto upon the charitable trusts of the Association. The deed was drafted by counsel who prior thereto gave two written opinions clearly showing that it was intended that the Association should hold the property and income as a trustee and deal with it in accordance with the charitable trusts of the Association and not that the Association should be absolutely entitled to it. Later a dispute arose between Sighismond and the other children as to whether or not the property and income was given absolutely to the Association. The wording of the deed was not disputed. P sought to adduce evidence in the form of counsel's opinions on the construction of the deed. Harman J. ruled the evidence to be inadmissible. P appealed. *Held,* dismissing the appeal, that the opinions constituted parol evidence of the intention of the children in executing the deed. The court was concerned to construe the words of the deed and not make findings about the intention of the children. The opinions could not be admitted generally on account of the rule against parol evidence in construing the terms of executed deeds. The opinions could not be admitted for the limited purpose of showing that the children were aware that an outright gift was disadvantageous from a taxation point of view, that they knew that the Association could take a gift absolutely, and that they were aware of the difference between making the Association a trustee and making an absolute gift to it under the rule permitting evidence to be adduced of the circumstances surrounding the execution of the deed. Evidence could be adduced to put the court in the same factual position as the persons executing the deed. In the present case P was seeking to adduce evidence as to the legal knowledge and intention of the person who drafted the deed. The evidence went to the aims and intentions of the children and not circumstances of objective fact surrounding the execution of the deed. There was no factual ambiguity in the wording of the deed so as to justify the admission of the evidence (*River Wear Commissioners* v. *Adamson* (1877) 2 App.Cas. 743, *Shore* v. *Wilson* (1842) 9 Cl. & F. 355 applied; *Atkinson's Will Trusts, Re; Atkinson* v. *Hall* [1978] C.L.Y. 3079 followed, *Prenn* v. *Simmonds* [1971] C.L.Y. 1711, *Reardon Smith Line* v. *Hansen-Tangen; Hansen-Tangen* v. *Sanko Steamship Co.* [1976] C.L.Y. 2582 considered; *Ofner, Re; Samuel* v. *Ofner* [1909] 1 Ch. 60 distinguished).

RABIN *v.* GERSON BERGER ASSOCIATION [1986] 1 All E.R. 374, C.A.

1514. Privilege—document—separate actions

In 1980 surveyors, who had been instructed by solicitors in contemplation of litigation, prepared a survey report on a vessel. That document was privileged in connection with that litigation. The vessel then suffered another casualty, and further separate litigation ensued. The plaintiffs in the later action sought discovery from the defendants of the survey report in the earlier action. D contended that their report was privileged. *Held,* allowing D's appeal, that the party claiming privilege in the subsequent action was the party entitled to privilege in the former action and was therefore entitled to assert such privilege in the second action: THE AEGIS BLAZE [1986] 1 Lloyd's Rep. 203, C.A.

1515. Privilege—legal professional privilege—communications between innocent assignee of fraudsman and solicitor

In this case the Court of Appeal held that where a fraudulent party communicated with his solicitor for the purpose of furthering a fraud or crime, such communication was outwith the normal scope of legal professional communications and would not be privileged. However, that principle does not to apply to the innocent communications between the assignee of a fraudsman and his solicitor: BANQUE KEYSER ULLMAN S.A. *v.* SKANDIA (U.K.) INSURANCE CO. [1986] 1 Lloyd's Rep. 336, C.A.

1516. Privilege—legal professional privilege—solicitor's attendance note—solicitor acting for purchaser and mortgagees—action between purchaser and mortgagees

Where legal professional privilege exists in connection with an attendance note prepared by a solicitor acting on behalf of P in the purchase of a property and on behalf of D in the mortgage of the property, P can restrain D by injunction from making any use of the note or information contained in it and compel its return to P from D.

In 1981 P purchased a house with the assistance of a mortgage from D. Prior to the purchase D's surveyor wrongly valued the house to the extent of £6,500 on account of his failing to properly appreciate the severity of certain defects in the structure of the house. G.E. and Co. acted on behalf of P in the purchase of the house and on behalf of D in connection with the mortgage of the house. In the course of the transaction G.E. & Co. prepared an attendance note of a conversation with P. P issued proceedings against D seeking to recover damages for the surveyor's negligence. Thereafter G.E. & Co., with knowledge of the proceedings, sent the attendance note to D. The substance of the note was pleaded in D's defence. P applied to strike out those parts of D's defence relating to the attendance note and sought an injunction to restrain D from using or relying in any manner on the note and require D to deliver up the note and any copies of it. The application was dismissed by the judge in chambers. *Held,* allowing P's appeal, that legal professional privilege attached to the attendance note and that privilege belonged exclusively to P. P was entitled to an injunction to restrain D from disclosing or making any use of the information contained in the note and entitled to delivery up of the note. D would be entitled to adduce the note in evidence or give secondary evidence of its contents at the trial of the action only if by that time P had made no application to restrain D from doing so, notwithstanding that legal professional privilege attached to it. It was crucial that a party who sought to avail himself of the protection of legal professional privilege vested in him must seek that protection before the other party had adduced the confidential communication in evidence or otherwise relied upon it at trial. Once a party's entitlement to that protection is established there is no discretion in the court to refuse relief outside the general principles applicable to discretionary relief by way of injunction, *e.g.* inordinate delay. The right of a party to such protection was not dependant in any way upon the conduct of the party against whom the protection was sought (*Lord Ashburton* v. *Pape* [1913] 2 Ch. 469 applied, *Calcraft* v. *Guest* [1898] 1 Q.B. 759, *Butler* v. *Board of Trade* [1970] C.L.Y. 1039 considered).

GODDARD *v.* NATIONWIDE BUILDING SOCIETY [1986] 3 W.L.R. 734, C.A.

1517. Privilege—without prejudice correspondence—claim for statutory compensation

"Without prejudice" privilege is not limited only to offers of compromise but extends to all documents so marked forming part of negotiations with a view to compromising a claim to be made by one party against the other whether or not proceedings between the parties had commenced.

The Council made a discontinuance order under the Town and Country Planning Act 1971, s.51 in respect of business use of certain premises by A. In consequence A became entitled to compensation under s.170 of the Act. A put forward an unquantified claim for compensation stating that he wished the amount of compensation to be negotiated with his agent. By a letter not marked "without prejudice" A's agents intimated their intention to submit a detailed claim at a subsequent meeting. At the meeting, document X was produced. It was a detailed submission of A's claim and marked "without prejudice." After correspondence, document A was superseded by an amended claim called document Y. Document Y was marked "without prejudice" as was the letter that accompanied it. The parties could not agree the proper amount of compensation and the matter was referred to

the Lands Tribunal for determination. The Council contended that documents X and Y were "open" claims and admissible in evidence. Gatehouse J. agreed with the Council and ordered that the documents be admitted in evidence. *Held,* allowing A's appeal, that the fact that a document is marked "without prejudice" does not conclusively or automatically render the document privileged. Where a claim to privilege is challenged the court is entitled to look at the document in order to determine whether "without prejudice" privilege can attach to it. "Without prejudice" privilege is not limited to documents which are offers but attaches to all documents so marked which form part of negotiations whether or not they are themselves offers. The privilege can attach to letters or documents seeking to initiate negotiations. Documents X and Y were clearly intended to be negotiating documents and were marked "without prejudice." Both documents were inadmissible (*Daintrey, Re, ex p. Holk* [1893] 2 Q.B. 116, *Cutts* v. *Head* [1984] C.L.Y. 2608 applied, *Norwich Union Life Insurance Society* v. *Waller Tony* [1984] C.L.Y. 1946 disapproved).
    SOUTH SHROPSHIRE DISTRICT COUNCIL *v.* AMOS [1986] 1 W.L.R. 1271, C.A.

1518. Security for costs—without prejudice negotiations
    [R.S.C., Ord. 23, r.1(1)(*a*).] On a summons for security of costs evidence of "without prejudice" negotiations is not admissible: SIMAAN GENERAL CONTRACTING CO. *v.* PILKINGTON GLASS (1986) 136 New L.J. 824, Judge John Newey Q.C.

1519. Witness summons—social worker—whether immunity
    [Adoption Agency Regulations 1983 (S.I. 1983 No. 1964), reg. 14(1).] There is no public interest immunity from giving evidence or producing documents which attaches to a social worker (*R.* v. *Greenwich Juvenile Court, ex p. Greenwich London Borough Council* [1978] C.L.Y. 1977, *D.* v. *N.S.P.C.C.* [1977] C.L.Y. 2324, *D. (Infants), Re* [1970] C.L.Y. 1359, *Gaskin* v. *Liverpool City Council* [1980] C.L.Y. 2139, *Campbell* v. *Tameside Metropolitan Borough Council* [1982] C.L.Y. 2467 considered): R. *v.* BOURNEMOUTH JUSTICES, *ex p.* GREY, *The Times,* May 31, 1986, Hodgson J.

EXECUTORS AND ADMINISTRATORS

1520. Probate
    NON-CONTENTIOUS PROBATE FEES (AMENDMENT) ORDER 1986 (No. 705) [45p], made under the Supreme Court Act 1981 (c.54), s.130; operative on May 30, 1986; introduces a distinction between fees on personal and postal applications for copies of documents.

EXTRADITION

1521. Arrest under warrant—delay in appearance before magistrate—abuse of process of court—photocopy of warrant admissible
    [Extradition Act 1870 (c.52), ss.10, 14, 15 and 26. Extradition Treaty between U.K. and Netherlands 1899.]
    Foreign warrants were issued for the arrest of the applicant, relating to offences said to have been committed by him in Holland. A provisional warrant was issued by the Bow Street Magistrates' Court. He was arrested and taken to Farnham Police Station, rather than Bow Street. At Farnham he was charged with firearms offences, pleaded guilty and was sentenced to eight weeks' imprisonment. On release he was re-arrested under the provisional warrant, taken to Bow Street and remanded in custody. The Secretary of State then signed Orders to Proceed. The applicant then re-appeared before the magistrate at Bow Street who heard for the first time of the applicant's earlier arrest. The magistrate found that the applicant had been held unlawfully since his re-arrest until the Secretary of State had acted but still ordered that the applicant be committed under s.10 of the Extradition Act. *Held,* refusing the application for judicial review, that the delay in bringing the applicant before the court was unjustifiable but could not be regarded as oppressive or inordinate. There was no bad faith or deliberate misconduct nor was there any deliberate manipulation of the court's procedure amounting to an abuse of the process of the court. Therefore, despite the serious irregularity, once the magistrate received orders to proceed from the Secretary of State he had no discretion to refuse committal if there was evidence to justify committal. The warrants produced by the Dutch authorities were adequate evidence. One was signed by the Prosecutor which meant that it was duly authenticated by an officer of the Netherlands. The second was an authenticated

photocopy of a warrant. The magistrate was entitled to regard the photocopy as sufficient compliance with s.15(1) of the Extradition Act 1870 (*R.* v. *Brentford Justices, ex p. Wong* [1981] C.L.Y. 1694, *R.* v. *Derby Crown Court, ex p. Brooks* [1985] C.L.Y. 2126, *R.* v. *Oxford City Justices, ex p. Smith* [1982] C.L.Y. 1979 considered, *R.* v. *Ganz* (1881) L.R. 9 Q.B.D. 93 applied.)

R. *v.* Bow Street Magistrates, *ex p.* Van der Holst (1986) 83 Cr.App.R. 114, D.C.

1522. Certification and authentication of evidence—whether affidavits sworn before competent authority

[Extradition Act 1870 (c.52), s.15(2).] Documents supporting a request by the U.S. Government for extradition of E were "certifications" under seal by a U.S. consul, the acting Secretary of State, the Attorney-General and the Director of the Office of International Affairs, U.S. Department of Justice. An affidavit of the Florida state attorney responsible for the relevant prosecutions deposing to affidavits of admitted accomplices of E was attached. *Held*, refusing a writ of *habeas corpus*, that in criminal matters in Florida a notary public accepts the oath of the maker of statement that the contents of a statement are true. The Florida state attorney was a competent authority for the purposes of extradition law. The accomplices' statements would be admissible as depositions or statements in Florida and could be regarded as depositions in extradition committal proceedings. Separate certification from a state official attesting to the power of a notary was not required for inter-state recognition of an affidavit. No formal incantation in the certification is necessary under s.15 of the 1870 Act. It was clear that the Florida state attorney had seen the original affidavits of the accomplices. The copies had been properly certified and were admissible: Espinosa, *Re* [1986] Crim.L.R. 684, D.C.

1523. Committal proceedings—identification from criminal records photographs—admissibility

[Extradition Act 1870 (33 & 34 Vict. c.52), s.10.]

Criminal records photographs of an accused are admissible at extradition committal proceedings to prove identity.

The French Government requested the extradition of the applicant, a Belgian, wanted for the attempted murder of two Germans on holiday in France. At committal proceedings evidence included signed statements by the victims and photographs from the Belgian Criminal Records Department by which the victims had identified their attacker. The applicant was committed to prison. *Held*, dismissing the application for habeas corpus, that the photographs were admissible as to proof of identity; they were not to be excluded in committal proceedings just because they tended to show the accused had a criminal record (*R.* v. *Dwyer and Ferguson* (1924) 18 Cr.App.R. 145; *R.* v. *Wainwright* (1925) 19 Cr.App.R. 52 distinguished).

R. *v.* Governor of Pentonville Prison, *ex p.* Voets [1986] 1 W.L.R. 470, D.C.

1524. Committal proceedings—sworn statements—taken in a foreign State—whether admissible evidence

[Extradition Act 1970 (c.52), ss.7, 10, 14; Federal Republic of Germany (Extradition) Order 1960 (S.I. 1960 No. 1375), Sched. 2, arts XI, XII: Federal Republic of Germany (Extradition) (Amendment) Order 1978 (S.I. 1978 No. 1403) art. 3.]

Sworn statements made in Bolivia were held to be admissible in extradition proceedings at the application of the West German Government requesting the extradition of a person who had allegedly held a West German national hostage in Bolivia.

Per curiam: (i) The weight to be given to such evidence is a matter for the magistrate. He would not be entitled to refuse to admit evidence obtained in a third State according to considerations such as the character of that State's regime, whether it is a friendly State, whether the U.K. has an extradition treaty with it, and the like; (ii) The purpose of article XII of the treaty is to prevent the government seeking extradition from causing a person to be held in custody for longer than two months while they seek to assemble sufficient evidence to justify extradition.

On March 3, 1984 a warrant was issued under s.8(2) of the Extradition Act 1970 by a magistrate at Bow Street for the arrest of the applicant who was suspected and accused of the "crime of detaining a hostage", a West German national at La Paz, Bolivia. He was arrested at Gatwick Airport the same day. On April 13, 1984 the

Home Secretary made an order under s.7 signifying that a requisition had been made by the West German Government for the surrender of the applicant for this crime. Statements and depositions were taken, many of them in Bolivia. The hearing took place on July 6, 1984, and a preliminary point was argued whether the Bolivian statements were properly to be received in evidence under article XI of the extradition treaty between the German Government and the U.K. Government. The magistrate ruled that they were admissible. Further untranslated documents later arrived, but a further hearing was adjourned. On July 25, 1984 the Secretary of State issued a further order to proceed under s.7 requiring the magistrate to issue his warrant for the same offence. No further requisition had been made by the German Government. On July 26, 1984 the magistrate terminated the part-heard proceedings and ordered the discharge of the applicant who was then re-arrested under the second warrant. The magistrate rejected a submission that the renewed proceedings were oppressive, vexatious, and an abuse of the process of the court. The applicant applied to judicially review the Secretary of State's order to proceed of July 25 and the magistrate's decision of July 26 to proceed, contending that the Bolivian statements were inadmissible in evidence, that the Secretary of State had no power to issue a second order, and that the proposed continuation of the proceedings was oppressive, vexatious, and an abuse of the court. The Divisional Court and the House of Lords on appeal dismissed the application. *Held,* that (1) the application of s.14 of the Extradition Act 1970 was not limited either by article XI of the extradition treaty or to proceedings for extradition under the agreement with West Germany without any saving by article 3 of the 1978 Order. There was no reason to construe the phrase in section 14 "in a foreign state" as impliedly restricting the depositions or statements that might be received in evidence to depositions or statements taken in the foreign State applying for the extradition. The Bolivian statements were admissible in evidence (*R. v. Governor of Brixton Prison* [1911] 2 K.B. 82 considered); (2) in extradition proceedings pursuant to s.10 of the Act of 1870 the magistrate was not concerned with the question whether the evidence produced by the requesting State would be available at the trial in the requesing State in admissible form according to the law of the requesting State; (3) s.7 of the Act of 1870 placed no express limitation on the number of orders to proceed that the Secretary of State might make pursuant to a requisition for the surrender of a fugitive and none could be inferred. He might make a further order whether or not the fugitive was already in custody and whether or not any further request had been received. Where a fugitive had been discharged from custody under an earlier order Article XII of the treaty did not prevent his re-arrest although the initiation of new proceedings might amount to an abuse of process (*R. v. Governor of Pentonville Prison, ex p. Sotiriadis* [1974] C.L.Y. 1605 considered); (4) in all the circumstances, the abandonment by the German Government of the earlier proceedings in which the new evidence was not available in order to replace them with proceedings in which it was, whereby difficult questions as to the form and authentication of the earlier evidence could be avoided, had not been an abuse of the process of the court.

R. v. SECRETARY OF STATE FOR THE HOME DEPARTMENT, *ex p.* REES [1986] 2 W.L.R. 1024, H.L.

1525. Fugitive offenders

FUGITIVE OFFENDERS (DESIGNATED COMMONWEALTH COUNTRIES) ORDER 1986 (No. 2022) [45p], made under the Fugitive Offenders Act 1967 (c.68), s.2(1); operative on January 1, 1987; designates, for the purposes of s.1 of the 1967 Act, Brunei, Maldives and Vanuatu.

1526. Genocide

EXTRADITION (GENOCIDE) (AMENDMENT) ORDER 1986 (No. 2011) [45p], made under the Extradition Act 1870 (c.52), ss.2, 17 and 21; operative on January 1, 1987; applies the Extradition Acts 1870–1935 as amended to the offence of genocide in the case of Spain being a state with which the U.K. has an extradition treaty.

1527. Hijacking

EXTRADITION (HIJACKING) (AMENDMENT) ORDER 1986 (No. 2012) [45p], made under the Extradition Act 1870 (c.52), ss.2, 17 and 21, and the Aviation Security Act 1982 (c.36), ss.9(2) and 39(1); operative on January 1, 1987; amends S.I. 1971 No. 2102.

1528. Internationally protected persons
EXTRADITION (INTERNATIONALLY PROTECTED PERSONS) (AMENDMENT) ORDER 1986 (No. 2013) [45p], made under the Extradition Act 1870 (c.52), ss.2, 17 and 21, and the Internationally Protected Persons Act 1978 (c.17), ss.3(2) and 4(1); operative on January 1, 1987; amends S.I. 1979 No. 453.

1529. Protection of aircraft
EXTRADITION (PROTECTION OF AIRCRAFT) (AMENDMENT) ORDER 1986 (No. 2014) [45p], made under the Extradition Act 1870 (c.52), ss.2, 17 and 21, and the Aviation Security Act 1982 (c.36), ss.9(2) and 39(1); operative on January 1, 1987; amends S.I. 1973 No. 1756.

1530. Suppression of terrorism
EXTRADITION (SUPPRESSION OF TERRORISM) (AMENDMENT) ORDER 1986 (No. 220) [40p], made under the Extradition Act 1870 (c.52), ss.2, 21; operative on March 13, 1986; amends S.I. 1978 No. 1106 by adding Belgium, The Netherlands, Portugal and Switzerland to the Schedule thereto.
EXTRADITION (SUPPRESSION OF TERRORISM) (AMENDMENT) (No. 2) ORDER 1986 (No. 1300) [45p], made under the Extradition Act 1870 (c.52), ss.2, 21; operative on August 26, 1986; applies the Extradition Acts 1870 to 1935 to Italy and Spain for the purposes of the European Convention on the Suppression of Terrorism.

1531. Taking of hostages
EXTRADITION (TAKING OF HOSTAGES) (AMENDMENT) ORDER 1986 (No. 2015) [45p], made under the Extradition Act 1870 (c.52), ss.2, 17 and 21, and the Taking of Hostages Act 1982 (c.28), s.5(1); operative on January 1, 1987; amends S.I. 1985 No. 751.

1532. Tokyo Convention
EXTRADITION (TOKYO CONVENTION) (AMENDMENT) ORDER 1986 (No. 2016) [45p], made under the Extradition Act 1870 (c.52), ss.2, 17 and 21, and the Civil Aviation Act 1982 (c.16), s.93(4); operative on January 1, 1987; applies the Extradition Acts 1870–1935 to offences committed on board aircraft in flight registered in Spain.

1533. Treaty between U.K. and U.S.A.
UNITED STATES OF AMERICA (EXTRADITION) (AMENDMENT) ORDER 1986 (No. 2020) [£1·40], made under the Extradition Act 1870 (c.52), ss.2, 17 and 21; operative on a date to be notified; applies the Extradition Acts 1870–1895 in the case of the U.S.A. in accordance with the treaty between the U.K. and the U.S.A. signed at London on June 8, 1972, as amended.

1534. Treaty between U.K. and Spain
The U.K. and Spain exchanged instruments of ratification on March 24, 1986 in respect of the extradition treaty signed on July 22, 1985. The treaty will come into force on July 1, 1986.
SPAIN (EXTRADITION) ORDER 1986 (No. 766) [£2·40], made under the Extradition Act 1870 (c.52), s.2; operative on July 1, 1986; applies the Extradition Acts 1870–1935 in the case of Spain in accordance with the extradition treaty between the U.K. and Spain concluded on July 22, 1985.

1535. Withdrawal of proceedings—whether discharge—whether bar to extradition
[Extradition Act 1870 (c.52), s.3(3).] S.3(3) of the Extradition Act 1870 provides that where a fugitive offender has also been accused of an offence in the U.K. he shall not be extradited "until after he has been discharged, whether by acquittal or by expiration of his sentence or otherwise". When proceedings against a fugitive offender are withdrawn from the court by the prosecution, the offender has been "discharged" within the meaning of the subsection (*R. v. Phipps, ex p. Alton* [1964] C.L.Y. 2283 and *Rex (McDonnell) v. Tyrone Justices* [1912] 2 I.R. 44 applied): R. *v.* GOVERNOR OF PENTONVILLE PRISON, *ex p.* HERBAGE (No. 3), *The Times,* November 15, 1986, D.C.

FACTORIES

1536. Fencing of machinery—experimental machine—whether within regulations
[Factories Act 1961 (c.34), s.14(1).] An experimental machine which has been installed in factory for testing is "any machinery" within s.14(1) of the Factories Act 1961, and must therefore be fenced (*Parvin v. Morton Machine Co.* [1952] C.L.Y.

1378 distinguished, *Irwin* v. *White Tomkins and Courage* [1964] C.L.Y. 1512 considered): TBA INDUSTRIAL PRODUCTS v. LAINE, *The Times*, June 23, 1986, D.C.

1537. Health and safety at work—enforcing authority
[Health and Safety at Work etc. Act 1974 (c.37), ss.10, 11(5), 15(2), 18(2); Health and Safety (Enforcing Authority) Regulations 1977 (S.I. 1977 No. 746), regs. 3, 5, Sched. 1.] Where the main activity at the premises altered so that it now came within the ambit of the local authority rather than the Executive, the local authority immediately became the enforcing authority notwithstanding that the procedure for formally transferring the responsibility for enforcement had not been followed: HADLEY v. HANCOX, *The Times*, November 18, 1986, D.C.

1538. Inspectors—prosecutions—time limits
[Health and Safety at Work Act 1974 (c.37), s.33(1)(*a*).] There is no time limit for bringing prosecutions for offences under this section: KEMP v. LIEBHERR—GREAT BRITAIN, *The Times*, November 5, 1986, D.C.

1539. Lighting—maintenance—duty of employer
[Factories Act 1961 (c.34), ss.5(1), 29(1).]
Section 5(1) of the Factories Act 1961 imposes the absolute duty on employers for the provision of sufficient lighting in factories, which will be breached even if a bulb fails immediately before an accident occurs.
E fell down the stairs in D Co.'s factory where he worked, because a light bulb had failed leaving the lower stairs in darkness. *Held*, that s.5(1) of the Factories Act 1961 imposed an absolute duty on D Co. which would be breached even by a light bulb failing immediately upon the accident. Although D Co. provided a reasonably efficient system of maintenance, that was not enough, and they were liable for E's injuries (*Thornton* v. *Fisher & Ludlow* [1968] C.L.Y. 1594 applied).
DAVIES v. MASSEY FERGUSON PERKINS [1986] I.C.R. 580, Evans J.

1540. Safe access—ice—reasonable precautions. See DARBY v. GKN SCREWS & FASTENERS, § 2266.

1541. Sex discrimination
FACTORIES ACT (HOURS OF EMPLOYMENT ORDERS AND REGULATIONS) REVOCATION AND AMENDMENT ORDER 1986 (No. 2312) [£1·40], made under the Factories Act 1961 (c.34), Pt. VI amended by the Sex Discrimination Act 1986 (c.59), s.7, Pt. III; operative on February 27, 1987; amend and revoke orders which relate to hours and holidays by removing references to women.

FAMILY ALLOWANCES

1542. Child benefit
CHILD BENEFIT (UP-RATING) REGULATIONS 1986 (No. 1172) [45p], made under the Child Benefit Act 1975 (c.61), s.22(3); operative on July 28, 1986; further amend S.I. 1976 No. 1267 by increasing the weekly rates of child benefit.

FIREARMS

1543. Fees.
FIREARMS (VARIATION OF FEES) ORDER 1986 (No. 986) [80p], made under the Firearms Act 1968 (c.27) s.43; operative on October 1, 1986; varies fees payable under the 1968 Act in connection with the grant, renewal or variation of a firearms licence.

1544. Possession—intent to commit indictable offence—length of sentence. See R. v. SHELDRAKE, § 862.

1545. Possession—temporary custody—whether transfer
[Firearms Act 1968 (c.27), ss.2(1), 3(2), 57(4).]
When a shotgun is left with a third party for custody or for cleaning, it is transferred to that person and that person possesses it for the purposes of ss.3(2) and 2(1) of the Firearms Act 1968.
D held a shotgun certificate for his two shotguns. He took them to X's house for safekeeping and for cleaning whilst he was on holiday. X held no certificate. D was charged with transferring the guns contrary to s.3(2) of the Firearms Act 1968; X was charged with possessing them contrary to s.2(1). The justices acquitted. *Held*, on appeal by the prosecutor, that in the circumstances there was a transfer contrary to

s.3(2) had possession contrary to s.2(1), and the case would be remitted to the justices with a direction to convict.

(*Sullivan* v. *Earl of Caithness* [1976] C.L.Y. 1252 applied).

HALL v. COTTON [1986] 3 W.L.R. 681, D.C.

1546. Prohibited weapon—incomplete sub-machine gun

[Firearms Act 1968 (c.27), ss.5(1)(2), 57(1) (as amended by Transfer of Functions (Prohibited Weapons) Order 1968 (S.I. 1968 No. 1200)).]

A firearm which ordinarily would be a prohibited weapon as being capable of continuous fire, but which lacks a necessary part can still be a prohibited weapon either on the basis that it is a component part of one, or that the necessary part can be replaced.

Per curiam: a weapon might be so damaged that it can no longer fairly be described as a weapon.

C was a registered firearms dealer who had in his possession a sub-machine gun designed for automatic fire only. The gun was incomplete: there was no trigger, pivot pin or magazine, but with a little work those omissions could be rectified. The trial judge ruled that the gun was still a prohibited weapon, and C thereupon pleaded guilty. *Held,* that the judge was right and the appeal would be dismissed. The evidence was that the gun could easily be made to fire, and in any event, by virtue of s.5(1)(*a*), when taken with the words of s.57(1)(*b*) clearly make it an offence to have in ones possession any component part of a prohibited weapon (*R.* v. *Pannell* [1982] C.L.Y. 1376 applied).

R. v. CLARKE (FREDERICK) [1986] 1 W.L.R. 209, C.A.

FISH AND FISHERIES

1547. Crabs and lobsters

CRAB CLAWS (PROHIBITION ON LANDING) ORDER 1986 (No. 496) [80p], made under the Sea Fish (Conservation) Act 1967 (c.84), s.6(1); operative on April 4, 1986; prohibits the landing of crab claws in the U.K. if they have been detached from crabs caught within British fishery limits.

UNDERSIZED CRABS ORDER 1986 (No. 497) [80p], made under the Sea Fish (Conservation) Act 1967, ss.1(1)—(4)(6), 15(3), 20(1); operative on April 4, 1986; prescribes the minimum sizes for the landing of edible crabs in the U.K.

1548. Diseases of fish

DISEASES OF FISH (AMENDMENT) REGULATIONS 1986 (No. 538) [80p], made under the Diseases of Fish Act 1937 (c.33), s.9; operative on March 17, 1986; amend S.I. 1984 No. 455.

1549. Fishing boats

FISHING BOATS (EUROPEAN ECONOMIC COMMUNITY) DESIGNATION (VARIATION) ORDER 1986 (No. 382) [40p], made under the Fishery Limits Act 1976 (c.86), ss.2(1), 6(2); operative on March 31, 1986; varies S.I. 1983 No. 253 to take account of the accession of Spain and Portugal to the EEC.

1550. Fishing vessels

MERCHANT SHIPPING (FISHING VESSELS) (RADIOS) (FEES) REGULATIONS 1986 (No. 680) [80p], made under the Merchant Shipping Act 1970 (c.36), s.84; operative on April 15, 1986; reinstate fees for inspections for compliance with or exemption from S.I. 1974 No. 1919.

1551. Importation of live fish

IMPORTATION OF LIVE FISH OF THE SALMON FAMILY ORDER 1986 (No. 283) [40p], made under the Diseases of Fish Act 1937 (c.33), s.1(6); operative on February 18, 1986; specifies a description of live fish of the salmon family for the purpose of excluding fish of that description from s.1(1) of the 1937 Act, *i.e.* fish from Northern Ireland which have not been outside of it.

1552. Prohibition of fishing

COD (SPECIFIED SEA AREAS) (PROHIBITION OF FISHING) (REVOCATION) ORDER 1986 (No. 2075) [45p], made under the Sea Fish (Conservation) Act 1967 (c.84), ss.5(1), 15(3) and 20(1); operative on December 2, 1986; revokes S.I. 1986 No. 1982.

HERRING (FIRTH OF CLYDE) (PROHIBITION OF FISHING) ORDER 1986 (No. 2122) [80p], made under the Sea Fish (Conservation) Act 1967 (c.84), ss.5(1) and 15(3); operative on December 5, 1986; prohibits fishing for herring by any British fishing boat, registered in the UK or the Isle of Man or any of the Channel Islands, within the sea area in the Firth of Clyde as specified.

SAITHE (CHANNEL, WESTERN WATERS AND BAY OF BISCAY) (PROHIBITION OF FISHING) ORDER 1986 (No. 1115) [80p], made under the Sea Fish (Conservation) Act 1967 (c.84), ss.5(1) and 15(3); operative on July 7, 1986; prohibits fishing for saithe by any British fishing boat registered in the U.K., the Isle of Man or the Channel Islands within that part of I.C.E.S. VII (Channel and Western Waters) and I.C.E.S. VIII (Bay of Biscay) which lies inside British fishery limits.

SOLE (SPECIFIED SEA AREAS) (PROHIBITION OF FISHING) ORDER 1986 (No. 2060) [80p], made under the Sea Fish (Conservation) Act 1967 (c.84), ss.5(1) and 15(3); operative on November 29, 1986; prohibits fishing for sole by any British fishing boat registered in the UK or the Isle of Man within any part of a specified sea area or by any British fishing boat registered in any of the Channel Islands within any part of such a sea area.

1553. **Safety at Sea Act 1986 (c.23)**
This Act promotes the safety of fishing and other vessels at sea and the persons in them.
The Act received the Royal Assent on June 26, 1986 and comes into force on a day to be appointed.

1553a. **Safety at Sea Act 1986—commencement**
SAFETY AT SEA ACT 1986 (COMMENCEMENT NO. 1) ORDER 1986 (No. 1759 (c.61)) [45p], made under the Safety at Sea Act 1986 (c.23), s.15(3); brings into force on October 30, 1986, sections 10, 11, 14(2)(3), 14(4) (so far as it relates to s.14(2)(3)), 15 of the 1986 Act.

1554. **Salmon Act 1986 (c.62)**
This Act makes fresh provision for the administration of salmon fisheries in Scotland. It provides for the licensing and regulation of salmon dealing in Scotland, England and Wales and deals with certain offences connected with salmon. It also introduces measures for the review of certain salmon net fishing.
The Act received the Royal Assent on November 7, 1986. Pts. I and II and s.42 extend to Scotland only. With the exception of s.21, which comes into force on a day to be appointed, the Act comes into force on January 7, 1987.

1555. **Sea fishing**
COD (SPECIFIED SEA AREAS) (PROHIBITION OF FISHING) ORDER 1986 (No. 1982) [£1·40], made under the Sea Fish (Conservation) Act 1967 (c.84), ss.5(1), 15(3); operative on November 22, 1986; prohibits fishing for cod by British registered fishing boats in specified sea areas.

HERRING AND WHITE FISH (SPECIFIED MANX WATERS) LICENSING (VARIATION) ORDER 1986 (No. 1439) [80p], made under the Sea Fish (Conservation) Act 1967 (c.84), ss.4, 15(3), 20(1); operative on August 27, 1986; amends S.I. 1983 No. 1204.

LANCASHIRE AND WESTERN SEA FISHERIES DISTRICT (ABOLITION OF METROPOLITAN COUNTY COUNCILS) ORDER 1986 (No. 454) [40p], made under the Local Government Act 1985 (c.51), s.101; operative on April 1, 1986; makes provision in connection with the constitution of the Lancashire and Western Sea Fisheries Committee following the abolition of Metropolitan County Councils by the 1985 Act.

NORTH-EASTERN SEA FISHERES DISTRICT ORDER 1986 (No. 647) [£1·40], made under the Sea Fisheries Regulation Act 1966, ss.1, 18(1); operative on April 1, 1986; makes new provision for the constitution of the North-Eastern Sea Fisheries Committee as a consequence of the abolition of the metropolitan county councils.

NORTH WESTERN AND NORTH WALES SEA FISHERIES DISTRICT ORDER 1986 (No. 1201) [£1·40], made under the Sea Fisheries Regulation Act 1966 (c.38), ss.1, 2(1), (5) and 18(1); operative on July 11, 1986; provides for the constitution of the local fisheries committee for the Lancashire and Western Sea Fisheries District in consequence of the abolition of metropolitan county councils.

NORTHUMBERLAND SEA FISHERIES DISTRICT (VARIATION) ORDER 1986 (No. 648) [45p], made under the Sea Fisheries Regulation Act 1966 (c.38), s.1; operative on April 1, 1986; varies the constitution of the Northumberland Fisheries Committee as a consequence of the abolition of the metropolitan county councils.

SAITHE (CHANNEL, WESTERN WATERS AND BAY OF BISCAY) (PROHIBITION OF FISHING) (REVOCATION) ORDER 1986 (No. 1620) [45p], made under the Sea Fish (Conservation)

Act 1967 (c.84), ss.5(1), 15(3); operative on September 23, 1986; revokes S.I. 1986 No. 1115.

SEA FISH LICENSING (VARIATION) ORDER 1986 (No. 1438) [80p], made under the Sea Fish (Conservation) Act 1967, ss.4, 15(3), 20(1); operative on August 27, 1986; varies S.I. 1983 No. 1206 by extending the scope of that Order so as to give effect to Council Regulation (EEC) No. 3777/85 as extended by Council Regulation (EEC) No. 114/86.

SEA FISH (MARKETING STANDARDS) REGULATIONS 1986 (No. 1272) [£1·40], made under the European Communities Act 1972 (c.68), s.2(2); operative on August 14, 1986; provide for the enforcement of community regulations laying down common marketing standards and related rules as to marketing for certain species of sea fis including shellfish.

SEA FISHING (ENFORCEMENT OF COMMUNITY CONTROL MEASURES) (AMENDMENT) ORDER 1986 (No. 926) [80p], made under the Fisheries Act 1981 (c.29), s.30(2); operative on July 1, 1986; amend S.I. 1985 No. 487 in consequence of Council Regulation (EEC) No. 3723/85.

SEA FISHING (ENFORCEMENT OF COMMUNITY CONSERVATION MEASURES) ORDER 1986 (No. 2090) [£1·90], made under the Fisheries Act 1981 (c.29), s.30(2); operative on January 1, 1987; replaces S.I. 1983 No. 256, as amended, and makes provision for the enforcement of community restrictions and obligations contained in Council Regulation (EEC) No. 3094/86.

SEA FISHING (ENFORCEMENT OF COMMUNITY CONSERVATION MEASURES) (AMENDMENT) ORDER 1986 (No. 251) [80p], made under the Fisheries Act 1981 (c.29), s.30(2); operative on March 10, 1986; further amends S.I. 1983 No. 256 so as to provide for the enforcement of Council Regulation (EEC) No. 171/83.

SEA FISHING (ENFORCEMENT OF COMMUNITY QUOTA MEASURES) ORDER 1986 (No. 250) [£1·35], made under the Fisheries Act 1981, s.30(2); operative on February 18, 1986; provides for the enforcement of certain restrictions and obligations contained in Council Regulation (EEC) No. 3721/85, as amended by Council Regulations (EEC) Nos. 3777/85 and 114/86.

SEA FSHING (ENFORCEMENT OF COMMUNITY QUOTA MEASURES) (No. 2) ORDER 1986 (No. 2329) [£1·40], made under the Fisheries Act 1981 (c.29), s.30(2); operative on January 1, 1987; makes provision for the enforcement of certain Community restrictions relating to sea fishing.

SEA FISHING (ENFORCEMENT OF COMMUNITY MEASURES FOR SPANISH AND PORTUGUESE VESSELS) ORDER 1986 (No. 110) [£1·35], made under the Fisheries Act 1981 (c.29), s.30(2); operative on February 1, 1986; provides for the enforcement of three community regulations concerned with fishing within community waters by vessels flying the flags of Spain and Portugal.

SEA FISHING (SPECIFIED WESTERN WATERS) (RESTRICTIONS ON LANDING) (VARIATION) ORDER 1986 (No. 1437) [80p], made under the Sea Fish (Conservation) Act 1967, ss.6(1), 15(3), 20(1); operative on August 27, 1986; amends S.I. 1980 No. 335.

SOLE (IRISH SEA AND SOLE BANK) (PROHIBITION OF FISHING) ORDER 1986 (No. 1936) [£1·40], made under the Sea Fish (Conservation) Act 1967 (c.84), ss.5(1), 15(3); operative on November 15, 1986; prohibits fishing for sole by British registered fishing boats in specified parts of the Irish Sea.

THIRD COUNTRY FISHING (ENFORCEMENT) ORDER 1986 (No. 779) [£1·40], made under the Fisheries Act 1981 (c.29), s.30(2); operative on May 28, 1986; makes breaches of specified articles of Community regulations offences for the purposes of U.K. law where they occur within British fishing limits.

1556. Shell fish

PORTCHESTER CHANNEL OYSTER FISHERY ORDER 1986 (No. 1901) [80p], made under the Sea Fisheries (Shellfish) Act 1967 (c.83), s.1; operative on December 5, 1986; confers on the Portsmouth Harbour Oyster Society Ltd. the right of several fishery for oysters over part of Portchester Channel.

RIVER NENE FISHERY ORDER 1986 (No. 1896) [£1·40], made under the Sea Fisheries (Shellfish) Act 1967 (c.83), s.1; operative on December 3, 1986; confers on the Eastern Sea Fisheries Joint Committee the right of several fisheries for oysters, mussels, cockles and clams in an area of the Wash adjacent to the River Nene.

SCALLOPS (IRISH SEA) (PROHIBITION OF FISHING) (VARIATION) ORDER 1986 (No. 988) [80p]; made under the Sea Fish (Conservation) Act 1967 (c.84), ss.5(1)(5), 15(3),

20(1); operative on July 1, 1986; extends the area to which the prohibition on fishing contained in S.I. 1984 No. 1523 applies.

FOOD AND DRUGS

1557. Butter

BUTTER (EEC SPECIAL SALE) (AMENDMENT) REGULATIONS 1986 (No. 1373) [45p], made under the European Communities Act 1972 (c.68), s.2(2); operative on September 1, 1986; amend S.I. 1986 No. 68 so as to reduce the maximum price of concentrated butter produced from butter sold out of intervention stocks.

BUTTER (EEC SPECIAL SALE) REGULATIONS 1986 (No. 68) [80p], made under the European Communities Act 1972 (c.68), s.2(2); operative on February 18, 1986; prescribe maximum retail prices for concentrated butter produced from butter sold out of intervention stocks at a reduced price in accordance with the provisions of EEC Regulation 3143/85 as amended.

1558. Complainants supplying food to health authority—whether a sampling case

[Food and Drugs Act 1955 (c.16), ss.2, 91, 92(2) and 108(1A).] X, who found some metal in cheese which he bought from A.S. Co., made a complaint to and took the cheese to ADC's health officer. The public analyst certified the cheese to contain foreign material. *Held*, allowing the prosecutor's appeal from dismissal of a charge under s.2 of the 1955 Act, that the justices had erred in deciding that the time limit for commencing proceedings two months from the date of handing the cheese to the health officer, provided by s.108(1A) applied. That limit applied in cases where an authorised officer had procured samples for analysis under s.91. X had taken the cheese to the authority for analysis pursuant to s.92(2). The time limit did not apply to such cases: ARUN DISTRICT COUNCIL *v.* ARGYLE STORES [1986] Crim.L.R. 685, D.C.

1559. Contaminated milk—method of laying information

[Food Act 1984 (c.30), ss.2, 3(2), 8(1)(*b*).] It was proper to lay an information under s.8 (unfitness for human consumption) where the body of a mouse or pieces of glass were found in a bottle of milk (*Miller* v. *Battersea London Borough Council* [1956] 1 Q.B. 43 distinguished): BARTON *v.* UNIGATE DAIRIES, *The Times,* October 27, 1986, D.C.

1560. Contamination

FOOD PROTECTION (EMERGENCY PROHIBITIONS) ORDER 1986 (No. 1027) [80p], made under the Food and Environment Protection Act 1985 (c.48), s.1(1)(*a*); operative on June 20, 1986; contains emergency provisions to prevent human consumption of food contaminated as a result of the Chernobyl disaster.

FOOD PROTECTION (EMERGENCY PROHIBITIONS) (No. 2) ORDER 1986 (No. 1059) [80p], made under the Food and Environment Protection Act 1985 (c.48), ss.1(1) and 24(3); operative on June 26, 1986; contains emergency prohibitions restricting various activities in order to prevent human consumption of food rendered unsuitable in consequence of the escape of radioactive substances from Chernobyl in the U.S.S.R.

FOOD PROTECTION (EMERGENCY PROHIBITIONS) (No. 3) ORDER 1986 (No. 1121) [80p], made under the Food and Environment Protection Act 1985 (c.48), s.1(1)(*a*); operative on July 4, 1986; contains prohibitions restricting various activities in order to prevent human consumption of food which has been or may have been rendered unsuitable for that purpose in consequence of the escape of radioactive substances from Chernobyl in the U.S.S.R.

FOOD PROTECTION (EMERGENCY PROHIBITIONS) (No. 3) (AMENDMENT) ORDER 1986 (No. 1185) [80p], made under the Food and Environment Protection Act 1985, s.1(1)(*a*); operative on July 11, 1986; amends S.I. 1986 No. 1121 by reducing the area to which that Order applies.

FOOD PROTECTION (EMERGENCY PROHIBITIONS) (No. 3) (AMENDMENT) (No. 2) ORDER 1986 (No. 1247) [80p], made under the Food and Environment Protection Act 1985, ss.1(1), 24(3); operative on July 18, 1986; amends S.I. 1986 No. 1121 so as to reduce the area to which that order applies.

FOOD PROTECTION (EMERGENCY PROHIBITIONS) (No. 4) ORDER 1986 (No. 1179) [80p], made under the Food and Environment Protection Act 1985, s.1(1)(*a*); operative on July 9, 1986; contains prohibitions restricting various activities in order to prevent human consumption of food rendered unsuitable in consequence of the escape of radioactive substances from Chernobyl.

FOOD PROTECTION (EMERGENCY PROHIBITIONS) (No. 4) (AMENDMENT) ORDER 1986 (No. 1232) [80p], made under the Food and Environment Protection Act 1985, s.1(1)(*a*); operative on July 15, 1986; amends S.I. 1986 No. 1179.

FOOD PROTECTION (EMERGENCY PROHIBITIONS) (No. 5) ORDER 1986 (No. 1294) [£1·40] made under the Food and Environment Protection Act 1985, ss.1(1)(*a*), 24(3); operative on July 25, 1986; revoke and replace S.I. 1986 No. 1121 and applies to a smaller area than the preceding Order.

FOOD PROTECTION (EMERGENCY PROHIBITIONS) (No. 5) REVOCATION ORDER 1986 (No. 1412) [45p], made under the Food and Environment Protection Act 1985, s.1(1); operative on August 14, 1986; revoke S.I. 1986 Nos. 1294, 1344 and 1384.

FOOD PROTECTION (EMERGENCY PROHIBITIONS) (No. 5) (AMENDMENT) ORDER 1986 (No. 1344) [80p], made under the Food and Environment Protection Act 1985, ss.1(1), 24(3); operative on August 1, 1986; amends S.I. 1986 No. 1294 so as to reduce the area of Wales to which that Order applies.

FOOD PROTECTION (EMERGENCY PROHIBITIONS) (No. 5) AMENDMENT No. 2 ORDER 1986 (No. 1384) [80p], made under the Food and Environment Protection Act 1985, s.1(1)(*a*); operative on August 7, 1986; amends S.I. 1986 No. 1294 by reducing the area to which that Order applies.

FOOD PROTECTION (EMERGENCY PROHIBITIONS) (No. 6) ORDER 1986 (No. 1331) [80p], made under the Food and Environment Protection Act 1985 s.1(1) and 24(3); operative on July 30, 1986; restricts various activities in order to prevent human consumption of food rendered unsuitable because of the escape of radioactive substances from Chernobyl in the U.S.S.R.

FOOD PROTECTION (EMERGENCY PROHIBITIONS) (No. 6) AMENDMENT ORDER 1986 (No. 1360) [45p], made under the Food and Environment Protection Act 1985, ss.1(1), 24(3); operative on August 4, 1986; amends the Schedule to S.I. 1986 No. 1331 thus reducing the designated area to which that Order applied.

FOOD PROTECTION (EMERGENCY PROHIBITIONS) (No. 6) (AMENDMENT No. 2) ORDER 1986 (No. 1410) [80p], made under the Food and Environment Protection Act 1985, s.1(1)(*a*); operative on August 13, 1986; amends S.I. 1986 No. 1331.

FOOD PROTECTION (EMERGENCY PROHIBITIONS) (No. 7) ORDER 1986 (No. 1422) [£1·40], made under the Food and Environment Protection Act 1985, ss.1(1)(*a*), 24(3); operative on August 19, 1986; revoke and re-enacts S.I. 1986 No. 1331, as amended, and re-designates areas in Scotland.

FOOD PROTECTION (EMERGENCY PROHIBITIONS) (No. 7) (AMENDMENT) ORDER 1986 (No. 1432) [80p], made under the Food and Environment Protection Act 1985, ss.1(1), 24(3); operative on August 21, 1986; amends S.I. 1986 No. 1422.

FOOD PROTECTION (EMERGENCY PROHIBITIONS) (No. 7) (AMENDMENT No. 2) ORDER 1986 (No. 1491) [45p], made under the Food and Environment Protection Act 1985, ss.1(1), 24(3); operative on August 29, 1986; exempts from the restrictions imposed by S.I. 1986 No. 1422 sheep remaining in the area specified in that Order on August 21, 1986.

FOOD PROTECTION (EMERGENCY PROHIBITIONS) (No. 7) (AMENDMENT No. 3) ORDER 1986 (No. 1508) [45p], made under the Food and Environment Protection Act 1985, ss.1(1), 24(3); operative on September 2, 1986; adds to the exceptions from the area designated in S.I. 1986 No. 1422.

FOOD PROTECTION (EMERGENCY PROHIBITIONS) (No. 7) (AMENDMENT No. 4) ORDER 1986 (No. 1552) [80p], made under the Food and Environment Protection Act 1985, ss.1(1), 24(3); operative on September 8, 1986; exempts from the restrictions imposed by S.I. 1986 No. 1422 sheep which remained in certain parts of the area designated in that Order on September 8, 1986.

FOOD PROTECTION (EMERGENCY PROHIBITIONS) (No. 8) ORDER 1986 (No. 1574) [£1·40], made under the Food and Environment Protection Act 1985, ss.1(1), 24(3); operative on September 11, 1986; revokes and re-enacts with amendments S.I. 1986 Nos. 1422, 1432, 1491, 1508, 1552 which applied to specified areas of Scotland.

FOOD PROTECTION (EMERGENCY PROHIBITIONS) (No. 8) (AMENDMENT) ORDER 1986 (No. 1595) [80p], made under the Food and Environment Protection Act 1985, ss.1(1), 24(3); operative on September 15, 1986; adds to exemptions from the provisions of S.I. 1986 No. 1574.

FOOD PROTECTION (EMERGENCY PROHIBITIONS) (No. 8) (AMENDMENT No. 2) ORDER 1986 (No. 1615) [80p], made under the Food and Environment Protection Act 1985, ss.1(1), 24(3); operative on September 18, 1986; adds to the exemptions from the provisions of S.I. 1986 No. 1574.

FOOD PROTECTION (EMERGENCY PROHIBITONS) (NO. 8) (AMENDMENT NO. 3) ORDER 1986 (No. 1664) [80p], made under the Food and Environment Protection Act 1985, ss.1(1), 24(3); operative on September 26, 1986; adds to the exception to the areas designated in S.I. 1986 No. 1574.

FOOD PROTECTION (EMERGENCY PROHIBITONS) (NO. 8) (AMENDMENT NO. 4) ORDER 1986 (No. 1765) [80p], made under the Food and Environment Protection Act 1985, ss.1(1), 24(3); operative on October 13, 1986; extends the exemption from the restrictions imposed in S.I. 1986 No. 1574 on the movement of sheep in areas designated in that Order.

FOOD PROTECTION (EMERGENCY PROHIBITIONS) (NO. 8) (AMENDMENT NO. 5) ORDER 1986 (No. 1837) [80p], made under the Food and Environment Protection Act 1985 (c.48), ss.1(1), 24(3); operative on October 30, 1986; exempts from the restrictions imposed in S.I. 1986 No. 1574, sheep, which remained in specified parts of the area designated in that Order on October 30, 1986.

FOOD PROTECTION (EMERGENCY PROHIBITIONS) (NO. 8) (AMENDMENT NO. 6) ORDER 1986 (No. 1900) [£1·40], made under the Food and Environment Protection Act 1985, s.1(1) and 24(3); operative on November 7, 1986; corrects amendments to S.I. 1986 No. 1574.

FOOD PROTECTION (EMERGENCY PROHIBITONS) (NO. 8) PARTIAL REVOCATION ORDER 1986 (No. 1688) [80p], made under the Food and Environment Protection Act 1985, ss.1(1), 24(3); operative on September 30, 1986; removes the restrictions imposed in S.I. 1986 No. 1574 on certain specified parts of the area designated in that Order.

FOOD PROTECTION (EMERGENCY PROHIBITONS) (NO. 8) PARTIAL REVOCATION (NO. 2) ORDER 1986 (No. 1720) [80p], made under the Food and Environment Protection Act 1985, ss.1(1), 24(3); operative on October 6, 1986; removes restrictions on specified parts of the areas in Scotland designated by S.I. 1986 No. 1574.

FOOD PROTECTION (EMERGENCY PROHIBITIONS) (NO. 9) ORDER 1986 (No. 1993) [£1·40], made under the Food and Environment Protection Act 1985, ss.1(1), 24(3); operative on November 24, 1986; prohibits the slaughter of sheep which were removed from designated areas in Scotland before specified dates.

FOOD PROTECTION (EMERGENCY PROHIBITONS) (NO 10) ORDER 1986 (No. 2248) [£1·40], made under the Food and Environment Protection Act 1985 (c.48), ss.1(1), 24(3); operative on December 18, 1986; replaces S.I. 1986 No. 1993 and designates areas in Scotland on respect of which the slaughter of sheep removed from those areas is prohibited.

FOOD PROTECTION (EMERGENCY PROHIBITIONS) (ENGLAND) ORDER 1986 (No. 1413) [£1.40], made under the Food and Environment Protection Act 1985 (c.48), ss.1(1), 24(3); operative on August 14, 1986; replaces in relation to an area of land in England S.I. 1986 No. 1294, as amended.

FOOD PROTECTION (EMERGENCY PROHIBITIONS) (ENGLAND) AMENDMENT ORDER 1986 (No. 1431) [80p], made under the Food and Environment Protection Act 1985, ss.1(1), 24(3); operative on August 21, 1986; amends S.I. 1986 No. 1413 so as to exempt from restrictions imposed by that Order sheep which were in the designated area on August 21, 1986.

FOOD PROTECTION (EMERGENCY PROHIBITIONS) (ENGLAND) AMENDMENT (NO. 2) ORDER 1986 (No. 1479) [80p], made under the Food and Environment Protection Act 1985, ss.1(1), 24(3); operative on August 29, 1986; exempts from restrictions imposed in S.I. 1986 No. 1413 sheep which were in a specified part of the area designated in that Order on August 29, 1986.

FOOD PROTECTION (EMERGENCY PROHIBITIONS) (ENGLAND) AMENDMENT (NO. 3) ORDER 1986 (No. 1540) [80p], made under the Food and Environment Protection Act 1985, ss.1(1), 24(3); operative on September 5, 1986; exempts from the restrictions imposed in S.I. 1986 No. 1413 sheep which were in the specified part of the area designated in that Order on September 5, 1986.

FOOD PROTECTION (EMERGENCY PROHIBITIONS) (ENGLAND) AMENDMENT (NO. 4) ORDER 1986 (No. 1592) [80p], made under the Food and Environment Protection Act 1985, ss.1(1), 24(3); operative on September 13, 1986; exempts from the restrictions imposed by S.I. 1986 No. 1413 sheep which were in a specified part of the area designated in that Order on September 13, 1986.

FOOD PROTECTION (EMERGENCY PROHIBITIONS) (ENGLAND) (NO. 2) ORDER 1986 (No. 1689) [£1·40], made under the Food and Environment Protection Act 1985 (c.48), ss.1(1), 24(3); Operative on September 30, 1986; replaces S.I. 1986 No. 1413, as amended, and designates an area in England from which the movement of sheep is prohibited.

FOOD PROTECTION (EMERGENCY PROHIBITIONS) (ENGLAND) AMENDMENT (NO. 5) ORDER 1986 (No. 1621) [80p], made under the Food and Environment Protection Act 1985, ss.1(1), 24(3); operative on September 22, 1986; amends S.I. 1986 No. 1413.

FOOD PROTECTION (EMERGENCY PROHIBITIONS) (ENGLAND) (NO. 2) AMENDMENT ORDER 1986 (No. 2208) [45p], made under the Food and Environment Protection Act 1985 (c. 48), ss.1(1), 24 (3); operative on December 18, 1986; amends S.I. 1986 No. 1689 by exempting from the prohibition on slaughter contained in that Order sheep which have been marked by an official of MAFF.

FOOD PROTECTION (EMERGENCY PROHIBITIONS) (WALES) ORDER 1986 (No. 1411) [80p], made under the Food and Environment Protection Act 1985, ss.1(1), 24(3); operative on August 14, 1986; designates an area in Wales in which the movement and slaughter of sheep is prohibited.

FOOD PROTECTION (EMERGENCY PROHIBITIONS) (WALES) AMENDMENT ORDER 1986 (No. 1435) [80p], made under the Food and Environment Protection Act 1985, ss.1(1), 24(3); operative on August 22, 1986; amends S.I. 1986 No. 1411 so as to reduce the area in Wales to which that Order applies.

FOOD PROTECTION (EMERGENCY PROHIBITIONS) (WALES) AMENDMENT NO. 2 ORDER 1986 (No. 1483) [80p], made under the Food and Environment Protection Act 1985, ss.1(1), 24(3); operative on August 29, 1986; amends S.I. 1986 No. 1411 so as to exempt from restrictions imposed by that Order sheep which were in the designated area on August 29, 1986.

FOOD PROTECTION (EMERGENCY PROHIBITIONS) (WALES) AMENDMENT NO. 3 ORDER 1986 (No. 1535) [£1·40], made under the Food and Environment Protection Act 1985, ss.1(1), 24(3); operative on September 5, 1986; exempts from the restrictions imposed in S.I. 1986 No. 1411 sheep which were in a specified part of the area designated in that Order on September 5, 1986.

FOOD PROTECTION (EMERGENCY PROHIBITIONS) (WALES) AMENDMENT NO. 4 ORDER 1986 (No. 1576) [£1·40], made under the Food and Environment Protection Act 1985, ss.1(1), 24(3); operative on September 12, 1986; exempts from the restrictions imposed in S.I. 1986 No. 1411 sheep which were in a specified part of the area designated in that Order on September 12, 1986.

FOOD PROTECTION (EMERGENCY PROHIBITIONS) (WALES) AMENDMENT NO. 5 ORDER 1986 (No. 1616) [£1·40], made under the Food and Environment Protection Act 1985, ss.1(1), 24(3); operative on September 19, 1986; exempts from restrictions imposed in S.I. 1986 No. 1411 sheep which were in a specified part of the area designated in that Order on September 19, 1986.

FOOD PROTECTION (EMERGENCY PROHIBITIONS) (WALES) AMENDMENT NO. 6 ORDER 1986 (No. 1662) [£1·40], made under the Food and Environment Protection Act 1985, ss.1(1), 24(3); operative on September 26, 1986; amends S.I. 1986 No. 1411.

FOOD PROTECTION (EMERGENCY PROHIBITIONS) (WALES) (NO. 2) ORDER 1986 (No. 1681) [£2·40], made under the Food and Environment Protection Act 1985, ss.1(1), 24(3); operative on September 30, 1986; replaces S.I. 1986 No. 1411, as amended, and designates areas in Wales from which the movement of sheep is prohibited.

FOOD PROTECTION (EMERGENCY PROHIBITIONS) (WALES) (NO. 2) AMENDMENT ORDER 1986 (No. 1707) [£1·40], made under the Food and Environment Protection Act 1985, ss.1(1), 24(3); operative on October 3, 1986; exempts from the restrictions imposed in S.I. 1986 No. 1681 sheep which were in a specified part of the area designated in that Order on October 3, 1986.

FOOD PROTECTION (EMERGENCY PROHIBITIONS) (WALES) (NO. 2) AMENDMENT NO. 2 ORDER 1986 (No. 1756) [£1·40], made under the Food and Environment Protection Act 1985, ss.1(1), 24(3); operative on October 10, 1986; exempts from the restrictions contained in S.I. 1986 No. 1681 sheep which were in a specified part of the area designated in that Order on October 10, 1986.

FOOD PROTECTION (EMERGENCY PROHIBITIONS) (WALES) (NO. 2) AMENDMENT NO. 3 ORDER 1986 (No. 1775) [£1·40], made under the Food and Environment Protection Act 1985, ss.1(1), 24(3); operative on October 17, 1986; exempts from restrictions imposed by S.I. 1986 No. 1681 sheep which were in specified parts of the areas designated in that Order on October 17, 1986.

FOOD PROTECTION (EMERGENCY PROHIBITIONS) (WALES) (NO. 2) AMENDMENT NO. 4 ORDER 1986 (No. 1849) [80p], made under the Food and Environment Protection Act 1985, ss.1(1), 24(3); operative on October 31, 1986; exempts from restrictions sheep which were in areas designated in that Order on October 31, 1986.

FOOD PROTECTION (EMERGENCY PROHIBITIONS) (WALES) (NO. 2) AMENDMENT NO. 5 ORDER 1986 (No. 2242) [80p], made under the Food and Environment Protection Act 1985 (c.48), ss.1(1), 24(3); excepts from the prohibition on slaughter and supply contained in S.I. 1986 No. 1681 sheep which have been identified by an offcial of MAFF or the Welsh Office.

1561. Dairy produce quotas. See AGRICULTURE, § 52.

1562. Eggs
EGGS AUTHORITY (RATES OF LEVY) ORDER 1986 (No. 441) [40p], made under the Agriculture Act 1970 (c.40), s.13(2)(*b*) and (6); operative on April 1, 1986; fixes the rate of levy payable to the Eggs authority by hatchers and importers of pullet chicks for the production of eggs.

1563. Food sales—fitness for consumption
[Food and Drugs Act 1955 (c.16), s.135.] Justices erred in dismissing informations preferred by the local authority for sale of food to the prejudice of a purchaser on the basis that there had been no sale: FLEMING *v.* EDWARDS, *The Times*, March 15, 1986, D.C.

1564. Handling food—smoking at market stall
[Food Hygiene (Markets, Stalls and Delivery Vehicles) Regulations 1966 (S.I. 1966 No. 791 Regs. 2(2), 8(*e*), 25, 26.] The handling of open food is not confined to actually touching it, but refers to any operation referred to in Reg. 2(2), and includes a person smoking a cigarette between serving customers: CUCKSON *v.* BUGG, *The Times*, June 26, 1986, D.C.

1565. Meat
MEAT PRODUCTS AND SPREADABLE FISH PRODUCTS (AMENDMENT) REGULATIONS 1986 (No. 987) [£1·40], made under the Food Act 1984 (c.30), ss.4, 7, 118; operative on July 1, 1986; amend S.I. 1984, No. 1566.

1566. Meat—found to contain percentages of other meats—prejudice to purchaser
[Food and Drugs Act 1955 (c.16), s.2.]
If a purchaser is sold meat described as minced beef or minced steak which contains a percentage of other meats he cannot be described as other than prejudiced.

R, a butcher, sold to a purchaser quantities of "minced beef" and "minced steak" which were found to contain other meats. R was charged with having sold to the prejudice of the purchaser meats which were not of the nature demanded contrary to s.2(1) of the 1955 Act. R contended that the informations should have alleged that the products were not of the substance demanded. The justices held that the informations were properly framed but found that there was no requirement that minced beef or minced steak should contain any particular meat. They dismissed the informations. *Held*, allowing the appeal, that (1) it was equally apt to describe what was sold as being not of the nature or substance so that the informations were not bad; (*Preston* v. *Greenclose* (1975) 139 J.P. 245 applied); (2) a purchaser who bought minced beef or minced steak was entitled to receive a mince composed wholly of beef or steak, and if he was sold such mince which contained other meats he was prejudiced within s.2.

SHEARER *v.* ROWE (1986) 84 L.G.R. 296, D.C.

1567. Milk
CONDENSED MILK AND DRIED MILK (AMENDMENT) REGULATIONS 1986 (No. 2299) [£1·40], made under the Food Act 1984 (c.30), ss.4, 7, 118, 119; regs. 1 and 4 operative on February 2, 1987, regs. 2 and 3 operative on February 2, 1988; implement Council Directive No. 83/635/EEC.

MILK AND DAIRIES (HEAT TREATMENT OF CREAM) (AMENDMENT) REGULATIONS 1986 (No. 721) [80p], made under the Food Act 1984 (c.30), ss.4, 33, 118; operative on June 1, 1986; amend S.I. 1983 No. 1509 by removing the restriction applying between England and Wales and Northern Ireland on trade in heat-treated cream and to allow milk produced in Northern Ireland to be used in connection with the heat treatment of cream.

MILK AND DAIRIES (SEMI-SKIMMED AND SKIMMED MILK) (HEAT TREATMENT AND LABELLING) REGULATIONS 1986 (No. 722) [£2·90], made under the Food Act 1984, ss.30, 74(3), 118; operative on June 1, 1986; replace S.I. 1973 No. 1064 as amended.

MILK-BASED DRINKS (HYGIENE AND HEAT TREATMENT) (AMENDMENT) REGULATIONS 1986 (No. 720) [80p], made under the Food Act 1984, ss.4, 13, 118; operative on June 1, 1986; amend S.I. 1983 No. 1508 by removing the restriction applying between England and Wales and Northern Ireland on trade in milk-based drinks and by allowing milk production in Northern Ireland to be used in connection with the heat treatment of milk-based drinks.

MILK MARKETING SCHEME (AMENDMENT) ORDER 1986 (No. 83) [80p], made under the Agricultural Marketing Act 1958 (c.47), s.2 and Sched. 1; operative on February 17, 1986; amends S.R. & O. 1933 No. 789.

MILK (SPECIAL DESIGNATION) REGULATIONS 1986 (No. 723) [£4·40], made under the Food Act 1984, ss.38, 74(3) and 118; operative on June 1, 1986; require the use of special designations (*e.g.* "untreated" and "sterilised") in relation to the sale of milk and require any person using such a designation to be the holder of the appropriate licence.

1568. Repricing

FOOD (PROHIBITION OF REPRICING) (REVOCATION) ORDER 1986 (No. 175) [40p], made under the Prices Act 1974 (c.24), s.2(1)(6)(8); operative on March 1, 1986; revokes S.I. 1978 No. 1014 and S.I. 1979 No. 660.

1569. Sugar

SUGAR BEET (RESEARCH AND EDUCATION) ORDER 1986 (No. 429) [80p], made under the Food Act 1984 (c.30), s.68(1) and (2); operative on April 1, 1986; provides for the assessment of contributions for 1986–7 and their collection from British Sugar p.l.c. and growers of sugar beet during that year, towards the cost of the programme of research and education set out in the schedule.

1570. Third party proceedings—whether necessary to serve analyst's report on third party—mode of trial—election

[Food and Drugs Act 1955 (c. 16) (as amended), s. 2 (now Food Act 1984 (c. 30), s. 2) and ss. 108 and 113(1).] C.R.S. were served with a summons alleging an offence under s. 2 of the 1955 Act, as amended. C.R.S. exercised their right to bring before the court under s. 113(1) an employee, G, whose act or default they alleged caused the contravention of s. 2. C.R.S. elected summary trial. The hearing was adjourned to allow G to obtain representation. Ultimately magistrates ruled that the summons had been served validly on G. *Held,* that (1) there was no obligation on C.R.S. to serve a copy of the analyst's certificate with the summons served on G. The duties under s. 108 only affected the prosecutor of an original defendant; (2) the correct procedure to be followed by magistrates was for pleas to be taken first and then for election re mode of trial to be put. If one defendant elects trial on indictment, the whole matter must go to the Crown Court: R. *v.* UXBRIDGE JUSTICES, *ex p.* GOW; R. *v.* UXBRIDGE JUSTICES, *ex p.* COOPERATIVE RETAIL SERVICES [1986] Crim.L.R. 177, D.C.

FORESTRY

1571. Forestry Act 1986 (c.30)

This Act empowers the Forestry Commissioners to require the restocking of land with trees after unauthorised felling.

The Act received the Royal Assent on July 8, 1986 and comes into force two months from that date. It does not apply to Northern Ireland.

FRAUD, MISREPRESENTATION AND UNDUE INFLUENCE

1572. Bribe accepted by solicitor—capacity as receiver of moneys—profits

A solicitor, D, received a bribe from the other side in a commercial dispute for settlement of it. His clients, ISL, now sought the payment to them of the money, together with the profits made from the use thereof, and an account of such use. *Held,* that the solicitor and his client were in a creditor/debtor relationship, not one of trustee and *cestui que trust*. The money was money had and received, but the profits on it were not recoverable (*Lister* v. *Stubbs* [1890] 45 Ch.D. 1 followed; *Phipps* v. *Boardman* [1966] C.L.Y. 11052, IDC v. Cooley [1972] C.L.Y. 361 considered): ISLAMIC REPUBLIC OF IRAN SHIPPING LINES v. DENBY, *Financial Times*, October 22, 1986, Leggatt J.

1573. Execution of second mortgage—wife's consent—fraudulent misrepresentation—failure to obtain independent advice. See KINGS NORTH TRUST v. BELL, § 2227.

1574. Fraud trials. See LAW REFORM, § 1949.

1575. Non-fraudulent misrepresentation—value of premises—whether liable for damages

P bought premises from D. D misrepresented, although not fraudulently, that no work needed to be done in respect of public health requirements. In fact work costing £8,200 was necessary. *Held*, that reliance upon the misrepresentation cost P £8,200, which was the proper sum to be awarded by way of damages. The value of the premises could also, in the absence of other evidence, be assumed to be £8,200 less than the price paid by P: JACOVIDES v. CONSTANTINOU, *The Times*, October 27, 1986, Jupp J.

FRIENDLY SOCIETIES

1576. Fees

FRIENDLY SOCIETY (FEES) REGULATIONS 1986 (No. 620) [80p], made under the Friendly Societies Act 1974 (c.46), s.104(1), and S.I. 1971 No. 1900; increase fees payable under the 1974 Act.

1577. Friendly Societies Act 1984—extension

FRIENDLY SOCIETIES ACT 1984 (ISLE OF MAN) ORDER 1986 (No. 768) [45p], made under the Friendly Societies Act 1984 (c.62), s.4(3); operative on May 29, 1986; extends the 1984 Act to the Isle of Man.

GAMING AND WAGERING

1578. Betting, Gaming and Lotteries (Amendment) Act 1984—commencement

BETTING, GAMING AND LOTTERIES (AMENDMENT) ACT 1984 (COMMENCEMENT) ORDER 1986 (No. 102 (C.4)) [40p], made under the Betting, Gaming and Lotteries (Amendment) Act 1984 (c.25), s.4(2); brings s.2 of the 1984 Act into force on March 10, 1986. The remaining provisions of the Act are already in force.

1579. Betting duty. See CUSTOMS AND EXCISE, § 956.

1580. Betting offices

LICENSED BETTING OFFICES REGULATIONS 1986 (No. 103) [80p], made under the Betting, Gaming and Lotteries Act 1963 (c.2), s.10(6) and Sched. 4, paras. 1 and 3; operative on March 10, 1986; provide for the advertisements which may be published outside a licensed betting office, restrict the hours during which offices may be open, and require the display of certain notices in them.

1581. Bingo

GAMING (BINGO) ACT (FEES) ORDER 1986 (No. 833) [45p], made under the Gaming (Bingo) Act 1985 (c.35), Sched., para. 5(1); operative on June 9, 1986; requires the payment of fees in respect of the issue of and continuing in force of a certificate of approval by the Gaming Board to an organiser of multiple bingo games under the 1985 Act.

GAMING CLUBS (MULTIPLE BINGO) REGULATIONS 1986 (No. 834) [45p], made under the Gaming (Bingo) Act 1985, s.3(1); operative on June 9, 1986; provide for the management and conduct of games of multiple bingo under the 1985 Act.

1582. Gaming (Amendment) Act 1986 (c.11)

This Act amends ss.16 and 22 of the Gaming Act 1968. S.16 is amended to make provision for the redemption of cheques and s.22 is amended as to records to be kept in relation to cheques.

The Act received the Royal Assent on May 2, 1986. It does not extend to Northern Ireland. It comes into force on a day to be appointed.

1583. Gaming (Bingo) Act 1985—commencement

GAMING (BINGO) ACT 1985 (COMMENCEMENT) ORDER 1986 (No. 832 (c.21)) [45p], made under the Gaming (Bingo) Act 1985 (c.35), s.5(2); brings the 1985 Act into force on June 9, 1986.

1584. Gaming machines

GAMING ACT (VARIATION OF MONETARY LIMITS) ORDER 1986 (No. 1981) [45p], made under the Gaming Act 1968 (c.65), ss.34(9), 51(4); operative on January 1, 1987; increases maximum amounts which may be offered as prizes in amusements by means of gaming machines provided at certain fairs, licensed clubs and other premises.

1585. Pool Competitions Act 1971—continuance

POOL COMPETITIONS ACT 1971 (CONTINUANCE) ORDER 1986 (No. 1234) [45p], made under the Pool Competitions Act 1971 (c.57), s.8(2)(3); operative on July 26, 1986; continues the 1971 Act in force until July 26, 1987.

GAS AND GASWORKS

1586. Connection charges

GAS (CONNECTION CHARGES) REGULATIONS 1986 (No. 1448) [45p], made under the Gas Act 1986 (c.44), ss.10(4), 47(3)(b); operative on September 13, 1986; provides for charges in relation to connecting a person requiring gas to the gas supply.

1587. Gas Act 1986 (c.44)

This act provides for the appointment and functions of a Director General of Gas Supply and the establishment and functions of a Gas Consumers' Council; abolishes the privilege conferred on the British Gas Corporation by section 29 of the Gas Act 1972; makes new provision with respect to the supply of gas through pipes and certain related matters; provides for the vesting of the property, rights and liabilities of the British Gas Corporation in a company nominated by the Secretary of State and the subsequent dissolution of that Corporation; and makes provision with respect to, and to information furnished in connection with, agreements relating to the initial supply of gas won under the authority of a petroleum production licence.

The Act received the Royal Assent on July 25, 1986.

1588. Gas Act 1986—commencement

GAS ACT 1986 (COMMENCEMENT No. 1) ORDER 1986 (No. 1315 (c.43)) [45p], made under the Gas Act 1986 (c.44), s.68(5); brings into force on August 18, 1986 sections 1, 65 and 68, and Sched. 1, and brings into force on August 23, 1986 sections 2, 63 and 64, and Sched. 2.

GAS ACT 1986 (COMMENCEMENT No. 2) ORDER 1986 (No. 1809 (c.65)) [45p], made under the Gas Act 1986 (c.44), s.68(5); brings into force on November 14, 1986 section 62 of the 1986 Act.

1589. Gas Act 1986—orders

GAS ACT 1986 (APPPOINTED DAY) ORDER 1986 (No. 1316 (c.44)) [45p], made under the Gas Act 1986 (c.44), s.3; the day appointed for the purposes of s.3 of the 1986 Act and specified provisions of Pt. I of that Act is August 23, 1986.

GAS ACT 1986 (NOMINATED COMPANY) ORDER 1986 (No. 1317) [45p], made under the Gas Act 1986 (c.44), s.49(2); vests all the rights and liabilities of the British Gas Corporation in British Gas PLC on a day to be appointed.

GAS ACT 1986 (TRANSFER DATE) ORDER 1986 (No. 1318) [45p], made under the Gas Act 1986 (c.44), s.49(1); appoints August 24, 1986 for the purposes of s.49 of the 1986 Act.

1590. Oilfield interests

BRITISH GAS CORPORATION (DISPOSAL OF WYTCH FARM OILFIELD RIGHTS) DIRECTION 1986 (No. 980) [45p], made under the Oil and Gas (Enterprise) Act 1982 (c.23), s.11(1); operative on July 1, 1986; requires the British Gas Corporation to transfer to the Treasury Solicitor its rights in the Wytch Farm Oilfield.

1591. Restrictive trade practices

RESTRICTIVE TRADE PRACTICES (GAS SUPPLY AND CONNECTED ACTIVITIES) ORDER 1986 (No. 1810) [£1·40], made under the Gas Act 1986 (c.44), ss.62(2)(c), 64; operative on November 14, 1986; specifies the further conditions which must be satisfied for an agreement which complies with s.62(2)(a)(b) of the 1986 Act to be excluded from the provisions of the Restrictive Trade Practices Act 1976.

GUARANTEE AND INDEMNITY

1592. Construction—extrinsic evidence

[Statute of Frauds 1677 (c.3), s.4.] Extrinsic objective evidence is admissible, notwithstanding the requirements of section 4, to explain the meaning of terms used in a guarantee and whether they relate to present or future liability: PERRYLEASE *v.* IMECAR AG (1986) 136 New L.J. 987, Scott J.

1593. Group liability—surplus funds—distribution. See BROWN *v.* CORK, § 2841.

1594. Summary judgment—stay of execution

It would only be proper to stay the execution of summary judgment based on a guarantee, where there were cross-claims, in exceptional circumstances, particularly if the guarantees were the equivalent of letters of credit (*Nova Jersey Knit* v. *Kammgarn Spinnerei GmbH* [1977] C.L.Y. 195, *Moutecchi* v. *Shimco (U.K.)* [1979] C.L.Y. 2143, *Cebora SNC* v. *SIP Industrial Products* [1976] C.L.Y. 2202, *Aries Tanker Corp.* v. *Total Transport* [1977] C.L.Y. 2741, *Intraco* v. *Notis Shipping Corp.* [1981] C.L.Y. 2160): CONTINENTAL ILLINOIS NATIONAL BANK AND TRUST CO. OF CHICAGO *v.* PAPANICOLAOU, *The Times*, July 15, 1986, C.A.

1595. Surety—discharge—breach of contract between creditor and debtor by creditor—non-repudiatory breach

P was N's bank. N carried on business in the motor trade including the sale of petrol. N was overdrawn and owed P money on its loan account. N's liabilities were guaranteed by D. The guarantee provided by clause 1 that "this guarantee shall not be discharged nor shall the guarantor's liability under it be affected by anything which would not have discharged or affected the guarantor's liability if the guarantor had been a principal debtor to the bank instead of a guarantor." N's petrol supplier was paid by way of direct debit on its account with P. P declined to pay two direct debits. In consequence N was forced to pay for further deliveries by bankers draft which meant that the supplier had to be paid before N obtained funds from selling the petrol to its customers. Shortly afterwards N went into liquidation. P entered judgment in default against D for £366,000. D applied to set aside the judgment. D contended he was discharged from his obligations under the guarantee on account of a breach by P of its contract with or by failing to meet the direct debits in respect of petrol supplies. D was successful, P appealed. *Held*, that a non-repudiatory breach of the principal contract by the creditor will not discharge a surety who has guaranteed that contract. A repudiatory breach by the creditor accepted by the debtor would discharge the surety. If the provision of the principal contract in question were embodied in the contract of guarantee a non-repudiatory breach by the creditor might amount to a departure by the creditor from the contract of guarantee thus discharging the surety. In the present case if there was a breach by P it was not a repudiatory breach. By virtue of clause 1 of the guarantee it was impossible for D to argue that anything occurred between the parties that discharged him from his obligations. Judgment reinstated (*Royal Bank of Canada* v. *Salvatori* [1928] 3 W.W.R. 501, *Cellulose Prods. Pty.* v. *Truda* (1970) 92 W.N. (N.S.W.) 561, *Vavasseur Trust Co.* v. *Ashmore* (Court of Appeal, April 2, 1976, unreported) considered).

NATIONAL WESTMINSTER BANK *v.* RILEY [1986] FLR 213, C.A.

HAWKERS AND PEDLARS

1596. Street trading from van—application for consent—notice of objections—reasons for refusal—natural justice. See R. *v.* BRISTOL CITY COUNCIL, *ex p.* PEARCE, § 2054.

HIGHWAYS AND BRIDGES

1597. Bridges

COUNTY COUNCIL OF HEREFORD AND WORCESTER (BEWDLEY BYPASS BRIDGE) SCHEME 1984 CONFIRMATION INSTRUMENT 1986 (No. 1429) [80p], made under the Highways Act 1980 (c.66), s.106(3); confirms a scheme for the construction of a bridge at Bewdley.

LONDON BOROUGH OF TOWER HAMLETS (WANSBECK ROAD BRIDGE) SCHEME 1985 CONFIRMATION INSTRUMENT 1985 (No. 731) [£1·40], made under the Highways Act 1980 (c.66), s.106(3); confirms a scheme to construct a bridge over the navigable waters of the Hertford Union Canal.

S.I. 1986 Nos. 351 (Warwickshire County Council—Grand Union Canal Bridge) [80p]; 1760 (Buckinghamshire County Council—Canal Footbridges) [£1·90]; 1902 (Lancashire County Council—Shuttleworth Canal Bridge) [£1·40]; 2264 (County Council of Avon-Temple Bridge) [£1·40].

1598. Draft order—Secretary of State's interference—whether correct exercise of authority

[Road Traffic Regulation Act 1984 (c.27), ss.6, 122.] The G.L.C. made a draft order pursuant to the Road Traffic Regulation Act 1984 banning the driving of heavy goods vehicles. The Secretary of State prohibited the order on the ground that no inquiry had been held. The G.L.C. sought judicial review of the direction. *Held,* that (1) the Secretary of State was empowered to interfere only if there was some default or impropriety in the way an authority exercised its powers; (2) in this case the decision of the G.L.C. was legitimate. The direction was improper. Appeal from the decision of McNeill J. dismissed: GREATER LONDON COUNCIL *v.* SECRETARY OF STATE FOR TRANSPORT [1986] J.P.L. 513, C.A.

1599. Excavation—whether offence

[Highways Act 1980 (c.66), s.131(1).] S.131(1) of the Highways Act 1980 makes it an absolute offence to make an excavation in a highway, which consists of or comprises a carriageway, without lawful authority or excuse. Proof of *mens rea* is unnecessary: GREENWICH LONDON BOROUGH COUNCIL *v.* MILLCROFT CONSTRUCTION, *The Times,* July 26, 1986, D.C.

1600. GLC lorry ban—abolition of GLC—status of restricted streets

[Local Government Act 1985 (c.51) Sched. 4, para. 53(1), (2); Metropolitan Roads (Trunking) Order 1986 (S.I. 1986 No. 153).] Where roads had been made restricted streets by the GLC, and the same roads had been designated trunk roads by the Secretary of State after the abolition of the GLC, those roads lost their restricted status (*Peart v. Stewart* [1983] C.L.Y. 524, *Att.-Gen. v. Edison Telegraph Co.* [1886] Q.B. 244 considered): RICHMOND BOROUGH COUNCIL *v.* SECRETARY OF STATE FOR TRANSPORT, (1986) 136 New L.J. 941, Sir Neil Lawson.

1601. Highways (Amendment) Act 1986 (c.13)

This Act amends the Highways Act 1980 by imposing penalties in cases where a user of a highway is injured, interrupted or endangered as a result of the lighting of a fire on the highway or elsewhere.

The Act received the Royal Assent on May 2, 1986. It extends to England and Wales only and comes into force two months after Royal Assent.

1602. Maintenance depot—transfer. See LOCAL GOVERNMENT, § 2026.

1603. New street byelaws

NEW STREET BYELAWS (EXTENSION OF OPERATION) VARIATION ORDER 1986 (No. 610) [45p], made under the Highways Act 1980 (c.66), Sched. 23, para. 11; amends S.I. 1983 No. 483.

1604. Obstruction—elements of offence

[Highways Act 1980 (c.66), s.137(1).] The elements of the offence of obstruction under s.137(1) of the Highways Act 1980 are: (1) there must be an actual obstruction, which must be more than *de minimis;* (2) it must be wilful or deliberate; (3) there must be no lawful authority or excuse. "Lawful authority" includes, for example, licenced traders. "Lawful excuse" embraces activities lawful in themselves, which are also reasonable. There can therefore be, *e.g.* a right to use the highway for reasonable protest (*Nagy v. Weston,* [1965] C.L.Y. 1778, *Hubbard v. Pitt* [1975] C.L.Y. 2453, and *Cooper v. Commissioner of Police for the Metropolis,* [1986] C.L.Y. 661 applied; *Waite v. Taylor* [1985] C.L.Y. 1600 not applied): HIRST *v.* CHIEF CONSTABLE OF WEST YORKSHIRE, *The Times,* November 19, 1986, C.A.

1605. Road—public footpath—whether a road. See LANG *v.* HINDHAUGH, § 2976.

1606. Road humps

HIGHWAYS (ROAD HUMPS) (LOCAL INQUIRIES) REGULATIONS 1986 (No. 1858) [45p], made under the Highways Act 1980 (c.66), s.90C(5); operative on December 1, 1986; amends the Local Government Act 1972, s.250(4)(5) in its application to inquiries held in pursuance of s.90C(4) of the 1980 Act.

HIGHWAYS (ROAD HUMPS) REGULATIONS 1986 (No. 1856) [£1·40], made under the Highways Act 1980, s.90C(1), 90D(1)(2); operative on December 1, 1986; revokes and replaces with amendments S.I. 1983 No. 1087.

1607. Special roads

S.I. 1986 Nos. 778 (M57—Huyton Spur) [45p]; 1434 (M67 Denton Relief Road Motorway) [45p]; 1558 (Wickham–Theale) [45p]; 1646 (M11 London–Cambridge) [45p]; 1736 (A102(M) Eastway Section) [45p]; 1987 (M40 London–Oxford–

Birmingham) [80p]; 1988 (M40 London–Oxford–Birmingham) [45p] 2321 (Crick—Doncaster Bypass) [45p].

1608. Trunk roads

S.I. 1986 Nos. 69 (Chevening-Hastings) [40p]; 70 (Chevening-Hastings) [40p]; 152 (Oxford–Market Deeping) [40p]; 153 (Metropolitan Roads) [£2·80]; 189 (Hanford–Hanchurch) [40p]; 190 (London–Great Yarmouth) [80p]; 257 (Carlisle–Sunderland) [40p]; 258 (Carlisle–Sunderland) [80p]; 349 (London—Great Yarmouth) [80p]; 350 (Felixstowe—Weedon) [80p]; 397 (Eastern Avenue, Redbridge) [40p]; 507 (Boroughbridge—Thirsk) [80p]; 511 (London—Edinburgh—Thurso) [80p]; 512 (London—Edinburgh—Thurso) [40p]; 521 (Doncaster—Kendal) [40p]; 557 (Oxford—Market Deeping) [40p]; 565 (Folkestone-Honiton) [45p]; 667 (London-Penzance) [80p]; 675 (Folkestone-Honiton) [80p]; 676 (Folkestone-Honiton) [45p]; 679 (Derby—Macclesfield—Stockport) [45p]; 682 (Sheffield—Grimsby) [45p]; 726 (Newcastle-Under-Lyme—Tarvin) [80p]; 897 (London—Fishguard) [45p]; 1017 (Swansea–Manchester) [45p]; 1018 (Swansea–Manchester) [80p]; 1064 (Norman Cross—Grimsby) [45p]; 1065 (Norman Cross—Grimsby) [45p]; 1106 (Folkestone—Honiton) [45p]; 1107 (Folkestone—Honiton) [45p]; 1149 (London—Portsmouth) [45p]; 1150 (London—Portsmouth) [45p]; 1151 (London—Portsmouth) [45p]; 1242 (London North Circular) [80p];1244 (Swansea–Manchester) [45p]; 1389 (London–Penzance) [80p]; 1400 (Winchester–Preston) [45p]; 1407 (Eastern Avenue, Havering) [80p]; 1408 (Winchester–Preston) [80p]; 1409 (Winchester–Preston) [45p]; 1415 (Bath-Lincoln, King's Lynn–Newark) [80p]; 1416 (Bath–Lincoln, King's Lynn–Newark) [45p]; 1451, (Newtown–Barnstaple) [45p]; 1452 (Exeter–Leeds, Taunton–Fraddon) [80p]; 1453 (London–Edinburgh–Thurso) [£1·40]; 1454 (Carlisle–Sunderland) [45p]; 1455 (Carlisle–Sunderland) [45p]; 1469 (King's Lynn–Newark) [80p]; 1512 (Chester–Bangor) [45p]; 1513 (Chester–Bangor) [45p]; 1514 (Chester–Bangor) [45p]; 1516 (Exeter–Leeds) [45p]; 1647 (Woodford–Barking) [45p]; 1737 (London—Great Yarmouth) [80p]; 1738 (London–Great Yarmouth) [45p]; 1791 (Birmingham–Great Yarmouth) [80p]; 1792 (Birmingham–Great Yarmouth) [45p]; 1800 (The Parkway, Hounslow) [45p]; 1807 (Hungerford–Hereford) [80p]; 1814 (A3–Malden Way, Kingston Upon Thames) [45p]; 1824 (Raglan-Llandovery) [80p]; 1967 (London–King's Lynn) [45p]. 2149 (Winchester—Preston) [45p]; 2156 (London—Brighton) [45p]; 2157 (London—Brighton) [45p]; 2158 (London—Brighton) [45p]; 2159 (London—Brighton) [80p]; 2160 (London—Brighton) [80p]; 2319 (Birmingham—Nottingham) [45p]; 2320 (Birmingham—Nottingham) [80p]; 2355 (london—Portsmouth) [45p].

1609. Trunk roads

TRUNK ROADS (CONSTRUCTION AND MAINTENANCE AGREEMENTS) ORDER 1986 (No. 278) [£4·70], made under the Local Government Act 1985 (c.51), Sched. 4, para. 56; operative on April 1, 1986; provides for the continuation after April 1, 1986, of trunk road construction and maintenance agreements under s.6 of the Highways Act 1960.

HOUSING

1610. Benefits

HOUSING BENEFITS AMENDMENT REGULATIONS 1986 (No. 84) [40p], made under the Social Security and Housing Benefits Act 1982 (c.24), s.28(1); operative on February 3, 1986; provide that, in ascertaining a person's weekly income for the purposes of calculating entitlement to housing benefit, any job start allowance payable under arrangements made by the Manpower Services Commission is disregarded.

HOUSING BENEFITS AMENDMENT (No. 2) REGULATIONS 1986 (No. 852) [80p], made under the Social Security and Housing Benefits Act 1982 (c.24), s.28(1); operative on June 6 and July 28, 1986; amend S.I. 1985 No. 677.

HOUSING BENEFITS AMENDMENT (No. 3) REGULATIONS 1986 (No. 1009) [£1·40], made under the Social Security and Housing Benefits Act 1982 (c.24), ss.28(1), 45(1) and the Social Security Act 1975 (c.14), s.166(2)(3); operative on July 28, 1986 save for regs. 2(1)(4) (in part), 5 which are operative on September 1, 1986; amend S.I. 1985 No. 677 in relation to students.

HOUSING BENEFITS AMENDMENT (No. 4) REGULATIONS 1986 (No. 1156) [£1·40], made under the Social Security and Housing Benefits Act 1982 (c.24), s.28(1);

operative on July 28, 1986; amend S.I. 1985 No. 677 which relates to the statutory schemes for the grant of rate rebates, rent rebates and rent allowances.

HOUSING BENEFITS (SUBSIDY) ORDER 1986 (No. 2042) [£1·40], made under the Social Security and Housing Benefits Act 1982 (c.24), s.32(2); operative on December 29, 1986; sets out the manner in which the subsidy payable to authorities under s.32 of the 1982 Act is to be calculated in respect of the year 1986/87.

HOUSING BENEFITS AMENDMENT (NO. 5) REGULATIONS 1986 (No. 2183) [£1·40], made under the Social Security and Housing Benefits Act 1982 (c.24), s.28(1); operative on March 30, 1987; contain provisions relating to rate rebates, rent rebates and rent allowances.

HOUSING BENEFITS (SUBSIDY) AMENDMENT ORDER 1986 (No. 430) [80p], made under the Social Security and Housing Benefits Act 1982 (c.24), ss.32(2), 36(1); operative on March 31, 1986; amends S.I. 1985 No. 440.

1611. Caravan sites—duty of local authority—"squatters proceedings" see WEST GLAMORGAN COUNTY COUNCIL v. RAFFERTY; R. v. SECRETARY OF STATE FOR WALES, ex p. GILHANEY, § 3281.

1612. Closing order—house unfit for human occupation—challenge by protected tenant—factors to be taken into account by the local authority

[Housing Act 1985 (c.68), Pts. VI, IX.] The applicant, who was 72 years old, was a protected tenant of premises which had fallen into very substantial disrepair and which he accepted were unfit for human occupation. The respondent authority's environmental health officer made a report which was considered by the Health and Recreational Services Committee. The committee also had before them an estimate by an independent surveyor to the effect that the cost of repairs would be greater than the value of the premises, on the basis that the tenant would remain. The committee were satisfied that the premises were not capable of being rendered fit for human habitation at a reasonable cost. In due course a closing order was made in respect of the property. The applicant challenged this decision initially on the ground that the respondent authority had not properly considered the question of valuation, then, at the hearing, on the alternative grounds that the authority had failed to consider (a) the possibility of the tenant paying increased rent if the property was repaired, (b) the availability of grant aid, (c) the desirability of maintaining property and not encouraging property owners to do nothing for years, thereby allowing the properties to fall into such disrepair so that they could not be repaired at reasonable cost. *Held,* dismissing the application that (1) the court would assume for present purposes that the applicant was not a "person aggrieved" under the Act and not therefore entitled to appeal to the county court; (2) all three matters relied upon by the applicant were relevant matters which the authority were bound to take into account: it could not be inferred from the fact that there was no express reference to these matters in the documents before the court that they had not been taken into account; it was quite possible that if the applicant had sufficiently identified the matters he was relying on, the authority would have adduced evidence to show they had been taken into account; (3) even if they had not been taken into account, it was at least highly probable that the authority would have reached the same conclusion; (4) in any event the court would have refused relief by reason of the delay in mounting the challenge: R. v. MALDON DISTRICT COUNCIL, ex p. FISHER (1986) 18 H.L.R. 197, Simon Brown J.

1613. Closing order—use of premises in contravention of closing order—prosecution—proof of knowledge.

[Housing Act 1957 (c.56), s.27, Law of Property Act 1925 (c.20), s.198, Local Land Charges Act 1975, (c.76) Sched. 1] In June 1977 a closing order was made in respect of the premises. The local authority made an entry of the closing order in the Local Land Charges Register. In February 1979 the respondent purchased the premises. He was not expressly told about the closing order either by the local authority or his solicitors. He was prosecuted under s.27 of the 1957 Act in that knowing a closing order had become operative and applied to the premises he permitted them to be used in contravention of the order. In the magistrates' court it was held that he was not guilty as it had not been proved that he had actual knowledge of the order. The prosecuting authority appealed. *Held,* dismissing the appeal, that notwithstanding the provisions of the Law of Property Act 1925, registration of a closing order does not constitute actual notice of the existence of the closing order sufficient to satisfy the Housing Act 1957: BARBER *v*. SHAH (1985) 17 H.L.R. 584, D.C.

1614. Defective dwellings

DEFECTIVE DWELLINGS (MORTGAGEES) REGULATIONS 1986 (No. 797) [£1·40], made under the Housing Act 1985 (c.68), s.568; operative on June 1, 1986; apply where an owner of a defective dwelling has defaulted on the mortgage and the mortgagee is entitled to sell the dwelling and is in possession.

1615. Disrepair—notice to execute works—block of flats—reversionary interest—rack rent

Housing Act 1957 (c.56), ss.9(1A), 11(1), 37(1), 39(2).]

A freeholder who let a building under a single lease at less than the rack rent or granted separate leases at ground rents which in aggregate were less than the rent, and so retained only a reversionary interest which conferred no right of occupation was not a "person having control" of the building within s.39(2) of the Housing Act 1957 and could not be served with a notice to repair.

P was the freeholder of a block of 42 flats, 10 of which were let on a block booking and 32 of which had been sold on long leases of 99 years at ground rents which in total were less than a rack rent for the building as a whole. Under the terms of the leases P was responsible for keeping the building in repair, but was entitled to recover the cost of doing so by way of a service charge. The local authority served a notice under s.9(1A) of the Housing Act 1957 requiring P to carry out specified repairs. They ignored the notice and did not appeal to the county court within 21 days as permitted by s.11(1) of the Act. The authority served notice that they intended to enter the building and carry out the repairs and charge P. P sought and were granted a declaration that the notice of repair was invalid since they were not a "person having control" of the building for the purposes of s.9(1A) and so were not required to carry out the repairs. The local authority appealed to the Court of Appeal which dismissed their appeal, and they further appealed to the House of Lords. *Held*, dismissing the appeal, that where the building was let under a single lease at least than the rack rent or under separate leases at ground rents which in aggregate were less than the rack rent, so that the freeholder retained only a reversionary interest which conferred no right of occupation, which could be disposed of to someone else, the freeholder was not the person who would receive the rack rent "if the building were let at a rack-rent" and accordingly he was not deemed by s.39(2) to be the "person having control" of the building. Since P was not the person having control of the building, the notice of repair was invalid (*Truman Hanbury Buxton & Co. v. Kerslake* [1894] 2 Q.B. 774 and *London Corp. v. Cusack-Smith* [1955] C.L.Y. 2711 applied). Since the 1957 Act required the service of a valid notice on the person having control of the building, if it was not served on that person, it had no statutory force or effect at all, so that the right of appeal under s.11. and the effect, under s.37(1) of not appealing (which was that the notice to repair became "final and conclusive" of the validity of the notice) were not relevant.

POLLWAY NOMINEES *v*. CROYDON LONDON BOROUGH COUNCIL [1986] 2 All E.R. 849, H.L.

1616. Grants

HOUSING DEFECTS (EXPENDITURE LIMITS) ORDER 1986 (No. 1494) [80p], made under the Housing Act 1985 (c.68), s.543(4) (5); operative on September 25, 1986; specifies expenditure limits for various categories of defective dwelling.

1617. Home loss payment—improvement and alteration of property—temporary decant

[Land Compensation Act 1973 (c.26), s.29.] T had lived for 14 years in a flat rented from L. The flat was a three-bedroomed ground floor flat in a large block. L decided to improve and upgrade the block, as a result of which T would have to move out temporarily. The works included alterations to the flat so that it would be reduced in size, its internal arrangement altered so that the bedrooms would be reduced to one, and the living accommodation increased. In addition there would be a communal staircase taking up part of the space gained from the flat. The address of the flat would also be changed, as part of a general renumbering of the whole housing provision in the area. T made an application for home loss payment. L determined that she did not qualify as she had not been permanently displaced from the dwelling and the dwelling has not become a different dwelling by reason of the alterations. T sought judicial review of the decision. *Held,* dismissing the application, that (1) having regard to the provisions of the Act the issue is whether a dwelling from which the applicant is displaced remains the same dwelling on return; in some cases there can be a displacement from a dwelling which is simply being improved; it may be that in an appropriate case improvements are so radical and far reaching as to cause the original dwelling to lose its identity; (2) in the present case, the authority had adopted the correct approach of considering each case on its own merits and had asked themselves the right question, namely whether the dwelling as altered could be regarded as the same dwelling or whether the alteration was so radical as to make it something new: CASALE *v.* ISLINGTON, LONDON BOROUGH OF (1985) 18 H.L.R. 146, Taylor J.

1618. Home purchase assistance

HOME PURCHASE ASSISTANCE (PRICE-LIMITS) ORDER 1986 (No. 1511) [80p], made under the Housing Act 1985 (c.68), s.445(2)(3) and the Home Purchase Assistance and Housing Corporation Guarantee Act 1978 (c.27), ss.1(2), 2(7); operative on September 25, 1986; prescribes limits for the purposes of home purchase assistance bonuses and loans.

HOME PURCHASE ASSISTANCE (RECOGNISED LENDING INSTITUTIONS) ORDER 1986 (No. 1489) [45p], made under the Housing Act 1985 (c.68), s.447(2) (3); operative on September 1, 1986; adds Swansea Building Society to the list of recognised lending institutions.

HOME PURCHASE ASSISTANCE (RECOGNISED SAVINGS INSTITUTIONS) ORDER 1986 (No. 1490) [45p], made under the Housing Act 1985, s.448(2)(3); operative on September 1, 1986; adds the Swansea Building Society to the list of recognised savings institutions.

1619. Homeless persons—accommodation—test

[Housing (Homeless Persons) Act 1977 (c.48), ss.1, 4).]

When considering whether or not a person is homeless, a local authority is not obliged to consider the suitability of any accommodation occupied by an applicant but it is required to consider whether the accommodation he occupies can properly be described as "accommodation" within the ordinary meaning of that word.

P and his wife lived with their two children in bed and breakfast accommodation consisting of a single room with no proper cooking or washing facilities. They applied to the local authority to be housed, contending that they were homeless because the accommodation they occupied was unsuitable for their needs. The authority concluded that they were not homeless because accommodation was available for them. *Held,* dismissing the appeal, that the authority had been entitled to find as they did, because the applicants did, in fact, have accommodation available for their use. The test to be applied was whether the accommodation in fact occupied could properly be described as "accommodation" within the ordinary meaning of that word. It was irrelevant that the accommodation might be described as unfit, or overcrowded, within the meaning of the Housing Act 1957, or that it might be unsuitable for the particular applicant.

PUHLHOFER *v.* HILLINGDON LONDON BOROUGH COUNCIL [1986] 1 All E.R. 467, H.L.

1620. Homeless persons—domestic violence—whether homeless

[Housing (Homeless Persons) Act 1977 (c.48), s.1.]

The applicant was the joint owner of the matrimonial home she occupied with her husband between 1980 and 1983. In January she left her husband and went to live with another man because of her husband's violence towards her. After three months she left the other man but did not seek to re-occupy her former home, believing that if she did so her husband and his family would harass and threaten her. She applied to the respondent authority as homeless who held, first, that she was homeless intentionally and then that she was not homeless at all. The applicant challenged the decision. *Held,* dismissing the application that to qualify as homeless the applicant had to show either that she could not secure entry to her former home or that it was probable that occupation of it would lead to violence or to threats of violence from some other person residing in it; there was no evidence to show that any attempt had been made to secure entry and only the most indirect evidence that if she did violence would result; the evidence therefore did not go as far as necessary to say that the authority ought reasonably to have been satisfied that the applicant was homeless: R. *v.* PURBECK DISTRICT COUNCIL, *ex p.* CADNEY (1985) 17 H.L.R. 534, Nolan J.

1621. Homeless persons—duty to rehouse—whether accommodation to be available indefinitely

[Housing (Homeless Persons) Act 1977 (c.48), s.4(2), (3), (5).] The local authority is obliged to rehouse a homeless person indefinitely even though that person was occupying a "short-life" property before being made homeless by a fire (*R. v. Slough Borough Council, ex p. Ealing Borough Council* [1981] C.L.Y. 1299, *Din v. Wandsworth London Borough Council* [1981] C.L.Y. 1296, *Puhlhofer v. Hillingdon London Borough Council* [1986] C.L.Y. 1619 considered): R. *v.* CAMDEN LONDON BOROUGH COUNCIL, *ex p.* WAIT, *The Times,* July 12, 1986, McCowan J.

1622. Homeless persons—intentional homelessness—domestic breakdown

[Housing (Homeless Persons) Act 1977 (c.48), s.17] In November 1982 E left the matrimonial home (armed services married quarters) having discovered that her husband had committed adultery. She then applied to the local authority who advised her to return to the matrimonial home, and if necessary to seek an injunction against her husband, as she had made reference to violence on his part during the interview. Shortly afterwards her husband was posted to Brize Norton, and E returned to the married quarters. On receiving a notice to quit she again approached the authority who found that she was not intentionally homeless. However before an offer of accommodation was made E had decided to attempt a reconciliation with her husband, and moved with him to Brize Norton. A month later she once again approached the authority who again advised her to return to married quarters. There was no allegation of domestic violence during this period. E did not accept this advice and remained with her sister until she was required to leave in September 1983. The authority concluded that E's last permanent address was the married quarters in Brize Norton and that she was homeless intentionally therefrom, as it was available for her occupation and would have been reasonable for her to remain there, even if only for a short period until the right to occupy was determined by the armed forces and this would relieve the pressure on the local authority in circumstances of general housing shortage. E challenged this decision. *Held,* dismissing the application, that (1) ignorance of the fact that occupation for a short period was of assistance to the authority is not ignorance of a relevant fact within s.17 of the Act; (2) the authority were entitled to take into account the possibility that matrimonial law would protect E for such period as she could remain in married quarters; (3) it was not unreasonable for the authority to conclude that it would have been reasonable for the applicant to remain in occupation of the quarters for such a period: R. *v.* EASTLEIGH BOROUGH COUNCIL, *ex p.* EVANS (1984) 17 H.L.R. 515; McNeil J.

1623. Homeless persons—intentional homelessness—meaning, of a "settled accommodation"

[Housing (Homeless Persons) Act 1977 (c.48), s.4(5).]

The applicant was a young woman with a dependent child. In January 1984 she applied to the respondent authority for assistance under the Act who accepted a responsibility towards her, and provided her with a bedsitting room in temporary accommodation managed by the authority themselves. A sink, cooker and refrigerator were provided in the room, and the applicant had the shared use of a bathroom and communal sitting room. She occupied the accommodation under a licence agreement. In June 1984 the applicant moved into a larger room in the same property. Subsequently there were complaints from other residents about the applicant's conduct and a petition submitted to the authority. The applicant's licence was determined, and in March 1985 a possession order was made. The applicant then reapplied to the authority under the Act, who responded that she was regarded as intentionally homeless. The applicant sought judicial review of this decision, and the question of whether the applicant had been in "secure" or "settled" accommodation was dealt with as a preliminary point. *Held* that (1) the local authority are entitled to discharge their duty to provide permanent accommodation under s.4(5) of the Act in stages, (2) the status of a person who is unintentionally homeless is not displaced unless and until he or she acquires "settled accommodation"; the word settled is not a statutory term but a word of convenience, and is a question of fact and degree depending on the circumstances of each individual case; in this case the provision of temporary accommodation pending the full discharge of its duty by the provision of permanent accommodation was such "settled" accommodation: R. *v.* EAST HERTFORDSHIRE DISTRICT COUNCIL, *ex p.* HUNT, (1985) 18 H.L.R. 51, Mann J.

1624. Homeless persons—intentional homelessness—enquiries—burden of proof

[Housing Act 1985 (c.68), ss.60, 62.] The applicant (who was married with two children) had been living in a flat in the Channel Islands, which was in a substantial state of disrepair and badly affected by damp. On losing his job he travelled with his family to Southampton to find work. He then moved on to Kent where he had been born, and where he was interviewed by the homeless persons officer. The sole reason for leaving was recorded as being that he had lost his job. The authority found that he was homeless intentionally. Solicitors acting for the family wrote to the authority in May, 1984 then again in August, stating first that they had not made appropriate enquiries, and then supplying further information on the accommodation in the Channel Islands, giving details of its disrepair. A further letter was written in October, enclosing a letter from a local magistrate confirming the description of the premises. The applicant sought judicial review of the authority's decision. *Held,* (dismissing the application), that (1) although criticism could be made of the authority's failure to carry out appropriate enquiries in relation to the decision in May, any deficiency arising from this was cured by October 1984; (2) that the principles applicable to the challenge were (a) that the burden lies on the authority to make appropriate enquiries in a caring and sympathetic way; these should be pursued rigorously and the applicant should be given an opportunity to explain matters which might weigh against him, (b) the burden is on the authority to be satisfied that the applicant is homeless intentionally; if there is any doubt or uncertainty the issue must be resolved in the applicant's favour, (c) the main question was whether the authority was satisfied that it would have been reasonable for the applicant to remain where he was, (d) accommodation need not be appropriate or reasonable provided that it can properly be described as accommodation, (e) the court's supervisory jurisdiction can only be invoked in exceptional circumstances: R. *v.* GRAVESHAM BOROUGH COUNCIL, *ex p.* WINCHESTER (1986) 18 H.L.R. 207, Simon Brown J.

1625. Homeless persons—intentional homelessness—whether accommodation "available"

[Housing (Homeless Persons) Act 1977 (c.48), ss.16, 17] The applicant separated from her husband in April 1982 and thereafter lived with her dependant child in a property provided for her under the terms of a separation agreement. The property was subject to a deed of trust held by herself and her husband, which provided that if the applicant re-married or cohabited, the power of sale was to be exercised. In May 1983 the applicant's prospective future husband moved into the property, and in March 1984 an order for sale was made in the county court. The applicant applied to the respondent authority who determined that she was intentionally homeless because she allowed her prospective husband to live with her. The applicant challenged this decision. *Held,* granting the application, that (1) the phrase "accommodation which is available for his occupation" is to be construed in accordance with s.16 of the Act, (2) the authority were required to consider whether the accommodation in question was available for the occupation of the applicant, and any person who might reasonably be expected to reside with her, (3) there was no evidence that the authority had considered whether the applicant's common law husband might reasonably be expected to live with the applicant, (4) consequently the authority had failed to direct themselves as to the question of whether accommodation was available for occupation within the meaning of s.16: R. *v.* WIMBOURNE DISTRICT COUNCIL, *ex p.* CURTIS, (1985) 18 H.L.R. 79, Mann J.

1626. Homeless persons—intentional homelessness—whether applicant party to surrender

[Housing (Homeless Persons) Act 1977 (c.48), s.17.] Until February 1983, the applicant, his wife and their children lived in a house belonging to the respondent authority, of which the applicant wife had become a tenant by succession. In February 1983 the applicant's wife left the house to live with another man. In April 1983 she surrendered the tenancy of the house. The applicant sought unsuccessfully, to transfer the tenancy into his own name. The applicant and his wife were then reconciled and applied jointly to the authority but were held to have become homeless intentionally, the applicant's wife because she knew she would lose the former matrimonial home and that it would not be transferred to the applicant; the applicant because he allowed his wife to surrender knowing that there was no possibility of transfer. The authority further concluded that there was no evidence that the applicant's wife was acting against his wishes and that it would have been reasonable for her to remain at the property. The applicant challenged the decision. *Held*, granting the application, that there was no material on which the authority could conclude that the applicant was a party to the surrender, or that it was a joint surrender or abandonment: R. *v*. PENWITH DISTRICT COUNCIL *ex p*. TREVENA (1984) 17 H.L.R. 527, McNeill J.

1627. Homeless persons—offer of accommodation unreasonably refused—application to second authority—whether duty to accommodate

[Housing (Homeless Persons) Act 1977 (c. 48), ss. 1(1), 2, 4(5), 5(3), 17(1).]

Where a local council's offer of accommodation under the Housing (Homeless Persons) Act 1977 has been unreasonably refused, the council has no obligation to consider a second application from the same person made homeless again.

The applicant, a single woman with a child, was forced to leave her accommodation. She applied to the council who accepted it was under a statutory duty to house her. The council found her temporary accommodation and then offered her a permanent place outside the area; she refused it and was evicted. She then applied to a second authority who referred her application to the original council under s. 5. The council informed her it had discharged their duty by the earlier offer. *Held*, dismissing the application for judicial review, that the council had fulfilled its obligation under s. 4(5), and would have been under no duty to consider her second application if it had been made. R. v. *Westminster City Council, ex p. Chambers* [1983] C.L.Y. 1807 followed).

R. *v*. HAMMERSMITH AND FULHAM LONDON BOROUGH COUNCIL, *ex p*. O'BRIAN (1985) 84 L.G.R. 202, Glidewell J.

1628. Homeless persons—refusal of accommodation—change of circumstances

[Housing (Homeless Persons) Act 1977 (c.48), s.4(1)(5).]

The duty of a housing authority to offer accommodation under the Housing (Homeless Persons) Act 1977 to someone who had earlier unreasonably refused an offer of suitable accommodation revived once the applicant for accommodation established a material change in circumstances such as a change in priority need which rendered the previous offer unsuitable.

The applicant was a single woman expecting her first child and temporarily residing with her sister. She applied to the local housing authority under the 1977 Act which offered her suitable accommodation. She unreasonably refused this offer. She continued to reside with her sister and her own child. Almost 18 months after her first application she was expecting a second child and re-applied to the council. They decided that they were under no further statutory duty unless there were a fresh incidence of homelessness and refused her application. It was subsequently accepted by the council that the accommodation previously offered would have been unsuitable for the applicant and two children. The judge dismissed the applicant's application for judicial review to quash the council's decision, but her appeal was allowed.

Held, that while a housing authority which had made an offer of accommodation which had been unreasonably refused had performed the statutory duty imposed on them by s.4(5) of the Act of 1977, their duty nevertheless revived once the applicant established a material change of circumstances such as a change in priority need which, having regard to the general circumstances prevailing in relation to housing in the area, rendered the previously offered accommodation unsuitable for himself and those persons who might reasonably be expected to reside with him. The council's decision was quashed. (*R. v. Westminster City Council ex p. Chambers* [1983] C.L.Y. 1807 distinguished.)

R. *v*. EALING LONDON BOROUGH COUNCIL, *ex p*. MCBAIN [1985] 1 W.L.R. 1351, C.A.

1629. House in multiple occupation—Service of notices by local authority—Whether occupation needs to be permanent

[Housing Act 1985 (c.68), s.352.] The applicants were the owners of a number of premises in the respondent authority's area. These offered bed and breakfast accommodation. All the rooms were fully furnished with towels and bed linen provided. Room cleaning was offered. Kitchens were available for the preparation of food for children only. In many cases breakfast was not actually provided. The rooms were let at a daily charge of £5·00 per person. Nearly all the residents were sent to the premises by the local authority as homeless families. The average length of stay per family, according to the authority, was approximately six months. The authority served notices under what was then the Housing Act 1961 limiting the number of households who could occupy particular premises. The applicant sought judicial review on the ground that occupation for the purposes of the Housing Act 1961 (now 1985) denotes a degree of permanence. The application was dismissed. *Held*, on appeal, that while it might be open to argument that a person with a regular home of his own who stays overnight in a hotel may not be occupying it as his home, it would be a misuse of language to say that a person who is homeless and whose only residence is such premises is not occupying or living at the premises: THRASYVOULOU *v*. LONDON BOROUGH OF HACKNEY (1986) 18 H.L.R. 370, C.A.

1630. Housing and Planning Act 1986 (c.63)
This Act makes further provision with respect to housing, planning and local inquiries. It provides financial assistance for the regeneration of urban areas and for connected purposes.

1631. Housing and Planning Act 1986—commencement
HOSING AND PLANNING ACT 1986 (COMMENCEMENT NO. 1) Order 1986 (No. 2262 (c.92)) [£1·90], made under the Housing and Planning Act 1986 (c.63), s.57(2); brings into force on January 7, 1987 sections 1–4, 10–14, 16, 17, 19, 20, 22, 23, 24(1), Pt. III, sections 44–49, 54, 55, Pt. VI (Scotland), Scheds. 5 (Pt. I), 11 (paras. 1–7, 10–14, 16–18, 20–22, 24, 25, 33, 34 38, 45–53, 59, 61), 12 (Pts. III & IV).

1632. Housing (Scotland) Act 1986 (c.65)
This Act amends the Tenants' Rights, Etc. (Scotland) Act 1980, the Housing Associations Act 1985 in its application to Scotland and the Building (Scotland) Act 1959.
The Act received the Royal Assent on November 7, 1986.

1633. Housing benefit—assessment of income during benefit period—whether income during earlier or later period relevant. See R. *v*. HOUSING BENEFITS REVIEW BOARD OF THE LONDON BOROUGH OF EALING, *ex p*. SAVILLE, § 3133.

1634. Housing benefit—exclusion of eligibility of owner-occupier—meaning of owner. See R. *v*. HOUSING BENEFIT REVIEW BOARD FOR SEDGEMOOR DISTRICT COUNCIL, *ex p*. WEADON, § 3134.

1635. Housing benefit—Minister's duty to consult—whether mandatory—whether request for advice and time limit sufficient consultation
[Social Security and Housing Benefits Act 1982 (c.24), s.36(1).]
Where a Minister is under a duty to consult interested bodies before making regulations he can discharge that duty only by genuinely seeking advice, and affording those whose advice is sought a reasonable time in order to express their views and reasonable information concerning the subject matter of the proposed regulations.
Under s.28 of the 1982 Act the Secretary of State has power to make certain regulations with regard to housing benefits, but before doing so he is obliged, by s.36, to consult with organisations appearing to him to represent the housing organisations likely to be affected. The AMA was such an organisation and the Secretary of State purported to consult them. The letter requesting their views was received on November 22, 1982 and a reply was sought by November 30. The department ignored a request for more time to consider the position. Subsequently further amendments to the regulations had to be considered but the AMA was not furnished with a copy of the draft amendments. The AMA applied to quash the regulations made by the Minister. *Held*, that a declaration would be granted that the Secretary of State had failed in his duty to consult, but that the regulations would not be quashed as the main complaint of the AMA had, in reality, been the failure to consult rather than the content of the regulations, which had in any event been acted on for some while. The duty to consult required the Minister to make a genuine request for advice, and to have a genuine desire to receive that advice. The body from whom the advice was sought had to have a reasonable time within which to formulate an answer, and had also to be given all the material information. Whilst the urgency of any proposed regulations being made was relevant, there was no degree of urgency which absolved the Minister from his duty to consult—of which duty he had, in this case, been in breach.
R. *v*. SECRETARY OF STATE FOR SOCIAL SERVICES, *ex p*. ASSOCIATION OF METROPOLITAN AUTHORITIES [1986] 1 W.L.R. 1, Webster J.

1636. Housing management—consultation procedures—whether lawful

[Housing Act 1985 (c.68) s.105.] The appellant was a secure tenant of premises on an estate owned by the respondents. As a result of bad structural disrepair a report was prepared for the respondent's Development Committee which recommended in July 1983 (after having considered a number of options) that in principle the Committee should agree to the disposal of the whole estate to a private developer in a package form, allowing for some of the existing tenants to remain on the estate as council tenants and that the appropriate officer should be authorised to market the estate to reputable developers. The recommendation was adopted. The tenants' Residents Committee then prepared a leaflet criticising the report. On the basis of this, the Housing Management Committee resolved that the recommendations be rejected and that full consultation should take place on the proposals. The Development Committee resolved to adhere to their previous decision. The appellant then complained that consultation in accordance with the Act had not taken place, to which the respondents replied that the decision to market the estate was a decision *in principle*, and that once the proposals from the developers were forthcoming, and once the Council had decided which were viable, then consultation would take place. It would be at this stage, too, that tenants would be able to suggest alternatives to the proposals under the option to sell to the private sector and under other options. In December 1984 the appellant issued proceedings to restrain the council from proceeding further with the proposed sale. It was common ground between the parties that since February 1985 proper consultation was carried out with the tenants so far as concerned the proposals to which the consultation was directed. The appellant, however, contended that there had been no consultation prior to the decision in July 1983. The claim was dismissed in the county court. The appellant appealed on two grounds, (a) that although the decision of July 1983 was a decision "in principle" and although it could be reversed before being put into effect it was in substance a decision to sell the estate, and (b) even if it was not a decision to sell it was a decision to take forward one option only. *Held,* dismissing the appeal, that (1) before a decision is a matter of housing management the authority must be satisfied, *inter alia*, that the matter must be likely substantially to affect its secure tenants as a whole or a group of them; (2) that this should read "is likely if implemented to affect secure tenants"; (3) that in July 1983 the Development Committee was not asked to decide upon the sale of the estate but to agree in principle to a particular form of sale and to authorise marketing; there was no evidence that the making of that decision and the carrying out of marketing could so affect the tenants; (4) the decision was not a matter of housing management since the decision not to pursue a policy of repair or rehabilitation could only represent "a new programme" or "a change in policy" if there was an existing programme or policy; further the decision not to repair or rehabilitate was not likely to affect secure tenants since the cost was too high to obtain permission from the Department of the Environment; (5) the matter was within the jurisdiction of the county court, but the jurisdiction to grant an injunction is discretionary, and the court can have regard to delay in making the application, the fact that consultation has since taken place, and the effect on other residents: SHORT v. TOWER HAMLETS, LONDON BOROUGH OF (1985) 18 H.L.R. 171, C.A.

1637. Local authority—power to fix rent levels—housing benefit implications

[Social Security and Housing Benefits Act 1982 (c.24), Housing Benefits Regulations 1982 (S.I. 1982 No. 1124), Housing Act 1957 (c.56), s.111] The City Council was concerned with the cost of repairing their stock. In 1983 it proposed a scheme whereby the tenants could opt to accept one or other of two possible levels of repair, namely the full service (when a higher rent would be paid) and the limited service (when a lower rent would be paid). Central government regarded the scheme as unacceptable and promulgated an amendment order changing the definition of rent for the purpose of housing benefit subsidy. The scheme was then revised so that tenants in receipt of housing benefit were excluded from the option choosing the limited repairs service and tenants not in receipt of housing benefit who opted to do the minor repairs themselves became entitled to a repairs grant which was not conditional on any repairs being done and was paid directly to the credit of the tenant's rent account. The Secretary of State promulgated a second amendment (the object of which was again to foil the scheme) to the definition of rent set out in the Housing Benefits Regulations so that amounts attributable to any services, facilities or rights which a tenant may choose not to be provided with were excluded from the definition of rent for the purpose of subsidy. In due course the council made a claim for subsidy for the year 1984/1985 based on the subsidy in that year during which the scheme was running. The Secretary of State turned down the claim. The council began proceedings by way of judicial review seeking a declaration that the Secretary of State was under a duty to pay the moneys claimed. *Held*, dismissing the application, that (1) where a money claim arose wholly in the field of public law, proceedings by way of judicial review were appropriate, (2) although it would be wrong to shut out the Secretary of State from arguing the point that the scheme was *ultra vires*, any relief which the court might grant would take into account the fact that innocent people had joined the scheme in the belief that it was a valid scheme and had altered their position accordingly; (3) the court would hesitate long before deciding in a field of policy that a local authority had failed to take into account something material or taken into account something immaterial; (4) in the present case a body charged with housing management duties might well be failing to take into account a material consideration if no attention was paid to the incidence of subsidy as it affected proposed schemes; the court was not at all satisfied that there was any error in failing to take into account something that was immaterial; (5) the adoption of a scheme solely in order to obtain an increased subsidy might well be an improper purpose as far as the exercise of discretion under the legislation was concerned, but there was no evidence that the consideration of legitimate housing management matters was merely a sham or that the scheme was adopted for an improper purpose, (6) on the proper construction of the amendment to the Housing Benefit Regulations introduced in 1984, the Sheffield scheme fell within its terms and accordingly the amount attributable to the services which the tenant was entitled to choose under the scheme had to be excluded from the amount defined as rent for purposes of housing benefit subsidy: R. *v.* SECRETARY OF STATE FOR HEALTH AND SOCIAL SECURITY, *ex p.* SHEFFIELD, (1985) 18 H.L.R. 6, Forbes J.

1638. Mobile home loans. See BUILDING SOCIETIES, § 243.

1639. Mobile home—protected site
[Caravan Sites and Control of Development Act 1960 (c.62), ss.1(1)(4), 3(3)(4); Caravan Sites Act 1968 (c.52), s.1(2); Mobile Homes Act 1983 (c.34) ss.1(1)(2), 5.]
A "protected site" for the purposes of section 1(2) of the Mobile Homes Act 1983 means one where planning permission has been granted for one or more mobile homes to be set up upon it.
D stationed their mobile home, a caravan, on part of P's land and occupied the caravan as their only residence. No planning permission had been granted for the stationing of the caravan. D occupied the site pursuant to a gratuitous and temporary permission granted by P. P later revoked their permission, and when D refused to move, obtained a county court order for possession. D appealed on the ground that their occupation of the caravan was protected by the Mobile Homes Act 1983 and that they were entitled to an agreement pursuant to the Act to continue to station their caravan there. *Held,* dismissing the appeal that the words "protected site" for the purposes of section 1(2) of the Mobile Homes Act 1983 meant a site in respect of which planning permission had been granted for the stationing of one or more caravans thereon. Since no such permission had been granted in respect of this land, D did not qualify for protection under the Act and there were no grounds for upsetting the order for possession (*National By-Products* v. *Brice* [1984] C.L.Y. 1914 distinguished).
BALTHASAR *v.* MULLANE (1986) 84 L.G.R. 55, C.A.

1640. Possession action—mortgage obtained by fraudulent misrepresentation—wife's consent—whether enforceable. See KINGS NORTH TRUST *v.* BELL, § 2227.

1641. Possession order—suspension on terms—execution—whether court has power to extend time for application to suspend
[C.C.R. Ord. 13, r.4] In February 1981 the Erewash Borough Council obtained an order for possession against the applicant for non-payment of rent under a secure tenancy. The order was suspended for seven days and thereafter for so long as the applicant paid rent. The applicant then failed to pay and the authority sought to execute the warrant for possession. Two days before the date set for eviction the applicant applied to the county court of suspension of the warrant. The county court held that there was no jurisdiction to entertain the applicant for a further suspension.

The applicant sought judicial review of the decision. *Held*, granting the application, that (1) an order for possession suspended on terms is not to be read as that as soon as the terms are not complied with the landlord is entitled to execute the order without the tennant being able to apply for a further extension; (2) the power of the county court to extend time under C.C.R., Ord. 13, r.4 includes power to extend time in which to apply for the suspension of an order for possession: R v. ILKESTON COUNTY COURT, *ex p.* KRUZA (1985) 17 H.L.R. 539, Tudor Evans J.

1642. Possession proceedings—whether summary proceedings appropriate—whether any evidence of surrender by the tenant

[C.C.R. Ord. 24.] In June 1981 the landlord let a flat to an Iranian student, and then arranged for the appellant tenant to share the flat. In September 1981 the original tenant left, and the appellant tenant remained in occupation. In March 1985 the landlord issued a summary proceedings for possession under C.C.R., Ord. 24 in which he also deposed to the following: (a) that in December 1984 he had been informed by the tenant's sister that the tenant had left for the U.S.A. The landlord had visited the flat and found both sets of keys, and very few belongings; (b) in January 1985 the landlord learnt that the tenant would be starting a job in the U.S.A.; (c) in February the tenant phoned the landlord's wife to say he was returning. He was then told that the tenant had broken into the ground floor flat; (d) subsequently, the tenant had broken into the top floor flat. The first hearing was adjourned in order for the tenant to seek legal advice (although this reason did not appear on the record of what happened). At the next hearing the tenant was unrepresented. He was asked by the judge if he understood what was being said. The tenant nodded. The tenant did not then raise any issue in dispute, nor did he make any comments when told that if the order was granted he would have to leave. An order for possession was made. The tenant appealed. Leave to appeal out of time was granted. *Held*, allowing the appeal, that it was doubtful whether the matters relied upon by the landlord were cabable of amounting to a surrender of the tenancy by operation of law, and there was certainly a triable issue on the question; bearing in mind that the tenant was an Iranian student with a poor grasp of English the judge should either have adjourned the hearing to allow him to be represented or should have proceeded to a normal hearing: COOPER v. VARZDARI (1986) 18 H.L.R. 300, C.A.

1643. Right to buy

HOUSING (RIGHT TO BUY) (DESIGNATED RURAL AREAS AND DESIGNATED REGIONS) (ENGLAND) ORDER 1986 (No. 1695) [45p], made under the Housing Act 1985 (c.68), s.157(1)(3); operative on October 29, 1986; designates certain parishes in the Borough of Scarborough as rural areas for the purposes of s.157 of the 1985 Act.

HOUSING (RIGHT TO BUY) (MAXIMUM DISCOUNT) ORDER 1986 (No. 2193) [45p], made under the Housing Act 1985 (c.68), s.131(2); operative on January 7, 1987, prescribes £35,000 as the maximum discount allowable under the right to buy provisions of the 1985 Act.

HOUSING (RIGHT TO BUY) (PRESCRIBED FORMS) REGULATIONS 1986 (No. 2194) [£2.40], made under the Housing Act 1985 (c.68), s.176(1) and (5); operative on January 7, 1987; prescribe the forms of notice for use in connection with the right to buy under ss.122(1) and 124(1) of the 1985 Act and the particulars to be contained in them.

HOUSING (RIGHT TO BUY) (SERVICE CHARGES) ORDER 1986 (No. 2195) [80p], made under the Housing Act 1985 (c.68), Sched. 6, Pt. III, para. 16D; operative on January 7, 1987; prescribes the method for calculating the inflation allowance in relation to the service charge a tenant with a lease of a flat granted under the right to by provisions of the 1985 Act has to pay.

1644. Right to buy—secure tenant—validity of avoidance device by local authority

[Housing Act 1985 (c.68), Pt. V, Housing (Extension of Right to Buy) Order 1983 (S.I. 1983 No. 672).] The applicant had been the tenant of a property set in parkland owned by Plymouth City Council and Cornwall County Council jointly. In 1980 the applicant sought the right to buy the house which was denied on the grounds that he was not a secure tenant in that (a) the premises were owned jointly, and that (b) the premises were not held for the purposes of Pt. V of the Housing Act 1957. The applicant accepted that (b) was a valid ground for refusal. On May 31, 1983 the right to buy was extended to include houses held by a local authority for purposes other than under Pt. V. The applicant again applied. The authorities were anxious to prevent the applicant buying and devised a scheme whereby the two councils jointly granted a lease of the propery and two other lodges for a term of 20 years less two days to Plymouth City Council (note; the right to buy only applies where the landlord owned an interest sufficient to grant a 21 year lease). No notice of their intention to grant a lease was given, and no objections were considered. The applicant sought judicial review on the ground that the lease was a sham or alternatively *ultra vires* their powers. *Held*, granting the application that (1) the landlord condition is satisfied if the premises belongs to one of the bodies mentioned in the relevant section, even if it belongs to a body not mentioned in them; (2) the premises formed part of an open space for the purposes of the Town and Country Planning Act as amended, accordingly the grant of the lease without advertisement and the consideration of objections was void; (3) the transaction was not a sham; so long as the motivation was not improper a local authority is entitled in the same way as a private individual to arrange their affairs to avoid the impact of future legislation; (4) if the lease had been lawful and effective, the landlord would have been Plymouth City Council as leaseholder, and accordingly the "landlord condition" would not have been fulfilled: R. *v.* COUNCIL OF THE CITY OF PLYMOUTH, *ex p.* FREEMAN (1986) 18 H.L.R. 243, Hodgson J.

1645. Right to buy—time for exercise of right to buy—whether possession order to be made
[Housing Act 1980 (c.51), ss.2(4) (*b*), 5(1), 10(1), 16(1), Sched. 1, Pt. II, Sched. 4, Pt. I.]
Notwithstanding that a council tenant may have claimed to exercise his "right to buy" his council home, the council may become entitled to possession at any time down to completion on any of the grounds specified in Part I of Sched. 4 to the Housing Act 1980.
ELB claimed possession of the council house occupied by M, as a secure tenant, on the ground that it was larger than was reasonably required for her use. M resisted the claim on the ground that she had already served a notice claiming to exercise her right to buy the house. *Held*, that the exercise by a tenant of the right to buy is not a once and for all step, but a continuing process. Thus, a council may be entitled to recover possession on any of the grounds in Part I of Sched. 4 to the 1980 Act, down to completion. This is so notwithstanding that the tenant may have served a notice claiming to buy the house, and that the tenant's right to buy may have been established within ss.10(1) and 16(1) of the 1980 Act.
ENFIELD LONDON BOROUGH COUNCIL *v.* McKEON [1986] 2 All E.R. 730, C.A.

1646. Secure tenant—right to buy—cessation of occupation prior to completion
[Housing Act 1985 (c.68), Pt. V.] T was the secure tenant of a flat owned by the local authority. In March 1982 T served a notice on L claiming the right to buy the flat. In July, following a valuation, L replied offering (subject to contract) a 125-year lease of the flat, and requesting further information from T, failing which the contract for sale would not be proceeded with. The county court found as a fact that T had not replied to that letter, and that by April 1983 he had moved to another property which was now his principal home. L, on discovering this, had served a notice to quit in September 1983 on T in respect of the flat. T sought to defend possession proceedings on the ground that he was entitled to buy the flat. T appealed against the order for possession. *Held*, dismissing the appeal, that (1) if a secure tenant does not respond to a landlord's offer under the Housing Act 1980 (now Housing Act 1985) after a reasonable time, the offer will lapse, as it did in the present case; (2) the status of a secure tenant must exist both at the time when a claim to exercise the right to buy is made and when the conveyance or grant is made: SUTTON, LONDON BOROUGH OF *v.* SWANN (1985) 18 H.L.R. 140, C.A.

1647. Statutory nuisance—condensation dampness—scope of magistrates' powers.
[Public Health Act 1936 (c.49), s.99] The tenants of the appellant authority took proceedings for statutory nuisance in respect of their premises. Each of the premises was constructed in accordance with the building regulations in force at the time. Each was a flat in a low rise building. The tenants used their own portable heating appliances in addition to the gas fire in the living room; there were defects to the windows in each flat; there was inadequate insulation and each flat suffered from mould growth. The magistrate found that the mould growth was prejudicial to the health of the occupants and was a result of condensation dampness and made a

nuisance order the terms of which were agreed between the parties, and included double glazing, improved ventilation and the provision of full central heating. The authority appealed on the grounds that (a) their obligations were limited to those they owed as landlords to their tenants and (b) that the works ordered went beyond those which the magistrate was empowered to require in that they were improvements rather than repairs. *Held,* dismissing the appeal, that (1) if it can be shown that the landlord is guilty of a statutory nuisance he is responsible for it and for abating it even if there is no breach of his obligations as landlord; (2) magistrates have a wide discretion as to the terms included in a nuisance order, which discretion must be exercised reasonably; it is not limited to making an order for repairs only but they must bear in mind the heavy duties imposed on authorities and such orders should not be used to give tenants benefits they did not have when they took up the tenancies; (3) in the present case the order had been agreed but it should not be considered as a precedent; in the ordinary case it would require compelling evidence to require such extensive works to abate a nuisance and even where the terms are agreed the magistrates must consider for themselves whether they are reasonably necessary: BIRMINGHAM DISTRICT COUNCIL *v.* KELLY (1985) 17 H.L.R. 573, D.C.

HUMAN RIGHTS

1648. Data protection

DATA PROTECTION (FEES) REGULATIONS 1986 (No. 1899) [45p], made under the Data Protection Act 1984 (c.35), s.9(2), 40; operative on December 15, 1986; prescribe a fee of £2 for the supply by the Data Protection Registrar of a copy of the particulars contained in any entry in the register of data users and computer bureaux which is maintained under s.4 of the Act.

1649. European Convention on Human Rights—transsexual's rights

Mr. Rees, a transsexual, claimed that the United Kingdom were in breach of Articles 8 and 12 of the Convention on Human Rights 1950. Mr. Rees was born with the physical and biological characteristics of a female baby. As a child he exhibited masculine behaviour and was ambiguous in appearance. Mr. Rees underwent treatment for sexual conversion and lived as a male. He claimed that the U.K. authorities' refusal to change his entry in the register of births or to issue a birth certificate so as to reflect his change of sexual identity was contrary to Art. 8. He also claimed that English law, which made it impossible for him to enter into a valid contract of marriage with a woman, was contrary to Art. 12 of the Convention. He referred to the fact that English law only permitted marriage between persons of the opposite sex and that biological criteria were used to determine a person's sex. *Held,* that (1) Art. 8 had not been violated as the mere refusal to alter the register of births or to issue birth certificates whose contents differ from those of the birth register could not be regarded as arbitrary interference by public authorities in a person's right to respect for his private and family life. This was an area in which Contracting States had a wide margin of appreciation; (2) Art. 12 had not been violated as the right to marry, which was enshrined therein, referred to the traditional marriage between persons of opposite biological sex.

REES *v.* UNITED KINGDOM (No. 2/1985/88/135) *The Times,* October 21, 1986, European Court of Human Rights.

1650. European Convention—property rights

[Leasehold Reform Act 1967 (c.88).] The provisions of the 1967 Act are not in breach of the European Convention on Human Rights since the Act is within the limits that a national legislature has in implementing social policies): JAMES *v.* U.K., 26 R.V.R. 139, European Ct. of Human Rights.

1651. Extradition—delay

The applicant was detained in Switzerland pending a decision on Argentina's request for his extradition. His two applications for release were refused by the Swiss Federal Court after 31 days on the one occasion and after 46 days on the other occasion. He complained that Switzerland had violated Art. 5(4) of the European Convention on Human Rights. *Held,* that (1) there had been violations of Art. 5(4) of the Convention because (i) the procedure followed did not fully meet the guarantees provided by Art. 5(4). Art. 5(4) required that the applicant should have been provided, in some way or another, with the benefit of an adversarial procedure; (ii) the decisions had not been reached "speedily" on the facts of this case; (2)

Switzerland was ordered to pay 6,868 Swiss francs in respect of the applicant's claim for "just satisfaction" under Art. 50 of the Convention. The claim covered lawyer's fees and travel and hotel expenses: SANCHEZ-REISSE *v.* SWITZERLAND (No. 4/1985/90/137), *The Times,* November 4, 1986, European Court of Human Rights, Strasbourg.

1652. Fair trial—evidence

Mr. Unterpertinger (the applicant) was convicted by the Innsbruck Regional Court of causing actual bodily harm to his ex-wife and stepdaughter. His ex-wife and stepdaughter made statements to the police, but refused to give evidence at trial. On appeal the applicant requested that additional evidence, in particular from various witnesses, should be taken to throw doubt on the credibility of his ex-wife and stepdaughter. The Court of Appeal refused such requests, save for one request that his sister-in-law should give evidence. *Held,* that the Court of Appeal (and the Regional Court) based the applicant's conviction mainly on the statements made by his ex-wife and stepdaughter which were treated as proof of the truth of the accusations made by the women at the time. The applicant was, thus, convicted on the basis of "testimony" in respect of which his defence rights were appreciably restricted. This meant that the applicant did not have a fair trial, contrary to paragraph 1 of the Art. 6 of the European Convention on Human Rights and the principles inherent in paragraph 3(*d*) of Art. 6. Austria was ordered to pay the applicant compensation pursuant to Art. 50 of the Convention: UNTERPERTINGER *v.* AUSTRIA (No. 1/1985/85/134), *The Times,* December 10, 1986, European Court of Human Rights.

1653. Interference with property rights—forfeiture order

The applicant, a German company, complained about a decision of the U.K. authorities to forfeit 1,500 Krugerrands belonging to it. Two individuals had attempted to smuggle these coins into the U.K. in contravention of English criminal law's prohibition on importation of gold coins. Commissioners of Customs and Excise decided to forfeit the coins. The applicant complained that the decision constituted a violation of its right to peaceful enjoyment of possessions contrary to Art. 1 of the First Protocol of the European Convention on Human Rights and of its rights under Art. 6. *Held,* that (1) there was no breach of Art. 1 of the First Protocol as the applicant had the opportunity to challenge the Commissioners' decision by way of judicial review, but chose not to do so; (2) the mere fact of the applicant's property rights having been adversely affected by measures consequential upon an act for which third parties (the smugglers) were prosecuted could not of itself lead to the conclusion that any of the procedures complained of were concerned with the determination of a "criminal charge" against the applicant. Thus, Art. 6 was not applicable under this head. The applicant had not raised Art. 6 in so far as it related to "civil rights and obligations" and the Court did not consider it necessary to examine that point. ALLGEMEINE GOLD-UND SILBERSCHEIDEANSTALT AG *v.* UNITED KINGDOM (No. 14/1984/86/133), *The Times,* October 25, 1986, European Court of Human Rights, Strasbourg.

1654. Right to respect for one's home—Guernsey

In 1956 the applicants built a house in Guernsey where they lived until they moved abroad in 1960. In 1978 they returned to Guernsey. The Guernsey housing authority informed the applicants that they had lost their residence qualifications by reason of the Housing Control (Guernsey) Law 1969 and that they required a licence to occupy their house. Their licence applications were refused and they were prosecuted for unlawful occupation of their house. *Held,* that (1) decisions by the Guernsey housing authority to refuse the applicants' licences to occupy their house, as well as the conviction and fining of Mr. Gillow, amounted to interferences with the exercise of their right to respect for their home which were disproportionate to the legitimate aim pursued. It was legitimate for the Guernsey authorities to try to keep the population within acceptable limits and to show preference to those people with strong ties to Guernsey or involved in essential employment. The manner in which that aim was pursued in this case was disproportionate and a breach of Art. 8 of the European Convention on Human Rights was established; (2) Art. 1 of Protocol No. 1 to the Convention was not applicable to Guernsey; (3) there were no breaches of Art. 14, not Art. 6 of the Convention; (4) the matter of just satisfaction under Art.

50 of the Convention was reserved: GILLOW *v.* UNITED KINGDOM (No. 13/1984/85/132), *The Times,* November 29, 1986, European Court of Human Rights.

HUSBAND AND WIFE

1655. Co-habitees—joint tenancy—apportionment of beneficial interest. See MARSH *v.* VON STERNBERG, § 1857.

1655a. Co-habitees—ouster injunction—jurisdiction

Supreme Court Act 1981 (c.54), s.37; County Courts Act 1984 (c.28), s.38; Guardianship of Minors Act 1971 (c.3).]

The court has no power to make the ouster order based on the relationship of co-habitees.

M and F lived together as husband and wife, with a child and having the joint tenancy of a council house. F was imprisoned. M married X who moved in. When F was released M and X and the child moved out, and F moved back in. On M's application, the judge granted her custody of the child. However, he held that he had no jurisdiction to grant an ouster injunction against F. *Held,* dismissing M's appeal, F and M were joint tenants of the council house, with equal rights of occupation, neither having such a right to the exclusion of the other. Accordingly, the judge was right to hold that he had no jurisdiction. (*Richards* v. *Richards* [1982] C.L.Y. 1520 applied; *Re W (A Minor)* [1981] C.L.Y. 354 distinguished.)

AINSBURY *v.* MILLINGTON [1986] 1 All E.R. 73, C.A.

1656. Financial provision—lump sum—anticipation of Army gratuity—whether order to be made. See ROBERTS *v.* ROBERTS, § 1087.

1657. Injunction—ouster order—balancing exercise

[Matrimonial Homes Act 1983 (c.19), s.1(3).] H and W had married when H was 16½ years and W was 20. They had three young children and lived in a three bedroomed council house. There were frequent quarrels. W left and applied for non-molestation and ouster orders. The judge found that both parties were equally to blame on conduct, that W's allegations of violence were exaggerated and there had been no instance of actual violence by H. He made an ouster order to allow for a period of peace to help effect a reconciliation but refused a non-molestation order. *Held,* allowing H's appeal, that the judge had not applied the right criteria under s.1(3) of the 1983 Act. The reason for making the ouster order was not the approach which the statute required the court to take. In addition, the judge had probably not included in the balancing exercise the draconian nature of an ouster order. In the circumstances having regard to past circumstances, the matter would be remitted to be heard by another judge (*Richards* v. *Richards* [1982] C.L.Y. 1520 considered): SUMMERS *v.* SUMMERS (1986) 16 Fam. Law 56, C.A.

1658. Marriage (Prohibited Degrees of Relationship) Act 1986 (c.16)

This Act makes provision with regard to the marriage of persons related by affinity.

The Act received the Royal Assent on May 20, 1986. S.2 and Sched. 2 extend to Scotland only but otherwise the Act does not extend to Scotland or to Northern Ireland. It comes into force on days to be appointed.

1659. Marriage (Prohibited Degrees of Relationship) Act 1986—commencement

MARRIAGE (PROHIBITED DEGREES OF RELATIONSHIP) ACT 1986 (COMMENCEMENT) ORDER 1986 (No. 1343 (c.48)) [45p], made under the Marriage (Prohibited Degrees of Relationship) Act 1986 (c.16), s.6(5); brings the 1986 Act into force on November 1, 1986.

1660. Marriage (Wales) Act 1986 (c.7)

This Act extends s.23 of the Marriage Act 1949 (Benefices held in plurality) to Wales.

The Act received the Royal Assent on March 18, 1986 and came into force on that date.

1661. Matrimonial home—beneficial interest—considerations

[Law of Property Act 1925 (c.20), s.53.] In 1951 H and W had married and lived in the home of H's mother. In 1953 that house was sold and the proceeds were put towards the cost of purchasing the matrimonial home ("the property") which was bought in the joint names of H and W's mother, the balance being secured by way of a building society mortgage. By 1970 the mortgage had been discharged. Following the mother's death in 1971 H had become sole owner of the title. Between 1951 and 1963 W did not work and between 1963 and 1970 she earned just over £1,000. She had a separate bank account, made no contribution to the purchase price of the property or to the discharge of the mortgage. She paid for household expenses and clothes. In 1978 H secured the property to the plaintiff bank ("the Bank") to purchase shares in the company of which he was a director. W signed a letter of consent postponing any interest she might have in the property in favour of the Bank. It was accepted by H that he had no defence to the Bank's claim for possession. W claimed a substantial beneficial interest in the property and that the circumstances of which she signed the letter of consent were such that it was not binding upon her. *Held,* allowing the Bank's appeal, that even if H and W had made an oral declaration that it was their common intention that the property should belong to them jointly (which the county court judge had found), that would not operate to create a trust because of the provisions of s.53(1)(*b*). Something more was necessary to create a resulting, constructive or implied trust, and that would only occur if the agreement between the parties was that W was to do something to her detriment in pursuance of the agreement. Equity would not come to the aid of a mere volunteer. Moreover, W had not demonstrated that she was induced to act to her detriment upon the basis of a common intention of ownership of the property or otherwise that there was any nexus between the acquisition of the property and something provided or foregone by W. She had not established any beneficial interest in the property and the question of the effect of the letter of authority did not arise (*Gissing* v. *Gissing* [1970] C.L.Y. 1243 and *Eves* v. *Eves* [1975] C.L.Y. 3110 considered): MIDLAND BANK *v.* DOBSON AND DOBSON (1986) 1 F.L.R. 171, C.A.

1662. Matrimonial home—charging order—position of creditor
[Charging Orders Act 1979 (c.53), ss.1, 3(5).]
Although a creditor is justified in expecting a charging order to be made in his favour, countervailing factors of sufficient weight, such as hardship to a wife, can displace his rights.
H and W purchased a house in their joint names in 1970. In January 1981 W petitioned for divorce and in March commenced ancillary relief proceedings for a property adjustment order. On May 20 she obtained a decree nisi. Meanwhile H's business had run into difficulties and his partner issued a writ against H on May 22 and obtained summary judgment. He then obtained a charging order absolute under s.1 of the 1979 Act over H's interest in the home but did not serve W with the application or give her notice of it. W applied for the order to be discharged and the registrar ordered that it was to be subject to any order made in the ancillary relief proceedings and that H's interest in the home be transferred to W. The partner appealed against the variation of the charging order. The judge dismissed the appeal. On appeal *Held*, dismissing the appeal, that (1) W was an interested person within s.3(5) of the 1979 Act who had *locus standi* to apply for the order to be varied or discharged and should have been given notice of the application; (2) the court ought to ensure that a wife's rights of occupation were adequately protected. In balancing the competing claims of the creditor and the wife the court had to consider (a) whether the equity in the home was sufficient to enable the order to be made absolute and realised at once even though it could result in the wife being less well housed than she could otherwise have expected to be, (b) whether only such an order as might be necessary to protect the wife's right to occupy the home should be made, (c) whether the wife's right to occupy could be defeated by making the husband bankrupt, (d) any hardship suffered by the creditor. On the evidence the judge was right to decide that the hardship to W outweighed the creditor's interest (*First National Securities* v. *Hegerty* [1984] C.L.Y. 1691 distinguished).
HARMAN *v.* GLENCROSS [1986] 1 All E.R. 545, C.A.

1663. Matrimonial home—former council house—repayment of discount on sale
[Housing Act 1985 (c.68), s.160; Matrimonial Causes Act 1973 (c.18), ss.23, 24, 24A.] The sale of a former matrimonial home when ordered by the court led, when the house had been purchased at a discount from a local authority, to the requirement to repay the proper proportion of the discount as required by conditions of the

discounted sale: R. *v.* Rushmoor Borough Council, *ex p.* Barrett, *The Times,* September 5, 1986, Reeve J.

1664. Matrimonial homes—injunction—validity of marriage
[Matrimonial Homes Act 1983 (c.19), ss.19.] Where the validity of a marriage was in dispute the judge could for the purposes of interlocutory relief under ss.1 and 9 treat the marriage as binding until the contrary was shown when the issue could be properly determined by the Court: Seray-Wurie *v.* Seray-Wurie, *The Times,* March 25, 1986, C.A.

1665. Matrimonial home—ouster injunction—considerations
[Matrimonial Homes Act 1967 (c.75), s.1(3).] Following the breakdown of the marriage H went to live with his parents and friends leaving W and their two daughters, aged 18 and 15, in the matrimonial home. He continued to pay the mortgage and the outgoings. H's living arrangements became unsatisfactory and he proposed that he should return to live in the matrimonial home and to raise £20,000 as a second mortgage to provide W with funds to purchase alternative accommodation. W objected but H moved back. A month later W left with the younger daughter. She sought an injunction under the 1967 Act alleging that H had made threats of violence against W and her father. *Held,* dismissing H's appeal against an ouster order that the terms of s.1(3) were of the widest possible form and the matters to be considered by the judge embraced all the circumstances of the case. The instant case fell within the parameters of *Richards* and the recorder was entitled to find that H could make a home with his parents and that W had had good reason to leave (*Richards* v. *Richards* [1982] C.L.Y. 1520 followed): Baggott *v.* Baggott (1986) 16 Fam. Law 129, C.A.

1666. Matrimonial injunction—breach—committal—application failing to set out specific acts
A non-molestation and ouster order had been made against H. In W's committal application no allegations as to the nature of the acts which were alleged to amount to a breach of the order were set out although such matters were set out in her supporting affidavit. The judge dismissed the application but gave no judgment. *Held,* dismissing W's appeal, that the application to commit had to set out *seriatim* the acts alleged to be in breach of the order or undertaking since the person whose liberty was in jeopardy was entitled to know the precise charges against him. (*Wooley* v. *Wooley* [1974] C.L.Y. 2909 followed): Dorrell *v.* Dorrell (1986) 16 Fam. Law 15, C.A.

1667. Ouster order—hearing—procedure—cross-examination—unrepresented party
[Matrimonial Homes Act 1983 (c.19), s.1(3).] W had applied under s.1(3) for an ouster order. In her affidavit she alleged that H had left the matrimonial home but had been returning, usually in her absence, and going through the house against her wishes, that he continued to visit when she was at home and had made a nuisance of himself, and that he was having an unsettling effect on the child and causing concern by his unexpected appearances and persistent questioning. H had been unrepresented. He did not cross-examine W nor did W's solicitor cross-examine H. Having agreed with the judge that he did not need to go to the house and having appeared to concede that he had no objection to the proposed order H was ordered not to enter the matrimonial home for three months. *Held,* allowing H's appeal, that it was a prerequisite for a valid order under s.1(3) that the court, in the exercise of its discretionary power, should have regard to the reasonableness or unreasonableness of W's attitude where there was merely an affidavit stating what that attitude was. It was essential, therefore, that there should at least be an opportunity for the opposite party to test that affidavit evidence. When that party appeared unrepresented the court ought to remind the unrepresented party of his right to challenge the affidavit evidence by cross-examination (*Richards* v. *Richards* [1982] C.L.Y. 1520 applied): Harris *v.* Harris (1986) 1 F.L.R. 12, C.A.

1668. Periodical payments—husband supporting cohabitee and her child—considerations
[Domestic Proceedings and Magistrates' Courts Act 1978 (c.22), ss.3(2)(*b*), 20(11).] H had been ordered to pay periodical payments for his wife and three children. He went to live with another woman and her son. He applied for variation of the order. The justices' dismissed the application, giving as their reasons their findings that H had no legal obligation to maintain his cohabitee and her son and there had been no decrease in H's income since the previous variation. *Held,* allowing H's appeal, that s.20(11) provided that the court must have regard to all the circumstances of the case first consideration being given to the welfare of any minor child of the family. By

s.3(2)(*b*) the court was required to have regard to the financial needs, obligations and responsibilities of each of the parties. There was nothing in that provision which restricted the obligations or responsibilities to those which were legally enforceable. The justices had adopted an unduly restrictive approach of s.3(2)(*b*) and had erred in law. There could be circumstances where a man did have responsibility for his cohabitee and child. The matter would be remitted for a re-hearing: BLOWER *v.* BLOWER (1986) 16 Fam. Law 56, Heilbron J.

IMMIGRATION

1669/70. Appeal—oral hearing—whether power to dispense with
[Immigration Act 1971 (c.77), ss.22(1)(*b*), 22(5)(*b*); Immigration Appeals (Procedure) Rules 1984 (S.I. 1984 No. 2041), r.20(*c*).] S.22(5)(*b*) of the Immigration Act 1971 grants the holder of entry clearance the right to appeal against the decision of an adjudicator, and rules of procedure for such appeals may be made under s.22(1)(*b*) of the Act. Rule 20(*c*) of the Immigration Appeals (Procedure) Rules 1984 allows an appeal tribunal to dispose of an appeal without an oral hearing: this rule was intended to weed out hopeless appeals. *Held,* that although the rule came close to derogating from s.22(5)(*b*), and therefore being *ultra vires,* it was made within the powers conferred by s.22(1)(*b*). The power to dispense with an oral hearing should, however, only be used where it is obvious that no advantage is to be gained by a hearing, either in the way of evidence or of legal argument: R. *v.* IMMIGRATION APPEAL TRIBUNAL, *ex p.* JONES (ROSS), *The Times,* October 10, 1986, Simon Brown J.

1671. Application to vary leave—refusal on two grounds—one mandatory the other discretionary—whether refusal on first precludes exercise of discretion under second ground
The issue was if the Secretary of State refused an application (as it was mandatory for him to do) because the relevant marriage was in his view one of convenience, could he at the same time exercise a discretion on the second issue, namely the removal of a time limit because the relevant marriage had broken down. *Held,* that it did not follow, that because refusal was on one ground which was mandatory, that the Secretary of State had not applied his mind to the second, and separate, issue which was discretionary: R. *v.* IMMIGRATION APPEAL TRIBUNAL *ex p.* MOHAN (SURINDER) [1985] Imm.A.R. 84, C.A.

1672. Certificate of patriality—issued in error—effect
A certificate of patriality was issued to two girls (both citizens of the U.S.A.) in error, and without fraud or misrepresentation on their part. The Secretary of State subsequently reviewed the matter and refused to incorporate the certificate in a new passport. *Held,* that (1) what the Secretary of State had done was to cancel the certificate and not to refuse a certificate; and (2) that neither the adjudicator nor the Immigration Appeal Tribunal had jurisdiction to hear an appeal against such cancellation or withdrawal: SECRETARY OF STATE FOR THE HOME DEPARTMENT *v.* GOLD AND GOLD [1985] Imm.A.R. 66, Imm.App.Trib.

1673. Citizenship—British overseas citizenship
[Burma Independence Act 1947 (c.4); Mauritius Independence Act 1968 (c.8); British Nationality Act 1981 (c.61).] A's father was born in 1908 in Mauritius when it was a Crown Colony. A herself was born in 1927 in Burma when it too was a Crown Colony. By the British Nationality Act 1914 A and her father were both British subjects at the time of their births. By virtue of its excepting provisions, A retained that status under the 1947 Act. However, under the 1968 Act, and the Order made under it, she became a citizen of Mauritius and ceased to be a citizen of the U.K. and Colonies. *Held,* that A did not come within the provisions of the 1981 Act and was not a British Overseas Citizen: R. *v.* SECRETARY OF STATE FOR THE HOME DEPARTMENT, *ex p.* BIBI (MAHABOOB) [1985] Imm.A.R. 134, Mann J.

1674. Citizenship—relevance of illiteracy of applicant
[British Nationality Act 1981 (c.61), s.8(1).] X sought registration as a British citizen under s.8(1) of the British Nationality Act 1981. Her application was refused because the Secretary of State was not satisfied that her marriage to a British citizen was genuine. She sought an order of *certiorari* on the ground that insufficient weight had been placed on the fact that, being illiterate and innumerate, she had had difficulty in accounting for admitted inaccuracies in dates and numbers. *Held,* that

her illiteracy should have been taken into account. An order of *certiorari* would therefore be made: R. *v.* SECRETARY OF STATE FOR THE HOME DEPARTMENT, *ex p.* DINESH, *The Times,* December 11, 1986, Russell J.

1675. Close connection—residence alone—whether sufficient
Z was a citizen of Iran. He was admitted in 1973 aged 17 as a student. He remained until 1982. He then left and applied in Sao Paulo for entry as a person of independent means. He met the financial requirements, but he was refused. The Tribunal concluded that residence alone, no matter how long, could not by itself establish a sufficiently close connection with the U.K. *Held,* that residence such as Z's was capable of amounting to a sufficient connection. Whether it did was a matter for the tribunal, to whom the question was referred: R. *v.* IMMIGRATION APPEAL TRIBUNAL, *ex p.* ZANDFANI [1984] Imm.A.R. 213, Woolf J.

1676. Consular fees
CONSULAR FEES (AMENDMENT) ORDER 1986 (No. 1881) [45p], made under the Consular Fees Act 1980 (c.23), s.1(1); operative on November 18, 1986; amends S.I. 1983 No. 1518 so as to increase fees.

1677. Deportation—appeal—existing facts
In a deportation case, an appellant can, in an appeal to an adjudicator or the Immigration Appeal Tribunal against a decision of the Secretary of State to make a deportation order against him, rely on facts or circumstances which existed at the time of the Secretary of State's decision, but which were not known to the Secretary of State (R. *v. Immigration Appeal Tribunal, ex p. Weerasuriya* [1982] C.L.Y. 1903 and *R.* v. *Immigration Appeal Tribunal, ex p. Kotecha* [1983] C.L.Y. 1927 distinguished): R. *v.* IMMIGRATION APPEAL TRIBUNAL, *ex p.* HASSANIN, KANDEMIR AND MOHAMED FAROOQ, *The Times,* October 18, 1986, C.A.

1678. Deportation—appeal—time limits
[Immigration Act 1971 (c.77), s.15.] The time for appealing against a deportation order made under s.15 of the Immigration Act 1971, or against a notice of intention to deport made by an adjudicator, begins to run when service of the order is effected: R. *v.* IMMIGRATION APPEAL TRIBUNAL, *ex p.* CHUMUN and BANO-OVAIS, *The Times,* December 3, 1986, Hodgson J.

1679. Deportation—events subsequent to decision to deport—effect
[H.C. 169, paras. 156, 158.] R's application for further extension was refused and his appeal dismissed. Notice of intention to deport was served. R applied for asylum which was refused. He appealed against the notice of intention to deport: the issue concerned what circumstances were to be considered at the hearing of the appeal. *Held,* that as R's claimed fear of persecution should he be returned was not known to the Secretary of State when the decision to deport was made, it was not a proper matter to be considered by the adjudicator or the Tribunal. It might constitute a "compassionate circumstance" and thus be taken into account under paras. 156 and 158 of H.C. 169: RANGANATHAM *v.* SECRETARY OF STATE FOR HOME DEPARTMENT [1984] Imm.A.R. 247, Immigration Appeal Tribunal.

1680. Deportation—fraudulent marriage—whether sufficient grounds
[Immigration Act 1971 (c.77), s.3(5)(*b*).] G was a Turkish citizen. He obtained indefinite leave to remain on the basis of his marriage in the U.K. in 1975. That marriage terminated in divorce in 1979. In 1982 G returned to the U.K. accompanied by a Turkish wife of 18 years standing. *Held,* that deportation under s.3(5)(*b*) has to relate to the continued presence of the individual and cannot be based on the original fraud; but the deceitful use of marriage in the U.K. as a means to obtain leave to remain formed a "positive and specific" ground for deportation: GENC *v.* SECRETARY OF STATE FOR HOME DEPARTMENT [1984] Imm.A.R. 180, Immigration Appeal Tribunal.

1681. Deportation—mentally ill alien—powers of Secretary of State
[Mental Health Act 1959 (c.72), s.90; Immigration Act 1971 (c.77), ss.5, 30.] When an alien is being treated for mental illness in a hospital in the U.K., and the Secretary of State wishes to make an order removing him from the country, he need not use the powers contained in s.90 of the Mental Health Act 1959 (as amended by s.30 of the Immigration Act 1971). He can issue a deportation order under s.5 of the 1971 Act instead. S.90 is not paramount to the powers of that Act: R. *v.* SECRETARY

OF STATE FOR THE HOME DEPARTMENT, *ex p.* ALGHALI, *The Times,* July 22, 1986, D.C.

1682. Deportation—offences so serious as to justify deportation without any previous history or propensity to commit further crimes

This was an appeal against the decision of McNeill J. dismissing an application for judicial review (see [1985] C.L.Y. 1714). A was a citizen of St. Lucia who married a U.K. citizen and settled in the U.K. The marriage broke down. He was later convicted of and imprisoned for wounding his wife but without any recommendation for deportation. The Secretary of State initiated deportation proceedings under the Immigration Act 1971; s.3(5)(*b*). The Tribunal dismissed A's appeal and the application for judicial review was dismissed by McNeill J. *Held,* by the Court of Appeal, that (1) some offences were of so serious a nature as to justify deportation even if there was no record of previous offences and no great likelihood of the individual re-offending; (2) there was nothing to show that the Secretary of State had acted contrary to the law or to the Immigration Rules in order to bring the case within s.19(1)(*a*) of the Immigration Act 1971; (3) the Tribunal had set out its reasons adequately; (4) to succeed in an application for judicial review, A had to show the Tribunal's review of the Secretary of State's discretion was so wrong as to be assailable on *Wednesbury* principles (*Associated Provincial Picture Houses* v. *Wednesbury Corporation* (1948) C.L.C. 8107 applied: R. *v.* IMMIGRATION APPEAL TRIBUNAL, *ex p.* FLORENT [1985] Imm.A.R. 141, C.A.

1683. Deportation—overstayer—knowledge of overstaying—whether necessary to be liable for deportation

A was admitted to the U.K. as a student. She applied for an extension of leave which was refused and not appealed. One month after that refusal she married a British citizen: that was bigamous so far as A's partner was concerned, and he was subsequently convicted. A formed another association. The Secretary of State did not know of that association when he decided to initiate deportation proceedings. *Held,* that (1) the liability to deportation set out in s.3(5) of the Immigration Act 1971 is not restricted to those overstayers who knowingly overstay; (2) ignorance of overstaying is a compassionate circumstance to be taken into consideration under H.C. 169, para. 156; (3) the adjudicator was correct not to take into consideration factors not known to the Secretary of State when he decided to initiate deportation proceedings; (4) when the Secretary of State reviews a decision he has already taken, and maintains that decision, he does not make a "second decision" within the meaning of the Immigration Rules: HANIF (HOOSHA KUMARI) *v.* SECRETARY OF STATE FOR THE HOME DEPARTMENT [1985] Imm.A.R. 57, Imm.App.Trib.

1684. Deportation—valued member of Sikh community—whether effect on third parties a relevant factor

[Statement of Changes in Immigration Rules (H.C. Paper (1982–83) No. 66), paras. 154, 156, 158.]

When considering the merits of deporting any person, the authorities are required to consider as a relevant factor third party interests, such as could extend to the public interest as a whole where the person sought to be deported was a particularly valued member of the community.

S overstayed his leave to enter the United Kingdom and became a valued member of the Sikh community through religious, charitable and cultural works. The Secretary of State ordered him to be deported, and on his appeals the question arose as to the relevance of his works for the community as a whole. *Held,* that when considering deportation the effect on the remainder of the community of the loss of the person to be deported was capable of being a relevant factor and should therefore have been considered.

R. *v.* IMMIGRATION APPEAL TRIBUNAL, *ex p.* SINGH (BAKHTAUR) [1986] 2 All E.R. 721, H.L.

1685. Deportation order—application to revoke—procedure

[Immigration Act 1971 (c.77), s.3.] A person applying to revoke a deportation order on him has no right to remain in the U.K. pending the outcome of his application: R. *v.* SECRETARY OF STATE FOR THE HOME OFFICE, *ex p.* ERDOGAN *The Times,* June 30, 1986, Nolan J.

1686. Discretion of Secretary of State—exceptional circumstances—application for permanent stay

[HC 241, para. 24A] B was a citizen of Pakistan. He arrived on October 2, 1979 with entry clearance for marriage and was admitted for three months. Following his marriage he applied to remain permanently: he was refused. The Adjudicator allowed the appeal finding that B's inability to consummate the marriage which led to its breakdown constituted an exceptional circumstance. The Sec. of State appealed: it was allowed by the Tribunal. *Held,* that the words "exceptional circumstances" could mean circumstances which very rarely occurred, or circumstances which simply did not follow a rule or norm. It would be better to ask whether there were circumstances which justified departure from the normal rule: R. *v.* IMMIGRATION APPEAL TRIBUNAL, *ex p.* BASHIR [1984] Imm. A.R. 165, Webster J.

1687. Entry clearance—application for admission of adopted son—whether a de facto adoption satisfies the requirements of the immigration rules

Held, that where, under the *lex loci* there is no legally recognisable adoptive process, there cannot be a *de facto* adoption that would satisfy the requirements of the Immigration Rules: ALI *v.* ENTRY CLEARANCE OFFICER, DACCA [1985] Imm.A.R. 33, Imm.App.Trib.

1688. EEC national—refusal of residence permit—application for review—status of applicant

Held, that the rules drew a clear distinction between the right to seek employment (for which a six month "free period" is provided: see H.C. 169), and the right of residence of a person who is in work (see H.C. 169 and Directive 68/360). Therefore, (1) any application based on the right to seek work is not based on a claim of acquired residence, and whether it is made while leave is current will depend on leave formerly granted or right of residence formerly acquired; (2) any application based on actual or even past work is based on a claim of acquired residence, and hence is also a claim that the applicant has limited leave at the time of the application, and is entitled to remain because of it: HOTH *v.* SECRETARY OF STATE FOR THE HOME DEPARTMENT [1985] Imm.A.R. 20, Imm.App.Trib.

1689. Examination—time and place

[Immigration Act 1971 (c.77), Sched. 2, para. 2.] Examination of an immigrant under sched. 2, para. 2 of the Immigration Act 1971 need not take place at the time or port of entry. It can take place later and at a different time, when (for example) the officer has further information causing him to enquire as to any of the matters set out in sub-paras. (a), (b) and (c) of para. 2: SINGH (BALJINDER) *v.* HAMMOND, *The Times,* November 10, 1986, D.C.

1690. False entry clearance—whether offence

[Immigration Act 1971 (c.77), ss.4(2), 26(1)(c), Sched. 2, para. 16(2).] The presentation of a passport with an entry clearance certificate, both obtained by false representation, was an offence rendering P an illegal immigrant (R. v. *Secretary of State for the Home Department, ex p. Addo* [1985] C.L.Y. 1731, R. v. *Secretary of State for the Home Department, ex p. Khawaja* [1983] C.L.Y. 1908 considered): R. *v.* SECRETARY OF STATE FOR THE HOME DEPARTMENT, *ex p.* PATEL, *The Times,* October 27, 1986, C.A.

1691. Illegal entrant—false statement—test

[Immigration Act 1971 (c.77), s.33(1)] When the proven facts establish that a person has a certificate of patriality which he knew or had reasonable cause to know was false but fell short of proving that he has made a statement or representation which he knew to be false or did not believe to be true, the Home Office is not entitled to treat him as an illegal immigrant: R. *v.* SECRETARY OF STATE FOR THE HOME DEPARTMENT, *ex p.* ROUSE, *The Times,* November 25, 1985, Woolf J.

1692. Illegal entrant—leave to enter on basis of false statement—intention to stay as refugee—refusal of application for asylum—jurisdiction of court to decide whether person is a refugee

[Immigration Act 1971 (c.77), ss.4(1), 33(1), Statement of Changes in Immigration Rules (1983) (H.C. 169), para. 16.]

The court has no jurisdiction to determine as a matter of fact whether or not a person is a refugee or entitled to be granted asylum, such matters are for the Secretary of State to decide.

B was allowed to enter the U.K. for three months, having informed the immigration officer that he wished to study English at a language centre in Manchester. Nine months later B was arrested whilst working in a restaurant. B admitted that he lied to the immigration officer at the outset and that he wanted to settle in the U.K. He made an application for asylum as he feared he would be arrested on account of his political activities if returned to Turkey from whence he came. A decision not to grant asylum was made in September 1984 and confirmed in December 1984 by the Secretary of State. The Secretary of State decided that B was to be treated as an illegal entrant. B's application for judicial review of that decision was refused. B appealed and contended (1) he was not an illegal entrant because in all probability he would have been given leave to enter had he claimed to be a refugee at the outset; (2) where the Secretary of State decided that a person was not a refugee the status of that person should be investigated by the courts having regard to the provisions of paragraphs 16 and 73 of the Statement of Changes in Immigration Rules (H.C. 169) and to the Handbook on Procedures and Criteria for Determining Refugee Status published by the U.N. High Commission for Refugees; (3) that the Secretary of State misdirected himself in deciding to remove B as an illegal entrant rather than deporting him. *Held*, dismissing the appeal, that (1) whether or not B was an illegal immigrant must be considered in the context of the leave to enter that was sought and given. B's statements of his intention were fundamentally different from the truth. The decision that he was an illegal immigrant was unassailable; (2) by s.4(1) of the Immigration Act the power to give or refuse entry was to be exercised by an immigration officer and the power to give leave to remain or vary any leave to enter was to be exercised by the Secretary of State. Paragraph 16 of H.C. 169 required that full account be taken of the provisions of the Convention and Protocol relating to the Status of Refugees but it did not give the court any jurisdiction to determine the question of whether a person was a refugee or entitled to a grant of asylum. Those matters were to be determined by an immigration officer or the Secretary of State; (3) the Secretary of State did not misdirect himself nor breach the rules of natural justice in deciding to remove B rather than deport him notwithstanding that by so doing B was unable to exercise the right of appeal made available in respect of deportation orders (*R. v. Secretary of State for the Home Department, ex p. Khawaja* [1983] C.L.Y. 1908 considered).

R. *v.* SECRETARY OF STATE FOR THE HOME DEPARTMENT, *ex p.* BUGDAYCAY [1986] 1 W.L.R. 155, C.A.

1693. Judicial review. See Administrative Law.

1694. Judicial review—extent of courts consideration—matters not relied upon by the Secretary of State

A (who was the founder of the Church of Scientology) applied for a letter of consent to allow him to visit the U.K. The Home Office indicated they wished to interview A, so that the immigration officer might be satisfied about those matters he had to be satisfied. A declined to be interviewed, and his application was refused. The adjudicator dismissed the appeal, concluding that he could not be satisfied on the evidence before him that A intended to make only a short visit to the U.K. The Tribunal dismissed a further appeal. Judicial review was sought, when it was argued that the adjudicator and the Tribunal were restricted to reviewing the facts and issues on which the Secretary of State had come to his decision. *Held*, that the appellate authorities were not confined to considering the matters on which the Secretary of State based his decision. Section 18(2) of the Immigration Act 1971 did not affect the scope of appeals from his decision: its purpose was to avoid any dispute about the basis of that decision: R. *v.* IMMIGRATION APPEAL TRIBUNAL, *ex p.* HUBBARD [1985] Imm.A.R. 110, Woolf J.

1695. Leave to enter—condition—failure to observe

[Immigration Act 1971 (c.77), s.24(1)(*b*)(ii).] Failure to observe a condition of leave to enter the U.K. contrary to s.24(1)(*b*)(ii) of the Immigration Act 1971 is a continuing offence: MANICKAVASAGAR *v.* COMMISSIONER OF POLICE OF THE METROPOLIS, *The Times*, July 16, 1986, D.C.

1696. Leave to enter—deception of third party—whether right to remain

[Immigration Act 1971 (c.77), s.33(1).] Where leave to enter was obtained by a deception there was no right to remain in the U.K., even where the immigrant played no part in the deception (*R. v. Governor of Ashford Remand Centre, ex p. Bonzagon*, [1984] C.L.Y. 1738, R. *v. Secretary of State for the Home Department, ex p. Khawaja* [1983] C.L.Y. 1908 considered): R. *v.* SECRETARY OF STATE FOR THE HOME DEPARTMENT, *ex p.* KHALED, *The Times,* November 13, 1986, Otton J.

1697. Leave to enter—primary purpose of marriage—evidence of devotion

The immigration officer and the adjudicator should take into account when deciding the primary purpose of the marriage evidence of the couple's devotion to each other (*R. v. Immigration Appeal Tribunal, ex p. Bhatia* [1985] C.L.Y. 1709 considered): R. *v.* IMMIGRATION APPEAL TRIBUNAL, *ex p.* KUMAR, *The Times,* August 13, 1986, C.A.

1698. Limited leave to remain—failure to give reasons—whether failure appealable

N was exempt from immigration control by reason of the nature of his employment. On the termination of that employment, he applied for indefinite leave to remain: he was given limited leave but was given no reason for that limitation. *Held,* that it was mandatory for the Secretary of State to give reasons, and the decision was therefore appealable, and on appeal found to be invalid: NOORHU *v.* SECRETARY OF STATE FOR HOME DEPARTMENT [1984] Imm.A.R. 190, Immigration Appeal Tribunal.

1699. Marriage of convenience—intent to live with spouse—Secretary of State's belief—exercise of discretion

The rules contained in H.C. 241, paras. 23, 24 and 24A, make a clear distinction between the situation where the Secretary of State has reason to believe (1) that a marriage is one of convenience, and (2) that one of the parties no longer has any intention of living with the other as his or her spouse. In the former case he is bound to refuse an extension of stay or leave to remain. However, in the latter case, although the normal rule is that there will be no extension, it is open to the Secretary of State within the rules to grant an extension. The Home Office statement did not expressly record that the Secretary of State considered whether or not to depart from the normal conclusion. *Held,* that, merely because the Home Office statement did not expressly record whether or not the Secretary of State considered departing from the normal rule, does not mean he did not consider the possibility. The adjudicator did—and was entitled to—assume that the Secretary of State had exercised his discretion under para 24A(*e*): MALIK (MAHBOOB IQBAL AHMED), APPLICATION FOR JUDICIAL REVIEW [1985] Imm.A.R. 96, C.A.

1700. Marriage—visitor married to non-British wife—whether relief

[HC 169, para. 126] A was admitted as a visitor. He married a citizen of Cyprus who had been granted indefinite leave to remain. As a result of his marriage, A met all the requirements for leave to remain save that his wife was not a British citizen. *Held,* that HC 169, para. 126 gave a relief to husbands where wives were British citizens. It gave no right to A nor any discretion to the Secretary of State: R. *v.* IMMIGRATION APPEAL TRIBUNAL, *ex p.* AKSOY [1984] Imm. A.R. 171, Nolan J.

1701. Marriage—whether primary purpose to gain admission to U.K.—evidence to be considered

A was a citizen of India and settled there. He applied for entry clearance to enter the U.K. and marry his fiancée, a divorcée with a child. The match followed an advertisement by the bride's father in the *Hindustani Times.* It was common ground that the parties had met, and that the proposed marriage was genuine in that the parties intended to live together as man and wife. The application was refused because the entry clearance officer was not satisfied that the primary purpose of the marriage was not for the bridegroom to gain admission to the U.K. It was held by Forbes J. that (i) an application for entry clearance under H.C. 169, para. 41 must satisfy the entry clearance officer on the balance of probabilities in respect of all the requirements of para. 41; and (ii) on a proper construction of rule 41, when it is accepted that the marriage is genuine, it does not follow prima facie that the primary purpose of the marriage is not for the applicant to gain admission to the U.K. *Held,* dismissing the appeal, that (1) on the straightforward and clear meaning of H.C. 169, para. 41, the rule presumes that the primary purpose of the intended marriage is for the applicant to gain admission to the U.K.; (2) in considering an application under that rule, the entry clearance officer is entitled to make enquiries of his own and to test the evidence put forward by the applicant, but is not limited to the evidence he may put forward; (3) what the applicant says will be of primary importance, but the history of the other party will be relevant, as will be the reasons of the parents for arranging the marriage; (4) those parts of the judgment of Forbes J. where he purported to give guidance to entry clearance officers on how they should do their work should be disregarded: BHATIA *v.* IMMIGRATION APPEAL TRIBUNAL [1985] Imm.A.R. 50, C.A.

1702. Opportunity to have case referred back to adjudicator—not taken—whether possible then to assert a denial of natural justice

The adjudicator both misdirected himself in law on the burden of proof, and also refused an application by A to call a witness. On appeal, A's counsel was offered the opportunity for the case to be remitted with a direction on the law and for the witness to be called if need be. Counsel elected to carry on before the Tribunal on the basis of the evidence before it. The appeal was dismissed. An application for judicial review was sought. *Held,* that in such circumstances it cannot be asserted that there was a denial of natural justice on the ground that A's case was not properly put: NESSA (NEWARUN) *v.* SECRETARY OF STATE FOR THE HOME DEPARTMENT [1985] Imm.A.R. 131, C.A.

1703. Ordinary residence—temporary or occasional absences abroad—whether breaks period of ordinary residence in U.K.

S was ordinarily resident on January 1, 1973. He made a number of visits abroad, in particular a period of casual work in the U.S.A. *Held,* that (1) because S could be ordinarily resident in more than one place at any material time, it was a question of fact whether in the circumstances he had remained ordinarily resident in the U.K.; (2) taking into account S's subsequent conduct, which showed that he had carried out his earlier expressed intention of returning to the U.K., he had remained ordinarily resident in the U.K. throughout the relevant period (*Shah v. Barnet London Borough Council* [1983] C.L.Y. 1157 applied): R. *v.* IMMIGRATION APPEAL TRIBUNAL, *ex p.* SIGGINS [1985] Imm.A.R. 14, Nolan J.

1704. Overstaying leave—time limit for prosecution—evidence

[Immigration Act 1971 (c.77), ss.24(1)(*b*)(i), 28(1).] "Evidence" sufficient to found a prosecution is more than mere information, and the time limit on prosecutions runs from the time when such evidence is in the hands of the prosecutor (*R. v. Osbourne,* [1973] C.L.Y. 559 considered): ENAAS *v.* DOVEY, *The Times,* November 25, 1986, D.C.

1705. Passport issued by entity not recognised as a state—distinction between transacting business as a visitor and admission as a businessman

A were citizens of North Korea, both employees of the Korean Foreign Insurance Company.

The carried on business in Paris; much of their work was with insurance companies in the U.K. They paid a number of visits to the U.K., when they were admitted as visitors and transacted business as allowed by H.C. 169, para. 19. They then sought admission as businessmen. They were refused on the grounds they held travel documents issued by a state not recognised by Her Majesty's Government. *Held,* that there was a fundamental difference between (1) admission as a short-term visitor and (2) admission as a businessman when a longer stay was envisaged. Further, the reason given by the Secretary of State touched on matters of state and the Tribunal would not enquire further into diplomatic and political factors which had led him to exercise his discretion as he had.

DJANG (OR CHANG) AND DJOU (OR JU) *v.* SECRETARY OF STATE FOR THE HOME DEPARTMENT [1985] Imm.A.R. 125, Imm.App.Trib.

1706. Person of independent means—whether businessman can so qualify

A was an Iranian citizen who applied for entry clearance to settle as a person of independent means. It was found that he would not have restricted his business activities to operations outside the U.K. *Held,* accordingly, that he would have been a businessman while in the U.K., and as such could not enter as a person of independent means: JAHANGARD (JAFAR) *v.* ENTRY CLEARANCE OFFICER, VIENNA [1985] Imm.A.R. 69, Imm.App.Trib.

1707. Political asylum—meaning of "persecution"—standard of proof

Held, in this appeal that (1) the standard of proof was, these being civil proceedings, evaluated on a balance of probabilities; (2) the material date was the date of the decision; (3) it was incorrect to submit that, if a person had to refrain from political activity in order to avoid persecution, he should qualify for political asylum: R. *v.* IMMIGRATION APPEAL TRIBUNAL, *ex p.* JONAH [1985] Imm.A.R. 7, Nolan J.

1708. Political asylum—standard of proof—whether necessary to establish probability of fear of persecution
Held, that M did not have to establish that it was more probable then not that his fear of persecution was well founded. The Tribunal had to consider not only whether he would face persecution if returned, but whether he would necessarily be returned at all. The possible danger caused by a refusal to vary leave to remain was less than that caused by a decision to deport. The onus of proof would be higher in the first case than in the latter: MAKURO *v.* SECRETARY OF STATE FOR THE HOME DEPARTMENT [1984] Imm.A.R. 198, Immigration Appeal Tribunal.

1709. Refugee—expulsion—whether lawful
[Convention Relating to the Status of Refugees, art. 32(2)] M was a visitor and a refugee. He was granted temporary admission pending consideration of his application for entry as a visitor. His application was refused, and a removal order was issued effective the following day. Before removal, M applied for asylum: he was refused. *Held,* that Art. 32(2) of the Convention only applied to persons to be expelled on grounds of natural security and/or public order, and thus has no application in the present case: R. *v.* IMMIGRATION APPEAL TRIBUNAL, *ex p.* MUSISI [1984] Imm. A.R. 175, Monn J.

1710. Refusal of entry—assistance from relative—whether relevant
The existence of a relative to turn to in his own country can only form a ground for refusing entry to the U.K. if that relative is willing and able to help with finance or a home: R. *v.* IMMIGRATION APPEAL TRIBUNAL, *ex p.* SINGH, *The Times,* February 20, 1986, D.C.

1711. Refusal of leave to enter—adequacy of reasons—judicial review—alternative remedies
[Immigration Appeals (Notices) Regulations 1984 (S.I. 1984 No. 2040), Immigration Act 1971 (c.77), s.13, Sched. 2, para. 16.]
An applicant, refused leave to enter the U.K. by an immigration officer, must normally pursue the remedy offered by s.13 of the Immigration Act before seeking judicial review.
S sought leave to enter the U.K. for one week. The officer refused stating "I am not satisfied you are genuinely seeking entry only for this limited period." The applicant did not avail himself of the alternative statutory appeal procedure as that would have required him to leave the U.K. first, but sought judicial review of the decision, on the grounds that the officer's statement was not a sufficient reason for the purposes of reg. 4(1)(*a*). The Divisional Court refused leave to apply. *Held,* dismissing the appeal, that (1) the statement was an adequate statement of reasons; and (2) in the absence of special circumstances an applicant must avail himself of the remedy available in s.13 before seeking judicial review (*R. v. Chief Immigration Officer, Gatwick Airport, ex p. Kharazi* [1980] C.L.Y. 1428 distinguished).
R. *v.* SECRETARY OF STATE FOR THE HOME DEPARTMENT, *ex p.* SWATI [1986] 1 All E.R. 717, C.A.

1712. Refusal of leave to enter—bail—jurisdiction of the court
The court declined to decide finally whether there was power to grant bail since in any event no exceptional circumstances were present to justify the granting of bail (*R. v. Secretary of State for the Home Department, ex p. Swati* [1986] C.L.Y. 1711 considered): R. *v.* CHIEF IMMIGRATION OFFICER, *ex p.* SURESHKUMAR, (1986) 83 L.S.Gaz. 1902, C.A.

1713. Refusal to extend stay—appeal—appellants untraceable—dismissal of appeal—whether error in law
[Immigration Appeals (Procedure) Rules 1972 (S.I. 1972 No. 1684, r.12(*a*)(*c*).]
Where appeals against a refusal to extend the appellants' stay in the U.K. were dismissed in the absence of the appellants, who were not aware of the appeal, and whose advisers could not contact then, the adjudicator ought not to have been satisfied that no person was authorised to represent them and should have heard the appeals.
In 1979 the principal applicant was admitted to the U.K. as a student with leave to stay for seven months, later extended to September 1980. On September 16, 1980 she applied for a further extension to stay so that she could look after her children

who were at school here. Their applications were refused. They appealed requesting an oral hearing. By the date of the hearing they had moved and their advisers had not recorded the new address. By letter of November 9, 1981 they informed the adjudicator that they had no instructions and invited him to "decide this case in such manner as he may deem it to be proper" but requested a hearing. In purported exercise of his power under rule 12 of the Immigration Appeals (Procedure) Rules 1972 the adjudicator determined the appeals without a hearing and dismissed them. The applicants applied for judicial review to quash that decision. Taylor J. did quash his decision and ordered him to hear the appeals and the adjudicator's appeal to the Court of Appeal was dismissed. He further appealed to the House of Lords. _Held_, dismissing the appeal, that the letter of November 9, 1981 had not stated that the applicants had withdrawn their instructions to the advisers to act for them in the appeals, and so the adjudicator was not justified in finding that they were not authorised to represent the applicants at the hearing. Rule 12 provides that the adjudicator could determine an appeal without a hearing only if satisfied that "no person is authorised to represent him at a hearing." The adjudicator had not on the evidence reason to be satisfied that no person was so authorised and the adjudicator had erred in law in proceeding under rule 12 without a hearing.

RAHMANI *v.* DIGGINES [1986] 2 W.L.R. 530, H.L.

1714. Right of abode—breach of immigration laws—effect

K was a citizen of the U.K. and colonies. He entered as a student and then married a person who was settled in the U.K. He was granted indefinite leave. He then applied for a certificate of entitlement to a right of abode: that was refused on the basis that he had been in the U.K. in breach of the Immigration Laws. _Held_, that as he had stayed without leave, he was in breach of the immigration laws, and thus subject to a sanction for failure to acquire leave: KWOK *v.* SECRETARY OF STATE FOR HOME DEPARTMENT [1984] Imm.A.R. 226, Immigration Appeal Tribunal.

1715. Right of abode—Indian citizen—marriage to British citizen in India

[Immigration Act 1971 (c.77), s.2(1)(*a*)(*b*) as substituted by British Nationality Act 1981 (c.61), s.39(2).] B was born in India and as an Indian citizen married a British citizen in India on January 25, 1983. Later she arrived in the U.K. without entry clearance. She was refused entry on the ground that she was without leave. _Held_, that as she was not a British citizen, she did not qualify for a statutory right of abode under the new s.2(1)(*a*) of the 1971 Act which came into force on January 1, 1983: BRAHMBHATT *v.* CHIEF IMMIGRATION OFFICER AT HEATHROW AIRPORT [1984] Imm.A.R. 202, C.A.

1716. Rules—dependent relative—judicial review

[Statement of changes in Immigration Rules (H.C. 169, para. 52.] The requirement that applicants who wish to settle in the U.K. as dependent relatives of a resident had to show that their standard of living was substantially below their own countries' average was invalid as unreasonable as it was partial and discriminated between different classes: R. *v.* IMMIGRATION APPEAL TRIBUNAL, *ex p.* BEGUM (MANSHOORA), *The Times,* July 24, 1986, Simon Brown J.

1717. Student—arrival without entry clearance—officer not satisfied of ability to follow intended course—exhibit to affidavits of representations to and response from Secretary of State

Held, that (1) the discretion in para. 24 of H.C. 169 does not extend to the admission of a would-be student who, the immigration officer concludes, lacks the necessary ability to pursue a particular course; (2) on applications for leave, candour must be displayed, and therefore representations to, and especially responses from, the Secretary of State should be placed before the Court: R. *v.* SECRETARY OF STATE FOR THE HOME DEPARTMENT, *ex p.* BHAMBRA [1985] Imm.A.R. 28, Mann J.

1718. Student—definition of "enrolled"

Held, that the term "enrolled" in H.C. 169, para. 107 means that the student in question shall have an unconditional confirmed place on a course: CHINWO *v.* SECRETARY OF STATE FOR THE HOME DEPARTMENT [1985] Imm.A.R. 74, Imm.App.Trib.

1719. Student—grasp of English

[Statement of Changes in Immigration Rules (H.C. 169) (1983) paras. 21–24.] In deciding whether to admit a student to the U.K. an Immigration Officer is entitled to take into account whether the applicant's grasp of English is sufficient to enable him to pursue his intended course: R. *v.* SECRETARY OF STATE FOR THE HOME DEPARTMENT, *ex p.* OZKURTULUS, *The Times,* February 20, 1986, Farquharson J.

1720. Temporary admission—treatment as an illegal immigrant—whether correct

On arrival A (a citizen of Pakistan) sought admission as a visitor. He was refused leave to enter, but was granted temporary admission subject to certain conditions. He then married a British citizen and went to ground. When discovered he claimed a right to remain on the basis of his marriage, and under H.C. 169, para. 126. The Secretary of State treated A as an illegal immigrant, to whom the Immigration Rules as to variation of lease had no application. *Held,* that (1) H.C. 169, para. 126 did not apply to persons admitted temporarily under Schedule 2 to the Act, after having been refused leave to enter; (2) that A had been treated properly as an illegal immigrant: R. *v.* SECRETARY OF STATE FOR THE HOME DEPARTMENT, *ex p.* KHAN [1985] Imm.A.R. 104, C.A.

1721. Visitor—passport stamp recording leave is unclear—whether leave is limited or indefinite

It was not possible to determine the period of leave to remain in the U.K. from the stamp in M's passport, because it was unclear and could not be deciphered. *Held,* that unless the specification of the duration of leave was either expressed or could be implied, a notice indicating leave to enter was a grant of indefinite leave: SECRETARY OF STATE FOR THE HOME DEPARTMENT *v.* MANSOUR [1985] Imm.A.R. 1, Imm.App. Trib.

1722. Working holiday—whether need to show realistic prospect of employment

[Statement of Changes in Immigration Rules 1983 (H.C. 169), para. 30.] Since the purpose of the rule was to prevent the visitor becoming a drain on public funds, if he visited for a holiday and could support himself or be supported, it made no difference whether his prospects of employment, should he wish to take employment out of boredom or for some other reason, were realistic or not. In those circumstances the visitor would be allowed to enter the U.K.: R. *v.* IMMIGRATION APPEAL TRIBUNAL, *ex p.* BARI, *The Times,* October 7, 1986, C.A.

INCOME TAX

1723. Appeal hearing—refusal to allow further evidence—judicial review

The applicants appealed against assessment to income tax. At the appeal hearing, the applicants were represented by accountants, and two of them were present and gave evidence. The General Commissioners decided in principle that the applicants were assessable to income tax in respect of trading profits, and adjourned the appeals so that the figures might be agreed between the Inspector and the applicants. Agreement on figures was not reached; the appeals were listed for further hearing. At that hearing, the applicants applied to call further evidence. The General Commissioners refused that application. The applicants then applied for judicial review. The judge in the Queen's Bench Division dismissed that application. *Held,* dismissing the appeal, that the judge had decided correctly that the Commissioners had not exercised their discretion unlawfully or unreasonably in refusing the application to call further evidence: R. *v.* ST. MARYLEBONE SPECIAL COMMISSIONERS, *ex p.* SHOKROLLAH HAY (1983) 57 T.C. 59, C.A.

1724. Assessment—date when "made"

[Taxes Management Act 1970 (c.9), ss.34, 40.] Some weeks before the time limit in T.M.A. 1970, s.40, expired, the Inspector raised assessments against the administrators of Emanuel Honig by signing certificates to that effect which were entered into the assessment book of his district. However, notices of the assessments were not received by the administrators until after the time limit had expired. *Held,* dismissing the administrators' appeal, that the assessments had been made within the prescribed time limits and were valid: HONIG *v.* SARSFIELD [1986] S.T.C. 246, C.A.

1725. Bank interest—deduction of tax

[Income and Corporation Taxes Act 1970 (c.10), s.54.] T Co. was a property dealing company, which in 1980 borrowed £350,000 from Savings and Investment Bank Ltd., which was an Isle of Man bank having its registered office in Douglas. T Co. made payments of interest to the bank without deducting interest under I.C.T.A. 1970, s.54. *Held,* dismissing T Co.'s appeal, that the bank, albeit making loans to U.K. residents, was not carrying on a bona fide banking business in the U.K., so that income tax should have been deducted by T Co. from interest paid: HAFTON PROPERTIES *v.* McHUGH, *The Times,* December 16, 1986, Peter Gibson J.

1726. Building society payments

INCOME TAX (BUILDING SOCIETIES) REGULATIONS 1986 (No. 482) [£1·35], made under the Income and Corporation Taxes Act 1970 (c.10), s.343(1A); operative on April 6, 1986; establish a scheme for the taxation of dividends, interest and other payments by building societies.

1727. Capital allowances

CAPITAL ALLOWANCES (CORRESPONDING NORTHERN IRELAND GRANTS) ORDER 1986 (No. 539) [40p], made under the Capital Allowances Act 1968 (c.3), ss.84(1), 95(6); operative on April 1, 1986; replaces S.I. 1984 No. 407.

1728. Capital gains tax—alternative assessments—validity

[Taxes Management Act 1970 (c.9), s.49(1).] T was assessed to capital gains tax in respect of certain transactions; alternative assessments to income tax were also raised. T allowed the capital gains tax assessment to become final and paid the tax assessed. He appealed against the income tax assessments on the basis that they were precluded, he having been assessed to, and having paid, the capital gains tax. *Held,* dismissing T's appeal, that the alternative income tax assessments were valid: BYE *v.* COREN [1986] S.T.C. 393, C.A.

1729. Cash equivalents

INCOME TAX (CASH EQUIVALENTS OF CAR BENEFITS) ORDER 1986 (No. 703) [45p], made under the Finance Act 1976, s.64(4); operative on April 6, 1987; prescribes new amounts of cash equivalents on which directors and higher-paid employees are chargeable to income tax in respect of the benefit of a car made available for private use.

INCOME TAX (CASH EQUIVALENTS OF CAR FUEL BENEFITS) ORDER 1986 (No. 702) [45p], made under the Finance Act 1976 (c.40), s.64A(4); operative on April 6, 1987; prescribes cash equivalents on which directors and higher-paid employees are chargeable to income tax in respect of the benefits of car fuel made available for private use.

1730. Construction industry

INCOME TAX (SUB-CONTRACTORS IN THE CONSTRUCTION INDUSTRY) REGULATIONS 1986 (No. 1240) [£1·90], made under the Finance (No. 2) Act 1975 (c.45), s.70 and Sched. 12; operative on November 6, 1986; prescribe new forms for sub-contractor certificates and sub-contractor vouchers for use in the construction industry.

1731. Corporation tax—penalties—appeals—misnomer of respondents—leave to amend

Two companies sought to appeal against penalties awarded against them under T.M.A. 1970, s.20(1). In the appeals they had misnamed the respondents, referring to the Kensington General Commissioners instead of to the Special Commissioners; this was not a mere clerical error, and had been pointed out to them by the Inland Revenue. Subsequently, they sought notice to amend. *Held,* dismissing originating motions by the two companies, that, in the circumstances of delay in correcting the error after it had been pointed out to them, that the applications to amend and to extend the time for service of notices of motion should be refused: WARDMAN PAUL *v.* KENSINGTON GENERAL COMMISSIONERS AND I.R.C.; WOODTREK *v.* SAME [1986] S.T.C. 545, Knox J.

1732. Deposit-taker

INCOME TAX (COMPOSITE RATE) (RELEVANT DEPOSITS) ORDER 1986 (No. 771) [45p], made under the Finance Act 1984 (c.43), Sched. 8, para. 3A; operative on May 20, 1986; reduces the period in which a deposit-taker under Sched. 8 must pay an amount payable.

1733. Discretionary trust—appointment of capital—income

[Finance Act 1973 (c.51), s.17.]

H. a beneficiary under a settlement lived in a nursing home from 1978 until her death in 1981. The trustees exercised their powers to appoint sums of £109,000 out of capital to be paid on H's behalf to defray her medical and nursing expenses. At no time was H in a position to divert these sums to another use. The trustees appealed against assessments to income tax in respect of the sums appointed to H. A Special Commissioner found for the trustees. *Held,* dismissing the Crown's appeal, that unless the combined effect of the power in the settlement and the manner in which the power was exercised produced an entitlement to income in H's hands, the sums appointed were capital as regards both the trustees and H. The payments were made under the power of appointment over capital without creating a right to income, and were not taxable as income.

STEVENSON *v.* WISHART [1986] 1 All E.R. 404, Knox J.

1734. Double taxation

DOUBLE TAXATION RELIEF (TAXES ON INCOME) (SOVIET UNION) ORDER 1986 (No. 224) [£2·30], made under the Income and Corporation Taxes Act 1970 (c.10), s.497; provides for double taxation relief in relation to the Soviet Union.

1735. Emoluments—duties performed abroad

[Finance Act 1977 (c.36), Sched. 7, para. 2]. T performed duties overseas not only on "qualifying days" (*i.e.* days when he was entirely absent from the U.K.) but also on days which were not "qualifying days", because he returned to the U.K. before midnight. *Held,* dismissing both the Crown's and T's appeals, that (1) for the purpose of calculating overseas earnings relief under F.A. 1977, Sched. 7, account could be taken of work done overseas on days which were not "qualifying days" within Sched. 7, para. 2(1), and (2) that the amount of the emoluments to be attributed to the duties performed abroad was to be determined by reference to the contract, but, if there was no contractual allocation, the Apportionment Act 1870 applied to allocate 1/365 of the annual salary to each day (*Varnum v. Deeble* [1984] C.L.Y. 1799 followed): PLATTEN *v.* BROWN [1986] S.T.C. 514, Hoffmann J.

1736. Estimated assessments—unreliable records—judicial review

T was a self-employed painter and decorator. Estimated assessment to income tax were made on him for the years 1976–77 to 1982–83. The General Commissioners examined T's records in detail for one year, and found them to be unreliable. They inferred from that that the accounts for the other years were understated. Accordingly, they made their own estimates of T's profits, and confirmed the assessments accordingly. T appealed, contending, *inter alia,* that he had not had a fair opportunity to present his case. *Held,* dismissing T's appeal, that (1) the Commissioners were entitled to make estimates for all years having satisfied themselves that one year's accounts were unreliable, and (2) the question whether T had had a fair opportunity to present his case could be raised only by way of judicial review (dictum of Goulding J. in *Read v. Rollinson* [1982] C.L.Y. 1569 applied): BRITTAIN *v.* GIBBS [1986] S.T.C. 418, Vinelott J.

1737. European schools—supplements and allowances from Community Budget—exemption from tax. See HURD *v.* JONES, § 1439.

1738. Fiduciary relationship—accountability—deduction in respect of tax

As a result of actions brought by them, P were awarded judgment against D requiring D to account to them for moneys retained by D or its associated companies in breach of fiduciary duty under certain publishing and recording agreements. At a later hearing P claimed compound interest on the sums found to be due to them. D claimed that in making payment to P it should be entitled to deduct (1) amounts in respect of U.K. tax and foreign tax paid by it or its associated companies on the moneys wrongfully retained, (2) amounts in respect of tax which P would have paid had they received the amounts when they fell due, and (3) amounts in respect of tax on the interest. *Held,* that (1) D should make no deduction in respect of taxes paid by it and its associated companies (*O'Sullivan v. Management Agency and Music* [1985] Q.B. 428 distinguished), (2) in view of the complexity and impractability of the matter no deduction should be made in respect of P's U.K. and foreign tax position (*British Transport Commission v. Gourley* [1955] C.L.Y. 724, distinguished; dictum of Brightman L.J. in *Bartlett v. Barclay's Bank Trust Co.* [1980] C.L.Y. 2404 followed); and (3) similarly no deduction should be made in respect of tax from the compound interest: JOHN *v.* JAMES [1986] S.T.C. 352, Ch.D.

1739. Foreign pension—Sched. D, Case V

[Income and Corporation Taxes Act 1970 (c.10), ss.108, 109]. T had lived and worked in the U.S.A. for some twenty years. He then retired to live in the U.K., and received regular pension payments from the U.S. Government. *Held,* dismissing T's appeal, that the pension payments were income chargeable under Case V of Schedule D (income arising from foreign possessions) (*Colquhoun v. Brooks* (1889) 2

T.C. 490, and *Oppenheimer* v. *Cattermole* [1975] C.L.Y. 1660 followed): ASPIN *v.* ESTILL [1986] S.T.C. 323, Ch.D.

1740. Incorrect returns—neglect—penalties—whether excessive
[Taxes Management Act 1970 (c.9), ss.93, 95.] T appealed against penalties in the sum of £41,880 awarded against him under T.M.A. 1970, ss.93 and 95, by General Commissioners in respect of negligent delivery of incorrect returns and failure to deliver returns. The grounds of the appeal were, *inter alia*, that the Commissioners had unreasonably refused an application by T for adjournment and that the penalties were excessive. *Held*, that the Commissioners had not acted unfairly in refusing an adjournment and their decision to impose maximum penalties could not be criticised: JOLLEY *v.* BOLTON GENERAL COMMISSIONERS AND I.R.C. [1986] S.T.C. 414, Scott J.

1741. Incorrect returns or accounts—penalties—whether amounts excessive
[Taxes Management Act 1970 (c.9), s.95.] T was assessed to income tax on the basis that for many years he had been earning profits in a business in respect of which he had put in nil returns. Appeals against those assessments were dismissed. Subsequently, the Inspector commenced penalty proceedings under T.M.A. 1970, s.95. The Commissioners awarded penalties which approximated to 40 per cent. of the maximum penalties. *Held*, dismissing T's appeal, that in the circumstances it could not possibly be said that the penalties imposed were disproportionate to the fault: LEAR *v.* LEEK GENERAL COMMISSIONERS AND I.R.C. [1986] S.T.C. 542, Vinelott J.

1742. Incorrect returns—penalties
The taxpayers appealed against penalties awarded against them by General Commissioner for the years 1980–81 to 1982–83 in respect of the negligent delivery of tax returns and negligently submitted accounts. *Held*, dismissing the appeals, that the Commissioners were the judges of fact, and the Court ought not to interfere with their findings or decisions, they having evidently paid attention to their judicial duty: KHAN *v.* FIRST EAST BRIXTON GENERAL COMMISSIONERS [1986] S.T.C. 331, Ch.D.

1743. Insurance business—profits—deduction for claims. See SOUTHERN PACIFIC INSURANCE CO. (FIJI) *v.* COMMISSIONER OF INLAND REVENUE, § 2743.

1744. Insurance company—profits
[Mal.] [Income Tax Act 1967 (Malaysia) (as amended), s.60.] T. Co. was an insurance company registered in Singapore. It carried on business in Malaysia through a permanent establishment, for the purposes of which it maintained a separate life fund. It also maintained, as it was required to do, a Singapore life fund, which was constituted in part by investments in Malaysia. It claimed that under the Income Tax Act 1967 (Malaysia) (as amended) it was taxable in Malaysia only on income from its Malaysian life fund. *Held*, dismissing T Co.'s appeal, that it was also taxable in Malaysia on the income from Malaysian investments allocated to the Singapore life fund or representing non-assigned funds: GREAT EASTERN LIFE ASSURANCE CO. *v.* DIRECTOR GENERAL OF INLAND REVENUE [1986] S.T.C. 447, P.C.

1745. Interest
INCOME TAX (INTEREST ON UNPAID TAX AND REPAYMENT SUPPLEMENT) (NO. 2) ORDER 1986 (No. 1832) [45p], made under the Finance Act 1967 (c.54), s.40(2), the Taxes Management Act 1970 (c.9), s.89(2) and the Finance (No. 2) Act 1975 (c.45), ss.47(7)(10), 48(6); operative on November 6, 1986; increases to 9·5 per cent. the rate of interest chargeable on unpaid specified taxes.

INCOME TAX (INTEREST ON UNPAID TAX AND REPAYMENT SUPPLEMENT) ORDER 1986 (No. 1181) [45p], made under the Finance Act 1967 (c.54), s.40(2), the Taxes Management Act 1970 (c.9), s.89(2), and the Finance (No. 2) Act 1975 (c.45), ss.47(7) and (10) and 48(6); operative on August 6, 1986; for periods beginning on August 6 this order reduces from 11 to 8½ per cent. per annum the rate of interest chargeable on unpaid income tax, surtax, capital gains tax, corporation tax, development land tax, profits tax, excess profits tax, excess profits levy and overpaid development land tax.

INCOME TAX (INTEREST RELIEF) (QUALIFYING LENDERS) ORDER 1986 (No. 386) [40p], made under the Finance Act 1982 (c.39), Sched. 7, para. 14(2); prescribes bodies for the purposes of Sched. 7, Pt. IV to the 1982 Act.

1746. Interest—deduction—apportionment—management fees

[Fiji] [Income Tax Act (Fiji), ss.16, 17, 19(f).] T Co. borrowed moneys to acquire the shares in F which in turn controlled BL. It was the intention of T Co. that, having acquired F, it would cause BL to pay substantial management fees to T Co. Interest charges on the borrowed moneys were acknowledged not to be deductible in so far as they related to the shares in F. However, T Co. claimed that the interest should be apportioned between dividends paid on the shares in F and the management fees, the interest apportioned to the latter being deductible. *Held,* dismissing T Co.'s appeal, that the interest was wholly attributable to the shares in F, and so was not deductible: MARINE MANAGEMENT *v.* DEPUTY COMMISSIONER OF INLAND REVENUE [1986] S.T.C. 251, P.C.

1747. Interest relief

INCOME TAX (INTEREST RELIEF) (QUALIFYING LENDERS) (No. 2) ORDER 1986 (No. 1440) [45p], made under the Finance Act 1982 (c.39), Sched. 7, para. 14(2); designates qualifying lenders so that interest on qualifying loans may be paid to them under deduction of tax.

INCOME TAX (INTEREST RELIEF) (QUALIFYING LENDERS) (No. 3) ORDER 1986 (No. 2191) [80p], made under the Finance Act 1982 (c.39), Sched. 7, para. 14(2); prescribes specified bodies as qualifying lenders so that interest on qualifying loans made by them may be paid to them under deduction of tax.

1748. Jersey partnership—U.K. resident partner—Double Taxation Convention—exemption from tax

[Income and Corporation Taxes Act 1970 (c.10), s.497; Double Taxation Relief (Taxes on Income) (Jersey) Order (S.I. 1952 No. 1216), para. 3(2).] T was a U.K. resident and a member of a partnership, the business of which was controlled and managed in Jersey. He claimed that, by virtue of I.C.T.A. 1970, s.497, and para. 3(2) of the Double Tax Treaty with Jersey, he was exempt from U.K. income tax in respect of his share of the partnership profits. *Held,* allowing T's appeal, that (1) the partnership was a "body of persons" and a "Jersey enterprise" for the purposes of para. 3(2) of the Treaty, and (2) by virtue of that paragraph, T's share of the partnership profits was exempt from U.K. income tax: PADMORE *v.* I.R.C., *The Times,* December 3, 1986, Peter Gibson J.

1749. Judicial review—close company—covenanted payments—apportionment—discretion

[Finance Act 1972, (c.41), Sched. 16, para. 3.] T Co. was a close company which in several accounting periods made covenanted donations to a charity. In 1984 the Inland Revenue served notices indicating that the payments would be apportioned among the participators in T Co. pursuant to F.A. 1972, Sched. 16, para. 3. The notices were issued on the footing that the apportionment was mandatory and that the word "may" in para. 3(1) did not import any discretion. T. Co. applied for judicial review, which application was granted by the High Court. *Held,* dismissing the Crown's appeal, that the notices should be quashed, since the power under Sched. 16, para. 3(1), was discretionary, and that power was not properly exercised where notices were issued on the footing that there was a mandatory obligation to do so: R. v. H.M. INSPECTOR OF TAXES, *ex p.* LANSING BAGNALL (1986) S.T.C. 453, C.A.

1750. Judicial review—evidence before Commissioner. See R. *v.* SPECIAL COMMISSIONER, *ex p.* STIPPLECHOICE (No. 2), § 2855.

1751. Land—trade

In June 1977 the taxpayers purchased a piece of land for £65,000, providing £35,000 of the purchase price from their own resources and borrowing the balance. One of the taxpayers gave evidence that he intended to make a medium or long-term investment, that he had no intention of developing the land or receiving an income from it. On September 15, 1977, on the advice of an estate agent, the taxpayers sold the land for £100,000. They were assessed to income tax under Case I of Schedule D. The General Commissioners discharged the assessments. *Held,* dismissing the Crown's appeal, that the Commissioners had not misdirected themselves in law and their decision ought not to be upset: MARSON *v.* MORTON [1986] S.T.C. 463, Ch.D.

1752. Land—whether capital or income receipts—extraction of timber

[Malaysia] [Income Tax Act (Malaysia) 1967, s.4.] In 1969 T. Co. was allocated 7,000 acres of jungle in consideration of a premium of $17,100 per acre, and subject to an obligation to develop the land as an oil palm plantation within a specified time and to clear the land by felling and logging the standing timber. The premium charged included an element in respect of the right to extract timber. T. Co. accordingly felled and sold timber from the land, and was then assessed to income tax, timber profits tax and development tax for the years 1971, 1972 and 1973. The Malaysian Special Commissioners upheld the assessments on the grounds that T. Co. was carrying on a separate business of timber operators. *Held,* allowing T. Co's appeal, that the extraction of the timber was inseparable from the activity of developing the 7,000 acres as an oil palm plantation, and that the proceeds of sale of the timber were capital receipts: MAMOR SDN BHD *v.* DIRECTOR GENERAL OF INLAND REVENUE [1985] S.T.C. 801, P.C.

1753. Maintenance payments

INCOME TAX (SMALL MAINTENANCE PAYMENTS) ORDER 1986 (No. 328) [40p], made under the Income and Corporation Taxes Act 1970 (c.10), s.65(5); operative on April 6, 1986; increases the monthly limits for small maintenance payments in respect of which income tax is not deductible at source.

1754. Partnership—trade—loss—limited partner

[Limited Partnerships Act 1907 (c.24), s.4(2); Income and Corporation Taxes Act 1970 (c.10), s.168(1).]

A limited partner, whose contribution was limited to £15,000, was entitled to tax relief, for losses incurred in excess of that sum, against her other income.

On March 28, 1978 the taxpayer became a partner in a limited partnership formed for producing motion pictures. She contributed a total of £15,000 in two stages. In its accounting period to March 31, 1978 the partnership incurred a trading loss of £650,073. The taxpayer's proportionate share of that loss under the partnership deed was £41,144. She claimed to be entitled to set off this sum as a tax loss, together with a sum of £279 representing her proportionate share of the partnership loss for the year to March 31, 1979 apportioned up to April 6, 1978, *i.e.* a total of £41,423 against her other income for that year pursuant to s.168(4) of the Income and Corporation Taxes Act 1970. The special commissioners allowed her appeal from the inspector of taxes, and the Crown's appeals to the single judge, the Court of Appeal, and the House of Lords were dismissed.

Held, that a partnership's trading losses for tax purposes were conceptually quite distinct from its debts and liabilities and the assets available to meet them. Under s.4(2) of the Limited Partnerships Act 1907 the taxpayer's legal liability if it had been called in could not have exceeded her capital contribution of £15,000. But this was immaterial in considering whether she "sustains a loss" for tax purposes within s.168 of the Income and Corporation Taxes Act 1970. The loss was to be assessed by reference to her share as set out in the partnership deed. Accordingly she was entitled to set off the £41,423 against her other income for the year in question.

REED (INSPECTOR OF TAXES) *v.* YOUNG [1986] 1 W.L.R. 649, H.L.

1755. Personal equity plan

PERSONAL EQUITY PLAN REGULATIONS 1986 (No. 1948) [£2·90], made under the Finance Act 1986 (c.41), Sched. 8; operative on January 1, 1987; set up a scheme for investment plans for individuals, the income and gains of which are exempt from tax.

1756. Production of documents—whether gains "derived from" business

[Taxes Management Act 1970 (c.9), s.20.] M Co. appealed against an award of nominal penalties by a Special Commissioner for its failure to comply with two notices served on it under T.M.A. 1970, s.20, requiring it to produce certain documents. The documents related to a scheme to which M Co. was a party whereunder C Co. had granted to some of its employees options to acquire shares in C Co.; subsequently, those options had been exchanged for options to buy shares in an Isle of Man company. The Inland Revenue considered that the documents it required might show that those options had been assigned, giving rise to taxable gains. However, for the notices under T.M.A. 1970, s.20, to be valid, it needed to be shown that such gains would have "derived from [the] business" of C Co. *Held,* dismissing M Co.'s appeal, that gains realised from dealings in securities (options) indirectly deriving their value from the business of C Co. could be said to be "derived from [that] business": MONARCH ASSURANCE CO. *v.* SPECIAL COMMISSIONERS [1986] S.T.C. 311, Ch.D.

1757. Reduced and composite rate

INCOME TAX (REDUCED AND COMPOSITE RATE) ORDER 1986 (No. 2147) [45p], made under the Finance Act 1984 (c.93), s.26; operative on April 6, 1987; determines the rate at 24·75 per cent. for the year 1987–88.

1758. Relief—charitable gifts

INCOME TAX (EMPLOYMENTS) (No. 16) REGULATIONS 1986 (No. 2212) [45p], made under the Income and Corporation Taxes Act 1970 (c.10), s.204; operative on April 6, 1987; provide the machinery for the relief from tax through the PAYE system of sums withheld at the request of employees to go to charity.

1759. Schedule E—benefits in kind

[Income and Corporation Taxes Act 1970 (c.10), ss.1, 181, 183 and 195; Finance Act 1976 (c.40), s.64.] T was an employee earning over £8,500 per annum. His employer provided him with cars for his private use, incurring costs of licensing, insuring and repairing the cars, as well as of running them. *Held,* dismissing T's appeal, that pursuant to I.C.T.A. 1970, s.195, and F.A. 1976, s.64, he was assessable to income tax under Schedule E on the benefit, and that the amount to bring in as emoluments included the costs incurred by the employer in licensing, insuring and repairing the cars (*Tennant* v. *Smith* (1890) 3 T.C. 158, distinguished): WILSON v. ALEXANDER [1986] S.T.C. 365, Harman J.

1760. Schedule E—emoluments—distribution of trust funds—relevant years of assessment

[Income and Corporation Taxes Act 1970 (c.10), s.181] In 1957 and 1963 a company set up trusts for the benefit of its employees. In 1979 the company was taken over; it was decided to wind up the trusts and distribute the funds. The trustees, exercising their discretions, decided to distribute the funds to the employees having regard to length of service and salary level. Accordingly, in 1979/80 T received two sums totalling £18,111. T was assessed to income tax under Schedule E in respect of those sums. *Held,* allowing the Crown's appeal, that (1) the sums were emoluments assessable under Schedule E (*Brumby* v. *Miller* [1976] C.L.Y 1441, followed), and (2) the case should be remitted to the Commissioners to determine the years to which the sums should be appointed and the basis of the appointment: BRAY v. BEST [1986] S.T.C. 96, Walton J.

1761. Schedule E—employment—part-time lecturing

T was a barrister, with chambers in Lincoln's Inn, who had ceased general practice in 1960. He derived part of his income from part-time lecturing on legal subjects at the Thames Polytechnic and for the ILEA. He claimed that the income derived from these sources was assessable under Schedule D, not Schedule E. *Held,* dismissing T's appeal, that the income was correctly assessed under Schedule E: SIDEY v. PHILLIPS, *The Times,* December 12, 1986, Knox J.

1762. Schedule E—payment in respect of loss of rights—whether emolument

[Income and Corporation Taxes Act 1970 (c.10), ss.181, 183(1).]

The £1,000 paid to G.C.H.Q. employees is an emolument from employment.

In 1983 civil servants employed at G.C.H.Q. lost their right to belong to a trade union. They were offered a payment of £1,000 expressed to be in recognition of this loss. The taxpayer was assessed to income tax in respect of the £1,000. The taxpayer appealed contending that the payment was a solatium. *Held,* dismissing the taxpayer's appeal, that the word "emoluments" had a wider meaning than remuneration; the employment was the source of the payment and the payment was therefore an "emolument."

HAMBLETT v. GODFREY (INSPECTOR OF TAXES) [1986] 2 All E.R. 513, Knox J.

1763. Tax avoidance—purchase of "tax loss" company

[N.Z.] [Income Tax Act 1976 (New Zealand), ss.99, 191.] T Co. was member of a group of companies. In February 1978, it purchased the whole of the issued share capital of P. Co., a company with tax losses, at a price which related to the availability of those losses. The purpose of the arrangement was to reduce the income tax liability of the T. Co. group by using the losses of P Co. against group company profits pursuant to s.191 of the Income Tax Act 1976. The Commissioner of Inland Revenue contended that the losses could not be utilised under s.191, as the general anti-avoidance provisions of s.99 applied. *Held,* (Lord Cliver dissenting), that the general anti-avoidance provisions of s.99 applied to prevent the T Co. group utilising purchased tax losses: I.R.C. *v.* CHALLENGE CORP. [1986] S.T.C. 548, P.C.

1764. Tax avoidance—transfer of assets abroad

[Income and Corporation Taxes Act 1970 (c.10), s.478.] T, a consultant chartered surveyor, resident in the U.K. in 1974 entered into arrangements with D (a Jersey company the shares in which were held by trustees for the benefit of T's family) whereunder T gave his services to D free of salary until 1979 after which he was to receive such remuneration as the directors of D thought proper. D derived fees from the exploitation of T's services in the U.K. *Held,* that (1) the service arrangements which T made with D constituted a "transfer of assets" for the purposes of I.C.T.A. 1970, s.478, and under that section T was able to be assessed on the income arising to D, and (2) in any event, D was able to be assessed to income tax under I.C.T.A. 1970, s.246(2), on the basis that it was carrying on its trade in the U.K. through the agency of T: I.R.C. *v.* BRACKETT; BRACKETT *v.* CHATER [1986] S.T.C. 521, Hoffmann J.

1765. Tax thresholds

INCOME TAX (INDEXATION) ORDER 1986 (No. 529) [40p], made under the Finance Act 1980 (c.48), s.24(9); specifies certain amounts which take account of the percentage increase in the retail price index.

1766. Taxpayer on half salary—arrears paid simultaneously—liability for tax

[Trinidad and Tobago.] [Income Tax Ordinance (Laws of Trinidad and Tobago, 1950 ed., c.33, No. 1) (as amended), ss.5(1)(*e*), 6; Public Service Commission Regulations 1966 (Government Notice No. 132 of 1966), regs. 89, 112.]

The payment of several years of half salary arrears to a government employee is not to be treated as his income for the year in which the arrears are paid, but as income in the year to which each payment relates.

A teacher, employed by the government was charged with criminal offences in 1970 and paid only half his salary. In 1976 all criminal proceedings were withdrawn and he was paid all the arrears. He was assessed for tax on all the arrears as income received in 1976. His appeal was allowed. *Held,* dismissing the appeal to the Judicial Committee, that the arrears for each of the years formed part of his assessable income for the years to which each payment related (*Dracup* v. *Radcliffe* (1946) 27 T.C. 188; *Heasman* v. *Jordan* [1954] Ch. 744 applied).

BOARD OF INLAND REVENUE *v.* SUITE [1986] 2 W.L.R. 1042, P.C.

1767. Trade—partnership—deduction of removal costs

A large professional partnership from time to time required partners to relocate their place of work. It was the practice of the firm to assist with removal expenses in such cases. The firm sought to deduct expenditure so incurred in the computation of its profits for tax purposes. *Held,* allowing the Crown's appeal, that the expenditure was not deductible, as it could not be regarded as incurred "wholly and exclusively" for the purposes of the partnership treating the benefit to the individual partners as merely incidental: MACKINLAY *v.* ARTHUR YOUNG MCCLELLAND MOORES & Co., *The Times,* October 13, 1986, Vinelott J.

1768. Trading in shares and land—hotel property

[Mal.] T Co., a company whose objects clause empowered it to deal in land and other property and which had previously dealt in land, acquired and developed a hotel site, which it financed on a sale and lease-back transaction, and operated the hotel through a subsidiary company. As part of the sale and lease-back transactions, it had an option to buy-back the hotel. After a number of years of successful operation, T Co. sold the re-purchase option for the hotel to the hotel operating company and sold some of its shares in that company to the public. It was assessed to tax on the basis that the resulting profits were trading profits. *Held,* allowing T Co.'s appeal, there was no evidence for holding that the interests in the hotel and its site and the shares in the hotel operating company were held by T Co. otherwise than as capital assets: LIM FOO YONG Sdn Bhd. *v.* COMPTROLLER-GENERAL OF INLAND REVENUE [1986] S.T.C. 255, P.C.

INDUSTRIAL SOCIETIES

1769. Fees

INDUSTRIAL AND PROVIDENT SOCIETIES (AMENDMENT OF FEES) REGULATIONS 1986 (No. 621) [80p], made under the Industrial and Provident Societies Act 1965 (c.12), ss.70(1), 71(1), and the Industrial and Provident Societies Act 1967 (c.48), s.7(2); operative on April 28, 1986; increase fees payable under the 1965 and 1967 Acts.

INDUSTRIAL AND PROVIDENT SOCIETIES (CREDIT UNIONS) (AMENDMENT OF FEES) REGULATIONS 1986 (No. 622) [80p], made under the Industrial and Provident Societies Act 1965 (c.12), ss.70(1), 71(1), as applied by the Industrial and Provident Societies Act 1967 (c.48), s.7(2), and the Credit Unions Act 1979 (c.34), s.31(2); operative on April 28, 1986; replace S.I. 1985 No. 345 and increase fees payable for matters transacted under the 1965, 1967 and 1979 Acts.

1770. Industrial assurance

INDUSTRIAL ASSURANCE (FEES) REGULATIONS 1986 (No. 608) [40p], made under the Industrial Assurance Act 1923 (c.8), s.43; operative on April 28, 1986; replace S.I. 1985 No. 338 and increase fees.

INSURANCE

1771. All risks policy—duty of assured to take reasonable care

A contract of insurance containing the ordinary sort of clause requiring the insured to take reasonable steps to prevent loss was held not to have been breached when the insured took her eye off her luggage at an airport for two to three seconds, during which time her handbag was stolen. The insurers had to pay the agreed value of the contents. (*British and Foreign Marine Insurance Company* v. *Gaunt* [1921] 2 A.C. 41 considered): PORT-ROSE v. PHOENIX ASSURANCE (1986) 136 New L.J. 333, Hodgson J.

1772. Breach of foreign law—proceeds of crime—whether enforceable

A contract legally made in England is not made unenforceable by breaches of foreign law, unless those breaches have contributed to the insured loss. However, the insured is not entitled to rely on his own illegal acts, even if performed abroad and legal in the United Kingdom, when making his claim against the insurer. He may also not sue on his contract of insurance where his claim is so closely connected with the proceeds of crime that to allow it would offend the conscience of the court (*Bowmakers* v. *Barnet Instruments* [1945] K.B. 45 distinguished; *Beresford* v. *Royal Insurance Co.* [1938] A.C. 586 applied): EURO-DIAM v. BATHURST, *The Financial Times*, October 28, 1986, Staughton J.

1773. Broker—breach of contract—damages

An insurance broker who in breach of contract had failed to secure comprehensive motor insurance for a client whose vehicle was destroyed was not liable for the hire of another vehicle as the necessity to do so was due either to the customer's impecuniosity or the broker's failure to pay damages promptly: RAMWADE v. EMSON (W.J.) & Co., *The Times*, July 11, 1986, C.A.

1774. Contingency insurance—construction of policy—whether loss fell within terms

D were Lloyd's underwriters who had insured P against certain contingencies including "forgery, irregularity, fabrication or duplication of any securities." X was employed by P, and for a period of 10 years he unlawfully abstracted sums by forging bank transfers. The fraud was discovered, and D accepted liability for the sums abstracted. P also claimed for loss of use of the moneys and extra interest paid. *Held*, that the assumed losses were not sustained on account of the forgery—this did not directly or indirectly result in the loss of interest and P failed on causation: COURTAULDS & COURTAULDS (BELGIUM) S.A. v. LISSENDEN [1986] 1 Lloyd's Rep. 368, Saville J.

1775. Contingency monetary losses—whether authorised business

[Insurance Companies Act 1974 (c.49), ss.2(1)(*a*), 11(1).] If an insurer carries on authorised monetary loss business within the "marine, aviation and transport" class, he may insure contingency monetary losses arising from adjustment to aircraft insurance premiums. Such insurance contracts will be valid even though excluded by statutory reclassification from the "aviation" class: PHOENIX GENERAL INSURANCE CO. GREECE S.A. v. ADMINISTRATIA ASIGURARILOR DE STAT, *The Financial Times*, October 15, 1986, C.A.

1776. Contract—whether available—whether equitable relief

[Misrepresentation Act 1967 (c.7), s.2(2)] The test for determining whether a non-marine insurance contract is avoidable for misrepresentation is whether a circumstance was undisclosed or misrepresented which a prudent insurer would take into account when deciding whether or not to accept the risk, and what premium to charge. Where a contract is avoided on that ground, it is most unlikely that equitable relief under s.2(2) of the Misrepresentation Act 1967 would be allowed (*Container Transport International Inc.* v. *Oceans Mutual Underwriting Association (Bermuda)* [1984] C.L.Y. 3193 applied): HIGHLAND INSURANCE COMPANY v. CONTINENTAL INSURANCE COMPANY, *The Times,* May 6, 1986, Steyn J.

1777. Employers' liability—whether assured covered—whether absence of cover due to the fault of brokers—causation

D, a company specialising in decorating, were required to take out employer's liability insurance in respect of personal injury to employees. D had been insured by X, but X dramatically raised their premia. In these circumstances D's brokers W placed the cover with E, stating in the proposal form that D had never been the subject of a request for increased premia. The policy was issued, and contained a provision that it was only to cover injuries sustained from work carried out less than 40 feet above floor level. P was injured, falling from a height a little over 40 feet. D agreed damages with P, and sought an indemnity from E, alternatively damages from W. The judge held that E were entitled to repudiate liability on the ground of material non-disclosure. He held W to be liable, as the sole ground on which E had sought to repudiate (the failure to disclose a previous increase in premia) was consequent upon the conduct of W. E would not, on the evidence, have repudiated had the "40 feet point" been the only point open to them. *Held,* dismissing W's appeal, that the judge was correct in assessing, on the evidence before him, the chances of E taking the height point, and in finding, on that evidence, that they would not have taken that point: DUNBAR (ALFRED JAMES) v. A. & B. PAINTERS AND ECONOMIC INSURANCE CO. LTD. AND WHITEHOUSE & CO. [1986] 2 Lloyd's Rep. 38, C.A.

1778. Fees

INSURANCE (FEES) REGULATIONS 1986 (No. 446) [80p], made under the Insurance Companies Act 1982 (c.50), ss.94A and 97; operative on April 1, 1986; set out the fees to be paid to the Secretary of State under s.94A of the 1982 Act by insurance companies when they deposit annually their accounts and other documents.

1779. Fire insurance—onus of proof

P's warehouse premises were severely damaged by fire. The buildings, fixtures and fittings and stock were insured by a policy issued by D. D sought to avoid the policy on the ground that, P's managing director, C, deliberately caused the fire. On the facts the judge was not satisfied that an electrical fault had caused smouldering woodwork (undetected by C and other occupants but which became a flaming fire at almost the precise moment C left the premises) as the fire damage was equally consistent with intentional ignition of stock. *Held,* that in all the circumstances, D had discharged the heavy onus resting on them (proving fraud to a high degree of probability). P's action was dismissed (*S. and M. Carpets (London)* v. *Cornhill Insurance Co.* [1982] C.L.Y. 1659 followed): BROUGHTON PARK TEXTILES v. COMMERCIAL UNION ASSURANCE CO., May 19, 1986; Simon Brown J., Manchester. (*Ex rel. G. F. Tattersall, Barrister.*)

1780. Insurance companies—winding up. See COMPANY LAW.

1780a. Marine insurance. See SHIPPING AND MARINE INSURANCE.

1781. Market traders' insurance—theft from vehicle—exclusions clause—whether vehicle left unattended

L, who were market traders, were insured with D. Some goods were stolen from her car whilst it was standing outside her home. There was a specific provision in the policy which excluded liability if the vehicle was not "attended by the insured". Mrs. L was in her home when the theft occurred, and D denied liability. *Held,* that on a practical commonsense view of the facts, the vehicle had not been left unattended and P was entitled to recover: LANGFORD v. LEGAL & GENERAL ASSURANCE SOCIETY [1986] 2 Lloyd's Rep. 103, Judge Hawser Q.C.

1782. Material damage and consequential loss—whether "explosion"

P operated a smelting plant and were insured by D pursuant to two policies of insurance. The first covered fire and explosion damage; the second consequential loss arising therefrom. An impeller shattered in the blower house causing substantial physical damage and consequential loss. P claimed that this was damage caused by an explosion. *Held,* dismissing P's appeal, that the damage was not caused by an explosion but rather by a failure of the impeller: COMMONWEALTH SMELTING *v.* GUARDIAN ROYAL EXCHANGE ASSURANCE [1986] 1 Lloyd's Rep. 121, C.A.

1783. Motor insurance—theft—indemnity

On March 26, 1980, P effected a policy of motor insurance with D, covering third party, fire and theft. An exclusion clause in the policy provided: "The [Insurers] shall not be liable in respect of (1) any . . . loss . . . occurring whilst any motor vehicle . . . is (a) being used otherwise than in accordance with the limitation as to use . . . except that (1) the exclusion of use for any purpose in connection with the motor trade shall not prejudice the indemnity to the insured whilst the motor car . . . is in the custody or control of a member of the motor trade for the purpose of its upkeep." . . . "(c) . . . or when being driven by, or for the purpose of being driven, is in charge of any person other than an authorised driver." Only P was an authorised driver, and the use was social, domestic and pleasure only. In June 1980, P delivered the car to F, a body repairer and sprayer, for repair work. F drove the car to collect some spare parts from an agent. While briefly unattended by F at the agent's premises, the car was stolen and not recovered. *Held,* on appeal by P to recover on indemnity from D, allowing the appeal, that (1) at the relevant time, the car was in the custody or control of a member of the motor trade for the purposes of its repair; (2) exception 1(c) of the policy did not apply on the facts, as the car was at the agent's premises for a particular purpose independent of being driven *viz.* to ascertain whether spare parts were available for the car: SAMUELSON *v.* NATIONAL INSURANCE GUARANTEE CORP. [1985] 2 Lloyd's Rep. 541, C.A.

1784. Professional indemnity policy—whether claim within policy terms—non-disclosure of material facts

In this action P sought to recover sums from their professional indemnity insurers, D. D contended that the complex facts pursuant to which the claim arose did not fall within the terms of the policy, and they further contended that P had failed to disclose material facts thereby entitling them to avoid the policies. *Held,* that (1) on the evidence and true construction of the policies the alleged claims did not fall within the policy wording, and that (2) there had been material non-disclosure of facts: JOHNS *v.* KELLY [1986] 1 Lloyd's Rep. 468, Bingham J.

1785. Reinsurance—brokers' duty of care—legal effect of signing indication

In December 1980, S was negotiating to purchase the Z, and instructed his brokers, D5, to place suitable insurance cover. D5 first obtained a quote from D1, a total loss underwriter. D1 signed a line of 10 per cent. of value at a total loss rate of 0·45 per cent. after having been given a one-third signing down indication by D5. D5 then proceeded to obtain quotes from all risks underwriters. On January 2, 1981, D5 confirmed that all the insurance cover requested was completed. On January 13, 1981, the Z was stranded and suffered serious damage. On January 19, and 20, the all risks underwriters gave notice of abandonment on the basis that the Z was a constructive total loss. D5 did not achieve the one-third signing down indication. D reinsurers refused to pay. The issue on appeal was the 1–4 liability of the brokers to pay damages to D 1–4 for breach of duty. *Held,* allowing the appeal, that (1) the signing indication, according to the practice of the market, implied acceptance of a responsibility to use best endeavours to procure the signing down by the date of inception; (2) the fault of the brokers lay in a continuing failure to perform a positive undertaking; (3) there was nothing in the decided cases to suggest that a bare promise given in circumstances where the parties stood in no relationship, save that one was speaking to another about a transaction effected between the other and a third party, was capable of creating a situation where the speaker must do what he conveyed he would do, or pay damages in default; (4) there was nothing in the terms of the promise embodied in the signing indication to suggest it was directed to anyone other than the total loss leading underwriter; (5) in the absence of an express signing indication, the brokers could not be held liable where nothing was said to the underwriter because the underwriter did not trouble to ask: GENERAL ACCIDENT FIRE & LIFE ASSURANCE CORP. *v.* TANTER (PETER WILLIAM); THE "ZEPHYR" [1985] 2 Lloyds Rep. 529, C.A.

1786. Reinsurance contract—original insurance governed by Norwegian law—reinsurance contract with Lloyds in London—law of reinsurance contract. See FORSIKRINGSAKTIESEL-SKAPET VESTA *v.* BUTCHER, § 366.

1787. Subrogation—rights of landlord against tenant—covenant by landlord to insure premises—premises destroyed by fire—fire caused by tenant's negligence

Where in a lease a landlord covenants to insure the demised premises against the risk of damage by fire any loss resulting from a fire is to be recouped from the insurance moneys and no further claim for damages in negligence can be made against the tenant.

P let certain premises to D. P covenanted to keep the premises insured against, *inter alia*, fire. D covenanted to pay P insurance rent in respect of the premiums paid by P to insure the premises. The lease provided for D to be relieved of his repairing obligations in the event that the premises were destroyed by fire. P covenanted in that event to re-instate the premises with the insurance moneys received. The premises were destroyed by a fire occasioned by negligence on the part of D. The premises were re-instated by P at a cost of £1,429,166 which was met by P's insurers. Thereafter P's insurers sought to recover their outlay from D. Proceedings were instituted in P's name claiming damages of £1,429,166 in consequence of D's negligence. D claimed that P could not recover any sums by way of damages as P's losses had been met by P's insurers and P had insured the premises for their joint benefit. The trial judge upheld D's contentions. *Held*, dismissing P's appeal, that although P and D were not co-insured D had an insurable interest in the premises. The provisions of the lease could not have effect so as to deprive D of that insurable interest. In the circumstances, the insurance affected by P enured for the benefit of D. By covenanting to insure the premises in return for insurance rent P lifted from D the risk of liability for fire arising from D's negligence and brought that risk under insurance cover. The intention of the parties must have been that in the event of damage by fire P's loss was to be recouped from the insurance moneys and that P would have no further claim against D for damages for negligence. P was fully indemnified in the manner envisaged by the lease. In the circumstances, P could not recover damages from D in addition. As P had no right to claim damages from D for negligence there was no right to which P's insurers could be subrogated so as to recover their outlay from D (*Mumford Hotels* v. *Wheeler* [1963] C.L.Y. 1960 applied, *Greenwood Shopping Plaza* v. *Buchanan (Neil J.)* (1979) 99 D.L.R. (3d) 289, *Eaton (T.) Co.* v. *Smith* (1977) 92 D.L.R. (3d) 425, *Agnew-Surpass Shoe Stores* v. *Cummer-Yonge Investments* (1975) 55 D.L.R. (3d) 676 approved, *Petrofina (U.K.)* v. *Magnaload* [1983] C.L.Y. 1991, *The Yasin* [1979] C.L.Y. 2472 distinguished).

ROWLANDS (MARK) *v.* BERNI INNS [1985] 3 W.L.R. 964, C.A.

INTERNATIONAL LAW

1788. Antarctica

ANTARCTIC TREATY (CONTRACTING PARTIES) ORDER 1986 (No. 2221) [45p], made under the Antarctic Treaty Act 1967 (c.65), ss.7(1) and 10(7); adds Cuba and the Republic of Korea to the list of contracting parties to the Antarctic Treaty.

1789. Consular conventions

CONSULAR CONVENTIONS (ARAB REPUBLIC OF EGYPT) ORDER 1986 (No. 216) [40p], made under the Consular Conventions Act 1949 (c.29), s.6(1); operative on a date to be published; provides for the application of sections 1 and 2 of the 1949 Act to Egypt.

1790. Consular relations

CONSULAR RELATIONS (MERCHANT SHIPPING AND CIVIL AVIATION) (ARAB REPUBLIC OF EGYPT) ORDER 1986 (No. 217) [40p], made under the Consular Relations Act 1968 (c.18), ss.4, 16(2); operative on a date to be published; provides for the limitation of jurisdiction of UK courts in relation to the crews of Egyptian ships and aircraft.

1791. Foreign compensation

FOREIGN COMPENSATION (FINANCIAL PROVISIONS) ORDER 1986 (No. 219) [40p], made under the Foreign Compensation Act 1950 (c.12), s.7(2) and the Foreign Compensation Act 1962 (c.4), s.3(3); operative on March 20, 1986; directs the Foreign Compensation Commission to make a payment into the Consolidated Fund in respect of its expenses.

FOREIGN COMPENSATION (UNION OF SOVIET SOCIALIST REPUBLICS) (REGISTRATION AND DETERMINATION OF CLAIMS) ORDER 1986 (No. 2222) [£1.90], made under the Foreign Compensation Act 1950 (c.12), s.3; operative on February 1. 1987; provides for the registration and determination of claims for compensation from sums received from the government of the USSR in respect of property claims arising before 1939.

1792. Immunities and privileges

INTERNATIONAL FUND FOR IRELAND (IMMUNITIES AND PRIVILEGES) ORDER 1986 (No. 2017) [45p], made under the International Organisations Act 1968 (c.48), s.1; operative on a date to be notified; confers the legal capacities of a body corporate and exemption from direct taxes on the International Fund for Ireland.

1793. Outer Space Act 1986 (c.38)

This Act gives licensing and other powers to the Secretary of State in respect of the launching and operation of space objects and the carrying on of space activities.

The Act received the Royal Assent on July 18, 1986, and comes into force on a day to be appointed. The Act extends to England and Wales, Scotland and Northern Ireland.

1794. Overseas development

INTERNATIONAL FINANCE CORPORATION (1985 GENERAL CAPITAL INCREASE) ORDER 1986 (No. 1587) [45p], made under the Overseas Development and Co-operation Act 1980 (c.63), s.4; operative on August 14, 1986; provides for the payment to the Corporation of an additional subscription of U.S. $30,500,000.

INTERNATIONAL FUND FOR AGRICULTURAL DEVELOPMENT (SECOND REPLENISHMENT) ORDER 1986 (No. 2328) [45p], made under the Overseas Development and Co-operation Act 1980 (c.63), s.4; operative on December 18, 1986; provides for payments to the said Fund.

1795. Self-defence—armed attack—assistance to rebels

The general rule governing the use of force by one State against another allows for an exception in the case of self-defence, but this must be exercised only in response to an armed attack. The concept of armed attack does not include assistance to rebels. There is no rule permitting the exercise of collective self-defence in the absence of a request from the State which has allegedly suffered an armed attack. States do not have the right of collective armed response to acts which do not constitute an armed attack: MILITARY AND PARAMILITARY ACTIVITIES IN AND AGAINST NICARAGUA (NICARAGUA *v.* UNITED STATES OF AMERICA) (NO. 2), *The Times,* June 28, 1986, International Court of Justice.

INTOXICATING LIQUORS

1796. Exeter Airport

EXETER AIRPORT LICENSING (LIQUOR) ORDER 1986 (No. 971) [45p], made under the Customs and Excise Management Act 1979 (c.2), s.22; operative on June 16, 1986; brings s.87 of the Licensing Act 1964 into operation in relation to Exeter Airport.

1797. Licence—application to renew—refusal

Where no objection was made to an application for the annual renewal of a liquor licence the licensing justices should not refuse the application without canvassing the ground or grounds in open court so that the applicant knew what was troubling the justices and had an opportunity to deal with it: R. *v.* LIVERPOOL LICENSING JUSTICES, *ex p.* FISHGOLD, (1986) 150 J.P.N. 316, Taylor J.

1798. Licensing

SOUTHEND AIRPORT LICENSING (LIQUOR) ORDER 1986 (No. 525) [40p], made under the Customs and Excise Management Act 1979 (c.2), s.22; operative on April 2, 1986; brings s.87 of the Licensing Act 1964 into operation at Southend Airport.

1799. Licensing—charge for entry

The justices granted a liquor licence on condition, *inter alia,* that drink was served only to those who had paid an admission fee. Y reduced the fee to the minimum legal tender (then ½p.). *Held,* that the minimum legal tender was valuable consideration and constituted an admission fee: R. *v.* BODMIN CROWN COURT, *ex p.* YOUNG, *The Times,* July 5, 1986, C.A.

1800. Purchase—adult purchaser—consumer under 18. See WOBY *v.* B AND O, § 632.

JURIES

1801. Possibility of bias—lack of challenge—whether verdict unsafe and unsatisfactory

Suspicion that a juror might have some personal reasons for bias towards prosecution or defence is normally no ground for his disqualification.

The applicant, a striking miner, was charged with criminal damage to a car being driven across a picket line. The applicant was convicted; he subsequently discovered that one of the jury was a working miner. He sought leave to appeal on the basis of a material irregularity there being a risk of bias, possibly influential, on the part of the juror. *Held*, dismissing the application, that there was no ground for disqualification that a juror might have some bias towards prosecution or defence; especially when it amounted to mere suspicion *R.* v. *Chapman and Lauday* [1976] C.L.Y. 614 *R.* v. *Mason* [1980] C.L.Y. 1556, considered).

R. *v.* PENNINGTON (1985) 81 Cr.App.R. 217, C.A.

1802. Selection—powers to give directions

McC applied for a direction that a jury be "racially balanced" or have at least two black members, on the ground that his defence to a charge of conspiracy to rob involved a substantial challenge to police evidence and only black jurors could appreciate fully how police treated young black people. *Held*, that there was no power to make such a direction: R. v. McCALLA [1986] Crim.L.R. 335, Stoke-on-Trent Crown Court.

1803. Verdict—alteration after discharge of defendant—discretion of trial judge. See R. *v.* ANDREWS, § 943.

1804. Verdict—disqualified juror—alleged bias

[Juries Act 1974 (c.23), s.18.] Following B's conviction of burglary it was discovered that a member of the jury knew and had fought with B's son. The juror had volunteered the information that he had been detained in custody pursuant to a youth custody sentence which had been varied on appeal to two years' probation. C swore an affidavit to the effect that he had first recognised B during the course of the trial. *Held*, dismissing B's appeal, that (1) by virtue of s.18(1)(*b*) of the 1974 Act, the verdict should not be stayed or varied by reason only of a disqualified juror being a party to it; (2) the test was whether there was evidence suggesting directly or from which it can be inferred that the defendant may have been prejudiced or may not have received a fair trial (*R.* v. *Chapman and Lauday* [1976] C.L.Y. 614 applied; *R.* v. *Box and Box* [1963] C.L.Y. 1916, *R.* v. *Hood* [1968] C.L.Y. 910; *R.* v. *Sawyer* [1981] C.L.Y. 1482; *R.* v. *Spencer* [1985] C.L.Y. 568; *R.* v. *Pennington* [1985] C.L.Y. 1829 and *R.* v. *Dubarry* [1977] C.L.Y. 685 considered): R. *v.* BLISS [1986] Crim.L.R. 467, C.A.

1805. Verdict—unanimous verdict required—foreman wrongly stating verdict unanimous—whether affidavits of jurors admissible

[Trinidad and Tobago.] [Jury Ordinance (c.4 No. 2) s.16(1); Constitution of the Republic of Trinidad and Tobago Act 1976 (No. 4 of 1976), Sched. s.4(*a*).]

There is a presumption that a verdict given in the sight and presence of all members of the jury is one to which they all assent, and no evidence, therefore, will be admitted which is directed toward showing that in fact the jury were not so agreed, or had misunderstood the directions of the judge.

N was tried for murder, which required a unanimous verdict. The judge did not direct the jury that such a verdict was required, but when the clerk of the court asked the foreman if the jury had agreed upon a verdict, he asked them whether they had reached a unanimous verdict. The foreman, in the presence and hearing of the entire jury, said that they had—guilty. No juror made any protest, and N was sentenced to death. The foreman and three other jurors subsequently swore affidavits stating that in fact only eight of the jury had agreed with the verdict. *Held*, dismissing N's appeal, that the evidence could not be admitted. There was a presumption that when a verdict was returned in the presence and hearing of all members of the jury, and was received without protest by any of them, it was the verdict of the whole jury, and one with which they all agreed. According to the law of Trinidad and Tobago there had been no irregularity, and so the appeal had to be dismissed.

NANAN (LALCHAN) *v.* THE STATE [1986] 3 W.L.R. 304, P.C.

LAND CHARGES

1806. Local land charges

LOCAL LAND CHARGES (AMENDMENT) RULES 1986 (No. 424) [40p], made under the Local Land Charges Act 1975 (c.76), s.14; operative on April 1, 1986; increase the fees payable in connection with the registration of local land charges by 6·8 per cent.

1807. Receivership order—whether registrable

[Land Registration Act 1925 (c.21), ss.54(1), 59(5); Land Charges Act 1925 (c.22), s.6(1)(*b*).

A receivership order can be registered under s.6 of the Land Charges Act 1925 and can be registered as a caution under s.54 of the Land Registration Act 1925.

The landlords owned a block of flats some of which were let on long leases and some of which were let under statutory tenancies. It fell into disrepair and the first defendant, a statutory tenant, started an action for himself and other tenants, against the landlords seeking specific performance of the landlords' repairing covenants. During the pendency of that action, an order was made appointing a receiver to receive the rents and profits under the leases and to manage the property. The first defendant lodged a caution against the landlords' title in the Land Registry under s.54(1) of the Land Registration Act 1925 in respect of that order. The landlords, who wanted to sell long leases at premiums when flats in the block became vacant, applied for the removal of the caution, contending that the order appointing the receiver was not of its nature registrable and that the first defendant had no standing to lodge a caution. The application of the landlords was dismissed, and the landlords appealed. *Held*, by the Court of Appeal, that for the purposes of s.6(1)(*b*) of the Land Charges Act 1925 an "order appointing a receiver or sequestrator of land" was specific and unqualified as regards such an order, and accordingly such orders were not limited to reciverships which could bind a purchaser, as the landlords contended, but applied to any receivership of land. Accordingly, the order appointing a receiver to manage the block of flats would be registrable under the Land Charges Act in the case of unregistered land and, applying s.59(5) of the Land Registration Act, which equated the systems of registered and unregistered land as regards land charges, the order was therefore capable of being protected by the lodging of a caution against dealing under s.54 of the Land Registration Act 1925. Furthermore, since the receivership was made for the first tenant's benefit as a tenant, he was a person interested in the property by virtue of the order for the purposes of s.54(1).

The appeal was therefore dismissed.

CLAYHOPE PROPERTIES *v.* EVANS [1986] 2 All E.R. 795, C.A.

LAND DRAINAGE

1808. Drainage authorities

ANGLIAN WATER AUTHORITY (ABOLITION OF THE FELIXSTOWE INTERNAL DRAINAGE DISTRICT) ORDER 1986 (No. 1266) [80p], made under the Land Drainage Act 1976 (c.70), s.11(1); operative on July 10, 1986; abolishes the Felixstowe Internal Drainage District and transfers its rights and obligations to the said Water Authority.

SEVERN-TRENT WATER AUTHORITY (RECONSTITUTION OF THE NEWARK AREA INTERNAL DRAINAGE BOARD) ORDER 1986 (No. 1919) [80p], made under the Land Drainage Act 1976 (c.70), ss.11(4), 109(6); operative on November 3, 1986; reconstitutes the said Internal Drainage Board.

1809. Drainage charges

GENERAL DRAINAGE CHARGE (ANGLIAN WATER AUTHORITY) (ASCERTAINMENT) ORDER 1986 (No. 447) [40p], made under the Land Drainage Act 1976 (c.70), s.49(1) and (2); operative on April 1, 1986; concerns general drainage charges which may be raised by the Anglian water authority in their local land drainage districts for the year ending March 31, 1987.

1810. Drainage committee

LOCAL GOVERNMENT ACT 1985 (NORTH WEST WATER AUTHORITY REGIONAL LAND DRAINAGE COMMITTEE) ORDER 1986 (No. 616) [45p], made under the Local Government Act 1985, ss.101, 103(6); operative on April 1, 1986; makes provision with respect to the appointment of members of the said Committee.

LOCAL GOVERNMENT ACT 1985 (NORTHUMBRIAN WATER AUTHORITY REGIONAL LAND DRAINAGE COMMITTEE) ORDER 1986 (No. 617) [45p], made under the Local

Government Act 1985, ss.101, 103(6); operative on April 1, 1986; makes provision with respect to the appointment of members of the said Committee.

LOCAL GOVERNMENT ACT 1985 (SEVERN-TRENT WATER AUTHORITY REGIONAL LAND DRAINAGE COMMITTEE) ORDER 1986 (No. 613) [80p], made under the Local Government Act 1985 (c.51), ss.101, 103(6); operative on April 1, 1986; makes provision with respect to the appointment of members of the said Committee.

LOCAL GOVERNMENT ACT 1985 (THAMES WATER AUTHORITY REGIONAL LAND DRAINAGE COMMITTEE) ORDER 1986 (No. 618) [80p], made under the Local Government Act 1985, ss.101, 103(6); operative on April 1, 1986; makes provision with respect to the appointment of members of the said Committee.

LOCAL GOVERNMENT ACT 1985 (YORKSHIRE WATER AUTHORITY REGIONAL LAND DRAINAGE COMMITTEE) ORDER 1986 (No. 615) [45p], made under the Local Government Act 1985, ss.101, 103(6); operative on April 1, 1986; makes provision with respect to the appointment of members of the said Committee.

1811. Lands Tribunal decision

ALFORD DRAINAGE BOARD *v.* MABLETHORPE (Ref./LVC/1/1983) (1986) 277 E.G. 867,987. (The Board appealed against a decision of the LVC in relation to an assessment to annual value made under s.67 of the Land Drainage Act 1976 in respect of 175.12 acres of agricultural land with buildings at Bilsby, Lincolnshire. R argued that the correct approach was, via s.64(1) of the Act, to update the annual value in respect of which the land had been assessed to income tax under Schedule A in 1962–3, whereas the Board contended that the proper approach was to adjust down the agreed annual rental value of £7,700 in 1980 (being the year in which the Board resolved to revalue agricultural hereditaments) to equate with values in 1935 (being the year in which it alleged that annual values had last been determined). The tribunal found that a determination under s.67 was not required to be (as R had contended) a mere adjustment of a pre-existing figure, but was intended to be a new assessment. Furthermore there was no presumption that the 1962–3 assessment had regard to changes in circumstances occurring since 1935. The tribunal therefore adopted the approach proposed by the Board and, applying a factor of 16.82, reduced the 1980 rental value to give a 1935 rounded-up annual value of £460.)

1812. Transfer of functions. See LOCAL GOVERNMENT, § 2029.

LAND REGISTRATION

1813. Fees

LAND REGISTRATION FEE ORDER 1986 (No. 1399) [£2·40], made under the Land Registration Act 1925 (c.21), s.145 and the Public Offices Fees Act 1879 (c.58), ss.2 and 3; operative on October 1, 1986; alters the land registration fee scales.

1814. Land Registration Act 1986 (c.26)

This Act amends the Land Registration Act 1925 in relation to the conversion of title and in relation to leases (compulsory registration, inalienable leases, gratuitous leases and leases granted at a premium). It also abolishes the Minor Interests Index.

The Act received the Royal Assent on June 26, 1986 and comes into force on a day to be appointed. It extends to England and Wales only.

1815. Land Registration Act 1986—commencement

LAND REGISTRATION ACT 1986 (COMMENCEMENT) ORDER 1986 (No. 2117 (c.82)) [45p], made under the Land Registration Act 1986 (c.26), s.6(4); brings the said Act into force on January 1, 1987.

1816. Official searches

LAND REGISTRATION (OFFICIAL SEARCHES) RULES 1986 (No. 1536) [£2·40], made under the Land Registration Act 1925 (c.21), s.144; operative on October 1, 1986; replace S.I. 1981 No. 1135 and make fresh provision relating to the time at which an application for an official search of the register is treated as having been delivered.

1817. Overriding interest—wife in occupation—whether payment referable to purchase

[Land Registration Act 1925 (c.21), s.70(1)(g).] H and W, a separated husband and wife, were directors of a company. The company bought for £70,000 (which sum was paid outright and in full) a house that W occupied. W paid £8,600 from the proceeds of sale of another property into the company's bank account. On the liquidation of the company, W claimed an overriding interest in the house under s.70(1)(g) of the Land Registration Act 1925, as a result of her payment of £8,600.

Held, that as the £8,600 was paid into the company's account well after the house was bought, and was not referable to the purchase, it did not give W an equitable interest in the premises. In the circumstances, equity would not compel, or even allow, the company to hold part of the house on trust for W to the detriment of the creditors (*Williams & Glyn's Bank* v. *Boland* [1980] C.L.Y. 1847 applied): WINKWORTH *v.* BARON (EDWARD) DEVELOPMENT CO., *The Times,* December 10, 1986, H.L.

1818. Rectification of register—errors of description
[Land Registration Act 1925 (c.21) ss.82(1) and 123.]
The court may order rectification of the register even though the errors are of description, so long as the whole transaction is not void.
X sold land and a house to Y. A plan was annexed to the conveyance. Y registered the title, and the plan. This reserved to X a right of way over a track marked on the plan and a boundary fence. Y then sold his property to P. X then sold the adjoining land to D, on the basis of an inaccurate plan, which misdescribed the track. P sought a declaration in the county court and rectification of the register. The judge granted the orders. *Held,* dismissing D's appeal, that the court, including the County Court, could order rectification of the register even though the errors were of description, so long as the whole transaction was not void. (*Eastwood v. Ashton* [1915] A.C. 900 and *Watts* v. *Waller* [1973] C.L.Y. 1683 applied).
PROCTOR *v.* KIDMAN (1986) 51 P. & C.R. 67, C.A.

1819. Rules
LAND REGISTRATION (COMPANIES AND INSOLVENCY) RULES 1986 (No. 2116) [£1·40], made under the Land Registration Act 1925 (c.21), s.144; operative on December 29, 1986; amend S.R. & O. 1925 No. 1093.
LAND REGISTRATION (DELIVERY OF APPLICATIONS) RULES 1986 (No. 1534) [45p], made under the Land Registration Act 1925 (c.21), s.144; operative on October 1, 1986; amend S.R. & O. 1925 No. 1093 to make fresh provision relating to the time at which applications for registration are treated as having been delivered.
LAND REGISTRATION (POWERS OF ATTORNEY) RULES 1986 (No. 1537) [45p], made under the Land Registration Act 1925, s.144; operative on October 1, 1986; amend S.R. & O. 1925 No. 1093 to take account of the new enduring form of power of attorney permitted under the Enduring Powers of Attorney Act 1985.
LAND REGISTRATION RULES 1986 (No. 2118) [80p], made under the Land Registration Act 1925 (c.21), s.144; operative on January 1, 1987; amend S.R. & O. 1925 No. 1093 to take account of the Land Registration Act 1986. Rule 45, as amended, now extends to leases containing an absolute probibition against all dealings therewith *inter vivos.*

LANDLORD AND TENANT

1820. Agricultural holdings. See AGRICULTURE.

1821. Appointment of receiver—covenant to repair—landlord's breach—powers of the court
[Supreme Court Act 1981 (c.54), s.37.]
The court may appoint a receiver to collect rents and manage property which has fallen into such a state of disrepair as to require urgent action, even though the landlord's default has not gone so far as to create a virtual vacuum in the management of the property.
T were lessees of 110 flats in a large block on long leases which required L to maintain, repair, redecorate and renew the structure, the cost being recoverable from T, together with contributions towards a reserve fund against future repairing liabilities. When L acquired the freehold reversion the block was already in serious disrepair, with the cost of necessary works estimated at £300,000. L collected rents and service charges, provided a competent caretaker and carried out minor emergency repairs, but repeatedly failed to heed T's requests to carry out major repairs. The building continued to deteriorate and T feared damage to their interests. T applied for the appointment of a receiver under s.37 of the Supreme Court Act 1981. It was doubtful whether L could fund the repairs, but T were prepared to do so. *Held,* granting the application, that although L's default had not gone so far as to create a virtual vacuum in the management of the property urgent action was required to deal with the disrepair, and a receiver should be appointed (*Hart* v. *Emelkirk* [1983] C.L.Y. 2088 applied).
DAICHES *v.* BLUELAKE INVESTMENTS (1986) 51 P. & C.R. 51, Harman J.

1822. Assignment—assignee intending to sublet premises—refusal of consent by landlord to assignment—whether refusal reasonable

It is unreasonable for a landlord to refuse consent to an assignment of a long lease of a flat on the ground that the assignee intends to sublet the flat for some years.

A was an American attorney who proposed to take an assignment of a long lease from P of a flat in a luxury block occupied mainly by middle-aged and elderly professional people. Under the terms of the lease the landlord's consent to the assignment was required, such consent not to be unreasonably withheld. The landlord's consent was also required before the tenant could sublet the flat. A intended to continue working in the U.S.A. and take up possession of the flat upon his retirement 20 years later. In the meantime he intended to sublet the flat. D, the landlord refused to consent to the assignment to A on the ground that A would thereafter create a number of short term sub-leases of the flat to persons who were likely to cause difficulties for other tenants of the block, *i.e.* young people with habits and attitudes not in keeping with the majority of the tenants. P sought a declaration that D's refusal to consent to the assignment was unreasonable. Falconer J. held the refusal to be reasonable. *Held*, allowing P's appeal, that given that the leave provided for the creation of underleases it was unreasonable to refuse consent to the assignment on the ground that A intended to sub-let the flat. So far as prospective sub-tenants were concerned, any underleases created required the consent of D so that D was able to exercise considerable control over the type of person who might become a sub-tenant of the flat. In the circumstances, D's refusal to consent to the assignment to A was unreasonable,

RAYBURN *v.* WOLF (1985) 50 P. & C.R. 463, C.A.

1823. Assignment—covenant against assigning or underletting part of premises without permission—whether permission necessary to underletting of the whole

A covenant against assigning or underletting any part of the premises let restrained the assigning or underletting of the whole of the premises.

P was the tenant of a farm. By clause 3(24) of the lease P covenanted not to assign or underlet any part of the premises without the consent in writing of the landlord. D was P's landlord. P sought a declaration that an assignment or underletting of the whole of the premises did not require D's consent. *Held*, dismissing P's claim, that the words of the clause were clear and unambiguous. An underletting or assignment of the whole of the premises constituted an underletting or assignment of any part (*Cook* v. *Shoesmith* (1951) C.L.C. 5391 considered).

FIELD *v.* BARKWORTH [1986] 1 W.L.R. 137, Nicholls J.

1824. Assignment—covenant against assignment without consent—refusal on grounds of detriment to reversion and proposed use—whether reasonable

Where a proposed assignment would on paper cause a detriment to the landlord's reversion but in the actual circumstances of the case that detriment would not arise a refusal of consent by the landlord to the assignment is unreasonable.

P was the tenant of a two-storey office block on Highbridge Industrial Estate under a lease for 30 years from December 25, 1981 which provided for an upwards review of the rent payable every five years. The lease provided that the premises should only be used for office accommodation and prohibited P from assigning the premises without the consent of the landlord, such consent not to be unreasonably withheld. D was the owner of the Estate and P's landlord. P being a tenant by way of an assignment, D had the benefit of two direct covenants to pay the rent due under the lease. P occupied the premises as a single office block for its own use but in May 1984 moved to new premises. In August 1984 P applied to D for consent to assign the premises to Euro Business Services. Euro wished to use the premises for the provision of serviced office accommodation to persons requiring office accommodation on a short-term basis. Consent was refused on the ground that the value of D's reversion would be diminished. The trial judge found that the proposed use would not affect the value of the land or building at the end of the lease and nor would it prejudice future rent reviews. There was no significant danger that the rent would not be paid throughout the term. The trial judge also held that it was reasonable to conclude that the proposed use might affect the value of the premises detrimentally if D sought to sell or mortgage them during the term of the lease but that there was no prospect of D taking that course of action. The trial judge declared D's refusal of consent to be unreasonable. *Held*, dismissing D's appeal, that although a landlord need usually only consider his own interests in deciding whether or not to consent to a proposed assignment the refusal of consent may be held to be unreasonable where the benefit to the landlord from his refusal is unreasonably disproportionate to the detriment to the tenant. Having regard to the fact that the detriment to D was restricted to the paper value of his reversion and not its actual value to him, consent to the proposed assignment was unreasonably withheld. Although it may be reasonable to refuse consent on the ground of a proposed use that is permitted by the lease where the user covenant restricts use to a specific type it is not reasonable to refuse consent on the grounds of the proposed use where the result would be that the premises are left vacant where the landlord is fully secured for payment of the rent. The court set out seven propositions of law applicable to the granting or withholding of consent to an assignment (*Sheppard* v. *Hongkong and Shanghai Banking Corp.* (1872) 20 W.R. 459, *Gibbs & Houlder Bros. & Co.'s Lease, Re* [1925] Ch. 575, *West Layton* v. *Ford* [1979] C.L.Y. 1644, *Bromley Park Garden Estates* v. *Moss* [1982] C.L.Y. 1710, *Leeward Securities* v. *Lilyheath Properties* [1984] C.L.Y. 1968 considered; *Premier Confectionery (London) Co.* v. *London Commercial Sale Rooms* [1933] Ch. 904 distinguished).

INTERNATIONAL DRILLING FLUIDS *v.* LOUISVILLE INVESTMENTS (UXBRIDGE) [1986] 1 All E.R. 321, C.A.

1825. Assured tenancies

ASSURED TENANCIES (APPROVED BODIES) (AMENDMENT) (NO. 2) ORDER 1986 (No. 1208) [45p], made under the Housing Act 1980 (c.51), s.56(4); operative on August 11, 1986; amends S.I. 1982 No. 1229.

ASSURED TENANCIES (APPROVED BODIES) (AMENDMENT) ORDER 1986 (No. 864) [45p], made under the Housing Act 1980 (c.51), s.56(4); operative on June 21, 1986; amends S.I. 1983 No. 1375.

ASSURED TENANCIES (APPROVED BODIES) (NO. 1) ORDER 1986 (No. 866) [45p], made under the Housing Act 1980, s.56(4); operative on June 21, 1986; approves three bodies for the purposes of s.56 of the 1980 Act.

ASSURED TENANCIES (APPROVED BODIES) (NO. 2) ORDER 1986 (No. 1209) [45p], made under the Housing Act 1980 (c.51), s.56(4); operative on August 11, 1986; approves eight bodies for the purposes of s.56 of the 1980 Act.

ASSURED TENANCIES (APPROVED BODIES) (NO. 3) ORDER 1986 (No. 1729) [45p], made under the Housing Act 1980 (c.51), s.56(4); operative on November 4, 1986; approves eight bodies for the purposes of s.56 of the 1980 Act.

ASSURED TENANCIES (APPROVED BODIES) (NO. 4) ORDER 1986 (No. 2240) [45p] made under the Housing Act 1980 (c.51), s.56(4); operative on January 28, 1987; approves 12 bodies for the purposes of s.56 (bodies approved to grant assured tenancies).

ASSURED TENANCIES (PRESCRIBED AMOUNT) ORDER 1986 (No. 2180) [45p], made under the Housing Act 1980 (c.51), s.56B(6); operative on January 7, 1987; prescribes the amount which must be spent on work attributable to the dwelling-house concerned under s.56B.

LANDLORD AND TENANT ACT 1954, PART II (ASSURED TENANCIES (NOTICES) REGULATIONS 1986 (No. 2181) [£1·90], made under the Landlord and Tenant Act 1954 (c.56), s.66 as applied by the Housing Act 1980 (c.51), s.58(2); operative on January 7, 1987; prescribes forms to be used for the progress of Pt. II of the 1954 Act in the case of assured tenancies.

1826. Bankruptcy—effect on protected tenancy—covenants in lease—whether onerous

[Bankruptcy Act 1914 (c.59); Bankruptcy Rules 1952 (1952 S.I. No. 2113), rule 278.] T took a protected tenancy of a dwelling-house for a fixed term, during which they became bankrupt. The lease vested in the trustee-in-bankruptcy, who purported to disclaim it without the leave of the court, pursuant to s.54 of the Bankruptcy Act 1914 and rule 278 of the Bankruptcy Rules 1952, on the grounds that it contained onerous convenants, including an absolute prohibition against assignment—or sub-letting of the whole or part of the premises, a restriction to use as a dwelling-house, and full tenants' repairing obligations. When L sought possession upon the expiry of the term, T contended that the lease had not contained onerous covenants within the meaning of s.54 of the Act, that the trustee had not therefore been entitled to disclaim without the leave of the court, and that they were accordingly entitled to a statutory tenancy. The judge upheld this content. *Held*, allowing L's appeal, that (1) the covenants were onerous within the meaning of s.54 and rule 278, and that the disclaimer had accordingly been valid (*Smalley* v. *Quarrier* [1975] C.L.Y. 1907 applied); (2) even if the disclaimer had not been valid, T could not have claimed a statutory tenancy upon effluxion of the term because, the lease having vested in the trustee, they were no longer the person who was, immediately before the termination of the protected tenancy, the protected tenant; (3) the proper tribunal for the determination of the validity of the disclaimer was the Bankruptcy Court: EYRE v. HALL (1986) 280 E.G. 193, C.A.

1827. Business tenancy—agreement for new tenancy—whether binding
[Landlord and Tenant Act 1954 (c.56), ss.28, 69(2).] L gave notice under the Landlord and Tenant Act 1954, Pt. II to terminate T's tenancy of business premises, and T duly served a counter-notice under the Act. Negotiations subsequently took place, ending in January 1982 with an exchange of correspondence between the parties' surveyors which purported to agree terms for a new lease to commence in March 1982. The agreement was not registered as an estate contract. In February 1982 L's reversionary interest was conveyed to F Co., who thus became T's landlord. The judge held that, although F Co. was not bound by the January agreement because it had not been registered, T was nonetheless precluded by ss.28 and 69(2) of the Act from applying under the Act for a new tenancy, because it had reached with its landlord an agreement "for the grant to the tenant of a future tenancy of the holding . . . on terms and from a date specified in the agreement . . ." On appeal T therefore argued that the "agreement" was not binding because the terms were not sufficiently clear or because it was subject to the execution of a formal lease, which had never taken place; and that the words "agreement" and "agreement in writing" in ss.28 and 69(2) respectively connoted an agreement made with due formality. *Held,* dismissing the appeal, that (1) the terms of the January agreement were sufficiently clear (dictum of Lord Wright in *Hillas & Co.* v. *Arcos* (1932) 147 L.T. 503 applied); (2) the agreement upon its true construction became binding immediately; (3) ss.28 and 69(2) connoted no more than a binding contractual agreement enforceable at law: STRATTON (R. J.) v. WALLIS TOMLIN & Co. (1985) 277 E.G. 409, C.A.

1828. Business tenancy—application for new tenancy—whether grounds (c) and (g) made out
[Landlord and Tenant Act 1954 (c.56), s.30(1)(c) and (g).] T, who ran a nature cure centre, applied under Pt. II of the Landlord and Tenant Act 1954 for a new tenancy of premises occupied in connection with her business. The holding consisted of a top-floor flat and a basement flat in a house owned and otherwise occupied by L. L opposed the application on the grounds specified in s.30(1)(c) and (g) of the Act, namely that there had been a substantial breach of covenant in connection with T's use or management of the holding, and that she intended to occupy the holding for the purposes of her business or as a residence. At trial she gave evidence that the top floor flat had been used as a massage parlour in breach of covenant, and that she proposed to let both flats for residential occupation, after dividing the basement flat into at least two. The judge held that L had made out both grounds of opposition, and therefore dismissed the application for a new tenancy. In so doing he mistakenly noted that three rooms in the basement flat had been used, in breach of covenant, as a laundry. *Held,* allowing T's appeal, that (1) L's proposed use for the flats could not amount to "occupation" by her within the meaning of s.30(1)(c) (*Bagettes* v. *G.P. Estates* (1956) C.L.Y. 4833 applied; *Lee-Verhulst (Investments)* v. *Harwood Trust* [1972] C.L.Y. 1981 and *Cam Gears* v. *Cunningham* [1982] C.L.Y. 1728 distinguished); (2) although the judge would have been entitled to refuse a new tenancy under ground (c) in view of the breach of covenant in relation to the user of the top-floor flat, he had in fact exercised his discretion on a false basis, since there was no evidence that the basement flat was being used as a laundry at all; (3) the only solution was to send back the case for a retrial: JONES v. JENKINS (1985) 277 E.G. 644, C.A.

1829. Business tenancy—holding partitioned off from surrounding building—removal of partitions—whether "occupation" of holding
[Landlord and Tenant Act 1954 (c.56), s.30(1)(g).] L sought to determine T's tenancy of business premises in Newcastle-upon-Tyne on the grounds that L intended to occupy the holding for the purposes of a business to be carried on by them within the meaning of s.30(1)(g) of the Landlord and Tenant Act 1954. The holding comprised a partitioned section of the ground floor of a three-floored building, the remainder of the ground floor being occupied by L. L's initial proposal was to remove the partitions and to install a staircase to the 1st floor, which would occupy some 50 per cent. of the holding. At the

hearing T objected that this proposal was defective for the purposes of s.30(1)(*g*), since it would not involve occupation by L of the whole of the holding, and an adjournment was granted. At the resumed hearing L submitted an alternative proposal, which would resite the staircase outside the holding, and their property manager gave evidence that the new proposal would be adopted. The judge held that L had accordingly made out their grounds of opposition within s.30(1)(*g*). On appeal T contended that L had not demonstrated a genuine bona fide intention to adopt the second scheme, and that the proposed demolition of the partitions did not amount to an intention to "occupy the holding" within s.30(1)(*g*), since the holding would lose its identity. *Held,* dismissing the appeal, that (1) the time at which L's intention to occupy had to be determined was that of the hearing (*Betty's Cafe* v. *Phillips Furnishing Stores* [1958] C.L.Y. 1818 applied); (2) there was at the resumed hearing sufficient evidence in support of the judge's finding that L had the requisite intention and ability to carry out the resumed scheme; (3) L's intention was to occupy the holding within the meaning of s.30(1)(*g*) (*Nursey* v. *Currie* [1959] C.L.Y. 821, *Method Development* v. *Jones* [1971] C.L.Y. 6588, *Cam Gears* v. *Cunningham* [1982] C.L.Y. 1778, and *Leathwoods* v. *Total Oil Great Britain* [1984] C.L.Y. 1879 considered): THORNTON (J. W.) v. BLACKS LEISURE GROUP (1986) 279 E.G. 588, C.A.

1830. Business tenancy—interim rent on application for new tenancy—date from which to take effect

[Landlord and Tenant Act 1954 (c.56), s.24A (as inserted by Law of Property Act 1969 (c.59), s.3).]

A landlord may apply to the county county for an interim rent to be fixed in his answer to an application by the tenant for a new tenancy and any order for an interim rent will take effect from the date of that answer.

In January 1983 the tenant applied for a new tenancy of business premises; in the answer (dated May 27, 1983) the landlord indicated that she would oppose the grant of a new tenancy and in that answer included an application that the Court determine an interim rent. In April 1985 the landlord issued an application for an interim rent to be fixed. The judge fixed a new rent to run from the date of the 1985 application. *Held,* allowing the appeal, that there was no reason why an application that an interim rent be fixed should not be included in an answer to an application for a new tenancy. It followed that the relevant date for the purpose of the determination of the interim rent was the date of the answer.

THOMAS v. HAMMOND-LAWRENCE [1986] 1 W.L.R. 456, C.A.

1831. Business tenancy—landlord's intention to reconstruct—whether possession of holding required

[Landlord and Tenant Act 1954 (c.56), ss.30(1)(*f*), 31A(1)(*a*)] T applied for a new tenancy of single-storey premises, consisting of three rooms and kennels, on which she operated a business of clipping poodles and also kept a large number of her own dogs. L opposed the application on the ground that he intended to demolish and reconstruct the premises within the meaning of s.30(1)(*f*) of the Landlord and Tenant Act 1954, and further argued that this could not be achieved by a grant to him of access and facilities under s.31A(1)(*a*) of the Act, since he could not reasonably carry out the work of reconstruction without obtaining possession of the holding and without substantial interference to the holding for the purposes of the business. The judge found that the premises were past economic repair and required rebuilding, that L had established an intention to demolish and reconstruct, and that s.31A did not apply. He therefore refused T's application. *Held,* dismissing T's appeal, that the only reasonable inference from the evidence and general circumstances was that L would have to clear the whole site, and could not reasonably carry out the works without obtaining possession of the holding and interfering for a substantial time or to a substantial extent with the business user. S.31A did not therefore apply, and the judge had correctly refused the application: MULARCZYK v. AZRALNOVE INVESTMENTS (1985) 276 E.G. 1064, C.A.

1832. Business tenancy—notice by landlord to terminate—time—"within 3 months"

The word "within", when used in the context of a period of time, is capable of meaning "during" or "before or at the expiry of" that period.

L was entitled by its terms to terminate a lease at any time during its term by giving T "not less than 3 months' previous notice in writing". L served a notice requiring T to vacate the premises "within a period of 3 months" from the date of service. T did not vacate and L was granted an order for possession. T appealed. *Held,* that the word "within" could mean "during" or "before or at the expiry of" that period and therefore the full amount of the three month period, and not some lesser period, had been available to T. The notice was valid and T's appeal would be dismissed.

MANORLIKE *v*. LE VITAS TRAVEL AGENCY AND CONSULTANCY SERVICES [1986] 1 All E.R. 573, C.A.

1833. Business tenancy—notice to terminate—mis-statement of landlord—validity

[Landlord and Tenant Act 1954 (c.56), s.25(1).]

Notices in the prescribed form terminating tenancies under the Landlord and Tenant Act 1954 required the name of the landlord to be properly stated and identified.

In 1980 G Co., whose sole director and controlling shareholder was D, granted two business tenancies for a term of three years to the tenant (T). In 1982 notices in the prescribed form terminating the tenancies in accordance with s.25 of the Landlord and Tenant Act 1954 were served on T. The notices stated that solicitors were acting as agents for D, the reference to landlord was deleted, and the address given was that of the solicitors. T served counter-notices, addressed to the solicitors as agents for D, stating that she would not give up possession. She then applied to the county court for the grant to her of new tenancies, naming D as the respondent. In November 1985 an order was made substituting N as the respondent on the ground that he had become landlord having purchased the premises from G Co. In December 1985 T amended her applications, seeking an order that the notices were invalid. The judge held that they were valid even though they failed to identify the landlord correctly, and that the tenant had waived any objection to their validity. *Held,* allowing T's appeal, that the form of notice prescribed by the Act of 1954 required the name of the landlord to be stated. The notices to T did not comply with the statutory requirements because the name of the landlord was misstated so that the tenant was misled, and the notices were invalid. Further, in the circumstances, T was not debarred by waiver from relying on their invalidity. (*Barclays Bank* v. *Ascott* [1961] C.L.Y. 4871 approved; *Tennant* v. *London County Council* [1957] C.L.Y. 1961 and *Tegerdine* v. *Brooks* [1978] C.L.Y. 1769, C.A. considered).

Quaere: Whether there might be an exceptional case in which, notwithstanding the inadvertent misstatement or omission of the landlord, any reasonable tenant would have known that there was a mistake and known clearly what was intended.

MORROW *v*. NADEEM [1986] 1 W.L.R. 1381, C.A.

1834. Business tenancy—premises voluntarily vacated by T—correct proceedings

[Landlord and Tenant Act 1954 (c.56), ss.25, 30(1)(*f*)] L granted to T a business tenancy of an airline desk in the terminal of a small airport, which was due for reconstruction. The lease expressly provided that, in such an event, L would offer and T would take temporary accommodation. Reconstruction duly took place and T moved out voluntarily into the temporary accommodation. However, L subsequently served notice on T to terminate the tenancy under s.25 of the Landlord and Tenant Act 1954. T duly applied for a new tenancy, relying upon the express provision of the lease with respect to temporary accommodation, and upon an implied term that T's lease would not be terminated upon reconstruction. The judge held that T's application for a new tenancy was properly brought. *Held,* allowing L's appeal, that L's notice of termination under s.25 of the Act and T's subsequent application were both misconceived, since T had already voluntarily vacated the premises and the Act could not apply. Whilst T might well have a remedy under the express and implied terms of the agreement, this could not be the subject of proceedings under the 1954 Act: AIREPS *v*. BRADFORD CITY METROPOLITAN COUNCIL (1985) 267 E.G. 1067.

1835. Business tenancy—redevelopment—improvements—covenants permitting landlord to enter

[Landlord and Tenant Act 1954 (c.56), s.30(1)(*f*), (*g*).]

The test of whether a landlord needs to obtain possession of a building for reconstruction under s.30(*f*) of the Landlord and Tenant Act 1954 is whether he could under the existing tenancy enter the premises without getting possession or terminating the lease.

L demised to T land with a filling and service station. The lease contained a covenant permitting the landlords to enter the premises and carry out "any improvement or addition or alteration." L gave notice terminating the tenancy and stating that they would oppose the grant of a new tenancy under ss.30(1)(*f*) and (*g*) of the Landlord and Tenant Act 1954, on the grounds that they proposed to redevelop the site with a filling station and office block, which they would occupy for the purposes of their own business. The work could be done by allowing the contractor sole physical occupation for 16 weeks. T argued that L could do the work by merely requiring a temporary period of exclusive occupation, and that they therefore did not need to terminate T's rights to possession. The deputy High Court judge found in favour of L. *Held,* dismissing T's appeal, that (1) the test under s.30(1)(*f*) was whether L could under the existing tenancy enter the premises without getting possession or terminating the lease. The proposed reconstruction, because of its nature, would infringe T's right to quiet enjoyment, and therefore could not be done under the existing tenancy, and L were entitled to object under s.30(1)(*f*); (2) on the facts they were also entitled to object under s.30(1)(*g*) (*Heath* v. *Drown* [1972] C.L.Y. 1983 applied; *Price* v. *Esso Petroleum Co.* [1981] C.L.Y. 1515 distinguished; *Nursey* v. *Currie (P.) (Dartford)* [1959] C.L.Y. 1821 doubted).

LEATHWOODS v. TOTAL OIL GREAT BRITAIN (1986) 51 P. & C.R. 20, C.A.

1836. Business tenancy—rent review clause—whether removed floor to be included in assessment

With the agreement of the landlords, the tenants of a "handyman's store" on the ground and lower ground floors of a building, removed a part of the ground floor (about 314 sq. metres) so that timber could be stored vertically. The lease provided for a rent review every two years. The valuer assessed the rent on a value per square foot and included in his calculations the 314 sq. metres which had been removed. The tenants appealed. *Held,* dismissing the appeal, that the valuer was entitled to consider the rent obtainable from a willing lessee having regard to the actual use of the disputed area, and also to the possible use which a lessee might make of the premises after restoring the 314 sq. metres to the ground floor: HUDSON (A.) v. LEGAL AND GENERAL LIFE OF AUSTRALIA, June 23, 1986, P.C. [*Ex rel Richard Walford, Barrister.*]

1837. Business tenancy—Secretary of State for Social Services as tenant—whether entitled to new tenancy

[Landlord and Tenant Act 1954 (c.56), ss.23(3), 56(3)(4), National Health Service Act 1977 (c.49), ss.13, 14.]

A house converted into flats that was leased to the Secretary of State for Social Services, managed by a district health authority and occupied by employees of the health authority was occupied by a government department for a purpose carried on by it and thus subject to the provisions of Part II of the Landlord and Tenant Act 1954.

P owned a terraced house converted into eight self-contained flats. The house was let to the Secretary of State for Social Services for a term of fourteen years expiring in June 1985. Pursuant to the lease the Secretary of State could only permit persons in his employment or control to occupy the flats. The management of the flats was delegated to the Paddington and North Kensington Health Authority (a district health authority). The flats were used to provide temporary low cost accommodation for employees of the Authority and were not always occupied. The flats were occupied by employees pursuant to a standard written agreement. By the agreement, possession, management and control of each flat remained vested in the Authority, and, the Authority was the occupier of the flats for all purposes with a right of entry at all times for the purpose of exercising management and control. The Authority was responsible for all repairs and decorations. No rent was reserved under the standard agreement but deductions were made from the salary of an employee occupying one of the flats. P sought declarations that the house was not premises occupied by the Secretary of State for business purposes within the meaning of s.23 of the Landlord and Tenant Act 1954, and that the Secretary of State was not entitled to the grant of a new tenancy persuant to the provisions of Part II of the Act. *Held,* dismissing P's action, that by virtue of s.56(3) of the Act, Part II of the Act applied to the tenancy if the house was or included premises occupied for any purposes of a government department. Subsection (4) of s.56 was of no application to the present case notwithstanding that no rent was paid to the Secretary of State for the use of the house. Subsection (4) dealt with the situation where one government department granted a rent free tenancy to another government department and applied the provisions of Part II of the Act to that tenancy whether or not the premises were occupied for the purposes of a government department.

Having regard to the facts that one or more flats was usually vacant and under the control of the Authority; that the flats were visited regularly by the Authority; that the occupants did not have exclusive possession; that the Authority provided everything required for living in the flats and carried out all repairs and redecorations the Authority occupied the house for the purposes of s.56(3) of the Act. The occupation of the house by the Authority was an occupation in furtherance of the functions of the Secretary of State under the National Health Service Act 1977. The occupation of the house by the Authority was an occupation for a purpose of a government department within the meaning of s.56(3) of the Act. Part II of the Act applied to the tenancy. By virtue of ss.13 and 14 of the National Health Service Act 1977 the Authority occupied the house as the agent of the Secretary of State. In the circumstances it could not be said that there was no holding within the meaning of s.23(3) of the Act in respect of which the Secretary of State could claim a new tenancy (*Pfizer Corp.* v. *Ministry of Health* [1965] C.L.Y. 2940, *Chapman* v. *Freeman* [1978] C.L.Y. 1770 applied; *Lee-Verhulst (Investments)* v. *Harwood Trust* [1972] C.L.Y. 1981, *Boyer (William)* & *Sons* v. *Adams* [1976] C.L.Y. 1538, *Town Investments* v. *Department of the Environment* [1977] C.L.Y. 2516, *Groveside Properties* v. *Westminster Medical School* [1984] C.L.Y. 1885 considered).

LINDEN *v.* DEPARTMENT OF HEALTH AND SOCIAL SECURITY [1986] 1 W.L.R. 164, Scott J.

1838. Business tenancy—security of tenure—agreements for short tenancies excluding statutory protection

[Landlord and Tenant Act 1954 (c.56), s.38 (as amended by Law of Property Act 1969 (c.59), s.5).]

Where there were a succession of short term agreements for letting business premises excluding the operation of Part II of the Landlord and Tenant Act 1954 the giving and acceptance of rent did not create a periodic tenancy.

The landlord had at all times the prospect of being able to develop business premises that it owned but at an uncertain date. Three successive joint applications were made to the county court by the landlord and tenant under s.38 of the 1954 Act as amended and orders were obtained allowing short term tenancies in respect of the business premises excluding the provisions of ss.24 to 28 of Part II of the Act of 1954 (which give a tenant security of tenure). In October 1983 immediately prior to the expiry of the third tenancy, negotiations were started for a further application to the county court for approval of a further short-term tenancy, and several extensions were agreed, the last being until September 15, 1985. During this time the tenant remained in occupation paying rent but the parties never reached final agreement as to their application to the county court. In September 1985 the tenant claimed for the first time to be protected by Part II of the 1954 Act.

Held, on the landlord's claim for possession, that each extension was negotiated subject to a condition that the extension should be the subject of a tenancy agreement approved by the county court excluding the operation of ss.24 to 28 of the 1954 Act. It was clearly intended by both parties that until approval of the county court was obtained, there was no legally binding agreement, each party being free to resile from the negotiations, although the words "subject to contract" were not specifically used. The giving and acceptance of rent during the holding over pending negotiations for a new tenancy did not create a periodic tenancy. Accordingly the landlord was entitled to possession (*Clarke* v. *Grant* (1950) C.L.C. 5551; *Wheeler* v. *Mercer* [1956] C.L.Y. 4861, and *Hagee (London)* v. *A. B. Erikson and Larson* [1975] C.L.Y. 1884 applied; *Strong* v. *Stringer* (1889) 61 L.T. 470 distinguished).

CARDIOTHORACIC INSTITUTE *v.* SHREWDCREST [1986] 1 W.L.R. 368, Ch.D. Knox J.

1839. Business tenancy—terms—interim rent

[Landlord and Tenant Act 1954 (c.56), s.24A.] T applied under Part II of the Landlord and Tenant Act 1954 for a new business tenancy of a block of flats in London NW8, requiring a term of 14 years at a rent of £13,500 p.a. with a rent review after seven years, and otherwise on the terms of the original lease. In March 1983 L issued a summons for an interim rent, and then contended for a term of 10 years at a rent of £25,000 p.a. with a five-year rent review. On being advised that the rent for such a 10 or 14-year term should be £57,000 p.a., T applied instead for a one-year term at £57,000, whilst L continued to contend for 10 years, but at £125,000 p.a. At the hearing it became clear that T's principal requirement was time to consider their position, whilst L offered to meet the difficulty by inserting a break clause exercisable on six months notice. *Held,* that (1) the new term should be for ten years, starting in four months' time, at £106,000 p.a.; but with an option to break on six months' notice, exercisable within a month of the commencement of the new tenancy; (2) exercising its discretion under s.24A of the Act, subject to the principles in *English Exporters (London)* v. *Eldonwall* [1973] C.L.Y. 1902, the court would have determined the interim rent at £40,000 p.a.; but that there would be no order upon Ts' undertaking to pay an interim rent of £25,000 p.a. for July 1983 to March 1986, and of £40,000 thereafter; (3) *mutatis mutandis* the rent review clause in the new lease should be in the same terms as that in the original lease: CHARLES FOLLETT *v.* CABTELL INVESTMENT CO. (1986) 280 E.G. 639, Mr. T. L. G. Cullen Q.C.

1840. Business tenancy—works of reconstruction by landlord—whether entitled to possession
[Landlord and Tenant Act 1954 (c.56), ss.30(1)(*f*), 31A(1)(*a*)] Where a landlord could carry out the proposed works of reconstruction by making use of a power of entry reserved to him in the lease, and the tenant had offered to facilitate the works, then the landlord was not entitled to possession (*Heath* v. *Drown* [1972] C.L.Y. 1983, *Redfern* v. *Reeves* [1979] C.L.Y. 1579, *Price* v. *Esso Petroleum* [1981] C.L.Y. 1515 considered): CEREX JEWELS *v.* PEACHEY PROPERTY CORP. *The Times,* May 12, 1986, C.A.

1841. Covenant to employ resident porter—whether specifically enforceable
A covenant by a landlord to provide a resident porter is not fulfilled by the employment of a non-resident porter, a breach which may be remedied by an order for specific performance.

D owned a block of flats, the terms of the leases requiring the employment of a resident porter. When the resident porter resigned and went to live in a nearby block, D arranged with him that he would return daily to perform his duties. P sought an order for specific performance of the covenant. *Held,* that the employment of a non-resident porter was not a sufficient compliance with the covenant because it ignored the feeling of enhanced security which the presence of a resident porter engendered in the residents. The covenant was specifically enforceable and damages would not be ordered in lieu.

POSNER *v.* SCOTT-LEWIS [1986] 3 W.L.R. 531, Mervyn Davies J.

1842. Covenant to maintain—lessor covenanting to maintain "subject to lessee paying maintenance contribution"—whether condition precedent
[Housing Finance Act 1972, (c.47), S.91A (as inserted by Housing Act 1974 (c.44), s.124.)]
Whether liability in respect of one covenant in a lease was conditional upon the performance of another was to be decided upon the true intentions of the parties to be gathered from the instrument as a whole.

P were sub-lessees of a block of flats one of which was let to D. He covenanted to pay a "maintenance contribution" in four quarterly instalments. P covenanted "subject to the lessee paying the maintenance contribution" to perform various works of maintenance and repair to the internal services, external structure, and gardens. D, with the other tenants, was dissatisfied with the level and cost of P's services and refused to pay the maintenance contributions. P claimed for arrears, and D pleaded a set-off and counterclaim for damages for failure to perform P's covenants. The judge *held,* that the payment of the maintenance contribution was a condition precedent to any liability on the part of P to perform their covenant. *Held,* allowing D's appeal, that the question whether liability in respect of one covenant was dependent upon the performance of another was to be decided on the true intentions of the parties to be gathered from the instrument as a whole. The court was entitled to look at the statutory background at the time of the lease (in this case s.91A of the Housing Finance Act 1972). In the present case it was clear from the lease that the parties did not intend the words "subject to the lessee paying the maintenance contribution" to be a condition precedent to the performance by the lessor of his obligation to maintain. D was entitled to pursue his counterclaim for damages.

YORKBROOK INVESTMENTS *v.* BATTEN (1986) 52 P & C.R. 51, C.A.

1843. Covenant to repair—breach
[Housing Act 1961 (c.65), s.32.] F, a musician, the tenant of a flat, brought a claim against H, his landlord, under s.32. The flat was immediately beneath the roof and from autumn 1980 it leaked. Damp penetrated the window frames, damaging

decorations, furnishings and carpets. F notified H several times. Work commenced in late 1983 and was completed in February 1984, three-and-a-half years after the leaks started. *Held,* that there had been clear breaches of s.32. The flat smelt like the crypt of a church. F did not know what condition the flat would be in when he returned and he could not entertain business clients there. The small bedroom was uninhabitable. An award of £2,250 was made for the cost of redecorating affected areas; £200 was awarded for damage to a carpet, blinds, sheets and blankets; £2,000 general damages were also awarded (*Calabar Properties* v. *Stitcher* [1984] C.L.Y. 174 applied): FRASER v. HOPEWOOD PROPERTIES, October 29, 1985; H.H. Judge Parker; West London County Ct. (*Ex rel. Philomena Harrison, Barrister*).

1844. Covenant to repair—breach—admission—forfeiture—whether possession to be ordered under Order 14 pending trial of counterclaim for relief

L brought proceedings for forfeiture against T for breach of repairing covenant contained in a 99-year sub-lease of a block of flats. T admitted the breach, but the parties were in dispute as to the cost of remedial work, T arguing for £80,000 and L for £500,000. T counter-claimed for relief against forfeiture, to which L conceded that T would be entitled subject to terms. When L claimed possession under R.S.C., Ord. 14 pending trial of the counterclaim for relief, the judge gave T unconditional leave to defend under Ord. 14, r.3. In giving judgment on L's appeal, the Court of Appeal noted that there was an element of manipulation in L's insistence on an order for possession, since it had the avowed purpose of putting pressure on T by depriving T of normal cash-flow from sub-letting. *Held,* dismissing L's appeal, that (1) the right to relief against forfeiture, although now statutory, was in origin a true equitable defence to the legal claim for forfeiture, and should therefore result in unconditional leave to defend being given (*Morgan & Son* v. *Johnson (Martin) & Co.* (1948) C.L.Y. 2855 applied); (2) that in any event there should be unconditional leave to defend under Ord. 14, r.3 (*Meadows* v. *Clerical, Medical and General Life Assurance Society* [1980] C.L.Y. 1578 considered); (3) that it was accordingly unnecessary to determine the precise status of a tenant under a lease subject to forfeiture when the breach is undisputed but a claim for relief is pending: LIVERPOOL PROPERTIES v. OLDBRIDGE INVESTMENTS (1985) 276 E.G. 1352, C.A.

1845. Covenant to repair—construction of lease—whether cost recoverable from tenants

Ts' lease of the second floor of an office building allowed them the shared use of various common parts, which did not include the roof and parapet wall of the building. L undertook extensive repairing obligations, and were entitled to recover in respect of compliance with those obligations," . . . without any deductions, by way of further and additional rent, a sum on account of expenses and outgoings 'The Services Rent' . . . calculated in manner specified in the Fourth Schedule hereto." The Fourth Schedule provided that the certificate of L's surveyor should be conclusive and binding as to the services rent, and defined the heads of expenditure to which that certificate could relate. L sought to recover from T a portion of the cost of repairing the roof and parapet wall, and claimed that this was covered by the Fourth Schedule either as "maintenance of the exterior" of "the first- and second-floor offices"; or as "any expenses or outgoings which . . . are attributable wholly to the first- and second-floor offices"; or as "expenses and outgoings incurred . . . in respect of all other parts of the building of which the tenants have the use in common with the landlords and tenants and occupants of other portions of the building." The judge held that the costs were not recoverable by L. *Held,* dismissing L's appeal, that (1) the parapets and the roof were not part of the exterior of the first- or second-floor offices, (*Douglas-Scott* v. *Scorgie* [1984] C.L.Y. 1908 distinguished); (2) total expenditure on the roof was not attributable wholly to the first- and second-floor offices; (3) upon the true construction of the lease, T did not have any "use" of the roof or parapets at all (*South-West Water Authority* v. *Rumble's* [1984] C.L.Y. 3643 distinguished): RAPID RESULTS COLLEGE v. ANGELL (1986) 277 E.G. 856, C.A.

1846. Covenant to return deposit—assignment of reversion—whether covenant touched and concerned land

A lease contained a covenant by L, the landlord, that at the end of the lease he would return a deposit to T, the tenant. L assigned the reversion to X, from whom at the end of the lease T sought the return of his deposit. *Held,* that the covenant was not one that touched and concerned the land, and X was therefore not bound by it (*Dollar Land Corp.* v. *Solomon, Re* [1963] 39 D.L.R. (2d) 221 applied): HUA

CHIAO COMMERCIAL BANK *v.* CHIAPHUA INDUSTRIES, *The Times,* November 27, 1986, P.C.

1847. "Destination" restaurant—rent review—assessment of revised rent

T appealed against an arbitrator's assessment, pursuant to a five-yearly rent review, of a revised rent for premises in Knightsbridge used as a "destination" restaurant, *i.e.* a restaurant of the kind which customers choose on account of its food or atmosphere rather than because of the convenience of its location. The arbitrator, relying on a number of established "destination" restaurants as comparables, including five outside the Knightsbridge area, had raised the rent from £24,000 p.a. agreed at the previous review to £98,885. T pointed out that the subject premises had only been used as a "destination" restaurant for a comparatively short time, and contended that, in relying upon established "destination" restaurants as comparables, the arbitrator had given L the benefit of T's commercial success, and had reached a decision to which "no person acting judicially and properly instructed as to the relevant law" could have come. *Held,* dismissing the appeal, that (1) the arbitrator had based his decision on two findings of fact, namely (i) the suitability of the premises for use as a "destination" restaurant and (ii) the fact that the market in the restaurant districts of central London for premises suitable for such use is a single market within which the general location of the premises does not appreciably affect the rent which a prospective tenant would be willing to pay; (2) given these findings, from which there was no appeal there was no illogicality in the arbitrator's selection of comparables: MY KINDA TOWN *v.* CASTLEBROOK PROPERTIES (1986) 277 E.G. 1144, Hoffmann J.

1848. Estate cottage—whether held on licence or tenancy

In 1957 W, the owners of an estate, granted to D, an employee, a licence to occupy a cottage on the estate for a payment of £1·50 per week, for the better performance of his duties. The licence was expressed to determine upon the termination of D's employment with W. In 1962 W sold the estate to G, whose manager told D to "carry on as usual." D accordingly continued to work on the estate and to live in the cottage, paying the £1·50 per week which was, as before, deducted from his salary and described as "rent." In 1983 P purchased the estate and brought proceedings for possession of the cottage, claiming that D had occupied it under a licence which terminated together with his employment, and that P had never been D's employer. The judge held that D was a tenant, and refused to order possession. *Held,* dismissing P's appeal that (1) whether D's original occupancy was under a licence or a tenancy, (which it was not necessary to decide) there was a new agreement between D and G in 1962, when W ceased to be D's employer and G came on the scene; (2) thereafter the fact that D was granted exclusive possession by G and paid a weekly sum as "rent" created a strong presumption in favour of a tenancy, which could only be displaced by clear and unequivocal evidence; (3) the instruction to "carry on as usual" was equivocal, and incapable of rebutting the presumption in favour of a tenancy: POSTCASTLE PROPERTIES *v.* PERRIDGE (1985) 276 E.G. 1063, C.A.

1849. Fair rent—caravan—whether "house"

[Rent Act 1977 (c.42), s.1.]

Whether a caravan was within section 1 of the Rent Act 1977 as being a "house" depended on the circumstances of the letting, and in particular whether the caravan was sometimes moved and the services disconnected.

Per curiam: (i) Rent officers will be on their guard against landlords who rent out caravans on a long-term basis and who seek to avoid the controls of the Rent Acts by superficial arrangements tending to show mobility when in reality they are permanently based; (ii) If the occupancy of the caravan is used as a permanent home there is a greater likelihood of the caravan being permanently in place; (iii) There is no power in the county court to order deletion of entries in the register. Landlords who wish to challenge a rent officer's findings as to jurisdiction should do so promptly and before the entries are made in the register. If the rent officer is of the view that there is substance in the challenge he can delay making the registration until the county court determines the question. Otherwise the most convenient solution is the present practice of allowing the entry to remain on the register with the rent officer's endorsement against it that there is no jurisdiction to act on it.

The applicant owned a caravan site with 38 caravans which were not affixed to their concrete bases. They rested on their own wheels and were connected to mains water and electricity and to a sewage pipe. These were easily disconnected, and the caravans were sometimes moved to carry out repairs or renovations. One caravan was let to a Mrs M. and the local authority applied for the registration of a fair rent to the rent officer, pursuant to s.68 of the Rent Act 1977. He fixed a fair rent and made the appropriate entry in the register. The applicant sought judicial review.

Held, allowing the application, that whether a caravan was within s.1 of the 1977 Act as being a "house" depended on the circumstances of the letting, and in particular on features that revealed elements of site permanence or mobility. In the present case the movement of the caravans from time to time and the impermanence of the various services established that they could not be described as "houses".

R. *v.* RENT OFFICER OF THE NOTTINGHAMSHIRE REGISTRATION AREA, *ex p* ALLEN (1986) 52 P & C.R. 41, Farquharson J.

1850. Fair rent—reasons for decision

Upon an application to the rent assessment committee for the registration of a fair rent for a flat, L contended for an increase in the rent from the existing agreed figure of £80 per month to £160 per month, and relied heavily upon the effects of inflation. The tribunal, "having regard to all the evidence put before us, to our inspection, to our knowledge and experience and to the provisions of s.70 of the Rent Act . . .", confirmed the figure of £100 per month fixed by the rent officer. L challenged the decision by way of judicial review, on the ground that the tribunal had not given satisfactory reasons for apparently dismissing his evidence as to inflation. The judge, following *Ellis & Sons Fourth Amalgamated Properties* v. *Southern Rent Assessment Panel* [1984] C.L.Y. 1898, noted that a challenge by way of judicial review is preferable to an appeal under s.33 of the Tribunals and Inquiries Act 1971 where it is the decision-making process rather than the actual decision that is under attack. *Held,* dismissing the application, that the tribunal's reasons were sufficient to enable an informed reader to know exactly what was and was not being taken account of and how the decision was reached (dictum in *Metropolitan Holdings* v. *Laufer* [1975] C.L.Y. 1916 applied): R. *v.* LONDON RENT ASSESSMENT PANEL, *ex p.* CHELMSFORD BUILDING CO. (1986) 278 E.G. 39, McNeill J.

1851. Forfeiture—relief—scope of ancient equitable jurisdiction

[Law of Property Act 1925 (c.20), s.146(2).] L, having duly served a notice under s.146 of the Law of Property Act 1925, forfeited T's lease for breach of repairing covenant and re-entered in accordance with the provisions of the lease, without any application being made for relief by T pursuant to s.146(2) of that Act. The forfeiture proceedings being complete, T, who was thereafter precluded from applying for relief under s.146(2), sought relief under the ancient equitable jurisdiction of the court as preserved by *Shiloh Spinners* v. *Harding* [1972] C.L.Y. 1946. *Held,* striking out the claim for relief, that *Shiloh Spinners* v. *Harding* did not deal with the area covered by s.146. In the case of leases and underleases covered by s.146 the ancient jurisdiction of the court had indeed been ousted by the specific statutory machinery of s.146 (*Official Custodian for Charities* v. *Parway Estates Developments* [1984] C.L.Y. 1091 considered; *Abbey National Building Society* v. *Maybeech* [1984] C.L.Y. 1931 not followed): SMITH *v.* METROPOLITAN PROPERTIES (1985) 277 E.G. 753, Walton J.

1852. Forfeiture—waiver—effect of service of s.146 notice

[Law of Property Act 1925 (c.20), s.146.]

The service of a s.146 notice is not an unequivocal affirmation of the existence of a lease.

N was the assignee with L's consent of a lease of a flat for nine years from 1980 to 1989. In 1984 L, in the mistaken belief that N had assigned the lease in breach of covenant, served a s.146 notice. L then by writ claimed forfeiture of the lease for, *inter alia,* arrears of rent, dating back to 1981. N contended that the notice by its terms unequivocally recognised the continued existence of the lease and that by serving the notice L had waived any right to forfeit the lease for arrears of rent. *Held,* that the failures to pay rent had been once-for-all breaches capable of waiver, but the purpose and effect of the notice was to operate as a preliminary to actual forfeiture and it was not an unequivocal affirmation of the existence of the lease; L had not waived its right to forfeiture (*London and County (A. & D.)* v. *Wilfred Sportsmen* [1970] C.L.Y. 1552 *Old Grovebury Manor Farm* v. *W. Seymour Plant Sales and Hire (No. 2)* [1979] C.L.Y. 1622 applied; *Marche* v. *Christodoulakis* [1948]

C.L.C. 8890, *Segal Securities* v. *Thoseby* [1963] C.L.Y. 1953, *Central Estates Belgravia* v. *Woolgar (No. 2)* [1972] C.L.Y. 1968, *Blackstone (David)* v. *Burnetts (West End)* [1973] C.L.Y. 1906 distinguished).

CHURCH COMMISSIONERS FOR ENGLAND v. NODJOUMI (1986) 51 P. & C.R. 155, Hirst J.

1853. Fresh evidence—whether obtainable with reasonable diligence for use at trial

JB Co. let a house in 1972 on a protected tenancy to T who, in 1981, went to America for three years. During his absence he paid the rent by standing order, but the premises were occupied by Mr. and Mrs. K; and this arrangement continued after T's return in 1984. L, who had acquired the reversion after T's departure, sought possession against T and Mr. and Mrs. K on the grounds that T had abandoned the premises, was not occupying any part of them, and had assigned or sub-let them in breach of covenant without permission. At trial T gave evidence that N, an employee of JB Co., had consented to the arrangement. Towards the end of the judgment L's counsel interrupted to seek an adjournment in order to call N as a witness, but the judge refused the application and gave judgment against L. On appeal L argued that N's evidence ought to be admitted as satisfying the requirements set out in *Ladd* v. *Marshall* [1954] C.L.Y. 2507, since it could not have been obtained with reasonable diligence for use at trial, would probably have had an important influence on the trial, and was apparently credible. Mrs. K swore an unchallenged affidavit stating that she had informed L of N's role in the matter before commencement of proceedings. *Held,* dismissing the appeal, that the first requirement of *Ladd* v. *Marshall* was not satisfied, since L must have known of the importance of N's evidence in time to obtain it for use at trial: SPITALIOTIS v. MORGAN (1985) 277 E.G. 750, C.A.

1854. Industrial unit—replacement of roof—whether "repair"

In the leases of two industrial units on an estate in Blackpool, T covenanted, ". . . well and substantially to repair, replace, cleanse, paint, maintain, mend and keep the demised premises and the . . . roof . . .," and further covenanted to allow L to enter and carry out repairs should T fail to do so, and to recover the cost of so doing. The larger unit had a pitched roof covered with galvanised steel sheets. Upon expiry of the lease of the larger unit in October 1984 the roof had deteriorated beyond repair, despite a bitumastic coating which had not been put on until the galvanising had to a large extent worn off. The cost of replacing the roof was estimated at £84,364. The judge found that the letting value of the unit in its state of disrepair was virtually nil, but would have been £140–150,000 once all the roof was replaced. Accordingly s.18 of the Landlord and Tenant Act 1927 had no application, because the cost of repairs was not greater than the diminution in the value of the reversion. The principal issue for consideration was whether replacement of the roof was a repair. The judge noted that, in comparison with the estimated cost of replacing the roof, the estimated cost of replacing the building would be nearly £1,000,000. *Held,* after consideration of the decisions in *Lurcott* v. *Wakeley and Wheeler* [1911] 1 K.B. 905, *Brew Bros.* v. *Snax (Ross)* [1969] C.L.Y. 2024, *Ravenseft Properties* v. *Davstone (Holdings) Ltd.* [1979] C.L.Y. 599, *Halliard Property Co.* v. *Nicholas Clarke Investments* [1984] C.L.Y. 1966, and *Post Office* v. *Aquarius Properties* [1985] C.L.Y. 1865, that replacement of the roof would involve giving back to L not something different, but simply an industrial property with a new roof: it was thus a "repair," and L was entitled to recover the cost of replacement from T; (2) a claim by L to recover the cost of repairs to the smaller unit (the lease of which had not expired) in anticipation of entering on the premises and doing the work failed through lack of evidence as to L's intentions. However the judge noted that he agreed with the view expressed in *Hamilton* v. *Martell Securities* [1984] C.L.Y. 1959 that such costs would be a debt rather than damages, and would not therefore be caught by the provisions of the Leasehold Reform Act 1938: ELITE INVESTMENTS v. BAINBRIDGE (T.I.) SILENCERS (1986) 280 E.G. 1001, HH Judge Paul Baker Q.C.

1855. Installation of double-glazing—whether repair or "amenity"

By a lease of a flat in a block and a deed of covenant, T undertook to reimburse to D a proportion of the costs and expenses incurred by D pursuant to carrying out repairing obligations in the lease, and "such further or additional costs which the company shall properly incur in providing and maintaining additional services and amenities to Maybourne Grange . . ." When D sought to recover from T a proportion of the cost of replacing wooden-framed windows with double-glazed and maintenance-free windows throughout the block, T sought a declaration that the cost was not recoverable. *Held*, giving judgment for T, that the new windows were neither "amenities" nor repairs, but were rather long-term improvements. MULLANEY *v.* MAYBOURNE GRANGE (CROYDON) MANAGEMENT CO. (1986) 272 E.G. 1350, Mr. J. Jeffs Q.C.

1856. Insurance—landlord's covenant to insure—whether subrogation. See ROWLANDS (MARK) *v.* BERNI INNS, § 1787.

1857. Joint tenancy—co-habitees—apportionment of beneficial interest—mortgage liability

In 1974 W had become the protected tenant of a flat. M and W met in 1980, became engaged and commenced living together in the flat. In 1982 they purchased a long lease of it for £18,350 in their joint names. W contributed a cash sum of £5,000 and the balance was raised by way of a joint mortgage. At this time W was unemployed but it was contemplated that when she obtained employment she would help with the payments. M made actual payments of £500 before the engagement was broken off in 1983. He claimed under s.17 M.W.P.A. 1882 and s.30 L.P.A. 1925 that he was entitled to a half-share in the flat, valued at £35,000 and subject to an outstanding mortgage of £12,865. The registrar concluded, after taking into account the parties' contributions, the discount on the purchase price and the current value that M's interest was not insignificant—but was only four per cent. and ordered that he should be paid £900. *Held,* allowing M's appeal, that as the purchase of the property was for the parties' joint benefit and there being no evidence to the contrary, the beneficial interests would be decided in proportion to their contributions. W's situation as a sitting tenant amounted to a contribution by reason of the discount obtained and a result of her status. M was entitled to credit, though, for a sum representing M's mortgage liability as opposed to his actual payments. Here this would be inferred as 50-50, so that it followed that M's contribution at the time of the setting-up of the trust was one-half of the mortgage. The result was a lump sum due to M of £2,552 based upon a beneficial interest of 25.67 per cent. As a matter of equitable accounting M was also entitled to recoup half of his actual payments, namely, £250. Subsequent conduct, here, did not throw any light on what the parties originally agreed; and in the absence of a new or varied agreement it cannot affect that original agreement (*Walker* v. *Hall* [1984] C.L.Y. 1675 followed; *Wilson* v. *Wilson* [1963] C.L.Y. 1690, *Bedson* v. *Bedson*]1965] C.L.Y. 1858, *Pettitt* v. *Pettitt* [1969] C.L.Y. 1639, *Gissing* v. *Gissing* [1970] C.L.Y. 1243, *Cowcher* v. *Cowcher* [1972] C.L.Y. 1684, *Crisp* v. *Mullings* [1977] C.L.Y. 1208, *Bernard* v. *Josephs* [1982] C.L.Y. 2675, *Gordon* v. *Douce* [1983] C.L.Y. 1834 and *Young* v. *Young* [1984] C.L.Y. 1677 considered): MARSH *v.* VON STERNBERG (1986) 16 Fam. Law 160, [1986] 1 F.L.R. 526, Bush J.

1858. Joint tenancy—purchase price and outgoings in unequal shares—effect of severance

[Sing.] Joint tenants in law may be presumed in equity to hold the beneficial interest as tenants in common in unequal shares if on the facts their outgoings paid in unequal shares are comparable to the payment of purchase money in unequal shares.

M and J were granted a five year lease of a floor in an office block in Singapore. They occupied an unequal share of floorspace and paid all outgoings pro rata. Following a dispute, J applied for sale of the lease and an equal share of the proceeds or equal partition of the premises. The lease contained no words of severance and operated as a grant to the parties as joint tenants at law. The question arose as to whether they held the beneficial interest as joint tenants in equity or as tenants in common in equal or unequal shares. The High Court in Singapore refused to order a sale, holding that they held as tenants in common in unequal shares. The decision was reversed on appeal. *Held*, on appeal to the Privy Council, allowing the appeal, that as all outgoings were in unequal shares, on these facts the inference was that the parties had taken the premises in equity as tenants in common in unequal shares. The order was for sale of the premises and a division of the proceeds in proportion to the parties' shares.

MALAYAN CREDIT *v.* JACK CHIA-MPH [1986] 1 All E.R. 711, P.C.

1859. Lease—assignment—whether consent unreasonably withheld

A lease of commercial premises contained a covenant against assignment without L's consent, which was not to be unreasonably withheld, and further restricted the user of the premises to the composite user of retail shop, hot-food take-away and restaurant/snack bar. T wished to assign the term to A for use as a steak-house, and A produced references from their accountants, bank, solicitor and estate agent, together with two trade references. They also produced unaudited accounts for their existing steak-house business. L refused consent to the assignment on the grounds that the proposed user might result in breach of the user covenant, and that the various references related to the fulfilment by A of easier obligations at their present premises, and did not necessarily mean that A could manage the more onerous obligations that would result from the assignment to them of the subject lease. *Held*, that (1) the test was objective: could a reasonable landlord have withheld consent for the reasons actually advanced by L; (2) an expectation of future breach of user covenant was not a valid ground for the withholding of consent (*Killick* v. *Second Covent Garden Property Co.* [1973] C.L.Y. 1890 applied); (3) however a reasonable landlord could properly take the view on the information available that there was a real doubt about A's ability to meet their obligations under the lease as they fell due, and that consent had therefore been reasonably withheld: BRITISH BAKERIES (MIDLANDS) *v.* TESTLER (MICHAEL) & CO. (1986) 277 E.G. 1245, Peter Gibson J.

1860. Lease—assignment—whether consent unreasonably withheld
L developed new restaurant premises in Hammersmith and granted a lease to T, a company forming part of a large catering group, with the intention subsequently of selling the reversion to an investor. The lease prohibited assignment without L's consent, which was not to be unreasonably withheld. When T subsequently sought L's consent to the assignment of the term to M, a new "off-the-peg" company with whom T had entered into a franchise agreement, L refused on the grounds that the financial standing of M and of those put forward as guarantors on its behalf was inadequate, and that an assignment to M would lessen the investment value of the reversion, notwithstanding that T would remain liable for the rent under the original covenant if M defaulted. T sought a declaration that L's consent had been unreasonably withheld. *Held*, dismissing the claim, that, (1) having regard to the incompleteness of references provided for M and its guarantors, L's doubts as to M's financial standing had been reasonable; (2) in view of L's intention, known from the outset to T, of selling the reversion, L had been entitled to take into account the possibility that an assignment from T to M would lessen the investment value of the reversion; (3) there would be no disproportionate detriment to T, because L was willing to consent to a sub-letting from T to M; (4) in all the circumstances consent had not been unreasonably refused (*International Drilling Fields* v. *Louisville Investments (Uxbridge)* [1986] C.L.Y. 1824 considered): PONDEROSA INTERNATIONAL DEVELOPMENT INC. *v.* PENGAP SECURITIES (BRISTOL) (1986) 277 E.G. 1252, Warner J.

1861. Lease—breach of covenant—breach committed prior to assignment
[Law of Property Act 1925 (c.20), ss.141 and 142.] S, a statutory tenant, was in arrears of reserved rent and P, the landlords, took legal action. S counterclaimed in respect of a breach of covenant by P's predecessors-in-title in failing in their duty to keep the structure and exterior of the premises in good repair, and also a failure in respect of installations for the supply of gas, water and electricity. The judge had to consider a preliminary point of whether, by virtue of s.142, P could be held liable for the default of their predecessors. *Held*, that the common law position is that the assignee of the lease is not liable for breaches of covenant which occurred before the assignment to him. This is reflected in s.142. It is not correct to compare s.142 with s.141 because this is not like with like. S could not counterclaim against P for damages for breaches committed prior to the assignment of the reversion: PETTIWARD ESTATES *v.* SHEPHARD, April 11, 1986; Assistant Recorder Rice; West London County Ct. (*Ex rel. Simon Webber, Barrister*).

1862. Lease—discrepancy from wording of agreement for lease—whether rectification to be granted
In 1974 the parties through their surveyors negotiated the terms of a 99-year lease to run from May 1974 with three-year rent reviews. An agreement for a lease was executed in 1974, and the lease itself was executed in 1980. The actual lease correctly reflected the agreement of the parties through their surveyors as to the formula for calculating the revised rent, but the 1974 agreement, contrary to both parties belief, proved to contain a slightly different formula, which was more favourable to T than that originally agreed and correctly reproduced in the lease itself. T sought

rectification of the lease on the basis (which the judge accepted) that both parties had intended the lease to contain the same terms as the agreement. *Held,* giving judgment for L, and refusing rectification, that (1) rectification required a mistake about the effect of the document sought to be rectified; (2) in this case both parties had specifically intended the formula in the lease to have the effect which it did have, and that the fact that they also mistakenly thought that some other document had the same effect was not a basis for rectification. *Per curiam*: Rent formulae can often be expressed much more simply and unambiguously in algebraic terms: LONDON REGIONAL TRANSPORT *v.* WIMPEY GROUP SERVICES (1986) 280 E.G. 898, Hoffmann J.

1863. Lease—guarantee of T's covenant to pay rent—whether guarantor liable to assignee of reversion

P took an underlease of commercial property from L, and subsequently assigned the term to A Co. The licence to assign contained a guarantee against non-payment of rent, given by D to L and to the head lessor, but not to P. L subsequently assigned the reversion to H. When A Co. subsequently went into liquidation and defaulted on payment of the rent, P, as original under-lessees, had to pay the shortfall to H. P sought to recover the sums so paid from D under the guarantee, arguing that D owed to H a primary liability to make good the shortfall, and that P accordingly had an implied right of indemnity against D; alternatively that P was entitled to be subrogated to H's rights under the guarantee. *Held,* giving judgment for D, that (1) in the absence of an express assignment of the covenant of guarantee to H, the fundamental question was whether that covenant ran with the land so that H could take the benefit of it pursuant to s.78 of the Law of Property Act 1925; (2) the covenant of guarantee did not touch or concern the land, and therefore did not run with the land; (3) accordingly D owed no primary liability to H, and P was not entitled to any right of indemnity or subrogation (*Smith & Snipes Hall Farm* v. *River Douglas Catchment Board* (1949) C.L.C. 10592; *Distributors and Warehousing, Re* [1986] C.L.Y. 1864 and *Pinemain* v. *Welbeck International* [1985] C.L.Y. 1882 considered: *Selous Street Properties* v. *Oronel Fabrics* [1984] C.L.Y. 1954 distinguished): KUMAR *v.* DUNNING (1986) 279 E.G. 223, Tucker J.

1864. Lease—leave to disclaim—whether benefit of guarantee assigned

L's predecessor-in-title granted a lease of commercial property to T Co., under the terms of which G1 and G2 each guaranteed payment by T Co. of one-half of the rent, the guarantee to subsist only so long as the lease remained vested in T Co. When the reversion was later assigned to L there was no express assignment of the benefit of the guarantee, but the guarantors, on the supposition that they remained liable under the guarantee despite the assignment of the reversion, participated in a deed which varied certain terms of the lease. When T Co. subsequently went into liquidation the liquidator sought leave to disclaim the lease, but L opposed the disclaimer on the grounds that the rights of G1 and G2 would be affected. The fundamental question was therefore whether the benefit of the guarantee had been assigned to L, and L advanced a number of arguments in support of their contention that this was the case. *Held,* rejecting L's arguments and giving leave to disclaim, that (1) the assignment of the reversion had not of itself carried with it the benefit of the guarantee (*Griffith* v. *Pelton* [1958] C.L.Y. 1844 distinguished), and that it made no difference that the deed of variation assumed the contrary; (2) the deed of variation did not constitute a new guarantee nor, in the absence of a clear and definite statement that the guarantors were liable to L, did it provide the material for an estoppel by deed (*Onward Building Society* v. *Smithson* [1893] 1 Ch. 1 applied); (3) the benefit of the guarantee had not passed to L by virtue of s.62 of the Law of Property Act 1925, since it did not touch or concern the land (*Rogers* v. *Hosegood* [1900] 2 Ch. 388 and *London & County (A & D)* v. *Wilfred Sportsman* [1970] C.L.Y. 1552 considered); (4) nor had the benefit passed under s.56 of the 1925 Act (*Beswick* v. *Beswick* [1967] C.L.Y. 641 applied); (5) nor were L entitled to rectification of the transfer of the reversion; (6) nor was it meaningful to argue that the benefit of the guarantee could still be assigned to L; (7) even if, contrary to the judge's findings, L were entitled to the benefit of the guarantee, leave to disclaim would still be granted in the particular circumstances of the case, since otherwise the lease would become *bona vacantia* and the guarantee would in any case determine, since the lease would no longer be vested in the company: DISTRIBUTORS AND WAREHOUSING, *Re* (1986) 278 E.G. 1363, Walton J.

1865. Leasehold enfranchisement—"low rent"—"letting value"—premium payable at commencement

[Leasehold Reform Act 1967 (c.88), s.4(1).]

The expression "letting value" in s.4(1) of the Leasehold Reform Act 1967 referred to the best annual return obtainable in the open market for the grant of a long lease whether by letting at a rack rent or at a lower rent plus a premium.

Per curiam: In any future case further consideration should be given to the basis upon which a premium is to be expressed in annual terms; it should be done on a purely actuarial basis rather than upon an agreed formula between the parties.

In 1948 four dwelling houses were let to tenants on long leases each at an annual rent of £200 and for a premium varying between £1,250 and £1,500. In 1983 one of the original tenants and the successors in title of the other three made applications in the county court under the Leasehold Reform Act 1967 to acquire the freehold of the properties. The landlords resisted on the sole ground that the houses were not let at a low rent within the meaning of s.4(1) of the Act in that at the commencement of the tenancies, the rent in each case payable exceeded two-thirds of the letting value. The judge, while accepting expert evidence that in 1948 the rent at which each of the premises could have been let would have been less than £300, held that the capitalised value of the premiums paid had to be added to the rent, thereby resulting in an annual letting value exceeding £300. He granted the tenants' applications. The Court of Appeal dismissed the landlords' appeals by a majority. The landlords' appeal to the House of Lords was dismissed. *Held,* that on its true construction, the expression "letting value" in s.4(1) referred to the best annual rent obtainable in the market for the grant of a long lease on the same terms whether by letting at a rack rent or at a lower rent plus the payment of a premium and that, accordingly, since the annual rents paid by the tenants plus the decapitalised value of the premiums exceeded £300, the rents of £200 per annum were less than two-thirds of the letting value, and they were entitled to purchase the freeholds (*Gidlow-Jackson* v. *Middlegate Properties* [1974] C.L.Y. 2096; and *Manson* v. *Duke of Westminster* [1981] C.L.Y. 1542 considered).

JOHNSTON *v.* DUKE OF WESTMINSTER [1986] 3 W.L.R. 18, H.L.

1866. Leasehold enfranchisement—extended lease—price payable for freehold—"subject to the tenancy"—meaning of "tenancy"

[Leasehold Reform Act 1967 (c.88), s.9(1A).]

Where a lease has been extended under s.14 of the Leasehold Reform Act 1967, that extended lease is the tenancy to which the freehold is subject for the purpose of valuing the freehold for enfranchisement purposes.

In September 1981 H was granted an extended lease of the house of which he was the tenant under s.14 of the Leasehold Reform Act 1967. In February 1982 H served notice on his landlord, pursuant to s.8 of the Act, of his desire to have the freehold of the house. The notice was accepted by his landlord. The freehold was to be valued in accordance with s.9(1A) of the Act and in particular the assumption set out in sub-para. (a) that the vendor was selling "an estate in fee simple subject to the tenancy". H contended that "tenancy" meant the extended tenancy he had been granted under s.14 of the Act. The landlord contended that "tenancy" meant the original tenancy. If the latter contention were correct the freehold would be of far greater value than if the former contention were correct. The determination of the amount to be paid by H for the freehold was referred to the Lands Tribunal. *Held,* that the only tenancy existing at the valuation date was the extended tenancy, the original tenancy having terminated by surrender by operation of law. The freehold would be valued on the basis that it was subject to the extended tenancy.

HICKMAN *v.* TRUSTEES OF THE PHILLIMORE KENSINGTON ESTATE (1985) 50 P. & C.R. 476, Lands Tribunal.

1867. Leasehold enfranchisement—whether rateable value exceeds £1,500 on 1st April 1973—whether subsequent reduction retrospective for purposes of enfranchisement

[Leasehold Reform Act 1967 (c.88), ss.1(5) and (6), 37(6); General Rate Act 1967 (c.9), s.79; Rent Act 1977 (c.42), s.25(1)(2) and (4).] T were the lessees under a long lease of a house in London W.8, and sought to purchase the freehold under the Leasehold Reform Act 1967 as amended. In order to succeed they had to show that the rateable value of the premises did not exceed £1,500 on April 1, 1973. The premises had been originally entered in the 1973 list at £1,784, but in May 1973 a new proposal had been made by the VO reducing the rateable value to £1,605. Furthermore in March 1984 T1 had been granted a certificate by the VO under s.1(4A) of the Leasehold Reform Act as amended and para. 3(ii) of Sched. 8 to the Housing Act 1974, to the effect that the rateable value for the purposes of the Leasehold Reform Act should be reduced by £113 on account of improvements made by a previous tenant: it was common ground that this second reduction related back to April 1, 1973 for the purposes of leasehold enfranchisement. T1 therefore argued that the earlier reduction could also be relied on for this purpose, and that the cumulative effect of the reductions was thus retrospectively to reduce the rateable value as at April 1, 1973 to below £1,500; whilst the freeholder argued that the retrospective effect of the earlier reduction was for rating purposes only. Similar considerations arose in the case of T2. The judge found in favour of T. *Held*, dismissing L's appeals, that (1) T were not assisted by s.79 of the General Rate Act 1967; (2) the reductions in rateable value made after April 1, 1973 as a result of new proposals were retrospective for the purposes of the Leasehold Reform Act 1973, whether by way of s.37(6) of that Act and s.25(1), (2) and (4) of the Rent Act 1977, or by way of s.1(5) and (6) of the Leasehold Reform Act 1967 as amended: MACFARQUAR *v.* PHILLIMORE; MARKS *v.* PHILLIMORE (1986) 279 E.G. 584, C.A.

1868. Leasehold reform—European Convention—public interest. See JAMES *v.* U.K., § 1650.

1869. Leasehold reform—valuation—effect of extended tenancy
   [Leasehold Reform Act 1967 (c.88), s.9(1A).] L appealed against the determination by the Lands Tribunal of the respective amounts payable for the purchase by T under the Leasehold Reform Act 1967 as amended of the freeholds of three houses in Kensington. In each case T had applied for and been granted an extended lease of 50 years pursuant to s.14 of the Act. The rateable value of each property exceeded £1,000 on April 1, 1973, and the prices payable were thus to be assessed under s.9(1A) of the 1967 Act (as inserted by s.118(4) of the Housing Act 1974), which provides, *inter alia*, that the amount payable is to be computed," . . . on the assumption that the vendor was selling for an estate in fee simple, subject to the tenancy . . ." The Lands Tribunal found that the words "subject to the tenancy)" referred to the extended tenancy, with the result that the prices payable for the freeholds were greatly reduced. L contended before the tribunal and on appeal that those words must be taken to refer to the original tenancy, since it would be unacceptable if a tenant who chose to take an extended lease prior to making his request for the freehold could thereby pay a substantially lower price for enfranchisement than a tenant who had failed to take such an extended lease. *Held*, dismissing the appeal, that the words "subject to the tenancy" could not refer to anything else than the extended lease, since s.14 of the Act expressly provides that an extended tenancy is to be in substitution for the original tenancy. Any anomaly would have to be corrected by Parliament: MOSLEY *v.* HICKMAN; SAME *v.* HAGAN; SAME *v.* FRANCIS (1986) 278 E.G. 728, C.A.

1870. Leasehold Valuation Tribunal decision
   BURFORD ESTATE AND PROPERTY CO. *v.* CREASEY (Ref./LON/LVT/203) (1985) 277 E.G. 73 (T's predecessor-in-title held a house in north London on a 99-year lease at a ground rent of £6·75 p.a. and, upon expiry of the term in 1978, duly claimed an extended lease of 50 years pursuant to the Leasehold Reform Act 1967. When L applied to the tribunal for the determination of a modern ground rent pursuant to s.15(2) of the Act and the terms of the extended lease T, who had taken an assignment of the premises in 1982, argued that the period for determination of a modern ground rent was restricted by virtue of s.15(2)(*c*) of the Act to a 12-month period immediately preceding and terminating at the date of expiry of the original lease; that, pursuant to Sched. 1, para. 10(4) to the Act, upon expiry of the original lease no obligation attached to T when he acquired the leasehold interest in 1982 to pay a modern ground rent; and that L, by demanding and accepting rent of £6·75 p.a. from T and his predecessor between the commencement of the extended lease and March 1983 had agreed that the rent for the first 25 years of the extended term should remain at that rate. The tribunal rejected these arguments, holding that (i) subsection 15(2)(*c*) provides at most a commencement date only for the period during which the parties or the tribunal may determine the new rent, and that 12 months would in any event have been an unreasonably short period; (ii) that T, as assignee of the original tenant, held on the terms of the extended lease, which

therefore governed his rights and obligations; and (iii) that L's demand for and acceptance of rent did not amount to the clear and unambiguous evidence necessary to establish that there had been an assignment to modify the terms of the lease. The tribunal assessed the modern ground rent at £435 p.a., adopting the standing house approach and applying a site value percentage of 27½ per cent. (reduced in the circumstances of the particular case from the 30 per cent. which it considered appropriate for London suburbs) and a ground rental percentage of 7 per cent.).

1871. PILGRIM *v.* CENTRAL ESTATES (BELGRAVIA) (Ref./LON/LVT/253) (1986) 278 E.G. 1373. (This was a reference to determine the price payable under s.9 of the Leasehold Reform Act 1967 as amended for the freehold interest in an end-of-terrace house in Pimlico, London SW1. T held the premises on an underlease of 63 years with 4½ years unexpired as at the date of valuation (December 16, 1983) and at a ground rent of £16 p.a. whilst the headlease had 118 years unexpired. Pursuant to para. 7(1)(*b*) of the First Schedule to the 1967 Act, separate prices were payable to the head-lessee and freehold reversioner. In the absence of any evidence of sales of sites, the tribunal adopted the standing house approach. It found for an entirety value of £90,000 and a site value of 35 per cent. (which made allowance for the trapezium shape of the site and its proximity to adjacent high buildings on one side) whilst the figure for deriving the s.15 rent and its capitalisation was agreed at seven per cent. The tribunal did not consider it necessary to include a stage III reversion to rack rent in its valuation, since it took the view that where there is a lengthy period such as 118 years before the expiry of the head-lease, the proper approach is to value in perpetuity. The price payable for the head leasehold interest was thus assessed at £23,055, whilst that payable for the freehold was assessed at ten years' purchase of the head rent, *i.e.* £156.)

1872. Leases—privity of contract. See LAW REFORM, § 1953.

1873. Licence agreement—exclusive possession—whether a tenancy
In an action to determine whether M was a tenant or a licensee, the facts were as follows: M and two student friends decided to look for accommodation. They saw an advertisement in C's shop. The three students viewed the accommodation and subsequently were taken on as occupiers of the property. It was C's intention not to create any tenancy. The agreement signed included the words "there shall be nothing in the relationship between the grantor and the licensee whether under this agreement or otherwise which shall create or be deemed to create a tenancy or the relationship of landlord and tenant." Later, M challenged the relationship of licensee/grantor and asked for a fair rent to be set. *Held*, that C did intend that the three should have occupation of the flat, and in effect they also got exclusive occupation. M was not a lodger. He did not have exclusive possession but joint possession with his friends. There was a grant of exclusive possession to the three students at a rent (*Street v. Mountford* [1985] C.L.Y. 1893 followed): CAPLAN *v.* MARDON, January 13, 1986; H.H. Judge Cotton; Sheffield County Ct. (*Ex rel. Peysner & Foley, Solicitors*).

1874. Licences—exceptional circumstances—repairs
[Landlord and Tenant Act 1985 (c.20), s.11.] D's mother was the controlled tenant of a privately rented property. She died in 1950 and D's father succeeded to the tenancy. In 1957 he died. D, who was in residence, asked the landlord's permission to take over the tenancy but was refused. He paid rent, however, which the landlord accepted. In 1964, by exchange of letters, D was granted a "weekly decontrolled tenancy." D sought a declaration that s.11 applied to his tenancy (previously s.32 of the Housing Act 1961). *Held*, granting the declaration, that D was not to be regarded for the period 1957–1964 as a tenant in view of the landlord's refusal to grant a tenancy. The facts of the case constituted "exceptional circumstances" thereby not falling within Lord Templeman's dictum (*Street v. Mountford* [1985] C.L.Y. 1893) that an occupier should normally be regarded as either a lodger or a tenant: DAVIES *v.* BRENNER, July 31, 1986; H.H. Judge Tibber, Edmonton County Ct. [*Ex rel. Graham Robson, Solicitor.*]

1875. Lock-up garages—whether occupied for the purposes of a business
[Landlord and Tenant Act 1954 (c.56), s.23(1).] L let to T land near Northampton, on which T erected 46 lock-up garages for sub-letting. Thereafter the majority of these garages were sub-let at any particular time, but some would be vacant and T retained one for use as a storeroom. T were in rateable occupation of the site,

inspected it twice monthly through their manager, and carried out cleaning and maintenance, although not strictly required by the terms of the sub-lettings to do so. They also kept access keys to all the garages, but the evidence demonstrated that each sub-tenant enjoyed exclusive possession of his garage. There was no living accommodation on the site, no office, no water, no electricity and no security guard. When T made a request under s.26 of the Landlord and Tenant Act 1954 for a new tenancy, L objected that T did not occupy the premises for the purpose of a business carried on by them within the meaning of s.23(1) of the Act. The judge, after considering *Bagettes* v. *GP Estates* [1956] C.L.Y. 4833, *Lee-Verhulst (Investments)* v. *Harwood Trust* [1972] C.L.Y. 1981, *Boyer (William) & Sons* v. *Adams* [1976] C.L.Y. 1538 and *Hancock & Willis* v. *GMS Syndicate* [1983] C.L.Y. 2111, held that T did so occupy the premises. *Held,* allowing L's appeal, that the judge had misdirected himself in purporting to apply the principles established by those cases, and should in all the circumstances have reached a decision on the other side of the borderline (*Linden* v. *Department of Health and Social Security* [1985] C.L.Y. 1855 considered): TRANS-BRITANNIA PROPERTIES *v.* DARBY PROPERTIES (1986) 278 E.G. 1254, C.A.

1876. Lock-up shop—user covenant—construction

A lease of a lock-up shop in a parade in Basildon, Essex contained a covenant by T to use the premises for the sale of groceries (including meat, bread and vegetables) and as an "off-licence." T further covenanted not to sell or otherwise deal in . . . "cigarettes, tobacco and confectionery where the total sales area devoted to such commodities exceeds 2 per cent. of the net retail area . . ." or ". . . any newspapers, stationery, toys, haberdashery or wools whatsoever." When T began to sell electrical goods and items more usually found in chemists' shops, L sought an injunction restraining the sale of such items. At the trial the judge held that, on the true construction of the covenant, T were entitled to sell articles of a kind which, as at the date of the lease, were in fact being dealt with in supermarkets for the sale of groceries and provisions. He further found that T had not adduced any evidence which in any way established their case that any of the disputed goods were usually so sold, and awarded an injunction restraining T from selling ". . . any items not as of November 21st 1980 usually sold in supermarkets for the sale of groceries and provisions." *Held,* allowing T's appeal and varying the injunction, that (1) the judge had reached the correct conclusion as to the construction of the covenant; (2) however, in relation to the question of what was normally sold in supermarkets for the sale of groceries and provisions, he had wrongly held the burden of proof to be on T, and had in any case ignored relevant evidence adduced by T; (3) the injunction granted was too wide, and should be replaced by an injunction restraining the sale of certain named items: BASILDON DEVELOPMENT CORPORATION *v.* MACTRO (1986) 278 E.G. 406, C.A.

1877. Long lease—maintenance covenant—whether breach—whether fraud

P purchased a long lease in a block of flats of which D2, a firm of estate agents, acted as managing agents. The building was already badly maintained at the date of the purchase, and D1 and D2 subsequently made no attempt to operate the system of maintenance provided in the lease. The building was eventually found to be badly affected by dry rot, originating from the incursion of water. The local authority served a dangerous structure notice and obtained a magistrates' court order. When this was not complied with, it instructed builders to do the works. The judge held that D1 was liable to P in damages for deceit, because there had been at the time of the purchase a fraudulent concealment of dry rot by A, a building contractor, in the course of work ordered by D2 on D1's behalf. He further found that D1 and D2 were in breach of their respective maintenance obligations under the lease, and made an order for specific performance under s.125 of the Housing Act 1974. He also awarded nominal damages in respect of the breaches. On appeal D1 and D2 did not contest the finding that A had been fraudulent and was liable in deceit, but argued that his conduct was not to be imputed to them. *Held,* dismissing the appeal and affirming the judge's decision on different grounds, that (1) D2 had, through its controlling shareholder, become party to A's fraudulent misrepresentation; (2) A's fraudulent misrepresentation was within the actual or ostensible authority conferred on D2 by D1; (3) the judge had correctly found D1 and D2 to be in breach of their respective maintenance obligations, in respect of which they had covenanted in the lease to act as trustees; (4) the court would order the payment of damages for deceit and breach of covenant, together with the execution of the maintenance trusts of the lease and specific performance of the lessor's covenants pursuant to s.125 of the Housing Act 1974; (5) all details of the various orders were to be worked out by the Chief Chancery Master: GORDON *v.* SELICO (1986) 278 E.G. 53, C.A.

1878. Maintenance charge—interest on borrowed money—whether recoverable

A lease of a flat in a large block provided that T would pay by equal quarterly payments in advance a fixed sum "as a contribution" towards L's "yearly costs, expenses and outgoings," including the cost of a number of extensive maintenance obligations imposed upon L by the lease and specified in a schedule. T was additionally liable to pay a proportion of the sum by which the total costs thus incurred by L exceeded a specified sum, and L was entitled to recover such anticipated excesses in advance upon one month's written notice. L contended that T's liability included the reimbursement to L of interest charged upon money borrowed by L, pending receipt of T's payments, in order to carry out its obligations. The judge upheld L's contention, and made no order as to costs by analogy with applications for the grant of a new tenancy under the Landlord and Tenant Act 1954. *Held,* allowing T's appeal, that upon the true construction of the lease it did not provide for the recovery by L of such interest charges; and that T should have the costs of the hearing in the court below: BOLDMARK *v.* COHEN (1985) 277 E.G. 745, C.A.

1878a. Notice to quit—issued by one of two joint owners—whether valid

A notice to quit is valid even though issued by one of two joint owners where, on the facts, that owner was not in any breach of trust in issuing it (*Doe d. Aslin* v. *Summersett* (1830) 1 B. & Ad. 135; *Leek and Moorlands Building Society* v. *Clark* [1952] C.L.Y. 1947. *Greenwich London Borough Council* v. *McGrady* [1983] 2099, *Parsons* v. *Parsons* [1984] C.L.Y. 1918 considered): LECKHAMPTON DAIRIES *v.* ARTUS WHITFIELD (1986) 83 L.S.Gaz. 875, Judge Fallon Q.C.

1879. Occupation agreements—whether licences or tenancies—whether Order 113 possession orders appropriate

R entered into separate but identical written agreements with A1 and A2 for occupation by them of rooms in a house. The agreements permitted A to occupy the rooms ". . . on each day between the hours of midnight and 10.30 a.m. and between noon and midnight but at no other times for 26 weeks . . . for the purposes of temporary accommodation and for the licensees' personal use only." The agreements further reserved "possession, management and control" to L, who was to be "the occupier for all purposes," could retain keys, and had ". . . an absolute right of entry at all times for the purposes of exercising such management and control . . . of effecting any repairs or cleaning . . . of providing . . . attendance . . .", or ". . . of removing or substituting such articles of furniture . . . as the licensor shall see fit." They further provided that the occupants could be required to vacate their rooms and to move to any other room of comparable size in the building. When A1 and A2 held over at the end of the 26 weeks R successfully obtained possession orders under R.S.C., Ord. 113, the judge in each case refusing to remit the matters to the county court for trial under s.40 of the County Courts Act 1984, or to adjourn them to enable A to produce evidence that the licence agreements were "shams." *Held,* allowing the appeals, that (1) on their face the agreements involved the provision by L of attendance or services which required L to exercise unrestricted access to and use of the rooms; and thus, in accordance with the principle stated by Lord Templeman in *Street* v. *Mountford* [1985] C.L.Y. 1893, they were such as to constitute A1 and A2 lodgers only; (2) however L's claim was not sufficiently clear or straightforward for possession to be ordered under Ord. 113, because the agreements contained provisions which were arguably "sham", namely that A were not entitled to occupy the rooms between 10.30 a.m. and noon daily, and that L could remove as well as substitute furniture; (3) claims by A that no cleaning had in fact been carried out raised a sufficient doubt as to whether L in fact required unrestricted access as likewise to make an Order 113 possession order inappropriate, as did a claim by A2 that the second agreement was subject to an oral collateral agreement made with the housekeeper: CRANCOUR *v.* DA SILVAESA; SAME *v.* MEROLA (1986) 278 E.G. 618 & 733, C.A.

1880. Occupation as single private residence—licences for occupation

T took a lease of a flat in a large block and covenanted, *inter alia,* ". . . not to occupy the flat otherwise than as a single private residence in one occupation only." When T granted occupational licences to visitors to reside in the flat in return for a monetary payment, L sought an injunction enforcing the covenant. In Order 14 proceedings the judge held that T was using the flat for the purpose of carrying on the business of granting licences for occupation, and that the covenant had been broken: he accordingly granted the injunction. *Held,* dismissing T's appeal, that (1) the judge had correctly considered the test to be whether T was using the premises as a private residence; (2) that T was not so doing. This was not a case of a company using property for its directors, staff or guests, but amounted to the business of providing service accommodation, and could not be considered residence user at all. The proper way for T to exploit the property would be by sub-letting, which was permitted by the lease subject to L's consent; (3) however the court would grant T unconditional leave to defend as to the question of whether L had waived the breach of covenant: FALGOR COMMERCIAL S.A. *v.* ALSABAHIA (1985) 277 E.G. 185, C.A.

1881. Occupation by prospective purchaser—sale abandoned—whether tenancy created

A, the owner of a dwelling-house, allowed R into occupation of the house in order for R to do some repairs and arrange a mortgage pending a contemplated sale of the property to her. Under an arrangement which the judge found to be legally enforceable R paid the rates and also paid a weekly sum of £1·20 as a contribution to the insurance premiums. When the proposed sale fell through, R claimed a protected tenancy, on the basis that there had been a grant to her of residential accommodation "for a term at a rent with exclusive possession," thus fulfilling the requirements for a tenancy laid down by the House of Lords in *Street* v. *Mountford* [1985] C.L.Y. 1893. The judge upheld this contention. It was conceded that, had a tenancy been so created, it would fall within the Rent Act 1977. On appeal, A contended that the ultimate intention of the parties was not the grant of a tenancy but the conclusion of a contract of sale and purchase; alternatively that the ultimate intention of the parties had never been embodied in an enforceable contract: in either case he submitted that the principle of *Street* v. *Mountford* was inapplicable. *Held,* dismissing the appeal, that there was an enforceable contract for occupation of the premises for a periodic term at a rent of £1·20 per week with exclusive possession, and that the requirements of *Street* v. *Mountford* for the creation of a tenancy had been fulfilled: BRETHERTON *v.* PATON (1986) 278 E.G. 615, C.A.

1882. Opposition to new business tenancy—"reason connected with the tenant's use or management of the holding"

[Landlord and Tenant Act 1954 (c.56), s.30(1)(c).] T occupied land and premises belonging to L for the purpose of breeding greyhounds, and originally lived in a van parked on that land. It was subsequently held in litigation that this occupation constituted a business tenancy subject to an express term that T should not live on the land. Thereafter T, who contended that he must live nearby in order to conduct his business, moved the van to a grass verge some 100 yards from the holding and outside L's premises. The positioning of the van was said to be unlawful, but no steps had been taken to have it removed. When L served a notice under s.25 of the Landlord and Tenant Act 1954 determining T's tenancy, and T duly requested a new tenancy, L opposed the application on the ground that the parking of the van was a ". . . reason connected with the tenant's use or management of the holding" within the meaning of s.30(1)(c) of the Act. The judge accepted this contention and refused to order a new tenancy. *Held,* allowing T's appeal, that (1) having regard to the nature of T's business and the precarious nature of T's living arrangements, the judge had correctly found that these arrangements constituted a matter that fell within the scope of s.30(1)(c); (2) however, he had failed properly to exercise his discretion as to whether a new tenancy should be ordered, because he appeared to have based his decision solely upon the consideration that the van might be illegally parked, which was immaterial, and had not asked himself whether L's interest was likely to be prejudiced by the occurrence of the matters relied on as falling within s.30(1)(c); (3) the Court of Appeal did not have sufficient material to exercise the discretion themselves, and that the matter should therefore be remitted for reconsideration by the judge: BEARD (FORMERLY COLEMAN) *v.* WILLIAMS (1986) 278 E.G. 1087, C.A.

1883. Option for renewal of lease—proper time for exercise

A lease of a shop and flat for a term of 35 years till March 25, 1984 gave T an option to take a further 21-year term "on the written request of the tenant made three months before the expiration of the term hereby created." The last date for such a written request to be made was therefore Christmas 1983. In 1980 T's solicitors suggested in correspondence to L1 and L2 that the words "made three months before" meant "made at any time before the date three months before," and L2 replied that he concurred with this construction. T's solicitors subsequently gave written notice in January 1981, whereupon Ls' surveyors replied in March 1981 that L2 withdrew his reply, which had been made without professional advice, and that he rejected T's construction of the option. T sought specific performance of the option. *Held,* giving judgment for L, that (1) upon the true construction of the option clause the written request had to be given a reasonably short time before Christmas 1983 (*Biondi* v. *Kirklington and Piccadilly Estates* (1947) C.L.C. 1691 considered; (2) January 1981 was not such a reasonably short time before Christmas 1983; (3) L were not estopped by convention from withdrawing the position created by L2's reply, since in the circumstances there was nothing unfair or unjust in allowing them to do so (dictum of Lord Denning M.R. in *Amalgamated Investment and Property Company* v. *Texas Commerce International Bank* [1981] C.L.Y. 1273 applied): MULTON *v.* CORDELL (1985) 277 E.G. 189, H.H. Judge Thomas.

1884. Possession—landlord's own use—retrospective effect of statute—appeal pending

[Rent Act 1977 (c.42), Sched. 15, Case 11; Rent (Amendment) Act 1985 (c.24), s.1(1)(4).]

The provisions of the Rent (Amendment) Act 1985 apply retrospectively to a pending appeal.

L occupied his house for 12 years, then went abroad. After a period of occupation by L's son, the house was let to a tenant who had been served with a notice under Case 11 of Sched. 15 to the Rent Act 1977. A county court judge refused an order for possession under Case 11 on the ground that L was not residing there immediately prior to the grant of the tenancy. L appealed. Before the appeal was heard the Rent (Amendment) Act 1985 came into force, whereby s.1(1) amended Case 11 whereby the landlord need only establish occupation at any time before the letting. By s.1(4) the Act applied to tenancies granted and Case 11 notices served before the commencement of the Act. *Held,* that L's appeal was by way of rehearing, and the Act applied retrospectively. The appeal would be allowed, and the matter remitted to the county court for rehearing (dictum of Lord Denning in *Att.-Gen.* v. *Vernazza* [1960] C.L.Y. 2580 applied; *National Real Estate and Finance Co.* v. *Hassan* [1939] 2 All E.R. 154 distinguished.)

HEWITT *v.* LEWIS [1986] 1 All E.R. 927, C.A.

1885. Possession—premises subject to rent control—consent judgment

[Sing.] [Control of Rent Act (Statutes of Singapore, 1970 rev., c.266), s.14.]

Where the parties to an action for possession agreed that the premises were outside the rent control legislation or that the defendant's occupation was not protected, the court had no duty to consider the facts before making a possession order, and a consent order was valid.

The owners of premises brought proceedings in the district court in Singapore for possession against the occupiers alleging that they were trespassers in unlawful occupation. By their defence the occupiers claimed to be lawful tenants entitled to protection under the Control of Rent Act which by s.14 restricted the right to recover possession of premises comprised in a tenancy, but they agreed to a consent judgment against them which specifically stated that they admitted the owners' claim. They were ordered to give up possession although execution was stayed. They subsequently instituted proceedings in the High Court of Singapore claiming that the consent order was a nullity and should be set aside since, having regard to the Control of Rent Act, the district court had no jurisdiction to grant the order for possession. The judge set aside the consent order and awarded agreed damages to the occupiers who had vacated the premises pursuant to the consent judgment. The Court of Appeal of Singapore dismissed the owners' appeal. The owners appealed to the Judicial Committee. *Held,* allowing the appeal, that where the parties agreed that either the premises were outside the rent control legislation or the defendant's occupation was not protected, the court had no duty to consider the facts before making a possession order. Its jurisdiction to make an order was not restricted by s.14 unless the premises were comprised in a tenancy, and since the occupiers had admitted the claim and accepted that they were trespassers and unprotected, the consent judgment was valid and the order for possession effective. The occupiers were not therefore entitled to damages (*Nanyang Gum Benjamin Manufacturing (Pte.) v. Tan Tong Woo* [1978] 1 M.L.J. 233 doubted; *Barton v. Fincham* [1921] 2 K.B. 291; *Thorne v. Smith* [1947] C.L.Y. 8637 and *Peachey Property Corp.* v. *Robinson* [1966] C.L.Y. 6938 considered).

Quaere: Whether special considerations might arise, if in subsequent proceedings the defendant established by evidence that his agreement that a claim was well founded was given in pursuance of a compromise involving his being paid a sum of money.

SYED HUSSAIN BIN ABDUL RAHMAN BIN SHAIKH ALKAFF *v.* A.M. ABDULLAH SAHIB & Co. [1985] 1 W.L.R. 1392, P.C.

1886. Possession proceedings—whether summary proceedings appropriate—whether surrender by tenant. See COOPER *v.* VARZDARI, § 1642.

1887. Protected tenancies

PROTECTED TENANCIES (EXCEPTIONS) REGULATIONS 1986 (No. 541) [80p], made under the Rent Act 1977 (c.42), s.8; operative on May 1, 1986; consolidate regulations specifying educational institutions for the purposes of s.8.

1888. Protected tenancy—fair rent—effect of scarcity value and of exceptional right to charge premium on assignment

[Rent Act 1977 (c.42), s.70(2).] This was an appeal against the determination by the London Rent Assessment Panel of a fair rent of £11,000 (against £18,250 sought by L and £7,200 by T) for a house forming part of the Crown's Regent Park Estate and let for a term of $9\frac{1}{2}$ years from July 1980 at a rack rent. Being leased by the Crown Estate Commissioners, the premises were ones to which, by virtue of s.73 of and Sched. 8 to the Housing Act 1980, the prohibition against the charging by tenants of a premium on assignment in part IX of the Rent Act 1977 did not apply before the end of the year 1990. On appeal, L's principal complaint was that the Panel had erred, in that they had, without hearing evidence, effectively found that scarcity of accommodation existed in relation to the premises; and had further found that, in the circumstances postulated by s.70(2) of the 1977 Act, the premium value of T's leasehold interest was nil; and that in any event the right to charge a premium was a personal circumstance within the scope of the decision of the House of Lords in *Mason v. Skilling* [1974] C.L.Y. 2114, and was thus to be disregarded in assessing a fair rent. *Held*, allowing the appeal, quashing the decision and remitting the matter for further consideration, that (1) there had been evidence before the committee on which it could form its views as to scarcity (*Metropolitan Property Holdings v. Finegold* [1975] C.L.Y. 2840 and *Palmer* v. *Peabody Trust* [1974] C.L.Y. 3177 considered); and that L had had every opportunity to adduce evidence and make submissions to the committee on the question of scarcity; (2) the right to assign at a premium was not a "personal circumstance" within the decision in *Mason v. Skilling*; (3) in any event, to assess the premium value as nil as well as discounting scarcity would be to give to T a windfall not envisaged by the legislature, since it would entitle T to charge a premium and at the same time to get the benefit of a discounted rent. It was to be assumed that, in exempting lessees of property owned by the Crown Estate Commissioners from the prohibition on premiums, Parliament's intention must have been that the right to charge a premium should be taken into account in fixing a fair rent: CROWN ESTATE COMMISSIONERS *v.* CONNOR (1986) 280 E.G. 532, McCowan J.

1889. Protected tenancy—premises required as landlord's residence—"greater hardship"

[Rent Act 1977 (c.42), Sched. 15, Case 9] L, a ship's cook, sought possession under Case 9 of Sched. 15 to the Rent Act 1977 of a dwelling-house let on a protected tenancy to T, on the grounds that he had married a Russian lady who was about to arrive from Odessa, and required the house for a family home, since his only existing accommodation was a caravan, the lease of which was about to expire. T resisted the proceedings on grounds of greater hardship, claiming that he needed the house as a home for himself, the lady with whom he was co-habiting, their six-month-old daughter, and his 15-year-old daughter by his previous marriage. The local authority acknowledged in a letter to T that, should he and his family be evicted by a possession order, they would be homeless for the purposes of the Housing (Homeless Persons) Act 1977, and would have a priority need for accommodation under s.2(1) of the Act, because of their young child. The recorder noted in his judgment that, ". . . it is not for the Court to assume other than that something of a bed-and-breakfast accommodation would be made available in the first place", and held that T had made out the greater hardship. He therefore refused to order possession. Since the hearing L's position had deteriorated, because his wife had arrived in England and, during his absence at sea, first lived in the caravan as a bare licensee, and subsequently took a job in a London hotel on a temporary basis until a more suitable home became available. *Held*, allowing L's appeal and ordering possession, that in making his assumption as to "bed and breakfast accommodation . . . in the first place" the recorder had doubly erred. First he had not applied the burden of proof which lay on T; and secondly he had looked only at the short-term effect of an order for possession, and had failed to consider the longer-term effect at all: MANATON *v*. EDWARDS (1985) 276 E.G. 1257, C.A.

1890. Protected tenancy—premises required as landlord's residence—material time—"greater hardship"

[Rent Act 1977 (c.42), Pt. I of Sched. 15, Case 9; Pt. VI of Sched. 15, para. 1.]
In considering whether a landlord reasonably requires accommodation occupied by a statutory tenant under Case 9 of Part I of Schedule 15 to the Rent Act 1977, the relevant time is the date of the hearing, and not the date of issue of the proceedings.

L sought possession of a flat let to T on a protected tenancy on the grounds of rent arrears, and under Case 9 of Sched. 15 to the Rent Act 1977 on the grounds that she required the premises as a residence for herself. At the hearing there was no real evidence as to the difficulties which T would face in finding other accommodation, since she had not looked for any. However, the judge held that although at the time of the hearing L did require the flat as a residence of her own, she had not done so at the time of issuing proceedings, and he further found that T had established that she would suffer greater hardship than L if a possession order was made, because there would be a real risk of herself and her daughter being made homeless. He therefore declined to order possession under Case 9 and made an order for possession suspended so long as the current rent and arrears were paid. *Held*, allowing L's appeal that (1) in considering whether a landlord reasonably required accommodation under Case 9, the relevant time was the date of the hearing, and (2), on the evidence T could not have discharged the burden of demonstrating greater hardship. The case would accordingly be remitted to the County Court to investigate L's financial ability to live in the flat (*King* v. *Taylor* [1954] C.L.Y. 2810 applied).
ALEXANDER *v*. MOHAMADZADEH (1986) 51 P. & C.R. 41, C.A.

1891. Protected tenancy—statutory succession—residence with relative

T died. Her daughter, E, had stayed with T on three or four nights each week for more than six months before her death to look after her. E also kept on her own premises, paying the outgoings and having her post sent there. *Held*, that the question of residence was one of fact and degree, and if E had intended to return to her own home, or had not made up her mind about her future, she was not residing with T at the date of death: SWANBRAE *v*. ELLIOTT, *The Times*, December 6, 1986, C.A.

1892. Protection from eviction—meaning of "does acts"

[Protection from Eviction Act 1977 (c.43), s.1(3).] A carried out works to a flat occupied by his tenant, C, thereby making the flat uninhabitable. A claimed that he believed that C had agreed to the work and the evidence did not establish otherwise. A was convicted, however, of doing acts calculated to interfere with C's peace and comfort, namely having commenced major structural alterations . . . "took no further steps to complete them and left the same unfinished so that the premises were not habitable" by C, with intent to cause C to give up occupation, contrary to s.1(3) of the 1977 Act. *Held*, allowing A's appeal, that A's failure to take steps to complete the work was not the doing of an act or acts within s.1(3): R. *v*. AHMAD [1986] Crim. L.R. 739, C.A.

1893. Protection from eviction—meaning of "give up occupation"

[Protection from Eviction Act 1977 (c.43), s.3.] A was the director of L Co., which owned the premises in which T, an elderly statutory tenant, had a room. During works of conversion L Co. installed a new bathroom above T's room, which necessitated the installation of additional joists in the floor. A offered T alternative accommodation in a hotel while the work was carried out, but she refused. A then carried out the work from above, in consequence of which the ceiling in T's room fell down, and the room was rendered uninhabitable. The magistrate found that A had intended T to leave her room for so long as it took to carry out the intended works, which could have been up to two weeks, and convicted A on a charge of doing acts interfering with the peace and comfort of T with intent to cause her to give up occupation of the premises within the meaning of s.3(1)(*a*) of the Protection from Eviction Act 1977. The Crown Court dismissed A's appeal. *Held*, allowing A's appeal, that the word "occupation" was to be given the same meaning as under the Rent Acts, and that "give up" meant to give up permanently. (*R.* v. *Yuthiwattana* [1985] C.L.Y. 1809 distinguished). *Per curiam*: A could have been charged in the alternative under s.3(1)(*b*), since s.3 provides for one offence with different intents: SCHON *v.* CAMDEN LONDON BOROUGH COUNCIL (1986) 279 E.G. 859, D.C.

1894. Protection from eviction—temporary exclusion
[Protection From Eviction Act 1977 (c.43), ss.1(2), 4] C had told X that she was to quit a flat rented from C by May 13. He had told Y to quit the flat by May 6. On May 9 he refused to allow X or Y to enter the flat but offered, an hour later (after police intervention) to allow X to return for the night. X collected her property and left. *Held*, allowing C's appeal against conviction of an offence contrary to ss.1(2) and 4 of the 1977 Act, that in the absence of a finding as to whether X was intended to be evicted only for a short time, the appeal had to be allowed (*R.* v. *Yuthiwattana* [1985] C.L.Y. 1809 applied and considered): COSTELLOE *v.* LONDON BOROUGH OF CAMDEN [1986] Crim.L.R. 249, D.C.

1895. Quiet enjoyment—breach by predecessor in title—liability
[National Conditions of Sale (20th Ed.), condition 14.]
A landlord cannot be in breach of a covenant for quiet enjoyment through the existence of the easement which was created by his predecessor in title.

X developed a site and granted long leases of flats and garages upon it. The leases included a right of way over another part of the site. Subsequently, X transferred the freehold to A who then leased the part subject to the rights of way to B, an oil company, to construct a filling station and car wash, the lease which was for 99 years contained a covenant for quiet enjoyment on terms that B should hold the premises without interruption by A or any person lawfully claiming through under or in trust for him. The tenants of the flats brought an action against A and B seeking an injunction to restrain the construction of the car-wash, which would interfere with their rights of way. By a contribution notice B claimed against A that the injunction would amount to a breach of the covenant for quiet enjoyment. The injunction was granted against both A and B but on the question of A's liability to B, *held*, that the covenant did not protect B against the acts of A's predecessors in title. Under condition 14 of the National Conditions of Sale, the purchaser must satisfy himself as to incumbrances, and B's claim against A would be dismissed.
CELSTEEL *v.* ALTON HOUSE Holdings (No. 2) [1986] 1 All E.R. 598, Scott J.

1896. Racehorse gallops—exclusive possession—whether licence or tenancy
In a series of documents expressed to be "licences," P granted to D the right to use racehorse gallops in Berkshire, which latterly included an area of scrubland that was of use neither to P's farming activities nor to D for the training or exercise of racehorses. Eventually a dispute arose as to whether or not a tenancy had in fact been created by the latest document. D gave evidence that he currently trained some 75–80 horses, spent some £8,000 per year on maintenance, and only permitted other trainers to use the gallops on payment of a fee. *Held*, giving judgment for D, that, (1) irrespective of whether the grant was expressed to be a licence or tenancy, the determining feature was whether D had the right to exclusive possession of the gallops and the scrubland (*Bracey* v. *Read* [1962] C.L.Y. 1722a and *Street* v. *Mountford* [1985] C.L.Y. 1893 considered; (2) the document created a tenancy. In reaching this conclusion, the court was weighed by the nature of the scrubland, and by provisions in the document to the effect that D would have no claim against P if third parties brought horses onto the gallops, that P would not grant rights to third parties so as to interfere with D's rights under the grant, and that P would not use or permit the use of the gallops otherwise than for training and exercising racehorses: UNIVERSITY OF READING *v.* JOHNSON-HOUGHTON (1985) 276 E.G. 1353, Leonard J.

1897. Re-entry—subtenancy

A landlord is not entitled to effect re-entry of premises occupied by a subtenant by means of an agreement with the subtenant that he will be substituted as tenant on the terms of his existing subtenancy: ASHTON v. SOBELMAN, *The Times*, May 20, 1986, Chadwick Q.C. sitting as deputy High Court Judge.

1898. Reasonable endeavours—burden

A covenant to use reasonable endeavours is less onerous than one to use best endeavours, and the covenantor is entitled to weigh up all relevant considerations and decide on balance to act one way or another: UBH (MECHANICAL SERVICES) v. STANDARD LIFE ASSURANCE CO., *The Times*, November 13, 1986, Rougier J.

1899. Receiver—management expenses—whether recoverable

When a court, acting under the powers conferred by *Hart* v. *Emelkirk*, appoints a receiver to manage a block of flats, collect the rents and carry out repairs, the receiver is not entitled on an interlocutory application to recover the amount by which his expenses exceed the moneys he has received in the course of his management (*Boehm* v. *Goodall* [1911] 1 Ch. 155; *Hart* v. *Emelkirk*, [1983] C.L.Y. 2088, applied): EVANS v. CLAYHOPE PROPERTIES, *The Times*, November 10, 1986, Vinelott J.

1900. Registered rent—whether re-registration possible

[Rent Act 1977 (c.42) s.67.] T, who occupied a room in Chelsea at a rent registered in 1980 of £14 per week applied to the rent officer to re-register that existing rent, in the mistaken belief that L could otherwise increase her rent without a further determination. The rent officer explained T's mistake to her, and told her that she could make a request in writing seeking to withdraw her application, in which case, provided that L consented, he would take no further action. No letter of withdrawal arrived from T, and the rent officer in due course determined the rent at £16 per week. T, who claimed that she had sent a letter of withdrawal, sought an order of certiorari to quash the determination, on the grounds that the Rent Act 1977 does not provide for an application to re-register an existing registered rent. The judge refused to make the order. *Held*, allowing T's appeal and making the order, that (1) upon its true construction s.67(1) of the 1977 Act does not enable an application to be made for the re-registration of an existing registered rent; (2) the defect was a fundamental one and the determination was therefore liable to be quashed (*Chapman* v. *Earl* [1968] C.L.Y. 3362 applied): R. v. CHIEF RENT OFFICER FOR ROYAL BOROUGH OF KENSINGTON AND CHELSEA, *ex p.* MOBERLY (1986) 278 E.G. 305, C.A.

1901. Rent arrears—whether L estopped from enforcement

L sought summary judgment against T in respect of arrears of rent under a commercial lease. There had previously been negotiations between the parties "subject to contract" in which L had offered a substantial financial inducement to T in return for T's agreement to vacate first part and later the whole of the subject premises prior to being granted a new lease of alternative refurbished premises. Although negotiations eventually broke down before a formal contract was signed, T had vacated part of the subject premises, and argued that they had done so in reliance upon a representation by L to the effect that there would be no difficulty in reaching final agreement. They also claimed that the proposed inducement had included a rent "holiday," and sought to raise a proprietary estoppel both by way of a defence and as a counter-claim. *Held*, that T had made out an arguable case that such a proprietary estoppel had arisen, and that the claim for summary judgment must therefore fail (*Swallow Securities* v. *Isenberg* [1985] C.L.Y. 1909, *Crabb* v. *Arun District Council* [1975] C.L.Y. 1191 and *Taylor Fashions* v. *Liverpool Victoria Friendly Society* [1979] C.L.Y. 1619 considered): CENTRAL STREET PROPERTIES v. MANSBROOK RUDD & CO. (1986) 279 E.G. 414, H.H. Judge Finlay.

1902. Rent assessment committee—fair rent—reasons for decision

L appealed against the assessment by a rent assessment committee of a fair rent, which included a substantial sum in respect of services. The committee stated in their reasons that, "in view of the fact that the committee were unable to gain access to the flat, they made an adjustment in the total rent to reflect the updated service schedule." *Held*, that the matter must be remitted for reconsideration. The committee had either failed to take into account evidence given by L's surveyor, or had failed to give any reason for rejecting it or for coming to the conclusion which they did, other than the insufficient reason that they had been unable to gain access to the premises: DAEJAN PROPERTIES *v.* CHAMBERS (1985) 277 E.G. 308, McNeill J.

1903. Rent review—actual provision for future review—whether to be included in terms of hypothetical lease
    A lease contained a number of rent reviews, the review clause providing that the revised rent was, in default of agreement, to be assessed by an independent arbitrator, and was to be a "fair yearly rent for the demised premises on the relevant date . . . but without a premium, with vacant possession, and on the provisions of this lease (other than the rent hereby reserved)." At the first review, the familiar question arose as to whether the revised rent should be assessed on the basis that the hypothetical lease contained no provision for future reviews. *Held,* that the actual provision for future reviews was to be taken account of by the valuer (*MFI Properties v. BICC Group Pensions Trust* [1986] C.L.Y. 1909 and *British Gas Corp.* v. *Universities Superannuation Scheme* [1986] C.L.Y. 1911 followed). *Per curiam*: The principle of construction "contra proferentem" carries little weight in the case of a lease: AMAX INTERNATIONAL *v.* CUSTODIAN HOLDINGS (1986) 279 E.G. 762, Hoffman J.

1904. Rent review—application to RICS—whether properly made
    An application to the RICS for the appointment of arbitrator is validly made even though it is contingent upon the failure of negotiations and the requisite fees remain unpaid.
    A rent review clause in a lease of commercial property provided that, in the event of a dispute as to the amount of the revised rent, the matter was to be referred to an arbitrator nominated by the President of the Royal Institute of Chartered Surveyors, ". . . upon the application of the landlord made not later than 3 months before the relevant review date. It was agreed between the parties that if L failed to make such an application, its "trigger" notices would, upon the true construction of the lease, become void. Having served an effective trigger notice, L's agents wrote to the President of the RICS while negotiations were still on foot, stating ". . . we are writing in accordance with the terms of the lease to make an in-time only application for the appointment of an expert surveyor to determine the revised rent . . ." T objected that this was not a genuine application in that it was not intended to put the machinery into effective operation, and that it was further invalidated because T had not been given notice of it, and because it had not been accompanied by the £40 "processing" fee. *Held,* that the application was valid; (1) there was no requirement in the lease that T should be given notice; (2) there was no reason why a valid application should not be made contingent upon the failure of negotiations, and (3) it did not matter that the requisite fees remained unpaid (*Aly* v. *Aly* [1984] C.L.Y. 2691 applied).
    STAINES WAREHOUSING CO. *v.* MONTAGU EXECUTOR AND TRUSTEE CO. (1986) 51 P. & C.R. 211, Knox J.

1905. Rent review—arbitration award remitted—whether interest on intervening shortfall recoverable
    A rent review clause in a lease of commercial premises provided that any dispute as to the amount of the revised rent was to be determined by an arbitrator; and the arbitrator, in an award dated May 1983, duly determined the revised rent (effective from December 25, 1982) at £251,000. The award was subsequently remitted on the grounds of technical misconduct within the meaning of s.23 of the Arbitration Act 1950, and the revised rent was reassessed at £220,000 in an award dated November 1984. On the question of whether L was entitled to interest on the shortfall between the old and revised rents, *Held,* that (1) the shortfall between the old and revised rents did not become payable until the quarter day following the arbitration determination (*South Tottenham Land Securities* v. *R & A Millett (Shops)* [1984] C.L.Y. 1938 applied); (2) since the only question at issue in the arbitration was the amount of the revised rent, the new award had effectively replaced the original one, and the date of the award was therefore to be taken as November 1984; (3) the shortfall itself accordingly became payable on the December 1984 quarter day, and that, in the absence of any specific provision in the lease, interest on the shortfall could only begin to accrue from that date, and was not therefore payable for the period between December 1982 and December 1984: SHIELD PROPERTIES AND

INVESTMENTS *v.* ANGLO OVERSEAS TRANSPORT CO. (No. 2) (1986) 279 E.G. 1088, Mr. Michael Wheeler Q.C.

1906. Rent review—arbitration—extension of time
[Arbitration Act 1950 (c.27), s.27.] A lease granted in 1968 specified a rent of £800 for the first seven years of the term, and of £850 for the subsequent seven years. Thereafter the rent was to be reviewed so as to be the sum notified by L to T, unless T should within three months of notification (time to be of the essence) refer the question of the revised rent to arbitration. In due course L specified an increase of rent from £850 to £6,000. Having failed within the specified time to initiate arbitration proceedings, T sought an extension of time under s.27 of the Arbitration Act 1950. The judge at first refused an extension, but almost immediately recalled his judgment and gave a fresh judgment for T. *Held*, allowing L's appeal, that (1) although the rent review clause conferred the right to initiate arbitration proceedings upon one party only, rather than bilaterally, it contained an "agreement to refer future disputes to arbitration" within the meaning of s.27 of the 1950 Act, which was therefore applicable (*Tote Bookmakers* v. *Development and Property Holding Co.* [1985] C.L.Y. 90 disapproved; *Woolf* v. *Collis Removal Service* (1948) C.L.C. 413 applied; *Baron* v. *Sunderland Corporation* [1966] C.L.Y. 385 considered); (2) in the circumstances the judge had been entitled to recall his judgment (*Re Barrell Enterprises* [1973] 1 W.L.R. 19 considered); (3) however that the judge had misdirected himself in the exercise of his discretion, by considering the increase from £850 to £6,000 proposed by L to be a "gross inflation" of the rent, since he had failed to take into account the fact that the figure of £850 had been assessed in 1968; (4) T had not demonstrated a case of undue hardship, and that an extension would be refused: PITTALLIS *v.* SHEREFETTIN (1986) 278 E.G. 153, C.A.

1907. Rest review—arbitration—guidelines for leave to appeal on a question of law
[Arbitration Act 1979 (c.42), s.1(4).]
The House of Lords' guidelines for granting leave to appeal against the decision of a commercial arbitration are not capable of direct application to arbitrations on rent review clauses: it is sufficient if the judge is left in real doubt whether the arbitrator has right in law.
A 25-year lease of commercial property provided for rent reviews every five years (the revised rent to be assessed in default of agreement by an independent arbitrator) but did not specify the terms of the hypothetical letting under which the revised rent was to be assessed. The active lease contained severe restrictions as to user and alienation, but by the time of the first review L had introduced a new standard form of lease containing restrictions which were much more lenient; the arbitrator found that the terms of the hypothetical letting under which the revised rent was to be assessed were those of the new standard form lease. T sought leave under s.1(3) of the Arbitration Act 1979 to appeal on the ground that the arbitrator had erred in law. *Held*, granting leave, (1) that the guidelines laid down by the House of Lords in *Pioneer Shipping* v. *B.T.B. Tioxide; the Nema* [1981] C.L.Y. 76 and in *Antaios Compania Naviera SA* v. *Salen Rederierna AB (The Antaios)* [1984] C.L.Y. 96 relating to appeals against the decisions of commercial arbitrators were not capable of direct application to arbitration on rent review clauses. It was sufficient if, as in this case, the judge was left in real doubt whether the arbitrator was right in law (*Pioneer Shipping* v. *B.T.B. Tioxide; the Nema* [1981] C.L.Y. 76 and *Antaios Compania Naviera SA* v. *Salen Rederierna AB (The Antaios)* [1984] C.L.Y. 96 considered).
LUCAS INDUSTRIES *v.* WELSH DEVELOPMENT AGENCY [1986] 3 W.L.R. 80, Sir Nicholas Browne-Wilkinson, V.-C.

1908. Rent review—arbitrator's decision—inter-related break-clause—whether time of the essence
A lease of commercial property provided for a rent review to take effect as from the end of the fourteenth year of the term, and for the revised rent to be determined if necessary by arbitration, ". . . provided always that the decision of such arbitrator shall be obtained before the expiration of the first half of the fourteenth year of the term." It was further provided that T could determine the lease at the end of fourteen years by three months notice in writing given, ". . . within the six months previous to the end of the said fourteenth year of the said term . . ." When L failed to obtain the arbitrator's decision as to the amount of the revised rent within the specified timetable, T argued

that L was debarred from operating the rent review, since the inter-relation between the machinery for determining the new rent and that for operating the break-clause was such as to displace the presumption in *United Scientific Holdings* v. *Burnley Borough Council* [1977] C.L.Y. 1758 that time was not of the essence. The judge found for T. *Held*, allowing T's appeal, that, although there was the "clearest possible inter-relation" between the timetable embodied in the rent review clause and that embodied in the break-clause this was not, in the context of the particular lease, a sufficient contra-indication to displace the presumption that time was not of the essence. First the date of the relevant event, namely the obtaining of the arbitrator's decision, was substantially outside L's control; and secondly the potential hardship to T which might otherwise arise through tardy action by L could be eliminated or substantially mitigated by T initiating such action itself: METROLANDS INVESTMENTS v. DEWHURST (J. H.) (1986) 277 E.G. 1343, C.A.

1909. Rent review—basis—"relating to rent"—whether including rent reviews—whether future rent reviews relevant
Where a rent review clause is capable of bearing more than one meaning it should be construed so as to have regard to the commercial realities of life which would require the fact that further rent reviews were to take place to be taken into account.
Two underleases requred a new rent to be fixed having regard to the terms of the underleases ". . . other than those relating to rent . . ." *Held*, on the question whether that provision required the fact that there were provisions for further future rent reviews to be disregarded, that the hypothetical lease included the terms and circumstances extant at the time of the rent review, which included the fact that there would be future rent reviews. If the clause was ambiguous the court was entitled to look at the commercial realities of the situation and the purpose of the lease and the clause. To ignore the fact that there were to be future rent reviews would be to ignore reality. Therefore the new rent would be assessed on the basis that there would be future rent reviews (*The Antaios* [1984] C.L.Y. 96 dictum applied).
MFI PROPERTIES v. BICC GROUP PENSION TRUST [1986] 1 All E.R. 974, Hoffmann J.

1910. Rent review—fixed by reference to market rent—future rent reviews
P was the lessee of a lease of office premises with a term of 25 years and rent reviews every five years. P sought a declaration that under the lease the rent to be paid at the next review was the greater of (i) the clear yearly rent and (ii) a yearly sum equal to the rent at which the property comprised in the lease could be let in the open market at the best rent reasonably obtainable subject to the provisions of the lease (other than the amounts of rent specified in a schedule to the lease) but including the provisions for revising the rent. *Held*, that the declaration would be granted.
DATASTREAM INTERNATIONAL v. OAKEEP [1986] 1 W.L.R. 404, Warner J.

1911. Rent review—fixed by reference to rack rent—future rent reviews
The underlying commercial purpose of a rent review provision is to enable a landlord to obtain the open market rental the premises could command if let on the same terms at the review date.
P was the lessee of office premises under a 35-year lease containing provision for five-yearly rent reviews. The rent payable from the review date was to be the higher of (i) the yearly rent presently payable and (ii) the rack rental value of the premises at the relevant date. The rack rent was to be calculated by reference to a hypothetical lease containing the same provisions (other than as to the yearly rent) as the actual lease. P sought a declaration that only the provisions relating to the rent actually payable at the relevant review date should be excluded from consideration. *Held*, that in the absence of clear words or special circumstances the words should not be construed so as to confer a benefit on the landlord which he could not obtain by an actual letting on the open market at the review date, the rack rent should be fixed on the basis that the hypothetical letting was on the terms of the actual lease, excluding the rent quantified and payable up to the review date but including provisions for five-yearly rent reviews.
BRITISH GAS CORP. v. UNIVERSITIES SUPERANNUATION SCHEME [1986] 1 W.L.R. 398, Browne-Wilkinson V.-C.

1912. Rent review—provision in lease—whether improvements to be disregarded
In 1973 L leased to T land for use as a golf course, upon which, pursuant to the terms of the lease, T built a clubhouse and laid out a 18-hole golf course. In 1978 an entirely new lease of the land was granted, the effect of which was to prolong the

term and to enlarge the premises to include an adjoining 9-hole golf course. The 1978 lease (as subsequently rectified by consent) contained rent review provisions, the revised rent to be the open market rental value ". . . disregarding (if applicable) those matters set out in paragraphs (a) (b) and (c) of the Landlord and Tenant Act 1974." These words had also been used in the 1973 lease. At the first review under the 1978 lease T contended that, in assessing the revised rent, the clubhouse and 9-hole course were to be disregarded as tenant's improvements, which in turn raised the question of whether the review clause was to be construed as referring to s.34 of the Act as originally enacted, or as amended by the Law of Property Act 1969 s.1(1). The judge held that, on the true construction of the review clause, the reference was to s.34 as originally enacted, that the decision in *"Wonderland" Cleethorpes Re* [1963] C.L.Y. 1973 was to be distinguished, and that the clubhouse and 9-hole course should be disregarded in assessing the revised rent. *Held,* allowing L's appeal, that (1) the review clause referred to s.34 as originally enacted; (2) upon the true construction of the review clause and of the original s.34 as incorporated in that clause, there should be disregarded only those improvements which had been carried out during the current term granted by the 1978 lease and by the tenant in his capacity as tenant of the premises demised by that lease (*"Wonderland" Cleethorpes Re* applied); (3) the 9-hole course and clubhouse should therefore be taken into account in assessing the revised rent: BRETT *v.* BRETT ESSEX GOLF CLUB (1986) 278 E.G. 1476, C.A.

1913. Rent review—service of notice—time

Whether the existence of a "deeming provision" in a rent review clause made time of the essence for the service of a notice depended on the nature of the deeming provision, and in particular whether it was a "one-way" provision in favour of one party only: if it was "one-way" time would not be of the essence.

A rent review clause provided that if the tenant should fail within a defined period to serve a counter-notice, "it shall be deemed to have agreed to pay the increased rent specified in the rent notice". On July 5, 1983 the landlords served a notice to increase the rent but the tenants did not serve a formal counter-notice within one month as required. The counter-notice was not served until December 19, 1983. The landlords claimed arrears of rent based on the increased notice claiming that the counter-notice was out of time and that time was of the essence of the contract. The tenants relied on the presumption established by *United Scientific Holdings* v. *Burnley Borough Council* [1977] C.L.Y. 1758 that time was not of the essence. Judgment was given for the tenants. *Held,* applying *Mecca Leisure* v. *Renown Investments (Holdings)* [1984] C.L.Y. 1950 that where there was a provision "one-way" in favour of one party only, as here, time for service of the counter-notice was not of the essence. Contra, where the deeming provisions were in favour of each party, as in *Henry Smith's Charity Trustees* v. *AWADA Trading and Promotion Services* [1984] C.L.Y. 1952). If the Mecca Leisure case and the Henry Smith's Charity case could not be reconciled, the former should be followed as the later decision in time.

TAYLOR WOODROW PROPERTY CO. *v.* LONRHO TEXTILES (1986) 52 P. & C.R. 28, B. A. Hytner Q.C.

1914. Rent review—terms of hypothetical lease

In 1967 L underlet to T for a term of 35 years a complex of premises including the Cafe Royal in Regent St., London W1, part of this complex being subject to an existing underlease of 54 years dating from 1949. The 1967 underlease provided for two rent reviews, at which the revised rent was to be determined in default of agreement by an independent surveyor, and was to be, ". . . the best economic open market rental value at that time of the whole of the demised premises for a term of eleven or seven years (as the case may be) and assuming the responsibility of the tenant for the repairs thereof and insurance contributions and as to user as hereinbefore provided, but disregarding the factors set out in subsections (a), (b) and (c) of s.34 of the Landlord and Tenant Act 1954." A number of questions arose as to the true construction of the review clause. *Held* that (1) the review provisions required the demised premises to be valued subject to the 1949 underlease (*Avon County Council* v. *Alliance Property Co.* [1981] C.L.Y. 1577 distinguished); (2) substantial improvements carried out by T pursuant to the Fire Precautions Act 1971 in order to obtain a fire certificate were not improvements carried out "otherwise than in pursuance of an obligation to his immediate landlord" within the meaning of s.34(c) of the 1954 Act, and were not therefore to be disregarded in assessing the revised rent; (3) T's contention that the valuer should construe narrowly a user clause in the lease, as permitting the premises to be used as a high-class restaurant only, was incorrect; and that the valuer was entitled to take into account the possibility that L would authorise other users (*Plinth Property Investments* v. *Mott, Hay and Anderson* [1979] C.L.Y. 1639 distinguished); (4) the valuer was to assume that T would be permitted to use and install only such engines and machinery as might be required for heating, lighting, ventilation, working the lifts, and for performing any other operation incidental to or connected with the business of a high-class restaurant; (5) it was not the court's function to tell the valuer what considerations to take into account, and it would therefore decline to direct the valuer to take into account, in considering the possibility that an alternative user might be authorised, the degree of likelihood that planning and listed building consent would be obtained, and the cost of necessary works of conversion and adaptation (*Crompton Group* v. *Estates Gazette* [1978] C.L.Y. 1811 applied): FORTE & CO. v. GENERAL ACCIDENT LIFE ASSURANCE (1986) 279 E.G. 1227, Peter Gibson J.

1915. Rent review—terms to be implied into hypothetical letting of bare site

A 99-year lease of a public house in Basingstoke provided for five-yearly rent reviews. In default of agreement the revised rent was to be fixed by an independent valuer acting as an expert, and was to be "the reasonable then current ground rental . . ." for the unexpired portion of the term or for a term of 20 years, whichever was the greater, on the assumption that the demised premises were a bare site only, clear of buildings, but not so as to permit consideration of a claim for a reduced rental or for a rent-free period during hypothetical development. There were to be disregarded any effect on rent of the fact of T's occupation, any goodwill enjoyed in consequence of T's business, and any increase in value attributable to any justices' on-licence. The parties were in dispute as to whether the terms and conditions of the hypothetical lease were to be the same as in the original lease, or such as the valuer should regard as reasonable for a lease of a bare site for development at the relevant date. *Held* that (1) there was no presumption that a valuer must, in the absence of contra-indication, have regard to the terms of the original lease (*Sterling Land Office Developments* v. *Lloyd's Bank* [1984] C.L.Y. 1944 and *Scottish & Newcastle Breweries* v. *Sir Richard Sutton's Settled Estates* [1985] C.L.Y. 1925 considered); (2) the covenants in the existing lease, looked at as a whole, were not appropriate to the lease of a bare site; and that the terms and conditions of the hypothetical lease should therefore be such as the valuer should in the circumstances then obtaining regard as reasonable. BASINGSTOKE AND DEANE BOROUGH COUNCIL v. HOST GROUP (1986) 279 E.G. 505, H.H. Judge Micklem.

1916. Rent review—time—time of essence

Time is of the essence when a clause in a lease specifies a date when a fair rent is to be assessed, agreed or submitted for arbitration.

A Co. let a dwelling-house to E in August 1975 for a term of seven years and thereafter from year to year, at a rent of £570 per year for the first three years and thereafter either the fair rent as at August 1, 1978 to be ascertained under the Rent Acts or if the Acts did not apply, the current market rent to be agreed or determined. A Co. did not activate the provision and sold the premises to M Co. in 1979. M Co. applied under the Acts for registration of a fair rent. E contended that M Co. was out of time. The judge found for M Co. *Held*, allowing the appeal, that parties had incorporated the Rent Acts procedure to determine a fair rent, since a rent officer was obliged to assess a fair rent as at the time of the application, he therefor had no power in September 1979 to assess what the fair rent would have been in August 1978; the application had to be made by August 1978; M Co. was not entitled to a higher rent.

MCLEOD RUSSEL (PROPERTY HOLDINGS v. EMERSON) (1986) 51 P. & C.R. 176, C.A.

1917. Rent review—whether more than one "trigger" notice could be served—whether time of the essence for reference to arbitration

A commercial lease for a 21-year term provided that L could call for a review of the rent by notice in writing given ". . . at any one time after the commencement of the fourteenth year of the term . . . ," and that, if the parties could not agree on the amount of the revised rent, L could "by notice in writing given to the Tenant within three months thereof but not otherwise . . ." refer the matter for decision by an expert. In August 1982 L's agents sent a letter stating, "We have been instructed by your landlords . . . to negotiate with you in connection with the rent review contained in your lease, which became effective as at September 29th 1982." However no agreement as to the revised rent was reached, nor was a notice to refer the matter to arbitration served within the prescribed time. L subsequently purported to serve another "trigger" notice in June 1983, followed by a notice of reference to arbitration in November 1983. T contended that the notices were invalid, and that L had irrevocably failed to comply with the requirements for operating the review clause. *Held*, giving judgment for T, that (1) the original letter of August 1982 was a valid "trigger" notice, since no reasonable reader could have construed it otherwise. (*Norwich Union Life Insurance Society* v. *Waller (Tony)* [1984] C.L.Y. 1946, *Nunes* v. *Davies, Laing and Dick* [1986] C.L.Y. 1923 and *Shirlcar Properties* v. *Heinitz* [1983] C.L.Y. 2136 considered); (2) having regard to the words "and not otherwise," time was of the essence for giving a notice of reference to arbitration, and that the notice of November 1983 was therefore out of time in relation to the "trigger" notice of August 1982 (*Drebbond* v. *Horsham District Council* [1979] C.L.Y. 1638 followed); (3) there was no sufficient reason for construing the words "at any one time" in any other than their literal sense, namely that only one "trigger" notice could be served (*Norwich Union Life Insurance Society* v. *Waller (Tony)* [1984] C.L.Y. 1946 not followed); (4) accordingly the purported "trigger" notice of June 1983 had been invalid; (5) L had accordingly lost the right to a rent review: NORWICH UNION LIFE INSURANCE SOCIETY *v.* SKETCHLEY (1986) 280 E.G. 773, Scott J.

1918. Rent review—whether permitted user to be considered unlawful in hypothetical lease
   A 20-year lease of business premises with five-yearly rent reviews contained a covenant that they should not be used otherwise than as a film or photographic studios and ancillary offices. Works were necessary in order to ensure compliance with the provisions of the Fire Precautions Act 1971, and the general scheme of the lease was that L would carry them out, but that T would reimburse L by paying ten per cent. in each of the first ten years of the lease. The rent review clause provided that the market rent was to be assessed on the basis and assumption that the fire precaution works had not been carried out on behalf of L, and would not be carried out during the whole of the five-year period. The question therefore arose as to whether (as contended by T) the revised rent was to be assessed on the basis that T would thus be in great difficulty in complying with the user covenant (since the activities there contemplated would be unlawful if the fire precaution works had not been carried out); or (as contended by L) whether it should be assessed on the alternative basis that T would be able to carry out the intended business without doing the works. *Held*, having regard to the fact that the lease evinced a clear intention that the lessee should use and be permitted to use the premises for the purposes of a film and photographic studios, that L's construction was correct (*Bovis Group Pension Fund* v. *G.C. Flooring and Furnishing* [1984] C.L.Y. 1940 and *Trust House Forte Albany Hotels* v. *Daejan Investments* [1981] C.L.Y. 1576 considered): EXCLUSIVE PROPERTIES *v.* CRIBGATE (1986) 280 E.G. 529, Knox J.

1919. Rent review—whether valuer to assume a willing lessee
   A 25-year lease of business premises provided for five-yearly rent reviews, at which the revised rent was to be the "yearly rent . . . at which the property might reasonably be expected to be let on the open market . . . for a term of 25 years with vacant possession and otherwise on the same terms and conditions of this lease, including the provisions for rent reviews." *Held*, rejecting a contention by L, that if the valuer's examination of the appropriate open market were to reveal no willing lessee at any price, he was not required by the formula to proceed on the false assumption that such a willing lessee could be found (*Evans (F.R.) (Leeds)* v. *English Electric Co.* [1978] C.L.Y. 1814 distinguished: *Law Land Co.* v. *Consumers' Association* [1980] C.L.Y. 1634 and *British Gas Corp.* v. *Universities Superannuation Scheme* [1986] C.L.Y. 1911 considered): DENNIS AND ROBINSON *v.* KIOSSOS ESTABLISHMENT (1986) 280 E.G. 200, Mr Michael Wheeler Q.C.

1920. Rent review—construction
   A lease contained a number of rent reviews, and provided that the revised rent was to be assessed as the open market rent on the assumption that the premises were ". . . vacant and let as a whole . . . for the residue of the term hereby granted, upon the terms of this lease other than as to duration and rent." The parties agreed that

this did not exclude from consideration all terms of the lease which in any way related to duration or rent, but differed as to the narrower construction to be placed upon the words. L argued that terms which quantified duration and rent were to be excluded, and that no account was therefore to be taken of future rent reviews in assessing a revised rent. T argued that the only terms to be excluded were terms giving the duration of the lease and the quantified amount of the rent initially reserved, so that future rent reviews were not excluded from consideration in assessing a revised rent. *Held*, (1) that there is no presumption as to whether a rent review clause is to be treated as included in or excluded from the terms of a hypothetical letting. (*National Westminster Bank* v. *Arthur Young McClelland Moores & Co.* [1985] C.L.Y. 86 followed); (2) a submission by T based on s.34 of the Landlord and Tenant Act 1954 failed; (3) L's construction was correct, and that the revised rent was to be determined on the assumption that the hypothetical lease contained no provision for reviewing the rent payable thereunder. EQUITY AND LAW LIFE ASSURANCE SOCIETY v. BODFIELD (1985) 276 E.G. 1157, Peter Gibson J.

1921. Rent review—construction

A lease of office accommodation at an initial yearly rent of £8,000 provided for five-yearly rent reviews, the revised rent to be "the amount (if any) by which the fair rack rental value . . . at the date of review shall exceed the sum of £8,000 or the yearly rent fixed at the previous date of review as the case may be . . . so that in no event shall the rent payable . . . after the date of review be less than the rent payable . . . before the date of review." T contended that, at the first review date, the revised rent was in effect to be the current rack rental value, but that at subsequent review dates it would comprise £8,000 plus the difference between the current rack rental value and the rent fixed at the previous review date: *i.e.* from the second review onwards the revised rent would always fall short of the actual rack rental value. The deputy judge rejected this contention and found that, in conformity to normal rent review clauses in commercial leases, the revised rent would be the current rack rental value, provided that this exceeded the rent fixed at the previous review date. *Held*, allowing T's appeal, that T's construction was correct. The words "as the case may be" did not mean whichever is the higher", nor could it be assumed that the commercial parties to a commercial lease invariably intend that the rent should not in real terms fall below the market rent originally agreed upon: PHILPOTS (WOKING) v. SURREY CONVEYANCERS (1985) 277 E.G. 61, C.A.

1922. Rent review—construction

A lease of premises situated on an industrial estate in Basingstoke provided for a rent review, at which the revised rent was to be calculated by applying a mathematical formula to the rack rent (calculated on a per square foot basis) at which "standard accommodation" could if vacant be let at the relevant time in the open market on the terms and conditions of the lease. "Standard accommodation" was defined as "a standard single-storey industrial building in the same locality as the demised premises a of like age . . ." At the time of the grant of the lease the industrial estate had comprised the subject premises, which were of 100,000 s.f. with 49 per cent. office accommodation, plus six other units of between 10,000 and 15,000 sq. ft. with only 20 per cent. office accommodation. At the review L argued that "standard accommodation" for the purposes of calculating the revised rent denoted these other units, whilst T argued that there was to be implied a term that the "standard accommodation" should be the same size as the subject premises, and that the words "in the same locality" were to be construed as denoting an area of up to three-quarters of a mile from the subject premises in which comparables could be sought. *Held*, that L's construction was correct. It accorded better with what the judge took to have been the intention of the parties, whilst T's construction involved writing words into the lease, and would not on the facts in any event throw up helpful comparables: STANDARD LIFE ASSURANCE CO. v. OXOID; OXOID v. STANDARD LIFE ASSURANCE (1986) 277 E.G. 1248, Peter Gibson J.

1923. Rent review—construction—counter-notice

A tenant will have duly exercised his right under a rent review clause to give a counter-notice if it is in sufficiently clear terms to show to the recipient that he is purporting to exercise that right.

A rent review clause provided that the revised rent was, in default of agreement, to be that specified in L's "trigger" notice or, ". . . determined at the election of the

lessee (to be made by counter-notice in writing . . . not later than the expiration of
. . . three months) by an independent surveyor." It was agreed that time was of the
essence. L's trigger notice duly specified a sum of £23,000, to which T's agent
replied, "I am instructed . . . to give you . . . formal notice that the open market
rental is £12,000 p.a. and call on you under the terms of the above lease to agree
this. Please confirm this is accepted as due notice." L argued that this was not a valid
counter-notice, since it lacked the requisite clarity and did not constitute the exercise
of an election. *Held,* that the counter-notice was valid; (1) the correct test of clarity
was whether or not it was in sufficiently clear terms to show to the recipient that the
tenant was purporting to exercise his right to give a counter-notice; (2) it must have
been clear to anyone knowing the terms of the lease that T's agent was purporting to
give formal notice (*Amalgamated Estates* v. *Joystretch Manufacturing* [1981] C.L.Y.
1589 applied; *Edlingham* v. *MFI Furniture Centres* [1981] C.L.Y. 1575 considered.)
    NUNES v. DAVIES LAING & DICK (1986) 51 P. & C.R. 310, Sir Nicholas Browne-
Wilkinson, V.-C.

1924. Rent review—construction—effect of licence to convert
    L granted to T a licence to convert premises used for retail shopping into a
dolphinarium. The only consideration for the licence was an undertaking by T to
reinstate the premises at the determination of T's licence. T argued that the
obligation to reinstate was to be taken into account in assessing the revised rent
payable pursuant to a rent review clause in T's under-lease. There was no specific
provision to this effect. The judge, giving judgment for L, held that, on the true
construction of the licence read in the light of the under-lease, the obligation to
reinstate was not to be taken into account in assessing the revised rent. *Held,*
dismissing T's appeal, that on the true construction of the deed of licence the parties
cannot have intended the covenant to reinstate to be taken into account, since T, for
whose sole benefit the licence was given, would otherwise reap an additional benefit
in the form of a reduction of the revised rent: PLEASURAMA PROPERTIES v. LEISURE
INVESTMENTS (WEST END) (1986) 278 E.G. 732, C.A.

**1925. Rent review—construction—whether provision for future reviews to be taken into
account**
    A 25-year lease provided for five yearly rent reviews, at which the revised rent was
to be calculated on the basis of an open market letting with vacant possession for 25
years, ". . . upon the terms of this lease, except as regards rent." The rent review
clause was contained in a schedule, which also provided for the initial rent payable
under the lease and contained a number of other rent-related provisions, including a
covenant to pay rent, a provision for interest on arrears, and a provision for re-entry
for non-payment. L contended that the revised rent was to be assessed at each
review upon the basis that all the provisions in the schedule, including the rent
review clause itself, were to be disregarded as being "terms . . . as regards rent";
whilst T contended that the only provision to be disregarded was that which fixed the
initial rent payable under the lease. *Held,* after consideration of a number of recent
authorities, that in the absence of clear wording to the effect that the parties
intended on review to do more than merely reflect any alteration in the value of
money or in the property market generally, T's construction was correct (*Safeway
Food Stores* v. *Banderway* [1983] C.L.Y. 2125, *National Westminster Bank* v. *Arthur
Young, McClelland Moores & Co.* [1985] C.L.Y. 86, and *Equity and Law Life
Assurance Society* v. *Bodfield* [1986] C.L.Y. 1920 distinguished; *British Gas Corp.* v.
Universities Superannuation Scheme [1986] C.L.Y. 1911 considered): ELECTRICITY
SUPPLY NOMINEES v. F.M. INSURANCE CO. (1986) 278 E.G. 523, Mr. Terence Cullen
Q.C.

1926. Rent review—hypothetical lease—length of unexpired period of term
    [Arbitration Act 1979 (c.42), s.1.] A lease provided for rent reviews after seven
years and thereafter at yearly intervals, the revised rent to be assessed upon the
assumption that the premises were being let in the open market "otherwise on
the terms and conditions of this lease." At the second review L contended that the
revised rent should be calculated as if the hypothetical lease were for a term of 22
years, whereas T argued that the hypothetical lease should be only for the 10 years
which remained unexpired from the actual term. The arbitrator having found for T,
L sought leave to appeal under the Arbitration Act 1979, and argued that the
guidelines laid down by the House of Lords in *Pioneer Shipping* v. *B.T.P. Tioxide*

("The Nema") [1981] C.L.Y. 76 did not apply with the same force to a domestic rent review arbitration as to international commercial arbitrations. *Held,* refusing leave, that (1) there is nothing in the judgments in *The Nema* to suggest that the guidelines are not of general application to all arbitrations subject to the 1979 Act; the arbitrator was plainly right, having regard to the presumption that the hypotheses upon which a revised rent is fixed should bear as close a resemblance to reality as possible: NORWICH UNION LIFE INSURANCE SOCIETY *v.* TRUSTEE SAVINGS BANK CENTRAL BOARD (1986) 278 E.G. 162, Hoffmann J.

1927. Rent review—hypothetical lease—whether rights of user and sub-letting restricted to actual tenant

A rent review clause provided that the revised rent was to be the equivalent of the rent at which the property could be let in the open market for a term equal to the unexpired residue of the lease "in the same terms in all other respects as these presents". The lease contained a covenant restricting the use of the premises to "the storage, sale and display of craftsman's work . . . in respect of such part of the demised premises as shall for the time being be occupied and used by the lessee (here meaning the British Craft Centre . . .)". A further covenant prohibited assignment, sub-letting and parting with possession, save that, ". . . only while the lessee is the British Craft Centre the lessee may share occupation of the demised premises . . . with a holding or subsidiary company". A dispute arose at the rent review as to whether, for the purposes of assessing the revised rent, the express references to the British Craft Centre were to be retained in the hypothetical lease, thereby severely restricting the class of potential lessees and consequently the rent obtainable under the hypothetical letting. *Held,* that (1) the nature of the user restriction was intended to grant a personal privilege to the British Craft Centre to use the premises for storage, sale and display of craftsman's work; and that it was not intended that anyone else should use the premises for that purpose. The hypothetical lease should accordingly contain a similar restriction; (2) however that the privilege of sharing occupation with subsidiary or holding companies was not intended to be personal to the British Craft Centre, and that the relevant clause in the hypothetical lease ought therefore not to specify the BCC, but ought to contain simply a reference to "the lessee" with the name left blank: JAMES *v.* BRITISH CRAFT CENTRE (1986) 277 E.G. 976, Scott J.

1928. Rent review—model forms

The Law Society and the Royal Institution of Chartered Surveyors have published a new edition of their *Model Forms of Rent Review Clause.* Copies of the booklet are available from Surveyors Bookshop, 12 Great George Street, London SW1P 3AD and from the Law Society, 113 Chancery Lane, London WC2A 1PL or by post from: Surveyors Publications, Norden House, Basing View, Basingstoke RG21 2HN.

1929. Repairs—submission of estimates—whether condition precedent to T's liability to reimburse L

An underlease contained no covenant by T's predecessor to execute any external or structural repairs, responsibility for which rested with L's predecessor GUS under the terms of its head-lease. A side agreement provided that T's predecessor would reimburse to GUS a proportion of the costs of such repairs, ". . . provided that GUS shall not accept any tender or estimate or enter into any contract or place any order for the carrying out of any such repairs or works without first submitting the same . . . to the Bank for approval (such approval not to be unreasonably withheld)". In due course L entered into contracts for the carrying out of extensive repair works, without ever consulting T or showing to T any tenders, estimates, orders or contracts. *Held,* that (1) upon its true construction, and having regard to the fact that the side agreement was intended to cast upon T an obligation which they did not have under the terms of the under-lease, the requirement that tenders, estimates, contracts and orders should first be submitted to T for approval was a condition precedent to T's liability to contribute to the cost of the repairs (*Finchbourne* v. *Rodrigue* [1976] C.L.Y. 1521 and *Barnes* v. *Isaacs* [1891] 1 Q.B. 417 considered); (2) that T had not waived compliance with the requirements of the clause: CIN PROPERTIES *v.* BARCLAYS BANK (1986) 277 E.G. 973, C.A.

1930. Right to buy—time for exercise of right to buy—whether possession order to be made.

See ENFIELD LONDON BOROUGH COUNCIL *v.* MCKEON, § 1645.

1931. Schoolmaster—occupation of "school" house—whether licence or tenancy
D was employed by the local authority on P's behalf as a houseparent at a school, and was granted a service licence of a furnished flat within the school building for the better performance of his duties. When D subsequently married in November 1981 and raised "the possibility of a school house," he was allowed to occupy such a house. No formal written agreement was entered into, but in correspondence and subsequent notices to quit there were regular references by the authority to a "tenancy," and also a reference to "a yearly rental of £256." When D's employment at the school terminated, P sought possession on the grounds that D occupied the house on the same basis as that on which he had previously occupied the flat, namely as a licensee only. The recorder found for P and made an order for possession. *Held*, allowing D's appeal, that (1) when residential accommodation is granted for a term at a rent with exclusive possession, the landlord providing neither attendance nor services, the grant is a tenancy save in exceptional circumstances (*Street* v. *Mountford* [1985] C.L.Y. 1893 applied); (2) neither the relationship of the parties, nor D's previous occupation of the flat (it not being suggested that his occupation of the house was a service occupancy), nor the low rent, nor the extreme informality of the paperwork, nor other features relied on by P were sufficient to render this an "exceptional case": ROYAL PHILANTHROPIC SOCIETY v. COUNTY (1985) 276 E.G. 1068, C.A.

1932. Secure tenancy—possession—death of tenant without transfer—homosexual relationship
[Housing Act 1980 (c.51), ss.30, 50(3).]
Mrs. R had been the tenant of a council house owned by H.B.C. In 1981 S had joined Mrs. R and they had lived together in the state of lesbian relationship. In February 1983 Mrs. R died leaving the house to S. H.B.C. brought possession proceedings which S defended on the basis that Mrs. R had wanted to put S's name on the rent book but had been too ill to get to the council offices. *Held*, dismissing S's appeal, that the relationship in question did not entitle S to succeed to the tenancy under s.30 and the expression "living together as husband and wife", forming part of the definition of "family" in s.50(3), did not include a homosexual relationship (*Dyson Holdings* v. *Fox* [1975] C.L.Y. 1909 considered): HARROGATE BOROUGH COUNCIL v. SIMPSON [1986] 2 F.S.R. 91, C.A.

1933. Secure tenancy—possession proceedings—whether valid notice served
[Housing Act 1980 (c.51), s.33; Secure Tenancies (Notices) Regulations 1980 (S.I. 1980 No. 1339)] S.33 of the Housing Act provides that the court cannot entertain proceedings for possession of a house let on a secure tenancy unless L has served a notice on T in prescribed form specifying the ground upon which the court is to be asked to order possession, and giving particulars of that ground. L sought possession of a council house let to T on a secure tenancy on ground 1 of Sched. 4 to the Act, namely arrears of rent. L had duly served a notice specifying the ground upon which possession was sought but, misled by the wording of the prescribed form contained in the Schedule to the Secure Tenancies (Notices) Regulations 1980, failed to give particulars of the arrears, and merely stated, "The reasons for taking this action are non-payment of rent." The registrar and judge each dismissed T's application to strike out the proceedings for possession on the grounds that no valid notice had been served. *Held*, allowing T's application and striking out the claim, that the notice was defective, since nothing short of a specification of the amount claimed as being in arrear could amount to a proper particular of the ground upon which possession was being sought (*Re O'Connor and Brewin's Arbitration* [1933] 1 K.B. 20 and *Jones* v. *Evans* [1923] 1 K.B. 12 distinguished): TORRIDGE DISTRICT COUNCIL v. JONES (1985) 276 E.G. 1253, C.A.

1934. Statutory repairing obligations—whether Crown bound
[Housing Act 1961 (c.65), ss.32, 33.] In an action brought by P for arrears of rent and possession of premises let to D, D sought to counterclaim on the grounds that P were in breach of statutory repairing obligations imposed by ss.32 and 33 of the Housing Act 1961 (now consolidated under ss.11–16 of the Landlord and Tenant Act 1985). *Held*, that (1) in the absence of express words or necessary implication, the provisions invoked by D did not bind the Crown; (*Magdalen College Case* (1615) 11 Co.Rep. 66b disapproved; *Bombay Province* v. *Bombay Municipal Corporation* [1947] C.L.C. 1655–6 considered); (2) the counterclaim should be struck out: DEPARTMENT OF TRANSPORT v. EGOROFF (1986) 278 E.G. 1361, C.A.

1935. Statutory tenancy—alternative accommodation—whether any finding of reasonableness
[Rent Act 1977 (c.42), s.98(1).]

L sought possession of a dwelling-house let on a statutory tenancy to T, on the grounds that suitable alternative accommodation was available within the meaning of s.98(1) of the Rent Act 1977. T objected that the proposed alternative accommodation was too noisy. In his judgment the judge observed that, ". . . the only matter is whether the property offered is not suitable accommodation because it is too noisy." He found that the noise was not excessive, and "therefore" made an order for possession. *Held,* allowing T's appeal and remitting the matter to the judge, that the judge had made no reference to the additional requirement of s.98 that the order for possession should be reasonable, and that it was not safe for the Court of Appeal to presume that he had had it in mind in reaching his decision (*R. v. Bloomsbury and Marylebone County Court, ex p. Blackburne* [1985] C.L.Y. 189 applied).
MINCHBURN *v.* FERNANDEZ (1986) 280 E.G. 770, C.A.

1936. Statutory tenancy—residence for landlord—requirements
[Rent Act 1977 (c.42), Sched. 15, Case 11 and Pt. V, para. (*a*).]

Schedule 15 of the Rent Act 1977 permits a landlord to recover possession if he requires the dwelling-house as his residence even though he only proposes to reside there from time to time.

L, who lived primarily in Johannesburg, sought under Case 11 of Sched. 15 to the Rent Act 1977 to recover possession of a dwelling-house let on a statutory tenancy, on the grounds that it was required as a residence for himself and his wife within the meaning of para. (*a*) of Pt. V of Sched. 15. He only needed the house to live in during business and holiday visits to the U.K. which took place once or twice a year. The judge made the order sought. *Held,* dismissing T's appeal, that the Schedule imposed no condition of permanence, and the judge was entitled to reach his conclusion on the question of fact before him.
NAISH *v.* CURZON (1986) 51 P. & C.R. 229, C.A.

1937. Statutory tenant—whether intention to return to a dwelling-house
[Rent Act 1977 (c.42), s.2(1).] T was statutory tenant of a cottage at Saffron Walden, and also owned freehold business premises nearby, which contained a flat. Upon the death of his wife in 1975 T took up residence in the flat, where his mother could assist him in looking after his small children, but visited the cottage frequently to tend to his animals and garden. In 1979 he sublet part of the cottage. In 1982 L sued for possession, on the grounds that T had ceased to occupy the cottage, and that accordingly s.2(1) of the Rent Act 1977 had no application. However the judge refused possession on the grounds that T still had a sufficient intention to return. In 1983 T removed the sub-tenant, and began to redecorate the cottage, but stopped when it appeared that L wished to modernise the premises. He did not move back in, but used the cottage primarily to store his furniture. In 1985 L again sued for possession, *inter alia,* on the same ground as before, whereupon T and his children physically moved back in. The judge found that T had abandoned his intention to return, and that his move back had come too late and was in any case a façade. He therefore ordered possession. *Held,* dismissing T's appeal, that (1) the judge had properly directed himself to the question of whether or not T had abandoned his intention to return; (2) there had been evidence on which he could properly find that that intention had been abandoned: DUKE *v.* PORTER (1986) 280 E.G. 633, C.A.

1938. Tenancy—whether determinable upon notice or upon a life
[Law of Property Act 1925 (c.20), s.149(6).]

L granted to T a tenancy of a public house for a term of three years, after which T held over from year to year. The agreement provided that the tenancy could be terminated by six months' notice in writing; but that if T died during the term of the agreement L could terminate the agreement by giving notice in writing of not less than 14 days which, if T left a widow, should not expire earlier than three months after T's death. When L gave six months' notice to quit, T claimed that the termination provisions of the agreement were such as to give rise to a term of 90 years pursuant to s.149(6) of the Law of Property Act 1925. The judge rejected T's contention, holding that T's tenancy was not granted for a life or lives or for any term of years determinable with life or lives, but was rather determinable by notice, notwithstanding that the dropping of a life was a condition precedent to the service of a 14-day notice. *Held,* dismissing T's appeal, that the judge's analysis was correct: BASS HOLDINGS *v.* LEWIS (1986) 280 E.G. 771, C.A.

1939. Third party rights—injunction. See CELSTEEL *v.* ALTON HOUSE HOLDINGS, § 1114.

1940. Waste—removal of tenant's fixtures—failure to reinstate premises—liability of director of tenant company

An act of waste was committed where a tenant removed his fixtures and fittings from the demised premises and failed to reinstate the premises thereafter.

L let a unit on an industrial estate to Pilot Chemical Co. Pilot made a number of holes in the walls of the premises to instal pipework and extractor fans. Garmanson acquired Pilot's business, including the lease, in February 1978, and thereafter went into occupation. Garmanson gave notice to L and delivered up possession of the premises on October 5, 1978. Before doing so Garmanson removed the pipework and extractor fans and other tenant's fixtures. In consequence there were a number of holes in the walls of the premises. Garmanson failed to repair the premises before giving possession to L. L sued Garmanson and its director Givertz for damages for waste. Givertz was held liable in the sum of £524·87 being the cost of repairing the holes in the walls of the premises. *Held,* dismissing Givertz's appeal, that where a director of a company gave instruction for the company to commit a tortious act he was personally liable for that act. Once affixed the fixtures became part of the freehold. By removing them Garmanson damaged the premises and injured L's reversion. At common law it was a condition of a tenant's right to remove fixtures and fittings that any damage caused in doing so would be made good. The removal of fixtures and fittings without repairing the premises afterwards was a tortious act of voluntary waste committed by Garmanson. As Givertz gave the instructions for that act to be committed he was liable (*Foley* v. *Addenbrooke* (1844) 13 M. & W. 174, *De Falbe, Re; Ward* v. *Taylor* [1901] 1 Ch. 523, *Performing Right Society* v. *Ciryl Theatrical Syndicate* [1924] 1 K.B. 1 considered).

MANCETTER DEVELOPMENTS *v.* GARMANSON [1986] 1 All E.R. 449, C.A.

LAW REFORM

1941. Civil justice review

The Lord Chancellor's Department has appointed three teams of consultants to carry out studies of commercial cases, debt, and housing cases as part of the Civil Justice Review. Their consultation papers will be published not later than January 1987.

1942. Commercial Court

The Commercial Court, the third in a series of six consultation papers, has been published. This document forms part of the Civil Justice Review and proposes an increase in the judicial strength of the Court, control of access to the Court and close monitoring of commercial cases by the Court, with a special procedure for complex cases. Copies of the Report are available from the Lord Chancellor's Department, Room 611, Trevelyan House, London SW1P 2BY. [£1·00.]

1943. Commercial Court Committee

The *Report of the Practitioner Members of the Commercial Court Committee Approved and Adopted by the Commercial Court Committee* has been published. The report calls for a number of changes in practice and procedure designed to speed up cases in the Commercial Court. Copies of the report are available from the Commercial Court, Royal Courts of Justice, Strand, London WC2.

1944. Conspiracy to defraud. See CRIMINAL LAW, § 515.

1945. Contract—implied terms—supply of services

The Law Commission has published a report which discusses the law relating to contracts for the supply of services. No recommendations for reform are made. The report, *Implied Terms in Contracts for the Supply of Services,* is available from H.M.S.O. (Law Com. No. 156, Cmnd. 9773) [£5·10.]

1946. Conveyancing—defect in title

The Law Commission has published a working paper which examines the rule of law that limits damages recoverable by a purchaser of land when the vendor cannot fulfil his contractual obligation to show good title. Working Paper No. 98, *Transfer of Land: The Rule in Bain* v. *Fothergill* is available from H.M.S.O. (ISBN 0 730179 5) [£1·75].

1947. Criminal justice
The Government has published a White Paper, *Criminal Justice: Plans for Legislation* which details proposals to be set out in a new Criminal Justice Bill. Matters discussed include sentencing, compensation for victims, extradition, fraud trials and jury reform. The White Paper, Cmnd. 9658, is available from H.M.S.O. [£2·80].
The Home Office has published two consultative documents associated with the white paper on criminal justice legislation. They deal with the distribution of business between the Crown Court and Magistrates Courts and with custodial sentences for young offenders. Both documents are available, free of charge, from the Home Office, Queen Anne's Gate, London SW1H 9AT, rooms 1102 and 323 respectively.

1948. Custody
The Law Commission has published a working paper entitled *Family Law Review of Child Law: Custody*. This is the second in a series of consultative papers about the law relating to the upbringing of children. It considers the statutory powers of the courts concerning the custody of children and makes suggestions for reform. Comments should be sent by December 31, 1986 to Miss J. C. Hearn, The Law Commission, Conquest House, 37/38 John Street, Theobalds Road, London WC1N 2BQ. Working Paper No. 96 is available from H.M.S.O. (ISBN 0 11 730177 9) [£7·50.]

1949. Fraud trials
The Report of the Fraud Trials Committee was published on January 10, 1986. The main emphasis of the committee's findings is concerned with large scale or complex fraud cases. Fundamental changes in the law are called for. The report is available from H.M.S.O. [£9·00].

1950. Illegitimacy
A second report on illegitimacy has been published by the Law Commission. The Commission makes recommendations to remove discrimination against children born to parents who are not married to each other. A draft Family Law Reform Bill is annexed to the report. Law Com. No. 157 (Cmnd. 9913) is available from H.M.S.O. [£6·50.]

1951. Land mortgages
The Law Commission has published a working paper on land mortgages. The Commission proposes that existing methods of mortgaging interests in land should be abolished and replaced by a single "formal land mortgage." Copies of the report are available from H.M.S.O. (Working Paper No. 99, ISBN 0 11 730180 9) [£9·90.]

1952. Landlord and tenant—distress for rent
The Law Commission has published a working paper which examines the law relating to distress for rent. The Law Commission provisionally recommends abolition but seeks the widest possible range of views on all aspects of reform. Working Paper No. 97 is available from H.M.S.O. (ISBN 0 11 730178 7) [£4·75.]

1953. Leases—privity of contract
The Law Commission has published a working paper (No. 95) which examines the extent of the liabilities of parties to leases. The paper is entitled *Privity of Contract and Estate: Duration of Liability of Parties to Leases* and is available from H.M.S.O. (ISBN 0 11 730176 0) [£3·35.]

1954. Legal aid
The National Consumer Council has published its response to the report of the Legal Aid Scrutiny Review Team. *The Reform of Publicly Funded Legal Services in England and Wales* is available from Legal Aid Reform, National Consumer Council, 20 Grosvenor Gardens, London SW1W 0DH [£2.50.]
The report of the recent efficiency scrutiny of legal aid was published by the Lord Chancellor on June 27, 1986. Comments on the recommendations should be sent to the Lord Chancellor's Department, Room 316, Neville House, Page Street, London SW1 to arrive by September 30, 1986. Copies of the report are available from the Lord Chancellor's Department, priced £5.

1955. Parole evidence rule
The Law Commission's report on the parole evidence rule was published on January 9, 1986. No recommendations for reform were made. The report is available from H.M.S.O. (Law Com. No. 154) (Cmnd. 9700) [£3·90].

1956. Personal injuries litigation
The Lord Chancellor's Department has published a consultation booklet reporting on the results of a study of personal injuries litigation. The document finds the present system inefficient, slow and expensive and recommends a series of proposals to remedy these factors. *Civil Justice Review. Personal Injuries Litigation* is available from the Lord Chancellor's Department, Room 604, Neville House, Page Street, London SW1P 4LS. [£1].

1957. Prostitution
The Criminal Law Revision Committee has published its *Seventeenth Report on Prostitution.* In consultation with the Policy Advisory Committee on Sexual Offences the CLRC makes recommendations about the law on prostitution relating to off-street offences. The report is available from H.M.S.O. (Cmnd. 9688) [£3·90].

1958. Psychopathic offenders
The Department of Health and Social Security and the Home Office have issued a joint consultation document on the question of tighter controls over the discharge from hospital of offenders suffering psychopathic disorder. *Offenders Suffering from Psychopathic Disorder* is available from the Home Office, C3 Division, 50 Queen Anne's Gate, London SW1A 0AA. Tel: 01 213-3206; or D.H.S.S., MHC Division, Room C516, Alexander Fleming House, Elephant and Castle, London SE1 6BY.

1959. Reparation
The Home Office has published a consultative document on the subject of reparation by offenders to the victims of their crimes. *Reparation—a Discussion Document* is available from Room 314, Home Office. 50 Queen Anne's Gate, London SW1H 9AT.

1960. Restrictive covenants
The Conveyancing Standing Committee has published a consultative paper entitled *What Should We Do About Old Restrictive Covenants?* Copies of the paper and further information are available from Caroline Lonsdale, Secretary of the Conveyancing Standing Committee, Conquest House, 37/38 John Street, Theobalds Road, London WC1N 2BQ.

1961. Rights of access to neighbouring land
Rights of Access to Neighbouring Land are the subject of a Law Commission report (Law Com. 151) published on December 19, 1985. The Commission recommends that property owners should be allowed access to next door properties to carry out repairs to their own property. The report is available from H.M.S.O. (Cmnd. 9692) [£6·30].

1962. Small claims in county courts
The *Lord Chancellor's Department Civil Justice Review Consultation Paper: Small Claims* has been published as part of the Civil Justice Review. The consultation paper is based upon a study of the small claims system which was carried out for the Lord Chancellor's Department by Touche Ross Management Consultants. The consultation paper makes recommendations aimed at reducing delay and improving consistency in the way cases are handled. Copies of the consultation paper are available from the Lord Chancellor's Department, Room 604, Neville House, Page Street, London SW1P 4LS. [£1.]

1963. Social security—abolition of independent appeals
The Council on Tribunals has published a special report criticising the Government's proposal to abolish the right of independent appeal. *Social Security—Abolition of Independent Appeals under the proposed Social Fund* is available from H.M.S.O. (Cmnd. 9722) [£1·55].

1964. Sports grounds—crowd safety and control. See PUBLIC ENTERTAINMENTS, § 2746.

1964a. Unsecured creditors—remedies
The Institute of Law Research and Reform at the University of Alberta, Canada has published a research paper on the operation of the unsecured creditors' remedies system in Alberta.

LEGAL AID

1965. Advice and assistance
LEGAL ADVICE AND ASSISTANCE (AMENDMENT) REGULATIONS 1986 (No. 275) [80p], made under the Legal Aid Act 1974 (c.4), s.20; operative on March 12, 1986; amend

S.I. 1980 No. 1898 by providing that powers exercisable under the Regs. by the general committees of the Law Society shall be exercised instead by the secretary of each legal aid area; provision is made for appeals against refusal of applications for assistance by way of representation and dependants' allowances in assessing eligibility for advice and assistance is reduced to 25 per cent. above supplementary benefit levels.

LEGAL ADVICE AND ASSISTANCE AT POLICE STATIONS (REMUNERATION) (AMENDMENT) REGULATIONS 1986 (No. 445) [40p], made under the Legal Aid Act 1974 (c.4), s.20(1) and the Legal Aid Act 1982 (c.44), s.1; operative on April 1, 1986; increase the rates of payment for the remuneration of solicitors who give assistance to suspects at police stations.

LEGAL ADVICE AND ASSISTANCE AT POLICE STATIONS (REMUNERATION) (AMENDMENT) (No. 2) REGULATIONS 1986 (No. 1559) [80p], made under the Legal Aid Act 1974 (c.4), s.20(1), and the Legal Aid Act 1982 (c.44), s.1; operative on October 1, 1986; increase the rates of payment for the remuneration which may be paid to solicitors who advise suspects at police stations.

LEGAL ADVICE AND ASSISTANCE (FINANCIAL CONDITIONS) REGULATIONS 1986 (No. 643) [45p], made under the Legal Aid Act 1974 (c.4), ss.1, 20; operative on March 27, 1986; increases disposable capital limit for assistance by way of representation under the 1974 Act to £3,000 and the limit for other assistance to £800.

1966. Annual reports

The 35th Annual Reports of the Law Society and the Lord Chancellor's Legal Aid Advisory Committee have been published. The reports are available from H.M.S.O. (HC 156) [£12·30].

The 36th Annual Reports of the Law Society and the Lord Chancellor is Legal Aid Advisory Committee for 1985–86 have been published. Copies are available from H.M.S.O. (HC87) [£12·50.]

1967. Awards of costs—principles

[Legal Aid Act 1974 (c.4), s.13.] The Court has no power, where it has ordered an unsuccessful first defendant to pay the costs of the second defendant, to order that those costs be paid out of the Legal Aid fund: LANDAU *v.* PURVIS, *The Times,* August 12, 1986, G. Godfrey Q.C.

1968. Certificate—ambit—whether solicitor entitled to payment from client

[Legal Aid (General) Regulations 1980 (S.I. 1980 No. 1894, reg. 65.]

A solicitor is entitled to receive payment from his client for work undertaken by him on his client's instructions outside the ambit of a legal aid certificate granted to his client.

P was sued by a bank. In the course of the action, P failed to comply with an order of the court and in consequence was found to be in contempt. P consulted D, a firm of solicitors, in connection with the action against him. P was granted a legal aid certificate to apply within the proceedings between the bank and himself to purge his contempt. P's application to purge his contempt was unsuccessful. D carried out other work on P's instructions in connection with the action that P knew was not covered by the legal aid certificate and for which P expected to be charged privately. After a dispute between P and D, P commenced an action against D seeking, *inter alia,* a declaration that D was precluded from receiving payment for work carried out outside the ambit of the legal aid certificate by virtue of regulation 65 of the Legal Aid (General) Regulations 1980. Regulation 65 provides "Where a certificate has been issued in connection with any proceedings" . . . D . . . "shall not receive or be a party to any payment for work done in those proceedings during the currency of that certificate (whether within the scope of the certificate or otherwise) except such payments as may be made out of the fund". P conceded that after his unsuccessful application the legal aid certificate ceased to have any force but argued that it remained current as it had not been discharged. *Held,* dismissing P's appeal, that there was no obligation upon D to seek a discharge of the legal aid certificate. The certificate was not a current certificate once it ceased to have any force. The word "proceedings" in regulation 65 was limited in its meaning to the proceedings for which the legal aid certificate was issued, namely, to proceedings for P to apply to purge his contempt. Therefore, regulation 65 did not prohibit D from receiving payment from P for the work carried out in the action generally that did not form part of P's application to purge his contempt (*Mills* v. *Mills* [1963] C.L.Y. 2747 applied).

LITTAUR *v.* STEGGLES PALMER [1986] 1 W.L.R. 287, C.A.

1969. Costs—discretion of court—both parties assisted—considerations

[Legal Aid Act 1974 (c.4), s.2(5)(*b*); Supreme Court Act 1981 (c.54), s.18(1)(*f*); Legal Aid (General) Regulations (S.I. 1980 No. 1894), reg. 119.] The county court judge had heard two applications in divorce proceedings relating to custody of the two children and to W's application for ancillary relief. As both H and W were legally aided and both had succeeded and failed in their applications approximately to the same extent the judge made no order for costs save legal aid taxation. Subsequently, it became apparent that H's share in the equity of the matrimonial home was subject to the statutory charge and would thereby be diminished by some £2,000. Accordingly on H's application the judge reconsidered the costs position by endorsing the original order with a further order that W should pay H £1,000 towards his costs. W, having been refused leave by the judge applied to the Court of Appeal. *Held,* allowing W's application for leave and the substantive appeal, that the present case was one of the unusual cases where the court was entitled to hear the application as the judge had fallen into error by using the device of varying the costs order so as to readjust the property order. That was outside his power and he had acted in excess of his jurisdiction; for by s.2(5)(*b*) the fact that a person was or was not assisted was not a factor to be taken into account so that the exercise of the judge's discretion should follow normal principles. Moreover, the fact that the source of such costs was the equity in the former home was wrong by reason of reg. 119 (*Scherer* v. *Counting Instruments* [1978] C.L.Y. 2341, *Infabrics* v. *Jaytex* [1985] C.L.Y. 425 and *Marshall* v. *Levine* [1985] C.L.Y. 2637 considered): PARRY *v.* PARRY [1986] 16 Fam. Law 211, C.A.

1970. Criminal proceedings

LEGAL AID IN CRIMINAL PROCEEDINGS (COSTS) (AMENDMENT) REGULATIONS 1986 (No. 273) [40p], made under the Legal Aid Act 1974 (c.4), ss.30(9A), 39; operative on March 12, 1986; amend S.I. 1982 No. 1197 so that remuneration may be paid for work done by solicitors before the making of a legal aid order in respect of proceedings in magistrates' courts and enabling the Lord Chancellor to make or intervene in an appeal to the High Court from any decision of a taxing master.

LEGAL AID IN CRIMINAL PROCEEDINGS (COSTS) (AMENDMENT) (NO. 2) REGULATIONS 1986 (No. 444) [£1·35], made under the Legal Aid Act 1974 (c.4), s.39; operative on April 1, 1986; increase rates of remuneration for legal aid work in criminal proceedings done on or after April 1, 1986.

LEGAL AID IN CRIMINAL PROCEEDINGS (COSTS) (AMENDMENT) (NO. 3) REGULATIONS 1986 (No. 1515) [£1·90], made under the Legal Aid Act 1974 (c.4), s.39; operative on October 1, 1986, introduce a new system of prescribed standard fees for certain items of work done by junior counsel in the Crown Court.

LEGAL AID IN CRIMINAL PROCEEDINGS (COSTS) (AMENDMENT) (NO. 4) REGULATIONS 1986 (No. 1835) [80p], made under the Legal Aid Act 1974 (c.4), s.39; operative on November 21, 1986; amended S.I. 1982 No. 1197.

LEGAL AID IN CRIMINAL PROCEEDINGS (GENERAL) (AMENDMENT) REGULATIONS 1986 (No. 274) [40p], made under the Legal Aid Act 1974, ss.11, 39; amend S.I. 1968 No. 1231 reducing dependants' allowances applied in assessing eligibility for legal aid in criminal proceedings to 25 per cent. above supplementary benefit limits.

1971. "Date fixed for trial"—review. See R. *v.* BURY JUSTICES, *ex p.* N, § 630.

1972. Determination of applications

LEGAL AID (GENERAL) (AMENDMENT) REGULATIONS 1986 (No. 272) [£1·35], made under the Legal Aid Act 1974 (c.4), s.20; operative on March 12, 1986; amend S.I. 1980 No. 1894 so that the power to determine applications for legal aid and to issue, amend, revoke, discharge certificates shall be exercised by the secretary of each legal aid area.

1973. Error on face of certificate—effect

Where P's legal aid certificate named D correctly but with the wrong initials, and the mistake had been noticed by D but not by anyone else, and D had not revealed it, D's conduct was sufficiently unattractive to prevent an immediate award of costs, and the proper award was D's costs not to be enforced without leave (*R. & T. Thew* v. *Reeves* [1981] C.L.Y. 1604 considered): BROWN *v.* BLACKIE, (1986) 136 New L.J. 632, Benet Hytner Q.C.

1974. Law reform. See LAW REFORM.

1975. Legal Aid (Scotland) Act 1986 (c.47)
This Act establishes the Scottish Legal Aid Board and the Scottish Legal Aid Fund, makes provision in connection with the availability of criminal legal aid in Scotland and repeals and re-enacts with modifications certain enactments relating to legal aid and to advice and assistance in Scotland.
The Act received the Royal Assent on July 25, 1986.

1976. Means and merits test
LEGAL AID (GENERAL) (AMENDMENT) (NO. 2) REGULATIONS 1986 (No. 1186) [45p], made under the Legal Aid Act 1974 (c.4), s.20; operative on August 1, 1986; provide that the means and merits tests and the contribution conditions which would otherwise apply under the 1974 Act are excluded in respect of persons who apply under the Hague and European Conventions under ss.3(2) and 14(2) of the Child Abduction and Custody Act 1985 and who require legal aid in connection with those applications.

1977. Regulations
LEGAL AID (GENERAL) (AMMEDENT) (NO. 3) REGULATIONS 1986 (No. 2135) [45p], made under the Legal Aid Act 1974 (c.4), s.20; operative on January 1, 1987; modify S.I. 1980 No. 1894 in connection with the means and merits tests and the contribution conditions

1978. Resources
LEGAL AID (ASSESSMENT OF RESOURCES) (AMENDMENT) REGULATIONS 1986 (No. 276) [40p], made under the Legal Aid Act 1974 (c.4), ss.11, 20; operative on March 12, 1986; amend S.I. 1980 No. 1630 by reducing dependants' allowances in assessing eligibility for legal aid to 25 per cent. above supplementary benefit limits.

1979. Revocation of certificate—validity of certificate
[Legal Aid Act 1974 (c.4), ss.28 and 31; Legal Aid Act 1982 (c.44), s.9; Legal Aid in Criminal Proceedings (General) Regulations 1968 (S.I. 1968 No. 1231), regs. 2 and 31.] D received from the magistrates' court a legal aid order bearing a facsimile of the clerk of the court's signature, D having applied for legal aid to appeal to the Crown Court against a conviction. After counsel was instructed, magistrates purported to revoke the certificate on the ground that it had been sent in error and had never been considered. D's solicitor was told that a Crown Court judge would consider whether legal aid should be granted and was later told that it had been refused. *Held,* quashing the purported revocation that (1) only the magistrates' court could deal with an application for legal aid for an appeal to the Crown Court; (2) a certificate could only be revoked on the grounds provided by statute. The ground stated was not one of the statutory grounds; (3) although the magistrates could have sought a declaration that the legal aid order was invalid, they had not done so and it therefore was valid and effective: R. *v.* HUNTINGDON MAGISTRATES' COURT, *ex p.* YAPP [1986] Crim.L.R. 689, D.C.

1980. Scrutiny report. See LAW REFORM, § 1954.

1981. Statutory charge—divorce settlement—whether exemption
In a divorce suit, W accepted a sum of £7,000 from H in commutation of all her rights to future maintenance. She claimed that this should be regarded as income and not capital, and was therefore exempt from the Legal Aid charge. *Held,* that to say that this sum was a periodical payment of maintenance would strain the use of ordinary language. It should be regarded as "property recovered or preserved", and was therefore subject to the statutory charge: STEWART *v.* THE LAW SOCIETY, *The Times,* July 19, 1986, Latey J.

1982. Taxation—separate representation—Court of Appeal. See D (A MINOR), *Re,* § 2163.

LIBEL AND SLANDER

1983. Defamation—comment by servant or agent—whether defence available
[Aus.] [Defamation Act 1974 (Australia) (No. 18 of 1974), ss.9(1)(2), 33(1)(2).]
L, the captain of the West Indies cricket team, sued S, the proprietor of a daily newspaper, for defamation over suggestions in an article that the result of a match had been fixed. L pleaded four imputations defamatory to himself, namely that he had committed, or was suspected of having committed in the past, and that he was prepared to commit, or was suspected of being prepared in the future to commit, a

fraud on the public for financial gain in pre-arranging in concert with other persons the result of a cricket match. S denied that the article was defamatory and alternatively relied on the defence under s.33(1) of the 1974 Act of comment by its servant or agent. S pleaded in answer to an interrogatory that it did not intend by publication of the article to convey any of the imputations pleaded. At trial the judge withdrew the defence from the jury which awarded L \$100,000 damages. The Court of Appeal allowed the appeal. *Held,* allowing L's appeal, that the words of comment in the article were capable of being defamatory as pleaded, and the jury was entitled to find that S in publishing the article had made the defamatory imputations; the defence of comment under s.33(1) would be defeated under subsection (2) unless S's servant or agent held the opinion represented by defamatory imputations; the answer to the interrogatory was an admission that the writer of the article did not hold that opinion; although the trial judge had improperly withdrawn the defence from the jury, it could not have succeeded; the jury's verdict would be restored.

LLOYD *v.* SYME (DAVID) & Co. [1986] 2 W.L.R. 69, P.C.

1984. Defamation—defence of justification—particulars to be pleaded

Where a defendant in a defamation action relies on the defence of justification the meaning that he seeks to justify must be clearly and explicitly pleaded in his defence.

P lived with an Italian man in London who was alleged to be a member of a right wing terrorist group and responsible for the bombing of Bologna railway station in 1980, the murder of an Italian police constable and several bank robberies. The man was arrested outside P's flat in January 1983 and extradited at the request of the Italian authorities in early 1985. In January 1983 and February 1983 the *Daily Mail* and *News of the World* respectively published stories about P and the Italian man. P claimed the *Daily Mail* story was defamatory in that it alleged she lived with a man she knew to be a ruthless killer, had assisted in a bank robbery in Spain, had assisted in the commission of various grave criminal offences and lied about the extent of her knowledge of the man. P claimed the *News of the World* article was defamatory in that it alleged she knowingly assisted terrorists and lied about the extent of her knowledge. Two years after their defences had been served the defendants sought leave to amend their defence to rely upon a plea of justification. Leave was granted and the defendants indicated that the extent of the justification relied upon was that P was careless about the friends she kept. Later it became apparent that the defendants' justification was put in the form that P knew the man was a terrorist. P unsuccessfully appealed against the order giving leave to amend and thereafter appealed to the Court of Appeal. *Held,* that where a defendant seeks to rely upon a defence of justification the defendant must make it clear to the plaintiff precisely what defamatory meaning he claims is justified. There was no special rule applicable to defamation cases that a defendant need not particularise fully in his defence the nature of the justification upon which he seeks to rely. Appeal allowed in part to put defendants' on terms as to further amendments and particulars to be supplied. (*Slim v. Daily Telegraph* [1968] C.L.Y. 2231 considered).

LUCAS-BOX *v.* NEWS GROUP NEWSPAPERS [1986] 1 All E.R. 177, C.A.

1985. Defamation—qualified privilege

[Aus.] [Defamation Act 1974 (Australia) (No. 18 of 1974), s.22(1).]

A was the trainer of a rugby league team. M published an article written by one of its journalists criticising A's methods and recommending his dismissal. A instituted proceedings for defamation and the jury found for A and assessed damages at \$60,000. The judge, who by s.23 of the 1974 Act had to determine the issue of qualified privilege, upheld the defence of qualified privilege under s.22 and gave judgment for M. A's appeal to the Court of Appeal was dismissed. *Held,* on appeal, that (1) "information" in s.22(1)(*a*) and (*b*) included both statements of fact and comment and "an interest" in s.22(1)(*a*) was to be construed in a wider sense than that given to interest in the subject matter that was an ingredient of qualified privilege at common law and, in the broad sense used in para. (*a*), it included the interest readers could have in the performance and training of a rugby league team; therefore M had satisfied the requirements of s.22(1)(*a*) and (*b*); (2) allowing the appeal, that since M was a company it could only act through its servants and agents, and in deciding whether its conduct in publishing the article was reasonable under s.22(1)(*c*) its acts were those of the journalist it employed; the journalist had failed to take reasonable care to check his facts and M, being bound by this, had failed to discharge the onus on it under s.22(1)(c) and so failed to establish the defence of qualified privilege.

AUSTIN *v.* MIRROR NEWSPAPERS [1986] 2 W.L.R. 57, P.C.

1986. Defamation—standard of proof—direction to jury

It is not generally necessary to direct the jury that the more serious the allegation made, the higher the standard of proof required, save in unusual cases (*R. v. Secretary of State for the Home Department, ex p. Khawaja* [1983] C.L.Y. 1908, *R. v. Hampshire County Council, ex p. Ellerton* [1984] C.L.Y. 1548, *Sutherland v. Stopes* [1925] A.C. 47 considered): LAWRENCE *v.* CHESTER CHRONICLE, *The Times*, February 8, 1986, C.A.

1987. Defence—justification—exemplary damages

The pleadings held sufficient allegations to enable D to plead justification, notwithstanding that part of D's case was not proved. On a separate point, where a libel was published it was not the law that exemplary damages could only be awarded if D had the necessary guilty mind before that publication—there may be a subsequent occasion with reference to further publication: MAXWELL *v.* PRESSDRAM (No. 2), *The Times*, November 22, 1986, C.A.

1988. False innuendo—particulars of justification—meaning

[Defamation Act 1952 (c.66), s.5.]

Where a plaintiff complains that parts of a publication are defamatory by way of false innuendo, the defendant is entitled to plead that in their context the words are true or are fair comment, and particulars of justification should not be struck out where the defendant relies on other words in the publication as giving the words a different meaning in their full context.

Per curiam: A defendant who pleads justification must state the meaning which he seeks to justify. In future where differences of meaning are proposed by the parties, the issues as to the possible meanings of the words complained of will be confined to those pleaded (*Lucas-Box* v. *News Group Newspapers* [1986] 2 C.L. 165a applied).

P claimed damages for libel from D in respect of the whole of one article and parts of two others published in a newspaper. P pleaded that the words meant that P4 had deceived or negligently misled shareholders, investors and the public as to the operation of P1, P2, P3, companies run but not controlled by him. D pleaded fair comment and justification, the particulars of which tended to support the whole of the three articles including assertions in the latter two of which no complaint was made but which bore the same innuendo as those complained of. P applied to strike out those particulars which supported assertions of which they did not complain. The master dismissed the application, and the judge in chambers dismissed P's appeal. P's further appeal was dismissed. *Held,* that where a plaintiff complained that the natural and ordinary meaning of selected words in a publication was defamatory of him, and pleaded the meaning which he said they bore by way of false innuendo, the defendant was entitled to plead that in their context the words complained of were true or fair comment. Where a publication contained several defamatory comments which had a common sting, and the plaintiff complained of one or more, but not all of them, the defendant was entitled to justify the sting or assert fair comment. In either case the particulars of such pleas could be derived from parts of the publication of which the plaintiff did not complain in so far as they were relevant to the meaning of the words complained of or to the sting of the alleged libel, provided that having regard to the facts of the case and the attitude of the plaintiff such particulars were not oppressive. But where separate and distinct defamatory allegations were made, if the plaintiff selected some only for complaint, the defendant was not entitled either at common law or under s.5 of the Defamation Act 1952 to assert the truth of others by way of justification. Whether a defamatory statement was separate and distinct from other defamatory statements in the same publication was a question of fact and degree in each case. Accordingly since the allegations in the parts of the second and third articles of which P did not complain were not separate and distinct allegations from those complained of, D were entitled to support their pleas of justification and fair comment with particulars supporting the other allegations, and none of the particulars pleaded should be struck out (*S and K Holdings* v. *Throgmorton Publications* [1972] C.L.Y. 2029 applied; *Brembridge* v. *Latimer* (1864) 12 W.R. 878 10 L.T. 816; 4 N.R. 285 and dictum of Blackburn J. in *Watkin* v. *Hall* (1868) L.R. 3 Q.B. 396, 402 disapproved; *Templeman* v. *Jones* [1984] N.Z.L.R. 448 considered).

POLLY PECK (HOLDINGS) *v.* TRELFORD [1986] 2 W.L.R. 845, C.A.

1989. Injunction—justification

A plaintiff will not normally be awarded an injunction to restrain a newspaper from repeating allegedly defamatory statements where the newspaper claims justification, unless (a) the remarks are manifestly untrue, or (b) the newspaper does not intend to repeat allegations it acknowledges are unjustifiable (*Hubbard* v. *Pitt* [1975] C.L.Y. 2453 applied) AL-FAYED *v.* THE OBSERVER, *The Times*, July 14, 1986, Mann J.

1990. Justification—plea based on "common sting"—interlocutory injunction

The principle that an injunction would not be granted to restrain publication of an alleged defamatory article where the defendant intends to advance a plea of justification extends to the situation where the defendant intends to justify the common sting of several allegations, including the one complained of, even though he might not be able to prove the particular facts contained in the allegation.

D, published *Woman's Own,* and published a trailer for an article, written by the D2, about P. She told them she would object to any publication. D, wrote saying that they would justify anything they published. In the following week's issue, they published an article purporting to be an account of P's life with her husband containing allegations about her sexual behaviour. She objected to an allegation that she had committed adultery with a friend of her husband, the president of a foreign nation. D were not then able to advance a plea of justification, and she obtained an injunction preventing further publication. Three days later D applied for the discharge of the injunction on the basis that they intended to justify the sting of the article as a whole. The application was refused. *Held,* allowing D's appeal, that since D intended to justify the common sting of the article, namely that P was promiscuous, even though they might not be able to prove the particular facts contained in the specific allegation, the injunction should be discharged (*Bonnard* v. *Perryman* [1891] 2 Ch. 269, C.A. and *Polly Peck (Holdings)* v. *Trelford* [1986] C.L.Y. 1988 applied).

KHASHOGGI *v.* I.P.C. MAGAZINES [1986] 1 W.L.R. 1412, C.A.

LIEN

1991. Subrogation—unpaid vendor's lien—part of purchase price lent to purchaser by plaintiff—failure by purchaser to repay loan

D was the purchaser of a property. P were a firm of solicitors acting for D in the purchase. On the day fixed for completion P received a cheque drawn upon D's bank account for part of the purchase price. D informed P that the account held insufficient funds to meet the cheque that day but that there would be sufficient funds by the time the cheque was presented to D's bank for payment. P agreed on the faith of that assurance to complete the transaction with banker's drafts drawn on P's bank to the same value as the cheque. The transaction was duly completed but D's cheque was dishonoured. D subsequently went into receivership. The property in question was sold. P claimed to have a lien over the net proceeds of the sale having acquired by subrogation the right to a lien vested in the vendor of the property. The receiver claimed that the arrangement between P and D was no more than one of a loan on an unsecured basis until D's cheque was cleared and in consequence P's only rights were those of a holder of a cheque, *i.e.* an unsecured creditor. *Held,* that where a third party to a contract for the sale of a property acting on behalf of and at the request of the purchaser uses his own money in paying part of the purchase price due under the contract, the third party is prima facie entitled by subrogation to the vendor's lien in respect of the property. The arrangement between P and D was not inconsistent with P acquiring the vendor's lien over the property. The fact that the question of security for the loan was neither raised nor considered by either party did not lead to the conclusion that it was the common intention of the parties that P should not be subrogated to the vendor's lien. The application of the doctrine of subrogation would not lead to an unjust result in the circumstances and accordingly P's claim succeeded (*Orakpo* v. *Manson Investments* [1977] C.L.Y. 1977 considered, *Paul* v. *Speirway* [1976] C.L.Y. 2860 distinguished): BOODLE, HATFIELD AND CO. *v.* BRITISH FILMS 1986 PCC 176, Nicholls J.

LIMITATION OF ACTIONS

1992. Accrual of cause of action—building defectively constructed—no "injury" to property

[Can.] A contracted with the various defendants for various aspect of the construction of a building in early 1978. By August that year the building was completed and occupied by A. At that time, defects in the construction existed for which A sued the defendants in 1982. The defendants applied to dismiss the action on the ground that it was statute-barred under local legislation. *Held,* that the action was not "for damages in respect of injury to . . . property", for which a two year limitation period was provided. It was therefore an action not specifically provided for in the local limitation Act, to which a six year period applied. In plain language, the building had not been "injured". The cause of action accrued when the building was completed and turned over to A, no actual injury being required: ALBERNI DISTRICT CREDIT UNION *v.* CAMBRIDGE PROPERTIES, 65 B.C.L.R. 297, British Columbia C.A.

1993. Accrual of cause of action—defective foundations in house—negligence

In a negligence action against a council for defective house foundations, the cause of action does not arise until the condition of the house is such as to cause danger to the health or safety of the occupiers, which is when the council is in breach of its duty.

In 1975 P purchased a house built in 1964. In 1976, following a drought, cracks appeared as a result of subsidence caused by defective foundations. P claimed against D council for the negligence of their predecessors in failing to inspect the foundations. The official referee held that the cause of action occurred outside the limitation period. *Held,* allowing the appeal, that until the condition of the house gave rise to danger the authority was not in breach of a duty; the cause of action did not arise therefore until some time after the drought of 1976 (*Pirelli General Cable Works* v. *Oscar Faber & Partners* [1983] C.L.Y. 2216 distinguished; dicta in *Ketteman* v. *Hansel Properties* [1984] C.L.Y. 2675 applied).

JONES *v.* STROUD DISTRICT COUNCIL [1986] 1 W.L.R. 1141, C.A.

1994. Accrual of time—whether continuing defence

[Limitation Act 1939 (c.21), s.21.] D, a potential defendant, was entitled to rely on an absolute limitation under s.21 of the Limitation Act 1939. After the limitation period accrued, the Act was repealed. *Held,* that the repeal did not affect limitation defences that had already accrued, and D was still protected: ARNOLD *v.* CENTRAL ELECTRICITY GENERATING BOARD, *The Times,* October 20, 1986, C.A.

1995. Carriage by road—whether goods "lost"

[Marine Insurance Act 1906 (c.41), s.57(1); Convention on the Carriage of Goods by Road, Articles 20, 32.] Art. 32 of the Convention on the Carriage of Goods by Road provides that when goods are damaged in transit, the limitation period of one year for claims starts to run from the date of delivery. When there is a total loss of goods in transit, and in the absence of other agreement, a similar limitation period starts to run from the 60th day from the date when the carrier took over the goods. "Total loss" means the same as "actual total loss" in s.57(1) of the Marine Insurance Act 1906: the concept of "constructive total loss" has no place in the Convention. A written claim suspends the limitation period until the carrier has rejected the claim. Art. 20 provides that the non-delivery of the goods within 30 days of the agreed date of delivery, or, in the absence of other agreement, within 60 days of the carrier taking them over, shall be conclusive evidence of their loss. If goods in transit are badly damaged, but still retain a salvage value, this is a case of damage rather than loss: however, the goods are conclusively deemed to be "lost" if they are not delivered within the time limit. The word "claim" in Art. 32 includes a general intimation of intention to hold the carrier liable, and a written unrejected claim suspends the limitation period as soon as it begins to run, if it has not already begun: ICI FIBRES *v.* MAT TRANSPORT, *The Financial Times,* December 2, 1986, Staughton J.

1996. Expert—solicitor

[Limitation Act 1980 (c.58), s.14(3)(*b*).] A party's solicitor is not an "expert" within the meaning of s.14(3)(*b*) of the Limitation Act 1980 for the purposes of helping his client to ascertain the identity of a defendant. That provision refers to experts in the sense of expert witnesses (*Simpson* v. *Norwest Holst Southern* [1980] C.L.Y. 1682 applied): FOWELL *v.* NATIONAL COAL BOARD, *The Times,* May 28, 1986, C.A.

1997. Latent Damage Act 1986 (c.37). See NEGLIGENCE, § 2273.

1998. Negligence—personal injury—discretion to extend time
[Limitation Act 1980 (c.58), s.33.]
P was injured on board a vessel in April 1980. Great delays were experienced by his solicitors in seeking the advice of Cypriot lawyers, P's contract of employment being governed by Cypriot law. P's solicitors omitted to commence proceedings in time, and in autumn 1983 they applied to the Court to extend time pursuant to s.33 of the Limitation Act 1980. Sheen J. allowed the action to proceed. *Held,* dismissing O's appeal, that the judge had properly weighed all the relevant factors, and that the Court of Appeal would not interfere with the exercise by him of his discretion: BRADLEY *v.* HANSEATIC SHIPPING [1986] 2 Lloyd's Rep. 34, C.A.

1999. Personal injury—whether claim should proceed
[Limitation Act 1980 (c.58) ss.11, 14, 33.]
P was employed on D's ship, and during the course of his employment contracted dermatitis in 1971. P was made permanently unfit for further sea work in October 1972. On August 2 1984, P issued a writ for damages for personal injury against D. P accepted the claim was time-barred under s.11 of the 1980 Act. *Held,* on the question whether s.33 of the 1980 Act applied, that (1) there was a very long delay not induced by D; (2) the delay affected D more than P; (3) there was no suggestion that D's conduct prejudiced P's cause of action; (4) P's disability was a continuing one. The 1980 Act was designed to stop stale claims. In this case it would not be equitable to allow the action to proceed: PILMORE *v.* NORTHERN TRAWLERS [1986] 1 Lloyd's Rep. 552, Eastham J.

2000. Public utilities—right to recover expenses—date when cause of action accrues
[Public Utilities Street Works Act 1950 (c.39), s.26(6).]
When one statutory undertaker causes damage to the equipment of another and in respect of which it is liable to make compensation for the reasonable expenses of repair, the cause of action accrues when the repairs are carried out and the expense is incurred, rather than when the damage is actually caused.
Contractors employed by BT's predecessors damaged equipment owned by YEB, who repaired the damage some seven years after it had occurred and subsequently claimed to recover the cost thereof under the 1950 Act, alternatively in negligence. *Held,* on the question of whether the claim was statute-barred, that YEB had to concede that the claim in tort was statute-barred, but the claim under the 1950 Act was not so barred for the cause of action there accrued when the repairs were effected, and not when the damage was caused.
YORKSHIRE ELECTRICITY BOARD *v.* BRITISH TELECOM [1986] 2 All E.R. 961, H.L.

LITERARY AND SCIENTIFIC INSTITUTIONS

2001. Imperial War Museum
IMPERIAL WAR MUSEUM (BOARD OF TRUSTEES) ORDER 1986 (No. 2239) [45p], made under the Imperial War Museum Act 1985 (c.14), s.1(2); operative forthwith; makes provision regarding the membership of the Imperial War Museum's board of trustees

2002. Libraries
PUBLIC LENDING RIGHT SCHEME 1982 (AMENDMENT) ORDER 1986 (No. 2103) [45p], made under the Public Lending Right Act 1979 (c.10), s.3(7); operative on December 31, 1986; amends the Public Lending Right Scheme so that the sum attributable to each loan is changed to 1·20p.

2003. Merseyside museums and galleries
MERSEYSIDE MUSEUMS AND GALLERIES ORDER 1986 (No. 226) [£1·85], made under the Local Government Act 1985 (c.51), s.46; operative on February 20, 1986; provides for the transfer to a Board of Trustees of the collection of works of art and objects of historical or scientific interest previously held by the Merseyside County Council.

2004. Museum of London Act 1986 (c.8)
This Act makes provision concerning the composition and functions of the Board of Governors of the Museum of London and for the funding of the Museum.
The Act received the Royal Assent on March 26, 1986.

2005. National Research Development Corporation

NATIONAL RESEARCH DEVELOPMENT CORPORATION REGULATIONS 1986 (No. 431) [80p], made under the Development of Inventions Act 1967 (c.32), s.1(4) and Sched., para. 2(1); operative on April 14, 1986; bring the provisions for dealing with the appointment of the members of the Corporation and their tenure of office into line with the provisions application to the NEB, contained in the Industry Act 1975.

2006. Transfer of functions

TRANSFER OF FUNCTIONS (ARTS, LIBRARIES AND NATIONAL HERITAGE) ORDER 1986 (No. 600) [£1·40], made under the Ministers of the Crown Act 1975 (c.26), s.1; operative of April 29, 1986; transfers to the Lord President of the Council functions relating to the arts, libraries and the national heritage and in relation to specified institutions.

LOANS

2007. Local loans

LOCAL LOANS (INCREASE OF LIMIT) ORDER 1986 (No. 129) [40p], made under the National Loans Act 1968 (c.13), s.4(1); operative on January 30, 1986; increases the limit of lending by the Public Works Loan Commissioners to local authorities to £35,000 million.

2008. Personal guarantee—terms liability

H's business was in a desperate financial state. He and W, his wife, gave personal guarantees backed by a charge on their home, to secure a loan from the bank of £25,000 for six months at 42 per cent. per annum. H's accountant explained to W what she was signing. She was also given the opportunity, which she declined, of seeking independent legal advice. Forty-two per cent. was the normal commercial rate for loans on such terms. *Held*, that W knew what she was doing, and was not under undue influence. The bargain had not been manifestly unfair to W, since it had been her only chance of keeping her home. Nor could the Court regard the rate of interest as extortionate, as on the evidence adduced it was normal for such a short-term loan (*National Westminster Bank* v. *Morgan* [1985] C.L.Y. 413 applied): WOODSTEAD FINANCE v. PETROU, *The Times*, January 23, 1986, C.A.

LOCAL GOVERNMENT

2009. Accounts and audit

ACCOUNTS AND AUDIT (AMENDMENT) REGULATIONS 1986 (No. 1271) [80p], made under the Local Government Finance Act 1982 (c.32), ss.23 and 35; operative on August 14, 1986; amend S.I. 1983 No. 1761.

2010. Accounts—direct labour accounts—construction or maintenance work

[Local Government Act 1972 (c.70), s.161(1); Local Government, Planning and Land Act 1980 (c.65), s.20(1)(2).]

On their natural and ordinary meaning "painting" comes within the definition of "construction or maintenance work".

The district auditor responsible for the authority's accounts sought a declaration under s.161(1) of the 1972 Act that by excluding direct labour painting transactions from the statutory accounts required by the provisions of the 1980 Act, the authority's direct labour expenditure account and income account were contrary to law. The judge held that the words "building or engineering work involved in the construction, improvement, maintenance or repair of buildings and other structures in s.20(1) of the 1980 Act included painting and granted the declaration. *Held*, dismissing the appeal, that painting came within the definition of "construction and maintenance work" on the natural and ordinary meaning of the words in the definition.

WILKINSON v. DONCASTER METROPOLITAN BORORUGH COUNCIL (1986) 84 L.G.R. 257, C.A.

2011. Accounts—inspection of wages books—documents revealed

[Local Government Finance Act 1982 (c.32), s.17(1)] The production of a summary extract of accounts is insufficient to comply with the Act where it only includes gross payments to employees: OLIVER v. NORTHAMPTON BOROUGH COUNCIL, *The Times*, May 8, 1986, D.C.

2012. Allowances to members

LOCAL GOVERNMENT (ALLOWANCES) REGULATIONS 1986 (No. 724) [£1·90], made under the Local Government Act 1972 (c.70), ss.173, 177(1)(*f*), 177(2)(*c*), 177A, 178; operative on May 13, 1986; consolidate S.I. 1974 No. 447 as amended and prescribe attendance allowances payable to members of local authorities who are councillors.

2013. Anglesey Marine Terminal Act 1972

ANGLESEY MARINE TERMINAL ACT 1972 (EXEMPTION FROM CESSATION) ORDER 1986 (No. 1190) [45p], made under the Local Government Act 1972 (c.70), exempts the Anglesey Marine Terminal Act 1972 from cessation under the Local Government Act 1972, s.262(9).

2014. Boundaries

DURHAM (DISTRICT BOUNDARIES) ORDER 1986 (No. 281) [£1·35], made under the Local Government Act 1972 (c.70), ss.51(2), 67(4)(5); operative on April 1, 1986 save for Art. 2(1) which is operative on March 24, 1986; alters the boundaries of districts and parishes in County Durham.

ESSEX (DISTRICT BOUNDARIES) ORDER 1986 (No. 2279) [£1·40], made under the Local Government Act 1972 (c.70), ss.51(2), 67(4); operative on April 1, 1987 save for Art. 2(1) which is operative on February 1, 1987; amends district boundaries in Essex.

HERFORDSHIRE (DISTRICT BOUNDARIES) ORDER 1986 (No. 2278) [80p], made under the Local Government Act 1972 (c.70), ss.51(2), 67(4); operative on April 1, 1987 save for Art. 2(1) which is operative on February 1, 1987; alters the boundaries between the district of East Hertfordshire and the borough of Stevenage.

LANCASHIRE (DISTRICT BOUNDARIES) ORDER 1986 (No. 1909) [£1·90], made under the Local Government Act 1972 (c.70), ss.51(2), 67(4)(5); operative on April 1, 1987 save for Art. 2(1) which is operative on December 10, 1986; alters district boundaries between specified boroughs in Lancashire.

SHROPSHIRE (DISTRICT BOUNDARIES) ORDER 1986 (No. 1619) [80p], made under the Local Government Act 1972 (s.70), ss.51(2), 67(4); operative on April 1, 1987 save for Art. 2(1) which is operative on October 31, 1986; alters the boundary between the district of The Wrekin to the borough of Shrewsbury and Atcham.

SURREY (DISTRICT BOUNDARIES) ORDER 1986 (No. 321) [£1·85], made under the Local Government Act 1972 (c.70), ss.51(2), 67(4); operative on April 1, 1986 save for Art. 2(1) which is operative on March 31, 1986; transfers areas between specified boroughs in Surrey.

2015. Committees—confidentiality—exclusion of council members

It is not lawful for a council, by allowing a subcommittee to be used for party political purposes, to justify a need for confidentiality and secrecy which would not otherwise arise. However, it is not prima facie unlawful for a majority party to exclude members of other parties from committees. If an excluded councillor reasonably requests information about committee meetings, the committee must provide that information, and if the most convenient way of supplying that information is by allowing him to attend the meeting, then he must be allowed to attend (*R.* v. *Birmingham City Council, ex p. O* [1983] C.L.Y. 2422 applied): R. v. SHEFFIELD CITY COUNCIL, *ex p.* CHADWICK, *The Times*, December 19, 1985, D.C.

2016. Communities

CARMARTHEN (COMMUNITIES) ORDER 1986 (No. 2008) [£2·40], made under the Local Government Act 1972 (c.70), s.67(4)(5), Sched. 10, paras. 7, 9; operative on April 1, 1987 save for Art. 2(1) which is operative on January 1, 1987, continues 36 communities and constitutes five new ones in the District of Carmarthen.

CEREDIGION (COMMUNITIES) ORDER 1986 (No. 1364) [£2·90], made under the Local Government Act 1972 (c.70), s.67(4)(5), Sched. 10, paras. 7, 9; operative on April 1, 1987 save for Art. 2(1) which is operative on January 1, 1987; continues 26 communities and constitutes 25 new communities in the District of Ceredigion.

DINEFWR (COMMUNITIES) ORDER 1986 (No. 2077) [£2·40], made under the Local Government Act 1972 (c.70), s.67(4) and (5), Sched. 10, para. 7; operative on April 1, 1987, except Art. 2(1) which comes into force on January 1, 1987; continues 17 communities, abolishes seven and constitutes six new ones in Dinefwr.

MONMOUTH (COMMUNITIES) ORDER 1986 (No. 4) [£2·30], made under the Local Government Act 1972 (c.70), s.67(4) and (5) and Sched. 10, para. 7; operative on January 28, 1986 for the purposes of art. 2, and April 1, 1986 for all other purposes;

continues 27 communities and constitutes five new communities in the district of Monmouth.
MONTGOMERYSHIRE (COMMUNITIES) ORDER 1986 (No. 2009) [£2·40], made under the Local Government Act 1972 (c.70), s.67(4), (5) and Sched. 10, para 7; operative on January 1, 1987; continues 7 communities, abolishes 28 and constitutes 16 new ones in Montgomeryshire

2017. Delay in making rate—loss caused by delay—role of auditor—penalty for loss
Local Government Finance Act 1982 (c.32), ss.19, 20, 22; Local Government Act 1972 (c.70), ss.111, 151; General Rate Act 1967 (c.9), (as amended) ss.1–5, 11, 12, 50, Sched. 10; Local Government, Planning and Land Act 1980 (c.65), ss.56, 59, 72, 78, Sched. 12, pt. 1.] The local authority councillors delayed setting a rate in an effort to force the national government to allow the authority access to more funds. *Held,* that (1) the auditor had properly carried out his duties; (2) the auditor had made sufficient provision for the councillors to be heard in their defence; (3) a local authority was bound to make a rate as soon as practicable, and if a valid reason for delay existed, in any event by June 20 each year; (4) the reason given for delaying the making of a rate was not valid or proper; (5) such a reason had to relate in some way to the rate making process or the rate itself; (6) the failure amounted to wilful misconduct since the authority was earlier advised of the risk being taken; (7) the wilful misconduct caused a loss to the authority by reason of loss of interest on payments that would have been made; (8) an appeal could properly be made in its present form; (9) the hearing was a complete re-hearing (*Asher* v. *Lacey* [1973] 1 W.L.R. 1412; *Asher* v. *Secretary of State for the Environment* [1974] C.L.Y. 2160; *Associated Provincial Picture Houses* v. *Wednesbury Corporation* (1947) C.L.C. 8107; *Bromley London Borough Council* v. *Greater London Council* [1982] C.L.Y. 1910; *Bushell* v. *Secretary of State for the Environment* [1980] C.L.Y. 1337; *CCSU* v. *Minister for the Civil Service* [1985] C.L.Y. 12; *Fairmount Investments* v. *Secretary of State for the Environment and Southwark London Borough Council* [1976] C.L.Y. 305; *Forder* v. *Great Western Railway* [1905] 2 K.B. 532; *Graham* v. *Teesdale* [1983] C.L.Y. 2289; *Hackney London Borough Council* v. *Secretary of State for the Environment*, May 2, 1985, unreported; *Horabin* v. *British Overseas Airways Corp.* [1952] C.L.Y. 202; *Jeff* v. *New Zealand Dairy Production and Marketing Board* [1966] C.L.Y. 29; *Ladd* v. *Marshall* [1954] C.L.Y. 2507; *Local Government Board* v. *Arlidge* [1915] A.C. 120; *O'Reilly* v. *Mackman* [1982] C.L.Y. 2603; *R.* v. *Carson Roberts* [1908] 1 K.B. 407; *R.* v. *Gaming Board for Great Britain, ex p. Benaim* [1970] C.L.Y. 1160; *R.* v. *Hackney London Borough Council, ex p. Fleming*, unreported; *R.* v. *St Edmundsbury Borough Council, ex p. Investors in Industry* [1985] C.L.Y. 3458; *R.* v. *Secretary of State for the Environment, ex p. Hammersmith and Fulham London Borough Council*, unreported; *R.* v. *Secretary of State for the Environment, ex p. Leicester City Council* [1985] C.L.Y. 2919; *R.* v. *Sevenoaks District Council, ex p. Terry* [1985] C.L.Y. 3459; *Ridge* v. *Baldwin* [1963] C.L.Y. 2667; *Russell* v. *Duke of Norfolk* (1949) C.L.C. 1764; *Steeples* v. *Derbyshire County Council* [1984] C.L.Y. 3496; *Wiseman* v. *Borneman* [1969] C.L.Y. 1748 considered: SMITH *v.* SKINNER; GLADDEN *v.* MCMAHON, (1986) 26 R.V.R. 45, D.C.

2018. Disabled Persons (Services, Consultation and Representation) Act 1986 (c.33)
This Act provides for the improvement of services for the mentally or physically handicapped and for those suffering from mental illness, with better co-ordination of resources. It provides further for assessment of needs and for consultative processes and representational rights for such people.
The Act received the Royal Assent on July 8, 1986 and comes into force on days to be appointed. It does not extend to Northern Ireland.

2019. District Auditor—surcharge—procedure
[Local Government Finance Act 1982 (c.32), s.20(1).] If the failure of the District Auditor to accord oral hearings to councillors whom he was surcharging for a loss or deficiency caused by their wilful misconduct, caused any unfairness, it had been cured by their appeal to the Divisional Court: HOOD *v.* MCMAHON, *The Times,* August 1, 1986, C.A.

2020. Documents
LOCAL GOVERNMENT (INSPECTION OF DOCUMENTS) (SUMMARY OF RIGHTS) ORDER 1986 (No. 854) [£1·40], made under the Local Government Act 1972 (c.70), ss.1009(3), 266; operative on September 1, 1986; specifies enactments in respect of which

principal councils are required to keep a written summary of the rights to attend meetings and inspect, copy and be furnished with documents.

2021. Electoral divisions
Orders made under the Local Government Act 1972 (c.70), ss.58(2), 67:
S.I. 1986 Nos. 237 (Borough of Thamesdown) [£2·80]; 280 (Borough of Halton) [£2·30]; 383 (District of West Lancashire) [40p]; 526 (Borough of Blaenau Gwent) [£1·35]; 533 (Borough of Brecknock) [80p]; 535 (Borough of Lliw. Valley) [80p]; 556 (District of Monmouth) [80p]; 645 (Borough of Torfaen) [80p]; 1063 (Borough of Llanelli) [45p]; 1841 (District of Mid Sussex) [40p]; 1912 (Borough of Taunton Deane) [£1·40], 1963 (District of South Pembrokeshire) [45p]; 1964 (District of Ceredigion) [80p]; 2333 (Borough of Cyron Valley) [45p]; 2334 (Borough of Merthys Tydfil) [45p].

2022. Expenditure—rate support grant—guidelines issued by Secretary of State—validity
[Local Government Planning and Land Act 1980 (c.65), s.59; Local Government Finance Act 1982 (c.32), s.8.]
The Secretary of State can properly issue guidelines for expenditure to local authorities based on principles which apply to all authorities notwithstanding that there might be individual authorities which were unable to comply.
The Secretary of State for the Environment, following discussions with the local authority associations, issued provisional guidelines for expenditure guidance for 1984/5. There was then correspondence between the Secretary of State and the applicant council from which it appeared that the Secretary of State took into account the representations made to him that the formula contemplated as appropriate would place the council in breach of their statutory or unavoidable obligations. The Rate Support Grant Report was laid before the House of Commons which detailed the grant entitlement of all local authorities according to a set formula. The council applied for judicial review of the expenditure guidance contending that the guidance under s.59 of the 1980 Local Government Act, as amended by the 1982 Act, was lawful only if it was possible for the recipient local authority to follow it without adversely affecting the reasonable discharge of their statutory obligations, and that the council could not comply with the guidance and fulfil all their statutory duties. The judge dismissed the application and the council appealed. *Held*, dismissing the appeal, that there was nothing on the face of section 59 of the Act of 1980 and section 8 of the Act of 1982 expressing that the Secretary of State, in exercising his power to give guidance, was obliged to consider individually the position of each local authority and to adjust the guidance according to the level of those commitments, provident or extravagant, wise or unwise, and these considerations were manifestly contrary not only to the purpose for which the provision was introduced and also to the way in which the parliamentary expression was expressed. Even on the evidence there was no case for saying that the Secretary of State had acted unreasonably or misdirected himself. He could properly issue guidance based on principles which applied to all authorities even though there might be individual authorities which were unable to comply (*Associated Provincial Picture Houses* v. *Wednesbury Corp.* (1948) C.L.C. 8107 considered).
R. v. SECRETARY OF STATE FOR THE ENVIRONMENT, *ex p.* HACKNEY LONDON BOROUGH COUNCIL (1986) 84 L.G.R. 32, C.A.

2023. Finance—expenditure—trust fund. See R. v. DISTRICT AUDITOR No. 3 AUDIT DISTRICT OF WEST YORKSHIRE METROPOLITAN COUNTY COUNCIL, *ex p.* WEST YORKSHIRE METROPOLITAN COUNTY COUNCIL, § 2804.

2024. Grants—eligibility—powers of grants committees
[Local Government Act 1985 (c.51), s.48(8), (11)] S.48 of the Local Government Act 1985 does not allow the London Boroughs Grants Committee to restrict eligibility for grants to voluntary bodies that operate in more than three London boroughs. The power to make supplementary provisions under s.48(11) does not include the power to introduce a qualification for eligibility not found in s.48(11):
R. v. LONDON BOROUGHS GRANTS COMMITTEE. *ex p.* GREENWICH LONDON BOROUGH COUNCIL, *The Times*, May 6, 1986, D.C.

2025. Greater London Council—abolition—allocation of surplus funds in advance—whether ultra vires
[Local Government Act 1972 (c.70), s.111 Local Government Act 1985 (c.51), s.97(1).]

A local authority is empowered only to expend funds on projects properly referable to the year in question; "forward funding" is *ultra vires*.

The G.L.C. was to be abolished as from April 1, 1986. The relevant Acts contained detailed provisions as to the winding up of the G.L.C. and transfer to successor bodies. A substantial surplus was projected in G.L.C. finances as at date of abolition; the G.L.C. passed resolutions allocating large sums of money to reserve funds for later allocation to approved sources and bodies. The applicants, various London borough councils, sought judicial review of the decisions as being *ultra vires*. Macpherson J. dismissed the application, but he was reversed on appeal. *Held,* on appeal to the House of Lords, dismissing the appeal, that the G.L.C. were not authorised by statute to act in the way they had; further a local authority had power to expend only those funds properly referable to the year in which they were levied; "forward funding" was *ultra vires* and unlawful (*Manchester City Council* v. *Greater Manchester County Council* [1981] C.L.Y. 2456 distinguished).

WESTMINSTER CITY COUNCIL, *Re* [1986] 2 W.L.R. 807, H.L.

2026. Highway maintenance

BIRDWELL HIGHWAY MAINTENANCE DEPOT (TRANSFER) ORDER 1986 (No. 211) [80p], made under the Local Government Act 1985 (c.51), s.100; operative on April 1, 1986; transfers the said Depot from the Metropolitan County Council of South Yorkshire to the Secretary of State for Transport.

2027. Housing transfers—payment for disposals—capital account

[London Government Act 1963 (c.33), s.23(3); Local Government Planning and Land Act 1980 (c.65), part VIII.] Transfers of housing are disposals for which the local authority is entitled to payment for as agreed or assessed by the Secretary of State, and they are capital receipts: R. *v.* SECRETARY OF STATE FOR THE ENVIRONMENT, *ex p.* NEWHAM LONDON BOROUGH COUNCIL, *The Times,* December 23, 1985, Taylor J.

2028. ILEA

PRECEPT LIMITATION (PRESCRIBED MAXIMUM) (INNER LONDON EDUCATION AUTHORITY) ORDER 1986 (No. 265) [40p], made under the Local Government Act 1985 (c.51), ss.18, 68(6) and the Rates Act 1984 (c.33), s.2; operative on February 14, 1986; prescribes a maximum precept of 77·25 pence in the pound for ILEA for the financial year 1986/7.

2029. Land drainage

LOCAL GOVERNMENT ACT 1985 (LAND DRAINAGE FUNCTIONS) ORDER 1986 (No. 208) [£1·35], made under the Local Government Act 1985 (c.51), ss.11(2), 101, 103(6); operative on April 1, 1986 save for Art. 1(1)(*a*) which is operative on February 14, 1986; provides for land drainage as it affects the GLC and the metropolitan counties.

2030. Local Government Act 1986 (c.10)

This Act requires rating authorities to set a rate on or before April 1, regulates local authority publicity, makes various provision in connection with the disposal of local authority mortgages, and deals with connected purposes.

It received the Royal Assent on March 26, 1986.

2031. Local statutory provisions

LLANDRINDOD WELLS URBAN DISTRICT COUNCIL ACT 1920 (PARTIAL EXEMPTION FROM REPEAL) ORDER 1986 (No. 2068), [45p], made under the Local Government Act 1972 (c.70), s.262(9)(*a*); operative on December 29, 1986; continues in force after December 31, 1986 certain provisions of the said 1920 Act.

NON-METROPOLITAN AND WELSH COUNTIES (LOCAL STATUTORY PROVISIONS) ORDER 1986 (No. 2106) [45p], made under the Local Government Act 1972, s.262(9)(*d*); operative on December 31, 1986; further postpones from December 31, 1986 in certain specified local government areas the date on which all local statutory provisions to which s.262(9) applies shall cease to apply.

NON-METROPOLITAN COUNTIES (LOCAL STATUTORY PROVISIONS) ORDER 1986 (No. 1133) [45p], made under the Local Government Act 1972 (c.70), s.262 (9)(*a*); operative on August 4, 1986; exempts from repeal the local statutory provisions listed in art. 2.

2032. London. See LONDON.

2033. London main rivers

LOCAL GOVERNMENT ACT 1985 (LONDON MAIN RIVERS) ORDER 1986 (No. 711) [45p], made under the Local Government Act 1985 (c.51), ss.101, 103(6); operative on May 14, 1986; provides for a number of rivers in the former G.L.C. area to be deemed to be main rivers of the Thames Water Authority.

2034. Maximum precepts

LOCAL GOVERNMENT ACT 1985 (POLICE AND FIRE AND CIVIL DEFENCE AUTHORITIES) PRECEPTS LIMITATION ORDER 1986 (No. 212) [40p], made under the Local Government Act 1985 (c.51), s.68(4) and the Rates Act 1984 (c.33), ss.1, 4(4); operative on February 14, 1986; prescribes the maximum precepts in respect of the year 1986/7 for such of the police, fire and civil defence authorities established under Pt. V of the 1985 Act which are specified.

PRECEPT LIMITATION (PASSENGER TRANSPORT AUTHORITIES) (PRESCRIBED MAXIMUM) ORDER 1986 (No. 230) [40p], made under the Rates Act 1984, ss.1, 4(4); operative on February 14, 1986; prescribes maximum precepts for specified transport authorities for the year 1986/7.

2035. Mersey Tunnels

MERSEY TUNNELS ORDER 1986 (No. 297) [80p], made under the Local Government Act 1985 (c.51), ss.52, 100, 101; operative on April 1, 1986; transfers the Mersey Tunnels to the Merseyside Passenger Transport Authority.

2036. Mortgages

LOCAL AUTHORITIES (DISPOSAL OF MORTGAGES) REGULATIONS 1986 (No. 1028) [80p], made under the Local Government Act 1986 (c.10), s.7(6); operative on July 21, 1986; prescribe the information which is to be given to a mortgagor by a local authority which seeks his consent to the transfer of his mortgage and prescribes the form of that consent and the time in which it must be obtained.

LOCAL AUTHORITY (MORTGAGES) (AMENDMENT) REGULATIONS 1986 (No. 282) [40p], made under the Local Government Act 1972 (c.70), Sched. 13, para. 4(1); operative on April 1, 1986; amend the definition of "local authority" in S.I. 1974 No. 518.

2037. Noise insulation

NOISE INSULATION AGENCY AGREEMENTS (WEST YORKSHIRE) ORDER 1986 (No. 256) [40p], made under the Local Government Act 1985 (c.51), s.100, Sched. 4, para. 57; operative on April 1, 1986; terminates an agreement between the Secretary of State and the Metropolitan County Council of West Yorkshire made pursuant to S.I. 1975 No. 1763.

2038. Open government

The Local Government Legal Society Trust in association with the Society of Town Clerks' Education and Research Trust have published a study by Patrick Birkinshaw on the subject of open government—*Open Government: Freedom of Information and Local Government* (ISBN 0 9511101 01) [£4·95].

2039. Parish—trustees—authority

[Local Government Act 1972 (c.70), s.13(4)] Notwithstanding the absence of express authority from a parish meeting, Parish trustees who have no Parish Council can take steps, including the advancement of proceedings, to protect Parish property: TAYLOR *v.* MASEFIELD, *The Times,* May 22, 1986, C.A.

2040. Powers—delegation to committee—chairman

[Town and Country Planning Act 1971, (c.78), s.81(1); Local Government Act 1972 (c.70) s.101.]

"Committee" in s.101(1) of the Local Government Act 1972 has its modern meaning of a body of more than one member.

The council's standing orders allowed for the delegation to the chairman of the planning committee of the function of authorising the service of enforcement notices under s.87(1) of the 1971 Act. The chairman authorised the service of a notice on a company requiring it to comply with the terms of a temporary planning permission. The company appealed to the Secretary of State who held that the council could not delegate its functions to a committee with only one member under s.101(1) of the 1972 Act. The council were refused judicial review, on the ground that "committee" under s.101(1) has its modern meaning of a body of more than one member. *Held,* dismissing the appeal to the Court of Appeal, that the judges decision was correct. (*Reynell* v. *Lewis* (1846) 15 M. & W. 517 distinguished; *R.* v. *Brent Health Authority, ex p. Francis* [1985] C.L.Y. 2164 considered).

R. *v.* SECRETARY OF STATE FOR THE ENVIRONMENT, *ex p.* HILLINGDON LONDON BOROUGH COUNCIL [1986] (NOTE) 2 All E.R. 273, C.A.

2041. Powers of ILEA—publication of information—desire to persuade public opinion— whether proper

[Local Government Act 1972 (c.70), s.142(2).]

Where a second, unauthorised, purpose materially influences a local authority in reaching a decision which would otherwise be perfectly proper, the whole decision is liable to be quashed on the basis that the authority has taken into account irrelevant factors.

Following publication of a government white paper on rate-capping, ILEA, who set the education rate for the inner London area, began a campaign designed to bring to public notice what it saw as the implications for educational spending within its area. An advertising agency was retained, at a budget of £651,000, to inform the public and persuade them round to the ILEA view on rate-capping. *Held,* that although the first purpose may have been proper the second was not. In such circumstances, where the second consideration had been of material importance, the decision of a local authority would be declared invalid as having been reached after taking into account irrelevant considerations. S.142 did not authorise ILEA to carry out a publicity campaign designed to influence ministerial decisions.

R. *v.* INNER LONDON EDUCATION AUTHORITY, *ex p.* WESTMINSTER CITY COUNCIL [1986] 1 All E.R. 19, Glidewell J.

2042. Rate-support grant—expenditure targets—principles to be applied. See NOTTINGHAM- SHIRE COUNTY COUNCIL *v.* SECRETARY OF STATE FOR THE ENVIRONMENT; CITY OF BRADFORD METROPOLITAN COUNCIL *v.* SECRETARY OF STATE FOR THE ENVIRONMENT, § 27.

2043. Rate Support Grants Act 1986 (c.54)

This Act validates the payment of rate support grants to local authorities under the Local Government, Planning and Land Act 1980, Pt. VI. It also clarifies various provisions of that Act and of the Local Government Finance Act 1982.

The Act received the Royal Assent on October 21, 1986.

2044. Records

LOCAL GOVERNMENT (RECORDS) ORDER 1986 (No. 803) [45p], made under the Local Government (Records) Act 1962 (c.56), s.2(6); operative on May 20, 1986; extends to the councils of specified cities the powers under the 1962 Act to acquire records and accept the deposit of records.

2045. Recreation grounds—byelaws. See OPEN SPACES AND RECREATION GROUNDS, § 2484.

2046. Reorganisation

BOBS LANE FERRY ORDER 1986 (No. 1774) [45p], made under the Local Government Act 1985 (c.51), s.67(3); operative on December 1, 1986; transfers to the Greater Manchester Passenger Transport Executive property, rights and liabilities relating to the Bobs Lane Ferry.

LOCAL GOVERNMENT (MAGISTRATES' COURTS ETC.) ORDER 1986 (No. 399) [£2·80], made under the Local Government Act 1985 (c.51), ss. 52, 101; operative on April 1, 1986; makes provision in relation to the reorganisation of magistrates' courts in outer London occasioned by the Local Government Act 1985.

LOCAL GOVERNMENT REORGANISATION (AIRPORTS) ORDER 1986 (No. 425) [£1·35], made under the Local Government Act 1985, ss.40, 52, 101; operative on April 1, 1986; makes provision in respect of the property rights and liabilities in relation to airports.

LOCAL GOVERNMENT REORGANISATION (CAPITAL MONEY) (METROPOLITAN COUNTIES) ORDER 1986 (No. 2063) [£1·40], made under the Local Government Act 1985 (c.51), ss.77, 101; operative on December 30, 1986; makes provision concerned with the distribution of capital receipts by residuary bodies to authorities in the metropolitan counties.

LOCAL GOVERNMENT REORGANISATION (CAPITAL MONEY) (WEST MIDLANDS) ORDER 1986 (No. 2093) [£1·40], made under the Local Government Act 1985, ss.77, 101; operative on December 30, 1986; provides for the distribution of capital receipts by the West Midlands Residuary Body.

LOCAL GOVERNMENT REORGANISATION (COMPENSATION) REGULATIONS 1986 (No. 151) [£2·30], made under the Superannuation Act 1972 (c.11), s.24; operative on February 28, 1986; provide for the payment of compensation to persons who suffer loss of employment or diminution of emoluments attributable to the provisions of the Local Government Act 1985.

LOCAL GOVERNMENT REORGANISATION (CROXTETH HALL AND PARK) ORDER 1986 (No. 573) [40p], made under the Local Government Act 1985 (c.51), ss.52, 62(4), 100; operative on April 1, 1986; amends S.I. 1986 No. 413 in relation to the said Hall and Park.

LOCAL GOVERNMENT REORGANISATION (DEBT ADMINISTRATION) (GREATER MANCHESTER) ORDER 1986 (No. 563) [£1·35], made under the Local Government Act 1985 (c.51), s.66(1); operative on April 1, 1986; transfers to the Tameside Borough Council the rights and liabilities of the Metropolitan County Council in respect of money borrowed.

LOCAL GOVERNMENT REORGANISATION (DEBT ADMINISTRATION) (SOUTH YORKSHIRE) ORDER 1986 (No. 437) [£1·35], made under the Local Government Act 1985, s.66(1); operative on April 1, 1986; transfers to the Rotherham metropolitan borough council the rights and liabilities of the South Yorkshire metropolitan county council in respect of money borrowed.

LOCAL GOVERNMENT REORGANISATION (DEBT ADMINISTRATION) (TYNE AND WEAR) ORDER 1986 (No. 501) [£1·35], made under the Local Government Act 1985, s.66(1); operative on April 1, 1986; transfers to the South Tyneside Metropolitan Borough Council the rights and liabilities of the Metropolitan County Council in respect of money borrowed for the purposes of the Tyne Tunnel.

LOCAL GOVERNMENT REORGANISATION (DEBT ADMINISTRATION) (WEST MIDLANDS) ORDER 1986 (No. 553) [£1·35], made under the Local Government Act 1985, s.66(1); operative on April 1, 1986; transfers to the Dudley Metropolitan Borough Council the rights and liabilities of the Metropolitan County Council in respect of money borrowed which would otherwise have to be transferred to the residuary body.

LOCAL GOVERNMENT REORGANISATION (DEBT ADMINISTRATION) (WEST MIDLANDS) (AMENDMENT) ORDER 1986 (No. 1398) [45p], made under the Local Government Act 1985 (c.51), s.66(1); operative on September 8, 1986; amends S.I. 1986 No. 553.

LOCAL GOVERNMENT REORGANISATION (DEBT ADMINISTRATION) (WEST YORKSHIRE) ORDER 1986 (No. 471) [£1·35], made under the Local Government Act 1985, s.66(1); operative on April 1, 1986; transfers to the Bradford City Council the rights and liabilities of the West Yorkshire metropolitan county council in respect of money borrowed which would otherwise have been transferred to the West Yorkshire residuary body.

LOCAL GOVERNMENT REORGANISATION (DESIGNATED COUNCILS) (PENSIONS) ORDER 1986 (No. 96) [80p], made under the Local Government Act 1985 (c.51), s.66; operative on April 1, 1986; transfers to the designated district councils the responsibilities for certain pension and compensation matters of Tyne and Wear, West Midlands and West Yorkshire county councils which are abolished on April 1, 1986.

LOCAL GOVERNMENT REORGANISATION (DESIGNATION OF METROPOLITAN COUNTY COUNCIL STAFF) ORDER 1986 (No. 523) [£2·80], made under the Local Government Act 1985, s.52; operative on April 1, 1986; designates employees of the metropolitan county councils automatic transfer to an authority inheriting functions or property.

LOCAL GOVERNMENT REORGANISATION (DESIGNATION OF STAFF) (No. 2) ORDER 1986 (No. 582) [£1·40], made under the Local Government Act 1985 (c.51), s.52; operative on April 1, 1986; amend S.I. 1986 Nos. 192 and 426.

LOCAL GOVERNMENT REORGANISATION (GREATER LONDON COUNCIL TRANSFERRED HOUSING AND NOMINATION RIGHTS) ORDER 1986 (No. 442) [£1·85], made under the Local Government Act 1985, ss.89(1), (2), 100(1), (2) and (4) and 101; operative on April 1, 1986; contains provisions relating to the transference of housing accommodation and housing land from the G.L.C. to London borough councils and district councils.

LOCAL GOVERNMENT REORGANISATION (MANPOWER INFORMATION) REGULATIONS 1986 (No. 867) [£1·40], made under the Local Government Act 1985 (c.51), s.56; operative on June 13, 1986; require London borough councils, metropolitan district councils and the Common Council of the City of London to furnish the Secretary of State with information about their manpower.

LOCAL GOVERNMENT REORGANISATION (MISCELLANEOUS PROVISION) ORDER 1986 (No. 1) [£1·35], made under the Local Government Act 1985 (c.51), s.101; operative on

April 1, 1986, and January 31, 1986; amends various Acts in consequence of the 1985 Act which abolishes the GLC and the metropolitan county councils on April 1, 1986.

LOCAL GOVERNMENT REORGANISATION (MISCELLANEOUS PROVISION) (No. 2) ORDER 1986 (No. 300) [40p], made under the Local Government Act 1985, s.101; operative on April 1, 1986; provides for the signing of the minutes of the last meetings of the GLC and the metropolitan county councils and makes provision in relation to certain redundancy payments.

LOCAL GOVERNMENT REORGANISATION (MISCELLANEOUS PROVISION) (No. 3) ORDER 1986 (No. 379) [80p], made under the Local Government Act 1985, s.101; operative on March 10, 1986; replaces S.I. 1986 No. 300.

LOCAL GOVERNMENT REORGANISATION (MISCELLANEOUS PROVISION) (No. 4) ORDER 1986 (No. 452) [£1·85], made under the Local Government Act 1985, ss.98(9) and 101; operative on April 1, 1986; contains provisions consequential on the 1985 Act which abolishes the G.L.C. and the metropolitan county councils.

LOCAL GOVERNMENT REORGANISATION (MISCELLANEOUS PROVISION) (No. 5) ORDER 1986 (No. 564) [80p], made under the Local Government Act 1985, ss.10, 98(9), 100 and 101; operative on April 1, 1986; makes provision consequential on the 1985 Act.

LOCAL GOVERNMENT REORGANISATION (MISCELLANEOUS PROVISION) (No. 6) ORDER 1986 (No. 1929) [45p], made under the Local Government Act 1985, s.101; operative on November 14, 1986; provides that the Public Bodies (Admissions to Meetings) Act 1970 is not to be construed as applying to residuary bodies.

LOCAL GOVERNMENT REORGANISATION (MISCELLANEOUS PROVISION) (No. 7) Order 1986 (No. 2293) [45p], made under the Local Government Act 1985 (c.51), ss.100(3), 101; operative on February 5, 1987; makes further provision consequential on the abolition of the GLC and the metropolitan county councils.

LOCAL GOVERNMENT REORGANISATION (PRESERVATION OF RIGHT TO BUY) ORDER 1986 (No. 2092) [£3·40], made under the Local Government Act 1985 s.101; preserves the right to buy for secure tenants of residuary bodies even after the property is disposed by that authority.

LOCAL GOVERNMENT REORGANISATION (PROPERTY ETC.) ORDER 1986 (No. 148) [£2·80], made under the Local Government Act 1985, ss.44, 47, 62(4), 98(9), 100, 101; operative on April 1, 1986 save for Art. 22(2)–(4) which is operative on February 27, 1986; make provision for the transfer of property, rights and liabilities of the GLC and the metropolitan county councils on their abolition.

LOCAL GOVERNMENT REORGANISATION (PROPERTY ETC.) (No. 2) ORDER 1986 (No. 413) [£2·80], made under the Local Government Act 1985, ss.10, 45, 100, 101; operative on April 1, 1986; supplements S.I. 1986 No. 148.

LOCAL GOVERNMENT REORGANISATION (PROPERTY ETC.) (LOCAL FISHERIES COMMITTEES) ORDER 1986 (No. 624) [45p], made under the Local Government Act 1985 (c.51), s.100; operative on April 1, 1986; makes provision in connection with the property, rights and liabilities of local fishery committees following the abolition of the metropolitan county councils.

LOCAL GOVERNMENT REORGANISATION (REPAYMENT OF LOANS) (GREATER LONDON) ORDER 1986 (No. 439) [£1·35], made under the Local Government Act 1985, s.58(2); operative on April 1, 1986; defines the sums which are to be paid to the London Residuary Body by the London borough councils, the I.L.E.A. and the London Fire and Civil Defence Authority for the purpose of enabling that body to discharge liabilities inherited from the G.L.C.

LOCAL GOVERNMENT REORGANISATION (REPAYMENT OF LOANS) (MERSEYSIDE) ORDER 1986 (No. 436) [£1·35], made under the Local Government Act 1985, s.58(2); operative on April 1, 1986; defines the amounts which are to be paid to the Merseyside Residuary Body by the district councils within the metropolitan county, by the Merseyside Police Authority, the Merseyside Passenger Transport Authority and the Merseyside Fire and Civil Defence Authority for the purpose of discharging liabilities inherited from the Merseyside Metropolitan county council.

LONDON GOVERNMENT REORGANISATION (DESIGNATION OF STAFF) ORDER 1986 (No. 426) [£1·35], made under the Local Government Act 1985, s.52; operative on April 1, 1986; makes provision in relation to the transfer of staff from the G.L.C. to other authorities.

TOWN AND COUNTRY PLANNING (LOCAL GOVERNMENT REORGANISATION) (MISCELLANEOUS AMENDMENTS) ORDER 1986 (No. 435) [£1·35], made under the Town and Country Planning Act 1971 (c.78), ss.24, 25, 31, 34, 36, 37, 42, 53, 92A, 287, Sched. 14, the

Land Compensation Act 1961 (c.33), s.20, the Local Government Act 1972 (c.70), Sched. 16, para. 20 and the New Towns Act 1981 (c.65), s.7; operative on April 1, 1986; amends various planning orders to take account of the abolition of the G.L.C. and the metropolitan county councils.

Town and Country Planning (Local Government Reorganisation) (Miscellaneous Amendments) Regulations 1986 (No. 443) [£1·35], made under the scheduled regulations; operative on April 1, 1986; make provision consequential on the Local Government Act 1985 which abolishes the G.L.C. and the metropolitan county councils on April 1, 1986.

2047. Sex establishments—licensing—panel of councillors

A panel of councillors appointed by a local authority to determine on behalf of the authority applications for licences was not a judicial body and accordingly its conduct was not susceptible of judicial review: R. *v.* Reading Borough Council, *ex p.* Quietlynn, *The Times*, October 7, 1986, Kennedy J.

2048. Sex establishment—licensing—publication of resolution—time limit—paper on sale before official publicaion date

[Local Government (Miscellaneous Provision) Act 1982 (c.30), s.2(1)(2)(3), Sched. 3.]

For the purposes of a notice given under s.2(3) of the Local Government (Miscellaneous Provisions) Act 1982 a newspaper is deemed to have an official publication date, notwithstanding) it may be on sale before then.

At 7 p.m. on March 7, 1984 the council resolved that Sched. 3 to the 1982 Act would apply in their area and come into force on April 16, 1984. Notices of the resolution were published in a local paper of March 8 and 15. Although the paper carried those dates it had been on sale the afternoon and evening before, *i.e.* prior to the passing of the resolution. The applicants applied for judicial review saying that in these circumstances the publication on March 8 was a nullity. Forbes J. dismissed the application. *Held*, dismissing the appeal, that the Act contemplated an official publication date; that the official date was March 8 and that on that date the notice had complied with all the requirements.

Sheptonhurst *v.* Newham London Borough Council (1985) 84 L.G.R. 97, C.A.

2049. Sex establishment—locality—meaning

[Local Government (Miscellaneous Provisions) Act 1982 (c.30), Sched. 3, para. 12(3)(*d*)(i).] In an application for a licence to use premises as a sex shop the relevant locality is the area surrounding the premises, which may be of mixed character and need not be defined by boundaries on a map. The Court should construe the plain meaning of the section notwithstanding that in practice earlier applications were considered after those received subsequent to the appointed day: R. *v.* Peterborough City Council, *ex p.* Quietlynn, *The Times*, July 28, 1986, C.A.

2050. Special responsibility allowances

Local Government (Special Responsibility Allowances) (New Authorities) Regulations 1986 (No. 299) [40p], made under the Local Government Act 1972 (c.70), ss.177A, 178, 266; operative on March 18, 1986; provides for the payment of special responsibility allowances in respect of membership of authorities established under the Local Government Act 1985.

2051. Standing orders—committee members—criteria for selection

[Local Government Act 1972 (c.70), s.94.] The authority was entitled to establish, subject to rationality, criteria on members to be elected to a committee: R. *v.* Newham London Borough Council *ex p.* Haggerty, *The Times*, April 11, 1986, Mann J.

2052. Statutory powers—lawful exercise—whether unlawful fetter of powers

A local authority cannot generally make declarations of policy binding on future councils: it cannot extinguish statutory powers in that way, but it can do so by the valid exercise of other statutory powers. If a statutory power is lawfully exercised so as to create legal rights and obligations between the council and third parties, the council for the time being is bound even if their exercise of other statutory powers is hindered, and the powers of the future council have not been unlawfully fettered: R. *v.* Hammersmith and Fulham London Borough Council, *ex p.* Beddowes, *The Times*, August 26, 1986, C.A.

2053. Stocks and bonds

LOCAL AUTHORITY (STOCKS AND BONDS) (AMENDMENT) REGULATIONS 1986 (No. 345) [40p], made under the Local Government Act 1972 (c.70), Sched. 13, para. 4(1) as extended by the Stock Transfer Act 1982 (c.41), s.1; operative on April 1, 1986; amend S.I. 1974 No. 519 so that the definition of "local authority" includes I.L.E.A., joint authorities residual bodies and authorities established under S.I. 1985 No. 1884.

2054. Street trading from mobile vans—application for consent—notice of objections—reasons for refusal—natural justice

[Local Government (Miscellaneous Provisions) Act 1982 (c.30), Sched. 4, paras. 2, 7.]

A local authority is not obliged to give reasons for refusing an application for consent to trade from a mobile vehicle in a street.

In 1984 Bristol City Council adopted the provisions of Schedule 4 to the Local Government (Miscellaneous Provisions) Act 1982 to provide a system of licensing and consents to govern street trading. Prior thereto, P ran a business selling hot food from mobile vans. Thereafter P applied to the Council for consent to trade from mobile vans in three streets in Bristol. P's application was considered by the Council's Public Protection Committee on October 24, 1984 and refused. No reasons were given for the refusal. P was not allowed to address the Committee. The Committee had before it letters from P's solicitors stating that a refusal would result in the closure of P's business with the loss of six jobs and P's livelihood. The Committee received objections to P's application of which P was not notified. The Committee were informed that there were outstanding allegations in respect of food hygiene offences against the business dating from before the business came into P's ownership. P applied for judicial review of the Committee's refusal contending that the rules of natural justice had been breached, that no consideration was given to the consequences of refusing consent for P's business and that the allegations of food hygiene offences had improperly been considered. *Held,* dismissing the application, that the Committee had P's representations before it and thus must be presumed to have considered them. The Committee had been advised that the public hygiene matters did not arise from P's ownership of the business and thus must be presumed to have disregarded those matters. The Committee was not obliged to hear oral representations on P's behalf. Unlike the system of control through licensing, Schedule 4 of the Act contained no provisions to limit the relevant considerations to an application for a consent nor the grounds for refusing such an application. The Act gave no right of appeal against the refusal of a consent. The local authority was not obliged to give reasons for refusing to grant a consent. P should have been notified of the objections to his application and given the opportunity to answer them. As any comment P might make on the objections was unlikely to make a material difference to the Committee's consideration of his application, the court would not exercise its discretion to grant judicial review of the Committee's refusal of his application (*McInnes* v. *Onslow-Fane* [1978] C.L.Y. 21, *R.* v. *Gaming Board for Great Britain, ex p. Benaim and Khaida* [1970] C.L.Y. 1160, *R.* v. *Huntingdon District Council, ex p. Cowan* [1984] C.L.Y. 2777 considered).

R. *v.* BRISTOL CITY COUNCIL, *ex p.* PEARCE (1985) 83 L.G.R. 711, Glidewell J.

2055. Street trading—unlicensed traders—injunctions

Although an unusual course, where it is shown that the criminal process has not been a sufficient deterrent and magistrates have imposed fines below the maximum available, a local authority is entitled to an injunction to restrain unlicensed street traders regularly convicted of the offence: WESTMINSTER CITY COUNCIL *v.* FREEMAN (1985) 135 New L.J. 1232, C.A.

2056. Superannuation. See PENSIONS AND SUPERANNUATION.

2057. Thames Barrier

THAMES BARRIER AND FLOOD PREVENTION ACT 1972 (AMENDMENT) ORDER 1986 (No. 227) [40p], made under the Local Government Act 1985 (c.51), ss.101, 103(6); operative on April 1, 1986; transfers to the Thames Water Authority functions under the 1972 Act that were formerly exercised by the GLC.

2058. Tyne Tunnel

TYNE TUNNEL ORDER 1986 (No. 298) [80p], made under the Local Government Act 1985 (c.51), ss.52, 100, 101; operative on April 1, 1986; transfers the Tyne Tunnel to the Tyne and Wear Passenger Transport Authority.

2059. Waste regulation. See PUBLIC HEALTH.

LONDON

2060. Greater London Council
GREATER LONDON COUNCIL HOUSING (STAFF TRANSFER AND PROTECTION) ORDER 1979 (AMENDMENT) ORDER 1986 (No. 918) [45p], made under the London Government Act 1963 (c.33), ss.84, 85; operative on June 30, 1986; amend S.I. 1979 No. 1737.

2061. ILEA. See LOCAL GOVERNMENT.

2062. London regional transport
LONDON REGIONAL TRANSPORT (LEVY) ORDER 1986 (No. 156) [80p], made under the London Regional Transport Act 1984 (c.32), s.13(4); operative on February 4, 1986; imposes a levy of 9·79 pence in the pound on all rating areas in Greater London for the year 1986/7.

2063. Main rivers. See LOCAL GOVERNMENT, § 2033.

2064. Museum of London Act 1986 (c.8). See LITERARY AND SCIENTIFIC INSTITUTIONS, § 2004.

2065. Roads
DESIGNATION OF ROADS IN GREATER LONDON ORDER 1986 (No. 154) [£1·85], made under the Local Government Act 1985 (c.51), Sched. 5, para. 5(1); operative on April 1, 1986; designates roads in Greater London for the purposes of Sched. 5, para. 5(1) to the 1985 Act.

2066. Taxicabs
LONDON CAB ORDER 1986 (No. 857) [80p], made under the Metropolitan Public Carriage Act 1869 (c.115), s.9, and the London Cab and Stage Carriage Act 1907 (c.55), s.1 as extended by the London Cab Act 1968 (c.7), s.1; operative on June 15, 1986; increases taxicab fares.

LONDON TAXIS (LICENSING APPEALS) REGULATIONS 1986 (No. 1188) [45p], made under the Transport Act 1985 (c.67), s.17(2) and (5); operative on August 1, 1986; provide for appeals against decisions to refuse the grant of a taxi licence.

2067. Woolwich ferry
WOOLWICH FERRY ORDER 1986 (No. 330) [80p], made under the Local Government Act 1985 (c.51), ss.100, 101; operative on April 1, 1986; provides for the transfer of the operation of the Woolwich ferry to the Secretary of State.

MAGISTERIAL LAW

2068. Appeal—judicial review—breach of natural justice—damages—enforcement proceedings
[Maintenance Orders Act 1958 (c.39), s.18; Powers of Criminal Courts Act 1973 (c.62), s.21; Justices of the Peace Act 1979 (c.55), s.44; Magistrates Courts Act 1980 (c.43), ss.76, 77, 93.] In 1973 an order had been made by the justices that H should pay £2·50 p.w. for W and £1·50 p.w. for each of five children of the family. No payments were made. In 1974 W assigned the order to the D.H.S.S. In 1978 the arrears amounted to £2,490 and a warrant was issued but it was returned unexecuted. In 1981, no further payments having been made, a further warrant was issued. H appeared at court. £1,713 of the arrears was remitted, leaving £1,000 outstanding. H was ordered to pay £10 off the arrears and the current order, by this stage, of £4 p.w. Following H's further default he was arrested. In 1982 a 42 day suspended committal order was made on terms. H made three payments. H applied for a variation following service of a notice of commitment under s.18 of the 1958 Act. The application was dismissed and he was sent to prison in 1983. H's further application under s.18(4) was also refused. In 1984 the order was reduced to 1p a year and the arrears were remitted. H applied by way of judicial review to quash the committal orders of 1982 and 1983 and for damages from the justices. *Held,* dismissing the application, that where complaint was made that justices had reached a conclusion without any or any sufficient evidence to support it, the proper course was to proceed by way of case stated. Whilst s.21(1) of the 1973 Act required that the existence of legal aid should be notified to the defendant in specific circumstances the procedure for enforcement set out under s.18 of the 1958 Act and ss.76, 77 and 93 of the 1980 Act provided ample safeguards for the recalcitrant payer. *Wednesbury* principles were applicable to administrative decisions and not to judicial decisions of courts of law. Accordingly the justices were entitled to make the orders for

committal. Equally there was no principle or rule that a man in receipt of state benefits should not be required to make periodical payments nor that he should be reduced below subsistence level. By s.44 of the 1979 Act justices were not liable to be sued for damages if acting within the scope of their jurisdiction unless malice or lack of reasonable or probable cause was alleged. There was no evidence here (*Associated Provincial Picture Houses* v. *Wednesbury Corporation* (1948) C.L.C. 8107 considered; *Freeman* v. *Swatridge* [1984] C.L.Y. 1105; *McC (A Minor) Re* [1985] C.L.Y. 2108 and *G.* v. *G. (Minors: Custody Appeal)* [1985] C.L.Y. 2594 followed): R. v. CARDIFF JUSTICES, *ex p.* SALTER (1986) 1 F.L.R. 162, Wood J.

2069. Bail—failure to surrender—conduct of trial
[Bail Act 1976 (c.63), s.6.]
Only the court which grants bail can try the breach of it. If bail from a magistrates' court is breached, the offence is not indictable and cannot be tried by the Crown Court.

D was granted bail in the magistrates' court pending summary trial for deception. He absconded. When he was brought before the court two years later on a warrant, he pleaded guilty to absconding and was committed to the Crown Court for sentence. In the Crown Court he argued that the magistrates' court had had no jurisdiction to try the matter, since no information had been laid within six months of the offences. He was allowed to change his plea and the matter was remitted for hearing by the magistrates. The magistrates assumed jurisdiction, D pleaded guilty and was committed for sentence to the Crown Court. *Held*, dismissing D's appeal, that (1) no information need be laid; the court heard the proceedings of its own motion; (2) the matter could be tried only by the court which granted bail, and the magistrate was right to convict him and committ him for sentence. (*R.* v. *Manchester Stipendiary Magistrate ex p. Hill* [1982] C.L.Y. 1963; *R.* v. *Harbax Singh* [1979] C.L.Y. 406 and *R.* v. *Tyson* [1979] C.L.Y. 572 considered).
SCHIAVO v. ANDERTON [1986] 3 W.L.R. 177, D.C.

2070. Binding over—reason for not imposing bind-over—discretion
[Magistrates' Courts Act 1980 (c.43), s.115.] It is wrong in principle not to bind-over a defendant simply because he will not stop the acts complained of. A reason for not binding-over in those circumstances might be that imprisonment would be unjust in relation to other penalties visited upon other defendants in the same case.
LANHAM v. BERNARD, *The Times*, June 23, 1986, D.C.

2071. Binding over—victim of wounding
[Justices of the Peace Act 1968 (c.69), s.1(7).] G was involved in a fight. Later he was struck by X in a separate incident. G was charged under s.5 of the Public Order Act 1936 re the first incident. He attended X's Crown Court trial pursuant to a prosecution unconditional witness order but X pleaded guilty to wounding G, who therefore did not have to give evidence. After the judge had asked G whether he had anything to say on the question of whether G should be bound over, the judge bound him over to keep the peace for two years in his own recognisance of £200. *Held*, quashing the order, that (1) since G was not a person "who or whose case" was "before the Court" within s.1(7) of the 1968 Act, there was no jurisdiction to bind him over; (2) the judge should not have dealt with matters which would have been dealt with at G's trial, which had been adjourned by magistrates, pending the outcome of X's trial; (3) the proceedings were contrary to natural justice. G had no legal representation or opportunity to adduce evidence. The earlier incident was unconnected with the incident involving X. The evidence against G was never disclosed to him; (4) the prosecution had not informed the judge of G's means, though they had suggested the bind-over and the judge had not enquired as to G's means. Accordingly, there was no proper evidence from which to assess a proper sum for the recognisance; (5) it was unnecessary to decide whether admissible evidence of a risk of further breach of peace was necessary before a binding over order could be made (*R.* v. *Central Criminal Court, ex p. Boulding* [1984] C.L.Y. 2091 applied; *Sheldon* v. *Bromfield* [1964] C.L.Y. 2279 and *R.* v. *South West London Magistrates, ex p. Brown* [1974] C.L.Y. 2255 distinguished): R. v. KINGSTON CROWN COURT, *ex p.* GUARINO [1986] Crim.L.R. 325, D.C.

2072. Binding over—young offender—refusal to be bound over—power of justices
[Magistrates' Courts Act 1980 (c.43), s.115(3); Criminal Justice Act 1982 (c.48), s.9(1)(c).]

A court may commit to custody a person under 21 for refusal to be bound over under s.9(1)(*c*) of the Criminal Justice Act 1981.

D, aged 19, appeared before magistrates who found he had behaved in a way likely to cause a breach of the peace. He refused to be bound over; the magistrates considered they had power to commit him to custody notwithstanding his age. On appeal to the Divisional Court the question was whether, by reason of the Criminal Justice Act 1982 a person under 21 could be committed to custody. *Held*, dismissing the appeal, that a refusal to be bound over came within s.12(1) of the Contempt of Court Act 1981, and the magistrates were right to commit under s.9(1)(*c*) of the 1982 Act and s.115(3) of the Magistrates' Court Act 1980. (*Veater* v. *G.* [1981] C.L.Y. 473 considered).

Howley *v.* Oxford (1985) 81 Cr.App.R. 246, D.C.

2073. Child abduction

Magistrates' Courts (Child Abduction and Custody) Rules 1986 (No. 1141 (L.7)) [80p], made under the Magistrates' Courts Act 1980 (c.43), s.144; operative on August 1, 1986; provide for the procedure to be followed in magistrates' courts in consequence of the Child Abduction and Custody Act 1985.

2074. Committal—maintenance arrears—case stated

[Maintenance Orders Act 1958 (c.39), s.18.] A committal order for non-payment of maintenance is a final order notwithstanding s.18, and the Stipendiary Magistrate should have stated a case at the request of one party. (*Streames* v. *Copping* [1985] C.L.Y. 2128): R. *v.* Horseferry Road Magistrates' Court, ex p. Bernstein, *The Times*, November 4, 1986, Arnold J.

2075. Committal for trial—no evidence offered by prosecution—whether magistrates' duty not to commit

D elected trial on indictment on a charge of assault occasioning actual bodily harm. Prior to committal proceedings, the prosecution indicated its intention not to proceed with the charge but to charge D instead with a purely summary offence under s.51(1) of the Police Act 1964. D's solicitor sent to the court formal admissions including one of contact with the police officer's face as he was trying to eject D from a football ground. As the prosecution offered no evidence, the magistrate discharged D at the committal hearing. *Held*, dismissing D's application for judicial review of the decision, that once the prosecution decides to offer no evidence at committal proceedings, examining justices are bound to discharge the defendant (*R. v. Canterbury and St. Augustine Justices, ex p. Klisiak* [1981] C.L.Y. 549 applied): R. *v.* Horseferry Road Magistrates' Court, *ex p.* O'Regan [1986] Crim.L.R. 679, D.C.

2076. Compensation order—garnishee proceedings to enforce—effect of pending appeal. See Gooch *v.* Ewing (Allied Irish Bank, Garnishee), § 411.

2077. Costs—acquittal of defendant—prosecution ordered to pay defence costs

Justices when considering an order for costs on an indictable matter tried summarily, must bear in mind the provisions of the relevant practice direction.

The accused was charged with theft (shoplifting) and tried summarily. The defence, accepting the prosecution facts, went to her state of mind. She was acquitted and the prosecution was ordered to pay defence costs of £250. An application was made by the Crown for certiorari, to quash the order. *Held*, allowing the application, that the justices had failed to bear in mind para. 4 of the Practice Direction; if those guidelines were borne in mind there was no basis for making the order (*Practice Direction: Magistrates' Courts* [1982] 1 W.L.R. 1447).

R. *v.* Horseferry Road Justices, *ex p.* Underwoods (Cash Chemists) (1985) 81 Cr.App.R. 334, D.C.

2078. Discontinuation of proceeding

Magistrates' Courts (Discontinuance of Proceedings) Rules 1986 (No. 367 (L.1)) [40p], made under the Magistrates' Courts Act 1980 (c.43), s.144 as extended by the Prosecution of Offences Act 1985 (c.23), s.23; operative on April 1, 1986; makes provision regarding the discontinuance of criminal proceedings in magistrates' courts by the DPP where he has conduct of these proceedings.

2079. Fixed penalties

MAGISTRATES' COURTS (FORMS) (AMENDMENT) RULES 1986 (No. 1333 (L.12)) [£1·40] made under the Magistrates' Courts Act 1980 (c.43), s.144; operative on October 1, 1986; relates to the new system of fixed penalties.

2080. Guilty plea by post—procedural defect—whether judicial review

Where a defendant submits a postal plea of guilty, and there is a procedural defect when the case comes to be heard in his absence, that defect may give rise to judicial review. If the Divisional court declares the proceedings to have been a nullity, this is equivalent to quashing the conviction. There can then be a rehearing before the justices: R. *v.* EPPING AND ONGAR JUSTICES, *ex p.* SHIPPAM (C.) AND BREACH, *The Times,* June 7, 1986, D.C.

2081. Justices

JUSTICES OF THE PEACE (SIZE AND CHAIRMANSHIP OF BENCH) RULES 1986 (No. 923 (L.5)) [£1·40], made under the Justices of the Peace Act 1979 (c.55), s.18; operative on July 1, 1986; consolidate with amendments S.I. 1964 No. 1107, as amended.

2082. Justices—discontinuance of summary trial—exercise of powers

[Magistrates' Courts Act 1980 (c.43), s.25(2).] Justices have the power under s.25(2) of the Magistrates' Courts Act 1980 to discontinue summary trial of a defendant in favour of committal proceedings. This power cannot, however, be exercised until the summary trial has actually started: R. *v.* SOUTHEND JUSTICES, *ex p.* Wood, *The Times,* March 8, 1986, D.C.

2083. Justices—identity—right to know

There is no entitlement for magistrates to preserve their anonymity when sitting, and any attempt to do so is inimical to justice: R. *v.* FELIXSTOWE JUSTICES, *ex p.* LEIGH, *The Times,* October 8, 1986, D.C.

2084. Justices—liability to action—whether in execution of office

[Justices of the Peace Act 1979 (c.55), s.52(1).]

The liability of justices who have acted in excess of their jurisdiction, or without jurisdiction, may be limited to one penny.

S was liable to make periodical payments to his wife for their children pursuant to an order of the High Court. Because of an administrative error the order was not registered with the local magistrates' court. Mistakenly, but quite genuinely, S refused to make the payments: he believed that as a matter of law he did not need to make the payments. The justices committed him to 42 days' imprisonment, although, because of the failure to register the order they had no jurisdiction at all to deal with the matter. S claimed damages. *Held,* that s.52 of the 1979 Act was apt to include actions by justices which were in excess of their jurisdiction, or which were done without jurisdiction. In such circumstances the damages were limited to one penny.

R. *v.* WALTHAM FOREST JUSTICES, *ex p.* SOLANKE [1986] 3 W.L.R. 315, C.A.

2085. Justices—powers to order joint trial

Even when prosecution and defence agree that offences should be tried separately, justices can still order joint trial (*Clayton* v. *Chief Constable of Norfolk* [1983] C.L.Y. 2376 considered): R. *v.* HIGHBURY CORNER MAGISTRATES' COURT, *ex p.* McGINLEY AND LYNCH, *The Times,* February 4, 1986, D.C.

2086. Justices—unlicensed vehicle—back duty—whether power to reduce. See CHIEF CONSTABLE OF KENT *v.* MATHER, § 2928.

2087. Justice's clerk—discretion to issue summons—delay in application

When an application is made to a justices' clerk for a summons, he can ask why there has been a delay in the application, and, if there is no good reason for the delay, he has discretion to refuse to issue the summons. Summonses should not be applied for merely to forestall the expiry of a limitation period: R. *v.* CLERK TO THE MEDWAY JUSTICES, *ex p.* DEPARTMENT OF HEALTH AND SOCIAL SECURITY, *The Times,* June 14, 1986, D.C.

2088. Justices' clerk—duty to record evidence—domestic proceedings

The clerk to the justices must record oral evidence given in domestic proceedings: GRAY *v.* GRAY, *The Times,* February 25, 1986.

2089. Justices' clerk—notes—whether duty to supply to defendant

[Legal Aid in Criminal Proceedings (General) Regulations 1968 (S.I. 1968 No. 1230), reg. 16.]

Where a defendant appeals to the Crown Court against his conviction by the justices, the justices' clerk is not under a duty to provide the defendant with any notes of evidence unless the defendant is legally aided.

H appeared unrepresented before the justices charged with contravening a noise abatement order. H was convicted and appealed to the Crown Court. H instructed solicitors who applied to the clerk to the justices for a copy of any notes taken at the hearing. The clerk refused to provide any copies of his notes. H applied for judicial review seeking an order of mandamus to compel the clerk to supply a copy of his notes. *Held*, dismissing the application, that there was no rule at common law which entitled H to a copy of the clerk's notes. Rule 17 of the Magistrates' Courts Rules 1981 did not require the clerk to send any notes of evidence to the Crown Court when a defendant appealed against conviction, unlike r.74, which required such notes to be sent to a Crown Court if the defendant was committed to the Crown Court after conviction. Had H been legally aided the clerk would have been obliged to provide a copy of his notes by reg. 16 of the Legal Aid in Criminal Proceedings (General) Regulations 1968. H was not legally aided. The court could not order the clerk to give a copy of his notes to H. However, it is desirable that there should be no difference in procedure as far as possible between appeals by legally-aided defendants and non-legally aided defendants. Requests for copies of notes of evidence should be viewed sympathetically by justices' clerks (*R.* v. *Clerk to Lancaster Justices ex p. Hill* [1983] C.L.Y. 540 followed, *Practice Note (Appeals and Committals to Quarter Sessions)* [1956] C.L.Y. 5415, *Hill* v. *Wilson* [1984] C.L.Y. 2100 considered).

R. *v.* CLERK TO HIGHBURY CORNER JUSTICES, *ex p.* HUSSEIN [1986] 1 W.L.R. 1266, D.C.

2090. Juvenile—committal with adult

[Magistrates' Courts Act 1980 (c.43), s.24(1)(*b*).] When deciding whether to commit a juvenile for trial to the crown court jointly with an adult both juvenile and adult must appear at the same time. However, that decision having been made it is not necessary for both to appear at the same time when considering the adequacy of the evidence against each: R. *v.* DONCASTER CROWN COURT, *ex p.* CROWN PROSECUTION SERVICE, *The Times*, December 2, 1986, D.C.

2091. Juvenile court—committal for trial—mode of trial—power to reverse previous decision

[Magistrates' Courts Act 1980 (c.43), s.24(1).]

Where a juvenile court has determined the mode of trial of an alleged juvenile offender, a differently constituted court, on an adjourned hearing, has no power to review or reverse the previous decision in the absence of a change of circumstances.

Per curiam: (i) A decision to proceed summarily is open to review at any time before the beginning of the trial if there is a change of circumstances since the original decision was taken or if circumstances are drawn to the attention of the court that had existed at the time but had not been drawn to the attention of the court on the earlier occasion; (ii) The justices could on a plea of not guilty decide during the summary trial to exercise their power under s.24(6) of the Magistrates' Courts Act 1980 to discontinue the trial and proceed as examining justices.

The applicant, aged 16, appeared before the juvenile court charged with robbery and the possession of an imitation firearm. The justices, having heard submissions for the applicant and the prosecution, decided not to exercise their power under s.24(1)(*a*) of the Magistrates' Courts Act 1980 to commit him for trial on indictment but to proceed summarily. No plea was taken, the case was adjourned, and bail was granted. He did not surrender to bail, was arrested, and charged with other offences committed both before the original charge and while on bail. He appeared before a differently constituted Bench which decided that the previous decision was not informed, and purported to reverse it and committed the applicant for trial on the original charges. In so deciding they took into account only those factors which were placed before the justices on the previous occasion. The applicant's application for judicial review was granted. *Held,* that once a properly constituted Bench had made a proper decision under s.24 considering all the relevant factors and ordered summary trial, that could not be re-examined later by a differently constituted Bench on the same facts. The order of committal was *ultra vires* and would be quashed. (*R.* v. *Dudley Justices, ex p. Gillard* [1986] C.L.Y. 2103 considered).

R. *v.* NEWHAM JUVENILE COURT *ex p.* F (A MINOR) [1986] 1 W.L.R. 939, D.C.

2092. Magistrates' courts

MAGISTRATES' COURTS (AMENDMENT) RULES 1986 (No. 1332 (L.11)) [45p], made under the Magistrates' Courts Act 1980 (c.43), s.144; operative on October 1, 1986; relate to the new system of fixed penalties.

MAGISTRATES' COURTS (CIVIL JURISDICTION AND JUDGMENTS ACT 1982) RULES 1986 (No. 1962 (L.15)) [£2·40], made under the Magistrates' Courts Act 1980 (c.43), ss.144, 145 as extended by the Maintenance Orders Act 1958 (c.39), s.2A(1), the Maintenance Orders (Reciprocal Enforcement) Act 1972 (c.18), ss.2(3), 8(5), 33(4) and the Civil Jurisdiction and Judgments Act 1982 (c.27), ss.12, 48; operative on January 1, 1987; provide for the procedure to be followed in dealing with certain claims under the Convention on jurisdiction and enforcement of judgments in civil and commercial matters signed at Brussels on September 27, 1968.

MAGISTRATES' COURTS (WELSH FORMS) RULES 1986 (No. 1079 (L.6)) [£7·00], made under the Magistrates' Courts Act 1980 (c.43), s.144 and the Welsh Language Act 1967 (c.66), s.2; operative on August 1, 1986; provide for the use of Welsh forms in magistrates' courts proceedings in Wales.

2093. Magistrates' courts—list of charges—whether lawful

[Magistrates' Courts Rules (S.I. 1981 No. 552), r.66; Magistrates' Courts (Forms) Rules (S.I. 1981 No. 553).] The practice of producing for a Bench of justices a list which sets out the matters to be dealt with on a particular day, and including all charges related or unrelated against a single defendant, is not wrong in law. The form of list prescribed by the Magistrates' Courts (Forms) Rules 1981 for the register to be kept pursuant to r.66 of the Magistrates' Courts Rules 1981 is unobjectionable, and although there may be occasions when it is undesirable for unrelated charges to be listed together, the clerk's good sense should enable him to identify those occasions (*R.* v. *Weston-super-Mare Justices, ex p. Stone*, unreported, November 19, 1984 applied; *R.* v. *Liverpool Justices, ex p. Topping* [1983] C.L.Y. 2305 not applied): R. *v.* WESTON-SUPER-MARE JUSTICES, *ex p.* SHAW, *The Times*, October 27, 1986, D.C.

2094. Maintenance—arrears—appeal

[Maintenance Orders Act 1958 (c.39), s.4(7); Domestic Proceedings and Magistrates' Courts Act 1980 (c.22), s.29(1); Magistrates' Courts Act 1980 (c.43), ss.95, 111.]

There is no right of appeal to the High Court from a decision by justices on an application to remit arrears of maintenance other than by case stated under s.111 of the Magistrates' Courts Act 1980 on the grounds that the justices have erred in law or acted in excess of jurisdiction.

W sought to enforce arrears of maintenance against H. H asked the justices to remit all arrears. The justices refused. The Divisional Court held that it had no jurisdiction to entertain H's appeal by notice of motion, either under s.4(7) of the Maintenance Order Act 1958 or under s.29(1) of the Domestic Proceedings and Magistrates' Courts Act 1978. *Held*, dismissing H's appeal, that there was no right of appeal, save by way of case stated under s.111 of the Magistrates' Courts Act 1980 on the ground that the justices had erred in law or acted in excess of jurisdiction. (*Fletcher* v. *Fletcher* [1985] C.L.Y. 1689 approved; *Allen* v. *Allen* [1985] C.L.Y. 2115 disapproved).

BERRY *v.* BERRY [1986] 3 W.L.R. 257, C.A.

2095. Maintenance order—power to rectify

In 1982 H had been ordered to pay maintenance to the three children of the marriage "until each child attained the age of 16 years." H complied with the order. In October 1984 H ceased payment to the eldest child on his sixteenth birthday. In January 1985 H received an "amended order" with a covering letter from the clerk to the justices informing him that he should have continued payments as the original order had been subsequently amended requiring him to pay maintenance "until the date of the birthday of the children next following their attaining the upper limit of compulsory school age." H applied for judicial review to quash the "amended order." In his affidavit the clerk to the justices stated that he had no recollection of what had been said by the chairman of the justices but his notes indicated that the original order had been drawn up incorrectly due to a clerical error and that he had sought to rectify it by amending the order. *Held*, allowing H's application, that there was no statutory power in the magistrates' court to rectify mistakes in civil proceedings. In a number of similar cases such a power had been recognised when, for example, the order did not accurately reflect what had been said in court and there was no dispute as to that fact; but here the only evidence came from the clerk's scanty notes. In those circumstances the 1982 order should be deemed to be accurate. Even if there was a power to rectify, it lay in the court and could not be dealt with administratively by the clerk. Finally, it was far too late to amend the order, the effect of which would be to put H into arrears with the consequent threat of enforcement proceedings. (*R.* v. *Chester Justices, ex p. Holland* [1984] C.L.Y. 2126 considered): R. *v.* BRIGHTON MAGISTRATES COURT, *ex p.* BUDD (1986) 16 Fam. Law 134, McNeill J.

2096. Maintenance order—variation—succession adjourned hearings before different justices—unsatisfactory

The order had been registered in the magistrates court. H did not make any payments and arrears accrued. He applied for a variation and remission of the arrears on the ground of unemployment. The case was adjourned after H had given evidence of his circumstances. During each adjourned hearing a differently constituted bench of justices heard the evidence. The justices found that H's testimony could not be relied upon and made an order exceeding his weekly income. *Held*, allowing H's appeal, that the whole hearing had been extremely unsatisfactory. None of the evidence had been heard collectively by the bench. Furthermore the ground upon which the justices proceeded involved an assessment of H's credibility. That finding had never been canvassed in evidence and was plainly unsatisfactory. Due to a change in H's circumstances in that he had ceased to receive unemployment benefit and would shortly be receiving supplementary benefit the matter would be remitted to the justices for reconsideration: DUNCAN *v.* DUNCAN (1986) 16 Fam. Law 136, D.C.

2097. Maintenance—variation of order—hearing—involvement of justices

H applied to the justices for a variation of a maintenance order and for remission of substantial arrears. At the hearing both parties gave evidence as to their means without interruption from the justices. They dismissed H's application and in their reasons stated that they had not believed his evidence on certain specified matters. H appeared contending that the justices had wrongly rejected his evidence without giving him sufficient notice as to their doubts and an opportunity to give further explanation of the areas in doubts. *Held*, allowing H's appeal, that it was incumbent upon the justices in the interests of justice before dismissing the applicant's evidence out of hand, to give him some warning of their doubts and where appropriate to invite some further explanation. In the present case an unwitting miscarriage of justice had occurred. The case would be remitted for a rehearing before a fresh panel: COMLEY-ROSS *v.* COMLEY-ROSS (1986) 16 Fam. Law 132, Sheldon J.

2098. Periodical payments—husband supporting cohabitee and her child—considerations.
See BLOWER *v.* BLOWER, § 1668.

2099. Petty sessional divisions

PETTY SESSIONAL DIVISIONS (CORNWALL) ORDER 1986 (No. 2113) [80p], made under the Justices of the Peace Act 1979 (c.55), s.23(3)(5); operative on January 1, 1987; combines the petty sessional divisions of East Middle, East South and Liskerrett to form the new division of South East Cornwall.

PETTY SESSIONAL DIVISIONS (DYFED) ORDER 1986 (No. 765) [£1·40], made under the Justices of the Peace Act 1979 (c.55), s.23(1); provides for the reorganisation of petty sessional divisions within the county.

PETTY SESSIONAL DIVISIONS (NORTHUMBERLAND) ORDER 1986 (No. 1057) [80p], made under the Justices of the Peace Act 1979 (c.55), s.23(3)(5); operative on September 1, 1986; provides for the combination of the divisions of Bellingham and Hexham to form a new petty sessional division of Tynedale.

PETTY SESSIONAL DIVISIONS (NORTHUMBERLAND) (No. 2) ORDER 1986 (No. 2114) [80p], made under the Justices of the Peace Act 1979 (c.55), s.23(3)(5); operative on January 1, 1987; creates a new division of Coquetdale from the existing divisions of West Coquetdale Ward and Bamburgh and East Coquetdale.

PETTY SESSIONAL DIVISIONS (OXFORDSHIRE) ORDER 1986 (No. 2192) [£1·40], made under the Justices of the Peace Act 1979 (c.55), s.23(3)(5); operative on January 1,

1987; provides for the creation of a new petty sessional division of Witney from those of Bampton East and Bampton West and for a new division of East Oxfordshire from the divisions of Bullingdon and Watlington.

PETTY SESSIONAL DIVISIONS (WEST GLAMORGAN) ORDER 1986 (No. 231) [40p], made under the Justices of the Peace Act 1979 (c.55), s.23(3); operative on March 1, 1986; renames the petty sessional division of Afan as Port Talbot.

2100. Probation

COMBINED PROBATION AREAS ORDER 1986 (No. 1713) [£2·40], made under the Powers of Criminal Courts Act 1973 (c.62), s.54(4), Sched. 3, para. 1; consolidates with amendments S.I. 1974 No. 529, as amended.

COMBINED PROBATION AREAS (CORNWALL) ORDER 1986 (No. 2316) [45p], made under the Powers of Criminal Courts Act 1973 (c.62), s.54(4); Sched. 3, para. 1; operative in January 1, 1987; amend S.I. 1986 No. 1713 to take account of the combination of the petty sessional divisions of East Middle, East South and Liskerrett.

COMBINED PROBATION AREAS (DYFED) ORDER 1986 (No. 945) [45p], made under the Powers of Criminal Courts Act 1973 (c.62), s.54(4), Sched. 3, para. 1; operative on July 1, 1986; amends S.I. 1974 No. 529 to take account of the reorganisation of the petty sessional divisions of Dyfed.

COMBINED PROBATION AREAS (NORTHUMBRIA) ORDER 1986 (No. 2318) [45p], made under the Powers of Criminal Courts Act 1973 (c.62), s.54(4), Sched. 3, para. 1; operative on January 1, 1987; amends S.I. 1986 No. 1713 to take account of the combination of the petty sessional divisions of Bamburgh and East Coquetdale and West Coquetdale Ward.

COMBINED PROBATION AREAS (OXFORDSHIRE) ORDER 1986 (No. 2317) [45p], made under the Powers of Criminal Courts Act 1973 (c.62), s.54(4), Sched. 3, para. 1; operative on January 1, 1987; amends S.I. 1986 No. 1713 to take account of the combination of the petty sessional divisions of Bampton East and Bampton West.

2101. Procedure—protection order—breach—hearing rules of natural justice

H had appeared before the magistrates for an alleged breach of a protection order. By the time the case was reached his solicitor had had to leave for another appointment and, on the solicitor's advice, H had applied, unsuccessfully for an adjournment. Having been unable to find alternative representation the magistrates proceeded to hear the matter and fined H the sum of £20. He now applied for an order of certiorari to quash the decision contending that there had been a breach of natural justice. *Held*, refusing the application, that it was clear from the affidavits that H had been fully informed by the justices' clerk of his rights in the proceedings and had been helped by him in questioning witnesses including W and her witness at some length. In the circumstances the issue before the magistrates had been a simple one as to who was telling the truth. Accordingly, H had had full opportunity adequately to present his case. The application would also have had to be refused as it had been brought nine months after the decision. Notwithstanding such delay being due to the time taken to obtain legal aid and incorrect legal advice the court would not have extended the time as the penalty imposed had involved no substantial hardship or prejudice to H (*R. v. Stratford-on-Avon District Council, ex p. Jackson* [1985] C.L.Y. 2691 distinguished): R. *v.* ECCLES JUSTICES, *ex p.* SOUTHGATE (1986) 16 Fam. Law 262; (1986) 2 F.L.R. 163, McNeill J.

2102. Statistics—domestic proceedings

The Home Office has published a statistical bulletin (Issue 36/86) which gives details of statistics of domestic proceedings in magistrates' courts in England and Wales during 1985. Copies of the bulletin are available from the Statistical Department, Home Office, Lunar House, Croydon, Surrey CR0 9YD. Tel.: 01-760-2850. [£2.50.]

2103. Summary proceedings—offence triable summarily or on indictment—guilty plea—subsequent committal to Crown Court

[Magistrates' Courts Act 1980 (c.43), s.25(2).]

Where a magistrates' court accepts a guilty plea to an offence triable summarily or on indictment the defendant cannot thereafter be committed to the Crown Court for trial.

G appeared before the justices jointly charged with T with an offence of assault occasioning actual bodily harm. Having heard representations from the prosecution and G's solicitor the justices decided the matter was suitable for summary trial. G elected summary trial and pleaded guilty. T elected trial on indictment. One week later G and T appeared before a differently constituted Bench. The justices acceded to an application by the prosecution to discontinue G's summary trial and commit him to the Crown Court for trial with T. The Divisional Court made an order prohibiting the justices from committing G for trial. The prosecution appealed. *Held,* dismissing the appeal, that the justices could only commit G for trial pursuant to s.25(2) of the Magistrates' Courts Act 1980 before the conclusion of the evidence for the prosecution once the court had begun to try the information summarily. The "evidence for the prosecution" meant the evidence tendered to prove a defendant's guilt in a trial following a not guilty plea. Where a defendant pleaded guilty, summary trial proceedings could not be discontinued and the defendant could not be committed for trial to the Crown Court. After a plea of guilty had been accepted the defendant could only be committed to the Crown Court for sentence pursuant to s.38 of the Act.

GILLARD, *Re* (*sub nom.* R. *v.* DUDLEY JUSTICES, *ex p.* GILLARD) [1985] 3 W.L.R. 936, H.L.

2104. Trial—procedure—preliminary point
D was charged with driving an overweight vehicle. The prosecution relied upon a police officer's certificate that D had admitted responsibility for the vehicle pursuant to s.181 of the Road Traffic Act 1972. D's solicitor wished to challenge the admissibility of the certificate but did not require the officer to be called to give evidence. The justices refused to hear evidence from D on the point as a preliminary issue and proceeded with the prosecution case. No defence evidence was called. *Held,* dismissing his application for judicial review of the decision to refuse to decide the issue of admissibility as a preliminary issue, that within statutory restraints, justices determine their own procedure. D not having required the officer to be called, the justices were entitled to accept the prosecution evidence as providing a prima facie case on the point for D to deal with (*S.J.F.* v. *The Chief Constable of Kent* (10th June 1982) applied): R. *v.* EPPING AND ONGAR JUSTICES, *ex p.* MANBY [1986] Crim.L.R. 555, D.C.

2105. Witness summons—production of document—earliest time of production
[Magistrates' Courts Act 1980 (c.43), s.97(1).]
The first time at which a witness summons can require someone to produce a document or thing is the beginning of the committal proceedings.

W, a solicitor, was served with a witness summons directing him to produce at court tape recordings lodged with him by his client G, who was in custody during police investigations. The date for production was a remand hearing. W applied for judicial review by way of certiorari to quash the witness summons. *Held,* granting the application, that s.97(1) of the 1980 Act laid down that the first time at which a witness summons can require someone to produce a document or thing is the beginning of committal proceedings, and it did not therefore apply to a remand hearing; the justice to whom the application is made must be satisfied that the evidence is likely to be material to the charges, and an application in other terms is defective.

R. *v.* SHEFFIELD JUSTICES, *ex p.* WRIGLEY [1985] R.T.R. 78, D.C.

MALICIOUS PROSECUTION AND FALSE IMPRISONMENT

2106. Damages. See DAMAGES.

MARKETS AND FAIRS

2107. Stalls in former department store—whether market—whether city council entitled to injunction to protect its markets
Where a number of separate stalls were set up in a former department store a market was established which might be restrained by injunction by an owner of a statutory market in whose area the department store was located.

Manchester City Council owned and operated seven statutory markets within its area. In 1982 W obtained a lease of what was previously Affleck and Browns, a large department store, with the intention of turning it into an emporium in which large numbers of small traders might set up shop. W granted monthly licences to traders who wished to set up a stall in the building. Each unit occupied was divided from those around it by flimsy wooden lattice work in most cases and in some cases by nothing. When closed the units usually had similar lattice work drawn across their fronts although some had more substantial metal shutters. The licences were granted orally, no references were given by applicants nor taken up by W although an applicant might be refused a licence if other traders already there had something against him. Approximately 60 traders traded there in articles which would also be offered for sale in the council's markets. In 1983 the council were granted an injunction restraining W from operating a retail market of any description in the premises so as to interfere with or prejudicially affect the council's rights as a market owner. W appealed. *Held*, dismissing the appeal, that (1) the same rights attached to a statutory market as were attached to a franchise market established by a charter granted by the Crown. The council were entitled to protect their markets by an injunction restraining the operation of any rival market within 6⅝ miles of one of their markets; (2) W's operations constituted a market. A market was constituted by the provision of facilities for a concourse of buyers and sellers. There was an invitation to the public to come and sell at the premises. The fact that some control was exercised over sellers by the grant of licences did not alter the fact that a concourse was provided. It is a question of fact in each case as to whether or not a concourse of buyers and sellers exists; (3) the units operated by the sellers could not be described as shops and thus outside the field of the council's exclusive market rights (*Pope* v. *Whalley* (1865) 6 B. & S. 303, *Greenwood* v. *Whelan* [1967] C.L.Y. 2482 applied, *Birmingham Corporation* v. *Perry Barr Stadium* [1972] C.L.Y. 2125, *Kingston upon Hull City Council* v. *Greenwood* [1984] C.L.Y. 2136 considered, *Hailsham Cattle Market Co.* v. *Tolman* [1915] 2 Ch. 1 disapproved).

MANCHESTER CITY COUNCIL *v.* WALSH (1985) 50 P. & C.R. 409, C.A.

MEDICINE

2108. Carbadox

MEDICINES (CARBADOX PROHIBITION) ORDER 1986 (No. 1368) [80p], made under the Medicines Act 1968 (c.67), s.62; operative on September 3, 1986; prohibits the sale or supply of medicinal products containing carbadox and animal feed stuffs in which such products have been incorporated.

2109. Chemical sterilants

MEDICAL (CHEMICAL STERILANTS) ORDER 1986 (No. 2177 [95p], made under the Medicines Act 1968 (c.67), s.130(5)(*c*); operative on January 8, 1987; specifies chemical substances used to sterilise animals which are neither domesticated nor held in captivity as being excluded from the application of the 1968 Act.

2110. Corneal Tissue Act 1986 (c.18)

This Act amends the Human Tissue Act 1961, s.1 so as to allow the removal of eyes or parts of eyes for therapeutic purposes and purposes of medical education and research by persons who are not medically qualified, subject to appropriate safeguards.

The Act received the Royal Assent on June 26, 1986 and comes into force on August 26, 1986. It does not extend to Northern Ireland.

2111. Court welfare officer—inquiry and report—practice direction. See PRACTICE DIRECTION (FAM. D.) (CHILDREN: INQUIRY AND REPORT BY A WELFARE OFFICER), § 2631.

2112. Dentists

DENTAL AUXILIARIES REGULATIONS 1986 (No. 887) [£1·90], made under the Dentists Act 1984 (c.24), s.45; operative on May 19, 1986; provide, *inter alia,* for the enrolment of dental auxiliaries and for the approval of courses of training.

2113. Fees

RESIDENTIAL CARE HOMES (AMENDMENT) REGULATIONS 1986 (No. 457) [40p], made under the Registered Homes Act 1984 (c.23), ss.5(1), 8 and 16(1)(*j*), (*k*) and (2); operative on April 1, 1986, increase fees payable under S.I. 1984 No. 1345.

2114. General Medical Council

GENERAL MEDICAL COUNCIL (CONSTITUTION OF FITNESS TO PRACTISE COMMITTEES) RULES ORDER OF COUNCIL 1986 (No. 1390) (£1·40), made under the Medical Act 1983 (c.54), Sched. 1, paras. 20, 21, 22; operative on September 1, 1986; regulate the constitutions of the fitness to practise committees of the G.M.C.

GENERAL MEDICAL COUNCIL (REGISTRATION (FEES) REGULATIONS) ORDER OF COUNCIL 1986 (No. 149) [£1·35], made under the Medical Act 1983 (c.54), s.32; operative on February 1, 1986; prescribes fees payable to the GMC under the 1983 Act in respect of entries in the register of medical practitioners.

2115. Hearings
MEDICINES ACT 1968 (HEARINGS BY PERSONS APPOINTED) RULES 1986 (No. 1761) [80p], made under the Tribunals and Inquiries Act 1971 (c.62), s.11; operative on November 10, 1986; prescribe the procedure to be followed in connection with hearings by persons appointed under the 1968 Act or under regulations made under s.60 of that Act.

2116. Hormone growth promoters
MEDICINES (HORMONE GROWTH PROMOTERS) (PROHIBITION OF USE) REGULATIONS 1986 (No. 1876) [80p], made under the European Communities Act 1972 (c.68), s.2(2); operative on December 1, 1986; prohibit the administration of both natural and synthetic hormone growth promoters to animals other than for those specified for therapeutic treatment or for use in relation to fertility and reproduction.

2117. Medical practitioner—charge of professional misconduct—whether bad for duplicity—admissibility of evidence—whether injustice to practitioner
[General Medical Council Preliminary Proceedings Committee and Professional Conduct Committee (Procedure) Rules Order of Council 1980 (S.I. 1980 No. 858), Appendix, rr.30(1), 56(1).]

A charge against a doctor of professional misconduct referring to "individual patients" is not bad for duplicity where the reality of the charge, and its treatment by the parties, amounts to an allegation of an improper course of conduct.

The GMC charged P, a doctor, with abusing his professional position by repeatedly supplying drugs to patients without adequately researching the patients' backgrounds. The charge did not particularise the patients concerned but witness statements were sent to the solicitors acting for P, and no objection was raised to the form of the charge. At the hearing, evidence was given as to nine patients, including two whose identities were not released to the doctor, that evidence being inadmissible in criminal proceedings. Before admitting that evidence the Professional Conduct Committee failed to comply with r.56 of the 1980 Procedure rules, which required them to consult the legal assessor. *Held,* dismissing the appeal, that (i) the parties had treated the charge as referring to a course of conduct over the years and the fact that the charge might be bad for duplicity was no ground in the circumstances for allowing the appeal (*R.* v. *General Medical Council, ex p. Gee* [1986] C.L.Y. 2118 distinguished); (ii) although the Committee had been wrong in failing to consult the legal assessor before receiving evidence referring to the unidentified patients, no objection had been taken at the time, and P had not been prejudiced thereby; (iii) sufficient reasons had been given by the Committee and P had not been prejudiced by the paucity thereof (*Fox* v. *General Medical Council* [1960] C.L.Y. 1200 applied).

PEATFIELD *v.* GENERAL MEDICAL COUNCIL [1986] 1 W.L.R. 243, P.C.

2118. Medical practitioner—charge of professional misconduct—whether charge bad for duplicity—addition of further matters—whether fresh charges required
[General Medical Council Preliminary Proceedings Committee and Professional Conduct Committee (Procedure) Rules Order of Council 1980 (S.I. 1980 No. 858), Appendix, rr.11, 17, 22, 30.]

A charge of professional misconduct based upon a course of conduct in the treatment of a number of individual patients is not void for duplicity.

The General Medical Council received complaints from four of G's patients indicating that G was guilty of serious professional misconduct. The complaints were referred to the Preliminary Proceedings Committee which determined to charge G with serious professional misconduct and that an inquiry should be held by the Professional Conduct Committee. The charge as formulated set out allegations of fact concerning the treatment of individual patients and stated that in relation to the facts alleged G was guilty of serious professional misconduct. By way of further particulars given by letter in June and September 1984 the identity of eight patients was disclosed to G with information as to which of the allegations of fact stated in the charge applied to each patient. G sought further detailed particulars of what the council alleged constituted serious professional misconduct and requested the Council to amend the charge as it was duplicitous. The Council refused to provide further particulars and refused to amend the charge. On G's application for judicial review the charge was held to be bad for duplicity, the additional complaints could not be put before the Professional Conduct Committee without first being considered by the Preliminary Proceedings Committee and that G was entitled to the particulars sought. The Council appealed. *Held,* allowing the appeal in part, that a charge that was duplicitous was a bad charge and could not be proceeded on. A single charge based on a course of conduct where the charge was "serious professional misconduct" was not duplicitous even though the facts relied upon might identify several different patients and several different occasions. In G's case the charge could fairly be read as alleging a course of conduct adopted by G. In those circumstances the complaints of the four additional patients were merely further particulars of the charge that could be added by way of amendment pursuant to r.22 of the Rules. The additional complaints did not have to be considered by the Preliminary Proceedings Committee before they could be put before the Professional Conduct Committee. G was entitled to the further detailed particulars he sought (*Peatfield* v. *General Medical Council* [1986] C.L.Y. 2117 considered).

R. *v.* GENERAL MEDICAL COUNCIL, *ex p.* GEE [1986] 1 W.L.R. 1247, C.A.

2119. Medicinal products

MEDICINES (STILBENES AND THYROSTATIC SUBSTANCES) (AMENDMENT) REGULATIONS 1986 (No. 1980) [45p], made under the European Communities Act 1972 (c.68), s.2(2); operative on December 18, 1986; increase the maximum fine which can be imposed for an offence under S.I. 1982 No. 626 from £1,000 to £2,000.

2120. Midwives

NURSES, MIDWIVES AND HEALTH VISITORS (MIDWIVES AMENDMENT) RULES APPROVAL ORDER 1986 (No. 786) [£1·90], made under the Nurses, Midwives and Health Visitors Act 1979 (c.36), s.22(4); operative on May 30, 1986; amends S.I. 1983 No. 873 in relation to midwifery training and practice.

2121. Nurses agencies

NURSES AGENCIES AMENDMENT REGULATIONS 1986 (No. 1414) [45p], made under the Nurses Agencies Act 1957 (c.16), ss.2(2) and 7; operative on September 30, 1986; increase fees payable to a licensing authority for a licence to carry on a nurses' agency.

2122. Nurses, midwives and health visitors

NURSES, MIDWIVES AND HEALTH VISITORS (PERIODIC REGISTRATION) AMENDMENT RULES APPROVAL ORDER 1986 (No. 1345) [£1·40], made under the Nurses, Midwives and Health Visitors Act 1979 (c.36), s.22(4); operative on August 21, 1986; amend S.I. 1984 No. 873.

2123. Nursing homes

NURSING HOMES AND MENTAL NURSING HOMES (AMENDMENT) REGULATIONS 1986 (No. 456) [40p], made under the Registered Homes Act 1984 (c.23), ss.23(3)(*b*), 27 and 56(4); operative on April 1, 1986; increase the fees payable (associated with the registration of nursing homes) to the Secretary of State.

2124. Opticians

GENERAL OPTICAL COUNCIL (MEMBERSHIP) ORDER OF COUNCIL 1986 (No. 309) [40p], made under the Opticians Act 1958 (c.32), Sched., para. 13(1); operative on April 1, 1986; makes provision in relation to the membership of the General Optical Council.

2125. Pharmacist—misconduct

[Pharmacy Act 1954 (c.61), s.8.] A single act or error can be misconduct for the purpose of disciplinary proceedings even without any moral censure: R. *v.* PHARMACEUTICAL SOCIETY OF GREAT BRITAIN, *ex p.* SOKOH, *The Times,* December 4, 1986, Webster J.

2126. Poisons

POISONS (AMENDMENT) RULES 1986 (No. 10) [40p], made under the Poisons Act 1972 (c.66), s.7; operative on April 1, 1986; amend S.I. 1982 No. 218 by adding magnesium phosphide to Sched. 1.

POISONS (AMENDMENT No. 2) RULES 1986 (No. 1704) [45p], made under the Poisons Act 1972 (c.66), s.7; operative on December 1, 1986; amend S.I. 1982 No. 218 by including in the general exemptions any form of flux for use in soldering.

POISONS LIST ORDER 1986 (No. 9) [40p], made under the Poisons Act 1972 (c.66), s.2; operative on April 1, 1986; amends the Poisons List by adding magnesium phosphide to Pt. 1.

2127. Prescription only medicine—whether strict liability offence. See PHARMACEUTICAL SOCIETY OF GREAT BRITAIN *v.* STORKWAIN, § 701.

2128. Prescriptions
MEDICINES (PRODUCTS OTHER THAN VETERINARY DRUGS) (PRESCRIPTION ONLY) AMENDMENT ORDER 1986 (No. 586) [£1·35], made under the Medicines Act 1968 (c.67), ss.58(1)(4); operative on April 25, 1986; amends S.I. 1983 No. 1212.

2129. Professions supplementary to medicine
PROFESSIONS SUPPLEMENTARY TO MEDICINE (REGISTRATION RULES) (AMENDMENT) ORDER OF COUNCIL 1986 (No. 660) [45p], made under the Professions Supplementary to Medicine Act 1960 (c.66), s.2; approve rules amending S.I. 1962 No. 1765 by omitting references to the profession of remedial gymnasts.
PROFESSIONS SUPPLEMENTARY TO MEDICINE (WINDING UP OF REMEDIAL GYMNASTS BOARD) ORDER OF COUNCIL 1986 (No. 630) [£1·40], made under the Professions Supplementary to Medicine Act 1960, s.10(1); operative on April 1, 1986; provides for the winding up of the Remedial Gymnasts Board.

2130. Qualifications
MEDICAL AND DENTAL QUALIFICATIONS (EEC RECOGNITION—SPAIN AND PORTUGAL) ORDER 1986 (No. 23) [80p], made under the European Communities Act 1972 (c.68), s.2(2); operative on January 15, 1986; amends the Medical Act 1983 and the Dentists Act 1984 by adding to the relevant Schedules to those Acts the appropriate Spanish and Portuguese qualifications required for the purposes of registration as a fully registered medical practitioner and of registration in the dentists register.

2131. Veterinary drugs
MEDICINES (EXEMPTIONS FROM LICENCES AND ANIMAL TEST CERTIFICATES) ORDER 1986 (No. 1180) [£1·90], made under the Medicines Act 1968 (c.67), ss.15(1), (2) and 35(8)(*b*) and (9); operative on August 1, 1986; grants exemptions from the restrictions imposed by ss.7 and 32 of the 1968 Act on certain dealings (*e.g.* sale, supply and administration) in veterinary drugs without a product licence or animal test certificate.
MEDICINES (EXEMPTIONS FROM RESTRICTIONS ON THE RETAIL SALE OR SUPPLY OF VETERINARY DRUGS) (AMENDMENT) ORDER 1986 (No. 982) [£3·40], made under the Medicines Act 1968 (c.67), ss.57(1)(2)(2A), 129(4); operative on July 1, 1986; amends S.I. 1985 No. 1823 by substituting new Scheds. for Scheds. 1–4.
MEDICINES (EXEMPTIONS FROM RESTRICTIONS ON THE RETAIL SALE OR SUPPLY OF VETERINARY DRUGS) (AMENDMENT) (NO. 2) ORDER 1986 (No. 1997) [£3·40], made under the Medicines Act 1968 (c.67), ss.57(1), (2), (2A) and 129(4); operative on January 1, 1987; amends S.I. 1985 No. 1823.
MEDICINES (VETERINARY DRUGS) (EXEMPTION FROM LICENCES) (IMPORTATION) ORDER 1986 (No. 228) [80p], made under the Medicines Act 1968 (c.67), ss.13(2)(3), 15(1)(2); operative on March 12, 1986; grants exemptions from the restrictions imposed by s.7 of the 1968 Act.

MENTAL HEALTH

2132. Detention as patient—extent of powers
[Mental Health Act 1983 (c.20), ss.3, 17, 20(3)(4).]
A person can be detained for treatment in a mental hospital only when he requires in-patient treatment. There is no power to detain a person to administer treatment to which he does not consent and which does not require in-patient treatment.
Per curiam: (i) There is a distinction between being "detained" in a hospital and being "liable to be detained" in a hospital. Someone on leave of absence from a hospital cannot be regarded as detained in a hospital; (ii) there is no power under the Act of 1983 to give treatment to a mentally disordered person who withholds his consent unless he is detained in a hospital or had first been detained and been given leave of absence under s.17; (iii) unless clear statutory authority to the contrary exists, no one is to be detained in hospital or undergo medical treatment or even to submit himself to a medical examination without his consent. This is as true of a mentally disordered person as of anyone else.

The applicants W and L had been admitted to mental hospital on many occasions. W was living in a hostel but refusing to take medication. Her G.P. and a consultant psychiatrist considered it necessary for her health to continue to take medication while remaining at the hostel and signed a recommendation under s.3 of the Mental Health Act 1983. She was admitted to hospital for one night and then granted leave of absence under s.17 in the belief that as she was then a person "liable to be detained" the powers in ss.56 to 64 of the Act of 1983 to override the patient's refusal to consent to treatment could be brought into operation. L was detained for treatment under s.3 in December 1984 and was granted leave of absence under s.17 in February 1985 and was living at home. He refused to continue to take essential medication. On May 17 his medical officer, purporting to act under s.20, reported to the hospital managers that it was necessary for his health to receive treatment which required his detention, and they purported to renew the authority for his liability to be detained which had been due to expire on June 17. He remained at home. Later, his medical officer, mistakenly believing that his liability to be detained was due to expire on September 26 wrote on September 23 telling him to return to hospital with the intention of interrupting his leave before the expiry of the six month period. He did not return to hospital. The applicants sought judicial review. *Held,* (1) granting W's application, that admission and compulsory detention under s.3 on the written recommendation of two doctors applied to those who required in-patient treatment, and did not authorise a nominal detention when no necessary in-patient treatment was required. Since it was intended that W receive treatment while living at a hostel, their recommendation for her admission overnight was unlawful, and relief was granted by way of a declaration; (2) granting L's application, that the medical officer should only furnish a report to the hospital managers for the renewal of authority to detain a patient under s.20 when the doctor believed that in-patient treatment and detention was required. Since L's treatment was to be given at home, the report of May 17, 1985 of the medical officer was unlawful, and a declaration was granted. Further, it was unlawful to recall to hospital a patient on indefinite leave of absence when the intention was merely to prevent him from being on leave of absence for six months continuously. S.17(4) empowered a recall by the medical officer only where it was necessary for the patient's health or safety or for the protection of other persons, and so the purported recall on September 23 would have been unlawful even if L had been liable to be detained after June 17.

R. *v.* HALLSTROM, *ex p.* W.; R. *v.* GARDNER, *ex p.* L. [1986] 2 W.L.R. 883, McCullough J.

2133. Displacement—test of reasonable man—welfare of patient
[Mental Health Act 1983 (c.20), s.29(3)(*c*).]
In an application by Liverpool City Council for the nearest relative of a "patient" to be displaced under s.29 on the grounds that he unreasonably objected to the making of a guardianship application, the issue was raised as to whether or not in deciding the matter the court had to be satisfied that the grounds for guardianship (as set out in s.7) were also established. *Held,* that the test to be applied is what a "reasonable" person would do in the circumstances. The reasonableness must be judged in relation to the criteria for a guardianship acceptance. If there is acceptable evidence of a relevant mental disorder of the appropriate degree and the welfare of the patient requires admission to guardianship, then an order for displacement would be made. It is not necessary for the court to be satisfied that the application for guardianship would be successful; B, *Re* November 29, 1985; Liverpool County Ct. (*Ex rel. D. F. B. Swallow, Barrister*).

2134. Leave to bring proceedings—judicial review—whether "civil proceedings"
[Mental Health Act 1983 (c.20), ss.3, 139.]
On a true construction of s.139(1) of the Mental Health Act 1983 "civil proceedings" does not cover proceedings for judicial review so that such proceedings can be brought even where no negligence or bad faith was alleged.
Under s.139(1) of the Mental Health Act 1983 no person shall "be liable" to any civil or criminal proceedings in respect of any act purporting to be done under the Act unless the act "was done in bad faith or without reasonable care." Under s.139(2) "No civil proceedings shall be brought against any person in any court in respect of any such act without the leave of the High Court." Two doctors recommended that the applicant, who suffered from schizophrenia, be admitted to

hospital for treatment under s.3 of the 1983 Act in order that they might exercise the power under s.17 to grant her conditional leave of absence from the hospital. She was compulsorily admitted and the following day granted leave of absence on condition that she received the necessary medication. She applied to the High Court for leave to apply for judicial review to quash the admission to hospital or an order that it was *ultra vires.* She did not allege bad faith or negligence. The judge ruled that applications for judicial review were civil proceedings which were barred by s.139 and dismissed the application. Her application to the Court of Appeal to grant leave to apply for judicial review was granted. *Held,* that on a true construction of s.139(1) the words "civil proceedings" did not, in the absence of any specific definition, cover proceedings for judicial review, and a respondent in such proceedings was not "liable to" them. S.139 did not contain the clear and explicit words necessary to exclude the court's jurisdiction to grant orders of certiorari, and accordingly the court would grant her leave to apply for judicial review (dictum of Denning L.J. in *R.* v. *Medical Appeal Tribunal ex p. Gilmore* [1957] C.L.Y. 2269 applied; *Shackelton* v. *Swift* [1915] 2 K.B. 304; *Everett* v. *Griffiths* [1920] 3 K.B. 163 and *Richardson* v. *London County Council* [1957] C.L.Y. 2084 considered).

Per Ackner L.J. The jurisdiction given to the mental health review tribunal by s.72 of the Act of 1983 is limited to entertaining applications by persons who are liable to be detained under the Act. It has no power to consider whether a person is so liable, and cannot be used as a route to the High Court where it is sought to challenge the validity of an application for admission. Therefore the applicant was not entitled to seek from the tribunal a decision as to the *vires* of her admission, and accordingly there was no remedy open to her other than an application for judicial review.

WALDRON, *Ex p.* [1985] 3 W.L.R. 1090, C.A.

2135. Mental health review tribunal—reasons for decision—adequacy

[Mental Health Act 1983 (c.20), s.72(1)(*b*)(*i*)(*ii*).]

It is essential that a mental health review tribunal's reasons for refusal of an application for discharge should be clear both to the patient and to the doctor treating him (who has frequently initiated the application in the prior place).

A the applicant, was committed to a secure hospital after being convicted of manslaughter. After 12 years he applied to a mental health review tribunal for his discharge. The tribunal refused the application, stating that they had not been satisfied as to any of the matters involved in s.72(1)(*b*) (i) or (ii) of the Mental Health Act 1983, and that they were not persuaded that because of A's improved behaviour within the strict origins in hospital it necessarily followed that such behaviour would be maintained in the community. A applied for an order of certiorari to quash the decision. *Held,* granting the order sought, that it was essential for the tribunal to bear in mind the distinction between the diagnostic question whether the patient was suffering from mental illness, psychopathic disorder etc., and the policy question whether further detention was necessary for the patients' health or safety or for the protection of others. It was also essential that the tribunal's reasons should be clear both to the patient and the doctor treating him, who had frequently initiated the application in the first place. In this case, the tribunal's reasons were inadequate, and the decision would be quashed. (dictum of Donaldson P in *Alexander Machinery (Dudley)* v. *Crabtree* [1974] C.L.Y. 1206 applied).

R. *v.* MENTAL HEALTH REVIEW TRIBUNAL, *ex p.* PICKERING [1986] 1 All E.R. 99, Forbes J.

2136. Mental illness supervening after prison sentence—sentence—judicial and executive powers. See R. *v.* CASTRO, § 852.

2137. Psychopathic offenders. See LAW REFORM, § 1958.

2138. Review tribunal—conditional discharge—patient to continue to stay in hospital—whether orders valid

[Mental Health Act 1983 (c.20), ss.72 (11(*b*)), 73(2)(7), 145(1).]

"Discharge" in ss. 72–75 of the Mental Health Act 1983 means discharge from hospital; that discharge can be deferred under s.73(7) only for arrangements to be made for that purpose.

The cases of two patients, in mental hospitals as a result of criminal proceedings, were referred to review tribunals. In the case of patient "S" the tribunal ordered his conditional release but deferred the order pending arrangements to treat him in another hospital, prior to eventual release; in the case of "G" the tribunal decided to discharge him on condition he continued to reside in the hospital. *Held*, allowing the appeals, that once a tribunal was satisfied that all conditions of s.73(2) applied, they had to discharge a patient; discharge meant release from hospital and not further treatment at another hospital.

SECRETARY OF STATE FOR THE HOME DEPARTMENT *v.* MENTAL HEALTH REVIEW TRIBUNAL FOR MERSEY REGIONAL HEALTH AUTHORITY [1986] 1 W.L.R. 1170, Mann J.

2139. Review tribunal—discharge of patient—whether tribunal empowered to reconsider decision

[Mental Health Act 1983 (c.20), s.73(2)(7).]

A mental health review tribunal's decision to conditionally discharge a patient can only be deferred for the purpose of making arrangements for that discharge.

In two separate cases the Secretary of State's application for review of a decision of a tribunal was dismissed. In both cases the tribunal having decided that a patient should be conditionally discharged deferred the direction for further review.

Held, allowing the appeals, that the provisions of s.73(2) were mandatory, and once a decision was made to conditionally discharge a patient they had to make the order, which was final; they could only defer under s.73(7) for arrangements to be made for that discharge.

R. *v.* OXFORD REGIONAL MENTAL HEALTH REVIEW TRIBUNAL, *ex p.* SECRETARY OF STATE FOR THE HOME DEPARTMENT [1986] 1 W.L.R. 1180, C.A.

2140. Tribunal—decision—failure to give reasons

[Mental Health Act 1983 (c.20), s.1(3).]

In 1967 C was convicted of two offences of indecent assault on two young girls. He had a history of such offences but, with the exception of an offence of attempted buggery, they were not of a serious nature. A hospital order was made and a restriction order imposed for a five year period on the ground that C was suffering from a psychopathic disorder. After the expiration of the order in 1972 C's detention was reviewed biennially. In 1984 C applied to the tribunal for a review of his case. The responsible medical officer recommended that there was no evidence that C was suffering with a psychotic illness, that the diagnosis of a psychopathic disorder was based on C's sexual offences and nothing else, his main problem being one of sexual deviance which by s.1(3) of the 1983 Act was not a "mental disorder" within s.1(2). A consultant pyschiatrist gave evidence that C's record of sexual offences did not establish that he was suffering from a mental disorder. The tribunal refused to order C's discharge. C sought judicial review of the decision. *Held*, quashing the decision, that reasons given by the tribunal for refusing to direct C's discharge were merely a bare traverse of a circumstance in which discharge could be contemplated. The grounds for the reasons did not show why the evidence of the responsible medical officer and of the consultant psychiatrist had not been accepted. The tribunal asserted that C had signs of sexual deviancy but the 1983 Act required sexual deviancy to be discounted. C had not been enabled to know why the case advanced on his behalf had not been accepted (dictum of Nolan J. in *Bone* v. *Mental Health Review Tribunal* [1985] C.L.Y. 2167 applied).

R. *v.* MENTAL HEALTH REVIEW TRIBUNAL, *ex p.* CLATWORTHY [1985] 3 All E.R. 699, Mann. J.

2141. Tribunals—powers—transfer of patent

[Mental Health Act 1983 (c.20), ss.72 and 73] A tribunal is not empowered when dealing with a restricted patient under s.73 to exercise powers conferred under s.72, which relates to unrestricted patients, save in so far as s.73 specifically provides for such power: GRANT *v.* MENTAL HEALTH REVIEW TRIBUNAL, *The Times,* April 28, 1986, McNeil J.

MINING LAW

2141a. Coal industry

COAL INDUSTRY (LIMIT ON PAYMENTS IN RESPECT OF REDUNDANT MINEWORKERS) ORDER 1986 (No. 631) [45p], made under the Coal Industry Act 1985 (c.27), s.3(3); operative on March 30, 1986; increases to £1,800 million the maximum sum permitted under s.3(3) of the 1985 Act.

REDUNDANT MINEWORKERS AND CONCESSIONARY COAL (PAYMENTS SCHEMES) ORDER 1986 (No. 625) [£3·80], made under the Coal Industry Act 1977 (c.39), s.7(1)(7); operative on March 30, 1986; establishes a scheme for the payment of benefits to miners and other industry workers made redundant between March 30, 1986 and March 28, 1987.

2141b. Subsidence—compensation—lands tribunal

The tribunal has jurisdiction to award interest from the date of the cause of action in resolving a dispute over compensation payable under the Coal Mining (Subsidence) Act 1957: KNIBB *v.* NATIONAL COAL BOARD, *The Times,* July 17, 1986, C.A.

2141c. Training—duty of employer—dangerous practices

[Mines and Quarries Act 1954 (c.70), s.88.] S.88 of the Mines and Quarries Act 1954 imposes an obligation to provide supervision, training and instruction to employees. It does not apply, however, to mining practices that the employer forbids as dangerous: ENGLAND *v.* CLEVELAND POTASH, *The Times,* July 1, 1986, C.A.

MINORS

2142. Access—enforcement—considerations

M and F had lived together for about five months until January 1978. In July 1978 M gave birth to a daughter. F exercised access about once every six weeks. In March 1979 a magistrates' court made a custody order in favour of M and granted F reasonable access which he continued to exercise on the previous basis. At the end of 1979 F ceased access visits but continued to pay maintenance for the child following his cohabitation with a white woman. About two years later M changed her address without notifying F who ceased making payments. In November 1982 M married a white man. They both were involved with the Jehovah's Witnesses and had a strict and somewhat narrow life-style. The child's surname was also changed to M's married name. Having traced M's whereabouts F issued a summons in 1985 for defined access. Following the preparation of a welfare report and a period of interim access the magistrates ordered that F should have access to the child once a month for two hours. In their reasons they stated that the child was aware that F was black like herself, that it was in her best interests to get to know F and his daughter (by first cohabitee), that such contact would give the child a broader perspective and that such advantages outweighed the disadvantages caused by the opposition of M and her husband to access, as demonstrated during the interim access visits. *Held,* dismissing M's appeal and allowing F's cross-appeal against Wood J.'s decision to restrict access to once every three months, that the fact that the attitude of M and her husband had led to a distress on the child's part could not in itself render an order which had been made in her best interests inadmissible to those interests. M could not rely on her failure to comply with the order as a ground for contending that the order should have not been made in the first place. It would not therefore be said that the magistrates and the judge were plainly wrong. The judge's direction that access should not take place in the presence of M and her husband should stand. The frequency would be restored to that order by the magistrates. No order would be made on F's application for an order restraining M and her husband in relation to their attitude towards access and the child's involvement in it although M was warned as to the consequences if she attempted to thwart the order in the future (*G. v. G.* [1985] C.L.Y. 2594 followed): EVANS *v.* JACKSON, (1986) 150 J.P.N. 702, C.A.

2143. Access—termination—care order—issue of formal notification

[Child Care Act 1980 (c.5), ss.12B(1), (5).]

A local authority must reach a decision with urgency as to whether to terminate access to a child in its care to its parents: so that the parents can, if access is terminated, apply to the juvenile court against that decision. Not to decide is to deny the parents their rights.

The applicants were parents of a boy born in October 1981 who was made the subject of a care order in January 1982. The baby was placed with short term foster parents and then with long term foster parents who were prospective adopters in March 1982. Following the transfer, the parents did not see the boy save once in June 1983. Adoption proceedings were pending. The parents were told that access was not being refused but no access arrangements were made. On March 26, 1984 the solicitor for the local authority intimated that a notice under s.12B(1) of the Child Care Act 1980 would be issued, but no notice was issued. The authority decided not to issue a notice until after the hearing of the adoption proceedings stating that there was no obligation on them to issue a notice terminating access, as they were entitled under s.12B(5) to defer the decision for a reasonable period. The parents applied for judicial review. *Held,* granting the application, that whether the issue was "terminating arrangements for access" or "refusing to make arrangements," which distinction was maintained in subsections (4) and (5) the local authority had a duty to reach a decision urgently, and in the former case 14 days, or quite exceptionally, 21 was more than sufficient, and having reached that decision, the authority had a duty to inform the parent without delay and serve an appropriate notice. This is what the present authority ought to have done. The reason given by the authority was not relevant. Accordingly mandamus would issue (*Associated Provincial Picture Houses* v. *Wednesbury Corp.* (1948) C.L.Y. 8107 applied). The course taken by the local authority was in effect a denial of the right given to parents by Parliament to apply to a juvenile court. The decision was one which no reasonable local authority acting reasonably could possibly have reached.

R. *v.* BOLTON METROPOLITAN BOROUGH COUNCIL, *ex p.* B (1986) 84 L.G.R. 78, Wood J.

2144. Access—termination—child in care

[Child Care Act 1980 (c.5), ss.12B–D.] The child, a girl, had been born in 1975. Following her parents' divorce she remained with M. In 1978 she was committed to the care of foster parents under a local authority care order. In 1983 that placement broke down. M visited the child monthly but the visits ceased. In 1984 the child went to live with the present foster parents as possible adopters. The local authority gave notice under s.12B terminating access. M applied under s.12C for an access order. The justices ordered access once a month. On appeal the access order was quashed upon further affidavit evidence being admitted to correct any misunderstanding as to the local authority's future plans. He accepted that there should be one or two final visits by M but left the arrangements to the local authority. *Held,* allowing M's appeal, that the effect of the judge's order was to deprive M of the right to limited final visits as recommended by the *guardian ad litem* and to apply for a variation under s.12D. The order would be set aside and access would be granted on two occasions within the following six months. (*C. (A Minor) Re* (1979) 9 Fam. Law 50 and *T., (A Minor) Re (Welfare Report Recommendation),* (1980) 1 FLR 59 considered): DEVON COUNTY COUNCIL *v.* C. (1986) 16 Fam. Law 20, C.A.

2145. Access order—appeal—considerations

In wardship proceedings M had applied for staying access by the grandmother of T, a girl aged 9, to be terminated on the basis that the grandmother's husband had been convicted of an offence of unlawful sexual intercourse with a child of 15 and therefore represented a moral danger to T. The grandmother had previously had staying access by consent and had had T to live with her for some three years. The judge granted staying access. M appealed contending that the judge had erred in the exercise of his discretion, first in his conclusion that the granting of staying access as distinct from visiting access was not a circumstance which increased the risk to T and, secondly, that if any impropriety took place the grandmother would report it. *Held,* dismissing M's appeal, that this was exactly the sort of case which in line with *G.* v. *G.* it was wholly impossible effectively to challenge the exercise of the discretion of the trial judge. The first matter lay well within the choice of reasonable conclusion open to the judge and on the second matter he had accepted the grandmother's evidence in preference to that of the welfare officer (*G* v. *G* [1985] C.L.Y. 2594 applied): T (A MINOR) *Re,* (1986) 16 Fam. Law 189, C.A.

2146. Access order—enforcement—considerations

The appeal concerned the contention by M that no access should be granted to F because of the distress caused to the child by the dispute. *Held,* dismissing M's appeal and allowing F's cross-appeal by restoring the frequency of access ordered by the justices, that M could not rely on what amounted to her failure to comply with the court's order for access as a ground for contending that the order should not have been made in the first place. The fact that the attitude of M and the child's stepfather caused the child distress could not of itself render access by F harmful as the order had been made in the best interests of that child: E (A MINOR), *Re The Times,* August 8, 1986, C.A.

2147. Adoption—dispensing with mother's consent—regular access by mother—whether adoption appropriate
[Children Act 1975 (c.72), ss.3, 8, 12(2)(*b*).]
Where the interests of a child require regular access by the natural parent an adoption order is inappropriate.
In the course of a short marriage the mother had a child, whom she took to live with the applicants, a married couple, when she left the father. When the child was two she left her with the applicants and went to live with a second husband. Upon leaving him a year later she requested the return of the child, but the applicants refused. They applied for adoption. The mother refused her consent to adoption because she wished in the long term to be reunited with the child. The judge made an adoption order dispensing with her consent as being unreasonably withheld, but made provision for regular access by the mother. The mother appealed contending the judge was wrong to dispense with consent and an adoption order was inappropriate. *Held*, allowing the appeal, that (i) on the facts the judge was wrong to dispense with consent; (2) the order was inappropriate where it was thought necessary in the child's welfare for the parent to have regular access. Such access would strengthen the bond with the natural parent and would be irreconcilable with the purpose of an adoption order.
V. (A MINOR) (ADOPTION: CONSENT), *Re* [1986] 1 All E.R. 752, C.A.

2148. Adoption—dispensing with parental consent—practice
[Children Act 1975 (c.72), s.12.] The proposed adopters appealed against the refusal by the county court judge to make an order under s.12 dispensing with the parents' agreement to the proposed adoption of the child, aged four and a half. The practice of that county court was to hear first, as a separate matter, the question—whether to dispense with the parents' agreement—and then to proceed to the adoption hearing. *Held*, dismissing the appeal, that the matters relevant to dispensing with parental agreements were better aired within the framework of the adoption proceedings. The practice of having two separate hearing was an unsatisfactory one:
K. (A MINOR: ADOPTION), *Re*, (1985) 15 Fam. Law 314, C.A.

2149. Adoption—freeing for adoption—practice direction. See PRACTICE DIRECTION (FAM. D.) (CHILDREN: ADOPTION AND FREEING FOR ADOPTION), § 2584.

2150. Adoption—illegitimate child—opposing father—wardship—jurisdiction
[Guardianship of Minors Act 1977 (c.3), s.9; Children Act 1975 (c.72), ss.14, 85(7), 107(1); Child Care Act 1980 (c.5), ss.12A to 12G, 87(1).]
An illegitimate child had been taken into care in 1980. F visited the child until early 1982 when access was stopped. In 1984 the local authority applied under s.14 to free the child for adoption. As F was not recognised as a "parent" under s.85(7) of the 1975 Act nor a "guardian" under s.107(1) he began proceedings for custody and also commenced wardship proceedings. The local authority applied for the wardship to be discharged. *Held*, that F submitted that the court should exercise its jurisdiction as there was a gap in the statutory scheme. The gap was said to be (a) that F had no right under ss.12A to 12G of the 1980 Act to apply for access and (b) that the only method of resisting an order under s.14 of the 1975 Act was by obtaining a custody order under s.9 of the 1971 Act. There was no such gap since (a) s.87(1) of the 1980 Act purposely excluded the putative father from the access provision and (b) that s.14(8) of the 1975 Act provided that the court could not make an order unless it was satisfied that the father (not being the guardian) had no intention of applying for custody or that would be likely to be refused. In reality F was attempting to persuade the court to review the local authority's decision as to access and in doing so to interfere with its discretionary power. The wardship would therefore be discharged (*M, Re* [1955] C.L.Y. 1319; *A.* v. *Liverpool City Council* [1981] C.L.Y. 1796 and *W. (A Minor) (Care Proceedings: Wardship), Re* [1985] C.L.Y. 2250 applied): T. D. (A MINOR) (WARDSHIP: JURISDICTION), *Re* (1986) 16 Fam.Law 18, Sheldon J.

2151. Adoption—interim order—whether appropriate
[Children Act 1975 (c.72), s.19(1).] In May 1980 M abandoned her illegitimate daughter, then aged one year, to F. He immediately handed the child over to his parents with whom the child had lived ever since. In May 1984 the grandparents had applied for her adoption. Both M and F agreed along with the guardian ad litem. The justices refused to make a full adoption order but made an interim order under

s.19(1) for a period of one year. In their reasons the justices stated that whilst the grandmother, aged 54, would be suitable the age of their grandfather (66 years) might be a problem in the future. They were also anxious about the proposed intention of the grandparents to appoint F as a testamentary guardian since he was a drug addict and about the success of their upbringing of F since he had taken to drugs at the age of 16. They considered an interim adoption order would enable them to reconsider the position again with fuller reports including Part II of the 1975 Act (Custodianship) which would, by then, be in force. *Held*, allowing the grandparents' appeal, that the question was whether the justices' findings of fact supported their conclusion that adoption was inappropriate. Their answer in effect was to postpone the decision for one year. This would not assist matters. The facts supported the making of a full adoption order. Therefore the possibility of custodianship was an inappropriate consideration: O (A MINOR) (ADOPTION BY GRANDPARENTS), *Re*, (1985) 15 Fam. Law 305, D.C.

2152. Adoption—non-patrial infant—factors to be taken into account
Where a citizen of the U.K. seeks to adopt an infant that is not a citizen of the U.K. the welfare of the infant is the most important consideration to making or refusing an adoption order.

W was born in China in 1968 of Chinese parents. W's paternal aunt came to the U.K. in 1970 and was registered as a British citizen in 1975. In 1981 W applied for a student entry visa to enable him to attend an independent school near the aunt's home. W went to live with the aunt and remained in the U.K. studying from that time. W had no home to return to in Hong Kong. The aunt applied to adopt W. The application was supported by W's mother and the guardian *ad litem* appointed for W and W himself. At that time W was 17 years old. The judge took the view that the adoption was designed to provide the aunt with someone to look after her in her old age and to ensure W remained in the U.K. outside the control of the immigration authorities, further that adoption was not needed to provide W with a secure and settled place in his aunt's family. The judge refused to make an adoption order. *Held*, dismissing the appeal, that where an application to adopt a foreign child is made by a British citizen the Home Office should be given notice of the application. In considering the application the court must give first consideration to the need to safeguard and promote the welfare of the child throughout its childhood. The fact that the adoption order would remove the child from the scope of control exercised by the immigration authorities was an important consideration of public policy to be taken into account and balanced against the welfare of the child. It was a less important consideration than the welfare of the child. The court should consider whether the welfare of the child could be equally well promoted by an order not affecting its nationality as by an adoption order. In the present case the judge's decision could not be criticised. An adoption order would have made little difference to W's welfare, having regard to his age and circumstances, but a great deal of difference to his immigration status (*H. (A Minor) (Adoption: Non-Patrial), Re* [1982] C.L.Y. 2020 approved).
W. (A MINOR) (ADOPTION: NON-PATRIAL), *Re* [1985] 3 W.L.R. 945, C.A.

2153. Adoption—notice of hearing—practice direction. See PRACTICE, § 2562.

2154. Adoption—order—condition—best interests of child
[Children Act 1975 (c.72), s.8(7).]
The child, a girl, was born in 1979. She had been taken into care when she was 10 months old and placed with foster parents. F was deeply attached to the child and had had access until she was 15 months old. His visits were then terminated since which time the child had had no contact with the natural parents. The foster parents applied to adopt the child. F asked that a condition be attached to the adoption order so that he could be informed of the child's progress and what her needs were so that he could decide whether to extend the insurance policy that he had taken out in the child's name which matured when she reached the age of 13. The judge found that there were exceptional circumstances justifying the imposition of a condition that the adopters sent an annual report as to the child's progress to F through the Official Solicitor. *Held*, allowing the adopter's appeal, that since the whole tenor of adoption law was that the adoption parents took over completely the role of parents of the child no condition should be imposed which could be regarded as detracting from the rights and duties of the adopters. The condition was bad since it was contrary to

the basic concept of adoption. It was also contrary to the interests of the child in so far as it undermined the feeling of security which the adoption parents should have (*S. (A Minor) (Adoption Order: Access), Re* [1975] C.L.Y. 2444 considered): C. (A MINOR) (ADOPTION ORDER: CONDITION) *Re,* (1986) 1 F.L.R. 315, C.A.

2155. Adoption—order—condition of access—natural parent

[Children Act 1975 (c.72), s.8(7).] The child had been born in 1979. In April 1981 following an assault by M's co-habitee the child had been placed with foster parents. M had exercised access regularly. At the adoption hearing in 1983 it was agreed by all parties that access was desirable and should continue although M opposed the adoption application. The judge, however, declined to make an access order as he had decided that it would present problems and also refused to grant the adoption. *Held,* dismissing the adopters' appeal, that it was only in unusual and, perhaps, exceptional circumstances that a combined order should be made. Here once the adoption order was made M's position would change and her attempts at enforcing the order would inevitably undermine the stability of the child. Adoption was therefore not appropriate in the best interests of the child (*C (T.J.) Re* [1963] C.L.Y. 1768; *B. (M.F.), Re* [1972] C.L.Y. 2163, *J., Re* [1973] C.L.Y. 2162 and *S, Re* [1975] C.L.Y. 2144 considered): M. (A MINOR) (ADOPTION ORDER: ACCESS), *Re,* (1985) 15 Fam. Law 321, C.A.

2156. Adoption—parental consent—reasonableness

[Children Act 1975 (c.72), s.12(2).] F and M had married in 1979 when both were very young. They had two sons G, now aged five and R, three and a half years. Six months after R's birth F was convicted of an assault upon him and both boys were taken into care. R was subsequently adopted whilst G remained in a hostel with M. F and M resumed cohabitation and C was allowed home on trial. A signed undertaking was obtained from both parents. The experiment failed and, after a while, G was placed with foster parents with a view to adoption. By the time of the adoption application F and M had matured considerably. They had a third child and opposed the application. *Held,* that the chances of a successful reintroduction of G into the lives of F and M were absolutely minimal. No reasonable parent applying his or her mind to the history of G's life, hearing the opinions of the psychiatrist and the social workers as to his future needs could possibly come to any conclusion other than that G should live with his adopting family: G.B. (ADOPTION: PARENTAL AGREEMENT) *Re,* (1985) 15 Fam. Law 309, Kingham J.

2157. Adoption—private fostering—arranging adoption

[Adoption Act 1958 (c.5), s.29(1)(3)(*c*) (as amended by Children Act 1975 (c.72), s.28).]

Proof of an offence under s.29(3)(*c*) of the 1958 Act requires evidence of the commission of an offence under s.29(1) of the Act.

Mr. and Mrs. R, who had been looking to adopt a child, met a pregnant woman and a third party, W, who acted on her behalf and arranged to foster her child on a private basis. Mr. and Mrs. R realised the difference between fostering and adoption. They received the child soon after its birth and notified the local authority that they had fostered the child privately. They were charged with an offence contrary to s.29(3)(*c*) of the 1958 Act. A charge against W for an offence under s.29(1) was adjourned *sine die.* The justices held that the prosecution had failed to establish that the child had been received for adoption and dismissed the charges. *Held,* dismissing the prosecutor's appeal, that (1) proof of the offence of receiving a child for the purposes of adoption under s.29(3)(*c*) required evidence of the commission of the offence of making arrangements for the adoption of that child under s.29(1); there was not sufficient evidence to conclude that W had committed an offence under s.29(1) and the justices were obliged to acquit Mr. and Mrs. R; (2) the justices should have asked what was the real purpose for which Mr. and Mrs. R received the child into their care; the justices erred in law in considering only Mr. and Mrs. R's intention for the immediate future of the child.

GATEHOUSE *v.* R. [1986] 1 W.L.R. 18, D.C.

2158. Adoption—procedure—parent refusing consent

[Children Act 1975 (c.72), s.12(2).] The child had been born in 1976 and placed in the care of the local authority within a few months of her birth. M saw the child once in 1976 but had made no subsequent attempt to see her. In 1984 the foster parents applied to adopt the child. M refused to give her consent. The judge ordered that the application to dispense with M's consent be adjourned to a later date, thus separating this application from the substantive application to adopt. At the adjourned hearing M's application for a further adjournment to obtain legal representation was refused. After hearing her evidence the judge found that M's desire for access after a gap of eight years was not reasonable and made an order dispensing with her consent. At a subsequent hearing the adoption order was made. *Held,* dismissing M's appeal, that in an appropriate case (and perhaps the majority of cases) it was desirable to arrange for the hearing of the application to dispense with parental agreement within the framework of the trial of the adoption application. However, the choice of procedure was a matter of discretion for the trial judge. Here the judge had not exercised that discretion on any wrong principles and, in any event, he would have come to the same conclusion even if he had heard the two applications together (*W. (An Infant), Re* [1971] C.L.Y. 5831; *M. (An Infant) Adoption: Parental Consent), Re* [1972] C.L.Y. 546; *B. (A Minor) (Adoption by Parent), Re* [1975] C.L.Y. 2145; *K. (A Minor) (Adoption: Procedure), Re* [1986] C.L.Y. 2148 considered). L. S. (A Minor) (Adoption: Procedure), *Re* [1986] 1 F.L.R. 302, C.A.

2159. Adoption—regulations—notification—parental consent

[Adoption Act 1958 (c.5), s.34(1); Adoption Agencies Regulations 1983 (S.I. 1983 No. 1969), regs. 11(2)(*a*), 12(2)(*b*).]

A parent is prevented by s.34(1) of the Adoption Act 1958 from taking the child away from proposed adopters if agreement has been given whether orally or in writing.

M, the mother, was adamant that she wanted her child adopted, and arrangements were made to place the child with foster-parents from birth. The local authority, however, failed to give M notice of its decision that adoption would be in the best interests of the child under reg. 11(2)(*a*) of the Adoption Agencies Regulations 1983, though a social worker told her that the adoption was going ahead. The authority also failed to notify M under reg. 12(2)(*b*) that the child had been placed with prospective adopters. Further, M furnished no written consent to the adoption. The DHSS circular which had been supplied to M stated, "Once you have given your written agreement you are not allowed to take your child away from his new family before the adoption hearing, unless the court says you may." M changed her mind, and sought the return of the child. She argued that "agreement" to the order under s.34(1) of the Adoption Act 1958 must be written. *Held,* that (1) Regs. 11(2)(*a*) and 12(2)(*b*) were directory, not mandatory, and non-compliance would not vitiate an adoption. M had not been prejudiced, and non-compliance did not alter the order's validity; (2) agreement under s.34(1) might be either written or oral. M had agreed orally, and she was not entitled to the return of the child (dicta of Lord Penzance in *Howard* v. *Bodington* (1877) 2 P.D. at 211, of Sir Arthur Channell in *Montreal Street Co.* v. *Normandia* [1917] A.C. at 175 and of Lord Hailsham L.C. in *London and Clydeside Estates* v. *Aberdeen D.C.* [1980] C.L.Y. 315 applied).
T. (A Minor) (Adoption: Parental Consent), *Re* [1986] 1 All E.R. 817, C.A.

2160. Adoption—review of decision—wardship proceedings

It is not possible to review an adoption decision by a local authority in wardship proceedings (*A.* v. *Liverpool City Council* [1981] C.L.Y. 1796, *W, Re* [1985] C.L.Y. 2255 followed): R. v. Buckinghamshire County Council, *The Times,* December 21, 1985, C.A.

2161. Adoption—welfare of child—severance of adopted child from natural parent

The child had been born in 1976. The family separated in 1977 when she was only four months old. In 1978 the marriage was dissolved with being given custody with reasonable access to F. In 1981 M re-married and she applied to adopt the child with her new husband. F regularly exercised access and all parties wished this to continue. F gave his consent to the adoption application. The judge requested his attendance to give evidence and, in the presence of all parties, heard from the child. *Held,* that the relationship between F and the child was that of two friends and that F regarded the new family as the proper place for the child even in the event of the death of M or divorce. The child gave evidence to the effect that M's husband and daughter could not be a real father and sister unless she was adopted. It was therefore in the best interests of the child that an adoption order should be made *(B (MF) Re* [1972]

C.L.Y. 2163, *J., Re* [1973] C.L.Y. 2162 and *H, Re* [1976] C.L.Y. 2899 considered): F (AK) (MINOR) (ADOPTION), *Re* [1986] 16 Fam. Law 134, H.H. Judge Kershaw.

2162. Affiliation. See BASTARDY AND LEGITIMATION.

2163. Appeal—separate representation—costs
    M had appealed from the judge's decision committing the child to the care of the local authority. F, the local authority and the guardian *ad litem* were separately represented by solicitors and counsel and, collectively, sought to uphold the judge's order. *Held,* granting a legal aid taxation of F's costs that where it was perfectly practicable the same counsel should be able to represent the respondents' respective cases. In general the situation in the Court of Appeal was entirely different than first instance since it was the decision of the judge that was being upheld rather than interested parties calling evidence and canvassing any kinds of submissions. It should be regarded, therefore, as most unusual for different solicitors and counsel to be remunerated by different public or local government funds in order to line up the Court of Appeal and make the same submissions (*per* Cumming-Bruce L.J.): D. (A Minor), *Re*, (1985) 15 Fam. Law 314, C.A.

2164. Care order—closure of home—duty of local authority
    [Child Care Act 1980 (c.5), s.18(1).] The Social Services Committee of the council had decided to close a community home with education owned and maintained by the council for the accommodation of girls in care. In its deliberations the committee had not given any consideration to the needs or proposed disposal of any of the individual girls who would, if the recommendation was implemented, have to be found alternative placements. The committee had also not been informed that the girls, whose views had been canvassed by the officer of the home, were opposed to its closure. An application was made on behalf of the girls to quash the committee's decision on the basis that it was in breach of s.18(1). *Held,* allowing the application, that it had been incumbent upon the council before reaching a decision to have given first consideration to the welfare of each individual child concerned having regard to her views and the closure (*Liddle* v. *Sunderland Borough Council* [1984] C.L.Y. 2247 and *R.* v. *Solihull Metropolitan Borough Council, ex p. C* [1984] C.L.Y. 2234 followed; *Bell* v. *Hammersmith and Fulham London Borough Council, The Times,* December 17, 1979, distinguished; *Att.-Gen.* v. *Clarkson* [1900] 1 Q.B. 156, *Cape Brandy Syndicate* v. *I.R.C.* [1921] 2 K.B. 403, *Ormond Investments Co.* v. *Betts* [1928] A.C. 143, *Associated Provincial Picture Houses* v. *Wednesbury Corporation* (1948) C.L.C. 8107 and *Ministry of Pensions* v. *Higham* [1948] 2 K.B. 153 considered: R. *v.* AVON COUNTY COUNCIL, *ex p.* K [1986] 1 F.L.R. 443, Heilbron J.

2165. Care order—returning child home—revoking decision—considerations
    In both cases the local authority had proposed allowing the children in care to return home to the natural parents for a trial period. Subsequently, the local authorities changed their minds solely because they had received unsubstantiated allegations concerning the suitability of the parents. *Held,* on applications for judicial review, that it was incumbent on the local authority to give the parent an opportunity of refuting the allegations before deciding not to allow the children home on trial. The procedure adopted had to be designed to be fair to allow the parent to make representations and call evidence (*O'Reilly* v. *Mackman* [1982] C.L.Y. 2603 and *R.* v. *Monopolies and Mergers Commission, ex p. Matthew Brown* [1986] C.L.Y. 3398 followed; *A.* v. *Liverpool City Council* [1981] C.L.Y. 1796 and *Re W* [1985] C.L.Y. 2255 considered): R. *v.* HERTFORDSHIRE COUNTY COUNCIL, *ex p.* B; R. *v.* BEDFORDSHIRE COUNTY COUNCIL, *ex p.* C, *The Times,* August 19, 1986, Ewbank J.

2166. Care proceedings—access—termination—appeal—re-hearing
    [Child Care Act 1980 (c.5), s.12C.] The local authority had served notice under s.12B terminating access. M applied to the juvenile court under s.12C. The justices, by a majority, decided that M should be allowed access. On appeal by the local authority, the Divisional Court (Sir John Arnold P.) held that the reasons for the decision of the majority could not be supported but, instead of merely allowing the appeal, ordered that the matter be remitted to the juvenile court to be reheard by the same justices. The local authority appealed contending that the President had erred in ordering a rehearing. *Held,* dismissing the appeal, save that the retrial should be heard by a different bench, that a fresh trial was not wrong in principle but it was inappropriate for the same justices to undertake that task. It would throw

them into confusion if, having already expressed their views, they were asked to perform the exericse afresh: HEREFORD AND WORCESTER COUNTY COUNCIL *v.* JAH (1985) 15 Fam. Law 324, C.A.

2167. Care proceedings—access application—production of children at court—practice
Children and Young Persons Act 1969 (c.54), s.1.; Child Care Act 1980 (c.5), s.12c.] The juvenile court had made care orders in relation to three children. Access by the parents had been terminated following which they made application under s.12c. At the hearing before the justices the children were produced in court. At the parents' appeal the matter was drawn to the attention of the judge. *Held,* that although s.1 of the 1969 Act provided the children could be brought before a juvenile court on an application for a care order there was no such suggestion under s.12c of the 1980 Act. The practice was of no benefit; and without any statutory obligation it was also undesirable: A. *v.* WIGAN METROPOLITAN BOROUGH COUNCIL (1986) 16 Fam. Law 162, Ewbank J.

2168. Care proceedings—advance disclosure—early delivery of reports
In care proceedings, the local authority and the *guardian ad litem* have a duty to give advance disclosure of their case, either by sending a detailed letter to the parents' solicitors, or by sending copies of their witnesses' statements. Early delivery of reports is particularly important (*E.* v. *E.* [1985] C.L.Y. 2241 applied): R. *v.* WEST MALLING JUVENILE COURT, *ex p.* K. (1986) 150 J.P.N. 542, D.C.

2169. Care proceedings—appointment of guardian ad litem
[Children and Young Persons Act 1969 (c.54), s.32A; Magistrates' Courts (Children and Young Persons) Rules (S.I. 1970 No. 1792), rr.21B, 21C.] Following the birth of the child in December 1983 there were allegations of violence by H, aged 18, towards W aged 16 and to the child, resulting in a place of safety order and subsequent care proceedings. An order had been made in February 1985 providing for separate representation of the child under s.32A and it appeared that there was a conflict of interest between those of the child and the parents. In judicial review proceedings of the care order, criticism was made that no notice of such order had been given to H and W. The main ground of the application was the failure of the juvenile court to appoint a *guardian ad litem* for the child and that such omission had prejudiced the parents and the child since there had been no-one with the duty to lodge an appeal to the Crown Court. *Held,* dismissing the application, that whilst there was no provision relating to an order under s.32A similar to that under rr.21B and 21C of the 1970 Rules there had been no breach of the *audi alteram* rule as the parents had not been deprived of their right to be heard in the care proceedings. There was no mandatory requirement for a *guardian ad litem* to be appointed and no such application had been made during the course of the proceedings. The present case was not an obvious case for such an appointment and the making of a care order was inevitable. However, justices having decided that it was in the best interests of the child to grant legal aid for the purposes of separate representation should also bear in mind that the appointment of a *guardian ad litem* would, in all probability, be in the best interests of the child as well. There was no gap in the law as to the right of appeal. The child's solicitor was not *functus officio* when the juvenile court made its decision but also had a duty to consider the question of appeal and to file the appropriate notice: R. *v.* PLYMOUTH JUVENILE COURT, *ex p.* F, *The Times,* August 8, 1986, Waterhouse J.

2170. Care proceedings—inadequate notice of allegations—breach of natural justice
In care proceedings F's solicitors had tried to ascertain from the local authority particulars of the allegations to be made against him but had only received a response, in the form of reports, on the morning of the hearing. The justices refused F's application for an adjournment. *Held,* allowing F's application for judicial review, that the rules of natural justice had been breached. F was entitled to know the way the case was being put against him with sufficient particularity for the proper preparation of his case: K. *v.* K., *The Times,* April 24, 1986, Wood J.

2171. Care proceedings—new baby—approach
[Children and Young Persons Act 1969 (c.54), ss.1(2)(*a*), 70(1).] The Council had applied for a care order in respect of a new-born baby girl whose parents were both registered drug addicts. The baby had been born suffering from severe withdrawal symptoms and had been placed in intensive care. A place of safety order was

obtained and the baby was placed with foster parents. The justices, at the full hearing of the care proceedings, took the view that they were entitled to have regard to M's abuse of drugs during pregnancy and the events in the child's life whilst still a foetus when deciding whether the condition in s.1(2)(a) had been satisfied, namely, that the child's proper development was being avoidably prevented or neglected or her health was being avoidably impaired or neglected. They made a care order. On appeal, the Divisional Court held that the conditions of s.1(2)(a) had not been satisfied since M had had no opportunity to care for the child since birth and therefore no conduct by her could have been said to have affected the child's health. *Held,* allowing the council's appeal that the Divisional Court had fallen into error by restricting its view of the child's development to events which had taken place since the birth. Whilst "person" under s.70(1) denoted someone living rather than a foetus, the situation before birth was relevant when considering the events which had had the effect of impairing the child's health which were "avoidable". The whole process, including the M's continuing ability to look after the child, had to be looked at as a whole. In the circumstances the primary condition was satisfied (*M* v. *Westminster City Council* [1984] C.L.Y. 2206 followed; *A* v. *Liverpool City Council* [1984] C.L.Y. 1796 and *W (A Minor) (Care Proceedings: Wardship)*, Re, [1985] C.L.Y. 2256 considered: BERKSHIRE COUNTY COUNCIL *v.* D-P (1986) 16 Fam. Law 264; (1986) 2 F.L.R. 276, C.A.

2172. Care proceedings—new baby—mother's conduct during pregnancy
[Children and Young Persons Act 1969 (c.54), s.1(2)(a), 70 (1).]
A care order can be made on the grounds of a mother's abuse of her own health during pregnancy.
The child had been born prematurely to a mother who was a heroin addict. At birth the child was suffering from drug withdrawal symptoms and she was kept in the intensive care unit of the hospital for several weeks. The local authority applied for a care order. The justices found that the mother had been taking drugs for the past 10 years and had been a registered drug addict since 1982. They considered that they were entitled to have regard to the mother's abuse of her own bodily health during pregnancy when deciding whether the conditions in s.1(2)(e)—the health or proper development of the child being avoidably impaired or neglected—were satisfied, and made a care order accordingly. On appeal the Divisional Court held that the conditions of s.1(2)(e) could not be satisfied, since the mother had had no opportunity to care for the child since birth; thus no conduct by her could have been said to have affected the child's health. *Held,* allowing the local authority's appeal, that events occurring when the child was a foetus were relevant matters for the court's consideration if they affected its health or proper development after its birth. (*N* v. *Westminster City Council* [1984] C.L.Y. 2206 applied;) D (A MINOR) *Re* [1986] 3 W.L.R. 85, C.A.

2173. Care proceedings—optional proceedings—wardship—speedy hearing
In both cases the local authority had the option of applying for a care order either in care proceedings in the juvenile court or in wardship proceedings. Wardship proceedings were initiated and there was a delay of 2½ years before the cases came to trial. They were heard on consecutive days before the same judge. In both cases the court had not controlled the wardship. In *B*, concerning two children aged 14 and 12, the local authority had acted as if it already had a care order and had altered and substantially reduced access by the mother. In *L*, the child, aged two, had spent more than half her life with foster parents and had become settled in their home. *Held,* that where the local authority had the option of taking care proceedings or wardship proceedings it had a duty to bring the case on for hearing within a reasonable time. The delay in this case was totally unacceptable; and District Registrars should ensure that such cases were brought before the judge speedily even if there was delay or resistance, bearing in mind that in the magistrates' court the local authority would have been under a 28 day surveillance by the court and in all likelihood the case would have been heard and determined within three months: STOCKPORT METROPOLITAN BOROUGH COUNCIL *v.* B; STOCKPORT METROPOLITAN BOROUGH COUNCIL *v.* L (1986) 16 Fam. Law 187, Ewbank J.

2174. Care proceedings—power to award costs
[Children and Young Persons Act 1969 (c.54), s.21(2); Magistrates' Courts Act 1980 (c.43), s.64(1); Magistrates' Courts (Childrens and Young Persons) Rules 1970

(S.I. 1970 No. 1792 (L.32).] M had applied successfully for the discharge of a care order in respect of her daughter and had sought an order for costs under s.64(1) of the Act 1980 Act. The justices dismissed her application, having decided that they had no jurisdiction under s.64(1) since that power was limited to proceedings initiated by complaint and the instant application under s.21(2) of the 1969 Act could not properly be so described. M appealed by way of judicial review contending that the procedure applicable was by way of complaint since no specific procedure was prescribed by the 1970 Rules. *Held*, that the clear inference to be gained from a consideration of the prescribed forms and the wording of s.21(2) was that the hearing was of an application rather than a complaint. Moreover, following the *Gravesham* case where an application was made under s.21(2) by the natural mother she was not a party to the proceedings and therefore would not be described as a complainant for the purposes of s.64 (*R.* v. *Gravesham Juvenile Court, ex p. B* [1982] C.L.Y. 1928 followed): R. v. SALISBURY AND TILSBURY AND MERE COMBINED JUVENILE COURT, *ex p.* BALL (1985) 15 Fam. Law 313, Kennedy J.

2175. Child abduction
CHILD ABDUCTION AND CUSTODY (PARTIES TO CONVENTIONS) ORDER 1986 (No. 1159) [80p], made under the Child Abduction and Custody Act 1985 (c.60), ss.2 and 13; operative on August 1, 1986; specifies the contracting states to the convention on the civil aspects of international child abduction, and to the European Convention on Recognition and Enforcement of Decisions concerning Custody of Children.

2176. Child abduction and custody. See MAGISTERIAL LAW, § 2073.

2177. Child Abduction and Custody Act 1985—commencement
CHILD ABDUCTION AND CUSTODY ACT 1985 (COMMENCEMENT) ORDER 1986 (No. 1048 (c.26)) [45p], made under the Child Abduction and Custody Act 1985 (c.60), s.29(2); brings the whole Act into force on August 1, 1986.

2178. Child abduction—removal from jurisdiction—practice direction. See PRACTICE, § 2672.

2179. Children and Young Persons (Amendment) Act 1986 (c.28)
This Act amends the law in relation to children and young persons in care. It amends the provisions for regulations as to accommodation of children in care, for appeals and for parties to care proceedings.
The Act received the Royal Assent on July 8, 1986 and comes into force on days to be appointed. It does not extend to Scotland or Northern Ireland.

2180. Children in care—contribution notice—service—discretion
[Child Care Act 1980 (c.5), s.46(4).] Under s.46(4) of the Child Care Act 1980, a local authority need not serve a contribution notice if it thinks fit. The section does not prohibit the serving of such a notice, but leaves service to the authority's discretion: R. v. ESSEX COUNTY COUNCIL, *ex p.* WASHINGTON, *The Times*, July 12, 1986, McCowan J.

2181. Children in care—wardship—appropriateness—foster parents
The children, twins, had been committed to the care of the local authority and had been placed with foster parents for some nine years. Following disputes between the foster parents and the local authority over the upbringing of the twins they were removed and placed in a children's home. The foster parents issued an originating summons in wardship seeking care and control of the children and contended that the act of removal had deprived them of the opportunity to seek a custodianship order. *Held*, dismissing the summons, that as the foster parents had submitted that the removal of the twins by the local authority was an abuse of its power this could only be done by way of judicial review (*Associated Provincial Picture Houses* v. *Wednesbury Corporation* (1948) C.L.C. 8107 and *T. (A.J.J.) (An Infant), Re* [1970] C.L.Y. 1360 considered; *A.* v. *Liverpool City Council* [1981] C.L.Y. 1796 and *W (A Minor) (Wardship: Jurisdiction), Re* [1985] C.L.Y. 2255 applied): M (MINORS) *Re*, (1985) 83 L.S.Gaz. 780, Sheldon J.

2182. Custodianship—consent of natural parents—whether prerequisite
[Children Act 1975 (c.72), ss.12, 33, 37.] The applicants, the foster parents of a young child placed in the care of the local authority, had applied to adopt her. At the hearing the judge found that the natural parents had not unreasonably withheld their consent but decided to make a custodianship order in favour of the applicants: *Held*, allowing the applicants' appeal, that whilst s.37 made provision for a court

hearing an application for adoption or guardianship to make a custodianship order instead it was a pre-requisite that either the natural parents consented to adoption or the court decided to dispense with their consent under s.12. It was clear that in finding that the natural parents' refusal was reasonable the judge had fallen into error. However, since the applicants had not applied for custodianship under s.33 nor been heard on the point the order should be set aside and a directive given that the consent of the natural parents to adopt had been unreasonably withheld in the best interests of the child. The matter should be remitted to a judge to decide whether an adoption order should be made (*G*. v. *G*. [1985] C.L.Y. 2594 considered): M (A MINOR), *Re, The Times*, October 13, 1986, C.A.

2183. Custody—access—illegitimate child in care of local authority—access sought by putative father—jurisdiction of justices

[Guardianship of Minors Act 1971 (c.3), s.9(1)(*b*).]

Justices have jurisdiction to make an order for access in favour of the putative father of an illegitimate child in the care of a local authority.

By an order made by a juvenile court on February 11, 1981 an illegitimate child was placed in the care of the local authority. At first the local authority granted access to the child's putative father. In August 1984 the local authority denied any further access to the putative father. The father applied for an order for custody of the child against the mother and an order for access against both the mother and the local authority. The justices refused to issue a summons against the local authority on the ground that they had no jurisdiction to make the order sought. The father applied for judicial review. *Held,* that the father's rights were limited entirely to those conferred by sections 9 and 14 of the Guardianship of Minors Act 1971. The justices had jurisdiction to make an order for access in favour of the father under those provisions of the Act. Accordingly the summons against the local authority must be issued (*H (K. and M.) (Infants), Re* [1972] C.L.Y. 2179 explained, *R*. v. *Oxford Justices, ex p. H* [1974] C.L.Y. 2409 considered).

R. v. OXFORD JUSTICES, *ex p.* D. [1986] 3 W.L.R. 447, Waite J.

2184. Custody—care and control—split order—inappropriateness

M and R had been divorced in 1976, custody of the three children was granted to M, by consent. They lived in the former matrimonial home. In 1979 the eldest child went to live with F, who had re-married a lady with two children aged eight and five. In 1985 the two younger children, aged 15 and 14 went to F's home. the welfare report recommended that the children should remain with F and that access should remain available to M. The judge had been concerned with M's right of occupation of the matrimonial home which was in F's sole name. Accordingly, he made an order granting care and control to F and custody to M to preserve the home in case the children changed their minds and returned to M. *Held,* allowing F's appeal, that the judge had erred in treating matter as a relevant consideration on the issue of custody. He was not entitled to attempt to inhibit or influence the position in relation to the matrimonial home. Split orders were undesirable. It was important that F, having the day-to-day burden of the children, should have their custody. Due to the bitterness between the parties a joint custody order was inappropriate (*Dipper* v. *Dipper* [1980] C.L.Y. 787 followed; *Jane* v. *Jane* [1983] C.L.Y. 2448 considered): WILLIAMSON v. WILLIAMSON (1986) 16 Fam. Law 217, C.A.

2185. Custody—change of parent—stay of execution pending appeal—consideration

On March 7, 1985 an order was made by the magistrates granting custody of the child, aged 2½ years, to M. A stay of execution for 21 days pending appeal was made. F lodged notice of appeal in June 1985. The stay was regarded as extending automatically until the hearing of the appeal. No directions were sought by either party for an expedited hearing and as a result, the appeal was not heard until October 1985. *Held,* that such a stay should be limited in time. At the end of the specified period the order should come into effect unless an extension had been ordered by a judge of the Family Division in which the appeal would be pending. In that way it was possible for the High Court to control the hearing of the appeal and to prevent the delay such as had occurred in this case which was wholly detrimental not only to the interests of the child but also to the interests of the parents (*K (A Minor) (Access Order: Breach) Re* [1977] C.L.Y. 1913, applied): S v. S (CUSTODY ORDER: STAY OF EXECUTION) [1986] 1 F.L.R. 492, Booth J.

2186. Custody—hearing—criminal record and drink problem—need for adequate information

M, who was Spanish, and F, who was Welsh, had married in 1973. The two children of the family were now aged 10 and 8½. The marriage ran into difficulties following the move of the family to Madrid in 1979. In 1981, after the return of the parties to England, M was awarded custody of the children in the Magistrates' court. In 1982 she took them to the Canary Islands without leave of the court. In May 1983 she returned to England and left the children with F whilst she looked for accommodation in London. F immediately began wardship proceedings. A welfare officer, who had only seen F and the children together, reported in August 1983. At the hearing before the judge in December 1983 the welfare officer sought an adjournment to obtain more up-to-date information. The judge found that there was nothing to prevent M from caring for the children but came to the conclusion that their lives would be more stable with F. The judge had information about F's criminal record. He also had information that F had a significant drink problem in 1979 but no indication as to how the problem had progressed. After the hearing F was removed from his accommodation and re-housed as a result of which the children had to change schools. He had also been charged with being drunk in charge of a pedal cycle. *Held,* allowing M's appeal, that in custody cases it was desirable, where a party had a criminal record, not only that the full antecedents should be before the court but also that any social inquiry reports should be made available. Where there was a drink problem any medical reports should be disclosed. Here the information before the judge was incomplete. The welfare officer had also not seen M with the children coupled with events since the hearing a re-trial would be ordered: R. (MINORS) (CUSTODY), *Re* (1986) 1 F.L.R. 6, C.A.

2187. Custody—interim order—appeal

F appealed against the decision of Wood J. granting interim custody of a child, aged nearly five, to M on appeal from the Havant Magistrates Court which had granted interim custody to F. It was submitted by F that the judge had come to the decision that the child should be moved when on the evidence before him it was impossible for him to make such a decision. That evidence related mainly to a series of hearings in the Magistrates' Court, that F's case was never fully investigated and that the judge had a wholly unbalanced presentation of the case. F also submitted that the judge had erred in accepting the truth of the facts told to him during the course of the hearing without F having the opportunity of being able to cross-examine M or to give or call evidence to contradict those facts. *Held*, dismissing F's appeal, that the judge had had before him a considerable body of written evidence comprising the notes and records of the hearings in the Magistrates' Court and affidavits lodged for the purposes of the appeal. Both parties had been present at the hearing before the judge but neither had given evidence or sought to do so. Nothing adverse had been established against M and, if there had been it had been open to F to swear an affidavit or seek to give evidence before the judge. Equally, there was no criticism of F. However, the child had been with M for most of his life and there was no reason to interfere with the decision of the judge pending the full determination of the case: EDWARDS *v.* EDWARDS (1986) F.L.R. 205, C.A.

2188. Custody—interim order—no welfare report

Allegations had been made against the mother of three children, the youngest of whom was aged eight, which, if made out, placed the children at risk. Owing to their work-load the social services had told the judge that they required three to four months to prepare reports. The judge made an interim custody order in favour of the mother. *Held,* allowing appeals by the two fathers, that the judge should have adjourned the case for a welfare officer to attend and for some kind of reports from social services as he could not have been satisfied that the children's welfare was safe by living with the mother. In the circumstances he was plainly wrong in law in making an interim custody order: W (A MINOR), *Re, The Times,* November 13, 1986, C.A.

2189. Custody—joint custody—care and control

The parties separated in 1981 and came to an arrangement whereby their daughter, then about four years old, spent alternate weeks with them. In 1984 the divorce judge found the arrangement satisfactory, granted a decree absolute and awarded custody jointly. In 1986 M. applied for sole custody. *Held,* that it was prima facie wrong for a child to have such an unsettled existence, and while the parents might have joint custody (and it was so ordered) care and control should vest with M, with reasonable access to F (*G. v. G. (Minors: Custody Appeal)* [1985] C.L.Y. 2594 considered): RILEY *v.* RILEY, (1986) 150 J.P. 439, C.A.

2190. Custody—mother and child living abroad—return to jurisdiction—undertaking

In both cases the parties obtained divorces under the special procedure. At the time of the dissolution of the marriages the wives were living abroad and intended to remain with the children outside the jurisdiction. Custody orders were sought with the consent of both husbands but were refused by the court. By the time of the hearing of the appeal the wives had given undertakings which had not been before the judges in the county court, that they would return the children if called upon to do so. *Held,* allowing the appeals, that it was settled law that there was jurisdiction in the Court of Appeal and in the courts of this country to make orders for custody even though the child or children were living outside the jurisdiction of the court. The general rule was that the court would require that an undertaking be given by the custodial parent to bring the child within the jurisdiction if called upon so to do. The justice of the situation required that the court should accede to these applications: ARMSTRONG *v.* ARMSTRONG; HUFF *v.* HUFF (1986) 16 Fam.Law 21, C.A.

2191. Custody—refusal of adjournment—whether denial of justice

In 1982 M had started divorce proceedings whilst the one child of the marriage remained in her care. In 1984 the care of the child was transferred to F under an interim order. M instructed her solicitors that she wished her case to be presented by counsel but it was only shortly before the main hearing that she was able to provide sufficient funds to cover counsel's fees. At the main hearing her solicitor applied unsuccessfully for an adjournment so as to instruct counsel. *Held,* allowing M's appeal, that the result of the course taken by the judge was to prevent M from putting forward her case properly which, if left unremedied, would have a harmful effect on the parties future relations and her attitude towards the courts. Moreover, the period of delay caused by an adjournment had it been granted, would not have affected the immediate care and control of the child since it would have remained with F. Expedited re-hearing ordered before a different judge: WILSON *v.* WILSON (1986) 16 Fam. Law 212, C.A.

2192. Custody—removal from jurisdiction—considerations

Custody of the two children, daughters aged 11 and 10, had been given to M. F, who lived locally, had frequent staying access and had a close relationship with them, as did his parents. M applied unsuccessfully to take the children to New Zealand to live permanently with her, their stepfather and two young half brothers. *Held,* allowing M's appeal, that in considering the welfare of the children the court had to bear in mind the risk of friction and bitterness resulting from the reasonable proposals and wishes of the custodial parent being interfered with. The stability of the daughters centred in the main, on M and the home where they lived. The judge had not applied the correct test in holding that the daughters' interests were incompatible with the wishes of M. He had not given sufficient weight to the risk that the disappointment that would be felt by M and the stepfather of not being able to go to New Zealand would have on the daughters: L. *v.* H. (1986) 83 L.S.Gaz. 1154, C.A.

2193. Custody—welfare report—hearsay rule—whether appropriate

In custody proceedings a welfare report had been ordered. When the parties received their copies they found that parts had been deleted by order of the judge. H applied to the court for an unexpurgated copy. The judge refused the application stating that if a welfare report contained hearsay evidence and referred to people who could not be identified or called as witnesses then the evidence was inadmissible, should not have been included in the report and that the judge had a discretion and a duty to expunge such inadmissible matters. *Held,* allowing H's appeal, that the judge had been wrong to apply the strict rules of evidence. The welfare officer could not do the work required of him and comply with the hearsay rule. Once the report was prepared the parties were entitled as of right to see the whole of it and could then test that material at the hearing and cross-examine the welfare officer, and the judge would then be able to weigh the evidence: WEBB *v.* WEBB (1986) 16 Fam. Law 155, [1986] 1 F.L.R. 462, C.A.

2194. Custody—young children—whether general principles

It is not a general principle in custody cases that, all other things being equal, a young child ought to be with its mother. Where a custody decision is so finely-balanced that it could go either way, it will be difficult to fault whichever decision is taken (*W (A Minor) (Custody), Re* [1983] C.L.Y. 2445 applied): THOMPSON *v.* THOMPSON (1986) 150 J.P. 686, C.A.

2195. Custody order—best interests of child—perspective

In custody proceedings the judge had awarded custody, care and control of the child to F. *Held,* dismissing M's appeal, that where it appeared that the solution which would be in the best interests of the child in a few years time was different from that at the time of the hearing it was wholly in accordance with the principle that the judge should decide the application by reference only to what was best for the child in the relatively short term: T *v.* T, *The Times,* August 4, 1986, C.A.

2196. Custody proceedings—interim order—judicial interview of children

The parties had been divorced in February 1985. M was granted interim custody of the two children, a girl and boy and took them to live in Dundee. In June 1985 F moved the boy to Norfolk where he lived and made arrangements for him to attend school there. In September F applied to reverse the existing custody order. The judge, during the course of the hearing, saw the children in his private rooms and promised them confidentiality of the interview. As a result of matters divulged he decided to grant interim custody to F with access to M during the school holidays. In his judgment he recorded that he had committed himself to the children not to divulge their confidences and that he had made his decision in the absence of a welfare report and evidence on the relative merits of the English and Scottish educational systems. As a result of the order both children were moved from Dundee and were now attending Norfolk schools. *Held,* allowing M's appeal, that it was plain that the judge had been influenced by what the children had told him and that he had been wrong to keep secret matters upon which the parties' advocates had had no opportunity to make submissions. The application by F had also been supported by wholly inadequate evidence to justify the alteration of the existing order. In all the circumstances interim custody would be given to M with reinforced access but leaving care and control with F since the children were now fully integrated into Norfolk living and it was wrong to move them yet again for a further interim period pending the substantive hearing (*Bellenden* v. *Sattersthwaite* (1948) C.L.C. 3046 and *G* v. *G* [1985] C.L.Y. 2594 applied): ELDER *v.* ELDER (1986) 16 Fam. Law 190, C.A.

2197. Detention of child by police—application for release

[Children and Young Persons Act 1969 (c.54), s.28.] Where a child is detained and an application is made for his release, the police are entitled to be notified of and heard on the application: R. *v.* BRISTOL JUSTICES, *ex p.* BROOME, *The Times,* December 6, 1986, Booth J.

2198. Family Law Act 1986 (c.55)

This Act implements the recommendations of three Law Commission reports dealing with the custody of children, the recognition of foreign nullity decrees and declarations in family matters.

Part I provides the U.K. courts with new powers to deal with cases of child abduction by estranged parents. It sets out new rules for child custody which will settle the particular U.K. country (England and Wales, Scotland or Northern Ireland) in which a custody case can be decided. It enables custody orders made in one U.K. country to be enforced in another and it establishes new procedures for the enforcement of custody orders within each country. The present jurisdiction rules will be replaced with uniform rules for each part of the U.K.

Part II assimilates the recognition of foreign nullity decisions to those grounds of recognition for divorces and legal separations which are contained in the Recognition of Divorces and Legal Separations Act 1971.

Part III applies to England and Wales only and relates to declarations of status. It proposes a new legislative code to determine declaratory relief in matters of matrimonial status, legitimacy, legitimation and adoption.

With the exception of ss.64–67, which came into force on January 7, 1987, the Act comes into force on days to be appointed.

2199. Guardian ad litem—practice direction. See PRACTICE DIRECTION (FAM.D.) (GUARDIAN AD LITEM OF A CHILD), § 2642.

2200. Guardians ad litem
GUARDIANS AD LITEM AND REPORTING OFFICERS (PANELS) (AMENDMENT) REGULATIONS 1986 (No. 3) [40p]. made under the Children Act 1975 (c.72), s.103(1)(a); operative on February 3, 1986; amend S.I. 1983 No. 1908.

2201. Joint custody—care and control to father—generous access to mother—balancing considerations
M and F had married in 1978 and had two sons aged eight and six. M had left the matrimonial home in December 1983 to live with another man and had taken the children with her. The welfare officer reported that the conflict was not as to the competence of either parent but as to different values. The judge gave joint custody to the parties with care and control to F and very generous access to M. M appealed against the care and control order contending that the judge had wrongly taken into account M's adultery and conduct at the time of the separation, that he had failed to make any necessary findings of fact particularly as to the capacity of the parties to provide educational stimulus and discipline for the children and that he had given undue weight to the limited differences that a transfer of care and control would make to the amount of time available to F to exercise his influence upon the children in view of the extensive access previously enjoyed by M under W's order. *Held,* dismissing M's appeal, that the court could find no error, let alone any blatant error, in the judge's decision. He had not based his decision upon the circumstances in which M had left. He had, however, been entitled to point out that the circumstances in which M had left in no way reflected upon the conduct or character of F. There was also no lack of finding of fact. The judge had thought it in the best interests of the children for them to be brought up with F's standards rather than those of M and her cohabitee which he did not criticise but which were different. The period before the children went to school and when they came home was a crucial period when a parent did have influence over the children which was distinct from any period of access. The judge had obviously thought it desirable that F should be given this crucial period (*G.* v. *G. (Minors: Custody Appeal)* [1985] C.L.Y. 2594 followed): MAY v. MAY (1986) 1 F.L.R. 325, C.A.

2202. Law Reform (Parent and Child) (Scotland) Act 1986 (c.9)
This Act (which applies to Scotland only) deals with the consequences of birth out of wedlock, the rights and duties of parents, the determination of parentage and the taking of blood samples in relation to such determination, and amends the law as to guardianship.

2203. Maintenance—school fees—periodical payments against custodial parent
[Matrimonial Causes Act 1973 (c.18), ss.23(1)(d), 25.]
H was given custody, care and control of the three children. He applied to the court for periodical payments orders to be made against him to pay each child an amount equivalent to the school fees after deduction of income tax at the basic rate. H's intention was that the sums paid would become separate income of the children, who would contract with the school for payment of the fees, thereby reducing H's tax burden. The judge refused the order on the ground that it was the policy of Family Division judges to refuse such applications made by a custodial parent. *Held,* dismissing H's appeal, that (1) although the court could make an order for periodical payments on the application of the custodial parent against himself, and although (2), the court when making an order was required to have regard to the tax position of the family, and would select the most tax-effective of a number of possible orders, (3) it would not make an order when the arrangement was no more than a sham. (*Ramsay (W.T.)* v. *I.R.C.* [1981] C.L.Y. 1385 and *Furniss (Inspector of Taxes)* v. *Dawson* [1984] C.L.Y. 270 applied: dictum of Evershed M.R. in *Whiteside* v. *Whiteside* (1949) C.L.C. 9380 distinguished.)
SHERDLEY v. SHERDLEY [1986] 2 All E.R. 202, C.A.

2204. Proceedings—affidavit evidence—hearsay—right of cross-examination
In children's cases where an allegation was made in affidavit evidence which was part of a charge against a parent then the rule which required the deponent to state his source of information and belief should be enforced and, in turn, the source of that information should depose to an affidavit in order that he too might be tendered for cross-examination: N (A MINOR) *Re, The Times,* June 19, 1986, Lincoln J.

2205. Protection of Children (Tobacco) Act 1986 (c.34)

This Act amends the Children and Young Persons Act 1933 and the Children and Young Persons (Scotland) Act 1937 and makes it an offence to sell any tobacco product to persons under the age of 16.

The Act received the Royal Assent on July 8, 1986 and comes into force on October 8, 1986. It does not extend to Northern Ireland.

2206. Secure accommodation

SECURE ACCOMMODATION (NO. 2) (AMENDMENT) REGULATIONS 1986 (No. 1591) [80p], made under the Child Care Act 1980 (c.5), ss.21A(7), 39 and 85(4); operative on October 15, 1986; provide for a child who is a ward of court to be placed or kept in secure accommodation only pursuant to the direction of a judge exercising wardship jurisdiction without the involvement of a juvenile court.

2207. Wardship—adopted child—allegation of ill-treatment—re-opening case

In 1976 the child, now aged nine-and-a-half, had been taken into care and placed with foster parents. The natural mother (M) was granted access and the child knew who she really was. In 1982 M started wardship proceedings and the foster parents commenced adoption proceedings. At the consolidated hearing the judge found that the foster parents were not to blame for certain bruising to the child. He dismissed M's application, de-warded the child and made an adoption order on the basis that the child needed the stable environment that only such an order would afford him. In November 1983, six months later, M snatched the child. The parents' made him a ward of court. He was returned by the police after three days. M's application for leave to have an investigation of new evidence of alleged ill-treatment was dismissed. *Held*, dismissing M's appeal, that following *Re O*, M had to show an extremely strong prima facie case that it was in the child's best interests to reopen the case and have a full investigation into the present circumstances after an adoption order had been made. Such evidence was not available here. (*O., Re*, [1977] C.L.Y. 1962 applied): C. (A MINOR) (WARDSHIP: ADOPTED CHILD) (1985) 15 Fam. Law 318, C.A.

2208. Wardship—adoption—balancing considerations

In cross-applications M. the mother of two young children, sought care and control of or access to them in wardship proceedings and FM, the foster mother who had cared for them for three years, sought an adoption order to which M did not agree. The children's early life had been extensively disrupted. The local authority had purported to pass a parental rights resolution the validity of which was doubtful. The children had been placed with foster-parents as prospective adopters, M's application to rescind the resolution had been dismissed on appeal. Following the breakdown of the foster-parents' marriage FM had proceeded with the adoption application. M initiated a series of proceedings, including wardship, to draw attention to what she saw as the injustices he had suffered and to gain access to the children. *Held*, on the wardship question, that it was in the best interest's of the children that they should remain in the care of FM for the foreseeable future. On the adoption question the evidence indicated that there was a narrow balance in favour of adoption to long-term fostering. However, on the consent question it was impossible to hold that M's veto was unreasonable. It followed that the adoption application should be dismissed. The wardship should continue and a care order would be made. However it would not be helpful to introduce access immediately and the matter should be reviewed in nine months time following a report from the guardian *ad litem* (*F., Re* [1982] C.L.Y. 2022 applied; *O'Connor* v. *A and B* [1971] C.L.Y. 5833. *W., Re* [1971] C.L.Y. 5831; *O., Re* [1977] C.L.Y. 1920 and *H, Re: W., Re (Adoption: Parental Agreement)* [1983] C.L.Y. 2424 considered: B.A. (WARDSHIP AND ADOPTION), *Re*, (1985) 15 Fam. Law 306, Waterhouse J.

2209. Wardship—care and control—non-accidental injuries

The mother had four children: M born in 1977, K born in 1980, (who were the children of her first husband). R born in 1982 who was the child of her second husband) and S born in January 1985 (who was the child of her current cohabitee, Mr. I. As a result of injuries to M and K these children were taken into care. In early summer 1983, with a view to rehabilitation, they were placed in the charge and control of the mother at a stage when she had begun living with Mr. I. In November 1983 R was admitted to hospital with burns as a result of which M and K were removed and a juvenile court care order was made in respect of R. The mother lodged an appeal. Before it was heard she gave birth to S who was made a ward of court by the mother and Mr. I. The child R was then joined in the wardship proceedings and the mother sought care and control of R and S. The judge found that the injuries to K and M were non-accidental but had not been caused by the mother. He found that the injuries to R were non-accidental and had been caused by Mr. I. The judge decided that the risks attendant to the children were too great to be acceptable and ordered that R should remain a ward of court and be committed to the care of the local authority. However, because S. was Mr. I's own child he was justified in taking the risk and returning the child to the parents subject to a supervision order. *Held,* allowing the local authority's appeal, that the fact that S was Mr. I's own child was not a sufficient reason for taking the formidable risk of placing him in the care of the mother and Mr. I. Therefore, the judge's treatment of the balancing process in ascertaining the proper course for the welfare of the child was faulty in a highly material factor. Accordingly, S would be committed to the care of the local authority: I. *v.* BARNSLEY METROPOLITAN BOROUGH COUNCIL (1986) 1 F.L.R. 109, C.A.

2210. Wardship—care and control—Rastafarian parents
In 1979 M, then aged 15 had given birth to an illegitimate baby boy, P, and lived with the grandmother. In 1980 M became a Rastafarian, fell out with the grandmother, and moved to London with P in 1983 where she formed a relationship with F, a Rastafarian, and became a member of his extended family. P was unable to fit in with the different dietary habits and cultural patterns and became very unhappy. Later that year P was admitted to hospital clinically dead but was revived. He had collapsed from severe hypothermia and malnutrition and had sustained extensive non-accidental injuries over a period of time. M was charged in criminal proceedings. P was made the subject of a care order and placed with the grandmother. In July 1984 M gave birth to F's baby, J. A place of safety order was obtained and J was placed with short-term foster parents. In September at the trial in the criminal proceedings M was sentenced to two years' imprisonment. She was released in January 1986. In January 1985 the local authority resolved to rehabilitate J with M and to place them in a mother and baby unit in prison. The *guardian ad litem* representing J, was concerned about the proposals and issued wardship proceedings, In July 1985 the local authority resolved that it would endorse the wardship application and to recommend to the court that there should be no rehabilitation. *Held,* confirming the wardship, that it was not feasible to move J to M and F's family against the background of non-accidental injuries to P, it was also unlikely that M and F would be able fully to co-operate with social services due to their anti-white and anti-establishment attitudes. Finally, it would not be in J's interests to move from his present family to a different culture, environment, parental figures and diet: J.T. (A MINOR) (WARDSHIP: COMMITTAL), *Re,* (1986) 16 Fam. Law 213, Butler-Sloss J.

2211. Wardship—care and control—removal of child—formal application
The local authority had commenced wardship proceedings with regard to a baby born the previous day. The six other children of M were already subject to wardship proceedings in a case, still in progress, concerned, *inter alia,* with whether M's co-habitee had been responsible for non-accidental injuries to two of these children. Because of disquiet the local authority had then removed the baby but without applying either for a place of safety order or an order for wardship. *Held,* discussing M's interim application for the baby to be returned to her, that in view of the unresolved questions raised in the wardship proceedings and in the affidavit evidence in the present proceedings, it would not be safe to return the baby until a decision had been reached on the primary facts after a full hearing. Accordingly, the wardship would continue, with interim care and control to the local authority. However, the costs would be paid by the local authority to mark the fact that they had acted unconstitutionally, albeit in good faith, in the way in which they had removed the baby: HAVERING LONDON BOROUGH COUNCIL *v.* S (1986) 16 Fam. Law 157, [1986] 1 F.L.R. 489, C.A.

2212. Wardship—child in care
M, aged 15, had requested that her new-born child be received into care by the local authority. The child was placed with short-term foster parents. The putative father, aged 16, initiated wardship proceedings, by his next friend, and asked that care and control be committed to his mother. The local authority were of the opinion

that the more appropriate course was long-term fostering with a view to adoption but were willing for the matter to be decided in the wardship proceedings. The matter was referred by the registrar to the judge to decide whether it was appropriate to continue a wardship when the child was in care and where the local authority was agreeable to such a continuation. *Held,* that where a local authority invited the intervention of the wardship court to assist them in the exercise of powers otherwise available to them, the court would accede to that request even if the case was such that if the local authority opposed the exercise of the court's power the court would yield to avoid the circuitous process of the local authority itself invoking wardship proceedings. Accordingly, if another interested person initiated those proceedings and the local authority did not oppose the exercise of that jurisdiction, the court was enabled to exercise its powers. The fact that the putative father had not had his status declared by a court of competent jurisdiction would not impede the wardship if the court found that he was the father (*A.* v. *Liverpool City Council* [1981] C.L.Y. 1976. *J. (A Minor) (Care Order: Wardship) Re* [1984] C.L.Y. 2211 and *W. (A Minor) (Care Proceedings: Wardship) Re* [1985] C.L.Y. 2255 distinguished: A. *v.* B. AND HEREFORD AND WORCESTER COUNTY COUNCIL (1966) 1 F.L.R. 289, Sir John Arnold P.

2213. Wardship—child in care—secure accommodation—review panel
    Child Care Act 1980 (c.5), s.21A; Secure Accommodation (No. 2) Regulations (S.I. 1983 No. 1308). The child, a boy born in 1969, had had a disastrously unsettled history. In December 1983, in wardship proceedings, he was committed to the care of the local authority and the judge directed that he be kept in secure accommodation. As a result of previous hearings ([1984] C.L.Y. 2251 and [1985] C.L.Y. 2263) the juvenile court authorised that the child be kept in secure accommodation until June 1985 which was extended, at a case conference, to his sixteenth birthday in August 1985. The review panel, however, were of the opinion that the boy should be released immediately. The matter was again referred to the High Court for directions. *Held,* that the review panel was no more than an agency of the local authority. It was therefore not obliged to follow panel's advice or to accept any findings or recommendations that it might make since it had no statutory function or duty in relation to the first placement of the child in secure accommodation. Section 21A and the Regulations did not affect the overriding jurisdiction of the High Court in respect of wards committed to the care of the local authority. In consequence it had the power to order that its conclusions be made known to the juvenile court to which the matter might then be referred. The decision to keep the child in secure accommodation until his sixteenth birthday was appropriate, there being overwhelming evidence for such continued placement (*A.* v. *Liverpool City Council* [1981] C.L.Y. 1796, *M.* v. *Lambeth Borough Council (No. 2)* [1985] C.L.Y. 2263 and *W. (A Minor) (Care Proceedings: Wardship) Re* [1985] C.L.Y. 2255 considered: M. *v.* LAMBETH BOROUGH COUNCIL (NO. 3) (1986) 16 Fam. Law 23, Sheldon J.

2214. Wardship—discharge—care order in matrimonial proceedings—no distinction
    [Matrimonial Causes Act 1973 (c.18), ss.43(1), 5(*a*).] In 1981 the child, a boy aged 7, had been committed to the care of the local authority under s.43(1), having previously been in voluntary care. He was subsequently placed with foster parents. In 1982 M, in the same proceedings, applied and later appealed unsuccessfully for the discharge of the care order and for access with a view to rehabilitation. In 1985 the foster parents commenced proceedings for adoption. M issued wardship proceedings asking for the same relief as before. The registrar refused to discharge the wardship proceedings on the application of the local authority. *Held,* allowing the local authority's appeal, that the same criteria applied in a case under s.43(1) as with ordinary care orders except that certain additional powers were granted to the court, *e.g.* to give directions to the local authority under s.43(5)(*a*). Those powers did not include making the child a ward of court. In any event it was appropriate here, to discharge the wardship since M was seeking the same relief as in the matrimonial proceedings (*A* v. *Liverpool City Council* [1981] C.L.Y. 1796, *Re W* [1985] C.L.Y. 2255 and *W.* v. *Nottinghamshire County Council* [1986] C.L.Y. 2218 applied): J. *v.* DEVON COUNTY COUNCIL (WARDSHIP: JURISDICTION) (1986) 16 Fam. Law 162, Swinton Thomas J.

2215. Wardship—girl over 17—local authority care—inherent jurisdiction
[Family Law Reform Act 1969 (c.46), s.7(2)] The minor, a girl aged 17 years and 4 months, lived with her parents. She had become rebellious, sexually active, dishonest, and had run away from home several times. Her parents made the girl a ward of court. The Official Solicitor (as guardian *ad litem*) supported the parents and, with the acquiescence of the local authority applied for care and control to be committed to the local authority and that she be placed in secure accommodation. *Held*, that the High Court could exercise the wardship jurisdiction until the minor reached the age of 18. Although under s.7(2) the court only had power, under the statutory provisions, to commit a ward to the care of the local authority if she was under the age of 17 the court's inherent jurisdiction was not to restrict. As the minor was awaiting sentence by the juvenile court her disposal, in the first instance should be left to the justices. If after regaining her freedom she re-offended or showed herself still to be beyond normal control the High Court would again consider whether she should be placed in secure accommodation: S.W. (A MINOR) (WARDSHIP: JURISDICTION), *Re*, (1985) 15 Fam. Law 322, Sheldon J.

2216. Wardship—jurisdiction—prospective care proceedings—no exceptional circumstances
M and F, an unmarried couple, had five children ranging from 10 to infancy. As a result of F's violence the three older children had been taken into care and the fourth child had been taken away at birth and placed for adoption with M's consent. The relationship between M and F improved and M became pregnant. Following the birth the local authority informed M and F that they intended to apply for a care order and placed the child on the "at risk" register but allowed the child to remain on a trial basis. M warded the child. *Held*, dismissing her appeal against a dismissal of the wardship, that there was nothing exceptional in the facts of the case. There was not the remotest likelihood of M gaining care and control in view of the background of violence and neglect. There was no distinction in principle between the situation in which an order had been made by the juvenile court and where one would inevitably be made if an application was made by the local authority. In both situations the choice facing the court was whether the child's interests were better left with the local authority, as Parliament intended, or whether there were special circumstances upon which the court should exercise a supervisory jurisdiction. The judge had therefore exercised his discretion correctly (*A* v. *Liverpool City Council* [1981] C.L.Y. 1796 applied; *W Re* [1981] C.L.Y. 354 and *E, Re* [1983] C.L.Y. 2469 considered): W. *v*. SHROPSHIRE COUNTY COUNCIL (1986) 16 Fam. Law 128, C.A.

2217. Wardship—local authorities—use of jurisdiction
Local authorities should resort to the wardship jurisdiction in cases of difficulty, complexity, possible notoriety or where a stalemate had been reached (*D., Re* [1977] C.L.Y. 1930, *A*. v. *Liverpool City Council* [1981] C.L.Y. 1796 and *M., Re* [1985] C.L.Y. 2253 considered): L. H. (A MINOR), *Re, The Times,* April 15, 1986, Sheldon J.

2218. Wardship—local authority care—jurisdiction and procedure
[Children and Young Persons Act 1969 (c.54), s.15; Child Care Act 1980 (c.5), ss.2, 3, 12A.] The two children, a girl aged three and a boy aged two, were the younger children of a family of five, born to different fathers. Due to the family history the council had obtained supervision orders soon after the birth of the younger children. In 1984 they were placed into voluntary care by M for short periods. In 1985 both children were received into voluntary care under s.2 of the 1980 Act after M reported that the girl had sustained non-accidental injuries. The council decided to keep the children in care. M was able to collect the girl and within an hour had warded both children. Half an hour after the issue of the wardship summons the council obtained a place of safety order, and with the aid of the police recovered the girl. The council applied for care orders and to discharge the wardship. M appealed against Hollis J.'s decision that he had no jurisdiction to continue the wardship, contending that he had an inherent discretion to continue the wardship in cases where proceedings under the statutory code were not yet in existence notwithstanding that parallel remedies were available under that code; and that once the council had elected the voluntary path into care they were committed to pass a parental rights resolution under s.3 of the 1980 Act and precluded from applying for substitute care orders under s.15 of the 1969 Act. *Held*, dismissing M's appeal, that the council had in fact taken the decision to act under the statutory code and by the

time of the wardship proceedings had acted under that code. The question of the welfare of the children therefore fell within the purview of the statutory code so that the court had no jurisdiction in the wardship procedure. S.12A of the 1980 Act embraced both paths into care, whether by voluntary or compulsory means. The approach of the statutory code did not embrace any element of election which would limit the subsequent exercise of the council's powers. Therefore it had been open to the council to proceed under s.15 of the 1969 Act (*A* v. *Liverpool City Council* [1981] C.L.Y. 1796 and *Re W (A Minor) (Wardship Jurisdiction)* [1985] C.L.Y. 2255 applied; *Lewisham London Borough Council* v. *Lewisham Juvenile Court Justices* [1979] C.L.Y. 1810 distinguished): W. *v.* NOTTINGHAMSHIRE COUNTY COUNCIL (1986) 16 Fam. Law 185, C.A.

2219. Wardship—local authority care—secure accommodation

[Family Law Reform Act 1969 (c.46), s.7(2); Child Care Act 1980 (c.5), s.21A; secure accommodation (No. 2) Regulations (S.I. 1983 No. 1308)] A local authority is not under a duty to seek directions from the High Court before applying to the juvenile court for an order authorising the placing or keeping of a ward in secure accommodation. Only if the facts were such that the local authority was uncertain whether to make an initial application should such directions be sought. Equally, if during the currency of a direction the local authority thought that the child should be transferred out of secure accommodation an application should be made at once (*K. (A Minor), Re* [1985] C.L.Y. 2262 distinguished): M. (A Minor), *Re, The Times,* January 24, 1986, C.A.

2220. Wardship—local authority care—secure accommodation—proper procedure

[Child Care Act 1980 (c.5), s.21A as substituted by Health and Social Services and Social Security Adjudications Act 1983 (c.41), s.6, Sched. 1, para. 5; Secure Accommodation Regulations (No. 2) (S.I. 1983 No. 1808), 1983.]

Where a local authority seeks to place a ward of court in secure accommodation, application ought to be made first to the juvenile court without recourse to the wardship jurisdiction.

The minor, a boy born on July 12, 1968, was received into voluntary care in June 1980 and placed in a children's home. He absconded and committed numerous offences. In November 1983 he was made a ward of court and placed in secure accommodation following the expiry of orders made by a juvenile court. The local authority wished to place him in secure accommodation for a further 12 months and sought guidance of the High Court. *Held,* that the application for an authority to place a ward of court in secure accommodation ought first to be made to the juvenile court without recourse to the wardship jurisdiction (*M.* v. *Lambeth London Borough Council* [1984] C.L.Y. 2251 not followed).

LIVERPOOL CITY COUNCIL *v.* H.K. (1985) 83 L.G.R. 421, Heilbron J.

2221. Wardship—ouster injunction—procedure

[Guardianship of Minors Act 1971 (c.3) and Guardianship Act 1973 (c.29); Matrimonial House Act 1983 (c.19).] It is quite proper for a judge to hear and determine an application about a ward of court before deciding on an ouster application by one of the parents: ESSEX COUNTY COUNCIL *v.* T, *The Times,* March 15, 1986, C.A.

2222. Wardship proceedings—child abuse—diagnostic interviews—evidential limitations

The two cases concerned conclusions drawn from diagnostic sessions held at the Great Ormond Street Hospital child abuse clinic. In the first case, E, the judge had seen a video recording of an interview between the child and a psychological social worker. There were leading questions and hypothetical questions and a lot of the answers were left in the air. The technique was of recent development and involved the use of anatomically explicit dolls. He had grave doubts about the evidential standing of the interview although it was not intended to have evidential value. The conclusion that there had been sexual abuse by the father was unjustified on the material evidence available to the social worker.

In the second case, *G,* M had made an allegation of sexual abuse by F two years after the alleged incident in support of her application to stop access by F to her two children. There had been no video recording of the interview with the child. The social worker had come to the firm conclusion that there had been sexual abuse but had failed to ask one more question as to where the incident had taken place. Had she done so she would have realised the child was not telling the truth. It had been a mistake to investigate a remark of a child, aged nearly three years, two years later: E (A MINOR) *Re*; G (A MINOR) *Re, The Times*, July 16, 1986, Ewbank J.

2223. Wardship proceedings—role of doctors

In wardship proceedings every expert should be careful not to become emotionally involved with the side on which he was called to give evidence as such bias would impede a judge from accepting his evidence, deduction and conclusions. It was also of the utmost importance that the medical profession understood (a) that no major step in a child's life could be taken without the leave of the court and that the official solicitor acted in an independent role, in consequence of which his investigations and those undertaken by experts acting on his behalf should not be impeded by those of the medical profession instructed by a parent: C (AN INFANT), *Re, The Times*, November 10, 1986, Butler-Sloss J.

2224. Welfare officer—conciliation and reporting—different functions

Whilst it is the duty of the court Welfare Officer to assist the court to resolve disputes that the parties cannot solve it is inappropriate for the same officer to become involved in conciliation and subsequent investigation for the purposes of preparing a report. These are different functions. It was also important that there be no undue delay in the preparation of welfare reports: H (CONCILIATION: WELFARE REPORTS). *Re*, [1986] 1 F.L.R. 476, Ewbank J.

2225. Welfare officer's report—contents of report

The welfare officer's report in contested custody proceedings should contain the results of an investigation into the minor(s) involved, and his/their relationship with any relevant adults, and their circumstances: SCOTT *v.* SCOTT, *The Times*, April 2, 1986, C.A.

MORTGAGES

2226. Bank mortgage—contingent liabilities—whether covered by mortgage

The companies borrowed money secured by mortgage on their properties. The lender, a bank, further provided performance bonds for the companies. The companies went into liquidation and the liquidator paid off all the moneys owing, and sought the re-conveyance of the mortgaged properties from the bank. The bank refused to re-convey, and subsequently the performance bonds were in fact called in. *Held*, that since it was perfectly proper for the bank to demand payment of the moneys outstanding during the currency of the mortgage, but still to retain the security for the contingent liability, the liquidator could not, upon payment of the outstanding moneys demand the re-conveyance of the properties while the contingent liability remained in existence: RUDD & SON, *Re;* FOSTERS & RUDD, *Re, The Times*, January 22, 1986, C.A.

2227. Execution of second mortgage—wife's consent—fraudulent misrepresentation—failure to obtain independent advice

Where a wife is induced to execute a second mortgage on the home by a fraudulent misrepresentation of her husband, the deed may be unenforceable against her. The defendants, H and W, agreed to execute a second mortgage for an advance to H for a partnership business in which W was not involved. In reliance on H's false representation she signed the deed without independent advice. On the plaintiff's claim to enforce the mortgage, the judge made an order for possession. *Held*, allowing W's appeal, that since the plaintiffs had entrusted to H the execution of the deed by W, H had acted as their agent; they could not enforce against her because of the fraudulent misrepresentation by him (*Chaplin* v. *Brammall* [1908] 1 K.B. 233 C.A. applied; *Avon Finance* v. *Bridger* [1985] C.L.Y. 1289 considered).

KINGS NORTH TRUST *v.* BELL [1986] 1 W.L.R. 119, C.A.

2228. Law Commission Working Paper. See LAW REFORM, § 1951.

2229. Local authority—disposal of mortgages—information. See LOCAL GOVERNMENT, § 2036.

2230. Notice of equitable interest—person in occupation—husband concealing wife's occupation

[Law of Property Act 1925 (c.20), s.199(1)(ii)(*a*).]

A wife who is separated from her husband but spends some part of virtually every day in the matrimonial home remains in occupation. A purchaser or mortgagee needs to carry out a full inspection of property in order to discover who other than a husband is in occupation, and has to look behind the husband's attempted concealment of his wife's occupation.

The marriage between a husband and wife broke down and the wife left the matrimonial home but returned there regularly, including sleeping there when the husband was away. The house was in the husband's name. The husband approached mortgage brokers to obtain a loan of £66,000 on the security of the house which was unregistered land. He signed the application form and stated that he was single. The brokers instructed a surveyor to carry out a survey and the husband arranged a time on a Sunday when the wife was away. The surveyor saw evidence of the occupation by the husband and his children, but no evidence of occupation by any other female. The husband told the surveyor that his wife had left many months ago, and was living with someone nearby. The plaintiffs made a loan offer which was accepted in the light of the surveyor's report. Shortly after, the husband and son emigrated. The plaintiffs sought to enforce their charge and the question arose whether the charge was subject to or overrode the wife's equitable interest. The plaintiffs contended that mere occupation in the case of unregistered land was not sufficient to protect a person claiming equitable rights against a purchaser or mortgagee of the legal estate unless the claimant was found in occupation or would have been found on proper inspection taking place. It was common ground that the surveyor was the plaintiffs' agent. *Held*, that for physical presence to amount to actual occupation it did not have to be either exclusive or continuous and uninterrupted. Nor was it negatived by regular or repeated absence. Since on the facts the wife spent some part of virtually every day in the former matrimonial home, it was clear she had been in occupation and her change of habits had not altered that (dictum of Lord Wilberforce in *Williams and Glyn's Bank* v. *Boland* [1980] C.L.Y. 1847 applied). When the surveyor discovered that the husband was married but separated he was under a duty to look for signs of occupation and to tell the plaintiffs. In any event, the reference in the report to the "son and daughter" itself should have put the plaintiffs on further inquiry which would have led them to discover the wife's beneficial interest by virtue of s.199(1)(ii)(*a*) of the Law of Property Act 1925. They had knowledge of her beneficial interest and the mortgage took effect subject to those rights. The husband's attempt to conceal the wife's occupation could not be relied on by the plaintiff as preventing the need for further inquiry. Where a purchaser or mortgagee made reasonable inquiries and inspections and did not find the claimant in occupation or evidence sufficient to give notice of it, they were not fixed with notice of the claimant's rights. In the case of residential property what was a reasonable inspection depended on all the circumstances. On the facts, the plaintiffs' pre-arranged inspection on a Sunday afternoon was not within the category of "such . . . inspections . . . as ought reasonably to have been made" under s.199(1)(ii) of the 1925 Act. The plaintiffs' claim for possession was dismissed.

KINGSNORTH TRUST *v.* TIZARD [1986] 2 All E.R. 54, His Honour Judge Finlay Q.C. sitting as a Judge of the High Court.

2231. Overriding interest—execution of charge by two trustees for sale—overreaching

[Law of Property Act 1925 (c.20), ss.2(1)(ii), 14: Land Registration Act 1925 (c.21), ss.3(xv)(*a*), 20(1)(*b*), 70(1)(*g*).]

The interest of an equitable tenant in common in actual occupation is not overreached by the execution of a legal charge on the property by two trustees for sale.

A married couple purchased a house to house themselves and the wife's parents who contributed half of the purchase price. The balance was raised by a mortgage and the property conveyed to the couple as beneficial joint tenants and registered in their names. The parents occupied the property. The couple executed second and third charges without the parents' knowledge, and finally consolidated all the mortgages with a charge to the Society, of which the parents knew nothing, and about whom the Society made no inquiries. The couple defaulted on the mortgage and the Society brought possession proceedings. The parents asserted that their interests in the property had priority to that of the Society. The judge made an order for possession. *Held*, allowing the appeal, that actual occupation of registered land by an equitable tenant in common converted what would otherwise be a minor interest into an overriding interest, and in the absence of inquiry, a legal disposition of the land, whether affected by one or more trustees for sale, took effect subject to such overriding interest; nor was the interest overreached by operation of s.2(1)(ii) of the Law of Property Act 1925 by execution of a legal charge on the property by two trustees for sale (*Bull* v. *Bull* [1955] C.L.Y. 2313 and *Williams & Glyn's Bank* v. *Boland* [1980] C.L.Y. 1847 applied).

CITY OF LONDON BUILDING SOCIETY v. FLEGG [1986] 2 W.L.R. 616, C.A.

2232. Sale by mortgagee in possession—valuation by surveyor—whether negligent

P fell into arrears with repayments in respect of a derelict bungalow mortgaged to D, who obtained an order for possession and decided to sell the property. D quickly negotiated a sale subject to contract for £5,500 to X, and then wrote to K, a surveyor, instructing him to carry out a "crash sale valuation" of the premises and adding that they had already had an offer to purchase subject to contract. Subsequently K was told on D's behalf that it was hoped to conclude the sale by the end of the month. K, interpreting his instructions as meaning that D wanted him to give the lowest valuation that he properly could, assumed a four-week sale exposure for the purposes of the valuation, and valued the bungalow at £5,750. D then concluded the sale to X for £6,000, and X shortly afterwards resold the bungalow for £10,000. P thereupon brought an action against D on the grounds that D had failed to exercise the power of sale so as to obtain the true market value of the property, and D joined K as third party. The judge found that D had failed to take reasonable care to obtain the true market value, that D should have exposed the bungalow to the market through local estate agents for three months, and that such exposure would have obtained a price of not less than £8,500. He thus awarded P damages of £2,500, but dismissed D's third-party claim against K. On appeal D contended that K had not correctly interpreted his instructions; alternatively that he had in any event owed a duty to advise D of the true market value irrespective of his instructions. *Held*, dismissing D's appeal, that (1) the language of the letter and the background circumstances all pointed to the conclusion that D wanted a quick sale, and that K had not misinterpreted his instructions; (2) the requirement of a quick sale having been crucial to those instructions, K had not been under a duty to advise as to the true market value (*Singer and Friedlander* v. *John D. Wood & Co.* [1977] C.L.Y. 2455 distinguished): PREDETH v. CASTLE PHILLIPS FINANCE CO. (1986) 279 E.G. 1355, C.A.

2233. Undue influence—charge ever wife's property—whether manifest and unfair disadvantage to wife. See PETROU v. WOODSTEAD FINANCE, § 425.

NATIONAL HEALTH

2234. Charges

NATIONAL HEALTH SERVICE (CHARGES TO OVERSEAS VISITORS) AMENDMENT REGULATIONS 1986 (No. 459) [£1·35], made under the National Health Service Act 1977 (c.49), s.121; operative on April 1, 1986; amend S.I. 1982 No. 863.

NATIONAL HEALTH SERVICE (CHARGES FOR DRUGS AND APPLIANCES) AMENDMENT REGULATIONS 1986 (No. 432) [40p], made under the National Health Service Act 1977 (c.49), ss.77(1)(2), 83(*a*); operative on April 1, 1986; increases charges for the supply of drugs and appliances.

2235. Dental services

DENTAL AUXILIARIES (AMENDMENT) REGULATIONS 1985 (No. 1850) [40p], made under the Dentists Act 1984 (c.24), s.45; operative on December 1, 1985; provide for increases in certain fees.

NATIONAL HEALTH SERVICE (GENERAL DENTAL SERVICES) AMENDMENT REGULATIONS 1986 (No. 1499) [45p], made under the National Health Service Act 1977 (c.49), ss.35(1), 36; operative on October 1, 1986; amend S.I. 1973 No. 1468 to enable dentists to provide as preventive treatment the application of topical fluoride to persons under 16.

2236. Health and Social Security Act 1984—commencement

HEALTH AND SOCIAL SECURITY ACT 1984 (COMMENCEMENT No. 2) ORDER 1986 (No. 974 (c.24)) [45p] made under the Health and Social Security Act 1984 (c.48), s.27(1); brings into force on July 1, 1986 section 1(3)(5)(*a*)(6)(7) and Scheds, 1, Pts. I and II, 8 (in part).

2237. Health Service Joint Consultative Committees (Access to Information) Act 1986 (c.24)

This Act provides for access by the public to meetings of, and to certain documents and information relating to, joint consultative committees and sub-committees constituted under s.22 of the National Health Service Act 1977.

2238. Health service supply council

HEALTH SERVICE SUPPLY COUNCIL (ABOLITION) ORDER 1985 (No. 1877) [40p], made under the National Health Service Act 1977, s.11; operative on January 1, 1986; abolishes the Health Service Supply Council.

HEALTH SERVICE SUPPLY COUNCIL (ABOLITION) REGULATIONS 1985 (No. 1876) [40p], made under the National Health Service Act 1977 (c.49), s.12 and Sched. 5, paras. 10 and 12; operative on January 1, 1986; make provisions consequent upon the abolition of the Health Service Supply Council.

2239. Hospitals

BROADMOOR HOSPITAL BOARD (ESTABLISHMENT AND CONSTITUTION) ORDER 1986 (No. 2004) [45p], made under the National Health Service Act 1977 (c.49), s.11; operative on January 1, 1987; provides for the establishment and constitution of a special health authority to be known as the Broadmoor Hospital Board for the purpose of exercising functions in relation to Broadmoor Hospital.

BROADMOOR HOSPITAL BOARD (FUNCTIONS AND MEMBERSHIP) REGULATIONS 1986 (No. 2005) [80p], made under the National Health Service Act 1977 (c.49), ss.12, 13, 18(1)(a) and Sched. 5, paras. 12 and 16; operative on January 1, 1987; give directions to the Broadmoor Hospital Board to exercise certain functions under the 1977 Act.

MOSS SIDE AND PARK LANE HOSPITALS BOARD (ESTABLISHMENT AND CONSTITUTION) ORDER 1986 (No. 2006) [45p], made under the National Health Service Act 1977 (c.49), s.11; operative on January 1, 1987; provides for the establishment of a special health authority for the purpose of exercising functions in relation to Moss Side Hospital and Park Lane Hospital.

MOSS SIDE AND PARK LANE HOSPITALS BOARD (FUNCTIONS AND MEMBERSHIP) REGULATIONS 1986 (No. 2007) [80p], made under the National Health Service Act 1977 (c.49), ss.12, 13, 18(1)(a), Sched. 5, paras. 12, 16; operative on January 1, 1987; provide for the appointment of members of, and the procedure of, the Moss Side and Park Lane Hospitals Board.

RAMPTON HOSPITAL BOARD (ESTABLISHMENT AND CONSTITUTION) ORDER 1986 (No. 963) [45p], made under the National Health Service Act 1977 (c.49), s.11; operative on July 1, 1986; provides for the establishment of the Rampton Hospital Board.

RAMPTON HOSPITAL BOARD (FUNCTIONS AND MEMBERSHIP) REGULATIONS 1986 (No. 964) [80p], made under the National Health Service Act 1977, ss.12, 13, Sched. 5, para. 12; operative on July 1, 1986; provide for the appointment and tenure of office of members of the said Board.

2240. National Health Service

NATIONAL HEALTH SERVICE (CHARGES TO OVERSEAS VISITORS) AMENDMENT (NO. 2) REGULATIONS 1986 (No. 950) [45p]; made under the National Health Service Act 1977 (c.49), s.121; operative on July 1, 1986; amend the definition of "Continental Shelf" in S.I. 1982 No. 863 and adds Australia to the list of reciprocating countries.

NATIONAL HEALTH SERVICE (GENERAL MEDICAL AND PHARMACEUTICAL SERVICES) AMENDMENT REGULATIONS 1986 (No. 381) [40p], made under the National Health Service Act 1977, ss.29, 41, 42; operative on April 1, 1986; amend S.I. 1974 No. 160.

NATIONAL HEALTH SERVICE (GENERAL MEDICAL AND PHARMACEUTICAL SERVICES) AMENDMENT (NO. 2) REGULATIONS 1986 (No. 916) [45p], made under the National Health Service Act 1977, ss.29, 41, 42; operative on July 1, 1986; add Pameton Tablets to Sched. 3A to S.I. 1974 No. 160.

NATIONAL HEALTH SERVICE (GENERAL MEDICAL AND PHARMACEUTICAL SERVICES) AMENDMENT (NO. 3) REGULATIONS 1986 (No. 1486) [45p], made under the National Health Service Act 1977 (c.49), ss.29, 41, 42; operative on April 1, 1987 save for reg. 2(2) (3) which is operative on October 1, 1986; amend S.I. 1974 No. 160 so as to vary the list of drugs which may not be prescribed.

NATIONAL HEALTH SERVICE (TRANSFER OF OFFICERS) REGULATIONS 1986 (No. 331) [80p], made under the National Health Service Act 1977, Sched. 5, para. 10(5); operative on March 24, 1986; provides for the transfer of officers employed by health authorities to other authorities where there has been a transfer of functions.

NATIONAL HEALTH SERVICE (TRANSFER OF OFFICERS) (NO. 2) REGULATIONS 1986 (No. 524) [80p], made under the National Health Service Act 1977, Sched. 5, para. 10(2); operative on March 24, 1986; replaces S.I. 1986 No. 331.

NATIONAL HEALTH SERVICE (VOCATIONAL TRAINING) AMENDMENT REGULATIONS 1986 (No. 1642) [45p], made under the National Health Service Act 1977 (c.49), s.32(1)(*f*); operative on October 20, 1986; further amend S.I. 1979 No. 1644.

2241. National Health Service (Amendment) Act 1986 (c.66)
This Act extends the application of certain food and health and safety legislation to health authorities and health service premises. The Act makes further provision as to pharmaceutical services and the remuneration of persons providing those services. Royal Assent was given on November 7, 1986.

2242. Nurses, midwives and health visitors
NURSES, MIDWIVES AND HEALTH VISITORS (PERIODIC REGISTRATION) AMENDMENT (No. 2) RULES APPROVAL ORDER 1986 (No. 2294) [£1·40], made under the Nurses, Midwives and Health Visitors Act 1979 (c.36), ss.22(4); operative on December 31, 1986; amends S.I. 1983 No. 873 in relation to registration periods.

NURSES, MIDWIVES AND HEALTH VISITORS (QUALIFICATION OF HEALTH VISITORS) AMENDMENT RULES APPROVAL ORDER 1986 (No. 1897) [80p], made under the Nurses, Midwives and Health Visitors Act 1979 (c.36), s.22(4); operative on December 3, 1986; provide for admission to part II of the register for persons with specified qualifications.

2243. Ophthalmic services
NATIONAL HEALTH SERVICE (GENERAL OPHTHALMIC SERVICES) REGULATIONS 1986 (No. 975) [£2·40], made under the National Health Service Act 1977 (c.49), ss.38, 39, 40, 50, 126(4), 127(a), 128(1) and the Health and Social Security Act 1984 (c.48), s.28(1); operative on July 1, 1986; provide for arrangements for general ophthalmic services under the National Health Service.

NATIONAL HEALTH SERVICE (PAYMENTS FOR OPTICAL APPLIANCES) REGULATIONS 1986 (No. 976) [£2·40], made under the National Health Service Act 1977, ss.39, 78(1), 81, 82, Sched. 12, paras. 2, 2A and the Health and Social Security Act 1984 (s.48), s.28; operative on July 1, 1986; provide for payments to certain categories of persons for the supply of optical appliances prescribed following a NHS sight test.

NATIONAL HEALTH SERVICE (PAYMENTS FOR OPTICAL APPLIANCES) AMENDMENT REGULATIONS 1986 (No. 1136) [80p], made under the National Health Service Act 1977 (c.49), s.78(1) and Sched. 12, paras. 2(1), (2) and 2A; operative on July 28; 1986; amend S.I. 1986 No. 976.

2244. Rural dispensing committee
RURAL DISPENSING COMMITTEE (ESTABLISHMENT AND CONSTITUTION) AMENDMENT ORDER 1986 (No. 440) [40p], made under the National Health Service Act 1977 (c.49), s.11; operative on April 1, 1986; amends S.I. 1983 No. 312.

2245. Standing advisory committees
NATIONAL HEALTH SERVICE (STANDING ADVISORY COMMITTEES) (AMENDMENT) REGULATIONS 1986 (No. 458) [40p], made under the National Health Service Act 1977 (c.49), Sched. 4, para. 2; operative on April 1, 1986; amend S.I. 1981 No. 101.

2246. Superannuation
NATIONAL HEALTH SERVICE (SUPERANNUATION—SPECIAL PROVISIONS) AMENDMENT REGULATIONS 1986 (No. 199) [40p], made under the Superannuation Act 1972 (c.11), ss.10, 12; Sched. 3; operative on March 11, 1986; corrects an error in S.I. 1985 No. 1492.

2247. Training authority
NATIONAL HEALTH SERVICE TRAINING AUTHORITY AMENDMENT REGULATIONS 1986 (No. 1014) [45p], made under the National Health Service Act 1977 (c.49), Sched. 5, para. 12; operative on August 1, 1986; amends S.I. 1983 No. 1352 by deleting references to National Staff Committees.

NATIONAL HEALTH SERVICE TRAINING AUTHORITY (ESTABLISHMENT AND CONSTITUTION) AMENDMENT ORDER 1986 (No. 1015) [45p], made under the National Health Service Act 1977 (c.49), s.11; operative on August 1, 1986; amends S.I. 1983 No. 1351 by deleting references to National Staff Committees.

NEGLIGENCE

2248. Bailee for reward—duty of care—fire to wool store—whether reasonable precautions
[Aus.] A wool broker retained in its store wool it had sold to another. The store, built of timber, some forty years old, was surrounded by a paling fence from which

several palings were missing. An intruder entered through the gaps and set light to the outside of the store, which was destroyed along with the wool. *Held,* that (1) the broker was a bailee, with duties analogous to those of a bailee for reward, namely to take such care of the wool as was reasonable in the circumstances, and it bore the onus of disproving negligence on its part; (2) that the broker had failed to show that it had taken reasonable precautions to keep the wool safe; (3) that the damage resulting from the broker's breach of duty was not too remote (*Lamb* v. *Camden London Borough Council* [1981] C.L.Y. 1855 and *Perl (P.) (Exporters)* v. *Camden London Borough* [1983] C.L.Y. 2531 distinguished): PITT SON & BADGERY v. PROULEFCO S.A. (1984) 153 C.L.R. 644, High Ct. of Australia.

2249. Burst pipe—council flat—whether duty upon council

P was tenant of a first-floor council flat in Prescot, Manchester, which was reached by an external staircase. Water was supplied by a rising main which reached P's flat through a tank in the loft. Although the loft did not form part of the demise, P had a right of access to it, but could not exercise that right because of her age. During a cold spell a workman told P that water was not flowing through her taps, and telephoned D on her behalf, asking them to call. The following day P herself telephoned, and was told to switch the water off, but not where to find the stopcock. The evidence was that D had no one available to send along themselves. P believed the stopcock to be in the loft, but could not get up there herself, and could not find anyone to go up for her. A burst pipe ensued, with damage to P's possessions. The judge found that D had owed P a duty of care, and that they were in breach of it in failing to turn the stopcock off themselves or to advise and authorise P to get someone in to turn it off for her. He awarded £75 special and £700 general damages. *Held,* allowing D's appeal in part, that (1) once they were apprised of the fact that a pipe was frozen and liable to burst, D were under a duty to do whatever was reasonable in the circumstances, having regard to their capacity to act and their ability to abate or deal with the hazard (*Goldman* v. *Hargrave* [1966] C.L.Y. 8145 applied); (2) in this case D were not under a duty to send someone along to turn off the stopcock; (3) there was material on which the judge could find that more cogent advice could and should have been given to P; (4) the general damages would be reduced to £250: STOCKLEY v. KNOWSLEY METROPOLITAN BOROUGH COUNCIL (1986) 279 E.G. 677, C.A.

2250. Bus company—third party acts—liability

In ordinary circumstances a bus company cannot be held liable for third parties who drive away a bus and cause damage to other people: DENTON v. UNITED OMNIBUS CO., *The Times,* May 6, 1986, C.A.

2251. C.i.f. contract—damaged goods—stevedores—whether liable to buyer

[Can.] A wished to buy steel coils from B. In order for A to finance the purchase, it arranged for C to buy the steel from D and resell it to A. The steel was loaded into a ship owned by E in South Africa and was unloaded at New Westminster by stevedores, F. Some of the coils were damaged and an action for damages was commenced. *Held,* that there should be judgment for A against F. The damage to the steel was caused by improper loading procedures on F's part. F was not liable to C or D in either contract or tort, since they had suffered no loss, but could not escape liability to A, even though A was not the owner of the steel at the time the damage occurred, it not having yet paid C in full. F knew or ought to have known that the goods were carried c.i.f., whereby the risk passes to the buyer on shipment, although the seller may retain the right of disposal until paid. In the circumstances, it is almost self-evident that the person at whose risk the goods are at the time in question is likely to suffer loss if the goods are damaged by the stevedore's negligence (*Leigh & Sillivan* v. *Aliakmon Shipping Co.* [1985] 1 C.L. 472 and *Margarine Union Gmbh* v. *Cambay Prince Steamship Co.* [1967] C.L.Y. 3608 distinguished): TRIANGLE STEEL & SUPPLY CO. v. KOREAN UNITED LINES INC., 63 B.C.L.R. 66, Supreme Ct. of British Columbia.

2252. C. & f. contract—title—whether damages for economic loss

In order for a plaintiff to claim in negligence for loss of or damage to property he had to have either the legal ownership or a possessory title to the property concerned, and it did not suffice for him merely to have contractual rights in relation thereto which had been adversely affected. Accordingly buyers under a c. and f. contract of sale had no right to sue shipowners in tort.

Per curiam: English law does, in all normal cases, provide a fair and adequate remedy for loss of or damage to goods the subject matter of a c.i.f. or c. and f. contract, and the buyers in this case could easily if properly advised at the time when they agreed to the variation of the original c. and f. contract, have secured to themselves the benefit of such a remedy. By the variation to which they agreed, the buyers were depriving themselves of the right of suit under s.1 of the Bills of Lading Act 1855 which they otherwise would have had.

In July 1976 the plaintiff buyers contracted to buy a quantity of steel coils to be shipped in Korea c. and f., free out, Immingham. The price was to be paid by a 180-day bill of exchange to be endorsed by the buyers' bank in exchange for a bill of lading. The buyers intended to resell the steel before the bill of lading was tendered but could not effect a resale and their bank declined to back the bill. After discussion by agreement, the bill of lading was sent by the sellers to the buyers, the goods to be at the disposal of the sellers until further notice, and sales by the buyers were to be notified to the sellers. Later the buyers forwarded the bill of lading to agents at Immingham telling them to clear the goods through customs and to place them in a warehouse to the sole order of the sellers, stating that the buyers would accept liability as the sellers' agents. The goods were loaded on the defendant ship owners' vessel, *The Aliakmon*, which was on time charter, the time charterers being responsible for the stowage of the cargo, with a power reserved to the master to intervene. Damage was caused to the goods owing to bad stowage. The buyers sued the defendants for the loss suffered as a result of the damage. The judge held that the shipowners were liable to the buyers in contract only. The Court of Appeal allowed the defendants' appeal. The buyers appealed to the House of Lords claiming that there existed a duty of care which had been broken by the shipowners. *Held*, that the appeal was dismissed. It was a long established principle that the plaintiff could only claim for negligence for loss of or damage to property if he had either the legal ownership of or a possessory title to the property concerned at the time when the damage occurred. It did not suffice for him merely to have contractual rights adversely affected by the damage. Since the plaintiff buyers under a c. and f. contract of sale were neither legal owners nor did they have any possessory title they had no right to sue the shipowners in tort (*Margarine Union GmbH* v. *Cambay Prince Steamship Co. (The Wear Breeze)* [1967] C.L.Y. 3608 approved; *Schiffahrt & Kohlen GmbH* v. *Chelsea Maritime (The Irene's Success)* [1982] C.L.Y. 2886 overruled; dictum of Sheen J. in *The Nea Tyhi* [1982] C.L.Y. 2851 disapproved; *Anns* v. *Merton London Borough Council* [1977] C.L.Y. 2030 and *Candlewood Navigation Corp.* v. *Mitsui O.S.K. Lines (The Mineral Transporter)* [1985] C.L.Y. 2310 considered).

LEIGH AND SULLIVAN v. ALIAKMON SHIPPING CO. [1986] 2 W.L.R. 902, H.L.

2253. Contributory negligence—concurrent tortious and contractual duties to take reasonable care—whether contributory negligence a defence to claim in contract. See FORSIKRINGSAKTIESELSKAPET VESTA v. BUTCHER, § 366.

2254. Contributory negligence—drunk pedestrian—damages

A male, aged 22 at the date of the accident was run over by a car as he lay in the road, drunk. He did not realise that he had been run over because he was so drunk. He sustained a fractured pelvis, concussion, injury to his lower spine and cuts and abrasions. The general damages, assessed at £6,000 were reduced by two-thirds to £2,000 because of the plaintiff's contributory negligence: DONOGHOE v. BLUNDELL, May 22, 1985, H.H. Judge Lewis Hawser, Q.C., O.R. (*Ex rel. Karen Rea, Barrister*).

2255. Contributory negligence—unfenced machinery—personal injuries

P was a mechanical shovel driver employed by D. He was an experienced employee. Part of D's operation required a chain mounted bucket elevator system to collect quantities of fish-meal and convey it to a higher level. The system became jammed at its base point which required D to operate a system for clearing blockages. The procedure was followed and attempts were made to start the bucket but it merely rocked and remained jammed. P waited near the base of the machine but then decided to recommence clearing meal and took off the plate which he maintained had only been replaced loosely by hand turning the set screw. The plate had provision for eight set screws to secure it but only one was in position at the relevant time, the others having become lost. While thus attempting to remove meal, another attempt was made to restart the elevator system causing P's forearm to become trapped and injured. He brought an action for damages alleging breaches of ss.14(1) and 29(1) of the Factories Act 1961. *Held,* giving judgment for D, that the system overseen by the foreman was a reasonable one. There could be no breach of ss.14(1) or 29(1) for failing to fence the dangerous parts of the bucket elevator because it was not in motion at the relevant time. One screw was deemed sufficient to hold such a fence secure despite there being provision for seven more. In the circumstances P had himself broken all the relevant rules for safe clearance of blockages and was 100 per cent. contributorily negligent: HEWSON *v.* GRIMSBY FISHMEAL CO., June 4, 1986; Mr. A. W. Hamilton, Q.C., sitting as deputy High Court Judge. [*Ex rel. Langleys, Solicitors.*]

2256. Contributory negligence—whether defence to claim in contract. See AB MARINTRANS *v.* COMET SHIPPING CO.; SHINJITSU MARU NO. 5, THE, § 389.

2257. Defective foundations—duty to inspect—accrual of cause of action. See JONES *v.* STROUD DISTRICT COUNCIL, § 1993.

2258. Duty of care—bankers duty—credit reports
Whether credit reports supplied by a bank to a potential investor constitute advice giving rise to a duty of care is a matter of fact for the trial judge to decide on the evidence: ROYAL BANK TRUST CO. (TRINIDAD) *v.* PAMPELLONE, *Financial Times,* November 18, 1986, P.C.

2259. Duty of care—compliance with building regulations—whether duty owed to original building owner
[Public Health Act 1936 (c.49), s.64.]
A local authority is under no duty of care to an original building owner to ensure compliance with building regulations.
Per curiam: Even in relation to a subsequent owner, any duty was based on the prevention of danger to health or safety of the occupier, and there would be no duty in favour of a non-resident owner.
P Co., property developers proposed to build warehouses on the site of a filled-in swimming-pool. P Co. instructed A Co., architects, who instructed E Co., structural engineers to design the foundations. The council approved the plans for building regulation purposes. However, the foundations were inadequate, and as soon as the warehouses was built they began to fall down. P Co. claimed damages against the council for negligence and breach of statutory duty. The council joined A Co. Proceedings were discontinued against E Co., who were uninsured. The judge found that the council was liable. *Held,* allowing the Council's appeal, that a local authority was under no duty of care to an original building owner to ensure compliance with the building regulations, especially when the owners were themselves in breach of the regulations (*Governors of Peabody Donation Fund* v. *Sir Lindsay Parkinson & Co.* [1984] C.L.Y. 2298 applied; dictum of May L.J. in *Davy-Chiesman* v. *Davy-Chiesman* [1984] C.L.Y. 1995 334 approved; *Anns* v. *Merton London Borough* [1977] C.L.Y. 2030, *Dennis* v. *Charnwood B.C.* [1982] C.L.Y. 2535 and *Acrecrest* v. *W. S. Hattrell & Partners* [1982] C.L.Y. 2133 considered).
INVESTORS IN INDUSTRY COMMERCIAL PROPERTIES *v.* SOUTH BEDFORDSHIRE DISTRICT COUNCIL (ELLISON & PARTNERS (A FIRM), THIRD PARTY) [1986] 1 All E.R. 787, C.A.

2260. Duty of care—council flat—flooding caused by vandals—whether council liable
Liability for the wrongdoings of a third party will attach only when there is some special relationship between the defendant and the third party.
P, the tenant of a council flat in a block, telephoned the council to report that the flat above hers was unoccupied and unprotected against trespassers and vandals, and asked the council to board it up. No effective steps were taken to do so. Vandals got in on three occasions, damaging the water-pipes and causing severe damage by flooding in P's flat. When P sued the council, *inter alia,* for negligence, the judge rejected the claim on the ground of absence of duty of care, finding that it would have been impossible to prevent the vandals' activities. *Held,* dismissing P's appeal, that liability for the wrongdoing of a third party would attach only when there was some special relationship between the third party and the defendant. Since it was impossible for the council to control the acts of the third party, there was no duty of care, and the council were not liable in negligence. *Perl (P.) (Exporters)* v. *Camden London Borough Council* [1983] C.L.Y. 2531 and dicta of Robert Goff L.J. in *Paterson Zochonis* v. *Merfarken Packaging* [1983] C.L.Y. 485 applied.)
KING *v.* LIVERPOOL CITY COUNCIL [1986] 1 W.L.R. 890, C.A.

2261. Duty of care—defective premises

[Ire.] In 1981 P purchased a house built by D1 in 1975 and occupied by him since then. The house was inspected by P who had no professional or other qualifications, but was not professionally surveyed prior to its purchase. D2, a housing authority which was required before making a loan on a house to satisfy itself that the house provided adequate security, appointed D3, a valuer who had no qualifications in building construction, to inspect the house. D3 reported it in good repair and valued it at £25,000. On going into occupation P found various defects and had it surveyed by an engineer who reported that it was structurally unsound. *Held,* that (1) P was entitled to damages against D1 as he owed a duty of care to avoid dangerous and hidden defects and defects in the quality of the work to anyone to whom he might sell the house; (2) P was entitled to damages against D2 as it was in the reasonable contemplation of D2 that carelessness on its part might cause damage to P and that D2 was in breach of its duty of care in failing to appoint a valuer with qualifications in building construction; and (3) P was not entitled to damages against D3 as the standard of care required of him was that of an ordinary skilled auctioneer and P had not established that D3's inspection of the house was carried out carelessly: WARD *v.* McMASTER [1985] I.R. 29, Costello J.

2262. Duty of care—employer—provision of safe system of work—employee injured by act of employer's independent contractor

[Aus.] During the manual extension of the jib of a crane, operated by S's independent contractor, part of the crane fell on to K. The contractor had deliberately dropped the part and was found to have failed to keep a proper look out or to have warned of his intention to drop the part. K's foreman had failed to instruct him not to stand under the jib during the extension operation. *Held,* that S was in breach of his duty to provide a safe system of work because the foreman had failed to direct K not to stand under the crane jib during the extension operation. Further, the contractor's failure to adopt a safe system of work constituted a failure by S to satisfy a non-delegable duty to provide a safe system: KONDIS *v.* STATE TRANSPORT AUTHORITY (1984) 154 C.L.R. 672, High Ct. of Australia.

2263. Duty of care—employer's duty—vicarious liability

Where an employer entrusts his duty of care to his employee to another he is liable to the employee where that other person fails to discharge the duty: McDERMID *v.* NASH DREDGING AND RECLAMATION CO., *The Times,* April 17, 1986, C.A.

2264. Duty of care—foreseeability of injury—supervision of playground

D's managed a children's adventure playground. Unbeknown to them the gates had been unfastened by undoing a rope tie, and an abandoned car left smouldering in the playground. P's two young children, ventured upon the playground. The car exploded and they were injured. *Held,* that D's owed a duty of care to the children, but the risk of the accident that occurred was outside their reasonable contemplation. There was no duty to inspect the playground when it was not in use (*The Wagon Mound* [1961] C.L.Y. 2343 considered): MORGAN *v.* BLUNDEN; REILLY *v.* BLUNDEN, *The Times,* February 1, 1986, C.A.

2265. Duty of care—ice on access road—factory

[Factories Act 1961 (c.34), ss.28(1), 29(1).] P was employed by D at their factory. He slipped on ice and injured himself while using a path in order to attend a union meeting at one of the factory canteens. The path was a means of access to places of work. P contended that D were negligent in failing to institute and/or maintain a system for ice-clearance and were in breach of ss.28(1) and 29(1). *Held,* that D were negligent. The path was not a "passage" but it was used as a means of access to a place of work and it was immaterial that P was using it in order to attend a union meeting: HEMMINGS *v.* BRITISH AEROSPACE, May 2, 1986; Swinton-Thomas J., Bristol. (*Ex rel. Jonathan Walter, Barrister*).

2266. Duty of care—ice on access road—factory—reasonable precautions

[Factories Act 1961 (9 & 10 Eliz. 2, c.34), s.29(1).]
A failure to salt all approaches to a factory by 7.45 a.m. after a night's snow, may not be a breach of s.29 of the Factories Act 1961.
The plaintiff arrived at the factory where he worked at 7.45 a.m. 1.5 cm. of snow had fallen during the night, and the plaintiff slipped and fell on a sheet of ice in front

of the entrance door that had not been salted. The gang whose duty it was to spread salt came on duty at 7.30 a.m., and would salt the most dangerous parts first. *Held,* dismissing the action, that the defendants had taken all such steps as were reasonably practicable and were not in breach of their statutory duty under s.29.

DARBY *v.* GKN SCREWS AND FASTENERS [1986] I.C.R 1, Pain J.

2267. Duty of care—occupier of Court House—class of persons to whom duty owed—remoteness

[Aus.] S, while seated as counsel at the bar table in the old Alice Springs Court House, was shot and injured by an assailant, who had entered intending to shoot another lawyer. The Commonwealth owned, occupied and exclusively controlled the building. S contended that control, together with knowledge of the high emotion generated by court proceedings, imposed upon the defendant a duty to protect persons required to work in the Court House. At first instance, it was held that, although the defendant owed a duty of care to the class of persons of which S was one, there was no breach of that duty. The foreseeable risk was remote and no action beyond that which was done would have been taken by a reasonable man. *Held,* on appeal, that there was no general duty of care arising by reason of the Commonwealth's role in the administration of justice and that no duty arose in the circumstances of the case: SKUSE *v.* COMMONWEALTH OF AUSTRALIA, 62 A.L.R. 108, Federal Ct. of Australia.

2268. Duty of care—pedestrian crossing road—whether duty to cross at light-controlled crossing

A pedestrian is not under a legal duty to cross a road only at a light-controlled crossing. He can cross where he likes, provided he takes reasonable care of his own safety. Furthermore, he is entitled to assume that traffic on the road will drive lawfully, and in accordance with road signs and signals: he therefore owes no duty to vehicles that, *e.g.* are speeding, or have crossed a red light: TREMAYNE *v.* HILL, *The Times,* December 11, 1986, C.A.

2269. Duty of care—whether owed to building contractor by architect. See SHUI ON CONSTRUCTION CO. *v.* SHUI KAY CO., § 215.

2270. Economic loss—liability—proximity—foreseeable harm

A manufacturer of defective goods can be liable in negligence for economic loss suffered by an ultimate purchaser if there is a very close proximity or relationship between the parties and the ultimate purchaser had placed real reliance on the manufacturer rather than the vendor.

Per curiam: Where a supplier of goods incorporates the products of another manufacturer into his goods and the contract for the supply of those products to the supplier includes a term excluding liability for damage consequent on defects in those products, the manufacturer is entitled to rely on that exclusion clause in an action for negligence arising out of such a defect brought directly against him by a purchaser from the supplier.

P was a fish merchant and decided to expand his lobster trade by purchasing them in the summer and storing them until Christmas when prices were higher. He bought a tank which required pumps to oxygenate the water 24 hours a day. Within a few days the pumps cut out and continued to do so and on one occasion he lost his entire stock of lobsters. P relied heavily on the firm which installed the tank and pumps but he was at no stage aware of or had contact with the manufacturers. He brought an action, *inter alios,* against the manufacturers claiming damages for loss of the lobsters and economic loss of profit on intended sales. The judge found that the cause of the cutting out was the unsuitability of the pumps for the English voltage system (they were manufactured in France) and he held that the manufacturers owed P a duty of care on the basis that they ought to have been tested to ensure their suitability for use in England. The judge also held that although the actual physical damage to the lobsters could not have been foreseen, the economic loss was reasonably foreseeable since the manufacturers knew that the pumps were sold for use at fish farms which required constant circulation of water in tanks. The manufacturers appealed. P contended on the appeal that the actual physical damage to the lobsters was reasonably foreseeable. *Held,* that a manufacturer of defective goods could be liable in negligence for economic loss suffered by an ultimate purchaser if there was a very close proximity or relationship between the parties and the ultimate purchaser had placed real reliance on the manufacturer rather than the vendor. On the facts there was no such proximity and reliance and there was nothing to distinguish P's situation from that of an ordinary purchaser of goods who having suffered financial loss could look only to the vendor and not to the ultimate manufacturer to recover damages for purely economic loss. The manufacturer's appeal on the issue of liability for economic loss would be allowed (*Junior Books* v. *Veitchi Co.* [1982] C.L.Y. 766 explained). Whether damages were recoverable by P for loss of his lobsters depended on whether damage of that type was reasonably foreseeable by the manufacturers, and not on whether they could have foreseen the physical damage actually suffered by him. On the facts, it was a necessary inference that damage of the relevant type, namely physical harm to fish, was reasonably foreseeable by the manufacturers, and they were accordingly liable to P in respect of the physical damage caused and any financial loss suffered in consequence of that physical damage.

MUIRHEAD v. INDUSTRIAL TANK SPECIALITIES [1985] 3 All E.R. 705, C.A.

2271. Employer—loading bay—liability to employee
[Factories Act 1961 (c.34), ss.28(4), 29(1)] P fell over the edge of a loading bay and suffered injury. *Held,* that (1) the loading bay did not constitute an opening in the floor; (2) P's place of work had not been made or kept safe since it was reasonably practicable to fence it; (3) P's damages would be reduced by 50 per cent. in respect of contributory negligence (*Bath* v. *British Transport Commission* [1954] C.L.Y. 885, *Phillips* v. *Robertson Thain* [1962] C.L.Y. 307, *Street* v. *British Electricity Authority* [1952] C.L.Y. 1383 ff., *Walker* v. *Bletchley Flettons* [1937] 1 All E.R. 170, *John Summers & Sons* v. *Frost* [1955] C.L.Y. 1082, *Coltness Iron Co.* v. *Sharp* [1938] A.C. 90, *Edwards* v. *National Coal Board* [1949] C.L.Y. 6274 considered): ALLEN v. AVON RUBBER CO., *The Times,* May 20, 1986, C.A.

2272. House conversion—dry rot specialist—scope of duty of care
In 1981 W wished to sell a house which had just been converted into three flats and P1 and P2 decided to buy the ground-floor flat. Dry rot had already been identified in some of the timbers of that flat, and these were replaced on the instructions of a surveyor acting for P1 and P2's bank. W then instructed D, a dry rot specialist, to inspect the ground floor flat. D prepared a report saying that he had found no evidence of dry rot, but he sprayed the ground-floor floor and under-floor timbers as a precaution, in accordance with an estimate which he had prepared. He also gave a guarantee against recurrence, limited to the cost of doing the work again. P1 and P2 then bought the ground-floor flat, and P3 bought the first-floor flat. When dry rot appeared in both flats, P sued D for negligent breach of a duty of care, and obtained judgment against him for the cost of replacing the offending timbers, namely £7,351·95. *Held,* allowing D's appeal, that (1) D had owed a duty of care to P1 and P2, and had been negligent, but that P1 and P2 had not proved that they had relied on D's report, guarantee or estimate in purchasing the ground-floor flat, so that it had not been proved that D's negligence had caused their loss; (2) D had not owed a duty of care to P3; (3) D was liable under the terms of the guarantee for the cost of respraying the ground-floor timbers, namely £250: SHANKIE-WILLIAMS v. HEAVEY (1986) 279 E.G. 316, C.A.

2273. Latent Damage Act 1986 (c.37)
This Act amends the law on limitation of actions in relation to actions for damages for negligence which do not involve personal injuries. It gives, in certain circumstances, a cause of action to those with an interest in property in respect of negligent damage to the property which occurs before taking that interest.

The Act received the Royal Assent on July 18, 1986 and comes into force two months from that date. It extends to England and Wales only.

2274. Local authority—inspection of building—whether negligent—failure by purchaser to inquire—lack of reliance—whether breach of duty
[Aus.] In 1975, H bought a house in Sutherland Shire. During 1976, serious structural defects appeared in it due to subsidence, the house having been erected with inadequate footings on a steep slope. S had approved plans and issued a building permit for the site in 1968. In the course of erection, the house was inspected by S's officers, who, if they directed their attention to the matter (as to which there was no evidence), failed to notice that fewer footings were installed than were contemplated by the plans and that those installed were structurally weak. H sought no statutory certificate of compliance from S and made no other inquiry of it about such matters. At first instance and on appeal ([1985] C.L.Y. 211) it was held

that S, having failed to exercise reasonable care in conducting the inspection, was in breach of a duty of care owed by it to H and was liable in damages. *Held,* allowing S's appeal, that (1) as a general rule, the ordinary principles of the law of negligence apply to public authorities so that they are liable for damage caused by a negligent failure to act when they are under a duty to act, or by a negligent failure to consider whether to exercise in the public interest a conferred power, or by a person's relying on the negligent exercise of such a power; (2) S was not in breach of any duty it owed to H because (a) there was no evidence that S had acted negligently in undertaking its discretionary power of inspection (*per* Gibbs C.J. and Wilson J.); (b) in the absence of inquiry made of, or reliance placed upon, it by H, S owed no relevant duty of care to H (*per* Mason, Brennan and Deane JJ.) (*Anns* v. *Merton London Borough Council* [1977] C.L.Y. 2030 not followed): SUTHERLAND SHIRE COUNCIL v. HEYMAN, 60 A.L.R. I, High Ct. of Australia.

2275. Medical negligence—duty to warn parent—sterilisation operation
A Health Authority which attempted to sterilise a woman by operation to prevent future conception was held to have been negligent in failing to warn her of the attendant risks of failure and to discuss alternative forms of contraception: GOLD v. HARINGEY HEALTH AUTHORITY, *The Times,* June 17, 1986, Schiemann J.

2276. Medical negligence—loss of a chance—whether damages
By D's negligence P lost the chance, assessed at 25 per cent., of avoiding serious long-term disability. The judge therefore awarded one quarter of the value of the disability on a full liability basis. *Held,* the approach was correct (*Mallett* v. *McMonagle* [1969] C.L.Y. 898, *Davies* v. *Taylor* [1972] C.L.Y. 819, *Chaplin* v. *Hicks* [1911] 2 Q.B. 786 considered): HOTSON v. EAST BERKSHIRE AREA HEALTH AUTHORITY, *The Times,* November 17, 1986, C.A.

2277. Medical negligence—no warning of possible failure of operation—pregnancy after vasectomy—damages. See THAKE v. MAURICE, § 422.

2278. Medical negligence—standard of care—whether inexperience a defence
In medical negligence cases the same standard of care was required of doctors irrespective of seniority and inexperience was not a defence to an action: WILSHER v. ESSEX AREA HEALTH AUTHORITY, *The Times,* August 6, 1986, C.A.

2279. Medical practitioner—patient not properly examined—subsequent stroke—whether damage foreseeable
P, who was suffering very severe stomach pains, was attended at three o'clock in the morning by D1, a doctor who was not P's regular medical practitioner. Without a full examination D1 injected P with a drug containing morphine but did not advise him to go to hospital. At nine o'clock on the same morning D2, another doctor who was not P's regular practitioner, gave P another injection and advised him to go to hospital. P refused. At noon the same day P suffered a stroke and was admitted to hospital where an operation was performed on him. On P's claim for damages the trial judge withdrew P's case from the jury on the ground that if either D1 or D2 had been negligent he could not reasonably have foreseen that his conduct would cause the stroke suffered by P. *Held,* allowing the appeal, that (1) there was evidence of negligence which should have been left to the jury; and (2) if either of the defendants was negligent, P's stroke was not an unforeseeable result of that negligence: REEVES v. CARTHY [1984] I.R. 348, Sup. Ct. in Ire.

2280. Nervous shock—foreseeability—rescuer
A railway guard negligently gave P, the driver, the signal to start the train. As a result, X was killed. P stopped the train, and got out to help X. As a result, P suffered nervous shock. P's employers said it was not foreseeable that a train driver of reasonable firmness would suffer nervous shock. *Held,* that each "nervous shock" case should be tried on its own merits. A rescuer was assumed to be a person of normal disposition. It was reasonably foreseeable that P would behave as he did: as there was a risk that a rescuer might suffer as he did, his employers owed him a duty of care, of which they were in breach: WIGG v. BRITISH RAILWAYS BOARD, *The Times,* February 4, 1986, Tucker J.

2281. Planning authority—alleged failure to disclose planning blight—whether negligent
In 1982 P Co's director F negotiated to buy property in Lambeth. In answer to inquiries by P Co's solicitor the Council correctly replied in writing that the property was within a "Proposed Future Action Area," which meant, as the solicitor duly

advised F, that the locality was proposed for light industry development and was already subject to certain development controls. F thereupon rang the Council's offices, and was apparently told by an unidentified person, after discussion with another such person, that the locality was a housing action area for which certain grants could become payable. In reliance upon this conversation, which he could at trial no longer remember in precise terms, F arranged for P Co to buy the property, which duly proved to be blighted and caused P Co to make a loss on redevelopment. P Co therefore sued the Council for negligent failure to disclose the existence of planning blight in response to inquiries. *Held,* dismissing P Co's claim, that (1) the Council's written replies had been correct; (2) the unconfirmed and imprecise telephone conversation could not be relied upon as proving negligence against the Council (*Shaddock L. & Associates Property* v. *Parramutta City Council* (1981) 36 A.L.R. 385 followed): JGF PROPERTIES *v.* LAMBETH LONDON BOROUGH (1985) 277 E.G. 646, HH Judge Rubin.

2282. Protective clothing—knowledge of risk—liability

An employer, E, provided an employee, W, with wellington boots to be worn when working in slippery conditions. W did so, but when the tread wore off the soles of the boots, he did not apply for a new pair. He slipped and injured himself, and sued E, claiming that E had not provided him with protective clothing. *Held,* that E would be liable in negligence only if he had known, or ought to have known, that W was exposing himself to a significant risk of slipping by failing to obtain new boots, and had failed to instruct him to do so: SMITH *v.* SCOT BOWYERS, *The Times,* April 16, 1986, C.A.

2283. Sale of car—odometer reading—whether misrepresentation

A seller of a car who is negligent in believing, wrongly, that the car's odometer reading is correct, makes no misrepresentation by stating that it is correct "to the best of his knowledge and belief."

H bought a second-hand car from a dealer. The odometer on the car read 34,900, but the car had travelled 80,000 miles. The dealer told H that there was no warranty as to the mileage. H, in selling the car on to H.M. Co., signed a document declaring that "to the best of [his] knowledge and belief" the odometer reading was correct. H.M. Co. claimed damages for breach of warranty and misrepresentation. The judge awarded damages on the basis that although H had acted in good faith, he had been negligent. *Held,* that in the light of the finding of good faith, the representation made was true, and negligence was irrelevant. The appeal would be allowed.

HUMMINGBIRD MOTORS *v.* HOBBS [1986] R.T.R. 276, C.A.

2284. Sewer laid by local authority's predecessor—transfer of ownership—electricity cables damaged by subsidence

[Water Act 1973 (c.37), s.34(1); Local Authorities (England) (Property) Order (S.I. 1973 No. 1861), arts. 8, 18.]

The Local Authorities (England) (Property) Order 1973 transferring ownership and liabilities from local authorities to water authorities operates to transfer potential liabilities arising from the local authority's negligence.

Predecessors to the local authority had laid sewers in a road; in 1964 the plaintiffs laid electricity cables at a slightly higher level. Ownership of the sewer passed from the local authority in 1974, to the relevant water authority. In 1975 the cables were damaged by subsidence caused by water leakage. The plaintiffs sued the local authority, and added the water authority, in a negligence action. *Held,* giving judgment against the water authority, that the transfer of ownership and liabilities in 1974 operated to transfer liability for negligence to the water authority for a cause of action that arose after the transfer (*Ketteman* v. *Hansel Properties* [1984] C.L.Y. 2675).

LONDON ELECTRICITY BOARD *v.* REDBRIDGE LONDON BOROUGH COUNCIL (1985) 84 L.G.R. 146, Stocker J.

2285. Solicitor and surveyor—failure to discover planning restriction—whether negligent

P, advised by D1 (a firm of solicitors) and D2 (a surveyor), took a lease of premises for use as offices which they subsequently refurbished. They later discovered that the premises were subject to a conditional planning consent (known neither to the freeholder or to their managing agents at the time of the grant), the terms of which rendered the use by P of a principal area of the premises unlawful. The judge found that W, the solicitor acting on behalf of D1, had been sent a search certificate which revealed the entry on the planning register, but had never bespoken or examined a copy of the planning permission. He further found that D2 had made a telephone enquiry to the planning authority, which had elicited a negative response, and that he had also raised with the managing agents the question of the previous user of the premises, and had been told that no established use certificate was necessary, since the premises had been used as offices for years past. P claimed in negligence against D1 and D2. *Held*, that (1) D1 had been negligent; (2) D2's duty depended upon the circumstances and the terms of his retainer. In this case D2 had been under a duty to take reasonable care to satisfy himself that the premises were suitable, and to make enquiries of the planning authority: whether further enquiries or action were called for would depend upon the answers obtained; (3) on the facts found by the judge, D2 had not been in breach of duty; (4) P would not have taken the lease and embarked on long-term and substantial expenditure if they had been advised by D1 of the restriction and its implications: they were therefore entitled to substantial and not merely nominal damages (*Sykes* v. *Midland Bank Executor and Trustee Co.* [1970] C.L.Y. 2710 considered); (5) P's losses, after giving credit for sums received on surrender of the lease and 18 months' occupational benefit, was £195,621; (6) in the circumstances of the case D2 were entitled to receive their costs from D1: GP & B v. BULCRAIG AND DAVIS (1986) 280 E.G. 356, Mr. John Gorman Q.C.

2286. Teacher—injury to pupil—fall from trampoline—foreseeable risk of injury—whether failure to take proper care

[Aus.] At a school, trampolining lessons were conducted under the supervision of an experienced teacher. At the end of the lesson, the teacher told the pupils taking part in the lesson to pack up and, believing no pupil to be on the trampoline, walked a short distance away. In fact a fifteen-year-old boy mounted the trampoline and, in consequence of the actions of another boy or boys, got out of control when high in the air, fell on the trampoline frame and was severely injured. At first instance, the controlling education authority was held liable for the negligence of the teacher and the boy was found not to have been contributorily negligent. *Held*, by a majority, allowing the appeal, that, on the facts, the teacher had not been negligent and the action should be dismissed: BILLS v. STATE OF SOUTH AUSTRALIA (1985) 38 S.A.S.R. 80, Supreme Ct. of South Australia (In Banco.).

NORTHERN IRELAND

2287. Administrative law

LANDS TRIBUNAL (SALARIES) ORDER (NORTHERN IRELAND) 1986 (No. 66) [40p], made under the Lands Tribunal and Compensation Act (Northern Ireland) 1964 (c. 29), s.2(5); operative on April 16, 1986; revises the annual salaries payable to members of the Lands Tribunal; revokes the 1984 (No. 262) Order.

LANDS TRIBUNAL (SALARIES) (No. 2) ORDER (NORTHERN IRELAND) 1986 (No. 291) [45p], made under the Lands Tribunal and Compensation Act (Northern Ireland) 1964 (c.29), s.2(5), and the Administrative and Financial Provisions Act (Northern Ireland) 1962 (c.7), s.18; operative on October 21, 1986; increases the salaries of members of the Lands Tribunal; revokes the 1986 (No. 66) Order.

2288. Agency—Commission on Disposals of Land (Northern Ireland) Order 1986 (S.I. 1986 No. 767 (N.I. 5))

This Order provides that any stipulation made on a disposal of land, requiring the person acquiring the land to pay any commission due to an agent of the person disposing of it, is void, and that any similar stipulation made in relation to the undertaking of a review of the rent payable under a letting, or in connection with the extension or renewal of a letting, is also void.

The Order comes into operation on August 30, 1986.

2289. Agriculture

FEEDING STUFFS REGULATIONS (NORTHERN IRELAND) 1986 (No. 67) [£5·20], made under the Agriculture Act 1970 (c.40), ss.66(1), 68(1)(1A)(3), 69(1)(3), 70(1), 73(3), 74(1), 74A, 84, 86; operative on April 25, 1986; re-enact with amendments and revoke the 1982 (No. 337) and 1984 (No. 27) Regulations.

FEEDING STUFFS (No. 2) REGULATIONS (NORTHERN IRELAND) 1986 (No. 334) [£6·00], made under the Agriculture Act 1970 (c.40), ss.66(1), 68(1)(1A)(3), 69(1)(3), 70(1), 73(3), 74(1), 74A, 84, 86, and the European Communities Act 1972 (c.68), s.2(2);

operative on December 10, 1986; re-enact the 1986 (No. 67) Regulations with amendments which implement certain directives relating to non-medicinal animal feeding stuffs and incorporate certain changes relating to the control of additives and premixtures.

GRASSLAND SCHEME (NORTHERN IRELAND) 1986 (No. 113) [£1·40], made under the Agriculture Act (Northern Ireland) 1949 (c.2), s.6(1); operative on May 1, 1986; provides for the payment of grants towards expenditure incurred in the reseeding and regeneration of grassland outside the less favoured areas.

GRASSLAND (AMENDMENT) SCHEME (NORTHERN IRELAND) 1986 (No. 254) [80p], made under the Agriculture Act (Northern Ireland) 1949 (c.2), s.6(1); operative on August 2, 1986; provides that claims made under the 1986 (No. 113) Scheme may relate to land in any area of Northern Ireland outside a severely disadvantaged area.

IMPORT AND EXPORT (PLANTS AND PLANT PRODUCTS) (PLANT HEALTH) (AMENDMENT) ORDER (NORTHERN IRELAND) 1986 (No. 24) [40p], made under the Plant Health Act (Northern Ireland) 1967 (c.28), ss.2, 3(1), 3B(1); operative on February 24, 1986; amends the 1981 (No. 38) Order by omitting the references to non-indigenous plant pests and diseases and certain other plant pests and diseases and by restricting the powers of inspectors to take remedial action under art. 12 of the 1981 Order.

IMPORT AND EXPORT (POTATOES) (PLANT HEALTH) (AMENDMENT) ORDER (NORTHERN IRELAND) 1986 (No. 25) [40p], made under the Plant Health Act (Northern Ireland) 1967, ss.2, 3(1), 3B(1); operative on February 24, 1986; amends the 1981 (No. 36) Order by omitting the references to non-indigenous plant pests and diseases and certain other plant pests and diseases and by restricting the powers of inspectors to take remedial action under art. 13 of the 1981 Order.

IMPORT AND EXPORT (WOOD AND BARK) (PLANT HEALTH) (AMENDMENT) ORDER (NORTHERN IRELAND) 1986 (No. 26) [40p], made under the Plant Health Act (Northern Ireland) 1967, ss.2, 3(1), 3B(1); operative on February 24, 1986; amends the 1981 (No. 37) Order by omitting the references to non-indigenous pests and diseases and certain other pests and diseases and by restricting the powers of inspectors to take remedial action under art. 14 of the 1981 Order.

IMPORT AND EXPORT (WOOD AND BARK) (PLANT HEALTH) (AMENDMENT No. 2) ORDER (NORTHERN IRELAND) 1986 (No. 295) [45p], made under the Plant Health Act (Northern Ireland) 1967 (c.28), s.2(1)(2); operative on December 1, 1986; amends the 1981 (No. 37) Order in relation to coniferous wood and bark and to redefine wood.

INTENSIVE LIVESTOCK INDUSTRIES (ASSISTANCE) SCHEME (NORTHERN IRELAND) 1986 (No. 246) [£1·40], made under the Agriculture (Temporary Assistance) Act (Northern Ireland) 1954 (c.31), ss.1(1), 2(1); operative on September 6, 1986; provides for payments to be made by the Department of Agriculture to employers in the pigmeat processing, egg packing and poultry meat processing industries.

MILK (COMMUNITY OUTGOERS SCHEME) REGULATIONS (NORTHERN IRELAND) 1986 (No. 299) [£1·40], made under the European Communities Act 1972 (c.68), s.2(2); operative on September 19, 1986; implement the scheme for the payment of compensation to persons who give up the whole of the milk quota registered in their names and who undertake to discontinue milk production definitively.

MILK (PARTIAL CESSATION OF PRODUCTION) SCHEME (NORTHERN IRELAND) 1986 (No. 300) [80p], made under S.I. 1985 No. 958 (N.I. 9), art. 3(3)(4)(5)(7); operative on September 19, 1986; fixes the compensation payable for the surrender of part of a producer's milk quota and lays down general rules for the application of the scheme.

PLANT PESTS (AMENDMENT) ORDER (NORTHERN IRELAND) 1986 (No. 27) [40p], made under the Plant Health Act (Northern Ireland) 1967, ss.3(1), 3B(1); operative on February 24, 1986; amends the 1982 (No. 79) Order in relation to non-indigenous pests and diseases.

SEEDS (FEES) REGULATIONS (NORTHERN IRELAND) 1986 (No. 261) [£1·90], made under the Seeds Act (Northern Ireland) 1965 (c.22), ss.1(1)(2A), 2(2)(4); operative on September 10, 1986; increase fees for seed certification and licences for seed testing; revoke the 1985 (No. 219) Regulations.

2290. Animals

ANIMALS AND POULTRY (QUARANTINE CHARGES) (AMENDMENT) ORDER (NORTHERN IRELAND) 1986 (No. 116) [45p], made under S.I. 1981 No. 1115 (N.I. 22), art. 50(1); operative on June 9, 1986; amends the 1983 (No. 99) Order by substituting a new schedule of charges for the feeding, housing and care of certain animals in quarantine stations.

ANIMALS (SCIENTIFIC PROCEDURES) (1986 ACT) (COMMENCEMENT No. 1) ORDER (NORTHERN IRELAND) 1986 (No. 364 (c.9)) [80p], made under the Animals (Scientific Procedures) Act 1986 (c.14), ss.29, 30(3); brought all the provisions of the 1986 Act, except ss.7, 10(3) and Sched. 2, into operation on January 1, 1987.

DISEASES OF ANIMALS (MODIFICATION) ORDER (NORTHERN IRELAND) 1986 (No. 79) [40p], made under S.I. 1981 No. 1115 (N.I. 22), art. 16(2); operative on May 12, 1986; modifies the lists of diseases in para. 10 of Pt. I and para. 12 of Pt. II of Sched. 2 to the 1981 S.I.

EXPORT OF SHEEP (PROHIBITION) ORDER (NORTHERN IRELAND) 1986 (No. 288) [45p], made under S.I. 1981 No. 1115 (N.I. 22), art. 32; operative on September 4, 1986; prohibits the export from Northern Ireland to a Member State of the European Communities of sheep moved from a farm or agricultural premises in a designated area in certain circumstances.

HORNED CATTLE (EXEMPTIONS) ORDER (NORTHERN IRELAND) ORDER 1986 (No. 2) [40p], made under the Agriculture (Miscellaneous Provisions) Act (Northern Ireland) 1965 (c.3), s.20(3); operative on February 10, 1986; exempts certain classes or descriptions of cattle from the provisions of s.20 of the 1965 Act; revokes the 1967 (No. 199) Order.

IMPORTATION OF ANIMALS ORDER (NORTHERN IRELAND) 1986 (No. 253) [£2·40], made under S.I. 1981 No. 1115 (N.I. 22), arts. 5(1), 19(e)(f)(i)(k), 20(1)(2), 21(a), 24(1)(1A), 29(1)(2), 60(1), Sched. 3, Pt. II, paras. 2, 3, Pt. III, para. 1; operative on September 1, 1986; replaces existing legislation regulating the importation of animals into Northern Ireland.

TUBERCULOSIS CONTROL (AMENDMENT) ORDER (NORTHERN IRELAND) 1986 (No. 48) [£1·35], made under S.I. 1981 No. 1115 (N.I. 22), arts. 5(1)(b), 44(a), 60(1); operative on June 1, 1986; amends the 1964 (No. 31) Order by modifying the provisions for the identification of bovine animals with ear tags and requiring the preparation of returns and notices in connection with these ear tags.

2291. Arrest—validity—false imprisonment

[Northern Ireland (Emergency Provisions) Act 1978 (c.5), s.14; European Convention for the Protection of Human Rights and Fundamental Freedoms, art. 5.] A party of five armed soldiers and D, a female soldier, arrived by landrover early one morning at M's home and asked her to get dressed. Before leaving the house D said to M "As a member of Her Majesty's Forces I arrest you." When asked under what section, D said "section 14". M was then taken to a screening centre where she was questioned, searched and, without her knowledge, photographed. M was released within four hours of her arrest without being charged with any offence. She claimed damages for trespass, wrongful arrest, wrongful imprisonment and breach of the European Convention for the Protection of Human Rights and Fundamental Freedoms. In reply to a letter from M's solicitors the Crown Solicitor stated that D suspected M of being involved in the purchase of weapons for the Provisional I.R.A. in the United States of America. *Held*, dismissing M's claim, that (1) s.14(2) of the Northern Ireland (Emergency Provisions) Act 1978 dispensed with the need to inform M of the precise statutory provision under which she was arrested; (2) the defendant had proved that D had at the time of the arrest a genuine suspicion that M had committed an offence connected with the purchase of arms for a proscribed organisation; (3) the power of arrest conferred by s.14 of the 1978 Act is not limited to an arrest for the purpose of enabling the authorities to establish the identity of a suspect; (4) art. 5 of the European Convention does not affect the construction of s.14 of the 1978 Act; (5) the taking of M's photograph without interfering physically with her person was not tortious; and (6) the searching of M was not unreasonable or unlawful: MURRAY v. MINISTRY OF DEFENCE [1985] 12 N.I.J.B. 1, Murray J.

2292. Assembly

NORTHERN IRELAND ASSEMBLY (DISSOLUTION) ORDER 1986 (No. 1036) [45p], made under the Northern Ireland Act 1982 (c.38), s.5(1); operative on June 23, 1986; dissolves the Northern Ireland Assembly.

2293. Atomic energy

RADIOACTIVE SUBSTANCES (CARRIAGE BY ROAD) (AMENDMENT) REGULATIONS (NORTHERN IRELAND) 1986 (No. 61) [40p], made under the Radioactive Substances

Act 1948 (c.37), s.5(2)(3) and S.R. & O. (N.I.) 1970 No. 332; operative on June 1, 1986; amend the 1983 (No. 344) Regulations in relation to the definition of "International Regulations" and in relation to units of measurement.

RADIOACTIVE SUBSTANCES (GASEOUS TRITIUM LIGHT DEVICES) EXEMPTION ORDER (NORTHERN IRELAND) 1986 (No. 10) [£1·35], made under the Radioactive Substances Act 1960 (c.34), ss.2(6)(7), 6(5), 7(4), 21; operative on April 1, 1986; provides for exemptions and exclusions under the 1960 Act in respect of articles containing tritium gas.

RADIOACTIVE SUBSTANCES (LUMINOUS ARTICLES) EXEMPTION ORDER (NORTHERN IRELAND) 1986 (No. 11) [80p], made under the Radioactive Substances Act 1960, ss.2(6)(7), 6(5), 7(4), 21; operative on April 1, 1986; provides for exemptions and exclusions under the 1960 Act in respect of radioactive luminous instruments and indicators.

RADIOACTIVE SUBSTANCES (TESTING INSTRUMENTS) EXEMPTION ORDER (NORTHERN IRELAND) 1986 (No. 12) [£1·35], made under the Radioactive Substances Act 1960, ss.2(6)(7), 4(2)(3), 6(5), 7(4), 21; operative on April 1, 1986; provides for exemptions and exclusions under the 1960 Act in respect of testing instruments and radioactive sources used in conjunction with such instruments.

2294. Bankruptcy—arrangement—failure to obtain requisite majority—adjudication—rescission

[Irish Bankrupt and Insolvent Act 1857 (c.60), s.343; Bankruptcy Amendment (Northern Ireland) Order 1980 (S.I. 1980 No. 561 (N.I. 4)), art. 36; Bankruptcy Rules (Northern Ireland) 1983 (S.R. 1983 No. 310).] JP and AP, who carried on business in partnership, presented a joint petition for arrangement under s.343 of the Irish Bankrupt and Insolvent Act 1857. A protection order was made and at a private sitting of the court JP and AP had procured the necessary statutory three-fifths majority in respect of the partnership creditors and the creditors of JP. Only two creditors of AP had proved debts and one voted for and one against the arrangement proposals. JP and AP were accordingly adjudged bankrupt. JP and AP applied to the Master for rescission of the bankruptcy order on the ground that a creditor of AP had not received a form of proof of debt which complied with the Bankruptcy Rules (Northern Ireland) 1983 and that, if he had, he would have voted in favour of the arrangement proposals thus giving the requisite three-fifths majority. The Master refused the application and JP and AP appealed. *Held*, exercising the discretion of the court under art. 36 of the Bankruptcy Amendment (Northern Ireland) Order 1980, that the bankruptcy order should be rescinded: JP AND AP (BANKRUPTS), *Re* [1985] 11 N.I.J.B. 9, Hutton J.

2295. Bankruptcy—conveyance by bankrupt to himself and wife—mortgage of property

In September 1981 P2, a building society, offered L an advance of £26,000 to be paid when a new house was built on land of which L was the registered owner. P1, L's wife, borrowed £5,000 from her father and applied the money towards the cost of building the house. The advance was paid on March 11, 1982, and on the same date L, on his solicitor's advice and at the request of P2, transferred the property to himself and P1 and both L and P1 executed a deed of charge in favour of P2. P1 undertook joint and several liability for the mortgage debt. L was adjudicated bankrupt in May 1982. P1 and P2 sought a declaration that the deed of transfer and deed of charge took priority over the interest of the Official Assignee. *Held*, that P2 was entitled to the declaration as it had given valuable consideration for the deed of charge but P1 was not entitled to the declaration as the equity of redemption had an appreciable value and the undertaking by P1 of liability for the mortgage debt was not valuable consideration: LEDLIE *v.* OFFICIAL ASSIGNEE [1985] 10 N.I.J.B. 12, Lord Lowry L.C.J.

2296. Building and engineering, architects and surveyors

BUILDING (PRESCRIBED FEES) (AMENDMENT) REGULATIONS (NORTHERN IRELAND) 1986 (No. 331) [£1·40], made under S.I. 1979 No. 1709 (N.I. 16), arts. 3, 5(1), 13(2)(*e*); operative on January 1, 1987; amend the 1982 (No. 392) Regulations to increase the plan fees and inspection fees payable to district councils in respect of the erection of small domestic buildings and certain extensions and alterations to domestic buildings.

2297. Building and engineering, architects and surveyors—building contract—delay—whether architect's certificate valid

P, who had entered into a contract in the Standard Form of Building Contract, Local Authorities Edition with Quantities, 1963 Edition (July 1972 Revision) to carry out certain works, sub-contracted in the Standard Form for use where the sub-contractor is nominated under the 1963 Edition of the R.I.B.A. Form of Main Contract part of the works to D. When the works were completed a dispute between P and D about the validity of certificates issued by the architects entitling P to recover losses and expenses arising from D's alleged delay was referred to an arbitrator. D claimed that the certificates did not comply with the requirements in the contracts. The arbitrator stated a special case for decision by the court. *Held,* that (1) as the certificates did not express the architects' opinion that the sub-contracted works ought reasonably to have been completed within the specified period or extended periods the certificates did not comply with the requirements of the contracts; (2) P's right to set-off was limited to sums which D was liable to pay to him under the contract but D was not liable to pay compensation for loss or damage caused by delay until a valid architect's certificate was given; and (3) the issue of the architects' certificate was a condition precedent to P's entitlement to claim loss or damage for delay and the failure of the architects to issue such a certificate was not a matter for arbitration under the sub-contract: SAVAGE BROTHERS *v.* SHILLINGTON (HEATING AND PLUMBING) [1985] 2 N.I.J.B., Higgins J.

2298. Charities—will—lapse—cy-près

T by his will made in April 1974 left one-fourth of his residuary estate to the Treasurer of a Building Fund in connection with a church hall then used by a self-governing body as a place of worship. The Fund was established in 1967 to rebuild the existing hall or to build a new hall. In 1974 planning permission to build a new hall on the existing site was refused. In 1975 the Fund was used to purchase the hall of a neighbouring church and the existing hall was sold. The balance of the Fund was carried forward to a new fund for the renovation and repair of the newly purchased hall. *Held,* that (1) the objects of the new fund did not represent the objects of the original fund and the gift to the Building Fund failed; (2) T had a general charitable intention and the gift should be applied *cy-près*: CURRIE, *Re,* McCLELLAND *v.* GAMBLE [1985] 7 N.I.J.B. 69, Carswell J.

2299. Company law

COMPANIES ACTS (PRE-CONSOLIDATION AMENDMENTS) ORDER (NORTHERN IRELAND) 1986 (No. 132) [£2·90], made under S.I. 1982 No. 1534 (N.I. 17), art. 112(1); operative on the day on which the Order consolidating the Companies Acts (Northern Ireland) comes into operation; amends certain provisions of the Companies Acts (Northern Ireland) 1960 to 1983 in order to enable a satisfactory consolidation of those Acts to be produced.

COMPANIES (DISQUALIFICATION ORDERS) REGULATIONS (NORTHERN IRELAND) 1986 (No. 304) [£1·40], made under S.I. 1986 No. 1032 (N.I. 6), arts. 309(1), 681(1); operative on October 27, 1986; require certain court officers to provide the Department of Economic Development with particulars of disqualification orders and the granting of leave in relation to, or the variation or quashing on appeal of, such orders; revoke the 1983 (No. 402) Regulations.

COMPANIES (FORMS) REGULATIONS (NORTHERN IRELAND) 1986 (No. 287) [£9·80], made under provisions of S.I. 1986 No. 1032 (N.I. 6) and S.I. 1986 No. 1035 (N.I. 9) cited in Sched. 1 to the Regulations; operative on September 24, 1986; prescribe forms and particulars for the purpose of the 1986 S.I.s and prescribe the ways in which translations and copies of documents required to be delivered to the registrar are to be certified or verified and the manner in which notice is to be given by a transferee company to dissenting shareholders; revoke the 1961 (No. 83), 1963 (No. 164), 1979 (Nos. 231, 232 and 355), 1981 (No. 358), 1983 (Nos. 139 and 140) and 1984 (No. 316) Regulations.

COMPANIES (REGISTERS AND OTHER RECORDS) REGULATIONS (NORTHERN IRELAND) 1986 (No. 306) [£2·40], made under S.I. 1986 No. 1032, art. 672(4); operative on October 27, 1986; specify the places where a company is to allow inspection of, or to furnish reproductions of, registers and other records which are kept in other than a legible form by the use of computers and provide for the giving of notice of such places to the registrar of companies; revoke the 1981 (No. 361) Regulations.

COMPANIES (TABLES A TO F) REGULATIONS (NORTHERN IRELAND) 1986 (No. 264) [£2·90], made under S.I. 1986 No. 1032 (N.I. 6), arts. 14, 19(1)(4), 681(1); operative on September 24, 1986; set out in Tables A to F the regulations and forms of memorandum and articles of association for the purposes of arts. 14 and 19 of the 1986 S.I.

COMPANIES (UNREGISTERED COMPANIES) REGULATIONS (NORTHERN IRELAND) 1986 (No. 305) [£1·40], made under S.I. 1986 No. 1032, arts. 667(1)(3), 681(1), Sched. 21; operative on October 27, 1986; provide for the application to unregistered companies of certain provisions of the 1986 S.I.; revoke the 1966 (No. 38) Regulations.

2300. Company law—Business Names (Northern Ireland) Order 1986 (S.I. 1986 No. 1033 (N.I. 7))
This Order consolidates certain statutory provisions relating to the names under which persons may carry on business in Northern Ireland.
The Order comes into operation on September 24, 1986.

2301. Company law—Companies Consolidation (Consequential Provisions) (Northern Ireland) Order 1986 (S.I. 1986 No. 1035 (N.I. 9))
This Order deals with transitional matters, savings, repeals and amendments consequential upon the consolidation of the Companies Acts (Northern Ireland) 1960 to 1983.
The Order comes into operation on September 24, 1986.

2302. Company law—Companies (Northern Ireland) Order 1986 (S.I. 1986 No. 1032 (N.I. 6))
This Order consolidates the greater part of the Companies Acts (Northern Ireland) 1960 to 1983.
Except for art. 251(3)(4) which comes into operation on a day to be appointed, the Order comes into operation on September 24, 1986.

2303. Company law—Company Securities (Insider Dealing) (Northern Ireland) Order 1986 (S.I. 1986 No. 1034 (N.I. 8))
This Order consolidates statutory provisions relating to insider dealing in company securities.
The Order comes into operation on September 24, 1986.

2304. Company law—voting on a show of hands—shares held on trust
[Companies Act (Northern Ireland) 1960 (c.22), Table A, art. 7] P, a governing director of a company under its articles of association, transferred 240 of his 250 shares to D1 and D2 to secure a loan. The loan was repaid but the 240 shares were not transferred back to P. D1 and D2 requisitioned a meeting of the company for the purpose of moving a special resolution to revoke the article conferring the position of governing director on P. D1 and another director attended the meeting but P did not attend having been advised that as the holder of only 10 shares he could not prevent the passing of the resolution. The resolution was carried on a show of hands. P's application to have the resolution set aside was granted by the High Court on the grounds that the 240 shares were held by D1 and D2 as bare trustees for P and, as it was not possible to split a vote on a show of hands, D1 had voted as the holder of both his own shares and the shares held on trust by him for P and he was to that extent in breach of trust in voting for a resolution which was detrimental to P's interests. D1 and D2 appealed. *Held,* dismissing the appeal, that (1) D1 and D2 were trustees and not legal mortgagees of the 240 shares; (2) by voting on a show of hands, instead of calling for a poll, D1 had put himself in a position where his personal interests conflicted with those of P; (3) the resolution would not have been carried on a poll if the votes in respect of the shares held on trust had been cast against the resolution; (4) P's failure to require a re-transfer of his shares did not affect D1's duty to avoid a conflict of interest; and (5) Art. 7 of Table A does not operate to prevent an equitable owner of shares obtaining a court order to protect his equitable interests: MCGRATTAN *v.* MCGRATTAN [1985] 2 N.I.J.B., C.A.

2305. Company law—winding-up—fraudulent trading
[Companies Act (Northern Ireland) 1960 (c.22), s.298.] Under an agreement to provide stocking facilities made between P, a finance company, and EB, a company of which D1 and D2 were directors, P paid to S the price of three tractors delivered by S to EB. EB sold the three tractors but did not repay P. Two years later EB went into voluntary liquidation and P brought an application under s.298 of the Companies

Act (Northern Ireland) 1960 to make D1 and D2 personally liable for the debt due to P by EB. *Held,* dismissing P's application, that (1) under the agreement the property in the three tractors passed to P and, accordingly, EB became a bailee with a power of sale and a consequent ability to give a good title to a purchaser; (2) nothing D1 or D2 did stepped beyond the bounds of honesty or could generally be regarded as dishonest; and (3) when the tractors were sold neither D1 nor D2 knew that EB was insolvent or that P would never be paid: E.B. TRACTORS, *Re;* LOMBARD AND ULSTER *v.* EDGAR [1986] 3 N.I.J.B. 1, Murray J.

2306. Compulsory purchase—Lands Tribunal decisions
    BEATTIE *v.* NORTHERN IRELAND HOUSING EXECUTIVE, R/6/1985 (a house owned by B and occupied by McB was compulsorily acquired. B had bought the house at McB's request and allowed McB to occupy it at a rent of £10 per month. A question arose as to whether McB was a tenant or licensee. *Held,* that McB was a tenant as he had exclusive possession, he did not occupy the house as a caretaker, he paid a fixed rent and that, as between him and B, there was no act of friendship or generosity which could be regarded as special circumstances (*Street* v. *Mountford* [1985] C.L.Y. 1893 considered)).

2307. KANE *v.* DEPARTMENT OF THE ENVIRONMENT, R/14/1974 and R/31/1983 (a small farm comprising 43·6 acres owned by DK and MK was compulsorily acquired in June 1966. Following negotiations the compensation was agreed in January 1976 by DK at £18,700 plus £250 for disturbance. DK died in February 1976 and the agreement was then repudiated by MK who was his personal representative. MK died in June 1980 and his representative referred the matter to the Tribunal. *Held,* that based on values in June 1966, the total compensation should be £16,955 plus £500 for disturbance).

2308. MULVENNA *v.* DEPARTMENT OF THE ENVIRONMENT FOR NORTHERN IRELAND, R/26/1984 (this was a reference to determine the amount of compensation payable on the compulsory acquisition, for the purposes of the construction of a new road, of part of off-licensed premises fronting on a busy main road which, following the construction of the new road, became a road used only by local traffic. The land acquired included half of a store used in connection with the business and the entire store had to be demolished. The acquiring authority undertook to carry out certain accommodation works including the construction of a wall and of temporary storage. The tribunal awarded £510 for the 102 square yards acquired, £11,741 for injurious affection and severance, £14,500 for loss of profits and £1,000 for architectural work carried out by one of the claimants).

2309. Compulsory purchase—surveyor's fees—lands tribunal decision. See MAHOOD *v.* DEPARTMENT FOR THE ENVIRONMENT FOR NORTHERN IRELAND, § 357.

2310. County court practice
    COUNTY COURT (AMENDMENT) RULES (NORTHERN IRELAND) 1986 (No. 75) [£2·80], made under S.I. 1980 No. 397 (N.I. 3), art. 46; operative on April 21, 1986; amend the 1981 (No. 225) Rules so as to (*a*) increase the remuneration of an assessor; (*b*) increase the amount to be paid or tendered to a witness at the time of service of a witness summons; and (*c*) amend the provisions as to costs.
    COUNTY COURT (AMENDMENT No. 2) RULES (NORTHERN IRELAND) 1986 (No. 218) [£1·40], made under S.I. 1980 No. 397 (N.I. 3), art. 47, and the Child Abduction and Custody Act 1985 (c.60), ss.10, 24; operative as to rules 1 to 5 on August 1, 1986 and as to the remaining two rules on September 1, 1986; amend the 1981 (No. 225) Rules in relation to proceedings involving persons suffering from mental disorder, proceedings under the 1985 Act, the form of notice to be given to insurers in road traffic accident cases and the procedure for making applications under art. 98 of the Road Traffic (Northern Ireland) Order 1981.
    COUNTY COURT (AMENDMENT No. 3) RULES (NORTHERN IRELAND) 1986 (No. 347) (£1·90), made under S.I. 1980 No. 397 (N.I. 3), art. 47; operative on January 1, 1987; amend the 1981 (No. 225) Rules to take account of the commencement of the Civil Jurisdiction and Judgments Act 1982 (c.27).
    COUNTY COURT (COSTS IN AFFILIATION AND SEPARATION AND MAINTENANCE APPEALS) (AMENDMENT) RULES (NORTHERN IRELAND) 1986 (No. 88) [45p], made under S.I. 1980 No. 397 (N.I. 3), art. 47; operative on May 1, 1986; amend the 1966 (No. 276) Rules so as to include appeals under the Domestic Proceedings (Northern Ireland)

Order 1980 and to increase to £180 the maximum amounts payable in certain cases for solicitors' costs and counsel's fees.

COUNTY COURT FEES (AMENDMENT) ORDER (NORTHERN IRELAND) 1986 (No. 195) [80p], made under the Judicature (Northern Ireland) Act 1978 (c.23), s.116(1); amends Sched. 1 to the 1981 (No. 174) Order to increase certain fees and to fix new fees to be taken under the Criminal Injuries (Compensation) (Northern Ireland) Order 1977 and the Criminal Damage (Compensation) (Northern Ireland) Order 1977.

COUNTY COURT FEES (AMENDMENT No. 2) ORDER (NORTHERN IRELAND) 1986 (No. 348) [45p], made under the Judicature (Northern Ireland) Act 1978 (c.23), s.116(1); operative on January 1, 1987; amends Sched. 1 to the 1981 (No. 174) Order so as to delete certain fees and to insert a new fee.

2311. Criminal law—binding over—witness
[Magistrates' Courts (Northern Ireland) Order 1981 (S.I. 1981 No. 1675 (N.I. 26)), art. 144(1).] C and others were charged with assaulting H during a fracas. The resident magistrate convicted C but took the view that H had been involved in the fracas and that there was evidence of provocation on H's part. He said that he proposed to bind H to keep the peace and asked H, who was not legally represented, whether he wished to say anything. H made no reply and was bound over. H appealed to the Belfast Recorder's Court serving notice of the application on the complainant and lodging a copy with the clerk of petty sessions. The Recorder held that he had no jurisdiction to hear the application as it had not been served on the other party as required by art. 144(1) of the Magistrates' Courts (Northern Ireland) Order 1981. H applied for judicial review. *Held*, quashing the binding over order, that there had been a breach of natural justice in that H was not given such explanation of what the resident magistrate had in mind as was reasonably necessary for H to understand the proposal to bind him over or how the proposal would affect him nor was H given an opportunity of dealing with the proposal in such manner as conferred on him a just measure of protection of his interests: HUGHES' APPLICATION, *Re* [1986] 1 N.I.J.B. 30, Lord Lowry L.C.J. and Carswell J.

2312. Criminal law—charge based on information given by an accomplice—habeas corpus
A was arrested in March 1984 and charged with murder on the basis of information given by an accomplice. He was remanded in custody from week to week. In January 1985 A applied for a writ of habeas corpus. *Held*, refusing the application, that (1), although a witness statement intended to be adduced at a preliminary inquiry or investigation against A had not yet been taken from the accomplice, the written and oral statements already made by the accomplice involving A in the murder constituted evidence against him; (2) the delay in bringing A to trial was not unreasonable in the circumstances; (3) the court had no jurisdiction to issue a writ of habeas corpus to overrule a magistrate's decision made within jurisdiction that there was evidence against an accused which justified his being remanded in custody; and (4) if the delay in bringing A to trial had been unreasonable, the court would, in certain circumstances, have had jurisdiction to issue the writ: MCALEENAN'S APPLICATION, *Re* [1985] 13 N.I.J.B. 49, Hutton J. and Lord Lowry L.C.J.

2313. Criminal law—committal for trial—depositions not endorsed
[Grand Jury (Abolition) Act (Northern Ireland) 1969 (c.15), s.2(2); Criminal Justice (Committal for Trial) Act (Northern Ireland) 1968 (c.32), s.3; Magistrates' Courts (Northern Ireland) Order 1981 (S.I. 1981 No. 1675 (N.I. 26)), art. 33.] C was convicted in March 1981 of offences arising out of the destruction of buses by incendiary devices. The convictions were quashed on appeal and a new trial ordered. He was again convicted and on further appeal contended that the statements of evidence at the preliminary enquiry were not, as required by s.3(2)(*c*) of the Criminal Justice (Committal for Trial) Act (Northern Ireland) 1968 or art. 33 of the Magistrates' Courts (Northern Ireland) Order 1981, endorsed by the person who recorded the statements or to whom they were made. *Held*, dismissing the appeal, that (1) to commit a person for trial on evidence which does not support the charge is an error of law in the exercise of jurisdiction and not an example of the absence or excess of jurisdiction and accordingly the committal was not void but voidable; (2) under s.2(2)(*a*) of the Grand Jury (Abolition) Act (Northern Ireland) 1969 an indictment can only be presented against a person who has been committed for trial; (3) a deficiency of admissible evidence to justify committal does not destroy the

jurisdiction to commit or render the committal void; and (4) no legal objection can validly be raised to the fact that the judge in the re-trial had read the judgment quashing the convictions: R. *v*. CAMPBELL [1985] 9 N.I.J.B. 17, C.A.

2314. Criminal law—criminal injury—compensation—previous convictions
[Criminal Injuries (Compensation) (Northern Ireland) Order 1977 (S.I. 1977 No. 1248 (N.I. 15)), art. 6(3)(*b*)] P was shot by an off-duty member of the security forces who was suffering from a mental break-down. P's claim for compensation under the Criminal Injuries (Compensation) (Northern Ireland) Order 1977 was rejected under art. 6(3)(*b*) of the Order by the county court as P had previously been convicted of arson and of throwing stones at police landrovers. P appealed. *Held*, allowing the appeal, that when P committed the arson he was not motivated by any serious political conviction and that the throwing of the stones could be described as violent hooliganism: KINNEAR *v*. SECRETARY OF STATE [1985] 6 N.I.J.B. 92, O'Donnell L.J.

2315. Criminal law—criminal injury—related offence—nervous shock
[Explosive Substances Act 1883 (c.3), s.2; Criminal Injuries (Compensation) (Northern Ireland) Order 1977 (S.I. 1977 No. 1248 (N.I. 15))] P, a schoolboy aged 15 years, when cycling to school saw at the side of the road what appeared to him to be a body and he believed that it was the body of a police constable who had been kidnapped a few days earlier. This was reported to the security forces who searched the area and found that what had appeared to P to be a body was a dummy made of straw. The following morning while the security forces were still searching the area a bomb exploded close to where the dummy had been lying. P claimed compensation under the Criminal Injuries (Compensation) (Northern Ireland) Order 1977 for nervous shock. The claim was rejected by the county court. P appealed, *Held*, allowing the appeal, that (1) the explosion while the security forces were searching the area was an offence under s.2 of the Explosive Substances Act 1883 and the placing of the dummy at the side of the road constituted the related offence, within the meaning of the 1977 Order, of counselling the substantive offence of causing the explosion; (2) P's nervous shock was directly attributable to the related offence; and (3) although P's claim did not mention the explosion it was known to the police and the Secretary of State who were, therefore, not taken by surprise or put at a disadvantage: BELLEW *v*. SECRETARY OF STATE [1985] 6 N.I.J.B. 86, Hutton J.

2316. Criminal law—Criminal Justice (Northern Ireland) Order 1986 (S.I. 1986 No. 1883 (N.I. 15))
This Order alters the mode of trial for certain offences, clarifies the duration of training school orders, enables courts to make compensation orders against offenders, increases the period for which an accused may be remanded in custody with his consent, provides for the removal of prisoners to hospital for investigation or observation, provides a continuing offence for wrongful possession or use of premises and amends the Food and Drugs Act (Northern Ireland) 1958 (c.27) in relation to the mode of trial for, punishment of, and time limits for prosecution of, offences.
The Order comes into operation on January 6, 1987.

2317. Criminal law—evidence—accomplice—corroboration
Several accused, including G, were convicted of various terrorist offences largely on the evidence of McG, an accomplice—see [1984] C.L.Y. 2366. *Held*, dismissing the appeals of certain of the accused and allowing others, that (1) where a trial judge has expressly stated his belief in the truth of evidence, an appellate court, having regard to the advantages which the trial judge had of discerning its truth, must have some reason arising from the evidence to justify rejection of a finding of guilt; (2) where the findings of the trial judge are of secondary facts which are not immediately dependent on what he saw or heard, the appellate court is free to apply its own judgment; (3) a consistent and detailed account of a crime by an accomplice does little to rehabilitate his credibility as he knows all the circumstances of its commission; and (4) the support drawn by the trial judge in this case from a confrontation between McG and G was at best equivocal and, as evidence which was merely supportive must be unequivocal to be regarded as corroborative, there was no corroboration in G's case: R. *v*. GIBNEY [1986] 4 N.I.J.B. 1, C.A.

2318. Criminal law—evidence—admissibility of affidavits sworn for use in Republic of Ireland
[Evidence Act 1851 (c.93), s.7; Ireland Act 1949 (c.41), s.3(2).] D was convicted of murder—see [1986] 1 C.L. 288. The evidence against him consisted largely of his

fingerprints on the getaway car and two affidavits sworn by him for use in extradition proceedings in the Republic of Ireland. In these affidavits D admitted that he was a member of a terrorist organisation operating in the South Derry area near to which the murder was committed. D appealed. *Held,* allowing the appeal, that (1) the two affidavits were, by virtue of s.3(2) of the Ireland Act 1949, properly admitted in evidence under s.7 of the Evidence Act 1851; (2) the ruling against the admissibility of evidence to establish that the terrorist organisation to which D belonged was the only terrorist organisation operating in the South Derry area removed a vital link from the chain of evidence against D; and (3) the affidavits should, accordingly, have been regarded as more prejudicial than probative: R. *v.* McGLINCHEY [1985] 9 N.I.J.B. 62, C.A.

2319. Criminal law—murder—accused a soldier—self-defence—right to silence
    T, a member of an army foot patrol, came upon a disorderly scene in which a group of young men were pushing and shouting abuse at another army patrol. Two soldiers of this patrol were struggling with one of the young men and someone was lying on the ground with an army beret beside him. D, one of the young men, ran off and one of the soldiers pointing at D shouted "Get him". T pursued him and called "Stop" three times. On the third call D looked back, turning his body so that his left arm moved out of T's sight. T then shot and killed D. T claimed that when D turned T thought that he was reaching for a gun and intended to use it. T was, however, unarmed. The trial judge, sitting without a jury, accepted that the onus rested on the Crown to prove beyond all reasonable doubt that T was not acting in self-defence and that T was entitled to succeed on this ground if he honestly believed that D was about to attack him and endanger his life. In convicting T of murder the judge placed great emphasis on the fact that immediately after the shooting T did not act as if D was armed and on the fact that neither then nor in the following twelve months did T ever suggest to anyone that he shot D because he believed that D was armed and was about to shoot at him. *Held,* dismissing T's appeal, that (1) the trial judge's findings on facts and his assessment of the evidence and credibility of witnesses must be accorded due deference; (2) the inferences which the trial judge drew from T's failure after the shooting to explain that he fired in self-defence had nothing to do with an accused's right to silence; (3) although T admitted that he did not fire at D to effect his arrest the trial judge did consider T's defence on this ground but rejected it on the facts; and (4) the question of T taking action beyond the necessity of the occasion and using excessive force did not apply in this case to reduce the offence to manslaughter. T's application for a certificate that points of law of general public importance were involved in the decision was refused: R. *v.* THAIN [1985] 11 N.I.J.B. 31, 76, C.A.

2320. Criminal law—offensive weapon—lock knife
    [Public Order (Northern Ireland) Order 1981 (S.I. 1981 No. 609 (N.I. 17)), art. 12(1)] P was charged with having with him in a public place without lawful authority or reasonable excuse an offensive weapon, namely a lock knife, contrary to art. 12(1) of the Public Order (Northern Ireland) Order 1981. The knife when found on P was in his pocket and closed. P said that he had it with him in case he was attacked on his way home. The resident magistrate upheld a submission by P that there was no prima facie case to answer as the knife was not in itself an offensive weapon, had not been adapted as such and there was no evidence of P's intention to use it at the time. On appeal by way of case stated, *held* that a prima facie case had been established as a weapon which is not offensive in itself may become an offensive weapon depending on the intention of the user and P's statement that he had the knife with him in case he was attacked could mean that he would use it to defend himself if attacked, thus making the knife an offensive weapon. The case was returned to the resident magistrate for reconsideration: JARDINE *v.* KELLY [1985] 6 N.I.J.B. 96, C.A.

2321. Criminal law—possession of explosives—withholding information—construction
    [Criminal Law Act (Northern Ireland) 1967 (c.18), s.5(1).] D discovered explosives on the farm on which he was residing and believed that they were probably used on the following day to murder members of the security forces. He was charged under s.5(1) of the Criminal Law Act (Northern Ireland) 1967 with the offence of withholding information. *Held,* that (1) D had a reasonable excuse within the meaning of s.5(1) in that any information which he could have given would have tended to incriminate him and make him liable to prosecution; and (2) the words "or

some other arrestable offence" in para. (*a*) of s.5(1) do not cover the situation where the accused believes that some offence has been committed by reason of facts of which he is aware but those facts are quite separate and distinct from the facts which constitute the actus reus of the offence actually committed by the principal offender: R. *v.* DONNELLY [1986] 3 N.I.J.B. 48, Hutton J.

2322. Criminal law—possession of firearms
[Firearms (Northern Ireland) Order 1981 (S.I. No. 155 (N.I. 2)), arts. 17, 23] D and another man were inside a hayshed surrounded by police. The prosecution gave evidence that the police called on the two men to throw out their weapons but there was no reply and that the police fired into the hayshed when they saw two men inside it pointing rifles towards the police. D was wounded and the other man killed. The police found three rifles in the shed but no ammunition and the rifles were of old vintage and heavily corroded with rust. D, who claimed that he had just found the rifles in the shed, was charged under art. 17 of the Firearms (Northern Ireland) Order 1981 with possession of firearms with intent to endanger life and under art. 23 of the Order with possession of firearms in such circumstances as to give rise to a reasonable suspicion that he did not have them in his possession for a lawful object. *Held,* that the firearms were not in D's possession with intent to endanger life but were in his possession in such circumstances as to give rise to a reasonable suspicion that he did not have them in his possession for a lawful object: R. *v.* McAULEY [1985] 2 N.I.J.B. 48, Kelly L.J.

2323. Criminal law—procedure—accused an informer—duty of Crown—statements to police—admissibility
The accused, who was charged with various terrorist offences, contended on a *voire dire* that oral admissions and written statements made by him after his arrest and later withdrawn should be excluded from evidence as they were made by him as an informer and because he had accepted an offer made by the police that if he turned Queen's evidence he would get a good deal. He claimed that he was entitled to see all documents held by the Crown or the police containing details of meetings between him and the police and that the Crown was under a duty to inform the court at the commencement of the trial that he was an informer. *Held,* that (1) while there was no rule of law giving the defence a right to information in the possession of the Crown or police which was relevant to issues which might arise on the trial, it was not appropriate for the Crown to furnish such information to the defence until the accused had completed his evidence in chief on the *voire dire* but that, having regard to the Attorney-General's guidelines, the Crown should as soon as this was completed furnish details of the information given by the accused to the police about his own involvement in criminal activities and furnish an edited version of the information given by him about the criminal activities of other persons; (2) the defence knew before the commencement of the trial that the accused was an informer and there was no question of this being concealed from the court; (3) there was no basis for excluding the accused's confessions from evidence on the ground that the statements containing the confessions were made pursuant to an agreement with the police and were withdrawn by the accused because the police broke that agreement; and (4) having regard to the public need to bring to conviction those who commit criminal offences and to the public interest in the protection of the individual from unlawful and unfair treatment, the oral admissions and written statements should not be excluded from evidence: R. *v.* McALLISTER [1985] 10 N.I.J.B. 21, Hutton J.

2324. Criminal law—procedure—delay—defective summons
[Magistrates' Courts (Northern Ireland) Order 1981 (S.I. 1981 No. 1675 (N.I. 26/1, arts. 19, 45.] Three accused were charged with planting a hoax bomb on September 8, 1981. On April 18, 1984, they made written statements admitting the offence and summonses were issued against them on foot of complaints made on December 12, 1984. The matter came on for hearing at a special sitting of the magistrates' court on September 3, 1985, when the accused submitted that (1) the offence was a summary offence no longer capable of being tried on indictment and that the court had accordingly no jurisdiction as the complaints were not laid within three months of the offence; (2) the excessive delay in making the complaints was an abuse of the process of the court; and (3) the summonses were defective in that the offence with which the accused were charged was not, as specified in the summonses, an offence specified in Sched. 2 to the Magistrates' Courts (Northern Ireland) Order 1981. The

resident magistrate rejected the submission on the grounds that the offence was triable on indictment and that he had power under art. 45 of the 1981 Order to refer the matter to the Crown Court at any time during the hearing. He declined to rule on the question of delay until he had heard all the evidence. *Held,* dismissing applications for judicial review, that (1) having regard to art. 19 of the 1981 Order the complaint was not out of time; (2) a magistrates' court had power to refuse jurisdiction on the ground of excessive delay but in this case the power had not been exercised; and (3) the defect in the summons was not important and was remediable: SIMMONS APPLICATION, *Re* [1985] 12 N.I.J.B. 81, Lord Lowry L.C.J. and Gibson L.J.

2325. Criminal law—procedure—warrants issued on a complaint to one justice—fresh warrants issued by another justice on same complaint

To obtain B's extradition from the Republic of Ireland an inspector of the Royal Ulster Constabulary made complaints on oath to P, a justice of the peace, who signed the complaints and issued warrants for B's arrest. The inspector was later advised to obtain fresh warrants as there was some doubt about the validity of the warrants issued by P. The complaints were then placed before M, another justice of the peace, who signed the complaints and issued fresh warrants. B applied for judicial review on the ground that the complaints were made to one justice and the warrants issued by another. *Held,* granting the application, that the complaints were merely placed before M and were not revived and made to him: BURN'S APPLICATION, *Re* [1985] 11 N.I.J.B. 92, Lord Lowry L.C.J. and Gibson L.J.

2326. Criminal law—procedure—written statements—refusal of witnesses to attend—similar facts

[Magistrates' Courts (Northern Ireland) Order 1981 (S.I. 1981 No. 1675 (N.I. 26)), art. 42(3)] M was convicted of terrorist offences arising out of two separate and unrelated incidents. The first incident involved the detonation of a bomb in a culvert under a road when two soldiers were killed. M's fingerprints were found on a bottle near the culvert. The second incident involved the attempted murder by five masked men of five men in a farmyard. At M's trial arising out of the second incident the written statements of five Crown witnesses were read in court under art. 42(3) of the Magistrates' Courts (Northern Ireland) Order 1981 on the ground that all reasonable efforts to secure the attendance of the witnesses had been made without success. Four of the witnesses feared that their lives would be at risk if they gave evidence and the fifth was outside the jurisdiction of the court. M appealed. *Held,* (1) dismissing the appeal as regards the second incident, that the trial judge had ample evidence upon which to be satisfied that the conditions of art. 42(3) had been fulfilled and that he had exercised his discretion properly in permitting the statements to be read in evidence; (2) allowing the appeal as regards the first incident, that the trial judge wrongly took the second incident into account as similar fact evidence and as showing a motive tending to rebut M's innocent explanation of his fingerprints on the bottle. There was not in the features of the second incident, either singly or in combination, a uniqueness sufficient to constitute strikingly similar facts or to create such an underlying link as to make M's guilt in the second incident of positive probative value in the first incident: R. *v.* MARTIN [1985] 7 N.I.J.B. 84, C.A.

2327. Criminal law—recorded sentence—guidelines on use—precedent—stare decisis

[Treatment of Offenders Act (Northern Ireland) 1968 (c.29), s.18.] In June 1985 R was sentenced to two years' imprisonment for robbery and a recorded sentence of three years' imprisonment imposed in October 1984 was also put into effect, both sentences to run concurrently. R appealed against the sentence of two years' imprisonment and he was given leave to appeal also against the recorded sentence although the time for such appeal had expired. *Held,* that (1) the decision of the Court of Criminal Appeal in *R.* v. *Wightman* [1950] (N.I. 124) that recorded sentences were valid was binding on the Court of Appeal under the *stare decisis* principle; (2) the common law power to impose recorded sentences had not been abolished by s.18 of the Treatment of Offenders Act (Northern Ireland) 1968 which provided for the passing of suspended sentences; and (3) the recorded sentence of three years' imprisonment was not invalid on the ground that it was neither salutary in operation nor conformable to reasonable standards or requirements of the criminal law. The recorded sentence of three years was reduced to two years and principles laid down for the guidance of courts considering the passing of recorded sentences: R. *v.* RUSSELL [1986] 5 N.I.J.B. 36, C.A.

2328. Criminal law—series of offences—evidence—accomplice
[Crown Court Rules (Northern Ireland) 1979 (S.R. 1979 No. 90), r.21.] The indictment contained 184 counts against 38 accused relating to terrorist offences alleged to have been committed between December 1980 and February 1982. The principal and in some cases the only evidence against 37 of the accused was that of B, an accomplice. Three of the accused were acquitted and 22 appealed against their convictions. *Held,* dismissing certain appeals and allowing others, that (1) the words "series of offences" in r.21 of the Crown Court Rules (Northern Ireland) 1979 indicates that there must be some nexus between the offences if they are to be joined in the same indictment; (2) an accurate description of a crime merely strengthens the inference that the witness giving the description took part in the crime; (3) the existence of evidence amounting to corroboration against one defendant does not provide support for a finding against another defendant arising out of either the same or different facts; (4) evidence detracting from the credibility of a prosecution witness is more important than evidence which enhances it; and (5) the trial judge greatly overestimated B's honesty as a witness: R. *v.* DONNELLY [1986] 4 N.I.J.B. 32, C.A.

2329. Criminal law—wrongful arrest—damages
W, an unmarried school teacher aged 23, was arrested under emergency powers at her home at 6.30 in the morning by soldiers and taken to a police station in an armoured car. There she was measured, weighed and photographed and released two hours later without any apology or explanation. No suggestion was made that she had committed any offence. P claimed damages for wrongful arrest and imprisonment. D admitted that the arrest was unlawful. *Held,* that the damages should include exemplary damages for oppressive and arbitrary action by servants of the government and that, including such damages, the total should be £4,000: WALSH *v.* MINISTRY OF DEFENCE [1985] 4 N.I.J.B. 1, Lord Lowry L.C.J.

2330. Customs and excise—betting duty
GENERAL BETTING DUTY REGULATIONS (NORTHERN IRELAND) 1986 (No. 404) [£2·80], made under the Betting and Gaming Duties Act 1981 (c.63), s.12(2) and Sched. 1, para. 2; operative on March 30, 1986; introduce new arrangements for the administration of general betting duty.

2331. Damages—quantum—mitigation of loss
In October 1983 P's car was extensively damaged in a collision with D's vehicle. D admitted liability on the day of the hearing of P's claim in the Recorder's Court where P was awarded £1,264. P had bought his car in December 1982 for £2,250 under a hire purchase agreement and could not afford to buy a new car for cash. The damaged car was removed to P's house but as he was told by the police that he could not leave it blocking the roadway he arranged to have it moved to a local service station at a cost of £35. Although P was informed by an insurance assessor and by the managing director of the service station that the cost of repair would exceed the value of the car in its pre-accident condition, he still hoped to have it repaired and paid off the hire purchase instalments as they fell due. Since the accident, P incurred hiring charges totalling £1,053. The car was sold for scrap after the decision of the Recorder's Court but realised only £40 although its scrap value immediately after the accident was assessed at £150. *Held,* allowing P's appeal against the Recorder's decision, that P was entitled to (1) £1,350 as the value of the car before the accident less £150 as its then scrap value; (2) £35 for the removal of the car to the service station and (3) £455 for loss of use, that figure being the interest on £1,350 for two years and three months at 15 per cent. per annum. Nothing was awarded for storage or hire charges as these would not have been incurred if P had acted reasonably and disposed of the car shortly after the accident: MURRAY *v.* DOHERTY [1986] 2 N.I.J.B. 56, Carswell J.

2332. Death duties
ESTATE DUTY (NORTHERN IRELAND) (INTEREST ON UNPAID DUTY) ORDER 1986 (No. 1943) [45p], made under the Finance Act (Northern Ireland) 1970 (c.21 (N.I.)), s.1(2); operative on December 16, 1986; provides that interest on unpaid estate duty will run at eight per cent.

2333. Divorce and matrimonial causes
MATRIMONIAL CAUSES FEES (AMENDMENT) ORDER (NORTHERN IRELAND) 1986 (No. 233) [45p], made under the Judicature (Northern Ireland) Act 1978 (c.23), s.116(1),

and the Public Offices Fees Act 1879 (c.58), ss.2, 3; operative on July 31, 1986; increases the fee payable on presentation of a petition.

2334. Education

COLLEGES OF EDUCATION SALARIES (AMENDMENT) REGULATIONS (NORTHERN IRELAND) 1986 (No. 34) [80p], made under S.I. 1972 No. 1263 (N.I. 12), arts. 57(1)(4), 125(1) and the Administrative and Financial Provisions Act (Northern Ireland) 1962 (c.7) s.18; operative on February 28, 1986, with effect from December 1, 1985; increase salaries and allowances of staff in colleges of education.

COLLEGES OF EDUCATION SALARIES (AMENDMENT NO. 2) REGULATIONS (NORTHERN IRELAND) 1986 (No. 281) [80p], made under the Administrative and Financial Provisions Act (Northern Ireland) 1962, s.18, and S.I. 1986 No. 594, arts. 69(1)(4), 134(1); operative on September 30, 1986, with effect from April 1, 1986; increase salaries and allowances for academic staff in colleges of education.

EDUCATION (SPECIAL EDUCATIONAL NEEDS) REGULATIONS (NORTHERN IRELAND) 1985 (No. 365) [£1·85], made under S.I. 1972 No. 1263 (N.I. 12), Sched. 7A, paras. 2(1)(3), 6(1)(2); operative on January 1, 1986; make further provision with respect to the assessment of special educational needs and to statements of such needs.

FURTHER EDUCATION TEACHERS' SALARIES (AMENDMENT) REGULATIONS (NORTHERN IRELAND) 1986 (No. 38) [80p], made under S.I. 1972 No. 1263, arts. 57(1)(4), 58(2), 125(1) and the Administrative and Financial Provisions Act (Northern Ireland) 1962, s.18; operative on February 28, 1986, with effect from December 1, 1985; increase the salaries and allowances of teachers in institutions of further education.

FURTHER EDUCATION TEACHERS' SALARIES (AMENDMENT NO. 2) REGULATIONS (NORTHERN IRELAND) 1986 (No. 280) [£1·40], made under the Administrative and Financial Provisions Act (Northern Ireland) 1962 (c.7), s.18, and S.I. 1986 No. 594 (N.I. 3), arts. 69(1)(4), 70(2), 134(1); operative on September 30, 1986, with effect from April 1, 1986; increase salaries and allowances for teachers in institutions of further education and make arrangements for the safeguarding of salaries of teachers whose salary or allowances are reduced as a result of closure or reorganisation of an institution of further education; revoke the 1976 (No. 236) Regulations.

GRAMMAR SCHOOLS (FEES) (AMENDMENT) REGULATIONS (NORTHERN IRELAND) 1986 (No. 205) [45p], made under S.I. 1986 No. 594 (N.I. 3), arts. 26, 134(1); operative on August 1, 1986; increase to £50 the maximum fee which a Group A voluntary grammar school may charge in respect of any pupil enrolled in its secondary department for the purpose of meeting building and equipment expenditure.

TEACHERS' SALARIES (AMENDMENT) REGULATIONS (NORTHERN IRELAND) 1986 (No. 81) [£2·30], made under S.I. 1972 No. 1263 (N.I. 12), arts. 57(1)(4), 58(2), 125(1), and the Administrative and Financial Provisions Act (Northern Ireland) 1962 (c.7), s.18; operative on April 29, 1986; give effect from April 1, 1985, and March 31, 1986, to increases of 6·9 per cent. and 1·6 per cent. respectively in salaries and allowances for teachers in primary, secondary and special schools and for peripatetic and supply teachers.

TEACHERS' SALARIES (AMENDMENT NO. 2) REGULATIONS (NORTHERN IRELAND) 1986 (No. 165) [£1·40], made under S.I. 1972 No. 1263 (N.I. 12), arts. 57(1)(4), 58(2), 125(1), and the Administrative and Financial Provisions Act (Northern Ireland) 1962 (c.7), s.18; operative on July 30, 1986, with effect from April 1, 1986; revise scales of salaries and allowances for teachers in primary, secondary and special schools and for peripatetic and supply teachers.

2335. Education—choice of school—parental wishes—school attendance order—statutory interpretation

[Education and Libraries (Northern Ireland) 1972 (S.I. 1972 No. 1263 (N.I. 12)), arts. 34, 35, Sched. 9, paras. 1, 2] B's parents wished her to attend F school in Enniskillen when she completed her primary school education but the Education and Libraries Board decided that she should attend C school in Lisnaskea. The Board sent her transfer report form to C school where she was accepted as a pupil and her parents were informed that a place was available for her there. Following some correspondence and telephone conversations between B's mother and the Board, the Board understood that she and B had moved to Enniskillen and B was accordingly enrolled at F school as she was then in the traditional intake area for that school. When it later became clear that this was only a temporary move the Board informed B's mother that F school had been instructed not to admit B and that a place was still available for her at C school. From that time B did not attend any school. A month later the Board served a school attendance notice on B's father. The Board asked the Department of Education for a direction that C school be named in the attendance order on the ground that B's attendance at F school would involve unreasonable expense to the Board. B's father claimed that the Board was acting in breach of its obligation under art. 34 of the Education and Libraries (Northern Ireland) Order 1972 which required it, so far as compatible with the provision of efficient instruction and training and the avoidance of unreasonable public expenditure, to have regard to the general principle that pupils shall be educated in accordance with the wishes of their parents. *Held,* that (1) the Board had not acted unlawfully as it was entitled to take into account the desirability of ensuring that a school such as C school was supported by an adequate intake of pupils from its surrounding area; (2) words should be read into paras. 1 and 2 of Schedule 9 to the 1972 Order to avoid repugnancy between those paragraphs and art. 34 of the Order and to give the Department power to direct that a child shall attend a school nominated by the Board if the Department considers that the child's attendance at a school selected by its parents would be in conflict with the policy of the Board; and (3) as the Board in its application to the Department had relied on the ground that B's attendance at F school would involve unreasonable expense to the Board and that ground had been shown to be invalid, the Department should be prohibited from naming C school in the school attendance order. B should, therefore, attend F school: BOGUE'S APPLICATION [1985] 4 N.I.J.B., 44 Hutton J.

2336. Education—Education and Libraries (Northern Ireland) Order 1986 (S.I. 1986 No. 594 (N.I. 3)

This Order consolidates and revokes the Education and Libraries (Northern Ireland) Order 1972 and amending provisions.

The Order comes into operation on June 27, 1986.

2337. Education—provision of school transport

[Education and Libraries (Northern Ireland) Order 1972 (S.I. 1972 No. 1263 (N.I. 12)), art. 41] A's son G was a pupil in J primary school which was the one nearest his home. A requested the Education and Libraries Board to provide G with transport to J school. The Board refused but offered transport to F primary school as a bus service to that school passed G's home each morning and afternoon. A claimed that the Board was required by art. 41 of the Education and Libraries (Northern Ireland) 1972 to provide transport for the purpose of facilitating the attendance of pupils at school and that it should provide that transport to the nearest school. The Board contended that it was entitled to have regard to existing bus routes and whether there was cheaper transport available to another suitable school. *Held,* that the Board was under a duty under art. 41 to provide G with transport to J school or to pay his reasonable travelling expenses to that school and that this duty overrode any transport policy which the Board might wish to implement: BROWNLEE'S APPLICATION, *Re* [1985] 7 N.I.J.B. 1, Hutton J.

2338. Election law

ELECTORAL LAW (REGISTRATION RULES) (VARIATION) ORDER (NORTHERN IRELAND) 1986 (No. 194) [£1·40], made under the Electoral Law Act (Northern Ireland) 1962 (c.14), s.28(5); operative on July 11, 1986; amend the Registration Rules in Sched. 3 to the 1962 Act.

EUROPEAN ASSEMBLY ELECTIONS (NORTHERN IRELAND) REGULATIONS 1986 (No. 2250) [£4·90], made under the European Assembly Elections Act 1978 (c.10), Sched. 1, para. 2; operative on December 31, 1986; provide for the conduct of the election of representatives in Northern Ireland to the European Assembly, the elections to be conducted in accordance with the single transferable vote system; revoke the 1984 (No. 198) Regulations.

NORTHERN IRELAND ASSEMBLY ELECTIONS (AMENDMENT) ORDER 1986 (No. 1811) [80p], made under the Northern Ireland Assembly Act 1973 (c.17), ss.2(5), 5(2); operative on November 23, 1986; amends S.I. 1982 No. 1135 in relation to the franchise and the documents necessary to obtain a ballot paper at a polling station.

REPRESENTATION OF THE PEOPLE (NORTHERN IRELAND) REGULATIONS 1986 (No. 1091) [£5·60], made under specified provisions of the Representation of the People Act 1983 (c.2) and the Representation of the People Act 1985 (c.50); operative when specified provisions of the 1985 Act come into force; provide for the representation of the people in Northern Ireland.

REPRESENTATION OF THE PEOPLE (NORTHERN IRELAND) (AMENDMENT) REGULATIONS 1986 (No. 105) [80p], made under the Representation of the People Act 1983 (c.2), ss.53 and 201(1) and Sched. 2, paras. 11 and 11A; operative on February 3, 1986; amend S.I. 1983 No. 436.

2339. Election law—absent voter—application not received in time—injunction
P claimed to be entitled by reason of illness to be treated as an absent voter in a Parliamentary by-election for which a writ was received by D2, the Chief Electoral Officer, on January 6, 1986. The polling date was fixed for January 23, 1986, and applications to be treated as an absent voter were required to reach D1, the Deputy Electoral Officer, by noon on January 8, 1986. P claimed that she completed the application on January 7, 1986, and instructed K to lodge it on her behalf. K set off at 11.13 a.m. on January 8, 1986, but was delayed so long by police at a road check that he was unable to lodge the application in time. K claimed that the delay was deliberate but this was denied by the police. By notice of motion P sought an injunction to compel D1 and D2 to receive the application or to postpone the polling date until the postal vote was received. *Held,* refusing the injunction, that (1) it was impossible to grant a final injunction without proceeding to trial of the action; (2) an interlocutory mandatory injunction requiring D1 and D2 to receive the application would not be granted as this would effectively determine the whole subject matter of the action; (3) the statutory provisions fixing the date of the poll were mandatory and in the circumstances the poll could not be postponed; (4) an injunction would not lie against D1 and D2 as they were officers of the Crown; and (5) P had a remedy available in the election court: BURKE v. PATTERSON [1986] 2 N.I.J.B. 47, Carswell J.

2340. Emergency provisions
NORTHERN IRELAND (EMERGENCY PROVISIONS) ACT 1978 (AMENDMENT) ORDER 1986 (No. 75) [40p], made under the Northern Ireland (Emergency Provisions) Act 1978, s.30(3); operative on January 21, 1986; adds kidnapping and false imprisonment, certain firearms offences and offences relating to malicious damage to or interference with railways and intimidation to the list of "scheduled offences" in Sched. 4 to the 1978 Act which are not be treated as scheduled offences if the Attorney General for Northern Ireland so certifies in any particular case.

NORTHERN IRELAND (EMERGENCY PROVISIONS) ACT 1978 (CONTINUANCE) ORDER 1986 (No. 74) [40p], made under the Northern Ireland (Emergency Provisions) Act 1978 (c.5), s.33(3)(*a*); operative on January 25, 1986; continue the temporary provisions of the 1978 Act, except s.12 and Sched. 1, in force for a further six months.

2341. Employment
INDUSTRIAL RELATIONS (MEDICAL SUSPENSION) ORDER (NORTHERN IRELAND) 1986 (No. 302) [45p], made under S.I. 1976 No. 2147 (N.I. 28), art. 9(3); operative on November 1, 1986; amends the list of specified provisions in Sched. 1 to the 1976 S.I.

INDUSTRIAL RELATIONS (VARIATION OF LIMITS) ORDER (NORTHERN IRELAND) 1986 (No. 54) [80p], made under S.I. 1976 No. 1043 (N.I. 16), arts. 70, 80(3), and S.I. 1976 No. 2147 (N.I. 28), arts. 5(5), 63(4); operative on April 1, 1986; varies certain limits under those S.I.s and the Contracts of Employment and Redundancy Payments Act (Northern Ireland) 1965 (c.19).

REDUNDANCY PAYMENTS (LOCAL GOVERNMENT ETC.) (MODIFICATION) ORDER (NORTHERN IRELAND) 1986 (No. 206) [£1·40], made under the Contracts of Employment and Redundancy Payments Act (Northern Ireland) 1965 (c.19), s.26(5)(*a*)(6); operative on August 18, 1986; modifies certain redundancy payments provisions of Pt. II of the 1965 Act in relation to certain employees with local government service.

REPORTING OF INJURIES, DISEASES AND DANGEROUS OCCURRENCES REGULATIONS (NORTHERN IRELAND) 1986 (No. 247) [£3·40], made under S.I. 1978 No. 1039 (N.I. 9), art. 17(1)(2)(3)(4)(6), Sched. 3, paras. 14(1), 15, 19; operative on November 1, 1986; re-enact with amendments and revoke the 1981 (No. 339) Regulations.

STATUTORY SICK PAY (GENERAL) (AMENDMENT) REGULATIONS (NORTHERN IRELAND) 1986 (No. 83) [£1·35], made under S.I. 1982 No. 1084 (N.I. 16), arts. 4(3A), 5(4A)(5), 7(5), 19(4), 20, 22 and S.I. 1985 No. 1209 (N.I. 16), art. 1(8); operative on April 6, 1986; amend the 1982 (No. 263) Regulations in relation to the linking of periods of incapacity for work, the ending of certain periods of entitlement, the maximum entitlement to statutory sick pay, the calculation of entitlement limits, the records to be maintained by employers, the provision of information by employers to employees, statements to be provided to employees who are leaving and a penalty for failing to provide such a statement.

2342. Employment contract—restraint of trade
P, a manufacturer and distributor of fertilisers and grass seed, carried on business through resspresentatives each operating in his own area. D, one of the representatives, commenced employment with P in 1979. In 1983 D, together with other representatives, without much time for consideration entered into a contract of employment with P in which he agreed not to solicit custom from or deal with persons who were P's customers during the period of his employment with P or twelve months afterwards in the area within which he represented P or in any area within a 20-mile radius. In 1985 D left P's employment and commenced employment as a representative for S, which carried on a similar business, in the same area in which he operated as P's representative. P sought an injunction to restrain D from carrying on business in breach of his agreement. *Held,* refusing the injunction, that by including the 20-mile addition to D's area with P the restraint extended more widely than was reasonably necessary for the protection of P's interests and the restraint which was a single indivisible one extending over a specified area could not be severed into one for the area in which D acted as representative for P and another for the 20-mile extension: N.I.S. FERTILIZERS *v.* NEVILLE [1986] 2 N.I.J.B. 70, Carswell J.

2343. Employment—equal opportunities—guidelines for employers. See NEW YORK CITY EMPLOYEES' RETIREMENT SYSTEM *v.* AMERICAN BRANDS, § 1188.

2344. Employment—health and safety
NOTIFICATION OF NEW SUBSTANCES (AMENDMENT) REGULATIONS (NORTHERN IRELAND) 1986 (No. 188) [80p], made under the European Communities Act 1972 (c.68), s.2, and S.I. 1978 No. 1039 (N.I. 9), art. 17(1)(2), Sched. 3, paras. 1(1), 14(1); operative on August 1, 1986; amend the 1985 (No. 63) Regulations in relation to notification procedures and the disclosure of information.

2345. Employment—health and safety at work
ASBESTOS (PROHIBITIONS) REGULATIONS (NORTHERN IRELAND) 1986 (No. 35) [80p], made under S.I. 1978 No. 1039 (N.I. 9), art. 17(1)(2)(5), Sched. 3, para. 1(1); operative on March 6, 1986; implement Council Directives Nos. 76/769/EEC and 83/477/EEC in relation to prohibitions concerning the asbestos mineral crocidolite and products containing it and in relation to the protection of workers from risks related to exposure to asbestos at work in so far as it concerns asbestos spraying.
CONTROL OF LEAD AT WORK REGULATIONS (NORTHERN IRELAND) 1986 (No. 36) [£1·85], made under S.I. 1978 No. 1039, arts. 17(1)–(6), Sched. 3, paras. 1(1), 5(1), 6–10, 12(1)(3), 13, 14(1), 15; operative on March 6, 1986; impose requirements for the protection of employees who may be exposed to lead at work and of other persons who may be affected by such work.

2346. Employment—Redundancy Rebates (Northern Ireland) Order 1986 (S.I. 1986 No. 1886 (N.I. 16))
This Order restricts the payment of redundancy rebates to employers with less than ten employees and abolishes payments equivalent to redundancy rebates.
The Order came into operation on December 18, 1986.

2347. Employment—unfair dismissal—failure to comply with employer's guidelines
P, a car park attendant, had been issued with (1) a manual for his guidance and instruction which reminded him to be polite to customers and to call the manager if a car was stolen; (2) a document setting out the disciplinary procedure to be observed when an employee was guilty of misconduct; and (3) a memorandum containing guidelines as to what he should do if a car was stolen. P was given one oral warning and two written warnings about discourtesy to customers. About five months later a car was stolen while P was in charge of the car park but P did not report the matter to his employers or to the police. Following an interview about the matter P was dismissed, the letter to him stating that the reason for his dismissal was his incompetence in carrying out his duties under the memorandum in connection with the theft of the car. P's claim that he was unfairly dismissed was rejected by the industrial tribunal which found that P was guilty of a disciplinary offence in not

complying with the memorandum. P appealed by way of case stated. *Held,* that the tribunal wrongly gave to the memorandum the significance of a directive. The case was remitted to a different tribunal for a re-hearing: MAGUIRE *v.* NATIONAL CAR PARKS [1985] 6 N.I.J.B. 36, C.A.

2348. Employment—unfair dismissal—misconduct investigated by employer—reasonableness
[Industrial Relations (Northern Ireland) Order 1976 (S.I. 1976 No. 1043 (N.I. 16)), art. 22(10).] S, who was employed by U as a bus inspector, was dismissed for misconduct founded on an indecent assault alleged to have been committed on B, a young woman, while he was on duty. A disciplinary investigation was carried out by U's area manager who concluded that S should be dismissed forthwith. S appealed to U's managing director who carried out his own investigation and then set the area manager's decision aside and suspended S on full pay until he reached a decision. He continued his investigation and eventually concluded that B's complaint was justified and dismissed S. The industrial tribunal to which S appealed ordered his reinstatement. U appealed by way of case stated. *Held,* allowing the appeal, that (1) the tribunal had pressed into service every conceivable argument for the purpose of annulling U's decision and had disregarded a number of relevant factors in support of it; (2) under art. 22(10) of the Industrial Relations (Northern Ireland) Order 1976 the question for the tribunal was whether the employer had satisfied it that he had acted reasonably and not whether the tribunal itself considered the reason to be sufficient and the decision fair. It was wrong for the tribunal to substitute its own decision for that of the employer: SCOTT *v.* ULSTERBUS [1985] 9 N.I.J.B. 1, C.A.

2349. Evidence
BLOOD TESTS (EVIDENCE OF PATERNITY) (AMENDMENT) REGULATIONS (NORTHERN IRELAND) 1986 (No. 301) [80p], made under S.I. 1977 No. 1250 (N.I. 17), art. 10; operative on November 1, 1986; increase charges for blood tests to determine paternity in civil proceedings.

2350. Evidence—expert witness
The drivers of two cars involved in an accident as well as three passengers in one of the cars were killed. P, the administratrix of one of the deceased passengers, claimed damages from D, the administratrix of the driver of the car in which the deceased was a passenger, and this claim was settled for £30,000. D claimed contribution from a third party, the administrator of the driver of the other car, and he was ordered to pay two-thirds of the damages. The third party appealed. *Held,* allowing the appeal, that the trial judge based his decision largely on the evidence of an expert witness which was speculative and part of which was so far contrary to the ordinary experience of motorists that conclusions based wholly or mainly on that evidence could have no validity. As there was no evidence from which negligence causing or contributing to the accident could be inferred against the driver of the other car, a new trial would not be ordered and judgment would be directed in favour of the third party: CLARKE *v.* BROWN, BARCLAY THIRD PARTY [1986] 2 N.I.J.B. 1, C.A.

2351. Fire service
FIRE SERVICES (FACTORIES) (REPEALS) ORDER (NORTHERN IRELAND) 1986 (No. 350) [45p], made under S.I. 1984 No. 1821 (N.I. 11), art. 47(2); operative on February 1, 1987; repeals provisions of the Factories Act (Northern Ireland) 1965 (c.20) and revokes instruments made thereunder relating to fire precautions.
FIRE SERVICES (FACTORY, OFFICE AND SHOP PREMISES) ORDER (NORTHERN IRELAND) 1986 (No. 355) [80p], made under S.I. 1984 No. 1821, arts. 22(2)(*f*), 52(1)(*b*), operative on February 1, 1987; designates for the purposes of art. 22 of the 1984 S.I. the use of factory, office and shop premises (with certain exceptions) in which persons are employed to work.
FIRE SERVICES (HOTELS AND BOARDING HOUSES) (AMENDMENT) ORDER (NORTHERN IRELAND) 1986 (No. 28) [40p], made under S.I. 1984 No. 1821 (N.I. 11), art. 22(2); operative on April 1, 1986; amends the 1985 (No. 138) Order by re-defining "boarding house" to include a guest house.
FIRE SERVICES (1984 ORDER) (COMMENCEMENT No. 2) ORDER (NORTHERN IRELAND) 1986 (No. 353 (c.71) [45p], made under S.I. 1984 No. 1821, art. 1(2), and the Northern Ireland Act 1974 (c.28), Sched. 1, para. 2(1); brought art. 31 of the 1984 S.I. into operation on February 1, 1987.

FIRE SERVICES (1984 ORDER) (MODIFICATIONS) REGULATIONS (NORTHERN IRELAND) 1986 (No. 354) [£1·40], made under S.I. 1984 No. 1821, art. 47(1); operative on February 1, 1987; preserve the effect of certain provisions of the Factories Act (Northern Ireland) 1965 and the Office and Shop Premises Act (Northern Ireland) 1966 which are repealed by the 1986 (Nos. 350 and 351) Orders.

FIRE SERVICES (NON-CERTIFICATED FACTORY OFFICE AND SHOP PREMISES) REGULATIONS (NORTHERN IRELAND) 1986 (No. 352) [80p], made under S.I. 1984 No. 1821, arts. 34(1)(3)(4), 52(1)(*b*); operative on February 1, 1987; provide for certain fire precautions to be taken in the factories, office and shop premises which do not require a fire certificate under the 1984 S.I.

FIRE SERVICES (OFFICE AND SHOP PREMISES) (REPEALS) (NORTHERN IRELAND) 1986 (No. 351) [80p], made under S.I. 1984 No. 1821, art. 47(2); operative on February 1, 1987; repeals provisions of the Office and Shop Premises Act (Northern Ireland) 1966 (c.26) and revokes instruments made thereunder relating to fire precautions.

2352. Firearms

FIREARMS (PRESCRIBED FORMS) REGULATIONS (NORTHERN IRELAND) 1986 (No. 268) (£3·40), made under S.I. 1981 No. 155 (N.I. 2), arts. 10, 14, 27, 28, 34, 58; operative on November 3, 1986; consolidate with minor amendments and revoke the 1969 (No. 32), 1973 (No. 192) and 1979 (No. 276) Regulations.

2353. Fish and fisheries

ANGLING (DEPARTMENT OF AGRICULTURE WATERS) BYELAWS (NORTHERN IRELAND) 1986 (No. 111) [£1·40], made under the Fisheries Act (Northern Ireland) 1966, s.26(1); operative on June 2, 1986; specify the methods of angling permitted on waters controlled by the Department of Agriculture and provide for a minimum length and maximum number of fish which may be retained on any one day; also contain provisions restricting the use of boats and times of fishing; revoke the 1981 (No. 415) and 1984 (No. 42) Byelaws.

COARSE FISHING ROD LICENCES BYELAWS (NORTHERN IRELAND) 1986 (No. 110) [80p], made under the Fisheries Act (Northern Ireland) 1966 (c.17), s.26(1); operative on June 2, 1986; list the waters on which holders of coarse fishing rod licences are authorised to fish for coarse fish.

DRIFT NET LICENCE CONTROL BYELAWS (NORTHERN IRELAND) 1986 (No. 112) [45p], made under the Fisheries Act (Northern Ireland) 1966, s.26(1); operative on June 2, 1986; amend the 1969 (No. 91) Byelaws in relation to the use of drift net licences by agents.

FOYLE AREA (CONTROL OF NETTING) (AMENDMENT) REGULATIONS 1986 (No. 143) [45p], made under the Foyle Fisheries Act 1952 (Rep. of Ire. No. 5), s.13(1), and the Foyle Fisheries Act (Northern Ireland) 1952 (c.5), s.13(1); operative on May 31, 1986; postpone for one year the coming into operation of the 1983 (No. 143) Regulations which impose further restrictions on the materials which may be used in the construction of commercial fishing nets for the capture of salmon or trout.

FOYLE AREA (CONTROL OF NETTING) (AMENDMENT NO. 2) REGULATIONS 1986 (No. 144) [45p], made under the Foyle Fisheries Act 1952 (Rep. of Ire. No. 5), s.13(1) and the Foyle Fisheries Act (Northern Ireland) 1952 (c.5), s.13(1); operative on June 20, 1986; prohibit fishing for salmon by drift net in the Foyle Area during certain hours.

FOYLE AREA (LICENSING OF FISHING ENGINES) (AMENDMENT) REGULATIONS 1986 (No. 22) [80p], made under the Foyle Fisheries Act 1952 (Rep. of Ire. No. 5), s.13 and the Foyle Fisheries Act (Northern Ireland) 1952 (c.5), s.13; operative on February 28, 1986; increase licence fees payable in 1986 in respect of each type of net used and game fishing licence issued in the Foyle Area.

FOYLE AREA (WEEKLY CLOSE TIME) (AMENDMENT) REGULATIONS 1986 (No. 145) [45p], made under the Foyle Fisheries Act 1952, ss. 13(1), 28(3)(4), and the Foyle Fisheries Act (Northern Ireland) 1952, ss.13(1), 27(3)(4); operative on June 20, 1986; prohibit during certain hours commercial fishing for salmon and trout in the River Foyle.

RAINBOW TROUT WATERS BYELAWS (NORTHERN IRELAND) 1985 (No. 367) [40p], made under the Fisheries Act (Northern Ireland) 1966 (c.17), s.26(1); operative on February 1, 1986; designate certain waters as rainbow trout waters for the purposes of Bye-law 51 of the 1969 (No. 91) Bye-laws; revoke the 1982 (No. 115) Bye-laws.

SCALLOPS (PROHIBITION OF FISHING) REGULATIONS (NORTHERN IRELAND) 1986 (No. 150) [45p], made under the Fisheries Act (Northern Ireland) 1966 (c.17), s.124(1)(2); operative on June 1, 1986; prohibits during June 1986 fishing for scallops by British-owned fishing boats in certain waters off the Northern Ireland coast.

2354. Fish and fisheries—repair of dam—whether dam rebuilt or reinstated—whether obligation to provide a fish pass

[Fisheries Act (Northern Ireland) 1966 (c.17), s.54] An inspector of the Fisheries Conservancy Board found a gap in the structure of a dam owned by B and built before 1842. He pointed out that, if it was intended to rebuild or reinstate the dam, B was required by s.54 of the Fisheries Act (Northern Ireland) 1966 to provide a fish pass. B restored the dam without providing a fish pass. On a summons for failing to do so, the resident magistrate found that B had repaired but not rebuilt or reinstated the dam and was accordingly not guilty of an offence under s.54. W appealed by way of case stated. *Held*, that the facts admitted of only one reasonable answer, namely that B had reinstated the dam. The case was remitted to the resident magistrate with a direction to convict: WEAVER *v.* BOYCE [1985] 8 N.I.J.B., 54, C.A.

2355. Food and drugs

CASEINS AND CASEINATES REGULATIONS (NORTHERN IRELAND) 1986 (No. 40) [£1·35], made under the Food and Drugs Act (Northern Ireland) 1958 (c.27), ss.4, 7, 68, 68A; operative as to part on March 24, 1986, and as to the remainder on March 24, 1987; implement Council Directive 83/417/EEC on the approximation of laws relating to certain lactoproteins intended for human consumption.

IMPORTATION OF MILK (AMENDMENT) REGULATIONS (NORTHERN IRELAND) 1986 (No. 21) [40p], made under the Importation of Milk Act 1983 (c.37), s.1; operative on March 10, 1986; amend the 1983 (No. 338) Regulations in relation to the meaning of standardised whole milk and to the importation of milk and cream.

IMPORTATION OF MILK (AMENDMENT) (No. 2) REGULATIONS (NORTHERN IRELAND) 1986 (No. 119) [80p], made under the Importation of Milk Act 1983 (c.37), s.1; operative on June 1, 1986; amend the 1983 (No. 338) Regulations in relation to milk brought from Great Britain and in relation to the processing and packaging of permitted imported milk and milk brought from Great Britain.

MEAT PRODUCTS AND SPREADABLE FISH PRODUCTS (AMENDMENT) REGULATIONS (NORTHERN IRELAND) 1986 (No. 227) [80p], made under the Food and Drugs Act (Northern Ireland) 1958 (c.27), ss.4, 7, 68; operative on August 25, 1986; amend the 1984 (No. 408) Regulations in relation to declarations of contents.

WELFARE FOODS (AMENDMENT) REGULATIONS (NORTHERN IRELAND) 1986 (No. 131) [80p], made under the Welfare Foods Act (Northern Ireland) 1968 (c.26), s.1(3); operative on June 9, 1986; amend the definition of "approved price" in the 1981 (No. 159) Regulations and make provision for welfare milk to be available in metric measures.

2356. Game

GAME BIRDS PRESERVATION ORDER (NORTHERN IRELAND) 1986 (No. 214) [45p], made under the Game Preservation Act (Northern Ireland) 1928 (c.25), ss.7C(1), 7F; operative on August 11, 1986; prohibits, subject to certain exemptions, the killing or taking of partridges, red-legged partridges and hen pheasants during the open season, restricts dealings in hen pheasants and prohibits dealings in grouse, partridge and red-legged partridges.

2357/8. Gaming and wagering

AMUSEMENT PERMIT (PRESCRIBED PREMISES) REGULATIONS (NORTHERN IRELAND) 1986 (No. 126) [45p], made under S.I. 1985 No. 1204, art. 110(1); operative on June 1, 1986; prescribe the premises in respect of which a person may be granted an amusement permit by a district council.

BETTING, GAMING, LOTTERIES AND AMUSEMENTS (1985 ORDER (COMMENCEMENT No. 1) ORDER (NORTHERN IRELAND) 1986 (No. 124 (C.3)) [80p], made under S.I. 1985 No. 1204 (N.I. 11), art. 1(2), and the Northern Ireland Act 1974 (c.28), Sched. 1, para. 2(1); brought into operation on June 1, 1986, provisions of the 1985 S.I. relating to gaming other than gaming on bingo club premises.

GAMING MACHINE (FORM OF AMUSEMENT PERMIT) REGULATIONS (NORTHERN IRELAND) 1986 (No. 127) [£1·40], made under S.I. 1985 No. 1204, art. 114(1); operative on June 1, 1986; prescribe the form of amusement permits.

GAMING MACHINE (FORMS OF CERTIFICATES AND PERMIT) REGULATIONS (NORTHERN IRELAND) 1986 (No. 125) [£1·40], made under S.I. 1985 No. 1204, arts. 86(1)(2), 97(1); operative on June 1, 1986; prescribe the form of gaming machine certificates, gaming machine permits and certificates of registration of clubs issued under the 1985 S.I. by the court or the clerk of petty sessions.

HORSE RACING AND BETTING (AMENDMENT) ORDER (NORTHERN IRELAND) 1986 (No. 204) [45p], made under S.I. 1976 No. 1157 (N.I. 17), art. 11(2); operative on September 1, 1986; increases certain charges payable by bookmakers; revokes the 1985 (No. 167) Order.

2359. Highways and bridges—personal injuries—statutory duty—maintenance of road
P sustained personal injuries when a car driven by D1 in which he was a passenger struck a pot hole and skidded off the road. D1 claimed that the accident was due to the faulty way in which D2 had repaired and maintained the road. In response to questions put to it by the trial judge, the jury found that D1 was guilty of negligent driving and, although evidence was given by a police sergeant that there was on the following day a pot hole at the side of the road where the accident occurred, found that D2 had not failed in its statutory duty to maintain the road. D1 appealed. *Held,* dismissing the appeal, that it was a question of fact and degree whether the pot hole was an example of failure to maintain the road, whether the hole was on the road or on the verge and whether it was on the part of the road where the accident occurred and that it was open to the jury both on the facts and in law to come to the decision that it did: ANDERSON *v.* WILSON AND THE DEPARTMENT OF THE ENVIRONMENT [1985] 4 N.I.J.B., 23, C.A.

2360. Highways and bridges—statutory duty—repair—causation
[Roads (Northern Ireland) Order 1980 (S.I. 1980 No. 1085 (N.I. 11)), art. 8.] During a serious civil disturbance on May 4, 1983, rioters tore up flagstones from a footpath and constructed a low barricade across a street. The barricade was partially removed by some person or persons to allow the passage of vehicles, the broken flagstones being piled up loosely on the footpath and side of the road. On May 9, 1983, P was making her way home along the street when one of the broken flagstones fell on her leg. P claimed damages from the Department of the Environment as the road authority on the ground that it was in breach of its duty under art. 8 of the Roads (Northern Ireland) Order 1980 in failing to take steps to remove the remainder of the barricade. *Held,* allowing D's appeal from a county court decision awarding £2,500 to P, that the cause of the accident to P was not the lack of repair of the road but the pile of broken flagstones which at most constituted an obstruction and D was not liable under the 1980 Order for failure to remove an obstruction. In any case balancing the risk to its men and vehicles from rioters and the possibility of risk to pedestrians, D had taken such care as was reasonably required in the circumstances to secure that the street was not dangerous to traffic: DEVENNEY *v.* DEPARTMENT OF THE ENVIRONMENT [1986] 1 N.I.J.B. 1, Carswell J.

2361. Housing
HOME PURCHASE ASSISTANCE (PRICE-LIMIT) ORDER (NORTHERN IRELAND) 1986 (No. 156) [45p], made under S.I. 1981 No. 156 (N.I. 3), art. 153(2); operative on July 2, 1986; increases to £26,300 the prescribed limit on the purchase price of house property for which financial assistance is available under the S.I.; revokes the 1985 (No. 168) Order.

HOME PURCHASE ASSISTANCE (RECOGNISED SAVINGS INSTITUTIONS) ORDER (NORTHERN IRELAND) 1986 (No. 19) [40p], made under S.I. 1981 No. 156 (N.I. 3), art. 154(1); operative on March 10, 1986; adds two credit unions to the savings institutions recognised for the purposes of art. 153 of the S.I.

HOUSING BENEFITS (AMENDMENT) REGULATIONS (NORTHERN IRELAND) 1986 (No. 158) [80p], made under S.I. 1983 No. 1121 (N.I. 14), art. 3(1)(2); operative as to part on June 6, 1986, and as to the remainder on July 28, 1986; amend the 1985 (No. 282) Regulations in relation to the amounts used to calculate a person's entitlement to a housing benefit and in relation to a person's benefit period.

HOUSING BENEFITS (AMENDMENT No. 2) REGULATIONS (NORTHERN IRELAND) 1986 (No. 159) [45p], made under S.I. 1983 No. 1121 (N.I. 14), art. 3(2); operative on July 1, 1986; provide that, in ascertaining a person's weekly income for the purpose of calculating entitlement to housing benefit, any job start allowance payable under arrangements made by the Department of Economic Development shall be disregarded.

HOUSING BENEFITS (AMENDMENT NO. 3) REGULATIONS (NORTHERN IRELAND) 1986 (No. 235) [£1·40], made under S.I. 1983 No. 1121 (N.I. 14), art. 3(2); operative as to part on September 1, 1986, and as to the remainder on July 28, 1986; amend the 1985 (No. 282) Regulations in relation to students.

HOUSING BENEFITS (AMENDMENT NO. 4) REGULATIONS (NORTHERN IRELAND) 1986 (No. 239) [80p], made under S.I. 1983 No. 1121, art. 3(2); operative on July 28, 1986; amend the 1985 (No. 282) Regulations in relation to eligibility for housing benefits, deductions for non-dependants and amounts to be disregarded when ascertaining weekly incomes for housing benefits.

HOUSING DEFECTS (EXPENDITURE LIMIT) ORDER (NORTHERN IRELAND) 1986 (No. 273) [45p], made under S.I. 1986 No. 1301 (N.I. 13), Sched. 1, para. 2; operative on September 26, 1986; specifies £24,000 as the expenditure limit for the purposes of ascertaining the amount of reinstatement grant payable under art. 8 of the 1986 S.I. in respect of a defective dwelling.

2362. Housing—compulsory purchase—validity of vesting order
[Housing (Northern Ireland) Order 1981 (S.I. 1981 No. 156 (N.I. 3)), art. 48.] P carried on business as a merchant of non-ferrous metals and machinery in premises in Shiels Street, Belfast. Scrap metal was brought in large lorries to the premises for processing. The Northern Ireland Housing Executive declared an area near the premises to be a proposed re-development area and this area contained a street which provided direct access to P's premises. The Housing Executive then submitted to the Department of the Environment a re-development scheme, which consisted of a number of documents and maps including a proposed land use map, and applied for a vesting order. When notice of the application was published P sought a guarantee that satisfactory access to his premises would be provided. A public local inquiry was held at which P challenged the validity of the application for the vesting order on the ground that it did not comply with art. 48(1)(*b*) of the Housing (Northern Ireland) Order 1981. The Department approved the re-development scheme on condition that the Housing Executive provided satisfactory access to D's premises and made the vesting order. P applied for an order quashing the vesting order. *Held,* refusing the application, that (1) in its context "scheme" meant no more than a set of proposals for re-development of an area and the documents and maps sent by the Executive to the Department constituted such a scheme; and (2) the scheme complied with art. 48 of the 1981 Order as it indicated in general terms the manner in which the area should be laid out: KANE *v.* NORTHERN IRELAND HOUSING EXECUTIVE [1986] 2 N.I.J.B. 84, Carswell J.

2363. Housing—Housing (Northern Ireland) Order 1986 (S.I. 1986 No. 1301 (N.I. 13))
This Order facilitates the provision of financial assistance to certain private owners of dwellings which have been sold by the Northern Ireland Housing Executive or certain other public bodies and which are defective by reason of their design or construction and which, as a result of those defects having become generally known, have been substantially reduced in value. The Order also extends the circumstances under which a secure tenant of the Housing Executive has the right to buy his home and amends other rights of secure tenants under Pt. I of the Housing (Northern Ireland) Order 1983. The Order also deals with the repayment of housing association grants, with the power of the Housing Executive to enter into indemnity agreements with recognised bodies and with statutory tenancies by succession.
The Order came into operation on September 26, 1986.

2364. Industrial societies
CREDIT UNIONS (AUTHORISED INVESTMENTS) REGULATIONS (NORTHERN IRELAND) 1986 (No. 129) [80p], made under S.I. 1985 No. 1205, art. 33(1); operative on June 1, 1986; prescribe the manner in which credit unions may invest funds not immediately required for their purposes.

CREDIT UNIONS (FEES) REGULATIONS (NORTHERN IRELAND) 1986 (No. 138) [80p], made under S.I. 1985 No. 1205, arts. 31(2), 78(1); operative on June 1, 1986; prescribe the scale of fees payable to the registrar of friendly societies for the inspection or the furnishing of copies of documents in his custody or in connection with the exercise of his functions under the 1985 S.I.

CREDIT UNIONS (FORMS AND PROCEDURES) REGULATIONS (NORTHERN IRELAND) 1986 (No. 137) [£3·40], made under S.I. 1985 No. 1205 (N.I. 12), arts. 4(2), 10(4), 31(2)–(4), 78(1); operative on July 1, 1986; prescribe the forms to be used and the procedures to be followed in matters affecting credit unions under the 1985 S.I. and provide for the keeping of documents by the registrar of friendly societies and the inspection of such documents by the public.
CREDIT UNIONS (LIMIT ON LOANS) REGULATIONS (NORTHERN IRELAND) 1986 (No. 130) [45p], made under S.I. 1985 No. 1205, art. 28(6); operative on June 1, 1986; prescribe a limit of 98 per cent. of the net assets of a credit union on the total amount outstanding on loan to members.
CREDIT UNIONS (LIMIT ON SHARES) ORDER (NOTHERN IRELAND) 1986 (No. 209) [45p], made under S.I. 1985 No. 1205 (N.I. 12), art. 14(4); operative on October 1, 1986; increases to £5,000 the limit on the interest in shares of a credit union which a member may have or claim under art. 14(3) of the 1985 S.I.
CREDIT UNIONS (1985 ORDER) (COMMENCEMENT) ORDER (NORTHERN IRELAND) 1986 (No. 108 (C.2)) [45p], made under S.I. 1985 No. 1205 (N.I. 12), art. 1(2); brought the provisions of the S.I., so far as they confer power to make regulations and orders, into operation on May 1, 1986, and for all other purposes into operation on June 1, 1986.
INDUSTRIAL AND PROVIDENT SOCIETIES (FEES) (AMENDMENT) REGULATIONS (NORTHERN IRELAND) 1986 (No. 349) [80p], made under the Industrial and Provident Societies Act (Northern Ireland) 1969 (c.24), s.97(1); operative on December 31, 1986; increase fees to be paid for certain matters transacted or arising under the 1969 Act; revoke the 1985 (No. 128) Regulations.

2365. Insurance—policy on husband's life—husband killed in robbery by husband and wife—causation—public policy
An attempted robbery of a farmhouse by H, W and two others failed when one of the occupants returned unexpectedly. The occupant sought help from C, a neighbouring farmer, who encountered H in a field near the farmhouse and, thinking that H was about to shoot at him, fired a shot from behind a tree not aimed at H in particular. H was killed. W claimed benefits under an insurance policy on H's life. The trial judge rejected the claim—see [1986] 2 C.L. 200. *Held,* dismissing W's appeal, that (1) H's death was caused by the robbery; (2) C's act in firing the fatal shot was not unreasonable in the circumstances and did not break the chain of causation; and (3) as W must be regarded as having caused H's death by his participation in the robbery and as the robbery was of an immoral and anti-social nature, it would be contrary to public policy to allow W's claim to the policy monies: HEWITSON v. PRUDENTIAL ASSURANCE CO. [1985] 12 N.I.J.B. 65, C.A.

2366. Intoxicating liquors—application for licence—adequacy of licensed premises in vicinity—subsisting licence
[Licensing Act (Northern Ireland) 1971 (c.13), s.5(2).] An application for a provisional on/off licence for premises in Botanic Avenue, Belfast, was refused by the Recorder who was not satisfied that the number of licensed premises in the vicinity was inadequate. The applicant appealed. *Held,* dismissing the appeal, that (1) there was a considerable and growing demand in the vicinity for facilities for the purchase of intoxicating liquor and the number of licensed premises was inadequate to meet this demand; (2) the licence which was surrendered as required by s.5(2) of the Licensing Act (Northern Ireland) 1971 should not have been renewed as trading had been discontinued before its renewal and was, accordingly, not a subsisting licence for the purposes of that section: WINE INNS v. LAVERY [1985] 11 N.I.J.B. 19, MacDermott J.

2367. Intoxicating liquors—application for licence—catering facilities—whether sale of liquor the principal business
[Licensing Act (Northern Ireland) 1971 (c.13), s.3(1)(a).] McC applied for a licence under s.3(1)(a) of the Licensing Act (Northern Ireland) 1971 in respect of premises in which he intended that the only or principal business carried on in the premises would be the sale of intoxicating liquor for consumption on or off the premises. Almost half the floor space was, however, to be devoted, though not exclusively, to the service of snacks and more substantial sit-down meals. The Recorder refused the application on the ground that the snacks and meals would provide the greater part of the profits and that the sale of intoxicating liquor would

not be the principal business carried on in the premises. *Held,* allowing McC's appeal, that the real nature of the business would be that of a public house with superior catering facilities and not that of a restaurant with a bar: McCLOSKEY'S APPLICATION, *Re* [1985] 11 N.I.J.B. 86, Lord Lowry L.C.J.

2368. Intoxicating liquors—application for provisional licence—notice defective—whether verbal or technical errors
[Licensing Act (Northern Ireland) 1971 (c.13), Sched. 1, para. 1: County Court Rules (Northern Ireland) 1981 (No. 225), Ord. 43, r.14(1), Ord. 48, r.2] On an application for the provisional grant of a liquor licence, notices (which were required by para. 1 of Sched. 1 to the Licensing Act (Northern Ireland) 1971 to be published and required by Ord. 48, r.2, of the County Court Rules (Northern Ireland) 1981 to contain certain information) contained errors as to the date of the court sitting and as to the situation of a subsisting licence. The county court judge held that notwithstanding these errors he had jurisdiction to hear the application. An objector's application for a judicial review of this decision was refused—see [1985] 12 C.L. 270. *Held,* dismissing an appeal against the refusal of judicial review, that in so far as the requirements were provided by the County Court Rules they were governed by all those Rules including the dispensing power in Ord. 43, r.14 and that the errors did not mislead or prejudice any of the parties: O'LOUGHLIN'S APPLICATION, *Re* [1985] 6 N.I.J.B. 101, C.A.

2369. Intoxicating liquors—off-licence—shopping centre—adequacy of licensed premises in vicinity
An application for the grant of an off-licence for a unit in a shopping centre was refused by the county court on the ground that it had not been shown that the existing off-licensed premises in the vicinity were inadequate. The applicant appealed. *Held,* dismissing the appeal, that (1) the shopping centre did not create a new and small vicinity and that three existing off-licensed premises outside the centre were in the vicinity; and (2) that, while the applicant had shown that it would be convenient for shoppers using the centre to have an off-licence in it, it had not been shown that the number of existing off-licences in the vicinity was inadequate: STEWARTS SUPERMARKETS *v.* STERRITT [1985] 5 N.I.J.B. 51, Hutton J.

2370. Intoxicating liquors—provisional licence—suitability of premises—adequacy of existing premises in vicinity
[Licensing Act (Northern Ireland) 1971 (c.13), s.5(2)] An application for the provisional grant of a licence to sell intoxicating liquor either on or off premises consisting of a terrace house was granted by the county court despite objections by various persons and bodies. The objectors appealed. *Held,* dismissing the appeal, that (1) the applicant had established for the purposes of s.5(2) of the Licensing Act (Northern Ireland) 1971 that the premises when completed in accordance with plans lodged would be suitable for the sale of intoxicating liquor and that there was a growing demand in the vicinity of the premises for facilities for the purchase of intoxicating liquor which was not satisfied by the existing licensed premises; and (2) on the facts there were no grounds for the exercise of the court's general discretion to refuse the application: DONNELLY *v.* REGENCY HOTEL [1985] 5 N.I.J.B. 27, Carswell J.

2371. Landlord and tenant
REGISTERED RENTS (INCREASE) ORDER (NORTHERN IRELAND) 1986 (No. 56) [40p], made under S.I. 1978 No. 1050 (N.I. 20), art. 33(1)(2); operative on March 10, 1986; increase the rents of certain regulated tenancies by 5 per cent.

2372. Landlord and tenant—business tenancies—Lands Tribunal decisions
BALL *v.* PICKEN, BT/65/1986 (T's application for a new tenancy of licensed premises was opposed by L on the ground that she required them for the purposes of a business to be carried on by her. *Held,* refusing the application, that L, who was 67 years old, had established that it was she and not her son, who had come home from abroad and would manage the business, who would be the licensee of the premises and owner of the business which she proposed to carry on in the premises.)

2373. BITTLE AND WILSON *v.* WALKER, BT/59/1986, BT/60/1986 (B and W carried on their respective businesses in sheds in a farmyard which formed part of an estate of which the respondents were executors. To maximise the value of the estate the executors applied for and were granted, subject to conditions, planning permission to use the farmyard and buildings for light industrial use. The executors served notices of determination of tenancy on B and W who then applied for new tenancies. Because of the expense involved in meeting the conditions the executors decided not to proceed with the conversion of the farmyard to light industrial use and began to investigate other possible uses including the erection of dwelling-houses. *Held,* that the executors had not established their grounds of objection to the grant of the new tenancies).

2374.   EASTWOOD *v.* LOUGHRAN, BT/70/1986 (T's application for a new tenancy of business premises was opposed by L on the ground that he intended to occupy the premises for his own use. The notice to determine T's tenancy was in L's name although L had transferred the premises to his wife in 1970. *Held,* that the notice was invalid (*Morrow* v. *Nadeem* [1986] C.L.Y. 1833 followed.))

2375.   McGIMPSEY *v.* McGIMPSEY, BT/38/1986 (T's application for a new tenancy of business premises was opposed by L on the ground that T did not occupy the entirety of the premises at all or for any business purpose and if he did carry on business in the premises the part occupied by him for this purpose was very small. T, who had been in occupation of the premises since August 1955, sub-leased the greater part to T and H Cars in 1982 and 1985. *Held,* that the part occupied by T and H Cars must be excluded from the holding. A new tenancy was granted for the part occupied by T.)

2376.   VARIOUS APPLICANTS *v.* BELFAST CITY COUNCIL, BT/1–21/1986 (the Belfast City Council owned premises in Smithfield, Belfast, in which a market was carried on in temporary premises erected by the Council on the site after the previous structures were destroyed by fire in 1974. In 1985 the Council acquired a new site for the market and sold the original site to a company for use as a shopping development. The Council served notices to determine the tenancies of the occupants of the market premises who then applied for new tenancies under the Business Tenancies Act (Northern Ireland) 1964. The Council served one series of notices opposing the applications on one ground and later served another series of notices opposing the applications on a different ground. *Held,* that (1) as the notices did not cause any hardship or confusion to the tenants and were in the required form and served within the required time, both series of notices were valid; (2) in selling the Smithfield site the Council was a public authority carrying out statutory functions and, accordingly, Part I of the 1964 Act did not apply to the tenancies; and (3) notwithstanding that the Council had served notices under the Act, it was not estopped from relying on the exclusion of the tenancies by s.2(1)(*g*) of the Act).

2377. Landlord and tenant—determination of rent—Lands Tribunal decision
    TOWERMILL PROPERTIES *v.* DRESSWELL (NEWTOWNARDS), R/35/1985 (L issued a notice increasing the rent of a shop in a shopping centre from £22,750 per annum to £37,500 per annum. The shop fronted an octagonal shaped area used for various displays which obscured the displays in the shop. *Held,* that having regard to the rent agreed for the adjoining shop, the rent should be £33,300 per annum).

2378. Landlord and tenant—non-payment of rent—tenant a trustee—relief from forfeiture
    R, without obtaining his landlord's consent, in June 1982 assigned premises to P for the unexpired residue of a term of ten years subject to the payment of a rent to Z, who in October 1982 assigned their interest in the premises to D. P took the assignment at the request of W who had in 1979 been in financial difficulties. Since June 1982 W used the premises as a hot food bar although the permitted user under the lease was as a newsagent's, confectionery and tobacconist's shop or such other use as may be approved by the landlord. The rent was demanded of and paid by W though not always on the due date. Rent was paid up to the end of April 1983 but since that date D wrote to W claiming wrong amounts for rent and insurance. W tendered a cheque for the correct amounts but this was returned by D who exercised the right of re-entry for non-payment of rent by locking W out of the premises. P applied for an order granting relief from forfeiture for non-payment of the rent. *Held,* granting the order, that having regard to the history of the premises D could not complain about the absence of written consent to the assignment by R to P or about the arrangement whereby W occupied and used the premises and paid the rent: DUNCAN *v.* MACKIN [1985] 10 N.I.J.B. 1, Lord Lowry L.C.J.

2379. Landlord and tenant—squatter—use and occupation payments—whether lease or licence

[Landlord and Tenant Law Amendment Act Ireland 1860 (c.154), s.3] In December 1982 D illegally entered into occupation of a house owned by P, the Northern Ireland Housing Executive, and was permitted on payment of a weekly sum for use and occupation to stay there while his circumstances and the circumstances of his entering into occupation of the house were investigated. A letter from P to D stated that payment of the weekly sum would not confer on him any title to or tenancy of the house or affect P's right to its possession. D was issued with a payments book which contained payment slips, repair notification cards, a rent rebate application card and a termination of tenancy notice. In June 1983 P informed D by letter that, following an investigation of the circumstances of his illegal occupation, he was not entitled to a tenancy of the house. After that letter P accepted payments made on D's behalf by the Department of Health and Social Services under a new housing benefit scheme. In November 1983 P brought ejectment proceedings and in May 1984 was awarded a decree for possession by the county court judge. *Held,* dismissing D's appeal, that (1) s.3 of the Landlord and Tenant Law Amendment Act Ireland 1860 required an express or implied contract that a tenancy should be created and the facts in this case were insufficient to give rise to an inference that a tenancy should be created; (2) the licence given to D was a revocable licence which was revoked by P's letter of June 1983; and (3) the acceptance by P, after that letter, of payments for use and occupation and for arrears of such payments did not show an intention to waive the demand for possession: NORTHERN IRELAND HOUSING EXECUTIVE *v.* DUFFIN [1985] 8 N.I.J.B., 62, Carswell J.

2380. Local government

BELFAST CITY COUNCIL (TEMPORARY PROVISIONS) ORDER (NORTHERN IRELAND) 1986 (No. 101) [45p], made under S.I. 1986 No. 221 (N.I. 1), art. 3; operative from April 15, 1986, to April 17, 1986; empowers the Department of the Environment to appoint a person to exercise the functions of Belfast City Council.

DISTRICT COUNCIL (MORTGAGES) REGULATIONS (NORTHERN IRELAND) 1986 (No. 76) [80p], made under the Local Government Act (Northern Ireland) 1972 (c.9), s.70; operative on May 1, 1986; provide for the terms upon which mortgages may be entered into by a district council for the purpose of borrowing.

DISTRICT COUNCIL (STOCKS AND BONDS) REGULATIONS (NORTHERN IRELAND) 1986 (No. 77) [£1·85], made under the Local Government Act (Northern Ireland) 1972, s.70; operative on May 1, 1986; provide for the terms upon which stock or bonds may be issued and dealt with for the purpose of borrowing by a district council; revoke the 1967 (No. 166) Regulations.

GENERAL GRANT (SPECIFIED BODIES) REGULATIONS (NORTHERN IRELAND) 1986 (No. 154) [45p], made under S.I. 1972 No. 1999 (N.I. 22), art. 4(3); operative on July 8, 1986; specify bodies for the purpose of art. 4(3) of the 1972 S.I.

LOCAL GOVERNMENT (COMPENSATION FOR REDUNDANCY AND PREMATURE RETIREMENT) REGULATIONS (NORTHERN IRELAND) 1986 (No. 80) [£1·35], made under S.I. 1972 No. 1073 (N.I. 10), art. 19; operative on May 15, 1986; provide for compensation in certain cases of redundancy and amend the 1983 (No. 30) Regulations.

LOCAL GOVERNMENT (GENERAL GRANT) ORDER (NORTHERN IRELAND) 1986 (No. 237) [45p], made under S.I. 1972 No. 1999 (N.I. 22), Sched. 1, Pt. I, para. 3(1); operative on September 4, 1986; specifies those districts which are to be taken into account in calculating the standard penny rate products for the year ending on March 31, 1987, for the purpose of computing the resources element of the grant from central funds to district councils.

SEALING OF CONTRACTS (FINANCIAL LIMITS) ORDER (NORTHERN IRELAND) 1986 (No. 39) [40p], made under the Local Government Act (Northern Ireland) 1972 (c.9), s.100(1) and the New Towns Act (Northern Ireland) 1965 (c.13), s.7(2), Sched. 4, para. 14; operative on March 25, 1986; increases the limit under which district councils and new town commissions may enter into certain contracts not under seal; revokes the 1980 (No. 283) Order.

2381. Local government—Anglo-Irish Agreement—resolution to adjourn council meetings and not to hold committee meetings—whether intra vires—striking of rate—whether planning permission required for protest banner

[Local Government Act (Northern Ireland) 1972 (c.9), s.129.] In protest against the Anglo-Irish Agreement the Belfast City Council resolved at its meeting on

December 2, 1985, not to hold any council or committee meetings and delegated the Council's functions to the Town Clerk. At a special meeting on January 2, 1986, the Council resolved that a banner with the words "Belfast Says No" be erected at the front of the City Hall. Although planning permission was not received the banner was erected on January 11, 1986. Several councillors applied for judicial review. *Held,* by the trial judge, that (1) the *ultra vires* doctrine applies to resolutions of a council; (2) as the working of the Anglo-Irish Agreement could affect the Council's functions and matters in which the Council had an interest, the resolutions expressing opposition to the Agreement and authorising the erection of the protest banner were not *ultra vires*; (3) the payment of the cost of erecting the banner was a payment for a purpose which was in the interests of the Council; (4) the decision by the Council to delegate its functions to the Town Clerk was taken as a protest against the Anglo-Irish Agreement and not taken to enable the Council to carry out its functions efficiently and effectively and was therefore invalid as a power given for one purpose cannot be exercised for a different purpose; (5) mandamus would issue to compel the Council to hold meetings which it was under a duty to hold and which were necessary for the discharge of its functions; (6) mandamus would issue to compel the Council to strike a rate as the power given by s.129 of the Local Government Act (Northern Ireland) 1972 to the Department of the Environment to strike a rate was not a sufficient, effective and appropriate remedy; (7) the resolution authorising the erection of the protest banner was invalid as the summons to attend the meeting at which it was passed did not specify the resolution but its erection was properly authorised by a resolution passed at an earlier meeting; and (8) an injunction would issue to restrain the Council from displaying the banner without planning permission. *Held,* dismissing the Council's appeal, that (1) the failure to specify the business to be transacted at the second meeting which authorised the erection of the protest banner did not invalidate that meeting but the erection of the banner was unlawful as the prior consent required by law to its erection was not obtained; (2) the Council was not entitled to refuse or deliberately neglect to discharge its statutory functions as the elected local authority for Belfast and thereby to deprive the ratepayers and citizens of Belfast of its services; and (3) the best way of performing the Council's functions was to have them discharged by the elected representatives to whom Parliament and the electors had entrusted those functions. Orders of mandamus were issued directing the Council to hold such meetings of the Council and such Committee meetings as were necessary for the transaction of business and to strike a rate on or before February 26, 1986; Cook's Application, *Re* [1986] 1 N.I.J.B. 43, C.A.

2382. Local government—declaration—exclusion of councillors

[Local Government Act (Northern Ireland) 1972 (c.9), s.7(1); Northern Ireland Constitution Act 1973 (c.36), s.21] A district council passed a resolution that a member should not be entitled to attend or participate in a meeting of the council until he signed a declaration that he would not use his position as councillor for the purpose of advancing the aims or objects of any organisation which engages in violence or acts of terrorism or whose aim is the subversion of the state. *Held,* on an application for judicial review, that the declarations made unlawful by s.21 of the Northern Ireland Constitution Act 1973 are not limited to declarations which would be offensive to a person's religious belief or political opinion and accordingly that the resolution was void under s.21. In any event (1) the inclusion of the statutory requirement of a declaration in s.7(1) of the Local Government Act (Northern Ireland) 1972 negatived any implication of a power of a council to require any other type of declaration; (2) the protective and self-defensive powers of a council do not include power to require a declaration on security grounds; and (3) the dominant purpose of the council in passing the resolution was not an improvement in security but the exclusion of the Sinn Fein members: French's Application, *Re* [1985] 7 N.I.J.B. 48, Carswell J.

2383/4. Local government—delegation of functions to special committee—exclusion of councillors

[Local Government Act (Northern Ireland) 1972 (c.9), s.18; European Convention on the Protection of Human Rights and Fundamental Freedoms, art. 17] A district council, in purported exercise of s.18 of the Local Government Act (Northern Ireland) 1972, appointed a special committee consisting of all the members of the council, except two Sinn Fein members, to exercise the council's functions. The two excluded members applied for judicial review. *Held,* granting the application, that (1) the court could take judicial notice of the support given by the Sinn Fein party to murder and other acts of terrorist violence in Northern Ireland; (2) the power given by s.18 to appoint a committee is a power to appoint a committee for the better regulation and management of the council's business and cannot be used for the different purpose of excluding a councillor from the activities of the council; (3) the protective and self-defensive powers of a council which are implied by common law do not include powers to exclude members of a party which proclaims a particular policy outside the council chamber. If they did the council would not have been acting unreasonably in excluding the members of such a party: the exclusion would have been in conformity with art. 17 of the European Convention on the Protection of Human Rights and Fundamental Freedoms as Sinn Fein was a group engaged in activities aimed at the destruction of many of the important rights and freedoms set out in the Convention and as by taking part in the normal political activities in the council chamber the Sinn Fein councillors were seeking to advance the terrorist policy and aims of the party: CURRAN AND McCANN'S APPLICATION, *Re* [1985] 7 N.I.J.B. 22, Hutton J.

2385. Local government—Local Government (Temporary Provisions) (Northern Ireland) Order 1986 (S.I. 1986 No. 221 (N.I.1))
This Order enables the head of the Department of the Environment to make provision for the exercise of the functions of any district council, or of any joint committee appointed by two or more such councils, where the council or committee fails, or is unable or unwilling, to exercise any of its functions duly and effectually.
The Order came into operation on February 16, 1986, and unless renewed, ceases to have effect on May 31, 1988.

2386. Local government—suspension of member until apology—whether unreasonable
A, who was an elected member of the Belfast City Council, made reference in the course of a meeting to "the Union Jack, also known as the butcher's apron". It was then resolved by the Council under Order 31 of its Standing Orders that unless A withdrew this reference "he be suspended from the Council and remain suspended" until he withdrew the reference. *Held,* that the power given by Order 31 to suspend a member indefinitely until he submitted an apology was not reasonably necessary for the protection and self-defence of the Council and was accordingly *ultra vires*: McANULTY'S APPLICATION, *Re* [1985] 2 N.I.J.B. 63, Hutton J.

2387. Local government—vacation of councillor's office—adjournment of meetings, as a political protest
H, a councillor for a ward in which she was registered as an elector, attended a council meeting on September 23, 1985, but did not attend any meetings during the following three months. At its October meeting the Council resolved that future meetings be adjourned as a political protest, that a meeting be held on November 18, 1985, and that no committee meetings be held in the interim period. A notice setting out the agenda was sent out for this November meeting. None of the items on the agenda was dealt with at this meeting and it was adjourned. The Council met again on December 2, 1985, and adjourned without dealing with any of the items on the agenda. On December 24, 1985, H was informed by the Town Clerk that as she had failed to attend any meetings during the three months from September 23, 1985, she had ceased to be a member of the Council. H's office was declared vacant by the Council at its meeting in January 1986. H applied for judicial review on the grounds that her office had been wrongly declared vacant and that the adjournments of the meetings were unlawful. *Held,* that (1) as it was open to the Council at each meeting to proceed with the business on the agenda and as it could not be said that each meeting was intended to be nothing more than a vehicle for public protest, the meetings were not unlawful or void; (2) accordingly H's office had been correctly declared vacant; (3) following *Re Cook's Application* [1986] C.L.Y. 2381, the decisions of the Council to adjourn its meetings as a political protest were unlawful and mandamus would lie to compel the Council to discharge its functions; and (4) as an elector H had a sufficient interest to claim the remedies sought: HOGAN'S APPLICATION, *Re,* [1986] 5 N.I.J.B. 81, Carswell J.

2388. Magisterial law
MAGISTRATES' COURTS (AMENDMENT) RULES (NORTHERN IRELAND) 1986 (No. 175) [45p], made under S.I. 1981 No. 1675 (N.I. 26), art. 13; operative on June 30, 1986;

amend the 1984 (No. 225) Rules by prescribing increased scale costs in ejectment proceedings in magistrates' courts.

MAGISTRATES' COURTS (BETTING, GAMING, LOTTERIES AND AMUSEMENTS) (No. 1) RULES (NORTHERN IRELAND) 1986 (No. 133) [£1·90], made under S.I. 1981 No. 1675 (N.I. 26), art. 13, and S.I. 1985 No. 1204 (N.I. 11), Sched. 7, para. 3, Sched. 11, para. 2, Sched. 12, para. 3, Sched. 13, para. 2, Sched. 14, para. 2; operative on June 1, 1986; make provision in relation to courts of summary jurisdiction for applications for the grant, renewal or revocation of gaming machine certificates, the grant of gaming machine permits and applications for the registration of clubs under the 1985 S.I. and for the renewal or revocation of such registration.

MAGISTRATES' COURTS (CHILD ABDUCTION AND CUSTODY) RULES (NORTHERN IRELAND) 1986 (No. 219) [80p], made under S.I. 1981 No. 1675 (N.I. 26), art. 13, as extended by the Child Abduction and Custody Act 1985 (c.60), ss.10, 24; operative on August 1, 1986; make provision for the procedure to be followed in magistrates' courts in consequence of the coming into force of the 1985 Act.

MAGISTRATES' COURTS (CIVIL JURISDICTION AND JUDGMENTS ACT 1982) RULES (NORTHERN IRELAND) 1986 (No. 359 [£2·40], made under S.I. 1981 No. 1675 (N.I. 26), art. 13, the Maintenance and Affiliation Orders Act (Northern Ireland) 1966 (c.35), s.11A(1), the Maintenance Orders (Reciprocal Enforcement) Act 1972 (c.18), ss. 2(3), 8(5) 33(4), and the Civil Jurisdiction and Judgments Act 1982 (c.27), ss.12, 48; operative on January 1, 1987, provide for the procedure to be followed in courts of summary jurisdiction when dealing with certain claims under the Convention on jurisdiction and enforcement of judgments in civil and commercial matters signed at Brussels on September 27, 1968.

MAGISTRATES' COURTS (COSTS IN AFFILIATION AND SEPARATION AND MAINTENANCE PROCEEDINGS) (AMENDMENT) RULES (NORTHERN IRELAND) 1986 (No. 89) [45p], made under S.I. 1981 No. 1675 (N.I. 26), art. 13; operative on May 1, 1986; amend the 1966 (No. 277) Rules so as to include proceedings under the Domestic Proceedings (Northern Ireland) Order 1980 and to increase to £130 the maximum amounts payable in respect of solicitors' costs and counsel's fees.

MAGISTRATES' COURTS FEES (AMENDMENT) ORDER (NORTHERN IRELAND) 1986 (No. 103) [80p], made under the Judicature (Northern Ireland) Act 1978 (c.23), s.116(1); operative on May 12, 1986; amends the 1983 (No. 206) Order by substituting a new Schedule of court fees to be taken in magistrates' courts.

MAGISTRATES' COURTS (GAMING MACHINE) FEES ORDER (NORTHERN IRELAND ACT) 1986 (No. 140) [45p], made under the Judicature (Northern Ireland) 1978, s.116(1); operative on June 1, 1986; fixes the fees to be taken in magistrates' courts in respect of applications for the grant and renewal of gaming machine certificates, the grant of gaming machine permits and the registration and renewal of registration of clubs.

2389. Magisterial law—liability of members of juvenile court—jurisdiction

[Magistrates' Courts Act (Northern Ireland) 1964 (c.21), s.15.] A training school order made against P by a juvenile court was quashed as P had not applied for legal aid or been informed of his right to apply for legal aid. P's claim for damages against the members of the juvenile court was dismissed by the High Court but allowed by the Court of Appeal on the ground that the juvenile court had acted without jurisdiction—see [1984] C.L.Y. 2421. *Held*, dismissing an appeal by the members of the juvenile court, that (1) where justices have duly entered upon the summary trial of a matter within their jurisdiction, only something quite exceptional occurring in the course of their proceedings can oust their jurisdiction so as to deprive them of protection from civil liability for a subsequent trespass; and (2) although the juvenile court had jurisdiction to try P, it had, by reason of its failure to inform P of his right to apply for legal aid, acted without jurisdiction within the meaning of s.15 of the Magistrates' Courts Act (Northern Ireland) 1964, and its members were, accordingly, liable for damages: McCANN v. MULLAN [1984] N.I. 186, H.L.

2390. Magisterial law—summons signed before and served after defendant's seventeenth birthday—whether juvenile court had jurisdiction

[Children and Young Persons Act (Northern Ireland) 1968 (c.34), s.66(2)] D, a minor, was unlawfully on licensed premises during permitted hours. A summons signed before and served after D's seventeenth birthday commanded him to appear before a juvenile court. The court held that the proceedings did not commence until the service of the summons and, accordingly, that it had no jurisdiction to hear the case. *Held,* on appeal by way of case stated, that the juvenile court correctly refused jurisdiction but on the wrong ground. For the purposes of s.66(2) of the Children and Young Persons Act (Northern Ireland) 1968 the proceedings commenced on the hearing in the juvenile court: DIXON *v.* McCANN [1985] 8 N.I.J.B. 78, C.A.

2391. Medicine

MISUSE OF DRUGS (NORTHERN IRELAND) REGULATIONS 1986 (No. 52) [£3·30], made under the Misuse of Drugs Act 1971 (c.38), ss.7, 10, 22, 31, 38; operative on April 1, 1986; re-enact with amendments and revoke the 1974 (No. 272) Regulations and amending regulations.

MISUSE OF DRUGS (SAFE CUSTODY) (AMENDMENT) (NORTHERN IRELAND) REGULATIONS 1986 (No. 53) [40p], made under the Misuse of Drugs Act 1971, ss.10(2)(*a*), 31, 38; operative on April 1, 1986; amend the 1973 (No. 53) Regulations so as to exempt certain substances from the requirements of those regulations.

NURSING HOMES (REGISTRATION FEES AND LASERS CONTROL) REGULATIONS (NORTHERN IRELAND) 1986 (No. 166) [45p], made under the Nursing Homes and Nursing Agencies Act (Northern Ireland) 1971 (c.32), ss.1(2), 6(1)(*c*)(v)(vi)(*e*); operative on July 14, 1986; prescribe fees payable on an application for registration of a nursing home or change of manager of a nursing home and amend the 1974 (No. 313) Regulations.

NURSING HOMES (SPECIALLY CONTROLLED TECHNIQUE) ORDER (NORTHERN IRELAND) 1986 (No. 18) [40p], made under the Nursing Homes and Nursing Agencies Act (Northern Ireland) 1971 (c.32), s.6(1)(3); operative on March 1, 1986; specifies techniques of medicine or surgery involving the use of class 3B or class 4 laser products as subject to control for the purposes of the 1971 Act.

NURSING HOMES (SPECIALLY CONTROLLED TECHNIQUE) (NO. 2) ORDER (NORTHERN IRELAND) 1986 (No. 167) [45p], made under the Nursing Homes and Nursing Agencies Act (Northern Ireland) 1971, s.10(1)(3); operative on July 14, 1986; specifies techniques of medicine or surgery involving the use of class 3B or class 4 laser products as subject to control for the purposes of the 1971 Act. This Order replaces the 1986 (No. 18) Order which is null and void.

2392. Medicine—Nursing Homes and Nursing Agencies (Northern Ireland) Order 1985 (S.I. 1985 No. 1775 (N.I. 19))

This Order (1) enables the Department of Health and Social Services to specify techniques of medicine or surgery, the use of which may create a hazard, as subject to control; (2) extends the registration requirement for nursing homes to premises used for the provision of treatment by a specially controlled technique; and (3) enables the Department to require records to be kept of the use of such techniques.

The Order came into operation on January 19, 1986.

2393. Mental health

MENTAL HEALTH (1986 ORDER) (COMMENCEMENT NO. 1) ORDER (NORTHERN IRELAND) 1986 (No. 107 (C.1)) [80p], made under S.I. 1986 No. 595 (N.I. 4), art. 1(2), and the Northern Ireland Act 1974 (c.28), Sched. 1, para. 2(1); brings certain provisions of the S.I. into operation on May 1, 1986, and certain other provisions of the S.I. and the provisions of S.I. 1986 No. 596 into operation on July 31, 1986.

MENTAL HEALTH (1986 ORDER) (COMMENCEMENT NO. 2) ORDER (NORTHERN IRELAND) 1986 (No. 330 (C.5)) [45p], made under S.I. 1986 No. 595 (N.I. 4), art. 1(2), and the Northern Ireland Act 1974 (c.28), Sched. 1, para. 2(1); brought art. 116 of and para. 8(1) of Sched. 4 to the 1986 S.I. into operation on December 1, 1986.

MENTAL HEALTH (NURSES, GUARDIANSHIP, CONSENT TO TREATMENT AND PRESCRIBED FORMS) REGULATIONS (NORTHERN IRELAND) 1986 (No. 174) [£3·40], made under S.I. 1986 No. 595 (N.I. 4), arts. 7(3), 26, 63(1)(*b*), 64(1)(*a*), 135(1); operative on July 31, 1986; deal with the exercise of compulsory powers in respect of persons liable to be detained in hospital or subject to guardianship under the 1986 S.I.

MENTAL HEALTH (PAYMENT OF FEES) (AMENDMENT) REGULATIONS (NORTHERN IRELAND) 1986 (No. 96) [45p], made under the Mental Health Act (Northern Ireland) 1961 (c.15), ss.90, 112, and the Administrative and Financial Provisions Act (Northern Ireland) 1962 (c.7), s.18; operative on May 26, 1986; increase with effect from June 1, 1985, the fees for consultant or specialist work and for medical work other than consultant or specialist work payable to medical practitioners for recommendations made under ss.12, 15 and 21 of the 1961 Act; revoke the 1985 (no. 98) Regulations.

MENTAL HEALTH REVIEW TRIBUNAL (NORTHERN IRELAND) RULES 1986 (No. 193) [£2·40], made under S.I. 1986 No. 595, art. 83; operative on July 31, 1986; provide a new code of procedure to be followed in proceedings before the Mental Health Review Tribunal; revoke the 1962 (No. 69) Rules.

2394. Mental health—Mental Health (Northern Ireland) Order 1986 (S.I. 1986 No. 595 (N.I. 4))

This Order consolidates with amendments and repeals the Mental Health Act (Northern Ireland) 1961 and amending provisions. It makes provision with respect to the detention, guardianship, care and treatment of patients suffering from mental disorder and for the management of the property and affairs of such patients.

The Order comes into operation on days to be appointed.

2395. Mining law

MINERAL DEVELOPMENT (APPLICATIONS, FEES AND MODEL CLAUSES) (AMENDMENT) REGULATIONS (NORTHERN IRELAND) 1986 (No. 152) [45p], made under the Mineral Development Act (Northern Ireland) 1969 (c.35), s.49(1); operative on July 1, 1986; amend fees payable or refundable for certain licences, leases, permissions and permits under the Act and limit the maximum area to which an application for a prospecting licence can relate; revoke the 1981 (No. 152) Regulations.

2396. Minors—adoption—refusal of consent by parents

[Adoption Act (Northern Ireland) 1967 (c.35), s.5(1)] The parties had two children before their marriage in April 1981 and three children born afterwards. H had a long criminal record and had served various terms of imprisonment. He had also used violence against W. All the children were made wards of court and were living with foster parents. The Health and Social Services Board applied for leave to place the children for adoption. H and W objected. *Held,* refusing the application, that (1) where parents do not give their consent to adoption, the court can only dispense with that consent on one of the grounds set out in s.5(1) of the Adoption Act (Northern Ireland) 1967, the only ground in this case being that the parents were withholding their consent unreasonably; (2) the provision in the last part of s.5(1) that the welfare of the child should be the paramount consideration relates to the power of the court to dispense with the consent of a parent after the court is satisfied as to one of the matters in s.5(1)(a) to (e); and (3) as H and W were now living in a satisfactory home, W was in steady employment and both were anxious to show that they could bring up the children properly, they were not withholding their consent unreasonably. The Board should embark on a programme of increased access to the children by H and W with the aim of enabling the children to return to live with H and W: E. B. (MINORS), *Re* [1985] 5 N.I.J.B. 1, Hutton J.

2397. Minors—adoption—wards of court

M, who was born in February 1984, was, in July 1984, committed to the care of a Health and Social Services Board under an order made by a juvenile court and was placed with foster parents. D, who was born in May 1985, was also taken into care and placed with foster parents. The Board applied for an order that the two children be confirmed as wards of court and that leave be given for them to be placed for adoption. *Held,* granting the application, that (1) it was in the best interests of the children that the foster parents should be encouraged to adopt them and the giving of the leave sought would encourage the foster parents to do so; and (2) if the natural parents objected to the adoption the dispute would, in effect, be between the natural parents and the Board and not between the natural parents and the foster parents: M. McC. and D. H., *Re,* [1986] 5 N.I.J.B. 1, Hutton J.

2398. Minors—wards of court—jurisdiction

In August 1984 a magistrates' court ordered, by consent, that custody of three children be given to their mother and that access to them be given to their father. In February 1985 the father applied to the High Court for an order that the children be confirmed as wards of court and that he be given their custody. *Held,* refusing the application, that, as the question of the custody of and access to the children was properly before a magistrates' court, the application should have been made to the magistrates' court for a variation of its order: D. MINORS, *Re,* [1986] 5 N.I.J.B. 19, Hutton J.

2399. Minors—wardship—care and control

M. who was born in Northern Ireland, married F, an American citizen, in 1974. After a year in London they moved to America where T was born in 1977. M and F separated in 1981 and in 1985 an American court, which had earlier given an interlocutory judgment of dissolution of the marriage, awarded custody of T to M. M sent T to stay with her sister, Mrs. McK, in Northern Ireland. Mr. and Mrs. McK for various reasons formed the view that T was emotionally disturbed. T became so upset when she heard that F was coming to visit her that Mrs. McK sought help from the Social Services. T was referred to a doctor who sent her to a special unit of Doctor Barnardo's Homes. Mr. and Mrs. McK felt that T needed a period of stability to continue with her treatment in Northern Ireland and applied for an order making T a ward of court. *Held*, that it was in T's best interests that she should return to live with M in America as M had always shown a well-balanced concern for T's welfare and as T might never derive anything of benefit from her treatment in Northern Ireland. Leave was given to take T out of the jurisdiction: C (A Minor), *Re* [1985] 13 N.I.J.B. 1, Hutton J.

2400. National health

Charges for Drugs and Appliances (Amendment) Regulations (Northern Ireland) 1986 (No. 68) [40p], made under S.I. 1972 No. 1265, arts. 98, 106, 107, Sched. 15; operative on April 1, 1986; increase charges for certain drugs and appliances and the sums prescribed for prepayment certificates of exemption.

General Medical and Pharmaceutical Services (Amendment) Regulations (Northern Ireland) 1986 (No. 65) [40p], made under S.I. 1972 No. 1265 (N.I. 14), arts. 56(2), 63(2), 106, 107(6); operative on April 1, 1986; amend the list of drugs and other substances for which a doctor may not issue a prescription for supply under pharmaceutical services and which may not be dispensed under those services.

General Medical and Pharmaceutical Services (Amendment) (No. 3) Regulations (Northern Ireland) 1986 (No. 289) [45p], made under S.I. 1972 No. 1265 (N.I. 14), arts. 56(2), 63(2), 106, 107(6); operative on April 1, 1987, save for reg. 2(a)(b) which is operative on October 1, 1986; amend the list of drugs for which a doctor may not issue a prescription for supply under pharmaceutical services and which may not be dispensed under those services.

General Medical and Pharmaceutical Services (Amendment) (No. 2) Regulations (Northern Ireland) 1986 (No. 170) [45p], made under S.I. 1972 No. 1265 arts. 56(2), 63(2), 106, 107(6); operative on July 1, 1986; amend the list of drugs and other substances in the 1973 (No. 421) Regulations for which a doctor may not issue a prescription and which may not be dispensed under pharmaceutical services.

General Ophthalmic Services Regulations (Northern Ireland) 1986 (No. 163) [£2·40], made under S.I. 1972 No. 1265 (N.I. 14), arts. 62, 95, 98, 106, 107(6), and S.I. 1984 No. 1158 (N.I. 8), art. 18(1); operative on July 1, 1986; provide for arrangements for general ophthalmic services under the Health Service.

Medical Practitioners (Vocational Training) (Amendment) Regulations (Northern Ireland) 1986 (No. 69) [40p], made under S.I. 1978 No. 1907 (N.I. 26), art. 8; operative on August 1, 1986; amend the 1979 (No. 460) Regulations by substituting an annual date by which a post may be approved as an educationally approved post for the purpose of training a practitioner in the provision of general medical services; revoke the 1981 (No. 205), 1982 (No. 210), 1983 (No. 383) and 1984 (No. 405) Regulations.

Medical Practitioners (Vocational Training) (Amendment No. 2) Regulations (Northern Ireland) 1986 (No. 309) [45p], made under S.I. 1978 No. 1907 (N.I. 26), art. 8; operative on October 20, 1986; amend the 1979 (No. 460) Regulations in relation to the circumstances in which medical practitioners are exempt from the need to have acquired the prescribed medical experience.

Payments for Optical Appliances Regulations (Northern Ireland) 1986 (No. 164) [£1·90], made under S.I. 1972 No. 1265 (N.I. 14), arts. 62(2), 98, 106, 107(6), Sched. 15 and S.I. 1984 No. 1158 (N.I. 8), art. 18(1); operative on July 1, 1986; provide for payments to be made by the Central Services Agency and Health and Social Services Boards in respect of the cost incurred by certain categories of persons for the supply of optical appliances prescribed following a sight test under the health service.

Welfare Foods (Amendment No. 2) Regulations (Northern Ireland) 1986 (No. 357) [45p], made under the Welfare Foods Act (Northern Ireland) 1968 (c.26), s.1(3)(*b*); operative on January 4, 1987; amend the 1981 (No. 159) Regulations by increasing the amount which a supplier of welfare milk may be reimbursed for pasteurised milk.

2401. National health—Health and Personal Social Services (Amendment) (Northern Ireland) Order 1986 (S.I. 1986 No. 2023 (N.I. 20))

This Order applies the food legislation and the health and safety legislation to Health and Social Services Boards thereby removing from them Crown Immunity under that legislation, amends arrangements for pharmaceutical services and makes further provision with respect to the determination of the remuneration of persons providing general medical services, general dental services, general opthalmic services and pharmaceutical services.

The Order came into operation on January 26, 1987, save for arts. 3 and 4 which come into operation on March 1, 1987, and art. 5 which comes into operation on a day to be appointed.

2401a. National health—Health and Personal Social Services and Public Health (Northern Ireland) Order 1986 (S.I. 1986 No. 2229 (N.I. 24))

This Order amends health legislation in relation to the temporary provision of general medical services, medical and dental practitioners whose registration is suspended, payments for residential accommodation, the treatment of persons affected with an epidemic, endemic or infectious disease, the power of the Department of Health and Social Services to acquire land by agreement, the limit on guaranteed loan principal for loans to general medical practitioners, the offence of selling tobacco and related products to persons under the age of 16 and the removal to or detention in hospital of persons with notifiable diseases. The Northern Ireland Health and Social Services Council is dissolved and the Northern Ireland Staffs Council for the Health and Social Services is renamed as the Northern Ireland Health and Social Services Training Council.

The Order came into operation on February 17, 1987, save for art. 10 which comes into operation on a day to be appointed.

2402. Negligence—mortgage—premises partly defective

P purchased premises from D1 who was successor in title to D2. D2 had built an extension to the premises which it was claimed would have to be replaced as it was defective. P claimed that the plans for this extension were not in accordance with Building Regulations and that its construction was not carried out in accordance with those Regulations. D3, the Belfast City Council, was the responsible authority for building control, approval of plans, inspection of building construction and foundations. P's purchase was financed by a loan from D4, the Northern Ireland Housing Executive, which engaged a surveyor, D5, to carry out a survey of the premises. P believed that D4 had taken all proper steps to ascertain the condition of the premises and that D4 had at one time made an improvement grant to D2 in connection with the extension. A preliminary point was raised as to whether there was any cause of action against D4. *Held,* that (1) it was not D4's intention that P should accept the information comprised in its valuation of the premises or assessment of their condition rather than seeking his own advice and there was not a sufficient assumption of responsibility for that information to give rise to a duty of care; and (2) it was not one of D4's functions to protect against loss the successors in title of recipients of grants when exercising its statutory duty of paying out such grants. There was, accordingly, no cause of action against D4: CURRAN v. NORTHERN IRELAND CO-OWNERSHIP HOUSING ASSOCIATION [1985] 8 N.I.J.B. 22, Carswell J.

2403. Negligence—personal injuries—cause of accident—one defendant convicted of careless driving

P and D3, two motor cyclists, taking a bend in a road too fast, strayed over to their wrong side of the road and P collided with a car coming in the opposite direction driven by D1 and owned by D2. P on seeing the car had attempted to return to his own side of the road but D3 remained close to his wrong side of the road and passed safely between the car and his right hand side of the road. D3 was convicted of careless driving. P's claim for damages was dismissed when the jury found that neither D1 nor D3 was guilty of negligence. P appealed against the decision in favour of D3. *Held,* allowing the appeal, that (1) the trial judge in his charge to the jury had not failed to give sufficient weight to the possible blame attaching to D3; but (2) it was the presence of both P and D3 on the road and the breach of their duty of care to other road users which caused D1 to brake sharply and his car to slide. A new trial was ordered between P and D3: LAFFEY *v.* McCLOSKEY [1986] 1 N.I.J.B. 9, C.A.

2404. Negligence—personal injuries—series of cases—whether action should be tried with a jury

[Judicature (Northern Ireland) Act 1978 (c.23), s.62(2).] P claimed damages for hearing loss induced by exposure to excessive industrial noise while working for D. The action was set down for trial with a jury but D applied for an order under s.62(2) of the Judicature (Northern Ireland) Act 1978 that the action should be tried without a jury. This was one of five similar cases where the defendants applied for similar orders. The trial judge found that, while the trial of the action would require technical or scientific investigation when the meaning of s.62(2)(*b*) of the 1978 Act, he was not satisfied that a jury would be unable to understand the evidence but that for the special reason that it was desirable in the interests of justice that there should continue to be some degree of uniformity in the amounts of damages awarded in a series of similar cases the action was unsuitable to be tried with a jury. *Held,* dismissing P's appeal, that the court would not interfere with the exercise of the trial judge's discretion in favour of a non-jury trial: COUBROUGH *v.* SHORT BROTHERS [1985] 13 N.I.J.B. 20, C.A.

2405. Negligence—personal injuries—street lights not operating

P suffered personal injuries when in the darkness she tripped over an obstacle on a public footpath. The street lighting was not operating and had not operated for four days. On a preliminary point of law D argued that where a public authority had a discretionary power to light a public highway, negligence does not arise unless the authority acted *ultra vires* the power. This was accepted by the county court judge who found that the authority had not acted *ultra vires* the power. *Held,* on appeal by way of case stated that, as P could succeed if she could show that the public authority was guilty of operational negligence or had made a very unreasonable policy decision or that the obstacle had been placed on the footpath by the authority or its servants or agents, the case should be remitted to the county court for a hearing on the merits: CHAMBERS *v.* DEPARTMENT OF THE ENVIRONMENT [1985] 3 N.I.J.B., 88, C.A.

2406. Northern Ireland Act 1974

NORTHERN IRELAND ACT 1974 (INTERIM PERIOD EXTENSION) ORDER 1986 (No. 1047) [45p], made under the Northern Ireland Act 1974 (c.28), s.1(4); operative on June 23, 1986; extends to July 16, 1987, the operation of the temporary provisions for the government of Northern Ireland contained in Sched. 1 to the 1974 Act.

2407. Northern Ireland Assembly

NORTHERN IRELAND ASSEMBLY (ALLOWANCES) (VARIATION) ORDER 1986 (No. 222) [40p], made under the Northern Ireland Constitution Act 1973 (c.36), s.26(2) (2A)(6); operative on February 12, 1986, amends S.I. 1984 No. 1823 by increasing allowances in respect of the use of a motor vehicle.

2408. Northern Ireland (Emergency Provisions) Act 1978—continuance

NORTHERN IRELAND (EMERGENCY PROVISIONS) ACT 1978 (CONTINUANCE) (NO. 2) ORDER 1986 (No. 1146) [45p], made under the Northern Ireland (Emergency Provisions) Act 1978 (c.5), s.33(3)(*a*); operative on July 25, 1986; continues the 1978 Act in force for a further six months.

2409. Nuisance—contempt of court—committal

Following frequent breaches of an injunction restraining D from so operating his business as to cause a nuisance by reason of the emission of offensive smells, an order was made committing D to prison if he did not within eight weeks cease to carry on his business. The period of eight weeks was extended until the determination of an appeal. *Held,* dismissing the appeal, that as it was more than two years since D consented to the injunction he had had sufficient time to abate the nuisance. The period was, however, extended to June 7, 1986, to enable D to comply with the injunction: P. J. HOLDINGS *v.* GILROY [1986] 3 N.I.J.B. 100, C.A.

2410. Pensions and superannuation

HEALTH AND PERSONAL SOCIAL SERVICES (INJURY BENEFITS) (AMENDMENT) REGULATIONS (NORTHERN IRELAND) 1986 (No. 151) [£1·40], made under S.I. 1972 No. 1073

(N.I. 10), arts. 12, 14, Sched. 3; operative on July 9, 1986; make miscellaneous amendments to the 1975 (No. 85) Regulations.

LOCAL GOVERNMENT (SUPERANNUATION) (AMENDMENT) REGULATIONS (NORTHERN IRELAND) 1986 (No. 294) [£2·40], made under S.I. 1972 No. 1073 (N.I. 10), arts. 9, 14(1); operative on November 1, 1986; make miscellaneous amendments to the 1981 (No. 96) Regulations.

OCCUPATIONAL PENSIONS (REVALUATION) ORDER (NORTHERN IRELAND) 1986 (No. 356) [45p], made under S.I. 1975 No. 1503 (N.I. 15), art. 53A(1); operative on January 1, 1987; specifies three per cent. as the revaluation percentage for the 1986 revaluation period.

OCCUPATIONAL PENSION SCHEMES (MISCELLANEOUS AMENDMENTS) REGULATIONS (NORTHERN IRELAND) 1986 (No. 362) [80p], made under S.I. 1975 No. 1503, art. 53C, Sched. 1A, para. 13, Sched. 3, paras. 9(2), 20, 21; operative on January 5, 1987; make miscellaneous textual amendments to the 1984 (No. 332) and 1985 (Nos. 356 and 358) Regulations.

PENSIONS INCREASE (REVIEW) ORDER (NORTHERN IRELAND) 1986 (No. 213) [£1·40], made under S.I. 1975 No. 1503 (N.I. 15), art. 69(1)(2)(5); operative on July 28, 1986; provides for increases in the rates of public service pensions.

PENSIONS (PRESERVATION OF BENEFITS) (AMENDMENT) ORDER (NORTHERN IRELAND) 1986 (No. 155) [45p], made under S.I. 1975 No. 1503 (N.I. 15), art. 61; operative on October 1, 1986; expands the definition of "full rate" in art. 2 of the 1977 (No. 167) Order to allow a judicial office holder's preserved pension to be calculated by reference to his last salary before retirement.

ROYAL ULSTER CONSTABULARY PENSIONS (LUMP SUM PAYMENTS TO WIDOWS) REGULATIONS 1986 (No. 278) [45p], made under the Police Act (Northern Ireland) 1970 (c.9), s.25; operative on December 1, 1986; provide for the payment of a gratuity of £10 to certain policemen's widows.

ROYAL ULSTER CONSTABULARY PENSIONS (WAR SERVICE) (TRANSFEREES) REGULATIONS 1986 (No. 200) (£2·40], made under the Police Act (Northern Ireland) 1970 (c.9), s.25; operative on August 1, 1986, with effect from April 1, 1978; make provision for certain members and former members of the R.U.C. who have been unable to reckon their war service for pension purposes.

ULSTER SPECIAL CONSTABULARY PENSIONS (LUMP SUM PAYMENTS TO WIDOWS) REGULATIONS 1986 (No. 279) [45p], made under the Special Constables Act 1914 (c.61), s.1, and the Constabulary (Pensions) Act (Northern Ireland) 1949 (c.9), s.4(4); operative on December 1, 1986; provide for the payment of a gratuity of £10 to certain widows of former members of the Ulster Special Constabulary.

2411. Police

POLICE CADETS (AMENDMENT No. 2) REGULATIONS (NORTHERN IRELAND) 1985 (No. 368) [40p], made under the Police Act (Northern Ireland) 1970, s.10; operative on February 1, 1986; increase the pay of police cadets from September 1, 1985, and the annual charge payable by cadets for board and lodging from February 1, 1986.

ROYAL ULSTER CONSTABULARY (AMENDMENT No. 3) REGULATIONS 1985 (No. 362) [80p], made under the Police Act 1970, s.25; operative on February 1, 1986; increase the pay and allowances of police officers.

POLICE CADETS (AMENDMENT) REGULATIONS (NORTHERN IRELAND) 1986 (No. 315) [45p], made under the Police Act (Northern Ireland) 1970, s.10; operative on December 1, 1986, save for reg. 3 which came into operation on September 1, 1986; increase the pay of cadets and the annual charge payable by cadets for board and lodging.

ROYAL ULSTER CONSTABULARY (AMENDMENT) REGULATIONS 1986 (No. 118) [80p], made under the Police Act (Northern Ireland) 1970 (c.9), s.25; operative on June 1, 1986; amend the 1984 (No. 62) Regulations in relation to removal allowances and compensatory leave.

ROYAL ULSTER CONSTABULARY (AMENDMENT No. 2) REGULATIONS 1986 (No. 284) [80p], made under the Police Act (Northern Ireland) 1970 (c.9), s.25; operative on October 1, 1986, save for reg. 11 which is operative on April 1, 1987; amend the 1984 (No. 62) Regulations in relation to annual leave, overtime and allowances.

ROYAL ULSTER CONSTABULARY (AMENDMENT No. 3) REGULATIONS 1986 (No. 314) [80p], made under the Police Act (Northern Ireland) 1970 (c.9), s.25; operative on December 1, 1986, save for regs. 3 and 4 which came into operation on September 1,

1986; increase the rates of pay for members of the Constabulary not higher in rank than chief superintendent and increase the dog handler's allowance.

ROYAL ULSTER CONSTABULARY (DISCIPLINE AND DISCIPLINARY APPEALS) (AMENDMENT) REGULATIONS 1985 (No. 359) [80p], made under the Police Act (Northern Ireland) 1970 (c.9), s.25; operative on February 1, 1986; amend the 1977 (No. 236) Regulations in relation to the delegation of functions by the chief constable and to disciplinary boards.

2412. Practice

JUDGMENT ENFORCEMENT (AMENDMENT) RULES (NORTHERN IRELAND) 1986 (No. 361) [45p], made under S.I. 1981 No. 226, art. 141(1); operative on January 1, 1987; amends the 1981 rules (No. 147) to take account of the enforcement of judgments registered in the High Court under s.4 of the Civil Jurisdiction and Judgments Act 1982.

JUDGMENTS ENFORCEMENT (1981 ORDER (APPLICATION TO NON-MONEY FOREIGN JUDGMENTS) ORDER (NORTHERN IRELAND) 1986 (No. 360) [45p], made under S.I. 1981 No. 226 (N.I. 6), art. 5(1); operative on January 1, 1987, applies the 1981 S.I. to certain non-money judgments given outside Northern Ireland which are enforceable in Northern Ireland under the Civil Jurisdiction and Judgments Act 1982 (c.27).

JUDGMENT ENFORCEMENT FEES (AMENDMENT) ORDER (NORTHERN IRELAND) 1986 (No. 369) [45p], made under the Judicature (Northern Ireland) Act 1978 (c.23), s.116(1); operative on January 21, 1987; provides for a fee of £2·00 to be taken on an application for a search in the register of judgments.

LEGAL ADVICE AND ASSISTANCE (AMENDMENT) REGULATIONS (NORTHERN IRELAND) 1986 (No. 47) [40p], made under S.I. 1981 No. 228, arts. 14, 22(1); operative on March 12, 1986; amend the 1981 (No. 366) Regulations in relation to deductions to be made in respect of the maintenance of a spouse and of any dependent child or dependent relative for the purposes of calculating the disposable income of an applicant for legal advice and assistance.

LEGAL ADVICE AND ASSISTANCE (FINANCIAL CONDITIONS) REGULATIONS (NORTHERN IRELAND) 1986 (No. 241) [45p], made under S.I. 1981 No. 228, arts. 3(2)(3), 22(1); operative on September 1, 1986; increase the disposable capital limit of eligibility for assistance by way of representation under the 1981 S.I.

LEGAL AID (ASSESSMENT OF RESOURCES) (AMENDMENT) REGULATIONS (NORTHERN IRELAND) 1986 (No. 46) [40p], made under S.I. 1981 No. 228 (N.I. 8), arts. 14, 22(1); operative on March 12, 1986; amend the 1981 (No. 189) Regulations in relation to the deductions to be made in respect of the maintenance of a spouse and of any dependent child or dependent relative for the purposes of calculating the disposable income of an applicant for legal aid.

LEGAL AID (GENERAL) (AMENDMENT) REGULATIONS (NORTHERN IRELAND) 1986 (No. 210) [45p], made under S.I. 1981 No. 228 (N.I. 8), art. 22(1); operative on August 1, 1986; exclude the means and merits test and the contribution conditions which would otherwise apply under the 1981 S.I. in respect of persons who make applications under certain Conventions pursuant to ss.3(2) and 14(2) of the Child Abduction and Custody Act 1985 and who require legal aid in connection with those applications.

LEGAL AID (GENERAL) (AMENDMENT) (No. 2) REGULATIONS (NORTHERN IRELAND) 1986 (No. 346) [45p], made under S.I. 1981 No. 288 (N.I. 8), art. 22(1); operative on January 1, 1987; modify the 1965 (No. 217) Regulations in their application to the means and merits test and the contribution conditions in relation to the registration of certain foreign orders and judgments.

RULES OF THE SUPREME COURT (NORTHERN IRELAND) (AMENDMENT) 1986 (No. 128) [80p], made under the Judicature (Northern Ireland) Act 1978 (c.23), s.55; operative on September 1, 1986; amend the 1980 (No. 346) Rules in relation to medical evidence and reports in actions for damages in respect of personal injury or death and in relation to the reception in evidence at a trial of maps, plans, photographs and models.

RULES OF THE SUPREME COURT (NORTHERN IRELAND) (AMENDMENT No. 2) 1986 (No. 184) [£3·40], made under the Judicature (Northern Ireland) Act 1978 (c.23), s.55; operative on July 31, 1986; amend the 1980 (No. 346) Rules so as to introduce new provisions relating to the management of the property and affairs of patients in consequence of the Mental Health (Northern Ireland) Order 1986.

RULES OF THE SUPREME COURT (NORTHERN IRELAND) (AMENDMENT No. 3) RULES 1986 (No. 203) [£1·40], made under the Judicature (Northern Ireland) Act 1978 (c.23), s.55, and the Child Abduction and Custody Act 1985 (c.60), ss.10, 24; operative on August 1, 1986; amend the 1980 (No. 346) Rules to introduce a procedure for applications under the 1985 Act.

SUPREME COURT FEES (AMENDMENT) ORDER (NORTHERN IRELAND) 1986 (No. 232) [£1·40], made under the Judicature (Northern Ireland) Act 1978, s.116(1), and the Public Offices Fees Act 1879 (c.58), ss.2, 3; operative on July 31, 1986; amend the 1984 (No. 14) Order so as to increase the fee payable on sealing a writ of summons and other forms of originating process and the fee payable on an application by originating summons for wardship or adoption and so as to prescribe the fees payable in the Office of Care and Protection in relation to the affairs of patients.

2413. Practice—appearance—withdrawal

[R.S.C. (N.I.), Ord. 21, r.1.] Arising out of an accident in October 1974 in which P's property was damaged, P brought an action against D1, D2 and D3. The writ was issued in April 1979 but then served only on D1. In December 1983 it was served on D3 but, as it had not been renewed and as no appearance had been entered on D3's behalf, an order was obtained setting it aside as being out of time. In September 1985 D3's insurers instructed solicitors to act on D3's behalf and, as neither the insurers nor the solicitors knew that service of the writ had been set aside, the solicitors entered an appearance on D3's behalf. When they discovered that service of the writ had been set aside, they brought an application under R.S.C. (N.I.), Ord. 21, r.1, for leave to withdraw the appearance but this was refused by the Master. *Held,* allowing D3's appeal, that the entry of the appearance was due to a genuine misapprehension of fact on the part of the solicitors and the insurers and that this brought the case within the bounds of the court's discretion under r.1 of Ord. 21: BRADFORD *v.* DEPARTMENT OF THE ENVIRONMENT [1986] 3 N.I.J.B. 29, Carswell J.

2414. Practice—application for medical examination of defendant

P sued D for damages arising out of a motor accident. In the county court D successfully raised the defence that at the time of the accident he suffered from a black-out of which he had no warning. On P's appeal the Master ordered D to submit to a medical examination. D appealed from the Master's order. *Held,* disallowing the appeal, that the court had power to direct that a defendant should submit to a medical examination and that on the evidence such an examination was necessary to ensure justice between the parties: HERBINSON *v.* O'NEILL [1985] 3 N.I.J.B., 84, O'Donnell L.J.

2415. Practice—compromise of action—repudiation before approval by court

[R.S.C. (N.I.) Ord. 80, r.8] P, a minor, brought proceedings against D for damages. The action was compromised by agreement between counsel for P and D with the consent of P's next friend. The next friend resiled from the agreement before its approval by the court. *Held,* that under R.S.C. (N.I.), Ord. 80, r.8 the agreement was not valid without the approval of the court and, until it was so approved, the parties were entitled to resile from it: DUFFY *v.* MACLARON [1985] 6 N.I.J.B. 1, O'Donnell L.J.

2416. Practice—costs—taxation

Following an action for damages heard before a judge and jury in which P was awarded £600 and an appeal which was settled before the hearing for £10,000, the costs were taxed on a party and party basis, P's costs against the legal aid fund being taxed on the common fund basis. The Taxing Master allowed £600 for the instructions and preparation for trial of the action and £400 for the appeal. In arriving at the figure of £600 he allowed the sum of £20 per hour as the cost of having the work done by a person of suitable skill and experience. *Held,* on an application for review of items in the bill of costs, that (1) the court was entitled to review questions solely relating to quantum; (2) the Taxing Master was correct in declining to allow a higher figure as a recompense for the trouble in explaining the case to a difficult client; (3) the Taxing Master was incorrect in refusing to take account of the Belfast Solicitors' Association guide; (4) the costs were substantially out of line with those which a solicitor would receive for county court work; and (5) the sum of £600 should be increased to £750 and the sum of £400 to £500: THOMPSON *v.* DEPARTMENT OF THE ENVIRONMENT [1986] 3 N.I.J.B. 73, Carswell J.

2417. Practice—costs—unsuccessful legally-assisted party

[Legal Aid, Advice and Assistance (Northern Ireland) Order 1981 (S.I. 1981 No. 228 (N.I. 8)), art. 16.] P sued D for damages in respect of a personal injury and his claim was dismissed by the Recorder. His appeal was also dismissed, costs being awarded to D, but, as P was legally assisted, it was ordered that there should be no execution for costs without the leave of the court. D applied under art. 16 of the Legal Aid, Advice and Assistance (Northern Ireland) Order 1981 for an order that the costs of the appeal be paid out of the legal aid fund. *Held*, refusing the application, that, even after losing at first instance, P had an arguable case, the result of which depended on the appellate court's opinion on a question of fact and degree and that the appeal involved a rehearing in the literal and not merely the technical sense: THOMPSON *v.* CITY OF BELFAST YOUNG MEN'S CHRISTIAN ASSOCIATION [1986] 5 N.I.J.B. 29, Lord Lowry L.C.J.

2418. Practice—Judgments Enforcement (Amendment) (Northern Ireland) Order 1986 (S.I. 1986 No. 1166 (N.I. 11))
This Order allows the clerical and administrative costs of institutional garnishees (such as banks or building societies), in complying with an attachment of debts order made by the Enforcement of Judgments office, to be deducted from the debt which is the subject of the order. The order comes into operation on September 9, 1986.

2419. Practice—Legal Advice and Assistance (Amendment) (Northern Ireland) Order 1986 (S.I. 1986 No. 1167 (N.I. 12))
This Order enables the Lord Chancellor by regulation to prescribe different sums as the disposable capital limit on eligibility for legal advice and assistance and for legal assistance by way of representation.
The Order came into operation on July 30, 1986.

2420. Practice—personal injury—complicated medical evidence—whether action should be heard by a judge alone
[Judicature (Northern Ireland) Act 1978 (c.23), s.62(2); R.S.C. (N.I.), Ord. 33, r.4] P, a minor, sustained serious personal injury while undergoing an operation under general anaesthetic for the removal of his appendix. He claimed damages against D1, the surgeon, D2, the anaesthetist, and D3, the Health and Social Services Board. D2 set down the action for trial without a jury. P applied under R.S.C. (N.I.), Ord. 33, r.4, for an order that the action be tried with a jury. *Held*, refusing the application, that (1) it was for the party seeking a trial without a jury to establish that a jury would be unlikely to be able to comprehend the evidence; (2) the defendants had established that the trial would require a technical or scientific investigation, within the meaning of s.62(2) of the Judicature (Northern Ireland) Act 1978, which could not conveniently be made with a jury; and (3) where the issue of medical negligence is being determined by a judge alone it would be contrary to the interests of justice to require the issue of damages to be heard by a jury and unfair to the defendants to require two trials (*Monteith* v. *Western Health and Social Services Board* [1985] 6 C.L. 252 followed): KELLY *v.* QUARTEY-PAPAFIO [1985] 5 N.I.J.B. 84, Hutton J.

2421. Practice—personal injury—interrogatories
[Statute of Limitations (Northern Ireland) 1958 (c.10), ss.9A, 9D] In an action by P for damages for personal injury caused by exposure to dust when employed by D, the Master gave D liberty to administer interrogatories to P seeking the source of P's first knowledge that his injury was significant and was attributable to D's negligence. *Held*, disallowing P's appeal, that the interrogatories were necessary to dispose fairly of the matter as the information sought was required by D to enable it to determine whether or not the claim was brought within the three-year period provided by s.9A of the Statute of Limitations 1958 and to enable it to counter any application made under s.9D of the Statute for the disapplication of s.9A: McMULLAN *v.* HARLAND AND WOLFF [1985] 4 N.I.J.B., 11, Murray J.

2422. Practice—security for costs
P brought an action in the Republic of Ireland against D for libel in a newspaper which circulated both in the Republic and in Northern Ireland. Judgment was given for D and P's appeal to the Supreme Court in the Republic was unsuccessful. D furnished a bill of costs totalling IR £50,389 for the High Court proceedings and IR £44,511 for the Supreme Court proceedings. P then brought an action in the Northern Ireland High Court claiming damages for the same libel. The Master ordered P to lodge £3,000 as security for D's costs. D applied for further security. *Held*, that (1) the court had a full discretion to vary the amount of the security to

meet the conditions prevailing at the time of the application; (2) taking into account the likelihood that P will succeed and the possibility that the application might stifle a genuine claim by P, the security should be increased; and (3) having regard to estimates of costs submitted by D, P should be ordered to provide further security of £20,000: DEIGHAN v. SUNDAY NEWSPAPERS [1985] 3 N.I.J.B., 18, Carswell J.

2423. Prisons—Board of Visitors—natural justice

P, a prisoner, was charged with an assault on a prison officer. The governor considered the charge and then referred it to the Secretary of State who delegated his authority to hear the matter to the Board of Visitors. When the Board comprising the chairman and another member met in March 1984 to consider the matter P asked for legal representation. To ascertain the seriousness of the offence the Board asked the injured officer to describe his injuries and as a result granted P legal assistance. The governor was also ordered to be legally represented and the meeting was then adjourned. When the adjourned hearing was held in August 1984 the Board was augmented by a third member and a representative of the Prison Officers Association was allowed to attend as an observer. P's application to have the public and press admitted was refused. The Board found P guilty as charged and awarded 50 days cellular confinement of which 30 were suspended and 100 days loss of remission of which 50 were suspended. On receiving advice through the Governor that the power to suspend an award only permitted a suspension of the award in its entirety the hearing was re-convened and P was awarded 30 days cellular confinement suspended for six months and 140 days loss of remission. P applied for judicial review. *Held,* dismissing the application, that the proceedings did not infringe the rules of natural justice as (1) the March hearing merely determined the right to legal representation and the August hearing in which the third member took part was a complete hearing of every aspect of the substantive issue; (2) the representative of the Prison Officers Association did not take part in the deliberations or decision of the Board; (3) the governor would have been failing in his duty if he had not transmitted to the Board the advice which he had received about the nullity of the first award; and (4) even if P was not given a further opportunity to make representations about the second award this was in the circumstances of no substance or significance: McNALLY'S APPLICATION, *Re* [1985] 3 N.I.J.B., 1, Gibson L.J.

2424. Prisons—disciplinary award—judicial review—whether available

An application for judicial review of a disciplinary award made by a prison governor against P, one of his prisoners, was dismissed by the High Court which treated the question of availability as a preliminary issue. P appealed. *Held,* allowing the appeal, that (1) the proposition that the chief officer of a force governed by discipline ought not to be subject to the prerogative jurisdiction does not apply in relation to the disciplinary functions of a prison governor when hearing charges against prisoners, as prisoners do not belong to the disciplined body of which the governor is the superior officer; (2) there is no logical distinction between a disciplinary hearing by a prison governor and one by a Board of Visitors; and (3) it is reasonable and in the public interest that a prison governor when adjudicating on a charge against a prisoner should proceed according to natural justice and prison rules and unreasonable that he should enjoy freedom from High Court supervision: McKIERNAN'S APPLICATION, *Re* [1985] 6 N.I.J.B. 6, Lord Lowry L.C.J. and O'Donnell L.J.

2425. Prisons—disciplinary offence—legal representation—judicial review

[Prison Rules (Northern Ireland) 1982 (S.R. 1982 No. 170), r.34(2).] It was reported to the governor of a prison that H, one of the prisoners, had assaulted a prison officer. The governor after inquiry referred the matter to the Secretary of State who delegated his authority to the Board of Visitors. H's application for legal representation was refused. After holding an inquiry the Board found the charge against H proved and awarded him 60 days loss of privileges of which 30 were to be in cellular confinement. H applied for judicial review. *Held,* refusing the application, that (1) in rejecting H's application for legal representation, the Board had not acted contrary to the rules of natural justice as H was competent to conduct his own defence, as no points of law were likely to arise and as the charge was not a serious one; (2) there was nothing inherently wrong with the practice of witnesses reading statements of their evidence provided that a prisoner can fully absorb it; and (3) cellular confinement can, under r.34(2) of the Prison Rules (Northern Ireland) 1982, be awarded before it is certified that a prisoner is in a fit state to undergo it but the award cannot be implemented until it is so certified: HONE'S APPLICATION, *Re* [1985] 9 N.I.J.B. 96, Gibson L.J.

2426. Prisons—governor's inquiry—fair hearing—judicial review

A governor's inquiry was held to hear two charges against P, a prisoner. No copies were given in advance to P of the statements of evidence against him and written statements, which the Governor had previously seen, were read out at the inquiry by the witnesses. P was not given an opportunity to cross-examine the witnesses. P applied for judicial review. *Held*, refusing the application, that (1) there was no obligation to give copies of the witnesses' statements to P in advance; (2) the reading of the witnesses' statements did not impeach the fairness of the proceedings; (3) the failure to give P an opportunity to cross-examine was a defect in the proceedings but on the evidence as a whole no injustice was done and P had a full opportunity to hear what was alleged against him and to meet it: CROCKARD'S APPLICATION, *Re* [1985] 13 N.I.J.B. 69, Lord Lowry L.C.J.

2427. Prisons—restriction on visits—whether unreasonable

[Prison Rules (Northern Ireland) 1982 (No. 170), r.83.] It was proposed to restrict to two the number of visits to each prisoner during Christmas week. P applied for judicial review. *Held*, refusing the application, that (1) while unrestricted visits are the prima facie right of untried prisoners, under r.83 of the Prison Rules (Northern Ireland) 1982, such limits as the Secretary of State may direct may be imposed; (2) in imposing the limit of two the Secretary of State was acting within the legal ambit of his discretion; and (3) the court would not on the information given to it pronounce on the reasonableness or unreasonableness of the restriction: MULVENNA'S APPLICATION, *Re* [1985] 13 N.I.J.B. 76, Lord Lowry L.C.J.

2427a. Public entertainments and recreation—Recreation and Youth Service (Northern Ireland) Order 1986 (S.I. 1986 No. 2232 (N.I. 25))

This Order consolidates the law relating to recreation and youth service in Northern Ireland with amendments increasing the powers of the Sports Council and empowering the Department of Education to recover a share of any enhanced value of grant-aided facilities consisting of land or buildings.

The Order came into operation on February 17, 1987.

2428. Public health

PUBLIC HEALTH (FEE FOR NOTIFICATION OF INFECTIOUS DISEASE) REGULATIONS (NORTHERN IRELAND) 1986 (No. 185) [45p], made under the Public Health Act (Northern Ireland) 1967 (c.36), ss.2(4), 23(1), and the Administrative and Financial Provisions Act (Northern Ireland) 1962 (c.7), s.18; operative on August 4, 1986; increase the fee payable by a Health and Social Services Board to a medical practitioner for the notification of a case or suspected case of notifiable disease; revoke the 1984 (No. 374) Regulations.

SMOKE CONTROL AREAS (AUTHORISED FUELS) REGULATIONS (NORTHERN IRELAND) 1986 (No. 313) [45p], made under S.I. 1981 No. 158 (N.I. 4), art. 2(2); operative on December 1, 1986; prescribe "Geocite" as an authorised fuel for the purposes of the 1981 S.I.

2429. Railways

Orders made under the Transport Act (Northern Ireland) 1967 (c.37), s.66:
S.R. 1986 Nos. 7 (Cullybackey South) [£1·35]; 115 (Lurgan (Bells Row)) [£1·40].

2430. Rating and valuation

RATES (REGIONAL RATE) ORDER (NORTHERN IRELAND) 1986 (No. 78) [40p], made under S.I. 1977 No. 2157 (N.I. 28), arts. 7(1), 27(4); operative on May 1, 1986; fixes the regional rate for the year ending on March 31, 1987, and the amount by which it is to be reduced for dwelling-houses.

2431. Rating and valuation—Lands Tribunal decisions

ALLEN *v.* COMMISSIONER OF VALUATION, VR/58/1985 (successful appeal against the valuation of a two-storeyed detached villa built in 1927 or 1928, the valuation being reduced by £40 to take account of its disrepair as compared with the other comparables put in evidence).

2432.   BALLYMENA COURSING CLUB *v.* COMMISSIONER OF VALUATION, VR/11/1985 (of 50 acres of land owned by the Ballymena Coursing Club, 22 acres, which were surrounded by a post and wire fence, were used for hare coursing. A grandstand which contained three rooms one of which was used as a bar, was erected on these, 22 acres. The whole of the 50 acres was let in conacre to a member of the Club who used it to graze sheep. Hare coursing meetings lasting two days each were held twice a year and hares were trained during the fortnight before each meeting. *Held,* that the use of the 22 acres for hare coursing was use for a substantial part of the time and could not be disregarded under para. 4 of Sched. 1 to the Rates (Northern Ireland) Order 1977 and that the 22 acres were kept or preserved mainly for the sport of hare coursing).

2433.   FLANIGAN *v.* COMMISSIONER OF VALUATION, VR/71/1984 (successful appeal against a valuation of £2,100 for off-licensed premises in Falls Road, Belfast, the valuation being reduced to £1,900, as representing £450 for the net annual value of the premises as unlicensed premises plus £1,450 for enhancement due to the off-licence at 0·91 per cent. on a figure of £162,750 for turnover excluding non-alcoholic sales).

2434.   FLYNN *v.* COMMISSIONER OF VALUATION, VR/19/1985 (the upper two floors of a three-storeyed building in a retail shopping street were used for the manufacture of water beds and the ground floor for the sale of the beds. *Held* that, although there was a factory in the premises, there was one unified business and the premises were used as a retail shop).

2435.   LYLE *v.* COMMISSIONER OF VALUATION, VR/9/1984 (the ground floor of a lock-up shop in a secondary shopping street was used as a printing works by L. The shop window was obscured by a venetian blind and there was no counter or till. Only 5·6 per cent. of the total turnover represented cash sales. Most customers gave orders by telephone, by post or by orders canvassed by L. Members of the public at large were not invited or encouraged to resort to the premises. *Held,* that the premises were a factory and not primarily used and occupied for the purposes of a retail shop and, accordingly, were entitled to be distinguished in the Valuation List as an industrial hereditament).

2436.   MCATEER *v.* COMMISSIONER OF VALUATION, VR/16/1985 (successful appeal against a valuation of £960 for on-licensed premises in Rathfriland, Co. Down, the valuation being reduced to £830, being 2·6 per cent. on an estimated turnover of £32,000).

2437.   MCAULEY *v.* COMMISSIONER OF VALUATION, VR/2/1985 (the valuation of a detached bungalow was assessed at £450 and of this amount £70 was apportioned to facilities for the disabled. *Held,* that to allow for additional passage width, additional bathroom, central heating, motor house, hardstanding for the turning of a mini-bus to take the disabled person to school, and other matters, the amount apportioned to facilities for the disabled should be increased to £120).

2438.   MACKENZIE *v.* COMMISSIONER OF VALUATION, VR/19/1986 (successful appeal against the valuation of a house and motorhouse, the valuation being reduced by £1 to take account of partial central heating which was less effective than the partial central heating in a comparable house).

2439.   MAYES *v.* COMMISSIONER OF VALUATION, VR/34/1985 (successful appeal against a valuation of £64 for a terrace house in Olympia Drive, Belfast, the valuation being reduced to £57 to take account of a new stand in a football ground at the rear of the house which kept the house in shadow, created a smoke nuisance caused by down-draughts which did not exist before the erection of the stand and increased pedestrian traffic at the front of the house).

2440.   MOYLE DISTRICT COUNCIL *v.* COMMISSIONER OF VALUATION, VR/26/1984 (on an application by the Department of Education the valuations of two schools in the area of the Moyle District Council were reduced by applying a multiplier which consisted of a fraction where the numerator was the number of pupils enrolled in the school and the denominator was the permanent capacity calculated for that school. Both figures were supplied by the Department and the Education and Library Board. *Held,* restoring the original valuations, that the formula used by the Commissioner in his revision of the valuations was used without statutory authority or general agreement and was inaccurate and not reflective of the actual situation in the schools).

2441.   MULHOLLAND *v.* COMMISSIONER OF VALUATION, VR/48/1985 (M's appeal against a valuation of £1,430 in respect of the first floor of a building in Antrim which was used as a snooker hall was rejected by the Commissioner of Valuation on the ground that the property was capable of alternative commercial use in its present state without any structural alteration. *Held,* on appeal, that having regard both to comparable office accommodation and comparable snooker halls, the valuation should be reduced to £1,000).

2442. PALLIN *v.* COMMISSIONER OF VALUATION, VR/40/1985 (the valuation of a three-storeyed, semi-detached house was reduced from £240 to £215 having regard to comparable two-storeyed houses and end of terrace houses, there being no comparable three-storeyed, semi-detached houses in the area. Regard was also had to the fact that there was no room for a motor house and no access wide enough for a motor car).

2443. SOFTWARE IRELAND *v.* COMMISSIONER OF VALUATION, VR/21/1984 (premises were used by a company to make computer software products, programs being designed by the company's staff and keyed into blank disks. *Held,* that the premises were not occupied and used as a factory as the manual work done by a programmer was merely incidental to the creative, original and innovative process carried out).

2444. SWEENEY *v.* COMMISSIONER OF VALUATION, VR/38–45, 49–51, 53–65/1984 (these were appeals against the valuations of shops in a shopping centre in Ballymena, Co. Antrim. *Held,* that finalised assessments for other shops in the shopping centre were comparables in the same state and same circumstances and that shops in two other shopping centres were not comparable as those shopping centres were not close to the retail shopping centre of any town).

2445. WALKER *v.* COMMISSIONER OF VALUATION, VR/47/1985 (premises were occupied in part by a Member of Parliament for interviewing constituents and in part by a Senior Citizens Club for social purposes. *Held,* that the premises were not entitled to exemption as the evidence fell short of what was required to show that the Club used the premises for purposes declared to be charitable by the Recreational Charities Act (Northern Ireland) 1958 and as the Member of Parliament could not as an individual qualify as a body that is not established or conducted for profit).

2446. WILKINSON *v.* COMMISSIONER OF VALUATION, VR/51/1985 (the valuation of a solicitor's offices in Enniskillen was reduced from £590, which was based on the valuations of shops in the same street, to £455, which was based on comparables in the same state and circumstances used for the same category of use, *viz.* use as solicitor's offices and estate agent's and surveyor's offices).

2447. Rating and valuation—Rates (Amendment) (Northern Ireland) Order 1986 (S.I. 1986 No. 2024 (N.I. 21))
This Order enables a process for the recovery of rates in a court of summary jurisdiction to be served by ordinary post.
The Order came into operation on December 26, 1986.

2448. Real property and conveyancing
REGISTRATION OF DEEDS (FEES) ORDER (NORTHERN IRELAND) 1986 (No. 358) [80p], made under the Registration of Deeds Act (Northern Ireland) 1970 (c.25), s.16(1); operative on February 2, 1987; specifies the fees to be taken in respect of documents lodged for registration in the registry of deeds and for other matters done in that registry under the 1970 Act; revokes the 1981 (No. 104) Order.

2449. Real property and conveyancing—covenant—Lands Tribunal decision
MCMULLEN *v.* REPRESENTATIVE BODY OF THE CHURCH OF IRELAND, R/5/1985 (under a fee farm grant dated March 18, 1969, the Church granted to McM a former rectory and an adjoining field, McM covenanting not to erect any building on or to subdivide the premises without the written consent of the Church. McM applied to have this covenant extinguished. *Held,* refusing the application, that there had not been a change in the character of the neighbourhood since 1969 and that the covenant continued to secure a practical benefit to the Church. It was not necessary to decide whether the word "lease" in art. 5(2) of the Property (Northern Ireland) Order 1978 included a fee farm grant).

2450. Revenue and finance
CONTROL OF BORROWING (AMENDMENT) ORDER (NORTHERN IRELAND) 1986 (No. 17) [80p], made under the Loans Guarantee and Borrowing Regulation Act (Northern Ireland) 1946 (c.18), s.2(1)(2); operative on February 25, 1986; amends the 1962

(No. 187) Order in relation to the exemption from the controls contained in Pt. I of that Order.

ULSTER SAVINGS CERTIFICATES (FOURTH INDEX LINKED ISSUE) REGULATIONS 1986 (No. 244) [80p], made under the Exchequer and Financial Provisions Act (Northern Ireland) 1950 (c.3), s.15(1); operative on August 1, 1986; prescribe the terms governing the issue of Ulster Savings Certificates of the Fourth Index Linked Issue and the maximum number which a person may hold.

ULSTER SAVINGS CERTIFICATES (INDEX LINKED) (SUPPLEMENT) REGULATIONS 1986 (No. 176) (45p), made under the Exchequer and Financial Provisions Act (Northern Ireland) 1950 (c.3), s.15(1); operative on August 1, 1986; provide for the addition of a supplement to the amount repayable on Ulster Savings Certificates of the Index Linked Retirement and Second Index Linked Issues.

ULSTER SAVINGS CERTIFICATES (THIRTY-FIRST ISSUE) (AMENDMENT) REGULATIONS 1986 (No. 286) [45p], made under the Exchequer and Financial Provisions Act (Northern Ireland) 1950 (c.3), s.15(1); operative on September 1, 1986; increase the maximum permitted holding of Ulster Savings Certificates of the Thirty-first Issue.

ULSTER SAVINGS CERTIFICATES (THIRTY-SECOND ISSUE) REGULATIONS 1986 (No. 332) [45p], made under the Exchequer and Financial Provisions Act (Northern Ireland) 1950, s.15(1); operative on November 12, 1986; prescribe the terms governing the issue of Ulster Savings Certificates of the Thirty-second issue and the maximum number which a person may hold.

2451. Revenue and finance—Appropriation (Northern Ireland) Order 1986 (S.I. 1986 No. 593 (N.I. 2))
This Order authorises the issue out of the Consolidated Fund of Northern Ireland of a further sum for the year ended March 31, 1986, and of sums on account for the year ending on March 31, 1987, and appropriates those sums for specified services; also authorises the application of certain further sums as appropriations in and for the year ended March 31, 1986, and reduces certain sums already authorised to be applied as appropriations in aid.
The Order came into operation on March 26, 1986.

2452. Revenue and finance—Appropriation (No. 2) (Northern Ireland) Order 1986 (S.I. 1986 No. 1165 (N.I. 10))
This Order authorises the issue out of the Consolidated Fund of Northern Ireland of further sums for the year ended on March 31, 1985, and the year ending on March 31, 1987, and appropriates those sums for specified services; also authorises the application of certain sums as appropriations in aid for the year ending on March 31, 1987, and decreases a sum authorised to be so applied for the year ended on March 31, 1985.
The Order came into operation on July 8, 1986.

2452a. Revenue and finance—Appropriation (No. 3) (Northern Ireland) Order 1986 (S.I. 1986 No. 2227 (N.I. 22))
This Order authorises the issue out of the Consolidated Fund of Northern Ireland of a further sum for the year ending March 31, 1987, and appropriates that sum for a specified service. It also reduces one sum already authorised to be applied as an appropriation in aid.
The Order came into operation on December 16, 1986.

2453. Revenue and finance—Financial Provisions (Northern Ireland) Order 1986 (S.I. 1986 No. 2021 (N.I. 19))
This Order increases the limit on certain outstanding advances from the Consolidated Fund of Northern Ireland, abolishes various funds under the Exchequer and Financial Provisions Act (Northern Ireland) 1950 (c.3), doubles the sums and the percentage used in the calculation of registration fees for catering establishments and outside caterers and extends the powers of the Department of Finance and Personnel in relation to the Consolidated Fund with respect to overdrafts and investments.
The Order comes into operation on March 31, 1987, save for certain provisions which came into operation on January 26, 1987.

2454. Road traffic
FIXED PENALTY (INCREASE) ORDER (NORTHERN IRELAND) 1986 (No. 3) [40p], made under S.I. 1981 No. 154 (N.I. 1), art. 203(2); operative on February 17, 1986;

increases to £12·00 the fixed penalty for the offences to which art. 203 of the S.I. applies; revokes the 1982 (No. 76) Order.

GOODS VEHICLES (CERTIFICATION) (AMENDMENT) REGULATIONS (NORTHERN IRELAND) 1986 (No. 231) [80p], made under S.I. 1981 No. 154, arts. 53(3)(*h*), 54(1), 58(1), 218(1); operative on September 1, 1986; increase fees payable in connection with applications and re-applications for certificates for goods vehicles; revoke the 1985 (No. 191) Regulations.

HEAVY GOODS VEHICLES (DRIVERS' LICENCES) (AMENDMENT) REGULATIONS (NORTHERN IRELAND) 1986 (No. 368) [£1·40], made under S.I. 1981 No. 154 (N.I. 1), arts. 71(3)(*c*), 72(1), 75(1), 76, 214(1), 218(1); operative on February 9, 1987; further amend the 1981 (No. 240) Regulations.

LARGE PRIVATE PASSENGER VEHICLES (CERTIFICATION) (FEES) (AMENDMENT) REGULATIONS (NORTHERN IRELAND) 1986 (No. 230) [45p], made under S.I. 1981 No. 154, arts. 67(3), 69, 218(1); operative on September 1, 1986; increase fees payable in connection with applications and re-applications for inspections of large private passenger vehicles; revoke the 1985 (No. 193) Regulations.

MOTOR CYCLES (PROTECTIVE HEADGEAR) (AMENDMENT) REGULATIONS (NORTHERN IRELAND) 1986 (No. 238) [45p], made under S.I. 1981 No. 154, arts. 129(1)(3), 218(1); operative on September 1, 1986; amend the 1981 (No. 141) Regulations to take account of a new British Standard for protective helmets.

MOTOR VEHICLES (DRIVING LICENCES) (AMENDMENT) REGULATIONS (NORTHERN IRELAND) 1986 (No. 161) [45p], made under S.I. 1981 No. 154 (N.I. 1), arts. 18, 218(1); operative on July 14, 1986; amend the 1981 (No. 239) Regulations in relation to the alteration or defacement of driving licences, the classification of vehicles by reason of changed weight limit for motor tricycles and licences that can be surrendered for Northern Ireland driving licences.

MOTOR VEHICLE TESTING (FEES) (AMENDMENT) REGULATIONS (NORTHERN IRELAND) 1986 (No. 228) [45p], made under S.I. 1981 No. 154 (N.I. 1), arts. 33(2)(6), 35(3), 36(4), 218(1); operative on September 1, 1986; increase fees payable for motor vehicle and motor cycle tests and examinations and the fees payable on appeals; revoke the 1985 (No. 190) Regulations.

MOTOR VEHICLES (TYPE APPROVAL) (AMENDMENT) REGULATIONS (NORTHERN IRELAND) 1986 (No. 105) [£1·40], made under S.I. 1981 No. 154 (N.I. 1), arts. 31A(1), 31D(1), 218(1); operative on May 26, 1986; amend the 1985 (No. 294) Regulations in relation to certain standards and requirements.

PUBLIC SERVICE VEHICLES (AMENDMENT) REGULATIONS (NORTHERN IRELAND) 1986 (No. 33) [80p], made under S.I. 1981 No. 154 (N.I. 1), arts. 66(1), 70(4)(5), 218(1); operative on March 10, 1986; increases fees payable in respect of certain public service vehicle drivers' licences and make further provision with respect to badges to be worn by taxi drivers.

PUBLIC SERVICE VEHICLES (FEES) (AMENDMENT) REGULATIONS (NORTHERN IRELAND) 1986 (No. 229) [80p], made under S.I. 1981 No. 154, arts. 61(1), 66(1), 218(1); operative on September 1, 1986; increase fees payable in connection with applications and re-applications for licences for taxis; revoke the 1985 (No. 192) Regulations.

ROAD TRAFFIC ACCIDENTS (PAYMENT FOR TREATMENT) ORDER (NORTHERN IRELAND) 1986 (No. 123) [45p], made under the Public Expenditure and Receipts Act (Northern Ireland) 1968 (c.8), s.5, Sched. 3; operative on June 9, 1986; increases to £1,892·50 the maximum amount to be paid by an insurer or owner of a motor vehicle for hospital in-patient treatment of each road traffic casualty in respect of whose death or injury the insurer or owner has made a payment to which art. 99 of the 1981 S.I. applies; revokes the 1985 (No. 83) Order.

ROAD VEHICLES (REGISTRATION AND LICENSING) (AMENDMENT) REGULATIONS (NORTHERN IRELAND) 1986 (No. 706) [80p], made under the Vehicles (Excise) Act (Northern Ireland) 1972 (c.10 (N.I.)), ss.12, 23, 34, 37(1), Sched. 9, Pt. I, para. 20; operative on May 14, 1986; further amends S.R. & O. (N.I.) 1973 No. 490.

ROAD VEHICLES (REGISTRATION AND LICENSING) (AMENDMENT) (No. 2) REGULATIONS (NORTHERN IRELAND) 1986 (No. 1178) [45p], made under the Vehicles (Excise) Act (Northern Ireland) 1972 (c.10), ss.12, 23, 34, 37(1), Sched. 9, Pt. I, para. 20; operative on September 1, 1986; amend the 1973 (No. 490) Regulations to increase the fees for the issue of replacements for trade plates.

ROAD VEHICLES (REGISTRATION AND LICENSING) (AMENDMENT) (No. 3) REGULATIONS (NORTHERN IRELAND) 1986 (No. 2102) [80p], made under the Vehicles (Excise) Act

(Northern Ireland) 1972 (c.10), s.16(1)(3)(10); operative on January 1, 1987; amend the 1973 (No. 490) Regulations in relation to trade licences.

TRAFFIC SIGNS (AMENDMENT) REGULATIONS (NORTHERN IRELAND) 1986 (No. 173) [80p], made under S.I. 1981 No. 154, art. 27; operative on July 27, 1986; amend the 1979 (No. 386) Regulations.

VEHICLES (DRIVERS' HOURS OF DUTY) (AMENDMENT) REGULATIONS (NORTHERN IRELAND) 1986 (No. 162) [45p], made under S.I. 1981 No. 154, arts. 56(5), 58, 218(1); operative on July 14, 1986; amend the 1985 (No. 293) Regulations to exempt from the Regulations public service vehicles seating not more than eight passengers in addition to the driver.

Orders made under S.I. 1981 No. 154:

Art. 21(1): S.R. 1986 Nos. 4 (Londonderry) [80p]; 5 (Newtownabbey) [40p]; 6 (Belfast) [£1·85]; 13 (Holywood) [40p]; 20 (Londonderry) [40p]; 59 (waiting in lay-bys) [40p]; 62 (Dungannon) [40p]; 102 (Portadown) [45p]; 117 (Enniskillen) [80p]; 177 (Londonderry) [45p]; 215 (Omagh) [80p]; 243 (Portadown) [45p]; 282 (Cookstown) [45p]; 312 (Belfast) [45p].

Art. 22(1): S.R. 1986 Nos. 171 (Campsie) [45p]; 216 (Omagh) [45p]; 283 (Enniskillen) [45p].

Arts. 28(1) and 218(1): S.R. 1986 No. 267 (variation of maximum speed limits for certain vehicles) [45p]..

Art. 50(4): S.R. 1986 Nos. 148 (Cos. Armagh, Down and Tyrone) [£1·40]; 292 (Cos. Antrim, Armagh, Down and Londonderry) [£1·90]; 293 (Cos. Armagh and Down) [45p].

Art. 105(1), S.R. 1986 Nos. 197 (off-street parking) [£2·40]; 271 (Craigavon) [80p]; 298 (Belfast, Newtownabbey and Ballyclare) [£1·40].

2455. Road traffic—disqualification—suspension pending appeal

[Road Traffic (Northern Ireland) Order 1981 (S.I. 1981 No. 154 (N.I. 1)), art. 194(3)]. A magistrates' court disqualified H for driving and, without stating its reasons, refused him permission to drive pending appeal. H applied under art. 194(3) of the Road Traffic (Northern Ireland) Order 1981 for a suspension of the disqualification pending the hearing of an appeal. *Held,* granting the application, that suspension of a disqualification ought to be granted where the person disqualified has any chance of escaping disqualification on appeal and ought never to be refused without stating the reasons for the refusal: HAMILL'S APPLICATION, *Re* [1985] 8 N.I.J.B. 74, Lord Lowry, L.C.J.

2456. Road traffic—driving under the influence of drink—breath test—signing of consent—irregularities

[Road Traffic (Northern Ireland) Order 1981 (S.I. 1981 No. 154 (N.I. 1)), art. 146.] F was stopped by Constable S for speeding and was required by S to provide a specimen of breath as he suspected that F had been drinking. S sent for a breathalyser machine which arrived 41 minutes later. F then provided a specimen of breath which was over the permitted limit and signed a consent form in accordance with art. 146 of the Road Traffic (Northern Ireland) Order 1981. F was convicted. *Held,* allowing F's appeal, that (1) there was no evidence before the court that S was an authorised constable and no evidence that the device used for the breath test was an approved device; (2) failure to provide such evidence vitiated F's consent; and (3) the conviction would otherwise have been proper notwithstanding that the breathalyser was not available until 41 minutes after F was required to provide a specimen of breath: MOORE *v.* FINGLETON [1986] 2 N.I.J.B. 98, C.A.

2457. Road traffic—fun bike—whether intended or adapted for use on roads

[Road Traffic (Northern Ireland) Order 1981 (S.I. 1981 No. 154 (N.I. 1)), art. 2]. D was convicted by a magistrates' court of careless driving of a motor vehicle, namely a motorised tricycle commonly known as a fun bike, on the ground that even if it was intended primarily for use on rough terrain it was perfectly capable of being used on a road. D appealed by way of case stated. *Held,* allowing the appeal, that the fun bike was neither intended nor adapted for use on roads within the meaning of art. 2 of the Road Traffic (Northern Ireland) Order 1981: SYMINGTON *v.* McMASTER [1985] 8 N.I.J.B. 84, C.A.

2458. Road traffic—Road Races (Northern Ireland) Order 1986 (S.I. 1986 No. 1887 (N.I. 17))

This Order makes fresh provision with respect to the use of roads for motor races. The Order comes into operation on January 6, 1987.

2459. Sale of goods—consumer protection

PERAMBULATORS AND PUSHCHAIRS (SAFETY) REGULATIONS (NORTHERN IRELAND) 1986 (No. 37) [40p], made under the Consumer Protection Act (Northern Ireland) 1965 (c.14), s.1; operative on June 1, 1986; revoke the 1978 (No. 329) Regulations so far as they relate to pushchairs.

2460. Sale of goods—title—mercantile agent

[Factor's Act 1889 (c.45), s.9; Sale of Goods Act 1979 (c.54), s.25(1).] P sold catering equipment to C, the owner of a restaurant, the property in the goods not to pass until the purchase price was paid in full. Before the purchase price was paid C sold the restaurant including the catering equipment to D, no separate value being attributed to the equipment. In proceedings by P for the goods or their value D, relying on s.9 of the Factor's Act 1889 and s.25(1) of the Sale of Goods Act 1979, claimed that he had received the goods in good faith and without notice of P's title or other right to the goods. *Held,* awarding P the value of the goods, that the transaction did not in any way resemble a sale by a mercantile agent: MARTIN *v.* DUFFY [1985] 11 N.I.J.B. 80, Lord Lowry L.C.J.

2461. Settlements and trusts—variation

Under H's will his son R became entitled to the estate for life with remainder to his children or remoter issue as he should by deed or will appoint and in default of appointment to his children equally. If R died without issue, H's son W became entitled on similar trusts. If W died without issue, each of H's daughters became entitled on similar trusts. If these trusts failed H's sister and her issue became entitled to the estate. If any of H's sons or daughters entered a religious order or convent connected with the Roman Catholic Church, they forfeited their life interests under the will. R applied for approval of an arrangement varying the trusts so as to reduce the liabilities to capital transfer tax. *Held,* approving the arrangement with certain amendments, that the arrangement was for the benefit of the persons on whose behalf approval was sought, and that, although there were adults with contingent interests in the estate who were not parties to the application, approval could be given on behalf of R's minor grandson, W's two minor children and of H's daughters (other than the eldest) and their respective issue born and unborn: HALL *v.* MULLAN [1985] 4 N.I.J.B., 93, Murray J.

2462. Shipping and marine insurance

LOUGH ERNE (NAVIGATION) (AMENDMENT) BYE-LAWS (NORTHERN IRELAND) 1986 (No. 1) [£1·35], made under S.I. 1973 No. 69 (N.I. 1), art. 41, Sched. 7; operative on February 24, 1986; amend the 1978 (No. 43) Bye-laws in relation to licensing and registration requirements and other matters.

NORTHERN IRELAND FISHERY HARBOUR AUTHORITY (ACCOUNTS) REGULATIONS (NORTHERN IRELAND) 1986 (No. 51) [80p], made under the Harbours Act (Northern Ireland) 1970 (c.1), s.30(1)(4); operative on April 1, 1986; prescribe the form of, the particulars to be contained in and the method of compilation of the annual statement of accounts of the Northern Ireland Fishery Harbour Authority; revoke the 1977 (No. 122) Regulations.

2463. Social security

CHILD BENEFIT (UP-RATING) REGULATIONS (NORTHERN IRELAND) 1986 (No. 221) [45p], made under S.I. 1975 No. 1504 (N.I. 16), art. 7; operative on July 28, 1986; increase the weekly rates of benefit payable under the 1975 S.I.

FAMILY INCOME SUPPLEMENTS (COMPUTATION) REGULATIONS (NORTHERN IRELAND) 1986 (No. 202) [80p], made under the Family Income Supplements Act (Northern Ireland) 1971 (c.8), ss.2(1), 3(1)(1A), 10(2B); operative on July 29, 1986; increase prescribed amounts for the purposes of s.1(2) of the 1971 Act and the maximum weekly rates of family income supplements payable under the Act; revoke the 1985 (No. 209) Regulations.

FAMILY INCOME SUPPLEMENTS (GENERAL) (AMENDMENT) REGULATIONS (NORTHERN IRELAND) 1986 (No. 160) [45p], made under the Family Income Supplements Act (Northern Ireland) 1971 (c.8), s.4(2)(a); operative on July 1, 1986; amend the 1980

(No. 375) Regulations in relation to the amounts to be deducted in calculating or estimating a person's normal gross income.

HEALTH AND SOCIAL SECURITY (1984 ORDER) (COMMENCEMENT NO. 2) ORDER (NORTHERN IRELAND) 1986 (No. 169 (C.4)) [45p], made under S.I. 1984 No. 1158 (N.I. 8), art. 1(2), and the Northern Ireland Act 1974 (c.28), Sched. 1, para. 2(1); brought certain provisions of the 1984 S.I. into operation on July 1, 1986.

OCCUPATIONAL PENSION SCHEMES (CONTRACTING-OUT) (AMENDMENT) REGULATIONS (NORTHERN IRELAND) 1986 (No. 57) [80p], made under S.I. 1975 No. 1503 (N.I. 15), arts. 2(4), 40(1)–(1C), 44, 45(4)(6), 47(1), 48(9A), 53, Sched. 2, para. 6; operative on April 6, 1986; amend the 1985 (No. 259) Regulations so as to provide that where an earner's service in contracted-out employment by reference to a scheme is terminated on or after April 6, 1987, the person liable to pay any contributions equivalent premium or limited revaluation premium shall be the trustees of the scheme instead of the earner's employer and so as to specify cases in which trustees may recoup limited revaluation premiums from transfer payments.

OCCUPATIONAL PENSION SCHEMES (DISCLOSURE OF INFORMATION) REGULATIONS (NORTHERN IRELAND) 1986 (No. 225) [£2·40], made under S.I. 1975 No. 1503 (N.I. 15), arts. 2(5), 58A(1)(3)(4), 58E(1)(3)(4), 71(4), Sched. 1A, para. 14(3); operative on November 1, 1986; specify the information that is to be made available to certain persons, in certain circumstances, by the trustees of occupational pension schemes.

OCCUPATIONAL PENSION SCHEMES (MANAGERS) REGULATIONS (NORTHERN IRELAND) 1986 (No. 320) [45p], made under S.I. 1985 No. 1209 (N.I. 16), art. 7; operative on November 1, 1986; make provision as to who is to be treated as a manager of an occupational pension scheme which is a public service pension scheme.

OCCUPATIONAL PENSION SCHEMES (REVALUATION AND TRANSFER VALUES) (AMENDMENT) REGULATIONS (NORTHERN IRELAND) 1986 (No. 114) [45p], made under S.I. 1975 No. 1503 (N.I. 15), Sched. 1A, paras. 14, 20; operative on May 29, 1986; correct errors in the 1985 (Nos. 357 and 358) Regulations.

PNEUMOCONIOSIS, ETC., (WORKERS' COMPENSATION) (DETERMINATION OF CLAIMS) REGULATIONS (NORTHERN IRELAND) 1986 (No. 207) [80p], made under S.I. 1979 No. 925 (N.I. 9), arts. 3(2), 4(2), 6(2), 11(1); operative on August 18, 1986; prescribe the manner in which claims for payment must be made for determination under the 1979 S.I.; revoke the 1979 (No. 271) Regulations.

PNEUMOCONIOSIS, ETC., (WORKERS' COMPENSATION) (PAYMENT OF CLAIMS) REGULATIONS (NORTHERN IRELAND) 1986 (No. 208) [£1·90], made under S.I. 1979 No. 925, arts. 3(3), 4(3), 11(1)(4); operative on August 18, 1986; prescribe the amount of payments to be made under the 1979 S.I. to persons disabled by a disease to which the S.I. applies or to dependants of such persons who die while so disabled.

SOCIAL SECURITY ADJUDICATIONS (1983 ORDER) (COMMENCEMENT NO. 3) ORDER (NORTHERN IRELAND) 1986 (No. 363 (c.8)) [45p], made under S.I. 1983 No. 1524 (N.I. 17), art. 1(2), and the Northern Ireland Act 1974 (c.28), Sched. 1, para. 2(1); brings the remaining provisions of the 1983 S.I. into operation on April 6, 1987.

SOCIAL SECURITY BENEFIT (PERSONS ABROAD) (AMENDMENT) REGULATIONS (NORTHERN IRELAND) 1986 (No. 72) [40p], made under the Social Security (Northern Ireland) Act 1975, s.126; operative on April 6, 1986; amend the 1978 (No. 114) Regulations in relation to the Class 2 contributions paid by volunteer development workers.

SOCIAL SECURITY BENEFIT (PERSONS ABROAD) (AMENDMENT NO. 2) REGULATIONS (NORTHERN IRELAND) 1986 (No. 303) 45p], made under the Social Security (Northern Ireland) Act 1975 (c.15), ss.51(1), 126; operative on October 1 1986; amend the 1978 (No. 114) Regulations in relation to invalidity benefit and to persons who sustain an industrial accident or contract a prescribed disease outside Northern Ireland.

SOCIAL SECURITY BENEFITS UP-RATING ORDER (NORTHERN IRELAND) 1986 (No. 211) [£1·90], made under the Social Security (Northern Ireland) Act 1975 (c.15), s.120; operative on July 28, 1986; increases the rates and amounts of certain benefits and other sums.

SOCIAL SECURITY BENEFITS UP-RATING REGULATIONS (NORTHERN IRELAND) 1986 (No. 212) [80p], made under the Social Security (Northern Ireland) Act 1975, ss.17(1)(a), 58(3), 126, Sched. 14, para. 2(1); operative on July 28, 1986; make provision consequential on the 1986 (No. 211) Order and increase certain earnings limits; revoke the 1985 (No. 278) Regulations.

SOCIAL SECURITY (CLAIMS AND PAYMENTS, HOSPITAL IN-PATIENTS AND MATERNITY BENEFIT) (AMENDMENT) REGULATIONS (NORTHERN IRELAND) 1986 (No. 157) [£1·40], made under the Social Security (Northern Ireland) Act 1975 (c.15), ss.22(1), 27(4), 85(1), 154A(1); operative on June 30, 1986; amend the 1975 (Nos. 107 and 109) and the 1977 (No. 351) Regulations.

SOCIAL SECURITY (CONTRIBUTIONS) (AMENDMENT) REGULATIONS (NORTHERN IRELAND) 1986 (No. 71) [80p], made under the Social Security (Northern Ireland) Act 1975 (c. 15), s.126; operative on April 6, 1986; modify the 1975 Act and the 1979 (No. 186) Regulations in relation to the contributions payable by certain voluntary workers employed abroad.

SOCIAL SECURITY (CONTRIBUTIONS, RE-RATING) CONSEQUENTIAL AMENDMENT REGULA-TIONS (NORTHERN IRELAND) 1986 (No. 45) [40p], made under the Social Security (Northern Ireland) Act 1975 (c.15), s.124(1); operative on April 6, 1986, immediately after the coming into operation of the 1986 (No. 16) Order; amend the 1979 (No. 186) Regulations by increasing the special rate of Class 2 contributions payable by share fishermen.

SOCIAL SECURITY (CONTRIBUTIONS, RE-RATING) ORDER (NORTHERN IRELAND) 1986 (No. 16) [80p], made under the Social Security (Northern Ireland) Act 1975 (c.15), s.120; operative on April 6, 1986; increases the weekly earnings figures for primary and secondary earnings brackets, the rate of, and small earnings exception from, Class 2 contributions, the amount of Class 3 contributions and the lower and upper limits for Class 4 contributions.

SOCIAL SECURITY (INDUSTRIAL INJURIES AND ADJUDICATION) (MISCELLANEOUS AMENDMENTS) REGULATIONS (NORTHERN IRELAND) 1986 (No. 270) [80p], made under the Social Security (Northern Ireland) 1975, ss.76, 77, 113; operative on September 1, 1986; amend the 1986 (No. 179) Regulations in relation to occupational asthma and occupational deafness and amend the 1984 (No. 144) Regulations to remove certain restrictions on rights of appeal to a medical appeal tribunal.

SOCIAL SECURITY (INDUSTRIAL INJURIES) (PRESCRIBED DISEASES) REGULATIONS (NORTHERN IRELAND) 1986 (No. 179) [£3·80], made under the Social Security (Northern Ireland) Act 1975, ss.76, 77, 78, 113, 146, and S.I. 1982 No. 1084 (N.I. 16), art. 32(5); operative on July 28, 1986; consolidate and revoke the 1983 (No. 19) and amending Regulations.

SOCIAL SECURITY REVALUATION OF EARNINGS FACTORS ORDER (NORTHERN IRELAND) 1986 (No. 139) [45p], made under S.I. 1975 No. 1503, art. 23; operative on June 5, 1986; increases the earnings factors relevant to the calculation of the additional component in the rate of any long-term benefit or any guaranteed minimum pension or any other calculation required under Pt. IV of the 1975 S.I. for certain tax years.

SOCIAL SECURITY (UNEMPLOYMENT BENEFIT) AND SUPPLEMENTARY BENEFIT (AMEND-MENT) REGULATIONS (NORTHERN IRELAND) 1986 (No. 266) [80p], made under the Social Security (Northern Ireland) Act 1975 (c.15), s.17(2)(*a*), and S.I. 1977 No. 2156, art. 7; operative on September 1, 1986; further amend the 1981 (No. 371) and 1984 (No. 245) Regulations.

SOCIAL SECURITY (UNEMPLOYMENT, SICKNESS AND INVALIDITY BENEFIT) (AMENDMENT) REGULATIONS (NORTHERN IRELAND) 1986 (No. 82) [80p], made under the Social Security (Northern Ireland) Act 1975 (c.15), ss.15A, 16(1); operative on April 6, 1986; amend the 1984 (No. 245) Regulations in relation to the days which may be treated, for the purpose of entitlement to invalidity pension, as days of entitlement to sickness benefit and in relation to the qualifying date for entitlement to invalidity allowance.

SOCIAL SECURITY (UNEMPLOYMENT, SICKNESS AND INVALIDITY BENEFIT) (AMENDMENT No. 2) REGULATIONS (NORTHERN IRELAND) 1986 (No. 275) [45p], made under the Social Security (Northern Ireland) Act 1975 (c.15), s.17(2)(*a*); operative on November 3, 1986; provide that, in the case of a student attending a course of full-time education, a day falling within a period for which his maintenance grant or award is or would be payable, or during a vacation other than the summer vacation, shall not be treated as a day of unemployment.

STATUTORY SICK PAY (ADDITIONAL COMPENSATION OF EMPLOYERS) (COMPUTATION) REGULATIONS (NORTHERN IRELAND) 1986 (No. 64) [40p], made under S.I. 1982 No. 1084 (N.I. 16), art. 11(1A)(*a*); operative on April 6, 1986; reduce to 8 per cent. the percentage rate by reference to which is calculated the additional compensation to which an employer is entitled under reg. 2 of the 1985 (No. 257) Regulations in respect of payments of statutory sick pay made during the 1985/86 tax year.

STATUTORY SICK PAY UP-RATING ORDER (NORTHERN IRELAND) 1986 (No. 23) [40p], made under S.I. 1982 No. 1084 (N.I. 16), art. 9(3); operative on April 6, 1986; increases the sums specified in art. 9(1) of the S.I.

SUPPLEMENTARY BENEFIT (CLAIMS AND PAYMENTS) (AMENDMENT) REGULATIONS (NORTHERN IRELAND) 1986 (No. 365) [45p], made under S.I. 1977 No. 2156 art. 19(1)(2)(*i*); operative on January 26, 1987; amend the 1981 (No. 368) Regulations in relation to mortgage payments.

SUPPLEMENTARY BENEFIT (CONDITIONS OF ENTITLEMENT) (AMENDMENT) REGULATIONS (NORTHERN IRELAND) 1986 (No. 276) [45p]; made under S.I. 1977 No. 2156 (N.I. 27), art. 7; operative on November 3, 1986; amend the 1981 (No. 371) Regulations to insert a definition of "a course of advanced education" and to substitute a new definition of "student."

SUPPLEMENTARY BENEFIT (MISCELLANEOUS AMENDMENTS) REGULATIONS (NORTHERN IRELAND) 1986 (No. 262) [£2·90], made under S.I. 1977 No. 2156, arts. 4(1)(1A), 5, 6, 15, 19(1)(2)(*a*)(*c*)(*g*), 41(4); operative on August 11, 1986; further amend the 1980 (No. 417), 1981 (Nos. 369, 372) and 1984 (No. 144) Regulations.

SUPPLEMENTARY BENEFIT (REQUIREMENTS AND RESOURCES) (AMENDMENT) REGULATIONS (NORTHERN IRELAND) 1986 (No. 240) [£1·90], made under S.I. 1977 No. 2156, arts. 3(3), 4(1A), 41(3)(4), Sched. 1, paras. 1(2), 2(1)(3)(4); operative on July 28, 1986; make miscellaneous amendments to the 1983 (No. 61) and 1984 (No. 54) Regulations.

SUPPLEMENTARY BENEFIT (REQUIREMENTS AND RESOURCES) (MISCELLANEOUS AMENDMENTS) REGULATIONS (NORTHERN IRELAND) 1986 (No. 236) [£1·40], made under S.I. 1977 No. 2156, Sched. 1, paras. 1, 2; operative as to regs. 1, 2(1)(3) and 3(7) on July 28, 1986, as to reg. 2(2) on September 1, 1986, and as to regs. 3(1)–(6)(8) on November 3, 1986; amend the 1983 (No. 61) and 1984 (No. 54) Regulations to make provision for students.

SUPPLEMENTARY BENEFIT (SINGLE PAYMENTS) (AMENDMENT) REGULATIONS (NORTHERN IRELAND) 1986 (No. 345) [£1·40], made under S.I. 1977 No. 2156 (N.I. 27), arts. 5, 19(2)(*a*), operative on December 11, 1986; amend the 1981 (No. 369) Regulations to make new provision for payments in respect of fuel costs.

SUPPLEMENTARY BENEFIT UP-RATING REGULATIONS (NORTHERN IRELAND) 1986 (No. 223) [80p], made under S.I. 1977 No. 2156 (N.I. 27), Sched. 1, para. 2(1)(4); operative on July 28, 1986; increase certain amounts specified in the 1983 (No. 61) Regulations for the purposes of determining entitlement to supplementary benefit under the 1977 S.I.

2464. Social security—Social Security (Northern Ireland) Order 1986 (S.I. 1986 No. 1888 (N.I. 18))

This Order makes provision for personal pension schemes, amends the law relating to social security and occupational pension schemes, abolishes maternity pay and provides for the winding-up of the Northern Ireland Maternity Pay Fund and empowers the Department of Health and Social Services to pay certain travelling expenses in connection with social security.

The Order came into operation as to certain provisions on November 20, 1986, and as to the remaining provisions on days to be appointed.

2465. Social security—supplementary benefit—entitlement—full-time education

[Child Benefit (Northern Ireland) Order 1975 (S.I. 1975 No. 1504 (N.I. 16)), art. 4(1)(*b*); Supplementary Benefits (Northern Ireland) Order 1977 (S.I. 1977 No. 2156 (N.I. 27)), art. 9(3).] From September 28, 1982, until his nineteenth birthday on February 19, 1983, N attended the College of Business Studies which was a recognised educational establishment for the purposes of art. 4(1)(*b*) of the Child Benefit (Northern Ireland) Order 1975. He claimed supplementary benefit on the ground that he was not receiving full-time education. The Insurance Officer found that N was receiving relevant education within the meaning of art. 9(3) of the Supplementary Benefits (Northern Ireland) Order 1977 and rejected his claim. The Supplementary Benefits Appeal Tribunal dismissed his appeal but the Local Tribunal, allowing his further appeal, *held* that he was not receiving relevant education and this decision was affirmed by the Social Security Commissioner. *Held*, dismissing the Insurance Officer's appeal, that in calculating the hours devoted weekly to receiving full-time education at a recognised educational establishment, time spent on voluntary study or preparatory work either on or off the school premises should be disregarded: INSURANCE OFFICER *v.* NOLAN [1985] 12 N.I.J.B. 90, C.A.

2466. Tort—breach of confidence—vicarious liability—liability of Crown

[Crown Proceedings Act 1947 (c.44), s.2(1)(*a*).] P, a spinster, when she became pregnant, went in person to an office of the Department of Health and Social Services to apply for a maternity clothing grant. She later suffered a miscarriage. She did not tell her family or her friends of her pregnancy or miscarriage. Some time after she had applied for the grant, H asked her about her pregnancy stating that the girl in the Department who dealt with her application was his sister. It was not established whether the information given to H by his sister was given deliberately or accidentally. However, P was caused a material degree of distress and annoyance and claimed damages. *Held,* dismissing P's claim, that (1) on the facts proved the conditions had been met for a claim for breach of confidence; (2) if there was a cause of action for breach of confidence the Department was not vicariously liable as the information was not disclosed by H's sister in the course of her employment; and (3) the Department was not liable under s.2(1)(*a*) of the Crown Proceedings Act 1947 as it was not acting as an agent of the Crown in the sense intended by that section: O'NEILL *v.* DEPARTMENT OF HEALTH AND SOCIAL SERVICES [1986] 5 N.I.J.B. 60, Carswell J.

2467. Town and country planning

PLANNING (FEES) (AMENDMENT) REGULATIONS (NORTHERN IRELAND) 1986 (No. 296) [45p], made under S.I. 1972 No. 1634 (N.I. 17), art. 105A; operative on October 20, 1986; reduce the fee payable for applications and deemed applications for planning permission for the winning and working of peat.

PLANNING (GENERAL DEVELOPMENT) (AMENDMENT) ORDER (NORTHERN IRELAND) 1985 (No. 366) [£1·35], made under S.I. 1972 No. 1634 (N.I. 17), art. 13(1)(2)(3), and the Telecommunications Act 1984 (c.12), Sched. 4, para. 56(1); operative on February 10, 1986; adds two new classes dealing with telecommunications apparatus to Part I of Schedule 1 to the 1973 (No. 326) Order and amends class 12 of that Schedule which relates to development by the Post Office.

2468. Town and country planning—Lands Tribunal decision

MAGILTON *v.* DEPARTMENT OF THE ENVIRONMENT, LDV/4/1977 (M owned a 15 acre holding which included a quarry. In 1965 M leased 6 acres of this holding to S for quarrying purposes. In March 1967 planning permission for quarrying was restricted to one acre only. S abandoned his quarrying operations and he and M submitted claims for compensation. In 1970 the development value of the entire holding was determined at £1,200. In July 1977 the Department decided that compensation amounting to £962 out of the £1,200 development value was payable and that all of it was payable to S. M challenged the decision by letter dated September 22, 1977, to the Lands Tribunal but did not, as required by the Lands Tribunal Rules, send a copy to the Department. In November 1977 the Department paid over the whole of the compensation to S. *Held* that this was not an appropriate case for the exercise by the Tribunal of its discretion to put either or both of the parties on terms for the further conduct of the proceedings).

2469. Town and country planning—purchase notice—whether property incapable of reasonably beneficial use

[Planning (Northern Ireland) Order 1972 (S.I. 1972 No. 1634 (N.I. 17)) art. 70]. In October 1969 C, who intended to transfer his car business from Portadown to Belfast, acquired premises in Great Victoria Street, Belfast. From 1971 onwards it seemed likely that part of these premises would be required for road purposes and C abandoned his proposal to transfer his business to the new premises. As the threatened acquisition of the premises had an adverse effect on the quality and quantity of the existing tenancies of the premises and it was almost impossible to attract new long-term tenancies, C applied for planning permission to enlarge the premises and change their use. Permission was granted in June 1981 for a period of two years only. In December 1981 C served a purchase notice on the Department of the Environment under art. 70 of the Planning (Northern Ireland) Order 1972. The Department then served a counter notice objecting to the purchase notice on the grounds that part of the premises was in reasonably beneficial use and that, if the planning permission was acted upon, the premises would be capable of reasonably beneficial use. In May 1984 the Lands Tribunal upheld the purchase notice—see

[1984] C.L.Y. 2456. The Department appealed by way of case stated. *Held,* dismissing the appeal, that (1) "reasonably beneficial" means not only beneficial, in the sense that a benefit of some kind is derived, but reasonably beneficial, in the sense that a reasonable degree of benefit is to be derived; (2) the planning permission, although it did not specifically mention the top floor of the premises, and the purchase notice related to the entire premises but in any event, following *Essex County Council* v. *Essex Incorporated Congregational Church Union* [1963] C.L.Y. 3432, this point could not, as it had not been mentioned in the counter notice, be taken into account to invalidate the purchase notice: ALLEN v. DEPARTMENT OF THE ENVIRONMENT [1985] 8 N.I.J.B. 1, C.A.

2470. **Town and country planning—registration of a club—whether material change of use—waiver of a procedural requirement—whether a determination**
[Planning (Northern Ireland) Order 1972 (S.I. 1972 No. 1634 (N.I. 17)), art. 30]
On an application by a club for a certificate of registration to enable it to supply intoxicating liquor to members for consumption in its premises, an objection was lodged by a residents' association. Before the hearing the Department of the Environment in response to a telephone call made by someone on behalf of the club sent the club's architects a letter stating that there was no material change in use from an unlicensed club to a licensed club. The association applied for judicial review of this ruling by the Department. *Held,* that the Department had waived the requirement under art. 30 of the Planning (Northern Ireland) Order 1972 that an application for a determination under that Article must be in writing and was estopped from relying on lack of formality and, accordingly, the letter sent to the club's architects was a determination under that Article. However, the Department in making the determination may have failed to take some relevant material factors into consideration and the determination should be remitted to the Department for reconsideration: THOMPSON'S APPLICATION, *Re* [1985] 5 N.I.J.B. 84, Carswell J.

2471. **Town and country planning—Social Need (Northern Ireland) Order 1986 (S.I. 1986 No. 1302 (N.I. 14))**
This Order enables the Department of the Environment to provide financial assistance for such matters as the promotion, development or regeneration of commercial, industrial or other economic activity and the improvement of the environment in local government districts in Northern Ireland where there exist areas of social need. The Department is also given power to carry out works for the improvement of the environment and to carry out or give financial assistance towards the carrying out of studies, investigations and research for the purposes of the Order.
The Order came into operation on September 26, 1986.

2471a. **Trade and industry—Enterprise Ulster (Continuation of Functions) (Northern Ireland) Order 1986 (S.I. 1986 No. 2228 (N.I. 23))**
This Order revives certain functions of Enterprise Ulster which had ceased on March 31, 1986, and abolishes the limitation on the duration of those functions.
The Order came into operation on December 30, 1986.

2472. **Trade and industry—industrial training**
S.R. 1986 Nos. 120 (distributive industry) [£1·40]; 141 (textiles industry) [£1·40]; 142 (food and drink industry) [£1·40]; 191 (engineering industry) [£1·40]; 192 (catering industry) [£1·40]; 224 (construction industry) [£1·40]; 265 (road transport industry) [£1·40]; 290 (clothing industry) [£1·40].

2473. **Transport**
ROAD TRANSPORT LICENSING (FEES) (AMENDMENT) REGULATIONS (NORTHERN IRELAND) 1986 (No. 55) [40p], made under the Transport Act (Northern Ireland) 1967 (c.37), ss.9, 23(2); operative on April 1, 1986; increase fees payable for road service licences.
VEHICLE LICENCES (DURATION OF FIRST LICENCES AND RATE OF DUTY) (NORTHERN IRELAND) ORDER 1986 (No. 1427) [80p], made under the Vehicles (Excise) Act (Northern Ireland) 1972 (c.10 (N.I.)), s.2A; operative on October 1, 1986; makes provision for the first licences for mechanically propelled vehicles.

2474. **Vendor and purchaser—counter offer—whether a binding contract**
On March 4, 1983, D accepted P's written offer to purchase certain property. On March 7, 1983, D sought to add a new clause as to interest to the contract. On March 15, 1983, P objected to the addition of the new clause stating that the interest

and apportionment position was adequately governed by the general conditions of sale which were incorporated in the original contract. This counter offer was never expressly accepted by D. The trial judge granted specific performance of the contract—see [1986] 4 C.L. 259. *Held,* dismissing D's appeal, that an offer can be accepted by conduct, that whether or not there has been an acceptance by conduct depends on the facts and the inferences to be drawn from them and that the evidence pointed overwhelmingly in the direction of a completed and agreed contract: ROYAL AVENUE HOTEL *v.* RICHARD SHOPS PROPERTIES [1986] 5 N.I.J.B. 45, C.A.

2475. Water and waterworks—pollution—compensation—Lands Tribunal decision
HEANEY *v.* DEPARTMENT OF THE ENVIRONMENT FOR NORTHERN IRELAND, R/25/1985 (in 1980 harmful effluent was discharged through a pipe in sewage treatment works which had been constructed by the Department of the Environment in 1977/1978. Since the construction of the works the Department had done no work to the pipe, there was no breakage or leakage in the pipe and no repairs were carried out. H claimed compensation. *Held,* that the expression "provide and maintain such works" in art. 13(1) of the Water and Sewerage Services (Northern Ireland) Order 1973 included the operation and management of the sewage treatment works and accordingly that the tribunal had jurisdiction to hear and determine the claim for compensation).

2476. Weights and measures
MEASURING EQUIPMENT (LIQUID FUEL BY ROAD TANKER) (AMENDMENT) REGULATIONS (NORTHERN IRELAND) 1986 (No. 307) [£1·40], made under S.I. 1981 No. 231 (N.I. 10), arts. 9(1)(3), 10(6), 13(1); operative on November 3, 1986; make miscellaneous amendments to the 1984 (No. 117) Regulations.

MEASURING EQUIPMENT (MEASURES OF LENGTH) REGULATIONS (NORTHERN IRELAND) 1986 (No. 308) [£1·90], made under S.I. 1981 No. 231, arts. 9(1)(3)(4), 13(1); operative on October 27, 1986; prescribe measures of length, which do not bear the mark of EEC initial verification, for the purposes of art. 9(1) of the 1981 S.I. so that it is unlawful to use such measures for trade purposes unless they have been tested, passed as fit for such use and stamped by an inspector of weights and measures.

WEIGHING EQUIPMENT (FILLING AND DISCONTINUOUS TOTALISING AUTOMATIC WEIGHING MACHINES) REGULATIONS (NORTHERN IRELAND) 1986 (No. 311) [£2·90], made under S.I. 1981 No. 231, arts. 9(1)(3), 10(6), 13(1); operative on November 10, 1986; prescribe filling and discontinuous totalising automatic weighing machines for the purposes of art. 9(1) of the 1981 S.I. and exclude them from the application of the 1967 (No. 237) Regulations; also make provision for the purposes for which such machines may be used and for their construction, marking, erection and testing.

WEIGHTS AND MEASURES (AMENDMENT) REGULATIONS (NORTHERN IRELAND) 1985 (No. 364) [£1·35], made under S.I. 1981 No. 231 (N.I. 10), arts. 9(1)(3), 13(1); operative on January 29, 1986; amend the 1967 (No. 237) Regulations to take account of the demonetisation of the halfpenny in so far as they relate to price computing weighing instruments including ancillary and connected equipment.

WEIGHTS AND MEASURES (INTOXICATING LIQUOR) ORDER (NORTHERN IRELAND) 1986 (No. 226) [£1·40], made under S.I. 1981 No. 231 (N.I. 10), art. 19(2)(3)(7); operative on August 25, 1986; deals with the sale by retail of intoxicating liquor, the pre-packing of wines and the quantity marking of containers.

2477. Wills—construction—remainder interests—whether vested
T, who died in 1967, was survived by his widow, one daughter who died in 1981 and one granddaughter who died without issue in 1984. By his will T left the residue of his estate to his widow for life with remainder to his daughter and granddaughter in equal shares absolutely but, if either died before his widow, leaving issue, such issue should take the share which the parent would have taken if living at his widow's death. *Held,* that both the daughter and granddaughter took vested remainder interests which might have been but since their deaths could not be divested: ULSTER BANK *v.* McCULLOUGH [1985] 11 N.I.J.B. 1, Murray J.

2478. Wills—family provision—illegitimate children—joint bank account
[Inheritance (Provision for Family and Dependants) (Northern Ireland) Order 1979 (S.I. 1979 No. 924 (N.I. 8)).] T, who was unmarried, had two illegitimate children born in February 1973 and paid a weekly sum of £2·00, later increased to £4·25, in respect of each child under a maintenance order. T died in September 1984 leaving an estate consisting mainly of a farm valued at £44,000, a sum of £838 in a bank

account in his own name and a sum of £10,000 in a bank account in the joint names of T and a nephew. No provision was made by T's will for the maintenance of the two children although as from his death a small pension became payable to the children's mother under a superannuation scheme. The two children made an application under the Inheritance (Provision for Family and Dependants) (Northern Ireland) Order 1979 for provision out of T's estate. *Held*, that (1) one-half of the money in the joint bank account should be treated as part of T's estate; (2) T had failed to make reasonable financial provision for the two children; (3) provision should not be ordered so as to enable a minor applicant to have a capital sum when he attains his majority; and (4) each of the children should receive a lump sum of £10,000 out of T's estate: PATTON'S ESTATE, *Re;* MCILVEEN *v.* PATTON [1986] 3 N.I.J.B. 35, Carswell J.

2479. Workmen's compensation

PNEUMOCONIOSIS, ETC., (WORKERS' COMPENSATION) (SPECIFIED DISEASES) ORDER (NORTHERN IRELAND) 1986 (No. 168) [45p], made under S.I. 1979 No. 925 (N.I. 9), art. 3(1); operative on July 31, 1986; specifies two diseases as diseases under the 1979 S.I. for which provision has been made for the payment of lump sums to or in respect of certain persons who are, or were immediately before they died, disabled by them.

WORKMEN'S COMPENSATION (SUPPLEMENTATION) (AMENDMENT) REGULATIONS (NORTHERN IRELAND) 1986 (No. 222) [80p], made under the Industrial Injuries and Diseases (Northern Ireland Old Cases) Act 1975 (c.17), ss.2, 4(1); operative on July 30, 1986; make adjustments to the intermediate rates of lesser incapacity allowance consequential upon the increase in the maximum rate of that allowance made by the 1986 (No. 211) Order.

NUISANCE

2480. Noise—shop open on a twenty-four hour basis—injunction—laches

[Ire.] In 1980 D acquired premises which since 1977 had been used as a "twenty-four hour shop" and he continued the business previously carried on unaware that there had been objections to the use of the premises for the purposes of such a shop. In October 1981 a local residents association of which P was a member, complained to D about the excessive noise caused by his customers late at night. In April 1982 P obtained an injunction restraining D from carrying on business between midnight and eight in the morning. *Held*, on appeal, that (1) in the circumstances, including the fact that the premises were situated in an old-established residential area, the noise made at night by the customers constituted an actionable nuisance; (2) there was no undue delay in seeking the injunction as P was collecting the signatures of objectors in 1980 and 1981 and D must have been aware of this; and (3) the injunction should be varied to restrain D from carrying on the business between midnight and six in the morning: O'KANE *v.* CAMPBELL [1985] I.R. 115, Lynch J.

2481. Nuisance by tenants—consent of landlords—whether landlords liable—whether injunction appropriate

Where a landlord expressly or impliedly gives his consent to a use of land which has as a necessary and natural consequence the cause of sufficient noise to be classed as a nuisance, the landlord can be liable in nuisance.

A local authority gave permission to a go-kart club to operate a go-kart track on certain land in its ownership, and subsequently granted a seven year lease to the club for the purpose of operating the track. T and others, who were ratepayers living near the track, sought an injunction and damages against the authority, based on the nuisance caused by the noise made by the track. *Held*, that the noise was a natural and ordinary consequence of the use of the track for go-karting and the council had given permission for that use, so the council was liable in nuisance. Damages alone were a wholly inadequate remedy and an injunction would also be granted. (*Kennaway v. Thompson* [1980] C.L.Y. 2007 distinguished; *Smith v. Scott* [1972] C.L.Y. 2532 considered).

TETLEY *v.* CHITTY [1986] 1 All E.R. 663, McNeill J.

2482. Statutory nuisance—condensation dampness—scope of magistrates' powers. See BIRMINGHAM DISTRICT COUNCIL v. KELLY, § 1647.

OPEN SPACES AND RECREATION GROUNDS

2483. Doncaster Common—whether open space
[Local Government Act 1972 (c.70), s.123(2A) (as amended).] Doncaster Common is an "open space" within the meaning of the Act (*Box Hill Common, Re* [1979] C.L.Y. 253, *Mounsey* v. *Ismay* [1863] 3 H. & C. 486, *Heddon, Re* [1932] 1 Ch. 133, *Ellenborough Park, Re* [1955] C.L.Y. 882, *Tyne Improvement Commissioners* v. *Imrie* [1899] 81 L.T. 174, *Goodman* v. *Mayor of Saltash* [1882] 7 App. Cas. 633, *Att.-Gen.* v. *Antrobus* [1905] 2 Ch. 188 considered): R. v. DONCASTER METROPOLITAN BOROUGH COUNCIL, *ex p.* BRAIM, *The Times*, October 11, 1986, McCullough J.

2484. Recreation grounds
RECREATION GROUNDS (REVOCATION OF PARISH COUNCIL BYELAWS) ORDER 1986 (No. 114) [80p], made under the Local Government Act 1972 (c.70), s.262(8)(*c*); operative on March 1, 1986, revokes specified byelaws.
RECREATION GROUNDS (REVOCATION OF PARISH COUNCIL BYELAWS (No. 2) ORDER 1986 (No. 1461) [45p], made under the Local Government Act 1972 (c.70) s.262(8)(*d*); operative on November 1, 1986; revokes specified byelaws made pursuant to the Local Government Act 1984, s.8(1)(*d*).

2485. Royal park—trading in park
[Royal and Other Parks and Gardens Regulations.] 1977 (S.I. 1977 No. 217), reg. 4(5); Parks Regulation (Amendment) Act 1926 (c.36), s.2(1) (as amended).] It is not necessary for a conviction for trading in a park for the goods to be present in the park at the time (*Newman* v. *Lipman* [1951] C.L.C. 5950 distinguished): BURGESS v. MCCRACKEN, *The Times*, June 26, 1986, D.C.

PARLIAMENT

2486. Disqualification
HOUSE OF COMMONS DISQUALIFICATION ORDER 1986 (No. 2219) [£1·40], made under the House of Commons Disqualification Act 1975 (c.24), s.5; operative on December 16, 1986; amends the list of offices which disqualifies holders from membership of the House of Commons.

2486a. Lord Chancellor's salary
LORD CHANCELLOR'S SALARY ORDER 1986 (No. 1169) [45p], made under the Ministerial and other Salaries Act 1975 (c.27), s.1(4); operative on July 8, 1986; increases the salary payable to the Lord Chancellor.

PARTNERSHIP

2487. Dissolution—assets—leased premises—whether held for benefit for partnership
[Aus.] A doctor carried on business at leased premises. In 1979, he entered into partnership with another doctor and a new lease was granted to them. In 1981, the "new" partner dissolved the partnership. Prior to the winding up of the partnership affairs, the "new" partner obtained an agreement to grant him alone a new lease of the premises. *Held*, by a majority, that the agreement for the new lease was held upon constructive trust for those entitled to the property of the dissolved partnership (*Keech* v. *Sandford*, 25 E.R. 223, *Biss, Re; Biss* v. *Biss* [1903] 2 Ch. 40 and *Thompson's Trustee in Bankruptcy* v. *Heaton* [1974] C.L.Y. 2740 applied): CHAN (KAK LOUI) v. ZACHARIA (1983–84) 154 C.L.R. 178, High Ct. of Australia.

2488. Restrictions on size—English partnership in excess of restriction trading in Isle of Man—whether entitled to register
[Isle of Man] [Manx Registration of Business Names Act 1918 ss.3, 10; Manx Companies Act 1931, s.325.]
The Manx Companies Act 1931 provides by s.325—No company, association or partnership consisting of more than twenty persons shall be formed for the purpose of carrying on any business . . . unless it is registered as a company . . ., the Manx Registration of Business Names Act 1918 provides by s.3(*a*)—Every firm having a place of business in the Isle of Man and carrying on business under a business name which does not consist of the true surnames of all the partners who are individuals . . . shall be registered . . . s.10 provides that any firm not registered shall not be

entitled to enforce its rights by action or other legal proceedings subject to a proviso granting relief from that restriction. B and M were a firm of London stockbrokers that operated an office in which one partner worked in the Isle of Man. The firm consisted of 36 partners. The firm obtained a judgment against Fado in the Isle of Man courts on a cheque. In the course of executing the judgment the question arose as to whether the firm was entitled to enforce its rights by legal proceedings having regard to the provisions of the Manx Companies Act 1931, s.325 and the Manx Registration of Business Names Act 1918, ss.3(*a*) and 10. The First Deemster held that on a proper construction of s.325 a partnership of more than 20 partners was illegal in the Isle of Man so that the firm was neither entitled to be registered nor entitled to relief against their failure to register under the Registration of Business Names Act. *Held*, allowing the firm's appeal, that the firm was a properly constituted partnership in accordance with English law. Pursuant to English conflict of laws principles that applied in the Isle of Man with regard to the recognition of foreign corporations, the firm fell to be recognised by Manx law. There was nothing in s.3(*a*) to prevent the firm from registering although the section was to be read as subject to the proviso that a firm seeking registration must be validly constituted. Accordingly the firm was entitled to be registered under the Act. In the circumstances of the case the firm was entitled to relief under the proviso to s.10 against their failure to register under the Act: BUCKMASTER AND MOORE (A FIRM) *v.* FADO INVESTMENTS [1986] PCC 95, s.6, I.O.M.

2489. Trade—loss—limited partner. See REED (INSPECTOR OF TAXES) *v.* YOUNG, § 1754.

PATENTS AND DESIGNS

2490. Application—divisional application—late filing—discretion
[Patents Act 1977 (c.37), s.15(4); Patents Rules 1982 (S.I. 1982 No. 717), r.24(1)(*b*)(1).] A decided to file a divisional application when responding to the second report on their existing application. The application in suit was filed shortly afterwards. The Comptroller's agreement was sought under r.24(1)(*b*)(1) for the late filing. This was refused. The applicants appealed. *Held*, dismissing the appeal that (1) the Comptroller had correctly exercised his discretion taking into account all relevant matters; (2) although the European Patent Office had allowed the late filing uniformity of procedure was not the main consideration: KIWI CODERS CORPORATION'S APPLICATION [1986] R.P.C. 106, Whitford J.

2491. Application—patent—amendment
[Patents Act 1977 (c.37), ss.15, 18, 19 Patents Rules 1982 (S.I. 1982 No. 717), r.36.] The Patent Office granted the application for a patent. Thereafter A sought to amend the application to create two patents. The office refused to entertain these requests. *Held*, on appeal, that (1) it was proper practice to notify that the application was in order and simultaneously that a patent had been granted; (2) an application to amend could be made only before the letter of notification: OGAWA CHEMICAL INDUSTRIES [1986] R.P.C. 63, Falconer J.

2492. Application—irregularity—discretion
[Patents Rules 1982 (S.I. 1982 No. 717), r.100.] The application was filed and an official letter conveying the first report was issued and amendments in response were filed. A second report containing objections to the amended specification was prepared by the examiner but by mischance a letter containing the report was not issued. No further action was taken until the four-and-a-half-year period prescribed under s.20 expired, when the application was treated as having been refused. Seven months later the patent agent made enquiries about the application. The superintending examiner cancelled the entry and granted the patent but imposed terms to protect members of the public who might have acted upon the declared refusal. *Held*, on appeal, that (1) the examiner had properly exercised his discretion; (2) the patent agents should have checked the progress of the application: COAL INDUSTRY (PATENTS) APPLICATION [1986] R.P.C. 57, Falconer J.

2493. Application—novelty—European application—withdrawal
[Patents Act 1977 (c.37), ss.2, 5, 78.] A European application was published after the priority date of the application in suit and was subsequently withdrawn. The applicants argued that it should not be taken into account in determining novelty. The hearing officer refused the application on the ground that the European

document was citable. *Held,* on appeal, that the Patents Act 1977, s.78(5), was clear and must be applied, although it led to unfortunate results; (2) accordingly the European patent ceased to be citable within s.2(3) as from the date of withdrawal, and the objection to novelty on the basis of disclosure was removed: L'OREAL'S APPLICATION [1986] R.P.C. 19, Whitford J.

2494. Designs

REGISTERED DESIGNS (FEES) RULES 1986 (No. 584) [£1·35], made under the Registered Designs Act 1949 (c.88), ss.36, 40; operative on April 21, 1986 save for Rules 1(2) and (3) which are operative on May, 26, 1986; replaces the provision for fees contained in S.I. 1984 No. 1989 and increases those fees.

2495. Fees

Patents (Fees) Rules 1986 (No. 583) [£1·85], made under the Patents Act 1977 (c.37), s.123(1)(2)(3), Sched. 4, para. 14; operative on April 21, 1986, save for Rules 1(2)–(5) and 3 which are operative on May 26, 1986; replace the provision for fees contained in S.I. 1982 No. 717 with self contained provision.

2496. Infringement—after date of publication but before letters patent—accrual of cause of action—limitation

[Patents Act 1949 (12, 13 & 14 Geo. 6, c.87), s.13(4); Limitation Act 1980 (c.58), s.2.]

Where acts of infringement occur after the date of publication of the complete specification, the cause of action and time for the purposes of the Limitation Act began to run from the date of those acts.

In June 1967 the plaintiffs applied for letters patent in respect of certain improvements to an electrical switch. The complete specification was filed on June 7, 1968 and published on April 7, 1974. The letters patent were sealed on October 6, 1982 but dated and "made patent as of" June 7, 1968. In February 1984 the plaintiffs issued a writ for infringements of the patent between 1974 and 1978. The defendants sought dismissal of the action relying on s.2 of the Limitation Act 1980. The judge found for the defendants and the appeal was dismissed. *Held,* dismissing the appeal to the House of Lords, that the applicant had rights immediately after the publication of the complete specification; accordingly a cause of action in relation to acts of infringement arose from the date of those acts. The claim was therefore statute barred (*General Tire and Rubber Co.* v. *Firestone Tyre and Rubber Co.* [1975] C.L.Y. 2503 applied; *Distillers Co. (Biochemicals)* v. *Thompson* [1971] C.L.Y. 1599 distinguished).

SEVCON v. LUCAS CAV [1986] 1 W.L.R. 462, H.L.

2497. Infringement—evidence—privilege

[Scot.] [Patents Act 1977 (c.37), ss.105,127,Sched. 2.] In an action for infringement, the pursuers claimed privilege when their naval architect was asked about expert evidence which he gave to the U.K. patent agent in connection with an application for amendment. The defenders claimed that s.105 was not retrospective and did not apply to the 1976 amendment. *Held,* that s.105 protected patents already in existence. The communication was privileged: SANTA FE INTERNATIONAL CORP. v. NAPIER SHIPPING S.A. [1986] R.P.C. 72, Court of Session.

2498. Infringement—practice—discovery

P manufactured and sold TAGAMET. There was evidence that D was marketing TAGAMET exported from Spain in breach of licence. The trial judge granted interlocutory relief and ordered D to disclose names and addresses of suppliers. D appealed. *Held,* that the court had jurisdiction to order the disclosure of the name of a wrongdoer erring according to the law of a foreign country provided that it was shown that it concerned the transaction in which D was involved: SMITH KLINE AND FRENCH LABORATORIES v. GLOBAL PHARMACEUTICS [1986] R.P.C. 394, C.A.

2499. Infringement—restrictions on importation—novelty

[Treaty of the European Economic Community, arts. 30 and 36.] Whether or not potential commercial or industrial property relies, for exemption from the prohibition on restrictions on importation within the EEC, on the invention being novel has yet to be determined by the European Court. In the meantime, defences based on that proposition in infringement of patent actions should not be struck out: THETFORD CORPORATION v. FIAMMA SpA, *Financial Times,* December 3, 1986, C.A.

2500. Infringement—threats

[Patents Act 1977 (c.37), s.70] P was the registered proprietor of a U.K. patent for drain covers. P contacted H with whom he was negotiating manufacture under licence and told him that if he agreed to manufacture or sell D's patented product he would be liable to be sued for infringement. P issued a writ and sought an injunction. P's proceedings were later struck out and dismissed. D counterclaimed for damages for the threats, which frustrated her negotiations. *Held*, that (1) the action of P amounted to threats. P's threats were not exempted by the provision of the Patents Act 1977, s.70(4). An injunction and inquiry as to damages would be ordered: NEILD *v.* ROCKLEY [1986] F.S.R. 3, Falconer J.

2501. Infringement—threats—jurisdiction

[Patents Act 1977 (c.37), s.70.] P and D manufactured small electric motors. D wrote to potential customers threatening infringement proceedings on the basis of some of their patents. P sought an injunction to restrain D from further threats. D argued that they were justified. *Held*, that (1) threats in patent cases were a grave mischief. It was wrong to refuse relief merely because D claimed that they would justify the threats: JOHNSON ELECTRIC INDUSTRIAL MANUFACTORY *v.* MABUCHI-MOTOR K.K. [1986] F.S.R. 280, Whitford J.

2502. Licence of right—application to settle terms of licence—jurisdiction.

[Patents Act 1977 (c.37), s.46(3)(*a*) Sched. 1, para. 4(1)(2)(*c*); E.E.C. Treaty (Cmmd. 5179—II), arts. 30, 36.]

The comptroller has power to settle the terms of a licence of right before the end of the sixteenth year after the grant of a patent.

B and A & H each owned the U.K. patents for certain drugs which had been granted under the 1949 Act and would have expired 16 years after the grant but under the provisions of the 1977 Act the terms were extended for 4 years. G-B wanted to obtain a licence in respect of B's patent from the date it would be available as of right in August 1985. They applied in December 1984 to the Comptroller-General under s.46 of the 1977 Act to settle the terms of the licence but the comptroller held that he had no jurisdiction before the end of the sixteenth year. G-B applied for an order of mandamus but the judge refused to grant it and the Court of Appeal upheld that decision, holding that an application to settle the terms of the licence had to be made after the sixteenth year but the licence took effect from the date of the application. G wanted to import into the U.K. a drug protected in the U.K. by A & H's patent in August 1984, having failed to negotiate terms with A & H for a licence, G applied to the comptroller to settle the terms of a licence of right and informed A & H that they intended to begin importing the drug and would pay whatever royalty was eventually fixed. A & H brought an action to protect their patent and the judge granted an injunction restraining importation of the drug. The Court of Appeal, following the decision in the other case, held that since G had applied to the comptroller to settle the terms of a licence of right after the sixteenth year, they were to be treated as holders of such a licence. The order for summary judgment was set aside but the Court held that Articles 30 and 36 of the E.E.C. treaty did not prevent a prohibition against the importation of the drug. *Held*, that (1) by s.46 of, and para. 4(2)(*c*) of Sched. 1 to, the 1977 Act, the comptroller had power to settle the terms of a licence of right before the end of the sixteenth year but it could not take effect until after the end of that year and after the terms on which it was granted were settled by agreement or by the Comptroller; (2) the terms of the licence could preclude or limit importation from any country except a Member State of the E.E.C.; but the questions about the effect of Articles 30 and 36 would be referred to the European Court of Justice; (3) that although the Comptroller had wrongly held that he could not hear G-B's application, the passage of time had rendered the prerogative order of no practical effect, so the Court of Appeal's decision would stand; in A & H's case, the setting aside of summary judgment would be affirmed but the other matters would be adjourned until after the European Court of Justice's determination.

R *v.* COMPTROLLER-GENERAL OF PATENTS, DESIGNS AND TRADE MARKS, *ex p.* GIST-BROCADES [1986] 1 W.L.R. 51, H.L.

2503. Licences of right—imports—comptroller general
[Patents Act 1977 (c.37), s.50.] The Comptroller General has wide powers in settling terms of licences of right in new existing patents and may ban imports of the patented product from non-EEC countries if the public interest requires it. AN APPLICATION BY GENERICS (U.K.) *Re, Financial Times,* March 26, 1986, Whitford J.

2504. Patent—amendment—disclaimer—covetousness
[Patents Act 1949 (c.87), ss.29, 31.] An application for amendment of the specification in relation to paper filter elements was opposed. The applicants sought to amend to distinguish from certain other patents, and were stated to be by way of disclaimer. Opponents alleged that the proposed amendments did not in fact distinguish and further that claim I was covetous in the light of the patentees awareness of other existing patents. The hearing officer found that on the facts the claim was covetous and amendment was refused. The patentees appealed. *Held,* that (1) it was wrong to consider the issue of obviousness in amendment proceedings; (2) the test of covetousness was whether the patentee had knowingly and deliberately obtained claims of undue width. The patentee need not have been aware that he was not entitled to the claims nor that the claim was invalid (*Imperial Chemical Industries (Whyte's) Patent* [1978] C.L.Y. 2215 applied); (3) the hearing officer had properly exercised his discretion in refusing amendment. Appeal dismissed: DONALDSON CO. INC'S PATENT [1986] R.P.C. 1, Falconer J.

2505. Patents, Designs and Marks Act 1986. See TRADE MARKS AND TRADE NAMES, § 3422.

2506. Procedure—patent agent—confidential documents
The applicants sought a licence of right. The patentees wished to be represented before the Comptroller. The applicants argued that the confidential documents should be seen only by an independent patent agent. *Held,* upon the patentee's legal advisor undertaking not to disclose any material save in connection with the present proceedings, that the legal advisor should be permitted to act for the patentees: SCHERING A.G.'S PATENT [1986] R.P.C. 30, Whitford J.

PEERAGES AND DIGNITIES

2507. Baronetcy—legitimacy
[Scot.] [Legitimation (Scotland) Act 1968 (c.22)] Where a baronetcy has descended to the junior stirps due to the illegitimacy of the member of the senior stirps, his subsequent legitimation did not cause a reversion of the baronetcy to the senior stirps: DUNBAR *v.* LORD ADVOCATE, *The Times,* April 18, 1986, H.L.

PENSIONS AND SUPERANNUATION

2508. Appeals tribunals
PENSIONS APPEAL TRIBUNALS (ENGLAND AND WALES) (AMENDMENT) RULES 1986 (No. 366) [40p], made under the Pensions Appeal Tribunals Act 1943 (c.39), s.6, Sched. paras. 5, 6, 6A and the Tribunals and Inquiries Act 1971 (c.62), s.10; operative on April 1, 1986; provides for a procedure by which a person resident in one part of the UK may have his appeal heard in another part.

2509. Armed forces
NAVAL, MILITARY AND AIR FORCES ETC. (DISABLEMENT AND DEATH) SERVICE PENSIONS AMENDMENT ORDER 1986 (No. 592) [£1·90], made under the Social Security (Miscellaneous Provisions) Act 1977 (c.5), s.12(1); operative on July 28, 1986; further amends S.I. 1983 No. 883 in relation to death and disablement pensions relating to service in the 1914–18 war.

2510. British Council and Commonwealth Institute Superannuation Act 1986 (c.51)
This Act enables schemes to be made under s.1 of the Superannuation Act 1972 (superannuation schemes as respects civil servants etc.) in respect of persons who are serving or have previously served in employment with the British Council or the Commonwealth Institute.
The Act received The Royal Assent on July 25, 1986.

2511. British Council and Commonwealth Institute Superannuation Act 1986—commencement
BRITISH COUNCIL AND COMMONWEALTH INSTITUTE SUPERANNUATION ACT 1986 (COMMENCEMENT NO. 1) ORDER 1986 (No. 1860 (c.66)) [45p], made under the British Council and Commonwealth Institute Superannuation Act 1986 (c.5), s.3(2); brings into force on November 10, 1986 the whole Act as it applies to the British Council.

2512. Children's pensions

SUPERANNUATION (CHILDREN'S PENSIONS) (EARNINGS LIMIT) ORDER 1986 (No. 814) [45p], made under the Judicial Pensions Act 1981 (c.20), s.21(5); operative on July 28, 1986; revokes S.I. 1985 No. 1691.

2513. Clergy pensions See ECCLESIASTICAL LAW, § 1118.

2514. Company group pension scheme—employees of subsidiary company in group transferring to new scheme—value of fund—certificate of valuation

The court is bound to accept a certificate of valuation given by an actuary as to the value of funds to be transferred from an existing pension scheme for the employees of a group of companies to a new pension scheme for employees of a particular company within the group unless it was proved that the actuary had erred in principle in making a mistake or acted from improper motives.

Imperial Foods organised a pension scheme for persons employed by it and its subsidiary companies. The scheme contained provision for the fund to be separated and part transferred to a new scheme in the event that any of the companies ceased to be a subsidiary. The scheme provided for the portion to be transferred to the new scheme to be determined by the scheme's actuary as such a portion as shall in all the circumstances appear to him to be appropriate at the time the company in question ceased to be a subsidiary. Imperial Foods sold two of its subsidiary companies to Hillsdown Holdings. The sale was completed on May 18, 1982. A new pension scheme was set up for the employees of the subsidiary companies in November 1982. In a certificate dated November 30, 1983 the actuary of the Imperial Foods scheme certified the value of the fund to be transferred to the new scheme as at May 18, 1982 and as at November 1982 when the new scheme commenced. The actuary arrived at the relevant values by applying a method of calculation known as past service reserve with a reasonable allowance for future increases in pay and pensions. The actuary of the new scheme contended that the appropriate method of calculation was to partition the fund in accordance with the proportion that the employees of the subsidiary companies formed of all the employees of the group prior to the sale of the subsidiaries. The latter method would have resulted in a greater share being transferred to the new scheme on account of the fact that the scheme, at the relevant times carried a notional surplus of funds. Hillsdown Holdings sought to be set aside the actuary's certificate and determine the value of the part to be transferred in the manner contended for by the actuary of the new scheme. *Held*, that the court was bound to accept the actuary's valuation unless it was proved that some mistake of a substantial character had been made or the actuary had acted from some improper motive. It could not be said that the actuary erred in principle or failed to take account of all the relevant circumstances in choosing and applying the method of calculation he used. In any event the method of calculation proposed by the new scheme's actuary was not correct. The notional surplus of funds in the scheme did not belong to the individual employees but belonged to the scheme. The proper date for determining the separation of the fund was November 1982 when the employees of the subsidiary companies left the Imperial Foods scheme to join the new scheme. The function of an actuary in any situation which is not governed precisely by the provisions of the trust deed is to achieve the greatest possible degree of fairness between the various persons interested under the pension scheme (*Collier* v. *Mason* (1858) 25 Beav. 200, *Dean* v. *Prince* [1954] C.L.Y. 470 applied).

IMPERIAL FOODS PENSION SCHEME, *Re* [1986] 1 W.L.R. 717, Walton J.

2515. Contracting-out

CONTRACTING-OUT (REQUISITE BENEFITS—CONSEQUENTIAL PROVISIONS) REGULATIONS 1986 (No. 1716) [80p], made under the Social Security Act 1973 (c.38), ss.66(7), 99(1)(3), Sched. 16, para. 9(3), the Social Security Act 1975 (c.14), s.168(1), Sched. 20, the Social Security Pensions Act 1975 (c.60), ss.31(1)(2)(5)(7), 32(2), 35(8), 38(1)(13), 45(1). 52, Sched. 2, paras. 1, 9, the Social Security (Miscellaneous Provisions) Act 1977 (c.5), ss.21(2), 22(13) and the Social Security Act 1986 (c.50), s.84(1); operative on November 1, 1986; make provision in relation to guaranteed minimum pensions as a consequence of s.8 of the 1986 Act.

2516. Contributory pension scheme—substituted principal company—surplus funds

Employees who contribute to a compulsory pension scheme are not entitled to a "contributions holiday" when there are surplus funds. Although they are not entitled to benefit from the surpluses while they are employed, they are entitled to have them dealt with by discussions and negotiations between their continuing employers and the committee of management, and not to be irrevocably parted from them by the unilateral decision of a take-over raider with only a transitory interest in the share capital of the companies that employ them. Therefore, substitution of a new company in such a pension scheme is invalid if its purpose is not to preserve the scheme for the benefit of the employees, but to enable the substituted company to hive off surplus funds for its own benefit: Courage Pension Schemes, Re, *The Financial Times,* December 16, 1986, Millett J.

2517. Firemen
Fireman's Pension Scheme (War Service) (Transferees) Order 1986 (No. 1663) [£2·40], made under the Fire Services Act 1947 (c.41), s.26; operative on November 1, 1986; supplements S.I. 1979 No. 1360.

2518. Increases
Pensions Increase (Local Authorities' etc. Pensions) (Amendment) Regulations 1986 (No. 391) [40p], made under the Pensions (Increase) Act 1971 (c.56), s.5(2); operative on April 1, 1986; amends S.I. 1974 No. 1740; so as to secure that the cost of increasing certain pensions is borne by appropriate authorities.
Pensions Increase (Review) Order 1986 (No. 1116) [80p], made under the Social Security Pensions Act 1975 (c.60), s.59(1)(2)(5); operative on July 28, 1986; specifies increases for public service pensions.

2519. Judicial pensions
Judicial Pensions (Preservation of Benefits) (Amendment) Order 1986 (No. 111) [40p], made under the Social Security Act 1973 (c.38), s.65 and S.I. 1975 No. 1503; operative on August 1, 1986; clarifies that a judicial office holder's preserved pension is to be calculated by reference to his last salary before retirement, subject to any increases made pursuant to pensions increase legislation, rather than by reference to the salary he would have been earning had he retired at the time when the pension became due for payment.
Judicial Pensions (Preservation of Benefits) (Amendment No. 2) Order 1986 (No. 946) [80p], made under the Social Security Act 1973 (c.38), s.65 and S.I. 1975 No. 1503 (N.I. 15); operative on July 1, 1986; amends S.I. 1977 No. 717 and S.I. 1978 No. 407 and revokes S.I. 1986 No. 111.

2520. Local government
Local Government Superannuation (Miscellaneous Provisions) Regulations 1986 (No. 380) [£1·35], made under the Superannuation Act 1972 (c.11), ss.7, 12; operative on April 1, 1986; makes provision in relation to the abolition of the GLC and the metropolitan county councils and the formation of public transport companies.
Local Government Superannuation Regulations 1986 (No. 24) [£9·60], made under the Superannuation Act 1972 (c.11), ss.7, 12, Sched. 7, para. 5(1) and the National Insurance Act 1965 (c.51), s.110; operative on March 1, 1986; consolidate some amendments specified in S.I.'s relating to local government superannuation.

2521. Local government—reckonable years—calculation
[Regulations D21(1)(*a*) Local Government Superannuation Regulations (S.I. 1974 No. 520).] This regulation does not operate to limit reckonable periods of service which were concurrent periods of employment as opposed to sequential periods: Severn, Trent Water Authority *v.* Cross, *The Times,* June 12, 1986, Simon Brown J.

2522. Miscellaneous offices
Pensions (Miscellaneous Offices) (Preservation of Benefits) (Amendment) Order 1986 (No. 465) [40p], made under the Social Security Act 1973 (c.38), s.65; operative on October 1, 1986; amends S.I. 1977 No. 1653.

2523. Museums and Galleries Commission
Superannuation (Museums and Galleries Commissions) Order 1986 (No. 2119) [45p], made under the Superannuation Act 1972 (c.11), s.1(5), (8)(*b*); operative on January 1, 1987; adds the Museums and Galleries Commission to Sched. 1 to the 1972 Act.

2524. National Health Service—special provisions. See National Health, § 2246.

2525. Occupational schemes
Occupational Pension Schemes (Contracting-out) Amendment Regulations 1986 (No. 317) [80p], made under the Social Security Act 1975 (c.14), s.168(1),

Sched. 20 and the Social Security Pensions Act 1975 (c.60), ss.38(1) to (1c), 42, 43(4)(6), 45(1), 47(9A), 52, 66(3), Sched. 2, para. 6; operative on April 6, 1986; amends S.I. 1984 No. 380.

OCCUPATIONAL PENSION SCHEMES (DISCLOSURE OF INFORMATION) REGULATIONS 1986 (No. 1046) [£2·90], made under the Social Security Act 1975 (c.14), s.168(1), Sched. 20 and the Social Security Pensions Act 1975 (c.60), ss.56A (1)(3)(4), 56E (1)(3)(4), 62(4), 66(4), Sched. 1A, para. 14(3); operative on November 1, 1986; specifies the information that is to be made available to persons in occupational pension schemes by the trustees of that scheme.

OCCUPATIONAL PENSION SCHEMES (DISCLOSURE OF INFORMATION) (AMENDMENT) REGULATIONS 1986 (No. 1717) [80p], made under the Social Security Act 1975 (c.14), s.168(1), Sched. 20 and the Social Security Pensions Act 1975 (c.60), ss.56A(1)(3), 56E(1)(4); operative on November 1, 1986; amend S.I. 1986 No. 1046.

OCCUPATIONAL PENSION SCHEMES (MANAGERS) REGULATIONS 1986 (No. 1718) [80p], made under the Social Security Act 1985 (c.53), s.5; operative on November 1, 1986; provide for who is to be treated as a manager of an occupational pension scheme which is a public service pension scheme.

OCCUPATIONAL PENSION SCHEMES (MISCELLANEOUS AMENDMENT) REGULATIONS 1986 (No. 2171) [80p], made under the Social Security Act 1973 (c.33), s.99(1) and (2) and Sched. 16, paras. 9(2), 20 and 21, the Social Security Act 1975 (c.14), s.168(1) and Sched. 20, and the Social Security Pensions Act 1975 (c.60), s.52C and Sched. 1A, para. 13; operative on January 5, 1987; amend S.I. 1984 No. 614 and S.I. 1985 Nos. 1929 and 1931.

OCCUPATIONAL PENSION SCHEMES (REVALUATION AND TRANSFER VALUES) AMENDMENT REGULATIONS 1986 (No. 751) [45p], made under the Social Security Act 1975 (c.14), s.168(1) and Sched. 20, and the Social Security Pensions Act 1975 (c.60), Sched. 1A, paras. 14 and 20; operative on May 29, 1986; correct errors in S.I. 1985 Nos. 1930 and 1931.

OCCUPATIONAL PENSIONS (REVALUATION) ORDER 1986 (No. 2070) [45p], made under the Social Security Pensions Act 1975 (c.60), s.52A(1); operative on January 1, 1987; specifies the revaluation percentage for the year January 1, 1986 to December 31, 1986 as being three per cent.

2526. Police

POLICE PENSIONS (WAR SERVICE) (TRANSFEREES) REGULATIONS 1985 (No. 2029) [£2·30], made under the Police Pensions Act 1976 (c.35), ss.1, 3, 4; operative on January 31, 1986; make provision in relation to policemen and former policemen who have been unable to reckon their war service for pension purposes under S.I. 1979 No. 1259.

POLICE PENSIONS (AMENDMENT) REGULATIONS 1986 (No. 1379) [80p], made under the Police Pensions Act 1976 (c.35), ss.1, 3 and 4; operative on September 8, 1986; amend S.I. 1973 No. 428.

POLICE PENSIONS (LUMP SUM PAYMENTS TO WIDOWS) REGULATIONS 1986 (No. 1380) [45p], made under the Police Pensions Act 1976 (c.35), ss.1, 3 and 5; operative on December 1, 1986; provide for the payment of a gratuity of £10 to certain policemen's widows.

2527. Preservation of benefits

PENSIONS (MISCELLANEOUS OFFICES) (PRESERVATION OF BENEFITS) (AMENDMENT NO. 2) ORDER 1986 (No. 940) [45p], made under the Social Security Act 1973 (c.38), s.65 and S.I. 1975 No. 1503 (N.I. 15); operative on July 1, 1986; amends S.I. 1977 No. 1653 and revokes S.I. 1986 No. 465.

2528. Reckonable days—absence through trade dispute

[Local Government Superannuation (Amendment) (No. 2) Regulations 1981 (S.I. 1981 No. 1509), reg. C 1A.] P was advised to strike for one day by his union although the instruction was not mandatory. He did so, and lost one day's superannuation. The superannuation agreement provided for reckonable days to include days lost through trade disputes. *Held,* that it mattered not that P was only advised to strike; the day lost was one lost through a trade dispute: POVEY *v.* SECRETARY OF STATE FOR THE ENVIRONMENT, *The Times,* July 17, 1986, C.A.

2529. Royal Irish Constabulary

ROYAL IRISH CONSTABULARY (LUMP SUM PAYMENTS TO WIDOWS) REGULATIONS 1986 (No. 1381) [45p], made under the Royal Irish Constabulary (Widows' Pensions) Act

1954 (c.17), s.1; operative on December 1, 1986; provide for the payment of lump sums to widows in receipt of pensions under S.I. 1971 No. 1469.

2529a. Teachers
TEACHERS' SUPERANNUATION (AMENDMENT) REGULATIONS 1985 (No. 1844) (£2·80), made under the Superannuation Act 1972 (c.11), ss.9 and 12, Sched. 3; operative on January 1, 1986; amend S.I. 1976 No. 1987.

2530. War pensions
INJURIES IN WAR (SHORE EMPLOYMENTS) COMPENSATION (AMENDMENT) SCHEME 1986 (No. 1095) [45p], made under the Injuries in War Compensation Act 1914 (Session 2) (c.18), s.1; operative on July 28, 1986; increases the weekly allowance payable to ex-members of the WAF.

PERSONAL INJURIES (CIVILIANS) AMENDMENT SCHEME 1986 (No. 628) [£1·40], made under the Personal Injuries (Emergency Provisions) Act 1939 (c.82), ss.1, 2; operative on July 28, 1986; amends S.I. 1983 No. 686.

PETROLEUM

2531. British National Oil Corporation
BRITISH NATIONAL OIL CORPORATION (DISSOLUTION) ORDER 1986 (No. 585) [40p], made under the Oil and Pipelines Act 1985 (c.62), s.3(5); dissolves BNOC on March 27, 1986.

2532. Foreign fields. See REVENUE AND FINANCE, § 2860.

2533. Licence fees
PETROLEUM (PRODUCTION) (AMENDMENT) REGULATIONS 1986 (No. 1021) [45p], made under the Petroleum (Production) Act 1934 (c.36), s.6; operative on July 11, 1986; increase fees for production licences in seaward areas.

2534. Oilfield rights—pipelines
[Petroleum Production Act 1934 (c.36), ss.3, 11, 12; Mines (Working Facilities and Support) Act 1923 (c.20), s.3; Pipe-Lines Act 1962 (c.58), s.57.] On a proper construction of the statutory provisions the court has the jurisdiction to grant rights relating to the use of pipe-lines for the passage of petroleum products: BP DEVELOPMENT, *Re Financial Times*, February 26, 1986, Warner J.

2535. Petroleum revenue tax. See also REVENUE AND FINANCE.

2536. Petroleum revenue tax—supplement to costs incurred for purpose of calculating receipts for taxation—cut-off date for supplement—entitlement to supplement. See I.R.C. *v*. MOBIL NORTH SEA, § 2861.

2537. Submarine pipe-lines
SUBMARINE PIPE-LINES SAFETY (AMENDMENT) REGULATIONS 1986 (No. 1985) [45p], made under the Petroleum and Submarine Pipe-lines Act 1975 (c.74), ss.26(1), 27(2)(*d*)(*g*), 32(4); operative on December 18, 1986; amend S.I. 1982 No. 1513 in relation to testing of, and works on, pipe-lines.

POLICE

2538. Abuse of powers—excessive force used in arrest—damages
P was a 26-year-old Rastafarian. He stated that in July 1982 two police constables asked if they could search him for drugs. He explained that he had already been searched. He ran to catch a bus, was pursued by the police, was pulled off the bus platform and pushed against a fence. He was subsequently punched, kicked and thrown into a police van. He claimed damages for swollen, bruised lips, a swollen nose and forehead, and bruises to his back. He suffered no lasting injuries. The defendant denied the assault and that any injuries had been sustained. In the alternative, it was claimed that any injuries were the result of P's own unlawful action in resisting arrest. *Held*, that on the evidence, the degree of force used was excessive and unreasonable. P had offered no violence but the police officers had behaved as if he were a violent criminal. It was strongly suspected that the motive of the police was prejudice against a black man with an outlandish costume and a strange accent. P would receive £200 compensatory damages and £1,000 exemplary damages to mark a flagrant abuse of the police's considerable powers: LEON *v*. COMMISSIONER OF POLICE FOR THE METROPOLIS, November 6, 1985; H.H. Judge Marder, Q.C.; Clerkenwell County Ct. (*Ex rel. Tim Owen, Barrister*).

2539. Annual Report
The Report of Her Majesty's Chief Inspector of Constabulary for the year 1985 has been published. It is available from H.M.S.O. (ISBN 0 10 243786 6) [£8·50].

2540. Cadets
POLICE CADETS (AMENDMENT) REGULATIONS 1986 (No. 2033) [45p], made under the Police Act 1964 (c.48), s.35; operative on December 31, 1986; increases the pay of police cadets.

2541. Disciplinary procedure—officer pleading guilty to criminal offence—conditional discharge—whether "conviction"
[Powers of Criminal Courts Act 1973 (c.62), s.13(1)(3); Police Act 1976 (c.46), s.11(1)(2), Police Discipline Regulations 1977, reg. 5, Sched. 2, para. 15.]
A police officer convicted of a criminal offence and given a conditional discharge, has been "found guilty of a criminal offence" for the purposes of the Police disciplinary regulations.
The applicant, a police officer, pleaded guilty to an offence of wasting police time; he had made a false report of theft of money from his locker. He was granted a conditional discharge. Disciplinary proceedings were instituted charging him with committing an offence, criminal conduct. He pleaded not guilty on the grounds that by receiving a conditional discharge he was deemed not to have been convicted. *Held,* dismissing the appeal to the Court of Appeal, that the words "found guilty of a criminal offence" in the discipline regulations did not carry the formal meaning attributed to them by s.13 of the P.C.C.A. 1973.
R. *v.* SECRETARY OF STATE FOR THE HOME DEPARTMENT, *ex p.* THORNTON [1986] 3 W.L.R. 158, C.A.

2542/3. Disciplinary procedure—two-year delay—officers' appeal against finding—whether judicial review available.
[Police (Discipline) Regulations 1977 (S.I. 1977 No. 580), reg. 7.]
Judicial review is not normally available where there is an alternative remedy by way of appeal, save in exceptional circumstances.
In June 1981 complaints were made against five officers of the Merseyside police. No notice of the complaint was given to the officers until December 1983. At a hearing in September 1984 the Chief Constable rejected submissions of prejudice caused by the delay, and the officers were found guilty and dismissed. They exercised their right of appeal through the statutory procedure, but before the appeal was heard they applied for judicial review. The Divisional Court found that the application was premature. *Held,* allowing the appeal, that judicial review would not normally be available where there was an alternative remedy by way of appeal, save in exceptional circumstances; these circumstances were exceptional in view of the initial two-year delay (*R.* v. *I.R.C., ex p. Preston* [1985] C.L.Y. 1782. *Ex p. Waldron* [1985] C.L.Y. 160 applied).
R. *v.* CHIEF CONSTABLE OF MERSEYSIDE POLICE, *ex p.* CALVELEY [1986] 2 W.L.R. 144, C.A.

2544. Disciplinary proceedings—judicial review
The Court declined to interfere with the decision of a Chief Constable in disciplinary proceedings who had been attended by his deputy during an adjournment where, although the deputy was the investigating officer, nothing had been said about the proceedings: R. *v.* CHIEF CONSTABLE OF SOUTH WALES, *ex p.* THORNHILL, *The Times,* May 12, 1986, D.C.

2545. Evidence—special procedure material—duty to specify details. See R. *v.* CENTRAL CRIMINAL COURT, *ex p.* ADEGBESAN, § 912.

2546. Grants
POLICE (GRANT) (AMENDMENT) ORDER 1986 (No. 455) [40p], made under the Police Act 1964 (c.48), s.31; operative on April 1, 1986; amends S.I. 1966 No. 223 by increasing the police grant to police authorities in England and Wales.

2547. Housing allowance—powers of Secretary of State
[Police Regulations (S.I. 1979 No. 1470), reg. 47(4)(*b*); Home Office Circular No. 90/1984.] Police Regulation 47(4) provides for the assessment of a police officer's housing allowance, by relation to "the maximum limit for his rank", to be calculated by reference to the rent to be paid for an unfurnished letting of a house to be assessed by the district valuer. By a circular published in 1984, the Home Secretary

declared that he would take into account the rateable value of the selected house and whether it was broadly in line with the average rateable value of the police authority's housing. When applying for the Home Secretary's approval for increases in maximum limits, the authority had to state whether the selected house met the description, given the rateable value of the selected house and the average rateable value of the authority's housing stock. *Held,* that this part of the circular was *ultra vires.* The Home Secretary had to judge each application on its merits. He was not entitled to prejudge his consideration by laying down in advance criteria by which he would exercise his discretion: R. *v.* SECRETARY OF STATE FOR THE HOME DEPARTMENT, *ex p.* BENNETT AND THORNTON, *The Times,* August 18, 1986, C.A.

2548. Metropolitan police—detention—requirement to explain reasons. See R. *v.* HAMILTON, § 638.

2549. Police Federation
POLICE FEDERATION (AMENDMENT) REGULATIONS 1986 (No. 1846) [80p], made under the Police Act 1964 (c.48), s.44; operative on December 1, 1986; amend S.I. 1969 No. 1787.

2550. Police National Computer—report
The independent Police Complaints Authority has published a report arising from allegations of misuse of the Police National Computer. The report was made to the Home Secretary under section 97(2) of the Police and Criminal Evidence Act 1984. Copies are available from H.M.S.O. (ISBN 0 10 242586 8) [£2·10].

2551. Police Regulations
POLICE (AMENDMENT) (No. 2) REGULATIONS 1986 (No. 2032) [80p], made under the Police Act 1964 (c.48), s.33; operative on December 31, 1986; amend S.I. 1979 No. 1470.
POLICE (AMENDMENT) (No. 3) REGULATIONS 1986 (No. 2241) [45p], made under the Police Act 1964 (c.48), s.33; operative on December 31, 1986; rectify an error in S.I. 1986 No. 2032.

2552. Policing policy—discretion of chief constables
Although the Divisional Court can review local policing policy on the application of a person affected by it, chief constables have the widest possible discretion in what policing methods to use, and the courts will very rarely interfere: R. *v.* OXFORD, *ex p.* LEVEY, *The Times,* November 1, 1986, C.A.

2553. Powers of entry—purpose of entry unrelated to Act empowering entry—whether entry valid. See FOSTER *v.* ATTARD, § 675.

2554. Regional crime squads
The steering group report of the *Review of the Regional Crime Squads* has been published.

2554a. Regulations
POLICE (AMENDMENT) REGULATIONS 1986 (No. 784) [80p], made under the Police Act 1964 (c.48), s.33; operative on June 1, 1986; amend S.I. 1979 No. 1470.

2554b. Riot
RIOT (DAMAGES) (AMENDMENT) REGULATIONS 1986 (No. 76) [40p], made under the Riot (Damages) Act 1886 (c.38), s.3(2); operative on April 1, 1986; amend the 1921 Regulation's prescribing the procedure for claiming compensation under the 1886 Act.

2555. Special police services—payment—whether duty to protect from fear of future crime
[Police Act 1964 (c.48), s.15(1).] The provision of policemen at a football ground to keep law and order is the provision of special services within s.15(1) of the Police Act 1964. Although the police authority has a duty to protect people and property against crime or threatened crime (for carrying out which duty no payment is due) there is no public duty to protect the public from the mere fear of possible future crime: HARRIS *v.* SHEFFIELD UNITED FOOTBALL CLUB, *The Times,* April 4, 1986, Boreham J.

2556. Street collections
STREET COLLECTIONS (METROPOLITAN POLICE DISTRICT) (AMENDMENT) REGULATIONS 1986 (No. 1696) [45p], made under the Police, Factories, etc. (Miscellaneous Provisions) Act 1916 (c.31), s.5; operative on November 17, 1986; amend S.I. 1979

No. 1230 increases to £400 the level below which a certified account need not be supplied to the Commissioner of Police.

2557. Tape recordings—interviews—code of practice. See CRIMINAL LAW, § 592.

PRACTICE

2558. Adjournment—costs
P sought an injunction to restrain the use in trade of KODA, KODAONLINE and EKOL. Prior to the hearing P sought to adjourn the motion to trial. *Held*, that no order should be made on the motion, and in relation to costs, the correct order was D's costs in cause: KODAK *v.* REED INTERNATIONAL [1986] F.S.R. 477, Harman J.

2559. Adjournment—judge's discretion
A Judge who, through irritation with solicitors' incompetence in failing to secure the attendance of material witnesses, refused an adjournment exercised his discretion improperly: MILLINGTON *v.* KSC & SONS, *The Times,* July 23, 1985, C.A.

2560. Administration of Justice Act 1982—commencement
ADMINISTRATION OF JUSTICE ACT 1982 (COMMENCEMENT No. 5) ORDER 1986 (No. 2259 (c.89)) [45p], made under the Administration of Justice Act 1982 (c.53), s.76(1); brings into force on January 2, 1987 sections 38–47 and 75 as they relate to the County Courts Act 1959.

2560a. Administration of Justice Act 1985—commencement
ADMINISTRATION OF JUSTICE ACT 1985 (COMMENCEMENT No. 1) ORDER 1986 (No. 364 (C.10)) [80p], made under the Administration of Justice Act 1985 (c.61), s.69(2); brings into operation on March 12, 1986 sections 2, 4, 5, 7, 8, 12, 46, 67(2), Scheds. 1, 3, 8, Pt. III (in part) and brings into operation on April 28, 1986, section 50.

ADMINISTRATION OF JUSTICE ACT 1985 (COMMENCEMENT No. 2) ORDER 1986 (No. 1503 (c.54)) [45p], made under the Administration of Justice Act 1983 (c.61), s.69(2); brings into force on October 1, 1986 sections 13, 22, 23, 38, 47, 51, 55, 67(1) (in part) (2) (in part) of the 1985 Act.

ADMINISTRATION OF JUSTICE ACT 1985 (COMMENCEMENT No. 3) ORDER 1986 (No. 2260 (c.60)) [45p], made under the Administration of Justice Act 1985 (c.61), s.69(2); brings into force on January 1, 1987 sections 1, 2 (in part) and 3; brings into force on January 12, 1987, section 48.

2561. Adoption—commencement of proceedings—practice direction
The following direction was issued by the Senior Registrar of the Family Division on June 25, 1986.

The President and Judges of the Family Division are of the opinion that, in suitable cases, when leave is given to commence adoption or freeing for adoption proceedings in respect of a ward, the Court may direct that such proceedings may be commenced in the appropriate county court. Such a direction is likely to be particularly appropriate where it is apparent that the substantive adoption or freeing for adoption application will not be contested by the natural parent or parents. Such an order should also include a direction that, in the event of the making of the adoption order, the wardship be discontinued.

In all cases in which adoption or freeing for adoption applications are commenced in the High Court and which are proceeding with the consent of the natural parent (but subject to the exceptions which follow) the Official Solicitor is no longer prepared to consent to act as Guardian ad Litem of the child or as Reporting Officer for the consenting parent. In such cases, an appointment or appointments should be made from the panels established by the Guardians ad Litem and Reporting Officers (Panels) Regulations 1983.

The exceptions referred to above are:
(a) those High Court cases in which the Official Solicitor has acted as the child's Guardian ad Litem in the wardship proceedings;
(b) those cases where the child or its parents are foreign nationals;
(c) those cases which are proceeding in the High Court because of the provisions of section 29 of the Adoption Act 1958 (unlawful placements for adoption);
(d) those consent adoptions which have particularly difficult or unusual features.

In those High Court cases which, having initially proceeded on a consent basis, subsequently become opposed, the Official Solicitor will, if the Court considers it appropriate, be prepared to accept appointment as the child's Guardian ad Litem.

PRACTICE DIRECTION (FAM.D.) (ADOPTION) (COMMENCEMENT OF PROCEEDINGS IN COUNTY COURT: INVOLVEMENT OF OFFICIAL SOLICITOR IN HIGH COURT) June 25, 1986.

2562. Adoption—notice of hearing—practice direction

The following practice direction was issued by the Senior Registrar of the Family Division on March 24, 1986.

In future when the Court has given notice to a natural parent asking if he or she wishes to be heard in the proceedings and such natural parent has not acknowledged the receipt of such notice within 21 days the Principal Registry will inform the Applicants' Solicitors and thereupon it will be the duty of the Applicants' Solicitors to serve any such natural parent at the latest address known to the Principal Registry with a Notice in the following form: "Notice has been sent to you of the hearing of an application made to the Family Division of the High Court for an order for the (freeing for) adoption of whom you are believed to be a natural parent. No acknowledgment has been received from you by the Court and this is to inform you that you have the right to attend Court when the application is heard by a Judge so that you may give your views to the Judge as to whether or not an order should be made. If you wish to give your views to the Judge will you please return the attached form to the Court within the next 10 days and you will then be informed of the day fixed for hearing. If the Court does not hear from you within the next 10 days it will be assumed that you do not wish to take any part in the proceedings and the application for the (freeing for) adoption order will be fixed for hearing by a Judge without any further notice to you."

The latest address known to the Principal Registry will be supplied to the Applicants' Solicitors together with a copy of the Notice with the relevant form attached for service on the natural parent. It will be for the Applicants' Solicitors to satisfy the Court at the hearing as to service of the Notice and attached form. If for some reason, such as the natural parent's absence from the jurisdiction or failure to locate that person, there is a problem in effecting personal service, the Applicants' Solicitors should apply to a Registrar for directions as to service.

PRACTICE DIRECTION (FAM.D.) (ADOPTION: NOTICE OF HEARING) March 24, 1986.

2563. Anton Piller order—assault by police—evidence

[S.A.] M and others alleged that they had been assaulted by members of the South African police. They described in affidavits electronic equipment used during the assaults. They sought an order to obtain access to the police stations in order to inspect the equipment. *Held*, that the court would order the examinations. The evidence in question was essential and if it were not available justice could not be done: MATSHINI, *Ex p.* [1986] F.S.R. 454, Supreme Court of South Africa.

2563a. Anton Piller order—foreign proceedings

An Anton Piller order obtained in this country can be used abroad in foreign proceedings, if the purpose of those proceedings is to prevent disposal of assets before judgment, rather than to litigate abroad the issue which is already before the English court: BAYER *v.* WINTER (No. 3) The *Financial Times*, March 21, 1986, Hoffmann J.

2564. Anton Piller orders—breach of duty on ex parte application to disclose all relevant matters—damages

Because of the potentially disastrous consequences to a defendant of an Anton Piller order, accompanied as it often is by a Mareva injunction, there is a very strict duty on the plaintiff's solicitors to make full and frank disclosure of all relevant matters, and not to act oppressively or improperly in its execution. Where solicitors did improperly obtain such an order the proper course was not to set aside the Anton Piller order (which would serve no purpose) but to compensate the defendant by damages.

Per curiam: (i) The court had begun to grant Anton Piller orders too readily, granting them with insufficient thought being paid to the interests of the respondents; (ii) the order should be no wider than absolutely necessary, and once documents had been seized, they should be copied and the originals returned, a detailed record being kept of all documents being seized; (iii) where ownership of the property seized was disputed, it should not be retained by the plaintiff's solicitors.

CPI claimed that R and his associates were video pirates; their solicitors obtained, *ex parte*, an Anton Piller order and a Mareva injunction. Items were seized, in execution of the order, which were not included in the order; the items were retained by the solicitors, and some of them were lost. As a result of the execution of the order, and the grant of the injunction, R ceased trading, something that CPI and the other plaintiffs had hoped to achieve. *Held*, that (i) there was a duty on a plaintiff's solicitor seeking an Anton Piller order to make full and frank disclosure of all matters which could be relevant; (ii) when executing the order they were under a duty not to act oppressively, nor to abuse their power; (iii) on the facts the plaintiff's solicitors affidavit in support was so seriously deficient as to be misleading; (iv) further they had acted oppressively and abused their position by seizing objects not covered by the order; (v) the foregoing matters would justify setting aside the order, but no useful purpose would be served by so doing and damages would therefore be awarded.

COLUMBIA PICTURE INDUSTRIES *v.* ROBINSON [1986] 3 W.L.R. 542, Scott J.

2565. Appeal—failure to lodge documents in time—duty of solicitors
[R.S.C., Ord. 59, r.9.]
The time limits for lodging of documentation in civil appeals must be adhered to.
A number of appeals were listed together in the Court of Appeal in which solicitors had not lodged the prescribed bundles of appeal documents within the required time. *Held*, dismissing the appeals, that it was mandatory that solicitors document their cases within the time limit; if there were likely to be difficulties they must seek an extension of time at the earliest opportunity.

H, *Re* (NOTE) [1986] 2 All E.R. 629, C.A.

2566. Appeal—no transcript of original hearing—rules of procedure
Where there is an appeal from a judicial hearing of which no transcript was taken at the time, and one of the grounds of the appeal is a criticism of the judge's conduct of the case, the following rules should be observed: (i) the notice of appeal ought to be submitted to the judge before the matter comes before the Court of Appeal; (ii) if reliance is to be placed on notes of evidence, these should be agreed between counsel, who should then submit them to the judge; and (iii) the trial judge should then communicate with the Court of Appeal and the parties if he has any comment on the notes of evidence: R. (A MINOR), *Re, The Times*, October 10, 1986, C.A.

2567. Appeal—opposed *ex parte* hearing
The Court of Appeal has jurisdiction to hear an appeal on an opposed *ex parte* basis, but such appeals are to be deprecated: HUNTER *v.* WELLING, *The Times*, October 16, 1986, C.A.

2568. Appeal—question of fact
Issues of fact should not be appealed against by way of case stated: JAMES *v.* CHIEF CONSTABLE OF KENT, *The Times*, June 7, 1986, D.C.

2569. Appeal—refusal of leave to appeal—jurisdiction to reopen
Once an order is made by the Divisional Court, that Court is *functus officio,* and there is no power to alter the order. Once leave to appeal to the House of Lords has been refused by the Divisional Court, that refusal cannot be reopened: MCWHIRTER, *Re, The Times*, May 13, 1986, D.C.

2570. Appeal from Official Referees—causation as element of negligence
[R.S.C., Ord. 58, r.5] P1, builders were engaged by P2, developers to construct a warehouse with a car park on its roof. P1 engaged D, structural engineers, to produce the engineering plans necessary for the construction of the building and they told D the weight of the material (CDS) which P1 intended to use as the weatherproofing finish on the car deck. D produced the relevant design. In the meantime, CDS became unavailable. Before deciding on alternatives P1 enquired of D what would be the maximum weight permissible and were given an answer which it was held by the Official Referee was too low. P1 then used a material which although within the weight limit identified by D was not warranted as an adequate finish by the manufacturers; the material failed. The Official Referee held that D had been negligent in giving a weight limit which was too low and that that had foreseeably caused P1 to risk using a finish which might not work and held D liable for damages to be assessed. D appealed. *Held*, that (1) the appeal was competent notwithstanding Ord. 58, r.5 because a finding of causation is an essential element of liability in negligence (*Moody* v. *Ellis* [1984] C.L.Y. 2575 distinguished), (2) the Official Referee had had the benefit of seeing the witnesses and therefore the finding of fact which he had made which formed the substance of his finding negligence

would not be overturned. The finding of negligence failed from the facts so found: LEACH (HUBERT C.) *v.* CROSSLEY (NORMAN) & PARTNERS (1984) 30 Build. L.R. 95, C.A.

2571. Appeal on costs only—no leave from trial judge—whether jurisdiction in Court of Appeal

[Supreme Court Act 1981 (c.54) s.18(1)(*f*); R.S.C., Ord. 62, rr.3(1), 5(*b*).]

Where an appeal is brought on costs only, and the judge has refused leave to appeal, the Court of Appeal can entertain the appeal only where the real and overriding reason for the judge's refusal of leave was his taking into account some matter which he ought not to have taken into account.

Before trial of an action D made a payment into court, which was increased a week after the trial (which eventually lasted 45 days) began. P eventually recovered less than the initial payment in. The judge considered that the payment in was defective but also considered that D's conduct was at fault. He ordered D to pay P's costs down to the payment in, and that thereafter there should be no order as to costs. He refused D leave to appeal against the costs order. *Held,* that it was only where a judge who refused leave to appeal on a question of costs had considered an improper matter as his main ground for the refusal of leave that the Court of Appeal could entertain an appeal. Here it was clear that the judge had considered that D's own conduct had been at fault and that was a permissible reason for the exercise of his discretion. Appeal dismissed (*Campbell (Donald) & Co.* v. *Pollak* [1927] A.C. 732 and *Wagman* v. *Vare Motors* [1959] C.L.Y. 2564 applied).

SMITHS *v.* MIDDLETON [1986] 1 W.L.R. 598, C.A.

2572. Appeal on costs only—no leave from trial judge—whether jurisdiction in Court of Appeal—whether material upon which judge could exercise discretion

Where no leave to appeal on costs only has been granted, and there is material before the judge upon which he can exercise his discretion, the Court of Appeal cannot interfere, but the situation is different where there is no such material.

In dismissing two motions by D to dismiss P's actions for want of prosecution, the judge declined to dismiss the actions, but nevertheless ordered P, who had been successful on the motions, to pay the costs thereof. P appealed (the leave of the judge not having been sought or given). *Held,* that if there had been material upon which the judge could properly have exercised his discretion, however slight that material might have been, the Court of Appeal could not intervene. On the facts of the present case however, there was no basis at all upon which the judge could properly have ordered P to pay D's costs of the motions. In those circumstances the judge could not be said to have exercised his discretion judicially and the appeal from his order would be allowed, with costs.

SCHERER *v.* COUNTING INSTRUMENTS [1986] 1 W.L.R. 615, C.A.

2573. Appeal—rehearing—admissibility of fresh evidence.

[H.K.] [R.S.C., Ord. 14] P, main contractors, undertook to execute works for D upon terms similar to the JCT RIBA standard form contract. The architect issued an interim certificate in P's favour which D did not honour. P applied for summary judgment. D claimed to set off an alleged entitlement to liquidated damages relying upon two purported clause 22 certificates. The master determined that the purported certificates failed to comply with clause 22 and gave P judgment. D appealed and sought to reply upon two further certificates issued after the hearing before the master. *Held,* allowing the appeal, that the last two clause 22 certificates were valid certificates. Since the appeal was by way of a rehearing it was proper to admit the certificates as evidence unless there were special circumstances. The timing of the issue of the later two clause 22 certificates which were valid certificates was not a special circumstance: KIU MAY CONSTRUCTION CO. *v.* WAI CHEONG CO. (1983) 29 Build.L.R. 137 H.K. High Ct. Clough J.

2574. Appeals—time limits

[R.S.C., Ord. 59] Time limits should be strictly observed (*Van Stillevoldt (C. M.) BV* v. *E. L. Carriers Inc.* [1983] C.L.Y. 2864, *Practice Note (Appeal: Documents)* [1983] 2 All E.R. 416 considered): HOLLIS *v.* JENKINS (R. B.) (A FIRM), *The Times,* January 31, 1985, C.A.

2575. Appeals to Court of Appeal—child cases—legal aid delays

[R.S.C., Ord. 59, r.9.] Further time would be allowed for filing documents where a delay had occurred by reason of an application for legal aid. It is important for the

Court of Appeal to have up-to-date information in an appeal involving a child or children: RIDGEWAY v. RIDGEWAY, *The Times,* June 13, 1986, C.A.

2576. Bankruptcy—substituted service—practice note

The following practice note was issued on December 18, 1986 by the Chief Bankruptcy Registrar.

Substituted service of Statutory Demands & Petitions

Insolvency Rules 6.3, 6.11, 6.14 & 6.15

Statutory Demands

1. The creditor is under an obligation to do all that is reasonable to bring the statutory demand to the debtor's attention and, if practicable, to cause personal service to be effected. Where it is not possible to effect prompt personal service, service may be effected by other means such as first class post or insertion through a letter box.

2. Advertisement can only be used as a means of substituted service where:—
   (a) the demand is based on a judgment or order of any court;
   (b) the debtor has absconded or is keeping out of the way with a view to avoiding service and
   (c) there is no real prospect of the sum due being recovered by execution or other process.

As there is no statutory form of advertisement, the Court will accept an advertisement in the following form:

STATUTORY DEMAND

(Debt for liquidated sum payable immediately following a Judgment or Order of the Court)

To (block letters)
of

TAKE NOTICE that a Statutory Demand has been issued by
Name of creditor
Address
The creditor demands payment of £   the amount now due on a
Judgment/Order of the (High Court of Justice   Division)
(...................... County Court dated the   day of   19

The Statutory Demand is an important document and it is deemed to have been served on you on the date of the first appearance of this advertisement. You *must* deal with this demand within 21 days of the service upon you or you could be made bankrupt and your property and goods taken away from you. If you are in any doubt as to your position, you should seek advice *immediately* from a solicitor or your nearest Citizen's Advice Bureau.

The Statutory Demand can be obtained or is available for inspection and collection from:

Name
Address
(Solicitor for) the creditor
Tel. No.   Reference

You have only 21 days from the date of the first appearance of this advertisement before the creditor may present a bankruptcy petition

3. In all cases where substituted service is effected, the creditor must have taken all those steps which would suffice to justify the court making an order for substituted service of a petition. The steps to be taken to obtain an order for substituted service are set out below. Practitioners are reminded that failure to comply with the requirements of this Practice Note may result in the Court declining to file the Petition (I.R. 6.11(a))

4. *Order for substituted service of a bankruptcy petition*

In most cases, the following evidence will suffice to justify an order for substituted service:—
   (a) one personal call at the residence and place of business of the debtor where both are known or at either of such places as is known. Where it is known that

the debtor has more than one residential or business address, personal calls should be made at all addresses

(b) should the creditor fail to effect service, a first class prepaid letter should be written to the debtor referring to the call(s) the purpose of the same and the failure to meet with the debtor, adding that a further call will be made for the same purpose of the   day of   19 at

hours at   (place). At least two business days notice should be given of the appointment and copies of the letter sent to all known addresses of the debtor. The appointment letter should also state that:—

(b) (i) in the event of the time and place not being convenient, the debtor is to name some other time and place reasonably convenient for the purpose.

(b) (ii) (Statutory demands) if the debtor fails to keep the appointment the creditor proposes to serve the debtor by [advertisement, see para. 2] [post] [insertion through a letter box] or as the case may be, and that, in the event of a bankruptcy petition being presented, the court will be asked to treat such service as service of the demand on the debtor.

(b) (iii) (petitions) if the debtor fails to keep the appointment, application will be made to the court for an order for substituted service either by advertisement, or in such other manner as the court may think fit.

(c) in attending any appointment made by letter, inquiry should be made as to whether the debtor has received all letters left for him. If the debtor is away, inquiry should also be made as to whether or not letters are being forwarded to an address within the jurisdiction (England and Wales) or elsewhere.

(d) if the debtor is represented by a solicitor, an attempt should be made to arrange an appointment for personal service through such solicitor. Practitioners are reminded that the rules provide for a solicitor accepting service of a statutory demand on behalf of his client but there is no similar provision in respect of service of a bankruptcy petition.

(e) the supporting affidavit should deal with all the above matters including all relevant facts as to the debtor's whereabouts and whether the appointment letter(s) have been returned.

5. Where the court makes an order for substituted service by first class ordinary post, the order will normally provide that service be deemed to be effected on the 7th day after posting. Practitioners serving a statutory demand by post may consider using the same method of calculating service.

PRACTICE NOTE (BANKRUPTCY) (No. 4/86) December 18, 1986.

2577. Bankruptcy petition—creditors—practice note

The following practice note was issued by the Chief Bankruptcy Registrar on December 18, 1986.

Bankruptcy Petitions—Creditors

Insolvency Act 1986 S.S.267–269

Insolvency Rules 6.6-6.12

Forms 6.7, 6.8 and 6.9

To help practitioners to complete the new forms of a creditor's bankruptcy petition, attention is drawn to the following points:

1. The petition does not require dating, signing or witnessing.

2. In the title it is only necessary to recite the debtor's name *e.g.* Re John William Smith or Re J. W. Smith (male). Any alias or trading name will appear in the body of the petition. This also applies to all other statutory forms other than those which require the "full title".

3. Where the petition is based on a statutory demand, only the debt claimed in the demand may be included in the petition, except that interest or other charges which have accrued since the date of the demand to the date of the petition may be added: see I.R. 6.8-(1)(c) read with 6.1-(4).

4. When completing paragraph 2 of the petition, attention is drawn to I.R. 6.8-(1)(a)-(c), particularly where the "aggregate sum" is made up of a number of debts.

5. Date of service of the statutory demand (paragraph 4 of the petition):—

(a) In the case of personal service, the date of service as set out in the affidavit of service should be recited and whether service is effected *before/after* 16.00 hours on Monday to Friday or *before/after* 12.00 hours on Saturday: see O.65 r.7 of the Rules of the Supreme Court.

(b) In the case of substituted service (otherwise than by advertisement), the date alleged in the affidavit of service should be recited. (As to the date alleged see Practice Note No. 4/86).

(c) In the strictly limited case of substituted service by advertisement under I.R. 6.3, the date to be alleged is the date of the advertisement's appearance or, as the case may be, its first appearance: See I.R. 6.3-(3) and 6.11-(8).

6. There is no need to include in the preamble to or at the end of the petition details of the person authorised to present the petition.

7. Certificates at the end of the petition:—

(a) The period of search for prior petitions has been reduced to *3* years.

(b) Where a Statutory demand is based wholly or in part on a County Court judgment, the following certificate, which replaces the affidavit of County Court search, is to be added:

"I/We certify that on the   day of   19 I/We attended on the   County Court and was/were informed by an officer of the Court that no money had been paid into Court in the action or matter   v.   Plaint No.   pursuant to the Statutory demand".

This certificate will not be required when the demand also requires payment of a separate debt, not based on a County Court judgment, the amount of which exceeds the bankruptcy level (at present £750).

8. Deposit on Petition:

The deposit will now be taken by the Court and forwarded to the Official Receiver. The petition fee and deposit should be handed to the Supreme Court Accounts Office, Fee Stamping Rooms, who will record the receipt and will impress two entries on the original petition, one in respect of the court fee and the other in respect of the deposit. Cheque(s) for the whole amount should be made payable to "H.M. Paymaster General".

PRACTICE NOTE (BANKRUPTCY) (No. 3/86) December 18, 1986.

2578. Bankruptcy petition—practice note

The following practice note was issued by the Chief Bankruptcy Registrar on November 25, 1986.

Proof of continuing debt on hearing of bankruptcy petition

Bankruptcy Act 1914 S.5(2)

Insolvency Act 1986 S.271(1)(L)

Bankruptcy Rule 167

Insolvency Rule 6.25(1)

On the hearing of a petition for a bankruptcy order, to satisfy the Court that the debt on which the petition is founded has not been paid or secured or compounded for, the Court will normally accept as sufficient a certificate signed by the person representing the petitioning creditor in the following form:

"I certify that I have/my firm has made inquiries of the petitioning creditor(s) within the last business day prior to the hearing/adjourned hearing and to the best of my knowledge and belief the debt on which the petition is founded is still due and owing and has not been paid or secured or compounded for (save as to   )

Signed........................Dated.................

For the convenience of practitioners this certificate will be printed on the attendance slips. It will be filed after the hearing. A fresh certificate will be required on each adjourned hearing.

This practice Note will take effect on the 29th December 1986, when the Act and Rules come into effect, in respect of all petitions heard on or after that date whether or not presented and filed earlier.

PRACTICE NOTE (BANKRUPTCY) (No. 1/86) November 25, 1986.

2579. Breach of confidence—security for costs—corporate plaintiff

[Companies Act 1948 (c.38), s.447; Companies Act 1985 (c.6), s.726(1).]

D sought an order that P company give security for costs and that until security was given all further proceedings in the action be stayed. The order was made. Six months later P was ordered to pay a sum and unless that sum was paid by a specified date the action would be dismissed. On appeal P argued that under the Companies Acts there was no power to dismiss the action. *Held*, that (1) although s.447(1) did not confer power to dismiss the action, the count had power under the inherent jurisdiction; (2) since there was no evidence that D was suffering prejudice, the Master's order would be varied so as to make the security for costs payable in May 1986 instead of November 1985: SPEED UP HOLDINGS *v.* GOUGH [1986] F.S.R. 330, Evans-Lombe Q.C.

2580. Bullock order—White Book note

[R.S.C., Note 62/2/46.] The note in *The Supreme Court Practice 1985* that a Bullock order will not be made where the causes of action against the separate defendants were separate and distinct or founded on different sets of facts is incorrect: GOLDSWORTHY *v.* BRICKELL, *The Times,* November 12, 1986, C.A.

2581. Chancery Division—index—practice direction

Practice Direction No. 1 of 1986 was issued by the direction of the Vice-Chancellor on December 8, 1986. This direction deletes those Chancery (other than Companies Court) directions which are no longer required as they are out of date or found elsewhere and indicates those still in force which the practitioner is most likely to encounter. The Direction is an index primarily of Chancery Practice Directions.

PRACTICE DIRECTION (CH.D.) (INDEX) (No. 1 of 1986) December 8, 1986.

2582. Chancery Division—unassigned cases—practice direction

The following practice direction was issued by the Vice-Chancellor on July 31, 1986.

In order to improve the use of judge time in the Chancery Division, the listing arrangements will be slightly amended as from October 1, 1986.

In addition to those cases listed to be heard by individual judges, the Daily Cause List for each day may list one or more motions by order or cases from the Non-Witness List be heard on that day but not assigned to a particular judge ('an unassigned case'). If on any day the case assigned to a particular judge proves to be ineffective, he will hear an unassigned case. It is hoped that the great majority of unassigned cases will be heard on the day that they are listed but this cannot be absolutely guaranteed.

Solicitors and counsel engaged in cases listed as unassigned should communicate with the Chancery listing officer who will notify them as soon as possible which judge is to hear the case.

PRACTICE DIRECTION (CH.D.) (UNASSIGNED CASES) [1986] 2 All E.R. 1002.

2583. Chancery division—winding-up petitions—practice direction

The following practice direction was issued by the direction of the Vice-Chancellor on October 22, 1986.

With effect from the commencement of the Hilary Sittings 1987, the list of winding-up petitions, at present heard by the Judge acting as Companies Court Judge of the term on a Monday, will be heard by the Companies Court Registrar on a Wednesday. The Registrar will sit in court on a Wednesday each week of the term when he will hear all unopposed petitions and related applications other than those for relief under Section 522 of the Companies Act 1985 or for the restraint of advertisement of a petition. In accordance with the Practice Direction of the Lord Chief Justice of May 9, 1986, Solicitors, properly robed, will be permitted rights of audience before the Registrar.

The Companies Court Judge of the term will continue to sit on a Monday each week of the term when he will deal with (1) Petitions to confirm reductions of capital and/or share premium account (2) Petitions to sanction schemes of arrangement (3) Motions and (4) opposed Winding-up petitions which have been adjourned to him by the Registrar.

PRACTICE DIRECTION (CH.D.) (No. 2 of 1986) (COMPANIES COURT: HEARING OF WINDING-UP PETITIONS IN LONDON) OCTOBER 22, 1986.

2584. Children—adoption and freeing for adoption—practice direction

The following practice direction was issued by the Senior Registrar of the Family Division on February 14, 1986.

The Practice Direction of June 19, 1985 [1985] 6 C.L. 278a, [1985] 2 All E.R. 832 provided, *inter alia,* that applications by local authorities for leave to place a ward with long term foster parents with a view to adoption should not be made until such time as the foster parents have been selected.

The President and Judges of the Family Division are now of the opinion that this requirement is unnecessarily restrictive. Application for leave may be made before the foster parents are known.

The Practice Direction is therefore hereby amended by deleting the second sentence of the third paragraph.

PRACTICE DIRECTION (FAM. D.) (CHILDREN: ADOPTION AND FREEING FOR ADOPTION) February 14, 1986.

2585. Civil Jurisdiction and Judgments Act 1982—commencement

CIVIL JURISDICTION AND JUDGMENTS ACT 1982 (COMMENCEMENT NO. 2) ORDER 1986 (No. 1781 (c.62)) [45p], made under the Civil Jurisdiction and Judgments Act 1982 (c.27), s.53(1), Sched. 13, Pt. I, para. 3; brings into force on November 14, 1986 section 35(1) of the 1982 Act.

2586. CIVIL JURISDICTION AND JUDGMENTS ACT 1982 (COMMENCEMENT NO. 3) ORDER 1986 (No. 2044 (C.78)) [45p], made under the Civil Jurisdictions and Judgments Act 1982 (c.27), s.53(1), Sched. 13, Pt. I, para. 3; brings the remaining provisions of the 1982 Act into force on January 1, 1987.

2587. Commercial Court Committee—report. See LAW REFORM, § 1943.

2588. Commercial Court guide

A new *Guide to Commercial Court Practice* for the assistance of users of the Commercial Court in London was published on September 9, 1986 by the Lord Chancellor's Department on behalf of the Commercial Court. Copies of the guide are available from the Lord Chancellor's Department, Room 604, Neville House, Page Street, London SW1P 4LS. [£2.]

2589. Companies Court—insolvency—practice direction

The following practice direction was issued by the direction of the Vice-Chancellor on December 10, 1986.

1. As from December 29, 1986 the following applications shall be made direct to the Judge and, unless otherwise ordered, shall be heard in open Court:—

    (i) Applications to commit any person to prison for contempt.

    (ii) Applications for urgent interlocutory relief (*e.g.* applications pursuant to section 127 of the Act prior to any winding-up order being made).

    (iii) Applications to restrain the presentation or advertisement of a petition to wind up.

    (iv) Petitions for administration orders or an interim order upon such a petition.

    (v) Applications after an administration order has been made pursuant to section 14(3) of the Act (for directions) or section 18(3) of the Act (to vary or discharge the order).

    (vi) Applications pursuant to Section 5(3) of the Act (to stay a winding-up or discharge an administration order or for directions) where a voluntary arrangement has been approved.

    (vii) Appeals from a decision made by a County Court or by a Registrar of the High Court.

2. Subject to 4 below all other applications shall be made to the Registrar in the first instance who may give any necessary directions and may, in the exercise of his discretion, either hear and determine it himself or refer it to the Judge.

3. The following matters will also be heard in open Court:—

    (i) Petitions to wind up (whether opposed or unopposed)

    (ii) Public examinations

    (iii) all matters and applications heard by the Judge except those referred by the Registrar to be heard in chambers or so directed by the Judge to be heard

4. In accordance with directions given by the Lord Chancellor the Registrar has authorised certain applications to be dealt with by the Chief Clerk of the Companies Court pursuant to Rule 13.2(2) of the Insolvency Rules 1986. The applications are:—

    (a) to extend or abridge time prescribed by the Rules in connection with winding-up (Rule 4.3)

    (b) for substituted service of winding-up petitions (Rule 4.8(6))

    (c) to withdraw petitions (Rule 4.15)

    (d) for the substitution of a petitioner (Rule 4.19)

(e) for directions on a petition presented by a contributory (Rule 4.22(2))
(f) by the Official Receiver for limited disclosure of a Statement of Affairs (Rule 4.35)
(g) by the Official Receiver for relief from duties imposed upon him by the Rules (Rule 4.47)
(h) by the Official Receiver for leave to give notice of a meeting by advertisement only (Rule 4.59)
(i) by a liquidator for relief from the requirement to send out forms of proof of debt (Rule 4.74(4))
(j) to expunge or reduce a proof of debt (Rule 4.85)
(k) to appoint a liquidator in either a compulsory or a voluntary winding-up (Rules 4.102 and 4.103)
(l) for leave to a liquidator to resign (Rule 4.111)
(m) by a liquidator for leave to make a return of capital (Rule 4.221)
(n) to transfer proceedings from the High Court to the County Courts (Rule 7.11)
(o) for leave to amend any originating application

5. The Practice Directions dated October 15, 1979 ([1979] 1 W.L.R. 1416; [1979] 3 All E.R. 613) and March 3, 1982 ([1982] 1 W.L.R. 389; [1982] 1 All E.R. 846) are hereby revoked.

PRACTICE DIRECTION (CH.D.) (COMPANIES COURT: INSOLVENCY ACT 1986) (NO. 3 OF 1986) December 10, 1986.

2590. Compromise agreement—whether void for maintenance or champerty
P employed D1 to build flues and stacks for incinerators at Guy's Hospital; D2 supplied the concrete rings wherewith the stacks were built; D3 were the architects for the project; D4 were the structural engineers; D5 were the heating and servicing engineers. In 1978 one of the stacks collapsed. P started proceedings against the Ds who issued contribution notices against each other. Before trial all the Ds except D5 compromised the claim on terms, *inter alia*, that D4 should take over and continue against D5 both P's and the Ds' claims against D5, D4 having paid that part of the overall settlement sum notionally referable to the liability of D5. In the subsequent proceedings D5 contended that that part of the compromise agreement that purported to assign rights against D5 was void for maintenance or champerty. *Held*, determining this plea as a preliminary issue, that the compromise agreement constituted a valid equitable assignment of choses in action; the agreement was not void for maintenance or champerty because D4 had a genuine commercial interest in the subject matter of the assignment, the possibility of D4 making a profit out of the transaction was so slight that it could not affect the justifiability of the agreement: SOUTH EAST THAMES REGIONAL HEALTH AUTHORITY *v.* LOVELL (Y J) (LONDON) (1985) 32 Build L.R. 127, H.H. Judge Newey, O.R.

2591. Conditional order—whether correct
When liability and quantum are still at large, a court should not make a party's right to defend conditional on his paying the plaintiff a sum on account of whatever damages might be awarded: NOBLE *v.* WAKEFIELD CITY METROPOLITAN COUNCIL, *The Times*, July 16, 1986, C.A.

2592. Contempt—breach—failure to identify
[C.C.R., Ord. 29, r.1(5).] Following the breach of a non-molestation order A was committed to prison for contempt but the committal order did not specify the reasons for the committal. *Held*, allowing A's appeal, that the form of a committal order under Ord. 29, r.1(5) clearly contemplated that the recipient should be told what the contempt was for which he was being committed. The warrant for committal did not cure this important defect: for whilst it recited the contempt alleged it was a document addressed to the relevant authorities and not to the contemnor. In the circumstances although there had been a serious contempt the court had no alternative but to discharge the order and to order that A be released: PARRA *v.* RONES (1986) 16 Fam. Law 262, C.A.

2593. Contempt—breach of negative undertaking
[R.S.C. Ord. 45] The order does not apply to proceedings to enforce a negative undertaking to the Court. The undertaking is a promise to the Court upon which the Court pursues a particular course of action. So long as the defendant has notice of the undertaking given on his behalf a breach of it can be punished as a contempt of

court; CAMDEN LONDON BOROUGH COUNCIL *v.* ALPENOAK (1985) 135 New L.J. 1209, Garland J.

2594. Contempt—breach of non-molestation injunction—adjournment—concurrent criminal proceedings

P and D had been living together and had one child; P was granted a non-molestation injunction. She applied to commit D for breach, alleging that he had come to her home, threatened to kill her, smashed her property and assaulted her with an iron bar. The county court judge adjourned P's application until the conclusion of the pending criminal proceedings against D arising out of the same incident. *Held,* allowing W's appeal, that the judge had not been referred to *Sczepanski* where the Court of Appeal had held that the jurisdiction of the court when exercising its jurisdiction in contempt proceedings was quite separate from any criminal proceedings. It was an inherent power which derived from the jurisdiction of the court to enforce its orders. The judge had therefore been in error (*Szczepanski* v. *Szczepanski* [1985] C.L.Y. 2632 followed): CAPRICE *v.* BOSWELL (1986) 16 Fam. Law 52, C.A.

2595. Contempt—committal for contempt—standard of proof

The appropriate standard of proof to be applied in committal proceedings in a civil action is the criminal standard of proof (*West Oxfordshire District Council* v. *Beratec* [1986] C.L.Y. 2601, *R.* v. *Secretary of State for the Home Department, ex p. Khawaja* [1983] C.L.Y. 1908, *Deborah Building Equipment* v. *Scaffco* [1986] C.L.Y. 2643, *Danchevsky* v. *Danchevsky (No. 2)* (unrep. November 10, 1977), *Re Bramblevale* [1969] C.L.Y. 2810 considered): DEAN *v.* DEAN, *The Times,* November 13, 1986, C.A.

2596. Contempt—committal—non-molestation order—period of imprisonment for breach

Contempt of Court Act 1981 (c.49), s.14(1).] The parties lived in Guernsey. Following the breakdown of their relationship M took their baby and went to live in England with her grandparents. Having learned that F had followed her to England M obtained an *ex parte* non-molestation order on behalf of the child and herself and an order preventing F from coming within a quarter-mile radius of the grandparents' home. A penal notice was attached. Subsequently, F waylaid M outside the home and assaulted her and, on a subsequent occasion, he had twice entered the home and assaulted both M and the grandparents. The judge found the breaches sufficiently serious to merit a prison sentence of nine months. *Held,* allowing F's appeal, that the two episodes were serious breaches and merited a penal sentence of three months' imprisonment. However it was impossible to lay down guide-lines in such cases since the family background and circumstances varied in each instance. The maximum sentences under s.14(1) of the 1981 Act were, though, worthy of note: H (A MINOR) (INJUNCTION: BREACH), *Re,* (1986) 16 Fam. Law 139, C.A.

2597. Contempt—committal order—indefinite period—whether valid

[Contempt of Court Act 1981 (c.49), s.14(1) Administration of Justice Act 1960 (c.65), s.13(3).]

A committal order for a contempt of court must be for a finite period.

In the course of civil litigation the defendant on numerous occasions failed to obey High Court Orders to produce documents. He was committed to prison for contempt "until further order." The defendant appealed contending that an order purporting to imprison him for an indefinite period was unlawful. *Held,* allowing the appeal, that the committal order was unlawful having regard to s.14(1) of the 1981 Act.

LINNETT *v.* COLES [1986] 3 W.L.R. 843, D.C.

2598. Contempt of court—libel proceedings—justification

[Contempt of Court Act 1981 (c.49), s.2.]

A plaintiff in libel proceedings cannot obtain an injunction restraining further publication of the alleged libel when the defence is one of justification unless there is a substantial risk of serious prejudice to the trial.

In 1984 the plaintiff began proceedings for libel against a newspaper which relied on the defence of justification. The case was set down for trial not earlier than March 1987. In April 1986 the defendants the owners of another newspaper, proposed to publish the same allegations. The Attorney-General brought proceedings to restrain the defendants under the strict liability rule in s.1 of the Contempt of Court Act 1981, *i.e.*, "the rule of law whereby conduct may be treated as a contempt of court as tending to interfere with the course of justice in particular legal proceedings regardless of intent to do so." However, under s.2 this rule only applied if the publication created a substantial risk that the course of justice in those proceedings would be seriously impeded or prejudiced and if such proceedings were "active", *i.e.* had been set down for trial. The defendants contended that where the publication could be justified the right of freedom of expression was to be balanced against the right to a fair trial and that up until three months before the trial the balance ought to be in favour of publication. They further contended that in any event there was no substantial risk of serious prejudice, since the trial was not until March 1987. The judge granted an injunction restraining publication, but the defendants' appeal was allowed. *Held*, that although normally no prior restraint would be ordered against a defendant pleading justification, the court would inevitably make an order under s.2 of the 1981 Act if there was a substantial risk of serious prejudice to the trial. These were stringent tests. Each case depended on its own facts, but factors of great importance were the place of trial, the nature of the proposed publication, and the proximity of it to the date of trial. In this case, although the proceedings were "active", the date fixed for trial was so far in advance of the proposed publication that it did not create a substantial risk of serious prejudice. The injunction was discharged . (*Bonnard* v. *Perryman* [1891–4] All E.R. Rep. 965 and dictum of Lord Reid in *Att.-Gen.* v. *Times Newspapers* [1973] 3 All E.R. 54 at 65; [1973] C.L.Y. 2618 considered).

ATT.-GEN. *v.* NEWS GROUP NEWSPAPERS [1986] 2 All E.R. 833, C.A.

2599. Contempt—picket of court by strikers—whether court has jurisdiction to prevent by injunction
[Can.] In Autumn 1983 a government employees' union began a legal strike against the executive branch of the government. They established picket lines at the entrances to various courts. Acting on his own motion, the Chief Justice of the Supreme Court issued an injunction restraining the union from further such picketing. *Held*, dismissing the union's appeal, that Canadian citizens have a constitutional right to unfettered access to the courts. Superior courts have an inherent jurisdiction to maintain their independent authority and to prevent abuse of their processes. Since the picketing was calculated to interfere with the lawful processes of the court it amounted to contempt and could be restrained by injunction: BRITISH COLUMBIA GOVERNMENT EMPLOYEES' UNION *Re* [1985] 5 W.W.R. 421, British Columbia C.A.

2600. Contempt—threat to barrister
B, a barrister, brought private criminal proceedings against D. While proceedings were still pending, S, D's solicitor, wrote to B threatening to report him to the Inner Temple authorities, and to sue him for malicious prosecution. *Held*, that the former threat amounted to contempt of court, but the latter, although close to the boundary of the permissible, was not. A party could take proper steps to defeat his opponent, but if pressure was applied, it had to be fair, reasonable and moderate. A party may not make unlawful threats, and in this context "unlawful" meant "unlawful". S would be fined £750 (*Att.-Gen.* v. *Times Newspapers* [1973] C.L.Y. 2618 applied): MARTIN (PETER), *Re, The Times*, April 23, 1986, D.C.

2601. Contempt—standard of proof
The standard of proof in proceedings for committal for breach of an injunction or undertaking is the civil, not the criminal, standard: WEST OXFORDSHIRE DISTRICT COUNCIL *v.* BERATEC, *The Times*, October 30, 1986, D.C.

2602. Contempt—wardship—suspended committal—formalities
[Contempt of Court Act 1981 (c.49), s.14(1).] The ward, who was in the care and control of M's stepfather and his wife (the plaintiffs), was not returned by M and F after a period of access and was taken by F to Italy. In proceedings it was ordered that the ward should be returned forthwith to the plaintiffs and that M should attend court. At that subsequent hearing on August 7, 1985 the judge ordered (i) M's committal to prison suspended for 21 days, a discharge of that order to be considered if the ward was returned within that time, (ii) the ward be returned within 10 days and (iii) M to surrender her passport. The child was not returned. On September 16, 1985, on the hearing of the plaintiffs' summons a committal order was made against M suspended for 14 days. The hearing took place in chambers and there was no public announcement of the judge's order. *Held*, allowing M's appeal, that the order of August 7 was fatally flawed in that it imposed a suspended sentence of

imprisonment that was not for a fixed term, contrary to s.14(1) of the 1981 Act. Furthermore, it failed to state the contempts and it was not clear to whom it was directed and what exactly M was required to do. The proceedings on September 16 should have been launched by notice of motion. The order of that date was flawed in that it was founded in part on a defective injunction and on an act of contempt which had already been punished. The sentence was also not for a fixed term. (*Att.-Gen.* v. *Staffordshire County Council* [1905] 1 Ch. 336 and *McIlraith* v. *Grady* [1967] C.L.Y. 3107 applied; *Morris* v. *Redland Bricks* [1969] C.L.Y. 2866 considered): C (A MINOR) (WARDSHIP: CONTEMPT), *Re*, (1986) 16 Fam. Law 187, C.A.

2603. Costs—application for solicitor to pay costs personally—whether trial judge should hear application

[R.S.C. Ord. 62, r.8.]

An application for an order that a solicitor pay the costs of a trial should be heard by the trial judge unless there are exceptional circumstances that require the application to be heard by another judge.

At the end of a hearing lasting 26 days the trial judge in giving judgment for D was highly critical of the conduct of H, P's solicitor. The judge formed a provisional view on what he had heard that H did on occasions invent or embellish evidence with a view to improperly furthering his client's case, and that H was unfit to remain on the Roll of Solicitors. The judge sent a copy of his judgment to the secretary of the professional purposes committee of the Law Society. D applied for an order that H be jointly and severally liable with P to meet D's costs in the action. H applied for an order that the application be heard by another judge and not the trial judge. The application was refused and H appealed contending that by reason of the comments made in the judgment the trial judge would have the appearnace of being biased against H and that H would wrongly be put in the position of having to persuade the trial judge to take a different view of his conduct than that which he had originally expressed. *Held*, dismissing the appeal, that D's application under R.S.C., Ord. 62, r.8 provided a summary remedy of a compensatory nature against H. Such an application should be heard by the trial judge unless there were compelling reasons to the contrary. Such cases would be exceptional. No such reasons existed in the present case. The procedure to be adopted on the hearing of the application was a matter for the judge. The judge should take account of any handicap caused to H through his inability to cross-examine witnesses who gave evidence in the trial and any claim to privilege asserted by his client. The burden of proof was on the applicant defendant and, the more serious the charges levelled against H the more difficult they would be for the applicant to prove (*Brendon* v. *Spiro* [1938] 1 K.B. 176 applied).

BAHAI v. RASHIDIAN [1985] 3 All E.R. 385, C.A.

2604. Costs—costs payable by solicitor—jurisdiction to order

[R.S.C., Ord. 62, r.8.] The defendant's solicitor will only be required to pay the costs of a successful plaintiff in clear cases, supported by evidence rather than inference, of serious misconduct or serious dereliction of duty by that solicitor (*Kelly* v. *L.T.E.* [1982] C.L.Y. 2447, *Rondel* v. *Worsley* [1968] C.L.Y. 3054, *Edwards* v. *Edwards* [1958] C.L.Y. 957, *Davy-Chiesman* v. *Davy-Chiesman* [1984] C.L.Y. 1995 considered): ORCHARD v. SOUTH EASTERN ELECTRICITY BOARD, *The Times*, November 14, 1986, C.A.

2605. Costs—matrimonial costs—judicial discretion

In matrimonial proceedings the trial judge had ordered, *inter alia*, that H should pay to W the sum of £31,000 assessed as costs recoverable by her from H. Without giving any indication of her intention to do so, the judge had elected to assess the figures for costs under R.S.C., Ord. 62, r.9 as a gross sum, instead of taxed costs so as to avoid the problems arising out of the taxation of such costs. *Held*, dismissing H's appeal, that there were no formal restrictions with which a judge had to comply when awarding a fixed sum other than such discretion had to be exercised in a judicial manner. There had been no miscarriage of justice in the instant case: LEARY v. LEARY, *The Times*, October 7th 1986, C.A.

2606. Costs—motions to remit arbitration awards—whether costs limited to parties to proceedings

[Supreme Court Act 1981 (c.54), s.51(1); R.S.C., Ord. 62, r.2(4).]

An order for costs under s.51(1) of the Supreme Court Act 1981 is not limited so as to be paid only by parties to the proceedings.

Following damage to their vessel, shipowners made a claim against the charterers; they claimed against the sub-charterers. Arbitration awards were ultimately submitted to the relevant tribunals, but owing to disputes as to the scope of remissions, the owners and the sub-charterers issued notices of motion. These were heard together, and an order for costs was made including costs paid by the charterers in the sub-charter proceedings. The appeal was allowed. *Held*, the House of Lords allowing the appeal, that the discretionary power to award costs was wide, and there was no justification for implying a limitation that costs could only be ordered to be paid by parties to the proceedings (*Forbes-Smith* v. *Forbes-Smith* [1901] P. 258; *Fairfax (John) & Sons,* v. *E.C. de Witt & Co.* [1958] 1 Q.B. 323 C.A. overruled).

AIDEN SHIPPING v. INTERBULK [1986] 2 W.L.R. 1051, H.L.

2607. Costs—overseas counsel—taxation. See TAI HING COTTON MILL v. LIU CHONG BANK (No. 2), § 2742.

2608. Costs—personal liability of solicitor—right to open

[R.S.C., Ord. 62, r.8.] There is no right or obligation on solicitor at risk of being made personally liable for costs to open proceedings by showing why the order should not be made: BAHAI v. RASHIDIAN (No. 2), *The Times,* June 11, 1986, Drake J.

2609. Costs—R.S.C., Ord. 62

THE RULES OF THE SUPREME COURT (AMENDMENT) ORDER 1986 (S.I. 1986 No. 632) brings into force on April 28, 1986 a new Order 62 of the Rules of the Supreme Court. The new Order 62 changes the basis for the award and taxation of legal costs between parties in the Court of Appeal and the High Court from recovering costs which are "necessary and proper" to recovering costs which have been "reasonably incurred."

2610. Costs—security for costs—third party—whether security for costs against plaintiffs

[R.S.C., Ord. 23, r.1(1)(3).]

Since a third party joined by a defendant is not in the position of being a defendant to the plaintiff's claim, there is no jurisdiction to order the plaintiff to provide security for the third party's costs.

The plaintiffs brought an action against several defendants claiming sums of money alleged to be due under a contract of insurance. The defendants joined the third party to the action claiming an indemnity from it. The plaintiffs obtained orders for specific discovery and interrogatories against the third party which then applied pursuant to R.S.C., Ord. 23, r.1 for an order that the plaintiffs provide security for the third party's costs. The judge dismissed the application on the ground that he had no jurisdiction to make such an order. *Held*, that the third party's appeal was dismissed. "Proceedings" in R.S.C., Ord. 23 r.1 referred to an action or to proceedings in the nature of an action; it referred to the whole matter and not to an interlocutory application in some other proceedings. Since the third party was not in the position of being a defendant to the plaintiff's claim, within the meaning of R.S.C., Ord. 23, r.1(3) there was no jurisdiction to order the plaintiffs to provide security for the third party's costs. Even if there were such a jurisdiction, the court would refuse to make such an order in its discretion since the defendants could be ordered to pay the third party's costs if they failed in their claim against the third party.

TALY N.D.C. INTERNATIONAL N.V. v. TERRA NOVA INSURANCE CO. (CHANDLER HARGREAVES WHITTAL & CO. THIRD PARTY) [1985] 1 W.L.R. 1359, C.A.

2611. Costs—taxation—practice direction

From April 28, 1986 until further direction The Masters' Practice Notes 1986 will apply to all bills of costs lodged for taxation in the Supreme Court Taxing Office, The Principal Registry of the Family Division and the Admiralty Registry accept such bills lodged in accordance with Rule 11(3) of the Rules of the Supreme Court (Amendment) 1986 (S.I. 1986 No. 632 (L.2)) to which the practice notes made under the Rules of the Supreme Court (Amendment) 1979 (S.I. 1979 No. 35 (L.I)) will continue to apply.

PRACTICE DIRECTION (SUP. CT. TAXING OFFICE) (NO. 1 OF 1986) April 9, 1986.

2612. Costs—taxation—standard basis
[R.S.C., Ord. 72, r.19(2).]
The new Ord. 62 is not a complete restatement of the costs rules; it is a rationalisation of the different bases for awarding costs, and a successful party is still not entitled to indemnity costs, save in exceptional cases.

A successful plaintiff invited the judge to take the opportunity to review the new costs rule and redress the imbalance whereby a successful party only recovered roughly two-thirds of his costs. *Held,* there had been a rationalisation not a complete restatement of the rules and this was not an occasion for reappraising what cases should be dealt with on the standard basis.

(Dictum of Brightman L.J. in *Bartlett* v. *Barclays Bank Trust Co. Ltd. (No. 2)* [1980] C.L.Y. 2403 applied.)

BOWEN-JONES v. BOWEN-JONES [1986] 3 All E.R. 163, Knox J.

2613. Counterclaim—whether liquidated claim
P sued D on a cheque. D counterclaimed £6,923, including unliquidated damages for breaches of conditions in a contract of sale. *Held,* that this did not constitute a liquidated or ascertainable claim entitling D, on P's application for summary judgment, to unconditional leave to defend (*Nova (Jersey) Knit* v. *Krammgarn Spinnerei* [1977] C.L.Y. 195 distinguished): CASE POCLAIN CORP. v. JONES, *The Times,* May 7, 1986, C.A.

2614. Court of Protection—appointment of public trustee as receiver—practice direction
The following practice direction was issued by the Master of the Court of Protection on December 9, 1986.

1. The Public Trustee and Administration of Funds Act 1986 will come into force on January 2, 1987. From that date, the Public Trustee will be able to be appointed Receiver under the Mental Health Act 1983.

2. However, in normal circumstances, the Public Trustee as Receiver will refer to the Court of Protection any applications made in connection with any of the following:—
    (1) paragraphs (e), (i) and (k) of s.96 of the Mental Health Act 1983, or paragraph (d) as regards substantial gifts;
    (2) applications under ss.98, 99, 100 and 104 of the Mental Health Act 1983;
    (3) applications under the Enduring Powers of Attorney Act 1985
    (4) applications under s.1(3) of the Variation of Trusts Act 1958, s.36(9) of the Trustee Act 1925 and s.54 of the Trustee Act 1925.

3. The Public Trustee will be appointed in all cases in which the Principal of the Management Division of the Court of Protection is at present Receiver and a separate order will be pronounced in respect of each of those patients.

4. In the case of First General Orders to be pronounced on or after 2 January 1987, the Public Trustee will be appointed in all cases in which the Principal of the Management Division would previously have been appointed.

5. The order appointing the Public Trustee in place of the Principal of the Management Division will be in the following form:—
"Court of Protection   No.
Order dated 2 January 1987
In the matter of (Patient's name) (in this order referred to as the Patient)
IT IS ORDERED
1. The Principal of the Management Division of the Court of Protection is discharged from the receivership and his final account as Receiver is dispensed with.
2. The Public Trustee of Stewart House, 24 Kingsway, London WC2B 6HD is appointed Receiver and in relation to the property and affairs of the Patient is authorised generally for the purposes of Part VII of the Mental Health Act 1983 to do or secure the doing of all such things as appear necessary or expedient.
3. The Public Trustee as Receiver is authorised to carry into effect all or any contracts entered into by the Principal of the Management Division of the Court of Protection on behalf of the Patient."

6. The First General Order appointing the Public Trustee as Receiver will be in the following form:—
"Court of Protection   No.
First General Order dated
In the matter of (Patient's name) (in this order referred to as the Patient)
Upon the application of
IT IS ORDERED
The Public Trustee of Stewart House, 24 Kingsway, London WC2B 6HD is appointed Receiver and in relation to the property and affairs of the Patient is authorised generally for the purposes of Part VII of the Mental Health Act 1983 to do or secure the doing of all such things as appear necessary or expedient."
7. The order which will be made where the Principal of the Management Division is at present Receiver *ad interim* will be:—
"Court of Protection   No.
Supplemental Order dated 2 January 1987
In the matter of (Patient's name)
1. This order is supplemental to an order dated
     (the Interim Order)
2. The Interim Order shall be read and construed as if the name of the Public Trustee were substituted therein as Receiver in place of the Principal of the Management Division of the Court of Protection but in all other respects the Interim Order is confirmed."
8. It has been agreed with H.M. Land Registry that no question will be raised as to the Public Trustee's power to dispose of or otherwise deal with land when he is acting under an order in one of the above forms.
9. All documents to be executed by the Public Trustee pursuant to an order in one of the above forms will be sealed with his Official Seal.
10. From January 2, 1987, all enquiries, applications and correspondence concerning cases in which the Public Trustee has been appointed Receiver should be sent to the Receivership Division, Stewart House, 24 Kingsway, London WC2B 6HD. All enquiries, applications and correspondence in cases where any other person or body is Receiver should continue to be sent to the Protection Division, Staffordshire House, 25 Store Street, London WC1E 7BP.
11. From January 2, 1987, the title "Court of Protection" will apply only to what is at present entitled the Judicial Division of the Court of Protection. The Management Division (which will be known in future as the Receivership Division) and the Protection Division will both become part of the new organisation, to be called the Public Trust Office. Until further notice, applications made to the Public Trust Office which concern matters solely within the province of the Court of Protection will be accepted as properly made, even if made in the wrong name, but time will be saved if the correct address is used. The address of the Court of Protection itself will remain Staffordshire House, 25 Store Street, London WC1E 7BP.
PRACTICE DIRECTION (COURT OF PROTECTION) (APPOINTMENT OF PUBLIC TRUSTEE AS RECEIVER) December 9, 1986.

2615. Court-martial. *See* ARMED FORCES.

2616. Declaratory relief—cause of action. See KINGDOM OF SPAIN *v.* CHRISTIE, MANSON & WOODS, § 1297.

2617. Defence and counterclaim—procedure—notes of judgment
P sued D, who filed a defence and counterclaim. At the beginning of the trial of the action, the judge was invited to enter judgment for P on the whole or part of his claim, and proceed to try the counterclaim. *Held,* that the principles for the judge to apply were the same as in an application for summary judgment under R.S.C., Ord. 14. Even in urgent cases, a judge should always be given the opportunity of approving (even if informally) notes of his judgment that are to be provided for the Court of Appeal: BELSHAM *v.* WILLIAM DAWSON & SONS, *The Times,* November 27, 1986, C.A.

2618. Discovery—Anton Piller order—solicitors' undertaking—VAT proceedings. See E.M.I. RECORDS *v.* SPILLANE, § 3480.

2619. Discovery—complex papers—use of co-ordinator
In an appropriate case a person not a party, nor a prospective witness, nor a legal advisor could be entrusted with the task of co-ordinating or collating the documents

available on discovery. However it was open to the party disclosing the documents to object for a good reason to a particular person: DAVIES v. ELI LILLY & CO. *The Times,* August 2, 1986, Hirst J.

2620. Discovery—disclosure of part of letter—whether waiver of privilege in respect of whole
The disclosure of part of a letter pursuant to a general order for discovery in the course of litigation between the parties constitutes a waiver of privilege in respect of the whole contents of that letter (*Great Atlantic Insurance Co.* v. *Home Insurance Co.* [1981] C.L.Y. 2522 and *General Accident Fire and Life Assurance Corp.* v. *Tanter* [1985] C.L.Y. 1804 applied): POZZI v. ELI LILLEY & CO., *The Times,* December 3, 1986, Staughton J.

2621. Discovery—documents leading to grant of search warrant—whether jurisdiction—whether public interest immunity
[Supreme Court Act 1981 (c.54), s.33; R.S.C., Ord. 29, r.7A.] In an action against a chief constable, P sought disclosure of documents leading to the grant of search warrants. *Held,* that the application would be refused because (1) there was no jurisdiction in either R.S.C., Ord. 29, r.7A or s.33 of the Supreme Court Act 1981; (2) the documents were covered by public interest immunity: TAYLOR v. ANDERTON, *The Times,* October 21, 1986, Scott J.

2622. Discovery—legal professional privilege—dominant purpose test
[N.Z.] When litigation is in progress or is reasonably apprehended, a report or other document obtained by a party or by his legal adviser is privileged from inspection or production in evidence if the dominant purpose of its preparation is to enable the legal adviser to conduct or advise regarding the litigation (*Waugh* v. *British Railways Board* [1979] C.L.Y. 2172 applied): GUARDIAN ROYAL EXCHANGE ASSURANCE OF NEW ZEALAND v. STUART [1985] 1 N.Z.L.R. 596, N.Z. C.A.

2623. Discovery—list of documents—privileged documents—mistaken inclusion
[R.S.C., Ord. 24, rr.5, 9.]
Copies must be provided of privileged documents mistakenly included in a list for discovery once the list has been inspected although notification of objection to production may be given until that moment.
The liquidator in proceedings to set aside a fraudulent preference mistakenly included in his list of documents a number of letters for which privilege could have been claimed. The respondent's solicitor saw them and made notes. He was then notified of the mistakes. He nevertheless requested copies. The liquidator served a revised list. *Held,* it was too late for the liquidator to correct his mistake, and the respondent was entitled to copies.
BRIAMORE MANUFACTURING (IN LIQUIDATION), *Re* [1986] 3 All E.R. 132, Hoffmann J.

2624. Discovery—personal injuries action—medical notes
Where a plaintiff sues a defendant for damages for personal injuries he is entitled to discovery of hospital notes and records against a health authority, even if it is not a party to the action: WALKER v. ELI LILLY & CO., *The Times,* May 1, 1986, Hirst J.

2625. Discovery—privilege—police questionnaires
[Police Act 1964 (c.48), ss.48, 49.]
Where police take statements both for the purpose of investigating a complaint under s.49 of the Police Act 1964 and also for the purpose of investigating the death of a member of the public, it will be the dominant purpose which determines whether the statements are subject to discovery.
The Metropolitan Police began an investigation into the death of Blair Peach during a public demonstration. They took witness statements and completed questionnaires. The statements were made available to the coroner at the inquest. Peach's mother claimed damages under s.48 of the Police Act 1964. The Commissioner refused to produce the statements for the purposes of the action, claiming privilege on the grounds of public interest in that they were obtained for the purpose of investigating a complaint under s.49 of the Police Act. *Held,* that the investigation was both the investigation of a complaint, and also for the purpose of ascertaining how the deceased had died. Had the statements been solely for the purpose of a s.49 inquiry, they would have been privileged. However, the dominant purpose had been to ascertain how the deceased had died, and their production would be ordered (*Nielson* v. *Laugharne* [1981] C.L.Y. 2142 distinguished; *Hehir* v. *Comr. of Police for*

the Metropolis [1982] C.L.Y. 2353 and *Conerney* v. *Jacklin* [1985] C.L.Y. 1998 considered.)

PEACH *v.* COMMISSIONER OF POLICE FOR THE METROPOLIS [1986] 2 All E.R. 129, C.A.

2626. Documents served on counsel—whether authority to accept
[Road Traffic Act 1972 (c.20), s.10(5), (8) (as substituted by Transport Act 1981 (c.56), s.25(3), Sched. 8.]

Counsel does not have general authority to accept service of documents in the way that a solicitor does; he does, however, have authority to accept, or to decline to accept, service of documents relevant to a matter in issue in the magistrates' court.

D was charged in the magistrates' court with a number of charges arising out of the same incident the charges all being dependent on an analyst's and a medical certificate. On an earlier hearing, after solicitors and D had left court, counsel accepted the certificates from the police officer. He then forgot about it, and at the trial of the charges took the point that they had not been served; on being reminded of the facts, he argued that they had not been validly served, he being counsel in the case. The justices upheld that submission. *Held,* allowing the prosecutor's appeal, that although counsel did not have general authority to accept service, he had authority to accept, or to decline to accept service of documents relevant to a matter in issue in the magistrates' court. (*Burt* v. *Kirkcaldy* [1965] C.L.Y. 3492 and *Anderton* v. *Kinnard* [1986] C.L.Y. 2866 applied.)

PENMAN *v.* PARKER [1986] 1 W.L.R. 882, D.C.

2627. Enduring power of attorney—grants of administration—practice direction
The following practice direction for grants of administration on death was issued by the Senior Registrar of the Family Division on March 14, 1986.

1. The Enduring Powers of Attorney Act 1985 came into force on March 10, 1986. The Act provides that an enduring power of attorney, within the meaning of the Act, is not revoked by the subsequent mental incapacity of the donor, but once the donor has become incapable the rights of the attorney are limited until the power of attorney has been registered with the Court of Protection. Even a registered enduring power of attorney may confer only limited powers on the attorney, so that it will be necessary to ensure that the power covers an application for a grant.

2. Effect on existing grants:
(a) If a sole, or sole surviving, grantee becomes mentally incapable his attorney under an enduring power of attorney is not able to continue the administration on behalf of the grantee in reliance on the power of attorney, whether or not it has been registered with the Court of Protection. Where the attorney subsequently applies for a grant in respect of any unadministered estate the grant to the donor should be lodged with the application for the grant and will be retained by the Court.

(b) If one of two or more grantees becomes mentally incapable, the attorney under an enduring power of attorney of the incapable administrator similarly will not be able to continue the administration with the capable grantee(s). The grant in these circumstances should be revoked and a fresh grant will be needed to continue the administration.

(c) Where a grant has issued to an attorney of a donor for the use and benefit of that donor and the donor becomes mentally incapable, the attorney will be able to continue with the administration, provided that the donor has also appointed the same attorney under a sufficient enduring power of attorney which has been registered with the Court of Protection, even if the power of attorney used on the grant application was a different power of attorney and it has been revoked by the donor's mental incapacity.

3. Applications for grants after March 10, 1986:
(a) Where the donor is mentally capable of managing his affairs, an application for a grant by an attorney may be made, as before, under rule 30 of the Non-Contentious Probate Rules 1954 in reliance on a power of attorney which is not an enduring power of attorney. The existing practice and procedure will apply.

(b) Where the donor is mentally incapable of managing his affairs and the application for a grant is supported by a power of attorney which is in the form of an enduring power of attorney but which has not been registered with the Court of Protection the application may proceed under rule 30 NCPR and the existing practice and procedure will apply, save that the original power of attorney should normally be produced on the application. If a copy of the power of attorney certified in accordance with section 3 of the Powers of Attorney Act 1971 is lodged, instead of the original, the oath to lead to the grant should confirm that no application has been made to the Court of Protection for the registration of the enduring power of attorney.

(c) Where the donor is mentally capable of managing his affairs and the application for the grant is supported by an enduring power of attorney which has been registered with the Court of Protection (the donor's incapacity being impending) it must be sworn in the oath to lead to the grant (and in the affidavit in support of any application for a direction under rule 30(2) NCPR) that the donor is mentally capable of managing his affairs. The original power of attorney sealed by the Court of Protection should be produced on the application.

(d) where the donor is mentally incapable of managing his affairs and the application for the grant is supported by an enduring power of attorney which has been registered with the Court of Protection it will not be apparent from the fact of registration whether the donor is mentally incapable or whether the incapacity is impending. It must be sworn in the oath to lead to the grant that the donor is mentally incapable of managing his affairs. No other evidence of mental incapacity will be called for. Notice of the application for the grant must be given to the Court of Protection as required by rule 33(3) NCPR and although rule 33 NCPR does not at present refer to an attorney, under a registered enduring power of attorney, of a person who is by reason of mental incapacity incapable of managing his affairs, such an attorney will normally be considered to be a suitable person to whom to direct the issue of a grant pursuant to an order made under the last line of rule 33(1)(*b*) NCPR. The original power of attorney, sealed by the Court of Protection, should be produced on the application. Practitioners' attention is also drawn to the provisions of rule 33(2) NCPR.

4. Unless there is a relevant restriction in the power of attorney, the limitation to be included in a grant issuing to an attorney under an enduring power of attorney should be "to AB the lawful attorney of CD for his use and benefit and until further representation be granted", whether the donor is capable and the application is made under rule 30 NCPR or whether the donor is mentally incapable and the application is made under rule 33 NCPR: Practice Direction (Fam.D.) (Enduring Power of Attorney: Grants of Administration), March 14, 1986.

2628. Enduring Powers of Attorney Act 1985—applications prior to registration—practice direction

The following practice direction was issued by the Master of the Court of Protection of March 18, 1986.

Where an attorney wishes to make some application to the Court of Protection under the above Act before having lodged the application to register, the original enduring power of attorney must accompany the first application: Practice Direction (Court of Protection: Enduring Powers of Attorney Act 1985) March 18, 1986.

2629. Execution—writ of fieri facias—erroneous setting aside of judgment subsequently reversed—priority of writ

[Supreme Court Act 1981 (c.54), s.138.] Where judgment was obtained and a writ of *fieri facias* issued and was delivered to the sheriff, and subsequently the judgment was erroneously overturned, and then restored, the writ of *fieri facias* regained its priority over all similar writs issued and delivered to the sheriff after its original delivery: Bankers Trust Co. *v.* Galadari, *The Times*, October 15, 1986, C.A.

2630. Experts' reports—medical negligence—discretion to order exchange

[R.S.C., Ord. 38, r.38.] The High Court has a discretion in actions for personal injuries alleging medical negligence to order disclosure and exchange of experts reports: Graham *v.* Watt-Smyrk, *The Times,* November 26, 1986, Tudor Evans J.

2631. Family Division—conciliation—report of court welfare officer—practice direction

The following practice direction was issued by the Senior Registrar of the Family Division on July 28, 1986 with the approval of the President and the concurrence of the Lord Chancellor.

A Judge or Registrar, before ordering an inquiry and report by a Court Welfare Officer, should, where local conciliation facilities exist, consider whether the case is a suitable one for attempts to be made to settle any of the issues by the conciliation process, and if so, a direction to this effect should be included in the order. If conciliation fails, any report which is ordered must be made by an officer who did not act as a conciliator.

Where the court directs an enquiry and report by a Welfare Officer, it is the function of the Welfare Officer to assist the court by investigating the circumstances of the child, or children, concerned and the important figures in their lives, to report what he sees and hears, to offer the court his assessment of the situation and, where appropriate to make a recommendation. In such circumstances, it is not the role of the Welfare Officer to attempt conciliation although he may encourage the parties to settle their differences if the likelihood of a settlement arises during the course of his enquiries.

PRACTICE DIRECTION (FAM. D.) (CHILDREN: INQUIRY AND REPORT BY A WELFARE OFFICER) [1986] 2 F.L.R. 171, July 28, 1986.

2632. Family Division—transfer of proceedings—practice direction

The following direction was issued by the President of the Family Division on April 28, 1986.

I. These directions are given under s.37 of the Matrimonial and Family Proceedings Act 1984 by the President of the Family Division with the concurrence of the Lord Chancellor, and apply to all family proceedings which are transferable between the High Court and county courts under ss.38 and 39 of that Act. They do not apply to proceedings under the following provisions (which may be heard and determined in the High Court alone):

(*a*) s.45(i) of the Matrimonial Causes Act 1973 (declaration of legitimacy or validity of a marriage);

(*b*) the Guardianship of Minors Acts 1971 and 1973 in the circumstances provided by s.15(3) of the Guardianship of Minors Act 1971;

(*c*) s.14 of the Children Act 1975 where the child is not in Great Britain (proposed foreign adoption);

(*d*) s.24 of the Children Act 1975 or s.6 of the Adoption Act 1968 (Convention adoptions);

(*e*) Pt. III of the Matrimonial and Family Proceedings Act 1984; or to an application that a minor be made, or cease to be, a ward of court.

2(1) Family proceedings to which these directions apply (including interlocutory proceedings) shall be dealt with in the High Court where it appears to the court seised of the case that by reason of the complexity, difficulty or gravity of the issues they ought to be tried in the High Court.

(2) Without prejudice to the generality of sub-para (i), the following proceedings shall be dealt with in the High Court unless the nature of the issues of fact or law raised in the case makes them more suitable for trial in a county court than in the High Court:

(*a*) petitions under s.1(2)(*e*) of the Matrimonial Causes Act 1973 which are opposed pursuant to s.5 of that Act;

(*b*) petitions in respect of jactitation of marriage;

(*c*) petitions for presumption of death and dissolution of marriage under s.19 of the Matrimonial Causes Act 1973;

(*d*) proceedings involving a contested issue of domicile;

(*e*) applications under s.5(6) of the Domicile and Matrimonial Proceedings Act 1973;

(*f*) applications to restrain a resident from taking or continuing with foreign proceedings;

(*g*) proceedings for recognition of a foreign degree;

(*h*) suits in which the Queen's Proctor intervenes or shows cause and elects trial in the High Court;

(*i*) proceedings in relation to a ward of court (i) in which the Official Solicitor is or becomes the guardian ad litem of the ward or of a party to the proceedings, (ii) in which a local authority is or becomes a party, (iii) in which blood tests are required, or (iv) where any of the matters specified in (j) below are in issue;

(*j*) proceedings concerning children in divorce and under the Guardianship Acts where (i) an application is opposed on the grounds of want of jurisdiction, or (ii) there is a substantial foreign element, or (iii) there is an opposed application for leave to take a child permanently out of the jurisdiction or where there is an application for temporary removal of a child from the jurisdiction and it is opposed on the ground that the child may not be duly returned;

(*k*) applications for adoption or for freeing for adoption (i) which are opposed on the grounds of want of jurisdiction, (ii) which would result in the acquisition by a child of British nationality;

(*l*) interlocutory applications involving (i) Anton Piller orders, (ii) Mareva injunctions, (iii) directions as to dealing with assets outside the jurisdiction.

3. In proceedings where periodical payments, a lump sum payment or property are in issue the court shall have regard in particular to the following factors when considering in accordance with para. 2(1) above whether the complexity, difficulty or gravity of the issues are such that they ought to be tried by a judge of the High Court:

(*a*) the capital values of the assets involved and the extent to which they are available for, or susceptible to, distribution or adjustment; or

(*b*) any substantial allegations of fraud or deception or non-disclosure; or

(*c*) any substantial contested allegations of conduct.

An appeal in such proceedings from a registrar in the county court shall be transferred to the High Court where it appears to the registrar, whether on application by a party or otherwise, that the appeal raises a difficult or important question of law.

4. Subject to the foregoing, family proceedings may be dealt with in a county court.

5. Proceedings in the High Court which under the foregoing criteria fall to be dealt with in a county court or a divorce county court, as the case may be, and proceedings in a county court which likewise fall to be dealt with in the High Court shall be transferred accordingly, in accordance with rules of court, unless to do so would cause undue delay or hardship to any party or other person involved.

PRACTICE DIRECTION (FAM.D.) (TRANSFER OF PROCEEDINGS) [1986] 2 All E.R. 703.

2633. Family Division—wards—secure accommodation—practice direction

The following practice direction was issued by the Senior Registrar of the Family Division with the approval of the President and the concurrence of the Lord Chancellor on October 14, 1986.

The Secure Accommodation (No. 2) (Amendment) Regulations 1986 (S.I. 1986 No. 1591), came into force on October 15, 1986 and provide, *inter alia*, that a ward of court may be placed and kept in secure accommodation only pursuant to the direction of a judge exercising wardship jurisdiction in the High Court or in wardship proceedings transferred to a county court under s.38 of the Matrimonial and Family Proceedings Act 1984.

In other secure accommodation applications, dealt with in the juvenile court, s.21A(6) of the Child Care Act 1980 governs the legal representation of children for the purpose of ensuring that the views and wishes of the child can be fully argued before, and taken into consideration by, the juvenile court.

Before making a direction to place or keep a ward in secure accommodation, the court should, unless the ward is already represented by a guardian ad litem or there are special reasons why the ward should not be so represented, join the ward as a party to the proceedings and appoint a guardian ad litem to protect his interests and ensure that his views are made known to the court.

PRACTICE DIRECTION (FAM.D.) (WARDS: SECURE ACCOMMODATION) [1986] 3 All E.R. 320.

2634. Fees

SUPREME COURT FEES (AMENDMENT) ORDER 1986 (No. 637) (80p), made under the Supreme Court Act 1981 (c.54), s.130; operative on April 28, 1986; increases fees Nos. 1, 8(a), 9, 13, 14, 23, 26(a), 27(a)(b) and introduces certain new fees.

SUPREME COURT FEES (AMENDMENT No. 2) ORDER 1986 (No. 2144) [80p], made under the Insolvency Act 1986 (c.45), ss.414 and 415, and the Supreme Court Act 1981 (c.59), s.130; operative on December 29, 1986) amends S.I. 1980 No. 321.

2635. Fees—matrimonial causes. See DIVORCE AND MATRIMONIAL CAUSES, § 1081.

2636. Foreign judgments

RECIPROCAL ENFORCEMENT OF FOREIGN JUDGMENTS (CANADA) ORDER 1986 (No. 2027) [£1·90], made under the Foreign Judgments (Reciprocal Enforcement) Act 1933 (c.13), ss.1, 3 and the Civil Jurisdiction and Judgments Act 1982 (c.27), s.9(2);

operative on January 1, 1987; extends Pt. I of the 1933 Act to the judgment of designated Canadian courts.

2637. Foreign proceedings—interpleader proceedings injunction
The Bank of Tokyo ("B.T.") was a Japanese Bank carrying on business in London. It owned as a wholly owned subsidiary the Bank of Tokyo Trust Co., ("B.T.T.C."), a New York corporation. Mr. Karoon was an Iranian who worked for an Iranian company, called Maritime Co. He maintained personal accounts both with B.T.T.C. and B.T. He left Iran and transferred all his money from B.T.T.C. to B.T. In February 1980 B.T. received a letter from Maritime stating that Mr. Karoon had been sentenced to prison *in absentia* and that his property had been confiscated by the Government of Iran. B.T. was asked to transfer all his balances to Iran. Mr. Karoon was advised of this and instructed B.T. to transfer his accounts to another bank. B.T. were concerned about their position, (particularly since Mr. Karoon had earlier transferred moneys from the company account in B.T. to his own account) and in March 1980 issued an interpleader summons, to determine whether it should pay the money it held to Mr. Karoon or to Maritime. Mr. Karoon then applied to strike out the interpleader summons. He claimed that the moneys were all personal moneys transmitted from New York to London. B.T.'s officer swore an affidavit giving evidence obtained from B.T.T.C. The judge refused to strike out the summons and eventually ordered B.T. to pay the money into court. Mr. Karoon then sued in New York claiming breach of B.T.T.C.'s duty of confidentiality to him in disclosing information to B.T. B.T. sought to restrain Mr. Karoon from proceeding with his actions in the American courts, but the court refused to do so. *Held*, that it was for American law to determine whether a breach of contract had taken place by B.T.T.C. which was a separate corporation from B.T., as being the *forum conveniens*. There were no reasons of public policy which required an injunction.
BANK OF TOKYO v. KAROON [1986] 3 W.L.R. 414, C.A.

2638. Foreign proceedings—joinder as third parties—whether unjust
English producers formed an association to sell their goods in the U.S.A., where the association were exposed to litigation of a sort that could only be commenced in that country. *Held,* that the association could join the producers as third parties in U.S. proceedings: BITMAC v. CREOSOTE PRODUCERS ASSOCIATION, *The Times,* June 14, 1986, C.A.

2639. Foreign proceedings—pre-trial discovery—whether unconscionable interference
[(Supreme Court Act 1981 (c.54), s.37(1).]
Although the court could grant an injunction to prevent an unconscionable interference with the procedure of English courts, it would not do so to prevent pre-trial discovery (which would not have been available in England) in the U.S.A. P were an American insurance company, and having reinsured the liability of another American insurance company, U.N.I., reinsured the risk with D in London. P claimed under the contract of reinsurance and brought proceedings in the Commercial Court. Before the defence was served, D lodged a petition in a United States district court seeking an order for pre-trial discovery of documents relevant to the claim and Ps' contract of reinsurance with U.N.I. against persons resident in the United States who were not parties to the English action. P applied in the Commercial Court to restrain D from taking any step in the American proceedings. The judge made such an order, and the Court of Appeal dismissed the defendants' appeal. They further appealed to the House of Lords. *Held*, allowing the appeal, that the power of the High Court under s.37(1) of the Supreme Court Act 1981 to grant an injunction was limited to two main situations (Lord Mackay of Clashfern and Lord Goff of Chieveley *dubitante*): (1) where one party threatened the legal or equitable right of another the enforcement of which was amenable to the jurisdiction of the court; (2) where one party to an action had behaved or threatened to behave in an unconscionable manner. In the circumstances P had failed to show either that Ds' conduct was amenable to the jurisdiction of the court or that it was unconscionable in the sense that it interfered with the due process of the High Court's jurisdiction. Accordingly the injunctions were discharged. (*Siskina (Owners of cargo laden on board)* v. *Distos Compania Naviera S.A.* [1977] C.L.Y. 2344; *Castanho* v. *Brown & Root (U.K.)* [1981] C.L.Y. 2200; and *British Airways Board* v. *Laker Airways* [1984] C.L.Y. 2641 applied). *Per* Lord Goff of Chieveley: I am reluctant to accept the proposition that the power of the court to grant injunctions is restricted to certain

exclusive categories. That power is unfettered by statute and it is impossible at the present time to foresee every circumstance in which it may be thought right to make the remedy available.

SOUTH CAROLINA INSURANCE CO. *v.* ASSURANTIE MAATSCHAPPIJ "DE ZEVEN PROVINCIEN" N.V. [1986] 3 W.L.R. 398, H.L.

2640. Funds

SUPREME COURT FUNDS (AMENDMENT) RULES 1986 (No. 1142 (L.8)) [45p], made under the Administration of Justice Act 1965 (c.2), s.7(1); operative on August 1, 1986; alter the rate of interest on money in court placed to a deposit account from eight to seven-and-a-half per cent. per annum.

SUPREME COURT FUNDS (AMENDMENT No. 2) RULES 1986 (No. 2115 (L.16)) [80p], made under the Administration of Justice Act 1965 (c.2), s.7(1); operative on January 1, 1987; alter the rate of interest on money in court placed to a deposit account under S.I. 1975 No. 1803 from 7½% to 8½% p.a. and on money placed to a short-term investment account from 11½% to 12¼% p.a.

2641. Garnishee order—jurisdiction

[R.S.C., Ord. 49.] The temporary presence of the garnishee within the jurisdiction at the time is sufficient to enable the Court to make the order. SCF FINANCE CO. *v.* MASRI (No. 2), *The Times,* August 12, 1986, Gibson J.

2642. *Guardian ad litem* **of a child—practice direction**

The following practice direction was issued by the Senior Registrar of the Family Division on March 10, 1986.

The attention of practitioners is drawn to Ord. 55, r.4(1)(*a*), Ord. 80 and Ord. 90, rr.28 and 29 of the Rules of the Supreme Court in relation to appeals to the Divisional Court where a child was a party to the proceedings in the court below and is affected by the appeal. The notice of motion should be served on the *guardian ad litem* of the child appointed in the court below and no order is required appointing that person *guardian ad litem* in the Divisional Court proceedings provided his consent to act and his solicitor's certificate, referred to in Ord. 80, r.3(8), are filed in the Principal Registry.

The heading of the notice of motion should show the child as a party to, and represented by his *guardian ad litem* in, the proceedings in the court below and the address at which the *guardian ad litem* was served with the notice should be shown in the certificate required by Ord. 90, r.29(4)(*b*).

The written consent of the *guardian ad litem* of the child in the court below to act as the child's *guardian ad litem* in the appeal proceedings and the certificate by the solicitor for the child, referred to in Ord. 80, r.3(8), should be filed in the Principal Registry by that solicitor, as soon as practicable after the notice of motion has been served.

If there was a legal aid certificate in respect of the child in the proceedings in the court below, the attention of practitioners is also drawn to reg. 47 of the Legal Aid (General) Regulations 1980. The certificate may not be extended to cover the appeal proceedings and an application for a separate certificate is required if legal aid is sought in respect of the appeal.

PRACTICE DIRECTION (FAM. D.) (*Guardian ad Litem* OF A CHILD) March 10, 1986.

2643. Injunction—breach—application to commit

An applicant who seeks to commit a person for breach of an injunction must establish a deliberate or wilful breach of a court order beyond reasonable doubt: DEBORAH BUILDING EQUIPMENT *v.* SCAFFCO, *The Times,* November 5, 1986, Potts J.

2644. Injunction—committal for breach—rehearing

The court granted an interim injunction. S was allegedly in breach but did not appear on the committal application where he was sentenced to 28 days in custody. When he later appeared he sought to set aside the order. The judge heard evidence from him and confirmed the order. *Held,* that the whole hearing should have been re-opened in order to give S an opportunity to cross-examine the witnesses called in support of the committal application: ASLAM *v.* SINGH, *The Times,* June 12, 1986, C.A.

2645. Injunction—confidential information—previous publication—whether to strike out claim for injunction restraining disclosure—counterclaim—actionable abuse of process of court

A claim based on an actionable abuse of the process of the court is sufficiently pleaded so as to be arguable where it is alleged (1) that allegations made in the process concerned are false and (2) that the allegations are made with a view to obtaining a benefit or advantage that cannot be secured in the proceedings themselves or for some wrongful purpose.

P claimed to be entitled to certain confidential information relating to couplings for pipes used on oil rigs and oil jetties. D had published the information to the world at large. P claimed damages against D and sought an injunction to restrain D from using the information or communicating it to anyone else. Upon D's application, the claim for an injunction was struck out on the ground that the information in question had already been published to the world. D was also granted leave to make a counterclaim based on an alleged actionable abuse of the process of the court in that the action was brought by P to damage D's business and not for the protection of any legitimate interests of P. D alleged that P had made false allegations in the statement of claim and that P had made use of the action to deter third parties from dealing with D. *Held,* allowing P's appeal in part, that it was not appropriate to strike out P's claim for an injunction by means of an interlocutory order. The evidence at trial might disclose that P's business required protection that might be obtained from such an injunction. The usefulness or otherwise of the injunctive relief claimed could only properly be gauged at trial after all the material facts had been found. D's counterclaim would be allowed to stand. If the allegations of fact pleaded were proved at trial the basis for an arguable case on actionable abuse of the process of the court was made out. It was not necessary that the proceedings complained of be determined and found to be brought without reasonable or probable cause before an actionable abuse could be claimed. There was an actionable abuse where a person used the process of the court to obtain some collateral advantage or benefit for himself beyond that which could properly be secured in the proceedings complained of (*Cranleigh Precision Engineering* v. *Bryant* [1964] C.L.Y. 1306, *Grainger* v. *Hill* (1838) 4 Brig.N.C. 212 considered).

SPEED SEAL PRODUCTS *v.* PADDINGTON [1985] 1 W.L.R. 1327, C.A.

2646. Injunction—confidentiality—publication of information relating to national security

From a decision by a judge to grant interlocutory injunctions restraining publication of information said to breach confidentiality, the appellant had to show that the judge had erred in principle. He had weighed the balance of the damage that might be caused by publication with the potential harm caused by the injunction. Damages could not compensate for wrongful publication. There was no error of principle. (*Lion Laboratories* v. *Evans* [1984] C.L.Y. 1325, *American Cyanamid Co.* v. *Ethicon* [1975] C.L.Y. 2640, *Att.-Gen.* v. *Jonathan Cape* [1975] C.L.Y. 2714, *Francome* v. *Mirror Group Newspapers* [1984] C.L.Y. 1321 considered): ATT.-GEN. *v.* THE OBSERVER, *The Times,* July 26, 1986, C.A.

2647. Injunction—interlocutory injunction—Mareva and Anton Piller orders—restraint from leaving jurisdiction sought—whether appropriate.

[Supreme Court Act 1981 (c.54), s.37(1).]

Where a plaintiff seeks relief in the form of a Mareva or Anton Piller order and the court grants it, the court has jurisdiction to grant further relief restraining the defendant's departure from the jurisdiction until the execution of the orders.

P began an action claiming damages for the wrongful worldwide distribution of counterfeit insecticide. They sought a Mareva injunction and an Anton Piller order, and a further injunction restraining the defendant from leaving the jurisdiction until the Anton Piller order had been executed. The judge granted the Mareva and Anton Piller orders but refused the further relief. *Held,* allowing the appeal, that s.37(1) of the 1981 Act gave the court a wide discretion to do what was just and reasonable; there was jurisdiction to grant the relief sought and it would be granted for a limited time to allow the execution of the Mareva and Anton Piller orders (*Astro Exito Navegacion SA* v. *Southland Enterprise Co.; The Messiniaki Tolmi* [1982] C.L.Y. 419 applied).

BAYER AG *v.* WINTER [1986] 1 All E.R. 733, C.A.

2648. Injunction—interim relief

The *American Cyanamid* principles do not apply to applications for interlocutory injunctions where there are no issues of fact: where the issue is one of law, the court ought to resolve the dispute before deciding whether to grant the application: (*American Cyanamid* v. *Ethicon* [1975] C.L.Y. 2640 distinguished), BRADFORD METROPOLITAN CITY COUNCIL v. BROWN, *The Times*, March 18, 1986, C.A.

2649. Injunction—locus standi

[R.S.C., Ord. 29, r.1(3).] Where a person has been displaced as liquidator by a provisional liquidator, the Court cannot restrain him by injunction in winding up proceedings from dealing with arrests under his control as he is not a party to the proceedings and interlocutory relief is ancillary to those proceedings: TURNER (P.) (WILSDEN), *Re, Financial Times*, November 12, 1986, C.A.

2650. Injunction—mandatory injunction—considerations where special factors. See CONCORDE CONSTRUCTION CO. v. COLGAN, § 224.

2651. Injunction—mandatory injunction in interlocutory proceedings—principles

The standard required for a mandatory injunction in interlocutory proceedings is higher than that required for a prohibitory injunction; the court must feel a high degree of assurance that it will turn out at trial to have been rightly granted.

P were mortgagees of a vessel being loaded at Bombay with a cargo purchased by D. Because of delays, D lent X, shipowners, money to pay their debts in Bombay, in order to free the vessel and cargo. D then agreed to subrogate their rights to T. D agreed with P not to arrest the vessel at the port of destination. P was unaware of D's agreement with T. On unloading, X were unable to pay D, who were unable to pay T, who arrested the vessel. P sought an interlocutory injunction requiring D to pay T, in order to have the arrest lifted. The judge held that P had a fully arguable case for implying a term that D would do anything in their power to pay T, to avoid T exercising their independent power of arrest. *Held,* allowing D's appeal, that the judge had applied the wrong test. The standard was higher than in a prohibitory injunction, and the court must feel a high degree of assurance that such an injunction would turn out at trial to have been rightly granted. D would be put into an irretrievable position if it were held that there was no such implied term, and damages were sufficient if P proved their case (dictum of Megarry J. in *Shepherd Homes* v. *Sandham* [1970] C.L.Y. 2293 applied).

LOCABAIL INTERNATIONAL FINANCE v. AGROEXPORT; THE SEA HAWK [1986] 1 All E.R. 901, C.A.

2652. Injunction—Mareva injunction—failure to disclose material facts

A Mareva injunction was improperly obtained by reason of material non-disclosure. P then discontinued the action and issued a new writ and obtained a further Mareva injunction in the new action on the same day as the discontinuance. The affidavit in support of the second application for a Mareva injunction attempted to explain the inaccuracies and non-disclosure in the first application as well as supporting the application. *Held,* that the second injunction would be discharged since P had had the considerable and unfair advantage of a continuous Mareva injunction since the outset, and the faults in the first application were not cured by the second (*Bank Mellat* v. *Nikpour* [1982] C.L.Y. 2506, *Yardley & Co.* v. *Higson* [1984] C.L.Y. 441 considered): EASTGLEN INTERNATIONAL CORP. v. MONPARE (1986) 136 New L.J. 1087, Gatehouse J.

2653. Injunction—Mareva injunction—transfer of assets out of jurisdiction—foreign assets—discovery in aid of injunction

Disclosure of foreign assets is not ancillary to the granting of a *Mareva* injunction, because that injunction is limited to assets within the jurisdiction and accordingly no order should be made requiring a defendant to disclose assets outside the jurisdiction.

P obtained a *Mareva* injunction restraining D from removing from the jurisdiction or otherwise disposing of his assets, and obtained a further order that D disclose his assets wherever situate. In compliance with that order D disclosed bank accounts in various European countries, which P then enjoined. D subsequently applied for the discharge of the injunction which was granted on his undertaking not to dispose of the assets within the jurisdiction. *Held,* dismissing P's appeal, that the Court had power to grant a *Mareva* injunction solely over assets within the jurisdiction. Disclosure of foreign assets could not be regarded as ancillary to the *Mareva* injunction, the jurisdiction to grant discovery related to the *Mareva* injunction being limited to assets within the jurisdiction.

ASHTIANI *v*. KASHI [1986] 2 All E.R. 970, C.A.

2654. Injunction—representation—proceedings—squatters

[R.S.C., Ord. 113.] P owned various substantial areas of land and quarries in Somerset. One area was occupied by squatters. An Order 113 proceeding and a writ of possession caused their move 17 days after the hearing to P's quarry a mile or so away. There was evidence of damage to P's quarry, considerable violence by the squatters, and the squatters' intention to move from one part of P's land to another. The squatters were not identified by name save one. They were too violent to effect personal service but most were of an identifiable appearance. Two sets of proceedings ensued: (1) Order 113 against named defendant and persons unknown relating to one quarry and adjoining quarry, with an *ex parte* application to abridge time; and (2) a writ action against named defendant in representative capacity with injunctions sought to recover land and prevent threatened occupation of P's land in Somerset over a radius exceeding 10 miles. *Held,* that, an injunction would be granted against defendants in representative proceedings (a) to recover land presently occupied by them, and (b) to prevent threatened trespass to and occupation of other land owned by the plaintiff in the vicinity (*Michaels (M.) (Furriers)* v. *Askew* [1983] C.L.Y. 2969 considered): AMEY ROADSTONE CORP. *v*. PURDEY AND PERSONS UNKNOWN, Swinton-Thomas J., Bristol. (*Ex rel. Malcolm D. Warter, Barrister.*)

2655. Injunction—restraint of payment of demand bond

In 1978 P undertook pursuant to three contracts to supply, erect and commission poultry slaughter-houses in Iraq. The employers were as to two contracts the General Poultry Company for the Central Zone (CZ) and as to the third the General Poultry Company for the Northern Zone; both were Iraqi state enterprises. Each contract was governed by Iraqi law and provided that P procure the issue to the employer by an Iraqi bank of a performance bond. P through their bankers. D1, duly procured D2, an Iraqi bank, to issue the guarantees. In 1979 CZ and NZ were cancelled by statute and for them were substituted as universal successors two State Enterprises for poultry (SEPS). In 1981 the SEP were cancelled and for them was substituted the State Establishment of Agricultural Design and Construction (SEADC). In 1984 SEADC sought payment of the bonds from D2 and D2 sought payment from D1. P sought an injunction restraining D1 and D2 from paying the bonds on the grounds that SEADC were not the proper beneficiary of the bonds and that payment by D1 would be breach of D1's contract with P and that presentation of a demand by D2 and payment by them would constitute a tort. *Held,* that (1) where a demand is made by the beneficiary on the local bank and by the local bank on the London confirming bank and by that bank on its customer so long as the demands fall within the terms of the documents which create the contracts between the parties, such demand must be paid irrespective of any dispute between principal and beneficiary save and except if there is fraud. In the present case there was no fraud but there was an arguable case that the demand did not tally with the documents as being made by a party not named; (2) The Court would not issue an injunction because if demand were good D1 and D2 would commit no actionable breach in paying but if the demand were bad damages would be an adequate remedy: GKN CONTRACTORS *v*. LLOYDS BANK (1985) 30 Build.L.R. 48, C.A.

2656. Interest—recovery of debt or damages—tender of sum claimed—whether interest can be claimed

[Supreme Court Act 1981 (c.54), s.35A (as inserted by Administration of Justice Act 1982 (c.53), s.15(1), Sched. 1).]

Where the full amount of the damages claimable is paid before the judgment, the plaintiff is entitled to claim interest thereon.

P claimed by way of damages sums due from D under contracts of reinsurance. After a delay of 29 months, D2 offered sums in full settlement of the whole claim which P accepted in settlement only of the principal claim and not of any claim for interest. P applied for summary judgment which D2 resisted on the ground that the claim for damages had already been settled and the court had no jurisdiction to award interest alone. The judge gave judgment for the full amount claimed including interest. *Held,* dismissing D2's appeal that on a claim for damages and interest the court had power to give judgment on liability, to assess damages, and to award interest pursuant to section 35A of the Supreme Court Act 1981. Although D's payment of a sum equal to the amount of the damages claimed was a matter to be taken into account by the court, the payment did not extinguish P's cause of action. Since D had no defence to P's claim for damages, the judge was entitled to award damages together with interest.

EDMUNDS *v.* LLOYDS ITALICO & L'ANCORA COMPAGNIA DI ASSICURAZIONE E RIASSICURAZIONE S.p.A. [1986] 1 W.L.R. 492, C.A.

2657. Interim payment—application
[R.S.C. Ord. 29, r.10.] P engaged H as an architect to design and supervise certain building works, principally the conversion of a basement into a restaurant and bar. H's design provided for the basement to be tanked with a waterproof membrane. D1 were the main contractors, D2 were the specialist tanking sub-contractors and the London Borough of Havering passed the plans and inspected the works for the purpose of the Building Regulations. After completion of the works the basement flooded. P sued all the persons concerned and issued a summons seeking an order for interim payment pursuant to R.S.C., Ord. 29, r.10. *Held,* that the application must fail because P had failed to discharge the onus imposed on them, on the true construction of the rule, of showing not only that one of several defendants must be liable for the damage but also which one of the defendants was so liable. Further, the evidence filed in support of the application by P did not in any event comply with R.S.C., Ord. 29, r.10(3)(*a*) or (*b*): BREEZE (BRIAN) *v.* McKENNON (R.) & SON (1985) 32 Build.L.R. 41, C.A.

2658. Interlocutory proceedings—cross-examination before service of statement of claim—Anton Piller order
The court will refuse an application for cross-examination of a defendant served under an Anton Piller order and restrained from leaving the jurisdiction since the judge ought not to preside over the interrogation of one party by another before service of the statement of claim.

P manufactured an insecticide and alleged that the defendant, W, and others, were responsible for the sale of a counterfeit form of it. They obtained an interlocutory injunction *ex parte* restraining him from removing from the jurisdiction or disposing of his assets, directions as to documentations and assets, and an Anton Piller order permitting P's solicitors to enter and search his premises. He was also restrained from leaving England and required to give up his passport. When the Anton Piller order was served and before any statement of claim had been served, his premises were searched and W was questioned for several hours in order to obtain the information he had been directed to disclose. P considered his answers unsatisfactory and applied for an order directing his attendance for cross-examination in regard to the whereabouts of his assets and the part he had played in the counterfeit transactions, and restraining his liberty to leave England until he had been cross-examined. P intended to apply to commit him for contempt if he did not answer fully. W resisted this application. *Held,* that in civil litigation it was the proper function of the judge to decide issues between the parties and not to preside in a supervisory capacity over an interrogation of one party by another. While the court had an *in personam* jurisdiction to subject a citizen to interrogatory process in order to enforce an order, it would not be often, if at all, that the court would exercise its discretion to do so. Having regard to the fact that no statement of claim had been served and W had had no opportunity to deal with the evidence put before the court when P obtained their order *ex parte,* and also that the answers were intended to be used on a committal application, the application for cross-examination would be refused. Nor would the court restrain his departure from England (*House of Spring Gardens* v. *Waite* [1985] C.L.Y. 2674 distinguished).

BAYER AG *v.* WINTER (No. 2) [1986] 2 All E.R. 43, Scott J.

2659. Judicial appointments
The policies and procedures followed by the Lord Chancellor when selecting candidates for judicial appointments and in recommending the appointment of Queen's Counsel have been set out in a booklet published on May 29, 1986. *Judicial Appointments, The Lord Chancellor's Policies and Procedures* may be obtained from Trevor Cook, Lord Chancellor's Department, Room 604 Neville House, Page Street, London SW1P 4LS. [£1.]

2660. Judicial review—application discontinued—costs

In the circumstances of this particular case the failure to write a letter before action had the consequence that the applicants failed to obtain an order for their costs against the respondent.

Opman International was a company based in the Netherlands and entitled to receive royalty payments from Tricentrol Thistle Developments, a British company. The payments were not subject to a deduction of U.K. tax so that Opman were entitled to receive them in full. From April 1, 1985 at the instigation of the Oil Taxation Office of the Inland Revenue Tricentrol began to deduct tax from the payments. By April 17, 1985 the Revenue had received an application from Opman to be exempted from the requirement to deduct tax on the payments. The application was pursued by Opman's accountants who formed the impression that the Revenue was unwilling to make a decision on the application. In consequence Opman commenced proceedings for judicial review of the decision that tax should be deducted from the payments. No letter before action was written to the Revenue. The proceedings were commenced in June 1985 and on July 26, 1985 the Revenue decided the matter in Opman's favour. Opman applied to discontinue the application and for an order for costs against the Revenue. *Held,* that the Taxes Management Act 1970 set out a procedure for appeals in Revenue matters. In consequence an application for judicial review in a Revenue matter should be a procedure of last resort. Opman had not adequately brought to the attention of the Revenue the urgency of their application. It was most likely that if a letter before action had been written the matter would have been resolved without the necessity to issue proceedings. In the circumstances of this particular case no order for costs was the appropriate order.

R. *v.* I.R.C., *ex p.* OPMAN INTERNATIONAL U.K. [1986] 1 All E.R. 328, Woolf J.

2661. Judicial review—conflict of evidence—factual issue

Where there was a doubt, but the probabilities pointed to one account rather than another being true, the court was entitled to act on the basis that it was true. It was not necessary for the court to give the benefit of any doubt to the applicant: R. *v.* SECRETARY OF STATE FOR THE HOME DEPARTMENT, *ex p.* MAJID, *The Times,* June 13, 1986, Simon Brown J.

2662. Judicial review—delay in application for leave to apply—whether good reason for extending time—meaning of "undue delay"

[Supreme Court Act 1981 (c.54), s.31(6); R.S.C., Ord. 53, r.4(1).]

The failure to make an application for leave to apply for judicial review promptly and in any event within three months constitutes undue delay that might result in the refusal of judicial review notwithstanding that there is good reason for the delay and that leave to apply out of time is granted.

On August 30, 1984, the district council resolved to grant planning permission for a supermarket. J applied for leave to apply for judicial review of the resolution on May 10, 1985. The delay in applying for leave was caused first, by an attempt to have the Secretary of State for the Environment call the matter in, secondly by difficulties in obtaining the grant of a legal aid certificate and thirdly by difficulties in obtaining permission from copyright holders for the use of plans and drawings material to the application for judicial review. Forbes J. dismissed J's application for leave to apply for judicial review. *Held,* allowing J's appeal, that although J's application had not been made promptly or within three months in accordance with R.S.C., Ord. 53, r.4(1), there was good reason for the delay so that the time for making the application would be extended. The application referred to in r.4(1) was the *ex parte* application for leave to apply for judicial review. Undue delay for the purposes of s.31(6) of the Supreme Court Act 1981 must be viewed objectively. Whenever there was a failure to act promptly or within three months there was "undue delay" even though there may have been good reason for the delay. It was for the court hearing the full application to consider whether the delay was such that the court ought not to grant judicial review in the exercise of its discretion having regard to the provisions of s.31(6) of the Act.

R. *v.* STRATFORD-ON-AVON DISTRICT COUNCIL, *ex p.* JACKSON [1985] 1 W.L.R. 1319, C.A.

2663. Judicial review—discovery. See R. *v.* GOVERNOR OF PENTONVILLE PRISON, *ex p.* HERBAGE (NO. 2), § 13.

2664. Judicial review—documents—practice direction
Applications will be struck out with costs unless the practice direction is faithfully followed (*Practice Direction (Evidence; Documents)* [1983] C.L.Y. 3059 considered): R. *v.* SECRETARY OF STATE FOR THE HOME DEPARTMENT, *ex p.* MEYER-WULFF, *The Times,* May 9, 1986, D.C.

2665. Judicial statistics
The Lord Chancellor's Department has published *Judicial Statistics* for the year 1985. The statistics relate to the criminal and civil business of those courts in England and Wales for whose administration the Lord Chancellor is responsible. They also cover some associated offices, the Judicial Committee of the Privy Council and certain tribunals. The statistics are available from H.M.S.O. (Cmnd. 9864) [£11·60].

2666. Jurisdiction
CIVIL COURTS (AMENDMENT NO. 2) ORDER 1986 (No. 1361) [45p], made under the Supreme Court Act 1981 (c.54), s.99(1), the Bankruptcy Act 1914 (c.59), s.96, and the Companies Act 1985 (c.6), s.512(4); operative on October 1, 1986; amends S.I. 1983 No. 713 by establishing district registries of the High Court at Basingstoke and Milton Keynes.

2667. Leave to defend—considerations
The major consideration in deciding whether to give a defendant leave to defend is whether he has a defence on the merits. This transcends any reasons he has given for his delay in entering an appearance, even if he has deliberately lied in giving his reasons (*Evans* v. *Bartram* [1937] A.C. 473 applied): VANN v. AWFORD, *The Times,* April 23, 1986, C.A.

2668. London Bar Arbitration Scheme
The London Common Law Bar Association launched the London Bar Arbitration Scheme on June 24, 1986. A guide to the scheme, including a set of model rules, is available from the Arbitration Secretary, London Common Law Bar Association, 11 South Square, Gray's Inn, London WC1.

2669. Mareva injunction—discharge—circumstances
The Court considered the circumstances in which a Mareva injunction will be discharged. It said (1) that even where such an injunction is obtained *ex parte,* there should be some originating process to sustain it, and if within a reasonable time of the grant of the injunction proceedings are not started, the injunction will be discharged; (2) a Mareva injunction will not be granted to a plaintiff unless he has a cause of action against the defendant; (3) the injunction will be discharged if the party seeking the injunction has not made a full and fair disclosure of its own position; (4) the plaintiff must show a good and arguable case against the defendant; and (5) the plaintiff must be able to identify assets which he can show are likely to be dissipated unless the defendant is restrained by injunction: SIPOREX TRADE v. COMDEL COMMODITIES, (1986) 136 New L.J. 538, Bingham J.

2670. Matrimonial causes—consent orders—practice direction
This Direction is issued with the concurrence of the Lord Chancellor.
1. Rule 9 of the Matrimonial Causes (Amendment No. 2) Rules 1985 amended the Matrimonial Causes Rules 1977 by substituting a new rule 76A.
2. That rule requires an application for a consent order under any of sections 23, 24, 24A or 27 of the Matrimonial Causes Act 1973 to be accompanied by minutes of the order in the terms sought indorsed with a statement signed by the respondent to the application signifying his agreement, together with a statement containing the information as required by the Rules.
3. It is considered that the rule is properly complied with if the statement indorsed on the minutes is signed by solicitors on record as acting for the respondent.
4. A suggested form of accompanying statement of information is set out in the Schedule hereto. [Not reproduced here.]
5. Although the rule does not require the statement of information to be signed by either party, practitioners may consider it appropriate for the form to be signed by or on behalf of both parties as a means of establishing the accuracy of the information relating to their respective clients.
PRACTICE DIRECTION (FAM.D.) (MATRIMONIAL CAUSES RULES 1977: RULE 76A: CONSENT ORDERS) February 17, 1986.

2671. Matrimonial causes—special procedure lists—practice direction

The following practice direction was issued by the Senior Registrar of the Family Division on March 26, 1986.

The hearing numbers of the above causes run from 1 to 9999 with a suffix letter. The suffix letter at present in use is K. In order to clear the lists of cases which have been set down for trial for some time, but in respect of which the date fixed by the court for pronouncement of the decree has been vacated, those cases listed with a suffix H have now been struck out of the lists.

Causes struck out of the special procedure lists under this notice may be restored to the current lists by filing Notice to Restore (Form D435A) in the Divorce Registry.

PRACTICE DIRECTION (FAM.D.) (MATRIMONIAL CAUSES IN THE SPECIAL PROCEDURE LISTS AT THE ROYAL COURTS OF JUSTICE) March 24, 1986.

2672. Minors—removal from jurisdiction—practice direction

The following practice direction was issued by the Senior Registrar of the Family Division on April 14, 1986.

The Child Abduction Act 1984 came into force in October 1984. Section 1 of the Act which relates to England and Wales provides that in relation to a child under 16 (and subject to certain exceptions) an offence is committed by

(a) a parent or guardian of the child, or

(b) a person to whom custody has been awarded by a court in England and Wales, or

(c) if the child is illegitimate, a person in respect of whom there are reasonable grounds for believing that he is the father

if that person takes or sends the child out of the United Kingdom

(i) without the consent of each person who is a parent or guardian or to whom sole or joint custody has been awarded by a court in England and Wales, or

(ii) if the child is the subject of a custody order, without the leave of the court which made the order, or

(iii) without leave of the court having been obtained under the Guardianship of Minors Act 1971 and 1973.

For the purposes of the 1984 Act, the term "custody" includes "care and control".

Under section 2 of the Act, an offence is also committed in relation to a child under the age of 16 by any person who is not a parent or guardian or a person to whom custody has been granted if without lawful authority or reasonable excuse he takes or detains the child (a) so as to remove him from the lawful control of any person having such lawful control or (b) so as to keep him out of the lawful control of any person entitled thereto.

With effect from May 2, 1986 ports will be informed directly by the police (instead of the Home Office) when there is a real threat that a child is about to be removed unlawfully from the country. The police will provide a 24 hour service and will liaise with Immigration Officers at the ports in an attempt to identify children at risk of removal. It is not necessary first to obtain a court order in respect of a child under 16 before police assistance is sought. If an order has been obtained, however, it should be produced to them. Where the child is between the ages of 16 and 18, it will be an essential prerequisite that an order is obtained which restricts or restrains removal, or confers custody.

No ward, however, may be removed from the jurisdiction without the leave of the court. Evidence will need to be produced to the police that the child is a ward. This may either be an order confirming wardship, an injunction, or if no such order has been made, in cases of urgency, a sealed copy of the originating summons.

Any application for assistance to prevent a child's removal from the jurisdiction must be made by the applicant or his legal representative to a police station. This should normally be the applicant's local police station. However, in urgent cases, or where the wardship originating summons has just issued or where the court has just made the order relied on, contact may be made with any police station. If it is considered appropriate by the police, they will institute the "port-alert" system to try to prevent removal from the jurisdiction.

Where the police are asked to institute a "port-alert", they will need first to be satisfied that the danger of removal is *real* and *imminent*. "Imminent" means within 24–48 hours and "real" means that the port-alert is not being sought by or on behalf of the applicant merely by way of insurance.

The request for assistance should be accompanied by as much of the following information as possible.

The child: names, sex, date of birth, description, nationality, passport number (if known)

The person likely to remove: names, age, description, nationality, passport number (if known), relationship to child and whether child likely to assist him or her

Person applying for a port alert: names, relationship to child, nationality, telephone number (and solicitor's name and number if appropriate)

Likely destination

Likely time of travel and port of embarkation

Grounds for port-alert (as appropriate)

1. Suspected offence under section 1 of Child Abduction Act 1984
2. Child subject to court order

Details of person to whom the child should be returned if intercepted

If the police decide that the case is one in which the port-alert system should be used, the child's name will remain on the stop list for four weeks. After that time, it will be removed automatically unless a further application for a port stop is made.

Another measure which an interested party may take is to give notice in writing to the Passport Department, Home Office, that passport facilities should not be provided in respect of the minor either without leave of the court, or in cases other than wardship, the consent of the other parent, guardian, or person to whom custody or care and control has been granted, or the consent of the mother in the case of an illegitimate child.

The Practice Notes of July 15, 1963 (1963] 3 All E.R. 66 and July 18, 1973 [1973] C.L.Y. 2194, [1973] 3 All E.R. 194 and the Practice Direction of July 20, 1977 [1977] 3 All E.R. 122 are hereby cancelled.

PRACTICE DIRECTION (FAM.D.) (CHILDREN: REMOVAL FROM JURISDICTION) April 14, 1986.

2673. Northern area—chancery business—listing—practice direction

The following practice direction was given by His Honour Judge Blackett-Ord, Vice-Chancellor of the County Palatine of Lancaster, on July 31, 1986. It has effect from October 1, 1986.

1. The Senior Chancery Clerk ("the Clerk") in the District Registries at Leeds, Liverpool, Manchester, Newcastle upon Tyne and Preston will each maintain separate lists of cases in the Chancery Division of the High Court proceedings in that Registry or intended to be tried at that centre namely:

(a) A *setting down list* comprising all cases for hearing by the Judge except cases entered in the Motion Day lists. In this list cases will be identified as 'witness' cases (involving the oral examination of witnesses of deponents) or 'non-witness' cases (not involving oral evidence).

(b) A list for each Motion Day at that centre, comprising motions, company petitions and all cases estimated to occupy the time of the Court for two hours or less.

2. *The Setting Down List*

(a) Cases will be entered when they are set down, adjourned into Court or otherwise ready for hearing or when transferred from a Motion Day list and will be deleted when disposed of.

(b) Each case will be given an identifying number. The Plaintiff's Solicitor will be sent a letter enclosing a blank Counsel's certificate of estimated hearing time and giving a date (which will normally be one month ahead) by which the certificate is required to be returned signed by all Counsel in the case.

(c) On receipt of Counsel's certificate the setting down list will be marked accordingly and the Clerk at each District Registry (except Manchester) will send to the Chancery Listing Officer at Manchester a photocopy of Counsel's certificate and a completed pro-forma.

(d) If Counsel's certificate is not lodged within the period specified or if it appears to the Clerk that through the default of any party the trial of the case may be delayed he will communicate with the party concerned. In the absence of a satisfactory reply the case will be referred to the District Registrar (under R.S.C., Ord. 34, r.5 or Ord. 28, r.10) or to the Judge for directions.

3. *Fixed Dates*

(a) The Chancery Listing Officer will maintain a list of cases from *all* the Chancery District Registries (including Manchester) where Counsel's certificate has been filed.

(b) Fixed dates will be allotted for all cases expected to last three days or more, the Chancery Listing Officer keeping the Judges' diaries and acting as co-ordinator. Applications for fixed dates at Leeds will continue to be made to the Clerk at Leeds. Now that there are usually three Judges sitting to hear Chancery cases in the Area, more cases are required at short notice to fill the gaps caused by settlements and it is intended to use the gaps to expedite the hearing of shorter cases. The Listing Officer will have a discretion whether or not to give a fixed date for any case with an estimated length of hearing of less than three days but initially fixed dates for such cases will not be given.

(c) A fixed date may be vacated by the Listing Officer if a revised certificate lengthening Counsel's estimate of the length of hearing is lodged, otherwise Vice-Chancellor Blackett-Ord's direction dated 14th July 1980 will apply with the addition of the words "or Judge O'Donoghue" after each reference to Judge Fitzhugh Q.C.

4. *Warned Cases*

(a) Cases not given a fixed date for trial (short cases) will be liable to be called on for trial at short notice.

(b) Parties or their solicitors in short cases will be notified as soon as practicable that their case is warned for a particular date (or dates).

(c) In the event of a short case not coming on for trial during the warned period the Listing Officer will then allocate a fixed date for trial.

5. *Motion Day Lists*

(a) Any case falling within 1(b) above may be entered on the list for any motion day at any centre, but Motions and Petitions with a time estimate of over two hours may (at the discretion of the Judge) be adjourned to another Motion Day or other date to be fixed as seems appropriate. In exercising his discretion the Judge will take into account the state of the lists generally and the relative urgency of the case.

(b) Subject to the above, motions will continue to be heard on any Motion Day and at any Centre named in the Notice of Motion and may be stood over or saved for hearing at any other centre.

6. *Papers for the Judge*

(1) In addition to any documents in the Court file legible copies must be provided as follows:

(a) *Writ actions.* On setting down, copies of the pleadings and other documents specified in Order 34 rule 3(1) R.S.C. and complying with Order 66.

(b) *Originating Summonses* and other cases involving affidavit evidence (other than simple creditors Winding-Up Petitions) when listed under paragraph 2(a) above.

(i) the Originating Summons or other Originating process.

(ii) the Affidavits and exhibits, which must comply with Practice Directions of the Lord Chief Justice dated July 21, 1983. Copies of exhibits which do not lend themselves to photographic reproduction may be omitted.

(iii) any Orders of the District Registrar which have been drawn up.

(iv) any requisite Legal Aid documents.

(c) *Motions*

(i) the Writ and any subsequent pleadings.

(ii) the Notice of Motion.

(iii) the affidavits and exhibits (see (b)(ii) above which applies).

(iv) in the case of Motions for Judgment, the documents referred to in the Supreme Court Practice 1985 paragraph 19/7/8 (with the exception of form E26 praecipe).

(2) The provision of these documents is the responsibility of the solicitor for the Plaintiff, the Petitioner, or the party moving the Court (as the case may be) except that

(a) The Court will provide copies of writs and orders on request.

(b) The solicitor for any Defendant or Respondent is responsible for copies of affidavits on which he relies and of their exhibits.

7. *Urgent Matters*

On a certificate of urgency (oral or in writing) by a solicitor or (if possible) counsel, arrangements will be made to communicate with the Judge without delay, by telephone if necessary.

8. In this Memorandum the expression "the Judge" means and includes His Honour Judge Blackett-Ord, Vice-Chancellor of the County Palatine of Lancaster, His Honour Judge Fitzhugh Q.C. and His Honour Judge O'Donoghue.

PRACTICE DIRECTION (NORTHERN AREA: HIGH COURT CHANCERY BUSINESS LISTING) July 31, 1986.

2674. Order requiring person to act—time limit—validity

[R.S.C., Ord. 42, r.2(1).] Order 42, r.2(1) provides that any order which requires a person to do an act must specify the time within which that act is to be done. If it does not, it is invalid, and the subject of the order is entitled as of right to have it set aside (*Van Houten* v. *Foodsave, The Times*, February 7, 1980 applied): HITACHI SALES (U.K.) v. MITSUI OSK LINES, *The Times*, April 16, 1986, C.A.

2675. Parties—company no longer existing

A company that has ceased to exist is not entitled to maintain a cause of action, and any action brought in its name must be struck out. Nothing in the law of subrogation overrides this principle, and therefore an insurer is not entitled to carry on an action in the name of an insured company that has been wound up: SMITH (M. H.) (PLANT HIRE) v. MAINWARING t/a INSHORE, *The Times*, June 10, 1986, C.A.

2676. Payment of debt—interest—power of the court

[Supreme Court Act 1981 (c.54), s.35A] P sued D for £x plus interest. Before trial, D paid P the sum of £x in full. P proceeded to trial, and was awarded judgment for £x plus interest. D appealed against the award of interest. *Held*, that if acceptance was not in full settlement of the claim to include interest, the court was entitled to exercise its discretion under s.35A of the Supreme Court Act 1981. The payment of £x could not give rise to a defence of tender, because it had been made after the start of proceedings: EDMUNDS v. ADAS, *The Financial Times*, February 12, 1986, C.A.

2677. Personal injuries litigation. See LAW REFORM, § 1956.

2678. Plaintiff or complainant convicted prisoner—production of plaintiff at court—considerations

[Criminal Justice Act 1961 (c.39), s.29(1).] Where a plaintiff or complainant is a convicted prisoner there is no obligation that he be produced to whatever court he is conducting litigation in at his demand free of charge, and if he is unable to afford the cost of his production the Secretary of State may decline to produce him from prison. (*Associated Provincial Picture Houses* v. *Wednesbury Corporation* [1948] C.L.Y. 8107, *Raymond* v. *Honey* [1982] C.L.Y. 2613, *R.* v. *Secretary of State for the Home Department, ex p. Anderson* [1984] C.L.Y. 2762, *Becker* v. *Home Office* [1972] C.L.Y. 2835 considered): R. v. SECRETARY OF STATE FOR THE HOME DEPARTMENT, *ex p.* GREENWOOD, *The Times*, August 2, 1986, Macpherson J.

2679. Pleadings—amendment

The general principle in the amendment of pleadings is that all amendments should be allowed so as to ensure that the real matters of controversy between the parties are before the court, provided that this can be done without injustice to the other side. Amendments alleging fraud are in this respect no different from any other amendments. There is no rule of practice that allegations of fraud have to be pleaded from the outset. (*Bentley & Co.* v. *Black* (1893) 9 T.L.R. 580 distinguished): ATKINSON v. FITZWALTER, *The Times*, August 21, 1986, C.A.

2680. Pleadings—contract—repudiation

Even though it took place subsequent to the date of the original pleading, it can be amended to include a claim of repudiation of contract and acceptance of it: TILCON v. LAND AND REAL ESTATE INVESTMENTS. *The Times*, October 29, 1986, C.A.

2681. Pleadings—further and better particulars—failure to provide

By a consent order, X agreed to give Y further and better particulars of his pleadings. He then refused to supply some of the particulars on the ground that, had the application been fought, he would not have been ordered to provide them. *Held,* that if X had wished to take this point, he should have contested the application, but that, having agreed to the order, he had waived his right to take it: FEARIS *v.* DAVIES, *The Times,* June 5, 1986, C.A.

2682. Possession order—writ of restitution—considerations
[R.S.C., Ord. 41, r.1, Ord. 113.]
Where an order for possession of land has been granted, a writ of restitution may be issued against occupants who were neither party to the proceedings nor dispossessed by this order, provided that there is a plain and sufficient nexus between the order and the need to effect further recovery of the land.
The Council and others owned land around Stonehenge. The appellants belonged to a cohesive group of nomadic squatters who habitually trespassed on one piece of land after another, defying the courts, and occasionally returning to sites from which they had already been dispossessed. In 1982 and 1983 possession orders were made against 66 members of the group; for the next two years trespassing by the group continued on the land. The Council then sought leave to issue a writ of restitution directing the sheriff to restore the land to the plaintiffs' possession. Only two of the present incumbents could be shown to be defendants to the original possession order. The master refused the application on the ground of lack of jurisdiction. The Council appealed. *Held,* allowing the appeal, that the writ might be issued against occupants who were neither party to the proceedings nor dispossessed by the order for possession, provided that there was a plain and sufficient nexus between the order and the need to effect further recovery of the land. There was a close nexus between the various unlawful occupiers, and the trespassers were part of the same series of events, and leave would be granted to issue the writ of restitution (dictum of Lord Widgery C.J. in *R.* v. *Wandsworth County Court, ex p. Wandsworth London Borough* [1975] C.L.Y. 475 applied).
WILTSHIRE COUNTY COUNCIL *v.* FRAZER [1986] 1 All E.R. 65, Simon Brown J.

2683. Practice form—document exchange—service
A Queen's Bench Masters' Practice Form was published on July 15, 1986 for use where service has been effected through a document exchange. [P.F. 136A (R.S.C., Ord. 65, r.5(1)(*c*)).]

2684. Precedent—ex parte application—Court of Appeal—service out of the jurisdiction
[R.S.C., Ord. 11, r.1(1)(*j*).]
A decision of the Court of Appeal on an *ex parte* application is binding on a single judge of the High Court unless it was arrived at *per incuriam* or is inconsistent with a later decision. A voluntary submission to a writ by D1 did not prejudice D2.
P were the consignees of cargo carried on D1's vessel. D2 were charterers of the vessel. The vessel suffered engine trouble and required salvage. By arbitration, payment was made to the salvors. P sought to recover their proportion of the salvage payments from the defendants. D1 agreed to submit to the jurisdiction of the English court, and proceedings were brought against D2. They sought to set aside the writ on the grounds that the action against D1 was not properly brought against a person within the jurisdiction. They claimed that the owners' voluntary submission to the jurisdiction did not make them a person duly served "within the jurisdiction" within Ord. 11, r.1(1)(*j*) because the owners had not been physically within the jurisdiction, and that they as proposed defendants should not be prejudiced by the actions of another defendant. P contended that the judge was bound by an *ex parte* decision of the Court of Appeal to hold that the owners had been properly served, D2 that he was not so bound. *Held,* that a judge of the High Court was bound by an *ex parte* decision of the Court of Appeal unless that decision was reversed by a later decision of the House of Lords, or there was a later decision of the Court of Appeal inconsistent with it, or the decision was *per incuriam.* The Court of Appeal decision here was binding. Even if it were not, it ought to be followed as being of persuasive authority. It followed that the court had power to permit service of the writ on the charterers because before the writ was issued the owners had authorised an agent within the jurisdiction to accept service and therefore the owners were themselves persons "within the jurisdiction" for purposes of r.1(1)(*j*) *Lister (R.A.) & Co.* v. *Thomson (E.G.) (Shipping)*; *Benarty, The* [1984] C.L.Y. 3213 followed. However, on the facts, it was not appropriate under R.S.C. Ord. 11, r.4(2) to serve the proceedings out of the jurisdiction since the case had a close connection with

Ethiopia and little connection with England (the second defendants were Ethiopian and the cargo was to be shipped from Europe to Ethiopia). It would be more convenient to hear it there. Service of the writ on the charterers was therefore set aside.

Quaere: Where a defendant out of the jurisdiction who voluntarily submits to the jurisdiction after the writ is served is a "person . . . within the jurisdiction": for the purpose of R.S.C., Ord. 11, r.(1)(*j*). *Russell (John) & Co. v. Cayzer Irvine & Co.* [1916–17] All E.R. Rep. 630; *Derby & Co. v. Larsson* [1976] C.L.Y. 2213 and *Lister (R.A.) & Co. v. Thomson (E.G.) (Shipping); Benarty, The* [1984] C.L.Y. 3213 considered).

AMANUEL *v.* ALEXANDROS SHIPPING CO., THE ALEXANDROS P [1986] 1 All E.R. 278, Webster J.

2685. Probate fees
NON-CONTENTIOUS PROBATE FEES (AMENDMENT NO. 2) ORDER 1986 (No. 2185) [45p], made under the Supreme Court Act 1981 (c.54), s.130; operative on January 12, 1987; amends S.I. 1981 No. 861.

2686. Public interest immunity—disclosure of information—consent
Although public interest immunity cannot be waived, it can evaporate if the relevant consents of persons involved in the giving and receiving of the information are given to its disclosure. If the immunity has been severely eroded by partial disclosure, this is a matter which can and should be taken into account, on the basis that a potential volunteer of information will not be deterred from giving information if he sees the court permitting disclosure of what is already largely disclosed: MULTI GUARANTEE CO. *v.* CAVALIER INSURANCE CO., *The Times*, June 24, 1986, Knox J.

2687. Public Trustee and Administration of Funds Act 1986 (c.57)
This Act provides for the reorganisation of the private assets work of the Public Trustee, the Court Funds Office and the management division of the Court of Protection. The work will be brought together in a single office to be headed by the Accountant-General and Public Trustee.
The Act comes into force on a day to be appointed. It extends to England and Wales only.

2688. Public Trustee and Administration of Funds Act 1986—commencement
PUBLIC TRUSTEE AND ADMINISTRATION OF FUNDS ACT 1986 (COMMENCEMENT ORDER 1986 (No. 2261 (C.91)) [45p], made under the Public Trustee and Administration of Funds Act 1986 (c.57), s.6(2); brings the 1986 Act into force on January 2, 1987.

2689. Recognition—State not recognised by the UK—whether locus standi
Whilst a certificate from the Foreign Office is conclusive that a State is not recognised as an independent state by the United Kingdom, the Court should take account of such local legislation as was not in conflict with the certificate.
South Africa declared that the territory of Ciskei should be a sovereign and independent state in 1981. Pursuant thereto a Department of Public Works was created, which contracted for the construction of a hospital and two schools. There was a limited bank guarantee in favour of Ciskei. P claimed for the return of the security, and the bank claimed to join Ciskei as thrd party. *Held*, that the certificate of the Foreign Office that Ciskei was not recognised as an independent State was conclusive. The court had thus to ignore any declarations or legislation by South Africa which conflicted with such certificate, but it could and should give effect to such acts as did not contravene the certificate. As South Africa was clearly entitled to exercise sovereignty over Ciskei, and was entitled to delegate legislative power to Ciskei, the court would regard Ciskei as being a subordinate body which had *locus standi* to sue and be sued. (*Carl Zeiss Stiftung v. Rayner & Keeler (No. 2)* [1966] C.L.Y. 1665 applied).

GUR CORP. *v.* TRUST BANK OF AFRICA [1986] 3 W.L.R. 583, C.A.

2690. Registration of English judgment—application out of time—extension
[Trinidad and Tobago] [Judgments Extension Ordinance (c.5 No. 9), s.3; R.S.C. (Trinidad and Tobago), Ord. 71.]
It is not necessary for the valid registration of an English judgment out of time for a formal application for an extension of time or a formal expression of an extension by the judge.

P obtained judgment for damages in the English Court for an accident in Trinidad. The application to register in Trinidad was made *ex parte* five days after the 12 month period allowed. There was no express application for or grant of an extension of time, but the judge ordered registration. A second judge refused *inter partes* to set aside the order. The Court of Appeal, however, reversed that decision. *Held*, allowing P's appeal, that the second judge had a discretion *inter partes* irrespective of the first judge's decision. No formal application for or grant of an extension was necessary, and the registration was valid.

QUINN *v.* PRES-T-CON [1986] 1 W.L.R. 1216, P.C.

2691. Reserved judgment—presentation

A reserved judgment should be given in open court and, save in exceptional circumstances, should not be delivered by post: SANDFORD *v.* EL ARIBI SERVICES (A FIRM), *The Times*, September 5, 1986, C.A.

2692. Restrictive practices—variation of court's decisions—practice direction

The following practice direction was issued by the direction of the President of the Restrictive Practices Court on December 11, 1986.

In circumstances where

    a. a variation of a previous decision of the Court is sought which would not in itself restrict or discourage competition to any material degree and

    b. the Director and any other party who appeared at the hearing of the previous proceedings consents to the variation

the application for leave together with the previous declaration or order of the Court may be lodged with the proper Officer of the Court for consideration by the Court.

The application for leave should be made by affidavit containing:

    i. (except in cases to which s.4(5) applies) a statement of the material change in the relevant circumstances and

    ii. a statement that the proposed variation would not in itself restrict or discourage competition

and exhibiting the signed consent of the Director to the variation and any other party who appeared at the hearing of the previous proceedings.

The proper Officer of the Court will then put the application for leave before the Court. If satisfied that leave may be given and that the application under s.4(1) should be granted the Court may grant leave and cause the proceedings to be listed: the decision will be given in open court without the parties or their representatives being required to attend.

If on the evidence, and on any other evidence required by the Court, the Court is not satisfied that it is proper for the matter to be dealt with in this way the application under s.4(1) will be listed for hearing in the normal way.

Wherever possible, parties and their advisers are asked to ensure that sufficient information is provided to enable the Court to be satisfied as to the propriety of making an order without hearing the parties since this Direction is designed to save time and costs.

PRACTICE DIRECTION (RESTRICTIVE PRACTICES COURT) (VARIATION OF COURT'S DECISIONS) December 11, 1986.

2693. Rights of audience—High Court of Justice—solicitors—discretion of the court

The High Court of Justice retained a general discretion to permit a solicitor to appear in open court on his client's behalf but that discretion would only be exercised in exceptional circumstances.

S was the defendant in a defamation action in the High Court the settlement of which was agreed and involved the reading in open court of a statement and apology. S and his solicitor objected to the cost of engaging a barrister to read out the statement and apology. S's solicitor applied for leave to appear in open court himself and read the statement. The application was refused and S appealed. *Held*, dismissing the appeal, that the court had inherent power to decide who should exercise rights of audience before it. Barristers have a general right of audience in the High Court. Solicitors have a general right of audience before the High Court when sitting in chambers. Barristers had no monopoly right of audience that prevented solicitors appearing in open court. The court had a general discretion to permit a solicitor to appear before it. That discretion should only be exercised in exceptional circumstances. There were no exceptional features in the present case and the application was properly refused by the judge. The established practice of the court could only be altered by an Act of Parliament or by the decision of all the judges of the court in question. The judges must be guided solely by their own view of what was required in the interests of the efficient and effective administration of justice (*Collier* v. *Hicks* (1831) 2 B. & Ad. 663, *Sergeants at Law, Re* (1840) 6 Bing. N.C. 235, *R.* v. *Denbighshire Justices, sub nom. ex p. Evans* (1846) 15 L.J.Q.B. 335 and (1846) 9 Q.B. 2791, *O'Toole* v. *Scott* [1965] C.L.Y. 2443, *Engineers' and Managers' Association* v. *Advisory Conciliation and Arbitration Service* (No. 1) [1980] C.L.Y. 2742 considered).

ABSE *v.* SMITH [1986] 1 All E.R. 350, C.A.

2694. Rights of audience—solicitors—practice direction

The following practice direction was issued by the Lord Chancellor, the Lord Chief Justice, the Master of the Rolls and the President of the Family Division on May 9, 1986.

In addition to the cases in which solicitors already have rights of audience in the Supreme Court, and without prejudice to the discretion of a judge to allow a solicitor to represent his client in open court in an emergency, a solicitor may appear in the Supreme Court in formal or unopposed proceedings, that is to say those proceedings where—

(a) by reason of agreement between the parties there is unlikely to be any argument and

(b) the Court will not be called upon to exercise a discretion.

A solicitor may also represent his client in the Supreme Court when judgment is delivered in open court following a hearing in chambers at which that solicitor conducted the case for his client.

PRACTICE DIRECTION (SOLICITORS: RIGHTS OF AUDIENCE) *The Times,* May 10, 1986.

2695. Rules of the Supreme Court

RULES OF THE SUPREME COURT (AMENDMENT) 1986 (No. 632 (L.2)) [£4·40]. Made under the Supreme Court Act 1981 (c.54); operative on April 28, 1986; amend the R.S.C. primarily in relation to costs under a new Order 62.

RULES OF THE SUPREME COURT (AMENDMENT No. 2) 1986 (No. 1187 (L.9)) [£2·90], made under the Supreme Court Act 1981 (c.54), s.84; amend S.I. 1965 No. 1776.

RULES OF THE SUPREME COURT (AMENDMENT No. 3) 1986 (No. 2289) [£2·90], made under the Supreme Court Act 1981 (c.54), s.84; operative on January 12, 1987; amends the R.S.C. relating to examinations and increases fees payable to examiners; appeals from VAT tribunals to the Court of Appeal; practice directions on arbitration proceedings; consequential upon the Merchant Shipping Act 1979; issuing of warrants of wrest in Admiralty actions; appeals to the High Court in relation to Stamp Duty Reserve Tax; inheritance tax; giving effect to the Administration of Justice Act 1985, s.48; consequential upon the Companies Act 1985; procedures for possession of land applications under the Drug Trafficking Offences Act 1986.

2696. Security for costs—defendant insurer seeking security in action on policy—relevant principles—discretion

[Aus.] In an action for indemnity under an insurance policy, where the existence of that policy is not in dispute, it is not ordinarily appropriate to grant security for costs in favour of a defendant insurer (*Parkinson (Sir Lindsay) & Co.* v. *Triplan* [1973] C.L.Y. 2632 and *Pearson* v. *Naydler* [1977] C.L.Y. 2393 followed): IRWIN ALSOP SERVICES *v.* MERCANTILE MUTUAL INSURANCE CO. [1986] V.R. 61, Supreme Ct. of Victoria.

2697. Security for costs—insolvent company in Northern Ireland

Security for costs can be ordered against an insolvent limited liability company incorporated and resident in Northern Ireland (*Raeburn* v. *Andrews* [1874] L.R. 9 Q.B. 118, *Wilson Vehicle Distributions* v. *The Colt Car Co.* [1983] C.L.Y. 2913 not followed; *Pray* v. *Edie* (1785) Durn. and E. 267, *Crozat* v. *Brogden* [1894] 2 Q.B. 30, *Wakely* v. *Triumph Cycle Co.* [1924] 1 K.B. 214 considered): D.S.Q. PROPERTY CO. *v.* LOTUS CARS, *The Times,* November 3, 1986, Millett J.

2698. Service of process—document exchanges

All document exchanges run by Britdoc Ltd., of Hays Wharf, Guildford, Surrey and Northern Document Exchange Ltd., of 9A Middlesbrough Wharf, Depot Road, Middlesbrough, Cleveland have been designated by the Lord Chancellor as document exchanges approved for service of documents in accordance with R.S.C., Ord. 65, r.5(1); C.C.R., Ord. 11, r.1(1) and M.C.R., r.118(1).

2699. Statement of claim—amendment—cause of action
[R.S.C., Ord. 20, r.5(5).]
P employed D1 as contractors, D2 as architects and D5 as structural engineers in connection with the construction of an office block. The works were completed in 1975. In 1977 and 1981 problems appeared in the air-conditioning system. In 1982 P issued a writ and seven months later served a statement of claim on all the Ds except D5. In 1985 defects in the walls of the building appeared, unrelated to the air-conditioning defect. In June 1985 notice of intent to proceed was served on D5 who applied for the action against them to be dismissed for want of prosecution. P applied for leave to amend the statement of claim served against the other Ds to plead the wall defects. *Held,* that (1) the action against D5 should be struck out pursuant to R.S.C., Ord. 18, r.19 as abuse of the process since a writ should not be issued against a party when it is not intended to serve a statement of claim against them but where the writ is issued only to protect the position; (2) the action against D5 should also be dismissed for want of prosecution; (3) whether a proposed amendment raised a new cause of action was a mixed question of fact and law and a question of degree; the amendments proposed by P did raise new causes of action; (4) whether a proposed amendment arose out of the same or substantially the same facts as the existing action within the meaning of R.S.C., Ord. 20, r.5(5) was also a question of degree; since in this case there was insufficient overlap there was no jurisdiction to exercise the discretion under R.S.C., Ord. 20, r.5(5).
Steamship Mutual Underwriting Assoc. *v.* Trollope & Colls (City) (1986) 33 Build.L.R. 77, C.A.

2700. Statement of claim—amendment—causes of action.
[R.S.C., Ord. 20, r.5(5)] P employed D to design and build a housing development. Defects appeared in the works. P issued a writ and served a statement of claim alleging only defective workmanship against D. P later applied to amend the statement of claim to plead defective design. The amendment was opposed upon the ground that it would add a new cause of action to the existing writ after the expiry of the relevant limitation period. The judge refused the amendment. *Held,* allowing the appeal, that although an allegation of defective design was a different cause of action from an allegation of defective workmanship (even though both arose out of the same contract) the amendment would be allowed since the amendment came within R.S.C., Ord.20, r.5(5) as arising out of the same or substantially the same facts as the existing pleaded cause of action: Circle 33 Housing Trust *v.* Fairview Estates (Housing) (1985) 4 Const.L.J. 282, C.A.

2701. Statement of claim—amendment—contribution—"if sued"
[Law Reform (Married Women and Joint Tortfeasors) Act 1935 (c.30), s.6(1)(c).]
P entered into an agreement with D whereby P undertook to construct a motorway service station, *inter alia,* in consideration of the grant of a 50-year lease thereof and associated franchise. In 1972 shortly after completion of the works the National Coal Board gave notice of proposed mining operations which in the event were carried out causing loss to P, part of whose service station was unusable during the course of the mining operations. P sued D for the consequent losses alleging misrepresentation at the tender stage constituted by D's failure to disclose the possibility or probability of mining works under the service station site. Alternatively that D were in breach of a duty to warn P. The writ was served in 1974, and the statement of claim in 1980. In 1981 the architects who had advised P discovered among their papers a letter from the consulting engineers who had acted at the time for D stating that the National Coal Board had no plans for extracting the coal beneath the site. P then applied to amend their pleadings to allege an express representation and negligent misstatement constituted by the letter. The judge at first instance, exercising his discretion pursuant to R.S.C., Ord. 20, r.5(5) disallowed the amendment. *Held,* allowing the appeal and the amendment, that (1) since on the evidence the letter could appear in some sort of context D would not be incapable of explaining the circumstances surrounding the letter and therefore they would suffer no irremediable prejudice through the absence of such evidence; (2) on the true construction of s.6(1)(c) of the Law Reform (Married Women and Joint Tortfeasors) Act 1935 the words "if sued" had no temporal connotation and therefore D would still be able to sue their former

consulting engineers as third parties notwithstanding the fact that by virtue of the expiry of the limitation period, the consulting engineers could not be successfully sued direct by D. In this respect too D suffered no prejudice such that the amendment should not be allowed: FORTES SERVICE AREAS *v.* DEPARTMENT OF TRANSPORT (1984) 31 Build.L.R. 5, C.A.

2702. Statement of claim—amendment—whether new cause of action. See IDYLL *v.* DINERMAN DAVISON & HILLMAN, § 205.

2703. Stay of action—collision—actions in Holland and England—balance of convenience

P's vessel "S" and D's vessel "I" were involved in a collision. D arrested "S" in Holland to found jurisdiction there. Later the same month P arrested D's vessel in the U.K. D applied for a stay of the English action on the grounds that the same matter was being litigated in Holland, and that justice could be done between the parties in that country at substantially less inconvenience and expense. *Held*, that (1) in this case there was no natural forum for the resolution of the disputes, and England and Holland were equally appropriate; (2) on the balance of convenience, there was not sufficient factors such as to deprive P of the right to bring his action in England: CORAL ISIS, THE [1986] 1 Lloyd's Rep. 413. Sheen J.

2704. Stay of action—forum non conveniens—vessel blacked in Sweden—owners commenced proceedings against I.T.F. in London—whether Sweden a more convenient forum

P's vessel, crewed by a Filipino crew, was detained in Sweden and blacked by the International Transport Workers Federation (who were based in England). The I.T.F. representatives insisted that the crew be paid I.T.F. rates and that P provide bank guarantees to the I.T.F. in London. In order to secure the release of the vessel P met the demands of the I.T.F. Once the vessel was released, P sued the I.T.F. in London, claiming recovery of the sums on the ground that they were paid under duress. The I.T.F. sought to stay the action on the ground of forum non conveniens, Sweden being a forum whose justice could be done at substantially less inconvenience and expense. *Held*, that (1) the dispute was between P and the I.T.F. It was a coincidence that it had occurred against a Swedish backdrop; (2) all the agreements made between P and the I.T.F. were governed by English law, and the I.T.F. campaign against flags of convenience was directed from England; (3) on the evidence, D had failed to show that Sweden was a more convenient forum: DIMSKAL SHIPPING CO. S.A. *v.* THE INTERNATIONAL TRANSPORT WORKERS FEDERATION [1986] 2 Lloyd's Rep. 165, Hirst J.

2705. Stay of action—jurisdiction—balance of convenience

D, a bank, entered into certain loan agreements with the P companies, all of whom were Greek/Liberian shipowners. Mortgages were taken, each of which was governed by Liberian and Greek law. Personal guarantees had been given by two Greek directors and D sued on those in the Piraeus courts. P brought an action in England contending that the bank was in breach of agreements, and that the Greek directors were released from their personal guarantees. The banks sought a stay of the action. *Held*, dismissing D's appeal, that (1) there was a legitimate juridical advantage in favour of the proceedings continuing in that all the various disputes could be ventilated in one hearing (not all of them were before the Greek courts); (2) the court would not interfere with the exercise of his discretion by the judge: HAWKE BAY SHIPPING CO. *v.* THE FIRST NATIONAL BANK OF CHICAGO; THE EFTHIMIS [1986] 1 Lloyd's Rep. 244, C.A.

2706. Stay of proceedings—foreign jurisdiction

A stay will generally be granted where the natural forum is a foreign jurisdiction. Only if the English court is the natural forum should the court carry out the necessary balancing exercise to determine whether to grant a stay.

P Co., incorporated in Northern Cyprus, contracted with the Libyan Directorate of Military Contracting to construct harbour works. Payment was to be in U.S. dollars and Libyan dinars. In exchange for an advance payment of 25 per cent. P Co. gave a performance bond of 10 per cent. in the event of termination of the contract, and a bank guarantee to cover the advance payment. In order to obtain a counter-guarantee from D, a Turkish Bank, they obtained the consent of the Turkish government to be treated as though they were a Turkish company. The contract was cancelled; D paid the guaranteeing bank and took possession of deposits furnished by P Co. P Co. claimed that the cancellation was unjustified, that they were not liable for repayment and took proceedings in England. On D's application for a stay, the judge held that the natural forum was Turkey, and the balance of convenience favoured trial in Turkey. *Held,* dismissing P Co.'s appeal, that the inquiry began with the search for the natural forum. If that was the foreign court the inquiry stopped there. The critical equation was only brought into play when the natural forum was found to be the English court (*St. Pierre* v. *South American Stores (Gath* v. *Chaves)* [1936] 1 K.B. 382, C.A., *The Atlantic Star* [1973] C.L.Y. 2702 and *MacShannon* v. *Rockware Glass* [1978] C.L.Y. 2390 applied; *Trendtex Trading* v. *Credit Suisse* [1981] C.L.Y. 298 considered).

MUDUROGLU *v.* T. C. ZIRAAT BANKASI [1986] 3 W.L.R. 606, C.A.

2707. Striking out—long and complex argument on law—whether striking out appropriate.
See WILLIAMS AND HUMBERT *v.* W. & H. TRADE MARKS (JERSEY), § 363.

2708. Summary judgment—hearing of application—consideration of issues. See SCHINDLER LIFTS (HONG KONG) *v.* SHUI ON CONSTRUCTION CO., § 217.

2709. Summary judgment—principles governing application—appeal from official referee.
See RAPID BUILDING GROUP *v.* EALING FAMILY HOUSING ASSOCIATION, § 233.

2710. Summary judgment—stay of execution—pending counterclaim
[R.S.C., Ord. 14, r.14/3–4/13.] A defendant is not entitled to a stay of execution of an Ord. 14 judgment when a counterclaim is pending, if there is no connection between the contractual transactions (*Shepphards* v. *Wilkinson & Jarvis* [1889] 6 T.L.R. 13 considered; *AB Contractors* v. *Flaherty Bros.* (unrep.) February 22, 1978, C.A. followed): DRAKE AND FLETCHER *v.* BATCHELOR, (1986) 83 L.S.Gaz. 1232, Sir Neil Lawson.

2711. Summary procedure under Order 14—arguable point of law—arbitration clause—stay
[Arbitration Act 1975 (c.3), s.1.]
On an application for summary judgment under R.S.C., Ord. 14 in a case with an arbitration clause if the defence depended on a point of law on which the plaintiff was clearly right, the court would give judgment for the plaintiff and would dismiss any cross-application for a stay under s.1 of the Arbitration Act 1975. If the plaintiff was not clearly right, the court would grant leave to defend and would stay the action, so as to refer the dispute to arbitration.
The buyers bought a consignment of sugar from the sellers f.o.b. a West Coast of India port under a contract of sale which provided that all disputes be submitted to arbitration. Despatch and demurrage at the port of loading was to be for the sellers' account. The sugar was sold on under a string of contracts. The buyers later claimed demurrage from the sellers which they resisted on the basis that their obligation was to indemnify the buyers only in respect of demurrage which they could prove they had incurred in relation to the sub-sale. The buyers applied under Order 14 for summary judgment and the sellers applied for a stay under s.1 of the Arbitration Act 1975. The buyers argued additionally that there had been a settlement whereby the sellers had agreed to pay the demurrage. The judge found there had been no settlement but gave judgment for the buyers under Order 14 and made no order on the application for a stay. The sellers appealed and both parties invited the Court of Appeal to determine finally the construction of the demurrage provisions, but did not agree to waive the arbitration. *Held,* allowing the appeal, that where under Order 14 proceedings the defence depended on an arguable point of law on which the plaintiff was clearly right, the court would give judgment for the plaintiff and dismiss any cross-application for a stay under s.1 of the 1975 Act, since there was no dispute to go to arbitration. But if the plaintiff was not clearly right, unless the parties agreed that the court should determine the point of law and waive any arbitration agreement in its entirety, the court would grant leave to defend without determining the point of law and would be bound to grant an application for a stay and refer the matter to arbitration. The court should not determine issues of law and refer only the facts to arbitration where there was an arbitration agreement. Since the construction of the demurrage clause was difficult the sellers should have leave to defend and in the absence of a waiver of arbitration, there should be a stay for the entire dispute to go to arbitration (*Pinemain* v. *Welbeck International* [1984] C.L.Y. 2719 applied).

S.L. SETHIA LINERS *v.* STATE TRADING CORP. OF INDIA [1985] 1 W.L.R. 1398, C.A.

2712. Summer vacation business—family division—practice direction

The following practice direction was issued with the approval of the President of the Family Division on May 16, 1986.

Business which will be taken at the Royal Courts of Justice during the Long Vacation will be

1. Injunctions.
2. Committals to, and release from, prison.
3. Custody, access or any other application relating to a child's welfare when the estimated length of hearing does not exceed one day.
4. Any other matter which has been certified by a Registrar as being fit for Vacation business.

In any case falling within category 3, the estimate must be signed by the solicitor making the application or by Counsel if instructed; it will only be in rare circumstances that a case, accepted for Vacation hearing on the basis of an estimate of not more than one day but which takes longer, will be continued to be heard during the Vacation after the first day.

In any case falling within category 4 a certificate signed by the solicitor making the application, or by Counsel if instructed, must be supplied to the Registrar that in his opinion (giving reasons) the matter is such that it must be dealt with during the Vacation.

Whether the Clerk of the Rules lists an application within category 3, or a Registrar accepts as Vacation business an application within category 4, will be entirely a matter for his discretion.

PRACTICE DIRECTION (FAM.D.) (SUMMER VACATION BUSINESS) May 16, 1986.

2713. Taxation—Admiralty costs—practice direction

The following practice direction was issued by the Chief Taxing Master on July 29, 1986.

At the request of Master Topley, Admiralty Registrar, all costs in Admiralty matters will be taxed in the Supreme Court Taxing Office.

The procedure for the commencement of taxation will be as set out in *The Supreme Court Practice 1985* Vol. I, paras 62/22/1–62/22/6.

A summons to review a taxation will follow the Queen's Bench Division procedure in accordance with the Practice Direction of Lord Lane CJ dated May 10, 1984 (see *Practice Note* [1984] C.L.Y. 2726 [1984] 2 All E.R. 288, [1984] 1 W.L.R. 856, *The Supreme Court Practice 1985* Vol. I, para. 62/35/3).

With the agreement of the Admiralty Registrar the Practice Direction of the Admiralty Registrar dated November 1, 1973 ([1973] C.L.Y. 3086 [1973] 3 All E.R. 896, [1973] 1 W.L.R. 1424) is cancelled.

PRACTICE DIRECTION (SUP. CT. TAXING OFFICE) (ADMIRALTY: COSTS) [1986] 3 All E.R. 178.

2714. Taxation—application out of time—practice direction

The following practice direction was issued by the Chief Taxing Master on June 27, 1986.

1. Parties wishing to begin proceedings for the taxation of any costs are reminded of the time limits imposed by R.S.C., Ord. 62, r.29(1) and (2).

2. A party who is unable to comply with one or more of the requirements of r.29(7)(*c*) and (*d*) should not delay beginning the proceedings for that reason but when taking the reference for taxation should apply to the taxing officer for any extension of time necessary to enable the requirements to be complied with.

3. If the proceedings are begun after the time limits have expired no formal application for extension of time need be made on taxing the reference. In such a case unless any other party entitled to be heard on the taxation makes a prior application, the question of an extension of time may be raised as a preliminary point on the substantive hearing of the taxation.

4. In any case where the time limits have not been complied with any other party entitled to be heard on the taxation may apply either before or as a preliminary point at the substantive hearing under the provisions of Ord. 62, r.28(4) for the bill to be reduced or wholly disallowed. An application under r.28(4) must be made to a taxing master or registrar.

5. Where the only taxation required is pursuant to Sched. 2 to the Legal Aid Act 1974 no application is required on taking a reference out of time. In any case where

he considers it appropriate so to do the taxing officer will, of his own motion, serve notice on the party entitled to the taxation under the provisions of reg. 104 of the Legal Aid (General) Regulations 1980 (S.I. 1980 No. 1894).

6. This direction supersedes Practice Direction No. 2 of 1984 dated February 9, 1984 which is hereby cancelled.

PRACTICE DIRECTION (SUP. CT. TAXING OFFICE) (No. 4 OF 1986) (APPLICATION FOR TAXATION OUT OF TIME) (1986) 136 New L.J. 706.

2715. Taxation—application to review—practice directions

The following practice direction was issued by the Chief Taxing Master on July 16, 1986.

Applicants for reviews of taxation are required to lodge with the Chief Clerk of the Supreme Court Taxing Office three bundles of documents for the use of the judge and assessors.

Upon receipt of the summons from the Queen's Bench or Chancery Divisions the Chief Clerk will send notice to the applicant requesting that the bundles be lodged, which should consist of copies of the following documents:

The summons to review.

Order/judgment or other instrument providing for the taxation.

Bill of costs.

Objections.

Respondent's answers (if any).

Master's answers and certificate.

Affidavits filed during the course of the taxation.

The legal aid certificate, any relevant amendments thereto and authority to apply for review where applicable.

Any correspondence or other documents to which reference is intended to be made at the hearing of the review.

Bundles must be clearly paginated with an index at the front of the bundle listing all the documents and giving a page reference for each one. The bundles must be bound together. Loose documents will not be accepted.

The bundles must be lodged within 21 days from the receipt of notice from the Chief Clerk or such other time as the Chief Clerk may direct.

PRACTICE DIRECTION (SUP.CT. TAXING OFFICE) (No. 5 of 1986) [1986] 1 W.L.R. 1053.

2716. Taxation—forms of bills of costs—practice direction

The Clerk of the Parliaments issued the following practice direction on July 25, 1986.

The House of Lords has ordered a revision of the Forms of Bills of Costs applicable to Judicial Taxation in the House of Lords (the Green Book, the last edition of which was issued on October 1, 1981).

The revision will apply to any entitlement to costs created by orders or judgments made on or after October 1, 1986.

The House of Lords has also ordered that the *standard basis* and *indemnity basis* be introduced as the basis for taxation of bills drawn in accordance with the new forms.

These revisions were approved by the Appeal Committee and agreed to by the House on July 24, 1986.

PRACTICE DIRECTION (H.L.) (TAXATION: FORMS OF BILLS OF COSTS) [1986] 2 All E.R. 984.

2717. Taxation of costs—delay in taxation—nominal award

[R.S.C., Ord. 62, r.7(5) (before the 1986 amendment), r.35.] The power to award a nominal or other sum in costs is exercisable where there has been delay in obtaining the taxation and where the paying party is prejudiced thereby. It is open to the taxing officer to form the opinion after great delay that prejudice exists without the paying party showing any specific instance thereof, although the party entitled to be paid was entitled to attempt to show that no prejudice existed, for example by showing that reliance on memory was unnecessary. (*Drake and Fletcher* v. *Clark* [1968] C.L.Y. 3079, *Chapman* v. *Chapman* [1985] C.L.Y. 2642, *Morelle* v. *Wakeling* [1955] C.L.Y. 2193, *Pamplin* v. *Fraser (No. 2)* [1984] C.L.Y. 2641 considered): JONES v. ROBERTS, *The Times*, August 2, 1986, C.A.

2718. Third party notice—refusal of directions—power of court
[R.S.C., Ord. 16, r.4.]
The court may refuse to give third party directions when the subject of the third party notice can show special circumstances where they ought not to be given.

P, solicitors, instructed A Co., architects, and E Co. engineers, to carry out alterations to their property. The plans were approved by and carried out under the supervision of the district surveyor of the GLC. P issued a statement of claim alleging defective works in January 1984. E Co. delivered a defence in May 1984. In October E Co. notified the GLC that third party proceedings would be issued against them. In April 1985 E Co. served a third party notice on the GLC. When E Co. sought third party directions, the GLC, relying on R.S.C., Ord. 16, r.4/7 argued that the third party proceedings should be ended since E Co. could have brought their claim for contribution much earlier, and that now that the remedial works were completed, the GLC could not instruct an independent expert. *Held,* that E Co. had delayed more than a year, and the GLC had proved special circumstances which caused the court to refuse to give third party directions.

COURTENAY-EVANS *v.* PASSEY (STUART) & ASSOCIATES (A FIRM) (GREATER LONDON COUNCIL, THIRD PARTY), [1986] 1 All E.R. 932, Judge John Newey Q.C.

2719. Tribunal award registered in county court—garnishee—High Court action pending— application for payment—whether payment out to be stayed
[County Court Rules 1981 (S.I. 1981 No. 1678 (L.20)) as amended, Ord. 30, r.6.]
The scope of the court's discretion to order or refuse to order a payment out under Ord. 30, r.6 of the County Court Rules is the same as the discretion of the High Court under R.S.C., Ord. 47, r.1(*a*).

The applicant was dismissed from his job and successfully brought a claim for unfair dismissal. The tribunal made a by consent award of some £7,391. After further enquiries the employers brought a High Court action for more than £8,000 alleged to have been stolen by the applicant during his employ. The tribunal's award meanwhile was registered with the County Court, and a garnishee order nisi was made. The employers then paid the judgment sum into court; the applicant applied for a payment out. The application was opposed but allowed on appeal. *Held,* allowing the defendants' appeal, that the County Court's discretion was analogous to the High Courts' as set out in R.S.C., Ord. 47, r.1(*a*); where there were "special circumstances" as here, the order for payment out should not have been made (*Wagner (Ferdinand) (a firm)* v. *Laubscher Bros. & Co. (a firm)* [1970] C.L.Y. 2305 C.A. considered).

SCHOFIELD *v.* CHURCH ARMY [1986] 1 W.L.R. 1328, C.A.

2720. Unless orders—practice note
The following practice note was issued on May 12, 1986 by the Senior Master of the Queen's Bench Division.

1. The Court of Appeal has again emphasised that an order that prescribes unpleasant consequences unless a particular act is done is an order that "requires a person to do an act" within the meaning of R.S.C., Ord. 42, r.2.

2. Rule 2(1) requires that (subject to important exceptions mentioned in para. 7 below) such an order must make clear to the party against whom it is made the precise period within which the act is to be done. A common form of such order provides that "unless" the act is done the unpleasant consequences are to follow, and is usually called an "Unless Order".

3. To comply with rule 2(1) such an order must either, (a), specify the time *after service of the order* within which the act is to be done *or,* (b), specify some other time for this purpose.

4. Accordingly an "unless" order should be worded either:
   (a) "Unless within [14] days of service of this order" . . . [the defendant serves his list of documents the defence be struck out and judgment entered for the plaintiff with costs (or as may be)]. This wording must be used if the affected party is not present or represented.
   or
   (b) "Unless by [4 p.m. on Friday 13th June 1986]" . . . [continue as above]. This is the clearest form but is suitable only where the affected party is present or represented and so has notice of the order. It is also suitable for consent orders. An alternative wording, which has been approved, and can be used where the party is present or represented is: "Unless within [14] days *from today*" etc., but

797

this sometimes leads to argument as to how the time is to be reckoned, and is not suitable for consent orders.

5. The same principles apply to the other form of peremptory order in common use and having the same effect. By it the party is, first, ordered to do the act and there is then added a clause that, in default of compliance, specified consequences will follow. That part that directs the act to be done *must* use wording (a) or (b) above, thus: (It is ordered that) "the [defendant] do within [14] days of service of this order" do the required act *or* "do by [4 p.m. on Friday June 1986]" do that act.

6. If an order of these types is made that does not fulfil either of these requirements a supplementary order should be obtained, fixing the time; until this is done the order cannot be enforced.

7. The exceptions to the foregoing provisions are set out in rule 2(2) and are judgments or orders: (a) to pay money to any person; (b) to give possession of land; (c) to deliver any goods. In these cases the judgment or order may be enforced immediately unless the Court (as it may) specifies a time for compliance or unless additional requirements for enforcement are imposed by some other rule (*e.g.* Ord. 45, r.3 relating to possession of land).

PRACTICE NOTE (Q.B.D.) (UNLESS ORDERS AND OTHER PEREMPTORY ORDERS) May 12, 1986.

2721. Winding-up petitions—advertisement—practice direction
The following practice direction was issued by the direction of the Vice-Chancellor on February 10, 1986.

Copies of *every* advertisement published in connection with a winding-up petition *must* be lodged with the Companies Court as soon as possible after publication and in any event not later than the day appointed by the Registrar pursuant to Rule 33 of the Companies (Winding-up) Rules 1949. This Direction applies even if the advertisement is defective in any way, *e.g.* is published at a date not in accordance with the Winding-up Rules, or omits or misprints some important words—or if the Petitioner decides not to pursue the Petition—*e.g.* on receiving payment.

PRACTICE DIRECTION (CH.D.) (No. 1 OF 1986) (COMPANIES COURT: ADVERTISEMENT OF WINDING-UP PETITIONS) February 10, 1986.

2722. Writ—amendments—limitation
[Limitation Act 1980 (c.58), s.35] In 1982 A.C.S. issued a writ against D, engineers, seeking damages in respect of alleged defects in three cold stores in Grimsby built between 1966 and 1970. In 1984 it was realized that A.C.S. had no interest in the cold stores and application was made to amend the writ to add as plaintiffs associated companies within the group of companies of which A.C.S. was a member. D opposed the application on the grounds that if it were allowed they would be deprived of a limitation defence. *Held*, that the amendment would not be allowed because the affidavit evidence showed that the damage may have occurred more than six years before the date of the application to amend, being the relevant date for the purposes of s.35 of the Limitation Act 1980, and therefore to allow the amendment might deprive D of a limitation defence. GRIMSBY COLD STORES *v.* JENKINS & POTTER (1985) 5 Const.L.J. 362, C.A.

2723. Writ—limitation period—grounds for extension
A court will not exercise discretion in favour of renewing a writ after the expiration of the time for service, in the absence of good and sufficient reason if the effect would be to deprive a defendant of a limitation defence: WILKINSON *v.* ANCLIFF (B.L.T.) (1986) 130 S.J. 766, C.A.

2724. Writ—ne exeat regno—Mareva injunction—alleged thief of money intending to leave jurisdiction
Where it is necessary to prevent a defendant leaving the jurisdiction with assets, thereby prejudicing a valid claim made by a plaintiff, the Court has jurisdiction to issue the writ *ne exeat regno* in conjunction with a Mareva injunction.

Per curiam: the writ should issue to the tipstaff, who should bring the arrested defendant forthwith before the judge so that consideration could be given at once as to the next step to be taken.

P suspected D, its sales manager, of corruption in Saudi Arabia. D nonetheless managed to leave Saudi Arabia with a large quantity of money and flew to the U.K. On arrival he was met by police and representatives of P but refused to hand over any money claiming it represented his savings. He told the police he intended to fly to the Far East the next day and P applied *ex parte* for leave to issue the writ *ne exeat regno* and a Mareva injunction. *Held,* that in the circumstances of a case such as the present the court could issue the writ *ne exeat regno* where necessary with a Mareva injunction. As the cause of action was one complying with s.6 of the repealed Debtors Act 1869, a requirement for the issue of the writ, and since D was about to leave the jurisdiction in possession of money allegedly stolen the court would grant leave to issue the writ (*Felton* v. *Callis* [1968] C.L.Y. 963 applied).

AL NAHKEL FOR CONTRACTING AND TRADING *v.* LOWE [1986] 2 W.L.R. 317, Tudor Price J.

2725. Writ—service—address of firm

[R.S.C., Ord 10, r.1(2)(3); Ord 81, r.3(1)(*a*)(*c*).]

Where a writ is sent to the previous address of a firm, and then forwarded to the present address, where it is received by a partner, there is proper service.

P issued a writ against D in December 1983. In December 1984, in purported compliance with R.S.C., Ord. 81, P placed a copy of the writ in the first class post addressed to the secretary of D at the address thought to be the firm's principal place of business within the meaning of Ord. 81, r.3(1)(*c*). In fact the firm had moved about three months before. The Post Office, as directed by D, redirected the copy writ to the firm's new address where it was received by a partner seven days before the expiry of the writ. D told P that they did not consider the writ to have been validly served on them, and P applied for the validity of the writ to be extended. The master granted the application, and the writ was served at the end of January 1985. D applied for the validity of the writ's extension to be discharged and a declaration that it had not been validly served. The Official Referee dismissed the application. D's appeal was dismissed. *Held,* by a majority, that although the reference to a firm's "principal place of business" in Ord. 81, r.3(1)(*c*) could not be construed with Ord. 10, r.1(2)(*a*) to mean the last known address of the firm, "sending" a copy of the writ by ordinary first class post for the purposes of Ord. 10, r.1(2)(*a*) and Ord. 81, r.3(1)(*c*) meant not merely putting it in the post, but the whole process of transmission from server to recipient. Since the writ had been received by D at its place of business, it had been validly served within the time limit notwithstanding that it had not been correctly addressed when posted (*Baker* v. *Bowketts Cakes* [1966] C.L.Y. 9987 considered). The Rules of service, combined with the operation of the Limitation Act 1980, must be strictly complied with, and the discretion to extend the validity of a writ is only to be exercised in exceptional circumstances. In this case there were no such circumstances and the validity of the writ ought not to have been extended (*Heaven* v. *Road and Rail Wagons* [1965] C.L.Y. 3252; *Afro Continental Nigeria* v. *Meridian Shipping Co. S.A.* [1982] C.L.Y. 2597; and *Leal* v. *Dunlop Bio-Processes International* [1984] C.L.Y. 2745 applied).

Per May L.J. The copy of the writ sent to the firm at its old address and received by a partner at the new address was served on the partner at his usual address for the purposes of Ord. 81, r.3(1)(*a*) construed with Ord. 10, r.1(2)(*a*).

AUSTIN ROVER GROUP *v.* CROUCH BUTLER SAVAGE ASSOCIATES [1986] 1 W.L.R. 1102, C.A.

2726. Writ—service abroad—tort within the jurisdiction

Camera Care (the plaintiff) sought leave to serve Victor Hasselblad outside the jurisdiction. The plaintiff sought leave on the ground that a tort had been "committed within the jurisdiction" under R.S.C., Ord. 11, r.1(1)(*h*). The plaintiff argued that the tort consisted of infringements of Arts. 85 and 86 EEC. The plaintiff's solicitors had made various procedural errors in seeking leave for such service. *Held,* that (1) the plaintiff had failed to show that the acts, which allegedly constituted the tort, had occurred within the jurisdiction. The fact that the European Court had found a concerted practice between Hasselblad and others to prevent, limit or discourage exports of Hasselblad equipment did not provide an indication of a tort in the U.K. The plaintiff had not demonstrated that this was a proper case for service out of the jurisdiction; (2) having regard to the errors of the plaintiff's solicitors, the Court's discretion should not be exercised in order to cure irregularities relating to service.

CAMERA CARE *v.* VICTOR HASSELBLAD AB [1986] E.C.C. 373, C.A.

2727. Writ—service—by post—unless contrary is shown
[R.S.C., Ord. 10, r.1(3)(*a*).]
The words "unless the contrary is shown" do not mean that it is open only to the defendant to show the contrary.
On February 21, 1984 H issued a writ against the council alleging negligence in the approval of plans and the supervision of construction work. On February 15, 1985 H's solicitor sent a copy of the writ by post to the council's chief clerk who received it on February 18. The council applied to have the writ set aside contending that under Ord. 10, r.1(3)(*a*) unless the contrary was shown by the defendant service of a writ by post was deemed to take place after seven days which was outside the period of validity of the writ. The judge upheld the council's contentions. *Held*, allowing the appeal, that "unless the contrary is shown" meant that it had to be shown by evidence to the satisfaction of the court. It did not mean that it was only open to the defendant to show the contrary. In this case the writ was valid since it had been established that it was served within the period of its validity.
HODGSON *v.* HART DISTRICT COUNCIL [1986] 1 All E.R. 400, C.A.

2728. Writ—service—deemed service—unless the contrary is shown
[R.S.C., Ord. 10, r.1(5), Ord. 18, r.1.]
A defendant can no longer appear gratis to a writ which had not been served.
P brought proceedings in Abu Dhabi as a result of an air collision, and also issued a writ against D in England within the two year limitation period applicable in Abu Dhabi to protect its position if Abu Dhabi law applied to its claim against D. P sent D a photocopy of the writ with a covering letter saying that it was sent for information only. D purported to acknowledge service and asked P to serve a statement of claim within 14 days. The master accepted P's contention that there had not been service. The judge allowed D's appeal. *Held*, allowing P's appeal that practice under previous rules of court whereby a defendant could appear gratis to a writ although it had not been served no longer applied; a writ could not be deemed to have been duly served under Ord. 10, r.1(5) if the contrary was shown by either the plaintiff or the defendant; P had shown that the writ had not been duly served (*The Gniezno* [1967] C.L.Y. 3093 considered).
ABU DHABI HELICOPTERS *v.* INTERNATIONAL AERADIO [1986] 1 All E.R. 395, C.A.

2729. Writ—service out of the jurisdiction—whether contract governed by English law—discretion
[R.S.C., Ord. 11(1)(*i*)(*f*).] P carried out substantial repairs to the vessel of X. X could not afford to pay for these repairs and assigned the proceeds of an insurance policy. D were Italian insurers. That policy provided that all the terms thereof were to be identical to that subscribed by English lead underwriters. The latter policy simply provided that the place of physical issue of the policy was the City of London and that all suits thereunder "may be brought against these insurers in any . . . competent court in the U.S." Leave to issue and serve proceedings against D were refused to P on an *inter partes* hearing. P appealed. *Held*, allowing P's appeal, that (1) the contract was not in fact made in London but in Italy. However, (2) P had established a good arguable case that the proper law was English law as the centre of gravity of the contract was English and the U.S. suable clause indicated that if the option to sue in the U.S. was not exercised, then the proper law would be English law; (3) in the circumstances it was appropriate for the court to exercise its discretion by allowing the claims to be brought in England: CANTIERI NAVALI RIUNITI S.p.A. *v.* N. V. OMNE JUSTITIA: THE STOLT MARMARO [1985] 2 Lloyd's Rep 428, C.A.

2730. Writ—service out of the jurisdiction—whether correct forum
When a party seeks leave to serve proceedings founded in contract on another party who is out of the jurisdiction, the onus is on the former to prove that English law governs the contract, and that an English court is the correct forum. The Court may give weight to the fact that similar litigation is already in progress in this country, and that the same lawyers and experts have already prepared and educated themselves to present similar issues to an English court. If the Court thought that this would contribute to the efficiency, economy and expedition of the litigation, it would militate in favour of the English courts retaining jurisdiction (*Amin Rasheed Shipping Corp.* v. *Kuwait Insurance Co.; Al Wahab, The* [1982] C.L.Y. 2914 applied): SPILIADA MARITIME CORPORATION *v.* CANSULEX, *The Financial Times,* November 25, 1986, H.L.

2731. Writ—service out of time—circumstances in which it may be renewed
[R.S.C., Ord. 6, r.8(2)] P's solicitors issued a writ on February 8, 1984, in respect of tenosynovitis, which it was alleged P had contracted in the course of her work in a chicken factory. On January 18, 1985, in an attempt to effect service, the writ was posted to the factory. This was not the registered office and had closed down. The writ was returned marked "gone away" on February 15 and on the same day was sent to the registered office. P sought an order extending its validity. On April 17 it was extended for three months from the date of the appeal. *Held,* on an application to discharge this order, that (1) the order was *ultra vires,* because under the rules validity may only be extended from the date of original expiry; (2) this was not a case in which extension could be permitted. Notwithstanding the fact that it was a mere mistake, that the insurers had full knowledge of the claim, that D knew that P was awaiting the outcome of another trial, and that she might be in a worse position than if no writ had been issued at all, there was no "good reason" or "exceptional circumstance" to justify extension (*Chappell* v. *Cooper* [1980] C.L.Y. 1676 followed): GULLIVER V. SUN VALLEY POULTRY, October 31, 1985; Wood J., Birmingham. (*Ex rel. Charles Harris, Barrister*).

2732. Writ—striking out—no reasonable cause of action
In this matter D sought to strike out P's points of claim on the grounds that it disclosed no reasonable cause of action in contract and/or that any tort was committed outside the jurisdiction. It was further alleged that D had been induced into accepting service of a writ in consequence of a misrepresentation by P as to the basis of P's claim. *Held,* on the singular facts of this case, that (1) D had submitted to the jurisdiction both in contract and in tort; (2) P had an arguable claim in contract and the points of claim would not be struck out: there was no operative misrepresentation on the part of P such as to induce D to submit to the jurisdiction: HISPANICA DE PETROLEOS S.A. v. VENCEDORA OCEANICA NAVIGACION S.A. [1986] 1 Lloyd's Rep. 211, C.A.

PRISONS

2733. Aiding a prisoner to escape—meaning of "prison"—escape from magistrates' court.
See R. v. Moss; R. v. HARTE, § 550.

2734. Annual report
The Home Office has published its *Report on the Work of the Prison Department* for 1985–86. Copies of the report are available from H.M.S.O. (Cm. 11) [£9·50.]

2735. Board of visitors—disciplinary proceedings—natural justice
A board of visitors of a prison had to perform administrative functions as well as adjudicating on cases of offences against discipline, and although it had a discretion not to continue with an adjudication, it should not readily regard background knowledge of a prisoner as a ground for not continuing.
A board of prison visitors found a prisoner guilty of having a controlled drug in his cell contrary to rule 47(7) of the Prison Rules 1964. After the adjudication, the prisoner realised that the chairman of the board had been a member of the local review committee which three weeks before had considered his application for release on licence on parole. The prisoner applied for judicial review on the grounds that there was a risk of bias in that the chairman would have known details of the prisoner, including details of an earlier drug related conviction. *Held,* dismissing the application that since Parliament required a board of visitors to perform administrative functions in a prison as well as adjudicating in cases of more serious offences against discipline, they would inevitably and frequently have knowledge of the background of a prisoner charged with a disciplinary offence. A board had a discretion not to proceed with an adjudication, but should not readily regard a general background knowledge of a particular prisoner as a reason for not proceeding. A reasonable and fair-minded bystander, with these considerations in mind, would not regard the chairman as being disqualified from adjudicating on the disciplinary charge.
R. v. BOARD OF VISITORS OF FRANKLAND PRISON, *ex p.* LEWIS [1986] 1 W.L.R. 130, Woolf J.

2736. Board of visitors—lesser offence—whether power to convict
[Prison Rules 1964 (S.I. 1964 No. 388), r.48(1) (as amended by Prison (Amendment) Rules 1974 (S.I. 1974 No. 713), r.5, Sched. and Prison (Amendment) Rules 1983 (S.I. 1983 No. 568), rr.5, 6.]

A board of visitors inquiring into an alleged offence have no power to convict of a lesser offence.

D, the prisoner, was charged with doing gross personal violence to a prison officer, under r.47(2) of the Prison Rules 1964. At the close of the prosecution case the board of visitors allowed a submission of no case, but directed that D be charged thereupon with the offence of assault as a lesser offence. On D's application for judicial review, the judge made an order of prohibition, declaring that the board had no jurisdiction to direct the lesser charge, and that the charge had not been laid "as soon as possible" under r.48(1). *Held,* dismissing the board's appeal, that alternative charges could have been brought and the board's action had been; (1) *ultra vires,* and (2) contrary to r.48(1); (3) the court heard the appeal on its merits, in its discretion, even though the board had now decided not to proceed further against D, since the matter involved questions of general public interest. (*Sun Life Assurance Co. of Canada* v. *Jervis* [1944] A.C. 111, distinguished.)

R. v. BOARD OF VISITORS OF DARTMOOR PRISON, *ex p.* SMITH [1986] 3 W.L.R. 61, C.A.

2737. Discipline

The Government has published its response to the Prior Committee report on the prison disciplinary system. The charges will be introduced in the Government's planned Criminal justice legislation. *The Prison Disciplinary System in England and Wales,* Cmnd. 9920 is available from H.M.S.O. [£3·80.]

2738. Inquiry into prisoner's escape

The Report of an inquiry into the escape of Alan Richard Knowlden from St. Mary's Hospital, Paddington by H.M. Chief Inspector of Prisons has been published. As a result of recommendations contained in the report, new instructions regarding the security of category A prisoners in outside hospitals have been issued. The Report is available from H.M.S.O. (HC 80) [£4·10.]

2739. Parole Board—annual report

The Parole Board has published its Annual Report for 1985. The Report is available from H.M.S.O. [£5·10]. (ISBN 0 10 242886 7.)

2740. Prison population—ethnic origins—statistics. See CRIMINAL LAW, § 920.

2741. Prison Rules—mother and baby unit—separation of mother from baby—authority of prison governor

[Prison Act 1952 (c.52), s.47(1); Prison Rules (S.I. 1964 No. 388), r.9(3).] M had been sentenced to 12 months' youth custody. She had been placed in a mother and baby unit in an open prison together with her four months' old baby girl. Whilst in the unit M's behaviour had been extremely disruptive; and after repeated warnings the governor gave instructions for the removal of the baby from the unit because of his concern for M's treatment of the baby and the unsettling effect on the baby and others in the unit. As a consequence M was returned to closed custody. In proceedings for judicial review Tudor Price J. found that there had been no breaches of natural justice since M had been repeatedly warned and had been given every opportunity to mend her ways and that the former had followed the right procedure. *Held,* dismissing M's appeal, under r.9(3) and Circular Instruction 51 of 1983 the Secretary of State had laid down general conditions for the admission and retention of a mother and child in a special unit. The practical application of such conditions was vested in the prison governor to the extent that he could make speedy decisions in urgent cases although it was not correct to treat the case as one where the Secretary of State had delegated his authority to terminate permission: R. v. SECRETARY OF STATE FOR THE HOME DEPARTMENT, *ex p.* HICKLING, (1986) 16 Fam. Law. 140, C.A.

PRIVY COUNCIL PRACTICE

2742. Costs—taxation—costs incurred in Hong Kong

[H.K.] Hong Kong (Appeal to Privy Council) Order in Council 1909 r.25; Judicial Committee (General Appellate Jurisdiction) Rules Order 1982 (S.I. 1982 No. 1676), Sched. 2, r.76.]

At the hearing of P.'s appeal to the Privy Council from the Court of Appeal in Hong Kong it was represented by English leading and junior counsel and junior counsel from Hong Kong. The appeal was allowed and D ordered to pay P's costs of the appeal including the costs of three counsel. Having been told by the registrar of the Supreme Court of Hong Kong that he doubted his power to tax the bill for costs for the appeal, P lodged with the Registrar of the Privy Council a main bill of costs for the work done in England and a supplementary bill for the work carried out in Hong Kong. The registrar refused to tax part of the supplementary bill but made full provision in the main bill for the work done by the Hong Kong counsel by including two fees for the work which he had neither done nor charged for. He also disallowed travel and hotel expenses and ordered that no further costs for that counsel be included in any bill submitted for taxation in Hong Kong. D appealed and P cross-appealed. *Held*, allowing the appeal that, (1) the jurisdiction of the registrar was limited by rule 76 of the Rules to costs incurred in England and since the two disputed fees had not been incurred they would be deleted; (2) when the Judicial Committee ordered a party to pay the costs of an appeal incurred in Hong Kong, rule 25 of the 1909 Order conferred jurisdiction to tax those costs on the proper officer of the Supreme Court of Hong Kong; the registrar's order prohibiting inclusion of any further costs for the Hong Kong counsel in any bill of costs submitted in Hong Kong would be set aside; D would be asked to pay P's costs of the appeal incurred and taxed in Hong Kong; (3) dismissing the cross-appeal, the registrar had properly disallowed the travelling and hotel expenses of P's Hong Kong counsel.

TAI HING COTTON MILL *v.* LIU CHONG HING BANK (No. 2) [1986] 1 W.L.R. 392, P.C.

2743. Insurance business—profits—deduction for claims
[Fiji] [Income Tax Act (Fiji), s.19(*g*).] T Co. carried on insurance business, including motor insurance. For the year to June 30, 1979, it sought to make a deduction in computing its profits in the sum of $85,000 in respect of claims incurred but not reported. The Supreme Court, on appeal from the Court of Review, allowed the deduction to the extent of 82.06% of $85,000 (an average of 17.94% of claims being found to be unsuccessful. The Court of Appeal reversed that decision on the grounds that (1) T Co.'s calculations were unreliable, and (2) that s.19(*g*) of the Income Tax Act (Fiji) precluded the deduction. *Held*, allowing T Co.'s appeal, that (1) the reliability of T Co.'s calculations was a matter of fact for the Court of Review and the Supreme Court which in the circumstances could not be disturbed (*Edwards v. Bairstow* [1955] C.L.Y. 1287 followed), and (2) that s.19(*g*) did not prevent the deduction in the calculation of profits (*Southern Railway of Peru v. Owen* [1956] C.L.Y. 4172 applied): SOUTHERN PACIFIC INSURANCE CO. (FIJI) *v.* COMMISSIONER OF INLAND REVENUE [1986] S.T.C. 178, P.C.

PUBLIC ENTERTAINMENTS

2744. Cinema—fees
FEES FOR CINEMA LICENCES (VARIATION) ORDER 1986 (No. 207) [40p], made under the Cinemas Act 1985 (c.13), s.3(8); operative on April 1, 1986; increases the maximum fees payable under s.3(7) of the 1985 Act.

2745. Safety of sports grounds
SAFETY OF SPORTS GROUNDS ACT 1975 (EXTENSION TO FOOTBALL GROUNDS) ORDER 1986 (No. 1044) [45p], made under the Safety of Sports Grounds Act 1975 (c.52), s.15; operative on July 21, 1986; extends the 1975 Act to all sports grounds at which Association Football, Rugby League Football or Rugby Union Football is played.

SAFETY OF SPORTS GROUNDS (AMENDMENT) REGULATIONS 1986 (No. 1045) [45p], made under the Safety of Sports Grounds Act 1975, s.6(1)(4); operative on July 28, 1986; amends S.I. 1976 No. 1263 as a consequence of S.I. 1986 No. 1044.

SAFETY OF SPORTS GROUNDS (DESIGNATION) ORDER 1986 (No. 1296) [80p], made under the Safety of Sports Grounds Act 1975 (c.52), s.1(1); operative on August 23, 1986; designates the sports stadia set out in Sched. 1 as stadia requiring safety certificates.

2746. Sports grounds—crowd safety and control
The final report of the Committee of Inquiry chaired by Mr. Justice Popplewell into crowd safety and control at sports grounds has been published. The report makes 15 recommendations to improve safety and crowd control. The report is available from H.M.S.O. (Cmnd. 9710) (ISBN 0 10 197 100 1). [£6·90.]

PUBLIC HEALTH

2747. Clean air

SMOKE CONTROL AREAS (AUTHORISED FUELS) REGULATION 1986 (No. 162) [40p], made under the Clean Air Act 1956 (c.52), ss.33, 34(1); operative on March 10, 1986; declare Calco Superheat to be an authorised fuel for the purposes of the 1956 Act.

SMOKE CONTROL AREAS (AUTHORISED FUELS) (NO. 2) REGULATIONS 1986 (No. 1480) [80p], made under the Clean Air Act 1956 (c.52), ss.33, 34(1); operative on September 25, 1986; authorise fuels for the purposes of the 1956 Act.

2748. Detergents

DETERGENTS (COMPOSITION) (AMENDMENT) REGULATIONS 1986 (No. 560) [40p], made under the European Communities Act 1972 (c.68), s.2(2); operative on March 30, 1986; amend S.I. 1978 No. 564.

2749. Drains—blockage—notice to remedy

[Public Health Act 1961 (c.64), s.17.]

A public health inspector can serve a valid notice on a landowner to remedy a sewer blockage even though it later transpires that the blockage is not on that person's land.

Per curiam: Where a notice has been served under s.17 and the defect turns out to be on someone else's land, s.17(3) of the 1961 Act enables the court to relieve either wholly or in part any liability of the person originally charged with the cost of remedying the defect.

In November 1981 sewage emerged onto the D's land. He called in the local authority whose public health inspector discovered an obstruction which he could not clear because there was no manhole at that point. Instead the inspector served a notice on D under s.17(1) of the Public Health Act 1961 requiring him to remedy the defect within 48 hours. The local authority and D then uncovered the bottom of the D's drive and after inserting a manhole discovered that the blockage was in fact not on D's land but under the highway. After clearing the blockage, the authority made a demand on D for payment of the cost of clearance but he refused to pay. They then commenced proceedings for payment in the county court. He denied he was liable, contending that the drain on his premises had not been "stopped up" within s.17(1) because the blockage was not on his land and that the notice served on him was invalid. The judge held that the notice was valid and that the authority was entitled to recover its expenses. *Held*, dismissing D's appeal, that a drain could be "stopped up" within s.17(1) even though the actual blockage was on someone else's land if the drain under the landowner's land was so full of matter that sewage was emerging from it. Because it created a public health hazard that had to be dealt with quickly, if there was information on which a local authority could form a view that a drain on the landowner's land was stopped up and it was not clear that the defect was elsewhere, the local authority could serve a notice under s.17 requiring the remedy of the defect within 48 hours even if it later transpired that the blockage was elsewhere. The notice served on the defendant was valid and he was liable to pay.

ROTHERHAM METROPOLITAN BOROUGH COUNCIL *v.* DODDS [1986] 2 All E.R. 867, C.A.

2750. Food contamination. See FOOD AND DRUGS, § 1560.

2751. Lawnmowers

LAWNMOWERS (HARMONISATION OF NOISE EMISSION STANDARDS) REGULATIONS 1986 (No. 1795) [£1·90], made under the European Communities Act 1972 (c.68), s.2(2); operative on November 18, 1986; implement Council Directive 84/538/EEC.

2752. Pollution

CONTROL OF POLLUTION (ANGLERS' LEAD WEIGHTS) REGULATIONS 1986 (No. 1992) [80p], made under the Control of Pollution Act 1974 (c.40), ss.100 and 104(1); operative on January 1, 1987; apply to lead weights, as defined, and prohibit the importation of lead in the form of lead weights.

CONTROL OF POLLUTION (ANTI-FOULING PAINTS) (AMENDMENT) REGULATIONS 1986 (No. 2300) [45p], made under the Control of Pollution Act 1974 (c.40), s.100; operative on January 30, 1987; reduces the maximum amount of tin permitted in copolymer paints to 5·5% by weight when dried.

CONTROL OF POLLUTION (EXEMPTION OF CERTAIN DISCHARGES FROM CONTROL) (VARIATION) ORDER 1986 (No. 1623) [80p], made under the Control of Pollution Act 1974 (c.40), ss.32(3)(*b*) and 104(1)(*a*), operative on October 15, 1986, as to arts 1, 2(*b*) and 3, and on October 15, 1987, as to art. 2(*a*), (*c*) and Sched.; varies S.I. 1983 No. 1182.

CONTROL OF POLLUTION (SUPPLY AND USE OF INJURIOUS SUBSTANCES) REGULATIONS 1986 (No. 902) [£1·40], made under the Control of Pollution Act 1974 (c.40), ss.100, 104(1); operative on June 30, 1986; re-enact with amendments S.I. 1980 No. 638 so as to give effect to certain provisions of Council Directive 85/467/EEC.

2753. Refuse—removal—definition of house

Public Health Act 1936 (c.49), ss.72–74.] Refuse produced by a university hall of residence is not refuse from a house: MATTISON *v.* BEVERLEY BOROUGH COUNCIL, *The Times,* July 8, 1986, MacPherson J.

2753a. Smoke abatement

SMOKE CONTROL AREAS (EXEMPTED FIREPLACES) ORDER 1986 (No. 638) [80p], made under the Clean Air Act 1956 (c.52), s.11(4); operative on May 1, 1986, exempts specified fireplaces from the provisions of s.11 of the 1956 Act.

PUBLIC OFFICES AND PUBLIC AUTHORITIES

2753b. Public Record Office

PUBLIC RECORD OFFICE (FEES) REGULATIONS 1986 (No. 697) [45p], made under the Public Records Act 1958 (c.51), s.2(5); operative on May 1, 1986; replace S.I. 1977 No. 288 and prescribe new fees for authentication of copies of records.

RAILWAYS

2754. Accidents

RAILWAYS (NOTICE OF ACCIDENTS) ORDER 1986 (No. 2187) [£2.40], made under the Regulations of Railways Act 1871 (c.78), s.6, the Railway Employment (Prevention of Accidents) Act 1900 (c.27), s.13(2), and the Road and Rail Traffic Act 1933 (c.53), s. 93(1); operative on January 1, 1987; specifies classes of accidents on railways which are to be reported to the Secretary of State for Transport.

2755. British Railways Board

BRITISH RAILWAYS BOARD (INCREASE OF COMPENSATION LIMIT) ORDER 1986 (No. 1891) [45p], made under the Railways Act 1974 (c.48), s.3(5); operative on November 20, 1986; increases to £10,000m. the amount payable to the said Board by the Secretary of State.

2756. Light railways

BLUEBELL EXTENSION LIGHT RAILWAY ORDER 1986 (No. 343) [£1·85], made under the Light Railways Act 1896 (c.48), ss.7, 9, 10, 11, 12 and the Transport Act 1968 (c.73), s.121(2); operative on February 26, 1986; provides for the extension of the said light railway.

BO'NESS AND KINNEIL LIGHT RAILWAY ORDER 1986 (No. 174) [£1·35], made under the Light Railways Act 1896 (c.48), ss.3, 7, 9–12; operative on January 30, 1986; provides for the operation of the said light railway.

BRITISH RAILWAYS BOARD (CENTRAL WALES RAILWAY) LIGHT RAILWAY (AMENDMENT) ORDER 1986 (No. 690) [45p], made under the Light Railways Act 1896 (c.48), ss.7, 9, 10, 11, 24; operative on April 9, 1986; makes provision for controlling single line working on the Central Wales Light Railway.

EAST LANCASHIRE LIGHT RAILWAY ORDER 1986 (No. 277) [£1·35], made under the Light Railways Act 1896, ss.3, 7, 9–12, 18, the Road and Rail Traffic Act 1933 (c.53), s.42 and the Transport Act 1968 (c.73), s.121(2); operative on February 18, 1986; provides for the operation of the said light railway.

NENE VALLEY LIGHT RAILWAY ORDER 1986 (No. 1000) [£1·40], made under the Light Railways Act 1896 (c.48), ss.7, 9–12; operative on June 11, 1986; makes provision in relation to the said light railway.

VICKERS SHIPBUILDING AND ENGINEERING LIMITED (BARROW-IN-FURNESS) LIGHT RAILWAY ORDER 1986 (No. 2150) [80p], made under the Light Railways Act 1896; makes provisions for the operation of the said light railway.

RATING AND VALUATION

2757/8. Agricultural land—pasturing of racing stock—whether agricultural operation

[General Rate Act 1967 (c.9), s.26(4); Rating Act 1971 (c.39), s.2.] "Agricultural land" in s.26 of the General Rates Act 1967 covers purposes contributing to human subsistence, and "livestock" in s.2 of the Rating Act 1971 means mammals and birds that contribute to human subsistence. The pasturing of racing stock in paddocks is not an agricultural operation within s.26(4) of the 1967 Act: HEMENS (VALUATION OFFICER) *v.* WHITSBURY FARM AND STUD, *The Times,* November 10, 1986, C.A.

2759. Appeal from rating authority—jurisdiction of Crown Court—unoccupied rate

[General Rate Act 1967 (c.9), ss.7, 9, Sched. 1, para. 3A.] (1) No appeal could lie against the levy of an unoccupied rate. Where the ratepayers had the prior opportunity to obtain a reduction in rateable value to a nominal figure but failed to do so; (2) no appeal could lie under s.9, which is concerned with refunds, where no part of the rates demanded have in fact been paid. (*R. v. Tower Hamlets Borough Council, ex p. Chetnik Developments* [1985] C.L.Y. 2791 considered): RIALTO BUILDERS *v.* BARNET LONDON BOROUGH COUNCIL, 26 R.V.R. 120, Wood Green Crown Court.

2760. Compensation—subsidence damage from mining—power to award interest in Lands Tribunal

[Law Reform (Miscellaneous Provisions) Act 1934 (c.41), s.3(1); Arbitration Act 1950 (c.27), s.20; Coal Mining (Subsidence) Act 1957 (c.59), s.13.] The Lands Tribunal has power to award interest upon damages awarded under the Coal Mining (Subsidence) Act 1957. The award should be in the form of an award of damages, not a declaratory judgment. Interest would run from the date by which the remedial works should have been carried out (*Att.-Gen.* v. *B.B.C.* [1980] C.L.Y. 2119, *Chandris* v. *Ibrandtsen-Moller Co. Inc.* (1950) C.L.C. 9921, *Hadley* v. *Baxendale* (1854) 9 Exch. 341, *President of India* v. *La Pintada Compania Navigacion SA* [1984] C.L.Y. 123 considered; *Monmouthshire County Council* v. *Newport Borough Council* [1947] C.L.Y. 5813, *Swift & Co.* v. *Board of Trade* [1925] A.C. 520 distinguished): KNIBB AND KNIBB *v.* NATIONAL COAL BOARD, 26 R.V.R. 123, C.A.

2761. Drainage Rates (Disabled Persons) Act 1986 (c.17)

This Act makes provision for reducing drainage rates in respect of premises used by disabled persons and invalids.

The Act received the Royal Assent on June 26, 1986 and comes into force on April 1, 1987. It does not extend to Scotland or Northern Ireland.

2762. Gas boards

RATING (PUBLIC GAS SUPPLIERS) ORDER 1986 (No. 1365) [45p], made under the General Rate Act 1967 (c.9), ss.33(1), 114; operative on August 23, 1986; applies s.33 of the 1967 Act to premises occupied by the British Gas Corporation.

2763. Lands Tribunal decisions

APPEAL OF BRYDON (V.O.), *Re* (Ref. LVC/613/1984) 26 R.V.R. 119. (The valuation officer's appeal was dismissed because bricking up a door and increasing the internal space from 100·6 sq. m. to 111·5 sq. m. amounted only to the alteration of an existing hereditament, not the creation of a new one).

2764. APPEAL OF COOPER, *Re* (V.O.) (Ref. LVC/673/1984) (1986) 26 R.V.R. 96. (A two storey semi-detached dwelling in good condition was extended at the rear, and a brick garage with a tiled roof was built on to the side of the property. The assessment was increased from £246 gross value to £292 gross value.)

2765. ARNOLD (PETER) *v.* RILEY (V.O.) (Ref./LVC/427/1985) (1986) 279 E.G. 1241 (The ratepayer appealed against the assessment of one of six shop units inside an Asda superstore on the Isle of Dogs in London Docklands. The premises had been let as a shell in 1984 to dry-cleaners for a 25-year term at a rent of £8,500 p.a. At the date of the proposal only one other unit was occupied; another was occupied shortly afterwards and two more a year later, one of which had subsequently been vacated. T contended that he had agreed to pay too high a rent, and that the correct rental value as at the date of the lease would have been £3,500 p.a. The tribunal accepted that, having regard to the fact that trading results had not come up to expectation, the actual rent was too high, but rejected the ratepayer's contention that it should for rating purposes be reduced by the proportion of actual to estimated customers in the

Asda store. Noting that direct comparison with local shops was difficult because of the differences in character, the tribunal estimated the correct figure for the rent at £5,000 p.a., and that the V.O.'s figure of £40 per sq. m. for Zone A should therefore be reduced to £25 per sq. m. On this basis, and making a deduction of 10 per cent. for poor position, the tribunal reached an assessment of £1,250 gross value, £1,013 rateable value.)

2766. Ascoli *v.* Tapper (V.O.) (LVC/672/1984) (1986) 26 R.V.R. 9. (A bungalow and garage were assessed at £320 r.v. having allowed £20 for a supermarket car-park and associated traffic. The assessment was reduced to £300. Any disrepair in the premises would be remedied by a hypothetical landlord.)

2767. Avila *v.* Salford City Council (Ref. 46/1983) (1985) 25 R.V.R. 198. (There was conflicting evidence about whether a claimant for owner occupier's supplement after compulsory purchase had lived in the property for the necessary two-year period. The tribunal preferred the claimant's evidence, and awarded the supplemental compensation.)

2768. Barlow (V.O.) *v.* Wiseville (LVC/599/1983, LVC/298/1985 consolidated) [1986] R.A.1. (A greyhound track was assessed at £3,450 on a turnover basis. The turnover at the date of the valuation was reduced by reference to the Retail Price Index, the assessment figure being 5·25 per cent. of the result. Profits were not used as a basis for valuation as the track was trading at a loss. The turnover basis reflected disadvantages inherent in the site.)

2769. Barnet London Borough Council *v.* Samuelson Group and Paynter (V.O.) (Ref. LVC/963/1984) [1986] R.A. 25 (whether or not premises comprise a single hereditament for rating purposes is a question of fact, and on the facts a number of film studios with associated facilities at one address was one hereditament).

2770. Bouton *v.* Bryden Smith (V.O.) (Reg. LVC/869/1984) 26 R.V.R. 119 (An allowance of 12½ per cent was increased to 17½ per cent. in view of the early morning noise from a vehicle depot as well as other noise, dust and fumes).

2771. Brown *v.* McGibbon (V.O.) (Ref. LVC/726/1984) 26 R.V.R. 119 (The ratepayer's appeal was dismissed since the diminution in light caused by an extension to a neighbouring property was not sufficient to cause a hypothetical landlord to reduce the rent).

2772. Chisem *v.* McLaurin (V.O.) (Ref. LVC/698/1984) 26 R.V.R. 118. (The assessment of £410 gross value was confirmed on a bungalow and garage in Stainton since the road noise complained of was not severe enough to have any effect on rental value, and the fact that an extension had been built and the rooms divided in a certain way could not work to reduce the rateable value).

2773. Confino *v.* Aluwihare (V.O.) (Ref. LVC/14–18/1985) [1986] R.A. 178. (The rateable value of two houses was reduced slightly by a small increase in the disability allowance already made in respect of derelict buildings nearby, squatters, building works and incomplete estate roads and lighting.)

2774. Cunningham *v.* Morrison-Bell (Ref./LRA/2/1985) (1986) 278 E.G. 741. (This was an appeal by T against the determination by the Leasehold Valuation Tribunal of the price payable under the Leasehold Reform Act 1967 for the freehold of a terraced two-bedroomed cottage in Shiremoor, near Newcastle. The property was held on a 99-year lease from November 1893 at a ground rent of £1·54, and the valuation date was July 13, 1984. The only matter in dispute was the value of the freehold interest in the land on which the property stood, which the leasehold valuation tribunal had assessed at £1,300. The tribunal, favouring the standing house approach contended for by L, found for an entirety value of £13,000 and for a deferred site value of £1,520. There being no cross-appeal by L, the assessment of £1,300 was upheld.)

2775. East Midlands Electricity Board *v.* Hudson (V.O.) [1986] R.A. 33 (the Board owned land used by an employees' sports and social club. The Tribunal found that the Board was not the "occupier" of the land for rating purposes, but that the committee of the club was the occupier, and that the premises had properly been assessed to rates).

2776. Frank Dee Supermarkets *v.* Lane (V.O.) (Ref. LVC/879/1984) 26 R.V.R. 136. (In order to assess the rateable value of a supermarket the premises should be zoned, and in view of the unusual position (behind the shops in the main shopping street) regard should then be had to similar premises which were local, but outside the town.)

2777.   HAYS BUSINESS SERVICES *v.* RALEY (V.O.) (Ref./LVC/881/1984) (1986) 278 E.G. 1101. (This was an appeal against the assessment of a six-storey former tea warehouse in Limehouse, East London, now used for the storing of important documents, records and other archive material including films and tapes. Because of the sensitive nature of such materials, part of the premises was protected by a special form of fire-fighting equipment, employing Halon gas. The V.O. contended that the principal function of this equipment was to protect the building from fire, and that it should therefore be brought into the valuation pursuant to s.21 and Sched. 3 to the General Rate Act 1967 and to the Plant and Machinery (Rating) Order 1960 as amended. The building also contained goods lifts, and the V.O. further contended that the valuation should assume that the lift shafts were part of the hereditament and the structure, and were to be considered as available for the hypothetical tenant in order for goods lifts to be installed as part of the tenant's equipment. It was agreed that the actual goods lifts themselves were not to be deemed part of the hereditament. The tribunal found that the fire-fighting equipment was not to be included in the assessment, since it was there primarily to protect the material stored in the building and not the building itself, and was in any case provided expressly for the purpose of the trade process being carried on there, within the meaning of Class 1B of the 1960 Order. As to the lift shafts, the tribunal accepted the V.O.'s approach. The ratepayer's comparables based on hereditaments without lift shafts were therefore rejected, and the assessment of £37,000 gross value £30,805 rateable value which had originally been agreed by previous owners in 1977 was confirmed).

2778.   HOLLISTER-SHORT *v.* GEARY (V.O.) (Ref. LVC/303/1982) (1986) 26 R.V.R. 95. (A property was assessed to rates. It was unoccupied and the ratepayer contended that it was uninhabitable. An extension was incomplete, and the building operations were defective in that there were now defective foul drains, and an arch was in danger of collapse. The valuation officer contended that the old part of the house could be put into habitable repair. The tribunal held that the new foul drainage system and the building works necessary to remedy the structural defects were not "repair" for the purposes of s.19 of the General Rate Act 1967, and accordingly the premises were incapable of beneficial occupation, and the assessment was reduced to nil.)

2779.   HUQUE *v.* GRIFFITHS (V.O.) (Ref. LVC/587/1984, 588/1984) (1986) 26 R.V.R. 95. (The ratepayer sought exemption from rates on the grounds that the first floor and ground floor of a house were uninhabitable, being in the process of conversion into flats. The basement, which had formed part of a maisonette being the basement and ground floors, was subject to a closing order. Work had been completed pursuant to the closing order, but the order was still in existence. In respect of the flats, approval had yet to be obtained, but the works in connection with it had been completed. The tribunal reduced the assessments (a) because the flats should be valued as they stood and (b) since the closing order was still in existence no hypothetical landlord would let and no hypothetical tenant would take property subject to a closing order, therefore the basement should be taken out of assessment.)

2780.   KELLY *v.* NATIONAL COAL BOARD (Ref. 220/1981) (1986) 26 R.V.R. 37 (K claimed compensation pursuant to the Coal Mining (Subsidence) Act 1957. He valued the property on the basis of its damaged condition, and attempts he had made to sell it. The tribunal found that the proper basis for valuation was as if the house was in good repair and decorative condition, and that K's efforts to sell were inadequate. The tribunal declined to award interest on the award made).

2781.   LONRHO TEXTILES (T/A BRENTFORDS) *v.* TRIPPIER (V.O.) (Ref. LVC/1042/1984) (1986) 278 E.G. 165. (The subject premises comprised a large retail corner unit in the Piccadilly Plaza in Manchester, opening out at the rear to more than double the width of the shop front; A storage area was partitioned off at the rear, and there was also a basement, which was largely unused. The 1973 assessment at £16,750 gross value, £13,930 was reduced by agreement in 1977 to £15,075 gross value, £12,534 rateable value, because of the effect of phase one of the Arndale development; and in 1983 the LVC further reduced the assessment for the same reason to £13,650 gross value, £11,347 rateable value, against which the ratepayer appealed. The tribunal noted that the exercise of comparing gross values with the later rents did not commend itself as a basis for valuation. It adopted the zone A price of £57 p.s.m. which had been applied to the adjoining units, and valued the main part of the basement at £6 p.s.m. and the rear of the basement at £5.50. It also applied an end allowance of 33·3 per cent., which covered any inherent disabilities in the ground floor, and in particular the fact that the total floor area was far too great to support sales space. The final figure was £13,000 gross value, £10,805 rateable value.)

2782.   MABBOTT *v.* KENT (V.O.) (Ref. LVC/837/1984) 26 R.V.R. 142. (The description of the rated hereditament was changed from "Apartment House" to "Guest House" as being a better description of a lodging house or hostel in use for bed and breakfast accommodation for homeless persons.)

2783.   MORTON (V.O.) *v.* JONES T/A JONES' CLOTHES (Ref. LVC/323–326/1985) (1986) 280 E.G. 207. (The Valuation Officer appealed against reductions of £75 in the assessments of four shops in a parade in Rugeley, Staffs., granted by the LVC on grounds of inconvenience and loss of trade during road-widening works. The tribunal found that the valuation date was that of the proposals for reduction, which had not been made until the works were almost at an end, by which time they would not have caused a prospective tenant to reduce his bid. It further found that the degree of disturbance suffered had not in any case quite reached the point at which the letting value of the premises had been depreciated. The appeals were thus allowed.)

2784.   MUSLIM *v.* ISLINGTON LONDON BOROUGH COUNCIL (Ref. 37/1982) (1986) 26 R.V.R. 19 (Premises consisting of a terrace house with basement in Islington, in multiple occupation, fell to be valued for compulsory purchase purposes. The tribunal preferred comparables involving properties similarly in multiple occupation, and evidence of actual rents rather than estimates of fair rents, and increased the value from the authority's offer of £15,000 to £23,000, based on eight years' purchase on the rental income less rates, water rates and drainage.)

2785.   NEWBRIDGE (KEN) *v.* IPSWICH BOROUGH COUNCIL (Ref. 204/1982) (1985) R.V.R. 200. (Compensation for the compulsory purchase of three unfit properties in the centre of Ipswich, the site of which was suitable for the erection of a pair of semi-detached houses, was assessed at a total of £4,500.)

2786.   NORTHUMBERLAND WATER AUTHORITY *v.* LITTLE (V.O.) (Ref. LVC/951, 952, 953, 955/1984) [1986] R.A. 61. (The authority owned sewers and associated premises on either side of a river, linked by a complex system of piping, or syphon. The authority sought exemption from rating saying that the syphon was a sewer, and that the associated premises were accessories belonging to a sewer. The tribunal upheld the authority's contentions, and further decided that the items on either side of the river formed two hereditaments in the light of the complexity of the syphon and the nature of the use of the respective premises.)

2787.   PAYNTER (V.O.) *v.* BUXTON (Ref. LVC/944, 945/1984) 26 R.V.R. 132. (Flats in a converted house were the subject of a programme of alteration and modernisation which was more than mere repair. The rateable value was therefore assessed at nil.)

2788.   RANK XEROX (U.K.) *v.* JOHNSON (V.O.) (Ref./LVC/572–575/1984) (1986) 279 E.G. 1096 (This was an appeal against the assessment of two out of three office blocks built above the shopping centre in Uxbridge. The appeal blocks, each of which had separate entrances from the pedestrian malls on the ground floor, were originally separately occupied and assessed, but were now both occupied by the ratepayer, which sought to have them assessed as one hereditament. Each block and a third in separate occupation, were passed by a covered walkway at second-floor level, over which the tenants of the appeal blocks only had a right to pass on foot, and which also served as a fire exit. This walkway was used by the ratepayers' employees primarily for access, and also for passage of a tea-trolley between blocks. A number of services were shared between the appeal blocks. The tribunal rejected the ratepayers' contention that the two blocks were contiguous and in the same curtilage, since the evidence fell far short of establishing that the ratepayer was in exclusive occupation of the walkway. Following consideration of the decisions in *Gilbert (V.O.) v. S. Hickinbottom & Sons* [1956] C.L.Y. 7297 and *Butterley Co. v. Tasker (V.O.)* [1961] C.L.Y. 7481, it also rejected the contention that the blocks were joined by an essential functional link, since many of the common services were provided as a matter of convenience or to avoid duplication, and it could not be said that there was a sufficient degree of propinquity to forge a link by means of the walkway. The tribunal further rejected the ratepayers' contention for an additional end allowance of 10 per cent. in respect of lack of access from the main road, access via two multi-storey car parks, and the lack of any prestigious entrance on the ground floor, since these disadvantages had been in existence when the assessments were originally agreed. The assessments were confirmed at £88,750 and £85,600 gross value respectively, including an existing end allowance of 10 per cent. for lack of car parking within the hereditaments.)

2789.   SHEERNESS STEEL CO. *v.* MAUDLING (V.O.) (Ref. LVC/412/1983) [1986] R.A. 45. (A steel-works was given a net annual value of £252,300 but became subject to production quotas. The ratepayer contended that the "state" of the plant included the legal impossibility of full production, and was upheld and the net annual value was reduced to £126,000.)

2790.   SMITH (V.O.) *v.* ELDERS OF THE UNITED REFORM CHURCH (LVC 540–541/1983) [1985] R.A. 279 (A church hall where the expenditure, including a notional allowance for the cost of labour in fact performed voluntarily and at no charge, exceeded the income from letting was exempted from an assessment to rates by s.39 of the General Rate Act 1967. The notional allowance was proper where the voluntary labour was not an essential feature of the premises: if it ceased the user would continue.)

2791.   SOBO *v.* YARWOOD (V.O.) (Ref. LVC/803/1984) (1986) R.V.R. 23 (a terraced house in South Shields was assessed at £220 gross value after the installation of partial central heating, with three radiators, and modernisation. The garage had been removed. The assessment was confirmed since partial central heating would be assessed broadly without fine distinction as to one radiator more or less, and in any event a small adjustment for one radiator would not affect the question of whether the gross value was excessive).

2792.   SOLENT LEISURE & PROPERTY DEVELOPMENTS *v.* HAYES (V.O.) (Ref. LVC/255/1985) 26 R.V.R. 139. (A maisonette in an unusual but awkward position was reduced in gross value from £800 to £750 having in mind the proportionate size of allowances made for smaller flats in the same building.)

2793.   TAYLOR *v.* BALL (V.O.) (Ref. LVC/246/1985) 26 R.V.R. 141. (An assessment of £100 rateable value in respect of an area of rough ground used for parking lettings was wrongly removed from the list and £300 substituted in the erroneous belief that the property was unassessed. The tribunal assessed the rateable value at £100 since the valuation officer had failed to discharge the heavy onus upon him to show that the assessment was wrong.)

2794.   THERMOGLOBE *v.* RAY (V.O.) (Ref. LVC/267/1984) (1986) 26 R.V.R. 97. (A disused warehouse was assessed at £22,900 gross value. The assessment was reduced to a nominal £1 because the building could not be used without substantial and significant improvement in order to obtain a fire certificate, and without such a certificate occupation would be unlawful. No such certificate existed. The works necessary would not be "repairs" within s.19 General Rate Act 1967.)

2795.   THORN EMI CINEMAS *v.* HARRISON (VO) (Ref./LVC/1048/1984) (1986) 279 E.G. 512. (This was an appeal against an assessment in respect of a cinema in Newcastle-upon-Tyne of £16,000 gross value, £13,305 rateable value, which had been agreed in 1978 as representing the correct value in 1973. The ratepayer argued that there had subsequently been substantial changes in the relative values of cinemas in Newcastle, with the result that the value of the appeal hereditament had been greatly reduced. In particular it contended that changes in the city centre had attracted a large part of the potential audience to rival cinemas, with a consequent downturn in admissions, that the area in which the appeal cinema was situated had become run down, and that further competition had arisen from video shops. It was agreed that the correct method of valuation was by taking a percentage of the gross receipts as an indication of the annual value of the hereditament, and that a valuation under s.20 of the General Rate Act 1967 (which produces a ceiling figure) produced a lower figure than a valuation under s.19. The tribunal found, rejecting a submission by the VO, that the element of value attributable to the volume of trade or business was to be taken into account, that s.20(2)(c) of the Act did not give rise to an implication to the contrary, and that the state of affairs existing in 1982, insofar as it affected the value of the appeal premises, must form an important part of the process of valuation (*Barlow (H) & Son* v. *Wellingborough Borough Council and James* (VO) [1984] C.L.Y. 2810 followed). By applying a percentage of 8.5 to adjusted estimated gross receipts of £90,000, the tribunal amended the assessment to £7,650 gross value, £6,347 rateable value).

2796. TOWER SHOES v. COMMISSIONER OF VALUATION FOR NORTHERN IRELAND (Ref. VR/2–4/1984) 26 R.V.R. 118. (The assessment on two shop units was reduced to allow for the particular frontage, but only by a small amount since by para. 1 of Part 1 of Sched. 12 to the Rates (Northern Ireland) Order 1977 (S.I. 1977 No. 2157 (N.I. 28) the estimated rent could not be less than the "shell rent" under the lease).

2797. T.S.B. v. SAUNDERS (V.O.) (Ref. LVC/999–1011/1984) [1986] R.A. 161. (The rateable value of nine shops was reduced because the plans for the area in which they were situated, and which were current in 1973 at revaluation, had not materialised, and the shops were not the excellent letting prospect that had been envisaged.)

2798. TYE (V.O.) v. CENTRAL ELECTRICITY GENERATING BOARD (Ref. LVC/876/1984) [1985] R.A. 273 (Premises used by the Board for the dissemination of information only and not on "operational" land were not within the category of office use, and accordingly were not liable to be rated by reason of the exemption contained in s.34(1) of the General Rate Act 1967. For these purposes the use of a photocopier was *de minimis*.)

2799. UNDERWOOD v. PRICE (V.O.) (Ref. LVC/369/1984) 26 R.V.R. 119 (After reviewing comparable property the value of an isolated house in Staffordshire, modernised and extended, was reduced from £274 rateable value to £245 rateable value).

2800. WILLACRE T/A LLOYD (DAVID) SLAZENGER RAQUET CLUB v. BOND (V.O.) (Ref./LVC/838/1984) (1986) 278 E.G. 629. (This was an appeal against the assessment under s.20 of the General Rate Act 1967 of a purpose-built tennis centre in Hounslow, comprising twelve indoor tennis courts in three halls, four squash courts, two raquetball courts, a small swimming pool, changing rooms with jacuzzis and saunas, bar, restaurant, gymnasium, office, shop, creche, nine outdoor all-weather tennis courts, three small-size junior courts, and 102 parking spaces. The ratepayer contended that the correct approach was by applying unit prices to the different courts and a price p.s.m. for the ancillary parts of the premises, whilst the V.O. relied on the "contractor's basis", starting with the evidence of the actual costs of construction. The tribunal found that, under the V.O.'s approach, a Sports Council grant of £90,000 was to be deducted, since it was reasonably to be expected by the hypothetical tenant; and that there should be a "pioneer's allowance" of 10 per cent. to reflect the greater-than-normal expectation of risk and uncertainty at the time of setting up the venture (which in the event had prospered). Both valuation approaches in fact led to the same assessment, namely £25,250 gross value, £21,013 rateable value.)

2801. Lands tribunal for Northern Ireland decision
WALKER v. COMMISSIONER OF VALUATION FOR NORTHERN IRELAND (Ref. VR/18/1984) (1986) 26 R.V.R. 24 (an hotel was enlarged and modernised. The ratepayer sought to apply the figure of 2.45 per cent. of annual turnover on a turnover of £340,000. The commissioner applied a figure of 3.2 per cent. on a turnover of £350,000, giving a valuation of £11,200. The tribunal agreed with his estimate of turnover, but reduced the figure of 3.2 per cent. to 3 per cent., giving a valuation of £10,500. The ratepayer at the hearing of the appeal had sought in addition to rely upon hitherto unmentioned difficulties with drainage to a septic tank. This was dismissed as it had at no time previously been mentioned and must therefore be trivial).

2802. Lands valuation appeal
[Scot] DUNDEE PORT AUTHORITY v. TAYSIDE ASSESSOR [1986] R.A. 15. (Ships' dues and goods' dues were paid to DPA for services, not in consideration of the occupation of land; likewise minimum guarantee payments were made to enable DPA to provide harbour services, and pursuant to bye-laws, not in consideration for the occupation of land. Consequently such income was part of the "relevant income" for assessing the rateable value.)

2803. Leasehold Valuation Tribunal decision
    OLIVER *v.* CENTRAL ESTATES (BELGRAVIA) (Ref./LON/LVT/230) (1985) 276 E.G. 1358. (A preliminary issue arose as to the assumptions applicable in calculating the price payable for the freehold of a house in Pimlico, S.W. London. T argued that the applicable assumptions were those contained in s.9(1) of the Leasehold Reform Act 1967, on the grounds that the relevant rateable value was that of March 23, 1965, namely £347. L contended for the assumptions contained in s.9(1A) of the Act as amended by the Housing Act 1974 s.118, on the grounds that the relevant rateable value was £1,347, being that in force on the date of the notice to enfranchise, namely March 30, 1984. The tribunal took the view that a clear distinction must be made between (i) eligibility under the Act to enfranchise or extend a long lease, and (ii) the price payable for the conveyance of the freehold, calculated in accordance with the assurances laid down by ss.9(1) and 9(1A) of the Act. Whilst eligibility depended upon the rateable value on the "appropriate day" as defined in the Act, being March 23, 1965, the relevant time for determining whether or not s.9(1A) applied was not the "appropriate day", but the date of T's notice to enfranchise. Since the rateable value of the subject premises exceeded £1,000 as at that date, s.9(1A) applied. The tribunal approved an extract to this effect in Woodfall, *The Law of Landlord and Tenant,* and also the decision in *Silverman* v. *Catherine Investments* [1984] C.L.Y. 2923.)

2804. Money raised from rates—unexpended balance—transfer to trust fund
    [Local Government Act 1972 (c.70) s.137; Local Government (Interim Provisions) Act 1984 (c.53), s.7.] The local authority transferred to a trust fund the unexpended balance of its revenue in order to avoid the limiting provisions provided by the 1984 Act. The beneficiaries of the trust were "any or all or some of the inhabitants of West Yorkshire." One of the purposes of the trust was to inform various bodies of the proposed abolition of the authority, and of other proposals affecting local government in West Yorkshire. *Held,* that since one of the purposes of the trust was not charitable, it could not be a charitable trust, and since there might be as many as two-and-a-half million beneficiaries the trust would not take effect as an express private trust because it would be unworkable, and since the proposed class was so wide as to be unascertainable in practical terms, the trust was a non-charitable purpose trust, and therefore void in law (*Manchester City Council* v. *Greater Manchester County Council* [1981] C.L.Y. 2456, *Gulbenkian's Settlements, Re* [1967] C.L.Y. 3068, *Baden's Deed Trusts, Re* [1969] C.L.Y. 2770, *Morice* v. *Bishop of Durham* 10 Ves. Jr. 522, *Baden (No. 2), Re* [1972] C.L.Y. 3163, *Manisty's Settlement, Re* [1973] C.L.Y. 2597, *Denley's Trust Deed, Re* [1968] C.L.Y. 3586, *Lipinski's Will Trusts, Re* [1976] C.L.Y. 2499 considered): R. *v.* DISTRICT AUDITOR NO. 3 AUDIT DISTRICT OF WEST YORKSHIRE METROPOLITAN COUNTY COUNCIL, *ex p.* WEST YORKSHIRE METROPOLITAN COUNTY COUNCIL (1986) 26 R.V.R. 24, D.C.

2805. Non-payment of rates—committal—delay—judicial review
    [General Rate Act 1967 (c.9), ss.102, 103.] S was allegedly in rateable occupation from 1973–1975. A distress warrant was issued in 1976. S alleged that he had no notice of and had never seen the summons. The warrant was not executed until 1981, and proved fruitless. In 1983 the authority sought a warrant of commitment. By that stage the authority had lost all its documents for the time in question, and S's former solicitors had shredded their files for that period. The justices nevertheless in 1985 made an order for commitment, suspended upon payment of the alleged rate arrears. *Held,* that leave to apply for judicial review would be granted despite the general rule that all other methods of appeal should have been exhausted, since the circumstances of this case were wholly exceptional: R. *v.* LAMBETH BOROUGH COUNCIL, *ex p.* STERLING (AHIJAH) (1986) 26 R.V.R. 27, C.A.

2806. Rate-capping—meaning of "Parliament"
    [Rates Act 1984 (c.33), s.4(1).] "Parliament" in s.4(1) of the Rates Act 1984 means the House of Commons alone: R. *v.* SECRETARY OF STATE FOR THE ENVIRONMENT, *ex p.* GREENWICH LONDON BOROUGH COUNCIL, *The Times,* December 19, 1985, C.A.

2807. Rate limit for expenses incurred—statutory report—remuneration of council officers
    [Local Government Act 1972 (c.70), ss.112, 137, 147; Local Government Finance Act 1982 (c.32), ss.15, 19.] The authority applied for declarations that their expenditure on s.137 items did not include the cost of staff engaged on such items but employed for ordinary authority duties. *Held,* that if the staff costs would not

have been incurred but for the authorisation of such expenses by s.137 then those costs were s.137 costs, and accordingly fell to be added to the total of monies spent up to the appropriate rate limit: R. *v.* DISTRICT AUDITOR FOR LEICESTER, *ex p.* LEICESTER CITY COUNCIL, (1985) 25 R.V.R. 191, Woolf J.

2808. Rate limitation

RATE LIMITATION (DESIGNATION OF AUTHORITIES) (EXEMPTION) ORDER 1986 (No. 344) [40p], made under the Rates Act 1984 (c.33), s.2(3)(8); operative on April 1, 1986; amends s.2(2)(*a*) of the 1984 Act so that it now specifies £11·1 million.

RATE LIMITATION (PRESCRIBED MAXIMUM) (RATES) ORDER 1986 (No. 329) [40p], made under the Rates Act 1984, ss.1, 4(4); operative on February 28, 1986; prescribes maximum rates for specified authorities for the financial year 1986/7.

2809. Rate product

RATE PRODUCT (AMENDMENT) RULES 1986 (No. 1236) [80p], made under the General Rate Act 1967 (c.9), ss.12, 14, 113 and 114; operative on August 14, 1986; amend S.I. 1981 No. 327.

2810. Rate rebate—provision of welfare services for disabled persons—part user

[Rating (Disabled Persons) Act 1978 (c.40) s.2.] The Samaritans sought a rate rebate as of right in respect of premises used by them in the carrying out of their charitable objects. The premises consisted mainly of a large room manned 24 hours a day with volunteers who answered a number of telephones. A substantial proportion of the callers were suicidal, and, *ex hypothesi,* suffering from mental disorders. *Held,* that the rules and objects of the charity did not provide for help only to the mentally disordered, nor was that a principal object to which other assistance and activities were ancillary, although in a large number of cases the charity undoubtedly assisted such persons as a result of its activities. The charity provided a befriending service and thus was not entitled to a rate rebate under the legislation in question (*Morgan* v. *Windsor and Maidenhead Royal Borough Council,* [1982] C.L.Y. 2648 considered): SAMARITANS OF TYNESIDE *v.* NEWCASTLE UPON TYNE CITY COUNCIL [1985] R.A. 219, C.A.

2811. Rateable value—reduction for improvements—leasehold enfranchisement

In order for T to purchase the freehold, pursuant to the Leasehold Reform Act 1967, of a house leased to him in London SW1, it was necessary for its rateable value not to exceed £1,500 as at April 1, 1973. The entry in the valuation list as at that date in fact showed a rateable value of £1,593, but T contended that this figure should be reduced to below £1,500 in consequence of his improvements. In April 1981 the V.O. determined the appropriate reduction at £88. There being no right of appeal, T sought to quash the determination by way of judicial review, on the ground that the V.O. had made no reduction on account of the conversion of a bedroom into a bathroom. *Held,* refusing the application, that (1), this being an application for judicial review and not an appeal, it was not sufficient for T merely to show that there were grounds for disagreeing with the V.O.'s conclusions on relevant matters: T had to show that the V.O. had not taken such matters into consideration at all; (2) apart from failing to look for some rating authority working papers in relation to the 1973 entry, which would have been difficult to find and would not in fact have been of assistance, the V.O. had taken all relevant matters into consideration: R. *v.* VALUATION OFFICER FOR WESTMINSTER AND DISTRICT, *ex p.* RENDALL (1986) 278 E.G. 1090, C.A.

2812. Rates relief—right of appeal—Crown Court

[General Rate Act 1967 (c.9), ss.7(1)(*c*), 53, Sched. 1, para. 3A (as amended by Courts Act 1971 (c.23), s.56(2), Sched. 9; Crown Court Rules 1971 (S.I. 1971 No. 1292) (L.33)), Sched. 1; Crown Court Rules 1982 (S.I. 1982 No. 1109) (L.22)), rr.1(2), 6(2), Sched. 1, Sched. 3, Pt. II, para. 4; Local Government Act 1974 (c.7), s.15(5).]

A right of appeal lies to the Crown Court against anything a rating authority does or omits to do.

A company owned a large office block unoccupied since its completion in 1976. The company were rated as owners of the block; they applied to the authority for remission on the grounds of hardship. The company appealed to the Crown Court, which held it had no jurisdiction. The rating authority appealed to the House of Lords. *Held,* dismissing the appeal, that the wording of s.7(1)(*c*) of the 1967 Act was of very wide application and it gave a right of appeal to the Crown Court in respect of anything a rating authority had done or omitted to do.

INVESTORS IN INDUSTRY COMMERCIAL PROPERTIES *v.* NORWICH CITY COUNCIL [1986] 2 W.L.R. 925, H.L.

2813. Receiver in occupation—rateable value—receiver empowered but not obliged to assume occupation—whether in rateable occupation
[General Rate Act 1967 (c.9). s.97(1).]
Where a debenture allows a receiver to take up occupation of a company's premises, but does not oblige him so to do, or of itself effect a transfer of possession, the receiver is only to be regarded as being in rateable occupation of the premises, where he is in actual occupation.

A receiver was appointed under a debenture which empowered, but did not require, him to take possession of the company's property; there was the usual agency provision. On the receivers notifying the local authority of their appointment, the local authority decided that they had entered into occupation of the premises, and in due course sent them a rate demand. The receivers refused to pay the rates and their appeal to the judge was dismissed. *Held,* allowing the appeal, that where receivers were not obliged by the terms of their appointment to take up occupation of the company's premises, they could only be liable for rates if they were in rateable occupation. Where the appointment contained the usual provisions that they acted as agents of the company it was only if they were in occupation as independent principals that they could be liable.

RATFORD *v.* NORTHAVON DISTRICT COUNCIL [1986] 3 All E.R. 193, C.A.

2814. Single unoccupied hereditament—part listed—whether whole entitled to relief
[General Rate Act 1967 (c.9) Sched. 1, para. 2; Town and Country Planning Act 1971 (c.78), s.54.] A single unoccupied hereditament consisted of two separate but interconnected buildings, one of which was referred to in a list of buildings of special architectural or historic interest pursuant to s.54 of the Town and Country Planning Act 1971. The buildings were linked by a bridge and a tunnel. On the question of whether the entire hereditament or only the listed part was, whilst unoccupied, entitled to exemption from rates pursuant to para. 2 of Sched. I to the General Rate Act 1977, the judge held that the entire hereditament was to be treated as included in the listing, and was therefore entitled to relief from rates in its entirety. *Held,* dismissing the rating authority's appeal, that (1) in all the circumstances the unlisted part was to be treated as included in the listing, since it was a "structure" which was "fixed" to the listed part of the rateable hereditament and further formed "part of the land" and was "comprised within the curtilage" of that part, within the meaning of s.54(9) of the 1971 Act (*Att.-Gen., ex rel Sutcliffe* v. *Calderdale Borough Council* [1984] C.L.Y. 3451 considered); (2) the entire hereditament was accordingly entitled to rating relief: DEBENHAMS *v.* WESTMINSTER CITY COUNCIL (1986) 278 E.G. 974, C.A.

2815. Substantial completion of new building—unoccupied rate thereafter—date from which rate to run
[General Rate Act 1967 (c.9), Sched. 1, paras. 7, 8, 9 (as amended).] A substantial and prestigious office development was erected and a dispute arose between the rating authority and the developer as to the date from which the unoccupied rate should run. *Held,* that (1) substantial completion is achieved when the building is broadly finished save for fitting out work. Minor matters of construction outstanding do not preclude substantial completion since fitting out could at that stage be started; (2) since para. 9 of the schedule is a "deeming" provision it is irrelevant that planning and organising the fitting out might in reality take several months from substantial completion until the sub-contractor started the fitting out work. Such work is deemed to start immediately upon substantial completion. In any event the planning for fitting out could take place before substantial completion; (3) what is customary in fitting out a building is a question of fact depending on the sort of building, its potential user or users, and their expectations as potential occupiers. Since the judge had failed to take account of some items that were customary, the time he allowed may have been too short, and the matter would be remitted for re-consideration (*J.L.G. Investments* v. *Sandwell District Council* [1977] C.L.Y. 2448, *Provident Mutual Life Assurance Association* v. *Derby City Council* [1981] C.L.Y. 2254, *Ravenseft Properties* v. *Newham London Borough Council* [1976] C.L.Y. 2270,

Watford Borough Council v. *Parcourt Property Investment Co.* [1971] R.A. 97 considered): LONDON MERCHANT SECURITIES v. ISLINGTON LONDON BOROUGH COUNCIL [1986] R.A. 81, C.A.

2816. Unoccupied hereditament—premises described in valuation list as offices—office use prohibited by planning condition

[General Rate Act 1967 (c.9), Sched. 1, paras. (1), (2).]

The fact that an owner of a hereditament described as offices in the valuation list cannot use the hereditament as offices because of a planning condition does not mean that the owner is prohibited by law from occupying the hereditament or allowing it to be occupied within the meaning of Sched. 1, para. 2 to the General Rate Act 1967.

H was the owner of certain hereditaments described in the council's valuation list as offices. The hereditaments were kept vacant on account of the fact that use as offices was prohibited by a planning condition attaching to them. H had been granted planning permission to use the hereditaments for residential purposes. The case was argued on the basis that there was no impediment to their occupation for residential purposes. H contended that as the hereditaments could not lawfully be used within their description in the valuation list, H was prohibited by law from occupying the hereditaments or allowing them to be occupied within the meaning of Sched. 1, para. 2 to the General Rate Act 1967 with the effect that no rates were payable to the council. H's argument was upheld by the Divisional Court but not by the Court of Appeal. *Held,* dismissing H's appeal, that the hereditament referred to in para. 2 of Sched. 1 to the Act was property sufficiently identified by an entry in the valuation list whether or not the description of that hereditament appropriately described the purpose for which the hereditament could lawfully be occupied. H was not prohibited by law from occupying the hereditaments but merely from using them for office purposes. Accordingly H was liable to pay rates to the council (*Ravenseft Properties* v. *Newham London Borough Council* [1975] C.L.Y. 2783, *Camden London Borough Council* v. *Herwald* [1978] C.L.Y. 2460a distinguished).

HAILBURY INVESTMENTS v. WESTMINSTER CITY COUNCIL [1986] 1 W.L.R. 1232, H.L.

2817. Unoccupied property—no entry in list—whether unoccupied rate payable.

[General Rate Act 1967 (c.9), ss.6, 17, Sched. 1.] The rating authority in June 1983 served a completion notice pursuant to para. 8 of Sched. 1 to the General Rate Act 1967 in respect of a recently completed office block in Islington owned by P, to the effect that the building be treated as completed on September 1, 1983. An appeal against the notice was pending in the Court of Appeal and the building remained unoccupied, the authority being unable to claim an unoccupied rate pursuant to s.17 and Sched. 1 to the Act because no rateable value had as yet been entered in the valuation list. In March 1984 the valuation officer made proposals to enter the premises in the list and the authority then made a rate demand, based on those proposals rather than on established rateable values, arguing that the Act applied as if the premises were occupied, that there had therefore been a notional coming into occupation of the premises, and that consequent upon the proposals it was accordingly entitled to demand rates pursuant to s.6(1)(c) and 6(2) of the Act. *Held,* that (1) occupation whether notional or actual was not a relevant circumstance for rating liability as regards unoccupied property; (2) the provisions of Sched. 1 as regards unoccupied rates superseded any other liability-imposing provision of the Act, including s.6 (*Hastings Borough Council* v. *Tarmac Properties* [1984] C.L.Y. 2933 applied; *Barr Hill Developments* v. *South Cambridgeshire District Council* [1979] C.L.Y. 2239 considered); (3) accordingly P were not liable to pay any unoccupied rate until the premises and their respective rateable values had been entered in the valuation list: TRENDWORTHY TWO v. ISLINGTON LONDON BOROUGH (1985) 277 E.G. 539, Mervyn Davies J.

2818. Unpaid rates—winding up petition—quantification of unpaid rates—unoccupied rate

[Companies Act 1948 (c.38), s.223; General Rate Act 1967 (c.9), Sched. 1, para. 13.] Where the starting point of a period of vacancy, which led to the levy of an unoccupied rate, was the subject of an as yet unheard appeal to the Court of Appeal, the rating authority cannot present a winding up petition in respect of the unpaid rates, since the amount owed is not ascertainable: TRENDWORTHY TWO v. ISLINGTON LONDON BOROUGH COUNCIL (1986) 26 R.V.R. 153, Michael Wheeler Q.C.

2819. Water rates—discrimination against a class of persons—commercial premises as against domestic premises

[Water Act 1973 (c.37), s.30(5).] R, as the proprietor of commercial premises, was not discriminated against in the assessment of payment of water rates since (a) those rates were not rates within the meaning of the General Rate Act 1967 and (2) Parliament had expressly provided for the system of reference to the general rate, and would not have detracted from that express provision save by express words. (*Daymond* v. *S.W. Water Authority* [1975] C.L.Y. 2788, *Northampton Corporation* v. *Ellen* [1904] 1 K.B. 299, *Att.-Gen.* v. *Wimbledon Corporation* [1940] Ch. 180 considered): South West Water Authority v. Rumbles (1986) 26 R.V.R. 144, C.A.

REAL PROPERTY AND CONVEYANCING

2820. Conveyance—"building"—greenhouse—whether included in conveyance

[Law of Property Act 1925 (c.20), s.62.]

Where a greenhouse was not affixed to land but lay in its own weight, it was not a "building" that was included in a conveyance of land with "buildings" thereon.

By a conveyance in 1980 P conveyed to D a parcel of land "together with the farmhouse and other buildings erected thereon." P had erected a large greenhouse on the land in 1979, consisting of a sectional frame bolted to large concrete plinths, which themselves rested unfixed on a concrete base. A dispute arose as to whether or not the greenhouse was included in the conveyance, and D refused P access to the land to remove it. P then brought an action claiming damages for conversion. *Held*, giving judgment for P, that "building" in the conveyance was to be given the same meaning as in s.62 of the Law of Property Act 1925; since the greenhouse was not in any way affixed to the land but lay on its own weight, it was a chattel and not a "building." (*Holland* v. *Hodgson* (1872) L.R. 7 C.P. 328, *H. E. Dibble* v. *Moore* [1969] C.L.Y. 3040 applied.)

Deen v. Andrews (1986) 52 P. & C.R. 17, Hirst J.

2821. Damages—breach of contract—defect in title. See Law Reform, § 1946.

2822. Discharge of water—occupier of low land—whether duty to accept

D owned some low land across which higher adjacent land drained. He filled in his land, preventing the draining of the higher land, which therefore flooded. P, the owner of the higher land, sued him. *Held*, that P had no cause of action. So long as D's actions constituted reasonable use of his own land, he was entitled to do as he did. An owner of high land has no right to discharge water over lower land: Home Brewery Co. v. Davis (William) & Co. (Loughborough), *The Times*, August 13, 1986, Piers Ashworth Q.C.

2823. Lands tribunal fees

Lands Tribunal (Amendment) Rules 1986 (No. 1322) [80p], made under the Lands Tribunal Act 1949 (c.42), s.3 and the Law of Property Act 1969 (c.59), s.28(6); operative on September 1, 1986; increase the fees payable in connection with proceedings before the Lands Tribunal, on average by about half.

2824. Mutual covenants—committee—whether bound to act reasonably or to give reasons

In 1895 53 tradesmen established by deed of mutual covenant a cooperative scheme for the acquisition, lotting and distribution amongst themselves for building purposes of an estate in Northumberland, and entered as mutual covenantors into a number of restrictive covenants as part of the scheme, which was to be administered by a committee appointed by them or their successors in title. The stipulations in the deed were thereafter democratically administered by successive committees appointed by a majority of the owners of the land, the committee itself having an express power to act by a majority. P were the successors in title to part of one of the original plots, on which they wished to build themselves a home, but their plans were rejected by the Committee as failing to comply with the committee's guidelines, and two amended sets of plans were rejected without reasons. P contended that it was an implied term of the deed of mutual covenant that such consent should not be unreasonably withheld, and that it was incumbent upon the committee to give reasons for refusing to approve a building plan submitted to them. It was conceded that the committee had duties to inspect and consider such applications, not to delegate, to act honestly and in good faith, and not to exclude relevant considerations or to take account of irrelevant ones. *Held*, rejecting P's contentions, that (1) whether a contract which required consent to be obtained by one party from the other contains an implied term that such consent is not to be unreasonably withheld, depends on the circumstances of the particular contract. In this case no such term was to be implied (*Wrotham Park Estate Co.* v. *Parkside Homes* [1974] C.L.Y. 3130 distinguished); (2) the committee was not bound to give reasons for its refusal of consent: PRICE *v.* BOUCH (1986) 279 E.G. 1226, Millett J.

2825. Possession order—writ of restitution—considerations. See WILTSHIRE COUNTY COUNCIL *v.* FRAZER, § 2682.

2826. Registered land—implied covenant of good title—interest under another title number
[Land Registration Rules (S.R. & O. 1925 No. 1093), r.77.] "The register" in rule 77 of the Land Registration Rules does not mean the global register of all registered land, but refers only to the register of the individual title in question. Therefore, on a conveyance of registered land, an implied covenant of good title takes effect subject to any other interest in the land appearing or protected on the register under that title number, but not to any interest in land which is the subject matter of another title number: DUNNING (A. J.) & SONS (SHOPFITTERS) *v.* SYKES & SON (POOLE), *The Times,* November 6, 1986, C.A.

2827. Restrictive covenant—freehold land—building of extension without prior consent
A and R were the freehold owners of adjoining properties and dwelling-houses erected thereon. A's predecessor in title had entered into a restrictive covenant in favour of R's predecessor that no additional building should be built "without the consent of the vendor or her successors in title." It was common ground that the covenant applied to A and R. In November 1983 A began to build an extension without consulting R. R objected and refused consent. A ceased work and began proceedings, seeking a declaration (a) that R's refusal was unreasonable, and (b) that he be permitted to put up the extension without R's consent. *Held*, that (1) the covenant was subject to an implied term that consent should not be unreasonably withheld, but (2) on the facts, R's consent had not been unreasonably withheld (*Wrotham Park Estate Co.* v. *Parkside Homes* [1974] 1 W.L.R. 798 considered): BOWER & BOWER *v.* GOODYEAR, February 25, 1986, Judge G. H. Wootton, Nuneaton County Ct. (*Ex rel. James Corbett, Barrister*).

2828. Restrictive covenants—conveyancing standing committee. See LAW REFORM, § 1960.

2829. Rights of access to neighbouring land. See LAW REFORM, §1961.

2830. River—boundary with land
P and D were freehold owners of adjoining properties. P's property consisted of a stretch of "the river Churnet" and D's property of land and houses thereon. D had bought his property in 1982 and P in 1983. In a boundary dispute, P claimed (a) the line of the boundary was the river bank and (b) the river bank was so much of the land adjoining or near to a river as performed or contributed to the performance of the function of containing the river. He sought a declaration accordingly. *Held*, dismissing the claim, that (1) no relevant conveyance defined the boundary; (2) as a matter of fact and common sense a river consisted of a river bed, banks and water, but (3) that factual description did not define the river owner's boundary which, as a matter of law, was the water's edge (*Smith* v. *Andrews* [1891] 2 Ch. 678 and *Jones* v. *Mersey River Board* [1957] C.L.Y. 1892 considered): BRIDDEN *v.* FENN, August 22, 1986; Judge Clive Taylor Q.C.; Stoke-on-Trent County Ct. [*Ex rel. James Corbett, Barrister.*]

2831. Vacant possession—fixtures and fittings—whether breach of obligations under contract. See HYNES *v.* VAUGHAN, § 3523.

RECEIVERS

2832. Administrative receivers
ADMINISTRATIVE RECEIVERS (VALUE ADDED TAX CERTIFICATES) RULES 1986 (No. 385) [40p], made under the Insolvency Act 1985 (c.65), ss.106, 226; operative on April 1, 1986; makes provision for the administrative receiver of a company to issue certificates under the Value Added Tax Act 1983, s.22.

2833. Appointment by debenture holder—company in liquidation—fixed charges paid off—whether balance to go to creditors or company

[Companies Act 1948 (c.38), s.94(1).] Surplus assets of a company in liquidation remaining after payment of fixed charges are payable to the liquidator and not to the preferential creditors.

A receiver was appointed under two debentures which had created fixed (and one floating) charges over the companies assets. After realising assets and paying off the charges the receiver found himself left with a substantial sum of surplus capital. An order for the compulsory winding up of the company was then made. The receiver issued a summons seeking directions. *Held,* that the surplus should go to the person entitled to the mortgaged property, in this case the liquidator of the company rather than to the company's preferential creditors (*Lewis Merthyr Consolidated Collieries, Re* [1929] 1 Ch. 498 applied).

G. L. SAUNDERS, *Re* [1986] 1 W.L.R. 215, Nourse J.

2834. Appointment by the court—landlord's covenant to repair—breach. See DAICHES *v.* BLUELAKE INVESTMENTS, § 1821.

2835. Contempt of court—application to discharge—discretion of court

The Court exercised a discretion to allow the NUM to apply to discharge the receivership notwithstanding its failure to purge its contempt to avoid hardship to the Union's members (*Hadkinson* v. *Hadkinson* [1952] C.L.Y. 2648 *considered*): CLARKE *v.* SCARGILL, *The Times,* October 25, 1985, Mervyn Davies J.

2836. Duty—disclosure of information to company

[Companies Act 1985 (c.6), ss.447(1), 499(1).]

Any right which a company may have to obtain information from a receiver is qualified by his primary responsibility to the debenture holder.

P, a group of companies, granted fixed and floating charges to a bank to secure various debts. The bank appointed receivers who realised various assets of the group. With some £11m. still owing P issued a notice of motion requiring the receivers to disclose full details of all disposals and proposed disposals; the reason given was that they, P, were entering into a contract with a third party whereby the debt might be discharged. *Held,* dismissing the motion, that the company's right to information was qualified by the receiver's primary responsibility to the debenture holder; the onus was on the company to prove their "need to know" and until then the receivers were entitled to refuse to make the disclosures.

GOMBA HOLDINGS UK *v.* HOMAN [1986] 3 All E.R. 94, Hoffmann J.

2837. Liability for rates—receiver empowered but not obliged to assume occupation—whether in rateable occupation. See RATFORD *v.* NORTHAVON DISTRICT COUNCIL, § 2813.

2838. Limited and disputed powers—removal—balance of convenience

P. Co. applied to remove a receiver appointed by D bank. The receiver had been appointed in a situation of some uncertainty as to the legality and enforceability of certain loan agreements, and with no provision as to his right of entry to the company's premises. The bank argued that a right of entry could be implied and the balance of convenience was in favour of allowing him to continue work. D appealed. *Held,* that the receiver must by implication have the power to enter premises and seize possession; further the potential loss to the bank far exceeded the potential loss to the Company, and this was a factor to be considered in deciding whether to remove the receiver: BYBLOS BANK S.A.L. *v.* RUSHINGDALE S.A. [1986] PCC 249, C.A.

2839. Personal liability—employee's contract of employment continuing after appointment—whether liable for employee's salary

[Companies Act 1948 (c.38), s.369(2).] N was the managing director of a company called Nocorrode under a five-year service contract at a salary of £7,500 per annum. In 1979 a receiver of the company was appointed by a bank holding a debenture issued by the company. Three weeks later the receiver gave N one month's notice to determine his service contract on May 20, 1979. N claimed that the receiver was personally liable to pay his salary from the date of his appointment until May 20, 1979. The trial judge dismissed N's claim. *Held,* dismissing N's appeal, that no personal liability on the part of the receiver arose by virtue of s.369(2) of the Companies Act 1948. By permitting N's contract of service to continue it could not be said that the receiver entered into a contract within the meaning of that section. The appointment of the receiver, being made out of court pursuant to a power in the debenture, did not operate as a dismissal of the company's employees. The receiver was the agent of the company so that there was no change in the personality of N's employer. N's salary could not be said to fall within the expression "costs and expenses of the receivership" so as to rank in priority in the subsequent liquidation of the company (*Gaskell* v. *Gosling* [1896] 1 Q.B. 669, *Foster Clark's Indenture Trusts, Re* [1966] C.L.Y. 1358, *Mack Trucks (Britain), Re* [1967] C.L.Y. 3396, *Griffiths* v. *Social Services Secretary* [1973] C.L.Y. 329 approved): NICHOLL v. CUTTS [1985] PCC 311, C.A.

2839a. Removal—dispute over appointment—limited powers—Appointment without notice—status quo—balance of convenience

The bank agreed to lend P £3 million. It was intended that the bank should be secured by charges over P's property. The bank prepared two charges, the first purported to be a fixed charge over specified plant and machinery and the second purported to be a floating charge over the company's stock-in-trade, work in progress and finished goods. The charges did not cover any other assets of the company nor its book debts, did not give the receiver a right of entry nor any power to write cheques on the company's bank account nor conduct the business of the company as a going concern. The documents prepared by the bank were signed by K, a director of the company, but were not sealed by the company. The documents bore the words "Signed, Sealed and Delivered", there was nothing else to indicate that the documents were intended to be deeds. On June 3, 1985, a receiver appointed by the bank appeared at P's premises and handed over a demand for £2·094 million and his appointment under the fixed charge. The receiver was appointed under the floating charge the next day. The appointment and demand were made without any prior notice to P. On June 7, 1985, P commenced action against the bank and applied by notice of motion to remove the receiver. *Held*, that the documents were not deeds. There was no sufficient indication that the documents were intended to be deeds. There was an arguable, albeit thin, case that the documents created an equitable mortgage of personalty under hand. Although it was conceded that the demand made was bad it was also just arguable that P had breached purported covenants in the documents creating the charges. The court had to consider whether the balance of convenience and maintenance of the status quo required the removal of the receiver pending the outcome of the action. The status quo to be considered was that before the appointment of the receiver. The bank could not by appointing a receiver without notice to P and in circumstances that gave P no opportunity to apply to the court for an injunction restraining the appointment of the receiver claim that the preservation of the status quo required the receiver to remain. Having regard to the limited extent of any powers the receiver might have, the balance of convenience required his removal pending the resolution of the action (*First National Securities* v. *Jones* [1978] C.L.Y. 793 distinguished).

RUSHINGDALE S.A. v. BYBLOS BANK S.A.L., 1985 PCC 342, Harman J.

2840. Remuneration agreed by debenture holder—attempt by liquidator to disallow remuneration—powers of court

[Companies Act 1948 (c.38), s.371.] A debenture holder is entitled to appoint a receiver to protect its interest and owes no duty to the company or unsecured creditors to refrain from so doing merely because that course might cause them some loss. Further the court had no right to interfere with the receiver's right to an indemnity in respect of disbursements, and should exercise its right to interfere with the receiver's contractual rate of remuneration, as agreed between him and the debenture holder, only where the rate can be seen to be clearly excessive.

Under the terms of debenture securing a loan of £200,000 made to a company for the purpose of buying some plant, LB, who had made the loan, were entitled to appoint a receiver, upon such terms as to remuneration as LB thought fit. Following a dispute between the company and the seller of the plant, an order for the winding up of the company was made. LB appointed a receiver. The liquidator applied under s.371 of the 1948 Act for a declaration that the appointment of the receiver was unnecessary, and that his fees and disbursements should be disallowed. *Held*, that the summons should be dismissed. LB was contractually entitled to protect its interest by the appointment of a receiver. When deciding whether or not to exercise that power LB was under no duty to have regard to the interests of the company or any unsecured creditors. On the facts there was nothing to show that the remuneration fixed was so clearly excessive as to justify the court in interfering; and the court had no right to negate the receiver's right to an indemnity in respect of his disbursements. *(Greycaine, Re* [1946] Ch. 269 considered).

POTTERS OILS, *Re* [1986] 1 W.L.R. 201, Hoffmann J.

2841. Surplus funds—cross guarantees and charges—whether set-off of trading debts between co-sureties

[Mercantile Law Amendment Act 1856 (c.97), s.5.] Company A was one of six subsidiary companies whose parent company was Sachs and Sherman. All the companies executed joint and several mutual guarantees in favour of the Midland Bank. Each company guaranteed the liability of the others to the Bank and was precluded from proving in the liquidation of any of the companies in competition with the Bank. All the companies executed debentures in favour of the Bank giving the Bank a right to appoint a receiver. In 1978 the Bank appointed a receiver when the groups overall indebtedness reached £314 million. The receiver set about realising the groups assets. After payment of the liabilities to the Bank the receiver was left with a surplus of £195,000. The surplus was referable to overpayments by the companies under their guarantees. By that time the companies were all in liquidation. The liquidator of company A and the receiver proposed to distribute the surplus on the footing that each company was deemed to have discharged its own indebtedness and to have borne so far as it was able to do so an equal share of the total liability to the Bank under the guarantees. The other liquidators contended that the liabilities incurred by each company in the course of trading with the others in the group should also be taken into account. The court at first instance determined that the surplus should be distributed without taking into account any inter-company indebtedness. *Held*, dismissing the liquidators' appeal, that the scheme of distribution proposed by the receiver and the liquidator of company A was the proper scheme and that any debts due from one company to another could not be set off against what was due to each company from the receiver. In the ordinary way such debts could be set off against the liability of any company that had underpaid its contribution to the guarantee sum to pay a company that had overpaid to the guarantee sum. That principle did not apply where the liabilities of the co-sureties to the creditor were secured. In such circumstances the overpaying co-surety was entitled to the benefit of the creditor's security against the under-paying co-surety pursuant to s.5 of the Mercantile Law Amendment Act 1856. The reference to recovery of a "just proportion" by the over-paying co-surety in the proviso to the section referred merely to the amount of contribution payable by the under-paying co-surety to the over-paying co-surety. It did not permit the under-paying co-surety to set off debts due from the over-paying co-surety against his liability to pay contribution to the over-paying surety (*Duncan, Fox & Co.* v. *North & South Wales Bank* (1880) 6 App. Cas. 1, *Re Parker, Morgan* v. *Hill* [1894] 3 Ch. 400, *Smith* v. *Wood* [1929] 1 Ch. 14, *Debtor, A. Re* (*No. 66 of 1955*) [1956] C.L.Y. 632 applied, *Dale* v. *Powell* (1911) 105 L.T. 291, *Kayley* v. *Hothersall* [1925] 1 K.B. 607 distinguished): BROWN *v.* CORK, 1986 PCC 78, C.A.

REGISTRATION OF BIRTHS, DEATHS AND MARRIAGES

2842. Marriage

MARRIAGE (AUTHORISED PERSONS) AMENDMENT REGULATIONS 1986 (No. 1444) [45p], made under the Marriage Act 1949 (c.76), s.74; operative on October 1, 1986; makes minor amendments to S.I. 1952 No. 1869.

REGISTRATION OF MARRIAGES REGULATIONS 1986 (No. 1442) [£3·40], made under the Marriage Act 1949 (c.76), ss.27(1)(2), 27A(3)(4)(7), 27B(2)(*b*), 31(2)(5), 32(2)(4), 35(1), 55(1), 57(2), 74, 76(5), the Registration Service Act 1953 (c.37), s.20(*a*) and the Marriage (Registrar General's Licence) Act 1970 (c.34), ss.2(1), 7, 18; operative on October 1, 1986 save for reg. 6 which is operative on November 1, 1986; prescribe the forms to be used for the preliminaries to marriage, the form of registration of particulars and the manner of registration by registrars.

REGISTRATION OF MARRIAGES (WELSH LANGUAGE) REGULATIONS 1986 (No. 1445) [£2·90], made under the Marriage Act 1949 (c.76), ss.27(1)(2), 27A(4), 27B(2)(*b*),

31(2)(5), 32(2)(4), 35(1), 55(1), 74 and the Registration Service Act 1953 (c.37), s.20(*a*) as extended by the Welsh Language Act 1967 (c.66), ss.2(2), 3(2); operative on October 1, 1986 save for reg. 4 which is operative on November 1, 1986; consolidates with minor amendments S.I. 1971 No. 129.

2843. Request for passpport—whether discrimination
[Race Relations Act 1976 (c.74), s.1.] Unless discrimination is "racial" as defined by the Race Relations Act 1976, it is not illegal under the Act. A Registrar of births, deaths and marriages asked an applicant for registration of marriage, who was born or residing abroad, to produce his passport. *Held,* that this was not racial discrimination within the meaning of s.1 of the Act: TEJANI *v.* SUPERINTENDENT REGISTRAR FOR THE DISTRICT OF PETERBOROUGH, *The Times,* June 10, 1986, C.A.

REVENUE AND FINANCE

2843a. Advance Petroleum Revenue Tax Act 1986 (c.68)
This Act provides for the repayment of certain amounts of advance petroleum revenue tax.
The Act received the Royal Assent on December 18, 1986.

2844. Appeal—judicial review—alternative remedy. See R. *v.* INSPECTOR OF TAXES, *ex p.* KISSANE, § 5.

2845. Appropriation Act 1986 (c.42)
The Act applies a sum out of the Consolidated Fund to the service of the year ending March 31, 1987 and deals with related matters. It received the Royal Assent on July 25, 1986.

2846. Borrowing control
CONTROL OF BORROWING (AMENDMENT) ORDER 1986 (No. 770) [45p], made under the Borrowing (Control and Guarantee) Act 1946 (c.58), ss.1 and 3(4); operative on May 20, 1986; amends S.I. 1958 No. 1208.

2847. Capital duty—increase in share capital of subsidiary company—assumption of liabilities—EEC Directive
[Finance Act 1973 (c.51), Sched. 19, para. 10]. T Co. owed £30m to banks. In 1983 it increased its share capital by issuing 30 million ordinary shares of £1 each to its parent company in consideration of that company assuming the liability to the banks. T Co. claimed exemption from capital duty under F.A. 1973, Sched. 19, para. 10. *Held,* dismissing T Co.'s appeal, that, (1) as the words of the statute were reasonably capable of more than one meaning, it was appropriate to have regard to the E.E.C. Directives, (2) in such circumstances it was correct to construe the words on the footing that Parliament did not intend to act in breach of international obligations, and (3) accordingly, the exemption in Sched. 19, para. 10, should be restricted to the transaction whereby the acquiring company became the beneficial owner of 75 per cent. or more of the capital of the acquired company: NATIONAL SMOKELESS FUELS *v.* I.R.C. [1986] S.T.C. 300, Ch.D.

2848. Consolidated Fund Act 1986 (c.4)
This Act applies £155,484,146·89 and £1,032,019,000 out of the Consolidated Fund to the service of the years ending March 31, 1985 and March 31, 1986 respectively.
The Act received the Royal Assent on March 18, 1986.

2848a. Consolidated Fund (No. 2) Act 1986 (c.67)
This Act applies £2,206,135,000 and £44,907,033,000 out of the Consolidated Fund to the service of the years ending March 31, 1987, and March 31, 1988 respectively.
The Act received the Royal Assent on December 18, 1986.

2849. Finance Act 1986 (c.41)
This Act grants certain duties, alters other duties, amends the law relating to the National Debt and Public Revenue and makes further financial provision in accordance with the Chancellor's budget.
The Act received the Royal Assent on July 25, 1986.

2850. Financial Services Act 1986 (c.60)
This Act regulates investment business. It defines investments and investment business, requires persons carrying on investment business in the U.K. to be authorised and provides for their regulation. It also makes changes to the law on

collective investment, listing of securities, offers of unlisted securities and insider dealing.

The Act comes into force on days to be appointed. It extends to Northern Ireland.

2851. Financial Services Act 1986—commencement

FINANCIAL SERVICES ACT 1986 (COMMENCEMENT NO. 1) ORDER 1986 (No. 1940 (c.69)) [45p], made under the Financial Services Act 1986 (c.60), s.211(1); brings into force on November 15, 1986 the following provisions of the 1986 Act: ss.177, 178(1)(2)(*a*) (6), 179 (in part), 180 (in part), 198(2)(*a*), 199(1)(*a*)(3)–(6)(8)(9) (in part), 200(1)(*b*) (in part), 201(1), 202, 203, 205, 207, 209, 210, Sched. 13, paras. 3, 4, 6, 7, 9, 10, 11, 13, 14 (in part).

FINANCIAL SERVICES ACT 1986 (COMMENCEMENT NO. 2) ORDER 1986 (No. 2031 (c.76)) [80p], made under the Financial Services Act 1986 (c.60), s.211(1); brings into operation on November 27, 1986, the provisions of the 1986 Act specified in the schedule.

FINANCIAL SERVICES ACT 1986 (COMMENCEMENT NO. 3) ORDER 1986 (No. 2246 (c.88)) [£1·40], made under the Financial Services Act 1986 (c.60), s.211(1); brings into force on December 18, 1986, ss.1, 2, 35, 42, 45, 105, 106, 174(1)(2), 179 (in part), 182, 198(1)(*b*)(2)(*b*), 200(1)(*b*)(5), 201(1), 202, 203, 205, 207, 209, 210, Scheds. 1 (except paras. 23, 25(2)(3)), 13; brings into force on January 12, 1987, ss. 5 (in part), 114, 115, 116, 118, 119, 121, 122 (in part), 123 (in part), 124, 126, 128, 129 (in relation to Sched. 10, paras. 1, 3(3), 4(6), 8(6), 10), 132(1)–(5), 132(6) (Pts. 1 and 2), 134, 137, 138(3)(5), 139(1)(*b*), 139(5) (in part), 140 (in part), 141, 173, 176, 178(10), 181, 187(3)(4), 188, 189, 192, 199(7), 200(1)(*b*)(5), 201(4), 204, 211(3) (in part), 212(2) (in part), 212(3) (in part), Scheds. 7, 8, 9, 10 (paras. 1, 3(3), 4(6), 8(6), 10), 11 (Pts. I–IV and paras. 40, 41, 44, 45), 14, 15 (para. 12), 16 (paras. 17, 28(*a*)(*b*), 32 (in part), 17 (in part); brings into force on April 30, 1987, ss.172, 212(2) (in part), 213(3) (in part), Scheds. 12, 16 (in part), 17 (in part); brings into force on February 16, 1987, s.212(3) (in part) and Sched. 17 (in part).

2852. Financial services—disclosure of information

FINANCIAL SERVICES (DISCLOSURE OF INFORMATION) (DESIGNATED AUTHORITIES) ORDER 1986 (No. 2046) [45p], made under the Financial Services Act 1986 (c.60), s.180(3), (4) and (5), and the Companies Act 1985 (c.6), s.449(1B), (1C) and (4); operative on November 28, 1986; designates certain authorities as authorities for the purposes of s.180 of the 1986 Act and s.449 of the 1985 Act in relation to particular functions.

2853. Judicial review—application discontinued—costs. See R. *v.* I.R.C., *ex p.* OPMAN INTERNATIONAL U.K., § 2660.

2854. Judicial review—commissioners—refusal to grant adjournment

Back-duty investigations culminated in a hearing before General Commissioners at which T's accountant, by reason of holiday and business commitments and short notice, was unable to attend. At the hearing, a member of the accountant's staff sought an adjournment; this was refused. The hearing proceeded, and the Commissioners decided against T. Dissatisfaction was expressed and a stated case requested. T then initiated proceedings for judicial review on the ground that the Commissioner had unreasonably refused the application for an adjournment. *Held,* that in tax cases where an appeal was available, judicial review should be granted only in exceptional circumstances, and that such circumstances did not obtain in the present case, since, in particular, T.M.A. 1970, s.56, gave the court wide powers to remit cases to commissioners for amendment or re-hearing: R. *v.* BRENTFORD GENERAL COMMISSIONERS, *ex p.* CHAN [1986] S.T.C. 65, Taylor J.

2855. Judicial review—evidence before Commissioner

Early in 1984 the Revenue made an application for leave under section 41 of the Taxes Management Act 1970 to make an assessment to corporation tax out of time on T Co. In February 1984 the Commissioner considered the application and granted leave. T Co. asserted that there was no rational basis for the Commissioner's decision and that there was no evidence of loss of tax to the Crown. In January 1985 the Court of Appeal granted leave to move for judicial review to quash the Commissioner's decision granting leave under section 41. In consequence, the Commissioner filed an affidavit disclosing the information which had been before her, which included (a) an allegation that T Co. had failed to comply with a notice requiring it to return its profits for the twelve months to January 31, 1978, (b) an allegation that it had ceased to trade on October 25, 1977, thus bringing an accounting period to an end, (c) an allegation that it had entered into a tax avoidance scheme, and (d) an allegation that it had profits of £732,850 falling into charge to tax. *Held,* refusing the application for judicial review, that T Co. had failed to make its case that the Commissioner's decision was without rational basis: R. *v.* SPECIAL COMMISSIONER, *ex p.* STIPPLECHOICE (No. 2) [1986] S.T.C. 4714, Nolan J.

2856. **Judicial review—Revenue documents—discovery.** See R. *v.* I.R.C., *ex p.* ROTHSCHILD (J.) HOLDINGS, § 18.

2857. **Judicial review—transactions in land—assessment—improper exercise of power.** See ADMINISTRATIVE LAW, §5.

2858. **Land—Malaysia—whether capital or income receipts—extraction of timber.** See MAMOR SDN. BHD. *v.* DIRECTOR OF INLAND REVENUE, § 1752.

2859. **Misapplication of statute—distortion of competition—locus standi**
    [European Economic Community Treaty, Arts. 92, 93.] A taxpayer does not usually have *locus standi* qua taxpayer to be heard on matters between the Inland Revenue and another taxpayer. Where the taxpayer comes to court, however, qua competitor whose particular and individual interests are inevitably affected by misapplication of statutory requirements, he does have *locus standi*. The Inland Revenue misapplied statutes, giving an unfair advantage to one oilfield operator and distorting competition to the disadvantage of others. *Held,* that this entitled a disadvantaged competitor to complain, not only under domestic law, but also under EEC law. Art. 92 of the EEC treaty forbids the distortion of competition by the favouring of certain undertakings. Art. 93 allows the Commission to abolish aid that it finds causes forbidden distortion, and says that the Commission must be told of plans to grant aid: proposed measures so to do shall not be put into effect until the Commission's decision. The persistence in the misapplication of the legislation with knowledge of its invalidity constituted an aid or a "plan to grant aid" or "proposed measure" within Art. 93: R. *v.* ATT.-GEN., *ex p.* I.C.I., *The Financial Times,* February 28, 1986, C.A.

2860. **Petroleum revenue tax**
    FOREIGN FIELDS (SPECIFICATION) (NO. 1) ORDER 1986 (No. 1644) [45p], made under the Oil Taxation Act 1983 (c.56), ss.9(5), 12(2); specifies part of the North Sea continental shelf subject to Norwegian jurisdiction, known as the Heimdalfield, as a foreign field for the purposes of the 1983 Act.
    FOREIGN FIELDS (SPECIFICATION) (NO. 2) ORDER 1986 (No. 1645) [80p], made under the Oil Taxation Act 1983 (c.56), ss.9(5), 12(2); specifies part of the North Sea continental shelf subject to Norwegian jurisdiction, known as the North East Frigg Field, as a foreign field for the purposes of the 1983 Act.

2861. **Petroleum revenue tax—relief**
    [Finance Act 1981 (c.35), s.11.] The court held that the defendant was not entitled to relief in respect of expenditure on an oil platform as, although the contract with C for the construction of the installation was made prior to 1981, the expenditure was due pursuant to contracts entered into subsequent to that date by C as the agent for the defendant: I.R.C. *v.* MOBIL NORTH SEA, *The Times,* November 21, 1986, C.A.

2862. **Religious or public benevolent institution—Scientology—whether exemption from pay-roll tax**
    [Aus.] A local statute exempted from tax wages paid or payable "by a religious or public benevolent institution, or a public hospital". In 1969 the Church of the New Faith was incorporated and registered in Victoria as a foreign company. Its members followed the writings of an American called Hubbard, who also had a substantial following in the U.S.A. and the U.K. Hubbard's ideas and practices were known as "Scientology" and his followers "scientologists". The Church claimed to be a religion and exempt from tax. *Held,* that the beliefs, practices of the Church were a religion in Victoria. *Per curiam,* the test of religion should not be confined to theistic religions (*Re South Place Ethical Society; Barralet* v. *Att.-Gen.* [1981] C.L.Y. 226 not followed): THE CHURCH OF THE NEW FAITH *v.* THE COMMISSIONER OF PAY-ROLL TAX (VICTORIA) (1982–1983) 154 C.L.R. 120, High Ct. of Australia.

2863. Stamp duties. see STAMP DUTIES.

ROAD TRAFFIC

2864. Accident

ROAD TRAFFIC ACCIDENTS (PAYMENT FOR TREATMENT) (ENGLAND AND WALES) ORDER 1986 (No. 368) [40p], made under the Public Expenditure and Receipts Act 1968 (c.14), s.5, Sched. 3; operative on April 1, 1986; varies amounts payable under the Road Traffic Act 1972, ss.154(1), 155(1), in respect of accidents.

2865. Accident—learner driver failing to stop—supervising driver aiding and abetting

[Road Traffic Act 1972 (c.20), ss.25(1)(4), 177(1), Sched. 4, pt. 1; Road Traffic Act 1974 (c.50), s.24(2), Sched. 6; Magistrates' Courts Act 1980 (c.43), s.44(1).]

The supervisor of a learner driver is not under a duty to ensure that the learner remains after an accident where he has stopped driving.

X, a learner driver supervised by D, had an accident which caused injury to a cyclist. X stopped and he and D both left the scene. Forty minutes later they were found by a police officer returning to the scene of the accident apparently in the hope that it was now safe to remove the car. X was convicted of failing to stop, contrary to s.25(1) of the Road Traffic Act 1972. D was prosecuted on the basis that he had aided and abetted X by failing to ensure that X remained. The justices acquitted him on the basis that X had stopped driving and that D's duty to supervise no longer existed. *Held,* allowing the prosecutor's appeal, that although that finding was correct D had nevertheless aided and abetted X on the facts found by the justices by walking away with him, then returning to collect the car with him. Accordingly, the case would be remitted to the justices with a direction to convict (*Att.-Gen.'s Reference (No. 1 of 1975)* [1975] C.L.Y. 2977 applied; *Rubie* v. *Faulkner* [1940] 1 K.B. 571 considered).

BENTLEY *v.* MULLEN [1986] R.T.R. 7, D.C.

2866. Analyst's certificate—service—whether authorised

[Road Traffic Act 1972 (c.20), ss.6(1), 8(1)(4)(6), 10(3)(4)(5)(8); Transport Act 1981 (c.56), s.25(3), Sched. 8.]

An analyst's or doctor's certificate may properly be served under s.10(5) of the Road Traffic Act 1972 if it is served on an authorised agent of the defendant who has authority to receive and deal with documents, such as his solicitor.

D gave a positive specimen of breath according to a Lion Intoximeter. He requested to supply blood instead, under s.8(6) of the Road Traffic Act 1972. The analyst's and doctor's certificates were not served on D. They were, however, served on D's solicitors at their request. D objected to their admissibility for lack of service within the terms of s.10(5). The justices upheld his objection. *Held,* allowing the prosecutor's appeal, that the documents could properly be served on an authorised agent who had authority to receive and deal with documents, such as the solicitors; furthermore, solicitors had authority to waive personal service, as they had done in this case (*R.* v. *Bott* [1968] C.L.Y. 2390 and *Burt* v. *Kirkcaldy* [1965] C.L.Y. 3492 applied).

ANDERTON *v.* KINNARD [1986] R.T.R. 11, D.C.

2867. Analyst's certificate—service—whether effective. See PENMAN *v.* PARKER, § 2626.

2868. Appeal against conviction—jurisdiction of Crown Court—appeal against one of several convictions. See DUTTA *v.* WESTCOTT, § 541.

2869. Blood specimen—breath analyser a reliable device—meaning

[Road Traffic Act 1972 (c.20), ss.5(1), 8(1) and (3) and 12(2).]

The words "a reliable device" in s.8(3) of the Act are to be construed as meaning "a device which the constable reasonably believes to be reliable" for the purpose of deciding whether a blood specimen may properly be required.

T provided two specimens of breath for analysis by a Camic Breath Analyser, and the readings recorded were 145 and 117 microgrammes of alcohol in 100 millilitres of breath. The constable was under instructions to treat a device whose readings varied by more than 10 per cent. as unreliable, and in the circumstances he required T to give a blood specimen. T was convicted under s.6(1) of the Act on the basis of the analysis of that sample. He appealed to the Crown Court, who found that the device in question was operating normally two days later. T contended that the device has been reliable and thus that the constable was not entitled to require a blood specimen. *Held*, that the words a "reliable device" in s.8(3) were to be given the meaning "a device which the constable reasonably believes to be reliable". The appeal would be dismissed.

THOMPSON *v.* THYNNE [1986] R.T.R. 293, D.C.

2870. Blood specimen—disqualification—special reasons
[Road Traffic Act 1972 (c.20), ss.6(1), s.8(1), 10, 12; Breath Analysis Devices (Approval) Order 1983.]
The court should not be drawn into detailed calculations, even when presented as expert evidence, as to a defendant's blood/alcohol level at the time of the alleged offence. Once a specimen of blood had been given, a printout from a Lion Intoximeter 3000 was not to be used to show a different concentration from that shown by analysis of the blood.
G drank a pint of lager and then a pint of shandy which, unknown to him, had been laced with half a pint of lager. Five minutes later, while driving his car, he was stopped by the police. About an hour and three-quarters later he provided a specimen of blood for analysis. The analysis showed 92 milligrammes of alcohol and it was agreed that half a pint of lager represented 15 milligrammes. On this basis the justices refused to disqualify. *Held*, that for the purpose of "special reasons" the court was concerned with blood/alcohol level at the time of the offence, but should not be drawn into detailed calculations. A printout from a Lion Intoximeter 3000 could not be used in evidence in cases where the defendant had provided a specimen of blood, and thus could not be used to show that blood/alcohol concentration was at one time higher than that shown by analysis of the specimen. The justices were correct in finding special reasons for not disqualifying (*Pugsley* v. *Hunter* [1973] G.W.I. 2917 and *Dawson* v. *Lunn* [1986] C.L.Y. 2924 applied).

SMITH *v.* GERAGHTY [1986] R.T.R. 222, D.C.

2871. Blood specimen—exercise of option to replace breath specimen—whether necessary to take test at hospital
[Road Traffic Act 1972 (c.20), as amended, ss.6(1)(*a*) and 8.] D provided a specimen of breath which registered 41 μg of alcohol per 100 ml. of breath. He exercised his option to replace this with a blood specimen under s.8(6) of the 1972 Act. *Held,* dismissing D's appeal against conviction under s.6(1)(*a*) of driving with excess alcohol in his blood, that "required" in s.8(6) did not bear the same meaning as in s.8(1). It was not necessary for the blood specimen to be taken at a hospital: SIVYER *v.* PARKER [1986] Crim.L.R. 410, D.C.

2872. Blood specimen—failure to provide—medical reason
[Road Traffic Act 1972 (c.20), ss.6(1)(*a*), 8(3)(*a*), 8(4) and 10] J provided two specimens of breath, the lower containing less than 50 μg of alcohol per 100 ml. of breath. He declined an opportunity to provide a blood specimen, saying that he disliked "needles" and had fainted years earlier following a blood test. He was not given an opportunity to provide a urine sample. *Held,* dismissing the appeal of the West Yorkshire Police, that (1) a repugnance to the taking of a specimen may amount to a reasonable excuse for failing to provide one if it amounts to a phobia recognised by medical science; (2) repugnance of such a degree is also capable of being a "medical" reason for failing to provide a specimen under s.8(3)(*a*); (3) if a suspect chooses to substitute a sample for breath, the officer is entitled to choose whether the sample be blood or urine, subject to any medical reason; (4) if there is a sound medical objection, the suspect is entitled to choose; (5) by virtue of s.8(4), the officer is not entitled to rule upon a medical issue (which must be decided by a medical practitioner), although he has power to decide whether a medical issue has been raised at all; (6) the officer had usurped the function of the medical practitioner in deciding that J's objection was invalid. Accordingly, the requisite conditions for admissibility of the breath specimen under s.10 were not satisfied (*R.* v. *Harding* [1974] C.L.Y. 3282, *R.* v. *Coates* [1976] C.L.Y. 2393 and *Sykes* v. *White* [1983] C.L.Y. 3220 applied; *Anderton* v. *Lythgoe* [1984] C.L.Y. 3003, *R.* v. *Sang* [1971] C.L.Y. 2605, *R.* v. *Trump* (1979) 70 Cr.App.R. 300 and *Fox* v. *Chief Constable of Gwent* [1984] C.L.Y. 3006 considered): WEST YORKSHIRE METROPOLITAN POLICE *v.* JOHNSON [1986] Crim.L.R. 64, D.C.

2873. Blood specimen—failure to provide—unavailability of breath test device—burden of proof

[Road Traffic Act 1972 (c.20), ss. 8(3)(*b*), 8(7).] At D's trial for failing to provide a specimen of blood, contrary to s.8(7) of the 1972 Act, the arresting police officer gave evidence that the station sergeant had told D that the approved breath test device could not be used because it was not available and that, accordingly, he required D to provide a specimen of blood for laboratory analysis. *Held,* allowing D's appeal against conviction, that the prosecution had failed to prove the facts required by s.8(3)(*b*). The officer's evidence was hearsay. The sergeant should have been called to give direct evidence that the device was not available: DYE *v.* MANNS [1986] Crim.L.R. 337, D.C.

2874. Blood specimen—independent analysis

[Road Traffic Act 1972 (c.20), ss.6(1), 8(3), 10(6).]

A person is not to be convicted upon evidence of a police analysis of a blood specimen unless he has had the opportunity of subjecting the part of the specimen given to him to independent analysis.

P was arrested and provided blood for analysis. She was given part of the specimen and took it away. Later that day P telephoned the police station and was informed that her specimen could not be submitted for analysis because it was not in an envelope with the flap sealed and signed by the station sergeant. P did not submit the specimen for analysis. The specimen retained by the police revealed an excess of alcohol: P submitted that this evidence was inadmissible because the right to have part of the specimen submitted to her had been frustrated. The justices rejected this and convicted her. *Held,* that the purpose of the right conferred by s.10(6) was to allow independent analysis. P had been misled, and deprived of this right, and the conviction would be quashed (*R. v. Anderson* [1972] C.L.Y. 2998 applied).

PERRY *v.* McGOVERN [1986] R.T.R. 240, D.C.

2875. Blood specimen—requirement for procedure

[Road Traffic 1972 (c.20), ss.6(1), 8.]

A prosecutor may rely on evidence of a blood specimen where the requirement for that specimen is made at one police station, and the specimen is taken at another station without establishing that no reliable breath analyser is available at the second station. There is no novation of procedure by repeating the requirement for a blood specimen at the second station.

B, an arrested motorist at a police station, was required to give two specimens of breath for analysis, but the device malfunctioned when the second specimen was given. The constable then required B to give a specimen of blood, and he was transferred to another police station for the purpose. There was a breath analyser at the second station but the constable took no steps to discover whether it was available, reliable or whether it was practicable to use it. Instead he repeated his request for a blood specimen and this was given. Before the magistrates, the defence contended that the operative request for a blood specimen was the second, and the prosecutor had not established that a reliable breath analyser was unavailable at the second station so the specimen could not be relied on in evidence. The information was dismissed. *Held,* on appeal, that that effective requirement for a blood specimen was made in accordance with statutory procedure at the first station. The evidence of the specimen could be relied on even though it was taken at a different station (*Pascoe v. Nicholson* [1981] C.L.Y. 2330 applied).

CHIEF CONSTABLE OF KENT *v.* BERRY [1986] R.T.R. 321, D.C.

2876. Blood specimen—whether valid requirement

[Road Traffic Act 1972 (c.20), s.8(3).]

A motorist is not to be required and cannot validly be required to give a specimen of blood unless the constable has reasonable cause to believe that for medical reasons a specimen of breath cannot be provided or should not be required.

B was arrested following a motor accident and taken to a police station. He was asked to give a specimen of breath and attempted to blow into the machine but no specimen was recorded. B said he was having difficulty blowing, due to a cut on his head. The constable did not believe the injury affected his ability to blow and did not think B was suffering from concussion, but accepted the excuse on the basis that B was the best judge of his injuries. The constable went to require a specimen of blood, which B refused to give. The justices found that the machine was working properly, and dismissed the charge under s.8(7). *Held*, that the appeal would be dismissed for lack of compliance with s.8(3).

HORROCKS *v.* BINNS [1986] R.T.R. 202, D.C.

2877. Breath specimen—admissibility
[Road Traffic Act 1972 (c.20), ss.6(1), 8, 10(2).]
Where for medical reasons only one breath specimen is given, evidence of this is admissible, and capable of being sufficient to ground a conviction.

B, an arrested motorist at a police station was required to give two specimens of breath. The giving of the second specimen was interrupted by a coughing fit. B suffered from asthma and the justices were of the opinion that he had a reasonable excuse for not providing a second specimen. The defence contended that evidence of the first sample was not admissible under s.10(2) of the Act, but B was convicted of driving with excess alcohol in his blood. *Held*, that evidence of the single specimen was both admissible and of sufficient evidential value to allow conviction.

BURRIDGE *v.* EAST [1986] R.T.R. 328, D.C.

2878. Breath specimen—analysis by Camic Breath Analyser—non-existent company named in Order approving Camic Breath Analyser—whether device properly approved
[Breath Analysis Devices (Approval) Order 1983, Sched.]
The Camic Breath Analyser is a device of a type approved by the Secretary of State notwithstanding that the Approval Order referred to it as being manufactured by a non-existent company.

D was asked to provide two specimens of breath for analysis by a Camic Breath Analyser machine. D was considerably over the limit and charged with driving a motor car when the proportion of alcohol in his breath exceeded the prescribed limit. D raised the defence that the machine was not a ". . . device of a type approved by the Secretary of State," in that the Breath Analysis Devices (Approval) Order 1983 approved a device called the Camic Breath Analyser manufactured by Camic Car and Medical Instrument Company. There was no such company, its proper name being Car and Medical Instrument Company. The justices felt that the manufacturer of the device was an integral part of its description for approval purposes and therefore as the machine was not manufactured by Camic Car and Medical Instrument Company the charge should be dismissed. The prosecution appealed by way of case stated. *Held*, allowing the appeal, that the insertion of the word "Camic" into the name of the manufacturer was a mistake. That mistake did not invalidate the approval as the material part of the Schedule to the Order was that which stated the type of device namely, "The device comprised of two components which are respectively known as the "Camic Simulator" and the "Camic Breath Analyser. . ." (*Hayward* v. *Eames* [1985] C.L.Y. 3045 considered).

CHIEF CONSTABLE OF NORTHUMBRIA *v.* BROWNE [1986] R.T.R. 113, D.C.

2879. Breath specimen—failure to provide—asking to speak to solicitor
[Road Traffic Act 1972 (c.20), s.8(1) and (7).]
A defendant may speak to a solicitor before deciding whether to provide specimens of breath, without committing an offence under s.8(7).

H, who was a motorist arrested and at a police station, was required by a constable to provide specimens of breath. He asked to speak to his solicitor first, and then offered to provide the specimens. He was charged with failing to provide a specimen, contrary to s.8(7) of the Act, and acquitted. *Held*, that since it was not clear whether H had asked to speak to his solicitor before deciding whether to provide specimens, or had refused to provide them until he had spoken to his solicitor, he should be given the benefit of the doubt, and the appeal should be dismissed (*Pettigrew* v. *Northumbria Police Authority* [1976] C.L.Y. 2391 considered.)

SMITH *v.* HAND [1986] R.T.R. 265, D.C.

2880. Breath specimen—failure to provide—medical reasons—validity of requirement of blood specimen
[Road Traffic Act 1972 (c.20), s.8.]
In considering whether a medical reason put forward by a motorist for not providing a specimen of breath was a proper one within the terms of s.8(3), a constable did not have to determine whether it was a medically recognised condition, only whether it could be and whether he had reasonable cause to believe that for medical reasons a specimen could not be provided or should not be required.

D, a motorist was arrested and while at a police station, was required by a constable, in accordance with s.8(1) of the Road Traffic Act 1972, to provide two specimens of breath for analysis by a Lion Intoximeter 3000. D put forward two medical reasons for not doing so. The first, agoraphobia, was rejected. The second, a phobia of machines, was accepted by the constable who then required a specimen of blood. When D refused this he was charged under s.8(7) with failing to provide a specimen without an excuse. The justices convicted, being of the opinion that a valid requirement for a specimen of blood had been made. *Held*, that a constable requiring a specimen of blood from a motorist was not obliged to determine as a matter of medical science whether the phobia put forward as an excuse was a recognised condition. All he could do was to consider whether it was capable of being such a condition, and if so whether he had reasonable cause to believe that a specimen could not be provided or should not be required. Provided there was sufficient material to justify the constable's decision, it was his alone and he need not summon a doctor to give his opinion. Accordingly the constable had made a valid requirement for a blood specimen. *Alcock* v. *Read* [1980] C.L.Y. 2299; *R.* v. *Harding* [1974] C.L.Y. 3282; *Sykes* v. *White* [1983] C.L.Y. 3220 and *Johnson* v. *West Yorks Police* [1986] C.L.Y. 2891 applied. *Horrocks* v. *Binns* [1986] C.L.Y. 2876 distinguished.

DEMPSEY v. CATTON [1986] R.T.R. 194, D.C.

2881. Breath specimen—failure to provide specimen—evidence—special reasons

[Road Traffic Act 1972 (c.20), ss.6(1), 8, 10, 12(2), 93(1), Sched. 4.]

Oral evidence of a reading on a Lion Intoximeter 3000 may only be relied on when it comes from someone trained to use the machine and to judge its reliability. Where a defendant is convicted of driving with excess alcohol on the evidence of one specimen, and is also convicted of failing to provide the second specimen, the circumstances do not constitute special reasons for failing to disqualify or endorse on the second offence.

D, an arrested motorist at a police station, provided a breath specimen in the presence of the arresting constable and the station sergeant. The constable noticed that the reading on the Lion Intoximeter was 75 microgrammes. D then failed to give a second specimen. Contrary to s.10(5) of the Act he was not provided with a printout. He was charged with driving with excess alcohol and failing to provide a specimen. The station sergeant was unavailable before the justices, and they would not admit the printout in evidence. D was convicted of driving with excess alcohol on the basis of the constable's evidence about the visual display on the Intoximeter. The justices then considered that the two offences arose from the same circumstances, that injustice would be caused by punishing for both, and for this special reason they ordered an absolute discharge without disqualification or endorsement for failing to provide a specimen. *Held,* that in circumstances where all the relevant provisions of 1972 Act had been complied with, a printout from a single specimen of breath was admissible. That oral evidence of the visual display on the Intoximeter was admissible if it came from an officer trained in how to judge the reliability of the device, and thus here there was no evidence of the amount of alcohol in the accused's breath, and the conviction must be quashed. That the justices were wholly wrong in considering that the offences arose out of the same circumstances, and no special reasons for not disqualifying or endorsing, so the case would be remitted to the justices on this point (*Whittall* v. *Kirby* [1947] C.L.Y. 9056 applied).

DENNENY v. HARDING [1986] R.T.R. 350, D.C.

2882. Breath specimen—failure to provide specimen—one specimen only

[Road Traffic Act 1972 (c.20), ss.6(1), 8(1)(*a*)(6)(7), 10(2), 12(2); Transport Act 1981 (c.56), s.25(3), Sched. 8.]

When a defendant provides only one specimen of breath the obligation to disregard the higher reading does not arise.

D was stopped and failed without reasonable excuse to provide a specimen of breath for a breath test under s.7(1)(*c*) of the 1972 Act. He was arrested and taken to the police station when he was required under s.8(1) to provide 2 specimens of breath. The first, as D knew, gave a reading of 55 microgrammes. He failed to blow sufficiently long or hard to provide a second reading. He was charged with driving with excess alcohol under s.6(1), failing to provide a specimen of breath for a roadside test under s.7(4) and failing to provide a specimen of breath at a police station under s.8(7). The justices admitted the evidence of the one breath specimen under s.10(2). D was convicted on all injunctions. He appealed against conviction for the s.6(1) and s.8(7) convictions. *Held,* dismissing the appeals, that (1) the breath analysis specimen was taken in accordance with necessary procedure under s.8 and was therefore admissible under s.10(2), and when only one specimen was provided the obligation under s.8(6) to disregard the higher reading did not arise; the justices were right to admit the evidence and convict D (*Howard* v. *Hallett* [1984] C.L.Y. 3024 distinguished); (2) D could properly be convicted under both s.6(1) and s.8(7).

DUDDY *v.* GALLAGHER [1985] R.T.R. 401, D.C.

2883. Breath specimen—failure to provide specimen—whether reasonable excuse
[Road Traffic Act 1972 (c.20), s.12(3).]
A defendant who made a genuine attempt to give a sample of breath for a Lion Intoximeter machine in accordance with the operator's instructions is guilty of failing to give a sample of breath without reasonable excuse contrary to s.8(7) of the Road Traffic Act 1972.
D was arrested, taken to a police station and asked to provide a sample of breath for analysis by a Lion Intoximeter machine. D blew into the machine which produced a printout recording "no sample". D was charged with failing to provide a specimen of breath contrary to s.8(7) of the Road Traffic Act 1972. D was acquitted. The prosecutor appealed by way of case stated. The justices stated that the operator of the machine gave evidence that he formed the impression that D was blowing round the mouthpiece instead of into it and that he was trying to defeat the machine. D gave evidence that he followed the operator's instructions, blew into the machine twice but not hard, his reading was zero and that he didn't realise the machine had not produced a satisfactory record. D stated he had never intended to defeat the machine. There was no evidence that the machine's visual display indicated "aborted". The justices preferred D as a witness to the machine's operator. If the prosecution evidence were correct the word "aborted" ought to have appeared on the machine's visual display. The defendant made a full and proper attempt to blow into the machine and thus had not in law failed to provide a specimen. In the alternative by acting to the best of his ability D had a reasonable excuse for failing to give a specimen of breath. *Held,* that the justices should have assumed, in the absence of evidence to the contrary, that the machine was in good working order. They were not entitled to draw upon their own experience of the machine nor draw inferences from the fact that no evidence was given that the machine displayed the word "aborted", but must decide the case on the evidence before them. Having regard to s.12(3) of the Act the justices could not properly conclude that D had not failed to provide a specimen. The fact that D made a genuine attempt to do so was not a reasonable excuse for that failure (*R.* v. *Lennard* [1973] C.L.Y. 2896 considered, *Castle* v. *Cross* [1984] C.L.Y. 3048 applied).

ANDERTON *v.* WARING [1986] R.T.R. 74, D.C.

2884. Breath specimen—failure to provide specimen—whether reasonable excuse
The fact that a breath test machine is difficult to use and that the defendant had made a genuine attempt to provide a specimen for analysis is not capable of constituting a reasonable excuse for failing to provide a specimen of breath for analysis.
D was asked to give a specimen of breath for analysis using an Alcometer S-L2 machine in the back of a police car. On his first attempt D failed to provide a sufficient sample to operate the machine and was charged with failing to provide a specimen of breath for analysis without reasonable excuse. D was convicted by the justices and appealed unsuccessfully to the Crown Court. D appealed by way of case stated. In the course of the Crown Court hearing, the court tested an Alcometer S-L2 and found it was difficult to operate properly at a first attempt. The court found that D was asked to blow into the machine whilst he was sitting in the back of a police car and the machine was held between the front seats of the car by the officer. The court found that D made a genuine attempt to operate the machine. It was contended by D that in the circumstances he had a reasonable excuse for failing to provide a specimen of breath. *Held,* dismissing the appeal, that D did not have a reasonable excuse for failing to provide a specimen of breath in the absence of any physical incapacity or failure to understand what was required of him (*R.* v. *Lennard* [1973] C.L.Y. 2896, *Beck* v. *Sager* [1979] C.L.Y. 2308 considered, *Anderton* v. *Waring* [1986] C.L.Y. 2883 applied).

DAWES *v.* TAYLOR [1986] R.T.R. 81, D.C.

2885. Breath specimen—failure to provide—whether reasonable excuse
[Road Traffic Act 1972 (c.20), ss.7, 8.]
The question of whether a defendant has a reasonable excuse for not providing a specimen of breath does not arise until and unless he attempts to provide one. The court may conclude that he has not so done his best without evidence of the reading on the device in question.

T was required to provide a specimen of breath by the roadside and refused. He was arrested, taken to a police station and required to provide two specimens of breath, and again he refused. He later sought to raise a defence of reasonable excuse on the grounds that he suffered from asthma. The justices convicted him. *Held*, that since T did not mention the asthma at the time no question of a reasonable excuse arose. Further that in the absence of an Intoximeter printout the justices were still entitled to conclude that T had provided insufficient breath for analysis (*Castle* v. *Cross* [1984] C.L.Y. 3048 applied).
TEAPE v. GODFREY [1986] R.T.R. 213, D.C.

2886. Breath specimen—failure to provide—whether requirement lawful
[Road Traffic Act 1972 (c.20), ss.6(1), 7(2)(4)(5), 8(1)(7); Transport Act 1981 (c.56), s.25(3) Sched. 8.]
D was involved in an accident and the constable who attended, having smelt her breath, required her to provide a specimen of breath which she refused. She was arrested and taken to the police station where the station officer informed her that she had been arrested for failure to take a breath test and was required to provide 2 specimens of breath under s.8(1) of the 1972. Act. D refused and was charged with contravening s.8(7). At trial a submission of no case to answer was upheld on the ground that the arresting officer was investigating an accident and not an offence under s.5 or s.6, so that the requirement to provide a specimen was unlawful. *Held*, allowing the prosecutor's appeal, that when the station officer required the specimens under s.8(1) he was investigating whether D had committed an offence under s.6(1) so that his requirement was lawful; the case would be remitted with a direction to continue the hearing.
GRAHAM v. ALBERT [1985] R.T.R. 352, D.C.

2887. Breath specimen—failure to provide specimen—unlawful arrest—relevance
[Road Traffic Act 1972 (c.20), ss.7(5), 8(7); Transport Act 1981 (c.56), s.25(3), Sched. 8.]
A prior lawful arrest is not a necessary ingredient of the offence of failing to provide a specimen.

B was charged with failing to provide a specimen of breath, contrary to s.8(7) of the 1972 Act, and various other offences. The justices acquitted him having found that he had not been driving the relevant motor car at the relevant time and that his admitted refusal to provide a specimen of breath had followed on from an unlawful arrest. On the question whether a lawful arrest under s.7(5) of the 1972 Act is an essential prerequisite to a conviction for an offence under either s.6 or s.8(7) of the 1972 Act. *Held*, allowing the appeal, that the question of whether or not a lawful arrest has been made is wholly irrelevant to the question whether when at the police station, no matter how he had come there, B had failed without reasonable excuse to provide a specimen of breath when required to do so (*Fox* v. *Chief Constable of Gwent* [1984] C.L.Y. 3006 applied).
BUNYARD v. HAYES (NOTE) [1985] R.T.R. 348, D.C.

2888. Breath specimen—failure to provide—whether evidence of calibration of device needed
[Road Traffic Act 1972 (c.20), s.8.]
No evidence of calibration of the breath analysis device is required to prove a charge under s.8(7).

O was required to give two specimens of breath for analysis. He gave one, but in giving the second breathed in short bursts, contrary to the officer's instructions and failed to provide a sufficient specimen. He was given a second opportunity, again failed to provide a sufficient specimen, and was charged under s.8(7) of the Act. The justices admitted the officers' oral evidence that the reading on the first occasion was 75 microgrammes of alcohol in 100 millilitres of breath, and convicted. O appealed on the grounds that this evidence was inadmissible and prejudicial, that the evidence of the officer should have been supplemented with evidence that the device used was properly calibrated. *Held*, that while it would have been better to exclude evidence of the reading, the justices treated it only as evidence that O was capable of giving a specimen, so no material irregularity had occurred to justify allowing the appeal. That since proof of a charge under s.8(7) depended on failure to provide a specimen, evidence of calibration was not required (*Owen* v. *Chesters* [1985] C.L.Y. 3054 and *Morgan* v. *Lee* [1985] C.L.Y. 3049 distinguished).

OLDFIELD *v.* ANDERTON [1986] R.T.R. 314, D.C.

2889. Breath specimen—50 microgrammes or below—specimen of blood—admissibility of breath specimen

[Road Traffic Act 1972 (c.20), ss.5(1), 8(1)(4)(6), 10(2); Transport Act 1981 (c.56), s.25(3), Sched. 8.]

S.8(6) of the Road Traffic Act 1972 takes precedence over s.10(2).

A provided a breath specimen which resulted in readings of less than 50 microgrammes of alcohol. He then provided a blood specimen which became contaminated and could not be analysed. A was charged with driving contrary to s.5(1) of the 1972 Act and at trial evidence of the breath specimen was adduced. A was convicted. *Held,* allowing the appeal, that when, pursuant to s.8(1) of the 1972 Act, an analysis of a specimen of breath produces a reading of less than 50 microgrammes and the motorist then provides a specimen of blood, then evidence of the breath analysis cannot be used, even though the blood specimen is incapable of analysis, since s.8(6) takes precedence over s.10(2) that evidence of alcohol in a specimen of breath should in all cases be taken into account.

ARCHBOLD *v.* JONES [1986] R.T.R. 178, D.C.

2890. Breath specimen—Lion Intoximeter—wide margin between readings—whether evidence of malfunctioning

[Road Traffic Act 1972 (c.20), ss.6(1), 10 and 12(2).]

A margin between two breath test readings which is merely unusually high does not provide sufficient evidence for magistrates to conclude that the device in question is malfunctioning.

M was arrested, taken to a police station and asked to provide two specimens of breath. The Lion Intoximeter 3000 gave readings of 88 microgrammes, and 76 microgrammes of alcohol in 100 millilitres of blood. A police officer gave evidence that this difference was unusually high, and although some readings produced wider differences, the usual margin was 2–3 microgrammes. The magistrates treated this as evidence that the device was malfunctioning, and M was acquitted. *Held*, that there was no evidential basis for finding that the device was malfunctioning.

LLOYD *v.* MORRIS [1986] R.T.R. 299, D.C.

2891. Breath specimen—option of blood specimen—medical reason for refusal

[Road Traffic Act 1972 (c.20), ss.6(1), 8(1), (3)(*a*), (4), (6), (7), 10(2)(4), 12(2)(*a*), Transport Act 1981 (c.56), s.25(3), Sched. 8.]

An aversion to needles is capable of being a medical reason within s.8(3)(*a*) of the Road Traffic Act 1972 for not providing a specimen of blood.

J provided a specimen of breath which contained less than 50 microgrammes of alcohol. He was offered the option of providing a specimen of blood under s.8(6) of the 1972 Act, but not of providing a specimen of urine. J said that he had an aversion to needles. The constable decided that this did not constitute a medical reason within s.8(4) for refusing to provide a specimen of blood and did not seek the opinion of a medical practitioner. J was charged with driving contrary to s.6(1) and was convicted, evidence of the printout having been produced. J appealed to the Crown Court which allowed the appeal. *Held*, dismissing the prosecutor's appeal, that J's expression of aversion to a blood test was capable of being a medical reason; when a motorist was offered the option to exercise his right under s.8(6) it was his choice whether to do so; thereafter the constable had the right to choose whether the motorist should provide a specimen of blood or urine; if the motorist raised a medical reason for refusing to comply with the constable's choice, the validity of that reason had to be determined by a medical practitioner; the procedural requirements of s.8(6) had not been followed which rendered the evidence of the printout inadmissible (*Anderton* v. *Lythgoe* [1985] C.L.Y. 2994 applied).

JOHNSON *v.* WEST YORKSHIRE METROPOLITAN POLICE [1986] R.T.R. 167, D.C.

2892. Breath specimen—provision after initial failure—admissibility
[Road Traffic Act 1972 (c.20), ss.6(1)(*b*), 8(1)(4)(6)(7), 12(2)(3), Transport Act 1981 (c.56), s.25(3), Sched. 8.]
Where a motorist has failed to provide a specimen of breath there is nothing to prevent an officer giving the motorist a second opportunity to provide a specimen.
M was required to provide a specimen of breath for analysis at a police station by a Lion Intoximeter 3000 device. She failed to do so. Shortly thereafter she was requested to try again and provided a specimen. Since the reading was less than 50 microgrammes she opted for a blood test. She was prosecuted on the evidence of the blood test with contravening s.6(1)(*b*) of the 1972 Act. The justices dismissed the information because the officer had given M a second opportunity to provide a breath specimen. *Held,* allowing the prosecutor's appeal, that when someone failed to provide a specimen of breath under s.8(1) nothing precluded the making of a further request for such a specimen (*Revel* v. *Jordan* [1984] C.L.Y. 2998 applied).
OWEN *v.* MORGAN [1986] R.T.R. 151, D.C.

2893. Breath specimen—refusal to supply—special reasons for refusal to order endorsement
[Road Traffic Act 1972 (c.20), s.8(7).]
D's car was parked in the car park of a public house. It was moved by a group of youths. When the police arrived they found D standing by his car, where he admitted to being the owner. He was asked for and refused to give a specimen of his breath and was arrested and charged under s.8(7) of the Road Traffic Act 1972. At trial he pleaded guilty. The justices decided that D was not going to drive his motor car and so they did not disqualify him but ordered his licence to be endorsed with the mandatory 10 points. *Held,* allowing the appeal, that the special reasons found for not disqualifying D related wholly to the offence in question and could amount to a special reason for not ordering endorsement. Accordingly the justices did have a discretion whether or not to order endorsement and the case would be remitted back to them (*R.* v. *Wickins* [1958] C.L.Y. 2988 applied).
McCORMICK *v.* HITCHINS (1986) 83 Cr.App.R. 11, D.C.

2894. Breath specimen—replacement by blood specimen—consent
[Road Traffic Act 1972 (c.20), ss.6, 8 (both as substituted).] Since the onus is on D to establish that he consents to a blood sample being taken where circumstances provide for the giving of such a sample he must give an unconditional assent. If he does not, and no blood sample can therefore be taken by a doctor, the specimens of breath given earlier can be used in evidence against him: RAWLINS *v.* BROWN, *The Times,* June 6, 1986, D.C.

2895. Breath test—analysis from two cycles of intoximeter—oral evidence of operator
[Road Traffic Act 1972 (c.20), ss.8(1)(6), 10.]
The oral evidence of an officer of readings given by a Lion Intoximeter machine that he was operating was admissible to prove an excess alcohol charge where the prosecution chose not to or could not rely upon a certified printout produced by the machine.
D was requested to provide two samples of breath for analysis by a Lion Intoximeter machine by an officer. The officer observed that the first sample produced a reading of 95 microgrammes of alcohol in 100 millilitres of breath. The second sample was not provided in time so that the machine completed its cycle by recording no sample in respect of the second sample. The machine produced a printout recording the details. D was asked to provide two further samples which were provided within one cycle of the machine's operation. The officer observed that the first reading was 98 microgrammes of alcohol. The printout produced by the machine on its second cycle was signed by the officer and D and a copy given to D. At the hearing the prosecution sought to rely upon the oral evidence of the officer of the readings of 95 and 98 microgrammes given by the machine that he observed. The justices dismissed the case on the ground that both readings were not obtained in one operating cycle of the machine. The prosecution appealed by way of case stated. *Held,* that the prosecutor was entitled to adduce evidence of two samples analysed in two separate operating cycles by the machine as the absence of a second sample within one operating cycle did not affect or prejudice the reading given by the machine with regard to the first sample produced. By virtue of s.8(1)(*a*) of the Act the prosecution could only rely upon the readings of 95 and 98 microgrammes of alcohol and the third reading, *i.e.* the second reading in the second cycle had to be

discarded as it could not have been validly required by the officer. Section 10 provided a method of proving the analyses made by the machine by production of a certified printout that had been served on the defendant. That mode of proof was not made the exclusive mode of proof by the Act. As such it was open to the prosecution to prove the analyses produced by the machine through the oral evidence of the officer of his observations of the readings given (*Howard* v. *Hallett* [1984] C.L.Y. 3024 considered, *Morgan* v. *Lee* [1985] C.L.Y. 3049 applied).

CHIEF CONSTABLE OF AVON AND SOMERSET CONSTABULARY *v.* CREECH [1986] R.T.R. 87, D.C.

2896. Breath test—erratic driving—excess breath alcohol—when suspicion of officer arose— whether breath test requirement valid

[Road Traffic Act 1972 (c.20), ss.6(1), 7(1) as substituted by Transport Act 1981 (c.56), s.25(3), Sched. 8.]

Under the Transport Act 1981 there is no longer a need for an officer's suspicion of alcohol to have been formed while a defendant was still driving.

D, who was driving erratically, was stopped by another motorist. Ten minutes later the police arrived and noticed that D smelt of alcohol and was unsteady. D refused a breath test and was arrested. A subsequent Intoximeter reading proved positive. He was charged, *inter alia*, with excess alcohol (s.6(1) as amended). The justices dismissed that charge as there was a clear break between the driving and the forming of the suspicion. *Held*, allowing the prosecutor's appeal, that the old requirement was not necessary under the new law; there need be no nexus between the driving and the arrival of the police and the forming of suspicion.

BLAKE *v.* POPE [1986] 1 W.L.R. 1152, D.C.

2897. Breath test—identical readings from specimens—admissibility of print-out

[Road Traffic Act 1972 (c.20), ss.8(6) and 10(3).] D provided two specimens of breath which yielded identical readings on a Lion Intoximeter print-out. *Held*, dismissing D's appeal against conviction of driving with excess alcohol in his breath, that it was plain from reading s.8(6) of the 1972 Act with s.10(3) that both readings were admissible in such circumstances. D's argument that neither was admissible could not be correct (*Burridge* v. *East* [1986] C.L.Y. 2877 considered): R. *v.* BRENTFORD MAGISTRATES' COURT, *ex p.* CLARKE [1986] Crim.L.R. 633, D.C.

2898. Breath test—print out with incorrect name—whether admissible

[Road Traffic Act 1972 (c.20), s.10(5).] T provided breath for a Camic device. The officer conducting the test mistakenly inserted an incorrect forename for T, who signed the form. T made no comment when served with a copy of the print-out which bore the incorrect name. *Held*, dismissing T's appeal against conviction of driving with excess alcohol in his breath, that the error was purely formal, caused no prejudice to T and did not render the result of the test inadmissible under s.10(5) of the 1972 Act (*Beck* v. *Scammell* [1985] Crim.L.R. 794 considered): TOOVEY *v.* CHIEF CONSTABLE OF NORTHUMBRIA [1986] Crim.L.R. 475, D.C.

2899. Breath test—procedure—non-compliance

[Road Traffic Act 1972 (c.20), s.6(1), as substituted by Transport Act 1981 (c.56), s.25(3) and Sched. 8.] Where an officer, having obtained two specimens of breath, wrongly demanded, rather than offered to accept, a specimen of blood or urine, neither the breath nor the other specimens were admissible in evidence as the statutory procedure had not been followed (*Anderton* v. *Lythgoe* [1985] C.L.Y. 2994; *Johnson* v. *West Yorkshire Metropolitan Police* [1986] C.L.Y. 2891 followed): WAKELEY *v.* HYAMS, *The Times,* November 11, 1986, D.C.

2900. Breath test—reliable device

[Road Traffic Act 1972 (c.20), s.8(3)(*b*).] D provided two samples of breath for analysis by an intoximeter. When the reading of the final check of the device was motivated by the officer conducting the test, about an hour and three-quarters later, he decided that the device was not reliable within s.8(3)(*b*) of the 1972 Act. *Held*, allowing the prosecutor's appeal against a finding of no case to answer on a charge of failing to provide a blood specimen, that although the justices had correctly found that the time in issue was the time when the request for blood was made, they had erred in finding that the evidence of unreliability of the device one and three-quarter hours before could not be sufficient evidence of its unreliability at the time of request for blood: OXFORD *v.* BAXENDALE [1986] Crim.L.R. 631, D.C.

2901. Breath tests—statistics

The Home Office has published a statistical bulletin (Issue 19/86) giving details of breath tests in England and Wales during 1985. Copies of the bulletin are available from: Statistical Department, Home Office, Tolworth Tower, Surbiton, Surrey, KT6 7DS. Tel. 01-399 5191, ext. 298.

2902. Breath test—whether practicable to use intoximeter device—no trained officer at police station

[Road Traffic Act 1972 (c.20), s.8(3)(*b*).] K was asked to provide a specimen of blood because there was no officer present at the police station who was trained in the use of the approved Intoximeter breath device. *Held,* allowing the prosecutor's appeal against dismissal of an information alleging failure by K to provide a specimen of blood, that at the relevant time it was "then . . . not practicable to use such a device there" within the wording of s.8(3)(*b*) of the 1972 Act. The relevant time was when the request for blood was made. The justices had erred in finding that it was "then" practicable to use the device because an officer could have been brought from a neighbouring station: CHIEF CONSTABLE OF AVON AND SOMERSET CONSTABULARY *v.* KELLIHER [1986] Crim.L.R. 635, D.C.

2903. Car tax

CAR TAX (AMENDMENT) REGULATIONS 1986 (No. 306) [40p], made under the Car Tax Act 1983 (c.53), s.8, Sched. 1, paras. 3(2), 12; operative on April 1, 1986; amend S.I. 1985 No. 1737 in relation to distress for unpaid tax.

2904. Careless driving—emergency—standard of care

D was driving a lorry along a motorway at night when, through no fault of his, its forward lights went out. He decelerated and pulled on to the hard shoulder, where he collided with a stationary unlit car. He was convicted of careless driving, and the Crown Court said in dismissing his appeal that he should have decelerated, put on a hazard sign, braked, and, when the lorry was almost stationary, pulled over on to the hard shoulder. *Held,* that this was a counsel of perfection. No motorist was called upon to achieve that standard when suddenly confronted with an emergency, especially when that emergency deprived him of forward light. A lower standard was to be applied in such circumstances. As it was not suggested that D ought to have known about the car, and as the emergency was not of D's making, the appeal would be allowed: JONES *v.* BRISTOL CROWN COURT (1986) 150 J.P. 93, D.C.

2905. Carriage by road

CARRIAGE OF GOODS BY ROAD (GUERNSEY) ORDER 1986 (No. 1882) [80p], made under the Carriage of Goods by Road Act 1965 (c.37), ss.9, 12; operative on January 7, 1986; revokes and replaces S.I. 1971 No. 1743, and extends to Guernsey with modifications the provisions of the 1965 Act as amended by the Carriage by Air and Road Act 1979.

INTERNATIONAL CARRIAGE OF DANGEROUS GOODS BY ROAD (FEES) REGULATIONS 1986 (No. 589) [40p], made under the Finance Act 1973 (c.51), s.56(1)(2); operative on May 1, 1986; prescribe fees payable in connection with the issue of an ADR certificate.

ROAD TRAFFIC (CARRIAGE OF DANGEROUS SUBSTANCES IN PACKAGES ETC.) REGULATIONS 1986 (No. 1951) [£2·90], made under the Health and Safety at Work etc. Act 1974 (c.37), ss.15(1)–(6), 82(3)(*a*) and Sched. 3, paras. 1(1)–(4), 3, 9, 12, 14, 15(1) and 16; operative on April 6, 1987, except for reg. 7 which is operative on April 6, 1988; impose requirements in relation to the carriage of dangerous substances by road in packages.

2906. Causing death by reckless driving—direction to jury—"obvious"

[Criminal Appeal Act 1968 (c.19), s.2(1); Road Traffic Act 1972 (c.20), s.1; Criminal Law Act 1977 (c.45), s.50(1).]

K was charged with causing death by reckless driving, contrary to s.1 of the 1972 Act. The judge, while directing the jury on the law regarding the risk involved, stated that it had to be serious but failed to state that it must be obvious. K was convicted. *Held,* dismissing the appeal, that the judge had misdirected the jury by omitting the word "obvious" but in the circumstances if the jury had been directed that the risk had to be both serious and obvious they would have inevitably concluded that it was obvious and convicted; there had been no miscarriage of justice and the proviso to s.2(1) of the 1968 Act applied (*R. v. Lawrence* [1981] C.L.Y. 2382 applied).

R. *v.* KHAN [1985] R.T.R. 365, C.A.

2907. Coach drivers—hours of work and rest—prescribed hours exceeded—whether defence of exceptional circumstances applicable

[European Agreement concerning the Work of Crews of Vehicles engaged in International Road Transport (AETR) (1971) Cmnd. 4858, art. 11.]

The fact that coach passengers on an international journey would otherwise be temporarily stranded in France which caused a coach driver to exceed his prescribed hours of driving and resting on account of the care and comfort of his passengers did not provide a defence to a charge of exceeding his prescribed hours.

The defendants were coach drivers engaged in returning their coaches and passengers to the U.K. from the Continent. In France one of the four drivers was dismissed by the coach company on the grounds that his driving was dangerous. In consequence if the coaches were to return to the U.K. the drivers would be required to take shorter rest periods and longer driving periods than those prescribed by the European Agreement concerning the Work of Crews of Vehicles engaged in International Road Transport (AETR). The drivers were instructed by the coach company to continue their journey having regard to the care and comfort of the passengers. The drivers were charged with exceeding their hours prescribed by AETR. The drivers sought to rely upon the defence provided by art. 11 of the AETR. Art. 11 provides: "Provided that there is no detriment to road safety, the driver may depart from the provisions of the Agreement in case of danger, in case of *force majeure*, to render aid, or as a result of a breakdown, to the extent necessary to ensure the safety of persons, of the vehicle or its load and to enable him to reach a suitable stopping place or, according to the circumstances, the end of his journey." The justices found that the decision that the coaches should return was taken after weighing up the alternatives, which were impracticable, having regard to the care and comfort of the passengers and that the drivers were entitled to rely upon the defence in art. 11. The drivers were acquitted. The prosecution appealed by way of case stated. *Held*, allowing the appeal, that art. 11 could not apply on the facts found by the justices. There was no danger at the time the decision to continue the journey was taken. At that time the coaches were already at a suitable stopping place. The factors of passengers' care and comfort could not be described as factors of safety. Art. 11 could only apply where there was a real emergency. There was no real emergency in this case but instead a difficult administrative problem for the coach company.

GELDART *v.* BROWN [1986] R.T.R. 106, D.C.

2908. Construction and use

MINIBUS (CONDITIONS OF FITNESS, EQUIPMENT AND USE) (AMENDMENT) REGULATIONS 1986 (No. 1813) [45p], made under the Road Traffic Act 1972 (c.20), s.40(1)(3) and the Public Passenger Vehicles Act 1981 (c.14), s.44(1)(*e*); operative on November 26, 1986; further amend S.I. 1977 No. 2103.

PUBLIC SERVICE VEHICLES (CONDITIONS OF FITNESS, EQUIPMENT, USE AND CERTIFICATION) (AMENDMENT) (NO. 2) REGULATIONS 1986 (No. 1812) [45p], made under the Road Traffic Act 1972, s.40(1)(3) and the Public Passenger Vehicles Act 1981 (c.14), s.6; operative on November 26, 1986; further amend S.I. 1981 No. 257.

ROAD VEHICLES (CONSTRUCTION AND USE) REGULATIONS 1986 (No. 1078) [£10·00], made under the Road Traffic Act 1972 (c.20), ss.34(5), 40(1)–(3) and 172; operative on August 11, 1986; consolidate S.I. 1978 No. 1017 and S.I. 1955 No. 990 (as respectively amended).

ROAD VEHICLES (CONSTRUCTION AND USE) (AMENDMENT) REGULATIONS 1986 (No. 1597) [45p], made under the Road Traffic Act 1972 (c.20), ss.40(1)(3), 41(3); operative on October 10, 1986; amend S.I. 1986 No. 1078 in relation to spray containment devices which must be fitted to certain categories of vehicles.

2909. Crown roads

CROWN ROADS (ROYAL PARKS) (APPLICATION OF ROAD TRAFFIC ENACTMENTS) (AMENDMENT) ORDER 1986 (No. 1224) [45p], made under the Road Traffic Regulation Act 1984 (c.27), s.131; operative on August 12, 1986; applies ss.104–106 of the 1984 Act (immobilisation of vehicles illegally parked) to Crown roads in Regent's Park.

2910. Disabled drivers

LOCAL AUTHORITIES' TRAFFIC ORDERS (EXEMPTIONS FOR DISABLED PERSONS) (ENGLAND AND WALES) REGULATIONS 1986 (No. 178) [£1·35], made under the Road

Traffic Regulation Act 1984 (c.27), ss.124, 134(2), Sched. 9 and the Chronically Sick and Disabled Persons Act 1970 (c.44), s.21(1)(*b*); operative on April 1, 1986; require orders made by local authorities to include an exemption from waiting prohibitions in certain circumstances, and from charges and time limits at places where vehicles may park and wait, in respect of vehicles displaying a disabled persons badge under s.21 of the 1970 Act.

2911. Disqualification—discretion—circumstances relating to offender
[Road Traffic Act 1972 (c.20), s.101(2), Sched. 4, Pt. III, para. 1; Transport Act 1981 (c.56), s.30, Sched. 9, Pt. I, para. 6.]
When a court exercises its discretion under s.19(2) of the Transport Act 1981 not to disqualify a motorist, circumstances relating to the offender as well as the offence may be taken into account as mitigating circumstances.

P, who already had eight penalty points endorsed on his licence for offences other than driving, hired a motor car on hire-purchase and sold it without telling the buyer of its ownership. He pleaded guilty to theft of the car and obtaining property by deception. He was sentenced to concurrent and suspended terms of imprisonment. In addition, an order was made under s.101 of the 1972 Act for endorsement of his licence coupled with an endorsement of eight penalty points under s.19(1) of the 1981 Act. He was also disqualified for six months under s.19(2) of the 1981 Act. He appealed against the imposition of the endorsement on the grounds that special reasons within s.101(2) existed and against the disqualification. *Held*, allowing the appeal in part, that (1) the reasons advanced for not endorsing, *viz.* that the case was not of taking someone else's car but of dishonest appropriation by sale, applied to all cases of theft by a hirer and were not special to the facts constituting the case, the endorsement would stand (*Whittall* v. *Kirby* (1947) C.L.C. 9056 applied); (2) under s.19(1) of the 1981 Act both disqualification and endorsement of penalty points were not to be ordered; (3) s.19(6) of the 1981 Act did not preclude the court from considering circumstances relating to the offender as well as the offence in exercising the discretion under s.19(2) not to disqualify; P's previous good driving record and the opportunity to assist his rehabilitation enabled the court to quash the disqualification.
R. *v.* PRESTON [1986] R.T.R. 136, C.A.

2912. Disqualification—disqualification until test passed—circumstances where appropriate.
See R. *v.* PEAT, § 821.

2913. Disqualification—evidence—computer printout
[Road Traffic Act 1972 (c.20), s.182(2A).] The Act rendered a computer printout admissible but not conclusive when the question whether D had applied for disqualification to be suspended pending appeal arose. Once challenged, the printout should not be acted upon without supporting evidence: TAYLOR *v.* COMMISSIONER OF POLICE OF THE METROPOLIS, *The Times*, November 3, 1986, D.C.

2914. Disqualification—excess alcohol—special reasons
[Road Traffic Act 1972 (c.20), s.93(1).]
There are seven factors to be considered in deciding whether there are special reasons for not disqualifying for driving with excess alcohol: (1) how far the vehicle was driven; (2) the manner in which it was driven; (3) the state of the vehicle; (4) whether the driver intended to drive any further; (5) road and traffic conditions; (6) whether there was any danger, and (7) the reason for the vehicle being driven.

D who had been drinking was a passenger in the car. The driver lost control and rolled the car into a field. The car had a flat tyre. D drove the car from the field a few yards into the road and parked it. He was charged with driving with excess alcohol. D pleaded guilty. The justices found special reasons for not disqualifying because of the short distance of and reason for driving. *Held*, dismissing the prosecutor's appeal that the shortness of the distance was not the only criterion, but the justices had taken other criteria into consideration as well. The matters which should be taken into account were, (1) how far the vehicle was driven; (2) the manner in which it was driven; (3) the state of the vehicle; (4) whether the driver intended to drive any further; (5) road and traffic conditions; (6) whether there was any danger, and (7) the reasons for the vehicle being driven (*James* v. *Hall* [1927] C.L.Y. 3031, *R.* v. *Agnew* [1969] C.L.Y. 3161, *Coombs* v. *Kehoe* [1972] C.L.Y. 3032, *R.* v. *McIntyre* [1976] C.L.Y. 2385 and *Haime* v. *Walklett* [1984] C.L.Y. 3028 considered).
CHATTERS *v.* BURKE [1986] 3 All E.R. 168, D.C.

2915. Disqualification—special reasons—distance driven
[Road Traffic Act 1972 (c.20), ss.5(1), 7(4), 93(1)(2), Sched. 4, Pt. 1, Transport Act 1981 (c.56), ss.25(3), 30, Sched. 8, Sched. 9, Pt. 1, para. 20.]

The fact that a motorist drives only a very short distance is capable of being a special reason for not disqualifying him from driving under s.93(1) of the 1972 Act.

R drove with his wife to a party and parked in the hotel car park. They had agreed that his wife would drive back. After the party R's wife did not want to reverse out of the place where the car was parked in the car park. R did so, travelling only a few feet, and hit another car. R pleaded guilty to charges under s.7(4) and 5(1) of the 1972 Act. He submitted that there were special reasons under s.93(1) for not disqualifying him, namely the short distance driven, the fact that he was not going to drive any further, and that he did not know he was committing an offence. The justices held that these did not amount to special reasons and disqualified R. *Held,* allowing the appeal, that a special reason had to be a mitigating or extenuating circumstance not amounting in law to a defence, connected with the commission of the offence which ought properly to be taken into account in sentencing; the fact that R drove only a very short distance was capable of amounting to a special reason.

REDMOND *v.* PARRY [1986] R.T.R. 146, D.C.

2916. Disqualification—totting up—penalty points—endorsement
[Transport Act 1981 (c.56), s.19.]

In ascertaining the total of penalty points for the purposes of a totting up disqualification the court must take account of any penalty points that would have been endorsed on the defendant's licence but for the fact that he was disqualified for the offence in question.

D was committed for sentence to Luton Crown Court on four charges and was sentenced to three years' imprisonment. The following orders were made: (1) driving without insurance—conditional discharge, eight penalty points to be endorsed on licence, one year's disqualification from driving; (2) taking a motor car without consent—eight penalty points; (3) a further six months' disqualification under the totting up provisions. On appeal the sentence of imprisonment was reduced to two years in total. The court identified unlawful sentences in respect of the disqualifications and penalty point endorsements. D had been disqualified from driving on two previous occasions within the three years preceding his appearance at Luton. *Held,* that it was wrong to impose penalty points and disqualify D at the same time. It was wrong to order the totting up disqualification to run consecutively to the disqualification for driving without insurance. By virtue of the provisions of s.19(3)(*a*) of the Transport Act 1981 the court in assessing whether D should be disqualified as a totter should take account of any points that would have been imposed had D not been disqualified. It was clear that the judge would have imposed 16 penalty points on D, the two offences being committed on separate occasions. As such D was liable to be disqualified as a totter. Having regard to his previous disqualifications he should have been disqualified for two years under the totting up provisions. As s.11(3) of the Criminal Appeal Act 1968 prevented the court from dealing with D more severely than he was dealt with by the court below the six months' totting up disqualification would be allowed to stand notwithstanding that it was unlawful but ordered to run concurrently with the 12 months' disqualification. The orders imposing penalty points would be quashed (*R. v. Kent (Peter)* [1983] C.L.Y. 3288 applied).

R. *v.* YATES [1986] R.T.R. 68, C.A.

2917. Disqualification—vehicle used for other offence—whether court to invite submissions before disqualifying. See R. *v.* POWELL (M.B.), § 819.

2918. Drivers' hours
COMMUNITY DRIVERS' HOURS AND RECORDING EQUIPMENT (EXEMPTIONS AND SUPPLEMENTARY PROVISIONS) (AMENDMENT) REGULATIONS 1986 (No. 1669) [45p], made under the European Communities Act 1972 (c.68), s.2(2); operative on October 26, 1986; further extends the exemption contained in S.I. 1986 No. 1456 in relation to drivers' rest periods.

COMMUNITY DRIVERS' HOURS AND RECORDING EQUIPMENT (EXEMPTIONS AND SUPPLEMENTARY PROVISIONS) REGULATIONS 1986 (No. 1456) [£1·46], made under the European Communities Act 1972 (c.68), s.2(2); operative on September 29, 1986;

make modifications to the provision relating to Community drivers' hours and recording equipment.

COMMUNITY DRIVERS' HOURS AND RECORDING EQUIPMENT REGULATIONS 1986 (No. 1457) [80p], made under the European Communities Act 1972, s.2(2); operative on September 29, 1986; make provision in relation to drivers' hours and recording equipment.

COMMUNITY DRIVERS' HOURS (PASSENGER VEHICLES) (TEMPORARY EXEMPTION) REGULATIONS 1986 (No. 1542) [45p], made under the European Communities Act 1972 (c.68), s.2(2); operative on September 29, 1986; exempt from the provisions of Council Regulation (EEC) No. 3820/85 until October 26, 1986 vehicles engaged in the national carriage of passengers on a regular service.

DRIVERS' HOURS (GOODS VEHICLES) (EXEMPTIONS) REGULATIONS 1986 (No. 1492) [45p], made under the Transport Act 1968 (c.73), s.96(10); operative on September 29, 1986; revoke and replace with amendments S.I. 1978 No. 1364 and S.I. 1982 No. 1554.

DRIVERS' HOURS (GOODS VEHICLES) (MODIFICATIONS) ORDER 1986 (No. 1459) [80p], made under the Transport Act 1968 (c.73), ss.96(12), 101(2), 157; operative on September 29, 1986; modifies the provisions of s.96 of the 1968 Act in relation to drivers of goods vehicles.

DRIVERS' HOURS (HARMONISATION WITH COMMUNITY RULES) REGULATIONS 1986 (No. 1458) [80p], made under the Transport Act 1968, s.95(1) (1A); operative on September 29, 1986; revoke and replace S.I. 1978 No. 1157 so as to take account of Council Regulation (EEC) No. 3820/85.

DRIVERS' HOURS (KEEPING OF RECORDS) (AMENDMENT) REGULATIONS 1986 (No. 1493) [£1·40], made under the European Communities Act 1972, s.22 and the Transport Act 1968, ss.98, 101(2); operative on September 29, 1986; amends S.I. 1976 No. 1447.

2919. Drivers' hours—public service vehicle—whether manned by two drivers

[Transport Act 1968 (c.73), s.96 as amended; Council Regulation (E.E.C.) 543/69, Art. 11.]

In art. 11(3) of Council Regulation (E.E.C.) No. 543/69, the expression "manned by two drivers" means that two drivers must be aboard so long as the vehicle is in motion.

Four drivers were each assigned to drive one of four public service vehicles and a fifth driver travelled with each in turn. All were charged with failing to take nine hours' daily rest period. The informations were dismissed on the grounds that these vehicles were "manned by two drivers" within art. 11(3) of Council Regulation (E.E.C.) No. 543/69. *Held*, that the case would be remitted with a direction to convict.

WILLIAMS *v*. BOYD [1986] R.T.R. 185, D.C.

2920. Driving instruction

MOTOR CARS (DRIVING INSTRUCTION) (AMENDMENT) REGULATIONS 1986 (No. 882) [£1·40], made under the Road Traffic Act 1972 (c.20), ss.131(4) and 135(1); operative on June 21, 1986; allow for the issue of revised forms of licence and certificate.

MOTOR CARS (DRIVING INSTRUCTION) (AMENDMENT) (No. 2) REGULATIONS 1986 (No. 1338) [45p], made under the Road Traffic Act 1972 (c.20), ss.126(1A), 131(4) and 135(1); operative on September 30, 1986; make provision as a consequence of the coming into operation of s.1 of the Road Traffic (Driving Instruction) Act 1984.

2921. Driving without due care and attention—emergencies

[Road Traffic Act 1972 (c.20), s.3; Road Vehicle Lighting Regulations 1971 (S.I. 1971 No. 694) regs. 22, 77; Motorway Traffic (England & Wales) Regulations 1982 (S.I. 1982 No. 1163) reg. 7; Highway Code, Rule 117.]

In considering a charge of driving without due care and attention proper regard should be given to any state of emergency which a driver finds himself in, and his knowledge regarding possible responses to that emergency.

J was driving an articulated lorry at night along a motorway at about 55 m.p.h. when the vehicle's headlamps failed. He took his foot off the accelerator and steered on to the hard shoulder where he collided with an unlit stationary vehicle. The justices convicted him under s.3 of the Road Traffic Act 1972. His appeal to the Crown Court was dismissed on the grounds that he should have switched on the hazard warning lights and slowed to a near halt before moving on to the hard shoulder. *Held*, allowing the appeal that J was faced with an emergency, and nothing suggested he should have been aware of any obstruction. Thus the Crown Court had failed to give sufficient regard to the emergency, and the conviction would be quashed.

R. *v.* BRISTOL CROWN COURT, *ex p.* JONES; JONES *v.* CHIEF CONSTABLE OF AVON AND SOMERSET CONSTABULARY [1986] R.T.R. 259, D.C.

2922. Excess alcohol—aiders and abettors

Provided it can be established that each of two occupants of a car knew or were reckless that the other was unfit to drive, each can be convicted as principal or abettor whether or not the prosecution can establish precisely which role each played: SMITH *v.* MELLORS, *The Times*, November 21, 1986, D.C.

2923. Excess alcohol—alcohol level at time of driving—burden of proof

[Road Traffic Act 1972 (c.20), ss.6(1), 8(1), 10(1)(2), 12(2); Transport Act 1981 (c.56), s.25(3), Sched. 8.]

Once a defendant admits having driven on a particular day, and once it is proved that he has given a specimen over the prescribed limit, the burden is on him to show that he was not driving whilst over the limit.

D was arrested near a parked car on suspicion of theft. D said that he was the owner, had driven it and parked it there that day. He smelt of alcohol, was required to take a breath test and the test proved positive. The justices allowed a submission of no case. *Held*, allowing the prosecutor's appeal, that once D had admitted to driving on that day, and it was proved that his specimen was over the limit, the burden was on him to displace this presumption that he was over the limit when he drove and the case would be remitted to the justices to continue the hearing.

PATTERSON *v.* CHARLTON [1986] R.T.R. 18, D.C.

2924. Excess alcohol—"hip-flask" defence—computation of alcohol concentration at time of offence

[Road Traffic Act 1972 (c.20) ss.6, 10(2) as amended.]

In deciding whether, on a balance of probabilities, a defendant may successfully rely on s.10(2) of the Road Traffic Act 1972 as amended, the justices should not assume that the results of analysis represent a peak blood concentration of alcohol when computing the concentration of alcohol at the time of the offence.

L gave evidence, which was accepted by the justices sitting at Colchester, that on the evening in question he drank a pint of beer at about 7.30 p.m., and a second at about 10.00 p.m. at a function which he then left by motor car. The car broke down shortly afterwards and he went to a nearby public house to telephone a garage and the police. While in the public house a friend, who gave evidence to the same effect, brought him a third pint of beer which he then drank. On the arrival of the police, L accompanied them, at their request, to Colchester police station, and at 23.24 p.m. provided two specimens of breath for analysis. The lower reading was 53 microgrammes of alcohol in 100 millilitres of breath, equivalent to 122 milligrammes in the blood. An extract from the *British Medical Journal* was adduced in evidence by the defence. This gave much complex information about the blood/alcohol levels resulting from drinking various quantities of beer and the rates at which the body deals with alcohol. In particular, it gave 122 milligrammes as the peak blood concentration after drinking three pints of beer, but said nothing of the period over which this would have to be drunk. On the basis of this, the justices concluded that without the third pint he would not have had excess alcohol in his blood, and thus L was entitled to be acquitted in accordance with s.10(2). *Held*, that there was no reason to assume that this was a case concerned with peak blood concentration. In the light of the facts found as to the time of drinking, there was no evidence on which the justices could properly reach the conclusion they did. They misconstrued and misunderstood the document before them.

DAWSON *v.* LUNN [1986] R.T.R. 234, D.C.

2925. Excess alcohol—"hip-flask" defence—consumption of alcohol after ceasing to drive

[Road Traffic Act 1972 (c.20), ss.6(1)(*a*), 10(2) and 12(2).]

In considering, on a charge under s.6(1)(*a*) of the Act, whether the statutory defence under s.10(2) is made out, the justices are not to be concerned with whether the defendant is in charge of the vehicle when the further alcohol is consumed.

R drank some beer in a public house. He came out, and drove his car into several other vehicles, and into the wall of the public house. He stopped driving and immediately consumed two double whiskies. One of the other drivers removed the keys of his car to ensure he did not leave the scene. At the time of the accident his blood alcohol level was less than the limit but exceeded it after the drinking of the whiskies. He was charged with driving with excess alcohol contrary to s.6(1)(*a*) of the Act, and the justices convicted on the grounds that he was still in charge of the vehicle when he drank the whisky, having done nothing to divest himself of responsibility for it. *Held*, that since R was charged under s.6(1)(*a*), the justices had erred in concerning themselves with whether he was in charge of the car, and the appeal would be allowed.

RYNSARD *v*. SPALDING [1986] R.T.R. 303, D.C.

2926. Excise duty

ROAD VEHICLES (EXEMPTIONS FROM DUTY) REGULATIONS 1986 (No. 1467) [80p], made under the Vehicles (Excise) Act 1971 (c.10), s.7(3A); operative on October 1, 1986; exempts from excise duty vehicles imported by a member of a visiting force.

2927. Excise licence

ROAD VEHICLES (EXCISE) (PRESCRIBED PARTICULARS) (AMENDMENT) REGULATIONS 1986 (No. 2100) [80p], made under the Vehicles (Excise) Act 1971 (c.10), ss.16(1), 37(2); operative on January 1, 1986; amend S.I. 1981 No. 931 by prescribing two new forms.

VEHICLE LICENCES (DURATION OF FIRST LICENCES AND RATE OF DUTY) ORDER 1986 (No. 1428) [80p], made under the Vehicles (Excise) Act 1971 (c.10), s.2A; operative on October 1, 1986; makes provision for the first licences for mechanically propelled vehicles.

2928. Excise licence—back duty—whether justices had power to reduce

[Vehicles (Excise) Act 1971 (c.10), ss.8(1), 9(1)(7); Magistrates' Courts Act 1980 (c.43), ss.34, 35, 150.]

Justices have no power to reduce vehicle excise back-duty in view of a defendant's means.

D pleaded guilty to two charges of keeping a vehicle on a road without an excise licence. The justices took the view that the back duty was a "fine" within ss.34 and 35 of the Magistrates' Courts Act 1980, and that having regard to D's means, the figure should be reduced. *Held*, allowing the prosecutor's appeal, that s.35 did not apply to back duty, and the justices had no power to reduce the sum (*Leach* v. *Litchfield* [1960] C.L.Y. 2064 applied).

CHIEF CONSTABLE OF KENT *v*. MATHER [1986] R.T.R. 36, D.C.

2929. Fixed penalties

FIXED PENALTY (INCREASE) ORDER 1986 (No. 56) [40p], made under the Road Traffic Regulation Act 1984 (c.27), Sched. 12, para. 4(2); operative on February 17, 1986; provides for an increase from £10 to £12 in the fixed penalty in respect of offences to which para. 2 of Sched. 12 applies (in connection with lights, reflectors, obstruction etc.) for which a person is liable on summary conviction to be fined £100 or more.

ROAD TRAFFIC (TEMPORARY PROVISIONS AS TO FIXED PENALTIES) ORDER 1986 (No. 1329) [45p], made under the Road Traffic Regulation Act 1984 (c.27), Sched. 12, para. 1; brings to an end on October 1, 1986, the interim period referred to in the said Schedule 12 (temporary provisions as to fixed penalties).

2930. Goods vehicle—working time—statutory breaks—whether on duty

[Transport Act 1968 (c.73), ss.95(3)(*a*), 96(3)(*a*)(*b*)(11)(13), 103(1)(*a*)(4); Road Traffic (Drivers' Ages and Hours of Work) Act 1976 (c.3), s.2(1)(*e*)(*f*); Council Regulation (EEC) No. 543/69, arts. 7(1), 8(1).]

The question whether a statutory break is or is not a period during which a driver is on duty is a question of fact to be determined from the circumstances of each case.

C, a driver within s.95(3) of the 1968 Act was charged under s.96(3)(*a*) and s.96(11) with having exceeded by 46 minutes the maximum driving time of 11 hours. The tachograph indicated that he had driven for 11 hours 46 minutes with 2 breaks of half an hour. The magistrate made no finding of fact about the employer's view whether C was on duty within s.103(4) during the breaks, but found that they formed part of the working day as they were required by statute and were not off duty periods within s.96(3)(*b*). C was convicted. *Held*, allowing the appeal, that whenever an employed lorry driver was not driving and was either inside or outside the lorry which was at a standstill, the court had to find on the evidence both why the driver was not driving and whether the employer would regard him as on duty, the question whether the driver was on duty during a statutory break being one of fact.

CARTER v. WALTON [1985] R.T.R. 378, D.C.

2931. Goods vehicles

GOODS VEHICLES (OPERATORS' LICENCES, QUALIFICATIONS AND FEES) (AMENDMENT) REGULATIONS 1986 (No. 666) [£1·40], made under the Transport Act 1968 (c.73), ss.89(1), 91(1)(2)(6) and the European Communities Act 1972 (c.68), s.2(2); operative on May 1, 1986; amend S.I. 1984 No. 176.

GOODS VEHICLES (OPERATORS' LICENCES, QUALIFICATIONS AND FEES) (AMENDMENT) (No. 2) REGULATIONS 1986 (No. 1391) [45p], made under the Transport Act 1968 (c.73), ss.69(4), 91(1)(2) and the European Communities Act 1972 (c.68), s.2(2); operative on September 12, 1986; amend S.I. 1984 No. 176 by redefining "international transport operation" and deleting the definition of "national transport operation."

GOODS VEHICLES (PLATING AND TESTING) (AMENDMENT) (No. 2) REGULATIONS 1986 (No. 1090) [45p], made under the Road Traffic Act 1972 (c.20), s.45(1)(6); operative on August 1, 1986; amends S.I. 1982 No. 1478.

2932. Goods vehicles—operator's licence—test certificate—tachograph requirements—showman's vehicle

[Transport Act 1968 (c.73), ss.60 and 97; Road Traffic Act 1972 (c.20), s.46(2); Goods Vehicles (Operators' Licences) Regulations 1977 (S.I. 1977 No. 1737), Sched. 1, para. 23; Goods Vehicles (Plating and Testing) Regulations 1982 (S.I. 1982 No. 1478), reg. 4 and para. 15 of Sched. 2; EEC Council Regulations 543/69; Community Road Transport Rules (Exemptions) Regulations 1978, reg. 4(3)(f).] Each defendant was charged with operator's licence offences contrary to s.60 of the 1968 Act, test certificate offences under s.46(2) of the 1972 Act and tachograph offences under s.97 of the 1968 Act. F was managing director and secretary of S Co. and employed E. He belonged to the Showman's Guild and was from a family of circus entertainers. F supplied a large tent with electric lighting and seating to the organiser of a music festival. A generator bolted to the trailer unit of S Co.'s articulated H.G.V. vehicle supplied the lighting. The vehicle was stopped when being driven back. The generator was in the vehicle; the tent was in the trailer. *Held*, that (1) the justices had wrongly decided that F was exempt from having an operators' licence by virtue of para. 23 of Sched. 1 to the 1977 Regulations as there was no evidence that the vehicle was being used solely for the business of a travelling showman. "Travelling showman" could not embrace the business of hiring equipment to another to stage a music festival; (2) the justices had erred in finding that the vehicle was exempt from requiring a test certificate by virtue of para. 15 of Sched. 2 to the 1982 Regulations as on the facts the use of the generator could not reasonably be found to be use for display purposes. Under para. 15 the equipment permanently fixed to the vehicle had to be used for an activity carried on at least partly on the vehicle and "display" meant some sort of mobile exhibition; (3) re the tachograph informations, the justices erred in finding that the vehicle was being used to transport "circus and fun-fair equipment" within the exemption under Article 4 of EEC Council Regulations 543/69 but had correctly decided that the music festival was a "cultural event" within the exempting provisions of reg. 4(3)(f) of the 1978 Regulations: CREEK v. FOSSETT, ECCLES AND SUPERTENTS [1986] Crim.L.R. 256.

2933. Hackney cab—regulations

[Road Traffic Regulation Act 1984 (c.27); City of Gloucester (Eastgate Street) (Waiting Regulation) Order 1982.] A hackney carriage which is not plying for hire is not entitled to the benefit of the regulation authorising carriages plying for hire to park at authorised stands: RODGERS v. TAYLOR, *The Times*, October 28, 1986, D.C.

2934. Hackney carriage—renewal of licence—fitness to drive—judicial review

A decision not to renew a taxi driver's licence on the ground that he is medically unfit made on the basis of medical evidence that is not disclosed to the driver and without giving the driver an opportunity to make representations is made in breach of the rules of natural justice and liable to be quashed in proceedings for judicial review.

H was a London taxi driver who had held a cab-driver's licence for 12 years. In 1983 H reached 50 years of age. It was the practice of the Assistant Commissioner of Police of the Metropolis to require a taxi driver to produce a suitable medical report on his fitness to drive a taxi cab. The London Cab Order 1934 gave the Assistant Commissioner a discretion to refuse to renew a licence if the applicant failed to satisfy him that he was fit to act as a cab driver. H was examined by C, his own doctor. C completed the Assistant Commissioner's standard form of medical report and certified H fit to drive. C mentioned on the form that H had an epileptic fit in 1979 which was investigated by Lewisham Hospital with inconclusive results. The Assistant Commissioner required H to be examined by K, another doctor. K contacted Lewisham Hospital and was informed that the hospital notes relating to the 1979 incident were scanty. The notes recorded that he had passed out whilst sitting next to a gas fire. The hospital stated that he had three similar attacks previously and diagnosed epilepsy. K concluded that there was evidence H had suffered from epilepsy but was not at that time suffering from the disease. Subsequently H was informed that his application for a renewal of his licence was refused on the ground that he could no longer be considered to meet the required medical standard for a taxi cab driver's licence. H was not given a copy of K's report nor advised of its contents. He was not given the opportunity to make representations about the prospective refusal of his application to renew his licence. H contended that he had not been diagnosed epileptic, that he had passed out in consequence of fumes from the gas fire in 1979 and that although he had passed out on two previous occasions, in neither case had epilepsy been diagnosed. H sought judicial review of the Assistant Commissioner's decision. His application was refused. H appealed. *Held*, allowing the appeal, that C having certified H to be fit to hold a cab driver's licence H had a legitimate expectation that the licence would be granted. When his licence was not renewed H had a justifiable grievance in that the adverse factors in K's report were not communicated to him, nor was he given an opportunity to make any representations regarding those factors. The decision to refuse to renew H's licence was based on a hearing diagnosis of an earlier complaint of which the hospital notes were scanty and the accuracy of the past recorded history was disputed. There was evidence from C and K that H was at the present time fit to drive. The decision made effectively deprived H of his livelihood. The decision-making process was defective and unfair. The decision not to renew H's licence would be quashed (*Council of Civil Service Unions* v. *Minister for the Civil Service* [1985] C.L.Y. considered).

R. *v.* ASSISTANT COMMISSIONER OF POLICE OF THE METROPOLIS, *ex p.* HOWELL [1986] R.T.R. 52, C.A.

2935. Heavy goods vehicles

HEAVY GOODS VEHICLES (DRIVERS' LICENCES) (AMENDMENT) REGULATIONS 1986 (No. 752) [45p], made under the Road Traffic Act 1972 (c.20), s.119; operative on May 29, 1986; amend S.I. 1977 No. 752.

HEAVY GOODS VEHICLES (DRIVERS' LICENCES) (AMENDMENT) (NO. 2) REGULATIONS 1986 (No. 868) [45p], made under the Road Traffic Act 1972, ss.119, 120(1), 124; operative on July 1, 1986; reduces the application fee for an HGV test to £40.

MOTOR VEHICLES (DRIVING LICENCES) (AMENDMENT) REGULATIONS 1986 (No. 748) [45p], made under the Road Traffic Act 1972, ss.88, 107; operative on September 1, 1986; amend S.I. 1981 No. 952 so as to increase fees for driving licences.

2936. Information—election by prosecutor—effect of dismissal—autrefois acquit

[Road Traffic Act 1972 (c.20), ss.6(1)(*a*), 8(1)(4)(6); Transport Act 1981 (c.56), s.25(3), Sched. 8.]

The doctrine of autrefois acquit does not apply when the prosecutor has properly been put to his election of which information to proceed on.

B provided two specimens of breath under s.8(1) of the 1972 Act which revealed a reading of 40 microgrammes of alcohol. He then provided a specimen of blood for analysis under s.8(6) which showed that he had exceeded the prescribed limit. He was charged under s.6(1) with driving with excess alcohol as ascertained by a specimen of breath. At court the prosecution added a second information which differed from the first only in stating that the blood-alcohol proportion was ascertained by a specimen of blood. B submitted that the prosecutor should be put to his election and he offered no evidence on the first information and it was dismissed. B then submitted that the second charge should not be heard as it was autrefois acquit. The submission was rejected and B pleaded guilty. *Held,* dismissing the appeal that the prosecutor had erred in drafting the first information but the

prosecutor had been properly put to his election which made the doctrine of autrefois acquit inapplicable; the doctrine of res judicata did not apply as there had been no trial on the merits (*Connelly* v. *D.P.P.* [1964] C.L.Y. 665 applied; *R.* v. *Swansea Justices ex p. Purvis* (1981) 145 J.P. 252 distinguished).
BROADBENT v. HIGH [1985] R.T.R. 359, D.C.

2937. Information—particulars
[Road Traffic Act 1972 (c.20), s.6(1).] An information under this section is more properly worded if it includes the words "as substituted by section 25(3) of the Transport Act 1981". JONES v. THOMAS (JOHN BARRIE), *The Times,* November 5, 1986, D.C.

2938. Intoximeter—blood test option—refusal
[Road Traffic Act 1972 (c.20), ss.6(1)(*a*), 8(1)(*a*) as substituted.] The option of providing a blood test on readings of 50 mg. or more on an Intoximeter was not to be equated with the statutory provisions, and magistrates were entitled to rely on the Intoximeter printout where the option of giving a blood sample had been refused by an officer who honestly believed that the scheme had ended (*Associated Provincial Picture Houses* v. *Wednesbury Corporation* (1948) C.L.C. 8107 considered): McGRATH v. FIELD, *The Times,* November 20, 1986, D.C.

2939. Intoximeter—calibration check—whether device unreliable
[Road Traffic Act 1972 (c.20), ss.6(1)(*a*), 8.] At a police station D was required to provide two breath specimens. The second calibration check of the Lion Intoximeter device registered 38° High, being 0.1 per cent. above the maximum laid down in the device's handbook. D was therefore required to provide a blood specimen on the basis that the device was unreliable. *Held,* allowing the prosecutor's appeal, that the justices had erred in dismissing the charge against D of driving with excess alcohol in his blood contrary to s.6(1)(*a*) of the 1972 Act on the basis that the device was reliable and there had therefore been no power under s.8 to request a blood specimen, that it is not permissible for justices to regard a device as reliable when there is evidence that it was operating outside the area of tolerance. The *de minimis* principle could not apply: WAITE v. SMITH [1986] Crim.L.R. 405, D.C.

2940. Intoximeter—challenge to reliability—discrepancy with blood sample reading
The results of a blood or urine test can be used to challenge the reliability of a reading produced by a Lion Intoximeter machine.
D was charged with driving a motor vehicle when the proportion of alcohol in his breath exceeded the prescribed limit. D provided two specimens of breath for analysis by a Lion Intoximeter machine. The machine produced readings of 58 and 54 microgrammes of alcohol to 100 millilitres of breath. One and a half hours later D gave a blood sample in accordance with the Home Office Circular No. 32/1984. The analysis of the blood sample produced by the prosecution showed 87 milligrammes of alcohol in 100 millilitres of blood. D's analysis gave an average reading of 80·50 milligrammes. D challenged the reliability of the readings produced by the Intoximeter machine by calling evidence of what he had drunk on the day in question and an account of the discrepancy between the reading produced by the analysis of his blood sample and the reading produced by the machine. D was acquitted. The prosecution appealed by way of case stated. *Held,* that the reliability of the machine could not be challenged by evidence of the amount of alcohol D had consumed prior to providing the specimens of breath nor by evidence of the way in which he had conducted himself. D was entitled to challenge the reliability of the readings produced by the machine by comparing them to the reading produced by analysis of his blood sample. There was sufficient evidence for the justices to find that the readings produced by the machine could not be relied upon to be accurate. The fact that the blood analyses indicated an excessive proportion of alcohol in D's blood did not assist the prosecution as D was charged with having excess alcohol in his breath. Appeal dismissed (*Hughes* v. *McConnell* [1985] C.L.Y. 3055 applied, *Castle* v. *Cross* [1984] C.L.Y. 3048 considered).
LUCKING v. FORBES [1986] R.T.R. 97, D.C.

2941. Intoximeter—reliability—assessment of evidence
[Road Traffic Act 1972 (c.20), s.10(2).] Where evidence is adduced before justices to show that a Lion Intoximeter machine was not functioning properly, it is still open to the justices to consider s.10(2) of the Road Traffic Act 1972 (as substituted), and

conclude that the evidence has not attacked the validity and accuracy of the machine's printout: NEWTON v. WOODS, *The Times,* June 16, 1986, D.C.

2942. Judicial review—irregularity in plea—no irregularity in actions of tribunal
[Road Traffic Act 1972 (c.20), ss.6(1), 8(1), 12(2).]
Where a defendant pleads guilty to driving with excess alcohol on the basis of inaccurate legal advice about the Intoximeter printout, certiorari is available to quash the conviction.

K was required to give two specimens of breath for analysis. The printout showed that one of the calibration checks was beyond the limits of tolerance, and recorded the level as 81 microgrammes. K was charged with driving with excess alcohol. His solicitor assured him that, on enquiry, a senior police officer had said that the device was functioning properly on the day in question. K pleaded guilty on his solicitor's advice and was fined and disqualified. On hearing the truth, K applied for judicial review. *Held,* that although certiorari was primarily a remedy for an error of the tribunal, and there was none here, there was a gross irregularity in the proceedings, which were initiated on no evidence. This vitiated K's plea, and the conviction would be quashed (*R. v. West Sussex Quarter Sessions, ex p. Johnson* [1973] C.L.Y. 2097 applied; *R. v. Ashford (Kent) Justices, ex p. Richley (No. 2)* [1955] C.L.Y. 685 and *R. v. Leyland Justices, ex p. Hawthorn* [1979] C.L.Y. 416 considered).
R. v. KINGSTON UPON THAMES JUSTICES, *ex p.* KHANNA [1986] R.T.R. 364, D.C.

2943. Licensing requirements—breakdown vehicle—recovery vehicle
[Transport Act 1968 (c.73), s.60(1): Vehicles (Excise) Act 1971 (c.10), ss.8(1), 12(4), 16; Road Traffic Act 1972 (c.20), ss.45(6), 46 as amended; Road Vehicles (Registration and Licensing) Regulations 1971 (S.I. 1971 No. 450), reg. 35(4); Goods Vehicles (Plating and Testing) Regulations 1982 (S.I. 1982 No. 1478), reg. 3(1).]
Appropriately constructed vehicles are not prevented from being breakdown vehicles or recovery vehicles by virtue of the fact that they are used to transport two disabled vehicles.

Two defendents on each of several occasions used a breakdown vehicle to transport two disabled vehicles, one up and one behind, and were charged with use without a goods vehicle test certificate and a plating certificate, and separately with use without a trade licence, on the grounds that the exemption from the requirements for these did not apply while more than one vehicle was being transported. *Held,* that the vehicles, first as "breakdown vehicles" and secondly as "recovery vehicles", were exempt from the licensing provisions (*Universal Salvage* v. *Boothby* [1984] C.L.Y. 3078 applied; *Gibson* v. *Nutter* [1984] C.L.Y. 3072 distinguished).
KENNET v. HOLDING & BARNES; HARVEY (T. L.) v. HALL [1986] R.T.R. 334, D.C.

2944. Lion Intoximeter—ambiguity of printout—evidence
[Road Traffic Act 1972 (c.20), ss.6(1), 8, 10(1).]
An ambiguity in the printout from a Lion Intoximeter goes to the weight of the evidence, not its admissibility.

Per curiam: It is important not to elide ss.8 and 10 of the Act. In considering admissibility of the printout, the court is not concerned with reliability of the machine in the same way as when considering s.8. Lack of reliability might entitle the court to reject the evidence of the printout, but does not make it inadmissible.

S was required to produce two breath specimens for analysis by a Lion Intoximeter 3000. The printout incorrectly stated the day on which the analysis was done, though the date was correct. The constable gave evidence that the device correctly calibrated itself both before and after analysis. The magistrates considered the device was unreliable and dismissed the charge of driving with excess alcohol. *Held,* that the error went to weight of the evidence not admissibility, and had been remedied by the constable's evidence. The evidence had been wrongly excluded (*Wright* v. *Taplin (Note)* [1986] C.L.Y. 2945 and *Owen* v. *Chesters* [1985] C.L.Y. 3054 applied; *Morgan* v. *Lee* [1985] C.L.Y. 3049 and *Burditt* v. *Roberts (Note)* [1986] C.L.Y. 2946 considered; *Slender* v. *Boothby (Note)* [1986] C.L.Y. 2951 explained).
FAWCETT v. GASPARICS [1986] R.T.R. 375, D.C.

2945. Lion Intoximeter—defect
[Road Traffic Act 1972 (c.20), ss.8(1), 10(3).]
Justices are entitled to convict on the basis of a printout from a defective breath analyser, where the evidence shows that the defects could result only in a lower-than-accurate reading.

T was charged with driving with excess alcohol on the basis of a Lion Intoximeter 3000 printout which showed a lower reading of 46 microgrammes. The prosecutor adduced evidence that the device was defective shortly after delivering the printout, but in a way which could only result in a lower reading than otherwise. T did not object to the printout at trial, and was convicted. *Held,* that the justices were entitled so to convict.

WRIGHT *v.* TAPLIN (NOTE) [1986] R.T.R. 388, D.C.

2946. Lion Intoximeter—errors in printout

[Road Traffic Act 1972 (c.20), ss.6(1), 8, 10(3).]

Spelling mistakes in the elements of a Lion Intoximeter printout which are entered by the operator are not evidence of the unreliability of the device.

B was required to give a specimen of breath at a police station. The printout included two spelling mistakes in the information entered into it by the police officer. The defence contended that this indicated that the device was unreliable. B was nonetheless convicted, but appealed. *Held,* that the appellant's contentions were impossible to sustain. The errors showed the fallibility of the operator, not the unreliability of the device.

BURDITT *v.* ROBERTS (NOTE) [1986] R.T.R. 391, D.C.

2947. Lion Intoximeter—printout—alteration of time shown—admissibility

[Road Traffic Act 1972 (c.20), s.10(3)(5); Transport Act 1981 (c.56), s.25(7), Sched. 8.]

An alteration in handwriting by an officer to show the time of a printout from an intoximeter in British Summer Time does not affect its admissibility.

S provided a specimen of breath for analysis by a Lion Intoximeter 3000 device. The printout recorded the time as Greenwich Mean Time. The Officer amended the statement to read British Summer Time, making a note to that effect on his copy, but not on that given to S. At trial the justices upheld a submission that the printout was inadmissible. *Held,* allowing the prosecutor's appeal, that the nature of the printout had not been materially altered and it remained for the purposes of s.10(3) of the 1972 Act a statement produced automatically by the device of which S had been handed a copy under s.10(5).

BECK *v.* SCAMMELL [1986] R.T.R. 162, D.C.

2948. Lion Intoximeter—printout—duty to hand to accused

[Road Traffic Act 1972 (c.20), ss.6(1), 8(1), 10(3)(5); Transport Act 1981 (c.56), s.25(3), Sched. 8.]

A Lion Intoximeter printout must be handed to the accused (or later served). It is not enough to put it on a desk and leave it there in front of him.

A provided specimens of breath for a Lion Intoximeter. The three printouts were explained to him and put on a desk for him to sign. He signed two but not the third, and then asked what he was signing. The officer removed the two signed ones, and left the third. The justices dismissed the charge on the basis that the printout had not been handed to D. *Held,* dismissing the prosecutor's appeal, that leaving the document on the desk did not amount to handing it to D, and the justices had reached the correct decision.

WALTON *v.* RIMMER [1986] R.T.R. 31, D.C.

2949. Lion Intoximeter—proper self-calibration—evidence to challenge

[Road Traffic Act 1972 (c.20), ss.6(1), 8(1), 10(2)(3), 12(2), Transport Act 1981 (c.56), s.25(3), Sched. 8.]

The readings produced by a device which has properly gone through its self-calibration, are conclusive where there is no evidence challenging the reliability of the device.

N provided a specimen of breath for analysis by a Lion Intoximeter 3000 device. The printout revealed that self-calibration was properly achieved and readings of 170 and 171 microgrammes of alcohol were recorded. N was tried on a charge of driving contrary to s.6(1)(a) of the 1972 Act. N gave evidence that in the $3\frac{1}{2}$ hours before driving he had drunk three glasses of barley wine and one glass of wine. He adduced a letter from the Home Office Forensic Science Laboratory that that amount of drink would be likely to result in a reading below the prescribed limit, and that the actual reading produced would have required a minimum rapid consumption of three-quarters of a bottle of spirits. The justices dismissed the information. *Held,* allowing the prosecutor's appeal, that when a device showed that it had properly gone through its self-calibration, the readings it produced were conclusive of the amount of alcohol in the motorist's breath unless there was direct evidence of some malfunction in the machine itself; there had been no such evidence (*Hughes* v. *McConnell* [1985] C.L.Y. 3055 followed).

PRICE *v*. NICHOLLS [1986] R.T.R. 155, D.C.

2950. Lion Intoximeter—reliability

[Road Traffic Act 1972 (c.20), ss.6(1), 8(1).]

Where the only evidence of unreliability of a Lion Intoximeter 3000 is disparity between the readings of two specimens given by a motorist, and the expert evidence clearly establishes that the breath alcohol level was not below a level above the legal limit, there are no grounds for dismissing an information alleging driving with excess alcohol.

T was required to provide two specimens of breath for analysis by a Lion Intoximeter 3000. The device appeared to be functioning normally but the readings given were 110 and 94 microgrammes. T was charged with driving with excess alcohol and at trial, expert evidence conflicted on the issue of the reliability of the device. However, T's expert conceded that the level of alcohol could not have been less than 40 microgrammes. The information was dismissed. *Held*, on appeal, that the prosecutor had established that the defendant's breath-alcohol level exceeded 35 microgrammes, and thus the justices had erred in law in dismissing the information (*R*. v. *Coomaraswamy* [1976] C.L.Y. 2413 and *Thomas* v. *Henderson* [1983] C.L.Y. 321a applied, *Lloyd* v. *Morris (Note)* unreported July 18, 1985 applied).

GORDON *v*. THORPE [1986] R.T.R. 338, D.C.

2951. Lion Intoximeter—reliability

[Road Traffic Act 1972 (c.20), s.8(1).]

An error in the date on the printout of a Lion Intoximeter 3000 is sufficient basis for the constable to decide that the device is unreliable, for the purpose of determining whether his subsequent request for a blood sample is valid or not.

T was required to produce two breath specimens late on February 28, 1984. The Lion Intoximeter printout showed the first to have been given at 11.59 on February 28 and the second at 00.01 on March 1, rather than on February 29. On this basis, the constable decided that the device was not reliable and required a specimen of blood, which T refused to give. The justices held that the constable was entitled to require the specimen of blood and T was convicted of failing to provide a specimen without reasonable excuse. *Held*, that the justices were correct in their conclusion and T's appeal would be dismissed.

SLENDER *v*. BOOTHBY (NOTE) [1986] R.T.R. 385, D.C.

2952. Motor cycle—driving

[Road Traffic Act 1972 (c.20), s.6(1).] Justices could properly conclude that a person who was appropriately garbed and propelled a motor cycle for a distance by standing astride it was driving it: McKOEN *v*. ELLIS, *The Times*, July 11, 1986, D.C.

2953. Motor-cycles

MOTOR CYCLES (PROTECTIVE HELMETS) (AMENDMENT) REGULATIONS 1986 (No. 472) [40p], made under the Road Traffic Act 1972 (c.20), ss.32(1), (2) and 33(1); operative on April 11, 1986; amend S.I. 1980 No. 1279.

2954. Motor insurance—theft—indemnity. See SAMUELSON *v*. NATIONAL INSURANCE GUARANTEE CORP., § 1783.

2955. Motor vehicle—intended use—application of regulations

[Road Traffic Act 1972 (c.20), ss.40, 190; Motor Vehicles (Construction and Use) Regulations 1978 (S.I. 1978 No. 1018), regs. 3(1), 107(1).]

In deciding what is a motor vehicle for the purposes of the Road Traffic Act 1972, an objective test should be applied, taking into account features of the vehicle in question and the actual use by its owners.

M Co. owned a fork lift truck registered for use on the road and taxed as a works truck. This vehicle had an enclosed glazed cab, lights, a horn and various other accessories making it suitable for road use. However, it had no speedometer, no wing mirrors, poor forward visibility, and had to be stopped every five miles or so to cool down. The vehicle travelled on public roads between premises of M Co., sometimes under its own power and sometimes on a low-loader. Its tyres contravened regulation 107(*f*) and (*g*) of the Motor Vehicles (Construction and Use) Regulations

1978. The justices convicted for this, taking into account their view that M Co. took advantage of its taxation to drive the vehicle on public roads when it suited them. *Held*, that there was ample material on which the justices might conclude that this was a "motor vehicle . . . intended . . . for use on roads" thus necessitating compliance with the regulations. Accordingly the justices had come to the right decision in the circumstances (dicta of Lord Parker C.J. in *Burns* v. *Currell* [1963] C.L.Y. 3038 applied; *O'Brien* v. *Anderton* [1979] R.T.R. 388 followed; *Daley* v. *Hargreaves* [1961] C.L.Y. 7765 considered; *MacDonald* v. *Carmichael* [1941] J.C. 27 not applied).
PERCY v. SMITH [1956] R.T.R. 252 D.C.

2956. Motor vehicle—meaning
[Road Traffic Act 1972 (c.20), s.190.] The burden of proof is on the prosecution to prove that any given vehicle is a motor vehicle intended or adapted for use on the road. The court gave guidance in general terms as to when a vehicle might fall within the Act (*O'Brien* v. *Anderton* [1979] R.T.R. 388; *Burns* v. *Currell* [1963] C.L.Y. 3038 considered): CHIEF CONSTABLE OF AVON AND SOMERSET v. F, *The Times*, November 3, 1986, D.C.

2957. Motor vehicle offences—statistics
The Home Office has published statistics of offences relating to motor vehicles in England and Wales during 1985. Copies of the statistical bulletin, Issue 81/86, are available from the Statistical Department, Home Office, Lunar House, Croydon, Surrey CR0 9YD. Tel. 01–760–2850. [£2·50.]

2958. Motor vehicles
MOTOR VEHICLES (AUTHORISATION OF SPECIAL TYPES) (AMENDMENT) ORDER 1986 (No. 313) [80p], made under the Road Traffic Act 1972 (c.20), s.42; operative on April 1, 1986; amends S.I. 1979 No. 1198.
MOTOR VEHICLES (DESIGNATION OF APPROVAL MARKS) (AMENDMENT) REGULATIONS 1986 (No. 369) [£1·35], made under the Road Traffic Act 1972, s.63(1); operative on April 1, 1986; further amends S.I. 1979 No. 1088.

2959. Motorway traffic—obstruction—stopping on motorway—whether offence
[Motorway Traffic (England and Wales) Regulations (S.I. 1982 No. 1163), Reg. 7(4).] Reg. 7(4) of the 1982 Motorway Traffic Regulations provides that a motorist forced by the presence of a stationary vehicle or object to stop on a motorway is not committing an offence. The regulation does not permit the motorist to remain at rest on the carriageway once the obstruction has gone: MAWSON v. CHIEF CONSTABLE OF MERSEYSIDE, *The Times*, July 21, 1986, D.C.

2960. Northern Ireland. See NORTHERN IRELAND.

2961. Notice of intended prosecution—charge—whether service
[Road Traffic Act 1972 (c.20), s.179(2).] A motorist was sufficiently served with a notice of intended prosecution where he was charged within 14 days of the offence and was given a copy of the notice of the charge: SAGE v. TOWNSEND, *The Times*, May 27, 1986, D.C.

2962. Parking
CONTROL OF OFF-STREET PARKING (APPEALS PROCEDURE) (ENGLAND AND WALES) (METROPOLITAN DISTRICTS) REGULATIONS 1986 (No. 264) [£1·85], made under S.I. 1986 No. 225; operative on April 1, 1986; prescribe the procedure for appeals against decisions of Metropolitan District Councils in connection with licences for the operation of off-street parking.
CONTROL OF OFF-STREET PARKING (ENGLAND AND WALES) (METROPOLITAN DISTRICTS) ORDER 1986 (No. 225) [£2·80], made under the Road Traffic Regulation Act 1984 (c.27), s.44(1)(*a*); operative on April 1, 1986; applies the provisions of s.43 and Sched. 4 to the 1984 Act, which are concerned with off-street parking, to the Metropolitan Districts.
CONTROL OF OFF-STREET PARKING IN GREATER LONDON (APPEALS PROCEDURE) REGULATIONS 1986 (No. 262) [£1·85], made under the Road Traffic Regulation Act 1984, Sched. 4, para. 17; operative on April 1, 1986; prescribes the procedure for appeals against decisions of local authorities in Greater London in connection with licences for the operation of off-street parking.
CONTROL OF PARKING IN GOODS VEHICLE LOADING AREAS ORDERS (PROCEDURE) (ENGLAND AND WALES) REGULATIONS 1986 (No. 181) [£1·85], made under the Road

Traffic Regulation Act, s.124, Sched. 9, Pt. III; operative on April 1, 1986; prescribe the procedure to be followed in relation to the making of orders under s.61(1) of the 1984 Act.

IMMOBILISATION OF VEHICLES ILLEGALLY PARKED (LONDON BOROUGHS OF CAMDEN, KENSINGTON AND CHELSEA, AND WESTMINSTER, AND THE CITY OF LONDON) ORDER 1986 (No. 1225) [£3·40], made under the Road Traffic Regulation Act 1984 (c.27), s.106(1) and (5); operative on August 12, 1986; revokes S.I. 1985 No. 464.

2963. "Pay and display" car park—notice requiring information as to identity of driver—time for compliance

[Road Traffic Regulation Act 1967 (c.76), ss.85(2)(*a*) and 85(3).] D was the registered keeper of a vehicle which he parked in a "pay and display" car park without displaying a valid ticket. When the excess charge ticket was not paid, a notice under s.85(2)(*a*) of the 1967 Act was served on him requiring him to provide information as to the identity of the driver within 14 days. D did not provide the information until the day of hearing of a charge against him of failing to supply the information, contrary to s.85(3). *Held*, dismissing his appeal against conviction, that, although no time-limit for complying with the notice was prescribed by statute or regulation, the information had to be given forthwith or within a reasonable time: LOWE *v*. LESTER [1986] Crim.L.R. 339, D.C.

2964. Police—discretion not to proceed against offending motorist. See R. *v*. COXHEAD, § 672.

2965. Procedure

LONDON AUTHORITIES' TRAFFIC ORDERS (PROCEDURE) REGULATIONS 1986 (No. 259) [£2·80], made under the Road Traffic Regulation Act 1984 (c.27), s.124, Sched. 9, Pt. III; operative on April 1, 1986; prescribes the procedure to be followed by the London Borough Councils and the City of London in connection with making road traffic regulations under the 1984 Act and s.36B of the Road Traffic Act 1972.

2966. Production of documents—driving licence—impossibility of production—whether defence

[Road Traffic Act 1972 (c.20), s.161(4).]

The fact that it is impossible for a defendant to produce his driving licence is not a defence to a charge of failing to produce his driving licence contrary to s.161(4) of the Road Traffic Act 1972.

D was issued with a form HORT/1 by a police officer requiring him to produce his driving licence for examination at a police station within five days. At that time D's licence was in the possession of the Driver and Vehicle Licensing Centre at Swansea. D's licence was not returned in time for D to produce it. D was charged with failing to produce his driving licence contrary to s.161(4) of the Road Traffic Act 1972. D was convicted and appealed. *Held*, dismissing D's appeal, that the fact that it was impossible for D to produce his driving licence was not a defence to the charge but was mitigation of the offence (*Davey* v. *Towle* [1973] C.L.Y. 2960 applied, *Harding* v. *Price* [1948] 1 K.B. 695 considered).

SPARKS *v*. WORTHINGTON [1986] R.T.R. 64, C.A.

2967. Proper control of vehicle—distribution of load

[Road Traffic Act 1972 (c.20), ss.40(5), 101(1), Sched. 4.]

The provisions of regulation 119 of the Motor Vehicles (Construction and Use) Regulations and s.40(5) of the 1972 Act are to be broadly construed.

S drove his vehicle with a sheepdog on his lap. He pleaded guilty to driving while in such a position that he could not have proper control over the vehicle, contrary to regulation 119 of the Motor Vehicles (Construction and Use) Regulations 1978 and s.40(5) of the Road Traffic Act 1972. The justices fined him and ordered his licence to be endorsed. His appeal in respect of the endorsement was dismissed by the Crown Court. *Held*, that the dog came within the spirit and letter of regulation 119 and s.40(5) as a badly distributed load causing danger within para. (*a*) in column 4 of Part 1 of Sched. 4 to the 1972 Act, and thus the courts below had arrived at the correct conclusion.

SIMPSON *v*. VANT [1986] R.T.R. 247, D.C.

2968. Public service vehicles

PUBLIC SERVICE VEHICLES (CONDITIONS OF FITNESS, EQUIPMENT, USE AND CERTIFICATION) (AMENDMENT) REGULATIONS 1986 (No. 370) [40p], made under the

Public Passenger Vehicles Act 1981 (c.14), ss.52(1)(*a*), 60(1), 61(2); operative on April 1, 1986; amends S.I. 1981 No. 257 so as to increase fees payable thereunder.

2969. Random stops of vehicles—breath test—whether improper
[Road Traffic Act 1972 (c.20), ss.6(1), 8(1)(*a*), 159.]
There is nothing to stop the police carrying out random stops of vehicles to see if people have been drinking.
Police were carrying out random stops to see if motorists had been drinking. They stopped D, smelt alcohol on his breath, and breathalysed him. On his appeal against a conviction for excess blood/alcohol, the Crown Court allowed the appeal on the basis that random stopping was malpractice. The prosecutor appealed. *Held,* allowing the appeal, that it was not. Malpractice meant oppression or capricious behaviour. The police could not require breath tests at random, but there was nothing to prevent them stopping cars at random to see if drivers had been drinking (*Winter* v. *Barlow* [1980] C.L.Y. 2306, *Such* v. *Ball* [1982] C.L.Y. 2718 and *Fox* v. *Chief Constable of Gwent* [1985] C.L.Y. 2986 considered; *R.* v. *Needham* (Note) [1974] C.L.Y. 3305 explained).
CHIEF CONSTABLE OF GWENT v. DASH [1986] R.T.R. 41, D.C.

2970. Reckless driving—defence of intention to assist lawful arrest of offenders
[Criminal Law Act 1967 (c.58), s.3(1).]
A defence under s.3(1) of the Criminal Law Act 1967 is open to a person charged with reckless driving in certain circumstances.
The appellant was working on the forecourt of his garage when another vehicle drew up, and the occupant hurled objects damaging his car's windscreen and hitting him. The appellant, having told his wife to telephone the police, set off in pursuit and forced the car on to the verge, ramming it when stationary. He was charged with reckless driving. His defence under s.3(1) of the 1967 Act was that he was using reasonable force to assist the lawful arrest of offenders. The judge directed that s.3(1) was incapable of affording him a defence. *Held,* allowing the appeal, that the defence was open on a charge of reckless driving and should have been left to the jury.
R. v. RENOUF [1986] 1 W.L.R. 522, C.A.

2971. Reckless driving—goods vehicle—unsecure load
[Road Traffic Act 1972 (c.20), s.1.]
A person who drives a goods vehicle with the knowledge that its load is unsafe and likely to fall off is guilty of reckless driving.
D was the driver of an articulated lorry. A piece of machinery weighing between three and five tons was loaded onto the trailer of D's lorry. The machinery was top heavy. D was advised to secure the machine with chains. D disregarded that advice and drove the vehicle on a public highway. The trailer hit a pot hole and the machine fell off. The machine fell on a pedestrian who was killed. D was charged with causing death by reckless driving. At the close of the prosecution case D submitted that although there was evidence that he was reckless as to the safety of his load he did not drive recklessly. D's submission was rejected. D changed his plea to guilty and thereafter appealed against his conviction. *Held*, dismissing D's appeal, that D was driving with the knowledge that by doing so he was putting other road users at risk of serious injury or death. In the circumstances D was driving recklessly (*R.* v. *Spurge* [1961] C.L.Y. 7780 considered).
R. v. CROSSMAN [1986] R.T.R. 49, C.A.

2972. Recording equipment
PASSENGER AND GOODS VEHICLES (RECORDING EQUIPMENT) (AMENDMENT) REGULA-
TIONS 1986 (No. 2076) [45p], made under the European Communities Act 1972 (c.68), s.2(2); operative on December 31, 1986; amend S.I. 1979 No. 1746 so as to provide that nominations or approvals issued under Reg. 4 shall expire on January 31.
PASSENGER AND GOODS VEHICLES (RECORDING EQUIPMENT) (APPROVAL OF FITTERS
AND WORKSHOPS) (FEES) REGULATIONS 1986 (No. 2128) [45p], made under the Finance Act 1973 (c.51), s.56(1) and (2); operative on January 30, 1987; revoke and re-enact S.I. 1977 No. 1413 and S.I. 1985 No. 1802.

2973. Registration and licensing
ROAD VEHICLES (REGISTRATION AND LICENSING) (AMENDMENT) REGULATIONS 1986
(No. 607) [80p], made under the Vehicles (Excise) Act 1971 (c.10), ss.12, 23, 37,

39(1), Sched. 7, Pt. I, para. 20; operative on April 28, 1986; amend S.I. 1971 No. 450.

ROAD VEHICLES (REGISTRATION AND LICENSING) (AMENDMENT) (NO. 2) REGULATIONS 1986 (No. 1177) [45p], made under the Vehicles (Excise) Act 1971 (c.10), ss.16, 23 and 37; operative on September 1, 1986; increase the fees for the issue of replacements of trade plates.

ROAD VEHICLES (REGISTRATION AND LICENSING) (AMENDMENT) (NO. 3) REGULATIONS 1986 (No. 2101) [80p], made under the Vehicles (Excise) Act 1971 (c.10), s.16(1)(2)(8); amend S.I. 1971 No. 450 in relation to trade licences.

2974. Removal of motor vehicle—driver under influence of drink
[Police Act 1964 (c.48), s.51(3).]
If a car is stopped by police and the driver found to be driving with excess blood/alcohol, the police must protect road users, for example by removing the car; but a responsible person who demonstrates the right and the capacity to look after the car may lawfully prevent them from removing it.

D was stopped and breathalysed. His breath test was positive, and he was arrested. The police sought to remove the car to the police station with or without D in it. There was an argument and D locked the car from inside. On a charge against D of obstructing the police, he argued that they had no right to remove the car. He was convicted. *Held*, dismissing the appeal, that the police were under a duty to protect the car and other road users, which was usually carried out by taking it to the police station. A responsible person who could demonstrate the right and the capacity to look after the car might lawfully prevent the police from removing it without being guilty of obstruction, but D did not fall into the latter category, and was therefore properly convicted (*Rice* v. *Connolly* [1966] C.L.Y. 9240, *Hills* v. *Ellis* [1983] C.L.Y. 726 and *Stunt* v. *Boston* [1973] C.L.Y. 2994 considered).

LIEPINS *v.* SPEARMAN [1986] R.T.R. 24, D.C.

2975. Removal of vehicles
REMOVAL AND DISPOSAL OF VEHICLES (LOADING AREAS) REGULATIONS 1986 (No. 184) [80p], made under the Road Traffic Regulation Act 1984 (c.27), s.103; operative on April 1, 1986; provide for the removal and disposal of vehicles in any part of a loading area when parking is prohibited.

REMOVAL AND DISPOSAL OF VEHICLES REGULATIONS 1986 (No. 183) [£2·30], made under the Refuse Disposal (Amenity) Act 1978 (c.3), ss.3, 4 and the Road Traffic Regulation Act 1984, ss.99, 101; operative on April 1, 1986; make provision for the removal and disposal of vehicles.

2976. Road—footpath impassable to cars—whether a road
[Road Traffic Act 1972 (c.20), ss.6(1), 99, 196(1), as amended.]
The very broad definition of "road" in s.196(1) is not to be narrowed by the ordinary meaning of the word.

L drove his motorcycle on a public footpath four to five feet wide, which was not designed for, and was impassable to motor cars. He was convicted by the magistrates of driving on a road with excess alcohol in his blood, and whilst disqualified. He appealed to the Crown Court, who found that the footpath was a highway, and dismissed the appeal. *Held*, that once it was established that the footpath was a highway it fell within s.196(1), and it was irrelevant that it was not a road within the ordinary meaning of the word.

LANG *v.* HINDHAUGH [1986] R.T.R. 271, D.C.

2977. Road Traffic (Driving Instruction) Act 1984—commencement
ROAD TRAFFIC (DRIVING INSTRUCTION) ACT 1984 (COMMENCEMENT NO. 2) ORDER 1986 (No. 1336 (c.47)) [40p], made under the Road Traffic (Driving Instruction) Act 1984 (c.13), s.5(3); brings into force on September 30, 1986, s.1 of the 1984 Act.

2978. Road Traffic Regulation (Parking) Act 1986 (c.27)
This Act amends the Road Traffic Regulation Act 1984 (c.27) in relation to parking.

The Act received the Royal Assent on July 8, 1986 and comes into force two months from that date. It does not extend to Northern Ireland.

2979. Road Traffic Regulation Act 1984—commencement
ROAD TRAFFIC REGULATION ACT 1984 (COMMENCEMENT NO. 1) ORDER 1986 (NO. 1147 (c.32)) [45p], made under the Road Traffic Regulation Act 1984 (c.27), s.145(2)(3); brings s.90 of the 1984 Act into force on July 31, 1986.

2980. Speed limit
MOTOR VEHICLES (VARIATION OF SPEED LIMITS) REGULATIONS 1986 (No. 1175) [45p], made under the Road Traffic Regulation Act 1984 (c.27), s.86(2), (3); operative on July 22, 1986; increase the speed limits for certain vehicles on motorways and dual carriageways.

2981. Speed limit—street lighting—defective light—error in distance between lamps
[Road Traffic Regulation Act 1967 (c.76), ss.71(1), 72(1), 78A(1), Road Traffic Act 1972 (c.20), s.203.]
An error of 12 yards between two street lamps can be regarded as *de minimis.*
S drove his motor car at a speed exceeding 30 m.p.h. on a road and was charged with driving contrary to ss.71 and 78A of the 1967 Act. The prosecution evidence was that the average distance between street lamps was 95 yards but that lamp number 8 was unilluminable and the distance between lamps 5 and 6 was 212 yards. The justices, being satisfied that the road had a system of street lighting by means of lamps placed not more than 200 yards apart and that the road was therefore restricted, convicted S. *Held,* dismissing the appeal, that (1) the fact that one of the lamps was unilluminable was irrelevant (*Walker* v. *Rawlinson* [1976] R.T.R. 94 applied); (2) in a system of 24 lamps an error of 12 yards or six per cent. between two lamps was *de minimis* (*Briere* v. *Hailstone* [1968] C.L.Y. 3506 applied).
SPITTLE *v.* KENT COUNTY CONSTABULARY [1986] R.T.R. 142, D.C.

2982. Supply of information—requirement served on company secretary
[Road Traffic Act 1972 (c.20), s.168; Companies Act 1948 (c.38), s.437.] A requirement to supply information is made satisfactorily if made on the company secretary: BLAKE *v.* CHARLES SULLIVAN CARS, *The Times,* June 26, 1986, D.C.

2983. Tachograph—exemption—burden of proof
[Community Road Transport Rules (Exemptions) Regulations 1978 (S.I. 1978 No. 1158) reg. 4] A defendant seeking to rely on the exemption from the requirement to use a tachograph had to prove on the balance of probabilities that the vehicle was a specialised one used for door to door deliveries: GAUNT *v.* NELSON, *The Times,* May 21, 1986, D.C.

2984. Tachograph—falsification of records—sentence. See R. *v.* PARKINSON, § 928.

2985. Taking a conveyance—evidence—case to answer. See CHIEF CONSTABLE OF AVON AND SOMERSET CONSTABULARY *v.* JEST, § 934.

2986. Television receiving apparatus—television used for showing videos in a motor coach—whether "television receiving apparaus"
[Motor Vehicles (Construction and Use) Regulations 1978 (S.I. 1978 No. 1017), reg. 143.]
An ordinary televison used for showing videos on a long distance motor coach was a television receiving apparatus within the meaning of reg. 143(2) of the Motor Vehicles (Construction and Use) Regulations 1978.
A coach owned by Target Travel was observed on the M.1 by a police officer. There was a television set in the coach that was on and, in the opinion of the officer, in a position where it was likely to distract the driver. Target Travel were charged with using a television receiving apparatus in a motor vehicle under circumstances and in a position such that it might cause distraction to the driver contrary to reg. 143(2) of the Motor Vehicles (Construction and Use) Regulations 1978. The television set was used for showing videos and was not connected to an aerial to enable it to receive television programmes. Target Travel was convicted and appealed by way of case stated. *Held*, dismissing the appeal, that the television set was designed and constructed to receive television signals. As such, it was a television receiving apparatus within the meaning of the regulation. It did not cease to be a television receiving apparatus merely because it was not attached to an aerial. The nature of the apparatus should not be confused with the use to which it was put.
TARGET TRAVEL (COACHES) *v.* ROBERTS [1986] R.T.R. 120, D.C.

2987. Testing of vehicles

GOODS VEHICLES (PLATING AND TESTING) (AMENDMENT) REGULATIONS 1986 (No. 371) [40p], made under the Road Traffic Act 1972 (c.20), s.45, 199(2); operative on April 1, 1986; amends S.I. 1982 No. 1478 so as to increase fees payable thereunder.

MOTOR VEHICLES (TESTS) (AMENDMENT) REGULATIONS 1986 (No. 372), [40p], made under the Road Traffic Act 1972, s.43(2)(6); operative on April 1, 1986; amends S.I. 1981 No. 1694 so as to increase the fees payable thereunder.

MOTOR VEHICLES (TESTS) (AMENDMENT) (NO. 2) REGULATIONS 1986 (No. 904) [45p], made under the Road Traffic Act 1972 (c.20), s.43(2)(6); operative on July 1, 1986; increase fees for MOTs.

2988. Traffic lights

LONDON TRAFFIC CONTROL SYSTEM (TRANSFER) ORDER 1986 (No. 315) [£1·35], made under the Local Government Act 1985 (c.51), Sched. 5; operative on April 1, 1986; transfers functions relating to traffic light signals conferred on London authorities to the Secretary of State.

MERSEYSIDE TRAFFIC CONTROL SYSTEM (TRANSFER) ORDER 1986 (No. 316) [£1·35], made under the Local Government Act 1985, Sched. 5; operative on April 1, 1986; transfer functions relating to traffic light signals conferred on Merseyside authorities to the Secretary of State.

2989. Traffic regulation

LOCAL AUTHORITIES' TRAFFIC ORDERS (PROCEDURE) (ENGLAND AND WALES) REGULATIONS 1986 (No. 179) [£2·80], made under the Road Traffic Regulation Act 1984 (c.27), ss.124, 134(4), Sched. 9, Pt. III; operative on April 1, 1986; lay down the procedure to be followed by local authorities in England (outside of Greater London) and Wales in connection with the making by them of traffic and parking orders under the 1984 Act and the Road Traffic Act 1972, s.36B.

SECRETARY OF STATE'S TRAFFIC ORDERS (PROCEDURE) (ENGLAND AND WALES) REGULATIONS 1986 (No. 180) [£2·30], made under the Road Traffic Regulation Act 1984, ss.124, 134(2), Sched. 9, Pt. III; operative on April 1, 1986; lays down the procedure to be followed by the Secretary of State in connection with the making of traffic orders under the 1984 Act and the Road Traffic Act 1972, s.36B.

2990. Traffic signs

TRAFFIC SIGNS (AMENDMENT) REGULATIONS 1986 (No. 1859) [45p], made under the Road Traffic Regulation Act 1984 (c.27), s.64(1)(2); operative on December 1, 1986; amends S.I. 1981 No. 859 to provide for a traffic sign to give warning of a humped zebra crossing.

2991. Traffic wardens

FUNCTIONS OF TRAFFIC WARDENS (AMENDMENT) ORDER 1986 (No. 1328) [45p], made under the Road Traffic Regulation Act 1984 (c.27), s.95(5); operative on October 1, 1986; amends S.I. 1970 No. 1958.

2992. Type approval

MOTOR VEHICLES (TYPE APPROVAL) (GREAT BRITAIN) (AMENDMENT) REGULATIONS 1986 (No. 739) [£1·40], made under the Road Traffic Act 1972 (c.20), ss.47(1), 50(1); operative on May 26, 1986; further amend S.I. 1984 No. 981.

MOTOR VEHICLES (TYPE APPROVAL FOR GOODS VEHICLES) (GREAT BRITAIN) (AMENDMENT) REGULATIONS 1986 (No. 427) [£1·35], made under the Road Traffic Act 1972 (c.20), ss.47(1), 50(1); operative on April 4, 1986; further amend S.I. 1982 No. 1271.

MOTOR VEHICLES (TYPE APPROVAL FOR GOODS VEHICLES) (GREAT BRITAIN) (AMENDMENT) (NO. 2) REGULATIONS 1986 (No. 1089) [45p], made under the Road Traffic Act 1972 (c.20), ss.47(1), 50(1); operative on August 1, 1986; further amend S.I. 1982 No. 1271.

MOTOR VEHICLES (TYPE APPROVAL) (AMENDMENT) REGULATIONS 1986 (No. 1501) [£1.40], made under the European Communities Act 1972 (c.68), s.(2); operative on September 29, 1986; amend S.I. 1980 No.1182 by substituting a new Sched. 2 for the one contained in that Order, as amended.

2993. Use of vehicle—meaning—vehicle on tow

[Road Traffic Act 1972 (c.20), ss44(1), 143(1).]

A vehicle being towed with its wheels and brakes locked is not being "used" on a road.

D was sitting in the driving seat of a van which was being towed, to give warning if danger arose. The steering was locked, and the brakes were jammed so that the wheels would not turn. D was convicted of 'using' the vehicle on a road without insurance or a current test certificate. *Held,* allowing the appeal, that the van was an inanimate hunk of metal like a sledge and incapable of being controlled, and D could not be said to have been using it (*Nichol* v. *Leach* [1973] C.L.Y. 3024 applied; *Elliott* v. *Grey* [1959] C.L.Y. 2903 and *Hewer* v. *Cutler* [1974] C.L.Y. 3397 distinguished).

THOMAS *v.* HOOPER [1986] R.T.R. 1, D.C.

2994. Various offences—sentencing—means of offender

The means of an offender are irrelevant to whether a monetary or custodial penalty should be imposed, but once a fine is decided upon, the means are of critical importance in deciding the amount of the fine.

B was of very limited means, had no driving licence and an appalling record of driving offences. He pleaded guilty before justices to a series of 10 offences, including driving with excess alcohol in the blood, careless driving and driving uninsured. He was fined £650, disqualified and ordered to pay costs. He appealed to the Crown Court on the grounds that the sentence was excessive in view of his means. The Crown Court substituted four months imprisonment for the £100 fine imposed in respect of driving with excess alcohol, and allowed the other fines to stand, with one day's imprisonment in default of immediate payments. *Held,* that determination of the appropriate type of penalty was to be made without regard to the means of the offender. Means were critical in determining the level of a particular fine. There had been an error of law in the process of sentencing and an order of certiorari would be granted to quash the sentence of imprisonment. B was conditionally discharged for two years.

R. *v.* LIVERPOOL CROWN COURT, *ex p.* BAIRD [1986] R.T.R. 346, D.C.

2995. Vehicle excise—time-limit for summary proceedings—when time commenced

[Vehicle Excise Act 1971 (c.10), ss.8 and 28.] A police officer saw D, who admitted having used on a public road a vehicle for which a licence was not in force, contrary to s.8 of the 1971 Act. The officer's report only came to the knowledge of the Secretary of State almost a month later, until when the Secretary of State did not have sufficient evidence to warrant a prosecution. *Held,* dismissing D's appeal against conviction, that (1) a constable discovering an offence under s.8 is not required to institute proceedings and follow the procedure in s.28; (2) if instead he informs the Secretary of State, the six-month time-limit under s.28(1) runs from when the Secretary of State has knowledge of the alleged offence and sufficient information within s.28(1): ALGAR *v.* SHAW [1986] Crim.L.R. 750, D.C.

SALE OF GOODS

2996. Breach of warranty—misrepresentation—whether liable. See HUMMING BIRD MOTORS *v.* HOBBS, § 2284.

2997. C. & f. contract—variation of contract—passing of title—whether action in tort. See LEIGH AND SILLAVAN *v.* ALIAKMON SHIPPING CO., § 2252.

2998. C.i.f. contract—export prohibition—whether seller can make subsequent appropriations—lateness of notice of appropriation

S sold a quantity of soya bean meal to B for shipment in June to September 1973, pursuant to the terms of GAFTA 100. In June 1973 the U.S. Department of Commerce imposed an embargo on the export of soya meal, and only licensed the export of 40 per cent. of the balance of contracted quantities. S invoked clause 21 of the contract, and claimed cancellation of 60 per cent. of the contract. S appropriated 40 per cent. S then purported to appropriate further cargo that had become available. B refused to take up the goods, contending that S had no right to appropriate further soya to the contract and further that the subsequent notices of appropriation were late. The GAFTA Board of Appeal found for S on both points. *Held,* that although the Board of Appeal was correct in finding for S on the first point, they ought to have permitted B to raise arguments as to the lateness of the appropriation. B had not, on the evidence, waived their right to raise such arguments: ANDRÉ ET CIE *v.* COOK INDUSTRIES INC. [1986] 2 Lloyd's Rep. 200, Bingham J.

2999. C.i.f. contract—whether parties intended contract to be enforceable
D agreed to sell P 300,000 M.T. of sugar pursuant to a c.i.f. contract. It was contemplated by the parties that D could execute a contract with B to sell the same sugar, but at a higher price. D was then to pass on to P a sum of money representing the difference between the contract price and that paid by B. B did not, however, buy any sugar and D insisted that P perform the contract. P refused, and declared that the contracts which he had signed were shams. He sought a declaration that he was not bound by them. *Held,* dismissing P's appeal, that the claim would be dismissed. The contracts had been signed by P and there was no evidence that either party had intended them not to be enforceable: HARYANTO YANI *v.* MAN (E. D. & F.) (SUGAR) [1986] 2 Lloyd's Rep. 44, C.A.

3000. Car odometer reading—knowledge and belief—whether breach of warranty or misrepresentation. See HUMMINGBIRD MOTORS *v.* HOBBS, § 2284.

3001. Consumer protection
CHILD RESISTANT PACKAGING (SAFETY) REGULATIONS 1986 (No. 758) [80p], made under the Consumer Safety Act 1978 (c.35), s.1(4); operative on December 1, 1987; prohibit the supply of specified products (*e.g.* toxic and corrosive products) where they are contained in packaging not approved by the British Standards Institution.
FIREWORKS (SAFETY) REGULATIONS 1986 (No. 1323) [45p], made under the Consumer Safety Act 1978 (c.38), s.1(4); operative on August 1, 1986; prohibits persons from supplying fireworks to any person apparently under 16.

3002. The National Consumer Council has published its Annual Report for 1985/1986. Copies of the Report are available free of charge from: Annual Report, National Consumer Council, 18, Queen Anne's Gate, London SW1H 9AA. (Please enclose S.A.E. with 31p stamps.)

3003. Consumer Safety (Amendment) Act 1986 (c.29)
This Act makes further provision with respect to the safety of consumers.
Royal Assent was given on July 8, 1986 and comes into force on August 8, 1986. Subject to specified sections, the Act extends to Scotland and Northern Ireland.

3004. Consumer Safety Act 1978—commencement
CONSUMER SAFETY ACT 1978 (COMMENCEMENT NO. 2) ORDER 1986 (No. 1297 (C.42)) [45p], made under the Consumer Safety Act 1978 (c.38), s.12(2); brings into operation on August 8, 1986 s.10(1) of, and Sched. 3 to, the 1978 Act.

3005. Fitness for purpose—manufacturers' instructions—defect
[Sale of Goods Act 1979 (c.54), s.14.] Where goods are retailed with misleading manufacturers' instructions they are sold in breach of the requirements for merchantability and fitness for purpose even though the retailer had insufficient knowledge to appreciate the defects: WORMELL *v.* RHM AGRICULTURAL (EAST) (1986) 130 S.J. 166. P. Ashworth sitting as deputy High Ct. Judge.
[Sale of Goods Act 1979 (c.54), s.14(2), (3).]
Goods which were unsuitable if used in accordance with the manufacturers' instructions which were misleading were not fit for their purpose within the meaning of the Sale of Goods Act 1979.
P was a farmer who needed to kill wild oats in his crop of winter wheat. Adverse winter conditions prevented him spraying his crop. By the end of March it was too late to use most herbicides, but D, who were agricultural suppliers, recommended a herbicide which P bought. The instructions stated that the herbicide was effective against wild oats at any stage, but if used late there was a danger of damage to the main crop. He used it in mid-June when conditions were finally suitable but the herbicide had little or no effect on the wild oats. He claimed against D that they were in breach of the terms implied by s.14 of the 1979 Sale of Goods Act that the herbicide was of merchantable quality and fit for its purpose. *Held,* giving judgment for P, that although it was suitable for killing wild oats the herbicide was only effective if it was supplied with the necessary instructions so that it could be applied properly and at the right time. When P purchased the goods, he purchased them with their instructions. Goods which were ineffective when applied in accordance with their instructions were not fit for their purpose. The instructions were misleading as understood by P and a reasonable user as they did not state that the herbicide was ineffective against wild oats if sprayed at a late stage in the main crop's growth. They were not therefore

fit for their purpose (*Willis* v. *FMC Machinery & Chemicals* (1976) 68 D.L.R. (3d) 127 considered).
WORMELL *v.* R.H.M. AGRICULTURE (EAST) [1986] 1 W.L.R. 336, Piers Ashworth Q.C.

3006. F.o.b. contract—condition as to time of nomination—enforcement
D agreed to sell sugar f.o.b. to P, with the port to be specified by D "at latest 14.11.83." On November 11, 1983, P reminded D of their obligations, but a nomination was not made until November 15, 1983. P contended that the contract was cancelled. D contended that P was in repudiatory breach. The Council of the Refined Sugar Association found for D. P appealed successfully. *Held,* dismissing D's appeal, that although a finding by the arbitrators demonstrated that strict punctuality was difficult in that trade, that was quite insufficient to displace the strict requirements as to time in a commercial contract: GILL & DUFFUS S.A. *v.* SOCIETE POUR L'EXPORTATION DES SUCRES [1986] 1 Lloyd's Rep. 322, C.A.

3007. F.o.b. contract—duty of seller to deliver—nature of duty
In an arbitration the GAFTA Board of Appeal held that an f.o.b. seller was in default of his obligations if on receiving a notice of readiness from a buyers' vessel he did not *at that moment* have the goods ready for delivery. Bingham J. upheld the award. *Held,* allowing an appeal, that the seller could not be held in default if he could load within either a reasonable time or the time laid down by the contract. The seller was under no obligation to load cargo other than when the vessel was able to receive them: TRADAX EXPORT S.A. *v.* ITALGRANI DI FRANCESCO AMBROSIO [1986] 1 Lloyd's Rep. 112, C.A.

3008. F.o.b.—payment against letter of credit
A seller of goods under a contract of sale providing for payment for goods f.o.b. by letter of credit against documents cannot recover the price if the documents are properly rejected due to his failure to comply with the credit: SHANSHER JUTE MILLS *v.* SETHIA LONDON, *Financial Times,* July 2, 1986, Bingham J.

3009. GAFTA 100—embargo—failure by sellers to deliver balance
S were sellers of soya bean meal pursuant to a contract made with B on the GAFTA 100 form. In mid-1973 the United States government imposed a 60 per cent. embargo on the export of soya. S claimed the protection of clause 21 as to the balance of 60 per cent. In order to succeed they had to establish that all other shippers were prevented from performing the contracts which made up that chain which culminated in the contract between S and B. *Held,* dismissing S's appeal, that S were bound by findings of the arbitrator and had failed to establish the unavailability of cargo: COOK INDUSTRIES *v.* TRADAX EXPORTS S.A. [1985] 2 Lloyd's Rep. 454, C.A.

3010. GAFTA 100—notice of appropriation—time for giving notice—clauses 10 and 25
The dispute in this case turned upon whether S, the sellers of soya bean meal pursuant to a GAFTA 100 contract, gave a timeous notice of appropriation. S relied upon clause 25 of the form and contended that notwithstanding clause 10 of the form, clause 25 applied to extend time when the expiry date for giving notice fell on a non-business day. *Held*, that the construction contended for by S was correct: GRANARIA B.V. *v.* LEIEVOEDERS B.V. [1986] 1 Lloyd's Rep. 373, Hirst J.

3011. Letter of credit—variations—whether implied term
On November 16, 1979, P agreed to buy from B (Libyan suppliers) a quantity of naphtha cargo from Zueitina, lifting to be completed by December 5, 1979. P subsequently agreed to sell the cargo to D. The quality of the cargo was described by a number of "in-tank typicals", and one of these was "colour Saybolt plus 30". Subsequently, B asked P to effect a number of changes in the letter of credit in B's favour, including a change in the description of cargo which was now to be "Libyan condensate usual quality loaded at Zueitina," and an extension of the shipment date. P's bankers forwarded the modifications to D. D accepted the alterations, but failed to instruct their bankers to alter the letter of credit in favour of P in the same corresponding respects. Loading of the cargo on board the M.T. *Gudermes* was delayed in consequence, and demurrage was paid by D. Delays occurred at the discharge port in locating a buyer as a result of D's failure to realize that the change in cargo description meant the naphtha was brown, not

colourless. P sued D for the balance of the price of the naphtha. *Held,* that (1) D had failed to prove an enforceable settlement agreement with P on the facts; (2) both the contract of sale and the letter of credit had been varied so as to substitute, *inter alia,* the quality of the cargo sold; (3) the quality of the cargo loaded was in accordance with the contract and letter of credit as varied; (4) there was no implied term that the quality of cargo loaded would not significantly differ from the quality originally contracted for before the variation; (5) D were still able to claim damages from P for any loss caused by delay as a result of the dilatoriness of P's bankers: CEDAR TRADING CO. *v.* TRANSWORLD OIL; THE GUDERMES [1985] 2 Lloyd's Rep. 623, Leggatt J.

3012. Merchantable quality—defect in car—whether entitled to rescission
[Sale of Goods Act 1979 (c.54), s.14.] P bought a new car which possessed a minor defect which was likely to (and eventually did) cause the car to break down while in use. *Held,* that although the purchaser of a new car ought to expect teething troubles, a defect of this kind meant that the car was neither of merchantable quality nor reasonably fit for its purpose under s.14 of the Sale of Goods Act 1979. Rescission would only be allowed, however, within a reasonable time of purchase (*Bartlett* v. *Sidney Marcus* [1965] C.L.Y. 3516 distinguished): BERNSTEIN *v.* PAMSONS MOTORS, *The Times,* October 25, 1986, Rougier J.

3013. Merchantable quality—negligence—scope of duty
[Sale of Goods Act 1979 (c.54), s.14.] A bought fluid from B which B stored and delivered to its customers in plastic containers made by C. The containers, full of liquid, were left stacked and exposed to very hot sunlight by A. They collapsed and all the fluid was lost. *Held,* that (1) the containers were of merchantable quality since the goods were fit for the purpose or purposes of normal use, and no special use or uses had been made known to C; (2) C was not liable in tort since the product complained of had merely become reduced in value and had not harmed or endangered any other property of the purchaser; (3) the type of damage and the conditions in which it occurred were not reasonably forseeable (*Muirhead* v. *Industrial Tank Specialities* [1985] C.L.Y. 2311, *Donoghue* v. *Stevenson* [1932] A.C. 562 considered): M/S ASWAN ENGINEERING ESTABLISHMENT *v.* LUPDINE, *The Times,* August 4, 1986, C.A.

3014. Merchantable quality—repairable defect—damages
[Sale of Goods Act 1979 (c.54), s.14(6).] The fact that a defect is repairable does not prevent it from making the thing sold unmerchantable. If the defect has been successfully put right, this will affect the right to reject the goods, but does not affect the question of merchantability, which falls to be judged at the moment of delivery. It is implicit in s.14(6) of the Sale of Goods Act 1979 that if goods do not satisfy the definition of merchantable quality, they are to be regarded as unmerchantable. So where the purchaser of a new £16,000 Land Rover found that it had defective engine, bodywork, gearbox and oil seals, *held,* that he was entitled to the return of his money. The vehicle had been sold as new, and the performance and finish to be expected of such a car when considering the "merchantable quality" test of s.14 was that of a model of average standard with no mileage. Defects that would be acceptable in a second-hand car were not to be expected of a new one. The fact that a new car came with a manufacturer's warranty should not lead the buyer to expect less of the car (*Lee* v. *York Coach and Marine* [1977] C.L.Y. 2665 applied): ROGERS *v.* PARISH (SCARBOROUGH), *The Times,* November 8, 1986, C.A.

3015. Non-payment—settlement—frustration
P exported potatoes on terms controlled by the Egyptian government. P claimed against D, buyers, in respect of non-payment for nine shipments of potatoes in 1981, alleged by D to have arrived in damaged condition. Payment under the terms of the potato agreement should have been made about one week after the arrival of the goods. In August 1981, P and D negotiated a settlement in which D agreed to pay for the nine shipments in instalments, and a further contract was entered into for the supply of potatoes from P to D from 1982–1984 on the same payment terms as the original potato agreement. In December 1981, the Egyptian government varied the payment mechanism for export—sales which was henceforth to be by confirmed letters of credit. D objected and refused to pay the instalments under the settlement agreement. *Held,* that (1) the potato agreement was governed

by Egyptian law, and the effect of the Egyptian regulation was to frustrate the contract for future supply plus the settlement agreement, as the matter had been concluded against the background of the former; (2) P could however recover the unpaid price of the nine shipments in damages & the damaged cargo could be counter-claimed by D: NILE CO. FOR THE EXPORT OF AGRICULTURAL CROPS *v.* BENETT (H. & J. M.) (COMMODITIES) [1986] 1 Lloyd's Rep. 555, Evans J.

3016. Passing of property—unascertained goods—wine held in bulk lots—crystallisation of floating charges

LWC was a company dealing in wines that had substantial stocks of wines stored in various warehouses. LWC ran a scheme whereby persons could purchase quantities of wine for investment or laying down. The purchaser bought wine from LWC which would remain in the warehouse in bulk. The customer's purchase would be entered in LWC's stock book as such and allocated a reference number identifying its current warehouse location. The wine remained in bulk storage at the warehouse and was not divided up or allocated to any particular purchase. LWC provided the purchaser with a document of title confirming the purchaser to be the sole and beneficial owner of the wine he had purchased. The contract for sale of the wine contemplated that the wine would belong to the purchaser and would be stored for him by the vendor. LWC's bank borrowings were secured by a floating charge over its assets. In August 1974 the bank appointed a receiver and the charge crystallised. The receiver sought directions from the court with respect to three categories of wines held for purchasers by LWC. In the first category S purchased a quantity of wine that at the time of purchase represented all LWC's stock of that particular wine. In the second category B and a number of others purchased wine of a particular description that exhausted LWC's stock of that wine held by a number of warehouses. The third category involved mortgages of the wine purchased by the purchaser. In such cases the warehouseman holding the wine in question provided an acknowledgment to the mortgagee that the wine purchased by the mortgagor would be held to the mortgagee's order. In each of the categories no appropriation had taken place and it was not possible to specify which particular cases of wine comprised in the bulk stored were attributable to any one contract of purchase. *Held*, that in each category the wine remained the property of LWC and thus formed an asset of LWC that the receiver was entitled to dispose of. The contention raised in all three categories that LWC held the bulk wine as a whole on trust in undivided shares for each of the purchasers failed. Such a trust could not be spelled out from the circumstances or the documents signed by LWC. To create such a trust it must be possible to ascertain with certainty not only what the interest of the beneficiary is to be but to what property it is to attach. It was impossible to identify which particular cases of wine were held for each purchaser. Similarly the purchasers had no right to specific performance exercisable against LWC or the receiver. The court could not decree specific performance of a contract for the sale of goods under the Sale of Goods Act or otherwise in respect of unascertained goods. The cases of wine for each particular purchase were unascertained. In the first category it could not be said that the existing stock purchased by S was appropriated to that contract in the absence of anything to identify those particular cases as the subject matter of S's contract. It was open to LWC to obtain more wine of the same description for delivery to S should it wish so to do. Similarly there was nothing in the contracts contained in the second category to identify which particular cases were appropriated to the collected purchases. The mere fact that LWC sold quantities of wine that exhausted its stock did not have the effect of passing a proprietary interest in those stocks to the various purchases. It was not possible to ascertain which cases belonged to which purchaser. With regard to the third category the acknowledgments of the warehousemen given to the mortgagees might raise an estoppel in the purchaser's favour. An estoppel merely had the effect that LWC and the warehouseman could not deny that the purchaser had title to the quantity of wine in question held by the warehouseman. It did not create any actual title to the wine vested in the purchaser. The fact that LWC was estopped from denying that it had sold and appropriated to the contract a given quantity of wine of a particular description could not affect the rights of the receiver who, under the floating charge, acquired goods of that description (*Woodley* v. *Coventry* (1863) 2 H. & C. 164, *Knights* v. *Wiffen* (1870) L.R. 5 Q.B. 660, *Wait, Re* [1927] 1 Ch. 606

applied, *Pooley* v. *Budd* (1851) 14 Beav. 34, *Simm* v. *Anglo-Am. Tel. Co.* (1879)
5 Q.B.D. 188, *Inglis* v. *Stock* (1885) 10 App.Cas. 263, *Healy* v. *Howlett & Sons*
[1917] 1 K.B. 337, *Eastern Distributors* v. *Goldring* [1957] C.L.Y. 1308 considered,
Wait & James v. *Midland Bank* (1926) Com.Cas. 172 distinguished): LONDON
WINE CO. (SHIPPERS), *Re*, 1986 PCC 121, Oliver J.

3017. Port discharge—suitability of ship—duty of seller
Under a contract of sale of goods afloat which provides for discharge at one of a
range of agreed ports it is the seller's obligation to establish that the ship is
capable of discharging at any of the ports. Demurrage cannot be claimed for time
lost due to the ship's unsuitability for discharging at the chosen port: ENRICO SpA
v. PHILLIP BROS., *The Financial Times*, June 13, 1986, Staughton J.

3018. Supply of services—implied terms. See LAW REFORM, § 1945.

3019. Trade descriptions
TEXTILE PRODUCTS (INDICATIONS OF FIBRE CONTENT) REGULATIONS 1986 (No. 26)
[£2·80], made under the Medicines Act 1968 (c.67), s.103(3); operative on March
1, 1986 and May 29, 1987; revoke and re-enact S.I. 1973 No. 2124, S.I. 1975 No.
928 and S.I. 1984 No. 1640.
TRADE DESCRIPTIONS (ORIGIN MARKING) (MISCELLANEOUS GOODS) (REVOCATION)
ORDER 1986 (No. 193) [40p], made under the Trade Descriptions Act 1968 (c.29),
ss.8, 9, 38(1); operative on March 8, 1986; revoke S.I. 1981 No. 121 and S.I. 1984
No. 91.

**3020. Trade descriptions—"act or default of some other person"—acting in course of
trade or business**
[Trade Descriptions Act 1968 (c.29) s.23.]
Where the commission of an offence under the Trade Descriptions Act 1968 is
caused by the act or default of some other person, that other person is guilty of
the offence pursuant to s.23 of the Act notwithstanding that he was not acting in
the course of trade or business.
R applied a false trade description to a motor vehicle contrary to s.1(1)(*b*) of
the Trade Descriptions Act 1968. The motor vehicle was sold to R, a garage, by O
in his capacity as a private individual. O deliberately misrepresented the mileage
of the vehicle to R. The mileage constituted the false trade description applied by
R. The local trading standards officer, K, preferred an information against O
alleging he was guilty of an offence under s.23 of the Act in that the commission
of the offence by R was due to his act or default. O contended that he could not
be convicted of the offence because he was not acting in the course of a trade or
business. O was convicted and appealed by way of case stated. *Held*, dismissing
the appeal, that s.23 of the Act was clear in its wording. It did not expressly
require that the "some other person" liable to conviction under it should be acting
in the course of a trade or business, nor was it possible to imply such a
requirement into the wording of the section (*Meah* v. *Roberts* [1977] C.L.Y. 1442
applied.)
OLGEIRSSON v. KITCHING [1986] 1 W.L.R. 304, D.C.

3021. Trade descriptions—defence of due diligence—evidence
[Trade Descriptions Act 1968 (c.29), s.24(1)(3).] The defendants, a Frozen
Food company were charged with two offences under the Trade Description Act
1968; namely that on March 6, 1982 they had supplied frozen meat described as
"rump steak," meat which was in fact silverside of beef. The defendants availed
themselves of the statutory defences of s.24(1)(3), and the justices dismissed the
information. The appellants appealed by case stated. *Held*, allowing the appeal,
that there was insufficient evidence given to the justices as to the nature of the
sampling carried out to support their finding: AMOS v. MELCON (FROZEN FOODS)
(1985) 4 T.L.R. 247, D.C.

3022. Trade descriptions—Law Society—meaning of trade
[Trade Descriptions Act 1968 (c.29), s.14.] The Law Society does not "trade"
within the meaning of the Trades Descriptions Act 1968, and cannot therefore be
in breach of, *inter alia*, s.14 of that Act, because (a) it does not offer services to
the public; (b) it does not carry out commercial functions offering services to the
public; and (c) it does not carry on matters in the course of trade or business: R.
v. BOW STREET MAGISTRATES' COURT, *ex p.* JOSEPH, (1986) 130 S.J. 593, D.C.

SAVINGS BANKS

3023. National savings bank

NATIONAL SAVINGS BANK (INTEREST ON ORDINARY DEPOSITS) Order 1986 (No. 2161) [45p], made under the National Savings Bank Act 1971 (c.29), s.5(5); operative on January 1, 1987; continues the two-tier interest rate structure for ordinary deposits in the N.S.B., contained in S.I. 1985 No. 1875.

NATIONAL SAVINGS BANKS (INVESTMENT DEPOSITS) (LIMITS) (AMENDMENT) ORDER 1986 (No. 1217) [45p], made under the National Savings Bank Act 1971 (c.29), s.4(1); operative on July 16, 1986; increases the limit on the aggregate amount which can be accepted by the Director of Savings from any person by way of investment deposit in the N.S.B. from £50,000 to £100,000.

3024. Trustee savings banks

TRUSTEE SAVINGS BANKS ACT 1981 (FUND FOR THE BANKS FOR SAVINGS) (CLOSURE) ORDER 1986 (No. 841) [45p], made under the Trustee Savings Banks Act 1981 (c.65), s.53(1)(4); appoints May 21, 1986 as the date for the closure of the Funds for the Banks for Savings.

TRUSTEE SAVINGS BANKS (INTEREST-BEARING RECEIPTS) ORDER 1986 (No. 453) [40p], made under the Trustee Savings Bank Act 1981, Sched. 5, para. 2(1); operative on April 2, 1986; increases the rate of interest payable on receipts issued under s.34(1) of the 1969 Act. The receipts relate to sums paid into the fund for the banks for savings by trustee savings banks before November 21, 1979.

3025. Trustee Savings Banks Act 1976—commencement

TRUSTEE SAVINGS BANKS ACT 1976 (COMMENCEMENT NO. 9) ORDER 1986 (No. 1221 (c.35)) [45p], made under the Trustee Savings Banks Act 1976 (c.4), s.38(3); brings into force on July 20, 1986 Sched. 5, paras. 19 and 20 to the 1976 Act.

3026/7. Trustee Savings Banks Act 1985—appointed day

TRUSTEE SAVINGS BANKS ACT 1985 (APPOINTED DAY) (NO. 1) ORDER 1986 (No. 1219) [45p], made under the Trustee Savings Banks Act 1985 (c.58), Sched. 1, para. 13; appoints July 20, 1986 for the purposes of Sched. 1, para. 13 to the 1985 Act.

TRUSTEE SAVINGS BANKS ACT 1985 (APPOINTED DAY) (NO. 2) ORDER 1986 (No. 1220 (c.34)) [45p], made under the Trustee Savings Banks Act 1985, s.4(3)(4); appoints July 20, 1986 for the repeal of specified provisions of the Trustee Savings Banks Act 1981 and other enactments.

TRUSTEE SAVINGS BANKS ACT 1985 (APPOINTED DAY) (NO. 3) ORDER 1986 (No. 1222) [45p], made under the Trustee Savings Banks Act 1985, s.1(4); provides that the vesting day for the purposes of the 1985 Act shall be July 21, 1986.

TRUSTEE SAVINGS BANKS ACT 1985 (APPOINTED DAY) (NO. 4) ORDER 1986 (No. 1223 (c.36)) [£1·40], made under the Trustee Savings Bank Act 1985, s.4(3)(4)(5); provides that July 21, 1986 shall be the appointed day for the repeal of specified provisions of the Trustee Savings Banks Act 1981 and other enactments.

SEA AND SEASHORE

3028. Offshore installations

Orders made under the Oil and Gas (Enterprise) Act 1982 (c.23), s.21(1)–(3):
S.I. 1986 Nos. 27 (Shell/Esso 49/26F and 49/269—operative on January 15, 1986) [40p], 36 (Sinbad Saxon—operative on January 16, 1986) [40p]; 37 (Treasure Seeker—operative on January 16, 1986) [40p]; 38 (Sedco 707—operative on January 16, 1986) [40p]; 39 (Bideford Dolphin—operative on January 16, 1986) [40p]; 40 (Ocean Benloyal—operative on January 16, 1986) [40p]; 41 (Sovereign Explorer—operative on January 16, 1986) [40p]; 42 (Dixilyn Field 96—operative on January 16, 1986) [40p]; 43 (Kingsnorth U.K.—operative on January 17, 1986) [40p]; 44 (Sedco 703—operative on January 17, 1986) [40p]; 45 (Ocean Bounty—operative on January 17, 1986) [40p]; 46 (Glomar Moray Firth—operative on January 17, 1986) [40p]; 47 (Penrod 92—operative on January 17, 1986) [40p]; 48 (Ocean Benarmin—operative on January 17, 1986) [40p]; 106 (Sean (PP) 49/25A—operative on January 25, 1986) [40p]; 107 (Santa Fe 135—operative on January 25, 1986) [40p]; 108 (Glomar Arctic II—operative on January 25, 1986) [40p]; 130 (Dyvi Omega—operative on January 30, 1986) [40p]; 131 (Western Pacesetter IV—operative on January 30, 1986) [40p]; 132 (Charles Rowan—operative on January 31, 1986) [40p]; 157 (Glomar Biscay II—operative on February 5, 1986) [40p];

163 (Sedco/BP 711—operative on February 6, 1986) [40p]; 200 (Aladdin—operative on February 7, 1986) [40p]; 201 (Sedco 704—operative on February 7, 1986) [40p]; 202 (Interocean II—operative on February 7, 1986) [40p]; 203 (Sedco 700—operative on February 8, 1986) [40p]; 236 (Dixilyn Field 96—operative on February 14, 1986) [40p]; 353 (High Seas Driller—operative on February 28, 1986) [40p]; 354 (Galveston Key—operative on February 28, 1986) [40p]; 355 (Drillstar—operative on February 28, 1986) [40p]; 356 (Dundee Kingsnorth—operative on February 28, 1986) [40p]; 357 (Benreoch—operative on March 1, 1986) [40p]; 358 (Ocean Nomad—operative on March 1, 1986) [40p]; 433 (Sovereign Explorer—operative on March 6, 1986) [40p]; 434 (Sea Explorer—operative on March 6, 1986) [40p]; 460 (Borgsten Dolphin—operative on March 12, 1986) [40p]; 546 (Dundee Kingsnorth—operative on March 19, 1986) [40p]; 605 (Arco 49/28 Thames A—operative on March 27, 1986) [45p]; 818 (Dundee Kingsnorth—operative on May 10, 1986) [45p]; 819 (Penrod 8—operative on May 10, 1986) [45p]; 820 (Dyvi Sigma—operative on May 10, 1986) [45p]; 821 (Sedco/BP 711—operative on May 10, 1986) [45p]; 822 (M.G. Hulme Jr.—operative on May 10, 1986) [45p]; 824 (Benreoch—operative on May 10, 1986) [45p]; 825 (Glomar Arctic II—operative on May 10, 1986) [45p]; 826 (Dixilyn Field 96—operative on May 10, 1986) [45p]; 827 (Santa Fe 140—operative on May 10, 1986) [45p]; 828 (Ocean Nomad—operative on May 10, 1986) [45p]; 829 (Apollo II—operative on May 10, 1986) [45p]; 830 (Pentagone 84—operative on May 10, 1986) [45p]; 889 (Britannia—operative on May 23, 1986) [45p]; 941 (Dundee Kingsnorth—operative on June 5, 1986) [45p]; 942 (Galveston Key—operative on June 5, 1986) [45p]; 943 (Benvrackie—operative on June 5, 1986) [45p]; 1007 (High Seas Driller—operative on June 14, 1986) [45p]; 1008 (Dyvi Omega—operative on June 14, 1986) [45p]; 1012 (Alwyn North B—operative on June 14, 1986) [45p]; 1092 (Interocean II—operative on June 28, 1986) [45p]; 1131 (Ocean Kokuei—operative on July 5, 1986) [45p]; 1132 (Cecil Provine—operative on July 5, 1986) [45p]; 1193 (Sedneth 701—operative on July 12, 1986) [45p]; 1194 (Drillstar—operative on July 12, 1986) [45p]; 1195 (Galveston Key—operative on July 12, 1986) [45p]; 1196 (Sedco 714—operative on July 12, 1986) [45p]; 1197 (Benvrackie—operative on July 12, 1986) [45p]; 1198 (Aladdin—operative on July 12, 1986) [45p]; 1199 (21/10—FE—operative on July 12, 1986) [45p]; 1281 (Benreoch—operative on July 24, 1986) [45p]; 1282 (Penrod 92—operative on July 24, 1986) [45p]; 1283 (Pentagone 84—operative on July 24, 1986) [45p]; 1284 (Zepata Nordic—operative on July 24, 1986) [45p]; 1392 (Sedco/BP 711—operative on August 9, 1986) [45p]; 1393 (Dyvi Sigma—operative on August 9, 1986) [45p]; 1394 (Penrod 80—operative on August 9, 1986) [45p]; 1395 (Apollo II—operative on August 9, 1986) [45p]; 1462 (Penrod 92—operative on August 23, 1986) [45p]; 1463 (Gilbert Rowe—operative on August 23, 1986) [45p]; 1464 (Penrod 85—operative on August 23, 1986) [45p]; 1465 (Rowan Gorilla II—operative on August 23, 1986) [45p]; 1577 (Aladdin, operative on September 12, 1986) [45p]; 1578 (Sea Explorer—operative on September 12, 1986) [45p]; 1579 (Treasure Seeker—operative on September 12, 1986) [45p]; 1580 (Dyvi Omega—operative on September 12, 1986) [45p]; 1581 (Benvrackie—operative on September 12, 1986) [45p]; 1582 (Bay Driller—operative on September 12, 1986) [45p]; 1583 (High Seas Driller—operative on September 12, 1986) [45p]; 1584 (Stadrill—operative on September 12, 1986) [45p]; 1585 (Sedco 700—operative on September 12, 1986) [45p]; 1665 (Petronella Wellhead—operative on September 27 1986) [45p]; 1666 (Scapa Template—operative on September 27, 1986) [45p]; 1740 (Bay Driller—operative on October 9, 1986) [45p]; 1741 (Dyvi Omega—operative on October 9, 1986) [45p]; 1742 (Drillstar—operative on October 9, 1986) [45p]; 1743 (Penrod 92—operative on October 9, 1986) [45p]; 1744 (Glomar Moray Firth I—operative on October 9, 1986) [45p]; 1745 (Benreoch—operative on October 9, 1986) [45p]; 1746 (Neddrill Trigon—operative on October 9, 1986) [45p]; 1839 (Dyvi Sigma—operative on October 31, 1986) [45p]; 1840 (Treasure Seeker—operative on October 31, 1986) [45p]; 1841 (Pentagone 84—operative on October 31, 1986) [45p]; 1842 (Penrod 92—operative on October 31, 1986) [45p]; 1843 (Ocean Benarmin—operative on October 31, 1986) [45p]; 1844 (Sedco 700—operative on October 31, 1986) [45p]; 1845 (M.G. Hulme Jr—operative on October 31, 1986) [45p]; 2051 (Benreoch—operative on November 29, 1986) [45p]; 2052 (Penrod 80—operative on November 29, 1986) [45p], 2053 (Kingsnorth U.K.—operative on November 29, 1986) [45p]; 2055 (High Seas Driller—operative on November 29, 1986) [45p]; 2056 (Morecambe Flame—operative on November 29, 1986) [45p]; 2057 (Ocean Nomad—operative on November 29, 1986) [45p]; 2058 (Safe Supporter—operative on November 29, 1986) [45p]; 2059 (Trident X—operative on November 29, 1986) [45p]; 2272 (Treasure Seeker—operative on December

20, 1986) [45p]; 2273 (Western Apollo I—operative on December 20, 1986) [45p]; 2274 (Sedco/BP 711—operative on December 20, 1986) [45p].

3029. Offshore installations—revocation

Orders made under the Oil and Gas (Enterprise) Act 1982 (c.23), s.21(1): S.I. 1986 Nos. 28 (S.I. 1985 No. 1648—Treasure Seeker—operative on January 15, 1986) [40p]; 29 (S.I. 1985 No. 946—Glomar Moray Firth—operative on January 15, 1986) [40p]; 30 (S.I. 1985 No. 1649—Dixilyn Field 96—operative on January 15, 1986) [40p]; 31 (S.I. 1985 No. 1512—Ocean Benloyal—operative on January 15, 1986) [40p]; 32 (S.I. 1985 No. 1435—Sinbad Saxon—operative on January 15, 1986) [40p]; 33 (S.I. 1985 No. 1226—Ocean Bounty—operative on January 15, 1986) [40p]; 34 (S.I. 1985 No. 1062—Bideford Dolphin—operative on January 15, 1986) [40p]; 35 (S.I. 1985 No. 1769—Sovereign Explorer—operative on January 15, 1986) [40p]; 49 (S.I. 1985 No. 1496—Glomar Arctic II—operative on January 17, 1986) [40p]; 50 (S.I. 1985 No. 1824—Benvrackie—operative on January 17, 1986) [40p]; 51 (S.I. 1985 No. 1768—Glomar Biscay II—operative on January 17, 1986) [40p]; 89 (S.I. 1985 No. 1720—KCA Sandpiper—operative on January 23, 1986) [40p]; 90 (S.I. 1985 No. 1497—Western Pacesetter IV—operative on January 23, 1986) [40p]; 91 (S.I. 1985 No. 1770—Dundee Kingsnorth—operative on January 23, 1986) [40p]; 92 (S.I. 1985 No. 928—Sea Explorer—operative on January 23, 1986) [40p]; 93 (S.I. 1985 No. 1868—Dyvi Omega—operative on January 23, 1986) [40p]; 109 (S.I. 1985 No. 1692—Aladdin—operative on January 25, 1986) [40p]; 117 (S.I. 1985 No. 793—Kingsnorth U.K.—operative on January 29, 1986) [40p]; 118 (S.I. 1985 No. 1433—Glomar Arctic I—operative on January 29, 1986) [40p]; 133 (S.I. 1985 No. 1431—Drillstar—operative on January 30, 1986) [40p]; 134 (S.I. 1985 No. 394—Charles Rowan—operative on January 30, 1986) [40p]; 164 (S.I. 1985 No. 1894—Interocean II—operative on February 6, 1986) [40p]; 165 (S.I. 1985 No. 1511—Sedco 700—operative on February 6, 1986) [40p]; 166 (S.I. 1985 No. 1895—Sedco 704—operative on February 6, 1986) [40p]; 204 (S.I. 1986 No. 42—Dixilyn Field 96—operative on February 8, 1986) [40p]; 205 (S.I. 1986 No. 40—Ocean Benloyal—operative on February 8, 1986) [40p]; 206 (S.I. 1985 No. 1950—M.G. Hulme Jr.—operative on February 8, 1986) [40p]; 215 (S.I. 1985 No. 1437—Cecil Provine—operative on February 12, 1986) [40p]; 359 (S.I. 1986 No. 131—Western Pacesetter IV—operative on February 28, 1986) [40p]; 360 (S.I. 1986 No. 41—Sovereign Explorer—operative on February 28, 1986) [40p]; 361 (S.I. 1985 No. 1510—Benreoch—operative on February 28, 1986) [40p]; 362 (S.I. 1985 No. 1949—Ocean Nomad—operative on February 28, 1986) [40p]; 363 (S.I. 1986 No. 47—Penrod 92—operative on March 1, 1986) [40p]; 461 (S.I. 1986 No. 157—Glomar Biscay II—operative on March 12, 1986) [40p]; 462 (S.I. 1986 No. 36—Sinbad Saxon—operative on March 12, 1986) [40p]; 548 (S.I. 1986 No. 44—Sedco 703—operative on March 15, 1986) [40p]; 549 (S.I. 1986 No. 356—Dundee Kingsnorth—operative on March 15, 1986) [40p]; 550 (S.I. 1984 No. 1268—Apollo I—operative on March 15, 1986) [40p]; 552 (S.I. 1986 No. 201—Sedco 704—operative on March 15, 1986) [40p]; 606 (S.I. 1985 No. 1523—Bideford Dolphin—operative on March 27, 1986) [45p]; 815 (S.I. 1984 No. 1045—Transocean 6, S.I. 1985 No. 764—Dyvi Sigman, S.I. 1985 No. 790—Arch Rowan, S.I. 1985 No. 1464—Dixilyn Field 97, S.I. 1985 No. 1771—Glomar Arctic III, S.I. 1985 No. 1810—Pentagone 84, S.I. 1985 No. 1972—Penrod 80, S.I. 1985 No. 1973—Glomar Main Pass 1, S.I. 1986 No. 38—Sedco 707, S.I. 1986 No. 39—Bideford Dolphin, S.I. 1986 No. 43—Kingsnorth U.K., S.I. 1986 No. 48—Ocean Bounty, S.I. 1986 No. 48—Ocean Beramin, S.I. 1986 No. 107—Santa Fe 135, S.I. 1986 No. 108—Glomar Arctic III, S.I. 1986 No. 130—Dyvi Omega, S.I. 1986 No. 163—Sedco/BP 711, S.I. 1986 No. 202—Interocean II, S.I. 1986 No. 236—Dixilyn Field 96, S.I. 1986 No. 357—Benreoch, S.I. 1986 No. 358—Ocean Nomad, S.I. 1986 No. 433—Sovereign Explores, S.I. 1986 No. 460—Borgsten Dolphin, S.I. 1986 No. 546—Dundee Kingsnorth—operative on May 8, 1986) [80p]; 816 (S.I. 1985 No. 108—Drillstarr, S.I. 1985 No. 970—Sedco 714, S.I. 1985 No. 1693—Sedco 714, S.I. 1985 No. 691—Trident X, S.I. 1985 No. 1752—Trident X, S.I. 1985 No. 692—Treasure Swan, S.I. 1985 No. 899—Treasure Swan, S.I. 1985 No. 969—Treasure Swan, S.I. 1985 No. 1867—Treasure Swan—operative on May 9, 1986) [45p]; 865 (S.I. 1985 No. 1948—Stadril, S.I. 1985 No. 1811—Ocean Liberator, S.I. 1986 No. 200—Aladdin—operative on May 18, 1986) [45p]; 915 (S.I. 1986 No. 354—Galveston Key, S.I. 1986 No. 353—High Seas Driller, S.I. 1986 No. 823—Dyvi Omega, S.I. 1986 No. 818—Dundee Kingsnorth—operative on May 31, 1986) [45p].

S.I. 1986 Nos. 1101 (S.I. 1986 No. 824—Benreoch, S.I. 1986 No. 825—Glomar Artic II, S.I. 1986 No. 826—Dixilyn Field 96, S.I. 1986 No. 941—Dundee Kingsnorth—operative on July 2, 1986) [45p]; 1130 (S.I. 1986 No. 46—Glomar Moray Firth, S.I. 1986 No. 355—Drillstar, S.I. 1986 No. 828—Ocean Nomad, S.I. 1986 No. 942—Galveston Key, S.I. 1986 No. 943—Benvrackie, S.I. 1986 No. 1007—High Seas Driller—operative on July 5, 1986) [45p]; 1200 (S.I. 1985 No. 1524—South East Forties Template, S.I. 1986 No. 203—Sedco 700—operative on July 12, 1986) [45p]; 1396 (S.I. 1986 No. 822—M.G. Hulme Jr., S.I. 1986 No. 1131—Ocean Kokuei; S.I. 1986 No. 1281—Benreoch—operative on August 9, 1986) [45p]; 1466 (S.I. 1986 No. 1092—Interocean II—operative on August 23, 1986) [45]; 1586 (S.I. 1986 No. 1196—Sedco 714—operative on September 12, 1986) [45p]; 1667 (S.I. 1986 No. 1581—Benvrackie, S.I. 1986 No. 827—Sante Fe 140—operative on September 27, 1986) [45p]; 1747 (S.I. 1986 No. 1583—High Seas Driller; S.I. 1986 No. 1585—Sedco 700—operative on October 9, 1986) [45p]; 1838 (S.I. 1986 No. 1463—Gilbert Rowe—operative on October 31, 1986) [45p]; 2050 (S.I. 1986 Nos. 1577—Aladdin, 1395—Apollo II, 132—Charles Rowan, 1742—Drillstar, 1195—Galveston Key, 1845—M. G. Hulme Jr, 1843—Ocean Benarmin, 1284—Zapata Nordic—operative on November 29, 1986) [45p]; 2271 (S.I. 1986 No. 1744—Glomar Moray Firth I—operative on December 20, 1986) [45p].

SETTLEMENTS AND TRUSTS

3030. Bank depositing trust money with itself as trustee—winding up—whether beneficiaries have priority over unsecured creditors. See SPACE INVESTMENTS *v.* CANADIAN IMPERIAL BANK OF COMMERCE TRUST CO. (BAHAMAS), § 285.

3031. Construction—class gift—issue—whether gift void for perpetuity
On the true construction of a settlement, the word "issue" meant issue through all degrees, not children; there was a possibility of the issue limitation taking effect outside the perpetuity period, and it was accordingly void for remoteness.

Under a settlement made in 1924 the settlor created trust funds in favour of his daughter. By clause (3)(c); "in case there shall be no such child who shall live to take a vested interest in such share upon trust to pay transfer and divide such share equally amongst such of the daughters who shall then be living and the issue of any of them who may be then dead such issue taking their parents share only on attaining the age of 21 years or marrying under such age."

The settlor had three daughters. They all attained 21, married and survived the testator, who died in 1963, but only the second daughter had children. The third daughter died in 1984. The trustees applied for the determination of the question whether the word "issue" referred to in clause (3)(c) was to be construed as issue and not as children, and if so whether the limitation in the clause was void for perpetuity. *Held*, that the word "issue" meant issue through all degrees not children, and that the issue intended to take on a daughter dying without leaving a child were any issue living at the death of a daughter; but issue intended to take on the failure of a child to attain 21 were those alive at the death of the child, and it followed, having regard to the possibilities as they existed before 1924, that since there might be issue born after the death of the daughter, but who were included in the issue class, which closed on the death of the child, that they would not necessarily take a vested interest within 2 years of the daughter's death. Therefore there was the possibility of the issue limitation taking effect outside the perpetuity period and accordingly it was void for remoteness; and there was a resulting trust in favour of the settlor's estate (*Re Cockle's Will Trusts* [1967] C.L.Y. 4074 and *Re Deeley's Settlement* [1974] C.L.Y. 3487 applied).

DRUMMOND, *Re*: FOSTER *v.* FOSTER [1986] 1 W.L.R. 1096, Mervyn Davies J.

3032. Constructive trust—misappropriation of funds from solicitor's client account—liability of bank as constructive trustee. See LIPKIN GORMAN *v.* KARPNALE AND LLOYDS BANK, § 170.

3033. Constructive trust—trust fund for benefit of family of murderer—conditional upon co-operation of murderer—payment of murderer's legal fees and debts out of trust fund—whether unjust enrichment
[Can.] The parents of children murdered by O, brought an action to set aside the payment of $100,000 by the Royal Canadian Mounted Police pursuant to a trust agreement, signed by O's solicitor, M, as trustee. O was involved in negotiating the

agreement, which stipulated that the money was payable on condition that O provide information as to the location of the murdered children and that the money was solely for the benefit of O's wife and child and not for the benefit of O. It was also agreed that O's solicitor's bill and other family debts should be paid out of the trust funds. *Held,* that the money paid to M was impressed with a constructive trust for the benefit of the plaintiffs. O had received the benefit as the money was used to pay his outstanding debts and had been permitted to benefit unjustly from his crimes. The plaintiffs had suffered a corresponding deprivation. It was not possible to sever the interest of O's wife and child and to deal only with the portion of the fund which benefited O, because the interests of those other parties arose from the killings. Accordingly, the defendants were accountable for the entire sum and the plaintiffs had a right in equity to claim the money: ROSENFELDT *v.* OLSON [1985] 2 W.W.R. 502, British Columbia Supreme Ct.

3034. Constructive trust—unmarried couple—property in man's name—woman's indirect contributions to household—whether beneficial interest

Indirect contributions to the purchase price of a house by substantial contributions towards the housekeeping and to the bringing up of children are sufficient to create a beneficial interest in favour of the woman where the property is in the name of the man and a common intention that she should have such an interest exists.

P and D commenced a casual relationship in 1967. In July 1969 P gave birth to a child of which D was the father. They decided to live together and in December 1969 a house was purchased. The house was conveyed into the names of D and his brother. D told P her name was not going onto the title because it would prejudice pending matrimonial proceedings between P and her husband. £1,043 of the purchase price of £5,490 was paid in cash by D. The remainder was raised by means of two mortgages. The mortgage repayments were made by D. After they moved into the house P paid D £6 per week. A second child was born on 13 July 1971. In addition there were two children from P's earlier marriage. From 1972 to 1980 when the relationship broke up P earned similar sums to D out of which she made very substantial contributions to the housekeeping and to the feeding and bringing up of the children. In September 1975 a sum of £1,037 was paid into a building society account in their joint names. The sum represented the balance of insurance moneys paid out for repairs to the house after a fire. P claimed a beneficial interest in the house. The trial judge rejected her claim. *Held,* allowing P's appeal, that the court would find a constructive trust giving P a beneficial interest if P was able to establish a common intention between her and D and acted on by her that she should have a beneficial interest in the property. In acting to her detriment the conduct required of P was conduct that she could not reasonably be expected to embark upon unless she was to have an interest in the house. In the present case the common intention of the parties that P was to have a beneficial interest in the house was established by the excuse given by D to P for not putting her name on the title of the house; such an excuse could only have been necessary if it was intended that P should have an interest in the house. It could properly be inferred that P made substantial contributions to the mortgage payments by her contributions towards the housekeeping given that the parties had barely sufficient money when they were both earning similar sums of money. P could not reasonably have been expected to give D such substantial assistance in making the mortgage payments unless she was to have an interest in the house. Accordingly P acted to her detriment on the faith of the common intention of the parties that she should have an interest in the house. P was entitled to a half interest in the house. Mustill L.J. set out a summary of the relevant propositions of law to be applied in such cases (*Pettitt* v. *Pettitt* [1969] C.L.Y. 1639, *Gissing* v. *Gissing* [1970] C.L.Y. 1243, *Eves* v. *Eves* [1975] C.L.Y. 3110 considered). GRANT *v.* EDWARDS [1986] 2 All E.R. 426, C.A.

3035. Discretionary trust—appointment of capital—whether income. See STEVENSON (INSPECTOR OF TAXES) *v.* WISHART, § 1733.

3036. Funding from rates—unexpended balance—validity. See R. *v.* DISTRICT AUDITOR NO. 3 AUDIT DISTRICT OF WEST YORKSHIRE METROPOLITAN COUNTY COUNCIL, *ex p.* WEST YORKSHIRE METROPOLITAN COUNTY COUNCIL, § 2804.

3037. Joint tenancy—severance—trust for sale—beneficial interests

Where a conveyance into joint names contains an express declaration that the parties are to hold the proceeds of sale on trust for themselves as joint tenants, then on severance a tenancy in common in equal shares is created, and the declaration is conclusive of the position.

In 1960 P and her husband purchased a house which was conveyed into the sole name of the husband, although it was agreed between them that P was entitled to a half share in the beneficial interest in the property. In 1971 P left the husband and later began living in the property with D. In 1978 the husband, in consideration of the cost of his share, conveyed the freehold to P and D as beneficial joint tenants on trust for sale "to hold the net proceeds of sale . . . UPON TRUST for themselves as joint tenants." In 1983 P severed the joint tenancy and issued a summons for the determination of their respective beneficial interests, contending that she was entitled to three-quarters of the beneficial interest on the basis that she already owned one-half and it was intended that the joint tenancy should only extend to the half share she received from the husband. The registrar held that they held as tenants in common in equal shares, and the judge, on appeal by the plaintiff, upheld this decision. P further appealed to the Court of Appeal. *Held,* dismissing the appeal, that where a conveyance into joint names contained an express declaration of trust that the parties were to hold the proceeds of sale of the property on trust for themselves as joint tenants, then on severance of the tenancy, a tenancy in common in equal shares was created. Furthermore, the doctrine of resulting implied or constructive trusts could not be invoked where there was an express declaration which comprehensively declared what were the beneficial interests in the property or its proceeds of sale since such a declaration was exhaustive and conclusive of the position unless and until the conveyance was set aside or rectified. D was therefore entitled to a half share of the beneficial interest in the property (*Wilson* v. *Wilson* [1963] C.L.Y. 1690, dicta of Lord Upjohn in *Pettitt* v. *Pettitt* [1969] C.L.Y. 1639, [1969] 2 All E.R. at 405; of Lord Diplock in *Gissing* v. *Gissing* [1970] C.L.Y. 1243, [1970] 2 All E.R. at 789; *Leake (formerly Bruzzi)* v. *Bruzzi* [1974] C.L.Y. 1778 and *Pink* v. *Lawrence* [1978] C.L.Y. 1785 followed. Dictum of Lord Denning M.R. in *Bedson* v. *Bedson* [1965] C.L.Y. 1858; [1965] 3 All E.R. at 314 disapproved).

GOODMAN *v.* GALLANT [1986] 1 All E.R. 311, C.A.

3038. Tracing trust funds—clearly identifiable—whether right to trace. See MAGENTA FINANCE AND TRADING CO. *v.* SAVINGS AND INVESTMENT BANK, § 167.

3039. Trustee investments

TRUSTEE INVESTMENTS (ADDITIONAL POWERS) ORDER 1986 (No. 601) [45p], made under the Trustee Investments Act 1961 (c.62), s.12; operative on April 29, 1986; adds ILEA and residuary bodies established under the Local Government Act 1985, s.57 to the list of authorities in Sched. 1, Pt. II, para. 9 to the 1961 Act.

3040. Trustees—removal—facts in dispute—court's jurisdiction

[Can.] P was a party to a joint venture agreement, AM being the trustee of the joint venturers. A dispute arose between the parties and P sought an order to remove AM as trustee and to appoint a new trustee on the basis of alleged mismanagement and partiality. Contradictory evidence was brought before the court. *Held,* that the court's jurisdiction to remove trustees is delicate and should not be undertaken in summary proceedings if the facts are in dispute. The court's statutory discretion to replace a trustee should only be exercised if the trustee is willing or if there is no dispute about the facts rendering his removal necessary (*Combs, Re,* (1884) 51 L.T. 45 and *Henderson, Re* [1940] Ch. 764 applied): POPOFF *v.* ACTUS MANAGEMENT [1985] 5 W.W.R. 660, Saskatchewan Q.B.

3041. Variation of trusts—class with remote contingent interests—whether persons who "may become entitled"

[Variation of Trusts Act 1958 (c.53), s.1(1)(b).]

On the true construction of s.1(1)(b) of the Variation of Trusts Act 1958 persons who have an actual, though contingent and very remote, interest under a trust are not persons who "may become entitled" to an interest.

Under a settlement dated 1937, the settlor's daughter, then aged four, was to receive the income for life at 21, on her death her share to be held for any appointees under her will, and in default to accrue to the share of the settlor's son. In the event of their failure or determination, the trustees were to pay the income to the settlor's wife for life or until remarriage, and thereafter to hold the capital and income for such of the settlor's four sisters as were living at the time of failure or determination and their issue then living and attaining the age of 21 *per stirpes.* The

settlor's daughter was now married with three children of full age. His wife and four sisters had died. The settlor's son and daughter sought to vary the trust. None of the numerous issue of the sisters was made a party since it was not practicable to obtain their approval. *Held*, that the sisters' issue had an actual, though contingent and very remote, interest under the trust, and were not persons who "duly become entitled" under s.1(1)(*b*) of the Variation of Trusts Act 1958. Accordingly, the court had no jurisdiction to approve the arrangement on their behalf. (*Suffert's Settlement, Re* [1960] C.L.Y. 2923 applied.)
KNOCKER *v.* YOULE [1986] 1 W.L.R. 934, Warner J.

SHIPPING AND MARINE INSURANCE

3042. Admiralty practice—arrest after judgment—whether permissible
[Sing.] *Held*, by the Singapore High Court, that a plaintiff in an action in rem could arrest a vessel after having obtained judgment in the action. Although the cause of action merged in the judgment, the right to security in the ship was not lost: *Aletta, The* [1974] 1 Lloyd's Rep. not followed: THE DAIEN MARU No. 18 [1986] 1 Lloyd's Rep. 387, Thean J., Singapore High Court.

3043. Admiralty practice—arrest—classification survey whilst under arrest—whether part of Admiralty Marshal's expenses
The vessel "H.G." was appraised and sold by the Admiralty Marshal after an action had been commenced against her by P, her mortgagees. Whilst under arrest, a classification society inspected and surveyed the vessel. The Admiralty Marshal ordered that the expenses of the survey be paid from the proceeds of sale of "H.G." P contended that such sums should not be paid out of the fund. *Held*, that the practice adopted by the Marshal was sensible, as it enabled the ship to be sold in class, and the classification fees could be paid out of the fund: HONSHU GLORIA, THE [1986] 2 Lloyd's Rep. 63, Sheen J.

3044. Admiralty practice—costs—taxation—practice direction. See PRACTICE DIRECTION (SUP. CT. TAXING OFFICE) (ADMIRALTY: COSTS), § 2713.

3045. Admiralty practice—exclusive jurisdiction clause stay of action
By an action in rem, P, cargo owners, sued D, shipowners, under a bill of lading issued in Cuba for short delivery and damage to a cargo of Cuban sugar carried on board D's vessel and delivered in Japan. The Bill of lading was governed by the Hague Rules and contained an exclusive jurisdiction clause in favour of Cuba. In the absence of agreement, P's claim would be time barred in Cuba. *Held*, that (1) the contract of carriage was clearly governed by Cuban law, but the validity of the jurisdiction clause would be determined by applying English law; (2) D had not shown that there was a dispute about their liability for all but a very small part of the claim; (3) in exercising its discretion whether or not to grant a stay, the Court should take into account all the relevant circumstances. On the facts it appeared that D did not genuinely seek trial in any country but were merely delaying; (4) P had shown strong grounds why a stay should not be granted, despite the Cuban jurisdiction clause. D's application for a stay was dismissed: THE FRANK PAIS [1986] 1 Lloyd's Rep. 529, Sheen J.

3046. Admiralty practice—sale of ship pendente lite—whether port authority preserved right to claim pre-arrest charges
The vessel F was arrested pursuant to certain claims brought by pilots. P, a harbour authority, sought an order that the vessel be moved from the drydock in which she was arrested, on the grounds that the vessel prevented them from using the dock for other ships. The vessel was in the event sold pendente lite. Certain other caveators contended that as the order for sale only preserved P's right to detain the vessel for pre-arrest charges and as they had allowed it to be sold, they had lost such a right. *Held*, that (1) P had consented to an order that the vessel be sold on the clear understanding that they would not be financially prejudiced; (2) therefore, P's right to pre-arrest charges pursuant to s.39 of the Port of London Act 1968 was preserved: THE FREIGHTLINE ONE [1986] 1 Lloyd's Rep. 266, Sheen J.

3047. Admiralty practice—salvage—non-tidal waters—award
The admiralty jurisdiction is exercised worldwide, and most of those courts recognised that there were no grounds for excluding from salvage services assistance rendered to a vessel in danger in non-tidal waters.

The *Goring*, a small passenger vessel, was seen by one of the plaintiffs to drift down a non-tidal stretch of the river Thames towards Reading bridge. The plaintiffs' claim was that the vessel was running into danger herself and to other craft. The plaintiffs managed to get a line aboard her and haul her to a vacant mooring. They issued a writ *in rem* against the *Goring* endorsed with a claim for salvage services. The owners applied to have the writ set aside on the ground that the action could not succeed as services rendered to a vessel in danger in non-tidal waters could not be salvage services in respect of which an award could be payable. *Held*, dismissing the application, that the jurisdiction exercised by the Admiralty court and by admiralty courts in other countries was worldwide, and most of these courts recognised that assistance rendered to ships at sea, in harbours, and in inland navigable waters could be salvage services. There were no grounds for excluding from salvage services assistance rendered to a vessel in danger in non-tidal waters, and so the defendants had shown no cause for setting aside the writ.
GORING, THE [1986] 2 W.L.R. 219, Sheen J.

3048. Admiralty practice—security for costs—refusal to grant—exercise of discretion
T made certain claims against the vessel G. She was appraised and sold after an arrest by T. G brought a separate action against the vessel's proceeds. G got judgment in default in their action although T were not informed of G's application. The judgment was set aside. Both T and G made applications against each other for security for costs. The judge refused these applications. *Held*, dismissing G's appeal, that the judge had properly exercised his discretion in refusing security for costs and that the Court of Appeal would not interfere with that exercise: THE GULF VENTURE [1986] 2 Lloyd's Rep. 129, C.A.

3049. Admiralty practice—writ—validity—costs of discharging cargo
[R.S.C., Ord. 6, r.8.] On December 21, 1976, the M was arrested at Sunderland, and was shortly thereafter ordered to be appraised and sold *pendente lite*. In May 1977, the Admiralty Marshal discharged the cargo, discharging costs exceeding £160,000. The Court ordered that the P mortgagees were to finance the costs of cargo discharge in the first instance, but that cargo was only to be released to cargo-owners on terms. The cargo was ultimately released on guarantees being furnished to the Admiralty Marshal. P claimed contributions for discharging costs from the D cargo-owners, and issued their writ on November 4, 1982. The writ was received on October 17, 1983. In 1984, the Court held that the costs of discharge should be borne by cargo-owners, and on October 19, 1984, the validity of the writ was extended for the purposes of service. D cargo-owners applied to set aside the writ. *Held*, dismissing the appeal from the Admiralty Registrar; that (1) the court was entitled to balance the hardship to the respective parties when exercising its discretion under R.S.C., Ord. 12, r.8. On the facts, the balance of justice clearly lay with P; (2) D were aware of the possibility of a claim since 1979, and none of D alleged they were prejudiced by the delay: MYRTO, THE (No. 3) [1985] 2 Lloyds Rep. 67, Sheen J.

3050. Arrest—release—injunction. See LOCOBAIL INTERNATIONAL FINANCE *v.* AGROEXPORT; SEA HAWK, THE, § 2651.

3051. Assessment of damages—currency. See LASH ATLANTICO, THE, § 971.

3052. "Bailee" clause—sue and labour costs—whether recoverable from underwriters
A insured R's consignment of plywood for a voyage from Singapore to Esbjerg. Some of the goods were short loaded or delivered damaged. R claimed against A but A denied liability. R then commenced proceedings against the carrier to preserve the timebar. R obtained judgment against A under the policy, but contended that they were entitled to claim the costs of suing the carrier under the "bailee" clause in the insurance policy. This provided that it was the duty of the assured "to ensure that all rights against carriers, bailees . . . are properly preserved. *Held*, dismissing A's appeal, that R was entitled to these expenses, as in order to give business efficacy to the contract, it was necessary to imply a term to the effect that expenses incurred by R in performing his obligation in circumstances where A was liable to him, were recoverable: NETHERLANDS INSURANCE CO. EST. 1845 *v.* LJUNGBERG KARL & CO. A.B. [1986] 2 Lloyd's Rep. 19, H.L.

3053. Beacons
GENERAL LIGHTHOUSE AUTHORITIES (BEACONS: HYPERBOLIC SYSTEMS) ORDER 1986 (No. 2285) [45p], made under the Merchant Shipping Act 1979 (c.39), s.34(3);

operative on January 11, 1987; provide for a reference to a beacon in the Merchant Shipping Act 1894, Pt. XI, to include certain Navigator transmitter chains in the British Isles operated by Racal-Decca Marine Navigation Ltd.

3054. Bill of lading—cargo claim—Italian law—liability of ship

Under an Italian law bill of lading P's cargo was carried on board D's vessel. Some of the cargo was damaged on discharge. *Held*, that (1) the goods were damaged as a result of faulty stowage and negligent discharge; (2) applying Italian law, that the exclusion clauses in the bill of lading did not exonerate D, who could not therefore rely upon the negligence of stevedores: THE SAUDI PRINCE (No. 2) [1986] 1 Lloyd's Rep. 347, Bingham J.

3055. Bill of lading—fraudulently misdated—reliance

P purchased 4500MT of rice extract from T on c.i.f. terms. It was a term of that contract that the bills of lading would be dated June 20—July 15. D were owners of the vessel which was to carry the goods. All bills issued by their agents were dated July 15 although in fact the cargo was not all loaded until July 26. The cargo was late arriving in Europe and P had to buy in in order to meet its commitments. P claimed damages for fraudulent misrepresentation, saying that they would have rejected the bills had they been correctly dated. *Held*, that D had fraudulently misrepresented the date of shipment and that P was induced to accept the bills in consequence thereof: THE SAUDI CROWN [1986] 1 Lloyd's Rep. 261, Sheen J.

3055a. Bill of lading—"Himalaya clause"—goods damaged prior to loading—whether terminal operator liable

P bought a consignment of motorcycles ex warehouse. S acted as P's agents in arranging transportation of the motorcycles to Canada. D operated a dock in Liverpool. They provided container services. S had always transported goods on ships owned by M and on all such occasions bills of lading containing "Himalaya" clause had been issued. Whilst awaiting the arrival of the vessel the consignment was damaged by the negligence of D. No bill of lading was ever issued, although D claimed the benefit of the "Himalaya" clause. *Held*, that (1) no act had been performed by D that was referable to the services provided for in any bill of lading that might be issued. Before such act the offer in the bill of lading had not been accepted; (2) as there was no concluded contract between P and D, no exclusion clause existed; (3) further the negligence was wholly collateral to the operation of loading and shipping the motorcycles: BURKE (RAYMOND) MOTORS *v.* THE MERSEY DOCKS AND HARBOUR CO. [1986] 1 Lloyd's Rep. 155, Leggatt J.

3056. Bill of lading—holders and endorsees—wrongful delivery to another

The holders and endorsees for value of bills of lading were entitled to the delivery of the shipped goods. If those goods were wrongfully delivered to another, the holders of the bills were entitled to damages, the measure of which was the market value of the goods at the time and place when possession should have been given (*Swire* v. *Leach* [1865] C.B. (N.S.) 479, *The Winkfield* [1902] P. 42, *London Joint Stock Bank* v. *British Amsterdam Maritime Agency* [1910] 16 Com.Cas. 102 considered): CHABBRA CORP. *v.* OWNERS OF JAG SHAKTI, (1986) 83 L.S.Gaz. 45, P.C.

3057. Bond put up by insurers of P and I club—effect of bond

Cargo-owners arrested a ship after the cargo was found to be damaged. The ship owners needed its release as quickly as possible. An insurance company gave a guarantee irrevocably to pay the cargo-owners any sum that may be due, on behalf of the P and I club with which the ship owners had entered the ship. *Held*, that the guarantee was a proper guarantee, not the payment of insurance, and consequently the insurance company were entitled to be reimbursed by the ship owners for the payment in fact made to the cargo-owners (*Owen* v. *Tate* [1975] C.L.Y. 1531, ZUHAL K, THE, *Financial Times*, November 11, 1986, Sheen J.

3058. British Shipbuilders (Borrowing Powers) Act 1986 (c.19). See TRADE AND INDUSTRY, § 3391.

3059. Carriage by sea. See CARRIERS.

3060. Carriage by sea—bill of lading subject to U.S. Carriage of Goods by Sea Act 1936—transhipment at Hong Kong—whether Hague-Visby rules applicable—package limitation

[H.K.] Two boilers were shipped from the U.S.A. pursuant to a through bill of lading which conferred a right on the carrier to tranship the cargo. D shipped the boilers from Baltimore to Hong Kong and arranged for them to be transhipped from Hong Kong to Shanghai. The boilers were damaged. P claimed for the full loss suffered by him. D relied upon the incorporation of the U.S.A. Carriage of Goods by Sea Act into the Bill of Lading and the package limitation therein. P contended that by reason of the transhipment in Hong Kong the final leg of the carriage was subject to the Hague-Visby rules as enacted in Hong Kong. *Held,* that (1) the U.S. Act applied to the whole of the carriage in that there was no reference to Hong Kong in the bill of lading. In transhipping there D was simply exercising a right under that bill of lading; (2) "shipment" under the Hague-Visby rules did not embrace transhipment. D was therefore entitled to limit his liability: ANDERS MAERSK, THE [1986] 1 Lloyd's Rep. 483, Supreme Ct. of Hong Kong, Mayo J.

3061. Carriage by sea—limitation of time—amendment of writ
This action concerned a cargo claim brought under three bills of lading. P, the cargo owners, did not specifically plead their causes of action under two bills in the writ, although the fact that the claim arose out of the carriage in D's vessel, was pleaded. D took no objection to the way in which the claim had been formulated in the writ until the trial, but then contended that, under the Hague Rules, P's claim was time barred. *Held,* that (1) P's claim was not time barred. The amendment made by P to correct the deficiency related back to the issuance of the writ: in any event D had acquiesced in the amendment: EMPRESA CUBANA IMPORTADORA DE ALIMENTOS *v.* OCTAVIA SHIPPING CO. S.A.; THE KEFALONIA WIND [1986] 1 Lloyd's Rep. 273, Bingham J.

3062. Carriage by sea—short landing—cargo claim—title to sue
P1 agreed to sell sugar to P2 c. & f. Apapa. P1 was described as the shipper and P2 the notify party on the bills of lading. Cargo was damaged on discharge and P1, P2 and P3 sued D, the vessel. D disputed the title of the plaintiffs to sue. *Held,* that on the facts and evidence P2 had proved title to sue: CZARNIKOW *v.* PARTENREEDEREI: MS JUNO: THE JUNO [1986] 1 Lloyd's Rep. 190, Leggatt J.

3063. Charterparty—cancellation—whether O could have loaded within laycan—burden of proof
O let their vessel to C for the carriage of cargo. The vessel looked to C as though she would miss the cancelling date so C cancelled the charter and fixed an alternative date. The dispute was referred to arbitration. O claimed dead freight and C contended that the vessel could not have commenced loading before the cancelling date. The arbitrators held that the burden of proof was on C. *Held,* allowing C's appeal, that the burden of proof was in fact on O and O had failed to discharge it: FERCOMETAL S.A.R.L. *v.* MSC MEDITERRANEAN SHIPPING Co. S.A. THE SIMONA [1986] 1 Lloyd's Rep. 171, Leggatt J.

3064. Charterparty—dispute—arbitration—whether binding settlement agreement—action on settlement
O chartered their vessel to C. Various disputes broke out between them and negotiations ensued between C and O's P & I Club. The club sent a letter to O's solicitors and the arbitrators stating "the responsibility for the cargo claim rests with our members" and inviting the arbitrators to close their file. The Club then sought to take various points on quantum. C commenced an action contending that there had been a binding admission of liability: *Held,* that on the facts and the evidence there was a binding admission of liability that amounted to a settlement agreement: NAVIERA MULTINACIONAL DEL CARIBE S.A. *v.* SPARTI COMPANIA NAVIERA S.A.; THE TRANSWORLD SAILOR [1986] 1 Lloyd's Rep. 151, Steyn J.

3065. Charterparty—indemnity—whether implied term
The Court will not construe a Gencon form charterparty as containing an implied term that the charterers must indemnify the shipowners for liabilities incurred to a third party under the bills of lading.
A vessel was chartered pursuant to a Gencon form charterparty. The cargo was spoiled. By cl. 2 as between shipowners and charterers, the owners were not liable for loss of or damage to cargo except for personal want of due diligence or default. However, the bill of lading clause made the shipowners liable under the Hague rules to third parties to whom the bills of lading were negotiated. The cargo owners were holders of the bills of lading, which contained the clause paramount, claimed damages from the owners. The charterers refused to take part in the proceedings.

The owners settled the claims, then claimed indemnity from the charterers. *Held,* there was no implied term in the charterparty that the charterers would indemnify the owners even though the act of the charterers of negotiating the bills of lading had exposed the owners to liability (*Krüger & Co.* v. *Moel Tryvan Ship Co.* [1907] A.C. 272 distinguished; *Dawson Line* v. *A.G. Adler für Chemische Industrie of Berlin* [1931] All E.R.Rep. 546, dictum of Buller J. in *Duffield* v. *Scott* [1775–1802] All E.R.Rep. at 623, *Smith* v. *Compton* (1832) 3 B & Hd. 407, *Jones* v. *Williams* (1841) 7 M. & W. 493 and *Parker* v. *Lewis* (1873) L.R. 8 Ch.App. 1035 considered.)

BEN SHIPPING CO. (PTE) v. AN BORD BAINNE; C JOYCE, THE [1986] 2 All E.R. 177, Bingham J.

3066. Charterparty—laytime—strike clause—strike period within laytime period—demurrage
O let their vessel to C for a voyage charter. The charter contained a general strike clause. When the vessel arrived there was a strike at Piraeus that was over before expiry of laytime. C contended that the period of the strike should be excluded from laytime. *Held,* an appeal from an arbitrator, that C was correct and that the award should be amended accordingly: ARMADA LINES CONTINENT-MEDITERRANEAN SERVICE v. NAVIERA MURUETA S.A.: THE ELEXALDE [1985] 2 Lloyd's Rep. 485, Hobhouse J.

3067. Charterparty—NYPE charter—"grates and stoves"
The phrase "grates and stoves" in relation to the cost of fuel should be interpreted as meaning any fuel consuming device used for the crew's domestic comfort: SUMMIT INVEST INC. v. B.S.C. (THE SOUNION), *The Times,* December 4, 1986, C.A.

3068. Charterparty—repudiation—whether D guaranteed performance of charterers
P were a one-ship company and used J brokers to fix their vessels. J used their contacts with N brokers to fix a one-year time charter with X Co. The charter was extended for a second year by agreement, but shortly thereafter X Co. repudiated the charter. P claimed that N had agreed with J that D would guarantee the performance under the charter. D contended that there was no such agreement and that in any event J had no actual or ostensible authority to reach such an agreement. *Held,* on the facts and the evidence that P had not discharged the burden of proving that such an agreement was made: POLARIS STEAMSHIP CO. S.A. v. TARGCONE (A.) INC.: "THE NEFELI" [1986] 1 Lloyd's Rep. 339, Bingham J.

3069. Charterparty—responsibility for stowage—whether contributory negligence defence to claim in contract. See AB MARINTRANS v. COMET SHIPPING CO.; SHINJITSU MARU NO. 5, THE, § 389.

3070. Charterparty—terms—loading time.
Where a contract for the sale of a cargo stated that loading time was to count "as per Centrocon charterparty . . ." this imported all provisions as to time in the charterparty. Consequently the sellers could not be made liable for delay caused by river obstruction as the terms provided that time ceased for obstructions beyond the charterers control: PAGNAN (R.) AND FRATELLI v. FINAGRAIN COMPAGNIE COMMERCIALE AGRICOLE ET FINANCIERE S.A., *Financial Times,* July 30, 1986, Staughton J.

3071. Charterparty—time charter—speed warranty—consumption warranty—meaning and effect of qualification "about"—"moderate weather"
O let their vessels to C pursuant to time charters. These charters contained speed and consumption warranties that were qualified by the word "about" and contained reference to "moderate weather." There was a dispute between the parties as to the correct performance obligations of O and this was referred to arbitration. O appealed. *Held,* that (1) "about" did import a range of obligations and O was only liable for failing to perform his minimum obligation; (2) the state of the margin to be imported by "about" depended upon the facts of the case: it was for the arbitrators to decide what was appropriate; (3) the required margin had to be allowed in all conditions up to moderate weather (re 4 knots): ARAB MARITIME PETROLEUM TRANSPORT CO. v. LUXOR TRADING PANAMA; ALBIDA, THE [1986] 1 Lloyd's Rep. 142, Evans J.

3072. Collision
COLLISION REGULATIONS (SEAPLANES) (GUERNSEY) ORDER 1986 (No. 1892) [80p], made under the Merchant Shipping Act 1894 (c.60), ss.418(1), 738, and the Civil Aviation Act 1982 (c.16), s.97(1); operative on January 1, 1987; revokes S.I. 1977 No. 982 and applies to seaplanes on the water within Guernsey or its territorial waters.

LAKE WINDERMERE (COLLISION RULES) (REVOCATION) ORDER 1986 (No. 1893) [45p], made under the Merchant Shipping Act 1894 (c.60), ss.421(2), 738(1); operative on December 4, 1986; revokes S.I. 1973 No. 1230.

3073. Collision—crossing vessels—bad lookout—apportionment

In December 1979 there was a collision between vessels A and G. A was proceeding out of the Eastern Petroleum anchorage in Singapore harbour on a course of 165 degrees whilst G was proceeding in a westerly direction along the Eastern Fairway. Both vessels saw each other at about a minute or less before the collision. A contended that G was the give-way ship under the crossing rule, and that G was displaying misleading lights. G contended that A should not have proceeded out into the fairway until the way was clear. *Held,* that the overriding cause of the collision was bad lookout on both vessels. Each vessel had an ample opportunity to see the other, and blame would be divided equally: THE GOLDEN MISTRAL [1986] 1 Lloyd's Rep. 407, Sheen J.

3074. Collision—crossing vessels—navigation—lookout—apportionment

On February 13, 1975, a collision occurred between P's vessel C and D's vessel S off Bombay during the hours of darkness. Each vessel claimed the other was to blame. *Held,* that (1) the situation of danger arose five minutes before the collision; (2) S was at fault in altering course 90° to starboard and increasing speed, thereby attempting to cross ahead of C at a time and in circumstances when it was unsafe to do so; (3) S's lookout was a subject of criticism; (4) S could have altered course to port at any time up to two minutes before the collision and thereby avoided it; (5) S should have put her engines full astern at an earlier stage; (6) C should have reduced speed, stopped her engines and gone astern as soon as S's red light became visible. The proportion of blame was S: 85 per cent.; C: 15 per cent.: STATE OF HIMACHAL PRADESH, THE [1985] 2 Lloyd's Rep. 573, Sheen J.

3075. Collision—liability—appeal—apportionment

This was an appeal from a judgment of Sheen J. in an action concerning a collision between two vessels, the K and the S, in the Bay of Algeciras. The K was at anchor at the time of the collision, and Sheen J. held the S solely to blame for the collision. *Held,* on a review of the evidence, that Sheen J. was amply justified in reaching the conclusion that he had. The collision was solely caused by the failure of those on board the S to use their radar: ST. LOUIS, THE [1986] 2 Lloyd's Rep. 125, C.A.

3076. Contract of affreightment—whether binding—lien—bill of lading

A were engaged in the liner trade. They had negotiations with R who wished to ship wastepaper to India. At the end of those negotiations A agreed to a "promotional rate" of freight and to hold that rate open for a period. R actually then presented some paper for shipment, a quantity of which was shortshipped. R refused to pay the freight and A exercised a lien and refused any further bookings. R claimed that A's agreement gave rise to binding legal obligations. *Held,* allowing A's appeal, that (1) A's agreement amounted to a quote only and did not create any legal obligations on the part of A to R; (2) by the terms of the bill of lading freight was earned upon receipt of goods. A was, therefore, entitled to exercise a lien over the goods: SCANCARRIERS A/S *v.* AOTEAROA INTERNATIONAL LTD., THE BARRANDUNA [1985] 2 Lloyd's Rep. 419, P.C.

3077. Conversion—measure of damages—bills of lading

The proper measure of damages for the conversion of a cargo is the full market value of the cargo at the time and place of the conversion.

A, a firm in Singapore, agreed to finance the purchase by buyers in Bangladesh of salt from India and expended S$275,620·82. The suppliers were paid for the salt which they shipped on board the *Jag Dhir* in India for carriage to Chittagong in Bangladesh. Two bills of lading were issued which were received by A after being endorsed generally by the suppliers. A endorsed them over to P for value. On arrival in Chittagong the buyers obtained delivery of the salt without presentation of the bills of lading in consideration of an indemnity signed on their behalf together with a counter signature on behalf of a bank in Bangladesh for which the buyers had deposited an indemnity the equivalent of S$389,117·62. P brought an Admiralty action *in rem* in the High Court of Singapore against a sister ship, the *Jag Shakti* claiming against the ship owners damages for breach of contract and conversion. The judge awarded P S$389,117·62. The Court of Appeal reduced the award to

S$275,620·82. P appealed. *Held,* that (1) the ship owners had wrongly converted the salt and the proper measure of damages was the full market value of the salt at the time and place of conversion, it being irrelevant that P might have to account to the buyers for part of the amount recovered; but (2) dismissing the appeal, P had failed to produce reliable evidence of the full market value and the bank deposit had been calculated without reference to the value of the salt, so that the award of S$275,620·82 would be upheld (*Swire* v. *Leach* (1865) 18 C.B.N.S. 479 and *The Winkfield* [1902] P.42 applied).

JAG SHAKTI, THE [1986] 2 W.L.R. 87, P.C.

3078. Court of formal investigation into collision—findings of fact—High Court action—whether bound by findings

[Merchant Shipping Act 1894 (57 & 58 Vict., c.60), s.466; Shipping Casualties and Appeals, Re-Hearings Rules 1923 (S.R. & O. 1923 No. 752), rr.3, 4, 11.]

A court of investigations set up by the Secretary of State under s.466 of the Merchant Shipping Act 1894 is not a court of competent jurisdiction on the question of civil liability.

In December 1982 two cross channel ferries collided at Harwich. A formal inquiry set up by the Secretary of State, concluded that the preponderance of blame fell on the defendant's vessel. The plaintiffs issued a writ to recover damages, claiming 80 per cent. of the damage sustained. The defendants denied liability. The plaintiffs pleaded that the defendants were precluded from reopening the findings of the court of investigation by reason of issue estoppel or abuse of process. *Held,* on a preliminary issue, that the defendants were not estopped from raising the defence, and were not abusing the process of the court.

EUROPEAN GATEWAY, THE [1986] 3 W.L.R. 756, Steyn J.

3079. Employer's liability—defective equipment—whether includes ship. See COLTMAN *v.* BIBBY TANKERS, § 1183.

3080. Fees

MERCHANT SHIPPING (FEES) (AMENDMENT NO. 1) REGULATIONS 1986 (No. 837) [45p], made under the Merchant Shipping (Safety Convention) Act 1949 (c.43), (s.33(2) and the Merchant Shipping Act 1979 (c.39), s.21(1)(3)(*r*); operative on June 5, 1986; amend S.I. 1985 No. 1607 by increasing fees in connection with the registration of ships and copies of documents.

3081. Fishing vessels. See FISH AND FISHERIES, § 1550.

3082. Harbours and docks

BRISTOL PORT AND HARBOUR REVISION ORDER 1986 (No. 1626) [80p], made under the Harbours Act 1964 (c.40), s.14; operative on October 1, 1986; authorises certain works to be carried out by the City Council of Bristol in the Bristol Port.

CATTEWATER HARBOUR REVISION ORDER 1986 (No. 137) [40p], made under the Harbours Act 1964 (c.40), s.14; operative on February 1, 1986; increases the borrowing powers of the Harbour Commissioners.

DOCKYARD SERVICES (DEVONPORT) (DESIGNATION AND APPOINTED DAY) ORDER 1986 (No. 2243) [45p], made under the Dockyard Services Act 1986 (c.52), s.1(1); operative on April 4, 1987; designates Devonport Royal Dockyard for the purposes of s.1(1) of the Act.

DOCKYARD SERVICES (ROSYTH) (DESIGNATION AND APPOINTED DAY) ORDER 1986 (No. 2244) [45p], made under the Dockyard Services Act 1986 (c.52), s.1(1); operative on April 4, 1987; designates Rosyth Royal Dockyard for the purposes of s.1(1) of the Act.

GLENSANDA HARBOUR REVISION ORDER 1986 (No. 2130) [£1·40], made under the Harbours Act 1964 (c.40), s.14; operative on December 4, 1986; authorises Foster Yeoman Ltd. to construct a berthing face from solid rock and to dredge and reclaim an adjacent area in substitution for certain works authorised by Glensanda Harbour Order 1985.

LITTLEHAMPTON HARBOUR REVISION ORDER 1986 (No. 124) [80p], made under the Harbours Act 1964, s.14; operative on February 1, 1986; amends the borrowing powers of the Littlehampton Harbour Board.

PORTS (FINANCE) ACT 1985 (INCREASE OF GRANTS LIMIT) ORDER 1986 (No. 714) [45p], made under the Ports (Finance) Act 1985 (c.30), s.1(3)(4); operative on March

26, 1986; increases the limit on the aggregate amount of grants that may be made to the National Dock Labour Board to £20 million.

PORTSEA HARBOUR REVISION ORDER 1986 (No. 2356) [45p], made under the Harbours Act 1964 (c.40), s.14; operative on January 14, 1987; substitutes new limits of jurisdiction for the Portsea Harbour Co. Ltd.

SUTTON HARBOUR REVISION ORDER 1986 (No. 301) [£1·35], made under the Harbours Act 1964, s.14; operative on February 21, 1986; changes the name of the Sutton Harbour Improvement Company and authorises further borrowing.

3083. Hovercraft

HOVERCRAFT (CIVIL LIABILITY) ORDER 1986 (No. 1305) [£3·40], made under the Hovercraft Act 1968 (c.59), ss.1(1)(*h*), (*i*) and (3)(*f*), (*g*); operative on December 1, 1986; provides for the limits of overall liability of hovercraft owners for personal injury and loss or damage to property.

3084. Light dues

MERCHANT SHIPPING (LIGHT DUES) (AMENDMENT) REGULATIONS 1986 (No. 334) [40p], made under the Merchant Shipping (Mercantile Marine Fund) Act 1898 (c.44), s.5(2); operative on April 1, 1986; increase light dues payable under the 1898 Act.

3085. Loss by fire—fire started deliberately—claim by mortgagee

An insurance policy covered total or constructive total loss by fire caused by "an occurrence". *Held*, that "occurrence" included fire, even when that fire was started deliberately by the insured. Although the insured could not claim under the policy, his mortgagee could: "fire" did not mean only accidental fire: THE ALEXION HOPE, *The Financial Times*, October 29, 1986, Staughton J.

3086. Loss or damage to vessel—two causes of loss—one only insured

[Marine Insurance Act 1906 (c.41), s.55(1), (2).] Where there are two causes of loss or damage of similar strength and only one is an insured risk the insurers must pay unless the uninsured risk is specifically excluded by the policy (*Harbutts Plasticine v. Wayne Tank and Pump Co.* [1970] C.L.Y. 362 considered): LLOYD (J. J.) INSTRUMENTS *v.* NORTHERN STAR INSURANCE CO., *Financial Times*, October 21, 1986, C.A.

3087. Marine insurance—brokers—whether liable for payments allegedly made by underwriters to sub-brokers

P were the owners of a vessel. D were London brokers who placed part of the insurance risk with Italian underwriters. D issued a cover note. Various claims arose out of an engine damage incident. Italian underwriters refused to pay up and P claimed against D, contending that D had received the insurance monies to their use, in circumstances where Italian "middlemen" had been credited with the sums. *Held*, that (1) the middlemen were not agents of D; (2) D were merely agents and P could not succeed against them: TRADING & GENERAL INVESTMENT CORP. *v.* GAULT ARMSTRONG & KEMBLE; THE OKEANIS [1986] 1 Lloyd's Rep. 195, Bingham J.

3088. Marine insurance—jurisdiction—service of writ outside jurisdiction. See CANTIERI NAVALI RIUNITI SpA *v.* N.V. OMNE JUSTITIA; STOLT MARMARO, THE, § 2729.

3089. Merchant shipping

LIMITATION OF LIABILITY FOR MARITIME CLAIMS (PARTIES TO CONVENTION) ORDER 1986 (No. 2224) [80p], made under the Merchant Shipping Act 1979 (c.39), Sched. 4, Pt. II, para. 13; operative on January 6, 1987; declares the states which are parties to the Convention on limitation of liability for maritime claims (1976).

MERCHANT SHIPPING (CARGO SHIP CONSTRUCTION AND SURVEY) REGULATIONS 1984 (AMENDMENT) REGULATIONS 1986 (No. 1067) [80p], made under the Merchant Shipping Act 1979 (c.39), ss.21(1)–(4) and 22(1); operative on July 1, 1986; amend S.I. 1984 No. 1217.

MERCHANT SHIPPING (CERTIFICATES OF COMPETENCY AS A.B.) (ISLE OF MAN) ORDER 1986 (No. 2220) [45p], made under the Merchant Shipping Act 1948 (c.44), s.5(4); operative on January 27, 1987; provides for the recognition in the U.K. of certificates of competency as A.B. granted in the Isle of Man.

MERCHANT SHIPPING (CERTIFICATION OF MARINE ENGINEER OFFICERS AND LICENSING OF MARINE ENGINE OPERATORS) REGULATIONS 1986 (No. 1935) [£2·90], made under the Merchant Shipping Act 1970, (c.36), ss.43 and 68, and the Merchant Shipping Act 1979 (c.39), s.21(1)(*a*), (3) and (6); operative on December 15, 1986; revoke and re-enact S.I. 1980 No. 2025.

MERCHANT SHIPPING (CHEMICAL TANKERS) REGULATIONS 1986 (No. 1068) [£1·40], made under the Merchant Shipping Act 1979 (c.39), ss.21(*a*), (*b*), (3), (5) and (6), and 22(1); operative on July 1, 1986; require chemical tankers to comply with the international code for the construction and equipment of ships carrying dangerous chemicals in bulk.

MERCHANT SHIPPING (DANGEROUS GOODS) (AMENDMENT) REGULATIONS 1986 (No. 1069) [£1·40], made under the Merchant Shipping (Safety Convention) Act 1949 (c.43), s.23 and the Merchant Shipping Act 1979 (c.39), ss.21(1)(*a*) and (*b*), (3), (4) and (6), and 22(1) and (3); operative on July 1, 1986; amend S.I. 1981 No. 1747.

MERCHANT SHIPPING (DISTRESS SIGNALS AND PREVENTION OF COLLISIONS) (GUERNSEY) ORDER 1986 (No. 1163) [80p], made under the Merchant Shipping Act 1979 (c.39), s.47(1); operative on October 1, 1986; extends to Guernsey and applies to ships registered there. S.I. 1983 No. 708.

MERCHANT SHIPPING (FIRE PROTECTION AND FIRE APPLIANCES) (AMENDMENT) REGULATIONS 1986 (No. 1070) [£1·40], made under the Merchant Shipping Act 1979 (c.39), ss.21(1)(*a*)(*b*), (3) and (4), and 22(1); operative on July 1, 1986; further amend S.I. 1984 No. 1218.

MERCHANT SHIPPING (GAS CARRIERS) REGULATIONS 1986 (No. 1073) [£1·40], made under the Merchant Shipping Act 1979 (c.39), ss.21(*a*), (*b*), (3), (5) and (6), and 22(1); operative on July 1, 1986; require gas carriers to comply with the international code for the construction and equipment of ships carrying liquefied gases in bulk.

MERCHANT SHIPPING (LIABILITY OF SHIPOWNERS AND OTHERS) (CALCULATION OF TONNAGE) ORDER (No. 1040) [45p], made under the Merchant Shipping Act 1979 (c.39), Sched. 4, para. 5, Pt. II; operative on December 1, 1986; implements the rules for measuring gross tonnage set out in the international convention on tonnage measurement of ships (1969).

MERCHANT SHIPPING (LIFE-SAVING APPLIANCES) REGULATIONS 1986 (No. 1066) [£9·10], made under the Merchant Shipping Act 1979 (c.39), ss.21(1)(*a*)(*b*)(3)(4)(5)(6), 22(1); operative on July 1, 1986; provide for the life-saving appliances which must be carried on United Kingdom ships of different classes.

MERCHANT SHIPPING (LIFE-SAVING APPLIANCES REGULATIONS 1980) (AMENDMENT) REGULATIONS 1986 (No. 1072) [£1·90], made under the Merchant Shipping Act 1894 (c.60), s.427 and the Merchant Shipping Act 1979 (c.39), ss.21(1)(*a*), (*b*), (3)–(6), and 22(1); operative on July 1, 1986; amend S.I. 1980 No. 538.

MERCHANT SHIPPING (MEDICAL STORES) REGULATIONS 1986 (No. 144) [£1·85], made under the Merchant Shipping Act 1979 (c.39), ss.2(1)(*a*)(3)(4)(5)(6), 22(1)–(3) and the Medicines Act 1968 (c.67), s.103(3); operative on March 10, 1986; replace S.I. 1974 No. 1193, as amended, and provide for the scales of medical stores required to be carried on U.K. registered sea-going ships.

MERCHANT SHIPPING (MUSTERS AND TRAINING) REGULATIONS 1986 (No. 1071) [£1·40], made under the Merchant Shipping Act 1979 (c.39), ss.21(1)(*a*) and (*b*), (3), (4) and (6), and 22(1); operative on July 1, 1986; give effect to the provisions concerning musters, drills and related training in Ch. III in the 1983 amendments to the International Convention for the Safety of Life at Sea 1974.

MERCHANT SHIPPING (PASSENGER SHIP CONSTRUCTION) (NEW AND EXISTING SHIPS) (AMENDMENT) REGULATIONS 1986 (No. 1074) [80p], made under the Merchant Shipping Act 1979 (c.39), ss.21(1)(*a*), (*b*), (3) and 22(1); operative on July 1, 1986; amend S.I. 1980 No. 535 and 1984 No. 1216.

MERCHANT SHIPPING (RADIO INSTALLATIONS) (AMENDMENT) REGULATIONS 1986 (No. 1075) [80p], made under the Merchant Shipping Act 1979 (c.39), s.21(*a*) (*b*), (3)–(5); operative on July 1, 1986; amend S.I. 1980 No. 529.

MERCHANT SHIPPING (STERLING EQUIVALENTS) (VARIOUS ENACTMENTS) (AMENDMENT) ORDER 1986 (No. 2038) [45p], made under the Merchant Shipping Act 1974 (c.43), s.1(7); operative on November 30, 1986; amends S.I. 1986 No. 1777 so as to give effect to an increased maximum liability of the International Oil Pollution Compensation Fund.

3090. Merchant Shipping Act 1970—commencement

MERCHANT SHIPPING ACT 1970 (COMMENCEMENT NO. 10) ORDER 1986 (No. 2066 (c.79)) [£1·40], made under the Merchant Shipping Act 1970 (c.36), s.101(4); brings into force on September 1, 1987 s.100(3) (in part) and Sched. 5 (in part) (repeals).

3091. Merchant Shipping Act 1979—commencement
MERCHANT SHIPPING ACT 1979 (COMMENCEMENT NO. 10) ORDER 1986 (No. 1052 (c.28)) [80p], made under the Merchant Shipping Act 1979 (c.39), s.32(2); bring into force on December 1, 1986 sections 17, 18, 19(1)(4), 50(4) (in part), Scheds. 4, 5, 7, Pt. I.

3092. Oil pollution
INTERNATIONAL OIL POLLUTION COMPENSATION FUND (PARTIES TO CONVENTION) ORDER 1986 (No. 2223 [80p], made under the Merchant Shipping Act 1974 (c.43), 1(2) and the Merchant Shipping Act 1894 (c.60), s.738; operative on January 27, 1987; declares States which are party to the International Convention on the Establishment of an International Fund for Compensation for Oil Pollution Damage 1971 (Cmnd. 7383).

MERCHANT SHIPPING (INDEMNIFICATION OF SHIPOWNERS) (AMENDMENT) ORDER 1986 (No. 296) [40p], made under the Merchant Shipping Act 1974 (c.43), s.5(4)(*a*)(6); operative on May 1, 1986 save for Art. 3 which is operative on August 1, 1986; amends S.I. 1985 No. 1665.

MERCHANT SHIPPING (OIL POLLUTION) (PARTIES TO CONVENTION) ORDER 1986 (No. 2225) [80p], made under the Merchant Shipping (Oil Pollution) Act 1971 (c.59), s.19(2) and the Merchant Shipping Act 1894 (c.60), s.738; operative on January 27, 1987; declares States which are parties to the International Convention on Civil Liability for Oil Pollution Damage 1969 (Cmnd. 6183).

3093. Owners claim lien against freight due by sub-charterer to charterer—assignment of freight—whether deductions permissible—interest
P let their vessel to X who sub-let in turn to D. X ceased trading and P claimed a lien against D in respect of balance of freight due from D to X. Upon the exercise of the lien there came into existence an equitable assignment of balance of freight by D to P. The parties reached an agreement as to the payments to be made. However, D then sought to deduct from the freight due overtime costs that would normally have formed part of the expenses of X. P claimed interest. *Held,* that (1) D could not deduct expenses from P's claim for freight, that claim for freight being sacrosanct; (2) the parties did not include interest within the scope of their agreement and P could not, therefore, claim it: FREEDOM MARITIME CORPORATION *v.* INTERNATIONAL BULK CARRIERS; KHIAN CAPTAIN (NO. 2) THE [1986] 1 Lloyd's 429, Hirst J.

3094. Pilotage
LONDON PILOTAGE (AMENDMENT) ORDER 1986 (No. 568) [80p], made under the Pilotage Act 1983 (c.21), s.9; operative on May 1, 1986; amends S.R. & O. 1937 No. 1122 by extending the limits of the London Pilotage District to include Chatham Docks.

PILOTAGE COMMISSION PROVISION OF FUNDS SCHEME 1986 (CONFIRMATION) ORDER 1986 (No. 402) [80p], made under the Pilotage Act 1983 (c.21), s.3(3); operative on April 1, 1986; confirms a scheme under which the Pilotage Commission may levy a charge of $\frac{3}{4}$% on the pilotage receipts of pilotage authorities.

3095. Pilotage Act 1983—appointed day
PILOTAGE ACT 1983 (APPOINTED DAY NO. 1) ORDER 1986 (No. 1051) [45p], made under the Pilotage Act 1983 (c.21), ss.55(4), 58(2); appoints December 1, 1986 for the purposes of ss.55(4) and 58(2) of the 1983 Act.

3096. Prevention of Oil Pollution Act 1986 (c.6)
This Act prohibits the discharge from vessels of oil or mixtures containing oil into certain U.K. waters.

The Act received the Royal Assent on March 18, 1986 and comes into force on May 18, 1986.

3097. Protection of wrecks
PROTECTION OF WRECKS (DESIGNATION NO. 1) ORDER 1986 (No. 1441) [45p], made under the Protection of Wrecks Act 1973 (c.33), s.1(1)(2)(4); operative on September 22, 1986; designates as a restricted area an area of Bracklesham near Selsey Bill.

PROTECTION OF WRECKS (REVOCATION) ORDER 1986 (No. 1020) [45p], made under the Protection of Wrecks Act 1973 (c.33), ss.1, 3(2); operative on July 18, 1986; revokes S.I. 1985 No. 699.

3098. Safety

MERCHANT SHIPPING (FIRE PROTECTION) (NON-UNITED KINGDOM) (NON-SOLAS SHIPS) RULES 1986 (No. 1248) [£1·90], made under the Merchant Shipping Act 1894 (c.60), s.427(1); operative on September 1, 1986; apply specified fire protection requirements to certain non-U.K. ships when in a port in the U.K.

3099. Safety at Sea Act 1986. See FISH AND FISHERIES, § 1553.

3100. Sale of ship—commission—settlement

P shipbrokers sued E shipbuilders for commission on three ship sales alleged to have been arranged by P, and also sued the buyers of the ships for damages for unlawfully inducing breaches of contract by E. P sued all the defendants for conspiracy to deprive P of commission. P and E entered into settlement negotiations early in 1984. P argued that on a true construction of the telex exchanges, a binding settlement had been reached at the latest by March 1, 1984. The case was decided on its own facts. *Held*, that no binding settlement had been reached, only an agreement in principle which was intended to be finalised when the parties had agreed on a contract which their solicitors had drafted: AUNE (CARL) AGENCIA MARITIMA AFRETAMENTOS *v.* ENGENHARIA E. MAQUINAS S.A. [1986] 1 Lloyd's Rep. 544, Steyn J.

3101. Salvage—sunken wreck—Crown's right—whether "derelict"—chattels brought to U.K.

[Merchant Shipping Act 1984 (c.60), ss.510, 518, 523; Merchant Shipping Act 1906 (c.48), s.72.]

Claimants who salvaged items from the wreck of the *Lusitania,* sunk outside U.K. territorial waters, and brought them to the U.K.; had a good title to them.

The *Lusitania,* outward bound for New York, was sunk by a German submarine on May 7, 1915 off Kinsale in Eire, outside U.K. territorial waters. She was abandoned and the owners were compensated by insurers for her loss, and the ship and its contents became the property of the insurers. In 1982 the vessel was located and the claimants salvaged items from the sea bed and brought them into the U.K. The Crown asserted a droit of Admiralty and title to these items. The claimants sought a declaration that they had a good title to the items which were part of the cargo and the passengers' personal property, in the absence of the true owner. *Held*, granting the declaration, that the ship had been abandoned and derelict whether she remained afloat or sunk. Being derelict, it was a "wreck" within section 510 of the Merchant Shipping Act 1894, and therefore Part IX of that Act applied to the retrieval of the contents as being wreck (*H.M.S. Thetis* (1835) 3 Hag.Adm. 228 and *The Tubantia* [1924] P.75 applied). By s.523 of the Merchant Shipping Act 1894 the Crown's right to claim a droit of Admiralty was limited to an unclaimed wreck found in U.K. territorial waters. Although s.518 had been extended by s.72 of the Merchant Shipping Act 1906 so that where a wreck lying outside U.K. territorial waters was found and brought within the U.K. the finder had a duty to deliver the wreck to the receiver of wrecks, the Act of 1906 had not altered or extended the Crown's right over wrecks. There was therefore no droit of admiralty over the wreck and the claimants had good title in the absence of the true owners.

PIERCE *v.* BEMIS; THE LUSITANIA [1986] 2 W.L.R. 501, Sheen J.

3102. Shipbuilders—borrowing powers

BRITISH SHIPBUILDERS BORROWING POWERS (INCREASE OF LIMIT) ORDER 1986 (No. 2258) [45p], made under the Aircraft and Shipbuilding Industries Act 1977 (c.3), s.11(7); operative on December 16, 1986; increases the borrowing limit of British Shipbuilders to £1400 million.

3103. Shipbuilding contract—commission agreement—entitlement to commission. See MOUNDEAS (GEORGE) & CO. S.A. *v.* NAVIMPEX CENTRALA NAVALA, § 418.

3104. Shipowners liability

MERCHANT SHIPPING (LIABILITY OF SHIPOWNERS AND OTHERS) (RATE OF INTEREST) ORDER 1986 (No. 1932) [45p], made under the Merchant Shipping Act 1979 (c.39), Sched. 4, Pt. II, para. 8; operative on December 1, 1986; provides that the rate of interest to be included in the limitation fund constituted by a person seeking to limit his liability by virtue of the Convention on Limitation of Liability for Maritime Claims 1976 shall be 12 per cent.

3105. Soviet Union

MERCHANT SHIPPING (PROTECTION OF SHIPPING AND TRADING INTERESTS) (USSR) ORDER 1986 (No. 310) [40p], made under the Merchant Shipping Act 1974 (c.43), s.14(2)(6); operative on March 28, 1986; requires the provision of information about carryings by Soviet shipping lines between the UK and specified destinations.

3106. Sterling equivalents
MERCHANT SHIPPING (STERLING EQUIVALENTS) (VARIOUS ENACTMENTS) ORDER 1986 (No. 1777) [45p], made under the Merchant Shipping Act 1974 (c.43), s.1(7); the Unfair Contract Terms Act 1977 (c.50), s.28(4), and the Merchant Shipping Act 1979 (c.39), Sched. 3, Pt. II, para. 5; operative on November 7, 1986; specifies the sterling amounts which are equivalent to amounts expressed in gold francs in the said Acts of 1974, 1977 and 1979.

3107. Time charter—hire—equitable set off—whether charterers prejudiced in use of vessel
O let their vessel to C under a time charter on the NYPE form. C suspected that the bunker consumption of the vessel was not as warranted and pressed, as they were entitled to do, for the vessel's logs. Once C had obtained the logs, an analysis by them led them to allege that O had been improperly dealing with the fuel. C therefore claimed an entitlement to make an equitable set off from hire. It was held in arbitration that they were so entitled. *Held,* allowing O's appeal, that (1) most of the allegations made by C amounted to failures that affected the use of the vessel or prejudiced C in their use of it; (2) accordingly although C had a cross-claim in respect of their allegations, they were not entitled in law to equitable set off: LEON CORPORATION *v.* ATLANTIC LINES AND NAVIGATION CO. INC.: THE LEON [1985] 2 Lloyd's Rep. 470, Hobhouse J.

3108. Time charter—NYPE form—(clause 8)—responsibility for stevedore damage to vessel— meaning of additional words "and responsibility"
By a time trip charter on the NYPE form O let their vessel to C. The charter (cl.8) provided that "Charterers are to load, stow and trim and discharge the cargo at their expense under the supervision and responsibility of the Captain". O alleged that the vessel was damaged by stevedores and claimed damages from C. Arbitrators allowed O's claim. C appealed. *Held,* that (1) cl.8 of the Charter made O prima facie responsible for stevedore negligence; (2) C could only be liable for stevedore negligence insofar as he interfered in stevedore operations. There was no evidence that he did and C's appeal was allowed: ALEXANDROS SHIPPING CO. *v.* MSC MEDITERRANEAN SHIPPING CO: ALEXANDROS P [1986] 1 Lloyd's Rep. 421, Steyn J.

3109. Towage contract—provisions relating to approval of seaworthiness—damage to tow— deviation
This case, which was decided upon its own particular facts and contractual provisions concerned the towage of a crane barge by P from Japan to Alexandria. The tow hit bad weather and had to deviate to Singapore. P incurred repair costs and demurrage, and sought to recover these from D, the owners of the barge. D contended that the crane barge had not been made fit for towage by P and that in breach of contract P had instructed a classification society other than those nominated to make the crane barge towworthy. *Held,* that (1) on the evidence D had agreed to a change of classification surveyors; (2) P was entitled to recover the repair, deviation and demurrage costs, in that they had undertaken their obligations to instruct leading marine surveyors of high repute—the fastening method adopted was not negligent in any event: GOLIATH TRANSPORT & SHIPPING B.V. *v.* GENERAL AUTHORITY OF THE PORT OF ALEXANDRIA; SALVIA, THE [1986] 1 Lloyd's Rep. 438, Bingham J.

3110. Voyage charter—cesser clause—charterers' liability for cargo claim
O chartered their vessel to C for the carriage of rice to Basrah. The charter provided that C were responsible for freight and demurrage but that all other liability would cease on shipment. There was a cargo claim against O at Basrah which O sought to pass on to C under the charterparty. C contended that the cesser clause excluded them from liability. *Held,* that although (1) prima facie C would appear to have a defence under the cesser clause; (2) the clause did not relieve C from liability because it did not only relieve C from liability where O was provided with an effective lien: ACTION S.A. *v.* BRITANNIC SHIPPING CORPORATION LTD.: THE AEGIS BRITANNIC [1985] 2 Lloyd's Rep. 481, Staughten J.

3111. Voyage charter—demurrage—construction of laytime provisions
O let two of their vessels to C for the performance of voyage charterparties. The charterparties provided that should the vessel be unable to give notice of readiness by reason of congestion at Calcutta, time would count for the day following notice of

the vessel's arrival off Sandheads. The vessels did not give notice off Sandheads but at a place much closer to Calcutta. C argued that the notices were not valid and that laytime did not commence running. O contended that it ought to be implied into the charter that a notice given at a place closer to Calcutta than Sandheads was valid. *Held,* upholding the arbitrator, that the notices given were valid, as it was obvious that reasonable commercial men would not require the vessel to made a substantial deviation in order merely to give a valid notice: MOSVOLDS REDERI A/S *v.* FOOD CORP. OF INDIA [1986] 2 Lloyd's Rep. 68, Steyn J.

3112. Voyage charter—freight—deduction

[R.S.C., Ord. 14.] O let their vessel to C for the carriage of livestock. It was a term of the charter that the holds would be properly ventilated with a floor space of 4,750 sq. m. In fact a vet did not approve all of the holds on the grounds of poor ventilation, thereby reducing the available floor space to 3,400 sq. m. C deducted sums from freight payable to reflect the reduced floor space. O sought recovery of the balance of freight by way of Ord. 14 proceedings. *Held,* that as (1) the case did not prove an exception to the rule that freight is payable without deduction; (2) judgment would be given for O: ELENA SHIPPING *v.* AIDENFIELD. THE ELENA [1986] 1 Lloyd's Rep. 425, Steyn J.

3113. Voyage charter—war risk insurance—whether loss of earnings insurance included

O let their vessel to C to carry cargo to Iran. The charter provided that additional war risk premiums charged were to be paid by C. O sought to charge C with both additional war risk premiums and also loss of earnings insurance. Arbitrators allowed this latter head of claim. C appealed. *Held,* allowing C's appeal, that loss of earnings insurance did not fall within the definition of war risk premiums provided for in the charter: ISLAMIC REPUBLIC OF IRAN SHIPPING LINES *v.* P. & O. BULK SHIPPING: THE DISCARIA [1985] 2 Lloyd's Rep. 489, Staughten J.

3114. Wrongful damage repair—other repairs—whether recovery of full cost of detention

Wrongful damage repair was needed to a ship, so O, the owner, withdrew it from use to carry it out. At the same time he had other desirable but not essential repairs done, although he would not have withdrawn the ship from use solely to have these carried out. *Held,* that O was entitled to recover the entire cost of detention from the wrongdoer without deduction, because but for the wrongful damage he would not have had to withdraw it at all. However, if the ship would in any event have been out of commission during that period, O would have only been entitled to recover any extra expense incurred by the wrongdoing (*The Ferdinand Retzlaff* [1972] C.L.Y. 3212 applied): ELPIDOFOROS SHIPPING CORPORATION *v.* FURNESS WITHY (AUSTRALIA) PROPERTY (THE OINOUSSIAN FRIENDSHIP), *The Times,* November 28, 1986, H.L.

SOCIAL SECURITY

3115. Adjudication

SOCIAL SECURITY (ADJUDICATION) REGULATIONS 1986 (No. 2218) [£4·90], made under the National Insurance Act 1974 (c.14), s.6(1)(3), the Social Security Act 1975 (c.14), ss.100(2)(4), 101(5A)(5B), 105(2), 106(1)(*b*)(*bb*) (2)(4), 108(2)(3), 109(2)(3), 110(5), 112(3)(5), 113(1)(2), 114, 115, 119(3)(4), 166, Scheds. 12, 13, 20, the Health and Social Services and Social Security Adjudication Act 1983 (c.41), Sched. 8, para. 31 and the Social Security Act 1986 (c.50), ss.52(4), 89(1), Sched. 7, para. 4(2); operative on April 6, 1987; make provision for the determination of claims and questions under serious specified social security enactments.

3116. Appeal to Social Security Commissioner—refusal of night time attendance allowance— no reasons given—judicial review

[Tribunals and Inquiries Act 1971 (c.62) s.12(1); Tribunals and Inquiries (Social Security Commissioners) Order 1980 (S.I. 1980 No. 1637), art. 2.]

Social Security Commissioners are specifically exempted from the requirement to give reasons for their decisions and accordingly it is only if an applicant can show that the Commissioner has acted on improper or insufficient reasons that his decision will be upset.

Per curiam: Commissioners may always give reasons if they think fit but the court would decline to suggest any general principle that reasons should be given.

An attendance allowance board did not consider that C, who was severely mentally retarded, fulfilled the requirements for a night time attendance allowance. The Social

Security Commissioner refused leave to appeal against that decision, but gave no reasons. The judge refused leave to apply for judicial review, but suggested that the case was sufficiently special that reasons should have been given. *Held,* that the Commissioner was specifically excluded from the usual requirement to give reasons for his decision and it would be improper to draw any adverse inferences from his failure so to do. An applicant must show that the Commissioner had acted improperly or had had insufficient reasons for his decision. The court was entitled to assume that the Commissioner had acted properly.

R. *v.* SECRETARY OF STATE FOR SOCIAL SERVICES, *ex p.* CONNOLLY [1986] 1 W.L.R. 421, C.A.

3117. Attendance allowance—child in care of foster parent—whether "boarded out"
[Child Care Act 1980 (c.5), s.21(1)(*b*).] When a child is in the care of a local authority, and the authority then places the child with foster parents selected by a scheme arranged by an organisation such as Dr. Barnardo's, the child has been "boarded out" by the authority, within the meaning of s.21(1)(*b*) of the Children Act 1980: KININMONTH *v.* CHIEF ADJUDICATION OFFICER, *The Times*, October 17, 1986, C.A.

3118. Attendance allowance—conditions—date of claim—Commissioner's decision
[Social Security (Attendance Allowance) (No. 2) Regulations 1975 (S.I. 1975 No. 598), reg. 5.] On February 20, 1983 a claim to attendance allowance was made, C having been admitted to a National Health Service hospital on February 11, 1983. He was maintained there free of charge until his death on March 9, 1983. The insurance officer decided attendance allowance was not payable and on appeal this decision was upheld by the Appeal Tribunal. C's widow appealed to the Commissioner. *Held,* that (1) applying *Insurance Officer* v. *McCaffrey* ([1985] C.L.Y. 3279), a claimant for attendance allowance who at a particular date earlier than the date of claim satisfied all the conditions for an award of the allowance was, for the purposes of reg. 5 of the Social Security (Attendance Allowance) (No. 2) Regulations 1975 entitled to the allowance at that earlier date; (2) in the present appeal, subject to the satisfaction of the medical conditions in s.35(1) and (2) of the Social Security Act 1975, attendance allowance was payable from the payment day following February 20, 1983 until the end of the payment week in which the claimant's death occurred (this latter date having occurred before the expiry of the four week period allowed by reg. 5): DECISION NO. R(A) 1/86.

3119. Benefits
SOCIAL SECURITY BENEFIT (PERSONS ABROAD) AMENDMENT REGULATIONS 1986 (No. 486) [40p], made under the Social Security Act 1975 (c.14), ss.131, 166 and Sched. 20; operative on April 6, 1986; amend S.I. 1975 No. 563.

SOCIAL SECURITY (UNEMPLOYMENT, SICKNESS AND INVALIDITY BENEFIT) AMENDMENT REGULATIONS 1986 (No. 484) [80p], made under the Social Security Act 1975, ss.15A, 16(1); operative on April 6, 1986; amend S.I. 1983 No. 1598.

SOCIAL SECURITY BENEFITS UP-RATING ORDER 1986 (No. 1117) [£1·90], made under the Social Security Act 1975 (c.14), ss.124, 126A; operative on July 28, 1986; alters benefits and increases benefits specified in Pts. I, III, IV and V of Sched. 4 to the 1975 Act.

SOCIAL SECURITY BENEFITS UP-RATING REGULATIONS 1986 (No. 1118) [80p], made under the Social Security Act 1975 (c.14), ss.17(1)(*a*) 58(3) and 131, Sched. 14, para. 2(1) and Sched. 20; operative on July 28, 1986; deal with the up-rating of benefit.

3120. Breach of duty—local authority—review powers of Secretary of State
[National Assistance Act 1948 (c.29), s.36(1); Chronically Sick and Disabled Persons Act 1970 (c.44), s.2] When the Secretary of State exercises his review powers under s.36(1) of the National Assistance Act 1948, he is not acting as a tribunal of fact, and he can therefore only exercise his powers if satisfied that the local authority has acted irrationally. There has only been a breach of s.2 of the Chronically Sick and Disabled Persons Act 1970 when an applicant can establish (i) a specific need for which he is alleging arrangements should be made; (ii) the arrangements required to satisfy that need; (iii) an express request to the local authority to satisfy the need; (iv) a clear failure by the local authority to satisfy that need: R. *v.* KENT COUNTY COUNCIL, *ex p.* BRUCE, *The Times*, February 8, 1986, D.C.

3121. Charges

NATIONAL ASSISTANCE (CHARGES FOR ACCOMMODATION) REGULATIONS 1986 (No. 861) [45p], made under the National Assistance Act 1948 (c.29), s.22(3) and (4); operative on July 28, 1986; supersede S.I. 1985 No. 1317.

3122. Child benefit. See FAMILY ALLOWANCES, § 1542.

3123. Claims

SOCIAL SECURITY (CLAIMS AND PAYMENTS) AMENDMENT REGULATIONS 1986 (No. 1772) [45p], made under the Social Security Act 1975 (c.14), s.79(3), Sched. 20; operative on November 18, 1986; further amend S.I. 1979 No. 628 so as to extend to 35 days the period for which a claim for unemployment benefit may be treated as made in regard to the Christmas and New Year holidays.

SOCIAL SECURITY (CLAIMS AND PAYMENTS, HOSPITAL IN-PATIENTS AND MATERNITY BENEFIT) AMENDMENT REGULATIONS 1986 (No. 903) [£1·40], made under the Social Security Act 1975 (c. 14), ss.22(1), 27(4), 85(1), 165A(1), 166; operative on June 30, 1986; further amend S.I. 1975 Nos. 553 and 555 and S.I. 1979 No. 628.

3124. Contributions

SOCIAL SECURITY (CONTRIBUTIONS) AMENDMENT REGULATIONS 1986 (No. 485) [80p], made under the Social Security Act 1975 (c.14), ss.131, 166(2), 168 and Sched. 20; operative on April 6, 1986; modify provisions of the 1975 Act in relation to the contributions payable by certain voluntary workers employed abroad.

SOCIAL SECURITY (CONTRIBUTIONS, RE-RATING) ORDER 1986 (No. 25) [80p], made under the Social Security Act 1975 (c.14), ss.120(5),(6), 121(2) and 123A(1) and (2); operative on April 6, 1986; increases specified amounts of weekly earnings under the 1975 Act.

SOCIAL SECURITY (CONTRIBUTIONS, RE-RATING) CONSEQUENTIAL AMENDMENT REGULATIONS 1986 (No. 198) [40p], made under the Social Security Act 1985 (c.14), ss.129(1), 168(1), Sched. 20; operative on April 6, 1986; further amend S.I. 1979 No. 591 by increasing the special rate of Class 2 contributions payable by share fishermen.

3125. Earnings factor

SOCIAL SECURITY REVALUATION OF EARNINGS FACTORS ORDER 1986 (No. 809) [80p], made under the Social Security Pensions Act 1975 (c.60), s.21; operative on June 5, 1986; made consequent upon a review under the 1975 Act which provides for the revaluation of earnings factors so that they maintain their value in relation to the general level of earnings in Great Britain.

3126. Family income supplement—claimant's husband in prison—whether single woman

[Family Income Supplements Act 1970 (c.55), s.1; Supplementary Benefits (Aggregate) Regulations (S.I. 1981 No. 1524), r.3(a).] C's husband had been sent to prison for 9 months. C was left to fend for herself and her son, then aged 7, on her earnings and child benefit. She applied for supplementary benefit under s.1(1). The supplement officer decided that she would not be regarded as a single woman for the purposes of the Act. On appeal the tribunal construed the word "household" under the 1970 Act by reference to the 1981 Regulations. Under r.3(a) a person in prison was not regarded as a member of the household for the period of his imprisonment. They allowed C's appeal. The social security commissioner, on appeal, concluded that the tribunal had erred in law by reference to the subordinate legislation. *Held,* dismissing C's appeal, that it had been clearly wrong for the tribunal to apply the 1981 Regulations, which related to the aggregation of resources to s.1 of the 1970 Act. On the undisputed facts C could not be considered a single woman and the commissioner had been right in her decision not to send the case back to the tribunal (*England v. Secretary of State for Social Services* (1982) 3 FLR 222 applied; *Santos v. Santos* [1972] C.L.Y. 1087 considered): TAYLOR *v.* SUPPLEMENTARY BENEFIT OFFICER (1986) 1 FLR 16, C.A.

3127. Family income supplement—composition of family—overpayment—Commissioner's decision

[Family Income Supplements Act 1970 (c.55), s.6(3)] C and a Mrs. G claimed and were awarded family income supplement for a family consisting of themselves and one child. Before that award had expired C had parted from Mrs. G and with a Mrs. B had claimed and been awarded family income supplement for a family consisting of themselves and four children. In completing this claim C did not declare the earlier claim. When this came to light the supplement officer (now adjudication officer) reviewed the second award and decided that family income supplement was not payable because a previous claim was in existence. He also decided that the Secretary of State was entitled to recover the overpayment of family income supplement resulting from the overlap of benefit paid on the two awards. On appeal the tribunal upheld the supplement officer's decision. *Held,* that (1) the decision of the supplementary benefit appeal tribunal (now the social security appeal tribunal) was not erroneous in law and accordingly the appeal failed; (2) under s.6(3) of the Family Income Supplements Act 1970 no review of an award can be made for any subsequent change of circumstance other than that prescribed in the Family Income Supplements (General) Regulations (reg. 4). If Mrs. G claimed supplementary benefit as C stated was her intention when he left her, the effect of reg. 4 in this case was that family income supplement would not have been payable to C but Mrs. G could have continued to be entitled to receive it; (3) although C had left Mrs. G and gone to live with Mrs. B, he could not be included in any family other than that formed by himself and Mrs. G until the award made to that family had expired; (4) under the provisions of reg. 10, overpayment of benefit was recoverable, by the Secretary of State, from the persons concerned if those persons cannot show that they had disclosed all the material facts. The burden of proof rests with the claimants. It is not necessary to show intention, malice or even negligence on the part of a claimant in failing to disclose a material fact. It is only necessary to show that a claimant either knew or with reasonable diligence ought to have known the true position; (5) C knew or ought to have known at the date of his second claim that family income supplement might still have been in payment to Mrs. G and it was his duty to alert the Department to the possibility. He had made no attempt to find out whether Mrs. G had surrendered the order book. By failing to do so he did not comply with the reasonable standard of care in giving the answers he did when making the second claim. The claimant failed to disclose a material fact and the overpayment was repayable: DECISION No. R(FIS) 3/85.

3128. Family income supplement—gross income—enterprise allowance—Commissioner's decision

Each of the claimants was running a separate business on a self-employed basis. The husband's business was trading at a profit but that of the wife, which had recently commenced, was operating at a loss. The wife was receiving £40 per week Enterprise Allowance. The adjudication officer assessed the family's normal gross weekly income as comprising the weekly amount of the husband's net business profit plus the full amount of the wife's Enterprise Allowance. On appeal the tribunal, by a majority, upheld the adjudication officer's decision. *Held,* that (1) the decision of the tribunal was erroneous in law and is set aside; (2) Enterprise Allowance payments are receipts of the business which they were paid to set up and accordingly fall to be treated under reg. 2(3) of the Family Income Supplement (General) Regulations as part of a person's earnings from any gainful occupation which do not comprise salary, wages or fees related to a fixed period. Expenses should be deducted from receipts (which include Enterprise Allowance) when ascertaining the net profits of the business, in the usual way: DECISION No. R(FIS) 7/85.

3129. Family income supplement—mature full-time student—whether remunerative full-time work—Commissioner's decision

[Family Income Supplement (General) Regulations 1980 (S.I. 1980 No. 1437), reg. 5.] Cs made a renewal claim to family income supplement in respect of themselves and four children. Although the husband had previously been self employed, and engaged in remunerative full-time work, at the date of the renewal claim he had become a mature student pursuing a full-time degree course at a university and was in receipt of a grant from the local education authority. His wife was not employed. The adjudication officer disallowed the claim on the ground that it did not include a man or woman engaged and normally engaged in remunerative full-time work within the terms of reg. 5 of the Family Income Supplements (General) Regulations 1980. On appeal the Social Security Appeal Tribunal upheld this decision. *Held*, dismissing Cs' appeal, that (1) while undertaking his course of studies C was, in a general sense, in full-time work but that work was not remunerative. The grant from the local authority was a contribution to his maintenance and that of his family and not a return for C's work on the course; (2) working for a degree is not analogous to being self employed and working with the desire hope and intention of claiming a reward or profit; (3) consequently Cs had no entitlement to family income supplement because their family was not a "family" within the special definition in s.1(1) of the 1970 Act: DECISION NO. R(FIS) 1/86.

3130. Family income supplement—normal gross income—strike—Tribunal decision
[Family Income Supplements Act 1970 (c.55); Family Income Supplements (General) Regulations 1980 (S.I. 1980 No. 1437), regs. 2, 3] C made a claim for family income supplement for a family consisting of husband, wife and their two children. At the date of the claim the wife was engaged and normally engaged in remunerative full-time work but the husband was on strike; the strike had been preceded by an overtime ban. Before the strike started the husband's earnings with or without overtime payments were such that, when added to those of his wife, entitlement to family income supplement was extinguished. The adjudication officer decided that in order to determine the husband's normal gross earnings it was necessary to have regard to a period other than the five weeks preceding the claim and it was decided that this should be to a period when he was working with overtime. On these grounds that adjudication officer disallowed the claim. On appeal C contended that his normal income, for the purpose of the claim, was NIL because he was, in the material period, on strike. The social security appeal tribunal concurred with C's submission and reversed the adjudication officer's decision. The social security appeal tribunal also decided that family income supplement was to be paid for a period of 17 weeks from the date of claim, reviewable thereafter at four weekly intervals to provide for the change in the claimants' financial circumstances should the strike cease. *Held,* that (1) the Family Income Supplements Act 1970 and reg. 2 of the Family Income Supplements (General) Regulations consistently direct attention to the origin of a person's normal gross income, and it follows that normalcy needs to be ascertained by reference to that origin or source, as at the date of claim; (2) in the present case, C's source of income was a gainful occupation under a contract of service with the National Coal Board. That contract was not abrogated by the strike action and it could not possibly be said that at the date of claim his "normal gross income" from his gainful occupation under his contract of service was NIL. In this case in order to properly determine C's normal weekly income from his gainful occupation it was imperative to select some period other than the 5 weeks preceding the claim. It was held that it was not necessary in this case to determine C's normal gross income with or without overtime as on any footing it was sufficient to extinguish entitlement at the date of claim; (3) reg. 3(1) of the Family Income Supplements (General) Regulations allows an award to be made for a period shorter than 52 weeks where the determining authority is satisfied that the benefit should be payable at least at a certain (minimum) rate. The regulation does not however enable the period of payment to be shortened where the determining authority is satisfied or believes that the rate fixed may become too high at some future time (as by the end of the miners' strike in the present case). The regulation does not by its language confer any such two-way flexibility; (4) the tribunal's decision was erroneous in law and is set aside: DECISION NO. R(FIS) 2/85.

3131. Family income supplement—self-employed person—remunerative work—Commissioner's decision
[Family Income Supplements (General) Regulations 1980 (S.I. 1980 No. 1437), reg. 5(1).] [Scot.] In claiming family income supplement C stated that she was employed as a part-time teacher and also self-employed as a silversmith. She had worked 7 hours, 20 hours, 17 hours and 22 hours in the 4 relevant weeks. The adjudication officer disallowed the claim on the ground that C was not engaged in remunerative full-time work within the terms of reg. 5(1) of the Family Income Supplements (General) Regulations 1980. On appeal to the social security appeal tribunal C stated that in connection with her work as a silversmith she had only included the hours spent on practical work at her bench. She had not included time spent on visits to and from clients, trips to retailers and wholesalers, at the craft centre and Assay Office and in working out ideas for a design competition. The tribunal, however, upheld the adjudication officer's decision taking the view that these activities did not constitute remunerative work. *Held,* that (1) the decision of the tribunal was erroneous in law and therefore set aside; (2) activities in the course of remunerative work are not, in respect of the self-employed, restricted only to those activities which are costed; (3) the activities described by the claimant are for

the most part essential to her self-employment and are therefore carried out with the desire hope and intention of claiming a reward or profit: DECISION NO. R(FIS) 6/85.

3132. Family income supplements

FAMILY INCOME SUPPLEMENTS (COMPUTATION) REGULATIONS 1986 (No. 1120) [80p], made under the Family Income Supplements Act 1970 (c.55), ss.2(1), 3(1) and (1A) and 10(3A); operative on July 29, 1986; increase the amounts prescribed for the purpose of determining family income supplements.

3133. Housing benefit—assessment of income during benefit period—whether income during an earlier or later period relevant

[Social Security and Housing Benefits Act 1982 (c.24), Housing Benefit Regulations 1985 (S.I. 1985 No. 677).] Between November 22, 1984 and December 12, 1984 the applicant and his cohabitee were taking part in an official strike for which period they received no salary. Their only income was £22·50 each in strike pay. On the day the strike began the applicant applied to the respondent authority for housing benefit. This claim was rejected by reference to reg. 14 of the Housing Benefit Regulations and further that it was considered reasonable, having regard to the short duration of the strike, to take account of the applicant's income both immediately before and after the strike. This decision was upheld by the housing benefit Review Board. The applicant sought judicial review of the Review Board's finding. *Held*, granting the application, that (1) the purpose of reg. 14 is to assess what is likely to be the income of the claimant during the benefit period, not to assess what income or resources he ought to have available to him; (2) the claimant was in gainful employment even though on strike but nonetheless "income" in the regulations refers to such income therefrom which is likely to continue in the benefit period; (3) where the actual income of a claimant in the benefit period is known there is nothing in reg. 14(4) which gives an authority power to have regard to the claimant's level of income during an earlier or later period.

R. v. HOUSING BENEFITS REVIEW BOARD OF THE LONDON BOROUGH OF EALING, *ex p.* SAVILLE (1986) 18 H.L.R. 349, Kennedy J.

3134. Housing benefit—exclusion of eligibility of owner-occupier—meaning of owner

[Social Security and Housing Benefits Act 1982 (c.24), Housing Benefit Regulations 1985 (S.I. 1985 No. 677).] The applicant and her two children lived in a house in the respondent authority's area. The house had been purchased in 1984 jointly with her parents, and she held one-half of the shares in the property. By a written agreement it was provided that the applicant and her parents would stand possessed of the property and proceeds of sale upon the terms of the trust for sale set out in the agreement. This also permitted the applicant and her children to have exclusive use and occupation of the property provided she paid all the rates, other outgoings and £30·00 per week to her parents. In September 1984 she applied to the local authority for housing benefit in respect of the sum of £30·00 per week. Her application was rejected by the authority and subsequently by the review board. In July 1985 she made an application for judicial review. *Held*, granting the application, that (1) the period for bringing the application would be extended, (2) since the Act and regulations themselves provided a definition of "owner" it was unnecessary to look elsewhere; applying the definition contained in reg. 2(2) the applicant did not fall within it because she was not entitled to dispose of the fee simple without the consent of the other trustees, accordingly she was not excluded from eligibility for a rent allowance: R. v. HOUSING BENEFIT REVIEW BOARD FOR SEDGEMOOR DISTRICT COUNCIL, *ex p.* WEADEN (1986) 18 H.L.R. 355, Schiemann J.

3135. Independent appeals—abolition under proposed social fund. See LAW REFORM, § 1963.

3136. Industrial disablement benefit—prescribed disease—occupational deafness—Tribunal's decision

[Scot.] A fabrication planner employed by a firm of marine engineers spent the greater part of his working day inside a hardboard hut (later changed to a Portacabin) within a workshop. He would, however, spend more than one hour each day within the workshop itself, allocating work to workmen who used pneumatic percussive tools as members of a fabrication unit. The hut was positioned 12 feet above the workshop floor but only 2 feet from the fabrication block in a horizontal measurement. *Held*, that (1) the presence of a particular requirement showing that work in the shipbuilding or ship-repairing industries has been wholly or mainly in the immediate vicinity of pneumatic percussive tools on metal does not prevent an employee in those industries from availing himself of the less restrictive terms of the more general requirement of showing that he has worked in the immediate vicinity of such tools for at least an average of one hour per working day; (2) in any case, the intervention of the hardboard walls of the hut, though a significant factor, did not in this case outweigh the pure distance factor which the Chief Commissioner had held (see *Decision R(1) 7/76*) may itself be decisive of the question whether work is in the immediate vicinity: DECISION No. R(I) 8/85.

3137. **Industrial disablement benefit—review—industrial accident—Commissioner's decision**
C claimed disablement benefit having suffered a heart attack which he said began while he was at work on November 16, 1976. The claim was disallowed by the adjudication officer and then on appeal firstly by the Social Security Appeal Tribunal and then the Commissioner. The Commissioner accepted that a pathological change for the worse had occurred in the course of C's employment but found that it did not arise out of that employment. C subsequently applied for a review of the Commissioner's decision. *Held,* that although a decision that no accident had occurred was capable of review by virtue of section 104 of the Social Security Act 1975, the effect of section 107(6)(*b*) was to prohibit review in any circumstances of a decision that an accepted accident had not arisen out of or in the course of employment (R(I) 11/62 considered): DECISION No. R(I) 9/85.

3138. **Industrial injuries**
SOCIAL SECURITY (INDUSTRIAL INJURIES AND DISEASES) MISCELLANEOUS PROVISIONS REGULATIONS 1986 (No. 1561) [£1·90], made under the Social Security Act 1986 (c.50), s.39; operative on October 1, 1986; contain provisions consequential upon the changes made to Pt. II of the Social Security Act 1975 by s.39 of the 1986 Act.

3139. **Industrial injuries benefit—disablement pension—calculation of arrears—Commissioner's decision**
Arrears of disablement pension became payable in 1982 when an original assessment by a medical board of three per cent. from 1962 was raised by a medical appeal tribunal to 53 per cent. (50 per cent. net) from 1962. An award was made based upon the rates appropriate for 50 per cent. from time to time in force since January 7, 1962, but C sought to establish that this should have been calculated by reference only to the rate appropriate to 50 per cent. in 1982. *Held*, that payment of arrears, calculated according to rates from time to time in force, was correct, this being the effect of section 57(6) of the Social Security Act 1975 and reviews by the Secretary of State authorised under section 125 of that Act; and also of preceding legislation appropriate to the period of arrears at issue: DECISION No. R(I) 1/86.

3140. **Invalidity benefit—review—varying medical opinion—Commissioner's decision**
On September 21, 1984, C's doctor advised him to refrain from work for three months by reason of low back pain. Invalidity benefit was awarded for the inclusive period September 27, 1984, to December 26, 1984, on the basis of that opinion. On October 9, 1984, a medical officer of the Department of Health and Social Security examined C and considered that whilst he was incapable of his previous occupation of laundry worker, he was fit for light work within certain specified limitations. On October 23, 1984, C's doctor advised him to refrain from work for four weeks by reason of low back pain and vertigo. On November 27, 1984, C was examined by a different medical officer of the Department who also expressed the view that C was capable of limited work. In the light of that medical opinion the adjudication officer purported to review the decision awarding invalidity benefit from September 27, 1984, to December 26, 1984, and to revise it in respect of the inclusive period from December 1, 1984, to December 20, 1984. *Held*, that (1) if there is a mistake as to a primary fact, then the possibility of review under the provisions of s.104(1)(*a*) of the Social Security Act 1975 presents itself. In the present case, C's capacity or incapacity for work is the ultimate issue, on the outcome of which an award is made or refused, and is a matter which must be inferred from primary facts. If there is no mistake as to a primary fact, but the mistake relates to how the fundamental issue has been decided on the basis of the primary facts, then there is no error as to some material fact. The adjudication officer had initially made an award based on a medical opinion, and he subsequently purported to review that decision by reason of a different medical opinion. But there was no mistake on his part as to some specific or primary fact and accordingly, there was no question of his original awarding

decision having been based on a mistake as to some material fact (*Decision R(I) 3/75* approved); (2) furthermore, there can be no question of a different medical opinion constituting a change of circumstances for the purposes of review under s.104(1)(*b*) of the Social Security Act 1975 (*R(S) 6/78* approved); (3) the adjudication officer was not entitled to review his decision under s.104(1) and the award of invalidity benefit must stand: DECISION NO. R(S) 4/86.

3141. Invalidity care allowance—sex discrimination—allowance not paid to married woman living with husband. See DRAKE *v.* CHIEF ADJUDICATION OFFICER (No. 150/85), § 1468.

3142. Invalidity pension—appeal—appeal out of time
[Social Security Act 1975 (c.14), ss.36(4), 82(2); Social Security Act 1980 (c.30), s.14(2)(*b*); Social Security (Adjudication) Regulations 1984 (S.I. 1984 No. 451), reg. 3(2), Sched. 2, para. 9.]
A social security commissioner's refusal to grant an extension of time to appeal cannot be appealed; it can be challenged by an application for judicial review if the commissioner fails to take into account some relevant consideration, or takes into account some irrelevant consideration or his decision is perverse.
A, the applicant, became unfit to do housework after being assaulted. She sought an invalidity pension. Her application and appeal were dismissed. The law was then changed after a decision of the House of Lords. The commissioner refused leave to appeal to the Court of Appeal out of time. A applied to the Court of Appeal for leave to appeal. *Held*, refusing the application, that the commissioner's refusal was not a decision for the purpose of s.14(2) of the Social Security Act 1980, and the court had no jurisdiction to hear the appeal; the commissioner's decision could be challenged by an application for judicial review if the commissioner failed to take into account some relevant consideration, or took into account some irrelevant consideration, or his decision was perverse (*Bland* v. *Chief Supplementary Benefit Officer* [1983] C.L.Y. 3482 applied: *Nancollas* v. *Insurance Officer* [1985] C.L.Y. 3262 considered).
WHITE *v.* CHIEF ADJUDICATION OFFICER [1986] 2 All E.R. 905, C.A.

3143. Lump sum payments
PENSIONERS' LUMP SUM PAYMENTS ORDER 1986 (No. 1119) [45p], made under the Pensioners' Payments and Social Security Act 1979 (c.48), s.4(1)(2); operative on December 1, 1986; provides for a lump sum payment of £10 to pensioners in the week commencing December 1, 1986.

3144. Maternity and funeral expenses
SOCIAL FUND MATERNITY AND FUNERAL EXPENSES (CLAIMS AND PAYMENTS) REGULATIONS 1986 (No. 2172) [£1·90], made under the Social Security Act 1986 (c.50), s.51(1)(*a*)–(*s*)(2), 54, 84(1) and the Social Security Act 1975 (c.14), s.114; operative on April 6, 1987; provides for claims for and payments of social fund payments for maternity and funeral expenses.
SOCIAL FUND MATERNITY AND FUNERAL EXPENSES (GENERAL) REGULATIONS 1986 (No. 2173) [£1·40], made under the Social Security Act 1986 (c.50), ss.32(2)(*a*), 34(1) and 89(1); operative on April 6, 1987; prescribe the circumstances in which maternity and funeral payments are to be made.

3145. Mobility allowance
MOBILITY ALLOWANCE AMENDMENT REGULATIONS 1986 (No. 1541) [80p], made under the Social Security Act 1975 (c.14), ss.37A and 114(1), and Sched. 20, and the Social Security Act 1986 (c.50), ss.51(1)(*b*)–(*e*), 84(1)(*c*) and 89(1); operative on October 1, 1986; amend S.I. 1975 No. 1573.

3146. Mobility allowance—assessment of immobility—burden on tribunal
A medical appeal tribunal had to assess the extent to which the pain and discomfort suffered by P affected his mobility. They decided that he was exaggerating or lying about his symptoms. *Held*, that it would be an intolerable burden on the tribunal to make specific findings about the distance he could walk, and the amount of pain that would make him stop walking. There was no breach of natural justice in the tribunal's not putting to P that he was exaggerating or lying: BARON *v.* SECRETARY OF STATE FOR SOCIAL SERVICES, *The Times*, March 25, 1986, C.A.

3147. Mobility allowance—decision of Medical Appeal Tribunal—effect on adjudicating authorities—Commissioner's decision

On March 23, 1983 a claim for Mobility Allowance was received by the Secretary of State. A Medical Board, sitting on August 12, 1983, determined the medical questions adversely to the claimant and on October 6, 1983 the insurance officer disallowed the claim. On appeal, a Medical Appeal Tribunal, sitting on January 31, 1985, decided the medical questions favourably to the claimant but only in respect of the period from and including June 1, 1984. On April 18, 1985 the Chief Adjudication Officer referred certain questions to the Social Security Appeal Tribunal concerning the effects of the decision of the Medical Appeal Tribunal for the lay adjudicator. The Appeal Tribunal decided on June 10, 1985 the decision of the insurance officer could be reviewed and revised and that the claimant was entitled to Mobility Allowance from and including June 1, 1984. The Chief Adjudication Officer then appealed to the Commissioner. *Held,* that (1) the adjudicating officer was obliged to give effect to the decision of the Medical Appeal Tribunal as it was not for him to enter into the merits of the medical questions which had been referred to the appropriate adjudicating medical authority or to consider the correctness or otherwise in law of the decision of such medical authority; (2) the conclusion of the tribunal that the provisions of s.104(1)(*b*) of the Social Security Act 1975 provided an appropriate statutory authority for the adjudication officer's review in the present case was correct as the decision of the Medical Appeal Tribunal is, like the case of retrospective legislation figured in para. 10 of *Decision R(G) 3/85,* the warrant for a revised decision under this section having effect from the appropriate earlier date established by that decision, in this case June 1, 1984: DECISION NO. R(M) 1/86.

3148. Overpayments

SOCIAL SECURITY (PAYMENTS ON ACCOUNT, OVERPAYMENTS AND RECOVERY) REGULATIONS 1986 (No. 2217) [£2·90], made under the Social Security Act 1986 (c.50), ss.27, 51(1)(*t*)(*u*), 53, 84(1), 89; operative on April 6, 1987; make provision in relation to the recovery of or the offset against of over payments of social security benefits.

3149. Persons abroad

SOCIAL SECURITY BENEFIT (PERSONS ABROAD) AMENDMENT (No. 2) REGULATIONS 1986 (No. 1545) [45p], made under the Social Security Act 1975 (c.14), ss.51(1), 131, 168(1) and Sched. 20; operative on October 1, 1986; amend S.I. 1975 No. 563.

3150. Retirement pension—increase in respect of a child—child commencing employment—Commissioner's decision

[Scot.] [Child Benefit (General) Regulations 1976 (S.I. 1976 No. 965), reg. 7.] C was in receipt of retirement pension together with an increase in respect of his grandson, in respect of whom he was also entitled to child benefit. The child, aged 17, left school on July 8, 1983 and commenced employment on July 11, 1983. He was excluded from the child benefit award from July 18, 1983. Increase of retirement pension continued in payment for a further seven weeks to September 7, 1983 but subsequently the insurance officer reviewed the award, decided that there was no entitlement during this period, declared an overpayment of £55.65 and required its payment. C appealed. *Held,* that (1) reg. 7(1) and (2) of the Child Benefit (General) Regulations 1976 applied to C's grandson in that although he ceased full-time education on July 8, 1983, he fell to be treated as a child up to the "terminal date"—September 5, 1983. Reg. 7(3) does not remove entitlement to child benefit for a child undertaking full-time employment but provides that such benefit shall not be payable; (2) C's entitlement to an increase of retirement pension depended upon his being entitled to child benefit for his grandson. Entitlement to child benefit continued to September 5, 1983 albeit that by the operation of reg. 7(3) child benefit was not payable after July 18, 1983. C must therefore be held to remain entitled to increase of retirement pension up to the week in which September 5, 1983 fell; (3) the decision awarding increase of retirement pension did not fall to be revised in respect of the period July 21, 1983 to September 7, 1983 and no overpayment of retirement pension had been made. In considering the concept of the claimants continued entitlement to child benefit notwithstanding the fact that the benefit was not payable, the Commissioner applied the reasoning of the House of Lords in *Insurance Officer* v. *McCaffrey* [1984] C.L.Y. 2452 and rejected that in R(S) 11/83: DECISION NO. R(P) 3/85.

3151. Severe disablement allowance

SOCIAL SECURITY (SEVERE DISABLEMENT ALLOWANCE) AMENDMENT REGULATIONS 1986 (No. 1933) [45p], made under the Social Security Act 1975 (c.14), ss.36(7)(*d*), 115(1), Sched. 13, para. 2, Sched. 20; operative on December 8, 1986; amend S.I. 1984 No. 1303 so that a person entitled to an allowance may undertake work as part of his medical treatment without losing benefit so long as his earnings do not ordinarily exceed £25·50 per week.

3152. Severe disablement allowance—previously entitled to invalidity pension—date of award—Commissioner's decision

[Social Security (Claims and Payments) Regulations 1979 (S.I. 1979 No. 628), reg. 11(1) (as amended); Social Security (Severe Disablement Allowance) Regulations 1984 (S.I. 1984 No. 1303), reg. 20(1).] C had been in receipt of non-contributory invalidity pension since February 14, 1981. Her claim was disallowed from and including December 18, 1981 because she had not proved that she was incapable of performing normal household duties by reason of some specific disease or bodily or mental disablement. In a decision dated April 22, 1984 the Commissioner held that such benefit was not payable from December 18, 1981 to January 1, 1983. On receipt of further evidence he subsequently determined the claim in respect of the period December 31, 1981 to November 28, 1984 and held that non contributory invalidity pension was payable and proceeded, by reference to the relevant transitional provisions, to determine whether he could and should award severe disablement allowance to the claimant from November 29, 1984 and if so when his award should terminate. *Held*, that (1) under the transitional provisions of the Severe Disablement Allowance Regulations, by reason of her entitlement to non contributory invalidity pension immediately before both September 10, 1984 and November 29, 1984. (a) C is entitled to severe disablement allowance for November 29, 1984 and any subsequent days which together with November 29, 1984 fall within a single period of interruption of employment even though she may not be disabled for the purpose of s.36 of the Social Security Act and whether or not the appointed day in respect of her is November 29, 1984; (b) the provisions of s.79(1) of the Social Security Act relevant at the time, that benefit must be duly claimed, are deemed satisfied by reason of the Secretary of State's acceptance of the claim for non-contributory invalidity pension as a claim for severe disablement allowance; (c) from September 2, 1985, when s.165A of the Social Security Act 1975 came into effect and provided that no person shall be entitled to any benefit unless he makes a claim for it, the claimant continued to be entitled as the necessary claim had been made, see paragraph 1(b) above: (2) severe disablement allowance is payable under the provisions of reg. 11(1) of the Social Security (Claims and Payments) Regulations, as the necessary conditions for such an award are satisfied, for a period down to the date of decision by the Commissioner and for 26 weeks thereafter; (3) C is entitled to severe disablement allowance for all subsequent days falling within the same single period of interruption of employment so long as she continues to satisfy the requirements for entitlement to such an allowance other than those referred to in para. (a) and (b) of reg. 20(1) of the Social Security (Severe Disablement Allowance) Regulations 1984: DECISION No. R(S)1/86.

3153. Sick pay. See EMPLOYMENT, § 1247.

3154. Sickness benefit—capacity for work—suitable employment—Commissioner's decision

C, a 26 year old machine operator with a history of back trouble, had been receiving sickness benefit. Medical reports by Divisional Medical Officers of the DHSS dated November 11, 1983 and January 23, 1984 indicated that C was incapable of his normal occupation but capable of work within certain limits. The adjudication officer disallowed the sickness benefit claim from December 5, 1983 and C appealed. *Held*, (1) in accordance with *Decision R(S) 2/78* it is normal practice not to assess C's capacity for work by reference to alternative occupations until a period of six months has elapsed; (2) the test to be applied is whether C was capable of any work which he could reasonably be expected to do and to consider his "employability" state *without* retraining; (3) except where it may be properly concluded from common knowledge that suitable employment exists of which C must have been capable, there are other cases where the medical and general circumstances require consideration to be given as to *what* work the claimant may have been capable of at the material time; (4) in the determination of an appeal the determining authority is assisted if the adjudication officer provides specific job descriptions for which the particular claimant was capable at the material time; (5) C had discharged the burden of proof and the appeal was allowed: DECISION NO. R(S) 6/85.

3155. Sickness benefit—incapacity—absence from Great Britain—Tribunal decision

[Social Security Benefit (Persons Abroad) Regulations 1975 (S.I. 1975 No. 563, reg. 2(1).] C suffered from hypertension and underwent coronary bypass surgery in November 1980 which resulted in a malunion of his sternum. Following a further operation in February 1982 to wire up the sternum he suffered a number of spells of incapacity ending on December 14, 1983 and on December 22, 1983. Having worked the preceding day, he went to the United States to seek further operative treatment. On February 6, 1984 he became incapable of work because of chest pains and on April 2, 1984 underwent another operation in California for the rewiring of his sternum as well as receiving treatment for his hypertension. Sickness benefit was disallowed by the adjudication officer because C did not satisfy the provisions of the Social Security Benefit (Persons Abroad) Regulations and disqualification for absence abroad required by s.82(5)(a) of the Social Security Act 1975 could not be avoided. The Social Security appeal tribunal upheld the decision and C appealed to the Commissioner. *Held,* by Mr. D. G. Rice and Mr. I. Edwards-Jones, Mr. J. N. B. Penny dissenting that (1) in the context of reg. 2(1)(b) of the Social Security Benefit (Persons Abroad) Regulations "incapacity" means "incapacity for work" and such incapacity must arise "by reason of some specific disease or bodily or mental disablement"; (2) to succeed in invoking reg. 2(1)(b) it is a basic requirement that (a) the claimant was immediately prior to his absence from Great Britain, incapacitated for work by reason of some specific disease or bodily or mental disablement; (b) his going abroad is for the purpose of having treatment for that condition; and (c) the condition giving rise to the incapacity abroad was capable of being identified with the condition giving rise to the incapacity subsisting at the date of departure abroad; (3) the claim failed because of the claimant's inability to demonstrate incapacity for work immediately prior to the commencement of his absence from Great Britain.

NB: The Tribunal referred to a number of reported and unreported Commissioners' decisions dealing with reg. 2(1) of the Social Security Benefit (Persons Abroad) Regulations which in their opinion contained material meriting reappraisal. In particular they expressed reservations about the dicta in *R(S) 6/61* and *R(S) 1/75* as to the meaning of "specific purpose" and directed that *CS/112/1982* (unreported) should not be followed: DECISION NO. R(S) 2/86.

3156. Social Security Act 1986 (c.50)

This Act makes provision in relation to personal pension schemes, amends the law relating to social security, occupational pension schemes and the provision of refreshments for school pupils, abolishes maternity pay under the Employment Protection (Consolidation) Act 1978 and provides for the winding-up of the Maternity Pay Fund and empowers the Secretary of State to pay the travelling expenses of certain persons.

The Act received the Royal Assent on July 25, 1986.

3157. Social Security Act 1986—commencement

SOCIAL SECURITY ACT 1986 (Commencement No. 1) ORDER 1986 (No. 1609 (C.58)) [80p], made under the Social Security Act 1986 (c.30), ss.83(1), 88(1); brings into force on October 1, 1986 sections 39 (in part), 51(1)(b)(c)(d)(e), 62, 67(1), 71(1)–(3), 86(1)(2) (in part), Sched. 3, paras. 1, 2, 3, 5(1) (in part) (2), 13, 14, 15, 17, Sched. 10, paras. 68, 83, 84, 88, 89, 90, 91, 92, 93, 95, 97, 100, 104, 105, Sched. 11 (in part) and brings into force on October 5, 1986 sections 42–44

SOCIAL SECURITY ACT 1986 (COMMENCEMENT No. 2) ORDER 1986 (No. 1719 (C.60)) [80p], made under the Social Security Act 1986 (c.50), s.88(1); brings into force on November 1, 1986 sections 8, 16, Scheds. 10 (in part) and 11 (in part), and brings into force on April 6, 1987 section 11 and Sched. 10, para. 13.

SOCIAL SECURITY ACT 1986 (COMMENCEMENT No. 3) ORDER 1986 (No. 1958 (c.72)) [45p], made under the Social Security Act 1986 (c.50), s.88(1) and (2); brings into force on April 6, 1987, ss.52, 82 and Schedules 5 and 9 of the 1986 Act.

SOCIAL SECURITY ACT 1986 (COMMENCEMENT No. 4) ORDER 1986 (No. 1959 (c.73)) [£1·40], made under the Social Security Act 1986 (c.50), s.88(1); brings into operation on March 15, April 6 and April 7, 1987, specified provisions of the 1986 Act.

3158. Statutory sick pay—entitlement—commencement of period of entitlement—Commissioner's decision

C claimed statutory sick pay for a period of incapacity commencing on December 1, 1983 during a stoppage of work due to a trade dispute at her place of employment which began on November 24, 1983 and ended on December 4, 1983. The adjudication officer decided that a period of entitlement to statutory sick pay did not arise because on December 1, 1983 there was a stoppage of work due to a trade dispute and C had not proved that at no time on or before December 1, 1983 she did not participate in, or have a direct interest in, the trade dispute. As a result, statutory sick pay was not payable throughout the period of incapacity from December 1, 1983 to December 31, 1983. On appeal, the social security appeal tribunal upheld the adjudication officer's decision and the claimant appealed to a Social Security Commissioner. *Held*, that (1) for the purposes of establishing a period of entitlement, the commencement of the period of entitlement cannot be deferred to a later date when a stoppage of work due to a trade dispute at the place of employment has come to an end; (2) in applying the provisions of the Social Security and Housing Benefits Act 1982, the adjudicating authorities are not concerned with the merits of the dispute or the manner in which the stoppage of work was called or the legal effect of such stoppage upon the contract of service, but with the question whether or not there was on the relevant date, within the meaning of section 19 of the Social Security Act 1975, a stoppage of work due to a trade dispute at the employee's place of employment: DECISION No. R(SSP) 1/86.

3159. Students

SOCIAL SECURITY (UNEMPLOYMENT, SICKNESS AND INVALIDITY BENEFIT) AMENDMENT (No. 2) REGULATIONS 1986 (No. 1011) [80p], made under Social Security Act 1975 (c.14), ss.17(2)(*a*), 166(1), Sched. 20; operative on November 3, 1986; provide that a student attending a full-time course of education shall not be treated as unemployed on any day in a period for which a maintenance grant is payable except during the summer vacation.

3160. Supplementary benefit

SUPPLEMENTARY BENEFIT (CLAIMS AND PAYMENTS) AMENDMENT REGULATIONS 1986 (No. 562) [80p], made under the Supplementary Benefits Act 1976 (c.71), ss.11, 14(1)(2)(*a*)(*g*)(*i*), 34(1), Sched. 1, para. 4; operative on April 21, 1986; further amends S.I. 1981 No. 1525.

SUPPLEMENTARY BENEFIT (CLAIMS AND PAYMENTS) AMENDMENT (No. 2) REGULATIONS 1986 (No. 2154) [45p], made under the Supplementary Benefits Act 1976 (c.71), ss.14(1)(2)(i), 34(1); operative on January 26, 1987; amends S.I. 1981 No. 1525 in relation to mortgage payments.

SUPPLEMENTARY BENEFIT (CONDITIONS OF ENTITLEMENT) AMENDMENT REGULATIONS 1986 (No. 1010) [45p], made under the Supplementary Benefits Act 1976 (c.71), ss.5, 34(1); operative on November 3, 1986; amend S.I. 1981 No. 1526 by inserting a definition of "a course of advanced education" and by amending the definition of "student."

SUPPLEMENTARY BENEFIT (MISCELLANEOUS AMENDMENTS) REGULATIONS 1986 (No. 1259) [£2·90], made under the Supplementary Benefits Act 1976 (c.71), ss.2(1), (1A), 3, 4, 11, 14(1), (2)(*a*), (*c*) and (*g*), 33(5) and 34(1)(*a*) and the Social Security Act 1975 (c.14), s.166(2) and (3); operative on August 11, 1986; amend S.I. 1981 No. 1528.

SUPPLEMENTARY BENEFIT (REQUIREMENTS AND RESOURCES) AMENDMENT REGULATIONS 1986 (No. 1292) [£5·40], made under the Supplementary Benefits Act 1976 (c.71), ss.1(3), 2(1A), (2), 33(5) and 34(1)(*c*) and Sched. 1, paras. 1(2), 2(1)–(4); operative on July 28, 1986; make further provision for boarders.

SUPPLEMENTARY BENEFIT (REQUIREMENTS AND RESOURCES) MISCELLANEOUS AMENDMENT REGULATIONS 1986 (No. 1293) [£1·90], made under the Supplementary Benefits Act 1976 (c.71), ss.2(2), 34(1)*b*), Sched. 1, paras. 1 and 2; make provisions for students.

SUPPLEMENTARY BENEFIT (SINGLE PAYMENTS) AMENDMENT REGULATIONS 1986 (No. 1961) [£3·80], made under the Supplementary Benefits Act 1976 (s.71), ss.3, 14(2)(*a*), 34(1) and the Social Security Act 1975 (c.14), s.166(2)(3); operative on December 11, 1986; further amend S.I. 1981 No. 1528 so as to make new provision for payments in respect of fuel costs.

SUPPLEMENTARY BENEFIT UPRATING REGULATIONS 1986 (No. 1173) [80p], made under the Supplementary Benefits Act 1976, ss.2(2), 34(1)(*a*) and Sched. 1, para. 2(1) and (9); operative on July 28, 1986; increase certain amounts specified in S.I. 1983 No. 1399.

3161. Supplementary benefit—backdated claim—good cause—Commissioner's decision
[Supplementary Benefit (Claims and Payments) Regulations 1981 (S.I. 1981 No. 1525), reg. 5(2)(*b*).] C claimed a supplementary allowance on August 22, 1984 and requested that the claim be backdated. A sickness benefit claim, previously made on March 12, 1984, had at that time not been determined. The adjudication officer refused to backdate the claim because he was not satisfied that good cause for delay in claiming had been shown, and reg. 5(2)(*b*) of the Claims and Payments Regulations could not apply, because the claim to supplementary allowance had been made before receipt of a decision on sickness benefit. Benefit was awarded from the prescribed pay week commencing August 27, 1984. The tribunal upheld the adjudication officer's decision and C appealed to the Commissioner. *Held,* that (1) the tribunal were entitled to conclude that continuous good cause for delay had not been established from May 15, 1984 or May 18, 1984 to the date of claim or for any other period in accordance with Claims and Payments Regulation 5(2)(*a*). (2) the purpose of reg. 5(2)(*b*) is to prevent the loss of supplementary benefit by a claimant who delays claiming until he knows the outcome of a claim for another benefit. The only restriction is that the claim must be made as soon as reasonably practicable after a decision on the other claim is received. There is nothing to prevent the claim for supplementary benefit being made before a decision on the other benefit is received. The appeal was allowed and the Commissioner decided that the claim for supplementary benefit was to be treated as made on March 12, 1984: DECISION NO. R(SB) 5/86.

3162. Supplementary benefit—backdated claim—whether good cause—Commissioner's decision
[Supplementary Benefit (Claims and Payments) Regulations 1981 (S.I. 1981 No. 1525), reg. 5(2)(*a*).] C had been unemployed and receiving unemployment benefit until February 14, 1984. On February 22, 1984 he claimed supplementary benefit on a form B1 which he had been given, on January 26, 1984, for that purpose. The adjudication officer decided that he was entitled to benefit from February 25, 1984. C appealed against this decision on the grounds that the award of supplementary benefit should have begun when his unemployment benefit ceased and that he had not claimed earlier due to an injury to his right arm and in any event he was unaware that there would be any difficulty in obtaining a back-dated award. The tribunal confirmed the adjudication officer's decision and the claimant appealed to a Social Security Commissioner. *Held,* allowing the appeal, that (1) the question whether "there was good cause for failure to make the claim before the date on which it was made" in reg. 5(2)(*a*) of the Supplementary Benefit (Claims and Payments) Regulations 1981 was a question of law, R(S) 2/63 affirmed; (2) it was vitally important for any tribunal considering "good cause" to segregate findings of primary fact from their conclusions and reasons upon such issues of law as arise for determination: DECISION NO. R(SB) 39/85.

3163. Supplementary benefit—board and lodging rules—whether ultra vires
[Immigration (Variation of Leave) Order (S.I. 1976 No. 1572; Supplementary Benefit (Conditions of Entitlement) Regulations (S.I. 1980 No. 1586), reg. 7] M, an immigrant, was granted leave to enter the U.K. on condition he did not seek work there. His leave to remain was subsequently extended under the Immigration (Variation of Leave) Order. *Held,* that he could not claim supplementary benefit for the period of extended leave, because during that period he could not have been treated as being available for employment under reg. 7 of the Supplementary Benefit (Conditions of Entitlement) Regulations, as his extended leave was granted on the same terms as the original leave, which prohibited working: ALI *v.* CHIEF ADJUDICATION OFFICER, *The Times,* December 24, 1985, C.A.

3164. Supplementary benefit—entitlement—period following commencement of work—Commissioner's decision
[Supplementary Benefits Act 1976 (c.71), s.6; Supplementary Benefit (Conditions of Entitlement) Regulations 1981 (S.I. 1981 No. 1526), regs. 9(2)(*a*), 10; Supplementary Benefit (Single Payments) Regulations 1981 (S.I. 1981 No. 1528),

reg. 4; Supplementary Benefit (Urgent Cases) Regulations 1981 (S.I. 1981 No. 1529), reg. 3.]

C, a 16 year old, had left school in June 1983 and started full-time employment on August 15, 1983. Her wages were not payable until September 27, 1983 and her employers were not prepared to give her an advance of wages. She therefore made a claim for supplementary benefit and for a single payment to meet travelling costs to and from work. The supplementary benefit officer refused both claims and on appeal this decision was confirmed by the appeal tribunal. C appealed to the Social Security Commissioner. *Held,* dismissing the appeal, that (1) C was not excluded from supplementary benefit by section 6(1) of the Supplementary Benefits Act 1976 during the 15 days after the commencement of her full-time employment because she was *not* to be treated as being in full-time employment by virtue of reg. 9(2)(*a*) of Supplementary Benefit (Conditions of Entitlement) Regulations 1981; (2) C was excluded from supplementary benefit by s.6(2) of the Supplementary Benefits Act 1976 because under the provisions of s.6(3) and reg. 10 of the Supplementary Benefit (Conditions of Entitlement) Regulations 1981 she fell to be treated as receiving relevant education until the terminal date, September 5, 1983; (3) C was not entitled to a single payment for travelling expenses because she was not a "claimant" for the purposes of the Supplementary Benefit (Single Payments) Regulations 1981; (4) C was not entitled to a payment under the Supplementary Benefit (Urgent Cases) Regulations 1981 up to September 5, 1983 because she was prevented from so qualifying by s.6(2) of the Supplementary Benefits Act 1976 but had a possible limited entitlement thereafter.

The appeal on the main issue, which was that of the claimant's entitlement to supplementary benefit in the 15 day period following the commencement of work, was dismissed. The Commissioner set aside the decisions relating to the Single Payments Regulations and Urgent Cases Regulations because of inadequate findings of fact and reasons. The Commissioner gave the decision under the Single Payments Regulations and remitted for rehearing by a different tribunal the issues arising under the Urgent Cases Regulations: DECISION No. R(SB) 34/85.

3165. Supplementary benefit—failure to maintain children—whether offence

[Supplementary Benefits Act 1976 (c.71), s.25] The prosecution does not have to prove that the defendant was capable of paying maintenance to establish the offence and the provisions of section 18 of the Act are not relevant to the proceedings: R. *v.* DAVIS, *The Times,* May 20, 1986, D.C.

3166. Supplementary benefit—nomination as claimant—failure to claim—Commissioner's decision

[Supplementary Benefit (Aggregation Regulations) 1981 (S.I. 1981 No. 1524), reg. 1A(2).] C was a married woman living with her husband and children. She registered unemployed and claimed both a supplementary allowance and a single payment for expenses in respect of her grandmother's funeral. A benefit officer (now the adjudication officer) rejected her claims on the ground that she was not the "relevant person" for the purposes of section 1(2) of the Act. On appeal the tribunal upheld the decision and C appealed to a Social Security Commissioner. *Held,* allowing the appeal, that (1) leaflets of the Department of Health and Social Security only indicated the official view of the interpretation of the regulations and were not available as an aid to construction. However the Social Security Advisory Committee reports on regulations before enactment were such an aid; (2) nomination as to who should be the claimant for the purposes of reg. 1A(2)(*a*) of the Aggregation Regulations 1981 was primarily a matter of choice for the married (or unmarried) couple concerned. Furthermore, evidence concerning that choice, or a completed form of nomination, may be forwarded after the time of the claim. Only if a couple failed to nominate could reg. 1A(2)(*b*) apply and the Secretary of State decide who should be the claimant; (3) in the light of the House of Lords' decision in the case of *Insurance Officer* v. *McCaffrey* [1985] C.L.Y. 3279, failure to claim supplementary benefit did not bar "entitlement" to that benefit—for the purposes of reg. 1A(*b*)(vii) and (viii)—at a date earlier than the one on which it was subsequently claimed; (4) for the purposes of reg. 1A(1)(*b*) in conditions (vii) and (viii) of that regulation "entitled to supplementary benefit . . ." should be read as if it said "excepted from disentitlement to supplementary benefit . . .": DECISION No. R(SB) 6/86.

3167. Supplementary benefit—overpayment—Commissioner's decision
In connection with his claim to supplementary allowance in July 1981 C declared that his wife's part-time earnings, after deductions, were £34·46 a week. In October 1983 he was asked to forward details of his wife's wages and it was ascertained that they had increased. The adjudication officer decided that supplementary allowance of £481·63 had been overpaid from April 24, 1982 to October 29, 1983 and was recoverable. On appeal the tribunal confirmed the decision subject to the sum of £481·63 being reassessed to take account of five weeks of underpayment falling within the overpayment period. C appealed to a Social Security Commissioner on the grounds that weeks of underpayment after October 29, 1983 should also be set-off against the amount of the overpayment. *Held,* that (1) the tribunal had erred in law because it had not complied with what is said in *R(SB) 9/85,* para. 6 and had failed to: (a) state expressly the sum which was recoverable by the Secretary of State; and (b) indicate clearly the manner in which that sum had been calculated; (2) it can be appropriate for an appeal tribunal to pass an issue of assessment or accounting back to the local adjudication officer for such an issue to be resolved between the adjudication officer and the claimant. But it is essential in such a case that the tribunal make it clear that in the event of disagreement the matter must be restored before them; (3) the phrase "at the material dates" in *R(SB) 10/85,* para. 9 can be properly applied to each and every date upon which benefit fell to be paid within the period of overpayment and extends the concept of "set-off" to underpayments made during that period; (4) those dates continue to be "material" down to the date when the adjudication officer is in possession of the material facts which have been concealed from him by reason of either misrepresentation or failure to disclose. But underpayments made after that date cannot be brought within the phrase "re-appraisal of entitlement to supplementary benefit at the material dates."
The Commissioner set aside the tribunal's decision and remitted the matter to a differently constituted tribunal solely for the purpose of determining the recoverable sum: DECISION NO. R(SB) 11/86.

3168. Supplementary benefit—person having conditional leave to remain in U.K.—whether available for employment
[Supplementary Benefits Act 1976 (c.71) s.2(1A); Supplementary Benefit (Requirements and Resources) Miscellaneous Provisions Regulations (S.I. 1985 No. 613), Sched. 1A, para. 6(2)] Sched. 2A, para. 5(3) s.2(1A) of the Supplementary Benefits Act 1976 is concerned with questions arising out of individual claims, and does not give a power to make regulations which would in themselves permit the Secretary of State (or any other person) to lay down rules or make decisions of general application. Accordingly, sched. 1A, para. 6(2) and sched. 2A, para. 5(3) of the 1985 Supplementary Benefits Regulations, which purport to be made under s.2(1A) are *ultra vires*: R. *v.* SECRETARY OF STATE FOR SOCIAL SERVICES, *ex p.* COTTON, *The Times,* December 14, 1985, C.A.

3169. Supplementary benefit—regulations—Parliamentary procedure
[Supplementary Benefits Act 1976 (c.71), s.33(3)(*c*).] S.33(3)(*c*) of the Supplementary Benefits Act 1976 contains a mandatory, not a directory, requirement that draft regulations be laid before Parliament. Draft regulations laid before Parliament contained references to a booklet which was an external document, and was not itself before Parliament. *Held,* that there was no authority which prevented reference to an external document, and it was not necessary to lay the document itself before Parliament: R. *v.* DEPARTMENT OF HEALTH AND SOCIAL SECURITY, *ex p.* LONDON BOROUGH OF CAMDEN, *The Times,* March 5, 1986, D.C.

3170. Supplementary benefit—relevant education—full-time—Commissioner's decision
[Supplementary Benefits Act 1976 (c.71), s.6; Social Security (Adjudication) Regulations 1984 (S.I. 1984 No. 451), reg. 69.] C, aged 16, was single and living in her parents' household. In September 1983 she was registering as available for employment and receiving a supplementary allowance while studying for 2 A level and one O level examinations. The benefit officer referred the question of whether she was receiving relevant education for the purposes of s.6(3) of the Supplementary Benefits Act 1976 to an insurance officer under reg. 5 of the Supplementary Benefit (Determination of Questions) Regulations 1980 ("Determination of Questions Regulations") which then applied, and, in the meantime he decided in accordance with that regulation that she was not entitled to supplementary benefit

on the assumption that the answer would be adverse to C. C appealed to a tribunal and provided evidence that the total of time required for instruction and homework was 14 hours. The tribunal confirmed the decision and C appealed to a Social Security Commissioner. *Held,* allowing the appeal, that (1) the expression "full-time" as used in s.6(3) should be construed in its ordinary everday sense; (2) the question of whether for the purposes of s.6 a person is receiving relevant education constitutes a question of fact; (3) "relevant education" in s.6(3) must be "full-time" education by attendance at an establishment recognised by the Secretary of State as being, or comparable to, a college or a school; (4) reg. 69 of the Social Security (Adjudication) Regulations 1984 provides that a tribunal shall not determined an appeal until the adjudication officer has given a substantive answer on the material question at which point the tribunal is to be seised of all the issues in the case; (5) since the insurance officer's decision had been given on the question referred to him by the benefit officer under reg. 5 of the Determination of Questions Regulations, it followed that, under the new procedure introduced by reg. 69, the tribunal were competent to decide the correctness or otherwise of that decision: DECISION NO. R(SB) 22/85.

3171. Supplementary benefit—resources—capital resource—Commissioner's decision
[Supplementary Benefits (Resources) Regulations 1981 (S.I. 1981 No. 1527), reg. 4(1).] C had been receiving supplementary benefit since 1980. In November 1982 he received £18,700 following the compulsory purchase of his house but claimed to have spent it all on repaying various loans. The adjudication officer decided that the money should be treated as still possessed by him and, because it exceeded the prescribed limit (at that time £2,500) he was not entitled to supplementary benefit. On appeal the tribunal confirmed the decision. Following an appeal to a Social Security Commissioner the appeal was reheard by a different tribunal which also confirmed the decision. C appealed again to a Social Security Commissioner. *Held,* allowing the appeal, that (1) once it had been shown that a capital resource had been received by the claimant the onus of proving that it was no longer possessed by him rested on the claimant and failing a satisfactory explanation it was open to the tribunal to find that the claimant still had that resource; (2) if it was found that the claimant still retained the resource and had not disposed of it so that his actual resources were above the prescribed limit, reg. 4(1) of the Supplementary Benefits (Resources) Regulations 1981 (notional resources) was not required to be considered. If on the other hand it had been disposed of, it was necessary to consider reg. 4(1); (3) the expression "Any resource of which a member of the assessment unit has deprived himself" in reg. 4(1) should be given its ordinary and natural meaning in the context in which it occurred; (4) any deprivation must have been for the purpose of securing supplementary benefit or increasing the amount of such benefit, but that purpose need not be the predominant motive; (5) if it was decided that the claimant had deprived himself of a capital resource for the purpose of securing supplementary benefit then the adjudication authority must exercise its descretion as to whether to treat the claimant as still possessed of the resource in question. This discretion is unlimited. It must, however, be exercised judicially, taking into account all the circumstances of the case; (6) if an adjudication authority found that reg. 4(1) fell to be applied against the claimant in circumstances where an actual resource was converted into another actual resource of lesser value, then they should only apply the regulation to treat the claimant as still possessed of the difference between the value of the new resource and the resource which it replaced: DECISION NO. R(SB) 38/85.

3172. Supplementary benefit—resources—capital sum repayable on demand—Commissioner's decision
C was a single woman who had lived in a Rest Home since 1977, the fees being met from her retirement pension and capital. Her capital consisted of £785·90 in the National Savings Bank and a National Savings Bond of £3,000 which she had purchased in 1978 using, in part, a £2,000 loan from a friend. The loan was made on the following terms: (a) the capital sum was repayable on demand; (b) C was not to use any of the capital sum; (c) C was entitled to use any interest produced by the capital sum, so long as the loan subsisted. On October 12, 1984 she claimed supplementary benefit as her friend required repayment of the loan, and she had sent the bond for encashment. The adjudication officer decided that C was not entitled to supplementary benefit as she had capital in excess of the prescribed limit (at the time £3,000). C appealed and the tribunal

upheld the appeal. The adjudication officer appealed to a Social Security Commissioner. *Held,* dismissing the appeal, that the loan was made on the express condition that C enjoyed only the use of the interest, the capital was not at her disposal and in consequence not her resource: DECISION NO. R(SB) 12/86.

3173. Supplementary benefit—resources—deprivation of capital—Commissioner's decision
[SUPPLEMENTARY BENEFIT (RESOURCES) REGULATIONS 1981 (S.I. 1981 No. 1527), regs. 4, 6.] C was made redundant on April 6, 1984 and received sums totalling over £8,000 in connection with the termination of his employment. He claimed supplementary benefit on July 10, 1984 and his actual capital resources at that time were assessed at £4,104·06. On July 19, 1984 they had reduced to £2,004·06 after a withdrawal of £1,500 on July 17, 1984. The adjudication officer considered that C had deprived himself of capital in order to receive supplementary benefit. He decided that C should be treated as still in possession of capital resources, including notional resources, exceeding £3,000, the prescribed limit and rejected the claim, On appeal the tribunal confirmed the decision and C appealed to a Social Security Commissioner. *Held,* allowing the appeal, that (1) for the purposes of the application of reg. 4(1) of the Supplementary Benefit (Resources) Regulations 1981 three things must be established, *viz* (i) that C has deprived himself of a resource; (ii) that he has done so for the purpose of securing or increasing supplementary benefit; and (iii) that it is appropriate to exercise the discretion to treat the resource as still possessed by C; (2) the word "deprive" is an ordinary English word whose meaning is not a question of law and does not change by reference to the consequences of deprivation. Any act, as a result of which a claimant no longer possessed the resource, whether or not he acquired another resource in its place, could be considered as a deprivation; (3) whether its purpose is to secure or increase benefit is ordinarily a matter of inference from the primary facts and facts for or against that conclusion must be included; findings were essential on the reasons tendered by the claimant for various items of expenditure and if in issue, on the extent of C's knowledge of the capital limits; (4) affirming para. 22 of CSB 858/84 (reported as R(SB) 38/85, the purpose of securing benefit, or increasing the amount thereof need not be the sole purpose, but it must be a significant operative purpose; (5) if it was found that a deprivation or conversion for either of the above reasons had taken place, it was necessary to consider first the effect of reg. 6(1)(c)(ii) of the Supplementary Benefit (Resources) Regulations 1981. Personal possessions would be included under reg. 5(a) at their current market value less any amount that would be attributable to the expense of sale. It was then necessary to consider the exercise of the discretion in reg. 4(1); (6) the discretion should be exercised to put C in the same position as is practicable had the transaction not been entered into, but not to penalise him further. If the inclusion of a notional resource would cause the claimant the hardship of living without supplementary benefit for a time, that hardship could not ordinarily be a ground for exercising the discretion in C's favour without nullifying the purpose of the regulation; (7) the discretion should not be exercised so to count the resource twice. If C has deprived himself of cash in the purchase of an item that was not disregarded, the discretion should be limited to the excess of the cash over the value of that item. The resource should also not be treated as possessed for all the time; had the claimant retained the capital resource he would have had to meet his requirements out of that resource: DECISION NO. R(SB) 40/85.

3174. Supplementary benefit—resources—maintenance arrears paid as lump sum—Commissioner's decision
[Supplementary Benefit (Resources) Regulations 1981 (S.I. 1981 No. 1527), reg. 13] C was a divorced woman who had received supplementary benefit since August 1, 1983. A court order requiring her ex-husband to pay her £10 per week maintenance was not paid regularly and he fell into arrears of some £400. On November 5, 1983 she received a cheque from him for £40, in respect of those arrears. She cashed it soon after and used the money to repay loans from relatives. On November 14, 1983 she notified the local office of the payment and on November 15, 1983 the adjudication officer decided that the £40 should be treated as an income resource at the rate of £10 per week for four weeks commencing November 7, 1983 and that she was not entitled to supplementary benefit for the period November 7, 1983 to December 4, 1983. C appealed against this decision and the tribunal decided that she was so entitled to benefit for that

period as the £40 represented arrears for a period prior to August 1, 1983. The adjudication officer appealed to a Social Security Commissioner. *Held,* allowing the appeal, that (1) the aggregate of the four weeks arrears was a "lump sum" as defined in reg. 13(5) of the Resources Regulations; (2) the weekly amount to be taken into account under reg. 13(3)(*a*) was the sum produced by dividing the lump sum by the number of weeks ascertained by applying the formula in that regulation; (3) in reg. 13(4) the words "in making periodical payments" and "ceases to make" fell to be applied in the everyday sense and constituted issues of fact; (4) in applying reg. 13(4)(*a*) the words "but excluding for this purpose the sum of £2.00 there mentioned" should be construed as if the words "the aggregate of £2.00 and" did not occur in reg. 13(3)(*a*)(i); (5) provision for attributing lump sums paid by liable relatives was to be taken as made by reg. 13 and no recourse to reg. 9 was required; (6) in reg. 13(2) the words "in which" were to be construed as meaning "as to which": DECISION No. R(SB) 32/85.

3175. **Supplementary benefit—resources—payment in lieu of concessionary coal—Commissioner's decision**

[Supplementary Benefit (Resources) Regulations 1981 (S.I. 1981 No. 1527), reg. 10.] C was a married man with three dependent children who stopped work due to a trade dispute on March 9, 1984. He claimed supplementary benefit on March 27, 1984. His personal requirements fell to be disregarded under s.8 of the Supplementary Benefits Act 1976, but he was entitled to benefit for his wife and children. He normally received tax-free payments of £133.60 a quarter from the National Coal Board in lieu of concessionary coal. On May 4, 1984 he received a payment of £89.07 for the quarter February 1, 1984 to April 30, 1984. This was a reduced amount of two-thirds because he had been on strike for part of the period. The adjudication officer treated the payment as earnings and attributed it forward over two months at a weekly rate of £10.26, subject to a disregard of £4. On appeal, the tribunal decided by a majority that the payment was not earnings and should not have been taken into account. The adjudication officer appealed to a Social Security Commissioner. *Held,* that (1) the payment constituted "remuneration or profit derived from any employment" for the purposes of reg. 10(1) of the Supplementary Benefit (Resources) Regulations 1981, because it would not have been made had the claimant not been an employee of the National Coal Board; (2) the provision of reg. 10(3)(*a*) (the disregard of one daily meal provided free at a person's place of work) was a further indication that reg. 10 was intended to cover miscellaneous remuneration or profit derived from employment; while the practice of the Inland Revenue though relevant, was not conclusive of the question under reg. 10; (3) although there were restrictions on the receipt of the money, which was in a sense "a heating allowance," it did not alter the fact that the sum was remuneration or profit from employment; (4) the exemption given to "the value of any benefit in kind in the form of a concession" under reg. 11(4)(*f*) could not apply to any payment which was caught by reg. 10; it can only apply to concessions which are not earnings: DECISION No. R(SB) 2/86.

3176. **Supplementary benefit—resources—student maintenance allowance—Commissioner's decision**

[Supplementary Benefit (Resources) Regulations 1981 (S.I. 1981 No. 1527), regs. 11(2), (4).] C lived with her two dependent children and had been in receipt of supplementary benefit since 1981. In August 1983 she was awarded a minor grant by the local education authority in connection with a full time course of business studies. The grant comprised her tuition fees, the fee for one examination and a maintenance allowance of £381 payable in three equal instalments at the beginning of each academic term. The terms occupied 38 weeks of the year. According to the Chief Education Officer the grant of £381 was deemed to include £105 for meals, the remainder covering sundry costs of equipment, books, travel, etc. The benefit officer first determined the grant was equivalent to £10·02 a week during term-time and that it attracted a disregard of £9·50 under reg. 11(4)(*e*) of the Supplementary Benefit (Resources) Regulations. Later, on review, the benefit officer decided that a disregard of £2 a week, and not £9·50, was appropriate under reg. 11(2)(*l*) of the Supplementary Benefit (Resources) Regulations. He further considered that, of the total maintenance allowance of £381, there should be disregarded, under reg. 11(4)(*j*), £85·65 representing the actual cost of books and equipment and £114 representing travelling expenses. This meant that £2·77 of the minor grant, instead of £0·52 as previously, was accounted as weekly income. The outcome of the review was a decision effective from the pay day in week commencing February 27, 1984 that C was entitled to supplementary benefit of £35·39 weekly. On appeal the tribunal confirmed that decision and C appealed to a Social Security Commissioner. *Held*, dismissing the appeal, that (1) where a maintenance allowance included a payment for the provision of equipment, books and travelling expenses essential to a course, it was not necessary for the purpose of regulation 11(4)(*j*) to have a specific breakdown of those various costs; (2) a claimant must demonstrate to the satisfaction of the benefit (adjudication) officer the expenditure actually incurred; (3) only a person who had not attained the age of 19 could ever be actually in receipt of "relevant education" in accordance with section 6(2) of the Supplementary Benefits Act 1976: DECISION No. R(SB) 8/86.

3177. Supplementary benefit—resources—valuation of joint interest in property—Commissioner's decision

[Supplementary Benefit (Resources) Regulations 1981 (S.I. 1981 No. 1527), reg. 5(a)(*i*).] In January 1984 C made a claim for supplementary benefit. He had capital assets consisting of £1,124·18 in a building society and he was joint owner of a bungalow with his nephew who lived in Tasmania. The adjudication officer decided that the value of C's capital resources exceeded the prescribed limit (at that time £3,000) and that he was not entitled to supplementary benefit. On appeal the tribunal confirmed the decision and C appealed to a Social Security Commissioner. *Held*, allowing the appeal, that (1) C's joint interest in the property was not an unobtainable asset but was difficult to realise, and that interest fell to be valued; (2) the market value of the property was the price that it would fetch in the market; (3) applying *R(SB) 21/83* the interest of a joint tenant, or tenant in common, lay not in the land itself but in the proceeds of sale of the land. As such the 10 per cent. deduction in the case of land under reg. 5(a)(i) of the Supplementary Benefit (Resources) Regulations 1981 did not fall to be made, but a deduction fell to be made for the expenses of sale. Such expenses were liable to be estimated and would normally be about 10 per cent.; (4) a tribunal can properly find only the minimum value of a claimant's interest in the property if that value, net of expenses, together with his other assets obviously exceeded the capital limit; (5) if the value of premises which were for sale was disregarded under reg. 6(1)(a)(iii), so too was the value of the claimaint's interest in those premises: DECISION No. R(SB) 14/86.

3178. Supplementary benefit—resources—whether reversionary interest—Commissioner's decision

[Supplementary Benefit (Resources) Regulations 1981 (S.I. 1981 No. 1527), reg. 6(1)(*a*)(*vi*).] C, a married man in his early 50's received supplementary allowance continuously from March 21 1980 to March 35, 1982. The supplementary benefit officer decided that C was not entitled to supplementary allowance from March 26, 1982 because the value of his wife's interest in a property, other than their home, was in excess of the capital limit at that time of £2,000. The benefit officer further decided that C had been overpaid benefit of £4,863·07 in consequence of the non-disclosure of the resource and that the overpayment was recoverable. On appeal, C argued that until his non-dependant son's death on April 6, 1981 the property had been jointly owned by his son and his wife and that during this period his capital resources, including the value of his wife's interest in the property did not exceed the prescribed capital limit. C conceded that there was an overpayment from when his wife became sole beneficial owner until the property became subject to tenancy, on or about June 3, 1981 but argued that from thenceforward it became a "reversionary interest" within the meaning of reg. 6(1)(*a*)(*vi*) of the Supplementary Benefit (Resources) Regulations 1981 and should be disregarded. The tribunal confirmed that C was not entitled to benefit and decided that there had been a recoverable overpayment of £2,852·40. C appealed to a Social Security Commissioner. *Held*, allowing the appeal, that (1) the wife's beneficial interest in the property did not at any time, including after she had granted the tenancy, qualify for disregard as a "reversionary interest" under reg. 6(1)(*a*)(*vi*); (2) the term "reversionary interest" had an everyday meaning. For a word to have an everyday use it was not necessary for it to have a "popular sense" and to be in daily use by the entire speaking population. It was sufficient if it had a meaning in everyday use amongst a spectrum of users needing to give it a broader meaning than when used in the context of a particular science or art. "Reversionary interest" was not a term of art; (3)

"reversionary interest" was something which did not afford any present enjoyment but carried a vested or contingent right to enjoyment in the future; (4) the wife's interest in the property was not purely reversionary at any time and, even though the granting of a tenancy technically gave it a reversionary *element*, the property was still readily realisable. The future right to physical possession did not warrant an apportionment of her interest under reg. 6(1)(*a*)(*vi*), which could only disregard an interest in property if reversionary in its entirety; (5) the tribunal needed to make express findings as ingredients in the causal chain necessary to establish liability for recovery of the overpayment (referred to *R(SB) 21/82* and *R(SB) 54/83*; (6) the "diminishing capital" principle in para. 14 of *R(SB) 15/85* had to be applied though there might be cases in which the capital was so substantial that no fully detailed application was required: DECISION No. R(SB) 3/86.

3179. Supplementary benefit—single claimant—whether a householder—Tribunal decision
[Supplementary Benefit (Requirements) Regulations 1983 (S.I. 1983 No. 1399), regs. 2(1), 5(6), 14(5).] C, a single parent with a one year old child and in receipt of a supplementary allowance, lived as a member of her parent's household. On April 23, 1984 C entered upon a tenancy of a local authority accommodation and became liable to pay rent in respect of that accommodation. C was however unable to enter into actual occupation of the accommodation until May 7, 1984. The adjudication officer refused to treat C as a householder until she occupied the new accommodation. C appealed to an SSAT which allowed her appeal. The adjudication officer appealed to a Social Security Commissioner. The appeal was heard by a Tribunal of Commissioners. *Held,* allowing the appeal, by Mr. Bowen Q.C. and Mr. Edwards-Jones Q.C., Mr. Goodman dissenting that: (1) the word "householder" is defined by para. 2(3) of Sched. 1 to the Act, and the prescribed conditions mentioned therein are those provided by regulation 5(6) of the Supplementary Benefit (Requirements) Regulations; (2) the meaning of "home" unless the context requires is prescribed by reg. 2(1) of the Requirements Regulations, and the material phrase for consideration in this appeal was "normally occupied", (3) a person could be said under the general law to occupy premises only where he physically resided there, albeit he also resided in other accommodation (*Herbert* v. *Byrne* [1964] C.L.Y. 3146 and *Elliott* v. *Camous* 66 TLR referred to and applied); (4) in the context of supplementary benefit, with the exception of express legislative provision, it is not possible for a person to have more than one "home" at a time *R(SB)30/83* applied; (5) that the words "other than regulation 23 (non-householder's contribution)" in reg. 14(5) of the Requirements Regulations (a provision excepting from the general rule that housing requirements will be met in respect only of a single home) did not exclude a "non-householder" from benefiting from the provisions of regulation 14(5) (*CSB/292/1983* and *CSB/399/1983* not followed); (6) the words "retain the accommodation" in reg. 14(4) of the Requirements Regulations did not cover a situation where a person sought to secure accommodation in advance by paying a retainer or entering into commitment to it (*CSB/292/1983* and *CSB/399/1983* disapproved). Actual residence was required; (7) that upon the proper construction of reg. 14(2), a person who has at a given time a housing requirement constituted by a non-householder's contribution is precluded from having any other housing requirement: DECISION No. R.(SB) 7/86.

3180. Supplementary benefit—single payment—adjudication officer's evidence—Commissioner's decision
C made a claim for a single payment for a set of bunk beds. She submitted three estimates from town-centre suppliers, the lowest being for £119·95 and £6 for delivery. The adjudication officer stated that he had contacted a store who quoted the price of £99·90 for two sets of bunk beds, and he awarded a single payment of £100. C appealed against the amount of the award to a tribunal, who expressly preferred the evidence given by the adjudication officer to that given by C and confirmed his decision. C then appealed to the Commissioner. *Held,* allowing the appeal, that (1) the adjudication officer did not give evidence; he had only made submissions. No tribunal should accept the contested statements made by the adjudication officer's representative if he does not adduce evidence in support of them or submit himself for questioning; (2) if the adjudication officer comes to the hearing unprepared to support his statement by evidence, the tribunal must either decide the appeal on the basis that the facts are unproved or adjourn to give the officer an opportunity of proving them. If the officer gives oral evidence he should be

prepared to answer relevant questions put to him by the claimant or his representative; (3) in general the adjudication officer should, if seeking to establish that an item is available at a particular store at a particular price, produce a letter from the store to that effect. In addition, someone who has seen the item should give evidence as to its quality; (4) whether or not a particular store is considered to be accessible to a claimant is a question of reasonableness. A claimant is not automatically entitled to the cost of an item of reasonable quality at the nearest or most convenient store if a substantial saving can be made by acquiring the item at another reasonably accessible store: DECISION NO. R(SB) 10/86.

3181. Supplementary benefit—single payment—evidence of claimant—Commissioner's decision

[Supplementary Benefits (Single Payments) Regulations 1981 (S.I. 1981 No. 1528), regs. 27, 30.] A man in receipt of supplementary benefit, made a claim for single payments in respect of clothing on the ground that he has gained weight rapidly as he had put on 4 stone in 12 months. The adjudication officer refused a single payment on the basis that the claimant had failed to satisfy regs. 27 and 30 of the Supplementary Benefits (Single Payments) Regulations 1982 as there was no evidence of a rapid weight gain. C appealed this decision to the tribunal who in turn confirmed the decision. C appealed to the Commissioner. *Held,* allowing the appeal, that (1) at the time a single payment is made the adjudication officer should determine and record the following: (i) what is claimed and (ii) whether or not the adjudication officer accepts that the claimant has established the need for the item or items claimed in accordance with reg. 3 of the Single Payments Regulations, it is only by so doing that the adjudication officer can effectively determine what circumstances require investigation and determination and what may be ignored as irrelevant; (2) reg. 27(1)(a) of the Single Payments Regulations merely gives examples which are not exhaustive but reg. 27 should be construed and applied in the light of the fact that supplementary allowance is intended to provide for replacement clothing; (3) under reg. 27(a)(i), what is "rapid" loss or gain falls for determination in accordance with the ordinary use of that word; (4) as the reference to rapid weight gain or loss is only by way of example a weight loss or gain which is other than rapid is not precluded from regulation 27 of the Single Payments Regulations; (5) there is no rule in English law that corroboration of the claimant's own evidence is necessary. *R(I) 2/51* commended; (6) when an adjudication authority rejects a claimant's evidence it must identify the grounds for such rejection; (7) reg. 27(1)(a) does not require that a need arising otherwise than by normal wear and tear must be a need arising from some medical condition: DECISION NO. R.(SB) 33/85.

3182. Supplementary benefit—single payment—exceptional need.

[Supplementary Benefits Act 1976 (c.71), ss.1(1) and 3(1).] "Single payment to meet exceptional need" does not cover regular, recurring need but is limited to exceptional expenditure over a limited period: VAUGHAN *v.* SOCIAL SECURITY ADJUDICATION OFFICER, *The Times,* July 17, 1986, C.A.

3183. Supplementary benefit—single payment—expenses arising from appearance in court—Commissioner's decision

[Supplementary Benefit (Single Payments) Regulations 1981 (S.I. 1981 No. 1528), reg. 6(2)(j)] C who was in receipt of supplementary benefit, owed £300 under a court order for money due to a hire purchase company in respect of furniture. He had not attended the court when the order was made but he claimed a single payment when the bailiff served a warrant for £50 arrears and £8 costs. The adjudication officer and later the tribunal disallowed the claim as the sum of £58 was held to be in respect of expenses arising from an appearance in court and therefore excluded under the provision of reg. 6(2)(j) of the Supplementary Benefit (Single Payments) Regulations 1981. C appealed to a Social Security Commissioner on the grounds that the sum of £50 was due in respect of his debt and was not as the result of a court appearance. *Held,* dismissing the appeal, that (1) it is the intention of reg. 6(2)(j) to cover the genus of expenses of any kind which resulted from court proceedings; (2) compliance with a bailiff's warrant is an expense arising from a court appearance; (3) reg. 6(2)(j) applies with equal effect to a claimant who appeared in court in person and one who did not; (4) the expression "expenses arising from an appearance in a Court" is a perfectly intelligible way of describing expenses arising from court proceedings: DECISION NO. R(SB) 37/85.

3184. Supplementary benefit—single payment—fuel costs—Commissioner's decision

[Supplementary Benefit (Single Payments) Regulations 1981 (S.I. 1981 No. 1528), reg. 26.] C and his wife moved to their present home in January 1983 when C was in work. At that time the home was heated entirely by electric fires. In February 1984 gas central heating was installed. In July 1984 C, then being unemployed, made a claim for a single payment to help with his fuel costs. The adjudication officer and, on appeal, the tribunal refused this claim. C appealed to a Social Security Commissioner. *Held,* that (1) reg. 26 is concerned with the "fuel costs" of the relevant assessment unit. It is, accordingly, necessary to have regard to *all* such fuel as is involved in the heating of the relevant premises; (2) it is for the claimant to establish that the relevant fuel costs are greater than the amount which has been put aside to pay for them. He can, however, do this by establishing that he put *no* amount aside. (See para. 15 of *R(SB) 22/84);* (3) the "need" in terms of reg. 3(2)(*a*) of the Single Payments Regulations is for money to pay outstanding fuel costs. It is not necessary for the claimant to have been entitled to a supplementary pension or allowance throughout the period in which the relevant fuel costs were incurred provided that he was so entitled (or entitled subject to claim, etc.) at the date of his claim for fuel costs; (4) the claimant must establish a causal link between: (i) the fact that the fuel costs were greater than the amount which had been put aside to pay for them, and (ii) unfamiliarity with the cost of running the heating system attributable to one or both of the prescribed circumstances. When nothing has been put aside, that causal link may be difficult to establish; (5) the word "recent" as used in reg. 26(1)(*b*) falls to be given its everyday meaning but manifestly relates to a period of not *less* than six months following the move to a new home or the installation of a new heating system; (6) reg. 26(1)(*b*) should be construed as though it read "(*b*) the members of the assessment unit *were* unfamiliar with the costs of running the heating system in their home because they *had* recently moved to that home or the system *had* recently been installed": DECISION No. R(SB) 1/86.

3185. Supplementary benefit—single payment—protective clothing—Commissioner's decision

[Scot.] [Supplementary Benefits (Single Payments) Regulations 1981 (S.I. 1981 No. 1528), reg. 30.] C made a claim for a single payment in respect of working clothes and tools, as he had started part-time work. The adjudication officer refused a single payment on the basis that C had failed to satisfy regs. 23 and 30 of the Supplementary Benefits (Single Payments) Regulations 1981 as in force at the date of claim. C appealed this decision to the tribunal who confirmed the decision on reg. 30 on grounds that although there was a serious risk to C's health and safety created by his lack of the necessary protective clothing, that risk could be prevented by C leaving the employment. He then appealed to the Commissioner. *Held,* that (1) a totally literal reading of the expression "the only means" as implying the absence of any other means whatsoever cannot have been intended by the legislature. The expression "the only means" is to be construed as implying only the absence of any other means which might reasonably be taken into account as being available in the circumstances of the case; (2) the word "means" in reg. 30(1) is not restricted in meaning to financial means and extends to cover other available expedients. The Commissioner in allowing the appeal set aside the decision of the appeal tribunal and gave his own decision that C was entitled to a single payment for working clothes, but not for working tools: DECISION No. R(SB) 4/86.

3186. Unemployment benefit—habitual residence—contributions paid in another Member State—Commissioner's decision

[Council Regulation (EEC) No. 1408/71, arts. 69, 71] C, being unable to find employment in the U.K., went to West Germany in the spring of 1981 and through a succession of employment agencies obtained about two years employment with the same employer. When this employment ended he was paid about two-and-a-half months of unemployment benefit by the West German authorities and this continued to be paid under Art. 69 of Council Regulation (EEC) No. 1408/71 on his return to the U.K. on June 30, 1983. Apart from a period in Spain from August 4–11, 1983, unemployment benefit under Art. 69 continued in payment until September 29, 1983. C made a claim to U.K. unemployment benefit from June 30, 1983 but this was disallowed on the ground that he did not satisfy the contribution conditions. C appealed on the ground that his West German insurance contributions should be counted, and the appeal tribunal accepting that he had been habitually resident in the U.K. whilst employed in Germany allowed his claim from September 30, 1983 on the basis of Art. 71 of the Regulation. The adjudication officer appealed to the Commissioner. *Held,* dismissing the appeal, that (1) the claimant needs to look for some exception (namely via Arts. 67 and 71) from the rule that the law does not provide for the right of an unemployed worker to claim unemployment benefit under the legislation of a Member State other than the State in which he became unemployed; (2) as the claimant has not completed lastly in this country periods of insurance against unemployment he could avail himself of Art. 67 only if he came within the exception of Art. 71(1)(*b*)(ii); (3) only if the claimant, during his last employment in West Germany, was habitually resident in the territory of a Member State other than West Germany—in this case the U.K.—can he invoke Art. 71(1)(*b*)(ii); (4) bearing in mind the concept of habitual residence considered by the European Ct. in Case 76/76 *Di Paolo* v. *Office National de l'Emploi* [1977] C.L.Y. 1349 C retained the U.K. as the centre of his interest; (5) "stable" employment in a Member State must be interpreted as meaning the same as permanent or steady. The degree of permanence has to be such as to be capable of outweighing the consideration that the person concerned may have left his wife and family in another State. C's last period of employment in West Germany was not stable and he was habitually resident in the U.K. during this period; (6) the suspension of benefit under the legislation of the State of residence for any period during which the unemployed person may make a claim under Act. 69 in the State to whose legislation he was last subject, lasts only while the benefit is being "claimed" under Art. 69; (7) C is entitled to unemployment benefit from the period from September 30, 1983 to April 25, 1984; (8) the first three days of the period September 30, 1983 were not waiting days unless the days for which C received West German unemployment benefit under Art. 69 were to be treated as not being days of unemployment; (9) loss of benefit under Art. 69 on account of receipt of West German benefit should not be treated as disqualification and reg. 7(1)(*b*) of the Social Security (Unemployment, Sickness and Invalidity Benefit) Regulations 1983 relates only to disqualification and not to other forms of disentitlement of non payability. DECISION NO. R(U) 7/85.

3187. Unemployment benefit—habitual residence—contributions paid in another Member State—Commissioner's decision

C, having resided in the U.K. for 25 years took up employment in West Germany on February 1, 1980 under a contract providing for three years' employment. His wife joined him in September 1980. He retained some links with the U.K. but lived and worked in West Germany throughout the period of his contract, which was extended for a further year to January 31, 1984. C returned to the U.K. on February 1, 1984, his wife having preceded him in August 1983. C had been insured under the West German insurance scheme but the West German authorities did not authorise the export of their unemployment benefit under Art. 69 of Council Regulation (EEC) No. 1408/7. On February 2, 1984 he claimed unemployment benefit in the U.K. The adjudication officer disallowed the claim because C did not satisfy the British contribution conditions. On appeal C contended that the contributions he paid in West Germany should be taken into account under Art. 67 of Regulation (EEC) 1408/71. This appeal was rejected by the appeal tribunal which considered that C had not been habitually resident in the U.K. during the relevant period for the purposes of Art. 71 of Regulation (EEC) No. 1408/71. *Held,* dismissing the appeal, that (1) C falls within Art. 1(a) of Regulation (EEC) No. 1408/71 because of his past employment in the U.K. and West Germany. He is not assisted by the convention between the U.K. and West Germany which is displaced as regards persons and matters covered by that regulation in pursuance of Art. 6 thereof; (2) C had to rely exclusively on Regulation (EEC) No. 1408/71 if he was to succeed in his claim for unemployment benefit, but, because he had not lastly completed a period of insurance in Great Britain immediately before the period for which he claimed, he could not rely on Art. 67 without also bringing himself within the scope of Art. 71; (3) in the absence of any entitlement to unemployment benefit under Art. 69 of Regulation (EEC) No. 1408/71, there is no question of any suspension of Art. 71; (4) for the purposes of Art. 71, West Germany was the competent State, and the competent institution was the West German social security authority; (5) to come within Art. 71 C had to show that he was residing, during his period of employment in West Germany, in another Member State, in this case, the U.K.; (6) it is for the adjudication officer to determine whether a claimant is habitually resident in the

U.K. during the relevant period; (7) it is a matter for the Secretary of State to determine whether or not, taking into account a claimant's contributions, he has sufficient contributions to meet the contribution conditions; (8) on the facts C could properly be regarded as habitually resident in West Germany throughout the relevant period; (9) whether or not C is "ordinarily resident" in the U.K. for tax purposes has no relevance as to whether or not C was "habitually resident" in the U.K. for the purposes of Art. 71(1)(*b*)(*ii*) of Regulation 1408/71: DECISION No. R(U) 4/86.

3188. Unemployment benefit—trade dispute—whether direct interest
[Social Security Act 1975 (c.14), s.19(1)(*a*) (as amended by Employment Protection Act 1975 (c.71), s.111(1).]

A worker who is prevented from working by pickets during a trade dispute is disqualified from receiving benefit since although he is not directly participating in the dispute he is directly interested since the result might affect his pay and redundancy payment.

The claimant applied to his employers, the N.C.B., for voluntary redundancy at a time when there was no industrial dispute. Later, trade disputes arose, and the union approved strike action. On March 10, as a result of his application, he was given 12 weeks notice terminating his employment on June 2. On March 23 the employees at his colliery came out on strike but the claimant went to work except from March 23 to April 13 when he was prevented from doing so by pickets. Thereafter he worked most days until June 2. On June 5 he claimed unemployment benefit. The adjudication officer decided he was disqualified from receiving benefit as long as the strike lasted, and his appeal was rejected by the Social Security Appeal Tribunal which found that the disqualification lasted from March 23 to August 20 when there was sufficient resumption of work. The Tribunal of Commissioners found on appeal that the stoppage came to an end on November 20 and that the claimant was not entitled to benefit until then since under section 19(1) of the Social Security Act 1975 he had lost employment by reason of a stoppage of work which was due to a trade dispute at his place of employment. *Held*, dismissing the claimant's appeal, that section 19(1) was not concerned with attitudes or motives but with a factual situation so that where a stoppage occurred due to a dispute, a claimant was disqualified, even though he was already under a redundancy notice and lost his job under that notice or had, despite redundancy, recovered his original job. The proviso to section 19(1) which states that the subsection does not apply in the case of a person who proves that he is not participating in or directly interested in the trade dispute which caused the stoppage did not apply to the claimant: although he was not participating in the dispute or a person interested in the issue of pit closures, both the issue of pit closures and of wages had caused the stoppage of work and therefore the claimant had lost employment in circumstances where he was directly interested in the trade dispute because its result would affect the amount of his pay and redundancy payment. Leave to appeal was granted.

CARTLIDGE *v.* CHIEF ADJUDICATION OFFICER [1986] 2 W.L.R. 558, C.A.

SOLICITORS

3189. Advertising
The National Consumer Council has published its response to the Law Society's Consultation Document on the Revision of the Solicitors' Practice Rules and a Solicitors' Advertising Code. The NCC favours moves to allow solicitors to advertise. Copies of their paper are available, free of charge, from: Response on Solicitors' Practice Rules and Solicitors' Advertising Code, National Consumer Council, 18, Queen Anne's Gate, London SW1H 9AA.

3190. Appeal to Court of Appeal—documents—duty of solicitors
The failure of a solicitor to properly document an appeal, which leads to the dismissal of the appeal, is not to be used deliberately as a cheap way of withdrawing an appeal. In seven separate appeals the appellant's solicitor was reported to the Law Society for breach of duty. (Note *re* documentation of appeals, *The Times,* June 13, 1986, C.A.)

3191. Conduct of proceedings—fairness—acting on both sides
A solicitor should not prosecute a case against a defendant he has previously advised on his defence: R. *v.* DUNSTABLE JUSTICES, *ex p.* COX, *The Times,* February 7, 1986, D.C.

3192. Costs—application for solicitor to pay costs personally—whether trial judge should hear application. See BAHAI *v.* RASHIDIAN, § 2603.

3193. Costs—taxation—basis for taxation
[Solicitors Act 1974 (c.47), s.74(3).] T, the mortgagee, had taken possession proceedings. The terms of the charge provided that the mortgagee should be entitled to his costs of enforcing the security so as to be afforded a "full, complete and unlimited indemnity." T's solicitors submitted their bill prepared upon the solicitor-and-own-client basis. On taxation, the registrar, applying s.74(3) allowed costs only upon a party-and-party basis. T applied to the judge for review. *Held,* that the normal rule is that a mortgagee is entitled to his costs of enforcing the security only upon a party and party basis. In the present case, however, the contract provided for a complete and unrestricted indemnity. This agreement is unaffected by the 1974 Act as that Act has to be construed in the light of the County Court Rules then in force (the 1936 Rules)—they provided for fixed items of costs save in so far as there was provision for the judge to exercise a discretion in respect of those items. The application was allowed and the taxation should proceed on a solicitor-and-own-client basis: TARRANT *v.* SPEECHLY BIRCHAM, May 19, 1986, H.H. Judge Birks, Slough County Ct. [*Ex rel. William Norris, Barrister*]

3194. Disciplinary proceedings—powers of tribunal
[Solicitors (Disciplinary Proceedings) Rules (1985 S.I. No. 226), rule 34.] Where the Solicitors Disciplinary Tribunal acquits a solicitor of conduct unbefitting a solicitor, and this is the only charge against him, rule 34 of the Solicitors (Disciplinary Proceedings) Rules does not empower them to reprimand him for failing adequately to supervise an unadmitted legal executive: SOLICITOR, A, *Re, The Times,* December 13, 1986, D.C.

3195. Duty to warn client—contract
A solicitor faced with an unusual clause in a contract should be put on notice and advise his clients of the implications of signing the agreement: COUNTY PERSONNEL *v.* PULVER (ALAN R.) & CO., *The Times,* October 29, 1986, C.A.

3196. Fiduciary duty—client—joint venture
Where a solicitor enters into a joint venture with a client he is not in breach of his fiduciary duty in failing to advise him on the business prudence of the venture so long as the terms of agreement were fair and the client was fully appraised of the nature and effect of the transaction: HANSON *v.* LORENZ & JONES, *Financial Times,* November 5, 1986, C.A.

3197. Lay Observer—annual report
The Eleventh Annual Report of the Lay Observer has been published. It is available from H.M.S.O. (ISBN 0 10 232386 0) [£3·10].

3198. Legal aid certificate—ambit—whether entitlement to payment. See LITTAUR *v.* STEGGLES PALMER, § 1968.

3199. Money deposit—terms of trust
Where no clear terms are laid down, money deposited in a joint solicitors account is held on resulting trust to the order of the depositor. Where that is a company placing money for no specified purpose but obtained under a warranty scheme it reverts to the liquidator on winding up: MULTI GUARANTEE CO., *Re, Financial Times,* June 24, 1986, C.A.

3200. Negligence—failure to discover planning restriction. GP & B *v.* BULCRAIG AND DAVIS, 199a.

3201. Professional negligence—sale of land—deposits
[Ire.] P1 and P2, who were negotiating for the purchase of two flats in a proposed building development, were informed by the builder's agent that booking deposits were required and that these deposits would be paid to the builder. D1, the solicitor for P1 and P2, warned them of the risks involved in paying the money to the builder, but on his advice they wrote cheques in favour of D2, the solicitor for the builder. D1 sent these cheques to D2 but did not make it clear that they were to be held by D2 as stakeholder and not as agent for the builder. The builder went into liquidation and P1 and P2 lost these deposits. *Held,* that P1 and P2 were entitled to recover their losses from D1 as he, by failing to put D2 on notice that the deposits were to

SOLICITORS

be held by him as stakeholder, had not exercised reasonable professional skill: DESMOND v. BROPHY [1985] I.R. 449, Barrington J.

3202. Rights of audience—High Court of Justice—discretion of the court. See ABSE v. SMITH, § 2693.

3203. Rights of audience—practice direction. See PRACTICE DIRECTION (SOLICITORS: RIGHTS OF AUDIENCE), § 2694

3203a. Undertaking—duty to third party
When a client gives his solicitor authority to give an undertaking to a third party, the solicitor owes that third party a duty of care in tort, although not in contract: AL KANDARI v. BROWN (J. R.) & Co., The Times, November 19, 1986, C.A.

STAMP DUTIES

3204. Avoidance scheme—preordained series of transactions
It is for the court to ascertain the substance of a transaction effected by an instrument to determine whether it falls within the charge to stamp duty.

In 1984 I negotiated the purchase of a freehold dwelling house for £145,500. On February 17, 1984, to reduce liability to stamp duty, the vendor made an agreement with I for a 999 year lease of the property at a premium of £145,000 and an annual rental of £25. On February 21 the vendor contracted to sell for £500 the property subject to the 999 year lease to H Co., a company owned and controlled by I's solicitors, which in February 23, agreed to subsell its reversionary interest to I for £600. The transactions were completed on March 16 and the Commissioners subsequently assessed I for stamp duty. Held, dismissing I's appeal, that although stamp duty was chargeable on instruments and not transactions, the court could ascertain the substance of a transaction to determine whether it fell within the charge to duty; when a preordained series of transactions was entered into solely to avoid the duty, the court would treat it as one transaction achieving the preordained result; the lease agreement had to be disregarded and the remaining transactions treated as a single transaction transferring the property to I with stamp duty chargeable (Ramsey (W.T.) v. I.R.C. [1981] C.L.Y. 1385; I.R.C. v. Burmah Oil Co. [1982] C.L.Y. 1516 and Furniss v. Dawson [1984] C.L.Y. 270 applied).
INGRAM v. I.R.C. [1986] 2 W.L.R. 598, Vinelott J.

3205. Conveyance on sale—conditional offer
On May 21, 1983 a final offer of shares or cash was made by T Co. for the shares in T. The offer was made conditional on no announcement being made convening a general meeting of T, on or before 21 days after the offer became unconditional, to effect a capital reorganisation. The offer was declared unconditional on June 8. On June 10 T announced that an extraordinary general meeting was to be held on June 29 to effect a capital reorganisation. Five block transfers in respect of irrevocable forms of acceptance and transfer received on various dates before June 29 were presented for stamping. Held, dismissing T's appeal, that irrevocable forms of acceptance and transfer delivered before the offer became unconditional on June 8, 1986 became effective transfers on that date and forms delivered after that date but before June 29, 1986 took effect on delivery and that stamp duty was payable accordingly: B.T.R. v. I.R.C. [1986] S.T.C. 433, Harman J.

3206. Reserve tax
STAMP DUTY RESERVE TAX (INTERESTS ON TAX REPAID) ORDER 1986 (No. 1710) [45p], made under the Finance Act 1986 (c.41), s.92(4)(5); operative on October 27, 1986; for the purposes of s.92 of the 1986 Act specifies the rate of interest as 8·5 per cent.
STAMP DUTY RESERVE TAX (INTEREST ON TAX REPAID) (No. 2) ORDER 1986 (No. 1833) [45p], made under the Finance Act 1986 (c.41), s.92(4)(5); operative on November 6, 1986; specifies that 9.5 per cent. per annum is the "appropriate rate" for the purposes of s.92 of the 1986 Act.
STAMP DUTY RESERVE TAX REGULATIONS 1986 (No. 1711) [£3·40], made under the Finance Act 1986, s.98; operative on October 27, 1986; provide for the management of stamp duty reserve tax.

STATUTES AND ORDERS

3207. Breach of statutory duty—contempt of statute—whether offence created. See R. v. HORSEFERRY ROAD JUSTICES, ex p. INDEPENDENT BROADCASTING AUTHORITY, § 496.

3208. Construction—trustee savings banks. See ROSS v. LORD ADVOCATE, § 171.

3209. Royal Assents

The following Act received the Royal Assent during 1986:

Advance Petroleum Revenue Tax Act 1986 (c.68), § 2843a
Agriculture Act 1986 (c.49) § 47
Agricultural Holdings Act 1986, (c.5), § 45
Airports Act 1986 (c.31), § 142
Animals (Scientific Procedures) Act 1986 (c.14), § 77
Appropriation Act 1986 (c.42), § 2845
Armed Forces Act 1986 (c.21) § 121
Atomic Energy Authority Act 1986 (c.3) § 133
Australia Act 1986 (c.2) § 187
British Council and Commonwealth Institute Superannuation Act 1986 (c.51),
    § 2510
British Shipbuilders (Borrowing Powers) Act 1986 (c.19), § 3391
Building Societies Act 1986 (c.53), § 236
Children and Young Persons (Amendment) Act 1986 (c.28), § 2179
Civil Protection in Peacetime Act 1986 (c.22), § 279
Commonwealth Development Corporation Act 1986 (c.25), § 190
Company Directors Disqualification Act 1986 (c.46), § 290
Consolidated Fund Act 1986, (c.4), § 2848
Consolidated Fund (Appropriation) Act 1986 (c.42), § 2845
Consolidated Fund (No. 2) Act 1986 (c.67), § 2848a
Consumer Safety (Amendment) Act 1986 (c.29), § 3003
Corneal Tissue Act 1986 (c.18), § 2110
Crown Agents (Amendment) Act 1986 (c.43), § 31
Disabled Persons (Services, Consultation and Representation) Act 1986 (c.33),
    § 2018
Dockyard Services Act 1986 (c.52), § 1184
Drainage Rates (Disabled Persons) Act 1986 (c.17), § 2761
Drug Trafficking Offences Act 1986 (c.32), § 546
Education (Amendment) Act 1986 (c.1), § 1130
Education Act 1986 (c.40), § 1129
Education (No. 2) Act 1986 (c.61), § 1131
European Communities (Amendment) Act 1986 (c.58), § 1372
Family Law Act 1986 (c.55), § 2198
Finance Act 1986 (c.41), § 2849
Financial Services Act 1986 (c.60), § 2850
Forestry Act 1986 (c.30), § 1571
Gaming (Amendment) Act 1986 (c.11), § 1582
Gas Act 1986 (c.44), § 1587
Health Service Joint Consultative Committees (Access to Information) Act 1986
    (c.24), § 2237
Highways (Amendment) Act 1986 (c.13), § 1601
Horticultural Produce Act 1986 (c.20), § 60
Housing and Planning Act 1986 (c.63), § 1630
Housing (Scotland) Act 1986 (c.65), § 1632
Incest and Related Offences (Scotland) Act 1986 (c.36), § 618
Industrial Training Act 1986 (c.15), § 3395
Insolvency Act 1986 (c.45), § 304
Land Registration Act 1986 (c.26), § 1814
Latent Damage Act 1986 (c.37), § 2273
Law Reform (Parent and Child) (Scotland) Act 1986 (c.9), § 2202
Legal Aid (Scotland) Act 1986 (c.47), § 1975
Local Government Act 1986 (c.10), § 2030
Marriage (Prohibited Degrees of Relationship) Act 1986 (c.16), § 1658
Marriage (Wales) Act 1986, (c.7), § 1660
Museum of London Act 1986 (c.8), § 2004
National Health Service (Amendment) Act 1986 (c.66), § 2241
Outer Space Act 1986 (c.38), § 1793
Parliamentary Constituencies Act 1986 (c.56), § 1156
Patents, Designs and Marks Act 1986 (c.39), § 3422

Prevention of Oil Pollution Act 1986, (c.6), § 3096
Protection of Children (Tobacco) Act 1986 (c.34), § 2205
Protection of Military Remains Act 1986 (c.35), § 130
Public Order Act 1986 (c.64), § 686
Public Trustee and Administration of Funds Act 1986 (c.57), § 2687
Rate Support Grants Act 1986 (c.54), § 2043
Road Traffic Regulation (Parking) Act 1986 (c.27), § 2978
Safety at Sea Act 1986 (c.23), § 1553
Salmon Act 1986 (c.62), § 1554
Sex Discrimination Act 1986 (c.59), § 1244
Social Security Act 1986 (c.50), § 3156
Statute Law (Repeals) Act 1986 (c.12), § 3210
Wages Act 1986 (c.48), § 1293

3210. Statute Law (Repeals) Act 1986 (c.12)
This Act repeals certain enactments which are no longer of any practical use and makes provision in connection with their repeal.
The Act received the Royal Assent on May 2, 1986.

STOCK EXCHANGE

3211. Financial services—disclosure of information. See REVENUE AND FINANCE, § 2852.

TELECOMMUNICATIONS

3212. Broadcasting
BROADCASTING (LOCAL SOUND BROADCAST PROGRAMME CONTRACTORS' ADDITIONAL PAYMENTS) ORDER 1986 (No. 629) [45p], made under the Broadcasting Act 1981 (c.68), s.32(8)(9); operative on April 1, 1986; amends s.32(4) of the 1981 Act so as to substitute for "40 per cent" the word "nil."

3213. Broadcasting—whether breach of statutory duty a criminal offence—contempt of statute—judicial review—time for application. See R. *v.* HORSEFERRY ROAD MAGISTRATES, *ex p.* INDEPENDENT BROADCASTING AUTHORITY, § 496.

3214. Broadcasting—wireless telegraphy—forfeiture of apparatus
[Wireless Telegraphy Act 1949 (c.54), ss.1(1), 14(3).] R having been convicted of using apparatus for wireless telegraphy, contrary to s.1(1) of the 1949 Act, the magistrates ordered forfeiture of the equipment seized from R, under s.14(3). *Held,* allowing R's appeal in part, that records and cassettes seized from R were not "apparatus for wireless telegraphy" but speakers seized from him were. (*King* v. *Bull* [1937] 1 K.B. 810 considered).
RUDD *v.* DEPARTMENT OF TRADE AND INDUSTRY [1986] Crim.L.R. 455, C.A.

3215. Cable and Broadcasting Act 1984—commencement
CABLE AND BROADCASTING ACT 1984 (COMMENCEMENT No. 2) ORDER 1986 (No. 537 (c.16)) [80p], made under the Cable and Broadcasting Act 1984 (c.46), s.59(4); brings into force on April 1, 1986 ss.37–41, 57(1) (in part) and Sched. 5 (in part).

3216. Cable television
CABLE (PRESCRIBED DIFFUSION SERVICE) ORDER 1986 (No. 900) [45p], made under the Cable and Broadcasting Act 1984 (c.46), s.2(3); operative on July 1, 1986; defines the meaning of "prescribed diffusion service."

3217. Interception of Communications Act 1985—commencement
INTERCEPTION OF COMMUNICATIONS ACT 1985 (COMMENCEMENT) ORDER 1986 (No. 384 (C.12)) [40p], made under the Interception of Communications Act 1985 (c.56), s.12(2); brings the 1985 Act into force on April 10, 1986.

3218. Licences
TELECOMMUNICATIONS ACT 1984 (EXTENSION OF RELEVANT PERIOD) ORDER 1986 (No. 1275) [45p], made under the Telecommunications Act 1984 (c.12), Sched. 5, para. 1; operative on August 9, 1986; extends the "relevant period" under the 1984 Act.

3219. Public telecommunication system
PUBLIC TELECOMMUNICATION SYSTEM DESIGNATION (EAST LONDON TELECOMMUNICA-TIONS LIMITED) ORDER 1986 (No. 1113) [45p], made under the Telecommunications

Act 1984 (c.12), ss.9, 104; operative on August 4, 1986; designates telecommunication systems operated by the said company as public telecommunication systems.

3220. Subliminal images—breach of statutory duty—whether offence. See R. *v.* HORSEFERRY ROAD MAGISTRATES, *ex p.* INDEPENDENT BROADCASTING AUTHORITY, § 496.

3221. Transfer of functions
TRANSFER OF FUNCTIONS (SECRETARY OF STATE AND TREASURY) ORDER 1986 (No. 2237) [£1·40], made under the Ministers of the Crown Act 1975 (c.26), s.1; operative on January 29, 1987; transfers functions relating the holdings of the government on British Telecommunications plc and Cable and Wireless plc.

3222. Wireless telegraphy
WIRELESS TELEGRAPHY (LICENCE CHARGES) REGULATIONS 1986 (No. 1039) [£1·40], made under the Wireless Telegraphy Act 1949 (C.54), s.2(1); operative on July 15, 1986; provide for the fees to be paid on the issue and renewal of 59 wireless telegraphy licences, broadcast relay stations and other licences relating to broadcasting.

TIME

3223. Summer time
SUMMER TIME ORDER 1986 (No. 223) [40p], made under the Summer Time Act 1972 (c.6), s.2(3); operative on February 26, 1986; provides for the periods of summer time in 1986, 1987 and 1988.

TORT

3224. Conversion—date of which damages fall to be assessed
[Torts (Interference with Goods) Act 1977 (c.32), s.6(1)] P, a finance company, owned a tractor worth £20,000. D, an agricultural machinery supplier, came into possession of the vehicle after it had been burnt out in August 1981 at the premises of a farmer to whom the tractor was to be leased by P. (The leasing agreement was due to be signed on the day after the fire had taken place.) D had been given permission by the engineering assessors of the farmer's insurance company to remove it. D made an offer of £1,000 to the assessors for the salvage. The offer was refused. Two months after the fire an independent salvage buyer, acting on the authority of the insurance company, visited D's premises to take away the tractor and assess its salvage value. D refused to surrender it, as he had an outstanding claim against the insurance company. A year elapsed and D began to rebuild it. Seven months later he sold the vehicle for £15,150. P agreed that they could select the date of the final act of conversion as the date at which damages were to be assessed, thereby taking advantage of the "windfall" value of the substantial improvements D had made. *Held,* that where there is a series of acts of conversion, it is not open to P to select the last date as the occasion upon which damages fall to be assessed. The refusal to release the vehicle was a clear act of conversion. The subsequent acts comprised a continuing course of conduct. It would be wrong to select isolated acts and to say damages flow from each act. S.6 did not change the common law rules. D honestly believed he had a valid claim against the insurance company which justified, in his mind, retention of the tractor. However he did not believe that he had "good title" to the tractor or salvage. He could not thus avail himself of s.6(1). As to the value of the goods at the date of the material act of conversion, this amounted to the salvage value of the vehicle in the aftermath of the fire. It was necessary to remember that a seller may not always get the top market value. Damages assessed at £3,000: HIGHLAND LEASING *v.* PAUL FIELD (T/A FIELD MACHINERY), December 6, 1985; R. M. Stewart Q.C. (*Ex rel.* T. P. *Barnes, Barrister*).

3225. Deceit—maintenance covenant—damages. See GORDON *v.* SELICO, § 1877.

3226. Trespass. See TRESPASS.

3227. Wrongful interference with contractual relations—use of clips from films after death of performer—whether liability in tort. See RICKLESS *v.* UNITED ARTISTS CORP., § 429.

TOWN AND COUNTRY PLANNING

3228. Agricultural land—enforcement notice—material change of use
D purchased in 1983 agricultural land in order to raise beef cattle. He brought a caravan on to the land where he stored cattle feed and which he used as a shelter.

An enforcement notice was served. *Held*, on appeal to the High Court by the council, that no material change in the use of the land had occurred. Appeal dismissed: WEALDEN DISTRICT COUNCIL *v.* SECRETARY OF STATE FOR THE ENVIRONMENT AND COLIN DAY [1986] J.P.L. 753, Kennedy J.

3229. Alteration to listed building—whether absolute offence
[Town and Country Planning Act 1971 (c.78), s.55(1) as amended by the Local Government, Planning and Land Act 1980 (c.65), Sched. 15, para. 6(1).]
S.55(1) of the Town and Country Planning Act 1971 creates an offence of strict liability.
M was instructed by a company that held a long lease of a Grade II listed building to remove various fixtures and fittings. The local authority laid informations against M that he did works without their consent contrary to s.55 of the Act. The magistrate accepted a submission that the offence required proof of *mens rea* and dismissed the information. *Held*, granting the application for judicial review, that the offence was one of strict liability (*R. v. Marsham* [1892] 1 Q.B. 371, C.A. applied).
R. *v.* WELLS STREET METROPOLITAN STIPENDIARY MAGISTRATE, *ex p.* WESTMINSTER CITY COUNCIL [1986] 1 W.L.R. 1046, D.C.

3230. Amusement centre—change of use from shop
[Town and Country Planning Act 1971 (c.78), s.36 and Sched. 9.] The Council refused planning permission to change the use of the ground floor of a shop to an amusement centre with ancillary snack bar. The appeal premises were a short distance from the prime shopping parade and in the middle of a short block of eight commercial properties, only two of which were used as shops. The premises had been used as a shop but were now vacant. Over 60 per cent. of the units in the short block, including the appeal premises were already used for non-retail purposes. The local plan permitted changes to non-retail use only where no more than 33 per cent. of the "units" in the "application frontage" were in non-retail use. The developer appealed to the Secretary of State. *Held*, by the Inspector following a public inquiry, that (1) the case turned on whether or not the proposed development would noticeably damage the attractiveness or vitality of the district shopping centre; (2) the proposal was in contravention of the statutory local plan but the statutory policy did not apply to this non-retail use. Appeal allowed, conditional permission granted: BIRMINGHAM CITY COUNCIL AND BRIDGENS (E.) AND CO. (Ref. T/APP/P4605/A/84/20649/P5) (1985) 1 P.A.D. 53.

3231. Amusement centre—non-retail use in secondary shopping street
[Town and Country Planning Act 1971 (c.78) s.36; Circular 22/80); Development Control Policy Note No. 11.] The Council refused planning permission for the change of use from a double-fronted shop to an amusement centre. The proposal was to instal a total of 35 machines. The developer appealed and at the public inquiry stated that the centre was intended to attract adults, mainly shoppers, with a lower age limit of 18 years. The shop was located in a secondary shopping street and the planning policy in the Central Area Plan approved in 1981 relating to loss of shops to non-retail uses was ambiguous. *Held*, by the Inspector, that to allow the appeal would be consistent with Development Control Policy Note 11 and the advice given in Circular 22/80 that development should only be prevented when to do so served a clear planning purpose. The Inspector stated that the provision of a range of ancillary services and facilities was an essential part of the attraction of the street. The appellant accepted strict conditions. Appeal allowed: IPSWICH BOROUGH COUNCIL AND CHARLES MANNING AMUSEMENT PARK (Ref:T/APP/R3515/A/84/023608/P7) (1985) 1 P.A.D. 56.

3232. Blight notice—counter-notice—date at which to be considered
The earliest date to which the Lands Tribunal had to consider the validity of a counter-notice to a blight notice must be the date of the counter-notice, but the Tribunal had to take account of subsequent events in determining the weight to be attached to the local authority's declared intentions.
The claimant owned a dwelling-house through the front garden of which a service road was due to be constructed, according to the local plan adopted by the planning authority in 1983. She served a blight notice and the authority served a counter-notice in March 1984 on the grounds that it did not intend to acquire any of her land unless compelled to do so. It relied on resolutions from its relevant committees, but the claimant relied on resolutions which indicated that the council might acquire the

land. It was accepted that the burden rested on the council to show that its counter-notice was well-founded. They contended that the earliest date to take into consideration on the question of whether the counter-notice was well-founded was the date of it, but suggested looking also at subsequent events. *Held*, that the counter-notice was not well-founded and that the blight notice must be upheld. The council were unable to justify a categorical assertion that it did not intend to acquire because it had supported the local plan which might require the acquisition. The earliest date to which the Tribunal had to consider whether the council had established a valid objection to the blight notice must be the date of the counter-notice, but that in judging the validity of the grounds in the notice and in particular the precise nature of the county council's declared intention, the Tribunal could not shut its eyes to subsequent events as an indication of the weight to be attached to that declared intention.

CHARMAN *v.* DORSET COUNTY COUNCIL (1986) 52 P. & C.R. 88. Lands Tribunal (Ref. No. 116/1984), J. H. Emlyn Jones Esq.

3233. Blight notice—whether jurisdiction to strike out. See BINNS *v.* SECRETARY OF STATE FOR TRANSPORT, § 349.

3234. Building for indoor training of ponies—Green belt—use appropriate to rural area
[Town and Country Planning Act 1971 (c.78), s.36.] WM wished to erect a building, measuring 200ft. by 85ft. and of a height of 25ft. to the ridge, to train 12 polo ponies. The appeal site was part of a house and land totalling some 12 acres including stables and ancillary buildings and a paddock and was located in the green belt within which the policy was that new buildings should only be permitted in very special circumstances. The Council refused permission. *Held*, on appeal by the Inspector, that (1) the recreational use proposed was appropriate to a rural area; but (2) green belt policies also required that any buildings to be erected for a recreational use should be of a design, siting and materials in sympathy with the character of the area, (3) the proposed building was the largest for some distance in a pleasant rural location and not dissimilar in appearance to an industrial building or warehouse. Appeal dismissed: WINDSOR & MAIDENHEAD DISTRICT COUNCIL AND WALTON MASTERS (Ref. T/APP/DO325/A/84/20012/P2) (1985) 1 P.A.D. 67.

3235. Building society office—non-retail use in retail location—effect on pedestrian flow—importance of window display
[Town and Country Planning Act 1971 (c.78), s.36.] The City Council refused planning permission for the change of use of the basement and ground floor of a listed building from retail to building society office. The premises were situated on the fringe of the primary shopping area and within an area where the draft City Plan would not normally permit non-retail uses. The developer appealed and contended that the office was capable of generating more activity than many kinds of retail use. *Held*, by the Inspector, that (1) the main issue was whether the proposal would significantly detract from the retail character and vitality of that part of the city centre; (2) the area in which the appeal premises were situated was quite different in character to the main shopping area; (3) the continuous retail frontage extended up to but not beyond the appeal premises; (4) the appeal premises were appropriately located in being at the end of a row of shops. Appeal allowed subject to conditions including one requiring the maintenance of a window display in the ground floor window: BATH CITY COUNCIL AND ANGLIA BUILDING SOCIETY (Ref: T/APP/P0105/A/85/028040/P7) (1986) 1 P.A.D. 175.

3236. Burial ground—agricultural land—officers' recommendation to grant permission—need
[Town and Country Planning Act 1971 (c.78), s.36, Sched. 9.] The Burial Committee of three parish councils made two applications for planning permission to use a 1.17 acre site as a burial ground. The site was an overgrown field together with a wooded strip and was well screened by hedges and established planting and was within the South Downs Area of Outstanding Natural Beauty. Despite the officers' recommendation to grant conditional permission the Council refused permission relying upon (a) those Structure Plan policies which sought the retention of the rural appearance and character of the area and (b) the unadopted local plan. The Burial Committee appealed. *Held*, by the Inspector following a public inquiry, that (1) the policies of severe restraint were well founded; but (2) a burial ground was a quite exceptional form of development; (3) there was a genuine need for the new burial

ground and the appeal site appeared to be the only suitable and available area of land; (4) the proposal would not be harmful in any way to the visual harmony and essential rural character of the area. Appeal allowed: HORSHAM DISTRICT COUNCIL AND BRAMBER PARISH COUNCIL (Ref. T/APP/Z3825/A/85/028692/P2 and A/85/033593/P2) (1986) 1 P.A.D. 300.

3237. Burial ground—site in rural setting—loss of agricultural land
[Town and Country Planning Act (c.78) s.36, Sched. 9.] Planning permission was refused to change the use of agricultural land to use as a burial ground. The site was of 0.86 acres in area and owned by the Burial Board and the field appeared to be good quality land which had been in recent arable use. The site was in a rural setting with only one dwelling overlooking it. In 1949 the Burial Board had been granted planning permission for the proposed use. The Board appealed by way of written representations. *Held*, by the Secretary of State, that (1) the visual impact of the proposal would be very slight; (2) the site was just outside the developed area in rural, tranquil and pleasant surroundings but within clear view of the Church; (3) the site could not be considered a serious loss to agriculture. Appeal allowed: CARRICK DISTRICT COUNCIL AND PROBUS BURIAL BOARD (Ref: APP/P0810/A/84/016464) (1986) 1 P.A.D. 297.

3238. Caravan site—protected site—mobile home. See BALTHASAR *v.* MULLANE, § 1639.

3239. Caravan sites—occupation—meaning
[Caravan Sites and Control of Development Act 1960 (c.62); Caravan Sites Act 1968 (c.52)] The definition of "occupation" contained in the Caravan Sites and Control of Development Act 1968 has no bearing on that word when it is used in the Caravan Sites Act 1968: R. *v.* BEACONSFIELD JUSTICES, *ex p.* STUBBINGS, *The Times,* May 7, 1986, D.C.

3240. Caravans—residential mobile homes—whether appropriate fee had been paid—change of use—further application needed for operational development—split decision
[Town and Country Planning Act 1971 (c.78), ss.36, 52, Sched. 9; Town and Country Planning General Development Order 1977 (S.I. 1977 No. 289); Town and Country Planning (Fees for Applications and Deemed Applications) Regulations 1983 (S.I. 1983 No. 1674); DoE Circular 23/85.] The applicant sought planning permission for two extensions of a total area of 9.49 acres to an existing caravan park which had started in 1952 on a 22 acre site. The Council failed to determine the application within the statutory period but argued that the applicants had not paid the proper fee and that therefore the Secretary of State had no jurisdiction. The applicant appealed and at the inquiry the Council contended on the merits that the proposal would result in loss of visual amenity of an otherwise undeveloped stretch of coastline and the loss of agricultural land. *Held*, by the Inspector, that (1) as no reference was made in the application to any operational development it should be treated as a straightforward change of use application for which the correct fee had been paid; to the extent that any operational development was proposed by the appellants a further application might have to be made; (2) the two elements of the proposals, 6.75 acres to the west and 2.74 acres to the north, were clearly identifiable; (3) the western extension would be visually intrusive and would materially detract from the appearance of the woodland; (4) the caravans would have no visual impact on the surrounding area for the northern extension nor would the area of farmland be reduced. Appeal allowed in part: ROCHESTER-UPON-MEDWAY CITY COUNCIL AND MARINA SERVICES MEDWAY (Ref: T/APP/Y2240/A/85/27198/P.5) (1986) 1 P.A.D. 276.

3241. Change of use—agricultural building—rural policies
[Town and Country Planning Act 1971 (c.78) s.36; Town and Country General Development Order 1977 (S.I. 1977 No. 289); DoE Circulars 22/80, 16/84, 1/85.] The Council refused planning permission for the change of use of an existing agricultural building to a bagging unit for sugar beet for seasonal use from October to March together with improvement to the existing access. Nearby was an unsightly concrete framed potato store. The proposal involved the removal of this. The scheme involved creating eight full-time and two part-time jobs. The issues were (a) whether the relaxation of the normally restrictive policies against industrial development in the countryside could be justified and (b) traffic, access and noise. *Held*, by the Secretary of State following a public inquiry, that (1) the proposed use would lead to the visual enhancement of the area because conditions could be imposed covering landscaping

and removal of the potato store (C22/80 and C16/84 referred to); (2) there would be an overall improvement in traffic conditions; (3) industrial development could occur without detriment to the environment. Appeal allowed subject to conditions: TAUNTON DEANE BOROUGH COUNCIL AND GILLARDS FARMS AND TRANSPORT (Ref. APP/D3315/A/84/U19906) (1986) 1 P.A.D. 124.

3242. Change of use—bank—local plan policy—effect on shopping centre
[Town and Country Planning Act 1971 (c.78), s.36 and Sched. 9; Town and Country Planning (Use Classes) Order 1972 (S.I. 1972 No. 1385); DOE Circulars 22/84, 14/85; Development Control Policy Note No. 11.] The council refused permission for change of use from retail to a bank in the central shopping area of Stafford. The property was an eighteenth century Grade II listed building flanked by a solicitor's office and building society and was last used as an electrical retail outlet. The local plan retail protection policy provided that permission for non-retail use should be granted only in exceptional circumstances, permission would not normally be granted where it would result in three or more adjoining retail uses becoming non-retail. The council considered the proposal to be detrimental to the character of the shopping centre. The appellants said that their current premises were inadequate and it was uncertain whether the shortly to expire lease would be renewed. *Held,* by the inspector following a public inquiry, that (1) the local plan objectives were in conformity with the guidance in D.C.P.N. No. 11 and were proper policies, but that he gave less weight to the policies because they had not been subject to public discussion: circular 22/84; (2) the inspection had regard to circular 14/85 and the importance of expansion and the creation of new jobs; (3) the number of callers likely and the retention of a "shop window" display would ensure that a "dead section" was not created in the shopping street, consequently there was no "demonstrable harm" caused by the development; (4) a condition was imposed restricting the use of the premises for the purposes of a bank. Appeal allowed: STAFFORD BOROUGH COUNCIL AND TRUSTEES SAVINGS BANK (Ref. T/APP/T 3425/A/85/036134/P4) (1986) 1 P.A.D. 344.

3243. Change of use—dwelling to offices—A.O.N.B.—structure plan policies
[Town and Country Planning Act 1971 (c.78), s.36 and Sched. 9; DOE circulars 22/84, 14/85.] The council refused permission for change of use of a cottage from residential to offices. The cottage fronted the A22 and was bounded on one side by a commercial garage and on another by a hotel. Access was through the garage premises. The house had been occupied by garage personnel but had been empty for some time and had been put on the market but had not attracted a purchaser. The property was within an Area of Outstanding Natural Beauty. It was the council's policy to restrict commercial uses to towns and villages in accordance with the rural restraint policies in the structure plan. *Held,* by the inspector following a public inquiry, that (1) the adverse factors affecting the property when taken together were sufficient to justify a change of use in spite of the council's policies, these factors included: noise and disturbance from heavy traffic, the nature of the adjoining uses, access and parking difficulties; (2) the physical appearance of the area would not be affected by the proposed occupier, a small consultancy firm, which was a suitable use; (3) the inspector did not agree with the council that it was necessary to make the permission personal to the appellant. Appeal allowed: WEALDEN DISTRICT COUNCIL AND MONTLAKE (Ref. T/APP/C1435/A/85/033119/P3) (1986) 1 P.A.D. 347.

3244. Change of use—guesthouse to elderly persons' home—policy restriction—limitation period
[Town and Country Planning Act 1971 (c.78), s.36, sched. 9; Town and Country Planning Use Classes Order 1972 (S.I. 1972 No. 1385); Development Control Policy Note 15.] The Council refused planning permission for use of a guesthouse to be changed to an elderly persons' home. The guesthouse was a nine-bedroomed semi-detached Victorian house situated a half mile from the town centre and bounded by properties of a similar size comprising hotels and guesthouses to the north-east and south-east and residential properties to the north and west. The Council did not object on amenity grounds nor in relation to the criteria set for homes for elderly people in D.C.R.N. No. 15. The developer appealed and relied, *inter alia,* upon *Rann* v. *Secretary of State for the Environment* [1980] C.L.Y. 2666 in arguing that the proposal did not involve a material change of use. *Held,* by the Inspector, that (1) in *Rann* v. *SOSE* the handicapped children's use was regarded as a Class XI use only

because of the temporary nature of their stay and that case did not apply here because there was no question of a mixed use in this case; (2) the appellant's recent use of the premises for the accommodation of long-term residents, including former mental patients, was not a use normally associated with a guesthouse; (3) the use as a home for the boarding and care of old people was within Class XIV of the Use Classes Order and the proposal entailed a material change of use; (4) the Council's policy of prohibiting loss of hotel accommodation to schemes for elderly people did not have the authority of one associated with an approved district or structure plan and it was only one factor; (5) the proposed use would be viable, ensure that the property continued to be kept in good repair and would not demonstrably harm the local environment; (6) as the proposal was intended for local people it would not result in the influx of more elderly people into the town. Appeal allowed subject to condition that permission is implemented within two years: TORBAY BOROUGH COUNCIL AND COUGHLAN (Ref: T/APP/MH140/A/85/030786/P5) (1986) 1 P.A.D. 269.

3245. Change of use—houses—change to private dwellings
[Town and Country Planning Act 1971 (c.78), ss.36, 53, Sched. 9; Town and Country Planning Act 1984 (c.10), s.5; DoE Circular 18/84.] Four houses had been built in the grounds of a hospital and used by resident hospital staff. The houses were now in separate ownership from the rest of the former hospital premises, the hospital having been closed in 1983. Three of the houses adjoined the former hospital buildings. It was intended to use the main hospital buildings as a private hospital. The Council refused planning permission for the change of use of the houses to private dwellings. The appellants contended that permission was not required. The Council disputed this and objected because the site was within the green belt and subject to policies severely restricting development. *Held,* allowing the appeal, that (1) *Winton* v. *Secretary of State for the Environment* [1983] C.L.Y. 3657 indicated that development requiring planning permission might well be involved so the application would be determined on its merits; (2) notwithstanding the greenbelt and rural policies the appeal premises already existed and there was no logical reason why they should remain empty; (3) the Council produced no evidence of any alternative demand for the use of the dwellings in association with the hospital buildings: STAFFORD BOROUGH COUNCIL AND MIDLAND COUNTIES SECURITIES (Ref. T/APP/Y3425/A/84/018365-8/P5) (1986) 1 P.A.D. 108.

3246. Change of use—small-scale businesses—presumption in favour—"bad-neighbour" development
[Town and Country Planning Act 1971 (c.78), s.36; Town and Country Planning (Use Classes) Order 1972 (S.I. 1972 No. 1385); DoE Circular 22/80; Development Control Policy Note 3.] The Council refused planning permission for the change of use from upholstery workshop to a collection depot with fridge for hides, fat and bones of a unit on an industrial trading estate. The proposed use would be within Class IX of the Use Classes Order 1972 and was a "bad neighbour" industry. The appeal premises were adjacent to a Chapel of Rest. *Held,* by the Inspector following a public inquiry, that (1) the proposed use need not be incompatible with other uses on the industrial estate; (2) it would be better if the proximity of the Chapel of Rest could be avoided but no other site had become available for the proposed development; (3) the Circulars constitute a presumption in favour of small businesses; (4) there had been no effective action taken by the authority to provide sites for "bad neighbour" industries. Appeal allowed, subject to conditions: RICHMONDSHIRE DISTRICT COUNCIL AND MARKENDALE—LANCASHIRE. (Ref. T/APP/E2720/A/84/24672/P2) (1986) 1 P.A.D. 130.

3247. Chemical fertiliser lagoons—whether permitted development on agricultural land—loss of good agricultural land
[Town and Country Planning Act 1971 (c.78), s.36; Town and Country Planning General Development Order 1977 (S.I. 1977 No. 289); DOE Circulars 22/84, 14/85.] The Council refused planning permission for the construction of two rubber-lined lagoons for the mixing and storage of chemical fertiliser for local use, on land situated in open countryside and surrounded by agricultural land. 200m to the south was a long-established industrial area. The smaller lagoon was to be some 20 × 15 yards with an average depth of 8 ft. and would be open tapped: the larger lagoon was to be about four times this size. The developer appealed and the Inspector

considered the main issues to be the effect of the proposal on the rural character and appearance of the area with regard to the approved and emerging rural settlement policies for the district and the impact of the traffic generated. *Held*, by the Inspector, that (1) the proposed use was not intended to be simply for the use of the agricultural unit on which it would be located: therefore the proposed development was not permitted by Art. 3(1) and Class VI of the GDO; (2) the relevant policy in the emerging local plan indicated a general presumption against development in the open countryside other than for specific purposes, including agriculture. The proposed development was an industrial undertaking; (3) the development would be noticeable; (4) the nearby country roads were already subjected to high numbers of heavy goods vehicles and the generated traffic from the development could not have a significant impact; (3) the development did not need to be located on the appeal site with the consequent loss of good agricultural land. Appeal dismissed: CHESTER CITY COUNCIL AND PROVEN CHEMICALS (Ref. T/APP/X0605/A/85/028950/PS) (1986) 1 P.A.D. 252.

3248. Chemical works—long established—extension—advice and guidance of HSE—local plan policy

[Town and Country Planning Act 1971 (c.78), s.36; Town and Country Planning General Development Order 1977 (S.I. 1977 No. 289); Control of Industrial Major Accident Hazard Regulations 1984 (S.I. 1984 No. 1902); Health and Safety Guidance Note C5/2; DoE C9/84.] The Council refused planning permission for the erection of three 40-tonne storage tanks on the site of a chemical works which had existed since the 1920s. The Council were of the view that it was their duty to exercise rigorous control over the intensification or extension of hazardous industries and the Local Plan stated that such industries would be permitted only in locations acceptable to the Health and Safety Executive where it could be shown beyond reasonable doubt that there would be no adverse effects. The developer appealed. The Inspector considered that there were three issues: (a) whether the tanks would result in an increase of emission from the plant; (b) whether they would be likely to result in an increase in potential hazards, and (c) the effect of the tanks on the appearance of the area. *Held*, by the Inspector following a public inquiry, that (1) the approval would not result in increased emissions resulting from higher production levels which would not otherwise be possible; (2) tank storage would not be likely to increase the adverse effects on local residents; (3) there was no evidence of special circumstances suggesting that the preference of the HSE for storage in fixed bulk tanks rather than drums was not applicable or appropriate in this case; (4) the Local Plan policy of showing beyond reasonable doubt that there would be no adverse effects on people, properties or sites was not justified for established industries, particularly where no major extension or intensification was proposed. The policy was misleading and obscured the need for existing firms to object to the plan at the appropriate preparation stage (reference to C9/84). Appeal allowed, subject to conditions: KIRKLEES METROPOLITAN BOROUGH COUNCIL AND WILLIAMS (HOUNSLOW) (Ref. T/APP/J4715/A/84/23376/P7) (1986) 1 P.A.D. 145.

3249. Coast protection—called-in application—conflict with structure plan

[Town and Country Planning Act 1971 (c.78) s.35; Coast Protection Act 1949 (c.74), s.5(1); Countryside Act 1968 (c.41), ss.11, 49; Town and Country Planning General Regulations 1976 (S.I. No.1419 reg.7(1).] The District Council proposed to construct a new sea wall berm and wave wall, to scarp the cliffs and to reconstruct an existing wall. There was a planning application by the Council in accordance with regulation 7 of the Town and Country Planning General Regulations 1976 and the application was called-in by the Secretary of State. The Council argued at the Inquiry that the works were needed to protect the vulnerable site. The site lay within a proposed Site of Special Scientific Interest which was of international importance. The approved structure and local plan policies permitted development only if it could be shown not to be harmful to the scientific interest. The Nature Conservancy Council withdrew its objection on the basis of agreements with the Council. *Held*, by the Secretary of State (the Inspector having sat with an Assessor at the inquiry) that the works were essential to prevent further cliff erosion and to protect adjoining coastal protection works. Permission granted: THANET DISTRICT COUNCIL AND NATURE CONSERVANCY COUNCIL (Ref: SE2/5283/42/12) (1985) 1 P.A.D. 99.

3250. Composite use—discontinuance of one component use—whether a material change of use

The discontinuance of a use of land cannot of itself amount to a change of use.

The subject land was since 1957 subject to an established use for two distinct purposes: the use and maintenance of vehicles and plant in connection with the extraction of sand and gravel from adjoining land, and the use of vehicles and plant unconnected with such extraction. The first use ceased in 1972. Enforcement notices were served, and upheld by the inspector, who found that he was not required to determine the lawful or established use of the land, and that the continued use of the land for vehicles and plant unconnected with the extraction of sand or gravel was a material change of use. The owners' appeals were rejected by the Secretary of State, and by the judge. *Held,* allowing the appeal to the Court of Appeal, that the inspector had erred in failing to consider whether there was a lawful and established use. He had not found any increase in intensity of the continued use, and therefore appeared to have found a change of use solely because one of the component uses had ceased. It would be absurd if the occupier had to obtain planning permission to discontinue an activity on his own land. Since this case had not been properly investigated, it would be remitted to the Secretary of State to do so (*Wipperman v. Barking London Borough Council* [1966] C.L.Y. 11382 applied).

PHILGLOW *v.* SECRETARY OF STATE FOR THE ENVIRONMENT (1986) 51 P. & C.R. 1, C.A.

3251. Concrete batching plant—previous permission expired—effect upon environment—increase in road traffic and rail link

[Town and Country Planning Act 1971 (c.78), s.36.] The County Council failed to determine within the prescribed period an application for planning permission to erect a concrete batching plant, an aggregate storage building, ancillary offices and other facilities together with associated car and lorry parking on land adjacent to an existing rail depot. The cement was to be conveyed to the site by tanker, and sand and gravel aggregate by rail to underground hoppers. The developer appealed. The Inspector identified three main issues: (a) whether existing dust problems in nearby properties would be exacerbated materially; (b) whether there would be unacceptable disturbance from the plant, vehicles or additional rail movements and (c) whether there would be serious highway congestion and dangers. *Held,* by the Inspector that (1) the county council's approved minerals criteria for the assessment of planning applications and the approved structure plan (alterations) contained no policies specifically concerned with the provision of concrete batching plants but the structure plan did deal with support for the establishment of rail depots for the import of aggregates. A structure plan consultation document indicated that the county council would encourage the provision of new rail depots; (2) although permission for a concrete batching plan granted on appeal in 1979 had expired, it remained a material consideration but required to be considered in the light of significant differences between the two proposals and material changes that had occurred since then; (3) the 12 ft. high concrete panel wall would attenuate noise levels and diminish visual distraction to nearby occupiers; (4) there was no other site in the area which could provide a rail service to a concrete batching plant; (5) a request by the council that if the appeal were to be allowed it should be contingent upon an agreement between the freehold owner and the mineral planning authority to establish arrangements for the operation of the depot was wholly unreasonable. Appeal allowed subject to conditions: HERTFORDSHIRE COUNTY COUNCIL AND TARMAC TOPMIX (Ref. T/APP/Y1945/A/84/21382/P7) (1986) 1 P.A.D. 246.

3252. Conservation area—inspector's decision—whether adequate reasons given

[Town and Country Planning Act 1971 (c.78), s.245] The planning authority sought under s.245 of the Town and Country Planning Act 1971 to quash a decision by the Secretary of State's Inspector allowing a company to establish an amusement centre in a conservation area in St. Ives, Cornwall, on the ground that the inspector had failed to take into account guidance issued by the Department of the Environment to the effect that amusement centres are out of place in a conservation area. *Held,* allowing the application, that (1), if the inspector was minded to depart from any such policies applicable to the conservation area, the authority were entitled to clear and intelligible reasons explaining why, in the circumstances of the particular case, it was appropriate so to depart; (2) whilst the inspector's general approach would have been appropriate had this not been a conservation area, he had failed to give such reasons; (3) in making his permission conditional upon the agreement of a scheme to cover "A. Noise Insulation. B. Shopfront type. C. Opening hours" the inspector had imposed conditions which, as expressed, were not reasonably practical to enforce: PENWITH DISTRICT COUNCIL *v.* SECRETARY OF STATE FOR THE ENVIRONMENT (1985) 277 E.G. 194, Woolf J.

3253. Conservation areas

TOWN AND COUNTRY PLANNING (NATIONAL PARKS, AREAS OF OUTSTANDING NATURAL BEAUTY AND CONSERVATION AREAS, ETC.) SPECIAL DEVELOPMENT (AMENDMENT) ORDER 1986 (No. 8) [40p], made under the Town and Country Planning Act 1971 (c.78), ss.24, 287(3) and (10); operative on March 1, 1986; amends S.I. 1985 No. 1012.

3254. Continuance of old development plan—new local plan—clerical error

[Town and Country Planning Act 1971 (as amended) (c.78), Sched. 7, paras. 5A, B, C] The Secretary of State had the necessary power to correct a clerical error where an old development plan which he had obviously intended to continue had been omitted from his order: R. *v.* SECRETARY OF STATE FOR THE ENVIRONMENT, *ex p.* GREAT GRIMSBY BOROUGH COUNCIL, *The Times,* May 12, 1986, Russell J.

3255. Control of advertisements—balloon advertising

[Town and Country Planning (Control of Advertisements) Regulations (S.I. 1984 No. 421), reg. 2(4).] When an advertisement is displayed on the side of a balloon tethered to a company's premises, for the purposes of reg. 2(4) of the 1984 Town and Country Planning (Control of Advertisements) Regulations the advertisement is treated as being displayed on the site to which it is tethered: WADHAM STRINGER (FAREHAM) *v.* FAREHAM BOROUGH COUNCIL, *The Times,* November 10, 1986, D.C.

3256. Costs—enforcement notice appeal—alternative to enforcement proceedings

[Town and Country Planning Act 1971 (c78), ss.36, 88 and Sched. 9; Local Government Act 1972 (c.70), s.250(5); Circulars 73/65; 69/71; 22/80.] The appeal site had been used as a builders' merchants yard for 30 years. It was a non-conforming use in a residential area. The site was in a conservation area and had previously had on it six untidy structures. The appellants decided to replace these with one large storage shed. Having commenced construction the appellants applied for planning permission. This was refused by the Council on the grounds that, (a) the appearance and location of the shed seriously detracted from the appearance of the adjoining property (which was of local architectural or historic interest) and (b) the proposal would intensify and consolidate a non-conforming activity in a predominantly residential area. The Council issued enforcement notices. At the Inquiry the appellant asked for costs against the Council. *Held,* by the Inspector, that (1) if the structure were completed so it blended with the neighbouring structures it would be acceptable, (2) there was no real harm done by the building to the amenities of local residents. Appeal allowed. *Held,* by the Secretary of State agreeing with the Inspector's recommendation, that since the Council admitted that some kind of building was necessary there was an alternative to the Council initiating enforcement proceedings (C22/80 and C69/71 referred to). The Council had, therefore behaved unreasonably. Costs awarded to the appellant: GREENWICH LONDON BOROUGH COUNCIL AND TRIDENT BUILDERS MERCHANTS (Refs: APP/5012/C/83/3323, APP/E5330/C84/286, APP/E5330/A/83/7343(PLUP 4C)) (1985) 1 P.A.D. 93.

3257. Deemed planning permission—award by planning authority to itself—whether defective

[Town and Country Planning General Regulations 1976 (S.I. 1976 No. 1419) regs. 4, 5; Town and Country Planning General Development Order 1977 (S.I. 1977 No. 289) Arts. 10, 11; Town and Country Planning (Development Plans) (England) Direction 1981] The authority awarded itself deemed planning permission, pursuant to regs. 4 and 5 of the Town and Country Planning General Regulations 1976, for the development of a retail superstore in Carlisle. CCS who had previously made an unsuccessful application for a similar development of their own in Carlisle, sought judicial review to quash the award, in the hope that an inquiry would result before an inspector, at which all extant applications for similar local developments could be heard and at which the local authority would not hold the trump card of planning permission. CCS argued (i) that the authority failed properly to report the existence and nature of CCS's own application, so that the sub-committee failed to have proper regard to a material planning consideration; (ii) that the authority had had regard to the irrelevant and immaterial consideration of its own substantial financial gain; (iii) that it had authorised the development with unreasonable haste and without allowing or taking account of public consultation replies on the relevant policy; (iv) that it had acted unfairly and unreasonably in requesting CCS to agree to a deferment of the determination of CCS's own application, without disclosing its own proposal to seek permission for such a development on a site within its own ownership; and (v) that it had failed properly to comply with a number of statutory consultative requirements. CCS further argued that the Secretary of State had acted unreasonably in refusing to call in the authority's case. *Held,* refusing the application, that (1) the first four grounds against the authority failed; (2) the fifth ground also failed, both as a matter of discretion and because the requirements in question were in any event directory rather than mandatory; (3) there were no grounds for complaint against the Secretary of State's decision: R. *v.* Carlisle City Council, *ex p.* Cumbrian Co-operative Society (1985) 276 E.G. 1161, Macpherson J.

3258. Deemed planning permission—procedure
[Town and Country Planning General Regulations 1976 (S.I. 1976 No. 1419), reg. 4(2)(*c*).] The local authority owned a 125 acre park which was within a conservation area, and proposed to construct an athletics track with spectator facilities on six acres. A notice was displayed at an entrance to the park. The local authority deemed permission granted. An objector sought judicial review. *Held,* that (1) only one notice was required to be displayed; (2) the form of the notice was invalid because it failed to state that objections should be lodged in writing and the period in which objections were to be made. Strict compliance with the notice procedure under r.4(2)(*c*) was essential; (3) the notice was further invalid because the authority had not considered the effect of the proposed development on the conservation area: R. *v.* Lambeth London Borough Council, *ex p.* Sharp [1986] J.P.L. 200, Croom-Johnson J.

3259. Dismissal of appeal contrary to Inspector's recommendation—whether sufficient evidence—whether reasons adequate
[Town and Country Planning Act 1971 (c.78), s.245; Town and Country Planning (Inquiry Procedure) Rules 1974 (S.I. 1974 No. 419), Rule 13.] A wished to construct a large shopping centre on a site of 109 acres some three and a half miles from the centre of Leicester, but were refused planning permission on the basis that the proposal was contrary to the shopping policies of the approved Leicestershire Structure Plan. Following a public inquiry the Inspector recommended to the Secretary of State in April 1982 that planning permission be granted. In May 1983 the Secretary of State issued a decision letter purporting to refuse permission, but this letter was subsequently quashed by consent. In 1984 and again in early 1985 he gave notice of intention to reopen the inquiry, but on each occasion the decision letter was again quashed. In October 1983 he issued a further letter, which dismissed A's appeal on the grounds that the proposed centre would be incompatible with one of the policies of the structure plan. A sought to quash that decision letter also, on the grounds that there was no material upon which the decision could properly be based, and that the Secretary of State had not complied with the requirement of Rule 13 of the Town and Country Planning (Inquiry Procedure) Rules 1974 that he should notify his reasons in writing. *Held,* dismissing the appeal, that (1) the Secretary of State was entitled to disagree with his Inspector and to change his mind on proper grounds between May 1983 and October 1985, and that there had been evidence on which he could properly do so (*Ashbridge Investments* v. *Minister of Housing and Local Government* [1965] C.L.Y. 522, *Seddon Properties* v. *Secretary of State for the Environment* [1981] C.L.Y. 2730, and *Sainsbury (J.)* v. *Secretary of State for the Environment and Colchester Borough Council* [1978] C.L.Y. 2898 considered; *Coleen Properties* v. *Minister of Housing and Local Government* [1971] C.L.Y. 1503 distinguished); (2) in the circumstances of the case the reasons given by the Secretary of State for this decision on a matter of planning judgment, although expressed briefly and in a manner liable to leave A with a sense of grievance, were nonetheless proper, adequate and intelligible (*Poyser and Mills' Arbitration, Re* [1963] C.L.Y. 43 considered); (3) in any event any failure by the Secretary of State to give adequate reasons could not, on the particular facts of this case, have caused A sufficiently substantial prejudice to justify setting aside the decision: Centre 21 *v.* Secretary of State for the Environment (1986) 280 E.G. 889, C.A.

3260. District shopping centre—new superstore—impact on other centres in neighbourhood
[Town and Country Planning Act 1971 (c.78) ss.36, 37; DoE Circular 22/80; Development Control Policy Note No. 13.] Appellants sought permission to erect a District Centre as part of Phase 2 of the Pheasant Wood Development of Thornton Cleveleys, Lancashire. The appeal was against the Council's deemed refusal. The new housing area at Pheasant Wood was nearing completion. *Held*, by the Secretary of State, agreeing with his Inspector's conclusions; that (1) there were no insuperable highway or parking problems associated with the site; but (2) the proposal would occupy an inappropriate urban site and would disturb and distort the present balance of retail trade between the existing main town centres of the North Fylde. Appeal dismissed: WYRE BOROUGH COUNCIL AND BROSELEY ESTATES (Ref. APP/U2370/A/84/012076) (1984) 1 P.A.D.

3261. Disused airfield—proposal for microlight aircraft—abandonment
[Town and Country Planning Act 1971 (c.78), ss.22, 33, 36, 53.] Bovingdon Airfield ceased full operational use in 1970. It straddles the boundary between two Councils and is located in the green belt. The Councils refused permission to use the airfield for the operation of microlight aircraft. The main planning issues were the effect of the proposal on (a) the amenities of local residents and (b) on the character of the green belt. The appellants argued that as the airfield had been used only for agriculture since 1970 the original use still subsisted. *Held*, by the Secretary of State, that (1) the original use ceased with no intention of resumption and was therefore abandoned, (2) provided microlight flying occurred for recreational purposes it might in principle take place in the green belt without any special need having to be established; (3) the noise likely to be generated would interfere with the tranquillity of the local homes and with the peaceful character of the green belt; (4) the microlight operations could pose security and safety problems for the new prison due to be completed in 1987 close to the runway. Appeal dismissed: CHILTERN AND DACORUM DISTRICT COUNCILS AND LONDON ULTRALIGHT FLYING CLUB (Refs. APP/XO4/15/A/83/009764, APP/A1910/A/009807) (1985) 1 P.A.D. 61.

3262. Doctors' surgery—need overriding policy presumption against development
[Town and Country Planning Act 1971 (c.78), s.36 and Sched. 9; Circular 1/85.] The proposal was for a doctors' surgery and access on land proposed for inclusion in the green belt in the County Council's draft green belt boundaries local plan which awaited a decision on the proposed alterations to the Structure Plan. The major part of the site was zoned for residential use in the 1958 Town Map and a small strip along the northern edge had been in the metropolitan green belt since 1972. The area surrounding the appeal site was in part open countryside. The Council refused planning permission. *Held*, by the Inspector that (1) there was a strong policy presumption against development on the appeal site; (2) the practice's present premises were inadequate, could not be redeveloped and no suitable alternative site was likely to become available in the foreseeable future; (3) on the basis of the strong community benefit to be gained from a new surgery the need for the facility outweighed any policy presumption against development. Appeal allowed. CHILTERN DISTRICT COUNCIL AND GIBBS (Ref: T/APP/XO4015/A/84/020070/P5) (1985) 1 P.A.D. 96.

3263. Draft local plans—inquiry
Three draft local plans were prepared by the district council. Each contained an identical draft policy section. The Council decided that an inspector would hold an inquiry into the policy sections of the plans, and two further inspectors would hold different inquiries into the specific aspects of the three plans. The further inspectors would attend the policy inquiry beforehand as observers. The applicants sought judicial review. *Held*, that the proposed arrangements were permissible. At this stage there was no breach of the rules of natural justice. Application refused: R. v. WAKEFIELD METROPOLITAN DISTRICT COUNCIL, *ex p*. ASQUITH [1986] J.P.L. 440, Woolf J.

3264. Educational building—green belt—traffic—not primary road
[Town and Country Planning Act 1971 (c.78) s.36, Sched. 9; Development Control Policy Note No. 6; Department of Transport Advice Note TA/4/80.] The appeal site was a former school. The Council refused outline planning permission for a new school and ancillary facilities. Ninety per cent. of the site would be left open. The site was allocated in the Town Map as being within the green belt and for school

purposes. The Structure Plan permitted a school in large grounds of it did not impair the rural character. Local residents expressed concern about traffic on the busy distributor road. *Held,* by the Secretary of State agreeing with his Inspector's recommendations, that (1) the highway objections did not justify refusal. The section of the road which passed the appeal site was not part of the primary road network and therefore para. 1.3 of TA/4/80 did not apply; (2) the scheme would not result in unacceptable visual intrusion; (3) the proposal was wholly appropriate to the area. Appeal allowed subject to conditions relating to trees and shrubs and restricting the height and floor area of the buildings: BRACKNELL DISTRICT COUNCIL AND SOCIETY OF LICENSED VICTUALLERS (Ref. APP/C0305A/84/12718) (1985) 1 P.A.D. 90.

3265. Enforcement notice—appeal—impropriety not raised before inspector
[Town and Country Planning Act 1971 (c.78), s.246.] The council served enforcement notices alleging (a) material change of use, and (b) erection of a portable building. The appellants contended that an objector who was legal officer to R2 had dissuaded a witness from giving evidence, and that this was a serious impropriety constituting a breach of the rules of national justice. *Held,* that (1) an appeal under s.246 was limited to the determining an appeal against a decision on a point of law; (2) new facts such as these could not be raised in such an appeal; (3) the enforcement notice would be upheld. Application dismissed: LONDON PARACHUTING *v.* SECRETARY OF STATE FOR THE ENVIRONMENT AND SOUTH CAMBRIDGESHIRE DISTRICT COUNCIL [1986] J.P.L. 428, Mann J.

3266. Enforcement notice—change of use—error in notice—correction
[Town and Country Planning Act 1971 (c.78), s.88A(2) (as inserted by Local Government and Planning (Amendment) Act 1981 (c.41), s.1, Sched. 1).]
A misrecital in an enforcement notice of the time within which a breach is alleged to have occurred goes to the substance of the matter.
H Co. owned a quarry and adjacent buildings. In 1983 the local authority issued an enforcement notice alleging a material change in the use of a building without planning permission. The notice recited a breach of planning control after the end of 1963. Under s.87(4)(c) of the 1971 Act, as amended, the alleged breach should have occurred within the last four years. On H Co.'s appeal the inspector held that no one had been misled, amended the notice and dismissed H Co.'s appeal. *Held,* allowing the appeal, that the misrecital in the enforcement notice went to the substance of the matter and correction could not be made without doing injustice to H Co. (*Miller-Mead* v. *Minister of Housing and Local Government* [1963] C.L.Y. 3406 and *Wealden D.C.* v. *Secretary of State for the Environment* [1983] C.L.Y. 3682 applied).
HUGHES (H. T.) & SONS *v.* SECRETARY OF STATE FOR THE ENVIRONMENT (1986) 51 P. & C.R. 134, D.C.

3267. Enforcement notice—condition relating to agricultural occupancy
R acquired land with the benefit of a permission for the erection of a dwelling specified to be an agricultural workers' dwelling and subject to an agricultural occupancy condition. The council took action for non-compliance with an enforcement notice as to the agricultural occupancy. The magistrates dismissed the summons. *Held,* that (1) the magistrates had wrongly considered the wording of the condition instead of the enforcement notice; (2) R, a builder who worked the land for vegetables at evenings, and weekends was not "solely or mainly employed in agriculture"; (3) the court would not define the term "employed in agriculture." EPPING DISTRICT COUNCIL *v.* SCOTT [1986] J.P.L. 603, D.C.

3268. Enforcement notice—egg packing—change of use
In 1973 permission was granted for the use of farm land as an egg packing station and distribution and servicing of vehicles used in that connection. In 1979 enforcement notices were served alleging a material change of use to the storage and repair of motor vehicles in connection with a business including paint spraying. The Secretary of State upheld the notices. On appeal to the High Court the notices were upheld. *Held,* on appeal to the Court of Appeal, that (1) it was appropriate to have regard to the terms of the planning permission; (2) the permission in this case was clear; (3) the use not in connection with egg packing was a material change of use; (4) use as an egg packing station was outside the scope of the Use Classes Order 1972 (*Miller Mead* v. *M.H.L.G.* [1963] C.L.Y. 3406, *Lewis* v. *Secretary of State for the Environment* [1972] C.L.Y. 3345 considered): KUXHAYS (ALEXANDER) AND WENBAN

(DAVID) *v.* SECRETARY OF STATE FOR THE ENVIRONMENT AND LEWES DISTRICT COUNCIL [1986] J.P.L. 675, C.A.

3269. Enforcement notice—existing use rights—appeal raising new point of law

The applicant challenged the inspector's decision in respect of enforcement notice A on the ground that it went too far in its requirement to discontinue the use altogether. This point had not been raised before the inspector. *Held,* that (1) the inspector had erred in law in failing to apply the principle in *Mansi* v. *Elstree District Council* [1964] C.L.Y. 3580; (2) the applicant could raise in court a point not raised at the inquiry:

JOHN PEARCY TRANSPORT *v.* SECRETARY OF STATE FOR THE ENVIRONMENT AND HOUNSLOW LONDON BOROUGH COUNCIL [1986] J.P.L. 680, David Widdicombe Q.C.

3270. Enforcement notice—Inspector's decision

An enforcement notice was served alleging the making of a material change of use to use for the purpose of retail sales and ancillary purposes. The annex to the notice gave reasons for its issue. The Inspector upheld the notice because of the unacceptable mix of traffic and pedestrians. He refused to grant permission. The appellants contended that it was not open to the Inspector to come to that conclusion as a result of his inquiry. *Held,* that (1) the planning authority is not required to give reasons in the enforcement notice itself; (2) the Inspector's observations on the site visit could be used in his decision; (3) if an allegation of *mala fides* is made the Inspector should deal with it, but failure to do so will not necessarily be fatal. Appeal dismissed: WASS (W. & J.) *v.* SECRETARY OF STATE FOR THE ENVIRONMENT AND STOKE ON TRENT CITY COUNCIL [1985] J.P.L. 120, Woolf J.

3271. Enforcement notice—non-service on owner—effect

[Town and Country Planning Act 1971 (c.78), ss.87(1)(4), 88(1)(*e*), 89(1), 91(1)(2), 243(1)(2).]

The Secretary of State is the forum for deciding all challenges to enforcement notices.

P, who had resided in the U.S.A. at all material times, owned a corner property immediately adjoining a property belonging to his sister-in-law, Mrs. P, who was allowed by him to use it for the purposes of her business which she carried on at her premises. She built a shed in his garden to use as a store. She applied for planning permission to retain the shed stating that she owned P's premises. The application was refused and her appeal dismissed. The council served an enforcement notice on Mrs. P to remove the shed. She neither appealed nor took any steps to remove the shed and the council gave notice under s.91 of the 1971 Act that it would enter the land to remove the shed. P applied for judicial review on the ground that he had not been served with the enforcement notice. The application was refused. *Held,* dismissing the appeal, that although the enforcement notice had not been served on P as required by s.87(4) of the 1971 Act, the effect of ss.88(1)(*e*), 88(4) and 243(2), made it impossible to contend that the failure rendered the enforcement notice a nullity; the Secretary of State was the forum for deciding all challenges to the validity of enforcement notices, and s.243 ousted the jurisdiction of the court to determine such challenges (*Davy* v. *Spelthorne Borough Council* [1983] C.L.Y. 3679 followed; *McDaid* v. *Clydesdale District Council* [1984] C.L.Y. 3422 not followed).

R. *v.* GREENWICH LONDON BOROUGH COUNCIL, *ex p.* PATEL (1986) 84 L.G.R. 241, C.A.

3272. Enforcement notice—retail shop—disturbance from delivery vehicles

[Town and Country Planning Act 1971 (c.78), s.88; DOE Circulars 22/80, 14/85; Development Control Policy Note 14.] The Council issued an enforcement notice alleging a material change in use from a retail shop selling to the public to use a wholesale warehouse for the wholesale supply of meat to colleges, restaurants, etc. Sales to retail customers represented 20 per cent. of total trade. The appeal premises consisted of the ground floor and basement of a two-storey terraced property which was surrounded by small terraced "turn-of-the-century" houses. There was an appeal under s.88(2)(*a*), (*b*), (*c*), (*g*) and (*h*) of the TCPA 1971. The appellant relied upon *LTSS Print and Supply Services* v. *Hackney London Borough Council* [1976] C.L.Y. 2691 and *MonoMart Warehouses* v. *Secretary of State for the Environment* [1978] C.L.Y. 2871 to support their contention that the primary purpose of the premises was for the cutting up and selling of meat and any storage was ancillary to that purpose. *Held,* by the Inspector, that (1) the notice would be correct by deleting that part of the allegation relating to a wholesale warehouse since a building would not be used as a wholesale warehouse if its primary use was the wholesale supply of meat (para. 3 of DCPN 14); (2) the premises in their present form did not look like a shop and they were not open during ordinary shopping hours. The appeal on grounds (b) and (c) failed; (3) the nature of the business disturbed neighbours to an unreasonable extent given the early arrival of meat delivery lorries. Encouragement of small businesses was subject to the proviso that such businesses should not cause harm to the neighbouring users (C22/80 and C14/85); this one did cause such harm. The appeal on ground (a) accordingly failed. The appeal on ground (b) was withdrawn and ground (g) was dismissed. Appeal dismissed: enforcement notice amended: CAMBRIDGE CITY COUNCIL AND HADJIOANNOU (Ref. T/APP/Q0505/C/84/3679/P6) (1986) 1 P.A.D. 256.

3273. Enforcement notice—whether ambiguous—whether void
The authority served an enforcement notice in respect of land in Cleethorpes, requiring A, ". . . to discontinue the use of the land for the holding of markets and associated car parking on Sundays which fall within the period of summer time in any year." Following an enquiry the Inspector found that the expression "the period of summer time" was ambiguous, but purported to uphold the notice in varied form. *Held*, allowing A's appeal, that (1) the expression "the period of summer time" was hopelessly ambiguous, and that the notice was accordingly a nullity; (2) the Inspector had accordingly not had jurisdiction to vary it (*Miller-Mead* v. *Minister of Housing and Local Government* [1963] C.L.Y. 3406 applied: DUDLEY BOWERS AMUSEMENT ENTERPRISES *v.* SECRETARY OF STATE FOR THE ENVIRONMENT (1986) 278 E.G. 313, Mr. David Widdicombe Q.C.

3274. Enterprise Zones
NORTH WEST KENT ENTERPRISE ZONES (DESIGNATION) ORDER 1986 (No. 1557) [80p], made under the Local Government, Planning and Land Act 1980 (c.65), Sched. 32, para. 5; operative on October 10, 1986; designated as an enterprise zone an area in North-West Kent.

3275. Established use certificate—enforcement notice
[Town and Country Planning Act 1971 (c.78), ss.12, 88, 94, 243.] C provided car parking facilities for users of Gatwick airport. The land was attached to a dwelling-house with warehouse and barn. An enforcement notice required discontinuance of car parking. An application for an established use certificate relating to land was rejected prior to the issue of the notice. The Secretary of State refused the appeals against the notice and the refusal. The company appealed to the High Court. *Held,* that the use of the land except for use of the barn under the temporary permission was not only non-conforming but illegal use. Consequently the application and appeal regarding the established use certificate was invalid: VAUGHAN *v.* SECRETARY OF STATE FOR THE ENVIRONMENT AND MID-SUSSEX DISTRICT COUNCIL [1986] J.P.L. 840, McNeill J.

3276. Estate agents' office—change of use from public house—retail use not implemented but permission remaining valid
[Town and Country Planning Act 1971 (c.78), s.36; Development Control Policy Note 11.] The Council refused to grant planning permission for the change of use of a public house to an estate agents' office. In 1984 permission had been granted for change of use of the ground floor of the property to retail use with office and storage accommodation over. The premises had subsequently been sold with a covenant restricting the sale of alcohol. This permission had not been put into effect but remained valid. The premises occupied a prime High Street position close to the centre of the shopping and commercial area and were adjacent to a solicitors' office and a china shop. *Held,* by the Inspector following a public inquiry, that (1) although DCPN 11 refers to the impact of "dead frontage" on the character of a shopping centre, the use of the premises as a public house would have rendered the frontage "dead" during a large proportion of normal shopping hours; (2) there was insufficient evidence that there would be a strong prospect of early occupation of the appeal premises by a retail trader; (3) the design of the premises and lack of rear access militated against successful retail use; (4) the proposed use would be likely to generate as much activity as would many shops. Appeal allowed: NEW FOREST DISTRICT COUNCIL AND MESSRS. AUSTIN AND WYATT (Ref:T/APP/B1740/A/85/028722/P4) (1986) 1 P.A.D. 172.

3277. Explosives factory—relevant considerations—encouraging new businesses

[Town and Country Planning Act 1971 (c.78), s.36; DoE Circulars 22/80 and 1/85.] The proposal was to erect buildings for the blending and storage of commercial explosives. The Council refused planning permission and were concerned about, *inter alia*, the safety and security of the factory and magazine, and disturbance to residents and livestock resulting from test explosions. The developer appealed. The Inspector considered the main issues were (a) the effect upon the rival locality and (b) the adequacy of the Class III roads. *Held,* by the Inspector following a public inquiry, that (1) the development could become an alien intrusion into a landscape whose visual quality could be favourably compared with the nearby designated Area of Great Landscape Value. Lighting would be required and this would be intrusive; (2) there would be a conflict with walkers and horseriders; (3) the appellants had underestimated the number of likely vehicular movements and the traffic likely to be generated could not be accommodated on the local Class III roads without increasing safety hazards to an unacceptable degree; (4) the objections were too serious to be overridden by the economic benefits (C22/80 referred to). Appeal dismissed: NORTH DEVON DISTRICT COUNCIL AND B.E.P. (Ref. T/AA/G1115/A/84/025282/P2) (1986) 1 P.A.D. 141.

3278. Factory unit—draft local plan—allocation for public car parking—previous action by council

[Town and Country Planning Act 1971 (c.78), s.36, Sched. 9; DOE Circulars 22/80, 16/84, 14/85; development control policy note no. 5.]

The council refused permission for a factory unit on a cleared site next to the appellant's existing factory between a public and a private car park. The site had been cleared as a result of demolition orders served on four houses by the council. The council proposed to allocate the site for public car parking in the draft local plan and the main issue was whether this was a sufficient reason to override the presumption in favour of industrial development. *Held,* by the inspector after a public inquiry; that (1) the council having proceeded by way of demolition order rather than compulsory purchase in 1984 revealed that earlier intentions to acquire for public car parking had been abandoned; (2) the proposed notation in the draft local plan was not an interest of acknowledged importance when considering the advice in Circulars 22/80, 16/84 and 14/85 and when weighed against the expected increase in employment from the proposal; (3) the small size of the site was taken into account in concluding that the proposal would not cause serious harm. Appeal allowed: EREWASH BOROUGH COUNCIL AND LUCKING (C. J. & D. J.) (Ref. /T/APP/N1025/A/85/34832/P2) (1986) 1 P.A.D. 338.

3279. Farmyard—use for storage and servicing of farm contracting plant—effect on residential amenities and rural character of area

[Town and Country Planning Act 1971 (c.78), s.36, Sched. 9; DOE Circulars 22/80, 1/85, 14/85.] The council refused permission for continuing use of part of an existing farmyard for parking and servicing farm contracting plant. There had been some industrial type of use on the site since the 1920s; before 1970 three people were employed there in a fencing business. The appellant accepted there had been a change of use in 1972 since when an average of 10 men full-time and three men part-time had been employed in a farm/construction contracting plant business. The appellant said there was no alternative site so that 13 jobs would be lost and local farmers would lose a contractor who dealt with their construction needs. The site was within a special landscape area designated in the adopted structure plan and was somewhat exposed. Some disturbance was caused to local residences by noisy lorries. *Held,* by the inspector after a public inquiry that (1) having regard to the advice in C22/80 and annex B relating to small businesses and local employment, the contribution of the appellant's well-established business to the local economy in jobs and agricultural requirements, outweighed the detrimental effects of the proposal on both residential amenities and local character; (2) it was appropriate to impose a condition limiting the number of lorries to be parked, and a further condition limiting the use to that applied for, *i.e.* parking and routine maintenance of farm contracting plant; (3) although the appellant would accept a personal condition limiting the use to his business the inspector did not feel that such a condition was justified having regard to the advice in C1/85. Appeal allowed: TUNBRIDGE WELLS

Borough Council and Boulding (Ref. T/APP/M2270/A/85/036704/P4) (1981) 1 P.A.D. 331.

3280. **Fish farm—security caravans—special landscape area—area of high ecological value**
[Town and Country Planning Act 1971 (c.78), s.36, Sched. 9.] The Council refused planning permission for the placing of two caravans (A and B) on land forming part of a Fish Farm, consisting of 99 trout ponds on about 55 acres. One of the caravans had been on the land for three years and the other for eight years and the farm had been in use since 1972. The developer appealed and contended that the caravans were used for caretakers/nightwatchman and blended in with the surrounding countryside. The Council argued that the development was not appropriate in a rural location, in an area of special landscape and of high ecological value. *Held,* by the Inspector, that (1) caravan A was necessary for the control of the water supply and security made it reasonable for supervision to be exercised from that point, some 700 yards from the main buildings: the need for that caravan outweighed the landscape policy objection; (2) the use of caravan B along with A was necessary for the proper running of a commercial enterprise and it could be permitted without additional significant harm to the rural nature of the area. Appeal allowed subject to the permission being a personal one: Salisbury District Council and Trafalgar Fisheries (Ref: T/APP/T3915/A/85/29345/P2) (1986) 1 P.A.D. 272.

3281. **Gipsies—accommodation—whether duty of local authority to provide—"squatters proceedings"**
[Caravan Sites Act 1968 (c.52), Part II, Caravan Sites and Control of Development Act 1960 (c.62).] Over a number of years gipsies had resided within the respondent authority's area. By June 1985 the authority were not providing any accommodation for the gipsies, whether permanent or temporary, pursuant to their duties under the 1968 Act. In September 1985 "squatters" proceedings were begun against a number of gipsies. The possession order was subsequently set aside on the ground that the authority were in breach of their duty to provide accommodation. This was appealed, and was the first appeal. Subsequently an application was made by way of judicial review to quash, *inter alia,* the decision to institute proceedings for possession. At first instance it was held (a) that the authority were clearly in breach, (b) the decision to evict was accordingly one that no reasonable authority could make. The council appealed. This was the second appeal. *Held,* allowing the appeal in part, that (1) the fact that the council were and are in breach of their duty to provide accommodation, and that this breach may have caused some of the gipsies to squat, did not of itself afford any defence to the possession proceedings or deprive the council of their right to possession; (2) however having regard to all the circumstances of the case the decision to evict without making any provision for alternative accommodation for any of the gipsies was a decision which was so unreasonable as to be perverse, and accordingly not open to the council; (3) the court should not make a declaration as to the circumstances in which a county council would be entitled to seek possession of the land; this was a matter for the council and any further decision would be open to challenge in the usual way: West Glamorgan County Council *v.* Rafferty; R. *v.* Secretary of State for Wales, *ex p.* Gilhaney (1986) 18 H.L.R. 375, C.A.

3282. **Gipsies—Mobile home—green belt—area of great landscape value**
[Town and Country Planning Act 1971 (c.78), s.36, sched. 9; DoE Circulars 42/55, 28/77, 57/78, 14/84; DCPN 8] The Council refused planning permission for the siting of one mobile home for a gipsy family on a site situated within an area of great landscape value on the town map and an area of special character in the Greater London Development Plan. The green belt policies of these plans did not permit residential development other than in specifically defined circumstances. The applicant appealed. *Held,* by the Inspector, that (1) the caravan would be seen as a consolidation of scattered developments, diminishing a valuable open break within the greenbelt; (2) the existing sites in the area did not meet the demand and the national guidelines emphasised the urgency of the need for sites (reference to C28/77 and C57/78 and DCPN 8); (3) but given the site's location in an area subject to special controls and in particular green belt policies the arguments for departing from these was not convincing; (4) no evidence had been presented to suggest that efforts had been made to find alternative accommodation. Appeal dismissed: Bromley London Borough Council and Jackson (Ref.T/APP/G5180/A185/025913/P2) (1986) 1 P.A.D. 144.

3283. Gipsy encampments
    GIPSY ENCAMPMENTS (DESIGNATION OF THE BOROUGH OF BROXBOURNE) ORDER 1986
(No. 688) [45p], made under the Caravan Sites Act 1968 (c.52), s.12(2); operative on
May 9, 1986; designates the said borough of Broxbourne as an area to which s.10 of
the 1968 Act applies.
    GIPSY ENCAMPMENTS (DESIGNATION OF THE BOROUGH OF DARLINGTON AND THE
DISTRICTS OF CHESTER-LE-STREET, DERWENTSIDE, EASINGTON, SEDGEFIELD, TEESDALE
AND WEAR VALLEY) ORDER 1986 (No. 1572) [45p], made under the Caravan Sites Act
1968 (c.52), s.12(2); operative on October 10, 1986; designated the said areas for the
purposes of section 10 of the 1968 Act.
    GIPSY ENCAMPMENTS (DESIGNATION OF THE BOROUGH OF WATFORD) ORDER 1986
(No. 2286) [45p], made under the Caravan Sites Act 1968 (c.52), s.12(2); operative
on January 29, 1987; designates Watford for the purposes of s.10 of the 1968 Act.
    GIPSY ENCAMPMENTS (DESIGNATION OF THE CITY OF CANTERBURY) ORDER 1986 (No.
1170) [45p], made under the Caravan Sites Act 1968 (c.52), s.12(2); operative on
August 8, 1986; designates Canterbury as an area to which s.10 of the 1968 Act
applies, thus making it an offence for any gipsy to station a caravan within the
designated area.
    GIPSY ENCAMPMENTS (DESIGNATION OF THE DISTRICT OF EAST NORTHAMPTONSHIRE)
ORDER 1986 (No. 2048) [45p], made under the Caravan Sites Act 1968 (c.52),
s.12(2); operative on December 26, 1986; designates East Northamptonshire for the
purposes of s.10 of the 1968 Act.
    GIPSY ENCAMPMENTS (DESIGNATION OF THE DISTRICT OF RYEDALE) ORDER 1986 (No.
1145) [45p], made under the Caravan Sites Act 1968 (c.52), s.12(2); operative on
August 8, 1986; designates the area of Ryedale as an area to which s.10 of the 1968
Act applies.

3284. Gravel pit—proposed hotel—whether planning appeal unlawfully refused by Secretary of State
    H, a gravel company, wished to build a hotel on surplus land left after a pit had
been worked out at Wraysbury, Berkshire, but permission was refused by the local
authority on the grounds that the site was within the metropolitan green belt. On
appeal the Inspector recommended that the application be approved, but the
Secretary of State did not accept the Inspector's recommendation and dismissed the
appeal. H sought to quash the Secretary of State's decision on the grounds that he
had possibly misunderstood the effect of the M25 on planning policy as regards
development in the green belt; that he had differed from the Inspector on a finding
of fact without giving H the opportunity to make representations; that he had
rejected the Inspector's "flexible" approach to green belt policy in favour of a strict
approach without giving reasons; that he had failed to take into account the grant of
planning permission in 1964 for a motel on green belt quarry land a quarter of a mile
to the south of the appeal site; and that he had failed to give proper or adequate
reasons for his decision. *Held*, that the application failed on all grounds. In particular
the refusal to endorse the "flexible" approach was a matter of planning policy, and
did not constitute a finding of fact. It had not been established that the Secretary of
State had exceeded his powers or broken one of the procedural rules: HALL
AGGREGATES (THAMES VALLEY) v. SECRETARY OF STATE FOR THE ENVIRONMENT (1986)
278 E.G. 308, Mr. David Widdicombe QC.

3285. Gipsies—camping on land—whether power to prohibit
    [Public Health Act 1936 (c.49), s.100.] The Public Health Act 1936 does not make
it an offence to create a statutory nuisance: the offence arises on non-compliance
with a nuisance order. A local authority has no power under s.100 of the Act to seek
orders prohibiting gypsies from camping on land within its area but which it does not
own: BRADFORD METROPOLITAN CITY COUNCIL v. BROWN, *The Times*, March 18, 1986,
C.A.

3286. Horticultural development—whether permitted development—article 4 direction
    [Town and Country Planning Act 1971 (c.78), ss.22, 36, 53, 290; Town and
Country Planning General Development Order 1977 (S.I. 1977 No. 259) Arts. 3, 4,
Sched. 1: Development Control Policy Note No. 1.] The Council refused permission
for the erection of a tool and implement shed, a glasshouse, two polytunnels and the
construction of a cesspool for horticultural purposes on land which had almost all
been cultivated to some degree and had been partly fenced with a water supply laid

on. The land was part of a larger area which was subject to a direction under Article 4, but the land, the subject of the proposal, did not fall within that Art. 4 direction. The developer appealed. *Held,* by the Secretary of State, that (1) the investment made by the appellant in the land, both financial and in effort, demonstrated that he was serious about his agricultural enterprise and that the land was used for the purposes of a business; (2) thus the proposed buildings were permitted under Class VI of Sched. 1 to the GDO on that part of the site not subject to the Art. 4 direction; (3) for that part of the land subject to the Art. 4 direction, pursuant to s.53 of the 1971 Act, the Secretary of State formally determined that given the substantial size of the polythene tunnels (each 20 ft. × 40 ft.) and the manner of fixing them to the ground they would constitute development comprising building operations. Permitted development—no further action on appeal: CANTERBURY CITY COUNCIL AND NODING (Ref. APP/J2210/A/85/025910) (1986) 1 P.A.D. 237.

3287. Horticultural distribution centre—change of use to high technology use of site—green belt

[Town and Country Planning Act 1971 (c.78) s.36 and Sched. 9; General Development Order 1977 (S.I. 1977 No. 289), art. 4 and Sched. 1; DoE Circulars 22/80, 16/84.] The Council failed to determine an application to change the use of a redundant horticultural distribution centre and warehouse to use as a Class X warehouse and the conversion of an existing barn to form an office suite and the retention of a building as a vehicle store. The site was within the green belt and the proposed high-technology use was not within any of the categories normally permitted in the green belt. The appellant sought assistance from Circulars 22/80 and 16/84. *Held,* by the Inspector, that (1) while Circular 22/80 encouraged economic activity the Circular made clear that this should not be taken as overriding policy for the green belts; (2) in relation to a site of 1h.a. the potential activity should be seen as large-scale business development and not a small business for the purposes of C22/80; (3) the one would be alien to the green belt and introduce an intrusive feature into an attractive rural setting; (4) the fragmentation of agricultural holdings should be resisted. Appeal dismissed: SURREY HEATH BOROUGH COUNCIL AND VDU INSTALLATION (Ref. T/APP/D3640/A/84/25692/P2) (1985) 1 P.A.D. 31.

3288. Hotel—green belt site—trunk road access—adjoining existing restaurant—relevance of draft local plan

[Town and Country Planning Act 1971 (c.78) s.36; Development Control Policy Note No. 12.] An application was made for planning permission for the erection of a 20 bedroom hotel on land adjoining an existing restaurant. This land had access onto a slip road which led to a trunk road near a motorway junction. The site was within an area which had long been defined as Metropolitan Green Belt, where new development would be permitted in very special circumstances only: the proposal did not fall within any of these exceptions. The draft local plan only permitted hotels and motels within the built-up area. The council refused permission and the applicant appealed. *Held,* by the Secretary of State agreeing with his Inspector, that (1) the local demand was not such as to be a determining issue in this case (reference to DCPN 12); (2) if a motel were to be built in the area it was preferable for it to occupy an area within the curtilage of an existing commercial building rather than for it to be located in unspoilt countryside (reference made to para. 16 of DCPN 12); (3) the appearance of the proposed building would not significantly increase the visual obtrusiveness of the site as a whole; (4) the local plan, being in draft form only, could be given comparatively little weight; (5) the additional traffic movements would not be significant; (6) the arguments were finely balanced but the proposal could be permitted as an exception to green belt policies. Appeal allowed subject to a landscaping condition: BRENTWOOD DISTRICT COUNCIL AND TRUST HOUSE FORTE CATERING (Ref.APP/H1515/A/84/020808) (1986) 1 P.A.D. 185.

3289. Hotel extension—green belt—near built-up area—small business

[Town and Country Planning Act 1971 (c.72), s.36, sched. 9; DoE Circulars 42/55, 22/80, 14/84, 16/35; Development Control Policy Notes 4 and 12.] The Council refused planning permission for the erection of an 11 bedroomed two storey hotel extension and car parking on land in the Outer Metropolitan Green belt and situated 200m from the edge of the main built-up area. The applicant appealed. *Held,* by the Inspector, that (1) despite the strong presumption against development in the green belt as reaffirmed in C14/84 it was also government policy to encourage the formation and expansion of small scale businesses, of which this enterprise was one (reference to C22/80 and C16/85); (2) additional employees would be accommodated in existing residential areas (reference to para. 6 of C42/55); (3) the extension would not appear as an intrusion or major intensification of development; (4) there were special circumstances unlikely to be duplicated elsewhere. Appeal allowed subject to car parking and landscaping conditions: CHELMSFORD BOROUGH COUNCIL AND BARTELLA (Ref.T/APP/W1525/A/84/023883/P5) (1986) 1 P.A.D. 187.

3290. Industrial development—extension in green belt—site of special scientific interest
[Town and Country Planning Act 1971 (c.78), s.36 and Sched. 9; Wildlife and Countryside Act 1981 (c.69), DOE Circular 14/85.] The council refused outline permission for warehouse and industrial development on an eight acre site within the green belt, 3·5 acres of which was notified as a site of special scientific interest (S.S.S.I.). The site adjoined the appellant's existing operation who claimed they needed to expand in order to survive and could not relocate. *Held,* by the inspector after a local inquiry, that (1) the appeal came within the exceptions to the application of a presumption against development in the green belt being for the expansion of a large established place of employment which could not be expected to locate elsewhere; (2) the S.S.S.I. was a valuable and recognised feature which should be retained; (3) the inspector was not entirely satisfied that the appellant had fully explored all available options; (4) it was noted that the appellant had planning permission to extract marl on the appeal site which would destroy the S.S.S.I. and thus remove the objection, but that the inspector trusted the appellant; (5) taking into account the advice in Circular 14/85 and the good record of the company such factors did not outweigh the harm in the loss of an irreplaceable S.S.S.I.: Appeal dismissed: WALSALL METROPOLITAN BOROUGH COUNCIL AND ROBERT M. DOUGLAS HOLDINGS (Ref. T/APP/V4630/A/85/026623/P7) (1986) 1 P.A.D. 341.

3291/2. Inquiries
TOWN AND COUNTRY PLANNING (VARIOUS INQUIRIES) (PROCEDURE) (AMENDMENT) RULES 1986 (No. 420) [£1·35], made under the Tribunals and Inquiries Act 1971 (c.62), s.11 applied by the Town and Country Planning Act 1971 (c.78), Sched. 9, para. 7; operative on April 1, 1986; amend S.I. 1974 Nos. 419 and 420 and S.I. 1981 No. 1743 as a consequence of the abolition of the GLC and the metropolitan county councils.

3293. Judicial review—whether proper to seek—special considerations
[Town and Country Planning Act 1971 (c.78), s.245] Appeal was by the G.L.C. against the Queen's Bench Master's decision to strike out the G.L.C.'s application under T.C.P.A. 1971, s.245. Application was to quash a decision made by an inspector on behalf of the Secretary of State dismissing an appeal by A against the failure of Harrow Borough Council to determine an application for planning permission. The Master accepted that the G.L.C. were not a "person aggrieved." *Held,* that (1) there were special considerations which made it desirable that the approach of the inspector in relation to the reasoning of his decision on the appeal should be tested; (2) leave should be given to apply for a judicial review: GREATER LONDON COUNCIL *v.* SECRETARY OF STATE FOR THE ENVIRONMENT AND HARROW LONDON BOROUGH COUNCIL [1985] J.P.L. 868, Woolf J.

3294. Lands tribunal decision
BELL *v.* CANTERBURY CITY COUNCIL (Ref. 166/1985) (1986) 279 E.G. 767. (This was a reference to determine the compensation payable under s.174 of the Town and Country Planning Act 1971 as a result of the refusal to allow grubbing up for grazing purposes of 39·1 acres of woodland near Canterbury under Tree Preservation Order No. 3 of 1982. The tribunal found (1) that the measure of compensation in s.174 is the loss or damage caused by the refusal of the application, without qualification, and that compensation could therefore take account of the loss of the proposed use for grazing, which had been a viable proposition; (2) that a post-dated resolution by the Council that, had consent to grub up been granted, an order to replant would have been made, was a device to avoid liability to pay compensation; (3) that the relevant date was that of the refusal of consent in June 1983. By deducting the capital value of the land in its current state and the cost of reclamation, deferred for one year, from the capital value of the land after reclamation, deferred for three years, the tribunal assessed compensation for loss of capital value at £32,600 and compensation for consequential loss and disturbance at £13,946·71.)

3295. CARROLL'S, GILLIN'S AND NORTH'S APPLICATIONS, *Re (*Ref LP/17–19 (1980) [1985] J.P.L. 135. (The 1920s covenant with Bradford Corporation provided that garden land was to be maintained as open space. The applicants sought to build two pairs of semi-detached houses on their section of the garden land. *Held,* that the covenants were not obsolete since the development would be of serious detriment to the enjoyment by the objectors of their rear gardens to whom the covenants secured practical benefits and effects).

3296. CHURCH COTTAGE INVESTMENTS *v.* HILLINGDON LONDON BOROUGH (Ref./127/1985) (1986) 280 E.G. 101. (On C Co.'s claim for compensation for refusal of planning permission in respect of a development claimed to fall within para. 3 of Sched. 8 to the Town and Country Planning Act 1971, a preliminary question arose as to whether the subject premises consisted of one or more buildings. The property, which was built in 1938 and consisted of 38 self-contained flats, was divided into five main sections each connected to the next, so that the front and rear elevations had a continuous aspect. It was agreed that the issue for the tribunal was one of fact. The tribunal, accepting a number of contentions put forward on behalf of C Co., and paying particular attention to the continuous bonding of the exterior brickwork, found that the property constituted a single building.)

3297. ISLINGTON LONDON BOROUGH'S APPLICATION, *Re* (LP/26/1984) [1986] J.P.L. 214 (Application was to discharge restrictions affecting 1·043 acres in Islington, imposed in 1968 with the G.L.C., that the land should be used as a public open space only. Residential and industrial development was proposed. *Held*, that although the restrictions were not obsolete the community would benefit and the restrictions would be discharged. Compensation to the G.L.C. was to be its original contribution to the purchase price with adjustments for inflation).

3298. WARD *v.* WYCHAVON DISTRICT COUNCIL (Ref./21/1984) (1986) 279 E.G. 77. (This was a reference under s.127 of the Town and Country Planning Act 1971 to determine the compensation (if any) payable for interruption by the Council to a right of way in fee simple over an unmade council-owned farm track 1,030 yards long, which led from a farm and bungalow to the centre of Evesham, and to the maintenance of which by the Council the claimants were required to make a contribution. In 1981 the lane was severed, and the lower part permanently closed to traffic, by the construction of a new main road; and the Council provided alternative access to the farm and bungalow by constructing a tarmacadamed road 280 yards long to the new main road: in consequence the distance from the farm and bungalow to schools and shops were increased. By the time of the closure, housing estates were under construction on either side of the lane. The claimants sought compensation on the grounds that the approach to the farm and bungalow was now longer and less convenient, and that there was an increased risk of trespass and vandalism. The tribunal, noting that the new arrangements relieved the claimants of the need to contribute to maintenance of the lower part of the lane, found that the value of the two interests had not been lowered by the new arrangements. In particular any trespass or vandalism (of which there was no evidence since 1981) would be properly attributable not to the new road but to the encroachment of the housing estates. The claim for compensation thus failed.)

3299. Leisure park—policies restricting development in open countryside
[Town and Country Planning Act 1971 (c.78), s.36.] The proposal was to develop nine acres of land in the open countryside for a model world, animal enclosures, picnic area, playground, parking, crazy golf, a restaurant and toilet block. The Council refused planning permission. The two main issues at the public inquiry were (1) whether the proposal represented intrusive development in the countryside and (2) whether it was possible to achieve an acceptable access. *Held,* by the Inspector, that there were strong national planning policies restricting development in the open countryside and these were reinforced by the structure and local plan policies. The components of the proposal would help to erode the rural character which these policies sought to preserve. Further, traffic to the site would have to use a road which had all the characteristics of a rural lane and which had no footpath. Appeal dismissed: DARLINGTON BOROUGH COUNCIL AND GIBBON (ref.T/APP/L1310/A/84/21736/P2) (1985) 1 P.A.D. 59.

3300. Licensed betting office—parade of shops—effect on area including schools and dwellings

[Town and Country Planning Act 1971 (c.78), s.36; Development Control Policy Note Nos. 3 and 11.] An application was made for planning permission to change the use of a shop to a licensed betting office and for the installation of a new frontage. The Council refused permission relying upon DCPN 3 and 11 and expressing concern about the effect upon people living nearby. The Council also relied upon the adopted Borough Plan which designated the area as predominantly residential with a presumption against development that would be detrimental to residential amenities. The applicant appealed. *Held,* by the Inspector, that (1) this appeal could be distinguished from an earlier one relating to premises with houses on either side; (2) there were no dwellings unrelated to the betting office in very close proximity to the appeal premises; (3) the proposed used would not be likely to have an impact on those living nearby any greater than any possible retail use of the premises. Appeal allowed subject to a condition requiring a window display to be provided and maintained: COLCHESTER BOROUGH COUNCIL AND MECCA BOOKMAKERS (Ref:T/APP/A1530/A/84/19893/P7) (1986) 1 P.A.D. 178.

3301. Light industrial development—in accordance with planning policy—relationship to larger industrial site—harm to residence from traffic

[Town and Country Planning Act 1971 (c.78), s.36, Sched. 9; DOE Circular 14/85.] The appeal related to an application for light industrial development on a site which had permission for warehousing within 1·2 ha of land owned by the appellant and largely occupied by a transport firm and a builders' merchants. The appeal site had access from two local roads each fronted by residential development and the main issue was disturbance from increased heavy traffic. *Held,* by the inspector, after a public inquiry, that (1) any improvement in the living environment was unlikely until the transport firm and appellant's builder's merchants relocated; (2) light industrial development did not usually give rise to much heavy traffic; (3) the proposed use was in accordance with the council's long term planning objective and would not be likely to cause any significant deterioration in residential amenities; (4) the inspector imposed a number of conditions but bearing in mind C14/85 it was not appropriate to restrict the use of the building to a named firm. Appeal allowed: LUTON BOROUGH COUNCIL AND FIRBANK (C.) AND SON (Ref. T/APP/A0210/A/85/035525/P5) (1986) 1 P.A.D. 334.

3302. Light industrial estate—second phase—effect on line of proposed relief road

[Town and Country Planning Act (c.78), s.36.] The developer wished to carry out the second phase of development of a small industrial estate. The Council refused permission for this solely because the development straddled the line of a proposed relief road. The road had been first proposed in the early 1970s but was not expected to be carried out before 1995–2000 and was not included in either the structure or local plan. *Held,* by the Inspector, that (1) the main issue was whether the proposal for the relief road was of sufficient firmness to justify refusal of permission; (2) it would be unreasonable in the circumstances to inhibit the development proposals on the basis of the current programming. Appeal allowed, subject to conditions to protect the amenities of nearby residents and the area: EAST HERTFORDSHIRE DISTRICT COUNCIL AND RAYNHAM HOUSE INVESTMENTS (Ref. T/APP/J1915/A/85/028356/P5) (1986) 1 P.A.D. 128.

3303. Listed building—alteration or extension—consent—fence

[Town and Country Planning Act 1971 (c.78), ss.54(9), 55(1).] A hotel and an adjoining coach-house were grade II listed buildings. They became separately owned and a fence was put up between them which was not physically attached to either of them. The Council issued a listed building enforcement notice demanding removal of the fence. The owners appealed to the Secretary of State who quashed the notice. *Held,* dismissing the appeal, that since the fence was neither an alteration nor extension of the listing building within s.54(9) of the 1971 Act, listed building consent under s.55(1) was not required for its erection.

COTSWOLD DISTRICT COUNCIL *v.* SECRETARY OF STATE FOR THE ENVIRONMENT (1986) 61 P. & C.R. 139, D.C.

3304. Manufacture of bricks and tiles—use of local clay—opportunity to control restoration of adjoining land by means of section 52 agreement—procedure for negotiations
    [Town and Country Planning Act 1971 (c.78), ss.36, 52.] The appellant applied for permission to erect a factory for the manufacture of bricks and tiles which was to be based upon clay extracted from land adjoining the appeal site. The appeal site was located within an attractive rural landscape where it was the policy to restrict development to that concerned with agriculture or forestry. Considerable development had taken place in the immediate vicinity of the appeal site. A large brickworks using clay extracted from adjoining land had been active between 1935 and 1970. *Held*, by the Secretary of State, that (1) it would be more appropriate to secure control of the restoration of the adjoining land by means of a formal agreement under s.52 of the 1971 Act than by conditions; (2) therefore the decision would be deferred for three months for negotiations. Such negotiations took place and in a second decision letter the Secretary of State noted that a s.52 agreement had been entered into. The appeal was therefore allowed subject to additional conditions requested by the Council. One of these prevented the use of imported materials without the authority's previous agreement: BUCKINGHAMSHIRE COUNTY COUNCIL AND FIRMIN (Ref. APP/5123/A/83/003033) (1986) 1 P.A.D. 136.

3305. Meeting hall—open land—relationship between meeting hall and leisure activities—presumption in favour of development
    [Town and Country Planning Act 1971 (c.78), s.36, Sched. 9; DoE Circular 14/85; White Paper 1985 "Lifting the Burden".] The Council refused planning permission for the use of a site situated one mile from the town centre for a meeting hall for the Jehovah Witnesses. The site was flat and open and subject to the Council's policy to use the land in that area for holiday and leisure associated purposes. The applicant had made three previous applications to build a meeting hall in the town but all had been refused. The applicants appealed and argued, *inter alia*, that the proposed activity of people attending a church meeting in their leisure time was not unrelated to people attending a meeting at a conference centre. *Held*, by the Inspector, that (1) the location of the site made it suitable; (2) there was a large area of adequate land vacant and available for further holiday and leisure activity; (3) the erection of a meeting hall was not so far removed from the activities envisaged by the Council for that area; (4) the project would contribute to economic activity and the provision of new jobs (reference to C14/85 and the White Paper "Lifting the Burden"). Appeal allowed: BRECKLAND DISTRICT COUNCIL AND DEREHAM CONGREGATION OF JEHOVAH'S WITNESSES (Ref: T/APP/F2605/A/85/031220/P3) (1986) 1 P.A.D. 286.

3306. Mineral extraction—extension of time limit for coal extraction—delay to restoration of area for agriculture
    [Town and Country Planning Act 1971 (c.78), ss.32 and 36, Sched. 9; Control of Pollution Act 1974 (c.40), s.72; DoE Circular 3/84.] The appeal site formed part of a much larger 50 acre site. The land had been the subject of mineral workings for over 100 years. The appellants took control of the excavations about 16 years ago and since then they had removed all but one of the derelict tips and restored about 20 acres in the most prominent areas in keeping with the surrounding landscape. In 1979 a slip occurred in the excavations close to some cottages causing part of their gardens to subside. A scheme was agreed whereby a buttress was formed to the unstable area using the overburden to the coal seam and coal was extracted with the void to be filled with imported waste material. Planning permission was granted in accordance with this subject to a condition that the coaling operations and formation of the buttress should be completed within 12 months of commencement. The appellants had asked for an extension of that time limit but the Council had refused this. *Held*, by the Inspector, that (1) the objectives of the county and borough councils to secure the early restoration of the land and its return to agriculture should be supported; but (2) the very large void south of the filled area had ample space for its filling with waste material and spoil from within the workings to proceed simultaneously with the proposed coal extraction. Appeal allowed: DERBYSHIRE COUNTY COUNCIL AND KELLY (D. P.) (SHEFFIELD) (Ref.T/APP/D1000/A/84/20223/P7) (1986) 1 P.A.D. 207.

3307. Minerals—extension of existing quarry—effects on employment
    [Town and Country Planning Act 1971 (c.78), s.36 and Sched. 9; Town and Country Planning (Minerals) Act 1981 (c.36); Town and Country Planning General

Regulations 1976 (S.I. No. 1419); Circulars 22/80; 38/81; 21/82; 16/84; 1/85.] The proposal was to extend existing sand and gravel workings in eight equal phases with progressive restoration to agriculture. The Council had extracted gravel and sand from the area since the 1920s. The appellants had purchased the land in 1983 and were granted a three-year planning permission expiring in June 1986. That consent related to extradition now nearing completion. Policy C4 of the Structure Plan stated that proposals for mineral workings would be considered in the light of their economic and employment effects, their effects on agriculture, the landscape and features of special interest, the transport network and the amenity of residents. Policy C5 required restoration proposals including satisfactory tree and hedgerow planting and ground contouring. *Held*, by the Inspector, that (1) proposed rate of extraction was no greater than in the past; (2) the closure of the quarry would depress the local economy and the proposal would give security of employment for at least nine to ten years; (3) the loss of employment from closing the quarry would not be compensated for by an increase in employment from tourism; (4) with proper supervision the site could appear as a natural part of the rural scene and would be well screened from the National Park authority's caravan park; (5) the amenity objections did not justify a refusal of planning permission: see Circular 22/80. Further, Circular 16/84 emphasised that the encouragement of industrial development was vital. Reference also made to para. 2 of Circular 21/82(6) the conditions attached were in the light of Circular 38/81 and Circular 1/85. Appeal allowed subject to conditions: NORTHUMBERLAND COUNTY COUNCIL AND NORTHERN AGGREGATES (Ref.T/APP/R2900/A/84/18860) (1985) 1 P.A.D. 76.

3308. Minerals—oil well—drilling of exploratory well—green belt
[Town and Country Planning Act 1971 (c.78), s.36; DoE Circulars 14/84, 2/85.] The Council refused to grant planning permission for the improvement of access, construction of an access road, the drilling of an exploratory oilwell and the subsequent testing in the event of oil being found on a site within the green belt. The proposed development was strongly objected to by local residents who were supported by their parish councils and Members of Parliament. The developer appealed and a public inquiry was convened. *Held*, by the Secretary of State who was in general agreement with his Inspector, that (1) the appeal fell to be determined in the light of C2/85; (2) subject to environmental considerations the exploitation of on-shore oil was in the national interest; (3) it was the quality of the environment and not the degree of national interest that varied from case to case; (4) the emphasis of C2/85 was on the resolution of possible objections, rather than on restriction; (5) having considered all the representations made there was no sound and clear cut reason for withholding permission. Appeal allowed subject to special conditions: SURREY COUNTY COUNCIL AND CONOCO (U.K.) (Ref. APP/B3600/A/84/20896/Part 2) (1986) 1 P.A.D. 197.

3309. Minerals—recovery of coal from disused colliery spoil heap—earlier decision quashed
[Town and Country Planning Act 1971 (c.78), s.36; Circular 1/82.] There had been an Inquiry into the County Council's refusal of permission for the recovery of coal from a disused colliery spoil heap and the subsequent landscape treatment of the site. The Secretary of State felt unable to accept his Inspector's recommendation that the appeals be allowed because he considered himself constrained by his policy on direct land grant either to impose conditions of the standard outlined in Appendix III to Circular 1/82 or to dismiss the appeals if those conditions could not be properly imposed. Subsequently the Secretary of State accepted that his decision was wrong in law and it was quashed by the High Court. The parties were given the opportunity of making further representations. The Opencast Executive maintained its objection. *Held*, by the Secretary of State, that (1) the appellants had put forward a case of need for the coal; (2) it was necessary that the conditions imposed should seek to ensure the satisfactory working of the land and its restoration to an acceptable level; (3) as agreed by all parties the restoration and aftercare in compliance with Appendix III of Circular 1/82 would render the proposals uneconomic; (4) with appropriate conditions a reasonable standard of restoration and aftercare could be achieved. Appeal allowed subject to conditions; MERSEYSIDE COUNTY COUNCIL AND OGDEN (A) AND SONS (Ref.APP/5093/A/82/106489) (1985) 1 P.A.D. 72.

3310. National parks

TOWN AND COUNTRY PLANNING (AGRICULTURAL AND FORESTRY DEVELOPMENT IN NATIONAL PARKS ETC.) SPECIAL DEVELOPMENT ORDER 1986 (No. 1176) [£1·40], made under the Town and Country Planning Act 1971 (c.78), ss.24, 287(3) and (4); operative on November 1, 1986; replaces S.I. 1950 No. 729.

3311. New towns

BASILDON DEVELOPMENT CORPORATION (TRANSFER OF PROPERTY AND DISSOLUTION) ORDER 1986 (No. 502) [40p], made under the New Towns Act 1981 (c.64), s.41, Sched. 10, paras 2, 3; operative on April 1, 1986; provides for the transfer of the property of the Basildon Development Corporation to the Commission for the New Towns.

DEVELOPMENT BOARD FOR RURAL WALES (EXTINGUISHMENT OF LIABILITIES) ORDER 1986 (No. 1509) [80p], made under the Development of Rural Wales Act 1976 (c.75), s.13A(1); operative on September 15, 1986; extinguishes certain liabilities of the Board in respect of sums borrowed from the Secretary of State in connection with the discharge by the Board of its functions in respect of the development of new towns.

NEW TOWNS (EXTINGUISHMENT OF LIABILITIES) ORDER 1986 (No. 1382) [£2·90], made under the New Towns Act 1981 (c.64), s.62A(1); operative on September 1, 1986; provides for the extinguishment of all liabilities in respect of certain advances made by the Secretary of State to four development corporations.

NEW TOWNS (SUSPENSION OF LOAN REPAYMENT) ORDER 1986 (No. 1436) [£2.40], made under the New Towns Act 1981, s.62B(1) and (3); operative on September 12, 1986; provides for the suspension of certain loans made by the Secretary of State to specified development corporations.

3312. Nursing centre—extension—Conservation Area—considerations

[Town and Country Planning Act 1971 (c.78) s.36, Sched. 9; DoE Circulars 22/80, 14/85; Development Control Policy Notes 1, 2, 7 and 10.] The Council refused planning permission for the extension of an existing nursing home to form a 60-bed nursing centre with two operating theatres. The site occupied a prominent position in a Conservation Area. The Council did not object in principle to the proposal but objected to the scale of the development. The developer appealed. *Held,* by the Inspector, following a public inquiry, that (1) the character of the area was in part attributable to the spacious setting of the buildings and their landscaping and the scheme would be overbearing and visually intrusive, as accepted by the appellant's planning witness; (2) the appellant's witness agreed that damage to trees could well result and this would have an adverse effect upon the amenities of the nearby block of flats: the material reduction in the present open aspect was a fact to be taken into account; (3) a condition restricting the times of admissions and the use of the operating theatres was not practicable on humanitarian and economic grounds and would be difficult to enforce; (4) the provision of car parking was inadequate; (5) the proposals did not satisfy para. 6 of D.C.P.N. 7 which required primary consideration in a Conservation Area to be given to whether the proposal would "preserve or enhance its character" (reference also to paras. 18, 19 and 20 of C22/80 and D.C.P.N.s 1, 2 and 10). Appeal dismissed: SHEFFIELD CITY COUNCIL AND ALDEROAK (Ref: T/APP/U4420/A/85/28855/P7) (1986) 1 P.A.D. 263.

3313. Office building—no objection by council on previous appeal on grounds of office policy—implication

[Town and Country Planning Act 1971 (c.78), s.36.] The appeal site comprised a single storey commercial building, nine lock-up garages and dilapidated sheds in the forecourt area. The existing premises on the site were not currently in use. The site had been the subject of a previous appeal which involved a mixed development including a two storey residential block and a three storey office development. That appeal was dismissed primarily on the grounds of overdevelopment. The current proposal was for the demolition of the existing industrial and storage buildings and the erection of a two storey office building. The Council refused planning permission on the ground that the scheme conflicted with their office development policy. There was also a lot of local concern as regards the effect on amenities. *Held,* by the Inspector following a public inquiry, that (1) the ground for refusal was not, as contended by the Council, new and materially different from the policy reason given for the refusal of the previous application; (2) the fact that the previous decision did not make specific reference to contravention of the statutory office policies indicated that the Council did not consider that any such contravention existed; (3) re-development rather than re-use would be a planning advantage; (4) development along the lines proposed would not be contrary to the objectives of the office policies nor materially detract from the environment but the actual building and layout proposed were unacceptable. Appeal dismissed : HILLINGDON LONDON BOROUGH COUNCIL AND BLACK (W.E.) (Ref.T/APP/R5510/A/84/25735/P5) (1986) 1 P.A.D.

3314. Office development—local business—regional and local policies of severe restraint—car parking space deficiency

[Town and Country Planning Act 1971 (c.78), s.36; DoE Circulars 22/80, 16/84.] Planning permission was sought for the demolition of an existing building and erection of a four storey office building with a car park. The Council failed to determine the application within the prescribed period. The developer appealed. The Inspector considered that the principal issues were whether the appellant's needs were such as to justify an exception to the severe restraint strategy applicable and whether the proposed design would be substantially out of scale or character. *Held,* by the Inspector that (1) the proposed design conflicted with the provisions of the approved structure plan as the amount of new office floorspace allowed for up to 1991 had been reached; (2) the structure plan was approved in 1980 and it was likely that the current review would make provision for some additional office development over the period 1982/96. That period had already begun and it was reasonable that some permissions should continue to be given if the circumstances were otherwise appropriate; (3) the council had accepted that the proposal would not result in pressure for additional housing or an existing highways; (4) the proposal would contribute significantly to the national and local economies; (5) there were no suitable alternative premises in the locality; (6) there was little to be gained by deferring the development until additional public car parking facilities had been provided; (7) an agreement had been entered into whereby the Council would be paid £90,000 in lieu of the provision of car parking spaces on site and that overcame the objection on grounds of insufficiency of car parking space. Appeal allowed subject to conditions: WINDSOR AND MAIDENHEAD ROYAL BOROUGH COUNCIL AND LAMBART COMPUTING (Ref.T/APP/D0325/A/84/16136/P2) (1986) 1 P.A.D. 162.

3315. Office development—replacing existing building

[Town and Country Planning Act 1971 (c.78), ss.36, 37.] The appellant sought outline planning permission to demolish an existing office building and to replace it with a new office building. The Council failed to determine the application and the appeal was against the deemed refusal. The main planning issues were—(*a*) whether office redevelopment of the site was appropriate notwithstanding the Town Action Area Plan policies which aim to locate industry in the area and (b) if the office use was appropriate whether the indicated details of the proposal were satisfactory with regard to usual, environmental and highway consideration. *Held,* by the Inspector, that (1) the appeal site was unlikely ever to be available for industrial purposes; (2) the site was not suitable for industrial use because of lack of surface parking and the proximity of existing housing; (3) the proposal was not in conflict with the Town Action Area Plan because it did not increase the existing stock of offices. The Inspector informally expressed his view on what form of development might be appropriate having held that the proposal before him was not acceptable. Appeal dismissed: BOROUGH OF RICHMOND-UPON-THAMES AND C. & A. PENSION TRUSTEES (Ref. T/APP/25810/A/84/18543/P5) (1985) 1 P.A.D. 44.

3316. Office development with some residential units—deemed refusal of permission—plot ratio

[Town and Country Planning Act 1971 (c.78), ss.36, 37.] The appellant proposed to erect a building comprising offices and residential units with ancillary plant and car parking space following the demolition of existing buildings. The scheme was amended and approved by the Westminster City Council. The Greater London Council issued a direction that permission should be refused because the office development was inconsistent with the criteria for the location of offices contained in the Greater London Development Plan. The appeal site was situated just outside the Central Activator Zone. The main planning issue was the question of the impact of the proposal on the neighbourhood. *Held,* by the Inspector that (1) the small amount of reduction of sunlight to two flats could be disregarded. No local resident appeared at the inquiry; (2) there was no reason to disagree with the conclusion of the City Council that the proposal was acceptable. The plot ratio of 3.94:1 as opposed to the 3.5:1 standard of the District Plan was not an overriding factor having regard to the benefits resulting from the scheme. Conditional planning permission granted: WESTMINSTER CITY COUNCIL AND EAGLE STAR PROPERTIES (Ref. T/APP/X5990/A/84/14192/P7) (1985) 1 P.A.D. 41.

3317. **Office, retail, residential development—deemed refusal—office location policies**
[Town and Country Planning Act 1971 (c.78), ss.36, 37 and 52 and Sched. 9; Town and Country Planning (Local Planning Authorities in Greater London) Regulations 1980 (S.I. 1980 No. 443): Circular 10/73.] The developer appealed against the deemed refusal of outline permission for office, retail and residential development of a site containing London Transport's Gloucester Road underground station. As the application proposed office space of more than 2,785 sq.m. it had to be submitted also to the Greater London Council (Town and Country Planning (Local Planning Authorities in Greater London) Regulations 1980). The main planning issue was whether the proposals conflicted with the Greater London Development Plan and the Royal Borough of Kensington and Chelsea District Plan. There was also an issue over highway considerations. The GLC argued that the scheme did not ensure that there would be residential development on the land south of the railway. The GLC also argued that the scheme of a third party would secure residential as well as office accommodation. *Held*, by the Inspector, that (1) the site was in a Preferred Office Location listed in the GLDP; (2) the scheme did not conflict with the approved development plans and there was no sound or clear cut objections and therefore permission should be granted: KENSINGTON AND CHELSEA ROYAL BOROUGH COUNCIL AND LEGAL AND GENERAL ASSURANCE SOCIETY (Ref. T/APP/K5600/A/84/20971/P5) (1984) 1 P.A.D. 35.

3318. **Offices—local firm occupancy condition—effectiveness of condition**
[Town and Country Planning Act 1971 (c.78), s.36; DoE Circulars 42/55, 22/80, 1/85, 14/85.] In 1982 the Council had granted planning permission for the erection of a high street banking hall and offices subject to a local firm occupancy condition. It was now sought to discharge that condition. The Council had refused to allow this contending that the aim was to reduce pressure for development in the Metropolitan Green Belt. *Held*, by the Inspector following a public inquiry, that (1) the permission for the commercial development should have been refused and not granted subject to the local firm occupancy condition; (2) Circular 1/85 states that an expansion of a local firm would not necessarily lead to less pressure for the development than the arrival of a firm from outside the area; (3) additional office floor space would tend to increase the demand for development for other purposes but that demand was created when the offices were permitted and could not be dissipated by a condition restricting their occupancy. Appeal allowed: SOUTH BUCKS DISTRICT COUNCIL AND HOLLAND AUTOMATION INTERNATIONAL (U.K.) (Ref.T/APP/N0410/A/85/027035/P2) (1986) 1 P.A.D. 159.

3319. **Offices and residential—acceptable land use—structure plan office allocation exhausted—development of remainder of site**
[Town and Country Planning Act 1971 (c.78), s.36.] The Council failed to determine within the prescribed period an application for planning permission for a mixed scheme of offices and housing with ancillary car parking with provision for bus stands on land at the Maidenhead Bus Station. The land was no longer required as a bus station. The consultation Draft Local Plan indicated that the site should be redeveloped for housing and offices. The office allocation in the approved Structure Plan had been fully taken up and the Borough Council's policy included an embargo on all major office development. The developer appealed. *Held*, by the Secretary of State, that (1) the office allocation guidelines in the approved structure plan had been fully taken up but; (2) that did not necessarily justify the refusal of further office development. However, it was not appropriate in this case to allow development which might seriously prejudice proper consideration of the proposals and objectives in the emerging replacement structure and local plan; (3) the level of office development might prejudice the redevelopment of the remaining part of the total site. Appeal dismissed: WINDSOR AND MAIDENHEAD ROYAL BOROUGH COUNCIL AND CITY AND NORTHERN (Ref.APP/D0325/A/84/021226) (1986) 1 P.A.D. 169.

3320. Peak district
> PEAK PARK JOINT PLANNING BOARD ORDER 1986 (No. 561) [£1·35], made under the Local Government Act 1972 (c.70), ss.241, 266 and Sched. 17, Pt. I and the Local Government Act 1985 (c.51), Sched. 3, para. 2(1); operative on April 1, 1986; alters the membership of the board and the apportionment of its expenses.

3321. Planning appeals
> TOWN AND COUNTRY PLANNING (DETERMINATION OF APPEALS BY APPOINTED PERSONS) REGULATIONS 1986 (No. 623) [45p], made under the Town and Country Planning Act 1971 (c.78), s.287, Sched, 9, para. 1; operative on May 1, 1986; amend S.I. 1981 No. 804 to prescribe further classes of appeal which may be determined by an Inspector.

3322. Planning authority—alleged failure to disclose planning blight—whether negligent. See JGF PROPERTIES *v.* LAMBETH LONDON BOROUGH, § 2281.

3323. Planning permission—application—alternative sites—Secretary of State's decision
> The Secretary of State called in applications to develop a site in Dockland. After the inquiry the Inspector recommended refusal. The Secretary of State nevertheless granted the applications. The local authority appealed to the High Court, who upheld the Secretary of State's decision. The authority further appealed to the Court of Appeal. *Held,* that (1) The Secretary of State had properly considered the development plan; (2) alternative sites were not relevant in this case; (3) an alternative site was relevant when, *inter alia,* the proposed development would have inevitable adverse effects or disadvantages to the public or to some section of the public; (4) the Minister had given adequate reasons for his decision: TOWER HAMLETS LONDON BOROUGH COUNCIL *v.* SECRETARY OF STATE FOR THE ENVIRONMENT [1986] J.P.L. 193, C.A.

3324. Planning permission—application to quash—relevant planning consideration
> The applicant sought permission to build water sewage works on his land. The local authority first failed to decide the matter within the relevant time and then resolved that they would have refused permission. The Secretary of State granted permission. The local authority sought to quash the permission. *Held,* that (1) the Secretary of State's reasoning was adequate; (2) it is for the planning authority or the Minister to decide whether the existence of an alternative site is a relevant planning consideration. The court would only interfere if they had been unreasonable: VALE OF GLAMORGAN BOROUGH COUNCIL *v.* SECRETARY OF STATE FOR WALES AND SIR BRANDON RHYS WILLIAMS [1985] J.P.L. 198, Woolf J.

3325. Planning permission—condition—road widening—validity
> [Town and Country Planning Act 1971 (c.78), s.52.] D were granted planning permission for residential development subject to conditions. One required the widening of an existing road by one metre with associated remedial works. The Secretary of State held that the condition was *ultra vires,* insofar as it related to land not owned or controlled by the developers.
> On appeal to the High Court Farquharson J. upheld the decision of the Secretary of State. The Council appealed to the Court of Appeal. *Held,* that the condition would probably not have been lawful even if it had been incorporated into a section 52 agreement. It might have been reasonable had the developer merely been required to contribute to the widening. A condition cannot positively require a developer to do an act of widening or building a highway (*Hall* v. *Shoreham by Sea Urban District Council* [1964] 1 W.L.R. 240 applied): CITY OF BRADFORD METROPOLITAN COUNCIL *v.* SECRETARY OF STATE FOR THE ENVIRONMENT AND MCLEAN HOMES NORTHERN [1986] J.P.L. 598, C.A.

3326. Planning permission—engineering operations on agricultural land—extraction of minerals—need to advertise application
> [Town and Country Planning General Development Order 1977 (S.I. 1977 No. 289), arts. 3, 8(1)(*b*), Sched. 1, Class VI, para. 1.]
> A development involving the extraction of minerals on a substantial scale in the course of engineering operations on agricultural land involved two activities and could not be described solely as engineering operations on agricultural land.
> A partnership of farmers wished to construct a reservoir covering 18 acres of land on their farm and 6·5 metres deep, for crop irrigation purposes. In the process large quantities of gravel would be extracted and sold by the farmers. The extent of mineral extraction was to be confined to that which was necessary for the construction

of the reservoir. No operations ancillary to the extraction of the gravel were to take place on the land. The county council directed the farmers to make an application for planning permission for the reservoir development and stated that the application must be advertised and the appropriate fee paid before any application would be entertained. The farmers contended that the development consisted solely of engineering operations requisite for the use of the land for the purposes of agriculture within art. 3 of and Schedule 1, Class VI, para. 1, to the Town and Country Planning General Development Order 1977 so that the application need not be advertised nor a fee paid in respect of it. In proceedings by the farmers for judicial review Nolan J. rejected that contention. *Held,* dismissing the farmers' appeal, that in deciding whether the proposed development consisted solely of engineering operations for the purposes of agriculture or whether it consisted partly of that activity and partly of winning or working minerals the development must be looked at objectively and without reference to the motive or purpose of the developer. Where both activities were recognisable in a substantial degree the development could not be described as one of engineering operations for the purposes of agriculture. A development involving the extraction of gravel on the scale proposed could not be described solely as an engineering operation. The development involved the winning or working of minerals within article 8(1)(b) of the Order.
WEST BOWERS FARM PRODUCTS *v.* ESSEX COUNTY COUNCIL (1985) 50 P. & C.R. 368, C.A.

3327. **Planning permission—housing development—consistency of Inspectors' decisions—circular 22/80**

Three applications for planning permission to develop a site were made in succession. Each went to appeal and the three Inspectors who rejected each appeal did so for different reasons. The appellants contended to the High Court that the Inspectors ought to be consistent in their decisions. They further contended that the Inspector had failed to apply circular 22/80. *Held,* that (1) each Inspector was entitled to exercise his own judgment provided that he applied the proper criteria; (2) it is important that the courts produce quick decisions where planning matters are at issue; (3) if the developer fails to identify the need for housing land, the Inspector need not balance any need against planning objections; (4) Circular 22/80 correctly applied. Decision upheld (*Pye (J.A.) (Oxford) Estates* v. *Wychavon District Council* [1982] C.L.Y. 3195 not followed): ROCKHOLD *v.* SECRETARY OF STATE FOR THE ENVIRONMENT AND SOUTH OXFORDSHIRE DISTRICT COUNCIL [1986] J.P.L. 130, Forbes J.

3328. **Planning permission—inquiry—correspondence between Minister and applicant—natural justice**

Application was to develop a site with offices, some residential units and parking and some shops. Permission was refused. The Inspector on appeal recommended that the appeal be allowed. The Council wrote to the Secretary of State before the decision, stating that the Inspector appeared to have overlooked certain matters. There was also correspondence between the applicant and the Minister. In October 1984 the Minister was informed that the s.52 agreement had been reached. He granted planning permission in January 1985. The Council alleged breach of natural justice and defective reasoning in the decision letter. *Held,* that the cases established that (1) the Inquiry Procedure Rules did not exhaust the requirements of natural justice; (2) there was no such thing as a technical breach of natural justice; (3) the complainant had to show "substantial prejudice." The decision in this case should be quashed (*George* v. *Secretary of State for the Environment* [1980] C.L.Y. 313; *Lake District Special Planning Board* v. *Secretary of State for the Environment* [1975] C.L.Y. 20 *applied*): READING BOROUGH COUNCIL *v.* SECRETARY OF STATE FOR THE ENVIRONMENT AND COMMERCIAL UNION PROPERTIES (INVESTMENTS) [1985] J.P.L. 115, D. Widdicombe Q.C.

3329. **Planning permission—inquiry—fresh evidence—duty to re-open inquiry—Secretary of State's decision**

[Town and Country Planning (Inquiries Procedure) Rules 1974 (S.I. 1974 No. 419) r.12.] M sought permission for a "Stolport" aerodrome in Dockland. An inquiry was held, subsequent to which the Inspector recommended that planning permission be granted, subject to conditions. The Secretary of State sought technical advice on the terminology to use in drafting the conditions. Fresh evidence was then submitted to the Secretary of State by the Department of Transport. The Secretary refused to re-open the inquiry. The councils sought judicial review of that decision not to re-open the inquiry. *Held*, that (1) on the evidence there was no obligation upon the Secretary of State to re-open the inquiry; (2) the Secretary of State had acted reasonably throughout; (3) there was no breach of Rule 12 of the Town and Country Planning (Inquiries Procedure) Rules 1974. R. *v.* SECRETARY OF STATE FOR THE ENVIRONMENT, JOHN MOWLEM & CO., LONDON DOCKLAND DEVELOPMENT CORPORATION, *ex p.* GREATER LONDON COUNCIL [1986] J.P.L. 32, Glidewell J.

3330. Planning permission—inspector's decision—material consideration

R were refused permission for the conversion of each of several two-storey houses into flats. On appeal the Inspector allowed each conversion. The Council appealed. *Held*, that the Inspector's decision was defective since he had failed to take into account sound insulation as a material consideration and the provisions of circular 1/85: LONDON BOROUGH OF NEWHAM *v.* SECRETARY OF STATE FOR THE ENVIRONMENT AND EAST LONDON HOUSING ASSOCIATION [1986] J.P.L. 605, Webster J.

3331. Planning permission—modification—extension to house

[Town Country Planning Act 1971 (c.78), ss.45, 164.] In June 1983 the planning authority granted permission for the erection of a single storey extension to a house. Growing along the boundary of the house was a line of cupressus trees which shielded adjoining properties. The authority previously made an order modifying that permission and now wished to revoke that order and make another modifying order. An inquiry was held in September 1985. *Held*, by the Secretary of State that the objective of the order to increase the chances of survival of trees was in accordance with the aims of national and local planning policies. The order was made before building work commenced and complied with s.45 of the 1971 Act. However, the order sought was modified so that the foundations were in part cantilevered so as to protect the roots of the trees. Order confirmed with modification: HERTSMERE DISTRICT COUNCIL AND DEEM (Ref. E1/5254/28/2) (1985) 1 P.A.D. 20.

3332. Planning permission—national considerations preferred over local considerations—misdirection

[Town and Country Planning Act 1971 (c.78), s.245.] Where the inspector failed to have regard to local employment conditions but promoted the national policy of encouraging employment by allowing new business development, he misdirected himself and his decision would be quashed: SURREY HEATH BOROUGH COUNCIL *v.* SECRETARY OF STATE FOR THE ENVIRONMENT, *The Times*, November 3, 1986, Kennedy J.

3333. Planning permission—objectors—natural justice

Neighbours to a property sought judicial review contending that when permission was granted the proper procedures had not been followed by the council. The permission was to rebuild 25 existing dog kennels. A revised application was made informally by letter. An objector requested a site meeting with the council. When he returned from holiday, permission had been granted. *Held*, that the council had been in dereliction of their duty to treat all parties fairly and had prejudiced the interests of the objectors by not giving them an opportunity to present their views on the accuracy of an amended plan. Application granted: R. *v.* TORFAEN BOROUGH COUNCIL (amended to MONMOUTH DISTRICT COUNCIL), *ex p.* JONES [1986] J.P.L. 686, Woolf J.

3334. Planning permission—outline permission—agricultural dwelling

[Town and Country Planning Act 1971 (c.78) s.36 and Sched. 9; DoE Circular 24/73; Development Control Policy Note 4.] The appeal site was within a 13h.a. agricultural holding located within an area where the structure plan policy prohibited residential development unless it was justified in connection with agriculture or forestry. The appellants argued at the inquiry that since acquiring the holding in 1982 the income they received from the keeping of beef cattle on it was not sufficient. The proposal was to establish an intensive calf rearing unit to make the holding viable. *Held*, the inspector dismissing the appeal, that para. 6 of the Annex to C24/73 referred to the need to provide "firm evidence" of what was proposed. This had not been provided. Further, where a holding, such as this one, resulted from land from an adjoining farm being sold off, any new dwelling would require full explanation and justification (para. 11 of Development Control Policy Note 4). Appeal dismissed: SALISBURY DISTRICT COUNCIL AND LEWIS (Ref. T/APP/T3915/A/84/023625/P4) (1985) 1 P.A.D. 29.

3335. Planning permission—outline permission—Inspector's regard to material planning consideration

Outline planning permission to build 48 houses on a seven acre site was refused. Subsequently outline permission for 35 houses was granted subject to various considerations. Thereafter the authority refused permission. An inquiry was held and the Inspector dismissed the appeal. *Held,* on appeal, that the Inspector had been aware of the earlier resolution and had had all relevant matters in mind: SUNLAND DEVELOPMENT CO. *v.* SECRETARY OF STATE FOR THE ENVIRONMENT AND LEWES DISTRICT COUNCIL [1986] J.P.L. 759, Hodgson J.

3336. Planning permission—outline permission—reserved matters—differences

An application for approval of reserved matters has to be within the ambit of an outline planning permission.

The owners of a site consisting mainly of a busy transport interchange applied to the council for an extensive redevelopment of the site involving certain features. Outline planning permission was granted subject to the condition that detailed plans could be submitted. Plans were submitted which did not include certain of the features but the council assumed that the application was still valid. The G.L.C. having been consulted as the highway authority concluded that the application was invalid and applied for judicial review of the decision. The judge refused the application. *Held,* dismissing the appeal, that if an applicant wished to depart significantly from the outline planning permission he must apply for a new planning permission; it was a question of fact whether a detailed plan was within the ambit of the outline permission; that on the evidence in the present case the council had been fully entitled to conclude that the departure from the outline permission was not sufficient to require a fresh application.

R. *v.* HAMMERSMITH AND FULHAM BOROUGH COUNCIL, *ex p.* GREATER LONDON COUNCIL (1986) 51 P. & C.R. 120, C.A.

3337. Planning permission—permitted change of use—effect on previous permission

[Town and Country Planning Act 1971 (c.78), s.23(8); Town and Country Planning General Development Order 1977 (S.I. 1977 No. 289), s.3(1) and Schedule 1; Town and Country Planning (Use Classes) Order 1972 (S.I. 1972 No. 1385).] Schedule 1 to the Town and Country Planning General Development Order 1977, read together with Article 3(1) of that Order and with Class 1 of the Schedule to the Town and Country Planning (Use Classes) Order 1972, permits in Column (1), ". . . subject to the limitations contained in the description of that development in column (1)," a change of use without planning permission from that of "a shop for the sale of hot food" to "use as a shop for any purpose except (i) the sale of hot food . . ." and other specified exceptions. In 1978 L acquired premises in Abercynon with planning permission for use as a fish and chip shop, but was forced through ill-health to let the premises to E, who used it as an antique shop pursuant to the above provisions. In 1983, having recovered her health and regained the premises, L sought to resume their old use as a hot food take-away shop, but was served with an enforcement notice by the council, on the grounds that such a resumption required planning permission. The Inspector allowed L's appeal against the notice, and the judge dismissed the council's appeal. *Held,* dismissing the council's further appeal, that (1) upon the change of use to an antique shop the previous permission for use as a fish and chip shop had become spent, and that resumption of the earlier use in principle required a fresh permission (*Young* v. *Secretary of State for the Environment* [1983] C.L.Y. 3676 applied; *Pioneer Aggregates (UK)* v. *Secretary of State for the Environment* [1984] C.L.Y. 3465 distinguished); (2) however the change to an antique shop permitted by s.3(1) and Schedule 1 to the 1977 Order was a permission to develop land granted by a development order subject to limitations within the meaning of s.23(8) of the Town and Country Planning Act 1971, and that L was thus entitled without further permission to resume use of that land as a hot food take-away shop, which was the "normal use of that land" within the meaning of s.23(8): CYNON VALLEY BOROUGH COUNCIL *v.* SECRETARY OF STATE FOR WALES (1986) 280 E.G. 195, C.A.

3338. Planning permission—permitted development—construction of irrigation reservoir for a farm

[Town and Country Planning Act 1971 (c.78), s.53; Town and Country Planning General Development Order 1977 (S.I. 1977 No. 289), Sched. I, Class VI.]

In a section 53 determination on whether the construction of an irrigation reservoir was permitted development under Class VI, it was held that the Secretary of State had wrongly concentrated on whether the operations were engineering operations as opposed to whether the result was a building.

The second respondent applied to the local planning authority under section 53 of the Town and Country Planning Act 1971 for a determination whether the construction of a 5,000,000 gallon farm irrigation reservoir would constitute development for which planning permission was required. The embankment to contain the water would use only excavated materials. The reservoir would exceed in area the permitted ground area for a "building" in paragraph 1(a) of Class VI of Schedule 1 to the General Development Order of 1977. The planning authority determined that planning permission was required, but the Secretary of State allowed an appeal by the second respondent against that determination, holding that the construction would amount to the carrying out of engineering operations within paragraph 1(a) of Class VI rather than building operations. The local authority sought judicial review, which was granted. *Held,* that the Secretary of State had failed to consider as he should have done whether the proposals would result in a "building" within paragraph 1(a) of Class VI, which was essentially a question of fact and degree, and the matter should be remitted to him for consideration of that question. *Quaere*: whether the excavation of the materials to make the embankment and dig the reservoir was an activity that of itself required planning permission, or was it merely ancillary to the building or engineering activity.

SOUTH OXFORDSHIRE DISTRICT COUNCIL *v.* SECRETARY OF STATE FOR THE ENVIRONMENT (1986) 52 P. & C.R. 1, McCullough J.

3339. Planning permission—reconsideration—Inspector's report—interpretation of structure plan

[Town and Country Planning Act 1971 (c.78), s.245] The Council applied to quash a decision of an Inspector to determine an appeal against the refusal of outline planning permission for sheltered housing for the elderly, which included 40 dwellings. An Inspector's decision had earlier been quashed by the court and reconsidered by the Inspector in the light of further representations. The Inspector then granted planning permission. The Council argued that the Inspector had misinterpreted the relevant policies of the structure plan. *Held,* that the Inspector had rightly concluded that the development did comply with the provisions of the structure plan, and planning permission was appropriate: CHELMSFORD BOROUGH COUNCIL *v.* THE SECRETARY OF STATE FOR THE ENVIRONMENT AND ALEXANDER (E. R.) [1985] J.P.L. 112, Glidewell J.

3340. Planning permission—resolution and letter—whether constitutes a grant

The applicants sought judicial review of the council's decision to refuse planning permission in September 1984 to construct two-storey elderly persons flats and convert and rebuild a property on the grounds that the site was of considerable archeological and historic significance and that the remains of a twelfth century palace were enhanced by their setting. Earlier the planning committee passed a resolution that planning permission be granted subject to the execution of a s.52 agreement. Details of the resolution were notified to the applicants by letter. *Held,* that the resolution and letter did not constitute a formal grant of planning permission: R. *v.* WEST OXFORDSHIRE DISTRICT COUNCIL, *ex p.* PEARCE HOMES [1985] J.P.L. 523, Woolf J.

3341. Planning permission—revocation—estoppel

[Town and Country Planning Act 1971 (c.75), ss.45, 51, 64; Local Land Charges Rules 1966 (S.I. 1966 No. 579).] The local authority granted conditional outline planning permission for two four-room dwellings in December 1981. In March 1982 the developer left detailed drawings of the proposal with the group planning officer. The officer wrote to the developer stating that he would have to submit an application for detailed approval but that the drawings were acceptable and that the developer could commence foundation work. The detailed plans were submitted and three or four weeks later the developer erected brickwork on the foundations to the level of the bottom of the ground floor windows. The foundations were not as indicated on the plans. The plans made no provision for vehicular access to the site. The Council made an order revoking the outline permission. *Held,* by the Secretary of State, that (1) no estoppel arises because the appellant did not dig the foundations as indicated (reference made to *Western Fish Products* v. *Penwith District Council* [1981] C.L.Y. 2732); (2) the lack of vehicular access to the site made the development unacceptable. Order confirmed: ISLINGTON LONDON BOROUGH COUNCIL AND KATSIAOUNIS (Ref. GLP/5020/28/12) (1985) 1 P.A.D. 22.

3342. Planning permission—status of government circulars—policy considerations
[Town and Country Planning Act 1971 (c.78), ss.29, 245, Circular 22 of 1980.] On appeal, an Inspector refused planning permission for residential development on the grounds that the planning objections were sufficiently strong to overcome the presumption in favour of development. The applicant appealed under s.245. *Held,* that if a particular factor is a material consideration and therefore must be taken into account as required by s.29, it cannot be excluded as a proper consideration by the directive of a government circular. A policy can decide the weight to be placed upon various considerations; (2) in this case the Inspector had failed to follow government policy. This did not affect the outcome of the Inspector's decision having regard to the fact that he would have come to the same decision even if he had not misinterpreted policy; (3) in some circumstances the courts would find a misinterpretation of policy a proper ground for quashing the decision: GRANSDEN (E. C.) & CO. AND FALKBRIDGE v. SECRETARY OF STATE FOR THE ENVIRONMENT AND GILLINGHAM BOROUGH COUNCIL [1986] J.P.L. 519, Woolf J.

3343/4. Play group/day nursery—extension to dwelling—conservation area—effect on amenities
[Town and Country Planning Act 1971 (c.78), s.36, Sched. 9; Development Control Policy Note 2; DoE Circulars 22/80, 14/85.] The Council refused planning permission for the erection of an extension to a dwelling and the change of use of the ground floor from residential to a shared residential and play group/day nursery. The site had a long frontage on to one road and contained a large two-storey detached house in well-kept landscaped grounds with tall boundary walls, hedges and trees. It was in a Conservation Area containing similar mature detached and semi-detached houses located near the town centre. The developer appealed. *Held,* by the Inspector, that (1) the project would provide a welcome service but the way the proposed play group/day centre is run could change in the future; (2) the noise from the extra vehicle movements would annoy and disturb the neighbours and the noise of children in the house and rear garden would harm the amenities of the neighbours. Appeal dismissed: GRIMSBY BOROUGH COUNCIL AND LATIMER (Ref: T/APP/T2025/A/84/25178/P7) (1986) 1 P.A.D. 284.

3345. Poultry rearing houses—smell resulting—balance between protecting the environment and economic food production
[Town and Country Planning Act 1971 (c.78), ss.36, 52; DOE Circulars 22/80, 14/85.] The Council refused planning permission for the erection of eight poultry rearing houses and one control shed on a woodland site on the grounds that (a) the proposal did not incorporate sufficient protection to residents in the locality from smell which was likely to arise and (b) it constituted an overconcentration of similar development in this part of the district. The developer appealed. *Held,* by the Inspector following a public inquiry, that: (1) it was apparent that nuisance by reason of smell had arisen from a similar plant; (2) but there has to be a practicable balance between the protection of the environment and economic food production and it was impossible to eliminate all complaints of bad smells (reference to the draft MAFF report "Guidelines for Housed Livestock"); (3) there was no evidence to conclude that there would be regular or persistent odour nuisance sufficient to justify refusal: smell could arise anywhere, within the countryside; (4) it was not necessary or practicable to impose a condition restricting the spreading of manure or spent matter within specified distances of dwellings; (5) the evidence of past smell from the similar operation was not sufficient to provide a sound and clear cut reason for refusal within the terms of C22/80 having regard to the particularly well screened and relatively isolated location; (6) although the provision of additional employment is not decisive it is a matter of concern for the Secretary of State as expressed in C14185: this would result in a significant number of additional jobs in the processing factory. Appeal allowed subject to special conditions: CHERWELL DISTRICT COUNCIL AND FACCENDA CHICKEN (Ref. T/APP/C3105/A/84/24404/P5) (1986) 1 P.A.D. 241.

3346. Proposed hotel refused—whether evidence to support inspector's findings
TFH applied to quash the Secretary of State's decision endorsing in full the inspector's decision to dismiss an appeal against the refusal of the planning authority

to grant planning permission for the construction of a Post House Hotel some five miles from the centre of Bristol on Green Belt land. The inspector had found that there was "overwhelming evidence" of the need for an additional hotel in the Bristol area, and that the proposed site was a splendid location for a hotel, especially having regard to its convenience for the M4 and M32 motorways. However he found that, ". . . if there is such a shortage of 3/4 star hotel accommodation . . . the natural market forces of supply and demand will operate and the demand will be met, given that it is the wish of the respondent authority for additional and improved hotel facilities in the Bristol area." He concluded that there was no justification for setting aside two of the most basic and stringent planning considerations against development, namely the Green Belt and the loss of high quality agricultural land. TFH argued that the inspector had been debarred as a matter of law from deciding that the accepted need could be satisfied on some alternative site; and that there was no evidence in any case on which he could have arrived properly at that conclusion. *Held*, dismissing the application, that (1) the inspector had been entitled as a matter of law to reach such a conclusion on the facts; (2) there had been evidence on which the inspector could reach his conclusion, and that, in so far as it expressed an opinion or judgment on the likely future course of events, it was well within the proper scope of his powers to form such a conclusion: TRUSTHOUSE FORTE HOTELS *v.* SECRETARY OF STATE FOR THE ENVIRONMENT (1986) 279 E.G. 680, Simon Brown J.

3347. Public house—enforcement notice—alleged change from hotel—composite use of site
    [Town and Country Planning Act 1971 (c.78), s.88, sched. 9; Hotel Proprietors Act 1956 (c.62); Town and Country Planning (Use Classes) Order 1972 (S.I. 1972 No. 1385).] The Council served an enforcement notice alleging a material change of use of a large sixteenth century house to use as a public house without planning permission. The notice required that that use cease within 28 days. The house stood in 1.3 acres of grounds on the edge of a built-up area. The owners of the house appealed against the notice on grounds (a) and (c) of s.88(2) of the 1971 Act and there was also the deemed application for planning permission. At the public inquiry evidence was given that the premises had been used to provide overnight accommodation and food since the 1930s. Also witnesses stated that they regarded the house as their local public house. In 1984 the owners had been granted a full justice's on-licence, there being no objection from the local authority. This was renewed in 1985 without objection. A restaurant licence was granted without objection in 1984 and the restaurant was open every day except Mondays. *Held*, by the Inspector, that (1) the notice was not, as the appellants contended, invalid because it had misdescribed the use of the premises as that of a public house; (2) all the elements of a hotel use as defined in the Hotel Proprietors' Act 1956 continued even though the old name of Temperance Hotel had been dropped; (3) the introduction of a public bar into an hotel did not alter its planning use as a hotel, since the same amount of sleeping, restaurant, cafe and tea room facilities had not altered (*Emma Hotels* v. *Secretary of State for the Environment* [1981] C.L.Y. 2675 considered) (4) the facts showed that although use of the premises had greatly intensified since 1983 the hotel use continued. Appeal allowed: BRADFORD CITY METROPOLITAN COUNCIL AND SHELLBRIDGE HOLDINGS (Ref:T/APP/W4705/C/84/2296/P6) (1986) 1 P.A.D. 181.

3348. Purchase notice—existing state of the land—no enforcement proceedings
    [Town and Country Planning Act 1971 (c.78), s.180.]
    If enforcement proceedings cannot be brought in respect of a breach of planning permission, "the existing state of the land" is to be taken as its state as it exists in fact.
    In 1979 B purchased land for use as a road haulage depot. It had been used for this purpose in the past but had been unused for some time and before 1964 hardcore had been laid over part of the site without planning permission. The local authority served two enforcement notices requiring B to discontinue that use. B's appeal was dismissed because the use had been abandoned and its application to continue the use was also dismissed. B then served a purchase notice under s.180 of the 1971 Act requiring the local authority to purchase its interest in the land, claiming that the land was incapable of reasonably beneficial use in its existing state because of the refusal of planning permission. The only lawful purpose for which the land could be used was for agricultural purposes but because of the hardcore this

could only be done at very considerable expense. The Secretary of State refused to confirm the notice on the grounds that the presence of the hardcore had to be disregarded since it had been laid without permission. B sought and was granted judicial review of the refusal. *Held,* dismissing the Secretary of State's appeal, that under s.180 of the 1971 Act, if the land had been affected by development carried out without planning permission but a valid enforcement notice could be or had been served requiring restoration of the land to its previous condition which would make it capable of reasonably beneficial use the owner was not entitled to serve a purchase notice. But this did not apply if enforcement proceedings could not be brought in respect of the breach of planning permission, in which case the "existing state of the land" was its state as it in fact existed. Since the hardcore had been laid more than 4 years before the date of service of the purchase notice, the Council no longer had power to issue or serve a valid enforcement notice requiring its removal and the existing state of the land was its state with the hardcore (dictum of Lord Scarman in *Pioneer Aggregates (U.K.)* v. *Secretary of State for the Environment* [1984] C.L.Y. 3465 applied).

BALCO TRANSPORT SERVICES *v.* SECRETARY OF STATE FOR THE ENVIRONMENT [1985] 3 All E.R. 689, C.A.

3349. Quarry—condition requiring restoration

Planning permission was granted in 1952 for the continuation of quarrying operations on the appeal site subject to conditions providing for restoration of the site following completion of quarrying. In 1984 owners applied to tip commercial waste into the quarry followed by a covering of topsoil. The question arose whether the planning authority was entitled to treat the 1984 application as approval of details arising out of the 1952 permission. *Held,* that upon application for declaration by a neighbouring landowner the local authority were correct in treating the application as approval of details of the 1952 permission: R. *v.* SURREY COUNTY COUNCIL and A. & J. BULL (SOUTHERN), *ex p.* MONK [1986] J.P.L. 828, McNeill J.

3350. Radio mast—appeal requiring joint decisions of two Secretaries of State—visual impact

[Town and Country Planning Act 1971 (c.78), ss.36, 225 and Sched. 9.] The Council refused two applications for planning permission by the South Western Electricity Board for the erection of a radio mast, 33 or 34.5 m high, on its depot which formed part of a small cluster of industrial buildings in an otherwise largely residential area. The depot could be seen from a large number of residential properties which were arranged in a series of tiers along the contours of the valley. The Board appealed by way of written representations and the appeal was determined jointly by the Secretary of State for the Environment and the Secretary of State for Energy. *Held,* agreeing with the Inspector's report, that while there were advantages for the Board of a mast erected on the depot site those advantages did not outweigh the harmful effects which had caused many local residents to express concern. Appeal dismissed: TORBAY BOROUGH COUNCIL AND SOUTH WESTERN ELECTRICITY BOARD (Ref: SW/APP/M1140/84/02001 and A/85/020911) (1986) 1 P.A.D. 266.

3351. Radio mast—council's policies—residential area

[Town and Country Planning Act 1971 (c.78) ss.36, 88; Sched. 9.] In January 1985 the Council issued an enforcement notice requiring the removal of a radio mast fixed to the flank wall of a semi-detached house. The mast was given additional support from guy ropes and stood 10 ft above the highest part of the house when not in use. It carried an aerial array on a pole mounted 'H' which could be rotated in azimuth and elevation to transmit and receive any signals from communication satellites. The householder appealed. *Held,* by the Inspector, that (1) no question of television or radio interference was raised; (2) the Council had argued that the mast was not within its own guidelines which were that no action was to be taken against masts attached to a dwelling and not affecting the front elevation or rising more than 10 ft above the roof ridge: the Council had not understood the implications or application of this policy; (3) the balance of public interest clearly indicated that the appellant should retain the mast; (4) a personal condition would ensure its removal when no longer required. Appeal allowed, enforcement notice quashed: ENFIELD LONDON BOROUGH COUNCIL AND LIMEBEAR (Ref. T/APP/Q5300/C/85/1127/P6) (1986) 1 P.A.D. 289.

3352. Radio mast—impact of street scene—effect of existing television aerials
[Town and Country Planning Act 1971 (c.78), ss.32, 36; Sched. 9.] The Council refused planning permission for the retention of an amateur directional beam aerial and a vertical antenna fixed to a house. There were many large aerials of a similar size and appearance but for television in the area. The applicant appealed. *Held*, by the Inspector following an informal hearing, that (1) he was not satisfied that there was any interference resulting from the appellants' installation, despite complaints from some residents. (2) the appellant's aerials were at the rear of his house and had no significant effect on the area. Appeal allowed: BASILDON DISTRICT COUNCIL AND MARSHALL (Ref: T/APP/U1505/A/85/028060/P2) (1986) 1 P.A.D. 289.

3353. Radio mast—telescopic—residential area
[Town and Country Planning Act 1971 (c.78) ss.36, 88; Sched. 9; Town and Country Planning General Development Order 1977 (S.I. 1977 No. 289).] In 1986 the Council issued an enforcement notice requiring the removal within one month of a radio mast and antennae for amateur radio use. The 18ft. mast (reaching 30ft. when raised) was in the back garden of a bungalow in a pleasant residential area in the village centre. In 1985 the Council refused planning permission for the mast. The applicant appealed. *Held*, by the Inspector, that (1) the proposal was not exempted from the need for permission by the G.D.O.; (2) the mast was required in connection with a legitimate home based hobby which could play a role of national importance in the field of communications; (3) some residents raised no objection and others found it an eyesore: it was not so ugly or oppressive to justify upholding the enforcement notice and requiring its removal. Enforcement notice quashed and planning appeal allowed: SOUTH STAFFORDSHIRE DISTRICT COUNCIL AND SMITH (Refs: T/APP/C3430/C/84/2825/P6 and A/84/29841/P6) (1986) 1 P.A.D. 289.

3354. Radioactive waste
TOWN AND COUNTRY PLANNING (NIREX) SPECIAL DEVELOPMENT ORDER 1986 (No. 812) [£3·40], made under the Town and Country Planning Act 1971 (c.78), ss.24 and 287(5); operative on July 7, 1986; grants planning permission for the carrying out of development for the purpose of investigating the suitability of land for the deposit of low level radioactive waste.

3355. Reconversion of flats—swimming pool—permitted development—effects on amenity
[Town and Country Planning Act 1971 (c.78) ss.36, 53, Sched. 9; Town and Country Planning General Development Order 1977 (S.I. 1977 No. 289) Sched. 1.] The appeal premises were originally a single dwelling. In 1968 this was converted into two flats. The appellant applied for planning permission to construct a swimming pool in the garden belonging to the ground floor flat which she owned. Since the application the appellant had purchased the upper flat and had substantially completed internal works to reconvert the house into a single dwelling. It was argued at the public inquiry that planning permission was no longer required because it came within Class 1 of Schedule 1 to the General Development Order 1977. The appellant relied upon *Lewis* v. *Secretary of State for the Environment* [1972] C.L.Y. 3345. The Council relied upon *Wakelin* v. *Secretary of State* [1983] C.L.Y. 3649 and *Jennings* v. *Secretary of State* [1982] C.L.Y. 2130. *Held*, dismissing the appeal that (1) he was not satisfied that development requiring planning permission was not included; (2) the pool would have effects on near neighbours but it would not be unduly intrusive; (3) the surrounding wall would be prominent and its austere appearance of concrete blocks would not be appreciably mitigated by the proposed use of trailing plants: LANCASTER CITY COUNCIL AND RUSHWORTH (Ref: T/APP/A2335/A/34/022747(P5) (1986) 1 P.A.D. 102.

3356. Residential development—adjacent to area of outstanding natural beauty—"planning gain"—sports ground
[Town and Country Planning Act 1971 (c.78), ss.36, 52, Sched. 9; Local Government Act 1972 (c.70), s.125; DoE Circulars 9/80, 22/83, 15/84; Development Control Policy Note 4.] The Council refused planning permission to develop a 2·7 ha site of grassland for eight houses and use of the remainder as a sports ground. The parish council supported the scheme. The Council contended that the proposal would be an extension into the countryside immediately adjacent to an area of outstanding natural beauty and would be contrary to the policies of the development, structure and district plans and to DCPN 4. *Held*, by the inspector after a public inquiry, that (1) residential development would intrude into the mainly rural character; (2) the

proposal clearly conflicted with the policy to maintain the site as a whole as a public open space or for playing fields; (3) the appellants had not shown any substantial deficiency in available housing land, nor that the Council was disregarding paragraphs 11–13 of C15/84 and C9/80; (4) financial considerations could be relevant (*Brighton Borough Council* v. *Secretary of State for the Environment* [1980] C.L.Y. 2674); (5) he was not convinced that some scheme could not be implemented by the parish council for the whole site; (6) the club's needs were not such as to override the fundamental planning objections. Appeal dismissed: WEALDEN DISTRICT COUNCIL AND BROAD OAK UNITED FOOTBALL AND BOYS CLUB (Ref. T/APP/E1435/A/84/017949/P6) (1986) 1 P.A.D. 111.

3357. Residential development—backland development—density—tree preservation order
[Town and Country Planning Act 1971 (c.78), s.36, Sched. 9; D.C.P.N.: No. 2; Circular 1/85.] A developer appealed against the council's failure to determine an outline application for 11 units on densely wooded land, subject to a tree preservation order behind existing residential development in London NW9. The principle of development was not in issue. *Held,* by the inspector after a public inquiry, that (1) the new houses would be well spaced detached and two-storey in keeping with the existing properties and the envisaged density was below that recommended in the Greater London Development Plan; (2) there would be some intrusion but overlooking could be minimised by internal design, positioning of windows and the ameliorating effect of existing and new trees; (3) the proposed access and landscaping would reduce and absorb noise and disturbance; (4) it was necessary to impose detailed conditions, as agreed, concerning the protection of trees during construction including the submission and approval of plans of underground works, and the approval of detailed landscaping plans; (5) the siting, number and density of the scheme's houses took into account the character of the area and the need to preserve trees and did not jeopardise the main planning interest in the maintenance of acceptable standards of amenity having regard to the area's character, though the quality of neighbour's lives would be affected; (6) a properly designed access would not appreciably add to congestion; (7) many conditions agreed between the council and the appellant were either unenforceable or unrelated to planning and were deleted, having regard to Circular 1/85. Appeal allowed subject to conditions: BRENT LONDON BOROUGH COUNCIL AND ASHTON HOMES (Ref. T/APP/T5150/A/85031344/P3) (1986) 1 P.A.D. 314.

3358. Residential development—calculating five-year land availability
[Town and Country Planning Act 1971 (c.78), s.36, Sched. 9; DoE Circulars 38/81, 15/84, 22/84 and 1/85.] The appellant sought outline planning permission for the residential development of a 2·5 h.a. site. An Inspector's decision following an earlier inquiry (in August 1983) had been quashed by the High Court. The site was not in the green belt. A second inquiry was held in March 1985 and the main issues were (a) deciding on the appropriate method of calculating whether a five-year supply of house building land existed and (b) if in this case there was a shortfall of housing land whether the amenity value of the site was such as to negate the presumption in favour of planning permission set out in Circular 15/84, Annex A para. 3. *Held,* by the Inspector that C15/84 precluded the use of the draft structure plan alterations' figure (see C15/84 Annex B paras. 3 & 4). The amenity of the site was not such as to fall within C15/84 Annex B para. 3. Appeal allowed subject to special conditions (provided prior to inquiry: see C38/81, Part 1, para. 17): WIGAN METROPOLITAN BOROUGH COUNCIL AND BROSELEY ESTATES (Ref: T/APP/5089/A/83/3093/P5) (1985) 1 P.A.D. 5.

3359. Residential development—club training area—residential area
[Town and Country Planning Act 1971 (c.78), s.36, Sched. 9; Fire Services Act 1947 (c.41), s.14; DOE Circular 15/84; Command paper 9585 of July 1985.] The Council refused outline planning permission for 30 two-bedroomed and seven three-bedroomed houses on a 0·77 ha site adjacent to the rugby ground in York. The site was the rugby club's training area and was sometimes used for car parking on match days. The applicant appealed and a public inquiry was held. The main issues were (a) the effects of the proposal on the residential amenities of the area, (b) highway safety, (c) suitability for housing, (d) whether the proposed layout was of an acceptable standard. *Held,* by the Inspector, that (1) the Popplewell Report suggested that wherever practicable roads within a quarter mile of a sports ground should be

kept entirely free of parked vehicles; (2) the nearby roads could always cope with the additional traffic from the development; (3) the cones and double yellow lines nearby gave easy and unobstructed access to the ground for emergency vehicles; (4) the loss of the club's car parking spaces could be accommodated for the most part in the nearby public car parks which were only some 350m away from the ground; (5) a member of the public had expressed concern that fire hydrants could be covered if streets were fully parked, this being an offence under s.14 of the Fire Services Act 1947; however, there were other powers to deal with such an obstruction; (6) the council conceded that if the rugby club were not present there would be no objection to developing the site for residential purposes; (7) but the submitted scheme did not provide a satisfactory layout and no consideration had been given to the protection of the proposed dwellings from noise arising from adjoining land. Appeal dismissed: YORK CITY COUNCIL AND YORK RUGBY LEAGUE FOOTBALL CLUB (Ref. T/APP/F2740/A/85/30349/P2) (1986) 1 P.A.D. 303.

3360. Residential development—competing sites—structure plan review
[Town and Country Planning Act 1971 (c.78), ss.35, 52; DoE Circular 9/80.] The appellant proposed to develop 120 houses on the edge of a village of some 650 dwellings. There was also an application by another developer who proposed 340 houses on a nearby site. The Secretary of State called in the smaller development proposal and the inquiry held also dealt with the second developer's appeal. The structure plan review came into full statutory force a few days after the inquiry. The main issues at the inquiry were (a) Whether either or both of the proposals should be permitted and (b) the highway implications given the existing substandard junction. *Held*, by the Secretary of State, that the smaller development should be permitted. The release of both sites could not be justified on the basis of housing need. Preserving the remaining village atmosphere conflicted with strategic policy grounds. The appellants should agree under s.52 of the 1971 Act to carry out road improvements: LICHFIELD DISTRICT COUNCIL AND WETENHALL COOPER (Ref. WMR/P/5370/219/1) (1985) 1 P.A.D. 10.

3361. Residential development—conversion of garage/stable block to dwellings—restricted to persons employed locally as sole or main residence
[Town and Country Planning Act 1971 (c.78), s.36; DOE Circular 5/68.] In 1981 the Lake District Council Special Planning Board granted planning permission for the conversion of a stable/garage block to dwelling units subject to a condition prohibiting their occupation except as a main residence (*i.e.* for more than half of every calendar year) for a locally employed person. The occupant of the house who let off parts of this as a holiday home appealed against this occupancy condition. The appeal was dealt with by way of written representations. The decision was held in abeyance pending that of the structure plan which was approved in 1983. One modification deleted a policy seeking to restrict the occupancy of housing development. The appellant was invited to say whether he wished the application to be regarded as one for short term holiday lettings and for ordinary private dwelling houses. *Held*, by the Secretary of State, that (1) preventing outsiders from occupying new dwellings might merely increase the demand for older houses for use as holiday homes or for retired people; (2) there was nothing inherently unlawful in granting permission subject to sole or main residence, or local people, conditions; (3) however only very exceptional circumstances would justify restricting the occupation of houses to particular classes of person, *e.g.* where a dwelling would not normally be permitted but where an overriding need for it had been established; (4) both types of condition would deprive householders of their normal rights of disposal of their properties; (5) as the Board accepted that the appeal site was suitable for the proposed development, a refusal of permission pursuant to s.36(3) of the 1971 Act was not appropriate; (6) a prohibition on holiday letting had not been shown to be necessary since it would not ensure that the building was converted to residential accommodation. Appeal allowed: LAKE DISTRICT SPECIAL PLANNING BOARD AND CAREY (Ref. APP/5941/A/82/01842) (1986) 1 P.A.D. 224.

3362. Residential development—derelict nursery land—whether within village boundaries—scale—conditions
[Town and Country Planning Act 1971 (c.78), s.36, Sched. 9; DOE Circular 1/85.] The council refused outline permission for a development of about 20 houses on the site of a nursery with glasshouses which was largely derelict at the edge of a village,

with open pasture to the south and east, the north and west being built up. The structure plan provided for small scale development and infilling in the village with a presumption against development outside the village. The council had not formally determined a boundary between the village and countryside. *Held,* by the inspector after a public inquiry, that (1) the purpose of defining the village boundary here was to decide which structure plan policy applied to the site and this was a matter of judgment for which it was relevant to consider the practical consequences of any such definition; (2) the site did not have the open countryside quality of the fields to the south and east; the derelict nursery made little or no contribution to the countryside and it would be prohibitively expensive to clear the site and return it to productive agriculture or horticulture and the practical consequence of excluding the nursery from the village would be to perpetuate an area of derelict and unusable land, accordingly the site was properly regarded as part of the village; (3) it is for the council to decide which forms of development are appropriate for the site, but due regard must be given to the consequences on the orderly and efficient use of land; development along the road frontage alone as accepted by the council would sterilise the remainder of the site and there was no evidence to show that a further 20 houses would be out of scale with the settlement nor put an undue strain on existing services; (4) any precedent argument failed; (5) the inspector rejected all proposed conditions save for requiring submission of reserved matters for approval. Appeal allowed: LEWES DISTRICT COUNCIL AND RENDELL AND ALDOUS (Ref. T/APP/P1425/A/85/036484/P2) (1986) 1 P.A.D. 321.

3363. Residential development—flats—"intensive" development—character of area
[Town and Country Planning Act 1971 (c.78), s.56; DOE Circulars 23/77, 12/81, 14/85.] The Council refused planning permission for residential development comprising 31 flats, garages and associated site works. The 4.6 acre appeal site lay within a residential area on a ridge of highland and was within a conservation area. The Greater London Development Plan described the site as being in an Area of Special Character and as in the vicinity of an Area of Metropolitan Open Land. On the site was a large Victorian house with two main storeys and an attic, with outbuildings and a cottage and a garden area and tennis court. Two months after the refusal of planning permission this house became a Grade II listed building. Two months later the Council approved a development brief for the site. This draft brief restricted the area for development to approximately the tennis court area. In the light of this, the developer amended the scheme to 26 flats and reduced the number of garages/parking spaces from 55 to 37. The developer appealed and a public inquiry was held. The Inspector decided that the extent and scope of the amendments were not such as to constitute new proposals requiring a fresh application as urged, not by the council, but by other objectors. *Held,* by the Inspector, that (1) in spite of recent developments the area was basically quiet and secluded consisting mainly of substantial houses in large grounds with a semi-rural feeling. The proposed development would be altogether too large and bulky in relation to its site and the listed building; (2) the development would result in loss of trees; (3) the listed building would be severed from an integral part of its landscaped setting; (4) although the proposal would not of itself overload the existing road system, the council were understandably concerned about the cumulative effects on traffic flow of several such developments; (5) the proposal would be out of keeping with the established character of the road. Appeal dismissed: HARROW LONDON BOROUGH COUNCIL AND BOVIS HOMES (Ref. T/APP/M5450/A/85/31367/P2) (1986) 1 P.A.D. 217.

3364. Residential development—former colliery waste site—amenity space for community
[Town and Country Planning Act 1971 (c.78), s.36, Sched. 9.] The council refused outline permission for seven detached houses on a former waste tip now used for the storage of rubber tyres which are clearly visible from nearby new housing estates. Some immediately surrounding land had been reclaimed and landscaped for amenity purposes. The District Plan showed the site and surroundings as proposed open space. *Held,* by the inspector, after a public inquiry, that (1) provision of recreation areas was fundamental to successful development, and if this site was removed from the proposed amenity sites the local community would have 7·4 acres per 1000 people, which nearly met the local plan requirement of eight acres per 1000 and bettered the structure plan requirement of seven acres per 1000. With the site included as open space the figure was 7·6 acres per 1000; (2) even taking into

account the high proportion of young people locally, the open space provision with the loss of the appeal site would not be unacceptable and was not a sufficiently great reason to dismiss the appeal; (3) the neighbouring occupants concerns about loss of privacy due to loss of trees would be met by mutually agreed conditions. Appeal allowed: TAMWORTH BOROUGH COUNCIL AND SIMPSON (R. A.) AND SON (TAMWORTH) (Ref. T/APP/Z3445/A/85/032993/P4) (1986) 1 P.A.D. 318.

3365. Residential development—houses on open land next to green belt
[Town and Country Planning Act 1971 (c.78), s.36, Sched. 9; DOE Circulars 22/85, 15/84, 14/85.] The council refused outline permission for residential development on open rough grassland bordered by houses on two sides and a cricket pitch and green belt on the remaining two. A public footpath ran along the boundary of the site between the A road to the north and the green belt land to the south. At the local plan inquiry the inspector had recommended that the appeal site would be designated for housing but the council decided that the plan should show it as remaining in open use. The council and appellants disagreed as to whether the house building targets in the approved structure plan up to 1986 would be met. *Held,* by the inspector, after a public inquiry, (1) that visual importance of the site had to be measured against the scarcity of other open land in the neighbourhood and that the road had other breaks in the built up frontage, there was also the cricket ground and visual contact with the countryside beyond the site; (2) although "openness" was an amenity in itself, the real amenity value of this site lay in its access to the green belt land behind; such access would be preserved in the proposed layout; (3) the inspector noted the disagreement as to whether there would be a shortfall in housing land in the modified structure plan period but relied upon Circular 15/84 Annex A paragraph 8 to find that the fact that housebuilding needs of an area could be met from identified sites was not in itself sufficient reason for refusing planning permission elsewhere; (4) there was a shortage of land in the area for the type of housing proposed here, the site had little intrinsic value as open space and lay within the urban environment of the town. The local and structure plan policies did not present sound and clearcut reasons to offset the objections of national policy set out in Circulars 22/80 and 14/85 and their presumption in favour of granting planning permission; (5) the footpath along the boundary of the site was of crucial importance and a condition was attached relating to it. Appeal allowed: SALFORD CITY COUNCIL AND AVANTI ENGINEERING (Ref. T/APP/V4230/A/85/36430/P2) (1986) 1 P.A.D. 328.

3366. Residential development—incursion into countryside—noise from nearby kennels
[Town and Country Planning Act 1971 (c.78), s.36 and Sched. 9; DoE Circulars 10/73, 9/80 and 15/84; British Standard BS4142.] Application for outline permission for 59 dwellings on 3·6 h.a. site. 18 of these dwellings would be on land not allocated for residential development on the proposed line of a by-pass abandoned in 1983 in the non-statutory local plan approved in 1974. 1 h.a. of the development would be on undeveloped grazing land. At the inquiry the appellants put forward an alternative involving a slightly reduced area and 56 dwellings. *Held,* by the Inspector that (1) the noise from nearby kennels was not a strong enough reason to refuse permission (Circular 10/73 paras. 24–34 and British Standard 4142); (2) the proposal would be a substantial incursion into still unspoilt countryside. Even though part of the site was allocated for residential development the local plan was prepared over 10 years ago. By para. 3 of C15/84 the Government remained committed to the need to conserve and improve the countryside. Appeal dismissed: STRATFORD-ON-AVON DISTRICT COUNCIL AND SEQUOIA PROPERTIES (Ref. T/APP/J. 3720/A/83/3136) (1985) 1 P.A.D. 14.

3367. Residential development—land availability—traffic and highway matters
[Town and Country Planning Act 1971 (c.78), s.36; DoE Circular 16/84; Technical Advice Note: TA20/81.] The Council refused an outline application to permit residential development on 31·7 acres at a gross density of seven dwellings per acre and accommodating 600 people. The site consisted of woodland and areas of open heath with numerous footpaths and was not allocated for development in the draft local plan. *Held,* by the Secretary of State following a public inquiry, that (1) he noted that the Inspector concluded that there ought to be a presumption in favour of development because of the deficit of housing land supply; (2) however he did not need to express a view on the Inspector's approach because in any event this consideration was heavily outweighed by serious planning objections; (3) in the

absence of an identified adequate supply of housing land the objection based on visual impact alone should not outweigh the need, if any, to make land available for housing; (4) there was no reason to disagree with the village limits as soundly defined in the local plan; (5) there was a strong structure plan policy against such development in this open area; (6) there must be the most serious highway objections despite the concessions of the district and county councils. Appeal dismissed: MID-SUSSEX DISTRICT COUNCIL AND CHARLES CHURCH DEVELOPMENTS (Ref. APP/D3830/A/84/017196) (1986) 1 P.A.D. 120.

3368. Residential development—loss of agriculture—need for land for housing—site identification
[Town and Country Planning Act 1971 (c.78), s.36, Sched. 9; DOE Circulars 75/76, 15/84, 22/84, 1/85, 15/85.] The council refused outline permission for 4·6 houses on 3 ha of land currently in use as an apple orchard but it was making a loss. The proposal was broadly in conformity with Hampshire County's Coast and Country Conservation Policy and the site was excluded from application of the policy in the emerging local plan. Proposed alterations to the structure plan established a presumption against development in the countryside. *Held,* by the inspector after a public inquiry, that (1) as the emerging local plan was still at stage (a) (as identified in the memorandum accompanying Circular 22/84) allowing this appeal would not prejudice the plan making process, and the provisions of the emerging plan should not be given great weight; it was not certain that the school sites would become available for housing as proposed, especially in the short term; (2) the structure plan housing provision figures could not be applied to administrative areas to enable the council to demonstrate a supply of land in accordance with Circular 15/84; (3) the proposal would not unacceptably harm the approved structure plan, nor its proposed alterations nor the Coast and Country Conservation Policy; (4) development on the site would not be an obvious and conspicuous erosion of the gap between two neighbouring towns such that permission should be refused; (5) the site was of good quality land, but the council agreed that it was a site where there was less objection to development and that further development in the plan area would inevitably be on good agricultural land; (6) the viability in agricultural or horticultural use was marginal and such considerations did not justify a refusal in accordance with the guidance in Circular 75/76; (7) a set of proposed conditions which was largely accepted by the appellants was rejected by the inspector on the basis that the normal "reserved matters" condition would cover all necessary details. Appeal allowed: FAREHAM BOROUGH COUNCIL AND TRURYN LEISURE SERVICES (U.K.) (Ref. T/APP/A1720/A/85/033780/P5) (1986) 1 P.A.D. 324.

3369. Residential development—near cathedral and university—high land—density
[Town and Country Planning Act 1971 (c.78), ss.36, 210, Sched. 9; Town and Country Planning General Development Order 1977 (S.I. 1977 No. 289); DoE Circular 1/85.] The Council refused planning permission for the erection of 28 one-bedroom houses, 20 two-bedroom houses, 1 one-bedroom bungalow and 65 parking spaces and a retaining wall. The site was bounded by higher undeveloped university and cathedral land to the north. The parties agreed that the question of land slippage was not a matter of planning concern (reference to *Stringer* v. *Minister of Housing and Local Government* [1972] C.L.Y. 3357). It was generally agreed that the site should be developed residentially. *Held,* by the Inspector following a public inquiry, that (1) the university campus had a far greater impact on the character of the hillside than this proposal; (2) the district plan had a practical contradiction between its recognition of this site as one for one- and two-bedroomed dwellings and its density limit of 20 dwellings; (3) the proposed density was comparatively low for a suburban area; (4) there was a significant local need for the type of housing proposed; (5) a condition should be imposed preventing the erection of garages within the curtilages, fences, gates or walls (C1/85 referred to). Appeal allowed: GUILDFORD BOROUGH COUNCIL AND DOWNLAND GENERAL HOUSING ASSOCIATION (Ref. T/APP/Y3615/A/84/17956/P5). (1986) 1 P.A.D. 116.

3370. Residential development—no presumption in favour—noise from steelworks
[Town and Country Planning Act 1971 (c.78), s.36; Town and Country Planning (Inquiry Procedure) Rules 1974 (S.I. 1974 No. 419); DOE Circulars 10/73, 15/84, 16/84; Design Bulletin 32.] The Council refused planning permission for the erection of 63 houses on 1 hectare of land which was designated for industrial use by the 1957

Town Map. The draft local plan did not indicate any particular use for the land which was still covered with concrete slabs and brick rubble. Adjacent to the land was a steelworks. The developer appealed and a public inquiry was held. The council relied upon the Town Map and contended that the site should not be developed separately but jointly with another site, that the disposition of the parking spaces would be unsatisfactory and that the development would be affected by noise from the steelworks. *Held,* by the Secretary of State, that (1) as there was a five year supply of housing land there was no presumption in favour of the development in terms of para. 12 of Circular 15/84; (2) the allocation in the Town Map was not a sufficient reason for refusal as no evidence was given that the land was a vital part of the area zoned in the Town Map; (3) no evidence was given that the site should be developed together with other land; (4) whilst some of the distances between houses and parking spaces might exceed those recommended in Design Bulletin 32, those deficiences did not warrant dismissal of the appeal; (5) if residential development were permitted the growth of the steelworks could be inhibited by complaints of noise (reference to C16184). This would be counter to the need to enhance the quality of residential surroundings (ref. to C10/73). The inspector was correct to assess the potential noise with the steel works operating at maximum capacity in accordance with para. 27 of C10/73. Appeal dismissed: SHEFFIELD (CITY) METROPOLITAN DISTRICT GROUP AND WIGGINS GROUP (Ref. A/44420/A/84/018093) (1986) 1 P.A.D. 210.

3371. Residential development—noise from existing factory

[Town and Country Planning Act 1971 (c.78), s.36, Sched. 9; Control of Pollution Act 1974 (c.40); DoE Circular 10/73; Development Control Policy Note No. 3.] Proposal to develop 0·4 h.a. site with 12 houses. To the north-west of the site was a grade 2 listed building in need of urgent repairs. The appellants proposed to use the housing development to fund these repairs. The planning issues were (a) the effect of noise from a nearby glassworks on the proposed development and (b) access for emergency vehicles given the length of the proposed cul-de-sac. The Chief Planning Officer recommended granting permission. The Council refused permission. *Held,* by Inspector, following Public Inquiry in Feb. 1985, that the noise from the factory was considerable. The advice in Circular 10/73 and Development Control Policy Note 3 is relevant where there is an existing industrial development. Appeal dismissed: DUDLEY METROPOLITAN BOROUGH COUNCIL AND DAVIES AND FIRMSTONE (Ref. T/APP/C4615/A/84/020675/P2) (1985) 1 P.A.D. 1.

3372. Residential development—outline application—housing land supply

[Town and Country Planning Act 1971 (c.78), s.36; DOE Circulars 22/80, 15/84, 22/84, 14/85.] The Council refused outline planning permission for development of a 35 acre site bounded by residential development on two sides and by natural constraint on the other two sides. The county development plan town map was approved some 27 years previously, with amendments 22 years ago. The structure plan was nearing the end of its period and the first alteration was awaiting the Secretary of State's decision. The local plan had not yet been published for consultation. The appeal site was unallocated in the Town Map. The developer appealed and following a public inquiry the Inspector recommended the dismissal of the appeal on the grounds of prematurity and the need to separate the urban areas. *Held,* by the Secretary of State, that (1) the assessment of housing land availability should be based upon the position at a particular date, the latest available being the most appropriate. The deductions for lapsed outline permissions or where permissions had been granted on sites which were not listed at the time of refusal for this proposal related to past events and were not relevant to the method of calculation laid down in C15/84; (2) by the residual method the Council's figures showed sufficient supply of land to satisfy C15/84 and therefore the presumption set out in C22/80 Annex A, para. 3 did not apply; (3) the proposal would not be an extension but more of a "rounding-off"; (4) the absence of a local plan, or one that is in the offing, is not, in itself, a reason for refusing planning permission (C22/84); (5) as there were no sound and clear cut reasons for refusal the appeal should be allowed (C14/85): Appeal allowed: CREWE AND NANTWICH BOROUGH COUNCIL AND NEED AND BEECROFT (Ref. APP/K0615/A/84/023059) (1986) 1 P.A.D. 228.

3373. Residential development—permission already given for part of site—loss of agricultural land

[Town and Country Planning Act 1971 (s.36); DOE Circulars 22/80, 15/84, 14/85.] The Council refused planning permission to develop 2.3ha of mainly grade 3A agricultural land. The land included a smaller parcel of land of about 1.5ha which already had outline planning permission for residential development. The site was immediately north of a residential area and otherwise surrounded by arable farmland. The developer appealed and a public inquiry was convened. *Held,* by the Inspector, that (1) if the Council and Ministry of Agriculture, Fisheries and Food were seriously concerned about the loss of agricultural land they would have resisted the earlier grant of permission for the smaller site; (2) there was a conflict between the "presumption against" residential development in the countryside in the structure plan and the "presumption in favour" in C14/85 but it was appropriate to place more weight on C14/85, (3) enlarging the area of new housing would adversely affect good farmland and the countryside but they would not be so demonstrably harmed as to outweigh the presumption in favour of development; (4) the preservation of the view from private houses was not a proper function of development control. Appeal allowed: KETTERING BOROUGH COUNCIL AND BURTON LATIMER SETTLED ESTATES AND SPRINGFIR ESTATES (Ref. T/APP/L2820/A2631/P6) (1986) 1 P.A.D. 214.

3374. Residential development—previous permission—green belt—local planning inquiry—supply of housing land

[Town and Country Planning Act 1971 (c.78), ss.36, 43, Sched. 9.] The council refused outline planning permission for residential development of a site situated in the green belt and in an area of special county value. Two tree preservation orders applied to the site which was some 600m from the village centre. The applicant appealed and a public inquiry was held. A preliminary issue was argued before the Inspector relating to a 1954 outline permission for land for the most part equating with the appeal site. Part of the roadline was pegged out by the appellants in 1955. The appellants relied upon *Malvern Hills District Council* v. *Secretary of State for the Environment* [1982] C.L.Y. 3187 and *Spackman* v. *Secretary of State for the Environment* [1977] C.L.Y. 2975 in arguing that the pegging out was a "specified operation" as defined in s.43(2)(*d*) of the 1971 Act. The council relied upon *Etheridge* v. *Secretary of State for the Environment* [1984] C.L.Y. 3462. *Held,* by the Inspector, that with regard to the preliminary issue (1) even if the pegging out of the road line did constitute a "specified operation" the appellants were in breach of the condition in not having previously supplied details in drawings. Here, the pegging out was unauthorised and could not preserve the outline permission; (2) the pegging out was not an operation in the course of laying out or constructing a road or part of a road. No application had been made within three years of April 1, 1969 and therefore the permission had lapsed; (3) *High Peak Borough Council* v. *Secretary of State for the Environment* [1981] C.L.Y. 2717 was not relevant to this case. With regard to the planning issues the Inspector held that (a) there was a small shortfall in the five year housing land supply, (b) although the local plan inquiry inspector recommended that the appeal site be deleted from the Green Belt it was up to the council to decide what action to take, (c) the site was of significant landscape importance, (d) as there appeared to be an inadequate supply of housing land a presumption in favour of granting permission would normally apply but that presumption should not prevail because the site was in the green belt. Appeal dismissed: MACCLESFIELD BOROUGH COUNCIL AND RIPPER (Ref. T/APP/C0630/A/85/28013/P2) (1986) 1 P.A.D. 306.

3375. Residential development—public open space—outline application approved previously—renewed application

[Town and Country Planning Act 1971 (c.78), ss.36, 52; DOE Circulars 22/80, 15/84, 22/84, 1/85.] The Council refused to renew an outline planning permission for residential development on a 5.2 acre site which was allocated in the 1970 Town Map for public open space with a residential frontage along a road. The local plan which was not yet approved allocated the whole site for public open space. In 1972 an outline permission had been granted for industrial development. Renewal of that permission having been refused in 1975, the outline application for residential development was approved in 1976. The application for renewal was made in 1979 but was not refused until 1983, after the developer had agreed to a number of extensions. The developer appealed. The Inspector considered that the planning issues were whether it was reasonable to refuse permission for renewal of a permission already granted and whether the proposal would unacceptably detract from the amenities of the area. *Held,* that (1) little weight should be given to the public open space allocation of the site, the Town Map having been disregarded twice and the local plan having completed only two of the four stages described in the Memorandum, para. 1.12 accompanying C22/84. The stated minimum requirement for open space in the local plan would still be met; (2) there had been no material change in planning circumstances since the original permission was granted other than in respect of housing policy (para. 48 of C.1/85). The appellant was not to blame for the delay; (3) a renewal of permission could have been granted in 1979 and it was unreasonable to keep on postponing a decision until new housing policies and the emerging local plan could be used as a reason for refusal; (4) on the Council's own figures there was not enough land to meet the five year requirement (ref. to para. 12 of C15/84 and para. 8 of C22/80); (5) the outlook of residents backing onto the site would be largely protected by the proposed strip of public open space: Appeal allowed subject to conditions: STAFFORDSHIRE MOORLANDS DISTRICT COUNCIL AND MACHIN DEVELOPMENTS (Ref. T/APP/L3435/A/84/014722/P7) (1986) 1 P.A.D. 221.

3376. Residential development—sheltered flats—likelihood of commercial use—conservation area

[Town and Country Planning Act 1971 (c.78), ss.36, 52, 277A, Sched. 9.] The council refused planning permission for 38 sheltered flats for the elderly on a site which had formerly housed a cinema but had been vacant since the 1970s and was in a conservation area. The site was allocated for retail and office use in the draft local plan. Several planning permissions had been granted for commercial use on the site. *Held,* by the inspector after a public inquiry, that (1) the site was not a prime shopping frontage; (2) the structure plan and draft local plan did not require the provision of more shops and offices and that employment provision and commercial activity was not likely to occur in the foreseeable future on this site; but if there was such demand it could be accommodated by the redevelopment of buildings or land in the town centre; (3) the open site currently detracted from the mixed character of the conservation area and the proposed building would be an improvement which would be likely to be achieved and would not conflict with national and local conservation area policies; (4) there was no sound objection on infrastructure grounds; (5) the proposal would meet a valid need by catering for elderly owner occupiers and would contribute to meeting the structure plan housing requirement; (6) car parking would be inadequate if the development were to be occupied by younger age groups but the section 52 agreement would prevent such occupation; (7) for all the above reasons the proposal would not cause demonstrable harm to interests of acknowledged importance. Appeal allowed: ROCHFORD DISTRICT COUNCIL AND MCCARTHY AND STONE (DEVELOPMENTS) (Ref. T/APP/B1550/A/85/032721/P2) (1986) 1 P.A.D. 311.

3377. Residential development—supply of housing land

[Town and Country Planning Act 1971 (c.78), s.36; DOE Circulars 14/84, 15/84; Technical Memorandum H12/76; Technical Document TD 11/82.] The council refused planning permission for development of a large greenfield site situated within the Metropolitan Green Belt for housing, a railway station and 10 acres of light industrial or warehousing with other facilities. There were two identical applications, A and B, except that for B permission for the construction of an omni-directional interchange onto the A3 trunk road was also sought. The developer appealed. The Inspector considered there to be three main planning issues, whether: (a) the green belt policies and the advanced state of preparation of the local plan created presumptions against development; (b) the proposals offered any planning advantages to justify the granting of planning permission; (c) there was any evidence of present or future housing need to justify the granting of planning permission. *Held,* by the Secretary of State agreeing with his Inspector, that (1) the proposals would extend the urban area perceptibly into a largely unspoiled local landscape; (2) there was no evidence as to whether land for two years' development was immediately available as required by para. 12 of C15/84, but the appeal land could not contribute to that requirement. A five years supply of housing land existed; (3) it was a matter of judgment whether the shortfall and the problems of developing urban sites were so great as to be overcome only by the release for phased development of an additional major site; (4) the planning advantages of developing the appeal land would have to be overriding; (5) there was no evidence of a need for a new railway station and the inclusion of this did not argue in favour of developing the site; (6) the Department of Transport's Direction of refusal for application B was rooted on the well-established general objection to the formation of additional access to trunk and principal roads. Appeal dismissed: GUILDFORD BOROUGH COUNCIL AND MARTIN GRANT HOMES (Refs. APP/5386/A/82/012131 and APP/Y3615/A/84/021620) (1986) 1 P.A.D. 231.

3378. Residential development—two applications—same site but different boundaries—conditions

[Town and Country Planning Act 1971 (c.78), ss.36, 37, Sched. 9; DoE Circulars 15/84, 1/85.] The Council refused planning permission for the erection of four detached houses and construction of an access road. The appellant then applied for permission to erect three detached houses. This was not determined within the prescribed period and the developer appealed after notice of which the Council notified the appellants of its refusal on this second application. Both proposals provided for high close boarded fences to screen the access road from neighbouring houses. The Council was concerned about the possible loss of trees, loss of privacy to neighbouring gardens and noise and disturbance. *Held,* by the Inspector that, (1) there was not a sufficient tree reason for refusal for either scheme; (2) the second scheme was worse than the first given the proposed position of the access road and the southernmost house; (3) the first scheme of four houses was not only less likely to lead to noise or disturbance to neighbours but also made more effective use of available land in accordance with C15/84; (4) a condition preventing the conversion of the garages would not be imposed because in the absence of exceptional circumstances it would be unreasonable (reference made to C1/85) and such conversion would require planning permission. Appeal for four houses allowed. Appeal for three houses dismissed: BARNET LONDON BOROUGH AND ASHTON HOMES (Ref. T/APP/N5090/A/84/023447/P2 and 025940/P2) (1986) 1 P.A.D. 105.

3379. Restaurant—change of use to—from shop—tourist area—existing premises unsatisfactory

[Town and Country Planning Act 1971 (c.78), s.36, sched. 9; DoE Circular 22/80; Development Control Policy Note 11.] The City Council refused planning permission to change the use of premises as a shoe shop to that of a restaurant. The applicant already operated a restaurant in adjacent premises. The premises were in the Strand, London, the shops of which mainly serve the needs of the working population in the area and the visitors and tourists. *Held,* by the Inspector, that (1) it had already been decided that the proposed use was acceptable in this location; (2) whether any particular non-retail service was already sufficiently represented was a matter of commercial judgment and was not material to a planning application; (3) a considerable increase in employment would result; (4) there was clearly a demand for the appellants' services which their present premises could not satisfy; (5) on balance the public would gain from the proposal and the retail character and function of the Strand would not be so significantly adversely affected as to justify a refusal of consent. Appeal allowed and personal planning permission granted: WESTMINSTER CITY COUNCIL AND MCDONALDS HAMBURGERS. (Ref.T/APP/X5990/A/84/0254265P5) (1986) 1 P.A.D. 191.

3380. Restaurant—condition—enforcement notice

[Town and Country Planning Act 1971 (c.78), s.246.] A permission for a restaurant was granted in 1978 subject to the condition that the restaurant should not be open after midnight or before 9 a.m. The stated reason was to protect the amenities enjoyed by the occupants of adjoining residences. An enforcement notice was served alleging that the restaurant was open to the public after midnight and before 9 a.m. and open to the public on Sundays. The Inspector upheld the notice. M appealed to the High Court. *Held,* that (1) no grounds arose under s.246(2). The condition meant that following closure of the restaurant to the public persons inside should be given a reasonable period to consume their food.

MIAH *v.* SECRETARY OF STATE FOR THE ENVIRONMENT AND HILLINGDON BOROUGH COUNCIL [1986] J.P.L. 756, Woolf J.

3381. Restaurant and residential—change of use from public house
[Town and Country Planning Act 1971 (c.78) s.36, Sched. 9.] The Council refused planning permission to change the use of a public house to that of a restaurant with two flats on the first floor and a ground floor extension. The Council refused on the ground that the change would result in a serious loss to the local amenity with some 1060 persons over the age of eighteen years living within a quarter of a mile of the appeal site. *Held,* by the Inspector following a public inquiry, that (1) if the Council's quarter mile standard was applied, a large proportion of the local populace would live outside the defined existing catchment areas; (2) as a public house was considered a desirable facility and some people could be up to three-quarters of a mile from the nearest one the loss of this facility was a disadvantage of the proposal; (3) the proposed restaurant would provide a welcome new facility with the creation of additional employment. Appeal allowed because of the absence of any policy or other significant planning objection: Barnet London Borough Council and Happy Eater (Ref. T/APP/N5090/A/84/022152/P5) (1985) 1 P.A.D. 50.

3382. Restrictive covenant—building for use by domestic staff—obsolete
In 1969 planning permission was granted for a single storey extension ("Sunnyside") some 19 feet from the house ("Belairs") for domestic staff accommodation. The owner's successor who farmed the land nearby wished to use Sunnyside as a home for an agricultural worker. He sought the discharge of the restrictive covenant. He then leased Belairs to a third party. The planning authority opposed the application, contending that it was against the county structure plan, and that although it was unlikely that it would ever again be used by domestic staff, it could be used as a granny flat. *Held,* that (1) the District Council would not be injured if the application were granted, and the applicant succeeded under para. (*c*) of s.84(1) of the Law of Property Act 1925; (2) he also succeeded under para. (*a*), on the ground that the restrictive was obsolete.
Cox's Application, *Re* (1986) 51 P. & C.R. 335, Lands Tribunal.

3383. Restrictive covenant—modification—compensation—Lands Tribunal
[Law of Property Act 1925 (c.20), s.84(1).]
A council which sold a house with a restrictive covenant forbidding the erection of a further structure was entitled to object to an application to modify the covenant and could claim compensation for the reduction of the purchase price due to the imposition of the restriction.
In 1981 the objector, the Council of the London Borough of Hillingdon, sold a house to the applicant and his wife. The cost after discounts was £22,575, although the market price was £27,750. The property included a large garden in respect of which the applicant later gained planning permission to erect a dwelling house. The transfer contained a covenant restricting the erection of any structure. The applicant sought to modify or discharge this restriction. The Council objected to the application in order to gain compensation. They originally claimed in respect of the increase in market value of the application site if development permission was granted, apparently under s.84(1) of the Law of Property Act 1925. At the hearing, however, they put their claim under para. (ii) of those provisions, *i.e.* a sum to make up for the reduction of the purchase price due to the imposition of the restriction. The claim in the notice of objection was for £9,000; the claim at the hearing was for £3,000. *Held,* that the application succeeded under para. (*aa*) of s.84(1). The claim for compensation also succeeded. On the evidence the sum of £700 represented the additional compensation which would have been paid if the restriction had not been imposed and that sum should be awarded. Since that sum was much less than either of the two amounts claimed by the objector, the objector must pay the applicant three-quarters of the costs of the proceedings taxed on County Court Scale 3.
Harper's Application, *Re* (1986) 52 P. & C.R. 104, Lands Tribunal (Ref. No. LP/43/1984), V. G. Wellings Esq., Q.C.

3384. Restrictive covenant—modification—money adequate compensation
[Law of Property Act 1925 (c.20), s.84(1).]
Where the freeholder of land held only a reversionary interest in it, he had the right to object to a proposed modification of a restrictive convenant benefitting the land, but money was an adequate compensation for any damage to his interest.
The owner of land sold part of it to the applicant taking a covenant that no structures or buildings should be built upon the application land. Some years later

the owner erected on part of the land he retained a house and garage which was occupied by a former employee who had security of tenure. This licensee carried on a small-holding and shop business on his land. The applicant sought to modify the restrictive covenant to enable him to build a bungalow for his own occupation: he had obtained planning permission. The application site was close to the land occupied by the licensee. The land owner and licensee opposed the application. *Held,* that the licensee had no estate or interest in the land and his application must be dismissed. The erection of the bungalow would injure the landowner as freeholder and the restriction was not obsolete. The application therefore failed under paras. (*a*) and (*c*) of s.84(1) of the Law of Property Act 1925. The proposed use of the application land was reasonable but the restriction did secure to the freeholder practical and substantial benefits of value. But since his interest was reversionary, money was a sufficient compensation for him for any damage to his interest. The application was therefore granted under para. (*aa*) of s.84(1), on payment of £2,500 compensation.

DA COSTA'S APPLICATION, *Re* (1986) 52 P. & C.R. 99, Lands Tribunal (Ref. No. L.P./40/1983), V. G. Wellings Esq., Q.C.

3385. Sports facilities—green belt—balancing of benefits against environmental harm
[Town and Country Planning Act 1971 (c.78), s.36.] The appeal site was an irregular shaped grassland of some 18 acres located within the green belt. The Council had refused planning permission on two successive pairs of applications. Each pair consisted of an application for change of use and the laying out of sports pitches and an application to erect a pavilion or club house. The parish council and local residents had objected on green belt policy grounds and also on grounds of congestion and danger from the additional traffic. The Structure Plan provided that as an exception to the prohibition of development in the green belt sports facilities which could not be expected to be located elsewhere might be permitted provided that in general such facilities would be directed towards suitable parts of the green belt, as allocated in local plans, unless they are to meet the needs of the immediate community. *Held,* by the Inspector, that application 1 was rejected because the bowling green and tennis courts could be properly located in a built up area. Application 3 did not include either and was allowed. The size of the building proposed in application 2 would result in environmental harm whereas that in application 4 was adequate. Appeals on applications 3 and 4 only conditionally allowed: METROPOLITAN BOROUGH OF SOLIHULL AND NEWCOMBE ESTATE Co. (Ref. T/APP/Q4625/A/84/14314–5/P7 and T/APP/Q4625/A/25/28864–5/P7) (1985) 1 P.A.D. 69.

3386. Stop notice—compensation—time limits for claim
[Town and Country Planning Act 1971 (c.78), s.177; Town and Country Planning General Regulations 1976 (S.I. 1976 No. 1419, reg. 14.]
A claim for compensation in respect of a stop notice need not be in any particular form but must be unequivocal.

T Co. owned premises in Lewes but the council refused its application for planning permission to use the premises for other purposes and served an enforcement notice and a stop notice. These were quashed by the Secretary of State. To claim compensation T Co. had to make a claim within six months of the Secretary of State's decision in January 1981. T Co. did not make a formal claim until August 1981 and admitted that it was out of time but a letter had been sent in January 1981 stating that a formal claim for compensation would be made in due course. *Held,* on the question whether the letter fulfilled the requirements as to time for service of a claim for compensation, that s.177 of the 1971 Act and reg. 14 of the 1976 Regulations did not require that a claim for compensation in respect of a stop notice should be in any particular form or that it should state the sum claimed or that it should be a detailed claim; it must merely be unequivocal that a claim was being made; the claims in August 1981 were further and better particulars of the claim already delivered; the claim was not out of time.

TEXAS HOMECARE *v.* LEWES DISTRICT COUNCIL (1986) 51 P. & C.R. 205, Lands Tribunal.

3387. Stop notice—effect—future use of residential caravan site
[Town and Country Planning Act 1971 (c.78), s.90(2)(*b*).] D purchased land with a view to development as a residential caravan site. They permitted a travelling showman to move his caravan on to the site in breach of planning control. In

September 1985 the council served enforcement notices to take effect in November 1985 and served stop notices. D continued to use the site as a residential caravan site, and more residential caravans arrived. The council sought an injunction. *Held,* that the Act restricted the operation of a stop notice so that it was ineffective to prohibit the future use of the site for caravans occupied as sole or main residences: RUNNYMEDE BOROUGH COUNCIL *v.* SMITH [1986] J.P.L. 592, Millett J.

3388. Storage—open storage in green belt—previous appeal—personal and temporary permission

[Town and Country Planning Act 1971 (c.78), s.32.] The appeal site comprised an area of fenced-off land with an inner compound used for the storage of cylinders. It formed part of a much larger holding of land which contained a large number of old buildings and machinery and decaying vehicles. The developer applied for planning permission to store liquid gas cylinders on the site. The use was already taking place. The Council refused permission. The same use had been the subject of an earlier appeal which was dismissed in January 1984. Since that appeal the District Plan had been adopted and the site was now within the green belt. The Structure and District Plan policies contained a strong presumption against development within the green belt except in very special circumstances. Prior to the District Plan being adopted the site had been designated for public open space: this now no longer applied. *Held,* by the Inspector following a public inquiry, that (1) the development did not fall within any of the exceptions to the presumption against development; (2) a permanent use of the site for the storage of liquid gas cylinders would be unacceptable; (3) the particular use in the location did not cause any significant harm to the area (4) visibility at the access was now adequate; (4) the granting of a temporary and personal permission would allow a search for a new site. Appeal allowed, a personal permission was granted for two years: DACORUM DISTRICT COUNCIL AND BERKHAMPSTEAD TOOL HIRE (Ref. T/APP/A1910/A/84/023290/P5) (1986) 1 P.A.D. 153.

3389. Structure plan—alteration—reason for Secretary of State's decision

[Town and Country Planning Act 1971 (c.78), s.9(8).]

The Secretary of State is under a duty to give reasons for his decision where alterations are proposed to a structure plan, or where his decision conflicts with policy guidance, pursuant to s.9(8) of the Town and Country Planning Act 1971.

In 1976 the county council prepared a structure plan which was approved by the Secretary of State in 1979. In 1980 the Council proposed an alteration as to housing development policy which the applicants objected to, pursuant to sections 9 and 10 of the 1971 Act. The Secretary of State promised that the objections would be fully considered. That was on May 2, 1984. On July 4, 1984 the Department of the Environment published Circular 15/84, paragraph 8 of which seemed to be difficult to reconcile with the policies adopted in the structure plan for housing development. On October 12, 1984 the Secretary of State published his decision letter on the county council's alteration proposals which by implication accepted the alteration in the policy. The applicants applied to the High Court under s.244(2)(*b*) of the Act of 1971 contending that the Secretary of State had failed to comply with s.9(8) of the Act in that he had given no reasons for his decision, and secondly that his decision was contrary to the advice contained in Circular 15/84. *Held,* allowing the application and quashing the proposed alteration of policy, that the point raised by the applicants in their objections had been substantial and it was necessary for the Secretary of State to give some reasons, however brief, for his decision, and to have made some reference to the policy contained in Circular 15/84 when explaining his endorsement of the county council's policy (*Poyser and Mills' Arbitration, Re* [1963] C.L.Y. 43 applied; *Edwin H. Bradley & Sons v. Secretary of State for the Environment* [1983] C.L.Y. 3745 applied).

BARNHAM *v.* SECRETARY OF STATE FOR THE ENVIRONMENT (1986) 52 P. & C.R. 10, Farquharson J.

3390. Tipping—established use certificate—appropriate conditions

[Town and Country Planning Act 1971 (c.78) ss. 36, 94, 95, Sched. 9; Control of Pollution Act 1974 (c.40); Circular 1/85.] The County Council refused the appellant's application for an established use certificate under s.94(1)(*a*) of the 1971 Act for the use of land as a tip for waste materials and for planning permission to restore the land to agriculture. The appellants referred to *Northavon D.C. v. Secretary of State for the Environment* [1980] C.L.Y. 2675. The planning issues were (a) the effects on the residential amenity of neighbours and (b) the conditions which might be imposed in the light of Circular 1/85. *Held*, by the Secretary of State agreeing with the recommendations of the Inspector, that (1) the Council's refusal of an established use certificate was well founded because it was not clear from the evidence that tipping on any part of the appeal site had continued since the end of 1963; (2) water pollution from tipping was a matter for consideration on an application for a waste disposal licence; (3) the balance of the highway factors might be against the development, but so slightly that it should not influence the decision; (4) the restored land would blend in acceptably in the area of outstanding natural beauty; (5) controls which would be exercised through the site licence should not be duplicated. Appeal allowed subject to conditions: HEREFORD AND WORCESTER COUNTY COUNCIL AND DUBBERIEY (Ref. APP/5058/D/83/75 and APP/F1800/A/84/14233) (1985) 1 P.A.D. 85.

3390a. Tower for clay shooting—already erected—effect on visual amenity
[Town and Country Planning Act 1971 (c.78), s.36; General Development Order 1977 (S.I. 1977 No. 289) art. 3, Sched. 1, Class III(2).] The appellant had erected a 100ft. tower painted white on the edge of a small wood almost in the centre of the Roundwood Estate. The tower projected about 50ft. above the trees. The tower was to be used (1) for providing two high platforms from which clay shooting targets would be launched and (2) to support a proposed water storage tank to be used for water taken from a borehole on the estate. The Council refused permission for both the tower and the storage tank. *Held*, on appeal by the Inspector that (1) the tower would be seen by comparatively few people given the size of the estate and the configuration of the landscape and it would stand out less if painted a different colour; (2) the water storage tank would add unacceptably to the visibility of the tower and therefore should not be permitted. The appeal was allowed so far as it related to the retention of the tower subject to it being painted a colour acceptable to the Council and subject to the tower not being used more than 28 days in total in any calendar year in accordance with Art. 3, Sched. 1, Class III(2) of the 1977 General Development Order; BASINGSTOKE & DEAN BOROUGH COUNCIL AND CHURCH, (Ref.T/APP/H1705/A/84/019340/P3) (1985) 1 P.A.D. 65.

3390b. Town and Country Planning (Minerals) Act 1981—commencement
TOWN AND COUNTRY PLANNING (MINERALS) ACT 1981 (COMMENCEMENT No. 3) ORDER 1986 (No. 760 (c.20)) [45p], made under the Town and Country Planning (Minerals) Act 1981 (c.36), s.35; brings into operation all the provisions of Pt. I of the 1981 Act which are not already in operation, and s.34 as it applies to those provisions, on May 19, 1986.

3390c. Unauthorised development—injunction proceedings—availability of criminal proceedings—whether civil proceedings justified
[Local Government Act 1972 (c.20), s.222.]
A local authority may institute civil proceedings under s.222 of the Local Government Act 1972 without first exhausting the process of the criminal law.
D began developing a caravan site without planning permission. They disregarded a series of enforcement notices and stop orders. The planning authority decided that criminal proceedings would take too long and brought proceedings for an injunction instead under s.222 of the Local Government Act 1972. The judge refused the injunction on the ground that criminal sanctions were available. *Held*, allowing the planning authority's appeal, that the authority was entitled to act under s.222 without first exhausting the process of the criminal law, and the injunction should be granted (dictum of Lord Templeman in *Stoke-on-Trent City Council* v. *B. & Q. (Retail)* [1984] C.L.Y. 3231 applied; *Gouriet* v. *Union of Post Office Workers* [1977] C.L.Y. 690 and dictum of Oliver J. in *Stafford Borough Council* v. *Elkenford* [1977] C.L.Y. 2874 considered).
RUNNYMEDE BOROUGH COUNCIL *v.* BALL [1986] 1 All E.R. 629, C.A.

3390d. Urban development corporation—listed building control—power to enforce planning powers—fiat of Attorney General
[Local Government Act 1972 (c.70), ss.222(1)(a), 270(1); Local Government, Planning and Land Act 1980 (c.65), s.136(3)(e).]
An urban development corporation established under the Local Government, Planning and Land Act 1980 does not have power to bring proceedings to enforce planning law without the fiat of the Attorney General.

The plaintiffs were an urban development corporation and constituted as the local planning authority for the area for the purpose of building control. The defendants were owners of a derelict building which they began to demolish, and continued to demolish despite a preservation notice. The plaintiffs obtained an injunction pending trial. *Held,* allowing the appeal, that the urban development corporation did not come within the definition of a "local authority" and could not take proceedings independently of the Attorney-General; the plaintiffs had no *locus-standi* and were not entitled to bring proceedings (*Gouriet* v. *Union of Post Office Workers* [1977] C.L.Y. 690 applied).

LONDON DOCKLANDS CORP. v. RANK HOVIS (1985) 84 L.G.R. 101, C.A.

3390e. War damage—section 53 determination—reinstatement of cottages—further subsequent collapse

[War Damage Act 1943 (6 & 7 Geo. (c.31), s.2; Town and Country Planning Act 1971 (c.78), ss.53, 290; Town and Country Planning General Development Order 1977 (S.I. 1977 No. 289), Sched. 1, Class XI; Building Regulations 1976 (S.I. 1976 No. 1676).] A pair of semi-detached cottages were badly damaged and rendered uninhabitable as a direct consequence of enemy action in 1941. Since that time the cottages had suffered further damage and dereliction. The cottages could be rebuilt to give the original appearance and much of the original stone could be re-used and suitable tiles could be obtained. An application was made under T.C.P.A. 1971, s.53 and the Council determined that the proposal to reinstate the cottages would require planning permission. The applicant appealed. *Held,* by the Secretary of State, that (1) as class XI of Sched. 1 to the G.D.O. did not prescribe any limitation in time for works for reinstatement the period of intervening years since the war damage occurred did not remove the rights under Class XI; (2) for purposes of Class XI a distinction should not be made between war damage and subsequent deterioration provided that the original damage was caused solely by enemy action during the war; (3) the current review of the G.D.O. was not a matter that should influence this appeal. Appeal allowed: SOUTH HEREFORDSHIRE DISTRICT COUNCIL AND MORRIS (Ref. APP/U1830/G/84/70) (1986) 1 P.A.D. 294.

3390f. Waste disposal licence—rejection—cessation of one of two uses—abandonment

[Town and Country Planning Act 1971 (c.78), ss.22, 23; Control of Pollution Act 1974 (c.40), ss.5, 10; Town and Country Planning General Development Order 1977 (S.I. 1977 No. 289).] The Council refused two applications for a waste disposal licence under the Control of Pollution Act 1974 because it considered that planning permission was required to dispose of waste on the site. The site had in 1948 been used for both waste disposal and as a sewage treatment works. By the mid 1960's the greater part of the site was just a sewage works. The waste disposal use finished no later than 1974 and in 1979 the site was decommissioned and cleared. In 1983 the superficial area of the deposit did not extend to the whole site and not all the area on which waste was to be deposited under either proposal was already covered with deposited material. The developer appealed, the main planning issues being (a) whether the site was still to be regarded as having a waste disposal use and (b) if so whether it would entitle the appellant to resume the depositing of waste on the scale proposed. *Held,* by the Secretary of State agreeing with the Inspector, that (1) the change from the mixed waste disposal and sewage treatment use to a single use as sewage treatment was not, on the evidence, a material change of use: there can only be a material change consequent upon the expansion of the surviving use; (2) the earlier waste disposal use was long since not merely discontinued but abandoned; (3) as both proposals involved extending the superficial area of deposit they involved a material change of use by virtue of T.C.P.A. 1971, s.22(3)(*b*); (4) T.C.P.A. 1971, s.23(3)(*b*) did not apply since its object was to protect an occasional use rather than one which existed continuously as part of a mixed use; (5) thus because of intensification and s.22(3)(*b*) planning permission was required for each proposal and the Council had no power to issue a disposal license by reason of s.5(2) of C.P.A. 1974: HEREFORD AND WORCESTER COUNTY COUNCIL AND NEWBOULD (Ref: LW/APP/HE/202) (1986) 1 P.A.D. 281.

TRADE AND INDUSTRY

3391. British Shipbuilders (Borrowing Powers) Act 1986 (c.19)

This Act increases the limit imposed by s.11 of the Aircraft and Shipbuilding Industries Act 1977 in relation to the finances of British Shipbuilders and its wholly owned subsidiaries.

The Act received the Royal Assent on June 26, 1986. It extends to Northern Ireland.

3392. Co-operative Development Agency and Industrial Development Act 1984—commencement

CO-OPERATIVE DEVELOPMENT AGENCY AND INDUSTRIAL DEVELOPMENT ACT (COMMENCEMENT) (AMENDMENT) ORDER 1986 (No. 128 (c.6)) [80p], made under the Co-operative Development Agency and Industrial Development Act 1984 (c.57), s.7(1)(*b*)(2)(3)(5); amends S.I. 1984 No. 1845.

3393. Industrial development

APPLE AND PEAR DEVELOPMENT COUNCIL ORDER 1986 (No. 1372) [£2·40], made under the Industrial Organisation and Development Act 1947 (c.40), s.8(1); operative on August 5, 1986; continues in being the development council with certain changes in its organisation.

CUTLERY AND STAINLESS STEEL FLATWARE INDUSTRY (SCIENTIFIC RESEARCH LEVY) (ABOLITION) ORDER 1986 (No. 995) [45p], made under the Industrial Organisation and Development Act 1947 (c.40), s.9; operative on June 30, 1986; abolishes the said levy.

3394. Industrial training

S.I. 1986 Nos. 475 (levy—plastics processing) [£1·35];901 (levy—hotel and catering) [£1·40]; 1013 (levy—engineering) [£1·90]; 1477 (clothing and allied products-levy) [£1·40]; 1610 (road transport—levy) [£1·40].

3395. Industrial Training Act 1986 (c.15)

This Act makes provision with respect to the functions of industrial training boards.

It received the Royal Assent on May 20, 1986 and comes into force two months from that date.

3396. Monopolies and mergers—investigation—disclosure of information

The Monopolies and Mergers Commission has a duty to investigate proposed mergers to see whether they are in the public interest. Information given to it by one party to a merger is not strictly confidential, and it can therefore disclose it to the other party if it considers that that disclosure will help its investigations: R. *v.* MONOPOLIES AND MERGERS COMMISSION, *ex p.* ELDERS IXL, *Financial Times*, May 2, 1986, Mann J.

3397. Monopolies and mergers—reference to commission—whether abandonment of merger proposals

[Fair Trading Act 1973 (c.41), s.75.]

It is a question of fact for the Monopolies and Mergers Commission, though not for the chairman alone, whether a merger proposal has been abandoned, or merely amended.

There was a takeover battle between Guiness and Argyll for Distillers. G's bid was referred to the Monopolies and Mergers Commission. This severely handicapped G in that the bid now automatically lapsed. G notified the chairman of the commission that it intended to make a new offer on different terms which it hoped would be acceptable to the Secretary of State. The chairman, acting alone, but with the consent of the Secretary of State decided therefore not to proceed with this reference on the ground that the proposal was the same one, but merely varied. A sought judicial review. The application was refused. *Held*, dismissing A's appeal, that (1) whether or not the merger proposal had been abandoned, or merely amended was a question of fact for the commission; (2) the chairman had no power to act on behalf of the commission; however, since the investigating group would have reached the same decision, and the Secretary of State had consented, the relief sought would be refused.

R. *v.* MONOPOLIES AND MERGERS COMMISSION, *ex p.* ARGYLL GROUP [1986] 2 All E.R. 257, C.A.

3398. Monopolies commission—hearing of reference—procedure

[Fair Trading Act 1973 (c.41), pt.5.] The court will not interfere with the Commission's procedure in order to force it to disclose each piece of evidence to all parties to an enquiry: R. *v.* MONOPOLIES AND MERGERS COMMISSION, *ex p.* MATTHEW BROWN, *The Times,* July 18, 1986, Macpherson J.

3399. Restraint of trade—doctor—partnership agreement

[National Health Service Act 1977 (c.49), Sched. 10, para. 2(2)(*a*).]

A covenant restraining the outgoing partner from practising medicine within a certain area is not void as contrary to public policy or para. 2(2) of Sched. 10 to the National Health Service Act 1977.

The three plaintiffs, partners in a National Health Service medical partnership served notice on D requiring him to leave the partnership within 12 months. D set up in practice a few doors away. P invoked a covenant in the partnership agreement barring practice within two miles for two years. D contended that the covenant was void for public policy, alternatively that such a covenant came within para. 2 of Sched. 10 to the National Health Services Act 1977 which provided that if any valuable consideration other than the performance of services in the partnership were given by a partner as consideration for being taken into partnership, there should be deemed to be a sale of the goodwill of the practice. *Held,* that (1) such a covenant was not inconsistent with the National Health Services scheme, and (2) there was no "valuable consideration" within para. 2 (*Hensman* v. *Traill* [1980] C.L.Y. 370 overruled; dicta of Evershed M.R. in *Whitehill* v. *Bradford* [1952] C.L.Y. 2271 applied).

KERR *v.* MORRIS [1986] 3 W.L.R. 662, C.A.

3400. Restrictive practices—public interest—licences—cars—spare parts

The Monopolies and Mergers Commission decided that Ford in refusing to grant licences to independent manufacturers to make replacement body parts was anti-competitive. Competition in this area was in the public interest. If the monopoly were broken the prices of spare body parts would be likely to decrease. The quantum of appropriate royalty was a vexed question which could only be resolved by changes in the law to reduce the period of protection to five years: FORD MOTOR CO.'S REPLACEMENT BODY PARTS POLICY, *Re* [1986] F.S.R. 147, U.K. Monopolies and Mergers Commission.

3401. Restrictive practices—Royal Charter

[Restrictive Trade Practices Act 1976 (c.34), ss.11(1), 16.]

The Charter of the Royal Institute of Chartered Surveyors is subject to the Restrictive Trade Practices Act 1976. It is not excluded by virtue of being a Royal Charter.

The Royal Institute of Chartered Surveyors was incorporated by Royal Charter in 1881, followed by a number of supplemental charters. The question arose whether on such supplemental charter, bye-laws and regulations constituted a registrable agreement or arrangement under s.1(1) of the Restrictive Trade Practices Act 1976. *Held,* that the institution was not only a corporation sole but also a creature of its members who had agreed to be bound by the Charter, bye-laws and regulations, and there was therefore an "agreement" under s.43(1) of the Act. The fact that the Institution was created by Royal Charter did not exempt it from being subject to the Act (*British Basic Slag* v. *Registrar of Restrictive Trading Agreements* [1963] C.L.Y. 3475 and *Fisher* v. *Director General of Fair Trading* [1982] C.L.Y. 3237 C.A. applied).

ROYAL INSTITUTION OF CHARTERED SURVEYORS' APPLICATION, *Re.* ROYAL INSTITUTION OF CHARTERED SURVEYORS *v.* DIRECTOR GENERAL OF FAIR TRADING [1986] I.C.R. 551, C.A.

3402. Restrictive practices—undertaking to court—agreement to 'like effect'—whether contempt

[Restrictive Trade Practices Act 1976 (c.34), s.2(2)(*b*).]

Where the Director General of Fair Trading seeks writs of sequestration for contempt of undertakings, the onus is on him to prove the new restrictions are of "like effect".

In 1966 four leading newspaper publishers agreed fixed discounts to wholesalers. The court declared the agreements were contrary to public policy, and undertakings were given not to enter into any agreement containing restrictions to "like effect." In

1982, on the brink of a rail strike, the publishers agreed to increase the previous separately agreed discounts by a uniform amount. The agreement never came into force. *Held,* on an application by the Director General of Fair Trading on the grounds that the publishers were in contempt, refusing the application, that the Director had not discharged the onus of proving that the restrictions in the 1982 agreement were to the "like effect."

NATIONAL DAILY AND SUNDAY NEWSPAPERS PROPRIETORS' AGREEMENT, *Re* [1986] I.C.R. 44, Restrictive Practices Ct.

3403. Restrictive trade practices

RESTRICTIVE TRADE PRACTICES (APPROVAL OF STANDARDS AND ARRANGEMENTS) (AMENDMENT) ORDER 1986 (No. 614) [45p], made under the Restrictive Trade Practices Act 1976 (c.34), ss.9(5), 42(2); operative on April 1, 1986; provides that terms in an agreement relating to standards of dimension, design, quality and performance or arrangements as to the provision of information or advice to purchasers, consumers or users are to be disregarded in deciding whether the 1976 Act applies to the agreement.

RESTRICTIVE TRADE PRACTICES (SERVICES) (AMENDMENT) ORDER 1986 (No. 2204) [45p], made under the Restrictive Trade Practices Act 1976 (c.34), s.15(2); operative on January 1, 1987; ends the restriction contained in S.I. 1976 No. 98 for certain agreements entered into by building societies.

3404. Unit trusts

A consultative document about the way Unit Trust schemes are authorised and regulated has been published by the Department of Trade and Industry. Comments on all aspects of the proposals should be sent by September 30, 1986 to: Mr. J. Clarke, DTI, Room 522, 10–18 Victoria Street, London SW1H 0NN. The consultative document is available from H.M.S.O. [£9·85].

TRADE MARKS AND TRADE NAMES

3405. Application

TRADE MARKS AND SERVICE MARKS (RELEVANT COUNTRIES) ORDER 1986 (No. 1303) [80p], made under the Trade Marks Act 1938 (c.22), s.39A(7); operative on October 1, 1986; specifies the countries in which an application for the registration of a trade or service mark will give priority in respect of an application made in the U.K. within the following six months.

3406. Application—distinctiveness

[Trade Marks Act 1938 (c.22), ss.9, 10, 17, 43; Trade Marks Rules 1938, rr.33–35.] Objection was made to applications to register marks "Always" in classes 3, 5 and 21 since the word was not distinctive.

The applicants appealed against the refusal to register in part B. *Held,* that it was wrong to register a general word used in trade: ALWAYS TRADE MARK [1986] R.P.C. 93, Falconer J.

3407. Application—distinctiveness—letter mark

[Trade Marks Act 1938 (c.22), ss.9, 10.] Application was to register a stylised form of the letters G.I. for metal goods. A appealed the refusal to register arguing that the stylised form suggested a coil of wire or metal. *Held,* that the mark did not have sufficient visual distinctiveness to qualify for registration as an unused mark: GI TRADE MARK [1986] R.P.C. 100, Board of Trade.

3408. Application—word and device

[Trade Marks Act 1938 (c.22), ss.9, 10, 17, 53; Trade Marks Rules 1983, r.131.] Application was to register a device and mark and "Telecheck". The composite mark was refused by the Registrar on the ground that the word was descriptive. On appeal, the applicants offered to disclaim the word although they had not offered this in their statement of case. *Held,* that it was not open to the appellants to offer a disclaimer if it had not been mentioned in their statement of case.

TELECHECK TRADE MARK [1986] R.P.C. 77, Board of Trade.

3409. Fees

TRADE MARKS AND SERVICE MARKS (FEES) RULES 1986 (No. 1447) [£1·40], made under the Trade Marks Act 1938 (c.22), ss.40, 41; operative on October 1, 1986; replace the provision for fees in S.I. 1986 No. 691.

TRADE MARKS (FEES) RULES 1986 (No. 691) [£1·40], made under the Trade Marks Act 1938 (c.22), ss.40, 41; rules 1(1), 2 and 4 operative on May 12, 1986 and rules 1(2)(3) and 3 operative on May 26, 1986; replaces the provision for fees contained in S.R. & O. 1938 No. 661 with self-contained provision.

3410. Forms

TRADE MARKS AND SERVICE MARKS (FORMS) RULES 1986 (No. 1367) [£6·50], made under the Trade Marks Act 1938 (c.22), s.40; operative on October 1, 1986; replace S.R. & O. 1938 No. 661 and prescribe new forms.

3411. Hallmarks

HALLMARKING (APPROVED HALLMARKS) REGULATIONS 1986 (No. 1757) [45p], made under the Hallmarking Act 1973 (c.43), ss.4(7), 21(1); operative on November 10, 1986; amend the 1973 Act, s.4 and Sched. 2 in relation to the conditions under which articles of precious metals may be struck with approved hallmarks.

HALLMARKING (EXEMPTED ARTICLES) ORDER 1986 (No. 1758) [45p], made under the Hallmarking Act 1973 (c.43), Sched. 1, Pt. IV, para. 1(1)(b); operative on November 10, 1986 save for Art. 2(c) which is operative on May 11, 1987; varies Sched. 1 to the 1973 Act in relation to the solder used in certain exempt articles.

3412. Infringement—computer programs and video games

[Fra.] The Court held that computer programs and video games were not intellectual works and did not come within the penal provisions of the Copyright Act 1957, that the Patents (Amendment) Act 1978 had abolished penal sanctions for infringement of patent and only an action for breach of competition law existed. Bad faith is presumed in matters of trade mark infringement. The convictions of D were quashed: ATARI IRELAND v. VALADON (ALAIN) AND TARAYRE CLAUDE GUILLEMIN [1986] F.S.R. 1., Cour d'Appel Paris.

3413. Infringement—discovery—use of documents for foreign proceedings. See BAYER A.G. v. WINTER, § 2647.

3414. Infringement—discovery of names of suppliers—privilege against self-incrimination

[Supreme Court Act 1981 (c.54), s.72] P sought discovery of the names and addresses of suppliers of allegedly infringing goods. D invoked the privilege against self-incrimination and submitted that it would impinge on D's right to silence in the pending criminal proceedings for conspiracy to defraud P. *Held,* that (1) the Supreme Court Act 1981, s. 72 applied where criminal proceedings had been commenced as well as where proceedings were likely; (2) it was not enough to show that the required disclosure was a disadvantage to D, unless there was a likelihood of injustice to D in addition. Discovery ordered (*Rank Film* v. *Video Information Centre* [1981] C.L.Y. 2148 considered; *Jefferson* v. *Bhetcha* [1979] C.L.Y. 2184 applied): CHARLES OF THE RITZ GROUP v. JORY [1986] F.S.R. 14, Scott J.

3415. Infringement—passing off—confusion

[Trade Marks Act 1938 (c.22), s.4.]
D produced OXBRIDGE marmalade. P2 was registered user of OXFORD marmalade and sought interlocutory relief alleging infringement and passing off. *Held,* that the injunction would be granted. Despite lack of similarity of get-up there was a clear risk of confusion especially since many purchasers were foreign: CPC (UNITED KINGDOM) v. KEENAN [1986] F.S.R. 527, Peter Gibson J.

3416. Infringement—summary judgment—whether frivolous counterclaim

[Trade Marks Act 1938 (c.22), ss.5, 26 R.S.C., Ord, 14.] P were proprietors of registered trade mark TOPAZ for wines, spirits, liqueurs and cocktails. D marketed a cocktail TOPAZ, and were sued by P. D defended on the ground of P's non-user and counterclaimed for rectification. D applied for summary judgment. *Held,* that (1) P must show that there is no triable issue on either defence or counterclaim; (2) since the counterclaim was not frivolous D should have leave to defend and pursue the counterclaim: WILLIAMS & HUMBERT v. INTERNATIONAL DISTILLERS AND VINTNERS [1986] F.S.R. 150, Whitford J.

3417. Infringement—unfair competition

[Ger.] [EEC Treaty. Arts. 30 and 36 Export Promotion Act 1959 (Ireland) Trade Mark Act (Germany) Arts. 15, 25, 31.] P registered in Germany a shamrock mark and "Kleeblatt" (clover) in respect of foods. D set up in Ireland to promote the export of Irish goods. They used the shamrock as their sign. They participated in fairs and exhibitions in Germany. P alleged infringement of trade mark and unfair competition. D appealed against the order granted. *Held,* that (1) the court should consider the extrinsic evidence that confusion would not occur; (2) in this case although the marks were the same the Irish goods were clearly indicated as originating from the Republic of Ireland; (3) it was not essential that the mark be registered since the D had a protectable interest in its mark: SHAMROCK TRADE MARK [1986] F.S.R. 271, Fed.Sup.Ct., Germany.

3418. Passing off—family name—circus—confusion
[S.A.] P had since 1963 run the Boswell-Wilkie circus, which was well known in South Africa. D formed "Brian Boswell's Circus." P obtained an interdict. D appealed. *Held,* that where a name had acquired a particular meaning it was incumbent upon another using the same name to ensure that the public is not confused. Reasonable steps are not enough: BOSWELL-WILKIE CIRCUS (PTY) *v.* BRIAN BOSWELL [1986] F.S.R. 479, Supreme Court of S. Africa, appellate division.

3419. Passing off—get-up—cigarette papers—market monopoly
P manufactured cigarette papers in packets of three colours named RIZLA. D were a match manufacturer and intended to launch cigarette papers called SWAN. P sought interlocutory relief, alleging passing off. *Held,* that D's packaging was sufficiently different to avoid confusion. P could not have a monopoly in particular colours. The fact that P had hitherto had a virtual monopoly of the market did not entitle them to complain when competition arose: RIZLA *v.* BRYANT & MAY [1986] R.P.C. 389, Walton J.

3420. Passing off—infringement of trade mark—breach of contract
D operated the fine art department at Harrods for 15 years, under a series of contracts. Harrods sought an injunction restraining D from advertising this fact when D was setting up his own showroom. *Held,* that D had committed no infringement of trade mark, nor passing off. D was, however, in breach of the contractual clause "not to advertise or indicate its association with Harrods or to use Harrods' name directly or by inference in its advertising . . .": HARRODS *v.* SCHWARTZ-SACKIN & Co. [1986] F.S.R. 490, Warner J.

3421. Passing off—trade libel—malicious falsehood
D advertised its "whopper" hamburger on cards saying "It's Not Just Big, Mac" continuing "Unlike some burgers, it's 100 per cent. pure beef, flame grilled never fried, with a unique choice of toppings." P argued that persons seeing the advertisement would think that they could get a "Big Mac" at D's establishment. P's goodwill would be diluted. P further alleged trade libel and malicious falsehood of P's hamburgers. *Held,* that (1) the public would think that the burger was an improved version of the "Big Mac," obtainable at D's premises. An injunction was granted restraining passing off; (2) readers of the advertisement would not reach the conclusion which P alleged, *i.e.* that the advertisement was libellous of P's goods. No case had been made out by P in this claim; (3) advertisements are not to be read like a will or contract, but broadly: McDONALD'S HAMBURGERS *v.* BURGERKING (U.K.) [1986] F.S.R. 45, Whitford J.

3422. Patents, Designs and Marks Act 1986 (c.39)
This Act amends the enactments relating to the registers of trade marks, designs and patents so as to enable them to be kept otherwise than in documentary form and so as to give the enactments due effect in relation to any portion of a register not kept in documentary form; amends the Trade Marks Act 1938 in relation to the use of the Royal Arms and other devices, emblems and titles and in relation to the protection of trade marks and service marks for whose protection application has been made overseas; and makes various amendments to the 1938 Act and other Acts in its application to service marks.
The Act received the Royal Assent on July 18, 1986.

3423. Patents, Designs and Marks Act 1986—commencement
PATENTS, DESIGNS AND MARKS ACT 1986 (COMMENCEMENT NO. 1) ORDER 1986 (No. 1274 (c.41)) [45p], made under the Patents, Designs and Marks Act 1986 (c.39), s.4(6); brings into force on October 1, 1986 sections 1, 3(1) (in part), Scheds. 1, paras. 1 and 2, 3, Pt. I (in part).

3424. Registration—goods associated with provision of service

[Trade Marks Act 1938 (c.22), s.68.] A life insurance company applied to register three marks for a wide range of goods in class 16. Objection was taken that the mark was not a trade mark within the Act. The applicants did not trade in goods and desired to put the mark on their insurance policy documents. *Held*, that the mark would not be a trade mark, since the goods were ancillary to the applicants' services: A.D.D.-70 TRADE MARK [1986] R.P.C. 89, Trade Marks Registry.

3425. Registration—letter mark—whether capable of distinguishing

[Trade Marks Act 1938 (c.22), ss.9, 10, 17, 53 Trade Marks Rules 1938, ss.129–133.]

A sought registration of the mark VEW with a semicircle. The registrar held that the mark lacked inherent distinctiveness. The applicants appealed to the Secretary of State for Trade. *Held*, that (1) although the appeal was not in proper form because of A's failure to state the grounds of appeal fully and state the case in documents accompanying the notice of appeal, the appeal would be considered; (2) whether a mark of three letters was an invented word was a question of fact. In this case there was no evidence that it was a word. Appeal dismissed: VEW TRADE MARK [1986] R.P.C. 82, Board of Trade.

3426. Service marks

TRADE MARKS AND SERVICE MARKS (RELEVANT COUNTRIES) (AMENDMENT) ORDER 1986 (No. 1890) [45p], made under the Trade Marks Act 1938 (c.22), s.39A(7); operative on November 14, 1986; specifies countries in which an application for the registration of a service mark will be given priority in respect of an application in the U.K. within the following six months.

TRADE MARKS AND SERVICE MARKS (RELEVANT COUNTRIES) (AMENDMENT No. 2) ORDER 1986 (No. 2236) [45p], made under the Trade Marks Act 1938 (c.22), s.39A(7); operative on January 27, 1987; lists Mexico as one those countries in which application for a service mark will be given priority following an application in the U.K.

TRADE MARKS AND SERVICE MARKS RULES 1986 (No. 1319) [£4·90], made under the Trade Marks Act 1938 (c.22), ss.36, 40 and 40A; operative on October 1, 1986; replace S.R. & O. 1938 No. 661 and apply the rules to service marks.

3427. Trade mark—bottle—whether registrable

[Trade Marks Act 1938 (c.22).]

A container or bottle cannot be registered as a trade mark.

Coca Cola had been sold in its distinctive bottle in the U.K. since the 1920s. The bottle's design was registered under the Patents and Designs Act 1907, but that registration expired in 1940. No protection was available under the Patents Act 1977 and the Copyright Act 1956, since the Coca Cola bottle was neither a novel product nor an artistic work. The Coca Cola Co. sought to register their bottle as a trade mark under the Trade Marks Act 1938. The registrar refused the application. His refusal was upheld by the High Court and the Court of Appeal. *Held*, dismissing the appeal to the House of Lords, that the function of the Act was to protect the mark, not the article marked, and the application had been properly refused (*Smith Kline and French Laboratories* v. *Sterling-Winthrop* [1975] C.L.Y. 3434 distinguished).

COCA-COLA CO.'S APPLICATIONS, *Re* [1986] 2 All E.R. 274, H.L.

3428. Trade Marks (Amendment) Act 1984—commencement

TRADE MARKS (AMENDMENT) ACT 1984 (COMMENCEMENT) ORDER 1986 (No. 1273 (c.40)) [45p], made under the Trade Marks (Amendment) Act 1984 (c.19), s.2(2); brings the 1984 Act into force on October 1, 1986.

TRADE UNIONS

3429. Action, short of dismissal—time limit for complaint—whether action continuing

[Employment Protection (Consolidation) Act 1978 (c.44), ss.23, 24(2).]

For the purposes of the time-limit under s.24(2) of the Employment Protection (Consolidation) Act 1978, an agreement as to pay may amount to the "action" on the day it first takes effect, and subsequent payments based upon it may not amount to a "series of similar actions" such as will extend the time limit.

Four cleaners at a college were members of the union; three were not. The union negotiated an agreement on pay and conditions on behalf of the four, to take effect on July 1, 1983. Subsequently, the three seemed to be doing rather better, so the four complained that they were being penalised for being members of a trade union. Their complaint was presented after September 30, 1983, *i.e.* outside the time limit. The industrial tribunal held that it had no jurisdiction to hear the complaint. *Held,* dismissing the appeal, that the tribunal were entitled to find that the continuing payments were a continuation of an action which took place on July 1, 1983, as opposed to a series of similar actions, and that therefore it had no jurisdiction.

ADLAM *v.* SALISBURY AND WELLS THEOLOGICAL COLLEGE [1985] I.C.R. 786, E.A.T.

3430. Certification officer

CERTIFICATION OFFICER (AMENDMENT OF FEES) REGULATIONS 1986 (No. 302) [40p], made under the Trade Union (Amalgamations, etc.) Act 1964 (c.24), s.7, the Trade Union and Labour Relations Act 1974 (c.52), s.8(4) and the Employment Protection Act 1975 (c.71), s.8(2); operative on April 1, 1986; increase specified fees.

3431. Collective agreement—binding in honour only—whether enforceable. See MARLEY *v.* FORWARD TRUST GROUP, § 1173.

3432. Constructive expulsion—resignation

[Employment Act 1980 (c.42), s.4(2)(*b*)] The Court was unable to find that a lorry driver who had resigned from his union following disputes with it could properly be held, on the natural meaning of the word, to have been "expelled" from it: McGHEE *v.* TRANSPORT AND GENERAL WORKERS UNION, (1985) 82 L.S.Gaz 3696. C.A.

3433. Consultation—new union—duty of employer

[Coal Industry Nationalisation Act 1946 (c.59), s.46; Trade Union and Labour Relations Act 1974 (c.52), s.18.] The NCB is under a duty to consult the Union of Democratic Mineworkers and the NUM in arranging a conciliation agreement; the National Reference Tribunal (NRT) no longer exists having been unilaterally ended by the NCB; and the NRT Scheme had at no time been legally binding on the parties thereto: NATIONAL COAL BOARD *v.* NATIONAL UNION OF MINEWORKERS, *The Times,* June 21, 1986, Scott J.

3434. Contempt of court—sequestration—whether funds held by a branch are the property of the union

[Trade Union and Labour Relations Act 1974 (c.52), ss.2(1)(*b*), 14.] SOGAT was found to be in contempt of Court and a writ of sequestration was issued directing Commissioners to take control of all of its property. In giving directions the High Court held that branch and chapel funds were subject to sequestration as property of the union. The union appealed to the Court of Appeal. *Held,* that the appeal would be allowed. The dispute related solely to that part of weekly contributions which represented a contribution to local funds. The judge at first instance had accepted that a branch could not, as a matter of law, own property. A proper consideration of the rules of the union made it clear that that was not the case. There were trustees of union branches and rules which regulated their powers. On a proper interpretation of those rules the beneficial ownership of the contested funds was that of the branch members. Such an arrangement was not a trust void for perpetuity because in the event of dissolution, the members of the branch would be entitled to the assets. The vesting of the branch assets in the branch trustees did not alter this analysis. There was no contrary evidence that the funds in dispute belonged to the branch the purposes of which were similar to, but did not include, all of the purposes of the union and most of them were limited in terms to expenditure on the branch or for the benefit of the members of the branch (*Neville Estates* v. *Madden* [1961] C.L.Y. 1002, followed): NEWS GROUP NEWSPAPERS *v.* SOCIETY OF GRAPHICAL AND ALLIED TRADES 1982 [1986] I.R.L.R. 227, C.A.

3435. Contempt—union immunity—whether an action for contempt of court is an action in tort.

[Employment Act 1982 (c.46), s.15(2).]

Contempt proceedings are not an action in tort even though they may arise out of an action in tort, and s.15(2) of the Employment Act 1982 has no application.

The NGA were in dispute with various newspapers. In the course of that dispute the newspapers obtained interlocutory injunctions against the NGA. In subsequent proceedings in the High Court it was found that the NGA had acted in flagrant breach of those interlocutory injunctions and had put down on paper resolutions which complied with the law whilst making it perfectly clear to its members its support for those acts of contempt. The NGA were held liable for those breaches of injunction committed by its officials and fined £15,000. The NGA appealed to the Court of Appeal arguing that it could rely on its immunity from an action for tort under s.15 of the Employment Act 1982 in relation to acts not authorised or endorsed by a responsible person. *Held,* dismissing the appeal, that the sole question before the court was whether the alleged contemnor had done the prohibited acts. Such proceedings were not an action in tort, even though they might arise out of an action in tort, and s.15(2) had no application.

EXPRESS AND STAR *v.* NATIONAL GRAPHICAL ASSOCIATION (1982) [1986] I.C.R. 589, C.A.

3436. Funds—disposition of funds—union seceding from federation of merged unions
[Trade Union and Labour Relations Act 1974 (c.52), s.2(1)(*b*).]
Although the court can help in making sense out of the obscure union rules, it cannot infer rules which do not exist.

In 1972 an amalgamated union and a national union agreed to merge to form the defendant union, D. In 1983 the plaintiff union, P wished to secede from D and take with it an equitable proportion of D's funds. D's rules made no provision for the payment out of assets to seceding constituent unions, and because of its size P could not change the rules. *Held,* dismissing P's application, that there was no provision in the rules for removal of assets on secession and since by s.2(1)(*b*) of the 1974 Act D's trustees held its funds and assets in trust for the union, it would be an unjustified intervention if the court made an order forcing the trustees to pay out funds to a seceding group (*Keys v. Boulter (No. 2), Williamson v. Bennett* [1972] C.L.Y. 3468 and *British Actors' Equity Association v. Goring* [1978] C.L.Y. 3003 distinguished).

BURNLEY NELSON ROSSENDALE AND DISTRICT TEXTILE WORKERS' UNION *v.* AMALGAMATED TEXTILE WORKERS'S UNION [1986] 1 All E.R. 885, Tudor Price J.

3437. Industrial action—ballot
[Trade Union Act 1984 (c.49), s.10(1) and (3).] Where a union has balloted its members to obtain sanction for industrial action, it does not need a further ballot to resume that action which it had suspended to the purposes of negotiation: MONSANTO *v.* TRANSPORT AND GENERAL WORKERS UNION, *The Times,* July 16, 1986, C.A.

3438. Injunction—picketing place of work
[Trade Union and Labour Relations Act 1974 (c.52), s.15.] The statutory protection did not apply to a person who, although formerly employed by a company at one place of work picketed another establishment owned by the employer, but after he had lost his job, and such establishment had never been his place of work (*Att.-Gen. v. P.Y.A. Quarries* [1957] C.L.Y. 2579, *Thomas v. NUM (South Wales)* [1985] C.L.Y. 3526 considered): NEWS GROUP NEWSPAPERS *v.* SOGAT 1982, *The Times,* August 1, 1986, Stuart-Smith J.

3439. Membership—deterrence—different rates of pay
[Employment Protection (Consolidation) Act 1978 (c.44), s.23(1)(*a*).] S.23(1)(*a*) of the Employment Protection (Consolidation) Act 1978 protects employees from action short of dismissal designed to deter them from being members of "an independent trade union". X employed members of two unions, and paid members of union Y more than those of union Z. It was found as a fact that this was to penalise union Z, which claimed that such action was outlawed by the subsection. *Held,* that the subsection was not directed towards inter-union disputes. The words "an independent trade union" mean "any union at all", and not "a specified union": X's action was not penalising union membership *per se,* but membership of union Z. Furthermore, the action taken against the members of Z was not taken against them as individuals, but as members of Z. Their claim therefore failed. The subsection as a whole covers inaction as well as action: NATIONAL COAL BOARD *v.* RIDGEWAY, *The Times,* August 14, 1986, E.A.T.

3440. Membership—exclusion—assessment of compensation as a remedy by the Employment Appeal Tribunal
[Employment Act 1980 (c.42), ss.5(2), 5(6).] S resigned from her membership of a Trade Union after an altercation with the union's district secretary following her action in passing a picket line during an unofficial strike. S applied to be readmitted to the union and her application was rejected. She exercised a right of appeal to the union's Executive Council in London but did not attend the hearing on the ground

that her expenses would not be recoverable and because she had no representation. Her appeal for readmission to membership was rejected. S applied to an Industrial Tribunal who found that the refusal of readmission to membership on the part of the union was unreasonable. The union maintained the refusal to readmit to membership and compensation fell to be assessed by the Appeal Tribunal under s.5(2) of the 1980 Act. *Held,* that compensation was assessed at £11,947. The Employment Appeal Tribunal confirmed that it had power to reduce the amount of compensation if it found that the refusal or expulsion was to an extent caused or contributed to by any action of the applicant. Such discretion was to be exercised most sparingly and only in the most exceptional cases. In this case having heard S cross-examined, it was clear that S had not caused or contributed to her dismissal by reason of provocation. However S should have attended the appeal meeting in London. The cost of a day return ticket would not have been beyond her and although it was not the cause of the union's refusal to readmit her to membership, it did to some extent contribute to that refusal. The appropriate percentage to attribute to that contribution was 20 per cent. and the award was abated accordingly. SAUNDERS *v.* BAKERS FOOD AND ALLIED WORKERS' UNION [1986] I.R.L.R. 16, E.A.T.

3441. Membership—exclusion—compensation
[Employment Act 1980 (c.42), ss.4, 5.]
A complainant's failure to pay union dues leading to expulsion from the union is not capable of being conduct which contributed to the union's refusal of reinstatement so as to justify making a reduction in compensation.
E was dismissed. He let his union dues fall into abeyance and was expelled. He was refused reinstatement until an industrial tribunal gave a declaration that he was entitled to be a member. E applied for compensation under s.5(1) of the Employment Act 1980. *Held,* that compensation (1) was payable for injury to E's feelings; (2) would be reduced for failure to inform the union when he had been offered a job, and also to reflect the poor prospects of employment in that type of work generally; but (3) his failure to pay union dues was not capable of being conduct which contributed to the union's refusal of reinstatement so as to justify making any reduction in compensation. (*Howard* v. *National Graphical Association*) [1985] C.L.Y. 3522 E.A.T. considered).
DAY *v.* SOCIETY OF GRAPHICAL AND ALLIED TRADES 1982 [1986] I.C.R. 640, E.A.T.

3442. Membership—severance pay—surrender of membership—reapplication—refusal—whether unreasonable
[Employment Act 1980 (c.42), s.4.]
The word "employment" in s.4(1) of the Employment Act 1980 is to be construed widely as meaning employment in a particular field of industry, rather than narrowly as referring to a specific job.
Between 1961–1976 the applicant was a member of a union in the printing industry. In 1976 he took voluntary redundancy, accepted severance pay, and ceased to be a member; in accordance with union rules he signed an undertaking not to seek employment in the printing industry. In 1979, unable to find work, he applied to rejoin the union. His application was refused and he complained to an industrial tribunal, which dismissed his complaint. *Held,* allowing the appeal, that "employment" in s.4(1) of the 1980 Act meant employment in a particular field of industry rather than a specific job.
CLARK *v.* SOCIETY OF GRAPHICAL AND ALLIED TRADES 1982 [1986] I.C.R. 12, E.A.T.

3443. Threatened strike—injunction to prevent strike—cause of action
[Trade Union and Labour Relations Act 1974 (c.52), s.13.] A group of abbatoir proprietors sought to prevent the union calling a series of threatened one day strikes. They sought to rely on the tort of interference with trade or business, or the tort of interference with contract. *Held,* that (1) the first tort required (a) the necessary interference, (b) by unlawful means and (c) that there should be an intention to injure P. As to the unlawful means P relied upon inducement of a breach of statutory duty or the breach of each contract of employment by each employee. The evidence showed no arguable case of a breach of statutory duty, and no arguable case that the predominant purpose of the proposed strikes was to injure P; (2) the second tort relied upon the same unlawful means as the first. Therefore no injunction would be granted since there was no arguable case to go to trial; (3) a third tort

relied upon by P, inducement of breach of statutory duty, failed *in limine* since there was no arguable case of such breach of duty (*Merkur Island Shipping Corp.* v. *Laughton* [1983] C.L.Y. 3704, *Meade* v. *Haringey London Borough Council* [1979] C.L.Y. 816 considered): BARRETTS & BAIRD (WHOLESALE) *v.* INSTITUTION OF PROFESSIONAL CIVIL SERVANTS, *Financial Times,* November 26, 1986, Henry J.

3444. Trade union rules—extent to which court will intervene in their application

H was the candidate who lost an election for a full-time post in the Boilermakers Union. He objected to the outcome of the election based on a breach of the union's own rules. H lodged objections to the outcome of the election but his opponent was declared elected. H applied to the Chancery Division and in the course of the proceedings sought leave to amend his statement of claim which sought to set aside the election. The union applied to strike out the statement of claim on the basis that it did not raise a cause of action. *Held,* that the statement of claim should be struck out for the following reasons: (1) it was not the function of the court to act as an appellate jurisdiction upon the decision of the members of a club or union. All a court was required to consider was that the rules of the organisation had been followed. In this case there was no allegation that the internal appeal open to H had not been followed; (2) on a construction of the rules, the union had a requirement to consider complaints about electoral irregularities and this appeared to have been done; (3) there was no breach of natural justice which arose by the fact that four members of the executive council sat upon the general council which heard an internal appeal. There was no rule of natural justice that a member of a body which had sat at first instance was thereby disabled from sitting upon an appeal. The action was dismissed with an order for costs. Leave to appeal was refused. (*Dawkins* v. *Antrobus* (1881) 17 Ch. 615, followed): HAMLET *v.* GENERAL MUNICIPAL BOILERMAKERS AND ALLIED TRADES UNION [1986] I.R.L.R. 293, Harman J.

TRANSPORT

3445. Community bus

COMMUNITY BUS REGULATIONS 1986 (No. 1245) [80p], made under the Public Passenger Vehicles Act 1981 (c.14), ss.52(1) and 60(1) and the Transport Act 1985 (c.67), s.23(2)(*b*) and (8); operative on August 11, 1986; provide for vehicles used under a community bus permit.

3446. Fixed penalties

FIXED PENALTY (INCREASE) ORDER 1986 (No. 1327) [45p], made under the Transport Act 1982 (c.49), s.29(5); operative on October 1, 1986; increases fixed penalties under Pt. III of the 1982 Act.

FIXED PENALTY (PROCEDURE) REGULATIONS 1986 (No. 1330) [£1·40], made under the Transport Act 1982, ss.49(1) and 73(5); operative on October 1, 1986; provide for the procedure to be followed under the new system of fixed penalties which relates to moving traffic offences.

3447. Inquiry—validity

As the purpose of a transport inquiry is to put before the Minister enough information to enable him to make a properly informed decision, the fact that the inspector's report fails to comment on government policy does not render it invalid: R. *v.* SECRETARY OF STATE FOR TRANSPORT, *ex p.* GWENT COUNTY COUNCIL, *The Times,* November 1, 1986, C.A.

3448. London regional transport. See LONDON, § 2062.

3449. Public passenger transport

PUBLIC PASSENGER TRANSPORT POLICIES (ANTICIPATORY EXERCISE OF POWERS) ORDER 1986 (No. 81) [40p], made under the Local Government Act 1985 (c.51), s.101; operative on February 13, 1986; enables the metropolitan county passenger transport authorities established under the 1985 Act to take specified steps which are required to be taken as a preliminary to the exercise of the powers necessary to perform the duties imposed by s.9A(1) and (7) of the Transport Act 1968.

3450. Public passenger vehicles

LOCAL SERVICES (OPERATION BY TAXIS) (LONDON) REGULATIONS 1986 (No. 566) [80p], made under the Transport Act 1985 (c.67), s.12(9) and (10); operative on April 16, 1986; contain provisions relating to the use of taxis to provide local services.

LOCAL SERVICES (OPERATION BY TAXIS) REGULATIONS 1986 (No. 567) [80p], made under the Transport Act 1985, s.12(9) and (10); operative on April 16, 1986; contain provisions relating to the use of taxis to provide local services.

3451. Public service vehicles

OPERATION OF PUBLIC SERVICE VEHICLES (PARTNERSHIP) REGULATIONS 1986 (No. 1628) [£1·40], made under the Public Passenger Vehicles Act 1981 (c.14), ss.58, 61(2); operative on October 26, 1986; replace S.I.1981 No. 259.

PUBLIC SERVICE VEHICLES (DRIVER'S LICENCES) (AMENDMENT) REGULATIONS 1986 (No. 753) [45p], made under the Public Passenger Vehicles Act 1981 (c.14), s.60(1); operative on May 29, 1986; further amend S.I. 1985 No. 214 to extend the time limit for producing a licence to the police from five to seven days.

PUBLIC SERVICE VEHICLES (DRIVERS' LICENCES) (AMENDMENT) (No. 2) REGULATIONS 1986 (No. 869) [45p]; made under the Public Passenger Vehicles Act 1981, ss.52(1)(*b*) and 60(1); operative on July 1, 1986; amend S.I. 1985 No. 214.

PUBLIC SERVICE VEHICLES (DRIVERS' LICENCES) (AMENDMENT) (No. 3) REGULATIONS 1986 (No. 972) [45p], made under the Public Passenger Vehicles Act 1981 (c.14), ss.52(1)(*b*), 60(1); operative on July 1, 1986; corrects an error in S.I. 1986 No. 869.

PUBLIC SERVICE VEHICLES (LONDON LOCAL SERVICE LICENCES) REGULATIONS 1986 (No. 1691) [£1·90], made under the Public Passenger Vehicles Act 1981, ss.5, 52(1), 57(3), 59, 60(1) and the Transport Act 1985 (s.67), s.42(10); operative on October 26, 1986; replace with modifications S.I. 1980 No. 1354.

PUBLIC SERVICE VEHICLES (OPERATORS' LICENCES) REGULATIONS 1986 (No. 1668) [£1·90] made under the Public Passenger Vehicles Act 1981, ss.14a(2), 16(1a)(3)(4), 18(1)(3), 52(1), 57(3), 59, 60(1), 81(1), 82(1) and the Transport Act 1985 (c.67), s.27(1)(3); operative on October 26, 1986; consolidate with certain modifications S.I.1981 No. 258 as amended.

PUBLIC SERVICE VEHICLES (OPERATORS' LICENCES) (AMENDMENT) REGULATIONS 1986 (No. 994) [45p], made under the Public Passenger Vehicles Act 1981, ss.18(3)(*a*), 59; operative on July 10, 1986; amend S.I. 1981 No. 258.

PUBLIC SERVICE VEHICLES (REGISTRATION OF LOCAL SERVICES) REGULATIONS 1986 (No. 1671) [£1·40], made under the Public Passenger Vehicles Act 1981, ss.52(1), 60(1)(*f*) and the Transport Act 1985 (c.67), ss.6(2)(*a*)(3)(*a*)(8)(*a*)(9), 8(6); operative on October 27, 1986; make provision in relation to registration of particulars of local services which is required under the 1985 Act, s.6.

PUBLIC SERVICE VEHICLES (TRAFFIC COMMISSIONERS: PUBLICATION AND INQUIRIES) REGULATIONS 1986 (No. 1629) [80p], made under the Public Passenger Vehicles Act 1981, ss.5(1)(2)(*b*), 54(3)–(6), 56(1), 60(1); operative on October 26, 1986; make provision for the publication of "Notices and Proceedings" by traffic commissioners and for inquiries.

PUBLIC SERVICE VEHICLES (TRAFFIC REGULATION CONDITIONS) REGULATIONS 1986 (No. 1030) [80p], made under the Public Passenger Vehicles Act 1981, ss.5(1), 60, 61(2) and the Transport Act 1985 (c.67), ss.7(6)(9)(11), 9(3); operative on July 14, 1986; make provision in connection with the determination and application of traffic regulation conditions which relate to local services subject to the registration under the 1985 Act.

3452. Public transport

NORTHAMPTON (REVOCATION OF RESTRICTION) ORDER 1986 (No. 1504) [45p], made under the Public Passenger Vehicles Act 1981 (c.14), s.78; revokes the restriction imposed by the Northampton Corporation Act 1922, s.33.

3453. Public transport executives—co-operation requirements

Orders made under the Transport Act 1985 (c.67), s.60(2)(4); all operative on October 25, 1986; provide that on October 26, 1986 the said executives are to cease to be under an obligation to co-operate with the National Bus Company and the Scottish Transport Group in relation to the provision of bus services: S.I. 1986 Nos. 1672 (West Midlands) [80p]; 1673 (West Yorkshire) [80p]; 1674 (Tyne and Wear) [80p]; 1675 (South Yorkshire) [80p]; 1676 (Greater Manchester) [80p]; 1677 (Merseyside) [80p].

3454. Public transport executives operating powers.

Orders made under the Transport Act 1985 s.60(5); all operative on October 26, 1986; provide that on November 4, 1986, the said executives are to cease to have the power to carry passengers by road, and that on October 26, 1988 they are to cease to have the power to let passenger vehicles on hire with or without trailers for the carriage of goods: S.I. 1986 Nos. 1648 (Tyne and Wear) [45p]; 1649 (Greater Manchester) [45p]; 1650 (Merseyside) [45p]; 1651 (South Yorkshire) [45p]; 1652 (West Midlands) [45p]; 1653 (West Yorkshire) [45p].

3455. Road humps—inquiries
ROAD HUMPS (SECRETARY OF STATE) (INQUIRIES PROCEDURE) RULES 1986 (No. 1957) [£1·40], made under the Tribunals and Inquiries Act 1971 (c.62), s.11; operative on December 15, 1986; regulate the procedure to be followed in connection with local inquiries caused by the Secretary of State for Transport to be held under the Highways Act 1980, s.90C(4), in relation to proposals to construct road humps.

3455a. School services
SCHOOL SERVICES (TRANSITIONAL PROVISIONS) REGULATIONS 1986 (No. 1253) [45p], made under the Transport Act 1985 (c.67), Sched. 6, para. 11(1); operative on August 7, 1986; provide for school buses during the transitional period which ends on October 25, 1986.

3456. Tachograph—falsification of records—sentence. See R. *v.* PARKINSON, § 928.

3457. Taxicabs
LICENSED TAXIS (HIRING AT SEPARATE FARES) ORDER 1986 (No. 1386) [80p], made under the Transport Act 1985 (c.67), s.13(1); operative on September 3, 1986; modify the taxi code relaxing a number of requirements.
LICENSED TAXIS (HIRING AT SEPARATE FARES) (LONDON) ORDER 1986 (No. 1387) [80p], made under the Transport Act 1985, s.13(1); operative on September 3, 1986; modifies the taxi code in its application to London taxis.
TAXIS (SCHEMES FOR HIRE AT SEPARATE FARES) REGULATIONS 1986 (No. 1779) [80p], made under the Transport Act 1985 (c.67), s.10(5)(*c*)(8); operative on November 14, 1986; apply to schemes made under s.10 of the 1985 Act outside of London and prescribe the provisions which must be included in those schemes.

3458. Taxis—levy of charge—British Airports Authority
The British Airports Authority has the power under its existing by-laws to levy a charge on taxi-drivers using the taxi feeder park at Heathrow Airport: R. *v.* BRITISH AIRPORTS AUTHORITY, *ex p.* LONDON TAXI DRIVERS ASSOCIATION, *The Times,* March 13, 1986, D.C.

3459. Transfer of undertaking
BURNLEY AND PENDLE JOINT TRANSPORT UNDERTAKING (TRANSFER) ORDER 1986 (No. 1702) [£2·40], made under the Transport Act 1985 (c.67), ss.69(7)(9), 70(1)(5); operative on October 26, 1986; provides for the transfer of the Burnley and Pendle joint transport undertaking to a company formed by those councils.
CLEVELAND TRANSIT (TRANSFER) (No. 2) ORDER 1986 (No. 1780) [£2·90], made under the Transport Act 1986, ss.69(7)(9), 70(1)(5); operative on October 26, 1986; provides for the transfer of the joint bus undertaking of the Langbaurgh, Middlesbrough and Stockton-on-Tees Borough Councils to a company formed by those Councils.
GRIMSBY-CLEETHORPES JOINT TRANSPORT UNDERTAKING (TRANSFER) ORDER 1986 (No. 1703) [£2·40], made under the Transport Act 1985, ss.69(7)(9), 70(1)(5); operative on October 26, 1986; provides for the transfer of the Grimsby and Cleethorpes joint transport undertaking to a company formed by those councils.

3460. Transport Act 1982—commencement
TRANSPORT ACT 1982 (COMMENCEMENT No. 6) ORDER 1986 (No. 1326 (c.45)) [45p], made under the Transport Act 1982 (c.49), s.76(2); brings into force in England and Wales on October 1, 1986, Pt. III (except s.39), ss.73, 75, 76, Scheds. 1, 3 of the 1982 Act.

3461. Transport Act 1985—commencement
TRANSPORT ACT 1985 (COMMENCEMENT No. 2) ORDER 1986 (No. 80(c.3)) [40p], made under the Transport Act 1985 (c.67), s.140(2) and (3); brings into force on February 14, 1986, the scheduled provisions of the 1985 Act, all of which relate to travel concessions.
TRANSPORT ACT 1985 (COMMENCEMENT No. 3) ORDER 1986 (No. 414 (C.13)) [80p], made under the Transport Act 1985 (c.67), s.140(2); brings into force on April 1, 1986 sections 57(6), 93(8)(*b*), 102, 108, 109, 116(1), 139(1)(2)(3) of, and Sched. 3,

paras. 8, 24, 26, Sched. 6 paras. 22, 23, Sched. 7, paras. 3, 9, 17, 19, 22, 24 and Sched. 8 to, the 1985 Act.

TRANSPORT ACT 1985 (COMMENCEMENT No. 4) ORDER 1986 (No. 1088 (c.30)) [£1·40], made under the Transport Act 1985 (c.67), s.140(2)(3); brings into force on July 14, 1986 sections 7–9, 126(3), brings into force on July 26, 1986 sections 114, 115, 116(2)(3), 139(3) Sched. 8 and brings into force on August 1, 1986 sections 10, 11, 13, 17, 18, 22, 23, 33, 126(1)(2), 127(1)(2)(4), 139(2), Sched. 7, paras. 2, 21(2).

TRANSPORT ACT 1985 (COMMENCEMENT No. 5) ORDER 1986 (No. 1450 (c.49)) [£1·40], made under the Transport Act 1985 (c.67), s.140(2)(3); brings into force on September 15, 1986 sections 31, 104, 117, 139(1)(2)(3) of, and Scheds. 4, 6, paras. 24, 25, Sched. 7, paras. 7, 8, 15, 21(3)(11), Sched. 8 to the 1985 Act.

TRANSPORT ACT 1985 (COMMENCEMENT No. 6) ORDER 1986 (No. 1794 (c.63)) [£1·40], made under the Transport Act 1985 (c.67), s.140(2)(3); brings into force on October 26, 1986 sections 1, 4, 6, 24–28, 32, 35–46, 111, 126, 127(4), 139(1)–(3) of, and Scheds. 1, 6, 7, 8 to the 1985 Act.

3462. Travel concession schemes

TRAVEL CONCESSION SCHEMES REGULATIONS 1986 (No. 77) [£2·80], made under the Transport Act 1985 (c.67), ss.93(4), 94(1), 96(1), (5), 97(6), 100(1), (6) and 134(4) and (5); operative on February 14, 1986; provide for the arrangements between authorities administering travel concession schemes and operators of public passenger transport services participating in such schemes.

3463. Tribunal rules

TRANSPORT TRIBUNAL RULES 1986 (No. 1547) [£2·90], made under the Transport Act 1985 (c.67), Sched. 4, para. 11(1); operative on October 1, 1986; prescribe the rules for tribunals set up to adjudicate in relation to specified sections of the 1985 Act.

TRESPASS

3464. To the person—battery—intentional hostile touching

A trespass to the person in the form of a battery is established where the defendant intentionally touches the plaintiff and that touching is hostile.

P and D were both 13-year-old boys attending the same school. P sued D for damages for personal injuries. P claimed D committed the tort of trespass to the person by intentionally jumping on P. D contended that P was carring a bag over his shoulder, D pulled the bag off his shoulder in an act of ordinary horseplay. He denied jumping on P. P applied for summary judgment under Order 14. The judge in chambers held that on the facts alleged by D P's claim in trespass was made out and entered judgment for P. *Held,* allowing D's appeal, that to found a claim in trespass to the person based on a battery it was necessary for P to prove that there was an intentional touching or contact in one form or another by D and that the touching was hostile. P did not have to prove that D intended to injure him. P's claim would fail if D could show that the physical contact in question was generally acceptable in the ordinary conduct of daily life. It was a question of fact whether the physical contact in question was hostile. Where the immediate physical contact does not itself demonstrate hostility P should plead the facts alleged to demonstrate hostility. In the present case there were a number of questions that required investigation in evidence at a trial, accordingly D should have unconditional leave to defend (*Turberville* v. *Savage* (1669) 1 Mod. Rep. 3, *Cole* v. *Turner* (1704) Holt K.B. 108, *Williams* v. *Jones* (1736) Lee *temp* Hard. 298, *Fowler* v. *Lanning* [1959] C.L.Y. 3380, *Letang* v. *Cooper* [1964] C.L.Y. 2149, *Collins* v. *Wilcock* [1984] C.L.Y. 506 considered).

WILSON *v.* PRINGLE [1986] 2 All E.R. 440, C.A.

UNIVERSITIES

3465. Fees—eligibility for lower rate—residency requirement

[Education (Fees and Awards) Regulations 1983 (S.I. 1983 No. 973), Sched. 2, para. 2(2)(*a*)] A New Zealand student who had spent the three preceding years in various European countries but had settled nowhere in particular was nevertheless entitled to be treated as having been ordinarily resident in the European Community, and eligible to pay fees at the lower rate: UNIVERSITY COLLEGE LONDON *v.* NEWMAN, *The Times,* January 8, 1986, C.A.

3466. Visitor—dismissal of lecturer—jurisdiction

While the visitor of a university has exclusive jurisdiction over purely domestic internal matters, a claim founded on an ordinary contract, such as a contract of employment, was justiciable at common law and was within the jurisdiction of the courts.

In 1973 P was employed as a lecturer at the University of Bradford and so became an employee of it. The university was founded by Royal Charter and was a corporation within a visitor's jurisdiction. The university dismissed P in 1983 and she brought an action claiming that the decision was null and void by reason of non-compliance with the disciplinary rules and procedures of the university's charter and statutes; she also claimed damages for breach of contract or alternatively arrears of salary. The university applied to stay the proceedings, under R.S.C., Ord. 18, r. 19 or the court's inherent jurisdiction on the ground that the proceedings concerned purely domestic matters within the visitor's exclusive jurisdiction and for the stay to continue until the visitor had adjudicated. The judge refused the application and the university's appeal was dismissed. *Held,* that contracts between a corporation subject to visitorial jurisdiction and a member which did not involve the internal relationship between them arising out of the constitution of the corporation were not within the jurisdiction of the visitor, which was confined to matters relating to the private regulations and constitution of the corporation. A common law claim for breach of a contract of service did not derive from membership of the corporation and the plaintiff, whose membership of the university was merely incidental to her contract, was not precluded from bringing an action in the courts. The fact that such a claim would involve questions of construction of the internal constitution of the corporation did not bring it within the exclusive jurisdiction of the visitor. *Thorne* v. *University of London* [1966] C.L.Y. 12308 distinguished; *Hines* v. *Birkbeck College* [1985] C.L.Y 3552.295a doubted; *Att. Gen.* v. *Magdalen College, Oxford* (1847) 10 Beav. 402; *Thomson* v. *University of London* (1864) 33 L.J. Ch. 625; *Patel* v. *University of Bradford Senate* [1979] C.L.Y. 2736; *Murdoch University* v. *Bloom and Kyle* [1980] W.A.R. 193 and *Norrie* v. *University of Auckland Senate* [1984] 1 N.Z.L.R. 129 considered). *Per* Fox L.J. The statements in the authorities as to the exclusivity of the visitor's jurisdiction are not made in relation to actions which the courts will entertain. His jurisdiction derives from status and where the issue does not derive from status he has no jurisdiction except that which the court may concede to him. *Per* Lloyd L.J. The only way in which the universities can exclude the jurisdiction of the courts in cases of wrongful dismissal is by incorporating an arbitration clause in their contracts of employment. In many ways, that would be a happy solution.

THOMAS *v.* UNIVERSITY OF BRADFORD [1986] 2 W.L.R. 111, C.A.

VALUE ADDED TAX

3467. Amendment regulations

VALUE ADDED TAX (GENERAL) (AMENDMENT) REGULATIONS 1986 (No. 71) [40p], made under the Value Added Tax Act 1983 (c.55), Sched. 7, paras. 2(1) and 6(4); operative on February 19, 1986; amend S.I. 1985 No. 886.

3468. Appeal—application out of time—service of notice—partnership

BLYTH ELFORDS *v.* CUSTOMS AND EXCISE COMMISSIONERS (1985) V.A.T.T.R. 204, V.A.T. Tribunal. (BE were a firm of solicitors. The firm was originally called "Elfords" but in 1980 several new partners were admitted and in 1981 another firm merged with Elfords. In 1982 Elfords was dissolved and two firms were formed therefrom one of which, BE, took over Elfords's VAT registration number. The Commissioners assessed BE in respect of periods between 1979 and 1984, such assessments being made on all persons who were at any time partners in BE or Elfords. The partners who had not joined BE were not notified directly of such assessments and appealed for an extension of the time within which they could (i) appeal against such assessments and (ii) serve an application for non-payment of tax on the grounds of hardship. *Held,* that justice would not be done by refusing the application and such partners would be given six weeks to make such further applications.)

3469. Appeal—procedure—late submission of case

DORMERS BUILDERS (LONDON) *v.* CUSTOMS AND EXCISE COMMISSIONERS (1986) V.A.T.T.R. 69, V.A.T. Tribunal (DB Co. appealed against an assessment to tax made on it by the Commissioners. The Commissioners agreed that the appeal should proceed without deposit of tax by DB Co. The Commissioners were 50 days late in providing their statement of case to the Tribunal, in breach of V.A.T. Tribunals Rules 1972, r.6 and DB Co. asked the Tribunal to allow its appeal on that ground. *Held,* that the Tribunal would follow the practice of the High Court. As no injustice would be caused by allowing the late submission by the Commissioners, the appeal would be allowed to proceed on the basis that if DB Co. lost its appeal it should not pay interest on unpaid tax in respect of the period of such delay.)

3470. Appeal—repayment of tax—overdeclaration

POTTER (R.) *v.* CUSTOMS AND EXCISE COMMISSIONERS (1985) V.A.T.T.R. 255, V.A.T. Tribunal. (P carried on business as a retailer of products called Tupperware by appointing dealers to sell Tupperware through private parties. He originally accounted for tax on the full price paid to the dealers by customers but later, on the basis that his sales were to the dealers. The Commissioners assessed him on the basis that he made supplies through the dealers as agents to customers at the full sale price. P appealed against such assessments and also claimed repayment of tax paid earlier on the basis that he made supplies to the ultimate customers. The Court of Appeal upheld P's appeal. He applied for a direction under V.A.T.A. 1983, s.40(4) that all tax overpaid by him should be repaid. *Held,* that under s.40(4) the Tribunal only had jurisdiction in respect of tax paid under an assessment made by the Commissioners, it did not have power to consider the earlier overdeclarations of tax made by P. Accordingly it could only order repayment of tax paid under the assessments made.)

3471. Assessment—accounting system—rounding down

CATCHLORD *v.* CUSTOMS AND EXCISE COMMISSIONERS (1985) V.A.T.T.R. 238, V.A.T. Tribunal (C Co. carried on business as hoteliers and restaurateurs. It employed a computerised accounting system under which tax on each item comprised in an invoice was rounded up if over ·6p, or rounded down if ·6p or under. No permanent record was kept of individual items in an invoice. The Commissioners determined that such accounting practice resulted in a shortfall in tax paid and assessed C Co. on an estimate of such shortfall. *Held,* that pursuant to C.E.C. Notice No. 700, C Co. was only entitled to round down whole invoices and not separate items. The appeal would be dismissed.)

3472. Assessment—underdeclared tax—licensed premises—line by line mark-up

CLARKE (H) *v.* CUSTOMS AND EXCISE COMMISSIONERS (1985) V.A.T.T.R. 138, VAT Tribunal (C carried on business as the proprietor of licensed premises. The Commissioners believed that the returns made by C underdeclared output tax due. They completed a line by line average mark-up exercise in relation to each beer sold over a three month period. After negotiating with C on the amount of wastage due to spillages, losses in pipes and beer left at the bottom of barrels, the Commissioners allowed a 5.09 per cent. wastage figure. This was not reduced by any figure for gains made where less than a full pint was served. C contended that the wastage allowed was insufficient. *Held,* that the Tribunal could not fault the 5.09 per cent. allowance made by the Commissioners, nor the principles on which it was calculated. The resulting increases in stock deemed to have been sold by C obtained by calculating what was bought from supplies were therefore correct and assessments to the output tax underdeclared would be upheld).

3473. Assessments—notification—onus of proof

[Value Added Tax Act 1983 (c.55), Sched. 7, para. 4.] T Co. sold scrap silver, a by-production of its film processing business, but did not include those sales in its V.A.T. returns. The Commissioners assessed V.A.T. on the basis of purchase notes which they had obtained from dealers in silver and which they alleged related to sales of silver by T Co. T Co. appealed against the assessment, contending (1) that the assessment was invalid as it had not been properly notified to them in accordance with V.A.T.A. 1983, Sched. 7, para. 4(2), and (2) that the burden of proving that the purchase notes related to sales by T Co. lay on the Crown. *Held,* dismissing T Co's appeal, that (1) the assessment was only unenforceable until properly notified, and any initial irregularity had been cured, and (2) it was for T Co. to show that the assessment ought to be reduced: GRUNWICK PROCESSING LABORATORIES *v.* CUSTOMS AND EXCISE COMMISSIONERS [1986] S.T.C. 441, Macpherson J.

3474. Bad debt relief—liquidation—recovery by Commissioner

THK Co. received goods from suppliers in respect of which tax was due. Before paying for such goods it went into liquidation. The suppliers paid the output tax due in respect of such supplies but after the liquidation commenced they recovered such tax from the Customs and Excise Commissioners, pursuant to VAT (Bad Debt) Regulations (S.I. 1978 No. 1129) Reg. 6. The liquidator subsequently obtained sufficient funds to pay all creditors in full. The Commissioners sought payment by the liquidator of an amount equal to the tax repaid to the suppliers. The suppliers had not proved in the liquidation for the output tax. *Held,* that the Commissioners were not entitled to be subrogated to the suppliers' right to payment and had no right of recovery: T.H. KNITWEAR (WHOLESALE), *Re, The Times,* 8 November 1986, Browne-Wilkinson V.-C.

3475. Bad debt relief—whether supply of goods or services—concessionaire agreement

WAYFARER LEISURE *v.* CUSTOMS AND EXCISE COMMISSIONERS (1985) V.A.T.T.R. 174, VAT Tribunal (WL Co., carried on business as a retailer. It operated a retail outlet in a store owned by X Co. and under its agreement with X Co. all trading receipts were handed over to X Co. daily and X Co. subsequently repaid WL Co. (less its commission) and accounted for value added tax directly to the Commissioners. In 1983, X Co. went into liquidation and the tax was never paid. WL Co. sought relief by deducting such tax as a bad debt pursuant to Value Added Tax Act 1983, s. 22. *Held,* that s. 22 only grants relief in respect of bad debts incurred for goods or services supplied to the debtor. Here there was no supply by WL Co. to X Co. The appeal would be dismissed).

3476. Certificates—administrative receivers. See RECEIVERS, § 2832.

3477. Composite supply—single charge—accommodation and heating

HAZELWOOD CARAVANS AND CHALETS *v.* CUSTOMS AND EXCISE COMMISSIONERS (1985) V.A.T.T.R. 179, VAT Tribunal (H Co. carried on the business of renting holiday homes for each of which it charged a price inclusive of gas and electricity. It accounted for tax on the basis that £10 per week weekly charges were for supplies of gas and electricity and thus zero-rated. The Commissioners determined that it made one supply only which was standard rated. *Held,* that asking the question what did H Co. supply for the price paid, the answer was it supplied accommodation including facilities such as heating and lighting. There was thus one composite supply on which tax had to be charged at standard rate).

3478. Consideration—market value—cash and other consideration—party plan sales

NATURALLY YOURS COSMETICS *v.* CUSTOMS AND EXCISE COMMISSIONERS (1985) V.A.T.T.R. 159 VAT Tribunal (N Co. carried on business as suppliers of cosmetics by selling them to independent contractors, called consultants, who supplied them on to persons holding parties, called hostesses, for sale to friends. Certain products were sold to the consultants at a reduced price, which were intended to be given by the consultants to hostesses as inducements to hold such parties. The Commissioners contended the output tax was payable in respect of such supply by N Co. not on the price paid by the consultant but on the proper wholesale price. *Held,* that as under Value Added Tax Act 1983, s.10(3) a supply is to be taken as made at market value if made for a consideration only partly consisting of money, the Tribunal had to see if there was other consideration. Here, the price was reduced so that the consultant could persuade hostesses to give parties thus providing more business for N Co. and this constituted the provision of further consideration by the consultant. Accordingly the appeal would be dismissed).

3479. Direction by Commissioner—Sixth Directive—value of supplies

LAUGHTONS PHOTOGRAPHS *v.* CUSTOMS AND EXCISE COMMISSIONERS (1986) V.A.T.T.R. 13, V.A.T. Tribunal (LP Co. carried on business as suppliers of photographs to parents of schoolchildren. Such supplies were made by LP Co. taking photographs at a school and agreeing with the headmaster for him to sell the photographs and remit the consideration, less a fee paid to the school by LP Co. The Commissioners took the view that such method of selling put LP Co. in a favourable position compared to its competitors. They issued a Direction pursuant to V.A.T.A. 1983, Sched. 4, para. 3, directing that the consideration for such supplies should be taken to be the open market value by a retail sale. Following the decision of the European Court in *Direct Cosmetics* v. *Customs and Excise Commissioners* [1985] C.L.Y. 1497, which held that the enactment of such provision was an unauthorised derogation under Art. 27, para. 2 of the Sixth Directive, the Commissioners obtained such derogation and the Direction here accorded therewith. LP Co. contended (i) that such Direction was invalid since it was not made to prevent tax evasion or avoidance within such Art. 27, and (ii) that such derogation itself was invalid. *Held,* that although the Tribunal accepted that LP Co. did not intend to evade or avoid tax the Tribunal was not able to decide the limits of Art. 27. This matter would be referred to the European Court under Art. 177 of the Treaty of Rome for an opinion thereon. The appeal would be adjourned.)

3480. Documents—Anton Piller order—solicitors' undertaking
[Value Added Tax Act 1983 (c.55), Sched. 7, para. 8(2)(3) (as amended by Finance Act 1985 (c.54), Sched. 7, para. 3.]

The Customs and Excise Commissioners are entitled to obtain documents from a defendant in relation to value added tax, even though they may be self-incriminating and though criminal proceedings have been commenced. Documents held by solicitors to the sole order of defendants under an undertaking to the court were also to be produced.

Per curiam: So long as documents are held solely as the result of discovery, particularly discovery under compulsion under an Anton Piller order, it would be quite wrong to authorise their use in criminal proceedings brought under fiscal laws and having no connection with the original cause of action (*Customs and Excise Commissioners* v. *A. E. Hamlin & Co.,* [1984] C.L.Y. 2560 not followed).

In 1982 and 1983 the court made Anton Piller orders authorising Ps to remove into their solicitors' custody alleged counterfeit records and documents belonging to Ds. The order contained undertakings by the solicitors to retain them in their custody until further order. In May 1984 the actions were settled and by a consent order Ds waived any title to any illicit goods and the solicitors undertook to return all goods of a non-illicit nature. In 1985 criminal proceedings were instituted against two of Ds by Customs and Excise Commissioners relating to the fraudulent evasion of value added tax. The commissioners under Sched. 7, para. 8, of the Value Added Tax Act 1983, as amended, served a notice on Ps' solicitors, requiring them to produce for inspection all documents in their possession relating to the business of two of Ds which they obtained under the Anton Piller order. The solicitors applied for directions. Ds resisted disclosure on the grounds that the law provided an exemption from the production of self-incriminating documents, particularly after the start of criminal proceedings. *Held,* that para. 8(2) of Sched. 7 to the 1983 Act enabled the Commissioners to obtain documents generally for the purpose of managing Value Added Tax and there was no room for an implied exception for documents which might be self-incriminating, notwithstanding that criminal proceedings had commenced. Had the documents been in Ds' possession, their production could have been required. However, under para. 8(3) production could not be required from a person who did not hold them to the sole order of a person falling within para. 8(2), and a solicitor holding documents seized under an Anton Piller order or under discovery did not hold them to the sole order of the person from whom they had been seized and could not be required to produce them under para. 8(3). After the consent order in May 1984 the documents were held by the solicitors to the sole order of Ds subject only to an implied undertaking not to use them or allow them to be used for any collateral purpose without Ds' consent. The notice requiring production was validly served on the solicitors under para. 8(3) but they could not disclose them without being in breach of the implied undertaking and being in contempt of court. But in the special circumstances of the consent order, the solicitors' undertaking would be relaxed to allow the documents to be produced to the commissioners. (*Home Office* v. *Harman* [1982] C.L.Y. 2433 applied; *A.* v. *H.M. Treasury* [1979] C.L.Y. 2274 considered).

E.M.I. Records *v.* Spillane [1986] 1 W.L.R. 967, Browne-Wilkinson, V.-C.

3481. Exempt supply—gaming facilities—casino operator
Seven (J.) *v.* Customs and Excise Commissioners (1986) V.A.T.T.R. 42, V.A.T. Tribunal (JS Co. carried on the business of operating casinos. It entered into an agreement with a company operating liners, P Co., under which P Co. provided shipboard facilities which JS Co. utilised in operating a casino. P Co. took a share of gross receipts after deducting staff costs but added a charge for victualling JS Co.'s

staff. The Commissioners assessed such amount to tax. *Held,* that the substance and reality of the agreement was that P Co. received consideration for the provision of facilities for the playing of games of chance. Such a supply being exempt pursuant to V.A.T.A. 1983, Sched. 6, Grp. 4, item 1, the appeal would be allowed.)

3482. Finance Act 1985
FINANCE ACT 1985 (VALUE ADDED TAX TRIBUNAL RULES) (APPOINTED DAY) ORDER 1986 (No. 934) [45p], made under the Finance Act 1985 (c.54), s.27(3); appoints July 1, 1985 as the day on which the power to make rules relating to VAT tribunals is transferred to the Lord Chancellor.

3483. Finance Act 1985—appointed day
FINANCE ACT 1985 (BREACHES OF REGULATIONS) (APPOINTED DAY) ORDER 1986 (No. 969) [45p], made under the Finance Act 1985 (c.54), s.12(8); the appointed day after which s.39(8) of the Value Added Tax Act 1983 shall not apply is October 1, 1986.
FINANCE ACT 1985 (DEFAULT SURCHARGE) (COMMENCEMENT) ORDER 1986 (No. 968 (c.23)) [45p], made under the Finance Act 1985, s.19(10); brings s.19 of the 1985 Act, which relates to default surcharges, into force on October 1, 1986.
FINANCE ACT 1985 (REPAYMENT SUPPLEMENT) (APPOINTED DAY) ORDER 1986 (No. 970) [45p], made under the Finance Act 1985, s.20(4); provides that s.20 of the 1985 Act shall have effect with respect to any prescribed accounting period ending after October 1, 1986.

3484. Finance Act 1985—commencement
FINANCE ACT 1985 (BAD DEBT RELIEF) (COMMENCEMENT) ORDER 1986 (No. 337 (c.9)) [40p], made under the Finance Act 1985 (c.54), s.32(2); brings s.32(2) of the 1985 Act into force on April 1, 1986.
FINANCE ACT 1985 (VALUE ADDED TAX TRIBUNALS) (COMMENCEMENT) ORDER 1986 (No. 365 (c.11)) [40p], made under the Finance Act 1985, s.30(2); brings into force on April 1, 1986 section 30 of, and Sched. 8 to, the 1985 Act.

3485. Input tax—intention to make taxable supplies—consideration—statutory levy
The Apple and Pear Development Council existed to promote the production and marketing of English fruits for which purpose it provided services to fruit growers. It was obliged to provide such services by statute and the growers were obliged by statute to pay levies to the council. It sought repayment of input tax suffered by it on supplies made to it but the commissioners contended that as it did not make taxable supplies it could not do so. A Value Added Tax Tribunal allowed an appeal by the Council but the Divisional Court allowed an appeal by the commissioners therefrom. The Court of Appeal held that the compulsory levy did not constitute consideration for a supply of services by the Council since an element of bargain rather than compulsion was a prerequisite to a sum constituting consideration. Since the Council's activities were not taxable it could not claim repayment of input tax. The Council appealed to the House of Lords. *Held,* that on the assumption that the Council's activities were not conducted for a consideration input tax attributable to such activities was not reclaimable. Since, however, it was unclear whether the meaning of "consideration" here bore its ordinary meaning in English law or a wider meaning, the question of whether it could include payment of a compulsory levy would be referred to the Court of Justice of the European Community. The appeal would be adjourned: CUSTOMS AND EXCISE COMMISSIONERS *v.* APPLE AND PEAR DEVELOPMENT COUNCIL [1986] S.T.C. 192, H.L.

3486. Input tax—management services—credit note—parent and subsidiary
LAURENCE SCOTT *v.* CUSTOMS AND EXCISE COMMISSIONERS (1986) V.A.T.T.R. 1, V.A.T. Tribunal (LS Co. was the parent of a group of companies. No group election for VAT purposes was in force. Because LS Co. was concerned about the cash holding position of its subsidiaries it adopted arrangements whereunder it paid all interest charges incurred by group members. It then charged subsidiaries an amount, described as a management charge, calculated as two per cent. per quarter of an amount broadly equal to the excess of net capital employed over interest charges. It charged output tax on such amounts. Where a subsidiary's interest charges exceeded net capital employed, LS Co. issued a credit note with a VAT credit shown thereon. It deducted such VAT credit as input tax. The Commissioners assessed LS Co. in order to obtain repayment of such "input tax" deducted by it and contended that there was no legal justification for LS Co. to claim such sum as input tax. *Held,* that

it was wrong for LS Co. to deduct such sums since they did not constitute "input tax" within the legislation.)

3487. Input tax—transfer of business as going concern—intention of purchaser
[Value Added Tax (Special Provisions) Order 1981 (S.I. 1981 No. 1741), Reg. 12(1).] D Co. purchased the stock, trade name, leasehold premises and goodwill of an insolvent company which carried on the business of retailing reproduction furniture. It purported to reclaim input tax in respect of such supply made to it. The Commissioners refused to allow it to do so, determining that the supply was one of a business as a going concern, which supply is not to be treated as a taxable supply pursuant to VAT (Special Provisions) Order 1981, Reg. 12(1). A Value Added Tax Tribunal upheld an appeal by D Co., holding that as D Co. intended to conclude the business of retailing reproduction furniture and concentrate on selling kitchens and bathrooms it had not taken over the insolvent company's business. The Commissioners appealed. *Held,* that the vital consideration was whether a purchaser had been put in possession of a going concern which he could carry on. Whether or not D Co. chose to carry on the business transferred was irrelevant. The appeal would be allowed: CUSTOMS AND EXCISE COMMISSIONERS *v.* DEARWOOD [1986] S.T.C. 327, McCowan J.

3488. Land
VALUE ADDED TAX (LAND) ORDER 1986 (No. 704) [45p], made under the Value Added Tax Act 1983 (c.55), ss.17(2), 48(6); operative on November 1, 1986; amends Sched. 6, Group 1 to the 1983 Act.
VALUE ADDED TAX (LAND) (No. 2) ORDER 1986 (No. 716) [45p], made under the Value Added Tax Act 1983, ss.17(2), 48(6); operative on June 1, 1986; adds to the supplies which we exempt under Group 1 of Sched. 6 to the 1983 Act the letting of facilities for playing any sport or participating in any physical recreation.

3489. Pawnbrokers
VALUE ADDED TAX (TREATMENT OF TRANSACTIONS) ORDER 1986 (No. 896) [45p], made under the Value Added Tax Act 1983 (c.55), s.3(3)(c); operative on July 1, 1986; removes from the scope of VAT disposals by pawnbrokers of goods to the pawnor within three months of the goods passing to the pawnbroker under the Consumer Credit Act 1974, s.120(1)(a).

3490. Penalty—failure to register—mitigation
RHODES (LEILA MARY) *v.* CUSTOMS AND EXCISE COMMISSIONERS (1986) V.A.T.T.R. 72, V.A.T. Tribunal (R carried on a debt collecting business. In November 1985 she applied to the Commissioners for registration. The Commissioners determined that, in view of her turnover, R should have been registered from July 21, 1985. They accordingly granted retrospective registration from that date. R sought to obtain tax due for the period from such July to November by sending further invoices to customers so that the Commissioners suffered no loss of tax. The Commissioners assessed R to a penalty pursuant to F.A. 1985, s.15(1). R appealed against the penalty and its quantum. *Held,* that as there was no evidence of any reasonable excuse for the non-notification in July, the Tribunal could not mitigate the penalty despite it being of the maximum amount.)

3491. Procedure—appeal dismissed—entertainment of second appeal
N carried on business in partnership with C until 1981. After the termination of the partnership he informed the Commissioners that C had made improper returns. As a result the Commissioners assessed C and N for underdeclared tax. C and N appealed to a Value Added Tax Tribunal but the appeal was dismissed. Subsequently the Commissioners sought payment of such tax from N and sought judgment under R.S.C., Ord. 14. N claimed that the Commissioners had broken an undertaking not to proceed against him. The Master hearing the Ord. 14 summons adjourned the hearing to allow N to appeal to another Tribunal. Such Tribunal ordered the fresh appeal to be struck out. *Held,* that the Tribunal acted properly in striking out the appeal as the matter had already been determined: NAWAZ *v.* CUSTOMS AND EXCISE COMMISSIONERS [1986] S.T.C. 484, Macpherson J.

3492. Procedure—hearsay evidence—lack of witness statement
F Co. appealed against an assessment to tax to a Value Added Tax Tribunal. At the hearing the Commissioners did not serve any witness statements. An officer of the Commissioners gave evidence of statements made to him by B, another such officer who had previously been concerned in the matter. B was not called. F Co.

contended that the Tribunal should not have allowed such hearsay evidence. *Held,* that if no objection to the admission of hearsay evidence is made at the hearing by the appellant or the Tribunal, no later complaint is possible. The appeal would be dismissed: FARLEY (WAYNE) *v.* CUSTOMS AND EXCISE COMMISSIONERS [1986] S.T.C. 487, Macpherson J.

3493. Proceedings by Commissioners—Crown debt—alternative to assessment

ILC Co. carried on the business of providing language courses. It returned certain amounts as being output tax due to the Commissioners on form VAT 1 but did not pay such tax. The Commissioners assessed ILC Co. for such tax. On appeal from a VAT Tribunal to the High Court, ILC Co. contended that it was not possible for the Commissioners to assess for tax due in the manner employed since they had issued a single assessment in respect of a number of accounting periods. The High Court agreed with such contention and discharged the assessment. The Commissioners considered that such tax was still due to them and sued for it as a debt to the Crown. ILC Co. contended that it was not open to the Commissioners to use the parallel courses of issuing assessments, which were subsequently discharged, and suing for a debt due in respect of ILC Co.'s VAT return. *Held,* that the Commissioners had a remedy open to them, in addition to the assessment procedure, of suing for output tax collected by ILC Co. and not paid over to them. There would be judgment for the plaintiff: CUSTOMS AND EXCISE COMMISSIONERS *v.* INTERNATIONAL LANGUAGE CENTRES [1986] S.T.C. 279, BENNETT, Q.C.

3494. Refunds

VALUE ADDED TAX (REFUND OF TAX) ORDER 1986 (No. 336) [40p], made under the Value Added Tax Act 1983 (c.55), s.20(3); operative on April 1, 1986; specifies bodies who will be entitled to claim refunds of VAT on supplies to or importations by them if not made for the purpose of business.

VALUE ADDED TAX (REFUND OF TAX) (No. 2) ORDER 1986 (No. 532) [40p], made under the Value Added Tax Act 1983, s.2(3); operative on April 1, 1986; specifies bodies established under s.10 of the Local Government Act 1985 for the purposes of s.20 of the 1983 Act.

3495. Registration

VALUE ADDED TAX (INCREASE OF REGISTRATION LIMITS) ORDER 1986 (No. 531) [40p], made under the Value Added Tax Act 1983 (c.55), Sched. 1, para. 12; operative on March 19, 1986 save for Art. 3 which is operative on June 1, 1986; increases the registration limit to £20,500 per annum and the single quarterly limit to £7,000, it also increases the cancellation limit to $20,500 in respect of past turnover and to £19,500 in respect of anticipated turnover.

3496. Registration—voluntary registration—exercise of discretion

HALL (J.) *v.* CUSTOMS AND EXCISE COMMISSIONERS (1985) V.A.T.T.R. 267, V.A.T. Tribunal. (H carried on the business of farming 22 acres. His turnover was well below the threshold for registration being always below £3,000 *per annum.* He applied for voluntary registration under V.A.T.A. 1983, s.11(1)(*b*) which the Commissioners have power to grant if they think fit. The Commissioners refused such voluntary registration, considering that since H's income came primarily from a pension, H's was not a hard or exceptional case warranting voluntary registration. H appealed. *Held,* that the Tribunal could only interfere with the exercise of such discretion where the decision of the Commissioners was wrong in principle or one which no reasonable Commissioners could have reached. As this was not the case, the appeal would be dismissed.)

3497. Regulations

VALUE ADDED TAX (GENERAL) (AMENDMENT) (No. 2) REGULATIONS 1986 (No. 305) [40p], made under the Value Added Tax Act 1983 (c.55), Sched. 7, para. 6(4); operative on Aoril 1, 1986; amend S.I. 1985 No. 886 in relation to distress for unpaid tax.

3498. Relief

VALUE ADDED TAX (BAD DEBT RELIEF) REGULATIONS 1986 (No. 335) [£1·35], made under the Value Added Tax Act 1983 (c.55), s.22(6)(7); operative on April 1, 1986; replace S.I. 1978 No. 1129 as amended by S.I. 1981 No. 1080.

VALUE ADDED TAX (SMALL NON-COMMERCIAL CONSIGNMENTS) RELIEF ORDER 1986 (No. 939) [80p], made under the Value Added Tax Act 1983 (c.55), s.19(1);

operative on July 1, 1986; increases to £27 the value of private non-commercial consignments of goods which are relieved from VAT on importation.

3499. Repayment supplement
VALUE ADDED TAX (REPAYMENT SUPPLEMENT) REGULATIONS 1986 (No. 909) [45p], made under the Finance Act 1985 (c.54), s.20(2); operative on October 1, 1986; provide for an extension of the 30 day period for a repayment supplement under s.20 of the 1985 Act in four specified sets of circumstances.

3500. Retailer—special scheme—turnover—energy stamps
PARR (T.) v. CUSTOMS AND EXCISE COMMISSIONERS (1985) V.A.T.T.R. 250, V.A.T. Tribunal. (P carried on business running a Post Office. P operated Special Scheme D pursuant to Customs and Excise Notice No. 727. Under V.A.T.A. 1983, Sched. 4, para. 6, a retailer is to exclude from turnover consideration given for the supply of a stamp which gives a right to receive services. P sold items called Energy Stamps, which a customer could use in payment of a gas or electricity bill. The Commissioners determined that such supplies fell to be excluded by such Sched. 4, para. 6. As a result of excluding such items from turnover in the operation of Scheme D, the output tax paid by P was increased. P appealed. *Held,* that the purchase of a stamp did not grant a right to receive goods or services and Sched. 4, para. 6 did not therefore apply to exclude energy stamps from P's turnover. The appeal would be allowed.)

3501. Return—furnishing of return by post—agency of Post Office
[Scot.] [Value Added Tax (General) Regulations 1980, (S.I. 1980 No. 1536) reg. 51(1).] W carried on business in Edinburgh and was registered for value added tax. By V.A.T. (General) Regs. 1980, reg. 51(1), she was required to furnish the Customs and Excise Commissioners with a quarterly return. One such return was completed by her and posted to the Commissioners at the proper time but the Commissioners never received it. W was charged with failing to furnish a return pursuant to such reg. 51(1). *Held,* that the requirement that a person should furnish a return meant he should put it into the possession of the Commissioners. By sending W a prepaid envelope in which a return was to be posted, the Commissioners had constituted the Post Office their agent for receipt of such return. By furnishing their agent with the return W had satisfied reg. 51(1) and could not be convicted of the offence: AIKMAN v. WHITE [1986] S.T.C. 1, J.C.

3501a. 6th V.A.T. directive. See EUROPEAN COMMUNITIES.

3502. Special scheme—exercise of discretion by Commissioners—refusal to permit use of scheme
The predecessor of B (1980) Co., B Co., carried on business as a retailer of furniture, much of which furniture it sold on instalment terms. Under Value Added Tax (Supplies by Retailers) Regs. 1972, (S.I. 1972 No. 1148) reg. 2(1), the Commissioners have power to permit a retailer to account for tax under a special scheme. B Co. used the "optional method," under which it accounted on the basis of sums received on a day plus sums receivable at a later date for bargains struck that day, less amounts received in respect of earlier sales. It wished to change to the "standard method," under which accounting is based on actual receipts, but was not allowed to do so. Accordingly a new company, B (1980) Co., was set up to carry on the retail business and collect debts owed to B Co. B (1980) Co. applied for permission to use the "standard method" but the Commissioners refused it. A Value Added Tax Tribunal allowed an appeal by B (1980) Co., holding that in the exercise of their discretion, the Commissioners had ignored the legal separation of B Co. and B (1980) Co. and had reached a decision which no reasonable Commissioners could have reached. The Commissioners appealed. *Held,* that as the Tribunal had correctly understood and applied the law and that as there was ample evidence to support the conclusion at which the Tribunal arrived, the appeal would be dismissed: CUSTOMS AND EXCISE COMMISSIONERS v. J. BOARDMANS (1980) [1986] S.T.C. 10, Kennedy J.

3503. Supply—food—consumption on premises
CROWNLION (SEAFOOD) v. CUSTOMS AND EXCISE COMMISSIONERS (1985) V.A.T.T.R. 188, VAT Tribunal (C Co. carried on business as suppliers of food from kiosks. The appeal related to events before May 1, 1984 when, pursuant to Value Added Tax Act 1983, Sched. 5, Grp. 1, item 1 and Note 3(a), supplies of food were zero-rated unless made in the course of catering which was deemed to include the supply of

food for consumption on the premises. C Co. supplied food from a kiosk situated in a shopping precinct. Such kiosk was situated near other kiosks offering different types of food and was adjacent to an area within such precinct offering seating at tables for 375 persons. The Commissioners accepted that so far as customers took food purchased from such kiosk out of the precinct, the supply thereof by C Co. fell to be zero-rated. They contended that in respect of customers who ate food at such tables, the supplies made to them by C Co. fell to be standard rated. *Held,* that although the supplies made to such customers were not in the course of catering in the normal sense, they were supplies made of food for consumption on the premises. The kiosks and the seating area were properly to be regarded as an enclave in which food was supplied and consumed. The appeal would be dismissed).

3504/5. Supply—nature of supply—timesharing—shares containing rights of occupation

COURT BARTON PROPERTY *v.* CUSTOMS AND EXCISE COMMISSIONERS (1985) V.A.T.T.R. 148, VAT Tribunal (C Co. owned a number of holiday cottages suitable for timesharing. Supplies of timeshares are subject to tax at standard rate. C Co. did not sell timeshares as such but made issues of ordinary shares in itself to persons requiring timeshare accommodation. Under its articles of association, each such share in C Co. carried the right to use of a cottage for a particular week in each of 25 years and the cost of shares varied from £1,500 to £4,000 depending on the type of cottage and week chosen. The Commissioners determined that C Co. was carrying on a business supplying holiday accommodation. C Co. contended that it was merely supplying ordinary shares and the Tribunal could go beyond a share to examine the rights thereunder. *Held,* that C Co. was clearly supplying holiday accommodation. As regards the share, the tribunal must look to what the consideration given was paid for. It was principally for holiday accommodation, with only £1 being attributable to the exempt supply of the share).

3506. Supply—time of supply—loan by supplier to customer

DOLOMITE DOUBLE GLAZING *v.* CUSTOMS AND EXCISE COMMISSIONERS (1985) V.A.T.T.R. 184, VAT Tribunal (D Co. carried on business as a supplier of double glazing. Such supplies were zero-rated but by Finance Act 1984, s.10 such zero-rating was ended with respect to supplies made on or after June 1, 1984. By Value Added Tax Act 1983, s.4(3) a supply of services is made when the service is performed or, if earlier, when payment is made. Before June 1, D Co. agreed to supply double glazing to a customer, the supply to be made after such date. In order to enable the customer to pay for such service before such date, D Co. lent him the sum free of interest and without security. Two days later the customer paid over a cheque for such sum in paying for the supply. The Commissioners submitted that such exchange of cheques was not genuine, that the purported repayment of the loan after June 1, 1984 was the true date of payment and thus the supply was standard rated. *Held,* that in the absence of evidence to the contrary the loan was genuine and the supply must be treated as made before such June 1).

3507. Supply of employees—parent and subsidiary—administrative convenience

T Co. owned a subsidiary, M Co., which carried on business as insurance brokers. For convenience, all of M Co.'s employees were hired and paid by T Co. M Co. did not pay T Co. but a debit was shown in respect of salaries of such employees in the consolidated accounts of the group. The Commissioners contended that T Co. was making a taxable supply of its staff to M Co. in consideration of M Co. defraying the salaries. A Value Added Tax Tribunal held that there was no taxable supply by T Co. and that the payment of salaries was merely a matter of administrative convenience. The Commissioners appealed. *Held,* that since the employees were employed by T Co., sums debited to M Co. constituted consideration paid for the supply to it of the employees by T Co. The appeal would be allowed: CUSTOMS AND EXCISE COMMISSIONERS *v.* TARMAC ROADSTONE HOLDINGS [1985] S.T.C. 830, Kennedy J.

3508. Supply of goods—agent—value of supply—party sales

SIMPLY CROSS-STITCH *v.* CUSTOMS AND EXCISE COMMISSIONERS (1985) V.A.T.T.R. 241, V.A.T. Tribunal. (S carried on business retailing embroidery kits. This they did by appointing persons described as agents who themselves arranged for the sale of products to customers by arranging for hostesses to hold private parties, to which the agent brought products. The agent had no real freedom to alter the selling price named by S. There was no Romalpa clause in the agency agreement and the agent was not responsible for bad debts. S contended that the agents were in law acting as principals and thus its only supply was to them at the ultimate sale price less commission. The Commissioners contended that S was making sales to the customers as the agents were truly agents. *Held,* that on the evidence, the agents were in law agents. The appeal would be dismissed.)

3509. Supply of goods—consideration—voucher—scheme
Boots Co. *v.* Customs and Excise Commissioners (1986) V.A.T.T.R. 49, V.A.T. Tribunal (B Co. carried on business as retail chemists. It operated Special Scheme A pursuant to Notice No. 727, under which it accounted for tax on its gross takings. It operated a discount scheme under which purchasers of one product obtained vouchers enabling them to purchase another product at a reduced price. The Commissioners contended that the supplies of the latter product were not made for a consideration wholly in cash, being cash and a voucher and that pursuant to V.A.T.A. 1983, s.10(3), such supplies should be treated as made at open market value. B Co. contended that the price reduction obtained by the use of vouchers was a discount within Sixth Directive Art. 11.A.1., para. 3(*b*). *Held,* that such s.10(3) did apply and the reductions obtained were not discounts within Art. 11. The appeal would be dismissed.)

3510. Supply of services—provision to employees—full cost thereof—depreciation of yacht
Teknequip *v.* Customs And Excise Commissioners (1985) V.A.T.T.R. 167, VAT Tribunal (T Co purchased a yacht with the intention of allowing its employees to use it, free of charge. The Commissioners determined that such supplies to employees were taxable and that pursuant to Finance Act 1972 Sched. 2, para. 5(3) and Sched. 3, para. 8 the supply was to be taken as having been made at the full cost to T Co. of providing such services. *Held,* that the contention of the Commissioners was correct. In calculating such full cost, this would not, as the Commissioners further contended, be done by adding in an amount on the basis of annual depreciation divided by the number of days of such use only, rather the depreciation must be taken as occurring throughout the year and each day of use represented depreciation of one 365th part in that year).

3511. Supply of services—time of supply—payment by cheque
Rampling (M. R.) *v.* Customs and Excise Commissioners (1986) V.A.T.T.R. 62, V.A.T. Tribunal (R carried on business as a joiner. He agreed to perform work on houses owned by H, commencing in April 1984. In the 1984 Budget Speech, the provisions of V.A.T.A. 1983 Sched. 5, Grp. 8, items 2 and 3, under which building work is zero-rated were amended from March 13, 1984 so as to remove from zero-rating works of building reconstruction. Under transitional provisions work performed after May 30, 1984 was zero-rated if the consideration was paid before then. R agreed with H that the contract price would be paid by cheque before such date but that the cheque would not be cashed until completion of the work. The Commissioners contended that the consideration was not paid until the cheque was cashed. *Held,* that as a cheque was only a conditional form of payment, the consideration was only received when it was presented and met. The appeal would be dismissed.)

3512. Tax evasion—criminal offence—cheating public revenue—absence of deceit
M carried on business trading in gold. He charged output tax on sales but never accounted for it to the Customs and Excise Commissioners. He was convicted of cheating the public revenue in the Crown Court and sentenced to six years' imprisonment. He appealed, contending that since F.A. 1972, s.38(1) provided for a less serious offence of fraudulent evasion of tax, where no deceit needed to be proved, the more serious offence of cheating must require proof of deceit, of which there was none in respect of M. *Held,* that cheating did not require any act of deceit. Further, since M had evaded over £629,000 of tax, the sentence was not wrong in principle: R. *v.* Mavji [1986] S.T.C. 508, C.A.

3513. Taxable supply—personal assets—Sixth Directive
Stirling (R.) *v.* Customs and Excise Commissioners (1985) V.A.T.T.R. 232, V.A.T. Tribunal. (S carried on the business of farming on the estate inherited from his father. Due to financial pressure he was forced to lease the mansion house furnished, together with sporting rights over the estate. Subsequently he was forced to sell an inherited stamp collection the proceeds of which sale he used to reduce the business overdraft. Later he sold the mansion house and certain valuable contents,

applying such proceeds for the purposes of the business. The Commissioners determined that the sales of the collection and such contents were made in the furtherance of the business pursuant to F.A. 1972, s.2(2)(*b*). S contended that since Sixth Directive, Art. 2, provided for a charge to tax by a taxable person when acting as such, these sales were not taxable. *Held,* that as S was merely selling personal assets, he was not acting as a taxable person. The appeal would be allowed.)

3514. Temporarily imported goods
VALUE ADDED TAX (TEMPORARILY IMPORTED GOODS) RELIEF ORDER 1986 (No. 1989) [£2·40], made under the Value Added Tax Act 1983 (c.55), ss.3(3)(*c*), 19(1), (1A) and 45(1) and (2); operative on January 1, 1987; replaces S.I. 1985 No. 1646.

3515. Tribunals
VALUE ADDED TAX TRIBUNAL RULES 1986 (No. 590) [£2·80], made under the Value Added Tax Act 1983 (c.55), Sched.8, para. 9; operative on May 1, 1986; prescribe the procedure to be followed in appeals to VAT tribunals.
VALUE ADDED TAX TRIBUNALS (AMENDMENT) RULES 1986 (No. 2290) [45p], made under the Value Added Tax Act 1983 (c.55), Sched. 8, para. 9; operative on January 12, 1987; amends S.I. 1986 No. 590 in relation to appeals to the Court of Appeal so that the certificate should be applied for at the conclusion of the tribunal hearing or within 21 days from that date.
VALUE ADDED TAX TRIBUNALS APPEALS ORDER 1986 (No. 2288) [45p], made under the Finance Act 1985 (c.54), s.26; operative on January 12, 1987; enables appeals to be made directly to the Court of Appeal from Value Added Tax Tribunals.

3516. Zero-rating
VALUE ADDED TAX (HANDICAPPED PERSONS AND CHARITIES) ORDER 1986 (No. 530) [80p], made under the Value Added Tax Act 1983 (c.55), ss.16(4) and 48(6); operative on April 1, 1986; extends the zero-rating provisions in the 1983 Act.

3517. Zero-rating—hot food—purpose of heating—pie manufacture
PIMBLETT (JOHN) *v.* CUSTOMS AND EXCISE COMMISSIONERS (1985) V.A.T.T.R. 210, V.A.T. Tribunal. (P Co. carried on business as bakers and retailers of pies. By V.A.T.A. 1983, Sched. 5, Grp. 1, Item 1, note 3(*b*) (as inserted by F.A. 1984) food sold for consumption off the premises does not fall to be zero-rated if it has been heated above the ambient air temperature and is supplied above such temperature. P Co. did not re-heat pies for sale but regularly sold pies while still warm. The Commissioners considered that the supply of such pies fell to be standard rated. P Co. contended that its purpose in heating them was to bake them, not to enable them to be sold warm. *Held,* that while determining P Co.'s purpose was a subjective test, it was relevant to consider the purpose of shop managers, who recognised that pies should be sold while still warm. The appeal would be dismissed.)

3518. Zero-rating—international services—retaining fee
EDDERY (PATRICK) *v.* CUSTOMS AND EXCISE COMMISSIONERS (1986) V.A.T.T.R. 30, V.A.T. Tribunal (PE Co. entered into an agreement to secure the sole right to the services of E, a jockey, to ride outside the U.K. It also agreed with O to supply such services to O in consideration of certain fees per race and £150,000 retaining fee. The Commissioners accepted that all riding fees were zero-rated under F.A. 1972, Sched. 4, Grp. 5, item 3, being supplies of sporting services outside the U.K. They contended that the retainer was paid for the right to obtain such services which was not within such item 3. *Held,* that the consideration paid for the services of riding by E consisted of riding fees and the £150,000. The appeal would be allowed.)

VENDOR AND PURCHASER

3519. Conveyance—"building"—greenhouse—whether included in conveyance. see DEEN *v.* ANDREWS, § 2820.

3520. Leasehold property—landlord's consent to assignment—delay by purchaser—vendor's right to rescind
[National Conditions of Sale, 20th ed., condition 11(5).] The question of whether a landlord's consent to an assignment could or could not be obtained was a question of fact in every case, depending on all the circumstances. If it could reasonably be obtained, the transaction would be ordered to go ahead. Appeal allowed: 29 EQUITIES *v.* BANK LEUMI (U.K.), *The Times,* October 16, 1986, C.A.

3521. Option to purchase—deposit to be paid within specified time—document exchange.
See WILLMOTT (JOHN) HOMES v. READ, § 405.

3522. Sale of land—exchange of parts—identity of counterparts—rectification
[Aus.] When the parties to a sale of land have agreed the terms of their bargain and agree on exchange of parts to seal that bargain, it will usually accord with their intention to treat that exchange as creating a binding contract, despite a lack of correspondence in the parts, provided that lack of correspondence can be remedied by rectification. If the parties do not conclude the terms of the bargain in the prior negotiations and look to the parts as exchanged to fix the terms or if it appears that the parties only intend to be bound by an exchange in identical terms, the position will be different (*Eccles* v. *Bryant* (1948) C.L.C. 10575, *Harrison* v. *Battye* [1974] C.L.Y. 3938 and *Domb* v. *Isoz* [1980] C.L.Y. 2796 considered) : SINDEL v. GEORGIO (1984) 154 C.L.R. 661, High Ct. of Australia.

3523. Sale of land—fixtures and fittings—vacant possession—whether vendor ready and willing to perform outstanding obligations
A vendor of property will not be in breach of his duty to give vacant possession of the property where rubbish remains on it at the time for completion unless the rubbish constitutes an impediment which substantially prevents or interferes with the purchaser's enjoyment of the right of possession.
D agreed to sell to P a dwelling-house, outbuilding and two acres of land for a price of £122,500. The agreement was in the form of the National Conditions of Sale, 20th ed. (December 1981). Condition 13 provided for the purchaser to buy with full notice in all respects of the actual state and condition of the property and to take the property as it was. Condition 22 permitted a party ready and willing to fulfil his obligations under the contract to serve a special notice to complete upon the other party. Thereafter if the defaulting party failed to complete the transaction the contract could be treated as repudiated. P failed to complete on time and was thereafter served with a special notice to complete by D under condition 22 on January 4, 1985. P claimed that D was not ready and willing to fulfil his outstanding obligations under the contract because a chrysanthemum growing frame and sprinkler alleged to be a fixture and fitting passing with the property on completion had been removed by D and because D could not give vacant possession on completion having regard to the quantity of rubbish left on the property. P contended the notice to complete was invalid and on January 28, 1985, commenced an action for specific performance with an abatement of the purchase price. P lodged a caution with the Land Registry against the property. D in the meantime found another purchaser and applied for an order that the caution be vacated. The chrysanthemum growing frame was to cover a bed 87 ft. long and 25 ft. wide. The frame supported the flowers as they grew and this required raising from time to time. It was removed completely at the end of the growing season to permit the bed to be worked over and planted for the next season. The sprinkler formed part of the frame and was attached to a tap by a length of hosepipe. D admitted removing the frame and sprinkler but claimed they were not fixtures and fittings. The rubbish complained of consisted of a small pile of garden rubbish near a bonfire site, a neat stack of concrete blocks and some corrugated sheet, an old tree stump, an area 30 ft. by 25 ft. covered with aggregate, bonfire remains, broken tiles, bricks and concrete and bits of wood, another area with some builder's rubbish, an old fire-extinguisher and an old dinghy trolley on it, a mound of earth with a few foreign objects in it at the back of the garage, and a quantity of rubbish and other useful items stored in some loose boxes. *Held,* vacating the caution, that the growing frame and sprinkler was not a fixture of the property. Debris making up old bonfire sites, garden rubbish piles, compost heaps and manure heaps merges into and becomes indistinguishable from the soil of the property. Such debris becomes a part of the property sold. By virtue of condition 13 of the contract P was obliged to take the property as it was with its existing garden and stable rubbish piles and bonfire sites. Things such as the fire extinguisher, dinghy trolley and other items or rubbish not forming part of the property that were present did not prevent D giving vacant possession. The presence of such materials on the property could only prevent D giving vacant possession if it substantially prevented or interfered with P's enjoyment of the right of possession of a substantial part of the property. No fair or arguable case in support of the caution had been made out (*Rawlplug Co.* v. *Kamvale Properties* [1969] C.L.Y. 1989, *Cumberland Consolidated*

Holdings v. *Ireland* [1946] K.B. 264 applied; *Norman* v. *Hardy* [1974] C.L.Y. 2002 considered).
HYNES *v.* VAUGHAN (1985) 50 P. & C.R. 444, Scott J.

3524. Sale of lease—balance of purchase money—whether payment into court
[National Conditions of Sale, 20th ed., condition 8.]
Where a vendor and purchaser contract that the purchaser may, pending completion, remain in possession on specified terms, it is not open to the vendor to seek a *Greenwood* v. *Turner* order, *i.e.* that the purchaser make payment into court of the remainder of the purchase price or else relinquish possession.
By a contract dated September 13, 1985 the vendors agreed to sell to the purchaser for £29,000 the leasehold interest in certain premises in their business as builders merchants, the sum to include goodwill, fixtures and fittings, and the stock in trade. The purchaser was let into possession on August 12, 1985 and had carried on business there ever since. The contract incorporated the terms of the National Conditions of Sale, 20th ed., condition 8 of which provided that if a purchaser was let into occupation before completion, he was entitled to remain there until completion or until discharge or rescission as a licensee, and upon discharge or rescission he had to give up possession on seven days' or more notice by the vendor. The contract provided for the payment of £2,900 on the date of the contract and for completion on September 26, 1985. No deposit was paid on the date of the contract, but £14,500, to be treated as including the deposit, was paid on September 16. Completion did not take place on September 26, and the vendors served a notice to complete, pursuant to condition 22 of the National Conditions of Sale requiring completion within 16 working days after service of the notice, a period expiring on October 31, and making time of the essence. On October 30 the purchaser paid a further £7,000 but could not pay the remaining £7,500. On January 21 the vendors claimed specific performance or alternatively an order that the purchaser give up possession. By a notice of motion of the same date they sought a *Greenwood* v. *Turner* order [1891] 2 Ch. 144 for payment into court of the remainder of the purchase price, with interest due under the contract, or alternatively that the purchaser should relinquish possession of every asset part of the subject matter of the contract, and an injunction restraining them from disposing of any such asset. The vendors' application for relief was dismissed. *Held*, that where the vendor and purchaser had contracted that the purchaser might remain in possession on terms, pending completion, it was not open to the vendor to seek a *Greenwood* v. *Turner* order. Further, since a substantial proportion of the price had been paid, and the sale included not merely the lease, but also goodwill and stock in trade, some of which had been sold and replaced in the ordinary course of business of the purchaser, the making of a *Greenwood* v. *Turner* order would be inappropriate (*Maskell* v. *Ivory* [1970] C.L.Y. 2892 distinguished).
ATTFIELD *v.* D.J. PLANT HIRE & GENERAL CONTRACTORS CO. [1986] 3 W.L.R. 432, Scott J.

3525. Specific performances—whether vendor entitled to resell land. See GKN DISTRIBUTORS *v.* TYNE TEES FABRICATION, § 406.

WATER AND WATERWORKS

3526. Boreholes
THAMES WATER AUTHORITY (AMENDMENT OF LOCAL ENACTMENTS) ORDER 1986 (No. 58) [40p], made under the Water Resources Act 1963 (c.38), s.133(1); operative on February 14, 1986; amends two orders in connection with the taking of water from boreholes on land at Gomshall in Surrey.

3527. Financial provisions
RICKMANSWORTH WATER (FINANCIAL PROVISIONS) ORDER 1986 (No. 1277) [80p], made under the Water Act 1945 (c.42), ss.23 and 50; operative on July 22, 1986; relates to the capital and borrowing powers of the Rickmansworth Water Company.

3528. Lands Tribunal decision
BATEMAN *v.* WELSH WATER AUTHORITY (Ref./84/1885) (1986) 279 E.G. 1367. (B operated a trout farm in Wales for which they took water from the River Eastern Cleddes, the amount effectively being controlled by a discharge consent limiting the amount that could flow back into the river. On July 2, 1984 the authority gave notice

of intention to apply for a drought order, which came into effect on August 3, reducing the permitted flow of the water in the river upstream of B's farm. In the meantime the authority made available facilities at its own trout farm 35 miles away, to which a large part of B's stock was moved. B subsequently claimed compensation pursuant to s.1 of the Drought Act 1976 in respect principally of the cost of moving the stock and the cost of adopting a policy of continuous pumping at their own farm before the making of the drought order, so as to improve the quality of such water as remained available. The tribunal noted that, following the decision in *Prasad* v. *Wolverhampton Borough Council* [1983] C.L.Y. 356, expenditure incurred before the making of the drought order could still be attributed to that order: the proper test was that laid down in *Harvey* v. *Crawley Development Corp.* [1957] C.L.Y. 476, namely whether the expenditure was not too remote and was the natural and reasonable consequence of the drought order. Applying that test the tribunal disallowed the whole claim, since the expenditure incurred on continuous pumping was attributable not to the drought order but to the actual drought itself; since the level of water actually available after imposition of the order was sufficient to enable B to operate within the limits of the discharge consent, and since the removal of stock to the authority's farm had in fact enabled B to continue operations at an appreciably higher level than would otherwise have been possible, even without a drought order. Assuming the availability of the authority's farm, all these items of expenditure would have been incurred irrespective of whether the order was imposed.)

3529. Reservoirs Act 1975

RESERVOIRS ACT 1975 (APPLICATION FEES) (AMENDMENT) REGULATIONS 1986 (No. 853) [45p], made under the Reservoirs Act 1975 (c.23), ss.4(2), 5; operative on June 1, 1986; increases fees in connection with applications by civil engineers to become members of panels constituted for the purposes of the 1975 Act.

RESERVOIRS ACT 1975 (CERTIFICATES, REPORTS AND PRESCRIBED INFORMATION) REGULATIONS 1986 (No. 468) [£2·30], made under the Reservoirs Act 1975 (c.23), ss.5, 20(1), 21(1) and 23; operative on April 1, 1986; prescribe the form in which reports are to be made and certificates given under the Act, wherever its provisions require the making of a report or the giving of a certificate by a civil engineer engaged on work in connection with a large raised reservoir.

RESERVOIRS ACT 1975 (REFEREES) (APPOINTMENT AND PROCEDURE) RULES 1986 (No. 467) [80p], made under the Reservoirs Act 1975, ss.19(5) and 23(2); operative on April 1, 1986; make provision relating to the appointment of a referee under s.19 of the 1975 Act.

3530. Reservoirs Act 1975—commencement

RESERVOIRS ACT 1975 (COMMENCEMENT No. 3) ORDER 1986 (No. 466 (C.15)) [£1·35], made under the Reservoirs Act 1975 (c.23), s.29 and the Local Government (Interim Provisions) Act 1984 (c.53), s.6(3); brings into force on April 1, 1986 in areas other than Greater London and the metropolitan counties sections 6–10, 12–14, 15(1)–(5), 19, 20, 21(1)–(6), 22, 23, 25–28, Sched. 2 of the 1975 Act and brings into force on April 1, 1986 in Greater London and the metropolitan counties sections 2, 3, 11, 15(4), 16, 17 (in part), 18, 21(5)(6), 22, 24 of the 1975 Act.

RESERVOIRS ACT 1975 (COMMENCEMENT No. 4) ORDER 1986 (No. 2202 (c.86)) [80p], made under the Reservoirs Act 1975 (c.23), s.29 and the Local Government (Interim Provisions) Act 1984 (c.53), s.6(3); brings into force on April 1, 1987, in relation to Greater London and the metropolitan counties, sections 6–10, 12–14, 15(1)(5), 17(1)(*b*)–(*d*) (3), 19, 20, 21(1)–(6), 22, 23, 25–28, Sched. 2 of the 1975 Act.

3531. Thames Barrier—transfer of functions. See LOCAL GOVERNMENT, § 2057.

3532. Water authorities

ANGLIAN WATER AUTHORITY (AMENDMENT OF LOCAL ENACTMENT) ORDER 1986 (No. 1670) [45p], made under the Water Resources Act 1963 (c.38), s.133(1); operative on October 28, 1986; confirms the licence to draw water from the River Great Ouse at the Seven Holes Sluice.

ANGLIAN WATER AUTHORITIES (MIDDLE LEVEL TRANSFER) ORDER 1986 (No. 1739) [45p], made under the Water Resources Act 1971 (c.34), s.1, operative on October 6, 1986; provides for the discharge of water into the Old Bedford River.

ANGLIAN WATER AUTHORITY (STOUR GROUNDWATER) ORDER 1986 (No. 1575) [£1·40], made under the Water Resources Act 1963 (c.38), s.67, the Compulsory Purchase

Act 1965 (c.56), s.36, and the Water Resources Act 1971 (c.34), s.1; operative on September 10, 1986; empowers the authority to acquire certain lands, make discharges of water and construct works.

SOUTHERN WATER AUTHORITY (NIGHTINGALE STREAM DISCHARGE) ORDER 1986 (No. 1690) [45p], made under the Water Resources Act 1971, s.1; operative on September 30, 1986; authorises the discharge of water into the Nightingale Stream.

WATER AUTHORITIES (RETURN ON ASSETS) ORDER 1986 (No. 1952) [80p], made under the Water Act 1973 (c.37), s.29(2)(a); operative on December 15, 1986; gives directions to the water authorities. It specifies the rate of return on the value of their net assets which the Secretary of State considers each water authority can reasonably achieve for 1987–88.

WELSH WATER AUTHORITY (PLAS YR ESGOB BOREHOLE) ORDER 1986 (No. 1986) [80p], made under the Water Act 1945 (c.45), s.23; operative on December 1, 1986; provides that the said authority may continue and maintain "the existing borehole" as defined.

WELSH WATER AUTHORITY (RUTHIN BOREHOLE) (DISCHARGE) ORDER 1986 (No. 1531) [45p], made under the Water Resources Act 1971 s.1; operative on September 1, 1986; authorises the authority to discharge water from the Ruthin borehole.

YORKSHIRE WATER AUTHORITY (DERRINGS BECK DISCHARGE) ORDER 1986 (No. 774) [45p], made under the Water Resources Act 1971 (c.34), s.1; operative on April 29, 1986; permits the said authority to discharge water from the Tholthorpe Borehole into Derrings Beck.

YORKSHIRE WATER AUTHORITY (GALE GATE DRAIN DISCHARGE) ORDER 1986 (No. 775) [45p], made under the Water Resources Act 1971 (c.34), s.1; operative on April 29, 1986; permits the said authority to discharge water from the Upper Dunsforth Borehole into Gale Gate Drain.

3533. Water charge—sewerage—assessment of charge. See SOUTH WEST WATER AUTHORITY v. RUMBLES, § 2819.

3534. Water orders
Orders made under the Water Act 1945 (c.42): s.19(6): S.I. 1986 Nos. 1618 (South West Water) [45p]; 1733 (West Kent Water) [80p]; 1776 (West Hampshire Water) [£1.40].

S.23: S.I. 1986 Nos. 2 (Eastbourne Water) [£1·35]; 13 (South Staffordshire Water) [40p]; 136 (Mid Southern) [£1·35]. 245 (Cambridge) [40p]; 246 (Cambridge) [80p]; 247 (Cambridge) [80p.]. S.32: S.I. 1986 Nos. 2 (Eastbourne Water) [£1·35]; 13 (South Staffordshire Water) [40p]; 136 (Mid Southern) [£1·35]; 249 (North Surrey) [80p]; 740 (Cambridge Water) [80p]; (c.42).

S.33: S.I. 1986 Nos. 136 (Mid Southern) [£1·35]; 249 (North Surrey) [80p].

S.50: S.I. 1986 Nos. 2 (Eastbourne Water [£1·35] South Staffordshire Water) [40p]; 136 (Mid Southern) [£1·35]; 249 (North Surrey) [80p].

Ss. 23, 32(1): S.I. 1986 No. 2136 (East Anglia Water) [45p], 2210 (Essex Water) [80p].

Ss.23, 32, 33 and 50: S.I. 1986 No. 401 (Hartlepool) [£3·30].

Orders made under the Water Act 1945: ss.23, 33, 50: S.I. 1986 No. 1532 (Portsmouth Water) [80p].

WEIGHTS AND MEASURES

3535. Fees
MEASURING INSTRUMENTS (EEC PATTERN APPROVAL REQUIREMENTS) (FEES) (AMENDMENT) REGULATIONS 1986 (No. 831) [45p], made under the Finance Act 1973 (c.51), s.56(1) and (2); operative on June 9, 1986; increase the fees for examiner staff time, equipment test unit staff time and use of an environmental testing chamber.

3535a. Intoxicating liquor—unstamped measures
[Weights and Measures Act 1963 (c.31), s.11(2).] The licensee of a public house used unstamped measures for serving drink. Held, that this was prima facie use by his employers for the purpose of charges against them under s.11(2) of the Weights and Measures Act 1963: EVANS v. CLIFTON INNS, The Times, March 18, 1986, D.C.

3536. Linear measures
WEIGHTS AND MEASURES (LOCAL AND WORKING STANDARD LINEAR MEASURES) REGULATIONS 1986 (No. 1684) [80p], made under the Weights and Measures Act 1985

(c.72), ss.4(5)(6), 5(9), 86(1), 94(1); operative on October 27, 1986; prescribe the methods of testing and adjusting, and the limits of error, working standard linear measurements used by inspectors, and make provision for local standard linear measurements.

3537. Measuring instruments

MEASURING EQUIPMENT (LIQUID FUEL DELIVERED FROM ROAD TANKERS) (AMENDMENT) REGULATIONS 1986 (No. 1210) [£1·40], made under the Weights and Measures Act 1985 (c.72), ss.11(1), (4), 12(12), 15(1), 86(1) and 94(1); operative on August 11, 1986; amend S.I. 1983 No. 1390.

MEASURING EQUIPMENT (MEASURES OF LENGTH) (AMENDMENT) REGULATIONS 1986 (No. 2109) [45p], made under the Weights and Measures Act 1985 (c.72), ss.11(1)(4)(7), 15(1), 86(1), 94(1); operative on December 5, 1986; corrects an error in S.I. 1986 No. 1682.

MEASURING EQUIPMENT (MEASURES OF LENGTH) REGULATIONS 1986 (No. 1682) [£1·40], made under the Weights and Measures Act 1985 (c.72), ss.11(1)(4)(7), 15(1), 86(1), 94(1); operative on October 27, 1986; prescribe measures of length, which do not bear the mark of EEC initial verification, for the purposes of s.11(1) of the 1985 Act that their trade use is unlawful unless they have been tested.

MEASURING INSTRUMENTS (EEC INITIAL VERIFICATION REQUIREMENTS) (FEES) (AMENDMENT) REGULATIONS 1986 (No. 1043) [45p], made under the Finance Act 1973 (c.51), s.56(1)(2); operative on July 28, 1986; increase fees payable under S.I. 1982 No. 811.

3538. Miscellaneous foods

WEIGHTS AND MEASURES ACT 1963 (MISCELLANEOUS FOODS) (AMENDMENT) ORDER 1986 (No. 1260) [£1·40], made under the Weights and Measures Act 1985 (c.72), s.86(2); operative on September 1, 1986; amends S.I. 1984 No. 1316.

3539. Packaged goods

WEIGHTS AND MEASURES (PACKAGED GOODS) REGULATIONS 1986 (No. 2049) [£5·60], made under the Weights and Measures Act 1985 (c.72), ss.47–49, 51, 54, 63, 65–68, 86 and 94(1); operative on January 1, 1987; consolidate S.I. 1979 No. 1613; as amended, which made provision for implementing the system of quantity control ("the average system") applicable to the packaging of goods sold by weight on volume.

3540. Passing of property

[Weights and Measures Act 1963 (c.31), s.22(6), Sched. 6, part 1.] For the purposes of an offence under the Act, where a dealer in items contracts their delivery to a sub-contractor who affords the customer the opportunity to select from a pool, property in the items passes when the buyer appropriates them to the contract by taking them into his home: CHURCH *v.* LEE & CO-OPERATIVE RETAIL SERVICES, (1986) 150 J.P.N. 335, D.C.

3541. Short measure—defences

[Weights and Measures Act 1963 (c.31), ss.14, 24, 26.] On three informations the justices acquitted D in the following circumstances: On the first D had boned the meat sold according to their normal practice; on the second D had delivered chickens without giblets, but there were no specific instructions about giblets; and on the third the weight of a delivery of meat was incorrectly stated as the result of misreading the foreman's writing, notwithstanding a system of double-checking for such mistakes. *Held,* that there was nothing to show that the justices had erred in some way and the appeal was dismissed: NORTH YORKSHIRE COUNTY COUNCIL *v.* HOLMESTERNE FARM CO. (1985) 150 J.P.N. 111, D.C.

3542. Testing equipment

WEIGHTS AND MEASURES (LOCAL AND WORKING STANDARD WEIGHTS AND TESTING EQUIPMENT) REGULATIONS 1986 (No. 1685) [£1·90], made under the Weights and Measures Act 1985 (c.72), ss.4(5)(6), 5(9), 86(1), 94(1); operative on November 1, 1986; replace S.I.1983 No. 1653 and prescribe the method of testing and adjusting, and the limits of error, working standard weights and test equipment used by inspectors.

3543. Units of measurement
UNITS OF MEASUREMENT REGULATIONS 1986 (No. 1082) [£1·90], made under the European Communities Act 1972 (c.68), s.2(2); operative on August 1, 1986; consolidate S.I. 1978 No. 484 and S.I. 1980 No. 1070, as amended.

3544. Weighing equipment
WEIGHING EQUIPMENT (FILLING AND DISCONTINUOUS TOTALISING AUTOMATIC WEIGHING MACHINES) REGULATIONS 1986 (No. 1320) [£2·90], made under the Weights and Measures Act 1985 (c.72), ss.11(1), (4), (7), 12(12), 15(1), 86(1) and 94(1); operative on September 1, 1986; prescribe filling and discontinuous totalising automatic weighing machines for the purposes of s.11(1) of the 1985 Act.

3545. Weights regulations
WEIGHTS REGULATIONS 1986 (No. 1683) [£2·90], made under the Weights and Measures Act 1985 (c.72), ss.11(1)(4), 15(1), 86(1), 94(1); operative on November 1, 1986 save for regs. 1(4) and 13 which are operative on September 1, 1988; replace S.I.1970 No. 1370 and apply to all weights used for trade purposes except for weighing coins or currency notes.

WILLS

3546. Administrator of estate—completion of sale by vendor administrator—letters of administration
[(Sing.) Probate and Administration Act, s.37(2).] A vendor administrator is not able to complete the sale of land comprised in the estate without extracting a grant of letters of administration: CHAY CHING HWA v. SEAH MARY, Sol. Jo. 860, P.C.

3547. Construction—meaning of "money"
The testatrix made a will without professional assistance. Having cancelled all other wills, appointed executors and given certain pecuniary legacies, she directed "remainder of money to be equally divided between" six named persons. She directed that her house was to be sold privately if possible, and that there was to be no sale of the house or furniture on the premises. She then made specific bequests of furniture and other chattels. The property in the estate consisted of stocks, shares, National Savings certificates, bank accounts, building society accounts, chattels and a freehold house. *Held,* that in the context "money" included the whole of her residuary estate (*Perrin* v. *Morgan* [1943] A.C. 399 applied; *Re Mellor* [1929] 1 Ch. 446 considered): GAMMON, *Re*; SHELTON v. WILLIAMS, February 27, 1986; Terence Cullen, Q.C., sitting as a Deputy High Court Judge [*Ex rel. Josephine Hayes, Barrister.*]

3548. Family provision—claim by widow—death of widow before hearing—whether action subsists for benefit of estate
[Law Reform (Miscellaneous Provisions) Act 1934 (c.41.), s.1(1); Inheritance (Provision for Family and Dependants) Act 1975 (c.63), s.1(2).]
An action by a widow under s.1 of the Inheritance (Provision for Family and Dependants) Act 1975 is personal and on her death prior to relief being granted does not subsist for the benefit of her estate.
H died in 1984 and his widow began proceedings against his estate for provision under s.1(2) of the 1975 Act; she died before the hearing of the application. Her personal representatives sought to continue the action. *Held*, that a widow claiming reasonable financial provision under s.1 of the 1975 Act had no cause of action capable of surviving her death. She had no enforceable right against the estate of the deceased, merely a right to apply to the Court for relief (*Sugden* v. *Sugden* [1957] C.L.Y. 1087 applied).
WHYTTE v. TICEHURST [1986] 2 W.L.R. 700, Booth J.

3549. Family provision—daughter—estranged mother—considerations
[Inheritance (Provision for Family and Dependants) Act 1975 (c.63), ss.1, 2, 3.]
The applicant was aged 58 and the daughter of the deceased. The estate amounted to £172,000. The legacy was £200. She had been taken to South Africa shortly after her birth, by her father and brought up by his parents. During her childhood and adolescence she had no contact with the deceased. In 1948 they met but the deceased stated that she wished to keep their relationship a secret. In 1953 the applicant settled in England but the deceased repulsed all her efforts to establish a relationship or to help her financially. However, she indicated that the applicant would be well

provided for in her will. In 1973 the deceased made a will leaving the applicant £500 and a chain. Following the applicant's marriage in 1977 the legacy was reduced to £200. The main beneficiaries under the will were six animal charities. The applicant and her husband (aged 63) had been made redundant. The applicant was physically disabled and had epilepsy. They had no capital apart from a small bungalow purchased from their redundancy monies. When they reached retirement age they would receive a state pension. *Held,* that *Re Coventry* did not support the view that an adult child had to show exceptional circumstances. Whilst the deceased owed no legal obligation to the applicant there was some moral obligation to help the applicant. It followed that the legacy was not reasonable provision. Taking all the factors into account under s.3 a small capital sum of £3,000 would be appropriate to enable the applicant to meet her immediate needs and to obviate the difficulty of backdating an order and a periodical payments order of £4,500 p.a. until further order during her lifetime. It might well be appropriate to reduce this order when the state pension became due for payment (*Coventry, Re* [1979] C.L.Y. 2807 considered): DEBENHAM DECD., *Re* (1986) 16 Fam. Law 101, Ewbank J.

3550. Family provision—death of applicant—abatement of cause
[Law Reform (Miscellaneous Provisions) Act 1934 (c.41), s.1; Inheritance Provision for Family and Dependants Act 1975 (c.63), s.3.] H and W had been divorced in 1977. In 1983 H had transferred his house into the joint names of himself and his housekeeper (D2) as joint tenants. H died in 1983 and the house passed by right of survivorship to D2. W applied under ss.2 and 9 of the 1975 Act. Before her application was determined she died on May 9, 1985. D2 applied to strike out W's application. W's personal representatives contended that her application was a cause of action capable of surviving her death for the benefit of her estate under s.1 of the 1934 Act. *Held,* that an application under the 1975 Act was a personal application and could not be continued by the applicant's personal representatives. The provisions of s.3 were intended to relate to the present needs of the applicant at the time of the hearing and the Act did not, therefore, anticipate a cause of action enforceable by the applicant's estate: R. (DECEASED), *Re*; R. *v.* O. (1986) 16 Fam.Law 58, Mr. Registrar Garland.

3551. Family provision—failure to provide for past mistress
P had met the deceased in 1967 and had become his mistress. She was 29 and unmarried. He was a married man aged 50 whose wife was in poor health. By a letter dated May 25, 1975 the deceased asked P to come and live with him offering "what emotional security I can give, plus financial security during my life and financial security after my death: He implied and P understood that the deceased would marry her after his wife died. She provided wifely services and was paid a salary of £100 p.m. rising to £120 p.m. plus £30 p.w. housekeeping. In 1977 the deceased's wife died but he did not in the event marry P. He made some provision for her in his wills, the last being in 1979 by way of a legacy of £15,000 with provisions relating to her continued residence with him until his death. Subsequently, the deceased cut P out of his will and gave her a written notice of dismissal in 1980. They parted though, without rancour and kept in touch until the deceased's death in April 1982. In 1983 P made a claim for financial provision based on the contents of the 1975 letter contending (i) that the deceased's representations amounted to a constructive trust; (ii) that under the doctrine of proprietary estoppel equity would subject the estate to such beneficial interest in her favour and would give effect to the representation upon which she relied and (iii) that there was a concluded contract between them. *Held,* dismissing P's application, that P had made no relevant contribution to the acquisition or preservation of any asset of the deceased so as to enable her to claim a beneficial interest therein and that a common intention in itself was insufficient. The doctrine of proprietary estoppel was also inappropriate since no specific assets could be identified. As far as the contractual argument was concerned the "offer" in the 1975 letter was no more than a statement of intent and it was questionable whether there was any intention to create a legally binding contract. The fact that P had not lived with the deceased continuously until his death meant that she was not entitled to bring any claim under the 1975 Act. (*Pettit* v. *Pettit* [1969] C.L.Y. 1639, *Gissing* v. *Gissing* [1970] C.L.Y. 1243, *Crabb* v. *Arun District Council*]1975] C.L.Y. 1191 and *Taylor Fashions* v. *Liverpool Victoria Trustees Co.* [1979] C.L.Y. 1619 considered): LAYTON *v.* MARTIN (1986) 16 Fam. Law 212, Scott J.

3552. Intestacy—movable and immovable property in three different countries—immovable property in United Kingdom—statutory legacy—"residuary estate of intestate"
[Administration of Estates Act 1925 (c.23), s.46.]

A surviving spouse's rights to a statutory legacy under s.46 of the Administration of Estates Act 1925 are not affected by the spouse's rights in the deceased's estate in another country.

D, the deceased, died intestate, survived by W, and his children by a previous marriage. His estate consisted of property in Trinidad and Tobago, Barbados and the United Kingdom. Part of the estate in the United Kingdom consisted of immovable property. W's benefit from the foreign property amounted to more than $1 million. she claimed a statutory legacy out of D's "residuary estate" in the United Kingdom under s.46 of the Administration of Estates Act 1925. The children contended that the "residuary estate" included the foreign property, and that W's claim has been thereby satisfied. *Held,* that s.46 could only impose a charge for the statutory legacy on English immovables, and there was no way in which the charge on the English immovable estate could be said to have been satisfied by the overseas assets; accordingly, W was entitled to claim her statutory legacy.

COLLENS, DECD., *Re*; ROYAL BANK OF CANADA (LONDON) *v.* KROGH [1986] 1 All E.R. 611, Browne-Wilkinson V.-C.

WORDS AND PHRASES

3553. The following words and phrases have been judicially considered in 1986:

accommodation, § 1619
available route, § 1145
building, § 500
by way of trade, § 437
collection, § 276
committee, § 2040
damage, § 530
does acts, § 1892
employment, § 3442
enrolled, § 1718
issue, § 3031
legal proceedings held in public, § 520
motor vehicle, § 2956
owner, § 3134
previously, § 341
prison, § 550
protected site, § 1639

purposes for which the land was acquired, § 353
released to public, § 410
reliable device, § 2569
road, § 2976
significant, § 521
so serious that a non-custodial sentence cannot be justified, § 897
state, § 2789
supply, § 646
tenancy, § 1866
the tenant, § 41
undue delay, § 2662
unless the contrary is shown, § 2727
vocation, § 1138
within, § 1832

WORKMEN'S COMPENSATION

3553a. Supplementation
WORKMEN'S COMPENSATION (SUPPLEMENTATION) AMENDMENT SCHEME 1986 (No. 1174) [80p], made under the Industrial Injuries and Diseases (Old Cases) Act 1975 (c. 16), ss. 2 and 4(2); operative on July 30, 1986; amends S.I. 1982 No. 1489.

BOOKS AND ARTICLES

INDEX OF BOOKS

The following books were published in 1986. They are listed under the appropriate Current Law heading. Books relating to Scotland are listed separately.

ADMINISTRATIVE LAW
Birkinshaw, P.—Open Government: Freedom of Information and Local Government. Paperback: £4·95: ISBN 0 951110 10 1.
Cane, P.—An Introduction to Administrative Law. First edition. Paperback: £9·95: ISBN 0 19 825485 7.
Foulkes' Administrative Law—by D. Foulkes. [Sixth edition.] Hardback: £27·50: ISBN 0 406 584 095. Paperback: £17·95: ISBN 0 406 584 109.
Galligan, D.—Discretionary Powers: a Legal Study of Official Discretion. Hardback: £30·00: ISBN 0 19 825498 9.
Yardley, D. C. M.—Principles of Administrative Law. Second edition. Paperback: £9·95: ISBN 0 406 68993 8.

AGENCY
Christou, R.—International Agency, Distribution and Licensing Agreements. [Longman Commercial Series]. Hardback: £42·50: ISBN 0 85121 188 7.
Markesinis, B. S. and Munday, R. J. C.—An Outline of the Law of Agency. Second edition. Paperback: £8·50: ISBN 0 406 62272 8.

AGRICULTURE
Card, R., Murdoch, J. and Schofield P.—Law for Estate Management Students. Second edition. Paperback: £16·95: ISBN 0 406 56291 1.
Gammie, M. and Bailey, J.—Land Taxation. Looseleaf: £125·00: ISBN 0 421 27540 5.
Rogers, C. P.—Agricultural Tenancies Law and Practice. Paperback: £28·00. ISBN 0 406 25840 6.
Tyler, E. L. G.—Cases and Statutes on Land Law. Second edition. Paperback: £10·95: ISBN 0 421 34350 8.

ARBITRATION
Dore, I.—Arbitration and Conciliation under the UNCITRAL Rules: a Textual analysis. Hardback: £37·50: ISBN 089838 913 5.
Lee, E.—Dictionary of Arbitration Law and Practice. Hardback: £34·50.
Lee, E.—Encyclopedia of International Commercial Arbitration. Looseleaf: £130·00: ISBN 0 850 440 59 X.
Lew, Dr. J. D. M.—Contemporary Problems in International Arbitration. Hardback: £40: ISBN 0 951 0664 12.
Williams, R.—Concilio—Arbitration Handbook. Paperback: £10.

AVIATION
Taylor, S. and Parmar, H.—Aviation Law for Pilots. Fifth edition. Paperback: £9·95: ISBN 0 00 3832 73 2.

BANKING
Abbott, K. and Pendlebury, N.—Business Law. Third edition. Paperback: £4·95: ISBN 0 905 435 67 2.
Allied Dunbar Investment Guide 1986–87—Edited by C. Robinson. Hardback: £12·50: ISBN 0 85121 166 6.
Gabriel, P.—Legal Aspects of Syndicated Loans. Hardback: £45·00: ISBN 0 406 10210 4.
Hedley, W.—Bills of Exchange and Bankers' Documentary Credits. Hardback: £52: ISBN 1 85044 084 0.
Higson, C. J.—Business Finance. Paperback: £12·95: ISBN 0 406 50141 6.
Islamic Banking and Finance.—Edited by the Butterworths Editorial Staff. Hardback: £40·00: ISBN 0 406 10034 9.
Kettell, B. and Magnus, G. A.—The International Debt Game. Paperback: £12·50: ISBN 0 86010 810 4.
Milnes Holden, J.—The Law and Practice of Banking: Vol. 2: Securities for Bankers' Advances [Seventh edition]. Paperback: £12·95: ISBN 0 273 02295 4.
Palfreman, D.—The Law of Banking. Third edition. Paperback: £6·50: ISBN 0 7121 0682 0.
Salinger, F. R.—Factoring and the Lending Banks. Paperback: £4·95: ISBN 0 85459 253 9.

BOOKS AND ARTICLES

BANKRUPTCY

Fletcher, I. F.—Insolvency Act 1985. [Current Law Statutes Annotated Reprints]. Paperback: £12·50: ISBN 0 421 34700 7.

Lingard, J. R.—Corporate Rescues and Insolvencies. Hardback: £25·00: ISBN 0 406 10043 3.

Totty and Jordan.—Insolvency. Hardback: £170. Looseleaf: ISBN 0 085121 142 9.

Totty, P. and Jordan, M.—Insolvency: An Introduction to the 1985 Act. Paperback: £6·95: ISBN 0 85121 216 6.

BOUNDARIES AND FENCES

Aldridge, T.—Boundaries, Walls and Fences. Sixth edition. Paperback: £11·95: ISBN 0 85121 234 4.

BRITISH COMMONWEALTH

Trindade, F. and Lee, H. (Editors).—The Constitution of Malaysia: Further Perspectives and Developments. Essays in Honour of Tun Mohamed Suffian. Hardback: £30·00: ISBN 0 19 582644 2.

BUILDING AND ENGINEERING, ARCHITECTS AND SURVEYORS

Building Law Reports, Vol. 30.—Edited by H. Lloyd and C. Reese. Hardback: £17·00: ISBN 0 7114 5808 1.

Building Law Reports Vol. 31.—Edited by C. Reese and N. Baatz. Hardback: £19·00. ISBN 0 582 49492 3.

Building Law Reports, Vol. 32.—Edited by H. Lloyd, C. Reese and N. Baatz. Hardback: £19·00: ISBN 0 582 494 93 1.

Elder, A. J.—Guide to the Building Regulations 1985. Paperback: £16·95: ISBN 0 85139 844 8.

Estates Gazette Law Reports 1985.—Two volumes. Edited by J. Muir Watt. Hardback: Vol. 1: £20·00: ISBN 0 72820 097 X: Hardback: Vol. 2: £20·00: ISBN 0 72820 098 8.

Furmston, M. and Powell-Smith, V.—Construction Law Reports, Vol. 3. 1985. Hardback: £18·50: ISBN 0 85139 782 4.

Hibberd, P. R.—Variations in Construction Contracts. Hardback: £17·95: ISBN 0 00 383191 4.

Lloyd, H.—The Liability of Contractors. Hardback: £39·95: ISBN 0 582 46368 8.

Meopham, B.—F.I.O.I.C. Conditions of Contract: A Commercial Manual. Hardback: £30.00: ISBN 0 08 039234 2.

Powell-Smith, V. and Billington, M. J.—The Building Regulations Explained and Illustrated. Seventh edition. Paperback: £12·95: ISBN 0 00 383226 0.

Ross, M.—Negligence in Surveying & Building. Paperback: £13·50: ISBN 0 7282 0095 3.

CAPITAL TAXATION

Butterworths Budget Tax Tables 1986—Edited by Bond, D., Grosse, C., Kronbergs, Z. and Parrington, S. 22nd edition. Paperback: £2·80: ISBN 0 406 50841 0.

Butterworths Orange Tax Handbook 1986–87.—Eleventh edition. Paperback: £17·00: ISBN 0 406 50832 1.

Butterworths Yellow Tax Handbook 1986–87.—Twenty-fifth edition. Paperback: £19·00: ISBN 0 406 51003 2.

Cox, C. and Ross, H.—Capital Gains Tax on Businesses. Second edition. Paperback: £17·50: ISBN 0 421 33960 8.

Gammie, M.—Tax Strategy for Directors, Executives and Employees. Second edition. Paperback: £25·00: ISBN 0 85121 076 7.

Kay, J. and King, M.—The British Tax System. Fourth edition. Hardback: £17·50: ISBN 0 19 877263 7. Paperback: £6·50: ISBN 0 19 877262 9.

Kingley, K. R.—Tolley's Guide to the New Inheritance Tax. Paperback: £4·95: ISBN 0 85459 256 3.

Moores & Rowland's Tax Guide 1985–86. Ninth edition. Paperback: £25: ISBN 0 406 35920 2.

Pritchard, W. E.—Taxation. Seventh edition. Paperback: £7·95: ISBN 0 7121 2037 8.

Ray, R.—Practical CTT Planning. Third edition. Paperback: £20: ISBN 0 406 53616 3.

Sinclair, W. and Silke, P.—Allied Dunbar Capital Taxes and Estate Planning Guide. Third edition. Hardback: £12·50: ISBN 0 85121 213 1.

Stoy Hayward.—Inheritance Tax. Paperback: £7·95: ISBN 1 85091 247 5.

Tolley.—(Ed. Maas, R.) Property Taxes. Paperback: £15·95: ISBN 0 85459 223 7.

Tolley's.—Capital Gains Tax 1986–87 [1986–87]. Paperback: £13·50: ISBN 0 85459 240 7.

Tolley's Capital Gains Tax Base Date Prices—compiled by Extel Statistical Services. Paperback: £15·00: ISBN 0 85459 244 X.

Tolley's.—Taxation in the Channel Islands and Isle of Man 1986 [1986]. Paperback: £11·50: ISBN 0 85459 225 3.

Tolley's Tax Cases 1986—By Victor Grant. Paperback: £15·50: ISBN 0 85459 229 6.

Tolley's Tax Computations 1985–86. K. M. G. Thomson McLintock. Paperback: £19·50: ISBN 0 85459 197 4.

Tolley's.—Taxwise Taxation Workbook No. 1 [1986/7]. Paperback: £13·95: ISBN 0 85459 2571.

BOOKS

CAPITAL TAXATION—*cont.*

Tolley's Tax Bumph 1985–86.—Edited by R. Wareham and N. Bowen. Paperback: £18·95: ISBN 0 85459 198 2.

Tolley's Tax Planning 1986. Paperback: £27·50: ISBN 0 85459 203 2.

Tolley's Tax Tables 1986–87.—Paperback: £4·95: ISBN 0 85459 213 X.

Walters, R. M.—Inheritance Tax. Paperback: £7·95: ISBN 0 7121 06928.

Wareham, R.—Tolley's Tax Data 1986–87. Paperback: £6·95: ISBN 0 85459 223 7.

Whillans's Tax Tables 1986–87.—Edited by S. Parrington. [Thirty ninth edition]. Paperback: £2·60: ISBN 0 406 54321 6.

White, P.—Tax Planning for the Family. [Practical Tax Series]. Third edition. Paperback: £18·95: ISBN 0 85120 920 3.

White, P.—Tax Planning on Marriage Breakdown. Fourth edition. Paperback: £25·00: ISBN 0 85121 074 0.

CHARITIES

Tolley's Charities Manual by Burgess, A., Crane, M. and Fox, R.—Hardback: £23·95: ISBN 0 85459 216 4.

COMMON LAW

Postema, G.—Bentham and the Common Law Tradition. First edition. Hardback: £40·00: ISBN 0 19 825505 5.

Poulter, S. M.—English Law and Ethnic Minority Customs. Paperback: £25·95: ISBN 0 406 18000 8.

COMPANY LAW

Abbott, K.—Company Law, Second edition. Paperback: £4·95: ISBN 0 905435 60 5.

Abbott, K. and Pendlebury, N.—Business Law. Third edition. Paperback: £4·95: ISBN 0 905 435 67 2.

Arora, A.—Jordans Guide to Company Administration. Paperback: £9·50: ISBN 0 85308 084 4.

Begg, P. F. C.—Corporate Acquisitions & Mergers. Second edition. Hardback: £40: ISBN 0 86010 813 9.

Butterworths.—Company Law Guide. Eds. Renshall, M. and Walmsley, K. Paperback: £18·95: ISBN 0 406 19700 8.

Cooke, T. E.—Mergers and Acquisitions. Hardback: £35·00: ISBN 0 631 14747 0.

Coopers and Lybrand—Form and Content of Company Accounts. Third edition. Paperback: £8·95: ISBN 1 85185 032 5.

Fletcher, I. F.—Insolvency Act 1985. [Current Law Statutes Annotated Reprints]. Paperback: £12·50: ISBN 0 421 34700 7.

Franks, J.—The Company Director and the Law. Fifth edition. Hardback: £14·95: ISBN 0 85121 321 X.

Gammie, M.—Tax Strategy for Directors, Executives and Employees. Second edition. Paperback: £25·00: ISBN 0 85121 076 7.

Gilpin, A.—Dictionary of Economics and Financial Markets. Fifth edition. Hardback: £17·95: ISBN 0 406 50230 7.

Gore-Brown on Companies.—Edited by A. J. Boyle and R. Sykes. Two volumes. 44th edition. Looseleaf: £150·00: ISBN 0 85308 082 8.

Higson, C. J.—Business Finance. Paperback: £12·95: ISBN 0 406 50141 6.

Jordans—Company Law Materials. Tenth edition. Paperback: £8·00: ISBN 0 85308 087 9.

Lingard, J. R.—Corporate Rescues and Insolvencies. Hardback: £25·00: ISBN 0 406 10043 3.

Lintott, D.—Handbook of Company Secretarial Practice. Paperback: £13·95: ISBN 0 902197 41 X.

Mascarenhas, A.—Current Accounting Law and Practice 1986. Eleventh edition. Paperback: £26·50: ISBN 0 906157 09 9.

Mayson, S. and French, D.—A practical approach to Company Law. Third edition. Paperback: £15·95: ISBN 1 85185 028 7.

Roberts, D.—How to Form a Company: a practical guide to the formation of private companies. Second edition. Hardback: £19·50: ISBN 0 902197 44 4.

Roberts, D.—Index to the Companies Act 1985 and Related Legislation. Paperback: £5·25: ISBN 0 902197 47 9.

Roberts, D.—The Administration of Company Meetings. First edition. Hardback: £19·50: ISBN 0 902197 45 2.

Smith and Keenan's Company Law—by D. Keenan. [Sixth edition]. Paperback: £10·95: ISBN 0 273 02487 6.

Stilling, P. J. Wild, K. and Sharp, D.—Company Accounting Requirements: a practical guide. Second edition. Paperback: £15·50: ISBN 0 85121 146 1.

Tiley, J. and Bailey, S.—Business Law. Longman Exam Guides. Paperback: £5·95: ISBN 0 582 29678 1.

BOOKS AND ARTICLES

COMPANY LAW—*cont.*

Tolley's Index to Companies Legislation—compiled by J. Stafford and N. Bowen. Paperback: £7·50: ISBN 0 85459 214 8.

Tolley's Share Options and Incentives for Directors and Employees—by Koppel, M. and Wolstenholme, P. Paperback: £7·95: ISBN 0 85459 180 X.

Tolley's Taxation of Insolvent Companies by Davis, A.—Paperback: £9·95: ISBN 0 85459 232 6.

Totty and Jordan.—Insolvency. Hardback: £170. Looseleaf: ISBN 0 085121 142 9.

Totty, P. and Jordan, M.—Insolvency: An Introduction to the 1985 Act. Paperback: £6·95: ISBN 0 85121 216 6.

Townsend, B.—The Financing of Countertrade. Hardback: £27·50: ISBN 0 406 10200 7.

[Ireland] Ussher, P.—Company Law in Ireland. Paperback: £18·95: ISBN 0 421 29750 6.

Walmsley, K.—Butterworths Company Law Handbook. Fifth edition. Paperback: £15·95: ISBN 0 406 14314 5.

Westby-Nunn's Company Secretarial Handbook. Ninth edition. Gorman, C. N. and Barker, A. V. Paperback: £17·95: ISBN 0 85121 068 6.

Wine, H.—Buying and Selling Private Companies and Businesses. [Third edition]. Paperback: £17·00: ISBN 0 406 42418 7.

Yates, D. and Hawkins, J.—Standard Business Contracts: Exclusions and Related Devices. Hardback: £58·00: ISBN 0 421 30760 9.

CONSTITUTIONAL LAW

Harden, I. and Lewis, N.—The Noble Lie. Hardback: £25·00: ISBN 0 09 164130 6.

Robilliard, St. J. and McEwan, J.—Police Powers and the Individual. Paperback: £10·50: ISBN 0 631 13996 6.

Sampford, C. and Galligan, D. (Editors)—Law, Rights and the Welfare State. Hardback: £25·00: ISBN 0 7099 3838 1.

Trindade, F. and Lee, H. (Editors).—The Constitution of Malaysia: Further Perspectives and Developments. Essays in Honour of Tun Mohamed Suffian. Hardback: £30·00: ISBN 0 19 582644 2.

CONSUMER CREDIT

Bennion, F.—Consumer Credit Act Manual. [Longman Practitioner Series]. Third edition. Paperback: £20·00: ISBN 0 85121 100 3.

Consumer Law Statutes.—Fifth edition. Paperback: £14·95: ISBN 0 906533 45 7.

Leder, M. J.—Consumer Law. Second edition. Paperback: £4·95: ISBN 0 7121 0677 4.

CONTRACT

Cheshire Fifoot & Furmston—Law of Contract. Eleventh edition. Paperback: £18·95: ISBN 0 406 56536 8.

Collins, H.—The Law of Contract. Hardback: £14·95: ISBN 0 297 787 845; Paperback: £7·50: ISBN 0 297 787 853.

Consumer Law Statutes.—Fifth edition. Paperback: £14·95: ISBN 0 906533 45 7.

Davies, F. R.—Contract Law. [Fifth edition]. Hardback: £9·50: ISBN 0 421 35090 3. Paperback: £6·75 ISBN 0 421 35100 4.

Gorton, L. and Ihre, R.—A Practical Guide to Contracts of Affreightment and Hybrid Contracts. Hardback: £24·50: ISBN 1 85044 060 3.

Lafili, L., Gevurtz, F. and Campbell, D.—Survey of the International Sale of Goods. Paperback: £28·95: ISBN 90 6544 241 3.

Lloyd, H.—The Liability of Contractors. Hardback: £39·95: ISBN 0 582 46368 8.

Meopham, B.—F.I.O.I.C. Conditions of Contract: A Commercial Manual. Hardback: £30·00: ISBN 0 08 039234 2.

Schofield, M. A.—Laytime and Demurrage. Hardback: £45·00: ISBN 1 85044 057 3.

Yates, D. and Hawkins, J.—Standard Business Contracts: Exclusions and Related Devices. Hardback: £58·00: ISBN 0 421 30760 9.

COPYRIGHT

Blanco White, T. A. and Jacob, R.—Patents, Trade Marks, Copyright and Industrial Designs. Third edition. Hardback: £12·95: ISBN 0 421 34960 3; Paperback: £8·95: ISBN 0 421 34970 0.

Edwards, C. and Savage, N.—Information Technology and the Law. Hardback: £35·00: ISBN 0 333 41393 8.

McFarlane, G.—Copyright through the Cases. Paperback: £15·00: ISBN 0 08 039208 3.

Phillips, J.—Introduction to Intellectual Property Law. Paperback: £13·95: ISBN 0 406 25832 5.

Sterling, J. A. L. and Carpenter, M. C. L.—Copyright Law in the United Kingdom. Hardback: £47·00: ISBN.

Williams, J.—A Manager's Guide to Patents, Trade Marks and Copyright. Hardback: £12·95: ISBN 0 85038 970 4.

BOOKS

CORPORATIONS

Cooke, T. E.—Mergers and Acquisitions. Hardback: £35·00: ISBN 0 631 14747 0.

Lingard, J. R.—Corporate Rescues and Insolvencies. Hardback: £25·00: ISBN 0 406 10043 3.

Tiley, J. and Bailey, S.—Business Law. Longman Exam Guides. Paperback: £5·95: ISBN 0 582 29678 1.

CORPORATION TAX

Butterworths Budget Tax Tables 1986—Edited by D. Bond, C. Grosse, Z. Krongbergs and S. Parrington, 22nd edition. Paperback: £2·80: ISBN 0 406 50841 0.

Butterworths Yellow Tax Handbook 1986–87.—Twenty-fifth edition. Paperback: £19·00: ISBN 0 406 51003 2.

Gammie, M.—Tax Strategy for Directors, Executives and Employees. Second edition. Paperback: £25·00: ISBN 0 85121 076 7.

Moores & Rowland's Tax Guide 1985–86. Ninth edition. Paperback: £25: ISBN 0 406 35920 2.

Pritchard, W. E.—Corporation Tax. Ninth edition. Paperback: £7·95: ISBN 0 7121 0694 4.

Pritchard, W. E.—Taxation. Seventh edition. Paperback: £7·95: ISBN 0 7121 2037 8.

Tolley's.—Corporation Tax 1986–87 [1986–87]. Paperback: £12·25: ISBN 0 85459 239 3.

Tolley's Tax Bumph 1985–86.—Edited by R. Wareham and N. Bowen. Paperback: £18·95: ISBN 0 85459 198 2.

Tolley's.—Taxation in the Republic of Ireland 1986–87. Paperback: £11·95: ISBN 0 85459 226 1.

Tolley's.—Taxwise Taxation Workbook No. 1. Paperback: £13·95: ISBN 0 85459 2571.

Tolley's Tax Cases 1986—By Victor Grant. Paperback: £15·50: ISBN 0 85459 229 6.

Tolley's Tax Computations 1985–86. K. M. G. Thomson McLintock. Paperback: £19·50: ISBN 0 85459 197 4.

Tolley's Tax Planning 1986. Paperback: £27·50: ISBN 0 85459 203 2.

Tolley's Tax Tables 1986–87.—Paperback: £4·95: ISBN 0 85459 213 X.

Wareham, R.—Tolley's Tax Data 1986–87. Paperback: £6·95: ISBN 0 85459 223 7.

Whillans's Tax Tables 1986–87—Edited by S. Parrington. [Thirty ninth edition]. Paperback: £2·60: ISBN 0 406 54321 6.

COUNTY COURT PRACTICE

Black, A.—Enforcement of a judgment. Seventh edition. Paperback: £12·95: ISBN 0 85121 023 6.

County Court Practice 1986, The—Edited by R. C. L. Gregory, Judge Peck and D. Lewis. Hardback: £70·00: ISBN 0 406 163 277.

CRIMINAL LAW

Amissah, A. N. E. [Ghana]—Criminal Procedure in Ghana. Paperback: £15·95: ISBN 9 964 72 009 2.

Ardis, P. and Comer, M.—Risk Management: Computers, Fraud and Insurance. Hardback: £19·95: ISBN 0 07 084926 9.

Banton, M.—Investigating Robbery. Hardback: £16·50: ISBN 0 566 051141.

Bottomley, K. and Pease, K.—Crime and Punishment. Interpreting the Data. Paperback: £7·95: ISBN 0 335 15389 5.

Bovey, K.—Misuse of Drugs: a Handbook for Lawyers. Paperback: £24·00 ISBN 0 406 10390 9.

Bucknell and Ghodse—Misuse of Drugs. Hardback: £35·00: ISBN 0 08 039203 2.

Burney, E.—Sentencing Young People: What went wrong with the Criminal Justice Act 1982. Hardback: £12·95: ISBN 0 566 05127 3.

Chatterton, C.—Bail: Law and Practice. Paperback £23·95: ISBN 0 406 10180 9.

Cross & Wilkins (ed. Tapper, C.)—Outline of the Law of Evidence. Sixth edition. Paperback: £10·95: ISBN 0 406 57081 7.

Fattah, E. A.—From Crime Policy to Victim Policy. Hardback: £29·50: ISBN 0 333 39994 3.

Feldman, D.—The Law Relating to Entry, Search and Seizure. Paperback: £28·95: ISBN 0 406 19910 8.

Gifford, Lord.—The Broadwater Farm Inquiry. First edition. Paperback: £4·95: ISBN 0 946918 59 7.

Harper, J. and Hamilton, P.—A Fingertip Guide to Criminal Law. Paperback: £15·00: ISBN 0 406 10380 1.

Heal, K. and Laycock, G.—Situational Crime Prevention from Theory into Practice. Paperback: £7·95: ISBN 0 11 340826 9.

Jones, T. MacLean, B. and Young, J.—The Islington Crime Survey. Hardback: £25·00: ISBN 0 566 05264 4.

Kinsey, R., Lea, J. and Young J.—Losing the Fight Against Crime. Paperback: £7·50: ISBN 0 631 13721 1.

May, R.—Criminal Evidence. Paperback: £19·50: ISBN 0 421 30290 9.

Morton, J.—Handling Criminal Cases: A Guide to Preparation and Defence. Paperback: £9·95: ISBN 0 08 039158 3.

[5]

BOOKS AND ARTICLES

CRIMINAL LAW—*cont.*

Murphy, D J. I.—Customers and Thieves: An Ethnography of Shoplifting. Hardback: £18·50: ISBN 0 566 00882 3.

Murphy, P. and Barnard, D.—Evidence & Advocacy. Second edition. Paperback: £7·95: ISBN 0 906322 96 0.

Pointing J. (editor)—Alternatives to Custody. Paperback: £7·95: ISBN 0 631 14702 0.

Radzinowicz, L. and Hood, R.—A History of English Criminal Law and its Administration from 1750, Vol. 5—The Emergence of Penal Policy. Hardback: £75·00: ISBN 0 420 46280 5.

Rutherford, A.—Growing out of Crime: Society and Young People in Trouble. Paperback: £3·95: ISBN 0 140 22383 5.

Ryan, C. and Scanlan, G.—Criminal Law. [SWOT series]. Paperback: £6·95: ISBN 0 906322 98 7.

Sargant, T. and Hill, P.—Criminal Trials—the Search for Truth. First edition. Paperback: £2.00: ISBN 0 7163 1348 0.

Smith & Hogan.—Criminal and Materials. Third edition. Paperback: £16·95: ISBN 0 406 65825 0.

Turnbell-Walker, A.—The Police and Criminal Evidence Act 1984: a Guide for Duty Solicitors. Booklet: £4·95: ISBN 1 85190 019 5.

Turner, A. and Marsh, M.—The New Fixed Penalty System (and Disqualification, Endorsement and Penalty Points). Paperback: £16·00: ISBN 0 870 08040 8.

Walker, C.—The Prevention of Terrorism in British Law. Hardback: £27·50: ISBN 0 7190 1782 3.

Wilkinson's Road Traffic Offences.—Second Cumulative Supplement to the Twelfth edition by Halnan, P. Paperback: £30·00: ISBN 0 85121 251 4.

Williams, D. B.—Criminal Injuries Compensation. Paperback: £9·95: ISBN 0 08 039244 X.

Wolchover, D.—The Exclusion of Improperly Obtained Evidence. First edition. Paperback: £18·00: ISBN 0 8599 2 380 0.

Kessler, K. and Goodfellow, G.—Inheritance Tax Planning. [Longman Intelligence Reports]. Paperback: £75·00: ISBN 0 85121 245 X.

DAMAGES

Brennan, D.—Provisional Damages—A guide to the new procedures. Paperback: £17·50: ISBN 0 907 822 83 5.

Furmston, M.—The Law of Tort: Policies and Trends in Liability for Damage to Property and Economic Loss. Hardback: £29·95: ISBN 0 7156 2012 6.

Kemp, D.—Damages for Personal Injury and Death. Second edition. Paperback: £16·95: ISBN 0 85121 117 8.

Pritchard, J.—Personal Injury Litigation. Fifth edition. Paperback: £22·00: ISBN 0 85121 203 4.

Ross, M.—Negligence in Surveying & Building. Paperback: £13·50: ISBN 0 7282 0095 3.

Stapleton, J.—Disease and the Compensation Debate. Hardback: £22·50: ISBN 0 19 825552 7.

Williams, D. B.—Criminal Injuries Compensation. Paperback: £9·95: ISBN 0 08 039244 X.

DEATH DUTIES

Way, P. and Soares, P. C.—Death and Taxes. Paperback: £18·50: ISBN 0 85120 931 9.

DIVORCE AND MATRIMONIAL CAUSES

Black, J.—A Practical Approach to Family Law. Paperback: £12·95: ISBN 0 906322 70 7.

Brown on Divorce—by George G. Brown. Second edition. Looseleaf: £75·00: ISBN 0 7219 1050 5.

Eekelaar, J. and Maclean, M.—Maintenance after Divorce. Hardback: £19·50: ISBN 0 19 825530 6. Paperback: £8·95: ISBN 0 19 825529 2.

Freeman, M. (editor)—Essays in Family Law 1985. [Current Legal Problems series]. Paperback: £13·50: ISBN 0 420 47510 9.

Goldrein, I. S. and de Haas, M. R.—Property Distribution on Divorce. Second edition. Paperback: £10·95: ISBN 0 85121 001 5.

Jackson, J. and Davies, D.—Jackson's Matrimonial Finance and Taxation. Fourth edition. Hardback: £45·00: ISBN 0 406 25447 8.

Pace, P. J.—Family Law. Third edition. Paperback: £6·50: ISBN 0 7121 0758 4.

Parkinson, L.—Conciliation in Separation and Divorce. Paperback: £12·95: ISBN 0 7099 4053 X.

Rakusen, M. L. and Hunt, D. P.—Distribution of Matrimonial Assets on Divorce. Supplement to second edition. Paperback: £10·95: ISBN 0 406 35102 3.

Rayden on Divorce—edited by J. Jackson, G. T. Marple and A. K. Biggs. Second cumulative supplement to fourteenth edition. Paperback: £47·50: ISBN 0 406 35175 9.

Smith, R. M.—Matrimonial Causes (Amendment No. 2) Rules 1985: a practical guide. Paperback: £5·95: ISBN 0 85121 206 9.

White, P.—Tax Planning on Marriage Breakdown. Fourth edition. Paperback: £25·00: ISBN 0 85121 074 0.

BOOKS

EDUCATION

Cox, B.—The Law of Special Educational Needs. Paperback: £7·95: ISBN 0 7099 3498 X.

Milman, D.—Educational Conflict and the Law. Hardback: £16·95: ISBN 0 7099 3521 8.

Nice, D. (editor)—Education and the Law. Paperback: £10·95: ISBN 0 900313 20 X.

EMPLOYMENT

Bowers, J.—A Practical Approach to Employment Law. Second edition. Paperback: £15·95: ISBN 1 85185 027 9.

Davidson, F.—A Guide to the Wages Act 1986. First edition. Paperback: £8·50: ISBN 185 185 047 3.

Dickens, L., Jones, M., Weekes, B. and Hart, M.—Dismissed: A study of Unfair Dismissal and the Industrial Tribunal System. Paperback: £8·50: ISBN 0 631 15219 9.

Evans, A. and Palmer, S.—Negotiating Shorter Working Hours. Hardback: £29·50: ISBN 0 333 38858 5.

Hepple, B. and Fredman, S.—Labour Law and Industrial Relations in Great Britain. First edition. Paperback: £17·95: ISBN 90 6544 2626.

Lewis, D.—Essentials of Employment Law. Second edition. Paperback: £13·95: ISBN 0 85292 357 0.

Lewis, R.—Labour Law in Britain. Paperback: £15·00: ISBN 0 631 13755 6.

Smith, I. T. and Wood, J. C.—Industrial Law. Third edition. Hardback: £26·00: ISBN 0 406 381 445. Paperback: £16·95: ISBN 0 406 381 453.

Stranks, J. and Dewis, M.—Health and Safety Practice. Paperback: £22·50: ISBN 0 273 02599 6.

Titman, B. and Camp, P.—Individual Employment Law. Second edition. Paperback: £9·95: ISBN 0 421 35320 1.

Tolley's Share Options and Incentives for Directors and Employees—by Koppel, M. and Wolstenholme, P. Paperback: £7·95: ISBN 0 85459 180 X.

Toulson, N.—Pensions for the Self-Employed. Hardback: £18·50: ISBN 0 566 02570 1.

Whincup, M.—The Right to Dismiss. Hardback: £17·50: ISBN 0 00 383244 9.

Williams, D. B. and Walker, D. J.—The Industrial Tribunal Practice. Second edition. Paperback: £24·00: ISBN 0 946700 18 4.

EUROPEAN COMMUNITIES

Cawthra, B. I.—Patent Licensing in Europe. Second edition. Hardback: £40: ISBN 0 406 14841 4.

Kelley, P. and Onkelinx, I.—EEC Customs Law. Looseleaf: £45·00: ISBN 0 906214 29 7.

Korah, V.—EEC Competition Law and Practice. Third edition. Paperback: £12·95: ISBN 0 906214 39 4.

Korah, V.—Patent Licensing and EEC Competition Rules Regulation 2349/84. Paperback: £17·95: ISBN 0 906214 36 X.

Korah, V.—R. & D. and the EEC Competition Rules Regulation 418/85. [European Competition Law Monographs]. Paperback: £21.50: ISBN 0 906214 45 9.

Tolley's.—Taxation in the Republic of Ireland 1986–87 [1986–87]. Paperback: £11·95: ISBN 0 85459 226 1.

Vaughan, D. (ed.)—Law of the European Communities Vol. I. First edition. Hardback: £60·00: ISBN 0406 003 017

Vaughan, D. (ed.)—Law of the European Communities Vol. II. First edition. Hardback: £60·00: ISBN 0406 003 025.

Völker, E. L. M. and Steenbergen, J.—Leading Cases and Materials on the External Relations Law of the E.C. Hardback: £73·75: ISBN 90 6544 2219.

EVIDENCE

Cross & Wilkins (ed. Tapper, C.)—Outline of the Law of Evidence. Sixth edition. Paperback: £10·95: ISBN 0 406 57081 7.

Curzon, L.—Law of Evidence [M & E Handbook Series]. Second edition. Paperback: £6·50: ISBN 0 7121 0675 8.

Murphy, P. and Barnard, D.—Evidence & Advocacy. Second edition. Paperback: £7·95: ISBN 0 906322 96 0.

Wilkinson, A.—The Scottish Law of Evidence. Paperback: £18·50: ISBN 0 406 26110 5.

Wolchover, D.—The Exclusion of Improperly Obtained Evidence. First edition. Paperback: £18·00: ISBN 0 8599 2 380 0.

EXECUTORS AND ADMINISTRATORS

Pettitt, D. M.—The Will Draftsman's Handbook. Fourth edition. Paperback: £17·50: ISBN 0 85121 140 2.

Ryan, M.—Executorship and Administration. [Lawyers Practice and Procedure Series]. Paperback: £12·95: ISBN 1 85190 003 9.

Woolf, E., Tanna, S. and Singh, K. (eds.)—Executorship and Trusts Law and Accounts. Second edition. Paperback: £14·95: ISBN 0 7121 0751 7.

[7]

BOOKS AND ARTICLES

FAMILY ALLOWANCES

Mesher, J.—CPAG's Supplementary Benefit and Family Income Supplement: The Legislation. Third edition. Paperback: £15·00: ISBN 0 421 35380 5.

FRAUD, MISREPRESENTATION AND UNDUE INFLUENCE

Rowell, R.—Counterfeiting and Forgery: A Practical Guide to the Law: Hardback: £26·95: ISBN 0 406 10110 8.

GAMING AND WAGERING

Pain, K. W.—Licensing Practise and Procedure. [Second edition]. Paperback: £12·95: ISBN 1 85190 009 8.

HIRE PURCHASE

Leder, M. J.—Consumer Law. Second edition. Paperback: £4·95: ISBN 0 7121 0677 4.

HOUSING

Arden, A.—Homeless Persons—The Housing Act 1985. Part III. [Second edition]. Paperback: £10·50: ISBN 0 90509099 12 5.

Arden, A.—Housing Act 1985. [Current Law Statutes Annotated Reprints]. Paperback: £16·95: ISBN 0 421 35370 8.

Arden, A.—Housing Consolidation 1985. [Current Law Statutes Annotated Reprints]. [Set of three titles]. Paperback: £25·00: ISBN 0 421 36080 1.

Arden, A. and Ramage, J.—Housing Associations Act 1985. [Current Law Statutes Annotated Reprints]. Paperback: £7·50: ISBN 0 421 35900 5.

Estates Gazette Law Reports 1985.—Two volumes. Edited by J. Muir Watt. Hardback: Vol. 1: £20·00: ISBN 0 72820 097 X; Hardback: Vol. 2: £20·00: ISBN 0 72820 098 8.

Ryde on Rating—edited by G. R. G. Roots and N. G. A. King. [Fourth cumulative supplement to thirteenth edition]. Paperback: £11·50: 0 406 36315 3.

HUMAN RIGHTS

Gulleford, K.—Data Protection in Practice. Paperback: £19·95: ISBN 0 406 17700 7.

Poulter, S. M.—English Law and Ethnic Minority Customs. Paperback: £25·95: ISBN 0 406 18000 8.

HUSBAND AND WIFE

Black, J.—A Practical Approach to Family Law. Paperback: £12·95: ISBN 0 906322 70 7.

Eekelaar, J.—and Maclean, M.—Maintenance after Divorce. Hardback: £19·50: ISBN 0 19 825530 6; Paperback: £8·95: ISBN 0 19 825529 2.

Freeman, M. (editor)—Essays in Family Law 1985. [Current Legal Problems series]. Paperback: £13·50: ISBN 0 420 47510 9.

Goldrein, I. S. and de Haas, M. R.—Property Distribution on Divorce. Second edition. Paperback: £10·95. ISBN 0 85121 001 5.

Jackson, J. and Davies, D.—Jackson's Matrimonial Finance and Taxation. Fourth edition. Hardback: £45·00: ISBN 0 406 25447 8.

Pace, P. J.—Family Law. [Third edition]. Paperback: £6·50: ISBN 0 7121 0758 4.

Parkinson, L.—Conciliation in Separation and Divorce. Paperback: £12·95: ISBN 0 7099 4053 X.

Rakusen, M. L. and Hunt, D. P.—Distribution of Matrimonial Assets on Divorce. Supplement to second edition. Paperback: £10·95: ISBN 0 406 35102 3.

Rayden on Divorce—edited by J. Jackson, G. T. Marple and A. K. Biggs. [Second cumulative supplement to fourteenth edition]. Paperback: £47·50: ISBN 0 406 35175 9.

Smith, R. M.—Matrimonial Causes (Amendment No. 2) Rules 1985: a practical guide. Paperback: £5·95: ISBN 0 85121 206 9.

IMMIGRATION

Bevan, V.—Development of British Immigration Law. Hardback: £29·95: ISBN 0 7099 0663 3.

Dummett, A. (editor)—Towards a Just Immigration Policy. Paperback: £7·95: ISBN 0 900137 26 6.

Fransman, L. and Webb, D.—Immigration Emergency Procedures. Paperback: £11·00: ISBN 0 905099 11 7.

Handsworth Law Centre.—Immigration Law Handbook. Third edition. Paperback: £2·50: ISBN 0 951 0745 0 4.

Pearl, D.—Family Law and the Immigrant Communities. Paperback: £7·50: ISBN 0 85308 102 6.

INCOME TAX

Butterworths Budget Tax Tables 1986—Edited by Bond, D., Grosse, C., Kronbergs, Z. and Parrington, S. Twenty-second edition. Paperback: £2·80: ISBN 0 406 50841 0.

Butterworths Yellow Tax Handbook 1986–87. Twenty-fifth edition. Paperback: £19·00: ISBN 0 406 51003 2.

Gammie, M.—Tax Strategy for Directors, Executives and Employees. Second edition. Paperback: £25·00: ISBN 0 85121 076 7.

Jackson, J. and Davies, D.—Jackson's Matrimonial Finance and Taxation. Fourth edition. Hardback: £45·00: ISBN 0 406 25447 8.

BOOKS

INCOME TAX—*cont.*

Kay, J. and King, M.—The British Tax System. Fourth edition. Hardback: £17·50: ISBN 0 19 877263 7. Paperback: £6·50: ISBN 0 19 877262 9.

Moores & Rowland's Tax Guide 1985–86. Ninth edition. Paperback: £25: ISBN 0 406 35920 2.

Ola, C. S.—Nigerian Income Tax Law and Practice. Paperback: £9·50: ISBN 0 333 40007 0.

Pritchard, W.—Income Tax. Fifteenth edition. Paperback: £7·95: ISBN 0 7121 0974 9.

Pritchard, W. E.—Taxation. Seventh edition. Paperback: £7·95: ISBN 0 7121 2037 8.

Tolley's—Income Tax 1986–87. Paperback: £14·95: ISBN 0 85459 238 5.

Tolley's Tax Bumph 1985–86.—Edited by R. Wareham and N. Bowen. Paperback: £18·95: ISBN 0 85459 198 2.

Tolley's Tax Cases 1986— By Victor Grant. Paperback: £15·50: ISBN 0 85459 229 6.

Tolley's Tax Computations 1985–86. K. M. G. Thomson McLintock. Paperback: £19·50: ISBN 0 85459 197 4.

Tolley's Tax Data 1986–87.—By Wareham, R. Paperback: £6·95: ISBN 0 85459 223 7.

Tolley's Tax Efficient Personal Investments—by Arthur Andersen & Co. Paperback: £11·95: ISBN 0 85459 262 8.

Tolley's Tax Planning 1986. Paperback: £27·50: ISBN 0 85459 203 2.

Tolley's Tax Tables 1986–87.—Paperback: £4·95: ISBN 0 85459 213 X.

Tolley's.—Taxation in the Channel Islands and Isle of Man [1986]. Paperback: £11·50: ISBN 0 85459 225–3

Tolley's.—Taxation in the Republic of Ireland 1986–87 [1986–87]. Paperback: £11·95: ISBN 0 85459 226 1.

Tolley's.—Taxwise Taxation Workbook No. 1 [1986/7]. Paperback: £13·95: ISBN 0 85459 257 1.

Whillans's Tax Tables 1986–87—Edited by S. Parrington. Thirty-ninth edition. Paperback: £2·60: ISBN 0 406 54321 6.

White, P.—Tax Planning for the Family. [Practical Tax Series]. Third edition. Paperback: £18·95: ISBN 0 85120 920 3.

White, P.—Tax Planning on Marriage Breakdown. Fourth edition. Paperback: £25·00: ISBN 0 85121 074 0.

INHERITANCE TAX

Kessler, J. and Goodfellow, G.—Inheritance Tax Planning. [Longman Intelligence Reports]. Paperback: £75·00: ISBN 0 85121 245 X.

Tolley's Inheritance Tax 1986–87—By Wareham, R. Paperback: £14·50: ISBN 0 85459 241 5.

Venables, R.—Inheritance Tax Planning. Paperback: £90·00.

INSURANCE

Ardis, P. and Comer, M.—Risk Management: Computers, Fraud and Insurance. Hardback: £19·95: ISBN 0 07 084926 9.

Bingham's Motor Claims Cases—By J. A. Taylor. Ninth edition. Hardback: £55·00: ISBN 0 406 11813 2.

Butterworths Insurance Law Handbook.—Second edition. Paperback: £19·95: ISBN 0 406 17637 X.

Hardy Ivamy, E.—General Principles of Insurance Law. [Butterworths Insurance Library]. Fifth edition. Hardback: £70·00: ISBN 0 406 25280 7.

Jess, D. G.—The Insurance of Commercial Risks: Law and Practice. Hardback: £32·00: ISBN 0 406 25711 6.

Tolley's National Insurance Contributions 1986–87—By Neil D. Booth. Paperback: £15·95: ISBN 0 85459 217 2.

INTERNATIONAL LAW

Bowman & Harris.—Multilateral Treaties—Index and Current Status. Third Cumulative Supplement. Paperback: £18·50: ISBN 0 406 25292 0.

Cassese, A.—International Law in a Divided World. Hardback: £45·00: ISBN 0 19 876194 5.

Christou, R.—International Agency, Distribution and Licensing Agreements. [Longman Commercial Series]. Hardback: £42·50: ISBN 0 85121 188 7.

Islamic Banking and Finance.—Edited by the Butterworths Editorial Staff. Hardback: £40·00: ISBN 0 406 10034 9.

Kettell, B. and Magnus, G. A.—The International Debt Game. Paperback: £12·50: ISBN 0 86010 810 4.

Lafili, L., Gevurtz, F. and Campbell, D.—Survey of the International Sale of Goods. Paperback: £28·95: ISBN 90 6544 241 3.

Lee, E.—Encyclopedia of International Commercial Arbitration. Looseleaf: £130·00: ISBN 0 850 440 59 X.

Lew, Dr. J. D. M.—Contemporary Problems in International Arbitration. Hardback: £40: ISBN 0 951 0664 12.

Mann, F. A.—Foreign Affairs in English Courts. Hardback: £25·00: ISBN 0 19 825564 0.

BOOKS AND ARTICLES

[10]

BOOKS

LANDLORD AND TENANT—*cont.*
Stapleton, T.—Estate Management Practice. Second edition. Paperback: £14·50: ISBN 0 7282 0094 5.
Tyler, E. L. G.—Cases and Statutes on Land Law. Second edition. Paperback: £10·95: ISBN 0 421 34350 8.

LAND REGISTRATION
Timothy, P. J.—Wontner's Guide to Land Registry Practice. Fifteenth edition. Paperback: £16·50: ISBN 0 85120 993 9.

LEGAL AID
The Law Society.—Legal Aid Handbook 1986. Seventh edition. Paperback: £7·95: ISBN 0 11 380001 0.

LEGAL HISTORY
Baker, J. and Milsom, S.—Sources of English Legal History: Private Law to 1750. Hardback: £30·00: ISBN 0 406 01640 2; Paperback: £18·95: ISBN 0 406 01641 0.
Cowper, F.—A Prospect of Gray's Inn. Second edition. Hardback: £10: ISBN 0 420 47330 0.
Davies, W. and Fouracre, P. (eds.)—The Settlement of Disputes in Early Medieval Europe. First edition. Hardback: £30·00: ISBN 0 521 307 880.
Falk Moore, S.—Social Facts and Fabrications. First edition. Paperback: £13·95: ISBN 0 521 30938 7. ISBN 0 521 31201 (pbk.)
Hamilton, R.—All Jangle and Riot. First edition. Hardback: £12·95: ISBN 086 205 0839.
Lee, R.—The Elements of Roman Law. Fourth edition. Paperback: £13·50: ISBN 0 421 01780 5.
Major, W. T.—Mastering Basic English Law. Paperback: £3.95: ISBN 0 333 37402 9.
Postema, G.—Bentham and the Common Law Tradition. First edition. Hardback: £40·00: ISBN 0 19 825505 5.
Radzinowicz, L and Hood, R.—A History of English Criminal Law and its Administration from 1750. [Set of five volumes.] Hardback: £235·00: ISBN 0 420 47520 6.
Stone, J.—Precedent and Law: Dynamics of Common Law Growth. Hardback: £34·00: ISBN 0 409 49304 X.
Twining, W. (editor).—Legal Theory and Common Law. Hardback: £22·50: ISBN 0 631 14477 3.

LIEN
Tetley, W.—Maritime Liens and Claims. Hardback: £45·00: ISBN 0 948406 00 3.

LIMITATION OF ACTIONS
Astle, W. E.—Limitation of Liability. Paperback: £12·00: ISBN 0 905045 63 7.
Josling, J. F.—Periods of Limitation. Sixth edition. Paperback: £13·95. ISBN 0 85121 145 3.

LITERARY AND SCIENTIFIC INSTITUTIONS
Ziman, J., Sieghart, P. and Humphrey, J.—The World of Science and the Rule of Law. Hardback: £19·50: ISBN 0 19 825516 0.

LOCAL GOVERNMENT
Arden, A.—Housing Act 1985. [Current Law Statutes Annotated Reprints]. Paperback: £16·95: ISBN 0 421 35370 8.
Arden, A.—Housing Consolidation 1985. [Current Law Statutes Annotated Reprints] [Set of three titles]. Paperback: £25·00: ISBN 0 421 36080 1.
Birkinshaw, P.—Open Government: Freedom of Information and Local Government. Paperback: £4·95: ISBN 0 951110 10 1.
Hughes, D.—Environmental Law. Paperback: £14·95: ISBN 0 406 01691 7.
Longman.—Directory of Local Authorities. 1986/87 edition. Paperback: £14·95: ISBN 0 85121 167 4.
Manchester, C.—Sex Shops and the Law. Hardback: £18·50: ISBN 0 566 05232 6.
Ryde on Rating—edited by G. R. G. Roots and N. G. A King. [Fourth cumulative supplement to thirteenth edition]. Paperback: £11·50: ISBN 0 406 36315 3.
Smith, G.—Local Government for Journalists. Second edition. Paperback: £5·50: ISBN 0 904677 28 1.

MAGISTERIAL LAW
Anthony and Berryman's Magistrates Court Guide 1986.—Edited by A. P. Carr. Paperback: £13·95: ISBN 0 406 10839 0.
Barker, K. and Sturges, J.—Decision Making in Magistrates' Courts. Paperback: £4·95: ISBN 1 85190 017 9.
Chatterton, C. M.—Procedure and Sentencing in the Magistrates' Courts. Hardback: £65·00: ISBN 0 85992 360 6.
Harris, B.—The Criminal Jurisdiction of Magistrates. Tenth edition. Hardback: £60·00: ISBN 0 903 39398 0. Paperback: £48·00: ISBN 0 870 08015 7.
McLean, I. and Morrish, P.—The Magistrates' Court. Seventh edition. Hardback: £22·50: ISBN 0 85992 369 X.

MAGISTERIAL LAW—*cont.*

Pain, K. and Whate, S.—Emergency Applications to Magistrates. Paperback: £12·95: ISBN 1 85190 001 2.

Stone's Justices' Manual—Edited by J. Richman and A. T. Draycott (three volumes). Hardback: £90·00: ISBN 0 406 386 722.

MEDICINE

Bucknell and Ghodse—Misuse of Drugs. Hardback: £35·00: ISBN 0 08 039203 2.

Nicholson, R.—Medical Research with Children: Ethics, Law and Practice. Hardback: £12·50: ISBN 0 19 261528 9.

MEETINGS

Janner, G.—Janner on Meetings. Hardback: £15·00: ISBN 0 566 02639 2.

Roberts, D.—The Administration of Company Meetings. First edition. Hardback: £19·50: ISBN 0 902197 45 2.

MENTAL HEALTH

Bean, P.—Mental Disorder and Legal Control. Hardback: £27·50: ISBN 0 521 30209 9.

Whitehorn, N.—Court of Protection Handbook. Seventh edition. Paperback: £11·95: ISBN 0 85120 992 0.

MINORS

Black, J.—A Practical Approach to Family Law. Paperback: £12·95: ISBN 0 906322 70 7.

Burney, E.—Sentencing Young People: What went wrong with the Criminal Justice Act 1982. Hardback: £12·95: ISBN 0 566 05127 3.

Franklin, B.—The Rights of Children. Paperback: £8·95: ISBN 0 631 14712 8.

Freeman, M. (editor)—Essays in Family Law 1985. [Current Legal Problems series.] Paperback £13·50: ISBN 0 420 47510 9.

Hayes, M. and Bevan, V.—Child-Care Law. Paperback: £7·50: ISBN 0 85308 100 X.

Nicholson, R.—Medical Research with Children: Ethics, Law and Practice. Hardback: £12·50: ISBN 0 19 261528 9.

Pace, P. J.—Family Law. [Third edition]. Paperback: £6·50: ISBN 0 7121 0758 4.

Pearce, N.—Custodianship: the Law and Practice. Paperback: £7·95: ISBN 0 85190 0 15 2.

Pearce, N.—Wardship: the Law and Practice. Paperback: £12·95: ISBN 0 906840 97 X.

Priest, J.—In Place of a Parent: A Guide to the Legal Framework. Paperback: £7·50: ISBN 0 85308 101 8.

Rutherford, A.—Growing out of Crime: Society and Young People in Trouble. Paperback: £3·95: ISBN 0 140 22383 5.

MISCELLANEOUS

Bradney, A., Fisher, V., Masson, A., Neal, A. and Newell, D.—How to Study Law. Hardback: £9·50: ISBN 0 421 34380 X; Paperback: £5·95: ISBN 0 421 34390 7.

Briskman, H.—Marketing Questions and Answers: English Business Law. Paperback: £7·95: ISBN 1 85185 010 4.

Chambers, M.—Managing Your Career in the Law. Paperback: £1·25: ISBN 0 85514 043 7.

Denning.—Leaves from my Library. An English Anthology. Hardback: £12·50: ISBN 0 406 17615 9.

Dobash, R. P., Dobash, R. E. and Gutteridge, S.—The Imprisonment of Women. Paperback: £7·95: ISBN 0 631 14319 X.

Goodrich, P.—Reading the Law: A Critical Introduction to Legal Method and Techniques. Hardback: £27·50: ISBN 0 631 14629 6. Paperback: £9·95: ISBN 0 631 14631 8.

Hazell's Guide 1986.—Second edition. Paperback: £15·00: ISBN 0 901718 38 6.

Logan, R. G. (editor).—Information Sources in Law. Hardback: £38·00: ISBN 0 408 11474 6.

McCormick, N. and Birks, P. (editors)—The Legal Mind: Essays for Tony Honoré. Hardback: £35·00: ISBN 0 19 876196 1.

Major, W. T.—Mastering Basic English Law. Paperback: £3·95: ISBN 0 333 37402 9.

Mandaraka—Sheppard, A.—The Dynamics of Agression in Women's Prisons in England. Hardback: £17·50: ISBN 0 566 00863 7.

Mothersole, B.—Citizen 16+. The Civil Law and You. Paperback: £6·95: ISBN 0 333 36794 4.

Reeves, P.—Are Two Legal Professions Necessary? Paperback: £11·95: ISBN 0 08 039218 0.

Rudden, B. and Wyatt, D. (eds.)—Basic Community Laws. Second edition. Paperback: £9·95: ISBN 0 19 876198 8.

Shrager, D. and Frost, E. (eds.)—The Quotable Lawyer. First edition. Hardback: £17·95: ISBN 0 8160 1184 2.

Smith and Keenan's English Law—By Denis Keenan. Eighth edition. Paperback: £11·50: ISBN 0 273 02342 X.

Wallington, P. and Merkin, R.—Essays in Memory of Professor F. H. Lawson. Hardback: £19·00: ISBN 0 406 50030 4.

Yearbook of Law Computers and Technology.—Edited by C. Arnold. Volume 2 1986. Hardback: £16·95: ISBN 0 406 18701 0.

Zaid, A. M.—The Islamic Law of Bequest. Hardback: £25·00: ISBN 0 905906 42 X.

BOOKS

MISCELLANEOUS—*cont.*
Ziman, J., Sieghart, P. and Humphrey, J.—The World of Science and the Rule of Law. Hardback: £19·50: ISBN 0 19 8255 16 0.

MONEY
Gatenby, J. K.—Recovery of Money. Sixth edition. Paperback: £19·95: ISBN 0 85121 003 1.

NEGLIGENCE
Butterworths—Leading Cases in the Law of Negligence for 'A' Level. Second edition. Paperback: £4·95: ISBN 0 406 01682 8.
Ross, M.—Negligence in Surveying & Building. Paperback: £13·50: ISBN 0 7282 0095 3.

PATENTS AND DESIGNS
Blanco White, T. A. and Jacob, R.—Patents, Trade Marks, Copyright and Industrial Designs. Third edition. Hardback: £12·95: ISBN 0 421 34960 3; Paperback: £8·95: ISBN 0 421 34970 0.
Cawthra, B. I.—Patent Licensing in Europe. Second edition. Hardback: £40: ISBN 0 406 14841 4.
Phillips, J.—Introduction to Intellectual Property Law. Paperback: £13·95: ISBN 0 406 25832 5.

PARLIAMENT
Van Mechelen, D. and Rose, R.—Patterns of Parliamentary Legislation. First edition. Hardback: £16·50: ISBN 0 566 053276.

PARTNERSHIP
Eastaway, N. and Gilligen, B.—Tax and Financial Planning for Professional Partnerships. Second edition. Paperback: £16·50: ISBN 0 406 50180 7.
Morse, G.—An Introduction to Partnership Law. Paperback: £6·95 ISBN 1 85185 025 2.
Underhill's Principles of the Law of Partnership—by E. R. Hardy Ivamy. [Twelfth edition]. Hardback: £14·95; Paperback: £10·95: ISBN 0 406 669 082.

PATENTS & DESIGNS
Cawthra, B. I.—Patent Licensing in Europe. Second edition. Hardback: $40: ISBN 0 406 14841 4.
Eisenschitz, T. and Phillips, J.—The Inventors' Information Guide. Second edition. Paperback: £6·50: ISBN 0 9510664 0 4.
Johnston, D.—Design Protection. Second edition. Hardback: £8·95: ISBN 0 85072 165 2.
Korah, V.—Patent Licensing and EEC Competition Rules Regulation 2349/84. Paperback: £17·95: ISBN 0 906214 36 X.
Phillips, J.—Patents in Perspective. Paperback: £12·75: ISBN 0 906214 37 8.
Williams, J.—A Manager's Guide to Patents, Trade Marks and Copyright. Hardback: £12·95: ISBN 0 85038 970 4.

PENSIONS AND SUPERANNUATION
Ellison, R.—Pension Fund Reform. Paperback: £8·50: ISBN 0 85121 182 8.
Toulson, N.—Pensions for the Self-Employed. Hardback: £18·50: ISBN 0 566 02570 1.

PERPETUITIES
Zaid, A. M.—The Islamic Law of Bequest. Hardback: £25·00: ISBN 0 905906 42 X.

PETROLEUM
Etikerentse, G. [Nigeria]—Nigerian Petroleum Law. Paperback: £7·45: ISBN 0 333 39357 0.

POLICE
English, J.—Police Training Manual [Fifth edition]. Paperback: £12·95: ISBN 0 07 084797 5.
Gifford, Lord.—The Broadwater Farm Inquiry. First edition. Paperback: £4·95: ISBN 0 946918 59 7.
Lambert, J. L.—Police Powers and Accountability. Hardback: £16·95: ISBN 0 7099 1660 4.
Robilliard, St. J. and McEwan, J.—Police Powers and the Individual. Paperback: £10·50: ISBN 0 631 13996 6.
Turnbull-Walker, A.—The Police and Criminal Evidence Act 1984: a Guide for Duty Solicitors. Booklet: £4·95: ISBN 1 85190 019 5.
Wegg-Prosser, C.—The Police and the Law. Paperback: £6·95: ISBN 0 085120 758 8.

PRACTICE
Berlins, M. and Dyer, C.—The Law Machine. Second edition. Paperback: £3·95: ISBN 0140 22 695 8.
Black, A.—Enforcement of a judgment. Seventh edition. Paperback: £12·95: ISBN 0 85121 023 6.
Brennan, D.—Provisional Damages—A guide to the new procedures. Paperback: £17·50: ISBN 0 907 822 83 5.
Butterworths.—All England Law Reports Annual Review 1985. Hardback: £15: ISBN 0 406 87962 1.
Colman, A. D.—The Practice and Procedure of the Commercial Court. Second edition. Hardback: £35: ISBN 0 85044 061 1.
Cook, M. J.—The Taxation of Legal Costs. Paperback: £19·50: ISBN 0 907 822 657.

BOOKS AND ARTICLES

PRACTICE—*cont.*

Cretney, S.—Enduring Powers of Attorney. [Guide and Practice Series.] Paperback: £7·50: ISBN 0 85308 103 4.

Dowell, J., Hall, A., Levin, J., Olley, S. and Wyld, N.—The Emergency Procedures Handbook. Paperback: £14·00: ISBN 0 905099 109.

Estates Gazette Law Reports 1986, vol. 1.—Edited by J. Muir Watt. Hardback: £21·50: ISBN 0 7282 0101 1.

Gatenby, J. K.—Recovery of Money. Sixth edition. Paperback: £19·95: ISBN 0 85121 003 1.

Heward, E.—Chancery Orders. Hardback: £35·00: ISBN 0 870 08020 3.

Jones, G. and Goodhart, W.—Specific Performance. Hardback: £35·00: ISBN 0 406 258 090.

Kelly's Draftsman.—Edited by Ramage, R. Fifteenth edition. Hardback: £60·00: ISBN 0 406 26315 9.

Lister, S. and Marshall, P.—The High Court. Hardback: £27·50: ISBN 0 85922 370 3.

O'Hare, J. and Hill, R.—Civil Litigation. [Longman Practitioner Series]. Fourth edition. Paperback: £15·95: ISBN 0 85121 222 0.

Mann, F. A.—Foreign Affairs in English Courts. Hardback: £25·00: ISBN 0 19 825564 0.

Morton. J.—Handling Criminal Cases: A Guide to Preparation and Defence. Paperback: £9·95: ISBN 0 08 039158 3.

Murphy, P. and Barnard, D.—Evidence & Advocacy. Second edition. Paperback: £7·95: ISBN 0 906322 96 0.

Pain, K. and White, S.—Emergency Applications to Magistrates. Paperback: £12·95: ISBN 1 85190 001 2.

Reid, B.—Confidentiality and the Law. Hardback: £20: ISBN 0 08 039236 9.

Stone, J—Precedent and Law: Dynamics of Common Law Growth. Hardback: £34·00: ISBN 0 409 49304 X.

Twining, W. (editor).—Legal Theory and Common Law. Hardback: £22·50: ISBN 0 631 14477 3.

Whitehorn, N.—Court of Protection Handbook. Seventh edition. Paperback: £11·95: ISBN 0 85120 992 0.

PUBLIC ENTERTAINMENTS

Robertson, G. and Nicol, A.—Media Law. Paperback: £8·50: ISBN 0 8039 9726 4.

RATING AND VALUATION

Ryde on Rating—edited by G. R. G. Roots and N. G. A. King. [Fourth cumulative supplement to thirteenth edition]. Paperback: £11·50: ISBN 0 406 36315 3.

REAL PROPERTY AND CONVEYANCING

Aldridge, T.—Boundaries, Walls and Fences. Sixth edition. Paperback: £11·95: ISBN 0 85121 234 4.

Card, R., Murdoch, J. and Schofield, P.—Law for Estate Management Students. Second edition. Paperback: £16·95: ISBN 0 406 56291 1.

Estates Gazette Law Reports 1985.—Two volumes. Edited by J. Muir Watt. Hardback: Vol. 1: £20·00: ISBN 0 72820 097 X; Hardback: Vol. 2: £20·00: ISBN 0 72820 098 8.

Farrand, J. T.—Emmet on Title. Nineteenth edition. Hardback: £175. Looseleaf 2 vols.: ISBN 0 85121 148 8.

Fysh, M. and Wilson Thomas, R.—The Industrial Property Citator: Supplement 1985. Paperback: £25: ISBN 0 907 451 14 4.

Gammie, M. and Bailey, J.—Land Taxation. Looseleaf: £125·00: ISBN 0 421 27540 5.

Gregory, R.—Stamp Duties for Conveyancers, Fourth edition. Paperback: £13·50: ISBN 0 85121 173 9.

Kenny, P—Licensed Conveyancing: The New Legislation. Paperback: £3·75: ISBN 0 421 35050 4.

Kenny, P. H. and Bevan, C. M.—Conveyancing Law. Third edition. Paperback: £6·50: ISBN 0 7121 0755 X.

Lewinson, K.—Drafting Business Leases. Second edition. Hardback: £23·50: ISBN 0 85121 024 4.

MacKenzie, J. and Phillips, M.—A Practical Approach to Land Law. Paperback: £14·95: ISBN 1 85185 024 4.

Maudsley & Burn.—Land Law Cases and Materials. Fifth edition. Paperback: £21·95: ISBN 0 406 62309 0.

Moeran, E.—Practical Conveyancing. [Longman Practitioner Series]. Tenth edition. Paperback: £15·95: ISBN 0 85121 223 9.

Simpson, A. W. B.—A History of the Land Law. Second edition. Paperback: £12·50 ISBN 0 19 825536 5.

Sinclair, J.—Handbook of Conveyancing Practice in Scotland. Paperback: £16·95: ISBN 0 406 20600 7.

Stapleton, T.—Estate Management Practice. Second edition. Paperback: £14·50: ISBN 0 7282 0094 5.

BOOKS

BOOKS AND ARTICLES

ROAD TRAFFIC—*cont.*
Turner, A. and Marsh, M.—The New Fixed Penalty System (and Disqualification, Endorsement and Penalty Points). Paperback: £16·00: ISBN 0 870 08040 8.
Wilkinson's Road Traffic Offences.—Second Cumulative Supplement to the Twelfth edition by Halnan, P. Paperback: £30·00: ISBN 0 85121 251 4.

SALE OF GOODS
Consumer Law Statutes.—Fifth edition. Paperback: £14·95: ISBN 0 906533 45 7.
Lafili, L., Gevurtz, F. and Campbell, D.—Survey of the International Sale of Goods. Paperback: £28·95: ISBN 90 6544 241 3.

SCOTLAND
Banking
Caskie, D.—Wallace and McNeil's Banking Law. Ninth edition. [Paperback: £24·00: ISBN 0 414 00782 4.]
Bankruptcy
McBryde, W. W.—The Bankruptcy (Scotland) Act 1985. [Paperback: £8·50: ISBN 0 414 00777 8.]
Children and Young Persons
McNeill, P. G. B.—Adoption of Children in Scotland. Second edition. [Paperback: £15·00: ISBN 0 414 00779 4.]
Company Law
Scots Mercantile Law Statutes 1986. [Paperback: £19·00: ISBN 0 414 00800 6.]
Criminal Law
Bovey, K.—Misuse of Drugs: a Handbook for Lawyers. [Paperback: £24·00: ISBN 0 406 10390 9.]
Harper, J. and Hamilton P.—A Fingertip Guide to Criminal Law. [Paperback: £15·00: ISBN 0 406 10380 1.]
Hume's Commentaries on Crimes. Reprint of Fourth edition. [Two volumes: Hardback: £55·00: ISBN 0 902023 160.]
Macdonald, Sir J.—A practical Treatise on the Criminal Law of Scotland. Reprint of Fifth edition. [Hardback: £16·00.]
Scots Criminal Courts Statutes 1986. [Paperback: £9·00: ISBN 0 414 00797 2.]
Divorce and Consistorial Causes
Macdonald, H. R. M.—A Guide to the Family Law (Scotland) Act 1985. [Paperback: £9·00: ISBN 0 86325 080 7.]
Nichols, D. I. and Meston, M. C.—The Matrimonial Homes (Family Protection) (Scotland) Act 1981. Second edition [Paperback: £10·50: ISBN 0 414 00778 6.]
Evidence
Wilkinson, A. B.—The Scottish Law of Evidence. [Paperback: £18·50: ISBN 0 406 26110 5.]
Heritable Property and Conveyancing
Halliday, J. M.—Conveyancing Law and Practice in Scotland. Volume II. [Hardback: £30·00: ISBN 0 414 00789 1.]
McDonald, A. J.—Conveyancing Manual. Third edition. [Paperback: £25·00: ISBN 0 947641 06 8.]
McDonald, A. J.—Registration of Title Manual. [Paperback: £19·00: ISBN 0 947641 09 2.]
Rankine on Land-Ownership. Reprint of Fourth edition. [Hardback: £39·50.]
Rights of Way: a Guide to the Law in Scotland. [Paperback: £2·00: ISBN 0 9502811 3 1.]
Scots Conveyancing Statutes 1986. [Paperback: £7·00: ISBN 0 414 00801 4.]
Sinclair, J.—Handbook of Conveyancing Practice in Scotland. [Paperback: £16·95: ISBN 0 406 20600 7.]
Housing
Himsworth, C. M. G.—Public Sector Housing Law in Scotland. Second edition. [Paperback: £7·95: ISBN 0 905011 22 8.]
Husband and Wife
MacDonald, H. R. M.—A Guide to the Family Law (Scotland) Act 1985. [Paperback: £9·00: ISBN 0 86325 080 7.]
Nichols, D. I. and Meston M. C.—The Matrimonial Homes (Family Protection) (Scotland) Act 1981. Second edition. [Paperback: £10·50: ISBN 0 414 00778 6.]
Scots Statutes: Family Law; Succession, Trusts, etc. 1986. [Paperback: £10·50: ISBN 0 414 00802 2.]
Landlord and Tenant
Duncan, A. G. M. and Hope, J. A. D.—The Rent (Scotland) Act 1984. [Paperback: £12·00: ISBN 0 414 00789 1.]
Himsworth, C. M. G.—Public Sector Housing Law in Scotland. [Paperback: £7·95: ISBN 0 905011 22 8.]
Rankine, J.—A Treatise on the Law of Leases in Scotland. Reprint of third edition. [Hardback: £37·00.]

BOOKS

SCOTLAND—*cont.*

Law Reform

Thomson, J. M.—The Law Reform (Miscellaneous Provisions) (Scotland) Act 1985. [Paperback: £6·50: ISBN 0 414 00788 3.]

Miscellaneous

Paterson, A. A. and Bates, T. St. J. N.—The Legal System of Scotland: Cases and Materials. Second edition. [Paperback: £16·50: ISBN 0 414 00738 2.]

Scotish Current Law Yearbook 1985. Scottish Current Law Case Citator 1985. Scottish Current Law Legislation Citator 1985. [Cloth: £73·00: ISBN 0 414 00792 1 (Yearbook); 0 414 00790 5 (Case Citator); 0 414 00791 3 (Legislation Citator).]

Scottish Law Directory 1986. [Hardback: £19·00: ISBN 0 85279 124 0.]

Parent and Child

McNeill, P. G. B.—Adoption of Children in Scotland. Second edition. [Paperback: £15·00: ISBN 0 414 00779 4.]

Practice

Compendium of Legal Aid 1986. [Paperback: £6·50: ISBN 0 414 00796 4.]

Graham Stewart on Diligence. Reprint. [Hardback: £29·00.]

St. Clair, J. and Davidson, N. F.—Judicial Review in Scotland [Hardback: £8·00: ISBN 0 414 00774 3.]

Scots Civil Courts Statutes 1986 [Paperback: £20·00: ISBN 0 414 00799 9.]

Revenue and Finance

Jones, M. and Mackintosh, S.—Revenue Law in Scotland [Paperback: £16·00: ISBN 0 406 50170 X.]

Sheriff Court Practice

Carmichael, I. H. B.—Sudden Deaths and Fatal Accident Inquiries: Scots Law and Practice. [Paperback: £15·00: ISBN 0 414 00775 1.]

Solicitors

Solicitors' Compendium 1986. [Paperback: £4·50: ISBN 0 414 00798 0.]

Succession

Scots Statutes: Family Law; Succession, Trusts, etc. 1986. [Paperback: £10·50: ISBN 0 414 00802 2.]

SEA AND SEASHORE

Calwell, B.—Sea Lawyer: A Guide for Yachtsmen. Second edition. Paperback: £6·95: ISBN 0 229 11762 7.

SETTLEMENTS AND TRUSTS

Courtney, B—Trust Taxation Manual. First edition. Paperback: £16·00: ISBN 0406 503 303.

Hayton, D. and Marshall—Cases and Commentary on the Law of Trusts. [Eighth edition]. Hardback: £34·00: ISBN 0 420 47370 X; Paperback: £24·00: ISBN 0 420 47380 7.

Todd, P.—An Introduction to the Law of Trusts. Paperback: £9·95: ISBN 1 85185 021 X.

Woolf, E., Tannu, S. and Singh, K. (eds.)—Executorship and Trusts Law and Accounts. Second edition. Paperback: £14·95: ISBN 0 7121 0751 7.

SHIPPING AND MARINE INSURANCE

Astle, W. E—Limitation of Liability. Paperback: £12·00: ISBN 0 905045 63 7.

Brodie, P. R.—Dictionary of Shipping Terms. Paperback: £14·50: ISBN 1 85044 069 7.

Brooke, H.—The Institute Cargo Clauses (AIR). Paperback: £9·00: ISBN 0 900886 27 7.

Denny, M.—Introduction to General Average. Paperback: £6·00: ISBN 0 948691 10 7.

Griggs, P. and Williams, R.—Limitation of Liability for Maritime Claims. Hardback: £24·00: ISBN 1 85044 083 2.

Henry, C. E.—The Carriage of Dangerous Goods by Sea. Hardback: £20·00: ISBN 0 86187 569 9.

Mankabady, S.—International Maritime Organisation Vol. 1: International Shipping Rules. First edition. Hardback: £45·00: ISBN 0 7099 3591 9.

Meeson, N.—The Practice and Procedure of the Admiralty Court: Forms and Precedents. Hardback: £35·00: ISBN 1 85044 087 5.

Pineus, K.—Ship's Value. Second edition. Hardback: £32·50: ISBN 1 85044 062 X.

Schofield, M. A.—Laytime and Demurrage. Hardback: £45·00: ISBN 1 85044 057 3.

Templeman/Lambeth.—Templeman on Marine Insurance. Sixth edition. Hardback: £50·00: ISBN 0 273 02537 6.

Tetley, W.—Maritime Liens and Claims. Hardback: £45·00: ISBN 0 948406 00 3.

Theunis, J. et al.—Arrest of Ships—2: Belgium, the Netherlands, India, Yugoslavia. [Arrest of Ships Series]. Hardback: £24·00: ISBN 1 85044 091 3.

SHOPS

Leder, M. J.—Consumer Law. Second edition. Paperback: £4·95: ISBN 0 7121 0677 4.

Murphy, D. J. I.—Customers and Thieves: An Ethnography of Shoplifting. Hardback: £18·50: ISBN 0 566 00882 3.

BOOKS AND ARTICLES

SOCIAL SECURITY

Bonner, D., Hooker, I., Smith, P. and White, R.—Non-Means Tested Benefits: The Legislation. Paperback: £12·75: ISBN 0 421 35390 2.

Cohen, R. and Lakhari, B.—National Welfare Benefits Handbook. Sixteenth edition. Paperback: £4·00: ISBN 0 903963 95 7.

Mesher, J.—CPAG's Supplementary Benefit and Family Income Supplement: The Legislation. Third edition. Paperback: £15·00: ISBN 0 421 35380 5.

Smith, R. and Rowland, M.—Rights Guide to Non-Means-Tested Social Security Benefits. Ninth edition. Paperback: £4·00: ISBN 0 903963 96 5.

Tolley's National Insurance Contributions 1986–87—By Neil D. Booth. Paperback: £15·95: ISBN 0 85459 217 2.

SOLICITORS

Hill, R. N.—How to survive your Articles. Paperback: £5·95: ISBN 0 08 033068 1.

King, A. and Barlow, J.—Solicitors and their Business Clients. Third edition. Paperback: £15·50: ISBN 1 85185 031 7.

Law Society—The Professional Conduct of Solicitors. Third edition. Looseleaf: £20·00.

Phelps, J. and Gizzi, J.—Solicitors and VAT. Paperback: £7·95: ISBN 0 406 50360 5.

Reuter Simkin.—The Young Solicitor's Guide. Paperback: £2·25: ISBN 0 95111 07 05.

STAMP DUTIES

Butterworths Orange Tax Handbook 1986–87.—Eleventh edition. Paperback: £17·00: ISBN 0 406 50832 1.

Gregory, R.—Stamp Duties for Conveyancers. Fourth edition. Paperback: £13·50: ISBN 0 85121 173 9.

Sergeant and Sims on Stamp Duties—[Fourth cumulative supplement to eighth edition]. Paperback: £11·50: ISBN 0 406 37040 0.

STATUTES AND ORDERS

Consumer Law Statutes.—Fifth edition. Paperback: £14·95: ISBN 0 906533 45 7.

Is It In Force? 1986.—Paperback: £14·95: ISBN 0 406 07281 7.

Roberts, D.—Index to the Companies Act 1985 and Related Legislation. Paperback: £5·25: ISBN 0 902197 47 9.

Totty, P. and Jordan, M.—Insolvency: An Introduction to the 1985 Act. Paperback: £6·95: ISBN 0 85121 216 6.

Tyler, E. L. G.—Cases and Statutes on Land Law. Second edition. Paperback: £10·95: ISBN 0 421 34350 8.

STOCK EXCHANGE

Allied Dunbar Investment Guide 1986–87.—Edited by C. Robinson. Hardback: £12·50: ISBN 0 85121 166 6.

Courtney, D. and Bettelheim, E. C.—An Investor's Guide to the Commodity Futures Markets. Hardback: £16·95: ISBN 0 406 10190 6.

TORT

Hodge, J. B.—Vicarious Liability. Paperback: £7·50: ISBN 01 948691 00 X.

Fleming, J. G.—An Introduction to the Law of Torts. Second edition. Hardback: £17·50: ISBN 0 198 761 546; Paperback: £8·95: ISBN 0 198 761 554.

Furmston, M.—The Law of Tort: Policies and Trends in Liability for Damage to Property and Economic Loss. Hardback: £29·95: ISBN 0 7156 2012 6.

Markesinis, B.—The German Law of Torts. First edition. Hardback: £55·00: ISBN 0198 255 314.

TOWN AND COUNTRY PLANNING

Elder, A. J.—Guide to the Building Regulations 1985. Paperback: £16·95: ISBN 0 85139 844 8.

Estates Gazette Law Reports 1985.—Two volumes. Edited by J. Muir Watt. Hardback: Vol. 1: £20·00: ISBN 0 72820 097 X; Hardback: Vol. 2: £20·00: ISBN 0 72820 098 8.

Hughes, D.—Environmental Law. Paperback: £14·95: ISBN 0 406 01691 7.

Manchester, C.—Sex Shops and the Law. Hardback: £18·50: ISBN 0 566 05232 6.

Telling, A.—Planning Law and Procedure. Seventh edition. Paperback: £12·50: ISBN 0 406 66522 2.

TRADE AND INDUSTRY

Schmitthoff, C.—Export Trade. Eighth edition. Hardback: £32·00: ISBN 0420 466 401.

TRADE MARKS AND TRADE NAMES

Blanco White, T. A. and Jacob, R.—Patents, Trade Marks, Copyright and Industrial Designs. Third edition. Hardback: £12·95: ISBN 0 421 34960 3; Paperback: £8·95: ISBN 0 421 34970 0.

Drysdale, J. and Silverleaf, M.—Passing Off: Law and Practice. Hardback: £28·50: ISBN 0 406 25340 4.

Narayanan, P.—Trade Mark Cases & Passing Off Cases (two volumes). Hardback: £95·00: ISBN 0 421 34460 1.

BOOKS

TRADE MARKS AND TRADE NAMES—*cont.*

Phillips, J.—Introduction to Intellectual Property Law. Paperback: £13·95: ISBN 0 406 25832 5.

Williams, J.—A Manager's Guide to Patents, Trade Marks and Copyright. Hardback: £12·95: ISBN 0 85038 970 4.

TRADE UNIONS

Dickens, L., Jones, M., Weekes, B. and Hart, M.—Dismissed: A Study of Unfair Dismissal and the Industrial Tribunal System. Paperback: £8·50: ISBN 0 631 15219 9.

Evans, A. and Palmer, S.—Negotiating Shorter Working Hours. Hardback: £29·50: ISBN 0 333 38858 5.

Hepple, B. and Fredman, S.—Labour Law and Industrial Relations in Great Britain. First edition. Paperback: £17·95: ISBN 90 6544 2626.

Lewis, R.—Labour Law in Britain. Paperback: £15·00: ISBN 0 631 13755 6.

Smith, I. T. and Wood, J. C.—Industrial Law. Third edition. Hardback: £26·00: ISBN 0 406 381 445; Paperback: £16·95: ISBN 0 406 381 453.

Williams, D. B. and Walker, D. J.—The Industrial Tribunal Practice. Second edition. Paperback: £24·00: ISBN 0 946700 18 4.

TRANSPORT

Kitchin's Road Transport Law.—Twenty-fifth edition. Ed. Duckworth, James. Paperback: £14·95: ISBN 0 406 26476 7.

VALUE ADDED TAX

Butterworths Budget Tax Tables 1986.—Edited by Bond, D., Grosse, C., Kronbergs, Z. and Parrington, S. 22nd edition. Paperback: £2·80: ISBN 0 406 50841 0.

Butterworths Orange Tax Handbook 1986–87.—Eleventh edition. Paperback: £17·00: ISBN 0 406 50832 1.

Kay, J and King, M.—The British Tax System. Fourth edition. Hardback: £17·50: ISBN 0 19 877263 7. Paperback: £6·50: ISBN 0 19 877262 9.

Moores & Rowland's Tax Guide 1985–86. Ninth edition. Paperback: £25: ISBN 0 406 35920 2.

Phelps, J. and Gizzi, J.—Solicitors and VAT. Paperback: £7·95: ISBN 0 406 50360 5.

Pritchard, W. E.—Taxation. Seventh edition. Paperback: £7·95: ISBN 0 7121 2037 8.

Tolley's.—Taxation in the Channel Islands and Isle of Man 1986 [1986]. Paperback: £11·50: ISBN 0 85459 225-3.

Tolley's.—Taxation in the Republic of Ireland 1986–87 [1986–87]. Paperback: £11·95: ISBN 0 85459 226 1.

Tolley's.—Taxwise Taxation Workbook No. 1 [1986/7]. Paperback: £13·95: ISBN 0 85459 2571.

Tolley's.—Value Added Tax 1986–87 [1986–87]. Paperback: £12·95: ISBN 0 85459 242 3.

Tolley's Tax Bumph 1985–86.—Edited by R. Wareham and N. Bowen. Paperback: £18·95: ISBN 0 85459 198 2.

Tolley's Tax Cases 1986—By Victor Grant. Paperback: £15·50: ISBN 0 85459 229 6.

Tolley's Tax Computations 1985–86. K. M. G. Thomson McLintock. Paperback: £19·50: ISBN 0 85459 197 4.

Tolley's Tax Planning 1986.—Paperback: £27·50: ISBN 0 85459 203 2.

Tolley's Tax Tables 1986–87.—Paperback: £4·95: ISBN 0 85459 213 X.

Tolley's VAT Planning.—Edited by Robert Wareham. Paperback: £14·95: ISBN 0 85459 208 3.

Whillans's Tax Tables 1986–87.—Edited by S. Parrington. [Thirty-ninth edition]. Paperback: £2·60: ISBN 0 406 54321 6.

WILLS

Wright, C. E.—Succession: Cases and Materials. Paperback: £17·95: ISBN 0 406 56311 X.

Pettitt, D. M.—The Will Draftsman's Handbook. Fourth edition. Paperback: £17·50: ISBN 0 85121 140 2.

Tristram and Cooke's Probate Practice.—Edited by G. A. Terian, J. S. Gowers and B. Kay. [Supplement to twenty-sixth edition.] Paperback: £6·00: ISBN 0 406 40322 8.

INDEX OF ARTICLES

The following articles were published in 1986. They are listed under the appropriate Current Law headings.

ARTICLES

ARTICLES

ARTICLES

ARTICLES

ARTICLES

COMPANY LAW—*cont.*

Insolvency Act 1985 as it affects directors and others (*E. Joseph and M. Tenzer*): 83 L.S.Gaz. 3333.

Insolvency Act's message to directors (*P. Farmery*): (1986) 4 Co. Law Dig. 56.

Introduction to U.S. anti-trust law (*S. Johnson and D. Rupert*): 83 L.S.Gaz. 112.

Liability of officers on company instruments (*D. Fox*): 4 Co. Law Dig. 107.

Lifting the veil between holding and subsidiary companies (*F. Rixon*): 102 L.Q.R. 415.

Minority remedy in section 459—first grapeshot (*N. Bourne*): (1986) 7 B.L.R. 181.

My body, myself: problems of identity in corporate crime (*P. von Nessen*): (1985) 3 C. & S.L.J. 235.

New administrator procedure—some overseas comparisons (*L. Sealy*): (1986) 2 Ins. L.P. 70.

"Not the act of the company" (*M. Burke*): (1985) B.L.R. 276.

Nullity of companies in English law (*R. Drury*): 48 M.L.R. 644.

Off-balance sheet financing (*G. Jones*): (1986) 4 Co. Law Dig. 62.

Perils of being a director (*R. Lowe*): 5 Lit. 240.

Piercing the corporate veil—a new direction? (*A. Domanski*): 103 S.A.L.J. 224.

Point on the companies consolidation (*F. Bennion*): 130 S.J. 736.

Problems of transferring shares in private companies (*D. Fox*): 130 S.J. 718.

Proposed legal changes in the regulation of auditors (*R. Leach*): 4 Co. Law Dig. 106.

Protection of minority shareholders after a take-over bid (*K. Kolodny*): 7 Co. Law. 17.

Qualifications in audit reports (*J. Parkinson*): (1985) 2 P.N. 105.

Recent developments in company law judicial decisions (*R. Pennington*): 130 S.J. 623.

Reform of the *ultra vires* rule: a consultative document (*M. Stamp*): 136 New L.J. 962.

Relative nature of a shareholder's right to enforce the company contract (*R. Drury*): [1986] C.L.J. 219.

Remedies for abuse of majority power (*P. Xuereb*): 7 Co.Law. 53.

Review of recent corporate insolvency decisions in the Scottish courts (*I. Fletcher*): (1986) 14 I.B.L. 67.

Set-off: its relevance to insolvency law (*B. Griffin*): [1985] Ins.L.P. 140.

Should floating charges and receivership be abolished? (*G. L. Gretton*): 1986 S.L.T.(News) 325.

Small private take-overs—the case for a national protocol (*M. Long and P. Johnson*): 83 L.S.Gaz. 1472.

Transfer of undertakings: recent judicial attitudes (*J. McMullen*): 6 Co. Law 254.

Ultra vires dividend payments in the light of recent legislation (*D. Fox*): (1986) 4 Co. Law Dig. 21.

Ultra vires rule (*S. Davis*): 136 New L.J. 907.

COMPANY LAW—*cont.*

Unfairly prejudiced directors (*R. Instone*): 136 New L.J. 973.

Unfit directors: a testing time ahead (*C. Grenville*): (1986) 2 Ins.L.P. 7.

Valuing minority holdings in private companies (*D. Fox*): 130 S.J. 476.

Voluntary arrangements: 1986 Admin. June i.

Were those old SI's included in the Companies Act 1985? (*B. Johnson*): 83 L.S.Gaz. 1130.

Who's winding up who? (*C. Grenville*): (1986) 2 Ins.L.P. 38.

COMPULSORY PURCHASE

Compensation—disturbance (*J. T. Aitken*): (1986) 19 S.P.L.P. 93.

Compensation for compulsory purchase: equivalence and the date for fixing interests (*E. Young and J. Rowan-Robinson*): [1986] J.P.L. 727.

Disturbance compensation: flexibility and the principle of equivalence (*E. Young and J. Rowan-Robinson*): [1986] J.P.L. 656.

What is deductible from compulsory purchase compensation? (*P. Smith*): 136 New L.J. 424.

CONFLICT OF LAWS

Arbitration—international aspects (*A. E. Anton*): 1986 S.L.T.(News) 45, 53.

Controlling forum-shopping: the impact of *MacShannon* v. *Rockware Glass (R. Schuz)*: 35 I.C.L.Q. 374.

Discretion to stay proceedings—the impact of *"The Abidin Daver"* on judicial chauvinism (*A. Mainsbridge*): II Sydney L.R. 151.

English proceedings and foreign limitation periods (*N. Jacobs*): 136 New L.J. 499.

Executive certificates in foreign affairs: prospects for review and control (*C. Warbrick*): 35 1 C.L.Q. 138.

Executive certificates in foreign affairs: the United Kingdom (*E. Wilmhurst*): 35 1 C.L.Q. 157.

Foreign marriages—some validity and immigration issues (*R. M. White*): (1986) 116 SCOLAG 79.

Matrimonial judgments as defences in the conflict of laws (*A. Jaffey*): [1986] 5 C.J.Q. 35.

Non-enforcement of foreign laws in England (*M. Jefferson*): (1986) 7 B.L.R. 138.

Problems of extraterritorial jurisdiction: economic sovereignty and the search for a solution(*A. Lowe*): 34 I.C.L.Q. 724.

Recent English decisions on recognition of talaq (*K. McK. Norrie*): (1986) 31 J.L.S. 158, 208.

Romalpa: international dimension (considering *Hammer and Sohne* v. *H.W.T. Realisations* [1985] C.L.Y. 3771; *Zahnrad Fabrik Passau GmbH* v. *Terex* [1985] C.L.Y. 4744 and *Armour* v. *Thyssen Edelstahlwerke A.G.* [1986] C.L.Y. 4630, 4631) (*H. Patrick*): 1986 S.L.T.(News) 265, 277.

Time limitation in the English conflict of laws (*P. Stone*): [1985] L.M.C.L.Q. 497.

ARTICLES

ARTICLES

ARTICLES

[29]

ARTICLES

ARTICLES

[31]

ARTICLES

ARTICLES

ARTICLES

ARTICLES

ARTICLES

ARTICLES

[37]

ARTICLES

ARTICLES

ARTICLES

ARTICLES

ARTICLES

HUSBAND AND WIFE—*cont.*

Custody appeals: House of Lords' approach (*S. de Cruz*): 130 S.J. 563.

Divorce and the children: the matrimonial home and maintenance (*M. Southwell*): 130 S.J. 196.

Divorce English style—a new way forward? (*J. Eekelaar*): [1986] J.S.W.L. 226.

Domestic violence and the county court: 5 Lit. 256.

Extra-judicial divorces revisited—a radical approach (*D. Gordon*): 37 N.I.L.Q. 151.

Family courts or family law reform—which should come first (*B. Hoggett*): (1986) 6 L.S. 1.

Family Law (Scotland) Act 1985 (*E. E. Sutherland*): 1986 S.L.T.(News) 85, 93.

Financial provision reformed—an abdication of responsibility? (*J. Dewar*): [1986] Conv. 96.

Foreign marriages—some validity and immigration issues (*R. M. White*): (1986) 116 SCOLAG 79.

Fresh approach—a summary of the Matrimonial Causes Procedure Committee Report (*E. Walsh*): 15 Fam. Law 299.

Interest analysis, false conflicts, and the essential validity of marriage (*P. Smart*): 14 Anglo-Am. 225.

Matrimonial *Mareva* (*R. Purdie*): 5 Lit. 183.

New law on property after divorce and on aliment (*M. Hall*): (1986) 112 SCOLAG 5.

Recognition in England of talaq divorces (*P. Stone*): 14 Anglo-Am. 363.

Registration and the Matrimonial Homes Act (*J. Treleaven*): 104 *Law Notes* 332.

Remission of arrears in matrimonial matters: the principles (*A. Samuels*): 129 S.J. 879.

Role of the court in family matters (*J. Graham Hall and D. Martin*): 5 Lit. 205.

Section 41 appointments—their place in a unified family court (*J. Graham Hall and D. Martin*): 150 J.P.N. 611.

Step-daughters and mothers-in-law (*D. Nichols*): 1986 S.L.T.(News) 229.

Taxation of the spouses: a comparison of Canadian, American, British, French and Swedish law (*L. Dulude*): 23 Osgoode Hall L.J. 67.

Transferable tax allowance (*S. Eden*): (1986) SCOLAG 138.

Whither the Family Court? (*J. Black*): 150 J.P.N. 422.

Whither the sanctity of marriage? (*B. Raisbeck*): 130 S.J. 117.

IMMIGRATION

Adoption and immigration (*A. Khan*): 130 S.J. 213.

Family settlement cases: a denial of statutory rights (*L. Fransman*): (1986) 1 Imm. and Nat. L. & P. 5.

Foreign marriages—some validity and immigration issues (*R. M. White*): (1986) 116 SCOLAG 79.

Immigration (Bail) Bill 1985 (*R. Scannel*): (1986) 1 Imm. and Nat. L. & P. 26.

IMMIGRATION—*cont.*

Immigration law and validity of marriages (*D. Pearl*): [1985] *Legal Action* 173.

New immigration rules (*J. Gillespie*): (1986) 1 Imm. and Nat. L. & P. 23.

Recent developments in immigration law and practice (*R. Scannell*): [1986] *Legal Action* 57.

Rights of appeal on refusal of an application for asylum (*E. Guild*): (1986) 1 Imm. and Nat. L. & P. 27.

Village enquiries in the Indian sub-continent (*D. Webb*): (1986) 1 Imm. and Nat. L. & P. 16.

INCOME TAX

A moving experience (*B. Carver*): 117 Tax. 278.

Budget 1986 (*J. Simpson*): (1986) 31 J.L.S. 193.

Buying own shares boosts net assets (*H. Stanton*): 193 Acct. (No. 5768) 12.

Deductibility of expenses for Schedule D income tax—the "all or nothing" rule (*R. Kerridge*): [1986] B.T.R. 36.

Discrimination in tax system between men and women (*E. M. Scobbie*): (1986) 119 SCOLAG 119.

Food for thought (*B. Carver*): 117 Tax. 138.

Lawyers' income tax deductions: neither sartorial nor gastronomic (*S. Foster*): 130 S.J. 600.

Maintenance payments—tax changes (*E. M. Scobbie*): (1986) 115 SCOLAG 60.

Mortgage interest relief (*D. Harris*): 116 Tax. 432.

Payments in advance (*A. Sellwood*): 117 Tax. 165.

Pitfall of gains taxed as income (*E. Bayfield*): 15 C.S.W. 979.

Transferable tax allowance (*S. Eden*): (1986) SCOLAG 138.

INDUSTRIAL SOCIETIES

Industrial and provident societies—time for a fresh approach? (*I. Swinney*): (1986) 4 Co. Law Dig. 30.

INSURANCE

Buildings insurance—description of buildings (*D. Jess*): 136 New L.J. 197.

Business interruption insurance: protecting the cash flow (*E. Gamlen*): 136 New L.J. 524, 571.

Commercial vehicles insurance (*D. Jess*): 136 New L.J. 243.

Conditions in policies of insurance—onus of proof (*Hon. Mr. Justice Derrington*: 59 A.L.J. 554.

Consumer guarantee and insurance contracts (*R. Parkash*): L.S. Gaz. 3547.

Contents insurance—burglar alarm conditions (*D. Jess*): 136 New L.J. 221.

Definition of crime in insurance contracts (*M. Wasik*): [1986] J.B.L. 45.

Illegality and the law of insurance (*P. Chai*): [1985] M.L.J. cxxix.

Increase of risk in insurance policies (*P. Chai*): [1985] 2 M.L.J. xci.

ARTICLES

ARTICLES

ARTICLES

ARTICLES

ARTICLES

ARTICLES

ARTICLES

ARTICLES

ARTICLES

ARTICLES

ARTICLES

ARTICLES

ARTICLES

ARTICLES

ARTICLES

ARTICLES

ARTICLES

RECEIVERS—*cont.*

Insolvency Act and the corporate "user": (*P. Farmery*): (1985) 6 B.L.R. 303, (1986) 7 B.L.R. 4.

Insolvency Act 1985 as it affects directors and others (*E. Joseph and M. Tenzer*): 83 L.S.Gaz. 3333.

Insolvency Act's message to directors (*P. Farmery*): (1986) 4 Co. Law Dig. 56.

Set-off: its relevance to insolvency law (*B. Griffin*): [1985] Ins.L.P. 140.

Voluntary arrangements: 1986 Admin. June i.

REGISTRATION OF BIRTHS, DEATHS AND MARRIAGES

Girl they named Manhattan: the law of forenames in France and England (*R. Munday*): (1985) L.S. 331.

REPARATION (SCOTLAND ONLY)

Road accidents in France and how to cope legally (*A. Cornec*): (1986) 31 J.L.S. 153.

REVENUE AND FINANCE

Acquisition by employees of shares on a flotation (*D. Cohen*): 83 L.S.Gaz. 2984.

Avoiding VAT traps (*V. Durkacz*): 117 Tax. 97.

Bondwashing made simple (*D. Stopforth*): 117 Tax. 373.

Bondwashing specialities (*D. Stopforth*): 117 Tax. 388.

Border issues (*M. Jones*): [1986] B.T.R. 75.

Bretton Woods and the British courts (*F. Davidson*): 1986 S.L.T.(News) 237.

Budget 1986 (J. Simpson): (1986) 31 J.L.S. 193.

Budget Review 1986 (*M. Gowar*): 83 L.S.Gaz. 1117.

Capital gains and valuation (*E. Bayfield*): 15 C.S.W. 735.

CGT and business assets (*B. Friedman*): 116 Tax. 191.

Capital Transfer Tax: a complaint with illustrations (*R. Oerton*): 130 S.J. 495.

Cars and aluminium (*C. Reece*): 117 Tax. 183.

Charitable covenants by individuals—a history of the background to their tax treatment and their cost to the exchequer (*D. Stopforth*): [1986] B.T.R. 101.

Cloud cuckoo land (*D. Harris*): 117 Tax. 172.

Commodity futures contracts and the Gaming Act (*D. Chaikin and B. Moher*): [1986] L.M.C.L.Q. 390.

Constitutionality of the *Ramsay* principle (*R. Bartlett*): [1985] B.T.R. 338.

Corporate ownership of United Kingdom property by a non-resident owner (*D. MacDonald Allen*): 129 S.J. 882.

Cost of capital and raising venture capital in a tax efficient manner (*R. Ashton*): (1986) 3 B.T.R. 176.

Deductibility of expenses for Schedule D income tax—the "all or nothing" rule (*R. Kerridge*): [1986] B.T.R. 36.

REVENUE AND FINANCE—*cont.*

Default in international loan agreements—I (*R. Youard*): [1986] J.B.L. 276.

Discrimination in tax system between men and women (*E. M. Scobbie*): (1986) 119 SCOLAG 119.

Distress for unpaid tax (*A. Davis*): 117 Tax. 118.

Double taxation treaties (*E. Tomsett*): 83 L.S.Gaz. 1450, 1783.

Enterprise zones (*B. Williams*): 116 Tax. 445.

Estate planning: belt or braces? (*M. Pettitt*): 130 S.J. 739.

Extension of consortium relief (*P. Yerbury*): 117 Tax. 211.

Finance Act 1985 (*A. Shipwright*): 129 S.J. 767, 786, 803.

Finance Bill 1986 (*P. Hockley*): (1986) Admin. July 2.

Form or fiscal fiction? (*M. Gunn*): 117 Tax. 175.

Furniss v. *Dawson*: 104 *Law Notes* 292.

How to reduce the tax burden (*E. Bayfield*): 15 C.S.W. 734.

How to tax an alien (*B. Nicholson and L. Campbell*): 118 Tax. 115.

Import duties on the value of software from non-EEC countries (*J. Borking*): Comp.L.P. 10.

Ingram v. *I.R.C.*: stamp duty after *Furniss* v. *Dawson* (*T. Lyons*): [1986] Conv. 257.

Inheritance tax and the general practitioner (*B. McCutcheon*): 83 L.S.Gaz. 2628.

Inheritance tax—the second coming (*B. McCutcheon*): 83 L.S.Gaz. 1778.

International taxation: extending the U.K. revenue network (*R. Deutsch*): 7 Co. Law. 3.

Investment business—Financial Services Bill (*T. N. Biggart*): (1986) 31 J.L.S. 98.

Investment trust companies (*J. Macleod*): [1985] B.T.R. 278.

Inward investment in the U.K. (*A. Cinnamon and M. Flynn*): 83 L.S.Gaz. 2634.

Is it an industrial building? (*D. Jeffrey*): 117 Tax. 75, 156.

Is it an industrial building? (*B. Williams*): 117 Tax. 8.

Leasing: the lessee's viewpoint (*R. de Metz*): [1986] 7 B.L.R. 221.

More on receivability and receipt (*J. Tiley*): [1986] B.T.R. 152.

Mortgage interest relief (*D. Harris*): 116 Tax. 432.

National insurance contributions (*I. Young*): [1986] 7 B.L.R. 41.

New approach and the views of the Law Society (*R. White*): [1986] B.T.R. 18.

New liability rules (*B. McCutcheon*): 118 Tax. 10.

New regulatory framework—the Financial Services Bill (*P. Farmery*): 4 Co. Law Dig. 111.

Non-rolling vans gather no tax (*C. Brand*): 17 C.S.W. 285.

Offshore companies: still as safe as houses? (*D. O'Connell and D. Johnson*): 83 L.S.Gaz. 2623.

[59]

ARTICLES

ARTICLES

ARTICLES

ARTICLES

[63]

ARTICLES

ARTICLES

ARTICLES

ARTICLES

ARTICLES

ARTICLES

ARTICLES

INDEX 1972–86

References are to the relevant Year Book and then the paragraph number, e.g. 80/1122 means para. 1122 in the Current Law Year Book 1980. References without a year are to the Consolidation Volume 1947–1951.
For references to pre-1972 material, see the Index to the Current Law Year Book 1976.

Burial and Cremation—*cont.*
human tissue, 76/223
injunction, 84/249
interment of ashes in church, 82/260
local authorities, 77/241
Northern Ireland. *See* NORTHERN IRELAND.
Parish Councils and Burial Authorities (Miscellaneous Provisions) Act 1970 (c. 29) ... 70/258
prevention of lawful burial 73/295; 83/288
registration of births, deaths and marriages. *See* REGISTRATION OF BIRTHS, DEATHS AND MARRIAGES.
tombstones. *See* TOMBSTONES.
Burma, 73/2542
Burma Independence Act 1947 (11 & 12 Geo. 6, c. 3) ... 5002
Bus Fuel Grants Act 1966 (c. 46) ... 66/12231
Business names, 80/250
Business Names Act 1985 (c. 7) ... 85/280
Butter, 77/1428; 78/1493; 79/1326; 80/1295. *See also* FOOD AND DRUGS.
By-laws—
breach by group, 78/2
forestry, 79/1340
local government, 72/2363; 73/296; 78/2; 79/2010
Byssinosis, 73/3496

Cable and Broadcasting Act 1984 (c. 46) ... 84/3379, 3380
Camping,
gypsy encampments, 73/3241; 74/3744; 75/3353
Canada, 72/229–40; 75/243, 2097, 2728, 3165; 77/203, 2730
Canada Act 1982 (c. 11) ... 82/221
Canals, 72/335; 73/296–7; 76/225; 86/253
Droitwich Canals Trust, 86/253
Firth and Clyde Canal (Extinguishment of Rights of Navigation) Act 1962 ... 62/325
local authority byelaws, 73/296
navigation, 73/297; 76/225
Northern Ireland. *See* NORTHERN IRELAND.
transport nationalisation and denationalisation. *See* TRANSPORT.
water. *See* WATER AND WATERWORKS.
Cancer. *See* WORKMEN'S COMPENSATION.
Capacity, 72/1082
Capital allowances, 73/1650–2; 75/1636–9; 77/1576; 78/357, 1634, 1635, 1696; 79/1441–3; 80/389, 390, 1441–3
Capital Allowances Act 1968 (c. 3) ... 68/1865
Capital gains, 72/1712–20; 73/1653–6; 74/1831–40; 75/1640–6; 76/1400–11; 77/423–5, 1577–90; 78/358–60, 1636–43; 79/370, 371, 1445–55; 80/1444–59
Capital Gains Tax Act 1979 (c. 14) ... 79/1456
Capital Taxation, 75/265–70; 76/226, 227; 77/242–46; 78/199–202; 79/229–33; 80/225–231; 81/206–212; 82/261–271; 83/289–298; 84/250–270; 85/235–252; 86/254–66
capital gains, 84/250–257; 85/235–243; 86/254–262
capital transfer tax, 75/265, 266, 269, 934, 1841, 2376; 76/266; 77/243; 79/230–232; 80/226–228; 81/207–211; 82/263–270; 83/290–296; 84/258–266; 85/244–249; 86/263

Capital Taxation—*cont.*
Capital Transfer Tax Act 1984 (c. 51) ... 84/267
company capital, 77/244
corporation tax, 84/268
double taxation, 79/233; 80/229
estate duty, 78/201; 85/250
Finance Act 1975 (c. 7) ... 75/270
Finance Act 1976 (c. 40) ... 76/227
Finance Act 1977 (c. 36) ... 77/245
Finance Act 1978 (c. 42) ... 78/202
Finance Act 1980 (c. 48) ... 80/230
Finance Act 1981 (c. 35) ... 81/212
gilt-edged securities, 84/269
increase in share capital, 86/265
Lands Tribunal decision, 85/251
National Heritage Act 1980 (c. 17) ... 80/2658
parallel pooling, 86/266
tax avoidance scheme, 84/270
transfer of property, 77/246
Capital Transfer Tax Act 1984 (c. 51) ... 84/267
Car, driving. *See* ROAD TRAFFIC.
Car tax, 73/2872; 80/2290. *See also* VALUE ADDED TAX.
Car Tax Act 1983 (c.53) ... 83/3234
Caravan Sites Act 1968 (c. 52) ... 68/2163
Caravan Sites and Control of Development Act 1960 (c. 62) ... 60/3113
Caravans,
gipsy, encampments, 73/3241; 74/3057, 3744; 75/3353
Mobile Homes Act 1975 (c. 49) ... 75/3355
sites, 80/2630
town and country planning, 72/3324, 3325; 73/3225–7; 75/3353, 3355; 78/2866
whether a dwelling-house, 77/1585
Care and protection, 73/2171; 74/2367; 75/2010, 2152, 2153; 76/1762–5
Careless driving, 72/2985–7; 73/2986; 75/3008; 3009
Caribbean Development Bank, 72/177
Carriage by Air Act 1961 (c. 27) ... 61–458
Carriage by Air (Supplementary Provisions) Act 1962 (c. 43) ... 62/146; 72/171
Carriage by Air and Road Act 1979 (c. 28) ... 79/234; 80/231a
Carriage by Railway Act 1972 (c. 33) ... 72/2878, 2879
Carriage of Goods by Road Act 1965 (c. 37) ... 65/406
Carriage of Goods by Sea Act 1971 (c. 19) ... 71/10892; 77/2769
Carriage of Passengers by Road Act 1974 (c. 35) ... 74/3880
Carriers, 72/336; 73/298–301; 74/291–8; 75/271–4; 76/228–34; 77/247–51; 78/203–7; 79/234–237; 80/231a–236; 81/213–219; 82/272–277; 83/299–303; 84/271–275; 85/253–260; 86/267–273
bailment, 76/228
canals. *See* CANALS.
carriage by air; 83/299, 300; 84/272; 85/140; 86/267. *And see* AVIATION.
Carriage by Air and Road Act 1979 (c. 28) ... 79/234; 80/231a
carriage by rail. *See* RAILWAYS.
carriage by road, 77/247–9, 1233; 78/203–205; 79/235; 80/232, 233; 81/213–218; 82/272–274; 83/301; 84/273; 85/254–6; 86/269, 270. *See also* ROAD TRAFFIC.

Fees—*cont.*
building societies, 74/286; 78/194; 79/224; 80/222
burial, 78/198; 79/228
commissioners for oaths, 72/3268
companies, 73/340; 75/292; 78/255; 80/264
consuls, 78/1720
coroners, 72/537; 73/428; 74/478; 75/456, 1810
counsel, 79/2134
county court, 74/496; 76/374; 77/436; 78/376; 79/381; 80/408
credit unions, 79/1496a
deeds of arrangement, 73/151
divorce and matrimonial causes, 75/956, 1381; 78/805; 79/759; 80/770, 771
executors and administrators, 78/2819
firearms, 75/1447; 78/1470; 79/1312
friendly societies, 77/1459; 78/1520; 79/1346a; 80/1309
gaming, 77/1466; 78/1529; 80/1314
industrial societies, 80/1507
inquiries, 80/5
land registration, 73/1880; 75/1844
licensing, 80/1550
medicine, 78/1939; 79/1751; 80/1761
merchant shipping, 77/2785; 78/2741; 79/2464; 80/2467
parochial, 79/800; 80/832
patents and designs, 73/2480, 2501; 75/2523; 78/2232; 80/2030
Privy Council, 77/2423a; 80/2202
Public Trustee, 79/2419
recording equipment installation, 77/2610
Registrar of Friendly Societies, 79/2404
registration of births, deaths and marriages, 77/2514; 80/2268
savings banks, 77/2678; 78/2656
sheriffs, 77/2714; 78/2626; 79/2424
solicitors, 77/2879; 78/2817–9; 79/1661, 2566, 2567; 80/2583–5
superannuation and trust funds, 79/2060a
Supreme Court, 72/2740–2; 74/1020, 2953; 75/2627–9; 78/2370; 79/2133; 80/2145
telecommunications, 78/2846
weights and measures, 77/3162; 79/2796; 80/2809
winding up, 79/288
Fences, 74/314
Fencing of machinery—
dangerous machinery, obligation to fence, 75/1424; 76/1232
Ferry, 77/3091
Fertilisers, 72/66; 73/63, 64; 76/57; 80/42
Festival of Britain (Additional Loans) Act 1951 (c. 47) ... 10236
Festival of Britain (Sunday Opening) Act 1951 (c. 14) ... 10237
Festival of Britain (Supplementary Provisions) Act 1949 (c. 102) ... 10238
Festival Pleasure Gardens Act 1952 (c. 13) ... 52/3450
Field, 77/2821
Field Monuments Act 1972 (c. 43) ... 72/2538
Fiji, 76/176, 1415, 1439; 79/182; 80/165
Fiji Independence Act 1970 (c. 50) ... 70/171
Film Levy Finance Act 1981 (c. 16) ... 81/2223
Films, 78/2438
Films Act 1960 (c. 57) ... 60/2623
Films Act 1964 (c. 52) ... 64/3055
Films Act 1966 (c. 48) ... 66/10097

Films Act 1970 (c. 26) ... 70/2367
Films Act 1979 (c. 9) ... 79/2203
Films Act 1980 (c. 41) ... 80/2207
Films Act 1985 (c. 21) ... 85/2772
Finance. *See* REVENUE AND FINANCE.
Finance Act 1947 (c. 35) ... 8968
Finance (No. 2) Act 1947 (11 & 12 Geo. 6, c. 9) ... 8969
Finance Act 1948 (c. 49) ... 8970
Finance Act 1949 (c. 47) ... 8971
Finance Act 1950 (c. 15) ... 8972
Finance Act 1951 (c. 43) ... 8973
Finance Act 1952 (c. 33) ... 52/3054
Finance Act 1953 (c. 34) ... 53/3172
Finance Act 1954 (c. 44) ... 54/2894
Finance Act 1955 (c. 15) ... 55/2398
Finance (No. 2) Act 1955 (4 & 5 Eliz. 2, c. 17) ... 55/2399
Finance Act 1956 (c. 54) ... 56/7715
Finance Act 1957 (c. 49) ... 57/3110
Finance Act 1958 (c. 56) ... 58/2944
Finance Act 1959 (c. 58) ... 59/2855
Finance Act 1960 (c. 44) ... 60/2777
Finance Act 1961 (c. 36) ... 61/7727
Finance Act 1962 (c. 44) ... 62/2621
Finance Act 1963 (c. 25) ... 63/3020
Finance Act 1964 (c. 49) ... 64/3166
Finance (No. 2) Act 1964 (c. 92) ... 64/3167
Finance Act 1965 (c. 25) ... 65/3419
Finance Act 1966 (c. 18) ... 66/10480
Finance Act 1967 (c. 54) ... 67/3431, 3432
Finance Act 1968 (c. 44) ... 68/3390
Finance Act 1969 (c. 32) ... 69/3094
Finance Act 1970 (c. 24) ... 70/2484
Finance Act 1971 (c. 68) ... 71/10091, 10092
Finance Act 1972 (c. 41) ... 72/2953
Finance Act 1973 (c. 51) ... 73/2859
Finance Act 1974 (c. 30) ... 74/484, 800, 1845
Finance Act 1975 (c. 7) ... 75/2878
Finance (No. 2) Act 1975 (c. 45) ... 75/2879
Finance Act 1976 (c. 40) ... 76/2354
Finance Act 1977 (c. 36) ... 77/245, 426, 708, 1598, 1599, 2533, 2534, 3115
Finance Act 1978 (c. 42) ... 78/202, 362, 688, 1651–3, 2525, 3032
Finance Act 1979 (c. 25) ... 79/2277
Finance (No. 2) Act 1979 (c. 47) ... 79/2278
Finance Act 1980 (c. 48) ... 80/230, 395, 618, 1468, 1469, 2070, 2277, 2594, 2650, 2774
Finance Act 1981 (c. 35) ... 81/212, 1406, 2303, 2351, 2692, 2840
Finance Act 1982 (c. 39) ... 82/2694
Finance Act 1983 (c. 28) ... 83/3195
Finance (No. 2) Act 1983 (c. 49) ... 83/3196
Finance Act 1984 (c. 43) ... 84/2978
Finance Act 1985 (c. 54) ... 85/2968
Finance Act 1986 (c. 41) ... 86/2849
Finance (Income Tax Reliefs) Act 1977 (c. 53) ... 77/1601
Fines—
enforcement, 73/617
Home Office Study, 78/1906
sentence, 73/617
Finland, 72/1819, 1820; 73/1750–2
Fire. *See also* FIRE SERVICE.
arson, 72/575; 75/503
liability for escape of, 75/2325
Fire insurance, 73/1693; 74/427, 1885; 75/391, 1641, 1713; 76/1455; 78/1700; 79/1509–12; 80/1514

Horticultural Produce Act 1986 (c. 20) ... 86/60
Horticulture, 72/68; 74/72, 73; 79/70; 80/45
Horticulture Act 1960 (c. 22) ... 60/77, 78
Horticulture (Special Payments) Act 1974 (c. 5) ... 74/73
Hospital Complaints Procedure Act 1985 (c. 42) ... 85/2283
Hospitals, 72/2132, 2133
  charities, 77/257
  national health, 72/2215–7; 73/2219, 2220; 74/122, 2454; 77/1990
  teaching hospitals, 79/1844
Hotel Proprietors Act 1956 (c. 62) ... 56/4377
Hotels. *See* INNKEEPERS.
House of Commons, 72/2543, 2544; 75/2470–2; 76/2012. *See also* PARLIAMENT.
House of Commons (Administration) Act 1978 (c. 36) ... 78/2208
House of Commons (Disqualification) Act 1957 (c. 20) ... 57/2593
House of Commons (Disqualification) Act 1975 (c. 24) ... 75/2471
House of Commons (Indemnification of Certain Members) Act 1949 (c. 46) ... 6998
House of Commons Members' Fund Act 1948 (c. 36) ... 6299
House of Commons Members' Fund Act 1957 (c. 24) ... 57/2595
House of Commons Members' Fund Act 1960 (c. 50) ... 60/2319
House of Commons Members' Fund Act 1962 (c. 53) ... 62/2239
House of Commons Members' Fund and Parliamentary Pensions Act (c. 7) ... 81/2010
House of Commons (Redistribution of Seats) Act 1947 (c. 10) ... 7000
House of Commons (Redistribution of Seats) Act 1949 (c. 66) ... 7001, 7002
House of Commons (Redistribution of Seats) Act 1958 (c. 26) ... 58/2446
House of Commons (Redistribution of Seats) Act 1979 (c. 15) ... 79/2014
House of Lords. *See also* PARLIAMENT.
  appeal, 72/2676, 2745; 73/2627; 74/2892
House Purchase and Housing Act 1959 (c. 33) ... 59/1448
House to house collections, 74/302
Housing, 72/1650–75; 73/1575–60; 74/1744–70; 75/1558–88; 76/1346–66; 77/1506–24; 78/1565–87; 79/1379–95; 80/1348–77; 81/1290–325; 82/1449–83; 83/1788–1827; 84/1623–1667; 85/1606–1664; 86/1610–47
  alteration of house, 83/1788
  alternative accommodation, 83/2060; 85/1606
  area of, 73/1575
  assured tenancies, 84/1623
  benefits, 83/1790; 85/1607; 86/1610
  building restrictions. *See* BUILDING AND ENGINEERING, ARCHITECTS AND SURVEYORS.
  caravan, 77/1585
  clearance areas, 72/1650; 75/332, 2006; 76/284, 285; 78/1565, 1566; 82/349; 83/1791; 84/1624
  closing orders, 73/1576; 85/1608; 86/1612, 1613
  compensation, 72/402; 81/1290; 84/1625
  compulsory purchase, 82/370. *See also* COMPULSORY PURCHASE AND REQUISITION.
  condensation dampness, 83/1792
  contributions, 73/1578

Housing—*cont.*
  control order, 78/1568, 1569; 79/1380; 83/1793
  cost of building, 75/2891
  council housing, 72/1653; 75/1860; 78/1570; 80/1349; 82/1452–4
  council tenancy, 79/1381
  covenant to repair, 73/1579; 85/1610
  defective dwellings, 86/1614
  defects, 83/1794
  demolition orders, 72/1654; 75/345, 2747; 76/1349
  design, 73/1580
  disrepair, 85/1611; 86/1615
  duty of local authority, 78/1571
  duty to rehouse, 74/1745; 77/1745; 85/1612
  dwelling-house, 82/1455
  fitness for habitation, 74/1746; 75/337, 1566, 1567, 2747; 76/300, 1351; 77/1508, 1509; 78/1572–4; 79/1382–4; 81/1292, 1293; 82/1456; 83/1795
  forms, 72/1655; 74/1747
  grants, 77/1510; 80/1350; 81/1294; 82/1457; 83/1796; 84/1626; 86/1616
  home insulation, 82/1458; 84/1627
  home loss payment, 84/1628; 85/1613; 86/1617
  home purchase assistance, 78/1575; 80/1351; 81/1295; 82/1459; 83/1799; 84/1629; 85/1614; 86/1618
  Home Purchase Assistance and Housing Corporation Guarantee Act 1978 (c. 27) ... 78/1576, 1577
  homeless persons, 79/1385–8; 80/1352–61; 81/1296–304; 82/1460–73; 83/1800–1813; 84/1630–1645; 85/1615–1632; 86/1619–28
  homes insulation, 80/1362; 81/1305; 83/1814
  Homes Insulation Act 1978 (c. 48) ... 78/1578
  hostel, 83/1815
  house in multiple occupation, 86/1629
  house purchase, 77/1511
  house refuse, 74/3078
  housing action area, 78/1579
  Housing Acts, 4480, 4486; 56/3931; 61/3951–4, 3957; 64/1714; 65/1824; 69/1613; 71/5345; 72/1664; 73/1581, 1582, 1586, 1587; 74/1749, 1750; 75/1568; 76/1352; 79/1389; 80/1363, 1364; 81/1306
  Housing Act 1985 (c. 68) ... 85/1641
  Housing (Amendment) Scotland Act 1981 (c. 72) ... 81/1307
  Housing and Building Control Act 1984 (c. 29) ... 84/1646
  Housing and Planning Act 1986 (c. 63) ... 86/1630
  housing associations, 72/1657; 73/1583–5; 74/1749–53; 75/1569; 79/1390; 80/1365; 81/1308; 82/1474, 1475; 83/1816, 1817; 84/1647, 1648
  Housing Association Act 1985 (c. 69) ... 85/1641
  housing benefits, 82/1476; 83/1818; 84/1649; 85/1636–40; 86/1633–5
  Housing (Consequential Provisions) Act 1985 (c. 71) ... 85/1641
  Housing Consolidation Acts 1985, 85/1641
  Housing Corporation, 74/1754; 75/2006; 76/1353; 79/1390a; 83/1819
  Housing Defects Act 1984 (c. 50) ... 84/1650
  housing finance, 72/1659–64; 75/1986
  Housing Finance Act 1972 (c. 47) ... 72/1660; 75/1572

[159]

[193]

[197]

Practice—*cont.*

divorce and matrimonial causes. *See* DIVORCE AND MATRIMONIAL CAUSES.

enforcement of foreign judgment, 74/397, 2892

evidence, 74/485

extension of time, 75/569; 79/2104; 81/2116

financial provisions, 78/795

House of Lords, 72/2676, 2745; 73/2627; 74/2892

immigration adjudicator, 72/2677. *See also* IMMIGRATION.

industrial tribunal, 72/1184; 73/2600; 76/2102

interpleader, 76/2103

jurisdiction, 72/109; 80/419

justices. *See* MAGISTERIAL LAW.

leapfrog, 72/2680

magistrates' court, from, 78/1895

minors, 78/2317

National Industrial Relations Court, 72/2681, 2682

notice of appeal, 79/2607; 81/2117

numerous previous appeals, 78/2318

Order 14, 78/2316

out of time, 76/2104; 77/1757

patents and designs, 78/2217. *See* PATENTS AND DESIGNS.

petitions for leave, 74/2893; 76/2105; 77/2278; 79/2106, 2107

point of law, 79/2741

preliminary issues, 77/2279

Privy Council, 76/2106

questions of fact, 72/2683

review of exercise of discretion, 76/2107

special verdict of Crown Court, 75/2588

transcript of evidence, 77/2280

transcript of judgment, 73/2601

appearance, 75/2589; 78/2320

applications and change of name, 84/2578

applications to a single Lord Justice of the CA, 85/2601

appointment as Queen's Council, 83/2873

arbitration, 83/124, 145; 85/2602

assignment of cause of action, 85/2603

assignment of joint rights, 85/2604

attachment of earnings, 75/1083; 76/2108; 78/2322; 79/2109

Attorney-General, 76/803

audience. *See* Audience, right of.

authorities, 77/2281; 83/2563

bankruptcy, 77/181; 84/178; 86/2576–8. *See also* BANKRUPTCY AND LIABILITIES ADJUSTMENT.

barristers, 72/2685–7; 73/2602; 74/2894; 75/2591; 76/2110, 2169, 2207; 77/2282, 2283, 2303; 78/2323; 79/2110, 2111; 81/2118–2120; 85/2605

bias, 77/2284

blood tests, 72/2688

breach of confidence, 82/3207; 83/2881, 2882; 84/2580; 85/2606

Bullock order, 86/2580

Central Criminal Court. *See also* CRIMINAL LAW.

certificate of estimated length of trial, 76/2131

certiorari, 77/2285; 78/2324, 2429; 79/535

chambers, 74/1585, 3018

champerty, 85/2607

Practice—*cont.*

Chancery Division, 7524–35; 72/2689–95; 73/2603–9; 74/2896–901; 75/2592–5; 76/2113, 2114; 77/2286–94; 78/2326–9; 79/2113, 2114; 80/2106–10; 81/2121–2123; 82/2409–15; 83/2883–6; 85/2608, 2609; 86/2581–3

Chancery of Lancaster, 73/2604

change of name, 74/2902; 83/2887

charging order, 73/2610; 75/2596, 2597; 77/2295; 81/2457; 82/2416

Charging Orders Act 1979 (c. 53) ... 79/2115; 80/2111

charities, 72/343

Chelmsford Crown Court, 85/2610

Chief Taxing Master, 77/2296

children, 82/2417; 85/2611; 86/2584

citation of cases, 83/2888

civil appeals, 83/2889

civil claim, effect of criminal conviction, 76/2133

civil courts, 83/2890; 84/2581

civil evidence, 72/1472; 74/1566

Civil Jurisdiction and Judgments Act 1982 (c. 27) ... 82/2418; 84/2582

civil liability, 84/2583

civil proceedings, 84/984

claim for declaration, 85/2612

claim for possession, 85/2613

commencement of proceedings, 84/2585

Commercial Court, 74/2904; 77/2297, 2298; 78/2330; 79/2116; 81/2125; 82/2419, 2420; 83/2891; 85/2614–16; 86/2588

committal order. *See* Committal orders.

committals for contempt, 84/2586

common defence, 84/2587

commons, 72/2698

community law, 77/1309

companies. *See* COMPANY LAW.

Companies Court, 77/280, 281, 2301; 78/2332; 79/286; 80/2112; 82/2422–4

compromise agreement, 86/2590

compromise of action, 83/2892, 2893; 85/2617, 2618

conditional order, 86/2591

conflicting decisions, 84/2588

consent order, 78/2333, 3093; 80/777, 2114; 81/2126; 82/2427, 2428; 84/2589, 2590

construction of documents, 85/2619

contempt, 72/2700–4; 73/935, 2613–20; 74/2907–14; 75/2599–601; 76/416, 417, 2116–9; 77/2303–10; 78/2335–40; 79/2119–22, 2699; 80/1385, 1813, 2115, 2119, 2120, 2134; 81/2127, 2128; 82/2430–9; 83/2896–902; 84/2591–97; 85/470, 2620–34; 86/2592–2602

Contempt of Court Act 1981 (c. 49) ... 81/2129; 82/2440

continuation of proceedings, 83/2903

contract, 83/432, 451

contribution, 84/2598

co-plaintiffs, 84/2599

costs, 72/2705–16; 73/102, 884, 2623–37; 74/2915–29; 75/346, 2602, 2603, 2606, 2680; 76/355, 759, 2030, 2120, 2122, 2123, 2125, 2127–30; 77/837, 1152, 1342, 2312, 2315–7, 2319–21, 3182; 78/2341–9; 79/37, 2124–7; 80/2121–4; 81/2130–6; 82/2442–52; 83/2910–17; 84/2601–2608; 55/2636–43; 86/2603–12. *See also* COSTS.

[215]

INDEX 1972–1986